THIRTY-THIRD EDITION

KOVELS'
ANTIQUES
& COLLECTIBLES

PRICE LIST

FOR THE 2001 MARKET

ILLUSTRATED

THREE RIVERS PRESS

NEW YORK

Published by Three Rivers Press, New York, New York.
Member of the Crown Publishing Group.

Random House, Inc. New York, Toronto, London, Sydney, Auckland
www.randomhouse.com

THREE RIVERS PRESS is a registered trademark and the Three Rivers Press
colophon is a trademark of Random House, Inc.

Printed in the United States of America

Library of Congress Catalog Card Number: 83-643618
ISBN 0-609-80571-1 (pbk.)
10 9 8 7 6 5 4 3 2 1

Books by Ralph and Terry Kovel

American Country Furniture 1780–1875

A Directory of American Silver, Pewter, and Silver Plate

Kovels' Advertising Collectibles Price List

Kovels' American Art Pottery: The Collector's Guide to Makers,
Marks, and Factory Histories

Kovels' American Silver Marks: 1650 to the Present

Kovels' Antiques & Collectibles Fix-It Source Book

Kovels' Book of Antique Labels

Kovels' Bottles Price List

Kovels' Collector's Guide to American Art Pottery

Kovels' Collectors' Source Book

Kovels' Depression Glass & Dinnerware Price List

Kovels' Dictionary of Marks—Pottery & Porcelain

Kovels' Guide to Selling, Buying, and Fixing
Your Antiques and Collectibles

Kovels' Guide to Selling Your Antiques & Collectibles

Kovels' Illustrated Price Guide to Royal Doulton

Kovels' Know Your Antiques

Kovels' Know Your Collectibles

Kovels' New Dictionary of Marks—Pottery & Porcelain

Kovels' Organizer for Collectors

Kovels' Price Guide for Collector Plates, Figurines,
Paperweights, and Other Limited Editions

Kovels' Quick Tips—799 Helpful Hints on
How to Care for Your Collectibles

Kovels' Yellow Pages: A Collector's Directory

The Label Made Me Buy It: From Aunt Jemima to Zonkers—
The Best-Dressed Boxes, Bottles and Cans from the Past

This is the 33rd year *Kovels Antiques & Collectibles Price List* has been published. And the book is still being written by the original authors, Ralph and Terry Kovel. It has changed from a book with no illustrations and typewriter-style letters to this edition with hundreds of pictures and logos, about 50,000 prices, dozens of tips about care, and a special color-picture report on holiday and special-event collectibles.

READ THIS BEFORE YOU USE THIS BOOK—IT WILL HELP

This is a book for the average collector. All year we check prices, visit shops and shows, read our mail, check online computer services and the Internet, and decide what antiques and collectibles are of most interest. We concentrate on the average pieces in any category. Sometimes one or two high-priced pieces are included in a category so you will realize that some of the rarities are quite valuable. For example, this year several rare pieces of pressed glass were sold. A Three Face champagne glass with hollow stem auctioned for $4,600 and a Lion (frosted) pitcher for $5,100.

Examples of furniture, silver, Tiffany, or art pottery may sell for more than $50,000; we list a few of those examples. The highest price in this book is $88,000 for a Handel lamp. The lowest price is 25 cents for an olive can label. Most pieces we list cost less than $10,000. We even list the weird and the wonderful. This year you can find prices for a jail door ($225), a gym locker ($250), a pair of women's clown shoes ($50), and an antique gum saver—a tin lithographed box for "chewed gum" made in 1898 ($145). The smallest object is a button. The largest is a wooden backbar that is 9 by 10 feet.

Prices are up in some categories. Prices for studio jewelry from the 1950s, such as pieces by Sam Kramer and Arthur Smith, have been rising. Probably the most active area of collecting this year is Arts & Crafts. There is continued interest in garden antiques, art pottery, tiles, and toys. The antiques malls that are springing up in all parts of the country and the auctions and sales found on the Internet are also influencing prices. Small pieces that are inexpensive and easy to identify sell quickly. At least 40 percent of the serious buyers of antiques now use computers. This percentage is increasing each year. The market online is getting larger and is international. Objects that are well known around the world, like pens, cigarette lighters, toys, Royal Doulton pottery, majolica, and oak furniture, are selling well.

Each year categories are added or omitted to make it easier for you to find your antiques. New categories this year are Peanuts (the comic strip) and Star Trek—Star Wars.

The book is kept at about 800 pages because it is written to go with you to sales. We try to have a balanced format—not too many glass, pottery, or collectible items, a variety of furniture from the 18th through the 20th centuries, not too many items that sell for over $5,000. The prices are *from* the

American market *for* the American market. Few European sales are reported. We take the editorial privilege of not including any prices that seem to result from "auction fever." The computer-generated index is so complete it amazes us. Use it often. An internal alphabetical index is also included. For example, there is a category for Celluloid. Most items made of celluloid will be found there, but if there is a toy made of celluloid, it will be listed under Toy and also indexed under Celluloid. There are also cross-references in the listings and in the paragraphs. But some searching must be done. For example, Barbie dolls are found in the Doll category; there is no Barbie category. And when you look at "doll, Barbie" you will see a note that tells you that Barbie is under "doll, Mattel, Barbie" because most dolls are listed by maker. We differentiate between doll furniture made to a scale suitable for displaying dolls and dollhouse furniture made in the small scale meant for a dollhouse. All pictures and prices are new every year, except pictures that are pattern examples shown in Depression Glass and Pressed Glass. The pictures have been computer-enhanced to make them as crisp as possible. Antiques pictured are items offered for sale, not museum pieces. We hate to waste space, so whenever computer-generated spaces appear, we fill them with tips about care of collections, security, and other useful information. These tips are set in special type, so they will not be confused with the prices. Leaf through the book and learn how to wash porcelains, store textiles, guard against theft, and much more. We use new tips every year. Don't discard this book when it is time to buy a new one next year. Old Kovels' price books should be saved for future reference, and for tax and appraisal information.

The prices in this book are reports from the general antiques market. Each year, every price in the book is new. We do not estimate or "update" prices. Prices are actual asking prices, although a buyer may have negotiated a price to a lower figure. No price is an estimate. We do not ask dealers and writers to estimate prices. Experience has shown that a collector of one type of antique is prejudiced in favor of that item, and prices are usually high or low, but rarely a true report. If a price range is given, it is because at least two identical items were offered for sale at different times. The computer prints the high and low figures. Price ranges are found only in categories like Pressed Glass, where identical items can be identified. If the price listed in this book is from an auction, it includes the buyer's premium, but like all the prices, it does not include sales tax. Some prices in *Kovels' Antiques & Collectibles Price List* may seem high and some may seem low because of regional variations. But each price is one you could have paid for the object.

If you are selling your collection, do not expect to get retail value unless you are a dealer. Wholesale prices for antiques are from 20 to 50 percent less than retail. Remember, the antiques dealer must make a profit or go out of business. Internet auction prices are less predictable. Because of the international audience and "auction fever," prices often are higher or lower.

THE RECORD PRICES HYPE

The media loves to report record prices, amazing auctions, high-priced discoveries, and other events that really have little to do with the antiques and collectibles market familiar to the average collector. This year, front-page stories told of a painting found in a garage that attracted an online bid of more than $100,000 (the painting's background was later questioned) and a Tiffany poppy table lamp stored in a basement for forty years that auctioned for $123,200. The strangest was a broken Baker & Cutting Glass & Pickle Mfrs. jar found in a dig in four pieces that sold at auction for $165. Unbroken, it probably would have set the record for an American bottle. Great stories, but—like winning the lottery—not likely to happen to everyone. So study the records, but remember that these are the prices for the rarest and best.

ADVERTISING

- **Single cartoon or promotional glass:** $1,792 for a 1977 Pepsi, Batgirl & Robin glass tumbler with a superhero theme, made by Brockway Glass.

BRONZE & OTHER SCULPTURES

- **Eames sculpture and a piece of mid-20th-century design:** $365,000 for a 1943 Ray and Charles Eames molded plywood sculpture, 37½ x 27 x 13 inches.
- **Eames sculpture and postwar design:** $143,000 for a splint sculpture by Ray Eames, c.1943, 43 inches.

CLOCKS & WATCHES

- **Any watch:** $11,002,500 for a Patek Philippe 18K-gold pocket watch, No. 198385, made for Henry Graves Jr., with 24 complications, including perpetual calendar, moon phases, sidereal time, power reserve, and indications for time of sunset and sunrise and the night sky of New York City, weighing 1 pound 3 ounces, 4¼ inches. Patek Philippe was commissioned in 1925 by Henry Graves to produce the most complicated watch in the world; started in 1928, completed in 1932, and delivered on January 19, 1933.
- **Patek Philippe Calatrava wristwatch:** $371,290 for an 18K–pink gold, 2-time-zone Patek Philippe Calatrava wristwatch with three hands; ref. 2597HS, c. 1962.
- **Patek Philippe "World Time" wristwatch, ref. 1415HU:** $868,065 for a Patek Philippe 18K–pink gold wristwatch with polychrome cloisonné enamel dial representing Europe, Africa, and Asia; made in 1949.
- **Patek Philippe astronomic wristwatch, ref. 2499:** $1,066,774 for a Patek Philippe 18K–pink gold wristwatch with round button chronograph, register, tachometer, perpetual calendar, and moon phases; c. 1960.
- **Patek Philippe wristwatch:** $1,918,387 for a Patek Philippe 18K–yellow gold, split-seconds wristwatch with enamel dial and Breguet numerals, made in 1922.
- **Piguet & Meylan "Le Coeur" watch:** $1,421,613 for "Le Coeur" by Piguet & Meylan—a gold, enamel, pearl-and-turquoise, heart-shape, quarter-repeating

musical, automaton watch with center-seconds; enamel work by J.A. Lissignol, c. 1820.

- **Singing-bird watch:** $541,613 for an 18K-gold-and-enamel, pearl-and-ruby set singing-bird watch, attributable to Jaquet-Droz, Geneva, No. I, c. 1785.

FOLK ART

- **Decoy at auction:** $684,500 for a c. 1917 sleeping Canada Goose carved by Elmer Crowell of East Harwich, Massachusetts, with fine painted detail, layered carved wing tips, fluted tail, sculpted head and neck, and the "Crowell" oval brand.

FURNITURE

- **American armchair:** $1,982,500 for an 18th-century, Waln-Large family, Queen Anne, carved, 42-inch-high walnut armchair, with serpentine crest and carved shell, solid vasiform splat over shaped arms with knuckle grips, and compass slip-seat on carved cabriole legs with trifid feet.
- **American card table:** $2,862,500 for a Cornelius Stevenson, Chippendale, carved mahogany card table, c. 1760; has a rectangular hinged top that opens to a baize-lined playing surface, wells for game pieces, thumbmolded drawer, and cabriole legs on ball-and-claw feet; 28½ x 36 x 17 inches.
- **American side chair:** $1,432,500 for a John Cadwalader Chippendale mahogany side chair, with a serpentine crest above a pierced splat, an over-upholstered and shaped saddle-seat, on C-scroll and acanthus-carved cabriole legs with hairy-paw feet; inscribed *I* and is 37 inches in height.
- **Arts & Crafts furniture:** $596,500 for a c. 1902 oak-and-wrought-iron, one-of-a-kind sideboard by Gustav Stickley, extending more than 10 feet in length, passed down through Gustav Stickley's daughter and grandson.
- **Double Marshmallow sofa:** $16,500 for the George Nelson Marshmallow extended version sofa with multicolored naugahyde cushions, brushed-steel and black-metal frame. Sofa was custom-made for ConEdison Building, New York City, 1958; 104 x 32 x 29 inches.
- **Eames and Saarinen armchair prototype:** $129,000 for Charles Eames and Eero Saarinen "Conversation" armchair prototype designed 1940 to 1941, with molded plywood shell, formed foam-rubber cushioning and custom upholstery, four tapered and angled wood dowel legs. Won first place in 1941 Museum of Modern Art "Organic Design Competition." One of two or three prototypes known to exist.
- **Gustav Stickley bookcase:** $60,500 for a Gustav Stickley bookcase that has two doors with single vertical mullions over two cabinet doors, original copper ring pulls, and an early red decal; 64 x 42 x 14 inches.
- **Gustav Stickley butterfly screen:** $22,000 for a three-panel Gustav Stickley butterfly screen, with original finish and a branded signature; 66 x 66¾ inches.
- **Gustav Stickley double-door bookcase:** $30,250 for a Gustav Stickley double-door bookcase with cabinets underneath, signed with red decal, c. 1904 to 1907, 64 x 42 x 14 inches.
- **Gustav Stickley table No. 410-L:** $38,500 for a Gustav Stickley leather-top table, model No. 410-L, with stack hexagonal stretcher and signed with red decal and Stickley in box; c. 1902, 30½ x 48 x 48 inches.

- **Josef Hoffman seven-ball chair:** $75,000 for a seven-ball bentwood high-back chair designed by Josef Hoffman; c. 1906.
- **L. & J. G. Stickley drink stand No. 22:** $17,600 for an L. & J. G. Stickley drink stand with original copper top and original finish; 28 x 18 inches.
- **Limbert table No. 139:** $28,600 for a Limbert octagonal table No. 139, with original dark finish, signature, and paper label; 29¼ x 48 x 48 inches.
- **Miniature painted chest:** $220,000 for a Pennsylvania, painted, miniature blanket chest with ivory panel with stylized red and green tulip tree on a blue reserve, sawtooth border, and wrought iron strap hinges and grab lock; dated 1777 and inscribed Barbara Emr—, 9 x 14¾ x 9½ inches.
- **Nathan Lombard furniture:** $365,300 for a Federal inlaid cherry chest of drawers by Nathan Lombard, with serpentine front, chevron stringing, mahogany banding, four cockbeaded drawers, faux keyholes, and bracket feet; c. 1800, 36 x 42¾ x 19¾ inches.
- **Pembroke table:** $226,500 for a Charleston, South Carolina, Federal, mahogany and kingwood-inlaid Pembroke table, 1790 to 1800, 28½ x 31¼ x 19⅝ inches.
- **Pottier and Stymus cabinet:** $104,500 for an American Aesthetic Movement Pottier and Stymus cabinet, maple and satinwood, with marble plaques on the doors.
- **Safari sofa:** $31,966 for the Archizoom Associati Safari Sofa—two rectangular and two square white fiberglass forms with scalloped seating areas, upholstered in synthetic leopard skin with corresponding carpet; designed 1968, 100 x 84 inches.
- **17th-century American furniture:** $2,422,500 for the Pope valuables cabinet made in 1679; 16⅜ inches. This cabinet was made to commemorate the marriage of Joseph and Bathsheba Pope, a Quaker couple who stood as accusers in the notorious Salem witchcraft trials.
- **Single chair:** $613,760 for a beechwood "throne chair," by Georges Jacob, carved by Rode, with stripped-down giltwood and open arms, twisted and pearl bands, berried laurels, and entrelac and guilloche patterns. Commissioned in 1784 by the Comte d'Artois, in preparation for a visit by his brother, King Louis XVI.
- **20th-century chair:** $640,500 for a cast bronze armchair by Armand Albert Rateau, 1919 to 1920.

LAMPS & LIGHTING

- **Dirk Van Erp milk can lamp:** $159,500 for a Dirk Van Erp hammered copper "milk can" lamp; 26 inches high.
- **Pairpoint puffy Begonia lamp:** $63,250 for a 16-inch puffy Begonia lamp with a bronze Pairpoint base.

MISCELLANEOUS

- **American Indian Art:** $684,500 for an American Indian Tsimshian wood spirit mask from the Northwest coast, created as a religious ceremonial icon 1790 to 1840.
- **Apple 1 computer:** $18,000 for the first Apple 1 computer, built by Steve Jobs in 1976, with original operating manual along with two checks made out to Apple Computer—one for $600 for the hardware with a note saying "purchased from Steve Jobs in his parents' garage in Los Altos (Calif.) and the other for

$193, dated August 5, 1976, for the software with the description "programmed by Steve Jobs."

- **Bayley-Lee fan:** $37,500 for an 1880s Bayley-Lee custom-built fan with brass plaque that reads: "Presented to Thomas Alva Edison by the designer Joseph Lee with the compliments of the New York Edison Co." The fan also features an etched portrait of Edison, miniature replicas of early light-bulb sockets, miniature Edison bulbs, and other miniature designs of early Edison inventions, including a voltmeter, ammeter, and chemical meter.
- **Folk art watercolor:** $687,500 for a pair of American folk art watercolors on paper, mounted together in a mahogany frame and inscribed, "Mr. and Mrs. Samuel Ensminger taken at Manheim 1831," by Jacob Maentel (American, 1763 to 1863). The watercolor portraits picture a husband and wife, the wife seated with a child on her lap, her husband standing at a desk writing with a quill pen; 17 x 21 inches.
- **Gothic flatiron:** $11,508 for a French Gothic-style flatiron, with pointed sole, parallel sides, and a "V"–shape, hanging ring at the rear; upper sole is decorated with a gallery of cut lily flowers; 1480 to 1520, 10⅝ inches.
- **Griswold skillet:** $1,800 for an Erie No. 8 Spider cast iron skillet, Seldon & Griswold Mfg. Co., pre-1890.
- **Metal lunch box:** $11,500 for a metal 1954 Superman lunch box with thermos and original packaging, made by Adco.
- **Single fraktur:** $181,500 for a watercolor-and-ink-on-paper fraktur, by Daniel Otto—a birth certificate for Georg Weber, October 22, 1794, with announcement written in script inside a big heart, with tulips, two parrots, and a dog-faced alligator; 13¼ x 16 inches.
- **Typewriter:** $57,538 for the world's first production typewriter, the so-called Writing Ball, patented by Danish inventor Rasmus Malling-Hansen in 1867.
- **Vermont License plate:** $14,850 for a Vermont automobile license plate with the number 9 in white on a blue enameled surface; 1905, 5¼ x 9¼ inches.

MOVIE & CELEBRITY MEMORABILIA

- **Lobby card:** $11,812 for a single lobby card from *The Mummy*, Universal, 1932.
- **Marilyn Monroe dress:** $1,267,500 for the full-length, flesh-colored gown, made of soufflé gauze with graduated rhinestones embroidered in a rosette design, worn by Marilyn Monroe when she sang "Happy Birthday, Mr. President" to John F. Kennedy on May 19, 1962.

MUSIC

- **Gagliano violin:** $200,500 for a rare 1709 violin by the Neapolitan maker Alessandro Gagliano of Naples, with the label "Alexander Gaglianus Fecit Neap 1709," a one-piece back of strong narrow curl and similar ribs, a plain scroll, and golden red varnish; 14 inches.

PAPER

- **Declaration of Independence broadside:** $415,000 for a copy of the Declaration of Independence referred to as the "Boston Printing" by Gill, Powars and Willis, 1776.

- *History of Oak Trees of America* **book:** $19,550 for a copy of André Michaux's book *History of Oak Trees of America*, from the Charles P. Berolzheimer Library Collection.
- **Printed book:** $8,802,500 for the Fox-Bute four-volume subscriber set of the first edition of Audubon's *Birds of America.*
- **Signed first edition of Dr. Seuss book:** $8,625 for the inscribed and signed first edition of Dr. Seuss's *And to Think that I Saw It on Mulberry Street,* New York, 1937; also $4,600 for the signed first edition of Dr. Seuss's *McElligot's Pool,* New York, 1947.
- **Titanic menu:** $74,750 for the April 14, 1912, menu for the last lunch served on the R.M.S. Titanic; 9½ x 7 inches. The menu was attached behind a framed oil-on-canvas painting of the *Titanic* signed by A. Dymott.

POTTERY & PORCELAIN

- **American market Chinese Export porcelain:** $90,500 for a cider jug and cover, painted with the medal "Order of the Cincinnati"; one side shows Cincinnatus receiving his sword from three Roman senators, and the other side shows Cincinnatus sowing seeds; both sides displayed on the United States eagle's breast; c. 1790, 10¼ inches.
- **Fiesta turquoise onion soup:** $11,000 for a Fiesta turquoise, covered, onion soup.
- **Harlequin duck:** $3,300 for a turquoise Harlequin duck.
- **Newcomb pottery at auction:** $82,500 for a monumental Newcomb College, art pottery, high glaze vase, sculpted, with morning glories in blue, green and yellow underglaze, Leona Nicholson's decorator mark, and Joseph Meyer's potter mark; registration number BX62, c. 1907, 16 x 9 inches.
- **Nippon vase:** $8,000 for a Nippon porcelain vase in cobalt blue, with roses; 24 inches.
- **Polacca Olla:** $28,750 for a Polacca Olla from the early 1840s, made by the Hopi Indians of the Southwest; globular, with high-shoulder-and-squat-neck form; brown-red and black on a cream ground with banded geometric designs; 10 inches.
- **Teco vase:** $66,000 for a tall vase with reticulated blade-shaped leaves around the foot and a smooth matte green with charcoal glaze; 18 x 6 inches.

SILVER & OTHER METAL

- **Archibald Knox cigarette box:** $206,000 for an enameled silver cigarette box designed by Archibald Knox for Liberty's, 1901.
- **Bombé censer:** $511,200 for a Ming Dynasty bombé censer decorated with lotus blossoms; 5½ x 9 inches.

SPORTS

- **Baseball stadium artifact:** $19,721 for an 8½-foot bronze Babe Ruth Plaza marker, which was installed outside Yankee Stadium following Ruth's death in 1948.
- **Baseball uniform:** $451,542 for the New York Yankee's uniform Lou Gehrig wore July 4, 1939, when he gave his "farewell speech."

- **Batting helmet:** $12,629 for Roberto Clemente's 1960s Pittsburgh Pirates batting helmet.
- **Bicycle:** $164,820 for an Otto "Diamond Frame" safety bicycle, with S-sprung tires; c. 1891.
- **Clemente signature baseball:** $9,609 for a baseball signed by Roberto Clemente in 1972.
- **Olympic torch:** $8,737 for the 1936 torch that carried the Olympic flame from Mt. Olympus in Greece to the games in Berlin (on the eve of World War II).
- **Souvenir sports pin:** $13,447 for a pinback button with the words "Boston Red Sox, American League 1915 Champions"; 2¼ in.

TOYS, DOLLS & GAMES

- **Britains Boy Scout display set:** $2,912 for a Britains Boy Scout display set—a two-tray, 44-piece set showing Boy Scouts engaged in various chores and activities.
- **East Kent Regiment soldiers:** $2,352 for a c. 1900 set of the East Kent Regiment soldiers in khaki service uniforms, in the original box.
- **Lionel 1912 Special locomotive:** $25,300 for a standard-gauge, brass, Lionel 1912 Special locomotive.
- **Lionel No. 101 trolley:** $25,300 for a standard-gauge, Lionel No. 101, summer trolley, painted blue, cream, and red, in the original box, c. 1910.
- **Robot toy:** $47,242 for a 15-inch, Machine Man robot toy, made by Masudaya c. 1958—one of the Gang of Five series, a battery-operated "bump-and-go," with lithographed tin plate, blue & silver details, green, translucent-plastic eyes, and amber, translucent-plastic, convex ear panels.
- **Soldier set:** $5,264 for a soldier set of British Army Infantry Officers, in the original box, c. 1940, by Britains Ltd.

A NOTE TO COLLECTORS

You already know that this is a great overall price guide for all sorts of antiques and collectibles. Each entry is current, every picture is new, all prices are accurate.

But in the collecting world, things change quickly. Important sales produce new record prices. Fakes appear. Rarities are discovered. To keep up with these developments, read *Kovels on Antiques and Collectibles*, a monthly newsletter with up-to-date information on the world of collecting. It is filled with color photographs, about forty to an issue. The newsletter reports prices, trends, auction results, Internet sales, and other pertinent, up-to-date news for collectors. For a free sample of *Kovels on Antiques and Collectibles*, fill out and mail the postage-paid postcard at the back of this book. We also have an informational Web site that gives pricing information and excerpts from our newsletter. Visit www.kovels.com to learn more.

KEEP READING—HOW TO USE THIS BOOK

There are a few rules for using this book. Each listing is arranged in the following manner: CATEGORY (such as Pressed Glass or Furniture), OBJECT (such as vase), DESCRIPTION (as much information as possible about size, age, color, and pattern). Some types of glass, pottery, and silver are exceptions to this rule. These are listed CATEGORY, PATTERN, OBJECT, DESCRIPTION. All items are presumed to be in good condition and undamaged, unless otherwise noted. If a maker's name is easily recognized, like Gustav Stickley, we try to include it near the beginning of the entry. If the maker is obscure, the name may be at the end. Because the descriptions are part of actual reports, we do not edit to make everything consistent in each entry. We try to edit enough to be sure that two items are not actually two descriptions of the same piece.

Several special categories were formed to make the most sensible listing possible. For instance, the Tool category includes ax, level, plane, slide rule, wrench, and the tools whose names you might not recognize, such as "adze." Many of the glass entries are in special categories: Glass-Art, Glass-Blown, Glass-Contemporary, Glass-Midcentury, and Glass-Venetian. Major glass factories are still listed under the factory names, and well-known types of glass, such as cut, pressed, Depression, Carnival, etc., can be found in their own categories. The silver listings are also a bit different. You will find silver flatware in either Silver Flatware Plated or Silver Flatware Sterling. You will also find a section for Silver Plate, which includes coffeepots, trays, and other plated pieces. Solid or sterling silver is listed by country, so look for Silver-American, Silver-English, etc. Silver jewelry is listed under jewelry. Pottery and porcelain are usually listed by factory name or item, but some are found in Art Pottery, Art Nouveau, Art Deco, Arts & Crafts, Dinnerware, Kitchen, Pottery, or Porcelain.

Sometimes we make arbitrary decisions based on the number of entries or interest in a subject. Fishing has its own category, but hunting is part of the larger category called Sports. We have eliminated all guns except toy types. It is not legal to sell weapons without a special license, and so guns are not part of the general antiques market. Airguns, BB guns, rocket guns, and others are listed in the Toy section. Several idiosyncrasies of style appear because the book is printed by computer. Everything is listed according to the computer alphabetizing system. This means words such as "Mt." are alphabetized as "M-T," not as "M-O-U-N-T." All numerals are before all letters; thus 2 comes before "A." A quick glance will make this clear, as it is consistent throughout the book.

We made several editorial decisions. A bowl is a "bowl" and not a "dish," unless it is a special dish, such as a pickle dish. A butter dish is a "butter." A salt dish is called a "salt" to differentiate it from a saltshaker. It is always "sugar and creamer," never "creamer and sugar." Political collectors often refer to "pinbacks," the round celluloid or tin pins that are decorated with candidates' names and faces. The word "button" is sometimes used in this book instead of the word "pinback." Of course, the word "button" is also used when referring to the fasteners used on clothing. Where one dimension is given, it is the height; or if the object is round, the dimension is the diameter. The height of a picture is listed before width. Glass is clear unless a color is indicated.

Every entry is listed alphabetically, but the problem of language remains. Some antiques terms, such as "Sheffield" or "Pratt," have two meanings. Be sure to read the paragraph headings to know the meaning used. All category headings are based on the language of the average person at an average show, and we use terms like "mud figures" even if not technically correct.

This book does *not* include price listings of fine-art paintings, antiquities, stamps, coins, or most types of books. *Big Little Books* and similar children's books *are* included. Comic books are *not* listed, but original comic art and cels *are* listed in their own categories.

All pictures in *Kovels' Antiques & Collectibles Price List* are listed with the prices asked by the seller. "Illus" (illustrated nearby) is part of the description if a picture is shown.

There have been misinformed comments about how this book is written. We *do* use the computer. It alphabetizes, ranges prices, sets type, and does other time-consuming jobs. Because of the computer, the book can be produced quickly. The last entries are added in June; the book is available in October. This is six months faster than would be possible any other way. But it is human help that finds prices and checks accuracy. We read everything at least three times, sometimes more. We edit from 80,000 entries to the 50,000 entries found here. We correct spelling, remove incorrect data, write category headings, and decide on new categories. We sometimes make errors. Information in the paragraphs is reviewed and updated each year. This year over thirty-three corrections and additions were made in the category headings.

Prices are reports from all parts of the United States and Canada (translated to U.S. dollars at the rate of $1.45 U.S. to $1 Canadian) between June 1999 and June 2000. Prices are from auctions, shops, and shows. Every price is checked for accuracy, but we are not responsible for errors.

We cannot answer your letters asking for specific price information. But please write if you have any requests for categories to be included in future editions or any corrections to information in the paragraphs or prices.

When you see us at the shows, stop and say hello. Don't be surprised if we ask for your suggestions for the next edition of *Kovels' Antiques & Collectibles Price List*. Or you can write us at P.O. Box 22200-K, Beachwood, Ohio 44122 or visit us at our Web site: www.kovels.com

RALPH & TERRY KOVEL
July 2000

ACKNOWLEDGMENTS

Special thanks should go to those who helped us with pictures and deeds: Allard Auctions, Inc.; Auctions Unlimited Inc.; Bill Bertoia Auctions; Bruce and Nicki Waasdorp; Buffalo Bay Auction Co.; Christie's; Cincinnati Art Galleries; Collectors Auction Services; Copake Auction; Cowan Pottery Museum Associates; Craftsman Auctions; Cyr Auction Company; David Rago Auctions, Inc.; DeFina Auctions; Dunbar Gallery; eWolfs.com; Fink's Off The Wall Auctions; Fontaine's Auction Gallery; Frank H. Boos Gallery; Garth's Auction, Inc.; Gary Metz's Muddy River Trading Co.; Gene Harris Antique Auction Center, Inc.; Glass-Works Auctions; Henry/Peirce Auctioneers; Jackson's Auctioneers & Appraisers; James D. Julia, Inc.; John Toomey Gallery; Lang's Sporting Collectibles, Inc.; Leland's Auctions; Los Angeles Modern Auctions; Lovely Things Antiques; McMasters; Michael Ivankovich Auction Co., Inc.; Neal Auction Company; New Orleans Auction Galleries, Inc.; Noel Barrett Antiques; Pacific Glass Auctions; Phillips; Phillips-Selkirk's; Randy Inman Auctions; Richard Opfer Auctioneering, Inc.; Robert C. Eldred Co., Inc.; Skinner, Inc.; Smith & Jones, Inc.; Sotheby's; Timeworn Treasures; Treadway Gallery, Inc.; Waddington's; William Doyle Galleries; and Wm. Morford. An extra thank-you for the special help given by Carmie Amata, Lee Markley, James Measell, and Ralph Meermans.

To the others in the antiques trade who knowlingly or unknowingly contributed to this book, we say "thank you": 20th Century Art & Design; A Squirrel's Nest; A.A. Antiques; Acorn Acres Antiques; Adamstown Antique Gallery; Alderfer Auction Company; Alexander Antiques; Alfred Cali; Alice & James Rose; American Carnival Glass; American Social History & Social Movements; Anderson Auction; Anderson's, Glass Dept.; Andre Ammelounx; Antique Advertising Auction; Antique Bottle & Glass Collector; Antique Doll Auction; Antique Jewelry Trojners; Antique Toy World; Antiques at O'Connors; Ark Antiques; AR's Scavenger Hunt Antiques & Collectibles; Arville Hornback; Ashley's Antiques & Interiors; Attenson's Coventry Antiques; Auction Team Köln; Autopia Advertising Auctions; B. Withey; Baker's International Antiques & Collectibles; Barbara Joyce Kaye; Barbara Rosen; Bedford on the Square; Be-hold, Larry Gottheim; Belfast Antiques & Books; Bertha Brown; Betty Stepp; Bill & Joan Lennon; Bill Smith; Bill Sweet; Bill Tanner; Billie Nelson Tyrrell; Bischoff Galleries; Blue & White Pottery Club; Bob Brady; Bob Jones; Bruno Matteo; C. E. Zambon; Carlton's Antique Toys; Carol Bakker; Carol Schulman; Carson/Bonnie Patterson; Cats Cradle Antiques; Cerebro; Charles E. Kirtley; Charles G. Richardson; Christopher Kenwood; Clarence & Betty Maier; Collectorholics; Continental Hobby House; Country Cousin Antiques; Crafts Auction; Crazyladycollectibles; Dan Leonard; David Campbell; Dee's Antiques; Dick Bowman; DJ's Antiques; Donald McKinsey; Dori Miles; Doug Brown; DuMouchelle's Art Galleries Co.; E & G Antiques; Earl Nydam; Early Adventure; East End Galleries; Eddie Hartwell; Eileen Josep; Erika Wilson; Evan Sommerfeld; Fern Bisel Peat; Flo-Blue Shoppe; Foundation Antiques; Frances Wilder; Freeman's; Gisela Antiques; Glen Campbell; Gloria Bodell; Gold Nugget Antiques; Grace Williams; Grandma's Attic; Green Valley Auctions, Inc.; Greg Manning Auctions, Inc.; Grey Flannel Auctions; Gus Kollitus; Helen & Bud Rarey; Helen Stemberg; Heritage Antique Maps; Hodge Podge Antiques; Hoosier Peddler; International Collectibles; Internet Antique Shop; J. R. Borchert; Jack Sullivan;

James McDonald; Jan-Tiques; Jennifer Sleeper; Jerry Stokes; Joel Goesch; John Rajpolt; Joyce Bee; Joyce Williams; June Greenwald Antiques; Ken Farmer Auctions & Appraisals; Ken Roberts; Kensington Antique Parlor; Keystone Toy Trader; Kinzua Country Antiques; Klaus Banke; L. H. Selman Ltd.; Lady A Antiques; Lazeski Antiques; Leann Delance; Leon Kaye; Leslie's Antique & Auctions; Linda J. Davey; Lloyd Bishop; Lynn Geyer's Advertising Auctions; M & L Toys; Manion's International Auction House, Inc.; Marie McClellan; Maritime Antiques & Auctions; Marsha's Antiques; Meg Carroll; Memories Galore; Mike Clum Inc. Auction Gallery; Mike Red Cloud; Miss Polly Peret; Necessaire & Auctions Unlimited Inc.; Nikel Enterprises, Inc.; Norm & Jan Thran; Norman C. Heckler & Company; Not For Kids Only, Inc.; Old Barn Auction; Old Storefront Antiques; Oldies but Goodies; P. C. Madison; Pascoe & Co., Inc.; Peter Vincent; Philip Norman; Pook & Pook, Inc.; Provenance; Publick House Antiques; R. G. Munn Auction; R. S. Goldberg; Red & Mary Ann Huston; Replacements, Ltd.; Rex Stark; Rhoda Curley; Richard A. Powell; Richard Antiques; Richard Commini; Richard Funk; Robert Hildreth; Roberta's Doll House; Roma & Dick Taylor; Ron Farley; Russ Cochran's Comic Art Auction; S. Burdette; Sandy Rosnick; Scott Carrasco; Scott Farrell; Serious Toy; Shannon Greenlee; Simmons and Company Auctioneers, Inc.; Slater's Americana; Sloan's Auction Galleries; Sophie Dryden; Southern Folk Pottery Collector's Society; St. Charles Gallery; Stanley Tessel; Steve & Cathy Sawchurk's Sales; Steve's Lost Land of Toys; Stitches In Time; Superior Galleries; Susan Levine; Susan Raisin; Sussex Antique Toy Shop; Swann Galleries, Inc.; Tarnan Blair Collector; Tea Leaf Club International; Team's Tiffany Treasures; Ted Kromer; Ted Poss; Temple's Antiques; The Finer Things; The Village Antiques; Theriault's; Therrie Sherwood; Three Centuries Antique Gallery; Tias Antiques & Collectibles; Tom Caniff; Tom Polansky; Tom Sage, Jr.; Tom Snook; Trader Fred's Toys of Yore; Truly Snooty Antiques; Turn of the Century Antiques; Utah Mouse Collector; Vicki Ticen; Wicker's Antiques; Win Burrell; Winter Associates; Woody Auction; Yankee Tools & Collectables; Yard's Antiques; Yesterdays South, Inc.; and York Town Auction Inc.

No one can write a price list like Kovels without help from many people. They comment, check facts, review artwork, solve computer problems, and much more. This is what makes an accurate book that's published on time every year. Pam Stinson-Bell of Crown Publishers read almost every word and every correction. She also supervised the staff who had to put the pieces together to get the color insert, cover, and main copy as perfect as possible. Chip Gibson, Laura Paczosa, Karen Minster, Liz Matthews, and John Sharp of Crown did more than their jobs. Merri Ann Morrell and Patricia Stenbeck of Precision Graphics unraveled computer mysteries to get the information to behave and form proper printed pages. Our daily companions at work—Kitty Busher, Grace DeFrancisco, Marcia Goldberg, Harriet Goldner, Evelyn Hayes, Katie Karrick, Karen Kneisley, Eleanore Melzak, Nancy Saada, Cherrie Smrekar, Edie Smrekar, Virginia Warner, and Ann Wochner—did their usual overtime work in writing and proofing to produce another good year for the *Kovels' Antiques and Collectibles Price List*. Benjamin Margalit took all the color photographs and even learned how to use new digital equipment. But Gay Hunter once again was the "mother of the book." She kept us all on schedule, read copy over and over again, solved problems, ran interference between departments, and watched the details. To all, thank you. There would be no book without you.

A. WALTER made pate-de-verre glass under contract at the Daum glassworks from 1908 to 1914. He started his own firm in Nancy, France, in 1919. Pieces made before 1914 are signed *Daum, Nancy* with a cross. After 1919 the signature is *A. Walter Nancy.*

Bowl, Yellow Flowers, Flanked By Green Leaves, Spotted Brown Salamander, 4 In.	3450.00
Figurine, Chickadee, Standing On Naturalistic Base, Cobalt Glass, 4 In.	1725.00
Vase, Inverted Bell Form, Maroon Stylized Flowers, Amber, Tan, Disk Foot, 4 In.	1495.00
Vase, Stylized Blue Trees, Yellow Flowers, Green, Bulbous, AW, 6 x 3 In.	935.00
Vase, Stylized Green Tree, Red Flowers, Yellow Ground, AW, 8 1/4 x 3 1/2 In.	990.00

ABC plates, or children's alphabet plates, were most popular from 1780 to 1860, but are still being made. The letters on the plate were meant as teaching aids for children learning to read. The plates were made of pottery, porcelain, metal, or glass. Mugs and other items were also made with alphabet decorations.

Bowl, Underplate, Nursery Rhymes, Sterling Silver, International, 4 & 6 In.	700.00
Loving Cup, The Enchanted Garden, Elf, Owls, Porcelain, 2 Handles, England	20.00
Mug, For A Dear Boy, Staffordshire, 2 1/4 In.	195.00
Plate, Capitol At Washington, D.C., 6 1/2 In.	243.00
Plate, Cat & Fiddle, Tin, 9 In.	35.00 to 85.00
Plate, Dog, 6 1/2 In.	110.00
Plate, Don't You Wish You May Get It, Monkey Taunting Dog, J & G Meakin, 7 1/4 In.	95.00
Plate, Franklin Proverb, 3 Removes Are As Bad As Fire, J & G Meakin, 7 1/4 In.	110.00
Plate, Franklin Proverb, Now I Have A Sheep & A Cow, Staffordshire, 1830	175.00
Plate, Girl Playing Piano, c.1860	25.00
Plate, Girl With Bee On Cheek, Pressed Glass, 6 1/2 In.	125.00
Plate, Harry Is Baiting His Line, For To Fish He Doth Incline, Staffordshire, 1853, 6 In.	175.00
Plate, Our Donkey And Foal, Enameled, Blue, Green, Red, Ocher, Black Transfer, 6 In.	145.00
Plate, Sancho Panza, Frosted, 6 In.	85.00
Plate, Swing Swong, Elsmore & Son, 8 1/8 In.	115.00
Plate, Wandering Pie, Birds, Staffordshire, Late 1800s	135.00 to 185.00
Plate, Who Killed Cock Robin?, Tin, 8 In.	250.00

ABINGDON POTTERY was established in 1908 by Raymond E. Bidwell as the Abingdon Sanitary Manufacturing Company. The company started making art pottery in 1934. The factory ceased production of art pottery in 1950.

Bowl, Console, Blue Leaf, Marked	25.00
Bowl, Scroll, c.1941, 3 3/4 x 14 1/2 In.	25.00
Bowl, Yellow, Handle, Marked, 3 3/4 x 14 In.	45.00
Cookie Jar, Bo Peep	285.00
Cookie Jar, Jack In The Box	500.00
Cookie Jar, Little Old Lady	500.00
Dish, Shell, Pink, 7 x 10 In.	45.00
Planter, Fan Shape Ribbon, Marked, 4 1/2 x 8 In.	45.00
Vase, 2 Handles, Blue, c.1948, 9 1/4 In.	75.00
Vase, Blue, c.1950, 10 5/8 In.	75.00
Vase, Cornucopia, Double, Pink	45.00
Vase, Fan, Salmon Color, Marked, 9 In.	25.00
Vase, Medium White Swirl, c.1950, 9 In.	50.00
Vase, Rose Color, Handles, Marked, 5 1/2 In.	50.00
Vase, Salmon, White Interior, Marked, 5 x 11 In.	35.00
Vase, Swirl, Blue, c.1940, 10 5/8 In.	75.00
Vase, Wedgwood Blue, 2 Handles, c.1939, 9 3/4 In.	58.00
Vase, White Swirl, Wide Top, c.1940, 9 In.	50.00

ADAMS china was made by William Adams and Sons of Staffordshire, England. The firm was founded in 1769 and became part of the Wedgwood Group in 1966. The name "Adams" appeared on various items through 1998. All types of tablewares and useful wares were made. Other pieces of Adams will be found listed under Flow Blue and Tea Leaf Ironstone.

Biscuit Jar, Jasper Dip, Blue, White Relief, Fox Hunting Scene, Handle, Cover, 6 1/2 In.	275.00

Bowl, Oriental Scene, Flow Blue, 10 1/8 In. 115.00
Cup & Saucer, Children & House, Blue, Handleless 120.00
Cup & Saucer, Children, Geese & Dog, Blue, Handleless 210.00
Cup & Saucer, Spatterware, Rose 330.00
Dish, Serving, Kyber, Ironstone, Flow Blue, 7 1/2 In. 165.00
Pitcher, Milk, Rose Type, Cornflowers, 8 1/2 In. 275.00
Plate, Bologna, Red Transfer, Marked, 9 1/2 In., Pair 137.00
Plate, Romantic Scene Of Castle, Bridge, Rowing Boat, Figures On Riverbank, 1825 . . . . 121.00
Plate, Rose, George Jones & Sons, 6 7/8 In., 3 Piece 250.00
Platter, Boy On Pony, Sheep, Grapevine & Fruit Border, 11 1/2 x 9 3/4 In. 605.00
Platter, Embossed & Cobalt Blue Feather Edge Design, 15 1/2 In. 40.00
Platter, Fairy Villas, Flow Blue, c.1891, 13 x 15 3/4 In. 495.00
Platter, Lyme Castle Kent, Floral Border, Blue, 16 1/2 x 21 1/4 In. 1056.00
Soup, Dish, Headwaters Of The Juniata, 10 1/2 In. 165.00
Teapot, Shells In Reserves, Blue, Signed, 8 1/2 In. 145.00
Vase, Pedestal, Jasper Dip, Blue, Classical & Leaf Relief, Impressed Mark, 13 3/4 In. 748.00
Vase, Pierced Cover, Dark Blue Jasperware, Acanthus & Flower Relief, c.1800, 8 3/8 In. . . 174.00
Wall Pocket, Jasper Ware, Blue, Cornucopia, White Classical Relief, Mark, 11 1/4 In. . . . 115.00

ADVERTISING containers and products sold in the old country store are
now all collectibles. These stores, with the crackers in a barrel and a
potbellied stove, are a symbol of an earlier, less hectic time. Listed
here are many of the advertising items. Other similar pieces may be
found under the product name, such as Planters Peanuts. We have tried
to list items in the logical places, so large store fixtures will be found
under the Architectural category, enameled tin dishes under Graniteware, paper items in the Paper category, etc. Store fixtures, cases, and
other items that have no advertising as part of the decoration are listed
in the Store category.

Ad, Chesterfield Cigarette, Bobby Riggs, Athletes, Matted, 1947, 7 x 10 In. 35.00
Apron, Reddy Kilowatt 10.00
Ashtray, Bear & Forbear, 2 Little Bears For Every Home, Pressed Chalk, 4 x 3 In. 80.00
Ashtray, Coors, Embossed Butter, Malted Milk, Beer 65.00
Ashtray, Crane Co. Casting Center, Rogers, Ark., Pig Features, 8 x 6 1/2 In. 60.00
Ashtray, Drink Dr Pepper, Good For Life, 1940, 8 1/2 In. 77.00
Ashtray, Firestone, Glass With Replica Tire 15.00
Ashtray, Goodrich Silverstone Tire, Green Glass Insert 45.00
Ashtray, Kraft Foods, Horse-Drawn Dairy Wagon, Gold Anniversary, 1953, 3 5/8 In. 1.00
Ashtray, Mack Truck, Bulldog, Chrome, Design Patent 87931, 7 x 4 In. 39.00
Ashtray, Smokey Bear, Aluminum, Round, 4 In., 4 Pieces 20.00
Ashtray, Streamline Bicycle, Daton, Speed Model, Chrome Tank, 1937 . . . . 3190.00
Ashtray, Whirlpool, Aluminum, October 1954, 11 In. 10.00
Automatic Cashier, Brandt, In Working Order 5.50
Bag, Paper, Stovene Polishing Mitten, Save Your Hands!, Portsmouth, N.H., 8 In. 12.00
Bag Rack, Thirsty Just Whistle, Soda, Tin, 37 x 16 1/2 In. 690.00
Banner, Alaskan Brewing Co., Vinyl, 2 x 6 Ft. 12.00
Banner, Baby Octopus, Smallest In World, Circus, Canvas, 6 Ft. x 11 Ft. 6 In. 2500.00
Banner, Ballantine Ale & Beer National Tavern Month, Satin, 1960s, 12 x 19 In. 15.00
Banner, Blue Coral Treatment, Salute To Quality!, Blue Ground, 34 1/2 In. 105.00
Banner, Chesterfield, Cigarette Pack On Front, Red, Black & Yellow, 42 x 19 In. 30.00
Banner, Dixie Minstrel Show, Black Face, Canvas, 4 x 6 Ft. 750.00
Banner, Dr Pepper, The Price Remains The Same To Us, 5 Cent, 8 x 22 In. 154.00
Banner, Drink Dr Pepper, Frosty, Man, Frosty!, Dog, 1950, 16 x 22 In. 357.00
Banner, Elwin Strong, Smashing Play, Painted, Red Ground, 1930, 50 x 86 In. 245.00
Banner, Esso Canvas, World's First Choice, Red Lettering, Black Ground, 36 In. 130.00
Banner, Frosty, Man Frosty!, Dr Pepper, Dogs, Friendly Pepper-Upper, 15 x 25 In. 192.00
Banner, Keep Your Motor Full Powered, Lady Driving Red Car, Black, 36 In. 365.00
Banner, Levi's, Dance Tonight, Multicolored Pastel, Corrugated, 1960s, 93 x 34 In. 500.00
Banner, Miller High Life Beer, Image Of Miller Girl, 19 1/2 x 15 1/2 In. 825.00
Banner, Space Saving, No Return, Drink Dr Pepper In Cans, Little Girl, 1960, 22 In. 33.00
Banner, Tomorrow's Fruit Depends On Today's Planting At Cultivation, 1930, 33 In. 247.00
Banner, Tony Lama Boots & Belts, El Paso, Texas, Gray Suede, 1960s, 45 In. 270.00
Banner, Valley Forge Beer, Satin, 1950s, 11 x 13 1/4 In. 22.00

Banner, We Redeem Coupons, Dr Pepper Good For Life, 14 x 15 In. 176.00
Banner, Winchester Ammo, Cowboy, The Linds, Yellow, Black, 49 x 57 In. 226.00
Banner, Wrangler Jeans, Worn By Champion Cowboys, Denim, 70 x 38 In. 165.00
Barrel, National Biscuit Co., Paper Lithograph, Cardboard, 8 In. 39.00
Barrel Cover, Holland Gin, Steamship Picture, Brass, Felt Backing, 18 In. Diam. 165.00
Bat, Baseball, Red Goose Shoes, Wooden, Stamped Logo, 32 In. 50.00
Bean Pot, Spirit Of '76, Boston The Home Of The Bean, Glazed Stoneware, 7 In. 154.00
Beer Scraper, Whalebone 65.00
Bench, Hamilton Brown Shoe Co., Wooden, 1920s, 6 Ft. 225.00
Bench, Poll-Parrot Shoes, Seat Cutouts, Horse, Donkey, Buffalo, Dog, 23 x 35 x 96 In. ... 2310.00
Bill Hook, Townsend West Cream Top Milk, Celluloid, 2 x 2 3/4 In. 44.00
Bin, Board Of Trade Tobacco, Stuart, Chapin & Co., Hinged Lid, Wooden, 10 In. 297.00
Bin, Cover, Tiger Chewing Tobacco, Blue, Black, Gold Lettering, 6 x 8 x 11 In. 42.00
Bin, E. Maginn's Excelsior Crackers, Pittsburgh, 2 Sides Glass, Tin, 11 1/4 In. 550.00
Bin, Ginger, Counter, Hinged Lid, Tin Lithograph, 9 In. 55.00
Bin, Ginger, Young Girl, Flowers, Top Opening Lid, Tin Lithograph, 9 In. 413.00
Bin, Gunpowder Tea, Store Counter, Hinged Lid, Tin Lithograph, 10 In. 99.00
Bin, Lorillard's Rose Leaf Tobacco, Cardboard, Wood Top & Bottom, 14 In. 231.00
Bin, Princess Salted Peanuts, Slip Lid, Tin Lithograph, 9 1/2 In. 330.00
Bin, Rose Leaf, Lithograph, Hinged Glass Lid, Round Counter, 8 1/2 In. 143.00
Bin, Sure Shot, Tobacco Store, Hinged Lid, Tin Lithograph, 15 1/4 In. 523.00
Bin, Sweet Burley Tobacco, Hinged Lid, Tin Lithograph, 11 1/4 In. 176.00
Bin, Sweet Cuba Fine Cut, Slant Front, 8 x 9 In. .... 195.00 to 500.00
Bin, Sweet Mist Tobacco, Cardboard, Hinged Lid, 11 In. 176.00
Bin, Thalhimers, Coffee, Tin Lithograph, Embossed, Slide Opening, 20 3/4 In. 468.00
Bin, Try Our Spices, 6 Labeled Bins, Removable Lids, Tin Lithograph, 33 In. 1595.00
Blanket, United Air Lines, Wool, Tan, Dark Brown Letters, 54 x 42 In. 31.00
Blotter, At 10, 2 & 4, Dr Pepper, Dark Green Ground, 1940, 9 1/2 In. 264.00
Blotter, Barney Oldfield, If Barney Trusts Them You Can, Green, Black, 3 x 6 In. 110.00
Blotter, Blue Coal, Lancaster, Pa., Woman On Phone, Unused, 1930s, 4 x 9 In. 6.00
Blotter, Firestone, Gum-Dipped Motorcycle Tires, 3 1/8 x 6 In. 110.00
Blotter, Gordon Keith Studio, Oakland, Cal., Unused, 4 x 9 In. 11.00
Blotter, Green River Whiskey Blots Out All Your Troubles, Man, Horse, Unused, 1899 .. 28.00
Blotter, Howards Sales Co., Belly Dancer, Earl Moran, Used, 1952 .... 7.50
Blotter, Miller's Leather Store, Waverly, Iowa, 1930s, 3 1/8 x 6 In. 4.00
Blotter, Pfaltzgraff Pottery Co., 12-Gal. Stoneware Crock 28.00
Blotter, Reichert Milling Co., Freeburg, Ill., Young Children, 1910, 3 x 6 In. 7.00
Blotter, Sun-Maid Nectars, Grapes & Product Picture, 3 1/2 x 5 3/4 In. 4.00
Blotter, Tucker Shoe Repair, Moultrie, Ga., Unused, 1930s, 3 x 5 In. 4.00
Blotter, Wampole's Preparation .... 5.00 to 7.00
Books may be included in the Paper category.
Booklet, Goes Art Advertising Blotters, Salesman's Sample, 1920s, 46 Pages 50.00
Booklet, Jell-O Girl Entertains, Rose O'Neill Pictures, 5 1/4 x 6 7/8 In. 35.00
Bookmark, Buckwalter Stove, Die Cut Teddy Bear, Stove On Back, Celluloid, 3 In. 110.00
Bookmark, Tapan Shoe Mfg. Co., Die Cut Feet, Celluloid, 3 In. 22.00
Bootjack, Lee Riders, Wooden, Black Leather Trim, 12 In. .... 20.00 to 32.00
Bottles are listed in their own category.
Bottle Openers are listed in their own category.
Bowl, Cereal, Wheaties, Breakfast Of Champions, Milk Glass, 1940s 48.00
Box, see also Box category.
Box, Aseptone Tablets, 2 Vials 7.50
Box, Battery Additive, Lee Petty Picture, Box, 1960s, 24 Piece 35.00
Box, Brantford Starch, Trunk, Dome Top, Wooden, Lithographed Paper Cover, 10 In. 135.00
Box, Candy, Heide's Colored Coons, c.1910, 10 1/4 x 6 3/4 x 1 3/4 In. 305.00
Box, Candy, Loft, Cardboard Hat Form, Textured Paper, Hatband Label, 13 In. 55.00
Box, Cash, Tutti-Frutti Gum, Adams & Sons Premium, Tin, 8 1/2 x 12 1/2 In. 40.00
Box, Cereal, Garden Rolled Oats, John Price & Co., Philadelphia, Pa., 1 Lb. 205.00
Box, Cereal, Leadway Quick Cooking Rolled Oats, Chicago, Ill., 3 Lbs. 28.00
Box, Cereal, Mamma's Choice Rolled Oats, Samuel Mahon Company, 1 Lb. 225.00
Box, Cereal, Morning Glory Quick Oats, Canister Form, 8 3/4 In. 77.00
Box, Cereal, Red Bird Quick Cooking Rolled Oats, Highland Grocery Co., 3 Lbs. 175.00
Box, Cereal, Wheaties, Cincinnati Reds, World Series Champions, 1990, 18 Oz. 25.00
Box, Cigar, Al Aimmons For Quality Cigar, 3 x 5 1/2 x 9 In. 445.00

Box, Cigar, College Days, Wooden, c.1890, 25 Count 66.00
Box, Cigar, Early Catch, Angler Standing In Boat Picture, Wooden, Paper Cover 55.00
Box, Cigar, King Of The Turf, Wooden, Liner, c.1890, 100 Count 77.00
Box, Cigar, Mohawk Chief, Wooden, c.1930s, 50 Count 72.00
Box, Cigar, Yellow Cab Sweets, Wooden, 8 1/2 x 5 1/4 x 2 1/2 In. 205.00
Box, Cigarette, Camel Cigarettes, For More Pure Pleasure, Blue, 1950, 11 x 3 In. 42.00
Box, Cigarette, Camel, Merry Christmas, Red, White Camel, Gold Foil, 1950 .... 40.00
Box, Cigarette, Chesterfield, Image Of Alexander Twins, Wooden Frame, 24 x 30 In. 39.00
Box, Cigarette, Clown Cigarettes, Multicolored Graphics, 1930s 85.00
Box, Cigarette, Death Cigarettes, Black, White, Empty Carton, 11 x 3 x 5 x 2 In. 26.00
Box, Cigarette, Hit Parade Cigarettes, Red, White, Gold, 10 1/4 x 3 1/2 x 2 In. 47.00
Box, Cigarette, Lucky Strike, Merry Christmas, White, Red, Green, 11 x 3 x 2 In. 40.00
Box, Cigarette, Pall Mall, Merry Christmas & Santa Claus Graphics 50.00
Box, Cigarette, Richfield Oil Co., Copper Over Chalkware, 1930s 675.00
Box, Cigarette, Tire Cover, Vinyl, Joe Camel In A Red Jeep In Desert, 28 In. 28.00
Box, Cigarette, Turkey Red Cigarettes, Woman Wearing Fez, 1910, 3 x 2 x 1/4 In. 500.00
Box, Cigarette, Walnut Mild Aromatic, Quality Since 1856 .... 45.00
Box, Clark's Spool Thread, Blind Man's Bluff, Wooden, c.1920, 4 1/2 x 3 1/4 In. 94.00
Box, Collar, Fitted Cover, E. Stone New York, Cardboard, Printed, 1900s, 13 x 5 In. 575.00
Box, Counter, Nabisco, Hinged Cover 28.00
Box, Display, Bear Brand, Bear & Children, 1933, Large 32.00
Box, Display, Goudey Indian Gum, 1 Cent, Indian Picture, 1933, 6 x 9 3/4 In. 1440.00
Box, Dr. J.B. Lynas Glycerine & Tar Soap, 1902, Unfolded 4.00
Box, Duryeas' Satin Gloss Starch, Paper Label, 9 1/2 x 6 1/2 In. 68.00
Box, Evening In Paris Powder, Cardboard, Peach Tan, 2 1/4 In. 10.00
Box, Fatima Cigarette, Nickel Silver, Arts & Crafts, Felt Lining 65.00
Box, Fun-To-Wash Washing Powder, Mammy Picture, 7 1/2 In. 55.00
Box, Goblin Soap, Cardboard, Contents, 2 1/2 x 1 1/2 x 4 In. 44.00
Box, Gold Dust Washing Powder, Contents, Sample 38.00
Box, Gum, Wrigley's Spearmint Gum, Unopened 20 Pack, 1950, 9 1/2 In. 88.00
Box, Hoover Electric Cleaner, Fabric Handle, NRA Eagle Label, 1930s, 9 x 14 In. 20.00
Box, Ivins Biscuit, Lithograph Paper, Dovetailed, Wooden, 21 1/4 In. 44.00
Box, Ivory Snow Detergent, 1st Time Baby Pictured, 1960s, Sample Size 30.00
Box, Jacquot & Co. Blacking, Dovetailed, Wooden, Litho Paper Labels, 8 3/4 In. 44.00
Box, Java Orange Pekoe Tea, Oriental Girl, 1/2 Lb. 4.00
Box, Jonteel Powder, Cardboard, Flesh, 3 1/4 In. 30.00
Box, Kennedy's Medical Discovery & Sure Cure, Wooden, 11 3/4 x 12 1/2 In. 40.00
Box, Kraft Cheese, Wooden 20.00
Box, Log Cabin Syrup, Cardboard, Shipping, c.1918, 16 1/2 x 11 x 10 1/2 In. 185.00
Box, McGregor Sportswear, Red & Green Plaid, Unicorns, 14 3/4 x 9 x 3 In. 20.00
Box, Morning Dew Toilet Soap, Paper Lithographed Labels, Wooden, 14 1/2 In. 132.00
Box, Pencil, Red Goose, School Scene, Tin 45.00
Box, Pencil, Star Brand Shoes, Paper On Wood, Tin End Cap, 11 1/2 In. 77.00
Box, Pepsin Tolu Fruit Gum, Cardboard, Glass Insert, Paper Litho Label, 8 1/2 In. 121.00
Box, Pointer Smokeless Powder Loaded Shells, Hunter & Dog, 4 In. 250.00
Box, Puritan Candy Figs, Weeks Brothers Company, Label, Round 475.00
Box, Robin Hood Shot Shell, Swanton, Vermont, 4 1/4 x 4 1/4 In. 1045.00
Box, Schoenhut Humpty-Dumpty Circus, Wooden Sides, Cardboard Top & Bottom 350.00
Box, Seed, Flower, Oak, Dovetailed Corners, Hinged Lid, Labels, Mandeville, 15 In. 75.00
Box, Stag Smoking Tobacco, Sunset, Moose, Countertop, Box, 13 x 4 x 17 In. 440.00
Box, Superior Condition Powders, Steer Head, Contents, c.1900, 3 1/2 x 7 In. 88.00
Box, Tut Fleurs Face Powder, Red & Black, Contents, 3 1/2 x 1 1/2 In. 30.00
Box, Vampire Shampoo, Witol's, Powder Type, Cardboard, 2 1/4 x 2 In. 10.00
Box, Webster's Seeds, Wooden, Paper Label, 8 3/4 x 6 x 3 In. 55.00
Box, William's Root Beer Extract, Dovetailed, Slide Lid, Paper Label, 7 1/2 In. 143.00
Bridge Scorer, Peter Doelger Bottled Beer, Celluloid, 2 Sides 44.00
Broadside, Smith's Egg & Health Producer, Have You Seen It, Hens, 22 x 14 In. 39.00
Broadside, Winchester, Topperweins, Western Ammunition & Guns, 12 x 9 In. 113.00
Brochure, McCormick Deering Threshers, Pictures, 1920s-1930s, 18 Pages 22.00
Broom Holder, Baker's Coconut, Wall Mount, Tin Lithograph, 2 1/2 x 6 1/4 In. 155.00
Brush, Shoe, Columbia Brewing, 1940s, 2 1/4 x 7 3/4 In. 60.00
Bucket, Bucket Brand Syrup, Tin Lithograph, No Lid, 1929, 4 1/4 In. 150.00
Bucket, Gold Stenciled Label, Davies Welsh Candy In Wreath, Tin, 3 3/4 In. 92.00

Cabinet, Beldings Silk, 1 Door, Revolving Thread Display, 3 Drawers, 61 1/2 In. 862.00
Cabinet, Choice Perfumery, Reverse Painting, Wooden, 4 Glass Shelves, 30 x 32 In. 495.00
Cabinet, Diamond Dyes, Children With Balloon, Tin Lithograph, 24 1/2 In. 1045.00
Cabinet, Diamond Dyes, Evolution Of A Woman ....1375.00 to 1550.00
Cabinet, Diamond Dyes, Governess, Tin Lithograph, 30 x 23 x 9 1/2 In. ....935.00 to 1705.00
Cabinet, Diamond Dyes, Washer Woman, Tin Lithograph Insert, Single Door, 30 In. 1485.00
Cabinet, Dr. A.C. Daniels Dog & Cat Remedies, Tin 2800.00
Cabinet, Dr. Lesure's Remedies, Tin Lithograph On Front Opening, 27 In. 3410.00
Cabinet, Elgin Watches, Front Opening, Reverse On Glass, Drawers Inside, 27 In. 990.00
Cabinet, Frank Tea & Spice, 5 Stenciled Drawers, Wooden, 26 In. 1980.00
Cabinet, Gem Damaskeen Blades, Tin Lithograph, Man Holding Child, Display 85.00
Cabinet, Humphrey's Remedics, Printed Tin Panel, 34 Rear Drawers, 27 3/4 x 22 In. 522.00
Cabinet, Humphrey's Specifics, Front & Back Lists Ailments, Tin, 17 3/4 In. 1725.00
Cabinet, Keen Kutter Knives, Counter Display, Wooden, Glass Front, 16 x 25 x 58 In. ... 1150.00
Cabinet, Needle, Milward's, Reverse On Glass, 2 Drawers, 13 In. 300.00
Cabinet, New Peerless Dye, Labeled Slots, Wooden, Paper Litho Labels, 20 1/4 In. 440.00
Cabinet, Putnam Dye, Tin, Original Packets Of Dye, 14 3/4 x 19 In. 137.00
Cabinet, Sauer's, Etched Glass, Wooden, Hinged Rear Door, 3 Shelves, 28 1/2 In. 550.00
Cabinet, Sergeant's Dog Medicine, Tin Lithograph, 1940, 7 x 12 x 14 In. 635.00
Cabinet, Spool, Brainerd & Armstrong, Carving, Mirror, 7 Drawers, Wooden, 24 In...... 1045.00
Cabinet, Spool, Brooks, Oak Front, Solid Panel Back, 25 In. 795.00
Cabinet, Spool, Carlile's, Mahogany, 2 Drawer, Decals, 21 3/4 In. 1073.00
Cabinet, Spool, Clark's, Slant Front, Oak, 4 Drawers, 1900, 14 1/2 In. 310.00
Cabinet, Spool, Corticelli, 8 Drawers, Walnut 750.00
Cabinet, Spool, George Clark Spool Co., 6 Drawers, Countertop, 24 x 16 In. 455.00
Cabinet, Spool, J. & P. Coats, Walnut, 6 Glass Insert Drawers, Refinished 1175.00
Cabinet, Spool, J.N. Leonard's Silk, Northampton, Ma., Walnut, 9 Drawers, 36 In. 4400.00
Cabinet, Spool, John Leonard's Silk & Twist, 18 Drawers, Glass Front, 36 x 82 In. 1870.00
Cabinet, Spool, John N. Leopards Silk & Twist, 36 Glass Front Drawers, 82 In. 1870.00
Cabinet, Spool, Merrick's, 4 Drawers, Decals, Wooden, 30 1/4 In. 413.00
Cabinet, Spool, Williamantic, 2 Drawers, Letters, Brass Scrolled Pulls 330.00
Cabinet, Spool, Williamantic, 4 Drawers, Panel Inserts Sides & Back, 14 1/2 In. 1210.00
Calendars are listed in their own category.
Calendar Holder, Dr Pepper, Aluminum, Plastic, Red Numbers, 1950, 8 1/2 In. 88.00
Calendar Holder, Dr Pepper, Aluminum, Plastic, Red Numbers, 6 1/2 In. 44.00
Can, Betty Zane Dwarf White Popcorn, Marion, Oh., Contents, Unopened, 10 Oz. 66.00
Can, Crispaco, Original Lid, Red Ground, 10 Lb. 247.00
Can, Dad's Root Beer, Orange Ground, 1950, 7 1/2 x 8 In. 154.00
Can, Donald Duck Pop Corn, Carnavon, Ia., Contents, Unopened, 10 Oz. 305.00
Can, Engine Lighter Fluid, Red, Black, White Lettering, 4 1/2 In. 20.00
Can, Giant Salted Peanuts, Red Ground, 10 Lb. 154.00
Can, Gilmore Lion Head Motor Oil, Red, White & Yellow, Lion Logo, 1 Qt. 210.00
Can, Gloria Jean Golden Mushroom Pop Corn, Paper Label, Contents, 10 Oz. 55.00
Can, Grady's Polish, Black Image, Paper Label, 3 1/2 In. 28.00
Can, Johnson's Powder Wax, For Dancing Floors, Tin, 5 5/8 In. 20.00
Can, Norva Peanut Butter, Black Lettering, Handle, Norfolk, Va., 1 Lb. 86.00
Can, Ronsonol Lighter Fluid, Yellow, Blue, Tin, 5 1/2 In. 21.00
Can Opener, Schlitz, Beer Can Shape, Steel, 1 3/4 In., Pair 23.00
Candy Dish, Trans World Airlines, Scalloped, Silver Plated, 1950s-1960s, 9 In. 66.00
Canisters, see introductory paragraph to Tins in this category.
Cap, Cork N Seal, Acme Beer, San Francisco, Ca., 1930s 14.00
Cap, Cork N Seal, Blitz Weinhard Beer, Portland, Or., 1940s 12.00
Cards are listed in the Card category as card, advertising.
Carrier, Can, Blatz Beer, 6-Pack, 1950s 20.00
Carrier, Dr Pepper, 12-Pack, Aluminum, 1940 .... 495.00
Carrier, Dr Pepper, 24-Pack, Cardboard Stripes, 1947 .... 100.00
Carrier, Dr Pepper, 24-Pack, Green, White Stripes, Cardboard, 1952 .... 154.00
Carton, Camel Cigarettes, 1940s, Empty, 11 In. 35.00
Carton, Chesterfield, Beautiful Woman With Many Cartons In Arms, 1940s 62.00
Carton, Lucky Strikes, Red Circle On Green, Metallic, 1940s 80.00
Carton, Lucky Strikes, Red Flower On Green, Metallic, 1940s 60.00
Case, Blough Remedies, Decal, Mirrored Sliding Rear Doors, Glass, Oak, 14 1/2 In. 385.00
Case, Eversharp Pen, Reverse Painted On Glass, Felt Lining, Wooden, 24 1/4 In. 121.00

Case, Great Scot Mountain Lake Country Bartletts, Wooden, 1940s, 19 x 9 In. 31.00
Case, Rex-Roy Cigars, Tin Lithograph Marquee, Wood & Glass, 5 x 9 In. 27.00
Chair, Duke's Cameo Cigarettes, Wood, Stenciling 2 Sides, Paper Litho, 30 In. 132.00
Chair, Piedmont The Virginia Cigarette, Folding, Wood & Metal, 30 1/2 In. 85.00
Chalkboard, Red Goose Shoes, Cardboard, 20 In. 88.00
Change Receiver, see also Tip Tray in this category.
Change Receiver, Baby Ruth Gum, Glass, Reverse Painted, 4 1/2 x 2 x 6 In. 150.00
Change Receiver, Boston Herald, Boy Running With Paper, 8 1/2 In. 66.00
Change Receiver, Broadway Brewing Co., Pure Beers, Red Ground, 9 1/4 In. 71.00
Change Receiver, Clark's Teaberry Gum, Glass, Reverse Decal, 9 1/2 x 2 x 6 In. 330.00
Change Receiver, Clysmic Table Water, 8 1/2 In. 220.00
Change Receiver, Cur-Ray Tampa Cigars, Reverse On Glass, 6 In. 170.00
Change Receiver, Drink Dr Pepper, King Of Beverages, 1915, 6 In. 3267.00
Change Receiver, Eversweet Deodorant, Courtesan In Middle, 9 1/4 In. 577.00
Change Receiver, Fairy Soap, Child Sitting In Middle, 9 In. 110.00
Change Receiver, Fry's Chocolate, Humorous Image Of Child, Glass, Label, 7 3/4 In. ... 154.00
Change Receiver, King's Puremalt With Nurse, Nursing Carrying Tray, 8 1/2 In. 77.00
Change Receiver, Universal Victor Havana Cigars, Reverse On Glass, 6 1/2 In. 165.00
Change Receiver, White Rock Table Water, Square, 7 In. 55.00
Change Receiver, White Rock Table Water, World's Best Table Water, 8 1/4 In. 77.00
Change Receiver, Whitehouse Ginger Ale, Purity Guaranteed, Red Rim, 9 3/4 In. 88.00
Child Seat, Red Goose Shoes, Black Saddle, Red, Orange, Tan, Fiberglass, 32 In. 523.00
Cigar Cutter, Brass, Key Wind, Erie Specialty Co., Pat. Feb. 19, 1888, 6 1/2 x 5 In. 115.00
Cigar Cutter, Brass, Ship's Telegraph Center, With Ashtray Base 330.00
Cigar Cutter, Dona Marina, Mexican Cigar, Clockwork, Mechanism, 3 1/4 In. 325.00
Cigar Cutter, Hermann Cigars, Clockwork Mechanism, 3 1/2 In. 450.00
Cigar Cutter, Home Run, Reverse Painted Glass, H.F. Kohler Pipe Mfg., 8 x 6 In. 1840.00
Cigar Cutter, J.U. Divelbiss, Clockwork Mechanism, c.1889 .... 450.00
Cigar Cutter, Lillian Russell Cigar 5 Cents, Cast Metal, 8 1/2 x 6 3/4 In. 315.00
Cigar Cutter, Parrot Shape, Brass Wings, Raise Head Up & Down, 11 In. 350.00
Cigar Cutter, Schneck, Cigars Of Quality Maker, Tabletop, 7 1/2 In. 1300.00
Cigar Cutter, Smoke Country Gentleman, 5 Cent, 3 In. 150.00
Cigarette Papers, Pyramid Brand, Egyptian Design, 50 Sheets 5.00
Cigarette Silk, University Of Michigan, Wolverine, Yell, 1912, 4 x 5 1/2 In. 35.00
Cigarette Silk, Zia, Louisiana State University, 1913, 4 x 5 1/2 In. 35.00
Clicker, Endicott-Johnson Shoes, Tin, 1 3/4 In. 20.00
Clocks are listed in their own category.
Clothes Brush, Wilson's Co-Re-Ga, Perfect Adhesive For Dentures, Celluloid, 3 3/8 In. ... 28.00
Coaster, Eblings Beer & Ale, New York, N.Y., 1940s, 4 1/4 In. 14.00
Coaster, Edel Brau Beer & Ale, Brooklyn, N.Y., 1940s, 4 In. 18.00
Coaster, Fort Schyler Beer & Ale, Utica, N.Y., 1940s, 3 1/2 In. 10.00
Coaster, Hamm's Beer, Bear, Resting Head, Big Bear Drinking Brotherhood, 3 3/8 In. ... 5.00
Coaster, Horlacher Beer, Allentown, Pa., 1940s, 4 1/4 In. 11.00
Coaster, Michelob Beer, St. Louis, Mo., 1940s, 4 In. 12.00
Coaster, Ming's Chinese Food, Palo Alto, Cal., 1950, Unused, 3 In. 4.00
Coaster, Ruppert Knickerbocker Beer, 6 Piece 130.00
Coaster, Star Beer, Lancaster, Pa., 1940s, 4 1/4 In. 42.00
Coaster, Waldech Beer, Square, 4 1/4 In., 12 Piece 22.00
Coffee Grinder, None-Such, Tin Lithograph, Cast Iron, Wooden, 9 In. 77.00
Coffee Set, Nescafe, World, 12 Mugs, 15 Piece 60.00
Container, Shipping, Horehound Drops, Formed Wood, 13 x 8 3/4 In. 110.00
Crate, Junghans, For 1/2 Hour Trenton Clock 5.50
Crate, United Wholesale Druggist, Shipping, Wooden, 1920s, 21 x 30 x 21 In. 33.00
Crock, Butterine, Stenciled Front & Back, Glazed, Stoneware, Lid, 6 3/4 In. 198.00
Crock, Heinz Apple Butter, Stoneware, Lid, Bail Handle, Paper Labels, 5 1/2 In. 253.00
Crock, Heinz's, Mustard, Dusseldorfer, Stoneware, Lid, Bail, 3 3/4 In. 120.00
Crock, Weidmann's Peanut Butter, Meridan, Miss., Incised, Pottery, c.1890, 4 In. 210.00
Cup, Armour's Vigoral Cup, Floral, Decorated, 3 1/2 In. 66.00
Cup, Cudahy's Rexsoma, Floral, Decorated, 3 1/2 In. 55.00
Cup, Pepsi, Light-Up, Plastic, 1950, 13 In. 522.00
Cup, Red Goose Shoes, Logo Front, Lettering Back, Ceramic, Czechoslovakia, 4 In. 17.00
Cup, Uneeda Biscuit, Boy With Slicker, 3 In. 33.00
Cuspidor, Red Skin Brant Cut Plug, Embossed Indian, Brass 50.00

Advertising, Dispenser, Chero
Crush, Ceramic, No Pump, 1910

Advertising, Dispenser,
CherriBon, Ceramic

Advertising, Dispenser, World's
Liquid Force, Planet Earth

Cutout, De Laval Cream Separators, Holstein Cows, Mother & Calf, Tin, 3 x 5 In. 130.00
Decal, Bob's Big Boy, Decalcomania Co., Los Angeles, 1950s, 3 x 4 1/4 In. 18.00
Decal Sheet, Orange Crush, Li'l Abner Characters, 1950 . . . . 30.00
Decanter, Dewar's Whiskey, Engraved Lettering, 11 In. 55.00
Decanter, Sunnybrook Whiskey, Engraved Lettering, Ground Stopper, 12 1/2 In. 38.00
Dispenser, Bromo-Seltzer, Cobalt Blue Bottle 195.00
Dispenser, Buckeye Root Beer, Original Pump, 1930s 1200.00
Dispenser, Chero Crush, Ceramic, No Pump, 1910 . . . . *Illus* 6900.00
Dispenser, CherriBon, Ceramic . . . . *Illus* 6325.00
Dispenser, Cherry Smash . . . . .2350.00 to 3080.00
Dispenser, Dainty Powder, J.R. Watkins Co., Mary King Green 18.50
Dispenser, Diamond Matches 1 Cent, 3 Books, Dark Brown, Metal, 13 x 10 In. 525.00
Dispenser, Dr Pepper, Light Green, Tombstone Shape, Plastic, 1960, 7 In. 385.00
Dispenser, Fowler's Cherry Smash, 5 Cent, Pump, Ceramic 3080.00
Dispenser, Fowler's Root Beer, Ceramic, 14 In. 110.00
Dispenser, Grape Crush, Fountain, Amethyst Glass 2530.00
Dispenser, Grape Ola, Porcelain & Glass, Original Spigot, 11 1/4 In. 330.00
Dispenser, Hav-A-Nut, Countertop, Plastic, Clear, Lime Green, Box, 6 1/2 In. 23.00
Dispenser, Heinz, Pickle Barrel With Spigot, Embossed Base, 2 Sides, 14 3/4 In. 660.00
Dispenser, Hires Munimaker Syrup, Onyx Ball Handle, 34 1/2 In. 6325.00
Dispenser, Hires, Drink Hires It Is Pure, Ceramic, Pump, 13 In. 605.00
Dispenser, Lash's Grapefruit, Green Glass Globe, Labels, 12 1/4 In. 220.00
Dispenser, Magnus California Pure Orangeade Boy & Girl, 1920, 7 In. 1705.00
Dispenser, Mission Orange, Black Porcelain Top, Stoneware Pot, 1940s, 26 In. 200.00
Dispenser, Mitchell's Old Heather Dew, Whiskey, Scotch, Glass, 1800s, 28 1/2 In. 1100.00
Dispenser, Nesbitt's Root Beer, Barrel, Wooden, 25 1/2 In. 715.00
Dispenser, Rochester Root Beer, Barrel On Stump, 12 In. 77.00
Dispenser, Scott's Root Beer, Barrel Shape 4255.00
Dispenser, Stearn's Root Beer, Ceramic, Barrel On Stump, Embossed Lettering, 15 In. 545.00
Dispenser, Susu Salted Nuts, Embossed Glass & Metal, 1923, 12 1/2 In. 154.00
Dispenser, Ward's Lemon & Orange Crush, Figural 2530.00
Dispenser, Ward's Orange Crush, Orange Shape, Flower & Grass Base, 9 1/2 In. 440.00
Dispenser, Ward's Orange Crush, Original Ball Pump, 1920s 1220.00
Dispenser, World's Liquid Force, Planet Earth . . . . *Illus* 6037.00
Display, Altes Lager Boy War Bonds, Cardboard, Stand-Up, 1940s, 10 1/2 x 13 In. 50.00
Display, Banthrico Win A Car, 4 Cars On Base 3750.00
Display, Beech-Nut Chewing Gum, 4 Sections, Countertop, 11 x 6 1/2 In. 140.00
Display, Campbell's Soups, Tomato Juice, Campbell Kids On Each End, 1930, 27 In. 253.00
Display, Chiclets, Five Cents The Ounce, Frank Fleer, 10 x 7 1/2 In. 315.00
Display, Chief Watta Pop, Chalk Bust, Countertop, 10 In. 230.00
Display, Dr Pepper Bottle, 10, 2 & 4, Plastic, 1950, 4 In. 577.00
Display, Eat-It-All Cone, Composition Cone Form, White, Tan, 23 In. 143.00
Display, Favorite Stove & Range Co., Window, Boy & Girl, Cardboard, Pair 650.00
Display, Hamm's Beer, Polar Bear, Mechanical, 22 In. 345.00
Display, Hoppe's Gun Cleaning Patches, Complete With Boxes, 1940s 55.00

Fray Check, a product found in sewing supply shops, is useful for repairing tears in cardboard signs.

Advertising, Display, Selby
Split Shot Sinker, Tin,
With Containers

Display, Li'l Smoky, Leather Holsters, Hubley Cap Guns, Halco, 1940s, 12 In.	125.00
Display, Man, Black Suit, Umbrella, Bergermeister German Beer, Metal, 1960s	300.00
Display, Miller Genuine Draft Beer, Plastic Bottle, Black Plastic Base, 1989, 12 In.	21.00
Display, Mule, Papier-Mache, Santa Rita Tequila, Mini Bottle, Shot Glass, 6 In.	15.00
Display, National Edison Mazda, Fan Form	2090.00
Display, Pabst Beer, Brass Automobile, Mechanical, Light-Up, Hits Bump	250.00
Display, Pabst Blue Ribbon, Bartender Holding 4 Foaming Mugs, 15 In.	115.00
Display, Pabst Bock Beer, Cardboard, Stand-Up, 1940s, 11 x 14 In.	40.00
Display, Paris Garters, Tin Lithograph Covered Wooden Case, Front Logo, 15 1/4 In.	66.00
Display, Poll-Parrot Shoes, Composition, Metal Stand, 48 1/2 In.	275.00
Display, Poll-Parrot Shoes, Parrot, Light-Up, Mechanical, Wooden, 45 In.	330.00
Display, Poll-Parrot Shoes, Reverse On Glass, Counter, Light-Up, Plastic, 13 1/4 In.	1100.00
Display, Red Goose Shoes, Goose With Buzzer, Drops Eggs	175.00
Display, Remington Inc., Die Cut, Hunter Smoking Pipe, Cardboard, Stand-Up, 29 In.	220.00
Display, Selby Split Shot Sinker, Tin, With Containers .... *Illus*	2145.00
Display, Shooting Linds, Winchester, Milesburg, Cardboard, Oct. 1947, 22 x 14 In.	339.00
Display, Star Brand Shoes, Light-Up, Metal Display Stand, Reverse On Glass, 40 In.	110.00
Display, Victorinox, Swiss Army Knife, Blades & Tools Move, Wooden Frame, 35 In.	195.00
Display, Weather-Bird Shoes, Die Cut Cardboard, Stand-Up Easel Back, 33 In.	165.00
Display, Weather-Bird Shoes, Mechanical, Electric, Composition, Rubber, 22 1/2 In.	468.00
Display, Weltman & Dwire Tobacco Co., Tipsy Granulated Smoking Tobacco, 32 x 22 In.	88.00
Display, Westinghouse Lamp, Light-Up Bulbs, Paper Decal, Tin Lithograph, 27 1/2 In.	660.00
Display, Winchester Fishing Lure, Trout, Bass, Walleye, Die Cut, 1954, 8 x 20 In., 4 Pc.	339.00
Display, Wrigley's Gum, Cardboard, Holds 20 Packages, Countertop, 12 In.	270.00
Display, Wrigley's, Arrow Figure, Stencil, Celluloid Face, Tin, 13 1/2 In.	825.00
Display, Zippo, Acrylic, Lighted, Tower, Rotates, Unassembled, Box, 67 x 19 In.	140.00
Display, Zippo, Plastic, Clear, Black Top & Base, Lighted, Tower, 13 x 23 In.	180.00
Dolls are listed in their own category.	
Door Push, Butter-Nut Bread, Tin, Bread Shape, 19 3/4 x 8 3/4 In.	330.00
Door Push, Crescent Flour, 9 1/2 x 3 3/4 In.	230.00
Door Push, Red Goose Shoes, Orange, Red, Porcelain, 7 In.	198.00
Door Push, Vicks, 2 Bottles Of Product, Porcelain, 1940s, 4 x 8 In.	488.00
Fans are listed in their own category.	
Figure, Actigall, First Pattern, Plastic, Green, 1989, 7 In.	65.00
Figure, Actigall, Gall Bladder, Green Plastic, 4 1/4 In.	37.00
Figure, Big Boy, First Model, Soft Plastic, Vinyl, 1950s, 9 1/2 In.	73.00
Figure, Big Boy, Second Model, Plastic, Vinyl, 1973, 8 1/2 In.	22.00
Figure, Coopers Old Bohemian Beer, Chalkware, 1930s, 7 x 15 1/2 In.	185.00
Figure, Count Chocula, Soft Plastic, Painted, In Bag, 8 In.	36.00
Figure, Cowboy, Guns & Ammo, Chalkware, Wooden Base, Iron Wheels, 58 x 14 In.	735.00
Figure, Elsie The Cow, Bernie, Plush, Vinyl Head, 1977, 15 In.	45.00
Figure, Firestone Rubber, Native Scouring Tree, Composition, 5 1/2 In.	35.00
Figure, Kentucky Fried Chicken, Colonel Sanders, Canada, 12 1/2 In.	38.00
Figure, Kentucky Fried Chicken, Colonel Sanders, Plastic, 9 1/2 In.	40.00
Figure, Lee Western Wear, Charles Russell's The Weaver, Bronzed Plastic, 14 In.	280.00
Figure, Mac Tonight, McDonald's, On Carton, 10 In.	32.00
Figure, Miller High Life, Composition, Crackled Paint Base, 1930s, 6 In.	105.00

Figure, Old Crow Whiskey, Composition, 36 In. . . . . .325.00 to 375.00
Figure, Poll-Parrot Shoes, Brownish Red, Plaster, 11 1/2 In. 50.00
Figure, Poll-Parrot Shoes, Green, Yellow, Tan, 11 In. 154.00
Figure, Poll-Parrot Shoes, Metal Hanger, Plaster, 13 In. 154.00
Figure, Poll-Parrot Shoes, Painted, Ceramic, Integral Label On Tree Base, 8 In. 121.00
Figure, RCA, Nipper, Chalkware 45.00
Figure, Red Goose Shoes, Ceramic, Integral Label, 1 1/2 In. 72.00
Figure, Red Goose Shoes, Painted, Plaster, 8 In. 110.00
Figure, Red Goose Shoes, Red, Orange, Plaster, 11 In. 88.00
Figure, Reddy Kilowatt, Translucent Pink Body, Plastic, 1950s, 6 In. 200.00
Figure, Ritalin Man, Brown 85.00
Figure, Rolling Rock Beer, Chalkware, 1950s, 10 1/2 x 11 In. 30.00
Figure, Sprite Lyman, Talking, Vinyl, Movable Arms & Legs, 1980s, 7 1/2 In. 35.00
Figure, Spuds Mackenzie, Bud Light, With Heart, 1987, 2 1/2 In. 26.00
Figure, Travelodge Sleep Bear, Plastic, Brown, Painted, In Bag, 1978, 5 1/2 In. 40.00
Figure, Weather-Bird Shoes, Black, Red, Orange, Painted, Chalk, 12 In. 303.00
Figure, Weather-Bird Shoes, Painted, Chalk, 14 In. 495.00
First Aid Kit, Indiana & Michigan Electric Co., White Metal, Hinged Lid 20.00
Flashlight, Green Giant, Little Green Sprout, Handle, Box, 5 x 9 In. 40.00
Foam Scraper, Adler Brau Beer, 2 Sides, 1950s 45.00
Foam Scraper, Gerhard Lang Brewing, Curved Style, 1930s 35.00
Foam Scraper, Stegmaier Gold Medal Beer, 2 Sides, Curved, Pre-Prohibition 68.00
Foam Scraper, Utica Club Beer & Ale, Curved, 1930s 35.00
Foam Scraper-Napkin Holder, Rheingold Beer, Metal, Plastic, 1950s 30.00
Frame, Kay, Horizontal Cardboard, Original Paint, 1940, 6 In. 110.00
Frame, Kay, Wooden, 1940, 7 In. 220.00
Glass, A & W Root Beer, 1963 . . . . 8.00
Glass, Adler Brau Beer, Red Painted Label, 1950s, 5 1/2 In. 37.00
Glass, Anthony & Kuhn Brewing Co., XXX Center, St. Louis, Embossed, 6 5/8 In. 265.00
Glass, Arby's, Head In Star, Sylvester 9.00
Glass, Barbarossa Beer, Red & Yellow Letters, 1950s, 7 1/2 In. 22.00
Glass, Beer, Pells Brewing & Ice Co., Trinidad, Colo., Etched, 3 5/8 In. 66.00
Glass, Borden Dairy, Aunt Elsie, Red, 1940-1950, 3 1/2 In. 55.00
Glass, Borden Dairy, Baby Beulah, Red & Blue, 1940-1950, 3 1/2 In. 55.00
Glass, Borden Dairy, Elsie, As Dutch Girl, Windmill, Yellow, 3 1/2 In. 47.00
Glass, Buffalo Brewing, Etched, Letters, 1910s, 4 In. 190.00
Glass, Coon Chicken Inn 10.00
Glass, Dayton Breweries Trademark, Different Brands Listed, Etched, 3 7/8 In. 115.00
Glass, Dose, J. Lindeman Druggist, Meadville, Pa. 22.00
Glass, Dose, Tebbetts & Soules Drug Store, Manchester, N.H. 22.00
Glass, Dr Pepper, 2-Tone Label, 1960, 9 1/2 In. 88.00
Glass, Enterprise Brewing Co., Yosemite Lager, San Francisco, Etched, 3 1/2 In. 85.00
Glass, Hires Root Beer, White Label, 1950, 9 1/2 In. 22.00
Glass, Kauffman Brewing Co., Cincinnati, Embossed In Shield, 6 1/8 In. 115.00
Glass, Louis Bergdoll Brewing, 60th Anniversary, 1909, 4 In. 70.00
Glass, Milwaukee Brewing Co., Milwaukee, Wis., Etched, Factory Scene, 3 3/8 In. 60.00
Glass, Old Heidelberg Beer, Sandstone Finish, Gold Letters, 1910s, 3 1/2 In. 35.00
Glass, Old Reading Beer, Red, Yellow & Black Letters, 8 In. 125.00
Glass, Phoenix Brewing Co., Ky., Embossed, The Phoenix, 1883-1911, 6 1/2 In. 255.00
Glass, Red Stripe Beer, Red & Black Painted Label, 1970s, 5 1/2 In. 10.00
Glass, Schlitz, After Hours, Light-Up, Concealed Bulb In Long Stem, Box, 9 In. 22.00
Glass, Standard Brewery, Embossed, Eagle Logo, Chicago, 3 1/2 In. 50.00
Glass, Walter Bros. Brewing Co., Etched Logo, Factory Scene, Menasha, Wis., 3 3/8 In. . . 35.00
Globe, Kentucky Fried Chicken, The Colonel In Center, Milk Glass, 1960, 10 In. 110.00
Globe, Red Goose Shoes, Etched Glass, Painted, 2 Images, 12 In. 715.00
Goblet, Sicks Rainier Brewing Co., Red Letters, 6 In. 8.00
Handkerchief, McDonald's, Baltimore Orioles, TV Station Logo, 17 In. 20.00
Hatchet, Red Goose Shoes, Wooden Handle, Stamped Steel Head, 13 3/4 In. 39.00
Holder, Chief Watta Pop Indian, Lollipop, Dark Brown Indian 410.00
Holder, Curtiss Lollipop, Play Safe!, Orange Ground, Metal, 19 In. 190.00
Humidor, Cremo Cigars, Tin Lithograph, Cigar Shop Display, 5 3/4 x 14 In. 275.00
Ice Pick & Bottle Opener, Alpen Brau Beer, Wooden, 1930s, 10 In. 15.00
Ice Scraper, Have You Made The Budweiser Beer Test, 1930s, 3 3/4 x 3 In. 94.00

Jar, Adams, Pepsin Tutti-Frutti, Glass Stopper, Wooden Box, Dovetailed, 11 1/2 In. 193.00
Jar, Barsam Brothers Peanut, Octagonal, Clear, 10 In. 100.00
Jar, Country Store Display, Ground Stopper, 21 In. 99.00
Jar, Cracker, Brass Fittings, S.F. Co. For Peek Frean Co. 80.00
Jar, Dr. Miles Anti-Pain Pills, Swirled Design On Lid, 16 1/2 In. 745.00
Jar, Dr. Pierce's Pleasant Purgative Pellets, 3 Packages, 6 1/2 In. 402.00
Jar, Dr. Simmon's Aspirin, Laxative Tablets For Pain, 12 In. 515.00
Jar, Heinz's Celery Sauce, Ground Stopper, 12 In. 550.00
Jar, Heinz's Keystone Onions, Ground Stopper, 9 1/4 In. 410.00
Jar, Orris Tooth Powder, Faceted Ball Knop Top, Teethers, 12 In. 58.00
Jar, Squibb's Brown Mixture Lozenges, Patent April 2, 1889, 8 1/2 In. 230.00
Jar, Squirrel Peanut, Tin Lithograph Lid, 8 1/2 In. 55.00
Jar, Sterling Gum, Oval, Glass, Embossed, Metal Lid, Number 7 Ghost, 7 In. 83.00
Jersey, Baseball, Reddy Kilowatt, Junior Baseball League, 1950s, Size 42 . . . . 385.00
Jug, Kola-Mint, Stoneware, Cork Stopper, Miniature, 5 In. 11.00
Jug, Miners Fruit Nectar Co., Boston, Mass., Albany & Bristol Glaze, c.1900, 11 In. 77.00
Jug, Syrup, Dr Pepper, Original Top, 1950, 7 In. 170.00
Keg, Rochester Root Beer, Wooden, Nickel Plated Spigot, Claw Feet 1100.00
Keg Tap, Lone Star Beer, Clear Acrylic Handle, 7 x 9 In. 25.00
Key Chain, Bartels Crown Beer, Syracuse, N.Y., Pre-Prohibition 13.00
Key Chain, Blatz Beer, Milwaukee, Wis., Brass, 2 Sides, Pre-Prohibition 16.00
Key Fob, Y-B, Cigar Shape, With Chain, 2 In. 30.00
Kick Plate, Dr Pepper, 1941, 12 x 29 In. 613.00
Kick Plate, NeHi, 1940s, 11 1/2 x 29 In. 200.00
Kick Plate, NuGrape, Bottle On Left, 1930s, 12 x 30 In. 207.00
Kick Plate, Orange Lemon & Lime, Bottle On Left, 1920s, 9 x 20 In. 833.00
Kooler-Keg Knob, King Cole Beer, Prototype, 1940s 140.00
Label, Airline, Paul Bunyan's, Peel Off Center, 1950s, 4 1/2 In. 19.00
Label, Beef, Home Packed, Hereford Cow, Woodcut, New York, c.1910, 12 x 4 In. 10.00
Label, Beer, Acme, Die Cut, Tax Stamp, 1940s, 11 Oz. 3.00
Label, Beer, General Gee Picnic, Tax Stamp, U Permit, 1/2 Gal. 18.00
Label, Beer, Iron City Bock, Pittsburgh, Pa., Tax Stamp, 1940s, 12 Oz. 20.00
Label, Beer, Old Abbey, Tax Stamp, 1930s, 1/2 Gal. 17.00
Label, Beer, Old Carnegie Bock, Cartiers Vall., Pa., 1930s, 12 Oz. 20.00
Label, Beer, Schmidt's Pilsener, Yellowed, 1900s 30.00
Label, Broom, Black Banjo Player Dixie, 1920, 3 1/2 In. 12.00
Label, Cigar, Cherokee Maid 385.00
Label, Cigar, Chief Joseph, Indian 295.00
Label, Cigar, Croaker, Outside 225.00
Label, Cigar, Edsonia, Phonograph 650.00
Label, Cigar, Forest Rose 275.00
Label, Cigar, Gettysburg Commanders, Interior & Outside 145.00
Label, Cigar, Honest Yankee 75.00
Label, Cigar, La Normandy, Interior 105.00
Label, Cigar, Leon De Oro 60.00
Label, Cigar, Old Abe, Outside 100.00
Label, Cigar, Paul Clay, Memory 60.00
Label, Cigar, Peerless 85.00
Label, Cigar, Porto Rico Specials 295.00
Label, Cigar, Puritan Leader, Inside, Knight 65.00
Label, Cigar, Red Dandies 245.00
Label, Cigar, Regalia Grande 185.00
Label, Cigar, Royal Perfectos 115.00
Label, Cigar, Royal Princess 155.00
Label, Cigar, Sam Houston, Embossed, Gold Trim, Square, 1910, 4 1/2 In. 15.00
Label, Cigar, Social Tips, Men At Table 550.00
Label, Cigar, Tioga Chief 445.00
Label, Cigar, Toreador 150.00
Label, Cigar, Trolley, Car Pictured 1950.00
Label, Cigar, Two Roses 115.00
Label, Cigar, Ultimatum, Lamb's 98.00
Label, Fertilizer, Lawn Grass, Weed Destroyer, Salt Lake City, 1910, 5 x 10 In. 18.00
Label, Food, Alpine Kidney Beans, Mountain Climber, Bowl Of White Beans, N.Y. 50

Label, Food, Blue Hill White Corn, House By River, Conifers 3.00
Label, Food, Cloth Of Gold Golden Bantam Corn, Large Red Bird, Gilt 3.00
Label, Food, Indian Weaver Brand Vegetables, Bluewater, N.M., 1938, 7 x 9 In. 7.00
Label, Food, Jonesport Fish Flakes, Old Lighthouse, Ship, Fish, 9 x 4 In. 1.00
Label, Food, La Perla, California Olives, Old-Fashioned Boy .... .25
Label, Food, Little Joe Crowed Peas, Whistling Black Youngster Going Fishing 2.00
Label, Food, Maryland Chief Green Beans, 2 Images Of Indian Chief 1.00
Label, Food, Mayfield Peas, Country Sunrise Scene, Dish Of Vegetable 1.00
Label, Food, Mellendale Lima Beans, Forest, Stream, Mountains, Lima Beans In Pods ... 1.00
Label, Food, Mt. Vernon Apple Butter, White Mansion, Va., 7 Lbs., 6 1/2 x 8 1/2 In. 1.00
Label, Food, Old Black Joe, Black-Eyed Peas, Elderly Black Man & Cabin 2.00
Label, Hotel, Brown Palace, Shipping, Denver, Col., Browns, Yellow, 1930s, 3 x 6 In. ... 14.00
Label, Hotel, Hot Springs, Ark., Arlington, Baths, Tower, 1930s, 4 x 3 1/2 In. 11.00
Label, Luggage, Challenger Inn, Sun Valley, Idaho, Skier, Tux, Top Hat, 1940s, 3 1/2 In. . 25.00
Label, Malt Tonic, Bon Ton, L Permit Prohibition, 13 Oz. 40.00
Label, Wine, Fountain Grove Vineyard, Sonoma Moselle, Santa Rosa, 1946, 4 x 5 In. 12.00
Label, Wine, Italian Swiss Colony California Sherry, Asti, Ark., 1940s, 3 x 4 1/2 In. 5.00
Lamps are listed in the Lamp category.
Letter Opener, Fuller Brush Man, Plastic 10.00
Light, Blatz Beer, Plastic, Metal, 1970s, 7 1/4 x 10 In. 196.00
Light, Budweiser Beer, Pocket Watch Shape, 1950s, 12 1/2 x 17 In. 95.00
Light, Calendar, Canadian Club Whiskey, Plastic, 1960s, 8 x 11 In. 5.00
Light, Canada Dry Ginger Ale, Plastic, Vacuum Formed, 1960s, 16 3/4 x 6 In. 55.00
Light, Cordova Wines, Glass & Metal, Wooden Frame, 1950s, 13 x 7 3/4 In. 9.00
Light, Duquesne Beer, Pocket Watch Shape, 1930s 48.00
Light, Iroquois Beer & Ale, Plastic, Wooden, 1950s, 11 1/2 x 17 1/2 In. 12.00
Light, Iroquois Beer, Neon, 1950s, 19 1/2 x 12 1/2 In. 135.00
Light, P.O.C. Beer, Plastic, 1950s, 11 1/2 x 9 In. 160.00
Light, With Sign, Trommer's White Label Beer, Reverse Glass, 1940s, 13 x 10 In. 116.00
Lighter, Cigar, Lamp, P. Hauptmann 5 Cents, Tin Shade, Cast Iron, Countertop, 18 In. ... 555.00
Lunch Boxes are listed in their own category.
Lunch Pail, Central Union Cut Plug, Gold Trim 125.00
Lunch Pail, Pedro Tobacco, Tin Lithograph, Hinged Lid, Tax Stamp, 1910, 8 In. 187.00
Lunch Pail, Penny Post Cut Plug, Strater Brothers Tobacco Co., Metal 250.00
Lunch Pail, U. S. Marine Cut Plug, Naval Ship, Lithograph, Hinged Lid, 7 1/2 In. 220.00
Lunch Pail, Union Leader Plug Tobacco, Wire Bail 48.00
Matchbook, Regal Pale Beer, San Francisco, Cal., 1940s 3.00
Matchbook Cover, Mammoth Cave Hotel, Picture, 1930s 6.00
Medallion, Hartford Fire Insurance Co., Bronze, Whitehead-Hoag, 1921, 4 In. 26.00
Megaphone, Dr Pepper, Frosty Man, Frosty, Paper, Metal Ring At Top, 1950, 8 In. 357.00
Menu Board, Bud Light Beer, White Plastic Center Panel, 1989, 32 x 19 In. 28.00
Menu Board, Drink Dr Pepper, Black Board, 1960, 20 x 28 In. 88.00
Menu Board, Drink Dr Pepper, Dark Green Board, 1960, 14 x 20 In. 275.00
Menu Board, Drink Dr Pepper, Distinctively Different, White, Plastic, 1960, 8 In. 66.00
Menu Board, Have A Pepsi, Black Board, Ivory Border, 1950, 20 x 30 In. 71.00

Advertising pocket mirrors range in size from 1 1/2 to 5 inches in
diameter. Most of these mirrors were given away as advertising pro-
motions and include the name of the company in the design.

Mirror, ABC Power Washer, Altorfer Bros. Co., Woman Wringing Clothes, 2 1/8 In. 253.00
Mirror, Adam Scheidt Brewing Co., Norristown, Pa., Bottle, Pocket, 2 3/4 In. 77.00
Mirror, American Line, Philadelphia, Ocean Liner, Round, 1 3/4 In. 132.00
Mirror, An Enameled Range, J. August Miller, Celluloid, Green, Oval, 2 3/4 In. 120.00
Mirror, Anderson's Soups, Camden, N.J., Man Eating Soup, Round, 2 1/8 In. 55.00
Mirror, Angelus Marshmallows, Cherubs & Box, Oval, 2 3/8 In. 50.00
Mirror, Anheuser-Busch Ginger Ale, Logo, Oval, 2 3/4 In. 154.00
Mirror, Anheuser-Busch, Reverse Painting On Glass, Bud Girl, 9 x 13 1/4 In. 20.00
Mirror, Aspeleiter Wines, Liquors & Cigars, Rochester, Buxom Woman, 2 3/4 In. 358.00
Mirror, Aunt Jemima Breakfast Club, 1960s, 3 In. 20.00
Mirror, Aurora Beer, Aurora, In., Round, 1930s, 2 In. 61.00
Mirror, Bagley Tobacco Pocket Wetstone, Product Pictured, Oval, 2 3/4 In. 50.00
Mirror, Beautyskin, Chichester Chemical Co., Phila., Woman, 2 3/8 In. 66.00
Mirror, Beehive Overalls Best Maid, Allentown, Pa., Woman In Overalls, 2 3/4 In. 132.00

Mirror, Beeman's Pepsin Gum, Man With Mustache, Black Field, 2 1/8 In. 176.00
Mirror, Bell's Coffee, Chicago, Bell, Round, 2 1/8 In. ....33.00 to 44.00
Mirror, Berry Brothers' Varnishes, Children With Dog Pulling Wagon, 2 1/8 In. ...154.00 to 187.00
Mirror, Biltmore Lunch, New Britain, Smiling & Grouchy Faces, 2 1/4 In. 105.00
Mirror, Blue Ribbon Canned Foods, O. & F.P.M., Peoria, Ill., Set Table, 2 1/8 In. 110.00
Mirror, Blue Ribbon, Monmouth, Ill., Woman, 2 1/4 In. 99.00
Mirror, Bortree Corset Co., Jackson, Mich., Form Fitting Corsets, Round, 2 In. 154.00
Mirror, Boston Herald, The Sunday Herald, Newsboy, 1 3/4 In. 330.00
Mirror, Bradley & Metcalf Co., Milwaukee, High Top Shoe, 1 3/4 In. 88.00
Mirror, Brotherhood Overalls, H.S. Peters, Dover, N.J., Seminude Woman, 2 1/8 In. 187.00
Mirror, Calox Tooth Powder, Your 32 Teeth Are 32 Reasons, Logo, 2 3/4 In. 50.00
Mirror, Campbell's Soup, 21 Kinds, 10 Cents A Can, 1 3/4 x 2 3/4 In. ....120.00 to 140.00
Mirror, Cascarets Candy Cathartic, Wheeling, W.V., Reclining Woman, 2 1/8 In. 99.00
Mirror, Cascarets, They Work While You Sleep, Cherub On Pot, 2 1/8 In. 28.00
Mirror, Ceresota Flour, Boy Cutting Bread, Black Border, 2 1/8 In. ....28.00 to 33.00
Mirror, Ceresota Flour, Pure, Wholesome, Not Bleached, Child, 2 1/8 In. 110.00
Mirror, Chew Beeman's Gum, Man With Mustache, 2 1/8 In. 308.00
Mirror, Columbia Tool Steel Co., Red & Blue, White Ground, Celluloid, Pocket 25.00
Mirror, Continental Cubes Pipe Tobacco, Sitting Woman, Red Dress, Pipe, 2 3/4 In. 275.00
Mirror, Continental Pipe Tobacco, Floozy Woman In Red Dress, Pipe, 2 3/4 In. 275.00
Mirror, Crystal White Laundry Soap, Peet Bros. Mfg. Co., Kansas City, 2 1/8 In. 28.00
Mirror, Cunningham Piano, The Matchless, Philadelphia, Windblown Nude, 2 3/4 In. 275.00
Mirror, Denta-Bleach, Eureka Chemical Co., Omaha, Neb., Woman's Head, 2 In. 94.00
Mirror, Denver Dry Goods Company, Factory, Oval, 2 3/4 In. 99.00
Mirror, Dr. Louis Goldberg, Optometrist, Blue On White, Pocket 60.00
Mirror, Drink Dr Pepper, Black, 1930, 8 x 16 In. 660.00
Mirror, Duffy's Pure Malt Whiskey, Aged Chemist, Oval, 2 3/4 In. ....33.00 to 66.00
Mirror, Dunham's Coconut, Waitress, 2 1/8 In. 94.00
Mirror, Dutch Java Coffee, Secret Of Happiness, Dutch Couple, Round, 2 1/8 In. 72.00
Mirror, Electric Renovator Mfg. Co., Pittsburgh, Pa., Woman Vacuuming, 2 3/4 In. 28.00
Mirror, Empire Cream Separator Co., Nothing Else Will Do, Milk Maid, 2 3/4 In. 99.00
Mirror, Enameled Range, Berwick, Pa., Stove, Oval, 2 3/4 In. 77.00
Mirror, Excelsior Motor Mfg. & Supply Co., Chicago, Motorcycle, 2 3/4 In. 440.00
Mirror, Featuring The Doctor, Wall, 1930, 4 x 8 1/2 In. 990.00
Mirror, Feigenspan's, Newark, Profile Of Woman With Ribbon In Hair, 2 3/4 In. 33.00
Mirror, Ferner Bros. & Co. Shoes, Somerset, Pa., Woman With Daisies, 2 3/4 In. 165.00
Mirror, Fleischmann's Yeast, Girl, 2 1/4 In. 77.00
Mirror, Franke Davis Fish Co., Gloucester, Mass., Fish & Lobster, Oval, 2 3/4 In. 176.00
Mirror, Friedman-Shelby Shoe Co., St. Louis, High Top Shoe, Round, 2 3/8 In. 88.00
Mirror, Frisco System, Train In Mountains, Round, 2 1/8 In. 88.00
Mirror, Garden City Tailoring, Chicago, Spirit Of '76, Round, 2 1/4 In. 22.00
Mirror, Garret's Baker Rye, Baltimore, Nude Woman On Riverbank, Oval, 2 3/4 In. 358.00
Mirror, Garrett's American Wines, Norfolk, Nude Angel & Fairy, 2 3/4 In. 220.00
Mirror, Garrett's American Wines, Virginia Dare, Nude Woman Archer, 2 3/4 In. 523.00
Mirror, Geo. Muehlebach Brewing Co., Kansas City, Mo., Bottle, 2 3/4 In. 121.00
Mirror, George Wm. Hoffman Co., Indianapolis, Ind., Nude Woman At Bar, 2 1/8 In. 358.00
Mirror, Gold Cross Milk, Product Can, Round, 1 3/4 In. 17.00
Mirror, Good Luck Bread, For Life, Bread, Folding Handle, 2 x 4 5/8 In. 88.00
Mirror, Goodyear's Rubber Glove Co., Gloves & Galoshes, Round, Pincushion, 2 1/4 In. .. 33.00
Mirror, Great Majestic, Modern Range, St. Louis, Mo., Woman, Stove, 2 1/8 In. 248.00
Mirror, Grennell Bros., Michigan, Store Front, Round, 2 In. 17.00
Mirror, Harvest King, Kansas City, Mo., Bare Breasted Woman & Big Hat, 1 3/4 In. 110.00
Mirror, Holland Furnace Co., Make Warm Friends, 2 3/4 In. 50.00
Mirror, Honesdale Chamber Of Commerce, Park Scene, Celluloid, Pocket 15.00
Mirror, Horlick's Malted Milk, Milk Maid & Cow, Logo, Round, 2 1/8 In. ....33.00 to 44.00
Mirror, Hotel Raymond, Fitchburg, Mass., Woman, 2 1/4 In. 55.00
Mirror, Humphrey's Witch Hazel Oil, Reverse On Glass, Beveled, Oak Frame, 11 1/2 In. . 44.00
Mirror, J.G. Seeger & Sons, Buffalo, N.Y., Building Scene, Pocket 26.00
Mirror, J.H. Bell & Co., Chicago, Mocha & Java Coffee, Bell, 2 1/8 In. 66.00
Mirror, J.I. Case Threshing Machine Co., Racine, Wis., Eagle, 2 3/4 In. 165.00
Mirror, J.W. Clarke, Dr. A.C. Daniels, Boston, Mass., Woman, Horse, Dog, 2 1/8 In. 220.00
Mirror, Jack's, Arcanum, Ohio, Bare Breasted Woman, Hand Colored, 2 1/4 In. 143.00
Mirror, Jesse E. Nichols Cafe, Auburn, N.Y., Old Woman Spanking Tot, 2 3/4 In. 330.00

Mirror, John Deere Plow Co., Omaha, Motor Pictured, Round, 2 1/4 In. 385.00
Mirror, John W. Crooks Chocolate Company, Boston, Bee & Flowers, 2 1/8 In. 94.00
Mirror, Kansas Expansion Flour, Product Sunflower, Round, 2 1/8 In. 50.00
Mirror, Keith's Vaudeville, Woman With Parasol, 2 3/4 In. 66.00
Mirror, King Arthur Flour, Minn., Knight On Horseback, 2 1/8 In. 154.00
Mirror, Kingan's Sausage-Lard, Sailor, 2 1/4 In. 94.00
Mirror, Knab's Lunch Rooms & Railroad Locator, Depot Listing, 2 3/4 In. 33.00
Mirror, Kobacher's, Coat Hooks, Oak Frame, Early 20th Century, 29 x 19 In. 345.00
Mirror, LaFrance Shoes For Woman, Green, Blue, Pink, Celluloid, Purse, 1 1/4 In. 41.00
Mirror, Lan-Tox Store Girl, Nurse, Oval, 2 3/4 In. 132.00
Mirror, Laurel Stoves, Art Stove Co., Woman, Laurel, 2 3/4 In. 176.00
Mirror, Levenson Hair Shop, Rochester, N.Y., Woman, Flowing Hair, 2 3/4 In. 17.00
Mirror, Lockport Light, Heat & Power Co., Woman, Hat, Round, Pincushion, 2 1/4 In. ... 99.00
Mirror, Malt Rainier Tonic, Seattle, Bottle, Off-Center, 2 3/4 In. 121.00
Mirror, Marston's Restaurant & Luncheon Rooms, Hatching Chick, 2 3/4 In. 55.00
Mirror, Martin Sporn's Place, Norfolk, Neb., Woman, 2 1/4 In. 248.00
Mirror, Mennen's Violet Talcum Toilet Powder, 1 3/4 x 2 3/4 In. 66.00
Mirror, Meyer-Wilms Co. Dry Goods, Quincy, Ill., Woman, 2 3/4 In. 50.00
Mirror, Molson Beer, Imported From Canada, Wooden Frame, 20 x 16 In. 20.00
Mirror, Morrell's Pride Meats, Delivery Man In Heart, Round, 2 1/4 In. 28.00
Mirror, Moyer's Clothing Store, Wooden Frame, 9 1/2 In. 154.00
Mirror, Nann & Kress, Syracuse, N.Y., Nude Woman With Anniversaries, 2 3/4 In. 121.00
Mirror, National Brewing Co., Saginaw, Mich., Logo, Round, 2 1/4 In. 88.00
Mirror, National Glass Corporation, Truck Photo, Celluloid, 1930s, 4 In. 100.00
Mirror, Nature's Remedy Tablets, Face, Pill On Tongue, Red Border, 2 1/8 In. 55.00
Mirror, New & True Brand Coffee, Binghamton, N.Y., 2 3/4 In. 110.00
Mirror, New Bridge, Eldora, La., Bridge Picture, Celluloid, 1 3/4 In. 20.00
Mirror, New England, Your Credit Is Good At, Puritan Woman Profile, 2 3/8 In. 33.00
Mirror, New Marsden Hotel, Alexandria Bay, N.Y., Woman, 2 1/4 In. 88.00
Mirror, Ohio Match Co., Factory & Product, Round, Paperweight, 3 1/2 In. 121.00
Mirror, Old Henry Whiskey, Barrel, Oval, 2 3/4 In. 149.00
Mirror, Old Reliable Coffee, Always Good, Man In Red Jacket, Round, 2 1/8 In. 44.00
Mirror, Old Reliable Coffee, Man In Fur Coat, Celluloid, Pocket 28.00
Mirror, Olt's Cream Ale & Superba Beer, Dayton, Ohio, Fairy With Beer, 2 In. 413.00
Mirror, Ondoca Delicious Food Drink, Woman On Beach, Beach Ball, 2 3/4 In. 220.00
Mirror, Osgood C. Cobb Jewelers, Iowa Falls, Good Luck, 2 3/4 In. 28.00
Mirror, Oxford Chocolate, Woman Scholar Profile, Oval, 2 3/4 In. ....28.00 to 33.00
Mirror, Parfumerie Ed. Pinaud, Woman, Bare Shoulders, 2 3/8 In. 44.00
Mirror, Peninsular Stove Co., Factory, Oval, 2 3/4 In. 121.00
Mirror, Perfection Wafers, Woman, 1902 Penny Inset, Round, 1 1/2 In. 77.00
Mirror, Philadelphia Bulletin, Woman With Auburn Hair, 2 3/4 In. 33.00
Mirror, Pildoritas De Reuter, Hummingbird & Woman, 2 1/8 In. 55.00
Mirror, Pittsburg Automatic Gas Water Heater, Quick Hot Water, 2 3/4 In. 77.00
Mirror, Please Help The Blind, Blind Man & Leggy Woman, Round, 1 3/4 In. 22.00
Mirror, Providence Car Fender, Providence, R.I., Streetcar, 2 1/8 In. 358.00
Mirror, Queen City Brewing Co., Old German Beer, Celluloid, Pocket 70.00
Mirror, Queen Quality Shoes, Portrait Of A Queen, Celluloid, Purse, 2 1/4 In. 35.00
Mirror, Queen Quality Shoes, Regal Lady In Red Cape, Oval, 2 3/4 In. 132.00
Mirror, Radcliffe Shoe For Women, Celluloid, Birthstone Border, 2 3/16 In. 17.00
Mirror, Rawson's Horse Remedies, Oak Frame, 20 1/2 In. 149.00
Mirror, Red Seal Lye, Product Pictured, Round, 1 3/4 In. 55.00
Mirror, Reliable Shoe Co., Orwigsburg, Pa., Woman's Profile, 2 3/4 In. 88.00
Mirror, Revlon, American Way Manicure, Red, Blue, White Ground, Celluloid, Pocket ... 70.00
Mirror, Royal Blend Roasted Coffee, Granger & Co., Product Pictured, 2 3/4 In. 105.00
Mirror, Royal Traders, Chicago, Looking Into This Mirror, Tiger, Round, 2 In. 215.00
Mirror, Ryan's Pure Beers, Syracuse, N.Y., Indian, Round, 2 1/8 In. 187.00
Mirror, Schoble Hats, Reverse On Glass Mirror, Swing Frame, 14 1/4 In. 185.00
Mirror, Scranton Stove Works, Old Style Stove, Round, 2 1/8 In. 22.00
Mirror, Sharples Tubular Cream Separators, Man Pouring Cream, Woman, 2 3/4 In. 143.00
Mirror, Sherwin-Williams Paints, Logo, Round, 2 1/8 In. 33.00
Mirror, Smith's Green Mountain Renovator, Woman In Powdered Wig, 2 1/8 In. 99.00
Mirror, Standard Oleomargarine, Indianapolis, Product Pictured, 2 3/4 In. 11.00
Mirror, Standard Remington Typewriter, Round, 2 1/8 In. 121.00

Mirror, Starrett Tools, Tools On Red Field, Round, 2 1/8 In. 39.00
Mirror, Sterling Range, Rome, N.Y., Stove, 2 1/4 In. 187.00
Mirror, Stonington, Furniture Co. Household Ranges, Black On White, Pocket 25.00
Mirror, Sullivan & Co., Philadelphia, Bare Shouldered Woman's Profile, 2 3/4 In. 22.00
Mirror, Surbrug's Tobacco, Bare Breasted Woman & Tobacco Leaves, 2 3/4 In. 1155.00
Mirror, Tailor Made Clothing Co., Chicago, Scissors & Tape Measure, 1 3/4 In. 39.00
Mirror, Taka Cola, Woman & Clock, Round, 2 1/8 In. 55.00
Mirror, Traveler's Insurance Company, Speeding Locomotive, 2 3/8 In. 88.00
Mirror, Ulmer Packing Co., Pottsville, Pa., Bacon & Eggs, Round, 2 1/8 In. 72.00
Mirror, United Commercial Travelers Convention, 1909, Wisconsin, 2 3/4 In. 11.00
Mirror, Use White Loaf Flour, Pretty Lady, Black Ground, Pocket 67.00
Mirror, Wabasha Roller Mill Co., Flour Bag, Birthstones, Oval, 2 3/4 In. 11.00
Mirror, Walter A. Lord Jewelry Co., Woman, Oval, 2 3/4 In. 132.00
Mirror, Wheeling Machine Products Co., Round, Paperweight, 2 1/2 In. 11.00
Mirror, Whiteford's Chewing Gum, Wooden Frame, Easel Back, 14 1/2 In. 198.00
Mirror, Whitehouse Coffee, Dwinel-Wright Co., Product Box Pictured, 2 In. 22.00
Mixer, Milkshake, Cole's, Cast Iron, 1910, 24 In. 4312.00
Mobile, Falls City Fishing Products, 5 Piece, Cardboard, 1950s 29.00
Mug, Anheuser-Busch, Display 110.00
Mug, Campbell Kid, Trademark Campbell Soup Co., Plastic, 2 3/4 In. 10.00
Mug, Drink Tomato Juice, Red Tomato, Green Leaves, Raised Relief, 3 x 2 In. 10.00
Mug, Frostie Old Fashioned Root Beer, Light Cardboard, 5 In. 99.00
Mug, Hires Root Beer, Boy Pointing, Drink Hires Root Beer, 4 x 3 1/2 In. 225.00
Mug, Hires Root Beer, Ugly Boy, Mettlach 225.00
Mug, Hires, Boy On Front, Word Hires On Back, 4 In. 297.00
Mug, Iroquois Beer & Ail, Painted Label, 1950s 6.00
Mug, Jos. Reiger's Pure Beer, Ceramic, Allover Crackle, 1890s 165.00
Mug, Nestle Quick, Rabbit, Hard Plastic, Ears As Handles, 4 In. ....15.00 to 20.00
Mug, Pitcher, Kool-Aid, Translucent, Embossed, Plastic, 1980, 3 In. & 6 In. .... *Illus* 20.00
Mug, Quaker Oats, Ounces Marked Inside, Plastic, 3 1/2 In. .... *Illus* 3.50
Mug, Robert Portner Brewing Co., Alexandria, Va., Pottery, Bristol Glaze, 5 In. 165.00
Mug, Tivoli Beer, Copper, Etched, Logo, 1930s, 4 In. 10.00
Mug, Valley Forge Beer, Franklin Min, 1985, Miniature 18.00
Noisemaker, Neligh Cigar Co., 2 Red Wooden Knockers At Side, Wooden, 6 In. 20.00
Pack, Cigarette, All American Cigarettes, Buy U.S. War Bonds, Red Eagle Flying 50.00
Pack, Cigarette, Barking Dog, Unopened, Wrapped In Plastic, 20 Pack 39.00
Pack, Cigarette, Chelsea Cigarettes, Edgeworth, Reed Tobacco Co. 30.00
Pack, Cigarette, Debs Rose Tips, Benson & Hedges Co., Sealed Package, 20 Pack 55.00
Pack, Cigarette, Domino Cigarette, Reed Tobacco Company, Sealed Package 35.00
Pack, Cigarette, Fatima Turkish Blend Cigarettes, Liggett & Myers Tobacco Co. 33.00
Pack, Cigarette, Home Run, Liggett & Myers Tobacco Co., Baseball Graphics 58.00
Pack, Cigarette, Lady Hamilton, World Renowned Cigarettes, Unopened 35.00
Pack, Cigarette, Listerine Cigarettes, Made Of The Finest Tobacco, Unopened 52.00
Pack, Cigarette, Marlboro Cigarettes, Philip Morris & Co. Ltd., Ivory Tipped 75.00

Advertising, Mug, Pitcher, Kool-Aid, Translucent, Embossed, Plastic, 1980, 3 In. & 6 In.

Advertising, Mug, Quaker Oats,
Ounces Marked Inside,
Plastic, 3 1/2 In.

Advertising, Pitcher, Nestle
Quik, Bunny's Ears Turn, Stir
Milk, Plastic, 1980, 9 1/2 In.

Pack, Cigarette, O-Nic-O Denicotinized, Unopened, Wrapped In Plastic, 20 Pack 25.00
Pack, Cigarette, Philip Morris & Co., Ltd., Sealed Package, 20 Pack 35.00
Pack, Cigarette, Sano Cigarettes, All That Joyous Aroma, But Less Nicotine, 20 Pack 35.00
Pack, Cigarette, Sweet Caporal, American Tobacco Co., Sealed Package, 20 Pack 30.00
Pack, Cigarette, Topper's, Tops Them All, Man Wearing Top Hat Smoking, 20 Pack 55.00
Pack, Old King Cole Smoking Mixture, Cellophane Cover, M. Parrish, 4 x 3 In. 230.00
Packet, Biggerhair Tobacco, African Figure With Earrings & Nose Ring . . . . .72.00 to 88.00
Pail, Armour's Veribest Peanut Butter, 3 13/16 In. 295.00
Pail, Armour's Veribest Peanut Butter, 4 1/2 In. 595.00
Pail, BB Coffee, Tin Lithograph, Slip Lid, Bail Handle, 10 1/2 In. 143.00
Pail, Campbell Coffee, Tin, 4 Lb. 75.00
Pail, Caraja Coffee, Paper Label, Tin, Slip Lid, Bail Handle, 10 1/2 In. 143.00
Pail, Cream Dove Peanut Butter, Tin Lithograph, Lid & Bail, 4 1/2 In. 22.00
Pail, Fashion Cut Plug Tobacco, 4 x 7 3/4 x 5 In. 210.00
Pail, Jolly Time Hulless Pop Corn, Boy & Girl, 16 Oz. 130.00
Pail, Jolly Time Pop Corn, No. 1, Images Of Boys & Girls, Good Housekeeping, 1927 . . .   55.00
Pail, Just Suits Cut Plug, Tin Lithograph, 4 1/2 x 8 In. 70.00
Pail, Kitte's Peanut Butter, 1 Lb. 50.00
Pail, Lard, Little Pig, Rhymes, Tin Lithograph 170.00
Pail, Lifesavers, Metal, 1950s, 11 In. 145.00
Pail, Lovell & Covel Pure Hard Candies, Lid, Red Riding Hood, 3 In. 340.00
Pail, McCormick's Jersey Cream, Tin Lithograph, Slip Lid, Bail Handle, 7 In. 143.00
Pail, Monarch Peanut Butter, 3 11/16 In. 475.00
Pail, Morris', Supreme Peanut Butter, Children & Beach, 1 Lb. 375.00
Pail, Nalley's Popcorn, Boy Eating Popcorn, Red Ground, Bail Handle, 9 Oz. 110.00
Pail, Niggerhair Tobacco, Smoke Or Chew, Handle 54.00
Pail, Niggerhair Tobacco, Tin, Lithograph, Bail Handle, No Lid, 6 1/2 In. 132.00
Pail, No. 16 Mixtures, Paper Label, Comical Frog, Wooden, Bail Handle, 12 In. 132.00
Pail, Schepp's Coconut, Lid, Tin Lithograph, Monkeys Drinking, 4 In. 230.00
Pail, Sears Roebuck Coffee, 5 Lb., 8 1/4 In. 120.00
Pail, Shedd's Peanut Butter 35.00
Pail, Sweetheart Pure Peanut Butter, Canada, 1 Lb. 100.00
Pail, Veteran Brand Peanut Butter, 1 Lb. 165.00
Pail, Wilson's Peanut Butter, Bail Handle, Tin, 12 Oz. 385.00
Pedestal, Soda Fountain, Glass, Chrome Connector, Pre-1916, 12 In., Pair 60.00
Pencil Holder, King Of Beverages, Bullet Shape, Celluloid Cover, 6 1/2 x 7 In. 1100.00
Pickle Fork, Heinz 57, Green Plastic 8.00
Pie Plate, Watkins Products, Danish Raspberry Cream 42.00
Pillbox, DM Postal Credit Union, Brushed Finish, Plastic Drawer, Zippo, 1970s 55.00
Pin, American Casualty Insurance Co., Celluloid, 1 1/4 In. 8.00
Pin, Barney & Berry, In Every Land Where Water Freezes, Ice Skate, 1 In. 23.00
Pin, Bell Phone, 1876-1926, 50 Years, Candlestick Phone, Blue Celluloid, 1 In. 35.00
Pin, Compliments Of Annie Oakley, U.M.C. Ammunition, Celluloid, Metal, 3/4 In. 379.00
Pin, Evinrude, Outboard Motor, Big Twin, Blue, Box, 3 1/2 In. 31.00
Pin, Meridian Fertilizers, Celluloid, 1902, 1 In. 6.00
Pin, Pan-Am Clipper, Airplane Shape, Stamped Brass, 2 1/4-In. Wingspan, Pair 48.00
Pin, Perk-Up With Dr Pepper, Yellow Ground, Celluloid, 4 In. 660.00
Pin, Poth's Beer, Angel & Cherub, Whitehead & Hoag, 1 1/4 In.   33.00
Pin, Telephone Pioneers Of America, George S. Ladd Chap. No. 27, Celluloid, 2 In. 18.00
Pin, Tivoli Export Beer, F.A. Poth & Sons, Bottle, Whitehead & Hoag, 1 1/2 In. 33.00
Pinball, Poll-Parrot Shoes, Wood, Metal, Stenciled Backboard, 17 1/2 In. 44.00
Pitcher, Gablinger's Beer, Painted Label, 1960s, 9 In. 14.00
Pitcher, Nestle Quik, Bunny's Ears Turn, Stir Milk, Plastic, 1980, 9 1/2 In. . . . .*Illus*   18.00
Plaque, Owl Drug Co., Plaster, Multicolored Paint, 12 3/4 In. Diam. 175.00
Plaque, Poll-Parrot Shoes, Hanging, Plaster, 18 In. 99.00
Plate, Budweiser Beer, World Famous Clydesdales, Porcelain, 1970s, 11 In. 15.00
Plate, Budweiser Bottles, Cheers, Metal, Norman Rockwell, 1980s 15.00
Plate, Dinner, Fort Pitt Beer-Old Shay Ale, Porcelain, 1940s, 9 3/4 In. 60.00
Plate, Dr Pepper, Red Roses, King Of Beverages, 7 1/2 x 8 In. 1331.00
Plate, Drink Dr Pepper, 10, 2 & 4, Red Ground, 10 In. 726.00
Plate, The Wertz Ice Cream, White, Blue Edge Trim, 6 1/4 In. 22.00
Plate, Watkins Products, Pumpkin Ride Country Kids 22.00
Pouch, Bride Rose Cut Plug Mixture, Harry Weissinger, Cloth, Contents 55.00

Puppet, H.R. Pufnstuf, Pop-Tarts Premium, 1970 .... 81.00
Puppet, Mr. Wiggles, Jell-O Premium 210.00
Push Bar, King Cole Tea, Coffee, Porcelain, 31 1/2 x 3 In. 220.00
Push Bar, Sunbeam Bread, Steel, Painted, 31 1/2 x 8 3/4 In. 440.00
Puzzle, Chase & Sanborn Coffee, Country Store Scene 78.00
Puzzle, Chase & Sanborn Coffee, Heart Shape Die Cut, Cardboard, String, 2 1/2 In. 22.00
Puzzle, Hood's Sarsaparilla, Horse & Wagon, Lowell, Ma., American, 1891, 10 x 15 In. ... 316.00
Radiator Cover, Shell Logo On Each Side, Yellow, Red Lettering, 13 x 18 In. 45.00
Razor Bank, Listerine, Donkey 25.00
Ribbon, Shaker Cloak, E.J. Neale & Co., Cloaked Woman, Woven Silk, 3 x 7 1/2 In. 258.00
Rolling Pin, Krispy Krust, Chrome Roller, Red Bakelite Handles, Box 35.00
Rug, Red Goose Shoes, Yellow Border, 57 In. 550.00
Rug, Weather-Bird, 56 In. 440.00
Salt & Pepper Shakers are listed in their own category.
Sample Kit, Eli Lilly & Co., Paper, Fold Out, 1915, 22 Sealed Ampules 220.00
Scales are listed in their own category.
Scooter, Poll-Parrot Shoes, Parrot, 3 Wheels, Painted Wood, Rubber Tires, 17 In. 963.00
Seed Bin, Landreths Seeds, Bristol, Pa., Tin, Oak Grained, Fruits Panel, 28 x 28 In. 520.00
Shoehorn, Martin Cigars, Giveaway, 4 1/4 In. 66.00
Shoehorn, Philip Martin Cigars, 40 Anos, 4 1/4 In. 66.00
Shoehorn, Shinola, The Wonderful Shoe Polish, Tin Lithograph, 4 In. 88.00
Shot Glass, Another Knockout, 2 3/8 In. 3.00
Shot Glass, Chicago, Black Amethyst, 2 3/8 In. 5.00
Shot Glass, I Don't Drink Much, Buxom Women In Red Dresses, 4 Oz. 10.00
Shot Glass, If You Drink Don't Drive, 2 3/8 In. 3.00
Shot Glass, Just A Swallow, Yellow & Red Painted Design 5.00
Shot Glass, Lord Calvert, The Whiskey Of Distinction 5.00
Shot Glass, Old Kentucky Tavern 5.00
Shot Glass, Reno Lake Tahoe & Virginia City, 2 3/8 In. 3.00
Shot Glass, Ronald W. Reagan 40th President, Head & Shoulders, Black Print 8.00
Shot Glass, Universal Studios Tour, Black, White Lettering, 2 Horizontal Bands 7.50
Sign, 7-Up, Bottle Shape, Tin, Embossed, 13 x 44 1/2 In.......................... 575.00
Sign, 7-Up, Curved Bottle, Die Cut, Tin, Embossed, 44 1/2 In. 275.00
Sign, A & P, Mother Love, Children, Chicks, Paper Lithograph, Framed, 27 x 13 In. 143.00
Sign, ABC Bohemian, King Of All Bottled Beers, Celluloid, 9 x 6 1/2 In. 385.00
Sign, Accent On Youth, Young Woman In Shorts Showing Cigarettes, 1940, 14 In. 36.00
Sign, Acme Beer, Tin Over Cardboard, Octagonal, 1930s, 15 1/4 x 15 1/4 In. 200.00
Sign, Alaga Syrup, Willie Mays, Paper, 1960s, 10 x 20 In. 385.00
Sign, Alta Mineral Water, Woman In Vintage Clothing, 19 1/2 x 13 1/2 In. 850.00
Sign, Ambassador Beer, Reverse Painting On Glass, 1950s, 10 x 7 In. 15.00
Sign, American Express Travelers Cheques Accepted Here, Porcelain, 18 x 13 In. 230.00
Sign, American Gentleman Shoe, Embossed, Tin Lithograph, 19 x 12 In. 121.00
Sign, Anchor Beer, Painted On Curved Glass, Wooden Frame, Inner Lights, 25 In. 850.00
Sign, Angelus Marshmallow, Die Cut Girl, Drumming, Cardboard, 11 x 5 1/2 In. 302.00
Sign, Anheuser-Busch, L.A. Beer, Neon, Dark Red, Blue, Gold, Plastic, 17 x 21 In. 36.00
Sign, Arden Milk, Milk Bottle, Porcelain, 2 Sides, 28 x 33 In. 635.00
Sign, Badger Farm Materials Handling Equipment On 2 Panels, Metal, 35 In. 48.00
Sign, Ballantine Ale, Paper, Glass, Frame, 1950s, 9 1/2 x 12 In. 25.00
Sign, Ballard's Obelisk Flour, Tin, Boy In Sailor Suit, 33 x 46 In. 2472.00
Sign, Barber Shop Pole, Barber Shop Logo, Porcelain, 24 x 17 In. 190.00
Sign, Barber Shop, Ask For Wildroot, White, Red, Blue Lettering, 39 x 13 1/2 In. 85.00
Sign, Bardenheier Wine & Liquors, Oval, Tin Litho, Embossed Frame, 19 x 23 In. 688.00
Sign, Between Bites Drink Squeeze, Man & Boy In Rowboat, Cardboard, Easel, 19 In. 193.00
Sign, Bireley's Soda, Price, Frame, 1930s, 15 x 19 In. 48.00
Sign, Blackwell's Bull Durham, Stone Litho, Man With Drinks, c.1880, 24 x 31 In. 350.00
Sign, Blanchard Brand Delicious Ice Cream, Good For Babies, Baby, 1950, 24 In. 357.00
Sign, Blanchard Ice Cream, Baby, Arms & Legs Swing, Battery, 1940s, 19 x 24 In. 515.00
Sign, Blatz Beer, Blatz, America's Great Light Beer, Brown Plastic Frame, 21 In. 36.00
Sign, Boone Kitchen Cabinet Store List, Tin Lithograph, Sliding Button, 12 3/4 In. 176.00
Sign, Borden's Ice Cream, Elsie In Daisy, Light-Up, 26 1/2 x 8 3/4 x 3 3/4 In. 240.00
Sign, Bradley Cigars, Tin Lithograph, c.1920, 13 1/2 x 19 1/2 In. 105.00
Sign, Brook's Six Cord Cotton, Reverse On Glass, Wooden Frame, 10 3/4 In. 55.00
Sign, Brookfield Rye, Tin Lithograph, Self-Framed, 32 3/4 In. 2530.00

Sign, Buckeye Premium Beer, Molded Plastic, Pheasant, 1950s, 11 x 14 In. 30.00
Sign, Budweiser Barley Malt Syrup, Couple Holding Malt Syrup, 1930, 13 x 21 In. 275.00
Sign, Budweiser Beer, Tin Over Cardboard, 1951 Calendar Pad, 1951, 18 1/4 In. 70.00
Sign, Budweiser Girl, Frame, 39 x 24 In. 1430.00
Sign, Budweiser, Bowtie Shape, Neon, Plastic, 12 x 20 In. 90.00
Sign, Budweiser, King Of Beers, 8 Clydesdales, Beer Wagon, 20 x 47 1/4 In. 55.00
Sign, Budweiser, King Of Bottled Beer, White Lettering, Red Ground, Embossed, 72 In. ... 715.00
Sign, Buffalo Club Rye Whiskey, Tin Lithograph, Buffalo Picture, 29 x 38 In. 990.00
Sign, Busch Beer, A & Eagle Logo, 1970s, 18 x 17 In. 17.00
Sign, Buscho, Non-Intoxicating Cereal Beverage, Tin, Prohibition Era, 10 In. 94.00
Sign, Buster Brown, Reverse On Glass, Easel Back, 12 3/4 x 7 3/4 In. 100.00
Sign, Butcher's, Sheet Iron, Pig's Head Shape, Gilt Traces, 19th Century, 8 In. 1540.00
Sign, Bydweuster Beer, Pocket Watch Shape, 12 1/2 x 17 In. 90.00
Sign, C.D. Kenny, Easter Surprise, Children, Easter Bunny, Litho, Frame, 13 x 27 In. 275.00
Sign, C.H. Bemann Watchmaker, Reverse On Glass, Wooden Frame, 72 In. 770.00
Sign, Cafe, Lever, Raises Arms & Mug To Sailor's Mouth, 1860, 33 x 26 3/4 In. 3500.00
Sign, Call For Philip Morris, Tin Lithograph, Self-Framed, 27 1/2 x 10 In. 110.00
Sign, Camel Cigarette, Old Tobacco Farmer, I Ought Know, I Grow Tobacco, 15 In. 35.00
Sign, Campbell's Soups, Ready In A Jiffy, Tin, 17 1/2 x 11 1/2 In. 155.00
Sign, Canadian Club, Paper, 3 Men With Cigars, 1930s, 11 x 16 In. 28.00
Sign, Canadian Trails, Motels Motor Courts, Porcelain, 2 Sides, 18 x 26 In. 35.00
Sign, Carnation Ice Cream, Tin, 1940s, 24 In. 125.00
Sign, Castrol, Red Lettering, Dark Green Ground, Porcelain, 15 3/4 x 23 3/4 In. 275.00
Sign, Centlivre Brewing Co., Lager Beer, Fort Wayne, Frame, 29 x 42 In. 710.00
Sign, Centlivre Tonic, For Sale Here, Nurse, Cardboard, Hanging, 22 x 12 In. 150.00
Sign, Century Cereal Beverage, Tin, 1920s, 7 x 4 In. 25.00
Sign, Champagne Velvet, Tin Over Cardboard, Frame, 1930s, 15 x 20 1/2 In. 350.00
Sign, Chancellor Cigar, Paper, 40 x 24 In. 3300.00
Sign, Charley Denby Cigar, Logo Boy, Carrying Box, Die Cut Cardboard, 10 In. 120.00
Sign, Chas. D. Clark House & Sign Painting, Wooden, 19 Century, 82 x 102 In. 3500.00
Sign, Chesterfield Cigarettes, Fred Waring, Henry James, Paper, 21 x 12 In. 55.00
Sign, Chesterfield Cigarettes, George Burns, Gracie Allen, Cardboard, 21 x 22 In. 50.00
Sign, Chesterfield Cigarettes, Pack Picture, Tin, 11 3/4 x 17 3/4 In. 150.00
Sign, Chew Mail Pouch Tobacco, With Thermometer, Red, White, Blue, Metal, 38 In. 87.00
Sign, Chief Oshkosh Beer, Tin, Flange, Indian Picture, 18 x 13 1/2 In. 1070.00
Sign, Clabber Girl Baking Powder, 2 Sides, Tin Lithograph, 34 In. 55.00
Sign, Clabber Girl, The Healthy Baking Powder, Red Lettering, Embossed, 12 In. 65.00
Sign, Clark's O.N.T. Spool Cotton, Raised Image, Self-Framed, Tin, Litho, 20 1/4 In. 50.00
Sign, Cloverdale Soft Drinks, Silver Embossed Dots Lettering, 1950, 9 x 13 In. 38.00
Sign, Coburger Beer, Curved Corners, Gold & Black, Tin, 17 x 21 In. 95.00
Sign, Colgate Dental Cream, 3 Panel, Wooden Frame, 36 x 62 In. 130.00
Sign, Comic Books Given Away, 6-Bottle Carton Of Dr Pepper, 1950, 22 x 34 In. 305.00
Sign, Concord Dairy, Milk, Cream, Porcelain, Round, 22 In. 255.00
Sign, Coors Light-Up Mirror, Silver, Neon, Brown Wooden Frame, 20 x 25 x 6 In. 41.00
Sign, Coverdale Soft Drinks, Tin Over Cardboard, 1950s, 9 1/4 x 13 In. 75.00
Sign, Crescent Watch Cases, Crescent Moon, Reverse On Glass, Frame, 25 1/2 In. 275.00
Sign, Crotzer's Bromo Mint, Buxom Lady, Color Litho, Cardboard, 17 1/2 x 36 In. 242.00
Sign, Curb Service Pepsi-Cola, Ice Cold Bigger-Better, Black Ground, 1940, 28 In. 467.00
Sign, Dad's Old Fashioned Root Beer, Black Lettering, 1950, 18 x 46 In. 275.00
Sign, Daily Half Dozen, Do These At Every Stop, Watch Your Sales Grow, 28 x 44 In. 385.00
Sign, De Laval Cream Separator, 2 Sides, 27 1/2 In. 4400.00
Sign, De Laval Separator, Authorized Agency, 1930, 26 x 18 In. 1277.00
Sign, Deering Ideal Mower, Deering Harvest Company, Frame, 20 x 30 In. 330.00
Sign, Demand Kayo It's Real Chocolate, Embossed, Wooden Frame, Tin, 29 1/2 In. 248.00
Sign, Denver Sandwich Candy 5 Cents, White Lettering, Red Ground, 1950, 2 x 22 In. 121.00
Sign, Dewry's Old Stock Ale, Composition, 10 1/2 x 16 1/2 In. 88.00
Sign, Diamond Dyes, A Busy Day In Dollville, Tin Lithograph Over Cardboard, 17 In. 3190.00
Sign, Double Cola, Double Measure, Double Pleasure, Embossed, 1940, 28 In. 495.00
Sign, Dr Pepper Bottling Co. Triangle, Red Ground, 1940, 21 x 12 In. 1573.00
Sign, Dr Pepper, Bottle Cap, At 10, 2 & 4, White Ground, 1959, 18 x 22 In. 1633.00
Sign, Dr Pepper, Accredited Route Salesman, Gold Ring, 1940, 7 In. 660.00
Sign, Dr Pepper, Certainly!, Drink Woman At Stadium, 1940, 9 1/4 In. ....385.00 to 660.00
Sign, Dr Pepper, Delivery Cycle, Yellow Body, 1960, 6 1/2 In. 330.00

Sign, Dr Pepper, Featuring Kid At Ball Game With Dr Pepper, 25 x 32 In. 2420.00
Sign, Dr. E.L. Graves Tooth Powder, Reverse Foil On Glass, Mirror Back, 22 In. 560.00
Sign, Dr. Jayne's Expectorant, Reverse On Glass, Wooden Frame, 11 In. 275.00
Sign, Dr. Morse's Indian Root Pill, Easel Back, Cardboard, 9 x 19 In. 130.00
Sign, Dr. Morse's Indian Root Plus, Die Cut Cardboard, Easel Back, 19 1/2 In. 61.00
Sign, Dr. Nix, Marvelous Fishing Act, Folded, Lithograph, 19 x 15 In. 1380.00
Sign, Drewry's Beer, Trademark Of Quality, Cardboard, 1950s, 17 x 25 In. 70.00
Sign, Drewry's Old Stock Ale, Composition, 3-D Plastic Bottle, 1940s, 12 x 15 In. 40.00
Sign, Drink Barq's, It's Good, Beveled Edge, 1950, 11x 14 In. 209.00
Sign, Drink Cello, Delicious Fruit Juice, Celery Flavor, 27 1/2 x 9 1/2 In. 125.00
Sign, Drink Chocolate Soldier In Bottles, Yellow, Red, Brown, 14 x 11 In. 27.00
Sign, Drink Dr Pepper, Bigger & Better, Turquoise, Black Ground, Neon, 1930, 9 In. 4400.00
Sign, Drink Dr Pepper, Glass Of Dr Pepper, 1940, 12 x 13 In. 550.00
Sign, Drink Dr Pepper, Good For Life!, At 10, 2 & 4, 5 Cents, Aluminum, 10 In. 1210.00
Sign, Drink Dr Pepper, Good For Life!, Thank You, Call Again, Red, 1940, 8 x 13 In. 4950.00
Sign, Drink Dr Pepper, King Of Beverages, Beveled Edge, Cardboard, 1910, 8 In. 4477.00
Sign, Drink Dr Pepper, White Lettering, Red Ground, 1930, 10 x 17 1/2 In. 2090.00
Sign, Drink Dr Pepper, Woman With Flowers, 1940, 6 In. 577.00
Sign, Drink Green River, All Ways Delightful, Cardboard, Tin Frame, 42 In. 193.00
Sign, Drink Hires Root Beer, Amber Color, 1950, 13 x 42 In. 440.00
Sign, Drink Mavis, Woman Sitting On Bench Drinking Mavis, 1930, 18 x 30 In. 825.00
Sign, Drink Nesbitt's California Orange, Kids With Clown, 1940, 9 1/4 In. 385.00
Sign, Drink Orange Crush, Sold Here Ice Cold, Carbonated Beverage, 1930, 18 In. 786.00
Sign, Drink Pepsi-Cola, Bottle Cap, Yellow Ground, 1954, 8 1/4 x 8 1/2 In. 192.00
Sign, Drink Polly's Soda Pop, Tin Lithograph, 25 1/4 In. 358.00
Sign, Drink Un 7-Up Anytime, Neon, Plastic, 1970, 24 x 32 In. 484.00
Sign, Dupont Powders, Hunters & Dogs, Tin Lithograph, Self-Framed, 33 In. 990.00
Sign, Dutch Boy Paints, Holding Giant Brush, Cardboard, 1920s, 8 1/4 x 8 1/2 In. 920.00
Sign, Dutch Boy, Painters Carrying Can, Die Cut, Easel Back, 1930s, 21 x 37 In. 375.00
Sign, Egyptian Straights, Face Of Woman, Frame, 35 1/2 x 25 1/2 In. 313.00
Sign, El-Mar-Mar Cafe, Reverse On Glass, 30 x 21 In. 165.00
Sign, Elgin Watch, Paper Lithograph, Frame Under Glass, 30 In. 220.00
Sign, Empire Cream Separators, Painted, Wooden, 12 In. 193.00
Sign, Enterprise Stove, Flange, Tin, 2 Sides, 18 In. 385.00
Sign, Eskay's Food, Die Cut, Cardboard Child, Easel Back, Stand-Up, 6 In. 88.00
Sign, Eslinger's Repeal Beer, Tin Lithograph Over Cardboard, 13 1/2 In. 176.00
Sign, F. Ruhstaller, Gilt Edge-Steam Beer, 26 x 24 In. 1320.00
Sign, Fairmont Ice Cream, Neon, Green & Red, 25 x 10 In. 245.00
Sign, Fame & Fortune & War Of Wealth Cigars, Tin, 1900, 7 1/2 x 14 In. 65.00
Sign, Feel Fresh!, Drink Orange Crush, Carbonated Beverage, Crush Figure, 40 In. 467.00
Sign, Fireman's Fund Insurance Co., Car Accident, Fire, Theft Scenes, Frame, 22 In. 550.00
Sign, Fitch's Standard Heart Chewing Gum, Cardboard, Frame, c.1910, 10 In. 175.00
Sign, Fitzgerald's Ale, Tin, 1940s, 13 x 8 1/2 In. 75.00
Sign, Fly Central Airlines, 2-Prop Airplane, Lithographed, 13 x 27 In. 40.00
Sign, Ford, Smart New Interiors, Smartest Ford Car Ever Built!, 1946, 35 x 46 In. 90.00
Sign, Foremost Ice Cream, Tin, Embossed, Carton Shape, 24 x 17 1/2 In. 120.00
Sign, Foremost So-Lo Low Fat Milk, Aluminum, Milk Carton Shape, 15 x 30 In. 165.00
Sign, Forest Castle, Hughs & Glennon Bry., Horseshoe Shape, Rubber, 24 x 28 In. 840.00
Sign, Fountain Pen, Cast Iron Figure Of Woman With Flower, 1900, 15 In. 412.00
Sign, Frank Fehr Brewing Co., Try Our Bock Beer, 1880, 30 x 40 In. 510.00
Sign, French Bauer Ice Cream Cone, Light-Up, Peach Ice Cream, Wooden Base, 8 In. 2662.00
Sign, Fresh 7-Up, Green Lettering, White Ground, 1951, 15 1/2 x 40 In. 575.00
Sign, Genesee Beer, Puppies, Tin Over Cardboard, Gold Frame, 1960s, 14 x 7 In. 25.00
Sign, Get The Break!, Kleanbore Shot Shells, Join The Remington Straight Club, 20 In. . . . 192.00
Sign, Gilillan Newtrodyne, Radio, Bring The World To Your Home, 1920s, 14 x 25 In. 75.00
Sign, Gillette Blades, Red Lettering, Yellow Ground, Porcelain, 1930, 19 x 22 In. 3080.00
Sign, Glass Of Dr Pepper With Fan, 1940, 12 x 12 In. 495.00
Sign, Good Humor Ice Cream, White Ground, 1940, 26 x 50 In. 634.00
Sign, Grain Belt Beer, Neon, Window Style, No Transformer, 1950s, 25 x 12 In. 105.00
Sign, Granger Pipe Tobacco, Red, Marine Smoking Pipe, 16 x 11 In. 35.00
Sign, Grapette Soda, White Lettering, Black Ground, 1950, 10 x 26 In. 132.00
Sign, Gravel Springs Mineral Water Gravel Springs Co., Tin, 1915, 13 x 19 In. 575.00
Sign, Green River Whiskey, Black Man Holding Horse, Jug, c.1900, 23 x 34 In. 165.00

Sign, Green River Whiskey, Black Man, Horse, Jug, Frame, 19 1/2 x 24 1/2 In. 250.00
Sign, Green Spot Orange-Ade, Oranges, Bottles, Glasses, Cardboard, c.1936, 21 In. 66.00
Sign, Green Spot Orange-Ade, Tin Lithograph, Embossed, Donaldson Art, 20 x 12 In. . . .   200.00
Sign, Groceries, World Soap, Teas & Coffees, Porcelain, Flange, 12 x 18 In. 1210.00
Sign, Gurd's Distilled Water, Be Good To Your Battery, Use Gurd's, Red, 21 In. 385.00
Sign, Hamilton Brown Shoes, Elegant Woman, Frame, c.1915, 19 3/4 x 16 In. 220.90
Sign, Hamilton Watch, Tin Lithograph Over Cardboard, Raised Image, 19 In. 1320.00
Sign, Hamm's Beer, Dancing Bear, On Barrel, Vacuformed Plastic, Round, 15 In. 21.00
Sign, Harding's Hardware, Girl With Roses, Paper Litho, Framed, Matted, 15 x 20 In. . . .   248.00
Sign, Harper's Whiskey, Here's Happy Days, Porcelain, Framed, 23 x 17 In. 550.00
Sign, Harrison Valley Mineral Water, Photograph Center, 1910, 17 x 14 In. 120.00
Sign, Have A Dad's Old Fashioned Root Beer, It's Delicious, On Black, 1950, 20 In. 110.00
Sign, Headlight Overalls, Porcelain, 1930s, 10 x 32 In. 745.00
Sign, Healthful Cleanliness, There's Nothing Like Old Dutch, Yellow, 1940, 18 In. 1028.00
Sign, Heidelberg Beer, Bar Scene, Plaque Type, 13 1/4 x 9 x 3 In.   165.00
Sign, Helmar Turkish Cigarettes, Helmar Cowgirl, Porcelain, 2 Sides, 23 x 16 In. 1246.00
Sign, Hendler's Ice Cream, Cardboard, Kewpie Kid, 1920s, 4 x 10 In. 17.00
Sign, Hercules Powder, Paper Lithograph, Framed Under Glass, 18 In. 300.00
Sign, Here's Luck!, Stroh's Bohemian Beer, Burnt Orange, Die Cut, 17 x 17 In. 82.00
Sign, Hires R-J Root Beer, So Good, With Real Root Juices, 1940, 13 x 39 In. 1045.00
Sign, Hires Root Beer, Couple In Speedboat, Die Cut, 1940, 10 x 12 In. 231.00
Sign, Hires, Early Store, Root Beer, With Owl, 9 In. 104.00
Sign, Hollywood Glo, Countertop, 3-Fold, Cardboard, c.1940, 18 x 12 In. 50.00
Sign, Honeymoon Tobacco, Moon, Tin, John Igelstroem Co., 9 3/4 x 6 3/4 In. 325.00
Sign, Horlick's Malted Milk, Maiden & Cow, Paper Lithograph, 19 In. 204.00
Sign, Hoster's Beer, Self-Framed, Tin Lithograph, 33 In. 990.00
Sign, Hub Clothing, Seated Black Boy Holding Sign, Dimensional, Metal, 53 In. 2310.00
Sign, Ice Cold Bludwine, For Your Health's Sake, 1920, 10 x 13 In. 726.00
Sign, Ice Cold Pepsi-Cola, Sold Here, Black Ground, 1940, 10 x 14 In. 755.00
Sign, It's Hood's Ice Cream The Flavor's There, Embossed, Tin Lithograph, 28 In. 633.00
Sign, J. & P. Coats, Lithograph, Wooden Frame, Tin, 21 3/4 In. 110.00
Sign, J. H. Gilmour, Clock, Cast Iron, Tin, 2 Sides, 32 In. 743.00
Sign, James L. Libby's Dead Shot Collar, Frame, 1800s, 11 1/2 x 14 1/2 In. 1540.00
Sign, John Deere Farm Implements, Porcelain, 72 x 24 In. 4950.00
Sign, Join Me!, Drink Dr Pepper, Girl In Car Holding Dr Pepper, 9 1/2 In. 495.00
Sign, Jumbo Beard Elephant, Die Cut, 1950, 15 x 13 In. 605.00
Sign, Kingsbury Pale Beer, Embossed Tin, Beer Bottle, 19 1/2 x 27 1/2 In. 143.00
Sign, Kis-Me Gum, Cardboard, Embossed, 7 In. 385.00
Sign, Knapp Calendar Co., Color Paper, Lithograph, Logo, 23 1/2 x 36 In. 475.00
Sign, Knickerbocker Beer, Priscilla, Foil Over Cardboard, 1950s, 17 3/4 x 14 In. 15.00
Sign, Knife Trade, Yellow Pine, Black Over White, Wooden, 1900, 6 x 36 In. 475.00
Sign, Kodak Verichrome Safety Film, Porcelain, 2 Sides, Box Shape, 21 x 14 In. 165.00
Sign, Koester's Fresher Bread, Blue, Yellow, Rolled Edges, Tin Lithograph, 30 1/2 In. . . .   176.00
Sign, Kotex, Nurse With Box, Tin Lithograph, Holes For Hanging, 19 In. 308.00
Sign, La Flor De Carvalho Cigars, Tin Lithograph, Oak Frame, c.1910, 15 x 21 In. 130.00
Sign, Lee Union-Alls Overalls, Whizits, Union Made, Yellow Ground, 1940, 13 x 27 In. . . .   453.00
Sign, Leesures By Lee, Cardboard, Motorized Venetian Blind Effect, 18 x 3 In. 155.00
Sign, Levi's 501, Clear Plexiglas, Orange, White, Blue, 24 x 18 In. 40.00
Sign, Levi's Jeans, Dance Tonight, Color, Plastic Laminated, 14 x 38 In. 90.00
Sign, Levi's Shoes & Boots, Pulpboard, Copper Leaf Letters, 12 In. 20.00
Sign, Levi's, Chuckwagon Scene, Plastic Coated, 14 x 36 In. 100.00
Sign, Livingston & Toney's Pool Parlor, Paper Lithograph, Under Glass, 18 In. 550.00
Sign, Lowenbrau Munich Beer, Cardboard, Frame, 1950s, 15 x 18 In. 5.00
Sign, Lucky Strike Cigarette, Tony Lazzeri, Cardboard, 21 x 12 In. 1120.00
Sign, Lucky Strike Cut Plug Tobacco, Pipe Shape, 2 Sides, 19 In.   3000.00
Sign, Lukes Music Store, Frigidaire, General Motors, Die Cut, Porcelain, 60 In. 495.00
Sign, Magic Yeast, Boy In Turban, Stone Lithograph, Cardboard Hanger, 1906, 15 In. 290.00
Sign, Magic Yeast, Harry Roseland Painting, Stone Lithograph, c.1909, 20 x 15 In. 445.00
Sign, Magnolia, White Flowers, Red Basket, 1953, 7 x 7 1/4 In., 5 Piece 2970.00
Sign, Maine Camp, Log Cabin, Names, Scroll Cut, 22 1/4 x 24 1/2 In. 290.00
Sign, Marlboro Cigarettes, Cowboy On Horse, Leading Other Horse, Tin, 17 x 22 In. 25.00
Sign, Marlin Firearms, Paper Lithograph, Framed Under Glass, 22 1/2 In. 110.00
Sign, Marvels Cigarette, Tin, Embossed 2 Packs, 3 1/2 x 16 In. 95.00

Sign, Mayo's Plug Tobacco, Logo Rooster Strutting, Cloth, 24 x 14 1/2 In. 275.00
Sign, McCormick, Derring Threshers, Frame, c.1931, 31 x 41 In. 150.00
Sign, Mechanical Woman's Head, Die Cut Litho, Eye & Mouth Movement, 27 In. 1045.00
Sign, Meerschaum Tobacco, Cat Using Box As Kittens Home, c.1900, 17 In. 145.00
Sign, Meissner Felsenkeller Bier, St. Afra Monk, Metal, Germany, 1930s, 21 In. 125.00
Sign, Mercurochrome, Cardboard, Die Cut, Easel Back, 22 In. 50.00
Sign, Michelin, Man On Bicycle, Smoking Cigar, France, 50 x 34 In. 935.00
Sign, Millbank Virginia Cigarettes, Porcelain, Mounted On Wooden Strips, 60 In. 248.00
Sign, Miller Lite, A Fine Pilsner Beer, Neon, Wooden Plastic Frame, 21 x 16 In. 25.00
Sign, Mission Orange, Bottle, Tin Lithograph, Self-Framed, 25 1/2 x 10 In. 130.00
Sign, Moosehead Canadian Lager Beer, Plastic, Green, Red, Gold, 14 In. 25.00
Sign, Morton's Salt, It Pours, White Lettering, Black, Tin, 9 3/4 x 27 1/2 In. 90.00
Sign, Murad Turkish Cigarettes, Porcelain, 22 x 3 1/2 In. 200.00
Sign, Musical Instruments, Wooden, Folk Art, 1909, 10 x 46 In. 250.00
Sign, National Fire Insurance Co., Helmeted Woman, Flag, Metal, 3 x 12 5/8 In. 31.00
Sign, National Premium Beer, Hanger, Round, Embossed, Tin Lithograph, 9 1/2 In. 44.00
Sign, Nesbitt's California Orange Sold Here, Black Ground, 1940, 13 x 18 In. 1089.00
Sign, Nestle Permanent Waving, Licensed Nestle Shop, Die Cut, Oval, 15 x 18 In. 1265.00
Sign, New Eddie Bracken Show, Sponsored By Texaco, 1946, 13 x 21 In. 43.00
Sign, Niagara Fire Insurance, New York, Safety Fund Policies, Black, 1915, 21 In. 3267.00
Sign, Nichol Kola, America's 5 Cent Taste Sensation, Tin, 1936, 8 x 24 In. 18.00
Sign, Nichol Kola, Bellhop Stretching Arms Out To Nichol Kola, Tin, 12 In. 30.00
Sign, Nichol Kola, Vitamin B1 Added, America's Taste Sensation, Tin, 28 In. 30.00
Sign, Norfolk Food Of Strength, Young Child, Paper, c.1900, 33 1/2 x 23 1/2 In. 325.00
Sign, NuGrape Soda, Embossed Tin, Paper Residue, 43 1/2 In. 413.00
Sign, Odin 5 Cent Cigar, Man Carrying Odin Briefcase, Yellow Ground, 10 x 28 In. 330.00
Sign, OFC Whiskey, Tin Lithograph, Frame, 1890s, 15 1/2 x 11 1/2 In. 495.00
Sign, Ohio Farmers Insurance Co., Heavy Porcelain, 2 Sides, 18 In. 413.00
Sign, Old Egypt Cigarettes, Bright Tin Lithograph Over Cardboard, 19 In. 176.00
Sign, Old Plough, Wrought Iron, Steel & Wood, Worn Paint, 45 x 48 In. 935.00
Sign, Old Reliable Coffee, Dutchman, Tin Lithograph, 9 1/4 x 6 1/2 In. 330.00
Sign, Old Taylor Whiskey, Reverse Painted Glass, Frame, 29 x 42 In. 2530.00
Sign, One-Wire Electric Fencer, Demonstrated Here, Yellow, Black, 20 x 7 In. 55.00
Sign, Onward Garden Soldiers!, Drink Dr Pepper, 1940, 6 x 6 1/2 In. 467.00
Sign, Optometrist, 3-Dimensional, Zinc, 35 In. 3200.00
Sign, Orangeine Powders, Die Cut, Easel Back, 13 3/4 In. 187.00
Sign, P-F Canvas Shoes, P-F Time Is Here, 16 x 8 1/2 In. 31.00
Sign, Pabst Blue Ribbon On Draft, Reverse On Glass, Frame, 1940s, 14 x 9 In. 85.00
Sign, Pabst Blue Ribbon, Brand Labels, Prices, Plastic, Light-Up, 11 x 36 In. 39.00
Sign, Pabst Blue Ribbon, The Original Is Here!, White, Metal, 12 In. 76.00
Sign, Pacific Coast Borax, Woman In Hat, Paper Lithograph, 1907, 19 3/4 In. 88.00
Sign, Paul Jones Rye, Tin Lithograph, Self-Framed, 28 1/2 In. 1540.00
Sign, Pennsylvania Dutch Old German Beer, Cardboard, 1950s, 10 3/4 x 6 3/4 In. 35.00
Sign, Peppy Party!, Drink Dr Pepper, Woman Playing Accordion, 7 1/2 x 8 In. 440.00
Sign, Pepsi Flag, Red Lettering, Black Border, 1940, 42 x 70 In. 99.00
Sign, Pepsi-Cola Bottle, Die Cut, 1940, 12 x 45 In. 1375.00
Sign, Pepsi-Cola Tops, Aluminum, 1940, 14 x 36 In. 990.00
Sign, Pepsi-Cola, 12 Ounces, 1930, 5 x 12 In. 665.00
Sign, Perry Davis, Pain Killers, Linen Cloth, 28 1/2 x 12 In. 350.00
Sign, Peters Cartridge Company, Hunters & Moose In Canoe, Frame, 20 x 31 In. 120.00
Sign, Peters Weather-Bird Shoes, Sidewalk, Painted Wood, 2 Sides, 43 1/2 In. 1650.00
Sign, Philip Morris Cigarettes, King Size & Regular, Cardboard, 18 x 23 1/2 In. . . . . .38.00 to 50.00
Sign, Philip Morris, Embossed, Tin Lithograph, 13 1/4 In. 154.00
Sign, Phillies Cigars, Only 5 Cents, Tin, Embossed, 17 1/4 x 10 1/2 In. 120.00
Sign, Pick A Pack Dr Pepper, Metal Frame, 1960, 12 x 16 In. 77.00
Sign, Piedmont Cigarette, Lithograph Paper, Under Glass, Wooden Frame, 16 1/2 In. 300.00
Sign, Piels Real Lager Beer, Porcelain, Black & Red Letters, 12 x 23 In. 200.00
Sign, Pioneer Suspenders & Garters, Papier-Mache Covered Wagon, 11 x 14 In. 440.00
Sign, Pittsburgh Provision & Packing Co., Girl, Cow, Paper Litho, Frame, 27 1/2 In. 176.00
Sign, Poll-Parrot Shoes, Easel Back, Embossed, Cardboard, Die Cut, 15 1/2 In. 99.00
Sign, Poll-Parrot Shoes, Electric, Light-Up, Plastic, 25 1/2 In. 275.00
Sign, Poll-Parrot Shoes, Hanger, Die Cut Cardboard, Wooden, Metal Perch, 15 1/4 In. . . . 275.00
Sign, Poll-Parrot Shoes, Sidewalk, Painted Wood, 2 Sides, 45 1/2 In. 605.00

Sign, Ponce De Leon Tobacco, Tin Lithograph, Self-Framed, 22 x 28 In. 440.00
Sign, Pontchartrain Beach, Tin, Face Of Clown, Roller Coaster, 20 x 26 3/4 In. 522.00
Sign, Post Toastie's Cereals, Flexible Cardboard, 1927, 27 x 21 In. 260.00
Sign, Potosi Beer, Aluminum, 1950s, 10 x 7 In. 55.00
Sign, Prior Tasty Beer, Reverse Painted, 3 1/2 x 10 In. 60.00
Sign, Purity Batter Pretzels, Die Cut, Smiling Boy, Carrying Giant Pretzel, 22 In. 70.00
Sign, Raleigh Cigarettes, Now At Popular Prices, Woman, Paper, 1939, 12 x 18 In. 40.00
Sign, Rally, Mowers, Reversible, Aluminum, 12 x 18 In. 65.00
Sign, Rams Head Ale, Tin Over Cardboard, 9 x 13 In. 55.00
Sign, Reach For Sunbeam, Energy Packed Bread, 1960, 18 x 54 In. 1210.00
Sign, Red Coon Chewing Tobacco, Raccoon Holding Product, Frame 88.00
Sign, Red Goose Shoes, Balloon, Die Cut, Easel Back, Embossed, Cardboard, 11 1/4 In. . . 66.00
Sign, Red Goose Shoes, Boston, Bronze, Counter, Fixed Easel Back, 6 1/2 In. 253.00
Sign, Red Goose Shoes, Girl, Cloth Dress, Die Cut, Cardboard, Easel Back, 20 In. 319.00
Sign, Red Goose Shoes, Goose, Die Cut, Easel, Embossed, Foil, Cardboard, 13 1/4 In. . . . 468.00
Sign, Red Goose Shoes, Stitched Felt, Stand, Metal Frame, Stand, 25 In. 44.00
Sign, Red Goose Shoes, Tin Lithograph, Embossed, 27 3/4 In. 253.00
Sign, Red Owl Store, Porcelain, 2 Sides, 56 In. 1870.00
Sign, Red Top Beer, Embossed Tin Lithograph, Die Cut, 21 In. 385.00
Sign, Reddy Kilowatt, Your Electric Service, Aluminum, Round, 23 3/4 In. 330.00
Sign, Remington Kleanbore Hi Speed, Longer Range, Higher Velocity, 13 x 20 In. 577.00
Sign, Remington, Hunter With Dog, Color Lithograph, Framed, Mounted, 17 x 23 In. 121.00
Sign, Rest Room Colored, Green Ground, Porcelain, 2 Sides, 12 x 8 In. 525.00
Sign, Rheingold Beer, Back Bar, Reverse On Glass Marquee, Light-Up, 11 x 10 In. 105.00
Sign, Rice & Co. Flower Seed, Fairies, Flowers, Young Woman, Paper Litho, 20 x 28 In. . . 176.00
Sign, Richardson Root Beer, Tin Lithograph, 2 Sides, 12 In. 93.00
Sign, Rock Creek Ginger Ale, Convex, Tin Lithograph, 12 In. 176.00
Sign, Royal Baking Powder, Gingerbread Man, Can & Book, Paper, 30 x 20 In. 125.00
Sign, Royal Crown Cola, Thermometer On Right Side, Black Ground, 1940, 9 x 12 In. . . . 330.00
Sign, Rush!, Rush!, For Orange Crush, Carbonated Beverage, Crush Figure, 48 In. 605.00
Sign, S.M. Hess & Brother, Young Girl, Paper, Lithograph, 23 1/2 In. 198.00
Sign, San Joaquin Power, Porcelain, Line & Pole, Round, 6 In. 205.00
Sign, Sanford's Inks, Tin On Cardboard, Beach & Meek Co., 1901, 13 x 6 In. 175.00
Sign, Satin Skin Cream, Woman, In Center, With Product, 1903, 28 x 42 In. 85.00
Sign, Satin Skin, Cherub Whispering To Young Lady, Easel Back, c.1911, 12 x 28 In. 675.00
Sign, Say Drink Hires, Boy Holding Mug, Light Green Ground, 1922, 9 x 9 1/4 In. 2860.00
Sign, Scarlet Flame Coal, Cover The Earth, Porcelain, 19 1/4 x 34 1/2 In. 605.00
Sign, Schlitz Beer, Cash Register Shape, Neon, Gold, Plastic, 12 x 10 x 6 In. 40.00
Sign, Schlitz Malt Syrup, Embossed, Tin Lithograph, 23 1/2 In. 110.00
Sign, Schoenling, Riverboat Scene In Cincinnati, Light-Up, Frame, 1960, 15 x 18 In. 48.00
Sign, School, Drive Slowly, Guard, Wearing Uniform, Standing, Tin, 60 x 18 In. 1045.00
Sign, Schultz & Co., Zanesville, O., Babies On Swing, Die Cut, 2 Sides, 5 3/4 In. 55.00
Sign, Seagram's Canadian Hunter Mellow Sipping Whiskey, 35 x 27 In. 37.00
Sign, Serve Coke At Home, 6-Pack, White Ground, 1947, 9 1/4 In. 550.00
Sign, Shamrock Dairy, Green Lettering, 1950, 22 x 56 In. 1210.00
Sign, Sherwin Williams Cover The Earth, Red Paint Covering Earth, 45 x 25 In. 450.00
Sign, Silver Fox Beer, Reverse Painted, Oval, 1930s, 8 1/2 x 10 1/4 In. 30.00
Sign, Smart Lift, Drink Dr Pepper, Woman Wearing Bathing Suit, 1940, 6 1/2 In. 412.00
Sign, Smart Lift, Drink Dr Pepper, Young Girl With Fishing Equipment, 7 1/2 In. 330.00
Sign, Smith & Wesson Revolvers, Cowboy On Horseback, Frame, 18 x 22 In. 315.00
Sign, Snowboy Picked For Flavor, Fruits, Vegetables, Porcelain, Round, 1940s, 20 In. 465.00
Sign, Solace Tobacco, Woman On Ladder, Stone Lithograph, 1884, 36 In. 660.00
Sign, Southern Brand, Pure White Lead Paint, Dutch Boy, Flange, 14 x 21 In. 765.00
Sign, Squirrel Brand Salted Peanuts, Squirrel On Top, Cardboard, 12 x 11 In. 230.00
Sign, Squirt, Switch To Squirt, Never An After-Thirst!, Red Lettering, 1958, 9 In. 200.00
Sign, Stafford's Universal Ink, 2 Children, Color, Tin, Framed, 20 1/2 x 20 In. 440.00
Sign, Streetcar, Wrigley's Gum, Cardboard, Gum, Man, Green & White, 1950s 90.00
Sign, Stroehmann's Bread, Embossed, Tin Lithograph, 25 1/2 In. 495.00
Sign, Sun Crest Soda, Baseball Equipment, Can't Lose, 1930s, 9 x 12 In. 385.00
Sign, Sunbeam Bread Girl, Look New Sunbeam Is Better, 1950, 11 x 24 In. 907.00
Sign, Sunbeam Bread It's Batter Whipped!, Embossed, Tin Lithograph, 29 1/2 In. 413.00
Sign, Sunbrite Cleanser, Porcelain, Curved Corner, 15 x 17 3/4 In. 575.00
Sign, Sunkist Grower, Porcelain, Self-Framed, 19 1/2 x 11 1/2 In. 220.00

Sign, Swift Lift!, Drink Dr Pepper, Woman Wearing Bathing Suit Reclining, 6 In. 467.00
Sign, Swift's Pride Soap, Boy, Wings On Hat & Feet, Cardboard, c.1900, 13 In. 330.00
Sign, Swift's Red Steer Brand Fertilizers, Porcelain, Flange, 18 x 27 1/2 In. 1320.00
Sign, Switch To Squirt, Open-Closed, Masonite, 2 Sides, 1955, 16 x 12 In. 190.00
Sign, Take Home A Carton Of Dr Pepper, 6-Pack, Yellow Ground, 1940, 20 x 28 In. 1045.00
Sign, Take Home A Carton Royal Crown Cola, 1941, 9 3/4 In. 2970.00
Sign, Take Home A Carton, Pepsi-Cola, Finer Flavor, 1940, 10 x 15 In. 440.00
Sign, Take Home A Handipack, Orange-Crush, 6-Pack, 1940, 12 x 28 In. 1430.00
Sign, Tecumseh, Aluminum, Embossed Lettering, 24 x 36 In. 150.00
Sign, The Bradley Shoe, Bradley & Metcalf Co., Milwaukee, Wis., Tin, 19 x 95 In. 495.00
Sign, This Business Is Operated By A Veteran Of World War II, Celluloid, 10 x 12 In. 302.00
Sign, Thristy?, Crush That Thirst!, Orange Crush Pop, White Lettering, 12 x 30 In. 176.00
Sign, Time To Eat Seapure Oysters, Clock, Card Stock, 2 Sides, 1930s, 19 In. Diam. 28.00
Sign, Tippecanoe, The Best For Malaria, Tired Feeling, Frame, 20 1/4 x 8 1/2 In. 220.00
Sign, Tobacco, Between The Acts, Paper, Donaldson Bros., c.1880, 12 x 29 In. 745.00
Sign, Tobacconist, Pipe Shape, Carved Wood, Polychrome, Gilt, 68 In. 2300.00
Sign, Tony's Market, Elsie's Logo, Red Lettering, Black, Tin, 56 x 51 x 9 In. 745.00
Sign, Trade, Butcher's, Standing Bull, Cast Iron, Late 19th Century, 11 1/2 In. 4830.00
Sign, Trade, Keys Made, Curtis Industries, Tin Lithograph, Key Form, 15 x 31 In. 120.00
Sign, Trade, Padlock, With Protruding Key, Wood, Metal, 1970, 14 x 22 In. 77.00
Sign, Triangle, Dr Pepper Bottling Co., Red Ground, 1930, 23 x 18 In. 1210.00
Sign, Try Whistle, Pop Bottle, Thirsty?, Orange Soda Pop, Die Cut, 1950, 11 1/2 In. 264.00
Sign, Twenty Grand Cigarettes, Race Horse, Heavy Cardboard Frame, 25 x 31 In. 100.00
Sign, Unbelievable Dad's Root Beer, White Ground, 1960, 12 x 30 In. 275.00
Sign, Union-Made Cigars, We Sell Union Label Cigars, Blue Label, Cardboard, 12 In. . . . 33.00
Sign, Van Houten's Cocoa, Lithograph, Cardboard, Wooden Frame, 24 x 34 In. 550.00
Sign, Veedol Skater, Young Lady, Figure Skating, Red Lettering, Tin, 14 x 5 In. 355.00
Sign, Velvet Tobacco, Tin Lithograph, Father, Son Child, 28 1/2 x 22 1/2 In. 825.00
Sign, Vigorator, Tin Lithograph, 9 In. 99.00
Sign, W.H. Glassick, Roofing, Spouting, Wooden, Weathered, 18 x 61 In. 110.00
Sign, Waitress Serving Dr Pepper, Drink Dr Pepper, At 10, 2 & 4, 1930, 7 x 15 In. 1155.00
Sign, Wake Up Your Taste With Dr Pepper, Couple Sitting With Dr Pepper, 1950, 7 In. . . . 550.00
Sign, Walk Over Shoes, Tin, 2 Sides, 19 12 x 13 1/2 In. 350.00
Sign, We Give S & H Green Stamps, Metal, Green Enamel, 42 x 35 In. 40.00
Sign, We Sell 7-Up, The Quality Drink, Glass, 1950, 8 x 7 In. 330.00
Sign, We Serve Gollam's Lebanon Ice Cream, White Lettering, Black, 1941, 8 In. 550.00
Sign, Wedding Bouquet Sugars, Embossed Tin Lithograph, 4 x 14 In. 135.00
Sign, Welch Junior's Grape Juice, Embossed, 1930s, 13 x 20 In. 400.00
Sign, Western Super X, Champions In Their Class!, Kid With Rifle, 1940, 19 x 26 In. 632.00
Sign, Western Union Telegraph Here, Porcelain, 2 Sides, 17 x 11 In. 165.00
Sign, Westminster Rye, Motoring Scene, Embossed Frame, Tin Litho, 25 1/2 x 38 In. 2530.00
Sign, What's A Potato Without Mortons?, 1950, 18 x 36 In. 187.00
Sign, Whistle, Morning-Noon-Night, Thirsty Just Whistle, Tin, Round, 1940, 14 In. 245.00
Sign, White Ribbon Beer, Self-Framed, Tin Lithograph, 24 In. 990.00
Sign, White Rock Sparkling Beverages, Red Lettering, White, 1950, 33 x 57 In. 550.00
Sign, White Rose In Center, Porcelain, 2 Sides, 18 x 17 1/2 In. 90.00
Sign, Wild Flower Cigar, Reverse On Glass, Frame, 25 3/4 x 9 1/4 In. 1100.00
Sign, Winchester, Paper On Cardboard, String Hung, 9 1/4 x 13 3/4 In. 2530.00
Sign, Wings Cigarettes, Let's Go U.S.A., Keep 'em Flying, World War II, 18 In. 110.00
Sign, Wiss Scissors, Genuine Wiss Stay Sharp, Tin, Easel Back, 36 In. 275.00
Sign, Witch Hazel Toilet Soap, Girl, Lithograph, Titled Frame, Paper, 14 1/2 In. 358.00
Sign, Wonder Bread, Tin, Embossed, Bread Shape, 35 1/4 x 26 In. 240.00
Sign, Wonder Orange, Embossed, Tin Lithograph, 27 1/2 In. 120.00
Sign, Wonder Orange, The Wonder Drink, 5 Cents In Bottles, 1930, 10 x 18 In. 357.00
Sign, Worcester Salt, Sepia, Paper, Stone Lithograph, c.1900, 14 x 18 In. 205.00
Sign, Wright, Logo In Center, Black Lettering, Porcelain, 18 x 36 In. 75.00
Sign, Wrigley's Gum, Pack Of Gum, Man, Green, White, Cardboard, 1950s, 21 x 11 In. . . 90.00
Sign, Wrigley's Gum, Present For You, Paperboard, 1950s, 21 x 11 In. 88.00
Sign, Yeast Foam, Paper, Metal Stripes, 15 x 10 In. 77.00
Sign, Your Fresh Up 7-Up, 2 x 19 1/2 In. 42.00
Sign, Zippo, Evolution Of Flame, Zippo Lighter, Ice Age To Metal Age, 30 x 18 In. 28.00
Spoon, Banner Buggies, Silver Plate, Double-Sided Handle, Rogers, 4 1/4 In. 38.00
Spoon, Quaker Oats, Silver Plate 15.00

Spoon, Rolex Bucherer Watches, Lion Monument In Bowl, Silver Plated, 4 In. 40.00
St. Lawrence Tobacco Co., Thos. Davidson, Quebec, 4 x 6 In. 145.00
Stove, Potbelly, Spark, Cast Iron, Poker, Grey Iron Casting, Salesman Sample 155.00
Stove Polish, Woman Suffrage, 2 Girls Fishing, c.1880, 3 3/4 x 2 3/4 In. 55.00
String Holder, Dutch Boy All Purpose Soft Paste White Lead, 1930, 14 x 26 In. 4400.00
String Holder, Red Goose Shoes, Painted, Cast Iron, 15 In. 688.00
Sugar & Creamer, Hotpoint, Metal, 1930s 30.00
Sweater, Budweiser, Bud Light, Spuds Mackenzie On Surfboard, 1987, Small 22.00
Swizzle Stick, Glass, Morgan's Tavern, Green River Whiskey, 1930s, 6 1/4 In. 6.00
Swizzle Stick, Kentucky Straight Bourbon Whiskey, Antique, Red Lettering, Plastic 12.00
Tap Knob, Acme Beer, Chrome, Plastic Insert, 1930s 50.00
Tap Knob, Blatz Old Heidelberg, Chrome, Enamel Insert, 1930s 38.00
Tap Knob, Clipper Beer, Bakelite, Aluminum Insert, 1940s 16.00
Tap Knob, Kaier's Special Beer, Plastic, Plastic Insert, 1950s 170.00
Tap Knob, Old Shay Ale, Bakelite, Metal Insert, 1950s 195.00
Tap Knob, Ortlieb's Beer, Bakelite, Plastic Insert, 1940s 16.00
Tap Knob, Silver Label Beer, Bakelite, Enamel Insert, 1940s 25.00
Tap Knob, Stoney's Beer, Bakelite, Enamel Insert, 1950s 52.00
Tap Knob, Trommers White Label, Bakelite, Enamel Insert, 1940s 60.00
Thermo-Pitcher, Campbell Soup, 1960s, 1/2 Gal. 50.00
Thermometers are listed in their own category.
Thimble, J.R. Watkins Co., Cinnamon 22.00
Time Book, Lee Overalls, Black & White Photos, 1949, 36 Pages 21.00

Advertising tin cans or canisters were first used commercially in the United States in 1819 and were called *tins*. The English language is sometimes confusing. Today the word *tin* is used by most collectors to describe many types of containers, including food tins, biscuit boxes, roly poly tobacco containers, gunpowder cans, talcum powder sprinkle-top cans, cigarette flat-fifty tins, and more. Beer cans are listed in their own category. Things made of undecorated tin are listed under Tinware.

Tin, 3 Twins Fine Cut Smoking Tobacco, Thos. Davidson Mfg. Co., 4 x 6 In. 85.00
Tin, Abbey Pipe Tobacco, Upright, Pocket, 4 x 2 In. 360.00
Tin, Adams Chewing Gum, 2 Victorian Women 95.00
Tin, Admiral Rough Cut, Canister, Knob Top Lid, A.C. Co., 6 x 5 In. 165.00
Tin, Airfloat Talcum Powder, Woman Picture, 4 1/2 x 2 1/2 x 1 1/4 In. 180.00
Tin, Arabian Coffee, Tone Bros., Des Moines, Lithograph, 10 In. 44.00
Tin, Arm-Chair Club English Mixture Pipe Tobacco, Canister, Screw Top, 4 1/4 In. 29.00
Tin, Armour's Peanut Butter, Lithograph, Nursery Rhyme, Bail Handle, 3 3/4 In. 44.00
Tin, Athlete Tobacco, D. Ritchie & Co., Montreal, Box, 4 x 6 In. 115.00
Tin, Babcock's Talc Powder, Liton, 1906, 4 1/4 In. 11.00
Tin, Bagley's Old Colony, Concave, Pocket 180.00
Tin, Baltimore Candy, Isley Lithograph, Hinged Lid, 6 In. 33.00
Tin, Bambino, Smoking Tobacco, Silhouette Of Babe Ruth, Pocket, 4 x 2 In. 3220.00
Tin, Bartoldi Mixture, S.C. Peter Hauptmann & Co., 4 x 3 x 2 In. 258.00
Tin, Bicycle Cough Drop, House Form, Lithograph, Paper Label, Hinged Lid, 7 In. 154.00
Tin, Big Ben Clock, Pocket, 4 x 2 In. 18.00
Tin, Bin, Chase's Tea, Roll Front, E.M. Chase Tea Co., Manchester, N.H., 9 x 7 In. 180.00
Tin, Blue Bird Confectionery, Red, Gold Trim, Harry Vincent Ltd., England, 6 x 5 In. 45.00
Tin, Blue Flame Coffee, Lithograph, Slip Lid, Bail Handle, 8 1/2 In. 187.00
Tin, Blue Jay Coffee, Rectangular, 1 Lb. 200.00
Tin, Bon-Air, Smoking Tobacco, Pocket, 4 x 2 In. 540.00
Tin, Borden's Bremil Powdered Infant Food, Key, 1950s 5.00
Tin, Bowey's Hot Chocolate Powder, Gold, Black, Orange, 7 x 7 x 10 1/2 In. 93.00
Tin, Buckingham Cigarettes, Season's Greetings, 150 . . . . 94.00
Tin, Buckingham Cut Plug Tobacco, Multicolored, Slip Top, 5 x 4 1/4 In. 30.00
Tin, Buckingham, Trial Package, Sample 56.00
Tin, Bull Dog Cut Plug Deluxe, Picture Of Dog, 4 1/4 In. 478.00
Tin, Bullock's Powder Mitt, Apple Blossom, Satin Mitt, Refill Pocket, 9 x 5 In. 30.00
Tin, Burley Boy, Bagley's, White Man's Hope, Boxer On Front, 3 x 1 x 4 In. 1095.00
Tin, Bus, Carr's Biscuits, Doubledecker Bus, Lithograph, Biscuit, 10 In. 1045.00
Tin, Bus, Crawford's Biscuits, Doubledecker, Disc Wheels, Biscuit, 11 In. . . . . .2500.00 to 4400.00

Tin, Bus, Gray Dunn's Biscuits, Lithograph, Spoked Wheels, Biscuit, 7 1/2 In. 7150.00
Tin, C.D. Kenny Coffee, Hotel Brand Coffee, Lithograph, 7 1/2 In. 132.00
Tin, Camel Cigarettes, Camel, Pyramids, Town, Slide Opener, 1930s, 3 1/4 In. 35.00
Tin, Camp Fire Cocoa, Lotos Tea Concern, Indian Woman Holding Pot, 8 Oz. 165.00
Tin, Campfire Marshmallows Supreme, Round, 7 3/4 In. 44.00
Tin, Canada Straight Cut Plug Pipe Tobacco, 4 1/4 x 3 In. 27.00
Tin, Cayenne, Woman's Portrait, Pink, Lithograph, 9 1/2 In. 88.00
Tin, Central Union New Cut Smoking, Pocket, 3 x 1 x 4 In. 266.00
Tin, Century Spices Mustard, Milwaukee, Wis., 2 Oz. 94.00
Tin, Century Tobacco, Pre-1901, 3 3/4 x 2 1/4 In. 325.00
Tin, Champagne Sparklets, Falk Tobacco Co., 3 1/2 x 1 1/2 x 3 1/4 In. 44.00
Tin, Chase & Sanborn High Grade Coffee, New York, Sample, 2 1/2 x 2 In. 88.00
Tin, Chicago Cubs Chewing Tobacco, 6 x 4 x 4 In. 375.00
Tin, Cigarette, Omar Cigarettes Turkish Blend, Pale Blue, 8 1/2 x 6 x 1 In. 20.00
Tin, Cinnamon Spice, J.R. Watkins Medical Co. 5.00
Tin, Cleveland Superior Baking Powder, 3 1/4 x 2 In. 30,00
Tin, Clubb's Best Perigue Mixture, Canada, 1 Lb. 37.00
Tin, Colgate's Baby Talc, Lithograph, 6 In. ....44.00 to 105.00
Tin, Colgate's La France Rose Talc Powder, Sample, 2 1/4 In. 180.00
Tin, Colgate's Monad Violet Talc, Embossed, Lithograph, 4 1/2 In. 50.00
Tin, Colonel Sanders Kentucky Kandie, Canister, 1960s, 1 Qt. 45.00
Tin, Colonial Coffee, Lithograph, Screw Top, 6 In. 66.00
Tin, Comfort Powder, Baby, Nurse, Lithograph, 1891, 3 1/2 In. 440.00
Tin, Coquette Smoking Tobacco, Dominion Tobacco Co., Montreal, 5 x 3 1/2 x 2 In. 30.00
Tin, Coronation Coach, W. & R., Jacob, Biscuit 345.00
Tin, Cracker, Nabisco Premium Saltines, 9 x 4 x 5 In. 20.00
Tin, Crown Baking Paper, East St. Louis, Il., Paper Label, 1 3/4 x 3 1/2 In. 94.00
Tin, Dan Patch Cut Plug, 4 x 6 In. 110.00
Tin, Darling Talcum Powder, Paper Label, Shaker Top, 3 1/2 In. 55.00
Tin, Devoe's Sweet Smoke, Pocket, 3 x 7/8 x 4 1/2 In. ....445.00 to 455.00
Tin, Dill's Best Rubbed Cube Tobacco, Yellow, New Girl, 3 1/2 x 3 In. 93.00
Tin, Dime Razor Bank, 1 x 3 1/8 In. 50.00
Tin, Dixie Kid, Cut Plug, Black Boy, Box 320.00
Tin, Dixie Queen Tobacco, Plug Cut, Woman In Hat, Lithograph, 6 1/2 x 3 3/4 x 3 In. ... 143.00
Tin, Dough-Boy, Prophylactics, Litho Cardboard Box, Contents, 3 1/2 In. 220.00
Tin, Dr. Herman's Foot Powder, Paper Label, 4 1/2 In. 50.00
Tin, Drip Sanico Coffee Method, Sanitary Grocery Co., 1 Lb. 128.00
Tin, Edgeworth Junior, Extra High Grade, Blue, Pocket, 3 x 7/8 x 4 1/2 In. 55.00
Tin, Edgeworth Junior, Light Mild Burley, Contents, Pocket 78.00
Tin, Egyptian Cigarettes, M. Melachrino & Co., 1910, 1 x 3 x 6 In. 25.00
Tin, El Teano Cigars, Cigar Graphics, 6 1/4 x 4 x 5 1/2 In. 72.00
Tin, Elba Queen Coffee, Oshkosh/Sheboygan, Key Wind, Paper Label, 1 Lb. 83.00
Tin, Elite Foot Powder, 4 1/8 x 2 1/8 x 1 1/4 In. 34.00
Tin, Ellis Coffee, Slip Lid, Tin, 8 1/2 In. 55.00
Tin, Ensign Perfection Cut Tobacco, Pocket, 3 x 7/8 x 4 1/2 In. 145.00
Tin, Epicure, Shredded Plug Tobacco, Pocket, 3 x 7/8 x 4 1/2 In. 110.00
Tin, Excelsior Coffee, Boston & Chicago, Key Wind, 1 Lb. 210.00
Tin, Fairmount, Mixture, Pocket, 3 x 7/8 x 4 1/2 In. 310.00
Tin, Farmer's Pride Pickling Whole Mixed Spices, Paper Label, 3 Oz. 55.00
Tin, Farmer's Pride Turmeric, Terre Haute, In., Paper Label, 1 1/2 Oz. 66.00
Tin, Fashion, Cut Plug, Vertical Box, 6 x 4 x 6 In. 390.00
Tin, First Pick Coffee, Image Of Coffeepot, Key Wind 1090.00
Tin, Fleishmann's Diamalt, Diamalt Man Logo, No Cap, 50 Lb. 30.00
Tin, Flor De Franklin Cigars, 5 1/4 x 3 In. 110.00
Tin, Folger's Coffee, Merchant Ship, Lithograph, 5 Lb. 35.00
Tin, Forest & Stream Tobacco, 1927 Tax Stamp 525.00
Tin, Forest & Stream, 2 Men, Pocket 425.00
Tin, Four Roses Smoking Tobacco, Flip Top 175.00
Tin, Four Roses, Green & Red Roses, Pocket, 3 x 7/8 x 4 1/2 In. ....410.00 to 600.00
Tin, Frescodor Baby Talc 525.00
Tin, Gate City Spices, Cream Of Tartar, Keokuk, Ia., 1 1/2 Oz. 50.00
Tin, Gensco Condoms, Contents, 2 1/2 x 1 3/4 In. 395.00
Tin, Gilmore, Christmas, 10 In. Diam. 145.00

Tin, Golden Rod Baking Powder, Contents, 3 1/4 x 2 In. 43.00
Tin, Good Luck One Spoon Baking Powder, Paper Label, Contents, 2 x 3 3/4 In. 77.00
Tin, Granger Rough Cut Pure Tobacco, Pocket 1590.00
Tin, Granulated 54 Free Sample, Tall, Pocket ....155.00 to 280.00
Tin, Green River, Smoking Tobacco, Paper Canister 90.00
Tin, Green's August Flower, Antacid Carminative Laxative 25.00
Tin, Hand Made, Globe Tobacco Co., Canister, 1901, 6 1/2 x 5 In. 435.00
Tin, Harp Plug Cut, Green, Pocket 135.00
Tin, Harvard Peanuts, Peanut Man, 10 Lb. 135.00
Tin, Haserot's Senora Coffee, Tall, 1 Lb. 46.00
Tin, Hawaiian Kona Coffee, Lime Green, 1 Lb. 93.00
Tin, Hi-Ho Smoking Mixture, Gold Can, Man Smoking, Pocket 4180.00
Tin, Hi-Plane, 4 Engine Sea Plane, Pocket, 3 x 7/8 x 4 In. 345.00
Tin, Hiawatha, Fine Cut, Absolutely The Best, Round 233.00
Tin, Hindoo, Strater Brothers, Louisville, Pocket, 3 1/2 x 1 x 3 1/2 In. 645.00
Tin, Honeymoon, Tobacco, Arum Flavored, 3 x 7/8 x 4 1/2 In. 280.00
Tin, Honeysuckle Bright Chewing Tobacco, W.C. MacDonald, Montreal, 4 x 5 1/4 In. 90.00
Tin, Hugh Campbell's Shag, Man With Pipe, Pocket, 3 x 7/8 x 4 1/2 In. 474.00
Tin, Huntley & Palmer's, Suitcase, Biscuit 195.00
Tin, J. Hungerford Smith Fountain Syrup, Contents, 1 Gal. 25.00
Tin, Jam-Boy Coffee, Lithograph, Screw Top, 6 1/4 In. 165.00
Tin, Jap Rose Talcum Powder, Lithograph, 6 In. 39.00
Tin, Jap Rose Tooth Silk Dental Floss 35.00
Tin, Jolly Time Giant Yellow Pop Corn, Contents, 10 Oz. 33.00
Tin, Jolly Time White Hulless Pop Corn, Contents, Unopened, 10 Oz. 66.00
Tin, Just Suits Cut Plug Tobacco, Red, Gold, Tin, 8 x 5 x 4 In. 21.00
Tin, Kar-A-Van Famous Coffee, Toledo, Ohio, Inset Lid, 1 Lb. 50.00
Tin, Keystone Ammonium Chloride Lump, Square, 5 Lbs., 7 x 4 1/2 In. 20.00
Tin, King Edward, Crimp Cut, Lithograph Lid, Tax Stamp, Pocket 1250.00
Tin, King Othon Coffee, Label, 1/2 Lb. 365.00
Tin, King Othon Coffee, Union City, N.J., Key Wind, Contents, 1 Lb. 275.00
Tin, King Syrup, Baltimore Paper Label, Classic Lion, 4 1/4 In. 61.00
Tin, Kingsbury Crest, Tobacco Mixture, Pocket, 3 x 7/8 x 4 1/2 In. 830.00
Tin, Klein's Japanese Cough Drops, 15 Cents, Dragon, Blue & White, 3 In. 24.00
Tin, Kodak Cut Plug Smoking Tobacco, Canada, 5 x 3 1/2 x 1 1/2 In. 235.00
Tin, Krip Peanut Brittle, Lummis & Co., Philadelphia, Slip Lid, 10 Lb. 48.00
Tin, La Palina Cigar, 10 Senators, Congress Cigar Co. Philadelphia, 1926, 5 x 3 In. 10.00
Tin, Lewis' American Lye, Indian Head, Paper Label, Contents, 2 3/4 x 4 1/4 In. 28.00
Tin, Life Pipe Tobacco, Pocket, 3 x 7/8 x 4 1/2 In. 1090.00
Tin, Light House Sardines, Arcadia Food Co., Litho & Paper Label, 3 1/4 x 4 In. 44.00
Tin, Log Cabin Coffee, Key Wind 990.00
Tin, Log Cabin, 4 Oz. 10.00
Tin, Long Tom Smoking Tobacco, Rock City Tobacco Co., 5 x 3 5/8 x 2 In. 70.00
Tin, Loving Cup, Flake Cut, Pocket, c.1900 .... 3509.00
Tin, Lowney's Cocoa, Tin Lithograph, Sample, Embossed Slip Lid, 1 3/4 In. 132.00
Tin, Lucky Strike, A. Patterson Tobacco Co., Rich'd Va., 8 Oz., 4 3/8 In. 44.00
Tin, Lucky Strike, Roll Cut Tobacco, Pocket, 4 1/2 In. 91.00
Tin, Lucky Strike, Tobacco, Flat, Early, 4 1/2 In. 28.00
Tin, Luzianne Coffee, 1926, 3 Lb. 65.00
Tin, Luzianne Coffee, Dated 1928, 3 Lb. .... 45.00 to 95.00
Tin, Luzianne Coffee, Mammy Picture, 1 Lb. 165.00
Tin, Make-A-Man Tablets, Lindsey's Remedy, 3 In., 2 Pieces 264.00
Tin, Mammy's Coffee, C. D. Kenny, Baltimore, Images Of Black Mammy, 11 In. 297.00
Tin, Mansion Inn Coffee, Cup & Saucer Picture 60.00
Tin, Marschall Needle, Zukunft Mittellaut, Turquoise, Square, 1930s 9.00
Tin, Master Workman Tobacco, Wright Co., Richmond, Va., 4 1/2 x 2 3/4 x 3/4 In. 82.00
Tin, Mazola Oil, Corn Girl, 1920s, 1 Qt. 50.00
Tin, Medaglia D'Oro Caffe, S.A. Schonbrunn & Co., Inc., Contents, 12 Oz. 34.00
Tin, Mennen Talcum For Men, Green Striped, 5 1/2 x 2 1/2 x 2 1/2 In. 46.00
Tin, Mennen's Toilet Powder, Classic Baby Image, Lithograph, 1906, 4 1/2 In. 99.00
Tin, Mi Waliki Cigars, 10 Count, 1926, 3 1/2 x 5 In. 77.00
Tin, Milady Coffee, 1 Rose Picture, H.P. Lau Co., 1 Lb. 135.00
Tin, Millar's Nut-Brown Coffee, E.B. Millar & Company, 1 Lb. 104.00

Tin, Mocha & Java Coffee, Lithograph, 6 1/2 In. 66.00
Tin, Model Smoking Tobacco, Extra Quality, Sample 145.00
Tin, Mount Cross Branch, J.S. Brown Mercantile Co., 1 Lb. 145.00
Tin, Mountain Cross Coffee, Denver, Colo., Pry Lid, 3 Lb. 195.00
Tin, Mustard, White Tie, J.R. Watkins Medical Co. 120.00
Tin, Napoleon Clipping Tobacco, Utica Tobacco Co., Napoleon On Front 88.00
Tin, Niggerhair Smoking Tobacco, Pail 300.00
Tin, North Pole, Cut Plug, Oval Top, 2 Polar Bears Playing, Canister 1535.00
Tin, Nylotis Baby Powder, Borated, 4 3/4 In. 295.00
Tin, O.K. Smoking Tobacco, L. Larue Jr., 5 x 3 5/8 x 1 7/8 In. 30.00
Tin, Ocean Blend Tea, Stock Image, Canadian, 8 1/2 In. 55.00
Tin, Oceanic Cut Plug, Yellow Ground, Ship, Waves, 6 x 4 x 3 In. 125.00
Tin, Old Colony, Sample 135.00
Tin, Old Rip, Smoking Tobacco, Rip With Cane, Long White Hair, Hobbling, 4 x 5 In. 335.00
Tin, Old Seneca Stogies, Tin Lithographed, Canister 350.00
Tin, Olde Tavern Coffee, Lee & Cady, Detroit, Mich., 1 Lb. 70.00
Tin, Ole King Cole Smoking Mixture, King, Jesters, Maxfield Parrish, 3 x 1 1/2 In. 465.00
Tin, Oromo Coffee, Bursley & Company, Inc., 1 Lb. 60.00
Tin, Our Jewel Roasted Coffee, Tin Lithograph, Knob Top, Canister, 6 In. 77.00
Tin, Palmy Days, Tobacco, Green With Red, Triangle On Front, Pocket 265.00
Tin, Parker's Foot Powder, 4 1/2 In. 33.00
Tin, Peanut, Harvard, Peanut Dressed As Harvard Student, 10 Lb. 150.00
Tin, Perfect Pipe Tobacco, Pocket 365.00
Tin, Peterson's Rum & Honey Tobacco, Tin Lithograph, Pocket, 3 1/2 x 3 In. 1100.00
Tin, Pickwick Coffee, Red, Yellow, White, 1 Lb. 31.00
Tin, Picobac, Hand, With Leaves, Pocket 139.00
Tin, Pinex Laxative, Black & Yellow, Hinged Cover 3.00
Tin, Pioneer Baking Powder, Man Chopping Wood, 2 1/2 x 4 1/2 In. 745.00
Tin, Pipe Major, English Smoking Mixture, Scotsman, Pocket ....300.00 to 440.00
Tin, Planters House Coffee, St. Louis, U.S.A., Slip Lid, 1 Lb. 345.00
Tin, Polo Cigarette Tobacco, Contents, 4 x 2 3/4 x 1 In. 64.00
Tin, Popcorn, Western Auto, Season's Greetings, Santa Claus, Model T Ford, 13 In. 20.00
Tin, Postmaster Smokers Cigar, 2 For 5 Cents, Orange, White, Black, 5 x 5 In. 55.00
Tin, Pride Of Virginia, Tobacco, Flat, 4 1/2 In. 28.00
Tin, Puck Cigarette Tobacco, Hockey Players, 3 1/4 x 4 In. 220.00
Tin, Punch Cigars, 25 Count 27.00
Tin, Puritan Cut Plug, Canister, 3 x 3 1/4 In. 105.00
Tin, Qboid, Cube Cut Tobacco, Pocket, Hinged Lid, 4 In. 77.00
Tin, Quality Inn Coffee, Sorver McEvoy & Co., 1 Lb. 170.00
Tin, Red Bell Coffee, Euclid Coffee Co., Cleveland, Ohio, Tall, 1 Lb. 96.00
Tin, Red Dragon Store Tea, J.E. Magness, Iowa City, Ia., Black, Gold Letters 67.00
Tin, Red Owl Coffee, Red Owl Stores, Inc., 1 Lb. 46.00
Tin, Revere Coffee, Paul Revere, Early Tin Lithograph, Ginna, Hinged Lid, 4 In. 88.00
Tin, Richeleau Cut Plug, Standard Tobacco Co., Quebec, Round, 2 3/8 x 3 1/2 In. 82.00
Tin, Rod & Reel Cut Plug Tobacco, Red & Black, Gold Trim, 3 1/4 x 4 1/4 In. 135.00
Tin, Ronsonol Lighter Fuel, Blue, Cream & Red, Lead Pour Spout, 1950s, 4 Oz. 30.00
Tin, Royal Blue Stores Coffee, Tall, 1 Lb. 85.00
Tin, S.S. Pierce Co., Perfect Pipe Tobacco 275.00
Tin, Scarless Gall Remedy, Winterset, Iowa, 1935, 2 1/2 x 1 In. 12.00
Tin, Sea Toast, Keebler, Sailboat Picture, 9 1/2 x 3 1/4 In. 130.00
Tin, Seidlitz Powders, Ottumwa, Iowa, Factory On Lid, 1 5/8 x 3 x 4 1/2 In. 22.00
Tin, Shell Household Insect Spray, 1 Gal. 176.00
Tin, Silvercup Coffee, Mogar Coffee Co., 1 Lb. 89.00
Tin, Sozodont Tooth Powder, Lithograph, Double Slip Lid, 2 3/4 In. 231.00
Tin, Sportsmen Tobacco, L. Landry & Co., Montreal, 5 x 3 5/8 x 3 1/2 In. 155.00
Tin, Standard Japan Tea, Red, Gold Letters, Canister 165.00
Tin, Staple Grain, Slide Top, Pocket 250.00
Tin, Star Razor, Includes Razor, Lithograph, 2 1/2 In. 94.00
Tin, Star Stove Polish, George Washington, Paper Label, 4 In. 83.00
Tin, Sunbeam Coffee, Francis H. Leggett & Co., 1 Lb. 60.00
Tin, Sunny Boy Peanut Butter, Brundage Bros. Co., Snap Lid, 25 Lb. 130.00
Tin, Sunoco Lighter Fluid, White & Blue, 1960s, 4 Oz. 26.00
Tin, Sunshine Coffee, Springfield Grocer Co., 1 Lb. 70.00

Tin, Swansdown Coffee, Snap Top, 3 Lb., 8 x 6 In. 305.00
Tin, Sweet Bouquet Smoking Tobacco, B. Houde & Co., Quebec, 5 3/4 In. 195.00
Tin, Sweet Cuba Fine Cut Tobacco, Wire Handle, Silver, Red, Green, 4 x 5 In. 30.00
Tin, Sweet Hart Mustard, Hart Food Stores, Rochester, N.Y., 2 Oz. 50.00
Tin, Sweet Mist Chewing Tobacco, Lift Top Lid, Canister, Cardboard, 11 x 8 In. 385.00
Tin, Sweetheart Talcum Powder, Lithograph, 1906, 4 1/2 In. 33.00
Tin, Sykes Comfort Powder Talcum, Children, Nurse, Lithograph, 3 1/2 In. 286.00
Tin, Tennyson 5 Cent Cigars, Pocket 85.00
Tin, Tetlow's Toilet Powder, Baby, Lithograph, 4 In. 17.00
Tin, Texaco Lighter Fluid, Star Logo, Red, White & Gold, 1960s, 4 Oz. 36.00
Tin, Thompson's Double Malted Milk, Red, White, Blue, 4 Sides, 9 x 9 x 15 In. 63.00
Tin, Three Cadets Condoms, 3 For 35 Cents, Contents 43.00
Tin, Three Feathers Plug Cut, Pocket 460.00
Tin, Tiger Brand, Picture Both Sides, Handles, 1 Lb. 28.00
Tin, Tiger Tobacco, Image Of Tiger, Lithograph, Store Bin, 11 1/2 In. 176.00
Tin, Times Square Smoking Mixture, Navy, Tall Buildings At Night 320.00
Tin, Tiny-Tot Toilet Powder, Lithograph, 3 3/4 In. 55.00
Tin, Tonka Smoking Mixture, 5 x 3 3/4 x 3 1/4 In. 405.00
Tin, Towle's Log Cabin Syrup, Girl, I Like Hot Cakes, 12 Oz. 110.00
Tin, Tracy & Wilson Pepper, Early Litho, Woman Portrait, Blue, 9 1/2 In. 440.00
Tin, Triangle Tooth Soap, Somers Bros., Tooth Shaped, 3 1/2 x 1 In. 99.00
Tin, Trolley, LMS, Tin Lithograph, Disc Wheels, Maroon, Biscuit, 9 In. 825.00
Tin, Trout-Line Smoking Tobacco, Pocket 770.00
Tin, Tuckett's Orinoco Cut Fine, 3 3/4 x 4 1/4 In. 50.00
Tin, Tussils Lozenge, Red, White & Green, The Chemists, Cromwall, England, 3 x 2 In. ... 35.00
Tin, Tuxedo, Patterson's, Pocket 5.00
Tin, U.S. Marine Flake Cut, Pocket, 3 x 7/8 x 4 1/2 In. 390.00
Tin, Union Leader Cut Plug, 1910s, 7 3/4 x 4 x 5 1/4 In. 55.00
Tin, Veteran Brand Coffee, Lithograph, Slip Lid, 5 1/2 In. 88.00
Tin, Veteran Long Cut Tobacco, Image Of Jackson & Civil War Drum 55.00
Tin, Victor Drip Grind Coffee, Ben Hur Style Chariot, 5 1/2 x 3 1/2 In. 33.00
Tin, Virginia Dare Coffee, Image Of Woman, Lithograph, 6 In. 358.00
Tin, Waverley Virginia Cigarettes, Lambert & Butler, England, Pocket 28.00
Tin, Wellington London Mixture, Orange, Pocket 290.00
Tin, Wild Rose Talcum Powder, 6 3/4 x 3 1/8 In. 108.00
Tin, Wing's Baby Powder, Lithograph, 1906, 4 In. 55.00
Tin, Wood's Improved Lollacapop, Mosquito, 3 1/4 x 1 3/4 x 1/2 In. 75.00
Tin, Woodfield's Oyster, Galesville, Md., 1935, 1 Gal. 125.00
Tin, Yankee Boy Plug Cut, Pocket 475.00

Advertising tip trays are decorated metal trays less than 5 inches in diameter. They were placed on the table or counter to hold either the bill or the coins that were left as a tip. Change receivers could be made of glass, plastic, or metal. They were kept on the counter near the cash register and held the money passed back and forth by the cashier. Related items may be listed in the Advertising category under Change Receivers.

Tip Tray, Baker's Cocoa, Tin, Woman Serving, House, Round, 6 In. 255.00
Tip Tray, Brading's Ale, Elk, Round, 4 3/8 In. 95.00
Tip Tray, C.D. Kenny, Chcon Tea, Woman, Green Dress, Tin Lithograph, Round, 4 1/4 In. 66.00
Tip Tray, Cottolene, Black Woman & Child, Picking Cotton, 4 1/4 In. 55.00
Tip Tray, De Laval, Mother Working Separator, Child, c.1906, 4 1/4 In. 330.00
Tip Tray, Deerfoot Farms Sausage, Porcelain, Round, Germany, 3 1/2 x 1/2 In. 55.00
Tip Tray, Domestic Sewing Machine, Miss Liberty, American Eagle, 6 In. 195.00
Tip Tray, Donald Duck Soda, Donald In Airplane, Spanish Wording, 7 x 5 In. 40.00
Tip Tray, Dr Pepper, Black Boy & Watermelon, 3 1/4 In. 2783.00
Tip Tray, Fairy Soap, Have You A Little Fairy In Your Home?, 4 1/4 In. ....80.00 to 115.00
Tip Tray, G.C. Roser, Young Woman With Roses, Tin Lithograph, Frederick, Md., 4 In. .. 44.00
Tip Tray, Garland Stoves & Ranges, Chicago, Round, 3 1/2 In. 50.00
Tip Tray, Goebel Beer, Dutchman, Pouring Beer, Wearing Wooden Shoes, 4 In. 41.00
Tip Tray, Gold Seal Champagne, Urbana Wine Co., 4 5/8 x 6 5/8 In. 135.00
Tip Tray, Heath & Milligan Paints, Paper Label, 4 1/4 In. 230.00
Tip Tray, Helvetia Milk Condensing Co., 3 1/2 In. 145.00

Tip Tray, Jap Rose Soap, Children, Tin Lithograph, Round, 4 In. 44.00
Tip Tray, Knapstein Brewing, Co., Special Brew, Woman, Round, 1910, 4 1/2 In. 127.00
Tip Tray, Maltosia Pure Food Beer, Round, 5 1/8 In. 195.00
Tip Tray, Maltosia, Bare-Breasted Woman Riding A Swan, Tin Lithograph, Round, 5 In. ... 77.00
Tip Tray, National Beer, Race Horse, Meek Co., National Brewing Co., 1908, 4 In. 115.00
Tip Tray, Oak Stove Co., Dowagiac, Mich., Round, 3 1/2 In. 50.00
Tip Tray, Olympia Beer, Black & White Musketeer Type Picture, Round 100.00
Tip Tray, Pennsey Select Beer, Woman With Bottle, 4 1/4 In. 94.00
Tip Tray, President's Suspenders, J.H. Jingle & Son, Tin Litho, Glass Insert, 4 In. 28.00
Tip Tray, Quandt's, Famous Beer & Ales, Electro-Chemical Engraving, N.Y., 4 1/4 In. ... 125.00
Tip Tray, Quick Meal Ranges, Tin Lithograph, Oval, 4 1/2 x 3 1/4 In. 205.00
Tip Tray, Red Raven Splits, Round, 4 1/8 In. 190.00
Tip Tray, Resinol Soap & Ointment, For All Skin Diseases, 4 1/4 In. 150.00
Tip Tray, Sen-Sen Throat Ease & Breath Perfume, 4 x 4 1/2 In. 45.00
Tip Tray, Stagmier Beer, Oval, 6 1/8 x 4 3/8 In. 195.00
Tip Tray, Velvet Champagne, Terre Haute Brewing Co., 4 1/4 In. 175.00
Tip Tray, White's Hotel, Rome, N.Y., Tin Lithograph, Round, 4 1/4 In. 28.00
Tip Tray, Woodland Whiskey, Victorian Woman, Tin Litho, Deep Dish, Round, 4 1/4 In. ... 143.00
Tobacco Cutter, Brown's Mule, Cast Iron, Countertop 27.50
Tobacco Cutter, Drummond's Good Luck Tobacco, Cast Iron, Countertop 44.00
Tobacco Cutter, Iron, Griswold Erie, No. 1, Pat. 1883 .... 90.00
Tobacco Cutter, Save The Tags, Cast Iron, Countertop 60.00
Tobacco Cutter, Triumph, Cast Iron, Countertop 27.00
Toy, Bear, Lee, Tan Plush, Blue Denim Bib Overalls, 14 In. 50.00
Toy, Car, American Motors-Nash Metropolitan, Red Plastic, Hubley, 1950s, 6 In. 115.00
Toy, Car, Racer, Alka-Seltzer, Plastic 33.00
Toy, Jumping Jack, Dan D. Cream, Wooden, 1915 .... 190.00
Toy, Naugie, Monster-Shaped Stuffed Naugahyde Samples, 3 Piece 405.00
Toy, Tastykake, Maneuver 4 Steel Balls Into Holes, Steel, 1940-1950, 1 1/4 In. 12.00
Toy, Tony The Tiger, Sitting In Car, Kellogg's, Friction 195.00
Toy, Train, Refrigerator Car, Ballantine Ale, HO Scale, 1970s 17.00
Toy, Whistle, Red Goose Shoes 5.00
Tray, Tip, see Tip Trays in this category.
Tray, A. Gettelman Beer Milwaukee Beer, Pie Plate, 1930s, 13 In. 30.00
Tray, Ale Wehle Beer, 1940s, 12 In. 85.00
Tray, Anheuser-Busch, Logo Center, Steel, 1970s, 18 x 9 In. 45.00
Tray, Beer Drivers Union 132, Philadelphia, Horses & Wagon, Oval, 16 1/2 In. 305.00
Tray, Bricker's O.K. Bread, Man's Portrait, Tin Lithograph, Round, 4 1/4 In. 44.00
Tray, Bull Brand Feeds, Maritime Milling Co., Buffalo, N.Y., Rectangular, 6 1/2 In. 44.00
Tray, Burger Beer, Oval, 1930s, 15 1/4 In. ....40.00 to 110.00
Tray, Canadian Ace Beer & Ale, Birds & Floral, 1950s, 13 In. 15.00
Tray, Chiclets Chewing Gum, Black Bakelite, Metal, 9 x 7 1/2 In. 55.00
Tray, Congress Beer, Embossed & Etched Plated, 1910s, 16 x 12 In. 60.00
Tray, Country Club, Pony Express, 13 In. 180.00
Tray, Dobler Lager, Pre-Prohibition, 16 1/2 x 13 1/2 In. 505.00
Tray, Dr Pepper At All Soda Fountains, 5 Cents, Oval, 1910, 13 1/2 x 16 1/2 In. 8800.00
Tray, Dr Pepper, King Of Beverages, 1906, 16 1/2 x 13 3/4 In. 800.00
Tray, Drink Dr Pepper, Bracing, Healthful, Invigorating Ideal Beverage, Round, 15 In. ... 3410.00
Tray, Dutch Club Beer, Pittsburgh Brewing Co., 1940s, 12 In. ....*Illus* 120.00
Tray, Edelweiss Beer, Tin Lithograph, Schoenhofen Brewing, 1913, 13 1/2 In. 165.00
Tray, Famous Narragansett Banquet Ale, Pie Plate, 1930s, 13 In. 35.00
Tray, Fehr's Famous Beers, Tin Lithograph, Romantic Couple, 1910, 13 In. 450.00
Tray, Fredricksburg Brewery, San Jose, Cal., Woman, Holding Tray, Round, 13 In. 175.00
Tray, Gold Medal Flour, Washburn Crosby Co., Minnesota, 15 5/8 x 11 1/8 In. 18.00
Tray, Golden State Beer, Milwaukee Brewery, San Fran., Eagle, Rectangular, 13 In. 100.00
Tray, Golden West Brewing Co., Oakland, Calif., 1911-1920, Round, 13 In. 550.00
Tray, Hamm's Preferred Stock Beer, Blue Border, 1960s, 13 In. 30.00
Tray, Harry Mitchell's Beer, Good Honest Beer, Pie Plate, 1930s, 13 In. 120.00
Tray, Hartford Insurance Co., Round, Tin, 13 1/4 In. 68.00
Tray, Hendrick Beer, Metal, Albany, N.Y., Round, 12 In. 15.00
Tray, Howerton Sanitary Dairy, Northhampton, Pa., 13 1/4 x 13 1/4 In. 150.00
Tray, Hull's Beer & Ale, Beautiful Woman, With Glass, 1940s, 12 In. 65.00
Tray, J.H. Cutter Whiskey, Ship Picture, 16 1/2 In. 715.00

Advertising, Tray,
Dutch Club Beer,
Pittsburgh Brewing
Co., 1940s, 12 In.

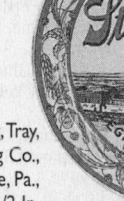
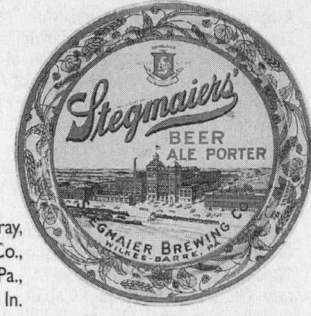

Advertising, Tray,
Stegmaier Brewing Co.,
Wilkes-Barre, Pa.,
1910s, 12 1/2 In.

Tray, Jas. E. Pepper Whiskey, Born With Republic, Colonial Scene, Round, 12 In. 100.00
Tray, Knickerbocker Beer, Metal, Round, 12 In. ....9.00 to 15.00
Tray, Land O'Lakes Sweet Cream Butter, Indian Maiden, 13 1/4 x 10 3/4 In. 25.00
Tray, Lebanon Valley Clothing, Woman With Fan, Tin Lithograph, 12 In. 149.00
Tray, Mathie Brewing Co., Los Angeles, Cal., Donkeys & Wagon, Bottle, 12 In. 175.00
Tray, Narragansett Ale, Indian Chief Gansett, Skating With Tray Of Beer, 12 In. 65.00
Tray, Narragansett Lager & Ale, Dr. Seuss Drawing, Chief Gansett, Metal, 12 In. ... .50.00 to 70.00
Tray, New Yorker Beer & Ale, Men Scene, 1930s, 12 In. 70.00
Tray, NuGrape, Woman In Victorian Outfit, Holding Bottle, 10 1/2 x 13 1/4 In. 130.00
Tray, Pabst Blue Ribbon Beer, Man, Pouring Beer, 1930s, 10 1/2 x 13 1/2 In. 68.00
Tray, Pacific Beer, Mount Tacoma Picture, Round, 12 In. 55.00
Tray, Peerless Nerve Tonic, Black Ground, Red Border, 1905, 12 In. 695.00
Tray, Pennsylvania Special Beer, Waitress, With Tray, 1900s, 13 In. 325.00
Tray, Pickwick Ale, Man Standing On Chair, 1930s, 12 In. 38.00
Tray, Purity Ice Cream, Deliciously Different, Canada, 15 3/4 x 12 In. 46.00
Tray, Regal Beer, Man, Large Hat, With Glass, 1950s, 13 In. 45.00
Tray, Roxo Sodas, Man In Top Hat, 1920s, 13 x 10 1/2 In. 75.00
Tray, Schaefer Beer, F & M Schaefer Brewing Co., Brooklyn, NY-Albany, 11 3/4 In. 20.00
Tray, Sparkling Pepsol, Dog Picture, 1930s, 12 In. 36.00
Tray, Staples & Griffin, Woman In White Dress, Tin Lithograph, 17 1/4 In. 193.00
Tray, Stegmaier Brewing Co., Wilkes-Barre, Pa., 1910s, 12 1/2 In. ....*Illus* 234.00
Tray, Stock, Girl With Pink Bonnet, Tin Lithograph, 16 1/2 In. 22.00
Tray, Tadcaster Beer & Ale, The Worcester Brewing Company, Mass., Round, 12 In. 155.00
Tray, Tobacco Satin Turkish Cigarette, Round, 14 In. 35.00
Tray, Tru-Blu Beer & Ale, Blue Boy Picture, 1940s, 12 In. 42.00
Tray, Uneeda Graham Crackers With Milk, Rosy Cheek Boy, 15 5/8 x 11 1/8 In. 18.00
Tray, Utica Club Is Where It Really Swings, Metal, Round, 13 1/8 In. 15.00
Tray, Valley Forge Special Beer, Blue Ground, 1930s, 12 In. 40.00
Tray, Wrigley's Soap, Black Cat, Tin Lithograph, Round, 3 1/2 In. 176.00
Tray, Yuengling's Beer, Ale & Porter, 13 In. ....17.00 to 40.00
Tumbler, National Biscuit Co., Chocolate Slag 130.00
Tumbler, National Biscuit Co., Uneeda Milk Biscuit, Caramel Slag 130.00
Vending Machine, All-Purpose, 5-Cent, Paper Label, Glass Reservoir, Acorn 22.00
Vending Machine, Arcade Exhibit, Exhibit Supply Co. Cards, Chicago, Pat 4-21-25 ..... 11.00

AGATA glass was made by Joseph Locke of the New England Glass
Company of Cambridge, Massachusetts, after 1885. A metallic stain
was applied to New England Peachblow and the mottled design char-
acteristic of agata appeared.

Finger Bowl Set, With Underplate, 12 Piece 1320.00
Toothpick 1100.00
Water Set, Pitcher, 6 Tumblers 8300.00

AKRO AGATE glass was made in Clarksburg, West Virginia, from 1932
to 1951. Before that time, the firm made children's glass marbles,
which are listed in this book in the Marble category. Most of the glass
is marked with a crow flying through the letter *A*.

Ashtray, Shell, Marbleized Orange 7.00

Ashtray, Square, Marbleized Blue, 2 7/8 In. 8.00
Cigarette Holder, Ashtray, Marbleized Blue 50.00
Creamer, Chiquita, Baked-On Royal Blue 9.00
Creamer, Chiquita, Transparent Cobalt 9.00
Creamer, Interior Panel, Marbleized Blue 42.00
Creamer, Interior Panel, Opaque Blue, Darts 95.00
Creamer, Miss America, White 135.00
Creamer, Octagonal, Opaque Dark Blue, 1 1/4 In. 28.00
Creamer, Raised Daisy, Marbleized Yellow 195.00
Creamer, Stacked Disc, Green 10.00
Creamer, Stippled Band, Transparent Green, 1 1/2 In. 27.00
Creamer, Stippled Band, Transparent Topaz, 1 1/4 In. 75.00
Cup, Chiquita, Opaque Purple 95.00
Cup, Chiquita, Transparent Cobalt 14.00
Cup, Interior Panel, Opaque Jade, Luster, 1 1/4 In. 17.00
Cup, Octagonal, Opaque Pumpkin, 1 1/4 In. 28.00
Cup, Stacked Disc & Interior Panel, Transparent Green 62.00
Cup, Stippled Band, Transparent Green, 1 1/2 In. 20.00
Cup & Saucer, Chiquita, Opaque Green 8.00
Cup & Saucer, Stippled Band, Transparent Cobalt, 1 1/2 In. Cup 35.00
Cup & Saucer, Stippled Band, Transparent Green, 1 1/2 In. Cup 29.00
Cup & Saucer, Stippled Band, Transparent Topaz, 1 1/4 In. Cup 29.00
Pitcher, Water, Stacked Disc, Opaque Green 10.00
Planter, Graduated Dart, Scalloped Edge, Oval, Opaque Blue, 8 1/2 In. 30.00
Plate, Chiquita, Opaque Green ....4.00 to 8.00
Plate, Interior Panel, Opaque Green, 4 1/4 In. 7.00
Plate, Interior Panel, Opaque Yellow, 3 1/4 In. 16.00
Plate, Interior Panel, Transparent Green ....6.00 to 7.00
Plate, J. Pressman, Baked-On Green 5.00
Plate, Miss America, White, Decal 50.00
Plate, Octagonal, Opaque Blue 14.00
Plate, Octagonal, Opaque Green, 3 3/8 In. 12.00
Plate, Raised Daisy, Opaque Blue 23.00
Plate, Stacked Disc, Opaque Blue ....6.00 to 22.00
Plate, Stacked Disc, Transparent Cobalt 18.00
Plate, Stacked Disc, White, Decal 85.00
Powder Dish, Scotty, Medium Opaque Blue 110.00
Powder Jar, Cover, Colonial Lady, White 98.00
Saucer, Chiquita, Opaque Green 3.00
Saucer, Chiquita, Opaque Yellow 12.00
Saucer, Interior Panel, Opaque Pink, 2 3/4 In. 14.00
Saucer, Octagonal, Opaque Pink, 2 3/4 In. 18.00
Saucer, Raised Daisy, Marbleized Yellow 16.00
Saucer, Stacked Disc, Opaque Green 5.00
Smoking Set, Marbleized Blue, Box, 5 Pieces 65.00
Sugar, Chiquita, Opaque Green ....7.00 to 9.00
Sugar, Cover, Miss America, White, Decal 215.00
Sugar, Interior Panel, Opaque Blue, Darts 95.00
Sugar, Raised Daisy, Marbleized Yellow 195.00
Sugar, Stacked Disc, Opaque Green 10.00
Sugar & Creamer, Stacked Disc, Opaque Pink 47.00
Teapot, Chiquita, Transparent Cobalt Blue 33.00
Teapot, Cover, Chiquita, Opaque Blue 39.00
Teapot, Cover, Interior Panel, Transparent Green 55.00
Teapot, Interior Panel, Opaque Green 25.00
Teapot, Miss America, White, Decal 350.00
Teapot, Stippled Band, Transparent Topaz 34.00
Tumbler, Interior Panel, Transparent Green, 2 In. 11.00
Tumbler, Raised Daisy, Opaque Blue 110.00
Tumbler, Stacked Disc & Panel, Transparent Green, 2 In. 11.00
Tumbler, Stippled Band, Transparent Green, 1 3/4 In. 12.00
Water Set, Stacked Disc & Interior Panel, Transparent Green, 7 Piece 125.00
Water Set, Stippled Band, Topaz, 5 Piece 90.00

ALABASTER is a very soft form of gypsum, a stone that resembles marble. It was often carved into vases or statues in Victorian times. There are alabaster carvings being made even today. Because the alabaster is very porous, it will dissolve if kept in water, so do not use alabaster vases for flowers.

Bowl, Neoclassical, Colorful Arrangement Of Dried Pomegranates, Floral, 16 In.	230.00
Bust, Augustus Caesar, Marked, L. Clerici, 19th Century, 21 1/4 In.	863.00
Bust, Sad Girl, Bye-Bye Birdie, c.1890, 18 In.	690.00
Bust, Veiled Woman With Lowered Eyes, On Columnar Ringed Pedestal, 17 In.	1725.00
Bust, Woman, Braided Hair, Envelope Resting In Laced Bodice, 21 In.	770.00
Bust, Woman, Lace In Hair, Dress Ruffle, Marble Pedestal, 41 In.	660.00
Column, Octagonal Top, Spiral Fluted Stem, Octagonal Plinth, Italy, c.1900, 42 In.	305.00
Figurine, Classical Maiden, Seated On Bench, White, Piuiole, 1920s, 13 1/2 In.	460.00
Figurine, Cupid & Psyche, 9 1/2 In.	220.00
Figurine, Naked Boy, Sitting On Naturalistically Carved Base, 14 In.	1035.00
Figurine, Sythean Slave, Seated, Sharpening The Blade, Eyes Turned Upward, 12 In.	1045.00
Figurine, Young Girl Stepping Into Pond, 1900, 21 In., 2 Piece	690.00
Figurine, Young Woman, Classical Style, 22 1/2 In.	385.00
Group, 2 Girls Reading, Seated On Stone Wall, Italy, 1875-1900, 24 In.	2640.00
Group, Ariadne & Panther, Nude, Italy, 1875-1900, 15 1/2 x 13 In.	1815.00
Group, Pauline Borghese As Venus, Italy, 1900, 22 In.	2530.00
Group, Young Romance, P.E. Fiaschi, 25 1/2 x 18 x 12 In.	2530.00
Lamp, Inverted Bell Shape, Square Plinth, 18 1/4 In.	335.00
Lamp, Neoclassical, Athenienne Form, Raised On Triangular Plinth, Italy, 28 In.	2860.00
Lamp, Vase Shape, Plinth, Art Deco, 24 3/4 In.	495.00
Miniature, Taj Mahal, Carved, Polychrome, Fitted Box, 5 1/8 In.	138.00
Obelisk, Square Tapered Column On 4 Tortoises, Bronze Mounts, c.1900, 26 In., Pair	2200.00
Pedestal, Intertwined Dolphins, 21 1/2 In.	242.00
Tazza, Neoclassical, Raised On Circular Plinth, 8 x 14 In.	935.00
Urn, Campana Form, Square Base, Flower & Foliage Band, 15 In.	748.00
Urn, Louis XVI Style, Ram's Mask Handles, Gilt Bronze Mounted, 24 In., Pair	1840.00
Vase, Neoclassical, Medusa's Mask Center, Scrolled Handles, Electricfied, 28 In.	10350.00
Vase, Neoclassical, Vintage Band, Stylized Griffin Handles, Stepped Foot, 22 In.	2530.00

ALEXANDRITE is a name with many meanings. It is a form of the mineral chrysoberyl that changes from green to red under artificial light. A man-made version of this mineral is sold in Mexico today. It changes from deep purple to aquamarine blue under artificial light. The Alexandrite listed here is glass made in the late nineteenth and twentieth centuries. Thomas Webb & Sons sold their transparent glass shaded from yellow to rose to blue under the name Alexandrite. Stevens and Williams had a cased Alexandrite of yellow, rose, and blue. A. Douglas Nash Corporation made an amethyst-colored Alexandrite. Several American glass companies of the 1920s made a glass that changed color under electric lights and this was also called Alexandrite.

Cordial Set, Facet Cut, Spire Stopper, c.1926, 7 Piece	635.00
Vase, Red Violet, Cut Panels, Scalloped Rim, Moser, 7 3/4 In.	1095.00

ALUMINUM was more expensive than gold or silver until the 1850s. Chemists learned how to refine bauxite to get aluminum. Jewelry and other small objects were made of the valuable metal until 1914, when an inexpensive smelting process was invented. The aluminum collected today dates from the 1930s through the 1950s. Hand-hammered pieces are the most popular.

Bowl, Chrysanthemum, Fluted, Continental, 11 In. . . . . .15.00 to 30.00
Bowl, Engraved Floral Center, Hand Forged Everlast Metal, 12 1/2 x 3 In.	10.00
Butter, Glass Insert, Buenilum	30.00
Coffee Urn, Chrysanthemum, Electric, Continental	60.00
Compote, Chrysanthemum, Leaves At Base, Continental	25.00
Compote, Tulip Finial, Ribbon & Flower Legs, Rodney Kent	23.00
Crumber Set, Rodney Kent, 2 Piece . . . . .26.00 to 35.00
Frame, Picture, Design On Back, Easel, Palmer-Smith	80.00
Ice Bucket, Hammered, Rodney Kent	45.00

Lamp, Daisy, Table, Wendell August Forge 910.00
Napkin Holder, Apple, Hawthorn, Everlast 15.00
Pitcher, Rodney Kent, Large 27.00
Plate, Engraved, Morning Glories, Hearth & Home Scene, Farberware, 15 In. 25.00
Plate, Wendell August Forge, Box, 4 1/2 In. 20.00
Sculpture, The Genius Of Man, Avard Fairbanks, 1940s Car, W.P.A. Style, 15 In. 2420.00
Silent Butler, Palm Leaves, Everlast 35.00
Silent Butler, Stamped Ivy Design, Oval, Everlast 5.00
Tray, Allover Design, August Forge, 12 1/2 x 7 In. 40.00
Tray, Grasshopper Design, Wendell August Forge, 5 1/2 In. 130.00
Tray, Hand Wrought, Handles, 12 In. 20.00
Tray, Handle, Rodney Kent, 12 x 7 In. 25.00
Tray, Pinecone, Handles, Everlast, 12 x 15 In. 25.00
Tray, Zodiac, Arthur Armour, 19 In. 60.00
Wastebasket, Map, Arthur Armour 205.00

AMBER, see Jewelry category.

AMBER GLASS is the name of any glassware with the proper yellow-
brown shading. It was a popular color just after the Civil War and
many pressed glass pieces were made of amber glass. Depression glass
of the 1930s–1950s was also made in shades of amber glass. Other
pieces may be found in the Depression Glass, Pressed Glass, and other
glass categories. All types are being reproduced.

Ashtray, Eagle, 9 1/4 In. 8.00
Candlestick, Dugan, 4 In. 12.00
Candy Dish, Cover, 6 x 6 In. 15.00
Compote, Whirling Star & Hobstar, 6 1/2 x 4 1/2 In. 15.00
Mug, Barrel, 2 1/2 x 3 In. 10.00
Pitcher, Clear Handle, 4 1/2 In. 8.00
Pitcher, Enameled, Flowers, Bird, 11 1/2 In. 225.00
Relish, 9 3/4 x 5 In. 5.00
Rose Bowl, 3-Footed, 8 3/4 In. 12.00
Sugar Shaker, Paneled, Footed 250.00
Tumbler, Daisy, 12 Oz., 6 1/2 In. 40.00
Tumbler, Flip, Molded Leaf Design, 19th Century, 8 1/4 In. 77.00
Tumbler, Whiskey, Leaf & Berry Etching, Bottom Straw Marks, 1 1/4 Oz., 2 In. 5.00
Tumbler, Whiskey, Slight Flair, Polished Pontil, 1 1/2 Oz., 3/8 In. 5.00
Vase, Bud, Pewter Overlay On Neck, 4 In. 770.00
Wine, Enameled White Grape Leaves, 5 1/4 In. 65.00

AMBERETTE pieces are listed in the Pressed Glass category under the pattern name
Amberette.

AMBERINA is a two-toned glassware made from 1883 to about 1900. It
was patented by Joseph Locke of the New England Glass Company,
but was also made by other companies. The glass shades from red to
amber. Similar pieces of glass may be found in the Baccarat and Plated
Amberina categories. Glass shaded from blue to amber is called *Blue
Amberina* or *Bluerina*.

Berry Bowl, Daisy & Button, Square, 5 In., Pair 55.00
Bowl, Flower-Form, Ruffled Edge, 3 3/4 x 7 In. 550.00
Bowl, Swirl, Ruffled Edge, 3 3/4 x 5 1/2 In. 187.00
Celery Vase, Diamond-Quilted, Scalloped Edge, 6 1/8 & 6 1/4 In., Pair 405.00
Celery Vase, Swirl, 6 In. 125.00
Compote, Cover, Swirl, Enameled Flowers, Silver Plate Ladle, 10 In. 325.00
Cordial, 4 3/4 In. 60.00
Creamer, Applied Amber Handle, 4 In. 300.00
Creamer, Reverse Thumbprint, Tricornered Edge, 4 In. 110.00
Cruet, Coin Spot, Square Base, Amber Handle, 7 1/2 In. 375.00
Cup, Reverse Thumbprint, Pair 60.00
Finger Bowl, Ruffled Edge, 2 1/2 x 5 1/2 In. 160.00
Hat, 3 In. 40.00
Pitcher, Diamond-Quilted, Square Base, 6 1/4 In. 50.00
Pitcher, Inverted Thumbprint, Square Handle, Late 19th Century, 9 In. 115.00

Pitcher, Reverse Thumbprint, 5 In.	25.00
Pitcher, Reverse Thumbprint, Square Mouth, 4 1/2 In.	90.00
Pitcher, Water, Reverse Thumbprint, Melon Ribs, 9 In.	90.00
Punch Cup, Diamond-Quilted, Reeded Amber Handle, 2 1/2 In.	50.00
Tankard, 10-Panels, Reeded Handle, 6 5/8 In.	315.00
Tankard, Diamond-Quilted, Handle, Flared Rim, 7 In.	430.00
Toothpick, Daisy & Button, 3-Footed, 2 3/4 In.	275.00
Toothpick, Mt. Washington	285.00
Toothpick, New England	80.00
Tumbler, Diamond-Quilted, 3 3/4 In.	60.00
Vase, Applied Floral & Rigaree, Brass Stand, 10 In.	500.00
Vase, Basket Weave, Ruffled Edge, 9 1/4 In.	105.00
Vase, Bulbous, Narrow Neck, Leaf & Cherry Design, 4 Ribbon Feet, Handle, 8 In.	275.00
Vase, Inverted Thumbprint, Wishbone Feet, 5 1/4 In., Pair	150.00
Vase, Lily, Trumpet, Ribbed, Tricornered Edge, Late 19th Century, 9 1/2 In.	405.00
Vase, Ribbed Body, Foliate & Wing Design, Ruffled Edge, 10 In.	46.00
Vase, Swirl, Applied Serpent, Footed, 8 1/2 In.	175.00
Water Set, Diamond-Quilted, Folded Rim, Applied Handle, 9 1/4 In. Pitcher, 5 Piece	210.00

AMERICAN DINNERWARE, see Dinnerware.

AMERICAN ENCAUSTIC TILING COMPANY was founded in Zanesville, Ohio, in 1875. The company planned to make a variety of tiles to compete with the English tiles that were selling in the United States for use in fireplaces and other architectural designs. The first glazed tiles were made in 1880, embossed tiles in 1881, faience tiles in the 1920s. The firm closed in 1935 and reopened in 1937 as the Shawnee Pottery.

Figurine, Colt, Blue Flambe Glaze, 10 1/2 In.	176.00
Paperweight, Ram, Base, Glossy Black Glaze, 3 x 5 1/2 In.	66.00
Tile, Arts & Crafts, Figural, Frame, 6 x 6 In., Pair	110.00
Tile, Benjamin Franklin, Square, Mid 1930s, 4 In., Pair	60.00

AMETHYST GLASS is any of the many glasswares made in the dark purple color of the gemstone called amethyst. Included in this category are many pieces made in the nineteenth and twentieth centuries. Very dark pieces are called *black amethyst* and are listed under that heading.

Bobeches, Paper Label, 8 Prism Holes, 1920s, 3/4 In.	60.00
Candleholder, 10 3/4 In.	15.00
Candleholder, Twisted Stem, 5 1/4 In.	14.00
Cordial Set, Decanter, 4 Cordials, Crystal Pedestal, Stopper	75.00
Goblet, Gold Design, Gilt Band, Rim & Foot	25.00
Vase, Enameled Flowers, Melon, 8 1/4 In.	245.00
Vase, Ruffled Edge, 4 3/4 In.	60.00

AMPHORA pieces are listed in the Teplitz category.

ANDIRONS and related fireplace items are included in the Fireplace category.

ANIMAL TROPHIES, such as stuffed animals, rugs made of animal skins, and other similar collectibles, are listed in this category. Collectors should be aware of the endangered species laws that make it illegal to buy and sell some of these items. Any eagle feathers, many types of pelts or rugs (such as leopard), ivory, and many forms of tortoiseshell can be confiscated by the government. Related trophies may be found in the Fishing category. Ivory items may be found in the Scrimshaw or Ivory categories.

American Eagle, Natural Fibers, Sneaky Pete, 25 x 34 In.	495.00
Bighorn Sheep Head, 32 In.	180.00
Black Bear Cub, 2 Outstretched Paws	400.00
Black Bear Head, 13 In.	145.00
Deer Hide, Indian Chief Painting, Framed, Tagged, 1890, 55 x 40 x 5 In.	440.00
Hugh Kudu, Head Mount, 36-In. Horns, Horn To Neck 59 In.	715.00
Lion Skin, Shield, African, 21 x 38 In.	303.00
Mountain Sheep Head, Full Curl	285.00
Reed Buck, Skull, Tanned Hide, 72 x 50 In.	61.00

Rug, Black Bear, Claws Intact, Felt Backed, 67 x 69 In. 550.00
Rug, Tiger Skin, Claws On Front Feet, 111 x 68 In. 908.00
Snakeskin, Rattlesnake, With Rattles, Felt Backing, 60 In. 58.00
Steer Horns, Longhorn, Tooled Leather Center, Oak Backboard, 48 In. 105.00
Thompson Gazelle Head, Tanned Hide, 81 x 58 In. 143.00
Warthog, Ivory Tusks, 24 In. 165.00
Water Buffalo Head, 42 x 47 x 34 In. 495.00

ANIMATION ART collectibles include cels that are painted drawings on celluloid needed to make animated cartoons shown in movie theaters or on TV. Hundreds of cels were made, then photographed in sequence to make a cartoon showing moving figures. Early examples made by the Walt Disney Studios are popular with collectors today. Original sketches used by the artists are also listed here. Modern animated cartoons are made using computer-generated pictures. Some of these are being produced as cels to be sold to collectors. Other cartoon art is listed in Comic Art and Disneyana.

Cel, Flash Gordon, Flash Must Evade Killer Robots On Planet Mongo, 1979 . . . . 190.00
Cel, Flash Gordon, Struggling To Get Free From Devil Vines, 1979 . . . . 190.00
Cel, High Diving Hare, Warner Brothers, Mounted, 9 1/4 x 12 1/4 In. 460.00
Cel, Kirk & Dr. Spock, Aboard The Enterprise, 1975 . . . . 110.00
Cel, Peter Pan, Peter Takes Wendy's Hand As They Fly, 1953, 10 x 13 In. 1440.00
Cel, Star Trek, Uhura, 1975 . . . . 70.00
Cel, Steel & America, Donald Duck, Rope Over Shoulder, Walt Disney, Frame 345.00
Cel, Teenage Mutant Ninja Turtles, April, Matted Cover, Bag, 1991, 8 x 9 In. 50.00
Cel, Teenage Mutant Ninja Turtles, Leonardo & April, MWS, Frame, 14 In. 25.00
Cel, Thumper & Miss Bunny, Bambi Film, 13 x 10 In. 120.00
Cel, Wendy & Peter Pan Telling Story To Children, 1953, 7 1/2 x 9 1/2 In. 900.00

ANNA POTTERY was started in Anna, Illinois, in 1859 by Cornwall and Wallace Kirkpatrick. They made many types of utilitarian wares, bricks, drain tiles, and giftware. The most collectible pieces made by the pottery are the pig-shaped bottles and jugs with special inscriptions, applied animals, and figures. The pottery closed in 1894.

Figurine, Dog, Brown Glaze, Molded Hair & Features 6900.00
Flask, Pig, St. Louis, Great Railroad River Guide, Stoneware, 1884, 6 1/4 In. 7425.00

APPLE PEELERS are listed in the Kitchen category under Peeler, Apple.

ARCHITECTURAL antiques include a variety of collectibles, usually very large, that have been removed from buildings. Hardware, backbars, doors, paneling, and even old bathtubs are now wanted by collectors. Pieces of the Victorian, Art Nouveau, and Art Deco styles are in greatest demand.

Art Deco, Panels, Plaster, Frieze, Reclining Woman, Flowers, Fruit, 28 x 98 In., Pair 1150.00
Backbar, Hutch, Inlaid Wood, Leaded Glass Cabinets, Lighting, 7 x 7 x 5 Ft. 7500.00
Backbar, Soda Fountain, Oak, 10 x 8 Ft. 5000.00
Backbar & Front Bar, Wooden, 9 x 8 Ft. & 9 x 10 Ft. 12500.00
Bathtub, Tin, Oak Rim, Hardware, Victorian, 68 x 27 x 22 In. 1025.00
Bathtub, Tin, Rounded Back, Arm Rests, 19th Century, 39 x 31 x 23 In. 140.00
Bracket, Ebonized & Gilt Wood, Satyr, 12 x 22 In., Pair 4400.00
Bracket, Griffin Support, Carved, Gilt, Italy, 20 x 17 x 12 In., Pair 3300.00
Bracket, Victorian, Louis XVI Style, Oak, Ivory Paint, 17 1/2 x 16 In. 550.00
Bracket, Wall, Giltwood, Composition, Stylized Dragon, Napoleon III, 11 In., Pair 6325.00
Bracket, Wall, Man Supporting Shelf, Wooden, Gesso, 24 In., Pair 3735.00
Bracket, Wood, Carved Scallop Shell, Fruit, Polychrome, Italy, 23 x 24 In. 1020.00
Bracket, Wrought Iron, Open Scrollwork, Quatrefoil, New Orleans, 34 In., Pair 770.00
Capital, Limestone, Weighing Of Souls, Romanesque Style, France, 18 1/4 x 16 In. 1375.00
Column, Beechwood, White Paint, Foliate Scrolls, Fruit, Leafage, 106 x 26 In. 3220.00
Column, Spar, Male & Female Bust On Stem, Stepped Base, 24 In., Pair 10925.00
Column, Teakwood, Fluted Standard, Sandstone Plinth, 93 1/2 x 14 1/2 In., Pair 5280.00
Column, Variegated Pink & White Marble, White Marble Socle, Italy, 49 In., Pair 6325.00
Cornice, Window, Interlocking Diamonds, Painted, Gilt, Victorian, 63 In., Pair 140.00
Cornice, Window, Walnut, Gilt, Renaissance Revival, 27 x 64 In., Pair 3080.00

Door, Beveled Leaded Glass, Circular Floral, Prairie School, 80 In., Pair 4675.00
Door, Elevator, Brass, 2 Geometric Panels, Floral, Art Deco, 84 3/4 In., Pair 2587.00
Door, Jail, Pulaski County, Arkansas, Brass Handle 225.00
Door, Mahogany, Nickeled Brass Hardware, 19th Century, 108 x 22 In., Pair 1380.00
Door, Oak, Louis XV, Carved Trophies, Foliage & Scrolls, 84 x 28 In., Pair 3220.00
Door Handle, Wrought Iron, Mid 18th Century, 3 Piece 522.00
Door Knocker, Hand Holding Ball, Iron 135.00
Door Knocker, Iron, 4-Pointed Plate, Heavy Ring Knocker, England 77.00
Door Knocker, Lion Mask, Brass, 10 In. 69.00
Eagle, Cast Iron, 32-In. Wingspan, Contemporary Walnut Base 595.00
Fan, Demilune Shape, Fluted, Rayed Louvers, Green Paint, 1800, 21 x 53 In. 745.00
Fence Section, Cast Iron, Footed, 26 x 24 In. 56.00
Figure, Cherub, Fruitwood, Baroque, Italy, 17th Century, 13 x 11 x 6 In. 490.00
Figure, Eagles, Concrete, 29 x 16 In., Pair 402.00
Finial, Reverse Acorn Shape, Painted White, Pair 1320.00
Gate, Bronze, Oval Rococo Style Base, Louis XIV, 6 1/2 In., Pair 4890.00
Gate, Cemetery, Edward R. Dolan, Willow, Doves, Lambs, Iron, c.1860, 41 x 29 In. 1380.00
Gate, Forged Iron, Scrolled Top & Panels, Basket Weave, 93 x 35 In., Pair 880.00
Gate, Iron, Old Green Paint, Stewart Iron Works, Cincinnati, Oh., 48 In. 335.00
Gate, Iron, Weathered Surface, 58 x 42 In., Pair 220.00
Gate Weight, Horse Shape, Iron, Late 19th Century, 16 x 17 In. 495.00
Grill, Cast Iron, Rusted White Repaint, 61 In. 190.00
Gym Locker, Wooden, Green Paint, 3 Joined Together 250.00
Lamp, Street, Detroit, Copper, Teardrop Type 275.00
Mailbox, Griswold 100.00
Mailbox, Top Slot, Crest, New York State Capitol 750.00
Mantel, Applied Fluted & Carved Columns, Flora Carving Over Opening, 52 In. 385.00
Mantel, Blue, Green Tulip Design, Pa., Early 19th Century, 53 1/2 x 58 In. 440.00
Mantel, Carrara Marble, Carved Pilasters, Paw Feet, 40 x 55 In. 2300.00
Mantel, Center Frieze, Cherubs Driving Chariot, 47 1/2 x 75 In. 8050.00
Mantel, Empire, Oak, Painted, 1/2 Columns, 19th Century, 48 x 53 x 7 In. 280.00
Mantel, Fluted Supports, Cast Iron Grate, Enameled Tiles, c.1880, 51 x 72 In. 620.00
Mantel, King Of Russia Marble, Fluted Pilaster Supports, 51 x 67 In. 1980.00
Mantel, Louis XVI Style, Marble, Bronze, 40 x 50 1/2 x 13 In. 1495.00
Mantel, Marble, Ogee Beveled Design, Stepped Back Feet, 41 x 41 1/2 In. 715.00
Mantel, Oak, Crown Molded, Beveled Rectangle Mirror, 80 x 53 In. 450.00
Mantel, Pine, Red Marbleized Paint, Cream Ground, Country, 8 3/4 x 66 x 49 In. 770.00
Mantel, Rouge Marble, Free-Standing Columns, c.1880, 50 x 72 In. 990.00
Mantel, Walnut, Cupboard Top, Victorian, 63 x 44 x 14 In. 935.00
Medallion, Ceiling, Silvered Bronze, 17 In. 135.00
Model, Mahogany, Spiral Staircase, Carved, 40 In. 2805.00
Panel, Cherry, Carved Interwoven Design, 2 Quarter Fans, 13 x 68 In. 460.00
Panel, Georgian Style, Cherry, Recessed Niche, Spiral Pilasters, c.1900, 98 In. 715.00
Panel, Wooden, Carved, Pendant Science & Art Trophies, 77 x 19 1/2 In., Pair 2300.00
Plaque, Giltwood, Neoclassical, Female Mask, Shield, 1800s, 13 x 32 x 4 1/2 In. 2530.00
Rondel, Marble, Bronze, Neoclassical Design, Fleur-De-Lis, France, 27 x 27 In. 1955.00
Soda Fountain, 6 Heads, Ice Cream Box, Sink Compartment, 9 Ft. 3500.00
Stairs, Corner Type, Blue Paint 2900.00
Supports, Bust, Figure Of Woman, Topping Bellflower, Walnut, 43 In., Pair 1540.00
Tile, Roof, Rooster, Mosaic Inlay, Unglazed Red Clay, 19 In. 550.00
Wallpaper Roll, Moon Landing, Rocket & Man 30.00

AREQUIPA POTTERY was produced from 1911 to 1918 by the patients
of the Arequipa Sanitarium in Marin County Hills, California. The
patients were trained by Frederick Hürten Rhead, who had worked at
the Roseville Pottery.

Bowl, Blue Matte Glaze, Low, 1912, 9 1/2 In. 210.00
Bowl, Brown Mottled Glaze, 1 1/2 x 5 1/2 In. 341.00
Bowl, Closed Form, Green To Black Glaze, Signed, 5 In. 176.00
Bowl, Green & Blue Matte Glaze, Eucalyptus Branches, Incised KH/11, 6 1/2 In. 880.00
Bowl, Purple Matte Glaze, 1912, 6 1/2 In. 410.00
Bowl, Purple Matte Glaze, Light Green, Blue Highlights, 1912, 6 1/2 In. 255.00
Figurine, Scarab, Covered In Maroon Matte Glaze, Signed, 3 In. 770.00

Vase, Blue Gray Matte Glaze, White Berries, Squat, Incised AP, 1911, 4 1/4 x 7 In. 660.00
Vase, Blue Matte Glaze, 8 In. 1760.00
Vase, Floral Design, Blue, Green Matte Glaze, 4 In. 655.00
Vase, Full-Length Leaves, Rose Matte Glaze, Dimpled, 8 x 4 1/4 In. 715.00
Vase, Heart Shaped Leaves, Squeezebag, Frothy Green Matte Glaze, 7 In. 4675.00
Vase, Organic Gourd Form, Green Matte Glaze, Signed, 1913, 7 1/2 In. 1540.00
Vase, Rose Matte Glaze, Swollen Shoulder, 5 1/2 In. 385.00
Vase, Squeezebag Design, Purple Matte Body, Signed, 6 In. 550.00

ARGY-ROUSSEAU, see G. Argy-Rousseau category.

ARITA is a port in Japan. Porcelain was made there from about 1616.
Many types of decorations were used, including the popular Imari
designs, which are listed under Imari in this book.

Bowl, Blue & White Genre Design, Raised Base, 4-Character Mark, 9 x 3 1/2 In. 55.00
Bowl, Central Dragon Roundels, Floral Border, Fuku Mark, 19th Century, 7 In., 4 Piece . .   977.00
Charger, Carp, 1850-1860 . . . . 24000.00
Charger, Landscape On Interior & Exterior, Marked On Base, Mid 19th Century, 17 In. . . .   517.00
Dish, Pomegranate Design, Blue, White, 19th Century 27.00
Ginger Jar, Cover, 19th Century, 15 In. 1800.00
Plate, Landscape Design, Blue, White, Octagonal, 19th Century, 6 1/4 In. 77.00
Vase, 6 Winged Horses, Abstract Bird & Greek Key Foot, 19th Century, 35 1/2 In. 977.00

ART DECO, or Art Moderne, a style started at the Paris Exposition of
1925, is characterized by linear, geometric designs. All types of furniture and decorative arts, jewelry, book bindings, and even games were
designed in this style. Additional items may be found in the Furniture
category or in various glass and pottery categories, etc.

Figurine, Female Nude, Hands On Head, Bisque, Germany, 11 In. 310.00
Fountain, Wrought Iron, Mosaic Glass Tile Basin, Illuminated, France, 42 x 26 In. 6900.00
Lamp Base, Black, White Silk Shade, 3 Lobed Tiers, Scalloped Foot, 1930, 13 1/4 In. . . .   835.00
Pedestal, Rosewood, Faux Ivory, 4 Spherical Supports, White Dots, 47 x 10 In. 3735.00
Tray, Metal, Reverse Painted Glass Insert, Geometric Shapes, Cream, Red, 18 In. 265.00
Vase, Glass, Architectural Form, Cobalt, American, 11 3/4 In. 173.00
Vase, Pottery, Grape Pattern, Green, Gray, Squeezebag, Charlotte Rhead, 6 3/4 In. 341.00

ART GLASS, see Glass-Art category.

ART NOUVEAU is a style of design that was at its most popular from
1895 to 1905. Famous designers, including Rene Lalique and Emile
Galle, produced furniture, glass, silver, metalwork, and buildings in
the new style. Ladies with long flowing hair and elongated bodies were
among the more easily recognized design elements. Copies of this
style are being made today. Many modern pieces of jewelry can be
found. Additional Art Nouveau pieces may be found in Furniture or in
various glass categories.

Vase, Glass, Enamel, Ruffled Edge, Yellow, Enamel Flower, Egg Shape, 5 3/4 In. 52.00
Vase, Patinated Metal, 4 Scroll Handles, Continental, 1900-1925, 12 In. 330.00

ART POTTERY was first made in America in Cincinnati, Ohio, during
the 1870s. The pieces were hand thrown and hand decorated. The art
pottery tradition continued until the 1920s when studio potters began
making the more artistic wares. American, English, and Continental art
pottery by less well-known makers is listed here. Most makers listed
in *Kovels' American Art Pottery*, such as Arequipa, Ohr, Rookwood,
Roseville, and Weller, are listed in their own categories in this book.
More recent pottery is listed under the name of the maker or in the
Pottery category.

Bowl, Byrdcliffe, Red, Blue & Yellow Flowers, White Ground, Blue Interior, 6 In. 330.00
Bowl, Fluted, Blue & Brown Crystalline Glaze, Arne Bang, 4 1/4 x 8 1/2 In. 330.00
Bowl, Raspberry & Green Drip Matte Glaze, Rose Valley, Wm. Jervis, 2 x 6 1/2 In. 660.00
Bowl, Stylized Flowers, White Ground, Rhead, Santa Barbara, Stamped, 2 x 8 1/2 In. 1100.00
Bowl, Stylized Sunlit Band, University City, Incised UC, 1 3/4 x 4 1/2 In. 3080.00
Bowl, White Crystalline Glaze, Arne Bang, 5 x 9 1/2 In. 330.00
Figurine, Woman's Bust, Art Deco, Caramel Glaze, American Art Clay Co., 8 x 6 In. 132.00

Jardiniere, Stylized Plants, Periwinkle Blue Glaze, University City, 8 x 9 1/4 In. 440.00
Jug, Dragon, Dark Green & Red, Green Ground, Rhead, Signed, 10 1/4 In. 172.00
Jug, Tulip Pattern, Luster Finish, Rhead, Signed, 9 1/4 In. 172.00
Pitcher & Mug Set, Pastoral Scene, Polychrome, 10-In., Pitcher, Avon, 5 Piece 66.00
Plaque, Painted Cherry Blossoms Oriental Design, Laura Fry, 1882, 15 x 11 In. 440.00
Tile, Stylized Peacock Feather Under Multicolored Glaze, Rhead, 5 1/2 In. 385.00
Vase, 3 Nudes Clinging To Shoulder, Anna Valentien, 1911, 16 3/4 In. 935.00
Vase, Broad Leaves, Olive, Ocher Mottled Glaze, Chicago Crucible, 5 1/2 In. 522.00
Vase, Bud, 4-Sided Neck, Leathery Glaze, Green & Turquoise, Chicago Crucible, 8 In. . . . 330.00
Vase, Celadon & Ochre Crystalline Glaze, University City, 9 x 3 In. 1760.00
Vase, Double Overlapping Leaves, Green, Tobacco Matte Glaze, 9 In. 415.00
Vase, Dragonflies, Green, Ivory Matte, 4 1/2 In. . . . . .120.00 to 175.00
Vase, Embossed Leaves, Frothy Green Semimatte Glaze, Chicago Crucible, 7 In. 550.00
Vase, Flame Painted Gold Iridescent, Bronze Neck, Footed, Brouwer, 12 In. 10450.00
Vase, Green, Brown Matte Glaze, 9 1/2 In. 165.00
Vase, Handles, Matte Green, Pennsylvania Museum School Of Industrial Arts, 11 In. 715.00
Vase, Ivory Flame Painted, Yellow & Umber Glaze, Brouwer, 3 3/4 x 3 In. 495.00
Vase, Landscape, Blowing Trees, Blue Shades, White, Incised Denver/DW, 3 1/2 In. 880.00
Vase, Light Lavender Ground, Crystalline Glaze, F.H. Robertson, Signed, 6 In. 6050.00
Vase, Mistletoe, Robin's-Egg Blue Glaze, Oval, Denaura Denver, 6 3/4 x 3 1/4 In. 1320.00
Vase, Molded Vertical Leaves, Buds On Stems, Green Matte Glaze, 9 1/2 In. 360.00
Vase, Mottled Celadon Crystalline Glaze, Bulbous, Grand Feu, 4 3/4 In. 4400.00
Vase, Multicolored Green Glaze, Shouldered Form, 13 In. 465.00
Vase, Multitoned Green Matte Glaze, Pedestal Foot, F.H. Robertson, 4 In. 440.00
Vase, Oriental Form, Tan To Green Matte Glaze, Rhead, 10 1/2 In. 1430.00
Vase, Pillow, Eagle & Swallows, Teal Ground, Gilded Rim, Matt Morgan, 14 In. 1045.00
Vase, Pink Dogwood, Chocolate Ground, Albert Valentien, 1901, 10 5/8 In. 4510.00
Vase, Repeating Leaf Blades, Green Matte Glaze, Early 20th Century, 5 7/8 In. 258.00
Vase, Scarab, Enamel Graffito, Sheer White Ground, Bulbous, Rhead, 10 x 10 1/2 In. . . . 15400.00
Vase, Squat, Mottled Brown, Green & Blue Flambe Glaze, Norweta, 3 1/4 x 3 3/4 In. 605.00
Vase, Thick Burgundy Matte Glaze, Low Closed Form, California Faience, 6 x 4 In. 935.00
Vase, Tulips & Leaves, Matte Green Glaze, Oval, Denaura Denver, 9 x 5 In. 2860.00
Vase, Turquoise Glossy Glaze, Bulbous, Durant Kilns, 1921, 7 In. 195.00
Vase, Winter Scene, Black, Gray, Ivory Ground, Cincinnati, 1880, 6 In. 220.00

ARTHUR OSBORNE plaques are found in the Ivorex category.

ARTS & CRAFTS was a design style popular in American decorative arts from 1894 to 1923. In the 1970s collectors began to rediscover Mission furniture, art pottery, metalwork, linens, and light fixtures from this period. The interest has continued. Today everything from this era is collectible, including jewelry, graphics, and silverware. Additional items may be found in the Furniture category, various glass categories, etc.

Box, Cigarette, Shield & Monogram Top, Dirk Van Erp, 1 3/4 x 5 x 3 3/4 In. 110.00
Box, Oak, Cutout Design, Brass Ormolu, Original Patina, 11 x 5 In. 525.00
Charger, Bronze, Hammered, Liberty & Co., 1905 . . . . 1200.00
Coat Rack, Make Yourself At Home, 11 x 40 In. 305.00
Lampshade, Leaded Glass, Square, 10 x 9 1/2 x 9 1/2 In. 495.00
Lampshade, Leaded, Geometric, Caramel, White, Green & Red 770.00
Smoking Set, Copper & Brass, Hammered, Rivets, Medallions, 4 Piece 385.00
Vase, Marbled Green Top, Bronze Base, Flared, Carl Sorenson, 8 In. 220.00
Woodblock, Geometric Design, Frame, 5 1/2 x 7 In. 385.00

AURENE glass was made by Frederick Carder of New York about 1904. It is an iridescent gold, blue, green, or red glass, usually marked *Aurene* or *Steuben*.

AURENE

Bowl, Blue Iridescent Glass, Inverted Lip, Steuben, 1904, 10 In. 920.00
Bowl, Ruffled Edge, Twist Turned Detail, Gold, Pink, Green, Iridescent, Haviland, 5 In. . . . 144.00
Candlestick, Twist Stems, Disc Feet, Gold Luster, Carder, 1920, 10 1/8 In., Pair 1092.00
Compote, Gold, 8 In. 715.00
Goblet, Diminutive Bowl, Iridescent Gold, Pink, Flat Circular Foot, 6 1/8 In., Pair 550.00
Goblet, Gold Glass, Twisted Stem, Signed, Steuben, 5 In., 5 Piece 1210.00
Lamp, Table, Pulled Gold Aurene Leaf, Gold Interior, Green, Brown, 1915, 21 In., Pair . . . 4025.00

Vase, Blue, Baluster, Rolled Rim, Footed, Signed, 9 In. 1190.00
Vase, Blue, Ruffled Rim, Steuben, 6 x 10 In. 1840.00
Vase, Green Pulled Loops, Gold Iridescent, Steuben, 4 3/4 In. 1035.00
Vase, Urn Shape, Blue, Signed, Steuben, 10 1/2 In. 920.00

AUSTRIA is a collecting term that covers pieces made by a wide variety of factories. They are listed in this book in categories such as Royal Dux, or Porcelain.

AUTO parts and accessories are collectors' items today. Gas pump globes and license plates are part of this specialty. Prices are determined by age, rarity, and condition. Signs and packaging related to automobiles may also be found in the Advertising category. Lalique hood ornaments will be listed in the Lalique category.

Badge, Shell Lubrication, Uniform, Cloisonne, Die Cut, Continental, 2 x 2 In. 495.00
Badge, Station Manager, Chevron, Uniform, 1 1/4 x 1 1/2 In. 255.00
Badge, Tydol, Flying A Gasoline, Hat, Cloisonne Over Nickel, 1 3/4 x 1 3/4 In. 550.00
Badge, Veedol Winged V, Painted, Promotion With Gene Autry's Ranch, 2 3/8 x 1 In. 110.00
Banner, Veedol Oil, Time To Change To Warm Weather Veedol, Cloth, 56 x 36 In. 53.00
Barometer, Veedol Motor Oil, Black Lettering, Gold Ground, 11 1/2 In. 110.00
Booklet, Advertising, Studebaker, See America First, Photos, 1941, 28 Pages 20.00
Booklet, Studebaker, See America First, Photos, 28 Pages 25.00
Brush, Socony-Polarine, Mohair, Wooden Handle, 7 In. 45.00
Can, Archer Lube, Indian, 5 Gal. 45.00
Can, Gargoyle Mobilgrease No. 4, Paper Label, Partial Contents, 4 In. 20.00
Can, Imperial Gas, 5 Gal. 22.00
Can, Mobil Jet Oil 254, Airplane On Label, Contents, 1 Qt. 20.00
Can, Powerized Gasoline Emergency, Sunburst Refining, 1 Qt. 220.00
Can, Reliance Anti-Freeze, Robot Looking Character Picture, Imperial Qt. 300.00
Charm Bracelet, Goodyear Service Award, 14K Gold, 5, 10, 15, 20, 25 & 30 Years 330.00
Clock, Waltham, Brass, Blue Face, Square, c.1920, 2 3/4 In. 53.00
Clothespin Bag, Ray's Mobil Station, Cloth, 2 Top Corner Holes, 10 1/2 x 13 In. 70.00
First Aid Kit, Pure Oil Company, Metal, Wall Mount, 9 3/4 x 9 3/4 x 2 3/4 In. 35.00
Flag, Mobil-Socony, Mounts On Truck's Cab, 1950s, 25 x 12 1/2 In. 75.00
Gas Pump, Bennett Good Gulf, Gulf Logo Sign On Top Of Pump, 52 x 15 x 15 In. 495.00
Gas Pump, Bennett Good Gulf, Red Lettering, 52 x 15 x 15 In. 440.00
Gas Pump, Bowser Red Sentry Filtered Gasoline, Dark Puce, 80 In. 1595.00
Gas Pump, Shell Premium, Logo, Red Lettering, 59 1/2 x 28 x 18 In. 550.00
Gas Pump, Shell Visible, Shell Logo On Each Side, 121 x 15 In. 1375.00
Gas Pump Front, Enco Extra Gasoline, Metal, Tiger Face, 1950 .... 145.00
Gas Pump Globe, American Gas 95.00
Gas Pump Globe, Frontier, Rarin' To Go, 13 1/2 In. 515.00
Gas Pump Globe, Kyso Green, Standard Oil Of Kentucky, 16 1/2 In. 855.00
Gas Pump Globe, Mobil Premium, Capcolite Body, 13 1/2 In. 275.00
Gas Pump Globe, Quick-Flash Hi-Grade, Milk Glass, Red Letters, Blue Flying Eagle ... 1870.00
Gas Pump Globe, Red Indian, 13 1/2 In. 980.00
Gas Pump Globe, Southland's Hercules, 17 1/2 x 17 In., 3 Piece 285.00
Gas Pump Globe, Standard Oil Gold Crown, Original Mount, Ring Base 495.00
Gas Pump Globe, Texaco Sky Chief, 1940, 8 In. 357.00
Gearshift Knob, Skull, Bakelite 98.00
Goggles, Driving, Amber Glass Lenses, Hinged Metal Frame, Elastic Strap, 1920s 45.00
Grill Badge, Farmers Mutual Automobile Ins. Co., Aluminum, Car, Painted, 4 x 3 In. 275.00
Hat, Mobilgas-Mobiloil, With Cloisonne Badge, Size 6 7/8 .... 330.00
Hat, Mobiloil, Service, Cloth, Size S 85.00
Headlight Lamps, Mazda, Eveready, 1930s, Box Of 10 .... 22.00
Hood Ornament, Nude Figure In Diving Position, Hair, Winged Form, Metal, 5 In. 55.00
Hood Ornament, Winged Woman Ornament Affixed To Metal Bracket, Chrome, 11 In. .. 73.00
Hubcap, A.B.C. Car Company, St. Louis, Mo. 700.00
Hubcap, Devaux 210.00
Key Chain, Texaco, Blimp 30.00
Key Ring & Key Blank, Mercury, Emblem, Red Ground, 1940s-1950s 25.00
Knife Sharpener, Humble Gasoline, Houston, Tex., Celluloid, Oval, 2 3/4 In. 25.00
License Plate, California, 1919, 13 x 4 1/2 In. 35.00
License Plate, Massachusetts, 1905, 5 1/4 x 9 1/4 In. 990.00
License Plate, Massachusetts, 1914, Ingirich Mfg. Co., Beaver Falls, Pa., 5 1/2 x 14 In. .. 90.00

License Plate, New York, 1920, Metal 40.00
License Plate, New York, 1964, World's Fair, Black, Yellow, 12 x 6 In. 25.00
License Plate, Oklahoma, 1907, Visit 1957, Red Lettering, 6 x 12 In. 25.00
License Plate, Passenger, Illinois, 1913 . . . .   375.00
License Plate, Pennsylvania, Judiciary, 1931, Black, Tin, 6 x 12 In. 90.00
License Plate Attachment, Boys Town, The Heart Of America, Tin, 6 1/4 x 5 3/4 In. 175.00
License Plate Attachment, Dr Pepper, Black Lettering, White Ground, Tin, 1940, 10 In. . .   770.00
License Plate Attachment, Go To Crystal Beach, Tin, 10 x 4 3/4 In. 70.00
License Plate Attachment, Let's Go Places, Elephant, Embossed, 1948, 6 x 5 3/4 In. 440.00
License Plate Attachment, Milwaukee Braves, Embossed, 4 3/4 x 5 1/4 In. 105.00
Manual, Packard Six, Photos, 1937, 61 Pages 20.00
Mirror, Side-Mounted Spare Tires, Leather Straps, Pair 70.00
Mirror, Visor, Sunoco, 10 x 3 1/2 In. 60.00
Model, Ford Motor Co., 1903 Model, Diamond & Ruby, Sterling Silver, 24 3/8 In. 5750.00
Mug, Coffee, Texaco, Ship's China, 3 5/8 In. 210.00
Oil Can, A-Penn Motor Oil, Contents, 1 Qt. 70.00
Oil Can, AA-1 Motor Oil, Phoenix Oil Co., Inc., Black, Tin, 1 Qt. 125.00
Oil Can, Activa Oil, New Alliance Oil Co., Red, White, Tin, 2 Sides, 8 1/4 In. 20.00
Oil Can, Aeroshell Oil, Red Lettering, Light Yellow, Tin, 9 1/2 x 6 1/4 x 2 In. 55.00
Oil Can, Agalion Motor Oil, Northern Oil & Fuel Corp., Watertown, N.Y., Tin, 1 Gal. 385.00
Oil Can, Amoco French Dry Cleaner, Purple Top, Bottom, Tin, 1 Gal. 50.00
Oil Can, Associated Motor Oil, San Francisco, Calif., White Lettering, Red, 1 Gal. 715.00
Oil Can, Boston Coach Axle, Standard Oil Co., 6 1/2 In. 190.00
Oil Can, Champlin Motor Oil, Screw Top, 1 Qt. 33.00
Oil Can, Conoco Super Motor Oil, SAE 30 Weight, 5 1/2 In. 23.00
Oil Can, Cruiser, Pennsylvania Motor Oil, Light Yellow, Tin, 2 Sides, 1 Qt. 125.00
Oil Can, Crystal Flash Motor Oil, Blue, White, Red Top, Bottom, 1 Qt. 90.00
Oil Can, Deep-Rock Motor Oil, Shaffer Oil Refining Co., 1/2 Gal 105.00
Oil Can, En-Ar-Co Penn., Imperial Qt. 175.00
Oil Can, Esso 2-T Motor Oil, Red Lettering, Tin, 2 Sides, 8 1/4 In. 60.00
Oil Can, Faultless Auto Oil, Hawkeye Oil Co., 1 Gal. 110.00
Oil Can, Gargoyle Mobil Oil, Socony-Vacuum Oil Co., Inc., White, Tin, 1 Qt. 90.00
Oil Can, Gold Seal Motor Oil, Red Paint, Tin, 1/2 Gal. 265.00
Oil Can, Golden Shell Auto Oil Co., Tin, 1 Gal. 440.00
Oil Can, Gulf Supreme Motor Oil, Gulf Refining Co., 1 Gal. 355.00
Oil Can, Indian Cylinder Motorcycle Oil, Indian Motorcycles, Dark Green, 1 Gal. 715.00
Oil Can, Indian Head Hydraulic Brake Fluid, Red Lettering, Blue, 1 Qt. 50.00
Oil Can, International Harvester, Presnall Implement Company, 7 1/2 In. 22.00
Oil Can, Iso-Vis, Standard Oil, Chicago, Ill., Contents, 1 Qt. 35.00
Oil Can, Kendall Rubber Lubricant, White Lettering, Red, Light Yellow, Tin, 1 Gal. 10.00
Oil Can, Kendall, Household Utility Oil, Sheet Metal, 5 In. 32.00
Oil Can, Keynoil Motor Oil, Red Lettering, Tin, 1/2 Gal. 525.00
Oil Can, Lion Head Motor Oil, Gilmore Oil Co., Los Angeles, Calif., Tin, 1 Qt. 175.00
Oil Can, Magnolene Motor Oil Co., Black Lettering, Light Green Ground, Tin, 1/2 Gal. . .   570.00
Oil Can, New York Coach Oil, Ornate Borders, Tin, 4 Sides, 6 3/4 In. 105.00
Oil Can, Para-Field Motor Oil, Contents, 1 Qt. 185.00
Oil Can, Penn-Rad Pour, Dark Green, Tin, 1/2 Gal. 20.00
Oil Can, Pennzoil Outboard Motor Oil Bottle, Bright Yellow, Red Label, Glass, 1 Qt. 20.00
Oil Can, Phillips 66 Marine HD Engine Oil, Contents, 1 Qt. 165.00
Oil Can, Polarine Cup Grease, Red Lettering, Metal Handle, Tin, 25 Lb. 100.00
Oil Can, Polarine Motor Oil, Light Yellow, Tin, 3 Sides, 1/2 Gal.   285.00
Oil Can, Quaker State Duplex Outboard Motor Oil, 2 Men In Motorboat, Green, 1 Qt. 25.00
Oil Can, Red Indian Aviation Motor Oil, Red Faced Indian On Front, 1 Qt. 100.00
Oil Can, Richlube Motor Oil, Richfield Oil Co., Los Angeles, Calif., 1/2 Gal. 440.00
Oil Can, Sentinel Rubbing Compound, Cover, 1 Gal. 15.00
Oil Can, Shell Motor Oil, Swing Spout, 1/2 Gal. 110.00
Oil Can, Signal Quality Lubricants, Contents, 1 Lb. 110.00
Oil Can, Sinclair Opaline Motor Oil, Black, Red, Metal, 1 Qt., 3 Piece 140.00
Oil Can, Socony Auto Spring Oil, With 21-In. Spout, 1 Qt. 70.00
Oil Can, Springear, Halstead Oil Co., Inc., Dark Green, Tin, 7 1/2 In. 25.00
Oil Can, Sunlight Axle Oil, Monarch Mfg. Co., Black Lettering, Tin, 6 3/4 In. 75.00
Oil Can, Super Galena Fortified Motor Oil 50.00
Oil Can, Texaco 574 Motor Oil, Screw Top, 1 Qt. 65.00

Oil Can, Texaco Motor Oil F, Clean, Clear, Golden, Handi-Grip, 1/2 Gal. 355.00
Oil Can, Texaco Oil, Dark Green, Tin, 1/4 Gal. 65.00
Oil Can, Valvoline Motor Oil, Best By Every Test, Dark Green, Black Lettering, 1 Qt. 445.00
Oil Can, Vico Motor Oil, Utah Oil Refining, 1/2 Gal. 195.00
Oil Can, Viscoline Automobile Cylinder Oil, Natrona Pipe Line & Refinery Co., 1 Gal. ... 135.00
Oil Can, White Lettering, Dark Green Ground, Tin, 1 Gal. 210.00
Oil Can, Yacco, Huile Minerale Stabilisee, Dark Green, Pale Yellow, 2 Sides, 8 x 8 1/2 In. 15.00
Plate, Mobiloil, AF, Certified Service, 8 In. 907.00
Poster, Automobile Needs, Family On Picnic Scene, 37 x 23 1/2 In. 90.00
Rack, Bottle, Mobil Oil, Porcelain Shield, With 6 Bottles, With Thimble Caps 355.00
Roof Lights, Taxicab, 1950s 75.00
Shop Coat, Sinclair Oils, Twill, White Herringbone, 4 Pockets, Lee, 1940s, Size 40 ..... 170.00
Sign, 100% Pure Pennsylvania Oil, Permit No. 1, Porcelain, 2 Sides, 12 x 10 In. 220.00
Sign, Ace High Motor Oil, Porcelain, Airplane Picture, 2 Sides, 23 1/4 x 17 1/4 In. 3740.00
Sign, Amilcar, Antique Car In Center, Red Lettering, Tin, 15 1/2 x 19 1/4 In. 330.00
Sign, Amoco Battery Cable Service, White Lettering, 1960, 10 x 17 In. 121.00
Sign, Amoco Courtesy Cards Honored Here, Red Lettering, 15 x 24 In. 105.00
Sign, Arret Autobus Stop, Flange, Black Lettering, Lime Green Ground, 20 x 14 In. 45.00
Sign, Ask For Gargoyle Mobil Oil Authorized Service, Black Lettering, 24 In. 395.00
Sign, Ask For Veedol Motor Oil, Red Lettering, Black, Porcelain, 28 x 22 In. 260.00
Sign, Atlantic With Hanger, White Lettering, Red Ground, 43 x 72 In. 230.00
Sign, Atlas Spark Plugs, Wooden, Rat Trap Shape, 7 1/2 x 17 1/2 x 3/4 In. 90.00
Sign, Atlas Tires & Batteries, Porcelain, Red Ground, 60 x 15 7/8 x 1 In. 360.00
Sign, Bear Quality Service, Happy The Bear, Metal, Bear Shaped, 35 x 27 In. 63.00
Sign, Blue Crown Husky Spark Plugs, Embossed Tin, 1946, 20 x 10 In. 310.00
Sign, Briggs & Stratton, Enamel, Reversible, 24 x 48 In. 125.00
Sign, Champion Spark Plugs, Wake Up Sleepy Motors, Paper, 11 1/4 x 10 1/2 In. 155.00
Sign, Chevrolet Bowtie, Dark Blue, Die Cut, Cardboard, 10 3/4 x 30 In. 90.00
Sign, Chevrolet Guardian Maintenance, We Airline Check, When We Chevy Tune, 44 In. .. 115.00
Sign, Cities Service National Charge Cards, Flange, Green, Red Lettering, 21 In. 105.00
Sign, Colonial Gas, Green Lettering, White Ground, Porcelain, 23 In. 200.00
Sign, Conoco, Hottest Brand Going, Conoco!, Wooden, 17 x 9 x 75 In. 45.00
Sign, Continental Trailways Bus Station, White, Maroon Lettering, Metal, 36 In. 65.00
Sign, Essolube Standard, Logo On Bottom Center, Red, Porcelain, 5 x 12 In. 145.00
Sign, Eyquem Spark Plug, Dark Blue, Porcelain, 38 3/4 x 12 In. 655.00
Sign, Firestone Tire, Flange, Red Lettering, Porcelain, 2 Sides, 36 x 28 In. 825.00
Sign, Fisk Tire, Small Boy, With Candle, Porcelain, Black Letters, 28 x 36 In. 900.00
Sign, Goodrich Garage Tires, 2 Sides, White, Black, Metal, Circular, 18 In. ......525.00 to 880.00
Sign, Goodyear Tire, Flange, Showing Tire, Die Cut, Porcelain, 34 x 21 1/2 In. 800.00
Sign, Greyhound Lines, Porcelain, 2 Sides, 36 x 20 1/4 In. 800.00
Sign, Greyhound Lines, Ticket Office, Black, Orange, White, Porcelain, 2 Sides, 30 In. 2530.00
Sign, Hartford Tires Give Tire Insurance, Die Cut, Metal, 19 1/2 In. 1320.00
Sign, Havoline Motor Oil, New & Improved Keeps Your Engine Clean, 21 In. 275.00
Sign, Jenney Gasoline, Winter Driving, 1934 Calendar, Cardboard, 2 Sides, 21 x 14 In. 95.00
Sign, Ladies' Rest Room, Sanitary Seat Covers, Porcelain, Flange, 10 x 9 3/4 In. 265.00
Sign, Marathon, Best In The Long Run, Man, Running, Red Ground, 72 In. 550.00
Sign, Michelin Tire, Michelin Man Riding On Motorcycle, Tin, 20 x 14 1/2 In. 475.00
Sign, Michelin, Michelin Man Riding Bicycle, Red Lettering, Tin, 29 1/2 In. 205.00
Sign, Mobil Oil, Gargoyle, Black Lettering, Porcelain, 24 x 19 In. 255.00
Sign, Mobil Oil, Gargoyle, CW For Gears, Porcelain, 8 3/4 x 10 3/4 In. 1210.00
Sign, Mobil Pegasus, Red Horse In Center, Prancing, Die Cut, Embossed, 45 In. 1565.00
Sign, Mother Goose Fisk Tire, Maxfield Parrish, 1920s, 14 1/2 x 25 3/8 In. 7480.00
Sign, Oldsmobile Service, White Lettering, Black Ground, Circular, 60 In. 550.00
Sign, Overland Motor Car, We Use An Overland Motor Car, Black Ground, 10 In. 185.00
Sign, Pennsylvania Vacuum Cup, Good Mile Tires, White Lettering, 22 x 16 In. 465.00
Sign, Pennzoil Courtesy Cards, Honored Here, Black Lettering, Flange, 14 x 18 In. 60.00
Sign, Pennzoil, Welcome To Our Service Department, Ask For Pennzoil, 18 In. 65.00
Sign, Perfection Asbestos Protected Tire, Flange, Die Cut, Metal, 23 x 16 In. 120.00
Sign, Polarine Oil & Greases, Motor Car & Motor Boat Lubrication, Tin, 19 x 4 3/8 In. ... 410.00
Sign, Power-Lube Motor Oil, Smooth As The Read Of A Tiger, Orange, Black, 28 In. 1665.00
Sign, Pump, Blue Sunoco 200, Diamond Shape With Arrow, Porcelain, 15 x 20 3/4 In. ... 355.00
Sign, Pump, Douglas Blend Gasoline, Embossed Aluminum, 14 x 10 In. 495.00
Sign, Pump, Flying A Gasoline, Porcelain, 10 x 10 In. 255.00

Sign, Pump, Sinclair Diesel, Porcelain, 12 x 13 1/2 In. 130.00
Sign, Pump, Time Super Gasoline, Clock Picture, Porcelain, 9 1/4 x 14 In. 660.00
Sign, Quaker State Outboard Oil, 100% Pure Pennsylvania Oil, Green, 12 In. 60.00
Sign, Red Crown Gasoline, Iron Hanging Frame, Porcelain, 1920s, 42 In. 488.00
Sign, Schenuit Aircraft Tires & Tubes, Red Lettering, Flange, 14 x 18 1/2 In. 140.00
Sign, Sealed For Your Protection, Porcelain, 14 x 9 In. 165.00
Sign, Shell Charge Cards Honored, Porcelain, 2 Sides, 14 x 19 1/4 In. 165.00
Sign, Shell Oil, No Admittance Except On Business, Porcelain, 15 x 6 In. 195.00
Sign, Shell Service Logo On Front, Man Driving Race Car, Red Lettering, 34 x 25 In. 175.00
Sign, Shell, Appointed Oil Fired Heating Installer, Frame, Porcelain, 13 x 18 In. 230.00
Sign, Shell, Flange, Shell Motor Oil Logo, Red Lettering, Porcelain, 15 3/4 In. 605.00
Sign, Shell, Saves On Stop & Go Driving, Super-Shell, Red Lettering, 33 x 57 In. 75.00
Sign, Shell, Sexy Lady And Shell Logo, Die Cut, Tin, 15 1/2 x 6 1/2 In. 1210.00
Sign, Signal Oil & Gas Co., Northern District, Porcelain, Die Cut, 24 x 15 In. 415.00
Sign, Sinclair, Dark Green Ground, Porcelain, 6 x 45 x 1 In. 330.00
Sign, Socony Vacuum, Shield Shape, Masonite, 8 1/4 x 8 1/4 In. 65.00
Sign, Standard Ethyl Gasoline, Silver Lettering, Black Ground, 2 Sides 330.00
Sign, Standard Heating Oils, Chevron, Porcelain, 15 3/4 x 20 In. 575.00
Sign, Texaco Farm Lubricants Sold Here, Porcelain, 42 x 30 In. 550.00
Sign, Texaco Motor Oil, Circular Logo, Flange, Red, Black Ground, Porcelain, 23 In. 330.00
Sign, Texaco, Easy Pour Can, Texaco Motor Oil, Red Ground, 27 1/2 x 17 In. 990.00
Sign, Texaco, No Smoking, Porcelain, White Ground, Star, 4 x 23 In. 395.00
Sign, That Good Gulf Gasoline, Gulf Refining Co., Black, Orange Center, 18 In. 330.00
Sign, Time For A Change?, Ask For Uniflo Motor Oil, Black Lettering, 1960, 10 x 17 In. . 187.00
Sign, Tiolene, The Pure Oil Co., U.S.A., Black Lettering, White, Round, 1940, 15 In. 330.00
Sign, Union Service Station, Stop Wear, Porcelain, 48 1/4 x 9 1/2 In. 1100.00
Sign, Veedol Motor Oil, 100 % Pennsylvania, SAE 20, Porcelain, 4 3/4 x 3 3/4 In. 265.00
Sign, Wolf's Head Oil, Tin, Self-Framed, 19 3/4 x 13 3/4 In. 440.00
Sign, Your Equipment Deserves The Best, Always Use Penn Drake, 27 In. 145.00
Spark Plug Cleaner, Champion, Minute, Glass Tube, Wooden Case, 6 1/2 In. 65.00
Sprayer, Standard Oil Company, Indian Quixpray, Aluminum, Pocket Type, 4 3/4 In. 40.00
Sticker, Windshield, Ship Design, Gulfport, Miss., Oval, 1930s, 4 In. 9.00
Tail Light, Bail Handle, Adams & Westlake, 1895 .... 125.00
Tin, Archer, Lubricants, Indian, Bow & Arrow 93.00
Tin, Chevron Handy Oil, 4 Oz. 33.00
Tin, Flying A Household Oil, Lead Top, Cap, 4 Oz. 55.00
Tin, Lindley's Motor Brand, American Can Co., 1 Lb. 120.00
Tin, Signal Products Household Oil, Contents, 4 Oz. 90.00
Tin, Standard Oil, Household Lubricating Oil, Oiler Type, 4 Oz. 40.00
Tin, Thermo Anti-Freeze, Snowman Walking, 1945, 1 Gal. 66.00
Tire Gauge, Schrader, Patent 1928 .... 40.00
Traffic Light, Rewired 85.00
Water Bag, Veedol, Eagle Brand, 150 Hour Tractor Oil 100.00

AUTUMN LEAF pattern china was made for the Jewel Tea Company
beginning in 1933. Hall China Company of East Liverpool, Ohio,
Crooksville China Company of Crooksville, Ohio, Harker Potteries
of Chester, West Virginia, and Paden City Pottery, Paden City, West
Virginia, made dishes with this design. Autumn Leaf has remained
popular and was made by Hall China Company until 1978. Some other
pieces in the Autumn Leaf pattern are still being made. For more information, see *Kovels' Depression Glass & Dinnerware Price List*.

Bowl, Gold, 9 1/2 In. 30.00
Bowl, Refrigerator, Stacking, 3 Piece 110.00
Bowl, Salad 16.00
Bowl, Stacking, 6 1/4 In. 25.00
Bowl, Vegetable, Cover, Oval, 10 In. 60.00
Bowl Set, 3 Piece 65.00
Cake Plate, Flat, 9 1/2 In. 22.00
Canister, Round, Large 45.00
Card, Playing, Double Deck, Unopened 225.00
Coffeepot, 8 Cup 70.00
Cup, St. Denis 38.00

Cup & Saucer, St. Denis 35.00
Custard Cup Set, 6 Piece 120.00
Hot Plate, Oval, 10 1/4 In. 25.00
Hot Plate, Round, 7 1/8 In. 20.00
Marmalade, Bowl, Tray & Cover, 3 Piece 95.00
Mustard, 3 1/2 In. 95.00
Percolator 200.00
Pitcher, Round, 2 1/2 Pt., 6 In. 20.00
Plate, 7 In. 8.50
Plate, Dinner, 10 In. 18.00
Platter, Oval, 11 1/2 In. 25.00
Salt & Pepper ....20.00 to 25.00
Saucer, St. Denis 20.00
Teapot, Aladdin, 10 1/2 In. 95.00
Teapot, Long Spout, 7 In. 40.00
Tumbler, 15 Oz. 35.00

AVON bottles are listed in the Bottle category under Avon.

AZALEA dinnerware was made for Larkin Company customers from 1918 to 1941. Larkin, the soap company, was in Buffalo, New York. The dishes were made by Noritake China Company of Japan. Each piece of the white china was decorated with pink azaleas.

NORITAKE
AZALEA PATT.
HANDPAINTED
JAPAN
NO. 19322
252627

Basket 180.00
Bowl, Gold Trim, 5 1/2 In. 20.00
Butter Tub, With Drainer 43.00
Cake Plate, 9 3/4 In. 34.00
Cup & Saucer 20.00
Cup & Saucer, Marked, Gold Trim 20.00
Dish, Pickle, Loop Handle 20.00
Gravy Boat, Attached Underplate, Gold Trim, Red Wreath Mark, 9 In. 42.00
Plate, 6 1/2 In. ....7.00 to 8.00
Plate, 7 5/8 In. 10.00
Plate, 8 1/2 In. 24.00
Plate, 9 3/4 In. 24.00
Plate, Gold Trim, 10 In. 25.00
Plate, Serving, Handles, 9 3/4 In. 35.00
Plate, Square, 7 In. 85.00
Platter, 11 3/4 In. ....50.00 to 55.00
Platter, Gold Trim, 13 3/4 In. 60.00
Salt & Pepper 24.00
Soup, Dish, 7 1/2 In. 25.00
Sugar & Creamer, Cover ....25.00 to 45.00

BACCARAT glass was made in France by La Compagnie des Cristalleries de Baccarat, located 150 miles from Paris. The factory was started in 1765. The firm went bankrupt and began operating again about 1822. Cane and millefiori paperweights were made during the 1860 to 1880 period. The firm is still working near Paris making paperweights and glasswares.

LES
VAPORISATEURS
M
PARIS
BACCARAT

Bottle, Swirl, Rose Teinte, Stopper, 7 1/2 x 4 In. 135.00
Bottle, Wine, Zipper, Rose Teinte, Cut Paneled Neck, 10 1/4 In. ... 225.00
Bowl, Free-Form, 8 In. 52.00
Candelabrum, 2-Light, Alfante, Frosted Lobe, Cherub, Holding Stem, Prisms, 24 In. 522.00
Candelabrum, 4-Light, Tulip-Shaped Cups, Emerald Headers, Prisms, 24 In., Pair 1540.00
Candelabrum, 5-Light, Swirl, Red Bobeches, Prisms, 23 1/2 In. ... 1570.00
Centerpiece, Berried Laurel Stem, Branch Feet, Signed, 19th Century, 20 1/4 In. 460.00
Champagne, Fluted, Knopped Tapered Stem, 4 1/4 In., 8 Piece 385.00
Decanter, Whiskey, 24K Gold Design, Square, 8 1/2 In. ....260.00 to 360.00
Figurine, Bird, Silhouette, Signed, 3 1/4 In. 75.00
Figurine, Hedgehog, 5 In. 80.00
Figurine, Puck, Brass Herald Horn, Signed, 5 3/4 x 4 In. 65.00
Figurine, Squirrel, Munching On Treat, Signed, 4 1/2 In. 95.00
Figurine, Stylized Human Profile, Triangular Section, 10 1/4 In., Pair 920.00

Figurine, Tennis Player, Label, Etched Logo, 9 In. 196.00
Figurine, Toucan, 6 1/2 In. 80.00
Figurine, Whale, 6 In. 50.00
Ice Bucket, Swirl, Rose Tiente, Brass Fittings, 5 1/4 In. 195.00
Lamp, Fairy, Rose Tiente, Silver Plated Base, 4 1/4 x 5 1/2 In. 295.00
Mustard, Spoon 85.00
Paperweight, Beetle & Primrose, Cog, Translucent Blue Ground, 1983, 3 1/16 In. 500.00
Paperweight, Butterfly Over Clematis, Flattened Millefiori Wings, 3 1/8 In. 4000.00
Paperweight, Clematis Vines, Star & Bull's-Eye Cane Centers, Red, White, Blue, 3 In. ... 10000.00
Paperweight, Concentric Millefiori, Star, Cog, Arrow & Stardust Canes, 2 1/16 In. 300.00
Paperweight, Dahlia, Millefiori, Translucent Aqua Ground, 1971, 3 1/8 In. 700.00
Paperweight, Dahlia, Overlapping Petals, Translucent Blue Ground, 1973, 3 1/16 In. 750.00
Paperweight, Double Clematis, Faceted Star-Cut Garland 430.00
Paperweight, Millefiori Garlands, Canes, Latticinio Ground, Faceted, 3 1/4 In. 345.00
Paperweight, Mountains Of The Moon, Tan Ground, Green & Mica Flecks, 3 1/4 In. 250.00
Paperweight, Pansy, Star-Cut Base, 2 1/2 In. 460.00
Paperweight, Rose, Ruby Petals, White Double Swirl Latticinio, 1976, 3 1/8 In. 550.00
Paperweight, Scrambled Millefiori, Blue, Pink, Green, White, 2 3/4 In. 200.00
Paperweight, Snake Coil, Quatrefoil, Chocolate, Emerald, Tan Ground, 3 1/8 In. 8000.00
Paperweight, Sulphide, Andrew Jackson, Green Base, Label, Case 35.00
Paperweight, Sulphide, Eleanor Roosevelt, Amethyst Base, Label, Case .... .75.00 to 295.00
Paperweight, Sulphide, Winston Churchill, Paris, 1966, 2 3/4 In. 200.00
Paperweight, Sulphide, Woman Holding Star, Blue Ground 60.00
Paperweight, Tan Snake, Green Mottled Ground, 1979 .... 330.00
Perfume Bottle, Ming Toy, Kneeling Geisha, 1923 .... 5225.00
Pitcher, Swirl, Amberina, 6 1/2 In. 225.00
Tankard, Water, Swirl, Amberina, 12 In. 250.00
Tumbler, Harmonie, 4 1/8 In. 67.00
Vase, Bow & Foliate Swag, Neoclassical Figures, 3 Curving Feet, 9 3/8 In. 690.00
Vase, Fan, Allover Landscape & Butterfly Design, Brass Frog, 6 x 5 1/4 In. 115.00
Vase, Fluted, Flared, Etched Mark, 9 3/4 x 8 1/2 In. 1100.00
Vase, Iris, Lavender, Rust, White, Flared, Enameled, 1900, 12 In. 345.00
Wine, Balloon, Faceted Stem, Signed, 12 Piece 550.00

BADGES have been used since before the Civil War. Collectors search
for examples of all types, including law enforcement and company
identification badges. Well-known prison or law enforcement badges
are most desirable. Most are made of nickel or brass. Many recent
reproductions have been made.

Alaska-Yukon-Pacific Exposition, Silver Plate, Shield Shape, 1 1/4 x 1 1/4 In. 25.00
Army, USSR Outstanding, Enamel & Gilt, Pinback 10.00
British Beret, Silver Finish, Airborne Unite, Eagle With Wreath 15.00
Chauffeur, Alabama, Eagle At Center, White Metal, 1932, 1 1/4 In. 138.00
Chauffeur, Arizona, Black Painted Decal, Bronze, 1937, 1/2 In. 24.00
Chauffeur, Arizona, Black Painted Lettering, Steel, 1943, 1/2 In. 95.00
Chauffeur, Arizona, Bronze, 1933, 1 3/4 x 1 In. 105.00
Chauffeur, Arizona, Bronze, Oblong, 1935, 1 3/4 In. 40.00
Chauffeur, Arizona, Red, White Celluloid, 1945, 1 1/4 In. 65.00
Chauffeur, California, Brass, Tin Plate, 1931, 1 3/4 In. 21.00
Chauffeur, Colorado, Brass, Black Matte Finish, 1916, 2 In. 180.00
Chauffeur, Colorado, Brass, White Metal, 1936, 1/2 x 5 In. 42.00
Chauffeur, Florida, Brass, Black Accents, 1936, 1 1/4 In. 140.00
Chauffeur, Idaho, Bronze, Cross Shape, 1923, 2 x 1/2 In. 100.00
Chauffeur, Illinois, Black Painted Lettering, Bronze, Oval, 1913, 2 In. 160.00
Chauffeur, Illinois, Eagle At Bottom, Brass, Nickel, 1921, 1 1/4 In. 38.00
Chauffeur, Indiana, Black Painted Number Decal, Brass, Shield Shape, 1916, 1 1/4 In. ... 130.00
Chauffeur, Kansas, Brass, Sunflower Design, 1930, 1/2 In. 23.00
Chauffeur, Louisiana, Nickel, 1941, 1 1/4 In. 65.00
Chauffeur, Maryland, Yellow Celluloid, Oval, 1915, 1 3/4 In. 610.00
Chauffeur, Minnesota, Green Painted Decal, Nickel, Diamond Shape, 1930, 2 In. 34.00
Chauffeur, Missouri, Black Painted, State Of Missouri Shape, Aluminum, 1932, 1/2 In. .. 64.00
Chauffeur, Missouri, Green Painted Decal, Aluminum, Diamond Shape, 1920 .... 28.00
Chauffeur, Missouri, Metal, Diamond Shape, Licensed Chauffeur, Expires 1/4/19, 2 In. .. 61.00

Chauffeur, New Mexico, Red Painted Decal, Brass, 1952, 2 x 1/2 In. 20.00
Chauffeur, New York, Black, Yellow Painted Decal, Brass, 1915, 1 1/4 In. 20.00
Chauffeur, Ohio, Diamond Shape, Nickel, Pinback, 1914, 1 3/4 In. 72.00
Chauffeur, Pennsylvania, Brass, Tin Plate, Oval, 1913, 2 1/2 In. 35.00
Chauffeur, Texas, Black Painted Decal, Brass, Oval, 1924, 1/2 In. 65.00
Chauffeur, Utah, Copper, 1940, 1/4 In. 140.00
Chauffeur, West Virginia, Black Painted Decal, Nickel, 1924, 1/2 In. 32.00
Deputy Sheriff, Monroe County, N.Y., State Crest, Eagle, Gilt Brass, 2 1/2 x 1 1/2 In. ... 30.00
Driver's License, Pennsylvania Licensed Driver, Blass, 1915, 1 3/4 x 2 1/2 In. 45.00
Eagle, Double-Headed, Chased Border, St. Petersburg, Gold, Enamel, 1871, 2 In. 1840.00
Employee, Crown Drug Stores, Name Plate, Red & Blue Logo, Brass, 2 In. 23.00
Employee, Rexall Drugs, Place For Employee's Name, Cloisonne, 2 1/4 x 1 1/2 In. 105.00
Forest Service, Issued To Retired Park Rangers, Shield Shape, Bronze, 1/2 In. 76.00
Hat, Curved Bottling Co., Gold Color, 1940, 3 1/2 In. 797.00
Hunting & License, Mississippi, 1942 .... 60.00
Inspector, Department Of Justice Immigration, Gold Tone, Blue, 1/2 In. 34.00
Naval Police Driver, Panama, Diving Helmet Over Anchor, Lucite, Brass, 1 1/2 In. 25.00
Parachutist, White & Blue Enamel, Gilt Airplane Affixed, Poland 10.00
Pilot, Rocky Mountain Airlines, Wings, Bronze Color, 2 In. 148.00
Pinbar, Red, White & Blue Ribbon, Trans-Mississippi Fair, Goddess, Fairgrounds 85.00
Police, Buffalo, Rushing Buffalo Scene, Black Lettering, 3 1/4 In. 50.00
Police, Cap, Lighthouse, Applied Brass Numbers 65.00
Police, Chief, Chillicothe, Ill., 7-Pointed Star, Gold Colored Metal, Blue Enamel, 3 In. ... 50.00
Police, Commonwealth Of Maine 45.00
Police, Detective, New Orleans, Star & Crescent Shape, Brass, 2 1/4 In. 41.00
Police, Mohawk Tribe, New York State Seal, Blackened Brass, 2 1/2 In. 60.00
Police, Nebraska City, Shield Shape, Star In Center, Eagle Top, 2 1/2 In. 44.00
Police, Officer, 7-Pointed Star, Sterling Silver, 1920s, 3 In. 400.00
Police, Old Fashioned, Nickel Tone, Round, 1 7/8 In. 103.00
Police, Patrolman, Ely Police Dept., Star Shape 185.00
Police, Sergeant, Montreal, Shield Shape, Beaver Top, Chromed, 3 In. 55.00
Police, Special Police, Frankfort, N.Y., Eagle Top, Brass, 2 1/5 In. 20.00
Police, State Of Pennsylvania, Eagle Top, Steel, 2 1/4 In. 26.00
Police, U.S. Secret Service Uniformed Division, White House, Gold Tone, 1/4 In. 109.00
Police, Warwick, Indiana State Seal, Gray Metal, 3 x 2 1/4 In. 30.00
Porter, Pullman Company, I.D., Celluloid, Photo Insert, 1 3/8 x 2 1/8 In. 38.00
Security, Indian Motorcycle Co., White, Metal, Shield, 2 1/2 In. 20.00
Security, Silver Nugget, Blue Enamel Lettering, Star Shape, 1950 .... 49.00
Special Agent, Wells Fargo Express Co., Shield, Eagle On Top, White Metal 35.00
Taxi Driver, Columbus, Ohio, Brass, Engraved, 1954, 1 1/2 In. 32.00
Treasury Dept., Collector Of Customs, Resigned, 10K Gold Finish, Blue Enamel 200.00
U.S. Air Mail, Pilot's Wings, Globe In Center, Pat. Applied For, Rolled Gold, 3 1/2 In. 385.00
U.S. Post Office, United States Mail Rural Farm Delivery, Metal, 3 In. 400.00
Uniformed Machine Gunner, Blue Ribbon, Medal, 350 Club MG Co. 7, 1938, 1 3/8 In. ... 36.00

BANKS of metal have been made since 1868. There are still banks, mechanical banks, and registering banks (those that show the total money deposited on the face of the bank). Many old iron or tin banks have been reproduced since the 1950s in iron or plastic. Some old reproductions marked Book of Knowledge or John Wright, or Capron are listed. Pottery, glass, and plastic banks are also listed here. Mickey Mouse and other Disneyana banks are listed in Disneyana. We have added the M-numbers based on *The Penny Bank Book: Collected Still Banks* by Andy and Susan Moore.

Aberdeen Angus Bull, Aluminum, M 555, 4 1/8 In. 99.00
Air Mail, Mailbox On Pedestal, Cast Iron, Dent, 1920, 5 x 6 3/8 In. 495.00
Alphabet, Polyhedron, Gold Paint, Embossed Letters, Cast Iron, M 1604, 3 7/8 In. 1575.00
Apollo 8, Moon & Space Capsule, Cast Iron, M 800, John Wright, 1968, 4 1/4 In. 17.00
Apple, Leaf Stem Base, Cast Iron, M 1621, Kyser & Rex, 1882, 3 In. ....715.00 to 1500.00
Apple, With Brown Twig Stem, Ceramic, 4 3/8 In. 451.00
Arabian Safe, Cast Iron, Embossed Camel, Kyser & Rex, 1882, 4 9/16 In. 200.00
Aunt Jemima, Mammy With Spoon, Cast Iron, A.C. Williams, 1905-1930s, 6 In. ..143.00 to 220.00

Aunt Jemima, Mammy With Spoon, Slot In Legs, Cast Iron, M 169, 5 7/8 In. 363.00
Bank Building, Bank Of New Glarus, Souvenir, White Metal 85.00
Bank Building, Birth Bank, With Clock, Brass, Steel, M 1141, England, 1840, 7 1/2 In. . .   242.00
Bank Building, Capitol Bank & Trust, White Metal, 4 1/4 In. 72.00
Bank Building, City Bank, Crown, Cast Iron, Thomas Swan, 5 1/2 In. . . . .*Illus*   4400.00
Bank Building, City Bank, With Teller, Cast Iron, M 1099, H.L. Judd, 5 1/4 In. 253.00
Bank Building, Columbia, Cast Iron, M 1077, Kenton, 1893-1904, 7 In. . . . . .352.00 to 605.00
Bank Building, Cook County Federal Savings, White Metal, 4 1/2 In. 83.00
Bank Building, County Bank, Brass, M 1110, John Harper, 1892, 4 1/4 In. 127.00
Bank Building, Crown, Gray Paint, Brown Roof, Cast Iron, J. & E. Stevens, 3 5/8 In. 360.00
Bank Building, Cupola Bank, Cast Iron, M 1145, J. & E. Stevens, 1872, 5 1/4 In. 396.00
Bank Building, Deposit Bank, Small Print, Cast Iron, M 1082, 4 1/4 In. 94.00
Bank Building, Domed, Cast Iron, M 1182, A.C. Williams, 1899-1934, 4 1/2 In. 60.00
Bank Building, Finial Bank, Brown, Cast Iron, Kyser & Rex, 1887, 5 3/4 x 4 3/8 In. 425.00
Bank Building, First National Bank Of Chicago, Metal, M 1222, Bonthrico, 1970, 8 In. . .   72.00
Bank Building, First Security Trust & Savings, White Metal, 2 1/4 In. 116.00
Bank Building, Globe Savings Fund, Cast Iron, M 1199, Kyser & Rex, 1889, 7 1/8 In. 6710.00
Bank Building, Home Savings Bank, Dog Finial, Cast Iron, M 1237, 5 3/4 In. . . . .182.00 to 231.00
Bank Building, Home Savings, Dog Finial, Cast Iron, J. & E. Stevens, 1891, 5 3/4 In. . . .   485.00
Bank Building, Home Savings, Red, Black Roof, Peoples Savings Bank, 10 In. 2665.00
Bank Building, Home Savings, Roof Casting, Embossed, Detroit, Mich., 10 In. 1210.00
Bank Building, Home Savings, White, Yellow Roof, Brown Trim, Cast Iron, 5 7/8 In. 215.00
Bank Building, International Credit Union Center, White Metal, 2 1/2 In. 95.00
Bank Building, Prudential, White Metal, 9 1/2 In. 450.00
Bank Building, Roof Bank, Double Door, Cast Iron, M 1124, Casting, 1903-1928, 5 In. . .   105.00
Bank Building, Second Ward Bank, Lead, 2 1/4 In. 255.00
Bank Building, State Bank, Cast Iron, M 1080, Kenton, 1900, 5 7/8 In. . . . . .138.00 to 215.00
Bank Building, State Bank, Cast Iron, M 1085, Kenton, 1890, 3 1/2 In. 1127.00
Bank Building, State, Bronze Trim, Cast Iron, M 1085, Kenton, 1890, 3 1/8 In. 265.00
Bank Building, State, Bronze Trim, Embossed Letterscast Iron, M 1079, Kenton, 7 In. . . .   510.00
Bank Building, State, Dormers On Roof, 4 Steps, Cast Iron, M 1078, Kenton, 8 In. 605.00
Bank Building, State, Gold, Bronze Trim, Cast Iron, M 1080, Kenton, 5 5/8 In. . . .305.00 to 385.00
Bank Building, Tower, Brown, Cast Iron, M1198, Kyser & Rex, 6 7/8 x 2 1/2 In. 1330.00
Bank Building, Triangular Building, Cast Iron, M 1235, Hubley, 1914, 6 In. 523.00
Bank Bungalow, Cast Iron, Grey Iron Casting, 1918-1928, 3 3/4 In. . . . . .255.00 to 660.00
Bank Of Industry, Safe, Cast Iron, 5 3/8 In. 120.00
Barrel, Walled City, Wooden, Pull-Off Metal Top, Painted, Russia, c.1910, 4 In. 140.00
Barrel, White City Barrel No. 1, Cast Iron, M 908, Nicol, 1894, 4 In. 176.00
Barrel, White City Puzzle Savings, Puzzle Savings No. 3, Silver, Cast Iron, 6 x 8 In. 265.00
Baseball, Jimmy Braves, Children's Cancer Research, Composition, 6 1/2 In. 61.00
Baseball, Tin Lithograph, Stand, 1950s 100.00
Baseball Player, Cast Iron, A.C. Williams, 1909, 5 3/4 In. 140.00
Basketball Shoe, Cloth Laces, Cast Iron, 7 3/8 In. 50.00
Basset Hound, Head, Cast Iron, M 380, 3 1/8 In. 1155.00
Battleship, Maine, Cast Iron, Grey Iron Casting, M 1441, Large, 1898-1903, 5 1/4 In. . . .   451.00
Battleship, Maine, White, Upper Deck Has Lifeboats, Cast Iron, J. & E. Stevens, 10 In. . .   11540.00
Battleship, Oregon, Cast Iron, M 1450, Small, J. & E. Stevens, 1891-1906, 3 7/8 In. 209.00
Beaky At Tree Trunk, White Metal, M 303, Moss Mfg., 1930s, 4 1/8 In. 100.00
Bear, Honey Bear, Cast Iron, U.S., 2 1/2 In. 935.00
Bear, Mean, Standing, Cast Iron, M 713, Hubley, 1906, 5 1/2 In. 100.00
Bear, Stealing Pig, Cast Iron, M 693, 5 1/2 In. . . . . .578.00 to 1760.00
Bear, Teddy Bear, Standing, Cast Iron, M 694, Arcade, 2 1/2 x 3 7/8 In. 180.00
Bearded Man In Vest, Painted, Tin, 6 In. 231.00
Beehive, On Base, White Metal, M 685, 3 3/4 In. 33.00
Beehive, Square, Bank For Savings, Lead, 3 In. 77.00
Bell, Liberty Bell With Yoke, Cast Iron, M 809, Arcade, 1925-1934, 3 1/2 In. 22.00
Big Boy, Hard Plastic, Head Rotates, In Bag, Taiwan, 8 1/2 In.   24.00
Big Boy, Vinyl, Uncut Coin Slot, 1950s, 9 1/2 In. 40.00
Billiken, On Throne, Cast Iron, M 73, A.C. Williams, 1909, 6 1/2 In. . . . . .154.00 to 165.00
Black Boy, 2 Faces, Cast Iron, M 83, A.C. Williams, 1901-1919, 4 1/8 In. . . . . . . .83.00 to 390.00
Black Boy, 2 Faces, Cast Iron, Painted, A.C. Williams, 1901-1919, 3 1/4 In. 245.00
Black Man, On Bale Of Cotton, Cast Iron, U.S. Hardware, 1898, M 37, 4 7/8 In. 462.00

Bank, Bank Building, City Bank, Crown,
Cast Iron, Thomas Swan, 5 1/2 In.

Bank, Building, Log Cabin,
Tin, 3 In.

Boat, Gunboat, Silver Paint, Red Accents, Cast Iron, M 1462, Kenton, 8 1/2 In. 2120.00
Book, Leather Covered, Life Insurance Savings Bank, 5 1/8 In. 30.00
Buffalo, Cast Iron, M 560, Arcade, 1920-1925, 3 1/8 In. 132.00
Buffalo, Standing, Amherst Stoves Embossed All Sides Of Bank, 5 x 8 In. 240.00
Building, 1876 Bank, Cast Iron, M 1011, Variation, Judd, 1895, 3 3/8 In. 231.00
Building, Bethel College, Building, Cast Iron, M 1196, Service Foundry, 2 7/8 In. .127.00 to 132.00
Building, Blackpool Tower, Cast Iron, M 984, Chamberlain & Hill, 1908, 7 3/8 In. 132.00
Building, Castle, Cast Iron, M 954, Kyser & Rex, 1882, 3 In. 633.00
Building, Church, Westside Presbyterian, Cast Iron, M 958, 1916, 3 3/4 In. 440.00
Building, Colonial House, Side Porch, Cast Iron, M 993, A.C. Williams, 1910-1934, 3 In. . 187.00
Building, Columbia Tower, Cast Iron, Columbia Gray Iron Casting Co., 1897, 7 In. 785.00
Building, Cone Shaped Dome, Cast Iron, Kenton, 1893-1913, 2 1/2 In. 418.00
Building, Domed Mosque, Gold, Bronze, Cast Iron, Grey Iron Casting Co., 5 1/8 In. 340.00
Building, Flat Iron Building, Cast Iron, M 1159, Kenton, 1904-1913, 8 1/4 In. 3520.00
Building, Flat Iron, Cast Iron, M 1161, No Trap, Kenton, 1912-1919, 5 1/2 In. 187.00
Building, Hansel & Gretel, Tin, Stollwerck, Germany, c.1890, 2 1/4 In. 140.00
Building, House With Chimney, Chimney Slot, Cast Iron, M 997, 2 7/8 In. 660.00
Building, Independence Hall, 3-In-1, Cast Iron, M 1211, 6 3/8 In. 1485.00
Building, Independence Hall, Glass, M 1207, Wm. R. Kirchner, Pat. 1876, 7 In. 77.00
Building, Lichfield Cathedral, Cast Iron, Chamberlain & Hill, England, 1908, 6 5/8 In. 430.00
Building, Log Cabin, Tin, 3 In. ....*Illus* 280.00
Building, Marquee Clock, Silver, Gold Trim, Cast Iron, Hubley, 6 In. 580.00
Building, Napoleon Bank, Rooster Finial, Brass, M 1152, France, 5 1/4 In. 633.00
Building, New England Church, Cast Iron, White, Steeple, M 986, 7 1/2 In. 578.00
Building, Oriental Building, Cast Iron, Oval, M 1005, Kyser & Rex, 1880, 3 In. 468.00
Building, Pavilion, Cast Iron, M 1004, Kyser & Rex, 1880, 3 1/8 In. 352.00
Building, Skyscraper, 6 Post, Cast Iron, M 1241, A.C. Williams, 1900-1909, 6 1/2 In. 550.00
Building, Town Hall, Cast Iron, M 998, Kyser & Rex, 1882, 4 5/8 In. 745.00
Building, Victorian House, Cast Iron, M 1143, J. & E. Stevens, 1883, 3 1/4 In. 350.00
Building, Victorian, Multiplying, Cast Iron, M 1184, J. & E. Stevens, 1883, 6 1/2 In. 1320.00
Building, Villa, Brown, Gold Roof, Cast Iron, M 1179, Kyser & Rex, 1894, 5 9/16 In. 3390.00
Building, Villa, Brown, Lattice Window, Cast Iron, M 959, Kyser & Rex, 1882, 5 7/8 In. . 605.00
Building, Westminster Abbey, Cast Iron, M 973, England, 1908, 6 1/4 In. ....154.00 to 187.00
Building, Westside Presbyterian Church, Cast Iron, M 958, c.1916, 3 3/4 In. ......305.00 to 440.00
Camel, Gold Paint, Cast Iron, M 767, A.C. Williams, 1917-1920s, 7 1/4 In. 455.00
Camel, Kneeling, Cast Iron, M 770, Kyer & Rex, 1889, 2 1/2 In. ....510.00 to 715.00
Canteen, Boyco, Kick In, Tin, M 1418, 4 1/4 In. 688.00
Capitalist, Cast Iron, M 5, U.S., c.1890, 5 In. 2310.00
Car, 4 Passengers, Red Paint, Gold Wheels, Cast Iron, A.C. Williams, 7 In. 2905.00
Car, 4 Passengers, Red, Gold Wheels, Cast Iron, M 1487, A.C. Williams, 6 In. 460.00
Car, Yellow Cab, Driver, Coin Trap, Arcade, 8 In. 1595.00
Cash Register, Junior, Cast Iron, J. & E. Stevens, 1920s, 5 1/2 In. 165.00
Cash Register, Junior, Cast Iron, M 930, J. & E. Stevens, 1920s, 4 1/4 In. 220.00
Cat, By House, Pottery, 2 7/8 In. ....*Illus* 297.00
Cat, Long Tail, Cast Iron, M 369, Grey Iron Casting, c.1910, 4 3/8 In. 1375.00

Chest, Decorated, Flowers, Tin, 3 1/2 In. 88.00
Chick, Hatching From Egg, Lead, 3 5/8 In. 176.00
Child On Chamber Pot, Pottery, 3 3/4 In. ....*Illus* 138.00
Christmas Roast Pig, Standing On All Fours, Cast Iron, 3 x 7 1/8 In. 405.00
Clown, Red Hat, Cast Iron, M 211, A.C. Williams, 1908, 6 3/16 In. ....121.00 to 198.00
Clown, With Crooked Hat, Cast Iron, M 210, U.S., 6 3/4 In. 1210.00
Coal Scuttle, Lead, M 1358, U.S., 3 1/4 In. 121.00
Cockatoo, Painted, White Metal, M 656, 5 In. 242.00
Col. Sanders, White Plastic, Margardt Corp., 1972, 10 In. 56.00
Cottage, Welsh, 2 Chimneys, Arbor Over Door, Blue Roof, Ceramic, 3 1/2 In. 100.00
Cottage With Balcony, Tin, 2 3/4 In. 100.00
Crosley Radio, Cast Iron, Tin, M 820, Kenton, 1931-1936, 4 5/16 In. 451.00
Crystal Bank, Cast Iron, Glass, M 926, Arcade, 1910-1925, 3 7/8 In. 105.00
Daffy Duck At Tree Trunk, White Metal, Painted, M 280, Metal Moss Mfg., 4 1/4 In. 110.00
Dancing Elephant, Pottery, 6 1/2 In. 60.00
Dancing Woman, White Metal, 7 In. 100.00
Devil, 2 Faces, Cast Iron, M 31, A.C. Williams, 1904-1912, 4 1/4 In. ....555.00 to 798.00
Devil's Head, Chalkware, Carnival Type, 1950, 6 1/2 In. 60.00
Dog, Boston Bull Terrier, Cast Iron, Brown, White & Black, Vindex, 1931, 5 1/4 In. 165.00
Dog, Boxer, Seated, Cast Iron, Worn Gold & Red Paint, 4 1/2 In. 38.00
Dog, Bulldog, Seated, Cast Iron, Variation, M 396, Canada, 3 7/8 In. 220.00
Dog, Collie, Walking, Ceramic, 3 5/8 In. 187.00
Dog, Fido, On Pillow, Cocked Head, Cast Iron, M 443, Hubley, 1920s, 7 3/8 In. ..143.00 to 240.00
Dog, Lost Dog, Sitting, Lifting Head, Howling, Cast Iron, Judd, 1890s, 5 3/8 In. ..459.00 to 484.00
Dog, Pug Dog, Cast Iron, Kyser & Rex, M 405, 1889, 3 1/2 In. 187.00
Dog, Scotty, Seated, Cast Iron, M 428, 3 1/8 In. ....180.00 to 231.00
Dog, Spaniel, Cast Iron, M 418, Variation, 3 3/4 In. 231.00
Dog, St. Bernard, Cast Iron, M 437, A.C. Williams, 1905-1930s, 5 1/2 In. 165.00
Dog, St. Bernard, Cast Iron, M 437, A.C. Williams, 1905-1930s, 3 3/4 In. 135.00
Dog, Water Spaniel, I Hear A Call, Cast Iron, M 438, U.S., 5 3/8 In. 198.00
Dolphin, Boy In Boat, Cast Iron, M 33, Grey Iron Casting, c.1900, 4 1/2 In. 561.00
Donkey, Saddle, Cast Iron, M 499, 4 1/2 In. ....110.00 to 165.00
Donkey, With Saddle Bags, Lead, M 503, Germany, 1920s, 5 In. 88.00
Doughboy, Cast Iron, Later Casting, M 48, 7 In. 100.00
Duck, Cast Iron, M 615, A.C. Williams, 1909-1935, 4 7/8 In. ....220.00 to 231.00
Duck, On Tub, Hat, Save For A Rainy Day, Cast Iron, M 616, Hubley, 1930s, 5 3/8 In. 121.00
Duck, Open Wings, Cast Iron, M 624, Hubley, 1930s, 4 3/4 In. ....132.00 to 187.00
Duck, Round, Cast Iron, M 619, Kenton, 1936-1940, 4 In. 264.00
Dutch Cleanser, Tin, With Tulips 135.00
Dutch Girl, Holding Flowers, Cast Iron, M 183, Key Locked Trap, Hubley, 5 1/4 In. 143.00
Eagle, Old Abe With Shield, Cast Iron, M 676, U.S., 1880, 3 7/8 In. 1430.00
Eisenhower, Bust, Original Box, White Metal, M 132, Banthrico, 1950s, 5 5/8 In. 127.00
Electrolux Vacuum Cleaner, Save 'n Pay, Model G, Plastic, Box, 1950s, 5 1/2 In. 37.00
Elephant, Cast Iron, M 454, Wing, c.1900, 2 1/2 In. 154.00
Elephant, On Tub, Cast Iron, M 483, A.C. Williams, 1920s, 5 3/8 In. 105.00

Bank, Cat, By House, Pottery,
2 7/8 In.

Bank, Child On Chamber
Pot, Pottery, 3 3/4 In.

Bank, Gingerbread House, Cast
Iron, France, 3 7/8 In.

Elephant, On Wheels, Cast Iron, M 446, A.C. Williams, 1920s, 4 1/8 In. . . . . .231.00 to 545.00
Elephant, Pulling Chariot, Cast Iron, M 479, Hubley, 1906, 4 3/4 In. 1045.00
Elephant, Seated On Bench, Turned Trunk, Cast Iron, M 445, U.S., 4 1/4 In. . . . . .363.00 to 545.00
Elephant, With Blanket, Cast Iron, M 487, Kenton, 1936-1940, 3 1/8 In. 1320.00
Elephant, With Howdah, Cast Iron, M 459, A.C. Williams, 1912-1934, 3 In. 72.00
Farmers & Merchants State Bank, Wakefield, Ks., Dime Savings, Celluloid, 2 1/4 In. . . . 30.00
Fat Man, Texaco, Green Uniform, Plastic, 4 7/8 In. 120.00
Feed The Kitty, Seated Cat, Lead, M 347, Hockswender, 1930s, 4 7/8 In. 55.00
Fidelity Safe, Dog Embossed On Box, Cast Iron, Kyser & Rex, c.1880, 3 5/8 In. 170.00
Fidelity Trust, Vault, Black Paint, Brass Combination Lock, Cast Iron, Hart Mfg., 8 In. . . 380.00
Figure, Red Goose Shoes, Goose, Cast Iron, M 612, Arcade, 1920s, 3 7/8 In. 418.00
Flying Saucer, White Metal, 4 In. 308.00
Foxy Grandpa, Cast Iron, M 320, Hubley, 1920s, 5 1/2 In. 418.00
Gas Stove, Old-Fashioned, Cast Iron, Tin, M 1349, U.S., 1901, 5 1/2 In. 110.00
Gas Tank Car, Glass, Tankard System Saves, 5 1/4 x 3 3/4 x 1 3/4 In. 80.00
Gem Stove, Cast Iron, M 1364, Abendroth, U.S., 4 3/4 In. 105.00
General Butler, Cast Iron, M 54, J. & E. Stevens, 1884, 6 1/2 In. . . . . .1100.00 to 3200.00
General Pershing, Cast Iron, Grey Iron Casting, 7 3/4 In. 230.00
George Washington, Bust, Lead, 6 1/2 In. 55.00
Gingerbread House, Cast Iron, France, 3 7/8 In. . . . . *Illus* 2530.00
Girl With Basket Of Flowers, White Metal, M 321, Vanio, 1938, 5 5/8 In. 94.00
Give Me A Penny, Black Figure, Red Shirt, Cast Iron, M 167, 5 5/8 In. 319.00
Globe On Arc, Cast Iron, Arcade, 1900-1913, 5 1/4 In. 210.00
Globe On Arc, Grey Iron Casting, 1900-1903, 5 1/2 In. 103.00
Golliwog, Cast Iron, M 85, John Harper, England, 1910-1925, 6 3/16 In. 314.00
Graf Zeppelin, Cast Iron, A.C. Williams, M 1428, 1920-1934, 6 3/4 In. . . . . .137.00 to 143.00
Graf Zeppelin, On Wheels, Cast Iron, A.C. Williams, 2 1/4 In. 250.00
Hat, Liberty Bell, Tin, M 1387, U.S., 1917, 2 In. 50.00
Hen, On Nest, Cast Iron, M 546, U.S., Early 1900s, 3 In. . . . . .800.00 to 825.00
Horse, Beauty, Black Paint, Cast Iron, M 532, Arcade, 4 1/8 x 4 3/4 In. 95.00
Horse, Prancing, Belly Band, Cast Iron, M 506, U.S., 4 1/2 In. 165.00
Horse, Prancing, Cast Iron, M 517, U.S., 1910-1930s, 4 1/4 In. . . . . .60.00 to 80.00
Horse, Prancing, Cast Iron, M 518, Canada, 4 1/8 In. 176.00
Horse, Rearing, Beauty, Oval Base, Cast Iron, M 514, U.S., 4 3/4 In. 286.00
Horse, Saddle Horse, Cast Iron, M 523, A.C. Williams, 1934, 2 3/4 In. 231.00
Horse, Tally Ho, Centered In Horseshoe, Chamberlain & Hill, M 535, 4 1/2 x 5 In. 116.00 to 375.00
Horse With Flynet, Cast Iron, M 527, 4 In. 341.00
Humpty Dumpty, Tin, Chein, 1934, 5 1/4 In. . . . . *Illus* 220.00
Ice Cream Freezer, North Pole, M 1371, Grey Iron Casting, 1928, 4 1/4 In. . . . . . .110.00 to 365.00
Indian, Oklahoma U., White Metal, 6 In. 110.00
Indian, With Tomahawk, Cast Iron, M 228, Hubley, 1915-1930s, 5 7/8 In. 187.00
Jack-In-Box, Green, Ceramic, M 248, U.S., c.1895, 4 1/2 In. 70.00
Kangaroo, Nodder, Wooden, Orange, Gimbels Store Sticker On Bottom, 1940s, 5 In. 55.00
Key, Cast Iron, William Somerville, 1905, 6 In. 425.00
Kris Kringle, Deposit A Penny To Call Santa, Tin, Plastic, Cloth, Japan, 7 In. 27.00
Lincoln High Hat, Cast Iron, U.S., c.1882, 2 3/8 In. 100.00
Lion, On Rock, Lead, M 752, England, 3 In. 253.00
Lion, On Wheels, A.C.Williams, 1920s, 4 1/2 In. . . . . .115.00 to 340.00
Lion, Standing, Gilt, Cast Iron, 6 1/2 In. 105.00
Little Thrifty, Child Depositing Coin, Ceramic, 5 In. 110.00
Locomotive, Safety, Cast Iron, Semimechanical 743.00
Lucie Attwell's Fairy Tree, Round, Inverted Cone Top, Tin, 13 3/4 In. 132.00
Lucky Lager Beer, 1940s 28.00
Lucky Penny, 2 3/4 In. 100.00
Mailbox, U.S. Mail, Eagle, Embossed, Green, Gold Accents, Cast Iron, Kenton, 4 In. 180.00
Mailbox, U.S. Mail, Victorian Pedestal Base, Cast Iron, M 861, Hubley, 1906, 7 3/4 In. . . 1815.00
Mailbox, U.S. Mail, With Eagle, Cast Iron, M 855, Hubley, 1906, 4 In. . . . . .100.00 to 185.00
Mailbox, White, Painted Scene, Ceramic, 3 In. 165.00
Mammy, Hands On Hips, Cast Iron, Gold, 5 1/4 In. 220.00
Mammy, Hands On Hips, Cast Iron, M 176, Hubley, 1914-1946, 5 1/4 In. . . . . .130.00 to 143.00
Marietta Silo, Cast Iron, U.S., 5 1/2 In. 1485.00
Mary & Lamb, Cast Iron, M 164, U.S., 1901, 4 3/8 In. 1018.00
Mascot, American League, Boy, On Baseball, Hubley, 1914, 5 13/16 In. . . . . . . .1595.00 to 1795.00

Mechanical banks were first made about 1870. Any bank with moving parts is considered mechanical. The metal banks made before World War I are the most desirable. Copies and new designs of mechanical banks have been made in metal or plastic since the 1920s. The condition of the paint on the old banks is important. Worn paint can lower a price by 90%.

Mechanical, Artillery, Cast Iron, Book Of Knowledge 88.00
Mechanical, Betsy Ross, Standing With Flag, Partial Original Box, Cast Iron 303.00
Mechanical, Boy On Trapeze, Cast Iron, Book Of Knowledge ....825.00 to 865.00
Mechanical, Boys Stealing Watermelons, Cast Iron, Kyser & Rex 3737.00
Mechanical, Bulldog, Blue Carpet, Cast Iron, Book Of Knowledge, Variation 132.00
Mechanical, Butting Buffalo, Book Of Knowledge, Cast Iron, Kyser & Rex .....200.00 to 325.00
Mechanical, California Raisins & Sun Maid, Hard Vinyl, 2 x 6 x 7 In. 31.00
Mechanical, Calumet Bank, Baking Powder Can, Baby's Head Moves, Tin, 4 In. ..105.00 to 120.00
Mechanical, Cat & Mouse, Black, White Balancing Cat, Cast Iron, Book Of Knowledge .. 187.00
Mechanical, Chief Big Moon, Cast Iron, J. & E. Stevens 5500.00
Mechanical, Clown On Globe, Cast Iron, J. & E. Stevens 905.00
Mechanical, Clown, Sticks Out Tongue, Arched Top, Tin 127.00
Mechanical, Coffin, Skull & Skeleton Hand, Tin, Plastic, Yoneya Toys, Japan, Box, 6 In. . 60.00
Mechanical, Creedmoor, Blue Pants, Cast Iron, Book Of Knowledge ....110.00 to 396.00
Mechanical, Creedmoor, White, Cast Iron, J. & E. Stevens 1050.00
Mechanical, Darktown Battery, Cast Iron, J. & E. Stevens ....1017.00 to 3650.00
Mechanical, Dentist, Blue Base, Cast Iron, Book Of Knowledge, Variation ....110.00 to 175.00
Mechanical, Dog On Turntable, Cast Iron, Judd, 5 1/2 In. 575.00
Mechanical, Donkey, Bobbing Head, Party Mascot In Blue Suit, Red Tie, 1960, 8 In. 100.00
Mechanical, Eagle & Eaglets, Cast Iron, Book Of Knowledge ....132.00 to 450.00
Mechanical, Elephant With Howdah, Cast Iron 625.00
Mechanical, Elephant, Cast Iron, Book Of Knowledge 350.00
Mechanical, Elephant, Pull Tail, White Elephant, Cast Iron, Capron 154.00
Mechanical, Frog On Rock, Cast Iron, Kilgore 561.00
Mechanical, Gem, Building With Dog, Cast Iron, Judd Mfg., 1870s-1880s 1320.00
Mechanical, Giant In Tower, Cast Iron, John Harper & Co., Patented 8-13-1892 .... 4950.00
Mechanical, Hall's Excelsior, Building, Cast Iron, J. & E. Stevens 165.00
Mechanical, Home Town Battery, White Faces, Cast Iron, Book Of Knowledge. 143.00
Mechanical, Hoop-La, Clown & Dog, Cast Iron, John Harper 1430.00
Mechanical, I Always Did 'Spise A Mule, Boy On Bench, Cast Iron, J. & E. Stevens 660.00
Mechanical, I Always Did 'Spise A Mule, Jockey, Book Of Knowledge 143.00
Mechanical, Indian & Brown Bear, Cast Iron, Book Of Knowledge ....226.00 to 450.00
Mechanical, Indian & White Bear, Cast Iron, J. & E. Stevens 2350.00
Mechanical, Jolly Nigger, High Hat, Red Shirt, Cast Iron, England 451.00
Mechanical, Jolly Nigger, Red Shirt, Black Face, Cast Iron, Shepard Hardware ....385.00 to 440.00
Mechanical, Leap Frog, Cast Iron, Book Of Knowledge ....187.00 to 395.00
Mechanical, Leap Frog, Cast Iron, Shepard Hardware, 1890s 2800.00
Mechanical, Lion & 2 Monkeys, Cast Iron, Kyser & Rex ....1400.00 to 3900.00
Mechanical, Monkey & Coconut, Cast Iron, J. & E. Stevens, 12 In. 3025.00
Mechanical, Monkey, Depositing Coin Into Organ, Blue Base, Hubley, 10 x 3 In. 5080.00
Mechanical, Monkey, Tips Hat, Tin, Chein, 4 7/8 In. 77.00
Mechanical, Monkey, With Organ Grinder, Cast Iron, Capron 143.00
Mechanical, Monument, Trick Door, Wooden 99.00
Mechanical, Mule Entering Barn, Cast Iron, J. & E. Stevens, 1880, 8 1/2 In. .....880.00 to 1575.00
Mechanical, Mule Entering Barn, Gray Barn, Cast Iron, Capron 176.00
Mechanical, Organ, Cat & Dog, Chime Of Bells, Cast Iron, Kyser & Rex, 15 In......... 4205.00
Mechanical, Organ, Monkey, Cast Iron, Kyser & Rex, Medium 1072.00
Mechanical, Owl, Glass Eyes, Trap, Cast Iron, 7 1/2 In. 330.00
Mechanical, Owl, Turns Head, Cast Iron, J. & E. Stevens, 1880 ....725.00 to 853.00
Mechanical, Paddy & The Pig, Coin On Pig's Nose, J. & E. Stevens, 10 In. ....3555.00 to 4200.00
Mechanical, Paddy & The Pig, Dark Blue Coat, Cast Iron, Book Of Knowledge. 176.00
Mechanical, Penny Pineapple, Cast Iron ....175.00 to 187.00
Mechanical, Presto, Pull Drawer & Deposit Coin, Cast Iron, Kyser & Rex, 1894, 3 In. ... 305.00
Mechanical, Punch & Judy, Coin In Plate, Shepard Hardware Co., 8 x 5 In. ....1870.00 to 3390.00
Mechanical, Rabbit In The Cabbage, White, Pink Eyes, Cast Iron, Kilgore 385.00
Mechanical, Reclining Chinaman, Cast Iron, J. & E. Stevens 2970.00
Mechanical, Southern Comfort, Confederate Soldier Shoots Coin, 20th Century, 6 In. 155.00

Mechanical, Speaking Dog, Cast Iron, J. & E. Stevens, 1888 .... 1900.00
Mechanical, Speaking Dog, Girl, Maroon Base, Cast Iron, 10 In. ....1575.00 to 4840.00
Mechanical, Tammany, Cast Iron, J. & E. Stevens ....484.00 to 690.00
Mechanical, Tammany, Cast Iron, Painted, Book Of Knowledge, 6 In. ....135.00 to 143.00
Mechanical, Teddy & The Bear, Cast Iron, Book Of Knowledge 350.00
Mechanical, Thrifty Animal Bank, Tin, Buddy L, 3 1/8 In. 286.00
Mechanical, Trick Dog, Solid Base, Cast Iron, Hubley, 1920s ....220.00 to 352.00
Mechanical, Trick Pony, Cast Iron, Book Of Knowledge ....138.00 to 325.00
Mechanical, Two Frogs, Cast Iron, Capron 286.00
Mechanical, Two Frogs, Cast Iron, J. & E. Stevens, 1882, 8 1/2 In. 4450.00
Mechanical, Uncle Remus, Log Cabin, Policeman, Cast Iron, Book Of Knowledge. 154.00
Mechanical, Uncle Sam & Arab, Uncle Sam Wearing Barrel, Cast Iron, 1970s 468.00
Mechanical, Uncle Sam, Cast Iron, Book Of Knowledge ....143.00 to 165.00
Mechanical, Uncle Sam, Cast Iron, Shepard Hardware 2650.00
Mechanical, William Tell, Cast Iron, Book Of Knowledge ....128.00 to 130.00
Mechanical, William Tell, Cast Iron, J. & E. Stevens, 10 x 6 3/4 In. 926.00
Mermaid, Cast Iron, M 34, Grey Iron Casting, c.1900, 4 9/16 In. 523.00
Minuteman, Standing, On Pedestal, White Metal, M 327, Banthrico, 1941, 8 1/8 In. 72.00
Missouri Tigers, Mascot Figure, Football, White Metal, 4 1/4 In. 110.00
Money Bag, $100,000, Cast Iron, M 1262, U.S., 3 5/8 In. 176.00
Monkeys, See, Hear, Speak No Evil, Cast Iron, M 743, A.C. Williams, 3 1/4 In. 253.00
Moody & Sankey, Cast Iron, Smith & Egge, 1870, 5 In. ....*Illus* 8470.00
Motor Bank, Early Street Trolley, Red, Gold Coin Slot, Cast Iron, Kyser & Rex, 5 In. ... 485.00
Mulligan, Policeman, Cast Iron, M 177, A.C. Williams, 1905-1932, 5 3/4 In. .....175.00 to 220.00
Mutt & Jeff, Cast Iron, M 157, A.C. Williams, 1912-1931, 4 1/4 In. 187.00
Nipper, Cast Iron, 6 In. 165.00
Officer, Cadet, Cast Iron, M 8, Hubley, 1905-1915, 5 3/4 In. 633.00
Oklahoma State U., Cowboy Figure, White Metal, 5 7/8 In. 94.00
Old Abe, Eagle In Pose With Shield, Cast Iron, M 676, 1880, 3 7/8 In. 605.00
Old Beggarman, White Metal, M 55, Germany, 7 1/2 In. 374.00
Old Doc Yak, Cast Iron, M 30, Arcade, 1911-1913, 4 1/2 In. 341.00
Old Lady In The Shoe, Nursery Rhyme, Metal, 1960s 75.00
Orange, Dimpled Surface, Ceramic, 3 3/8 In. 11.00
Our Empire, Cast Iron, M 1320, England, 1911, 6 5/8 In. 132.00
Our Kitchener, Cast Iron, M 1313, England, 1914, 6 5/8 In. 90.00
Owl, Be Wise Save Money, Gold Paint, Red Trim, Cast Iron, A.C. Williams, 5 In. 170.00
Owl, Orange, White Paint, Cast Iron, M 597, Vindex, 4 1/4 In. 305.00
Owl On Stump, Cast Iron, U.S., 3 5/8 In. 110.00
Pay Phone, Crank, Cast Iron, M 857, J. & E. Stevens, 7 3/16 In. 644.00
Pig, Drinking, Ceramic, M 636, 2 1/2 In. 72.00
Pig, In Coin Purse, Ceramic, 3 In. 88.00
Pig, Pink, Black Feet, Norco Foundry & Specialty Co., Pottstown, Pa. 28.00
Pig, Pottery, Brown & White Slip Glaze, 19th Century, 3 1/2 In. 44.00
Pig, Seated, With Cap, Ceramic, 5 3/8 In. 195.00
Pig, Standing, Spotted, Chalkware, Carnival Type, 1950, 11 In. 55.00
Pig In Well, Pottery, 3 3/8 In. ....*Illus* 170.00
Pirate, Pistol Packing Pirate, On Chest, White Metal, M 341, U.S., 6 1/4 In. 116.00

Bank, Moody & Sankey,
Cast Iron, Smith & Egge,
1870, 5 In.

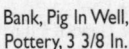

Bank, Pig In Well,
Pottery, 3 3/8 In.

Pirates Treasure Chest, Metal, 1960s 55.00
Pocahontas, Head, Painted, Lead, M 226, Continental, 3 1/8 In. 72.00
Policeman, Hombergers Boys Dept Mulligan, Cast Iron, M 179, 5 3/4 In. 286.00
Policeman, Round, Tin Lithograph, Germany, 2 1/4 In. 245.00
Porky Pig, Cast Iron, M 264, Hubley, 1930, 6 In. 550.00
Porky Pig, Standing On Embossed Base, White, Red Jacket, Cast Iron, Hubley, 6 In. 95.00
Possum, Cast Iron, M 561, Arcade, 1910-1913, 2 3/8 In. ....385.00 to 688.00
Professor Pug Frog, Gold Paint, Cast Iron, M 311, A.C. Williams, 3 1/4 In. ......145.00 to 308.00
Purdue Boilermakers, Mascot Figure, Football, White Metal, 7 In. 171.00
Purse, Yellow Drawstring, Painted Man With Walking Stick, Ceramic, 3 5/8 In. 429.00
Puzzle Pail, White City, Cast Iron, M 911, Nicol, 1893, 2 5/8 In. 149.00
Rabbit, Begging, Iron, Gold & Red Paint, M566, A.C. Williams, 1908-1920s, 5 In. 160.00
Rabbit, Lying Down, Cast Iron, M 565, U.S., 2 1/8 In. 264.00
Rabbit, Standing, Cast Iron, A.C. Williams, M 574, 1908-1920s, 6 1/4 In. ....154.00 to 231.00
Radio, 3 Dials, Cast Iron, Tin, Kenton, 1927, 3 In. 200.00
Radio, Crosley, Red, Gold Highlights, Cast Iron, M 820, Kenton, 1931-1936, 5 1/8 In. ... 605.00
Radio, GE, Cast Iron, M 822, Arcade, 1932-1934, 3 7/8 In. ....132.00 to 135.00
Radio, Majestic, Floor Model, Steel Back, Cast Iron, M 827, Arcade, Box, 4 1/2 In. 510.00
Radio, Templeton, Cast Iron, Red Paint, Steel Sides, Gold Trim, M 826, Kenton, 4 1/4 In. 605.00
Record Player, Save For Your Brunswick, Steel, M 825, U.S., 5 In. 94.00
Recruit, Cutie, Unbuttoned Pants, Suspenders, Cast Iron, M 40, John Harper Ltd., 6 In. .. 265.00
Red Goose School Shoes, Goose Figure, Cast Iron, M 628, Arcade, 3 3/4 In. 330.00
Red Goose Shoes, Cast Iron, Red Paint, M 610, Arcade, 1920s, 3 3/4 In. 143.00
Red Goose Shoes, Goose Figure, Cast Iron, M 612, Arcade, 1920s, 3 7/8 In. 418.00
Red Goose Shoes, Save For A Rainy Day, Goose, Cast Iron, 5 1/2 In. 95.00
Refrigerator, GE, Cast Iron, Small, M 1330, Hubley, 1930-1936, 3 3/4 In. ....66.00 to 143.00
Refrigerator, Kelvinator, Cast Iron, M 1338, Arcade, 1932-1934, 3 7/8 In. ....88.00 to 94.00
Register, Building, Recording Bank, Cast Iron, M 1062, U.S., 1891, 6 5/8 In. 220.00
Register, Clown & Monkey, Painted, Daily, Tin, 2 1/2 In., Dime 132.00
Register, Columbian Mogie Savings, Cast Iron, 6 1/2 In., Dime 176.00
Register, Cowboy, Daily, Painted, Tin, 2 1/2 In., Dime 175.00
Register, GE, Painted, Tin, 2 1/2 In., Dime 297.00
Register, Jackie Robinson, Daily, Painted, Tin, 2 1/2 In., Dime 578.00
Register, Mercury Dime, Painted, Tin, 2 5/8 In. 240.00
Register, Piggy, Daily, Painted, Tin, 2 1/2 In., Dime 105.00
Register, Prince Valiant, Painted, Tin, 2 1/2 In., Dime 300.00
Register, Prudential, Cast Iron, 7 In., Dime 127.00
Register, South Side State Bank, Dimeometer, Tin, 5 In., Dime 198.00
Register, Thrifty Elf, Dime A Day, Tin, M 1570, 2 5/8 In., Dime ....94.00 to 175.00
Register, Treasury, Union Savings & Loan, Cleveland, Tin, 2 1/2 In., Dime 18.00
Register, Trunk, Phoenix, Cast Iron, Piaget, U.S., M 947, 1890, 4 1/4 In., Dime 77.00
Register, Uncle Sam, Tin, Black, 6 1/4 In. ....38.00 to 65.00
Register, Vacation, Girl & Ducks, Daily, Painted, Tin, Mc 241, 2 1/2 In., Dime 100.00
Reindeer, Iron, Hand Painted, John Wright, 1960s 150.00
Rhino, Cast Iron, M 721, Arcade, 1910-1925, 2 5/8 In. ....319.00 to 523.00
Roly Poly, Monkey, Tin, M 1277, Chein, 1940s, 6 In. ....*Illus* 310.00
Rooster, Black, Red Highlights, White Eyes, Cast Iron, M 547, Arcade, 4 5/8 In. ..297.00 to 305.00
Round Man, With Mug, Tin, M 271, 2 3/8 In. ....61.00 to 198.00
Royal, Cast Iron, M 1329, England, 1910, 5 1/4 In. 209.00
Rudolph The Red Nosed Reindeer, Aluminum, Red Light Bulb Nose 135.00
Rumpelstiltskin, Cast Iron, M 75, U.S., 1910, 6 In. 385.00
Safe, Animals, On Front Panel, Embossed, Gold Trim, Cast Iron, Pat. 1881, 3 In. 155.00
Safe, Arabian Scene, Cast Iron, M 882, Kyser & Rex, 1882, 4 5/8 In. 121.00
Safe, Bank Of Columbia, Uncle Sam & Miss Liberty, Embossed, Cast Iron, 5 1/2 In. 120.00
Safe, Bank Of Industry, Vault, Man, Holding Anvil, Red Paint, Cast Iron, Kenton, 6 In. ... 530.00
Safe, Child's, Fireproof, Tin, M 900, Chein, 5 7/16 In. 61.00
Safe, Coin, Cast Iron, M 875, Variation, 4 1/4 In. 165.00
Safe, Combination Lock, Baby Bank, Original Box, Tin, 4 1/4 In. 39.00
Safe, Combination Lock, Broadway Savings Bank, Tin, 3 7/8 In. 55.00
Safe, Combination Lock, Cupid, Cast Iron, 4 5/8 In. 85.00
Safe, Combination Lock, Ideal Bank, Cast Iron, 6 3/8 In. 88.00
Safe, Combination Lock, Junior Safe Deposit, Cast Iron, Tin, 4 1/2 In. 143.00
Safe, Combination Lock, National Safe, Cast Iron, Tin, 4 3/4 In. 88.00

Never repaint an old bank.
It lowers the resale value.

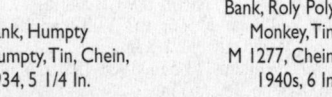

Bank, Humpty
Dumpty, Tin, Chein,
1934, 5 1/4 In.

Bank, Roly Poly,
Monkey, Tin,
M 1277, Chein,
1940s, 6 In.

Safe, Combination Lock, Safe Deposit, Cast Iron, 3 7/8 In.	77.00
Safe, Combination Lock, Safe Deposit, Cast Iron, 5 1/4 In.	495.00
Safe, Combination Lock, State, Cast Iron, Tin, 4 1/8 In.	90.00
Safe, Combination Lock, Sun Dial Bank, Tin, 4 1/2 In.	198.00
Safe, Combination Lock, Treasure, Cast Iron, 5 In.	132.00
Safe, Diamond, Vault, Embossed Diamond Safe On Front Panel, Cast Iron, 7 3/8 In.	350.00
Safe, Egyptian Scene, Cast Iron, 4 5/8 In.	825.00
Safe, Fidelity Trust Vault, Lord Fauntleroy, Cast Iron, M 903, J. Barton Smith, 6 1/2 In.	523.00
Safe, Floral Design, Cast Iron, M 885, 4 5/8 In.	231.00
Safe, Globe, Hinged Door, Brown, Nickel Combination Lock, Cast Iron, M 812, 5 In.	180.00
Safe, Ideal Trust, Combination, 7 1/4 In.	155.00
Safe, Japanese, Bronze Accents, Embossed, M 883, Kyser & Rex, 5 1/2 In.	193.00 to 265.00
Safe, Jewel, Grill, Cast Iron, 5 3/4 In.	95.00 to 132.00
Safe, Kodak, Cast Iron, M 875, J. & E. Stevens, 1905, 4 1/4 In.	149.00
Safe, Little Red Riding Hood, Basket, Wolf By Her Side, Cast Iron, M 25, Harper, 5 In.	3870.00
Safe, National Iron, Cast Iron, Variation, 4 3/8 In.	264.00
Safe, Red Ball, Cast Iron, M 873, U.S., 3 In.	253.00
Safe, Security Safe Deposit, Cast Iron, 4 1/8 In.	105.00
Safe, Security Safe Home Deposit, Cast Iron, Tin, 6 3/4 In.	138.00
Safe, Sports, Cast Iron, M 886, Kyser & Rex, 1882, 3 In.	176.00
Safe, Vault, Embossed Flowers On Paneled Sides, Cast Iron, 1890, 4 1/2 In.	180.00
Safe, White City Puzzle Safe No.12, Cast Iron, M 910, Nicol, 1893, 4 7/8 In.	230.00
Safe, Young America, Cast Iron, M 881, Kyser & Rex, 1882, 4 3/8 In.	187.00
Sailor, Seaman's Bank, Ceramic, 5 5/8 In.	11.00
Santa Claus, Entering Chimney, White Metal, M 105, 6 1/4 In.	99.00
Santa Claus, Oriental, Pack, Lead, M 97, Japan, 4 In.	88.00
Santa Claus, Pack, Cast Iron, M 63, Harper, 4 1/8 In.	2310.00
Santa Claus, Standing, Holding Tree, Cast Iron, M 61, Hubley, 5 7/8 In.	575.00
Satchel, Cast Iron, M 1268, U.S., 3 3/8 In.	121.00
Satchel, Pacific Coast Savings Society, Lead, 4 In.	83.00
Satellite, Duro Molde, Die Cast, 11 In.	100.00
Save & Smile, Money Box, Cast Iron, M 24, England, 4 1/4 In.	220.00
Savings Chest, Nickel Steel, Key, M 948, U.S., 1892, 4 5/16 In.	245.00
Scholar, Leaning On Globe, Lead, 6 3/8 In.	121.00
Sea Lion, Cast Iron, Black, Red, M 732, Arcade, 1910-1913, 3 3/8 In.	297.00 to 1020.00
Sesquicentennial Liberty Bell, Cast Iron, M 782, Grey Iron Casting, 1928, 3 3/4 In.	40.00
Sesquicentennial Liberty Bell, With Clock, White Metal, M 816, Variation, 6 7/8 In.	330.00
Sharecropper, Darkey, Cast Iron, M 173, A.C. Williams, 1901, 5 1/2 In.	144.00 to 165.00
Shell Out, Conch Shell, Cast Iron, White Paint, J. & E. Stevens, 1882, 2 1/2 x 5 In.	365.00
Sinclair Dinosaur, Plastic, 1960s	48.00
Sinclair Dinosaur, White Metal, M 777, Variation, 8 1/2 In.	100.00
Singer Sewing Machine, Cast Iron, Tin, M 1369, Germany, 1925, 5 1/8 In.	605.00
Smokey Bear, Ceramic, Smiling, Hat In Hand, Sitting On Tree Trunk, 1950s, 6 In.	75.00 to 95.00
Sniffles, Tree Trunk, White Metal, M 289, 5 1/8 In.	99.00
Soldier, Minuteman, Cast Iron, M 44, Hubley, 1905-1906, 6 In.	155.00 to 418.00
Space Needle, Base, White Metal, 5 1/2 In.	66.00
Spiderman, Gumball Machine, Coin, Superior, 1984	85.00
St. Louis Cardinals, Mascot Figure, Baseball, 6 1/2 In.	176.00

Statue Of Liberty, Cast Iron, M 1166, 9 5/8 In. 1705.00
Statue Of Liberty, Silver Paint, Coin Slot On Base, Cast Iron, Kenton, 10 In. 460.00
Stop Sign, Green Paint, Gold Accents, Cast Iron, M 1481, Dent, 5 5/8 x 2 1/2 In. 980.00
Stove, Champion Heater, Combination Lock, Cast Iron, M 1355, 4 1/8 In. 110.00
Stove, Marshall Stove, Red Paint, Scale, Embossed, Cast Iron, U.S., 3 7/8 In. 145.00
Stove, Reliable, Parlor Stove, Red Inserts, Cast Iron, Schneider & Trenkamp, 6 1/4 In. . . . 970.00
Stove, Space Heater, Bird, Cast Iron, M 1087, England, 1892, 6 1/2 In. . . . . .77.00 to 395.00
Stove, Space Heater, Cupid, Cast Iron, M 1090, England, c.1895, 6 1/2 In. 506.00
Stove, York Stove, Cast Iron, M 1351, 4 In. 176.00
Stove, Young America, Gold Trim, Embossed, Cast Iron, M 881, Kyser & Rex, 4 3/8 In. . . 240.00
Street Clock, Cast Iron, Tin, M 1548, A.C. Williams, 1920s, 6 In. 430.00
Teepee, Indian Standing Next To Teepee, Lead, M 223, 3 3/4 In. 495.00
Thing, Addams Family TV Show, Plastic, Box, 1964 . . . . 150.00
Tombstone, Stone, Granite Finish, W.H. Collins, 7 3/4 In. 165.00
Topo-Gigio, Farmer, Hard Vinyl, Red Yarn Hair, Movable Head, 1970, 11 In. 26.00
Train, Safety Locomotive, Cast Iron, Semimechanical 770.00
Train, Travel To Success By Thrift, Lead, M 1477, 2 In. 55.00
Transvaal Money Box, Cast Iron, Bronze Finish, 6 In. 550.00
Treasure Chest, Tin Lithograph, Chein, 1930, 4 In. 80.00
Trolley, Main Street Trolley, People, Cast Iron, M 1471, A.C. Williams, 1920s, 3 In. 385.00
Trolley, Main Street, Gold Paint, Cast Iron, M 1471, A.C. Williams, 1920s, 6 3/4 In. 345.00
Trolley, Marquee On Roof, Cast Iron, 1889, 4 5/8 In. 545.00
Trust Bank, Banker, Seated, Dark Suit, Cast Iron, 1890, J. & E. Stevens, 7 In. 580.00
Turkey, Cast Iron, M 587, A.C. Williams, 1905-1935, 3 3/8 In. . . . . .121.00 to 308.00
Twinkies Shoes, Paper Label, 2 In. 88.00
Uncle Sam, Bust, Ceramic, 4 In. 44.00
Uncle Sam Hat, Tin, M 1383, Chein, 1941, 3 1/4 In. .65.00 to 132.00
Urn, Pitcher Finial, Coiled Handles, Ceramic, 6 1/4 In. 44.00
Vending, Hand Shadows, Tin, Stollwerk, 6 1/4 In. 225.00
Weatherbird Shoes, Figural, Plastic, Smiling Rooster Holding Umbrella, 1960s, 4 In. 4.00
Weight, 50 Lb., White, Ceramic, 2 3/8 In. 44.00
Whizzor Clown, White Metal, M 249, Banthrico, 6 1/2 In. 55.00
Wisconsin Badgers, Mascot Figure, White Metal, 6 In. 155.00
Yogi Bear, Leaning Against Building, Plastic, 1973, 11 In. 35.00
Young Negro, Cast Iron, M 170, England, 4 1/2 In. . . . . .55.00 to 132.00
Zeddy Teddy Bear, Holds Placard, Let's Start Saving Together, Plastic, Canada, 10 In. . . . 26.00

BANKO, Korean ware, and Sumida are terms that are often confusing. We use the names in the way most often used by antiques dealers and collectors. Korean ware is now called *Sumida Gawa* or *Sumida* and is listed in this book in the Sumida category. Banko is a group of rustic Japanese wares made in the nineteenth and twentieth centuries. Some pieces are made of mosaics of colored clay, some are fanciful teapots. Redware and other materials were also used.

Sugar, Cranes & Flowers 95.00
Tea Set, Millefiori, Bamboo Handle On Teapot, 5-In. Teapot . . . .*Illus* 350.00
Wall Pocket, Glazed & Unglazed, Early 1800s 75.00

Banko, Tea Set,
Millefiori, Bamboo
Handle On Teapot,
5-In. Teapot

BARBED WIRE was first patented in 1867. Collectors want eighteen-inch samples.

Brotherton Parallel, 2 Barbs, 1878, 17 In.	3.50
Cline's Rail, 5 Barbs, 1883, 18 In.	6.00
Crandal Zigzag, 1879, 18 In.	4.00
Gliddens' Cable, Seven Strands, 2-Point Barbs, 1874, 18 In.	5.50
Hearst Ranch Copper, 3 Diamonds Per Cut	10.00
Hodges Spur Rowel, 5 Rowels, 1887, 18 1/2 In.	5.00
Kelly Diamond Point, 4 Spikes On It, 1868, 20 In.	5.50
Stubbe Plate, 2 Plates, 1883, 18 In.	3.50
Vosburgh Clinch Wire, 1893, 18 In.	16.00

BARBER collectibles range from the popular red and white striped pole that used to be found in front of every shop to the small scissors and tools of the trade. Barber chairs are wanted, especially the older models with elaborate iron trim.

Backbar, Barber Shop, Walnut	1000.00
Blade Set, Steel, Celluloid, Marked Monday To Saturday, John Williams, 6 Piece	58.00
Chair, Koken, Leather, Steel, Porcelain, Light Green Pedestal, 43 x 27 x 40 In.	105.00
Chair, Koken, Oak & Iron, Green Upholstery	1900.00
Chair, Koken, Oak, Leather Upholstery	2540.00
Chair, Koken, Wood, Leather, Embossed Filigree Sides, Head Rest, Child's Seat, 46 In.	920.00
Mug, Use Tonique DeLuxe The Liquid Headrest	145.00
Pole, Electric, Spins, Cast Iron Mounting Bracket, c.1940, 25 1/2 x 8 In.	225.00
Pole, Koken, Porcelain & Glass, Wall Mount, 33 In.	2700.00
Pole, Oak Wood, Faded Red, White & Blue Paint, Bracket, 1925, 33 In.	330.00
Pole, Stripes, Blue & Gold Balls, Wall Mount, 19th Century, 47 In.	1955.00
Pole, Turned Wood, Weathered Blue, Silver, Red & White Repaint, Steel Base, 95 In.	1045.00
Pole, Wooden, Red & White Stripes, Blue Balls At Top & Bottom, 58 In.	455.00
Rack, Shaving Mug, Oak, Carved Top, 35 Holes, 45 x 41 x 8 In.	910.00
Seat, Child's, For Barber's Chair, Plated Iron Rods, Padded Seat, 9 x 24 In.	35.00
Shoeshine Stand, Koken, Marble	5000.00
Sign, Ask For Wildroot, Barber Pole Picture, Tin, Embossed, 27 3/4 x 9 3/4 In	100.00
Sign, Hair Bobbing Our Specialty, Porcelain, 2 Sides, 24 x 12 In.	165.00
Sign, Journeymen Barbers Union Shop, Eagle & Shield, Metal, Chain, 8 x 9 In.	75.00
Sign, Pole Shape, Globe Top, Modern Service, Porcelain, Curved, 12 x 48 In.	355.00
Sign, Pole Shape, Look Better, Feel Better, Porcelain, Curved, 16 x 24 In.	85.00
Sign, White Lettering, Black, Red, White Stripes, 2 Sides, 12 x 24 In.	132.00

BAROMETERS are used to forecast the weather. Antique barometers with elaborate wooden cases and brass trim are the most desirable. Mercury column barometers are also popular with collectors. It is difficult to find someone to repair a broken one, so be sure your barometer is in working condition.

2 Thermometers, Hayden & Gibbard	2310.00
Agricultural, Case	357.00
Aneroid, L. Cassio & Co., French Dore, Bronze, Floral Wreath, Enamel Dial	1265.00
Aneroid, Walnut, Round Face, Brass Bezel, Germany, 44 In.	1152.00
Banjo, A. Corte, Thermometer & Mirror, Mahogany Inlay, Glasgow, 38 In.	660.00
Banjo, Hygrometer, Thermometer, Black Lacquer, Mother-Of-Pearl Inlay, 43 In.	865.00
Banjo, I.M. Teddinghaus, Mahogany Veneer, Early 19th Century, 37 1/2 In.	2575.00
Banjo, Nautical, Mercury, Rosewood Veneer, Inlaid Mother-Of-Pearl, 8 In.	550.00
Banjo, Rofs & Co., Mahogany Veneer, Line Inlay, c.1820, 38 1/4 In.	420.00
C. Tagliabue, Hygrometer Thermometer, Inset Ivory Urn, Satinwood, 44 In.	9775.00
Canterbury, G. Arzoni, Mahogany Case, 38 In.	385.00
Gerlan, Ebonized Case, Inlaid Mother-Of-Pearl Plaques, Arts & Crafts, 17 3/4 In.	200.00
Kendall Brothers, Brass, Nautical	2530.00
Pocket, Altimeter, Pillischer, London, Leather Case	145.00
Pocket, Cooke & Sons, Gilt	85.00
Round Dial, Oak, Leaf Carved Crest & Pendant, England, 1875, 26 1/2 In.	230.00
S.A. Sperry, Woodruff's Patent, Gold Stenciled Label, Silvered Face Plate, 41 In.	2145.00
Slade & Keast, Wooden, Nautical, Brass Scales, Cistern & Gimbal	1320.00
Stick, Central Eagle Design, Floral, Leaf Pediment, Octagonal Frame, France, 35 In.	86.00

Stick, Cornelius Knudsent, Mahogany & Ebonized Wood, 36 1/2 In. 85.00
Stick, E.C. Spooner, Silvered Scale, Thermometer, Mahogany Base, 39 1/2 In. 5517.00
Stick, Ipswich, Walnut, Reed, 38 1/2 In. 300.00
Stick, J. & W. Martin, Mahogany, Veneers, Broken Arch Top, London, 17 x 5 In. 1025.00
Stick, John M. Merrick & Co., Worcester, Mass., Walnut, Cased, 38 1/2 In. 605.00
Stick, Nautical, Mercury, Mahogany, Ship's Wheel, Wall, 1935, 43 In. 550.00
Stick, Precision Thermometer & Instrument Co., U.S. Navy, Weather Station, 9 In. 1100.00
Stick, R & J Beck, Figured Walnut Veneer, 1825, 36 1/2 In. 868.00
Stick, Timby, Rosewood, No Mercury, Pat. 1857, 39 x 2 In. 175.00
Stick, W & S Jones, Swan's Neck Crest, Mahogany, Early 1820s, 14 1/2 In. 1955.00
Storm King, Walnut, E.C. Spooner, 42 In. 632.00
Stormograph, Atmospheric Pressure, Drawer For Charts, 8 1/2 x 9 In. 750.00
Thermometer, Louis XVI, Giltwood, Carved, Painted, Birds, Scrolls, 41 x 17 In. 3960.00
Wheel, C.J. Verga, Mahogany, 19th Century, 37 1/2 In. 290.00
Wheel, Giltwood, Bellflower Frame, Painted Dial, France, 19th Century, 38 In. 690.00
Wheel, Giltwood, Louis XVI, Ebonized, Leaf Pendant, 43 x 12 x 3 In. 1610.00
Wheel, Louis Philippe, Mahogany, Round With Wright Thermometer, 34 1/2 In. 575.00
Wheel, Moses Levi, Level & Humidity Dials, Convex Mirror, Mahogany, 37 In. 258.00
Wheel, Toniere, Mahogany, Thermometer & Mirror, c.1840, 38 1/2 In. 632.00

BASEBALL collectibles are in the Sports category, except for baseball cards, which
are listed under Baseball in the Card category.

BASKETS of all types are popular with collectors. American Indian,
Japanese, African, Shaker, and many other kinds of baskets can be
found. Of course, baskets are still being made, so the collector must
learn to tell the age and style of the basket to determine the value.

Bee Keep, Rye Straw, 16 x 15 1/4 In., Pair 605.00
Burl Wood, Carved, Oval, 5 x 9 In. 300.00
Bushel, Brown Paint, Stave Construction, Bentwood Swivel Handle, 15 In. 135.00
Buttocks, Splint, 34 Ribs, Bentwood Handle, Varnished, 15 x 17 In. 80.00
Buttocks, Splint, 37 Ribs, Bentwood Handle, Ohio State Fair, Woven, 1938, 5 In. 302.00
Buttocks, Splint, 38 Ribs, Woven, 6 x 6 1/4 x 2 3/4 In. 165.00
Buttocks, Splint, Fixed Handle, 21 x 14 1/2 In. 255.00
Buttocks, Splint, Oak, 3 x 2 3/4 In. 123.00
Buttocks, Splint, Oak, 11 In. 45.00
Buttocks, Woven Splint, 20 Ribs, Bentwood Handle, 7 1/2 x 7 1/2 In. 165.00
Buttocks, Woven Splint, 22 Ribs, Bentwood Handle, 5 1/2 x 5 3/4 x 3 1/2 In. 150.00
Egg, Oak Splint, Woven Construction, 6 In. 66.00
Egg, Splint, 2 Handles, Oval, 5 3/4 In. 145.00
Flower Gathering, New England, Early 19th Century, 23 In. 285.00
Gathering, Splint, Square, Loop Handle, 9 In. 66.00
Gathering, Splint, Swing Handle, J. Folger, Nantucket, 19th Century, 9 1/2 In. 145.00
Gathering, Splint, Swing Handle, New England, 19th Century, 7 1/2 In. 175.00
Indian, Coiled Form, Spiraling Vertical Bands, 4 1/4 x 7 1/4 In.   97.00
Laundry, Reed & Cane, Wood & Wire Handles, Stars & Border Stripes, 9 x 25 In. 440.00
Melon, Double, Handle, 21 In. 330.00
Melon, Double, Long, 19th Century, 7 1/2 x 16 x 9 In. 99.00
Melon, Hickory Handle, 8 In. 65.00
Nantucket, Bail Handle, Copper Rivet & Burr, Jose Formoso Reyes, 1940s, 15 In. 4830.00
Nantucket, Carved Ivory Whale On Cover, Ivory Pin Closure, Oval, 9 x 7 In. 690.00
Nantucket, Carved Swing Handle, Metal Anchoring Pins, 5 x 5 3/4 In. 2185.00
Nantucket, Swing Handle, Bird's-Eye Maple Base, 3 Concentric Rings, 4 x 9 1/2 In. 880.00
Nantucket, Swing Handle, Wooden Base, 3 Deep Rings, 8 1/2 x 13 In. 6820.00
Nantucket, Swing Handle, Wooden Base, Ferdinand Sylvaro, 4 x 9 1/2 In. 935.00
Parfleche, Splint & Raffia Geometric Design, Polychrome, Square, 8 In. 44.00
Pine Needle, Cover, Pinecone Finial, California, Early 20th Century, 4 In. 22.00
Porcupine & Birchbark, Cover, Cylindrical, Maple Leaf Design, 3 1/4 In. 55.00
Rye Straw, Oval, 15 x 21 x 5 1/4 In. 85.00
Splint, 11 Melon Ribs, Diamond Handles, 10 1/2 x 6 In. 176.00
Splint, 2 Handles, Oak, Flared Rim, Bulbous, 25 In. 195.00
Splint, Bamboo, Crescent Form, Early 20th Century, 13 In. 550.00
Splint, Bentwood Handle, Dark Patina, Round, 12 x 6 In. 245.00
Splint, Bentwood Handle, Green Paint, 11 Ribs, 9 x 4 1/2 In. 220.00

Splint, Bentwood Handle, Stave, Old Dark Red, 19 x 11 In. 385.00
Splint, Bentwood Rim Handles, Round, 16 x 12 1/2 In. 110.00
Splint, Bentwood Swivel Handle, Dark Brown Varnish, 16 x 7 1/2 In. 190.00
Splint, Bulbous, Flat Back, Open Handle, Hanging, 12 1/2 In. 110.00
Splint, Continuous Hickory Handle, 9 1/2 In. 55.00
Splint, Gathering, Oak, Hoop Handle, Tapered To Base, 16 x 22 In. 220.00
Splint, Imbricated, Loop Handle, Relief Banded Design, 9 1/2 In. 255.00
Splint, Nailed Rim, Handle, Marked Genoa Apple Basket, Oval, 12 x 20 1/2 x 8 In. 165.00
Splint, Oak, Brown Highlights, 1900, 12 x 6 1/2 x 8 1/2 In. 90.00
Splint, Oak, Curved & Notched Handle, Oval Rim, 2 Bands Color, 15 1/2 x 16 In. 90.00
Splint, Oak, Forked Handle, Southwest Va., Early 20th Century, 7 1/2 x 16 x 8 In. 950.00
Splint, Oak, Swing Handle, Pennsylvania, 19th Century, 11 1/2 In. 1760.00
Splint, Old Green Paint, Round, 12 x 7 3/4 In. 520.00
Splint, Oval, Alternating Yellow, Red Flowers, Dark Blue, Red, 4 x 13 x 8 In. 635.00
Splint, Oval, Wall, Red, Blue Geometric Flowers, Dots, 19th Century, 4 x 12 x 6 In. 430.00
Splint, Rectangular, Wooden Handle, Deep, 14 1/2 In. 30.00
Splint, Round, Bentwood Rim Handles, 20 x 11 In. 195.00
Splint, Round, Old Gray, White Paint, Woven, 12 x 10 1/2 In. 82.00
Splint, Square, Wooden Handle, Dark Stays For Pattern, 13 In. 70.00
Splint & Macrame, Handle, Wave Design, 12 In. 66.00
Splint Feather, Cover, Salmon Traces On Stays, 24 In. 70.00
Storage, Rattan, Bamboo, Decorative Handle, Oval, Ching Dynasty, 15 x 11 x 13 In. 144.00
Storage, Woven Splint, 4 Handles, Porcupine & Plain Weaving, 28 In. 460.00
Wedding, Elm, Carved Dragon Handle, Round, Ching Dynasty, 15 x 15 x 12 In. 115.00
Wedding, Fir, Carved Phoenix Handle, Oval, Chinese, 10 x 12 x 8 In. 230.00
Wicker, Oval, Zoar, Ohio, 26 1/2 x 32 In. 220.00
Wicker, Round, Zoar, Ohio, 22 In. 165.00
Wire, Loop Handle, Bulbous Base, 7 x 14 In. 70.00

BATCHELDER products are made from California clay. Ernest Batchelder established a tile studio in Pasadena, California, in 1909 and expanded until 1916. Then he built a larger factory with a new partner. The Batchelder-Wilson Company made all types of architectural tiles, garden pots, and bookends. The plant closed in 1932. In 1936 Batchelder opened Batchelder Ceramics, also in Pasadena, and made bowls, vases, and earthenware pots. He retired in 1951 and died in 1957. Pieces are marked *Batchelder Pasadena* or *Batchelder Los Angeles*.

BATCHELDER
LOS ANGELES

Bookends, Incised Vertical Design, Light Gray, 6 In. 220.00
Tile, 3 Flowers With Leaves In Vase, Brown, Blue Ground, 5 1/2 x 8 In. . . . . .230.00 to 275.00
Tile, Blue, Brown Matte Glaze, 7 1/2 x 3 1/2 In. 355.00
Tile, Brown Poppy Pods, Blue Ground, Square, 2 1/2 In. 275.00
Tile, Brown Trees, Blue Ground, Square, 4 1/2 In. 440.00
Tile, Cockatoos In Trees, Brown, Blue, Metallic Rose, 4 In., 2 Piece 285.00
Tile, Embossed, Bouquet Of Flowers, Birds, Beige Bisque Clay, Stamped, 6 x 8 In. 415.00
Tile, Floral Design In Center, Brown, Blue Ground, Square, 5 1/2 In. 220.00
Tile, Floral Design, Brown, Red, Blue, Cat, Bird, 6 x 1 In., 3 Piece 135.00
Tile, Floral, Brown & Blue, Signed, Square, 4 In., 6 Piece 310.00
Tile, Knight On Horseback, Rust, Light Blue Ground, Square, 8 In. 330.00
Tile, Poppy, Blue Ground, Signed, Square, 6 In. 253.00
Tile, Stylized Floral Design, Brown, Blue, Buff, Square, 3 In. 275.00
Tile, Stylized Floral Design, Indian Design, Brown Matte Glaze, 3 1/2 In. 330.00
Tile, Stylized Floral, Blue, Brick Ground, Signed, Square, 6 In. 230.00
Tile, Stylized Flowers, Leaves In A Vase, Brown, Blue Ground, 6 1/2 x 8 1/2 In. 355.00
Vase, Cobalt Blue & Teal Glaze, Bulbous, Incised OLB/R, 5 x 3 3/4 In. 550.00
Vase, Green & Multitoned Blue Matte Glaze, 3 1/2 In. 410.00

BATMAN and Robin are characters from a comic strip by Bob Kane that started in 1939. In 1966, the characters became part of a popular television series. There have been radio and movie serials that featured the pair. The first full-length movie was made in 1989. The third movie was made in 1995.

Bank, 8 1/4 In. 15.00
Bank, Caped Crusader, Plastic, Full Color 65.00

Batcycle, Batman & Robin 700.00
Book, Color By Number, Large Format, Unused, Whitman, 1966 .... 95.00
Clock, Alarm, Batman & Robin, Color 25.00
Clock, Talking 145.00
Cookie Jar, 11 1/2 In. 48.00
Costume, Robin, Action Boy, Ideal, Box 1200.00
Executive Set, Calendar, 1977, Figural, With Stapler & Sharpener, Janex 175.00
Figure, Batgirl, Comic Heroine Series, 1967 .... 4500.00
Figure, Batman Forever, Hand Painted, Resin, Box 225.00
Figure, Batman, Bendy, Flex-A-Toy, Wonder, 1960s, 8 In. 115.00
Figure, Penguin, Parachute, Ahi, 1974 .... 28.00
Flag, Bike Safety, Batman Super Friends, Cycle Safety, 1974 .... 20.00
Game, Batman & Robin, Hasbro, Board, 1965 .... 61.00
Game, Batman & Robin, Hassenfeld, Board, 1965 .... 65.00
Game, Batman, 50th Anniversary Edition, University Games, 1989 .... 25.00
Game, Batman, With Robin & Batmobile, Hasbro, Board, 1974 .... 38.00
Game, Card, Robin, Boy Wonder, Russell's, Box, 1977 .... 20.00
Lithograph, Batman & Robin, Autographed Bob Kane, 1979, 28 x 22 In. 575.00
Lunch Box, Batman & Robin, Metal, Aladdin, 1966 .... 65.00
Mug, Robin Running On Front, Logo On Reverse, Milk Glass, 1960s 5.00
Paint Set, Oil, By Number, Original Shrink-Wrap, Hasbro, 1973 .... 100.00
PEZ, Black, On Card 5.00
Soaky, Batman, Blue, Yellow, Violet, 1966, 10 In. 68.00
Tile, Joker, Frame, Warner Bros. 50.00
Toy, Flying Batman, Battery Operated, Plastic, Box 35.00
View-Master, Purr-Fect Crime, Shrink-Wrap, Sawyers, 1966 .... 45.00
Wallet, Plastic, 1966 .... 50.00

BATTERSEA enamels, which are enamels painted on copper, were made
in the Battersea district of London from about 1750 to 1756. Many
similar enamels are mistakenly called *Battersea.*

Box, 2 Gents On Hobbyhorses On Hinged Lid, Oval, 19th Century 467.00
Box, Courting Couple On Top, 3 In. 45.00
Box, Face Of Clock & Viking Ships, 3 In. 300.00
Box, Family With Parasols, Cover, 1 3/4 In. 80.00
Box, Mirror, I Love Well To Kiss & Tell, 1 1/2 In. 75.00
Box, Mirror, May Thy Hand & Mine Forever Entwine, 1 3/4 In. 75.00
Box, White Raised Bird Scene, Love The Giver, Blue, Mirror, 1 3/4 x 1 1/4 x 3/4 In. 295.00
Mirror Knobs, Dr. Benjamin & Governor Morris, Esq., 2 x 1 1/2 In., Pair 5462.00

BAUER pottery is a California-made ware. J.A. Bauer moved his Kentucky pottery to Los Angeles, California, in 1909. The company made
art pottery after 1912 and dinnerwares marked *Bauer* after 1929. The
factory went out of business in 1962.

Atlanta, Batter Bowl, Pink, Green 85.00
Atlanta, Tumbler, Green 20.00
Figurine, Swan, White Matte Glaze, 4 x 9 In. 85.00
Free-Form Design, Bowl, Blue & 2-Tone Brown Matte Glaze, Russel Wright, 24 In. 1540.00
Hand Thrown, Bowl, Celadon Microcrystalline, Gunmetal Interior, Wright, c.1950, 10 In. ... 660.00
Plainware, Mixing Bowl, Yellow, No. 3, 2 Gal. 425.00
Plate, Artist Signed, J. Galan 125.00
Ring, Bread Plate, Blue, 6 In. 8.50
Ring, Mixing Bowl, No. 12, Green 65.00
Ring, Plate, Green, 12 In. 100.00
Twist, Bean Pot, Delph Blue, Matt Carlton 200.00
Twist, Vase, Delph Blue, Handle, Matt Carlton, 12 1/4 In. 3000.00

BAVARIA is a region in Europe where many types of porcelain were
made. In the nineteenth century, the mark often included the word
Bavaria. After 1871, the words *Bavaria, Germany,* were used. Listed
here are pieces that include the name *Bavaria* in some form, but major
porcelain makers, such as Rosenthal, are listed in their own categories.

Ashtray, 3 Birds, Gerold Poezellen, 5 1/4 In. 18.00

Bowl, Boy Using Camera, Girl & Dog, Cat, Toys, Stamped, Child's, 7 1/2 In. 65.00
Bowl, Pedestal, Sylvia, Pink Flowers, Gold Accent Trim, Artist's Initials, 10 In. 45.00
Bowl, Tilly, 8 1/2 In. 30.00
Bowl, White Roses, Hand Painted, Marked DM Bavaria, 10 In. 62.50
Breakfast Set, Eberthal, Black & Gold, Paisley Band, 7 1/2 In. 50.00
Cup & Saucer, Thomas, Ivory, Gold Rim, Blue Mark & Shield 17.50
Cup & Saucer, Yellow Roses, Purple Flowers, Taeger & Co., 3 3/4 & 5 3/4 In. 850.00
Dish, Pink & Yellow Flowers, Gold Speckled Trim, 2 Handles, Stamped, Z.S. & C. 65.00
Frame, White, Gold Crown Stamp, Bavaria Germany, 4 x 4 In., Pair 8.00
Plate, Augustia, Maiden, Yellow, Pastel, Gold Trim, 9 In. 63.00
Plate, Black Knight, Notched Gilt Rim, Ivory Center, 11 In., 11 Piece 172.00
Plate, Dogwood, Pink, Lilac, Green, Hand Painted, Bareuther Waldsassen, 5 3/4 In. 25.00
Plate, Hand Painted, Ink Mark, C & J Louise, Jaeger & Co., c.1902 . . . . 19.00
Plate, Moose, Cobalt Blue & Gold Design Rim, 10 In. 60.00
Plate, Plums & Grapes, Gold Trim, Schumann Arzberg Germany, 7 3/8 In. 20.00
Plate, Service, Floral Center, Gold Rim, 6 Piece 305.00
Plate, Wild Roses, Hand Painted, Schumann Arzberg, 7 1/4 In. 22.00
Relish, 10 In. 45.00
Sugar & Creamer, Hand Painted, Monogram, Pogers-Martini Co., 3 & 2 1/4 In., Pair 55.00
Tankard, Hand Painted, Red & Pink, Gilt, Artist, P.T., 1800s, 13 In. 365.00
Tea Set, Silver Over White, Stamped Porcellan Bavaria 225.00
Vase, Potato Harvest Prayer Scene, Brown Glaze, W. Dvay, T.S.& Co., 6 1/4 In. 65.00

BEADED BAGS are included in the Purse category.

BEATLES collectors search for any items picturing the four members of the famous music group or any of their recordings. Because these items are so new, the condition is very important and top prices are paid only for items in mint condition. The Beatles first appeared on American network television in 1964. The group disbanded in 1971. Ringo Starr, George Harrison, and Paul McCartney are still performing. John Lennon died in 1980.

Charm Set, LP Photo Record, Capitol Records, 1960s, 4 Piece 95.00
Coat, John Lennon, Sleeveless, Japanese Style, Silk, Letter Of Authenticity 4025.00
Doll, Paul McCartney, 10 In. 65.00
Doll Set, 1964, 5 In., 4 Piece 696.00
Doll Set, Applause, 4 Piece 595.00
Doll Set, Plastic, Hamilton, 1991, 4 Piece 295.00
Doll Set, Sgt. Pepper, 4 Piece 595.00
Figure, With Instruments, Box, 9 1/2 In., 4 Piece 165.00
Figurine, Paul McCartney, Royal Doulton, Medium 250.00
Flicker Set, 4 Rings, Uncut, In Acrylic, 1960s, 2 x 3/4 In. 75.00
Game, Flip Your Wig, Milton Bradley, Board, Box 100.00
Grocery List, John Lennon, Handwritten On Envelope 1035.00
Guitar, Autographed Paul McCartney, Ariana Mocel No. AW-71, 1980 . . . . 2035.00
Lunch Box, Yellow Submarine, Steel, Yellow Plastic Cup, Thermos, 1969, 8 x 7 In. 380.00
Pen, Float About, Beatles Abby Road, Silver & Black Brickwork 6.00
Pen, Float About, Yellow Submarine, Passes, Portraits, Fishes 6.00
Phonograph, NEMS Enterprises, Ltd., London, Blue Leatherette Cover, 3-Speed 805.00
Photograph, Fab 4 With Guitars, John Lennon Autograph, 7 x 9 In. 920.00
Pin, Tie Tack, Faces Of The Fab 4 Surrounding A Guitar, Gray Metal, 1964 . . . . 20.00
Poster, Hard Day's Night, United Artists, 1964, 24 Sheet 1955.00
Poster, Help, Yellow Ground, 1965, 40 x 60 In. 230.00
Poster, Let It Be, United Artists, 1970, Three Sheet 460.00
Poster, Yellow Submarine, Il. Sottomarino Giallo, United Artists, 1968, 39 x 54 In. 747.00
Poster, Yellow Submarine, Yellow Lettering, Purple Ground, 1968, 40 x 60 In. 460.00
Puzzle, Illustrated, Box, 1970, 800 Piece 95.00
Puzzle, Jigsaw, Beatles In Pepperland, Box, 100 Piece 200.00
Record, Yesterday & Today, Butcher Coats, Decapitated Baby Heads, LP, Vinyl 2985.00
Ticket, Shea Stadium Concert, Full Ticket, Lime Green, Group Picture, Aug. 23, 1966 . . . 465.00
Wristwatch, Yellow Submarine, Fossil 85.00

BEEHIVE, Austria, or Beehive, Vienna, are terms used in English-speaking countries to refer to the many types of decorated porcelain

bearing a mark that looks like a beehive. The mark is actually a shield, viewed upside down. It was first used in 1744 by the Royal Porcelain Manufactory of Vienna. The firm made porcelains, called *Royal Vienna* by collectors, until it closed in 1864. Many other German, Austrian, and Japanese factories have reproduced Royal Vienna wares, complete with the original shield or *beehive* mark. This listing includes the expensive, original Royal Vienna porcelains and many other types of beehive porcelain. The Royal Vienna pieces include that name in the description.

Charger, Amor's Triumph Scene, Geometric Border, Signed, 13 1/4 In. 905.00
Charger, Cephalese & Aurora, Late 19th Century, 14 In. 1080.00
Charger, Scenes From Shakespeare Plays, 1902, 19 3/4 In. 865.00
Chocolate Set, Elegant Couples In Country, Gilt, Weimar Germany Mark, 3 Piece 900.00
Ewer, Portrait, Maiden, Gilt Winged Female Bust Handle, Wagner, c.1900, 15 In. 3160.00
Figurine, Gazelle, Lying, Royal Vienna, 8 In. 295.00
Plaque, Chariot Scene, Cupid & Bow, Women, 8 1/2 In. 265.00
Plate, Cabinet, Foliate Design, Cobalt Ground Border, 9 1/2 In. 520.00
Plate, Cabinet, Nude Woman In Landscape, Deep Burgundy Border, 9 1/2 In. 1840.00
Plate, Gleaners In Center, Scenes Around Rim, 9 1/2 In. 125.00
Plate, Lovers Scene, Scenes Around Edge, Pastel, Gold Trim, Marked, 10 1/2 In. 175.00
Plate, Maiden Guiding 2 Soldiers Toward Lake, Flower Medallions, Signed, 9 3/4 In. . . . 690.00
Plate, Maiden In Drapery, In Garden, Vignettes Of Animals, Signed, c.1900, 9 1/2 In. . . . 805.00
Plate, Monk Tuning Violin, Mark Under Glaze, 8 1/2 In. 34.00
Plate, Portrait Of Young Girl, Blue Ground, Leaves & Floral Panels, 9 3/4 In. 690.00
Plate, Portrait, Queen Louise, Gilt, Green & Blue Borders, 9 3/4 In. 880.00
Plate, Portrait, Woman Center, Enamel, Cobalt Blue Border, Gilt Trim, 10 In. 315.00
Plate, Young Girl, Titled Angelina, Scroll Work, Graf, 1880s, 9 3/8 In. 1380.00
Stein, 2 Women, Putti Watching, Cobalt Blue, Gold, Porcelain Inlaid Lid 2200.00
Stein, Monks With Tankard & Barrel, Cobalt Blue, Gold Ground, 1/5 Liter 2420.00
Sugar & Creamer, Floral 75.00
Tray, Bacchic Procession, Leopard-Drawn Chariot, 2 Handles, 24 3/4 In. 2450.00
Tureen, On Stand, Domed Cover, Allegorical Figural Panels, Gilt Borders, 17 In. 7475.00
Vase, Cover, Nude Figures, Winged Cherubs, 9 1/4 In., Pair 1650.00
Vase, Cover, Stand, Figural Panels, Jeweled & Gilt Borders, Red Ground, 20 In., Pair 7475.00
Vase, Heart Shape, Fluted, Maiden & Cupid In Landscape, c.1900, 12 In. 2585.00
Vase, Maiden & Cupid In Garden, Cylindrical, Painted, Wagner, 3 1/2 In. 575.00
Vase, Woman Portrait, Oval Cartouche, Applied Turquoise Beading, Wagner, 12 In. 800.00
Vase, Woman, Flowing Hair, Blue Ground, Laurel Branch Handle, Baluster Shape, 10 In. . . 600.00

BEER BOTTLES are listed in the Bottle category under Beer.

BEER CANS are a twentieth-century idea. Beer was sold in kegs or returnable bottles until 1934. The first patent for a can was issued to the American Can Company in September of that year; and Gotfried Kruger Brewing Company, Newark, New Jersey, was the first to use the can. The cone-top can was first made in 1935, the aluminum pop-top in 1962. Collectors should look for cans in good condition, with no dents or rust. Serious collectors prefer cans that have been opened from the bottom.

American Dry, Flat Top, 1950s, 16 Oz. 90.00
Ballantine Beer, Flat Top, 1950s 20.00
Black Pride Beer, Pull Tab, 1960s 3.00
Bonanza Premium Beer, Pull Tab, 1970s 4.00
Burgermeister Pale Beer, Flat Top, 1950s 32.00
Chief Oshkosh Beer, Flat Top, 1950s 40.00
Eastside Keglined Beer, Gold, Red Logo, Eagle In Center, 1930s, 8 1/4 In. 65.00
Ebling Premium Beer, Growler Style, Steel, Orange & Red Logo, 5 In. 30.00
Edelweiss Beer, Cone Top, 1940s 114.00
Falstaff, Cone Top, 1950s 16.00
Fitzgerald's, Crown, Enamel, 1940s 45.00
Fox Deluxe Beer, Flat Top, 1950s 78.00
Gipps Amberlin Beer, Flat Top, 1950s 12.00
Hudson House Beer, Pull Tab, 1960s 15.00

Jet Malt Liquor, Pull Tab, 1960s 15.00
Labbat's IPA Pale, Flat Top, 1950s 73.00
Maier Select Beer, Cone, 1940s 60.00
Master Premium Beer, Flat Top, 1950s 90.00
Muehlebach's Pilsner, Cone Top, 1940s 33.00
National Bohemian Light Beer, Flat Top, 1950s 23.00
Old Bohemian Draft Beer, Pull Tab, 1970s 50.00
Old Timers Ale, Flat Top, 1950s 68.00
Old Topper Snappy Ale, Crown, 1950s 4.00
Ox Bow Beer, 1970s 18.00
Pilser's Beer, Flat Top, Gold, 1950s 11.00
Rainier Ale, Flat Top, 1950s, 11 Oz. 13.00
Regal Pale, Flat Top, 1950s 12.00
Schlitz Draft Beer, Pull Tab, 1970s 42.00
Schmidt Draft Beer, 1960s, 16 Oz. 18.00
Senator's Club Beer, Flat Top, White & Gold, 1960s 75.00
Storz Gold Crest Beer, Flat Top, 1940s 110.00
Van Dyke Beer, Zip Top, 1960s 10.00
Whale's White Ale, Pull Tab, 1970s 9.00

BELL collectors collect all types of bells. Favorites include glass bells, figural bells, school bells, and cowbells. Bells have been made of porcelain, china, or metal through the centuries.

Brass, Mexico, c.1860, 7 x 6 In. 200.00
Brass, Woman, Clapper Feet, 4 In. ....*Illus* 15.00
Brass, Wooden Handle, Signed RW 1 Interior, England, 1765 .... 495.00
Bronze, 13-In. Throat 225.00
Cast Iron, Iron Fittings, A. Fulton, Pittsburgh, 1848, 24 1/2 x 21 In. 3465.00
Cast Iron, With Yoke, 18 x 18 In. 69.00
Ceramic & Brass, From The Belmont In Harwich, 5 1/2 In. 88.00
Conestoga Wagon, Wrought Iron, Frame, Brass, Mid 19th Century 150.00
Cranberry Swirl, Clear Handle, Early 20th Century, 14 In. 115.00
Dinner Gong, Arts & Crafts, Hammered Brass, 5 Feet, Posts, Arched Crest Rail, 38 In. 770.00
Dinner Gong, Arts & Crafts, Wooden, Top Roof, 21 x 12 1/2 In. 990.00
Gong, Hammer, Chinese, Brass, c.1900 .... 85.00
Horse Collar Mount, Eagle Finial, Horsehair Tassels, 4 Bells 125.00
Liberty Bell, Sterling Silver, Towle, c.1976, 3 3/4 In. 69.00
Monastery, Brass, Figures In Quatrefoils, Fleur-De-Lis, Dutch, 20th Century, 9 In. 35.00
Pottery, Peasant Woman, 4 1/4 In. ....*Illus* 12.00
Sleigh, 15 Graduated Bells, Strap 120.00
Sleigh, 19 Graduated Bells, Strap 350.00
Sleigh, 20 Graduated Bells, Brass, 1900s 165.00
Sleigh, 23 Bells, Leather Strap, Pair 95.00
Sleigh, 31 Graduated Polished Bells, New Leather Strap 190.00
Sleigh, 42 Bells, Brass, Leather Strap, 84 In. 340.00
Table, Brass, England, Late 18th Century, 4 1/4 In. 225.00
Table, Oriental Man, Movable Arms, Seated On Top, Bronze, 7 3/4 In. 2990.00
Temple, Teak, Domed, Fabric Wrapped Handle, Indonesia, 1900s, 25 x 32 In., Pair 345.00

Bell, Brass, Woman, Clapper Feet, 4 In.

Bell, Pottery, Peasant Woman, 4 1/4 In.

Billy Beer cans are not worth hundreds of dollars even though this myth appears in newspapers about every six months.

BELLEEK china was made in Ireland, other European countries, and the United States. The glaze is creamy yellow and appears wet. The first Belleek was made in 1857. All pieces listed here are Irish Belleek. The mark changed through the years. The first mark, black, dates from 1863 to 1890. The second mark, black, dates from 1891 to 1926 and includes the words *Co. Fermanagh, Ireland*. The third mark, black, dates from 1926 to 1946 and has the words *Deanta in Eirinn*. The fourth mark, same as the third mark but green, dates from 1946 to 1955. The fifth mark, green, dates from 1955 to 1965 and has an R in a circle added in the upper right. The sixth mark, green, dates after 1965 and the words *Co. Fermanagh* have been omitted. The seventh mark, gold, was used from 1980 to 1993 and omits the words *Deanta in Eirinn*. The eighth mark, introduced in 1993, is similar to the second mark but is printed in blue. The word *Belleek* is now used only on the pieces made in Ireland even though earlier pieces from other countries were sometimes marked *Belleek*. These early pieces are listed by manufacturer, such as Ceramic Art Co., Haviland, Lenox, Ott & Brewer, and Willets.

Basket, Flowers, 2nd Mark, Black, 5 1/2 x 8 In. 2750.00
Cake Plate, Limpet, 2nd Mark, Black, 10 In., Pair 55.00
Candlestick, Celtic, 3rd Mark, Black, 5 In. 200.00
Card Holder, Shell Form, Coral Base, 2nd Mark, Black, 2 3/4 In. 250.00
Cup & Saucer, Shamrock, Harp Handle, 3rd Mark, Black 110.00
Ewer, Applied Floral, Enameled, 6th Mark, Green, 7 3/8 In., Pair 110.00
Ewer, Floral, 6th Mark, Green, 9 In., Pair 135.00
Figurine, Belgian Hawkers, 6th Mark, Green, 6 3/4 In. 175.00
Figurine, Greyhound, 3rd Mark, Black, 6 1/2 In. 375.00
Matchbox, Tea Ware, Cover, 1st Mark, Black, 3 1/2 In. 140.00
Pitcher, Blackberries & Blossoms, 3rd Mark, Black, 10 1/4 x 5 In. 440.00
Shaving Cup, Enameled Acorns, Oak Leaves, 7th Mark, Gold, 4 1/4 In. 247.00
Sugar & Creamer, Artichoke, 3rd Mark, Black 150.00
Sugar & Creamer, Lily Pattern, 3rd Mark, Black 145.00
Sugar & Creamer, Shell, Luster Trim, 5th Mark, Green, 3 5/8 In. 50.00
Teapot, Clover Form, 3rd Mark, Black, 7 In. 253.00
Teapot, Shell Form, 4th Mark, Green, 3 1/2 In. 165.00
Teapot, Tridacna, Luster Handle, 8th Mark, Blue 150.00
Vase, Aberdeen, Left Handed, 5th Mark, Green, 6 1/2 In., Pair 150.00
Vase, Molded Urn Shape, Applied Floral Design, 5th Mark, Green, 10 1/2 In. 140.00
Vase, Ram's Head, 5th Mark, Black, 5 1/4 In. 550.00
Vase, Spill, Ivory, Brown Wash, 1st Mark, Black, 5 In. 90.00
Vase, Swan, 2nd Mark, Black, 8 In. 1100.00

BENNINGTON ware was the product of two factories working in Bennington, Vermont. Both the Norton Company and the Lyman Fenton Company were out of business by 1896. The wares include brown and yellow mottled pottery, Parian, scroddled ware, stoneware, graniteware, yellowware, and Staffordshire-type vases. The name is also a generic term for mottled brownware of the type made in Bennington.

Basin, Dark Brown Glaze, 3 1/4 x 13 In. 100.00
Bottle, Monk, Allover Mottled Brown Glaze, Lyman Fenton, 1849, 10 1/2 In. 825.00
Bowl, Sponge Pattern Glaze, Brown, Tan, Molded Rim, 19th Century, 12 1/2 In. 86.00
Bowl & Pitcher, Enameled, Flint, 13 1/2 In. 3195.00
Bowl Set, Graduated, 8 Piece 300.00
Candlestick, Amber & Green Running Glaze, 7 7/8 In., Pair 1705.00
Candlestick, Mottled Glaze, c.1849, 9 1/2 In. 795.00
Canister, Rockingham, Glazed, Alternate Rib, Lid, Impressed 1849 Mark, 9 1/4 In. 431.00
Churn, Norton, Stoneware, Cobalt Blue, Stylized Leaves, Lid, Dasher, 1800s, 17 In. 431.00
Coffeepot, Game Scenes, Hound Handle, Pierced Spout 50.00
Creamer, Cow, Allover Mottled Brown Glaze, 1875, 5 1/2 x 7 In. 220.00
Creamer, Cow, Cover, c.1849, 5 1/2 x 7 In. 695.00
Cuspidor, Allover Mottled Brown Glaze, Lyman Fenton, 1849, 4 1/4 x 9 1/2 In. 85.00
Figurine, Poodle, Basket Of Flowers In Mouth, Brown Mottled Glaze, 8 1/2 In. . .2900.00 to 3100.00
Flask, Book, Enamel, Impressed Round Mark, 19th Century, 1 Pt., 6 In. 316.00

Footbath, Enamel, Handles, Impressed Oval Mark, 1800s, 9 x 14 x 19 In. 3738.00
Jug, Norton & Fenton, Cobalt Blue, Floral, Salt Glaze, 19th Century, 3 Gal., 15 In. 230.00
Paperweight, Dog, Round 1949 Mark, 6 1/2 x 4 3/4 In. 200.00
Pitcher, 2 Rabbits, Medium To Dark Brown Glaze, Hound Handle, 8 x 7 In. 55.00
Pitcher, Anchor & Chain, Floral Fan Under Spout, Rope Border Lip, Handle, 10 In. 90.00
Pitcher, Peacock With Columns & Florals, Medium Brown Glaze, 8 x 6 In. 90.00
Pitcher, Rabbit & Stag On 1 Side, Medium Brown Glaze, Branch Handle, 9 In. 90.00
Pitcher, Raised Stag Design, Boar & Birds, White Ground, 9 1/4 x 12 In. 192.00
Snuff Jar, Toby Shape, Hat Lid, 1849 .... 695.00
Soap Dish, Enamel, Rib Pattern, Lid, Impressed Mark, 1800s, 5 x 4 x 5 In. 546.00
Teapot, Medium Dark Brown Glaze, Beaded Band At Rim, Handle, 9 x 7 In. 55.00
Teapot, Rib Pattern, 1849 .... 995.00

BERLIN, a German porcelain factory, was started in 1751 by Wilhelm
Kaspar Wegely. In 1763, the factory was taken over by Frederick the
Great and became the Royal Berlin Porcelain Manufactory. It is still in
operation today. Pieces have been marked in a variety of ways.

Bowl, Arms Of Russian Empire, Double Headed Eagle, Gilt Rim, Signed, c.1778, 9 In. .. 4887.00
Candlestick, 2 Cherubs, Lower, Floral Sprigs, Blue & Gilt Base, c.1810, 12 In., Pair 1610.00
Coffeepot, Swan Neck Spout, 1830s, 10 1/4 In. 112.00
Cup, Das Universitats Gebaunde, Gilt Floral Design, 4 1/2 In. 405.00
Cup, Military Figure, Seated On Wall, Battle In Ground, Signed, 1850s, 4 1/4 In. 345.00
Cup & Saucer, Cabinet, Relief Portrait, Princess Louise Of Prussia, c.1915, 4 5/8 In. 1150.00
Cup & Saucer, Raised Gilt Floral Design 86.00
Plaque, Bird Flying Beneath Berry Branches, Jeweled Border, 1882, 14 1/2 In., Pair 6900.00
Plaque, Psyche, Kneeling On Rock, Peering Into Pond, Signed, 7 x 5 In. 2990.00
Urn, Cover, Ormolu Mounted, Pair` 4890.00
Vase, Cover, Park Scenes, Laurel Design, Lion Masks, Blue, 1900, 27 In. 5175.00
Vase, Topographic, Market, Town Hall & Bourse In Danzig, Gilt, Oval, 1850, 10 In. 1980.00
Wall Pocket, Cherub Reserve Center, Flower, 1870s, 13 1/4 In. 365.00

BESWICK started making earthenware in Staffordshire, England, in
1936. The company is now part of Royal Doulton Tableware, Ltd. Figurines of animals, especially dogs and horses, Beatrix Potter animals,
and other wares are still being made.

Character Jug, Mr. Bumble The Beadle, No. 2032 .... 75.00
Creamer, Pecksniff, No. 1117 .... 70.00
Figurine, Amiable Guinea Pig, No. 2061 .... 500.00
Figurine, Benjamin Bunny, No. 1105/1 .... 325.00
Figurine, Benjamin Wakes Up, No. 3234 .... .35.00 to 45.00
Figurine, Cat, Cheshire, No. 2480 .... 575.00
Figurine, Cat, Siamese, Lying, No. 1559, 7 1/4 In. 55.00
Figurine, Dog, Bulldog, Bosun, No. 1731, White & Tan, Small, 2 1/2 In. .... .35.00 to 50.00
Figurine, Dog, Dachshund, Begging 75.00
Figurine, Flopsy, Mopsy & Cottontail, No. 1274 .... 180.00
Figurine, Grouse, Gloss Finish, Albert Hallam, No. 2063, 5 1/2 In., Pair 449.50
Figurine, Horse, Black Beauty, Large, No. 2466 .... 135.00
Figurine, Horse, Galloping, No. 1374 .... 325.00
Figurine, Hunca Munca Spills The Beads, No. 3288 .... 60.00
Figurine, Jemima Puddleduck, No. 1092 .... 225.00
Figurine, Jemima Puddleduck, No. 3373 .... 85.00
Figurine, John Joiner 40.00
Figurine, King Of Hearts, No. 2489 .... 90.00
Figurine, Little Pig Robinson, Stripes, No. 1104/1 .... 175.00
Figurine, Mother Ladybird, No. 2966 .... 45.00
Figurine, Mr. Alderman Ptolemy, No. 2424 .... .40.00 to 160.00
Figurine, Mr. Tod, No. 3091/1 .... 85.00
Figurine, Mrs. Alderman Ptolemy, No. 5224 .... 200.00
Figurine, Mrs. Tiggy Winkle, Platinuminon, No. 1107 .... .40.00 to 275.00
Figurine, Peter With Daffodils, No. 3597 .... 40.00
Figurine, Pickles, No. 2334, 4 1/2 In. .... .285.00 to 300.00
Figurine, Pigling Bland, Purple Jacket, No. 1365/1 .... .385.00 to 500.00
Figurine, Poorly Peter Rabbit, No. 2560 .... 35.00

Figurine, Sally Henny Penny, No. 2452 .... 80.00
Figurine, Shire Foal, Brown, 6 1/4 In. 85.00
Figurine, Simpkin, c.1979, No. 2508 .... 335.00
Figurine, Tom Kitten & Butterfly, No. 3030 .... 150.00
Jug, Hamlet, Embossed, Polychrome Glazes, Marked, 8 1/4 In. 77.00
Salt & Pepper, Benjamin Bunny, Peter Rabbit 10.00
Tankard, Carol Singers, Yule 1972, 5 In. 95.00
Teapot, Peggoty, No. 1116 .... 135.00
Teapot, Sairey Gamp, No. 691 .... 135.00

BETTY BOOP, the cartoon figure, first appeared on the screen in 1931. Her face was modeled after the famous singer Helen Kane and her body after Mae West. In 1935, a comic strip was started. Her dog was named Bimbo. Although the Betty Boop cartoons ended by 1938, there was a revival of interest in the Betty Boop image in the 1980s and new pieces are being made.

Bank, Betty Sitting On Roof Of Building, Painted Ceramic, K.F.S., 1981 .... 30.00
Clock, Alarm, Holding Head 125.00
Cookie Jar, Cleopatra, 15 In. 200.00
Cookie Jar, Juliet, 14 In. 200.00
Doll, Jointed, 1930s, 13 In. 255.00
Figurine, Bisque, Crepe Paper Dress, Hat, 6 3/4 In. 45.00
Light Bulb, Bisque, Hand Painted, 1931 .... 350.00
Lunch Box, Tin 14.00
Ornament, Christmas Tree, Betty, Bathtub, 5 1/2 x 5 1/2 In. 45.00
Pen, Float About, Betty Dresses-Undresses To Her Bikini 3.50
Pen, Float About, Biker Betty, Rides Motorcycle, USA Map 3.50
Pen, Float About, Santa Betty, Ice Skates, Snowflakes 3.50
Pin, Brass, Red & Black Enamel, Pinback, 1940s, 1 1/2 In. 55.00
Wristwatch 35.00

BICYCLES were invented in 1839. The first manufactured bicycle was made in 1861. Special ladies' bicycles were made after 1874. The modern safety bicycle was not produced until 1885. Collectors search for all types of bicycles and tricycles. Bicycle-related items are also listed here.

American Cycle Manufacturers, Woman's, Cork Grips, Red Paint, No Saddle, 1915 ..... 3450.00
Bombard Industries, Bowden Spacelander, Futuristic Molded Case, Red, c.1960 .... 4025.00
Boneshaker, Iron Frame, Wooden Spokes, Spring Iron Seat, Black Paint, 1870 .... 1840.00
Boneshaker, Wooden Handle Grips, Spool Pedals, Brown Leather Seat, 1840 .... 2070.00
Borg-Warner, Ingersoll Steel & Disc. Co., Ingo-Bike, Red Paint, 1925 .... 345.00
Brownell, Boneshaker, Patented Nov. 20, 1866, Signed & Dated 6050.00
Colson, Commander, Red Head, Battery Box Built Into Head, 1938 .... 2970.00
Columbia, All Bright, c.1885 .... 4125.00
Columbia, RX5, Spring Fork, Green, Cream, Whitewall Tires, 20th Century 690.00
Columbia, Special Deluxe, Red & White, Rear Basket, Original Labels, c.1940 .... 330.00
Columbia, Tandem, Model 43, Woman's & Man's, Front Brakes, 1898 .... 3025.00
Columbia High Roadster, Pinstriped, c.1882 .... 3190.00
Columbine, High Wheel, c.1889 .... 33850.00
Crypto, 2-Speed, Planetary Hub Gears, Pneumatic Tires, England, 1889 .... 19550.00
Davis Sewing Machine Co., Wood Rims, Leather Grip, Leather Seat, Dark Blue, 1930 ... 1035.00
Elgin, Black Hawk, Headlight, 26-In. Steel Overlay Rims, 1934 .... 2200.00
Elgin, Miss America, Girl's, Deluxe, 1939 .... 1320.00
Elgin, Woman's, Twin Headlights, Skirt Guard, Green, White Paint, 1939 .... 747.00
Elliot Hickory, Brake Hardware, Chain, Wooden Spoke Wheels, 1888 .... 7700.00
Evinrude, Streamflow, Aluminum Frame, Bright Blue, Delta Headlight, 1937 .... 10350.00
Gendron Wheel Co., Fixed Gear, Green Paint, 1910 .... 460.00
Gormully & Jeffery, American Light Safety, Swinging Tubular Rod, 1888 .... 19550.00
Gormully & Jeffery, Scout, Child's, Front Brakes, Wire Grid Skirt 2750.00
Herbert, Hillman & Cooper, Kangaroo, High Wheel Safety, 1889 .... 9350.00
Howe Machine Co., Huntington Leatherwork, Green Finish, Gilt, 1880, 52 In. 4025.00
Huffman, Top Flite, Boy's, 1941 .... 3530.00
Macmillan Replica, Pedals Used For Propulsion, 1989 .... 7475.00

Mercedes-Benz, Cruiser, Modern, Aluminum, Chrome, Disc Brakes 1265.00
Michaux, Boneshaker, Velocipede, 1870 .... 6960.00
Monarch, Silver King, Boy's, 1946, 26 In. 825.00
Monark, For Firestone, 1940-1950 .... 1760.00
Monark, Silver King, Aluminum Frame, 1930 .... 977.00
Monark, Silver King, Girl's, Aluminum Wingbar, Butterfly Kickstand, 1937 .... 5175.00
Monark, Silver King, Model D, 1930 .... 805.00
Peugeot, Hard-Tired Safety Bike, Front Spoon Brakes, X-Frame Design 11500.00
Punnett, Companion, Side-By-Side, Red Finish, 1896 .... 1430.00
Ranger, Boy's Juvenile, Tank Tool Box, Mead Leather Saddle, 26-In. Wheel, 1924 ...... 805.00
Ranger, Spring Fork Middle Weight, Horn Tank, Whitewall Tires Allstate, 1959 .... 460.00
Roadmaster, Luxury Liner, Boy's 495.00
Roberts, Race Bike, Blue, White Lettering, 1970 .... 920.00
Rouse, Hazzard & Co., Overland, Convertible Frame, Original Paint, Nickel Plate, 1891 .. 1955.00
Schwinn, 50th Anniversary Paramount Fork & Frame, 14K Gold Fork, 1989 .... 1150.00
Schwinn, Ace, Red, White Neck 1045.00
Schwinn, American Beauty, Boy's, Half-Tooth Design, Passenger Rack, 1930 .... 488.00
Schwinn, Auto Cycle, Built-In Light For Night Riding, Streamlined Tank, 1936 .... 4887.00
Schwinn, Black Phantom, Front Headlight, Chrome Fenders, Red Highlights, 1952 ...... 3737.00
Schwinn, Black Phantom, Red, Black Paint, 1950 .... 3162.00
Schwinn, Common Sense, Tandem, Wood, Metal Rim, Carbide Light, 1891 .... 17250.00
Schwinn, Continental Racer, 10-Speed, Coppertone Paint, 1959 .... 632.00
Schwinn, Deluxe Stingray, Cooper, 1965 .... 316.00
Schwinn, Girl's, B-6, Sturmey-Archer 3-Speed Drum Brake, Fender Light, 1947 .... 1725.00
Schwinn, Girl's, Fender Light, Horn Tank, Navy Blue, Highlight, Red, Cream, 1953 ..... 172.00
Schwinn, Horn Tank, Hanging, Headlight, Green, Cream Paint, Saddle, 1938 .... 1150.00
Schwinn, Mini-Twinn Tandem, Green Paint, 1968 .... 575.00
Schwinn, New Old Stock Sting-Ray, Fair Lady, Green Paint, Pink Floral, 1970 .... 805.00
Schwinn, Panther, Horn Tank, Generator, White Lined Schwinn Tires, 1968 .... 575.00
Schwinn, Paramount, Front Hub, Double-Sided Rear Hub, Orange Paint, 1939 .... 1610.00
Schwinn, Shelby, Orange, Taupe Paint, Speedometer, Clock, 1948 .... 862.00
Shelby, Air Flow, Woman's, Aluminum Rack & Chain Guard, Taillight 3530.00
Shelby, Flying Cloud, Boy's, Balloon, 1938 .... 6875.00
Silver King, Woman's, Deluxe Model, Complete, 1934 .... 750.00
Singer Xtraordinary, 59-In High Wheel, 1887 .... 13750.00
Standard Union, Brass Badge, Backbone Astride Saddle, 1880, 54 In. 2875.00
Stearns, Racing Tandem, Front-To-Rear Chain Rings, Original Orange Paint, 1900 ...... 862.00
Tandem, Red, Black Paint, 1925 .... 632.00
Tricycle, Child's, Molded Grips, Seat, Aluminum, Red Stripping, 1920 .... 373.00
Tricycle, Fairy Tiller, 18-In. Rear Wheel, Elyria, Ohio, 1890s 247.00
Tricycle, Hayfork, Rack & Pinion Rear Wheel Steering, Black Iron Frame, 1885 .... 11500.00
Tricycle, Invalid, Foot & Level Pump Action, Oak Cane Seat & Foot, c.1910 .... 715.00
Tricycle, Junior Toy Corp., Sky Skipper, Streamlined Pedals, Grips, 1937 .... 1840.00
Tricycle, Large Sprocket, Adjustable Handle Bars, c.1900 .... 467.00
Tricycle, Racing, Cripper Type, Sprung Front & Rear Differential, 1890, 40 In. 6050.00
Union, Hard Tire Safety, Unusual Front, Rear Suspension, 1892 .... 11550.00
Union Manufacturing & Co., Man's, Adjustable Slotted Crank Pedestals, Black 1840.00

Bicycle, Victor, Model C, Man's,
Hard Tire Safety, 1885

Bicycle, White Cycle Co., Bronco,
Pneumatic Rear Wheel Gear

Bicycle, White Cycle Co., White Flyer,
Westboro, Mass., 1890

Clean chrome with a commercial
chrome cleaner or an acidic
cleaner. Rinse, then rub it shiny
with a dry cloth.

Old newspapers can be used to
polish water spots off chrome.

Velosolex, Motorized, Serial No. 7220989, France, 1975 .... 690.00
Victor, Model C, Man's, Hard Tire Safety, 1885 ....*Illus* 9900.00
Warmanschub Cycle House, Boy's, Cork Grips, Leather Seats, Red Paint, 1915 .... 977.00
Western Flyer, Woman's, Airflow Balloon Tire, Art Deco Industrial Design 2530.00
Western Wheelworks, Leather Seat, Green, Red Paint, Chicago, 1940, Pair 575.00
White Cycle Co., Bronco, Pneumatic Rear Wheel Gear ....*Illus* 5500.00
White Cycle Co., White Flyer, Westboro, Mass., 1890 ....*Illus* 33000.00
Whizzer, Motor Bike, Spring Fork Frame, 1950 .... 1430.00

BING & GRONDAHL is a famous Danish factory making fine porcelains
from 1853 to the present. Underglaze blue decoration was started in
1886. The annual Christmas plate series was introduced in 1895. Dinnerwares, stoneware, and figurines are still being made today. The firm
has used the initials B & G and a stylized castle as part of the mark
since 1898.

B & G
KØBENHAVN
MADE IN
DENMARK

Figurine, Bird, Standing, 4 1/2 In. 58.00
Figurine, Else, No. 1574, 6 3/4 In. 250.00
Figurine, Little Girl, No. 1526, Head Bowed, Cradles Doll In Lap, 3 1/2 In. 57.00
Figurine, Mary, No. 1721, 7 1/4 In. 250.00
Figurine, Penguin, No. 1822, 10 In. 400.00
Figurine, Seated Nude Male, Embracing Cluster Of Grapes, 1912, 5 In. 575.00
Plate, Christmas, 1901, Three Wise Men From The East, 7 In. 287.00
Plate, Christmas, 1902, Interior Of A Gothic Church, 7 In. 632.00
Plate, Christmas, 1903, Happy Expectation Of The Children, 7 In. 126.00
Plate, Christmas, 1904, View Of Copenhagen From Frederiksberg Hill, 7 In. 172.00
Plate, Christmas, 1905, Anxiety Of The Coming Christmas Night, 7 In. 143.00
Plate, Christmas, 1907, Little Match Girl, 7 In. 170.00
Plate, Christmas, 1909, Happiness Over The Yule Tree, 7 In. 517.00
Plate, Christmas, 1913, Bringing Home The Yule Tree, 7 In. 90.00
Plate, Christmas, 1923, Royal Hunting Castle, The Eremitage, 7 In. 105.00
Plate, Christmas, 1953, Boat Of His Majesty, King Of Denmark, 7 In. 125.00
Plate, Christmas, 1959, Christmas Eve, 7 In. 75.00
Plate, Christmas, 1960, Danish Village Church, 7 In. 200.00
Plate, Christmas, 1965, Bringing Home The Christmas Tree, 7 In. ....20.00 to 55.00
Plate, Mother's Day, 1969, Dogs & Puppies 325.00
Plate, Mother's Day, 1970, Birds & Chicks, Box, 6 In. 20.00
Plate, Mother's Day, 1979, Fox & Cubs 18.00

BINOCULARS of all types are wanted by collectors. Those made in the
eighteenth and nineteenth centuries are favored by serious collectors.
The small, attractive binoculars called *opera glasses* are listed in their
own category.

Dienstglas, No. 12440, Brown Case, Germany, 5 x 4 5/8 In. 56.00
Field, Day & Night, Signal Glass, Black Paint, Vendome, Paris, 5 1/2 x 4 1/2 In. 105.00
Grande Puissance Extra, Brass, Field Glasses 55.00
Warner & Swazey, Marked US Navy, Case, Booklet 235.00
Zeiss Starmorbi, Multi-Power, Tripod, 3 Pairs Eye Pieces, Leather, 5 x 19 x 7 In. 1375.00

BIRDCAGES are collected for use as homes for pet birds and as decorative objects of folk art. Elaborate wooden cages of the past centuries can still be found. The brass or wicker cages of the 1930s are popular with bird owners.

Brass, Pullout Tray, Hanging From Brass Stand, 65 In.	120.00
Finch, Wooden, Pottery Bowl, Rectangular, China, 5 In., Pair	115.00
Gilt & Bronze, Elaborate Pierced Design, Signs Say Invisible Birds, 38 In., Pair	12650.00
Mansion, France, 19th Century, Large	4200.00
Metal, House, Painted, Peaked Roof, Scrolls On Frame, 65 x 33 x 17 In.	288.00
Pine, Rustic Turreted House, 3-Story, Hand Sawn Birds, Flowers, 1909, 28 In.	1035.00
Tole & Wire, Conservatory Form, 26 x 20 In.	460.00
Tole & Wire, Queen Anne Style House, 19th Century, 15 3/4 x 17 3/4 In.	214.00
Turned Wood, Wire, Dark Paint, Gold, With Leatherized Parrot, Floor Stand, 72 In.	495.00
Wire, House With Grand Entrance, Front Porch, Green Paint, 21 x 19 x 18 In.	230.00
Wire, Wooden Fret Work, Worn White Paint, Folk Art, Victorian, 13 x 18 x 15 In.	330.00
Wire, Wooden, Eastlake Style House, Gingerbread Trim, Red, Blue Paint, 18 In.	345.00
Wirework, Central Tower, Carousel Beside Wooden Turrets, 19th Century, 41 In.	1955.00
Wooden, Carved, Stained, Palace, 3 Steeples, Continental, 1875-1900, 44 x 31 In.	3740.00
Wooden, Serpent Head Handle, 3 Hand Carved Birds & Duck Inside, 16 1/2 x 16 In.	440.00
Wooden, Starburst Glass Feeders, Victorian	445.00

BISQUE is an unglazed baked porcelain. Finished bisque has a slightly sandy texture with a dull finish. Some of it may be decorated with various colors. Bisque gained favor during the late Victorian era when thousands of bisque figurines were made. It is still being made. Additional bisque items may be listed under the factory name.

Bust, Maiden, Signed, A. Carrier, France, 14 1/2 In.	633.00
Figurine, Bonzo Dog, Germany, Marked, 1920s, 3 In.	45.00
Figurine, Maiden, Seated With Birds, Alfred Pensky, Germany, 4 In.	46.00
Figurine, Nude Bathing Beauty, Germany, 3 In.	195.00
Figurine, Young Child Riding Elephant, Gray, Yellow, Pink, Blue, Germany, 5 x 4 1/2 In.	85.00
Humidor, Face, 7 1/4 In.	385.00
Planter, Uncle Walt & Skeezix, 1930s	75.00
Plaque, Cherub, Flowers & Butterflies, White, Dark Green Ground, 5 1/2 In.	29.00
Plaque, Courting Couple, High Relief, 7 1/2 In., Pair	22.00
Tobacco Jar, Boy's Head, Side-Glancing Eyes, Head Scarf Cover, Germany	495.00
Vase, Figures, Boy & Girl, Musical Instruments, Germany, 5 1/2 In., Pair	39.00
Vase, White Clay, Incised Collar Rim, Odell & Booth Bros., 11 In.	55.00

BLACK memorabilia has become an important area of collecting since the 1970s. The best material dates from past centuries, but many recent items are also of interest. F & F is the mark used on plastic made by Fiedler & Fiedler Mold & Die Works, Inc. in the 1930s and 1940s. Objects that picture a black person may also be listed in this book under Advertising, Tins; Banks; Bottle Openers; Cookie Jars; Salt & Pepper; Sheet Music; Toys; etc.

Ashtray, Native Woman Head, Stand	13.00
Badge, Slave, Tax, Copper, Charleston 998, Servant 1857, 1 x 1 In.	2185.00
Badge, Slave, Tax, Copper, Charleston 1851, Servant 2376, 1 x 1 In.	1840.00
Badge, Slave, Tax, Copper, Charleston 2083, Servant 1836, 2 x 2 In.	1840.00
Banner, Martin Luther King Memorial, Black On White, 40 x 46 In.	439.00
Book, Little Black Sambo, Golden Book, 1948	145.00
Book, Little Black Sambo, Whitman, Small Format, 1953	90.00
Button, Brierfield Plantation, Carriage Driver	50.00
Button, Star Plantation, Straw Boss, Louisiana	50.00
Clothes Whisk, Figure On Handle, Wooden, Blue Paint, Red Nylon Bristles, 7 1/2 In.	22.00
Cookie Jars are listed in the Cookie Jar category.	
Creamer, Googly-Eyed Girl, Japan	165.00
Display, Golliwog, Countertop, Stand-Up, 1960s	60.00
Doll, Boy, Closed Mouth, Paperweight Eyes, Molded Black Hair, 18 In.	995.00
Doll, Cloth, Hooked Hair, Embroidered Face, Polka Dot Dress, 1800s, 16 In.	925.00
Doll, Girl, Molded Face, Painted Face, 15 In.	695.00
Doll, Mammy, Blue Dress & Petticoat, Antebellum, 19 In.	455.00

Doll, Papier-Mache, Child, Sculpted Hair, Straw-Filled Muslin Body, Germany, 20 In. ... 900.00
Doll, Topsy Turvy, Composition, 8 1/4 In. 275.00
Figure, Black Boy, Fishing, Straw Hat, Wooden, Cutout, Original Paint, 1940s, 17 In. 130.00
Figure, Blackamoor, With Cornucopia, Polychrome, Gilt, 58 1/2 In., Pair 1760.00
Figurine, Black Man Eating Watermelon, Inscription, Billy Ray Hussey, 8 In. 209.00
Handbill, Save Our Lives-They Must Not Burn, 1934, 5 1/2 x 8 1/2 In. 244.00
Letter, Scottsboro-Herndon Emergency Fund, International Labor Defense, 8 x 11 In. ... 288.00
Marionette, Dancing Dan, Wood, Spring Neck & Legs, Paper Face, 1938, 11 1/4 In. 72.00
Notepad Holder, Mammy, Plastic, White, Black Trim 55.00
Plaque, Martin Luther, Bust, Brass, Tin Frame, 2 5/16 x 3 In. 72.00
Plate, Coon Chicken Inn, 10 In. 430.00
Postcard, Happy Fiddler From Dixie Land 8.00
Poster, Defend Our Civil Rights, Judge Hubert T. Delany, 1952, 4 x 9 In. 18.00
Poster, Mrs. McGee's Own Story, Harlem Civil Rights Cong. Speech, 5 x 8 1/2 In. 20.00
Poster, Sing Out!, People's Artists, Satchel Paige On Cover, 1954, 5 1/2 x 8 1/2 In. 63.00
Poster, Sing Out!, Songs For Negro History Week, 1951, 5 1/2 x 8 1/2 In. 31.00
Poster, Vote Against Jim Crow!, Socialist Party Attacking FDR & GOP, 4 x 5 In. 42.00
Poster, What Makes Johnny Bad?, Statement On Juvenile Delinquency, 1942, 4 x 6 In. .. 25.00
Song Booklet, Negro Spirituals, 1923 .... 6.00
Spice Set, Mammy, Metal Rack, F & F, 4 Piece 185.00
Stein, Character, Black Man, Arms Folded On Stomach, Porcelain 900.00
String Holder, Domed Lid, Black Man's Face, Painted, Iron, 19th Century, 8 x 6 In. 633.00
String Holder, Mammy, Pottery 235.00
Syrup, Mammy 60.00
Table Card, Coon Chicken Inn, 2 Sides 33.00
Tile, Mammy, Yellow, Mosaic 500.00
Tumbler, Old Fashioned, Gold, Red Calypso Dancer, 8 Piece 48.00

BLACK AMETHYST glass appears black until it is held to the light, then a dark purple can be seen. It has been made in many factories from 1860 to the present.

Bowl, Enameled Flowers, 8 In. 47.00
Bowl, Mt. Pleasant, Turned-Up Edges, Handles, 10 In. 10.00
Compote, Grape, Pedestal, 6 /12 In. 17.00
Flowerpot & Frog, 6 In. 40.00
Ice Bucket, Diamond-Quilted Interior, Silver Handle, 6 x 5 In. 35.00
Toothpick, Hand Etched Floral Band At Top, 2 5/8 In. 35.00
Vase, Applied Crystal Decoration, Hand Blown, 4 1/4 In. 55.00
Vase, Grape & Vine Cutting, 9 In. 495.00
Vase, Ruffled Top, 8 1/2 In. 15.00
Vase, Snake Dance, 2 Handles, 7 In. 35.00

BLOWN GLASS, see Glass-Blown category.

BLUE GLASS, see Cobalt Blue category.

BLUE ONION, see Onion category.

BLUE WILLOW, see Willow category.

BOCH FRERES factory was founded in 1841 in La Louviere in eastern Belgium. The wares resemble the work of Villeroy & Boch. The factory is still in business.

Figurine, Keramis Rooster, Beige, Blue, Green, Crystalline Matte Glaze, 6 1/4 In. 77.00
Lamp Base, Table, Vines & Fruits Design, Yellow, Brown, Blue, 1928, 24 In. 316.00
Vase, Bands Of Flying Birds, Art Deco, Charles Catteau, c.1925, 9 3/4 In. 1100.00

BOEHM is the collector's name for the porcelains of Edward Marshall Boehm. In 1953 the Osso China Company was reorganized as Edward Marshall Boehm, Inc. The company is still working in England and New Jersey. In the early days of the factory, dishes were made, but the elaborate and lifelike bird figurines are the best-known ware. Edward Marshall Boehm, the founder, died in 1961, but the firm has continued to design and produce porcelain. Today, the firm makes both limited and unlimited editions of figurines and plates.

Bottle, White, Swirling Ribs, Glossy Finish, Stopper, Green Stamp Mark, 6 1/4 In., Pair . 77.00

Figurine, Audubon Trumpeter Swan, No. 40266, 15 In. 1265.00
Figurine, Baby Blue Bird, No. 442, 4 1/2 In. ....92.00 to 115.00
Figurine, Baby Blue Jay, No. 436, 4 1/2 In. 115.00
Figurine, Baby Cedar Waxwing, 3 1/4 x 2 3/4 In. 77.00
Figurine, Baby Crested Flycatcher, Hand Painted, Stamped, 5 1/4 x 3 1/4 In. 88.00
Figurine, Baby Goldfinch, Hand Painted, Stamp Mark, 4 1/4 x 3 1/2 In. 77.00
Figurine, Black Cat Chickadee, Hand Painted, Stamped, 9 x 5 3/4 In. 165.00
Figurine, Blue Grosbeak, No. 489, 11 1/4 In. 1035.00
Figurine, Bluebird, No. 4026, 4 3/4 In. 69.00
Figurine, Brown Thrasher, No. 400-26, 8 x 11 1/4 In. 575.00
Figurine, Elephant, Faux Diamond Eyes, 8 In. 515.00
Figurine, Fledgling Brown Thrasher, 5 1/4 x 5 1/4 In. 99.00
Figurine, Fledgling Kingfisher, Hand Painted, Stamped Mark, 6 1/2 x 4 In. 88.00
Figurine, Fledgling Magpie, Hand Painted, Stamped, 5 1/2 x 3 3/4 In. 77.00
Figurine, Fledgling Red Poll, 3 3/4 x 3 3/4 In. 66.00
Figurine, Hooded Merganser, No. 496, 10 5/8 In., Pair 690.00
Figurine, Indigo Bunting, Hand Painted, Stamp Mark, 9 1/2 x 5 1/4 In. 143.00
Figurine, Kirtlands Warbler, No. 40169, Signed, 1980, 9 In. 515.00
Figurine, Mockingbirds, Feeding Young, Nasturtium, Green Leaves, No. 182, 10 In. 440.00
Figurine, Northern Oriole, 12 In. 110.00
Figurine, Nuthatch, Hand Painted, Stamp Mark, 10 x 5 1/4 In. 176.00
Figurine, Peregrine Falcon, No. 200-10, 6 In. 170.00
Figurine, Prairie Chicken, No. 464, 10 In., Pair 1207.00
Figurine, Saw-Whet Owl, No. 200-38, 6 1/2 In. 200.00
Figurine, Supreme Orchid Cactus With Horned Toad, No. 69, 1976, 6 1/2 In. 455.00
Figurine, Tree Sparrow, 8 x 6 1/2 In. 99.00
Figurine, Tufted Titmire, Signed, No. 482G, 13 In. 305.00
Figurine, Tumbler Pigeons, No. 416, 8 1/2 In., Pair 630.00
Figurine, White Rabbit, Glossy Finish, Green Stamp Mark, 2 1/4 x 2 1/2 In., Pair 132.00
Figurine, White Throated Sparrow, Hand Painted, Stamped Mark, 9 1/4 x 5 3/4 In. 143.00
Urn, Bisque, Fluted, Cover, Stamped, 7 1/4 In. 33.00

BOHEMIAN GLASS, see Glass-Bohemian.

BONE DISHES were considered a necessary part of a table setting for
the Victorian table. The crescent-shaped dish was kept at the edge of
the dinner plate so the bones removed from the fish could be stored
away from the uneaten food. Some bone dishes were made in more
fanciful shapes and many resemble fish.

Albany, Johnson Bros., 6 x 3 1/2 In. 88.00
Blue Danube, 6 1/2 x 3 In. 21.00
Butterflies, Yellow On White, Herend, Hungary, 8 1/4 x 5 1/4 In. 175.00
Clarence, Grindley, 7 1/4 x 4 In. 75.00
Royal Crown, Knife, Original Box, 4 1/2 In. 96.00
Wentworth, Meakin, 6 1/2 x 3 1/4 In. 68.00

BOOKENDS have probably been used since books became inexpensive.
Early libraries kept books in cupboards, not on open shelves. By the
1870s bookends appeared, especially homemade fret-carved wooden
examples. Most bookends listed in this book date from the twentieth
century. Bookends are also listed in other categories by manufacturer
or material.

Abraham Lincoln, Bronze 150.00
Aged Man On Library Steps, Open Book, Cold Painted Metal, G.S. Allen, 7 1/2 In. 143.00
Arts & Crafts, Craftsman Co., No. 279 .... 350.00
Bird, Cockatoo Perched On Book, Copper, Polychrome, 1930, 9 1/4 In. 287.00

Don't cut the price off a book's dust jacket. It will affect the value.

Bookends, Eagle, With Shield,
E Pluribus Unum, Cast Iron,
7 1/8 x 5 1/8 In.

Bookends, Girls,
Under Tree, Iron,
5 5/8 x 4 1/8 In.

Bookends, Pagoda, Ivory,
Brass, Potter Mellen,
6 1/2 x 2 1/2 x 6 In.

Brass, Copper, Hammered, Round, Die Stamp Mark, Karl Kipp, 4 x 4 In. 275.00
Cherubs, Copper, Bronzed, 4 7/8 In. 165.00
Children On Sled, Brass, Jennings, 1930, 5 In. 115.00
Cockatoos, Brass, Jennings Brother, 6 In. 115.00
Copper, Hammered, Arts & Crafts, 3 1/4 x 4 1/2 In., Pair 2765.00
Cottage, Cast Iron, Bradley & Hubbard, 4 In. 165.00
Cowboys, On Rearing Horses, Painted Metal, c.1925, 10 3/4 x 4 1/2 x 6 1/2 In. 385.00
Dog, Bulldog, Cast Iron, Brass Plate 130.00
Dog, German Shepherd, Bronze, B & H, 6 In. 172.00
Dog, German Shepherd, Cast Metal, Germany 105.00
Dog, Hunting, Looking To The Side, Raised Paw, Green Marble, Bronze, 4 In. 230.00
Dogs, At Gate, Bronze, B & H, 1920, 5 1/4 In. 460.00
Dutch Boy & Girl, Spelter, Gilt, 5 x 5 1/2 In. 230.00
Eagle, With Shield, E Pluribus Unum, Cast Iron, 7 1/8 x 5 1/8 In. . . . . *Illus* 50.00
Elephant, Metal, c.1920, 4 5/8 In. 69.00
Elephants, Sitting, Brass, Jennings, 1930, 4 1/2 In. 92.00
Eve, Cast Iron, Signed Roma, c.1925, 6 3/4 In. 145.00
Fisherman, In Stream, Rod Raised Above Head, Bronze 145.00
Flower Stalks, Etched, Brass, Carence Crafters, 20th Century, 5 In. 290.00
Flowers, Leaves, Vines, Etched Brass, Arts & Crafts, George W. Frost, 3 3/4 x 5 In. 300.00
George Washington, Bronze, 1928, 4 3/8 In. 135.00
Girls, Under Tree, Iron, 5 5/8 x 4 1/8 In. . . . . *Illus* 35.00
Horse, Jumping, Clear Glass, American Glass 55.00
Horses, Mare & Foal, Syroco 45.00
Indian, Asleep, On Horse, Cast Iron, Stainless Steel, Remington Style, 6 x 3 In. 36.00
Indian Brave, Bronze, B & H, 1930, 5 1/2 In. 172.00
Ivy Design, Bronzed Metal, McClelland Barclay, 4 3/4 In. 145.00
Kneeling Nude, Draped, Art Nouveau, Spelter, Copper Finish 385.00
Liberty Bell, Sesquicentennial, Bronze, 1926, 6 1/4 In. 57.00
Man, Ivory Head, Seated On Library Steps, 6 1/2 In. 400.00
Mushroom, Copper, Old Mission Kopperkraft, 3 3/4 x 5 In. 175.00
Nude Maidens, Dancing, Patinated Metal, Art Deco, c.1930, 6 1/2 In. 230.00
Nude Maidens, Seated, White Metal, Green Finish, 8 1/4 In. 140.00
Owl, Art Nouveau, Brass, Adjustable 130.00
Pagoda, Ivory, Brass, Potter Mellen, 6 1/2 x 2 1/2 x 6 In. . . . . *Illus* 175.00
Pan, Figural, Silver Plate, Green Marble Base, France, 8 x 6 1/2 x 2 1/2 In. 520.00
Peacocks, At Archway, Bronze, Werner Bros., 6 In. 100.00
Peacocks, Bronze, 1930, 6 In. 90.00
Plank, Rounded Edge, Leather Matte, Arts & Crafts, G. Stickley, Branded, 6 x 6 In. 660.00
Puppy, Bronze, Barking & Prize, F.B. Parsons, 6 7/8 In. 690.00
Scotties, Syroco 35.00
Scotty, Cast Iron, Hubley 140.00
Storks, Cold Painted, Ivory Beaks, Black Marble, Bronze, 1930, 5 x 3 In. 345.00
Stylized Bees, Motto, Brass, Rectangular, Carence Crafter, 4 3/4 x 7 In. 396.00

Washington Crossing The Delaware, Brass, Jennette, 1930, 6 In. 92.00
Waves, Etched, Motto, There Is No Past, Brass, Arts & Crafts, George W. Frost, 6 In. 325.00
Wolfhound, Silver Plate, c.1930, 4 1/2 In. 85.00
Woman's Head, Art Nouveau Design, Bradley & Hubbard, 5 1/2 x 8 1/2 In., Pair 110.00

BOOKMARKS were originally made of parchment, cloth, or leather.
Soon woven silk ribbon, thin cardboard, celluloid, wood, silver, tortoiseshell, and metals were used. Examples made before 1850 are
scarce, but there are many to be found dating before 1920.

Belle Of Lipton's Ceylon Tea Gardens, 1904, 6 In. 12.00
Capitol Building, Capitol Washington D.C., 3 In. 6.00
Clover, Arts & Crafts Sterling Silver Flower, Signed, 3 1/8 x 1 1/8 In. 41.00
Dr. Price's Baking Powder, 1920 . . . . 16.00
Girl Skipping Rope, Paper, Miller Organ & Piano, Lebanon, Pa. 5.00
Gold Seal Champagne, Urbana Wine Co., Urbana, N.Y., 2 1/2 x 1 1/2 In. 25.00
Hagley's Chocolates, Chicago, Wolf & Co., Philadelphia, 6 x 2 In. 15.00
Lipton Tea Ladies In Native Costume, Paper, 1905 . . . . 20.00
Memorial Commemorating Grant's Death, 1885, 2 3/4 x 11 1/4 In. 12.00
Mohair Teddy Bear, Celluloid, Whitehead & Hoag Co., 3 x 2 3/4 In. 63.00
National Tuberculosis Assoc., 1955 . . . . 7.00
Pears Soap, Mint Die Cut, 1890 . . . . 15.00
Poll Parrott Shoes, 5 1/2 In. 13.00
Poole Piano Co., Boston, Mass., Celluloid 18.00
Scottish Widows Fund, Word Funds On Back, 1890, 4 x 1/2 In. 20.00
Silk, Rt. Hon. W.E. Gladstone, T. Stevens, Coventry 187.00
Stollwerck Gold Grand Chocolate & Cocoa, Celluloid, Bastian Bros. Co., N.Y. 20.00
Teddy Bear, Aluminum, Seaside Aluminum Novelty Co., Atlantic City, N.J. 46.00
Waltham Crayons Celluloid, Whitehead Hoad, N.J. 26.00

BOSSONS character wall masks, plaques, figurines, and other decorative pieces are made by W.H. Bossons, Limited of Congleton, England.
The company was founded in 1946 and is still working.

Abdhul, Head, 8 In. 165.00
Betsey Trotwood, Head, 5 3/4 In. 85.00
Bill Sikes 65.00
Birds On Branches, Other Feeding 3 Babies 110.00
Bretonne Lady, Head, 1982, 5 1/2 In. 85.00
Coolie, Head, 1963, 6 3/4 In. 68.00
Desert Hawk, 7 /12 In. 145.00
Dog, Labrador Retriever, Head, 1968 . . . . 50.00
Dog, Syrian Boxer 65.00
Eskimo Head 125.00
Himalayan, Head, 1971 . . . . 55.00
Kurd's Head 60.00
Pathan, 10 In. 175.00
Plaque, Chrysanthemum, Hand Painted, 14 In. 65.00
Tony Weller, Head, 4 1/2 In. 55.00
Uriah Heep, Head, 1964 . . . . 55.00

BOSTON & SANDWICH CO. pieces may be found in the Sandwich Glass category.

BOTTLE collecting has become a major American hobby. There are
several general categories of bottles, such as historic flasks, bitters,
household, and figural. Pyro is the shortened form of the word
pyroglaze, an enameled lettering used on bottles after the mid-1930s.
ABM means the bottle was made by an automatic bottle machine after
1903. For more bottle prices, see the book *Kovels' Bottles Price List* by
Ralph and Terry Kovel.

Apothecary, Aq. Menth. V., Round, Blown, 1860s, 8 3/4 In. 55.00
Apothecary, Carminum, Reverse Painted Label, 1880s, 9 In. 17.00
Apothecary, Cobalt Blue, Bay Water, Frank E. Morgan, 7 1/2 In. 77.00
Apothecary, Cumin Semences, Blown, Cobalt Blue, Painted Tin Cover, 9 1/2 In. 230.00
Apothecary, Gilt, Amethyst Glass, Black Label, England, 19th Century, 15 In., Pair 770.00

Apothecary, Label Under Glass, Cover, Late 19th Century, 9 1/2 In., 4 Piece 130.00
Apothecary, Porcelain, Medieval Type Design, Isis, Italy, 10 In. 220.00
Apothecary, WT Co., Acid Benzoic, Recessed Label, Square, 4 1/2 In. 22.00

Avon started in 1886 as the California Perfume Company. It was
not until 1929 that the name *Avon* was used. In 1939, it became Avon
Products, Inc. Avon has made many figural bottles filled with cosmetic
products. Ceramic, plastic, and glass bottles were made in limited
editions.

Avon, 1760 Dueling Pistol, Box, 1973 .... 10.00
Avon, 1850 Pepperbox Pistol, Box, 1979 .... 8.00
Avon, Alaskan Moose, Aftershave, 1974 .... 9.00
Avon, Bell, Good Luck, 1983 .... 5.00
Avon, Candleholder, Cape Cod, 1983, 3 3/4 In., Pair 12.00
Avon, Goblet, Hummingbird, 1987, Pair 25.00
Avon, Noble Prince, Aftershave, German Shepherd, 1975, 4 Oz. 4.00
Avon, Snoopy, WWI Flying Ace, Bubble Bath, Blue Helmet, 1968 .... 23.00
Avon, Stein, Gold Rush, 1987 .... 25.00
Avon, Stein, Great American Baseball, 1984 .... 25.00
Avon, Stein, Ship Builders, Box, 1986 .... 45.00
Avon, Stein, Tall Ships, Box, 1982 .... 45.00
Barber, 3 Segmented Body, Molded Ribs, Cranberry, White & Blue Spatter, 1900s 440.00
Barber, Bay Rum, Milk Glass, Floral, Mallet Shape, 8 In. 55.00
Barber, Cologne, Bark Composition Cover, Portrait Panel, Girl, Fox Stopper, 10 In. 210.00
Barber, Cranberry Opalescent, Satin Finish, Stars & Stripes, Polished Pontil, 7 In. 176.00
Barber, Floral Enamel Design, Rolled Lip, Amethyst, Open Pontil, 7 1/2 In. 110.00
Barber, Gold Painted Floral, Olive Yellow, White Splotches, Long Neck, 6 In. 77.00
Barber, Mary Gregory Type, Bay Rum, Amethyst, Gristmill Picture, Pontil, 7 3/4 In. 300.00
Barber, Mary Gregory Type, Light To Medium Blue, Gold Girl & Bird, 2 3/4 In. 275.00
Barber, Sapphire Blue, Pink & Yellow Bird On Branch, Bulbous, 1870-1920, 8 1/8 In. 715.00

Beam bottles were made to hold Kentucky Straight Bourbon, made by
the James B. Beam Distilling Company. The Beam series of ceramic
bottles began in 1953.

Beam, Antique Telephone, 1978 .... 50.00
Beam, Democrat Donkey, Standing, Clown Outfit, 1968, 12 In. 22.00
Beam, Democrat, Computer Shape, Donkey On Screen, 1984 .... 85.00
Beam, Democratic Convention, Donkey Head, 1956, 10 1/2 In. 45.00
Beam, Louisiana Super Dome, 1975 .... 28.00
Beam, Republican Convention, Elephant Head, Place For Cocktail Glass, 1956, 10 1/2 In. 45.00
Beam, Republican Elephant, Standing, Boxing Gloves, 1964, 12 3/4 In. 50.00
Beam, Republican Elephant, Standing, Raised Trunk, Clown Outfit, 1968, 12 In. ....20.00 to 25.00
Beam, Republican Elephant, Wearing Helmet, On Football, 1972 .... 35.00
Beer, Angel's Brewery & Soda Works, Ernst F. Hubler Prop., Amber, Cork 130.00
Beer, Anheuser-Busch Bock Beer, Label, 1930s 33.00
Beer, Frank Jones Holden Ale, Label, 1900s 16.00
Beer, Henry Weinhard Export Beer, Portland, Or., Light Amber, Foil Top 145.00
Beer, Johns English Brew, Stoneware, 1890s 15.00
Beer, Philadelphia XXX Porter & Ale, Emerald Green, Applied Top, Graphite Pontil 165.00
Beer, San Diego Brewing Co., San Diego, Cal., Dark Amber, Blob Top 11.00
Beer, Schlitz, Royal Ruby, Original Labels, c.1950, 1 Qt. 75.00
Beer, Schmidt's, Buy U.S. War Bonds & Saving Stamps, World War II, 9 1/2 In. ....58.00 to 65.00
Beer, Thomas Downing, Hanford, Cal., Amber, Crown Top, Split 45.00
Beer, Wonder Bottling Works, Oakland, Cal., Amber, Tooled Top, Split 55.00
Bininger, A.M. & Co., Old Kentucky Bourbon, Yellow, Amber, Open Pontil, 9 1/4 In. ... 420.00
Bitters, Brown's Celebrated Indian Herb, Indian Queen, Black Amber, 12 1/4 In. 349.00
Bitters, Buffalo Old Bourbon, Geo. E. Dierssen & Co., Sacramento, Cal., Amber 330.00
Bitters, California Fig & Herb, Wichmann 44, Gold Amber 55.00
Bitters, Canton, Star, Lady's Leg, Amber, 12 1/4 In. 405.00
Bitters, Congress, Amber, Panels, 9 1/4 In. 175.00
Bitters, Congress, Amethyst, Pontil, From Gardner Collection, 7 3/4 In. 830.00
Bitters, Crookes's Stomach, Olive Green, Cream Top, Sloping Shoulder, 10 1/8 In. 577.00
Bitters, Doyle Hop Bitters, Red, Amber, 1872, 9 5/8 In. 30.00

Bitters, Dr. C.W. Warner's German Hop Bitters, Amber, 1880, 9 1/2 In. 45.00
Bitters, Dr. Corbett's Renovating Shaker, Green, Open Pontil, 9 1/2 In. 1870.00
Bitters, Dr. Harter's Wild Cherry, Dayton, Ohio, Amber, Label, c.1880, 2 3/4 In. 150.00
Bitters, Dr. J. Hostetter's Stomach, Amber, 8 3/4 In. 25.00
Bitters, Dr. J. Hostetter's Stomach, Graphic Front, Amber, Square, 9 In. 45.00
Bitters, Dr. J. Hostetter's Stomach, Olive Amber, Square, 1880, 9 1/2 In. 185.00
Bitters, Dr. Langley's Root & Herb, Blue Green, 8 7/8 In. 122.00
Bitters, Dr. Loew's Celebrated Stomach Bitters & Nerve Tonic, Yellow Green, 3 1/2 In. . . . 440.00
Bitters, Dr. Loew's Celebrated Stomach, Yellow Green, c.1880, 9 1/4 In. 330.00
Bitters, Dr. Mackenzie's Wild Cherry, Chicago, Rectangular, 8 1/2 In. 175.00
Bitters, Dr. Shepard's Compound Wahoo Bitters, Brand Rapids, Mi., Aqua, Dug, 7 1/2 In. 140.00
Bitters, Dr. Soule's Hop, Yellow Amber, Square, 9 1/4 In. 125.00
Bitters, Drake's Plantation, 6-Log, Dark Puce, 10 In. 295.00
Bitters, Drake's Plantation, 6-Log, Patented 1862, Amber 100.00
Bitters, Greeley's Bourbon, Medium To Deep Puce, Barrel, 9 3/8 In. 330.00
Bitters, Highland Bitters & Scotch Tonic, Red Copper, 9 5/8 In. 2265.00
Bitters, Lithauer Stomach, Hartwig Kantorowicz, Milk Glass, 3 3/4 In. 95.00
Bitters, Moulton's Oloroso, Fluted Shoulders & Base, Aqua, 1880, 11 1/4 In. 330.00
Bitters, National, Ear Of Corn, Deep Strawberry Puce, Patent 1867, 12 5/8 In. 2035.00
Bitters, Old Hickory, Celebrated Stomach, Amber, Smooth Tooled Mouth, c.1880, 9 In. . . . 88.00
Bitters, Perrine's Apple Ginger, Orange Amber, 9 1/2 In. 265.00
Bitters, Sanborn's Kidney & Liver Vegetable Laxative, Amber, 10 In. 120.00
Bitters, Star Kidney & Liver, Amber, Square, 8 3/4 In. 80.00
Bitters, W. Chilton & Co., Romaine's Crimean, Cabin, Amber, Square, 10 1/4 In. 660.00
Bitters, White's Stomach, Deep Amber, 9 1/2 In. 96.00
Bitters, Yerba Buena, San Francisco, Calif., No. 2, Amber, Square, 9 5/8 In. 95.00
Bitters, Yochim Bros. Celebrated Stomach, Amber, Square, 8 3/4 In. 75.00
Black Glass, Boot Shape, c.1760, 17 In. 495.00
Black Glass, Dutch Onion, Deep Olive, Laid On Ring, Open Pontil, 6 1/2 In. 130.00
Blown, Cobalt Blue, Ribbed, Swirl Fluted Stopper, 10 1/2 In. 330.00
Blown, Globular, Deep Yellow Olive, Applied Collared Ring, 1830, 10 In. 440.00
Coca-Cola bottles are listed in the Coca-Cola category.
Cologne, 12 Sides, Plum Amethyst, Tooled Flared Mouth, 1860-1880, 4 1/16 In. 146.00
Cologne, Bunker Hill Monument, c.1855, 8 1/8 In. 1815.00
Cologne, Pale Blue, Basket Weave, Sheared Lip, Baluster, Open Pontil, 3 In. 22.00
Cologne, Pale Blue, Floral Spray, Stopper, Rectangular, 6 In. 66.00
Cordial, Crown Cordial & Extract Co., New York, Lid, Clamp, 1/2 Gal. 75.00
Cordial, Wishart's Pine Tree Tar, Yellow Green, 7 3/4 In. 215.00
Cosmetic, Brugeline Hair Restorer, Amber, 6 1/2 In. 45.00
Cosmetic, C.E. Brigg's, Russian Hair Restorer, Cobalt Blue, 6 In. 100.00
Cosmetic, Corolla's Hair Tonic, Aqua, 7 1/2 In. 24.00
Cosmetic, Fountain Of Youth Hair Restorer, Cobalt Blue, Applied Top, 7 1/4 In. 1430.00
Cosmetic, Harry D. Haber's Magic Hair Coloring, Deep Cobalt Blue, 6 In. 145.00
Cosmetic, Mrs. S.A. Allen's World's Hair Restorer, Straw Yellow, Smooth, 7 1/4 In. 46.00
Cosmetic, Oldridge's Balm Of Columbia For Restoring Hair, Ice Blue, 1826, 6 3/4 In. . . . 180.00
Cosmetic, Phalon's Chemical Hair Invigorator, Aqua, Open Pontil, 5 1/2 In. 60.00
Cosmetic, Rhode's, Hair Rejuvenator, Lowell, Mass., Amber, 6 1/2 In. 42.00
Cure, Ayer's Cherry Pectoral, Aqua, Open Pontil, 7 In. 65.00
Cure, Celery Compound, Embossed Stalk Of Celery, Amber, 10 In. 120.00
Cure, Dr. B.W. Hair's Asthma Cure, Hamilton, Ohio, Aqua, Square, 7 3/4 In. 40.00
Cure, Dr. Frazier's Quick Cure, 5 3/4 In. 32.00
Cure, Dr. Kilmer's Swamp Root Kidney Liver & Bladder, London, E.C., 5 3/4 In. 25.00
Cure, Dr. Larookah's Indian Vegetable Pulmonic Syrup, Green Aqua, 8 1/2 In. . . . . .60.00 to 130.00
Cure, Dr. Samuels World's Dyspepsia's Cure, 4 1/4 In. 15.00
Cure, Healy & Bigelow's Indian Kickapoo Cough, Aqua, 6 1/4 In. 15.00
Cure, Rosewood Dandruff, J.R. Reeves Anderson, Ind., 6 3/8 In. 25.00
Cure, Sanford's Radical, Cobalt Blue, Drip Top, 7 1/2 In. 33.00
Cure, Warner's Safe Kidney & Liver, Rochester, N.Y., Amber 44.00
Decanter, Cone, Art Deco, Michelin Man Tube-Style Stopper, 12 In. 150.00
Decanter, Old Government Whiskey, Gold Writing, Backbar 175.00
Demijohn, Amethyst, Applied Top, 5 Gal. 355.00
Demijohn, Blown, Chestnut, Yellow Green, Flattened Sides, String Lip, 1830, 3 1/2 In. . . . 275.00
Demijohn, Citron, Applied Top, 14 1/2 In. 55.00

Demijohn, Green, 19th Century, 26 x 16 In. 250.00
Demijohn, Olive Green, Bubbles, Sloping Collar, Open Pontil, 10 In. 95.00
Demijohn, Pale Green, Applied Top, Smooth Base, Whittled, 12 1/2 In. 75.00
Elk-O-Lene Motor Oil, Clear, Red Baked Finish, Screw Cap, 1 Qt. 110.00
Figural, Atterbury Duck, Milk Glass, Sheared Mouth, 1880, 11 5/8 In. 165.00
Figural, Baseball, Flask, Take Me Out To The Ball Game & Get Drunk 120.00
Figural, Book, Departed Spirits Flask, Brown & Yellow, 5 5/8 In. 360.00
Figural, Book, Wonders Of The Earth, Flask, Brown & Black, 6 3/4 In. 440.00
Figural, Bust, Napoleon, Hat As Closure, Glass Pedestal, 1911, 10 3/4 In. 2530.00
Figural, Bust, Poincare, Milk Glass, Wide Mouth, Tin Cap Base, 13 1/2 In. 825.00
Figural, Cherub Holding Clock, Milk Glass, Topaz, Ruffled Mouth, 1900, 13 3/4 In. 231.00
Figural, Chinese Man, Seated, Sapphire Blue, Metal Head Stopper, 1890, 5 1/2 In. 605.00
Figural, Christmas Tree, Tooled Mouth, Glass Star Stopper, 1900, 13 1/2 In. 209.00
Figural, Dice, Double, Milk Glass, Card's Pictures Each Side, Dice Stopper, 8 1/4 In. 90.00
Figural, Eiffel Tower, Depose, Pontil, 13 3/4 In. 80.00
Figural, Jim Crow, Seated On Barrel, Flask, Bennington Pottery, 9 1/4 In. 302.50
Figural, John Bull On Stump, Brown Albany Slip, 9 1/2 In. 200.00
Figural, Locomotive, Machined Mouth, 1920, 11 1/2 In. 230.00
Figural, Man, With Scroll, Pottery, 19th Century, 7 5/8 In. 170.00
Figural, Owl, Jar, Milk Glass, Ground Mouth, Lid, 1905, 1 Pt. 110.00
Figural, Pig, Philbrook & Tucker, Gold Amber, 1875, 10 1/4 In. 635.00
Figural, Queen Victoria, Pottery, 19th Century, 8 1/4 In. 185.00
Figural, Skeleton, Sitting On Barrel, White Ceramic, Brown, Tan, Red, Orange, 13 In. ... 231.00
Flask, Anchor & Sheaf Of Wheat, Aqua, 1850-1860, 1 Pt. 195.00
Flask, Chestnut, Light Yellow Olive, Blown, Crude Rolled Mouth, 1783-1830, 5 5/8 In. .. 205.00
Flask, Chestnut, Yellow Olive, Blown, Tooled Collared Mouth, 1830, 7 7/8 In. 210.00
Flask, Clasped Hands & Eagle, Pittsburgh District, Citron, Applied Mouth, 1880, 1 Pt. ... 715.00
Flask, Columbia & Eagle, Portrait, Aqua, Pontil, 1840, 1 Pt. 165.00
Flask, Corn For The World, Monument, Baltimore, Blue Aqua, 1 Qt. 190.00
Flask, Cornucopia & Urn, Pictorial, Lancaster Glass Works, Aqua, 1850, 1/2 Pt. 165.00
Flask, Double Eagle, Stoddard Glasshouse, Yellow Olive Amber, 1860, 1/2 Pt. 175.00
Flask, Double Eagle, Stoddard, N.H., Reverse, Dark Olive Green, 1 Pt. 155.00
Flask, Eagle & Cornucopia, Aqua, Sheared Mouth, Pontil, 1850, 1 Pt. 125.00
Flask, Eagle & Flag, Coffin & Hay Manufactory, Aqua, Pontil, 1847, 1 Pt. 100.00
Flask, Eagle & Indian Shooting Bird, Blue Aqua, 1880, 1 Qt. 145.00
Flask, Emil Larsen, N.J., 12 Diamond, Amethyst, Molded, Pocket, c.1930, 5 1/4 In. 230.00
Flask, For Pike's Peak, Eagle, Pittsburgh, Pa., Aqua, 1/2 Pt. 95.00
Flask, For Pike's Peak, Prospector & Hunter, Aqua, 1 Pt. 100.00
Flask, General Washington & Eagle, Kensington, Aqua, 1820-1840, 1 Pt. 220.00
Flask, Hip, Sterling Silver, Machine Tooled, Screw Cap, England, 1869, 3 3/4 In. 192.00
Flask, Hunter & Fisherman, Calabash, Amber 187.00
Flask, Lowell Railroad & Eagle, Yellow Amber, Olive Tone, 1848, 1/2 Pt. 275.00
Flask, Masonic & Eagle, Yellow Olive, Amber Tone, 1830, 1/2 Pt. 230.00
Flask, Merry Christmas & Happy New Century, Clock Reverse, Milk Glass 77.00
Flask, Pretzel, Pottery, Foust Distillery, Glen Rock, Pa. 210.00
Flask, R. Blackington & Co., Vertical Engine Turning, Flattened Knop Lid, 14K Gold ... 1265.00
Flask, Sam's Johnson Bar, Reno, Nevada, Coffin, Interior Stain, 1 Pt. 1760.00
Flask, Semimatte Glaze Dripping Over Mustard, Fantoni, 8 3/4 In. 300.00
Flask, Sheaf Of Grain, Pictorial, Aqua, Applied Mouth, 1880, 1 Pt. 99.00
Flask, Sheaf Of Wheat & Star, Calabash, Aqua, 1 Qt. 45.00
Flask, Stag & Willow Tree, Coffin & Hay, Aqua, 1848, 1 Pt. 175.00
Flask, Success To The Railroad, Yellow Olive, 1848, 1/2 Pt. 255.00
Flask, Summer & Winter, Aqua, Double Collar, 1 Pt. 180.00
Flask, Traveler's Companion & Star, Olive Amber, 1 Qt. 230.00
Flask, Union Clasped Hands & Eagle, Aqua, 1 Pt. 200.00
Flask, Washington & Sheaf, Aqua, Open Pontil, 1/2 Pt. 145.00
Flask, Washington & Taylor, Never Surrenders, Medium Puce, 1880, 1 Pt. 110.00
Flask, Washington, Father Of His Country, Aqua, 1 Pt. 110.00
Flask, Washington, Father Of His Country, Ice Blue, 1/2 Pt. 260.00
Flask, White Drag Loops, Pocket, Pontil, 5 3/4 In. 165.00
Food, Brand Clover Honey, Pure Honey, Embossed, 1852 .... 17.00
Food, Fine Table Salt, J.T. Morton, London, Blue, Wax Sealer 253.00
Food, French's Perfect Mustard, Repro Schies Wire, Glass Lid, 1/2 Pt. 23.00

Food, H.J. Heinz Co. Ketchup, Pittsburgh, Pa., No Cap, 5 In. 75.00
Food, Jumbo Apple Butter, Embossed Elephant, c.1930 . . . . 110.00
Food, Oil Of Cloves, Cobalt Blue, Early Shield Label, 1870, 11 1/2 In. 66.00
Food, Pure Horseradish, H.D. Geer, Three Rivers, Mass., Aqua, Pickle Style, 7 In. 10.00
Fruit Jar, A. Dufour & Co., Gray, France, Gray, Pewter Collar & Cap, Lid 5 1/2 In. 255.00
Fruit Jar, A. Stone & Co., Phila., Aqua, Applied Mouth, 1880, 1 Qt. 1045.00
Fruit Jar, A.B.C., Aqua, Iron Yoke Clamp, Glass Lid, 1880-1900, 1 Qt. 990.00
Fruit Jar, A.P. Donaghho, Parkersburg, W.Va., Stoneware, Blue Stencil, 9 3/4 In. 1100.00
Fruit Jar, Acme, Shield, Clear, Selenium Tin, Lid, Clamp, Square, 1/2 Gal. 14.00
Fruit Jar, Aggee Victory, Clear, Glass Lid, Wire Bail, 1 Pt. 22.00
Fruit Jar, Air-Tight, Medium To Deep Blue, Barrel, Pat. April 13, 1858, IP, 1 Qt. . . . . *Illus* 880.00
Fruit Jar, Air-Tight, Ravenna Glass Works, Green, Iron Pontil, 1860, 1 Qt. 2750.00
Fruit Jar, Anchor Mason's Patent, Ghost Anchor, Clear, 1 Pt. 32.00
Fruit Jar, Atlas E-Z Seal, Aqua, Lid, Clamp, 1 Pt. 15.00
Fruit Jar, Atlas E-Z Seal, Cornflower Blue, Lid, 1 Qt. 20.00
Fruit Jar, Atlas Good Luck, Clear, Stopper, Lid, Clamp, 1/2 Pt. 23.00
Fruit Jar, B.B. Wilcox, Aqua, Glass Lid, Ground Mouth, 1880, 1 Qt. 110.00
Fruit Jar, Baltimore Glass Works, Aqua, Square Collar, Willoughby Stopple, 1 Qt. 990.00
Fruit Jar, BBGMCo., Amber, Glass Lid, Zinc Band, 1/2 Gal. *Illus* 8250.00
Fruit Jar, Beaver, Facing Right, Log, Gold Amber, Glass Lid, Cylindrical, 1900, 1 Qt. . . . 660.00
Fruit Jar, Blue, Tooled Drawn Mouth, Cork Stopple, Iron Pontil, 1845-1860, 1 Pt. 165.00
Fruit Jar, Brookfield, Aqua, Glass Lid, Iron Yoke Clamp, 1880, 1 Qt. 2640.00
Fruit Jar, Canton Domestic, Clear, Clamp, 1 Qt. 75.00
Fruit Jar, Canton Domestic, Cobalt Blue, Glass Lid, Wire Bail, 1900, 1 Qt. 13200.00
Fruit Jar, Carroll's True Seal, Screw Lid, Frame, 1 Pt. 30.00
Fruit Jar, Cohansey, Sun-Colored Amethyst, Wire Clamp, Glass Lid, 1890, 1/2 Pt. 440.00
Fruit Jar, Common Sense, Gregory's Patient, Aqua, Glass Immerser Lid, 1 Qt. 605.00
Fruit Jar, Cunningham & Co., Pittsburgh, Blue Green, Iron Pontil, 1860, 1 Qt. 230.00
Fruit Jar, Cunningham & Co., Pittsburgh, Pa., Aqua, Embossed Base, Iron Pontil, 1 Qt. . . 385.00
Fruit Jar, Cutting & Co., San Francisco, Pale Blue Green, Cylindrical, 1880, 1/2 Gal. 660.00
Fruit Jar, D.A. Knowlton, Saratoga, N.Y., Dark Yellow Olive, Wide Mouth, 1870, 1 Qt. . . 6050.00
Fruit Jar, Dunkley Preserving Co., Kalamazoo, Sept. 20th 1898, Repro Clamp, 1 Pt. 32.00
Fruit Jar, Ecliron Pontilse, Light Green, Amber Striations, Glass Lid, 1900, 1/2 Gal. 360.00
Fruit Jar, Espy Phil, Aqua, Open Pontil, 1840-1860, 10 5/8 In. 100.00
Fruit Jar, Excelsior, Basket Of Fruit, Aqua, Milk Bottle Shape, Glass Lid, 1880, 1/2 Gal. . 770.00
Fruit Jar, Flaccus Bros., Milk Glass Lid, Screw Band, 1900, 1 Pt. 77.00
Fruit Jar, Flaccus Bros., Steers Head, Grass Green, Milk Glass Lid, 1905, 1 Pt. 935.00
Fruit Jar, Flaccus Bros., Steers Head, Table Delicacies, Amethyst, Square, 1/2 Pt. 88.00
Fruit Jar, Forster Jar Atlas Type, Clear, Glass Lid, Band, England, 1 Pt. 25.00
Fruit Jar, Franklin, Ground Mouth, Aqua, Zinc Band, Glass Lid, 1890, Midget Pt. 440.00

Bottle, Fruit Jar, Patent Sept. 18, 1860, Blue Aqua, Wax Sealer, 1 Qt.
Bottle, Fruit Jar, Potter & Bodine, Aqua, Barrel, 1/2 Gal.
Bottle, Fruit Jar, Air-Tight, Medium To Deep Blue, Barrel, Pat. April 13, 1858, IP, 1 Qt.
Bottle, Fruit Jar, Gem, Light Green, Lid & Insert, 1 Qt.

Fruit Jar, Gem, Aqua, Glass Lid, Zinc Band, 1890, 1 Gal. 1760.00
Fruit Jar, Gem, Cross, Aqua, Glass Lid, Zinc Band, 1890, 1 Gal. 1650.00
Fruit Jar, Gem, HGW, Aqua, Yellow Olive, Zinc Band, Glass Lid, 1890, Midget Pt. 300.00
Fruit Jar, Gem, Light Green, Lid & Insert, 1 Qt. . . . . *Illus* 132.00
Fruit Jar, Gilberd's Improved, Star, Aqua, Glass Lid, Wire Clamp, 1890, 1 Pt. 660.00
Fruit Jar, Gilberd's, Star, Aqua, Glass Lid, Ground Mouth, 1 Qt. 303.00
Fruit Jar, Hampden Creamery, Aqua, Wire Clamp, Glass Lid, 1890, 1 Pt. 550.00
Fruit Jar, Imperial Trademark, Aqua, Glass Lid, Ground Mouth, 1900, 1 Pt. 1980.00
Fruit Jar, Johnson & Johnson, New York, Cobalt Blue, Screw Band, Square, 1 Qt. 300.00
Fruit Jar, La Lorraine, Green, Yellow Tone, Glass Lid, 1890-1920, 1 Liter 121.00
Fruit Jar, Ludlow's Patent, Aug. 6, 1861, Aqua, Glass Lid, Iron Cage Clamp, 1870, 1 Pt. . 605.00
Fruit Jar, Magic, Amber, Glass Lid, Repro Clamp, 1 Qt. . . . . *Illus* 1430.00
Fruit Jar, Marion, Mason's Patent Nov. 30th, 1858, Aqua, 1 Pt. 30.00
Fruit Jar, Mascot Trademark Pat'd Improved, Milk Glass Lid, 1/2 Gal. 210.00
Fruit Jar, Mason's 1, Patent Nov. 30th 1858, Aqua, Wrench Lugs, Zinc Lid, 1/2 Gal. 1320.00
Fruit Jar, Mason's 2, Patent Nov. 30th 1858, Aqua, Zinc Lid, 1890, Midget Pt. 77.00
Fruit Jar, Mason's 3, Patent Nov. 30th 1858, Aqua, Zinc Lid, 1890, Midget Pt. 470.00
Fruit Jar, Mason's 4, Patent Nov. 30th 1858, Aqua, Zinc Lid, 1890, Midget Pt. 77.00
Fruit Jar, Mason's 5, Patent Nov. 30th 1858, Aqua, Zinc Lid, 1890, Midget Pt. 61.00
Fruit Jar, Mason's Patent Nov. 30th 1858, Aqua, Zinc Lid, 1900, 1 Qt. 121.00
Fruit Jar, Mason's Patent Nov. 30th 1858, Gold Yellow, Zinc Lid, 1890, 1 Qt. 990.00
Fruit Jar, Mason's Union, Shield, Aqua, Zinc Lid, 1890, 1 Qt. 550.00
Fruit Jar, Mason's, Cross, Patent Nov. 30th 1858, Fink & Nasse, Aqua, 1890, 1 Qt. 1430.00
Fruit Jar, Mason's, Cross, Patent Nov. 30th 1858, Yellow, Olive Tone, 1890, 1/2 Gal. 1210.00
Fruit Jar, Mason's, Patent Nov. 30th 1858, Aqua, Zinc Band, Glass Lid, 1900, 1 Pt. 120.00
Fruit Jar, Mason's, Patent Nov. 30th 1858, Citron, Olive Tone, Zinc Lid, 1/2 Gal. 410.00
Fruit Jar, Mason's, Patent Nov. 30th 1858, Light Green To Aqua, Zinc Lid, 1/2 Gal. 200.00
Fruit Jar, Mason's, Patent Nov. 30th 1858, Yellow, Zinc Lid, 1870-1890, 1 Qt. 715.00
Fruit Jar, McMechens Always The Best Old Virginia, Wheeling, W.Va., 1900, 1 Pt. 110.00
Fruit Jar, Millville Atmospheric, Amber, Glass Lid, Iron Clamp, 1/2 Gal. . . . . *Illus* 11000.00
Fruit Jar, Millville Atmospheric, Cobalt Blue, Glass Lid, Iron Clamp, 1 Qt. . . . . *Illus* 24200.00
Fruit Jar, Patent Sept. 18, 1860, Blue Aqua, Wax Sealer, 1 Qt. . . . . *Illus* 165.00
Fruit Jar, Patented Oct. 19, 1858, Amethyst, Glass Lid, 1 Qt. . . . . *Illus* 1210.00
Fruit Jar, Petal, Aqua, Rolled Mouth, Iron Pontil, 1860, 1 Qt. 240.00
Fruit Jar, Potter & Bodine, Aqua, Barrel, 1/2 Gal. . . . . *Illus* 990.00
Fruit Jar, Puritan, L S Co., Apple Green, Ramped Iron Ring, Wire Clamp, 1 Qt. 525.00
Fruit Jar, Royal, Black, Glass Lid, Zinc Band, 1 Qt. . . . . *Illus* 7150.00
Fruit Jar, Scranton Jar, Aqua, Glass Lid, Ground Mouth, 1890, 1 Qt. 935.00
Fruit Jar, Star, Encircled By Fruit, Aqua, Cylindrical, 1890, 1 Qt. 55.00
Fruit Jar, Steven's Tin Top, Lewis & Neblett, Cin., Oh., Aqua, 1890, 1 Qt. 275.00
Fruit Jar, Trademark, Lightning, Yellow Amber, Putnam Base, Patd. Date On Lid, 1 Qt. . . 85.00
Fruit Jar, Union No. 5, Aqua, Tin Lid, Wax Sealer, 1860-1880, 1 Qt. 210.00
Fruit Jar, Van Vliet Jar Of 1881, Aqua, Glass Lid, Metal Yoke, 1890, 1 Qt. 880.00
Fruit Jar, Veazey Forbes & Co., Wheeling W.V., Deep Aqua, 1880, 1/2 Gal. 1760.00
Fruit Jar, Victory, Pacific Glass Works, Deep Aqua, Glass Lid, 1880, 1 Qt. 412.00
Fruit Jar, W.H. Glenny Son & Co., Buffalo N.Y., Aqua, Square Collar, Glass Lid, 1 Qt. . . 155.00
Fruit Jar, Wallaceburg Gem, Clear, Glass Lid, Band, 1 Qt. 14.00
Fruit Jar, Webster's, Patent Feb. 16, 1864, Deep Aqua, Metal Band Lid, 1880, 1/2 Gal. . . 2750.00
Fruit Jar, Whitney, Aqua, Threaded Glass Lid, Cylindrical, 1880, 1 Qt. 825.00
Fruit Jar, Wm. L. Haller, Carlisle, Pa., Aqua, Willoughby Stopple, 1870, 1 Qt. 1100.00
Fruit Jar, Yeoman's, Patent Applied For, Aqua, Cork Stopple, 1/2 Gal. 55.00
Gemel, Double Jug, I.D. Richards, No. 25 Elm Street, Albany Glaze, c.1860, 9 In. 305.00
Gin, Case, Olive Amber, Blown, Applied Top, Open Pontil, 10 In. 110.00
Ginger Beer, American Ginger Beer, Matheson's Detroit Distill Water Co., Keep Cool . . . 300.00
Glue, Mucilage, Clear, Bell Shape, Flip, 1870s, 3 1/2 In. 22.00
Household, Ammonia, S.F. Gaslight Co., Blue, Applied Top, 10 In. 100.00
Household, Ivory Blacking, Cobalt Blue, Sunken Panels, 5 1/4 In. 28.00
Household, Original E.C. Hazard's Liquid Bluing, New York, Hinge Mold Top, 6 3/8 In. . . 20.00
Household, P.R.R. Disinfectant, Amber, 6 In. 55.00
Household, SS Newton's Patent Dec. 20-76, Green, 5 1/4 In. 33.00
Ink, Blown, Clear, Screw Down To Seal, 2 1/8 In. 225.00
Ink, Carter's, Cathedral, Cobalt Blue, Master, 1930, 9 3/4 In. . . . . 90.00 to 110.00
Ink, Carter's, Ma & Pa, Porcelain, White, Germany, 1915, 3 5/8 In., Pair 160.00

Bottle, Fruit Jar, Royal, Black, Glass Lid, Zinc Band, I Qt.
Bottle, Fruit Jar, BBGMCo., Amber, Glass Lid, Zinc Band, 1/2 Gal.
Bottle, Fruit Jar, Millville Atmospheric, Cobalt Blue, Glass Lid, Iron Clamp, I Qt.
Bottle, Fruit Jar, Millville Atmospheric, Amber, Glass Lid, Iron Clamp, 1/2 Gal.
Bottle, Fruit Jar, Magic, Amber, Glass Lid, Repro Clamp, I Qt.
Bottle, Fruit Jar, Patented Oct. 19, 1858, Amethyst, Glass Lid, I Qt.

Ink, Carter's, Teal, Pour Spout, Master, 3/4 Pt. 125.00
Ink, Chaulin Bervete, Opalescent, Cut Panels, France, Pontil, 4 1/8 In. 155.00
Ink, Harrison's Columbian, Aqua, Ground Lip, 2 1/8 In. 440.00
Ink, House, Jet Black Ink, Aqua, Tooled Lip, 2 3/4 In. 385.00
Ink, Olive Green, Cylinder, Flared Lip, Open Pontil, 4 3/8 In. 60.00
Ink, Pitkin, 36 Ribs, Swirled To Left, Medium Olive Yellow, Pontil, 1830, 2 In. 522.00
Ink, Pitkin, 36 Ribs, Swirled To Left, Teal Blue Stripes, White Specks, 1890, 1 3/4 In. . . . 412.00
Ink, S.S. Stafford's, Cobalt Blue, Spout, Tooled Mouth, 1910, 9 1/2 In. 50.00
Ink, Sanford's, Clear, Glass Lid, Patent, 1900, Master, 1 Qt. 45.00
Ink, Stickwell & Co., Umbrella, Aqua Blue, 3 In. 75.00
Ink, Teakettle, Cobalt Blue, Brass Neck Ring & Hinged Lid, 1895, 2 1/2 In. 575.00
Ink, Teakettle, Double Font, Pottery, White, Bird's Nest, Snakes, 1900, 2 In. 230.00
Ink, Teakettle, Woman & Children Scene, Brass Neck Ring, Hinged Lid, 1875, 2 5/8 In. . . 605.00
Ink, Thaddeus David's Co., Blue Green, Cylinder, 2 3/4 In. 65.00
Ink, Umbrella, 8 Sides, Olive Amber, Pontil, 2 1/2 In. 230.00
Ink, Umbrella, Green, Rolled Mouth, Ground Pontil, 2 3/8 In. 500.00
Ink, Yellow Olive, Sheared Lip, 1840, 2 3/8 In. 330.00
Inkwell, End-Of-Day, Clear Over Color, Pontil, 4 In. 55.00
Jar, Battery, L.C. & E. Co., Aqua, Glass Lid, 1 Qt. 37.00
Jar, Battery, Western Electric Co., Aqua, Glass Lid, Pour Lip, 1 Qt. 25.00
Jar, Producers Creamery, Benton Harbor, Mich., Sour Cream, Embossed, 12 Oz. 12.00
Jar, Storage, Tin Cover, 6 Sides, 12 In. 200.00
Jar, Wesson Mayonnaise, Whip . . . . .16.00 to 75.00
Jug, Golden Hill, 520 Monroe, Toledo, O., Brown, White, Blue Stencil, c.1900, 4 1/2 In. . . 130.00
Medicine, A.M. Cole, Virginia City, Cobalt Blue, Applied Top 770.00
Medicine, A.P. Wilkes Druggist, Seven Corners, St. Paul, Minn., Yellow Amber, 5 1/8 In. . . 15.00
Medicine, Armour Powdered Calves Tonsils, Amber, Cork, Label, Contents, 1900s, 4 In. . . 22.00
Medicine, B.F. Shaw, Virginia City, Nev., Tooled Top, 7 1/2 In. 22.00
Medicine, Cauch's Drug Store, Camphorated Oil, Blue Tint, Brown Label, 4 1/2 In. 24.00
Medicine, Couley's Fountain, Of Health, No. 38, Baltimore, Aqua, 9 3/4 In. 715.00
Medicine, Doctor Henry's Botanic Preparations, Aqua, Applied Top, 6 1/4 In. 176.00
Medicine, Dr. Blumer's Catarrh-Killer, Cobalt Blue, Red & Blue Paper Label, 5 In. 24.00
Medicine, Dr. E.D. Wardes, Corry, Pa., Modern Miracles Price 25 Cents, 5 3/8 In. 20.00
Medicine, Dr. Fitler's Rheumatic Remedy, Philada., 7 In. 25.00
Medicine, Dr. W.R. Merwin & Co., N.Y., Aqua, Applied Top Hinge, 5 3/4 In. 20.00
Medicine, E.E. Bruce Skunk Oil, Amber, Label, Cork, Round, Late 1800s, 4 1/2 In. 17.00
Medicine, Ebenezer A. Pearl's Tincture Of Life, Aqua, 7 3/4 In. 20.00
Medicine, Eli Lilly & Co., Pharmaceutical Chemists, Laxative Tablets, 8 1/2 In. 200.00
Medicine, Evans Eye Lotion, S.F. Durst, Philadelphia, Cobalt Blue, Eyecup, Box, 6 In. . . . 11.00

Medicine, G.C. Baxter Druggist, Carson, Light To Medium Amber, 8 1/4 In. 1650.00
Medicine, G.S. Cheney Co., Boston, Mass., Tincture Capsicum, Cork, Contents, 5 In. 25.00
Medicine, H.H. Stebbins Druggist, Black Hawk, Col., 4 7/8 In. 35.00
Medicine, Hamlin's Wizard Oil, Chicago, Ill., Aqua, Applied Top, 3 7/8 In. 240.00
Medicine, Healy & Bigelow Kickapoo Indian Oil, Cylinder, 5 3/8 In. 15.00
Medicine, J.M. Speer & Co., Wilkinsburg, Pa., Embossed Eagle, 7 1/2 In. 15.00
Medicine, John Wyeth & Bro., Morphine Sulphate Triturates, Amber, Cork, Square, 3 In. . 11.00
Medicine, Lactopeptine, Best Remedial Agent In All Digestive Disorders, Blue, 7 In. 66.00
Medicine, Lydia E. Pinkham's Vegetable Compound, Aqua, Oval, 8 1/4 In. 9.00
Medicine, Macortys Cimicifuga Specific Strength Medicine, Lloyd Brothers, 4 Oz. 15.00
Medicine, Morgan Cold Capsules, Amber, Screw Cap 17.00
Medicine, Morgan, Prescription, Cobalt Blue, Embossed, Stopper, Pre-1916, 3 1/2 In. 46.00
Medicine, Mrs. Dinsmore's Cough & Croup Balsam, Clear, 6 In. 12.00
Medicine, Osborne & Shoemaker, Reno, Nev., Teal Green, Rectangular 66.00
Medicine, Paine's Celery Compound, Amber 22.00
Medicine, Paul Rieger's Jamaica Ginger, San Francisco, Calif., Aqua 20.00
Medicine, Smelling Salts, Amethyst, Double Waisted, Metal Cap, 1888, 3 1/8 In. 66.00
Medicine, Smelling Salts, Amethyst, Rectangular, Corset, 2 1/2 In. 255.00
Medicine, Smelling Salts, Corset, Citron, Rectangular, 1860-1888, 2 1/4 In. 80.00
Medicine, Smelling Salts, Corset, Teal Green, Metal Screw Cap, 3 1/4 In. 110.00
Medicine, Smelling Salts, Double Corset, Deep Sapphire Blue, 1888, 3 1/8 In. 125.00
Medicine, Stearns & White Co., Cachous Aromatic, Flask, Label, 1930s, 2 1/4 In. 8.00
Medicine, Stockton Drug Co., Citrate, Stockton, Cal., Green, 7 3/4 In. 55.00
Medicine, Will A. Showalter Pharmacist, Latrobe, Pa., 4 7/8 In. 8.00
Milk, Arden Farm Inc., Red Pyro, Arden Boy, Round, 1/2 Pt. . . . . .18.00 to 28.00
Milk, Bowmont Farms Jersey Milk, Embossed, 1 Qt. 18.00
Milk, Cereal Milk, Vertical, 2 Sides, Amber, Glass Lid, 1 Qt. 20.00
Milk, Clark Dairy, Kirkwood, N.J., 1 Gill 12.00
Milk, Community Holland, Zeeland, Mich., 10 Oz. 15.00
Milk, Consumers Co-Op Dairy, Astoria, Ore, Embossed, Round, 1 Qt. 16.00
Milk, Gold Crest, Ludington, Mich., 2 Guards, 1/2 Gal. 38.00
Milk, Ideal Dairy, Manistee, Mich., 1 Qt. 25.00
Milk, Lincoln Dairy Co., Lincoln's Head, Red, Round, 1 Qt. 30.00
Milk, Mills Creamery, Grand Rapids, Mich., Sour Cream, Embossed, 12 Oz. 18.00
Milk, Palmerton Dairy, Palmerton, Pa., 1 Qt. 18.00
Milk, Plains Dairy System, Cheyenne, Wyo., Black, Cowboy, Round, Squat, 1 Qt. 38.00
Milk, Silver Seal Dairy, San Diego, Green Label, 1/2 Gal. 35.00
Milk, Stewarts Dairy, Highland Center, Wis., Juice, Embossed, 1 Pt. 12.00
Milk, Treasure State Dairy, Butte, Montana, Red, Sunrise, Round, Squat, 1 Qt. 32.00
Mineral Water, Aetna Mineral Spouting Spring, Aqua, Saratoga, N.Y. 2300.00
Mineral Water, Chase & Co., San Francisco, Stockton, Marysville, Cal., Green, 7 1/4 In. . . 550.00
Mineral Water, Clarke & White, New York, Yellow Olive, Collared Mouth, 1 Pt. 175.00
Mineral Water, Congress & Empire Spring Co., Deep Olive Green, 1 Qt. 118.00
Mineral Water, Congress & Empire Spring Co., Hotchkiss' Sons, Green, 1 Qt. 136.00
Mineral Water, Congress & Empire Spring Congress Water, Saratoga, N.Y., Teal Blue . . . 39.00
Mineral Water, Congress Empire Spring Co., Hotchkiss' Sons, Green, Whittled, 1 Pt. 44.00
Mineral Water, D.A. Knowlton, Saratoga, N.Y., Olive, Green, 1 Qt. 110.00
Mineral Water, D.J. Whelans, Troy, N.Y., Aqua, Hutchinson, 1881 . . . . 6.00
Mineral Water, Dorchester & Weymouth Mineral Water, Aqua, 6 1/2 In. 35.00
Mineral Water, Empire Spring Co., Emerald Green, 1 Pt. 122.00
Mineral Water, Empire Spring Co., Emerald Green, 1 Qt. 105.00
Mineral Water, Franklin Spring, Saratoga, N.Y, Yellow Green, 1 Qt. 585.00
Mineral Water, Highrock Congress Spring, Saratoga N.Y., Teal Blue, 1880, 1 Pt. 470.00
Mineral Water, John Ryan Excelsior, Savannah, Ga., Cobalt Blue, Iron Pontil, 7 In. 187.00
Mineral Water, Kissingen Waters, Teal Green, Open Pontil, Oval, 7 3/4 In. 245.00
Mineral Water, Middletown Mineral Springs Nature's Remedy, Green, 1 Qt. 100.00
Mineral Water, Pavilion & United States Spring Co., Emerald Green, 1 Pt. 310.00
Mineral Water, Saratoga Star Spring, Emerald Green, 1 Qt. 280.00
Mineral Water, Thompson's, Union Soda Works, San Francisco, Aqua, Tenpin 140.00
Mineral Water, Vichey Water, Hanbury Smith, Emerald Green, 1 Pt. 70.00
Miniature, Jug, Hanse & Orevlos, Canton, S.P., 2 Colors 500.00
Miniature, Jug, Newport Bar & Grill, Merry Christmas, 1911, 4 1/2 In. 450.00
Miniature, Kellogg's Bourbon Whiskey, Amber, Tooled Top, 5 In. 90.00

Nursing, Morgan, Turtle, Horn Nipple Shell, Box, Pre-1916, 3 1/2 In. 82.00
Nursing, Teddy's Pet Peaceful Nights For Your Baby, 4 In. 75.00
Oil, Polaris Snowmobile Oil, Plastic, Figural Shape, White, Red, Blue, 10 In. 40.00
Oil, Shell Oil, Caps & Rack, Embossed, Metal Rack, Clear, Set Of 10 . . . .   1700.00
Pepper Sauce, Cathedral, Lime Green, Applied Top 155.00
Pepper Sauce, Cathedral, Slag Striations Through Neck, 1845, 10 In. 165.00
Pepper Sauce, Ghirardelli & Co., San Francisco, Aqua, Applied Top, Bubbles 66.00
Pepper Sauce, Spanish, Beehive Rings, Partial Label 25.00
Pepper Sauce, W & E, Blue, Open Pontil, 9 In. 220.00
Perfume bottles are listed in their own category.
Pickle, Bunker Hill, Skilton Foote & Co., Amber, Cylinder, 7 In. 48.00
Pickle, Bunker Hill, Skilton Foote & Co., Yellow Green, 8 In. 175.00
Pickle, Cathedral, 8 Sides, Aqua, Arches, 1860s, 13 In. 1100.00
Pickle, Cathedral, Blue Green, Applied Mouth, Open Bubbles, c.1865, 9 1/4 In. 235.00
Pickle, Sanborn Parker & Co., Boston, Amber, Ground Top, Tapered, 7 1/4 In. 295.00
Poison, Arsenic Trioxide, Amber, 1/3 Grain, Paper Label, Cork, 3 1/4 In. 50.00
Poison, Davis & Geck, Brooklyn, N.Y., Cobalt Blue, Tooled Mouth, 3 1/8 In. 660.00
Poison, Gift Flasche, Skull & Crossbones, 6 Sides, Amber, Germany, 9 1/4 In. 415.00
Poison, Lattice & Diamond, Cobalt Blue, Tooled Mouth, 1910, 11 1/4 In. 415.00
Poison, Norsicht Gift, Skull & Crossbones, Sapphire Blue, 6 Sides, Germany, 6 3/4 In. 275.00
Poison, Owl Drug Co., 3 Sides, Cobalt Blue, Owl, 4 5/8 Ins 120.00
Poison, Skull, Pat. June 26th, 1894, Cobalt Blue, 4 1/8 In. 3520.00
Poison, Sugar Of Lead, Blue Tint, Skull & Crossbones, Red & White Paper Label, 4 In. . . .   28.00
Sarsaparilla, Dana's, Belfast, Maine, Aqua, Brown Glaze, 9 In. 30.00
Sarsaparilla, Dr. Townsend's, Albany, N.Y., Teal Blue, M On Base, 9 1/2 In. 176.00
Sarsaparilla, Dr. Townsend's, Emerald Green, c.1845, 9 1/2 In. 230.00
Sarsaparilla, Dr. Tutt's Sarsaparilla Queens Delight, Aqua, 7 1/2 In. 65.00
Sarsaparilla, John Bull's Extract, Louisville, Ky., Aqua, 9 1/2 In.   42.00
Sarsaparilla, Old Dr. J. Townsend's, Blue Green, Square, 1860, 9 3/8 In. 360.00
Scent, Honeycomb Pattern, Mixed Colors, 18th Century, 3 1/2 In. 250.00
Seal, De A. Delpit, Tabac, Nouvelle, Orleans, Yellow Olive, String Rim, 1880, 10 In. 770.00
Seal, I.L.M. Smith, Wine Mercht., Baltimore, Yellow Olive, 9 3/4 In. 1760.00
Seal, Revd. J.B. Melhuish, Dense Yellow Olive, Mold Blown, 1830, 11 In. 305.00
Seal, S. Lee, Deep Yellow Olive, String Rim, Pontil, 1735, 8 1/8 In. 2750.00
Seltzer, Artesian Mfg. & Bottling Co., Waco, Tex., 8 In. 825.00
Seltzer, Dark Green, Fluted, Shreveport, Louisiana, 8 1/2 In. 935.00
Seltzer, Dr Pepper Bottling Co., Springfield Seltzer, Red Lettering, 7 In. 385.00
Seltzer, Dr Pepper Bottling Works, New Braunfels, Tex., 8 In. 412.00
Seltzer, Dr Pepper, Clear, Round, Memphis, Tenn., 8 In. .360.00 to 465.00
Seltzer, Dr Pepper, Memphis, Tenn., 7 1/2 In. . . . . .300.00 to 385.00
Seltzer, Dr Pepper, Red Label, Austin, Tex., 7 1/2 In. 1320.00
Snuff, Amber Glass, Elephant, Dressed, Stopper, 2 1/8 In. 220.00
Snuff, Amber, Spade Shape, Dark Inclusions, Agate Stopper, 19th Century, 2 In. 302.00
Snuff, Glass, Bird, Flower Medallions, Turquoise Floral Ground, Metal Stopper, 2 In. 550.00
Snuff, Glass, Green, Tear Drop, Rose Quartz Stopper, 20th Century, 2 5/8 In. 231.00
Snuff, Glass, Reverse Painted, Landscape, Bird & Flowers On Reverse, 2 5/8 In. 770.00
Snuff, Glass, Travelers On Country Road, Teardrop, Gilt Metal Stopper, 3 In. 165.00
Snuff, Ivory, Mandarin On Ram, Painted, Head Stopper, Japan, 3 In. 220.00
Snuff, Ivory, Noble Woman On Ram, Painted, Head Stopper, Japan, 3 In. 220.00
Snuff, Jade, Green, Spade Shape, Floral Carving, Amethyst Stopper, 1900, 2 1/2 In. 165.00
Snuff, Jade, White, Flattened Shape, Coral Stopper, 2 3/4 In. 330.00
Snuff, Jade, White, Mask, Mock Ring Handles, Brown, Amber Stopper, 2 1/4 In. 275.00
Snuff, Lapis Lazuli Carving Of Foo Lion, Sodalite Stopper, 20th Century, 2 In. 66.00
Snuff, Milk Glass, Cat & Flower Garden, Simulated Coral Stopper, 2 1/8 In. 1100.00
Snuff, Mother-Of-Pearl, Spade Shape, Peacock On 1 Face, Pine Tree, Jadeite Stopper 165.00
Snuff, Peking Glass, Brown Overlay, Fisherman, Malachite Stopper, Chinese, 2 1/4 In. . . .   1045.00
Snuff, Porcelain, 5-Color Dragons, White Ground, Jadite Stopper, 2 1/2 In. 1375.00
Snuff, Porcelain, 6 Characters, Blue, White, Yung Cheng Mark On Base 88.00
Snuff, Porcelain, Blue, Sage & Bat, Cylindrical, Red Glass Stopper, 3 1/2 In. 77.00
Snuff, Porcelain, Famille Rose, Ocean Deities Scene, Land Officials, 19th Century, 2 In. . . .   110.00
Snuff, Porcelain, Folded Lotus Leaf Shape, Erotic, Coral Stopper, 2 3/4 In. 660.00
Snuff, Porcelain, Green Dragons, Imperial Yellow Ground, Jade Stopper, 1 5/8 In. 110.00
Snuff, Porcelain, Horse Trader, Dragon 1 Face, Scholar, Reverse, 20th Century, 2 In. 110.00

Snuff, Porcelain, Horse, Pine Tree, Red, Snowflake Ground, Jadeite Stopper, 2 1/2 In. 192.00
Snuff, Porcelain, Landscape, Famille Rose, Cylindrical, Jade Stopper, 3 In. 55.00
Snuff, Porcelain, Man As Woman When Turned Upside Down, Jade Stopper, 2 1/2 In. ... 275.00
Snuff, Porcelain, Mandarin Woman & Servant, Floral, Bird, Iron Red Ground, 3 In. 345.00
Snuff, Pottery, Dragons In Clouds, Carved, Yi Hsing, Oval, Coral Stopper, 2 1/4 In. 495.00
Snuff, Reverse Painted, Reclining Scholar, Scholar In Boat On Reverse, 2 1/4 In. 110.00
Snuff, Rock Crystal, Prunus & Iris Design, Agate Stopper, 2 3/8 In. 357.00
Snuff, Stoneware, Pewter, Floral, Woman's, England, 19th Century, 6 x 2 3/4 In. 405.00
Snuff, Stoneware, Woman, Grapevine Design, Plaque, England, 9 3/4 In., Pair 1150.00
Snuff, Tortoiseshell, Double Square, Gilt Calligraphy, Chinese, 2 In. 1100.00
Snuff, Tortoiseshell, Flattened Oval, Conforming Stopper, 2 3/4 In. 302.00
Soaky, Atom Ant, Orange Plastic, White Helmet, Hanna Barbera, 9 In. 38.00
Soaky, Felix The Cat, 1960s 20.00
Soaky, Frankenstein 100.00
Soaky, Speedy Gonzales, Box 15.00
Soda, 7-Up, Dark Green, 1976, 10 Oz. 6.00
Soda, A. Barabas, Mt. Carmel, Pa., Blob Top, Pony 12.00
Soda, A.B. Brimmer, Newton, N.J., Hutchinson 10.00
Soda, A.P. Moresi, Jeanerette, La., Hutchinson 10.00
Soda, Acme Club, Elyria, Ohio, Green, 1959, 32 Oz. 21.00
Soda, Barq's, Zelienople, Pa., 1969, 32 Oz. 5.50
Soda, Big Chief, Florence, Co., 12 Oz. 16.00
Soda, Bolen & Byrne Aerated Beverages, New York, Yellow Green, Round, Dug 68.00
Soda, C. Bowen & Co., Bottlers, Cincinnati, Sapphire Blue, Iron Pontil, 1860, 1/2 Pt. 195.00
Soda, C.A. Cole, C.F. Brown, Blue, Tenpin, Whittled 495.00
Soda, C.F. Plitt Bottler, York, Pa., Hutchinson 5.00
Soda, Christian Trade Star, Mark Wagner XXX Ginger Ale, Aqua, Blob Top, Pony 23.00
Soda, Clarke & Co., New York, Forest Green, Saratoga, 1 Qt. 165.00
Soda, Cohasset, Youngstown, Ohio, Green, 32 Oz. 5.50
Soda, Congress & Empire, Hotchkiss Sons, Emerald Green, Saratoga, 1 Qt. 136.00
Soda, Crystal Soda Water Co., Cobalt Blue 275.00
Soda, D.A. Knowlton, Saratoga, N.Y., Olive Green, Saratoga, 1 Qt. 110.00
Soda, Dad's Root Beer, Chicago, Ill., 1959, 10 Oz. 7.50
Soda, Donald Duck Cola, 1952, 10 Oz 21.00
Soda, E.L. Billings, Sac City, Geyser Soda, Aqua 30.00
Soda, Eagle, Emerald Green, Whittled, Cleaned 145.00
Soda, Eureka Spring, Saratoga, N.Y., Aqua, Torpedo, 1 Pt. 365.00
Soda, Excelsior Spring, Saratoga, N.Y., Green, 1 Qt. 145.00
Soda, G. Eland's Potash Water, Cross Street, Westgate Rd., New Castle, Blue, Torpedo ... 265.00
Soda, G.P. Morrill, Aqua, Bubbles, Whittled, 7 In. 1045.00
Soda, Hanford Soda Works, J.S., Hutchinson 25.00
Soda, Harmony Club, Cleveland, Ohio, Green, 1969, 32 Oz. 5.00
Soda, Henry Haussling, Newark, N.J., Hutchinson 10.00
Soda, Henry Winkle, Sac City, Aqua, Iron Pontil 200.00
Soda, John Hessler, Mark Bottling Works, Aqua, Hutchinson, 6-Sided Mug Base, 6 In. ... 25.00
Soda, John Ryan 1866, Excelsior Soda Works, Savannah, Ga., Cobalt Blue, 7 1/8 In. 90.00
Soda, Kickapoo Joy Juice, Green 8.00
Soda, Lancaster Glass Works, N.Y., Blue, Cleaned 66.00
Soda, M.O. Bennett, Cheyenne, Wyo., Aqua, Hutchinson 105.00
Soda, McCrudden Campbell & Co., Philada., Deep Aqua, Applied Top, Hinge Mold 25.00
Soda, Pavilion & United States Spring Co., Emerald Green, Saratoga, 1 Pt. 310.00
Soda, Queen City Soda Works, Seattle, W.T.A. Wolff, Blue, Hutchinson, 6 7/8 In. 300.00
Soda, Root Beer, I. Sutton & Co., Covington, Ky., Cobalt Blue, 8 1/2 In. 1045.00
Soda, Squirt, Painted Label, 1960s, Miniature 5.00
Soda, Star Bottling Works, Houston, Texas, Star, Hutchinson, 7 3/8 In. 50.00
Soda, Taylor, Never Surrenders, Union Glass Works, Sapphire Blue, 1860, 7 1/8 In. 2530.00
Soda, Theiler, Morristown, N.J., Hutchinson 6.50
Soda, Virginia Dare, New Kinsington, Pa., Green, 1973, 32 Oz. 12.60
Soda, Weymouth Soda Water Works, London, Aqua, 6 1/2 In. 35.00
Soda, White Eagle, Chicopee Falls, Ma., Green, 1965, 28 Oz. 6.00
Target Ball, Amber, Allover Diamond, Beads On Corner, Germany, 1890, 2 5/8 In. 265.00
Target Ball, Amber, Flared Lip, Refired Pontil, 3 x 2 1/2 In. 249.00
Target Ball, Bogardus Type, Cobalt Blue, Flared Lip, 3 1/4 x 2 1/4 In. 181.00

Target Ball, Bogardus, Patd. Apr. 10, 1877, Olive Yellow, Diamond, 2 3/4 In. 685.00
Target Ball, Charlottenburger Glashutten, Yellow Olive, Allover Diamond, 2 5/8 In. 660.00
Target Ball, Cobalt Blue, Ground Lip, 2 1/4 In. 260.00
Target Ball, Ira Paine, Amber, Blown, Feather Stuffing, Cork, 3 Piece, 3 x 2 1/2 In. 413.00
Target Ball, Ira Paine, Amber, Feathers, Cork, Flared Lip, Refired Pontil, 3 x 2 1/2 In. 424.00
Target Ball, Ira Paine, Amber, Patent October 23, 1877, Contents, 2 3/4 In. 300.00
Target Ball, N.B. Glass Works, Perth, Cobalt Blue, Diamond, England, 2 3/4 In. 165.00
Target Ball, N.B. Glass Works, Perth, Green Aqua, Diamond, England, 2 3/4 In. 150.00
Target Ball, Pat. Sep. 1880, March 1893, Cobalt Blue, Lip, Canada, 2 1/4 x 2 1/4 In. 396.00
Target Ball, W.W. Greener, St. Mary's Works, London, Amethyst, 2 5/8 In. 255.00
Target Ball, Yellow Amber, 3-Piece Mold, 1890, 2 5/8 In. 110.00
Tonic, Baume Tranquille, Opium Wine, Cork, Label, France, 11 In. 11.00
Tonic, Reed & Carnrick, Roboline, Amber, Cork, Contents, Box, 8 1/2 In. 105.00
Tonic, Sargon, Threaded Lid, Paper Label, Partial Contents, Box, 1940s, 3 3/4 x 8 In. 27.00
Vinegar, Jones Bros. & Co., Manufacture's Blue Bell, Stoneware, 3 1/4 In. 75.00
Vinegar, Maple Sap & Boiled Cider Vinegar, Cobalt Blue, Tooled Top 495.00
Wheaton, Apollo II, Cobalt Blue, 8 1/2 In. 12.00
Wheaton, Christmas, 1979, Cobalt Blue, 7 In. 55.00
Wheaton, Democratic, 1968, Green, 7 In. 12.00
Wheaton, John Garfield, Amethyst, 3 In. 6.00
Wheaton, Martin Van Buren, Green, 3 In. 3.00
Wheaton, Sky Lab I, Blue & Frost, 8 1/2 In. 18.00
Whiskey, 3 Feathers Reserve Whiskey, Wooden Bottle Cap, 30 In. 110.00
Whiskey, Aromatic Schnapps, Amber, 1 Pt. 143.00
Whiskey, Carnegie Brea Aberdeen Finest Scotch Malt, Jug, Pottery, Beige, 6 3/4 In. 185.00
Whiskey, Chapin & Gore, Sour Mash, Barrel, Amber, 1867 . . . . 95.00
Whiskey, Choice Old Cabinet Kentucky Bourbon, San Francisco, Amber 935.00
Whiskey, Cutter Old Bourbon, Flask, C.P. Morman Only Manf'r, Amber, 1 Pt. 550.00
Whiskey, Dewar's Perth, Jug, Pottery, Brown, Sepia Transfer, 9 3/4 In. 205.00
Whiskey, E.G. Booz's Old Cabin, Yellow Amber, 1 Qt. 65.00
Whiskey, Franklin's Whiskey House, Cairo, Illinois 320.00
Whiskey, Hilderbrandt Posner & Co., SF, Monogram, Amber 525.00
Whiskey, J.W. Kelly & Co Distillers, Chattanooga, Tenn., Square, 10 In. 25.00
Whiskey, M.P. Pollen & Zoon Aromatic Schnapps, Green, 1 Qt. Plus 65.00
Whiskey, Meredith's Diamond Club Pure Rye, Jug, Pottery, Transfer, KT&K, 7 1/8 In. . . . 55.00
Whiskey, Merry Christmas & Happy New Year, Label, Unused, Nip, 1900, Pair 90.00
Whiskey, Murdock Brand Scotch, Jug, Pottery, Cream Color, Transfer, 1910, 7 3/8 In. . . . 175.00
Whiskey, Pride Of Kentucky, Flask, 1/2 Pt. 121.00
Whiskey, Spruance Stanley & Co. Wholesale Liquor, San Francisco, Cal., Amber, Fifth . . 55.00
Whiskey, Udolpho Wolfe Aromatic Schnapps, Peach Puce, 1 Qt. 185.00
Whiskey, White Cross Aromatic Schnapps, Olive Green 65.00
Whiskey, Wise's Old Irish, Jug, Pottery, Cream Color, 1910, 7 3/8 In. 60.00
Whiskey, Wolter's Bros. & Co., San Francisco, Amber, 12 In. 660.00
Wine, Champagne, Olive Green, Blown, String Lip, Kick Up, 11 1/2 In. 75.00
Wine, Dark Olive Green, Applied Seal With Comet, Tapered Neck, Cylindrical, 13 In. . . . 170.00
Zanesville, J. Shepard & Co., Flask, Amber, Backwards, 1 Pt. 550.00

BOTTLE CAP collectors search for the printed cardboard caps used during the past 80 years. Unusual mottoes, graphics, and caps from dairies that are out of business bring the highest prices.

Breckenridge Lumber Co., Allover Yellow, Plastic, 1 1/2 In. 10.00
Easter Eggnog, Easter Bunny Picture 1.00
Milk & Juice, Variety Of Dairies, Assorted, 25 Piece 4.00
Sprite, Sprankelfris, Green Lettering, White, Green Ground, 1970, 16 In. 135.00

BOTTLE OPENERS are needed to open many bottles. As soon as the commercial bottle was invented, the opener to be used with the new types of closures became a necessity. Many types of bottle openers can be found, most dating from the twentieth century. Collectors prize advertising and comic openers.

14K Gold, Stainless Steel, Moderne, Cartier 100.00
2 Quails, Cast Iron, Hubley, 1930, 3 x 1 3/4 x 2 3/4 In. 205.00
Bat, Yankees, Ballantine Beer, 1960, 12 In. 32.00

Long-neck decanters and whiskey bottles are hard to dry. The water is often trapped in the lower part of the bottle. Roll up a paper towel and insert it into the bottle but do not let the towel touch the bottom of the glass. The towel will absorb the extra moisture and dry the inside of the bottle.

Bottle Opener,
Freddie Frosh, 4 1/4 In.

Bathing Beauty, Fresno Brewing Co., Fresno, Ca., 2 7/8 In.	38.00
Beck's Beer, Stylized Plated Steel, Germany, 3 1/2 In.	5.00
Betty Joe Carry Out	15.00
Black Caddy, Holding Tee Marker, Golf Bag, Iron, 5 3/4 In.	220.00
Black Man's Face, Large Mouth, Cast Iron, 1950s, 4 In.	125.00
Champagne, Ebonized Handle, c.1890	250.00
Chipmunk, Seven Falls On 1 Side, Cast Iron, 3 In.	108.00
Cowboy With Guitar, Wooden Head, White Cotton Hair, Bowtie, 6 In.	16.00
Dice, Bakelite Handle, Large	35.00
Dog, Scotty, Handle, White, Green Layer, 3 1/4 x 1 3/4 In.	37.00
Donkey, Cast Iron, Tan & Black Paint, 3 3/4 In.	20.00
Drink Gay-Ola, Improved Cola, Woman's Foot & Calf Shape, Steel, 3 1/8 In.	15.00
Drunk, Tuxedo, Leaning On Lamppost, Souvenir Of Weston, W. Va.	55.00
Drunk, Tuxedo, Leaning On Palm Tree, Cast Iron, Wilton	50.00
Fox Head 400 Beer, Bottle Shape, Wooden, Metal, 1950s	26.00
Freddie Frosh, 4 1/4 In. ....*Illus*	242.00
Gallagher & Burton Whiskies, Baltimore, Md., Corkscrew, Steel, 2 7/8 In.	6.00
Game Bird, Head, Cast Alloy, 3 1/2 x 4 In.	35.00
Gay-Ola, 5 Cents	7.50
Grapette, Thirsty Or Not, Enjoy Grapette	15.00
Happy Face Shape, Large	60.00
Harvard Export Beer On Sides, 3 1/4 In.	41.00
Hawaiian Woman, Kona, Pewter, 8 In.	21.00
Horse's Head, Brass	45.00
Horse's Rear, Cast Iron, 1 1/4 x 5 In.	35.00
Hotel Claridge, Memphis, Tenn., Steel, Foldout Corkscrew, 2 7/8 In.	7.00
International Breweries, Inc., Buffalo, N.Y., Findlay, Oh., Covington, Ky.	7.00
Lion Mask, Stylized, 2-Finger Pull, c.1920	80.00
Lucky Lager, San Francisco, Ca., 1930s	6.00
Mule's Head, Cast Iron, 3 1/4 x 4 In.	30.00
Old Manhattan Beer, Chicago, Ill., 1930s	3.00
Oshkosh	4.00
Parrot, On Stand, Mouth Open, Cast Iron, 2 x 5 In.	30.00
Parrot, On Stand, Mouth Open, Cast Iron, 3 x 5 1/4 In.	40.00
Pelican, Beak Down, Cast Iron, 4 x 4 In.	50.00
Salem Beer, Salem, Oh., 1940s	14.00
Schlitz Beer, 1930s, Miniature	21.00 to 22.00
St. Claire Beer, San Jose, Ca., 1930s	6.00
Starr, Falstaff Beer In Box, Gray, Red Lettering, Metal	20.00
Swordfish, Ohn Wright Co., Wrightsville, Pa., 6 In.	282.00
Waiter, Mugs, Composition, 5 1/2 In.	60.00

BOW is an English porcelain works started in 1744 in East London. Bow made decorated porcelains, often copies of Chinese blue and white patterns. The factory stopped working about 1776. Most items sold as Bow today were made after 1750.

Dish, Sweetmeat, White Shell, Alternating Concave, Convex Ribs, Oval, 1752, 7 In.	1380.00

Dish, Sweetmeat, White Shell, Various Shells Exterior, Conch-Shell Feet, 1752, 5 In. 2530.00
Figurine, Poultry Cook, Carrying A Tray Of Poultry, White Ground, 1760, 6 In. 3220.00

BOXES of all kinds are collected. They were made of thin strips of inlaid wood, metal, tortoiseshell, embroidery, or other material. Additional boxes may be listed in other sections, such as Advertising, Battersea, Ivory, Shaker, Tinware, and various Porcelain categories. Tea Caddies are listed in their own category.

Actor's, Traveling, Bayley & Blew, Wood, Leather, Mirror, Fitted, 1890, 9 x 14 x 10 In. . . .   1265.00
Ancient Sailing Scene, Incised, Painted, Hinged Lid, Wooden, Russia, 7 1/2 x 4 In. 140.00
Apple, Poplar, Old Red Repaint, 7 x 10 1/2 In. 355.00
Bakelite, Green, Hinged Lid, Applied Ends, Footed, Divided Center, Cylindrical, 7 In. . . .   605.00
Ballot, Drawer, Poplar, Dovetailed, Late 18th Century 250.00
Ballot, Old Red Paint, 8 1/2 x 16 In. 65.00
Band, Wallpaper Covered, Hardwood, White Pine Bottom, 19th Century, 3 1/2 x 7 7/8 In.   140.00
Band, Wallpaper Covered, Landscape & Figures, Castle Garden, Joel Post, 23 In. 3300.00
Band, Wallpaper Covered, Oriental Design, Dome Top, Casters, 13 1/2 x 30 In. 110.00
Band, Wallpaper Covered, Promenade, Figural Scene, 19 x 16 x 12 In. 1650.00
Band, Wallpaper Covered, Promenade, Figural Scene, 20 1/2 x 17 1/2 x 12 In. 2475.00
Bentwood, Bold Tulips, Green Leaves, Red, Green Curlicues On Sides, Oval, 3 x 10 In. . .   935.00
Bentwood, Dark Green Paint, Lapped Seams, Iron Tacks, Branded Label, 9 7/8 x 5 In. . . .   440.00
Bentwood, Finger Construction, Old Blue Paint, Round, 7 1/2 In.   330.00
Bentwood, Green Paint, Lapped Seams, Iron Tacks, 6 3/4 x 2 3/4 In. 245.00
Bentwood, Varnish, Lapped Seams, Iron Tacks, 8 5/8 x 4 1/8 In.   190.00
Bible, Oak, Chip Carved, Turned Legs, Continental, c.1740, 15 1/2 x 18 x 12 In. 935.00
Bible, Oak, Floral Carving, Forged Hasp, Lock, England, 1700s, 7 3/4 x 28 x 18 In. 805.00
Bible, Walnut, Lift Lid, 2 Drawers, William & Mary, 1750, 10 x 17 x 14 In.   4510.00
Black Japanned, Gilt, Hinged Lid, Side Handles, Early 19th Century, 11 x 16 x 12 In. . . .   1540.00
Black Paint Over Blue Stain, White Striping, Floral, Poplar, 6 x 8 x 13 In. 1100.00
Black Spot Design, Pine, Wallpaper Lined, Bail Handle, 19th Century, 16 x 8 In. 170.00
Bonbonniere, Cover, Engine Turned Sunrise, Laurel, Berry Border, Round, 1810, 3 In. . . .   1840.00
Bone, Inscribed Jane Hopkin Top, Ballymoney On Base, England, 19th Century, 3 In. 230.00
Book, Hearts, Incised Design, Pine, Carved, Painted, 19th Century, 7 x 4 x 1 1/2 In. 460.00
Book, Oak, Carved, Hinged Cover, 1920s, 6 1/2 x 9 1/2 x 3 In. 160.00
Book, Walnut, Inlay All Sides, Spine Pulls Out, 1890, 7 1/2 x 5 7/8 x 1 7/8 In. 155.00
Boulle, Inlays Of Silver, Brass & Ivory, Rectangular, 6 x 4 In. 170.00
Bride's, Figural Design, Hinged Lid, Germany, 15 x 10 In. 330.00
Bride's, Hearts, Hex Signs, Pinwheels, Maple & Pine, Chip Carved, 19th Century, 15 In. . .   3737.00
Bride's, Pine, 2 Hunters With Rifles, Polychrome Floral, Initials K.E. In Heart, 18 In. 1320.00
Brown Graining, Black Trim, Applied Molding, Poplar, 20 3/4 x 11 x 9 In. 165.00
Brown Wash, Initials H.A.B., Poplar, 13 x 9 1/4 x 5 5/8 In. 355.00
Buildings, Trees, Figures, Cover, Laced, Wooden, Oval, Scandinavia, 1800s, 9 x 20 In. . . .   977.00
Burl, Square Top, Painted, Ivory Cartouche, France, 3 1/2 x 8 x 8 In. 173.00
Burl Walnut, Brass Inlay, Continental, 9 In. 115.00
Butter, 2 Sections, Hinged Lids, Red Paint, Upright Handle, Poplar, 13 x 21 x 14 In. 275.00
Camphorwood, Brass Hardware, Chinese, 16 In., Pair 145.00
Candle, Beveled Edge, Dovetailed Case, Handle, Walnut, 10 3/4 x 8 1/2 x 5 3/8 In. 275.00
Candle, Black Stenciled Initials, J.P.F., Pine, Sliding Lid, Till 302.00
Candle, Dark Red Paint, Salmon Rose Lid, Dovetailed, Poplar, Zoar, Oh., 17 3/4 In. 357.00
Candle, Gray Paint, Sliding Lid, Pine, 5 x 5 3/4 x 11 1/4 In. 135.00
Candle, Mahogany, Beveled Slide Lid, Dovetailed Case, 19th Century, 6 x 8 x 12 In. 335.00
Candle, Sliding Lid, Red & Black Traces, Pine, 8 1/2 x 15 1/2 x 6 1/2 In. 110.00
Candle, Wall, Arched Crest, Walnut, Ohio, 13 1/2 x 7 1/4 x 10 In. 495.00
Candle, Wall, Blue Green Painted, Scalloped Crest, Poplar, 4 1/2 x 10 1/4 x 4 1/2 In. 200.00
Candle, Wall, Compass Designs, Pine & Chestnut, Carved, 12 x 8 1/2 x 15 In. 1045.00
Candle, Wall, Drawer, Pine, Dovetailed Case, 13 3/4 x 6 1/4 x 7 7/8 In. 467.00
Candle, Wall, Green, Poplar, 13 1/2 In. 440.00
Candle, Worn Red Flame Grained, Sliding Lid, Pine, 9 1/2 x 15 x 7 1/2 In. 330.00
Carved Dog Handle On Cove, Wooden R, 6 1/2 x 8 1/4 x 5 In. 635.00
Carved Grapes Front, Walnut, Gilens, 21 x 17 x 10 In. 175.00
Cherry, Dovetailed, Hinged Lid, Divided Interior, Grain Painted, 19th Century, 13 In. 4890.00
Cherry, Lid, 17 x 10 3/4 x 8 1/2 In. 385.00
Chip Carved, Maple, Early 20th Century, 4 1/2 x 11 x 6 In. 220.00

Box, Document, Multicolor Rainbow Design,
Pine, 8 x 16 x 6 1/2 In.

Box, Dome Top, Vinegar Grained, Sponged,
Label, Lucy M. Newton, Mass., 13 x 29 In.

Cigar Dispenser, Rosewood, Brass, Urn Filial, Holds 10 Cigars, Victorian, 13 In. 175.00
Cigarette, Balkan Sobranie Cigarettes Transfer, Pottery, 6 x 3 3/4 x 2 1/4 In. 60.00
Cigarette, Shagreen, Ebonized Edges, Early 20th Century, 2 3/4 x 8 1/4 x 3 3/8 In. 470.00
Cigarette, Shagreen, Green Stripes, Early 20th Century, 2 1/2 x 4 1/2 x 3 1/2 In. 360.00
Coffer, Carved Guilloche Frieze, Oak, Hinged Top, Molded Legs, England, 42 x 20 In. 990.00
Coffin, Carved 1 Block Of Wood, Slide Top, 2 7/8 x 1 1/4 In. 125.00
Collar, Traveling, Leather, England, 19th Century, 6 x 3 3/4 In. 185.00
Country Girl Gathering Mushrooms, Painted, Carved, Wooden, Russia, 4 x 6 In. 140.00
Cover, Wooden, Dovetailed, Wrought Iron End Handles, 31 1/2 x 15 1/2 x 15 In. 192.00
Crayon, Yellow, Black, Green Geometric Design, Poplar, Varnish Ground, 10 x 13 In. . . . 412.00
Curly Maple, Walnut Edge, Dovetailed, Beveled Lid, 10 3/4 x 6 x 5 1/8 In. 385.00
Cutlery, Banded, Mahogany, Hinged Lid, George III, 15 x 9 x 11 In., Pair 8050.00
Cutlery, Knife Slots On Side, Painted, Inscribed On Bottom, 1864, 15 x 10 x 7 In. 1050.00
Desk, Mahogany, Marquetry, Commode Shape, Louis XVI Style, Belle Epoque, 9 x 14 In. 605.00
Desk, Pine, Slant Lid, 19th Century, Child's, 4 x 8 1/2 x 6 1/2 In. 403.00
Document, Calamander, Hinged Lid, Paper Lined Interior, Regency, 9 1/2 x 16 x 8 In. . . . 495.00
Document, French Courtyard Scene, Dome Top, 12 1/2 x 8 3/4 x 4 1/2 In. 110.00
Document, Gold Stenciled Design, Dark Brown Grained Paint, 5 x 12 x 6 In. 190.00
Document, Multicolor Rainbow Design, Pine, 8 x 16 x 6 1/2 In. . . . .*Illus* 8250.00
Document, Oriental, Mahogany, Brass Trim, Lift Top, 19th Century, 11 x 12 In. 110.00
Document, Painted Figures In Village, Red Lacquer Ground, 25 In. 175.00
Document, Painted Flowers & Geometric, Leather Over Pine, 18th Century, 14 x 8 In. . . . 475.00
Document, Pine, Black Shagreen, Brass Fittings, 9 5/8 In. 440.00
Document, Quill, Straw Work, Dome Top, 1804 Newspaper Lined, 8 1/2 In. 120.00
Document, Rectangular, Burlwood, 19th Century, 5 x 12 1/2 In. 65.00
Document, Red & Black, Wooden, Grain Painted, Round, 17 1/2 x 10 1/2 x 8 1/2 In. 300.00
Document, Red Cherries, Green Leaves, White Border, Swags, Dome Top, 5 1/2 x 8 In. . . . 230.00
Document, Red, Yellow, Green Fruit & Leaves, Dome Top, 19th Century, 6 x 9 x 5 In. 5465.00
Dome Top, Hide Cover, Bail Handle, Newspaper Lining, 1829, 13 In. 145.00
Dome Top, Vinegar Grained, Sponged, Label, Lucy M. Newton, Mass., 13 x 29 In. . .*Illus* 8250.00
Domestic Scene, 7 Figures, Bark & Wood, England, 4 1/4 x 2 1/4 In. 115.00
Donation, Iron, Shaped Iron Strapping Sides, Continental, 18th Century, 11 3/4 x 8 In. . . . 230.00
Dresser, Cherubs & Birds, Beveled Crystal, Brass, 1950, 5 1/2 In. 60.00
Dresser, Embroidered, Silver Metallic Thread, Silk Lining, France, 1590-1640, Round . . . 3500.00
Dresser, Engraved, Heavy Gauge Brass, 7 1/2 In. 250.00
Dresser, Heart Shape, Wooden, 7 x 5 1/2 x 3 In. 550.00
Dresser, Mahogany, Inlay Lift Lid, Hepplewhite, 1800, 5 3/4 x 10 In. 2750.00
Dresser, Scene Of Prince Ivan, Painted, Hinged Lid, Russia, c.1910, 10 x 6 3/4 In. 225.00
Dresser, Serpentine Front, Mahogany, Ball Feet, Lift Lid, 19th Century, 5 3/4 x 9 In. 250.00
Dresser, Silver Metallic Thread & Silk, Salmon Silk Lining, Early 17th Century 1450.00
Dresser, Tear Shape, Smoked Glass Panels, Brass Frame, Round Lid, 5 1/4 x 8 In. 45.00
Dresser, Walnut, Late 19th Century, 6 1/2 x 18 In. 220.00
Dry Measure Set, Bentwood, Oak, E.B. Frye & Sommers, 1, 2, 4 & 8 Qt., 4 Piece 195.00
Figured Veneer, Inlay, Harlequin Banded Base, Hidden Sections, 12 x 7 x 5 In. 415.00
Fir, Floral Painted Cover, Secret Side Drawer, Ching Dynasty, 10 x 7 x 6 In. 105.00
Flint, Brass Floral Inlay, Steel Inlay, Spring Lock, 18th Century, 2 1/4 x 1 1/2 In. 335.00
Floral, Black Ground, Wooden, Tin Hasp, Lancaster, 1790, 2 1/4 x 9 1/4 In. 7700.00
Floral, Putti Designs In Relief, Stamp, Brass, 20th Century, 1 1/4 x 3 x 1 3/4 In. 287.00

Floral, Seashells, Maple, Dovetailed, Bun Feet, Painted, Signed, 3 x 10 x 6 In. 4025.00
Fruit, Yellow & Brown Graining, Canted Rectangular Shape, 17 In. 70.00
Fruitwood, Inlaid Rosewood, Leaf Scrolls, Victorian, Felt Lined, c.1880, 12 In. 316.00
Galuchat, Ivory, Cover, Jean Michael Frank, 1935, 2 In. 4600.00
General Lafayette Bust, Bird's-Eye Maple, Bronze Insert, Sept. 1757, 5 x 3 In. 290.00
Glass, Enameled Scrolls & Dots, Hinged Cover, Gilt Metal Rim, 19th Century, 5 x 4 In. ... 225.00
Glass, French Bulldog On Cover, Dome Top, France, 2 In. 1955.00
Glass, Lavender, Swirl, Egg Shape, Flashed, Hinged Cover, 6 1/2 In. 165.00
Glass, Winter Landscape, Enameled Hinged Cover, 19th Century, 3 x 2 1/4 In. 165.00
Grain Painted, Dome Top, 11 x 6 x 5 In. 295.00
Gunner's, Metal, Leather Cover, 6 Sections, 11 x 15 x 32 In. 40.00
Hardwood, Applied Silver Men Drinking, Continental, 19th Century, 5 1/4 In. 175.00
Hardwood, Repainted, Striping, Sponging, Yellow Ground, Dome Top, 11 5/8 In. 330.00
Hat, Traveling, Cunard Line Sticker, Wooden, Leather Strap, 11 x 15 In. 175.00
Hat, Wallpaper, Painted Floral Top 90.00
Hat, Wooden, Some Wallpaper Covering, Oval, 16 1/2 x 8 1/2 In. 185.00
Honor, Brass, T-Shaped Coin Slot, Ball Feet, Spring-Latch Lid, 4 1/2 x 9 x 8 3/4 In. 550.00
Horn, Cover, 18th Century, 3 1/4 In. 350.00
Horse, Dogs, Leaves, Wallpaper Interior, Rectangular Lid, Poplar, Penn., 6 In. 770.00
Hunter In Winter Forest, Incised, Painted, Hinged Lid, Wooden, Russia, 7 1/4 x 4 In. 90.00
Inlaid Scroll, Hinged Top, Paw Feet, Baroque, Walnut, Continental, 12 x 6 In. 535.00
Jewelry, 9 Paris Miniatures, Gilt Brass, Louis XVI Style, Oval, 1850-1875, 4 1/4 In. 990.00
Jewelry, Allover Needlework Figural, Leaf Panels, Hinged Top, 14 x 14 1/2 In. 635.00
Jewelry, Courting Figure Scene, Gilt, Bronze, Cover, Louis XV, 4 x 6 x 6 In. 920.00
Jewelry, Daisies & Leaves, Scrolls, Lime Green, Ormolu Handles & Feet, 4 x 5 x 3 In. ... 345.00
Jewelry, Frolicking Figure On Doors, Tooled Leather, Brass, 12 1/2 x 13 In. 1265.00
Jewelry, Geometric, Marquetry, Removable Tray, Lining, Mirrored Cover 95.00
Jewelry, Lacquered Wood, Shrine Shape, 2 Center Doors, 15 3/4 x 12 x 7 3/4 In. 145.00
Jewelry, Landscape Scenes, Micromosaic, Casket, Gilt Metal Frame, Italy, 5 x 6 In. 4830.00
Jewelry, Painted Log Cabin, Green, Red, 1930, 7 1/4 x 5 1/2 x 7 3/8 In. 175.00
Jewelry, Tortoiseshell, Ivory, Mother-Of-Pearl Lid, Anglo-Indian, 1900-1925, 6 x 3 In. ... 525.00
Jewelry, Woman Bust & Floral On 3 Sides, Bakelite, Deep Brown Black, Cover 165.00
Knife, Brass, Paw Feet, Reticulated Sides, Divider, 10 3/4 x 15 In. 770.00
Knife, Curly Maple, Walnut Bottom, 11 1/4 x 14 x 4 In. 415.00
Knife, Dovetailed, Divided, Cutout Handle, 11 x 16 In. 138.00
Knife, Eagle, Hunter, Deer, Leaves, Pine, Dovetailed, Brass Ring Handle, 4 x 5 In. 375.00
Knife, Heart Shape Cutout, Walnut, Dovetailed Drawer, 13 x 22 x 11 1/2 In. 1375.00
Knife, Mahogany Veneer, Inlay, Interior Baffles, Hepplewhite, 9 1/2 x 12 In., Pair 2310.00
Knife, Mahogany Veneer, Silver Fittings, Slant Lid Cover, Fitted Interior, Federal, 15 In. . 1095.00
Knife, Mahogany, Figured Veneer, Banded, Hepplewhite, 9 x 10 1/2 x 14 3/4 In. 1045.00
Knife, Mahogany, Urn Shape, Stand, Lift Top, England, 19th Century, 11 x 22 In., Pair ... 1570.00
Knife, Poplar, Hinged Lid, Blue Traces, Refinished, 12 In. 165.00
Knife, Scrolled Ends, Pine, Dovetailed, Divider, Handle, Early 19th Century, 11 In. 145.00
Knife, Serpentine Front, Mahogany, Brass Hardware, Continental, 16 x 15 In., Pair 1840.00
Knife, Serpentine Front, Mahogany, Fitted Interior, Georgian, 14 x 9 In., Pair 3450.00
Knife, Serpentine Front, Maple, Slant Lid Cover, Fitted Interior, Federal, 15 1/2 In. 690.00
Knife, Shell Inlay, Silver Fittings, Slant Top, Mahogany, 15 x 11 In., Pair 3740.00
Lacquer, Warrior, Hinged Lid, Russia, 1950s, 8 x 5 1/2 In. 170.00
Letter, Figured Walnut, Slant Front, Hinged Doors, Edwardian, 10 x 12 In. 195.00
Letter, Tortoiseshell & Quill, Ivory Crest On Lid, England, 4 x 10 x 5 In. 880.00
Mahogany, Dovetailed, Paw Footed, Brass Corners, 28 3/4 x 13 x 10 1/2 In. 245.00
Mahogany, Wall, Hinged Slant Lid, Open Over Pigeonholes, 1 Drawer, 18 In. 305.00
Mahogany Veneer, Hinged Lid, Fitted Drawer, Brass Ball Feet, 1820s, 8 In. 575.00
Make-Up, Elm, 2 Drawers, Folding Mirror, Ching Dynasty, 13 x 10 x 8 In. 230.00
Maple & Walnut, Bird's-Eye Maple Cover, Brass Handle, 7 1/4 x 12 x 5 In. 60.00
Metal, Rectangular, Riveted Strapwork, Includes Lock & Key, Alf Daguet, Paris, 4 In. 1265.00
Money, Girl In Basket, Peeking Out, Money Slot On Top Of Basket, 2 1/2 x 2 3/4 In. 75.00
Moon & Stars, Brown Graining, Dovetailed, Wooden, 21 1/4 x 10 3/4 x 10 1/2 In. 852.00
Musician's, Brassbound, Plaque, S. Krafft, Civil War Era, 7 x 16 x 9 1/2 In. 165.00
Old Red Paint, Black & Yellow Striping, Transfer, Wooden, Penn., 15 x 9 1/2 x 9 In. 605.00
Optic Block Pattern, Gilt, Red, Black, Wooden, Rectangular, 1800s, 6 1/2 x 13 x 11 In. . 3738.00
Orange Paint, Rose Mulling, Dome Top, Interior Till Wooden, 7 1/2 In. 865.00
Original Brown Vinegar Graining Wooden, Original Brass Handle, 6 x 8 x 14 In. 1980.00

Paint, Poplar, Red Paint, Striping & Medallion, Painted Interior, 15 1/2 x 12 x 4 In. 330.00
Painted Design, Fabric On Wood, Dome Top, Paper Lined Interior, 19 In. 415.00
Pantry, Bentwood, Wire Bail, Wooden Grip Handle, 1800s, 11 1/2 In. 110.00
Pantry, Black Daubs, Gray Ground, Dot Border, 9 x 4 In. 330.00
Pantry, Stacking, Wooden, Round, 5 To 10 In., 4 Piece 165.00
Paper, Archer & Dog, Reverse Painted Glass, Brass, 19th Century, 3 1/4 In. 215.00
Patch, Playing Cards Painted Panel, Ivory, Copper Inlay, Continental, 1 1/4 In. 550.00
Patch, Portrait Of Elegant Woman Cover, Cut Glass, Porcelain, 19th Century, 2 In. 140.00
Peasant House, Incised, Painted, Hinged Lid, Wooden, Russia, 7 1/2 x 5 1/4 In. 135.00
Peasant Woman With Cream Jar, Cow, Wooden, Russia, c.1917, 7 3/4 x 5 In. 110.00
Pencil, Jackie Coogan, Tin 40.00
Pencil, Marilyn Monroe, Vinyl, Wooden Base 80.00
Pencil, Pistol Shape, Plastic 30.00
Pencil, Titanic, Boat Picture, Empty, 1940s 15.00
Pencil, Wooden, Jack & Jill 20.00
Perfume, Rose Design, Amber Beveled Glass Panels, Pierced Brass, 12 1/2 x 3 1/2 In. 34.00
Perfume, Shalimar, Victorian 103.00
Perfume, Textured Twisted Ribbon, Beveled Smoked Glass Panels, 1950, 9 In., Pair 69.00
Pine, Red Paint, White Ground, Yellow Striping, Turned Feet, Lehnware, 7 In. 605.00
Pine, Striping, Black Ground, Dome Top, New England, 1810, 12 x 26 In. 415.00
Pipe, Applied Pinwheel On Crest, Cherry, Carved, Dovetailed Drawer, Conn., 20 In. 3850.00
Pipe, Crest With Backboard, Mahogany Finish, 1 Drawer, 17 1/2 In. 121.00
Pipe, Cutout Hearts, Pine, 1 Drawer, Compartments, Carved January 13, 1813, 17 In. 4950.00
Pipe, Lollipop Crest, Cherry, Dovetailed Drawer, Scrolled Top Edge, 18 1/2 In. 2915.00
Pipe, Mahogany, Single Drawer, Extended Backboard, Brass Knob, 22 x 4 x 5 In. 2645.00
Pipe, Pierced Heart & Diamond Design, Wooden, White Paint, 10 In. 4180.00
Pipe, Wall, Pine, Canted Sides, Pierced, 1 Drawer, American, 1800s, 18 x 6 x 5 In. 1955.00
Pipe, Walnut, Chip Carved, Scalloped Back, Sections, Secret Compartment, 21 3/4 In. ... 2610.00
Poplar, Dovetailed, Green Over Light Green, 15 3/4 x 9 3/8 x 9 1/2 In. 440.00
Poplar, Red & Black Grained Repaint, Lift Lid, Slant Top, 15 x 9 x 12 In. 605.00
Poplar, Striping, Red Paint, Black Border, Says Nell, 6 x 8 x 10 In. 605.00
Poplar, Worn Flame Graining, Dome Top, Incomplete Hasp, 10 x 22 x 9 In. 220.00
Powder, Yellow & Green Marble, Bluebird Powder Puff, Bakelite, 3 1/4 In. 230.00
Pressed Horn, Silhouette Black Man Top, Initials OP, Round, England, 3 5/8 In. 520.00
Red Line & Floral Top, Black Paint, Poplar, New York, 1820, 5 x 11 In. 250.00
Red Swags, Red & Black Cardinal, Painted, Green Ground, Wooden, 5 x 11 x 5 In. 4890.00
River Scene, Floral Design Sides, Incised, Painted, Russia, Round, 6 x 3 1/2 In. 125.00
Rosewood Veneer, Nacre Inlay, No Interior Tray, 12 1/2 x 9 1/2 x 6 3/4 In. 110.00
Rural Village, Children, Incised, Painted, Hinged Lid, Wooden, Russia, 7 1/4 x 4 In. 85.00
Seed, Walnut & Maple, Lid, Early 20th Century, 5 x 21 x 10 In. 135.00
Shirtwaist, Oak, Cedar Lined, Copper, Hammered, Lift Handles, Gustav Stickley, 16 In. . 9775.00
Slide Lid, Wooden, Signed, F.S. Newler, Gardiner, Me., 18 1/2 x 10 1/2 x 12 In. 70.00
Spice, Cherry, Slide Lid, Sections, Penn., 1800, 9 In. 1045.00
Spice, Ocher & Red Graining, Poplar, Slide Lid, Penn., 19th Century, 2 3/4 x 10 In. 990.00
Spice, Pine, Dovetailed, Dark Green Paint, 14 In. 110.00
Spice, Red, Black Graining, Pine, Slide Lid, 6-Section Interior, 4 x 8 1/4 x 11 In. 412.00
Spice, Scalloped Backboard, Cherry, 19 Drawers, Penn., 1820, 25 x 19 3/4 In. 6600.00
Spice, Tin, Black Paint, 6 Cans, Grater, 9 5/8 x 6 7/8 x 3 1/2 In. 130.00
Spice, Wall, Heart Shape Back, Pine, Slanted Lift Top, 1 Drawer, 1800s, 13 x 8 In. 489.00
Square Cover, Baroque, Walnut, Ring Handle, Italy, 4 3/8 x 6 x 5 3/4 In. 110.00
Storage, Bird In Flight, Crouching Cat Handle, Rectangular Hinged Top, 11 x 9 In. 26450.00
Storage, Birds & Flowers, Hand Painted, Laced Lap Joints, Oval, 16 1/2 x 5 3/4 In. 770.00
Storage, Compass Star Design, Pine, Dome Top, 19th Century, 9 1/2 x 34 In. 330.00
Storage, Painted Vine, Maple, Pine, Initials, Round, Early 19th Century, 6 1/4 x 14 In. .. 7475.00
Storage, Painted, Decals, Applewood, Dome Top, Penn., 19th Century, 5 x 10 x 6 In. 330.00
Storage, Pine, Grain Painted, Dome Top, Gold Trim, Brass Handle, 1800s, 6 x 12 x 6 In. . 230.00
Storage, Pine, Green Paint, Interior Sliding Panel Opens To Compartment, 18 In. 460.00
Storage, Tin, Grain Painted, Oval, 12 x 13 1/2 x 10 In. 110.00
Storage, Wallpaper Covered, Blue, Green, White Flowers, Oval, 5 x 10 x 7 In. 154.00
Storage, Wallpaper Covered, Buildings, Leaves, Animals, Blue, Hinged Lid, 1841, 16 In. . 255.00
Storage, Wallpaper Covered, Green & White Floral Design, 14 x 16 x 12 In. 1320.00
Storage, Wallpaper Covered, Leaf Print, Blue, Brown, Hinged Lid, 14 In. 60.00
Storage, Wooden, Lapped Construction, 12 In. 412.00

Strong, Steel, Brass Bound, Elaborate Mechanism Top, Continental, 6 3/4 x 4 1/4 In. 375.00
Tantalus Set, Walnut, Mother-Of-Pearl, Ormolu Tray, France, 11 x 12 In., 20 Piece 2035.00
Tea, Satinwood, Mahogany, Thomas Sheraton Style, Georgian, 5 x 8 1/4 x 4 1/4 In. 305.00
Tiger Maple & Walnut, Lift Lid, Penn., c.1860, 8 x 15 In. 605.00
Tobacco, Biblical Scenes, Brass, Oval, Dutch, 18th Century, 5 x 3 In. 860.00
Tobacco, Brass, Tin, 3 Sections, Japanned, 19th Century, 4 3/4 x 1 5/8 In. 90.00
Tobacco, City View Top, Horn, Laville De Rouen, Oval, 18th Century, 5 1/4 x 2 3/4 In. ... 750.00
Tobacco, Crossed Pipes On Reverse, Engraved Florals Panels, Side Handles, 1858, 5 In. ... 345.00
Tobacco, Domestic Scenes, Brass, Inscriptions, Dutch, Oval, 5 1/8 x 3 In. 1265.00
Tobacco, Engraved Agricultural Scene, Brass, Copper, Dutch, 18th Century, 6 1/2 In. 290.00
Tobacco, Engraved Domestic, Round, Joseph Browne, England, 1698, 3 1/2 In. 460.00
Tobacco, Engraved Man, Smoking Pipe On Cover, Tis Miyn Tabaak, 5 In. 235.00
Tobacco, Engraved Pitcher & Clay Pipes, Steel, England, 19th Century, 2 3/8 x 2 In. 260.00
Tobacco, Engraved Railroad Engine Lid, Brass, Copper, Dutch, 19th Century, 7 x 2 In. ... 290.00
Tobacco, Floral & Bird Design, Brass, England, 18th Century, 3 1/4 x 3 In. 375.00
Tobacco, Gentlemen Smoking & Drinking, Napoleon Finial, c.1790, 5 In. 300.00
Tobacco, Honor, Bell Hotel, Brass, No Key, 1816, England, 9 1/8 x 4 5/8 x 8 1/8 In. 345.00
Tobacco, Honor, Engraved Peacock, Brass, Allen Borman, England, 18th Century, 9 In. .. 980.00
Tobacco, Hunter Recoiling From Snake, Etched Brass, Oval, 18th Century, 5 3/4 In. 230.00
Tobacco, Ice Skating Scene, Horn, Oval, 18th Century, 5 1/4 x 2 7/8 In. 575.00
Tobacco, Incised Figures & Verses, Brass, Oval, Dutch Inscription, 18th Century, 5 In. ... 230.00
Tobacco, Iron, R. Prichard & Date 1772 Inside Cover, 18th Century, 4 3/4 In. 595.00
Tobacco, John Waugh Attorney At Law, Steel, Doulton, England, 18th Century, 4 x 2 In. . 315.00
Tobacco, Man In Boat, Books, Painted, 19th Century, 3 1/2 In. 110.00
Tobacco, Mother-Of-Pearl, Mahogany, Brass Border, Hinged Cover, Rectangular, 4 In. ... 115.00
Tobacco, Paktong, Engraved Design, Rectangular, England, 18th Century 195.00
Tobacco, Treen, Cherry, Mother-Of-Pearl Inlay, 4 1/2 In. 295.00
Tobacco, Wreck Of Royal George, Wooden, 1782, England, 4 3/4 x 2 3/8 In. 175.00
Toiletry, Rosewood, Cut Glass Bottles, Jars, Toothbrush Box, Hinged Lid, 6 3/4 x 12 In. . 825.00
Travel, Dressing, Walnut, Hinged Lid, Inset Oak Mirror 155.00
Twig, Slab Wood, Stencil Base, 20th Century, 21 x 12 x 18 1/2 In. 110.00
Utility, Floral Design, Oblong Octagonal Form, Hinged Lid, Ball Feet, Poplar, 5 In. 1725.00
Vanity, Floral & Scrolling Leaf Design, Mother-Of-Pearl Inlay, Chinese, 12 In. 260.00
Vanity, Velvet Lined, Fitted, Hinged Lid, Zebra Wood, Mechi, 1872, 12 x 14 In. 860.00
Village Scene, Landscape, Painted, Paper Cover, Snipe Hinges ....*Illus* 9350.00
Vinegar Grained Wood, Black Latch, Augusta, Maine, 10 x 23 x 12 In. ....*Illus* 1375.00
Wall, Grain Painted, Red & Black, Bronze Stencil, 1 Drawer, Dovetailed, 13 In. 1840.00
Wall, Shaped Back, Hangers, Yellow, Cover, American, 1800s, 8 x 13 x 5 In. 374.00
Wall, Shaped Backboard, Pine, Wire Loop Hanger, 6 x 5 x 2 1/4 In. 1495.00
Wall, Wallpaper Covered, Man & Child Interior Scene, 21 1/2 x 16 1/2 In. 495.00
Wall, Walnut, Tasseled Pendants, Vines & Leaves, Red-Brown Stain, 20 x 4 In. 1955.00
Wallpaper Covered, Blue, Brown & Red Cover, Oblong, 6 x 10 x 8 1/4 In. 135.00
Wallpaper Covered, Blue, Slide Lid, Wooden, 6 In. 145.00
Wallpaper Covered, Dark Blue, Black & Salmon, Oval, 4 In. 385.00
Wallpaper Covered, Slide Lid, Wooden, Pennsylvania, 19th Century, 5 In. 1980.00
Walnut, Dovetailed, Molded Edge Base & Lid, Wallpaper Lined, 12 x 8 x 8 In. 110.00
Walnut, Dovetailed, Sliding Lid, Fitted Interior, Iron Handle, 12 1/2 In. 357.00
Walnut, Parquetry, Hinged Lid, Italy, 1650-1700, 22 x 33 1/2 In. 2070.00
Waste, For Chewed Gum, Tin Lithograph, Cover, E. H. Lunken, 1898 .... 145.00

Box, Village Scene, Landscape, Painted,
Paper Cover, Snipe Hinges

Box, Vinegar Grained Wood, Black Latch,
Augusta, Maine, 10 x 23 x 12 In.

Watchmaker's Kit, Dovetailed Case, 238 Mainspring Packets, c.1900, 15 x 11 x 7 In. 320.00
Wedding Dress, Stand, Lacquer, Silk Lining, Oriental, 28 1/2 x 28 1/2 x 4 In. 385.00
White, Red Striping, Stencil, Black Paint, Poplar, Warren E. Utton, 5 x 9 x 11 In. 440.00
White Floral Transfer, Fitted Interior, Tin Latch, Pine, Paint, 6 1/2 In. 315.00
Work, Figured Veneer, Marquetry Inlay, Drawer Interior & Tray, 14 x 10 x 6 In. 275.00
Writing, Mahogany, Fitted Interior, Dovetailed Drawer, Bail Handles, 16 x 10 In. 385.00
Writing, Mahogany, Fitted, Old Finish, New York, 16 In. 275.00
Writing, Mahogany, Tabletop, Dovetailed Case, Tambour Top, Drawer, 16 x 10 In. 660.00
Writing, Pine, Lift Top, Slant Lid, Dovetailed, Mirror, American, 1800s, 9 x 12 x 13 In. . . 173.00
Writing, Pine, Painted, Dovetailed, Fitted Interior, Pigeon Holes, Drawers, 20 x 10 In. . . . 275.00
Writing, Walnut, Slant Top, Interior Drawer, 6 1/2 x 19 3/4 In. 412.00

BOY SCOUT collectibles include any material related to scouting, including patches, manuals, and uniforms. The Boy Scout movement in the United States started in 1910. The first Jamboree was held in 1937. Girl Scout items are listed under their own heading.

Backpack, Camping, Canvas, Olive Drab, BSA Emblem, 1940s, 20 x 17 In. 20.00
Badge, Hat, Jr. Asst. Scoutmaster, 1st Class, 3 Green Bars, Gilt Finish, 1940s, 1 In. 29.00
Badge, Kiwanis Patrol '54, 6-Pointed Star, Silver-Colored Metal, 1 1/2 In. 46.00
Badge, Patrol Leader, 1st Class, Stars Up, Silver Finish, 1910s, 1 1/2 In. 35.00
Bank, Buckle & Scarf, Cast Iron, M 47, Hubley, 1912, 5 3/4 In. 605.00
Bank, Cast Iron, M 46, Canada, 5 11/16 In. 495.00
Bank, Figural, Cast Iron, 5 7/8 In. 143.00
Book, On Motorcycles, 1912 . . . . 25.00
Bookends, BSA Emblem Shape 250.00
Bugle, Emblem, Rexcraft 75.00
Cane, Robert Baden-Powell Bust, Ivory, Handle, Hat & Uniform, 38 1/2 In. 1540.00
Cap, Air Scout, Garrison Style, Blue, World War II Era, Size Medium 42.00
Cap, Campaign, Scout Master, Band, 1930s 40.00
Cup, Folding, 50th Anniversary, National Jamboree, Colorado Springs 75.00
Handbook, For Boys, Norman Rockwell Cover, 39th Printing, 1946 . . . . 30.00
Handbook, Wolf Cub Scout, 1967 . . . . 15.00
Kit, Ancient Craft Arrowhead Flint Chip, BSA Emblem On Lid, Box, 1940s 38.00
Knife, Folding, 4 Blades, Lanyard Loop, Ulster Brand, 4 In. 22.00
Magazine, Scouting, Article On 1935 National Jamboree, July, 1935, 34 Pages 21.00
Medal, Eagle Scout, 3rd Type, Sterling Silver, 2 Sides, Blue Coffin-Style Case 90.00
Medal, Eagle Scout, Flat-Backed Eagle, Sterling Silver, Red, White & Blue Ribbon 35.00
Medal, Eagle Scout, Sterling Silver, Full Feathered Back, Era Stange Co., 1970 . . . . 40.00
Medal, Eagle, Flat Back, S Scroll, Single Knot, Sterling Silver, Robbins, 1950s-1960s . . . 40.00
Medal, Marked Eagle Across Chest, Late 1960s 45.00
Patch, National Jamboree, Washington, D.C., 1937 . . . . 85.00
Patch, Old Scout Leader Bullion Blazer, Dark Blue Velvet, Silk Embroidery 52.00
Patch, Philmont Kit Carson Treck, Light Blue Twill, Round, 1960s-1970s, 3 In. 24.00
Patch, Philmont Orienteering Federation, Square, 1973-1974, 3 In. 27.00
Patch, Philmont Scout Ranch, Cimarron, N.M., 50, Arrowhead Shape, 1988, 5 In. 60.00
Patch, Philmont Training Center, 25, Orange Twill, Round, 1974, 3 In. 20.00
Sash, Merit Badge, Eagle Scout, 24 Different Merit Badges, 1940, 6 In. 110.00
Sash, Merit Badge, Tan, Tenderfoot, 2nd & 1st Class Patches, 12 Badges, 1960 . . . . 35.00
Shirt, Brown Beaver, Yellow Twill, Red Border, Arrow Of Light Patch, 1960 . . . . 127.00
Signal Set, 1948 . . . . 30.00
Wallet, Top Grain Cowhide, Official, Box 40.00

BRADLEY & HUBBARD is a name found on many metal objects. Walter Hubbard and his brother-in-law, Nathaniel Lyman Bradley, started making cast iron clocks, tables, frames, andirons, lamps, chandeliers, sconces, and sewing birds in 1854 in Meriden, Connecticut. The company became Bradley & Hubbard Manufacturing Company in 1875. Charles Parker Company bought the firm in 1940. Their lamps are especially prized by collectors.

Andirons, Diamond Shape Finial, 21 x 10 In. 195.00
Desk Set, Cutout With Glass Underneath, Signed, 4 Piece 440.00
Desk Set, Owls, 4 Piece 575.00
Fender, Fire, Arts & Crafts, Brass 250.00

Inkwell, Arts & Crafts, 2 x 4 In. 60.00
Lamp, 10-Sided Slag Panels Shade, Garland Base, 28 1/2 In. 1725.00
Lamp, Banquet, 6 Brass Bent Scrolls, Domed Shade, 24 In. 625.00
Lamp, Banquet, Rose Ball Shade, Pierced Font, Electrified, 1880s, 32 In. 1195.00
Lamp, Bent Panel Shade, Bronze Metal Frame, 2 Sockets, 21 1/2 In. 977.00
Lamp, Boudoir, Riveted Strapwork, Slag Shade, 18 1/2 In. 1035.00
Lamp, Brass, 2-Light, 8-Panel Green Slag Floral Shade, 19 In. 245.00
Lamp, Desk, Double, Square Stepped Base, 17 1/2 In. 465.00
Lamp, Domed Shade, Slag Panels, Gilt Frame, 2 Sockets, 1930s, 22 In. 430.00
Lamp, Electric, Reverse Painted, Iris, Ice Chip Finish, 18 In. 3850.00
Lamp, Gone With The Wind, Yellow Ground, Red Rose Clusters, 30 In. .... .590.00 to 645.00
Lamp, Green, Cherry Slag Shade, Painted Metal Base, 18 x 16 In. 1840.00
Lamp, Kerosene, Gone With The Wind, Opal, Green, Large Lilies, 30 In. 700.00
Lamp, Metal, Brass Finish, Filigree White & Amber Slag Glass, 23 In. 660.00
Lamp, Organ, Floral Painted Shade, Orange, Brass Filigree Base, 34 In. 385.00
Lamp, Overlay Design, Green Border, Hanging 1210.00
Lamp, Table, Figure Of Nude, Metal Overlay, Slag Shade, 24 In. 2645.00
Lamp, Table, Ribbed Glass Shade, Water Lily Border, Olive, Tan, 21 In. 865.00
Lantern, Candle, Sheet Copper, Pierced, Applied Jewels, Stamped, 12 In. 385.00
Letter Holder, Brass, Leaves, 2 Part 47.00
Letter Rack, Brass, Pierced Scroll 415.00
Letter Stand, Iron, Fire Gilt, Lovebirds, Accessories 75.00
Sconce, Iron, Beveled Mirror, Prisms, Victorian, Marked 130.00
Sconce, Overlay, Yellow, Green Border 415.00
Stand, Smoking, Brass, 5 Accessories, 24 1/2 In. 110.00

BRASS has been used for decorative pieces and useful tablewares since ancient times. It is an alloy of copper, zinc, and other metals. Additional brass items may be found under Bell, Candlestick, Tool, or Trivet.

Bed Warmer, Copper, Engraved Bird Design, Turned Wooden Handle, 42 In. 240.00
Bed Warmer, Cover, Floral Design, Turned Wooden Handle, 11 1/2 x 33 In. 220.00
Bed Warmer, Cover, Floral Design, Turned Wooden Handle, Black Paint, 43 In. 357.00
Bed Warmer, Cover, Floral, Turned Wooden Handle, 11 1/2 x 36 In. 220.00
Bed Warmer, Embossed Lip, Salesman's Sample, 10 In. 430.00
Bed Warmer, Engraved Design, Turned Wooden Handle, 42 In. 155.00
Bed Warmer, Engraved Floral Design, Turned Wooden Handle, 19th Century, 40 In. 165.00
Bed Warmer, Etched Floral Design, Iron, 18th Century, 40 1/2 In. 121.00
Bed Warmer, Floral Design, Engraved Lid, Turned Maple Handle, 43 In. 468.00
Bed Warmer, Floral Engraved Cover, Turned Wooden Handle, 43 In. 220.00
Bed Warmer, Pierced Lid, Turned Wooden Handle, England, 19th Century 247.00
Bed Warmer, Pierced, Brass Handle, England, c.1750, 42 x 12 1/2 In. 1275.00
Bed Warmer, Pierced, Turned Wooden Handle, 42 In. 185.00
Bed Warmer, Raised Star, Pierced Design, Wooden Handle, Iron, c.1800, 51 In. 165.00
Bed Warmer, Tooled Lid, Starflower & Cross, Cast & Turned Brass Handle, 41 1/2 In. .. 525.00
Bed Warmer, Tooled Lid, Starflower, Wooden Handle, 42 In. 275.00
Bed Warmer, Tooled Sunburst Design Cover, Turned Handle, 44 In. 185.00
Bowl, Centerpiece, Glass Liner, Silvered, Hans Ofner, c.1905, 12 3/4 In. 9200.00
Bowl, Chromed, Marianne Brandt, c.1928, 13 1/4 In. 6325.00
Bowl, Hammered, Ribbed, Scalloped Rim, Flower Form, Casa Grande, Italy, 6 In. 45.00
Box, 4 Pivoting Sections, Engraved Girolamo & Initials, 19th Century, 2 1/2 In. 145.00
Box, Allover Engraved, 12 Sections, 19th Century, 6 3/4 x 2 7/8 In. 11.50
Box, Animal & Floral, Iron Mount, Lift Top, 2 Drawers, Asia, 11 x 7 1/2 x 6 1/4 In. 85.00
Box, Dome Top, Eagle, Crown Relief, England, 19th Century, 4 In. 175.00
Box, Engraved Coat Of Arms, Jacob Zeberer, England, Round, 3 3/4 In. 2300.00
Box, Hammered, Arts & Crafts, 6 x 5 In. 55.00
Box, Honor, Turned Feet, T-Shaped Slot, Engraved Design, Inscription, England, 6 In. 4620.00
Box, Middle East, 20th Century, 7 3/8 x 3 7/8 x 3 In. 30.00
Box, Steel, Slide Top, Floral Silver, Handle, Korea, 3 5/8 x 2 x 1 3/4 In. 65.00
Bridle Rosette, Horse & Carriage, White Ground, Nickel, Plastic Dome, 1 3/4 In., Pair .. 65.00
Bucket, Peat, Walnut, Brass Liner, Bail Handle, 1900, 12 x 12 In. 977.00
Bucket, Regency, Navette Form, Mahogany Peat, Bail Handle, 12 1/2 x 13 1/2 In. 920.00
Bucket, Russia, 19 x 8 3/4 In. 200.00

Calendar, Wheel, Moving To Set Month & Year, Whiz Wheel, 1931-1985 . . . . 22.00
Case, Writing, Mycock, England, Early 19th Century, 4 In. 175.00
Cauldron, 19th Century, 12 x 19 In. 100.00
Chalice, Cover, Pedestal, England, Mid 18th Century, 5 1/2 In. 225.00
Chamberstick, Handled Underplate With Center Candlestick, Rectangular, 4 3/4 In. 115.00
Chamberstick, Push-Up, Iron Thumb Piece, 4 1/2 In. 138.00
Chamberstick, Seaside Souvenir, Mother-Of-Pearl, Spiral Loop Handle, 2 1/2 In. 192.00
Charger, Adam & Eve With Serpent, Continental, 15 3/4 In. 520.00
Cigar Cutter, Pin Fire Type Pistol, Partly Nickel Plated, Wooden Grips 249.00
Cigar Cutter, Spring Loaded V-Cut, Siemens, Pocket, 1940s, 2 1/2 In. 55.00
Cigar Cutter, With Ashtray, Sword Type, Push Down 225.00
Clock, Lantern, William & Mary, Openwork Cresting & Bell, Wall Bracket, 13 In. 690.00
Coal Bin, Metal, Slant Front, Removable Interior Bin, Early 20th Century, 11 x 16 In. . . . 85.00
Coffeepot, Dovetailed Construction, c.1790, 8 1/4 In. 150.00
Cup & Saucer, Cast & Turned, England, 1760 . . . . 350.00
Curtain Ring, Gilt, Raised Beads, Victorian, Mid 19th Century, 4 In., Set Of 8 . . . . 200.00
Dish, Baroque, Nautical Allegory Center, Italy, 1900, 7 In. 172.00
Door Knocker, Sunburst Back Plate, 18th Century, 5 1/2 In. 225.00
Door Knocker, Urn, Acorn Form, Original Fastenings, 7 3/4 x 4 1/4 x 1 In. 115.00
Door Pull, 18th Century, Pair 195.00
Eagle, Open Winged, Standing On Ball, 5 Ft. Wingspan, 20 In. 1430.00
Figure, William Wallet, Jester, Standing On Ball, Tonkinson, Frame, 15 x 19 In. 345.00
Figurine, 2 Greyhounds, Dark Patina, 38 x 32 In., Pair 1100.00
Figurine, Bear In Robes, Oriental, 10 In. 80.00
Figurine, Indian, Hand On Hip, 23 1/2 In. 1210.00
Figurine, Phoenix Bird, With Oriental Accents, Black Finish, 10 In. 126.00
Frame, Amber Jewels, Pearls, Filigree, Enamel Scrolls, c.1900, 9 1/2 x 7 1/4 In. 1870.00
Girandole, Shakespearean Dressed Figure, Center Candle Sockets, 2 Arms, 17 In., Pair . . 220.00
Horse, Black Leather, Silver Buckle, Nobs & Horse Center Medallion, 7 x 3 In. 40.00
Horse, Scalloped Brown Leather Trim & Back, 4 1/4 In. 40.00
Humidor, Copper, Hammered, Arts & Crafts, Finial Top, 5 1/2 In. 77.00
Incense Burner, Heart Shape, On Trivet 45.00
Jardiniere, Hammered, Foo Lion Design, Loose Ring Handles, 15 1/2 In. 60.00
Jardiniere, Iron Wirework, Round Basket, Tole Insert, Continental, 12 x 10 In., Pair 2990.00
Jardiniere, Louis XVI, Kingwood, Tulipwood, Gilt, Brass Pendants, Toupie Feet, 7 In. . . . 1092.00
Jardiniere, Molded Leaf Design, Lion Mask & Ring Handles, 3 Paw Feet, 15 x 16 In. . . . 460.00
Jardiniere, Neoclassical, Mahogany, Diagonal Ebony, Boxwood Inlay, 30 1/2 In. 2300.00
Jardiniere, Regency, Galvanized Liner, Lion Mask Handles, 8 1/2 x 9 In. 488.00
Jug, Ale, Early 19th Century, 8 In. 150.00
Kettle, Domed Top, Riveted Brass Handle, England, 19th Century 425.00
Kettle, Spun, Iron Bail Handle, Hayden's Patent Label, 24 1/2 x 18 In. 190.00
Kettle, Wrought Iron Handle, Tulip Form Support, 1800, 10 3/4 In. 355.00
Ladle, Round Bowl Riveted To Handle, Impressed Richard Lee, American, 11 In. 518.00
Lock, Key, Adams Express Company, San Francisco 220.00
Map Case, 19th Century, Large 95.00
Martingale, Leather, 2 Hearts, Oval Medallion, Sleigh Bell, 1870, 40 In. 84.00
Mold, For Pewter Spoon, 18th Century, Pair 330.00
Obelisk, Incised Hieroglyphics, Square Base, 21 In., Pair 488.00
Padlock, Good Luck, Horseshoe Shape, Barnes Mfg. Co., 1879, 1 1/4 In. 40.00
Padlock, Lever Style, Key, Romer & Co., Newark, N.J., 19th Century 49.50
Padlock, Steel Loop, Dial Face On Bottom, United Inventors, Niagara Falls, N.Y. 26.00
Padlock, U.S. Bureau Of Indian Affairs, With Key, 3 In. 85.00
Pail, Jelly, Iron Bail, Rattailed End, 8 x 12 In. 60.00
Pail, Market, Dovetailed, Woman's Name & 1766, France, 18th Century 495.00
Pail, Wrought Iron Handle, Mid 19th Century, 13 In. 85.00
Pepper Castor, Baluster, England, 18th Century, 4 In. 395.00
Pitcher, Water, Hammered, Vase Form, Looped Handle, Arts & Crafts, 10 x 8 3/4 In. 125.00
Placecard Holder, Filigree, Jeweled, Austria, Set Of 12 . . . . 195.00
Plate, Painted American Ship Portrait, 14 In. 825.00
Plinth, Rococo Style, Molded Flower & Leaves Design, 4 Scrolled Feet, 14 3/4 In. 115.00
Pot, Hot Water, Turned Wooden Handle, 6 1/2 In. 77.00
Pot, Wrought Handle, Signed, Hiram W. Hayden, 1851, 9 1/2 x 6 1/2 In. 80.00
Samovar, Domed Cover, Cockerel, Standing On 2 Claw Feet, Ivory Handles, 25 In. 8625.00

Samovar, Treen Handles, Spout Finial, Tile Stand, 21 In.	150.00
Samovar & Tray, 16 1/2 In.	88.00
Shade, Lamp, Conical, Iris, Pierced, Hammered, Newcomb College, c.1905, 3 1/2 In., Pr.	140.00
Shelf, Kettle, Round, Sliding Shelf, Wrought Iron Hood, 7 1/2 In.	85.00
Spill Holder, Man, Taking Snuff, Other Man Taking Chew, 4 3/8 In., Pair	80.00
Spill Holder, Seamed Construction, 18th Century	195.00
Tazza, Hammered, Triangular, Bronze Eagle Supports, Art Deco, Kayser, 13 In. . . . .200.00 to	358.00
Teapot, Christopher Dresser, Scotland	950.00
Teapot, Engraved Floral Design, Scroll Handle, Tapered Body, 20th Century, 8 3/8 In.	165.00
Teapot, Secessionist, Impressed Design, Rattan Handle, Stand, Austria, 14 x 8 1/2 In.	110.00
Tobacco Jar, Cover, Finial, Bun Feet, England, c.1850, 7 3/4 x 4 In.	750.00
Tobacco Jar, Cover, Heavy Cast, England, c.1850, 4 1/2 x 2 3/4 x 5 1/4 In.	650.00
Tobacco Jar, Lead Press, Heavy Cast, England, c.1800, 3 1/4 x 2 3/4 x 6 In.	750.00
Tray, Edwardian, Mahogany, Low Brassbound Gallery, 1900, 1 3/4 x 17 In.	230.00
Umbrella Stand, Lion Mask & Ring Form Handles, 3 Paw Feet, 24 3/4 In.	345.00
Umbrella Stand, Scenic Repousse, Lion Handles, Paw Feet, Ovoid, 26 1/4 In.	192.00
Urn, Baluster Form, Flared Rim, Josef Hoffman, 1925, 6 1/4 In., Pair	1380.00
Urn, Molded Flower & Leaf Band, Square Base On 4 Round Knobs, 8 5/8 In., Pair	145.00
Vase, Copper Patina, 2 Handles, WMF, 11 x 6 In.	193.00
Vase, Embossed Scarab, Benedict, 3 1/2 In.	40.00
Vase, Hand Tooled, Copper Wash, Arts & Crafts, Green Enameled, 11 In.	110.00
Violin, Miniature, Bow, Black Leatherette Fitted Case, 5 In.	22.00
Watch Holder, Rooster, Wooden Brass Banded Base, c.1840	750.00
Wick Trimmers, Scissors, Scrolled Edge, 9 1/2 In.	193.00

BRASTOFF, see Sascha Brastoff category.

BREAD PLATE, see various silver categories, porcelain factories, and pressed glass patterns.

BRIDE'S BASKETS OR BRIDE'S BOWLS were usually one-of-a-kind novelties made in American and European glass factories. They were especially popular about 1880 when the decorated basket was often given as a wedding gift. Cut glass baskets were popular after 1890. All bride's baskets lost favor about 1905. Bride's baskets and bride's bowls may also be found in other glass sections. Check the index at the back of the book.

BRIDE'S BASKET, Cased, Rust, Yellow, Clear Ruffled Edge, Hobbs Brokunier Style, 9 In.	100.00
Cream, Blue & Red Ruffled Edge	275.00
Dancing Figures On Sides, Grape Vines Handle, Silver Plate, 1930s, 20 In.	138.00
Lavender, Ruffled Edge, Twist Handle, Flowers, 9 In.	175.00
Peachblow, Rose, White Opaque, Silver Plated Holder, Handle, 10 x 13 In.	840.00
BRIDE'S BOWL, Blue Overlay, Enameled White Flowers, Ormolu Holder, 8 1/4 In.	325.00
Cased, Tomato Red Interior, Lemon Yellow Exterior, Drape, 3 1/2 x 10 3/4 In.	110.00
Enameled Flowers & Leaves, Clear & Opaque Ruffled Edge, 9 3/4 In.	210.00
Mother-Of-Pearl, Pink, Herringbone, 9 1/2 x 5 In.	605.00
Pink Satin, Enameled Flowers, Shell Shape, Replated Stand, 10 1/2 In.	295.00
Satin Blue Over White, Gold Enameled Florals, Ruffled Edge, 10 In.	275.00

BRISTOL glass was made in Bristol, England, after the 1700s. The Bristol glass most often seen today is a Victorian, lightweight opaque glass that is often blue. Some of the glass was decorated with enamels.

Dish, Multicolored Floral Spray, Enameled Gold & Roundel, Dentil Edge, 10 In.	865.00
Honey Jar, Enameled Floral, Custard Ground, Brass Cover, Flop Handle, 5 In., Pair	70.00
Lamp, Light Blue, Enameled Floral, Kerosene Burner, H. Hinks & Sons, 16 1/4 In.	115.00
Lamp, Oil, Modeled Bronze Base, Registry On Font, Electrified, 36 In.	247.00
Lamp, Urn Shape, Round Stepped Base, White & Pink Flowers, Leaves, 16 In., Pair	395.00
Plate, Chinoiserie Figural Landscape, Mac-Cookworthy & Champion, 1800, 8 1/2 In.	121.00
Vase, Blue, White Enameled	70.00
Vase, Enameled Florals, Pink Ground, White Lining, Footed, 10 1/2 In.	55.00
Vase, Enameled Flowers, Cobalt Blue, White, 8 In.	75.00
Vase, Enameled, Birds In Moonlit Sky, 12 In., Pair	287.00
Vase, Victorian, Enameled Gold Floral & Leaf Sprays, 19th Century, 11 1/4 In., Pair	143.00

BRITANNIA, see Pewter category.

BRONZE is an alloy of copper, tin, and other metals. It is used to make
figurines, lamps, and other decorative objects. Bronze lamps are listed
in the Lamp category. Pieces listed here date from the eighteenth, nineteenth, and twentieth centuries.

Aquarium, Girl With Geese On A Stone, Honking Goose At Other End, Frame, 21 In. . . .	6325.00
Ashtray, 2 Polychromed Parrots Perched Over Round Ashtray, Onyx, 3 x 5 In.	143.00
Basket, Butterfly, Blue Opaline Glass Liner	165.00
Bowl, Basket Form, Crab, Cicada Relief, 3 Lotus Legs, Meiji Period, 5 1/2 In.	385.00
Bowl, Gurschner, Gustave, 2 Handles Each Side, Flattened, 1900, 6 In.	1610.00
Bowl, High Relief Of Rats, Signed, Meiji Period, 5 x 9 In.	687.00
Bowl, Phoenix In Branches, Japan, 11 In.	175.00
Bowl, Reticulated Side, Floral Band, 3 Claw Feet, 8 In.	660.00
Box, Trinket, Nude Woman Snake Charmer, Kneeling, Polychrome Rug, 6 1/2 x 6 In.	1320.00
Box, Turtle, Box On Back, Calligraphy, Dragons, Chinese, Early 20th Century, 5 1/2 In. . . .	145.00
Bust, Ajax, Black Patinated, Parcel Gilt, Italy, 16 1/8 In.	990.00
Bust, Apel, Marie, Woman, Reddish Brown Patina, 18 1/4 In.	315.00
Bust, Athena, Wearing Full Regalia, Tapered Socle, 19th Century, 15 In.	805.00
Bust, Baker, B., Jane W. Hobbs, Marble Base, 1923, 16 x 9 1/2 In.	373.00
Bust, Bofill, A., Sommeil De La Jeunesse, 14 In.	880.00
Bust, Carrier-Belleuse, A., Beethoven, Stamped Tiffany & Co., France, 8 1/2 In.	392.00
Bust, Diana, After Houdon, Stepped Black Marble Plinth, France, 19th Century, 24 In. . . .	550.00
Bust, Egaze, Emile, Male Elf, Pointed Ears, Beard, Signed, Bronze Sockle, 1880, 15 In. . . .	1955.00
Bust, Falguiere, Jean Alexandre Joseph, Diana, Brown Patina, Marble Base, 23 In.	4310.00
Bust, Fromme, Hans, Lord Byron, Marble Base, 15 1/4 In.	755.00
Bust, Gale, L., Chief Sitting Bull, c.1968, 20 x 8 In.	345.00
Bust, Lamertine, Leaning Head On Hand, France	110.00
Bust, Mengin, Paul, Femme, Ivory Cutout, Yellow Gold Patina, France, 7 3/4 In.	1380.00
Bust, Muller, H., Abraham Lincoln, Marble Socle, Rubbed Dark Brown Patina, 20 In. . . .	6900.00
Bust, Nock, Leo, Gentleman, Dark Brown Patina, Signed, 1919, 22 In.	952.00
Bust, Rimbez, Z., Bust Of Egyptian Maiden, Square Plinth, 22 1/4 In.	3450.00
Bust, Rolle, Pensive Maiden With Flowers In Hair, Signed, 1900, 23 x 11 In.	1150.00
Bust, Taverna, F.P. De, Fisherman, Brown Patina, Signed, 4 x 8 In.	130.00
Cachepot, Carrier-Belleuse, A., Bacchanal Scenes, High Relief, 12 1/2 x 11 3/4 In.	6900.00
Candlestand, Mythological Figures, Gilt, Cylindrical, Crown Top, 31 1/2 In.	935.00
Candlestand, Votive, Paste Stones, Gilt, 19th Century, 5 In., Pair	56.00
Casket, Gilt, Oval, Mirrored Lid, Paris Monuments On Ivory, Napoleon III, 6 In.	1210.00
Centerpiece, Cherub Heads Sides, Goat Head Handles, Neoclassical, Gilt, 12 1/2 In.	977.00
Compote, Brass Liner, Garland, Bust Design, Twisted Handles, Fluted Pedestal, 4 1/2 In. .	66.00
Desk Set, Gornik, Freidrich, Pen Tray, Inkwell, Letter Opener, Pheasant Design, 3 Piece .	880.00
Desk Set, Lanceray, Evgeni, G., Barnyard Geese Form, Marble Base, 1912, 5 Piece	6900.00
Desk Tray, Barclay, McClelland, Open Leaf, Mushrooms & Frog, 9 1/4 In.	248.00
Ewer, Nymph Hauling Net With Fish, Cast Tree Handle, Gilt, 1890, 16 1/2 In.	6325.00
Ewer, Relief Allegorical Figures, Brass, Onyx Base, 30 1/2 In.	575.00
Flagon, Ale, Chinoiserie Handle, France, 17th Century, 10 1/4 In.	850.00
Flower Holder, Jewett, Maude Sherwood, 2 Dancers, Brown Patina, 1924, 10 1/2 In.	5225.00
Garniture, Empire, Gilt & Silvered Bronze, Clock, Woman, Slate Base, 3 Piece	5750.00
Garniture, Gilt Bronze, Champleve, Clock, Arabesques, c.1900, 3 Piece	3450.00
Garniture, Gilt Bronze, Champleve, Clock, Candelabra, 22 3/4 In., 3 Piece	13800.00
Garniture, Hand-Painted Courting Scene, Dolphin Mounts, c.1920, 25 In., 3 Piece	400.00
Garniture, Urn Shape, Fruit Finials, Swag Handles, Onyx Base, France, 20 In.	410.00
Incense Burner, Urn Shape, Molded Hunt Scene, Monkeys On Tree, Japan, 22 In.	520.00
Ink Blotter, Bull Terrier Walking By Tree Stump, Early To Mid 20th Century, 5 In.	290.00
Koro, Bird & Duck, 2 Mask Handles, Foo Dog Finial, Japan, 23 In.	345.00
Koro, Birds, Dragons & Peacocks, Mask & Claw Legs, 19 In.	1095.00
Koro, Horse & Sea Animals, 3 Mask & Claw Legs, Japan, 15 In.	405.00
Mirror, Nude Woman Frame, Torso Forms Handle, Art Nouveau, Oval, 11 In.	305.00
Model, Arc De Triomphe, Black Marble Plinth, France, 8150-1875, 6 1/4 In.	550.00
Model, Napoleon's Column, Black Marble Plinth, France, 1850-1875, 10 3/4 In.	715.00
Mortar, Molded Rim & Base, Satyr Handles, Bell Form, 1772, 17 In.	920.00
Pin Tray, Center Sculpture, Art Deco, Signed E.H.T.	125.00

Plaque, Bardedienne, Frieze, Classical Figures, Late 19th Century, 7 1/2 x 28 In. 2090.00
Plaque, Carurro, E., Horse Race, 1941 . . . . 2090.00
Plaque, Chapu, Henri Michel, La Pensee, Gilt, Green Marble Back & Base, 27 In. 7475.00
Plaque, Classical, Baccantes Leading Silenus Disguised As Goat, 1910, 9 x 14 In. 440.00
Plaque, Napoleon & Josephine, Easel Support, 19th Century, 12 In., Pair 1035.00
Plaque, Satyr & Nymph, Wild Bacchic Dance, France, 19th Century, 7 1/4 x 15 3/4 In. . . . 495.00
Sculpture, 2 Boys Playing Piggy Back, Victorian Clothes, Ivory Plinth, 2 In. 290.00
Sculpture, 2 Classical Maidens Reading Letter, After J.L. Gregoire, Patinated, 19 In. 4620.00
Sculpture, Acteon, Nude Hunter Holding Pheasant, After A. Gaudez, c.1970, 45 In. 1150.00
Sculpture, Anthonisen, George, Creation, Man Pulling Woman Up, Marble Base, 25 In. . . . 1380.00
Sculpture, Anyz, Franta, Rearing Horse, Red Marble Plinth, 16 x 17 1/2 In. 1540.00
Sculpture, Archer, Onyx Base, 20 3/4 In. 260.00
Sculpture, Athlete, Brown Patina, Marble Plinth, Schmidt Hotel, Germany, 16 In. 504.00
Sculpture, Avalokitesvara, Standing, Stepped Headdress, Southeast Asia, 21 1/2 In. 290.00
Sculpture, Baizelin, Eugene Antoine, Woman, Partially Clad, Red Marble Base, 29 In. . . . 3450.00
Sculpture, Barbedienne, F.B., 2 Wrestling Bears, Octagonal Base, 8 1/2 In. 11500.00
Sculpture, Barbedienne, F.B., Senegal Elephant, Number 676/44, 5 1/2 In. 10925.00
Sculpture, Barrias, Louis-Ernest, Fame, Turquoise Jewels, Onyx Plinth, 33 1/2 In. 9200.00
Sculpture, Barrias, Louis-Ernest, Woman, Standing, Nature Revealing Herself, 23 In. 26450.00
Sculpture, Barye, Antoine Louis, Bull, Dark Brown & Golden Patina, 11 3/4 In. 3450.00
Sculpture, Barye, Antoine Louis, Panther Attacking Elk, Dark Brown Patina, 16 In. 5175.00
Sculpture, Barye, E., Alsatian, Seated, Golden Brown Patina, Marble Base, 4 x 5 In. 490.00
Sculpture, Bassin, Libellule, Dragonfly Girl, 21 In. 260.00
Sculpture, Bergman, Franz, Arabs, On Oriental Rug, Lamp, Monogram Base, 8 In. 1540.00
Sculpture, Bergman, Franz, Kangaroo, Monogram On Tail, 7 1/2 In. 935.00
Sculpture, Beschutz, Frog, Playing Golf, 19th Century, 7 1/2 In. 925.00
Sculpture, Bitter, Carl, Nude Woman & Deer, Sitting On Marble Base, 29 In. 3450.00
Sculpture, Blackamoor, Plumed Headdress, Polished, Polychrome, 55 In., Pair 3025.00
Sculpture, Blackamoor, With Walking Stick, Marked, 9 1/2 In. 880.00
Sculpture, Bologna, G., Winged Mercury, Foot On Child, Putti, Marble Base, 29 1/2 In. . . 385.00
Sculpture, Boucher, Alfred, Farm Girl Leaning On Pitchfork, 17 1/4 In. 920.00
Sculpture, Bouraine, Marcel, Nude Woman Holding Tray, Gilt, 19 1/4 In. 4600.00
Sculpture, Bouraine, Marcel, Penthesilia, Queen Of The Amazons, 31 In. 5750.00
Sculpture, Boy Holding Fishing Pole, Dangling Fish, Lava Rock Base, 30 In. 2300.00
Sculpture, Bright, Clayton, Cow, 1984, 5 x 13 In. 1320.00
Sculpture, Carrier-Belleuse, A.E., Woman, Fruit Basket On Head, 24 1/2 In., Pair 5750.00
Sculpture, Carrier-Belleuse, Albert Ernest, Festival Bound, 22 In. 2530.00
Sculpture, Cartier, Thomas-Francois, 2 Lions Fighting On Rockery, 13 3/4 x 20 1/2 In. . . 545.00
Sculpture, Cartier, Thomas-Francois, Pointer On The Scent, 12 1/4 x 25 1/2 In. 1495.00
Sculpture, Charpentier, J., 2 Wrestlers, Naked Figures Raised On Rocky Base, 25 In. 9775.00
Sculpture, Chronos, Black Patina, Marble Plinth, France, 19th Century, 13 In. 1925.00
Sculpture, Clara, Juan, Baby In Walker, Arms Outstretched, Stamped, 9 1/2 In. 1210.00
Sculpture, Clara, Juan, Little Girl, Seated, 2 Cats, Signed, 11 3/4 In. 373.00
Sculpture, Clark, Allan, Woman Holding Vase, Black Plinth, 8 5/8 In. 575.00
Sculpture, Clark, J.L., Bear Fighting Buffalo, c.1928, 16 In. 360.00
Sculpture, Clark, James L., Elk, Dark Brown Patina, 16 1/4 In. 7475.00
Sculpture, Clodion, C., Nude, Running, Scarf, Art Nouveau, Marble Base, 13 In. 100.00
Sculpture, Dancer, Art Deco, Painted, 11 In. 200.00
Sculpture, Dancing Satyr, Patinated, Sienna Marble Base, Italy, 1825-1850, 13 In. 660.00
Sculpture, Davis, Mare & Foal, 9 x 11 In. 546.00
Sculpture, De Longa, Girl With Parasol, Brown Patina, 26 In. 825.00
Sculpture, Debut, Jean Didier, La Moisson, Rubbed Dark Brown Patina, 30 In. 8050.00
Sculpture, Delabrierre, Paul Edouard, Sandpiper With Frog, 8 3/8 x 9 3/8 In. 1495.00
Sculpture, Descamps, Joseph, Naughty Dutch Girl, Ducks Around Bottom, 13 In. 1495.00
Sculpture, Devolterra, S.M., Roman Warrior On Horse, Marble Base, 19 1/2 In. 1045.00
Sculpture, Diana, After H. Muller, Green Patina, Marble Base, 12 1/4 In. 330.00
Sculpture, Dog, Irish Setter, Forest Green Enamel, Black-Hawk Foundry, 15 In. 280.00
Sculpture, Dubois, Paul, Charity, Greenish Brown Patina, 18 3/4 In. 3740.00
Sculpture, Eischer, Fisherman & Mermaid, Black Slate Base, 17 1/2 In. 1100.00
Sculpture, Elephant, Japan, 8 In. 260.00
Sculpture, Fayral, Dancer, Art Deco, 15 In. 375.00
Sculpture, Foch, B., American Indian Warrior, Charging Horse, Marble Base, 19 In. 1320.00

Sculpture, Fournier, Standing Woman Nude, Black Patina, Marble Plinth, 15 1/2 In. 475.00
Sculpture, Fraser, End Of The Trail, 14 In. 200.00
Sculpture, Fredericks, Marshall M., African Woman With Child, 22 In. 3750.00
Sculpture, Fredericks, Marshall M., Asian Woman With Deity, 25 In. 4255.00
Sculpture, Fredericks, Marshall M., Eagle, 44 x 63 In. 35000.00
Sculpture, Fredericks, Marshall M., Grouse, 28 1/2 In. 15000.00
Sculpture, Fredericks, Marshall M., Hawk, 30 In. 15000.00
Sculpture, Fredericks, Marshall M., Neck Shot, Polo Player On Horse, 1932, 15 In. 10925.00
Sculpture, Fredericks, Marshall M., Woman With Planet, Black Marble Base, 16 In. 7480.00
Sculpture, Fremiet, Emmanuel, Credo, Barbidienne Foundry Mark, 15 In. 920.00
Sculpture, Fremiet, Emmanuel, Roman Charioteer, 1870s, 16 1/2 In. 2990.00
Sculpture, Fremiet, Emmanuel, Standing Hound, Brown & Black Patina, 9 1/4 In. 2760.00
Sculpture, Gaudez, A., Le Belluaire, 1880s, 18 5/16 In. 2750.00
Sculpture, Gerome, Jean Leon, Caesar Franchissant Le Rubicon, 1900, 15 1/2 In. 7475.00
Sculpture, Goetz, Johannes, The Young Athlete, Signed, 10 x 14 In. 784.00
Sculpture, Gornik, Freidrich, 2 Camels, 1 With Rider, Marble Base, 12 x 7 x 12 In. 880.00
Sculpture, Gory, A., Dancer, Bent Leg, Gilt, Italy, 26 In. 9775.00
Sculpture, Gregoire, Jean Louis, Young Mozart, Dark Brown Patina, 28 In. 6325.00
Sculpture, Gustatson, Dancing Nude, Brown Patina, Signed, 1914, 22 In. 2600.00
Sculpture, Hagenauer, W., Giraffe, Prancing, Black Finish, Austria, 7 5/8 In. 345.00
Sculpture, Hancz, E., Troika, Black Patina, Signed, 18 x 11 1/4 In. 2375.00
Sculpture, Hart, Jonathan Scott, Joy Of Life, Rubbed Dark Brown Patina, 1910, 17 In. ... 6900.00
Sculpture, Hebe, Holding Ewer, Patinated, Continental, Late 19th Century, 25 In. 1210.00
Sculpture, Hegenbarth, Ernst, Eternal Woman, 1908, 14 1/2 In. 1320.00
Sculpture, Holand, C., Shield Of Medusa, Marble Pedestal, 18 In. 690.00
Sculpture, Hubert, Raphael, Young Shepherd, Medium Brown, Marble Base, 13 In. 575.00
Sculpture, Huntington, Anna Vaughn Hyatt, Reaching Jaguar, 6 1/2 In. 3105.00
Sculpture, Jacquemart, Henri Alfred, Seated Dog & Turtle, Golden Patina, 6 x 7 In. 2035.00
Sculpture, Janson, C.H., Dancer, Seminude Woman, 20th Century, 26 In. 1695.00
Sculpture, Jeannest, L., Bacchante Riding Goat, Hair Set With Grape Leaves, 16 In. 2875.00
Sculpture, Kauba, Carl, Bison, Dark Brown Patina, 10 3/4 x 16 7/8 In. 3165.00
Sculpture, Kauba, Carl, Indian Chief On Horse With Tomahawk, Cold Painted, 17 In. ... 2185.00
Sculpture, Kauba, Carl, St. George & Dragon, Marble Base, 15 In. 5750.00
Sculpture, Kelly, James Edward, Gentleman Saddling Horse, 1907, 21 In. 5750.00
Sculpture, Knight, Charles Robert, Recumbent Lioness, Rubbed Patina, 1911, 24 In. 4025.00
Sculpture, Kowlaczewski, P., Man, Tooth Necklace, Loin Cloth, Leggings, Spear, 21 In. . 660.00
Sculpture, Kraider, Erik, Lion, Sitting On Hind Legs, Marked, 49 1/2 In., Pair 5462.00
Sculpture, Lambert-Rucki, J., Mounted On Iron Stand, 8 3/8 In. 7475.00
Sculpture, Lanceray, Yevgeny-Alex, Bear Hunt With Cossacks, 12 x 24 In. 2310.00
Sculpture, Lanceray, Yevgeny-Alex, Charging Cossack, Foundry Mark, 11 x 15 In. 1495.00
Sculpture, Lanceray, Yevgeny-Alex, Cossack & Pack Mules, 8 x 8 1/2 In. 1900.00
Sculpture, Lanceray, Yevgeny-Alex, Cossack Rider, Foundry Seal, 10 x 10 1/2 In. 1035.00
Sculpture, Lanceray, Yevgeny-Alex, Troika, Sled, 3 Figures, 19th Century, 12 In. 3160.00
Sculpture, Larche, R., Young Warrior With Sword, 14 In. 605.00
Sculpture, Lechesne, Auguste, Pheasants, Brown Patina, 21 3/4 In. 3735.00
Sculpture, Leonard, Lambert Alexandre, Spaniel With Pheasant, 9 1/4 x 13 In. 2645.00
Sculpture, Lieberich, Nicholas, Samoyed Driving Team Of 4 Reindeer, 36 1/2 In. 9200.00
Sculpture, Lorenzl, Dancer, Ivory Head & Hands, Art Deco, Green Onyx Base, 13 In. ... 2200.00
Sculpture, Loucguenelf, P., Grizzly Bear, 6 x 8 In. 175.00
Sculpture, Lugerth, Ferdinand, The Gladiator, Signed, Austria, 11 1/2 In. 420.00
Sculpture, Madrassi, Luca, Lovers, Rubbed Dark Brown Patina, 28 1/2 In. 4600.00
Sculpture, Maenad & Young Bacchus, Gilt, Continental, 19th Century, 11 1/2 In. 635.00
Sculpture, Malissard, George, Military Officer, Horseback, Marble Base, 1927, 22 In. ... 1725.00
Sculpture, Matscheko, Nude Woman, Seated, Green Marble Plinth, Continental, 11 In. ... 546.00
Sculpture, Mene, Pierre Jules, Dog, Greyhound, Light Brown Patina, 9 In. 805.00
Sculpture, Mene, Pierre Jules, Nanny Goat, 8 1/2 In. 805.00
Sculpture, Mene, Pierre Jules, Valet De Chasse, Marble Base, 28 In. 1840.00
Sculpture, Mene, Pierre, Dog, Whippet & Ball, Brown & Black Patina, 6 x 7 In. 862.00
Sculpture, Mercie, A., David, Foot On Goliath's Head, Patinated, 29 3/4 In. 3520.00
Sculpture, Merculiano, Giacomo, 2 German Shepherds, Black Patina, 13 In. 2070.00
Sculpture, Mercury, Paul, Nude, Sitting On Rocky Ledge, Patinated, 17 x 15 In. 1320.00
Sculpture, Mercury, Paul, Seated God With Pan Pipe, Tree Stump, Marble Base, 23 In. .. 1265.00

Sculpture, Mignon, L., Lady Godiva, On Horse, Marble Plinth, 19th Century, 20 3/4 In. . . . 2990.00
Sculpture, Millet, Bull, Standing, 6 x 11 In. 850.00
Sculpture, Miner, Green Marble Round Base, 12 In. 990.00
Sculpture, Moigniez, Jules, 2 Fighting Sparrows, Brown Patina, 5 1/4 x 8 3/4 In. 750.00
Sculpture, Moigniez, Jules, Eagle, Brown Patina, Marble Base, 31 In. 1495.00
Sculpture, Moigniez, Jules, Golden Pheasant & Salamander, 20 x 10 3/4 In. 2300.00
Sculpture, Moigniez, Jules, Heron, Black, Golden Patina, 19 1/2 In. 5460.00
Sculpture, Moigniez, Jules, Mare, Saddle, Marble Base, 14 x 14 In. 200.00
Sculpture, Moigniez, Jules, Partridges & Their Young, Brown Patina, 15 x 14 In. 1725.00
Sculpture, Moigniez, Jules, Wild Boar Attacked By Hounds, 13 x 21 In. 2640.00
Sculpture, Montagne, Pierre, Marius, Cherub Seated On Log, Holding Pan Flute, 24 In. . . . 2640.00
Sculpture, Moreau, Mathurin, Woman, Allegorical, Butterfly On Hand, 43 1/2 In. 7475.00
Sculpture, Moret, Woman Nude, Sword, Marble Plinth, France, 7 In. 112.00
Sculpture, Nakian, Rueben, Leda & Swan, Signed & Dated 1963, 13 x 16 1/2 In. 3737.00
Sculpture, Ober, A., Cossack, On Rearing Horse, Marble Base, 1875, 15 3/4 In. 5175.00
Sculpture, Omerth, G., Girl Feeding Chickens, Marble Base, Signed, 8 1/4 In. 325.00
Sculpture, Paillet, Charles, Lion, Dark Patina, 1880, 6 In. 880.00
Sculpture, Paris, Roland, Serenade, Man Serenading Woman, Ivory Base, 12 In. 3680.00
Sculpture, Parsons, Edith, Dog, Chasing His Tail, 4 1/4 In. 345.00
Sculpture, Parzinger, H., Nude Man, Brown & Green Patina, Germany, 19 1/4 In. 952.00
Sculpture, Pautrot, Ferdinand, Pointer & Partridge, Brown Patina, 12 In. 3165.00
Sculpture, Pautrot, Ferdinand, Quail Feeding Its Young, Paris, 1869, 12 1/2 In. 1840.00
Sculpture, Pautrot, Ferdinand, Sparrows & Insects, Gilt Patina, 6 x 9 In. 1095.00
Sculpture, Peiffer, Putto, 22 In. 3737.00
Sculpture, Pernot, Henri, Boy Atop Bell, 1903, 15 1/4 In. 980.00
Sculpture, Perseus, Slaying Lion With Spear, 1930, 2 Piece 1265.00
Sculpture, Perseus, With Head Of Medusa, Patinated, Marble Base, 1875-1900, 20 In. . . . 2090.00
Sculpture, Pflug, O., Dog, Foxhound, Marble Base, 6 1/2 In. 495.00
Sculpture, Pigalle, Putto Beside Bird, 1870s, 18 3/4 In. 7475.00
Sculpture, Pilet, Leon, Violinist, 12 In. 460.00
Sculpture, Pinedo, Arabe En Marche, Middle Eastern Soldier, Red Patina, 25 In. 3735.00
Sculpture, Powers, Preston, Native American Hunter & Buffalo, 1893, 18 In. 4600.00
Sculpture, Pozene, Peasant, 2 Bullocks Pulling Cart, Ducks, 19th Century, 20 In. 10350.00
Sculpture, Quan Yin, Seated In Wheel Of Law Position, Silver Inlaid, 7 In. 1155.00
Sculpture, Reclining Girl, Bird, Art Deco, Green Marble Base, c.1900, 6 x 14 1/2 In. 250.00
Sculpture, Remington, Frederic, Horse Thief, Dark Brown Patina, 27 x 28 In. 690.00
Sculpture, Remington, Frederic, Man In Fringed Buckskins With Weapons, 29 In. 195.00
Sculpture, Rona, Lilly, Young Girl, 16 1/4 In. 247.00
Sculpture, Rose, Adam, Reclining Bison, Brown Patina, Marble Base, Signed, 15 x 9 In. . 1650.00
Sculpture, Rude, Francois, Education Of Achilles By Centaur Chiron, 18 x 17 1/2 In. 4025.00
Sculpture, Salmson, Jean Jules, Pandora, Seated On Broken Column, 22 In. 2990.00
Sculpture, Sanford, Dog, Greyhound, Patinated, 1913, 5 1/2 x 9 In. 495.00
Sculpture, Schaffert, Butcher, Marble Base, 9 In. 460.00
Sculpture, Schmidt, N., Grecian Woman Standing, Scale, Marble Base, 14 In. 525.00
Sculpture, Schmidt-Felling, Warrior On Horseback, 24 x 17 In. 2090.00
Sculpture, Schmidtcassel, G., Woman Balancing On Right Toe, Left Leg Bent, 14 In. 5462.00
Sculpture, Schwatenberg, Amazon Warrior, Brown Patina, Marble Plinth, 12 3/4 In. 330.00
Sculpture, Schwatenberg, Archer, Greenish Brown Patina, 9 5/8 In. 405.00
Sculpture, Seated Man, Art Deco Style, c.1930.14 1/2 In. 1265.00
Sculpture, Sheba, Thailand, 24 3/4 In. 155.00
Sculpture, Simon, Bernard, Women Torsos, Wooden Base, 26 In. 1035.00
Sculpture, Simone, E., Recumbent Hound, Brown Patina, 16 x 7 3/4 In. 1150.00
Sculpture, Siva Nataraja, India, 11 1/2 In. 170.00
Sculpture, Somme, Theophile, Harem Dancer, Ivory, Stepped Marble, 1895, 10 In. 2760.00
Sculpture, Stag, Austria, Forelegs On Marble Base, Cold Painted, 11 In. 935.00
Sculpture, Steiner, Clement-Leopold, Temptation, Reddish Brown Patina, 25 1/2 In. 2875.00
Sculpture, Steiner, Nude Man, Rising From Sea, Gilt, Rubbed Patina, 41 In. 6325.00
Sculpture, Tereszczuk, P., 2 Young Girls Riding Sled, Black Marble Base, 4 3/4 In. 440.00
Sculpture, Tereszczuk, P., Pierrot & Woman, Dancing, Ivory, Lamp Mounted, 14 In. 1840.00
Sculpture, Tereszczuk, P., Woman, Wearing Large Shawl, 1895, 6 In. 1955.00
Sculpture, Tharel, Leon, Boy, Resting, With Violin, 12 In. 150.00
Sculpture, Thomas, E., Fisherboy With Salamander, Brown, Green Patina, 14 1/2 In. 977.00

Sculpture, Troubetzkoy, Paul, Portrait Of A Lady, 1915, 16 1/2 In. 5175.00
Sculpture, Valton, Dog Straining On Chain, 23 1/2 In. 1430.00
Sculpture, Vanetti, A., Picador On Horse, Attacking Bull, Brown Patina, 28 In. 2585.00
Sculpture, Vidal, Louis, Lion Walking, Dated 1874, 14 1/2 x 27 In. 2415.00
Sculpture, Vienna, Lion, Crouched, Worn Paint, 9 1/2 In. 330.00
Sculpture, Vienna, Lizard, 19th Century, 7 In. 195.00
Sculpture, Vienna, Tortoise & Hare, Tan Agate Base, Plaque, 4 1/4 x 8 1/4 In. 1430.00
Sculpture, Wolff, A.M., Camel & Man, Red & Brown Marble Base, 6 3/4 In. 550.00
Sculpture, Young Shepherd With Sheep, France, 19th Century, 7 1/2 x 9 In. 415.00
Sculpture, Zocchi, Arnaldo, Christopher Columbus, Marble Vase, 16 1/4 In. 1380.00
Tazza, Barbedienne, F., Floral & Leaf Open Handles, Caryatid Classical Head, 10 In. 980.00
Tazza, Bird's Heads, Yellow Marble Base, Scrolling Loop Handles, 12 1/2 In., Pair 1955.00
Tazza, Black Marble, Snake Handles, Napoleon III, Gilt, Square Pedestal, 12 In., Pair ... 1320.00
Tazza, Cheuret, Albert, 2 Branches Of Cherries, 2 Branches Of Small Blossoms, 16 In. 287.00
Tazza, Diamond & Linear Design, Cut Glass Dish, Gilt, Pedestal, Continental, 13 In. 1610.00
Tazza, Kneeling Putto, Cut Glass Bowl, Black Glass Plinth, Gilt, Empire, 8 1/4 In. 605.00
Tazza, Toilette Of Venus In Temple, Patinated, Gilt, Renaissance Style, Oval, 21 x 12 In. . 1980.00
Tray, Putti In Garden, Gilt Border, Porcelain, Handle, 5 x 8 In. 275.00
Tray, Sorensen, Carl, Gilt Berry & Leaf Handles, 14 1/4 In. 58.00
Tureen, Cover, Lion's Heads, Patinated, Gilt, Reeded, Applied Ribbon, 14 x 24 In., Pair .. 2860.00
Urn, Barbedienne, F., Classical Scenes, Masks, Late 19th Century, 22 In., Pair 4312.00
Urn, Barbedienne, F., Continuous Figural Frieze, Scrolled Handles, Gilt, 16 In., Pair 2875.00
Urn, Berry Laurel, Round Foot, Cylindrical Marble Plinth, 7 3/8 In., Pair 490.00
Urn, Campana Form, Bearded Men Masks Handles, Empire, Gilt, Footed, 20 3/4 In. 690.00
Urn, Centaurs, Bacchic Celebration Patinated, Marble Pedestal, 9 In. 360.00
Urn, Domed Lid, Cast Bulrushes, Louis XVI, Gilt, Oval, Square Base, 18 In., Pair 2875.00
Urn, Grape & Vine Bands, Star & Floral Onyx Base, 9 In., Pair 200.00
Urn, Lid, Children With Turtle Medallion, Napoleon III, Dore, Eagle, 11 In., Pair 863.00
Urn, Pegasus & Bellerophon, Marble Socle, Tripod Base, 20th Century, 18 In., Pair 22185.00
Urn, Phoenix Opposed By Scrolling Dragon, Lappet Borders, Scrolled Handles, 21 In. ... 345.00
Urn, Picard, Putto Holding Swan, Classical Scenes, Gilt & Silvered, 14 1/2 In. 1650.00
Urn, Putti, Floral Garland, Ring Handles, Lion Heads, Baluster Shape, 30 7/8 In. 1380.00
Urn, Regency, Onyx Plinth, Handles, Lamp Mounted, 19th Century, 17 In., Pair 2070.00
Vase, 6-Lobed Panels, Galvanized Liner, Dark Brown Patina, 12 1/2 In. 517.00
Vase, Applied Dragon Design, Japan, 19th Century, 9 1/2 In. 176.00
Vase, Archaistic Hu Form, Animal Handles, 22 In. 80.00
Vase, Band With Panther Design, Neoclassical, Stepped Marble Base, 22 In., Pair 1725.00
Vase, Bigot, A., Gilt Bronze Ribbon Tied With 2 Large Bows, Dark Blue, 13 1/2 In. 2585.00
Vase, Bird On Flowering Prunus Tree, Japan, 11 1/2 In. 488.00
Vase, Cock On Branch, Copper & Mixed Metal Inlay, Signed, 6 In. 185.00
Vase, Embossed Turtle, Cranes, Asia, 10 1/2 x 13 1/2 In. 660.00
Vase, Flowering Branches, Birds, Patinated, Mixed Metal, Band, Japan, Meiji, 17 In. 4840.00
Vase, Fruiting Vines On Round Base, Gilt, Art Nouveau, 13 1/2 x 7 In. 2070.00
Vase, Gurschner, Sack, Stylized Leaf Tips, Hammered, Black Patina, 2 Handles, 7 In. 3795.00
Vase, Iris, Gilt, Early 20th Century, 10 1/4 In. 517.00
Vase, Profile Of Bird Of Paradise, Meiji Period, 6 In., Pair 230.00
Vase, Raised Bird On Tree, Molded Peacock-Shaped Loop Handles, Japan, 10 In. 86.00
Vase, Sorenson, Carl, Arts & Crafts, Green Patina, Flared, Footed, 6 3/4 In. 165.00
Vase, Sorenson, Carl, Flared, Verdigris Patina Bands, Interior, Impressed Mark, 7 In. 110.00
Vase, Vibert, A., Tulip Bulb With 3 Blooms, Floriform, Gilt, Signed, France, 9 In. 517.00
Wine Container, Cherub Mask, Leaf-Cast Handle, Patinated, Oval, 5 1/4 x 8 1/2 In. 360.00

BROWNIES were first drawn in 1883 by Palmer Cox. They are charac-
terized by large round eyes, downturned mouths, and skinny legs.
Toys, books, dinnerware, and other objects were made with the
Brownies as part of the design.

Brownie Blocks, Lithographed Paper, Palmer Cox, Box, 1891 .... 1200.00
Doll Set, Different, Names Stitched On Back, Palmer Cox, 1892, 8 In., 12 Piece 760.00
Game, Ring Toss, Wood & Paper Lithograph 525.00
Game, Ten Pin, Paper On Wooden Figures, 2 Mallets, 3 Balls, Box, Palmer Cox 1892 ... 1150.00
Trade Card, Dixon's Stove Polish, Brownies On Stove, 1888, 3 1/2 x 5 In. 55.00
Trade Card, Sea Island Coffee, Brownies Tobogganing, 1890s, 5 1/2 x 3 1/2 In. 40.00

BRUSH Pottery was started in 1925. George Brush first worked in 1901 in Zanesville, Ohio. He started his own pottery in 1907, but it burned to the ground soon after. In 1909 he became manager of the J.W. McCoy Pottery. In 1911, Brush and J.W. McCoy formed the Brush-McCoy Pottery Co. After a series of name changes, the company became The Brush Pottery in 1925. It closed in 1982. Collectors favor the figural cookie jars made by this company. Because there was a company named Brush-McCoy, there is great confusion between Brush and Nelson McCoy pieces. See McCoy category for more information.

MARK

Bowl, Onyx, 2 x 6 In.	55.00
Cookie Jar, Covered Wagon	700.00
Cookie Jar, Elephant With Ice Cream Cone	100.00
Cookie Jar, Hillbilly Frog	3700.00
Cookie Jar, Humpty Dumpty, Cowboy Hat	275.00
Cookie Jar, Laughing Hippo	725.00
Cookie Jar, Peter Pumpkin Eater	375.00
Cookie Jar, Sitting Hippo	400.00
Garden Dish, Stagecoach, 12 In.	95.00
Umbrella Stand, Old Ivory, 20 In.	1400.00
Urn, Onyx, 6 In.	85.00
Vase, Pastelware, Pink Flowers, Green Ground, 4 In.	1540.00

BRUSH MCCOY, see Brush category and related pieces in McCoy category.

BUCK ROGERS was the first American science fiction comic strip. It started in 1929 and continued until 1965. Buck has also appeared in comic books, movies, and, in the 1980s, a television series. Any memorabilia connected with the character Buck Rogers is collectible.

Comic Strip, Buck Rogers, Murphy Anderson, September 5, 1958, 4 1/2 x 15 In.	195.00
Crayon Ship, 1930s	125.00
Figure, Lead Casting, 1930, 3 Figures	16.00
Gun, Atomic Disintegrator, 1936, Box	1705.00
Gun, Atomic Disintegrator, Hubley	650.00
Gun, Disintegrator, Daisy, Copper Plated, Black Details, Sparks	395.00
Helmet, Space, Cloth	350.00
Helmet Mask, Sip's Ice Cream, 1940s, 8 x 9 In.	8.00
Jacket, Worn By Gil Gerard	920.00
Kite, Paper, 1950s	125.00

BUFFALO POTTERY was made in Buffalo, New York, after 1902. The company was established by the Larkin Company, famous manufacturers of soap. The wares are marked with a picture of a buffalo and the date of manufacture. Deldare ware is the most famous pottery made at the factory. It has either a khaki-colored or green background with hand painted transfer designs.

BUFFALO POTTERY, Bowl, Sauce, Willow, 4 3/4 In.	30.00
Bowl, Vegetable, Willow, Oval, 8 1/2 In.	130.00
Bowl, Willow, 1911, 9 1/4 In.	145.00
Bowl, Willow, 4 3/4 In.	24.00
Bread Plate, Willow, 6 3/8 In.	29.00
Casserole, Willow, Cover	50.00
Cup, Willow	80.00
Cup & Saucer, Willow	90.00
Cup & Saucer, Willow, 1916	72.00
Gravy Boat, Willow	240.00
Gravy Boat, Willow, 1911	227.00
Nappy, Willow, 4 3/8 In.	38.00
Pitcher, Blue & White Marine Scene, Lighthouse, 1907, 9 In.	275.00
Pitcher, Melon Shape, Gold At Handle, Panels, 1909, 8 3/4 In.	660.00
Pitcher, Roosevelt Bears, 10 In.	2145.00
Pitcher, Washington, Several Poses, Mount Vernon, c.1906, 7 In.	605.00
Plate, Christmas, 1956	35.00
Plate, Roycroft, Dinner	220.00

Plate, Willow, 3 1/2 In.	9.00
Plate, Willow, 4 1/2 In.	9.00
Plate, Willow, 7 In.	35.00
Plate, Willow, 9 1/4 In.	40.00
Plate, Willow, 10 1/4 In.	100.00
Plate, Willow, 1917, 8 3/8 In.	35.00
Platter, Willow, 1909, 9 5/8 In.	100.00
Platter, Willow, Oval, 10 3/4 In.	150.00
Platter, Willow, Oval, 16 3/8 In.	265.00
Salt & Pepper, Stylized Green & Brown Geometric Design, Roycroft, 3 In.	394.00
Soup, Coupe, Willow, 7 3/4 In.	60.00
Sugar, Cover, Willow	140.00
Sugar, Cover, Willow, 1907	140.00
Teapot, Cover, Willow, 4 In.	50.00
Tureen, Cover, Willow	415.00
BUFFALO POTTERY DELDARE, Bowl, Fruit, Ye Village Tavern, 1924	300.00
Bowl, Nut, Ye Lion Inn, Interior Tavern Scene, Green Glaze, 8 In.	880.00
Chop Plate, Fallowfield Hunt, The Start, Signed, 14 In.	522.00
Compote, Dard Hunter Geometric, Footed, Orb & Cross, Emerald, 9 In.	1430.00
Cup & Saucer, Ye Lion Inn, 6 In.	75.00
Eggcup, Street Scenes, Emerald, 3 3/4 x 2 In.	1230.00
Humidor, Ye Lion Inn, 7 In.	385.00
Mug, At The Three Pigeons, Dogs At Doorway, 4 In.	110.00 to 225.00
Mug, Dr. Syntax, With The Dairy Maid, Emerald, 3 1/2 In.	525.00
Mustard, Scenes Of Village Life In Ye Olden Days, Signed, 3 In.	1870.00
Pitcher, Dr. Syntax Bound To Tree By Highwaymen, Emerald, 8 In.	1950.00
Pitcher, Ye English Village, 8 Sides, 1908, 10 In.	995.00
Plaque, Landing, Group Of Mallards, Green Border, Signed, 12 In.	3300.00
Plate, Fallowfield Hunt, The Start, 9 1/4 In.	110.00 to 350.00
Plate, Ye Olden Times, 9 1/4 In.	250.00
Plate, Ye Village Gossips, 10 In.	100.00
Platter, Dr. Syntax Advertisement For A Wife, c.1909, 14 1/8 In.	415.00
Platter, Monk, Pair	3000.00
Punch Cup, Fallowfield Hunt, 1909, 2 1/4 In.	154.00
Stein, At Three Pigeons, Seattle Hotel, E. Dowman	1100.00
Tankard, Dr. Syntax, To Becky's Hand, Gave Squeeze, Emerald, 12 In.	1650.00
Teapot, Scenes Of Village Life In Ye Olden Days, Signed, 4 3/4 In.	395.00
Tile, Breaking Cover, Dog To Forefront, 6 In	220.00
Tray, Heirlooms, Women Modeling Jewelry, Signed, 13 1/2 In.	660.00

BUNNYKINS, see Royal Doulton category.

BURMESE GLASS was developed by Frederick Shirley at the Mt. Washington Glass Works in New Bedford, Massachusetts, in 1885. It is a two-toned glass, shading from peach to yellow. Some pieces have a pattern mold design. A few Burmese pieces were decorated with pictures or applied glass flowers of colored Burmese glass. Other factories made similar glass also called *Burmese*. Related items may be listed in the Fenton category, the Gunderson category and under Webb Burmese.

Bowl, Diamond-Quilted, Glossy, Footed, 6 In.	1500.00
Bowl, Ivy, Rolled Edge, 3 In.	225.00
Cruet, Yellow Body, Mushroom Stopper, 7 In.	1250.00
Cup, Applied Yellow Handle, Satin, 2 3/4 x 2 1/2 In.	265.00
Cup & Saucer, Paper Label	585.00
Ewer, Dragon & Floral, Handle, 10 3/4 In.	125.00
Finger Bowl, Octagonal, Fluted, 6 In.	280.00
Pitcher, Water, Applied Handle, 9 1/2 In.	180.00
Rose Bowl, Acorn, 2 1/2 In.	275.00
Rose Bowl, Violet, 2 1/2 In.	275.00 to 325.00
Rose Bowl, World's Fair, 1893, 3 1/2 In.	125.00
Salt & Pepper, Ribbed Pillar, Geometric, Silver Plated Holder, 4 In.	475.00
Sherbet, Footed, 4 In.	200.00

Vase, Acorn, Glossy, 3 In. 550.00
Vase, Bird & Floral, Handle, 4 3/4 In. 200.00
Vase, Bud, Floral Design, Gold & Enamel, Hand Painted, Bulbous, 8 In. 248.00
Vase, Floral & Bird, 5 1/2 In. 140.00
Vase, Floral, Crimped Edge, Glossy, 4 In. 275.00
Vase, Floral, Square Top, 3 1/4 In. 350.00
Vase, Ivy & Yellow Floral, 2 Handles, 3 In. 275.00
Vase, Stick Form, Trailing White, Pink, Yellow Roses, White Dot Border, 10 In. 575.00
Vase, Trumpet Form, Raised Round Foot, Brass Stand, 14 1/2 In. 345.00
Vase, Violet, Pedestal, Crimped, 4 In. 450.00

BUSTER BROWN, the comic strip, first appeared in color in 1902. Buster and his dog, Tige, remained a popular comic and soon became even more famous as the emblem for a shoe company, a textile firm, and others. The strip was discontinued in 1920, but some of the advertising is still in use.

Bank, Buster & Tige, Cast Iron, 5 1/2 In. 550.00
Bank, Buster Brown & Good Luck Horseshoe, Black, Cast Iron, Arcade, 4 In. 510.00
Bank, Buster Brown & Tige, Cast Iron, A.C. Williams, 1910-1932, 5 1/2 In. 440.00
Bank, Horseshoe, Good Luck, Cast Iron, 4 1/4 In. 363.00
Bill Hook, Picture Of Boy & Dog, Celluloid 27.00
Comic Strip, Color, Full Page, R.F. Outcault, 1909 .... 85.00
Cup & Saucer 65.00
Display, Kids In Pond, Frog & Fish, Mechanical 695.00
Doll, Rolly Dolly, Papier-Mache, Schoenhut, 10 In. 590.00
Doll, Stuffed, Advertising Shoes, 1910, 14 In. 95.00
Figurine, Buster Brown Standing Next To Tige, Red Scarf, Cast Iron, 5 1/2 In. 365.00
Mannequin, Girl, Buster Brown On Base, Store 145.00
Mirror, Buster Brown Winking, Tige Grinning, Round, Pocket, 1 3/4 In. 187.00
Plaque, Fold-Out, Authorized Dealer, Pulpboard, Counter Display, 14 In. 130.00
Playing Cards, Complete, 1906 .... 45.00
Postcard, Advertising, Cartoon, 1950s 3.00

BUTTER CHIPS, or butter pats, were small individual dishes for butter. They were the height of fashion from 1880 to 1910. Earlier as well as later examples are known.

Billingsley Rose, Spode, 1926, 3 3/4 In. 15.00
Blue, White, Scalloped Edge, John Maddock & Sons, 3 x 5/8 In. 10.00
Chicago, Rock Island & Pacific Railroad, Richard Lukin, 3 1/2 In. 160.00
Dan & Louie's Oyster Bar, Tan, Light Green 19.00
Floral Wreath Design, Flow Blue, Gold Highlights, Scalloped Edge 26.00
Flowers, Hand Painted, Royal Worcester, 3 1/4 In. 37.00
Flowers, Scrolls, Diamond Outer Edge, Blue Transfer, Grindley, 3 1/4 In. 10.00
Pansy, Majolica, 3 In. 114.00
Regina, Delft, Holland, 3 In. 7.00
Santa Fe Railroad, Red, Black, Ivory Body, Atchison, Topeka, 1959, 3 3/8 In. 102.00
Savoy, Johnson Bros. 77.00
Shenango China, 1940, 3 1/2 In. 7.00
St. Louis & San Francisco Railroad 25.00
Tiny Pink Flowers, Green Leaves, Theodore Haviland 22.00
U.S. Army Medical Dept., Shenango China, 1941 .... 28.00
Union Pacific, Winged Streamliner, Sterling China, East Liverpool, Ohio 13.00
Waldorf, New Wharf Pottery, England 62.00

BUTTER MOLDS are listed in the Kitchen category under Mold, Butter.

BUTTON collecting has been popular since the nineteenth century. Buttons have been known throughout the centuries, and there are millions of styles. Gold, silver, or precious stones were used for the best buttons, but most were made of natural materials, like bone or shell, or from inexpensive metals. Only a few types are listed for comparison.

Brass, Mother-Of-Pearl, Czechoslovakia, 11 Piece 20.00
Enamel & Gilt, Blue Enamel, White Stripes, 1/2 In., 6 Piece 55.00
Glass, Card, 7 Piece 10.00

Glass, Millefiori, Cut Blue To White Windows, John Gooderham, Canada 65.00
Jet, Rhinestone, Doll Size, Czechoslovakia, 14 Piece 20.00
Lady Washington Pearls, Doctor & Nurse Picture, On Card, 3 Piece 4.00
Paperweight, 6 Piece 26.00
Plastic, Bows, Red, On Original Card, Washable, 3/4 In. 5.00
Rhinestone, Black Plastic Rim, B. Blumenthal & Co., New York, Card, 3/8 In., 4 Piece . . 8.00
Stamped Metal, Silvered Finish, Bulldog, Avery, Farm Tractors, 3/4 In. 24.00
Sterling Silver, Various Raised Designs, Hand Made, Mexico, 6 Piece 50.00

BUTTONHOOKS have been a popular collectible in England for many
years but only recently have gained the attention of American collectors. The buttonhooks were made to help fasten the many buttons of
the old-fashioned high-button shoes and other items of apparel.

Sterling Silver, Glove 18.00
Sterling Silver, Glove, Retractable, Unger Bros., 3 In. 125.00
Sterling Silver, Shoehorn Set, Lady's, 2 Piece 75.00
Sterling Silver, Woman's, Retractable, Unger Bros., 3 In. 150.00

BYBEE POTTERY was started in 1845 and is still working. The Lexington, Kentucky, firm makes pottery that is sold at the factory. Pieces are
marked with the name or with the name enclosed by the outline of the
state of Kentucky.

Baker, Pink Spatter, 12 3/4 In. 27.00
Bowl, Burgundy, 10 1/2 In. 18.00
Candleholder, Green 15.00
Pitcher, Blue, Handle, 6 In. 37.00
Pitcher, Blue, Handle, 7 1/4 In. 45.00
Vase, Green Matte Glaze, Stoneware, Gold Foil Label, 3 3/4 In. 5.00
Vase, Reed Design, Mauve, Beige Ground, Bulbous, 6 1/2 In. 275.00
Vase, Ribbed Neck, Blue Microcrystalline Glaze, Bulbous, 5 In. 88.00

CALENDARS made to hang on the wall or to be displayed on a desk top
have been popular since the last quarter of the nineteenth century.
Many were printed with advertising as part of the artwork and were
given away as premiums. Calendars with guns, gunpowder, or Coca-
Cola advertising are most prized.

1883, Peerless Tobacco Works, Rochester, N.Y., Folding Trade Card 40.00
1888, Graves Cornstarch, Glued On Label, Full Pad, Cardboard 28.00
1892, Lau & Beck, Wine Merchant, Gypsies Playing Instruments, 18 x 15 In. 175.00
1897, X-Salia, 3 Pictures Of Actresses, 15 x 11 In. 230.00
1899, Youth Companion, 5-Fold, Young Women, 10 3/4 x 22 In. 50.00
1901, Quaker Oats, Fortune Telling 148.00
1903, Grand Union Tea Company, Mounted Under Plexiglas, 13 x 29 In. 605.00
1904, Deep Rock Spring Co., Oswego, N.Y., Celluloid Cover 10.00
1904, Roessle Brewery, Factory Picture 127.00
1907, Bristol Steel Fishing Rods, Outdoor Camping Scene, Frame 4950.00
1907, Henry Heeren, Farm Machinery, Full Pad, Frame, 11 1/2 x 5 3/4 In. 88.00
1907, Scherling Bros., Little Girl Talking To Doll, Cardboard, 17 x 10 1/2 In. 272.00
1909, Goodrich Tires, Arab With Camel, Palm Trees, Ink Blotter, 4 x 6 1/2 In. 55.00
1909, Pepsi-Cola, Woman, Dark Green Dress, Brown Ground, 10 x 19 In. 2530.00
1910, Osborne Harvesting, Frame With Glass, 15 1/2 In. 440.00
1910, Wm. Eichberg Fine Footwear, Die Cut, Full Pad, Frame, 7 3/4 x 14 In. 99.00
1910, York Gazette, Puppies, Mice & Kittens 22.00
1912, H. Clarke & Sons, Girl In Pink Dress, 35 x 24 1/2 In. 325.00
1912, Interboro Beer, 13 x 15 In. 75.00
1913, Household Family Magazine & Story Paper, Yard Long 880.00
1913, Selby Loads, Edward Wilson Currier, December Only, 27 1/2 x 21 In. 4455.00
1914, Red Goose Shoes, Cardboard, 20 In. 88.00
1915, Prudential Insurance, Lovely Woman, Warde Traver, 11 1/4 x 7 1/4 In. 45.00
1916, Little Girl, Standing Next To Flowers, Sailboat Ground, Geo. Weiss 395.00
1916, Winchester, Phillip R. Goodwin Aft 1750.00
1917, Hercules Powders, Frame With Glass, 33 1/2 In. 300.00
1917, Pabst Extract, Frame, 25 x 33 In. 230.00

1917, Prudential Insurance, Lovely Woman, Haskell Coffin, 11 1/4 x 7 1/4 In. 45.00
1918, Banca F. Pitocchelli, Massachusetts Merchant, Pretty Woman, 15 1/2 In. 110.00
1919, Edison Mazda, Spirit Of The Night, Maxfield Parrish, Small 2145.00
1919, Hercules Powders, Matte, Frame, 28 1/2 In. 385.00
1921, Edison Mazda, Primitive Man, Maxfield Parrish, 21 1/2 x 11 1/4 In. 965.00
1922, Edison Mazda, Egypt, Maxfield Parrish, 8 1/2 x 18 1/2 In. 4510.00
1924, Edison Mazda, Venetian Lamplighter, Maxfield Parrish, 18 x 7 3/8 In. 1265.00
1925, Dodge, Prince Agib, Maxfield Parrish, 8 x 6 In. 155.00
1926, Edison Mazda, Enchantment, Maxfield Parrish, Pocket, 3 3/4 x 2 1/4 In. 220.00
1927, Dodge, Circe's Palace, Friendship, Maxfield Parrish, Box, 5 1/4 x 4 In. 155.00
1927, Helf Hardware, Lithograph Cardboard, 16 In. 38.00
1929, Edison Mazda, Golden Hours, Maxfield Parrish, 19 x 8 1/2 In. 770.00
1929, Sacony Gasoline, Land-Water-Air, Partial Pad, 13 1/4 x 26 1/2 In. 465.00
1930, Edison Mazda, Ecstasy, Maxfield Parrish, Pocket, 3 3/4 x 2 1/4 In. 230.00
1931, Edison Mazda, Waterfall, Maxfield Parrish, 38 1/2 x 18 1/2 In. 2530.00
1931, Kansas City Coal Co., Aluminum Plate, 4 x 5 In. 20.00
1933, Edison Mazda, Sunrise, Maxfield Parrish, 8 1/2 x 19 1/8 In. 770.00
1934, Magnolia Trail, Mobil, 22 In. 165.00
1935, Nehi, Girl In Yellow Dress, Rolf Armstrong Artwork, 11 1/2 x 24 In. 575.00
1937, Phillip R. Goodwin, Mother Bear & Cubs, 16 x 20 In. 275.00
1937, Ulster Fuel Oil, Heat & Power Co., 7 1/2 x 15 In. 140.00
1938, Lucky Strike Green Pack, Pinup Girl, Bradford Crandell, 11 x 14 In. ....8.00 to 18.00
1940, 2 Women By Table Drinking Dr Pepper, 15 x 31 In. 1936.00
1941, Drink Dr Pepper, Woman In Yellow Vest, Frame, 11 1/2 x 24 In. 847.00
1942, Thy Templed Hills, Maxfield Parrish, 9 x 7 In. 90.00
1943, Woman, Blond Hair, Holding Turquoise Bag, 13 1/2 x 24 In. 1694.00
1944, Drink Dr Pepper, Woman Wearing Hat, 8 In. 385.00
1945, Drink Dr Pepper, Woman With White Star, 8 In. 220.00
1945, Essex Rubber Company, The American Way, Norman Rockwell 125.00
1946, Girls In Compromising Positions, 9 1/2 x 7 1/2 In. 86.00
1947, Drink Dr Pepper, Woman Wearing White Fur Muff, 8 In. 522.00
1947, Esquire Girl, 12 Different Pinups, 12 x 9 In. 75.00
1947, Esso Dealer, Old Man Holding Globe Out For Young Boy, 16 x 9 3/4 In. 35.00
1949, Douglas MacArthur Portrait, 25 5/8 x 16 In. 25.00
1949, Jones Auto Supply, Maid In Baltimore, Earl Moran, 16 x 39 1/2 In. 55.00
1950, Drink Dr Pepper, Woman In Center Holding Dr Pepper, 7 3/4 x 8 In. 275.00
1951, Esquire Girl, Pinup, 12 Luscious Lovelies, 4 1/4 x 3 1/4 In. 59.00
1951, Franklin Pure Milk Company, Wall Type, Full Year 10.00
1952, Gay Products Co, Grace Type Pinup Picture, If It's Gay, Its O.K. 10.00
1953, Drink Dr Pepper, Woman In Center, 6 1/2 x 7 In. 412.00
1954, Drink Dr Pepper, 10, 2 & 4, 9 1/2 In. 275.00
1957, Dr Pepper, Woman In Center Dancing, 7 x 7 1/2 In. 412.00
1966, Texaco, Railroad Insignia, 17 1/4 x 31 1/2 In. 175.00
1967, Horlacher Brewing 50.00
1969, Playboy, Pictures Girls Each Month, Spiral Bound, Envelope 25.00
1977, Canton Market, Chinese Girl, San Francisco, Ca., 11 x 17 In., 6 Pages 22.00
1983, Lugall Corporation, Different Girl & Hoist Each Page, 16 x 12 In. 16.00
1987, John F. Kennedy Medical Center, Family Pictures, Chicago, Ill. 10.00

CALENDAR PLATES were very popular in the United States from 1906
to 1929. Since then, plates have been made every year. A calendar and
the name of a store, a picture of flowers, a girl, or a scene were featured on the plate.

1908, European Country Estate Center, Monthly Calendars At Rim, 9 In. 45.00
1909, Border Scenes, Monthly Calendars Around Edge, 8 1/4 In. 25.00
1910, Clover Design Between Calendars, Purple Lettering, 7 1/4 In. 35.00
1910, Indian, Full Headdress 35.00
1910, Sleepy Eye 400.00
1911, Sea & Shoreline Scene, Small Boat On Beach, Storm Clouds, 7 5/8 In. 55.00
1912, Indian Maiden 50.00
1919, Heasho Co-Operative Co., Peace With Honor, 9 1/4 In. ....*Illus* 40.00
1921, Center Mountain Scene, Lake In Center, Sailboat, Gold Outer Band, 8 In. 30.00
1967, Fox Terrier, Compliments Of Walter's Auction Gallery, 9 In. 22.00

Calendar Plate, 1919, Heasho Co-Operative Co., Peace With Honor, 9 1/4 In.

Calendar Plate, 1976, 200th Anniversary, 1776-1976, E Pluribus Unum, Japan, 9 1/4 In.

1973, Zodiac, Gold Trim, 10 In. 15.00
1976, 200th Anniversary, 1776-1976, E Pluribus Unum, Japan, 9 1/4 In. ....*Illus* 25.00
1981, 4 Seasons Around Numbers, Month Design Center, 10 1/2 In. 18.00
1981, Children, Animals & Flowers, 10 3/4 In. 32.00
1983, Hail Columbia, Spencer Gifts, 9 In. 15.00

CAMARK POTTERY started in 1924 in Camden, Arkansas. Jack Carnes founded the firm and made many types of glazes and wares. The company was bought by Mary Daniel. Production was halted in 1983.

Ashtray Set, L Large, 4 Small, Poppy 22.00
Basket, Bird On Top, Blue, 8 In. 25.00
Basket, Iris, Hand Painted, 9 1/2 In. 185.00
Candlestick, Black, Candle Bowl, Black, 3 3/4 In. 6.00
Ewer, Paper Label, 14 In. 295.00
Ewer, Pastel Blue, Spiral Handle, 6 3/4 In. 40.00
Planter, Double Swan, Gold Trim, 6 In. 20.00
Planter, Strawberry Pot, Hanging, Ribbed Design, 7 In. 45.00
Tea Set, Demitasse, 6 Cups, 6 Saucers, Sugar & Creamer, Teapot, 15 Piece 575.00
Vase, Basket, Turquoise, 4 In. 12.00
Vase, Water Lily, Paper Label, Marked, 7 1/2 In. 195.00
Window Box, Pottery, Green Matte Glaze, 2 3/4 x 8 In. 18.00

CAMBRIDGE GLASS Company was founded in 1901 in Cambridge, Ohio. The company closed in 1954, reopened briefly, and closed again in 1958. The firm made all types of glass. Their early wares included heavy pressed glass with the mark *Near Cut*. Later wares included Crown Tuscan, etched stemware, and clear and colored glass. The firm used a C in a triangle mark after 1920. Some Cambridge patterns may be included in the Depression Glass category.

American Beauty, Sherbet, Airtrap Stem 95.00
Apple Blossom, Bowl, 2 Handles, Gold Trim, Gold Krystol 100.00
Apple Blossom, Candlestick, Keyhole, Green, 4 1/2 In., Pair 120.00
Apple Blossom, Cocktail, Flared, Amber, 3 Oz. 12.00
Apple Blossom, Cordial, Amber, 1 Oz. 9.00
Apple Blossom, Cup & Saucer, Emerald, After Dinner 100.00
Apple Blossom, Decanter, Amber, 14 Oz. 88.00
Apple Blossom, Finger Bowl, Gold Krystol 95.00
Apple Blossom, Ice Bucket, Green 165.00
Apple Blossom, Jar, Honey 495.00
Apple Blossom, Martini Jug, 60 Oz. 950.00
Apple Blossom, Nut Dish, Gold Krystol, 3 In. 65.00
Apple Blossom, Relish, 4 Sections, Gadroon, Pink 48.00
Apple Blossom, Sherbet, Tall, 7 Oz. ....18.00 to 30.00
Apple Blossom, Tray, Center Handle, 11 In. 75.00
Apple Blossom, Tumbler, Water, Amber, 9 Oz. 25.00
Apple Blossom, Tumbler, Whiskey, Footed, 2 Oz. ....65.00 to 85.00
Arcadia, Candy Dish, Cover, 6 In. 45.00

Bacchus, Sherry, Amethyst Flashed, 2 Oz. 45.00
Block Optic, Bowl, Rubina, 11 1/4 In. 150.00
Blue Jay, Candle Peg, 5 1/2 In. 110.00
Blue Willow, Plate, Green Enamel, 8 1/2 In. 125.00
Bourbon, Decanter, Square, 28 Oz. 65.00
Buddah, Lamp, Light Emerald 325.00
Cambridge Arms, Centerpiece, Candlebase, Candlearm, Peg Epergnes 65.00
Caprice, Ashtray, Moonlight Blue, Triangle, 3 In. ....10.00 to 15.00
Caprice, Ashtray, Pink, 3 In. 50.00
Caprice, Bonbon, Footed, Oval, 6 In. 15.00
Caprice, Bowl, 2 Handles, Alpine, 11 In. 88.00
Caprice, Bowl, Footed, Emerald, 13 1/2 In. 70.00
Caprice, Bowl, Fruit, Crimped, Moonlight Blue, 5 In. 85.00
Caprice, Box, Cigarette, Cover, Moonlight Blue, 3 1/2 x 2 1/2 In. ....30.00 to 45.00
Caprice, Cake Plate, Footed, Blue, 14 In. 125.00
Caprice, Cake Salver, 2 Piece 200.00
Caprice, Candlestick, 2-Light, Pair 135.00
Caprice, Candlestick, Prisms, 7 In., Pair 45.00
Caprice, Candy Dish, Cover, Footed, 6 In. ....45.00 to 55.00
Caprice, Candy Dish, Cover, Moonlight Blue, 6 In. 125.00
Caprice, Celery Dish, Moonlight Blue, 11 In. 225.00
Caprice, Centerpiece, 12 In. 20.00
Caprice, Cheese Stand, Moonlight Blue 350.00
Caprice, Cigarette Holder, Triangular, 3 x 3 In. 15.00
Caprice, Claret, 4 1/2 Oz. 60.00
Caprice, Coaster, Pink, 3 1/2 In. 55.00
Caprice, Cocktail, Oyster, Pink 85.00
Caprice, Cruet, Stopper, 5 Oz., 4 3/4 In. 90.00
Caprice, Cup & Saucer 15.00
Caprice, Ice Bucket 250.00
Caprice, Oil, Stopper, 3 Oz. 25.00
Caprice, Plate, 7 1/2 In. 15.00
Caprice, Plate, 9 1/2 In. 40.00
Caprice, Relish, 2 Sections, Moonlight Blue, 6 3/4 In. 35.00
Caprice, Salt & Pepper, Moonlight Blue 125.00
Caprice, Sherbet, Low, 5 Oz. 10.00
Caprice, Sugar & Creamer, Individual 24.00
Caprice, Torte Plate, Moonlight Blue, 14 In. 95.00
Caprice, Tray, Moonlight Blue, Oval, 9 In. 50.00
Caprice, Tumbler, Footed, Moonlight Blue, 5 Oz. 45.00
Caprice, Tumbler, Iced Tea, Moonlight Blue, 12 Oz. 120.00
Caprice, Tumbler, Mushroom, Pistachio, 12 Oz. 150.00
Caprice, Tumbler, Water, 9 Oz. 15.00
Caprice, Tumbler, Water, Footed, Mocha, 10 Oz 25.00
Caprice, Vase, Ball, 8 1/2 In. 550.00
Carmen, Ashtray, Top Hat 55.00
Carmen, Cigarette Holder, Clear Foot 135.00
Carmen, Muddler, Twist 125.00
Carmen, Sugar & Creamer, Individual 50.00
Carmen, Swan, 3 In. 110.00
Cascade, Centerpiece, Oval, 9 1/2 In. 50.00
Cascade, Dish, Mayonnaise, Underplate, Gold Krystol 55.00
Cascade, Vase, 9 1/2 In. 68.00
Chantilly, Bowl, 12 In. 95.00
Chantilly, Goblet, Water, 10 Oz. 34.00
Chantilly, Relish, 3 Sections, 12 In. 75.00
Chantilly, Relish, 5 Sections, 12 In. 110.00
Chantilly, Vase, Bud, Footed, 10 In. 45.00
Chantilly, Vase, Sterling Silver Base, 8 1/2 In. 110.00
Cleo, Bouillon, Underplate, Green 25.00
Cleo, Candlestick, Green, Pair 78.00
Cleo, Candy Dish, Cover, Amber 85.00
Cleo, Compote, Amber, 5 1/2 In. 15.00

Cleo, Cup, Moonlight Blue 20.00
Cleo, Ice Tub, Metal Handle, Amber 55.00
Colonial, Sugar & Creamer, Cover 55.00
Colonial, Water Set, Child's, Royal Blue, 6 Piece 60.00
Crown Tuscan, Ashtray, Shell, Footed 15.00
Crown Tuscan, Bowl, Shell With Nude, Gold Trim, 10 In. 325.00
Crown Tuscan, Candlestick, 2-Light, Keyhole, Rose Point, 6 In., Pair . . . . .220.00 to 275.00
Crown Tuscan, Candy Dish, Cover, 3 Sections 75.00
Crown Tuscan, Centerpiece, Shell, 7 1/2 In. 75.00
Crown Tuscan, Compote, Nude Stem, Shell, 7 In. 140.00
Crown Tuscan, Ivy Ball, Keyhole, 8 In. 55.00
Crown Tuscan, Swan, 8 1/2 In. 70.00
Crown Tuscan, Vase, Cornucopia, 10 1/2 In. 45.00
Crown Tuscan, Vase, Shell, 7 1/4 In. 95.00
Daisy, Basket, Near Cut, 5 In. 75.00
Daisy, Dish, Banana Split, Oval, 6 In. 30.00
Dance Of The Nudes, Sherbet, Pink 65.00
Dance Of The Nudes, Vase, Fan, Satin, 15 1/2 In. 125.00
Decagon, Almond Dish, Footed, Amber, 2 1/2 In. 16.00
Decagon, Bonbon, Ebony, Gold Encrusted, Floral Interior, 2 Handles, 6 1/4 In. 20.00
Decagon, Bowl, Amethyst, 8 1/2 In. 65.00
Decagon, Bowl, Flat Rim, Pink, 5 In. 18.00
Decagon, Cream & Sugar, Amber 20.00
Decagon, Creamer, Pink 15.00
Decagon, Cup & Saucer, Willow Blue 12.00
Decagon, Goblet, Water, Amethyst, 9 Oz. 30.00
Decagon, Ice Tub, Cobalt 120.00
Decagon, Server, Center Handle, Emerald, 12 In. 58.00
Decagon, Soup, Cream, Pink 27.00
Decagon, Tumbler, Footed, Amethyst, 2 1/2 Oz. 25.00
Decagon, Tumbler, Juice, Royal Blue, 5 Oz. 30.00
Diane, Bowl, Footed, Amber, 6 In. 85.00
Diane, Celery Dish, 11 In. 50.00
Diane, Compote, Blown, 5 1/8 In. 88.00
Diane, Console, Footed, 12 In. 110.00
Diane, Cup & Saucer, Amber 10.00
Diane, Goblet, Gold Krystol, 9 Oz. 75.00
Diane, Plate, Pink, Square, 10 1/2 In. 225.00
Diane, Tumbler, Iced Tea, Footed, Gold Krystol, 12 Oz. 75.00
Diane, Vase, Bud, 10 In. 65.00
Diane, Wine, 3 1/2 Oz. 45.00
Draped Lady, Flower Frog, Pink, 8 1/2 In. 160.00
Eagle, Bookends . . . . .60.00 to 105.00
Ebony, Basket, Clear Handle, 7 In. 80.00
Ebony, Candlestick, 4 In., Pair 40.00
Ebony, Cup & Saucer, After Dinner 25.00
Elaine, Ashtray, 4 1/4 In. 45.00
Elaine, Cake Plate, 13 In. 210.00
Elaine, Console, Footed, 12 In. 195.00
Elaine, Cup & Saucer 35.00
Elaine, Nut Dish, 4-Footed, 3 In. 65.00
Elaine, Plate, 7 1/2 In. 24.00
Elaine, Relish, 2 Sections, 2 Handles, 6 In. 25.00
Elaine, Relish, Center Handle, 3 Sections 125.00
Elaine, Tumbler, 7 Oz. 35.00
Empire, Compote, Emerald 48.00
Empire, Pitcher, Emerald 95.00
Empire, Vase, Emerald, 12 In. 135.00
Everglade, Candlestick, 2-Light, Moonlight Blue 250.00
Everglade, Candlestick, Moonlight Blue 80.00
Everglade, Creamer, Emerald 40.00
Everglade, Plate, Willow Blue, 8 1/2 In. 20.00
Everglade, Sherbet, Satin 20.00

Everglade, Vase, Violet, 12 In. 425.00
Feather, Pitcher, Near Cut, 10 1/2 In. 75.00
Fernland, Jug, Near Cut, 1 Qt. 55.00
Fernland, Rose Bowl, Near Cut, 6 In. 40.00
Gadroon, Basket, Minerva, Footed, 2 Handles, 7 In. 25.00
Gadroon, Relish, 3 Sections, Amethyst 95.00
Gadroon, Relish, 3 Sections, Royal Blue 90.00
Georgian, Tumbler, Carmen, 5 Oz. 30.00
Georgian, Tumbler, Peach-Blo, 9 Oz. ....10.00 to 30.00
Georgian, Tumbler, Willow Blue, 2 1/2 Oz. 20.00
Gloria, Cocktail Shaker, Amber, Clear Top 350.00
Gloria, Ice Bucket, Metal Handle 110.00
Gloria, Pitcher, Silver Overlay, Ebony, Oval 950.00
Gloria, Tumbler, 7 Oz. 75.00
Gloria, Vase, 10 In. 250.00
Grape, Bowl, Light Emerald, 9 1/2 In. 55.00
Gyro Optic, Jug, Ball, Silver Overlay, Roses, Leaves, Thorns, 32 Oz. 275.00
Gyro Optic, Sherbet, Pistachio, 7 Oz. 105.00
Ham Bone, Ashtray, The Cambridge Glass Co. In Gold On Edge, 10 In. 275.00
Helio, Candlestick, Doric, Pair 100.00
Helio, Compote, Stemmed, 6 In. 50.00
Imperial Hunt Scene, Bridge Set, Peach-Blo, 5 Piece 475.00
Imperial Hunt Scene, Goblet, Gold Incrusted, Peach-Blo, 9 Oz. 80.00
Imperial Hunt Scene, Parfait, Emerald, 5 1/2 Oz. 75.00
Imperial Hunt Scene, Sherbet, Gold Incrusted, Peach-Blo, 6 Oz. 55.00
Jenny Lind, Basket, Dark Amber, 8 1/2 In. 155.00
Krystolshell, Sugar & Creamer, Shell Footed 20.00
Lily Of The Valley, Candlestick 40.00
Lynbrook, Sherbet, Low 10.00
Mardi Gras, Vase, 10 In. 750.00
Martha Washington, Bowl, Royal Blue, 10 In. 115.00
Martha Washington, Plate, 7 1/2 In. 30.00
Martha Washington, Plate, Emerald, 8 1/2 In. 15.00
Minerva, Goblet, Water 32.00
Mt. Vernon, Candlestick, Dolphin, Peach-Blo, 9 1/2 In. 160.00
Mt. Vernon, Candy Dish, Cover, Urn, Emerald, 9 In. 100.00
Mt. Vernon, Celery Dish, 12 In. 25.00
Mt. Vernon, Coaster 8.00
Mt. Vernon, Compote, Heatherbloom 110.00
Mt. Vernon, Cup & Saucer 14.00
Mt. Vernon, Goblet, Water 15.00
Mt. Vernon, Ice Tub 75.00
Mt. Vernon, Plate, 6 In. 5.00
Mt. Vernon, Plate, 7 1/2 In. 8.00
Mt. Vernon, Salt & Pepper 40.00
Near Cut, Syrup Jug, Signed, Nickel Top 160.00
Near Cut, Vase, 2 Handles, 11 In. 110.00
No. 628, Candlestick, Etched Foot, Green, 3 1/2 In., Pair ....*Illus* 40.00
Nude, Brandy, Emerald 175.00
Nude, Champagne, Emerald, 6 Oz. 225.00
Nude, Champagne, Peach-Blo, 6 Oz. 500.00
Nude, Claret, Amethyst, 4 1/2 Oz. 135.00
Nude, Cocktail, Amethyst, 3 Oz. ....140.00 to 180.00
Nude, Cocktail, Mocha, 3 Oz. 320.00
Nude, Cocktail, Moonlight Blue, 3 Oz. 335.00
Nude, Compote, Carmen, 7 In. 300.00
Nude, Sauterne, Royal Blue, Clear, 3 Oz. 475.00
Nude, Wine, 3 Oz. 250.00
Pinch, Decanter Set, Amethyst, 7 Piece 110.00
Portia, Bowl, 11 1/2 In. 55.00
Portia, Candlestick, 2-Light, Pair 75.00
Portia, Candy Box, Cover 75.00
Portia, Cheese & Cracker Set 85.00

Cambridge, No. 628, Candlestick, Etched Foot,
Green, 3 1/2 In., Pair

To clean wax from glass candlesticks, scrape with a wooden stick,
then wash off the remaining wax
with rubbing alcohol.

Portia, Decanter, 28 Oz.	300.00
Portia, Marmalade, Cover, 8 Oz.	125.00
Portia, Relish, 4 Sections, Center Handle	95.00
Portia, Sherbet, Low, Emerald, 5 Oz.	65.00
Portia, Tumbler, Iced Tea, 12 Oz.	35.00
Pouter Pigeon, Bookends	100.00
Primrose, Basket, Plainware, 5 1/2 In.	125.00
Pristine, Ashtray, Mandarin Gold, 4 1/2 In.	55.00
Rondo, Cocktail Shaker, Stopper, 32 Oz.	200.00
Rondo, Sherbet, Low, 5 Oz.	10.00
Rosalie, Goblet, Carmen, Clear Stem, 8 Oz.	225.00
Rose Lady, Flower Frog, Green Satin, 8 1/2 In.	250.00
Rose Marie, Candlestick, 3-Light, Pair	45.00
Rose Point, Bell, Dinner	177.00
Rose Point, Bonbon, Crimped, Shallow, 7 In.	175.00
Rose Point, Bowl, 3-Footed, 10 1/2 In.	100.00
Rose Point, Bowl, Handle, 4-Toed, 12 In.	125.00
Rose Point, Butter, Cover, Round, 5 In.	235.00
Rose Point, Cake Plate, Tab Handles, 13 1/2 In.	55.00
Rose Point, Candlestick, 3-Light, 6 In., Pair	250.00
Rose Point, Candlestick, Calla Lily, 6 1/2 In., Pair	500.00
Rose Point, Candlestick, Ram's Head, 4 In., Pair	150.00
Rose Point, Candy Dish, Cover, 3 Sections, 8 In.	45.00
Rose Point, Cocktail Icer, 2 Piece	95.00
Rose Point, Compote, 7 In.	165.00
Rose Point, Condiment Set, 2 Cruets, Salt & Pepper, Tray, 5 Piece	350.00
Rose Point, Cordial, 1 Oz.	75.00
Rose Point, Creamer, Individual	25.00 to 30.00
Rose Point, Cruet, 6 Oz.	130.00
Rose Point, Cup & Saucer	45.00
Rose Point, Finger Bowl, Underplate	175.00
Rose Point, Goblet, Wine, 3 1/2 Oz.	40.00
Rose Point, Jug, Ball, 80 Oz.	200.00
Rose Point, Lamp Base, Hurricane	55.00
Rose Point, Parfait, 5 Oz.	95.00
Rose Point, Pitcher, 80 Oz.	375.00
Rose Point, Plate, 6 In.	18.00
Rose Point, Plate, 8 In.	20.00
Rose Point, Plate, 2 Handles, 11 In.	50.00
Rose Point, Relish, 3 Sections, 10 In.	50.00
Rose Point, Relish, 3 Sections, Ring Handle, 6 In.	60.00
Rose Point, Server, Center Handle	150.00
Rose Point, Sherbet, Pressed, 5 Oz.	60.00
Rose Point, Sherbet, Tall, 7 Oz.	35.00

Rose Point, Sugar & Creamer, Individual 25.00
Rose Point, Tumbler, 9 Oz. 40.00
Rose Point, Tumbler, Juice, Pressed, Footed, Carmen, 5 Oz. 150.00
Roselyn, Bowl, Flared, Footed, 12 In. 80.00
Roselyn, Candlestick, 2-Light 95.00
Roselyn, Candy Dish, Cover 75.00
Scotty Dog, Bookends 95.00
Seagull, Flower Frog, 8 1/2 In. 50.00
Shell, Candlestick, Dolphin Footed, 4 In. 60.00
Swan, 4 1/2 In. 60.00
Swan, 6 1/2 In. 55.00
Swan, Amber, 3 In. 85.00
Swan, Clear Satin, Red & Black Enamel, 4 1/2 In. 350.00
Swan, Emerald, 3 1/2 In. 45.00
Swan, Milk Glass, 4 1/2 In. 95.00
Swan, Peach-Blo, 8 1/2 In. 300.00
Swan, Peach-Blo, 10 In. 400.00
Talisman Rose, Goblet, 9 Oz. 28.00
Talisman Rose, Goblet, Gold, 9 Oz. 27.00
Tally-Ho, Pitcher, Emerald, 88 Oz. 65.00
Tulip, Jug, Willow Blue, 64 Oz. 150.00
Turkey, Candy Dish, Cover, Blue 950.00
Wheat Sheaf, Punch Bowl, Child's, Near Cut 45.00
Wildflower, Basket, Royal Blue, 7 In. 175.00
Wildflower, Bowl, Flared, 12 In. 55.00
Wildflower, Butter, Cover, Round, 5 In. ....140.00 to 195.00
Wildflower, Candy Box, Cover, 3 Sections, 8 In. 160.00
Wildflower, Celery Dish, 12 In. 40.00
Wildflower, Cocktail Shaker, Metal Top, 46 Oz., 13 1/2 In. 165.00
Wildflower, Corn Dish, 9 1/2 In. 55.00
Wildflower, Cruet 85.00
Wildflower, Lamp, Hurricane, GE Shade, H-Prisms, Bobeche & Collar, Gold Trim, Pair .. 1100.00
Wildflower, Relish, 5 Sections, 12 In. 75.00
Wildflower, Tumbler, Juice, Royal Blue, 5 Oz. 15.00
Willow, Sandwich Server, Center Handle, Oval, Amber, 12 x 10 In. 20.00
Windsor, Bowl, Cutting, 12 In. 75.00
Windsor, Candlestick, Shell, Blue, 2 1/2 In. 185.00
Yardley, Jar, Plastic Lid, 3 In. 15.00

CAMBRIDGE POTTERY was made in Cambridge, Ohio, from about 1895 until World War I. The factory made brown glazed decorated art wares with a variety of marks, including an acorn, the name *Cambridge*, the name *Oakwood*, or the name *Terrhea*.

Pitcher, Marked, 7 1/2 In. 1200.00
Plate, Grosvenor, 8 In. 22.00
Teapot, Ivory Body, Flowers, 6 In. 42.00

CAMEO GLASS was made in much the same manner as a cameo in jewelry. Parts of the top layer of glass were cut away to reveal a different colored glass beneath. The most famous cameo glass was made during the nineteenth century. Signed cameo glass pieces are listed under the glasswork's name, such as Daum or Galle.

Basket, Wide Weave, Footed, Atterbury, 8 In. 60.00
Bowl, Fruit, Blue, Rose Border, Stourbridge, 8 x 11 1/2 In. 300.00
Bowl, Iris Design, Vessiere, 4 1/2 In. 175.00
Box, Cover, Boat, Wooded Shore, Flat Diamond Shape, Gray, Pink, 1900, 7 3/4 In. 2300.00
Console, Green, Gilt Flower Design, 11 1/2 x 7 In. 308.00
Night-Light, Ferns, Umbrella Cover, Gray, Russet, Squat, Footed, 1900, 4 In. 2415.00
Shaker, Amber Leaves Cut To White, St. Louis, 4 In. 300.00
Vase, 2 Figures, Burgun & Schverer, Verrerie D'Art De Lorraine, c.1895, 12 In. 13750.00
Vase, Bayou Scene At Sunset, Yellow, Orange, Brown, Michel, France, 14 In. 980.00
Vase, Cabinet, Brown Floral, Leaf Design, 2 1/8 x 6 1/8 In. 1725.00
Vase, Floral, Green Cut To Rose, Oblong, 5 x 10 In. 350.00

Vase, Floral, Vesserie, 2 1/4 In. 275.00
Vase, Flower Heads, Cushion Foot, Tangerine, Violet, France, 1928, 26 In. 2587.00
Vase, Flower, Yellow & Purple, Egg Shape, 3 1/4 In. 430.00
Vase, Hydrangeas & Leaves, Gray, Pink, Baluster Shape, 1900, 19 3/4 In. 4500.00
Vase, Iris Design, Square, St. Louis, 4 In. 250.00
Vase, Landscape Scene, Brown Cut To Burnt Orange, LaRochere, 14 In. 660.00
Vase, Landscape Scene, Etched, LaRouchere, 11 1/2 In. 385.00
Vase, Landscape, Blue, Green, 17 In. 550.00
Vase, Leaves, Enameled, Gilt, Burgun & Schverer, 1900, 9 1/4 In. 9200.00
Vase, Nasturtium Blossom Trailing, Amethyst, Burgun, Schverer & Cie, 7 In. 2760.00
Vase, Pink & Brown, Rose Leaves & Rose Hips, Arsall, 14 In. 1100.00
Vase, Purple Flared Vine Design, Opaque Ground, Footed, Mabut, 13 3/4 In. 200.00
Vase, Purple, Gray Ground, Long Neck, LaRochere, 11 In. 550.00
Vase, Roses On Thorny Branches, Yellow, Russet, Gray, Paul Nicolas, 25 In. 4140.00
Vase, Songbird, 2 Butterflies, Floral Border, Deep Red Glass, White, 10 In. 2185.00
Vase, Stick, Morning Glory, Stourbridge, 8 In. 600.00
Vase, Stick, Stylized Flowers & Leaves, Bulbous Bottle Shape, 6 3/4 In. 575.00
Vase, Stylized Leaves, Pink, Blue, Purple, Mauve, Yellow, Burgun & Schverer, 9 In. 3450.00
Vase, Tulip Shape, City On Island Scene, J. Michel, 7 In. 450.00

CAMPAIGN memorabilia is listed in the Political category.

CAMPBELL KIDS were first used as part of an advertisement for the
Campbell Soup Company in 1906. The kids were created by Grace
Drayton, a popular illustrator of the day. The kids were used in magazine and newspaper ads until about 1951. They were presented again
in 1966; and in 1983, they were redesigned with a slimmer, more contemporary appearance.

Bank, Iron, Gold Repaint, 4 In. 190.00
Doll, Girl & Boy, Box, 1970s, Pair 135.00
Doll, Jointed Body, Store Tag 550.00
Doll, Plastic, Painted, Blond Hair, Red Dress, Head Rotates, 7 In. 25.00
Figurine, Pair Walking In Stride Together, Gold, Cast Iron, A.C. Williams, 4 In. 340.00
Mug, Campbell Soup Co., Plastic, 2 3/4 In. . . . . *Illus* 10.00
Napkin, Illustrated, 1950s, 4 1/2 x 4 1/2 In. 8.50
Puzzle 4.00

CAMPHOR GLASS is a cloudy white glass that has been blown or
pressed. It was made by many factories in the Midwest during the mid-
nineteenth century.

Baby's Shoe, Figural, Covered With Daisies, 1930, 4 In. 100.00
Decanter, Stopper, Painted Blue Forget-Me-Nots 165.00
Dresser Jar, Hinged Lid, Floral, Enameled 145.00
Vase, 2 Handles, Fluted & Ruffled Edge, White Interior, 4 1/2 In. 175.00

CANDELABRUM refers to a candleholder with more than one arm to
hold many candles; a candlestick is designed to hold one candle. The
eccentricity of the English language makes the plural of candelabrum
into candelabra.

2-Light, Leaves, Floral Bands, Cylindrical Faceted Stem, E. Caber, 15 In., Pair 5750.00

Go to antique shows early; there
may be plenty of antiques left at
the end of the show but the
dealers are tired and not as eager
to talk to the customers.

Campbell Kids, Mug, Campbell Soup Co.,
Plastic, 2 3/4 In.

2-Light, Marble, White, Entwined Laurel Leaves On Beaded Base, 11 In., Pair 975.00
2-Light, Silver, Spiraled Leaf Arms, Georg Jensen, 116 Oz., Pair 34500.00
3-Light, Brass, Clear & Tinted Glass Prisms, Linked Glass Swags, 18 In., Pair 520.00
3-Light, Bronze, Empire Revival, Ormolu, Reeded Column, Bobeche, 21 In., Pair 1870.00
3-Light, Bronze, Empire, Winged Classical Maiden, Marble Base, 23 In., Pair 1380.00
3-Light, Bronze, Gilt, Louis XV, Berried Finials, Cornucopia Arms, 18 In., Pair 2185.00
3-Light, Bronze, Girandole & Glass, Petal Branches, Glass Prisms, 19 In., Pair 3105.00
3-Light, Bronze, Marble, Napoleon III, Cluster Of Arrows, Gilt, 11 x 6 In., Pair 1380.00
3-Light, Bronze, Peasant Woman, Cornucopia, Prisms, Electrified, 22 In., Pair 635.00
3-Light, Gilt Brass, Scroll Arms, 3-Tier Bulbous Standard, Victorian, 23 In. 880.00
3-Light, Gilt, Bronze, Louis XVI, Cut Glass, Lyre Cage Support, 30 In., Pair 1610.00
3-Light, Silver On Copper, Scrolled Leaves, Convertible, Sheffield, 21 In., Pair 980.00
3-Light, Silver Plate, Converts To Single 12-In. Candlestick, 21 1/2 In., Pair 350.00
3-Light, Silver Plate, Reeded Swirl Arms, Gadrooned, Sheffield, 19 In., Pair 550.00
3-Light, Silver Plate, Removable Arms, Weighted, Empire Silver Co., 9 In., Pair 165.00
3-Light, Silver Plate, Scrolled Leaves, Knop Stem, Gorham, 16 In., Pair 575.00
3-Light, Silver, Central Finial, Drip Pans, R. Comyns, England, 1960, 14 In., Pair 4887.00
3-Light, Silver, Stylized Floral, Julius O. Randahl, Arts & Crafts, 7 x 10 In., Pair 1200.00
3-Light, Sterling Silver, 10 1/2 In., Pair .... 330.00 to 415.00
3-Light, Sterling Silver, Adjustable Center Standard, Scrolled Arms, 10 In., Pair 220.00
3-Light, Sterling Silver, Marked Sterling .950, 12 In., Pair 650.00
3-Light, Sterling Silver, Rococo Style, Leafy Scrolled Standard, 17 In., Pair 5940.00
3-Light, Sterling Silver, Weighted, Turned Shaft, Preisner, 16 1/2 In., Pair 920.00
3-Light, Sterling Silver, Wild Rose Pattern, International, 13 1/2 In., Pair 305.00
3-Light, Tapering Stem, 2 Branches, Vase Form Sconces, Silver, 10 1/4 In. 170.00
4-Light, Brass, Glass Swags & Chains, 3-Tier Standard, 21 In., Pair 715.00
4-Light, Brass, Leaf Base, Rope Twist, Crystal Bobeche, 14 x 14 In., Pair 170.00
4-Light, Bronze, Gilt & Patinated, Louis Philippe, 22 1/2 In., Pair 3080.00
4-Light, Bronze, Louis XV, Swirling Leaves Support, Rocaille Feet, 22 In., Pair 2120.00
4-Light, Cut Glass, Frosted, 2 Tiers, Spike Finial, Spear Prisms, Britain, 27 In. 385.00
4-Light, Gilt Brass, Rococo, Ape, Prisms, Electrified, 18 In., Pair 1540.00
4-Light, Silver Plate, Applied Leaves, Detachable Bobeches, 18 1/2 In., Pair 405.00
4-Light, Silver Plate, Triangular Base, 3 Caryatids, Leaves, Continental, 23 In. 1495.00
4-Light, Wood, Carved, Nude Boy With Fish, Goose, 3 Claw Feet, 35 In., Pair 2530.00
5-Light, Brass, Marble, C-Scroll, Pineapple, Lion's Head, 26 1/4 In. 465.00
5-Light, Brass, Scrolled Floral Arms, Flower-Shaped Cups, Prisms, 17 In. 115.00
5-Light, Bronze, Gilt, Leafy Feet, 4 Scroll Leaf Arms, 19 1/4 In., Pair 400.00
5-Light, Bronze, Louis XV, Garlands, Putto Holding Leafy Stem, 23 In., Pair 4600.00
5-Light, Bronze, Reeded Stem, Stepped Leaf Tip Tripartite Plinth, 29 In., Pair 6325.00
5-Light, Gilt Bronze, Bacchus Holding Cornucopia, 19th Century, 29 In. 2200.00
5-Light, Gilt Bronze, Cobalt Blue Porcelain, Urn Shape, 29 1/2 In., Pair 1840.00
5-Light, Gilt Bronze, Empire, 3 Fluted Round Columns, Triangular Base, 23 In. 515.00
5-Light, Gilt Bronze, Louis XV, Floral Garlands, C-Scroll Feet, 21 1/2 In., Pair 1840.00
5-Light, Gilt Bronze, Louis XVI, Pair Of Cupids, Round Base, 21 In., Pair 1725.00
5-Light, Gilt Bronze, Neo-Grecque, Tapered Column, Griffins, Electrified, 41 In. 495.00
5-Light, Porcelain, Sevres Vase, Gilt Bronze Handles, Floral Branches, Pair 5750.00
5-Light, Silver, Rococo, Scroll Design, Fluted Cut Glass Bowl, 16 x 15 In., Pair 1150.00
6-Light, Bronze, Gilt, Patinated, Marble, Empire, Winged Woman, 31 In., Pair 5750.00
6-Light, Bronze, Louis XV, Ribbon Tied Swags, Ram's Head Standard, 21 In., Pair 3737.00
6-Light, Gilt Bronze, Louis XVI, S-Scroll Arms, Electrified, c.1900, 35 In. 470.00
6-Light, Gilt Bronze, Louis XVI, Twist-Fluted Column, Cherub, 25 In. 2875.00
6-Light, Gilt Porcelain, Glass, 3 Men Figures, Continental, 40 In., Pair 3735.00
6-Light, Ormolu, Black Marble, Renaissance Style, Continental, 20 In., Pair 520.00
6-Light, Silvered & Gilt Bronze, Empire, Caryatid, Cherubs, 33 1/2 In. 1045.00
6-Light, Silvered Metal, Woman Holding Branches, Prisms, 48 In., Pair 4025.00
7-Light, Brass, Blue Glass Flowers, 36 In. 325.00
7-Light, Bronze, Louis XVI, Leaves, Spiral C Scrolls, Marble Base, 21 In., Pair 4600.00
7-Light, Gilt Bronze, Flowers & Leaves, Grape Clusters, Victorian, 31 In., Pair 1495.00
7-Light, Gilt Bronze, Louis XV, C-Scroll Stem, Dolphin, Electrified, 36 In., Pair 6325.00
7-Light, Gilt Bronze, Malachite Porcelain, Urn, Flowers, 22 In., Pair 3080.00
7-Light, Porcelain, Gilt, Cherub Musicians, Naples, 19 In., Pair 1495.00
8-Light, Gilt Bronze, Empire Style, Caryatid, Tripod Base, Cherubs, 32 In. 1185.00
8-Light, Gilt Bronze, Patinated, Bulbous Urn, 1900, 33 1/4 In., Pair 10350.00

10-Light, Gilt Bronze, Napoleon III, Louis XVI Style, Mounted As Lamp, 31 In. 2200.00
Garniture, 2-Light, Bronze, Candlesticks, Argand, Prisms, 23 In., 3 Piece 4890.00
Girandole, 1-Light, Gilt Brass, Marble, Rococo, 2 Girls, Goat, c.1855, 14 In., Pair 110.00
Girandole, 2-Light, Brass, Marble, Man, Kneeling Woman, Prisms, 3 Piece 120.00
Girandole, 2-Light, Bronze, Napoleon & Wellington, Prisms, 9 x 11 In., Pair 1430.00
Girandole, 2-Light, Giltwood, Gesso, Grape Leaves, Early Victorian, 40 In. 4180.00
Girandole, 3-Light, Mirror, Architectural Crest, Wood, Glass, Italy, 32 x 15 In., Pair 4025.00
Girandole, Brass, Prisms, Marble Base, 3 Piece 525.00
Girandole, Hung Beadwork, Electrified, 20 In., Pair 263.00
Girandole, Woman & Child Picking Flowers, 3-Light, Ormolu, Marble Base, 17 In. 385.00
Pierced Foliate Base, Bun-Form Feet, Silver, Reed & Burton, 1939 .... 1500.00

CANDLESTICKS were made of brass, pewter, glass, sterling silver, plated silver, and all types of pottery and porcelain. The earliest candlesticks, dating from the sixteenth century, held the candle on a pricket (sharp pointed spike). These lost favor because in times of strife the large church candlesticks with prickets became formidable weapons, so the socket was mandated. Candlesticks changed in style through the centuries, and designs range from classic to rococo to Art Nouveau to Art Deco.

Bell Metal, Neoclassical, Urn Top, Square Beaded Base, Push-Up, 10 In., Pair 545.00
Bell Metal, Urn Top, Round Tapered Shafts, Push-Up, England, 1810, 9 In., Pair 490.00
Blown Glass, Cobalt Blue Cut To Clear, Hollow Stem, 14 In., Pair 465.00
Brass, 17th Century Spanish Style, Mounted As Electric Lamp, 15 In., Pair 385.00
Brass, Altar, Gilt, Onyx, Triangular Plinth Cast, Scroll Feet, 24 1/2 In., Pair 1495.00
Brass, Altar, Pricket, Knop Standard, Tripod Feet, 18th Century, 16 1/4 In. 1320.00
Brass, Beehive Shape, Square Base, Push-Up Inserts, 10 1/2 In. 220.00
Brass, Beehive Shape, Square Base, Push-Up, 12 In. 140.00
Brass, Belted Shafts, Round Petal Base, Push-Up, England, 8 1/4 In., Pair 575.00
Brass, Colonial Style, 19th Century, 12 3/4 In., Pair 225.00
Brass, Cup Above Brass Design, Animals, Pedestal, 19th Century, 18 In., Pair 55.00
Brass, Cupped Swirl Base, 8 x 4 1/4 In., Pair 935.00
Brass, Cutout Base, Secessionist Style Bobeche, Brevete S.G.D.G., 6 1/2 In., Pair 100.00
Brass, Cylindrical, Side Push Knob, Push-Up, England, 7 1/2 In., Pair 90.00
Brass, Diamond & Beehive Design, Push-Up, 19th Century, 11 In., Pair 60.00
Brass, Diamond In Center, Turned Stems, Marked, Push-Up, 9 3/4 x 4 In., Pair 85.00
Brass, Diamond, Prince, Push-Up, Victorian, 11 3/4 In., Pair 245.00
Brass, Diamond, Princess, Push-Up, England, 11 In., Pair 155.00
Brass, Double Beehive, Square Base, Push-Up, 11 In. 190.00
Brass, Faceted & Beehive Stem, Push-Up, 9 In., Pair 225.00
Brass, Figural, Art Nouveau Woman, Marble Base, Erte, 1891 .... 190.00
Brass, Futuristic Cup, Jessie Preston, Anderson Mark, Arts & Crafts, 12 1/2 In. 925.00
Brass, Gamma, Round Base, Squat Top, Jarvie, 13 In. 1210.00
Brass, Hand Crafted, Rectangular Drip Pan, Push-Up, 5 x 6 3/4 x 5 In. 175.00
Brass, Inverted Beehive, Push-Up, Smith Company, 9 In. 120.00
Brass, King Of Diamonds, Push-Up, Victorian, 12 1/4 In., Pair 220.00
Brass, Neoclassical, Square Base, Round Stem, Push-Up, Pair 190.00
Brass, Octagonal Base, Bulbous Stem, 7 1/4 In., Pair 120.00
Brass, Paneled Shape, Chased Design, 8 3/4 In. 550.00
Brass, Petal Form Base, England, Mid 18th Century, 7 1/2 In., Pair .... 800.00 to 980.00
Brass, Picket, Ball Feet, Bulbous Stem, Wide Drip Pan, 15 In., Pair 3300.00
Brass, Pricket, 3 Paw Form Feet, Continental, 19 1/2 In., Pair 345.00
Brass, Pricket, Tripartite Base, Stylized Paw Feet, Continental, 22 In., Pair 90.00
Brass, Queen Anne, 6-Petal Base, Baluster Stem, 8 1/2 In., Pair 960.00
Brass, Queen Anne, Scalloped Base & Rim, 7 7/8 In. 660.00
Brass, Queen Anne, Scrolled Foot, Push-Up, 8 1/2 In., Pair 935.00
Brass, Queen Of Diamonds, Push-Up, 11 1/4 In., Pair 250.00
Brass, Round Base, Early 19th Century, 12 In., Pair 90.00
Brass, Round Dish Foot, Dutch, 17th Century, 6 In. 165.00
Brass, Round Scalloped Base, Tulip Socket, 5 3/8 In., Pair 385.00
Brass, Scalloped Base, Filled In Push-Up, 8 In. 155.00
Brass, Square Foot, Baluster Turnings, Continental, 5 In. 90.00
Brass, Vase & Ring Turnings, Mid 19th Century, 9 In., Pair 100.00

Brass, William & Mary Style, Barley Twist Stem, Wooden, 12 In., Pair 230.00
Bronze, Charles X, Gilt, Palm Tree Support, Figure Of A Warrior Maiden, 15 In. 1090.00
Bronze, Delta, Jarvie, 14 In. 1100.00
Bronze, Hammered Stepped Round Base, Early 20th Century, 2 3/4 In., Pair 230.00
Bronze, Leaf Running Length Of Stick, Tulip Form, Jesse Preston, 14 In. 3575.00
Bronze, Napoleon III, Reeded Shaft, Trefid Claw Feet, 10 7/8 In., Pair 400.00
Bronze, Ormolu, Cylindrical Stem, Tripartite Paw Feet, Charles X, 17 In., Pair 7475.00
Bronze, Parrot, Cold Paint, Vienna, 12 In. 465.00
Bronze, Patinated, Gilt, Egyptian Caryatid, Continental, 1825-1850, 13 In., Pair 3740.00
Bronze, Patinated, Regency, Gothic Windows, Architectural Designs, 9 In., Pair 1870.00
Bronze, Pharaoh, Standing, Egyptian, Napoleon III, 11 1/4 In., Pair 1840.00
Bronze, Pricket, Elephant Head Handles, Sentoku, Meiji Period, 7 In., Pair 165.00
Bronze, Putti Holding Torch Aloft, Leaves Border, 19th Century, 10 In., Pair 1380.00
Bronze, Renaissance Revival Style, Sphinx Supports, Prisms, 9 In., Pair 375.00
Bronze, Round Base, Egg Shaped Bobeches, Marked, Jarvie, 11 1/2 In, Pair 1610.00
Bronze Dore, Louis XV, Leaf Feet, Cartouche, Scrolls, Acanthus, 6 1/4 In., Pair 115.00
Canary, Fluted Column, Hexagonal Petal Socket, Square Stepped Base, 9 1/4 In. 110.00
Chrome, Variente, Interchangeable Tripods, 10 & 15 In., Pair ....*Illus* 50.00
Clambroth, Square Stepped Base, 9 1/8 In. 300.00
Copper, Arts & Crafts, Rolled Design, Brass Washed, Round Base, 8 In., Pair 165.00
Copper, Chamberstick, Enamel Overlay, Art Crafts Shop, 4 1/4 x 5 x 6 1/2 In. 440.00
Copper, Hammered, Bark Texture, Repousse Celtic Rose, Arts & Crafts, 6 1/2 In. 330.00
Copper, Hammered, Chamberstick, Gustav Stickley, 9 x 7 In. 525.00
Copper, Hammered, Trefoils, Tapered Bobeche, Arts & Crafts, 9 1/2 In., Pair 305.00
Copper, Square, Bowknot & Bellflower Swag, Arts & Crafts, 9 In., Pair 145.00
Copper, Twisted Shaft, Dark Patina, Arts & Crafts, Old Mission Kopper Kraft, 9 In. 165.00
Cut Glass, Diamonds & Ovals, Square Base, England, 20th Century, 11 1/2 In. 2670.00
Gilt, Altar, Crimson, Leaf Carved Shaft, Spreading Acanthus Base, Italy, 35 In. 825.00
Gilt, Altar, Knop Form, Standard Inset With Mirrored Segments, 32 In., Pair 1540.00
Gilt, Altar, Silver, Leaf Carved Knop Support, 3-Part Base, Scroll Feet, 28 In. 495.00
Gilt, Rectangular Plinth, Leaf Prism Frame, George IV, 8 1/4 In., Pair 1725.00
Gilt Brass, Leafy Design, H.N. Hopper & Co., Boston, 1850-1875, 6 1/4 In., Pair 305.00
Gilt Bronze, Altar, Pricket, Fluted Shaft, Acanthus, France, 1875-1900, 36 In., Pair 1210.00
Gilt Bronze, Elephant's Head, Opaline Vase, Marble Base, William IV, 8 1/2 In., Pair 2640.00
Gilt Bronze, Napoleon III, Fluted Shaft, Wreath Border Base, 12 In., Pair 1840.00
Gilt Bronze, Porcelain, Putto, Painted Flowers, France, c.1900, 9 In., Pair 920.00
Gilt Metal, Art Nouveau, Flower & Leaf Design, 8 In., Pair 345.00
Giltwood, Altar, Pricket, Bobeche, Polychrome, Mexico, 18th Century, 16 1/2 In. 275.00
Giltwood, Altar, Pricket, Giltwood, Knop Standard, 18th Century, Italy, 41 In., Pair 3520.00
Giltwood, Altar, Pricket, Knop Standard, Gray Painted Base, Italy, 30 1/2 In. 400.00
Giltwood, Altar, Pricket, Leaf, Fluted Standard, Round Plinth, Italy, 44 In., Pair 3680.00
Giltwood, Altar, Pricket, Round Drip Pan, Beaded Pedestal, Italy, 35 x 9 In. 515.00
Giltwood, Altar, Pricket, Urn & Leaf Standard, Continental, 18th Century, 44 In. 1100.00
Giltwood, Baroque Style, Urn Shaped Bobeche, Reeded Column, 13 In., Pair 880.00
Giltwood, Pricket, Gray Paint, Renaissance Style, Italy, 19th Century, 11 In., Pair 660.00

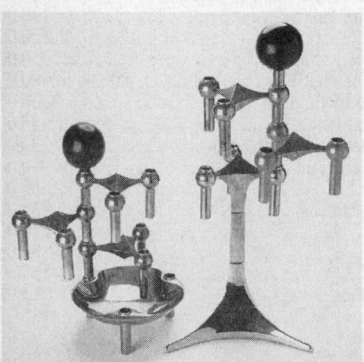

Candlestick, Chrome,
Variente, Interchangeable
Tripods, 10 & 15 In., Pair

Candlestick, Porcelain, Mars,
Early 18th Century, 10 In.

Glass, Amber, Enameled, Oval Body, Raised Flowers, Gilt Border, 9 1/2 In., Pair 200.00
Glass, Baluster Standard, Dome Base, Modernist Style, 12 1/2 In., Pair 250.00
Glass, Hollow Baluster Form, Flared Round Base & Bobeche, 9 In., Pair 260.00
Glass, Monogram, Bobeches, Prisms, 9 1/2 In., Pair 110.00
Glass, Side Drip Pan, Cut Stem, Cobalt Blue Overlay, Bohemian, 14 In., Pair 2185.00
Iron, Forged, Tripod Base, Spring Holder, Scrolled Handle, 11 In. 330.00
Iron, Hog Scraper, 19th Century, Push-Up, 7 1/4 In., 4 Piece 316.00
Mahogany, Brass Mounted, Open Spiral Shaft, Late Victorian, 12 1/2 In., Pair 605.00
Marble, Black, White, Verdigris Corinthian Capital, 22 1/2 In., Pair 375.00
Oak, Copper Trim, Rohlfs, 1902, 11 x 6 x 6 In. 990.00
Ormolu, Voluted Stem, Stepped Domed Base, Auguste Meissonier, 12 In., Pair 2530.00
Paktong, Gadrooned Bobeche, Stop Fluted Columns, 1765, 11 1/2 In., Pair 4025.00
Pewter, Tooled Rope Design, Push-Up, 10 7/8 In., Pair 385.00
Porcelain, Figural, Man & Woman, Robes, Turban, Continental, 11 3/8 In., Pair 575.00
Porcelain, Mars, Early 18th Century, 10 In. ....*Illus* 375.00
Porcelain, Putto, Floral Bocage, Scrollwork Base, Gold Anchor Mark, 11 In., Pair 360.00
Porcelain, Rococo, Applied Putto & Floral Design, Sitzendorf, 7 In., Pair 115.00
Porcelain, Young Child With Bird, Seated Beneath Tree, Germany, 8 In., Pair 90.00
Pressed Glass, Canary, Petal & Loop, American, Mid 19th Century, 6 In., Pair 345.00
Pressed Glass, Dolphin Shape, Hurricane Shade, 16 In., Pair 315.00
Redware, Black Glaze, Urn Top, Flared Stem, Ben Owen, 1960s, 13 1/2 In., Pair 335.00
Rock Crystal, Napoleon III, Baluster Shaped Stem, Scrolled Toes, 14 In., Pair 13800.00
Rock Crystal, Napoleon III, Leaf Tip Divided Stem, Serpentine Base, 16 In., Pair 6325.00
Sheet Brass, Trumpet Base, Mid-Drip Pan, 8 1/4 In. 1045.00
Silver, Baluster Stem, Acanthus Design, Black, Starr & Frost, 10 In., Pair 1320.00
Silver, Band Of Pyramid Beading, Stepped Base, George III, England, 12 In., Pair 3220.00
Silver, Embossed Baskets & Swags Of Flowers, England, 13 1/2 In., Pair 2875.00
Silver, Galleried Base, Tapered, Chased Dragon, Foo Dog Finial, 11 In., Pair 1380.00
Silver, Georgian, Stepped Armorial Base, Simon Jouet, 1757, 7 1/4 In., Pair 3740.00
Silver, Grapes Supporting Large Bell Shaped Base, Minsk, Russia, 12 In., Pair 980.00
Silver, Landgraaff, Trailing Flowers, Shells, Germany, c.1765, 9 1/2 In., Pair 5175.00
Silver, Oval Stem, Detachable Nozzle, George Eadon, England, 1799, 11 In., Pair 2185.00
Silver, Princess Patricia, Gorham, American, 10 In., Pair 332.00
Silver, Reed & Flute Band, J. Roberts, England, George III, 1812, 6 3/4 In., Pair 1035.00
Silver, Square Base, Swags, Lion Masks, Winter & Co., 1776, 11 In., 4 Piece 9200.00
Silver, Strapwork, Removable Nozzles, Odiot, France, 10 1/4 In., Pair 2760.00
Silver, Stylized Wheat Grass Fronds, Gadrooned Rim, George III, Ireland, 11 In., Pair ... 7475.00
Silver, Telescopic, T. Wallis & J. Hayne, England, 1816, 11 In., Pair 1840.00
Silver On Copper, Scrolls & Leaves, Double Knop Stems, Sheffield, 11 In., Pair 315.00
Silver On Copper, Stepped Base, Corinthian Column, Sheffield, 14 1/2 In., Pair 750.00
Silver Plate, 5-Light, Art Nouveau, Morning Glories, c.1910, 12 1/2 In. 200.00
Silver Plate, Acanthus Scones, Detachable Bobeches, Sheffield, 12 1/2 In., Pair 298.00
Silver Plate, Ornate Column, Blown Hurricane Shade, Sheffield, 24 In., Pair 415.00
Silver Plate, Reeded Design, Tapered Fluted Stems, Sheffield, 11 3/4 In., Pair 345.00
Silver Plate, Scrolled Leaves, Ellis-Barker Silver Co., 5 1/4 In., 4 Piece 175.00
Silver Plate, Tapered Knop Stem, Gadroon & Scroll Band, Sheffield, 12 In., Pair 520.00
Silver Plate, Telescopic, Applied Scrolls & Leaves, Sheffield, 9 3/4 In., Pair 230.00
Silver Plate, Telescopic, Detachable Bobeche, c.1830, 9 In., Pair 245.00
Sterling Silver, Applied Leaves, Scroll Base, Campana Sconce, 1820, 12 In., Pair 2070.00
Sterling Silver, Baluster Shaft, Scalloped Base, Belgium, 1740, 10 1/2 In., Pair 1100.00
Sterling Silver, Band Of Acanthus & Beading, Bombe Socket, 11 In., Pair 2300.00
Sterling Silver, Beaded Rim, Foliage, Garlands, Corinthian Columns, 11 In., Pair 1495.00
Sterling Silver, Charles X, Square Tapered Shaft, Round Base, 1819-1838, 9 3/4 In. 3960.00
Sterling Silver, Leaves, Fluted Stem, Flower & Leaf Garlands, Webster, 10 In., Pair 260.00
Sterling Silver, Stylized Shell Corners, Square Base, Ebenezer Coker, 9 In., Pair 2990.00
Sterling Silver, Table, Trumpet Form, Gilt Interior, Georg Jensen, 24 Oz., Pair 4600.00
Sterling Silver, Turned Shaft, Swirled Base, Belgium, 1740, 11 In., Pair 1430.00
Tin, Hog Scraper, Side, Lip Hanger, Push-Up, 7 In. 60.00
Tin, Painted, Round Weighted Base, Push-Up, 9 1/2 In. 210.00
Walnut, Brass, Open Spiral Base, c.1860, Pair 170.00
Wooden, Altar, Gilt, Baroque, Continental, 30 In., Pair 1495.00

CANDLEWICK items may be listed in the Imperial and Pressed Glass categories.

CANDY CONTAINERS have been popular since the late Victorian era. Collectors have long favored the glass containers, but now all types, including tin and papier-mache, are collected. Probably the earliest glass container sold commercially was the Liberty Bell made in 1876 for sale at the Centennial Exposition. Thousands of designs were made until the cost became too high in the 1960s. By the late 1970s, reproductions were being made and sold without the candy. Containers listed here are glass unless otherwise described. A Belsnickle is a nineteenth-century figure of Father Christmas.

Airplane, Liberty Motor, Clear, Original Tin	2200.00
Amos & Andy, In Open Air Taxi, Yellow Wheels, Victory Glass Co., 5 In.	580.00
Baby, Wax, Taufling, Lace Borders, Blue Ribbons, France, 1890, 10 1/2 In.	467.00
Bank, Buddy, Figure Of Boy Resting Arm On Lid, Marx Toy Co., 4 1/8 In.	365.00
Barney Google & Ball, Standing On Pedestal, King Features, 4 In.	240.00
Baseball Player, Bat In Hand, Standing Next To Barrel, 3 3/8 In.	530.00
Bell, Liberty Bell, Gilt	35.00
Belsnickle, Bisque, Cardboard, Papier-Mache, Flannel Coat, Feather Tree, 11 In.	660.00
Belsnickle, Green Feather Tree In Arm, Red Flannel Coat, Fur Beard, 9 In.	660.00
Belsnickle, Papier-Mache On Wood Base, Icicle Beard, 10 1/2 In.	1870.00
Birdcage, With Bail, Original Closure	275.00
Boat, Remember The Maine, Milk Glass, 7 1/4 In.	350.00
Boy, Pouty Expression, Hollow Torso, Gebruder Heubach, 8 1/2 In.	1050.00
Bus, Jitney, Dark Green Body, Red Tin Spoke Wheels, West Spec. Co., 4 In.	510.00
Bust, Irish Man, Smoking Pipe, Composition, Germany, 3 3/4 In.	120.00
Camel, Standing, Dromedary, Glass Eyes, Composition, Germany, 6 1/2 In.	320.00
Candlestick, Colonial, Original Closure	305.00
Cannon, Rapid Fire Gun, Original Tin, Original Closure, 7 3/4 In.	590.00
Car, Coupe With Long Hood, Clear, Original Closure, 5 1/4 In.	83.00
Carpet Sweeper, Dolly Sweeper, Original Tin, Original Closure	525.00
Cat, Black, Stretch Neck	2950.00
Chick, Glass Eyes, Wire Legs, Germany, 4 1/2 In.	300.00
Chick, Nodder, Blue Jacket, Orange Pants, Composition, Germany, 6 In.	130.00 to 135.00
Chick In Shell Car, Red Wheels, Tin Enclosure, Victory Glass Co., 5 In.	500.00
Chicken, On Nest, Glass, Paper Bottom, J.H. Millstein Co., 5 In.	20.00
Chicken, On Stump, Feather Tail, Composition, Germany, 4 1/2 In.	175.00
Coal Car, Overland Limited, Original Wheels, Original Closure, 4 1/2 In.	440.00
Daisy Duck, Long, Red Dress, Black Hat, Composition, Germany, 7 In.	240.00 to 340.00
Dirigible, Los Angeles, Paint Traces, Original Closure, 5 3/4 In.	165.00
Dog, Bulldog, Brown, Glass Eyes, Collar, Composition, Germany, 5 1/2 In.	530.00
Dog, Bulldog, Glass	45.00
Dog, Bulldog, Round Base, Brown Paint, Original Closure	72.00
Dog, Scotty, Head Up, Millstein	25.00
Dog, With Umbrella, Glass	75.00
Donkey, Pulling Cart	15.00
Duck, Large Bill, Paint Traces, Original Closure	185.00
Duck, Spring-Jointed Wings, Germany, 6 1/4 In.	165.00
Easter Egg, Papier-Mache, Hen, Chicks, Rooster, Dirigible, 1920s, 5 3/8 In.	200.00
Elephant, Walking, Glass Eyes, Composition, Germany, 5 3/4 In.	210.00
Fat Boy On Drum, Happifat, Standing On Drum, George Borgfeldt, 4 In.	360.00
Gas Pump, Gas 23¢ Today Embossed On Front Panel, Tin Enclosure, 5 In.	390.00
George Washington, Papier-Mache, Cardboard Cabin, 4 1/2 In.	165.00
Golf Bag, Bottom Closure	2500.00
Gun, Colt, Type 1, Partial Paint, Original Closure	44.00
Hat, Uncle Sam, Paint, No Closure, 2 1/2 In.	77.00
Hen, On Nest, Disc Lid For Woven Nest, Composition, Germany, 4 In.	230.00
Hen, On Nest, Papier-Mache, 7 In.	95.00
Hen, On Nest, Woven Straw Nest, Germany, 5 In.	300.00
Horn, 3-Valve, Tin Mouthpiece, Paint Traces, Original Closure, 5 In.	385.00
Iron, Flat Iron, Paint, Original Closure, 3 1/2 In.	690.00
Jack-O'-Lantern In Tree, Papier-Mache, 6 1/2 In.	990.00
Joan Of Arc, Doll, Candy Drawer In Base, Bisque Head, c.1875, 17 In.	3300.00
Lamp, Library Lamp, Original Fringe, Original Closure, 4 1/4 In.	825.00
Lantern, Beveled Panel Square, Candleholder, Original Closure, 4 1/8 In.	145.00

Lantern, Victory Glass Co. 30.00
Lawn Swing, Original Tin, Original Closure 965.00
Limousine, Westmoreland Specialty Co., Red Tin Spoke Wheels, Tin Roof 95.00
Locomotive, 999 With Man In Window, Original Candy, Original Closure 185.00
Man, Bisque, Folklore Costume, Cardboard Torso, Separates At Waist, 16 In. 4000.00
Man, Character Head, Fez Hat, Papier-Mache, 6 In. 210.00
Man, Character Head, Papier-Mache, Blue Uniform, 6 In. 265.00
Man, Red Jacket, Black Jacket, Cotton Batting, 3 1/4 In. 465.00
Man On Motorcycle, On Indian Model, Side Car, Spoke Wheels, 5 In. 500.00
Milk Carrier, Anco, Candy Milk Carrier, 4 Creamers With Caps 94.00
Moon Mullins, Black Cap, Original Closure 28.00
Mug, Kiddies Drinking Mug, No Closure 11.00
Opera Glass, Swirl Ribs, Original Tin, Original Closure 165.00
PEZ, Astronaut 1, Silver 875.00
PEZ, Bambi 60.00
PEZ, Bullwinkle, Brown Stem 535.00
PEZ, Clown, Whistle 10.00
PEZ, Donald Duck 15.00
PEZ, Foghorn Leghorn, With Feet 95.00
PEZ, Fred Flintstone, Zephyr 45.00
PEZ, Indian Brave, Red Face 185.00
PEZ, Indian Whistle, On Card 30.00
PEZ, Lamb, White Head, 4 1/4 In. 24.00
PEZ, Lion, Roar The Lion 185.00
PEZ, Mimic The Monkey 50.00
PEZ, Policeman 65.00
PEZ, Road Runner 20.00
PEZ, Smurf A, Feet, White Hat 5.00
PEZ, Space Gun, Red, 1980s 90.00
PEZ, Tinkerbelle 295.00
PEZ, Uncle Sam 235.00
PEZ, Zorro, Logo 85.00
Pheasant On Tree Stump, Polychromed, Germany, 3 3/4 In. 155.00
Phonograph, Glass Record Type, Horn, Original Closure 385.00
Policeman, Pumpkin Head, Paint Traces, Original Closure 2970.00
Rabbit, Amber Glass Eyes, Papier-Mache, Germany, 1900, 14 In. 412.00
Rabbit, Composition, White, Black Spots, Carrot In Mouth, Germany, 7 In. 200.00
Rabbit, Glass Eyes, Trembler Ears, Germany 130.00
Rabbit, Holding Carrot, Turtleneck, Shorts, Hat, Glass Eyes, Germany, 7 In. 345.00
Rabbit, On Log, Blue Dress, Guarding Egg, Composition, Germany, 3 In. 310.00
Rabbit, Papier-Mache, Glass Eyes, Wooden Cart, Germany, 10 In. 225.00
Rabbit, Peter Rabbit, Millstein, 6 1/4 In. 30.00
Rabbit, Pulling Cart, Brown Rabbit, Moss Covered Cart, Germany, 7 In. 319.00
Rabbit, Pulling Cart, Gray Wool Cover, Glass Eyes, Wheels, Germany, 12 In. 385.00
Rabbit, Seated, Glass, Millstein 25.00
Rabbit, Squatting, Caramel Painted Eyes, Moss Covered, Germany, 4 In. 155.00
Rabbit, Standing, White Felt Cover, Holding Carrot, Glass Eyes, Germany, 10 In. 165.00
Rabbit, Turtleneck, Shorts, Holding Carrot, Composition, Germany, 8 x 6 In. 415.00
Rabbit, White, Black Spots, Seated, Holding Carrot, Glass Eyes, Germany, 7 In. 195.00
Rabbit, With Wheelbarrow, Partial Paint, Original Closure 330.00
Rabbit Family, Painted, Original Closure 910.00
Refrigerator 5600.00
Road Sign, Don't Park Here, Orange Pole, Top, Tin Enclosure, 4 1/2 In. 170.00
Rocking Horse, Clown, Riding, White, Red, 4 1/4 In. 365.00
Rolling Pin, Original Closure 275.00
Rooster, Dressed, Metal Feet, Moving Head, Papier-Mache 415.00
Rooster, Spring Legs, Composition, Germany, 5 1/2 In. 175.00
Rooster, Young Chicks In Basket On Back, c.1900, 6 In. 500.00
Santa Claus, Blowing Horn, Red & Yellow Plastic, 5 1/2 In. 25.00
Santa Claus, Brown Suit, Feather Tree, Sled, Box 1045.00
Santa Claus, Composition Face & Hands, Mohair Beard, Germany, 26 In. 2785.00
Santa Claus, In Boot, Tree, Flocked Paper, Japan, 6 In. 60.00
Santa Claus, On Sled, Composition, Felt Clothes, Germany, 3 1/2 In. 210.00

Santa Claus, Papier-Mache, Cloth, Wire, Basket, Boots Open, Germany, 12 In. 1100.00
Santa Claus, Papier-Mache, Mica Flecked Pointed Hat, 14 In. 715.00
Santa Claus, Red & White, Plastic, B On Belt Buckle, Irvin, 6 1/2 In. 15.00
Santa Claus, Seated On Reindeer, Papier-Mache, Removable Head, 14 In. 2700.00
Santa Claus, Standing, Opens At Waist, Germany 695.00
Santa Claus, White Flannel & Fur, Separated At Waist, Papier-Mache, 10 1/2 In. 330.00
Skookum, By Tree Stump, Tin Enclosure, George Borgfeldt 360.00
Taxi, Black, White, Tin Spoke Wheels, Westmoreland Speciality Co., 4 In. 460.00
Taxi, Yellow, Tin Roof, Red Tin Spoke Wheels, West Spec. Co., 4 1/8 In. 365.00
Telephone, Candlestick, Glass 34.00
Telephone, Victory Glass Co. Dial Type, Original Candy, Original Closure . . . . .45.00 to 50.00
Toonerville Trolley, Whimsical, Fontaine Fox, 1922, 3 3/4 In. 580.00
Top, Spinning, Original Wooden Winder, Original Closure . . . . .83.00 to 110.00
Uncle Sam By Barrel, Standing By Barrel, Tin Coin Slot, 3 3/4 In. 300.00
VooDoo, Black Witch 25.00
Witch Rooster In Shoe, Papier-Mache, 6 In. 1540.00
World Globe, On Stand, Original Closure 525.00

CANES and walking sticks were used by every well-dressed man in the
nineteenth century, but by World War I the style had changed. Today
canes are used by few but the infirm. Collectors prize old canes made
with special features, like hidden swords, whiskey flasks, or risqué pictures seen through peepholes. Examples with solid gold heads or made
from exotic materials, such as walrus vertebrae, are among the higher
priced canes.

40 Inlaid Faceted Rubies In Knob Handle, Horn Ferrule, c.1900, 34 1/2 In. 7560.00
Alligator Grip, Pa., 1900 . . . .   192.00
Animal Claw Handle, Ebonized, Late 19th Century, 34 1/2 In. 230.00
Anna Dickinson Bust, Leather Belt, Buckle, Pewter, Partridgewood Shaft, 34 1/2 In. 550.00
Antler Handle, Silver Ferule, Hand Chased Fox, Wooden Shaft, Woman's, 34 In. 100.00
Bamboo, Iron Spike Tip, c.1900, 36 In. 92.00
Bartender's, Gadget, Shot Measure & Hidden Corkscrew, 1910 . . . .   425.00
Bird Claw & Egg, Sterling Silver, Tropical Wood Shaft, Brass Ferrule, c.1880, 35 In. 523.00
Boxer Dog, Glass Eyes, Birch Shaft, Bone Finial, 36 In. 230.00
Bulldog Head, Illuminated, Glass Eyes, Batteries In Handle, Hardwood Shaft, 35 1/4 In. .   605.00
Carved Head Of Black Man, Glass Eyes, Metal Ferrule, Early 20th Century, 35 1/4 In. . . .   200.00
Carved Snake, Star, Half Moon, Initials S.O., Date, 1918, 34 3/4 In. 440.00
Dagger, Ivory Handle, Iron Tip, Concentric Leather Circles, 11-In. Blade 310.00
Dagger, Staghorn, Glass-Eyed Man, Silver Collar, Rosewood Shaft, c.1830, 39 In. 395.00
Ebony, Gold Plated Handle, Presentation Inscription, 35 In. 83.00
Gold, Bark Malacca, Horn Ferrule, Tiffany, c.1920, 35 1/2 In. 3630.00
Gold Plated, Inscribed Elmer Williams, Employees Of Sioux 3, Mt. Carmel, Pa. 55.00
Gold Plated, Ronson Cigarette Lighter 6160.00
Gun, Dog Head, Gutta-Percha Handle, Silver Collar, 1860s, 36 1/2 In. 7840.00
Hawk Perched On Stump, Silver Collar, Glass Eyes, Walnut, c.1890, 35 In. 385.00
Horn, Fist Holding Truncheon, Wooden, 19th Century, 38 In. 120.00
Horse Measure, Swaine & Adency, England, 1920 . . . .   625.00
Ivory, Boxer Dog's Head Handle, Wooden, 35 In. 385.00
Ivory, Carved Dog's Head, Bamboo, 19th Century 275.00
Ivory, Dr. Watson, Smoking Pipe, Elephant Ivory Handle, Ebony Shaft, 36 In. 1870.00
Ivory, Fist, Narwhal Shaft, c.1860, 37 In. 6270.00
Ivory, Girl's Head, Silver Collar, Mahoganized Hardwood, c.1880, 35 1/2 In. 3740.00
Ivory, Grimacing Man, Bee On Forehead, Malacca Shaft, 36 1/4 In. 1870.00
Ivory, Horse's Hoof Handle, Wooden, 34 In. 220.00
Ivory, Leaves, Open Blossom, Hardwood Shaft, Horn Ferrule, c.1900, 36 In. 2420.00
Ivory, Melon Handle, Rosewood, 36 In. 340.00
Ivory, Monkeys, Mother, 3 Babies, Malacca Shaft, Japan, 37 1/4 In. 85.00
Ivory, Phrenology Head, c.1850, 36 3/4 In. 3025.00
Ivory, Rabbit Head, Teeth & Ears, Pierced For Wrist Cord, c.1870, 38 In. 4510.00
Ivory, Silver Mounted, Thorn Shaft, 19th Century, 35 1/4 In. 288.00
Ivory, Skull, Gold Collar, Malacca Shaft, 34 1/2 In. 990.00
Ivory, Tiger & Dog, Art Nouveau, Bamboo Shaft 5265.00
Ivory, Whale Handle, Rosewood, 36 In. 430.00

Ivory Handle, Jewels, Barely Twist Whalebone Shaft, c.1890 .... 6270.00
Ivory Skull, Articulated Jaw, 1880, 35 1/4 In. 2750.00
Lion's Body & Stag's Head Handle, Carved, Fruit & Leaf Shaft, 19th Century, 39 In. 495.00
Pocahontas, John Smith, Savers Of Early Virginia, Gibson Facet, 1932, 34 In. 260.00
Porcelain, Flowers, Ebonized Hardwood Shaft, Horn Ferrule, c.1890, 36 In. 525.00
Presentation, Jade Ball, Rock Crystal Ring, Brigg, 1908, 36 In. 2530.00
Remington, Doghead Gun, 1860 .... 7700.00
Shepherd's Stick, Wood, Carved Like Chain, Iron Tip, 50 In. 55.00
Silver Repousse, Bird & Deer, Hunting Scene, 19th Century 110.00
Snuffbox & Dagger, Side Button, 12-In. Blade Appears, Tortoiseshell, Ivory, c.1870 ..... 2100.00
Sword, Ebony, Carved, Ball In Cage, Folk Art, 19-In. Blade, 1900 .... 895.00
Sword, White, Engraved Round Handle, Sun & Zodiac Symbols, 22-In. Blade 195.00
Turk's Head Knot, Rosewood, Whale Ivory Baleen Spacers, c.1830 .... 975.00
Walking Stick, Bamboo & Pearl, Geisha Girl & Cherry Blossom, Japan, 1912, 35 In. 185.00
Walking Stick, Boar's Tusk, Sterling Silver Collar, Walnut Shaft, c.1880 .... 495.00
Walking Stick, Bone, Mastiff, Silver Mounted, Ebonized, Carved Beast's Head, 36 In. 345.00
Walking Stick, Boxer Dog, Crutch Handle, Carved Ivory Knob, Malacca, 37 In. 400.00
Walking Stick, Braided Root, Late 19th-Early 20th Century, 35 1/4 In. 58.00
Walking Stick, Chinoiserie Design Silver Knob, Wooden, c.1900, 36 In. 260.00
Walking Stick, Cleaved Hoof, Sterling Overlay, Crook Handle, Vienna Secession, 1800s . 230.00
Walking Stick, Ebonized, Chinese Silver Knob, Raised Prunus Designs, 32 In. 145.00
Walking Stick, Ebonized, Gold Filled Knob, 19th Century, 34 In. 175.00
Walking Stick, Ebonized, Repousse Scrollwork Curved Handle, 37 In. 230.00
Walking Stick, Ebonized, Sterling Silver, Marked, Birmingham, 1894, 34 In. 93.00
Walking Stick, Ebony & 14K Gold Handle, Inscribed H.A. Hamilton, 31 1/2 In. 237.00
Walking Stick, Ebony & Ivory, Stylized Alligator Head 325.00
Walking Stick, Ebony, Handle, Head, Fur Hat, Glass Eye, Early 1800s, 36 1/2 In. 230.00
Walking Stick, Edwardian, Ebonized, Gold Filled Knob, c.1910, 36 In. 200.00
Walking Stick, Fluted Ivory Handle, Sterling Silver, Rosewood Shaft 750.00
Walking Stick, Georgia Marble Head, Green, Red & White Swirl, 33 In. 225.00
Walking Stick, Glass, Aqua, Bright Yellow, Red, White Stripes, 66 In. 242.00
Walking Stick, Glass, Aqua, Dark Red, Blue, White Stripes, 1870, 66 In. 88.00
Walking Stick, Glass, Aqua, Parade Whimsy, 1870, 53 In. 121.00
Walking Stick, Glass, Aqua, Sapphire Blue Stripes, 1870, 48 In. 121.00
Walking Stick, Glass, Aqua, Yellow, Blue, Magenta Stripes, 66 In. 121.00
Walking Stick, Glass, Deep Aqua, Parade Whimsy, 1860, 38 In. 110.00
Walking Stick, Glass, Pigeon Blood Spiral Stripes, Parade Whimsy, 50 In. 209.00
Walking Stick, Glass, Red, White, Blue, Parade Whimsy, 1870, 71 In. 253.00
Walking Stick, Ivory Knob, Baby Crawling Out Of Pumpkin, Gold Band, 19th Century .. 1100.00
Walking Stick, Ivory Knob, Growling Dog's Head, Glass Eyes, 19th Century 605.00
Walking Stick, Ivory Knob, Man's Head, Retractable Tongue, Sterling Silver Band 770.00
Walking Stick, Ivory Knob, Medieval Village Idiot's Head, 19th Century 1320.00
Walking Stick, Knob Handle, Inked Diamond Pattern, Tricolor Bamboo Shaft, 32 1/2 In. . 115.00
Walking Stick, Knobby Sapling Type Shaft, Ivory Handle, 32 In. 55.00
Walking Stick, Lacquer, Black & Red, Allegorical Panels, Far East, 37 1/2 In. 80.00
Walking Stick, Mahogany, Ivory Spherical Knob, c.1900, 34 1/2 In. 145.00
Walking Stick, Monkey Head, Beaded Glass Eyes, Braided Collar, London, 33 1/4 In. 420.00
Walking Stick, Pewter Finish, Organic Form, L-Shape, Congo, Brass Finial, 36 In. 81.00
Walking Stick, Presentation, Floral Design, Gold Plated Top, Engraved, 1854, 36 1/2 In. . 170.00
Walking Stick, Rattlesnake, Brown, Black Spots, 36 In. 300.00
Walking Stick, Rosewood, Fitted Compass Knob, Sterling Silver, London, 1919, 35 In. ... 175.00
Walking Stick, Staghorn, Silver, 1900, 35 In. 115.00
Walking Stick, Stalactites, Silver Knob, Birch Stick, Marked, RFS & Co., 34 3/4 In. 115.00
Walking Stick, Sterling Silver Crook, Snakewood, c.1890 .... 650.00
Walking Stick, Sterling Silver Mounted, Ebonized, Hallmarked Chester, 1871, 35 1/2 In. . 105.00
Walking Stick, Sterling Silver, Wooden, December 25, 1905, Inscription, 33 3/4 In. 170.00
Walking Stick, Stylized Intertwining Sterling Vine, Jugenstil, Crook Handle, Brass Finial . 86.00
Walking Stick, Stylized Phallic Rhino Horn Handle, c.1850 .... 495.00
Walking Stick, Twined Snakes On Vines Form Medical Symbol, 20th Century, 45 In. 120.00
Walking Stick, Walrus Ivory Alligator, Snakewood Shaft, c.1900 .... 450.00
Walking Stick, Whalebone, Mahogany, Spiral Top, American, 19th Century, 37 In. 374.00
Walking Stick, Woman's, L-Shape, Carved Ivory Handle, Floral Guilloche, 35 In. 316.00
Walking Stick, Wood, Floral Silver Collet Beneath Knob, England, 1900, 35 1/2 In. 145.00

Water Buffalo Horn, c.1910 .... 325.00
Whale Ivory, Turk's Head Knot, Coin Silver Collar, Whalebone Shaft, c.1840, 37 In. 1540.00
Whale Tooth, Ebony, Ivory & Rosewood Separators 795.00
Whalebone, Carved Handle, Wooden Shaft, Brass Tip, 19th Century, 32 In. 100.00
Whalebone, Naughty Nellie Leg, Copper Ferrule.............................. 1075.00
Whalebone & Ivory, L-Shape Handle, 3 Baleen Spacers, Engraved J.M.C., 35 1/2 In. 400.00
Whistle, Bear, Ivory Handle, 1915, 35 1/4 In. 2200.00
Wood, Carved Bird, Schtockschnitzler Simmons, 19th Century, 36 3/4 In. 1045.00
Wood, Long-Billed Duck, Carved Bone Beak, Continental, 2 3/4 In. 259.00
Wood, Maple, Yellow & Black Barber Pole Paint, 36 In. 45.00
Wood, Pirate, Carved, Painted Eyes, American, Late 19th Century, 33 1/4 In. 300.00
Wood, Poacher's, Iron Barrel, Disguised Gun, England, 19th Century, 36 In. 935.00
Wood, Snake Ascending Tree Limb, Green Paint, Folk Art, 19th Century, 34 1/2 In. 550.00
Wood, Snake Handle, 2 Intertwined Snakes Shaft, Carved, Folk Art, 19th Century, 35 In. . 495.00
Wood, Walnut, Parrot Head, Silver Collar, Staghorn Ferrule, Walnut, c.1890, 35 1/4 In. ... 55.00

CANEWARE is a tan-colored, unglazed stoneware that was first developed by Josiah Wedgwood about 1770. It has been made by many
companies since that time and is often used for cooking or serving
utensils.

Jug, Gray, Tapered, Rope Banding, Loop Handle, 19th Century, 7 In. 55.00
Teapot, Cover, Bamboo Rims, Handle & Spout, Bacchanalian Boys, 1780s, 5 1/2 In. 1265.00
Vase, Bamboo Form, 3 Spills, Anthemion Banding, Late 18th Century, 9 1/2 In. 5750.00

CANTON CHINA is a blue-and-white ware made near the city of Canton,
in China, from about 1785 to 1895. It is hand decorated with Chinese
scenes. Canton is part of the group of porcelains known today as
Chinese Export Porcelain.

Basket, Pierced, 8 3/4 In. 305.00
Basket, Pierced, Blue & White, Undertray, 2 3/4 x 8 1/4 x 7 1/4 In. 880.00
Basket, Pierced, Undertray, Blue & White, 9 1/2 In. 880.00
Bottle, 8 1/2 In. 225.00
Bowl, 19th Century, 8 In. 55.00
Bowl, Blue & White, Cut Corner, 4 3/4 x 9 1/4 In. 880.00
Bowl, Blue, White, 9 3/4 In. 315.00
Bowl, Cover, Boar's Head Handles, 6 1/2 In. 475.00
Bowl, Pagoda, Blue & White, Scalloped, Shallow, 9 1/2 In. 685.00
Bowl, Reticulated Sides, Oval, 8 1/2 In. 135.00
Bowl, River Landscape & Fishing Boats, Blue, White, Geometric Blue Border, 16 In. 2530.00
Bowl, Scalloped Rim, Orange Peel Glaze, Blue, White, 10 x 2 3/4 In. 495.00
Bowl, Shallow, Blue & White, Scalloped Rim, 9 1/2 In. 360.00
Bowl, Square, Cut Corner, 19th Century, 9 1/2 In. 495.00
Bowl, Sunflower, 1850, 10 In. 850.00
Bowl, Vegetable, Blue & White, Modified Oval, 9 In. 220.00
Bowl, Vegetable, Cover, Blue & White, Rectangular, Pomegranate Finial, 9 1/2 In. 330.00
Bowl, Vegetable, Cover, Rectangular, 19th Century, 5 x 9 x 8 In. 85.00
Bowl, Vegetable, Diamond Shape, 19th Century, 4 x 10 1/2 x 8 1/4 In., Pair 635.00
Bowl, Vegetable, Oval, Pinecone Finial, 19th Century, 9 1/2 In. 250.00
Bowl, Vegetable, Rectangular, 19th Century, 4 1/2 x 8 x 7 In., Pair 490.00
Candlestick, 19th Century, 7 1/2 In., Pair 2640.00
Candlestick, 9 3/4 In. 1265.00
Chamber Pot, Cover, Blue, White 230.00
Compote, 5 1/2 In. 405.00
Creamer, 19th Century, 3 1/2 In. 130.00
Creamer, 3 1/2 In. 250.00
Cup & Saucer, Handleless, 19th Century, 6 Piece 75.00
Dish, Cover, Blue & White, Modified Oval Form, Pomegranate Finial, 10 1/2 In. 275.00
Dish, Hot Water, 19th Century, 10 3/4 In. 350.00
Dish, Leaf Shape, 7 3/4 In. 145.00
Dish, Leaf Shape, Landscape Design, Early 19th Century, 7 1/2 In. 255.00
Dish, Oval, Early 19th Century, 8 3/4 In. 230.00
Dish, Rectangular, Cover, 19th Century, 9 1/2 In. 275.00
Dish, Shrimp, Blue & White, 10 1/2 In., Pair 315.00
Dish, Shrimp, Blue & White, 10 1/4 In. 580.00

Ginger Jar, 3 1/2 In. 195.00
Ginger Jar, 4 1/2 In. 195.00
Ginger Jar, Cover, Blue & White, 6 1/2 In. 140.00
Jug, Cider, Blue, White, 9 1/4 In. 200.00
Jug, Cider, Cover, Blue & White, Foo Dog Finial, Twist Handle, 8 x 6 1/2 In. 1485.00
Jug, Cider, Cover, Flower Ends, Double Woven Strap Handle, 8 In. 1955.00
Jug, Cream, Blue & White, Spout, 3 1/2 In. 250.00
Mug, Blue, White, 3 1/2 In. 345.00
Mug, Twined Handle, 18th Century, 5 3/4 In. 245.00
Pitcher, Handle, 19th Century, 7 3/4 x 6 1/2 In. 490.00
Plate, 19th Century, 7 1/2 In., 12 Piece 415.00
Plate, 19th Century, 9 3/4 In., 8 Piece 635.00
Platter, Blue & White, 17 In. 375.00
Platter, Grilled Meats, Blue, White, Oblong, 1800, 9 1/2 x 7 In. 200.00
Platter, Meat, Rectangular, 15 1/2 In. 495.00
Platter, Oblong, 19th Century, 18 1/2 x 15 3/4 In. 745.00
Platter, Octagonal, Blue & White, 14 In. 190.00
Platter, Octagonal, Blue & White, 14 x 11 In. 415.00
Platter, Oval, 8 1/2 In. 110.00
Platter, Oval, Blue & White, 18 1/2 In. . . . . .770.00 to 825.00
Relish, Leaf Form, 19th Century 150.00
Sauceboat, 19th Century, 8 In. 110.00
Sauceboat, 7 1/2 In. 145.00
Sugar, Cover, 19th Century, 5 1/2 In. 330.00
Tea Caddy, Cover, Octagonal, 19th Century, 5 1/2 In. 2645.00
Teakettle, Stand, Globular Form, Continuous Figural Scenes, 12 1/4 In. 975.00
Teapot, Blue & White, Iron Handle, 6 In. 40.00
Teapot, Cover, Blue & White, Entwined Handle, 7 In. 825.00
Teapot, Cover, Blue & White, Underplate, 8 x 10 1/2 In. 1485.00
Teapot, Drum Form, 19th Century, 5 3/4 In. 440.00
Teapot, Drum Form, Entwined Handle, 19th Century 315.00
Teapot, Foo Dog Cover, Barrel Form, 19th Century, 6 1/2 In. 860.00
Tureen, Cover, Blue & White, Boar's Head Handles, 10 In. 770.00
Tureen, Soup, Cover, Handle, Rectangular, 19th Century, 7 1/2 x 12 x 8 In. 490.00
Tureen, Soup, Cover, Rectangular, 19th Century, 7 x 11 x 7 1/2 In. 230.00
Vase, Blue, 19th Century, 10 1/2 In. 230.00
Vase, Bluster Form, Blue & White, 15 1/2 x 10 In. 1870.00
Warming Dish, Last Half 19th Century, 9 1/2 In. 290.00

CAPO-DI-MONTE porcelain was first made in Naples, Italy, from 1743
to 1759. The factory moved near Madrid, Spain, reopened in 1771, and
worked to 1834. Since that time, the Doccia factory of Italy acquired
the molds and is using the crown and N mark. Societe Richard Ceram-
ica is a modern-day firm often referred to as Ginori or Capo-di-Monte.
This company uses the crown and N mark.

Basket, Flowered Edge, 4 In. 22.00
Bowl, Classical Design, Gilt, Applied Handles, Off-White Ground, 12 x 5 In. 69.00
Bowl, Molded Putto Design, Floral Interior, 8 3/4 In. 260.00
Bowl, With Undertray, Molded Putto, 7 1/4 In. 175.00
Box, Bronze Trim, Woman & Children Scene, Floral Border, 2 x 2 In. 132.00
Box, Cherub & Goat Cameo 1 Side, Tiger & Cherub Other, 8 x 5 1/2 In. 110.00
Box, Cover, Round, Ginori, 5 1/2 In. 58.00
Box, Molded Putto, Griffin & Leaf Design, Oval, 6 3/4 In. 490.00
Box, Mythological Scene On Cover, Putto Sides, Painted Interior, 3 In. 375.00
Casket, Panels Of Psyche & Cherubs, 7 1/2 x 9 1/2 In. 517.00
Centerpiece, Line Of Fancifully Clad Youth Musicians, 30 In. 1380.00
Figurine, 18th Century Woman, Seated, Parasol, 8 1/2 In. 85.00
Figurine, Bacchante Standing Beside An Urn On Stand, 9 In. 115.00
Figurine, Dwarf Woman, 1950, 4 5/8 In. . . . .*Illus* 300.00
Figurine, Girl In Ball Gown, With Flower Basket, 9 1/2 In. 30.00
Figurine, Old Beggar Woman, Polychrome & Gilt, Signed, 10 3/4 In. 190.00
Figurine, Victorian Woman, Marked, 5 In. 50.00
Figurine, Woman In Large Chair, Lace, 6 In. 90.00

Figurines are often damaged. Examine the fingers, toes, and other protruding parts for damage or repairs.

Capo-Di-Monte,
Figurine,
Dwarf Woman,
1950, 4 5/8 In.

Lamp, Lace Shade, Stepped Brass Plinth, 34 In., Pair 115.00
Pitcher, Bacchanalian & Mythological Scenes, 8 1/4 In. 402.00
Pitcher, Bacchanalian Scene, Grapevines, Lizard Form Handle, 8 3/4 In. 200.00
Pitcher, Blue Underglaze, 8 1/2 In. 520.00
Plaque, Battle Scenes, Octagonal, 20th Century, 6 1/2 x 5 1/2 In. 920.00
Plaque, Dolphins, Shell Shape Boat, Cherubs, Gilded Frame, Marked 525.00
Plaque, Oval, Zeus Overseeing 4 Seasons, Relief, 17 1/4 x 15 In. 485.00
Plaque, Relief Scene, Courting Couple, 11 In., Pair 165.00
Stein, Bacchanalian & Mythological Scenes, Figural Handle, Finial, 16 In. 750.00
Stein, People Commuting On Donkey, Carriage, Walking, 1/2 Liter 290.00
Stein, People Holding Hands With Vines Around Body, 1 Liter 577.00
Stein, Young Bacchantes On Goats, Figural Handle, 17 1/2 In. 1725.00
Tankard, Cover, Bacchanalian & Mythological Scenes, 10 1/2 In. 70.00
Urn, Baluster, 3 Winged Putti, Garland, Champleve, Green Onyx Base, 13 In. 425.00
Urn, Continuous Mythological Figural Frieze, Putti Finial, 15 3/4 In. 520.00
Urn, Cover, Blue Underglaze, 6 In. 140.00
Urn, Crown Finial, Slender Body, 19 1/2 In., Pair 1725.00
Vase, Allover Floral Design, Ginori, Italy, 13 In. 170.00
Vase, Relief Of Figures At A Feast, 8 7/8 In. 143.00

CAPTAIN MARVEL was introduced in February 1940 in Whiz comic books. An orphan named Billy Batson met the wizard, Shazam, and whenever he said the magic word he was transformed into a superhero. A movie serial was released in 1940. The comic was discontinued in 1954. A second Captain Marvel appeared in 1966, a third in 1967. Only the original was transformed by shouting *Shazam*.

Bank, Register, Magic Dime Saver, Painted, Tin, 2 1/2 In. 330.00
Glass, Shazam, Colorful Image On Front, 1976, 6 1/4 In. 12.00
Pennant, Blue Felt, 1946 .... 125.00
Poster, Adventures Of Captain Marvel, Buster Crabbe, 1941, One Sheet 425.00
Racer, Red Keywind, Fawcett 150.00

CAPTAIN MIDNIGHT began as a radio show in September 1940. The first comic book appeared in July 1941. Captain Midnight was really the aviator Captain Albright, who was to defeat the Nazis. A movie serial was made in 1942 and a comic strip was published for a short time. The comic book Captain Midnight ended his career in 1948. The radio premiums are the prized collector memorabilia today.

Cup, Ovaltine, Decal 125.00
Decoder, Silver Dart, S.Q., 1957 .... 225.00
Patch, Secret Squadron, 1956 .... 75.00

CARAMEL SLAG, see Imperial Glass category; see also Chocolate Glass category.

CARDS listed here include advertising cards (often called trade cards), greeting cards, baseball cards, playing cards, and others. Color pictures were rare in the nineteenth century, so companies gave away colorful cards with pictures of children, flowers, products, or related scenes that promoted the company name. These were often collected and stored in albums. Baseball cards also date from the nineteenth century when they were used by tobacco companies as giveaways. Gum cards were started in 1933, but it was not until after World War II that the bubble gum cards favored today were produced. Today over 1,000 cards are issued each year by the gum companies. Related items may be found in the Postcard and Movie categories.

Advertising, Alden Fruit Vinegar, C.H. Ross & Co. Groceries, 1885, 3 1/2 x 5 In.	15.00
Advertising, Alden Vinegar, Boy In Apple Tree, J.A. Thompson, 1880s, 3 x 5 In.	17.00
Advertising, Arbuckle Brothers, Alaska, Eskimos & Seals Scene, 3 x 5 In.	9.00
Advertising, Arbuckle's Coffee, Glucose Factory, Corn, Color, 1889, 3 x 5 In.	10.00
Advertising, Ayers Cathartic Pills, Doctor With Young Child, 1883, 12 1/2 x 7 1/4 In.	270.00
Advertising, Burdock Blood Bitters, Woman Looking Through Horseshoe	6.00
Advertising, Cinderella Trophy Baking Powder, 1900, 2 1/4 x 2 3/4 In., 4 Part	14.00
Advertising, Clark's Thread, Cliff House, Seal Rocks, San Francisco, 1890, 5 x 7 In.	16.00
Advertising, Community Church Of Garberville, Cal., Sunday School, 1920, 5 1/2 In.	8.00
Advertising, D.C. Eberhart, Dentist, Shrewsbury, Penn., 1883, 2 x 3 1/4 In.	12.00
Advertising, Dr. A.F. Bragg Dentist, Ornate Quill Pen, Floral, 1880s, 2 3/4 In.	12.00
Advertising, Duke's, Type A, Floral Beauties, 47 Piece	230.00
Advertising, F.T. Howell & Co., Paper Hangings, Witch Carrying Child	20.00
Advertising, Goodkind & Co., N.Y.C., Artificial Plants & Flowers, 1880s, 3 x 4 1/4 In.	10.00
Advertising, Hye & Guenther Dry Goods, Girl Pictured, 1880s, 3 x 5 In.	15.00
Advertising, J. & P. Coats, Little Witch, Black Cat & Spool	12.00
Advertising, J. Monroe Taylor's Gold Medal Baking Powder, Rat Biting Man's Behind	6.00
Advertising, James Meyer, Jr's. Girondin Extra Strength, Angel & Devil Scene	35.00
Advertising, Kinney Bros., Type A Cigarette, Naval Vessels Of The World, 22 Piece	57.00
Advertising, Kumysgen Food Additive, Full Color, 1890s	15.00
Advertising, Ludwigs Fancy Dry Goods, 38 West 14th St., N.Y., Drum Shape, 9 x 7 In.	45.00
Advertising, Magic Yeast Cakes, Die Cut, 10 x 5 In.	77.00
Advertising, Nestle's Mother Goose Series, Little Miss Muffet	12.00
Advertising, Peters Weatherbird Shoes, Trading, Framed, 16 In., 4 Piece	963.00
Advertising, Shaw Footwear, Floral, Canton, Maine, 1885, 4 1/2 x 7 In.	11.00
Advertising, Singer Manufacturing Co., And The Devil Came & Sowed Tares	16.00
Advertising, Solar Tips Shoes, John Mundell & Co., Devil, Warning About Cheap Shoes	30.00
Advertising, W.A. Batsford Dealer In Milk In Orange Co. Milk, Floral, 1880s, 2 x 3 In.	6.00
Baseball, Babe Ruth, Goudey, No. 149, 1933	2000.00
Baseball, Bob Feller, Bowman, No. 27, 1949	75.00
Baseball, Bob Feller, Bowman, No. 43, 1952	75.00
Baseball, Bob Feller, Bowman, No. 132, 1954	25.00
Baseball, Bob Feller, Topps, No. 88, 1952	30.00 to 100.00
Baseball, Campanella, Wilson Weiners, No. 1, 1954	275.00
Baseball, Carl Yastrzemski, Topps, No. 148, 1960	125.00
Baseball, Casey Stengel, Play Ball, No. 141, 1940	135.00
Baseball, Dom DiMaggio, Play Ball, No. 63, 1941	100.00
Baseball, Ed Mathews, Topps, No. 37, 1953	10.00
Baseball, Frank Robinson, Kahn's Wieners, No. 26, 1958	100.00
Baseball, Hank Aaron, Topps, No. 300, 1960	80.00
Baseball, Hank Greenberg, Goudey, No. 62, 1934	375.00
Baseball, Hank Greenberg, Goudey, No. 253, 1938	250.00
Baseball, Jackie Robinson, Running The Bases, Penny Arcade	20.00
Baseball, Joe DiMaggio, 1939	240.00
Baseball, Joe DiMaggio, Play Ball, No. 1, 1940	500.00
Baseball, Larry Doby, Bowman, No.151, 1951	20.00
Baseball, Leo Durocher, Goudey, No. 147, 1933	110.00
Baseball, Lou Gehrig, Goudey, No.92, 1933	550.00
Baseball, Mark McGwire, Topps, No. 401, 1985, Pair	450.00
Baseball, Mickey Mantle, 1963	86.00
Baseball, Mickey Mantle, Bowman, Color, No. 59, 1953	700.00
Baseball, Mickey Mantle, Bowman, No. 253, 1951	5200.00
Baseball, Reggie Jackson, Topps, No. 260, 1969	120.00
Baseball, Satchel Paige, Negro League & Organized Ball, 1981	70.00
Baseball, Tigers Team, Topps, No. 198, 1957	45.00

Baseball, Ty Cobb, 8 In. 1100.00
Baseball, U.S.A. Olympics Baseball Team, Topps, 1984 .... 200.00
Baseball, Willie Mays, Red Man Tobacco, No. 25N, 1954 .... 115.00
Basketball, Bill Russell, Boston Celtics, Rookie, 1957 .... 1437.00
Basketball, Michael Jordan, Chicago Bulls, Rookie, 1986 .... 862.00
Boxing, Chavez, De La Hoya, Autographed, Promotional 20.00
Boxing, Jack Dempsey, Sport Kings, No. 17, 1933 .... 225.00
Boxing, James J. Braddock, 1937 .... 230.00
Boxing, Mecca Cigarettes 100.00
Football, Bart Starr, Green Bay Packers, Topps, No. 86, 1963 .... 20.00
Football, Dan Marino, AFC Pro Bowl, Topps, Plastic Holder, 1984 .... 52.00
Football, Dan Marino, Dolphins, Rookie, Topps, 1984 .... 48.00
Football, Frank Gifford, Topps, No. 20, 1959 .... 35.00
Football, Jack Kemp, Topps, No. 35, 1965 .... 200.00
Football, Knute Rockne, Sport Kings, No. 35, 1933 .... 300.00
Football, Otto Graham, Rookie, 1950 .... 805.00
Football, Y.A. Tittle, New York Giants, Topps, No. 49, 1963 .... 40.00
Football, Y.A. Tittle, Topps, No. 130, 1959 .... 200.00
Golf, Walter Hagen, Sport Kings, No. 8, 1933 .... 75.00
Greeting, Adam Scheidt Brewing, Happy New Year, 1919 .... 16.00
Greeting, Birthday, Hula Dancer, On Beach, 1958, Envelope, Unused 5.00
Greeting, Chinatown Happy New Year, English & Chinese, San Fran., 3 1/2 x 5 1/2 In. ... 15.00
Greeting, Valentine, Black Child, Dice Attached, Mailing Box 35.00
Greeting, Valentine, Cut Paper, Round Design, Verse, Mennonite, Gilt Frame, 16 In. 465.00
Greeting, Valentine, Die Cut, Fold-Up, Honeycomb Tissue, Germany, 13 x 8 In. 285.00
Greeting, Valentine, Newspaper Boy, Scalloped, 1919, 6 1/2 x 5 1/4 In. 16.00
Greeting, Valentine, Snow White 28.00
Ice Skating, Bobby McLean, Sport Kings, No. 12, 1933 .... 50.00
Playing, Eastern Airlines 100.00
Playing, Marilyn Monroe, Famous Pose, 1976 .... 15.00
Playing, Pall Mall Cigarettes 8.00
Playing, Vargas, 52 Pinups, Box 130.00
Swimming, Johnny Weissmuller, Sport Kings, No. 21, 1933 .... 100.00
Veterans, Bradley S. Davis, Rawlins Post, No. 23, Stockton, Cal., Infantry, 1890, 4 In. ... 7.00

CARDER, see Aurene and Steuben categories.

CARLSBAD is a mark found on china made by several factories in Germany, Austria, and Bavaria. Many pieces were exported to the United States. Most of the pieces available today were made after 1891.

Ewer, Painted Floral Sprays, Rocaille Molded In Relief, c.1900, 11 In. 230.00
Fernery, Yellow Fuchsia, Red & Green Leaves, Ivory Ground, Silver Plated Rim, 10 In. ... 195.00
Sugar Shaker, Hand Painted Flowers, Gold Trim, Egg Shape, 4 3/8 x 3 1/4 In. 125.00
Vase, Royal Blue Flowers, Leaves, Vines, Ribbon Handles, 9 3/4 In. 130.00

CARLTON WARE was made at the Carlton Works of Stoke-on-Trent, England, beginning about 1890. The firm traded as Wiltshaw & Robinson until 1957. It was renamed Carlton Ware Ltd. in 1958. The company went bankrupt in 1995, but the name is still in use.

Bowl, Dragonfly, Waterlily, Burgundy Ground, 2 3/4 x 6 In. 88.00
Dish, Jelly, Primrose, 5 1/4 In. 40.00
Dish, Jelly, Windflower, 4 1/2 In. 40.00
Ginger Jar, England, 11 In. 121.00
Pitcher, Bird, Gold Branches & Flowers, Gold Handle & Foot, Signed, 6 3/4 In. 525.00
Toast Rack, 4 Slice 75.00
Vase, Bleu Royale, Turquoise Enamel, Gold Trim, Mottled Blue, 1930s, 7 1/4 In. 160.00
Vase, Cover, Foo Dog Finial, Pink Blossoms On Branches, Gold Trim, 8 3/4 In. 375.00
Vase, Cover, Rouge Royale, Foo Dog Finial, Enameled Gold Lake Scene, 1930, 22 In. 1380.00

CARNIVAL GLASS was an inexpensive, iridescent, pressed glass made from about 1907 to about 1925. More than 1,000 different patterns are known. Carnival glass is currently being reproduced. Additional pieces may be found in the Northwood category.

Acanthus, Bowl, Smoke, 9 1/2 In. 65.00

Acorn, Compote, Marigold, Ruffled Edge 3750.00
Acorn Burrs, Tumbler, Amethyst 70.00
Acorn Burrs & Bark pattern is listed here as Acorn Burrs.
Apple Blossom, Plate, Marigold, 8 1/2 In. 66.00
Apple Blossom, Plate, Peach Opalescent, Ruffled Edge 295.00
Battenburg Lace No. 1 pattern is listed here as Hearts & Flowers.
Battenburg Lace No. 2 pattern is listed here as Captive Rose.
Beaded Cable, Rose Bowl, Marigold, Ruffled Edge, 3-Footed ....85.00 to 95.00
Blackberry B pattern is listed here as Blackberry Spray.
Blackberry Bramble, Compote, Amethyst 125.00
Blackberry Rays, Compote, Green, Ruffled Edge 250.00
Blackberry Spray, Bonbon, Marigold, 6 In. 22.00
Blackberry Spray, Vase, Hat Shape, Red 450.00
Blackberry Wreath, Bowl, Amethyst, Ruffled Edge, 10 1/4 In. 250.00
Blackberry Wreath, Bowl, Green, Ruffled Edge, 10 1/2 In. 155.00
Blackberry Wreath, Bowl, Marigold, Ruffled Edge, 6 In. 80.00
Bo Peep, Mug, Marigold 75.00
Boggy Bayou, Vase, Green, 9 In. 175.00
Bouquet, Water Set, Marigold, 7 Piece 245.00
Boutonniere, Compote, Green, Ruffled Edge 85.00
Brocaded Acorns, Champagne, Ice Blue, 6 In. 135.00
Brocaded Acorns, Vase, Fan, Ice Blue, Footed 215.00
Brocaded Daffodils, Tidbit, Ice Green, Heart Shape, Handle 125.00
Brocaded Palms, Console Set, Pink, 3 Piece 250.00
Broken Arches, Punch Set, Marigold, 8 Piece 550.00
Brooklyn Bridge, Bowl, Marigold, 9 In. 250.00
Butterfly, Bonbon, Blue, 2 Handles, 7 1/2 In. 39.00
Butterfly, Bonbon, Green, 2 Handles, 7 1/2 In. ....80.00 to 115.00
Butterfly & Berry, Creamer, Blue 80.00
Butterfly & Berry, Hatpin Holder, Marigold 1800.00
Butterfly & Fern, Water Set, Blue, 7 Piece 425.00
Butterfly & Grape pattern is listed here as Butterfly & Berry.
Butterfly & Plume pattern is listed here as Butterfly & Fern.
Butterfly & Stippled Rays pattern is listed here as Butterfly.
Butterfly Bush, Bowl, Amethyst, Ruffled Edge, Australian, 6 1/2 In. 85.00
Cactus Leaf Rays pattern is listed here as Leaf Rays.
Captive Rose, Bowl, Green, Ruffled Edge, 8 1/2 In. 150.00
Captive Rose, Bowl, Marigold, 8 1/2 In. 135.00
Carolina Dogwood, Bowl, Amethyst Opalescent, Ruffled Edge, 8 1/2 In. 90.00
Cattails & Water Lily pattern is listed here as Water Lily & Cattails.
Cherry, Plate, Amethyst, Ruffled Edge, 6 1/2 In. 225.00
Cherry, Sugar & Creamer, Marigold, Large 200.00
Cherry Wreathed pattern is listed here as Wreathed Cherry.
Christmas Cactus pattern is listed here as Thistle.
Christmas Plate pattern is listed here as Poinsettia.
Cobblestones, Bowl, Amethyst, Ruffled Edge, 9 In. 260.00
Coin Dot, Bowl, Amethyst, 7 1/2 In. 45.00
Concave Diamonds, Tumbler, Blue 25.00
Concord, Bowl, Amethyst, Ruffled Edge, 9 In. 400.00
Corn, Vase, Ice Green 650.00
Courthouse, Bowl, Ice Cream, Amethyst, 7 1/2 In. 900.00
Daisy & Plume, Candy Dish, Ice Blue, Footed, Ruffled Edge 400.00
Daisy & Plume, Rose Bowl, Amethyst 100.00
Daisy Squares, Compote, Marigold, Ruffled Edge 300.00
Dandelion, Bowl, Green, Ruffled Edge, 8 In. 90.00
Dandelion, Mug, Marigold 350.00
Dandelion Variant pattern is listed here as Panelled Dandelion.
Diamond & Rib, Vase, Green, 12 In. 70.00
Diamond Lace, Pitcher, Water, Amethyst ....175.00 to 395.00
Diamond Points, Vase, Lavender, Tricornered, 9 3/4 In. 135.00
Diamond Ring, Bowl, Smoke, 5 In. 35.00
Dogwood & Marsh Lily pattern is listed here as Two Flowers.
Drapery, Rose Bowl, Aqua Opalescent 75.00

Elks, Bowl, Blue, Atlantic City, 1911, 8 In. 1710.00
Embroidered Mums, Plate, Ice Green, 9 In. 650.00
Fan, Gravy Boat, Peach Opalescent, Footed 65.00
Fan, Sugar, Peach Opalescent 50.00
Fan & Arch pattern is listed here as Persian Garden.
Fantasy pattern is listed here as Question Marks.
Fashion, Punch Cup, Marigold 10.00
Fenton's Butterfly pattern is listed here as Butterfly.
Fine Cut & Roses, Candy Dish, Ice Blue 115.00
Fine Cut & Roses, Rose Bowl, Ice Blue 210.00
Finecut & Star pattern is listed here as Star & File.
Fish & Flowers pattern is listed here as Trout & Fly.
Floral & Diamond Point pattern is listed here as Fine Cut & Roses.
Florentine, Candlestick, Celeste Blue, Small, Pair 195.00
Flowering Almonds pattern is listed here as Peacock Tail.
Fluffy Bird pattern is listed here as Peacock.
Fruits & Flowers, Bonbon, 2 Handles, Green 400.00
Fruits & Flowers, Bonbon, Basketweave, 2 Handles, Ice Blue 800.00
Fruits & Flowers, Bonbon, Basketweave, 2 Handles, Marigold 95.00
Good Luck, Bowl, Amethyst 100.00
Good Luck, Bowl, Basketweave, Green 335.00
Good Luck, Bowl, Marigold 200.00
Good Luck, Bowl, Ruffled Edge, Basketweave, Green, 9 In. 300.00
Grape, Compote, Smoke Carnival 350.00
Grape, Plate, Cobalt Blue, 6 In. 1900.00
Grape, Plate, Marigold, 9 In. 100.00
Grape & Cable, Banana Boat, Marigold, Banded 250.00
Grape & Cable, Berry Set, Green, 5 Piece 165.00
Grape & Cable, Bowl, Amethyst, 9 In. 95.00
Grape & Cable, Bowl, Basketweave, Amethyst, 9 1/2 In. 270.00
Grape & Cable, Bowl, Fruit, Marigold 145.00
Grape & Cable, Bowl, Ruffled Edge, Marigold, 9 In. 50.00
Grape & Cable, Bowl, Ruffled Edge, Marigold, 11 In. 125.00
Grape & Cable, Candle Lamp, Green, 2 Piece 650.00
Grape & Cable, Cracker Jar, Cover, Amethyst 275.00
Grape & Cable, Cup & Saucer, Ice Green 400.00
Grape & Cable, Decanter, Whiskey, Stopper, Marigold 300.00
Grape & Cable, Hatpin Holder, Amethyst ....225.00 to 395.00
Grape & Cable, Hatpin Holder, Marigold 225.00
Grape & Cable, Nappy, Ice Blue 800.00
Grape & Cable, Plate, Basketweave, Green, 9 In. 250.00
Grape & Cable, Plate, Marigold 95.00
Grape & Cable, Punch Bowl & Base, Amethyst 2500.00
Grape & Cable, Punch Cup, Aqua 200.00
Grape & Cable, Punch Cup, White 25.00
Grape & Cable, Spooner, Green 85.00
Grape & Cable, Sugar, Cover, Green 165.00
Grape & Cable, Sweetmeat, Cover, Amethyst ....200.00 to 225.00
Grape & Cable, Tumbler, Amethyst 30.00
Grape Arbor, Water Set, Marigold, 5 Piece 850.00
Grape Delight pattern is listed here as Vintage.
Grapevine Diamonds pattern is listed here as Grapevine Lattice.
Grapevine Lattice, Plate, Marigold, 6 In. 50.00
Greek Key & Scales, Bowl, Marigold, Domed Foot, 7 1/2 In. 50.00
Hanging Cherries, Compote, Amethyst 2100.00
Hanging Cherries, Compote, Marigold 700.00
Heron & Rushes pattern is listed here as Stork & Rushes.
Hobnail pattern is listed in this book as its own category.
Hobstar, Cracker Jar, Marigold 65.00
Hobstar & Arches, Bowl, Marigold 35.00
Holly, Bowl, Blue, Ruffled Edge 125.00
Holly, Compote, Amethyst, Ruffled Edge, 5 3/4 In. .... 50.00 to 65.00
Holly, Compote, Green, Ruffled Edge 275.00

Holly, Compote, Lime Green Opalescent 150.00
Holly, Compote, Marigold, Ruffled Edge 25.00
Holly Spray pattern is listed here as Holly Sprig.
Holly Sprig, Nappy, Green, Tricornered, Handle 160.00
Horse Medallions pattern is listed here as Horses' Heads.
Horses' Heads, Bowl, Amethyst, Ruffled, 7 1/2 In. 195.00
Horses' Heads, Rose Bowl, Marigold, Footed 105.00
Horses' Heads, Rose Bowl, Sapphire Blue, Footed 4000.00
Imperial Grape, Plate, Green, 12 In. 140.00
Imperial Grape, Water Set, Marigold, 7 Piece 300.00
Imperial Grape, Wine Set, Amethyst, 7 Piece 450.00
Inverted Strawberry, Cuspidor, Woman's, Marigold 800.00
Irish Lace pattern is listed here as Louisa.
Jeweled Heart, Bowl, Amethyst, 5 In. 45.00
Jeweled Heart, Tumbler, Marigold ....50.00 to 85.00
Kangaroo, Bowl, Amethyst, Ruffled Edge, Australian, 10 In. 600.00
Kangaroo, Bowl, Marigold, Ruffled Edge, Australian, 9 1/2 In. 220.00
Kimberly pattern is listed here as Concave Diamonds.
Kingfisher, Bowl, Amethyst, Ruffled Edge, Australian, 9 3/4 In. 450.00
Kittens, Banana Boat, Marigold 150.00
Kittens, Cup, Marigold ....110.00 to 200.00
Kittens, Toothpick, Celeste Blue, 4 Sides 400.00
Labelle Elaine pattern is listed here as Primrose.
Lattice & Grape, Pitcher, Blue 675.00
Lattice & Grape, Tumbler, Marigold ....10.00 to 30.00
Lattice & Grapevine pattern is listed here as Lattice & Grape.
Lattice & Points, Vase, White, 7 1/2 In. ....150.00 to 165.00
Leaf & Beads, Rose Bowl, Floral Interior, Amethyst, Footed 135.00
Leaf & Beads, Rose Bowl, Rays Interior, Green, Footed 95.00
Leaf Chain, Bowl, White, 9 In. 125.00
Leaf Medallion pattern is listed here as Leaf Chain.
Leaf Pinwheel & Star Flower pattern is listed here as Whirling Leaves.
Leaf Rays, Nappy, Amethyst 85.00
Lined Lattice, Vase, Marigold, 9 In. 50.00
Little Beads, Compote, Amethyst Opalescent 45.00
Little Flowers, Bowl, Marigold, Ruffled Edge, 10 In. 30.00
Little Stars, Bowl, Amethyst, 7 1/2 In. 180.00
Looped Petals pattern is listed here as Scales.
Lotus & Grape, Bowl, Blue, 9 In. ....165.00 to 175.00
Louisa, Rose Bowl, Amethyst 50.00
Louisa, Rose Bowl, Aqua 95.00
Lustre Flute, Sugar & Creamer, Green 40.00
Lustre Rose, Water Set, Marigold 160.00
Magnolia & Poinsettia pattern is listed here as Water Lily.
Many Stars, Bowl, Amethyst, Ruffled Edge, 10 In. 525.00
Maple Leaf, Spooner, Marigold 35.00
Maple Leaf, Tumbler, Amethyst 55.00
Maryland pattern is listed here as Rustic.
Melinda pattern is listed here as Wishbone.
Melon & Fan pattern is listed here as Diamond & Rib.
Memphis, Berry Bowl, Marigold, Large 110.00
Morning Glory, Vase, Funeral, Marigold, 17 In. 275.00
Morning Glory, Vase, Smoke, 6 In. 50.00
Mums & Greek Key pattern is listed here as Embroidered Mums.
Nesting Swan pattern is listed here as Swan, Carnival.
Oak Leaf & Acorn pattern is listed here as Acorn.
Oak Leaf Brocade pattern is listed here as Brocaded Acorns.
Octagon, Decanter, Stopper, Marigold 85.00
Omnibus, Tumbler, Marigold 200.00
Open Rose, Plate, Amber, 9 In. 350.00
Open Rose, Sauce, Blue, Ruffled Edge, 5 3/4 In. 800.00
Orange Tree, Fruit Bowl, Blue, Footed, 10 In. 225.00
Orange Tree, Mug, Blue ....25.00 to 40.00

Orange Tree, Powder Jar, Cover, Blue 140.00
Orange Tree, Powder Jar, Marigold 65.00
Orange Tree, Punch Set, Base, Bowl, Marigold, 10 Cups 395.00
Orange Tree, Sherbet, Green, 5 In. 65.00
Orange Tree, Tumbler, Blue 60.00
Orange Tree & Scroll, Pitcher, Blue 1000.00
Orange Tree & Scroll, Tumbler, Blue 150.00
Orange Tree & Scroll, Tumbler, Marigold ....60.00 to 85.00
Oriental Poppy, Water Set, Green, 7 Piece 1600.00
Oriental Poppy, Water Set, Marigold, 7 Piece 995.00
Palm Beach, Pitcher, Honey, Amber 300.00
Panelled Dandelion, Pitcher, Amethyst, 12 1/2 In. 550.00
Panelled Dandelion, Tankard, Green 275.00
Panelled Dandelion, Tumbler, Marigold 35.00
Pansy, Bowl, Amethyst, Ruffled Edge, 8 1/2 In. 220.00
Pansy, Dish, Pickle, Amethyst 90.00
Pansy, Dish, Pickle, Marigold 35.00
Pansy, Nappy, Marigold 35.00
Panther, Bowl, Blue, Footed, 5 In. 120.00
Panther, Bowl, Marigold, Ruffled Edge, 5 In. 50.00
Peach, Bowl, Ice Cream, Marigold 55.00
Peacock, Bowl, Amethyst, 9 In. 300.00
Peacock, Bowl, Electric Blue, Ruffled Edge, Stippled, 8 3/4 In. 700.00
Peacock, Plate, Blue 250.00
Peacock, Sauce, Blue, Ruffled Edge, 6 In. 1050.00
Peacock & Grape, Bowl, Marigold, Bearded Berry Exterior, Ruffled Edge 55.00
Peacock & Urn, Bowl, Blue, Ruffled Edge ....175.00 to 195.00
Peacock & Urn, Bowl, Celeste Blue, 8 1/2 In. 235.00
Peacock & Urn, Bowl, Ice Cream, Marigold, 10 In. 1700.00
Peacock & Urn, Bowl, Marigold, Ruffled Edge, 8 1/2 In. 145.00
Peacock & Urn, Bowl, White, Ruffled Edge, 8 1/2 In. 175.00
Peacock At The Fountain, Compote, Amethyst, Ruffled Edge 1600.00
Peacock At The Fountain, Compote, Green, Ruffled Edge 1400.00
Peacock At The Fountain, Pitcher, Water, Marigold 250.00
Peacock On Fence pattern is listed here as Peacock.
Peacock Tail, Compote, Green 32.00
Peacock Tail, Nappy, Green, 2 Handles 42.00
Peacocks On Fence, Bowl, Blue, 8 1/2 In. 600.00
Pearly Dots, Compote, Amethyst Opalescent, Ruffled Edge 65.00
Pepper Plant, Nut Dish, Green 28.00
Persian Garden, Bowl, Amethyst, Ruffled Edge, 10 In. 400.00
Persian Medallion, Bonbon, Amethyst 17.00
Persian Medallion, Bowl, Blue, 5 In. 30.00
Persian Medallion, Bowl, Green, 10 In. 225.00
Peter Rabbit, Bowl, Marigold 2000.00
Poinsettia, Pitcher, Milk, Marigold 85.00
Poinsettia, Pitcher, Milk, Smoke 260.00
Poinsettia & Lattice pattern is listed here as Poinsettia.
Pond Lily, Bonbon, Green 45.00
Pony, Bowl, Amethyst, Ruffled Edge, 8 1/2 In. 325.00
Pony, Bowl, Marigold, 8 1/2 In. 70.00
Pony Rosette pattern is listed here as Pony.
Poppy, Compote, Marigold, Flared 475.00
Poppy, Dish, Pickle, Blue 375.00
Poppy Scroll pattern is listed here as Poppy.
Primrose, Bowl, Green, 9 1/2 In. 65.00
Princess Lace pattern is listed here as Octagon.
Question Marks, Bonbon, Amethyst, 2 Handles, 3 3/4 In. 45.00
Question Marks, Bonbon, Marigold, 2 Handles, 3 3/4 In. 17.00
Question Marks, Cake Plate, Peach Opalescent, Ruffled Edge, Footed 135.00
Rainbow, Bowl, Basketweave, Amethyst, 9 In. 35.00
Rainbow, Bowl, Green, 9 In. 75.00
Raindrops, Bowl, Peach Opalescent, Footed, 9 1/4 In. 250.00

Raspberry, Pitcher, Milk, Marigold ....150.00 to 175.00
Raspberry, Water Set, Marigold, 5 Piece 200.00
Ribbon Tie, Bowl, Marigold, Fluted, 8 1/4 In. 15.00
Ripple, Vase, Amber, 10 In. 35.00
Roll, Water Set, Marigold, 5 Piece 210.00
Rose & Ruffles pattern is listed here as Open Rose.
Rose Spray, Compote, Marigold ....50.00 to 65.00
Roses & Fruit, Bonbon, Marigold, Handle, Footed 550.00
Rustic, Vase, Funeral, Amethyst, 20 In. 1500.00
Scales, Banana Boat, Amethyst Opalescent 100.00
Scales, Plate, Peach Opalescent, 9 In. 95.00
Scroll, Plate, Embossed, Amethyst, 9 In. 525.00
Seaweed, Bowl, Green, Flared, 9 In. 1900.00
Shell, Bowl, Amethyst 260.00
Shell, Bowl, Amethyst, Ruffled Edge 345.00
Shell & Sand pattern is listed here as Shell, Carnival.
Singing Birds, Mug, Blue 95.00
Singing Birds, Mug, Blue Opalescent 350.00
Singing Birds, Mug, Green 200.00
Soda Gold, Tumbler, Marigold 5.00
Soda Gold, Water Set, Smoke, 7 Piece 175.00
Spider Web pattern is listed here as Soda Gold.
Spring Flowers pattern is listed here as Bouquet.
Stag & Holly, Bowl, Marigold, Ruffled Edge, 10 1/2 In. 125.00
Star & File, Compote, Marigold 50.00
Star Medallion, Pitcher, Milk, Marigold ....20.00 to 55.00
Star Medallion, Pitcher, Milk, Smoke 25.00
Star Of David, Bowl, Amethyst, Ruffled Edge, 9 In. 185.00
Stippled Clematis pattern is listed here as Little Stars.
Stippled Diamond & Flower pattern is listed here as Little Flowers.
Stippled Leaf & Beads pattern is listed here as Leaf & Beads.
Stippled Rays, Bowl, Amethyst 85.00
Stork & Rushes, Mug, Black Amethyst 295.00
Strawberry pattern is listed here as Wild Strawberry.
Stream Of Hearts, Compote, Marigold 100.00
Strutting Peacock, Sugar & Creamer, Amethyst 60.00
Sunflower pattern is listed here as Dandelion.
Swan, Bowl, Marigold 165.00
Swan, Teal 195.00
Swirl, Powder Jar, Marigold 28.00
Teardrops pattern is listed here as Raindrops.
Thin Rib, Vase, Amethyst 60.00
Thin Rib, Vase, Marigold, 11 In. 10.00
Thistle, Banana Boat, Blue 525.00
Thistle, Banana Boat, Marigold 350.00
Thistle, Bowl, Amethyst, Ruffled Edge, 8 In. 225.00
Thistle & Thorn, Bowl, Marigold, Footed 40.00
Thistle & Thorn, Creamer, Marigold 35.00
Thistle & Thorn, Plate, Marigold, Ruffled Edge 45.00
Three Fruits, Bowl, Green 160.00
Three Fruits, Bowl, Green, Stippled 850.00
Three Fruits, Bowl, Ruffled Edge, Basketweave, Amethyst 300.00
Three Fruits, Plate, Amethyst, 12 Sides 150.00
Three Fruits Medallion, Bowl, Marigold, Footed 95.00
Tree Trunk, Vase, Amethyst, 8 1/2 In. 150.00
Tree Trunk, Vase, Ice Green, 11 In. 295.00
Trout & Fly, Bowl, Ice Cream, Marigold, 8 1/4 In. 525.00
Two Flowers, Bowl, Blue, Spatula Footed 90.00
Vintage, Fernery, Blue ....65.00 to 85.00
Vintage, Powder Jar, Cover, Marigold 85.00
Vintage, Rose Bowl, White 75.00
Vintage Leaf, Bowl, Green, Ruffled Edge 50.00
Waffle Band pattern is listed here as Lustre Flute.

Waffle Block, Basket, Marigold 55.00
Waffle Block, Punch Bowl, Marigold 150.00
Water Lily, Bonbon, Marigold 45.00
Water Lily, Bowl, Red, Footed, 6 In. 800.00
Water Lily & Cattails, Berry Bowl, Master, Amethyst, 9 In. 70.00
Water Lily & Cattails, Butter, Cover, Marigold 370.00
Whirling Leaves, Bowl, Amethyst, 9 1/2 In. 300.00
Wide Swirl pattern is listed here as Swirl.
Wild Strawberry, Bowl, Marigold 130.00
Wild Strawberry, Bowl, Marigold, Ruffled Edge 125.00
Wild Strawberry, Compote, Marigold, Ruffled Edge 175.00
Wild Strawberry, Plate, Marigold, 9 In. 175.00
Windmill, Bowl, Amethyst, 9 In. 65.00
Windmill, Dish, Pickle, Marigold 15.00
Windmill Medallion pattern is listed here as Windmill.
Wishbone, Chop Plate, Marigold, 10 In. 1600.00
Wishbone & Spades, Plate, Black Amethyst, 6 In. 1000.00
Wreathed Cherry, Water Set, Marigold, 6 Piece 775.00

CAROUSEL or merry-go-round figures were first carved in the United States in 1867 by Gustav Dentzel. Collectors discovered the charm of the hand-carved figures in the 1970s, and they were soon classed as folk art. Most desirable are the figures other than horses, such as pigs, camels, lions, or dogs. A jumper is a figure that was made to move up and down on a pole; a stander was placed in a stationary position.

Billy Goat's Gruff, Wooden, Carved Saddle, Long Horns, 1920 .... 1600.00
Chariot Car, Car Type, Carved Wood, Front & Back Seat 2750.00
Deer, Outside Row, Carved Saddle, Rocking Stand, Dentzel, 1900, 61 In. 7475.00
Fish, Carved, Painted, Glass Eyes, Carpeted Seat, Late 19th Century, 16 x 48 In. 1725.00
Goat, Jumper, Full-Bodied, Glass Eyes, Curled Horns, 19th Century, 56 In. 2300.00
Goat, Outside Row, 3 Medallions On Front Of Strap, Loff, 1885, 60 In. 7475.00
Horse, Black & White, Leather Saddle & Reins, Hand Carved, 24 x 47 In. 315.00
Horse, Brown & Yellow, Hair Tail, 43 x 44 In. 690.00
Horse, Inside Row, Carved Wood, 56 x 53 In. 1090.00
Horse, Jumper, Galloping, Head Lunging Forward, Green Saddle, Wood, 1917, 37 In. ... 8050.00
Horse, On Original Rockers, Charles Dare, c.1880 .... 4400.00
Horse, Polychrome, Contemporary, 48 In. 530.00
Horse, Prancer, Carved, Painted, Charles Loof, Early 20th Century, 55 x 55 In. 3450.00
Horse, Prancer, Carved, Polychrome, Glass Eyes, Armitage Herschell Co., 41 x 48 In. ... 12650.00
Panel, Jester Center, Dark Green Outline, 28 1/2 x 21 In. 1400.00
Pig, Runner, Painted, Protruding Tongue, Glass Eyes, Early 20th Century, 16 x 44 In. 2300.00
Rabbit, Glass Eyes, 55 x 63 In. 1450.00
Ram, Carved Wood, Continental 1265.00
Taxi, Yellow, France 2310.00
Tiger, Glass Eyes, Original Paint, Wood, 23 x 49 In. 7700.00

CARRIAGE means several things, so this category lists baby carriages, buggies for adults, horse-drawn sleighs, and even strollers. Doll-sized carriages are listed in the Toy category.

Baby Buggy, 4 Wheels, Single Seat, Yellow Paint, Green Pinstriping, 32 x 37 In. 825.00
Baby Buggy, Green, Black, Red, 10 Wooden Spoke Wheels, 19th Century, 40 In. 335.00
Baby Buggy, Heywood, 1870s 525.00
Baby Buggy, Original Paint, 19th Century 165.00
Baby Buggy, Wicker, Old White Repaint, 31 x 28 In. 110.00
Baby Buggy, Wicker, Original Condition, c.1900 .... 250.00
Child's, Push, 2 Prancing Full-Bodied Horse Pulling Coach, Pinstriping, 1890 .... 2200.00
Donkey Cart, Sicily, 32 x 47 In. ....*Illus* 2420.00
Sleigh, Horse Drawn, Velvet Upholstery, 74 In. 220.00
Sleigh, Push, Wooden, Chicken Heads & Winter Scenic Panels 630.00
Sleigh, Push, Worn Red Paint, Black Striping, Child's, 51 In. 410.00
Stroller, Amish, Blue Painted Body, Canvas Seat & Canopy, 42 1/2 In. 440.00
Stroller, Wicker, White 80.00
Wagon, Goat, Wooden, Old Red Paint, 4 Wheels 325.00

Some collectors want carousel horses that have been completely restored. Some buy only pieces with original paint. This is one type of collectible that can be restored without a loss in value. The work should be done by an expert.

Carriage, Donkey Cart, Sicily, 32 x 47 In.

CASH REGISTERS were invented in 1884 because an eye on the cash was a necessity in stores of the nineteenth century, too. John and James Ritty invented a large model that resembled a clock and kept a record of the dollars and cents exchanged in the store. John Patterson improved the cash register with a paper roll to record the money. By the early 1900s, elaborate brass registers were made. About World War I, the fancy case was exchanged for the more modern types.

9 Drawers, Oak Case, Cast Iron, Panel Base, 67 x 27 In.	575.00
Hallwood, Brass, $20 Key, Rare, 21 x 22 1/2 In.	275.00
Hallwood, Polished	600.00
McCaskey System, Slide-Out Ledger & Receipt Board Over Drawer, 21 In.	130.00
Michigan, Nickel Plated, Candy Store, 17 In.	190.00
National, 39 1/2-2-2, Brass, Polished, Embossed, Double Drawer, 24 In.	580.00
National, Brass & Nickel Plated, Registers Up To $5.95, 17 x 16 x 18 In.	275.00
National, Brass, $7 Key, Receipt, Grand, No Marquee, 17 In.	415.00
National, Brass, $10 Key, Receipt, Reproduction Amount Tendered, 17 In.	330.00
National, Mahogany Plinth, 65 x 27 In.	745.00
National, Marble Top Counter, Art Brass, 16 x 17 In.	690.00
National, Model 95, Brass, Oak Base, 21 In.	440.00
National, Model 100, Chrome, Coca-Cola Decals	850.00
National, Model 1064-G, Brass, Oak Base, Marble Counter, 27 In.	360.00
National, Model 240, Brass, Oak Base, 21 3/4 In.	95.00
National, Model 317, Nickel Plated, 17 In.	550.00
National, Model 348-2-2, Brass, Oak Base, Marble Counter, 18 In.	415.00
National, Model 349, Brass, Oak Base, Marble Counter, Marquee Missing, 17 In.	300.00
National, Model 412, Electric Sign, Restored	2300.00
National, Model 420, Brass, Oak Base, Marble Counter, Marquee Missing, 21 In.	470.00
National, Model 441, Brass, Oak Base, Counter & Marquee Missing, 21 1/2 In.	385.00
National, Model 442, Nickel-Plated Brass, Oak Base, Marble Counter, 22 In.	250.00
National, Model 452, Brass, Oak Base, Marble Counter, Marquee Missing, 28 In.	470.00
National, Model 522-EL-2C, Electric, Brass, Oak Base, Marble Counter, 27 1/2 In.	800.00
National, Model 532-3, Brass, Oak, Marble Counter, Marquee Missing, 29 In.	495.00
National, Model 552-4F, Brass, 9 Drawer, Oak Stand, 62 x 29 x 21 In.	1345.00
National, Queens, Brass, Oak Base, 23 1/2 In.	440.00
Sign, Amount Purchased, 2 Sides, Embossed, Nickel Plated Brass, 14 In.	99.00
St. Louis, Model 102	125.00

CASTOR JARS for pickles are glass jars about six inches in height, held in special metal holders. They became a popular dinner table accessory about 1890. Each jar had a top that was usually silver or silver plate. The frame, also of a silver metal, had a handle that arched above the jar and a hook that held a pair of tongs. By 1900, the pickle castor was out of fashion. Many examples found today have reproduced glass jars in old holders. Additional pickle castors may be found in the various Glass categories.

Pickle, Albertine, Mt. Washington Glass	3080.00
Pickle, Cobalt Blue, Enameled Flowers, Frame & Tongs	295.00

Pickle, Cranberry Glass, Cucumber Each Side, Derby Silver Plating, 10 3/4 In. 545.00
Pickle, Cranberry Glass, Drape Pattern, Silver Plate, Butterflies, Flowers, Tongs, 8 In. . . .   260.00
Pickle, Cranberry Glass, Thumbprint, Ornate Frame & Tongs 475.00
Pickle, Cranberry Glass, Thumbprint, Silver Plated Frame, Tongs 240.00
Pickle, Daisy & Button, Frame & Tongs 225.00
Pickle, Daisy & Button, Tongs, Tufts 475.00
Pickle, Daisy & Button, Vaseline, James Tufts Frame, Tongs 475.00
Pickle, Diamond Panel Bottom, Amber, Frame & Tongs 295.00
Pickle, Enameled, Butterflies & Ivy, Frame & Tongs 225.00
Pickle, Etched Floral, Silver Plated, Victorian 60.00
Pickle, Panel, Etched Flowers & Fern, Frame & Tongs 225.00
Pickle, Silver Frame 250.00
Pickle, Silver Plated Frame, Floral Filigree, Cranberry Glass, Enameled Daisies, 14 In. 465.00
Pickle, Thumbprint, Enameled Flowers, Tonge, Ornate Frame 465.00

CASTOR SETS holding just salt and pepper castors were used in the seventeenth century. The sugar castor, mustard pot, spice dredger, bottles for vinegar and oil, and other spice holders became popular by the eighteenth century. These sets were usually made of sterling silver. The American Victorian castor set, the type most collected today, was made of silver plated Britannia metal. Colored glass bottles were introduced after the Civil War. The sets were out of fashion by World War I. Be careful when buying sets with colored bottles; many are reproductions. Other castor sets may be listed in various porcelain and glass categories in this book.

2 Cruets, 2 Shakers, 1 Condiment Bottle, Floral, Silver Frame, Victorian, 14 In. 145.00
3 Bottles, 2 Castors, Condiment, Scallop Shaped Stand, Silver Plate, c.1910, 9 1/2 In. . . .   525.00
4 Bottles, 3-Part Mold, Pewter Frame, 9 In. 80.00
4 Bottles, Cranberry Glass, Flashed, Glass Stand, Metal Handle, 9 1/2 In. 260.00
4 Bottles, Silver Plated Holder, 9 1/2 x 5 In. 195.00
5 Bottles, Etched Flowers Pierced Handle, Silver Plate, 19th Century, 16 3/4 In. 145.00
5 Bottles, Pewter, Blown Molded Bottles, American, 19th Century, 8 1/4 In. 45.00
5 Bottles, Pressed Glass, Original Tops, Silver Plated Revolving Stand 65.00
5 Bottles, Silver Fittings, London, 1844, 8 In. 495.00
6 Bottles, Cut Glass, Silver Plated Holder 145.00
6 Bottles, Cut Glass, Silver Plated Holder, Pontils On Bottles 130.00
6 Bottles, Renaissance Revival Style Holder, Rogers & Co., Meriden, Conn., 17 In. 150.00
Daisy & Button Pattern, Cut Glass Bottles, Stand, Ball Feet, Silver Plated Holder 330.00

CATALOGS are listed in the Paper category.

CAULDON Limited worked in Staffordshire, Great Britain, and went through many name changes. John Ridgway made porcelain at Cauldon Place, Hanley, until 1855. The firm of John Ridgway, Bates and Co. of Cauldon Place worked from 1856 to 1859. It became Bates, Brown-Westhead, Moore and Co. from 1859 to 1862. Brown-Westhead, Moore and Co. worked from 1862 to 1904. About 1890, this firm started using the words *Cauldon* or *Cauldon ware* as part of the mark. Cauldon Ltd. worked from 1905 to 1920, Cauldon Potteries from 1920 to 1962. Related items may be found in the Indian Tree category.

CAULDON
ENGLAND

Creamer, Blue Romantic Transfer, 6 In. 100.00
Plate, Dessert, Rose & Floral Spray, Ivory Ground, Mint Green Rim, Gilt, 9 In., 8 Piece   .   230.00
Plate Set, Different Noblewoman Center Medallion, 12 Piece 4890.00
Platter, Turkey, Blue Transfer, Border, Marked, 1870 . . . .   750.00

CELADON is the name of a velvet-textured green-gray glaze used by Chinese, Japanese, Korean, and other factories. The name refers both to the glaze and to pieces covered with the glaze. It is still being made.

Bowl, Incised Phoenix Design, Koryo Dynasty, 6 3/4 In. 690.00
Bowl, Phoenix Design Interior, 6 1/4 In. 520.00
Bowl, Plum Blossom Design, Late 19th Century, 6 3/4 In. 25.00
Charger, Carp & Peony Design, Blue, White, Late 19th Century, 17 In. 467.00
Cup, Crane Design, 2 3/4 In. 90.00
Cup, Kingfisher Blue Glaze, Koryo Dynasty, 3 1/4 In. 605.00

Dish, Foliate Rim, Pale Blue Green, 5 3/4 In., Pair 115.00
Dish, Incised Floral & Leaves Design, Chinese, 9 3/4 In. 260.00
Dish, Incised Linear Design, Chinese, 11 1/2 In. 115.00
Figurine, Elephant, Chinese, 19th Century, 9 1/4 In. 795.00
Tureen, Nesting Hen Shape, Crackle Glaze, 12 x 12 1/2 x 9 In. 175.00
Vase, Baluster Shape, Figural Scene, Chinese, 19th Century, 16 1/2 In. 1600.00
Vase, Blue & White Immortals, Attendants, Wooden Cover, 19 In. 500.00
Vase, Blue Floral, Oriental, 16 1/2 In. 190.00
Vase, Chinese Shape, Losanti, 6 1/4 x 4 In. 440.00
Vase, Peony Design, 1800, 15 1/4 In. 465.00
Vase, Raised Figures Of Exotic Birds, Fish, Dragons, S-Scroll Handles, 16 3/4 In. 1035.00
Vase, Swelling Form, Mask & Ring Handles, Fitted As Lamp, 10 1/2 In. 115.00

CELLULOID is a trademark for a plastic developed in 1868 by John W.
Hyatt. Celluloid Manufacturing Company, the Celluloid Novelty Company, Celluloid Fancy Goods Company, and American Xylonite
Company all used Celluloid to make jewelry, games, sewing equipment, false teeth, and piano keys. Eventually, the Hyatt Company
became the American Celluloid and Chemical Manufacturing Company, the Celanese Corporation. The name *Celluloid* was often used to
identify any similar plastic. Celluloid toys are listed under Toys.

Album, Autograph, Couple Working On Farm Scene, Horse, 1906, 6 1/4 x 4 1/2 In. 120.00
Album, Photograph, Cottage Scene, Woods, 8 x 10 1/2 In. 295.00
Album, Photograph, Girl In Canoe Picture, Ornate Clasp, 1906, 8 x 10 1/2 In. 265.00
Box, Collar, Woman, Flowers In Hair, Hot Pink Lid, 5 x 6 1/4 In. 310.00
Box, Glove, Deer Scene, Mountain, Red Silk Lining, 12 1/2 x 3 3/4 x 4 1/4 In. 285.00
Box, Handkerchief, Courting Couple, Paper Top, 1905 .... 65.00
Box, Handkerchief, Woman, Ice Skating, 6 x 6 x 2 3/4 In. 170.00
Box, Pipe, Man & Woman, On Garden Fence, 6 1/2 x 2 1/4 In. 170.00
Box, Town Scene, Lithograph Paper, Silk Lining, 9 x 7 x 3 1/2 In. 195.00
Carving Set, Knife, Fork, Fake Horn Handles, Lamson & Goodnow, 3 Piece 35.00
Cigarette Case, 1930s, 3 1/2 x 3 In. 195.00
Comb, Openwork Pattern, Pale Green, Green Rhinestones, 1910-1920, 7 3/4 x 4 In. 110.00
Comb, Rhinestones, Swirl, Black, 1910-1920, 6 x 4 In. 110.00
Figurine, Reindeer, Cream, Glitter, Red Ribbon, Japan, Pat. 97485, 6 3/8 In. 35.00
Frame, Glass Cover, Oval, Easel Back, 1900-1920, 5 1/4 x 3 1/4 In. 90.00
Hair Receiver, Ivory Pyralin, DuBarry, Round, 1920s, 4 3/4 x 2 In. 22.00
Jewelry Box, White & Pink Floral Lithograph, 6 1/2 x 4 1/2 x 2 In. 150.00
Ornament, Hat, Rhinestone 25.00
Pin, Carnival, Pinback, 1 In. 5.00
Pin, Red Cross, Pinback, 3/4 In. 4.00
Pin, Seckatary Hawkins Club, Pinback, 1 In. 8.00
Placecard, Fortune, Cut Floral Design, Black Base, Box, Japan, 1930s, 23 Piece 50.00
Powder Box, With Puff, 3 Ivory Knob Legs, France, 1930s, 2 x 1 In. 80.00
Powder Box, Yellow, 6 Sides, Flat Footed, Halex, England, 1930s, 4 1/2 x 2 1/4 In. 42.00
Vanity Box, Victorian Woman, Floral Surround, New Satin Lining, 1900, 7 1/2 In. 65.00

CELS are listed in this book in the Animation Art category.

CERAMIC ART COMPANY of Trenton, New Jersey, was established in
1889 by J. Coxon and W. Lenox and was an early producer of American Belleek porcelain. It became Lenox, Inc. in 1906. Do not confuse
this ware with the pottery made by the Ceramic Arts Studio of Madi-
son, Wisconsin.

Jar, Cover, Stylized Trees, Blue, Green, Yellow, Gilt, White Ground, 5 In. 140.00
Spoon Warmer, Apple Blossoms, Ivory Ground, 7 x 6 In. 412.00
Vase, Landscape, Trees, Brown, Tan Ground, 10 x 4 1/2 In. 880.00

CERAMIC ARTS STUDIO was founded about 1940 in Madison, Wisconsin, by Lawrence Rabbett and Ruben Sand. Their most popular
products were expensive molded figurines. The pottery closed in 1955.
Do not confuse these products with those of the Ceramic Art Co. of
Trenton, New Jersey.

Figurine, Adonis & Aphrodite, Brown, 9 x 7 3/4 In. 650.00

Figurine, Benny Elephant, 3 1/2 In.	30.00
Figurine, Cinderella & Prince, 6 5/8 In., Pair	165.00
Figurine, Collie Dog Puppy, Sitting, 2 In.	34.00
Figurine, Drummer Girl, 4 In.	49.00
Figurine, Dutch Boy & Girl, Dancing, 5 1/2 In., Pair	59.00
Figurine, Dutch Couple, Kissing, 5 In.	49.00
Figurine, Dutch Girl, Green Trim, 5 In.	28.00
Figurine, Lamp, 2 3/4 In.	25.00
Figurine, Man With Violin, Girl With Tambourine, Pair	125.00
Figurine, Monkey, 3 1/2 In.	45.00
Figurine, Oriental Couple, 5 3/4 In., Pair	65.00
Figurine, Pomeranian, Standing, 3 In.	175.00
Figurine, Rumba Dancers, Man & Woman, Gold Trim	155.00
Figurine, Skunks, Inky & Dinky, 2 3/8 In., Pair	65.00
Figurine, Southern Colonel Jackson & Miss Lucindy	120.00
Figurine, Spanish Rumba Dancers, Green, Blue & Gold, 7 1/4 x 7 In.	145.00
Figurine, Toadstool, 3 In.	20.00
Figurine, Wee Eskimos, Boy & Girl, 3 1/4 x 3 In.	75.00
Figurine, Zebra, 5 In.	60.00
Salt & Pepper, Bear & Cub	85.00
Salt & Pepper, Boy In Chair, Boy Is Pepper, Chair Is Salt, 2 In.	60.00
Salt & Pepper, Gorilla & Baby	100.00
Salt & Pepper, Mouse & Cheese	37.00 to 40.00
Salt & Pepper, Oriental Boy & Girl	50.00
Salt & Pepper, Penguin, 3 3/4 In.	55.00
Salt & Pepper, Siamese Cat & Kitten, 4 1/4 x 3 1/4 In.	175.00
Salt & Pepper, Wee Eskimo, Boy & Girl, 3 1/4 x 3 In.	95.00
Shelf Sitter, Birds, Pudgie & Budgie, Pair	125.00
Shelf Sitter, Greg, 7 In.	40.00
Wall Pocket, African Man, African Woman, Titles, Signed, 8 1/8 In., Pair	275.00

CHALKWARE is really plaster of Paris decorated with watercolors. One type was molded from Staffordshire and other porcelain models and painted and sold as inexpensive decorations in the nineteenth century. Figures of plaster, made from about 1910 to 1940 for use as prizes at carnivals, are also known as chalkware. Kewpie dolls made of chalkware will be found in their own category.

Ashtray, 1936, 8 1/2 In.	35.00
Ashtray, Bikini Girl, Hula Skirt Forms Bowl, 1940	20.00
Ashtray, Dog, German Shepherd	22.00
Bookends, Indian Chief, Headdress, On 1 Knee, Figural, 1940	75.00
Box, Desk, Richfield Oil Co., Auto On Top	745.00
Bust, Putti, Molded Base, Unpainted, 19 In.	120.00
Cat, Sitting, 5 1/2 In.	1725.00
Cigar Box, Richfield, Dragster Shape, Copper Flashed, 1920-1930	675.00
Cowboy, Gun Belt, Hat, Vest, Says Guns & Ammunition, Pedestal, 60 In.	2850.00
Figurine, Baby, Black Kewpie Type, 1935-1940, 12 In.	110.00
Figurine, Clown, 12 In.	48.00
Figurine, Deer, Facing Pair, Signed Susie D. Cord, 8 1/2 In., Pair	935.00
Figurine, Deer, Lying, Raised Head, Tan, Black Markings, 10 In.	550.00
Figurine, Dog, Bulldog, White & Black, Orange Collar, 14 x 17 In.	410.00
Figurine, Dog, Poodle, Standing, Black Ears & Tail, Leash, 8 x 7 In.	525.00
Figurine, George Washington, On Horse, Carnival Type, 1940, 11 In.	40.00
Figurine, Gloomy Gus, 1920s, 11 In.	375.00
Figurine, Happy Hooligan, 1920s, 11 In.	375.00
Figurine, Hula Girl, Standing In Oyster Shell, Red Brushed Nipples & Lei, 1930s	120.00
Figurine, Pirate, Swashbuckling Pirate In Classic Regalia, 1953, 9 1/2 In.	25.00
Figurine, Rabbit, Yellow, Red & Black, 5 3/8 In.	550.00
Figurine, Sailor, 1940s, 9 In.	24.00
Figurine, Squirrel, Seated, Red & Green Highlighted Tail, Penna, 19th Century, 7 In.	415.00
Figurine, Squirrel, Seated, Yellow, Red, Green, Black Tail & Legs, 19th Century, 7 In.	550.00
Garniture, Mantel, Fruit Compote, Round Foot, 19th Century, 15 In.	1265.00
Garniture, Mantel, Fruits & Leaves On Base, Inscription, 19th Century, 14 In.	3450.00

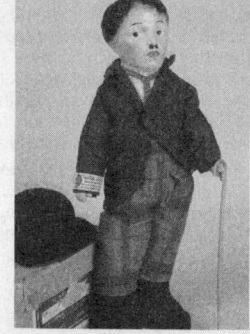

Charlie Chaplin, Doll, Composition
Head, Louis Amberg, 14 In.

If you have an alarm system, set
it each time you leave the house,
not just at night. Most home
burglaries take place during the
day or early evening.

Nodder, Hula Girl, Straw Skirt, 1940s, 10 In.	145.00
String Holder, Apples	60.00
String Holder, Baby Face	230.00
String Holder, Cat, Ball Of String	80.00
String Holder, Dutch Girl	85.00
String Holder, Mammy	235.00
String Holder, Mexican Man	75.00
String Holder, Pear	65.00

CHARLIE CHAPLIN, the famous comic and actor, lived from 1889 to
1977. He made his first movie in 1913. He did the movie *The Tramp*
in 1915. The character of the Tramp has remained famous, and in the
1980s appeared in a series of television commercials for computers.
Dolls, candy containers, and all sorts of memorabilia picture Charlie
Chaplin. Pieces are being made even today.

Candy Container, Charlie, Standing Along Side, Tin Enclosure, Borgfeldt, 4 In.	265.00
Card, Peep Show, The Tramp, 1920s, 2 1/2 x 14 3/4 In.	45.00
Comic Strip, Illusteret Familie-Journal, 12 Views, 1917-1920, Full Sheet	25.00
Corkscrew, Figural, 1930s	110.00
Doll, Composition Head, Louis Amberg, 14 In. ....*Illus*	725.00
Doll, Vinyl, Cloth Body, Box, 1972, 19 In.	55.00
Figurine, Plaster, Painted, Cero, 6 3/4 In.	50.00
Lobby Card, Great Dictator, United Artists, 1940	240.00
Salt & Pepper	35.00

CHARLIE MCCARTHY was the ventriloquist's dummy used by Edgar
Bergen from the 1930s. He was famous for his work in radio, movies,
and television. The act was retired in the 1970s.

Bank, Charlie Seated On His Suitcase, White Metal, Vanio, 5 1/2 In.	305.00
Bank, Charlie, Composition, Crown, 9 3/8 In.	66.00
Bank, Charlie, Monocle, With Trunk, White Metal, U.S., 1930s, 7 1/2 In.	55.00
Book, A Day With Charlie McCarthy & Edgar Bergen, 36 Pages, 1938	21.00
Card, Birthday, Edgar Bergen, You Can't Escape Birthdays, Charlie, 5 x 4 In.	16.00
Doll, Composition, Germany, 13 In.	375.00
Doll, Mortimer Snerd, Composition, Wire, Ideal, 13 In.	495.00
Dummy, Composition Socket Head, Muslin Body, Effanbee, c.1937, 19 In.	625.00
Figure, Wooden, 13 In.	75.00
Toy, Benzine Buggy, Windup, Tin, Marx	475.00 to 577.00
Toy, Benzine Mobile, Charlie Seated At Wheel, Tin, Louis Marx, 7 In.	485.00
Toy, Car, Pair Peering Through Roof Top, Tin, Louis Marx, 15 In.	3870.00
Toy, Drummer, Wearing Colorful Parade Uniform, Tin, Louis Marx, 9 In.	1030.00
Toy, Mortimer Snerd Hometown Band, Windup, Marx, 1930s	750.00
Toy, Walker, Charlie Wearing Black Tuxedo Getting Ready To Walk, Tin	340.00

CHELSEA porcelain was made in the Chelsea area of London from about 1745 to 1784. Some pieces made from 1770 to 1784 may include the letter *D* for *Derby* in the mark. Ceramic designs were borrowed from the Meissen models of the day. Pieces were made of soft paste. The gold anchor was used as the mark but it has been copied by many other factories. Recent copies of Chelsea have been made from the original molds. Do not confuse Chelsea porcelain with Chelsea Grape, a white pottery with luster grape decoration.

Basket, Leaf Shape, Puce Veined Leaf In Center, Green Edge, 1760, 11 In., Pair	1380.00
Candlestick, Flowers, Perched Songbird, Lower Songbird, 1765, 9 1/4 In., Pair	3450.00
Chamberstick, Scattered Sprays & Sprigs Of Flowers, Blue Border, 1765, 5 In., Pair	4890.00
Clock, Ship's Bell, Camel Back, Gold Plated, 6-In. Dial	3500.00
Dish, Fruits & Nuts In Center, Brown Border, Crenellated Edge, 1759, 10 In., Pair	1150.00
Dish, Kidney Shape, Large Exotic Bird Standing On Rock, 1765, 11 In., Pair	1610.00
Dish, Kidney Shape, Lobed Rim, Brown Edge, 1765, 11 3/4 In.	460.00
Dish, Spray & Scattered Sprigs Of Flowers, Brown Edged Lobed Rim, 1755, 10 In.	750.00
Dish, Tiger Entwined Around Bamboo Cane, Petal Shaped Rim, 1752, 6 7/8 In.	9775.00
Figurine, Cherub With Goat, Gilt Oval Base, Gold Anchor Mark, 3 In., Pair	230.00
Figurine, Hound, Spotted, Sitting, Brown, Tan, Gold Anchor Mark, 3 1/2 In., Pair	460.00
Figurine, Little Girl, Gold Dress, Floral Clusters, Lace Trim, Signed, 5 In.	28.00
Figurine, Sheep, Lying, 2 x 2 1/2 In.	155.00
Figurine, Squirrel Nibbling A Leafy Nut Or Berry, White, Delineated Paws, 1746, 5 In.	14950.00
Plate, Fruiting Branch Of Grapes, Currants, Birds Perched On Branches, 9 In., Pair	920.00
Platter, Sprays & Sprigs Of Flowers In Center, Exotic Birds, Scrolled Rim, 14 In.	865.00
Platter, Sprays Of Colorful Flowers In Center, Sprigs, Rectangular, 1755, 13 In., Pair	1755.00
Tray, Floral Sprays, Sprigs Of Flower In Center, Puce, Blue, Red, Purple, Yellow, 16 In.	1725.00
Tureen, Melon Form, Lobed Oval Fruit, Curled Vine Stem Knop, c.1755, 6 3/4 In.	3450.00
Vase, Exotic Birds Amidst Shrubbery, Mazarine, Blue, Entwined Handles, 10 In.	750.00

CHELSEA GRAPE pattern was made before 1840. A small bunch of grapes in a raised design, colored with purple or blue luster, is on the border of the white plate. Most of the pieces are unmarked. The pattern is sometimes called *Aynsley* or *Grandmother*. Chelsea Sprig is similar but has a sprig of flowers instead of the bunch of grapes. Chelsea Thistle has a raised thistle pattern. Do not confuse these Chelsea patterns with Chelsea Keramic Art Works, which can be found in the Dedham category, or with Chelsea porcelain, the preceding category.

Cup & Saucer	50.00
Sugar & Creamer, Cover, c.1830, 8 In.	82.00

CHINESE EXPORT porcelain comprises all the many kinds of porcelain made in China for export to America and Europe in the eighteenth, nineteenth, and twentieth centuries. Other pieces may be listed in this book under Canton, Celadon, Nanking, and Rose Medallion.

Basket, Chestnut, Reticulated Sides, Leaves, Butterflies, c.1800, 10 1/4 In.	800.00
Basket, On Stand, Overall Grape, Leaf Design, 1800, 4 1/2 In.	1870.00
Bowl, 5 People Exercising Tai Chi, Flow Blue, c.1840, 8 7/8 x 3 3/4 In.	190.00
Bowl, Circus Performer, Jugglers, Rope Walker, Famille Rose, 5 1/2 In.	70.00
Bowl, Domed Lid, Pine Trees, Flowering Shrubs, Famille Rose, 9 1/2 In.	935.00
Bowl, Figural & Floral Reserves, Famille Rose, Early 19th Century, 11 In.	1100.00
Bowl, Flared, 18th Century, 2 x 5 1/4 In.	75.00
Bowl, Floral & Bird Panels, Alternating Panels, Famille Verte, 5 3/4 In.	490.00
Bowl, Floral Design, Turquoise Ground, Famille Rose, 9 In.	90.00
Bowl, Floral Sprays, Gilded Interior Rim, Spearhead Border, c.1780, 10 In.	230.00
Bowl, Lake Scenes, Cut Corners, Square, c.1800, 4 1/2 x 10 In.	770.00
Bowl, Lotus Form, Bird, Floral Design, Famille Verte, 8 In.	910.00
Bowl, Mandarin Palette, Interior Floral Sprays, Red Rim, c.1785, 10 1/4 In.	490.00
Bowl, Procession Of Notables, Famille Rose, Woodem Stand, Late 1800s, 14 In.	550.00
Bowl, Rectangular, Landscape, Blue & White, Cover, Mid 1800s, 8 1/2 In.	385.00
Bowl, Vegetable, Cover, Oval, Polychrome, Peacock, 19th Century, 9 x 11 In.	400.00
Box, Game, Hinged Top, Chessboard & Backgammon Board, 19th Century	1495.00
Charger, Bamboo, Floral Urn, Ax-Form Lappet Border, Blue, White, c.1780, 12 In.	600.00

Charger, Central Floral Spray Design, Famille Rose, 14 In. 460.00
Charger, Flower Sprays, Diaper & Lappet Borders, Blue, White, c.1780, 13 3/8 In. 880.00
Charger, Overall Stemmed Flowers, Fruit Clusters, Blue, White, c.1780, 13 3/4 In. 440.00
Charger, Stylized Floral & Leaves, Famille Verte, 16 3/4 In. 370.00
Charger, Willow Tree, Flowers, Floral Border, Blue, White, c.1780, 13 3/4 In. 1100.00
Chocolate Pot, Mandarin, Side Handle, c.1785 .... 600.00
Coffeepot, Entwined Strap Handle, Gilt Grapevine Border, 9 3/4 In. 315.00
Coffeepot, Peacock Amid Figures, 1750s, 11 1/2 In. 9775.00
Compote, Diamond Shape, Raised Base, Famille Rose, 8 1/2 x 11 In. 140.00
Compote, Lobed Sides, Celadon Ground, Birds, Insects, c.1850, 11 x 14 In. 260.00
Compote, Reticulated Sides, Rope Twist Handles, Famille Rose, 11 x 9 1/2 In. 305.00
Condiment Set, Famille Rose, Lacquered Base Dishes, 12 In., 9 Piece 400.00
Creamer, Helmet Shape, Cobalt Blue, Gilt, 5 In. 125.00
Creamer, Helmet Shape, Floral Design, Famille Rose, 4 1/2 In. 50.00
Cup, Handleless, Polychrome, Monogram, 18th Century 90.00
Cup & Saucer, Chariot Design, Black & Flesh Tones, 18th Century 140.00
Cup & Saucer, Figures, Iron Red & White, Demitasse 60.00
Cup Plate, Figural Design, Blue & White Border, Famille Rose, 4 3/4 In., Pair 115.00
Cuspidor, Blossoming Peonies, Pink Diaper Border, c.1745, 4 1/2 In., Pair 1840.00
Dish, Central Floral Spray, Fish Scale & Turquoise Panel Border, 10 7/8 In., Pair 935.00
Dish, Curry, Heraldic Design, Lions, Motto, Oval, Footed, 12 1/4 x 9 1/2 In. 1045.00
Dish, Deep, Polychrome, Gilt, Martial Scene, Gilt Border, 19th Century, 10 In. 385.00
Dish, Deep, Western Figural & Landscape Design, Spearhead Border, 1800s, 9 In. 110.00
Dish, Floral Design, Famille Rose, 18th Century, 5 In. 290.00
Dish, Floral Panels, Divided By Diapering, Blue, White, Round, c.1720, 8 In. 470.00
Dish, Flower Form, Central Chrysanthemum, Rose Border, 18th Century, 6 In. 440.00
Dish, Flower Form, Green Ground, Polychrome Flowers, 18th Century, 6 In. 440.00
Dish, Green Fitzhugh, 6 In. 80.00
Dish, Hot Water, Armorial, Mandarin Interior, Famille Rose, 1820, 10 In., Pair 4025.00
Dish, Leaf Shape, Handle, Flower Clusters, Famille Rose, c.1770, 12 In. 1150.00
Dish, Painted Ibis Amid Flowering Shrubbery, c.1745, 11 1/4 In. 605.00
Dish, Shrimp, Oval, Flat Lip, Water Scene, Daoguang, c.1850, 10 In. 360.00
Dish, Warming, Lake Scene, 1800, 10 1/2 In., Pair 740.00
Ewer, Dragon Spout, Famille Verte, 19th Century, 14 In. 155.00
Figurine, Cockerel, 16 In., Pair .... 630.00 to 700.00
Figurine, Kingfisher, Tree Stump Base, Folded Feathers, Famille Rose, 8 In. 3680.00
Figurine, Lovebirds, 1860, 6 In. 895.00
Figurine, Parrot, Multicolored, 1895, 8 1/4 In. 395.00
Figurine, Peacocks, Famille Rose, 13 In. 315.00
Figurine, Pheasant, On Rocky Outcrop, Polychrome, 12 In., Pair 605.00
Garden Seat, Barrel, Maidens, Pierced, Famille Rose, 19 In., Pair 715.00
Garden Seat, Reeds & Flowers, Blue & White, 19th Century, 18 1/2 In. 660.00
Garniture, With 2 Beaker Vases, Famille Rose, 18th Century, 5 Piece 7150.00
Ginger Jar, Cover, Floral, Butterfly Design, Famille Verte, 10 In. 115.00
Jar, Baluster, Domed Cover, Vines, Flowers, Blue, White, c.1800, 24 1/2 In. 2640.00
Jar, Bird, Floral Design, Famille Rose, 16 In. 230.00
Jar, Cover, People In Scenic Panels, Famille Verte, 11 1/2 In. 460.00
Jar, Cover, Woman Figure Emerging From Flower Blossom, Famille Rose 750.00
Jardiniere, Flared, Children In Landscape, 1862-1874, 8 x 9 1/2 In. 385.00
Jardiniere, Lotus & Leaves, 1875-1908, 12 3/4 x 14 In. 495.00
Jug, Cream, Floral, 18th Century 185.00
Jug, Cream, Lake Scene, 19th Century, 5 In. 160.00
Lantern, Hexagonal, Pierced, People, Flowers, Famille Rose, 15 1/2 In., Pair 460.00
Mug, Crisscross Handle, Fitzhugh Rim, Blue & White, 5 In. 1650.00
Mug, Dragon Handle, Blue & White, c.1760, 5 1/4 In. 1850.00
Mug, Figural Design, 18th Century, 6 In. 440.00
Mug, Mandarin Scenes, Dragon Handle, c.1780, 5 1/2 In. 2200.00
Mug, Scenes In Multicolors, c.1720, 4 1/2 In. 1500.00
Planter, Oriental Landscapes, Blue, White, Bronze Mounted, 10 In., Pair 2530.00
Plaque, 4 Seasons, Bird & Flowers, Famille Rose, Frame, 24 x 14 In., 4 Piece 375.00
Plate, 3 European Women Picking Cherries From Tree, 9 In. 1035.00
Plate, Armorial, Double Crest Center, Floral Garland, Gilt Banding, 9 1/2 In. 165.00
Plate, Butterfly & Flower, Famille Rose, 8 In. 120.00

Plate, Central Floral, Flying Cranes & Floral Sprays Border, 9 In., Pair 230.00
Plate, Chop, Armorial, Grapevine Border, 18th Century, 14 In. 1100.00
Plate, Crane, Peony & Bamboo, Blue & Sepia, 18th Century, 9 In. 155.00
Plate, Fable Of Youth, Beauty & Folly, Blossoms On Rim, c.1765, 9 In. 3680.00
Plate, Famille Rose, Flowers, Treasured Antiques, Late 18th Century, 11 In. 1210.00
Plate, Fish Roe Band, Order Of Cincinnati Within Husk Band, c.1785, 9 In. 520.00
Plate, Floral Sprays Within Diapering, Floral Center, Famille Rose, 9 In., Pair 460.00
Plate, Flower & Garland Design, 18th Century, 9 In., Pair 185.00
Plate, Flower Basket, Polychrome, Early 19th Century, 8 3/4 In. 220.00
Plate, Flowers, Blue & White, 18th Century, 9 1/4 In. 175.00
Plate, Flowers, Polychrome, 18th Century, 8 3/4 In. 110.00
Plate, German Crest & Cipher Center, c.1745, 8 3/4 In., 8 Piece 460.00
Plate, Harbor Shipping Scene In Center, 18th Century, 9 In. 520.00
Plate, Jesuit-Type, Lowestoft, Black & Gold Crowned Virgin Center, 1700s, 9 In. 495.00
Plate, Landscape & Figural Design, 18th Century, 9 In. 825.00
Plate, Long Lady, Maidens In Garden, c.1780, 9 3/8 In., Pair 1045.00
Plate, Octagonal, Figural Scene, Famille Rose, Blue Border, 8 3/4 In., 4 Piece 220.00
Plate, Shield Design, Black & Gold, 18th Century, 8 In. 110.00
Plate, Western Style Figural Design, Spearhead Variant Border, Gilt, 1700s, 9 In. 468.00
Platter, Blue Medallion, Gray, Blue Border, Oval, Fitzhugh, 15 x 12 In. 575.00
Platter, Boats & Pagodas, Mountainous Landscape, 1770s, 15 In. 660.00
Platter, Butterflies, Insects & Chrysanthemums, Monogrammed, 17 In. 1265.00
Platter, Central Panel Of 5 Children Playing, Famille Rose, c.1920, 13 In. 140.00
Platter, Deer In Garden, 12 1/8 In. 370.00
Platter, Flower Garden & Willow Tree, 18th Century, 16 1/2 In. 795.00
Platter, Gilt Armorial Rim, Blue & White, Orange Peel Glaze, 13 In. 400.00
Platter, Gold, Red, Blue, Green Glaze, Lion Crest Rim, Oval, Fitzhugh, 12 x 9 In. 345.00
Platter, Lake Scenes, Blue, White, Rectangular, Chamfered Corners, 1700s, 18 In. 1540.00
Platter, Landscape, Brook, Building, Blue, White, c.1780, 13 1/4 x 10 1/2 In. 605.00
Platter, Landscape, Modified Fitzhugh, c.1800, 15 1/2 In. 825.00
Platter, Oblong, Watery Landscape, Sampans, Bridge, 1825-1850, 16 x 14 In. 550.00
Platter, Octagonal, Houses By River, Floral Border, Blue, White, c.1780, 12 In. 525.00
Platter, Pagoda & Riverscape, Blue, White, Fitzhugh, Oval, 14 1/2 In. 375.00
Platter, Pagoda, 18th Century, Oval, 11 1/2 In. 385.00
Platter, Roast, Fitzhugh, Oval, 1800, 12 3/4 In. 495.00
Platter, Stylized Floral Armorial, Famille Rose, Egg Shape, 1760, 14 1/4 In. 1430.00
Platter, Well & Tree, Blue & White, Fitzhugh, 16 In. 920.00
Platter, Well & Tree, Blue & White, Fitzhugh, 19 In. 1430.00
Platter, Well & Tree, Rose Mandarin, 18 In. 980.00
Punch Bowl, Arms Of Wood Of Complanthorpe, Famille Rose, 14 1/4 In. 2070.00
Punch Bowl, Judgement Of Paris, Spearhead Border, c.1750, 11 1/4 In. 1150.00
Punch Bowl, Oval Reserve, Famille Rose Scenes, Birds, 1780s, 15 1/2 In. 6110.00
Rose Bowl, Exterior Floral Scrolling, 3 Sheep Interior, 19th Century, 9 1/2 In. 370.00
Salt, Lake Scene, Blue & White, c.1780, 3 1/4 In. 495.00
Soup, Dish, Flower & Garland Design, 18th Century, 9 In. 120.00
Soup, Dish, Willow, Latticework Zigzag Fence, Blue, White, 9 In., 5 Piece 770.00
Spoon Tray, Oval, Fan-Shaped Landscape Cartouches, Blue, White, c.1800, 5 In. 130.00
Tankard, Oval, Tree, Hanging Flower Basket, Birds, Butterflies, 6 In. 400.00
Tea Set, Landscape Design, Gilt, Drum Shape, 1800, 3 Piece 1320.00
Tea Set, Orange Design, c.1750, 6 Piece 3250.00
Tea Set, Ribbed Body, Flowers, Berry Finial, 3 Piece 660.00
Teapot, Drum Shape, Red Floral Design, Entwined Handle, Fruit Finial, 6 In. 250.00
Teapot, Genre Scene, Woman, Troupe Of Musicians, Famille Rose, c.1775, 6 In. 895.00
Teapot, Mandarin Design, Silver Spout, Globular, 18th Century, 8 1/2 In. 330.00
Teapot, Monkey Shape, 1830, 6 1/2 In. 595.00
Teapot, Puzzle, Continuous Landscape, Blue Underglaze, 7 In. 950.00
Teapot, Sparrow Beak, Blue & White, Silver Mount, 5 1/2 In. 690.00
Teapot, Woman Figures Before Fence, Verso Jardiniere & Plant, 3 3/4 In. 400.00
Tile, Polychrome, Pierced Wooden Frame, 15 x 12 1/2 In. 220.00
Tray, Butterfly & Cabbage, 4-Lobed Shape, 19 1/4 In. 575.00
Tray, Notched Corners, Rim Fruits, Mid 19th Century, 16 3/16 In. 505.00
Tray, Rose Floral Scene, Yellow, Blue, Red Glaze, Famille Rose, 10 x 4 In. 520.00
Tureen, Floral Design, Blue & White, 14 In. 980.00

Tureen, Sauce, Flower Finial, Orange, Fitzhugh, 1795, 7 1/2 In. 2090.00
Tureen, Soup, Cover, Orange Fitzhugh, Strap Handle, 14 1/2 In. 16100.00
Tureen, Stand, Overlapped Leaves, Sprig Knop, Spray To Reverse, c.1775, 15 In. 9775.00
Umbrella Stand, Allover Fans & Butterflies, Contemporary, 18 In., Pair 355.00
Umbrella Stand, Cabbage & Butterfly Pattern, 25 In. 460.00
Vase, Allover Flower, Bird & Butterfly, Famille Rose, 1850s, 24 In., Pair 2645.00
Vase, Baluster, White Crackled Glaze, 19th Century, 15 1/2 In. 290.00
Vase, Bird & Chrysanthemums, Blue, Flared Neck, Pierced Handles, 1890s 175.00
Vase, Bluebird & Flower, Famille Rose, 19th Century, 11 In. 330.00
Vase, Bottle Shape, Mounted As Electric Lamp, 1900, 20 In. 355.00
Vase, Bottle, Swirling Coral Glaze, Banded Neck, Early 19th Century, 13 In. 1100.00
Vase, Brown Glaze, Polychrome Sampans, Mounted As Lamp, 22 1/2 In., Pair 1870.00
Vase, Butterfly, Kylins Circling Necks, Famille Rose, 11 1/2 x 4 In., Pair 490.00
Vase, Court Figures, Fish Border, Ormolu Mounts, Fitted As Lamp, 25 In., Pair 3740.00
Vase, Court Scene Front, Nobleman Back, Serpents, c.1825, 24 In., Pair 5520.00
Vase, Cover, Serpent Handles, Painted Mountain Villas, c.1785, 12 3/4 In., Pair 9775.00
Vase, Enameled Objects On Yellow Ground, Famille Rose, 12 1/2 In., Pair 546.00
Vase, Figural & Bird Scenes, Cobalt Floral Surrounds, 10 In., Pair 1495.00
Vase, Figures In Landscape, Famille Verte, 17 1/2 In. 862.00
Vase, Figures Picking Fruit, Butterflies On Verso, Famille Rose, 17 1/2 In. 115.00
Vase, God Of Longevity, Children With Peach On Bridge, Famille Rose, 18 In. 175.00
Vase, Hexagonal, Crane & Lily Design, 12 1/2 In., Pair 465.00
Vase, Iris, Blue & White, Cylindrical, With Lamp Insert, 14 1/2 In. 110.00
Vase, Panels Between Prunus Blossoms, Blue & White, 19th Century, 15 In. 515.00
Vase, Panels Of Precious Object & Animal, Floral Border, 22 1/2 In. 115.00
Vase, Pear Shape, Peacock & Peony Design, Famille Jaune, 12 1/2 In. 55.00
Vase, Pilgrim, Flask Shape, Outdoor Family Scenes, Tongzhi, 14 1/4 In. 770.00
Wall Pocket, Landscape Design, Famille Verte, Late 19th Century, 7 1/2 In. 55.00
Washbasin, Children & Mandarin Center, Floral Border, Rose Famille, 11 In. 465.00
Washbasin, Medallion, 2 Women, Floral Border, Bamboo, Rose Famille, 16 In. 465.00
Washbowl, Famille Rose, Figures & Dragon, Chinese House, 11 1/2 In. 440.00

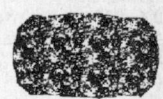

CHINTZ is the name of a group of china patterns featuring an overall design of flowers and leaves. The design became popular with English makers about 1928. A few pieces are still being made. The best known are designs by Royal Winton, James Kent Ltd., Crown Ducal, and Shelley. Crown Ducal and Shelley are listed in their own sections.

Ascot, Plate, 1905, 8 3/4 In. 395.00
Blue Tulip, Creamer, Royal Winton 145.00
Butterfly Chintz, Creamer, Wade Ceramics Ltd. 200.00
Butterfly Chintz, Teapot, Wade Ceramics Ltd. 300.00
Delphinium, Syrup, 5 x 6 In. 545.00
Festival, Vase, Bittersweet Color Under Rim, 6 1/4 In. 225.00
Floral Feast, Cheese Keeper 495.00
Floral Feast, Plate, 10 1/4 In. 220.00

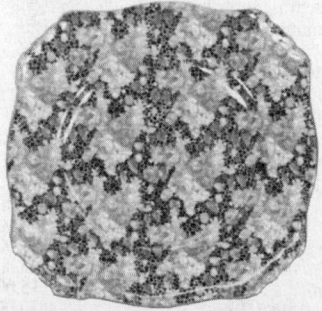

To remove an unwanted gummed price sticker, try heating it with a hair dryer. The glue will melt a bit, and it will be easier to peel off the sticker.

Chintz, Hazel, Plate, Royal Winton, 10 In.

Gatineau, Plate, Radford, England, 8 In. 24.00
Gatineau, Saucer, Radford, England, 5 1/2 In. 15.00
Hazel, Creamer, Royal Winton 140.00
Hazel, Plate, Royal Winton, 10 In. ....*Illus* 175.00
Hazel, Sugar & Creamer, Royal Winton 150.00
Kromer, Plate, Hand Painted Over Transfer, 1934, 9 In. 135.00
Lorna Doone, Tray, 3 Sections 135.00
Marina, Jug, Lord Nelson, 5 In. 300.00
Marina, Teapot, Stacking, 6 1/2 In. 995.00
Nantwich, Jug, Hot Water, 5 1/2 In. 398.00
Old Cottage Chintz, Salt & Pepper, Tray, 3 Piece 170.00
Paisley, Cup & Saucer, Radford, England 45.00
Red Roof Cottage, Woodland Scene, Wildflowers, Pond, Breakfast Set, 6 Piece 850.00
Red Spatter Glaze, Cheese Keeper 45.00
Red Spatter Glaze, Cup & Saucer 45.00
Rock Garden, Plate, 6 In. 115.00
Royalty, Plate, Royal Winton, Square, 9 In. 185.00
Somerset, Platter, Royal Winton, Round, 11 1/2 In. 385.00
Summertime, Cake Plate, Royal Winton, Open Handles ....110.00 to 125.00
Summertime, Teapot, Royal Winton, 5 In. 425.00

CHOCOLATE GLASS, sometimes mistakenly called caramel slag, was made by the Indiana Tumbler and Goblet Company of Greentown, Indiana, from 1900 to 1903. It was also made at other National Glass Company factories. Fenton Art Glass Co. also made chocolate glass from about 1907 to 1915. More recent pieces have been made by Imperial and others.

Cactus, Pitcher 395.00
Cactus, Tumbler, Greentown, 5 1/8 In. ....30.00 to 65.00
Cord Drapery, Butter, Cover, 4 3/4 In. 475.00
Cord Drapery, Compote, 7 /12 In. 500.00
Cord Drapery, Syrup 85.00
Daisy, Mustard, Cover, Spoon, Greentown 525.00
Geneva, Bowl, 8 3/8 In. 250.00
Geneva, Bowl, 10 1/2 In. 380.00
Geneva, Bowl, Oval, 8 1/4 x 5 1/4 In. 145.00
Geneva, Butter, Cover 500.00
Geneva, Creamer 170.00
Indoor Drinking Scene, Mug, 8 1/2 In. 300.00
Leaf Bracket, Creamer 130.00
Leaf Bracket, Sugar, Cover 190.00
Serenade, Mug 175.00
Shuttle, Mug 75.00
Wild Rose With Bowknot, Bowl, 8 1/2 In. 235.00

CHRISTMAS collectibles include not only Christmas trees and ornaments listed below, but also Santa Claus figures, special dishes, and even games and wrapping paper. A Belsnickle is a nineteenth-century figure of Father Christmas. A kugel is an early, heavy ornament made of thick blown glass, lined with zinc or lead, and often covered with colored wax. Christmas cards are listed in this section under Greeting Card. Christmas collectibles may also be listed in the Candy Container category and. Christmas trees are listed in the section that follows.

Belsnickle, Belt, Fur Trim, Germany 1650.00
Belsnickle, Holding Feather Tree, Basket On Back, Red Felt Coat, Wool Trim, 9 In. 220.00
Belsnickle, Papier-Mache, White, 1890s, Large 980.00
Belsnickle, Papier-Mache, Yellow 1150.00
Belsnickle, Papier-Mache, Yellow, Copper Flakes 980.00
Booklet, Rudolph The Red Nosed Reindeer, Montgomery Ward, 1930s 40.00
Candy Box, Sled, Santa Claus, Germany 395.00
Coaster, Porky Pig, Ringing Bell, Christmas, 1950s, 3 3/4 In. 15.00
Display, Santa In Autogyro, Store Type, Wood, Glitter, Painted, 16 1/2 In. 630.00
Doll, Santa Claus, Red Flannel Outfit, Tree In Hand, Papier-Mache, 14 1/2 In. 374.00

Fence, Tree, Cast Iron, Steel, Green, Gold, 8 Sections, 2 Gates, 104 In. 385.00
Figure, Angel, Winter Clothing, Book Of Carols, Die Cut, Germany, 1900s, 5 x 8 In. 22.00
Figure, Merrie-Merrie Christmas Tree, Lights Up, Roto-Vue, Box, 1950s, 11 In. 25.00
Figure, Santa Claus, Composition, Cloth, Spun Cotton Beard, Germany, 6 1/2 In. 65.00
Figure, Santa Claus, Composition, Molded Head, Red Flannel Suit, 1930s, 19 In. 315.00
Figure, Santa Claus, Papier-Mache, Cone, 2 Miniature Santas Inside, 5 In. 45.00
Figure, Santa Claus, Sleigh, Pulled By Pigs, Composition, Wood, 1900s, 29 In. 1430.00
Greeting Card, Designed By E.T. Hurley, 5 Piece 550.00
Greeting Card, Santa Claus, Fringed, 1880s, 4 x 6 In. 47.00
Placecard Ornament, Cast Metal, Best Wishes, Merry Christmas, 8 Piece 185.00
Planter, Santa Claus, Pottery, Betty Lou Nichols, 9 In. 175.00
Plates that are limited editions are listed in the Collector Plate category or in the correct fac-
tory listing.
Santa Claus & Sleigh, Die Cut, Paper, 1890s 1155.00
Toy, Merry Christmas, Carousel, Santa Claus, Key Wind, Celluloid, Japan, Box, 6 In. 125.00
Toy, Rudolph The Red Nosed Reindeer, Vinyl Face, Stuffed, Gund, 1940s 78.00
Toy, Rudolph The Red Nosed Reindeer, Walking, Battery Operated, 1970s 40.00
Toy, Santa Claus On Pig, Pull Toy, 10 3/4 In. 577.00
Toy, Santa Claus, Bell Ringer, Alps, 7 In. 135.00
Toy, Santa Claus, Bell Ringer, Holds Merry Christmas Sign, Windup, Tin, 7 In. 200.00
Toy, Santa Claus, Bell Ringer, Windup, Alps 75.00
Toy, Santa Claus, In Car, Japan 295.00
Toy, Santa Claus, Lifts Jumping Jack Out Of Bag, Paper, Wood, Clockwork, 16 In. 4400.00
Toy, Santa Claus, Long Neck, Tin, Rubber, Felt, Bell Ringer, Japan, Box, 7 In. 180.00
Toy, Santa Claus, Moves Up & Down Chimney, Metal, Windup 155.00
Toy, Santa Claus, On Sled, Reindeer, Key Wind, Celluloid, Metal, Japan, 8 1/4 In. 87.00
Toy, Santa Claus, Reindeer Pulling Cloth Santa Claus In Sleigh, Celluloid, 24 In. 145.00
Toy, Santa Claus, Riding Donkey, Basket On Back, Papier-Mache, Wire, 18 In. 1430.00
Toy, Train Hand Car, Santa Claus, Christmas Tree, Lionel 1100.00
Toy, Walker, Santa Claus, Battery Operated, Celluloid, Box 395.00
Wreath, Electric Candle, Red Chenille Wrapped, 2 Foil Leaves, 9 3/4 In. 35.00

CHRISTMAS TREES made of feathers and Christmas tree decorations of
all types are popular with collectors. The first decorated Christmas tree
in America is claimed by many states, including Pennsylvania (1747),
Massachusetts (1832), Illinois (1833), Ohio (1838), and Iowa (1845).
The first glass ornaments were imported from Germany about 1860.
Dresden ornaments were made about 100 years ago of paper and tinsel. Manufacturers in the United States were making ornaments in the
early 1870s. Electric lights were first used on a Christmas tree in 1882.
Character light bulbs became popular in the 1920s, bubble lights in the
1940s, twinkle bulbs in the 1950s, plastic bulbs by 1955. In this book
a Christmas light is a holder for a candle used on the tree. Other forms
of lighting include light bulbs. Other Christmas memorabilia is listed
in the preceding section.

Feather, 24 In. 115.00
Feather, 36 In. 475.00
Feather, Gooseberry Tipped, Silver Balls, Wooden Base, c.1890, 11 In. 400.00
Light, Grapes, Deep Cobalt Blue, Hearn Wright & Co., London, 3 7/8 In. 120.00
Light, Harlequin, Cobalt Blue, Diamond, Sheared Rim, England, 1910, 3 1/2 In. 125.00
Light, King Edward, Cobalt Blue, Ground Lip, England, 1910, 4 1/8 In. 825.00
Light, Queen Victoria, Puce, Hearn Wright & Co., London, 1890, 3 7/8 In. 1210.00
Light, Tulip, Turquoise Blue, Hearn Wright & Co, London, 1910, 3 1/2 In. 175.00
Light Bulb Set, Mickey Mouse, Noma, Box, 1930s . . . . .225.00 to 265.00
Light Bulb Set, Silly Symphony, Box, 1930s 315.00
Ornament, Angel & Child, Molded Glass 240.00
Ornament, Angel, Treetop, Spun Glass 25.00
Ornament, Arab On Camel, Dresden 950.00
Ornament, Baby In Bed, Waxed, Cotton, Wire, Sebnizt 385.00
Ornament, Baby On Beaded Ball, Cotton, Wire, Sebnizt, 2 1/2 In. 90.00
Ornament, Barbie, Hallmark, No. 1, Box 50.00
Ornament, Bicycle Built For 2, Dresden, 1890s 8250.00
Ornament, Bird In Nest, Wire Wrapped, Victorian 90.00

Ornament, Donald Duck, Figural, Lighted, 16 In. 21.00
Ornament, Girl, Wire Wrapped, Victorian 130.00
Ornament, House, Felt Cover, Mica, Hand Made, Czechoslovakia 15.00
Ornament, Indian Chief, Molded Glass 210.00
Ornament, Kugel, Green, Round, Embossed Cap 175.00
Ornament, Little Red Riding Hood, Glass, 1920s 120.00
Ornament, Mushroom Man, Clip-On 150.00
Ornament, Peacock, Pressed Cotton 12.00
Ornament, Phantom Of The Opera, 6 1/2 In. 45.00
Ornament, Prizefighter, Molded Glass 205.00
Ornament, Rudolph The Red Nosed Reindeer, Blinking Nose, Hallmark, 1989 .... 65.00
Ornament, Santa Claus, Clip-On, 1920s 125.00
Ornament, Santa Claus, On Reindeer, Dresden 1500.00
Ornament, Skeezix, Glass 200.00
Ornament, Smokey The Bear, 6 1/2 In. 40.00
Ornament, Space Man, Box 18.00
Stand, Musical, Manger Scene, Key Wind 660.00

CHROME items in the Art Deco style became popular in the 1930s. Collectors are most interested in high-style pieces made by the Connecticut firms of Chase Brass and Copper Company, and Manning Bowman.

Candleholder, Lucite, Farberware, 3 1/2 In. 45.00
Candlestick, Lucite, 3 1/2 In. 50.00
Candlestick, Scrolled Shaft, Reimann, Chase, 8 3/4 In. 275.00
Candy Dish, Cover, Rockwell Kent 12.00
Cocktail Set, Ribbed Shaker, Red Bakelite Handle, 5 Red Glass Goblets, 6 Piece 175.00
Cocktail Shaker, Bakelite Cap, Relief Scowling Face, 11 In. 220.00
Cocktail Shaker, Chrome Finish, Art Deco, 12 In. 22.00
Cocktail Shaker, Coffeepot Shape, Turning Top Shows The Recipe For 14 Drinks 35.00
Cocktail Shaker, Farberware 40.00
Cocktail Shaker, Fire Extinguisher Shape, Recipes, 11 In. 90.00
Coffee Set, Urn, Butterscotch, Catalin Handles, Continental Silver Co., 3 Piece 80.00
Decanter Set, Art Deco, Amethyst Insert, Farber Bros., 6 Stemmed Goblets, 10-In. 200.00
Ice Bucket, Bacchus, In Embossed Panel, Ring Handles, Rockwell Kent, Chase, 9 In. ... 360.00
Pitcher, Water, Catalin Handle, Ice Spout 60.00
Samovar Set, Percolator, Sugar, Creamer & Tray, Manning Bowman, 12 1/2 In. 715.00
Sauce, Tray & Ladle, Viking, Chase 60.00

CIGAR STORE FIGURES of carved wood or cast iron were used as advertisements in front of the Victorian cigar store. The carved figures are now collected as folk art. They range in size from counter type, about three feet, to over eight feet high.

Blackamoor, Polychrome Over Early Paint, 19th Century, 27 In. 5460.00
Holding Tobacco Pouch, Flat, 1840s, 57 In. 4125.00

Cigar Store Figure, Indian Princess, Headdress, Holding Cut Plug Tobacco & Cigars, Base

Electric toasters, coffeepots, and even some furniture are made with chrome, a plated metal. The plating is soft and very thin, so abrasives should not be used in cleaning. Clean chrome with a mild soap or detergent and a soft cloth, then use an all-metal cleaner to improve the shine.

Indian, Blue Coat 2475.00
Indian, Chief, 1900, 66 In. 14850.00
Indian, Feathered Headdress, Carved Pine, Holding A Rifle, Cigars, 81 In. 3960.00
Indian, Full Headdress, Cigars 5 Cents, 69 In. 450.00
Indian, Full Headdress, Holding Cigars & Box, 20th Century, 70 In. 2200.00
Indian, Headdress, Leaf Design Tunic, Arm Raised, 1900, 66 In. 14850.00
Indian, Mahogany, Polychrome, 1970s, 72 In. 360.00
Indian, Maiden, Headdress, Carved Pine, Holding Tobacco Leaves, 78 In. 715.00
Indian, Man, Headdress, Ceremonial Attire, Staff In Right Hand, 87 3/4 In. 975.00
Indian, Plaster, Brown Paint, Square Base, 1900, 20 5/8 In. 425.00
Indian, Polychrome Over Gesso, 19th Century, 17 1/2 In. 2300.00
Indian, Woman, Headdress, Holding Cigars, Polychrome, 74 1/2 In. 1265.00
Indian Chief, Standing, Holding Bunches Of Cigars, Pine, 1880, 66 In. 17250.00
Indian Princess, Headdress, Holding Cut Plug Tobacco & Cigars, Base . . . .*Illus* 6050.00
Napoleon, Bundle Of Cigars In Hand, Wooden, 27 1/4 In. 3300.00
Napoleon, Holding Cigars, Wooden, Countertop, 27 3/4 In. 3300.00
Performer, Rising Star, Wearing Fringed Costume, Pine, 57 In. 20700.00
Princess, Standing, Raised Right Arm, Pine, 62 In. 12650.00
Scotsman, Iron Bracket, 19th Century, 36 In. 3738.00
Scotsman, Tobacco, Snuff & Cigars Base, Polychrome Over Gesso, 38 In. 4140.00
Turk, Polychrome Over Gesso, 19th Century, 27 In. 3220.00
Turk, Smoking Pipe, Polychrome, 19th Century, 19 In. 2300.00

CINNABAR is a vermilion or red lacquer. Pieces are made with tens to hundreds of thicknesses of the lacquer that is later carved. Most cinnabar was made in the Orient.

Cup & Saucer 40.00
Jar, Vase, Continuous Scenic Design, 10 In. & 6 1/2 In., 2 Piece 70.00
Plate, Dinner 45.00
Vase, Bulging Body, Waisted Neck, Landscapes, People, Guangxu Period, 19 In. 770.00
Vase, Figural Design, Fitted As Lamp, 13 1/2 In. 57.00
Vase, Scenic Design, Clay Base, Bronze Foot & Rim, 19th Century, 7 1/2 In. 22.00

CIVIL WAR mementos are important collectors' items. Most of the pieces are military items used from 1861 to 1865. Be sure to avoid any explosive munitions.

Ballot Box, Hand-Planed Pine, Nails, Turned Handle, 10 x 6 1/2 x 4 1/4 In. 110.00
Banner, GAR Encampment, With 13 Star Flag, Cotton, 36 1/2 x 23 1/2 In. 275.00
Bayonet, Barrel Band, Medium Gray Blade, Brass Handle, 22 1/2-In. Blade 241.00
Belt, Leather, U.S. Brass Buckle & 1864 Musket Cartridge Box 275.00
Bit, Halter, U.S. Cavalry 975.00
Boot Pull, Ivory Handle, 7 In. 65.00
Box, Cartridge, Leather, With Web Belt 300.00
Box, Wood Inlay, Bone, Made By P.O.W., 12 1/8 x 5 1/8 x 5 1/4 In. 240.00
Broadside, Recruiting, African-American, Color 2145.00
Buckle, Brass, U.S., Lead Backed, 3 x 1 1/2 In. 176.00
Buckle, U.S., Brass Front, Lead Back, Oval 66.00
Bugle, L.E. Hodges, Company G., 3rd Maine Cavalry 925.00
Camp Chair, Folding 330.00
Canteen, Bull's-Eye, Pewter Spout, Phila., 7 1/2 In. 165.00
Canteen, GAR, Black Glass, Lettering, M.W. Elliott Co., F 101st Reg, PA VI, Stopper . . . 385.00
Canteen, Garrison, Wood Binding Pine, 10 Slats, 8 1/2 In. x 13 1/2 In. 264.00
Canteen, Grand Army Of Republic Emblem, Ironstone, 7 1/4 In. 750.00
Canteen, Wagon, Iron Band, Walnut Staves, Oval, Marked 64-65, 7 x 11 In. 290.00
Carpet Bag, Linen Lining, Lock & Key, A. Litchfield, 21 x 15 1/2 In. 265.00
Cartridge Pouch, Confederate, Flap, Leather, Brass Star, Oval CSA Plate, 6 x 7 In. 688.00
Chevron, Sergeant, Pair 204.00
Cutlass, Naval Officer's, Marked U.S.A., 1862, 32 In. 2695.00
Cutlass, Naval, Brass Guard, Ames Co., 26-In. Blade 600.00
Cutlass, Naval, Confederate, Fish Scale Handle, Dark Brown Patina, 1841 . . . . 1725.00
Cutlass, Naval, Confederate, Leather Scabbard, Brass Tip, 18 5/16-In. Blade 1380.00
Diary, F. Lobdell, Agent For Christian Commission, June 17, 1864, 117 Pages 1015.00
Dipper, Beer, Gourd, Dated 1862, Craven Co., N.C. 75.00

Discharge Papers, John Grate, Last Ohio Soldier, F Co. 5th Reg. Petersburg, 1865 ...... 385.00
Domino Set, Bone, Ebony, Mahogany, 3/8 x 1 3/16 In. 140.00
Dressing Kit, Mahogany, Mother-Of-Pearl Handle, Mirror, 3 3/4 x 8 In., 10 Piece 485.00
Drum, Eagle, Red Wooden Rims, Nickel Head Tensioner Brackets, A. Rogers, 16 In. 5175.00
Drum, Eagle, Veneer Body, Flag, E Pluribus Unum Banner, 1863, 15 x 10 In. 805.00
Drum, Engraved Shield, Nicholas Duley, Co., I, 127th N.Y.V. 2420.00
Drum, Military, Veneer Body, Wood, Nickel Finish, Rust Brown Patina, 16 x 11 In. 345.00
Drum, Military, Veneer Body, Wood, Stretcher Rings, Ropes, 19 1/2 x 20 In. 747.00
Drum, Snare, 13 Gold Stars In An Arch Above Hubert O. Moore 36th Reg., 1862 .... 4370.00
Envelope, Confederate, Charleston To Spartanburg, S.C., 5 Cent Stamps, Aug. 1862 ..... 209.00
Forage Cup, Confederate 1980.00
Glasses, Sharp Shooters 65.00
Hat, GAR, Felt, Black, Brass Braid Cord, Copper Pin, Pot Over Campfire, 8 1/4 In. 325.00
Horn, Brass, Marked Henry Pourcelte, Paris, 31 In. 165.00
Horse Bit, Marked Gettysburg Battlefield, U.S., Brass 88.00
Knapsack, Soft Pack Style, Waterproof Canvas 340.00
Knife, Bowie, Black Leather Sheath, Round Wooden Handle, 11 15/16-In. Blade 5750.00
Knife, Confederate, D-Guard Side, Incised Wooden Grip, 17 3/4 In. 895.00
Marker, Grave, 44 3/4 In. 450.00
Mirror, Shaving, Compartment For Straight Edge Razors, Tin 125.00
Music, Parade March, 22nd Regt. N.Y.S.M. Union Greys, 1863-1864, 6 Pages 125.00
Musket, Wm. Mason, 58 Cal., Strap & Bayonet, 1862 .... 1325.00
Pouch, Doctor's, Leather, Fitted With 48 Medicine Filled Vials 460.00
Powder Horn, Engraved, Trees, Deer, Hunters & Dogs, 18th Century 575.00
Razor Kit, Bone Handle, J. Rogers, Sheffield, Leather Strop, Box 115.00
Saddlebags, McClellan, Original Straps & Buckles 485.00
Salt Horn, Bone, Carved, Bone Cap, Brass Chain, 3 3/8 In. 160.00
Salt Horn, Wooden, Carved, Mother-Of-Pearl Base Plug, Brass Chain, 3 5/8 In. 110.00
Shell Jacket, Union, 11 Front Buttons, Butternut Color, Burlap, Yellow Piping 2200.00
Soap Box, Cover, With Mirror, 4 x 1 In. 120.00
Soldier's Hymn Book, Owned By H.M. Watters, 2nd Ohio Cav. 39.00
Sword, Confederate, 45th Virginia Volunteers, Boyle & Gamble 12500.00
Sword, Confederate, Pommel Leaf Design, Leather Scabbard, Leech & Rigdon 14087.00
Sword, Etched, Thomas Griswold & Co., New Orleans, CSA, 1861, 33 1/2 In. 935.00
Sword, Foot Officer's, Brass Wire Wrap, Fish Skin Handle, Brown Patina, 31 In. 1780.00
Sword, Foot Officer's, Floral Guard, Gun Metal Scabbard, 1861, 30 1/2-In. Blade 2010.00
Sword, Leather & Wire Grip, Brass Hilt, Engraved Blade, 34 3/4 In. 260.00
Sword, Officer's, US Militia, Gilt Brass Hilt, Gold Guard, 24-In. Blade 250.00
Valise, Officer's, Tooled Leather Exterior, Patriotic Hardware, 13 x 21 1/2 In. 575.00

CKAW, see Dedham category.

CLARICE CLIFF was a designer who worked in several English factories
after the 1920s. She is best known for her brightly colored Art Deco
designs. She died in 1972.

Alpine, Pitcher, Trees & House, Orange, Black Borders, 1930, 6 3/8 In. 1725.00

Clarice Cliff, Teepee, Teapot, Brave Spout,
Totem Handle, 1930s, 6 5/8 In.

Alpine, Shaker, Orange, Black Borders, Trees, Green Grass, Rooftop, 1930, 6 In. 1380.00
Autumn, Bizarre, Plate, Marked, 8 3/4 In. 660.00
Autumn Crocus, Coffee Set, c.1930, 7 1/2-In. Coffeepot, 18 Piece 1840.00
Balloon Trees, Pitcher, Blue, Yellow, Green, Orange, Black, Purple, 1932, 5 1/8 In. 920.00
Balloon Trees, Plate, Blue, Yellow, Green, Trees, Purple, 1932, 10 In. 1725.00
Beehive, Bizarre, Honey Pot, Red Gardenia 1060.00
Bizarre, Cup, Orange, Brown, Black Glaze, Chintz Handle, 1932, 3 5/8 In. 460.00
Bizarre, Teapot, Cover, Inverted Conical Form, Orange, Yellow, Angle Handle, 4 In. 2185.00
Blue Firs, Honey Pot, Restored Bee's Wing 2125.00
Delicia, Vase, Molded, Entwined Rope & Key Borders, 1930s, 8 3/4 In. 870.00
Delicia, Vase, Stamped Mark, 7 In. 415.00
Double V, Isis, Vase, 10 In. 3035.00
Floral, Vase, Hand Painted, Newport Pottery, England, Numbered, 6 1/2 In., Pair 150.00
Forest Glen, Bowl, Mottled Orange Interior, c.1936, 7 1/2 In. 290.00
Honolulu, Bizarre, Jug, Stylized Trees, Green & Black Trunks, 11 3/4 In. 575.00
Honolulu, Bookends 6070.00
Honolulu, Honey Pot 1640.00
House & Bridge, Honey Pot, Restored Finial 1545.00
Melon, Candlestick, Band Of Overlapping Fruit, Orange, Yellow, Blue, 3 In., Pair 1380.00
Melon, Jam Pot, Cover, Band Of Overlapping Fruit, Orange, Yellow, Blue, 4 In. 690.00
Rudyard, Bon Jour, Candlestick, 2-Light 5795.00
Taormina, Charger, Trees On Cliff Top, Sea In Distance, Stamped, 1937, 17 In. 1090.00
Teepee, Teapot, Brave Spout, Totem Handle, 1930s, 6 5/8 In. . . . . *Illus* 800.00
Tonquin, Bone Dish, Blue & White, Signed, 6 3/4 In. 25.00
Tonquin, Platter, Turkey, Deep Blue Landscape, Marked, 18 In. 330.00

CLEWELL ware was made in limited quantities by Charles Walter
Clewell of Canton, Ohio, from 1902 to 1955. Pottery was covered with
a thin coating of bronze, then treated to make the bronze turn different
colors. Pieces covered with copper, brass, or silver were also made.
Mr. Clewell's secret formula for blue patinated bronze was burned
when he died in 1965.

Bowl, Copper Clad, Brass J Monogram, Embossed Circle Mark, 3 1/2 In. 140.00
Bowl, Copper Clad, Faux Rivets, Impressed Mark, 2 x 3 1/2 In., Set Of 4 . . . . 230.00
Bowl, Fowler-Simpson Advertising Co. Cleveland, Copper Clad, 3 3/4 In. 140.00
Candlestick, Copper Clad, 4 Sides, Dark Bronzed Patina, 7 x 3 1/2 In., Pair 1430.00
Vase, 2 Buttressed Handles, Bronze Verdigris Patina, 5 1/2 x 7 In. 770.00
Vase, Bronze Verdigris Patina, Copper Clad, 6 1/4 x 3 1/2 In. 605.00
Vase, Bronze Verdigris Patina, Copper Clad, 7 1/2 x 3 1/2 In. 660.00
Vase, Bronze Verdigris Patina, Copper Clad, 14 1/2 x 6 1/4 In. 2530.00
Vase, Bud, Copper Clad, Verdigris Patina, Incised Mark, 10 x 3 1/4 In. 715.00
Vase, Bulbous, Footed, Copper Clad, Bronzed & Verdigris Patina, Incised, 4 1/2 x 5 In. . . 495.00
Vase, Copper Clad, Applied Nude On Vase With Vertical Leaves, 11 In. 715.00
Vase, Copper Clad, Bronzed Finish, Bulbous, Incised Mark, 11 x 5 In. 550.00
Vase, Copper Clad, Chalice Shape, Partial Verdigris Patina, 5 In. 165.00
Vase, Copper Clad, Green To Orange Patina, 7 In. 715.00
Vase, Copper Clad, Green, Blue, Brown Patina, Incised Mark, 13 In. 1540.00
Vase, Copper Clad, Verdigris To Bronze Patina, Oval, Incised Mark, 7 1/2 x 4 In. 1100.00
Vase, Copper Clad, Verdigris To Bronze Patina, Round, Incised Mark, 5 x 4 1/2 In. 825.00
Vase, Gold, Green, Copper Striated Patina, 11 x 7 3/4 In. 1045.00
Vase, Green, Brown Patina, Bronze, 2 Handles, 9 In. 1540.00
Vase, Stylized Poppies, Copper Clad, Bottle Shape, Original Patina, 7 x 2 1/2 In. 770.00

CLEWS pottery was made by George Clews & Co. of Brownhills Pottery, Tunstall, England, from 1890⑥ to 1961. Additional pieces may be
listed in the Flow Blue category.

Bowl, Landing Of General Lafayette, Blue & White, Oval, Staffordshire, 11 x 8 In. 2990.00
Bowl, Vegetable, Blue, Wilkie Series, Letter Of Introduction, 10 3/4 x 7 3/4 In. 440.00
Bowl, Vegetable, Cover, English Castle, Blue & White Transfer, Staffordshire, 6 x 12 In. . . 3565.00
Cheese Stand, Pagoda Design, Blue, White, 14 1/2 In., Pair 1265.00
Cup Plate, Landing Of Lafayette, Blue, 4 1/2 In. 550.00
Dish, Soup, Picturesque Views Near Fishkill, Hudson River, 10 1/4 In. 100.00
Pitcher, Coronation, Blue, 8 In. 605.00

Pitcher, View Of Insane Asylum, New York, Blue, 6 1/2 In.	715.00
Pitcher & Bowl, Dark Blue, Allover Pattern	2950.00
Plate, America & Independence, Dark Blue, 8 In.	275.00 to 330.00
Plate, Canterbury Cathedral, Blue, Leaves & Scroll, 10 1/2 In.	210.00
Plate, Dr. Syntax Disputing His Bill With Landlady, Dark Blue, 10 5/8 In.	145.00
Plate, Dr. Syntax, Taking Possession Of His Living, Blue, 10 In.	220.00
Plate, Hunter & 2 Dogs, Shooting Birds, Blue, 6 3/4 In.	175.00
Plate, Independence, Sheep On Lawn Center, James, Ralph Clews, 9 In.	412.00
Plate, Landing Of General Lafayette, Blue, Floral Border, 9 In.	155.00 to 355.00
Plate, Peace & Plenty, Dark Blue Transfer, 10 1/4 In.	275.00
Plate, Picturesque Views, Bakers Falls, Blue, 9 In.	130.00
Plate, Winter View Of Pittsfield, Mass., Blue & White, Staffordshire, 14 1/2 x 12 In.	490.00
Platter, Dr. Syntax Amused With Pat In Pond, Blue & White, 18 3/4 In.	1760.00
Platter, Landing Of General Lafayette, 19 x 14 1/4 In.	2200.00
Platter, Landing Of General Lafayette, Castle Garden, 12 1/2 x 9 In.	1380.00
Platter, Windsor Castle, Scroll Border, Blue, 17 In.	1045.00
Sugar, Coronation, Blue, 5 1/2 In.	155.00
Sweetmeat, Name & Gilt, Birds & Flowers, Oval, 3 Sections, 8 In.	316.00
Tureen, Boar Hunting Scene, Blue, Marked	880.00
Vase, Oval, Stylized Flowers, Yellow, Ochre & Brown, Chameleon Ware, 1930s, 6 In.	160.00
Vase, Tapered, Leaves, Geometric Border, Blue, Chameleon Ware, 1930s, 25 1/2 In.	690.00
Washbowl, States, Mansion, Flag & Boat, 13 1/4 x 4 1/4 In.	990.00

CLIFTON POTTERY was founded by William Long in Clifton, New Jersey, in 1905. He worked there until 1908 making a line called *Crystal Patina*. Clifton Pottery made art pottery. Another firm, Chesapeake Pottery, sold majolica marked *Clifton ware*.

Teapot, Indian Ware, Red Clay, Brown Geometric Design, Stamped, 4 In.	55.00
Vase, Bottle Shape, Crystal Patina, Incised, 9 1/2 x 4 1/2 In.	385.00
Vase, Crystal Patina, 2 Angular Handles, Marked, 1905, 4 3/4 x 5 1/5 In.	247.00
Vase, Crystal Patina, Angular Handles, Incised Mark, 10 x 7 In.	495.00
Vase, Crystal Patina, Light Green, 1905, 9 In.	247.00
Vase, Geometric Design, Dark Brown, Terra-Cotta Ground, Bulbous, 4 In.	140.00
Vase, Indian, Homolobi, Geometric Designs, Terra-Cotta Ground, Incised, 8 x 11 In.	495.00
Vase, Indianware, Stylized Geometric Design, Four Mile Run Arizona, c.1909, 2 1/4 In.	115.00

CLOCKS of all types have always been popular with collectors. The eighteenth-century tall case, or grandfather's clock, was designed to house a works with a long pendulum. In 1816, Eli Terry patented a new, smaller works for a clock, and the case became smaller. The clock could be kept on a shelf instead of on the floor. By 1840, coiled springs were used and even smaller clocks were made. Battery-powered electric clocks were made in the 1870s. A garniture set can include a clock and other objects displayed on a mantel.

Advertising, 7-Up, Plastic, Light-Up, Rectangular, In Packaging, 1960s	72.00
Advertising, 7-Up, Rotating, Privilege Panel, 10 1/2 x 16 x 5 1/2 In.	175.00
Advertising, Arrow Beer, Pam Electric, Wooden Frame, Metal Face, Stencil, 5 1/2 In.	154.00
Advertising, Blacksburg Bar & Grill, Drink Dr Pepper, Electric	155.00
Advertising, Blatz Beer, Gray Metal, 3-D Blatz Man In Barrel Coat, Bar, 11 x 3 In.	140.00
Advertising, Budweiser, Bill Elliott, Thunderbird Race Car, Red, Plastic, Alarm, 9 In.	28.00
Advertising, Budweiser, Light Beer, Light-Up, Plastic Frame, Bar, 12 x 12 x 5 In.	40.00
Advertising, Bulova, Seawright Jewelers, Light-Up	235.00
Advertising, Calumet Baking Powder, Reverse Painted Front, Oak Case, 39 x 16 In.	495.00
Advertising, Calumet, Reverse Painted Bottom, 2 Medallions, c.1900, 39 In.	740.00
Advertising, Champion Steering Wheel, Die Cut, Plastic, 11 1/2 In.	380.00
Advertising, Chevrolet, Super Chevrolet Service, White, Blue, Metal, 15 1/8 In.	340.00
Advertising, Clicquot Club, Light-Up, Square, c.1959, 15 In.	195.00
Advertising, Continental Airlines, Proud Bird, Golden Tail, Wood, Pressboard, 13 In.	23.00
Advertising, Coors Extra Gold, Wall, 110 Volt, 12 x 17 In.	33.00
Advertising, Cuckoo, Frostie Root Beer, Frostie Elf, Wooden, Electric, 19 x 10 In.	58.00
Advertising, Dawson's Ale & Beer, Plastic, Metal, Glass, Frame, 1950s, 24 1/2 x 18 In.	155.00
Advertising, Dr Pepper, Neon, Red Octagonal Frame, 1930, 18 In.	755.00
Advertising, Dr Pepper, Neon, Yellow Ground, Square, 1940, 15 In.	907.00

Advertising, Duquesne Pilsener Beer, Metal & Foil, Composition, 1940s, 13 x 10 In. 85.00
Advertising, Erie, Up To Time, Skillet Shape, Iron 6500.00
Advertising, Evinrude, Authorized Evinrude Parts & Service, Blue, Light-Up, 15 In. 1045.00
Advertising, Fort Pitt Beer, Metal, Glass, 1940s, 17 1/4 x 10 1/2 In. 135.00
Advertising, GMC Trucks, Sales GMC Trucks Service, Neon, White, Tin Face 880.00
Advertising, Grand Prize Lager, Reverse On Glass, 20 1/2 x 14 1/4 In. 660.00
Advertising, Hudson Super Six, Dealer's Desk, 1920s 325.00
Advertising, Joe Camel, Leather Jacket, Jeans, Display 70.00
Advertising, Kendall Spinner, Neon, Light Green, Red, White Lettering, 20 In. 1100.00
Advertising, Kickapoo Joy Juice, Figures In Exploding Barrel, Electric, c.1965, 16 In. ... 304.00
Advertising, Mayo Tobacco Co., Paper Label, Baird Clock Co. 2300.00
Advertising, Miller Lite Beer, Lite A Fine Pilsner Beer, Neon, Chrome Plastic, 12 In. 30.00
Advertising, Mobil Pegasus, Electric, Light-Up, Round, 15 In. 690.00
Advertising, Mobil Tire, Gold Paint, Black Trim, Metal Back, Germany, 4 In. 230.00
Advertising, Old Drum Brand, Blended Whiskey, 90 Proof, Electric, Tin Face, 12 In. 230.00
Advertising, Old Mr. Boston Fine Liquors, Gilbert Works, 8-Day, 21 1/2 x 10 x 15 In. ... 248.00
Advertising, Orange Crush, Taste Orange Crush, Plastic, 15 x 15 In. 192.00
Advertising, Pabst Blue Ribbon, Product Bottle, Bar Tender, Metal, 11 3/4 x 7 In. 55.00
Advertising, Peoples Beer, Plastic, Metal, 1960s, 12 1/2 x 6 1/2 In. 80.00
Advertising, Peters Shoes, Wind-Up, Alarm, Metal Case, 1923, 4 1/4 In. 50.00
Advertising, Pride Of Rochester, Reverse On Glass, 32 1/2 In. 605.00
Advertising, Raid, Bug Leaning On Radio Dial, Digital Clock Display, Plastic, 7 In. 52.00
Advertising, RCA Victor Big Color Television, Plastic, Light-Up, Square Face 350.00
Advertising, Red Goose Shoes For Boys & Girls, Plastic Base, Light-Up, 16 In. 160.00
Advertising, Red Goose Shoes, Light-Up, Composition Base, 14 3/4 In. 440.00
Advertising, Red Goose Shoes, Spinning Message, Light-Up, 18 1/2 In. 853.00
Advertising, Red Goose Shoes, They're Half The Fun Of Having Feet, Light-Up 468.00
Advertising, Red Goose Shoes, Wind-Up, Alarm, Brass Case, 1923, 4 1/4 In. .... .28.00 to 50.00
Advertising, Regal Beer, Light-Up, 1950s, Round, 14 In. 225.00
Advertising, Roberts Dairy Products, White Plastic, Aluminum Frame, 1950s, 17 In. 153.00
Advertising, Sapolin Paint, Old Town Canoe Factory, Rectangular, Back Lighted 160.00
Advertising, Sauer's Extract, Flavoring, Wooden 2100.00
Advertising, Schmidt's Light Beer, Light-Up, Box, 1960s, 13 1/2 In. 40.00
Advertising, Star Brand Shoes, Windup, Alarm, Embossed Metal, Decal Face, 4 1/2 In. .. 40.00
Advertising, Tung-Sol Authorized Distributor, Light-Up, Round, 15 In. 305.00
Advertising, U.S.G. Harness Oil, Oak Case Regulator, Paper Dial, 24 In. 853.00
Advertising, Ulster Manures, Reverse On Glass Front Panel, Wooden Case, 33 1/2 In. ... 300.00
Advertising, Vess Double Bubble Gum, Lettered Dial, Round, 15 In. 545.00
Advertising, Weatherbird Shoes, Black Rooster, Light-Up, Metal Base, 14 3/4 In. 350.00
Advertising, Winston Cigarettes, Surgeon General Warning, Plastic, Battery, 16 x 18 In. .. 26.00
Advertising, Winston, Fisherman, Light-Up, 20 x 16 1/2 In. 55.00
Advertising, Zeno Chewing Gum, Reverse On Glass Front Panel, 19 1/2 In. 575.00
Alarm, Golden Nov. Mfg.Co., Victorian House, Cast Iron, Brass, 1885 .... 90.00
Alarm, Hammered, 6 Enameled Panels, Sterling Silver, Liberty & Co., c.1900, 6 In. 4125.00
Anniversary, Brass, Green Onyx, Beveled Glass, Pendulum, 14 x 8 1/2 In. 935.00
Ansonia, 8-Day, Floral, Mohican Pattern, Porcelain Dial, Time & Strike, 11 x 11 1/4 In. .. 355.00
Ansonia, Art & Commerce, 8-Day, Time & Strike, Open Escapement, Statue, 21 In. 1870.00
Ansonia, Calendar, Walnut Veneer Case, Terry's Patent Calendar, 26 In. 468.00
Ansonia, Cavalier Stands At Right, 22 In. 880.00
Ansonia, Chased Design, Ball Feet, Brass, 11 1/2 In. 275.00
Ansonia, Crown, Crystal Regulator, Time & Strike, Open Escapement, 15 1/2 In. 880.00
Ansonia, Elysian, Crystal Regulator, 8-Day, Time & Strike, Open Escapement, 16 1/2 In. . 880.00
Ansonia, Kitchen, Oak, Gingerbread, 8-Day, Time & Strike, Calendar, Silk Screen Door .. 155.00
Ansonia, La Roca, Florals, 8-Day Time & Strike, Royal Bonn Case, 11 1/2 In. 1870.00
Ansonia, Mantel, 8-Day, Mahogany Veneer, Glass Tablet Showing Albany, N.Y., 19 In. ... 330.00
Ansonia, Mantel, 8-Day, Rococo Style, Glass Panel, Gilt Brass, c.1900, 12 1/2 In. 275.00
Ansonia, Mantel, Cartouche Shape, Dutch Scene, Waterway, Royal Bonn Case, 12 In. 355.00
Ansonia, Mantel, Cast Iron, Porcelain Dial, Faux Ivory Columns, Brass Swag, 13 x 9 In. . 110.00
Ansonia, Mantel, Figural, Woman, Metal, Time & Strike, 28 In. 748.00
Ansonia, Mantel, Green Edged Porcelain, Floral Spray Design, Rococo Style, 12 1/2 In. .. 260.00
Ansonia, Mantel, Metal, Woman, Time & Strike, 28 In. .... *Illus* 748.00
Ansonia, Mantel, Spelter, Allegorical Figures Of Air & Water, c.1885, 19 x 21 In. 1150.00
Ansonia, Monarch, Walnut, 8-Day, Time & Strike, Drawer, 24 3/4 In. .... *Illus* 990.00

A damaged porcelain clock face is difficult to repair. It will lower the price of a clock by 20% to 30%.

Clocks that are wound from the back should be wound counterclockwise because that is really clockwise from the front of the clock. Never wind an old clock counterclockwise from the front.

Clock, Ansonia, Mantel, Metal, Woman, Time & Strike, 28 In.

Clock, Ansonia, Monarch, Walnut, 8-Day, Time & Strike, Drawer, 24 3/4 In.

Ansonia, Ophelia, 8-Day, Time & Strike, Art Nouveau, 16 In.	715.00
Ansonia, Porcelain, Scroll & Scallop Shape, Blue, White, Fired Gold, c.1882, 11 In.	290.00
Ansonia, Regulator, Gillies Flavoring Extracts, 12 x 20 In.	800.00
Ansonia, Victorian Style, Walnut, Incised, Brass Mask, Foliage, c.1930, 20 x 18 In.	150.00
Art Nouveau, Gilt Metal, Swirl Form, Seminude Woman, Flowers, c.1904, 15 In.	230.00
Art Nouveau, Spelter, Woman In Diaphanous Dress, Above Clock, c.1910, 24 1/2 In.	1150.00
Art Nouveau, Woman's Head, Flowing Hair, Leaves, Thistles, Spelter, 12 1/2 In.	290.00
Artel, Ribbon Tied Bough, Eagle, Dolphins, Parcel Gilt, E. Ingel Brechten, 35 In.	6325.00
Atkins & Downs, Shelf, Reverse Painted Mt. Vernon, Gilt, Verre Eglomise, 36 1/4 In.	430.00
Atmos, LeCoultre, Brass, Glass Panel, Round Dial, Engraved Name Plate, Box, 9 In.	520.00
Automaton, Windmill, Gunmetal Case, 2 Thermometers, Barometer, 16 In.	1625.00
B.B. Lewis & Son, Calendar, Walnut, Carved Top, Sides & Bottom, Label, 29 1/2 In.	3080.00
Banjo, Federal, Giltwood, Verre Eglomise, Naval Battle Scene On Base, 41 1/2 In.	1095.00
Banjo, Federal, Mahogany, Brass Bezel, Painted Iron Dial, Eglomise, c.1820, 41 In.	5460.00
Banjo, Federal, Mahogany, Gilt Gesso, White Painted Iron Dial, 1820, 34 In.	4312.00
Banjo, Federal, Mahogany, Gilt Gesso, White Painted Metal Dial, 8-Day, 1820, 22 In.	1495.00
Banjo, Ingraham, Time Only, Mahogany Case, 34 In.	805.00
Banjo, Inlaid Mahogany Dial, Acorn Finial, Reverse Painted Rustic Landscape, 34 In.	2760.00
Banjo, Maiden & Battle Of Hull Scene, White Dial, Eglomise Throat, 1825, 41 In.	1650.00
Banjo, New Haven, Brass Works, Pendulum & Key, Chime, 25 In.	137.00
Banjo, Reverse Painted Victory On Lake Erie, Gilt Trim, 43 In.	3565.00
Banjo, Sessions Revere, Mahogany, 8-Day, Brass Side Frets, Eagle Finial, 35 In.	165.00
Banjo, Seth Thomas, No. 5, Mt. Vernon Scene, Mahogany Case, 30 In.	220.00
Banjo, Willard, Aaron, Painted Dial, Female In Chariot, Winged Horse, 1790s, 46 In.	2760.00
Banjo, Willard, Reverse Painted Naval Scene, 10 In.	4140.00
Banjo, Willard, White Painted Iron Dial With Floral Design, 8-Day, 1790, 87 In.	8050.00
Banjo, Willard, White Painted Iron Dial, 8-Day, Fan, Oak Leaf, Acorn, 1815, 29 1/4 In.	17250.00
Berge & Fuller, Mantel, Empire, 2 Weights, 32 x 29 In.	495.00
Biedermeier, Musical, Portico, Fruitwood, Temple Form, Fluted Columns, 19 In.	3680.00
Black Forest, Boar's Head, Walnut, 19th Century, 29 In.	3200.00
Black Forest, Mantel, Carved Eagles & Deer, 37 x 30 In.	4070.00
Blakeslee, H., Shelf, Fruit, Leaf Design, Bun Feet, 16 3/4 x 27 In.	460.00
Blinking Eye, Man, Movable Eyes Attached To Clock Face Set In Stomach, Iron, 16 In.	1495.00
Blinking Eye Mechanism, Mounted In Stomach, Standing Gentleman, Steel, 16 In.	575.00
Bracket, Beehive, Blue Opaline, 2 Birds, Flowering Vine, Mid 20th Century, 10 In.	1610.00
Bracket, Louis XIV, Enameled Dial, Surmounted By Father Time, 42 In.	3162.00
Bracket, Louis XV Style, Silvered Bronze, Boulle Marquetry, Cartouche Shape, 63 In.	2300.00
Bracket, Louis XV, Boulle Marquetry, Gilt Bronze, Cartouche Shape, Lenoir, 57 In.	7475.00
Bracket, Mahogany Case, Floral, Scroll Inlay, Tapered Full Columns, Bun Feet, 14 In.	173.00
Brandt, Marianne, Chromium Plated, Painted Black & White Metal, c.1930, 5 5/8 In.	3220.00
Brass, Mythological Figure Battling Lion, Rectangular Base, 19th Century, 13 In.	750.00
Brass, Novelty, 3 Stacked Rifles Supporting Drum Form Pendant, Copper, 1880, 11 In.	345.00
Bretby, Figural, Woman's Head, Flowing Hair, Painted Birds, Bronze, Pottery, 10 In.	1495.00
British United Clock Co., Walnut, Brass, Arched Pediment, Columns, Putto, 16 In.	200.00

Brocot, A., Mantel, Perpetual Calendar, Escapement, Adjustable, 1865, 20 In. 8625.00
Bronze, Crab Over Porcelain Face, Shell, 1900, 5 1/2 x 9 1/2 In. 258.00
Bronze, Green Marble, Circular Enamel Dial, Goat Standing On Grape, Leaf Vine, 23 In. . 4025.00
Bronze, Napoleon III, Gilt, Enameled Dial, Garland Sides, Mahogany Plinth, 44 In. 5520.00
Bronze, Sevres, Cylinder Form Dial, Putto With Garland, 19th Century, 14 3/4 In. 2300.00
Bronze & Gold Dome, Glass Enclosed Pendulum, Rococo, 1865, 19 In. 1705.00
Bronze & Onyx, Classical Maiden Seated On Plinth, 23 In. 2415.00
Brown, J.J., Skeleton, Silvered Dial, Openwork Floral, Time & Strike, 16 1/4 In. 900.00
Burl Walnut, Round, White Enamel Dial, Roman Numerals, Mid 19th Century, 17 In. . . . 200.00
Burr & Crittenden, Shelf, Stenciled, Turned Split Balusters, Painted Dial, 34 x 16 In. . . . 138.00
Caldwell, J.W., Mantel, Mercury Pendulum, Enameled Dial, 10 1/8 In. 240.00
Calendar, Octagonal Case, Brass Fittings & Works, Rosewood Veneer, 24 1/2 In. 275.00
Carriage, 3 Beveled Glass Panels, Key, Velvet Lined Carrying Case, 7 In. 363.00
Carriage, A. Stowell & Co., Brass, 5 In. 330.00
Carriage, Brass Borders & Base, Mercury Pendulum, Paris, c.1900, 9 In. 288.00
Carriage, Brass, 8-Day, Beveled Glazed Panels, Ball Feet, Leather Case, France, 4 1/8 In. 195.00
Carriage, Cloisonne, Brass, Corinthian Columns, Beveled Glass Sides, 7 x 4 In. 165.00
Carriage, Enameled Dial, Leather Case, France, Late 19th Century, 4 5/8 In. 253.00
Carriage, Enameled Face, Roman Numerals, Bail Handle, Brass, 4 1/2 In. 259.00
Carriage, Foliate Molded Borders & Panel, Gilt Metal, Late 19th Century, 6 In. 460.00
Carriage, Gilt Bronze, Repeating, Swing Handle, Late 19th Century, 5 x 2 1/2 In. 495.00
Carriage, Mappin & Webb, Brass, Beveled Glass, c.1900, 4 In. 330.00
Carriage, Shreve, Crump & Low, Brass, Rectangular Glass Case, 9 In. 489.00
Carriage, Time & Strike, Brass, France, 5 1/2 In. 290.00
Carriage, Waterbury Clock Co., Brass, Beveled Glass Panels, Alarm, c.1891, 4 1/4 In. . . . 145.00
Cartel, 12-Piece Dial, C-Scrolls & Floral Case, France, c.1850, 29 In. 6325.00
Cartel, Brass, Metal Face, Enamel Roman Numerals, Continental, 34 x 17 In. 2530.00
Cartel, Louis XV, Enamel White Dial, Roman, Arabic Numerals, Tortoiseshell, 12 In. . . . 1150.00
Cartier, Alarm, Travel, Gold Tone, Faux Lapis Dial, 2 1/2 In. 115.00
Chelsea Clock Co., Bronze, Desk, Art Nouveau, Gilt Metal, Enamel, Boston, 4 x 3 In. . . . 460.00
Chicago, Revolving, Metal, Standard Globe, 1930, 13 In. 275.00
Cockatoo, Leaf & Avian Design, Pinecone Weights, 15 In. 35.00
Cottage, Rosewood, Octagonal Top, 30-Hour, Time & Strike, Rectangular Tablet 105.00
Cuckoo, Poplar, Center Dial Surrounded By French Horn, Pheasant, Oak Leaf, 50 In. 3410.00
D'Aureville & Lallier, Mantel, 12-Piece Dial, Bell Striking, Heads Of Putti, 31 In. 2875.00
D'Ore, Figures Of Bacchus & Goat, Grapes On Base, Bronze, 13 x 10 In. 2055.00
Dasson, Henry, Mantel, Louis XV Style, Gilt Bronze, Foliage, Cabriole Legs, 17 3/4 In. . . 5175.00
DeLabrue, E., Mantel, Figural, Maiden, Bronze, Black, Vente Antico Base, 1900, 23 In. . . 345.00
Delarue Rue Commines, Mantel, Brass, Drum Case, 8-Day, 1/2-Hour Strike, 15 1/2 In. . . 320.00
Deluxe Clock Mfg. Co., Rabbit, Pendulum, Key Wind, Germany, 1920, 9 1/2 In. 550.00
Desk, Diana The Huntress, Seated, Jeweled Eagle, Silver, Vienna, 1885, 11 In. 7475.00
Desk, Enamel, Brass, Cobalt Blue, Stylized Monogram, 4 3/4 In. 160.00
Desk, Hardstone, Enameled, Rock Crystal Snail, Silver, Vienna, 1880, 3 1/2 In. 4255.00
Dolphin Mounts, Bronze & Marble, Scrolled Marble Base, 14 1/2 In. 990.00
Dual Globe, Barometer & Thermometer, Gilt Bronze, 16 1/2 In. 3750.00
Dubois Fils, Mantel, Empire, Young Woman At Well, Brass Works, A Paris, 17 1/4 In. . . . 1980.00
Durfee, Walter, Lyre, Wall, Time Only, Eglomise Glass Panels, Walnut Case, 41 In. 1840.00
Ebel, Boudoir, Gold Plated, Square, Round Celluloid Face, Lake Scene, c.1920, 4 In. 30.00
Ebonized Wood, Time & Strike, Eglomise Dial, Lake Scene, Continental, Wall, 11 In. . . . 185.00
Edward F. Caldwell & Co., Mantel, Lapis Lazuli, Silver Mounted, Art Deco, 11 In. 15400.00
Empire, Fruitwood, Brass Trim, Battery Operated, France, 12 3/4 In. 80.00
Empire, Pillar, String Suspension, Time, Strike & Chime, France, 24 3/4 In. . . . . *Illus* 990.00
Fashion, Victorian, Double Dial, Walnut, Carved, Seconds Dial, Calendar Dial, 32 In. 1610.00
Figural, Classical Scenes, Bronze Figure Of Seated Maiden, Black Marble Plinth, 21 In. . . 920.00
Figural, Gardener Support, Within Tree Branches, Garden Tools, Gilt Bronze, 17 1/2 In. . . 4312.00
Figural, Lion, Clock In Mouth, Gilded, Black Marble Base, Magnifying Lens, France 990.00
Figural, Mermaid, Regency, Bronze, Gilt Mermaid With Upswept Hand, 1840, 17 In. 3450.00
Figural, Sailor Standing In Rowboat, Rocky Base, Spelter, Early 20th Century, 28 In. 460.00
Flaconer, G., Regulator, Oak, Silvered Dial, Hours & Seconds, Glazed Case, c.1870 . . . . . 6325.00
Forrestville Clock Co., Shelf, Mahogany Veneer, Eagle Crest, Eglomise Panel, 1840 . . . . . 495.00
Fox, Eagle Top, Fox Running On Base, 19th Century, 22 In. 3200.00
Freiburg, Becker, Gustav, Bronze, Creatures, Scrolled Vines, Roman Numerals, 13 In. . . . 1495.00
French Empire, Bronze, Gold Dore, Glass Dome, Music Box Base, 1855, 20 x 15 In. 3905.00

To set the time, push the minute hand clockwise, never counterclockwise. If the clock chimes, be sure to wait until it stops striking before you advance the hands again.

Clock, Empire, Pillar,
String Suspension,
Time, Strike & Chime,
France, 24 3/4 In.

French Picture Frame, 8-Day Time & Strike, Shell Inlay, 1850, Moine, Bordeaux	265.00
Gilbert, Hickory Dickory Dock, White Mouse, Painted Case, 41 In.	2200.00
Gilbert, Pagoda Shape, Glass Case, Brass Pendulum, Ebonized Finish, 19 x 13 In.	165.00
Gilbert, Washington, Regulator, Oak, 8-Day	305.00
Gilbert, William, Regulator, Wall, Time Only, 35 In.	170.00
Gilbert & Clark, Wall, Ogee, Mahogany, 2 Paneled Doors, Rectangular Case, 26 In.	145.00
Gilbert & Co., Wall, Mahogany, Eagle Crest, Label, Marsh, Mirrored Door, 1840s, 34 In.	375.00
Gingerbread, Time & Strike, Gilt Design On Glass Door, 23 In.	55.00
Glass Dark Walnut Face, Mother-Of-Pearl Spandrels, Late 19 Century, 20 In.	500.00
Golay Fils & Stahl, Shelf, Silver, Black Onyx, 8-Day, 1925, 8 5/8 In.	5750.00
Gothic Revival, Bronze Dore, Architectural, Bell Tower, France, 19th Century, 22 In.	2300.00
Greek Revival, Marble, Bronze, Kneeling Slaves Holding Clock Face, 19 1/2 In.	7475.00
Herbert, E., Onyx, Marble & Bronze, Queen Figure, Hieroglyphics Inner Circle, 24 In.	2185.00
Herschede, Mahogany, Pineapple Finial, Cincinnati, Mid 20th Century, 19 In.	260.00
Howard, E., Lyre, Carved Leaf Finial, Reverse Painted Glass, 42 In.	2530.00
Howard, E., Regulator, Wall, Time Only, Walnut Case, 60 In.	5290.00
Howard Miller, Oak Frame, Numbers, Hexagonal Face, George Nelson, 12 1/2 In.	120.00
Howard Miller, Wall, Basket Weave Face, Enamel Numerals, George Nelson, 11 3/4 In.	165.00
Hunter & Animals, Black Forest, Walnut, 40 x 20 In.	18000.00
Ingraham, Kitchen, Walnut, 8-Day, Applied Medallions, Brass Pendulum Bob	110.00
Ingraham, Mantel, 8-Day, Figure-8 Door, Reverse Painted Gold Star, 15 1/2 x 9 1/2 In.	120.00
Ingraham, Mantel, Electra Model, Black, 1895	135.00
Ingraham, Shelf, Walnut, Grecian Type, 8-Day, Metal Dial, Time & Strike, 14 In.	355.00
Ingraham, Steeple, Mahogany, 8-Day, Time & Strike	75.00
Ithaca, Calendar, Bank, No. 2, Rosewood Case, Pat. 1865 & 1866, 48 x 20 In.	1980.00
Ithaca, Cottage, Double Dial, Calendar, Oak Case, 22 1/4 In.	660.00
Japy Freres, Bronze, Filigree, Urn Finial, Woman Bust Center, 19 x 6 1/2 x 9 1/2 In.	605.00
Japy Freres, Graniteware, White & Maroon Stripes, 8-Day, Wall, 11 1/2 x 8 In.	95.00
Japy Freres, Mantel, Gilt Chased Design, Time & Strike, 12 1/4 In.	400.00
Junghans, Shelf, Mahogany Veneer, Silvered Dial, Beveled Glass, Brass Works, 18 In.	385.00
Kitchen, Walnut, Time & Strike, 22 In.	200.00
Kroeber, F., Mantel, Arabic Chapters, Time & Strike, 8-Day, 20 In.	373.00
Kroeber, Florence, Parlor, American Aesthetic, 20 x 12 x 5 In.	715.00
Lamy, Joseph, Mahogany, Pierced Carved, Weight, 54 x 16 In.	2475.00
Le Roy, Charles, Mantel, Paris, Gilt Bronze, Cherub, Marble Plinth, Onyx Base, 14 In.	3760.00
Leaning Woman, Leaves, Shells & Scrolls Plinth, Metal, 19th Century, 19 1/4 In.	2760.00
LeCoultre, Atmos, Brass Case, Switzerland, 20th Century, 9 1/4 In.	315.00
LeCoultre, Atmos, Glass & Brass Case, 9 1/4 In.	410.00
LeCoultre, Mantel, Perpetual Motion, Brass, Glass, 8 x 9 In.	345.00
LeCoultre, Perpetual Motion, 9 1/4 In.	290.00
Louis-Phillippe, Bronze-Dore, Cherubs, Woman, Floral Wreath, 1830s, 18 x 14 In.	2300.00
Lux, Avon, Red, Black, Butterscotch Laminated, Brass Ball Handle, Bakelite, 4 In.	230.00
Lux, Cat, Eyes & Tail Move	650.00
Mahogany Case, Gold Etched Scroll & Floral Design, Silver Face, Germany, 16 In.	345.00
Mahogany Veneer Case, Silvered Dial, Beveled Glass, Brass Works, Chime, 9 1/4 In.	275.00
Mantel, 3-Train Movement, Striking Bells, Putto, Mermaid Supports, Bronze, 16 In.	4887.00
Mantel, 8-Day, Time & Strike, Mirror Sides, Cherubs, Walnut Case, 15 1/2 In.	355.00

Mantel, Arts & Crafts, Original Dark Case, Keywind Mechanism, 7 x 9 x 2 1/4 In. 330.00
Mantel, Arts & Crafts, Trapezoid, Parchment & Brass Face Under Glass, 7 x 9 In. 165.00
Mantel, Baroque Style, Walnut, Marquetry, Bronze Dore, Brass Dial, France, 45 In. 2070.00
Mantel, Black Marble, Column Form Stiles, Late 19th Century, 16 1/2 x 12 1/2 In. 520.00
Mantel, Black Marble, Rectangular Case, Projecting Base, France, c.1880, 12 x 9 In. 415.00
Mantel, Black Marble, Rectangular, Round Dial, Brass Border, 19th Century, 10 In. 200.00
Mantel, Black Marble, Roman Chapters, Time & Strike, Cherub Panels & Mask, 16 In. . . 200.00
Mantel, Black Numerals, Case Enclosing Birds, Bee In Basket, 1820s, 10 3/4 In. 2875.00
Mantel, Black Onyx, Brass Dial, Block Form, Plinth, 13 x 11 In. 125.00
Mantel, Brass, Marble Plinth, Reclining Neoclassical Woman, Continental, 18 In. 200.00
Mantel, Brass, Mercury Pendulum, Domed Top, Floral Finial, Square, France, 16 1/2 In. . 575.00
Mantel, Brass, Pierced, C-Scroll & Urn, France, 21 1/2 In. 410.00
Mantel, Bronze, 4 Marble Columns, Flower Basket Pendulum, Marble Base, 14 In. 467.00
Mantel, Bronze, Urn Shaped Finial, Painted Face, Ornate Pierced Scroll, France, 22 In. . . 660.00
Mantel, Champleve, Onyx, Glass Housing, Round Dial, Pendulum, 11 1/2 In. 1150.00
Mantel, Charles X, Figure Of Mercury Seated On Rockwork, Green Marble Base, 27 In. . 2300.00
Mantel, Chime, Heraldic Revival, Walnut, Faces, Animal Head Columns, 22 In. 730.00
Mantel, Chinese Woman Pouring Tea, Boats On Base, Gilt Bronze, France, 16 1/4 In. . . . 2365.00
Mantel, Classical Revival Style, Onyx, Architectural Case, Early 20th Century, 12 In. 190.00
Mantel, Dancing Bacchantes, After Clodion, Patinated & Gilt Bronze, Marble, 33 In. 5460.00
Mantel, Daubref, Louis XVI, White Marble, Ormolu, Striking, Drum Shape, 15 x 7 In. . . . 1210.00
Mantel, Dessille, Portico, Louis XVI, Marble, Bronze, Patinated, Gilt, Paris, 25 In. 6325.00
Mantel, Empire Style, Aurora With Male & Putto, Gilt & Patinated Bronze, 28 1/2 In. . . . 4025.00
Mantel, Empire, Gilt, Black Marble, Pendulum, France, 19 3/4 In. 1815.00
Mantel, Empire, Mahogany, Mother-Of-Pearl & Ivory Inlay, France, 20 In. 2310.00
Mantel, Empire, Marble, Ormolu, White Classical Cherubs, Pendulum, 21 1/4 In. 1650.00
Mantel, Empire, Ormolu, Woman, Cherub With Anchor, Pendulum, 17 1/4 In. 1760.00
Mantel, Empire, Patinated & Gilt Bronze, Rectangular, Woman Bust, Paw Feet, 18 In. . . . 2875.00
Mantel, Empire, Seated Woman With Fruit Basket, Gilt Bronze, France, 16 In. 710.00
Mantel, Enameled Dial, Count Wheel, Roman Warriors, Bun Feet, 1780s, 16 In. 7475.00
Mantel, Enameled Dial, Couple Playing Instruments, Spelter, Coquillage Base, 16 In. 405.00
Mantel, Enameled Dial, Lyre Form, 4 Pine Finials, Terrestrial Globe, 1870s, 13 3/4 In. . . . 2875.00
Mantel, Figural, Bronze, Fire Gilded, Woman, Porcelain Dial, Pat'd 1890-1894, 13 In. . . . 245.00
Mantel, Figural, Charles X, Round Steel Face, Surmounted By Joan Of Arc, 16 In. 1495.00
Mantel, Figural, Men & Women, Porcelain, Continental, 17 x 10 In. 374.00
Mantel, George III, Mahogany, Fluted Quarter Columns, Steel Face, Square Feet, 18 In. . . 977.00
Mantel, Grecian Design, Victorian, 22 x 12 1/2 In. 210.00
Mantel, Ivory & Marble, Classically Dressed Maiden, Masks, c.1900, 13 1/2 In. 2760.00
Mantel, Louis Philippe, Gilt Bronze, Figural, Woman With Torch, Ormolu Dial, 23 In. . . . 3450.00
Mantel, Louis XV Style, Gilt Bronze, Flowering Branches, Winged Putto, 27 3/4 In. 2875.00
Mantel, Louis XV Style, Gilt Bronze, Rocaille Case, Flower Urn, 1875-1900, 18 1/2 In. . . 2640.00
Mantel, Mahogany Veneer, Reverse Paint Flowers, Brass Movement, Alarm, 17 x 10 In. . . 110.00
Mantel, Mahogany, Double Steeple, 2 Glazed Doors, Painted Zinc Dial, 8-Day, 27 In. . . . 3105.00
Mantel, Mask Design, Enameled Numerals, Cast Brass, France, 16 In. 385.00
Mantel, Mourey, P.H., Greek Revival, Gilt Bronze, Victory Figure, Urn, 24 x 12 1/2 In. . . 2200.00
Mantel, Napoleon III, Allegorical Figures, Gilt Bronze, Tortoiseshell Veneer, 23 In. 5750.00
Mantel, Porcelain, Cherubs & Flowers, Telescope & Globe, Gilded Metal Frame, 20 In. . . 825.00
Mantel, Porcelain, Men & Women, Continental, 17 x 10 In. . . . .*Illus* 374.00
Mantel, Porcelain, Mythological Figures, Zephyr & Flora, France, 11 x 11 In. 550.00
Mantel, Portico, 2nd Empire, Mahogany, Gilt Bronze, France, 18 1/2 x 9 1/2 x 6 In. 1035.00
Mantel, Portico, Louis XVI Style, Gilt Bronze, Marble Columns, 19th Century, 29 In. . . . 3735.00
Mantel, Scrolled Canopy, Masks & Scrolls, Griffin Form Feet, c.1855, 18 1/2 In. 1150.00
Mantel, Temple Form, Metal Columns, Copper Pediment Plaque, 11 In. 172.00
Mantel, Thomas, Seth, Rosewood Veneer, 13 1/2 In. 66.00
Mantel, Tiffany, Grapes & Vines On Lattice Housing, Roman Numerals, 11 In. 2760.00
Mantel, White Marble, Lyre Case, Garlands Of Flowers, Oval Base, c.1900, 19 In. 4025.00
Mantel, Woman Reading, Leaning On Table, Gilt Bronze, Napoleon III, 18 1/2 x 15 In. . . 935.00
Marble, Louis XVI, Gilt Metal, Lyre Form Support, Drum Shaped Case, 27 1/2 In. 2530.00
Mare, Henry, Mantel, Hunter & Dog, Woman Busts, 10 x 15 In. 770.00
Marti, Samuel, Regulator, Brass, Beveled Glass, 8-Day, Strike, Made For Tiffany, 11 In. . 495.00
Menneville, Mantel, Woman, Sitting, Rectangular Clock, Gilt Metal, Onyx, 1925, 22 In. . . 2070.00
Miniature, Sterling Silver, Baroque Style, Ivory, Mother-Of-Pearl, France, 4 3/8 In. 575.00
Moir, William, Porcelain, Black Onyx, French Movement, New York, 9 1/2 x 8 x 5 In. . . . 175.00

Clock, Mantel, Porcelain,
Men & Women, Continental,
17 x 10 In.

Clock, Seth Thomas,
Man & Woman Each Side, 8-Day,
Time & Strike, 13 3/4 In.

Clock, Seth Thomas, Shelf,
Mahogany, Eglomise Floral,
Double-Decker, 32 3/4 In.

Mornaud, I., Bracket, Boulle Marquetry, Female Finial, Military Trophy, 42 In. 6900.00
Moucin, Shelf, Spelter Putti & Floral, Cobalt Blue Porcelain, 8-Day, France, 17 1/2 In. . . .   530.00
National Clock Co., Wall, Oak Case, Square Oak Face, 21 1/2 In.   125.00
Nelson, G., Chronopak Electric, White Wire Feet, Walnut, Marquetry Numerals, 7 In. 5500.00
New Haven, Mantel, Steeple, Reverse Glass, 19th Century, 2 1/2 x 11 In. 335.00
New Haven, Regulator, Crystal, Time & Strike, Brass Case, Beveled Glass, 10 In. 345.00
New Haven, Regulator, Oak, 8-Day, Cutout Pressed Crest & Skirt, Wall, 36 In. 330.00
New Haven, Steeple, Time & Strike, Reverse Painted Lower Door, 20 1/2 In. 200.00
New Haven, Steeple, Walnut, Brass Works, Reverse Glass With Rose, Label, 19 3/4 In. . .   192.00
Oak, French Style, Arched Case, Bronze Ormolu, Late 19th Century, England, 15 In. 345.00
Onyx, Napoleon III, Rectangular Base, Roman Numerals, Claw Feet, 18 3/4 In. 863.00
Oscar Onken Co., Mantel, Peaked Roof, Green Slag Insert, Brass Pendulum, 19 In. 140.00
Pillar & Scroll, Mahogany Veneer, Wooden Works, Weights, Pendulum, Key, 36 1/2 In. . .   1155.00
Pillar & Scroll, Mahogany, Painted Dial, Eglomise Door Panels, Conn., 31 In. 3850.00
Porcelain, Reclining Partial Nude, Putto, Germany, 12 In. 770.00
Portico, Giltwood, Ivory, Putti As Science, Mid 19th Century, 19 3/4 x 9 x 6 1/2 In. 1610.00
Pratt, Jr., Daniel, Shelf, Mahogany, Reading, Mass., c.1840, 31 1/2 In. 145.00
Pratt & Frost, Shelf, Time & Strike, Stenciled Splat, Mirrored Lower Panel, 34 3/4 In. . .   230.00
Pyramid, Louis XVI Style, Marble, Gilt Bronze, Classical Frieze, 19th Century, 21 In. . . .   2300.00
Raingo Fres., Reclining Muse, Cherubs, Bronze, Black Marble, France, 19 x 24 In. 2530.00
Ranlet, Noah, Dwarf, Pine, Painted Dial, 8-Day, Thumb Molded Door, 48 In. 6325.00
Regulator, Mahogany, Crest, Turned Half Columns, 3 Weights, 51 In. 770.00
Regulator, Rosewood, Ebonized Columns & Molding, 8-Day, Vienna, 33 In. 330.00
Regulator, Wall, Walnut, Thermometer, Barometer, France, 1800s, 35 In. 336.00
Royal Bonn, China Case, Porcelain Face, Cherub, Ribbons, Flowers, 15 In. 660.00
Sambo, With Banjo, Blinking Eye Style, Cast Iron, Replaced Clock, 15 1/2 In. 520.00
Sauer, Regulator, Gold Leaf Design, New Haven, 16 x 43 In. 2180.00
Sessions, Calendar, Regulator, Oak, Engraved Lattice & Scroll Design, c.1905, 39 In. 315.00
Sessions, Mantel, Key Wind, Chimes, Mahogany, c.1940, 21 In. 60.00
Sessions, Shell & Scroll Feet, Corinthian Columns, Cast Handles, 11 3/4 In. 172.00
Seth Thomas, Drop Regulator, 8 Sides, Walnut, 15 x 7 1/2 In. 330.00
Seth Thomas, Mahogany Veneer, Brass Works, Reverse Glass, Basket Of Flowers, 25 In. .   137.00
Seth Thomas, Mahogany Veneer, Glass Tablet, Duck & 2 Ducklings, Signed, 25 1/4 In. . .   135.00
Seth Thomas, Mahogany, Painted Glass Door, Gilt Accented Columns, c.1890, 33 In. 316.00
Seth Thomas, Mahogany, Pillar & Scroll, 30-Hour Weight Driven Movement, 32 In. 2185.00
Seth Thomas, Man & Woman Each Side, 8-Day, Time & Strike, 13 3/4 In. . . . .*Illus*   660.00
Seth Thomas, Mantel, Chiming, Inlaid Mahogany, Steel Dial, Bun Feet, 1925, 14 In. 175.00
Seth Thomas, Oak, Brass Works, Windup Alarm, Pendulum, Hanging, 29 1/4 In. 245.00
Seth Thomas, Ogee, Mahogany, Reverse Painted Glass Door, House, c.1850, 26 In. 290.00
Seth Thomas, Pillar & Scroll, Mahogany, Bracket Feet, 19th Century, 31 x 17 x 4 In. 670.00
Seth Thomas, Rosewood Steeple, Roman Numerals, Time & Movement, 8 x 21 In. 70.00
Seth Thomas, Shelf, Empire, Mahogany Veneer, Reverse Glass Painting, 25 In. 165.00
Seth Thomas, Shelf, Mahogany, Brass Works, Mercury Pendulum, 10 1/4 In. 160.00

Seth Thomas, Shelf, Mahogany, Eglomise Floral, Double-Decker, 32 3/4 In. . . . . . . *Illus* 345.00
Shelf, Art Nouveau, Cast Iron, Gold Repaint, Patent Applied For, 15 In. 80.00
Shelf, Hardwood Veneer, Brass Works, Brass Face, Strike Mechanism, Germany, 22 In. . . 275.00
Shelf, Kitchen, Pressed Oak, Brass Works, Alarm, Reverse Gold Scroll, Victorian, 22 In. . 95.00
Shelf, Oak, Rectangular Top, Time, Strike Movement, 13 x 20 In. 81.00
Shelf, Rosewood Veneer, Ebonized Pilasters, Brass Works, Pendulum, Key, 17 1/2 In. . . . 165.00
Shelf, Time, Strike & Chime, Moon Phase, Burlwood Case, Pineapple Finials, 11 In. . . . 373.00
Shelf, Under Globe, Figural, Gilt, Man Hold Birds, Hunting Design, 19 1/4 In. 1320.00
Side-Wheeler, Allover Carved Fretwork, Music Box, 1882, 17 x 9 x 27 In. 1650.00
Singing Ball, Fisherman & Wife, Carrying Floral Wreath, Dolphin Feet, 1920s, 23 In. 1500.00
Skeleton, Brass, 30-Hour Movement, Under Dome, 13 1/2 In. 825.00
Skeleton, Brass, Square Glass Case, 15 x 8 In. 935.00
Skeleton, Copper & Iron, Roman Numerals, Gold Hands, 19th Century, 36 In. Diam. 2640.00
Skeleton, Scroll Shape Frame, Brass, Glass Dome, England, Late 19th Century, 13 In. . . . 805.00
Skeleton, Stand, Time Only, Brass Open Works, 63 3/4 In. 2350.00
Smith & Goodrich, Shelf, Empire, Mahogany Veneer, Ogee, Broadway View, 26 In. 110.00
Spelter, Gilt Bronzed Ormolu Rococo Case, Victorian, 7 1/2 In. 62.00
Steeple, Mahogany, Ripple Front, American Flags, Balloon, Painted Dial, 16 In. 1265.00
Steeple, Rosewood, 8-Day Movement, 1875, 20 x 11 x 4 1/2 In. 175.00
Steeple, Time & Strike, Mahogany Case, 16 In. 92.00
Tall Case, Allan, Jo. B, Levers For Strike, Silent & Chime Selection, 9 Tubes, 78 In. 2580.00
Tall Case, Art Deco, Oak, Carved, Brass Dial, Foliate Crest, Germany, 76 1/2 In. 430.00
Tall Case, Arts & Crafts, Slatted Sides & Back, Brass Numerals, Pendulum, 79 In. 550.00
Tall Case, Arts & Crafts, Square Posts, 4 Lower Shelves, Brass Face, Glass Door, 76 In. . . 1045.00
Tall Case, Brass Numerals, 3 Shelves, Brass Pendulum, Mission Oak, c.1912, 68 In. 460.00
Tall Case, Brokaw, Isaac, Mahogany, Bonnet Top, Fluted Columns, Line Inlay, 93 In. 17050.00
Tall Case, Brownhill, Satin Wood Veneer, Brass Rosettes & Eagle, 98 In. 3360.00
Tall Case, Caldow, W., Enamel Dial, Arched Hood & Door, Mahogany, 89 1/4 In. 2150.00
Tall Case, Cherry, Carved Rosettes, Star Design Door, Red Paint, Pa., 1830, 101 In. 6600.00
Tall Case, Cherry, Fan Carved Bonnet, 30-Hour Brass Works, Pa., 1790, 96 In. 4400.00
Tall Case, Cherry, Maple Case, Sarcophagus Top, Brass Dial, Mass, 1780, 84 In. 7975.00
Tall Case, Cherry, Musical & Mechanical Works, Bun Feet, Pa., 1820, 94 In. 4950.00
Tall Case, Cherry, Pierced Fretwork, 3 Reeded Plinths, Painted Iron Dial, 89 1/8 In. 4600.00
Tall Case, Cherry, Star Rosettes Surrounded By 5 Finials, 8-Day Brass Works, 96 In. 6325.00
Tall Case, Cherry, Urn Finials, Pendulum Door, Paneled Base, c.1810, 94 1/2 In. 3360.00
Tall Case, Chippendale, Cherry, Steel Face, Brass Works, Calendar Movement, 91 In. 3920.00
Tall Case, Chippendale, Fluted Quarter Columns, Ogee Feet, 8-Day Brass Works, 93 In. . . 16500.00
Tall Case, Chippendale, Walnut, Bonnet Flame Finials, Fluted Columns, 91 In. 6050.00
Tall Case, Chippendale, Walnut, Osborne Dial, 8-Day Brass Works, c.1800, 91 In. 6325.00
Tall Case, Claggett, William, Cherry, Arched Cornice, Brass Dial, Newport, R.I., 100 In. . . 9200.00
Tall Case, Coxall, Samuel, Chapter Ring, Seconds Dial, Strike & Silent, 1750s, 91 In. . . . 3105.00
Tall Case, Dobbie, Thomas, 3 Stenciled Panels, Calendar Dial, 8-Day, 97 In. 3025.00
Tall Case, Empire, Mahogany, Beveled Glass Front, Moon Dial, 1900, 103 1/2 In. 3450.00
Tall Case, Farrar, Jonathon, Brass Dial, Putti, Spiral Twist Columns, Inlaid Star, 83 In. . . . 1295.00
Tall Case, Federal, Cherry, Walnut, Masonic Emblems, Painted Dial, 94 In. 3740.00
Tall Case, Federal, Mahogany, Brass Urn Finial, White Enamel Dial, 1800, 90 In. 12650.00
Tall Case, Federal, Mahogany, Pierced Fretwork Crest, French Feet, 1795, 97 In. 10350.00
Tall Case, Federal, Mahogany, White Painted Dial, Splayed Bracket Feet, 97 In. 18400.00
Tall Case, Fisher, John, Queen Anne, Pewter Dial, Pennsylvania, Walnut, 88 In. 4950.00
Tall Case, Flower On Wood Case, Mobier 7-Day Movement, France, 1860s, 90 In. 4500.00
Tall Case, Galrath, Waltham, Oak, Moon Phase, West Minister Chimes, 106 In. . . . . *Illus* 25300.00
Tall Case, George II, Green Lacquer, Pair Of Spherules Above Columns, 101 1/2 In. 8050.00
Tall Case, George III, Mahogany, Oak, Rectangular Brass Dial, Leaf Arabesques, 92 In. . . 4025.00
Tall Case, George III, Oak, Silvered Urn On Pediment, Arched Bonnet, 89 In. 1100.00
Tall Case, George III, Painted Posies, Basket Of Fruit, Bracket Feet, 1820s, 98 1/2 In. . . . 920.00
Tall Case, Georgian, Roman, Time & Strike, Tombstone Door, 62 In. 1840.00
Tall Case, Glazed Door, Enameled Dial, Farming Scene Around Dial, Oak, 108 In. 1430.00
Tall Case, Godshalk, Jacob, Federal, Mahogany, Arched Door, Brass Plaque, 114 In. 18400.00
Tall Case, Harland, Thomas, Federal, Mahogany, White Enameled Dial, 95 In. 18400.00
Tall Case, Hepplewhite, Cherry, Coastal Scene Dial, Dovetail Bonnet, 1807, 88 In. 2200.00
Tall Case, Herschede, Second & Date, Time & Strike, Moon Phase, Walnut, 80 3/4 In. . . . 3450.00
Tall Case, Houghton, Mahogany, Astronomical, Regulator, London, 1820, 86 In. 8800.00
Tall Case, J.E. Caldwell & Co., Walnut, Brass Dial, Roman Numerals, 90 In. 2415.00

Tall Case, Kerner, Alexander, Painted, Dial Signed, 1850s, 96 In. 1320.00
Tall Case, Krause, John, J., Cherry, 30-Hour, Broken Arch, Painted Dial, Pa., 94 In. 6600.00
Tall Case, Long, George, Flat Top, Hanover, 30-Hour Works, Walnut 2750.00
Tall Case, Louis Philippe, Fruitwood, Arched Door, Brass, Enamel Dial, 90 In. 1725.00
Tall Case, Louis Philippe, Provincial, Pine, Arched Bonnet Door, Ionic Pilaster, 98 In. ... 3080.00
Tall Case, Louis XVI, Oak, Enameled Dial, Brass Repousse, Plinth Base, 95 1/2 In. 3220.00
Tall Case, Louis XVI, Provincial, Polychrome, Glazed Door, 102 1/2 In. 1650.00
Tall Case, Mahogany Veneer, Tombstone Door, Turned, Reeded Columns, 94 x 19 In. 2240.00
Tall Case, Mahogany, 2-Train Movement, Fluted Columns, Plinth Base, 90 3/4 In. 4600.00
Tall Case, Mahogany, 8-Day, Silvered Dial, Brass Spandrels, England, 85 In. 2950.00
Tall Case, Mahogany, Brass Ball & Spire Finials, Painted Dial, American, 93 1/2 In. 1760.00
Tall Case, Mahogany, Inlay, Broken Arch Top, Quarter Columns, England, 95 In. 2090.00
Tall Case, Mahogany, Masonic Symbols & Calendar Dial, 8-Day, Scotland, 89 In. 1980.00
Tall Case, Mahogany, Round Hood & Dial Door, Bombay Waist, Victorian 990.00
Tall Case, Mahogany, Square Dial, 2-Train & 4-Pillar Movement, Inlaid Door, 90 In. 5175.00
Tall Case, Newcomber, W.G., Cherry, Swan's Neck Pediment, 20th Century, 68 In. 1345.00
Tall Case, Oak, Elliot Of London, 2-Train Quarter Striking Movement, Gongs, 104 In. ... 13800.00
Tall Case, Oak, Reeded Column, Bonnet Top, Brass, Painted Dial, England, 77 In. 715.00
Tall Case, Painted, Molded Hood, Square Glazed Door, 19th Century, France 1725.00
Tall Case, Parke, Solomon, Philadelphia Style, Mahogany, Shell & Fan Carving, 101 In. ... 5500.00
Tall Case, Pine Case, Arch Top, Roman Numerals, Ivory Face, 88 In. 1925.00
Tall Case, Pine, Arched Bonnet, 4 Turned Columns, Painted Dial, Country House, 80 In. .. 495.00
Tall Case, Pine, Poplar Veneer, Swan's Neck, Enamel Face, 1840, 89 1/4 In. 365.00
Tall Case, Pine, Red, Black Grained, Maine, 87 In. 2200.00
Tall Case, Poplar, Chamfered Corners, 30-Day, Moon Phase Dial, c.1835, 84 1/2 In. 1100.00
Tall Case, Poplar, Freehand Design, Tombstone Panel Door, Mew England, 84 In. 1845.00
Tall Case, Porthouse, John, Walnut, Maple Chamfered Corners, Brass Movement, 78 In. .. 2200.00
Tall Case, R. Whiting Winchester, Pine, Grain Painted, 81 In. ....*Illus* 7700.00
Tall Case, Schutz, Peter, Painted Face, Brass Name Box, Arched Door, Pa., 1956, 90 In. .. 3300.00
Tall Case, Smith, Aaron, Pine, Iron & Brass Works, Silvered Brass Face, 1781, 84 In. 7150.00
Tall Case, Solliday, B., Cherry, Broken Arch Bonnet, 30-Hour Brass Works, 1800, 91 In. . 5170.00
Tall Case, Sutherland, John, Mahogany, Bonnet, Rosettes, 8-Day Brass Works, 83 In. 3740.00
Tall Case, Thomas & Hoadley, Pine Case, White Painted Face, Roman Numerals 17600.00
Tall Case, Thompson, James, Mahogany & Maple, 8-Day, Pittsburgh, c.1815, 90 In. 6050.00
Tall Case, Tideswell, R.P., Oak, Mahogany, Broken Arch Pediment, 8-Day, Scene, 1833 .. 3520.00
Tall Case, Todd, John, Figured Mahogany Veneer, Inlay, Bonnet, Glasgow, 88 1/2 In. .. 2530.00
Tall Case, Tombstone Door, Brass 8-Day Movement, J & R Banbridge, 1830s, 94 In. 2240.00
Tall Case, Walnut Case, 8-Day, Pa., c.1790, 94 In. 4290.00
Tall Case, Walnut, 8-Day, Fluted Supports, Cornice, Lamb & Webb Dial, 1790-1810 ..... 10175.00
Tall Case, Walnut, Acorn Weights, Time & Strike, Carved Medallions, Germany, 90 In. .. 1100.00
Tall Case, Walnut, Gooseneck Pediment, Stars, 1700-1800, 100 In. ....*Illus* 1725.00
Tall Case, Watson, L., Poplar, Red & Black Grained, Scroll Crest, Cincinnati, 90 In. 4400.00
Tall Case, Weiss, Joseph, Cherry, Painted Face, 30-Hour, Bell & Strike, 98 In. 6950.00
Tall Case, Willard, Alex, T., Cherry, Broken Arch Pediment, Brass Movement, 97 In. 1870.00
Tall Case, Wooden Dial, Fluted Quarter Columns, French Feet, c.1820, 83 In. 710.00
Temple, Leaf Carved Designs, Brass Face, Glass Dome, Alabaster, 15 In. 345.00
Terry, Eli, Mahogany Veneer, Federal, Gold Eagle & Flowers, Wooden Works, 28 3/4 In. .. 825.00

Left to right: Clock, Tall Case, Galrath, Waltham, Oak, Moon Phase, West Minister Chimes, 106 In.; Clock, Tall Case, R. Whiting Winchester, Pine, Grain Painted, 81 In.; Clock, Tall Case, Walnut, Gooseneck Pediment, Stars, 1700-1800, 100 In.

Terry, Eli, Shelf, Mahogany, Reverse Painting Of House, Wooden Works, 29 In. 302.00
Terry, Samuel, Mahogany, Pillar & Scroll, Glazed Door, Gilt Wooden Dial, 1825, 31 In. ... 4255.00
Tiffany clocks are listed in the Tiffany category.
Tower, Brass & Iron Works, Bronze Bell, Painted Dial, 1787, 10-Ft. Pendulum 6050.00
Travel, Gorham, Engine Turned Case, Black, Starr & Frost, 3 x 2 In. 373.00
Travel, Mapin & Webb, Silver, Enamel, Ivory Dial, Kissing Couple, Putti, c.1930, 5 In. ... 2530.00
Travel, Octagonal Gold Engine Turned Face, Black Roman Numerals, 8-Day, 4 In. 172.50
Urn Top, Flanked By 2 Classical Maidens, Gilt Metal, c.1810, 18 x 15 In. 1450.00
Varnie, R., Mantel, Figural, Lion Attacking Snake, Bronzed Metal, Marble Base, 18 In. ... 365.00
Viennese, Enameled 18th Century Lover's Scene, Disk Shaped Case, 8 1/2 In. 2990.00
Wag-On-Wall, Porcelain Dial, Roman Numerals, 8-Day, Wreath Sheath, France, 17 In. ... 465.00
Wainright, J.J., Cast Brass, Aneroid Barometer & Thermometer, 26 In. 300.00
Wall, Art Deco, Oak, Leaded Glass Door, White Metal Dial, c.1920, 10 1/2 x 25 In. 260.00
Wall, Continental, Mahogany, Roman Numerals, Gilt Scrolls, Lake Landscape, 63 In. 1495.00
Wall, Walnut, Fruitwood, Inlaid Circles, Banding, Early 20th Century, 26 In. 290.00
Wall, Walnut, Glazed Door, Fluted Columns, 3 Urn Finials, Vienna, 19th Century, 43 In. . 200.00
Wall, Waterbury, Ship's Bell, Wood & Brass Wheel Mount, 16 In. 220.00
Walnut, Rectangular Pediment, 3 Finials, Beveled Glass Door, c.1900, 17 1/2 In. 245.00
Waterbury, Boy Figure Top, Gilt Metal, Dated 1890s, 7 3/4 In. 200.00
Waterbury, Calendar, Oak, Brass Works, Pendulum, Pat. July 30th, 1889, 29 In. 905.00
Waterbury, Carriage, Brass, 8-Day, Glazed Panels, Porcelain Dial, 1890-1891, 4 1/4 In. .. 165.00
Waterbury, Carriage, Repeating, Brass, 8-Day, Bracket Feet, 1/2-Hour Strike, 4 1/2 In. .. 250.00
Waterbury, Crystal Regulator, 8-Day, Time & Strike, Open Escapement, 14 In. 825.00
Waterbury, Cylindrical, Spider Model, Gilt Brass Frame, 1900s, 3 In. 230.00
Waterbury, Desk, Gilt Brass, Cylindrical, Spider Model, 3 In. 225.00
Waterbury, Drop Regulator, Walnut, Geometric Inlay, 27 1/2 In. 440.00
Waterbury, Oak, Brass Fittings, Brass Works, Pendulum, Key, Wall, 24 In. 165.00
Waterbury, Regulator, Brass, Glass, 8-Day, Strike, Faux Mercury Pendulum, 9 1/2 In. ... 175.00
Waterbury, Rosewood Veneer, Brass Trim, Eglomise Glass, Hanging, 19 In. 110.00
Waterbury, Shelf, 8-Day, Time & Strike, Open Escapement, Metal 220.00
Waterbury, Steeple, Mahogany Veneer, 19 In. 155.00
Waterbury, Steeple, Mahogany, Glass Door, Triangular Case, c.1860, 19 In. 230.00
Welch, E.N., Calendar, Rosewood Veneer, Octagonal, Hanging, 24 In. 245.00
Welch, E.N., Mantel, Walnut, 2 Dials, 8-Day, Calendar, 27 x 17 In. 1430.00
Welch, E.N., Shelf, Rosewood, 8-Day, Ogee, Metal Dial, Time & Strike 145.00
Westminster, Wall, Regulator, 8 x 23 In. 58.00
Whitelaw, James, Mantel, Gothic Revival, Walnut, Arch-Shaped Dial, Spires, 35 In. 2365.00
William IV, Brass Inlaid Mahogany, Mangle, Hour Strike, 1830, 23 In. 1955.00
Wise, John, Lantern, Alarm Dial, Brass, London, 15 1/2 In. 2433.00
Woody Woodpecker, Celluloid, Windup, Wall 325.00

CLOISONNE enamel was developed during the tenth century. A glass
enamel was applied between small ribbons of metal on a metal
ase. Most cloisonne is Chinese or Japanese. Pieces marked *China* are
twentieth-century examples.

Bowl, Floral, Fauna Design, Fitted Box, Blue Ground, 9 1/4 x 3 1/4 In. 104.00
Bowl, Shield Panels On Rust Reserve, 1900, 8 x 11 1/2 In. 192.00
Box, Cover, Allover Floral, Japan, 2 1/2 x 2 In. 210.00
Box, Cover, Dragon & Phoenix Alternating Panels, 4 1/2 In. 1495.00
Box, Floral & Butterfly Design, Blue & White Ground, Chinese, 10 1/4 In. 145.00
Box, Hinged Lid, Fish Scale Design, Bats At Rim, Chinese, 7 1/4 In. 230.00
Box, Music, Lift Lid, Bird, Flower Design, Black Ground, 5 1/2 In. 275.00
Charger, Fan Shaped Cartouches, Egret & Goose On Floral Reserves, 12 In., Pair 302.00
Charger, Man With Demonic Face In Landscape, Japan, 18 In. 430.00
Compote, Bird, Flower Design, Silver, Black Ground, 6 1/2 In. 220.00
Hatpin Holder, Red Stone, Silver Mounted, Steel Stem 200.00
Jar, Inverted Pear Shape, Butterfly, Flower Reserves, Aventurine Ground, 4 In. 120.00
Jardiniere, Chrysanthemum & Rose, Black Ground, 14 x 10 In. 358.00
Plate, Butterfly, Flower Design, Late 19th Century, 9 1/2 In. 190.00
Plate, Chrysanthemum Garden Surrounded By Floral Border, 9 3/4 In. 190.00
Plate, Flower Design, Black Ground, Enamel, 6 In. 143.00
Plate, Turquoise Dragon, Deep Blue Ground, 7 1/4 In. 220.00
Spice Jars, Yellow Ground, Flower Design, Pair 88.00

Teapot, Flower Design, Dark Blue Ground, Enamel, Late 19th Century, 4 3/4 In. 66.00
Vase, Bird, Flower Design, Green Ground, Enamel, 10 In. 357.00
Vase, Birds, Iris, 4 1/2 x 5 1/2 In. 55.00
Vase, Cabinet, Bird, Floral Design, Enamel, Late 19th Century, 3 3/4 In. 660.00
Vase, Chinese Peasant, Flowers, Butterflies, Melon Ribbed, 6 1/2 In. 75.00
Vase, Dragon, Flowers, 7 1/2 In. 44.00
Vase, Egyptian Pattern, Dark Ground, Green Interior, 8 x 3 1/2 In. 595.00
Vase, Green 3-Toed Dragon, Cobalt Blue Ground, Japan, 5 In. 86.00
Vase, Iris Design, Enamel, Globular, Late 19th Century, 6 In. 1650.00
Vase, Lappets & Bands Of Blue Polychrome, Dragon Handles, 33 In., Pair 632.00
Vase, Melon, Allover Multicolored Flowers, Silver Wires, Japan, 5 3/4 In. 235.00
Vase, Palace, Allover Polychrome Avian, Floral Design, Wooden Base, 39 1/2 In. 460.00
Vase, Pear Shape, Lavender Enamel, Late 19th Century, 3 1/2 In. 632.00
Vase, Red, White Peony Design, Enamel, Early 20th Century, 5 In. 220.00
Vase, Ruffled Rim, Allover Floral Ground, Scatted Fans, 6 1/2 In. 545.00
Vase, Seasonal Flowers, Trumpet Mouth, Late 19th Century, 9 3/4 In. 287.00
Vase, Seed Form, Bird, Wisteria, Green Aventurine Ground, Enamel, 10 In. 385.00
Vase, Seed Form, Floral Rondels, Black Ground, 7 3/8 In. 220.00
Vase, Seed Form, Wisteria Design, Midnight Blue Ground, 3 1/4 In. 357.00
Vase, Slender Neck, Blooming Rose Branches, Geometric Border Foot, 9 3/4 In. 385.00
Vase, Urn Shape, Black Ground, Colorful Dragons, Brass, 13 3/4 In., Pair 225.00
Vase, Yellow Flowers, Green Leaves, Black Ground, Copper Wiring, Japan, 9 3/4 In. 385.00

CLOTHING of all types is listed in this category. Dresses, hats, shoes,
underwear, and more are found here. Other textiles are to be found in
the Coverlet, Movie, Quilt, Textile, and World War I and II categories.

Bandanna, 101 Ranch, Brand Markings, Blue, Cotton, Signed Swagger, 24 x 24 1/2 In. . . . 283.00
Bandanna, Blue, White Polka Dots, Oshkosh B'gosh, Square, 22 In. 23.00
Belt, Bakelite, Red Cherries, Green Leaves, Red Chain, 39 In. 110.00
Belt, Leather, Black, Horsehair, Nickel Buckle, Western Design, Mexico, 32 In. 28.00
Belt, Leather, Tooled, Sterling Silver Stirrup Buckle, Circle R Western Wear, Size 36 . . . . 50.00
Belt, Silver, Marriage, Niello, Hebrew Mazel Tov, Early 20th Century 690.00
Belt Buckle, Lady's Head On Each Side, Clasp Style, Brass, Art Nouveau, 3 x 2 In. 25.00
Blazer, Mohair, Navy Blue, Silver Buttons, U.S. Air Force Academy, Size 40 . . . . 31.00
Blouse, Homespun Indigo, Child's, 1830s 125.00
Blouse, Lace, White, Embroidered Trim, Edwardian 25.00
Bonnet, Mourning, Black Silk, Feathers & Chin Ties, Lined, Mid 1800s 145.00
Bonnet, Woven Straw, Blue Velvet Ribbons, Baby's, France, 1865, 4 In. 467.00
Boots, Ankle, Suede, Red, Original Box, Playboy, 1980, Size 10 . . . . 30.00
Boots, Cowboy, Alligator, Imitation, Dark Brown, Tan Leather Uppers, Frye, Size 10 B . . 22.00
Boots, Cowboy, Leather, 2-Tone Brown, Tan Inserts, Red Diamonds, Acme, Size 8 1/2 D . 22.00
Boots, Cowboy, Leather, Biltrite, Butterfly, Tooled, 101 Ranch, Mike J. Sokoll 848.00
Boots, Cowboy, Leather, Black, Flower Petal & Leaf Design, Acme, Size 6 1/2 D 35.00
Boots, Cowboy, Leather, Black, White Stitching, Goodyear Chemigum Heel, Size 8 D . . . 35.00
Boots, Cowboy, Leather, Brown, Scroll Designs, Roy Cooper, Size 12 D 25.00
Boots, Cowboy, Leather, Brown, Stitched Leaf Design, Zodiac U.S.A., Size 12 . . . . 50.00
Boots, Cowboy, Leather, Brown, Tan Design, Acme Boot Co., Woman's, Size 11 D 30.00
Boots, Cowboy, Leather, Walnut, Green, Yellow Stitching, Frye, Size 11 D 28.00
Boots, Leather, Black, White Uppers, Embroidery, Cowtown, 1950s, Size 11 1/2 . . . . 24.00
Boots, Work, High Top, Leather, Brown, Capped Toes, Herman Shoes, 1940s, Size 6 . . . . 65.00
Breeches, Green Calico, Lace Calfs, Button Fly, 1900 . . . . 130.00
Camisole, White, Wide Hand Crocheted Edge 20.00
Cap, Chauffeur's, Black, Leather Tin, Embossed 1915 Touring Car On Front 415.00
Cap, Leather, Dark Brown, 1950, Size 6 1/2 . . . . 21.00
Cap, Pilot's, Gabardine, Navy Blue, Black Felt Visor, Trans World Airlines, Medium 76.00
Cape, Bishop's, Velvet, Beige, Gold Thread Embroidery, Flared, 1900s, 52 In. 460.00
Chaps, Cowboy, Batwing, C. Koler, Elko, Nev., 1940s, 36 x 32 In. 165.00
Chaps, Suede, Dark Brown, Rust, Riveted, Boy's 25.00
Chaps, Western, Batwing, Nickel Conchas, c.1930, 37 x 17 In. 305.00
Coat, Brown Finish, Dark Brown Pile Lining, 2 Slash Pockets, Size 42 . . . . 30.00
Coat, Buckskin Leather, Brown Suede, Fringed, 2 Patch Pockets, Berman, Size 40 . . . . . . 27.00
Coat, Chore, Denim, Blue, 4 Patch Pockets, Oshkosh B'gosh, Size 44 . . . . 70.00
Coat, Chore, Denim, Blue, Tan Corduroy Collar, Brass Lee Buttons, Lee, Size 44 . . . . 55.00

Coat, Chore, Denim, Corduroy Collar, Blanket Lining, Wear Well, Size 38 .... 30.00
Coat, Cut Velvet, Blue, Coral Beaded, Metallic Embroidery, Bonwit Teller, 1920s 1045.00
Coat, Denim, Fleece Lining, 2 Snap Pockets, Snap Front, Sears Roebuck, Size 42 R 23.00
Coat, Duffel, Wool Navy Blue, Zipper, Fieldmaster, YKK, Man's, Small 36-38 .... 41.00
Coat, Faux Fur, Leopard Print, Double Breasted, Woman's, 1960s, Small 45.00
Coat, Flying, Leather, Fleece Collar, Plaid Wool Lining, Button Front, 1930s, Size 38 .... 105.00
Coat, Hunter's, Wool, Red & Black Plaid, Masland Sportsman, Size 44 .... 25.00
Coat, Raccoon, Woman's 77.00
Coat, Wool, Dark Green Plaid, White Striping, Talon Zipper, Woolrich, 1948 .... 38.00
Coat, Wool, Red & Black Plaid, 2 Slot Pockets, Plastic Buttons, Penn-Rich, 1940 .... 32.00
Coat, Wool, Tan, Brown Fleece Lining, Leather Buttons, 3/4 Length, Pendleton, Size 42 .. 25.00
Collar, Jet Black Beaded, 18 In. 125.00
Coveralls, Big Smith, Twill, Blue, White Herringbone, Boy's, Size 10-12 .... 22.00
Coveralls, General Motors, Chevrolet, Twill, Herringbone, 1950s, Size 40 .... 62.00
Coveralls, Khaki, Polyester & Cotton, Zipper Front, Snaps, Union-Alls, Lee, Size 36 .... 30.00
Coveralls, Twill, Blue, United States Department Of Agriculture, Uniform, Medium 20.00
Dress, Cocktail, Taffeta, Black, Hubert De Givenchy, 1950s 4310.00
Dress, Cotton, Floral Print, Gray, Yellow, Orange, Junior Frocks, 1940, Size 13 .... 21.00
Dress, Cotton, Lace, Satin, White, 2-Piece, Victorian, c.1880 .... 250.00
Dress, Fawn Crepe Overlay, Beaded Bodice, Drop Waist, 1920s 90.00
Dress, Mourning, Silk Taffeta, Black, Victorian, c.1889 .... 250.00
Dress, Silk, Wool, Victorian, Child's 72.00
Dungarees, Denim, Indigo, Gripper Zipper Fly, Sanforized, Sears, 44 x 30 In. 68.00
Dungarees, Denim, Talon Zipper Fly, Tags, Boss Of The Road, Lee, Size 34 x 28 .... 50.00
Dungarees, Denim, Yellow Stitching, Copper Rivets, Tags, Madewell, 1950s, 42 In. 45.00
Dungarees, Old Kentucky, Cotton, White, Well Made, Label, Tag, 1950s, Size 33 x 34 ... 68.00
Hat, Daisy Mae Style, Denim, Blue, Cummins Diesel Engines Patch, Medium 30.00
Hat, Farmer's, Big Smith, Denim, Blue, Bill, Metal Air Vent Grommets, Size 8 .... 30.00
Hat, Highway Patrol Officer, Wool, Blue, Patent Leather Visor, 1940s-1950s 35.00
Hat, Police Chief, Wool, Brown, State Of New Jersey, Patent Leather Visor, Size 8 ...... 22.00
Hat, Shako, Wool Felt, Guard Sergeant Major's, Red, Black Pompom, 1840, 7 1/4 In. ... 575.00
Jacket, Air Jordan, Nylon, Black, Blue Mesh, Red Logo, Nike, Large 36.00
Jacket, Anti-Freeze, Nylon, Dark Brown, 2 Slash Pockets, McGregor, Size 40 L 35.00
Jacket, Big Yank, Denim, Indigo, 2 Snap Flap Patch Pockets, XL 30.00
Jacket, Bolero, Faux Leopard, Peach Satin Finish Lining, 1960s, Medium 40.00
Jacket, Brocade, Gilt, Silver Droplets, Framed, Indo-Persia, Child's, 1800s, 23 In. 140.00
Jacket, Buckskin, Dark Russet, Pullover, Fringed Cuffs, City Brand, Size XL 23.00
Jacket, Buckskin, Leather, Black, Fringed Yoke, Barjo Zipper, 2 Pockets, Size 44 ...... 20.00
Jacket, Carhart, Denim, Light Brown, Wool Lining, Zipper Front, 1930s, Size 38 .... 96.00
Jacket, Coach's, All Star 1969 Arizona, Cotton, Tan, Talon Zipper, Champion, Large 30.00
Jacket, Copper Snaps, Yellow On Black Label, 4 Pockets, Wrangler, Size 42 .... 22.00
Jacket, Corduroy, Dark Blue, Future Farmers Of America, Idaho Assn., Size 42 .... 30.00
Jacket, Dark Indigo, 2 Pockets, Black, Gold Neck Label, Sanforized, 1950, Size 46 R ... 180.00
Jacket, Denim, Blue Bell, Wheat, Pleated, Tags, Wrangler, Woman's, Size 14 .... 110.00
Jacket, Denim, Blue, 2 Flapped Pockets, Blank Orange Levi's Tab, Medium 30.00
Jacket, Denim, Blue, 2 Pockets, Brass Button Front, Madewell, Size 40 .... 40.00
Jacket, Denim, Blue, Brass Carhart Buttons, Belt With Metal Buckle, Size 42 .... 730.00
Jacket, Denim, Blue, Copper Buttons, Gray Blanket Lining, Wrangler, Size 38 .... 50.00
Jacket, Denim, Blue, Tan Plush Lining, Corduroy Collar, Tag, Maverick, Size 36 .... 22.00
Jacket, Denim, Dark Blue, Copper Finish Buttons, 2 Pockets, Levi's, Size 16 .... 23.00
Jacket, Denim, Indigo, 2 Pockets, Sanforized, Black Label, Yellow Lee Logo, Lee Rider . 26.00
Jacket, Denim, Indigo, Big E, 2 Pockets, Red Tab, Levi's, Size 38 .... 85.00
Jacket, Denim, Indigo, Big E, Second Edition, Button Front, Levi's, Size 40 .... 490.00
Jacket, Denim, Indigo, Black Maverick Blue Bell Label At Neck 20.00
Jacket, Denim, Indigo, Pleated Front, Lee Rider, Child's, 1950 .... 33.00
Jacket, Denim, Red Quilted Lining, Talon Zipper, On The Job Wear, Big Smith, Size 40 .. 39.00
Jacket, Desert Valley Electric, Elastic Knit Collar, Mort Satin, Large 30.00
Jacket, Drizzler, Dark Blue Water Repellent, 2 Pockets, McGregor, Size 38 .... 25.00
Jacket, Drizzler, Tan, Talon Zipper, 2 Slot Pockets, McGregor, Scotland, Size 38 .... 28.00
Jacket, Embroidered, Dragons Pagoda Scene, Silk, Black, Gold, Japan, 1940, Small 340.00
Jacket, Evening, Wool, Navy Blue, Glass Beaded Wheat Design, Banff Ltd., Size 12 .... 28.00
Jacket, Farm, Denim, Blue, 2 Patch Pockets, Brass Buttons, Big Smith, Size 46 .... 115.00
Jacket, Farm, Denim, Blue, White Stitching, Copper Metal Buttons, Blue Bell, Size 38 ... 23.00

Jacket, Farm, Denim, Dark Blue, Yellow Stitching, 4 Pockets, Dee Cee, Size Medium ... 38.00
Jacket, Flight, B-15, Army, Airforce, Alpaca, Gray, Brown Wool Collar, Size 40 .... 400.00
Jacket, Flight, Green Knit Trim, 2 Flap Pockets, Plush Collar, Ralph Lauren, Medium ... 41.00
Jacket, Flight, Horsehide, Brown, Fake Fur Collar, Knit Cuffs, Size 44 .... 26.00
Jacket, Flight, Poplin, U.S.A.F., Type N-3B, Wool Lining, Fur Trim, 1969, Medium 235.00
Jacket, Gabardine, Tan Rayon, Zipper, Dogs On Lining, 1950s, Medium 100.00
Jacket, Golf, Light Blue, White, Blue Striped Knit Collar, Talon Zipper, 1960, Medium .. 30.00
Jacket, Horsehide, Brown, Mouton Collar, Talon Zipper, 1940 .... 700.00
Jacket, Jogging, Snoopy, WW1 Flying Ace, Kunsan, Korea, Green, Zipper, XS 29.00
Jacket, Leather, Black, Fringed, Black, Blue Rose, Walter Dyer, Woman's, Size 14 ...... 29.00
Jacket, Leather, Braided Leather Buttons, 2 Flap Pockets, Schott Bros., Size 40 .... 20.00
Jacket, Leather, Brown, 2 Flap Pockets, Schott Brothers, Size 40 .... 35.00
Jacket, Leather, Wooden Buttons, Wool Lining, W.B. Place & Co., Pre-1930, Size 34 .... 370.00
Jacket, Leopard, Faux Print, Black Satin Lining, 1950, Woman's, Medium 60.00
Jacket, Letter, Black Wool Shell, Yellow Vinyl Sleeves, Snap Front, 1980s, Medium 20.00
Jacket, Navy Blue, White, Reversible, Skajum, Japan, Mt. Fuji, Deer, Medium 440.00
Jacket, Nylon Blue Lining, Red Trim, General Dynamics, Extra Large 35.00
Jacket, Safari, Light Blue, Snap Front, 4 Snap Pockets, Lee Rider, 1970s, Size 34 .... 21.00
Jacket, Satin, Blue, Embroidered Dragon, Tiger, Mt. Fuji, Late 1940s, Small 80.00
Jacket, Sharkskin, Cotton, Gray Green, Brown Streaks, Lined, Tom Sawyer, 1950s 32.00
Jacket, Sheepskin, Light Brown, Dark Brown Fur Lining, Brown Leather Buttons 57.00
Jacket, Silk, Matching Vest, Blue, Green, Red Rose Edge Design, Cream Ground 250.00
Jacket, Silk, Quilted, Embroidery, Brown, Ivory, Black, Blue, Cap, Chinese, 1930s, Large 34.00
Jacket, Sport, Clemson, Rayon, Blue, Orange Knit Trim, Brass Button Front, 1950 ...... 55.00
Jacket, Steerhide, Hercules, Reddish Brown, Conmar Zipper, Sears, Size 38 .... 65.00
Jacket, Suede, Chamois Color, Snap Front, 2 Flap Pockets, Pioneer, Size 12 .... 25.00
Jacket, Suede, Gold, Button Front, 2 Flap Pockets, Lee Rider, Medium 195.00
Jacket, Twill, Company, B-15, Conmar Zipper Front, Plush Lining, Medium 73.00
Jacket, Twill, Olive Green, Quilted, Front Zipper, 1950s-1960s, Child's, Medium 25.00
Jacket, U.S. Air Force Academy, Satin, White, Blue, White Stripes Knit Collar, Artex 40.00
Jacket, Western, Gabardine, Wool, Small Check, Blue, White, New Mexico, Small 23.00
Jacket, Western, Suede, Dark Brown, Fringe, 2 Pockets, K-Bar-Z, Size 16 .... 33.00
Jacket, Wool, Gray, Zipper, Taffeta Lining, 3 Pockets, Pendleton, 1940s, Medium 55.00
Jacket, Wool, Houndstooth, Navy Blue, Single Breasted, 1950s, Woman's, Small 40.00
Jacket, Wool, Nylon, Red & Black Checks, 2 Button Pockets, Sears Roebuck, Size 42 ... 50.00
Jeans, 505, Red Big E Tab, Talon Zipper, Paper Tags, Levi's, 1960s, 27x 28 In. 235.00
Jeans, Bell Bottom, Denim, Green, Gripper Zipper Fly, Levi's, Size 14 x 25 In. 30.00
Jeans, Boot Cut, Indigo Denim, Talon Zipper Fly, Lee Rider, 29 x 30 In. 29.00
Jeans, Buckle Back, Donut Button Fly, Stronghold Brownstein, 1903, 36 x 32 In. 1100.00
Jeans, Copper Rivets, Brass Button Fly, Lee Rider, 1950s, 33 x 36 In. 340.00
Jeans, Cowboy, 101-Z, Denim, Indigo, Talon Zipper, Tags, Lee Rider, 36 x 32 In. 430.00
Jeans, Cowboy, 200-Z, Denim, Indigo, Paper Tags, Lee Rider, 1960s, 33 x 30 In. 220.00
Jeans, Denim, Akamimi, 505, Talon Zipper Fly, Small E, Levi's, 42 x 34 In. 250.00
Jeans, Denim, Black, Tapered Fit, Paper Tags, Wrangler, 1960s, 32 x 34 In. 71.00
Jeans, Denim, Blue, Dark Yellow Stitching, Crown, 1950, Woman's, 40 x 29 In. 30.00
Jeans, Denim, Blue, Sanforized, Washington Dee Cee, 32 x 30 In. 22.00
Jeans, Denim, Blue, Yellow Stitching, 5 Pocket, Brass Talon Zipper, Fly Westerns, 31 In. .. 38.00
Jeans, Denim, Buckaroo, Paper Labels, Big Smith, Child's, 26 x 26 In. ....21.00 to 29.00
Jeans, Denim, Buckle Back, Steel Donut Buttons, Long L, Lee, 1940s, 32 x 29 In. 760.00
Jeans, Denim, Coral, Blue Bell, Scovill Zipper Fly, Silver Metal Rivets, 1970, 16 In. 35.00
Jeans, Denim, Indigo, Bell Bottom, Zipper Fly, Paper Tags, Levi's, 1970s, 30 x 38 In. ... 50.00
Jeans, Denim, Indigo, Conmar Zipper Fly, Red Tab, Akamimi, Big E, Levi's, 33 In. 289.00
Jeans, Denim, Indigo, Copper Rivets, Talon 42 Zipper Fly, Lee Rider, 1970, 32 In. 25.00
Jeans, Denim, Indigo, Donut Button, Talon Zipper, Lee Rider, 1940s, 32 x 35 In. 350.00
Jeans, Denim, Pale Blue, Zipper Fly, Silver Rivets, Sanforized, Wrangler, 34 x 34 In. 213.00
Jeans, Denim, White, Copper Rivets, White Tab, Big E, Levi's, 29 x 34 In. 30.00
Jeans, Denim, Zipper Fly, Copper Rivets, Wrench Pocket, Tags, Cowden, 38 x 32 In. 70.00
Jeans, Indigo, 501, Copper Rivets, Red Small E Tab, Levi's, 1970s, 32 x 36 In. 125.00
Jeans, Standard Cut Pockets, Zipper Fly, Black, Gold Bevo Pocket, Lee Rider, 27 In. 88.00
Jeans, Talon 42 Zipper, Paper Label, Lee, 1960s, 29 x 43 In. 21.00
Jeans, Western Cut, Maverick, Automaticks, Denim, Blue, Tags, 34 x 32 In. 34.00
Jersey, Motorcross, Honda, Nylon Mesh, Red, White, Blue, Viking, 1970s, Small 25.00
Jogging Suit, Blue Green, Drawstring Pants, Zipper Front, Nike, Medium 22.00

Jumpsuit, Seaquest, Original Patches, Worn On TV Show 375.00
Kepi, Indian Wars, Brass Bugle Strap Buttons, Sam Yarmer, E.G. Short & Co. 340.00
Kepi, Massachusetts Infantry, Insignia, Brass Bugle, Star Buttons, Post-Civil War 495.00
Kimono, Embroidered Front & Back, Metal Threads, Silk, 1850s 850.00
Kimono, Silk, Flower Design, Blue Ground, Sash 55.00
Kimono, Silk, Flowing Purple Lines, Cream Ground, Mottled Blue Hem 33.00
Kimono, Silk, Red, Embroidered Longevity Emblems, Late 19th Century 575.00
Kimono & Obi, Wedding, Peacock, Silk, 20th Century 880.00
Lab Coat, Twill, Gray, 3 Patch Pockets, 3 Button Front, Size 42 .... 20.00
Mittens, Bearskin, U.S. Army, 1880s 71.00
Mittens, Knit, New England, 1800-1820, 3 In. 185.00
Neckerchief, Carhart, Dark Blue, Rail Car & Heart Logo, 22 x 22 In. 300.00
Neckerchief, Carhart, Dark Blue, Rail Car & Heart Logo, 24 x 22 In. 230.00
Overalls, Ace Of Spades, Blue & White Pinstripes, Sweet Orr, Size 38 x 30 .... 100.00
Overalls, Bib, Blue & White Stripes, Tag, Big Smith, Child's, Size 0 .... 35.00
Overalls, Bib, Denim, Indigo, Donut Button Fly, Big Mac, JCPenney 42.00
Overalls, Bib, Denim, Indigo, Donut Button Fly, Lee, 32 x 34 In. 40.00
Overalls, Bib, Denim, Donut Button Fly, Sanforized, Washington Dee Cee, 38 x 34 In. ... 43.00
Overalls, Cotton, Scovill Zipper, White, Blue Striped, Patch Pockets, Burlington, 1960 ... 43.00
Overalls, Denim, Blue, White Stitching, Washington Dee Cee, 38 x 34 In. 39.00
Overalls, Denim, Dark Blue, Yellow Stitching, 5 Pockets, Crown Brand, Size 10 .... 51.00
Overalls, Denim, Indigo, Wreath Design, Big B Brotherhood 114.00
Pajamas, 2-Tone Green, Permanent Press, Ely & Walker, Man's, B Medium 20.00
Pants, Bell Bottom, Plaid, Wide Cuffs, Brown, Gray, White, Levi's, 1970s, Size 30 ..... 21.00
Pants, Corduroy, Brown, Copper Rivets, Talon 42 Zipper Fly, Lee Riders, Size 34 ...... 43.00
Pants, Cotton, Gray, Sanforized, Big Smith, 32 x 32 .... 28.00
Pants, Cowboy, Westerner, Khaki, Talon Zipper Fly, Paper Label, Lee, 1958, 33 In. 165.00
Pants, Denim, Light Blue, Blue Bell, Gripper Zipper Fly, Wrangler, Boy's, Size 14 ..... 23.00
Pants, Leather, Chocolate Brown, Zipper Fly, Hugo Buscati, Italy, Woman's, Size 6 ..... 26.00
Pants, Painter's, Cotton, White, Gripper Zipper, Sanforized, Old Kentucky, 42 In. 40.00
Pants, Ranch, Hot Pink, Commar Side Zipper, California, 1950, Levi's, 28 x 31 In. 26.00
Pants, Work, Cotton, Light Tan, Sanforized, Big Smith, 33 x 31 In. 27.00
Pants, Work, Cotton, Olive Drab, Buckle Back, Metal Button Fly, 1940s, Size 40 .... 92.00
Pants, Work, Twill, Cotton, Light Khaki, Sanforized, Lee Chetopa, 31 x 30 In. 27.00
Pants, Work, Twill, Gray, Gripper Zipper Fly, Cuffs, 1960, N & W, 34 x 32 In. 42.00
Petticoat, Cotton, Silk, Diamond Quilted, Deep Gray Green, Brown Print Lining, 34 In. .. 300.00
Petticoat, Cotton, White, Meandering Feathers Quilted, Machine Sewn, 26 In. 220.00
Petticoat, Homespun, Blue & White, Turkey Red Wool Border Bottom, 19th Century ... 295.00
Petticoat, Quilted, Blue 1 Side, Pumpkin Other, Early 19th Century 250.00
Petticoat, Sateen, Black, Feather Quilted, 36 In. 165.00
Pith Helmet, England, 1910 .... 175.00
Pith Helmet, U.S. Post Office Carrier, Blue & Gray, Vinyl Band, Cap Badge 25.00
Poncho, Felt, Turquoise, Gold Embroidered Floral, Fringe, Mexico, Child's, 4-6 .... 21.00
Robe, Brocade, 5 Clawed Dragon Roundels, Floral, Apricot Ground, 19th Century 862.00
Robe, Ceremonial, Velvet, Blue, Embroidered Gold Metallic Thread, Japan, 57 In. 375.00
Robe, Chain & Satin Stitch, Gold Threads, Figures, Garden, Woman's, 19th Century 1265.00
Robe, Embroidered, Dragon Clouds, Bats & Waves, 53 1/2 In. 545.00
Robe, Gilt Thread, Embroidered Dragon, Clouds, Bats, Buddhist Symbols, 56 1/4 In. 488.00
Robe, Priest's, Brocade Kesa, Gold Material, Dragon & Phoenix Design, 20th Century ... 747.00
Robe, Silk, Black & Gold Silk Ribbon, Plum Blue Cuffs, c.1910 .... 200.00
Robe, Silk, Blue Flowers & Birds, Embroidered, Chinese, c.1920 .... 520.00
Robe, Silk, Blue, Embroidered Peonies & Butterflies, Chinese, 19th Century, 51 In. 615.00
Robe, Silk, Dragon Amid Cloud, Maroon Ground, Gilt & Silvered Thread, 56 In. 1725.00
Robe, Summer, Official's Gauze, Rank Badge, Dragon Roundels, 19th Century 1610.00
Robe, Theatrical, Embroidered Falling Dragon, Buddhist Emblems, 52 In. 402.00
Robe, Wedding, Afghan, Floral Design, Maroon Ground 82.00
Sari, Silk, Magenta, Gold Embroidered Thread, India 52.00
Scarf, Churchill, Picture & Quotes, Rayon, Filmyra Fabrics, 33 1/2 In. ....*Illus* 50.00
Scarf, Faces, Flowers, Silk Twill, Peter Max, 42 x 14 In. ....*Illus* 95.00
Scarf, Flowers, Turquoise, Lime, Rayon, Vera, 43 x 13 3/4 In. ....*Illus* 20.00
Scarf, Hunting Dogs, Silk, Square, Occupied Japan, 36 In. 25.00
Scarf, Jacquard, Rayon, Maroon, White, Black Gray, 1940s, 46 x 13 In. 45.00
Serape, Blue, Red, Black, White, Mexico, 75 x 40 In. 140.00

Clothing, Scarf,
Faces, Flowers,
Silk Twill, Peter
Max, 42 x 14 In.

Clothing, Scarf, Churchill, Picture &
Quotes, Rayon, Filmyra Fabrics, 33 1/2 In.

Clothing, Scarf,
Flowers, Turquoise,
Lime, Rayon, Vera,
43 x 13 3/4 In.

Shawl, Chantilly Lace, Black, Allover Floral Design, Triangular, 77 x 115 In. 220.00
Shawl, Kashmir, Red & Burgundy, Gold & Blue Trim, Attached Fringe, 18th Century 2400.00
Shawl, Paisley, Bright Colored Stripes, Fringe, England, c.1850, 133 x 66 In. 880.00
Shawl, Paisley, Hand Embroidered, Red, 19th Century 467.00
Shawl, Paisley, Handmade, Border, Fringed, 74 x 74 In. 880.00
Shawl, Paisley, Wool, Woven Stripe Design, 62 x 64 In. 50.00
Shawl, Reversible, Tag, Pendleton, c.1920, 60 x 66 In. 132.00
Shawl, Silk, Embroidered, Passion Flower 1 Side, Quilted Reverse, 19th Century, 60 In. . . . 55.00
Shawl, Wedding, Silk Needlework, Floral, Red Ground, 19th Century, 78 x 56 In. 75.00
Shirt, Beach, Amusement Park Designs, Short Sleeves, McGregor, 1970s, Large 25.00
Shirt, Bowling, Blue, Yellow Chain Lettering On Back, League, Medium 31.00
Shirt, Bowling, Polyester, Black, Harbour Lights, Short Sleeves, King Louie, Size 36 . . . . 20.00
Shirt, Bowling, Rayon Blend, Yellow, Display Sample, Angeltown, 1960s, Medium 57.00
Shirt, Bowling, Turquoise, Bartlome's Ins., Short Sleeve, 1950s-1960s, Large 30.00
Shirt, Chambray, Blue, White Plastic Buttons, 1940, Size 12 . . . . 40.00
Shirt, Cotton, Tropical, Palm Trees, Fishermen, Station Wagon, Bluewater, 1950s 20.00
Shirt, Cowboy, Blue Denim, 2 Flap Pockets, Wrangler, 1960s, Boy's, Size 12 . . . . 20.00
Shirt, Cowboy, Gabardine, Burgundy, Snap Front, Town Topic, 1940s, Collar Size 14 . . . . 30.00
Shirt, Cowboy, Pale Turquoise, Yoke Accents, Pearlized Snaps, Tem-Tex, Medium 40.00
Shirt, Cowboy, Tan, Dark Brown Panels, Long Sleeves, 1950, H Bar C, Large 46.00
Shirt, Denim, Blue, Snap Front, 2 Snap Flap Patch Pockets, Big Yank, Medium 30.00
Shirt, Denim, Tan, Pullover, 2-Button Top, 4 Pockets, Early 1900s, Medium 390.00
Shirt, Flannel, Brown Cotton, Fleetline, 1950s, Medium 30.00
Shirt, Gabardine, Red Wine, 2 Patch Pockets, New Era, 1940 . . . . 40.00
Shirt, Hawaiian, Aloha, Natives, Cotton, Pocket, Wood Buttons, Kamehameha, XL 160.00
Shirt, Hawaiian, Aloha, Polyester, Blue, Flowers, Hilo Hattie's, Women's, Medium 27.00
Shirt, Hawaiian, Aloha, Polyester, White, Bird Scenes, Sears, Medium 21.00
Shirt, Hawaiian, Aloha, Purple, Black, Strawberry, White, Catalina, 1950, Medium 51.00
Shirt, Hawaiian, Aloha, Silk, Blue & Turquoise, Shaheen's Of Honolulu, Medium 20.00
Shirt, Hawaiian, Cotton, Hula Girls, Palm Trees, Boats, 1 Pocket, Hookano, Medium 75.00
Shirt, Hawaiian, Rayon, Purple, Japanese Drums, Coconut Buttons, 1950 . . . . 135.00
Shirt, Pullover, Chambray, Light Blue, 3 Button Placket, 1930 . . . . 50.00
Shirt, Red Flannel, Long Sleeve, 2 Flap Pockets, Sears, Medium 32.00
Shirt, Sport, Blue, Black Print Design, White Ground, Van Heusen, 1950, Large 21.00
Shirt, Twill, Light Brown, Long Sleeve, 2 Patch Pockets, Big Yank, Medium 200.00
Shirt, Uniform, Driver's, Acme Truck Line Inc., Gray, Half Sleeve, Extra Large 25.00
Shirt, Western, Blue, White Weave, Tan, Aqua Pinstripes, Rockmount, Size 15 1/2 In. . . . 20.00
Shirt, Western, Denim, Indigo, Copper Snap Front, Maverick, Small 22.00
Shirt, Western, Gabardine, Dark Green, 2 Flap Pockets, Town Topic, Medium 20.00
Shirt, Western, Gabardine, Mauve, Black, White Cord Trim, H Bar C, Size 15 1/2 . . . . . . 20.00
Shirt, Western, Pullover, Corduroy, Red, 4 Silver Colored Conchas, 1950s, Size 10 . . . . . 25.00
Shirt, Western, Wool, Plaid, Long Sleeves, Pearlized Snap Front, Pendleton, Medium 20.00
Shirt, White, Polyester, Blue Flowers, Gray Leaves, Mr. California, 1970s, Large 28.00
Shirt, Work, Blue, 2 Button Flap Pockets, King Kole, Size 16-16 1/2 . . . . 27.00

Shirt, Work, Cotton, Gray, 2 Flap Pockets, Tags, On Cardboard, Lee, 1940s, Small 90.00
Shirt, Work, Dark Gray, Cardboard Label, Dickies Shape Set, 1965, Medium 31.00
Shirt, Work, Gray, Permanent Press, Cardboard Label, Dickies Shape, 1965, Size 15 .... 32.00
Shirt, Work, Twill, Gray, Short Sleeve, 2 Flap Pockets, King Kole, Size 16 1/2 .... 23.00
Shoes, All Star, Suede, Red, White Star & Stripes, Converse, 11 1/2 In. 40.00
Shoes, Basketball, Black Canvas, White Soles, Frank Leahy, US Keds, Size 10 .... 40.00
Shoes, Basketball, High Top Canvas, White, Tred-Lite, 1950, Size 6 1/2 .... 55.00
Shoes, Basketball, High Top, Shotmakers, White Leather, Keds, Size 8 .... 25.00
Shoes, Basketball, Red & Gray Suede, Rubber Sole, Converse, 1970s, Size 12 .... 95.00
Shoes, Blue Suede, Lace-Ups, Playboy, 1980, Men's, Size 10 .... 73.00
Shoes, Canvas, Black, White Rubber Soles, Box, P.F. Flyer's, 1960, Boy's, Size 11 ...... 20.00
Shoes, Chukka Style, Leather, Green & Black, Red Wing, Box, Size 7 1/2 D 150.00
Shoes, Clown, LaRay, New York, Woman's, Size 9 .... 50.00
Shoes, Com-Pac, Green Suede, Red Wing, Box, Size 9 1/2 E...................... 72.00
Shoes, Dark Green Suede, Playboy, 1980, Box, Size 10 .... 76.00
Shoes, Dress, Brown Leather Oxford, Wolverine, 1960, Man's, Size 6 1/2 D 40.00
Shoes, Dress, Dead Stock, Leather, 1950s, Boy's, 10 1/2 In. 55.00
Shoes, Dress, Oxford, 2-Tone, Oxblood Leather, Gray Linen Insert, Jarman, 1950s, Size 9 96.00
Shoes, Gold Canvas, Black Toe Caps, Soles, Box, Bata Super Bullets, Men's, Size 10 In. . 42.00
Shoes, High Platform, Red Leather, Brass Studs, Woman's, 1940s 40.00
Shoes, High Top, Black Leather, Upper Laces, 1910, Woman's Size 8 .... 75.00
Shoes, High Top, Lace-Up, Brown Leather, White Cotton Lining, 2-In. Heels, Woman's .. 40.00
Shoes, High Top, Leather, Lace-Up, 17 Eyelets, High Heels, c.1910, Woman's, 9 In...... 65.00
Shoes, Jack Purcell, Black Canvas, White Rubber, P.F., B.F. Goodrich, Box, Size 7 1/2 ... 51.00
Shoes, Leather, High Top, Pointed Wing Tip, Lace-Up, Early 19th Century 45.00
Shoes, Leather, White & Blue, Playboy, 1980, Men's, Size 9 .... 103.00
Shoes, Leather, White, Ventilitated, Step Master, Box, 1947, Child's, Size 4 D 21.00
Shoes, Leather, Wooden Soles, Red Trim Base, Brass Toe Plates, Child's, 5 1/2 In. 72.00
Shoes, Penny Loafer, Black Leather, G.H. Bass & Co., Me., Weejuns, Bass, Size 8 ...... 23.00
Shoes, Red & White Leather, Playboy, 1980, Men's Size 10 1/2 .... 114.00
Shoes, Running, White Leather, Red Swoosh, Block Lettering, Nike, 1981, Size 10 ..... 36.00
Shoes, Skylarks, White Leather, High Top, Nike, Box, 1985, Size 8 .... 30.00
Shoes, Sneakers, Black Canvas, White Rubber, P.F., By B.F. Goodrich, Box, Size 8 1/2 .. 50.00
Shoes, Sneakers, High Top, Black Canvas, White Rubber Soles, Tuffs, 1960s, Size 9 .... 34.00
Shoes, Sneakers, La Crosse Pro-Am, White, Red, Blue Horizontal Stripes, 1960, Size 14 . 40.00
Shoes, Sport, All Star Basketball, Oxford, White Canvas, Converse, Box, 1970s, Size 12 . 40.00
Shoes, Sport, Black Canvas, Jack Purcell, P.F. Flyer, Boy's, Size 5 1/2 .... 36.00
Shoes, Sport, Blue Nylon Shell, Blue Suede Trim, Nike, 1981, 8 1/2 In. 50.00
Shoes, Sport, Chuck Taylor, Oxford, Black Canvas, Converse, 1970s, Size 9 1/2 .... 60.00
Shoes, Sport, High Top, White Canvas, Sportking, Converse, 1950s, Child's, 12 1/2 ..... 35.00
Shoes, Sport, High Top, White Leather, Cat Eye On Tongue, Puma, Men's, 6 1/2 .... 30.00
Shoes, Sport, Leather, Cleats, Little League, Gotham Athletic Footwear, 1940s, Size 8 ... 32.00
Shoes, Sport, Oxford, White Canvas, Red & Blue Trim, Rubber Toe Caps, 1960s, Size 8 . 61.00
Shoes, Sport, P.F. Flyers, High Top, Black, B.F. Goodrich, Box, Size 10 1/2 .... 74.00
Shoes, Tennis, Pale Blue Canvas, White PVC Sole, 1950, Woman's, Size 7 1/2 .... 22.00
Skirt, Poodle, Gray Felt, Pink & Black Poodle, Sequin Collar, Chain, 1950s, Small 25.00
Snowsuit, Rosy Beige, Talon Zipper, Tie Belt, Knit Cuffs, 1940s, Child's, Size 1 .... 22.00
Suit, Denim, Brushed Blue, Vest, Pants, Talon Zipper Fly, Levi's, Size 44 Coat, 3 Piece .. 51.00
Suspenders, Hickock Braces, Brown, Color Stripes, Elastic, Window Box 25.00
Sweater, Cowachin, Figure Skaters, Red, White, Blue, Pullover, Hood, Medium 75.00
Sweater, Cowachin, Wool, Blue, Red & White Ships, Zipper Front, Cowl Collar, Large .. 40.00
Sweater, High School Letter, Cardigan, Wool, Gold, 1950, Medium 42.00
Sweater, Hooded, Wool, White, Brown & Red Design, Zipper, Woman's, Medium 18.00
Sweater, Letter, IG, Pullover, Wool, Cream, Size 42 .... 55.00
Sweater, Letter, T, Football, Wool, Blue, Buffalo On Sleeve, 1964, Size 38-40 .... 30.00
Sweater, Navy, Big N On Front, Men's, 1920s................................. 120.00
Sweater, Shetland Wool, Gray, Zipper, Suede Elbow Pads, Jantzen, 1960s, Medium 46.00
Sweater, Wool, Ivory, Duck In Flight, Green Accents, Zipper, 1950s, Small 85.00
Sweater Vest, Chimayo Indian Type, Wool, Trader Dicks, Roswell, N.M., Medium 130.00
Sweatshirt, Brahms Portrait, Light Gray, Allison Products, Medium 155.00
Sweatshirt, Breezeshield, Powder Blue, Cotton, Hanes, Size 38-40 .... 60.00
Sweatshirt, Breezeshield, Short Sleeves, White, Black Trim, 3 Buttons, Hanes, Large 43.00
Sweatshirt, Cotton & Polyester, NASA Logo, White, Fruit Of The Loom, Large 22.00

Sweatshirt, Cotton, Light Gray, 1950, Small 61.00
Sweatshirt, Cotton, Navy Blue, Long Sleeves, Tag, Mayo Spruce, Large 31.00
Sweatshirt, Coughlin Crusaders, Navy Blue, Red Crusader Logo On Front, Large 21.00
Sweatshirt, Notre Dame, Gray, Blue, Gold Lettering, Champion, Adult's, XL 25.00
Sweatshirt, Olympics, Dark Blue, USA 1980 Olympic Games, Levi's 32.00
Sweatshirt, Panatela, Dark Blue, Orange Stitching, Patch, Levi's, Large 20.00
Sweatshirt, St. Cecilia Bobcats, Dark Blue, Yellow Letters, Cotton, Paper Tag, Small 79.00
Sweatshirt, Sweet Briar College, Dove Gray, Navy Blue Lettering, Champion, Large 25.00
Sweatshirt, Transylvania University, Red, White Lettering, Champion, Large 25.00
Sweatshirt, University Of Arizona, Gray, Navy Blue Lettering, Adult, Large 22.00
Sweatshirt, University Of Kentucky, Gold Cotton, Short Sleeves, 1960s, Medium 25.00
Sweatshirt, University Of Louisville, Black, Red Lettering, Champion, Medium 20.00
Sweatshirt, V Style, White, Cotton, 1940, 4-In. Cuffs 140.00
Swimsuit, Chartreuse, Rose Marie 38.00
Teddy, Batiste, White, Embroidered, 1 Piece 15.00
Uniform, Cavalry, Jacket & Trousers, 1872 .... 2000.00
Uniform, Delivery Man's, Wool, Brown, 3-Leaf Clover, 1940, Size 40 .... 60.00
Uniform, National Park Service Ranger, Blouse, Shirt, Hat, 1949, Large 72.00
Uniform, Nursing, 1939, Man's, Large, 2 Piece 60.00
Uniform, Police, Overland Park, Kansas, Black, Thinsulate Lining, Size 46 .... 45.00
Uniform, Volunteer, Red Cross, Seersucker, Blue, White, Size 14 .... 40.00
Veil, Red, Mirrored Discs, Brass, Glass Bead Fringe, Indo-Persia, 1800s, 10 x 11 In. 140.00
Vest, Corduroy, Wildfire, Dark Brown, Tan Satin Back, Plastic Buttons, Levi's, Size 34 .. 20.00
Vest, Gambler's, Brocade, Bronze Roulette Wheel Buttons, Levi's, 1950s, XL 46.00
Vest, Geometric Beadwork, Horned Creatures, Shell Collar, West Africa, 25 x 18 In. 770.00
Vest, Silk, Cream, Embroidered Leaves & Flowers, France, 18th Century, Man's 815.00
Vest, Sweater, Cashmere, Light Gray, Alan Paine, 1970, Medium 30.00

CLUTHRA glass is a two-layered glass with small air pockets that form white spots. The Steuben Glass Works of Corning, New York, made it in 1920. Kimball Glass Company of Vineland, New Jersey, made Cluthra from about 1925. Victor Durand signed some pieces with his name. Related items are listed in the Steuben category.

Lamp Base, Moderne, Flowers, Cream, White, Fleur-De-Lis Base, Steuben, 12 In. 2070.00
Vase, Amber, Red, Mustard, Blue Striations, Spherical, 8 5/8 In. 490.00
Vase, Blue Powder, Trapped Bubbles, Blue, Green Mottled, Yellow Neck, 8 In. 632.00
Vase, Controlled Bubbles, Silver Enamel, Inscribed, 4 In., Pair 230.00
Vase, Ivory, Baluster, Signed, 10 In. 1185.00
Vase, Mottled Blue, Baluster, 10 3/4 In. 1295.00
Vase, Mottled Royal Blue, White, Urn Shape, Signed, 1925, 6 1/4 In. 1035.00
Vase, Orange, White Mottled, Inverted, Durand & Kimble, 1930, 17 In. 575.00
Vase, Spring Green, Flared Rim, 12 In. 175.00
Wall Pocket, Black, White, Leaves Gilt Metal Frame, Pontil, 8 In. 490.00

COALPORT ware has been made by the Coalport Porcelain Works of England from 1795 to the present time. Early pieces were unmarked. About 1810–1825 the pieces were marked with the name *Coalport* in various forms. Later pieces also had the name *John Rose* in the mark. The crown mark has been used with variations since 1881. The date 1750 is printed in some marks, but it is not the date the factory started.

Basket, Serving, Painted Darker Tone Border, 1800, 14 1/2 In. 2645.00
Box, Lake Scene On Cover, Fan Form, 6 In. 405.00
Cup & Saucer, Sevres Style Floral Panels, Gilt, Pink Ground, c.1855, 5 In. 335.00
Dinner Service, Partial, Scalloped Rim, Blossoming Tree Border, 28 Piece 345.00
Dish, Alternating Panels Of Flowering Trees, Red, Blue, Green, Oval, 1810, 12 In. 865.00
Dish, Butterflies, 3-Dimensional, Flowers, Leaves, 4 x 1 In. 34.00
Dish, Cover, Armorial, Oval, Mottled Border, 1800, 9 3/4 In. 3162.00
Dish, Rocktree, Oval, 1805, 11 1/4 In. 920.00
Dish, Shell Shape, Crowned Rose Flanked By Shamrock, Thistle, Green Border, 9 In. 1035.00
Dish, Union Embossed, Botanical Subject, Scroll Handle, Signed, 1825, 9 In., Pair 4025.00
Ewer, Snake Head Handle, Flowers, Beaded Turquoise Enamel, Crown Mark, 10 In. 1375.00
Plate, Center Willow Tree, Rock, Peonies, Floral Border, 1895, 9 In., 12 Piece 1725.00
Plate, Flowers, Gilt Blue Ground Border, Gilt Rim, 1825, 9 5/8 In., Pair 865.00

Plate, Service, Gold Snowflake Center, Gold & Red Scalloped, 6 Piece 275.00
Tureen, Sauce, Cover, Stand, Crested, Inscribed Motto, 1820, 7 5/8 In., Pair 2875.00
Vase, Gilt Handle, Shape Of Ram's Heads, Butterflies, c.1891, 8 1/4 In. 1050.00
Vase, Gilt Handles, Rams' Heads Handles, Gilded Butterflies, c.1891, 8 1/4 In. 1050.00
Vase, Molded Flowering Branches On Front, Floral Swags, 6 1/4 In., Pair 550.00

COBALT BLUE glass was made using oxide of cobalt. The characteris-
tic bright dark blue identifies it for the collector. Most cobalt glass
found today was made after the Civil War. There was renewed interest
in the dark blue glass in the late 1930s and dinnerwares were made.

Butter, Crisscross, 1 Lb. 110.00
Cocktail Shaker, Dumbbell, Chrome Cap, 13 In. 160.00
Creamer, Gold Enameled Flowers, Gold Trim, Clear Handle, 3 1/2 In. 165.00
Decanter, Enameled Floral Medallions, Stopper, 17 x 7 1/2 In. 525.00
Dish, Refrigerator, Cover, Crisscross, 1 Lb. 125.00
Salt, Double, Openworked Silver Plated Holder, Bow At Top, 5 1/4 In. 115.00
Salt & Pepper, Tin-Plated Screw Tops, Label, Frank Tea & Spice Co., 5 1/2 In. 26.00
Vase, Applied Flower & Leaves, Vaseline Branch & Leaves, Long Neck, 7 3/4 In. 175.00
Vase, Enameled Winter Scene, Castle, Flattened Shape, 10 1/4 In. 165.00
Vase, Sawtooth Band, Bronze Rim, 3 Scrolls, Leaf Feet, 9 In. 385.00

COCA-COLA was first served in 1886 in Atlanta, Georgia. It was adver-
tised through signs, newspaper ads, coupons, bottles, trays, calendars,
and even lamps and clocks. Collectors want anything with the word
Coca-Cola, including a few rare products, like gum wrappers and cigar
bands. The famous trademark was patented in 1893, the *Coke* mark in
1945. Many modern items and reproductions are being made.

Ashtray, Drink Coca-Cola In Bottles, The Pause That Refreshes, Red Glass, 4 In. 25.00
Bag, Bowling Ball, Red Vinyl, Zipper Closure, 1950s, 13 x 7 In. ....105.00 to 110.00
Bank, Airplane, 1929 Model Lockheed Air Express, Metal, Ertl Toys, Box 65.00
Bank, Truck, 1923 Model Chevy Delivery, Metal, Ertl Toys, Box 75.00
Belt Buckle, 30 Year Safe Driver, Cloisonne Emblem, 2 3/4 x 1 1/2 In. 130.00
Big Bear Supermarkets, 50 Years, 1984 .... 8.00
Blotter, 3 Girls, 1944 .... 8.00
Blotter, Snow Scene, 1947 .... 9.00
Booklet, Know Your War Planes, William Heaslip Drawings, 1943, 42 Pages 71.00
Bookmark, Die Cut Heart, Woman With Pen, Celluloid, 2 1/4 In. 468.00
Bookmark, Drink Coca-Cola, 5 Cents, 1903, 2 x 6 In. 907.00
Bookmark, Drink Coca-Cola, Plastic, 1960 .... 3.00
Bottle, 75th Anniversary, Bottlers, 24 Assorted 66.00
Bottle, Atlanta, Small Label, 1975 .... 190.00
Bottle, Bear Bryant, 1981 .... 7.00
Bottle, DC Salutes Glamour Women Of The Year, Diet Coke, 1977, 8 Oz. 50.00
Bottle, Denver, Light Burgundy, Straight-Sided, Crown Top 85.00
Bottle, Ft. Collins, Colo., Aqua, Hobbleskirt, 1915 .... 85.00
Bottle, Georgia Bulldogs, Champs, 1980 .... 3.00
Bottle, Hawaii, Mickey Mouse, Toontown, Contents, 1994 .... 14.00
Bottle, Kansas City, Mo., Aqua, Hobbleskirt, 1915 .... 50.00
Bottle, Knoxville, Tenn., Arrow, Amber 125.00
Bottle, Little Rock, Ark., Dec. 25, 1923, Hobbleskirt, Aqua 12.00
Bottle, Paris, Ill., Pat'd. Nov. 16, 1915, Aqua, May West 24.00
Bottle, Philippine Islands Commemorative, Inauguration, Tropical Plant, 1994 .... 500.00
Bottle, Plastic, Experimental, Not Marketed 150.00
Bottle, Roanoke, Va., Amber 50.00
Bottle, Rod Carew, Baseball, 1987 .... 30.00
Bottle, Santa Rosa Bottling, Philippines, Commemorative 10.00
Bottle, Savannah, Ga., Aqua, Straight-Sided, Crown Top 60.00
Bottle, Seltzer, Cobalt Blue, 10 Sides, 12 1/4 In. 440.00
Bottle, Seltzer, Dark Green, Fluted, Winona, Minn., 8 In. 99.00
Bottle, Seltzer, Susanville Bottling Company, 11 3/4 In. 325.00
Bottle, Sonny's Real Pit Bar-B-Q, 1998, 8 Oz. ....*Illus* 75.00
Bottle, St. Petersburg, Fl., Hobbleskirt 7.00
Bottle, Straight-Sided, Original Stopper, 1910, 7 In. 88.00

Coca-Cola, Bottle,
Sonny's Real Pit
Bar-B-Q, 1998, 8 Oz.

Coca-Cola, Calendar,
1909, Girl, Drinking,
Glass

Bottle, Syrup, Apothecary Style, Nausea & Vomiting, Morgan & Sons, 7 1/2 In.	44.00
Bottle, Tampa, 80 Years, 1983	28.00
Bottle, Washington Redskins, 1983	10.00
Bottle, Washington Redskins, 1986	12.00
Bottle Opener, Cast Metal, Wall Mount, Starr X, Partial Box	20.00
Bottle Opener, Olympics	21.00
Bottle Opener & Cap Catcher, Fishtail Logo, 2 1/2 x 6 x 1 3/8 In.	55.00
Bottle Topper, Drink Coca-Cola, Coke, Plastic, 7 x 7 1/4 x 1 5/8 In.	745.00
Bowl, Pretzel, 1930, 3 x 4 In.	165.00
Calendar, 1908, October, Matted & Framed Under Glass, 6 3/4 x 13 3/4 In.	4620.00
Calendar, 1909, Girl, Drinking, Glass ....*Illus*	16100.00
Calendar, 1914, Betty, Wearing Pale Pink Dress, 13 x 32 In.	847.00
Calendar, 1918, Beach Beauties, Blue Ridge Bottling, Color Litho, 12 x 25 In.	1980.00
Calendar, 1919, Lithograph, Full Pad, 31 x 12 In. Image Size, 38 In.	242.00
Calendar, 1922, February, Frame, 17 x 35 In.	845.00
Calendar, 1922, Woman Wearing Summer Dress Drinking Coke, 9 x 9 1/4 In.	6050.00
Calendar, 1935, Out Fishing, Linton, Ind., 16 x 12 In.	825.00
Calendar, 1936, Woman, White Ruffled Dress, Holding Coke Out On Tray, 33 In.	1694.00
Calendar, 1944, Woman Drinking Coke, Wearing Hat, 6 1/2 In.	187.00
Calendar, 1947, Woman Leaning On Post, Drinking Coke, Matted, Framed, 7 1/2 In.	187.00
Card, Playing, 4th National Convention, San Diego, Silhouette Girl	20.00
Card, Playing, Collector's Club, 5 Different Decks	20.00
Card, Playing, Full Deck, 1928	2300.00
Carrier, 4-Bottle, Cardboard, With 4 Bottles, New Classic Caps	55.00
Carrier, 6-Bottle, Collapsible, Cardboard, 1939	93.00
Carrier, 6-Bottle, Delicious Coca-Cola Refreshing, Aluminum	50.00
Carrier, 6-Bottle, King-Size Coca-Cola, Die Cut, 1960, 30 x 36 In.	687.00
Carrier, 6-Bottle, Red Paint, 1930	187.00
Carrier, 6-Bottle, Red Paint, Cardboard, 1920	110.00
Carrier, 6-Bottle, Red Paint, Die Cut, 1951, 8 1/4 x 8 1/2 In.	1100.00
Carrier, 6-Bottle, White Paint, 1940	66.00
Carrier, 6-Bottle, Wire Handle, Red Paint, Die Cut, 1950, 11 x 13 In.	1375.00
Carrier, 6-Bottle, Wire Rack, Folding, Storage, 1940, 56 In.	432.00
Carrier, 6-Bottle, Yellow Paint, Wooden, 1940	231.00
Carrier, 8-Bottle, Yellow Paint, Wooden, 1940, Double	11.00
Carrier, 12-Bottle, Aluminum, Coca-Cola In Red, Vicksburg Stamp, 11 x 9 In.	300.00
Carrier, 12-Bottle, White Lettering, Red Paint, Die Cut, 1954, 13 x 19 In.	2640.00
Carrier, 12-Bottle, Yellow Ceramic, Bill Novelties, Original Box, 1950, Miniature	550.00
Carrier, 18-Bottle, Ballpark Type, Metal, 1930s	650.00
Carrier, 20-Bottle, Red Metal, 1950	215.00
Chair, Lawn, White Paint, Red Slogan, Child's, 1935	60.00
Clock, Betty, Plastic, 1970s	65.00
Clock, Drink Coca-Cola 10 Cent Bottles, Light-Up, Metal, 18 1/2 x 27 x 4 In.	660.00
Clock, Drink Coca-Cola Bottles, Pale Yellow Numbers, 1930, 14 x 17 1/2 In.	4620.00
Clock, Drink Coca-Cola, Glass Dome, Plastic, Logo, Light-Up, 13 1/4 x 13 1/4 In.	230.00
Clock, Drink Coca-Cola, Gold Numbers, GE Movement, c.1960, Round, 18 In.	265.00
Clock, Mirror, Litho Lettering, Wooden Frame, Battery Powered, 13 x 25 In.	56.00
Clock, Please Pay Cashier, Red Ground, Countertop, Light-Up, 1950, 7 In.	816.00

Clock, Please Pay When Served, Countertop, Light-Up, 1950, 6 1/2 x 7 In. 937.00
Clock, Reverse Painted Lower Panel, Coca-Cola In Bottles, 17 3/4 In. 860.00
Clock, School, 1972 . . . . 60.00
Clock, Silhouette Girl, Neon, Square 1900.00
Clock, Things Go Better With Coke, Plastic, Light-Up, 16 x 16 In. 240.00
Cookie Jar, Coke Bottle, Doranne 100.00
Cookie Jar, Polar Bear, Box 25.00
Cooler, Cover, Drink Coca-Cola On Sides, Red Paint, Steel, 1950, 13 x 18 In. 100.00
Cooler, Drain Spout, Lift-Out Gray, 17 x 17 In. 250.00
Cooler, Picnic, Cavalier, Red Paint, Original Box, 1950, 13 x 18 In. 440.00
Cooler, Picnic, Red Enamel, Removable Cover, Bail Handle, Aluminum, 1950, 18 In. 80.00
Cooler, Picnic, Red, White Vinyl Cover, Red Plastic, Holds 6 Bottles, Carry Straps 24.00
Cooler, White Lettering, Red, 1930, 4 x 5 In. 742.00
Cuff Link, 10K Gold, Bottle Shape, 3/4 In. 55.00
Dispenser, Ceramic, 1896, 18 In. 5000.00
Dispenser, No Drip Protectors, 17 Sleeves, Original Paint & Decal, 7 3/4 In. 525.00
Dispenser, Syrup, Wheeling Pottery, 1896 . . . . 5000.00
Display, Bottle, Rubber, 42 In. 412.00
Display, Counter, Bottle Shape, Christmas, 1930, 20 In. 200.00
Display, Counter, Santa Claus, Die-Cut Cardboard, 9 x 18 In. 230.00
Display, Navy Service Girl, Easel Back, Cardboard, 6 3/8 x 17 1/2 In. 1100.00
Doll, Barbie, Picnic Doll 15.00
Doll, NFL Girl, Band Uniform, Plush, Sticker, 17 In. 49.00
Door Push, Coca-Cola Bottle Shape, Die Cut, 12 3/8 x 4 In. 240.00
Doorknob, Brass 440.00
Festoon, Drink Coca-Cola, Delicious & Refreshing, 1918, 8 1/4 x 8 In. 5060.00
Flange, Enjoy Coca-Cola In Bottles, Red Ground, Oval, 1954, 7 1/4 x 18 In. 3300.00
Flashlight, Black, Plastic, Bottle Shape, Mexico, 3 1/2 In. 23.00
Flyswatter, Wooden Handle, Wire Mesh, 1942 . . . . 10.00
Game, Ping-Pong Set, Drink Coca-Cola, 4 Paddles, Ball 85.00
Glass, 5 Cents, 1912, 9 In. 770.00
Glass, 50th Anniversary, Gold Dipped, 8 Oz. 40.00
Glass, Collegiate Crest, Miami Hurricanes 11.00
Glass, Modified Flair, Etched, 1923-1925, 3 7/8 In. 40.00
Glass, Stars & Stripes 10.00
Golf Bag, Black Nylon & Red Leather, Belding Sports, 1960s 65.00
Hat, Soda Jerk, Boy, Bottle-Cap Hat, Paperboard, Folded, 7 Piece 26.00
Hatpin, 1930 . . . . 8.00
Ice Pick 4.00
Kick Plate, Drink Coca-Cola, Bottle, Porcelain, 1928, 30 x 10 In. 1100.00
Light Fixture, Globe, Milk Glass, 1930, 14 In. 968.00
Lighter, Bottle Shape, Drink Coca-Cola, Plastic, 2 1/2 In. 24.00
Lighter, Hard Plastic, Opens In Middle, 2 3/4 In. 64.00
Matchbook, Drink Coca-Cola, Woman Holding Coke, 1912, 9 1/4 x 9 1/2 In. 990.00
Menu Board, Bottle Top, Kay Displays, Wooden, 2 Sides, 34 1/2 x 16 1/2 In. 2060.00
Menu Board, Sign Of Good Taste, Blank With White Lines, Black, 19 In. 110.00
Mirror, Cat's Head, Die Cut Cardboard, 1920s, 2 1/2 x 2 1/2 In. 660.00
Mirror, Coca-Cola Girl, Woman With Wide Brim Hat, Oval, 1910, 2 3/4 In. . . . . . .275.00 to 578.00
Mirror, Drink Delicious Coca-Cola, Woman, Celluloid, Whitehead & Hoag, 2 3/4 In. 33.00
Mirror, Elaine, Oval, 1916, 2 3/4 In. 413.00
Needle Case, Drink Coca-Cola In Bottles, Cardboard, 1924, 2 x 3 In. 40.00
Patch, Driver's, Red Twill, Gauze Backing, 1950s, 6 1/2 In. 20.00
Patch, Iron-On, Always Coca-Cola 7.00
Pencil, Red Ground, 6 Doz., 1940, 9 In. 187.00
Pencil Holder, 1900s Syrup Urn Shape, Ceramic, 1960s, 7 1/4 In. 210.00
Pin, Bottle Club, Celluloid, Hand Holding Bottle Of Coke, 1 1/4 In. 65.00
Pin, Bottle In Center, White Lettering, Red Ground, 1950, 2 In. 357.00
Pin, Set, Country Flags, Olympics, Box, 1984, 5 Piece 175.00
Poster, 2 Women & 1 Man Drinking Coke, Refresh Yourself, 1955, 7 1/2 In. 1155.00
Poster, Beautiful Woman In Center, Wearing Hat, With Coke, Red Ground, 1941, 23 In. . . 2428.00
Poster, Coca-Cola Refreshing, Bottle, Under Icicles, Frame, 57 1/4 x 18 3/4 In. 495.00
Poster, Hanger, Grumman Wild Cat, U.S. Navy Fighter, 1943, 15 x 13 In. 50.00
Poster, Let's Watch For 'Em, Slow School Zone, Red Ground, 1956, 8 x 8 1/4 In. 1028.00

Poster, North American B-25 Mitchell Bomber, U.S. Army, 1943, 15 x 13 In. 50.00
Poster, Pause For Coke, Original Frame, 1948, 30 In. 900.00
Poster, Woman Holding Coke, Entertain Your Thirst, Drink Coca-Cola, 1941, 7 x 8 In. . . 495.00
Poster, Woman Holding Coke, Entertain Your Thirst, Drink Coca-Cola, 1951, 7 In. 330.00
Poster, Young Man Holding Coke, Drink Coca-Cola, Come & Get It!, 1956, 9 1/4 In. . . . 357.00
Purse, Change, Plastic, Squeeze To Open 3.00
Radio, Cooler Form, 9 1/2 x 12 In. . . . . .770.00 to 935.00
Radio, Crystal, Miniature Cooler Shape, Plastic, 2 3/4 x 2 1/4 x 1 5/8 In. 355.00
Radio, Transistor, Vending Machine Shape, Plastic, 7 1/2 x 3 x 1 1/4 In. 55.00
Salt & Pepper, Bottle Machine Shape, Metal, Red Plastic Base, Chinese, 5 In. 20.00
Service Award, Salesman Of The Month, Driver Shape, 1930s, 6 3/8 In. 745.00
Sign, 6-Pack Shape, Tin, Embossed, 11 x 13 In. 575.00
Sign, Betty, Full-Figure Form, With Pale Pink Dress, Blue, Green, Brown, 1914, 41 In. . . . 6490.00
Sign, Bottle In Center, Red Ground, Round, 1938, 45 In. 770.00
Sign, Bottle In Center, White Ground, 16 x 54 In. 385.00
Sign, Bottle In Center, White Ground, 9 1/2 In. 495.00
Sign, Bottle, Die Cut, 1951, 8 1/4 In. 325.00
Sign, Bottle, Porcelain, Coke Color, 5 x 6 1/2 In. 230.00
Sign, Bottle, White Lettering, Die Cut, 1956, 17 In. 88.00
Sign, Button, Coca-Cola, Convex, Tin, 24 In. 303.00
Sign, Button, Drink Coca-Cola, 1953, 16 x 54 In. 1430.00
Sign, Button, Drink Coca-Cola, Serve Yourself, Red, White Lettering, 1950, 12 In. 550.00
Sign, Button, Drink Coca-Cola, Sign Of Good Taste, Red, Attached To Wood, 1948, 12 In. 990.00
Sign, Button, Drink Coca-Cola, White Lettering, Red Ground, 1956, 12 In. 385.00
Sign, Button, Fishtail, White Lettering, Red Ground, Dec. 1962, 16 In. 357.00
Sign, Button, Tin, Red, Gray, Aluminum Die Cut Arrow, 12 In. 850.00
Sign, Christmas Bell, Die Cut, 12 x 12 In. 2530.00
Sign, Cigars Candy, Drink Coca-Cola, Porcelain, 1930s, 96 In. 1000.00
Sign, Coca-Cola At Soda Fountain, 5 Cents, Woman With White Dress, 1905, 46 In. 15400.00
Sign, Coca-Cola Belongs, Hot Dog Cookout Scene, Horizontal, 1942 . . . . 515.00
Sign, Coca-Cola Bottling Company, Red Ground, 1950, 11 x 21 In. 997.00
Sign, Coca-Cola, Have A Coke!, Neon, 1950, 23 x 14 In. 1028.00
Sign, Coke In Red Neon, White Wave, Green Ground, 27 x 14 x 6 1/2 In. 265.00
Sign, Curtis Hell Diver Airplane, Cardboard, 1950s, Frame 70.00
Sign, Delicious & Refreshing, Drink Coca-Cola, 5 Cents In Bottles, 1905, 10 x 20 In. 385.00
Sign, Drink Coca Cola, Refresh!, Iron Frame, 2 Sides, 1939, 30 In. 277.00
Sign, Drink Coca-Cola Here, Red Ground, Canada, 1940, 17 x 20 In. 665.00
Sign, Drink Coca-Cola In Bottles, Delicious & Refreshing, Red Ground, 1931, 28 In. 1155.00
Sign, Drink Coca-Cola, Bottle In Middle, 1931, 4 1/2 x 12 1/2 In. 907.00
Sign, Drink Coca-Cola, Diamond Shape, Red Ground, 1948, 42 x 42 In., Pair 330.00
Sign, Drink Coca-Cola, Die Cut, 1930, 5 1/2 x 18 In. 850.00
Sign, Drink Coca-Cola, Familiar Refreshment, With Hamburger, 1940, 14 x 31 In. 525.00
Sign, Drink Coca-Cola, Fountain Service, 1950, 12 x 28 In. 635.00
Sign, Drink Coca-Cola, Greetings, 1939, 7 1/2 In. 575.00
Sign, Drink Coca-Cola, Ice Cold, White Lettering, Red Ground, 1950, 27 x 28 In. 2750.00
Sign, Drink Coca-Cola, Ice Cold, White Lettering, Red Ground, 1953, 18 x 22 In. 513.00
Sign, Drink Coca-Cola, Pause Refresh, Lunch, Yellow Ground, Porcelain, 1950, 28 In. . . . 3850.00
Sign, Drink Coca-Cola, Pick Up 6 For Home Refreshment, 1954, 16 x 50 In. 1155.00
Sign, Drink Coca-Cola, Porcelain, 60 x 48 In. 690.00
Sign, Drink Coca-Cola, Red Ground, White Lettering, Embossed, 1948, 18 x 54 In. 630.00
Sign, Drink Coca-Cola, Scandinavian Sprite Boy With Coke Bottle, Red Ground, 54 In. . . 1150.00
Sign, Drink Coca-Cola, Sidewalk, Vertical Courtesy Panel, 2 Sides, 1950, 7 x 28 In. 1815.00
Sign, Drink Coca-Cola, Sold Here Ice Cold, Red Ground, 1932, 18 x 54 In. 1595.00
Sign, Drink Coca-Cola, Take Home A Carton, Big King Size, 6-Pack, 1961, 20 x 28 In. . . 1375.00
Sign, Drink Coca-Cola, White Ground, 1947, 9 1/4 In. 990.00
Sign, Drive-In Theater Marquee Shape, Plastic & Metal, 12 x 12 x 14 In. 965.00
Sign, Easy To Carry, Take Home A Carton, Sets Of 6-Packs, Die Cut, 8 x 8 1/2 In. 660.00
Sign, Eddie Fisher Standup, Wearing Dark Suit, Die Cut, 1954, 68 In. 390.00
Sign, Fountain Service, Drink Coca-Cola, 1936, 23 x 25 In. 2420.00
Sign, Fountain Service, Drink Coca-Cola, Pale Yellow Ground, 1950, 12 x 28 In. 850.00
Sign, Fountain Service, Drink Coca-Cola, Porcelain, 2 Sides, 1936, 22 3/4 x 25 1/2 In. . . . 855.00
Sign, Fountain Service, Drink Coca-Cola, Red Ground, Porcelain, 1950, 14 x 27 In. 1760.00
Sign, Fountain Service, Drink Coca-Cola, White Lettering, Red Ground, 1930, 27 In. 1030.00

Sign, Fountain Service, Drink Coca-Cola, White Lettering, Red Ground, 1941, 41 In. 1870.00
Sign, Girl & Boy On Stairs Enjoying Lunch & Coke, Under Glass, 16 x 27 In. 735.00
Sign, Ham Salad Sandwich & Coca-Cola, Cardboard, 12 x 16 3/4 In. 55.00
Sign, Hand Holding Bottle, Cardboard, Shadowbox Frame, 9 1/4 x 11 1/4 In. 305.00
Sign, Have A Coke, Bust Of Woman, Holding, Tilting Coke, 1948, 8 1/4 x 8 1/2 In. 1090.00
Sign, Have A Coke, Sprite Boy, Die Cut, 1944, 14 x 18 In. 4730.00
Sign, I Think It's Swell, Girl, On Stomach, Coke In Hand, Frame, 28 x 10 3/4 In. 935.00
Sign, Ice Cold Coca-Cola Sold Here, Yellow Lettering, Red Ground, 1930, 20 x 28 In. ... 1100.00
Sign, Pause, Drink Coca-Cola, Countertop, Light-Up, 1950, 8 1/2 In. 1815.00
Sign, People Standing Beside Red Boat, Matted, Framed, 1936, 9 1/4 In. 1452.00
Sign, Policeman Wearing Blue Uniform, Raised Hand, Slow School Zone, 1950 .... 3300.00
Sign, Refreshing Coca-Cola, Light Blue, Plastic, Light-Up, 1960, 24 x 20 x 4 In. 385.00
Sign, Serve Coke At Home, 6-Pack On Front, White, Tin, Self-Framed, 16 x 40 In. 205.00
Sign, Serve Coke At Home, Tin, Painted, Pilaster, With Button, 16 x 54 In. 205.00
Sign, Sidewalk, Dispenser, 1939, 25 x 26 In. 847.00
Sign, Sidewalk, Ice Cold Coca-Cola Sold Here, Red Ground, 1936, 20 x 28 In., Pair 440.00
Sign, Sprite Boy's Head & Face Pointing At 6-Pack, Die Cut, 1947, 42 x 33 In. 740.00
Sign, Sugar Ray Robinson, Frame, 1952, 12 x 15 In. 1495.00
Sign, Take A Case Home Today!, $1 For Deposit, Coca-Cola, Red Ground, 1950, 14 In. .. 220.00
Sign, Take A Case Home Today, Drink Coca-Cola, Quality Refreshment, 1959, 20 x 28 In. 880.00
Sign, The Pause That Refreshes, Drink Coca-Cola, 1937, 13 x 33 In. 525.00
Sign, Things Go Better With Coke, Ice Cold Coca-Cola, White Ground, 1960, 20 x 28 In.. 770.00
Sign, Tingling Refreshment, Girl, Hand Up, Cardboard, Frame, 1931, 23 x 40 In. 1650.00
Sign, To Be Refreshed, Woman Holding Coke, 1948, 8 1/2 x 8 3/4 In. 1331.00
Sign, Truck Cab, Drink Coca-Cola Ice Cold, Red Ground, 10 x 50 In. 665.00
Sign, Umbrella Girl With Cooler, Cardboard, Under Glass, 1942, 16 x 27 In. 990.00
Sign, Woman Wearing Suit, Holding 6-Pack, 1940, 64 In. 330.00
Sign, Yes, Woman Being Served Bottle, Cardboard, 1948, 20 x 36 In. 135.00
Sign, Young Couple, 6-Pack Of Coke, Sandwiches, Cardboard, 1942, 16 x 27 In. 735.00
Soda Cart, Japan, Box, 1960 .... 750.00
Thermometer, Bottle Shape, Tin, 5 1/4 x 17 In. ....30.00 to 44.00
Thermometer, Bottle Shape, Tin, 8 1/2 x 29 1/4 In. ....75.00 to 95.00
Thermometer, Button At Top, Embossed, Shipping Box, 1950s, 9 x 3 In. 860.00
Thermometer, Cigar Shape, Tin, Red & White, 8 1/4 x 30 In. 575.00
Thermometer, Die Cut, Embossed Tin Lithograph, Glass, 16 1/2 In. 88.00
Thermometer, Drink Coca-Cola In Bottles, Round, 1960s, 12 In. 100.00
Thermometer, Embossed Tin Lithograph, Glass, Manufacturing Defect Bottle, 16 In. 242.00
Thermometer, Silhouette Girl, Tin, Embossed, 6 3/4 x 16 In. 440.00
Thermometer, Things Go Better With Coke, Dial, White, Red Letters, 12 In. 250.00
Tip Tray, 1903, Hilda, 4 In. 4255.00
Tip Tray, 1906, Juanita, 7 1/4 In. 385.00
Tip Tray, 1907, Drink Coca-Cola, 7 1/2 In. ....121.00 to 410.00
Tip Tray, 1908, Topless Woman, Holding Bottle 7475.00
Tip Tray, 1909, Exhibition Girl, 8 1/2 In. ....270.00 to 360.00
Tip Tray, 1910, Coca-Cola Girl, 7 1/2 In. ....165.00 to 220.00
Tip Tray, 1913, Hamilton King Girl, 6 In. ....110.00 to 220.00
Tip Tray, 1914, Betty, 6 3/4 In. ....155.00 to 245.00
Tip Tray, 1916, Elaine, 7 In. ....100.00 to 250.00
Tip Tray, 1920, Golfer Girl, 5 In. ....165.00 to 275.00
Tip Tray, 1921, Autumn Girl, 7 In. 220.00
Tip Tray, 1922, Summer Girl, 7 In. 230.00
Tip Tray, 1922, Summer Girl, 8 1/2 In. ....430.00 to 935.00
Tip Tray, 1923, Flapper Girl, 8 1/2 In. ....170.00 to 220.00
Tip Tray, 1924, Smiling Girl, 6 1/2 In. 165.00
Tip Tray, 1925, Party Girl, 7 In. 110.00
Tip Tray, 1926, Golfers, Black Ground, 7 1/2 In. 410.00
Tip Tray, 1926, Golfers, Green Ground, 10 1/2 x 13 1/4 In. 1045.00
Tip Tray, 1927, Soda Jerk, Square, 7 In. 220.00
Tip Tray, 1929, Girl With Bobbed Hair, 6 1/2 In. ....75.00 to 110.00
Tip Tray, 1930, Bather Girl, 7 In. 245.00
Tip Tray, 1930, Telephone Girl, 6 1/2 In. ....100.00 to 220.00
Tip Tray, 1931, Barefoot Boy, 6 1/2 In. 230.00
Tip Tray, 1932, Girl In Bathing Suit, 5 1/2 In. 130.00

Most Coca-Cola trays had green or brown borders in the 1920s, red borders in the 1930s.

Coca-Cola, Tray, 1907, Relieves Fatigue,
16 1/2 x 13 1/2 In.

Tip Tray, 1933, Frances Dee, 8 In. 245.00
Tip Tray, 1934, Tarzan, 7 In. 360.00
Tip Tray, 1935, Madge Evers, 7 1/2 In. 255.00
Tip Tray, 1936, Hostess, 8 In. 385.00
Tip Tray, 1937, Running Girl, 6 1/2 In. 100.00
Tip Tray, 1938, Girl In Yellow Hat, 7 In. 110.00
Tip Tray, 1939, Springboard Girl, 7 In. . . . . .100.00 to 145.00
Tip Tray, 1940, Sailor Girl, 6 In. 100.00
Tip Tray, 1941, Skater Girl, 6 In. 80.00
Tip Tray, 1942, Two Girls At Car, 7 In. . . . . .110.00 to 200.00
Tip Tray, 1960, Woman Drinking Coke, 7 1/2 x 6 1/4 In. 30.00
Toy, Case, Wooden, With 12 3-In. Bottles 45.00
Toy, Hot Dog Cart 850.00
Toy, Picnic Set, Cooler, Plastic, 2 Bottles, Thermos, Accessories, 5 1/2 x 5 x 4 In. 415.00
Toy, Shopping Cart, Red Wheels, Handle, 1950, 8 1/2 x 9 In. 410.00
Toy, Truck, Buddy-L, Box, 1970, 9 In. 75.00
Toy, Truck, Delivery, Red Body, Rubber Wheels, Windup, Tin, Goso, 1952, 7 x 8 1/4 In. . . 1100.00
Toy, Truck, Delivery, Red Lettering, Yellow Body, Marx, 1954, 11 In. 121.00
Toy, Truck, Delivery, Red Lettering, Yellow, White Body, Sanyo, 1960, 12 1/2 In. 88.00
Toy, Truck, Delivery, Yellow Body, Marx, 1956, 12 1/2 In. 214.00
Toy, Truck, Delivery, Yellow Body, Rubber Wheels, Metalcraft, 1933, 11 In. 770.00
Toy, Truck, Delivery, Yellow Body, Tin, Rosko, 1950, 8 In. 242.00
Toy, Truck, Pick-Up, Volkswagen, Europa 165.00
Toy, Truck, Red Cab, 10 Glass Coke Bottles, Pressed Steel, Metalcraft, 11 In. 785.00
Toy, Truck, Red Cab, Yellow Body, 10 Glass Coke Bottles, Sheet Metal, 11 In. 2420.00
Trash Can, Red Ground, White Lettering, 1950, 7 In. 522.00
Tray, 1907, Relieves Fatigue, 16 1/2 x 13 1/2 In. . . . .*Illus* 5060.00
Tray, 1913, Hamilton King Girl, 9 1/4 In. 360.00
Tray, 1927, Curb Service, 13 1/4 x 10 1/2 In. 230.00
Tray, 1930, Telephone Girl 375.00
Tray, 1931, Barefoot Boy, 10 1/2 x 13 1/4 In. . . . . .675.00 to 1045.00
Tray, 1932, Girl In Bathing Suit, 8 1/4 In. 715.00
Tray, 1936, Hostess, 10 1/2 x 13 1/4 In. . . . . .385.00 to 400.00
Tray, 1938, Girl In Yellow Hat, 10 x 13 3/8 In. 210.00
Tray, 1939, Springboard Girl 400.00
Tray, 1940, Sailor Girl, 10 1/2 x 13 In. . . . . .170.00 to 210.00
Tray, 1941, Skater Girl, 10 5/8 x 13 In. . . . . .165.00 to 265.00
Tray, 1942, Two Girls At Car 225.00
Tray, 1948, Girl With Red Hair 120.00
Tray, 1950, Menu Lady, 10 1/2 x 13 In. 68.00
Tray, 1958, Picnic Basket 80.00
Tray, 1958, Picnic Basket, 13 1/4 x 10 1/2 In. . . . . .45.00 to 75.00
Tray, 1963, Christmas, Santa Claus Reading Children's Note, 14 x 10 1/2 In. 40.00
Tray, 1975, Atlanta Anniversary 10.00

Tray, 1975, Nashville Anniversary 20.00
Tray, 1982, Enjoy Coca-Cola 18.00
Vending Machine, Mills, Model G5 .... 1295.00
Vending Machine, Model 27A 1195.00
Watch Fob, Engraved Brass, 1 1/2 In. 121.00

COFFEE GRINDERS of home size were first made about 1894. They lost favor by the 1930s. Large floor-standing or counter-model coffee grinders were used in the nineteenth-century country store. The renewed interest in fresh-ground coffee has produced many modern electric and hand grinders, and reproductions of the old styles are being made.

American Duplex, Big Pot, Aluminum, Cast Iron 375.00
American Duplex, Big Pot, Electric, Stainless Steel, 29 1/2 In. ....*Illus* 770.00
Arcade, Crystal No. 3, Cast Iron, Wall Mount 230.00
Brass, Iron, 19th Century, 7 1/2 In. 77.00
Cast Iron, Clear Glass Jar, Wall Mount 40.00
Cherry, Iron Fitting, Dot Design, 1 Drawer, Small D On Handle, 1828 .... 1045.00
Cherry, Iron Fittings, Dovetailed Drawer, D. Small, York, Pa., 1828 .... 950.00
Clark, Cast Iron & Brass, Wolverhampton, England 100.00
Coles, Countertop, Stencil, 30 In. 450.00
Elgin National, Eagle Finial, Red, Woodruff & Edwards, 33-In. Wheel ......*Illus* 303.00
Elgin National, Floor, Woodruff & Edwards, 64 In. 500.00
Elgin National, Stencil, Eagle Finial, Woodruff & Edwards, 33 In. 275.00
Elma, Gold & Red Paint, Spain, Small 550.00
Elma, Spain, 11 1/2-In. Wheel 110.00
Enterprise, 24 In. 475.00
Enterprise, Double Wheel, 17-In. Wheels 300.00
Enterprise, Double Wheel, 19-1/2 In. Wheels 375.00
Enterprise, Flywheels, Drawer, Cast Iron, Wooden Base, 1873, 18 In. 150.00
Enterprise, Iron, Transfer, Worn Paint, Pat. Dec. 9, 1873, 34 1/2 In. 1375.00
Enterprise, No. 7, Red Paint, Stencil, Table Model ....*Illus* 468.00
Enterprise, No. 7, Stencil, 22 In. 425.00
Enterprise, No. 9, Cast Iron, Paint, Decals, 19th Century, 27 In. 1430.00
Enterprise, No. 12, Painted, Decals, Eagle Finial 4200.00
Enterprise, No. 112, 24 1/2-In. Wheel 200.00
Enterprise, Stenciled Pinstripe, Cast Iron, 68 In. 2750.00
Enterprise Mfg. Co., Philadelphia, Pat. Dec. 9, 1873, Cast Iron, 13 In. 1450.00
Fisher, Wooden, 1 Drawer, Tin Well 90.00
Golden Rule, Viewing Window, Iron, Wall Mount, 9 x 5 In. 440.00
Griswold, Tabletop 1500.00
Hobart, Electric, Stencil 50.00
Hollands, No. 1, Cast Metal Body, Wooden Base 220.00

Coffee Grinder, American
Duplex, Big Pot, Electric,
Stainless Steel, 29 1/2 In.

Coffee Grinder, Elgin National,
Eagle Finial, Red, Woodruff &
Edwards, 33-In. Wheel

Coffee Grinder, Enterprise,
No. 7, Red Paint, Stencil,
Table Model

Izone, Metal & Cast Iron 90.00
Jorgensen, Copper Funnel, Wood Body, Denmark, 10-In. Wheel 300.00
Landers Frary & Clark, Universal, No. 014, Wall Mount 10.00
Landers Frary & Clark, Universal, No. 110, Tin Body, Cast Iron Handle 70.00
National Coffee, Iron, Red Repaint, Gold Trim, Eagle Finial, 24 3/4 In. 410.00
Parker, Dovetail Corners, Acanthus Dome, Gadroon Border, c.1890-1900, 10 In. 175.00
Poplar, Nailed Drawer, Pewter Hopper, Iron Handle, 9 1/2 In. 130.00
Poplar, Worn Brown Flame Graining, 1 Dovetailed Drawer, 9 x 9 x 10 In. 135.00
Swift, Lane Bros., Repainted, 19 1/2 In. 350.00
Wooden Case, Embossed Top & Handle 40.00

COIN SPOT is a glass pattern that was named by the collectors for the
spots resembling coins, which are part of the glass. Colored, clear, and
opalescent glass was made with the spots. Many companies used the
design in the 1870–1890 period. It is so popular that reproductions are
still being made.

Cruet, Ball Shape, Cranberry 365.00
Pitcher, Cranberry Opalescent, Applied Clear Handle, 8 1/2 In. 435.00
Pitcher, Opalescent, 9 In. 165.00
Sugar Shaker, Cranberry Opalescent, 9 Panels, 5 In. 350.00
Vase, Jack-In-The-Pulpit, Clear, Cranberry Opalescent Crimped Rim, Bulbous, 4 In. 485.00
Water Set, Ruby Stain, Twisted Shape, 6 1/2-In. Pitcher, 5 Piece 220.00

COIN-OPERATED MACHINES of all types are collected. The vending
machine is an ancient invention dating back to 200 B.C. when holy
water was dispensed in a coin-operated vase. Smokers in seventeenth-
century England could buy tobacco from a coin-operated box. It was
not until after the Civil War that the technology made modern coin-
operated games and vending machines plentiful. Slot machines, arcade
games, and dispensers are all collected.

Candy, Chocolate, Art Nouveau, Germany ....*Illus* 2909.00
Candy, Chocolate, Cast Iron Hen, Tin, Germany, 1920 ....*Illus* 415.00
Candy, Well Here We Are, Nickel Plate, R.D. Simpson Co., 14 In. 275.00
Change Maker, Cast Iron & Brass, Hopkins & Robinson, 19 In. 715.00
Chuck Aluck, Large Cage, 1890 .... 395.00
Cigarette, 6 Brands, 10 Cents, Mirror Front, 1930s-1940s, 35 In. 275.00
Cigarette, Dial A Smoke, Red, Metal, Center Knob, 18 x 27 In. 150.00
Cigarette, Elephant, Dark Brown, Cast Iron, 5 1/2 x 8 1/4 In. 130.00
Cigarette, Mule, Front Ear Forward, Tail Lifts Up, Tin, 10 x 8 In. 120.00
Cigarette, Wooden, Mechanical, Dispenser Woman's Face, 6 1/2 In. 200.00
Cigars, Robert Burns, c.1960, 30 x 10 In. 160.00
Cigars, Roi-Tan, Counter, 1950s, 24 x 9 In. 160.00
Cough Drops, Glycerin Tablets, Die Cut Tin, 5 Column, 17 In. 635.00
Cup, 1 Cent Matchbox, Cigar Clipper, Iron, c.1912 .... 1350.00
Fare Box, Johnson, 20 In. 88.00
Fortune Teller, Ask Me Another, Arcade, Countertop, 1939, 15 x 21 In. 210.00
Gambling, Bajazzo, Jentzsch & Meertz, Germany, 1904 ....*Illus* 2656.00
Gum, 2 Columns For Peppermint & Spearmint, One Cent 66.00
Gum, Adams Pepsin Tutti-Frutti, 1894, 31 1/2 In. 750.00
Gum, Advance, No. 4 Mechanism, Aug. 1916, 12 In. 110.00
Gum, Beech-Nut Chewing Gum, 1947, 13 1/2 In. 450.00
Gum, Bubble Gum, Pillsbury Doughboy Top, Happy 25th Anniversary 800.00
Gum, Bubble Gum, Victor, 1 Cent, Wooden, Plastic, 12 x 7 x 5 In. 58.00
Gum, Mansfield Automatic Clerk, 5 Cent Rings Bell, 12 In. 990.00
Gum, Mansfield Automatic Clerk, Peppermint, 1902, 12 In. 650.00
Gum, Master No. 2, Gooseneck Masters, 1925, 16 In. 325.00
Gum, Metal, 15 3/4 x 9 3/4 In. 30.00
Gum, Northwestern 33, Orange, 1933, 14 1/2 In. 145.00
Gum, Paper Label, Vendo Silver Products Co., 18 In. 88.00
Gum, Pick-A-Pack, Bubble Gum, Art Deco, 14 1/4 x 10 In. 480.00
Gum, Pulver Chewing, Porcelain, 21 x 9 In. 825.00
Gum, Pulver, Kola-Pepsin Gum, 1910, 24 In. 1600.00
Gum, Roth's Pansy Gum, Your Fortune, 1905 .... 1400.00

Gum, Tab, Mills, 1 Cent 75.00
Gumball, Baker Boy, Black Man Version, 1929, 16 In. 1525.00
Gumball, Columbus Model 14, Green, 15 In. 575.00
Gumball, Hit The Target, 1950s, 19 In. 98.00
Gumball, Vendor Derby 2510.00
Lotion, Frostilla, Merchandise Dispensers, Inc., 1950s 240.00
Matches, 1 Cent, Cigar Cutter On Front, Cast Iron, 1912 .... 925.00
Matches, 1 Cent, Granite, 16 In. 125.00
Matches, Diamond Book Matches, 1928, 13 In. 240.00
Matches, Diamond Match, Penny, 13 x 4 1/2 In. 220.00
Matches, Mills, Owl, Oak Case, 20 In. 125.00
Matches, Ohio Blue Tip, Original Painted Label, 13 In. 88.00
Matches, Ohio Blue Tip, Penny, Key & Works, 1928 .... 132.00
Matches, Ohio Book Matches, 9 x 10 1/2 x 6 1/4 In. 210.00
Matches, The Number 4 Perfection, Specialty Mfg. Co., 1920 .... 725.00
Nickelodeon, Seeburg, Golden Oak, Leaded Glass Panel On Doors 4950.00
Nickelodeon, Seeburg, Mahogany Case, 2 Stained Glass Doors 7800.00
Peanut, Cebco, Electric, 2 Globes, 1930, 18 In. 500.00
Peanut, Fenachen Mfg., Wall Mount, 1930, 18 In. 100.00
Peanut, Kingery Mfg. Co., 4-Wheel Cart, 41 x 27 x 39 In. 2875.00
Peanut, Northwestern 33 Peanut, Brown, White, 14 In. 290.00
Peanut, Pix, Albert Pick & Co., Cast Iron, Ornate, Restored 9350.00
Peanut, Silver King Hot Nut, Ruby Glass, c.1947, 16 In. 155.00
Pinball, Deluxe World Series, 1950s 1800.00
Pinball, Jigsaw, Rock-Ola 1300.00
Pinball, Lucky Ace, Williams, No. 448, 1960s 900.00
Pinball, World Series, Rock-Ola 750.00
Slot, Caille, Sphinx, 5 Cent, 1930s ....1750.00 to 2200.00
Slot, Mills, Black Cherry, 5 Cent, 1940s 1400.00
Slot, Mills, Castle Front, 5 Cent 1500.00
Slot, Mills, Castle Front, 10 Cent, c.1933-1936 ....1495.00 to 1595.00
Slot, Mills, Cherry Falls, 1937 Model, 25 Cent, 25 1/2 In. 1910.00
Slot, Mills, Hightop, 5 Cent 1500.00
Slot, Mills, Nickel, Bursting Cherry, Lock Removed, Not Working 880.00
Slot, Novelty Mystery Golden, 5 Cent, 1933, 26 In. 1018.00
Slot, Sphinx Caille Bros., Detroit, Egyptian Design, 1930s 1650.00
Slot, Turn Knob, 50 Cent, Art Deco Case, 26 x 19 In. 575.00
Slot, Watling, Rol-A-Top, 10 Cent, 1930s Checkerboard 3900.00
Slot, Watling, Rol-A-Top, 25 Cent, 1930s Coin Front 4500.00
Stamp, Standard-Harvard Metal Type, Inc., 1920s, 39 In. 545.00
Stamp, U.S. Postage Stamps, 13 x 20 x 8 1/2 In. 305.00
Trade Stimulator, Mills Perfection, 5-Cent 5-Card Poker, 1901, 13 In. 2250.00
Trade Stimulator, Poker, Cigars, Oak, Rewards 2 To 100 Cigars, 20 In. 2260.00

Coin-Operated
Machine, Candy,
Chocolate,
Art Nouveau,
Germany

Coin-Operated Machine,
Candy, Chocolate, Cast Iron
Hen, Tin, Germany, 1920

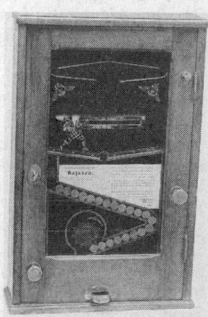

Coin-Operated Machine,
Gambling, Bajazzo, Jentzsch
& Meertz, Germany, 1904

COLLECTOR PLATES are modern plates produced in limited editions. Some may be found listed under the factory name, such as Bing & Grondahl, Royal Copenhagen, Royal Doulton, and Wedgwood.

Avon, Bouquet Of Love, 1987	10.00
Avon, Christmas, 1976	8.00
Avon, Classic Wedding, 1986	18.00
Avon, Currier & Ives, 1977	10.00
Avon, Hollywood Chorus Line, 1986	20.00
Avon, Hollywood, Easter Parade, Box, 1986, 8 In.	22.00
Avon, Jesus Feeds The Multitude, 1993	25.00
Avon, Liberty Bell	10.00
Avon, Tenderness Commemorative, 1974	10.00
Boehm, American Redstart, Flowering Dogwood, 1975	70.00
Bradford, At Storm's Passage, H. Schaare, 1993	6.00
Coheleach, Afternoon Shade, Box, 8 In.	25.00
Currier & Ives, Farmer's Home In Winter, 8 In.	20.00
Currier & Ives, Old Homestead In Winter, 8 In.	20.00
Franke, Hammond Harwood House, 10 1/2 In.	49.00
Franke, Joseph Webb House, 10 1/2 In.	40.00
Franke, Old Court House, Newcastle, Delaware, 10 1/2 In.	40.00
Franke, Tidewater, Virginia, 10 1/2 In.	40.00
Henriette Bonner, Frisky Felines, Box, Certificate, 1991	50.00
Kathy Wallace, Squeezing In Young Innocence, 8 1/4 In.	20.00
Mary Rhyner-Nadig, Moo Moo's Indian Cow, 1998, 3 1/4 x 2 In.	10.00
Motton, Napoleon's Image, Certificates, Box	34.00
Norman Rockwell, Antique Shop	25.00
Norman Rockwell, Music Maker, 1981, 8 1/2 In.	22.00
Reco, We Three Kings, Box, Certificate, 1989	30.00
Redlin, Elk At Marsh Lake, Snow Capped Mountain, 1990, 9 1/4 In.	32.00
Rhodes Studios, Main Street, Box	25.00
Rorstrand, Winter Country Scene, Windmill, Snowman, Boy, 1970, 7 1/2 In.	28.00
Schmid, Sacred Journey, Stained Glass, 1976	50.00
Schmid, Tranquility, Sister Berta Hummel, 1978	150.00
Stetson, Abraham Lincoln's Christening, 1953, 10 1/4 In.	18.00
W.S. George, Kittens At Play, Box, Certificate, 1991	45.00
W.S. George, Mischief With Hat Box, Box, Certificate	45.00

COMIC ART, or cartoon art, is a relatively new field of collecting. Original comic strips, magazine covers, and even printed strips are collected. The first daily comic strip was printed in 1907. The paintings on celluloid used for movie cartoons are listed in this book under Animation Art.

Drawing, Bugs Bunny, Black Ink, Fritz Freiling, Signed, 4 x 8 In.	94.00
Drawing, Mammy, Li'l Abner Strip, Al Capp, 19 3/4 x 15 1/2 In.	355.00
Drawing, Microscopic Giants, Pen & Ink, Virgil Finlay, 4 x 5 1/2 In.	600.00
Drawing, Robin, Black Ink, Bob Kane, Signed, 7 x 10 In.	100.00
Drawing, Weird Science, Al Williamson, 1953, 4 1/2 x 6 1/2 In.	181.00
Strip, Andy Capp, Reg Smythe, January, 2, 1983, 3 1/2 x 13 1/2 In.	165.00
Strip, Andy Gump, Sidney Smith, Matted, 1925, 5 1/2 x 20 In.	110.00
Strip, Apartment 3G, Alex Kotzky, December 30, 1969, 5 1/2 x 18 1/2 In.	55.00
Strip, B.C. Sunday, Johnny Hart, 1985, 11 x 16 In.	247.00
Strip, Blondie, Chic Young, Alex Raymond, 1932, 4 x 19 1/2 In.	572.00
Strip, Buz Sawyer, Roy Crane, 1945, 17 x 25 In.	594.00
Strip, Cisco Kid, Jose Louis Salinas, December 29, 1951, 5 1/2 x 20 In.	250.00
Strip, Dickie Dare, Milton Caniff, October 29, 1934, 5 x 24 1/2 In.	770.00
Strip, Dixie Dugan, Unpacked, J.H. Striebel, 6 x 19 1/2 In.	198.00
Strip, Dr. Kildare, Ken Balk, February 5, 1959, 5 1/2 x 18 1/2 In.	50.00
Strip, Johnny Comet, Frank Frazetta, Matted, Frame, 1952, 4 1/2 x 17 In.	1331.00
Strip, Johnny Hazard, Frank Robbins, 1966, 5 1/2 x 18 In.	143.00
Strip, Kevin The Bold, Signed Kreigh Collins, Best Wishes To Tex Lowell, 8/19/62	180.00
Strip, Li'l Abner, Al Capp, Sunday, May 8, 1938, 26 1/2 x 19 In.	495.00
Strip, Nancy, Ernie Bushmiller, February 10, 1941, 5 x 22 In.	205.00

Strip, Pogo, Walt Kelly, 1954, 16 x 23 1/2 In. 1210.00
Strip, Pogo, Walt Kelly, 1965, 16 x 23 In. 1320.00
Strip, Pogo, Walt Kelly, 1972, 5 x 17 In. 440.00
Strip, Rip Kirby, Alex Raymond, August 5, 1947, 5 1/2 x 18 1/2 In. 600.00
Strip, Rip Kirby, Alex Raymond, June 1, 1947, 5 1/2 x 18 1/2 In. 385.00
Strip, Secret Agent Corrigan, Al Williamson, 1978, 6 x 19 In. 275.00
Strip, Secret Agent Corrigan, Al Williamson, May 3, 1968, 5 x 18 In. 585.00
Strip, Secret Agent Corrigan, George Evans, 1985, 4 x 13 In. 55.00
Strip, Steve Roper, Sunday, March 6, 1961, 14 x 20 1/2 In. 220.00
Strip, Tarzan, Burne Hogarth, Feb. 5, 1950, 19 x 27 1/2 In. 5860.00
Strip, Tarzan, Lone Raider, Hal Foster, 1937, 26 1/2 x 19 1/2 In. 4845.00
Strip, Terry & The Pirates, Milton Caniff, 1938, 5 1/2 x 20 In. .... 484.00 to 847.00
Strip, Terry & The Pirates, Milton Caniff, August 15, 1935, 5 1/2 x 20 In. 1760.00
Strip, Tim Tyler's Luck, Lyman Young, Alex Raymond, 1933, 20 x 25 1/2 In. 797.00
U.S. Treasury Bond Savings Certificate, Al Capp, Shmoos, 1960, 8 1/2 x 10 1/2 In. 95.00

COMMEMORATIVE items have been made to honor members of royalty
and those of great national fame. World's fairs and important historical
events are also remembered with commemorative pieces. Related collectibles are listed in the Coronation and World's Fair categories.

Beaker, Edward VII & Alexandra, Stoneware, Doulton, 5 In. 245.00
Beaker, Queen Victoria 60th Anniversary, White, 1837-1897, 4 In. 195.00
Bread Tray, George Washington, Glass, Oval, Handles, 1876 .... 70.00
Bread Tray, Glass, Centennial, George Washington, Oval, Handle 72.00
Jug, Public Inauguration, Ronald Reagan, U.S. 40th President, 1985, 16 In. 88.00
Jug, Southern Heritage Honor Land Faith Family Confederate Memorial, 11 In. 88.00
Mug, Queen Victoria, Young & Older Portrait, Blue Pottery, Doulton 150.00
Pitcher, President Garfield, Stoneware, 8 1/4 In. 46.00
Plate, Prince Of Wales, Lady Diana, Royal Doulton 80.00
Towel, Wedding, Princess Diana & Prince Charles, Color Portrait 22.00

COMPACTS hold face powder. A woman did not powder her face in
public until after World War I. By 1920, the beauty parlor, permanent
waves, and cosmetics had become acceptable. A few companies sold
cake face powder in a box with a mirror and a pad or puff. Soon the
compact was designed by jewelers and made of gold, silver, and precious materials. Cosmetic companies began to sell powder in attractive
compacts of less valuable metal or plastic. Collectors today search for
Art Deco designs, commemorative compacts from world's fairs or
political events, and unusual examples. Many were made with companion lipsticks and other fittings.

Bakelite, Metal Lid, Black, Ivory, 3 In. 35.00
Bakelite, Yellow, Carved Floral Center, 1930s, 3 In. 295.00
Brass, Ball Shape 70.00
Brass Color, Filigree Design, 4 Blue Rhinestones, Ornate, Round, 2 In. 135.00
Cartier, Art Deco, Demilune Shape, Gold, 3 Rows Of Sapphires, Pave Diamonds 1035.00
Celluloid, Dance, Floral, Silk Cord & Tassel, 3 1/4 In. 175.00
Celluloid, Foil Back, Reverse Painted Man & Woman Lift Cover, 3 In. 42.00
Celluloid, Ivory Color, Puff, Oval, 1920s, 1 3/4 x 1 1/2 In. 70.00
Celluloid, Rhinestones, Black Cord, Loop At Base, Round, 1930s, 2 In. 310.00
Celluloid, Woman, Figural, Red Dress Front, Cream Dress Back, 3 5/8 In. 220.00
Ciner, Goldtone, Lipstick, Faux Pearls, Gold & Black Thread Design, Square, 3 In. 180.00
Coty, Buckle, Goldtone, Black Wavy Belt, Rouge & Powder, 3 3/4 x 2 1/4 In. 25.00
Coty, Memo, Chypre Perfume Tube, Goldtone, Box, 2 1/2 x 3 1/2 In. 195.00
Dorothy Gray, Goldtone, Black Mask, Oval, 3 3/4 In. 160.00
EBM Co., Silver Plate, Black Enamel Birds, 1930s, 2 1/4 x 1 3/4 In. 295.00
Eisenberg Original, Henriette, Gilt Metal, Rhinestone Ring, Applicator Pad, 3 In. 320.00
Elephant, Triangular Shape, Box 80.00
Elgin, Teardrop Shape, Sterling Silver 225.00
Elgin, Woman Enjoying Outdoor Sports In 4 Different Seasons, 2 3/4 In. 29.00
Elgin American, Art Deco, Ivory Enamel, Silvertone, Octagonal, 2 1/4 In. 245.00
Enamel, Cover, Spanish Village Scene, Black Enamel, 3 x 1 3/4 In. 31.00
Enamel, Elizabethan Scene On Lid, Black Enamel, 2 In. 30.00

Enamel, Floral Design On Lid, Blue Finish Bottom, White Metal Case, 2 x 1 1/4 In. 65.00
Enamel, Pink Floral Design On Lid, Brass, Square, 2 1/4 In. 35.00
Enamel, Rhinestone Accents, Billion Jubilee KC Life, 1954, 3 x 1/2 In. 30.00
Enamel, Women's Faces, Red, Black, 2 1/4 In. 35.00
Engine Turned, 14K Yellow Gold, 2 Stacked Compartments, Octagonal 517.00
Evans, Blue Enamel, Tango Chain, Lipstick, Rouge, 2 x 2 In. 225.00
Evans, Mesh, Red Enamel, Silver Plate Flowers, Round, 2 1/2 In. 100.00
Evans, Nickel Silver, Vanity Case, On Chain, 4 x 2 1/2 In. 135.00
Evans, Silver Plate, Black Enamel Flowers, Round, 2 1/4 In. 130.00
Evening In Paris, Cardboard, Square, Unused, 2 1/4 In. 170.00
Eversmart Manicure, Silver Plate, Greek Key Design, Pat. 1924, 2 3/4 In. 25.00
Flato, Goldtone, Raised Carriage, Rhinestones, Lipstick, Box, 2 1/2 x 2 1/4 In. 155.00
Flato, Green Pear-Shaped Stones, Powder Well, Puff, Mirror, Lipstick, 2 1/2 In. 200.00
Girey, Green Pearlized USN, Box 35.00
Gold Plate, Mother-Of-Pearl Squares, Rectangular, c.1920, 3 In. 35.00
Gorham, Silver, Enameled Floral Medallion, Pink Ground, Box 145.00
Helena Rubenstein, Gold Colored Metal 37.00
K & K, Sterling Silver, 10 Etched Stars, 2 3/4 x 2 3/4 In. 70.00
Lentheric, Bal Masque, Black Enamel, Gold Mask, Round, 2 1/2 In. 175.00
Locket Type, Woman Silhouette, Goldtone, Silk Ribbon, Oval, 1 1/2 In. 230.00
Mondaine, Petit Point Enamel, Brown Strap, 3 x 4 In. 225.00
Plastic, Ladybug Top, 1930s 150.00
Pygmalion, Suitcase, Happy Landing, Goldtone Straps & Handle, 3 In. 120.00
Revlon, Brushed Gold, Rhinestone, Ruby Trim, Puff, 1 3/4 In. 45.00
Rex 5th Avenue, Brass Woman Golfer, White Lucite Lid, Square, 3 3/4 In. 175.00
Rex 5th Avenue, Celluloid, Pastel Pansies On Side 65.00
Richard Hudnut, Art Deco, Pressed Powder, Lid Spring 200.00
Richard Hudnut, Deuville, Art Deco, Silver Plate, Face Profile, Rouge, Chain, Box 295.00
Ritz, Gold Basket Weave, Pouch, Round, 3 In. 50.00
Rosenfeld, Black Suede, Lace Type, Goldtone Clasp, Spain, 1940s, 5 In. 225.00
Serpentine Shape, Maiden Portrait On Lid, Turquoise Inserts, Silver, Germany 420.00
Silver, Cover With Mirror, Blue Stone, 2 x 1/4 x 1/4 In. 22.00
Silver, Enamel, Musician Serenading 2 Women, Marked 800, Germany 121.00
Silver Plate, Rhinestones, Spiders & Web Design, Chain, Finger Ring, Round, 2 In. 275.00
Sterling Silver, Chain Handle, Sterling Silver 87.00
Sterling Silver, Deep Monogram, Chain, 3 1/2 In. 50.00
Sterling Silver, White Enamel, Pastel Flower Basket Center, Round, 1 1/2 In. 325.00
Sterling Silver & Gold, Art Deco 175.00
Stratton, Enamel Pheasant On Cover 60.00
Telephone Dial Shape, I Like Ike In Holes, United States Map Center, Metal, Round 225.00
Tiffany & Co., Silver, Reeded, 14K Gold Geometric Clasp, Oval, 3 Rubies, Retro 260.00
Tortoiseshell Enamel, Gold Metal, Cigarette Case & Music Box, Box, 4 x 2 In. 240.00
Virginia Tech Medallion, 6-Cent Stamp, Envelope Shape, Folding, 3 1/2 x 2 1/4 In. 70.00
Volupte, Hand, Lace Glove, Hand Painted, Lacquered, 4 5/8 In. 130.00
Volupte, Spider Web 150.00
Volupte, Vanity Table, Goldtone, Lift Up Section, Black Case, 4 1/4 x 3 In. 155.00
Wadsworth, Vanity Table, Goldtone, Filigree Border Lid, 3 x 2 In. 345.00
Wedgwood, Blue Jasper Mounted Ivory, Beaded Trim, Fitted Interior, 1820s, 3 In. 430.00
Zell, With Lipstick, Box 24.00

CONSOLIDATED LAMP AND GLASS COMPANY of Coraopolis, Pennsyl-

vania, was founded in 1894. The company made lamps, tablewares, and art glass. Collectors are particularly interested in the wares made after 1925, including black satin glass, Cosmos (listed in its own category in this book), Martele (which resembled Lalique), Ruba Rombic (1928–1932 Art Deco line), and colored glasswares. Some Consolidated pieces are very similar to those made by the Phoenix Glass Company. The colors are sometimes different. Consolidated made Martele glass in blue, crystal, green, pink, white, or custard glass with added fired-on color or a satin finish. The company closed for the final time in 1967.

Banana Boat, Lovebirds 845.00
Bowl, Leaves & Berries, Blue On Cream, 4 In. 130.00

Candlestick, Catalonian, Pair	135.00
Candlestick, Ruba Rombic, Green, 4 3/4 In., Pair	520.00
Decanter Set, Ruba Rombic, Transparent Forest Green, 8 Cordials, Tray	6600.00
Plate, Dancing Nymph, 10 In.	265.00
Plate, Ruba Rombic, Transparent Forest Green, 9 In., 5 Piece	520.00
Sherbet, Dancing Nymph	95.00
Sugar & Creamer, Ruba Rombie, Smoky Topaz, c.1928, 2 1/8 & 3 1/2 In.	1265.00
Syrup, Bulging Loops, Pink Cased	260.00
Tumbler, Cocktail, Dancing Nymph	145.00
Tumbler, Dancing Nymph	200.00
Vase, Brown Chickadees, White Ground, Blue Flower, Leaves, 6 1/2 In.	185.00
Vase, Chickadee, 6 1/2 In.	495.00
Vase, Con-Cora, White, Painted Violets	130.00
Vase, Dogwood, Ivory, Baluster Shape, 11 In.	355.00
Vase, Fan, Catalonian, 6 In.	135.00
Vase, Martele, Satin Floral Design, Clear Ground, 10 1/4 In.	258.00
Vase, Ruba Rombic, Silver, 6 1/2 In.	632.00
Vase, Sweet Pea, Catalonian, 8 In.	135.00
Water Set, Ruba Rombic, Transparent Forest Green, 7 Piece	3300.00

CONTEMPORARY GLASS, see Glass-Contemporary.

COOKBOOKS are collected for various reasons. Some are wanted for the recipes, some for investment, and some as examples of advertising. Cookbooks and recipe pamphlets are included in this category.

600 Selected Recipes, H.K. Fairbanks & Co., 130 Pages, 1890	20.00
Art Of Cookery, Hannah Glasse, 1748, Rebound Brown Morocco Leather	595.00
Betty Crocker, Dinner For Two, Hardcover, 205 Pages, 1958	3.00
Blondie & Dagwood	55.00
Elsie's Instant Starlac Recipes, Elsie, Borden Cow, 12 Recipes, 1950s	6.00
Gold Medal Flour, 1909, 80 Pages	24.00
Gold Medal Flour, Gold Medal Cookbook, Washurn-Crosby Co., 1904, 72 Pages	25.00
Gone With The Wind, Pebco Tooth Paste, Scarlett & Tara Cover, 52 Pages	40.00
Gone With The Wind Southern Recipe, Scarlett O'Hara On Cover, 50 Pages	60.00
Henkels Flour, Good Things To Eat, Commercial Milling Co., Detroit, 1934, 64 Pages 8.00 to	10.00
Jell-O, Robinson Crusoe's Rescue, 8 1/2 x 2 1/4 In.	7.50
Kate Smith, Cake Recipes, 1952	10.00
Maple Leaf Milling Co., Cooking Made Easy, Anna Lee Scott, Canada, 1947, 132 Pages	8.00
National Seafood Recipes, Book Of A Thousand Cooks, Canada, 1927, 32 Pages	7.00
National Seafood Recipes, National Fish Co. Ltd., Halifax, Canada, 1924, 32 Pages	10.00
New York Times Cookbook, Craig Claiborne, Illustrated, 1961, 700 Pages	35.00
Virginia Cookery, Mary Stuart Smith, 1885, 7 1/2 In.	60.00

COOKIE JARS with brightly painted designs or amusing figural shapes became popular in the mid-1930s. Many companies made them and collectors search for cookie jars either by design or by maker's name. Listed here are examples by the less common makers. Major factories are listed under their own names in other categories of the book, such as Abingdon, Brush, Hull, McCoy, Red Wing, and Shawnee. See also the Disneyana category.

After School Cookies, Bell In Lid, American Bisque	55.00
Apple, 2 Green Leaves On Both Sides	275.00
Baby Elephant, American Bisque	120.00
Bart Simpson With Cookie, Treasure Craft, 12 In.	40.00
Baseball Boy, Treasure Craft	14.00
Bear, With Cookie, American Bisque	125.00
Bear, With Hat, American Bisque	75.00
Benjamin Franklin, Flag At Side, Treasure Craft	175.00
Big Dumb Clown, California Originals	150.00
Bowling Ball, Treasure Craft	75.00
Bubbles The Hippo, Blue, Metlox	750.00
Bulldog, Glass Eyes, Fierce Looking Dog, Glass Eyes, Italy	350.00
Christmas Tree, California Originals	290.00

Churn Boy, Regal 250.00
Clown, New Rose Collection 95.00
Clown, Pan American Art 22.00
Cookies, Blue & White, Wood Cover, Monoonth-Western 110.00
Cookies Of The World, Motto On Ship, Treasure Craft 175.00
Corvette, 1954, North American Ceramics 200.00
Cow Jumped Over The Moon, Yellow, Doranne Of California 185.00
Derby Dan, Mugsie, Pfaltzgraff 105.00
Dino, American Bisque 600.00
Drum, Drum Form, Rope Handled Lid, 7 3/4 In. 35.00
Elf, Sitting On Stump, Cookie In Hand, Sack On Back, Twin Winton 55.00
Emmett Kelly, Jr., Flambro 400.00
Ernie The Keebler Elf, Fitz & Floyd 125.00
Fire Hydrant, Doranne Of California 95.00
Flintstones, Wilma, On Telephone, American Bisque 600.00
French Poodle, American Bisque 100.00
Frog, Bouquet Of Flowers, Metlox 275.00
Gingerbread House, Curtains In Windows, Snow On Roof 30.00
Granny, Yellow & Pink, Brown Hair, American Bisque 200.00
Hampshire Hog, Fitz & Floyd 90.00
Hippo, Doranne Of California 145.00
Hobbyhorse, Regal 285.00
Horse, American Bisque 800.00
Hound Dog, Doranne Of California 55.00
Ice Cream Freezer, American Bisque 100.00
Lamb, American Bisque, 11 1/2 In. 75.00
Lion, Metlox 350.00
Little Red Riding Hood, Full Skirt, Regal 1200.00
Little Red Riding Hood, Open Basket, Regal 475.00
Luzianne Mammy, Carol Gifford 500.00
Majorette, American Bisque 450.00
Majorette, Regal 425.00
Mammy, Brayton Laguna 1000.00
Mammy, Googly-Eyed, Japan 900.00
Mammy, Pearl China 800.00
Mammy, Yellow, Mosaic Tile 375.00
Matilda, Brayton Laguna 800.00
Metlox Rose, Metlox 300.00
Milk Wagon, Pulled By Donkey, American Bisque 125.00
Mohawk Indian, American Bisque 1100.00
Monk, Twin Winton 30.00
Mother-In-The-Kitchen, Pink, Enesco 400.00
Noah's Ark, Treasure Craft 70.00
Owl, 10 1/2 In. 60.00
Penguin, Metlox 75.00
Pig, Metlox 95.00
Pig With Barrel Of Pork, Doranne Of California 65.00
Pink Cadillac, Expressive Designs, Miami, Florida, 1st Edition 325.00
Pinocchio, California Originals 900.00
Poodle, Pink, American Bisque 175.00
Poodle, Sierra Vista, 12 1/2 In. 150.00
Potbelly Stove, American Bisque 13.00
Rabbit On Cabbage, Metlox 150.00
Raggedy Andy, Metlox 115.00
Rolls-Royce Santa, Marked, Fitz & Floyd, 1987 .... 1000.00
Rooster, American Bisque 100.00
Santa Reading List, Marked Dayton Hudson 90.00
Tasmanian Devil, In Tornado, Good Co. 250.00
Tat-L-Tale, Helen Hutula Originals 750.00
Turkey, Morton 25.00
Turnabout Bear, Boy 1 Side, Girl On Other, Ludowici Celadon, 12 In. 145.00
Watermelon, Metlox 425.00
Yogi Bear, American Bisque, 1961 .... 400.00

COORS ware was made by a pottery in Golden, Colorado, owned by the Coors Beverage Company. Dishes and decorative wares were produced from the turn of the century until the pottery was destroyed by fire in the 1930s. The name *Coors* is marked on the back. For more information, see *Kovels' Depression Glass & Dinnerware Price List.*

COORS
U.S.A.

Ashtray, Orange, Raised Lettering On Bottom	15.00
Ashtray, Raised Lettering On Bottom	15.00
Mug, Marked, 1 1/2 In.	6.00
Pitcher, Chefsware, Yellow, 2 3/4 In.	12.00
Saltshaker, Rosebud, Green, Tapered	10.00
Teapot, Vase, Chefsware, 3 1/2 In.	20.00
Tray, Square, 5 In.	12.00
Vase, Blue Matte Glaze, White Interior, Marked, 1930s, 10 In.	100.00
Vase, Green Matte Glaze, c.1930, 12 In.	100.00

COPELAND pieces listed here are those that have a mark including the word Copeland used between 1847 and 1976. Marks include Copeland Spode and Copeland & Garrett. See also Copeland Spode and Royal Worcester.

Bowl, Byron View Series, Landscape Center, Mulberry, Marked, 12 1/2 In.	245.00
Bowl, Figural, Female Figures, Waves, 4 Shell-Shaped Base, c.1880, 13 In.	345.00
Bowl, Serving, Floral, Pale Lilac Rim, Copeland-Garnett, 1835, 11 In.	185.00
Centerpiece, 2 Cherubs Lugging Fishing Net, Majolica, c.1875, 14 In.	1840.00
Coffee Set, Lazy Susan, Pink & White, England, c.1860, 14 x 16 In., 11 Piece	1995.00
Figurine, Sabrina, Goddess Of Silver Lake, Parian, 19th Century, 12 In.	1800.00
Pedestal, Fluted Column, Anthemion Borders, New Fayence, c.1845, 35 In., Pair	2300.00
Pitcher, Baluster, Molded Rim, Acanthus Spout & Handle, Imari Style, 7 5/8 In.	201.00
Pitcher, Geometric Design, 9 1/2 In.	75.00
Pitcher, Jasper Ware, 6 1/2 In.	35.00
Pitcher & Bowl, Colored Large Leaves, 1861, 12 5/8 In.	230.00
Seat, Garden, Fluted Sides, Panels, Butterflies, Flowers, c.1850, 17 7/8 In., Pair	4890.00
Teapot, Fruit, Flowers, Vine, Brown, 6 In.	750.00
Tureen, Soup, Undertray, India Tree, Polychrome, Ironstone, 15 1/2 In.	275.00
Vase, Mask, Multicolored, 2 Handles, 10 1/2 In.	300.00
Vase, Multicolored, Cobalt Highlights, 8 1/2 In.	350.00

COPELAND SPODE appears on some pieces of nineteenth-century English porcelain. Josiah Spode established a pottery at Stoke-on-Trent, England, in 1770. In 1833, the firm was purchased by William Copeland and Thomas Garrett and the mark was changed. In 1847, Copeland became the sole owner and the mark changed again. W.T. Copeland & Sons continued until a 1976 merger when it became Royal Worcester Spode. Pieces are listed in this book under the name that appears in the mark. Copeland Spode, Copeland, and Royal Worcester have separate listings.

COPELAND
SPODE
ENGLAND

Bowl, Vegetable, Chinese Rose, Pair	225.00
Cake Plate, Christmas, On Stand, 12 1/2 x 3 In.	172.00
Dinner Set, Cowslip, Oval, Square Vegetable, Gravy, Tray, Relish, 56 Piece	308.00
Pitcher, Acanthus Leaf Handle & Spout, Classical Figures, Bulbous, 8 1/4 In.	220.00
Pitcher, European Landscape Transfer, 5 1/2 In.	100.00
Plate, Fish, Scenes Of Different Fish, 8 3/4 In., 4 Piece	175.00
Plate, Game Birds, Basket & Floral Sprig Border, 10 In., Set Of 12	2110.00
Plate, Gilded Bird & Floral, Claret Ground, 10 1/2 In., 12 Piece	510.00
Plate, Grisaille Transfer, Riverscape, 10 1/2 In., 6 Piece	50.00
Plate, Ivory, Scalloped Gilt Edged Rim, 6 In., 12 Piece	500.00
Plate, Pheasant Amid Blue Scalework Border, Floral Sprays, 9 In., 12 Piece	488.00
Plate, Scenes Of Dogs, 10 1/2 In., 12 Piece	412.00
Plate, Stanford University, 10 1/2 In.	185.00
Platter, Blue Country Scene, Farms, Floral Border, 17 x 13 3/8 In.	135.00
Platter, Blue Transfer, Label, 15 In.	165.00
Platter, Tower Pattern, 17 1/4 x 13 3/4 In.	190.00
Platter, Tower Pattern, Blue & White, 19 1/4 x 14 1/4 In.	245.00
Sugar & Creamer, Cover, Hunt Scene, Blue, 2 Handles, 4 1/4 In.	173.00

Tea Set, Heritage, 4-In. Teapot, 3 Piece 305.00
Tureen, Soup, Heritage, Undertray, Ladle, 3 Piece 690.00

COPPER has been used to make utilitarian items, such as teakettles and cooking pans, since the days of the early American colonists. Copper became a popular metal with the Arts & Crafts makers of the early 1900s, and decorative pieces, like desk sets, were made. Other pieces of copper may be found in the Arts & Crafts, Bradley & Hubbard, Kitchen, and Roycroft categories.

Arm Band, Marked Hopewell Md., Monroe Co., Mich., 4 x 3 In. 209.00
Ashtray, Horse, Standing, Hammered, Arts & Crafts, 5 1/2 x 7 In. 11.00
Basin, Hammered, Brass Handles, 23 1/2 In. 195.00
Basket, Canoe Shape, Hammered, Reticulated Handle, Dirk Van Erp, 9 x 10 1/2 In. 825.00
Basket, Waste, Hammered, Signed, Dirk Van Erp, 16 x 13 In. 1650.00
Basket, Wicker, Fern, Dirk Van Erp, 5 x 10 In. 1925.00
Beaker, Dovetailed Construction, 18th Century 210.00
Bed Warmer, Cover, Floral Designs, Wooden Handle, 45 1/2 In. 192.00
Bed Warmer, Engraved, Turned Wooden Handle 145.00
Bookstand, Folding, Hammered, Weighted Base, Apollo, 9 1/2 x 9 In. 88.00
Bowl, Cover Rooster Stone Finial, Hammered, Rebecca Cauman, 5 x 5 In. 1430.00
Bowl, Hammered, Avon Coppersmith, 3 x 12 In. 125.00
Bowl, Hammered, Bronze Eucalyptus Pod, Old Mission Kopper Kraft, 8 In. 1000.00
Bowl, Hammered, Flower Shape, Karl Lienenen, Handicraft Shop, 2 1/2 x 5 3/4 In. 165.00
Bowl, Hammered, Fluted Rim, Brown Patina, Arts & Crafts, 1 3/4 x 5 3/8 In. 125.00
Bowl, Hammered, Original Patina, Dirk Van Erp, 5 1/2 In. 355.00
Bowl, Ribbed, Scalloped Rim, Hammered, Marie Zimmerman, 1912, 7 x 9 3/4 In. 1495.00
Bowl, Scalloped, Windmill Mark, Dirk Van Erp, 7 3/4 In. 385.00
Box, Brass, Enamel Design On Top, Original Patina, Arts & Crafts, 5 1/2 x 3 In. 220.00
Box, Enamel Plaque, Peacock, Lanterns, Gold Foil, Cover, Marshall, Round, 2 x 4 In. .. 3200.00
Box, Hammered, Original Patina, Arts & Crafts, 10 x 6 In. 220.00
Box, Hammered, Signed, Dirk Van Erp, 5 In. 355.00
Box, Peaked Cover, Brass Band, Late 19th Century, 10 1/4 In. 115.00
Cachepot, Cover, Brass Handles, 12 x 10 In. 330.00
Chafing Dish, Cover, Original Patina, Wooden Handle, Heinrichs, 6 x 10 In. 193.00
Chafing Dish, Hammered, Lined, Wooden Pull Handle, 12 x 20 In. 1495.00
Chafing Stand, Finial Cover, Tray, Arts & Crafts, Shreve Crump & Low, 11 In. 495.00
Chamberstick, Riveted Handles, Flaring Bobeche, Marked, Gustav Stickley, 9 x 7 In. ... 605.00
Chamberstick, Rounded Handle, Jarvie, 2 1/2 x 6 In. 605.00
Charger, Hammered, Embossed, Sea Serpents, Salamanders, John Pearson, 1901, 24 In. ... 5225.00
Charger, Hammered, Embossed, Wave Pattern, Arts & Crafts, 21 In. 1540.00
Coal Scuttle, Hammered, Closed Box Mark, Dirk Van Erp, 10 1/2 In. 5500.00
Coffeepot, Hammered, Brass, Tin Lined, Wood Grain Pattern, Lubincraft, 8 1/2 In. 88.00
Compote, Center Classical Scene, 2 Handles, Brass, 19 3/4 x 13 1/4 In. 210.00
Desk Set, Hammered, Gustav Stickley, 7 Piece 4950.00
Dish, Fern, Hammered, Applied Feet, Benedict, Impressed Mark, 8 In. 190.00

Copper, Jardiniere, Embossed, Riveted Handles, Gustav Stickley, 12 x 11 1/2 In.

Copper, Jardiniere, Stylized Grape Clusters, Stickley Brothers, 8 x 13 In.

Copper, Tray, Hammered, Cutout Handles, Gustav Stickley, 19 1/2 In.

Dish, Hammered, Pewter Dog Handle, Avon, Marked, 4 3/4 In. 176.00
Ewer, Hammered, Arts & Crafts, 7 1/2 In. 88.00
Ewer, Hammered, Split Riveted Handle, Stickley Brother, Impressed 73, 14 x 6 1/2 In. . . .   770.00
Frame, Arts & Crafts, Pebbly Texture, Cutout Leather Panels, 19 x 14 In. 1760.00
Gong, Chased Dragon Design, Chinese, 24 In. 88.00
Holder, Bud Vase, Hammered, Stamped, Karl Kipp, 1 1/4 x 2 1/2 In. 154.00
Humidor, Hammered, Leaf Handle, Riveted Base, Cedar Box, Benedict Studios, 7 In. 1540.00
Jardiniere, Embossed, Riveted Handles, Gustav Stickley, 12 x 11 1/2 In. . . . .*Illus*   2090.00
Jardiniere, Hammered, Arts & Crafts, 2 Handles, Original Patina, 11 1/2 x 12 In. 300.00
Jardiniere, Hammered, Arts & Crafts, 4 Handles, Ball Feet, 9 x 8 In. 385.00
Jardiniere, Hammered, Embossed, Grapes, Stamped Stickley Brothers 302, 8 x 13 In. 2090.00
Jardiniere, Hammered, Handles, Gustav Stickley, 12 x 11 1/4 In. 3850.00
Jardiniere, Hammered, Riveted Bands, 8 1/2 x 11 In. 1073.00
Jardiniere, Regency, Chinoiserie Design, Bamboo Turned Tripod Base, 36 In. 715.00
Jardiniere, Ring Handles, Embossed Grapes, Stamped Stickley Brothers 301, 9 x 15 In. . . .   2200.00
Jardiniere, Stylized Grape Clusters, Stickley Brothers, 8 x 13 In. . . . .*Illus*   2090.00
Jug, Round Brass Foot, Handle, Removable Cover, Tibetan, 18th Century, 13 In. 460.00
Kettle, Maple Sugar, Hand Hammered, c.1870, 16 1/4 In. 135.00
Lamp Shade, Hammered, 4 Mica Panels, Vented Cap, Flared, Dirk Van Erp, 18 In. 4675.00
Letter Holder, Hammered, Sailing Ship, Arts & Crafts, Gertrude Twichell, 4 x 5 In. 375.00
Letter Opener, Hammered, Bone Handle, Arts & Crafts, Die Stamp AA, 11 1/4 In. 385.00
Log Carrier, Hammered, Arts & Crafts, 10 x 19 x 11 In. 275.00
Molds are listed in the Kitchen category.
Notepad Holder & Letter Opener, Hammered, Vine Medallion, Harry Dixon 605.00
Paper Spindle, Hammered, Bronze Eucalyptus Pod, Old Mission Kopper Kraft, 7 In. 330.00
Pen Tray, Etched Flowers, Carence Crafters, Arts & Crafts, 8 3/4 x 5 In. 235.00
Pen Tray, Hammered, Original Patina, Impressed Mark, Dirk Van Erp, 11 1/2 In. 110.00
Pipe Tamper, Silvered, Bust Victorian Man Shape, England, 2 3/4 In. 50.00
Pitcher, Hammered, 2 Handles, 2 Spouts, Dark Patina, Russia, 7 1/2 In. 33.00
Pitcher, Molded Fish Handle, Portugal, 9 In. 258.00
Plaque, Lincoln's Head, Hammered, Mission Oak Border, 14 In. 45.00
Plate, Enameled Red Poppies, Art Crafts Shop, 7 1/2 x 5 1/4 In. 385.00
Plate, Enameled Stylized Blue Flowers, Art Crafts Shop, Square, 6 In. 605.00
Plate, Enameled Stylized Border, Art Crafts Shop, Square, 6 1/2 In. 770.00
Plate, Enameled, Arts & Crafts, Stylized Flowers, Marked, Square, 7 1/2 In. 495.00
Pot, Brass Spigot, Footed, 30 x 22 In. 300.00
Pot, Swing Handle, 21 x 16 In. 220.00
Saucepan, Hinged Finial Lid, Wooden Handle, 18th Century 250.00
Stand, Smoking, Hammered, 4 Rods, Hemispherical Base & Top, Dirk Van Erp, 32 In. . .   2530.00
Tankard, Cover, 1800, 7 In. 295.00
Tea Set, Tray, Silver Bands At Edges, Ear-Form Handles, Joseph Heinrich, 3 Piece 1150.00
Tea Set & Tray, Hammered, Tapered Quatrefoil, Silver Bands, c.1900, 3 Piece 1150.00
Tea Urn, Floral Finial, 2 Leaf Handles, 13 1/2 In. 150.00
Teakettle, Dovetailed Construction, 11 1/2 In. 61.00
Teakettle, Gooseneck Spout, Acorn Finial, Dovetailed, 6 In. 85.00
Teakettle, Gooseneck Spout, Brass Handle & Finial, Dovetailed, 19th Century, 11 In. 190.00
Teakettle, Gooseneck Spout, S.A. Wassberg, 6 1/2 In. 85.00
Teakettle, Gooseneck Spout, Swing Handle, John Getz, 8 In. 1320.00
Teakettle, Oval, Dovetailed Joints, 11 In. 130.00
Tray, Applied Silver Flower, Butterflies, Bird, Square, Gorham, c.1883, 10 In. 1995.00
Tray, Frieze Of Cubist Figures, Del Campo, 11 1/2 x 11 1/2 In. 402.00
Tray, Hammered, Art Nouveau, Benedict, 24 x 11 In. 660.00
Tray, Hammered, Arts & Crafts, Original Patina, 2 Handles, 24 In. 440.00
Tray, Hammered, Cutout Handles, Gustav Stickley, 19 1/2 In. . . . .*Illus*   2200.00
Tray, Hammered, Gustav Stickley, Rolled Edge, Impressed Mark, 12 x 18 In. 1870.00
Tray, Hammered, Original Red Patina, Harry Dixon, 4 In. 120.00
Tray, Hammered, Raised Border, Round, Arts & Crafts, Falick Novick, 11 3/4 In. 350.00
Tray, Hammered, Scalloped & Lobed Rim, New Patina, Dirk Van Erp, 11 3/4 In. 360.00
Tray, Handles, Darcy Gaw Stamp, Round, Dirk Van Erp, c.1911, 18 3/4 In. 5500.00
Tray, Old Mission Copper Kraft, Oval, 6 In. 330.00
Tray, Sailboat Scene, Carence Crafters, 8 x 12 In. 70.00
Umbrella Stand, Riveted Band At Top & Base, Ring Handles, 1930s, 26 1/2 In. 287.00
Urn, Black Painted Base, Art Deco, c.1935, 19 1/2 In. 330.00

Vase, 3 Horizontal Crimped Tubes, Verdigris, Flattened Circular, 15 x 7 In. 86.00
Vase, Arts & Crafts, Green Matte Glaze, 9 x 11 In. 415.00
Vase, Footed, Henrichs, 16 In. 385.00
Vase, Hammered, Baluster, Closed Rim, Closed Box Mark, Dirk Van Erp, 10 In. 5500.00
Vase, Hammered, Baluster, Rolled Rim, New Dark Patina, Open Box Mark, 12 In. 880.00
Vase, Hammered, Broad Shouldered, Stickley Brothers, 8 1/2 In. 500.00
Vase, Hammered, Closed-In Rolled Rim, Leathery Texture, Dirk Van Erp, 15 In. 12100.00
Vase, Hammered, Cylindrical, Ruffled Rim, Original Patina, Albert Berry, 5 In. 470.00
Vase, Hammered, Dragon Relief, Gold Inlay, 3-Footed, Meiji Period, 5 x 11 In. 550.00
Vase, Hammered, Karl Kipp, 6 x 3 In. 412.00
Vase, Hammered, Original Patina, San Francisco, Harry Dixon, 10 In. 990.00
Vase, Hammered, Red Warty, Original Red Patina, Dirk Van Erp, 8 x 7 In. 15400.00
Vase, Hammered, Red, Yellow Enamel Flower, 2 Handles, 7 1/4 x 2 3/4 In. 209.00
Vase, Lotus Shape, Hammered, Molded Lobes, Scalloped, Marie Zimmermann, 10 In. ...   3160.00
Vase, Ribbed, Scalloped Rim, Dark Brown, Green Patina, Marie Zimmermann, 7 In. 4315.00
Wash Basin, Cover, Interior Rack 85.00
Wastebasket, Hammered, 2 Ring Handles, Arts & Crafts, 18 1/2 x 11 In. 357.00
Watering Can, 18th Century, Large 1450.00

COPPER LUSTER items are listed in the Luster category.

CORALENE glass was made by firing many small colored beads on the outside of glassware. It was made in many patterns in the United States and Europe in the 1880s. Reproductions are made today.

Vase, Cranberry, Leaf Pattern, 6 1/2 In. 80.00
Vase, Cranberry, Leaf Pattern, 9 1/2 In. 85.00
Vase, Yellow, 10 In., Pair 500.00

CORDEY China Company was founded by Boleslaw Cybis in 1942 in Trenton, New Jersey. The firm produced gift shop items. In 1969 it was acquired by the Lightron Corp. and operated as the Schiller Cordey Co., manufacturers of lamps. About 1950 Boleslaw Cybis began making Cybis porcelains, which are listed in their own category in this book.

Figurine, Neapolitan, Carrying Bread, 9 1/2 In. 110.00
Figurine, Woman In Bonnet, Holding Basket Of Roses, 10 1/4 In. 190.00

CORKSCREWS have been needed since the first bottle was sealed with a cork, probably in the seventeenth century. Today collectors search for the early, unusual patented examples or the figural corkscrews of recent years.

Angular Handle, Sterling Silver, Cartier, 6 3/4 In. 170.00
Black Cat, 1930s 110.00
Bone Handle, Thomason 550.00
Cork Puller, Champion, Bar Mount, Screw Clamp, Cast Iron, Wooden-Handled Lever ...   127.00
Drunken Scotsman, 1930 ....   90.00
Listerine, Embossed, Late 19th Century 9.00
Rosewood Handle, Barrow & Jackson, England 490.00
Royal Coat Of Arms, Bone Handle, Thomason, England 575.00
Welch's Grape Co. 16.00

CORONATION souvenirs have been made since the 1800s. Pottery, glass, tin, silver, and paper objects with a picture of the monarchs and date have been sold at many coronations. The pieces that mention King Edward VIII, the king who was never crowned, are not rare; collectors should be sure to check values before buying. Related pieces are found in the Commemorative category.

Bank, George V, Cast Iron, England, 1911, 6 5/8 In. 88.00
Bank, George V, English Flags, Variation, White Metal, 1911, 6 3/4 In. 330.00
Bank, Throne, Elizabeth II, Cast Iron, John Harper, 1953, 8 1/8 In. 88.00
Box, Monarch Design Top, White Metal, Souvenir Base, 9 1/2 x 6 x 4 1/2 In. 60.00
Cup & Saucer, Queen Elizabeth, Shelley, 1953 ....   60.00
Figurine, Queen Victoria, On Her Golden Jubilee, Staffordshire, 1877, 17 1/2 In. 275.00

Lighter, Elizabeth, Bust Of Queen Elizabeth 11, Bronze, 1953 . . . . 50.00
Menu, Coronation Banquet, Emperor Nicholas II & Alexandra, Vasnetsov, 1896 . . . . 5710.00

COSMOS is a pressed milk glass pattern with colored flowers made from 1894 to 1915 by the Consolidated Lamp and Glass Company. Tablewares and lamps were made in this pattern. A few pieces were also made of clear glass with painted decorations. Other glass patterns are listed under Consolidated Lamp and also in various glass categories. In later years, Cosmos was also made by the Westmoreland Glass Company.

Cologne Bottle, Stopper 275.00
Creamer, 5 In. 56.00
Lamp, Oil, Westmoreland, 8 In. 75.00
Mustard Jar, 2 1/2 In. 86.00
Pickle Castor, With Frame 795.00
Spooner, 5 In. 144.00
Tumbler, 3 1/2 In. 26.00

COVERLETS were made of linen or wool during the nineteenth century. Most of the coverlets date from 1800 to the 1880s. There was a revival of hand weaving in the 1920s and new coverlets, especially geometric patterns, were made. The earliest coverlets were made on narrow looms, so two woven strips were joined together and a seam can be found. The weave structures of coverlets can include summer and winter, double weave, overshot, and others. Jacquard coverlets have elaborate pictorial patterns that are made on a special loom or with the use of a special attachment. Quilts are listed in this book in their own category.

4 Roses & Stars Medallions, Borders, D. Cosley, Xenia, Ohio, 1859, 91 x 82 In. 425.00
Floral Design On Body, Blue & White, Corner Block Dated 1848, 82 x 78 In. 775.00
Jacquard, 4 Colors, Bird & Tree Border, Elizabeth Town, S.H., 1836, 76 x 70 In. 330.00
Jacquard, 4 Rose Medallions, Foliage, Stars, John Smith, 1838, 76 x 99 In. 935.00
Jacquard, 4 Rose Medallions, J. Armbruster In Corners, 1838, 70 x 78 In. 1430.00
Jacquard, Bird & Tree Border, Red, Blue, White & Gold, 2 Piece, 1836, 76 x 70 In. 365.00
Jacquard, Blue, White, Red & Green, Emmanual Meilly, 1841, 76 x 90 In. 440.00
Jacquard, Capitol Washington, Navy, Red, Natural, 2 Piece, 1846, 76 x 83 In. 355.00
Jacquard, Center Floral Medallion, Red, Green, Navy, H.F. Stager & Son, 80 x 84 In. 440.00
Jacquard, Central Star Medallion, Flowers, Eagle Spandrels, 80 x 102 In. 135.00
Jacquard, Compass Star, 4 Rose Medallions, Peter Lorenz, 1839, 80 x 88 In. 475.00
Jacquard, Double Weave, 4 Rose Medallions, Eagle & Fox Border, 96 x 112 In. 275.00
Jacquard, Double Weave, Floral Medallions, Stylized Flower Border, 85 x 97 In. 230.00
Jacquard, Double Weave, Flower Baskets, Peacocks Feeding Young, 76 x 88 In. 910.00
Jacquard, Double Weave, Geometric Floral, Red, Teal, Natural, 2 Piece, 72 x 86 In. 220.00
Jacquard, Double Weave, Medallions, Flowers, Birds, 1835, 75 x 86 In. 4180.00
Jacquard, Double Weave, Peacocks, Turkeys, Navy Blue & White, 76 x 82 In. 1980.00
Jacquard, Eagles With Liberty, Peacocks, Floral Border, Red, White & Blue, 70 x 83 In. . . 3080.00
Jacquard, Floral Medallions, Bird Borders, Gabriel Rausher, May 10, 1855, 72 x 43 In. . . . 385.00
Jacquard, Floral Medallions, Building & Floral Borders, 66 x 80 In. 220.00
Jacquard, Floral Medallions, Houses, Sailboats Corners, Blue, White, 1841, 74 x 91 In. . . 2420.00
Jacquard, Floral Medallions, Star Flowers, Bird Border, J.H. March, 1841, 80 x 97 In. . . . 495.00
Jacquard, Floral Medallions, Vine Borders, Navy, Salmon, Natural, 1849, 60 x 94 In. 165.00
Jacquard, Floral Stripe, Navy, Olive, Pink & Natural, 1855, 70 x 88 In. 440.00
Jacquard, Floral, Navy & White, Fringe, Double Weave, 2 Piece, 80 x 90 In. 520.00
Jacquard, Floral, Railroad Border, Navy, Natural, M.B. Finney, 2 Piece, 78 x 88 In. 3630.00
Jacquard, Floral, Weeping Willow Border, F.E. Hesse, Logan, Ohio, 1859, 37 x 86 In. 880.00
Jacquard, Flower Urns, Lilies Border Navy, James Pearson Chatham, Ohio, 66 x 84 In. . . . 1320.00
Jacquard, Flowers, Birds, Red, Blue & Green, Michael Weand, 2 Piece, 92 x 81 In. 440.00
Jacquard, Flowers, Red, White, Blue, Signed Emanuel Ettinger, Penn., 1837, 96 x 76 In. . . 175.00
Jacquard, Geometric Foliage, Rose & Leaf Border, Absalom Kinger, 76 x 94 In. 205.00
Jacquard, Grid, Bouquets Of Flowers, American Eagles, Signed, 1830, 87 x 92 In. 2875.00
Jacquard, Houses, Man, Plough, Horses, Farmer Fancy Label, Navy, White, 70 x 82 In. . . . 6930.00
Jacquard, Medallions, Eagle, Independence Hall Border, Blue, White, 78 x 100 In. 400.00
Jacquard, Medallions, Eagle, Tree Border, Blue Wool, White Cotton, 80 x 86 In. 430.00

Jacquard, Medallions, Floral Border, Fringe, Blue Wool, White Cotton, 76 x 92 In. 375.00
Jacquard, Poinsettias, Medallions, Eagle & Tree Border, Red, Blue, 2 Piece, 86 x 74 In. . . 305.00
Jacquard, Rose Medallions, Birds, Floral, G. Heibronn, Lancaster, Oh. 1851, 74 x 88 In. . 660.00
Jacquard, Single Weave, 4 Rose Medallions, Grape Border, Meily, Oh., 72 x 83 In. 330.00
Jacquard, Single Weave, Central Floral Medallion, Floral Borders, 74 x 90 In. 165.00
Jacquard, Star Flower Medallion, Border, Navy, White, D.L. Myers, 1844, 62 x 97 In. . . . 880.00
Jacquard, Star Medallions, Red, Navy, Daniel Bury, New Portage, Oh., 1846, 76 x 90 In. . 880.00
Overshot, Center Floral Medallion, Stylized Floral Borders, 89 x 82 In. 405.00
Overshot, Diamond & Cross, Red & White, 60 x 88 In. 115.00
Overshot, Handwoven In Plymouth, Edison Students, 82 x 100 In. 88.00
Overshot, Reversible Geometric, Wool & Linen, 78 x 70 In. 635.00
Overshot, Roses, Indigo, Natural, Reversible, Lucy Gilbert, Reading, 1833, 86 x 94 In. . . 880.00
Overshot, Star & Floral Chain, Daniel Bordner, 1841, 98 x 83 In. 317.00
Star Medallion, Hearts, Blue & White, Elizabeth U. Parker, 88 x 80 In. 495.00
Summer & Winter, Snowball Variant, Pine Tree Border, 73 x 87 In. 287.00

COWAN POTTERY made art pottery and wares for florists. Guy Cowan made pottery in Rocky River, Ohio, a suburb of Cleveland, from 1913 to 1931. A stylized mark with the word *Cowan* was used on most pieces. A commercial, mass-produced line was marked *Lakeware*. Collectors today search for the Art Deco pieces by Guy Cowan, Viktor Schreckengost, Waylande Gregory, or Thelma Frazier Winter.

Ashtray, Clown, April Green, 3 In. 88.00
Ashtray, Ship, Turquoise, 2 1/2 In. 145.00
Bookends, Boy & Girl, Ivory Glaze, Stamped, 6 1/4 x 4 In. 385.00
Bookends, Elephant, Ivory Glaze, Stamped Mark, Art Deco, 6 1/2 x 3 In., Pair 517.00
Bookends, Flying Fish, Antique Green Glaze, 8 1/2 x 6 In. 550.00
Bookends, Kicking Horse, Waylande Gregory, Egyptian Blue, 9 In. 1980.00
Bookends, Polar Bear, Modern Style, Margaret Postgate 1210.00
Bookends, Pouter Pigeon, Art Deco, Elmer Novotny 1800.00
Bookends, Push-Pull Elephant, Bronze, Margaret Postgate 1980.00
Bookends, Unicorn, Leaves, 7 1/4 In. 187.00
Bowl, Apple Blossom, 9 3/4 x 13 1/2 In. 55.00
Bowl, Cream, Green Interior, Pterodactyl Handles, Pedestal, 15 In. 165.00
Bowl, Cream, Rose Interior, Scalloped, 12 1/2 In. 55.00
Bowl, Delphinium, 11 3/4 In. 77.00
Bowl, Handles, Apple Blossom, Pterodactyl Handles, 15 x 8 3/4 x 5 3/4 In. 295.00
Bowl, Handmade, Waylande Gregory, 2 1/2 x 4 In. 110.00
Bowl, Spattered Green, Red & Black Exterior, Gold Interior, W. Gregory, 4 x 7 1/2 In. . . . 175.00
Bust, La Reveuse, Albert Drexler Jacobson, 1930 . . . . *Illus* 11000.00
Candleholder, Wildwood, Gazelle, Caramel, Waylande Gregory, Pair 325.00
Candlestick, Rowfant, Frank Nelson Wilcox 1200.00
Candlestick, Unicorn, Carel, Waylande Gregory, 5 1/2 In., Pair 740.00
Compote, Hyacinth, 3 3/4 x 7 1/2 In. 66.00
Compote, Mint Green, Ivory, Classical Shape, Mark, 3 1/4 x 6 In., Pair 55.00
Console, Hyacinth, 10 x 9 In. 83.00
Decanter, King, Queen Of Clubs, Oriental Red Glaze, Waylande Gregory, 10 In., Pair . . . 825.00

Cowan, Bust,
La Reveuse,
Albert Drexler
Jacobson, 1930

Cowan, Figurine,
Chinese Horse,
Ralph Howard
Cowan, 1931

Cowan, Fountain
Head, Seahorse,
Oriental Red Glaze,
11 1/4 In.

Cowan, Vase, Jet
Cover & Base,
Terra-Cotta
Glaze, R. Guy
Cowan, 13 1/2 In.

**Never leave your
house keys on the car
ring when you park
the car with an
attendant.**

Figurine, Bird & Wave, Melon Green, Alexander Blazys, 14 1/2 In. 1320.00
Figurine, Boy With Fawn, Waylande Gregory, c.1930, 16 1/2 In. 4840.00
Figurine, Chinese Horse, Ralph Howard Cowan, 1931 . . . .*Illus* 2640.00
Figurine, Fan-Tail Pigeon, Gold, Waylande Gregory, 7 x 9 1/4 In. 330.00
Figurine, Fish, Gilded Design, Orange Ground, Waylande Gregory, 8 1/4 x 12 In. 465.00
Figurine, Flamingo, Special Ivory, 11 In. 1210.00
Figurine, Fountain Of Atoms, 1939 World's Fair 7920.00
Figurine, Girl With Fawn, Boy With Fawn, Waylande Gregory, 15 & 16 1/2 In., Pair 6300.00
Figurine, Introspection, Sleeping Bird, A. Drexler Jacobson, Black, 8 1/2 In. . . . .1980.00 to 2200.00
Figurine, Madonna & Child, Brushed Gold, Waylande Gregory, 7 1/2 x 3 1/4 In. 145.00
Figurine, Margarita, Waylande Gregory, 1929, 16 In. 7290.00
Figurine, Mary, Margaret Postgate, Terra-Cotta, 1929, 10 1/4 In. 3970.00
Figurine, Persephone, Waylande Gregory, c.1930, 14 In. 1980.00
Figurine, Pierette, Primrose, 8 In. 1045.00
Figurine, Pierrette, Old Ivory, Stamped, 8 In. 275.00
Figurine, Swirl Dancer, Art Nouveau, R. Guy Cowan 1760.00
Figurine, Torso, Waylande Gregory, c.1930, 17 1/2 In. 3600.00
Finger Bowl, Melon Green, 4 1/4 In. 72.00
Flower Figure, Diver Woman, R. Guy Cowan 1980.00
Flower Figure, Pavlova, Walter Sinz & R. Guy Cowan 357.00
Flower Figure, Triumphant Lady, R. Guy Cowan, 16 In. 2420.00
Flower Figure, Wildwood Stag, Waylande Gregory 1430.00
Flower Frog, Awakening, Ivory Glaze, Stamped, 8 x 3 3/4 In. 352.00
Flower Frog, Figurine, Duet, Couple Dancing, Ivory Glaze, Stamped, 7 3/4 x 6 1/4 In. 495.00
Flower Frog, Figurine, Loveliness, Ivory Glaze, Incised B., 11 3/4 x 5 1/4 In. 770.00
Flower Frog, Grace, Old Ivory Glaze, Stamped, 6 1/2 x 4 1/4 In. 633.00
Flower Frog, Heavenward, Special Ivory, R. Guy Cowan, 8 In. 630.00
Flower Frog, Lady, Repose, Ivory, 6 In. 550.00
Flower Frog, Laurel, Old Ivory Glaze, Marked, 10 In. 396.00
Flower Frog, Nude, Heavenward, 8 In. 460.00
Flower Frog, Oriental Red, 2 3/4 In. 80.00
Flower Frog, Repose, Ivory Glaze, Stamped, 6 1/2 x 3 In. 231.00
Flower Frog, Scarf Dancer, Original Ivory Glaze, Marked, 7 1/2 In. 154.00
Flower Frog, Scarf Dancer, Special Ivory Glaze, Stamped Mark, 8 x 5 1/4 In. 231.00
Flower Frog, Toadstool, Hand Painted, Waylande Gregory 1485.00
Flower Holder, April Green, 2 3/4 In. 50.00
Fountain Head, Seahorse, Oriental Red Glaze, 11 1/4 In., Pair . . . .*Illus* 2700.00
Lamp, Woodland Nymph, Figural, Waylande Gregory 2920.00
Lamp Base, Beaver Holding Book, Green Matte Glaze, 9 1/2 In. 660.00
Lamp Base, Mottled Gray, Orange Semimatte Glaze, Spherical, Ridged, 8 x 8 In. 99.00
Lamp Base, Oriental Red Glaze, Bulbous, 11 1/2 x 9 1/2 In. 330.00
Nut Cup, Clown, Special Ivory, 3 In. 360.00
Ornament, Fountain, Seahorse, Waylande Gregory, Pair 2700.00
Paperweight, Elephant, Dark Blue, Emerald, Semimatte Glaze, 4 3/4 In. 319.00
Paperweight, Elephant, Gunmetal Black Glaze, 4 1/2 In. 305.00
Paperweight, Elephant, Ivory Glaze, Stamped, 4 1/2 x 3 1/4 In. 330.00
Paperweight, Elephant, Oriental Red, Margaret Postgate, 4 1/2 In. 330.00

Pitcher, Larkspur, 5 1/2 In. 88.00
Plaque, Polo, Viktor Schreckengost 1125.00
Plaque, Thunderbird, Egyptian Blue, Alexander Blazys 1210.00
Plate, Cactus Pattern, Red & Gold, Waylande Gregory, 10 3/4 In. 72.00
Reception Set, Sugar, Creamer, Tray, Turquoise, 3 Piece 105.00
Strawberry Jar, Saucer, Azure, 7 1/2 In. 360.00
Tea Tile, Floral, Special Ivory 77.00
Trivet, Fish, Thelma Frazier, Polychrome, 6 1/2 In. 385.00
Trivet, Lady's Head, 6 1/2 In. 165.00
Trivet, Molded Scene Of Fish, Shades Of Blue, 6 1/2 In. 13.00
Vase, Abstract Design, Several Shades Of Green On White, 8 1/2 In. 1400.00
Vase, Blue, Green, & Yellow Overlapping Circles, Ivory Matte, Hummel, 1928, 6 In. 415.00
Vase, Brown Neck, Dark Turquoise, 5 In. 55.00
Vase, Buff Clay, Sea Green Luster Over Larkspur Blue, R. Guy Cowan, 1917 .... 1760.00
Vase, Chinese Pillow, Dragon, Persian Blue Glaze, 11 1/2 In. 440.00
Vase, Cicadas, Orange Luster Glaze, Ink Mark, 13 1/2 In. 360.00
Vase, Covered Grape, Claire De Lune, 10 In. 440.00
Vase, Dragonfly, 9 In. 326.00
Vase, Dusty Pink, Signed, 5 1/4 In. 55.00
Vase, Flared, Green Mottled Matte Glaze Interior, Mottled Pink Interior, 4 x 6 In. 363.00
Vase, Floor, Oriental Red, Metal Stand, 20 In. 3960.00
Vase, Floral Curio, Larkspur, 5 In. 66.00
Vase, Fluted, Blue Luster Glaze, 11 1/2 In. 550.00
Vase, Jet Cover & Base, Terra-Cotta Glaze, R. Guy Cowan, 13 1/2 In., Pair .... *Illus* 1760.00
Vase, Larkspur, 7 1/2 In. 99.00
Vase, Larkspur, Lakewood Ware, Sea Green Drip, 13 In. 1960.00
Vase, Marigold, 7 x 8 1/4 In. 99.00
Vase, Oriental Red, 7 1/4 In. 130.00
Vase, Ribbed, Feathery Vermilion Glaze, Spherical, Stamped, 10 x 10 In. 135.00
Vase, Seahorse, Large Fan, Delphinium, 8 In. 99.00
Vase, Silhouetted Flowers, Yellow & Green Ground, Black Swirls, Signed, 8 1/2 In. 1210.00
Vase, Teal Base, Brown Top, 5 In. 55.00
Vase, Turquoise Mottled, Green Glaze, Bulbous, 10 3/4 In. 137.00
Vase, Turquoise, Green Mottled Semimatte Glaze, 9 1/2 In., Pair 550.00

CRACKER JACK, the molasses-flavored popcorn mixture, was first made in 1896 in Chicago, Illinois. A prize was added to each box in 1912. Collectors search for the old boxes, toys, and advertising materials. Many of the toys are unmarked.

Banjo, Tin 12.00
Beanie, Green Felt, With Cracker Jack & Cereal Tokens, Pins, 1940s 1000.00
Bookmark, Dog, Die Cut Tin, 1930, 2 1/2 In. 29.00
Bookmark, Tin 15.00
Car, Tin, No. 348 .... 80.00
Marshmallow & Louis In Boat, Sun Rubber 65.00

CRACKLE GLASS was originally made by the Venetians, but most of the ware found today dates from the 1800s. The glass was heated, cooled, and refired so that many small lines appeared inside the glass. It was made in many factories in the United States and Europe.

Cruet, Sapphire Blue, Blue, Reeded Handle, Stopper, 7 1/2 In. 150.00
Figurine, Fish, Open Mouth, Green, 12 In. 50.00
Pitcher, Cover, Cranberry, Reeded Handle, 11 In. 295.00
Pitcher, Cranberry, Amber Handle, 7 1/2 In. 50.00
Vase, Amber, 6 1/4 In. 8.00
Vase, Amethyst, 4 1/2 In. 40.00
Vase, Ruby, Clear Ruffled Edge, Kanawha, 5 In. 80.00

CRANBERRY GLASS is an almost transparent yellow-red glass. It resembles the color of cranberry juice. The glass has been made in Europe and America since the Civil War. It is still being made, and reproductions can fool the unwary. Related glass items may be listed in other categories, such as Northwood, Rubena Verde, etc.

Ashtray, 4 Leaf Clover, 7 x 8 1/4 In. 45.00

Biscuit Jar, Oval, Thumbprint, Enameled Leaves, c.1880, 10 1/2 In. 315.00
Bottle, Enameled White Dots, Gold Bands, 8 1/2 In. 165.00
Bowl, Diamond-Quilted, Clear Center, Silver Plated Stand, 6 3/4 x 9 In. 195.00
Bowl, Hobnail, Applied Milk Glass Rim, Ground Pontil, Hobbs Brokunier 132.00
Bowl, Thumbprint, Enameled Floral Sprays, Beaded Border, Rolled Rim, 6 In. 145.00
Cheese Dome, Thumbprint, Enameled Daisies, Quadruple Plate Stand, 9 In. 460.00
Decanter, Ribbed, Handle, Stopper, 10 In. 175.00
Epergne, 2 Handing Baskets, 14 x 9 In. 253.00
Jewelry Box, Enameled Dove On Cover, Wreath At Base, 2 1/2 x 4 1/2 In. 1235.00
Jug, Claret, Faceted Finial, Cut Handle, 17 In., Pair 805.00
Lamp, Globe, Opalescent Swirl, 5 1/4 In., Pair 110.00
Lamp Shade, Brass Fixture, America, 1870-1920, 16 In. 135.00
Lemonade Set, Mary Gregory Style, Clear Handle, 7 Piece 310.00
Liqueur Set, Gold, Enameled, Decanter & 4 Glasses 176.00
Muffineer, Silver Plated Top, 6 In. 190.00
Night-Light, Ball Shape, Brass, Clear Candle Insert, Brass Foot, 6 1/2 In. 175.00
Pitcher, Clear Handle, Stippled, 11 1/4 In. 225.00
Pitcher, Corset Shape, Floral, Gold Enamel, Scalloped, 9 In. 350.00
Pitcher, Milk, Rippled Thumbprint, Clear Handle, 6 1/8 In. 110.00
Pitcher, Optic Ribbed, Clear Handle, 8 In. 145.00
Pitcher, Slight Ribbing, Gold Trim, Clear Handle, Wafer Foot, 9 3/4 In. 225.00
Pitcher, Water, Mary Gregory Style, Clear Reeded Handle 231.00
Sugar Shaker, Silver Plated Cover, 19th Century, 6 1/4 In. 170.00
Sugar Shaker, Umbrella, White Spatter 345.00
Vase, Bulbous, Twisted Neck & Top, Drip Form Front, 12 3/4 In. 195.00
Vase, Clear To Cranberry, Looped Stem, Star Foot, 8 1/2 In. 250.00
Vase, Cylindrical, Gilt & Flower Bands, Scrolls, Beaded, 13 1/4 In. 431.00
Vase, Opalescent Petal Top, Green Foot & Stem, 11 1/2 In. 190.00
Vase, Satin White Design, Gold Trim, 5 1/8 x 3 In. 110.00
Vase, Tapered Neck, Flared Top, Black Free-Form Lines, Spiral Band, 11 In. 130.00
Vase, Trumpet, Cut To Clear, Pedestal Base, 19th Century, 13 In. 345.00
Water Set, Thumbprint, Round Pitcher, Beaumont Glass Co., 7 Piece 495.00

CREAMWARE, or queensware, was developed by Josiah Wedgwood
about 1765. It is a cream-colored earthenware that has been copied by
many factories. Similar wares may be listed under Pearlware and
Wedgwood.

Box, Screw Cover, Rural Landscape, Woman, Standing Alone, Floral, 1775, 3 In. 1495.00
Bust, William Augustus, Duke Of Cumberland, Full Face, Gorgon's Head, c.1760 ...... 3450.00
Coffeepot, Cover, Pear Shape, Black Transfer, Tea Party, Shepherd Prints, 10 In. 345.00
Compote, Undertray, Fenestrated, c.1800, 4 1/2 x 8 1/2 In. 580.00
Creamer, Cow, Cover, Manganese Patches, Milkmaid Seated Below, 6 5/8 In. 1207.00
Creamer, Domed Cover, Overlapping Leaves, Green, White Florets, 6 In. 1150.00
Jar, Cover, Urn Shape, Floral Swag, Lion Handles, 17 In. 144.00
Juvenile, Mug, Puddle Duck 168.00
Lamp, Nursery, Pierced Heater, Handles, Double Boiler, Candleholder, Cover, 10 In. 8650.00
Mug, Commemorating Battle Of Trafalgar, c.1805, 5 1/8 In. 1035.00
Mug, Floral Design, Floral Border At Rim, Early 19th Century, 4 x 3 In. 230.00
Pitcher, 2 Humorous Scenes, Dentist At Work, Early 19th Century, 7 In. 1035.00
Pitcher, Black Transfer, Washington In Glory, America In Tears, Eagle, 10 In. 1705.00
Pitcher, Copper Luster Pleated Top, Scalloped Rim, Green, Blue, Pink, 7 In., Pair 115.00
Pitcher, Odd Fellows, Text Both Sides, 4 1/2 In. 207.00
Plate, Fern Border, 9 1/2 In. 44.00
Plate, King's Rose, Wood, 19th Century, 7 3/4 In. 145.00
Plate, Manganese, Brown, Teal, Yellow, Green, Staffordshire, 10 In., 4 Piece 1380.00
Platter, Green, Gray, Yellow, Teal Blue, Gadroon Rim, Staffordshire, 1770, 19 In. 2645.00
Platter, Manganese Patches Sponged Ground, Staffordshire, c.1770, 19 In. 546.00
Platter, Scalloped Edge, Oval, England, 19th Century, 14 1/2 x 18 In. 200.00
Punchpot, Cover, Success To The City & Trade Of Cork, 18th Century, 8 In. 990.00
Sauce, Gray Center, Silver Luster, Band Of Stiff Leaves, Staffordshire, 8 In. 515.00
Sugar, Cover, Shackled Woman Slave Praying, Floral Handles, 4 3/8 In. 1725.00
Teapot, Cover, Landscape, Rising Sun, Purple Brocade Border, Greatbatch, 5 In. 1380.00
Teapot, Domed Cover, Manganese, Brown, Flowering Vine, Staffordshire, 5 In. 575.00

Teapot, Flower Knop, Floral Entwined Reeded Handle, Gilt, 6 1/2 In. 230.00
Tureen, Cover, Undertray, Pierced Cover, Floral Finial, Late 18th Century, 6 1/2 In. 745.00
Vase, Garniture, Flowers, Birds, Dolphin Handles, Nove, Venice, 27 1/2 In., Pair 1210.00

CREDIT CARDS, credit tokens, metal charge plates, phone cards, and other similar collectibles that replace money are now part of the numismatic collecting hobby.

Phillips 66, Paper, Green, White, Red Trim, 1940, 3 1/2 x 2 1/4 In. 50.00
Signal Oil Company, Paper, 1938, 3 1/2 x 2 1/4 In. 120.00
Socony-Vacuum White Eagle Division, Paper, White, Red, 1940, 3 3/4 x 2 In. 35.00
Standard Oil Company Of California, Paper, Red, White & Blue, 1931, 3 x 2 In. 185.00
Texaco, Paper, Gray Ground, Black Lettering, 1947, 3 1/2 x 2 1/4 In. 50.00
Texaco, The Texas Company, Paper, 1931, 3 3/4 x 2 1/2 In. 500.00
Texas Company, Paper, 1932, 3 3/4 x 2 1/2 In. 240.00
Union Oil, Paper, 50th Anniversary, 1940, 3 3/4 x 2 3/8 In. 55.00

CROWN DERBY is the name given to porcelain made in Derby, England, from the 1770s to 1935. Pieces are marked with a crown and the letter *D* or the word *Derby*. The earliest pieces were made by the original Derby factory, while later pieces were made by the King Street Partnerships (1848–1935) or the Derby Crown Porcelain Co. (1876–1890). Derby Crown Porcelain Co. became Royal Crown Derby Co. Ltd. in 1890. It is now part of Royal Doulton Tableware Ltd.

Butter, Cover, 1944 . . . . 125.00
Chop Plate, Beaumont 325.00
Coffeepot, Imari 595.00
Creamer, Imari 185.00
Creamer, Vine 150.00
Cup, Saucer & Plate, Tab Handles, No. 7875, Green Mark, 1920s 85.00
Cup & Saucer, Demitasse, Gilt Butterflies & Flowers, c.1888 . . . . 125.00
Dish, Soup, Beaumont 108.00
Jug, Avesbury, Cann Shape, 4 In. 75.00
Jug, Cream, Derby Posies, 1947, 3 1/2 In. 85.00
Paperweight, Barn Owl 150.00
Paperweight, Piglet, 2 1/2 In. 80.00
Paperweight, Puffin, 5 In. 160.00
Pin Tray, Flower, Gold Accents 40.00
Plate, Asian Rose, 9 In. 16.00
Plate, Beaumont, 6 1/4 In. 33.00
Plate, Derby Posies, 9 3/4 In. 75.00
Plate, Honeysuckle, 6 1/4 In. 20.00
Plate, Imari, Gilded Rim, 1902, 9 1/2 In. 110.00
Plate, Red Aves Design, c.1960, 10 1/2 In. 110.00
Sugar, Cover, Derby Posies, 1964, 2 x 3 1/2 In. 65.00
Teapot, Imari 595.00
Vase, Allover Raised Floral, Butterflies, c.1884, 5 x 6 1/2 In. 675.00
Vase, Japan, Stylized Oriental Flowers, Blue Glaze, Red, Green, 1815, 8 In. 687.00

CROWN DUCAL is the name used on some pieces of porcelain made by A. G. Richardson and Co., Ltd., of Tunstall and Cobridge, England. The name has been used since 1916.

Creamer, Atlanta 30.00
Cup & Saucer, Atlanta 30.00
Cup & Saucer, Chintz, Blue 95.00
Cup & Saucer, Rosalie 20.00
Gravy Boat, Bristol 165.00
Plate, Atlanta, 9 3/4 In. 20.00
Plate, Florentine, 6 1/4 In. . . . . .9.00 to 15.00
Plate, Florentine, 7 In. 20.00
Plate, Florentine, 9 3/4 In. 30.00
Plate, Rosalie, 6 1/4 In. 14.00
Plate, Rosalie, 8 1/2 In. 18.00

Plate, Rosalie, 10 1/4 In. 34.00
Sugar, Cover, Atlanta 45.00
Vase, Fruit & Leaves, Green Matte Ground, England, 10 1/2 x 5 1/2 In. 137.00

CROWN MILANO glass was made by Frederick Shirley at the Mt. Washington Glass Works about 1890. It had a plain biscuit color with a satin finish. It was decorated with flowers and often had large gold scrolls.

Biscuit Jar, Butterfly Finial Cover, Hobnail, Gold Chrysanthemums, Signed 1250.00
Biscuit Jar, Jeweled Seaweed, Underwater Scene, Textured Ground 2200.00
Biscuit Jar, Peach, Tree & Blossom, 7 In. 600.00
Biscuit Jar, Rose, Blossom, Melon Ribbed, 6 In. 875.00
Biscuit Jar, Yellow & Rose, Gold Enameled Leaf Design, 7 1/2 In. 800.00
Dish, Gold Floral, Mottled Ground, Square, 4 In. 200.00
Rose Bowl, Leaf Branch Design, 4 1/2 In. 200.00
Sugar & Creamer, Floral 300.00
Vase, Enameled Pink & Blue, 2 Handles, 7 In. 225.00
Vase, Free-Form Gold Accents, 10 1/2 In. 850.00
Vase, Queen's Design, Scrolled Acanthus, Flowers, Gilt, 8-Petal Rim 476.00
Vase, Scottish Thistle, Leaf & Vein Raised In Gold, 8 1/2 In. 1450.00
Vase, Stick, Grape Leaves, Sepia Wash, Gilt, 7 1/2 In. 728.00
Vase, Stick, Raised Segments, Beading, Mottled Ground, 15 In. 1600.00

CROWN TUSCAN pattern is included in the Cambridge glass category.

CRUETS of glass or porcelain were made to hold vinegar, oil, and other condiments. They were especially popular during Victorian times and have been made in a variety of styles since the eighteenth century. Additional cruets may be found in the Castor Set category and also in various glass categories.

Amber Glass, Enameled Flowers, Handle, Ball Stopper, 9 1/2 In. 150.00
Amber Glass, Inverted Thumbprint, Pewter Foot, Handle, Stopper, 10 3/4 In. 175.00
Blue Glass, Enameled Rows Of White Flowers, Bubble Stopper, 6 In. 125.00
Cranberry Glass, Enameled Daisies, Clear Handle, Ball Stopper, 8 In. 195.00
Cranberry Glass, Enameled Flowers & Buds, Dimpled, 8 3/4 In. 225.00
Cranberry Glass, Enameled Gold Branches, Clear Handle, Stopper, 5 3/4 In. 165.00
Cut Glass, Lotus Pattern Variation, Stopper, 6 In. 95.00
Green Glass, White Enamel, Handle, Bubble Stopper, 9 1/2 x 3 1/4 In. 165.00
Lime Green Glass, Enameled Flowers, Blue Leaves, Handle, Ball Stopper, 9 3/4 In. 150.00
Periwinkle Blue Glass, Orange & White Flowers, Handles, Bubble Stopper, 9 1/2 In. 145.00
Sapphire Blue Glass, Enameled Flowers, Amber Handle & Stopper, 8 In. 165.00
Sapphire Blue Glass, Wafer Foot, Gold Flowers, Clear Handle, 8 1/8 In. 175.00

CT GERMANY was first part of a mark used by a company in Altwasser, Germany, in 1845. The initials stand for C. Tielsch, a partner in the firm. The Hutschenreuther firm took over the company in 1918 and continued to use the *CT*.

C.T.

Bowl, Flowers, Gold On Cream Ground, Molded & Pierced Edge, No. 5295, 12 1/2 In. .. 190.00
Plate, Hand Painted, 8 1/4 In. 55.00

CUP PLATES are small glass or china plates that held the cup while a diner of the mid-nineteenth century drank coffee or tea from the saucer. The most famous cup plates were made of glass at the Boston and Sandwich factory located in Sandwich, Massachusetts. There have been many new glass cup plates made in recent years for sale to gift shops or limited edition collectors. These are similar to the old plates but can be recognized as new.

Abolitionist, Leaf Border, Black Transfer, Slave Man, Bundle On Back, 5 7/8 In. 345.00
Castle Garden Battery, New York, Border, Blue, Enoch Wood, 3 5/8 In. 440.00
Castle Garden Battery, New York, Dark Blue Transfer 285.00
Creamware, Praying Slave Man, 6 In. 1725.00
European Scene, Dark Blue, Burslem, Enoch Wood 165.00
Glass, Benjamin Franklin, Lacy Border, Cobalt Blue 1100.00
Glass, Eagle, Medium Sapphire Blue ....440.00 to 605.00

Glass, Fort Pitt Glass Works, 3 5/8 In.	138.00
Glass, Harp, Cobalt Blue	14300.00
Glass, Heart, Amethyst, 19th Century	935.00
Glass, Henry Clay, Peacock Blue, 19th Century	77.00
Glass, Lacy, Amethyst	275.00
Glass, Log Cabin, Yellow Honey Amber, 19th Century	495.00
Glass, Opalescent, Scalloped, Stippled, 3 9/16 In.	500.00
Glass, Roman Rosette, Honey Amber	522.00
Glass, Rope Border, Opaque Blue	990.00
Glass, Rosette & Sheaf Of Wheat, Medium Sapphire Blue	205.00
Glass, Rosette & Sheaf Of Wheat, Stippled, Scalloped Edge, Peacock Blue	66.00
Glass, Ship, Chancellor, Livingstons, Stippled Border, Light Bluish Green	230.00
Glass, Star, Alternating Scalloped & Pointed Border, Sapphire Blue	231.00
Glass, Sunburst, Smaller Sunbursts, Serrations, Scalloped Edge, Honey Amber	55.00
Hunting Scene, Dog, Blue Transfer, Enoch Wood & Sons	90.00
Ironstone, Dark Blue Marbleized, Marked, Pair	65.00
Lafayette, Black Transfer, Black Enamel Stripes, Pearlware, 3 3/4 In.	605.00
Landing Of Lafayette, At Castle Gardens, Blue Transfer	500.00

CURRIER & IVES made the famous American lithographs marked with their name from 1857 to 1907. The mark used on the print included the street address in New York City, and it is possible to date the year of the original issue from this information. Earlier prints were made by N. Currier and use that name from 1835 to 1847. Many reprints of the Currier or Currier & Ives prints have been made. Some collectors buy the insurance calendars that were based on the old prints. The words *large, small,* or *medium folio* refer to size. The original print sizes were very small (up to about 7 x 9 in.), small (8.8 x 12.8 in.), medium (9 x 14 in. to 14 x 20 in.), large (larger than 14 x 20 in.). Other sizes are probably later copies. Other prints by Currier & Ives may be listed in the Card category under Advertising and in the Sheet Music category. Currier & Ives dinnerware patterns may be found in the Adams or Dinnerware categories.

American Homestead, Spring, Trimmed Margins, Frame, 12 x 16 In.	385.00
American Homestead, Summer, Frame, 10 x 14 7/8 In.	220.00
American Railroad Scene, Frame, 9 5/8 x 14 In.	1100.00
California Wonder, Occident, 1873, 11 11/16 x 16 1/16 In.	200.00
Clipper Ship Sweepstakes, Frame, 25 x 31 In.	1250.00
Crack Trotter, 9 1/4 x 14 In.	110.00
Dairy Farm, Frame, 12 x 16 In.	165.00
Darktown Fire Brigade, Last Shake, Frame, 18 3/4 x 22 3/4 In.	247.00
Darktown Fire Brigade Saved, Matted, Frame, 13 3/4 x 17 3/4 In.	355.00
Farmer's Home, Winter, 1863, 16 1/4 x 23 1/8 In.	12000.00
First Care, The Young Mother, Matted, Frame, 22 1/2 x 18 1/2 In.	165.00
Garden Orchard & Vine, Frame, 16 1/2 x 20 1/2 In.	140.00
George Washington, N. Currier, c.1850, 27 1/2 x 21 1/2 In.	1250.00
Great Fight Between The Merrimac & Monitor, Frame, Small Folio	450.00
Great Fire At Boston, 1872, 10 3/4 x 14 1/2 In.	315.00
Great Ocean Yacht Race, Between Henrietta, Fleetwing & Vesta, 1867, 28 In.	1650.00
Halt By The Wayside, 13 1/2 x 17 5/8 In.	385.00
Harvest, Trimmed Margins, Frame, 12 x 15 In.	220.00
Home Of Washington, Mt. Vernon, Frame, 13 3/16 x 17 11/16 In.	275.00
Indian Falls, Frame, 12 3/4 x 15 3/4 In.	55.00
Inviting Dish, Still Life, Frame, 1879, 10 1/2 x 14 1/4 In.	225.00
Ivy Glad Ruins, Framed, Medium Folio	137.00
James K. Polk, Frame, 20 1/2 x 15 3/4 In.	99.00
Lake George, N.Y., Framed, 12 3/4 x 16 3/4 In.	192.00
Lakeside Home, Frame, 13 x 20 1/2 In.	275.00
Little Snowbird, Frame, 19 3/4 x 16 1/8 In.	137.00
Maj. Gen. William T. Sherman, Matted, Frame, 21 x 17 1/2 In.	220.00
Moonlight, The Ruins, 11 x 14 1/8 In.	160.00
My Three White Kitties, Learning Their ABC's, Frame, 11 x 14 In.	165.00

O'Sullivan's Cascade, Lake Of Killarney, Frame, 12 1/2 x 16 1/2 In. 165.00
Partridge Shooting, Matted, Frame, 12 x 15 7/8 In. 165.00
Race On The Mississippi, Frame, 1870, 11 1/2 x 15 1/2 In. 630.00
Ross Trevor, Frame, 13 x 15 3/4 In. 121.00
Sailor's Adieu, N. Currier, Beveled Frame, 16 1/4 x 12 1/4 In. 165.00
Sperm Whale In A Flurry, 1852, Small Folio 880.00
Tomb Of Washington, Frame, 13 7/8 x 17 7/8 In. 165.00
Tribute Of Autumn, Frame, 1870, 12 1/2 x 16 1/2 In. 245.00
Trotting Stallion, Phallas, 24 x 35 In. 962.00
Vigilant & Valkyrie In A Thrash To Windward, Frame, 1893, 19 3/8 x 26 1/2 In. 515.00

CUSTARD GLASS is a slightly yellow opaque glass. It was first made in
England in the 1880s and was first made in the United States in the
1890s. It has been reproduced. Additional pieces may be found in the
Cambridge, Fenton, Heisey, and Northwood categories. Custard glass
is called Ivorina Verde by Heisey and other companies.

Argonaut Shell, Berry Bowl, Master 225.00
Argonaut Shell, Butter 350.00
Argonaut Shell, Pitcher, Water 465.00
Argonaut Shell, Spooner 140.00
Argonaut Shell, Sugar 225.00
Argonaut Shell, Tumbler, Gold 95.00
Banded Ring, Berry Set, Gold Trim, 3 1/2-In. Bowl, 5 Piece 330.00
Beaded Circle, Berry Bowl, Gold, Master 585.00
Beaded Circle, Sauce, 4 3/4 In. 185.00
Chrysanthemum Sprig, Compote, Jelly 60.00
Chrysanthemum Sprig, Tumbler, Blue Design 200.00
Intaglio, Berry Bowl, Master 250.00
Intaglio, Butter .... .300.00 to 400.00
Intaglio, Creamer .... .125.00 to 325.00
Intaglio, Cruet, Gold & Green, 6 1/4 In. 285.00
Intaglio, Jelly Dish, Gold & Green, 4 1/2 In. 235.00
Intaglio, Pitcher .... .395.00 to 585.00
Intaglio, Salt & Pepper, Gold & Green, 3 1/4 In. 275.00
Intaglio, Sauce, Gold & Green, 21 3/4 In. 134.00
Intaglio, Spooner .... .125.00 to 265.00
Intaglio, Sugar .... .175.00 to 385.00
Intaglio, Water Set, Green & Gold, 9 1/2 In. 1495.00
Inverted Fan & Feather, Table Set, 3 Piece 375.00
Louis XV, Creamer 85.00
Louis XV, Water Set, Gold Trim, 7 1/2- In. Pitcher, 5 Piece 500.00
Maize is its own category in this book.
Nautilus, Sugar & Creamer 175.00

CUT GLASS has been made since ancient times, but the large majority
of the pieces now for sale date from the brilliant period of glass design,
1880 to 1905. These pieces have elaborate geometric designs with a
deep miter cut. Modern cut glass with a similar appearance is being
made in England, Ireland, and the Czech and Slovak republics. Chips
and scratches are often difficult to notice but lower the value dramati-
cally. A signature on the glass adds significantly to the value. Other cut
glass pieces are listed under factory names.

Banana Bowl, Hobstar & Daisy, 11 In. 190.00
Banana Bowl, Napoleon's Hat, Crosshatch Vesicas, 8 1/2 x 12 In. 775.00
Basket, Daisies, Geometric, Twisted Handle, 9 1/2 x 7 1/2 In. 395.00
Basket, Palm, Taylor Bros., 4 3/4 x 8 1/4 In. 435.00
Biscuit Jar, Canes, Lavender To Clear, England, 7 In. 225.00
Bonbon, 24-Point Hobstar, Strawberry-Diamond & Fan, 2 1/2 x 5 1/2 In. 150.00
Bottle, Scent, Flower & Leaf Design, 14K Gold Screw Cap, Collar, 3 3/4 In. 770.00
Bottle, Whiskey, Vertical Ribbons Of Bull's-Eyes, 12 In. 425.00
Bowl, 4 Floral Panels, Pinwheel Bands, Oblong, 10 x 6 1/4 In. 165.00
Bowl, Berlyn, 20-Point Hobstar Base, Quaker City, 5 3/4 In. 350.00

Bowl, Canes, Square, 9 In. 30.00
Bowl, Carolyn, Crossed Ovals, Rolled Edge, Signed, Hoare, 7 1/4 In. 395.00
Bowl, Central Star, Allover Diamonds, Linear & Crosshatch, Scalloped Edge, 10 In. 75.00
Bowl, Elite, Expanding Star, 9 1/4 In. 395.00
Bowl, Fans, Feathered Buzzsaws, Brilliant, 8 In. 112.00
Bowl, Fern, Hobstar, Star, Brilliant, 9 In. 450.00
Bowl, Fruit, Hobstars, Caned & Notched Diamonds, Gundy Chapperton, 8 3/4 In. 230.00
Bowl, Hobstars, Framed Hobnail Design, 9 x 4 In. 450.00
Bowl, Marie, Hobstars In Diamond Chain, Octagonal, 10 x 3 1/2 In. 365.00
Bowl, Pinwheels, Bull's-Eye Handles, 4 Sections, 11 1/2 In. 250.00
Bowl, Prisms, Rayed Fans, Hobstars & Strawberry-Diamonds, Alford, 9 1/2 x 4 In. 440.00
Bowl, Roses & Geometric Bands, c.1895, 8 In. 195.00
Bowl, Star & Pineapple, Sawtooth Scalloped Edge, 20th Century, 17 In. 85.00
Bowl, Sterling Silver Rim, Beddy & Whitmore, 8 In. 395.00
Bowl, Stylized Star, Sawtooth Scalloped Edge, Brilliant, 8 In. 63.00
Box, Silver Mounted, Geometric Design, Hinged Cover, Germany, 6 1/4 In. 635.00
Cake Plate, Cover, Star & Hobstars, 10 In. 75.00
Cake Plate, Geometric Star, Scalloped Edge, 12 In. 440.00
Candlestick, Flute, Hobstar Base, 8 In., Pair 475.00
Candlestick, Hobstar Base, 8 In., Pair 275.00
Candlestick, Panel Cutting, Teardrop Stem, 6 1/4 In., Pair 250.00
Carafe, Pillar & Prism, Sterling Silver Top, Gorham, 8 1/2 In., Pair 850.00
Celery Vase, Fans, Horseshoe & Diamond, 9 1/2 In. 200.00
Celery Vase, Fans, Linear Cuts, 9 3/4 In. 110.00
Celery Vase, Hobstar, Cane, Strawberry-Diamond & Fan, 13 x 5 In. 200.00
Centerpiece, Russian, Starburst, 20 x 8 In. 575.00
Champagne, Colonial, Repousse Silver Rim, Gorham, 3 1/2 In., 6 Piece 975.00
Champagne, Fluted, Gravic Floral, Cut Panels, Diamond Point, 8 1/2 In. 17.00
Champagne, Rosebud & Ribbon, Dorflinger, Pair 130.00
Claret, Hinged Cover, Scrolled Leavese, Victorian, 10 In. 489.00
Cologne Bottle, Hobstars, Canes & Fans, Strawberry-Diamond, 6 x 5 1/2 In. 255.00
Compote, Bell Shape, Allover Geometric, Brilliant, Sawtooth Edge, 5 x 6 In. 195.00
Compote, Cover, Crosshatch Ovals, Flame Finial, 6 Sides, 17 In., Pair 1540.00
Compote, Cover, Diamonds, Trumpet Shape, c.1895, 14 1/2 In. 330.00
Compote, Cover, Underplate, Crosshatch Ovals, Flame Finial, 9 1/2 In., Pair 770.00
Compote, Fan & Diamond, Flat Edge, Crosshatch Diamonds On Foot, 9 In., Pair 1100.00
Compote, Magnet, Footed, Blackmer, 8 x 6 In. 125.00
Compote, Paneled, Brilliant, 16 1/2 x 8 In. 100.00
Compote, Pineapple, Paneled, Scalloped Edge, 12 1/2 x 8 In. 220.00
Cooler, Champagne, Dogwood & Floral Spray, Silver Plated Liner, 1890, 7 x 8 In. 155.00
Cruet, Feathered Pinwheel, Stars, Fans, Double Ring Neck, Teardrop Stopper, 7 1/2 In. .. 305.00
Cruet, Hobstars, Notched Diamonds & Fans, Stopper, 6 1/4 In. 70.00
Decanter, Allover Stars, Crosshatch, Stopper, 16 1/4 In., 3 Piece 600.00
Decanter, Croesus, Turquoise To Clear, Stopper, J. Hoare, 13 In. ....*Illus* 30000.00
Decanter, Diamond-Point, Mushroom Finial, Faceted Neck, England, 11 In., Pair 195.00
Decanter, Faceted Body, Stepped Shoulder, Mallet Shape, Domed Stopper, 9 In. 220.00
Decanter, Faceted Ovals & Diamonds, Oval Stopper, England, 13 In, Pair 3450.00
Decanter, Florence Stars, Prisms, Fan & Hobstars, Rayed Star Base, Stopper, 11 In. 725.00
Decanter, Hobstars, Beaded Miters, Hour Glass Shape, Triple Notched Handle, 13 In. ... 395.00
Decanter, Hobstars, Fans, Crosshatch, Chartreuse To Clear, Tapered, 18 In. 335.00
Dish, Ice Cream, Arabian, Egginton, 6 In. 225.00
Dish, Pinwheel, Strawberry-Diamond, Notched Handles, 4 Sections, 11 In. 275.00
Glove Box, Engraved Flowers & Leaves, Satin, Bull's-Eye, 6 x 4 x 3 1/2 In. 765.00
Goblet, Flared, Thumbprint, Ruby To Clear, Germany, 1930, 5 1/2 In., 12 Piece 500.00
Goblet, Water, St. Louis, 7 1/2 In., 12 Piece 518.00
Goblet, Wheeler Pattern, Mt. Washington, 6 1/2 In. 85.00
Humidor, Tobacco, Hobstar, Notching, Fans, Ground Stopper, 4 x 4 1/2 In. 295.00
Hurricane Shade, Star, Rosettes, Wheat Stalks, Cylindrical, 23 1/2 In. 2185.00
Ice Bucket, Hobstar, Strawberry-Diamond & Fan, Signed, 5 In. 120.00
Jar, Prisms, Silver Sterling Cover, 7 x 6 1/2 In. 775.00
Jewelry Box, Cover, Bull's-Eye Around Top & Base, 6 x 3 1/4 In. 540.00
Jug, Claret, Leaves, Silver Mounted, Continental, 11 3/4 In., Pair 2640.00

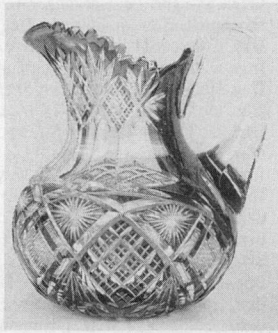

Cut Glass, Decanter,
Croesus, Turquoise To Clear,
Stopper, J. Hoare, 13 In.

Cut Glass, Punch Bowl, Stand,
Dauntless, Blue To Clear,
Bergen, 14 In.

Cut Glass, Pitcher,
Water, Harvard, Emerald To Clear,
8 1/2 In.

Jug, Claret, Stars, Silver Plate, Ornate Mounts, Rampant Lion Finial, England, 12 In.	605.00
Jug, Claret, Swirl, Silver Mounted, Leaves & Grapevines, P.B. & Co., 13 1/4 In.	935.00
Jug, Hobstar & Fan, Scalloped Edge, Handle, Hobstar Cut Base, Brilliant, 11 In.	805.00
Jug, Whiskey, Strawberry-Diamond & Fan, Sterling Silver Stopper	510.00
Lamp, Boudoir, Mushroom Shade, Butterfly & Floral Design, Prisms, 20 In.	575.00
Lamp, Hall, Floral Design	412.00
Muffineer, Sterling Silver Top, Watson, 7 1/2 In.	231.00
Pitcher, Creswick, Sterling Silver Rim, Egginton, 9 1/2 In.	975.00
Pitcher, Electra, Geometric, Bergen, 9 In.	3305.00
Pitcher, Hobstars, Strawberry-Diamond & Fan, Triple Cut Handle, 28 Oz.	496.00
Pitcher, Ice Water, Notched Flutes, Hobstars, Silver Collar, Wilcox Silver Co., 9 In.	1210.00
Pitcher, Russian, Cut Handle, Meriden, 10 In.	695.00
Pitcher, Sawtooth, 8 3/4 In.	135.00
Pitcher, Water, Cut Hobstars, Fans & Notched Diamonds, 9 In.	275.00
Pitcher, Water, Harvard, Emerald To Clear, 8 1/2 In. ....*Illus*	3000.00
Pitcher, Water, Pineapple, Spear & Diamond Pattern, 4 1/2 In.	450.00
Plate, Ice Cream, Snowflake, c.1905, 8 In., 9 Piece	165.00
Plate, Open Petal Design, Hobstar Banding, Pitkin & Brooks, 6 In., 5 Piece	400.00
Plate, Pointed Loops, Brilliant, Square, 7 In.	175.00
Plate, Snowflake Center, Hobstar Border, Iorio, 1969, 8 In.	80.00
Platter, Ice Cream, Daisy & Button, Double Sunburst, 9 x 16 In.	300.00
Punch Bowl, Stand, Dauntless, Blue To Clear, Bergen, 14 In. ....*Illus*	5500.00
Punch Bowl, Stand, Large Starburst Design, Scalloped Rim, 11 1/2 x 12 In.	2290.00
Punch Set, Daisy & Thistle Allover, 13 3/4 In., 9 Piece	920.00
Punch Set, Monarch, Footed Pedestal Cups, Hoare, 13 1/2 x 13 In., 13 Piece	1700.00
Relish, Floral & Laurel Festoons, 3 Sections, Silver Rim, Wallace, c.1930, 10 3/4 In.	105.00
Rose Bowl, 2 Pinwheels, Harvard Type, 6 In.	325.00
Rose Bowl, Monarch, Hoare, 7 In.	275.00
Salt, Cranberry To Clear, Rayed Base, 1 1/8 x 2 In.	125.00
Salt, Diamond & Fan, Scalloped Sawtooth Edge, 1900-1920, 3 1/4 In., 8 Piece	100.00
Sherbet, Diamonds & Fans, c.1915, 4 3/4 In., 5 Piece	110.00
Shot Glass, Thistle Shape, Thistle Border, Ireland, 2 In.	50.00
Spooner, 2 Large Hobstars, Elongated Diamonds, 4 1/2 In.	190.00
String Holder, Engraved Initials, Prism Base, Sterling Silver Cover, Gorham, 3 In.	4495.00
Sugar, Creamer & Spooner, Empress, Pitkin & Brooks	675.00
Sugar & Creamer, Strawberry-Diamond & Fan, Prisms, Triple Notched Handle, 2 In.	225.00
Sweetmeat, Cover, Diamond, Diamond Border, Star Cut Foot, Urn Shape, 11 In., Pair ...	1100.00
Syrup, Caned Diamonds, Separated By Fans, Silver Plated Top, 5 In.	250.00
Syrup, Cover, Crosshatch, Brass Covered Handle, Mid 19th Century, 8 In.	355.00
Tankard, Hobstars, Canes, Cut Handle, 9 x 8 In.	560.00

Tankard, Pinwheel & Fan, 12 In.	100.00
Tazza, Pinwheel & Harvard, 9 1/2 x 8 In.	395.00
Toothpick, Hobstar Cuttings, Heavy Foot, 3 3/4 In.	225.00
Tray, Crosscut Diamond, Strawberry-Diamond & Hobstar, 15 1/2 x 8 1/2 In.	850.00
Tray, Diamond Cut Band, Star Cut Center, Oval, c.1960, 8 x 14 In.	115.00
Tray, Hobstars & Fans, Heart Shape, 8 x 9 1/4 In.	250.00
Tray, Ice Cream, Hobstar, 17 1/2 In.	1050.00
Tray, Ice Cream, Hobstar, Strawberry-Diamond & Fan, 13 1/2 In.	170.00
Tray, Russian, Barge Shape, 11 In.	325.00
Tray, Wheat, Oval, Hoare, 10 12 x 7 In.	895.00
Tumbler, Diamond, Claret Cut To Clear, c.1890, 4 1/2 In., 6 Piece	305.00
Urn, Cover, Allover Diamond, 14 In., Pair	865.00
Urn, Diamond, Blaze Star Base, Bell Shape, St. Louis, 15 In.	2070.00
Urn, Diamond, Blaze Star, Thick Base, Medici, 10 1/2 x 7 1/4 In., Pair	1320.00
Urn, Diamond, Sawtooth Edge, Domed Lid, Finial, Round Foot, 1800s, 17 In., Pair	863.00
Urn, Hobstar, Strawberry-Diamond, 7 3/4 x 9 1/4 In.	1690.00
Urn, Neoclassical Style, Diamond, Bronze Dore, 16 1/2 In., Pair	1760.00
Vase, Allover Geometric, Early 20th Century, 7 x 15 7/8 In.	86.00
Vase, Column Of Hobstars, Bordered By Caned Vesicas, Hobstar Base, 15 In.	385.00
Vase, Cranberry Cut To Clear Satin, Bulbous, 12 In., Pair	175.00
Vase, Engraved Floral, Elongated Neck, Imperial Glass Mfg., 1912, 23 In.	6900.00
Vase, Floral, Scalloped, Round Foot, White To Clear, Gold, 13 1/2 In., Pair	880.00
Vase, Geometric, Ribbed Neck, Brilliant, 10 In.	935.00
Vase, Geometric, Smoke Glass, Art Deco, Mona France, 12 1/2 In.	69.00
Vase, Green Cut To Clear, Honesdale, 6 x 8 In.	1250.00
Vase, Hobstar, Strawberry-Diamond, Cane & Fan, Black, Starr & Frost Sterling, 12 In.	2200.00
Vase, Hobstars Within Diamonds, Surrounded By Flowers, c.1900, 12 In.	105.00
Vase, Pansy Floral, J. Hoare & Co., 1853, 12 In.	220.00
Vase, Trumpet, Daisies, Notched Base, 19th Century, 12 1/4 In.	120.00
Vase, Trumpet, Geometric, Rayed Base, Brilliant, 8 In.	165.00
Vase, Trumpet, Star & Pinwheel, 14 x 6 In.	195.00
Vase, Tulip Shape, Flowers, c.1915, 9 1/2 In.	220.00
Wine, Cranberry To Clear, Band Foot, 4 1/2 In.	190.00
Wine, Ornate, Cobalt Blue To Clear, St. Louis, 8 1/8 In., 5 Piece	288.00
Wine, Ornate, Red To Clear, St. Louis, 8 1/8 In., 5 Piece	345.00
Wine, Royal, Notched Stem, 20-Point Hobstar Foot, Dorflinger, 5 In.	50.00
Wine, Strawberry-Diamond & Fan, Cranberry To Clear, Dorflinger	250.00

CUT VELVET is a special type of art glass, made with two layers of blown glass, which shows a raised pattern. It usually had an acid finish or a texture like velvet. It was made by many glass factories during the late Victorian years.

Creamer, Blue	128.00
Cruet, Robin's-Egg Blue, Diamond-Quilted, Burmese, 9 In.	385.00
Vase, Stick, Diamond-Quilted, 19th Century, 6 In.	115.00

CYBIS porcelain is a twentieth-century product. Boleslaw Cybis came to the United States from Poland in 1939. He started making porcelains in Long Island, New York, in 1940. He moved to Trenton, New Jersey, in 1942 as one of the founders of Cordey China Co. and started his own Cybis Porcelains about 1950. The firm is still working. See also Cordey.

CYBIS

Figurine, Baby Egret	65.00
Figurine, Betty Blue, Young Girl In Victorian Dress, Marked, 8 1/2 In.	165.00
Figurine, Bunny, Pat-A-Cake, 4 1/2 In.	100.00
Figurine, Carousel Pony, Sugar Plum., 12 1/2 In.	885.00
Figurine, Cat With Ribbon, 9 x 5 3/4 In.	345.00
Figurine, Duckling, Baby Brother, Stamped, 4 In.	55.00
Figurine, First Flight, Girl With Blue Bird, Wooden Base, 4 1/2 In.	55.00
Figurine, Lotus Blossom, Oriental Girl Head, 14 In.	245.00
Figurine, Oceania, Sea King's Steed, 14 In.	985.00
Figurine, Owl, Baby, 4 1/2 In.	125.00
Figurine, Sir Henry Escargot, Snail, 1968, 3 In.	425.00
Figurine, Wendy, Young Girl In Nightgown Holding Doll, Signed, 6 1/2 In.	132.00

Czechoslovakia Pottery, Plate, Romantic
Couples, Yellow Panels, 10 3/4 In.

**When you move, remember that
there is no insurance coverage for
breakage if the items are not
packed by the shipper.**

CZECHOSLOVAKIA is a popular term with collectors. The name, first used as a mark after the country was formed in 1918, appears on glass and porcelain and other decorative items. Although Czechoslovakia split into Slovakia and the Czech Republic on January 1, 1993, the name continues to be used in some trademarks.

CZECHOSLOVAKIA GLASS, Bowl, Yellow, Black & Blue Enamel Band, 3 1/2 x 8 In.	935.00
Goblet, Cobalt Blue Cut To Clear, 5 1/2 In., 12 Piece	355.00
Lamp, Boudoir, Orange & Yellow Spatter	125.00
Powder Jar, Cobalt Blue Cut To Clear, Round, 4 x 2 1/2 In.	120.00
Tray, Pinwheel Design, 11 In.	115.00
CZECHOSLOVAKIA POTTERY, Charger, Classical Women, Border, B. Bloch & Co., 15 In.	275.00
Figurine, Nymph On Shell, Multicolored, Signed, 20 1/4 In.	862.00
Flower Holder, Bird & Stump	23.00
Plate, Iridescent, Blue Band, Roses, Alfrohlian, 11 In.	65.00
Plate, Romantic Couples, Yellow Panels, 10 3/4 In. ....*Illus*	35.00
Vase, Blue, Black Trim, Bulbous, 6 3/4 In.	48.00
Vase, Orange Iridescent Glaze, Porcelain, c.1940, 8 In.	12.00
Vase, Red Mottled, Jet Rim, Applied Serpentine Case, 8 In.	70.00
Wall Pocket, Orange Parrot, On Branch, 3 Openings	40.00

D'ARGENTAL is a mark used in France by the Compagnie des Cristalleries de St. Louis. The firm made multilayered, acid-cut cameo glass in the late nineteenth and twentieth centuries. D'Argental is the French name for the city of Munzthal, home of the glassworks. Later they made enameled etched glass.

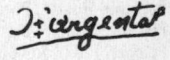

Box, Cover, Flowers, Green To Pink, 4 1/2 x 7 In.	1485.00
Vase, Cameo, Etched Flower Buds & Leaves, Signed, 9 1/2 In.	990.00
Vase, Cameo, Floral, Brown To Cream, 6 In.	1045.00
Vase, Flowing Branch & Leaves, Tulip Shape, Marked, 13 1/2 In.	2100.00
Vase, Lake, Mountains, Trees, Shoreline, Etched, 7 1/8 x 3 1/4 In.	695.00
Vase, Landscape, Palm Trees & Mountains By Water, Brown, Amber, 1910, 14 In.	1495.00
Vase, Leaves, Blue Cut To Clear Satin, 6 In.	880.00
Vase, Ocean Sunset, Oak Leaves, Gray, Amethyst, Light Blue, 13 3/4 In.	3696.00
Vase, Trees, Purple Cut To Deep Pink, 12 In.	1210.00

DANIEL BOONE, a pre-Revolutionary War folk hero, was a surveyor, trapper, and frontiersman. A television series, which ran from 1964 to 1970, was based on his life and starred Fess Parker. All types of Daniel Boone memorabilia are collected.

Book, Children's, Hard Bound, Color Illustrations, 60 Pages	30.00
Book, Comic, 1968	5.00
Knife & Canteen Set, Fess Parker, Box, Shrink Wrapped, 1964	35.00
Reel, View-Master, 4-Leaf Clover	17.00
Salt & Pepper	22.00

DAUM, a glassworks in Nancy, France, was started by Jean Daum in 1875. The company, now called *Cristalleries de Nancy*, is still working. The *Daum Nancy* mark has been used in many variations. The name of the city and the artist are usually both included.

Bowl, Blackberries On Thorny Vines, Gray, Green, Pink, Cameo, Signed, c.1910, 6 In. . . .		2800.00
Bowl, Coreopsis Daisies, Yellow, Green, White, Pink Mottled, 1910, 7 3/4 In.		2070.00
Bowl, Grapes On Vine, 2 Applied Glass Snails, Signed, Early 20th Century, 5 1/4 In.		1092.00
Bowl, Gray, Yellow, Green, Pink & Purple, Blackberries, Cameo, Oval, 1910		2800.00
Bowl, Ice Crystal Design, Pale Yellow, Orange, Etched, 3 x 8 In.		520.00
Bowl, Leaves & Berries, Ruffled Edge, Square, Cameo, 3 x 8 In.		1705.00
Bowl, Leaves, Scalloped Edge, Gray Infused With Crimson, Signed, c.1915, 3 1/4 In.		2070.00
Bowl, Purple Tiger Lilies, White, Brown, Inverted Rim, Round Foot, Cameo, 1914, 8 In. .		3450.00
Bowl, Rosehip Branches, Flowers, Yellow, White, Dark Cranberry, Cameo, 4 1/2 In.		1495.00
Bowl, Spring Landscape, Green, Brown, Black, Gray, 1910, 8 In.		1380.00
Box, Cover, Ivy, Berries, Dark Purple, Orange, Brown, Green, Cameo, 1910, 4 In.		1725.00
Box, Cover, Pink Star Flowers, Green Leaves, Yellow, Dark Purple, Cameo, 4 In.		2070.00
Candy Dish, Trees By A Lake, Yellow, Red Mottled, Dark Green, Square, 1910, 5 1/4 In. .		632.00
Centerpiece, Ice Crystal Design, Square, 1950, 3 3/8 In.		172.00
Chandelier, 2-Tone Yellow, 2 Tiers, Etched, 1925, 33 In.		13800.00
Chandelier, Floral Design, Ram's Head Hardware, Signed, 16 x 6 1/2 In.		2860.00
Chandelier, Flowers, Wrought Iron, Signed, 1900, 26 x 15 In.		4600.00
Chandelier, Gray Shade, Silver Metal, Etched, 1925, 26 In.		8050.00
Cologne Bottle, Floral, Green Cut To White, Stopper, Cameo, 6 1/2 In.		175.00
Ewer, Pink, Orange & Green Powder Overlay, Signed, c.1920, 10 In.		1035.00
Figurine, Bugatti, Frosted Interior, 1980s, 4 x 15 1/2 In.		1250.00
Figurine, Cat, 8 1/2 In.		330.00
Figurine, Dolphin, Long Sweeping Tail, Metal Stand, 6 1/4 x 18 In.		373.00
Figurine, Sailboat, On Shaped Square Base, Signed, France, 25 3/8 In.		460.00
Lamp, Gray, Orange, Lemon, Blue Domed Shade, Wrought Iron, 1900, 24 1/3 In.		2300.00
Lamp, Landscape, Dark Brown Trees, Sunset, Cameo, Wrought Iron, 1900, 17 In.		11500.00
Lamp, Landscape, River & Sunset Scene, Leafy Trees, Wrought Iron, 1900, 35 In.		14375.00
Lamp, Leaves, Wrought Iron, Signed, 1900, 17 In.		18400.00
Lamp, Orange, Purple, Bell Shade, Wrought Iron, 1925, 14 3/4 In.		2300.00
Lamp, White, Cobalt Blue, Mushroom Shade, Ball Feet, Wrought Iron, 11 In.		1265.00
Lamp Base, Flowering Magnolia Branches, Gold, Yellow, Orange, Cameo, 10 In.		3450.00
Lamp Base, Trumpet Flowers Rising From Broad Leaves, Orange, Brown, 1910, 23 In. . . .		1380.00
Letter Opener, Debussy, Pate-De-Verre Handle, 2 Musicians, Box, Signed, 10 1/2 In. . . .		287.00
Letter Opener, Wagnerian Figure, Lavender, Pate-De-Verre, Signed, 11 1/2 In.		1045.00
Night-Light, Black Trees In The Rain, Enameled, Pale Pink, Green, 8 3/4 In.		3450.00
Perfume Bottle, Daisy Spray, Red Ground, Gold Enamel, Silver Base, Stopper, 5 In.		1035.00
Perfume Bottle, Purple Violets, Orange Centers, Flattened Round Stopper, 4 In.		2300.00
Pitcher, Orange, Dark Pink Tulip Sprigs, Dark Pink Floral Border, Loop Handle, 4 In. . . .		2300.00
Pitcher, Pink Flowers On Brown Branches, White, Orange, Ear Shape Handle, 3 In.		2990.00
Salt, Black Tree Lined Shore, Distant Ruins, 2 Upright Handles, 1 3/8 In.		575.00
Torchere, Pink, Yellow Shade, Wrought Iron, Spreading Foot, Electrified, 67 In.		2875.00
Vase, 4 Blossoming Crocuses, Crimson, Gray, Flared Rim, Cameo, 1900, 5 3/4 In.		2700.00
Vase, Bell Shape, Deep Emerald, Square Foot, 1925, 10 1/4 In.		3162.00
Vase, Berries & Leaves, Cameo, 12 In. . . . .*Illus*		8680.00
Vase, Blue, Enameled Floral, Butterfly Mark, 12 1/2 In.		1750.00
Vase, Blue, Purple, Green Mottled, 25 1/2 In.		1955.00
Vase, Burgundy Berry Branch, Mottled Ground, Mounted As Lamp, 14 3/4 In.		1955.00
Vase, Cyclamen, Purple, Red, Green Leaves, 8 In.		2415.00
Vase, Daisy, White Enameled Berries, Gilt Silver Mounted, Cameo, 1900, 5 In.		400.00
Vase, Dark Purple, Orange, Red Lady Slippers, Green Stems, Yellow, Purple, 1895, 5 In. .		2415.00
Vase, Dutch Lowland Scenes, Sailboats & Windmills, 1890, 5 x 3 1/2 In.		805.00
Vase, Elongated & Pulled Rim, Free-Form Handles, c.1950, 9 In.		345.00
Vase, Enameled Sailing Ships, Rocky Shore, Square, 3 1/4 In.		1155.00
Vase, Engraved Wild Roses, Gold Enameled Borders, Signed, 19th Century, 7 1/4 In. . . .		805.00
Vase, Fall Landscape, Trees By The Water, Yellow, Green, Brown, Cameo, 2 1/2 In.		1495.00
Vase, Floral, Pale Pink, Purple, Carved, 1900, 5 1/2 In.		4600.00
Vase, Floral, Wheat Sheafs, 4 Colors, Cameo, Marked, 19 1/2 In.		2900.00

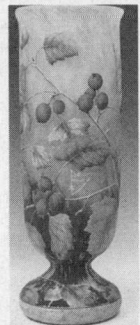

Shallow nicks and rough edges on glass can sometimes be smoothed off with fine emery paper.

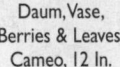

Daum, Vase,
Berries & Leaves,
Cameo, 12 In.

Daum, Vase, Wine Trees,
Sunset Ground, Cameo,
Signed, 12 1/2 In.

Vase, Flowers, Pink, Gold Design, Etched, Signed, 5 3/8 x 6 1/4 In. 1500.00
Vase, Grass Green Flowering Thistle, Martele Ground, Bell Shape, 1900, 9 In. 1610.00
Vase, Green Grape Clusters, Vines, Narrow Neck, Flared, Satin Base, Signed, 15 In. 1210.00
Vase, Hunting & Fishing Scene, Smoky Blue Ground, Footed, Bulbous, 5 In. 5175.00
Vase, Iris, Green, Gold Enameled Highlights, Cylindrical, Square, Cameo, 4 7/8 In. 460.00
Vase, Iris, Purple, Chipped Ice Ground, Gilt, Cameo, 4 1/2 In. 448.00
Vase, Irises, Emerald, Burgundy, Gold, Wavy Ground, Cameo, 4 1/2 In. 448.00
Vase, Lady Slippers, Joined By Cobwebs, Purple, Burgundy, Green, 4 In., Pair 3450.00
Vase, Lakeshore, Yellow Amber Overlay, Chinese Red, 15 In. 5320.00
Vase, Landscape Vista, Deep Green Etched To Mottled Orange Round, Cameo, 7 In. 4400.00
Vase, Landscape, Black Trees, Blue Sky, Green, Intaglio Etched, Cameo, Square, 11 In. .. 4885.00
Vase, Landscape, Cottage Scene, 2 Windmills, Steepled Church, Cameo, 1900, 4 3/4 In. .. 4600.00
Vase, Landscape, Falling Autumn Leaves, Gray, Yellow, Cameo, 15 In. 3737.00
Vase, Landscape, River, Autumn Scene, Cameo, 18 3/4 In. 7762.00
Vase, Landscape, River, Red, Orange, Green, Olive, Barrel Shape, Cameo, 4 7/8 In. 865.00
Vase, Leaves & Branches, Burnt Orange Leaves, Dark Green Base, Cameo, 1900, 20 In. . 4600.00
Vase, Leaves & Branches, Pale Yellow, Olive Green Base, Cameo, 1900, 16 1/4 In. 6900.00
Vase, Leaves & Branches, White Leaves, Pale Yellow, Dark Green Base, Cameo, 16 In. .. 4600.00
Vase, Orange, Dark Pink Tulips, Tulip Handles, Gray, Dark Amber, Cameo, 1895, 7 In. .. 3450.00
Vase, Orange, Red Poppies, Green Stems, Yellow, Pink, Orange, Cameo, 1914, 7 In. 3735.00
Vase, Pendant, Leafy Branches, Cranberry, Orange, Yellow, Gray, Cameo, 1914, 8 In. 2875.00
Vase, Pink Flowers, 6 Petals, White, Yellow, Raspberry Ground, Cameo, 1910, 12 In. 3450.00
Vase, Pink, Yellow Violets, Pink, Green, Yellow, Mottled Gray, Cameo, 1910, 4 1/4 In. ... 2645.00
Vase, Purple Star Flowers, Yellow Centers, Gray, 1910, 4 In. 1725.00
Vase, Purple Violets, Orange Centers, Gray, White, Purple, Cameo, 1910, 4 In. 1725.00
Vase, Purple Violets, Yellow Centers, White, Purple, Gray, Cameo, 5 In., Pair 2875.00
Vase, Purple, Pink Fuchsia Blossoms, Brown Stems, Cameo, 1910, 3 In. 2530.00
Vase, Red, Orange Poppies, Green Stems, Leaves, Yellow, Orange, Cameo, 1910, 4 In. ... 2875.00
Vase, Rose Hip, Yellow, Light Greens, Rose Pink, Rose Hips Among Leaves, 4 1/2 In. ... 1150.00
Vase, Seascape, Sailboats On The Water, Yellow, Orange, Blue, Gray, Cameo, 16 In. 3735.00
Vase, Ship In Harbor Scene, 16 1/2 In. 4000.00
Vase, Snowy Meadow, Blackbirds, 6 3/4 In. 3000.00
Vase, Stars, Opalescent, Enameled Chrysanthemums, Stars, Baluster, Cameo, 10 In. 1695.00
Vase, Trees In Rain, Gray, Pink, Enameled, Waisted, Signed, 19 3/4 In. 17050.00
Vase, Trees On Sunset Ground, Baluster, Signed, 12 1/2 In. 1430.00
Vase, Water Lilies & Herons, Silver Mounts, Light Green, Pale Red, 1894, 4 1/4 In. 3105.00
Vase, Wine Trees, Sunset Ground, Cameo, Signed, 12 1/2 In. ....*Illus* 1430.00
Vase, Winter Landscape, Leafless Trees, White, Brown, Black, Cameo, 1900, 7 1/8 In. ... 3735.00
Vase, Wooded & Lake Vista, Green To Mottled Orange, Cameo, Signed, 7 x 6 1/2 In. 1595.00
Vase, Wooded Lake Scene, Trees, Mottled Ground, 11 1/2 x 4 1/4 In. 8800.00
Vase, Wooded Winter Scene, Pumpkin Orange Mottled, Yellow, Etched, 6 In. 1840.00

Vase, Yellow Irises, Green, Bulbous, Yellow Mottled, 15 In. 3737.00
Vase, Yellow Orchids, Red, Brown, Green Stems, Yellow, Green, Cameo, 1910, 4 5/8 In. . 1725.00
Whiskey, Yellow, Brown, Amethyst, Bell Flowers, Red, Green Enamel, Cameo, 2 In. 784.00
Wine, Violet, Pale Rose, Green, Gilt Rim, Sea Green, Etched, 7 3/4 In., Pair 2185.00

DAVENPORT pottery and porcelain were made at the Davenport factory in Longport, Staffordshire, England, from 1793 to 1887. Earthenwares, creamwares, porcelains, ironstone, and other ceramics were made. Most of the pieces are marked with a form of the word *Davenport*.

DAVENPORT
LONGPORT
STAFFORDSHRE

Jar, Chutney, Abolitionist, Slave Producing Chutney, 4 3/4 In., Pair 4460.00
Pitcher, Presentation, Capt. N.J. Julius, Gilt Upper Half, 9 1/2 In. 275.00
Pitcher, Water, Castle Scene, Blue Transfer 245.00
Plate, Floral Arrangement On Table Center, Floral Border, Blue, 1850, 10 In. 245.00
Platter, Flow Blue, 21 x 16 In. 285.00
Platter, Flower Sprigs, Green Ground, c.1840, 18 3/4 In., Pair 4600.00
Platter, Rustic Scene, Blue & White, 16 1/2 In. 395.00
Platter, Willow, Ironstone, 15 1/4 In. 90.00
Vase, Cover, Scroll Handles, Lion Finial, 19 1/4 In. 1870.00

DAVY CROCKETT, the American frontiersman, was born in 1786 and died in 1836. The historical character gained new fame in 1954 when the Walt Disney television show ran a series of episodes featuring Fess Parker as Davy Crockett. Coonskin caps and buckskins became popular and hundreds of different Davy Crockett items were made.

Bank ....*Illus* 390.00
Belt & Buckle 30.00
Book, Little Golden Book, 1st Issue 22.00
Card, Birthday, Kit Carson, Webster & Columbus, 1950s 15.00
Card, Happy Birthday Grandson, 1950s 10.00
Clock, Wall, Box 215.00
Cookie Jar, American Bisque 200.00
Cookie Jar, Brush 300.00
Cuff Links, Metal, 1950s 38.00
Doll, Hat & Pouch, Hard Plastic, Box, 8 In. 225.00
Frontier Wagon, 2 Horses, Friction, Linemar 150.00
Jacket, Leather, Child's 100.00
Lamp, Davy, Bear, Tree, Pottery, Cardboard Shade, Premco Mfg., 1950s, 14 In. 150.00
Neckerchief, Red, Yellow 25.00
Nodder 170.00
Pencil Case, Flocked, Disney 50.00
Penknife, Fess Parker Picture, WDP, Imperial, 2 1/4 In. 57.00
Record, Ballad Of Davy Crockett, 78 RPM 45.00
Sheet Music, Ballad Of Davy Crockett, Fess Parker, 1954 .... 15.00
Shirt, Child's, Red Cotton, Short Sleeve, Black, White, 1950, Size 10 .... 31.00
Songbook, Ballad Of Davy Crockett, Piano, 1955 .... 38.00
Wallet, Vinyl, Bust Picture, c.1955, 3 1/4 x 4 1/2 In. 75.00

You can list only your phone number and not your street address in the local phone book. Ask your phone company. Good idea for a known collector.

Davy Crockett, Bank

DE VEZ was a signature used on cameo glass after 1910. E. S. Monot founded the glass company near Paris in 1851. The company changed names many times. Mt. Joye, another glass by this factory, is listed in its own category.

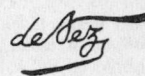

Lamp, Lake, Cottages, Yellow, Orange & Brown, Conical Shade & Base, 16 In.	4400.00
Vase, Castle Scene, Cameo, Marked, 14 In.	2300.00
Vase, Castle, Lake, Mountain, Boat Scene, Pink, Green & Clear, Signed, 9 3/4 In.	900.00
Vase, Cottage Scene, Mother & Child Under Tall Trees, Maroon, Amber, Oval, 6 In.	865.00
Vase, Island & Pine Trees, Light Green, Blue & Dark Brown, Signed, 10 In.	1300.00
Vase, Scenic, Silhouetted Trees Overlooking Water, Distant Villages, Signed, 10 In.	1150.00
Vase, Tree & Lake Scene, Cameo, Marked, 6 In.	850.00
Vase, Wooded Castle, Scene, Blue & Green, 8 In.	440.00

DECOYS are carved or turned wooden copies of birds, fish, or animals. The decoy was placed in the water or propped on the shore to lure flying birds to the pond for hunters. Some decoys are handmade; some are commercial products. Today there is a group of artists making modern decoys for display, not for use in a pond.

Bittern Drake, H. Gibbs, 2 3/4 x 2 1/2 In.	375.00
Black Drake, A. Elmer Crowell, East Harwich, Mass., 3 1/2 x 4 3/4 In.	630.00
Black Drake, James Lapham, Dennisport, Mass., 2 1/2 x 4 In.	285.00
Black Duck, Carved, Painted, 20th Century, 4 1/2 In.	260.00
Black Duck, Full-Bodied, Feather Dappling, Carved Bill, A. Elmer Crowell	2585.00
Black Duck, Glass Eyes, A. Elmer Crowell, East Harwich, Mass., 5 3/4 In.	515.00
Black Duck, Glass Eyes, A. Elmer Crowell, East Harwich, Mass., 7 In.	460.00
Black Duck, Hollow Carved, Glass Eyes, Scratch Painted, Ontario	120.00
Black Duck, Old Repaint, Ira Hudson, Chincoteague, Virginia	195.00
Black Duck, Premier Grade, Mason Decoy Factory, Detroit, Michigan	385.00
Black-Bellied Plover, Glass Eyes, Lead Base, 20th Century, 12 1/2 In.	2530.00
Black-Bellied Plover, Painted Eyes, Replaced Bill, Massachusetts	330.00
Bluebill Duck, Hollow Carved, Pair	2420.00
Bufflehead Drake, James Lapham, Dennisport, Mass., 3 x 4 1/2 In.	345.00
Bustard, Black Bellied, H. Gibbs, 1957, 3 1/2 x 4 In.	230.00
Canada Goose, A. Elmer Crowell, East Harwich, Mass., 4 x 6 In.	745.00
Canada Goose, Capt. Charles DeQuilefelt, Amityville, New York	220.00
Canada Goose, Carved, Painted, Early 20th Century, 23 In.	11500.00
Canada Goose, Cork Body, Elliot Brothers	220.00
Canada Goose, Field, Nova Scotia	360.00
Canada Goose, Preening Form, Tack Eyes, Cape Cod, Massachusetts	485.00
Canada Goose, Preening, Hollow Block, 23 In.	470.00
Canada Goose, Tin, Flat, Movable Neck & Stake, Working Paint	105.00
Canada Goose, Turned Head, Painted, 1920-1930	660.00
Canvasback Drake, Glass Eyes, Mason, 16 3/4 In.	440.00
Canvasback Drake, In Feeding Position, A. Elmer Crowell, East Harwich, Mass., 5 In.	860.00
Canvasback Drake, Laminated Walnut, Glass Eyes, Mike Geary Label, 13 In.	410.00
Canvasback Drake, Old Paint, Glass Eyes, Harry Ackerman, 22 1/2 In.	55.00
Canvasback Drake, Tack Eyes, Working Repaint	200.00
Canvasback Duck, Backbay, Mason	495.00
Canvasback Duck, Delaware River, Harry Gennimore	4675.00
Canvasback Hen, Glass Eyes, Gus Mook, 15 In.	125.00
Canvasback Hen, Standard Grade, Glass Eyes, Mason Decoy Factory, Detroit, Mich.	495.00
Coot, Original Paint, Robert McGaw	520.00
Crow, Balsa Wood, Glass Eyes, Black Paint, Wire Legs, 17 In.	275.00
Crow, Glass Eyes, Original Paint, Midwest	55.00
Crow, Midwest	360.00
Duck, Carved, Painted, Tack Eyes, 19th Century, 13 In.	230.00
Duck, Flying, Gus Wilson, Green, Gray, Blue, Black, Orange, 25-In. Wingspan, 20 In.	3025.00
Duck, Glass Eyes, Hand Carved & Painted, Signed F.B.H., 14 In.	210.00
Duck, Glass Eyes, Lead Weight, Palmer House, Pine, 13 1/4 In.	50.00
Duck, Iron, American, Late 19th Or Early 20th Century, 5 1/2 x 14 In.	460.00
Duck, Ward Brothers, c.1940	4675.00
Duck, Wooden, 1 Glass Eye, Signed B.C.SP, 17 In.	440.00

Eider, Juvenile, Original Paint, Nova Scotia 250.00
Eider Drake, Juvenile, Nova Scotia 90.00
Fish, Brook Trout, Ice Spearing, Carl Christensen, Painted, Box, 6 1/2 In. 110.00
Fish, Metal Tail & Fin, Hand Carved & Painted, 9 In. 45.00
Fish, Pike, Ice Spearing, Bud Stewart, Metal Spinner Blade, 10 In. 190.00
Fish, Pike, Pine, Gary I. Miller, Original Paint, 36 In. 190.00
Goldeneye Drake, A. Elmer Crowell, East Harwich, Mass., 2 1/4 x 4 In. 805.00
Goldeneye Drake, Inletted Head, Tack Eyes, Southern Maine 195.00
Goldeneye Hen, Amos Wheaton, South Seaville, New Jersey 910.00
Goldeneye Hen, Hollow Carved, Original Paint, Massachusetts 130.00
Goldeneye Hen, White Wing Speculums, Stipple Painted Breast, Sides, Joe Lincoln 3735.00
Goldeneye Whistler Drake, Wood Base, James Lapham, Dennisport, Mass., 3 x 4 In. 285.00
Goose, Cork, Wooden Head, Swimming Position, Glass Eyes, 26 1/2 In. 110.00
Green-Winged Teal, Full-Bodied, Joe Lincoln, 20th Century 690.00
Green-Winged Teal, Glass Eyes, H. Whittington, 6 3/4 In., Pair 275.00
Green-Winged Teal Drake, A. Elmer Crowell, East Harwich, Mass., 2 1/2 x 4 In. 860.00
Harlequin, Drake, Half-Sized, James Lapham, Dennisport, Mass. 330.00
Loon, Glass Eyes, Chas. Moore 1975, 20 3/4 In. 190.00
Loon, Swimming Form, Primitive, Old Repaint, New England 105.00
Mallard, Mason Back Bay, Harry Wilder, 1910, 32 In. x 11 1/2 In., Pair 1200.00
Mallard, Polychrome, Glass Eyes, W.V. Leonard Bureau, 6 1/2 In., Pair 110.00
Mallard, Standing, On Wood Base, Spread-Winged, Blue Bill, Pine, 3 Piece 805.00
Mallard Drake, Hollow Body, Glass Eyes, Lead Weight, Henry Perdew, 16 In. 300.00
Mallard Drake, Hollow Body, Tack Eyes, Lead Weight, Henry Perdew, 17 In. 520.00
Mallard Drake, Hollow, Glass Eyes, Wildfowler Stamp, Pair 245.00
Mallard Drake, James Lapham, Dennisport, Mass., 4 x 5 In. 430.00
Mallard Drake, Laminated Walnut, Varnished, Glass Eyes, Mike Geary Label, 16 1/2 In. . 135.00
Mallard Drake & Hen, Inletted Head, Glass Eyes, Hollow, Pair 340.00
Mallard Hen, Carved, Original Paint, Glass Eyes, Ed One Arm Kelly, Monroe, Mi. 660.00
Mallard Hen, Pratt Decoy Co., Repainted By George K. Barto, Tiskilrod, Illinois 90.00
Meadowlark, 4 Piece 40070.00
Merganser, Glass Eyes, Hollow, Chas. Moores, 1974, 18 In. 190.00
Merganser Drake, Glass Eyes, Bob Miller, 6 3/4 In. 165.00
Merganser Drake, Hooded, H. Gibbs, 2 1/2 x 2 3/4 In. 290.00
Merganser Drake, Red Breasted, A. Elmer Crowell, East Harwich, Mass., 2 1/2 x 6 In. 980.00
Merganser Hen, Hollow Carved, Barnegat Bay, New Jersey 485.00
Mouse, Ice Fishing, Glass Eyes, Wire Tail & Whiskers, Stamped DED, 5 1/4 In. 410.00
Owl, Metal, Folding, Dewey, 19 In. 165.00
Parrot, Carved & Painted Wood, Schnockschnitzler Simmons, Pa., 8 In. 19000.00
Pigeon, Shot Scars, Glass Eyes, Wood, 14 1/2 In. 495.00
Pintail, Polychrome, Glass Eyes, Cork Bottom, Mailing Label, 7 7/8 In., Pair 240.00
Pintail Drake, A. Elmer Crowell, East Harwich, Mass., 3 1/4 x 5 1/4 In. 920.00
Plover, Repainted, Joe King, Cape May, New Jersey 120.00
Rainbow Trout, Carved & Painted, Weathered Wooden Board Mount, 12 1/2 In. 75.00
Red-Breasted Merganser Drake, New England 250.00
Redhead Drake, A. Elmer Crowell, East Harwich, Mass., 2 1/2 x 4 In. 545.00
Redhead Drake, Wooden Base, H. Gibbs, 1965, 2 1/4 x 3 1/4 In. 230.00
Redhead Hen, Glass Eyes, 16 1/4 In. 180.00
Roothead Peep, Primitive, Original Paint, Virginia 145.00
Ruddy Drake, 2 x 2 3/4 In. 690.00
Ruffed Grouse, Wooden Base, A. Elmer Crowell, East Harwich, Mass., 3 1/2 x 4 1/2 In. ... 860.00
Shorebird, Carved & Painted, Black Stand, American, 1900, 13 x 8 1/2 In. 825.00
Shorebird, Dovetailed Removable Head, Glass Eyes, Hand Carved, Signed JS, 10 In. 110.00
Shorebird, Driftwood Base, Hand Carved, Painted 465.00
Shorebird, Feeding, Yellow Legs, Bead Eyes, 13 1/2 In. 220.00
Shorebird, Glass Eyes, Iron Beak, Root Base, Hand Carved & Painted, 14 In. 255.00
Shorebird, Metal Beak, Bullet Hole In Side, Before 1871 .... 350.00
Shorebird, Stand, Hand Carved & Painted, 8 1/2 In. 280.00
White-Winged Scoter, Full-Bodied, Inlet Head, Bill Against Breast, Aaron Wilson 1380.00
White-Winged Scoter, Original Paint, Nova Scotia 90.00
Yellowlegs, Chip Carved, Original Bill & Paint, Virginia 330.00
Yellowlegs, Running Form, Split Carved Tail, Old Replaced Bill, New England 170.00
Yellowlegs Shorebird, New Jersey 220.00

DEDHAM Pottery was started in 1895. Chelsea Keramic Art Works was established in 1872 in Chelsea, Massachusetts, by members of the Robertson family. The factory closed in 1889 and was reorganized as the Chelsea Pottery U.S. in 1891. The firm used the marks *CKAW* and *CPUS*. It became the Dedham Pottery of Dedham, Massachusetts. The factory closed in 1943. It was famous for its crackleware dishes, which picture blue outlines of animals, flowers, and other natural motifs.

Azalea, Cup	55.00
Azalea, Marmalade Bowl & Saucer, Cover, 6-In. Saucer	470.00
Azalea, Pitcher, Angular Handle, 5 x 4 In.	550.00
Birds In Potted Orange Tree, Plate, Impressed Rabbit Mark, 8 1/2 In.	520.00
Birds In Potted Orange Tree, Plate, Signed, 10 In.	440.00
Butterfly, Bowl, Repeat Stripes & Swirls, Signed, 4 1/2 In.	410.00
Dolphin, Upsidedown, Plate, Impressed CPUS Clover Mark, 8 5/8 In.	575.00
Duck, Plate, Blue Rabbit, Impressed Rabbit Mark, 8 1/2 In.	330.00 to 440.00
Duck, Plate, Square Blue Stamp, 8 1/2 In.	220.00
Duck, Tufted, Plate, Impressed Rabbit Mark, 8 5/8 In.	100.00 to 300.00
Elephant, Saucer	535.00
Elephant & Baby, Plate, Signed, 8 1/3 In.	770.00
Floral, Butter Chip, Floral Interior, Overlapping Petals, Signed, 3 1/2 In.	410.00
Grape, Plate, Impressed Rabbit Mark, 6 1/4 In.	140.00
Grape, Platter, Round, Blue Stamp, 12 In.	200.00
Horsechestnut, Plate, Blue Mark, Early 20th Century, 6 In.	170.00
Horsechestnut, Plate, Blue Rabbit, Impressed Rabbit Mark, 8 1/2 In.	110.00
Iris, Plate, Blue Rabbit & Impressed Rabbit Mark, 8 1/4 In.	220.00
Iris, Plate, Impressed Rabbit Mark, 6 1/8 In.	55.00 to 140.00
Lion Tapestry, Plate, Repeat Full Moon Above, Signed, 8 1/2 In.	990.00
Magnolia, Plate, 8 1/2 In.	190.00
Magnolia, Plate, Blue Rabbit, Impressed Rabbit Mark, 8 1/2 In.	250.00
Magnolia, Plate, Impressed Rabbit Mark, 6 In.	45.00
Moth, Plate, Blue Rabbit, Impressed Rabbit Mark, 8 1/2 In.	605.00
Mushroom, Plate, Bluc Stamp, 6 In.	375.00
Mushroom, Plate, Cobalt Blue Ground, Signed, 10 In.	495.00
Night & Day, Pitcher, Owl & Rooster Design, White, 5 In.	600.00
Pineapple, Plate, Impressed CPUS Clover Mark, Impressed EEX Mark, 8 5/8 In.	250.00 to 360.00
Polar Bear, Cup & Saucer, Signed, 2 1/8-In. Cup, 6-In. Saucer	385.00
Polar Bear, Plate, Blue Rabbit Mark, 8 1/2 In.	1018.00
Pond Lily, Plate, Blue Mark, Maude Davenport, 6 1/4 In.	1150.00
Pond Lily, Plate, Blue Rabbit, Impressed Rabbit Mark, 8 1/2 In.	120.00
Pond Lily, Plate, Impressed Rabbit Mark, 8 1/2 In.	165.00
Rabbit, Creamer	275.00
Rabbit, Cup & Saucer, Demitasse	325.00
Rabbit, Mug, Gray Crackle, Bulbous, Blue Stamp, 4 3/4 In.	800.00
Rabbit, Mug, Gray Crackle, Handle, Bubbles, Blue Stamp, 5 1/4 In.	715.00
Rabbit, Plate, Blue Stamp, 6 In.	175.00
Rabbit, Tray, Blue, White, 6 1/2 x 10 In.	550.00
Rabbit, Two Ear, Plate, 8 1/2 In.	100.00
Rabbit, Two Ear, Plate, Blue Rabbit, Impressed Rabbit Mark, 8 1/2 In.	360.00 to 440.00
Rabbit, Two Ear, Plate, Bread & Butter, Impressed Rabbit Mark, 6 1/8 In.	65.00 to 100.00
Rabbit, Two Ear, Sugar & Creamer, Blue Rabbit Mark, 2 x 4 In.	525.00
Scotty Dogs, Plate, Ear Perked Upward, Head Tilted, Signed, 8 1/2 In.	1650.00
Snowtree, Bowl, Large & Small Trees, Signed, 2 x 5 1/4 In.	190.00
Snowtree, Plate, Impressed Rabbit Mark, 6 1/8 In.	65.00
Thistle, Plate, Hugh Robertson, Signed, 8 1/2 In.	2970.00
Turkey, Plate, Blue Rabbit, Impressed Rabbit Mark, 8 1/2 In.	580.00
Turkey, Plate, Blue Stamp, 8 1/2 In.	360.00
Turkey, Plate, Square Blue Stamp, 8 1/2 In.	140.00
Vase, 4 Sides, Flowers, White Crackled Glaze, Rabbit Stamp, 8 1/2 x 5 1/4 In.	550.00
Vase, Brown Drip, Green Glaze, Experimental, Hugh Robertson, 10 3/4 x 4 3/4 In.	990.00
Vase, Classical Urn Form, 2 Leaf Form Handles, Terra-Cotta, CKAW, 1880, 6 In.	630.00
Vase, Frothy Brown, Green Glaze, Hugh Robertson, 9 3/4 x 5 In.	1980.00
Vase, Oxblood Orange Peel Semimatte Glaze, Bottle Shape, CKAW, 8 1/4 In.	1760.00
Vase, Sea Green Glaze, Raised Rim, Marked, Hugh Robertson, 8 1/2 x 9 1/2 In.	2100.00

DEGUE is a signature acid-etched on pieces of French glass made in the
early 1900s. Cameo, mold blown, and smooth glass with contrasting
colored rims are the types most often found.

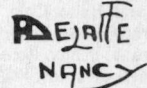

Vase, 3 Sunflowers, Trifid Leaves, Blue, Orange, Dark Purple, Tapered, Cameo, 8 In.	690.00
Vase, 5 Stems Of Stylized Chrysanthemums, Red, Pale Pink, Gray, Orange, 21 In.	3735.00
Vase, Black Cut To Matte Yellow, Orange, Green, Metal Base, 16 1/2 In.	154.00
Vase, Central Band Of Flowers, Narrow Leaves, Ivory, Red, Blue, Gray, 17 In.	1610.00
Vase, Desert Oasis Scene, Camels & Palm Trees, Orange, Dark Brown Layers, 5 In.	750.00
Vase, Maple Leaves, Purple Mottled, Crimson, Amber, 1925, 14 1/4 In.	1150.00
Vase, Morning Glory Vines, Purple, Red, Orange, Ocher, Flared Lip, 1925, 13 1/4 In.	2300.00
Vase, Purple, Blue Mottled, Signed, 15 In.	880.00
Vase, Raspberry, Orange, Cream Mottled, Signed, 12 1/2 In.	935.00
Vase, Stylized Bellflowers, Leaves, Blue Flared Rim, Gray, Cameo, 15 In.	1610.00
Vase, Stylized Floral Design, Taupe, Baluster, 1925, 18 In.	2300.00
Vase, Stylized Morning Glory Vines, Lappet Border, Orange, Brown, Yellow, 14 In.	2300.00
Vase, Stylized Petals Around Neck, Lavender Mottled, White, Gray, 1925, 17 In.	690.00
Vase, Stylized Vines, Metallic Design Interior, 1925, 10 1/4 In.	287.00

DELATTE glass is a French cameo glass made by Andre Delatte. It was
first made in Nancy, France, in 1921. Lighting fixtures and opaque
glassware in imitation of Bohemian opaline were made. There were
many French cameo glass makers, so be sure to look in other appropriate categories.

Lamp Shade, Light Purple, Deep Amethyst Overlay, Fruit & Vines, 5 In., Pair	672.00
Vase, Egg Shape, Mold Blown, Matted, c.1925, 7 In.	345.00
Vase, Floral, Brown, Tan, Nancy, 8 In.	770.00
Vase, Pink, Blue, Silver, Handles, Signed, 18 In.	1955.00
Vase, Scenic, Tree Lined Shore, Rocky Distant Hills, Raised Leaf, Brown, 1920, 6 In. . . .	515.00

DELDARE, see Buffalo Pottery Deldare.

DELFT is a tin-glazed pottery that has been made since the seventeenth
century. It is decorated with blue on white or with colored decorations.
Most of the pieces sold today were made after 1891, and the name
Holland appears with the Delft factory marks. The word *delft* also
appears on pottery from other countries. Delft was made in England in
the eighteenth century.

Bowl, Serving, Windmill Scene, Lobed, RC Versailles, 8 1/2 In.	55.00
Bowl, Shallow, Polychrome, 13 In.	715.00
Butter Chip, Sailing Ship, Signed	31.00
Charger, Blue, Green, Yellow, Fluted Edge, Dutch, c.1690, 13 In.	3500.00
Charger, Central Urn Of Flowers, Bells & Fruit Border, c.1720, 13 3/4 In.	2530.00
Charger, Elderly Lady Reading, Old Salt, Scalloped Rim, 15 In., Pair	143.00
Charger, Flower Heads & Leaves, 18th Century, 13 1/2 In.	546.00
Charger, Flowers & Birds, 13 1/4 In.	495.00
Charger, Flowers & Leaves, Blue, White, Claw Mark, L. Sanderus, c.1760, 11 In.	1170.00
Charger, Winter Landscape, Floral, 15 3/4 In.	230.00
Garniture Set, Oriental Figure & Floral, 9 1/2 In., 3 Piece	977.00
Inkstand, Rococo Form, Figural & Harbor Reserves, Allover Floral, Van Einhorn, 9 In. . .	488.00
Jar, Blue Floral, Avian Design, White Ground, 20 In.	315.00
Jar, Cover, Wide Central Band, Bird On Flowering Branch, c.1930, 10 In., Pair	545.00
Jar, Storage, Blue & White, London, c.1650, 3 1/2 In.	850.00
Jug, Figural, Man Smoking Pipe, Polychrome, 17th-18th Century, 10 In.	475.00
Jug, Puzzle, Here Gentlemen Come Try Your Skill, Flowering Plants, c.1760, 7 In.	1150.00
Jug, Windmill Scene, Blue & White, Silvered Base Mount, T&L, 10 In.	168.00
Pitcher, Peacock, 18th Century, 8 1/2 In.	470.00
Plaque, Hand Painted Seascape, Sailing Ships, 19th Century, 15 1/2 In.	488.00
Plaque, Harbor Scene, Hanger, Artist Signed, 11 x 12 In.	154.00
Plate, Flower Garden Design, England, 9 In.	220.00
Plate, Peacock Strutting Amongst Manganese Sponge Trees, Shrubs, 1740, 8 3/4 In.	1610.00
Plate, Woodsman Carrying Ax Over His Shoulder, Sprays, Brown Edge Rim, 9 In.	2070.00
Punch Bowl, Blue & White, England, 1720, 8 5/8 In.	1350.00

Salt, Blue, Green & Brown Sponged, White Ground, Oval, 4 1/8 In. 27.00
Standish, Heart Shape, Inkpot & Sander, 18th Century 495.00
Stein, Lithophane Bottom, Blue & White, Signed, 6 In. 220.00
Tile, Blue Cat Center, Mid 18th Century, Square 195.00
Tile, Church, Other With House By Sea, Frame, Square, 5 1/8 In., Pair 115.00
Tile, Dog Jumping Center, Stylized Border, 1630 . . . .   195.00
Tile, Dutch Windmill, 5 x 5 In. 45.00
Tile, Flowers & Fruit In Basket, Tulip, Black Frame, Holland Label, 6 1/4 x 6 1/2 In., Pair   165.00
Tile, Form Star Flower When Laid Together, Corner Flowers, 5 x 5 In., 4 Piece 55.00
Tobacco Jar, Brass Cover, Indians Smoking Next To Urn Marked Havana, 10 1/2 In. 2420.00
Tobacco Jar, Indians Smoking Next To Urn Marked Tonka, Blue, White, 10 1/2 In. 2970.00
Tobacco Jar, Seated Indian, Arms Of Amsterdam, Mounted As Lamp, 14 1/2 In. 3450.00
Toby Jug, Man Holding Pitcher, Polychrome Flowers, 18th Century, 10 In. 560.00
Vase, Allover Landscape & Figural Panels, Floral Borders, Blue & White, 28 In., Pair . . .   3735.00
Vase, Continuous Band Of Birds Of Paradise In Leaves, Late 18th Century, 19 In., Pair . .   1380.00
Vase, Courting Couple, Sailing Ships, Diaperwork, Ormolu Base, Cover, 18 3/4 In., Pair .   3450.00
Vase, Dancing Couple, Horn Player, On Barrel, 18th Century, 17 In., Pair 2300.00
Vase, Domed & Pierced Cover, Waterside Landscape, 19th Century, 17 1/2 In., Pair 3220.00
Vase, Domed Cover, Chinese Style Panels, Birds & Figures, 19th Century, 17 In., Pair . . .   2990.00
Vase, Octagonal, Ribbed, Blue & White, Flower & Bird Design, Lion Finial, 22 In., Pair .   1495.00
Vase, Windmill, 5 1/4 x 4 3/4 In. 25.00

DENTAL cabinets, chairs, equipment, and other related items are listed
here. Other objects may be found in the Medical category.

Tool Set, Box 121.00
Toothbrush, Celluloid, Morgan & Sons, 1900s 11.00

DEPRESSION GLASS was an inexpensive glass manufactured in large
quantities during the 1920s and early 1930s. It was made in many colors and patterns by dozens of factories in the United States. Most patterns were also made in clear glass, which the factories called *crystal*.
The term *crystal* is used here. The name *Depression glass* is a modern
one. For more descriptions, history, pictures, and prices of Depression
glass, see the book *Kovels' Depression Glass & Dinnerware Price List*.

Adam, Ashtray, Green, 4 1/2 In. 25.00
Adam, Bowl, Green, 4 3/4 In. 20.00
Adam, Bowl, Pink, 7 3/4 In. 30.00
Adam, Bowl, Vegetable, Oval, Pink, 10 In. . . . . .35.00 to 40.00
Adam, Cake Plate, Footed, Green, 10 In. . . . . .25.00 to 30.00
Adam, Candlestick, Green, 4 In. 55.00
Adam, Candy Jar, Cover, Green 110.00
Adam, Creamer, Green . . . . .20.00 to 25.00
Adam, Cup & Saucer, Green 30.00
Adam, Grill Plate, Green, 9 In. 20.00
Adam, Pitcher, Round Base, Crystal, 32 Oz., 8 In. . . . . .45.00 to 60.00
Adam, Plate, Green, 7 3/4 In. 18.00
Adam, Plate, Pink, Square, 9 In. . . . . .30.00 to 40.00
Adam, Platter, Pink, 11 3/4 In. 30.00
Adam, Salt & Pepper, Footed, Pink, 4 In. 85.00
Adam, Sherbet, Green 40.00
Adam, Tumbler, Iced Tea, Green, 5 1/2 In. . . . . .48.00 to 60.00
Adam, Tumbler, Water, Pink, 4 1/2 In. 30.00
Alice, Cup & Saucer, Jadite . . . . .4.50 to 12.00
American Pioneer, Cup & Saucer, Green 20.00
American Pioneer, Goblet, Pink, 4 In. 35.00
American Sweetheart, Berry Bowl, Monax, 9 In. 60.00
American Sweetheart, Bowl, Cereal, Pink, 6 In. 15.00
American Sweetheart, Bowl, Pink, 3 3/4 In. 75.00
American Sweetheart, Bowl, Vegetable, Oval, Monax, 11 In. . . . . .75.00 to 85.00
American Sweetheart, Console, Blue, 18 In. 1795.00
American Sweetheart, Console, Monax, 18 In. 650.00
American Sweetheart, Creamer, Blue 145.00
American Sweetheart, Creamer, Pink 10.00

American Sweetheart, Cup & Saucer, Monax ....12.00 to 15.00
American Sweetheart, Cup, Pink 15.00
American Sweetheart, Lamp Shade, Monax 850.00
American Sweetheart, Pitcher, Pink, 80 Oz., 8 In. ....855.00 to 875.00
American Sweetheart, Plate, Monax, 8 In. 8.00
American Sweetheart, Plate, Pink, 8 In. 10.00
American Sweetheart, Plate, Pink, 9 3/4 In. ....38.00 to 40.00
American Sweetheart, Plate, Red, 8 In. 125.00
American Sweetheart, Platter, Monax, Oval, 13 In. 75.00
American Sweetheart, Salt & Pepper, Monax 400.00
American Sweetheart, Salver, Pink, 12 In. 22.00
American Sweetheart, Sherbet, Monax 25.00
American Sweetheart, Soup, Cream, Monax, 4 1/2 In. 125.00
American Sweetheart, Soup, Cream, Pink, 4 1/2 In. 90.00
American Sweetheart, Sugar & Creamer, Blue 180.00
American Sweetheart, Sugar & Creamer, Monax ....18.00 to 20.00
American Sweetheart, Sugar, Cover, Monax 400.00
American Sweetheart, Tumbler, Pink, 5 Oz., 3 1/2 In. 100.00
Anniversary, Butter, Crystal 25.00
Anniversary, Cake Plate, Crystal, 12 1/2 In. 10.00
Apple Blossom pattern is listed here as Dogwood.
Aunt Polly, Butter, Cover, Blue 205.00
Aunt Polly, Nappy, Blue, 4 3/8 In. 20.00
Aunt Polly, Tumbler, Blue, 9 Oz., 3 3/4 In. 40.00
Aurora, Bowl, Blue, 4 1/2 In. ....20.00 to 50.00
Aurora, Creamer, Blue 28.00
Avocado, Bowl, 2 Handles, Green, 5 1/4 In. 36.00
Avocado, Bowl, 2 Handles, Pink, 5 1/4 In. 18.00
Avocado, Saucer, Pink ....22.00 to 25.00
Avocado, Sugar, Green 32.00
Ballerina pattern is listed here as Cameo.
Banded Rib pattern is listed here as Coronation.
Banded Rings pattern is listed here as Ring.
Basket pattern is listed here as No. 615.
Beaded Block, Bowl, Flared, Cobalt Blue, 6 1/2 In. 95.00
Block pattern is listed here as Block Optic.
Block Optic, Candlestick, Green, 1 3/4 In., Pair 120.00
Block Optic, Console, Pink, 11 1/2 In. 125.00
Block Optic, Cup & Saucer, Green 12.00
Block Optic, Ice Bucket, Green 65.00
Block Optic, Mayonnaise, Green, 4 In. 35.00
Block Optic, Pitcher, Green, 54 Oz., 8 1/2 In. 80.00
Block Optic, Plate, Green, 9 In. 22.00
Block Optic, Saltshaker, Footed, Pink 35.00
Block Optic, Sherbet, Green, 4 3/4 In. 18.00
Block Optic, Sugar, Round, Crystal 3.00

Depression Glass,
Anniversary

Depression Glass,
Beaded Block

Depression Glass,
Bubble

Depression Glass, Cameo

Put a silver spoon in a glass before pouring in hot water. It will absorb heat and keep the glass from cracking.

Block Optic, Tumbler, Iced Tea, Green, 10 Oz., 5 In.	22.00
Block Optic, Tumbler, Juice, Footed, Green, 3 Oz., 2 3/4 In.	35.00
Block Optic, Tumbler, Juice, Pink, 5 Oz., 3 1/2 In.	28.00
Block Optic, Whiskey, Pink, 1 5/8 In.	45.00
Boopie, Sherbet, Royal Ruby, Footed, 6 Oz.	10.00
Boopie, Tumbler, Royal Ruby, Beaded Crystal Foot, 4 Oz.	14.00
Bouquet & Lattice pattern is listed here as Normandie.	
Bow Knot, Sherbet, Green	17.00
Bubble, Berry Bowl, Blue, 8 3/8 In.	10.00
Bubble, Berry Bowl, Crystal, 8 3/8 In.	5.00
Bubble, Berry Bowl, Green, 8 3/8 In.	35.00
Bubble, Bowl, Cereal, Green, 5 1/2 In.	20.00
Bubble, Bowl, Fruit, Red, 4 1/2 In.	10.00
Bubble, Bread Plate, Blue, 6 3/4 In.	2.50 to 3.00
Bubble, Cup & Saucer, Blue	6.00 to 8.00
Bubble, Cup & Saucer, Green	16.00
Bubble, Cup, Red	11.00
Bubble, Goblet, Green	15.00
Bubble, Pitcher, Water, Red	65.00
Bubble, Plate, Blue, 9 3/8 In.	9.00
Bubble, Soup, Dish, Blue, 7 3/4 In.	15.00
Bubble, Sugar & Creamer, Blue	50.00
Bubble, Sugar & Creamer, Green	25.00
Bubble, Tidbit, 2 Tiers, Red	60.00
Bubble, Tumbler, Crystal Footed, Green, 16 Oz.	15.00
Bubble, Tumbler, Juice, Red, 6 Oz.	10.00
Bubble, Tumbler, Water, Footed, Green, 12 Oz.	12.00
Bullseye pattern is listed here as Bubble.	
Butterflies & Roses pattern is listed here as Flower Garden With Butterflies.	
Buttons & Bows pattern is listed here as Holiday.	
Cabbage Rose pattern is listed here as Sharon.	
Cameo, Bowl, Cereal, Green, 5 1/2 In.	35.00
Cameo, Bowl, Salad, Green, 7 1/2 In.	55.00 to 58.00
Cameo, Butter, Cover, Green	240.00 to 280.00
Cameo, Console, Footed, Green, 11 In.	98.00
Cameo, Goblet, Wine, Green, 4 Oz., 4 In.	76.00
Cameo, Grill Plate, Yellow, 10 1/2 In.	10.00
Cameo, Pitcher, Water, Green, 56 Oz., 8 1/2 In.	60.00
Cameo, Plate, Green, 8 In.	9.00
Cameo, Plate, Square, Green, 8 1/2 In.	45.00
Cameo, Platter, Closed Handles, Yellow, 12 In.	45.00 to 65.00
Cameo, Syrup, Green, 5 1/2 In.	375.00
Cameo, Tumbler, Green, 5 In.	35.00
Cameo, Vase, Green, 8 In.	65.00
Candlewick pattern is listed in the Imperial Glass category.	
Caprice pattern is included in the Cambridge Glass category.	
Carolyn, Bowl, Handles, Pink, 9 In.	45.00
Carolyn, Plate, Handles, Yellow, 12 In.	40.00
Charm, Saucer, Jadite	1.50
Checkerboard, Berry Bowl, Green, 4 1/2 In.	6.00

Cherry Blossom, Bowl, 3-Footed, Pink, 10 1/2 In. 93.00
Cherry Blossom, Child's Set, Delphite, 14 Piece 325.00
Cherry Blossom, Creamer, Child's, Pink 45.00
Cherry Blossom, Cup & Saucer, Pink 20.00
Cherry Blossom, Mug, Green, 7 Oz. 210.00
Cherry Blossom, Mug, Pink, 7 Oz. 485.00
Cherry Blossom, Pitcher, Green, 36 Oz., 6 3/4 In. 60.00
Cherry Blossom, Plate, Green, 7 In. ....24.00 to 27.00
Cherry Blossom, Platter, Divided, Crystal, 13 In. 60.00
Cherry Blossom, Platter, Oval, Pink, 11 In. 55.00
Cherry Blossom, Sandwich Server, Handles, Pink, 10 1/2 In. 30.00
Cherry Blossom, Sherbet, Green ....18.00 to 20.00
Cherry Blossom, Soup, Dish, Crystal, 7 3/4 In. 95.00
Cherry Blossom, Sugar & Creamer, Child's, Pink 46.00
Cherry Blossom, Tumbler, Footed, Delphite, 9 Oz., 4 1/4 In. 25.00
Chinex Classic, Cake Plate, Center Design, Ivory, 11 1/2 In. 5.00
Chinex Classic, Sandwich Server, Ivory, 11 1/2 In. 4.00
Circle, Cup, Green 5.00
Circle, Plate, Pink, 6 In. 2.50
Cloverleaf, Plate, Black, 8 In. ....14.00 to 16.00
Cloverleaf, Saucer, Green 3.00
Cloverleaf, Sherbet, Green, 6 In. ....6.00 to 10.00
Cloverleaf, Sugar & Creamer, Footed, Green, 3 5/8 In. 18.00
Cloverleaf, Tumbler, Green, Footed, 10 Oz., 3 3/4 In. 90.00
Colonial, Grill Plate, Green, 10 In. 25.00
Colonial, Plate, Pink, 10 In. 60.00
Colonial, Soup, Dish, Pink, 7 In. 90.00
Colonial, Tumbler, Water, Pink, 9 Oz., 4 In. 22.00
Colonial, Whiskey, Pink, 1 1/2 Oz., 2 1/2 In. 15.00
Colonial Fluted, Berry Bowl, Crystal, 7 1/2 In. 20.00
Colonial Fluted, Plate, Crystal, 6 In. 2.50
Columbia, Bowl, Ruffled, Crystal, 10 1/2 In. 20.00
Columbia, Cup & Saucer, Pink 30.00
Columbia, Plate, Crystal, 9 1/2 In. 12.00
Columbia, Tumbler, Crystal, 4 Oz. 12.00
Coronation, Plate, Pink, 6 In. 6.00
Coronation, Tumbler, Footed, Pink, 10 Oz., 5 In. 35.00
Cracked Ice, Sugar & Creamer, Cover, Pink 65.00
Cremax, Cup, Cream Colored 3.00
Cube pattern is listed here as Cubist.
Cubist, Butter, Pink 70.00
Cubist, Candy Jar, Pink, 6 1/2 In. 38.00
Cubist, Creamer, Green, 3 In. 7.00
Cubist, Pitcher, Green, 8 3/4 In. 250.00
Cubist, Plate, Green, 8 In. 14.00
Daisy pattern is listed here as No. 620.
Dancing Girl pattern is listed here as Cameo.

Depression Glass,
Cherry Blossom

Depression Glass,
Chinex Classic

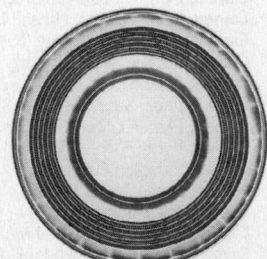

Depression Glass,
Circle

Depression Glass,
Cloverleaf

Depression Glass,
Colonial

Depression Glass,
Cubist

Decagon, Bonbon, Oval, Metal Holder, Green, 5 1/2 In. 30.00
Della Robbia, Bowl, Footed, Crystal, 12 In. 45.00
Della Robbia, Bowl, Heart, Handle, Crystal 175.00
Della Robbia, Bread Plate, Crystal, 6 1/2 In. 5.00
Della Robbia, Butter, Cover, Crystal 50.00
Della Robbia, Compote, Footed, Crystal, 6 1/2 In. 30.00
Della Robbia, Cup & Saucer, Crystal 14.00
Della Robbia, Nappy, Handle, Crystal, 7 1/2 In. 11.00
Della Robbia, Plate, Crystal, 10 1/2 In. 13.00
Della Robbia, Saltshaker, Crystal 10.00
Della Robbia, Sugar & Creamer, Cover, Crystal 45.00
Della Robbia, Torte Plate, Crystal, 14 In. 45.00
Dewdrop, Tray, Lazy Susan, Crystal, 13 In. 17.00
Diamond Pattern is listed here as Miss America.
Diana, Bowl, Scalloped, Crystal, 12 In. 15.00
Diana, Console, Amber, 11 In. 20.00
Diana, Cup & Saucer, Pink, After Dinner 39.00
Diana, Plate, Amber, 11 3/4 In. 18.00
Diana, Sandwich Server, Amber, 11 3/4 In. 10.00
Diana, Sherbet, Amber 10.00
Diana, Tumbler, Crystal, 9 Oz., 4 1/8 In. 22.00
Dogwood, Bowl, Cereal, Pink, 5 1/2 In. 30.00
Dogwood, Bowl, Fruit, Pink, 10 In. 750.00
Dogwood, Cake Plate, Pink, 13 In. 165.00
Dogwood, Creamer, Thick, Pink, 3 In. . . . . .15.00 to 20.00
Dogwood, Creamer, Thin, Pink, 2 3/4 In. . . . . .20.00 to 22.00
Dogwood, Cup & Saucer, Thick, Pink . . . . .15.00 to 27.00
Dogwood, Cup & Saucer, Thin, Pink 22.00
Dogwood, Grill Plate, Allover Pattern, Pink, 10 1/2 In. 20.00
Dogwood, Grill Plate, Crystal, 10 1/2 In. 28.00
Dogwood, Pitcher, Green, 80 Oz., 8 In. 575.00
Dogwood, Pitcher, Pink, 80 Oz., 8 In. . . . . .225.00 to 240.00
Dogwood, Plate, Pink, 9 1/4 In. . . . . .35.00 to 40.00
Dogwood, Salver, Pink, 12 In. 30.00

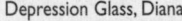

Depression Glass, Diana

Depression Glass, Dogwood

Depression Glass,
Doric

Depression Glass,
Fire-King

Depression Glass,
Floragold

Dogwood, Sherbet, Low Footed, Yellow	23.00
Dogwood, Sugar & Creamer, Thick, Pink, 3 1/2 In.	35.00
Dogwood, Tumbler, Pink, 12 Oz., 5 In.	65.00
Dogwood, Tumbler, Plain, Pink, 11 Oz., 4 In.	20.00
Doric, Berry Bowl, Green 4 1/2 In.	9.00
Doric, Berry Bowl, Pink, 4 1/2 In.	11.00 to 14.00
Doric, Bowl, Cereal, Pink, 5 1/2 In.	85.00
Doric, Bowl, Vegetable, Oval, Pink, 9 In.	30.00
Doric, Cake Plate, Pink, 10 In.	35.00
Doric, Candy Jar, Green, 8 In.	50.00
Doric, Plate, Pink, 9 In.	22.00
Doric, Sherbet, Green, 6 In.	12.00 to 16.00
Doric & Pansy, Butter, Cover, Ultramarine	455.00
Doric & Pansy, Cup & Saucer, Ultramarine	58.00
Doric & Pansy, Saucer, Child's, Ultramarine	10.00
Doric & Pansy, Tumbler, Ultramarine, 9 Oz., 4 1/2 In.	125.00
Double Shield pattern is listed here as Mt. Pleasant.	
Dutch Rose pattern is listed here as Rosemary.	
Early American Rock Crystal pattern is listed here as Rock Crystal.	
English Hobnail, Cordial, Crystal	12.00
English Hobnail, Cup & Saucer, Crystal	9.00
Fairfax, Creamer, Footed, Azure	15.00
Fairfax, Goblet, Cocktail, Pink, 3 1/2 Oz.	20.00
Fairfax, Sugar, Cover, Footed, Azure	40.00
Fairfax, Tumbler, Water, Topaz, 10 Oz.	26.00
Fine Rib pattern is listed here as Homespun.	
Fire-King, Bowl, Apple, Ivory, 9 1/2 In.	38.00
Fire-King, Bowl, Cereal, Blue, 5 3/8 In.	22.00
Fire-King, Bowl, Jadite, 5 3/8 In.	15.00
Fire-King, Casserole, Knob Cover, Blue, 2 Qt.	25.00
Fire-King, Flowerpot, 3 Bands, Jadite, 4 In.	25.00
Fire-King, Grease Jar, Cover, Ivory, Stripes	35.00
Fire-King, Pie Plate, Blue, 8 3/4 In.	10.00
Fire-King, Plate, Jadite, 7 1/4 In.	25.00
Fire-King, Platter, Jadite, 9 1/2 In.	35.00 to 59.00
Fire-King, Roaster, Cover, Blue, 10 3/8 In.	80.00
Fire-King, Sugar & Creamer, Jadite	12.00
Fleurette, Sugar & Creamer, Cover, White	14.00
Floragold, Berry Bowl, Square, Iridescent, 8 1/2 In.	10.00
Floragold, Bowl, Ruffled, Square, Crystal, 8 1/2 In.	12.00
Floragold, Candy Dish, Cover, Crystal, 6 3/4 In.	45.00
Floragold, Coaster, Iridescent	4.00
Floragold, Creamer, Footed, Iridescent	7.00
Floragold, Cup & Saucer, Iridescent	24.00
Floragold, Pitcher, Water, Iridescent, 64 Oz.	35.00
Floragold, Plate, Crystal, 13 1/2 In.	20.00

Floragold, Plate, Iridescent, 8 1/2 In. . . . . .40.00 to 45.00
Floragold, Saucer, Iridescent . . . . .9.00 to 12.00
Floragold, Sugar, Cover, Iridescent 17.00
Floragold, Tray, Indentation, Iridescent, 13 1/2 In. 24.00
Floragold, Tumbler, Footed, Iridescent, 10 Oz. 14.00
Floral, Bowl, Pink, 7 1/2 In. 22.00
Floral, Butter, Cover, Pink . . . . .95.00 to 110.00
Floral, Candlestick, Green, 4 In. 27.00
Floral, Candy Jar, Cover, Green 50.00
Floral, Coaster, Pink, 3 1/4 In. . . . . .12.00 to 15.00
Floral, Cup & Saucer, Green 22.00
Floral, Cup, Pink 7.00
Floral, Pitcher, Cone, Crystal, 32 Oz., 8 In. 38.00
Floral, Pitcher, Lemonade, Pink, 10 1/4 In. 285.00
Floral, Plate, Green, 6 In. 8.00
Floral, Relish, Oval, 2 Sections, Pink 25.00
Floral, Tumbler, Footed, Green, 5 1/4 In. 55.00
Floral, Tumbler, Iced Tea, Pink, 5 1/4 In. . . . . .60.00 to 65.00
Floral, Tumbler, Juice, Footed, Green, 3 1/2 In. 27.00
Floral & Diamond Band, Pitcher, Green, 42 Oz., 8 In. 150.00
Floral & Diamond Band, Tumbler, Iced Tea, Pink, 5 In. 50.00
Floral & Diamond Band, Tumbler, Water, Green, 4 In. 20.00
Florentine No. I, Creamer, Ruffled, Blue 65.00
Florentine No. I, Cup, Green 9.00
Florentine No. I, Plate, Green, 10 In. 25.00
Florentine No. I, Sherbet, Footed, Yellow 10.00
Florentine No. I, Sugar & Creamer, Ruffled, Crystal 50.00
Florentine No. 2, Ashtray, Green, 5 1/2 In. . . . . .12.00 to 14.00
Florentine No. 2, Bowl, Yellow, 6 In. 45.00
Florentine No. 2, Candy Dish, Cover, Pink 155.00
Florentine No. 2, Compote, Ruffled, Crystal, 3 1/2 In. 25.00
Florentine No. 2, Pitcher, Footed, Cone, Yellow, 7 1/2 In.   34.00
Florentine No. 2, Plate, Yellow, 8 1/2 In. . . . . .10.00 to 15.00
Florentine No. 2, Sherbet, Footed, Yellow 12.00
Florentine No. 2, Soup, Cream, Crystal, 4 3/4 In. 10.50
Florentine No. 2, Tray, Condiment, Round, Yellow, 8 1/2 In. 100.00
Florentine No. 2, Tumbler, Juice, Footed, Crystal, 5 Oz., 3 1/4 In. 18.00
Florentine No. 2, Tumbler, Water, Footed, Yellow, 9 Oz., 4 In. 18.00
Flower & Leaf Band pattern is listed here as Indiana Custard.
Flower Garden With Butterflies, Candy Dish, Cover, Blue 430.00
Flower Garden With Butterflies, Candy Dish, Heart, Yellow 1100.00
Flower Garden With Butterflies, Cup & Saucer, Green 110.00
Flower Rim pattern is listed here as Vitrock.
Forest Green, Ashtray, Hexagonal, 5 1/4 In. 6.00
Forest Green, Punch Set, 12 Cups, 14 Piece 95.00
Forest Green, Tumbler, Long Boy, 15 Oz. 5.00
Fortune, Berry Bowl, Pink, 4 In. 3.00

Depression Glass,
Floral

Depression Glass,
Florentine No. I

Depression Glass,
Holiday

Fortune, Bowl, Pink, 4 1/2 In. 9.00
Fortune, Cup, Pink 9.00
Fortune, Tumbler, Pink, 9 Oz., 4 In. 7.50
Fruits, Berry Bowl, Crystal, 5 In. 15.00
Fruits, Cup & Saucer, Blackberry, Crystal 19.00
Fruits, Cup & Saucer, Green, Crystal 10.00
Fruits, Cup & Saucer, Pear, Crystal 15.00
Fruits, Cup & Saucer, Strawberry, Crystal 19.00
Georgian, Bowl, Cereal, Green, 5 3/4 In. 21.00
Georgian, Bowl, Green, 4 1/2 In. 9.00
Georgian, Butter, Cover, Green 85.00
Georgian, Cup & Saucer, Green . . . . .10.00 to 12.00
Georgian, Plate, Green, 6 In. 7.00
Georgian, Tumbler, Iced Tea, Green, 12 Oz. 140.00
Hairpin pattern is listed here as Newport.
Harp, Cake Stand, Crystal, 9 In. 18.00
Harp, Cake Stand, Light Blue, 9 In. 45.00
Heritage, Bowl, Fruit, Crystal, 5 In. 15.00
Heritage, Cup & Saucer, Crystal 9.50
Heritage, Plate, Crystal, 9 1/2 In. 12.00
Hex Optic pattern is listed here as Hexagon Optic.
Hexagon Optic, Sugar & Creamer, Pink 12.00
Hobnail pattern is listed in the Hobnail category.
Holiday, Butter, Pink 45.00
Holiday, Candlestick, Pink, 3 In., Pair . . . . .110.00 to 115.00
Holiday, Console, Footed, Pink, 10 3/4 In. 55.00
Holiday, Plate, Pink, 9 In. . . . . .25.00 to 65.00
Holiday, Tumbler, Footed, Pink, 10 Oz., 4 In. 50.00
Homespun, Bowl, Cereal, Pink, 5 In. 17.00
Homespun, Pitcher, Ball, Tilted, Blue, 42 Oz. 60.00
Homespun, Platter, Oval, Tab Handles, Pink, 13 In. .22.00 to 25.00
Homespun, Sugar, Footed, Pink 10.00
Homespun, Tea Set, Child's, Crystal, Box, 4 Piece 325.00
Homespun, Tumbler, Juice, Pink, 5 Oz., 4 In. 7.00
Honeycomb pattern is listed here as Hexagon Optic.
Horizontal Ribbed pattern is listed here as Manhattan.
Horseshoe pattern is listed here as No. 612.
Indiana Custard, Bowl, Vegetable, Oval, Ivory, 9 1/2 In. 27.00
Indiana Custard, Butter, Cover, Ivory 60.00
Indiana Custard, Plate, Ivory, 9 3/4 In. 28.00
Iris, Berry Bowl, Beaded Edge, Crystal, 4 1/2 In. . . . . .38.00 to 45.00
Iris, Bowl, Ruffled, Crystal, 9 1/2 In. 20.00
Iris, Bowl, Ruffled, Iridescent, 11 In. 13.00
Iris, Candlestick, Crystal, Pair . . . . .40.00 to 42.00
Iris, Candy Jar, Cover, Crystal 185.00
Iris, Coaster, Crystal . . . . .110.00 to 115.00
Iris, Creamer, Iridescent . . . . .13.00 to 14.00
Iris, Cup & Saucer, Crystal 33.00
Iris, Goblet, Iridescent, 8 Oz., 5 3/4 In. 24.00
Iris, Goblet, Wine, Crystal, 4 Oz., 4 1/2 In. . . . . .14.00 to 27.00
Iris, Pitcher, Water, Footed, Crystal, 9 1/2 In. 42.00
Iris, Plate, Crystal, 9 In. 55.00
Iris, Sandwich Server, Iridescent, 11 3/4 In. 35.00
Iris, Sherbet, Footed, Crystal, 2 1/2 In. 10.00
Iris, Tumbler, Footed, Crystal, 6 In. . . . . .19.00 to 27.00
Iris, Vase, Crystal, 9 In. . . . . .25.00 to 45.00
Iris & Herringbone pattern is listed here as Iris.
Jadite, Canister, Coffee, Round, 40 Oz. 300.00
Jadite, Canister, Pepper, Open, 3 In. 90.00
Jadite, Canister, Sugar, 28 Oz. 300.00
Jadite, Canister, Tea, Round, 16 Oz. 175.00
Jadite, Measuring Set, 4 Piece 200.00
Jadite, Pitcher, Milk, 20 Oz. 85.00

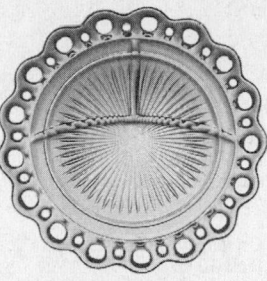

Depression Glass,
Jane-Ray

Depression Glass,
Lace Edge

Depression Glass,
Mayfair Federal

Jamestown pattern is listed here as Tradition.
Jane-Ray, Bowl, Dessert, Fruit, Jadite, 4 7/8 In. 15.00
Jane-Ray, Creamer, Jadite .... 15.00 to 18.00
Jane-Ray, Cup & Saucer, White 12.00
Jane-Ray, Cup, Jadite, After Dinner 45.00
Jane-Ray, Plate, Jadite, 9 1/8 In. 14.00
Jane-Ray, Platter, Oval, Jadite, 9 x 12 In. 42.00
Jane-Ray, Platter, Oval, White, 9 x 12 In. 30.00
Jane-Ray, Salt & Pepper, Jadite 60.00
Jane-Ray, Saucer, Jadite, After Dinner 50.00
Jane-Ray, Soup, Dish, Jadite, 7 5/8 In. .... 20.00 to 32.00
Jubilee, Bowl, 3-Footed, Yellow, 11 1/2 In. 350.00
Jubilee, Plate, Yellow, 7 In. 15.00
Jubilee, Sugar & Creamer, Footed, Yellow 50.00
Jubilee, Tray, Center Handle, Yellow, 11 In. 275.00
June, Bowl, Bouillon, Topaz 18.00
Kings Crown, Candy Dish, Cover, Crystal, Ruby Flashed, 6 In. 25.00
Knife & Fork pattern is listed here as Colonial.
Lace Edge, Bowl, Cereal, Pink, 6 3/8 In. .... 24.00 to 39.00
Lace Edge, Bowl, Crystal, 9 1/2 In. .... 25.00 to 45.00
Lace Edge, Bowl, Ribbed, Pink, 9 1/2 In. 34.00
Lace Edge, Butter, Cover, Pink 85.00
Lace Edge, Cup & Saucer, Pink 36.00
Lace Edge, Flower Bowl, Crystal Frog, Pink 25.00
Lace Edge, Grill Plate, Pink, 10 1/2 In. .... 20.00 to 22.00
Lace Edge, Plate, Pink, 10 1/2 In. .... 30.00 to 33.00
Lace Edge, Plate, Solid Lace, 4 Sections, Pink, 13 In. 60.00
Lace Edge, Relish, 3 Sections, Pink, 7 1/2 In. .... 25.00 to 95.00
Lace Edge, Tumbler, Pink, 9 Oz., 4 1/2 In. 20.00
Lake Como, Salt & Pepper, White 40.00
Lincoln Inn, Goblet, Water, Footed, Red, 2 Oz. 25.00
Lincoln Inn, Plate, Crystal, 8 In. 9.00
Lincoln Inn, Wine, Cobalt Blue, 5 Oz. 30.00
Line 300 pattern is listed in the Paden City category as Peacock and Wild Rose.
Lorain pattern is listed here as No. 615.
Lorna pattern is included in the Cambridge Glass category.
Louisa pattern is listed here as Floragold.
Lovebirds pattern is listed here as Georgian.
Madrid, Butter, Cover, Amber .... 70.00 to 75.00
Madrid, Candlestick, Amber, 2 1/4 In., Pair .... 22.00 to 23.00
Madrid, Coaster, For Lazy Susan, Crystal 25.00
Madrid, Console, Crystal, 11 In. 12.00
Madrid, Cookie Jar, Cover, Amber .... 45.00 to 55.00
Madrid, Creamer, Footed, Green 11.00
Madrid, Cup, Blue 18.00
Madrid, Mold, Gelatin, Amber, 2 1/8 In. .... 16.00 to 20.00

Madrid, Pitcher, Square, Green, 60 Oz., 8 In. . . . . .135.00 to 155.00
Madrid, Plate, Amber, 7 1/2 In. 13.00
Madrid, Salt & Pepper, Amber, 3 1/2 In. 55.00
Madrid, Salt & Pepper, Footed, Amber, 3 1/2 In. 150.00
Madrid, Soup, Cream, Amber, 4 3/4 In. 16.00
Madrid, Soup, Dish, Amber, 7 In. . . . . .16.00 to 18.00
Madrid, Sugar & Creamer, Cover, Amber 65.00
Madrid, Tumbler, Amber, 5 Oz., 3 7/8 In. 18.00
Manhattan, Bowl, Handles, Pink, 5 3/8 In. 26.00
Manhattan, Pitcher, Juice, Crystal, 42 Oz. 30.00
Manhattan, Plate, Crystal, 6 In. 9.00
Manhattan, Tumbler, Footed, Crystal, 10 Oz. 15.00
Manhattan, Tumbler, Footed, Pink, 10 Oz. 25.00
Many Windows pattern is listed here as Roulette.
Martha Washington pattern is included in the Cambridge Glass category.
Mayfair Federal, Creamer, Amber 12.00
Mayfair Federal, Plate, Amber, 9 1/2 In. 20.00
Mayfair Open Rose, Bowl, Vegetable, Oval, Blue, 9 1/2 In. . . . . .70.00 to 80.00
Mayfair Open Rose, Bowl, Vegetable, Oval, Pink, 9 1/2 In. 35.00
Mayfair Open Rose, Cake Plate, Footed, Pink, 10 In. 35.00
Mayfair Open Rose, Cake Plate, Handle, Crystal, 12 In. 57.00
Mayfair Open Rose, Candy Dish, Cover, Blue . . . . .275.00 to 320.00
Mayfair Open Rose, Cookie Dish, Cover, Pink 52.00
Mayfair Open Rose, Creamer, Footed, Pink 30.00
Mayfair Open Rose, Cup, Pink 18.00
Mayfair Open Rose, Decanter, Pink, Stopper, 32 Oz. . . . . .198.00 to 250.00
Mayfair Open Rose, Goblet, Cocktail, Pink, 4 In. 115.00
Mayfair Open Rose, Goblet, Water, Pink, 5 3/4 In. 85.00
Mayfair Open Rose, Grill Plate, Pink, 9 1/2 In. 37.00
Mayfair Open Rose, Pitcher, Blue, 80 Oz., 8 1/2 In. . . . . .195.00 to 325.00
Mayfair Open Rose, Pitcher, Pink, 37 Oz., 6 In. 57.00
Mayfair Open Rose, Pitcher, Pink, 60 Oz., 8 1/2 In. 55.00
Mayfair Open Rose, Plate, Blue, 6 In. . . . . .25.00 to 27.00
Mayfair Open Rose, Plate, Off-Center Ring, Blue, 6 1/2 In. . . . . .25.00 to 45.00
Mayfair Open Rose, Plate, Pink, 9 1/2 In. . . . . .53.00 to 65.00
Mayfair Open Rose, Platter, Oval, Blue, 12 1/2 In. 75.00
Mayfair Open Rose, Sandwich Server, Center Handle, Pink . . . . .55.00 to 57.00
Mayfair Open Rose, Sherbet, With Plate, Blue, 2 Piece 235.00
Mayfair Open Rose, Tumbler, Iced Tea, Footed, Blue, 15 Oz., 6 1/2 In. 250.00
Mayfair Open Rose, Vase, Sweet Pea, Pink . . . . .225.00 to 250.00
Miss America, Bowl, Curved, Crystal, 8 In. 90.00
Miss America, Candy Jar, Cover, Pink 165.00
Miss America, Celery Dish, Oblong, Crystal, 10 1/2 In. 15.00
Miss America, Compote, Crystal, 5 In. . . . . .14.00 to 16.00
Miss America, Compote, Pink, 5 In. 30.00
Miss America, Cup & Saucer, Crystal 14.00
Miss America, Goblet, Water, Pink, 10 Oz., 7 1/2 In. 43.00
Miss America, Goblet, Wine, Pink, 5 Oz., 4 3/4 In. 85.00
Miss America, Pitcher, Pink, 65 Oz., 8 In. 195.00
Miss America, Plate, Crystal, 10 1/4 In. 20.00
Miss America, Relish, 4 Sections, Crystal, 8 3/4 In. 11.00
Miss America, Sherbet, Pink 25.00
Moderntone, Berry Bowl, Cobalt Blue, 5 In. 22.00
Moderntone, Butter, Metal Cover, Cobalt Blue 125.00
Moderntone, Cup & Saucer, Cobalt Blue 15.00
Moderntone, Cup, Pink 10.00
Moderntone, Custard Cup, Cobalt Blue . . . . .20.00 to 22.00
Moderntone, Ice Bowl, Bail, Cobalt Blue 35.00
Moderntone, Plate, Cobalt Blue, 5 3/4 In. 6.00
Moderntone, Plate, Cobalt Blue, 7 3/4 In. 10.00
Moderntone, Platter, Oval, Cobalt Blue, 11 In. 45.00
Moderntone, Sandwich Server, Cobalt Blue, 10 1/2 In. 60.00
Moderntone, Sherbet, Cobalt Blue 13.00

Moderntone, Soup, Cream, Cobalt Blue, 5 In. 25.00
Moderntone, Sugar & Creamer, Cobalt Blue 58.00
Moderntone, Tumbler, Whiskey, Cobalt Blue, 1 1/2 Oz. 46.00
Moderntone Little Hostess Party Set, Cup, Gold 8.00
Moderntone Little Hostess Party Set, Plate, Turquoise, 5 1/4 In. ....7.00 to 8.00
Moderntone Little Hostess Party Set, Sugar & Creamer, Rust 20.00
Moderntone Little Hostess Party Set, Tea Set, Maroon, Box, 16 Piece 310.00
Moderntone Little Hostess Party Set, Teapot, Maroon, Box 275.00
Moderntone Little Hostess Party Set, Teapot, Turquoise 53.00
Moderntone Platonite, Creamer, Dark Blue 5.00
Moderntone Platonite, Cup, Dark Blue ....4.50 to 5.00
Moderntone Platonite, Plate, Black, 8 7/8 In. 13.00
Moderntone Platonite, Plate, Dark Blue, 6 3/4 In. ....4.00 to 4.50
Moderntone Platonite, Plate, Green, 8 7/8 In. 13.00
Moderntone Platonite, Plate, White, Green Stripe, 8 1/8 In. 8.00
Moderntone Platonite, Platter, Oval, Yellow, 11 In. 5.75
Moderntone Platonite, Salt & Pepper, Light Blue 25.00
Moderntone Platonite, Salt & Pepper, White 20.00
Moderntone Platonite, Saucer, White, Red Stripes 2.00
Moderntone Platonite, Sherbet, Yellow 5.50
Moderntone Platonite, Soup, Cream, White, Dark Blue 7.50
Moderntone Platonite, Sugar & Creamer, White, Rust 14.00
Moderntone Platonite, Tumbler, Cone, Footed, White 7.00
Moondrops pattern is listed in the New Martinsville category.
Moonstone, Bowl, Crimped, Crystal, 9 1/2 In. 22.50
Moonstone, Bowl, Crimped, Handle, Crystal, 6 1/2 In. 10.00
Moonstone, Candleholder, Crystal, Pair ....15.00 to 18.00
Moonstone, Cup & Saucer, Crystal 14.00
Moonstone, Goblet, Blue, 10 Oz., 5 1/2 In. 22.00
Moonstone, Goblet, Yellow, 10 Oz., 5 1/2 In. 22.00
Moonstone, Plate, Crystal, 8 In. 16.00
Moonstone, Puff Box, Cover, Crystal ....24.00 to 25.00
Moonstone, Relish, Cloverleaf, 3 Sections, 7 In. 12.00
Moonstone, Sandwich Server, Ruffled, Crystal, 10 In. 27.00
Mt. Pleasant, Grill Plate, Cobalt Blue, 9 In. 12.00
Mt. Pleasant, Tumbler, Footed, Cobalt Blue 50.00
Mt. Vernon pattern is included in the Cambridge Glass category.
New Century, Tumbler, Cobalt Blue, 5 Oz., 3 1/2 In. ....10.00 to 15.00
New Century, Tumbler, Cobalt Blue, 10 Oz., 5 In. 15.00
Newport, Berry Bowl, Cobalt Blue, 5 In. 25.00
Newport, Berry Bowl, Cobalt Blue, 8 1/2 In. 65.00
Newport, Cup, Amethyst 10.00
Newport, Plate, Cobalt Blue, 6 In. 7.00
Newport, Plate, Cobalt Blue, 8 13/16 In. ....18.00 to 40.00
Newport, Salt & Pepper, Amethyst 50.00
Newport, Sherbet, Platonite 2.50
Newport, Sugar & Creamer, Cobalt Blue, 4 3/4 In. 32.00

Depression Glass, Miss America

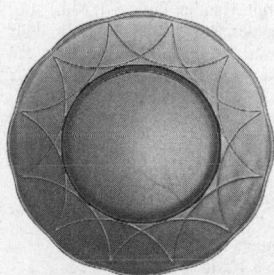

Depression Glass, Newport

Depression Glass,
No. 612

Newport, Tumbler, Water, Cobalt Blue, 9 Oz., 4 1/2 In. 42.00
No. 601 pattern is listed here as Avocado.
No. 610, Berry Bowl, Pink, 4 3/4 In. 65.00
No. 610, Pitcher, Pink, 1/2 Gal. 495.00
No. 610, Pitcher, Yellow, 1/2 Gal. 750.00
No. 612, Bowl, Cereal, Yellow, 6 1/2 In. 38.00
No. 612, Cup & Saucer, Green 8.00
No. 612, Grill Plate, Green, 10 3/8 In. 215.00
No. 612, Plate, Green, 6 In. 9.00
No. 612, Relish, 3 Sections, Footed, Yellow 35.00
No. 612, Sherbet, Yellow 14.00
No. 612, Tumbler, Green, 9 Oz., 4 1/2 In. 25.00
No. 615, Basket, Platter, Oval, Yellow 45.00
No. 615, Bowl, Oval, Yellow, 9 3/4 In. 75.00
No. 615, Cup & Saucer, Yellow, 11 1/2 In. 25.00
No. 615, Cup, Green 10.00
No. 615, Plate, Yellow, 7 3/4 In. 16.00
No. 618, Plate, Crystal, 8 3/8 In. 8.00
No. 618, Saucer, Crystal 4.00
No. 618, Tumbler, Crystal, 10 Oz., 4 1/2 In. ....38.00 to 45.00
No. 620, Bowl, Amber, 7 3/8 In. 20.00
No. 620, Grill Plate, Crystal, 10 3/8 In. 3.00
No. 620, Plate, Amber, 8 3/8 In. 6.00
No. 620, Plate, Crystal, 8 3/8 In. 5.50
No. 620, Plate, Green, 9 3/8 In. 6.00
No. 620, Sandwich Server, Crystal, 11 1/2 In. 15.00
No. 620, Sugar & Creamer, Amber 16.00
No. 620, Tumbler, Water, Footed, Amber, 9 Oz. 20.00
Normandie, Bowl, Iridescent, 6 1/2 In. 8.00
Normandie, Cup & Saucer, Pink 15.00
Normandie, Grill Plate, Iridescent, 11 In. 10.00
Normandie, Pitcher, Pink, 80 Oz., 8 In. 185.00
Normandie, Plate, Pink, 8 In. 16.00
Normandie, Platter, Iridescent, 11 3/4 In. 12.00
Normandie, Tumbler, Iced Tea, Pink, 12 Oz., 5 1/4 In. 175.00
Old Cafe, Candy Dish, Crystal 9.00
Old Cafe, Plate, Pink, 10 In. 55.00
Old Colony pattern is listed here as Lace Edge.
Old English, Tumbler, Green, 4 3/4 In. 24.00
Old Florentine pattern is listed here as Florentine No. 1.
Open Lace pattern is listed here as Lace Edge.
Open Rose pattern is listed here as Mayfair Open Rose.
Orchid, Sandwich Server, Center Handle, Square, Yellow 110.00
Ovide, Creamer, Blue Flowers, White 9.00
Ovide, Creamer, Green 3.00
Ovide, Plate, White, 9 In. 8.00
Ovide, Plate, Yellow, 8 In. 5.00
Ovide, Salt & Pepper, Green 35.00
Oyster & Pearl, Bowl, Fruit, Handle, Pink, 5 1/2 In. 25.00
Oyster & Pearl, Candleholder, Royal Ruby, 3 1/2 In., Pair 55.00
Palm Optic, Oyster Cocktail, Aqua, 2 1/2 In. 20.00
Palm Optic, Parfait, Aqua, Footed, 5 Oz. 20.00
Panelled Aster pattern is listed here as Primo.
Parrot pattern is listed here as Sylvan.
Patrician, Berry Bowl, Amber, 8 1/2 In. 20.00
Patrician, Berry Bowl, Crystal, 5 In. 12.00
Patrician, Bowl, Cereal, Amber, 6 In. ....25.00 to 28.00
Patrician, Butter, Cover, Amber 100.00
Patrician, Cup & Saucer, Crystal 17.00
Patrician, Grill Plate, Amber, 10 1/2 In. ....3.50 to 12.00
Patrician, Nappy, Amber, 8 1/2 In. 9.00
Patrician, Pitcher, Molded Handle, Amber, 75 Oz., 8 In. 120.00
Patrician, Plate, Amber, 9 In. 13.00

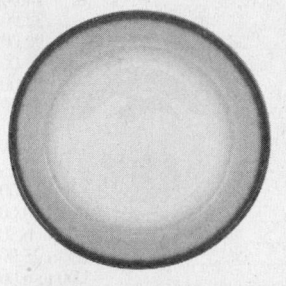

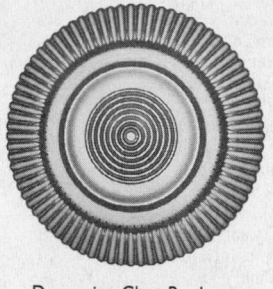

Depression Glass, Ovide   Depression Glass, Petalware   Depression Glass, Ring

Patrician, Plate, Crystal, 9 In. 9.00
Patrician, Platter, Oval, Crystal, 9 1/2 In. 30.00
Patrician, Salt & Pepper, Amber ....55.00 to 60.00
Patrician, Saltshaker, Pink 45.00
Patrician, Sherbet, Green 16.00
Patrician, Soup, Cream, Pink, 4 3/4 In. 18.00
Patrician, Tumbler, Footed, Amber, 8 Oz., 5 1/4 In. 49.00
Patrick, Tray, 2 Handles, Topaz, 11 In. 55.00
Peacock & Wild Rose pattern is listed in the Paden City category.
Petal Swirl pattern is listed here as Swirl.
Petalware, Berry Bowl, Monax, 9 In. 20.00
Petalware, Bowl, Cremax, Gold Trim, 9 In. 18.00
Petalware, Cup & Saucer, Cremax, Gold Trim 8.00
Petalware, Cup & Saucer, Monax 9.00
Petalware, Lamp Shade, Cremax, 8 1/2 In. 7.00
Petalware, Mustard, Underplate, Cobalt Blue 10.00
Petalware, Pitcher, Pink, 80 Oz. 28.00
Petalware, Plate, Crystal, 9 In. 9.00
Petalware, Plate, Monax, 9 In. 12.00
Petalware, Platter, Oval, Pink, 13 In. 20.00
Petalware, Salver, Pink, 11 In. 18.00
Petalware, Soup, Cream, Pink, 4 1/2 In. 18.00
Petalware, Sugar & Creamer, Cremax, Gold Trim 15.00
Philbe, Plate, Blue, 8 In. 130.00
Philbe, Tumbler, Blue, 5 In. 135.00
Pineapple & Floral pattern is listed here as No. 618.
Pinwheel pattern is listed here as Sierra.
Poinsettia pattern is listed here as Floral.
Popeye & Olive, Candy Dish, Low Pedestal, Red 24.00
Poppy No. 1 pattern is listed here as Florentine No. 1.
Poppy No. 2 pattern is listed here as Florentine No. 2.
Pretty Polly Party Dishes, see also the related pattern Doric & Pansy.
Primo, Cake Plate, Footed, Green, 10 In. 30.00
Primo, Plate, Green, 7 1/2 In. 9.00
Princess, Ashtray, Green, 4 1/2 In. 95.00
Princess, Bowl, Cereal, Green, 5 In. 40.00
Princess, Bowl, Hat, Green, 9 1/2 In. 50.00
Princess, Bowl, Octagonal, Green, 9 In. ....40.00 to 52.00
Princess, Butter, Cover, Green, 7 1/2 In. 125.00
Princess, Candy Dish, Cover, Green 65.00
Princess, Cookie Jar, Cover, Green 56.00
Princess, Cup & Saucer, Pink 28.00
Princess, Cup & Saucer, Yellow 8.00
Princess, Grill Plate, Green, 9 1/2 In. 20.00
Princess, Pitcher, Pink, 37 Oz., 6 In. ....75.00 to 90.00
Princess, Plate, Green, 9 1/2 In. 22.00
Princess, Plate, Pink, 8 In. 15.00

Princess, Plate, Topaz, 9 1/2 In. 14.00
Princess, Relish, 2 Sections, Green, 7 1/2 In. 32.90
Princess, Salt & Pepper, Yellow 90.00
Princess, Sherbet, Footed, Green ....15.00 to 24.00
Princess, Sugar & Creamer, Cover, Green 56.00
Princess Feather, Sauce, Crystal 35.00
Prismatic Line pattern is listed here as Queen Mary.
Provincial pattern is listed here as Bubble.
Pyramid pattern is listed here as No. 610.
Queen Anne, Coaster, Crystal, 3 1/2 In. 12.00
Queen Mary, Berry Bowl, Pink, 4 1/2 In. ....5.00 to 10.00
Queen Mary, Bowl, Cereal, Crystal, 6 In. 6.50
Queen Mary, Bowl, Cereal, Pink, 6 In. ....23.00 to 25.00
Queen Mary, Bowl, Handle, Pink, 4 In. ....5.00 to 6.00
Queen Mary, Butter, Crystal 25.00
Queen Mary, Candlestick, Double Branch, Crystal, 4 1/2 In. 7.50
Queen Mary, Compote, Crystal, 5 3/4 In. 8.00
Queen Mary, Creamer, Pink, Oval 7.50
Queen Mary, Cup & Saucer, Pink 18.00
Queen Mary, Plate, Crystal, 9 3/4 In. 18.00
Queen Mary, Plate, Pink, 6 In. 7.00
Queen Mary, Plate, Pink, 9 3/4 In. 58.00
Queen Mary, Sherbet, Footed, Crystal 5.00
Queen Mary, Sherbet, Footed, Pink 8.50
Queen Mary, Sugar, Oval, Crystal 7.50
Queen Mary, Tumbler, Water, Pink, 9 Oz., 4 In. ....14.00 to 25.00
Ring, Goblet, Crystal, Platinum Trim, 9 Oz., 7 1/4 In. 10.00
Ring, Pitcher, Crystal, 80 Oz., 8 1/2 In. 45.00
Ring, Plate, Crystal, Platinum Trim, 8 In. 3.50
Ring, Tumbler, Juice, Green, 5 Oz., 3 1/2 In. 7.00
Rock Crystal, Cake Stand, Green, 11 In. 48.00
Rock Crystal, Candlestick, Red, 5 1/2 In. 190.00
Rock Crystal, Console, Footed, Yellow, 12 1/2 In. 65.00
Rock Crystal, Cordial, Footed, Red, 1 Oz. 65.00
Rock Crystal, Finger Bowl, With Plate, Red, 5 & 7 In., 2 Piece 80.00
Rock Crystal, Pitcher, Cover, Pink, 9 In. 350.00
Rock Crystal, Sherbet, Footed, Crystal, 3 1/2 Oz. 4.00
Rope pattern is listed here as Colonial Fluted.
Rose Point, Relish, 3 Sections, Crystal, 10 In. 55.00
Rosemary, Berry Bowl, Amber, 5 In. 10.00
Rosemary, Cup & Saucer, Amber 11.00
Rosemary, Plate, Amber, 6 3/4 In. 5.50
Rosemary, Plate, Pink, 9 1/2 In. 20.00
Rosemary, Sugar & Creamer, Amber ....17.00 to 20.00
Roulette, Plate, Green, 8 1/2 In. 8.00
Roulette, Tumbler, Cone, Footed, Green, 10 Oz., 5 1/2 In. 30.00
Royal Lace, Bowl, 3-Footed, Ruffled, Crystal, 10 In. 45.00
Royal Lace, Bowl, 3-Footed, Ruffled, Pink, 10 In. 150.00
Royal Lace, Bowl, Vegetable, Oval, Cobalt Blue, 11 In. 65.00
Royal Lace, Butter, Cover, Cobalt Blue ....800.00 to 875.00
Royal Lace, Candlestick, Ruffled, Cobalt Blue, Pair 600.00
Royal Lace, Candlestick, Straight, Cobalt Blue, Pair ....160.00 to 215.00
Royal Lace, Cookie Jar, Cover, Pink 80.00
Royal Lace, Creamer, Cobalt Blue 60.00
Royal Lace, Cup & Saucer, Cobalt Blue 45.00
Royal Lace, Cup & Saucer, Pink 30.00
Royal Lace, Nut Bowl, Pink 650.00
Royal Lace, Pitcher, Green, 64 Oz, 8 In. 120.00
Royal Lace, Pitcher, Ice Lip, Green, 68 Oz., 8 In. 130.00
Royal Lace, Plate, Crystal, 9 7/8 In. 25.00
Royal Lace, Salt & Pepper, Green ....135.00 to 150.00
Royal Lace, Sherbet, Metal Holder, Cobalt Blue 45.00
Royal Lace, Soup, Cream, Green ....32.00 to 40.00

Depression Glass,
Sandwich Indiana

Depression Glass,
Sharon

Depression Glass,
Sierra

Royal Lace, Sugar, Cover, Pink 70.00
Royal Lace, Tumbler, Cobalt Blue, 5 Oz., 3 1/2 In. 50.00
Royal Lace, Tumbler, Crystal, 9 Oz., 4 1/8 In. 10.00
Royal Ruby, Berry Bowl, Round, 4 1/2 In. 18.00
Royal Ruby, Cup, Square 6.00
Royal Ruby, Goblet, Ball Stem 15.00
Royal Ruby, Pitcher, Water, Upright, 3 Qt. 43.00
Royal Ruby, Soup, Dish, 7 1/2 In. 13.00
Royal Ruby, Tumbler, 9 Oz., 4 1/8 In. ....5.00 to 6.50
S Pattern, Cup & Saucer, Crystal 5.00
S Pattern, Plate, Crystal, 8 1/4 In. 4.00
Sail Boat pattern is listed here as Sportsman Series.
Sandwich Anchor Hocking, Berry Bowl, Amber, 4 7/8 In. 4.00
Sandwich Anchor Hocking, Bowl, Cereal, Forest Green, 6 1/2 In. 70.00
Sandwich Anchor Hocking, Bowl, Oval, Crystal, 8 1/4 In. 75.00
Sandwich Anchor Hocking, Bowl, Royal Ruby, 5 1/4 In. 25.00
Sandwich Anchor Hocking, Cup & Saucer, Amber 7.00
Sandwich Anchor Hocking, Cup, Forest Green 43.00
Sandwich Anchor Hocking, Pitcher, Juice, Forest Green, 6 In. 250.00
Sandwich Anchor Hocking, Punch Bowl, Crystal 20.00
Sandwich Anchor Hocking, Tumbler, Forest Green, 9 Oz., 4 1/2 In. ....6.00 to 10.00
Sandwich Indiana, Candlestick, Amber, 8 1/2 In., Pair 26.00
Sandwich Indiana, Candlestick, Green, 3 1/2 In., Pair 45.00
Sandwich Indiana, Cup, Crystal 3.50
Sandwich Indiana, Decanter, Stopper, Crystal 30.00
Sandwich Indiana, Plate, Green, 10 1/2 In. 18.00
Sandwich Indiana, Plate, Oval, Indentation, Crystal, 8 In. 5.00
Sandwich Indiana, Sherbet, Footed, Amber, 3 1/4 In. 5.00
Sandwich Indiana, Tray, Round, Green, 10 In. 27.00
Saxon pattern is listed here as Coronation.
Sharon, Berry Bowl, Amber, 8 1/2 In. ....6.00 to 10.00
Sharon, Berry Bowl, Pink, 5 In. 14.00
Sharon, Berry Set, Amber, 7 Piece 50.00
Sharon, Bowl, Fruit, Amber, 10 1/2 In. ....18.00 to 21.00
Sharon, Bowl, Vegetable, Oval, Pink, 9 1/2 In. 35.00
Sharon, Bread Plate, Pink, 6 In. 9.00
Sharon, Butter, Cover, Green 104.00
Sharon, Cake Plate, Footed, Crystal, 11 1/2 In. 15.00
Sharon, Cake Plate, Footed, Pink, 11 1/2 In. ....38.00 to 45.00
Sharon, Cheese Dish, Amber ....195.00 to 225.00
Sharon, Cup & Saucer, Amber 10.00
Sharon, Cup & Saucer, Pink 16.00
Sharon, Jam Dish, Green 75.00
Sharon, Plate, Pink, 9 1/2 In. ....15.00 to 25.00
Sharon, Platter, Oval, Amber, 12 1/2 In. 19.00
Sharon, Platter, Oval, Green, 12 1/2 In. 35.00

Sharon, Platter, Oval, Pink, 12 1/2 In. 33.00
Sharon, Salt & Pepper, Green 75.00
Sharon, Sherbet, Footed, Amber 12.00
Sharon, Soup, Cream, Pink, 5 In. 40.00
Sharon, Soup, Dish, Amber, 7 1/2 In. ....50.00 to 58.00
Sharon, Sugar & Creamer, Cover, Amber 55.00
Sharon, Sugar, Cover, Green 61.00
Sharon, Sugar, Cover, Pink 55.00
Sharon, Tumbler, Iced Tea, Footed, Amber, 15 Oz., 6 1/2 In. 138.00
Sharon, Tumbler, Thick, Pink, 12 Oz., 5 1/4 In. 150.00
Sharon, Tumbler, Thin, Pink, 9 Oz., 4 1/8 In. ....45.00 to 48.00
Shell, Platter, Oval, Jadite, 9 1/2 x 13 In. 90.00
Sierra, Bowl, Cereal, Pink, 5 1/2 In. 15.00
Sierra, Bowl, Green, 5 1/2 In. 20.00
Sierra, Butter, Green 65.00
Sierra, Cup & Saucer, Pink ....15.00 to 24.00
Sierra, Pitcher, Green, 32 Oz., 6 1/2 In. 130.00
Snowflake, Cake Plate, Pink, 12 1/2 In. 25.00
Spiral, Pitcher, Green, 58 Oz., 7 5/8 In. 30.00
Spiral Flutes pattern is listed in the Duncan Miller category as Swirl.
Spoke pattern is listed here as Patrician.
Sportsman Series, Pitcher, White Ship, Cobalt Blue, 8 In. ....56.00 to 65.00
Sportsman Series, Plate, White Ship, Cobalt Blue, 9 In. 27.00
Sportsman Series, Tumbler, White Ship, Roly Poly, Cobalt Blue 12.00
Starlight, Sugar, Crystal 15.00
Stippled Rose Band pattern is listed here as S Pattern.
Strawberry, Sugar, Cover, Green, Large 100.00
Sunflower, Ashtray, Center Design, Green, 5 In. 15.00
Sunflower, Ashtray, Pink, 5 In. 7.00
Swirl, Bowl, Pink, 10 In. 20.00
Swirl, Bowl, Salad, Blue, 9 In. 18.00
Swirl, Bowl, Ultramarine, 9 In. 30.00
Swirl, Butter, Pink 200.00
Swirl, Console, Footed, Pink, 10 1/2 In. 95.00
Swirl, Lamp, Oil, Pink, 12 In. 65.00
Swirl, Plate, Crystal, 9 1/8 In. 6.00
Swirl, Plate, Ultramarine, 9 1/4 In. ....19.00 to 20.00
Swirl, Salt & Pepper, Ultramarine 45.00
Swirl, Sandwich Server, Ultramarine, 12 1/2 In. 35.00
Swirl, Soup, Dish, Lug Handle, Ultramarine 48.00
Swirl, Sugar & Creamer, Ultramarine 30.00
Swirl, Tumbler, Footed, Ultramarine, 9 Oz. 42.00
Swirl, Vase, Footed, Ultramarine, 8 1/2 In. 37.00
Swirl Fire-King, Cup & Saucer, Golden Shell, After Dinner 15.00
Swirl Fire-King, Cup & Saucer, Iridescent Luster, After Dinner 15.00
Swirl Fire-King, Cup & Saucer, Jadite, After Dinner 90.00
Swirl Fire-King, Soup, Dish, Jadite, 7 5/8 In. 110.00
Sylvan, Butter, Green 400.00
Sylvan, Grill Plate, Round, Green, 10 1/2 In. ....32.00 to 40.00
Sylvan, Jam Dish, Amber, 7 In. 33.00
Sylvan, Sugar & Creamer, Cover, Green 260.00
Tea Room, Bowl, Salad, Green, 8 3/4 In. 150.00
Tea Room, Goblet, Pink, 6 1/8 In. 80.00
Tea Room, Lamp, Cobalt Blue 70.00
Tea Room, Pitcher, Footed, Crystal, 64 Oz. 155.00
Tea Room, Pitcher, Footed, Green, 64 Oz. 175.00
Tea Room, Salt & Pepper, Pink 70.00
Tea Room, Sherbet, Footed, Pink 60.00
Tea Room, Sugar & Creamer, Green 42.00
Tea Room, Tray, Center Handle, Green 200.00
Tea Room, Tray, Center Handle, Pink 50.00
Tea Room, Tumbler Service, Amber, 9 Oz., 5 1/8 In. 200.00
Thistle, Plate, Crystal, 8 In. 9.00

Sometimes glasses get a cloudy look from the lime deposits in hard water. Cover the cloudy part with wet potato peelings for 24 hours. Rinse, dry.

Depression Glass,
Windmill

Threading pattern is listed here as Old English.
Tradition, Goblet, Wine, Green, 4 Oz. 15.00
Tradition, Goblet, Wine, Pink, 4 Oz. 22.00
Tulip, Cup & Saucer, Blue 18.00
Tulip, Nappy, Blue, 9 1/2 In. 14.00
Turquoise Blue, Creamer 8.00
Turquoise Blue, Cup & Saucer 7.00
Turquoise Blue, Plate, 9 In. 22.00
Turquoise Blue, Sugar 8.00
Twentieth Century, Cup & Saucer, Child's, Crystal 4.50
Twentieth Century, Cup & Saucer, Child's, Crystal, Blue Stripe 6.00
Twentieth Century, Plate, Crystal, Blue 8.00
Twisted Optic, Cup, Pink 5.00
Twisted Optic, Plate, Green, 8 In. 5.00
Vertical Ribbed pattern is listed here as Queen Mary.
Victory, Cup & Saucer, Cobalt Blue 50.00
Victory, Goblet, Cobalt Blue, 7 Oz., 5 In. ....75.00 to 85.00
Victory, Plate, Pink, 8 In. 8.00
Vitrock, Bowl, Cereal, White, 7 1/2 In. 20.00
Vitrock, Creamer, White 5.50
Waffle pattern is listed here as Waterford.
Waterford, Berry Bowl, Pink, 4 3/4 In. ....18.00 to 24.00
Waterford, Bowl, Cereal, Crystal, 5 1/2 In. 18.00
Waterford, Butter, Cover, Crystal 22.00
Waterford, Creamer, Crystal ....3.50 to 4.00
Waterford, Pitcher, Tilted, Crystal, 42 Oz. 22.00
Waterford, Sugar, Cover, Crystal ....6.00 to 10.00
Wheat, Cup & Saucer, White 10.00
White Ship pattern is listed here as Sportsman Series.
Wild Rose pattern is listed here as Dogwood.
Windmill, Tumbler, Water, Cobalt Blue, 9 Oz., 4 5/8 In. 8.00
Windsor, Berry Bowl, Pink, 8 1/2 In. 20.00
Windsor, Cake Plate, Footed, Green, 13 1/2 In. 38.00
Windsor, Candlestick, Crystal, 3 In., Pair 20.00
Windsor, Chop Plate, Pink, 13 In. 45.00
Windsor, Console, Pink, 12 1/2 In. 150.00
Windsor, Cup & Saucer, Crystal 8.00
Windsor, Pitcher, Pink, 52 Oz., 6 3/4 In. 30.00
Windsor, Plate, Green, 7 In. ....25.00 to 30.00
Windsor, Salt & Pepper, Green 45.00
Windsor, Tray, Handles, Pink, 8 1/2 x 9 3/4 In. 40.00
Windsor, Water Set, Pink, 5 Piece 40.00
Windsor Diamond pattern is listed here as Windsor.

DERBY has been marked on porcelain made in the city of Derby, England, since about 1748. The original Derby factory closed in 1848, but others opened there and continued to produce quality porcelain. The Crown Derby mark began appearing on Derby wares in the 1770s.

Candlestick, Birds In Branches, 2 Birds, Orange, Purple Plumage, Perched, 10 In. 3165.00
Candlestick, Birds In Branches, Brown, Yellow Plumage, Perched, 9 1/2 In., Pair 6035.00

Dish, Japan, Heart Shape, Leaf Medallions, Puce Spirals, Peony Sprays, Blue, 10 In. 690.00
Dish, King's Pattern, Center Prunus Tree, Flowers, Leaf Border, Signed, c.1825, 11 In. ...   805.00
Dish, King's Pattern, Flowering Tree, Peonies, C-Scroll Handles, c.1825, 12 1/2 In. 1380.00
Dish, King's Pattern, Oval, Flowering Prunus Tree, Leaf Border, Signed, 1825, 11 In. 805.00
Figurine, Tiger Crouching, With 1 Paw Raised On Grassy Base, 2 1/4 In. 1035.00
Inkwell, Garden Gate, Gold Highlights, Blue, Red, Green, 2 1/8 x 6 x 4 In. 75.00
Jug, Cream, Helmet Shape, Summer Flower Bouquet, Twig Handle, 1760, 5 In. 1265.00
Plate, Clover, Red & Gilt Scrolls, Early 19th Century, 9 1/2 In., 6 Piece 385.00
Plate, Japan, Stylized Flowering Tree, Vines, Iron Red, Blue, Gold, 1800-1825, 8 In. 660.00
Plate, King's Pattern, Center Prunus Tree, Barr, Flight & Barr, c.1810, 9 In., 6 Piece 3450.00
Platter, Center Crest Of Hope, Leaning Against Anchor, Motto, c.1786, 6 1/8 In. 5520.00
Platter, Imari, Cobalt Blue, Red & Gold, Signed, 21 1/2 x 18 In. 577.00
Sauceboat, Allover Floral Sprays, Iron Red, Purple, Yellow, Green, 1765, 6 3/4 In., Pair ..   1380.00
Saucer, Chubby Cupid Sitting On Cloud, Puce Flower Sprigs, 1785, 4 7/8 In. 230.00
Teacup, Flared Saucer, Scroll Handle, Roses, Cornflowers, William Duesbury, 1810 .....   58.00
Tureen, Soup, Underplate, Imari, Blue Mark & 563 In Red, 19th Century 550.00
Vase, Allover Raised Floral Gilding, Butterflies, Yellow Ground, c.1884, 6 1/2 In. 675.00
Vase, River Landscape, Allegorical Figure, Noon & Evening, Gilt Ground, 10 In., Pair ...   3450.00

DICK TRACY, the comic strip, started in 1931. Tracy was also the hero of movies from 1937 to 1947 and again in 1990, and starred in a radio series in the 1940s and a television series in the 1950s. Memorabilia from all these activities are collected.

Ad, Comic Strip, Ford-Autolite, Dick, Diamond Thief, Chester Gould, 1966, 7 x 10 In. 5.00
Car, Squad, 6 3/4 In. 75.00
Car, Squad, 11 In. 170.00
Card, Caramel, Johnson Candy Co., Chicago, 1940, 12 Piece 200.00
Comic Book, Popped Wheat, 1940 ....   13.00
Comic Strip, Chester Gould, 1944, 6 x 20 In. 1760.00
Crime Stoppers Set, Nightstick, Handcuffs, Badge, 1930s, 10 1/2 x 8 In. ....110.00 to 125.00
Dart Gun, With Magnifier, Larami, On Card, 1969, 6 x 8 1/4 In. 65.00
Doll, Bonnie Braids, Ideal, 1950s 145.00
Glass, Black Logo On Front, Name On Reverse, Frosted, 5 1/2 In. 14.00
Knife, B.O. Plenty, Whistle, Magnify Glass, Red Cord, Pocket 70.00
Plate & Mug Set, 2 Piece 450.00
Soaky, Dick Wearing Trench Coat & Fedora, 1960s 110.00
Suspenders, On Card 85.00

DICKENS WARE pieces are listed in the Royal Doulton and Weller categories.

DINNERWARE used in the United States from the 1930s through the 1950s is listed here. Most was made in potteries in southern Ohio, West Virginia, and California. A few patterns were made in Japan, England, and other countries. Dishes were sold in gift shops and department stores, or were given away as premiums. Many of these patterns are listed in this book in their own categories, such as Autumn Leaf, Azalea, Coors, Fiesta, Franciscan, Hall, Harker, Harlequin, Red Wing, Riviera, Russel Wright, Vernon Kilns, Watt, and Willow. For more information, see *Kovels' Depression Glass & Dinnerware Price List.*

Amberstone, Coffeepot, Homer Laughlin 95.00
Amberstone, Teapot, Homer Laughlin 95.00
Antique Grape, Bowl, Metlox, 6 1/2 In. 10.00
Antique Grape, Casserole, Cover, Metlox, 2 Qt. 100.00
Antique Grape, Creamer, Metlox 22.00
Antique Grape, Cup & Saucer, Metlox 13.00
Bamboo, Bowl, Blair, Large 80.00
Bird, Bowl, Teardrop, Blair 45.00
Bird, Plate, Salad, Blair, 4 Piece 180.00
Boots & Saddle, Plate, Wallace China, 7 In. 55.00
Crab Apple, Casserole, Cover, Southern Potteries 95.00
Currier & Ives, Berry Bowl, Blue, Royal China, 5 1/2 In. 3.50
Currier & Ives, Bowl, Cereal, Blue, Royal China, 6 In. 8.50

Currier & Ives, Bowl, Vegetable, Blue, Royal China, 9 1/4 In. 15.00
Currier & Ives, Bread Plate, Royal China 3.00
Currier & Ives, Casserole, Cover, Blue, Royal China 85.00
Currier & Ives, Casserole, Cover, Royal China 100.00
Currier & Ives, Chop Plate, Blue, Royal China, 12 In. 15.00
Currier & Ives, Cup & Saucer, Blue, Royal China .... 2.50 to 5.00
Currier & Ives, Gravy Boat, Tab Handles, Royal China 30.00
Currier & Ives, Plate, Blue, Royal China, 10 In. 6.00
Currier & Ives, Plate, Blue, Royal China, 6 In. 1.50
Currier & Ives, Plate, Royal China, 10 In. 5.00
Currier & Ives, Platter, Blue, Royal China, 13 In. 22.00
Currier & Ives, Soup, Dish, Blue, Royal China 8.50
Currier & Ives, Sugar, Blue, Royal China 12.50
Currier & Ives, Sugar, Cover, Royal China 15.00
Debutante, Pie Server, Homer Laughlin 30.00
Eggshell Nautilus, Cup & Saucer, Homer Laughlin. 2.50
Eggshell Nautilus, Platter, Homer Laughlin, 11 In. 20.00
Friendly Village, Tureen, Platter, Johnson Bros., 20 In. 286.00
Gay Plaid, Cup & Saucer, Blair 2.00
Gay Plaid, Sugar, Blair 10.00
Liberty Blue, Butter, Cover 65.00
Liberty Blue, Gravy Boat, Liner 65.00
Liberty Blue, Plate, 8 3/4 In. 28.00
Liberty Blue, Plate, 10 In. .... 7.50 to 16.00
Liberty Blue, Platter, Meat, 12 In. .... 45.00 to 65.00
Liberty Blue, Sugar & Creamer, Cover .... 50.00 to 65.00
Liberty Blue, Tureen, Soup, Underplate, Cover 350.00
Lu-Ray, Bowl, Persian Cream, Oval, Taylor, Smith & Taylor, 10 In. 12.00
Lu-Ray, Bowl, Vegetable, Surf Green, Round, Taylor, Smith & Taylor 50.00
Lu-Ray, Bowl, Windsor Blue, Taylor, Smith & Taylor, 5 In. 8.00
Lu-Ray, Cup & Saucer, Sharon Pink, Taylor, Smith & Taylor 10.00
Lu-Ray, Plate, Chatham Gray, Taylor, Smith & Taylor, 15 In. 35.00
Lu-Ray, Plate, Persian Cream, Taylor, Smith & Taylor, 6 1/2 In. 7.00
Lu-Ray, Plate, Sharon Pink, Taylor, Smith & Taylor, 6 1/2 In. 7.00
Lu-Ray, Plate, Sharon Pink, Taylor, Smith & Taylor, 9 In. 15.00
Lu-Ray, Plate, Sharon Pink, Taylor, Smith & Taylor, 15 In. 45.00
Lu-Ray, Plate, Surf Green, Taylor, Smith & Taylor, 10 In. 20.00
Lu-Ray, Platter, Sharon Pink, Taylor, Smith & Taylor, 11 1/2 In. 12.00
Lu-Ray, Salt & Pepper, Sharon Pink, Taylor, Smith & Taylor 20.00
Mexicana, Canister, Round, Homer Laughlin 310.00
Mulberry, Bowl, Homer Laughlin, 5 In. 34.00
Orange Tree, Bowl, Green, Homer Laughlin, 10 In. 60.00
Plantation Ivy, Tumbler, Iced Tea, Blue Ridge 85.00
Plantation Ivy, Tumbler, Juice, Footed, Blue Ridge 45.00
Provincial Blue, Sugar, Metlox 15.00
Renaissance, Cup & Saucer, Dark Green, Fitz & Floyd 40.00
Renaissance, Plate, Dinner, Dark Green, Fitz & Floyd 45.00
Rooster, Tureen, Basket Weave, With Ladle, Metlox, 1940s, 16 In. 450.00
Tulip, Mug, Fitz, Floyd 27.00
Westward Ho, Mug, Wallace China 45.00
Westward Ho, Pitcher, Water, Wallace China 50.00

DIONNE QUINTUPLETS were born in Canada on May 28, 1934. The
publicity about their birth and their special status as wards of the Canadian government made them famous throughout the world. Visitors
could watch the girls play; reporters interviewed the girls and the staff.
Thousands of special dolls and souvenirs were made picturing the
quints at different ages. Emilie died in 1954, Marie in 1970. Yvonne,
Annette, and Cecile still live in Canada.

Book, 1930s 35.00
Calendar, 1935, 5 3/4 x 12 In. 17.00
Doll Set, On Ferris Wheel, Composition, Madame Alexander, 1936, 18 In. 1035.00
Doll Set, On Seesaw, Cotton Play Suits, Madame Alexander, 8 In. Each 3250.00

Doll Set, Seated In Bed, Extra Sets Of Clothing, Madame Alexander 1995.00
Magazine, Life, Cover Of The 3rd Birthday, May 17, 1937, 8 Pages 25.00
Spoon, Cecile, Silver Plate 22.00
Teaspoon Set, Silver Plate, Set Of 5 . . . . 200.00

DISNEYANA is a collector's term. Walt Disney and his company introduced many comic characters to the world. Collectors search for examples of the work of the Disney Studios and the many commercial
products modeled after his characters, including Mickey Mouse, Donald Duck, and recent films, like *Beauty and the Beast* and *The Little
Mermaid.*

Alarm Clock, Mickey Mouse, Red Metal, Brass Bells, WDP, Bradley, 4-In. Face 42.00
Ashtray, Tinker Bell, Disneyland, Porcelain, Gilt Trim, 1950s, 6 In. 33.00
Badge, World Of Motion, Pressed Tin, Giveaway, 1980 . . . . 3.00
Bank, Big Al, Figural, WDP 50.00
Bank, Donald Duck, Plastic 25.00
Bank, Donald Duck, Register, Painted, Dime, 2 1/2 In. 297.00
Bank, Dopey, Composition, Crown, U.S., 1938, 7 In. 143.00
Bank, Dopey, Registered, Painted, Tin, Dime, 2 1/2 In. 143.00
Bank, Mickey Mouse . . . . *Illus* 650.00
Bank, Mickey Mouse, In Castle, Wooden 154.00
Bank, Mickey Mouse, Vinyl, WDP, PAL Plastic, 11 In. 25.00
Bank, Mickey Mouse, With Trunk, Composition, M 202, 6 In. 110.00
Bank, Pinocchio, Composition, 5 1/4 In. 260.00
Bank, Pinocchio, Composition, Crown, U.S., 5 1/8 In. 77.00
Bank, Pinocchio, Figural Head, Disney 125.00
Bank, Register, Snow White, Tin, Dime, 2 1/2 In. 176.00
Book, Adventures Of Mickey Mouse, Book 1, 1931 . . . . 150.00
Book, Big Red, Little Golden Book, 1963 . . . . 10.00
Book, Cinderella, McLoughlin, 1887 . . . . 85.00
Book, Desert Inn Mystery, Annette, Whitman, 1957 . . . . 8.00
Book, Disneyland On The Air, Little Golden Book, 1959 . . . . 8.00
Book, Donald Duck & Mouseketeers, Little Golden Book, 1956 . . . . 14.00
Book, Donald's Lucky Day, Paperback, 1939, 16 Pages 39.00
Book, Encyclopedia Of Animated Characters, Aladdin On Cover, Dust Jacket 20.00
Book, Epcot Center, Walt Disney World, Richard Beard, 1982 . . . . 53.00
Book, Here They Are, Mickey Mouse, Walt Disney & Ardra Wavle, 1940, 56 Pages 22.00
Book, Jungle Book, Baloo, Soaky Cover, 1966 . . . . 12.00
Book, Scamp, Adventures Of A Little Puppy, Little Golden Book, 1957 . . . . 15.00
Book, Story Of Disneyland, D50001, Soft Cover, 1955 . . . . 175.00
Book, Story Of Donald Duck, Hardback, 1938, 96 Pages 25.00
Book, Walt Disney Magic Moments, 1973 . . . . 20.00
Book, Walt Disney World & EPCOT Center Crescent, Hardcover, 1987 . . . . 18.00
Book, Walt Disney's Disneyland, 1969 . . . . 42.00
Book, Walt Disney's Disneyland, Soft Cover, 1987 . . . . 15.00
Book Bag, Snow White & Seven Dwarfs, 1950s 155.00

**To remove a musty odor from a
book, sprinkle talcum powder
between the pages, then wrap the
book and store it for a few
months. When you open it again,
brush out all the powder and the
musty smell will be gone.**

Disneyana, Bank, Mickey Mouse

Bookmark, Ruler, Bambi, Thumper, Flower, Prevent Forest Fires, Paper, 1944, 6 In. 20.00
Bowl, Donald Duck, Setting Up Picnic, Luster Ware, 1950s, 6 In. 23.00
Bracelet, Charm, Sterling Silver, 1932, 26 Charms 125.00
Bumper Sticker, Disneyland, Star Tours, 1986 . . . . 8.00
Candy Container, Daisy Duck, Long Bill, Red Dress, Black Hat, Germany, 6 1/2 In. 240.00
Canister, Mickey Mouse & Characters, Hand Painted, Name Gloria, Cardboard 100.00
Car, Parade, Marx 295.00
Car, Roadster, Mickey Mouse, Silver, Blue, Hong Kong, 5 In. 7.00
Card, Mickey Mouse, No. 2, Cats & Dogs, Mickey Mouse Bubble Gum Co. 67.00
Card, Valentine, Caricature, Mickey & Minnie, Mechanical, 1930s, 4 1/2 In. 55.00
Cel, see Animation Art category.
Clock, Alarm, Pinocchio & Jiminy Cricket, WDP 50.00
Clock, Wall, Mickey Mouse, Giant Wristwatch Shape, Elgin 125.00
Clock Radio, Mickey Mouse, Alarm, White Plastic, G.E. Youth Electronics 45.00
Coloring Book, Disneyland, Golden Book, No. 1136-20, 1983 . . . . 10.00
Coloring Book, Rescuers, Golden Book, 1977 . . . . 6.00
Comic Art, Chef Donald, Huey, Dewey, Louie, Watercolor & Ink, Hank Porter, 1941 . . . . 6930.00
Cookie Jar, Mickey Mouse, Treasure Craft, 12 In. 50.00
Cookware Set, Pan, Pot, Spoon, Metal, On Card, 1960s, 7 3/4 x 9 1/4 In. 45.00
Costume, Mickey Mouse, Mask, Box, 1940s 165.00
Coverlet, Mickey & Minnie Mouse, Crib, 1930s 125.00
Disneyland Disney Dollar, 1987 . . . . 8.00
Doll, Bashful, Snow White & Seven Dwarfs, Ideal, 7 In. 160.00
Doll, Doc, Snow White & Seven Dwarfs, Hard Rubber, Seberling, 6 In. 65.00
Doll, Donald Duck, Stuffed, 1950s, 9 In. 125.00
Doll, Ludwig Von Drake, Vinyl, Squeezable, 7 1/2 In. 60.00
Doll, Mickey Mouse Club, Wearing Mouse Ears, Molded Vinyl, WDP, 12 In. 27.00
Doll, Mickey Mouse, Cloth, George Borgfeldt Co., c.1931, 16 In. 545.00
Doll, Mickey Mouse, Clown, Swivel Head, Cloth Body, Knickerbocker, 15 In. 2000.00
Doll, Mickey Mouse, Gund, 24 1/2 In. 145.00
Doll, Mickey Mouse, Marching Mickey, Hasbro, 1976 . . . . 15.00
Doll, Minnie Mouse, Cloth, 12 In. 85.00
Doll, Peter Pan & Tinker Bell, Set No. 815, Box, 1952, 8 In. 180.00
Doll, Sleepy, Snow White & Seven Dwarfs, Composition, Knickerbocker, 9 In. 120.00
Doll, Sleepy, Snow White & Seven Dwarfs, Ideal, 12 In. 250.00
Doll, Snow White, Cloth Face Mask, Ideal, 15 In. 300.00
Doll, Snow White, Composition Head, Sleep Eyes, Madame Alexander, 15 In. 600.00
Doll Set, Snow White & Seven Dwarfs, Ideal, Box, 1939, 8 Piece 2000.00
Dominoes, Mickey Mouse, Pluto, Woodem, Walt Disney Enterprises, Balsam Box 74.00
Door Push, Embossed Brass On Wood, c.1955, 11 x 6 1/2 In. 120.00
Drawing, Mickey Mouse, At The Piano, 1929, 6 x 6 In. 2200.00
Drawing, Zorro, Walt Disney, 1958, Small Board 85.00
Dresser Set, Snow White, Walt Disney Prod., 3 Piece 20.00
Drum, Mickey Mouse, Sticks, 1930s, 6 1/2 In. 195.00
Drum Set, Mickey & Minnie Mouse, Tin Lithograph, Ohio Art, 1940s, 6 1/2 In. 95.00
Drum Set, Mickey Mouse Club, 27 In. 235.00
Egg Timer, Doc, Snow White & Seven Dwarfs, Porcelain, 1930-1940 . . . . 395.00
Figurine, Bear, Song Of The South 45.00
Figurine, Cinderella, Japan, 5 1/2 In. 45.00
Figurine, Dalmatian Pup, Japan, 2 1/4 In. 30.00
Figurine, Donald Duck, In Rowboat, Die Cut, Tin, 5 In. 785.00
Figurine, Donald Duck, Nodder, On Metal Base, Celluloid, Japan, 6 1/4 In. 1090.00
Figurine, Donald Duck, Waddling, Clockwork, Japan, 6 In. 545.00
Figurine, Dopey, Snow White & Seven Dwarfs, Soft Plastic, WDP, 1950s, 8 In. 50.00
Figurine, Dumbo, Pottery, Painted, WDP, Japan, 3 3/4 In. 21.00
Figurine, Ferdinand The Bull, Wooden, Jointed, 9 In. 245.00
Figurine, Geppetto, Syroco, 2 1/2 In. 30.00
Figurine, Goofy, Standing, Pink, Blue, Red Mouth, Carved, Wooden, Zoratti, 11 In. 132.00
Figurine, Maleficent, Evil Queen, Sleeping Beauty, Walt Disney 450.00
Figurine, Mickey & Minnie Mouse, Bisque, Borgfeldt, Box, 4 In., Pair 1450.00
Figurine, Mickey & Minnie Mouse, Bisque, Pie-Eyed, Label, c.1930, 3 1/2 In., Pair 80.00
Figurine, Peter Pan, Sitting Cross-Legged, Plastic, 1950s 25.00
Figurine, Pinocchio, Celluloid, Painted, Jointed, 8 1/2 In. 195.00

Figurine, Sneezy, Snow White & Seven Dwarfs, Soft Plastic, WDP, 1950s, 8 In. 60.00
Figurine, Three Little Pigs, Bisque, Painted, 3 1/2 In., 3 Piece Set 185.00
Figurine, Tramp, Lady & The Tramp, Ceramic, Walt Disney Productions, Japan, 6 In. 24.00
Game, Donald Duck Party Game, Parker, 1938 . . . .   50.00
Game, Frontierland, Walt Disney Official, 1955 . . . . .50.00 to 55.00
Game, Mary Poppins Carousel, Parker Brothers, 1964 . . . .   28.00
Game, Sleeping Beauty, 1958 . . . .   55.00
Game, Snow White & Seven Dwarfs, Cadaco, 1977 . . . .   20.00
Game, Walt Disney's Disneyland, Transogram, Box, 1950s 28.00
Game, Walt Disney's Zorro, WDP, Parker Brothers, Box, 1966 . . . .   25.00
Game, Walt Disney's Zorro, Whitman, 1958 . . . .   38.00
Guide Book, Disneyland, Complimentary, 25th Family Reunion, 1980 . . . .   12.00
Guide Book, Disneyland, Complimentary, Summer '69, Castle Picture 18.00
Guide Book, Spring, Castle Picture, 1975 . . . .   14.00
Handkerchief, Mickey Mouse, Fireman, Square, 8 In. 85.00
Hat, Mouseketeer Ears, Mickey Mouse Club, 1950s 90.00
Hot Plate, Donald Duck, Ceramic, 1940s 40.00
Hurdy-Gurdy, Mickey Mouse, Tinplate Band Organ, Lithograph 4600.00
Knife, Mickey Mouse Handle, World's Fair, 1933 . . . .   250.00
Lamp, Donald Duck, Figural, 1950s, 8 In. 150.00
Lamp, Mickey Mouse, 1936 . . . . 1496.00
Lamp, Mickey Mouse, Cardboard Candlestick, Wooden Base, Flicker Bulb, 9 In. 61.00
Lighter, Mickey Mouse, Brushed Finish, WDP, 1978 . . . .   240.00
Lighter, Mickey Mouse, Brushed Finish, Zippo, Black & Gold Box, 1980 . . . .   380.00
Lighter, Mickey Mouse, Red, Yellow, Black Enamel, Zippo, 1979 . . . .   198.00
Lobby Card, Pete's Dragon, Envelope, 1977, 11 x 14 In., 9 Piece 50.00
Lunch Box, Minnie Mouse Head, Hair Bow Handle, Plastic, Aladdin, 10 x 11 In. 35.00
Lunch Box, Woody Woodpecker, Scenes & Characters From Show, 1972, 8 x 4 In. 16.00
Lunch Box, Zorro, With Thermos, 1958 . . . .   150.00
Map, Disneyland, Dial, 1983 . . . .   35.00
Map, Disneyland, Folded, 1984 . . . .   16.00
Map, Disneyland, Folded, 1989 . . . .   18.00
Matchbook, Disneyland, America On Parade, 1976 . . . .   5.00
Mold, Mickey Mouse, Porcelain, Holland, 1930s, 7 In. 465.00
Music, Box, Snow White & Seven Dwarfs, Schmid 500.00
Napkin Ring, Mickey Mouse, Celluloid, Hand Painted, 1930s 295.00
Night-Light, Mickey Mouse, Chad Valley, Box 450.00
Nodder, Donald Duck, Ceramic, Japan 75.00
Organette, 16-Note, Instructions In Lid, Lithographed Characters, 1 Roll, Chein 70.00
Pail, Mickey Mouse & Donald Duck, 4 In. 375.00
Pail, Three Little Pigs 65.00
Paint Box, Donald Duck, 8 Colors, Water Pan, Tin, Transogram, 5 3/4 x 4 1/2 In. 20.00
Paper Doll, Donald Duck & Daisy, Box, 1984 . . . .   10.00
Paper Doll, Mickey & Minnie Mouse, Stepping Out, 1977, Uncut 25.00
Parking Ticket, Disneyland, 25 Cents, Gray With Red Stripe, c.1955 . . . .   35.00
Patch, Mickey Mouse, Playing Baseball, Twill, Bread Company Premium, 2 In. 20.00
Pattern, Cinderella's Apron, J.C. Penney Co., Uncut, 1950 . . . .   25.00
Pencil, Mechanical, Disneyland, Underwater Scene, Submarine, Green Plastic 21.00
Pie Bird, Donald Duck, Walt Disney 1500.00
Pin, 15 Years, Walt Disney World, 1986, 3 In. 10.00
Pin, Disneyland Hotel, Mickey's Face, 1980s, 1 1/8 In. 4.00
Pin, Disneyland, 30th Year Official Birthday Party, 1985, 3 In.   7.00
Pin, Disneyland, Blast To The Past, 1988, 3 In. 8.00
Pin, Disneyland, Splash Mountain, Mickey, Donald, Goofy, 1989, 3 In. 5.00
Pin, Disneyland, Star Tours, Logo, Black Ground, 1986, 3 In. 8.00
Pin, Disneyland, Star Tours, Logo, Blue Ground, 1986, 3 In. 5.00
Pin, Dumbo, Walt Disney Productions, Pinback, 1 1/2 In. 5.00
Pin, Official Mickey Mouse Store, Celluloid, Kay Kamen Ltd., 1937, 1 1/4 In. 20.00
Pin, State Fair '88, Mickey Mouse With Pig, 1988, 3 In. 5.00
Pin, Tron, 1982, 3 1/2 In. 10.00
Pin, Zorro, 7-Up, Walt Disney Productions, 1957, 1 1/4 In. 10.00
Pitcher, Dumbo Shape, 8 In. 105.00
Planter, Snow White, American Bisque . . . . .95.00 to 115.00

Disneyana, Postcard, Peter Pan, 3-D, 1966, 4 x 5 In.

Disneyana, Postcard, Pinocchio, 3-D, 1966, 4 x 5 In.

Disneyana, Tumbler, Donald Duck, Blue

Plate, Castle, Blue Ground, Porcelain, 1960s	14.00
Plate, Fantasia, Autumn Ballet, Vernon Kilns, 9 1/2 In.	195.00
Postcard, Disneyland, Moon Rocket, Tomorrowland, 1950s	20.00
Postcard, Disneyland, Street Car On Main Street, 1950s	10.00
Postcard, Mad Hatter's Tea Party, 1950s	5.00
Postcard, Peter Pan, 3-D, 1966, 4 x 5 In. ....*Illus*	15.00
Postcard, Pinocchio, 3-D, 1966, 4 x 5 In. ....*Illus*	15.00
Postcard, Sleeping Beauty Castle, 1950s	10.00
Postcard, Submarine Ride, Mermaids, 1960s	8.00
Poster, Jungle Book, Buena Vista, 1967, One Sheet	220.00
Poster, Song Of The South, RKO, 1946, Insert	205.00
Print, A Gentleman's Gentleman, 1936, 7 1/2 x 11 In.	35.00
Print, New Tales, Mother Goose Hickety Pickety, This Red Hen, 1944, 6 3/4 x 10 In.	24.00
Print, Snow White & Seven Dwarfs, Frame, 1962, 25 x 31 In.	395.00
Puppet, Hand, Donald Duck, Cloth Body, Soft Plastic Head, Squeaker	21.00
Puppet, Hand, Donald Duck, Latex Rubber Heat, Felt Body, Gund	125.00
Puppet, Hand, Donald Duck, Walt Disney Production, 1970s	10.00
Puppet, Hand, Jiminy Cricket, Cloth Body, Soft Plastic Head, Squeaker, 6 In.	21.00
Puppet, Hand, Minnie Mouse, Gund, 1960s	22.00
Puzzle, Jigsaw, Bugs Bunny Licking Lollipop, 65 Pieces, 1960, 7 x 9 In.	20.00
Puzzle, Jigsaw, Mary Poppins & Children, Sliding, Banister, Tray, Whitman, 1966	10.00
Record, Adventures Of Zorro, Little Golden, No. D448, 1958	15.00
Record, Disneyland, It's A Small World, In Package, 1970s	16.00
Record, Fantasia, Pastoral Symphony, 1961	12.00
Record, Fantasia, Vista, 1957	42.00
Record, Island At The Top Of The World, Album & Book, 1974	10.00
Record, Pirates Of Caribbean, No Book, 1970s	40.00
Record, Prince & The Pauper, LP, 1961	8.00
Record, Walt Disney Presents It's A Small World, 45 RPM, 1966	10.00
Record & Book, Disneyland, Great Moments With Mr. Lincoln, 1964	75.00
Reel, View-Master, Tomorrowland, Sawyer, 1956	35.00
Rocker, Child's, Pluto, Vinyl, 1950s	125.00
Rocker, Mickey Mouse, Wooden, Mengel Playthings, 35 1/2 In.	635.00
Rug, Mickey Mouse, Flying Rocket Kite, With Thumper	310.00
Salt & Pepper, Barrel Shape, Walt Disney World, Castle Picture, WDP, 1980s	15.00
Salt & Pepper, Donald Duck, Ceramic, 1950s	50.00
Salt & Pepper, Goofy & Teepee	15.00
Sheet Music, Big Bad Wolf, Disney	25.00
Sheet Music, Blue Shadows On The Trail, Melody Time, 1948	12.00
Sheet Music, Der Fuehrer's Face, Donald Duck	61.00
Sheet Music, Spoonful Of Sugar, Mary Poppins, 1965	6.00
Sheet Music, Step In Time, Mary Poppins, 1965	6.00
Shirt, Disco, Mickey Mouse, Sorcerer's Apprentice, Kennington Ltd., 1970s, Small	39.00
Shirt, Mickey & Minnie Mouse, Light Blue, Long Sleeves, Kennington, Medium	23.00
Shirt, Zorro, Black, Long Sleeved, Z Design, WDP Label, Child's, 5-6 Years	27.00
Shopping Bag, America On Parade, 1976	6.00

Snow Shovel, Donald Duck, Tin Lithograph, 1930-1940, 27 In. 360.00
Soaky, Pinocchio, 1960s 15.00
Soap Figure, Mickey Mouse, Box, W.D.E., 1930s, 5 In. 245.00
Sweeper, Donald Duck, Tin Lithograph, Ohio Art, 1940s, 7 1/2 x 27 In. 120.00
Tea Set, Mickey & Minnie Mouse, Sugar & Creamer, 4 Cups & Saucers, Japan 75.00
Teaspoon, Mickey Mouse, Silver Plate 35.00
Telephone, Mickey Mouse 80.00
Telephone, Mickey Mouse, Molded Plastic, Rotary Dial, WDP, AT&T, 15 In. . . . . .110.00 to 120.00
Ticket, Disneyland, Mark Twain, 1955 . . . . 50.00
Tin, Snow White & Seven Dwarfs, Biscuit, Belgian, 1930s 225.00
Toothbrush Holder, Donald Duck, Arms Around Mickey & Minnie, Bisque 350.00
Toothbrush Holder, Donald Duck, Long-Billed, Bisque, Bogfeldt & Co., 1930s 750.00
Toothbrush Holder, Mickey Mouse, Bisque, Movable Arm, 5 In. 350.00
Toothbrush Holder, Three Little Pigs, With Instruments, Bisque, Japan, 4 In. 68.00
Toy, Donald Duck & Goofy, Mounted On Round Bases, Tin, Marx, 10 1/4 In. 510.00
Toy, Donald Duck Duet, Donald & Goofy, Drum-Top Dancers, Tin, Marx, Box 1100.00
Toy, Donald Duck, Clockwork, Schuco, 6 In. 2100.00
Toy, Donald Duck, Dapper Donald, Rubber, Fisher-Price, 9 x 6 1/4 In. 600.00
Toy, Donald Duck, Doing Acrobatics, Gym, Celluloid, Clockwork, Linemar, 4 1/2 In. 230.00
Toy, Donald Duck, Jack-In-The-Box, Spear 225.00
Toy, Donald Duck, Trike, Tin, Celluloid Arms, Windup, 1950s 450.00
Toy, Donald Duck, Walker, Composition, Windup, Borgfeldt, 1938, 11 1/2 In. 950.00
Toy, Donald Duck, Xylophone Player, Fisher-Price 495.00
Toy, Goofy, Riding Tricycle, Hard Plastic, Mechanical, Gabriel, 1977 . . . . 45.00
Toy, Goofy, Tin, Windup, Tail Spins, Head Moves, Linemar 585.00
Toy, Handcar, Mickey Mouse & Minnie Mouse, Windup, 1930s 925.00
Toy, Huey, Dewey & Louis In Boat, Sun Rubber 65.00
Toy, Jump-Up Box, Nosey, Pinocchio, Composition, 11 In. 195.00
Toy, Ludwig Von Drake, Drives Go-Cart, Friction, 1961 . . . . 275.00
Toy, Mickey & Minnie Mouse, Handcar, Windup, Track, Lionel, 1930s . . . . .850.00 to 965.00
Toy, Mickey Mouse & Tractor, Sun Rubber, 1930s 70.00
Toy, Mickey Mouse, Choo-Choo, Fisher-Price, 1939 . . . . 825.00
Toy, Mickey Mouse, Drummer, Pull Toy, Paper, Wood, Fisher-Price, 1950s, 8 In. 110.00
Toy, Mickey Mouse, Engineer, Pull Toy, Wood, Paper Lithograph, Fisher-Price 195.00
Toy, Mickey Mouse, Fun-E-Flex Figure, 4 In. 165.00
Toy, Mickey Mouse, Fun-E-Flex, Box, Borgfeldt, 7 In. 2860.00
Toy, Mickey Mouse, Magic Show, Plastic Figure, Durham, Box, 1976, 12 In. 125.00
Toy, Mickey Mouse, On Tricky Trapeze, Hard Plastic, Gabriel 45.00
Toy, Mickey Mouse, On Tricycle, Hard Plastic, Mechanical, Gabriel, 1977 . . . . 45.00
Toy, Mickey Mouse, Plays Xylophone, Linemar, 6 1/2 In. 495.00
Toy, Mickey Mouse, Plush, Stuffed, Red Short Pants, WDP, Knickerbocker, 17 In. 26.00
Toy, Mickey Mouse, Racing Kart, Marx 395.00
Toy, Mickey Mouse, Squeak, Rubber, 1965 . . . . 75.00
Toy, Mickey Mouse, Train, Pull Toy, Fisher-Price, 1939 . . . . 625.00
Toy, Mickey Mouse, With Balloon Vendor, Tinplate, Lithograph, Windup, 1939 . . . . 805.00
Toy, Mickey Mouse, Yo-Yo, Wooden, Walt Disney Productions, 2 1/4 In. 24.00
Toy, Mickey Mouse, Zylotone Player, Linemar 575.00
Toy, Minnie Mouse Knitter 575.00
Toy, Pinocchio, Acrobat, Tin, Windup, Marx, 1938 . . . . 575.00
Toy, Pinocchio, Walker, Moving Eyes, Battery Operated, Marx 1200.00
Toy, Pluto The Pup, Articulated Wood, Borgfeldt, Box, 6 In. 920.00
Toy, Pluto, Mysterious, Walt Disney, Box 695.00
Toy, Pluto, Windup, Tin, Tin Lithograph, Marx, Box, 8 In. 395.00
Toy, Professor Von Drake, Linemar, Box 875.00
Toy, Thumper, Friction, Linemar 85.00
Toy, Top, Disney Characters, Chein, 1940s, 6 1/2 In. 165.00
Toy, TV Set, Automatic Toy Co., Box 395.00
Toy, Wristwatch, Peter Pan, On Card, 1950s 60.00
Tray, Disneyland, California, Map, Black Metal, Lithograph, Souvenir, WDP, 11 In. 21.00
Tray, Serving, Disneyland, 6 Scenes, Black Metal, 1970s 18.00
Tumbler, Donald Duck, Blue . . . .*Illus* 186.00
Tumbler, Rescuers, Madame Medusa, Pepsi, 1977 . . . . 10.00
View-Master Packet & Booklet, Disneyland, Main Street, GAF, In Package, 1970s 25.00

Watch, Donald Duck, Ingersoll 90.00
Watch, Mickey Mouse, Ingersoll, Watch Fob, Leather Strap, Mickey's Arms 440.00
Watch, Pinocchio, Ingersoll 70.00
Watch Fob, Three Little Pigs 125.00
Wristwatch, Mickey Mouse, 50th Anniversary, Bradley, Box, 1983 .... 95.00
Wristwatch, Mickey Mouse, Chromed Case, Leather Band, Battery Powered, 1 In. 31.00
Wristwatch, Mickey Mouse, Ingersoll 100.00
Wristwatch, Mickey Mouse, Ingersoll, Box, Price Tag, Instructions, 7 x 3 3/4 In. 275.00
Wristwatch, Minnie Mouse, Bradley 85.00
Wristwatch, Pluto, Silver Toned Case, Black Face, Brown Leather Band, U.S. Time 100.00

DOCTOR, see Dental; Medical

DOLL entries are listed by marks printed or incised on the doll, if possible. If there are no marks, the doll is listed by the name of the subject or country or maker. Notice that Barbie is listed under Mattel. G.I.
Joe figures are listed in the Toy section.

A.M., 323, Bisque, Googly, Mohair Wig, Original Costume, 7 In. 1275.00
A.M., 323, Bisque, Googly, Sleep Eyes, Mohair Wig, Original Dress, 10 In. 1975.00
A.M., 341, Baby, Bisque Flange Head, Closed Mouth, Molded Hair, Cloth Body, 13 In. 185.00
A.M., 341, Baby, Bisque, Molded Hair, Sleep Eyes, Cloth Body, 16 In. 110.00
A.M., 341-151, My Dream Baby, Bisque Head, Sleep Eyes, Painted Hair, 7 In...... 115.00
A.M., 370, Bisque Shoulder Head, Sleep Eyes, Open Mouth, Teeth, Kid Body, 25 In. 135.00
A.M., 390, Bisque Socket Head, Open Mouth, 4 Teeth, Sailor Suit, 9 In., Twins 325.00
A.M., 390, Bisque, Ball-Jointed, New Wig & Clothes, 22 In. 325.00
A.M., 390, Bisque, Blue Sleep Eyes, Lashes, Ball-Jointed Body, 11 In. 495.00
A.M., 390, Bisque, Brown Wig, Blue Eyes, Open Mouth, Jointed Body, 11 In. 120.00
A.M., 390, Bisque, Mohair Wig, Sleep Eyes, 27 In. 1275.00
A.M., Baby, Bisque Head, Sleep Eyes, Painted Hair, Cloth Body, 11 In. 55.00
A.M., Bisque, Blond, Sleep Eyes, Kid Body, Dress, 21 In. 220.00
A.M., Bisque, Sleep Eyes, Kid Gusset Body, Jointed, Dressed, 30 In. 575.00
A.M., Floradora, Bisque, Brunette, Sleep Eyes, Teeth, Composition, Clothes, 26 In. 305.00
A.M., Queen Louise, Bisque Socket Head, Sleep Eyes, 4 Teeth, Human Hair, 22 1/2 In. 225.00
Advertising, Burger King, 1970s 10.00
Advertising, Cerasota Flour, Fabric, 16 In. 95.00
Advertising, Elsie The Cow, Turn Me Over & I Moo, Ribbon, 1950 .... 275.00
Advertising, General Electric, Drum Major, Radio Character, Jointed, 19 In. ......*Illus* 1155.00
Advertising, Phillips 66, Buddy Lee, Uniform With Logo On Pocket & Cap, 13 In. 425.00
Advertising, Ralston Purina, Scarecrow, Vinyl Head, Cloth Body 45.00
Advertising, RCA Radiotrons, Wooden, Jointed, 16 In. ....*Illus* 1210.00
Advertising, Snap, Crackle & Pop, Vinyl, 3 Piece 95.00
Advertising, Tony The Tiger, Cloth, 1973 .... 29.00
Alabama Baby, Painted Blue Shoes, Applied Ears, 11 In. 1650.00
Alexander dolls are listed in this category under Madame Alexander.
Alma, Girl, Pressed Felt Swivel Head, Side-Glancing Eyes, Mitten Hands, 11 In. 200.00
Alt Beck & Gottschalck, 83/35, Bisque, Blue Sleep Eyes, Blond Wig, Box, 5 In. 350.00
Alt Beck & Gottschalck, 1000, China Shoulder Head, Blond Hair, Cloth Body, 26 In. 325.00

Doll, Advertising, General
Electric, Drum Major, Radio
Character, Jointed, 19 In.

Doll, Advertising, RCA
Radiotrons, Wooden,
Jointed, 16 In.

**Don't store a rubber doll in a
plastic bag. Wrap it in a white
cotton pillowcase.**

Alt Beck & Gottschalck, Baby, Happy Face, Blue Sleep Eyes, Mohair Wig, 22 In. 895.00
Alt Beck & Gottschalck, Sleep Eyes, Feathered Brows, Mohair Wig, Child, 22 In. 895.00
Amberg, Newborn, Bisque Flange Head, Sleep Eyes, Cloth Body, No Crier, 13 In. 290.00
American Character, Tiny Tears, Case, Outfits, 16 In. 50.00
Armand Marseille dolls are listed in this category under A.M.
Arranbee, Girl, Hard Plastic Head, Fuchsia Formal Gown, Fur Trim, Box, 1950s, 20 In. ... 550.00
Arranbee, Littlest Angel, Plastic Head, Sleep Eyes, Brunette Saran Wig, 1954, 10 In. 155.00
Automaton, 2 Dolls, Bisque Head, Musical, c.1910, 10 In. 630.00
Automaton, Black Minstrel Group, Carved Gesso Figures, Polychrome, 1800s 29325.00
Automaton, Figure, Smoker, Bisque Head, Composition Hands & Legs, 11 1/2 In. 460.00
Automaton, French, Woman, Teaching In School Room, 2 Tunes 1895.00
Automaton, Jumeau Bisque Head, Moving Arms & Neck, 18 1/4 In. 1150.00
Automaton, Lambert, Chinese Tea Drinker, Musical, Bisque Head, Amber, 1890, 18 In. .. 5750.00
Automaton, Lambert, Girl With Bird In Cage, Field Glasses, Musical, c.1890, 18 In. 7750.00
Automaton, Lambert, Smiling Girl With Bird In Cage, Cherries, Musical, 18 In. 15500.00
Automaton, Steiff, Max & Moritz, Window Display, Peeking Over Fence 1495.00
Automaton, Tea Drinker, Metal Head, Cardboard Wrapped Torso, Label, c.1870, 12 In. .. 4300.00
Automaton, Vichy, Mandarin Opium Smoker, Papier-Mache, Silk Robe, c.1890, 28 In. .. 10250.00
Averill, Allie Dog, Bisque, Glass Eyes, Pink Mustache, Tremble Tongue, 13 In. 550.00
Averill, Beloved Belindy, Cotton, White Button Eyes, c.1940, 18 In. 1200.00
Averill, Uncle Wiggily, Muslin Stuffed Cloth, Mask Face, 19 In. 500.00
Avon, Fashion, Soft Plastic, Black, Jointed, Pink Evening Gown, Box, 11 1/2 In. 21.00
Babyland Horsman, Rag, Hand Painted Face, Original Clothes, 1900, 14 In. 800.00
Babyland Horsman, Rag, Topsy-Turvy, White & Black Faces, Mitten Hands, 12 In. 405.00
Bahr & Proschild, 224, Bisque, Sleep Eyes, Mohair Wig, Composition Body, 14 In. 1250.00
Bahr & Proschild, 585, Toddler, Bisque Socket Head, Brown Glass Sleep Eyes, 9 In. 825.00
Bahr & Proschild, 604, Bisque, Sleep Eyes, Auburn Mohair Wig, 8 In. 895.00
Bahr & Proschild, Bisque, Fully-Jointed Body, Wistful Expression, Child, 1890, 17 In. ... 2000.00
Barbie dolls are listed in this category under Mattel.
Bebe Mascotte, Bisque Head, Paperweight Eyes, Composition, Impressed M2, c.1900 ... 1610.00
Belton, Baby, Bisque Head, Mohair Wig, Composition, Christening Dress, 10 1/2 In. 500.00
Belton, Bisque Socket Head, Replaced Mohair Wig, Wood, Composition, Child, 11 In. .. 425.00
Belton, Bisque, Feathered Brows, Sienna Paperweight Eyes, Original Clothes, 16 In. 2995.00
Bergmann dolls are also in this category under S & H and Simon & Halbig.
Bergmann, Bisque Socket Head, Blue Sleep Eyes, Open Mouth, 4 Teeth, Blond, 24 In. ... 325.00
Bergmann, Bisque Socket Head, Blue Sleep Eyes, Original Mohair Wig, 25 In. 395.00
Bergmann, Bisque Socket Head, Sleep Eyes, Open Mouth, 4 Teeth, 1916, 35 In. 800.00
Bergmann, Bisque Socket Head, Sleep Eyes, Open Mouth, 4 Teeth, 23 In. 325.00
Bergmann, Bisque, 4 Porcelain Teeth, Ball-Jointed Body, Child, c.1900, 28 In. 650.00
Bing, Pressed Cloth Head, Muslin Body, Folklore Costume, c.1920, 12 In. 750.00
Bisque, 3-Face, Wooden & Composition, Antique Dress, Child, 11 In. 975.00
Bisque, Baby, Seated In Antique Bathing Tub, 7 In. 595.00
Bisque, Boy & Girl, Boy Holding Toy, Girl Holding Doll, 1880, 14 In., Pair 770.00
Bisque, Flapper, Sleep Eyes, Closed Mouth, Mohair Wig, Long Stockings, 7 In. 795.00
Bisque, Girl, Bisque Shoulder Head, Painted Blue Eyes, Painted Blond Hair, 25 In. 350.00
Bisque, Googly, Original Mohair Wig, Original Costume, 6 1/2 In. 650.00
Bisque, Googly, Painted Side-Glancing Eyes, Painted Hair, Jointed, 4 1/2 In. 400.00
Bisque, Molded Hair, Brown Sleep Eyes, Composition, 18 In. 247.00
Bisque, Sleep Eyes, Open Mouth, Teeth, Wig, Kid Body, Clothes, 22 In. 305.00
Bisque Head, Blue Sleep Eyes, Open Mouth With Teeth, 21 In. 105.00
Black dolls are included in the Black category.
Blossom, Cloth Swivel Head, Mask Face, Pierrot, Boudoir, 1920s, 30 In., Pair 350.00
Borgfeldt, Bisque Socket Head, Brown Sleep Eyes, Open Mouth, 4 Teeth, 24 In. 350.00
Borgfeldt, Bisque Socket Head, Brown Sleep Eyes, Open Mouth, Human Hair, 21 In. ... 325.00
Boudoir, Smoking, Composition Swivel Head, Painted Features, Open Mouth, 25 In. 375.00
Boy, China Head, Black Hair, Kid Body, Velvet Suit, Stockings, 14 In. 55.00
Boy, Composition, Jointed Arms, Legs, Molded Cap, Cloth Body, 20th Century, 15 In. ... 81.00
Bru Jne, 1, Bisque Swivel Head, Blue Enamel Eyes, Closed Mouth, Bebe, 1886, 11 In. .. 6270.00
Bru Jne, 2, Bisque Socket Head, Dark Blue Glass Eyes, Closed Mouth, 11 In. 2750.00
Bru Jne, 2, Bisque Swivel Head, Brown Enamel Glass Eyes, Bebe, 1882, 12 In. 7700.00
Bru Jne, Bisque Swivel Head, Kid-Edged Shoulder Plate, Wooden Body, 14 In. 7250.00
Bruno Schmidt, 2072, Bisque, Hand Painted Features, Jointed Toddler Body, 20 In. 4495.00
Buddy Lee, Composition Head, Denim Shirt, Overalls, 12 In. 375.00

Buddy Lee, Composition, Labeled Lee Bib Overalls, 6 1/2 In. 137.00
Buddy Lee, Cowboy, Coveralls, Red Scarf, Hat, 6 In. 121.00
Buddy Lee, Engineer, 13 In. 200.00
Buddy Lee, Plastic, Denim Overalls, Shirt, Hat With Scarf, 8 1/2 In. 154.00
Buddy Lee, Plastic, Painted Hair, Denim Jeans, Plaid Shirt, Hat, 13 In. . . . . .400.00 to 850.00
Buddy Lee, Plastic, Striped Overalls, Denim Shirt, Lee Hat, 9 In. 165.00
Buddy Lee, Plastic, Striped Overalls, Striped Denim Shirt, 7 1/2 In. 55.00
Bugs Bunny, Plastic Head, Talking, Pink Vinyl Ears, Stuffed Cloth Body, 1971, 12 In. . . . 23.00
Buttercup, Cloth, Printed Features, From Toots & Casper Comic Strip, 1924, 18 In. 230.00
Bye-Lo, Bisque Flange Head, Brown Eyes, Closed Mouth, Germany, 18 In. 195.00
Bye-Lo, Bisque Flange Head, Sleep Eyes, Closed Mouth, Cloth Body, Long Dress, 16 In. . 350.00
Bye-Lo, Bisque Head, Blue Sleep Eyes, Cotton Body, Grace Putnam, c.1923, 10 In. 1550.00
Bye-Lo, Bisque Head, Blue Sleep Glass Eyes, Grace Storey Putnam, 1920s, 13 In. 375.00
Bye-Lo, Bisque, Painted Eyes, Label, 4 In. 395.00
Bye-Lo, Bisque, Paper Sticker, 4 In. 295.00
Bye-Lo, Bisque, Sleep Eyes, Celluloid Hands, Cloth Body, Mark, 1920s, 21 In. 460.00
Bye-Lo, Dome Bisque Flange Head, Sleep Eyes, Cloth Body, Grace S. Putnam, 11 In. . . . 275.00
Bye-Lo, Dome Bisque Flange Head, Sleep Eyes, Cloth Body, Grace S. Putnam, 13 In. . . . 185.00
Celluloid, Baby, Boy With Toys, Jointed Arms & Legs, Painted Hair, c.1915, 8 In. 400.00
Chad Valley, Bo Peep & Boy Blue, Pressed Felt Mask Face, Cloth Body, 14 In., Pair 800.00
Chad Valley, Pirate, Felt Body, Glass Eyes, Painted Features, 20 In. . . . . .1210.00 to 1410.00
Character, Pete, Composition, Wooden, Jointed, 9 In. . . . . *Illus* 330.00
Chase, Beehive Hair, Comb, Stippling, Original Wig, Original Clothes & Shoes 1495.00
Chase, Painted Stockinet Head, Painted Blue Eyes, Closed Mouth, Cloth Body, 24 In. . . . 650.00
Chase, Woman, Stockinet, Coiled Bun At Back, Cotton Sateen Body, 15 In. 2800.00
Chimney Sweep, Wood, Original Clothing & Broom, Late 18th Century 195.00
China Head, Braided Bun, Antique Clothes, Shoes, 15 In. 2550.00
China Head, Brown Hair, Antique Dress, 22 In. 4950.00
China Head, Glass Eyes, Exposed Ears, Clothes, 1850s, 14 1/2 In. 3200.00
China Head, High Brow, Black Hair, Cloth Body, Black Taffeta Dress, 23 In. 275.00
China Head, Patented July 15, 1862, Kid Body, Walking, Metal Feet, Key, 10 In. 650.00
China Head, Woman, Painted Snood, Silk Gown, Cloth Body, Leather Hands, 18 In. 2200.00
Clothespin, Early 19th Century 325.00
Dehors, Bisque Swivel Head, Portrait, Glass Eyes, Kid Fashion Body, c.1866, 21 In. 3900.00
Denamur, Bisque, Blue Eyes, French Body 3495.00
Denamur, Bisque, Cobalt Blue Eyes, Mohair Wig, Bebe, 15 In. 3495.00
Denamur, Black Bisque Socket Head, Amber Glass Eyes, 4 Teeth, Jointed Body, 20 In. . . 1800.00
Dennis The Menace, Soft Vinyl Head, Stuffed Cloth Body, Red Pajamas, 1960s, 10 In. . . . 22.00
DEP, 2, Bisque Socket Head, Open Mouth, Human Hair, Wood, Composition, 24 1/2 In. . . 650.00
DEP, 8, Bisque Socket Head, Sleep Eyes, Open Mouth, 4 Teeth, Human Hair, 20 In. 650.00
DEP, 154, Bisque Shoulder Head, Sleep Eyes, Open Mouth, Kid Body, 25 In. 245.00
DEP, Bisque Head, Human Hair, Jointed Arms & Legs, Composition, Kid Body, 29 In. . . . 350.00
Dolly Parton, Original Box, 16 In. . . . . .60.00 to 145.00

Doll, Character,
Pete, Composition,
Wooden, Jointed,
9 In.

Check wooden dolls for insect damage and infestation. Isolate the doll until you have chemically treated it to remove the insects.

Doll, French, Nurse,
World War I,
Composition, Wood,
Jointed, 14 In.

Dorothy Lamour, Cloth, Open-Close Mouth, Film Star Creations, Hollywood, 14 In. 135.00
Dressel, Bisque Head, Painted Eyes, Mohair Wig, Composition, c.1910, 13 In. 2300.00
Dressel, Bisque Socket Head, Open Mouth, 4 Teeth, 1914, 22 In. ....210.00 to 475.00
Dressel, Boy, Open Mouth, Brown Sleep Eyes, Mohair Wig, Jointed Body, 13 In. 795.00
Dressel, Uncle Sam, Bisque, Inset Eyes, Prominent Nose, Smile, Mohair Wig, 14 In. 1400.00
Duchess Doll Corp., Alice In Wonderland, Blond, Purple & White Gown, 1951, 8 In. 190.00
Effanbee, American Child, Composition, Closed Mouth, 19 In. 1000.00
Effanbee, Baby Dainty, Composition, Cloth, 19 In. 150.00
Effanbee, Composition Head, Sleep Eyes, Human Hair Wig, Child, c.1937, 20 In. 700.00
Effanbee, Dy-Dee Baby, Painted Lashes, Original Body & Boots, Paris Label, 22 In. 425.00
Effanbee, Green Sleep Eyes, Human Hair Wig, 4 Teeth, 5 Piece Body, c.1938, 21 In. 475.00
Effanbee, Historical, 1720, Composition Socket Head, Human Hair, Box, 14 In. 700.00
Effanbee, Historical, 1777, Composition Socket Head, White Mohair Wig, Box, 14 In. ... 750.00
Effanbee, Historical, 1872, Composition Socket Head, Human Hair, Box, 14 In. 425.00
Effanbee, Honey, Bride, Blue Sleep Eyes, Blond Saran Wig, Walker, 1954, 15 In. 345.00
Effanbee, John Wayne, 18 In. 95.00
Effanbee, Martha & George Washington, Composition, All Original, 10 In., 1930s, Pair .. 450.00
Effanbee, Patsy Ann, Composition, Blue Tin Sleep Eyes, Painted Hair, Bent Arm, 19 In. .. 325.00
Effanbee, Patsy Joan, Composition, Green Sleep Eyes, Painted Hair, Romper, 16 In. 300.00
Effanbee, Patsy, Babyette, Boy & Girl, Original Rompers, Twin Set 895.00
Effanbee, Patsy, Composition Head, Green Sleep Eyes, Closed Mouth, Wig, 19 In. 250.00
Effanbee, Peggy Lou, Bow-Shaped Lips, Human Hair Wig, Composition Body, 15 In. ... 525.00
Effanbee, Plastic, Sleep Eyes, Blond Floss Wig, Schiaparelli Dress, c.1952, 18 In. 2000.00
Effanbee, Puzzy, Original Clothes 595.00
Fashion, Bisque, Hand Painted, Paperweight Eyes, Redressed, 12 In. 1995.00
Fashion, Kidskin Face, Painted Features, Silk Walking Gown, France, 1912, 14 In. 435.00
Fred Flintstone, Original Outfit, Hanna Barbera, 1961, 19 In. 75.00
French, Bisque Head, Glass Eyes, Papier-Mache Body, Mechanical, Brass Crank, 16 In. ... 488.00
French, Bisque Socket Head, Blue Paperweight Eyes, Closed Mouth, Box, 19 In. 5610.00
French, Bisque Socket Head, Blue Paperweight Eyes, Original Costume, Bebe, 11 In. 6050.00
French, Bisque Socket Head, Bright Blue Enamel Eyes, Closed Mouth, Bebe, 19 In. 4730.00
French, Bisque Socket Head, Brown Glass Eyes, Blond Mohair Bobbed Wig, 29 In. 935.00
French, Bisque Socket Head, Cobalt Blue Glass Eyes, Brunette Mohair Wig, 15 In. 2310.00
French, Bisque Swivel Head, Blue Almond Glass Eyes, Closed Mouth, 1867, 18 In. 3850.00
French, Bisque Swivel Head, Blue Glass Enamel Eyes, Brunette Mohair Wig, 17 In. 6875.00
French, Bisque Swivel Head, Blue Glass Enamel Eyes, Closed Mouth, 1880, 20 In. 5830.00
French, Bisque Swivel Head, Blue Glass Paperweight Eyes, Closed Mouth, 17 In. 5280.00
French, Bisque Swivel Head, Blue Glass Sleep Eyes, Blond Mohair Wig, 1890, 4 1/2 In. .. 412.00
French, Bisque Swivel Head, Brown Glass Enamel Eyes, Closed Mouth, 1878, 11 In. 5500.00
French, Bisque, Blue Glass Almond-Shape Eyes, Brunette Mohair Wig, 1869, 21 In. 6325.00
French, Bisque, Chinese Woman, Socket Head, Brown Sleep Eyes, 17 In. 1320.00
French, Bisque, Fortune Teller, Swivel Head, Kid & Wood Body, c.1870, 15 In. 4535.00
French, Bisque, Hand Painted Features, Molded Eyelids, 12 In. 995.00
French, Bisque, Mignonette, Presentation Basket, Swivel Head, Painted Stockings, 5 In. .. 1400.00
French, Bisque, Mignonette, Swivel Head, Accessories, Velvet & Silk Box, c.1890, 4 In. . 1300.00
French, Bisque, Mystery Child, Brown Paperweight Eyes, Flocked Hair, 15 In. 1495.00
French, Bisque, Pale Blue Enamel Inset Eyes, Closed Mouth, Wooden Body, 17 In. 4640.00
French, Bisque, Socket Head, Blue Glass Sleep Eyes, Brunette Mohair Wig, 1920, 17 In. . . 1540.00
French, Bisque, Swivel Head, Blue Enamel Inset Eyes, Blond Mohair Wig, 13 In. 4290.00
French, Bisque, Swivel Head, Blue Enamel Inset Eyes, Blond Mohair Wig, 17 In. 5200.00
French, Bisque, Swivel Head, Cobalt Blue Glass Enamel Eyes, Blond Mohair Wig, 18 In. . 6390.00
French, Bisque, Swivel Head, Painted Blue Eyes, Closed Mouth, Jointed Body, 17 In. ... 9900.00
French, Composition, Glass Eyes, 6 Teeth, World War I Nurse's Uniform, 14 In. 575.00
French, Fashion, Hand Painted Features, Molded Eyelids, Bisque Lower Arms, 12 In. 995.00
French, Fortune Teller, Bisque, Swivel Head, Kid & Wood Body, c.1870, 15 In. 4535.00
French, Mechanical, Clockwork, Turns Head, Walks, Says Mama Papa, 23 In. 4500.00
French, Nurse, World War I, Composition, Wood, Jointed, 14 In. ....*Illus* 575.00
French, Pale Bisque Swivel Head, Cobalt Blue Glass Enamel Eyes, Closed Mouth, 16 In. . 2530.00
French, Paperweight Eyes, Auburn Wig, Ball-Jointed Body, 15 1/2 In. 2800.00
French, Papier-Mache, Glass Eyes, Bamboo Teeth, 13 In. 1350.00
French, Porcelain, Black Painted Hair, Blue Painted Eyes, Closed Mouth, 1860, 14 In. ... 1320.00
French, Porcelain, Blue Painted Eyes, Closed Mouth, Jointed, 1860, 16 In. 3190.00
French, Porcelain, Swivel Head, Blue Glass Enamel Eyes, Closed Mouth, 1858, 16 In. 3300.00

French, Porcelain, Swivel Head, Blue Painted Eyes, Brunette Mohair Wig, 18 In. 2750.00
French, Porcelain, Swivel Head, Blue Painted Eyes, Closed Mouth, 1858, 13 In. 3300.00
Freundlich, General MacArthur, Jointed Body, Composition, Original Tag, 1950s 275.00
Frozen Charlotte, China, Deep Pink, Close Mouth, Painted Hair, Germany, 10 In. 235.00
Frozen Charlotte, White Body, Painted Blue Eyes, Closed Mouth, Germany, 15 In. 325.00
Fulper, Bisque Head, Lithograph-Metal Eyes, Human Hair Wig, Bent Limb, 1918, 19 In. .. 230.00
G.I. Joe figures are listed in the Toy category.
Gans & Seyfarth, Bisque Socket Head, Sleep Eyes, Open Mouth, 5 Teeth, 22 1/2 In. 275.00
Gans & Seyfarth, Bisque, Molded Brows, Blue Eyes, Ball-Jointed, Child, 21 In. 895.00
Gaultier, 7, Bisque Swivel Head, Poupee, Paperweight Eyes, Kid Body, c.1870, 22 In. ... 3500.00
Gaultier, 8, Bisque Swivel Head, Glass Eyes, Stockinet Torso, Posable, c.1872, 17 In. ... 4200.00
Gaultier, Bisque Socket Head, Almond Brown Glass Eyes, Closed Mouth, Bebe, 9 In. ... 6160.00
Gaultier, Bisque Socket Head, Amber Brown Glass Eyes, Closed Mouth, Bebe, 16 In. ... 5940.00
Gaultier, Bisque Socket Head, Brown Paperweight Eyes, Synthetic Hair, 24 In. 1000.00
Gaultier, Bisque, Brown Eyes, Blond Hair, Old Dress, Hat & Shoes, F.G., 15 In. 4850.00
Gaultier, Bisque, Kid Shoulder, Enamel Eyes, Closed Mouth, Blond Wig, c.1870, 18 In... 2400.00
Gaultier, Bisque, Paperweight Eyes, Composition & Wood, Jointed Body, 25 In. 4600.00
Gaultier, Fashion, Bisque Swivel Head, Paperweight Eyes, Antique Dress, 14 In. 1000.00
Gebruder Heubach dolls are also in this category under Heubach.
Gebruder Heubach, 6969, Bisque, Sleep Eyes, Pouty Mouth, Ball-Jointed, c.1912, 13 In. .
Gebruder Heubach, 7246, Character, Pouty, Sleep Eyes, Jointed, Wig & Pate, 16 In. 2995.00
Gebruder Heubach, 7602, Bisque, Intaglio Eyes, Ball-Jointed Body, 20 In. 1495.00
Gebruder Heubach, 7604, Bisque, Character, Laughing, Solid Dome, Jointed, 15 In. 995.00
Gebruder Heubach, Bisque, Boy, Painted Brown Shoes, Clothes, 9 In. 1495.00
Gebruder Heubach, Bisque, Character, Pouty, Sleep Eyes, Ball-Jointed, 16 In. 2995.00
Gebruder Heubach, Bisque, Downcast Pouty Expression, Child, c.1915, 28 In. 3800.00
Gebruder Heubach, Bisque, Intaglio Eyes, Fleeced Hair, Basket, Layette, c.1915, 6 In. ... 2900.00
Gebruder Heubach, Dome Head, Boy, Molded Features, Intaglio Eyes, Jointed, 15 In. ... 995.00
Gebruder Kuhnlenz, Bisque, Pouty Expression, Ball-Jointed Body, Child, 13 In. 6500.00
Gebruder Ohlhaver, Revalo, Bisque Socket Head, Sleep Eyes, Teeth, Human Hair, 26 In. .. 350.00
Georgene Novelties, Raggedy Ann, Cotton, Tin Eyes, Printed Heart, Box, c.1948, 19 In. . 950.00
Georgene Novelties, Raggedy Ann, Outline Nose, Cloth Label, 1930s, 19 In. 595.00
Gerb's, Poupee, Pressed Felt Swivel Head, Painted Brown Eyes, Blond Mohair, 12 In. ... 350.00
German, Bisque Head, Shoulders, Blue Glass Eyes, Kid Leather Body & Limbs, 16 In. .. 1095.00
German, Bisque Shoulder Head, Molded Hair, Muslin Body, Box, c.1870, 9 In. 600.00
German, Bisque Socket Head, Glass Eyes, Open Mouth, 4 Teeth, c.1900, 18 In. 450.00
German, Bisque Socket Head, Sleep Eyes, Open Mouth, 4 Teeth, Mohair, 23 1/2 In. 195.00
German, Bisque, Amber-Tinted Socket Head, Open Mouth, Black Mohair Wig, 21 In. ... 2090.00
German, Bisque, Brown Sculpted Hair, Blue Glass Eyes, Antique Dress, 19 In. 880.00
German, Bisque, Brown Socket Head, Brown Glass Eyes, Black Mohair Wig, 20 In. 2420.00
German, Bisque, Brown Wig, Brown Eyes, 4 In. 93.00
German, Bisque, Googly Eyes, Yellow Sunbonnet, c.1915, 5 In. 225.00
German, Bisque, Sleep Eyes, Open Mouth, Blond Mohair Wig, Toddler, c.1915, 5 In. 550.00
German, Brown Sleep Eyes, Open Mouth, Bisque Lower Arms, 20 In. 193.00
German, Character, Boy, Bisque Head, Molded Hair, Kid Body, c.1900, 13 In. 750.00
German, Girl, Bisque, Flirty Glass Eyes, Molded Hair, Jointed, 9 1/2 In. 920.00
German, Porcelain Shoulder Head, Sculpted Hair, Muslin Body, c.1885, 19 In. 850.00
German, Porcelain Upper Half, Straw-Filled Muslin, Gypsy Costume, c.1915, 14 In. 1400.00
German, Queen Louise, Bisque Head, Sleep Eyes, Articulated Body, 23 In. 330.00
German, September Morn, Bisque, Grace Drayton, Label Front, 5 In. 3850.00
German, Waltzing, Celluloid Head, Wearing White Dress, Tin Hands, Body, 9 In. 2060.00
Gesland, Bisque Socket Head, Paperweight Eyes, Open-Close Mouth, Bebe, 22 In. 1350.00
Goetz, Sasha Boy, Light Brown Socket Head, Painted Eyes, Blond Hair, 1960s, 17 In. ... 2900.00
Goetz, Sasha Girl, Light Brown Socket Head, Painted Eyes, Blond Hair, 1960s, 17 In. ... 2250.00
Gre-Poir, Cloth Swivel Head, Mask Face, Mohair, Jointed Cloth Body, 17 In. 180.00
Half Dolls are listed in the Pinchushion category.
Halso, Plastic Head, Flirty Sleep Eyes, Cloth Body, Composition Arms & Legs, 29 In. ... 375.00
Hamburger & Co., Viola, Bisque, Sleep Eyes, Blond, Teeth, Composition, Jointed, 23 In. .. 165.00
Handwerck, 7 1/2, Bisque, Open Mouth, Jointed, Composition Body, Clothes, 23 In. 440.00
Handwerck, 99, Bisque Socket Head, Open Mouth, White Dress, 22 1/2 In. 305.00
Handwerck, 99, Bisque Socket Head, Sleep Eyes, Open Mouth, 4 Teeth, c.1900, 22 In. ... 900.00
Handwerck, 99, Huge Sleep Eyes, Human Hair Wig, Original Dress, 28 In. 1275.00
Handwerck, 109, Bisque Head, Composition, Ball-Jointed, Plaid Dress, 17 In. 165.00

Handwerck, 109, Bisque Head, Sleep Eyes, Composition, Human Hair, 30 In. 775.00
Handwerck, 109, Bisque, Human Hair Wig, Dress, Shoes, Coat, Leather Gloves, 16 In. .. 1550.00
Handwerck, 109, Bisque, Mohair Wig, Old Dress & Bonnet, Signed Body, 22 1/2 In. 1375.00
Handwerck, 119, Bisque Head, Glass Sleep Eyes, Jointed, Composition Body, 26 In. 288.00
Handwerck, 119, Bisque, Antique Clothes, 21 In. 950.00
Handwerck, Bisque Head, Glass Sleep Eyes, Mohair Wig, Composition Body, 24 In. 489.00
Handwerck, Bisque Head, Sleep Eyes, Brown Wig, Open Mouth, Composition, 25 In. ... 275.00
Handwerck, Bisque Socket Head, Brown Sleep Eyes, Human Hair Wig, Jointed, 28 In. ... 350.00
Handwerck, Bisque Socket Head, Brown Sleep Eyes, Open Mouth, Mohair Wig, 23 In. .. 675.00
Handwerck, Bisque, Human Hair Wig, Sleep Eyes, Original Dress, 32 In. 1750.00
Handwerck, Bisque, Painted Eyes, Dimples, Completely Original, 11 In. 450.00
Handwerck, Bisque, Sleep Eyes, Human Hair Wig, Signed, 32 In. 1750.00
Handwerck, Sleep Eyes, Ball-Jointed Body, School Girl Outfit, Shoes, 18 In. 750.00
Handwerck, Sleep Eyes, Human Hair Wig, Ball-Jointed Body, Old Clothes, 19 1/4 In. ... 695.00
Happifats, Girl, Painted Eyes, Germany, 4 In. 250.00
Hartmann, Bisque Head, Sleep Eyes, Open Mouth, Blond, Composition, Dress, 26 In. ... 220.00
Hasbro, Flying Nun, Box, Shrink Wrap, 2 1/2 x 5 1/2 In. 85.00
Herman Munster, Remco, 1960s 1980.00
Hermann Steiner, 128, Girl, Brown Eyes, Toddler Body, 15 In. 895.00
Hertel Schwab, 151, Bisque, Character, Boy, Aqua Sleep Eyes, 18 In. 995.00
Hertel Schwab, 151, Dome Bisque Socket Head, Sleep Eyes, 2 Teeth, Toddler, 22 In. 800.00
Hertel Schwab, 179, Bisque Head & Torso, Chubby Face, Painted Features, 7 In. 750.00
Hertel Schwab, Bisque Socket Head, Carrot Red Hair, Brown Googly Eyes, 1914, 10 In. . 3960.00
Heubach dolls are also in this category under Gebruder Heubach.
Heubach, 250, Bisque Head, Brown Sleep Eyes, Open Mouth, Composition, 21 In. 275.00
Heubach, 250, Brown Sleep Eyes, Open Mouth With Teeth, Original Wig, 19 In. 220.00
Heubach, 250/8, Bisque Head, Sleep Eyes, Mohair Wig, Jointed, Composition, 28 In. 405.00
Heubach, 320, Bisque Socket Head, Sleep Eyes, Open Mouth, 2 Teeth, 15 In. 375.00
Heubach, 7246, Bisque, Character, Pouty, 28 In. 6500.00
Heubach, 7345, Character, Blond Hair, 13 In. 1850.00
Heubach, 7679, Bisque, Whistler, Original Body, 16 In. 1995.00
Heubach, Baby Stuart, Kidskin Body, Jointed, 16 In. 1295.00
Heubach, Bisque Head, Molded Hair, Jointed Body, Celluloid Hands, 19 In. 460.00
Heubach, Bisque Socket Head, Intaglio Side-Glancing Eyes, Closed Mouth, 7 In., Pair ... 1045.00
Heubach, Dancing Girl, 13 In. 1550.00
Heubach Koppelsdorf, 312, Bisque, Open Mouth, Teeth, Composition, Jointed, 14 In. ... 330.00
Heubach Koppelsdorf, 320-321, Twins, Girl & Boy, Sleep Eyes, 16 In. 795.00
Heubach Koppelsdorf, Bisque, Brown Sleep Eyes, Ball-Jointed Body, Child, 33 In. 1295.00
Horsman, Baby Dimples, Steel Sleep Eyes, Teeth, Tongue, Cloth Body, 1927, 22 In. 115.00
Horsman, Bright Star, Party Dress & Hat, Paper Tag, 1938, 27 In. 300.00
Horsman, Composition, Tin Sleep Eyes, Open Mouth, 4 Teeth, Toddler, Box, 18 In. 255.00
Horsman, HEbee-SHEbee, Bisque, Charles Twelve Trees, Painted, 1923, 8 1/2 In. 430.00
Horsman, Indian Girl, Composition Flange Head, Painted Eyes, Cloth Body, Tag, 13 In. .. 225.00
Horsman, Jackie Coogan, Cloth Label, Original Pin, 14 In. 795.00
Horsman, Pudgie Baby, Plastic & Vinyl, 1979, 12 In. 45.00
Horsman, Tynie Baby, Bisque Head, Closed Mouth, Cloth Body, 1924, 11 In. 800.00
Horsman, Tynie Baby, Bisque, Swivel Head, Loop-Jointed Limbs, 1924, 8 1/2 In. 1400.00
Horsman, Tynie Baby, Composition Head, 1924, 19 In. 425.00
Huret, Bisque Shoulder Head, Blue Downcast Eyes, Closed Mouth, 16 In. 3410.00
Huret, Bisque, Swivel Head, Painted Blue Eyes, Blond Lamb's-Wool Wig, 1867, 17 In. .. 9900.00
Ideal, Abbott & Costello, Who's On First, Baseball Uniforms, 1984, 10 In. 150.00
Ideal, Action Boy, Space Suit, Box 825.00
Ideal, Bamm Bamm, 1962 .... 76.00
Ideal, Bonnie Braids, Unused, Box, 15 In. 400.00
Ideal, Chrissy, Growing Hair, Green Coat, Tag, 15 In. ....25.00 to 35.00
Ideal, Deanna Durbin, Composition Head, Hazel Sleep Eyes, Open Mouth, 20 In. .275.00 to 550.00
Ideal, Fanny Brice, Baby Snooks, Painted Eyes, Composition, Blue Dress, 12 In. 285.00
Ideal, Little Miss Marker, Sara Stimson, 1980, Box 20.00
Ideal, Little Miss Revlon, Vinyl, Blue Sleep Eyes, Dark Blond Hair, 1960, 10 In. 110.00
Ideal, Miss Liberty, Socket Head, 6 Teeth, Mohair Wig, Composition Body, 21 In. 700.00
Ideal, Mr. Magoo, Vinyl Head, Cloth, 1962, 16 In. 135.00
Ideal, Patty Playpal, Honey Blond Wig, Original Dress, 1960, 35 In. 300.00
Ideal, Toni, Bride, Plastic Head, Blue Sleep Eyes, Platinum Blond Wig, 1953, 15 In. 1200.00

Ideal, Toni, Plastic Head, Tagged Dress, Wrist Tag, c.1949, 14 In. 700.00
Ideal, Toni, Walker, Plastic Head, Blue-Green Sleep Eyes, Curled Red Wig, 1956, 16 In. .   1200.00
Indian dolls are listed in the Indian category.
Italian, Girl, Composition, Dark Hair, Windup Legs, 18 In. 175.00
Italian Girl, Composition, Life-Like Eyes, Cryer, 21 In. 145.00
J.D.K. dolls are also listed in this category under Kestner.
J.D.K., 257, Baby, Bisque, Open Mouth, 2 Teeth, Tongue, Composition, 22 In. 275.00
J.D.K., 260, Original Wig, Dress, Shoes, Toddler Body, 13 In. 795.00
J.D.K., Hilda, Baby, Antique Clothes & Wig, 14 In. 3450.00
Jensen, Gladdie, Bisque Head, Sleep Eyes, Teeth, Cloth Body, Clothes, 17 1/2 In. 425.00
Jumeau, 1, Bisque Socket Head, Baby, Glass Eyes, Ball-Jointed, c.1898, 11 In. 6000.00
Jumeau, 1, Bisque Socket Head, Blue Glass Enamel Eyes, Closed Mouth, Bebe, 11 In. . . .   4290.00
Jumeau, 2, Bisque Socket Head, Blue Glass Enamel Eyes, Bebe, 1878, 10 In. 3300.00
Jumeau, 2, Bisque Swivel Head, Poupee, Glass Eyes, Kid Body, c.1880, 10 1/2 In. 1500.00
Jumeau, 3, Bisque Socket Head, Brown, Brown Paperweight Eyes, Jointed, Bebe, 12 In. .   7480.00
Jumeau, 5, Bisque Socket Head, Blue Paperweight Eyes, Jointed, Bebe, 1886, 14 In. 5060.00
Jumeau, 5, Pressed Bisque Socket Head, Blue Glass Eyes, Ball-Jointed, c.1898, 14 In. . . .   5250.00
Jumeau, 7, Bisque Swivel Head, Paperweight Eyes, Kid Fashion Body, c.1880, 19 In. . . .   2500.00
Jumeau, 8, Bisque Socket Head, Bebe, Blue Glass Eyes, Pierced Ears, c.1878, 18 In. 6000.00
Jumeau, 8, Bisque Socket Head, Brown Paperweight Eyes, Closed Mouth, Bebe, 19 In. . . .   7920.00
Jumeau, 9, Bisque Socket Head, Blue Paperweight Eyes, Auburn Wig, Bebe, 1890, 20 In.   4730.00
Jumeau, 9, Bisque Socket Head, Blue Paperweight Eyes, Closed Mouth, Bebe, 20 In. 3850.00
Jumeau, 9, Bisque Socket Head, Brown Glass Paperweight Eyes, Bebe, 1885, 20 In. 4290.00
Jumeau, 9, Bisque Swivel Head, Paperweight Eyes, Kid Gusset-Jointed Body, 21 In. 4500.00
Jumeau, 10, Portrait, Bisque Socket Head, Blue Glass Eyes, Ball-Jointed, c.1882, 23 In. . . .   9000.00
Jumeau, 11, Upper Teeth, Jointed Body, Pink Silk Dress, 1907, 31 In. 2530.00
Jumeau, 12, Bisque Socket Head, Deep Blue Paperweight Eyes, Jointed, Bebe, 26 In. 6600.00
Jumeau, 12L, Bebe Louvre, Bisque Socket Head, Brown Paperweight Eyes, 1892, 26 In. . .   5250.00
Jumeau, Bisque Head, Cork Pate, Paperweight Eyes, Closed Mouth, Jointed Body, 14 In. .   2875.00
Jumeau, Bisque Head, Paperweight Eyes, Mohair Wig, Composition Body, 10 1/2 In. 4830.00
Jumeau, Bisque Socket Head, Amber Brown Glass Eyes, Closed Mouth, Bebe, 18 In. 6600.00
Jumeau, Bisque Socket Head, Amber Brown Paperweight Eyes, Bebe, 1890, 9 1/2 In. 5500.00
Jumeau, Bisque Socket Head, Blue Paperweight Eyes, Blond Mohair Wig, Bebe, 28 In. . . .   5170.00
Jumeau, Bisque Socket Head, Blue Paperweight Eyes, Closed Mouth, Bebe, 19 In. 4400.00
Jumeau, Bisque Socket Head, Blue Paperweight Eyes, Jointed, Bebe, 1892, 17 In. 4510.00
Jumeau, Bisque Socket Head, Glass Eyes, Human Hair, Ball-Jointed, c.1880, 17 In. 3400.00
Jumeau, Bisque Socket Head, Paperweight Eyes, Jointed Body, c.1890, 20 In. 4100.00
Jumeau, Bisque Socket Head, Replaced Human Hair, French Body, 1907, 23 In. 1125.00
Jumeau, Bisque Swivel Head, Blue Paperweight Eyes, Closed Mouth, 1880, 26 In. 5500.00
Jumeau, Bisque Swivel Head, Kid Fashion Body, Mitten Hands, c.1878, 11 In. 4100.00
Jumeau, Bisque Swivel Head, Paperweight Eyes, Kid Body, Human Hair Wig, 14 1/2 In. .   3975.00
Jumeau, Bisque, Enamel Eyes, Brunette Wig, Straight Wrists, Fully-Jointed Body, 10 In. .   7600.00
Jumeau, Bisque, Enamel Eyes, Closed Mouth, c.1878, 16 In. 7700.00
Jumeau, Bisque, Fashion, Blue Paperweight Eyes, Mohair Wig, Kid Body, 18 In. 3200.00
Jumeau, Bisque, Paperweight Eyes, Straight Wristed Body, French Clothes, 20 In. 9200.00
Jumeau, Bisque, Swivel Head, Pale Blue Paperweight Eyes, Original Costume, 20 In. . . .   3850.00
Jumeau, Blue Paperweight Eyes, Walker Body, E.D., 28 In. 4950.00
Jumeau, Brown Paperweight Eyes, Ball-Jointed Body, 1907, 30 In. 3000.00
Jumeau, Cork Pate, Paperweight Eyes, Closed Mouth, 26 In. 3080.00
Jumeau, Emile, Bisque Socket Head, Brown Glass Enamel Eyes, 1895, 19 In. 18700.00
Jumeau, Paris Bebe, Bisque Socket Head, Brown Glass Sleep Eyes, Open Mouth, 16 In. .   1760.00
Jumeau, Paris Bebe, Bisque Socket Head, Brown Glass Sleep Eyes, Open Mouth, 22 In. .   3960.00
Jumeau, Portrait, Paperweight Eyes, Closed Mouth, Human Hair Wig, 19 1/2 In. 5900.00
Jutta, 1349, Bisque Socket Head, Sleep Eyes, Open Mouth, 4 Teeth, 27 In. 500.00
Jutta, 1349, Bisque Socket Head, Teeth, Human Hair, Wood, Composition, 30 In. 500.00
Jutta, Dominican Nun, Blue Sleep Eyes, Wool, Habit, Cord Belt, Rosary, 28 In. 1695.00
K * R, 23, Bisque Socket Head, Sleep Eyes, Open Mouth, 3 Teeth, Mohair, Walker, 9 In. .   325.00
K * R, 62, Bisque Socket Head, Flirty Sleep Eyes, Open Mouth, 4 Teeth, 24 1/2 In. 450.00
K * R, 73, Bisque Socket Head, Flirty Sleep Eyes, Open Mouth, 4 Teeth, c.1910, 28 In. . . .   1050.00
K * R, 100, Molded Hair, Blue Eyes, Composition Body, White Gown, 10 In. 165.00
K * R, 101, Bisque Socket Head, Blue Painted Eyes, Pouty, Closed Mouth, 1912, 7 In. . . .   1540.00
K * R, 101, Bisque Socket Head, Painted Eyes, Pouty Mouth, Velvet Suit, 18 In. 2700.00
K * R, 101, Bisque, Character, Painted Eyes, Pouty Lips, Ball-Jointed, c.1912, 12 In. 2600.00

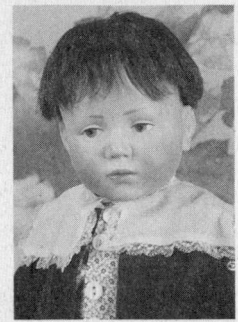

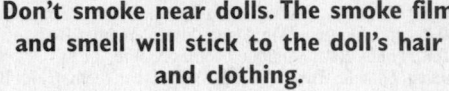

Don't smoke near dolls. The smoke film and smell will stick to the doll's hair and clothing.

Doll, K * R, 101, Boy, Bisque Socket
  Head, Redressed, 18 1/2 In.

K * R, 101, Bisque, Marie, Pouty Expression, Blond Wig, 18 In.	3900.00
K * R, 101, Boy, Bisque Socket Head, Redressed, 18 1/2 In. ....*Illus*	2700.00
K * R, 101, Character, Original Wig, Antique Clothes, 19 In.	5250.00
K * R, 101, Marie, Flowered Hat, 17 In.	3300.00
K * R, 114, Bisque, Gretchen, Closed Mouth, Ball-Jointed Body, c.1910, 18 In.	4700.00
K * R, 114, Gretchen, Bisque Socket Head, Painted Eyes, Ball-Jointed, c.1910, 19 In.	7250.00
K * R, 115, Bisque Socket Head, Sleep Eyes, Pouty, Jointed Toddler Body, c.1910, 16 In.	4900.00
K * R, 116A, Baby, Flirty Eyes, Antique Clothes & Wig, 16 In.	2650.00
K * R, 117N, Bisque Socket Head, Brown Glass Sleep Eyes, Child, 1912, 32 In.	3410.00
K * R, 121, Bisque, Azure Blue Sleep Eyes, Blond Wig, Jointed Body, Toddler, 25 In.	1995.00
K * R, 121, Dimpled Darling, Original Clothes, 17 In.	1480.00
K * R, 121, Sleep Eyes, Human Hair, Dimples, Baby Dress, 16 In.	950.00
K * R, 122, Bisque, Wig, 5-Piece Body, Romper, Toddler, 14 In.	1575.00
K * R, 122, Upper Teeth, Tongue, Blond Wig, Bent Limb Body, c.1915, 19 In.	1000.00
K * R, 126, Baby, Bisque Socket Head, Sleep Eyes, Dressed, 15 1/2 In.	400.00
K * R, 126, Bisque Socket Head, Sleep Eyes, Open Mouth, Bent Limb, Baby, 27 In.	490.00
K * R, 126, Bisque Socket Head, Sleep Eyes, 2 Teeth, Wobble Tongue, Baby, 16 In.	450.00
K * R, 126, Bisque, Sleep Eyes, Open Mouth, Tongue, Composition Body, Baby, 16 In.	440.00
K * R, 126, Flirty Eyes, 5-Piece Body, Toddler, 20 In.	950.00
K * R, 126, Jointed, Antique Clothes, Toddler, 28 In.	1995.00
K * R, 192, Bisque Socket Head, Sleep Eyes, Open Mouth, 4 Teeth, Ball-Jointed, 30 In.	1400.00
K * R, 257, Bisque, Pink, Blue Sleep Eyes, Antique Clothing, 21 In.	1295.00
K * R, Bisque Head, Pouty Mouth, Jointed Body, Cotton & Lace Dress, 11 1/2 In.	1150.00
K * R, Bisque Socket Head, Sleep Eyes, Jointed Wood, Composition, Child, 7 1/2 In.	370.00
K * R, Bisque, 4 Porcelain Teeth, Brunette Wig, Wooden-Jointed Body, Child, 27 In.	850.00
K * R, Bisque, Brown, Mohair Wig, 11 In.	995.00
K * R, Bisque, Brunette Wig, Composition & Wooden Ball-Jointed Body, 17 In.	4100.00
K * R, Bisque, Dreamy Sleep Eyes, Mohair Wig, Old Dress, Child, 21 In.	1150.00
K * R, Bisque, Flirty Eyes, 4 Porcelain Teeth, Ball-Jointed Body, Dressed, Child, 17 In.	1000.00
K * R, Bisque, Sleep Eyes, Original Shoes & Romper, 5-Piece Body, Toddler, 14 In.	1575.00
K * R, Boy, Bisque Socket Head, Blue Glass Sleep Eyes, Pouty, Closed Mouth, 14 In.	4070.00
K * R, Gretchen, Bisque, Closed Mouth, Mohair Wig, Composition & Wood, 19 In.	5600.00
K * R, Mother, Bisque Socket Head, Brown Glass Sleep Eyes, Brunette Wig, 1912, 19 In.	4070.00
K * R, Sleep Eyes, Human Hair Wig, Baby Gown, Dimples, Baby, 16 In.	950.00
Kathe Kruse, Annchen, Signed, Tag, 14 In.	2500.00
Kathe Kruse, Boy, Swivel Head, Painted Features, Muslin Body, Sailor Suit, 1930, 20 In.	1725.00
Kathe Kruse, Character, Boy, Series 1, Oil Painted Face, Cloth, 1915, 17 In.	2100.00
Kathe Kruse, Fenzi, Boy, Paper Label, c.1940, 17 1/2 In.	2000.00
Kathe Kruse, Girl, Brown Hair Waved Across Forehead, Painted Blue Eyes, 17 In.	6820.00
Kathe Kruse, Girl, Plastic Head, Mohair Wig, Cloth Body, Period Outfit, 1950s, 20 In.	750.00
Kestner dolls are also in this category under J.D.K.	
Kestner, 4 1/2, Bisque, Paperweight Eyes, Kid Body & Legs, Red Wool Dress, 15 1/2 In.	490.00
Kestner, 7, Boy, Mohair Wig, Paperweight Eyes, Hand Painted Face, 13 In.	2495.00
Kestner, 13, Bisque, Fixed Open Eyes, Closed Mouth, Jointed Composition Body, 19 In.	2645.00
Kestner, 15, Bisque Socket Head, Sleep Eyes, Row Of Teeth, Jointed, c.1885, 23 In.	3000.00

Kestner, 117, Daisy, Dress, Shoes, 28 In. 1100.00
Kestner, 126, Bisque, Sleep Eyes, Open Mouth, Starfish Hands, Toddler, 1920s, 10 In. 575.00
Kestner, 129, Bisque Socket Head, Brown Glass Sleep Eyes, Open Mouth, Child, 19 In. . 2640.00
Kestner, 143, Bisque Socket Head, Sleep Eyes, Open Mouth, Row Of Teeth, 1915, 9 In. . 750.00
Kestner, 143, Character, Bisque Socket Head, Sleep Eyes, 4 Teeth, Jointed, 1915, 7 In. 700.00
Kestner, 143, Character, Bisque Socket Head, Sleep Eyes, 4 Teeth, Jointed, c.1915, 9 In. . 900.00
Kestner, 143, Character, Human Hair Wig, Ball-Jointed Body, 20 In. 1395.00
Kestner, 146, Bisque, Blue Eyes, Antique Clothes & Shoes, 30 In. 1495.00
Kestner, 146, Bisque, Long Curls, Original Dress, Shoes & Undies, Signed, 25 In. 1675.00
Kestner, 148, Bisque Shoulder Head, Sleep Eyes, Open Mouth, 4 Teeth, Kid Body, 23 In. 280.00
Kestner, 152, Girl, Bisque Socket Head, Brown Sleep Eyes, Open Mouth, 11 In. 750.00
Kestner, 154, Bisque Head, Sleep Eyes, Blond, Kid Body, White Dress 495.00
Kestner, 161, Bisque, Sleep Eyes, Brunette, Composition, Jointed, 13 In. 1250.00
Kestner, 164, Bisque Head, Brown Sleep Eyes, Open Mouth, Jointed, 17 In. 415.00
Kestner, 164, Bisque, Blue Sleep Eyes, Mohair Wig & Pate, Signed, 12 In. 1175.00
Kestner, 164, Bisque, Mohair Wig, Original Dress & Shoes, 29 In. 2250.00
Kestner, 164, Open Mouth, 4 Teeth, Composition & Wooden Ball-Jointed Body, 27 In. .. 850.00
Kestner, 167, Bisque Socket Head, Sleep Eyes, Open Mouth, 4 Teeth, c.1910, 18 In. 850.00
Kestner, 167, Bisque, Sleep Eyes, Human Hair Wig, Feathered Brows, 20 In. 1550.00
Kestner, 167, Bisque, Sleep Eyes, Mohair Wig, Original Dress, Signed, 19 In. 895.00
Kestner, 168, Bisque Socket Head, Sleep Eyes, Open Mouth, 4 Teeth, Jointed, 19 In. ... 400.00
Kestner, 171, Bisque, Sleep Eyes, Mohair Wig, Original Costume, Signed, 27 In. 1450.00
Kestner, 172, Gibson Girl, Bisque, Blond Wig, Kid Body, Bisque Forearms, 18 In. 1700.00
Kestner, 174, Bisque Socket Head, Blue Glass Sleep Eyes, Open Mouth, Child, 10 In. ... 495.00
Kestner, 182, Bisque Socket Head, Blue Painted Eyes, Closed Mouth, 1910, 14 In. 3190.00
Kestner, 196, Bisque Socket Head, Blue Sleep Eyes, Open Mouth, Mohair Wig, 17 In. ... 185.00
Kestner, 211, Bisque Socket Head, Brown Glass Sleep Eyes, Open Mouth, 1912, 26 In. .. 2100.00
Kestner, 211, Sammy, Skin Wig Over Plaster Pate, 20 In. 1150.00
Kestner, 214, Azure Blue Sleep Eyes, Feather Brows, Luster Pate, Blond Wig, 19 In. 995.00
Kestner, 221, Bisque Socket Head, Googly Eyes, Toddler Body, c.1912, 12 In. 4800.00
Kestner, 221, Bisque, Human Hair Wig, Googly, Fully Jointed, Toddler, 11 In. 8000.00
Kestner, 243, Chinese Baby, Bisque Socket Head, Sleep Eyes, 2 Teeth, c.1912, 19 In. 7750.00
Kestner, 257, Baby, Pink Bisque, Blue Sleep Eyes, 26 In. 1995.00
Kestner, 260, Bisque, Starfish Hands, Sleep Eyes, Human Hair Wig, Dress, 6 1/2 In. 995.00
Kestner, Baby Jean, Painted Hair, 18 In. 1495.00
Kestner, Baby, Bisque, Bent-Limb Body, Antique Costume, 13 In. 525.00
Kestner, Bisque Head, Sleep Glass Eyes, Mohair Wig, Impressed P, 30 In. 518.00
Kestner, Bisque Socket Head, Brown Glass Eyes, Blond Mohair Wig, Child, 1890, 9 In. . 605.00
Kestner, Bisque Socket Head, Sleep Eyes, 2 Upper Teeth, Organdy Ruffled Dress, 16 In. . 4800.00
Kestner, Bisque, Pouty, Paperweight Eyes, Braided Wig, Costume & Shoes, 12 In. 3550.00
Kestner, Bisque, Swivel Head, Sleep Eyes, Open Mouth, 2 Teeth, c.1890, 8 1/2 In. 2500.00
Kestner, Century Baby, Bisque Socket Head, Sleep Eyes, Muslin Torso, c.1918, 19 In. 1000.00
Kestner, Character, Boy, Closed Mouth, Paperweight Eyes, 13 In. 2495.00
Kestner, Chinese Baby, Bisque, Sleep Eyes, 2 Teeth, Composition Body, 13 In. 5000.00
Kestner, Gibson Girl, Bisque, Blue Sleep Eyes, Closed Mouth, 20 In. 990.00
Kestner, Gibson Girl, Sleep Eyes, Original Body & Hands, Dressed, 20 In. 3600.00
Kestner, Hilda, Bisque Socket Head, Sleep Eyes, 2 Teeth, Baby Gown, c.1915, 24 In. 1500.00
Kestner, Hilda, Bisque, Painted Hair, Open Mouth, Tongue, Teeth, c.1914, 14 In. 2600.00
Kestner, Original Wig, Closed Mouth, Silk Dress, 18 In. 950.00
Kewpie dolls are listed in the Kewpie category.
Kley & Hahn, 167, Bisque Socket Head, Sleep Eyes, 2 Teeth, Toddler, 15 1/2 In. 1150.00
Kley & Hahn, 169, Bisque, Closed Mouth, Mohair Wig, Sleep Eyes, Toddler, 14 1/2 In. .. 3200.00
Kley & Hahn, 525, Bisque Socket Head, Sleep Eyes, Molded Hair, Sailor Suit, 21 In. 950.00
Kley & Hahn, 546, Girl, Bisque Socket Head, Sleep Eyes, Human Hair In Braids, 20 In. .. 2100.00
Kley & Hahn, Bisque, Blond Human Hair Wig, Antique Dress, 24 In. 1050.00
Kley & Hahn, Bisque, Dimples, Brunette Bobbed Wig, Wooden-Jointed Body, 25 In. ... 1600.00
Kley & Hahn, Bisque, Sleep Eyes, Human Hair Wig, Dressed, 24 In. 675.00
Kley & Hahn, Walkure, Bisque, Blond, Ball-Jointed, Replaced Clothes, 26 In. 600.00
Kley & Hahn, Walkure, Bisque, Sleep Eyes, Human Hair, Antique Dress, 24 In. 1050.00
Kling, Bisque, Pouty, Mohair Wig, Muslin Body, c.1880, 14 In. 1500.00
Knickerbocker, Bamm Bamm, Box, 1972, 6 In. 45.00
Knickerbocker, Beloved Belindy, Black Button Eyes, Cotton, Tag, Box, c.1965, 15 In. ... 850.00
Knickerbocker, Beloved Belindy, Painted Eyes, Cloth, Bobbs Merrill Co., 1962, 15 In. 935.00

Knickerbocker, Bozo The Clown, Vinyl Head, Yellow Feet, 1973, 11 1/2 In. 18.00
Knickerbocker, Raggedy Ann, 1963, 19 In. 395.00
Koenig & Wernicke, Bisque Socket Head, Sleep Eyes, 2 Teeth, Toddler, 1920, 22 In. 950.00
Koenig & Wernicke, Bisque, Open Mouth, 4 Porcelain Teeth, c.1910, 34 In. 2700.00
Lanternier, Bisque, Sleep Eyes, Open Mouth, Teeth, Wig, Composition, Jointed, 22 In. . . 605.00
Lenci, Boy, Pressed Felt Swivel Head, Applied Ears, Ethnic Costume, Tag, 11 In. 375.00
Lenci, Bride, Blond Mohair, Felt Clothing, 9 In. 255.00
Lenci, Character, Pouty, Tag On Dress, Child, 16 In. 1995.00
Lenci, Chinese, Pressed Felt Swivel Head, Painted Oriental Eyes, Mohair, 16 In. 1700.00
Lenci, Cloth & Felt Outfit & Cap, Basket On Back, 17 In. 1150.00
Lenci, Fad-Ette Smoker, Pressed Felt Swivel Head, Blond Mohair, Cloth Body, 25 In. 375.00
Lenci, Felt Swivel Head, Painted Brown Eyes, Closed Mouth, Red, Green Bow, 18 In. . . . 325.00
Lenci, Girl With Umbrella, Swivel Head, Closed Mouth, Bobbed Curly Hair, 21 In. 2650.00
Lenci, Girl, Hungarian, Jointed, Yellow-Trimmed Outfit, 1930s, 14 In. 490.00
Lenci, Girl, Polish, Jointed At Neck, Shoulders & Hips, Coil Basket, Dressed, 14 In. 373.00
Lenci, Girl, Rose, Swivel Head, Side-Glancing Eyes, Blond Wig, Ringlet Curls, 11 In. . . . 950.00
Lenci, Girl, Side-Glancing Eyes, Blond, Swivel Head, Hip-Jointed Legs, 20 In. 3800.00
Lenci, Girl, Side-Glancing Eyes, Brunette, Curls, Felt Body, Patchwork Dress, 20 In. 4500.00
Lenci, Girl, Spanish, Jointed At Neck, Shoulders & Hips, Pink Dress, Apron, 14 In. 460.00
Lenci, Girl, Swivel Head, Painted Side-Glancing Eyes, Mohair, Straw Hat, 14 In. 375.00
Lenci, Girl, Tuscany, Swivel Head, Closed Mouth, Felt Arms & Legs, c.1940, 19 In. 850.00
Lenci, Girl, Zurigo, Pouty, Swivel Head, Curly Wig, Muslin Torso, 1930, 14 In. 550.00
Lenci, Hiker, Girl, Swivel Head, Pouty, Long Curled Wig, Jointed Limbs, 19 In. 6600.00
Lenci, Lady, Long Limbs, All Original, Tag, 30 In. 2495.00
Lenci, Skier, Felt Swivel Head, Painted Brown Eyes, Felt Hair, Mascotte, 8 1/2 In. 375.00
Lenci, Swivel Head, Closed Mouth, Mohair Wig, Muslin Torso, c.1940, 11 In. 1200.00
Lenci, Woman, Spanish, Felt Swivel Head, Original Clothes, 19 In. . . . .*Illus* 1500.00
Levi, Big E, Rag, Blue Denim, Red Mop Hair, 16 In. 75.00
Levi, Big E, Rag, Blue Denim, Yellow Yarn Hair, Painted Face, 17 In. 250.00
Levi, Big E, Rag, Light Blue Denim, Yellow Yarn Hair, 12 In. 130.00
Levi, Red Cotton Mop Hair, Brass Button Nose, Light Blue Denim, 9 In. 50.00
Madame Alexander, Alice In Wonderland, Pinafore, 13 In. 550.00
Madame Alexander, Argentina, Plastic, Jointed, Sleep Eyes, Black Hair, 7 1/2 In. 135.00
Madame Alexander, Babs, Skater, Plastic, Blue Sleep Eyes, Blond Wig, c.1949, 14 In. . . . 650.00
Madame Alexander, Bride, Bow-Shaped Lips, Human Hair In Curls, 21 In. 850.00
Madame Alexander, Bride, Plastic, Sleep Eyes, Blond Wig, Walker, Tag, c.1958, 8 In. 150.00
Madame Alexander, Bride, Vinyl, Straight Leg, Original Tagged Clothing, Box, 14 In. . . . 90.00
Madame Alexander, Cissette, Plastic Head, Blue-Green Eyes, Blond Wig, 1957, 10 In. . . . 440.00
Madame Alexander, Cissy, Plastic, Vinyl Arms, Original Dress, 20 In. . . . .*Illus* 500.00
Madame Alexander, Clarabelle, Clown, Tagged Suit, Cloth 325.00
Madame Alexander, Glamour Girl, On Picnic, Plastic Head, Sleep Eyes, 18 In. 425.00
Madame Alexander, Groom, Plastic, Sleep Eyes, Auburn Wig, Walker, c.1956, 8 In. 150.00
Madame Alexander, Jane Withers, Open Mouth, 4 Teeth, c.1935, 17 In. 1050.00
Madame Alexander, Kate Greenaway, Brown Sleep Eyes, Composition, Tag, 13 In. 550.00

Doll, Lenci, Woman,
Spanish, Felt Swivel Head,
Original Clothes, 19 In.

**Vinyl dolls should not be
put in a hot attic. Heat
may darken the vinyl.**

Doll, Madame Alexander,
Cissy, Plastic, Vinyl Arms,
Original Dress, 20 In.

Doll, Mattel, Barbie, Brunette,
Ponytail, Orange Blossom
Clothes

Doll, Mattel, Barbie, Bubble
Cut, Titian Hair, Swimsuit,
Plastic Stand

Doll, Moravian, Cloth,
Painted Face, Stitch-Jointed
Shoulder, 18 In.

Madame Alexander, Little Shaver, Cloth Mask Face, Stockinet Body, Tag, 9 1/2 In. 325.00
Madame Alexander, Little Women, Tag, c.1947, 14 In., 5 Piece 1800.00
Madame Alexander, McGuffey Ana, Composition, Original Costume, 12 In. 165.00
Madame Alexander, McGuffey Ana, Composition, Sleep Eyes, Tag, c.1940, 15 In. 600.00
Madame Alexander, McGuffey Ana, Curly Bangs, Organdy Dress, Boots, c.1935, 11 In. . .   1250.00
Madame Alexander, Melinda, Portrette, Plastic, Blue Sleep Eyes, Tag, Box, 10 In. 275.00
Madame Alexander, Peter Pan Set, With Teddy Bear, Label 795.00
Madame Alexander, Pip, Pressed Felt Suede Mask Face, Cloth Body, Tag, 16 In. 525.00
Madame Alexander, Princess Elizabeth, Tagged Clothes, 17 In. 795.00
Madame Alexander, Scarlett O'Hara, Costume, Box, 18 In. 2100.00
Madame Alexander, Scarlett, Plastic Head, Sleep Eyes, Walking, 1965, 8 In. 500.00
Madame Alexander, Scarlett, Plastic, Sleep Eyes, Blond Wig, Walker, Tag, c.1955, 8 In. . .   375.00
Madame Alexander, Sonja Henie, Row Of Teeth, Smiling, Dimples, c.1939, 21 In. 1400.00
Madame Alexander, Tommy, Plastic Head, Green Sleep Eyes, Blond Wig, 1962, 12 In. . .   110.00
Madame Alexander, Wendy, Bride, Plastic, Sleep Eyes, Walking, Satin Dress, 15 In. 950.00
Marotte, Baby, Bisque Head, Playing Recessional, 13 1/2 In. 230.00
Marotte, Harlequin, Bisque Head, Green Costume, 13 In. 575.00
Marotte, Harlequin, Bisque Head, Multicolored Costume, Bells, 13 In. 862.00
Marseille, 550, Bisque Socket Head, Sleep Eyes, Boy, Sailor Suit, c.1912, 18 In. 1600.00
Marseille, 590, Bisque Socket Head, Sleep Eyes, Auburn Mohair, c.1912, 10 In. 500.00
Marseille, Just Me, Bisque, Blue Sleep Eyes, Sewn Mohair Wig, 11 In. 995.00
Martin, Washer Woman, Bent Over Washtub, Scrubs Clothes, c.1899, 7 1/2 In. 1380.00
Mattel, Allan, Red Hair, Beige Lips, Swim Trunks, Cork Sandals 110.00
Mattel, Barbie & Ken, Little Theatre Gift Set, Box, 1964 . . . .   7500.00
Mattel, Barbie, 35th Anniversary Gift Set, Blond, Box 75.00
Mattel, Barbie, 35th Anniversary, Blond 40.00
Mattel, Barbie, After The Walk, Box 100.00
Mattel, Barbie, American Girl, Blond Hair, Blue & White Striped Dress 325.00
Mattel, Barbie, Astronaut, 1985 . . . .   125.00
Mattel, Barbie, Black Hair, Bubble Cut, Sophisticated Lady Dress, Tiara 330.00
Mattel, Barbie, Black, 1989 . . . .   45.00
Mattel, Barbie, Brunette, Ponytail, Orange Blossom Clothes . . . .*Illus*   530.00
Mattel, Barbie, Bubble Cut, Blond Hair, White Lips, Red Swimsuit 70.00
Mattel, Barbie, Bubble Cut, Titian Hair, Swimsuit, Plastic Stand . . . .*Illus*   135.00
Mattel, Barbie, Calvin Klein Jeans, Box 45.00
Mattel, Barbie, Dreamtime, Pink Teddy Bear, 1984 . . . .   75.00
Mattel, Barbie, Easy-As-Pie Cookbook, Cynthia Lawrence, 1964 . . . .   135.00
Mattel, Barbie, Golden Dream, Quick-Curl Hair, Gold Dress, 1980 . . . .   85.00
Mattel, Barbie, Happy Holidays, 1988 . . . .   260.00
Mattel, Barbie, Happy Holidays, Special Edition, White Gown, Fur Trim, 1989 . . . .   85.00
Mattel, Barbie, In Japan, Red Kimono, Hair Ornament, Gold Foil Fan, Box 120.00
Mattel, Barbie, Lunch On The Terrace, Green & White Checked Skirt, Hat 95.00
Mattel, Barbie, Mardi Gras, American Beauties Collection, 1987 . . . .   40.00
Mattel, Barbie, No. 1, Blond, Ponytail, Black & White Swimsuit, Box 4800.00

Mattel, Barbie, No. 3, Blond, Box, 1960 .... 4400.00
Mattel, Barbie, No. 3, Blond, Ponytail, Hoop Earrings, Black & White Swimsuit, Box ... 1025.00
Mattel, Barbie, No. 3, Ponytail, Black, Black & White Swimsuit, Box 950.00
Mattel, Barbie, No. 4, Brunette, Black & White Swimsuit, Box 800.00
Mattel, Barbie, No. 5, Titian Hair, Ponytail, Black & White Swimsuit, Box 775.00
Mattel, Barbie, Nurse, White Dress & Cap, Blue Cape, Diploma, Glass 85.00
Mattel, Barbie, Opening Night 100.00
Mattel, Barbie, Ponytail, Top Knot, Gay Parisienne Dress, Gloves, Tag 2600.00
Mattel, Barbie, Scarlett O'Hara, Red Party Dress, Hollywood Legends Collection 65.00
Mattel, Barbie, Solo In Spotlight, Brunette, Box 40.00
Mattel, Barbie, Spring Bouquet, Box 95.00
Mattel, Barbie, Sun Gold Malibu, 1963 .... 40.00
Mattel, Barbie, Sunset Malibu, Blond, Box 145.00
Mattel, Barbie, Tropical Miko, 1985 .... 25.00
Mattel, Barbie, Twist 'n' Turn, Blond Hair, Orange 2-Piece Swimsuit, 1967 .... 135.00
Mattel, Barbie, Twist 'n' Turn, Brunette, Yellow Top, Flower Trim, Pants 255.00
Mattel, Barbie, Winter Princess, Box 145.00
Mattel, Buffy & Mrs. Beasley, 6 1/2 In. 150.00
Mattel, Chatty Cathy, Vinyl, Sleep Eyes, 2 Teeth, Dress Patterns, Shoehorn, Box, 20 In. .. 425.00
Mattel, Donny Osmond, Movable, Box, 1976, 12 In. 36.00
Mattel, Ken, 50th Ice Capades, 1989 .... 45.00
Mattel, Ken, American Airlines Captain, Blue Jacket, Silver Wings, Flight Bag 85.00
Mattel, Ken, Busy Ken, Brown Hair, Painted Teeth, Wrist Tag, Plastic Stand, Box 135.00
Mattel, Ken, Campus Hero, Striped Knit Sweater, White Pants, State Banner, Box 40.00
Mattel, Ken, Dream Glow, 1983 .... 75.00
Mattel, Ken, Dreamdate, Black Jacket, Lapel Carnation, 1982 .... 75.00
Mattel, Ken, King Arthur, Brunette 175.00
Mattel, Ken, Malibu, Surf's Up Gift Set, Painted Blond Hair, Swim Fins, Snorkel, Box .. 370.00
Mattel, Midge, Brunette, Red Swimsuit, Box 105.00
Mattel, Ricky, Skipper's Friend, Painted Red Hair, Swim Trunks, Wire Stand, Box 105.00
Mattel, Scooter, Red Hair, Pink Dress & Shoes, 1960s, 9 In. 62.00
Mattel, Skipper, Blond, Metal Headband, Wire Stand, Booklet, Box 115.00
Mattel, Skipper, Blond, Posable, Box, 1970, 9 In. 50.00
Mattel, Skooter, Skipper's Friend, Titian Hair, Wire Stand, Box 65.00
Mattel, Stacey, Titian Hair, Pink Lips, Talking, Blue & Silver Swimsuit 275.00
Mattel, Steffie, Walk Lively, Brunette Hair, Box 250.00
Mego, Cher, 1976 .... 83.00
Mego, Farrah, Posable, On Stand, 1977, 12 In. 55.00
Michael Jackson, Push Button To Sings & Move Arms, France, Box, 13 In. 170.00
Mignonette, Bisque, Peg-Jointed Arms & Body, Antique Costume, 5 In. 700.00
Molly'es, Raggedy Ann & Andy, Muslin Face, c.1934-1937, 18 In., Pair 2400.00
Moravian, Cloth, Painted Face, Stitch-Jointed Shoulder, 18 In. ....*Illus* 1525.00
Morimura, Porcelain Head & Body, Jointed Arms & Legs, Sleep Eyes, Japan, 24 In. 220.00
Nancy Ann Storybook, Queen Of Hearts, Box 35.00
Nancy Ann Storybook, Style-Show Formal, Plastic, Sleep Eyes, Tag, c.1950, 17 In. 1300.00
Norah Wellings, Black, Painted Facial Features, Overalls 110.00
Norah Wellings, Canadian Mountie, Velvet Shirt, Pants, Boots, England, 8 3/4 In. 55.00
Paper dolls are listed in their own category.
Papier-Mache, Blond Mohair Wig, Muslin Body, Bare Feet, c.1885, 21 In. 1600.00
Papier-Mache, Fashion, Inset Eyes, Double Row Of Teeth, Braided Hair, 25 In. 2000.00
Papier-Mache, Glass Eyes, Original Wig, Clothes & Hat, 16 In. 1300.00
Parian, Blond Hair, Pink Ribbon Band, Black Snood Over Hair, 20 In. 750.00
Parian, Boy, Molded Hair, Painted Eyes, Cloth Body & Legs, Kid Hands, 17 In. 632.00
Parian, Man, Bisque Shoulder Head, Painted Eyes, Cloth Body, Shirt & Tie, 27 In. 425.00
Pee-Wee Herman, Talking, Molded Plastic, Box, 17 In. 35.00
Pincushion dolls are listed in their own category.
Poured Wax, Shoulder Head, Glass Eyes, Closed Mouth, Mohair, Cloth Body, 14 In. 250.00
Princess Elizabeth, Madame Alexander 80.00
Puppet, Hand, Bozo, Talking, Display Box, Mattel, 11 x 7 In. 132.00
Puppet, Hand, Cockie, White & Brown Mohair, Steiff 40.00
Puppet, Hand, Little Audrey, Squeaker Voice, Box, 1950s 125.00
Puppet, Hand, Mr. Ed, Knickerbocker, 1962 .... 250.00
Puppet, Hand, Punch & Judy, Papier-Mache Heads & Hands 143.00

Puppet, Hand, Topo Gigio, Rubber Head, 1963 . . . . 85.00
Puppet, Katnip, Hand, Squeaker Voice, Box, 1950s 125.00
Queen Elizabeth II, Porcelain Shoulder Head, 1953, 22 In. 600.00
Rabery & Delphieu, Bisque Socket Head, Paperweight Eyes, Jointed, c.1885, 24 In. 3700.00
Rabery & Delphieu, Bisque, Painted Features, Paperweight Eyes, 25 In. 3995.00
Rag, Ink Face, Rag Wig, Original Clothing, 1870s 1200.00
Rag, Wellington Type, Painted, 13 In. 1950.00
Raynal, Poupee, Pressed Felt Swivel Head, Painted Eyes, Blond Mohair, 18 In. 475.00
Recknagel, 33, Bisque, Googly, Blue Intaglio Eyes, Fully Jointed Body, 10 In. 995.00
Recknagel, 100 9/0, Boy, Bisque Shoulder Head, Painted Hair, Kid Body, Clothes, 10 In. . 330.00
Revalo, 8, Bisque Socket Head, Sleep Eyes, Open Mouth, Teeth, Blond Mohair, 23 1/2 In. 450.00
S & H dolls are also listed here as Bergmann and Simon & Halbig.
S & H, 1303, American Indian, Sienna Bisque Socket Head, Painted Eyes, c.1900, 20 In. . 6500.00
S.F.B.J., 2, Bisque Socket Head, Paperweight Eyes, Open Mouth, 4 Teeth, c.1900, 11 In. . . 3400.00
S.F.B.J., 236, Boy, Bisque, Sleep Eyes, Open-Close Mouth, Composition, Jointed, 13 In. . . 770.00
S.F.B.J., 236, Toddler, Bisque Socket Head, Sleep Eyes, 2 Teeth, Human Hair, 27 In. 1700.00
S.F.B.J., 245, Bisque Socket Head, Glass Googly Eyes, c.1920, 11 In. 8750.00
S.F.B.J., 247, Baby, Bisque Socket Head, Glass Eyes, Blond Mohair, c.1917, 6 In. 1100.00
S.F.B.J., 247, Bisque Socket Head, Blue Glass Eyes, Closed Mouth, 1912, 8 In. 1210.00
S.F.B.J., 247, Bisque Socket Head, Flirty Sleep Eyes, 2 Teeth, Toddler, c.1920, 15 In. 1350.00
S.F.B.J., 252, Bisque Socket Head, Brown Glass Sleep Eyes, Closed Mouth, 8 In. 3520.00
S.F.B.J., 252, Bisque, Pouty Expression, Original Body, c.1912, 13 In. 4400.00
S.F.B.J., Bisque Head, Glass Sleep Eyes, Open Mouth, Tremble Tongue, 19 In. 1150.00
S.F.B.J., Bisque Socket Head, 2-Faced, Smiling, Crying, Paperweight Eyes, c.1900, 17 In. . 7250.00
S.F.B.J., Bisque Socket Head, Brown Glass Sleep Eyes, Open Mouth, Bebe, 1917, 8 In. . . . 990.00
S.F.B.J., Bisque, Sleep Eyes, Original Dress, Shoes, Jointed Body, Toddler, 10 1/2 In. 7500.00
S.F.B.J., Boy, Bisque, Fat Chubby Cheeks, Dimples, Sleep Eyes, Green Velvet Suit, 28 In. . 2995.00
S.F.B.J., Eden Bebe, Bisque, Brunette Human Wig, Paperweight Eyes, 20 1/2 In. 3200.00
S.F.B.J., Kiss-Throwing, Bisque Head, Flirty Eyes, Teeth, Pull String, Dress, 22 In. 950.00
Sailor, Arms Move When String Pulled, Composition, Wooden, Wire, 8 In. 27.00
Schmitt, Bisque, Flirty Eyes, Teeth, Human Hair Braids, Ball-Jointed Body, Child, 20 In. . 750.00
Schmitt & Fils, Bisque Socket Head, Blue, Enamel Eyes, Composition, Bebe, 13 In. 8250.00
Schmitt & Fils, Bisque Socket Head, Glass Eyes, Blond Mohair, c.1880, 16 In. 5000.00
Schmitt & Fils, Bisque Socket Head, Pale Blue Enamel Eyes, Bebe, 1880, 17 In. 5225.00
Schoenau & Hoffmeister, Bisque Head, Sleep Eyes, Open Mouth, Teeth, 22 In. 850.00
Schoenau & Hoffmeister, Bisque, Pansy, Sleep Eyes, Pansy III, Germany, c.1915, 22 In. . . 316.00
Schoenau & Hoffmeister, Carmencita, Bisque Socket Head, Sleep Eyes, 4 Teeth, 22 In. . . 560.00
Schoenau & Hoffmeister, Hanna, Bisque Socket Head, Sleep Eyes, 2 Teeth, 13 In. 600.00
Schoenhut, Baby, Wooden Socket Head, Painted Eyes, Spring Joints, Romper, 13 In. 275.00
Schoenhut, Cobalt Blue Eyes, Dimples, Straight Wrist, Oily Sheen, Pre-1900, 18 In. 695.00
Schoenhut, Girl, Wooden Socket Head, Painted Blue Eyes, Closed Mouth, 1919, 11 In. . . 990.00
Schoenhut, Girl, Wooden, Blond Mohair, Jointed, 4 Outfits, Label On Back, 22 In. 440.00
Schoenhut, Happy Hooligan, Wood, Composition, Jointed, 1924, 9 In. 985.00
Schoenhut, Maggie & Jiggs, Jointed, Tin, Pair . . . . *Illus* 440.00
Schoenhut, Rolly Dolly, Papier-Mache Head, Open-Close Mouth, 1908, 14 In. 800.00

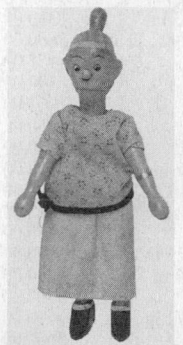

Doll,
Schoenhut,
Maggie & Jiggs,
Jointed, Tin

Doll, Simon & Halbig, 1078,
Bisque Socket Head, Sleep Eyes,
Open Mouth, 11 1/2 In.

Doll, Tete
Jumeau, Bisque
Socket Head,
Sleep Eyes,
Open Mouth,
20 1/2 In.

Schoenhut, Wooden Socket Head, Painted Blue Eyes, Jointed, Toddler, 1913, 13 In. 600.00
Schoenhut, Wooden, Spring Jointed, Clothes, Toddler, 14 In. 385.00
Shirley Temple dolls are included in the Shirley Temple category.
Simon & Halbig dolls are also listed here under Bergmann and S & H.
Simon & Halbig, 6 1/2, Bisque, Sleep Eyes, Open Mouth, Composition, Jointed, 18 In. . . .   415.00
Simon & Halbig, 110, Bisque Socket Head, Painted Eyes, 2 Teeth, Toddler, 1912, 14 In. . .   600.00
Simon & Halbig, 110, Bisque Socket Head, Pale Blue Upper Glancing Eyes, 15 In. 880.00
Simon & Halbig, 126, Brown Glass Eyes, Open Mouth With Movable Tongue, 15 In. 357.00
Simon & Halbig, 570, Bisque, Socket Head, Sleep Eyes, Open Mouth, 4 Teeth, 20 In. 375.00
Simon & Halbig, 719, Bisque Socket Head, Glass Eyes, Pierced Ears, 1888, 24 In. 4000.00
Simon & Halbig, 719, Bisque Socket Head, Paperweight Eyes, 4 Teeth, 1890, 21 In. 1100.00
Simon & Halbig, 719, Bisque, Bulging Eyes, Old Dress, Original Shoes, 23 In. 2850.00
Simon & Halbig, 719, Brown Sleep Eyes, Open Mouth, 4 Teeth, Jointed, 1890, 21 In. 1400.00
Simon & Halbig, 739, Bisque Socket Head, Brown, Glass Eyes, 4 Teeth, c.1895, 20 In. . . .   3300.00
Simon & Halbig, 886, Bisque, Mignonette, 4 Teeth, Red Silk Suit, Jointed, c.1890, 6 In. . .   1040.00
Simon & Halbig, 929, Bisque Socket Head, Paperweight Eyes, Human Hair, 17 1/2 In. . . .   2050.00
Simon & Halbig, 949, Bisque, Swivel Head, Paperweight Eyes, Kid Body, 17 1/2 In. 2700.00
Simon & Halbig, 979, Bisque Socket Head, Blue Glass Eyes, Open Mouth, Child, 17 In. .   990.00
Simon & Halbig, 1009, Bisque Head, Sleep Eyes, 4 Teeth, Mohair Wig, Clothes, 12 In. . .   180.00
Simon & Halbig, 1009, Bisque Socket Head, Sleep Eyes, 4 Teeth, Kid Body, 26 In. 600.00
Simon & Halbig, 1009, Bisque, Brown Mohair Wig, Original Head To Toe, 15 In. 1500.00
Simon & Halbig, 1019, Bisque Socket Head, Open Mouth, Swivel Waist, 1890, 18 In. . . .   2000.00
Simon & Halbig, 1039, Brown Eyes, Brown Wig, Walking, Kissing, Flirting, 22 In. 855.00
Simon & Halbig, 1078, Bisque Socket Head, Blue Sleep Eyes, Open Mouth, 11 In. 875.00
Simon & Halbig, 1078, Bisque Socket Head, Composition & Wood Body, 13 1/2 In. 450.00
Simon & Halbig, 1078, Bisque Socket Head, Sleep Eyes, Open Mouth, 11 1/2 In.   . . .*Illus*   75.00
Simon & Halbig, 1078, Bisque, Mohair Wig, Sleep Eyes, Jointed French Body, 10 In. 995.00
Simon & Halbig, 1079, Bisque Head, Jointed, Mohair Wig, Composition, Dress, 19 In. . . .   410.00
Simon & Halbig, 1079, Bisque Socket Head, Open Mouth, 4 Teeth, 31 In. 700.00
Simon & Halbig, 1079, Bisque Socket Head, Open Mouth, 4 Teeth, Human Hair, 19 In. . .   425.00
Simon & Halbig, 1079, Bisque Socket Head, Sleep Eyes, Open Mouth, 4 Teeth, 28 In. . . .   675.00
Simon & Halbig, 1079, Blond Mohair Wig, Azure Blue Eyes, Antique Clothes, 30 In. 1495.00
Simon & Halbig, 1159, Bisque Socket Head, Blue Sleep Eyes, Wooden-Jointed, 81 In. . . .   3190.00
Simon & Halbig, 1249, Bisque Socket Head, Child, Sleep Eyes, 4 Teeth, c.1900, 26 In. . .   1000.00
Simon & Halbig, 1250, Bisque Shoulder Head, Open Mouth, Kid Body, 19 In. 325.00
Simon & Halbig, 1279, Bisque Socket Head, Sleep Eyes, Antique Costume, Child, 29 In. .   6250.00
Simon & Halbig, 1299, Bisque Socket Head, Sleep Eyes, 2 Teeth, Jointed, c.1912, 20 In. . .   1500.00
Simon & Halbig, 1300, Mechanical, Shakes Tambourine, Head & Eyes Move, 21 In. 6900.00
Simon & Halbig, 1428, Bisque Socket Head, Closed Mouth, Blond Mohair Wig, 12 In. . . .   5720.00
Simon & Halbig, 1488, Bisque Socket Head, Sleep Eyes, Baby, c.1912, 19 In. 5100.00
Simon & Halbig, Bisque Head, Sleep Eyes, Ball-Jointed Composition Body, 21 In. 310.00
Simon & Halbig, Bisque Shoulder Head, Sculpted Hair, Alsatian Costume, c.1880, 12 In. .   550.00
Simon & Halbig, Bisque Swivel Head, Light Brown Sculpted Hair, Closed Mouth, 11 In. .   4400.00
Simon & Halbig, Bisque, Child, Fully-Jointed Body, Antique Frock & Bonnet, 19 In. 5400.00
Simon & Halbig, Bisque, French Human Hair Wig, Original Dress, Shoes, 24 In. 850.00
Simon & Halbig, Bisque, Original Wig, Dressed, 32 1/2 In. 1495.00
Simon & Halbig, Brown Glass Eyes, Open Mouth With Teeth, Original Wig, 23 In. 330.00
Simon & Halbig, Fashion, Bisque Swivel Head, Twill Over Wooden Body, c.1885, 11 In. . .   3600.00
Skookum, Indian Squaw, Composition, Original Costume, 9 In.   55.00
Skookum, Indian, 1930s, 14 1/2 In. 390.00
Skookum, Indian, c.1930, 9 In. 61.00
Skookum, Indian, Felt Leggings, Wool Blanket Robe, Suede Moccasins, 12 In. 150.00
Skookum, Indian, With Papoose, Apple Face, Beaded Necklace, 1920, 10 1/2 In. 110.00
Skookum, Papoose & Child, Composition Head, Sawdust Body, Wood Feet, 11 In. 39.00
Sonneberg, Marquis, Marquise, Bisque, 5-Piece Papier-Mache Body, c.1890, 10 In., Pair   .   3300.00
Space Boy, Space Outfit, Helmet, 8 In. 225.00
Steiff, Boy, Cream & Blue Knit Outfit, Blond Mohair Wig, 11 In. 1100.00
Steiner, Bebe Premier Pas, Bisque, Paperweight Eyes, Teeth, Walker, c.1890, 23 In. 6750.00
Steiner, Bisque Socket Head, Almond Blue Glass Eyes, Open Mouth, Bebe, 14 In. 4290.00
Steiner, Bisque Socket Head, Bebe, Blue Glass Eyes, Turkish Costume, c.1890, 14 In. . . .   3300.00
Steiner, Bisque Socket Head, Bebe, Blue Glass Paperweight Eyes, c.1890, 8 1/2 In. 3500.00
Steiner, Bisque Socket Head, Blue Paperweight Eyes, Jointed Body, 1885, 19 In. 5600.00
Steiner, Bisque Socket Head, Glass Eyes, Blond Mohair, Jointed Body, c.1890, 17 In. . . .   4100.00

Steiner, Bisque Socket Head, Paperweight Eyes, Blond Mohair, Jointed, c.1889, 23 In. 4000.00
Steiner, Bisque, Inset Eyes, Open Mouth, 2 Rows Teeth, Jointed Body, 16 In. 3700.00
Steiner, Bisque, Lever Sleep Eyes, Fully Jointed Body, Silk Gown, 16 In. 7500.00
Steiner, Bisque, Mohair Wig, Lever Sleep Eyes, Signed, 22 1/2 In. 8900.00
Steiner, Bisque, Paperweight Eyes, Blond Wig, Wooden-Jointed Body, 21 In. 8000.00
Steiner, Blue Paperweight Eyes, Long Human Hair Wig, Signed, 24 In. 6500.00
Steiner, Chinese Boy, Bisque Socket Head, Amber Brown Tinted, 10 In. 2310.00
Steiner, Clown, White Bisque Socket Head, Glass Eyes, Painted Face, c.1890, 9 In. 2600.00
Swaine & Co., Character, Boy, Bisque Head, Open Close Mouth, 10 In. 995.00
Terri Lee, Jerri Lee, Plastic, Painted Brown Eyes, Skin Wig, Tag On Shirt, Box, 16 In. . . . 275.00
Tete Jumeau, 8, Bisque Socket Head, Sleep Eyes, Open Mouth, Teeth, Mohair, 20 1/2 In. 2200.00
Tete Jumeau, Bisque Head, Pinafore, 24 In. 4895.00
Tete Jumeau, Bisque Socket Head, Sleep Eyes, Open Mouth, 20 1/2 In. . . . . *Illus* 2200.00
Tete Jumeau, Bisque, Paperweight Eyes, Mohair Wig, Straight Wrist, Dress, 21 In. 6500.00
Tete Jumeau, Closed Mouth, Blue Paperweight Eyes, Antique Clothes, 26 In. 5950.00
Uneeda, Rita Hayworth As Carmen, Sleep Eyes, Red Mohair, Composition, Tag, 14 In. . . 275.00
Unis France, 301, Bisque Socket Head, Blue Sleep Eyes, Open Mouth, 4 Teeth, 23 In. . . . 275.00
Ventriloquist Dummy, Billy Baloney, Pee-Wee Herman's Pal, Plastic, Fabric, 18 In. 50.00
Ventriloquist Dummy, Charlie McCarthy, 1968, 26 In. 55.00
Ventriloquist Dummy, Lester 35.00
Ventriloquist Dummy, Willie Talk 25.00
Venus, Poupee, Pressed Felt Swivel Head, Painted Eyes, Mohair, Paris, Tag, 16 In. 425.00
Vichy, Waltzing Lady, Bisque Socket Head, Blue Glass Eyes, 1875, 20 In. 7975.00
Vogue, Ginny, Blond, Blue Sleep Eyes, Molded Lashes, Walker, Tagged Clothes, 7 In. . . . 175.00
Vogue, Ginny, Dutch Boy & Girl, Plastic, Sleep Eyes, Wooden Shoes, Box, 7 1/2 In., Pair 625.00
Vogue, Ginny, Plastic Head, Auburn Hair, Tagged Dress, Toddler Body, 1953, 8 In. 1000.00
Vogue, Ginny, Plastic, Blue Sleep Eyes, Walker, Formal, Fur Hat, Tag, c.1957, 8 In. 200.00
Vogue, Ginny, Sleep Eyes, Blond Hair, Walker, Dutch Outfit, Tag, 1954, 9 In. 400.00
Vogue, Toddles, Dutch Boy & Girl, Composition, 5 Piece Body, 7 In., Pair 300.00
Vogue, Wee Imp, Plastic, Sleep Eyes, Orange Hair, Walker, Box, 1959, 7 1/2 In. 425.00
Volland, Percy The Policeman, Center Seam, Shaped Nose, Muslin, Label, c.1931, 15 In. . 3700.00
Volland, Raggedy Ann, Cloth Head, Black Shoebutton Eyes, Jointed, Blue Hat, 17 In. . . . 750.00
Volland, Raggedy Ann, Cloth Head, Black Shoebutton Eyes, Red Nose, 1915, 16 In. 1350.00
Volland, Raggedy Ann, Muslin Face, Painted Features, Original Dress, c.1918, 17 In. 4700.00
Volland, Raggedy Ann, Muslin Face, Printed Features, Original Dress, c.1920, 16 In. 2000.00
Volland, Uncle Clem, Muslin, Center Seam, Shaped Nose, c.1931, 16 In. 3100.00
Wax, Baby, Glass Eyes, Closed Mouth, Blond Hair, Cloth Body, Mid 19th Century, 12 In. 172.00
Wax, Infant, Blue Enamel Eyes, Downcast Pouty Lips, Muslin Body, c.1880, 22 In. 750.00
Wax, Mother, Baby In Arms, Wax Hands & Feet, Wood Base, 15 In. 1695.00
William Goebel, Bisque Socket Head, Sleep Eyes, Open Mouth, 4 Teeth, 22 1/2 In. 250.00
Wooden, Original Clothes, Late 18th-Early 19th Century, 10 1/2 In. 925.00

DONALD DUCK items are included in the Disneyana category.

DOORSTOPS have been made in all types of designs. The vast majority
of the doorstops sold today are cast iron and were made from about 1890
to 1930. Most of them are shaped like people, animals, flowers, or ships.
Reproductions and newly designed examples are sold in gift shops.

Basket Of Flowers, Cast Iron, 8 1/2 In. 120.00
Basket Of Tulips, Yellow Tulips, Brown Wicker, Green Base, Cast Iron, 13 x 9 In. 2180.00
Bathing Girls, Cast Iron 1750.00
Bird, Cockatoo, Perched On Branch, On Round Base, Cast Iron, 7 1/4 In. 460.00
Bird, Heron, Cast Iron, Albany Foundry, 7 1/2 x 5 1/8 In. 132.00
Bird, Heron, Painted, Cast Iron, 7 3/8 In. 215.00
Bird, Heron, Perched On The Rocks, Long Necked, Cast Iron, 10 In. 385.00
Bird, Parrot, Red, Green, Yellow, Cast Iron, 8 x 3 7/8 In. 365.00
Bird, Pheasant, Craning Neck, Looking Back, Cast Iron, Fred Everett, 8 1/2 x 7 In. 725.00
Bird, Quail, 2 Birds Standing Side By Side, Cast Iron, Fred Everett, 7 1/4 x 6 1/4 In. 605.00
Boat, 3-Masted Sailing Ship, Cast Iron, 9 In. 28.00
Boat, Galleon, Full Sail, Cast Brass, 10 3/4 In. 58.00
Boat, Sailing Ship, Don Fernando, Brass, 20 In. 110.00
Boat, Sailing Ship, Painted, Cast Iron, Albany Foundry Co., 12 In. 50.00
Brick, Molded Star Flower, Yellow & Brown Glaze, 3 x 4 3/4 In. 330.00
Buffalo Bill On Horse, Bronze, Cactus Ground, Pat. Pend., 12 x 10 1/2 In. 565.00

Bullfrog, Garden, Cast Iron, 9 1/2 In. 105.00
Cat, Arched Back, Curled-Up Tail, Cast Iron, 12 In. 3630.00
Cat, Arched Back, Full Figure, Yellow Eyes, Cast Iron, 10 1/2 In. 253.00
Cat, Arched Black, Raised Tail, Paint Remnants, Cast Iron, 20th Century, 11 x 8 In. 690.00
Cat, Full Figure, White & Gray Paint, Cast Iron, Hubley, 9 In. 165.00
Cat, Persian, Sitting, Gray & White Paint, Cast Iron, Hubley 330.00
Cat, Seated, Full Figure, Yellow Eyes, Cast Iron, 6 3/4 In. 22.00
Cat, Sitting, Painted, Cast Iron, 9 7/8 In. 160.00
Cat, Sleeping, Gold Paint, Cast Iron, National Foundry Co., 9 1/2 In. 247.00
Chinaman, Cast Iron, 8 3/4 In. 110.00
Conestoga Wagon, Blue Body, Orange Spoke Wheels, Cast Iron, 1930, 12 In. 380.00
Confederate Soldier, Standing, Painted, Cast Iron, 7 3/8 In. 100.00
Cottage, Fence, Flowers Growing On All Sides, National Foundry Co., 5 x 8 In. 365.00
Cottage, Flowers Growing Along Walls, White, Hubley, Cast Iron, 5 3/4 x 7 1/2 In. 365.00
Cottage, In The Woods, Smoke Out Of Chimney, Cast Iron, 8 1/4 x 7 1/4 In. 700.00
Cottage, Towering Trees, Front Yard Birdhouse, Red Roof, Cast Iron, 7 x 8 1/2 In. 365.00
Cottage, With Fence, Painted, Cast Iron, 5 3/4 In. 145.00
Covered Wagon, Painted, Cast Iron, 3 5/8 In. 165.00
Daisy Bowl, Green Vase, Black Base, Hubley, 7 1/8 x 5 7/8 In. 365.00
Daisy Bowl, Multicolored Daisies, White Bowl, Hubley, Cast Iron, 7 1/2 x 6 In. 425.00
Daisy Bowl, Painted, Cast Iron, 6 7/8 In. 125.00
Dog, 2 Scotty Dogs 150.00
Dog, Boston Terrier, 2-Tone Brown Paint, Cast Iron, 10 1/2 In. 165.00
Dog, Boston Terrier, Black & White Paint, Cast Iron, 9 1/2 In. 155.00
Dog, Boston Terrier, Black & White, Cast Iron, 10 In. 125.00
Dog, Boston Terrier, Cast Iron, 10 In. 130.00
Dog, Boston Terrier, Full Figure, With Paw Up, Black, White, Cast Iron, 9 1/2 In. 725.00
Dog, Boston Terrier, Original Polychrome, Cast Iron, 8 3/4 In. 196.00
Dog, Boston Terrier, Painted, Cast Iron, 9 x 8 In. 175.00
Dog, Boston Terrier, Standing, Cast Iron, c.1900, 9 1/2 In. 2257.00
Dog, Boxer, Full Figure, Standing, Brown, Cast Iron, Hubley, 8 1/2 x 9 In. 725.00
Dog, Boxing Puppy, Cast Iron, 6 1/4 In. 250.00
Dog, Bulldog, Full Figure, Standing, Cast Iron, Hubley, 4 5/8 x 5 1/2 In. 725.00
Dog, Dachshund, Full Figure, Standing, Short Hair, Cast Iron, Hubley, 5 x 9 In. 1210.00
Dog, English Bulldog, Glass Eyes, Cast Iron, 1928, 13 In. 225.00
Dog, German Shepherd, Standing, Cast Iron, 1930s, 9 In. 138.00
Dog, Hunting Dog With Bird, Original Paint, Cast Iron, 7 x 12 In.   275.00
Dog, On Pillow, Cast Iron, 4 1/2 In. 140.00
Dog, On Stool, Cast Iron, 9 In. 515.00
Dog, Police Dog, Standing, Cast Iron 85.00
Dog, Russian Wolfhound, Cast Iron, 10 In. 110.00
Dog, Scotty, Cast Iron, 16 1/4 In. 245.00
Dog, Scotty, Cast Iron, 8 In. 275.00
Dog, Scotty, Full Figure, Black Paint, Cast Iron, 8 1/2 In. 198.00
Dog, Sealyham, Cast Iron, Hubley, 7 In. 165.00
Dog, Setter, Cast Iron, Hubley, 9 In. 325.00
Dog, Terrier, White, Black, Sitting Up, Cast Iron, Signed, Spencer, 4 In. 1090.00
Dog, With Duck, Cast Iron, A.M. Greenblatt, Boston, Mass., 1925, 10 x 9 In. 1320.00
Door Caddy, Painted, Cast Iron, 16 1/8 In. 160.00
Duck, Full Figure, Cast Iron, 13 1/2 In. 1100.00
Duck, Profile, Head Turned, Wedge Base, Cast Iron, 13 1/2 In., Pair 275.00
Elephant, On Base, Painted, Cast Iron, 7 1/4 In. 165.00
Elephant & Baby Rhino, Painted, Cast Iron, 5 1/4 In. 140.00
Fantail Fish, Painted, Cast Iron, 19 1/2 In. 185.00
Fat Man, Cast Iron, 9 1/2 In. 1450.00
Fireplace Scene, Woman, Spinning Wheel, Seated, Fireplace, Cast Iron, 6 x 8 In. 365.00
Fireside, Gray & White Paint, Cast Iron, Hubley 300.00
Fish, Herring In Rocks, Cast Iron, 9 1/2 In. 85.00
Fisherman With Yellow Rain Coat, Cast Iron, 14 1/2 In. . . . . *Illus*   95.00
Flamingo, Painted, Brass, 13 5/8 In. 170.00
Flapper, Umbrella, Cast Iron, 1920s 2430.00
Floral, Art Nouveau, Painted, Cast Iron, 7 7/8 In. 185.00
Flower Basket, Calla Lilies, Blue Urn, Black Base, Cast Iron, Hubley, 7 1/2 x 7 In. 365.00

Doorstop,
Fisherman With
Yellow Rain Coat,
Cast Iron, 14 1/2 In.

Doorstop, Hare,
Upright, Iron,
Bradley &
Hubbard,
15 3/8 x 8 3/8 In.

Doormats at every door catch the dirt and keep it from creating dust and pollution in the house. Shake out, wash, or vacuum the mats frequently.

Flower Basket, Cast Iron, 7 1/2 In. 88.00
Flower Basket, Embossed Flower Dropped From Bunch, Cast Iron, Hubley, 17 In. 2055.00
Flower Basket, Gladiolus, Pastel Orange, Yellow, Cast Iron, Hubley, 10 x 7 3/4 In. 425.00
Flower Basket, Lilies Of The Valley, White Bow Top, Cast Iron, Hubley, 10 x 7 In. 425.00
Flower Basket, Marigolds, White Vase, Stripes, Cast Iron, Hubley, 7 1/2 x 8 In. 510.00
Flower Basket, Narcissus, Embossed, Cast Iron, Hubley, 7 1/4 x 6 3/4 In. 605.00
Flower Basket, Poinsettias, Red, Green, Terra-Cotta Pot, Blue, Cast Iron, 10 x 5 In. 845.00
Flower Basket, Poppies & Cornflowers, Cast Iron, Hubley, 7 1/4 x 6 1/2 In. 365.00
Flower Basket, Wicker, Bow Tied On Handle, Green Base, Cast Iron, 10 x 6 1/2 In. 665.00
Flower Basket, Wicker, Red, Pink, Yellow, Handle, Blue Base, Cast Iron, Hubley, 7 In. .. 365.00
Flower Basket, Zinnias, Gray, Blue Vase, Cast Iron, Hubley, 7 1/4 x 7 In. 510.00
Flower Basket, Zinnias, White, Green, Cast Iron, 9 1/4 x 6 In. 605.00
Fox Hunt, Cast Iron, 11 In. 200.00
Frog, Political, I Croak For Jackson Wagon, Green, Cast Iron 165.00
Frog, Standing, Painted, Cast Iron, 5 1/4 In. 225.00
Fruit Basket, Apples & Grapes, 3 Fruits As Centerpiece, Cast Iron, 4 7/8 x 7 In. 2060.00
Fruit Basket, Multi Fruits, Cast Iron, Albany Foundry, 10 1/8 x 7 1/2 In. 305.00
Fruit Basket, Multi Fruits, Round Handle, Cast Iron, 9 7/8 x 8 1/4 In. 365.00
Fruit Basket, Wicker, Bow Draping Into Arrangement, Green Base, Cast Iron, 7 In. 545.00
Fruit Basket, Wicker, Multi Fruits, Pineapple, Fallen Cherries, Cast Iron, 11 In. 1090.00
Fruit Basket, Wicker, Pink Bow, Cast Iron, 9 3/4 In. 240.00
Geisha Girl, Cast Iron, 7 In. 200.00
Girl, With Beanie, Cast Iron, 8 3/4 x 3 In. 154.00
Gnome, Cast Iron, 11 In. ....110.00 to 340.00
Gnome, Cast Iron, 11 x 5 In. 176.00
Gnome, Painted, Cast Iron, 12 5/8 In. 230.00
Golfer, Partial Paint, Cast Iron, 8 1/2 In. 660.00
Grapes & Leaves, Cast Iron, 7 3/4 In. 495.00
Hare, Upright, Iron, Bradley & Hubbard, 15 3/8 x 8 3/8 In. ....*Illus* 3300.00
Horse, Grazing, Painted, Cast Iron, 8 5/8 In. 185.00
Horse, Jumping Fence, Cast Iron 250.00
Horse, Percheron, Cast Iron, Hubley, 9 x 7 3/4 In. 66.00
Horse, With Dog, Lead, 6 1/2 In. 240.00
House, Cape Cod, Cast Iron, 5 3/4 In. 120.00
House, Cape Cod, Eastern Specialty Mfg. Co., 5 1/4 x 8 1/4 In. 99.00
Indian, Polychrome Paint, Cast Iron, 13 In. 412.00
Kitten, Bow, Cast Iron, 7 1/2 In. 195.00
Latin Rumba Dancer, Cast Iron, 11 In. 1485.00
Lighthouse, Bronze, 5 In. 120.00
Lighthouse, Cape Henry, Cast Iron, 24 3/4 In. 920.00
Lion, Raised On Hind Legs, Cast Iron, 15 In. 125.00
Little Southern Belle, Cast Iron, National Foundry Co., 6 3/4 x 3 3/4 In. 66.00
Mammy, Aunt Jemima With Hands On Hips, Black Dress, Cast Iron, Hubley, 12 In. 280.00
Mammy, Cast Iron, Painted, Polka Dot Bandanna, Apron, Hubley Co., 12 In. 1265.00
Man, In Chair, Bronze, 10 1/8 In. 215.00
Man, Spanish Guitar, Cast Iron, 11 In. 300.00
Mary Quite Contrary, Holding Garden Tools, Bouquet Of Flowers, Cast Iron 1045.00
Messenger Boy, With Flower Bouquet, Cast Iron, Hubley 1320.00

Oriental Girl, Cast Iron, 7 1/2 In.	285.00
Owl, Double, Cast Iron, 8 1/2 In.	450.00
Parrot, In Ring, Cast Iron, 8 x 7 In.	154.00
Parrot, Orange, Green Feathers, Cast Iron, Albany Foundry Co., 12 1/2 x 7 1/2 In.	187.00
Penguin, Top Hat, Cast Iron, 10 1/2 In.	845.00
Pirate, Sitting On Chest, Cast Iron	150.00
Poppies, Cornflower, No. 265, Cast Iron, Hubley, 7 1/4 x 6 1/2 In.	132.00 to 165.00
Putting Golfer, Red Shirt, Cast Iron, Hubley, 8 3/8 x 7 In.	285.00
Rabbit, Brae, Painted, Cast Iron, 6 1/4 In.	185.00
Rabbit, Cast Iron, 8 In.	230.00
Rabbit, March Hare, Painted, Cast Iron, 10 1/4 In.	165.00
Rabbit, Standing, Painted, Cast Iron, 6 In.	190.00
Redcap, Bearing Floral Bouquet, Fish, Cast Iron	1320.00
Rooster, Crowning, Full Figure, Cast Iron, 12 In.	220.00
Rose Basket, Cast Iron	250.00
Rumba Dancer, Green Hula Skirt, Yellow Tips, Cast Iron, 11 1/8 x 6 3/8 In.	1430.00 to 1485.00
School Bus, Cast Iron, 18 In.	100.00
Slipper, Cast Iron, 9 In.	315.00
Spanish Guitarist, Iron, CLVZ, Pat Pend., 11 x 3 1/2 In.	1760.00
Squirrel, On Tree Branch, Holding Nut, Cast Iron, 9 1/2 In.	375.00
Stagecoach, Cast Iron	65.00
Swan, Cast Iron, 7 In.	110.00
Texas, Long Horn Steer, Cast Iron, 10 1/2 In.	1450.00
Tiger Lilies, Cast Iron, 10 1/2 In.	265.00
Vase, Tulips, Orange, Pink, Hubley, 10 x 8 In.	425.00
Vase, White, Pink Flowers, Cast Iron, Hubley, 10 3/8 x 6 1/8 In.	545.00
Woman, Painted, Cast Iron, 6 1/2 In.	94.00

DORCHESTER POTTERY was founded by George Henderson in 1895 in Dorchester, Massachusetts. At first, the firm made utilitarian stoneware, but collectors are most interested in the line of decorated blue and white pottery that Dorchester made from 1940 until it went out of business in 1979.

DORCHESTER POTTERY WORKS BOSTON, MASS.

Bowl, Blue Geometric Design, White Ground, 2 Handles, 6 In.	77.00
Bowl, Lily-Of-The-Valley, White Lily Blossoms, Striped Leaves, 6 1/4 In.	275.00
Bowl, Pinecone, Incised Clusters Of Pine Needles, 4 In.	137.00
Casserole & Bowl, Blueberry, Striped Handles, Commemorative Panels, Pair	275.00
Mug, Blueberry Painting, Ivory Ground, Charles Hill, Signed, 4 1/2 In., Pair	192.00
Mug, Whale & Clown Happy Day, Commemorative, 3 In., Pair	137.00
Pitcher, Stylized Ship, Flared, Pumpkin Body, Knesseth Denisons, 6 3/4 x 8 In.	302.00
Pot, Hobo Scene, Cooking Over Camp Fire, Motto Pot Luck, R. Trotter, 6 1/4 In.	137.00
Syrup, Stylized Vine, Free-Form, Jackie Burn Callder, 4 3/4 In.	165.00

DOULTON pottery and porcelain were made by Doulton and Co. of Burslem, England, after 1882. The name *Royal Doulton* appeared on their wares after 1902. Other pottery by Doulton is listed under Royal Doulton.

Biscuit Jar, Flow Blue, Gloire-De Dijon, Burslem, 6 1/2 In.	175.00
Cracker Jar, Flowers, Tapestry Textured Ground, Nickeled Brass Handle, Lid, 7 1/2 In.	195.00
Ewer, Loop Handle, Faience, Yellow, Brown & Green, Daisies, Lambeth, c.1895, 14 In.	465.00
Hot Plate, Willow, Flow Blue, Burslem, 14 3/4 In.	195.00
Jar, Cameo Hunting Scene, Brown & Beige, Silver Cased Rim, Lambeth, 5 In.	165.00
Liquor Barrel, 6 Brown Bands, English Crest, 10 1/2 x 9 1/2 In.	115.00
Loving Cup, 3 Handles, Winged Dragon Handles, Scrolled Base, Burslem, 7 In.	110.00
Pitcher, 2-Tone Brown, Men, Windmill & Tree, Deer, Dog & Horse, Lambeth, 6 In.	495.00
Pitcher, Good Is Not Good Enough, Putto, Grape Vines, Stoneware, Burslem, 8 In.	230.00
Pitcher, Willow, Flow Blue, Incised & Printed Mark, 7 1/4 x 5 In.	175.00
Pitcher & Bowl, Chelsea, Burslem, 15-In. Pitcher	90.00
Pitcher & Bowl, Woman's Neck & Shoulders, Floral Design, Ironstone, 18 In.	490.00
Punch Bowl, Green Transfer Bird & Floral, Gilt Highlights On Foot, Watteau, 16 In.	375.00
Tobacco Jar, Cover, Applied Frieze, Flowers, Ribbed Border, Lambeth, c.1900, 6 In.	145.00
Toothpick, Burslem, Cream, Floral, 2 1/2 In.	75.00
Vase, Art Nouveau Design, Frank A. Butler, Lambeth, 13 3/4 In.	850.00
Vase, Blue Figural Scene, Winter, Lady In Snow, Spring, Lady Instrument, 18 In.	450.00

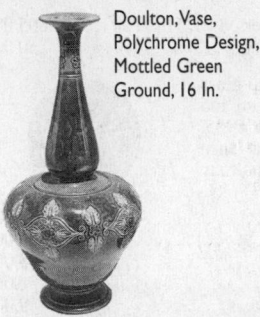

Doulton, Vase,
Polychrome Design,
Mottled Green
Ground, 16 In.

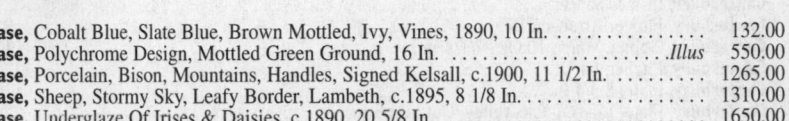

Don't put china with gold designs in the dishwasher. The gold will wash off.

Don't put pottery or porcelain with crazed glaze in the dishwasher. It will crack even more.

Vase, Cobalt Blue, Slate Blue, Brown Mottled, Ivy, Vines, 1890, 10 In.	132.00
Vase, Polychrome Design, Mottled Green Ground, 16 In. ....*Illus*	550.00
Vase, Porcelain, Bison, Mountains, Handles, Signed Kelsall, c.1900, 11 1/2 In.	1265.00
Vase, Sheep, Stormy Sky, Leafy Border, Lambeth, c.1895, 8 1/8 In.	1310.00
Vase, Underglaze Of Irises & Daisies, c.1890, 20 5/8 In.	1650.00
Vase, Wading Birds, Gilt Borders, Elephant Head Handles, Burslem, c.1882, 8 In.	3737.00

DRESDEN china is any china made in the town of Dresden, Germany. The most famous factory in Dresden is the Meissen factory. Figurines of eighteenth-century ladies and gentlemen, animal groups, or cherubs and other mythological subjects were popular. One special type of figurine was made with skirts of porcelain-dipped lace. Do not make the mistake of thinking that all pieces marked *Dresden* are from the Meissen factory. The Meissen pieces usually have crossed swords marks, and are listed under Meissen. Some recent porcelain from Ireland, called *Irish Dresden*, is not included in this book.

Bootie, Elfin Ware, Present From Lladgollen On Side, 1 1/2 In.	75.00
Cachepot, Floral Design, Scrolled Handles, 4 3/4 In.	75.00
Candy Container, Heart, Cupid	195.00
Centerpiece, Basket, Putti On Stem, Allover Leaves, 19th Century, 13 1/4 In.	460.00
Chocolate Pot, Hand Painted, Peasants Washing, Green Ground, Florals, 9 1/2 In.	1495.00
Clock, Scrolling Leaf Form, Gilt Highlights, White Ground, Applied Flowers, 10 1/2 In.	130.00
Compote, Floral, Reticulated, 7 1/2 x 8 1/2 In.	220.00
Figurine, Love Letter, 7 1/2 In.	135.00
Figurine, Man & Woman, Large Tree, Seated Nude Youth, 17 1/2 In.	385.00
Figurine, Milkmaid, Holding Letter, Late 19th Century, 8 In.	115.00
Figurine, Woman, In Lacy Skirt, Adjusting Stocking, Marked Dresden-Art, 6 3/4 In.	115.00
Figurine, Woman, In Lacy Yellow Skirt, Seated, Playing Lute, 6 In.	120.00
Figurine, Woman, Lounging In Chair, Lace, 8 In.	170.00
Group, Courtship, Man In Louis XV Costume, Lady Holding Lap Dog, 5 1/2 In.	345.00
Group, Shepherd Playing Pipes, 2 Young Women On Garden Bench, 8 1/2 In.	245.00
Luncheon Set, Pierced Floral Border, Summer Flowers, Gilt Highlights, 32 Piece	545.00
Placecard, Gilt Floral Garland, Rectangular, 4 x 1 3/4 In., 6 Piece	120.00
Plaque, Madonna & Child, After Rafael, Round, Frame, 6 In.	320.00
Plaque, Madonna Sedia, After Raphael, Ormolu Mount, Porcelain, Brodel, 3 In.	504.00
Plate, Floral, Gilt Trim, Reticulated, Germany, 8 1/4 In., 6 Piece	330.00
Plate, Green Dragon, Signed, 10 1/2 In.	70.00
Plate, Tannhauser, Act II, Pink, Cranberry, Blue & Green Borders, Gilt, 9 1/2 In.	495.00
Ramekin, Stand, Central Figure, Green Ground Border, 4 7/8 In., 10 Piece	430.00
Tea Caddy, A. Lamm, c.1880	285.00
Tray, Condiment, Floral & Gilt, Central Handle, 12 In.	260.00
Urn, Floral & Lovers In Garden Panels, Signed, 6 In.	105.00
Urn, Painted Figures In Reserve, Blue Ground, Gilt, Pedestal, 2 Handles	4480.00
Urn, Stand, Twisting Form, Encrusted Flowers & Putti, Branch Handles, 44 12 In.	3565.00
Vase, Alternating Panels Of Figures, Floral Bouquet, Yellow Ground, 13 1/4 In.	115.00
Vase, Cover, Alternating Panels Of Lovers, Floral Bouquet, Turquoise, 14 In., Pair	375.00
Vase, Cover, Gilt Border, Winged Female Term Handles, Signed, 16 1/2 In., Pair	1840.00
Vase, Cover, Stand, Lovers In Landscape, Cherubs, Flowers, Potschappel, 28 1/4 In.	4600.00

Vase, Rose Pompadour, Couples, Floral Bouquets, Gilt Scroll Borders, 14 1/2 In., Pair ... 605.00
Wall Bracket, Cherub & Floral Design, Porcelain, Late 19th Century, 8 1/2 In. 250.00

DUNCAN & MILLER is a term used by collectors when referring to glass made by the George A. Duncan and Sons Company or the Duncan and Miller Glass Company. These companies worked from 1893 to 1955, when the use of the name *Duncan* was discontinued and the firm became part of the United States Glass Company. Early patterns may be listed under Pressed Glass.

Canterbury, Basket, Crimped, Long Handle, 5 In.	45.00
Canterbury, Bowl, Crimped, Cape Cod Blue, 10 1/4 In.	59.00
Canterbury, Candlestick, 3-Light	35.00
Canterbury, Candy Dish, Cover, 3 Sections	36.00
Canterbury, Champagne, Footed, 6 Oz.	9.00
Canterbury, Cup & Saucer	15.00
Canterbury, Flower Arranger, Blue	95.00
Canterbury, Goblet, Water, 10 Oz., 7 1/4 In.	17.00
Canterbury, Pitcher, 64 Oz.	125.00
Canterbury, Plate, 8 3/4 In.	10.00
Canterbury, Plate, Lily-Of-The-Valley, Cutting, 8 In.	20.00
Canterbury, Plate, Salad, 9 In.	15.00
Canterbury, Rose Bowl	25.00
Canterbury, Sugar & Creamer, Chartreuse	30.00
Canterbury, Sugar & Creamer, Individual	17.00
Canterbury, Tumbler, Juice, Footed, 5 Oz., 4 1/4 In.	8.00
Caribbean, Ashtray, 6 In.	15.00
Caribbean, Candy Dish, Blue	135.00
Caribbean, Cigarette Holder, Cover	20.00
Caribbean, Cordial, 1 Oz.	75.00
Caribbean, Pitcher, Blue, 16 Oz., 4 3/4 In.	275.00
Caribbean, Punch Cup, Red Handle	12.00
Diamond Ridge, Punch Cup, 6 Piece	50.00
Festive, Creamer, Green	25.00
Festive, Tray, Green	85.00
Figurine, Fat Goose, 6 1/2 In.	200.00 to 275.00
First Love, Cocktail, 13 Oz., 4 1/4 In.	20.00
First Love, Iced Tea, Footed, 14 Oz., 6 3/4 In.	28.00
First Love, Relish, 3 Sections, Rectangular	48.00
First Love, Relish, 3 Sections, Sterling Base	45.00
First Love, Relish, 5 Sections	45.00
Hobnail, Candlestick, Pair	42.00
Hobnail, Cologne & Powder Jar, Cover, Green, 2 Piece	105.00
Hobnail, Sherbet, 5 Oz., 3 In.	9.00
India Tree, Rose Bowl, 5 In.	100.00
Pall Mall, Duck, Ashtray, 4 In.	35.00
Pall Mall, Swan, Open Back, Crystal, 7 In.	15.00
Pall Mall, Swan, Open Back, Crystal, 10 1/2 In.	40.00
Sandwich, Berry Bowl, 5 In.	10.00
Sandwich, Bowl, Fruit, Flared, 12 In.	38.00
Sandwich, Bowl, Grapefruit, Green, 1 1/2 x 6 In.	14.00
Sandwich, Cheese Dish, Cover, Round, 4 3/4 In.	105.00
Sandwich, Cocktail, 30 Oz.	6.00
Sandwich, Cup & Saucer	13.00 to 15.00
Sandwich, Deviled Egg Plate, 12 In.	60.00 to 65.00
Sandwich, Pitcher, Ice Lip, 1/2 Gal.	110.00 to 135.00
Sandwich, Plate, Hostess, 16 In.	65.00
Sandwich, Tumbler, Juice, Footed, 5 Oz.	9.00 to 12.00
Sanibel, Dish, Shell, Blue, 7 In.	40.00
Star In Square, Berry Set, Ruby Stained, Gold, 7 Piece	275.00
Swirl, Candlestick, Amber, 11 1/2 In., Pair	150.00
Swirl, Cornucopia, Red, 12 In.	275.00
Swirl, Dish, Grapefruit, Green, 6 3/4 In.	15.00
Swirl, Finger Bowl, Green	12.00

Swirl, Finger Bowl, Underplate, Amber 25.00
Swirl, Goblet, Water, Green, 7 Oz., 6 1/4 In. 15.00
Swirl, Lamp, Green, 10 1/2 In. 595.00
Swirl, Nut Cup, Amber 12.00
Swirl, Parfait, Amber, 4 1/2 Oz., 5 5/8 In. 25.00
Swirl, Soup, Cream, Amber 20.00
Swirl, Tumbler, Cocktail, Footed, Green, 2 1/2 Oz., 3 3/8 In. 10.00
Swirl, Tumbler, Water, Green, Footed, 7 Oz., 5 1/4 In. 10.00
Swirl, Vase, Green, 8 3/4 In. 25.00
Sylvan, Swan, Pink, 6 1/2 In. ....40.00 to 95.00
Teardrop, Ashtray, 5 In. 10.00
Teardrop, Cake Plate, 2 Handles, 13 1/2 In. 20.00
Teardrop, Claret, 4 Oz., 5 1/2 In. 18.00
Teardrop, Cup & Saucer 10.00
Teardrop, Goblet, 9 Oz., 7 In. ....8.00 to 9.00
Teardrop, Marmalade, Cover, Underplate 40.00
Teardrop, Plate, Lazy Susan, Grape Leaf Cutting 125.00
Teardrop, Tumbler, Juice, Footed, 4 1/2 Oz. 12.00
Terrace, Ashtray, Cobalt Blue, 3 1/2 In. 25.00
Terrace, Ashtray, Cobalt Blue, 4 1/4 In. 45.00
Terrace, Ashtray, Red, 3 1/2 In. 30.00
Terrace, Tumbler, Water, Red 45.00
Zippered Block, Salt & Pepper, Ruby Stained 200.00

DURAND art glass was made from 1924 to 1931. The Vineland Flint Glass Works was established by Victor Durand and Victor Durand, Jr., in 1897. In 1924 Martin Bach, Jr., and other artisans from the Quezal glassworks joined them at the Vineland, New Jersey, plant to make Durand art glass.

Jar, Cover, King Tut, Green, Amber, 7 1/4 In. 3105.00
Lamp, King Tut, Iridescent Silver Swirls, 6 1/2 In. 690.00
Torchere, Table, Crackle Pulled Feathers, Green, Striated, Electrified, 12 In., Pair 1725.00
Vase, Beehive, Blue Iridescent, Signed, 6 1/2 In. 1320.00
Vase, Beehive, Stepped Amber, Gold Iridescent Surface, 1925, 13 In. 920.00
Vase, Blue Iridescent, Light Blue, Polished Pontil, 1925, 7 In. 431.00
Vase, Blue, Purple Luster, Gold Threading, Marked, 1812, 6 1/2 x 4 In. 660.00
Vase, Gold Iridescent, Flared Rim, 1990, 5 3/4 In. 515.00
Vase, Iridescent Gold, Threads, 6 1/2 In. 952.00
Vase, King Tut, Iridescent Silver Swirls, Green, Signed, 6 3/4 In. 1000.00
Vase, King Tut, White Swirls, Gold Iridescent, Signed, 8 1/2 In. 900.00
Vase, Lady Gay Rose, Pink Coiled Iridescent, White, Yellow Interior, Flared, 12 In. 2875.00
Vase, Pulled Feathers, Gold Threads, Tapered, 9 1/2 In. 1500.00
Vase, Silver Threads, Blue Iridescent Ground, Signed, 6 In. 165.00
Vase, Spider Webbing, Gold Threads, Peach, Gold Iridized, White, 7 In. 460.00
Vase, Trailing Hearts & Vine, Green, Orange Ground, Signed, 8 In. 825.00
Vase, Trailing Hearts & Vine, Silver, Cobalt Blue Iridescent, Pontil, 1925, 9 In. 1955.00
Vase, White Opaque, Iridescent Blue & Gold, Gold Luster Interior, 8 1/4 In. 504.00

ELFINWARE is a mark found on Dresden-like porcelain that was sold in dime stores and gift shops. Many pieces were decorated with raised flowers. The mark was registered by Breslauer-Underberg, Inc., of New York City in 1947. Pieces marked *Elfinware Made in Germany* had been sold since 1945 by this importer.

Elfinware

Basket, White, Fruits, Flowers, Footed, 4 1/8 In. 57.00
Basket, White, Spinach Moss, Flowers, 1 1/2 In. 37.00
Bowl, Moss, Flowers, 3 Handles, 1 3/4 In. 70.00
Box, Terrier Dog On Cover, Spinach Moss, Blue & White Flowers, 2 x 2 In. .....213.00 to 250.00
Figurine, Dachshund, Spinach Moss, Blue Forget-Me-Nots, White Rose, 2 1/2 In. 250.00
Figurine, Pig On A Ladder, Flowers, 3 1/2 In. 29.00
Vase, Cover, Allover Spinach Moss, Flowers, Large, Rosebud, Footed, 4 In. 46.00
Vase, Figural, High Heel Shoe, Spinach Moss, Flowers, Handles, 2 1/2 In. 87.00
Vase, Pink Flowers, Leafy Vines, Bird, 5 1/2 In. 125.00
Vase, Spinach Moss, Blue Flowers, Pink Rose, 3 In. 64.00

ELVIS PRESLEY, the well-known singer, lived from 1935 to 1977. He became famous by 1956. Elvis appeared on television, starred in twenty-seven movies, and performed in Las Vegas. Memorabilia from any of the Presley shows, his records, and even memorials made after his death are collected.

Anklet, Dog Tag, Silver Tone, On Card, 1956	47.00
Book, Candidly Elvis, Soft Cover, Photographs, 1978	20.00
Book, Soft Cover, 127 Pages, 1985	7.00
Bracelet, Charm, Elvis Photo, Guitar, Broken Heart, Hound Dog, RCA, 1956	55.00
Charm Bracelet, Photo, Guitar, Heart, Hound Dog, RCA Emblem, Gold Tone, 1956	54.00
Menu, Sahara Tahoe, Elvis Presley On Back, 78 RPM Record Shape, 10 In.	75.00
Mirror, Pocket	3.00
Ornament, Hallmark, Box, 1992	33.00
Painting, Velvet, Portrait Of Elvis At The Mike, Wooden Frame, 1970, 16 x 20 In.	20.00
Pen, Float About, Great Pretenders, 3 Elvis Impersonators	3.75
Photograph, Elvis On Stage, May 1957, Small	12.00
Photograph, Elvis, Jailhouse Rock, Autographed, 1950s, 8 x 10 In.	1310.00
Pin, Love Me Tender, Photo	20.00
Poster, Flaming Star & Love Me Tender, 1956, 28 x 22 In., Half Sheet, Pair	287.00
Poster, King Creole, Frame, 81 x 41 In.	690.00
Poster, That's The Way It Is, MGM, 1971, One Sheet	230.00
Record, Elvis & Marilyn, Paradise, 45 RPM, 1978	25.00
Record, Good Rockin' Tonight, 45 RPM	1090.00
Record, Let's Play House, 45 RPM, Sun Records	1265.00
Record, Mama Liked The Roses, Wonder Of You, RCA, 45 RPM, Pair	23.00
Record, Mystery Train, 45 RPM, Sun Records	1150.00
Record, RCA, 1977 & 1978, Pair	5.00
Record, Separate Ways, Victor, 45 RPM, Autographed, 1972	190.00
Shirt, White Cotton, Thin Blue Stripe, Letter Of Authenticity	2070.00
Speedway, RCA Victor, LP, Bonus Photo	805.00
Ticket, Concert, August 22, 1977, Illustrated Folder	12.00

ENAMELS listed here are made of glass particles and other materials heated and fused to metal. In the eighteenth and nineteenth centuries, workmen from Russia, France, England, and other countries made small boxes and table pieces of enamel on metal. One form of English enamel is called *Battersea* and is listed under that name. There was a revival of interest in enameling in the 1930s and a new style evolved. There is now renewed interest in the artistic enameled plaques, vases, ashtrays, and jewelry. Enamels made since the 1930s are usually on copper or steel, although silver was often used for jewelry. Granite-ware is a separate category, and enameled metal kitchen pieces may be included in the Kitchen category.

Beaker, Coronation, Porcelain, Nicholas & Alexandra, 1896, 4 x 3 1/2 In.	1725.00
Blood Cup, Imperial Double-Headed Eagle & Cipher Of Nicholas & Alexandra, 1896	1568.00

Enamel, Dish, Tribal Figures,
Stenciled, Dane Burr,
4 1/2 In.

Enamel, Kovsh, Floral,
Animal Center, Feodor Ruckert,
4 1/2 In.

Enamel, Plate, Island Scene,
Symbolic Figures, Betty John,
1968, 8 1/2 In.

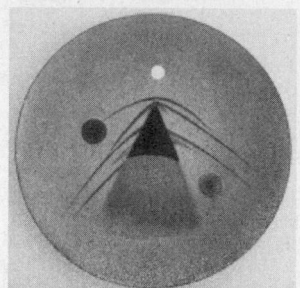

Enamel, Plate,
Rocket, NBC,
Wide Wide
World, Feb. 17,
1957, 7 1/2 In.

Enamel, Tray, Gold, Green Ground,
Multicolored Floral, Rectangular, 6 1/4 x 4 In.

Blood Cup, Nicholas II Coronation, Imperial Eagle & The Cipher Of Nicholas, 4 In. 840.00
Bowl, Burgundy & White, Marked Winter, 10 In. 45.00
Bowl, Floral Design, Lime Green, Salmon Pink Ground, 12 1/2 In. 165.00
Bowl, Raised, Copper Flute, Petals, Orange & Red, Arts & Crafts, 1 5/8 x 5 3/4 In. 450.00
Bowl, Stylized Coral, Blue, Green Design, Copper, 2 x 3 In. 145.00
Box, Lid, Medallion, Maiden By A Tree, Acanthus Border, Late 19th Century, 3 In. 173.00
Box, Pastoral Scene, Spiraling Sunray Ground, Cased Scrolls, Silver, 3 x 2 1/8 In. 978.00
Candy Dish, Copper, Signed Winter, 1960s, 7 1/2 In. 33.00
Cornucopia, Allegorical Scenes, Raised On Wings Of Pegasus, Silver, 1880, 10 In. 13800.00
Cup, Allegorical Scenes, Spreading Circular Base, Knop Standard, 14 In. 4600.00
Dish, Tribal Figures, Stenciled, Dane Burr, 4 1/2 In. ....*Illus* 20.00
Kovsh, Floral, Animal Center, Feodor Ruckert, 4 1/2 In. ....*Illus* 4200.00
Nef, Ship, Allegorical Scenes, Raised On Tails Of Dolphins, 1880, 13 1/2 In. 10350.00
Plaque, Cavalier, Copper & Oak Frame, Limoges, 8 1/4 x 4 3/4 In. 632.00
Plaque, Victory, Flesh Tones, Gilt, Round, Square Frame, Hans Bastanier, 1903, 12 In.... 4200.00
Plate, Bird Scene, Nekrasoff, c.1960, 4 1/2 In. 80.00
Plate, Copper, Peacock Feathers, Green Leaves, Arts Crafts Shop, 8 In. 550.00
Plate, Copper, Red Berries, Green Leaves, Arts Crafts Shop, Square, 6 In. 195.00
Plate, Copper, Red Strawberries, Green Stems, Arts Crafts Shop, 8 3/4 In. 935.00
Plate, Island Scene, Symbolic Figures, Betty John, 1968, 8 1/2 In. ....*Illus* 12.00
Plate, Rocket, NBC, Wide Wide World, Feb. 17, 1957, 7 1/2 In. ....*Illus* 95.00
Plate, Taito, Blue Ground, 7 1/2 In., Pair 55.00
Portrait, Young Beauty, On Copper, Limoges, c.1890, 4 x 3 1/4 In. 4460.00
Tray, Gold, Green Ground, Multicolored Floral, Rectangular, 6 1/4 x 4 In. ....*Illus* 6.50
Tureen, Undertray, Chrysanthemum, Transfer, Gilt, C.J. & Sons, 15 1/4 In. 135.00
Vase, Abstract Fan Design, Red, Pink, Black & White Enamel, Camille Faure, 4 In. 2875.00
Vase, Allegorical Scenes, Knop, 7 In. 1840.00
Vase, Bamboo Design, Pigeon's Blood, Late Meiji Period, 2 3/4 In. 275.00
Vase, Champleve, Mythical Creatures, Jewels, Lamp Mounted, Oriental, 15 In. 545.00
Vase, Classical Reserve Scenes, Baroque Scrolls, Figural Handles, 13 In. 9775.00
Vase, Cobalt, Ice Blue Scrolls, Black Enamel, Camille Faure, 1925, 4 3/8 In. 2645.00
Vase, Fish, Urn Form, Amber, Overall Multicolored, Dragonfly, Harrach, 1890, 9 In. 172.00
Vase, Floral Design, Blue, Cream, Red, Gilt, Bronze, France, 10 In. 402.00
Vase, Geometric Design, Green, White, Black Enamel, Camille Faure, 1925, 7 In. 3105.00
Vase, Geometric, Floral, Green, Japan, 20th Century, 13 In. 550.00
Wedding Cup, Musician Scene, Cavalier & People Dancing, Windmill, 1900, 4 In. 1760.00

ERPHILA is a mark found on Czechoslovakian and other pottery and
porcelain made after 1920. The mark was used on items imported
by Ebeling & Reuss, Philadelphia, a giftware firm that is still operating in Pennsylvania. The mark is a combination of the letters *E* and *R*
(Ebeling & Reuss) and the first letters of the city, Phila(delphia). Many
whimsical figural pitchers and creamers, figurines, platters, and other
giftwares carry this mark.

Creamer, Cat 65.00
Reamer, Marked 80.00
Teapot, Cat, 8 In. 195.00
Teapot, Cow, 7 1/4 In. 225.00

Teapot, Dog, 7 1/2 In. 225.00
Teapot, Dog, 8 In. 195.00

ES GERMANY porcelain was made at the factory of Erdmann
Schlegelmilch from 1861 to 1937 in Suhl, Germany. The porcelain,
marked *ES Germany* or *ES Suhl*, was sold decorated or undecorated.
Other pieces were made at a factory in Saxony, Prussia, and are
marked *ES Prussia.* Reinhold Schlegelmilch made the famous wares
marked *RS Germany.*

Bowl, Purple-Throated Warbler In Blue Berry Tree, Pierced Handles, 13 x 8 In. 73.00
Dish, Divided, Lobster, Tail Forms Handle, Flowers, Gilt, Blue Mark, 10 In. 84.00
Plaque, Bird In Landscape, Gilt Edging, Provsaxe, 1920, 12 1/2 In. 35.00
Plate, Bird On Tree Limb, Hand Painted, Pierced Handles, Green Mark, 10 In. 50.00
Plate, Robin In Mulberry Tree, Handle, Green Mark, 7 x 8 In. 67.00
Tankard, Yellow Roses, Blue Green Ground, Art Nouveau Mold, 15 In. 225.00

ESKIMO artifacts of all types are collected. Carvings of whale or walrus teeth are listed under Scrimshaw. Baskets are in the Basket category. All other types of Eskimo art are listed here.

Ax, Walrus Ivory, Primitive, 12 In. 110.00
Banner, Eskimo Child, Totem Pole, Paper, 1939, 3 x 7 In. 6.00
Basket, Baleen, Ivory Bear Figure, 1960s, 4 In. 715.00
Basket, Blue Beads On Lid & Neck, c.1920, 8 x 7 In. 330.00
Basket, Cover, Banded Polychrome Design, 1960s, 5 x 3 In. 66.00
Basket, Cover, Faded Polychrome Design, 1940s, 7 x 6 In. 165.00
Belt Buckle, Ivory, Dot Design, 3 In. 55.00
Boots, Salmon Skin 165.00
Boots, Sealskin, 19th Century 66.00
Bowl, Awl & Spoon, Wooden, Alaska, 9 x 11 x 7 In. 145.00
Cigarette Holder, Ivory, Totem Pole Shape, 19th Century, 4 In. 175.00
Comb, Bone, Engraved, 2 5/8 In. 49.00
Comb, Ivory, 4 1/2 In. 155.00
Cribbage Board, Walrus Ivory, Carved Fish & Whale, 15 1/2 In. 525.00
Cribbage Board, Walrus Tusk, With Eskimo, Dogsled, Polar Bear, 5 Seals, 18 1/2 In. 385.00
Dish, Coiled Grass, Yu'pik, Oblong, 1940, 12 x 5 1/2 In. 49.00
Doll, Drummer & Dancer, Ethel Washington, Late 1950s, Pair 2750.00
Doll, Hide, Rabbit Skin Coat, Wooden Face, 1970s, 13 In. 80.00
Drum, Hand, Ivory Handle, c.1920, 20 x 1 1/2 In. 330.00
Figurine, 2 Walruses, Peter Nuwya, 1974, 12 In. 470.00
Fish Hook, Fossil Ivory 50.00
Fork, Ivory, 3 Tines, 8 In. 55.00
Goggles, Snow, Ivory, 5 In. 440.00
Harpoon, Bone, Steel Point, Alaska, 5 7/8 In. 110.00
Harpoon, Walrus Tusk, Stone Point, 7 3/4 In. 385.00
Harpoon, Walrus, Hand Forged, St. Lawrence Island, 19th Century, 6 5/8 In. 110.00
Harpoon Head, Bone, Alaska, 7 In. 60.00
Harpoon Head, Fossil Bone 55.00
Jar, Coiled Basketry, Rye Grass, Dyed Sealskin Trim, 6 x 6 1/2 In. 250.00
Knife, Caribou, Scrimshaw, Hunting Scene, Leather Handle, c.1895, 23 In. 220.00
Knife, Inuit, Walruses, George Wostenholm IXL Cutlery Sheffield, Ivory, 1890s, 7 In. 460.00
Letter Opener, Ivory, Scrimshaw 28.00
Lure, Bone Hook, Sinew Forms Hook, 7 In. 175.00
Moccasins, Sealskin, Beads On Trade Cloth, c.1890, 4 1/2 In. 120.00
Mukluks, Beaded, c.1880, 15 1/2 In. 120.00
Parka, Seal Gut, 1900 . . . . 247.00
Picture, Northwest Coast, Frame, 5 In. 5.00
Plaque, Yu'Pik, Coiled Seagrass, Polychrome, c.1920, 6 In. 66.00
Scraper, Flint, 5 3/8 In. 99.00
Sculpture, Whale, Bone, c.1920, 2 1/2 x 10 x 3 In. 275.00
Spear, Wooden, Alaska, 85 In. 385.00
Spoon, Wooden 11.00
Toy, Boat, Baleen, Deck Insert, 2-Masted, Alaska, 10 1/2 In. 110.00
Walrus Tusk, Scrimshaw, Hunting Scene, 2 Seals, Polar Bear, 9 1/4 In. 135.00

FABERGE was a firm of jewelers and goldsmiths founded in St. Petersburg, Russia, in 1842, by Gustav Faberge. Peter Carl Faberge, his son,
was jeweler to the Russian Imperial Court from about 1870 to 1914.
The rare Imperial Easter eggs, jewelry, and decorative items are very
expensive today.

Bangle, Facing Lion Heads, Gold, Leather Case, 1900, 2 1/2 In.	3735.00
Beaker, Fluted Design, Profile Of Catherine The Great, Handle, Silver Gilt, 5 In.	13800.00
Beaker, Red Enamel Band Over Guilloche, Champleve Rim, Silver Gilt, 2 In.	4025.00
Beaker, Silver, Reeded Body, Cylindrical, Stephan Wakeva, 1890, 1 3/4 In.	2530.00
Bell Push, Enameled Rose, Ribbon Tied Leaf Branches, 3 Bun Feet, 1900, 2 1/4 In.	4600.00
Bell Push, Silver Gilt, 6-Pointed Star Chased With Acanthus Leaves, 2 In.	3680.00
Bonbonniere, Hinged Cover, Pannier Form, Cushion-Cut Amethyst, Gold, 2 In.	10350.00
Bowl, Dolphin Handle, Silver, Oval, Moscow, 1890, 2 1/2 In.	5175.00
Bowl, Geometric Design, Floral Band, Notched Rim, 4 Paw Feet, Circular, 9 In.	4600.00
Bowl, Glass, 2 Handles, Silver Rim & Handles, Marked, 1890, 10 1/2 In.	3680.00
Bowl, Silver, Empress Catherine The Great Coin Base, J. Rappoport, 1890, 2 3/4 In.	4885.00
Box, Presentation, Hinged Cover, Intertwined With Cabochons, 1908, 2 x 4 In.	4760.00
Box, Stylized Foliage, Muted Colors, Cabochon Sapphire Thumbpiece, 1910, 3 In.	5175.00
Cane Handle, Figural, Tau Form, Dark Green, Laurel Leaves Between Reeded Border	7475.00
Cane Handle, Hook Form, White Greek Key, Rose Cut Diamond Border, 8 In.	12650.00
Centerpiece, Anthemion, Laurel Wreath, 2 Scroll Handles, 4 Bun Feet, 1900, 12 In.	6900.00
Cigarette Case, Cover, Cabochon Sapphire Thumbpiece, Moscow, 1896, 3 1/8 In.	2300.00
Cigarette Case, Cover, Flowering Orange, Yellow, Green, Moscow, 1890, 4 In.	11500.00
Cigarette Case, Cover, Imperial Eagle, Silver, Moscow, 1915, 3 3/4 In.	3450.00
Cigarette Case, Sunray Design, Cabochon Ruby Thumbpiece, St. Petersburg, 1890, 3 In.	8050.00
Egg, Gold, Enamel, Eagle, Double-Headed, St. Petersburg, 1890, 7/8 In.	8050.00
Egg, Overall Cobalt Blue, Stylized Gold Clouds, Rose Cut Diamonds, 9/16 In.	9775.00
Egg, Overall Translucent Purple, Gold Laurel Leaf Border, c.1890, 7/8 In.	3220.00
Figurine, Hare, Feldspar, Rose Cut Diamond Eyes, St. Petersburg, c.1890, 1 7/8 In.	9200.00
Frame, Silver, Gadrooned, Ribbon Bow Top, Hardstone, Pink Quartz, 1890, 6 In.	9775.00
Jug, Claret, Art Nouveau, Double Gourd, Silver Mounted, Marked, 1900, 11 3/4 In.	8050.00
Kovsh, Enameled Leaves Interior, Flat Shaped Handle, 1900, 3 3/8 In.	9775.00
Kovsh, Gilt Silver, Plique-A-Jour Enameled Border, 1900, 3 3/4 In.	9775.00
Kovsh, Overall Translucent Red Over Guilloche Ground, Hook Handle, Silver, 3 In.	6900.00
Letter Opener, Mounted With Coin Of Reign Of Empress Elizabeth, Silver, Fitted Case	4600.00
Locket-Pendant, Gold, Enameled Pink, Guilloche Ground, Wooden Case, 1900, 2 In.	4140.00
Match Case, Silver, Gold, Red Translucent Enamel, Guilloche, 1900, 1 3/8 In.	8910.00
Match Holder, Varicolored Gold, Red Stone Thumbpiece, Marked, 1900, 1 3/4 In.	1725.00
Scent Flask, Gold, Translucent Apple Green, H.W., 1900, 2 In.	4310.00
Spoon, Silver, Enamel, Marked K. Faberge In Cyrillic, C. 1915, 4 1/4 In.	1680.00
Tazza, Tied Laurel Swags, Foliate, Geometric Design, Gadrooned Base, 3 Feet, 7 In.	9200.00
Tea & Coffee Set, Ivory Handles, Gilt Interior, 1910, 5 Piece	10350.00
Teapot, Hinged Cover, Hammered, Vegetable Form Finial, Moscow, 1894, 4 In.	2875.00
Vanity Case, Chased Overall With Engine Turned Reeded Bands, 2-Tone Gold, 4 In.	8050.00
Vase, Red Ceramic, Applied Gilt Silver Scrolls & Flowers, 1890, 3 1/2 In.	9200.00

FAIENCE refers to tin-glazed earthenware, especially the wares made in
France, Germany, and Scandinavia. It is also correct to say that faience
is the same as majolica or Delft, although usually the term refers only
to the tin-glazed pottery of the three regions mentioned.

Bowl, Green Semimatte Glaze, California Faience, 5 In.	110.00
Bowl, Hand Painted, Reticulated, Square, Signed Lille 1737, France	120.00
Bowl, Serving, Naturalistic Slip Design, Yellow & Tan Glaze, 12 In., 5 Piece	220.00
Box, Floral Design, Butterflies & Insect, Handles, Square, Emile Galle, 2 1/2 In.	230.00
Cachepot, Scrolls, Foliage Suspending From Flowering Branches, 8 In., Pair	258.00
Dish, La Liberte, Hand Painted Cherub, Flying From Birdcage, 1792	108.00
Ewer, Cathedral 1 Side, Lion & Wreath Other, Signed, 19th Century, 11 In.	110.00
Figurine, Man & Woman In Country Dress Seated, 19th Century, 7 In., Pair	115.00
Figurine, Man In Country Attire, Woman Holding Bundles Of Wheat, 7 In., Pair	230.00
Figurine, Smoking Pipe, Floral Clothing, Blue & White, Continental, 18 1/2 In.	115.00
Garniture, Art Nouveau, Gilt, Flowering Branch, Cobalt Blue Ground, 14 In., 3 Piece	545.00
Inkstand, 3 Ink Reservoirs, Triangular, 6 In.	55.00
Inkstand, Harbor Scene, Tower & Knight Inkpots, Raised Pawed Lion, 13 1/2 In.	745.00

Jardiniere, Figural, Cockerel, Scrolled Acanthus Base, Nove, Venice, 27 x 17 1/2 In. 1980.00
Jardiniere, Flowers & Foliage, Blue, White, Continental, 9 3/4 In. 920.00
Plate, Bird & Fruit Design, Octagonal, Continental, 9 In. 115.00
Plate, Cabinet, Mythological, Dragon-Like Beast With Stag Horns, France, 10 In. 140.00
Plate, Commemorating French Corsair Revenant, 19th Century, 9 1/4 In. 145.00
Plate, Peasant Scenes, France, 19th Century, 10 In., 11 Piece 310.00
Plate, Rose & Violet Floral Spray, Continental, 5 1/2 In., Pair 115.00
Tile, Southwest Scene, Multicolored, Red Clay, Signed, 5 1/2 In. 412.00
Urn, Scenic Design, Ram's Head Handles, 7 1/2 In., Pair 690.00
Vase, Applied Coral Rose, Orange Blossoms, Gray, Black Barbitine Ground, 6 1/2 In. ... 99.00
Vase, Applied Flowers & Leaves, White Glaze, Blue, Green, Black Ground, 10 In. 165.00
Vase, Applied Gilded Roses, Burgundy, Gold Ground, 8 1/4 In. 88.00
Vase, Applied Red Roses, Black Rim, Gilt Ground, 6 In. 33.00
Vase, Blue & Turquoise Semi-Matte Glaze, California Faience, 6 1/2 In. 275.00
Vase, Glossy Turquoise, Bulbous, Incised Mark, California Faience, 3 1/2 In. 195.00

FAIRINGS are small souvenir china boxes and figurines that were sold
at country fairs during the nineteenth century. Most were made in
Germany. Reproductions of fairings are being made, especially of the
famous *twelve months of marriage* series.

Box, Trinket, Cat On Bed, Who Said Rats?, Germany, 3 1/2 In. 150.00
Box, Trinket, Child On Bureau, 4 In. 40.00
Box, Trinket, Floral Painted, Nail Design, Dome Top, Folk Art, Penn., 4 1/2 x 5 1/2 In. 5945.00
Box, Trinket, Girl In Canoe, Kate Greenaway Style 97.00
Box, Trinket, Little Red Riding Hood, Begging Dog, 2 3/4 x 2 1/2 In. 45.00
Box, Trinket, Place For Photo Or Mirror, 5 x 3 In. 295.00
Box, Trinket, Romantic Painted Scene, Tin, Red Ground, Hinged Lid, Oval, 7 x 4 In. 70.00
Box, Trinket, Stork In Grass With Baby In Beak, 4 x 3 In. 30.00
Candlestick, Last In Bed To Put Out The Light, 3 1/2 In. 55.00
Figurine, Couple In Bed, Will We Sleep First Or How?, 3 1/2 x 4 In. 65.00
Figurine, Mother, Nurse, Baby, 3 x 4 In. 350.00
Figurine, Woman In Bed, Man Getting In, 3 x 3 5/8 In. 350.00

FAIRYLAND LUSTER pieces are included in the Wedgwood category.

FAMILLE ROSE, see Chinese Export category.

FANS have been used for cooling since the days of the ancients. By the
eighteenth century, the fan was an accessory for the lady of fashion,
and very elaborate and expensive fans were made. Sticks were made
of ivory or wood, set with jewels or carved. The fans were made of
painted silk or paper. Inexpensive paper fans printed with advertising
were giveaways in the late nineteenth and early twentieth centuries.
Electric fans were introduced in 1882.

Advertising, Glueks Beer, Cardboard, 1930s, 8 x 14 In. 30.00
Advertising, Lord & Taylor, Cardboard, Lithograph, Turned Wood Handle, 18 x 9 In. 143.00
Advertising, National Brewing Co., 1877 Calendar, Die Cut, Women, Framed, 22 In. 1980.00
Bamboo Sticks, Cloth, Traveling Musician, Lithograph, Victorian, 24 In. 17.00
Black Lacquer Ribs, Gouache Paper Figures, Ivory Faces, Fabric Costume, 11 1/4 In. 145.00
Bone Ribs, Silver & Gilt, Embroidered Paper, Painted Courting Couple, 10 3/4 In. 115.00
Bone Sticks, Gilt Paper, Court Scenes, Brass Trim, Mirror Insert, Frame, 13 x 21 In. 165.00
Electric, General Electric, Rotating, Brass & Iron, c.1920, 16 1/2 In. 90.00
Electric, Hot Air, Floor Model, Sterling Cycle, 45 In. 6500.00
Electric, Wall, Wooden, Metal Floral, Leaf Design, 34 1/2 x 24 In. 58.00
Electric, Westinghouse, 4 Blades, Brass, 1906, 13 In. 80.00
Electric, Westinghouse, 4 Blades, Cast Iron, 1910s-1920s, 18 In. 75.00
Electric, Westinghouse, 4 Blades, Heavy Iron Housing, Replacement Cord, 1920s, 13 In. .. 32.00
Gessoed Frame, 3 Women & Man Near Fountain, 14 1/4 In. 230.00
Giltwood Handle, Beaded, Geometric & Flowers, Round, Silk Fringe, 16 In., Pair 365.00
Ivory, Carved, In A Chinoiserie Design Lacquer Box, Late 19th Century, 10 In. 258.00
Ivory Panels, Pierced Work, Figures In Garden Scenes, Box, c.1850 .... 632.00
Ivory Sticks, Figures With Ivory Faces, Landscape, Box, China 126.00
Ivory Sticks, Silk Leaf, Mother & Newborn, Gilt, Glazed Case, 19th Century, 17 In. 112.00
Ivory Sticks, Silk, 18th Century, 14 x 24 In. 247.00

Ivory Sticks, Silk, Frame, 18th Century, 14 x 24 In.	495.00
Lacquer, Watercolor, Figures In Garden, 2 Sides, Chinese Export, 19th Century, 7 1/2 In.	190.00
Lacquered Sticks, Namban Style, Foreign Ships & Europeans, 19th Century	345.00
Mother-Of-Pearl Sticks, Painted Figures, Landscape, Gilt Highlighted, Frame, 22 In.	300.00
Mother-Of-Pearl Sticks, Painted Paper, Courting Couples, Continental, 9 In.	115.00
Mother-Of-Pearl Sticks, Painted, Couples In Park, Gilt Scrolls, c.1790, 22 1/2 x 14 In.	364.00
Mother-Of-Pearl Sticks, Painted, Court Scene, Lithographed, Case, c.1840, 23 x 13 In.	308.00
Mother-Of-Pearl Sticks, Persian Court Scene, Lithograph, Case, c.1870, 12 x 7 In.	112.00
Mother-Of-Pearl Sticks, Silk, Sequins, Leather & Satin Box, Paris, France, 12 In.	200.00
Painted, Garden & Waterfall Scenes, Gilt Borders, Case, c.1790, 24 x 15 In.	560.00
Painted & Gilt Silk, Group Of Women Dancing, Black Ground, Frame, 19 1/2 x 27 In.	200.00
Paper, Fisherman Admiring Landscape, Ink & Colors, Frame, 19th Century	115.00
Plastic, Indianapolis 500, Folding, 1960s	25.00
Polychrome Sticks, Sequined, Medallion Scene, Gilt Mesh, Case, c.1850, 18 x 10 In.	336.00
Sandalwood Sticks, Feather, Central Scene Of Couple Under Pine Tree, Guards, 1880	286.00
Sandalwood Sticks, Mandarins, Ivory Faces, Silk Clothes, Chinese Export, 1840, 11 In.	275.00
Silk, Hand Painted, Cherubs, Rose Swing Over Lake, Gilded Frame, 30 x 9 1/2 In.	286.00
Wooden Sticks, Carved, Painted, Romantic Roman Scene, Case, 1700s, 22 x 12 In.	560.00

FAST FOOD COLLECTIBLES may be included in several categories, such as Advertising, Coca-Cola, Toy, etc.

FEDERZEICHNUNG is the very strange German name for a pattern of mother-of-pearl satin glass. The pattern had irregularly shaped sections of brown glass covered with a pattern of gold squiggle lines. It was first made in the late nineteenth century.

Vase, Dark Brown, Gold Squiggles, Pinched Top, 7 In.	2500.00
Vase, Orange Ground, White Design, Gold Tracery, Cased White Interior, 9 In.	2600.00

FENTON Art Glass Company, founded in Martins Ferry, Ohio, by Frank L. Fenton, is now located in Williamstown, West Virginia. It is noted for early carnival glass produced between 1907 and 1920. Some of these pieces are listed in the Carnival Glass category. Many other types of glass were also made. Spanish Lace in this section refers to the pattern made by Fenton.

Aqua Crest, Creamer, Ruffled Edge	60.00
Aqua Crest, Vase, Hat Shape, 6 1/2 In.	25.00
Aqua Crest, Vase, Ruffled Edge, Bulbous, 12 In.	90.00
Autumn Acorn, Bowl, Blue Carnival	150.00
Bicentennial, Bell, Chocolate, 1976	45.00
Bicentennial, Plate, Independence, Blue, Commemorative Scenes, 8 In., 4 Piece	50.00
Blackberry, Compote, Milk Glass, Miniature	350.00
Blackberry, Plate, Marigold, 8 In.	450.00
Blue Ridge, Pitcher Set, 5 Piece	250.00
Burmese, Creamer, Leaf Decorated	70.00
Burmese, Fairy Light, Blue Flowers, 1985	125.00
Burmese, Lamp, Jacobean Floral, 23 1/2 In.	495.00
Burmese, Pitcher, Melon Ribbed	60.00
Burmese, Pitcher, Rose Decorated, 5 In.	65.00
Burmese, Plate, Farmyard, 10 1/2 In.	50.00
Burmese, Rose Bowl, Brass Stand	40.00
Burmese, Vase, Blue Flowers, 1984, 4 1/2 In.	60.00
Burmese, Vase, Rose Decorated, 7 In.	35.00
Burmese, Water Set, Raspberries, 7 Piece	445.00
Butterfly & Fern, Tumbler, Green Carnival	110.00
Cape Cod, Plate, Blue Opalescent, 1938, 6 In.	40.00
Chinese Yellow, Pitcher, Juice, 1925, 6 In.	78.00
Coin Dot, Basket, Mulberry, 1988	45.00
Coin Dot, Pitcher, Water, Cranberry Opalescent	295.00
Coin Dot, Vase, Hat Shape, Lime Opalescent	85.00
Colonial, Salt & Pepper, Blue	30.00
Colonial, Salt & Pepper, Pink	30.00
Diamond Lace, Bride's Bowl, Blue Opalescent, 10 In.	70.00

Diamond Optic, Bowl, Dolphin, Flared 50.00
Dot Optic, Creamer, Blue Opalescent, 1924 .... 40.00
Dot Optic, Cruet, Cobalt Blue Opalescent 75.00
Dot Optic, Cruet, Cranberry Opalescent 75.00
Dot Optic, Pitcher, Water, Cranberry Opalescent 295.00
Dragon & Lotus, Plate, Marigold Carnival 3000.00
Drapery, Cruet, Cranberry Opalescent 75.00
Elephant, Decanter, Sherry, Ball Stopper, 9 1/2 In. 350.00
Emerald Crest, Plate, 6 1/4 In. 40.00
Emerald Crest, Vase, 4 In. 40.00
Figurine, September Morn Nymph, Pink, 6 1/4 In. 125.00
Figurine, September Morn Nymph, Ruby, 6 1/4 In. 175.00
Flame Crest, Cake Plate, 12 3/4 In. 95.00
Garland, Rose Bowl, Blue 60.00
Garland, Rose Bowl, Green Carnival 600.00
Georgian, Mug, Beer, Pink, 8 Oz. 20.00
Gold Crest, Bonbon, Triangle 22.00
Gold Crest, Bowl, Ruffled Edge, 7 1/2 In. 35.00
Gold Crest, Hat 20.00
Hanging Heart, Bowl, Iridescent Green, 9 In. 65.00
Hanging Heart, Vase, Custard, Pinched, 8 In. 145.00
Hobnail, Ashtray Set, Nesting, Blue Opalescent, 3 Piece 50.00
Hobnail, Basket, Cranberry Opalescent 120.00
Hobnail, Basket, Topaz Opalescent, 8 1/2 In. ....45.00 to 75.00
Hobnail, Bowl, Blue Opalescent, 11 1/2 In. 85.00
Hobnail, Candlestick, Blue Opalescent, Flat, Pair 75.00
Hobnail, Candy Dish, Cover, Milk Glass, 6 1/2 x 6 1/2 In. 40.00
Hobnail, Candy Jar, Milk Glass 10.00
Hobnail, Creamer, French Opalescent, 2 3/4 In. 15.00
Hobnail, Cruet, Pink Opalescent 75.00
Hobnail, Epergne, 3-Lily, Cranberry Opalescent 140.00
Hobnail, Jam Jar, Underplate, Spoon 100.00
Hobnail, Jug, Blue Opalescent, Squat, 5 1/2 In. 60.00
Hobnail, Napkin Ring, Milk Glass, 4 Piece 200.00
Hobnail, Nappy, Blue Opalescent 22.00
Hobnail, Perfume Bottle, Blue Opalescent, Button Top 45.00
Hobnail, Plate, Milk Glass, 13 1/2 In. 80.00
Hobnail, Punch Set, Milk Glass, 14 Pieces 575.00
Hobnail, Salt & Pepper, Milk Glass 25.00
Hobnail, Slipper, Amberina, Label 30.00
Hobnail, Sugar & Creamer, Milk Glass 22.00
Hobnail, Tumbler, Blue Opalescent, 9 Oz., 6 Piece 90.00
Hobnail, Vase, Amber, 5 In. 20.00
Hobnail, Vase, Blue Opalescent, Cone Shape, 6 In. 40.00
Hobnail, Vase, Blue Opalescent, Hand Holding Horn, 6 In. 95.00
Ivory Crest, Rose Bowl 60.00
Mosaic Inlaid, Vase, Cobalt Blue, Yellow, Red, Black Threading, 1925, 5 In. 1092.00
Peach Crest, Basket, 7 In. 40.00
Peach Crest, Bowl, 10 In. 35.00
Peking Blue, Candlestick, 3 In., Pair 150.00
Polka Dot, Salt & Pepper, Cranberry Opalescent, 1955 .... 100.00
Poppy, Lamp, Gone With The Wind, Cameo Satin, 24 In. 250.00
Rib Optic, Tumble-Up Set, Blue Opalescent, Pitcher, Tumbler 119.90
Rib Optic, Vase, Blue Opalescent, Square Top, 6 In. 55.00
Rosalene, Candy Box, Cover, Chessie Cat, 1970s 500.00
Rosalene, Compote, 1970s, 7 In. 60.00
Rosalene, Tobacco Jar, Grape & Cable 195.00
Rosalene, Vase, Basket Weave, 8 In. 75.00
Rosalene, Vase, Fan, 1970s, 7 In. 195.00
Rose Crest, Basket, 6 In. 20.00
Rose Crest, Bowl, Flared, Crimped, 7 In. 45.00
Rose Crest, Top Hat, 1924, 5 In. 35.00

Rose Crest, Vase, 7 In. 65.00
Silver Crest, Banana Stand, Footed, 13 In. 95.00
Silver Crest, Basket, Butterflies, 7 In. 55.00
Silver Crest, Box, Cigarette, Design On Bronze, Signed, 4 1/2 In. 100.00
Silver Crest, Cake Stand, Footed, 13 In. ....45.00 to 55.00
Silver Crest, Candlestick, Crest On Base 100.00
Silver Crest, Candlestick, Ruffled Edge, 3 In., Pair 30.00
Silver Crest, Candy Dish, Cover ....55.00 to 100.00
Silver Crest, Compote, Low Footed 28.00
Silver Crest, Cup & Saucer 28.00
Silver Crest, Dish, Mayonnaise, Underplate, Spoon 45.00
Silver Crest, Epergne, 1-Lily, 13 In. 165.00
Silver Crest, Goblet 30.00
Silver Crest, Plate, 8 1/2 In. 28.00
Silver Crest, Relish, Heart, Handle, 7 In. 26.00
Silver Crest, Server, Center Handle, 12 1/2 In. 40.00
Silver Crest, Sherbet 10.00
Silver Crest, Tidbit, 2 Tiers, 8 x 12 In. 30.00
Silver Crest, Tidbit, 3 Tiers, 13 In., 8 In., 6 In. 45.00
Silver Crest, Torte Plate, 15 1/2 In. 335.00
Silver Crest, Vase, 6 In. 25.00
Silver Crest, Vase, Fan, 12 In. 110.00
Silver Crest, Vase, Flowering Branches, Sterling On Bronze, Cleaned Patina, 9 3/4 In. ... 140.00
Silver Crest, Vase, Fuchsia Blossom, Sterling On Bronze, Dark Patina, 7 1/4 In. 195.00
Snow Crest, Lamp, Hurricane, Cranberry 75.00
Snow Crest, Vase, Cranberry, 8 In. 95.00
Spanish Lace, Compote, Tall, Pink 75.00
Tulip, Bowl, Cobalt, 9 In. 25.00
Vasa Murrhina, Basket, Aventurine Green, 7 In. 70.00
Vasa Murrhina, Vase, Autumn Orange, 8 In. 45.00
Vasa Murrhina, Vase, Aventurine Green, 5 In. 38.00
Violets In The Snow, Bowl, 10 In. 125.00
Violets In The Snow, Vase, Fan, 6 In. 125.00

FIESTA, the colorful dinnerware, was introduced in 1936 by the Homer
Laughlin China Co., redesigned in 1969, and withdrawn in 1973. It
was reissued again in 1986 in different colors and is still being made.
The simple design was characterized by a band of concentric circles,
beginning at the rim. Cups had full-circle handles until 1969, when
partial-circle handles were made. Harlequin and Riviera were related
wares. For more information and prices of American dinnerware, see
the book *Kovels' Depression Glass & Dinnerware Price List*.

Chartreuse, Bowl, Fruit, 4 3/4 In. 25.00
Chartreuse, Chop Plate, 13 In. 90.00
Chartreuse, Coffeepot ....525.00 to 585.00
Chartreuse, Creamer, Ring Handle 30.00
Chartreuse, Cup & Saucer 44.00
Chartreuse, Cup & Saucer, After Dinner ....530.00 to 625.00
Chartreuse, Mug ....25.00 to 90.00
Chartreuse, Pitcher, Disk 275.00
Chartreuse, Plate, 7 In. 13.00
Chartreuse, Plate, 10 In. 50.00
Chartreuse, Sauceboat 85.00
Chartreuse, Soup, Cream ....60.00 to 95.00
Chartreuse, Vase, 10 In. 95.00
Cobalt Blue, Bowl, Fruit, 4 3/4 In. 35.00
Cobalt Blue, Carafe 495.00
Cobalt Blue, Chop Plate, 13 In. 45.00
Cobalt Blue, Coffeepot 325.00
Cobalt Blue, Creamer, Stick Handle 70.00
Cobalt Blue, Cup & Saucer, After Dinner ....90.00 to 95.00
Cobalt Blue, Eggcup 75.00

Cobalt **Blue,** Jar, Cover, Kitchen Kraft, Small 495.00
Cobalt **Blue,** Jug, 2 Pt. 90.00
Cobalt **Blue,** Mixing Bowl Cover, No. 1 .... 850.00
Cobalt **Blue,** Mixing Bowl, No. 1 .... 375.00
Cobalt **Blue,** Mixing Bowl, No. 2 .... 195.00
Cobalt **Blue,** Pitcher, 2 Pt. 120.00
Cobalt **Blue,** Pitcher, Disk ....125.00 to 185.00
Cobalt **Blue,** Plate, Deep, 8 1/4 In. 70.00
Cobalt **Blue,** Salt & Pepper ....30.00 to 60.00
Cobalt **Blue,** Soup, Cream 44.00
Cobalt **Blue,** Soup, Onion, Cover 925.00
Cobalt **Blue,** Spoon, Kitchen Kraft ....150.00 to 195.00
Cobalt **Blue,** Teapot, Cover, Large 75.00
Cobalt **Blue,** Teapot, Cover, Medium ....125.00 to 300.00
Cobalt **Blue,** Tumbler, Juice 40.00
Cobalt **Blue,** Tumbler, Water 95.00
Cobalt **Blue,** Vase, 8 In. 585.00
Cobalt **Blue,** Vase, 12 In. 1100.00
Forest Green, Bowl, 6 In. 44.00
Forest Green, Casserole, Cover 435.00
Forest Green, Coffeepot, Cover 285.00
Forest Green, Creamer 30.00
Forest Green, Cup & Saucer ....20.00 to 45.00
Forest Green, Eggcup 75.00
Forest Green, Mug ....80.00 to 90.00
Forest Green, Plate, 6 In. 13.00
Forest Green, Plate, 9 In. 19.00
Forest Green, Plate, 10 In. 65.00
Forest Green, Soup, Cream ....60.00 to 95.00
Gray, Bowl, Dessert, 6 In. 40.00
Gray, Bowl, Fruit, 4 3/4 In. 35.00
Gray, Casserole, Cover 375.00
Gray, Chop Plate, 13 In. 95.00
Gray, Coffeepot 750.00
Gray, Cup 36.00
Gray, Cup & Saucer ....20.00 to 44.00
Gray, Cup & Saucer, After Dinner 875.00
Gray, Jug, 2 Pt. 125.00
Gray, Mug ....80.00 to 95.00
Gray, Plate, 9 In. 30.00
Gray, Plate, Deep, 8 1/4 In. 45.00
Gray, Sauceboat 48.00
Gray, Saucer, After Dinner 195.00
Gray, Soup, Cream 60.00
Gray, Tumbler, Juice ....200.00 to 375.00
Ivory, Bowl, Fruit, 4 3/4 In. 20.00
Ivory, Casserole, Cover 150.00
Ivory, Cup & Saucer 10.00
Ivory, Mixing Bowl Cover, No. 1 .... 250.00
Ivory, Mixing Bowl, No. 3 .... 165.00
Ivory, Mixing Bowl, No. 4, Cover 1400.00
Ivory, Pitcher, Disk 175.00
Ivory, Plate, 6 In. ....6.00 to 7.00
Ivory, Plate, 7 In. 10.00
Ivory, Plate, 10 In. 80.00
Ivory, Plate, Calendar, 1954, 10 In. ....20.00 to 38.00
Ivory, Relish 185.00
Ivory, Saucer 4.00
Ivory, Soup, Onion, Cover ....800.00 to 950.00
Ivory, Tumbler, Juice 40.00
Ivory, Vase, 12 In. 1500.00
Light Green, Bowl, Fruit, 4 3/4 In. 28.00

Light Green, Bowl, Salad, Footed, 11 1/4 In. 475.00
Light Green, Chop Plate, 15 In. ....40.00 to 45.00
Light Green, Chop Plate, Metal Base 65.00
Light Green, Coffeepot, Cover 235.00
Light Green, Cup & Saucer 30.00
Light Green, Jar, Cover, Kitchen Kraft 130.00
Light Green, Mixing Bowl, No. 1 .... 230.00
Light Green, Mixing Bowl, No. 4 .... 195.00
Light Green, Mixing Bowl, No. 5 .... 225.00
Light Green, Mixing Bowl, No. 7 .... 475.00
Light Green, Pitcher, Disk 85.00
Light Green, Plate, 6 In. ....5.00 to 9.00
Light Green, Plate, 7 In. 9.00
Light Green, Plate, 9 In. 18.00
Light Green, Plate, 10 In. ....28.00 to 30.00
Light Green, Platter, Oval, 12 In. 32.00
Light Green, Soup, Onion, Cover ....750.00 to 850.00
Light Green, Teapot, Cover, 6 Cup 225.00
Light Green, Teapot, Cover, 8 Cup 255.00
Light Green, Vase, 8 In. 540.00
Medium Green, Ashtray 260.00
Medium Green, Bowl, Cereal, 5 1/2 In. 65.00
Medium Green, Bowl, Fruit, 4 3/4 In. 425.00
Medium Green, Cake Plate ....625.00 to 1950.00
Medium Green, Chop Plate, 13 In. 650.00
Medium Green, Cup & Saucer ....60.00 to 70.00
Medium Green, Cup, Tea 50.00
Medium Green, Mixing Bowl Cover, No. 2 .... 800.00
Medium Green, Mug 115.00
Medium Green, Plate, 6 In. 35.00
Medium Green, Plate, 7 In. 30.00
Medium Green, Plate, 9 In. 65.00
Medium Green, Plate, 10 In. ....80.00 to 175.00
Medium Green, Platter, Oval, 12 In. ....125.00 to 175.00
Medium Green, Sauceboat ....175.00 to 250.00
Medium Green, Sugar & Creamer 95.00
Medium Green, Teapot, Cover, 6 Cup 400.00
Red, Bowl, Salad, Footed, 11 1/4 In. 650.00
Red, Carafe, Cover ....195.00 to 475.00
Red, Carafe, Ivory Stopper 225.00
Red, Coffeepot 325.00
Red, Coffeepot, After Dinner 725.00
Red, Creamer, Individual 370.00
Red, Creamer, Stick Handle 85.00
Red, Cup & Saucer, After Dinner 95.00
Red, Jar, Marmalade 400.00
Red, Mixing Bowl, No. 1 .... 275.00
Red, Mixing Bowl, No. 3, Cover 1550.00
Red, Mixing Bowl, No. 4 .... 200.00
Red, Pitcher, Disk 750.00
Red, Plate, 9 In. 15.00
Red, Plate, 10 In. ....40.00 to 50.00
Red, Sauceboat ....60.00 to 65.00
Red, Soup, Cream 65.00
Red, Soup, Onion, Cover 835.00
Red, Spoon, Kitchen Kraft 90.00
Red, Syrup, Dripcut ....525.00 to 725.00
Red, Teapot, Cover, 6 Cup 125.00
Red, Tumbler, Juice 30.00
Red, Tumbler, Water 85.00
Red, Vase, 12 In. 805.00
Red, Vase, Bud, 6 1/2 In. 110.00

Rose, Ashtray, Basket Weave 50.00
Rose, Bowl, Fruit, 4 3/4 In. ....25.00 to 40.00
Rose, Casserole, Cover 225.00
Rose, Cup & Saucer 44.00
Rose, Mug 80.00
Rose, Pitcher, Disk 190.00
Rose, Plate, 7 In. 14.00
Rose, Plate, Compartment, 10 1/2 In. 95.00
Rose, Teapot, 6 Cup 275.00
Turquoise, Bowl, Fruit, 4 3/4 In. 20.00
Turquoise, Bowl, Nappy, 5 1/2 In. 25.00
Turquoise, Carafe, Cover 220.00
Turquoise, Casserole, Cover 135.00
Turquoise, Coffeepot 250.00
Turquoise, Cup & Saucer 29.00
Turquoise, Cup & Saucer, After Dinner ....95.00 to 115.00
Turquoise, Mixing Bowl, No. 1 ....240.00 to 385.00
Turquoise, Mixing Bowl, No. 4 ....175.00 to 240.00
Turquoise, Mixing Bowl, No. 6 .... 350.00
Turquoise, Mug 55.00
Turquoise, Nappy, 8 1/2 In. 25.00
Turquoise, Pitcher, Disk 110.00
Turquoise, Pitcher, Ice Lip 195.00
Turquoise, Plate, 6 In. ....5.00 to 8.00
Turquoise, Plate, 7 In. 9.00
Turquoise, Relish Tray 300.00
Turquoise, Salt & Pepper 135.00
Turquoise, Soup, Cream 45.00
Turquoise, Sugar, Cover ....35.00 to 40.00
Turquoise, Syrup, Dripcut 285.00
Turquoise, Teapot, 8 Cup 255.00
Turquoise, Tumbler, Juice 55.00
Turquoise, Tumbler, Water ....50.00 to 85.00
Turquoise, Vase, 8 In. 975.00
Turquoise, Vase, 10 In. 900.00
Yellow, Bowl, Salad, Footed, 11 1/4 In. ....225.00 to 470.00
Yellow, Calendar Plate, 1955, 10 In. 22.00
Yellow, Candleholder, Bulb, Pair 75.00
Yellow, Candleholder, Tripod, Pair ....400.00 to 695.00
Yellow, Casserole, Cover, Individual 140.00
Yellow, Coffeepot ....125.00 to 160.00
Yellow, Cup & Saucer, After Dinner ....55.00 to 95.00
Yellow, Jar, Cover, Kitchen Kraft 25.00
Yellow, Jar, Marmalade ....250.00 to 360.00
Yellow, Mixing Bowl, No. 1 .... 325.00
Yellow, Mixing Bowl, No. 2 ....120.00 to 140.00
Yellow, Mixing Bowl, No. 2, Cover 1275.00
Yellow, Mixing Bowl, No. 3 .... 135.00
Yellow, Mixing Bowl, No. 4 .... 145.00
Yellow, Mixing Bowl, No. 5 .... 185.00
Yellow, Mixing Bowl, No. 7 .... 325.00
Yellow, Mug 45.00
Yellow, Pitcher, Disk ....100.00 to 125.00
Yellow, Pitcher, Juice 40.00
Yellow, Plate, 6 In. 5.00
Yellow, Plate, 9 In. 11.00
Yellow, Plate, 10 In. ....25.00 to 28.00
Yellow, Sauceboat 22.00
Yellow, Soup, Onion, Cover 650.00
Yellow, Teapot, 6 Cup 195.00
Yellow, Tumbler, Juice 40.00
Yellow, Vase, 10 In. ....750.00 to 860.00

FINCH, see Kay Finch category.

FINDLAY ONYX AND FLORADINE are two similar types of glass made by Dalzell, Gilmore and Leighton Co. of Findlay, Ohio, about 1889. Onyx is a patented yellowish white opaque glass with raised silver daisy decorations. A few rare pieces were made of rose, amber, orange, or purple glass. Floradine is made of cranberry-colored glass with an opalescent white raised floral pattern and a satin finish. The same molds were used for both types of glass.

Creamer	650.00
Spoon	350.00
Sugar, Cover	400.00 to 675.00
Sugar Shaker	395.00 to 485.00
Tumbler	185.00
Tumbler, Barrel Shape, Orange	2500.00

FIREFIGHTING equipment of all types is wanted, from fire marks to uniforms to toy fire trucks. It is said that every little boy wanted to be a fireman or a train engineer 75 years ago and the collectors today reflect this interest.

Alarm, Clockwork Motor, Electric Bell, Instruction Plaque, Reset Lever, 13 In.	125.00
Badge, Beatrice, Neb. Volunteer Fire Dept., Metal Shield, 2 In.	20.00
Badge, Delegate, Pennsylvania State Firemen's Convention, Metal, 1914, 4 In.	25.00
Badge, Wyandotte Fire Dept., Eagle At Top, Brass, 2 1/4 In.	55.00
Bucket, Leather, Gilt Inscribed, City Of Boston, Ward No. 11, c.1826, 13 1/4 In.	1495.00
Bucket, Leather, Massachusetts, W. Crook, 1791, Pair	440.00
Bucket, Leather, Powder, Black Leather, Gold Lettering, Leather Handle, 9 1/2 In.	920.00
Bucket, Leather, Red Band Interior, Green Ground, Waltham Fire Club, 1824, 13 In.	460.00
Bucket, Leather, Yellow, Black Ground, B-Stone, Handle, 19th Century, 14 3/4 In.	978.00
Bucket, Protector 17, Painted Leather, 19th Century, 13 3/4 In.	373.00
Cap, Fire Brigade, Essex County, Cloth, Plastic Brim	50.00
Extinguisher, Captain Fire, Nickel Plated, 20 In.	85.00
Extinguisher, Copper, Full Size	40.00
Extinguisher, Liberty, Dry Powder Type, Cylinder, 2 x 22 In.	40.00
Extinguisher, Tube Type, 1899	90.00
Grenade, Autofyrstop, Ball Mount Bracket, Camphored Glass, 1900s	132.00
Grenade, F.L. Fleury Legrand, Amber, Allover Vertical Pattern, Contents, 5 1/2 In.	1100.00
Grenade, Harden's Hand, Deep Cobalt Blue, Contents	75.00
Grenade, Harden's Hand, Light Blue, Contents	130.00
Grenade, Imperial, Barrel, Amber, Canada, 1900, 1/2 Gal., 11 3/8 In.	685.00
Grenade, L'Incomustibilite, Paris, Amber, Circles Around Shoulder, 1895, 5 3/8 In.	355.00
Grenade, S.F. Hayward Broadway N.Y., 4 Panels, Embossed, Lavender, 6 In.	715.00
Grenade, Star Harden Hand, Cobalt Blue, Contents	100.00
Hat, Firefighter's, Windham	245.00
Helmet, Cairns, Model 900P, Yellow Molded Polycarbonate, Salesman's Sample	222.00
Horn, Brass, Silver Plated Inside Of Bell, 20 1/2 In.	247.00
Nozzle, Brass, Red Cord, Chicago, Pair	225.00
Nozzle, Ear Of Horse Drawn Wagons, Brass, Handles, 15 In.	77.00
Overcoat, St. Paul Fire Dept., Blue Wool, Silver Buttons, Lined	23.00
Pail, England's Coat Of Arms, Painted, 9 3/4 In.	168.00
Postcard, Fire Hall View, Cloquet, Minn., 1918	5.00
Sign, Fire Alarm, When Bell Rings Call Fire Dep't., Porcelain, Round, 12 In.	130.00
Sign, Fire Escape, Hand With Pointing Finger, Porcelain, 18 x 4 In.	200.00
Sign, Report Forest Fire To The Warden By Phone, Porcelain, Flange, 12 x 20 In.	160.00
Watch Fob, Fink Brewing, Fireman's Association, Harrisburg, Pa., Metal, 1914	75.00

FIREPLACES were used to cook food and to heat the American home in past centuries. Many types of tools and equipment were used. Andirons held the logs in place, firebacks reflected the heat into the room, and tongs were used to move either fuel or food. Many types of spits and roasting jacks were made and may be listed in the Kitchen category.

Andirons, Acanthus Leaves, Flame Finial, Female Masks, Lion Paw Feet, 23 In.	495.00
Andirons, Ball Top, Hearth Tongs, Early 19th Century, 14 1/2 In.	345.00
Andirons, Bell Metal, Ball Top Finals, Spurred Legs, Ball, Claw Feet, 18 In.	1610.00

Andirons, Bell Metal, Chippendale, Acorn Finial, Iron Log Guard, 1780, 19 1/2 In. 615.00
Andirons, Brass & Iron, Ball Topped, 19th Century, Miniature, 6 In. 1095.00
Andirons, Brass & Iron, Brass Urn Finials, Brass Shield At Bottom, 18 In. 1035.00
Andirons, Brass & Iron, Turned Columns, Iron Feet, Early 19th Century, 20 In. 225.00
Andirons, Brass & Wrought Iron, Knife Blade, Iron Bowed Legs, Footed, 16 In. 115.00
Andirons, Brass & Wrought Iron, Swags Above Square Plinth, Phil., 1785, 26 In. 6325.00
Andirons, Brass, Ball Finial, Octagonal Band, Cabriole Legs, Ball Feet, 23 In. 575.00
Andirons, Brass, Baluster Form, 19th Century, 15 In. 195.00
Andirons, Brass, Baluster Shape, Annulated Ball Finial, Arched Foot, Federal, 18 In. 405.00
Andirons, Brass, Baluster Standard, Sphere, Large Paw Feet, 26 In. 2750.00
Andirons, Brass, Belted Ball Finials, Spurred Legs, Ball Feet, 22 In. 1265.00
Andirons, Brass, Belted Ball Top, Circular Molded Posts, 18 In. 515.00
Andirons, Brass, Belted Ball Top, Turned Baluster Shaft, 15 In. 545.00
Andirons, Brass, Belted Double Lemon Top, Early 19th Century, 20 In. 865.00
Andirons, Brass, Belted Lemon Finial, Tapered Columns, 18 In. 1495.00
Andirons, Brass, Cannon Ball Finial, Arched Foot, 22 1/4 In. 100.00
Andirons, Brass, Chippendale Style, 19th Century, 23 x 20 In. 170.00
Andirons, Brass, Chippendale, Beehive Top, Turned Base, 16 1/2 In. 275.00
Andirons, Brass, Chippendale, Turned, Spurred Legs, 17 In. 245.00
Andirons, Brass, Chippendale, Urn & Flame Finial, Down Curved Legs, 1775, 24 In. 825.00
Andirons, Brass, Coat Of Arms, Lion & Unicorn Supported, 22 1/2 In. 2530.00
Andirons, Brass, Double Urn Top, Early 19th Century, 15 1/2 In. 375.00
Andirons, Brass, Elongated Acorn Finials, Spurred Arched Legs, 18 In. 1725.00
Andirons, Brass, Faceted Plinths, Spurred Legs, Ball Feet, 19th Century, 22 In. 1495.00
Andirons, Brass, Federal, Arched, Spurred Base, Ball Feet, 16 In. 115.00
Andirons, Brass, Federal, Spurred Arched Legs, Ball Feet, 1810, 25 In. 3735.00
Andirons, Brass, Federal, Spurred Arched Legs, Slipper Feet, 1800, 18 x 13 In. 4600.00
Andirons, Brass, Flaming Urn On Plinth, 1840s, 17 In. 1400.00
Andirons, Brass, Fluted Corinthian Columns, Scrolled Supports, 40 3/4 In. 920.00
Andirons, Brass, Fox Head, Mounted To Downswept Supports, 16 1/4 In. 2875.00
Andirons, Brass, George Washington Leaning On Column, 19th Century, 19 In. 110.00
Andirons, Brass, Lemon Log Stops, Hoofed Feet, 19 1/2 In. 1092.00
Andirons, Brass, Lemon Top, 19th Century, 19 1/2 In. 920.00
Andirons, Brass, Lemon Top, Faceted Plinths, Early 1800s, 17 In. 633.00
Andirons, Brass, Louis XVI, Floral Cast Scrolled Base, 15 In. 1265.00
Andirons, Brass, Napoleon III, Baroque Style, Lattice Work Plinth, Urn, 12 1/2 In. 200.00
Andirons, Brass, Owl, Angled Geometric Features, Art Deco, 1930, 15 7/8 In. 115.00
Andirons, Brass, Ring Turned Finials & Sl. . . . . 19 3/4 In. 488.00
Andirons, Brass, Ring Turned Ribbed Supports, Mid 19th Century, 23 In. 220.00
Andirons, Brass, Spurred Legs, Ball Feet, Shovel, Tongs, 17 3/4 In. 517.00
Andirons, Brass, Square Plinths, Spurred Cabriole Legs, Ball, Claw Feet, 26 In. 1955.00
Andirons, Brass, Steel, Baluster Shape, Scrolled Legs, Belle Epoque, 22 1/2 In. 980.00
Andirons, Brass, Stylized Floral Design, Arched Legs, Penny Feet, 1800, 22 In. 2875.00
Andirons, Brass, Tapered Shafts, Spurred Legs, Ball, Claw Feet, 27 In. 4715.00
Andirons, Brass, Turned Baluster Shafts, Stepped Bases, 1795, 14 In. 632.00
Andirons, Brass, Urn Finial, Spread Winged Eagle, Penny Feet, J. Bailey, 26 In. 6325.00
Andirons, Brass, Urn Shape, Triangle Base, Winged Heads, 19th Century, 16 1/2 In. 345.00
Andirons, Brass, Urn Shape, Willow Punchwork, Spurred Legs, 1790, 26 In. 5750.00
Andirons, Bronze, Foliate, Flower Heads, Pierced Scrolls, Louis XV, 12 3/4 In. 259.00
Andirons, Bronze, Pinwheel On Spear Support, Art Deco, France, 1925, 8 In., Pair 860.00
Andirons, Bronze, Putti & Sea Monsters, Italy 10925.00
Andirons, Cast Iron & Brass, Brass Ball Finial, Scrolled Base, 15 In. 46.00
Andirons, Cast Iron & Forged Steel, Cannon Ball Finial, Acorn Drop, 24 1/2 In. 200.00
Andirons, Cast Iron, Baseball Players, Standing, 20th Century, 19 In. 4600.00
Andirons, Cast Iron, Cat, P.S. & W. Co., 17 1/2 In. 1035.00
Andirons, Cast Iron, Duck, Four Seasons Shop 1430.00
Andirons, Cast Iron, Dutch Boy & Girl, Black Paint, 15 3/4 In. 55.00
Andirons, Cast Iron, George Washington, Late 19th Century, 20 In. 355.00
Andirons, Cast Iron, Gooseneck, Polyhedron Finials, 3 Spit Hooks, 20 x 18 1/4 In. 1610.00
Andirons, Cast Iron, Hessian, Mid-Late 19th Century, 20 In. . . . . .275.00 to 316.00
Andirons, Cast Iron, Kitten, Half-Round, Articulated Ears, Painted Eyes, 10 In. 1495.00
Andirons, Cast Iron, Sailing Ship, c.1910, 19 x 22 In. 120.00
Andirons, Cast Iron, Spiral Twist Standard, Scroll Top & Supports, 1870s, 27 In. 4025.00

Andirons, Cast Iron, Tweedledee & Tweedledum, 21 In. 1955.00
Andirons, Engraved, Ball, R. Wittingham, N.Y., Early 1800s, 24 In. 14950.00
Andirons, Figural, Youth Supporting Cavorting Cherub, Pierced Base, 20 1/4 In. 8625.00
Andirons, Gilt Bronze, Owl Form, Perched On Entwined Serpents, 21 x 14 In. 6325.00
Andirons, Gilt Bronze, Triple Acorn Finials, Tapered Feet, 12 x 17 In. 2650.00
Andirons, Parcel Gilt, Ball Finial, Angular Double Scroll, 1940, 20 1/2 In. 545.00
Andirons, Steel, Art Deco, Tall Struts, 6-Sided Medallion, Floral Finial, 20 In. 195.00
Andirons, Wrought Iron & Brass, Acorn Finial, Wirework Screen, 1810, 19 1/2 In. 3735.00
Andirons, Wrought Iron & Brass, Chippendale, Spurred Cabriole Legs, 20 In. 6325.00
Andirons, Wrought Iron & Brass, Knife Blade, Arched Legs, Penny Feet, 25 In. 690.00
Andirons, Wrought Iron & Brass, Spurred Arched Supports, 1810, 25 x 24 In. 4310.00
Andirons, Wrought Iron, Brass Ball Finial, Arched Legs, Penny Feet, 1750, 17 In. 880.00
Andirons, Wrought Iron, Brass Medallions At Base, Penny Feet, 18 In. 385.00
Andirons, Wrought Iron, Gooseneck, E.W. Wade, 19th Century, 17 In. 316.00
Andirons, Wrought Iron, Heart Design Center, Penna., Signed EL, 1795 .... 750.00
Andirons, Wrought Iron, Knife Blade, Brass Trim, Penny Feet, 23 In. 632.00
Andirons, Wrought Iron, Pineapple Top, Knife Blade Shaft, Penny Feet 385.00
Andirons, Wrought Iron, Serpentine, Ram's Head Finials, 13 In. 192.00
Andirons, Wrought Iron, Thistle, Brass Finials, Arts & Crafts, England, 25 In. 80.00
Andirons, Wrought Iron, Tongs, Shovel, 18th Century, 20 In. 715.00
Bellows, Cast Iron, Brass, Adjustable Wheel, Wooden Base, 19th Century, 21 5/8 In. 210.00
Bellows, Leather, Turtle Back, Rosewood Grained, Stencil, Brass Nozzle, 18 3/4 In. 210.00
Bellows, Multicolored Fruit & Flower Design, Mustard Ground, Original Paint 150.00
Bellows, Red Paint, Floral, Torn Leather, Tin Spout, 17 1/2 In. 300.00
Bellows, Turtle Back, Gold Stenciled Floral, Dark Ground, Brass Nozzle, 17 1/4 In. 165.00
Bellows, Turtle Back, Stenciled & Freehand Design, Brass Nozzle, 18 In. 440.00
Bellows, Wood & Leather, Fruit Design, 20 In. 44.00
Box, Tinder, 2-Part Cover Swivels One End, 1810, 2 1/8 x 2 1/2 In. 175.00
Box, Tinder, Strike-A-Light, Sheet Metal 350.00
Broiler, Adjustable Rack, Wrought Iron, Tripod Base, 6 Sets Of Tines, 26 1/2 In. 990.00
Bucket, Peat, Ribbed Body, 2 Brass Bands, Brass Handle, Mahogany, 17 x 14 1/2 In. 4887.00
Coal Bin, Hand Beaten Finish, Copper, c.1890, 20 1/2 In. 495.00
Coal Bin, Mirrored Backboard, Shelf, Hinged Front, Zinc Interior, 36 1/2 In. 230.00
Coal Bin, Pullout Storage Container, Decoupage Painted, 2 Side Handles, Victorian 195.00
Coal Hod, Cherry, Victorian 550.00
Coal Hod, Edwardian, Brass, Serpentine Galleried Top, Rosewood, 32 In. 1495.00
Coal Hod, Mahogany, Pullout Liner, Carved Floral Spray, Hinged Door, 12 1/4 In. 85.00
Coal Hod, Polychrome Floral, Brass Trim, Sheet Metal Insert & Shovel, 16 In. 258.00
Coal Scuttle, Brass, Helmet Shape, Swing & Tip Handles, Late 19th Century, 15 In. 86.00
Coal Scuttle, Scoop, Copper, c.1880, 9 In. 110.00
Coal Scuttle, Swing Handle At Rim, Man With Mandolin, Copper, Brass, 20 1/4 In. 115.00
Coal Scuttle, Toleware, Black, Floral Side Hooks, 11 x 20 x 14 In. 145.00
Coal Scuttle, With Scoop, Scroll, Reeded Design, Paw Feet, Brass, 19 In. 907.00
Crane, Wrought Iron, Twisted Ironwork, 18th Century 495.00
Fender, Brass & Iron Wire, Curved Ends, 3 Bun Feet, 19th Century, 9 x 48 x 9 In. 290.00
Fender, Brass & Iron Wire, Spiral Iron Vertical Wires, 3 Brass Finials, 1830, 12 In. 2875.00
Fender, Brass & Wire, Brass Rim, 4 Ball Feet, Iron Base, 17 x 47 3/4 x 16 In. 920.00
Fender, Brass & Wire, Brass Rim, Diamond Wirework, 12 1/4 x 28 1/2 x 9 In. 230.00
Fender, Brass & Wire, Brass Rim, Vertical Wirework, 3 Ball Feet, 11 3/4 x 36 In. 1495.00
Fender, Brass & Wire, Brass Top Rim, Scroll Design, 17 3/4 x 39 3/4 In. 1495.00
Fender, Brass & Wire, Brass Top Rim, Vertical Wirework, Iron Base, 9 1/2 x 29 In. 1495.00
Fender, Brass & Wire, Ribbed Brass Rim, 2 Ball Feet, 12 1/2 x 35 1/2 x 14 1/4 In. 1035.00
Fender, Brass Pull Heart, Cast Brass, Early 19th Century, 17 In. 150.00
Fender, Brass Rim, Wirework, Scrolls, American, Late 1800s, 10 x 41 x 14 In. 750.00
Fender, Brass, Central Convex Band, Stylized Paw Feet, 19th Century, 44 1/4 In. 290.00
Fender, Brass, Central Urn & Ribbons, 48 1/4 In. 175.00
Fender, Brass, Engraved Decoration, Paw Feet, England, 1790s, 6 x 40 1/2 x 6 In. 259.00
Fender, Brass, George III, Reticulated, 10 1/2 x 42 In. 275.00
Fender, Brass, Pierced Band Of Fruiting, Vine, Convex, Folding, 35 1/4 In. 150.00
Fender, Brass, Pierced Iron, 3 Ball Feet, Early 19th Century, 10 x 32 x 12 In. 460.00
Fender, Brass, Pierced, Convex Bosses, Ribbed Feet, 48 3/4 In. 295.00
Fender, Brass, Pierced, Convex Molding, Urn Form Finials, 39 1/4 In. 515.00
Fender, Brass, Pierced, Demilune, Early 19th Century, 5 3/4 x 33 3/4 x 14 In. 230.00

Fender, Brass, Rail On Swelled Reeded Supports, Stepped Base, 19th Century 182.00
Fender, Brass, Serpentine, Pierced, Beaded Edge, Molded Base, 5 x 36 x 8 1/2 In. 248.00
Fender, Brass, William IV, Pierced Front, Melon Lobed Feet, 10 3/4 x 33 x 14 In. 345.00
Fender, Brass, Wirework, Federal, Serpentine, 1800, 12 x 66 In. 1100.00
Fender, Bronze, Louis XV Style, Bird's Nests, Mother & Baby Birds, 43 x 20 In. 3080.00
Fender, Cast Brass, Rope Turned Design, Pineapple 385.00
Fender, Cast Iron, Brass, Cavetto-Molded Base, Pierced Arabesques, Victorian, 54 In. ... 980.00
Fender, Copper, Hammered, Arts & Crafts, 5 x 4 In. 220.00
Fender, Gilt & Patinated Bronze, Ormolu Medallions, Charles X, 11 x 43 In. 1320.00
Fender, Steel, Wire Grill, Brass Top Rail, 29 x 10 x 12 In. 495.00
Fender, Wire Grill, Brass Top Rail, Iron, 50 1/2 In. 687.00
Fender, Wirework, Serpentine, Brass Rail, Finials, 20th Century, 49 In. 467.00
Fender, Wirework, Serpentine, Brass Rail, Turned Finials, C-Scroll, 53 x 15 In. 1155.00
Fender, Wirework, Serpentine, Brass Rim, Early 1800s, 9 x 35 1/4 x 7 5/8 In. 460.00
Fender Seat, Red Button Tufted, Steel & Brass Supports, Victorian, 83 In. 5750.00
Fireback, Cast Iron, Relief Heraldic Crest, 24 x 21 1/2 In. 110.00
Fireback, Tulip & Heart, Arches, Columns, Gotes Brin Lein Ha, 1764, 28 x 24 In. 300.00
Firedog, Wrought Iron, Penny Feet, Gooseneck Finials, Tooled Detail, 7 In. 715.00
Foot Warmer, Wood, Tin, 5 3/4 x 9 x 7 1/2 In. 130.00
Footman, Brass & Wrought Iron, Wooden Turned Handle, 19th Century 247.00
Frame, American Encaustic Tiling Co. Tile Inserts, Cast Iron 187.00
Front, Cast Iron, Classical Style, Openwork, Crossed Cornucopias, 26 x 21 In. 99.00
Front, Gilt Bronze, Steel, Louis XVI Style, Columns, Latticework, 14 x 24 1/2 In. 1540.00
Grate, Cast Brass, Iron, Shell, Scroll Design, Serpentine Front, Tapered Legs, 24 1/2 In. ... 575.00
Grate, Cast Iron, 15 x 27 x 13 In. 165.00
Holder, Scottish Terrier Top, 3 Tools 85.00
Mantel is listed in the Architectural category.
Meat Spit, Iron, Adjustable, Penny Feet 220.00
Rail, Brass Top, Wire Mesh, 12 x 41 In. 525.00
Rail, Brass, Pierced, Center Panel, Rope Twist Bands, Footed, 10 x 48 x 13 In. 355.00
Rail, Brass, Wire Grid, Scrolls & Scallops, Curved, 41 x 24 In. 660.00
Rail, Brass, Wire, 40 1/2 In. 440.00
Screen, 3-Panel, Floral, Scroll Gilt Crest, Floral Scroll Panels, 68 1/2 In. 2760.00
Screen, 4-Panel, Black Lacquer, Semiprecious Stones, Early 20th Century, 72 In. 1725.00
Screen, 4-Panel, Leather, Carved Crest Centered By Cabochon, Birds, 102 1/4 In. 10450.00
Screen, 4-Panel, Leather, Gilt, Polychrome, Early 18th Century, 84 1/4 x 113 In. 4180.00
Screen, 4-Panel, Putti Depicting 4 Seasons, Gilt, Italy, 55 x 38 In. 3960.00
Screen, 4-Panel, Sultan, His Concubine & Their Attendants, 86 x 27 In. 5462.00
Screen, 4-Panel, Teakwood, Exotic Birds & Flowers, Cream, Silk, 72 x 84 In. 2310.00
Screen, 6-Panel, Ash, Plywood, Canvas Hinges, Charles & Ray Eames, 60 x 68 In. 3300.00
Screen, 6-Panel, Leather, Parcel Gilt, Garden Pavilions Design, 98 3/4 x 38 In. 9350.00
Screen, 8-Panel, Figural Design, Alabaster, 19th Century, 23 x 38 In. 247.00
Screen, Arched Leaf, Tubular Frame, Bail Handle, Gilt Brass, 34 1/4 x 53 In. 110.00
Screen, Brass, Gilt, Mesh Screen, Applied Design, Shaped Leaf Type Frame 385.00
Screen, Cast & Wrought Iron, Allover Vine & Leaf Design, Green Paint, 28 x 31 In. 460.00
Screen, Cherry, Ebonized, Embroidered Panel, Biedermeier, c.1830, 48 x 28 In. 2145.00
Screen, Chippendale, Mahogany, Adjustable, Downswept Legs, Snake Feet, 48 In. 1725.00
Screen, Empire, Mahogany, Gilt, Gabled Crest, Outcurved Legs, 42 3/4 In. 1150.00
Screen, Folding, Wire, Brass Top Rail, C-Scroll & Drape Design, 42 x 24 In. 410.00
Screen, Galle, Fruitwood, Mahogany, Irises, Marquetry, 1900, 33 x 22 In. 2875.00
Screen, Gothic, 5 Panel, Painted Courtly Figure, Wire, 13 1/2 x 27 In. Panel 750.00
Screen, Iron, Chrome Metal, 2 Stylized Parrots Set Within Leafage, France, 82 In. 3162.00
Screen, Leaf Carved Borders, Trellis Work, Gobelins Tapestry Panel, 44 1/4 In. 8050.00
Screen, Louis XV, Faux Marble, Leaf, Scroll Design, 63 x 12 x 47 In. 115.00
Screen, Louis XV, Giltwood, Flanked By Volutes, Cabriole Legs, 41 x 24 In. 546.00
Screen, Louis XVI Style, Scroll & Foliate, Pair Of Doves, Bronze, c.1900, 27 x 29 In. ... 690.00
Screen, Mahogany, 2 Movable Panels, Regency, 22 x 40 In. 550.00
Screen, Mahogany, Carved, Embroidered Panel, Morris & Co., c.1890, 42 x 22 In. 6050.00
Screen, Mahogany, Chippendale, Needlework Panel, Snake Feet, c.1760, 60 In. 3100.00
Screen, Mahogany, Needlepoint, Stylized Shell & Acanthine Crest, c.1820, 43 In. 385.00
Screen, Mahogany, Tapestry Type Center Panel, Turned Stretcher, 31 1/2 x 28 In. 335.00
Screen, Mesh, Riveted Brass Bands, Arts & Crafts, 32 x 48 In. 465.00
Screen, Metal, Floral, Branch Design, Mid 20th Century, 20 In. 1725.00

Screen, Needlework, Silk Crewel Acorns & Oak Leaves, Monogram, 36 x 26 1/2 In. 2420.00
Screen, Painted Leather, California Mission Scene, Iron Base, 35 x 34 In. 990.00
Screen, Pole, Ash, Beadwork & Needlepoint, 1825-1850, 54 In. 550.00
Screen, Pole, Hepplewhite, Mahogany, Tripod Base, Oval Screen, Adjustable, 52 1/2 In. ... 1980.00
Screen, Pole, Mahogany, Leather, Chinese Landscape, Urn Finial, 58 1/4 In. 515.00
Screen, Pole, Paint, Parcel Gilt, c.1830, 60 In., Pair 2760.00
Screen, Pole, Regency, Mahogany, Floral Needlework, Scrolled Feet Platform 135.00
Screen, Pole, Rosewood, Needlepoint Panel, Twist Turned Column, 65 1/2 In. 865.00
Screen, Pole, Tole Flowers, Center Fountain, Bird, Black Background, Cast Iron Base ... 275.00
Screen, Renaissance Figure Partially Clad, Draped With Leopard Skin, 90 In. 1495.00
Screen, Rosette Chamfered Stiles, Silk-On-Silk Needlework, Pictorial, 42 1/2 In. 1840.00
Screen, Rosewood, Beadwork Panel, Birds, Flowers, Victorian, 56 3/4 x 35 In. 990.00
Screen, Scrolled Crest Over Eglomise Panel, Silk Work Court Scene, 41 In. 690.00
Screen, Silk, Mahogany, 4 Downcurved Legs, Brass Casters, 1835, 43 x 22 In. 770.00
Screen, Stick & Ball, Large Claw Feet 660.00
Screen, Tapestry, Girl Feeding Chicken, Fruitwood Surround, Cheval Feet, 42 In. 1150.00
Screen, Tapestry, Napoleon III, Giltwood, Floral Design, Pineapple Finials, 37 1/4 In. ... 345.00
Screen, Tapestry, Young Girl Gathering Flowers, Floral Crest, 38 1/2 x 24 1/2 In. 2415.00
Screen, United Kingdom Map, Embroidered, Silk On Linen, 19th Century, 36 In. 115.00
Screen, Village Folk Scene, Road At Center, Pine, 1985, 37 x 46 In. 450.00
Screen, Walnut, Beaded Panel, Pheasant Amid Foliage, c.1880, 37 In. 460.00
Screen, Walnut, Floral, Scroll Design, Cabriole Legs, Pad Feet, 24 1/2 x 36 In. 345.00
Screen, Wrought Iron, Applied Birds & Dogs On Wire Mesh, Arts & Crafts 385.00
Shovel, Ember, Brass, England, 1680 .... 295.00
Shovel & Tongs, Brass, Wrought Iron, O. Phillips, N.Y., 19th Century, 30 In. 935.00
Skimmer, Iron, Brass, 1812, Pair 1045.00
Striker, Brass, Leather, Iron, Cutout Paktong Design, Asia, 19th Century, 3 1/4 In. 45.00
Striker, Brass, Leather, Iron, Reticulated, 2 Birds, Leaves, Asia, 19th Century, 3 3/4 In. .. 70.00
Surround, Carved Wood, Rectangular Mantel, Beveled Edge, 20th Century, 71 In. 315.00
Surround, Edwardian, Oak, Upper Frieze Center By 3 Concealed Doors, 58 1/2 In. 1650.00
Surround, Flower & Leaf Borders, Egyptian Pharaoh, Arts & Crafts, 30 1/2 In. 230.00
Surround, Incised Ribbon, God Bless Us Everyone, Brass Supports, 34 1/4 In. 275.00
Surround, Rococo, Marble Top, Mesh Center Section, Gilt, Bronze, 40 In. 4312.00
Toaster, Rotating, Penny Feet, 20th Century, 6 1/2 x 9 In. 90.00
Tongs, Pipe, Wrought Iron, 18th Century, 19 1/2 In., Pair 1150.00
Tool Set, Brass, Forged Steel, Shovel, Poker, Tongs, Log Carrier, Stand, 5 Piece 545.00
Tool Set, Brass, Steel, Tongs, Poker, Shovel, Stick Stand, c.1900, 4 Piece 545.00
Tool Set, Brass, Steel, Tongs, Shovel, Brush, Log Hook, Stand, Belle Epoque, 41 In. 1265.00
Tool Supports, Central Floral Motif, Diaperwork Field, 1814, 6 In., Pair 1035.00
Trammel, Chain, Wrought Iron, Adjustable, Min. 10 In. To Max. 37 3/8 In. 110.00
Trammel, Chain, Wrought Iron, Adjustable, Min. 15 In. To Max. 62 In. 125.00

FISCHER porcelain was made in Herend, Hungary, by Moritz Fischer. The factory was founded in 1839 and continued working into the twentieth century. The wares are sometimes referred to as *Herend* porcelain.

MF

Box, Round, Reticulated, Allover Floral Design, 3 1/2 In. 200.00
Dish, Pierced, Butterfly, Gold, 3 3/4 In. 37.00
Figurine, Bear, 3 3/4 In. 140.00
Figurine, Bear, Black & White, 3 1/2 x 3 1/2 In., Pair 345.00
Figurine, Bunny, Black & White, 2 1/4 In. 115.00
Figurine, Cat, Blue & White, 6 In., Pair 920.00
Figurine, Cat, With Ball, Orange & White, 5 1/4 In. 145.00
Figurine, Dog, With Ball, Yellow & White, 3 1/2 In. 115.00
Figurine, Duck, Pair, Green & Multicolored, 15 In. 980.00
Figurine, Elephant, Blue Fish Net, 10 In. 805.00
Figurine, Elephant, Green & White, 4 1/2 In. 260.00
Figurine, Fox, Green & White, 7 In. 345.00
Figurine, Frog, Green & White, 3 In. 86.00
Figurine, Giraffe, Green & White, 8 1/4 In., Pair 920.00
Figurine, Goose, With Golden Egg, Green & Multicolored, 7 1/2 In. 200.00
Figurine, Jaguar, Black & White, 6 1/2 In. 375.00
Figurine, Kangaroo & Baby, Green & White Mother, Orange & White Baby, 6 In. 374.00

Figurine, Mouse, Black & White, 2 1/4 In.	145.00
Figurine, Panther, Blue Fish Net, 16 In.	805.00
Figurine, Peacock, Hand Painted, 6 In.	175.00
Figurine, Rabbit, Green & White, 5 1/4 In., Pair	374.00
Figurine, Rabbit, Orange & White, 4 1/4 In.	200.00
Figurine, Rabbit, Yellow & White, 3 In.	145.00
Figurine, Ram, Blue & White, 4 1/2 In.	175.00
Figurine, Rhinoceros, Black & White, 5 1/8 In.	200.00
Figurine, Rooster, Black & Multicolored, 4 1/2 In.	175.00
Figurine, Sea Otter, Green & White, 7 1/2 In.	430.00
Figurine, Seal, Green, Multicolored, 7 1/2 In.	345.00
Figurine, Unicorn, 1 Reclining, Blue & White, 5 In., Pair	230.00
Figurine, Unicorn, Black & White, 5 In.	200.00
Jardiniere, Swirl Body, Sprays Of Green Flowers, Gilt Undulating Rim, 6 x 8 In.	287.00
Smoking Set, Covered Box, Matchbook Cover, Cigarette Stand, Tray, 4 In., 4 Piece	200.00
Tea & Coffee Set, Rothschild Pattern, 15 Piece	1585.00

FISHING reels of brass or nickel were made in the United States by 1810. Bamboo fly rods were sold by 1860, often marked with the maker's name. Lures made of metal, or metal and wood, were made in the nineteenth century. Plastic lures were made by the 1930s. All fishing material is collected today and even equipment of the past thirty years is of interest if in good condition with original box.

Bag, Hardy Bros. Ltd., Almwick, England, Shoulder Strap, Canvas, 13 x 15 In.	200.00
Bait, South Bend, Vacuum, Box	2420.00
Banner, Wright & McGill, Eagle-Claw Fishhooks, Silk, 18 x 29 In.	70.00
Bottle, Fly Oil, Boardman & Norton Apothecaries, Portsmouth, N.H.	150.00
Bottle, Meek Reel Oil, Horton Mfg. Co., For Fishing Reels & Many Other Used	190.00
Box, Chicago Wobbler, W.J. Jamison Co., Cardboard, 2 Piece	770.00
Box, Display, Shurkatch Baits, Sure Catch Fish, Cardboard, 11 x 16 In.	405.00
Box, Famous Pikie Minnow, Creek Chub Bait Co., 11 x 6 x 2 1/2 In.	355.00
Box, Fly, Cedar Drawers, Locking Fold Down Front, Contents, 17 x 20 x 19 In.	395.00
Box, Fly, Mahogany, Pine, 8 x 17 1/2 x 7 1/2 In.	355.00
Box, Hardy Neroda Fly, 140 Flies, Pipe Cleaner Clips, 4 x 6 In.	120.00 to 165.00
Box, Heddon's Dowagiac Surface Minnow, White, No. 302, Wooden, Sliding Lid	385.00
Box, Heddon, No. 5000 Tad Polly, Cardboard	440.00
Box, Michigan Life-Like Minnow	*Illus* 2860.00
Box, Pflueger's Monarch Minnow, Sliding Lid, Wooden, 2 3/4 In.	465.00
Box, Rod, Plywood, Belt & Latch Cover, 4 3/4 x 5 3/4 x 46 In.	27.00
Box, Tackle, Mahogany, Fitted Canvas Cover, 7 1/2 x 21 x 9 In.	795.00
Box, Tackle, Metal, Green Finish, Divided Lift-Out Tray, Contents, 6 x 20 x 6 In.	130.00
Bucket, Minnow, Falls City Air-Breather, Green Paint, Lift-Out Composition Insert	50.00
Bucket, Minnow, Galvanized, Torpedo Shape, Sliding Lid, Green Paint, 5 x 28 In.	143.00
Bucket, Minnow, Paragon Floating, Tin, Green Paint, Lift-Out Interior, Oval	550.00
Canoe Seat, Wicker, Folding, Strap Back, Compartment Under Seat, 17 x 26 In.	165.00 to 185.00
Catalog, Creek Chub, 1940, 35 Pages	165.00
Catalog, Heddon Deluxe, 1954, 76 Pages	120.00

Fishing, Box, Michigan Life-Like Minnow

Fishing, Creel, Woven Reed,
Canoe, Maine Indian

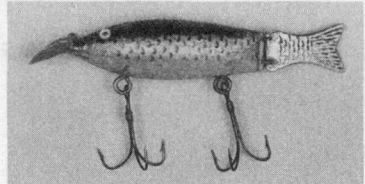

Fishing, Lure, C.W. Lane, Musky Wonder
Wagtail Wobbler, 1920, 5 1/4 In.

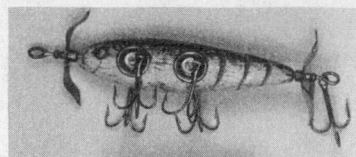

Fishing, Lure, Minnow, Michigan Life-Like

Catalog, Heddon, 1938, 40 Pages 330.00
Catalog, Heddon, 1939, 43 Pages 220.00
Catalog, Heddon, 1962, 63 Pages 75.00
Catalog, Pflueger, 1926, 116 Pages 115.00
Catalog, Shakespeare, 1925, 39 Pages 220.00
Chest, Fly, Mahogany, 7 Drawers, 15 x 20 x 11 In. 385.00
Chest, Tackle, Teakwood, Brass Hardware, Folding Leather Handle, 9 1/2 x 21 x 9 In. 165.00
Creel, Birchbark, Dyed Lashing, Leather Strap, Indian, Oval, 11 x 13 In. 2750.00
Creel, Birchbark, Shoelace Sewn, Front Picture, Leather Straps, 5 x 10 In. 1100.00
Creel, Harness, Horsehide, Brass Hardware, Unused 95.00
Creel, Jos. Schnell, Portland, Ore., Split Willow, Tooled Leather Trim, 7 1/2 x 13 In. 770.00
Creel, Mahogany, Barrel Shape, Brass Bound, Salmon On Plaque, 12 1/2 x 11 In. 990.00
Creel, Porcelain, Cover, Embleton Arms, A & S, Stoke-On-Trent, Arcadian, 2 x 3 In. 55.00
Creel, Split Willow, Leather Pocket, 8 x 12 In. 330.00
Creel, Whole Willow, Hole In Lid, 9 x 14 In. 135.00
Creel, Wicker, Leather Strap, Metal Fished-Shaped Lid Latch, Net, Small 130.00
Creel, Wicker, Worn Leather Fittings & Strap, Some Accessories, 13 In. 55.00
Creel, Willow, Belt & Buckle Lid Latch, 10 x 15 x 12 In. 110.00
Creel, Woven Reed, Canoe, Maine Indian . . . .*Illus* 2750.00
Creel, Woven Twig, Football Shape, 15 x 13 In. 190.00
Creel, Woven, Designed To Be Worn At Waist, 1920s, 13 x 8 In. 30.00
Dryer, Line, Collapsible Umbrella-Style Wooden Arms, Box 50.00
Float, Montague Automatic, Black & White, Decal, Box 100.00
Float, Net, Aqua Glass, Japan, 3 1/2 In. 13.00
Float Balls, Fishnet, Green Glass, Rope Mesh, Hand Blown, 12 In. 90.00
Fly, Box, Brass, Hammered Floral Top, 18th Century, 5 1/2 x 1 3/4 In. 300.00
Fly, Hardy Dry, DT-6, Blued Finish, 3 3/8 In. 245.00
Gaff, Brass, Collapsible, Ribbed Walnut Handle, Butt Cap, 13 To 24 In. 93.00
Gaff, Brass, Collapsible, Walnut Handle, Folding Hook Guard, 13 To 36 In. 70.00
Hair Mouse, Striped, Black Bead Eyes, Leather Ears, Rubber Tail 65.00
Lure, Bar Perch, Heddon, Spin Diver, L-Rig Hardware, Glass Eyes 825.00
Lure, Bud Stewart, Crippled Mouse, White Finish, Yellow & Black Dots, 3 In. 110.00
Lure, C.W. Lane, Musky Wonder Wagtail Wobbler, 1920, 5 1/4 In. . . . .*Illus* 3025.00
Lure, Creek Chub Deluxe, Wagtail Chub, Goldfish, Glass Eyes, Double-Line Tie 115.00
Lure, Creek Chub, Black Sucker, Glass Eyes, Corrugated Diving Lip, 4 1/4 In. 355.00
Lure, Creek Chub, Surface Dingbat, Black, Yellow Dots 300.00
Lure, Creek Club Bait Co., Wooden, Yellow, Green, 2 Hooks, 2 1/4 In. 24.00
Lure, Creek Club, Wiggler, No. 100, Gold Finish, Glass Eyes, Double Line Tie 440.00
Lure, Heddon, Black Sucker Minnow, No. 1300, Glass Eyes, 5 3/4 In. 3300.00
Lure, Heddon, Crab Wiggler, No. 1800, L-Rig Hardware, Glass Eyes 300.00
Lure, Heddon, Crazy Crawler, Yellow, Red, Aluminum Wings, 2 Hooks, Box, 2 1/2 In. . . . 355.00
Lure, Heddon, Dowagiac Minnow, No. 20, Cup-Rigged Hardware, Glass Eyes 165.00
Lure, Heddon, Vamp, No. 7500, Glass Eyes, Pike Scale Finish, Box 110.00
Lure, Lane's Automatic, Minnow, Metal Fins, 1913, 3 1/4 In. 1375.00
Lure, Louis Rhead, Minnow, Wooden, Line & Tinsel, 2 1/2 In. 100.00
Lure, Minnow, Manco, With Jersey Rig, S.H. Friend, Ohio, 1903 . . . . 3100.00
Lure, Minnow, Michigan Life-Like . . . .*Illus* 415.00
Lure, Minnow, White, Red Stripe, Glass Eyes, German Silver Props, 1910 . . . . 220.00
Lure, Mouse, Folk Art, Gray Finish, Red Tin Ears, 3 In. 145.00
Lure, Pepper, Minnow, Underwater, 5 Hooks, Painted Gill Marks, 1905 . . . . 55.00

Fishing, Reel, Edward Vom Hofe,
Trout, Perfection, No 1, German
Silver, Hard Rubber

Fishing, Reel, Geo. W. Gayle &
Son, Frankfort, Ky., No. 4,
German Silver, Bait Casting

Fishing, Reel, Hardy Bros., Ltd.,
Salmon, Cascapedia

Lure, Pflueger, Never Fail Minnow, Chub Scale Finish, Glass Eyes, 3 Hooks 190.00
Lure, Pflueger, Pippin Wobbler, 1 1/4 In., Pair 35.00
Lure, Springfield Novelty Co., Revolving, Box, 2 In. 247.00
Lure, Weller Classic, 2-Piece Body, Glass Eyes, 4 In. 27.00
Lure, William Crutchfield, Crutch's Lizard, White Bead Eyes, Box, 5 In. 70.00
Lure, Winchester, Underwater Minnow, Cup Rigged Bait, 3 Hooks 410.00
Minnow Trap, C.F. Orvis, Manchester, Vt., Glass, Wire Harness 160.00
Minnow Trap, Camp, Checotah, Okla, Pat. Pend., Aqua Glass, 3 Funnels 110.00
Minnow Trap, Glass, Green, Wire Handle Forms Feet, Funnel Opening, Screw Lid 165.00
Minnow Trap, Glass, Metal Bands, Handle Top, Swinging Cap Opening 105.00
Net, Folding, Aluminum, Triangular, Collapsible 19-In. Handle, Belt Clip 50.00
Net, Folding, Hardy Bros., England, Wooden Arms, Cane Handle, 30 In. 200.00
Net, Wooden & Cork, Float In 5 Ft. String 20.00
Plaque, Fish, Hardened Rubber, Wooden, 1900, Oval, 11 x 28 In. 70.00
Reel, Anson, Hatch, Side Mount, Horsehair Line, 1866, 3 7/8 In. 6600.00
Reel, B.C. Milam & Son, Frankfort, Ky., Bait Casting, German Silver, No. 3, 2 In. 1430.00
Reel, B.F. Meek & Sons, Trout Fly, Model No. 44, German Silver, 1900 .... 4510.00
Reel, Billinghurst, Fly, Birdcage, Fixed Handle, 1859 Patent, 3 In. 2750.00
Reel, Bogdan Nashua, N.H., Size No. O, Handmade, 3 1/4 In. 1430.00
Reel, Brass-Clamp Type, 40 Yard 110.00
Reel, Catino, Fresh Or Saltwater Fly, Florida, 3 1/2 In. 300.00
Reel, Clark, Horrocks & Co., Birdcage, Side Mount, Brass, Folding Handle, 1902, 3 In. .. 825.00
Reel, Clinton, Fly, Nickel Silver, Side Mount, 2 5/8 In. 6820.00
Reel, Edward Vom Hofe, Model 621, 6/0 Size, German Silver, Rubber, 4 1/4 In. 220.00
Reel, Edward Vom Hofe, Peerless No. 2, Trout, Pat. Jan. 23, 83, 2 3/4 In. 2475.00
Reel, Edward Vom Hofe, Peerless No. 3, Trout, 2 1/2 x 3/4 In. 3300.00
Reel, Edward Vom Hofe, Peerless, Model 7M, Gold & Black Finish, Left-Hand Wind 715.00
Reel, Edward Vom Hofe, Perfection Model, Size 1, Jan. 23, '83, Silver, Rubber 8525.00
Reel, Edward Vom Hofe, Salmon, German Silver, 1902 Patent, Size 2/0 .... 1925.00
Reel, Edward Vom Hofe, Trout, Nickel Silver, Crank Handle, 1870 .... 7810.00
Reel, Edward Vom Hofe, Trout, Perfection, No 1, German Silver, Hard Rubber .....*Illus* 8525.00
Reel, Geo. W. Gayle & Son, Frankfort, Ky., No. 4, German Silver, Bait Casting .....*Illus* 4400.00
Reel, Hardy Bros., Ltd., Salmon, Cascapedia ....*Illus* 7920.00
Reel, Hardy Bros., Ltd., Featherweight Silent Check, 2 Spare Spools 220.00
Reel, Hardy Golden Princess, Case & Paper, Box 160.00
Reel, Haywood, Trout, Brass, Crank Handle, 1845, 1 5/8 In. 455.00
Reel, Heddon Imperial, 125 Fly, Hinged Display Box 210.00
Reel, J.W. Young & Sons, Redditch, England, Unused, Box, 3 1/2 In. 100.00
Reel, Julius Vom Hofe, Trout, Click Switch, Size 4, 2 1/8 In. 220.00
Reel, Lionel Corp., Spinning, Chrome Metal, 2 3/8 In. 32.00
Reel, Malloch's Patent, Brass, Fixed Spool, Click Type, 4 In. 190.00
Reel, Mitchell 300, Third Model, Spinning, France 55.00
Reel, Montague City Rod Co., Amherst, Mass., Pat'd. Nov. 19, 1899, Combo Handle 1100.00
Reel, Morgan James, Pillbox Style, Side Mount, Brass, 1860, 2 5/8 In. 9350.00
Reel, Pflueger, Akron No. 1893L, Polished Metal, 2 Green Reel Knobs, 2 In. 40.00
Reel, Pflueger, Summit No. 1993L, Polished Metal, 2 Yellow Knobs, 2 In. 45.00

Reel, Seamaster Model, Handmade, Anti-Reverse, 3 1/2 In. 740.00
Reel, Sellers, Fly, Chrome Plate, Side Mount, Bas-Kit, Fixed Handle, 1935, 3 3/4 In. 990.00
Reel, Thos. J. Conroy, Trout, Aluminum, German Silver Handle, 1889, 3 1/4 In. 3300.00
Reel, Trout, Brass, Spike Mount, Crank Handle, Original Wing Nut, 2 In. 410.00
Reel, Wm. Shakespeare Jr., Nickel, Ivory-Colored Reel Knob, 2 In. 40.00
Rod, B.F. Nichol, Boston, Mass., 5 Tips, 1880s, 10 1/2 Ft. 355.00
Rod, Edward Vom Hofe, N.Y., Big Game, Wooden, 6 Ft. 9 In. 165.00
Rod, Fly, Orvis, Battenkill, 2 Tips, Aluminum Screw, 9 Ft. 275.00
Rod, Fly, Orvis, Shooting Star, 2 Tips, Aluminum Screw, 9 Ft. 330.00
Rod, Garrison 212, 2 Tips, 2 Piece, Bag & Tube, 8 Ft. 4180.00
Rod, Gillum, Detachable Conical Aluminum Extension Butt, 9 Ft. 3 In. 555.00
Rod, Hardy, Palakona, 1 Tip, Slide Band Over Cork Seat, Canvas Case & Tube, 7 Ft. 440.00
Rod, J.S. Sharpe, Ltd., Aberdeen, 2 Tips, Canvas Case & Tube, 7 Ft. 355.00
Rod, Leonard, 2-Handed, 3 Tips, Case, Aluminum Tip Tube, 12 Ft. 330.00
Rod, Leonard, Model 361 Baby Catskill, 15/16 Ounce, 6 Ft. 3025.00
Rod, Mills Standard, 2 Tips, 9 Ft. 440.00
Rod, Orvis, Midge, 2 Tips, 7 1/2 Ft. 495.00
Rod, Parker-Hawes, Meriden-Canterbury, Conn., 9 Ft. 990.00
Rod, Poachers, Hollow Walking Stick, Allover Carved Floral & Leaves, 10 Ft. 495.00
Rod, Salmon, Payne, Locking Seat, 9 1/2 Ft. 220.00
Rod, Spinning, Leonard, Fiberglass, Bag & Aluminum Tube, 7 Ft. 135.00
Rod, Spinning, Orvis Superlight, 1 Tip, Reel Seat, 2 Piece, 6 Ft. 355.00
Rod, Thomas & Thomas, Fountainhead, 2 Tips, 3 Piece, 1983, 7 1/2 Ft. 3300.00
Rod, Trout, Cortland 444 Ltd., 1 Tip, Cork Reel Seat, 2 Piece, 6 1/2 Ft. 190.00
Rod, Trout, Dickerson, 2 Tips, Walnut Spacer Reel Seat, 2 Piece, 8 Ft. 4180.00
Rod, Trout, Edwards Deluxe, Jim Payne Type Reel Seat, 8 Ft. 385.00
Rod, Trout, G.H. Howells, Seat, 2 Piece, 8 Ft. 2200.00
Rod, Trout, Leonard, 2 Tips, 3 Piece, Bag & Newer Tube, 1920s, 8 Ft. 770.00
Rod, Trout, Orvis, Model 99, 1 Tip, Atwood Seat, 2 Piece, 7 Ft. 495.00
Rod, Trout, Payne, 2 Tips, 3 Piece, Bag & Tube, 8 1/2 Ft. 880.00
Sign, Agents For The H.L. Leonard Rod Co., Shield Shape, Wooden, 14 x 20 In. 520.00
Sign, Horrocks-Ibbotson, Utica, N.Y., Makers, Fine Fishing Tackle, Frame, 16 x 22 In. 165.00
Spear, Eel, 5 Prongs 420.00
Trophy, Silver Atlantic Hen Salmon, Carved & Painted, Half Round, Plaque, 45 In. 1925.00

FLAGS are included in the Textile category.

FLASH GORDON appeared in the Sunday comics in 1934. The daily strip started in 1940. The hero was also in comic books from 1930 to 1970, in books from 1936, in movies from 1938, on the radio in the 1930s and 1940s, and on television from 1953 to 1954. All sorts of memorabilia are collected, but the ray guns and rocket ships are the most popular.

Colorform Set, 1980 .... 25.00
Comic Strip, Alex Raymond, 1937, 16 x 20 In. 10670.00
Poster, Flash Gordon's Trip To Mars, Buster Crabbe, 1938, One Sheet 260.00
Radio Gun, Repeater 450.00
Ray Gun 500.00
Record, 1949 .... 65.00
Rocket Fighter, Tin Lithograph, Windup, Marx 230.00
Space Compass, On Card, 1940s, 8 x 2 3/4 In. ....110.00 to 125.00
Space Gun, Max 495.00

FLORENCE CERAMICS were made in Pasadena, California, from World War II to 1977. Florence Ward created many colorful figurines, boxes, candleholders, and other items for the gift shop trade. Each piece was marked with an ink stamp that included the name *Florence Ceramics Co.* The company was sold in 1964, and although the name remained the same the products were very different. Mugs, cups, and trays were made.

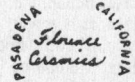

Figurine, Annabel, Pink, 8 In. 400.00
Figurine, Camille, 8 1/2 In. 200.00
Figurine, Chinese Boy & Girl, Green, 7 3/4 In., Pair 85.00
Figurine, Delia, 7 1/4 In. 175.00

Figurine, Eugenia, 9 In. . . . . .340.00 to 395.00
Figurine, Laura, Blue, 7 1/2 In. 65.00
Figurine, Marie Antoinette, 10 In. 280.00
Figurine, Melanie, Gray & Maroon, 7 1/2 In. 110.00
Figurine, Wood Nymph, Pink Dress 395.00

FLOW BLUE was made in England and other countries about 1830 to
1900. The dishes were printed with designs using a cobalt blue coloring. The color flowed from the design to the white body so that the finished piece has a smeared blue design. The dishes were usually made
of ironstone china.

Biscuit Jar, Flowers & Grain, Brass Collar, Bail Handle, 6 x 5 1/2 In. 336.00
Bowl, Cover, Scinde, Alcock, c.1840, 10 In. 995.00
Bowl, Floral, Upper Manley Pottery, 10 In. 75.00
Bowl, La Belle, Helmet, 4 x 8 x 6 In. 225.00
Bowl, Lorne, W.H. Grindley, 5 In. 22.00
Bowl, Melbourne, W.H. Grindley, 5 In. 50.00
Bowl, Oriental Woman, Holding Rose, Scalloped, J.P.F., Germany, 10 1/2 In. 75.00
Bowl, Osborne, Flanged, 9 In. 65.00
Bowl, Shanghae, Furnival, 9 In. 200.00
Bowl, Vegetable, Cover, Renown, Arthur Wilkinson 240.00
Bowl, Whompoa, Mellor & Venables, 13 1/2 In. 305.00
Butter Chip, Argyle, W.H. Grindley, 1896 . . . . 56.00
Butter Chip, Dresden, Burgess & Leigh, 1896 . . . . 23.00
Butter Pat, Montana, Johnson Bros., 10 Piece 99.00
Chamber Pot, Flosstine 195.00
Chamber Pot, Garland 195.00
Chamber Pot, Lily 195.00
Chamber Set, Carro, Grimwades, Stoke-On-Trent, 4 Piece 415.00
Coffeepot, Abbey, George Jones & Sons, c.1900, 6 1/4 In. 145.00
Compote, Holland, Johnson Bros. 350.00
Creamer, Kyber, Paneled, 5 1/2 In. 70.00
Creamer & Sugar, La Belle, Wheeling Pottery 450.00
Cup & Saucer, La Belle, Wheeling Pottery 195.00
Cup & Saucer, Mongolia 60.00
Cup & Saucer, Oriental, Hilditch & Son, 1822-1830 . . . . 80.00
Dish, Martha, Bridgett & Bates, 8 Piece 121.00
Dish, Sobraon, Reticulated, Footed, 13 1/2 x 10 1/4 x 4 In. 1200.00
Gravy Boat, Argyle, W.H. Grindley, c.1890, 4 x 7 3/4 In. 70.00
Gravy Boat, Manhattan, Liner, Alcock 55.00
Pitcher, Flowers In Relief, Gold Accents, 6 1/4 In. 146.00
Pitcher, Milk, Amoy, 7 1/2 In. 270.00
Pitcher, Water, York, C-Scrolls, Floral, 13 1/2 In. 75.00
Pitcher & Bowl, Campion, W.H. Grindley 1300.00
Pitcher & Bowl, Floral 280.00
Plate, Amoy, 9 In. . . . . .95.00 to 115.00
Plate, Argyle, W.H. Grindley, 10 In. 100.00
Plate, Asiatic Pheasants, 7 7/8 In., 12 Piece 247.00
Plate, Chusan, Clementson, 8 In. 185.00
Plate, Detroit, Campus Martius, Floral Border, 9 3/4 In. 110.00
Plate, Flower Center, 9 1/2 In. 35.00
Plate, Hong Kong, 10 In. 195.00
Plate, Indian Tree, 8 In. 40.00
Plate, Indian, F.&R. Pratt, 9 1/2 In. 150.00
Plate, Landscape, Avonware, 9 1/4 In. 20.00
Plate, Manilla, Podmore, Walker, 9 1/2 In. 185.00
Plate, Melbourne, W.H. Grindley, 8 In. 65.00
Plate, Pelew, Chandler, 9 14 In. 185.00
Plate, Temple, 8 In. 125.00
Plate, Tower, Turret, Waterfall, Fountain, Picnickers, 9 1/2 In., Pair 90.00
Platter, Albany, W.H. Grindley, 16 x 11 3/4 In. 185.00
Platter, Flower Border, W.H. Grindley, 16 x 11 1/2 In. 121.00
Platter, Indian Jar, Jacob & Thom. Furnival, 10 3/4 x 13 3/4 In. 255.00

Platter, Leicester, Hancock, Sampson, 14 3/4 In. 275.00
Platter, Lorne, W.H. Grindley, 13 x 18 In. 195.00
Platter, Oregon, T.J. & J. Mayer, 15 1/2 x 12 In. 400.00
Platter, Oriental, Center Pagoda, Floral Border, Scalloped, Oval, 17 1/4 In. 220.00
Platter, Oxford, Meakin, 18 1/2 x 13 In. 225.00
Platter, Palace Of St. Cloud, R. Hall, 17 x 13 1/4 In. 420.00
Platter, Persian, Johnson Brothers, 10 3/4 x 14 1/2 In. 157.00
Platter, Scinde, 13 In. 275.00
Platter, Scinde, Alcock, c.1839, 14 x 18 1/2 In. 1200.00
Platter, Tonquin, Rectangular, J. Heath, 13 3/4 x 10 1/4 In. 170.00
Relish, Trent, Scalloped, New Wharf, 10 1/2 x 7 3/4 In. 65.00
Sauce, Scinde, Light Blue 150.00
Shaving Mug, Gilt, Warwick, 3 1/2 In. 70.00
Soup, Dish, Asiatic, Pheasants, 8 5/8 In., 12 Piece 175.00
Soup, Dish, Conway, New Wharf ....110.00 to 125.00
Soup, Dish, Formosa, 10 In. 195.00
Soup, Dish, Watteau 120.00
Sugar, Cover, Fallow Deer, John Rodgers, 3 3/4 In. 95.00
Sugar & Creamer, Nonpareil, Burgess & Leigh 360.00
Tea Set, Child's, Stroke Pattern, 3 Piece 465.00
Tureen, Cover, Pekin, Pedestal, Leaf & Twig Handles, Thomas Dimmock, 9 In. 245.00
Tureen, Saucer, Kiota, Matching Ladle, 5 x 7 1/2 In. 225.00
Vase, Dutch Farm, Windmill, Ship, Beaker, George Jones & Sons, c.1890, 7 1/2 In. 138.00
Vase, Ship & Lighthouse, H.G. Harley Jones, 8 In. 125.00
Waste Jar, Campion, W.H. Grindley 500.00

FLYING PHOENIX, see Phoenix Bird category.

FOLK ART is also listed in many categories of this book under the actual
name of the object. See categories such as Box, Cigar Store Figure,
Paper, Weather Vane, Wooden, etc.

Aardvark, Beige, Red Tack Eyes, Pangoe Zoratti, 1986, 4 x 15 1/2 In. 165.00
Angel, Pine, Black Hair, Wooden Peg Feet, Arms, 19th Century, 12 1/2 In. 420.00
Ark, 30 Animals, Hand Carved, c.1880 .... 3250.00
Ashtray, Cigar Bands, Center Girl On Bike, 5 3/8 In. 120.00
Banner, Little Lulu, Fat Girl, Sideshow, Canvas, 4 x 6 Ft. 650.00
Banner, Pig Boy, Sideshow, Canvas, 4 x 6 Ft. 675.00
Birdhouse, 2-Story, Wooden, Overhanging Roof, On Tall Legs 395.00
Block, Chopping, Ax Head Carved From Block, Handle, Adirondack, 1931, 7 1/2 In. 75.00
Bottle, Battle Scene Inside, Figure, Wooden, Carved Stopper, 11 In. ....*Illus* 395.00
Box, Ballot, Bird's-Eye Maple, Inlaid, 1 Drawer, Brass Crest Handle, 5 1/2 x 11 3/4 In. .. 355.00
Bust, Thomas Jefferson, Carved Stone, Otis Shinn, West Virginia, 1932, 33 1/2 x 24 In. .. 605.00
Cage, Squirrel, Riverboat, 3 Tiers, 2 Smoke Stacks, Tin, Painted, 20 1/2 x 28 1/2 x 15 In. . 6900.00
Cannon, Mounted On Weighted Wooden Box, Cast Iron, 19th Century, 12 In. 230.00
Carriage, Black, Red, Mustard, Carved Wood, Metal, 1900, 7 x 10 In. 125.00
Carriage, Horse & Black Man, Driver With White Gloves, Wooden, 1900, 9 x 20 In. 450.00

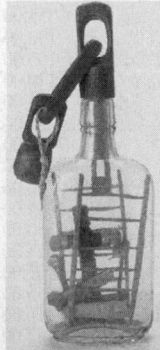

Folk Art, Bottle,
Battle Scene
Inside, Figure,
Wooden, Carved
Stopper, 11 In.

**Beware of fire. Never put a heavy
object on top of an electric cord.
Never put the cord under a rug.**

Folk Art, Retablo, Infant
Jesus, Road Scene, Tin,
Marked, 1936, 9 x 6 3/4 In.

Folk Art, Retablo, Virgin
Mary, Bandit Killing Man, Tin,
1940, 10 1/2 x 8 3/4 In.

Chair, Folding, Forked Tree Branch, Engraved, Liberty Indiana, March, 1892, 30 In. 13750.00
Conch Shell, Cameo Carved Busts, E Pluribus Unum, Garland, 1885, 8 1/2 In. 990.00
Cradle, Made From Gold Dust Crate, Wooden 115.00
Cross, Carved, Castle Turret Enclosure, Hanging Ball, Painted, 19th Century, 14 In. 55.00
Cup, Engraved Horn, Proposal, Toasting & Wedding Scene, 5 1/2 In. 320.00
Cup, Horn, Queen Anne, Inscribed WB 1704, 4 3/4 In. 325.00
Curtain Screen, Beads, Valance Over 2 Side Panels, Floor Type 2950.00
Deer Head, Wooden, With Real Antlers, Late 19th Century 1430.00
Diorama, Sailing Ship, Oak Shadowbox 595.00
Dog, Pink, Zoratti, 9 1/4 x 4 In. 55.00
Dog, Terrier, Pine, Mid 19th Century, 10 x 15 In. 467.00
Eagle, Spread Wings, Wooden, Gold & Red Paint Traces, 1860, 12 x 6 In. 385.00
Fruit, Pear, Peach, Pear, Twig Stems, Stone, 4 1/2 To 6 In., 3 Piece 850.00
Fruit, Stone, 8 Piece 595.00
Fruit, Stone, Box, 25 Piece 600.00
Gorilla, Wood Carving, Lorises Bashful, Signed, S.P. Zoratti, 1969, 9 1/2 x 5 In. 176.00
Happy Jack, Painted, Early 20th Century, 13 In. 688.00
Head, Bearded Man With Cap, Burl Wood, Painted, 21 In. 550.00
Head, Man's, Carved From Tree Trunk, 36 In. 192.00
Hummingbird, On Stump, Tack Eyes, Green, White, Red Body, Wood, Zoratti, 3 1/2 In. . . 66.00
Indian Head, Carved, Sandstone, Signed E. Reed, 9 1/2 In. 525.00
Jiggs, Wooden, Cutout, On Stand, 22 In. 50.00
Kangaroo, Joey In Pouch, Tack Eyes, Gray & White Paint, Zoratti, 13 x 7 3/4 In. 143.00
Ladle, Horn, Shaped Deer Head, Antlers, 13 In. 140.00
Man, Nude, Standing, Articulated Limbs Rotating On Steel Rollers, Pine, 20 In. 1265.00
Man On Turtle, Black Painted Suit, Yellow Shoes, Red & Black Turtle, 23 1/2 In. 1320.00
Model, Double-Decker Bus, Scroll Sawn, Lanterns, Glass Case, 1920, 11 x 20 In. 935.00
Model, Touring Car, Convertible, Scroll Sawn, Glass Case, 1920, 6 1/2 x 15 In. 275.00
Model Barn & Barnyard, Wooden, Separated Stalls, 2 Oxen, 39 x 19 1/2 x 15 1/2 In. 495.00
Monkey, Tack Eyes, Painted Pink, Zoratti, 8 1/4 x 3 1/2 In. 55.00
Penwipe, Hand Shape, Attached Felt 1750.00
Picture, 200 Cigar Labels, Walnut Frame, Victorian, 26 x 32 In. 355.00
Plaque, 2 Carved Deer Heads, Twig Antler, Pinecone, 13 1/2 In. 190.00
Plaque, Log Cabin, Birch Bark, Twigs, Moss, 12 In. 165.00
Rack, Doves Top, Cutout Design, 2 Drawers, Pigeonholes, Pine, 33 x 35 In. 170.00
Retablo, Infant Jesus, Road Scene, Tin, Marked, 1936, 9 x 6 3/4 In. . . . .*Illus* 75.00
Retablo, Virgin Mary, Bandit Killing Man, Tin, 1940, 10 1/2 x 8 3/4 In. . . . .*Illus* 85.00
Rooster, Carved & Painted, Stippled, Pine, Wilhelm Schimmel, 8 In. 7150.00
Rooster, Carved, Painted, Base 4885.00
Rooster, Raised On Black Metal Base, Red Paint, Pine, 18 1/2 x 18 In. 9200.00
Rooster, Red, Yellow, Orange & Black Paint, Late 19th Century, 5 In. 1045.00
Shelf, Candlestick, 2 Heart Cutouts, Pine, Walnut, 1800, 30 In. 1350.00
Shelf, Hanging, Mirror, Layered Green & Cream Paint, Acorn Caps, 23 x 16 In. 675.00
Shell, Carved, Deeply Engraved, Our Father, 19th Century, 3 1/2 In. 101.00
Shrine, Carved, Madonna & Christ Child, Flowers, Leaf Frame, Mexico, 31 x 24 In. 1035.00
Sideboard, Incised Flowerpots, Mirror, 1 Drawer, 2 Doors, Sam Blesse, 1897, Miniature . 110.00
Squirrel, Silvio Zoratti, Tack Eyes, Inscribed Jerboa, 1969, 9 3/4 x 9 1/2 In. 187.00

Squirrel, Standing, Incised Fur, Raised On Tree Bark Base, 1930, 6 In.	805.00
Squirrel Cage, Tin, Painted, Peaked Building, Chimney, Wire Wheel, 23 x 27 x 12 In. . . .	518.00
Stag, Reclining, Incised Fur, Large Antlers, Seated On Rectangular Base, 17 In.	4310.00
Table, Chip Carved, 3 Tops, Black Forest, 1900, 30 x 20 x 20 In.	895.00
Uncle Sam, 2-Board, Applied Arms To Hold Some Object, 1930, 75 In.	550.00
Wall Pocket, Walnut, Carved Leaves, Composition Minerva Head, Victorian, 14 x 23 In. . .	80.00
Whale, Smiling, Carved Wood, 19th Century, 6 1/2 x 9 1/2 In.	385.00
Whirligig, 2 Men Turning Fan, Articulated Limbs, 13 x 18 In.	690.00
Whirligig, Black Woman Washing Clothes, Wood, Tin & Wire, 26 In.	110.00
Whirligig, Indian In Canoe, Red, Ocher Paint, Late 19th Century, 44 In.	550.00
Whirligig, Man Sawing Wood, On Stand, 43 In.	165.00
Whirligig, Man Wearing Black Jacket, Blue Trousers, Early 20th Century, 12 In.	1380.00
Whirligig, Man Wearing Peaked Cap, Blue Jacket, Red Vest, Pine, 21 In.	6325.00
Whirligig, Man, Wooden, Wire, Sheet Metal, 9 1/4 In.	880.00
Whirligig, Policeman 1 Arm, Band Leader Other Arm, Old Paint, Wooden, 20 In.	3300.00
Whirligig, Soldier, Rotating Arms, Blue Hat, Red Jacket, White Pants, 18 1/4 In.	880.00
Whirligig, Woman Churning Butter, Painted, Michael H. Hutton, 24 In.	175.00

FOOT WARMERS solved the problem of cold feet in past generations. Some warmers held charcoal, others held hot water. Pottery, tin, and soapstone were the favored materials to conduct the heat. The warmer was kept under the feet, then the legs and feet were tucked into a blanket, providing welcome warmth in a cold carriage or church.

Punched Tin, Mortised Poplar Frame, Wrought Iron Pan, 6 1/4 x 14 In.	330.00
Punched Tin, Mortised Walnut Frame, 6 x 7 1/2 x 8 1/2 In.	137.00
Punched Tin, Single Wire Handle, Wooden Frame, Turned Spindles	205.00
Punched Tin, Starflower & Circle, Walnut Frame, 6 x 18 1/2 In.	192.00
Tin, Poplar Hinge, Diamond, Wrought Iron Pan, 5 1/2 x 7 1/2 x 8 1/2 In.	192.00
Tin, Soapstone Lid, Whale Oil Burner Interior, 9 3/4 In.	110.00
Walnut, Drilled Holes In Heart, Butterfly Shape, Brass Handle, 7 x 8 x 10 In.	330.00
Wooden Frame, Heart Design Tin, Turned Supports, 5 In.	192.00

FOOTBALL collectibles may be found in the Card and the Sports categories.

FOSTORIA glass was made in Fostoria, Ohio, from 1887 to 1891. The factory was moved to Moundsville, West Virginia, and most of the glass seen in shops today is a twentieth-century product. The company was sold in 1983; new items will be easily identifiable, according to the new owner, Lancaster Colony Corporation. Additional Fostoria items may be listed in the Milk Glass category.

American, Appetizer Set, 7 Piece . . . . .250.00 to 325.00
American, Ashtray, Square, 3 In.	7.50
American, Ashtray, Square, Large	90.00
American, Basket, Reed Handle . . . . .90.00 to 110.00
American, Biscuit Jar	800.00
American, Bottle, Ketchup, 6 3/4 In.	135.00
American, Bottle, Water	750.00
American, Bowl, 3-Toed, 10 1/2 In.	37.00
American, Bowl, 8 1/2 In.	200.00
American, Bowl, Cupped, 7 In.	75.00
American, Bowl, Flared, 10 x 4 In.	35.00
American, Bowl, Floating Garden, 10 In.	50.00
American, Bowl, Oval, 12 In.	50.00
American, Bowl, Salad, 10 In.	50.00
American, Bowl, Wedding, Cover, Large	1000.00
American, Box, Cosmetic, Cover, Round, 1 1/2 In.	750.00
American, Box, Handkerchief, Cover, Canary Yellow, 5 5/8 x 4 5/8 In.	695.00
American, Butter, Cover, Round	95.00
American, Cake Plate, 3-Toed, 12 In. . . . . .25.00 to 45.00
American, Cake Stand, Round, 10 In.	100.00
American, Candlestick, 2-Light, 4 1/8 x 8 1/2 In.	50.00
American, Candlestick, Bell Shape	125.00
American, Candy Dish, 3 Sections, Cover	80.00
American, Candy Dish, Open, 7 x 5 In.	500.00

American, Cheese & Cracker Set 65.00
American, Cigarette Box, Cover 40.00
American, Creamer, 9 1/2 In. 15.00
American, Decanter, Stopper 75.00
American, Dish, Ice Cream 70.00
American, Dish, Jelly, Cover 30.00
American, Dish, Lemon ....35.00 to 58.00
American, Dish, Mayonnaise, Underplate 30.00
American, Finger Bowl, Underplate 140.00
American, Goblet, Hexagonal Foot, 7 In., 10 Oz. 15.00
American, Ice Bucket 70.00
American, Ice Tub, Underplate, 5 1/2 In. ....33.00 to 45.00
American, Ice Tub, Underplate, 6 1/2 In. ....55.00 to 90.00
American, Lamp, Candle, 4 Piece 140.00
American, Lamp, Hurricane, Chimney ....325.00 to 450.00
American, Marmalade, Cover 125.00
American, Nappy, 8 x 4 3/4 In. 150.00
American, Pitcher, 1/2 Gal. 75.00
American, Plate, 7 1/2 In. 15.00
American, Plate, 14 In. 40.00
American, Platter, 10 1/2 In. 40.00
American, Platter, Oval, 12 In. 50.00
American, Puff Box, Cover, 3 In. 175.00
American, Punch Bowl, Base, 18 In. 350.00
American, Punch Bowl, Tom & Jerry 175.00
American, Ring Holder, Soap Dish 750.00
American, Rose Bowl, 3 1/2 In. 20.00
American, Salt & Pepper 25.00
American, Sherbet, Footed, Handle 150.00
American, Sherbet, Low, Footed 10.00
American, Syrup, Metal Handle 63.00
American, Toothpick 23.00
American, Torte Plate, 18 In. 125.00
American, Torte Plate, 20 In. 129.90
American, Tray, 5 Sections, Metal Frame 160.00
American, Tray, Cloverleaf 250.00
American, Tray, Dresser, 11 In. 250.00
American, Tray, Oval, Green, 10 1/2 In. 185.00
American, Tumbler, Iced Tea, 12 Oz. 22.00
American, Tumbler, Juice, 5 Oz. 14.00
American, Tumbler, Whiskey, 2 Oz. 15.00
American, Vase, Bud, Cupped, 6 In. 15.00
American, Vase, Bud, Flared, 8 In. 25.00
American, Vase, Cupped, 10 In. 225.00
American, Vase, Flared, 9 1/4 In. 100.00
American, Vase, Square Foot, 10 In. 40.00
American, Vase, Straight, 10 In. 85.00
American, Vase, Swung, 9 1/2 In. 250.00
American, Vase, Swung, 14 In. 235.00
American, Washbowl, 19 1/4 In. 2000.00
American, Water Set, Ice Lip, 6 Flared Tumblers, 7 Piece 100.00
American Lady, Cocktail, Amethyst, 3 1/2 Oz. 20.00
American Lady, Cordial, Regal Blue, 1 Oz. 85.00
American Lady, Goblet, 10 Oz. ....15.00 to 18.00
American Lady, Sherbet, 5 1/2 Oz. ....10.00 to 12.00
American Lady, Tumbler, Footed, 10 Oz. 12.00
American Lady, Tumbler, Juice, Footed, 5 Oz. 20.00
Baroque, Bowl, Azure, Handles, 8 1/2 In. 95.00
Baroque, Bowl, Flared, Pink, 12 In. 159.00
Baroque, Bowl, Rolled Rim, Azure, 11 In. 129.00
Baroque, Cup & Saucer, Azure ....30.00 to 39.00
Baroque, Dish, Mayonnaise, Underplate, Topaz 45.00
Baroque, Dish, Pickle, Azure 55.00

Baroque, Ice Bucket, Topaz 139.00
Baroque, Pitcher, Ice Lip 70.00
Baroque, Plate, Azure, 6 In. 12.00
Baroque, Plate, Azure, 7 1/2 In. 15.00
Baroque, Plate, Azure, 8 1/2 In. 20.00
Baroque, Plate, Topaz, 9 1/2 In. 59.00
Baroque, Relish, 3 Sections, Topaz 45.00
Baroque, Salt & Pepper, Topaz 119.00
Baroque, Soup, Cream, Underplate, Azure ....250.00 to 325.00
Baroque, Sugar & Creamer, Topaz, Individual 55.00
Baroque, Tidbit, 3-Toed 15.00
Baroque, Torte Plate, Azure, 14 In. 99.00
Baroque, Tumbler, Iced Tea, Topaz 69.00
Baroque, Tumbler, Juice, Azure, 5 Oz. 45.00
Bookends, Eagle 95.00
Bookends, Owl 195.00
Carmen, Celery Dish, Gold Trim 55.00
Century, Bowl, Handled, 8 In. 23.00
Century, Bowl, Rolled Rim, 11 In. 45.00
Century, Candlestick, 4 In., Pair 355.00
Century, Cup & Saucer ....15.00 to 16.00
Century, Pitcher, 7 In. 75.00
Century, Relish, 2 Sections, 7 3/8 In. 12.00
Century, Relish, 3 Sections, 11 1/8 In. 27.00
Century, Salt & Pepper 18.90
Century, Sugar & Creamer 25.00
Chintz, Bell, Dinner 125.00
Chintz, Bowl, 2 Handles, 10 1/2 In. 55.00
Chintz, Bowl, Flared, 11 1/2 In. 80.00
Chintz, Cake Plate, Handle, 10 1/2 In. 40.00
Chintz, Candlestick, 5 1/2 In., Pair 70.00
Chintz, Candy Dish, Cover 150.00
Chintz, Champagne, 6 Oz. 15.00
Chintz, Console Set, 2-Light Candlesticks, 3 Piece 125.00
Chintz, Cordial, 1 Oz. 43.00
Chintz, Cup & Saucer 25.00
Chintz, Plate, 7 In. 17.00
Chintz, Relish, 3 Sections 40.00
Chintz, Salt & Pepper 95.00
Chintz, Sandwich Server, Center Handle 55.00
Chintz, Torte Plate 55.00
Coin, Ashtray, Olive, 5 In. 8.00
Coin, Ashtray, Red, Small 18.00
Coin, Bowl, Footed, Olive, 8 1/2 In. 50.00
Coin, Bowl, Olive, 8 In. 28.00
Coin, Bowl, Oval, Olive, 9 In. 30.00
Coin, Bowl, Oval, Red, 9 In. 80.00
Coin, Bowl, Wedding, Cover, Blue, 8 1/4 In. 200.00
Coin, Bowl, Wedding, Cover, Emerald Green, 8 1/4 In. 135.00
Coin, Cake Stand, Amber, 10 In. ....110.00 to 150.00
Coin, Candleholder, Ruby, 4 1/2 In. Pair 50.00
Coin, Candlestick, Olive, 8 In. 25.00
Coin, Candy Jar, Cover, Ruby 100.00
Coin, Cigarette Urn, Footed, Blue 68.00
Coin, Condiment Set, Tray, Salt & Pepper, Cruet, Olive, 4 Pieces 215.00
Coin, Cruet Set, 4 Pieces 185.00
Coin, Decanter, Olive, Stopper, 1 Pt. 135.00
Coin, Lamp, Courting, Handle, Amber, 9 3/4 In. 60.00
Coin, Lamp, Patio, Electric, Shade, Amber, 16 1/2 In. 175.00
Coin, Nappy, Blue, 4 1/2 In. 20.00
Coin, Punch Set, Bowl, Base, Cup, Satin Coins, 14 Pieces 500.00
Coin, Salt & Pepper, Blue, 3 1/2 In. 85.00
Coin, Sugar, Cover, Red 70.00

Coin, Toothpick, Amber	5.00
Coin, Urn, Cover, Amber, 12 3/4 In.	68.00
Coin, Vase, Bud, Olive, 8 In.	25.00
Colony, Bonbon, 3-Toed	8.00
Colony, Bowl, 3-Toed, 5 1/4 In.	12.00
Colony, Bowl, Flared, 11 In.	30.00
Colony, Bowl, Flared, Footed, 6 1/2 In.	100.00
Colony, Bowl, Footed, 10 In.	125.00
Colony, Cake Salver, 12 In.	40.00
Colony, Celery Dish, Oval, 11 1/2 In.	30.00
Colony, Centerpiece, 13 In.	45.00
Colony, Cocktail, Oyster, 4 Oz.	12.00
Colony, Compote, Cover, 6 In.	30.00
Colony, Console, Rolled Edge, 14 In.	45.00
Colony, Cruet, Stopper	45.00
Colony, Cup & Saucer	8.00 to 10.00
Colony, Dish, Mayonnaise, Underplate	25.00
Colony, Finger Bowl	75.00
Colony, Goblet, Water, 9 Oz.	14.00 to 20.00
Colony, Goblet, Wine, 3 1/4 Oz.	25.00
Colony, Pitcher, 1 Pt.	100.00
Colony, Plate, 7 1/4 In.	9.00
Colony, Plate, 8 In.	13.00 to 15.00
Colony, Plate, 9 In.	35.00
Colony, Plate, 15 In.	70.00
Colony, Platter, 15 In.	40.00
Colony, Punch Bowl, Footed	1000.00
Colony, Punch Cup	12.00
Colony, Relish, Oval	12.00
Colony, Salt & Pepper	30.00
Colony, Sandwich Server, Center Handle	28.00
Colony, Sherbet, 5 Oz.	8.00
Colony, Sherbet, Flared, 5 Oz.	10.00
Colony, Soup, Cream, 5 In.	75.00 to 115.00
Colony, Tidbit, Plain Side, 6 In.	75.00
Colony, Torte Plate, 15 In.	60.00
Colony, Tray, Muffin, 2 Handles, 8 3/8 In.	35.00
Colony, Tumbler, Juice, Footed, 5 Oz.	24.00
Colony, Urn, Cover, Footed	75.00 to 85.00
Colony, Vase, 12 In.	300.00
Colony, Vase, 14 In.	400.00
Contour, Candlestick, 4 1/2 In., Pair	45.00
Contour, Goblet, Water, 10 1/2 Oz.	16.00
Coronet, Relish, 3 Sections	19.50
Coronet, Sandwich Server, Center Handle, 11 1/2 In.	18.00
Corsage, Cordial, 1 Oz.	50.00
Corsage, Cup & Saucer	23.00
Drape, Creamer, Gold Trim	22.00
Edgewood, Toothpick	60.00
Fairfax, Bouillon, Underplate, Rose	30.00
Fairfax, Bowl, Green, 12 In.	85.00
Fairfax, Cocktail, Icer, Rose	30.00
Fairfax, Cup & Saucer, Green	7.50 to 12.00
Fairfax, Cup & Saucer, Green, After Dinner	22.00
Fairfax, Decanter, Green	145.00
Fairfax, Nut Cup, Green	12.00
Fairfax, Nut Cup, Spiral, Green	22.00
Fairfax, Platter, Oval, Green, 12 In.	78.00
Fairfax, Platter, Oval, Green, 15 In.	145.00
Fairfax, Sauceboat, Underplate, Green	145.00
Fairfax, Sherbet, Green, Tall, 6 Oz.	22.00
Fairfax, Sherbet, Low, 6 Oz.	18.00
Fairfax, Sugar & Creamer, Cover, Blue	55.90

Fairfax, Tray, Center Handle, Topaz 20.00
Fairfax, Tumbler, Water, Footed, Green, 9 Oz. 24.00
Fairfax, Wine, Green, 3 Oz. 18.00
Figurine, Colt, Standing, 3 7/8 In. 45.00
Figurine, Madonna, 10 In. 55.00
Frisco, Candy Dish, Aqua Milk Glass, 6 1/2 In. 45.00
Grape, Candlestick, Orchid, Pair 45.00
Heather, Cake Plate 35.00
Heather, Candy Dish, Cover, Footed 55.00
Heather, Cordial, 1 Oz. 45.00
Heather, Salt & Pepper 48.00
Heather, Sugar & Creamer, Individual ....20.00 to 35.00
Heirloom, Candlestick, Pink, 3 1/2 In., Pair 35.00
Heirloom, Vase, Green, 11 In. 20.00
Heirloom, Vase, Pink, 11 In. 27.00
Hermitage, Bowl, Cereal, Amber 28.00
Hermitage, Bowl, Cereal, Cupped, Topaz 28.00
Hermitage, Bowl, Flared, Topaz, 4 1/4 In. 16.00
Hermitage, Bowl, Fluted, Azure, 6 In. 45.00
Hermitage, Bowl, Footed, Amber, 9 1/2 In. 65.00
Hermitage, Coaster, Topaz 8.00
Hermitage, Cocktail, Fruit, Amber, 5 Oz. 12.00
Hermitage, Cup & Saucer, Azure 25.00
Hermitage, Goblet, Water, Amber, 9 Oz. 22.00
Hermitage, Pitcher, Amber, 1 Pt. 65.00
Hermitage, Plate, Amber, 6 In. 7.00
Hermitage, Sherbet, Amber 14.00
Hermitage, Tumbler, Footed, Amber, 5 Oz. 14.00
Hermitage, Tumbler, Footed, Topaz, 9 Oz. 12.00
Holly, Cordial, 1 Oz. 35.00
Holly, Tray, Center Handle 20.00
Holly, Wine, 3 1/2 Oz. 25.00
Jamestown, Goblet, Water, Amber, 9 1/2 Oz. 6.00
Jamestown, Goblet, Water, Blue, 9 1/2 Oz. ....20.00 to 22.00
Jamestown, Pitcher, Ice Lip, Pink, 3 Pt. 150.00
Jamestown, Sherbet, Green, 6 1/2 Oz. 15.00
Jamestown, Tumbler, Iced Tea, Footed, Blue, 12 Oz. 24.00
Jamestown, Tumbler, Juice, Green, 5 Oz. 15.00
Jamestown, Tumbler, Water, 9 Oz. 17.00
June, Ashtray 75.00
June, Bowl, 3-Footed, Azure, 12 In. 145.00
June, Bowl, Topaz, 4 1/2 In. 28.00
June, Celery Dish, Topaz 60.00
June, Console Set, Grecian, Rose, 3 Piece 350.00
June, Cruet, Footed, Topaz 700.00
June, Cup, Rose, After Dinner 72.90
June, Goblet, Water, Topaz, 10 Oz. 55.00
June, Goblet, Wine, 3 Oz. 120.00
June, Parfait, Rose, 5 1/4 In. 130.00
June, Salt & Pepper 225.00
June, Sugar & Creamer, Cover 400.00
June, Tumbler, Whiskey, Footed, Topaz, 2 1/2 Oz. 65.00
June, Vase, Topaz, 8 In. 575.00
June, Whipped Cream Tub, Rose 295.00
Kashmir, Gravy Boat, Underplate, Blue 180.00
Kingsley, Compote, Azure, 4 3/4 In. 45.00
Lafayette, Celery Dish, Topaz, 11 1/2 In. 18.00
Lafayette, Chop Plate, Rose, 13 In. 75.00
Lafayette, Dish, Pickle, Amber 18.00
Lafayette, Grill Plate, Rose, 13 In. 75.00
Lafayette, Plate, Topaz, 7 1/2 In. 16.00
Lafayette, Plate, Wisteria, 7 1/2 In. 27.00
Lafayette, Relish, 2 Sections, Topaz 20.00

Lafayette, Sauceboat, Underplate, Green 65.00
Lafayette, Torte Plate, Green, 13 In. 68.00
Lafayette, Torte Plate, Ruby, 14 In. 145.00
Lamp, Oil, Cosmos, 1896, Miniature 275.00
Manor, Cordial, Topaz, 1 Oz. 75.00
Maypole, Torte Plate, Topaz 26.00
Meadow Rose, Candlestick, 2-Light, Pair 70.00
Meadow Rose, Champagne, 6 Oz. 17.00
Meadow Rose, Cocktail, 6 Oz. 28.00
Meadow Rose, Sauceboat, Underplate 170.00
Midnight Rose, Jug, Ice Lip, 1/2 Gal. 175.00
Midnight Rose, Vase, 9 1/2 In. 260.00
Minuet, Decanter, Footed, Fleur-De-Lis Stopper, Topaz 2200.00
Navarre, Candlestick, 2-Light, 6 3/4 In. 20.00
Navarre, Champagne, 6 Oz. 40.00
Navarre, Champagne, Flute, 6 Oz. 110.00
Navarre, Claret, Azure, 6 1/2 In., 6 1/2 Oz. 50.00
Navarre, Cocktail, 6 Oz. 25.00
Navarre, Cocktail, Oyster, 4 Oz. 28.00
Navarre, Cup & Saucer 25.00
Navarre, Pitcher, Contour, 1 Qt. 465.00
Navarre, Plate, 7 1/2 In. 12.00
New Garland, Bottle, Oil, No Foot 275.00
Oak Leaf, Bowl, 12 In. 45.00
Oak Leaf, Candy Dish, Cover, 3 Sections 65.00
Oak Leaf, Console Set, Rose, 3 Piece 116.00
Oriental, Compote, Blown, 6 In. 150.00
Pioneer, Platter, Amber, 15 In. 40.00
Plymouth, Sherbet, Ruby, 6 Oz. 13.00
Priscilla, Butter, Cover, Green, Gold Trim 53.00
Priscilla, Sugar & Creamer, Green 35.00
Romance, Champagne, 6 Oz. 23.00
Romance, Console, Round 45.00
Romance, Cup & Saucer 27.00
Romance, Goblet, Water, 9 Oz. 25.00
Romance, Sherbet, 6 Oz. 14.00
Romance, Tray, Center Handle 35.00
Romance, Tumbler, 6 In. 25.00
Romance, Tumbler, Juice, Footed, 5 Oz. 14.00
Royal, Console, Amber, 10 1/2 In. 25.00
Royal, Ice Bucket, Green 65.00
Seville, Cup & Saucer, Amber 12.00
Shirley, Sugar & Creamer, Individual 35.00
Spiral Optic, Vase, Green, Handle, 8 In. 60.00
Sunray, Coaster Set, 5 Piece 20.00
Sunray, Ice Bucket 35.00
Trojan, Bowl, Combination, Candleholder Handles, Topaz 265.00
Trojan, Sherbet, Tall, Topaz, 6 Oz. 22.00
Trojan, Tumbler, Azure, 9 Oz. 30.00
Vernon, Plate, Orchid, 10 In. 65.00
Versailles, Bonbon, Rose 20.00
Versailles, Cocktail, Oyster, Topaz 25.00
Versailles, Cup & Saucer, Green, After Dinner 95.00
Versailles, Plate, Topaz, 10 In. 40.00
Versailles, Sandwich Server, Fleur-De-Lis Handle, Topaz 55.00
Versailles, Sherbet, Tall, Rose, 6 Oz. 38.00
Versailles, Soup, Cream, Underplate, Topaz 40.00
Versailles, Soup, Dish, Topaz 70.00
Versailles, Tumbler, Water, Footed, Topaz, 9 Oz. 23.00
Versailles, Vase, Fan, Blue, 8 3/4 In. 825.00
Versailles, Whipped Cream Tub, Handle 95.00
Vesper, Console, Amber, Rolled Rim, 11 In. 30.00
Vesper, Cup, Amber, Footed 15.00

Vesper, Platter, 15 In.	55.00
Vesper, Soup, Cream, Amber	30.00
Victorian, Tumbler, Whiskey, Burgundy, Footed, 5 Piece	30.00
Virginia, Salt & Pepper, Amber	20.00
Wakefield, Cordial, 1 Oz.	18.00
Wakefield, Goblet, Water, 9 Oz.	18.00
Wedding Ring, Goblet, Platinum Band, 10 1/2 In.	15.00
Wedding Ring, Plate, Platinum Band, 7 In.	6.00
Willow, Cake Plate, Handles	35.00
Willow, Candlestick, 4 In., Pair	95.00
Willow, Cordial	50.00
Willow, Creamer	25.00
Willow, Cup & Saucer	25.00
Willow, Dish, Mayonnaise, Underplate	40.00
Willow, Goblet, 9 Oz.	22.00
Willow, Sherbet, 5 Oz.	18.00
Willow, Sugar	25.00
Willow, Torte Plate, 14 In.	100.00
Willow, Tumbler, Iced Tea, 12 Oz.	20.00
Willowmere, Cake Plate, Handles	38.00
Willowmere, Cup & Saucer	28.00
Willowmere, Plate, 7 In.	18.00
Willowmere, Sugar & Creamer	38.00
Willowmere, Torte Plate, 14 In.	45.00
Willowmere, Tumbler, Footed, 9 Oz.	22.00
Willowmere, Tumbler, Juice, Footed, 5 Oz.	12.00

FOVAL, see Fry category.

FRAMES are included in the Furniture category under Frame.

FRANCISCAN is a trademark that appears on pottery. Gladding, McBean and Company started in 1875. The company grew and acquired other potteries. They made sewer pipes, floor tiles, dinnerwares, and art pottery with a variety of trademarks. In 1934, dinnerware and art pottery were sold under the name Franciscan Ware. They made china and cream-colored, decorated earthenware. Desert Rose, Apple, El Patio, and Coronado were best-sellers. The company became Interpace Corporation and in 1979 was purchased by Josiah Wedgwood & Sons. The plant was closed in 1984 but a few of the patterns are still being made. For more information, see *Kovels' Depression Glass & Dinnerware Price List*.

Apple, Ashtray, Square	295.00
Apple, Bowl, 8 1/2 In.	32.00
Apple, Bowl, Sherbet, Footed	30.00
Apple, Bowl, Vegetable, 8 1/2 In.	45.00 to 50.00
Apple, Bowl, Vegetable, Divided, 10 1/2 In.	38.00 to 80.00
Apple, Butter Chip	15.00
Apple, Butter, Cover, 1/4 Lb.	8.00
Apple, Casserole, Cover, Individual	45.00
Apple, Chop Plate, 12 In.	40.00
Apple, Chop Plate, 14 In.	150.00
Apple, Cup & Saucer	53.00
Apple, Mixing Bowl, 7 1/2 In.	60.00
Apple, Mug, 12 Oz.	95.00
Apple, Pitcher, Milk, 7 In.	95.00
Apple, Plate, Child's, 3 Sections, 7 1/4 In.	175.00
Apple, Platter, 12 1/4 In.	65.00
Apple, Platter, 14 In.	85.00
Apple, Porringer, 6 In.	20.00
Apple, Relish, 3 Sections, 11 3/4 In.	85.00
Apple, Relish, Oval, 10 In.	50.00
Apple, Salt & Pepper	30.00
Apple, Tumbler, 6 In.	40.00

Apple, Tumbler, 10 Oz. 40.00
Bountiful, Saucer 7.00
Cafe Royale, Ashtray, Square 125.00
Cafe Royale, Compote, Low 165.00
Cafe Royale, Cookie Jar 225.00
Cafe Royale, Cup & Saucer 20.00
Cafe Royale, Mug, Small 20.00
Cafe Royale, Plate, Salad, 8 In. 20.00
Cafe Royale, Vegetable, Cover 125.00
Coronado, Casserole, Yellow, Handles, 1 1/2 Qt. 45.00
Coronado, Sherbet, Maroon 12.00
Daisy, Teapot, 5 In. 55.00
Desert Rose, Ashtray, Divided, 9 In. 50.00
Desert Rose, Ashtray, Square 295.00
Desert Rose, Bank, Piggy 295.00
Desert Rose, Bell, Danbury 75.00
Desert Rose, Bowl, Bouillon, Cover 395.00
Desert Rose, Bowl, Vegetable, Divided, 10 3/4 In. ....42.00 to 55.00
Desert Rose, Butter 45.00
Desert Rose, Casserole, 2 1/2 Qt. 695.00
Desert Rose, Coffeepot, Individual 395.00
Desert Rose, Compote, Large 75.00
Desert Rose, Cookie Jar 175.00
Desert Rose, Cup & Saucer 16.00
Desert Rose, Dish, Heart, 5 3/4 In. 145.00
Desert Rose, Mug, Large 50.00
Desert Rose, Pitcher, Water, 2 Qt. 100.00
Desert Rose, Plate, Child's, Square 125.00
Desert Rose, Platter, 12 In. 45.00
Desert Rose, Relish 150.00
Desert Rose, Salt & Pepper Mill 275.00
Desert Rose, Salt & Pepper, Tall 65.00
Desert Rose, Sherbet, 4 In. 25.00
Desert Rose, Sugar & Creamer 50.00
Desert Rose, Sugar & Creamer, After Dinner 30.00
Desert Rose, Syrup, 1 Pt. 75.00
Desert Rose, Tidbit, 2 Tiers 175.00
Desert Rose, Tidbit, 3 Tiers 95.00
Desert Rose, Trivet 100.00
Desert Rose, Tumbler, 6 Oz. 55.00
Forget-Me-Not, Bowl, 5 1/4 In. 20.00
Forget-Me-Not, Creamer 20.00
Forget-Me-Not, Cup & Saucer 25.00
Forget-Me-Not, Platter, 14 In. 65.00
Ivy, Bowl, 8 In. 52.00
Ivy, Bowl, Salad, 11 In. 95.00
Ivy, Bowl, Vegetable, Divided, 12 1/4 In. 55.00
Ivy, Butter ....80.00 to 85.00
Ivy, Chop Plate, 12 1/2 In. 70.00
Ivy, Creamer ....25.00 to 35.00
Ivy, Pitcher, 8 In. 80.00
Ivy, Sugar & Creamer ....80.00 to 85.00
Ivy, Teapot 50.00
Ivy, Tumbler 45.00
Meadow Rose, Pitcher 425.00
Meadow Rose, Tumbler, Water, 10 Oz. 30.00
Merry-Go-Round, Relish 28.00
Poppy, Butter, Cover 80.00
Poppy, Chop Plate, 12 In. 75.00
Poppy, Sugar 30.00
Starburst, Chop Plate, 12 In. 65.00
Wildflower, Bowl, 4-Footed 90.00
Wildflower, Bowl, Bonbon, 2 Handles 25.00

FRANKART, Inc., New York, New York, mass-produced nude *dancing lady* lamps, ashtrays, and other decorative Art Deco items in the 1920s and 1930s. They were made of white lead composition and spray-painted. *Frankart Inc.* and the patent number and year were stamped on the base.

Ashtray, Golfer, c.1900, 8 1/2 In.	230.00
Ashtray, Twin Fish, 5 In.	225.00
Bookends, Lady Head, Modernistic, 7 In.	275.00
Bookends, Spaniel, Pair	195.00
Figurine, Nude Female, On Brass Globe, Raising Dish Overhead, 25 1/2 In.	805.00

FRANKOMA POTTERY was originally known as The Frank Potteries when John F. Frank opened shop in 1933. The factory is now working in Sapulpa, Oklahoma. Early wares were made from a light cream-colored clay from Ada, Oklahoma, but in 1956 the company switched to a red burning clay from Sapulpa. The firm makes dinnerwares, utilitarian and decorative kitchenwares, figurines, flowerpots, and limited edition and commemorative pieces.

Ashtray, Arrowhead, 7 In.	30.00
Ashtray, Cocker Spaniel	125.00
Ashtray, Kansas	6.00
Bank, Piggy	25.00
Bookends, Boot	30.00
Bowl, Crescent, 12 1/2 In.	20.00
Bowl, Red Bud, 10 In.	125.00
Butter, Cover, Mayan-Aztec	35.00
Cup & Saucer, Plainsman	15.00
Dish, Baker, 2 Qt.	18.00
Figurine, Woman, Orange Glossy Glaze, Impressed Mark, 10 In.	110.00
Honey Pot, Beige	18.00
Mask, Indian, Pair	50.00
Mug, Elephant, Nixon & Agnew, 1968	55.00
Mug, Elephant, Nixon & Agnew, 1973	25.00
Mug, War God	95.00
Pepper, Teepee, 2 Holes	12.00
Pitcher, Ringed	75.00
Plaque, Angel	15.00
Plaque, Will Rogers	125.00
Plate, Christmas, 1965	195.00
Plate, Easter, 1972	11.00
Plate, Herbert Hoover	22.00
Plate, Oklahoma State	8.00
Plate, Plainsman, Green Glaze	15.00
Plate, Wagon Wheel, 5 In.	5.00
Salt & Pepper, Aztec, 2 1/2 In.	15.00
Salt & Pepper, Bull	250.00
Salt & Pepper, Elephant, Mirror Black	315.00
Salt & Pepper, First National Of Tulsa	50.00
Salt & Pepper, Horseshoe	55.00
Salt & Pepper, Oil Derrick	35.00 to 40.00
Salt & Pepper, Plainsman, 3 In.	12.00
Salt & Pepper, Sheaf Of Wheat	40.00
Sugar, Aztec	8.00
Sugar & Creamer, Cover, Wagon Wheel	25.00
Trivet, Beige	35.00
Trivet, Flycatcher	12.00
Trivet, Kansas Centennial	7.50
Trivet, Liberty Bell	7.50 to 10.00
Trivet, Rooster	15.00
Vase, Bud, Crocus, 8 In.	10.00
Vase, Bud, Snail, Ada Clay	75.00
Vase, Bud, Snail, Desert Gold	20.00
Vase, Shell, 6 In.	40.00

Wall Pocket, Phoebe 190.00
Wall Pocket, Woman's Head, Green & Brown Crystalline Glaze, Signed, 7 In. 120.00

FRATERNAL objects that are related to the many different fraternal organizations in the United States are listed in this category. The Elks, Masons, Odd Fellows, and others are included. Furniture is listed in the Furniture category. Shaving mugs decorated with fraternal crests are included in the Shaving Mug category.

Eastern Star, Badge, Enameled, 14K Gold 66.00
Eastern Star, Spoon, Sterling Silver, 1950s 40.00
Elks, Fan, Paper, Elks Reunion, 1909 .... 45.00
Elks, Pin, Our Guests, Hamm Brewing Co., Elk Head, Flag Ribbon, 1897, 2 x 1 In. 105.00
Elks, Plate, Atlantic City, Carnival Glass, Blue, 1911, 8 In. 1710.00
Elks, Shaving Mug, Emblem, Dell J. Olmstead, W. Austria, 1925, 3 5/8 In. 145.00
Elks, Stein Set, Pitcher, 6 Mugs, Transfer Decal, 11 1/2 In. 330.00
Elks, Watch Fob & Link Chain, 14K Gold, Gold Filled Bar, Elks Lodge 75.00
Knights Of Pythias, Sword, Leather Handle, Nickel Scabbard, 28 1/4-In. Blade 57.00
Knights Of The Maccabees, Mirror, Detroit, Lodge House, 2 3/4 In. 11.00
Knights Templar, Ribbon, Silk, Holyrood Commandery No. 32, Cleveland, 1883, 7 In. 45.00
Knights Templar, Sword, Steel Scabbard, Ivory Handle, Civil War, 27 In. 170.00
Ladies Of The Maccabees, Mirror, Michigan, Group Symbol, Oval, 2 3/4 In. 22.00
Masonic, Badge, Steward, 1950 .... 20.00
Masonic, Badge, Steward, 1958 .... 16.00
Masonic, Box, Collar, Wooden, Gutta-Percha Cover, Masonic Symbols 75.00
Masonic, Box, Mother-Of-Pearl, Black Lacquer, Floral Design, 5 x 16 x 12 1/2 In. 920.00
Masonic, Chalice, Cranberry Glass, Sword Handles, St. Paul, Pittsburgh, 1906 .... 75.00
Masonic, Emblem, Compass & Square, Gilt Bronze, 19th Century, 23 3/4 In. 690.00
Masonic, Goblet, Symbols, Engraved WM, English 1817 Coin In Stem, 5 1/4 In. 805.00
Masonic, Helmet, Lodge Spike, Tan Body, Brass Side Buttons, Red Interior, 1881 .... 20.00
Masonic, Humidor, Figural, Goat In Cape, Emblem, Gilt Metal, Glass, 8 1/2 In. 260.00
Masonic, Jug, F. & A.M., Emblem, Pottery, c.1870, 10 3/4 In., 1 Gal. 1760.00
Masonic, Master Mason's Certificate, Washington Remembered Lodge, Ribbon, 1803 .... 275.00
Masonic, Paperweight, Medal Center, 1969 Supreme Council, 3 1/4 In. 3.00
Masonic, Picture, Needlework, All-Seeing Eye, Square & Compass, 1827, 11 In. 747.00
Masonic, Pin, Grand Lodge F. & A.M. Florida, 25 Years Mason, Sterling Silver, 3/4 In. .. 15.00
Masonic, Postcard, Masonic Cemetery, Virginia City, Nev., Linen, Unused, 1930s 6.00
Masonic, Print, Our Flag & Its History 55.00
Masonic, Print, Our Mission, 1891 .... 55.00
Masonic, Ribbon, Triannual Conclave San Fran. Columbus Commandery, 1883, 8 In. 37.00
Masonic, Ring, Man's, 14K Yellow & White Gold, Diamond, 32nd Degree 1235.00
Masonic, Seal, Symbols, 19th Century, 5 In. 145.00
Masonic, Shield, Walnut, Square & Compass Framing, Early 20th Century, 19 In. 230.00
Masonic, Sword, Ames, Chicopee, Mass., 29 In. 110.00
Masonic, Watch Fob, Double Headed Eagle On 1 Side, 10K Rose Gold 374.00
Odd Fellows, Glass, Whiskey, Symbols, Wreath Reverse, J. & E. Hall, 4 1/2 In. 288.00
Odd Fellows, Needlework, Symbols, In God We Trust, 19th Century, 21 x 16 In. 245.00
Odd Fellows, Shaving Mug, Emblem, W.M. Mell, Gold Base, 1925, 3 1/2 In. 90.00
Odd Fellows, Sign, Shaking Hands & Eye In Horseshoe, Eagle, Iron, Painted, 6 1/2 In. 86.00
Shriner, Liquor Container, I Joined, Man With Crutch & Arm In Sling, 11 In. 20.00
Shriner, Pin, Garnets, Brass, Protector, 2 In. 95.00
Shriner, Shaving Mug, Gold Name 85.00

FRY GLASS was made by the H. C. Fry Glass Company of Rochester, Pennsylvania. The company, founded in 1901, first made cut glass and other types of fine glasswares. In 1922, they patented a heat-resistant glass called *Pearl Ovenglass*. For two years, 1926–1927, the company made Fry Foval, an opal ware decorated with colored trim. Reproductions of this glass have been made. Depression glass patterns made by Fry may be listed in the Depression Glass category. Some pieces of cut glass may also be included in the Cut Glass category.

FRY, Bonbon, Floral Cutting, 8 1/4 In. 45.00
Bowl, Hobstars Cutting, 7 3/4 In. 92.00
Casserole, Cover, Punched Nickel Holder 35.00

Cup & Saucer, Azure Blue 25.00
Cup & Saucer, Cobalt 40.00
Dish, Loaf, Ovenware, 9 1/2 In. 45.00
Plate, Azure Blue, 7 1/2 In. 10.00
Plate, Cobalt, 6 In. 10.00
Plate, Cobalt, 8 1/2 In. 15.00
Snack Plate, Cobalt 65.00
Tray, Sugar Cube, Floral Cutting 30.00
FRY FOVAL, Beverage Set, Jug, Tumblers, Teapot, Jade Handles, Silver Overlay, 8 Piece ... 1380.00
Jug, Hot Water, Jade Handle, Spout & Finial, 10 In. 260.00
Sherbet, Delft Blue Rim & Beads, 3 x 3 3/4 In. 120.00
Tea Set, Pearl, Silver Overlay, 1920, 9 Piece 862.00

FULPER Pottery Company was incorporated in 1899 in Flemington,
New Jersey. They made art pottery from 1910 to 1929. The firm had
been making bottles, jugs, and housewares from 1805. Doll heads were
made about 1928. The firm became Stangl Pottery in 1929. Fulper art
pottery is admired for its attractive glazes and simple shapes.

Bookends, Female Figures, Black Dress & Bonnet, Mark, Fish, 7 In., Pair 176.00
Bookends, Sleepy Reader, Green, Gunmetal Matte Glaze, 5 1/2 In., Pair 357.00
Bookends, Stylized Mask, Speckled Blue Matte Glaze, 5 1/2 x 6 In. 275.00
Bottle, Cat's-Eye Flambe Glaze, Embossed Salamander, 8 x 4 In. 1760.00
Bowl, 2-Tone Blue Drip Over Red Glaze, Stamped, 6 1/2 In. 187.00
Bowl, Apple Green, Turquoise Crystalline Glaze, 2 1/4 x 8 3/4 In. 165.00
Bowl, Blue & Green Flambe Glaze, Raised Rectangular Mark, 7 1/2 In. 88.00
Bowl, Brown, Pale Blue Glaze, 2 1/4 x 8 3/4 In. 225.00
Bowl, Cat's-Eye Flambe Glaze, Blue Interior, Angular Handles, 3 x 9 In. 138.00
Bowl, Cat's-Eye Flambe Glaze, Flared, Fluted, Mark, Label, 10 1/2 x 16 1/2 In. ... 143.00
Bowl, Cat's-Eye Flambe Glaze, Peacock Feather, Mustard Matte Glaze, 3 1/4 x 8 In. 192.00
Bowl, Centerpiece, Blue & Olive Green Crystalline Flambe Glaze, Lotus Shape, 11 In. ... 165.00
Bowl, Centerpiece, Footed, Lotus Shape, Turquoise Crystalline Glaze, 6 1/4 In. 140.00
Bowl, Centerpiece, Rose Famille Glaze, 3-Footed, Paper Label, 5 x 11 1/4 In. 415.00
Bowl, Centerpiece, Scalloped Rim, Famille Rose Glaze, 13 In. 140.00
Bowl, Charcoal, Multitone Green Matte Glaze, Ribbed, 11 In. 110.00
Bowl, Dark Wisteria Matte Glaze, 4 x 11 In. 275.00
Bowl, Effigy, Chinese Blue Flambe Glaze Over Blue Matte, 8 1/2 x 10 In. 660.00
Bowl, Effigy, Chinese Blue Glossy & Matte Glaze, Rectangular Ink Mark, 7 x 10 In. 415.00
Bowl, Embossed, Fish, Butterscotch Flambe, Leopard Skin Crystalline Glaze, 3 x 11 In. ... 1210.00
Bowl, Green Crystalline Glaze, Tan, Green Interior, Scalloped, 11 x 4 In., Pair 220.00
Bowl, Green, Blue & Gold Crystalline Glaze, 2 Handles, Ink Racetrack Mark, 7 In. 110.00
Bowl, Green, Butterscotch Flambe Glaze, Embossed Fish, 3 x 11 In. 1100.00
Bowl, Ibis, Flemington Green Flambe Glaze, Caramel Matte Exterior, 5 1/2 x 11 In. 1100.00
Bowl, Leopard Skin Crystalline Glaze, Ink Racetrack Mark, 1 1/2 x 8 3/4 In. 140.00
Bowl, Leopard Skin Crystalline Glaze, Ivory Interior, Rectangular Ink Mark, 10 In. 110.00
Bowl, Leopard Skin Crystalline Glaze, Squat, Ink Racetrack Mark, 5 3/4 x 8 3/4 In. 550.00
Bowl, Low Sides, Multicolored Flambe Glaze, Chinese Blue, Famille Rose, Mark, 9 In. ... 175.00
Bowl, Mahogany & Ivory Flambe Glaze, Mustard Matte Base, 4-Footed, 8 1/2 In. 385.00
Bowl, Mottled Green Exterior, Blue Flambe Interior, Closed-In Rim, 5 1/4 x 13 1/4 In. ... 440.00
Bowl, Turquoise Crystalline Glaze, Beige Clay, 6 x 15 In. 4675.00
Candleholder, Cat's-Eye Flambe Glaze, 3 Buttresses, Low, 6 In., Pair 138.00
Candleholder, Copper Dust Flambe Glaze, Low, Oval, 7 In., Pair 110.00
Candleholder, Flemington Green Glaze, Rectangular Ink Mark, 4 1/2 In. 135.00
Candlestick, Cucumber Crystalline Glaze, Rectangular Ink Stamp, 10 In., Pair 770.00
Candlestick, Gunmetal, Mahogany Flambe Glaze, 2 1/4 In., Pair 137.00
Candlestick, Twisted, Cat's-Eye Flambe Glaze, Ink Racetrack Mark, 8 In. 77.00
Centerbowl, Famille Rose Glaze, Scalloped, Racetrack Mark, 3 1/4 x 16 1/4 In. 176.00
Centerbowl, Gray & Black Glaze Over Blue Matte, Closed-In Rim, 5 x 12 In. 470.00
Centerpiece, Blue & Ivory Crystalline, Scalloped Roped Rim, Racetrack Mark, 15 In. ... 415.00
Chamberstick, Blue Crystalline Flambe Over Green, 7 In. 230.00
Chamberstick, Mottled Gray Matte Glaze, Incised Racetrack Mark, 7 1/2 In. 195.00
Charger, Footed, Blue & Ivory Flambe Glaze, Japanese Shape, 12 3/4 In. 660.00
Cider Set, Pitcher, 4 Mugs, Speckled Umber Glaze, Ink Racetrack Mark, 5 Piece 330.00
Console, Oval, Fluted, Cat's-Eye Flambe Glaze, Ink Racetrack Mark, 17 x 3 1/2 In. 165.00

Console, Scalloped, Blue Crystalline Glaze, Ink Racetrack Mark, 16 1/4 x 3 1/2 In. 140.00
Crock, No. 6, Cobalt Blue Floral, Gray Ground, Salt Glaze, 10 In. 165.00
Doorstop, Butterscotch Flambe Crystalline Glaze, 3 1/2 x 9 In. 1045.00
Doorstop, Cat, Figural, Moss To Rose Glaze, Stamped Mark, 6 1/2 x 8 1/2 In. 660.00
Doorstop, Cat, Figural, Turquoise Crystalline Glaze, 7 1/4 In. 440.00
Figurine, Dog, Butterscotch & Blue Flambe Glaze, 8 In. 374.00
Flower Frog, Fish Form, Blue Over Green Glaze, 5 In. 115.00
Flower Frog, Green, Turquoise Flambe Glaze, John Kunzman, 7 1/2 x 3 In. 770.00
Flower Frog, Pelican, Gunmetal & Black Glaze, Impressed Mark, 7 In. 195.00
Flower Frog, Penguin, Seated, Brown Matte Textured Base, 7 In. 440.00
Flowerpot, Butterscotch Flambe Glaze, No Mark, 14 x 16 In. 363.00
Humidor, Cat's-Eye Flambe Glaze, In Wooden Pipe Stand, Ink Racetrack Mark, 6 In. 250.00
Inkwell & Pen Tray, Vasekraft, Matte Ocher Glaze, Ink Racetrack Mark, 5 x 4 x 4 3/4 In. . 550.00
Jug, Blue, Green, Ivory Flambe Glaze, 9 3/4 x 7 In. 2530.00
Jug, Cobalt Blue Floral, Brown & Gray Ground, Salt Glaze, Incised Mark, 11 In. 245.00
Jug, Cobalt Blue Writing, A.J. Hedcomb Cider, Gray Ground, Salt Glaze, 11 In. 275.00
Jug, Musical, Flemington Green Flambe Glaze, Stopper, Red Paper Label, 10 In. 88.00
Jug, Spongeware, Blue & White, Filter No. 8, 2 Gal. 200.00
Jug, Wine, Mottled Green & Blue Glaze, Lavender, Ritz Music Box, Stopper, 10 In. 140.00
Lamp, Chinese Blue Flambe Glaze, Mushroom Shade, Leaded Glass Insets, 16 In. 13200.00
Lamp, Frothy Elephant's Breath, Mouse Gray Flambe Glaze, Bell-Shaped Shade, 16 In. .. 8800.00
Lamp, Mushroom Form, Green Crystalline Matte Glaze, Signed, 17 x 19 In. 23100.00
Lamp, Oil, Shade, Electrified, Signed, 17 x 14 In. ....850.00 to 1600.00
Lamp, Parlor, Ceramic Shade, Tiger's-Eye Glaze, Amber Glass Inserts, Vasekraft, 16 In. ... 3850.00
Lamp, Pavlova, Pink, Ivory, 15 In. 451.00
Lamp, Perfume, Ballerina, Blue, Stamped, 6 1/4 In. 275.00
Lamp, Perfume, Parrot Sitting On Stump, Light Heats Perfume, 9 1/4 In. 880.00
Lamp, Urn, Chinese Blue Crystalline Glaze, 9 1/2 In. 140.00
Lamp Base, Grecian Urn, Handles, Drip Glaze, Lavender, Original Hardware, 20 In. 252.00
Night-Light, Parrot, Bisque, 10 In. 605.00
Night-Light, Seated Girl, Yellow, Black Glaze, 6 1/2 In. 198.00
Pitcher, Colonial Ware, Green, Gunmetal Glaze, Handle, 5 1/2 In. 110.00
Pitcher, Cucumber Crystalline Glaze, Scrolled Handle, Ink Racetrack Mark, 4 In. 55.00
Pitcher, Water, Stylized Indigo Grapes, John Kunzman, 1908, 9 x 7 In. 1980.00
Powder Jar, Stylized Female Figure, Purple, Red, Ivory Glaze, 6 1/2 In. 143.00
Urn, Art Deco, Stylized Flowers, Embossed, Under Turquoise Crystalline Glaze, 14 In. ... 415.00
Urn, Black Mirror Glaze, Classic, Racetrack Mark, 13 x 8 In. 465.00
Urn, Cafe-Au-Lait Glaze, 4 Faceted Footed, Racetrack Mark, 16 1/4 x 5 1/2 In. 770.00
Urn, Chinese Blue To Famille Rose, Flat Shoulders, 2 Handles, Racetrack Mark, 9 In. 415.00
Urn, Chinese, Black Mirror Glaze, 2 Handles, Raised Racetrack Mark, 9 x 8 In. 770.00
Urn, Frothy Cucumber Matte Glaze, Hammered Surface, Ink Racetrack Mark, 12 In. 880.00
Urn, Gray, Blue, Amber Flambe Glaze, Lion Head Handles, 5 3/4 In. 264.00
Urn, Green & Cobalt Blue Flambe Mirror Glaze, Bulbous, Racetrack Mark, 11 1/2 In. ... 990.00
Urn, Green Leopard Skin Crystalline Glaze, Ink Racetrack Mark, 12 x 11 In. 2530.00
Urn, Scrolled Handles, Black Mirror & Copper Dust Crystalline Glaze, Ink Mark, 14 In. . 660.00
Urn, Speckled Matte Green Glaze, 2 Handles, Racetrack Mark, 10 1/4 x 5 3/4 In. 835.00
Urn, Stylized Flowers, Moss To Famille Rose Glaze, 2 Handles, Mark, No. 895, 13 In. ... 743.00
Vase, Apple Green, Turquoise Flambe Glaze, Handles, 7 1/2 In. 110.00
Vase, Ashes Of Rose Glaze, 12 In. 800.00
Vase, Black Mirror & Brown Flambe Glaze Over Caramel, 6 In. 220.00
Vase, Black Mirror & Crystalline Glaze, 2 Handles, 8 In. 990.00
Vase, Black Mirror & Ivory Flambe Glaze, Buttressed, Ink Racetrack Mark, 8 x 5 3/4 In. . 825.00
Vase, Black Mirror Flambe Glaze, 6 x 9 In. 605.00
Vase, Black Mirror Glaze, 2 Handles, Horizontal Mark, 6 1/2 x 9 1/4 In. 195.00
Vase, Black Mirror Glaze, 2 Handles, Squat, 3 In. 110.00
Vase, Black Mirror, Mahogany, Ivory Crystalline Flambe Glaze, 7 1/4 In. 357.00
Vase, Blue & Beige Flambe Glaze, Bulbous, Racetrack Mark, 5 1/4 In. 297.00
Vase, Blue & Beige Flambe Glaze, Oval, Impressed Fulper, 6 1/2 In. 187.00
Vase, Blue & Green Crystalline, Squat, Closed-In Shoulder, Racetrack Mark, 6 x 9 In. ... 440.00
Vase, Blue & Green Flambe Over Blue Matte Glaze, Flared Rim, 3 Buttresses, 7 In. 360.00
Vase, Blue & Green Luster Glaze, Bulbous, Raised Fulper Mark, 5 3/4 In. 195.00
Vase, Blue Green Flambe Dripping Over Blue Matte Glaze, 7 In. 413.00
Vase, Blue Green Flambe Over Famille Rose Glaze, Corseted, 2 Ribbed Handles, 8 In. ... 250.00

Vase, Blue Green Flambe To Rose Matte Glaze, Bulbous, 4 Handles, 13 x 11 In. 1430.00
Vase, Blue Matte Glaze, 2 Ring Handles, Raised Vertical Mark, 13 In. 525.00
Vase, Blue, Black Crystalline Flambe Glaze, Frothy Ivory, 11 3/4 x 7 In. 300.00
Vase, Blue, Gray, Ivory Flambe Glaze, 3 Ribbon Handles, 7 In. 220.00
Vase, Blue, Green, Purple Flambe Glaze, 2 Handles, Art Deco, 9 1/4 In. 220.00
Vase, Blue, Mahogany & Ivory Flambe Glaze, Racetrack Mark, 10 x 5 1/4 In. 525.00
Vase, Blue, Ocher, Green, Purple Flambe Glaze, 7 1/4 In. 412.00
Vase, Bluish Brown Flambe Glaze Over Taupe, 7 Sides, 8 1/2 In. 168.00
Vase, Brown, Green & Blue Flambe Glaze, Bulbous, Incised Mark, 8 1/2 In. 220.00
Vase, Buckle Molded Over Top, 5 In. 175.00
Vase, Bud, Butterscotch Flambe Glaze, Racetrack Mark, 5 In. 230.00
Vase, Bud, Dripping Green & Blue Matte Glaze, Racetrack Mark, 8 1/4 In. 253.00
Vase, Bud, Green Flambe Over Green Matte Glaze, 4 Sides, Ink Racetrack Mark, 8 In. . . . 415.00
Vase, Butterscotch Flambe Glaze, Baluster, Racetrack Mark, 12 x 4 1/2 In. 550.00
Vase, Butterscotch Flambe Glaze, Ink Racetrack Mark, 11 3/4 x 5 3/4 In. 990.00
Vase, Cat's-Eye Flambe & Black Mirror Glaze, Oval, Racetrack Mark, 7 In. 230.00
Vase, Cat's-Eye Flambe Glaze, 16 x 5 In. 2750.00
Vase, Cat's-Eye Flambe Glaze, 2 Scrolled Handles, Ink Racetrack Mark, 9 x 5 1/4 In. . . . 195.00
Vase, Cat's-Eye Flambe Glaze, 3 Buttresses, 6 1/2 In. 303.00
Vase, Cat's-Eye Flambe Glaze, Flared, 9 In. 137.00
Vase, Cat's-Eye Flambe Glaze, Handles, 7 1/2 x 6 1/2 In. 248.00
Vase, Cat's-Eye Flambe Glaze, Tapered, Rectangular Mark, 3 1/2 x 3 1/4 In. 195.00
Vase, Celadon, Green Drip On Rose Purple Glaze, 3 Buttresses Shoulder, 6 1/2 In. 385.00
Vase, Charcoal, Green Crystalline Glaze, 3 Handles, 7 In. 100.00
Vase, Chinese Blue Flambe Glaze, 2 Ring Handles, 13 x 7 1/2 In. 715.00
Vase, Chinese Blue Flambe Glaze, Bottle Shape, Incised Racetrack Mark, 8 In. 165.00
Vase, Chinese Blue Flambe Glaze, Oval, Raised Mark, 7 In. 220.00
Vase, Chinese Blue Flambe Glaze, Trumpet Shape, Ink Mark, 14 x 7 In. 770.00
Vase, Chinese Blue Over Black Mirror Flambe Glaze, Barrel, Vertical Mark, 4 x 3 In. . . . 165.00
Vase, Chinese Blue To Cat's-Eye Flambe Glaze, Buttressed Sides, 13 x 10 1/2 In. 3575.00
Vase, Chinese Blue To Flemington Green Flambe Glaze, Incised Racetrack Mark, 13 In. . . 770.00
Vase, Chinese Blue, Amber Mottled Glaze, 7 1/4 In. 100.00
Vase, Chinese Blue, Elephant's Breath Flambe Glaze, Corset, Racetrack Mark, 9 1/2 In. . . 495.00
Vase, Chinese Blue, Ivory & Mahogany Flambe Glaze, Tapered, Racetrack Mark, 10 In. . . 385.00
Vase, Chinese Blue, Olive Green Crystalline Glaze, Bullet, 3 Buttresses, 6 1/2 In. 300.00
Vase, Copper Dust Crystalline & Green Flambe Glaze, Corset, 2 Handles, 10 x 7 In. 935.00
Vase, Copper Dust Crystalline, Flemington Green Flambe, 2 Handles, Racetrack, 10 In. . . 465.00
Vase, Copper Dust Crystalline, Flemington Green Flambe, Racetrack Mark, 9 1/2 In. 495.00
Vase, Copper To Cucumber Crystalline Green Glaze, Buttress Handles, Squat, 9 In. 385.00
Vase, Crystalline Glaze, Avocado, 2 Handles, 6 1/2 In. 325.00
Vase, Crystalline Textured Glaze, Tiger's-Eye Flambe, Rose Bowl Shape, Mark, 5 1/2 In. . 440.00
Vase, Cucumber Crystalline Glaze, Bulbous, Incised Racetrack Mark, 8 x 6 In. 385.00
Vase, Cucumber Crystalline Glaze, Ring Handles, 125th Anniversary Paper Label, 12 In. . 245.00
Vase, Cucumber Crystalline Glaze, Shouldered Shape, Collared Rim, Ink Mark, 8 In. 825.00
Vase, Cucumber Crystalline Matte Glaze, Spherical, Racetrack Mark, 6 x 7 In. 825.00
Vase, Cucumber Matte Glaze, Incised Racetrack Mark, 10 1/2 x 3 3/4 In. 440.00
Vase, Dark Green Glaze, Stilt-Pull To Base, Bulbous, 3 Handles, Oval Mark, 7 In. 415.00
Vase, Dripping Brown Flambe, Ivory Glaze, 6 Sides, Rectangular Ink Mark, 9 In. 305.00
Vase, Elephant's Breath Flambe Glaze, Corseted, Ink Racetrack Mark, 7 1/2 In. 195.00
Vase, Famille Rose Matte Glaze, Bottle Shape, Squat, Incised Racetrack Mark, 8 In. 220.00
Vase, Flemington Green Crystalline Glaze, Oval, Closed-In Rim, 8 x 5 1/4 In. 495.00
Vase, Flemington Green Flambe Glaze, Buttressed, Rectangular Ink Mark, 8 In. 440.00
Vase, Flemington Green Flambe Glaze, Corset Waist, Racetrack Mark, 10 In. 440.00
Vase, Flemington Green Flambe Glaze, Gourd Shape, 2 Handles, Incised Mark, 7 In. 330.00
Vase, Flemington Green Glaze, 4 Buttresses, Rectangular Ink, 8 x 5 3/4 In. 525.00
Vase, Flemington Green Glaze, Buttresses, Converted To Lamp, 13 In. 1100.00
Vase, Flowing Green Matte Crystalline Glaze, Incised Racetrack Mark, 17 x 8 In. 2090.00
Vase, Frothy Green & Mauve Flambe Glaze, Bullet Shape, Incised Racetrack, 12 In. 1650.00
Vase, Frothy Green Over Speckled Beige Glaze, Spherical, 5 In. 330.00
Vase, Frothy Green Over Speckled Mauve Glaze, 5 In. 412.00
Vase, Frothy Rouge Flambe Glaze, 12 x 7 In. 715.00
Vase, Glossy Green & Chinese Blue Flambe, Oval, Incised Racetrack Mark, 5 1/4 In. 275.00
Vase, Glossy Rose To Crystalline Taupe Flambe Glaze, Raised Racetrack Mark, 12 In. . . . 550.00

Vase, Gold Crystalline Glaze, Brown, Cream, Blue Drip, 6 In. 220.00
Vase, Green & Blue Microcrystalline Glaze, Buttressed Sides, Tapered, 8 1/2 In. 360.00
Vase, Green & Mauve Flambe Over Famille Rose Matte Glaze, Racetrack Mark, 12 In. ... 525.00
Vase, Green & Raspberry Flambe, Squat, 2 Handles, Impressed Mark, 3 In. 88.00
Vase, Green & Turquoise Crystalline Glaze, Oval, Raised Racetrack Mark, 7 In. 195.00
Vase, Green Crystalline Glaze, 2 Handles, 6 In. 286.00
Vase, Green Crystalline Glaze, 3 Handles, 6 1/2 In. 225.00
Vase, Green Crystalline Glaze, Reticulated Neck, 2 Curled Handles, Signed, 8 1/2 In. 330.00
Vase, Green Crystalline Over Caramel Glaze, 7 In. 550.00
Vase, Green Drip Over Oatmeal Spotted Base, 6 In. 198.00
Vase, Green Flambe Glaze, Blue, Bottle Shape, 8 1/4 In. 300.00
Vase, Green Flemington Glaze, 2 Angular Handles, Squat, 3 1/2 In. 192.00
Vase, Green Luster To Blue Flambe Glaze, 3 1/2 In. 140.00
Vase, Green Matte Glaze, Frothy Caramel, White Glaze, 10 1/4 x 5 1/2 In. 880.00
Vase, Green Mirror & Umber Flambe Glaze, Barrel Shape, 4 3/4 In. 250.00
Vase, Green, Blue Flambe Glaze, 2 Angular Handles, Squat, 3 1/2 In. 303.00
Vase, Green, Blue Flambe Glaze, Blue Crystals, 11 In. 770.00
Vase, Green, Blue Flambe Glaze, Original Label, 3 1/2 In. 385.00
Vase, Green, Blue, Purple Flambe Glaze, 2 Handles, 6 1/2 In. 286.00
Vase, Green, Brown Flambe Glaze, Brown, Salmon High Glaze, Paper Label, 6 In. 286.00
Vase, Green, Brown Flambe, Brown, Salmon High Glaze, 6 In. 176.00
Vase, Green, Brown, Black, Vertical Ink Mark, 8 In. 440.00
Vase, Gunmetal & Green Mirror Glaze, Buttressed Rim, Spherical, 5 In. 385.00
Vase, Gunmetal, Green Matte Glaze, 2 Coiled Handles, Stamped, 8 1/2 In. 88.00
Vase, Inverted Pear Shape, Crystalline Glaze, Signed, 6 3/4 In. 440.00
Vase, Ivory, Cat's-Eye Flambe & Chinese Blue Glaze, Corseted Shoulders, 10 x 6 In. 550.00
Vase, Leather Famille Rose Matte Glaze, Ink Racetrack Mark, 5 3/4 x 8 1/2 In. 355.00
Vase, Leopard Skin Crystalline Glaze, 3 Handles, Round, Ink Racetrack Mark, 8 In. 1210.00
Vase, Leopard Skin Crystalline Glaze, Ink Racetrack Mark, 9 1/2 x 6 In. 990.00
Vase, Leopard Skin Crystalline Glaze, Rectangular Ink Mark, 6 x 7 In. 715.00
Vase, Mahogany, Ivory & Gunmetal Flambe, Corset Waist, Rectangular Ink Mark, 7 In. ... 330.00
Vase, Maroon, Green, Blue Flambe Glaze, Ribbed, 2 Handles At Top, 8 1/2 In. 165.00
Vase, Mauve, Rose Crystalline Glaze, Bulbous, 7 1/2 x 5 In. 247.00
Vase, Moss-To-Rose Glaze, 10 x 8 In. 605.00
Vase, Mottled Blue Matte Glaze, Cornucopia, Impressed Mark, 7 1/2 In. 110.00
Vase, Mottled Blue Matte Glaze, Corset Waist, Incised Racetrack Mark, 7 1/2 In. 275.00
Vase, Mottled Brown, Green & Ivory Flambe Mirror Glaze, Racetrack Mark, 17 x 9 In. ... 495.00
Vase, Mottled Gray-Green Flambe Glaze, Closed-In Rim, Incised Racetrack, 5 x 7 In. ... 275.00
Vase, Mottled Green, Brown & Blue Glaze, Cream To Pink Base, Handles, c.1915, 9 In. ... 655.00
Vase, Multicolored Flambe Glaze, Handles, Rectangular Mark, 12 In. 1045.00
Vase, Multitone Pink Matte Drip Glaze, Shouldered, 6 1/2 In. 130.00
Vase, Pillow, Flemington Green To Cat's-Eye Flambe Mirror, Rectangular Mark, 10 In. ... 550.00
Vase, Pillow, Green Crystalline, Rose Famille Glaze, 2 Scrolled Handles, Flared, 8 In. ... 250.00
Vase, Puce Green Over Sky Blue Flambe Glaze, 2 Handles, Racetrack Mark, 8 In. 248.00
Vase, Purple Matte Glaze, 3 Handles, Signed, 8 In. 385.00
Vase, Purple, Blue Matte Glaze, Bulbous, 7 1/2 In. 385.00
Vase, Purple, Rose Famille Glaze, 2 Angular Handles, Squat, 4 1/2 In. 275.00
Vase, Rose Crystalline Glaze, Bulbous, 9 In. 275.00
Vase, Turquoise & Apple Green Flambe Glaze, Tapered, Buttressed, 8 1/2 In. 165.00
Vase, Turquoise Crystalline Glaze, 2 Handles, Squat, Label, Racetrack Stamp, 7 In. 385.00
Vase, Turquoise, Amber Crystalline Glaze, Bullet Shape, 6 1/2 x 4 1/2 In. 247.00
Vase, Turquoise, Moss, Rose Flambe Glaze, 4 Buttressed Handles, 8 1/2 x 8 1/2 In. 2530.00
Vase, Violet Matte Glaze, 3 Handles, Squat, Raised Racetrack Mark, 6 In. 275.00
Vase, Wisteria Matte Glaze, Scrolled Handles, 8 1/2 In. 415.00
Washing Pot, Stylized Indigo Grapes, Salt Glaze, John Kunzman, 1908, 7 x 9 1/2 In. 770.00
Water Cooler, Indigo Band Design, Salt Glaze, John Kunzman, 1908, 11 x 8 In. 495.00

Be sure you have photographs and descriptions of your collections in case of a robbery. Keep them in a safe place away from your house.

FURNITURE of all types is listed in this category. Examples dating from the seventeenth century to the 1970s are included. Prices for furniture vary in different parts of the country. Oak furniture is most expensive in the West; large pieces over eight feet high are sold for the most money in the South, where high ceilings are found in the old homes. Condition is very important when determining prices. These are NOT average prices but rather reports of unique sales. If the description includes the word *style*, the piece resembles the old furniture style but was made at a later time. It is not a period piece. Garden furniture is listed in the Garden Furnishings category. Related items may be found in the Architectural, Brass, and Store categories.

Armchairs are listed under Chair in this category.
Armoire, 2 Doors, Painted, 1850, Holland 1195.00
Armoire, Anglo-Indian, Padouk, Double Doors, 19th Century, 72 x 51 In. 1320.00
Armoire, Art Deco, Teakwood, Ebonized Trim, 2 Drawers, Paneled Doors, 79 x 39 In. 518.00
Armoire, Art Deco, Walnut, Serpentine Top, 2 Doors, Rectangular Base, 65 In. 2070.00
Armoire, Bird's-Eye Maple, Faux Bamboo, Mirrored Door, Shelves, 84 In. 3162.00
Armoire, Chestnut, Paneled Doors, Brass Fiche Hinges, Late 18th Century, 95 In. 2860.00
Armoire, Classical, Mahogany, Carved, Half Columns, 2 Doors, Baltimore, 91 x 64 In. 3300.00
Armoire, Classical, Mahogany, Carved, Paneled Doors, Cased Drawers, 86 x 60 In. 4930.00
Armoire, Directoire, Oak, Stop Fluted Pilasters, Cream Paint, 99 1/4 x 65 1/2 In. 4620.00
Armoire, Flush Paneled Doors, Shelves, Storage Well, Red Lacquer, 70 1/2 In. 860.00
Armoire, French Provincial, Cherry, Paneled Door, Cabriole Legs, 89 x 39 x 24 In. 2530.00
Armoire, French Provincial, Shaped Paneled Doors, 1775-1800, 82 x 53 In. 2200.00
Armoire, Hardwood, Foliate Scrolled Borders, Bracket Feet, 68 1/2 In. 10350.00
Armoire, Louis Philippe, Fruitwood, Paneled Doors, Bracket Feet, 91 1/2 In. 2640.00
Armoire, Louis Philippe, Mahogany, 4 Doors, Gothic Panels, 102 In. 6600.00
Armoire, Louis Philippe, Walnut, Cyma Molded Cornice, Paneled Doors, 75 3/4 In. 1210.00
Armoire, Louis XV Style, Pine, Door, Cartouche Carving, 89 3/4 In. 2100.00
Armoire, Louis XV, Oak, 2 Asymmetrical Panels, Flat Cornice, 88 3/4 x 26 In. 2760.00
Armoire, Louis XV, Oak, Leaf Carved Frieze, 3 Shaped Panels, Cabriole Legs, 90 In. 575.00
Armoire, Louis XV, Walnut, Cornice, Frieze Over 2 Paneled Doors 3450.00
Armoire, Louis XVI Style, Walnut, Star Inlay, 2 Doors, 101 x 65 In. 3960.00
Armoire, Louis XVI Transitional, Elm, Paneled Doors, Brass Escutcheons, 91 In. 1430.00
Armoire, Louis XVI Transitional, Oak, Floral Medallion, 84 x 59 In. 3740.00
Armoire, Louis XVI, Cherry, Steel Hinges, Escutcheons, 88 1/2 x 61 In. 1980.00
Armoire, Louis XVI, Kingwood, Ribbon Trailing Foliage, 3 Drawers, 98 x 20 In. 11212.00
Armoire, Louis XVI, Mask Of Woman Within Sunburst, Gilt Medallion, 94 In. 1385.00
Armoire, Louis XVI, Walnut, Cornice Over Frieze, Scalloped Apron, 93 x 23 In. 4370.00
Armoire, Mahogany, 2 Drawers, 2 Beveled Glass Doors, 94 1/2 In. 1870.00
Armoire, Mahogany, Classical Columns, Scrolled Feet, 88 1/2 In. 2420.00
Armoire, Mahogany, Molded Cornice, Frieze, Cabriole Legs, 95 x 59 x 23 1/2 In. 1380.00
Armoire, Neoclassical, Burl Elm, Birch, Dentil Frieze, 2 Doors, 86 3/4 In. 2200.00
Armoire, Oak, Arched Cornice, 2 Paneled Doors, Ball Feet, 78 1/2 In. 1980.00
Armoire, Oak, Floral Frieze, 2 Paneled Doors, Scrolled Feet, 88 In. 4115.00
Armoire, Oak, Molded Cornice Over 2 Paneled Doors, Base Drawer, Bun Feet, 75 In. ... 575.00
Armoire, Pale Green Paint, Polychrome Flowers, Germany, 70 3/4 In. 1540.00
Armoire, Pine, Arched Top, Mirrored, England, 81 x 55 x 25 1/2 In. 575.00
Armoire, Pine, Drawer, Door, Floral Urns, Blue Paint, 39 x 41 x 69 In. 275.00
Armoire, Pine, Paneled Frieze, Star Over 2 Doors, Suspended Drawers, 72 In. 1150.00
Armoire, Renaissance Revival, Oak, 2 Doors, 2 Drawers, Continental, 60 x 96 In. 1870.00
Armoire, Rococo, Rosewood, Mirrored Doors, 107 1/4 x 71 1/2 In. 18700.00
Armoire, Walnut, Carved, Arched Cornice, Pierced Crest, Victorian, 119 x 69 In. 6900.00
Armoire, Walnut, Cornice Over 2 Long Doors, 2 Short Base Drawers, Holland, 78 In. ... 1980.00
Armoire, Walnut, Double Mirrored Doors, Urn Finials, Foliate Carved Frieze, 99 In. 327.00
Bed, Art Deco, Birch, Cream, Shagreen, Blond Wood Border, 1930, 39 1/2 In. 9775.00
Bed, Art Deco, Brass, Stylized Sunburst, Side Rails, c.1930, 48 3/4 x 42 1/2 In. 290.00
Bed, Art Deco, Palm Wood, Rectangular Head Board, Curved Footboard, 55 In. 2875.00
Bed, Belle Epoque, Brass, Reeded Latticework, Plaque With Putti, 3/4 Size, 79 In. 460.00
Bed, Biedermeier, Fruitwood, Scrolled Head & Footboard, 41 In., Pair 3450.00
Bed, Bird's-Eye Maple, Rope, Paneled Head Board, Acorn Ends, 52 x 72 x 79 1/2 In. 1650.00
Bed, Brass, Acorn Finials, 3 Spindles In Headboard & Footboard, 1900, 54 In. 225.00
Bed, Brass, Arched Head Board, Foliate Scrolled Panel, Vase-Form Finials, 48 x 54 In. .. 660.00

Furniture, Bed, Four-Poster, Birch, 81 x 71 In.

Furniture, Bed, Four-Poster, Chippendale, Mahogany, 84 x 79 In.

Bed, Brass, Square & Turned Tubes, 53 x 57 1/2 In. 155.00
Bed, Campaign, Scrolls, Pierced Plaque, Casters, Painted, Victorian, Pair 290.00
Bed, Charak, Federal Style, Mahogany, Crossbanded, Head Board, 40 x 40 In., Pair 750.00
Bed, Charles X, Mahogany, Folding Campaign, X-Shaped Legs, 21 x 86 In. 5750.00
Bed, Cherry, Poplar, Rope, Paneled Head Board, Red Paint, 75 1/2 x 55 1/2 In. 415.00
Bed, Christian Krass, Rosewood, Rectangular Head & Footboard, 1930, 67 1/2 In. 1380.00
Bed, Curly Maple, Spindles, Finials, Gate, Child's, 36 x 49 In. 495.00
Bed, E. Wormley, Mahogany, Rosewood, Dunbar, 80 x 39 In. 550.00
Bed, Empire, Mahogany, Arched, Scrolled, Carved Flowers, 77 x 50 In. 800.00
Bed, Empire, Mahogany, Doric Columns, Ring Turned Feet, 44 1/2 In., Pair 1095.00
Bed, F. Loeser & Co., Four-Poster, Empire Style, Mahogany, Carved, 81 x 67 In. 1035.00
Bed, Federal, Rope, Head Board, Floral, Red Painted Eagle, Pa., 1840, 50 x 84 In. 660.00
Bed, Field, Eldred Wheeler, Sheraton Style, Mahogany, Twin, Pair 1100.00
Bed, Field, Sheraton Style, Mahogany, Turned & Reeded Headposts, 41 In. 935.00
Bed, Four-Poster, Birch, 81 x 71 In. . . . . *Illus* 2300.00
Bed, Four-Poster, Birch, Pine, Rope, Urn Finials, 54 1/4 In. 360.00
Bed, Four-Poster, Black Walnut, Yellow Pine, Tester, Twisted Base, 90 1/2 In. 2875.00
Bed, Four-Poster, Brass, Whitcomb Metallic Bedstead Co., Queen 660.00
Bed, Four-Poster, Cherry, Scrolled Head Board, Straight Tester, 1825, 90 In. 1955.00
Bed, Four-Poster, Chippendale, Mahogany, 84 x 79 In. . . . . *Illus* 2300.00
Bed, Four-Poster, Classical, Mahogany, Rope Twist, Pineapple Finials, 88 In. 4125.00
Bed, Four-Poster, Curly Maple, Scrolled Head Board, Rope Rails, 57 x 74 1/2 x 79 In. . . . 1650.00
Bed, Four-Poster, Dutch Colonial, Hardwood, Cartouche, Tester, 1850, 60 x 85 In. 1760.00
Bed, Four-Poster, Federal Style, Mahogany, Carved Eagle, 78 In. 1380.00
Bed, Four-Poster, Federal, Birch, Reeded Posts, c.1815, 69 x 48 x 68 In. 1955.00
Bed, Four-Poster, Federal, Mahogany, Cherry, Reeded Baluster Posts, 81 1/2 In. 5520.00
Bed, Four-Poster, Federal, Mahogany, Rope Fitted Rails, 1800s, 86 x 58 x 78 In. 2070.00
Bed, Four-Poster, Federal, Walnut, Pine, Baluster, Urn Posts, Tester, Casters, 86 In. 2875.00
Bed, Four-Poster, Field, Sheraton, Curly Maple, Scrolled Head Board, 68 In. 3520.00
Bed, Four-Poster, Hardwood, Twisted Posts, Bulbous Turned Legs, 84 In. 3300.00
Bed, Four-Poster, Louis XVI, Beechwood, Square Sectioned Posts, 37 3/4 In., Pair 750.00
Bed, Four-Poster, Mahogany, Carved, Tester, Casters, 19th Century, 81 x 56 x 75 In. 560.00
Bed, Four-Poster, Mahogany, Pineapple Top, Acanthus, Feather Poles, 80 x 62 In. 1870.00
Bed, Four-Poster, Maple, Arched Head Board, Straight Tester, 83 x 46 x 72 In. 3737.00
Bed, Four-Poster, Rope, Maple, Grain Paint, Early 19th Century, Double, 49 In. 165.00
Bed, Four-Poster, Rope, Mixed Woods, Cutout Head Board, Quilt Roll, 32 x 72 In. 65.00
Bed, Four-Poster, Rope, Poplar, Acorn Finials, 19th Century, 47 x 56 In. 170.00
Bed, Four-Poster, Sheraton, Cherry, Pine Headboard, 1810, 74 x 54 In. 605.00
Bed, Four-Poster, Sheraton, Walnut, Scalloped Pine Head Board, 86 x 61 1/2 In. 1790.00
Bed, Four-Poster, Walnut, Carved, Arched Egg & Dart Tester, Victorian, 125 x 76 In. 9075.00
Bed, Four-Poster, Walnut, Paneled Head Board, Tapered Posts, Tester, c.1850, 102 In. . . . 4840.00
Bed, G. Stickley, 5 Broad Vertical Slats, Tapered Posts, Red Decal, 48 x 57 In. 7150.00
Bed, Half-Tester, Renaissance Revival, Walnut, Burl Walnut, 1875, 114 x 83 In. 3200.00
Bed, Hardwood, Brass Mounted, Spiral Twist Finials, Bun Feet, 19th Century, 60 In. 20700.00
Bed, Heywood-Wakefield Co., Maple, Sliding Doors, Twin, Pair 230.00
Bed, Joseph Bruno, Four-Poster, Federal Style, Mahogany, Urn Finials, 90 x 65 In. 1870.00
Bed, Louis Philippe, Sleigh Shape, Winged-Lion Stiles, 43 1/2 x 57 x 82 1/4 In. 4400.00
Bed, Louis XV, Walnut, Pierced Flower Head Footboard, 64 1/2 In. 345.00

Bed, Low-Post, Rope, Grain Painted, 35 1/2 x 74 In. . . . . *Illus*   805.00
Bed, Low-Post, Rope, Rectangular Head Board, Hinged Rail, Painted, 36 x 51 In. 1380.00
Bed, Low-Post, Rosewood, Carved, Scrollwork, Garlands, Victorian, 68 1/2 x 88 In. 5465.00
Bed, Mahogany, Fluted, Angled Head Board, Square Legs, 79 x 55 x 85 In. 2300.00
Bed, Maple, Rope, Peaked Head & Footboard, Ball Finials, c.1820, 50 x 75 In. 330.00
Bed, Murphy, Oak, Top Beveled Mirror, Doors, Bowfront, 77 1/2 In. 1350.00
Bed, Painted Classical Scene, 19th Century, 114 In. . . . . *Illus*   1500.00
Bed, Poplar, Low-Post, Rope, Patented Boyd Bed Rails, Red Paint, 37 x 72 In. 250.00
Bed, Poplar, Rope, Square Posts, Tapered Legs, 70 3/4 x 51 In. 440.00
Bed, Poplar, Rope, Turned & Paneled Posts, Goblet Finial, 70 x 53 x 59 In. 55.00
Bed, Regency, Mahogany, Burl Veneer, Carved Eagle & Shield, 72 x 66 In. 8960.00
Bed, Renaissance Revival, Walnut, Veneer, Domed Head Board, 102 x 65 x 84 In. 3360.00
Bed, Rococo Style, Arched Crest, Flowers, Gilt, Painted Cherubs, 45 x 53 In. 690.00
Bed, Rope, Red Paint, Pa., 19th Century, 3/4 Size 660.00
Bed, Shaker, Maple, Pine, 4 Block Turned Legs, First Half 19th Century, 30 1/4 x 64 In. . .   690.00
Bed, Sheraton, Curly Maple, Reeded Posts, Pine Head Board, 67 11/2 In. 1760.00
Bed, Sheraton, Mahogany, Acorn Finial, Brocade Hangings, Queen 2690.00
Bed, Sheraton, Mahogany, Carved, Scrolled Head Board, Pineapple Posts, 83 In. 4290.00
Bed, Sleigh, Charles X, Rosewood, Scrolling Foliate Marquetry, c.1830, 89 In. 3960.00
Bed, Sleigh, Mahogany, Paired Scrolled Ends, c.1835, 46 1/2 x 53 In. 1633.00
Bed, Sleigh, Mahogany, Scrolled Head & Footboard, 41 1/4 x 88 1/2 In. 518.00
Bed, Sleigh, Mahogany, Veneer, Scrolled Sides, Carved Feet, Casters, 102 In. 4025.00
Bed, Spool Turned, Spindle Head & Footboard, Side Rails, Child's 38.00
Bed, Stickley Brothers, Paneled, Glasgow Rose Inlay, Full Size, 60 x 56 1/2 In. 6600.00
Bed, Tiger Maple, Rope, 9 Spindles, Mattress & Springs, 55 x 51 In. 465.00
Bed, Trundle, Blue Over Red, Square Posts, Finial, 36 x 57 x 15 In. 330.00
Bed, Trundle, Square Posts, Cutout Head Board, Red Paint, Child's, 52 x 32 x 17 In. 55.00
Bed, Walnut, Rosewood Grained, Finials, Victorian, 88 x 72 In. . . . . *Illus*   825.00
Bed, Wedding, Mahogany, Carved, Canopy Top, Reverse Painted, Chinese, 80 x 70 In. 670.00
Bed Steps, Edwardian, Mahogany, Turned Legs, Potty 220.00
Bed Steps, Federal Style, Mahogany, Hinged Compartment Top Step, 19 1/2 x 17 In. 80.00
Bed Steps, Mahogany, Leather Inlay, Turned Legs, Ball Feet, 30 x 17 x 27 In. 518.00
Bedroom Set, Berkey & Gay, Burl Walnut, Incised Panels, Marble Tops, 3 Piece 8800.00
Bedroom Set, Chippendale Style, Mahogany, Reeded, 20th Century, 5 Piece 465.00
Bedroom Set, Eastlake, Walnut, Marble Tops, 3 Piece 1760.00
Bedroom Set, Empire, Mahogany, Scrolled Feet, 68 x 50 In., 3 Piece 1345.00
Bedroom Set, Empire, Mahogany, Spool Bed, 1800s, 4 Piece 390.00
Bedroom Set, Gilbert Rhode, Highboy, Lowboy, Vanity, Stool, Bed 1725.00
Bedroom Set, Marble Top, Floral Carved Panels, c.1880, 4 Piece 7150.00
Bedroom Set, Renaissance Revival, Burl Walnut, Marble Top, Victorian, 3 Piece 8500.00
Bedroom Set, Renaissance Revival, Maple, Ebonized, Gilt, Tufted Panels, 3 Piece 7425.00
Bench, 6 Barley Twist Legs, Spreaders, Upholstered, 18 x 43 In. 248.00
Bench, Arts & Crafts, Cast Iron, 2 Bronze Panels, Spanish Galleons, 1880s 805.00
Bench, Biedermeier, Fruitwood, Scrolling Sides, Saber Legs, 19th Century, 70 In. 3335.00
Bench, Blue Stripes, Turned Legs & Posts, Plank Seat, Half-Spindle Back, 71 1/2 In. 302.00

Furniture, Bed, Low-Post, Rope,
Grain Painted, 35 1/2 x 74 In.

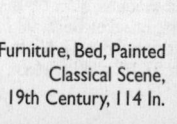

Furniture, Bed, Painted
Classical Scene,
19th Century, 114 In.

Furniture, Bed, Walnut,
Rosewood Grained, Finials,
Victorian, 88 x 72 In.

Bench, Bucket, Geometric, Pinwheel Design, Pa., 30 x 33 In. 4675.00
Bench, Bucket, Pine, Scrolled Sides, 2 Shelves, Red Paint, Pa., 30 In. 550.00
Bench, Cherry, Bootjack Ends, Base Shelf, 23 1/2 x 30 In. 170.00
Bench, Classical, Mahogany, Ogee Molded Seat Rail, Scrolled Legs, 17 x 36 In. 1870.00
Bench, Deacon's, 2-Board Seat, 24 Turned Spindles, 8 Legs, Stenciling, 31 x 96 In. 890.00
Bench, Deacon's, Half-Spindle Back, Plank Seat, Gilt, Fruit Design, 72 In. 935.00
Bench, Dragon Carved, Mother-Of-Pearl & Horn Inlay, Japan, 19th Century, 49 In. 1210.00
Bench, E. Wormley, Blond Wood, Long-John, Hairpin Legs, 59 In. 770.00
Bench, E. Wormley, Upholstered Top, 2 H-Frame Bases, 67 In. 1150.00
Bench, Elm, Rattan Corners, Ribbon Carved, 19th Century, 21 x 32 3/4 In. 1150.00
Bench, Fireside, Pine, High Back, 4 Vertical Panels, Lift Top Seat, 64 x 62 In. 1760.00
Bench, G. Nelson, Blond Wood, Ebonized Base, Herman Miller, 48 In. 550.00
Bench, Giltwood, Cane Back, Shaped Seat, Stop Fluted Legs, 2 Seats, 30 x 41 1/2 In. 460.00
Bench, Half Spindles, 3 Seats, Scrolled Arms, Painted, Pennsylvania, 80 In. 275.00
Bench, Hall, Arts & Crafts, Paneled Sides, Hinged Lift Top, Cushion, 56 In. 195.00
Bench, Hall, Cutout Tulip Back, Umbrella Stands On Sides, England, 35 x 17 In. 660.00
Bench, Hall, Limbert, Mahogany, 6 Vertical Slats, Lift Seat, 41 1/4 x 42 x 18 In. 4675.00
Bench, Hardwood, Paneled Base, Slat Seat, Rail Back, Chinese, 88 In. 550.00
Bench, Knoll, Vinyl Cushions, Chrome Legs, 3 Seats, 82 In. 1320.00
Bench, Limbert, Wide Slat Base, 18 x 20 x 15 In. 770.00
Bench, Louis XV Style, Carved Scallop Shell, Cabriole Legs, Tapestry, 28 x 18 In. 595.00
Bench, M. Breuer, Tubular Chrome, White Laminate Top, 1960, 14 In. 286.00
Bench, Mammy's, Pine, Poplar, Arrow Back, Rocking, 1820, 75 In. 192.00
Bench, Mammy's, Pine, Spindle Back, Scrolled Arms, New England, c.1810, 30 x 50 In. . . 825.00
Bench, Mammy's, Spindle Back, Gilt Floral Stencil, Black Paint, c.1830, 49 1/2 In. 880.00
Bench, Mammy's, Stenciled Design, Grain Painted, 48 In. 660.00
Bench, Neoclassical, Walnut, Padded Seat, Saber Legs, 30 x 51 x 20 In. 1610.00
Bench, Oak, Monk's, Hinged Top, Turned Feet, Lion-Shaped Arms, 28 x 41 3/4 In. 577.00
Bench, Oak, Paneled Back, Rectangular Mirror, Box Seat, Hinged Lid, 87 In. 1725.00
Bench, Pine, Bootjack Ends, Painted, 12 1/2 x 87 x 19 In. 185.00
Bench, Pine, Brown Graining, Yellow Ground, Cutout Legs, 15 x 35 1/2 In. 300.00
Bench, Pine, Forged Iron, Arched Backrest, 2 Seats, Scrolled Arms, c.1900, 40 In. 200.00
Bench, Pine, Green Paint, 17 x 39 x 19 In. 305.00
Bench, Pine, High Back, Grain Painted Surface, Early 19th Century, 37 1/2 In. 660.00
Bench, Pine, Lift Top, Storage Areas, Dovetailed Case, Bracket Feet, c.1830, 61 In. 285.00
Bench, Pine, Walnut Top Rail, Fitted Cushions, 62 x 16 x 33 In. 245.00
Bench, Poplar, Silver Gray Patina, Wire Nails, Cutout Feet, 9 1/2 x 87 x 18 In. 55.00
Bench, Queen Anne, Mahogany, Pad Feet, Brass Tacked Upholstery, 16 x 37 In. 440.00
Bench, Queen Anne, Oak, 5-Panel Back, 3-Board Seat, Curved Arms, 43 x 74 In. 895.00
Bench, Regency Style, Red Lacquer, Gilt, Curule Shape, Muslin Seat, 25 x 47 In. 880.00
Bench, Regency, Gilt, Metal, Salmon & Floral Stripes, Cut Velvet, 20 x 17 In. 315.00
Bench, Roycroft, Ali Baba, Half Ash Log, Keyed Tenon, Oak Trestle, 19 x 42 x 15 In. 7150.00
Bench, Roycroft, Oak, 2 Back Slats, Slat Seat, Orb & Cross Mark, 31 x 71 In. 2750.00
Bench, Satinwood, Pierced Ends, Brass Cup Casters, Victorian, Child's, 18 x 21 In. 1430.00
Bench, Scalloped Legs, Salmon Paint, Pa., 19th Century, 10 x 13 In. 3300.00
Bench, Scrolled Back, Sheep's Head, Arms, Continental, 19th Century, 28 x 30 In. 505.00
Bench, Spindle Back, Shaped Back, S-Scroll Seat, Removable Body Guard, 82 In. 1100.00
Bench, Spring, Brown Lacquer, Carved, Cut Down, Chinese, 17 x 53 x 22 In. 165.00
Bench, Walnut, 6 Cabriole Legs, Scrolled Toes, Upholstered, 19 x 53 1/2 In. 2070.00
Bench, Walnut, Classical X Shape, Carved Animal Heads, Continental, 25 x 27 In. 770.00
Bench, Walnut, Lift Top, Inlaid Scalloped Back, Continental, 46 x 55 In. 1650.00
Bench, Water, Poplar, Open Top, Shelf Base, Drawer, 42 x 59 In. 2420.00
Bench, William & Mary, Oak, Acanthus S-Scrolled Legs, Cane Seat, 18 x 46 1/2 In. 440.00
Bench, William IV, Mahogany, Stylized X-Shaped Base, Fleur-De-Lis, 23 x 15 In., Pair .. 1005.00
Bench, Windsor, Pine, Turned Back Supports, Curved Arms, 33 1/2 x 71 x 20 In. 560.00
Bench, Wrought Iron, Gilt, Tassel Finials, Scrolled Arms, 31 x 49 x 51 In. 431.00
Bench, Yellow Pine, Porch, Gothic Arched Trestle Feet, 34 x 71 In. 330.00
Bench-Table, Tilt Top, Lift Seat, Pinstripes, Late 19th Century, 30 x 53 In. 880.00
Bibliotheque, Napoleon III, Neoclassical Style, Sevres-Style Plaques, 42 x 66 In. 1760.00
Bibliotheque, Renaissance Revival, Walnut, 4 Short Drawers, Bracket Base, 98 In. 4890.00
Bookcase, 2 Glass Doors, Carved Oak Leaves, Acorns, Victorian, 73 x 37 1/2 In. 450.00
Bookcase, 2 Glazed & Mullioned Doors, Late 19th Century, 53 1/2 x 40 5/16 In. 460.00
Bookcase, Arts & Crafts, 3 Doors, Copper Star Pulls, 55 In. 1980.00

Bookcase, Arts & Crafts, Chestnut, Oak, 2 Doors, Large & Small Panes, 55 x 42 In. 2310.00
Bookcase, Arts & Crafts, Double Doors, Gallery Top, 3 Interior Shelves, 48 In. 1650.00
Bookcase, Biedermeier, Walnut, Gothic Glazed Bar On Paneled Doors, 72 In. 4400.00
Bookcase, Cherry, Glazed Doors, 4 Shelves Over Short Drawers, c.1790, 62 1/2 In. 4312.00
Bookcase, Eastlake, Walnut, Step Back, 2 Paneled Doors, 90 x 60 In. 2200.00
Bookcase, G. Stickley, 2 Doors, 16 Panes, Gallery Top, 56 1/2 x 48 In. 5225.00
Bookcase, G. Stickley, 2 Doors, 16 Panes, Gallery Top, Label, 35 x 25 In. 9350.00
Bookcase, G. Stickley, 2 Doors, 16 Panes, Gallery Top, Label, 56 x 13 In. 7975.00
Bookcase, G. Stickley, 2 Doors, 16 Panes, Gallery, Tenon Sides, Label, 56 x 35 In. 6050.00
Bookcase, G. Stickley, Mahogany, 2 Doors, 2 Oak Divided Panels, 58 In. 21850.00
Bookcase, G. Stickley, No. 719, 2 Doors, Glass Panes .... *Illus* 10450.00
Bookcase, George II, Mahogany, 6 Doors, Dentil Molded Cornice, 1800, 93 1/2 In. 11000.00
Bookcase, George II, Walnut, Mirrored Door, Slant Front, 4 Drawers, 81 In. 5500.00
Bookcase, Georgian Style, Mahogany, Glass Doors, Busts Of Diana 104 In., Pair 6050.00
Bookcase, Georgian, 4 Glazed Doors With Rosettes, Fretter Drawers, 87 In. 3300.00
Bookcase, Herter Bros., Walnut, 3 Adjustable Shelves, 2 Base Drawers, 66 x 57 In. 2310.00
Bookcase, L. & J.G. Stickley, No. 643, Mahogany, 2 Doors, 16 Panes, 56 In. 6900.00
Bookcase, Lawyers, Stacking, Oak, Beveled & Leaded Glass, 5 Sections, 68 x 34 In. 3465.00
Bookcase, Lifetime, 3 Glass Doors, Shelves, Decal, 54 x 54 x 12 In. 2145.00
Bookcase, Lifetime, No. 7242, 3 Drawers Over 2 Doors, Wood Squares, 55 In. 3100.00
Bookcase, Limbert, 2 Shelves Over 2 Doors, Heart-Shaped Cutouts, 47 x 31 In. 2860.00
Bookcase, Limbert, No. 314, Leaded Glass Door, Paper Label, 54 x 21 In. 7700.00
Bookcase, Limbert, No. 358, Corbel Supports, Copper Pulls, Arched Apron, 57 In. 2875.00
Bookcase, Limbert, No. 359, 2 Doors, Gallery, Branded, 57 x 66 1/2 x 14 In. 10450.00
Bookcase, Mahogany, 2 Glazed Doors, Adjustable Shelves, 56 3/4 x 53 1/4 In. 1155.00
Bookcase, Mahogany, Arched Frieze, Glazed Doors, Adjustable Shelves, 88 In. 5060.00
Bookcase, Mahogany, Glazed Doors, Egg-And-Dart Molding, 2 Drawers, 33 In. 5175.00
Bookcase, McCobb, Maple, 2 Shelves, Platform Stand, 60 x 18 x 34 In. 230.00
Bookcase, Neoclassical, Fruitwood, 2 Paneled Doors, Ormolu Mounts, 86 In. 2640.00
Bookcase, Neoclassical, Pine, Double Glazed Doors, Germany, 77 x 35 In. 1430.00
Bookcase, Onondaga, No. 320, Door Opposite Open Shelves, 42 x 35 In. 4400.00
Bookcase, Oriental, Bamboo, 3 Shelves, Red Lacquer, 44 x 14 x 57 In. 495.00
Bookcase, Plexiglas, Rounded Top, 5 Shelves, 48 x 12 1/2 x 84 In. 460.00
Bookcase, Regency Style, Mahogany, 3 Open Shelves, 2 Grilled Doors, 61 In. 3000.00
Bookcase, Regency, Mahogany, 2 Paneled Doors, Molded Edge Plinths, 84 In., Pair 1320.00
Bookcase, Regency, Mahogany, 4 Graduated Shelves, 57 In. 1150.00
Bookcase, Regency, Mahogany, 6 Doors, Rectangular Cornice, Key Border, 102 In. 14950.00
Bookcase, Regency, Rosewood, Spiral Brass Molding, Paw Feet, 33 3/4 In. 4025.00
Bookcase, Renaissance Revival, Oak, Rectangular Top, 3 Aligned Drawers, 48 In. 1035.00
Bookcase, Revolving, Mahogany, 1910s, 44 x 20 x 20 In. 247.00
Bookcase, Revolving, Mahogany, Inlay, 33 Shakespeare Volumes, c.1904, 6 In. 690.00
Bookcase, Rococo, Rosewood, Fruit, Foliate Carving, Mid 19th Century, 89 1/2 In. 5520.00
Bookcase, Roycroft, 4 Shelves, Base Drawer, Light Finish, 65 x 14 x 9 1/4 In. 7150.00
Bookcase, Stacking, Globe-Wernicke, Mahogany, Leaded Glass, 4 Sections, 34 x 67 In. .. 800.00
Bookcase, Stickley Brothers, Hammered Copper Ring Pull, 50 x 35 1/2 x 12 In. 3850.00
Bookcase, Walnut, 2 Dovetailed Drawers, 2 Paneled Doors, Zoar, Ohio, 73 1/2 In. 1100.00
Bookcase, Walnut, 2 Sections, 2 Glass Doors, Carved, 1870s, 103 In. 3300.00
Bookcase, Walnut, Maple, Carved Fretwork, Birds On Top, 1900, 79 x 47 x 15 In. 1150.00
Bookcase-Cabinet, Aesthetic Revival, Mahogany, Metal Inlay, England, 94 In. 5775.00
Bookcase-Desk, Federal, Cherry, Glazed Doors Over 4 Drawers, c.1820, 69 x 38 In. 5460.00
Bookrack, Arts & Crafts, Wooden, Folding, Open Sides, 6 x 16 x 7 In. 220.00
Bookrack, Arts & Crafts, Wooden, Inlay Ends, Expandable, 6 x 27 x 6 In. 110.00
Bookrack, Gustav Stickley, No. 90, Wooden, Rotating, 9 1/2 x 13 x 13 In. 2200.00
Bookrack, Oak, Telescopic Action, Foliage Base, Cast Iron, Casters, 44 In. 316.00
Bookshelf, Arts & Crafts, Oak, Slat Sides, Attached Mirror, 70 1/2 In. 1265.00
Bookshelf, Elm, Open Shelf, 2 Paneled Doors, Chinese, 39 1/2 x 60 In. 865.00
Bookshelf, Inlaid Tulipwood, Marble Top, Double Sided, Drawers, 32 x 24 In. 1035.00
Bookstand, Arts & Crafts, 3 Keyed Through-Tenon Shelves, 34 x 27 In. 360.00
Bookstand, Arts & Crafts, Mahogany, V-Shaped Top Rail, 32 x 10 x 29 In. 550.00
Bookstand, Carved Portrait Of Pocahontas, 14 x 9 3/4 In. 230.00
Bookstand, G. Stickley, Drop Leaf, Half-Moon Cutouts, 2 Shelves, 37 1/2 In. 825.00
Bookstand, Revolving, 2 Round Shelves, Victorian, 40 x 30 In. 145.00
Bookstand, Revolving, Mahogany, 4 Tiers, Faux Leather Books, Paw Feet, 45 In. 8050.00

Furniture, Bookcase,
G. Stickley, No. 719,
2 Doors, Glass Panes

Furniture, Bureau,
Federal, Bowfront,
Mahogany, 1810,
37 x 37 3/4 x 20 In.

Bookstand, Roycroft, Little Journeys, 3 Keyed Through-Tenon Shelves, 14 In. 600.00
Bookstand, Stickley Brothers, No. 4708, Oak, Gallery Top, 3 Open Shelves, 38 In. 1035.00
Box, Blanket, 1-Board Top, Pine Till, Dovetailed, Painted, 22 x 50 x 21 In. 1230.00
Box, Blanket, Lift Top, Brown Finish, Dovetailed, 19 x 37 1/2 x 18 In. 300.00
Box, Blanket, Oak, Domed Top, Wrought Iron Hinges, 1781, 32 x 54 x 26 In. 670.00
Box, Blanket, Poplar, 2-Board Top, Dovetailed, Till, 22 x 18 x 21 In. 560.00
Box, Blanket, Poplar, 6-Board Top, Till, Red Paint, Child's, 10 x 24 x 10 1/2 In. 155.00
Box-On-Stand, Anglo-Colonial, Hardwood, Brass, Mahogany Stand, 23 x 17 In. 715.00
Breakfront, Beacon Hill, Mahogany, 4 Drawers, Drawer Is Desk, 79 x 65 x 17 In. 2750.00
Breakfront, Chinoiserie, Overall Flower & Bird Design, 55 x 16 x 80 In. 805.00
Breakfront, George III, Chinoiserie, Figures Within Landscape, 90 x 74 In. 3960.00
Breakfront, Georgian Style, Mahogany, Glazed Doors, Gothic Arched Mullions, 89 In. . . 6325.00
Breakfront, Hepplewhite, Mahogany, Broken Arch Pediment, 4 Doors, 97 x 48 In. 6050.00
Breakfront, Kingwood, Tulipwood, Marble Top, Shaped Skirt, 33 1/4 In. 950.00
Breakfront-Bookcase, 4 Astragal Doors, 4 Paneled Doors, Victorian, 100 In. 10350.00
Breakfront-Bookcase, George III, Mahogany, Rectangular Cornice, 81 In. 1725.00
Breakfront-Bookcase, Mahogany, 3 Grillwork Doors, 3 Cupboard Doors, 84 In. 5175.00
Breakfront-Bookcase, Mahogany, Carved Bands, Ogee Bracket Feet, Ireland, 80 In. 2420.00
Breakfront-Bookcase, Regency, Mahogany, Crossbanded Frieze, 99 x 99 1/4 In. 17250.00
Buffet, Charles X, Mahogany, Long Lower Drawer, Cupboard Doors, c.1825, 48 In. 3500.00
Buffet, Empire, Mahogany, Marble Top, 2 Frieze Drawers, 2 Doors, 42 x 21 1/2 In. 2300.00
Buffet, Empire, Mahogany, Rectangular Top, 3 Drawers, Ball Feet, 48 x 59 x 21 In. 2415.00
Buffet, French Provincial, Cherry, Banded Top, 2 Drawers, 39 1/2 In. 1380.00
Buffet, French Provincial, Oak, 2 Drawers, 2 Doors, Carved, 1775-1800, 36 x 51 In. 2100.00
Buffet, Louis XV Style, Oak, Recessed Shelves, Doors, 89 x 66 In. 5500.00
Buffet, Louis XV, Fruitwood, 3 Frieze Drawers, Rectangular Marble Top, 39 In. 2875.00
Buffet, Louis XV, Oak, Rounded Molded Cornice Over 2 Doors, 96 x 24 1/4 In. 5060.00
Buffet, Louis XVI, Stained Elm, 4 Doors, 3 Drawers, Arched Cornice, 84 1/2 In., 2 Piece . 3740.00
Buffet, Louis XVI, Walnut, 2 Doors, 4 Bowfront Drawers, 39 x 71 In. 5500.00
Buffet, Rosewood, Carved Cornucopia, Marble Top, Beveled Mirror, 76 1/2 In. 880.00
Bureau, 2 Short Over 3 Drawers, Line Inlay, French Feet, Pa., c.1810, 44 1/2 In. 2530.00
Bureau, Art Deco, Mahogany, 3 Drawers, Zigzag Pulls, c.1935, 35 1/2 In. 1840.00
Bureau, Chippendale, Bowfront, Cherry, 4 Graduated Drawers, 1810, 37 x 42 In. 4600.00
Bureau, Empire, Mahogany, 4 Drawers, Reeded Edge Top, 1820, 34 1/2 x 45 1/2 In. 770.00
Bureau, Empire, Rectangular Top, 2 Glove Drawers, Blue Paint, Child's, 12 x 13 In. 690.00
Bureau, Federal, Bird's-Eye Maple, Scalloped Crest, 6 Drawers, 1825, 49 x 43 In. 770.00
Bureau, Federal, Bowfront, Mahogany, 1810, 37 x 37 3/4 x 20 In. . . . . *Illus* 14750.00
Bureau, Federal, Bowfront, Mahogany, Birch Veneer, Salem, Mass., 1810, 37 In. 14950.00
Bureau, Federal, Mahogany, 2 Cock-Beaded Short Drawers, Turned Legs, 1825, 44 In. . . . 1495.00
Bureau, Federal, Mahogany, Rectangular Top, Ring Turned Columns, 38 1/4 In. 2185.00
Bureau, George II, Walnut, Slant Front, 5 Drawers, Bracket Feet, 42 1/2 In. 5500.00
Bureau, George III Style, Mahogany, Slant Front, 4 Drawers, 96 1/2 In. 4840.00
Bureau, Hepplewhite Style, Pine Top, 4 Mahogany Drawers, 36 x 41 1/2 In. 825.00
Bureau, Hepplewhite, Bowfront, Maple, 4 Drawers, 38 1/2 x 21 1/2 In. 2860.00
Bureau, Louis XV, Mahogany, Leather Lined, Brass Top, Sabot Feet, 30 In. 3080.00
Bureau, Louis XV, Oak, 3 Graduated Drawers, Cabriole Legs, 17 x 50 1/2 In. 2300.00
Bureau, Louis XV, Rectangular Top, Shelved Compartments, Green Paint, 53 In. 4890.00
Bureau, Louis XVI, Mahogany, Molded Rectangular Top, 2 Short Drawers, 29 In. 1380.00

Bureau, Mahogany, Long Drawer Flanked By 2 Drawers, Inset Leather Top, 70 3/4 In. . . . 2875.00
Bureau, McCobb, Maple, 6 Drawers, Fitted Stand, 33 x 18 In. 430.00
Bureau, Neoclassical, Kingwood, Tulipwood, Diamond-Shaped Top, 36 In. 4143.00
Bureau, Queen Anne, 2 Short Drawers Over 2 Long Drawers, Cream Paint, 38 In. 1725.00
Bureau, Rococo, Mahogany, 3 Serpentine Drawers, Cream Painted Interior, 96 In. 2640.00
Bureau, Rococo, Oak, Rectangular Top, Leather Writing Surface, Bun Feet, 40 In. 5750.00
Bureau, Rococo, Slant Front, Burl Walnut, Bombe, Paw Feet, 1900, 40 1/2 In. 3080.00
Bureau, Sheraton, Bowfront, Mahogany, 2 Over 4 Drawers, 48 x 39 x 19 In. 990.00
Bureau, Sheraton, Mahogany, 2 Glove Boxes Over 3 Drawers, 13 x 12 x 8 In. 300.00
Bureau, Sheraton, Mahogany, 2 Over 4 Drawers, Scrolled Backsplash, 49 1/2 In. 935.00
Bureau, Sheraton, Mahogany, Bird's-Eye Maple Drawer, Turned Legs, 27 x 17 x 19 In. . . 303.00
Bureau, Slant Front, Cubbyhole, Drawer, Hidden Compartments, c.1780, 42 In. 4840.00
Bureau, Walnut, Rectangular Top, Fitted Interior, 7 Drawers, Bracket Feet, 42 In. 4025.00
Bureau, Walnut, Slant Front, Fitted Interior, Pigeonhole, 4 Drawers, 1750s, 41 In. 5250.00
Cabinet, Aesthetic Revival, Walnut, Kimbel & Cabus, 49 x 27 x 13 In. 1485.00
Cabinet, Art Deco, Rosewood, 2 Bifold Doors, Raised On Plinth, c.1935, 45 In. 1610.00
Cabinet, Art Deco, Rosewood, Rectangular Top, 4 Doors, Splayed Feet, 98 In. 3450.00
Cabinet, Art Nouveau, Walnut, 2 Cabinets, Beveled Glass, 62 x 26 x 15 In. 1045.00
Cabinet, Arts & Crafts, 2 Doors, 6 Shelves, Grand Rapids, Michigan, 55 x 45 x 13 In. . . . 1760.00
Cabinet, Arts & Crafts, 2 Drawers, 2 Glass Doors Over 2 Wood Doors, 62 x 49 In. 2310.00
Cabinet, Bar, Chippendale, Mahogany, Fold Front, 3 Drawers, 76 x 36 In. 770.00
Cabinet, Baroque, Oak, Ebony, Overhanging Rectangular Cornice, Bun Feet, 72 In. 8625.00
Cabinet, Biedermeier, Walnut, Rectangular Top, 2 Drawers, 1845, 55 x 16 x 45 In. 935.00
Cabinet, Black Lacquer, Bamboo, Spindle Gallery, 81 1/4 x 22 In. 3000.00
Cabinet, Bowfront, Oak, Marble Serpentine Foliate, 19th Century, 70 1/2 In., Pair 7475.00
Cabinet, Cherry, Cyma Cornice, 3 Shelves, Lower Doors, Storage, 78 In. 2860.00
Cabinet, Cherry, Poplar, Carved Hunt Scene, Fox Inlay, Carved Shells, 54 1/2 In. 575.00
Cabinet, China, French Provincial, Oak, 6-Tier Plate Rack, 3 Drawers, 79 x 69 In. 2640.00
Cabinet, China, Gallery, Top Glass Doors, Bell Furniture Co., 61 x 44 x 15 In. 1540.00
Cabinet, China, Hanging, Louis XVI, Walnut, Scalloped Crest, 53 x 40 In. 1320.00
Cabinet, China, Heywood-Wakefield Co., Solid Maple, 3 Drawers, Door, 26 x 45 In. 345.00
Cabinet, China, L. & J.G. Stickley, 2 Doors, 8 Panes, Backsplash, 56 1/2 In. 6600.00
Cabinet, China, Larkin, Oak, Claw & Ball Feet, Curved Glass Sides, 62 x 40 In. 800.00
Cabinet, China, Lifetime, 2 Doors, Through Tenon Top, Gallery, 54 x 55 x 16 In. 4400.00
Cabinet, China, Limbert, Arched Backsplash, Copper Hardware, 58 In. 3850.00
Cabinet, China, Limbert, Oak, Door, 3 Over 1 Large Pane, Signed, 59 In. 6600.00
Cabinet, China, Louis XVI, Fruitwood, 2 Shaped Doors, 81 x 53 In. 3740.00
Cabinet, China, Oak, Carved, Barley Twist Posts, Quartersawn, c.1895 . . . . 2310.00
Cabinet, China, Oak, Curved Glass Doors, Glass Sides, Queen Anne Feet, 41 x 63 In. . . . 840.00
Cabinet, China, Oak, Leaves & Acorns, Beveled Center Door, 72 x 48 x 17 In. 2015.00
Cabinet, China, Oak, Mythical Beast, Fruit & Vine Carving, Glazed Doors, 78 In. 2180.00
Cabinet, China, Tudor Style, Walnut, 3 Shelves, Early 20th Century, 62 In. 405.00
Cabinet, Corner, 4 Paneled Doors, Teal Paint, New England, 79 x 48 In. 7200.00
Cabinet, Corner, Biedermeier, Willow, Frieze Drawer, Cabinet Door, 58 1/4 In. 1380.00
Cabinet, Corner, Chippendale, Walnut, 8-Pane Astragal Doors, 83 In. 5465.00
Cabinet, Corner, George III Style, Mahogany, Geometric Glazed Doors, 85 In. 2640.00
Cabinet, Corner, Hanging, Louis XV Style, Oak, 2 Shelves, Doors, 37 In. 1625.00
Cabinet, Corner, Hanging, Mahogany, Mother-Of-Pearl Inlay, England, 35 In. 290.00
Cabinet, Corner, Louis XV, Oak, Floral Carved Doors, 86 1/4 x 62 In. 3520.00
Cabinet, Corner, Mahogany, Carved Feet, Mirrored Center, 84 1/2 x 34 In., 2 Piece 3850.00
Cabinet, Corner, Mahogany, Glass Door Over Paneled Door, Shelf, c.1850, 79 x 36 In. . . 1210.00
Cabinet, Corner, Pine, 2 Paneled Doors, Short Bracket Feet, 82 1/2 x 42 x 20 In. 1230.00
Cabinet, Corner, Stylized Foliage, Painted, Scandinavia, 1814, 77 In. 1955.00
Cabinet, Curio, Bird's-Eye Maple, Glass Pane In Door, 2 Shelves, c.1920, 41 In. 430.00
Cabinet, Curio, Ebonized, Gilt, Arched Panels, Square, Victorian, 104 x 36 In. 3740.00
Cabinet, Curio, French Style, Glass Shelf, Dentil Molding, Lighted, 75 x 50 In. 330.00
Cabinet, Curio, Giltwood, Mansard Roof, Glass Archways, Italy, 16 1/2 x 11 1/2 In. 495.00
Cabinet, Curio, Inlaid Mahogany, 2 Doors, 26 Panes, Late Victorian, 46 x 68 In. 1955.00
Cabinet, Curio, Louis XV Style, Ebonized, Ormolu Mounts, 39 x 22 In. 165.00
Cabinet, Curio, Louis XV, Bowed Glass Door, Painted Scenes, France, 44 x 21 In. 1320.00
Cabinet, Curio, Marquetry, Glass Door & Sides, Floral, Lighted, 27 x 14 x 62 In. 1100.00
Cabinet, Curio, Mythological Figure & Deities, Mother-Of-Pearl Inlay, 82 In. 9200.00
Cabinet, Curio, Overall Landscape Design, 4 Scrolled Legs, 32 1/2 x 15 x 58 In. 978.00

Cabinet, Curio, Pine, Crown Molding, Fluted Columns, Rectangular, 80 In. 290.00
Cabinet, Curio, Quartersawn Oak, 2 Glass Doors, Cornice, Flemish, 58 x 80 In. 935.00
Cabinet, Curio, Queen Anne, Mahogany, Step-Down, Door, Drawer, 70 x 29 In. 1210.00
Cabinet, Curio, Tulip, Fruitwood Spray On Door, Curved Glass, 80 x 47 In. 6000.00
Cabinet, Curio, Vernis Martin, Base Panels, 2 Glass Shelves, 26 x 64 In. 1150.00
Cabinet, Curio, Vernis Martin, Flowers, Ormolu Mounts, 41 In. 275.00
Cabinet, Curio, Vernis Martin, Ormolu Mounts, Painted, 34 In. 715.00
Cabinet, Display, Rococo, Acanthus, Scroll, Hanging, Continental, 18th Century, 26 In. . . 995.00
Cabinet, Dome Top, Glazed Doors, Interior Shelves, Lower Doors, Drexel, 91 1/2 In. 1035.00
Cabinet, E. Wormley, Black Lacquer, 4 Walnut Drawers, 33 x 28 In. 500.00
Cabinet, E. Wormley, Mahogany, 2 Rosewood Drawers, 33 x 24 In. 825.00
Cabinet, Eames, ESU 400, Colored Masonite Panels, 1952, 58 In. 15400.00
Cabinet, Ebonized, Brass, Ivory Inlay, Edward & Roberts, Victorian, 45 x 35 In. 1760.00
Cabinet, Ebony, 2 Doors, 20 Panes, Beveled Glass, Bracket Feet, 83 x 47 x 15 In. 977.00
Cabinet, Egyptian Revival, Mahogany Veneer, Marble, Door & Drawer, 30 In. 1210.00
Cabinet, Elm, Bamboo, 2 Sliding Doors, Ching Dynasty, 36 x 17 x 71 In. 2300.00
Cabinet, Federal, Crown Molding Over Glass Paneled Door, 16 x 68 In. 115.00
Cabinet, Fir, Black Lacquer, Gold Floral Inside Drawers, Ching Dynasty, 48 x 76 In. 2300.00
Cabinet, Folio, Mahogany, Tooled Leather Top, 2 Paneled Doors, Victorian, 38 In. 2070.00
Cabinet, Fornasetti, 2 Doors, Transfer Print, 1950s, 24 3/4 In. 5175.00
Cabinet, Frank Lloyd Wright, 2 Doors, Recessed Handles, Signed, 25 x 31 In. 2970.00
Cabinet, French Provincial, Gilt, Arched Door, 4 Shelves, 65 3/4 x 35 x 13 3/4 In. 1150.00
Cabinet, French Revival, Fruitwood, Brown Marble Top, 2 Drawers, 1920, 52 In. 488.00
Cabinet, French Style, Mahogany, Beveled Glass Door & Sides, Cabriole Legs, 58 In. . . . 546.00
Cabinet, Fruitwood, Parchment, Italy, 1940s, 57 3/4 x 62 In. 6900.00
Cabinet, G. Nakashima, Cherry, Pandanus Cloth, 2 Doors, 84 In. 7475.00
Cabinet, G. Nelson, Black Steel, 6 Birch Front Drawers, 34 x 48 In. 1210.00
Cabinet, G. Nelson, Rosewood Veneer, Thin Edge, Cast Aluminum Legs, 41 In. 4125.00
Cabinet, G. Nelson, Steel, Walnut Veneer Drawer, Masonite Doors, 30 In. 1150.00
Cabinet, G. Stickley, 2 Doors, 16 Panes, Shelves, Decal, 62 x 42 In. 12650.00
Cabinet, George III, Bowfront, Mahogany, 4 Cock-Beaded Drawers, 72 x 38 In. 7475.00
Cabinet, George III, Mahogany, Concealed Safe In Lower Section, 32 1/2 x 20 In. 250.00
Cabinet, George III, Mahogany, Rectangular Top, 2 Drawers, 1810, 24 In. 2530.00
Cabinet, George III, Mahogany, Rectangular Top, Molded Square Legs, 29 In. 1610.00
Cabinet, George III, Square Cove Molded Top, Pedestal, 42 x 17 1/2 In., Pair 1595.00
Cabinet, Georgian, Mahogany, 3 Paneled Doors, Plinth Base, 72 x 19 x 85 In. 2875.00
Cabinet, Gothic Revival, Rosewood, White Marble Top, 2 Drawers, 36 1/4 In. 5060.00
Cabinet, Hepplewhite Style, Fruitwood, Oak, c.1900, 39 1/2 In. 1345.00
Cabinet, Italian Neoclassical, Grissaille, Parcel Gilt, Face Of Mercury, 34 In. 3300.00
Cabinet, James I, Oak, Shell Frieze, Geometric, Flower Heads, Block Feet, 57 In. 920.00
Cabinet, Jelly, 5 Shelves, Screen & Knobs, Eagles, Painted, Late 1800s, 72 In. 525.00
Cabinet, Jewelry, G. Nelson, Teakwood, Walnut Fronts, White Enameled Base, 27 In. . . . 3080.00
Cabinet, Key, Dark Finish, Hinged Door, Carved Leaves & Letter E, Hanging, 18 In. 110.00
Cabinet, Kingman & Murphy, Renaissance Revival, Oak, N.Y., 39 1/2 x 41 1/4 In. 935.00
Cabinet, Liquor, Stickley Brothers, 2 Doors, Pullout Copper Tray, 51 x 27 x 16 In. 2970.00
Cabinet, Louis XIV, Marquetry Marble Top, Tortoiseshell, Brass, 43 x 44 x 16 In. 977.00
Cabinet, Louis XV Style, Mahogany, Giltwood, S Scrolls, 2 Doors, 18 x 28 x 10 In. 316.00
Cabinet, Louis XV, Serpentine Marble Top, Black Lacquer Chinoiserie, 38 1/2 In. 1760.00
Cabinet, Louis XVI Style, Walnut, Rectangular White Marble Top, 30 1/4 In., Pair 920.00
Cabinet, Louis XVI, Mahogany, Gilt Metal Top, Beveled Glass, 63 In. 2300.00
Cabinet, Louis XVI, Walnut, White Marble Top, Carved Apron, 41 1/2 In., Pair 2990.00
Cabinet, M. Breuer, Birch, Overhanging Top, 4 Drawers, Cutout Handles, 50 In. 3160.00
Cabinet, Mahogany, 2-Tone Alligatored Finish, 3 Drawers, Pa., 10 x 8 x 8 In. 275.00
Cabinet, Mahogany, Glazed Doors, Adjustable Shelves, 3 Drawers, 1830, 93 1/2 In. 4000.00
Cabinet, Mahogany, Maple, Ebonized, Carved, Doors, Drawers, A. Smith 1881, 30 In. . . . 4200.00
Cabinet, Mahogany, Mirror, Column Sides, 5 Glass Shelves, 20th Century, 81 In. 580.00
Cabinet, Mahogany, Mullioned Doors, Wood Shelves, Glazed, 19th Century, 91 In. 3450.00
Cabinet, Mahogany, Specimen, 18 Drawers, Locking Mechanism, c.1815, 38 In. 9775.00
Cabinet, Map, Walnut, 12 Drawers, Brass Pulls, Paneled Sides, 52 x 28 x 33 In. 1345.00
Cabinet, Metal, Black, White Laminate Top, Chrome Tab Pulls, 2 Doors, 36 In. 165.00
Cabinet, Mixed Woods, 2 Doors, Backsplash, Scalloped, 45 x 34 x 13 In. 715.00
Cabinet, Music, Edwardian, Mahogany, Rectangular Molded Top, 42 x 14 1/2 In. 460.00
Cabinet, Music, G. Stickley, No. 70W, Gallery Top, Rectangular Door, 46 In. 7475.00

Cabinet, Music, Rococo, Rosewood, Marble Top, Mirrored Door, 38 In. 1320.00
Cabinet, Music, Rosewood Slate Top, Gilt & Bronze Putti, 1860, 44 In. 2200.00
Cabinet, Napoleon III, Rosewood, White Marble Top, Concave Sides, 41 In. 13200.00
Cabinet, Neoclassical Revival, Mahogany, Marble Top & Columns, 47 x 89 In. 8030.00
Cabinet, Neoclassical, Walnut, Pyramidal Cornice, 2 Doors, Plinth Base, 94 In., Pair 2990.00
Cabinet, Oak, Flower Carved Glass Door, Reeded Molding, Flared Feet, 1900, 86 In. 5175.00
Cabinet, Oriental, Mother-Of-Pearl Inlay, 19th Century, 67 x 42 x 14 In. 335.00
Cabinet, Pine, 2 Plank Doors, Flat Top, 19th Century, 49 x 42 x 15 1/2 In. 55.00
Cabinet, Pine, Flat Top, 2 Paneled Doors, Bracket Feet, 19th Century, 73 In. 1455.00
Cabinet, Pine, Glazed & Paneled Doors, Shelved Interior, Lower Drawer, 74 In. 2750.00
Cabinet, Pine, Reticulated Iris Gallery, Plain Feet, Victorian, 66 1/2 x 35 In. 690.00
Cabinet, Polychrome Wood, 11 Panels, Dragons On Center, Tibet, 1880s, 40 In. 2185.00
Cabinet, Portfolio, Walnut, Drop Front, Portable Stand, Folding Supports, 42 3/4 In. 1515.00
Cabinet, Print, 4 Bird's-Eye Maple Lined Drawers, c.1870, 33 x 38 3/4 In. 865.00
Cabinet, Red Lacquer, Rectangular Top, 2 Doors, Round Legs, 42 x 22 x 75 In. 460.00
Cabinet, Renaissance Revival, Oak, Gothic Architecture, Knights, c.1890, 34 x 40 In. ... 1100.00
Cabinet, Renaissance Revival, Oak, Rectangular Top, Geometric Paneled Door, 44 In. ... 920.00
Cabinet, Robert Adam Style, Giltwood, Willow Mesh Door, Painted, 63 In., Pair 4400.00
Cabinet, Rococo, Demilune, Rouge Marble Top, Carved Scrollwork, Italy, 41 x 64 In. ... 5500.00
Cabinet, Rococo, Gilt, Gray Flecked Black Marble Top, Floral Pendants, 60 3/4 In. 4140.00
Cabinet, Rococo, Mahogany, Bombe Doors, Cornice On Raised Support, 88 In. 1955.00
Cabinet, Rococo, Walnut, Molded Cornice, 2 Doors, Canted Stiles, Bun Feet, 76 In. 4887.00
Cabinet, Rosewood, 2 Doors, Raised Panels, Interior Drawers, 19th Century, 78 In. 1200.00
Cabinet, Rosewood, Bronze Mythological Center Panel, 1875, 78 In. 5462.00
Cabinet, Rosewood, Hinged Lid, 4 Front Panels, c.1980, 20 x 72 In. 258.00
Cabinet, Saarinen, 2 Doors Over 4 Drawers, Aluminum Pulls, Curved Legs, 48 In. 1760.00
Cabinet, Saarinen, Maple, 5 Drawers, Aluminum Handles, 36 In. 1438.00
Cabinet, Sacristy, Spanish Baroque, Parcel Gilt, Polychrome, 22 1/4 x 34 3/4 In. 9900.00
Cabinet, Satinwood, Marquetry, Bronze Mounted, 2 Cupboard Doors, 1940, 58 In. 3160.00
Cabinet, Serpentine, Lacquered, Gilt, Late 19th Century, 46 x 22 x 10 In. 403.00
Cabinet, Ship's, Drawers, Stencil, Cunard, White Star, M & M Line, 71 x 22 In. 1017.00
Cabinet, Side, Baroque, Paneled Doors, Extended Paw Feet, 45 x 44 In. 1495.00
Cabinet, Side, Biedermeier, Oak, Ebonized, Serpentine, 83 x 52 x 24 3/4 In. 2185.00
Cabinet, Side, Regency, Ebony, Ormolu Mounted, Bronze Gallery, Drawer, 56 In. 5775.00
Cabinet, Side, Regency, Mahogany, 2 Doors, Brass Sunburst Grillwork, 38 x 74 In. 5060.00
Cabinet, Side, Satinwood, 5 Panels On Door, 3 Deep Interior Shelves, 78 x 22 In. 1210.00
Cabinet, Side, Vernis Martin, Mahogany, Couple On Panel, 71 In. 8050.00
Cabinet, Simulated Rosewood, Marble Top, Casters, Victorian, 30 x 18 In. 635.00
Cabinet, Specimen, Mahogany, 2 Paneled Doors, Multiple Doors Inside, 53 x 44 In. 1320.00
Cabinet, Spice, Pine, 12 Drawers, Scrolled Crest, Painted, 20 x 11 x 16 In. 2860.00
Cabinet, Tambour Top, 5 Drawers With Wavy Fronts, Edmond Spence, 1950, 48 In. 1980.00
Cabinet, Teakwood, Dragon Crest, Glazed Doors, Chinese, Late 1800s, 38 x 30 x 18 In. ... 345.00
Cabinet, William IV, Rosewood, Gray Marble Top, 2 Cabinet Doors, 1840, 39 In. 9200.00
Cabinet, Writing, George III, Mahogany, Rectangular Top, 4 Document Drawers, 38 In. ... 4025.00
Cabinet-Bookcase, Edwardian, Mahogany, 13-Pane Astragal Doors, 99 In. 2300.00
Cabinet-On-Stand, Empire Style, Mahogany, Gilt Bronze, Mirrored Back, 68 In. 2875.00
Cabinet-On-Stand, Georgian Style, Mahogany, 2 Doors, 2 Drawers, 40 x 53 1/2 In. 1760.00
Cabinet-On-Stand, Ivory Columns, 6 Open Shelves, 3 Drawers, 71 x 37 1/2 In. 9350.00
Cabinet-On-Stand, Paneled Doors, Shelves, Drawers, Red Lacquer, 65 In. 575.00
Cabinet-On-Stand, Renaissance Revival, Oak, Medieval Maiden, Saints, 56 x 34 In. 715.00
Cabinet-On-Stand, William & Mary, Walnut, Oyster Veneer, Glazed Doors, 67 1/4 In. ... 8000.00
Candle Screen, Lydia A. Atkins, 13 Years Old, Nov. 18, 1839, Wooden Stand, 7 x 17 In. .. 385.00
Candlestand, 2 Brass Cups, Drip Pans, Cast Iron, Brass, 18th Century, 48 1/4 In. 3100.00
Candlestand, Birch, Octagonal Top, 3 Cabriole Legs, Snake Feet, N.H., 1800, 27 In. 360.00
Candlestand, Birch, Rectangular, Urn & Baluster, New England, 1810, 29 x 15 In. 220.00
Candlestand, Brass, Gilt, Family & Interior Within Scrolled Frame, 12 x 4 In. 490.00
Candlestand, Cherry, Octagonal Top, Ring Turned Base, Late 18th Century, 25 In. 2300.00
Candlestand, Cherry, Octagonal, Urn Pedestal, Cabriole Legs, 19th Century, 23 x 14 In. ... 615.00
Candlestand, Cherry, Poplar, Hickory, Tripod Base, Bentwood Legs, 26 3/4 In. 550.00
Candlestand, Cherry, Round Top, Ring Turned Post, Pad Feet, 25 x 15 In. 800.00
Candlestand, Cherry, Shaped Top, Turned Pedestal, Tripod Base, 17 1/2 x 19 x 27 In. ... 415.00
Candlestand, Cherry, Square Top, Pedestal, Tripod Base, Pa., 1790, 25 1/2 In. 550.00
Candlestand, Cherry, Tripod Base, Snake Feet, 25 3/4 In. 385.00

Candlestand, Chippendale, Cherry, Round Top, Tripod Base, Snake Feet, 17 x 27 In. 990.00
Candlestand, Chippendale, Dish Top, Turned Pedestal, Mass., 18th Century, 27 In. 2070.00
Candlestand, Chippendale, Mahogany, Snake Feet, 15 1/2 x 26 In. 2860.00
Candlestand, Chippendale, Mahogany, Turned Pedestal, c.1770, 29 x 16 In. 8050.00
Candlestand, Curly Maple, Tripod Base, Cutout Legs, 30 In. 550.00
Candlestand, Dish Top, Hepplewhite, Cherry, Spider Legs, 18 x 28 In. 495.00
Candlestand, Dish Top, Mahogany, Birdcage Support, Phila., 1760, 20 In. 2860.00
Candlestand, Dish Top, Mahogany, Inlaid, New York, 1780, 28 x 19 In. 2530.00
Candlestand, Dish Top, Mahogany, Tripod Base, Pad Feet, 1780, 28 In. 1900.00
Candlestand, Dish Top, Queen Anne, Walnut, Tripod Base, 29 x 20 In. 3200.00
Candlestand, Dish Top, Queen Anne, Walnut, Tripod Base, Pa., 1790, 28 In. 1430.00
Candlestand, Dish Top, Sheraton, Mahogany, Turned Pedestal, 27 In. 320.00
Candlestand, Empire, Walnut, Cock-Beaded Top, Twist Turned Standard, 27 1/2 In. 290.00
Candlestand, Federal, Cherry, Rectangular Top, Drawer, Cabriole Legs, 25 In. 750.00
Candlestand, Federal, Cherry, Square Top, Beaded Edge, Cabriole Legs, 27 In. 1380.00
Candlestand, Federal, Cherry, Square Top, Ring Turned Post, Pad Feet, 28 x 16 In. 1495.00
Candlestand, Federal, Cherry, Stringing, Nathan Lombard, Mass., 1800, 26 x 17 In. 10350.00
Candlestand, Federal, Cherry, Turned Pedestal, Splayed Legs, New England, 28 In. 415.00
Candlestand, Federal, Mahogany, Birch, Octagonal Inlaid Top, 29 1/2 In. 4315.00
Candlestand, Federal, Mahogany, Dish Top, Tripod Base, 1800, 26 1/2 x 15 In. 660.00
Candlestand, Federal, Mahogany, Square Top, Ring Turned Support, Pad Feet, 28 In. 1265.00
Candlestand, Federal, Maple, Square Top, Ovolo Corners, Late 1700s, 25 x 14 x 15 In. .. 800.00
Candlestand, Federal, Ring Turned Post, Gilt, Black Paint, 1820, 28 x 15 1/4 In. 490.00
Candlestand, Federal, Square Top, Cutout Corners, 3 Feet, 25 1/2 x 16 1/2 In. 265.00
Candlestand, George III, Mahogany, Square Top, Cabriole Legs, 1900, 35 In. 920.00
Candlestand, Georgian, Mahogany, Vase-Form Standard, 3 Cabriole Legs, 28 In. 290.00
Candlestand, Hepplewhite, Birch, Spider Legs, Cut Corners, 14 x 20 In. 385.00
Candlestand, Hepplewhite, Cherry, 1-Board Top, Tripod Base, Snake Feet, 17 x 28 In. ... 1870.00
Candlestand, Jeremiah Gooden, Federal, Cherry, Maple, Label, c.1800, 28 x 16 In. 4600.00
Candlestand, Mahogany, Rope Twist, Scrolled Legs, Victorian, 29 x 20 1/2 In. 250.00
Candlestand, Mahogany, Scalloped Top, Tripod Base, Padded Snake Feet, 26 3/4 In. 5750.00
Candlestand, Maple, Mahogany, Notched Corner Top, Splayed Feet, 1820, 30 In. 495.00
Candlestand, Queen Anne, Cherry, Square Top, Turned Shaft, Cabriole Legs, 28 In. 798.00
Candlestand, Queen Anne, Maple, Curly Maple, Shaped Top, 26 x 18 1/2 x 15 In. 358.00
Candlestand, Queen Anne, Maple, Poplar, Round Top, Tripod Base, 1800, 27 1/2 In. 550.00
Candlestand, Queen Anne, Maple, Round Top, Tripod Base, Pa., 1800, 26 x 16 In. 715.00
Candlestand, Sheraton, Tiger Maple, Bird's-Eye Maple, Drawer, 27 x 18 1/2 x 18 In. 1210.00
Candlestand, Sheraton, Tiger Maple, Rounded Corners, Grain Painted, 26 1/2 In. 470.00
Candlestand, Softwood, Round, Vase-Form Pedestal, Tripod Base, Black Paint, 27 In. ... 165.00
Candlestand, Tilt Top, Birch, Octagonal, 3 Spider Legs, 1790, 28 3/4 x 21 In. 715.00
Candlestand, Tilt Top, Cherry, Birdcage Support, Tripod Base, 19 1/2 x 30 In. 385.00
Candlestand, Tilt Top, Cherry, Ring Turned Support, Pad Feet, 28 x 21 In. 1495.00
Candlestand, Tilt Top, Cherry, Square Chamfered Top, Cabriole Legs, Pad Feet, 27 In. ... 575.00
Candlestand, Tilt Top, Cherry, Tiger Maple, Oval Top, Bulbous Pedestal, 25 x 24 In. 775.00
Candlestand, Tilt Top, Cherry, Turtle-Shaped Top, Baluster Pedestal, Spider Legs, 28 In. .. 467.00
Candlestand, Tilt Top, Cherry, Vase-Form Shaft, Tripod Base, 27 x 16 1/4 In. 900.00
Candlestand, Tilt Top, Chippendale, Mahogany, Tripod Base, Snake Feet, 21 x 28 In. 430.00
Candlestand, Tilt Top, Empire, Mahogany, Rectangular Top, 27 x 23 1/4 x 18 In. 225.00
Candlestand, Tilt Top, Federal, Cherry, Rectangular, Tripod Base, Splayed Feet, 28 In. ... 115.00
Candlestand, Tilt Top, Federal, Mahogany, 3-Board, Vase-Form Base, 29 In. 390.00
Candlestand, Tilt Top, Federal, Mahogany, Baluster Shaft, Tripod Base, c.1820, 27 In. ... 355.00
Candlestand, Tilt Top, Federal, Mahogany, Oblong, Scrolled Legs, 1835, 29 In. 330.00
Candlestand, Tilt Top, Federal, Mahogany, Octagonal Top, c.1800, 28 x 18 In. 2070.00
Candlestand, Tilt Top, Federal, Mahogany, Oval, Mass., c.1810, 29 x 13 x 21 1/2 In. 1380.00
Candlestand, Tilt Top, Federal, Mahogany, Serpentine Top, Pad Feet, 25 x 19 1/2 In. 2300.00
Candlestand, Tilt Top, Hepplewhite, Cherry, 1-Board Top, Tripod Base, 17 x 20 In. 770.00
Candlestand, Tilt Top, Hepplewhite, Mahogany, Cut Corner Top, 13 x 20 In. 1375.00
Candlestand, Tilt Top, Mahogany, Birdcage, Tripod Base, Spider Legs, 15 x 22 In. 525.00
Candlestand, Tilt Top, Mahogany, Carved Vase-Form Pedestal, Carved Legs, 29 In. 355.00
Candlestand, Tilt Top, Mahogany, Turned Pedestal, Tripod Base, 27 1/2 In. 470.00
Candlestand, Tilt Top, Mahogany, Urn Pedestal, Paw Feet, 1886, 27 In. 845.00
Candlestand, Tilt Top, Mahogany, Vase-Form Pedestal, Spider Feet, 24 x 18 x 28 In. 495.00
Candlestand, Tilt Top, Mahogany, Vase-Form Turned Pedestal, Spider Legs, 28 1/2 In. ... 300.00

Candlestand, Tilt Top, Maple, 2-Board Top, Bulbous Pedestal, New England, 19 In. 165.00
Candlestand, Tilt Top, Maple, Mahogany, Rectangular, Tripod Base, c.1830, 29 In. 330.00
Candlestand, Tilt Top, Queen Anne, Mahogany, Oval, Vase-Form Pedestal, 1780, 28 In. . . 990.00
Candlestand, Tilt Top, Queen Anne, Mahogany, Snake Feet, 29 x 13 In. 2015.00
Candlestand, Tilt Top, Queen Anne, Walnut, Tripod Base, Pa., 1770, 23 In. 3575.00
Candlestand, Tilt Top, Walnut, Cherry, Birdcage, Pedestal, Cabriole Legs, 27 x 25 In. . . . 1320.00
Candlestand, Tilt Top, Walnut, Round, Turned Standard, Cabriole Legs, 27 x 19 In. 4400.00
Candlestand, Twig, Bent Vines, Heart Design On Base, Green Paint, Brown, 33 In. 140.00
Candlestand, Vase Turned Pedestal, Spider Legs, 27 1/2 x 17 In. 340.00
Candlestand, Wallace Nutting, Windsor, No. 17 . . . . 495.00
Candlestand, Walnut, Round Top, Pa., 1740, 25 1/2 x 17 In. 3410.00
Candlestand, Wrought Iron, 2-Light, Spring Mechanism, Tripod Pedestal, 22 x 12 In. 715.00
Canterbury, Burl Walnut, Drawer, 3 Sections, Porcelain Casters, 20 In. 1600.00
Canterbury, Legs Ending In Brass Caps, Casters, 20 x 18 In. 1035.00
Canterbury, Louis XV, Beechwood, Rectangular Top, Floral Cabriole Legs, 33 In. 316.00
Canterbury, Mahogany, 4 Scroll Cut Dividers, Drawer, Casters, Victorian, 18 In. 1320.00
Canterbury, Mahogany, Baluster-Shaped Splats, Drawer 245.00
Canterbury, Mahogany, Drawer, Ring Pulls, Casters, 20th Century 415.00
Canterbury, Mahogany, Rosewood, Turned Posts & Spindles, 19 x 17 1/4 In. 880.00
Canterbury, Pierced Sides, Ebonized & Gilt Incised, Hoof Feet, 29 In. 1840.00
Canterbury, Walnut, Divided Upper Section, Shelf, c.1860, 18 In. 1092.00
Cellarette, Arts & Crafts, Oak, Flat Top Over Door, 1912, 30 x 26 In. 400.00
Cellarette, Brass Strap Hinges, Cutout Legs, Lakeside Craft Shop, 19 x 29 In. 285.00
Cellarette, Chippendale, Mahogany, Hinged Top, Brass Escutcheon, 14 1/2 In. 1840.00
Cellarette, Federal, Hinged Top, Walnut, Storage Well, Late 18th Century, 28 1/4 In. 5175.00
Cellarette, Federal, Inlaid Mahogany, Hinged Top, Drawer, 36 x 21 In. 4315.00
Cellarette, Federal, Mahogany, Oval Brass-Banded Top, Tapered Legs, 1795, 30 In. 10925.00
Cellarette, G. Stickley, Drawer, Door, Hammered Copper Pulls, 29 x 20 x 15 In. 4400.00
Cellarette, George III Style, Mahogany, Brassbound, Octagonal, c.1900, 25 1/2 In. 1210.00
Cellarette, George III, Bowfront, Mahogany, Brass Handles, Casters, 27 1/2 In. 3300.00
Cellarette, George III, Japanned, Hexagonal, 28 x 17 1/2 In. 290.00
Cellarette, George III, Mahogany, Leopard's-Head Brass Handles, 27 1/4 In. 1840.00
Cellarette, George III, Mahogany, Trunk Shape, Bale Handles, 17 x 14 x 25 1/2 In. 800.00
Cellarette, George IV, Mahogany, Hinged Lid, Paw Feet, 21 x 25 1/4 x 19 In. 5750.00
Cellarette, Georgian, Mahogany, Octagonal Top, Lead Lined Interior, Scroll, 26 In. 545.00
Cellarette, L. & J.G. Stickley, Drawer, Door, Hammered Copper Pulls, 29 In. 3850.00
Cellarette, L. & J.G. Stickley, No. 25, 2 Doors, Gallery, 35 1/2 x 32 x 16 In. 7700.00
Cellarette, Mahogany, Carved Flowers & Waves, Claw Feet, c.1885 . . . . 1980.00
Cellarette, Oak, Sarcophagus Shape, Zinc Lined Well, Paw Feet, 26 x 36 In. 1695.00
Cellarette, Quarter-Fan Corner, 6 Bottle Compartments, c.1790, 24 1/2 In. 9775.00
Cellarette, Regency, Mahogany, Rectangular Domed Top, Canted Corners, 19 In. 2530.00
Cellarette, Rosewood, Brass Filigree, 4 Decanters, 16 Cordials, 11 x 13 In. 220.00
Cellarette, William I, Mahogany, Octagonal Paneled Well, Paw Feet, 17 x 30 In. 2420.00
Cellarette, William IV, Mahogany, Stepped Lid, Carved, 24 In. 6325.00
Chair, A. Girard, Cushion, Upholstered, Herman Miller, 27 In. 2310.00
Chair, A. Lorenz, Nickel Plated Steel, Cane Back & Seat, Arms, 29 x 23 3/4 In. 7475.00
Chair, Aalto, No. 37, Bent Laminated Supports, Upholstered Seat, Arms, 29 In. 3165.00
Chair, Aalto, No. 44, Bent Laminated Supports, Arms, 25 x 22 x 29 In. 2070.00
Chair, Acanthus Carved Crest, Pierced Baluster Splat, Needlepoint 520.00
Chair, Adams Style, Cane Seat, Painted, Arms, Boston 6875.00
Chair, Adirondack, Twig, Child's 600.00
Chair, Aesthetic Revival, Walnut, Needlepoint, 34 In., Pair 2185.00
Chair, Airline, Kem Weber, Cantilevered, 1930s, Arms . . . . *Illus* 8960.00
Chair, Andre Arbus, Rectangular Backrest, Down-Swept Arms, 1945, Pair 2070.00
Chair, Anglo-Colonial, Mahogany, Tub, Cane Seat, Back, Tapered Legs, 34 In., Pair 2860.00
Chair, Arched Crest Rail, Rectangular Splat, Paneled Seat, Red Lacquer, Scrolled Arms . . 175.00
Chair, Arched Crest, Carved Cartouche, Padded Arms, France, Victorian, 40 In. 165.00
Chair, Arrow Back, Plank Seat, Splayed Legs, Painted, Pa., 1810-1820, 33 In. 375.00
Chair, Arrow Back, Yellow Ochre Grained, Late 19th Century, Child's 220.00
Chair, Art Deco, Ebonized, Square Upholstered Back, Padded Arms, 1930s 690.00
Chair, Art Deco, Limed Oak, Raffia, Bun Feet, Slat Arms, Pair 1265.00
Chair, Art Deco, Oak, Tubular Steel, Upholstered Seat, Arms, 1930 . . . . 2875.00
Chair, Art Deco, Rattan, Black Paint, Orange & Green Lashing, 44 x 29 In., Pair 110.00

Cover scratches on dark cherry or mahogany by rubbing them with a bit of cotton dipped in iodine. Scratches on lighter woods can be covered by rubbing with a solution of equal parts iodine and alcohol.

Furniture, Chair, Airline, Kem Weber,
Cantilevered, 1930s, Arms

Chair, Art Deco, Rosewood, Upholstered, Stepped Plank Arms, France, 1930, Pair	8050.00
Chair, Art Deco, Walnut, Leather, Casters, 1930s, England, Pair	1380.00
Chair, Art Nouveau, Walnut, Pierced Back, Upholstered, Arms, Italy, 1900, Pair	1380.00
Chair, Arts & Crafts, 5 Vertical Slats, Brown Paint, Vinyl Seat, 35 In.	1540.00
Chair, Arts & Crafts, 5 Vertical Slats, V-Shaped Crest Rail, Leather Seat, 37 x 22 In.	690.00
Chair, Arts & Crafts, Mahogany, 2 Vertical Slats, Leather Seat, Arms, 20 x 37 In.	275.00
Chair, Arts & Crafts, Mahogany, 5 Vertical Slats, Saddle Seat, Arms, 37 1/2 In.	275.00
Chair, Arts & Crafts, Upholstered Seat, Splayed Slab Legs, 28 x 20 x 32 In.	465.00
Chair, Arts & Crafts, Wicker, Upholstered Seat, Arms, 35 x 32 In.	110.00
Chair, Balloon Back, Crescent Cutout & Scalloped Base, Plank Seat, Moravia, Pair	770.00
Chair, Ballroom, Walnut, Spindle Gallery, Pierced Crest, Overstuffed Seat, Victorian	375.00
Chair, Baltimore, Medallion Center Spindle, Matching Stretcher, Black Paint, Pair	1200.00
Chair, Bamboo, Elm, Geometric Designs, Arms, Shanxi, China, 19th Century, Pair	1035.00
Chair, Bamboo, Spindle Supports, Bamboo Turned Legs, 19th Century	175.00
Chair, Banister Back, Scrolled Handholds, Splint Seat, Red Stain, Late 1700s, 48 In.	4025.00
Chair, Baroque Style, Cartouche-Shaped Back, Pierced Splat, Scrolled Arms, Italy	1150.00
Chair, Baroque Style, High Back, Carved Female Figures, Arms, 19th Century	4400.00
Chair, Baroque Style, Open Back, Bone Hunt Scene Inlay, Italy, 19th Century, Pair	1265.00
Chair, Baroque Style, Walnut, Serpentine, Padded Back, Arms, Venice, 50 In.	3300.00
Chair, Baroque Style, Walnut, Upholstered, Spiral Twist Arms, Flemish, 24 x 34 In.	990.00
Chair, Baroque, Giltwood, Rectangular Cloth Top, Dolphin Feet, 1900, 24 1/2 In.	2420.00
Chair, Baroque, High Arched Upholstered Back, Bun Feet, 47 In., Pair	345.00
Chair, Baroque, Oak, Floral Medallions, 2 Maiden Heads, Paw Feet, Arms, 36 In.	1100.00
Chair, Baroque, Oak, Turned Legs, Needlepoint Seat, 1900, 58 In., Pair	920.00
Chair, Baroque, Walnut, Open Back, 5 Spindles, Cross Bars, Rush Seat, Spain	230.00
Chair, Beechwood, Cane, Cartouche Back Within Arched Frame, Cushion, Pair	1265.00
Chair, Beechwood, Cane, Serpentine Seat, Horse-Bone Front Legs, 1732, 46 In.	460.00
Chair, Beechwood, Stained, Banister Back, Woven Rush Seat, 18th Century	290.00
Chair, Belter, Henry Clay Pattern, Pair	5700.00
Chair, Belter, Rosalie With Grapes, Foliate Crest, Arms, 42 In.	5060.00
Chair, Biedermeier Style, Fruitwood, Fanned Splat, Cushion, Open Arms, c.1900, Pair	660.00
Chair, Biedermeier, Ebonized Wreath Splat, Padded Seat, Arms, 34 In., Pair	3450.00
Chair, Biedermeier, Fruitwood, Ebonized Wood, Saber Legs, 1830, Pair	930.00
Chair, Biedermeier, Pierced Splat, Center Crown, Drop-In Seat, Pair	660.00
Chair, Biedermeier, Rosewood, Walnut, Padded Back, Scrolled Feet, Arms, 41 In., Pair	4400.00
Chair, Billiard, Heywood-Wakefield Co., Paper Label, 42 In.	3200.00
Chair, Bird's-Eye Maple, Turned Legs, Concave Back Support, 33 1/2 In., Pair	250.00
Chair, Black Forest, Inlaid Panels & Seat, 37 In., Pair	715.00
Chair, Black Wrought Iron, Angular, Yacht Cord Back & Seat, 28 In.	1035.00
Chair, Cane Backrest, Ribbon Twist, White Paint, Cushion, Pair	1150.00
Chair, Captain's, Elm, Arms, England	140.00
Chair, Captain's, Firehouse, 8 Spindles, Plank Seat, Turned Legs, Refinished	90.00
Chair, Captain's, Scroll Back, 8 Turned Spindles, Plank Seat, Continuous Arms	120.00
Chair, Cartouche-Shaped Back, Carved Foliage, Cabriole Legs, Padded Arms, Pair	860.00
Chair, Cartouche-Shaped Cane Backrest, Leaf Carved Armrests, 40 In., Pair	4140.00
Chair, Carved Double Rose & Ribbon Crest, Upholstered Back, Seat & Arms, France	605.00
Chair, Carved Dragon, Dragon Arms, Japan, 19th Century	550.00
Chair, Carved, Padded Oval Back & Arms, Painted, Cushion, Pair	3575.00

Chair, Cast Iron, Spring Steel, Centripetal, Cane Seat, American Chair Co., 44 In. 1980.00
Chair, Chamfered Crest, Vase-Form Splat, Ring Turned Legs, 1750 . . . . 2185.00
Chair, Charles II Style, Walnut, Foliate Pierced Crest, Upholstered, Arms, c.1930 . . . . 345.00
Chair, Charles II, Walnut, Pierce Carved Crest, Foliage, Rope Twist Legs, Pair 1440.00
Chair, Cherry, Roundabout, Shaped Backrest, Rush Seat, Scrolled Arms, 30 x 17 In. 520.00
Chair, Chippendale Style, Mahogany, Pierced Splat, Claw & Ball Feet, c.1920 . . . . 145.00
Chair, Chippendale, Acanthus Leaf, Bellflower Accents, Eagle, Cabriole Legs, Arms 2530.00
Chair, Chippendale, Dark Stain, Serpentine Crest, Upholstered Slip Seat, 39 In. 800.00
Chair, Chippendale, Lolling, Mahogany, Carved, Upholstered, Arms, c.1780, 43 x 15 In. . . 4885.00
Chair, Chippendale, Mahogany, Arched Supports, Straight Legs, Upholstered 605.00
Chair, Chippendale, Mahogany, Balloon Seat, Ears, Crest & Splat, Cabriole Legs 465.00
Chair, Chippendale, Mahogany, Carved & Pierced Splat, Slip Seat, 39 5/8 In. 5500.00
Chair, Chippendale, Mahogany, Carved, Pierced Splats, Cabriole Legs, 41 In., Pair 5750.00
Chair, Chippendale, Mahogany, Carved, Upholstered Seat, Mass., c.1770, 37 In. 3735.00
Chair, Chippendale, Mahogany, Claw & Ball Feet, South Portland, Maine 3575.00
Chair, Chippendale, Mahogany, Fret Carved, Mortised Sides, Leather, Arms, 39 In. 1400.00
Chair, Chippendale, Mahogany, Pierced Splat With Heart, Lift Seat, Straight Legs 85.00
Chair, Chippendale, Mahogany, Pierced Splat, Cabriole Legs, 1770, 33 x 39 In. 6875.00
Chair, Chippendale, Mahogany, Ring Turned Posts, Sheaf Splats, Drop-In Seat 800.00
Chair, Chippendale, Mahogany, Roundabout, Scrolled Crest, 18th Century, 30 1/2 In. 2645.00
Chair, Chippendale, Mahogany, Serpentine Back, Straight Seat, 45 x 19 In. 980.00
Chair, Chippendale, Mahogany, Serpentine Crest, Carved, Upholstered, 37 In., Pair 8625.00
Chair, Chippendale, Mahogany, Serpentine Crest, Stretcher, 48 x 14 In. 3738.00
Chair, Chippendale, Mahogany, Straight Legs, Open Splat, Slip Seat, Pair 1100.00
Chair, Chippendale, Mahogany, Upholstered, Out-Scrolled Arms, Late 1700s, 46 In. 1265.00
Chair, Chippendale, Maple, Tiger Maple, Rush Set, Splat Back, Spanish Feet, 16 In. 360.00
Chair, Chippendale, Raked Molded Ears, Pierced Splat, Gilt, Late 1700s, 39 In. 316.00
Chair, Chippendale, Shaped Crest, Vase-Form Splat, Upholstered Seat 110.00
Chair, Chippendale, Walnut, Carved Crest, Slip Seat, Shell Carved Knees, c.1780 . . . . 1210.00
Chair, Chippendale, Walnut, Crest Rail, Trapezoidal Seat, 18th Century, 36 In., Pair 2520.00
Chair, Chippendale, Walnut, Ruffled Carved Crest, Square Legs, 1780, Pair 8625.00
Chair, Chippendale, Walnut, Ruffled Crest, Slip Seat, Claw & Ball Feet, 40 1/2 In. 4600.00
Chair, Chippendale, Walnut, Serpentine Crest, Splat, Scrolled Arms, Pa., 1770 . . . . 5500.00
Chair, Chippendale, Walnut, Vase-Form Splat, Claw & Ball Feet, 1730, 39 In. 4600.00
Chair, Christopher Wilk, Bentwood, Mahogany, Cane Back & Seat, 1980 . . . . 750.00
Chair, Classical, Mahogany, Carved, Saber Legs, Padded Seat, c.1820, Pair 1320.00
Chair, Classical, Scroll Carved Balloon Back, Upholstered Panel, Boston, 34 In., Pair 935.00
Chair, Cockfighting, Upholstered, High Upholstered Arms, Victorian 1980.00
Chair, Corner, Applied Crest, Baluster & Ring Posts, Rush Seat, Paint 330.00
Chair, Corner, Arts & Crafts, L-Shaped Legs, Rail, Leather Seat, 26 1/2 x 20 In. 137.00
Chair, Corner, Carved Wood, Inset Mounted Plaques In Splats, Chinese 155.00
Chair, Corner, Chippendale Style, Mahogany, 2 Vase-Form Tracery Splats 865.00
Chair, Corner, Chippendale Style, Mahogany, Cabriole Legs, Scrolled Arms 865.00
Chair, Corner, Chippendale Style, Mahogany, Carved, c.1890, 31 In. 1350.00
Chair, Corner, Chippendale, Mahogany, 2 Pierced Splats, Square Legs, 1770, 31 In. 550.00
Chair, Corner, Chippendale, Walnut, Birch, Vase-Form Splats, Out-Curved Arms 1095.00
Chair, Corner, Federal, Cherry, Diamond-Shaped Seat, Scalloped Skirt, 1810, 27 In. 495.00
Chair, Corner, George III, Pine, 2 Pierced Splats, Leather Seat 345.00
Chair, Corner, Georgian, Walnut, Pierced Splats, 1 Cabriole & 3 Turned Legs 600.00
Chair, Corner, Louis XV, Beechwood, Arched Molded Back, Scrolled Arms, 36 In. 1760.00
Chair, Corner, Mahogany, 3 Columnar Posts, Vase-Form Splats, Headrest, Rush Seat 1380.00
Chair, Corner, Mahogany, Arched Back Panels, Floral Marquetry, Bun Feet, Holland 400.00
Chair, Corner, Maple, Rush Seat, Turned Legs, New England, Late 1700s, 31 In. 2185.00
Chair, Corner, Maple, Square Rush Seat, Spanish Feet, Horseshoe Armrest, 29 In. 770.00
Chair, Corner, Marquetry, Flower Inlay, Cornucopias, Arms, Holland, 18th Century 2100.00
Chair, Corner, Oak, Padded Back, Cushion, Casters, Scrolled Spindle Arms 230.00
Chair, Corner, Queen Anne, Maple, Vase-Form Splats, Slip Seat, Early 1800s, 28 In. 2185.00
Chair, Corner, Rosewood, Cane Back Panel & Seat, Brass Mounts, 19th Century, Pair . . . 6900.00
Chair, Cube, Spindle, Paper Label, Michigan Chair Co., 36 x 21 In. 2050.00
Chair, Curly Maple, Vase-Form Splat, Turned Front Legs, Cane Seat, 1830-1840 . . . . 230.00
Chair, Curved Button Back, Casters, Low Arms, Victorian, Pair 1095.00
Chair, Curved Plate Glass, Upholstered Seat, Pittsburgh Plate Glass, 1930 . . . . 10450.00
Chair, Deck, Aluminum, Webbed Back & Seat, 1952, Pair 2070.00

Chair, Dutch Neoclassical, Elm, Balloon Back, Pierced Splat, Padded Arms, Pair 3740.00
Chair, E. Dieckmann, Nickel Plated Steel, Cane Back & Seat, Wood Arms, 1931 .... 5520.00
Chair, E. Wormley, Curved Seat, Dark Mahogany Legs, Janus, 26 x 29 In. 935.00
Chair, E. Wormley, Ebonized Wood, Leather Seat Pad, Arms, 31 In. 1265.00
Chair, Eames, Aluminum Group, Ribbed Vinyl, Wheels, Arms 635.00
Chair, Eames, Bentwood, Birch, Herman Miller, c.1950, 26 1/2 In. 1045.00
Chair, Eames, Eiffel Tower, Wire Grid Construction, 19 x 29 In. 120.00
Chair, Eames, Fiberglass, Birch, Wire, Swivel, c.1951, 31 In. 6900.00
Chair, Eames, LCW, Ash Plywood, Herman Miller, 22 x 26 In. 1045.00
Chair, Eames, LCW, Black Aniline Dyed Plywood Seat, Herman Miller, 22 x 26 In. 935.00
Chair, Eames, Plywood, Molded Seat, Red Aniline Dye, c.1946, Child's 8625.00
Chair, Eames, Pony, Cowhide Back & Seat ....*Illus* 38500.00
Chair, Eames, Steel Wire, Wire Grid Back & Seat, 2-Piece Vinyl Pad 345.00
Chair, Eastlake, Walnut, Architectural Crest Rail, Overstuffed Seat, Scrolled Arms 230.00
Chair, Eastlake, Walnut, Arms, 36 1/2 In., Pair ....*Illus* 140.00
Chair, Eastlake, Walnut, Carved Rectangular Crest, Velour, c.1880, Pair 375.00
Chair, Easy, Mahogany, Barrel Back, Leather 1150.00
Chair, Easy, Mahogany, Cushion, Out-Curved Arms, 32 In. 1090.00
Chair, Easy, Upholstered Seat, Chamfered Legs, Scrolled Arms, 45 In. 750.00
Chair, Easy, Walnut, Carved, Button Back, Flower & Fruit Crest, Low Arms, Victorian ... 200.00
Chair, Ebony, Cane Seat, Cushions, Casters, Arms, Victorian 805.00
Chair, Ebony, Rectangular Backrest, Scrolled Legs, Toes, Victorian, Pair 4255.00
Chair, Edwardian, Mahogany, Ivory, Tapered Legs, Splayed Feet, Arms, 34 In., Pair 1725.00
Chair, Egyptian Revival, Gilt Winged Serpent Crest, Red & Green Paint, Arms 600.00
Chair, Eileen Gray, Transatlantique, Leather Seat, Headrest, 1980 .... 690.00
Chair, Elm, Curved Rectangular Crest Rail, Splayed Legs, Arms, Continental 1150.00
Chair, Elm, Red & Black Lacquer, Mortised, Arms, Chinese, 39 In., Pair 600.00
Chair, Empire Style, Mahogany, Bowfront, Scrolled Back, Stuffed Seat, France, Pair 315.00
Chair, Empire, Bowfront Seat, Turned Legs, Down-Swept Padded Armrests 9200.00
Chair, Empire, Mahogany Finish, Ormolu, Gilt, Saber Legs, Upholstered, Arms 495.00
Chair, Empire, Mahogany, Dolphin's-Head Terminals, Scrolled Feet, 31 In., Pair 3135.00
Chair, Empire, Mahogany, Padded Back, Foliate Crest, Dolphin Arms, 36 3/4 In. 1725.00
Chair, Empire, Mahogany, Rectangular Crest, Carved Seat Rail, Tapered Legs, 35 In. 770.00
Chair, Empire, Mahogany, Rectangular Padded Back, Paw Feet, 34 3/4 In. 715.00
Chair, Empire, Mahogany, Round Granite Top, Gilt Metal Eagle Legs, 30 In. 3450.00
Chair, Erwine & Estelle Laverne, Tulip, White Fiberglass, 1960, 46 x 50 In. 2680.00
Chair, F. Albini, Wood, Upholstered Foam-Filled Back & Seat, 31 In. 490.00
Chair, Federal, Mahogany, Brass Caps, Casters, Scrolled Arms, 43 In. 460.00
Chair, Federal, Mahogany, Serpentine Crest, Fitted Cushion, 18 1/2 In. 3450.00
Chair, Federal, Mahogany, Serpentine Crest, Upholstered, Scroll Arms, 1800s, 60 In. 5000.00
Chair, Federal, Mahogany, Shaped Seat, Molded Legs, Upholstered, 27 In. 2645.00
Chair, Federal, Mahogany, Shieldback, 5 Leaf Carved Splats, H-Stretcher, Pair 800.00
Chair, Federal, Mahogany, Tapered Legs, Scrolled Arms, 46 In. 1725.00
Chair, Federal, Serpentine Crest, Upholstered, Flared Arms, c.1815, 47 1/2 In. 4600.00
Chair, Federal, Shieldback, Vase-Form Splat, Trapezoidal Slip Seat, 38 In., Pair 1850.00
Chair, Federal, Splayed Rectangular Back, Cane Seat, Tapered Legs 86.00
Chair, Federal, Walnut, Vase-Form Splat, Cane Seat, Box Stretcher, Ball Feet 150.00
Chair, Fiddleback, Rush Seat, Arms, Hudson River Valley, 18th Century, 61 In. 2530.00

Furniture, Chair,
Eames, Pony,
Cowhide Back
& Seat

Furniture,
Chair, Eastlake,
Walnut, Arms,
36 1/2 In., Pair

Furniture, Chair,
G. Stickley,
No. 335,
Tiger Maple,
3 Slats, Rush Seat

Chair, Figures Of Dolphin, Putti & North Winds, Hairy Paw Feet, Ram's-Head Arms 825.00
Chair, Flame & Ring Finials, 3 Spindles, Bun Grips, Cylindrical Arms, 38 In. 8050.00
Chair, Flower Heads At Knees, Gray Paint, Upholstered Arm & Back 7475.00
Chair, Flower Heads, Leaf Carved Bead Inset, Fluted Legs, Upholstered Back, Pair 4025.00
Chair, Folding, Arts & Crafts, Church, Carved Flowers, X-Base, Boston, 1895, 35 In. 1650.00
Chair, Folding, Elm, Rectangular Splat, Rope Seat, Northern China, 18th Century, Pair ... 490.00
Chair, Folding, Hunzinger, Walnut, Turned, New York, c.1870 .... 605.00
Chair, Frank Gehry, Cardboard, Corrugated, Masonite Sides, 28 In. 2300.00
Chair, Frank Lloyd Wright, 8-Sided Back, Cantilevered Seat, 28 In., Pair 285.00
Chair, Frank Lloyd Wright, Mahogany, Upholstered Back & Seat, 29 x 25 In., Pair 3190.00
Chair, Frank Lloyd Wright, Slab Back, Square Pierced Cutouts, Child's 4675.00
Chair, French Empire Style, Mahogany, Leather, Bronze Mounts, Arms 460.00
Chair, French Provincial, Ladder Back, Rush Seat, Celadon Paint, Pair 385.00
Chair, French Provincial, Walnut, Triple Rail Ladder, Rush Seat, Child's, 25 In. 345.00
Chair, French Revival, Mahogany, Foliate, Upholstered, Arms, 43 In., Pair 635.00
Chair, French Style, Carved, Upholstered, Open Arms, 20th Century, 43 In. 110.00
Chair, French Style, Cupid Painted On Woven Wood Medallion, 35 In. 375.00
Chair, French Style, Tapestry, Carved Skirt, Legs & Arms, 19th Century 1960.00
Chair, French Style, X Stretcher, Upholstered, Carved Skirt, Legs & Arms, 43 In. 785.00
Chair, Fruitwood, Shells & Swags, Cane Back & Seat, Arms, 20th Century, Pair 2760.00
Chair, G. Nakashima, Conoid, Carved From One Piece Of Wood, 1981 .... 1800.00
Chair, G. Nakashima, Walnut, 11 Spindles, Curved Crest Rail, Plank Seat, 32 In., Pair ... 4600.00
Chair, G. Nelson, Birch, Sculptured, Upholstered Seat, Herman Miller, c.1954 .... 600.00
Chair, G. Nelson, Coconut, White Enamel Metal Shell, Herman Miller, 1956 .... 4675.00
Chair, G. Nelson, DAF, Fiberglass Back & Seat, Steel Legs, 27 In. 1300.00
Chair, G. Nelson, Pretzel, Molded Birch, Walnut Seat, Arms, 1955, 30 In. 2970.00
Chair, G. Stickley, 3 Vertical Slats, Vinyl Seat, H. Ellis, 39 In., Pair 1320.00
Chair, G. Stickley, 5 Vertical Slats, Leather Cushion, Decal, Arms, 27 In. 770.00
Chair, G. Stickley, H-Back, Leather Seat, Red Als Ik Kan Mark, 39 x 16 In. 550.00
Chair, G. Stickley, Ladder Back, Hard Leather Seat, Branded, 36 In., Pair 990.00
Chair, G. Stickley, No. 306, 3 Slats, Woven Seat, 36 1/2 In. 600.00
Chair, G. Stickley, No. 324, Slat Arms, Red Decal, 39 x 29 x 30 In. 2750.00
Chair, G. Stickley, No. 335, Tiger Maple, 3 Slats, Rush Seat ....*Illus* 4400.00
Chair, G. Stickley, No. 353, Oak, 3 Vertical Slats, Rush Slip Seat, 39 In. 460.00
Chair, G. Stickley, No. 380, Oak, Leather Back & Seat, c.1904 .... 2300.00
Chair, Galle, Carved Mahogany, Marquetry Inlay, c.1890, 35 1/2 In., Pair 6760.00
Chair, George II Style, Mahogany, Carved, Gothic Tracery Splat, Cabriole Legs 200.00
Chair, George III, Beechwood, Gesso, Concave Round Back, Silk, Arms, 35 In. 3450.00
Chair, George III, Elm, Pierced Sheaf Splat, Drop-In Seat, Box Stretcher, Arms 1610.00
Chair, George III, Giltwood, Wreath Of Husks, Tapered Legs, Ball Feet, Arms 25300.00
Chair, George III, Mahogany, Padded Back, Back-Curved Supports, Arms 2185.00
Chair, George III, Mahogany, Pierced Splat, Curved Arms, 30 In. 525.00
Chair, George III, Mahogany, Pierced Splat, Scrolled Terminals, Arms, 1770 .... 2185.00
Chair, George III, Mahogany, Ribbonback, Carved, Overstuffed Seat, Pair 2875.00
Chair, George III, Mahogany, Serpentine Padded Back, Gainsborough, 39 1/4 In. 1760.00
Chair, George III, Mahogany, Serpentine Top Rail, Cabriole Legs, 40 In., Pair 5520.00
Chair, George III, Mahogany, Tub, Concave Back, Acanthus Columns, 33 3/4 In. 750.00
Chair, George III, Oak, Shaped Crest Rail, H-Frame Stretcher, Square Legs, Pair 345.00
Chair, George IV, Mahogany, Undulating Crest, Pierced Splat, Arms, 38 In., Pair 3910.00
Chair, Georgian Style, Mahogany, Scrolled Splat, Straight Legs, Plaid Seat 345.00
Chair, Georgian, Mahogany, Hoop Back, Serpentine Front Seat Rail, 1780 .... 165.00
Chair, Georgian, Open, Fluted Square Tapered Legs, Upholstered, Arms 69.00
Chair, Gilt Gesso, Serpentine Seat, Cushion, Victorian, 39 3/4 In., Pair 3080.00
Chair, Giltwood, Arched Padded Back Continuing To Arms, Paw Feet, 28 In. 2420.00
Chair, Giltwood, Padded Backrest & Arms, Arched, Cushion, c.1775 .... 5750.00
Chair, Globe-Wernicke, Aluminum, Vinyl, Metal Tag, 34 In., Pair 55.00
Chair, Golden Oak, Vinyl, Composition Lion's-Head Arms, 41 In. 132.00
Chair, Gothic Revival, Mahogany, Pierced Crest, Barley Twist Stiles, New York, Pair 605.00
Chair, Gothic Revival, Oak, Carved Griffin Crest, Open Foliate, Pair 990.00
Chair, H. Bertoia, Black Steel Rod Base, White Wire Grid Seat, Child's 488.00
Chair, H. Bertoia, Diamond, Chrome Wire, Upholstered, Arms, Knoll, 43 In. 360.00
Chair, Half Spindle, Dark Ground, Faux Tiger Maple Seat, 1830, 35 In., Pair 247.00
Chair, Hans Vollner, Oak, Tub Shape, Curved Back, Cane Seat, Square Legs, Arms 2185.00

Chair, Harden, Vertical Slats On Back & Under Arms, Drop-In Seat, 37 x 27 In. 470.00
Chair, Hardwood, Abstract Geometric Design, Turned Legs, Stretchers, Pair 13800.00
Chair, Hardwood, Carved, Red Lacquer, 19th Century, Pair 600.00
Chair, Hardwood, Yoke Back, Arched Crest Rail, Out-Curved Arms, 47 In., Pair 290.00
Chair, Heart-Shaped Back, Carved & Pierced Crest, Upholstered Arms, 41 In., Pair 600.00
Chair, Hepplewhite, Mahogany, Crest, Pierced Splat, Upholstered Seat, 1800, Pair 1980.00
Chair, Hepplewhite, Mahogany, Shieldback, Carved Wheat, Upholstered Seat, 36 In. 495.00
Chair, Heywood Bros. & Co., Wicker, Arms, Victorian, 37 x 27 x 20 In. 990.00
Chair, Hickory, Butternut, Splayed Back, 7 Tapered Rods, Slab Seat 80.00
Chair, Hickory, Maple, Turned Spindles, Rush Seat, Pilgrim Century, 44 1/2 In. 9775.00
Chair, Hitchcock, Arched Crest Rail, Spindle Gallery, Slab Seat, 19th Century, Pair 160.00
Chair, Hitchcock, Black, Stenciled Slat, 19th Century 40.00
Chair, Hitchcock, Curved Crest Rail, Parcel Gilt, Black Paint, P.B. Prentis 2300.00
Chair, Hitchcock, Rush Seat, Gilt & Stencil Decoration, Pair 155.00
Chair, Hitchcock, Splayed Rectangular Back, Woven Rush Seat, Black, Pair 200.00
Chair, Hitchcock, Stencil, Fruit Design, Cane Seat, 19th Century, 34 x 17 In. 40.00
Chair, Hitchcock, Stencil, Rush Seat, Turned Legs, 19th Century, 35 x 19 In. 40.00
Chair, Horseshoe-Shaped Back, Square Legs, Out-Curved Arms, Chinese, 37 In., Pair 650.00
Chair, Hunzinger, Oak, Scrolled Top, X-Shaped Legs, Painted, 1878, 38 x 24 In. 280.00
Chair, Ice Cream, Twisted Wire, Wood Seat, Child's 72.00
Chair, Italian Provincial, Beechwood, Rush Seat, Arms, 37 In., Pair 1540.00
Chair, J. & J.W. Meeks, Laminated Rosewood, Hawkins, c.1850 . . . . 7700.00
Chair, J. Hoffman, Bentwood, Fledermaus, Arms, c.1907 . . . . 2300.00
Chair, J.M. Young, Leather Back & Seat, Slat Sides, Label, 48 x 28 In., Pair 2200.00
Chair, J.M. Young, No. 186, 5 Slats Under Arm, Spring Cushion, 41 x 32 In. 3850.00
Chair, Jacobean Style, Oak, Carved, Padded Crest, Overstuffed Seat, 19th Century 140.00
Chair, Jacobean, Floral, Leaf Crest Rail, Cane Back, Rope Twist, Block Legs, Pair 290.00
Chair, Jacobean, Scroll, Crown Crest Rail, Block, Turned Legs, Scrolled Arms 545.00
Chair, Jacobean, Slanted Paneled Back, Arched Crest, Scrolled Arms, Pair 3165.00
Chair, Jacobsen, Egg, Tilting Chrome Base, Upholstered, F. Hansen 2750.00
Chair, Jacobsen, No. 3107, Steel Rod Legs, Pink Paint, Plastic Arms 315.00
Chair, Jacobsen, No. 3320, Fiberglass, Upholstered 1265.00
Chair, Jean Prove, Auditorium, Painted Steel, Leatherette, 1956, 36 1/2 In. 2300.00
Chair, John Jelliff, Walnut, Incised Gilt, Ebonized, Arms, c.1865, Pair 1270.00
Chair, L. & J.G. Stickley, Ladder Back, Upholstered Drop Seat, Arms, Label, 40 x 28 In. . 470.00
Chair, L. & J.G. Stickley, Mahogany, 10 Spindles, Drop-In Seat, Arms, 42 In. 990.00
Chair, L. & J.G. Stickley, No. 422, 6 Vertical Slats, Spring Cushion, 1912, 38 In. 460.00
Chair, Ladder Back, 2 Slats, Woven Cane Seat, Child's, 24 In. 275.00
Chair, Ladder Back, 3 Arched Curved Crossbars, Woven Rush Seat, Painted, Child's 260.00
Chair, Ladder Back, 3 Arched Slats, Sausage Turning, Finial, New England, Arms, 44 In. . . 165.00
Chair, Ladder Back, 3 Pinned Slats, Red Paint, Child's 330.00
Chair, Ladder Back, 3 Scrolled Slats, Rush Seat, Continental 190.00
Chair, Ladder Back, 4 Arched Slats, Acorn Finial, Rush Seat, Black Over Red Paint 145.00
Chair, Ladder Back, 5 Arched Slats, Finials, Shaped Arms, Mid-Atlantic, 1800 . . . . 550.00
Chair, Ladder Back, 5 Arched Slats, Needlepoint Seat, Adolph Loos, 30 In. 770.00
Chair, Ladder Back, Arched Slats, Black Paint, New England, Early 1800s, 23 x 9 In. 345.00
Chair, Ladder Back, Birch, Hickory, Woven Rush Seat, Double Box Stretcher, Arms 490.00
Chair, Ladder Back, Gray Patina, Rush Seat, Child's, 20 1/2 In. 220.00
Chair, Ladder Back, Maple, 3 Backrests, Mushroom Finials, Pilgrim Century, 19 In. 8050.00
Chair, Ladder Back, Maple, 4 Graduated & Arched Slats, Pa., 1800, 43 In. 1210.00
Chair, Ladder Back, Maple, 5 Arched Slats, Rush Seat, Arms, Pa., 1790, 48 In. 1320.00
Chair, Ladder Back, Maple, 5 Arched Slats, Rush Seat, Pa., 1800, 43 In. 1540.00
Chair, Ladder Back, Maple, Rush Seat, Horse Bone Legs, 44 1/4 In. 3740.00
Chair, Ladder Back, Maple, Rush Seat, Turned Front Legs, 43 x 19 In. 1870.00
Chair, Ladder Back, Mixed Wood, 4 Slats, Urn Finials, 18th Century, 40 In. 495.00
Chair, Ladder Back, Mixed Woods, 3 Slats, Turned Finial, Posts, Arms, 1800, 37 In. 140.00
Chair, Ladder Back, Rush Seat, Sausage Turning, Double Stretcher, Early 1700s, Pair 440.00
Chair, Ladder Back, Splint Seat, Red Paint, Arms, Early 18th Century 350.00
Chair, Ladder Back, Tiger Maple, 5 Reverse-Graduated Slats, Scrolled Arms, Pair 1980.00
Chair, Laminated Birch Legs, Suspended Seat Continues To Arms, 1965 . . . . 2530.00
Chair, Laminated Plywood Back & Seat, 4 Chrome Steel Rod Legs, Komai, 1949 . . . . 920.00
Chair, Late Classical, Mahogany, Carved, Leather, Horsehair, c.1840 . . . . 5720.00
Chair, Le Corbusier, Tubular Steel, Leather Bascule Seat, Arms 3450.00

Chair, Leather Buttoned Back & Seat, Padded Reading Support, c.1815 .... 4315.00
Chair, Limbert, Fixed Back, Heart-Shaped Cutout Slat, Arms, 40 1/2 x 29 1/2 In. 990.00
Chair, Limbert, Horizontal H Slat, Leather Seat, Michigan, 1912, 35 In. 545.00
Chair, Limbert, Mahogany, 4 Vertical Slats, Cushion, 28 x 36 In. 935.00
Chair, Limbert, No. 847, Leather Cushions, Arms, 32 x 31 x 32 In. 2145.00
Chair, Limbert, No. 931, 3 Vertical Slats, Drop-In Seat, 36 In. 770.00
Chair, Limbert, Oak, Cutout Back & Sides, Leather Seat, 41 x 27 x 21 In. 2475.00
Chair, Limbert, Twin Crest Rail, Front Stretcher, Rush Seat, Child's, 26 1/2 x 16 In. 220.00
Chair, Lolling, Chippendale, Mahogany, Square Back, Down-Swept Arms, 1780 .... 1100.00
Chair, Lolling, Chippendale, Mahogany, Straight Legs, Upholstered, Padded Arms 1400.00
Chair, Lolling, Federal, Mahogany, Birch, Serpentine Crest, 1795, 44 1/2 In. 9775.00
Chair, Lolling, Federal, Mahogany, Square Legs, Cushion, 1810, 43 x 15 In. 3450.00
Chair, Lolling, Mahogany, Carved Crest, Padded Back & Seat, 46 1/2 In. 1725.00
Chair, Lolling, Sheraton, Mahogany, Upholstered Serpentine Back, 1820, 43 In. 6600.00
Chair, Louis Philippe, Mahogany, Scrolled Crest, Toes & Arms, 39 1/4 In., Pair 1840.00
Chair, Louis Philippe, Walnut, Stuffed Back, Bowed Seat, Shaped Feet, c.1830, Pair 4125.00
Chair, Louis XIV Style, Burl Walnut, Shaped Back, Cushion, Arms, 39 In. 1760.00
Chair, Louis XIV, Mahogany, Molded Down-Swept Armrests, Pair 865.00
Chair, Louis XV Style, Beechwood, Arched Padded Back, Curved Arms, c.1900 .... 600.00
Chair, Louis XV Style, Beechwood, Cabriole Legs, Arms, c.1900, 39 1/2 In. 600.00
Chair, Louis XV Style, Beechwood, Padded Back & Sides, Serpentine Seat, Arms 275.00
Chair, Louis XV Style, Flower Crest, Painted, Padded Back, Velvet, Pair 635.00
Chair, Louis XV Style, Walnut, Arched Back, Serpentine Seat, Arms, c.1900, 39 In. 1210.00
Chair, Louis XV, Beechwood, Cabriole Legs, Needlepoint Back & Seat, 34 In. 660.00
Chair, Louis XV, Beechwood, Carved Crest, Padded Back, Painted, Arms 1035.00
Chair, Louis XV, Carved Crest, Upholstered, Serpentine Arms, 19th Century, 34 In. 220.00
Chair, Louis XV, Cream Paint, Cushion, Needlework, Arms, 38 In. 6325.00
Chair, Louis XV, Gilt, Padded Backrest, Carved Flower Heads, Arms, 39 In., Pair 3450.00
Chair, Louis XV, Giltwood, Carved Shells & Flowers, Upholstered Backrest, Pair 5750.00
Chair, Louis XV, Padded Backrest, Floral Top Rail, Cabriole Legs, Arms, 41 3/4 In. 1150.00
Chair, Louis XV, Serpentine Seat Rail, Velvet Back & Seat, 33 In., Pair 3025.00
Chair, Louis XV, Walnut, Cartouche Padded Back, Serpentine Seat, Arms, 44 In. 690.00
Chair, Louis XV, Walnut, Molded Back, Cabriole Legs, Knuckled Armrest 3520.00
Chair, Louis XVI Style, Arched Crest Rail, Flowers, Ribbons, Serpentine Seat, Pair 440.00
Chair, Louis XVI Style, Giltwood, Marquise, Carved Rosettes, Late 19th Century, Pair ... 7475.00
Chair, Louis XVI Style, Giltwood, Padded Cushion, Scrolled Arms, c.1900, 38 In. 1540.00
Chair, Louis XVI Style, Walnut, Padded Back, Bowed Seat, Arms, 35 In. 440.00
Chair, Louis XVI, Giltwood, Padded Arched Top & Seat, Arms, 39 In., Pair 4830.00
Chair, Louis XVI, Giltwood, Trophy-Shaped Crest Rail, Padded Back, Ball Feet 301.00
Chair, Louis XVI, Pair Of Crossed Torches, Floral Wreath, Foliate Legs, Pair 400.00
Chair, Louis XVI, Rectangular Back, Cane Panel, Down-Curved Arms, Pair 546.00
Chair, Louis XVI, Walnut, Floral, Ribbon Carved, Trumpet Legs, Arms, 39 In., Pair 3450.00
Chair, Louis XVI, White Paint, Green Highlights, Arms, 18th Century, 31 In. 2640.00
Chair, Lounge, Cantilevered Structure, Sling Back & Seat, 1920s, 40 1/2 In., Pair 402.00
Chair, Lounge, E. Wormley, Bentwood, Cane, Adjustable Back & Seat, 1950s, Pair 1380.00
Chair, Lounge, Eames, Ash Veneer Back & Seat, Rubber Shock Mounts, 1945 .... 1840.00
Chair, Lounge, Eames, Red Aniline Dye, c.1950, 26 1/2 In. 6325.00
Chair, Lounge, G. Nakashima, Black Walnut, Free-Form Right Arm, 1962, 33 1/2 In. 4025.00
Chair, Lounge, G. Nakashima, Conoid, Hickory, Spindles, Cushion 7150.00
Chair, Lounge, Ottoman, Eames, No. 670, Rosewood, Aluminum Base 3165.00
Chair, Lounge, Ottoman, Plycraft, Bentwood, Chrome Base, Vinyl, 36 In. 110.00
Chair, Lounge, Paulin, Bent Plywood, Steel Legs, Orange, 31 In. 1150.00
Chair, Lounge, Tapered, Dowel Back & Seat, Tubular Steel Legs, Martine 1840.00
Chair, Lounge, Walnut, Split Cane Back & Seat, D. Johnson, 1958, 28 In. 3450.00
Chair, Lounge, Warren McArthur, Tubular Aluminum, Upholstered Back & Seat, 32 In. .. 2300.00
Chair, Lounge, Wrought Iron, Tubular, Boucle, Swirl Design, 25 x 26 In. 195.00
Chair, M. Breuer, Chrome, Canvas Back & Seat, Wood Arms, 32 In. 3680.00
Chair, M. Breuer, Chrome, Tubular, Black Stretchers, Armrests, 28 In. 495.00
Chair, M. Breuer, Chrome, Tubular, Wassily, 1925, 26 3/4 In. 8050.00
Chair, M. Breuer, Solid Wood Seat, Plywood Sides, Bryn Mawr, 1938 .... 6600.00
Chair, M. Breuer, Tubular Chrome, Leather Straps, Wassily, 29 In. 880.00
Chair, Mahogany, Arched Crest Rail, Carved, Tobey, Chicago, c.1870, Pair 6600.00
Chair, Mahogany, Balloon Back, Arched Cross Bar, Scrolled Toes, Overstuffed Seat 40.00

Chair, Mahogany, Barrel Back, Carved Leaves, 20th Century 55.00
Chair, Mahogany, Carved Back, Carved Knees, Upholstered Seat, 41 In., Pair 490.00
Chair, Mahogany, Cherry Crest Rail, Pierced Splat, Needlepoint Seat, Victorian, Pair 172.00
Chair, Mahogany, Cock-Fighting, Pierced Comb Splat, Scrolled Arms, c.1825 .... 3160.00
Chair, Mahogany, Directoire, Bowed Seat, Tapestry, Turned Arms, Pair 4315.00
Chair, Mahogany, Flower Inlay, Birds & Insects, Drop-In Seat, Holland, 44 In., Pair 865.00
Chair, Mahogany, Leaf Carved Crest Rail, Pierced Gothic Back Splat, Pair 672.00
Chair, Mahogany, Martha Washington, Upholstered Arms, 40 In. 895.00
Chair, Mahogany, Metamorphic, Hinged Seat, Locking Mechanism, 1810 .... 8625.00
Chair, Mahogany, Metamorphic, Leather Seat, Scrolled Arms, 46 1/2 In. 1380.00
Chair, Mahogany, Padded Arched Back Continuing To Seat, 41 1/2 In., Pair 920.00
Chair, Mahogany, Padded Backrests, Fetlock Cabriole Legs, c.1740 .... 5750.00
Chair, Mahogany, Reclining, Adjustable Reading Stand, Leather, 1850s 9200.00
Chair, Mahogany, Rosewood Crest Rail, Cane Seat, Reeded Legs, 33 In., Pair 300.00
Chair, Mahogany, Shaped Back, Gothic Splat, Upholstered Seat, 38 In., Pair 400.00
Chair, Mahogany, Shieldback, Applied Scrolls, Beaded Edge, 1800 .... 1265.00
Chair, Mahogany, Spanish Carved Feet, Scrolled Arms, 1800, 35 In. 8050.00
Chair, Mahogany, Upholstered Back, Padded Hound's-Head Arms, Pair 4600.00
Chair, Majestic Chair Co., Arts & Crafts, 3 Vertical Slats, Rush Seat, 49 In. 2090.00
Chair, Majestic Chair Co., Tall Back, Tacked On Leather Back Panel, 49 x 17 In. 990.00
Chair, Maple, 15 Spindles, Finials, Padded Seat, Scrolled Arms 170.00
Chair, Maple, Ash, Ring Turned Supports, Double Stretchers, Arms, 41 In. 865.00
Chair, Maple, Birch, Pierced Splat, Rush Seat, Spanish Feet, 38 x 17 In., Pair 1380.00
Chair, Maple, North-Wind Face Carved Crest, Turned Spindles, Cabriole Legs 66.00
Chair, Maple, Poplar, Vase-Form Splat, Rush Seat, Turned Legs, 41 1/4 In. 220.00
Chair, Maple, Raked Splat, Ring Turned Legs, c.1875, 40 x 17 In. 575.00
Chair, Maple, Slat Back, Turned Finials, Posts, Rush Seat, Mid-1700s, 33 1/2 In. 1610.00
Chair, Maple, Vase-Form Splat, Trapezoidal Splint Seat, Arms, 1790, 41 x 17 1/2 In. 860.00
Chair, Martin, Cantilevered, Hinged Adjustable Back & Seat, 32 In. 9200.00
Chair, Mission, Plank Back To Floor, Cutout Heart, Chicago Mission Furniture, 42 In. ... 385.00
Chair, Molded Continuous Back & Seat, Brass Legs, Ico Parisi, c.1950, 38 In., Pair 1000.00
Chair, Molded Crest Rail, Upholstered Seat, Out-Curved Arms, 43 In. 4480.00
Chair, Morris, Arts & Crafts, Oak, Adjustable Slat Back, Arm Compartments, 39 In. 1320.00
Chair, Morris, Arts & Crafts, Prairie School, Paneled Sides & Back, 40 In. 715.00
Chair, Morris, Arts & Crafts, Vertical Slats, Cutout Sides, Child's, 28 In. 165.00
Chair, Morris, G. Stickley, Drop-In Spring Seat, Bow Arms, 36 1/2 x 30 In. 6050.00
Chair, Morris, G. Stickley, Flared Legs, Corbels, Leather Back & Seat, 44 In. 9350.00
Chair, Morris, G. Stickley, No. 332, Flat Arms Over 5 Wide Slats, 38 In. 8250.00
Chair, Morris, G. Stickley, No. 2340, Bow Arms, Red Decal, 1904, 23 3/4 In. 19550.00
Chair, Morris, J.M. Young, Corbels, Arched Apron, Arms, 38 x 31 In. 3575.00
Chair, Morris, J.M. Young, Slats To Floor, Leather Back & Seat, 38 x 30 In. 3300.00
Chair, Morris, L. & J.G. Stickley, 6 Slats Under Each Arm, Label, 39 x 32 In. 3300.00
Chair, Morris, L. & J.G. Stickley, No. 367, Mahogany, Woman's, 1907, 27 1/2 In. 5750.00
Chair, Morris, L. & J.G. Stickley, No. 774, 5 Long Vertical Slats, Woman's, 39 In. 2415.00
Chair, Morris, Lifetime, Leather Cushions, Bow Arms, Label, 38 x 31 x 34 In. 4675.00
Chair, Morris, Limbert, Mahogany, Leather Seat, Back Cushions, Arms, 36 In. 550.00
Chair, Morris, Oak, Curbed Legs, Wheel Casters, Upholstered, Shaped Arms 190.00
Chair, Napoleon III, Ebonized, Parcel Gilt, Padded Back, Center Plume Crown 125.00
Chair, Napoleon III, Giltwood, Padded Back, Arms, 43 In., Pair 1430.00
Chair, Napoleon III, Scrolled Top Rail, Rectangular Seat, Green, Red Apron, Pair 9200.00
Chair, Neoclassical Style, Mahogany, Winged Caryatid Arm Supports, 40 In., Pair 2860.00
Chair, Neoclassical, Fruitwood, Concave Back, Upholstered, Arms, 30 3/4 In. 1095.00
Chair, Neoclassical, Mahogany, Drop-In Cushion, Scrolled Arms, Russia, 38 In., Pair 4400.00
Chair, Neoclassical, Oak, Curved Crest, Padded Seat, Round Legs, 32 1/4 In., Pair 546.00
Chair, Neogothic, Arched Back, Trefoil Splat, Drop-In Seat 125.00
Chair, Neogothic, Walnut, Cutout Back, Rope Twist Posts, Needlepoint, Child's 385.00
Chair, Neogrecque, Gilt, Green, Vermilion Polychrome, 33 In. 3380.00
Chair, Neogrecque, Walnut, Vine Bearing Leaves & Berries, N.Y., 38 In. 920.00
Chair, Nursing, Oak, Elm, Crest Rail, Spindles, Rush Seat, Low Arms, Scotland, 40 In. .. 220.00
Chair, Oak, Carved Crest Over Molded Stiles, Cabriole Legs, France, 1900 .... 1100.00
Chair, Oak, Foliate Pierced Top Rail, Cabriole Legs Overstuffed Seat, 49 In. 575.00
Chair, Oak, Jacobean, Arched Solid Back, Box Seat, Drawer, Down-Swept Arms 1725.00
Chair, Oak, Open Back, Pierced Foliate Splat, Padded Seat, 1860s 100.00

Chair, Oak, Rectangular Padded Back, Overstuffed Seat, Leather, Pair 316.00
Chair, Oak, Scrolled Back, Molded Seat, Ball Legs, Bun Feet, Victorian, Pair 632.00
Chair, Oak, Shaped Crest, Plank Seat, H-Stretcher, Ball Feet, England, 17th Century 110.00
Chair, Oak, Top Rail, Square Legs, Wainscoting, Scrolled Arms, 53 x 29 x 23 In. 1840.00
Chair, Oak, U Shape, Carved, Anthemia, Leaves, Spindle Arms 495.00
Chair, Open Back, Arched & Shaped Crest Rail, Cane Seat, Child's, 1850s 75.00
Chair, Oriental, Teakwood, Shaped Splat With Tassel, Stretchers, 1875-1900, Pair 2200.00
Chair, Oscar Niemeyer, Vertebrae, Interlocking Metal Clips, Upholstered, 1970s 1840.00
Chair, Out-Curved Tufted Back, Overstuffed Seat, Curved Tufted Armrests, 34 In. 405.00
Chair, Padded Backrest & Arms, Down-Swept Supports, Gray Paint, 1880s, Pair 4025.00
Chair, Palazzo, Claw Feet, Undulating Curved Arms, Italy, 50 In., Pair 1035.00
Chair, Papier-Mache, Mother-Of-Pearl Inlay, Shaped Rails, Black Ground, Pair 3162.00
Chair, Paul Iribe, Black Lacquer, D Shape, Upholstered, Curved Arms, 1925 . . . . 805.00
Chair, Paul Tuttle, Banded Chrome, Z Shape, Canvas & Leather Sling 920.00
Chair, Pine, Top Runners, Stile Feet, Molded Edge Seat, 28 1/4 In. 690.00
Chair, Plank Seat, Stenciled Design, Grain Painted, Pair 66.00
Chair, Polychrome Design, Rush Seat, Painted, Black Ground, 1820s, Pair 385.00
Chair, Potty, Maple, 1840, 40 1/2 x 21 x 18 In. 115.00
Chair, Potty, Yellow & Gold Stenciling, American Flag, Eagle, Shield, 41 In. 55.00
Chair, Queen Anne Style, Painted Flowers & Fruit 1760.00
Chair, Queen Anne, Carved Crest, Rush Seat, Painted, 41 In. 1495.00
Chair, Queen Anne, Cherry, Ash, Ring Turned Stiles, Front Stretchers, 41 In. 750.00
Chair, Queen Anne, Fiddleback, Black Paint, Oriental, 20th Century, 72 x 21 In. 225.00
Chair, Queen Anne, Japanned, Upholstered Slip Seat, 1900, 37 In., Pair 1045.00
Chair, Queen Anne, Mahogany, Balloon-Shaped Seat, Out-Curved Arms, 1760 . . . . 9775.00
Chair, Queen Anne, Mahogany, Pierced Vase-Form Splat, Padded Seat 920.00
Chair, Queen Anne, Maple, Poplar, Nut Brown Finish, Turned Legs, 17 x 40 In. 2090.00
Chair, Queen Anne, Maple, Vase-Form Splat, Baluster Legs, 18th Century, 39 x 17 In. . . . 1035.00
Chair, Queen Anne, Maple, Vase-Form Splat, Trapezoidal Seat, 37 x 18 In., Pair 4885.00
Chair, Queen Anne, Rush Seat, Yoke Crest, Spanish Feet, Black Paint, 41 In. 2420.00
Chair, Queen Anne, Turned Stretcher, Spanish Feet, Rush Seat, 18th Century 360.00
Chair, Queen Anne, Vase-Form Splat, Padded Duck Feet, Rush Seat, Pair 3840.00
Chair, Queen Anne, Vase-Form Splat, Rush Seat, Hudson Valley, 1760, 42 In., Pair 275.00
Chair, Queen Anne, Vase-Form Splat, Serpentine Crest Rail, Rush Seat 330.00
Chair, Queen Anne, Vase-Form Splat, Yoked Crest, Duck Feet, Rush Seat 600.00
Chair, Queen Anne, Walnut, Double Arched Crest, Upholstered Seat, 40 In. 8050.00
Chair, Queen Anne, Walnut, Shaped Crest, Cabriole Legs, Trifid Feet, 42 In. 3335.00
Chair, Queen Anne, Walnut, Shell, Volute Crest, Claw & Ball Feet, Phila., 18 x 43 In. 9775.00
Chair, Queen Anne, Walnut, Trapezoidal Slip Seat, Cabriole Legs, 38 x 17 In., Pair 8625.00
Chair, Queen Anne, Walnut, Vase-Form Splat, Cabriole Legs, 18th Century, Pair 770.00
Chair, Queen Anne, Walnut, Vase-Form Splat, Compass Seat, 1760, 40 x 17 In. 2875.00
Chair, Queen Anne, Walnut, Vase-Form Splat, Slip Seat, Upholstered, Mass., Pair 11550.00
Chair, R. Shultz, Aluminum, Supporting Back & Seat, c.1966, 26 1/2 In. 920.00
Chair, Reclining, Tapered Turned Legs, Upholstered, Late 19th Century 145.00
Chair, Rectangular Back, Cabriole Legs, Green Paint, Arms, Pair 1840.00
Chair, Rectangular Splat, Cane Seat, Angular Scrolled Arms, Hongmu, 35 In. 1150.00
Chair, Regency Style, Gilt, Painted, Tapestry, Feather Carved Arms 770.00
Chair, Regency Style, Mahogany, Scrolled Back, Floral Splat, Cane Seat, Cushion 633.00
Chair, Regency Style, Walnut, Shell Carving, Arched Padded Back & Seat, Arms, Italy . . . 1495.00
Chair, Regency, Beechwood, Bamboo, Rectangular Cane Seat, 37 In., Pair 1980.00
Chair, Regency, Continuous Arms Scrolled To Rectangular Seat, 36 In., Pair 3220.00
Chair, Regency, Corinthian Legs, Gilt, Painted, Upholstered Back, Arms, Pair 980.00
Chair, Regency, Ebonized, Seat Rail, Gilt Carved Ormolu, Reeded Legs, 35 In., Pair 1035.00
Chair, Regency, Ebony, Gilt Ball Finials, Carved Flower Heads, Saber Legs, Arms, Pair . . 750.00
Chair, Regency, Klismos Shape, Ebonized, Gilt, Cane Seat, Arms, 32 1/4 In. 3220.00
Chair, Regency, Laburnum, Scroll-Shaped Back, Plank Seat, c.1820 . . . . 2530.00
Chair, Regency, Mahogany, Crosshatched Design, Saber Legs, Arms, Pair 550.00
Chair, Regency, Mahogany, Molded Crest, Down-Swept Arms, 35 In., Pair 1150.00
Chair, Regency, Mahogany, Molded Crest, Padded Seat, Saber Legs, 34 In., Pair 500.00
Chair, Regency, Neoclassical Scrolls, Urns & Greek Key, Cane Seat, Arms, c.1800 . . . . . . 3850.00
Chair, Regency, Padded Cartouche Back, Serpentine Seat, Cabriole Legs, Child's 135.00
Chair, Regency, Rosewood, Brass Inlay, Cane Seat, Velvet Tufted Cushion 385.00
Chair, Renaissance Revival, Burl Walnut, Shieldback, Carved, Hinged Seat, Pair 825.00

Chair, Renaissance Revival, Ebonized, Gilt Design, Upholstered, Victorian 175.00
Chair, Renaissance Revival, Ebonized, Ivory Inlay, 42 In. 300.00
Chair, Renaissance Revival, Walnut, Coat Of Arms, Leather Seat, Italy, 57 In., Pair 6037.00
Chair, Renaissance Revival, Walnut, Fluted Legs, Button Tufted, 31 In. 575.00
Chair, Risom, Teakwood, Flared Legs, Upholstered Seat, Splayed Arms, 29 In. .... .110.00 to 275.00
Chair, Robert Thompson, Oak, Hand Carved, Inset Panel, Leather Seat, Arms, Pair 1500.00
Chair, Robert Venturi, Laminated Plywood, Upholstered, c.1982, 38 1/2 In. 8050.00
Chair, Rocker, is listed under Rocker in this category.
Chair, Rococo, Cartouche-Shaped Button Back, Padded Scrolled Arms, Pair 1150.00
Chair, Rococo, Giltwood, Upholstered, Arms, Italy, 19th Century, 42 x 26 In., Pair 2530.00
Chair, Rococo, Polychrome Scenes, Yellow Ground, 19th Century, Italy, Pair 2310.00
Chair, Rococo, Rosewood, Pierce Carved Arabesques, Floral Crest, Arms, 47 In. 9200.00
Chair, Rococo, Rosewood, Shieldback, Arms, France, 40 3/4 In., Pair 1100.00
Chair, Rococo, Shell, Foliate Carved Top Rail, Serpentine Upholstered Seat, Pair 4600.00
Chair, Rococo, Simulated Rosewood, Cartouche Button Back, Arms 920.00
Chair, Rococo, Walnut, Crest, Upholstered, Casters, Open Arms, 34 In. 275.00
Chair, Rococo, Walnut, Padded Back, Rectangular Seat, Arms, Italy, 55 In. 2200.00
Chair, Rococo, Walnut, Scrolled Crest & Feet, Foliate, Cabriole Legs 920.00
Chair, Rose Valley, Dark Finish, Turned Legs, Leatherette Back & Seat, 35 In. 990.00
Chair, Rosewood, Arched Back, Pierced Splat, Paneled Seat, Scrolled Arms, Pair 345.00
Chair, Rosewood, Arched Crest, Cabriole Legs, Casters, Upholstered, Arms, Victorian ... 330.00
Chair, Rosewood, Carved, Cartouche Back, Needlepoint, Casters, Victorian 260.00
Chair, Rosewood, Carved, Pierced Splat, Open Arms, Chinese, Late 19th Century 290.00
Chair, Rosewood, Open Tracery Back, Scrollwork, Overstuffed Seat, Victorian 1150.00
Chair, Rosewood, Pierced Crest Rail, Fruit & Vines, Rectangular Seat, 4 Piece 345.00
Chair, Rosewood, Pierced Crest, Upholstered, Arms, 1870, 47 In. 2310.00
Chair, Rosewood, Shieldback, Casters, Overstuffed Seat, Open Arms, Victorian 1035.00
Chair, Round Back, Floral Crest, Needlepoint, Padded Arms, 1880s, Pair 690.00
Chair, Roycroft, 2 Slats, Alligatored Leather Seat, Orb & Cross Mark, Arms 3300.00
Chair, Roycroft, 2 Slats, Leather Seat, Arms, 38 x 25 x 22 1/2 In. 2860.00
Chair, Roycroft, Hard Leather Panels, Curved Back, Inventory Mark, 41 x 19 In. 1430.00
Chair, Roycroft, Ladder Back, Leather Seat, Orb & Cross Mark, 36 1/2 In., Pair 1320.00
Chair, Roycroft, Mahogany, 4 Vertical Slats, Leather Seat, Child's 2200.00
Chair, Roycroft, Mahogany, Hourglass Slat, Leather Seat, Orb & Cross, 43 In. 1540.00
Chair, Roycroft, Slat Back, Alligatored Leather Seat, Orb & Cross Mark, 41 In. 2530.00
Chair, Sack Back, 9 Spindles, Saddle Seat, Scrolled Arms, 1860s, 38 1/2 In. 1150.00
Chair, Sausage Turning, Brown Paint, Arms, New England, 18th Century, Child's 695.00
Chair, Savonarola, Walnut, Acanthus Capped Rams, Sleigh Feet, Lion Paws 375.00
Chair, Savonarola, Walnut, Acanthus Crest, Center Lion Mask, Down-Swept Arms 150.00
Chair, Scrolled Arms & Legs, Tapestry Back & Seat, Continental 495.00
Chair, Sedan, Louis XV Style, Giltwood, Canvas, Cartouches, Figures, 72 In. 8050.00
Chair, Shaker, No. 1, Maple, Taped Seat, Early 20th Century, Child's, 28 x 11 In. 1092.00
Chair, Shaker, Rod Back, Upholstered Seat, Enterprise Chair Mfg. Company 275.00
Chair, Shaped Crest Rail, Black, Red Paint, Scrolled Arms, 42 In. 805.00
Chair, Sheraton, Barrel Back, Acanthus Carved Legs, 20th Century, 33 In. 410.00
Chair, Sheraton, Mahogany, Cane, Silk Brocade, Late 19th Century, 36 In. 385.00
Chair, Sheraton, Maple, Slat Back, Rush Balloon Seat, 19th Century, 33 In., Pair 170.00
Chair, Sheraton, Rush Seat, Stenciled Decoration, Balloon Seat, Splayed Legs, Pair 138.00
Chair, Simulated Rosewood, Padded Crest Rail, Scrollwork, Arms, Victorian 750.00
Chair, Slat Back, Gold Stenciled Legs, Taped Seat, Painted, 23 1/2 In. 750.00
Chair, Slipper, E. Wormley, Lacquered, Upholstered Back & Seat, 23 In. 1035.00
Chair, Slipper, Mahogany, Grape & Leaf Cluster Crests, Lyre Splats, 1840s, Pair 970.00
Chair, Slipper, Mahogany, Oval Pierced Back, Cabriole Legs, Mid 19th Century 195.00
Chair, Slipper, Robsjohn-Gibbings, Cabriole Legs, Upholstered Seat & Back, 30 In. 860.00
Chair, Slipper, William IV, Saber Legs, Carved Rails, Upholstered, 30 In., Pair 285.00
Chair, Steer Horn, Cowhide Leather Seat, Texas, 1940s, Arms 1400.00
Chair, Steer Horn, Upholstered Seat, c.1890, 37 1/2 In. 550.00
Chair, Stickley Brothers, 4 Horizontal Slats, Mackmurdo Feet, Arms, 40 In. 490.00
Chair, Stickley Brothers, 4 Vertical Slats, Drop-In Seat, Open Arms, 47 In. 412.00
Chair, Stickley Brothers, Mahogany, 38 x 18 1/2 x 16 1/2 In., Pair 935.00
Chair, Stickley Brothers, Memsie, Leather Seat, Carved Arms, 39 In. 1760.00
Chair, Stickley Brothers, Narrow Paneled Back, Cutout Rail, Mackmurdo Feet, 39 In. 440.00
Chair, Stickley Brothers, No. 479 1/2, 3 Vertical Slats, Drop-In Cushion, 37 In. 990.00

Chair, Stickley Brothers, No. 577 1/2, 6 Vertical Slats, Cane Seat, Arms, 25 x 40 In. 295.00
Chair, Stickley Brothers, No. 616 1/2, Chromewald Type, Cane Panel, Arms, 39 In. 165.00
Chair, Stickley Brothers, No. 887 1/2, 5 Vertical Slats, Saddle Seat, Arms, 27 x 35 In. 385.00
Chair, Stickley Brothers, Oak, Rope Twist Legs & Arm Supports, Upholstered Seat 205.00
Chair, Stickley Brothers, Tapered Back Splat, Reticulated Crest Rail, 39 In. 440.00
Chair, Stickley Brothers, Vertical Slats, Corbels, Leather Cushion, Arms, 39 In. 990.00
Chair, Studio Club, P. Evans, Metal, Cubic Swivel Base, Leather Seat, 27 In. 2760.00
Chair, Sue Et Mare, Carved Mahogany, Arms, 1925, Pair 5750.00
Chair, Tablet Crest, 2 Opposing Griffins, Rush Seat, Painted Slats, 33 In. 920.00
Chair, Teakwood, Pierced Back & Arms, Silk Brocade Cushion, 20th Century, 42 In. 456.00
Chair, Teakwood, Slat Back, Apron Pierced With Lozenges, Arms, Pair 2185.00
Chair, Tete-A-Tete, Dragon Carved, Winged Dragon Feet, Japan, 19th Century, 45 In. 725.00
Chair, Tiger Maple, Shaped Crest Rail, Horizontal Splat, Slip Seat, Pair 747.00
Chair, Turned Spindles, Pierced Horizontal Splat, Bamboo Turned Legs, Arms, 35 In. 316.00
Chair, Turner & Co., Oak, 4 Vertical Slats, Plank Seat, 1910, 35 In. 520.00
Chair, V. Panton, Cone, Upholstered, Chrome Base, 24 x 33 In. 1045.00
Chair, V. Panton, Wire Cone, Veneer, Round Seat, Upholstered, 1960s, 30 x 5 In. 1430.00
Chair, Valet, Wegner, Walnut, Coat Hanger Backrest, 3 Tapered Legs 2300.00
Chair, Van Der Rohe, Barcelona, Steel, Leather, 30 1/4 In. 3737.00
Chair, Van Der Rohe, Chromium Plated, Canvas, 1927, 31 In., Pair 5520.00
Chair, Van Der Rohe, Stainless Steel, Leather Straps, Tufted Cushion, Pair 7150.00
Chair, Van Der Rohe, Steel, Leather Seat, Back & Arms, 31 In. 880.00
Chair, Van Der Rohe, Tufted Leather Seat, Knoll, 29 x 30 x 29 In. 4675.00
Chair, Vertical Slats, Crest, Cabriole Legs, Paw Feet, Upholstered, 34 In. 100.00
Chair, Wallace Nutting, No. 408, Windsor, Sack Back, Arms 935.00
Chair, Wallace Nutting, No. 464, Carver, Arms 965.00
Chair, Wallace Nutting, Pennsylvania Comb Back, Arms 1045.00
Chair, Wallace Nutting, Windsor, Fanback, Arms, Paper Label, 44 In. 1100.00
Chair, Wallace Nutting, Windsor, Fanback, Vase-Form Legs, Scrolled Ears, 15 In. 300.00
Chair, Wallace Nutting, Windsor, Sack Back, Arms 935.00
Chair, Walnut, Anthemion Crest, Padded Armrests, Continental, Pair 660.00
Chair, Walnut, Arched Back, Ribboned Myrtle Wreath, Incurved Arms, 1860s, Pair 2300.00
Chair, Walnut, Arched Padded Back, Hairy Paw Feet, Down-Swept Scrolled Arms, Pair .. 805.00
Chair, Walnut, Banister Back, Woven Rush Seat, Crest Rail, 45 In. 1875.00
Chair, Walnut, Burl Veneer, Upholstered, Arms, Victorian, 45 In., Pair .... *Illus* 300.00
Chair, Walnut, Burl Veneer, Upholstered, Arms, Victorian, Pair 495.00
Chair, Walnut, Carved Crest, Upholstered, Open Arms, Victorian .... *Illus* 495.00
Chair, Walnut, Carved Horizontal Splat, Plank Seat, 18th Century, Continental, 38 In. 55.00
Chair, Walnut, Carved, Cartouche Back, Crest, Tufted, Arms, Victorian 490.00
Chair, Walnut, Carved, Cartouche Back, Tracery, Casters, Tapestry, Victorian 460.00
Chair, Walnut, Carved, Grotto, c.1880 .... 1500.00
Chair, Walnut, Carved, Horsehair, Victorian, Pair 660.00
Chair, Walnut, Carved, Padded Back, Dog's-Head Terminals, Casters, Arms, Victorian ... 805.00

Furniture, Chair, Walnut, Burl
Veneer, Upholstered, Arms,
Victorian, 45 In.

Furniture, Chair, Walnut,
Carved Crest, Upholstered,
Open Arms, Victorian

Furniture, Chair, Walnut,
Medallion Back, Horsehair,
Victorian, 38 In.

Chair, Walnut, Coin De Feu, Leaf & Vine Design, Petit-Point, c.1860-1870 .... 375.00
Chair, Walnut, Fantasy, Scrolled Back Rail, Bird & Feather, Removable Seat, 31 In. 2035.00
Chair, Walnut, Floral Carved, Needlepoint, Victorian, 40 1/2 In. 275.00
Chair, Walnut, Grape Bunch At Crest, Upholstered, Open Arms, c.1870 .... 200.00
Chair, Walnut, Invalid, Swiveling Directional Knobs, 2 Front & 1 Back Wheel, 43 In. 1210.00
Chair, Walnut, Medallion Back, Horsehair, Victorian, 38 In. ....*Illus* 150.00
Chair, Walnut, Open Carved Top, Arms, Victorian, 39 x 23 x 36 In. 385.00
Chair, Walnut, Open Rectangular Back, Pierced Splat, Casters, Victorian 86.00
Chair, Walnut, Pierce Carved Center Crest, Upholstered, c.1900 .... 358.00
Chair, Walnut, Pierced Splat, Shell Carved Side Rails, 1760, 40 In. 3720.00
Chair, Walnut, Pierced Stretcher, Velvet Backrest & Slung Seat, Scrolled Arms 450.00
Chair, Walnut, Pierced Vase-Form Splat, Damask Seat, 18 x 37 In. 1430.00
Chair, Walnut, Pine, Low Back, Brass Tapered Feet, Upholstered, 27 In. 115.00
Chair, Walnut, Rectangular Padded Back, Ring Turned Crossbar, 17th Century, Pair 431.00
Chair, Walnut, Scroll Carved Crest Rail, Arms & Legs, Silk, 29 1/2 In. 335.00
Chair, Walnut, Shieldback, Rampant Lion, Scroll Carved Seat 115.00
Chair, Walnut, Upholstered Back, Casters, Down-Swept Arms, Victorian 405.00
Chair, Walnut, Upholstered Backrest, Scrolled Toes, Padded Armrests, 1740s, Pair 9775.00
Chair, Walnut, Upholstered Backrest, Twist Turned Legs, Flemish, 1600s 5750.00
Chair, Walnut, Vase-Form Splat, Slip Seat, Trifid Feet, Pa., 17 x 41 1/2 In. 3080.00
Chair, Wegner, Peacock, Ash, Woven Rush Seat, Teakwood Armrests, 42 In., Pair 4400.00
Chair, Wegner, Wishbone, Woven Rope Seat, Pink Paint, Carl Hansen, 29 In. 495.00
Chair, White Fiberglass, Shape Of Man, 1968, 23 x 56 In. 1495.00
Chair, Whittled, Limb Type, White Pickled, Upholstered, Open Arms, 40 In., Pair 230.00
Chair, Wicker, Recliner, Upholstered, Early 20th Century, Child's 155.00
Chair, William & Mary, Maple, Upholstered Seat, Ring Turned Legs, 47 1/2 In. 490.00
Chair, William & Mary, Walnut, Rectangular Back, Ball Feet, 1900, 39 1/2 In., Pair 330.00
Chair, William & Mary, Walnut, Scrolled Top Rail, Cane Back & Seat, Arms, 55 In. 1760.00
Chair, William IV, Mahogany, Carved Shell Shield, 19th Century, 33 x 15 x 12 In. 635.00
Chair, William IV, Mahogany, Gondola Shape, Leather, 36 In. 4620.00
Chair, William IV, Oak, Upholstered Top Rail, Padded Seat, 29 1/2 In. 715.00
Chair, Windsor, 5 Spindles, Medallion Back, Bamboo Turning, Yellow Paint, Child's 465.00
Chair, Windsor, 7 Spindles, Rectangular Crest, Bamboo Turning, Arms, 36 In. 545.00
Chair, Windsor, 7 Spindles, Saddle Seat, Painted, Continuous Arms, c.1800, 35 In. 3105.00
Chair, Windsor, 7 Spindles, Shaped Crest Rail, Turned Stiles, 1795-1810, 36 x 21 In. 220.00
Chair, Windsor, 7 Spindles, Simulated Bamboo Turning, H-Stretcher, Arms 465.00
Chair, Windsor, 9 Spindles, Crest Rail, Painted, Scrolled Arms, c.1800, 37 x 17 In. 2300.00
Chair, Windsor, A. Houck, Brace Back, Red Paint, 1785 .... 6710.00
Chair, Windsor, Arched Comb Back, Black Over Red Paint, Scrolled Arms 2415.00
Chair, Windsor, Arrow Back, Grape, Leaf Stencil, Yellow Paint, Arms, Pa., 1820 .... 275.00
Chair, Windsor, Arrow Back, Weaver's, Black Paint, c.1830, 36 In. 190.00
Chair, Windsor, Ash, Birch, Pine, 9 Spindles, Arched Crest Rail, H-Stretcher, Arms 545.00
Chair, Windsor, Ash, Pine, Maple, Shaped Slab Seat, Splayed Legs, Child's 143.00
Chair, Windsor, Bamboo Turning, Stepped Crest, 34 In. 165.00
Chair, Windsor, Bamboo Turning, Yellow Pinstripes, 1830, 34 In. 5750.00
Chair, Windsor, Birdcage, 6 Spindles, Bamboo Turning, Black Paint, 33 x 16 1/2 In. 230.00
Chair, Windsor, Bow Back, 7 Spindles, Dark Varnish, New England, 19th Century 110.00
Chair, Windsor, Bow Back, 7 Spindles, Saddle Seat, Splayed Base, 37 3/4 In. 330.00
Chair, Windsor, Bow Back, 7 Spindles, Splayed, Bulbous Turned Legs, Saddle Seat 275.00
Chair, Windsor, Bow Back, 9 Spindles, Saddle Seat, Bamboo Turning, Pa. 415.00
Chair, Windsor, Bow Back, 9 Spindles, Shield-Shaped Seat, Mortised Arms, Pa. 600.00
Chair, Windsor, Bow Back, Ash, Poplar, Birch, 7 Tapered Spindles, H-Stretcher, Arms ... 865.00
Chair, Windsor, Bow Back, Bamboo Turning, Black Paint, Continuous Arms, 36 In. 715.00
Chair, Windsor, Bow Back, Bowed Crest, Plank Seat, Black Paint, Child's, 20 In. 800.00
Chair, Windsor, Bow Back, Mahogany, Brace Back, Arms, Pair 6325.00
Chair, Windsor, Bow Back, Maple, Ash, 9 Tapered Spindles, Splayed Legs, 1790 .... 1095.00
Chair, Windsor, Bow Back, Oak, Ash, Birch, Spindles, Scrolled Arms 690.00
Chair, Windsor, Bow Back, Poplar, Hickory, 9 Spindles, Saddle Seat, c.1780, 36 In. 330.00
Chair, Windsor, Bow Back, Saddle Seat, H-Stretcher, Brown Paint, Turned Arms 440.00
Chair, Windsor, Bow Back, Shield-Shaped Seat, Pa., c.1810, 37 In., Pair 1540.00
Chair, Windsor, Bow Back, Spindles, H-Stretcher, Black Over Green Paint, Arms 770.00
Chair, Windsor, Bow Back, Splayed Base, Shaped Seat, Arms, 37 3/4 In. ....*Illus* 525.00
Chair, Windsor, Bow Back, Splayed Base, Turned Legs, Black Paint, Arms, 17 x 37 In. ... 1430.00

Chair, Windsor, Bow Back, Splayed, Saddle Seat, Red Varnish, Arms, 35 In. 600.00
Chair, Windsor, Brace Back, 9 Spindles, Shield Seat, Black Paint, 1790 . . . . 385.00
Chair, Windsor, Chestnut, Maple, Incised Splayed Legs, Continuous Arms, 37 In. 1095.00
Chair, Windsor, Comb Back, 5 Flared Spindles, Plank Seat, Black Paint, Arms, 17 In. 4600.00
Chair, Windsor, Comb Back, 6 Spindles, Drawer, Writing Arm, c.1775, 46 In. 5175.00
Chair, Windsor, Comb Back, Barrel Crest Rail, Bamboo Turning, Arms, 1815, 41 In. 1380.00
Chair, Windsor, Comb Back, Blunt Arrow Feet, Green Paint, Pa., 1770, 42 In. 4125.00
Chair, Windsor, Comb Back, Ear Crest, Scrolled Arms, Philadelphia, 1755, 39 In. 4090.00
Chair, Windsor, Comb Back, Extended Serpentine, Continuous Arms, 1780, 42 In. 2530.00
Chair, Windsor, Comb Back, Red Paint, Yellow Pinstripes, Arms, Pa., 1780 . . . . 7425.00
Chair, Windsor, Crest Rail With Ears, Turned Legs, Ringed Stretcher, 1760 . . . . 1760.00
Chair, Windsor, Elm, Spindles, H-Stretcher, Scrolled Arms, Child's 290.00
Chair, Windsor, Fanback, 10 Spindles, Saddle Seat, Salem, Mass., 1849, 35 In. 470.00
Chair, Windsor, Fanback, 11 Spindles, 2 Stiles, D-Shaped Seat, Arms, 1800, 46 In. 880.00
Chair, Windsor, Fanback, 7 Spindles, Arrow Feet, Black Over Blue Paint, 1800s 3850.00
Chair, Windsor, Fanback, 7 Spindles, Concave Crest Rail, 1790, 37 In. 7475.00
Chair, Windsor, Fanback, 7 Spindles, Scalloped Seat, Pa., 1780 . . . . 880.00
Chair, Windsor, Fanback, 7 Spindles, Scrolled Ears, Reddish Brown Finish, 16 In. 880.00
Chair, Windsor, Fanback, 7 Spindles, Shaped Seat, Pa., 1780, 34 In. 3850.00
Chair, Windsor, Fanback, 7 Spindles, Shield Seat, Baluster Legs, 1790, 37 In., Pair 1650.00
Chair, Windsor, Fanback, 7 Spindles, Shield Seat, Pa., 1790, 36 x 23 In. 825.00
Chair, Windsor, Fanback, 7 Spindles, Shield Seat, Rhode Island, 19th Century 715.00
Chair, Windsor, Fanback, 8 Spindles, Scalloped Seat, Pa., 1780 . . . . 715.00
Chair, Windsor, Fanback, 9 Spindles, Saddle Seat, Painted, c.1780, 43 1/2 In. 5465.00
Chair, Windsor, Fanback, 9 Spindles, Simulated Bamboo, Red Paint 200.00
Chair, Windsor, Fanback, Bamboo Turning, Black Paint, 1800, New England 2310.00
Chair, Windsor, Fanback, Brace Back, 5 Spindles, Arms, c.1780, 43 In. 7475.00
Chair, Windsor, Fanback, Spindles, Serpentine Crest, Splayed Legs, Conn., 40 In. 3450.00
Chair, Windsor, High Back, Shaped Seat, Spindle Arms, 39 3/4 In. 330.00
Chair, Windsor, Hoop Back, 7 Spindles, H-Stretcher, Pair 495.00
Chair, Windsor, Hoop Back, 7 Spindles, Shaped Seat, Bamboo Turning, Black Paint 120.00
Chair, Windsor, Hoop Back, 9 Spindles, Bamboo Turning, Green Paint 175.00
Chair, Windsor, Hoop Back, 9 Spindles, H-Stretcher, Down-Swept Arms 400.00
Chair, Windsor, Hoop Back, 9 Spindles, Saddle Seat, Bamboo Turning 240.00
Chair, Windsor, Hoop Back, Bamboo Turning, Splayed, Arms 230.00
Chair, Windsor, Hoop Back, Elm, 11 Spindles, Dish Seat, Scrolled Arms, 1830s 460.00
Chair, Windsor, Hoop Back, Hickory, 7 Spindles, Sloping Spindle Supported Arms 315.00
Chair, Windsor, Hoop Back, Hickory, 7 Tapered Spindles, Saddle-Shaped Slab Seat 145.00
Chair, Windsor, Hoop Back, Pine, 9 Spindles, Bamboo Turning, Slab Seat, 1850 . . . . 230.00
Chair, Windsor, Kentucky Maple, Bamboo Turning, Signed Gibson 550.00
Chair, Windsor, Low Back, 11 Spindles, Oval Seat, 1785, 32 x 33 1/2 In. 2860.00
Chair, Windsor, Low Back, D-Shaped Seat, Blunt Arrow Feet, Pa., 1775 . . . . 880.00
Chair, Windsor, Mahogany, Bamboo Turning, Floral, Shaped Seat, Arms, 35 In. 385.00
Chair, Windsor, Rod Back, Dish Seat, Drawer, Right-Hand Writing Arm 215.00
Chair, Windsor, Rod Back, Plank Seat, Bamboo Turning, Red Paint, Arms, 1815 . . . . 4125.00
Chair, Windsor, S. Tracy, Bow Back, Saddle Seat, Bamboo Turning, c.1815, 36 x 17 In. . . 690.00

**If your wicker furniture is very
dusty, take it to the gas station
and blow the dust away with
the air hose.**

Furniture, Chair,
Windsor, Bow Back,
Splayed Base, Shaped
Seat, Arms, 37 3/4 In.

Chair, Windsor, Sack Back, 6 Spindles, Saddle Seat, Ring Turned Legs, 37 x 17 In. 430.00
Chair, Windsor, Sack Back, 7 Spindles, Bowed Crest, Saddle Seat, Arms, 1780 .... 1610.00
Chair, Windsor, Sack Back, 7 Spindles, Elliptical Seat, Arms, Pa., 1785 .... 770.00
Chair, Windsor, Sack Back, 7 Spindles, Rain Gutter Saddle Seat, Arms 1100.00
Chair, Windsor, Sack Back, Black Paint, Arms, Pa., Late 19th Century 1320.00
Chair, Windsor, Sack Back, H-Stretcher, Black Paint, Knuckle Arms, 38 1/4 In. 2860.00
Chair, Windsor, Sack Back, Scalloped Seat, Green Paint, Arms, Pa., 1790 .... 1650.00
Chair, Windsor, Sack Back, Scalloped Skirt, Turned Legs, Dark Surface, Arms, 1800 .... 3300.00
Chair, Windsor, Step-Down, Fruit Design, Yellow Paint, Early 19th Century, Pair 440.00
Chair, Windsor, Step-Down, Stenciled Leaves & Fruit On Top Rail, Yellow Paint 165.00
Chair, Windsor, Turned Spindles, Black, Red Grain, Arms, 31 1/2 x 24 x 19 In., Pair 335.00
Chair, Windsor, Yew Wood, Arched Spindles, Plank Seat, Spindle Arms, 40 In. 250.00
Chair, Wing, Barrel Back, Square Beaded Legs, 1780, 45 1/2 x 34 In. 3300.00
Chair, Wing, Carved Acanthus Leaves, Fluted Legs, Upholstered 530.00
Chair, Wing, Chippendale, Mahogany, Scalloped Crest, 1780 .... 2200.00
Chair, Wing, Chippendale, Mahogany, Upholstered, 45 x 30 In. 2475.00
Chair, Wing, Chippendale, Square Base, Upholstered, 18th Century 3850.00
Chair, Wing, Empire, Mahogany, Philadelphia, Late 19th Century 550.00
Chair, Wing, Empire, Raised Chinoiserie Floral, Arms, 1835, 41 In. 4480.00
Chair, Wing, Federal, Mahogany, Carved, Reeded Front Legs, Brass Casters, c.1820 ..... 5775.00
Chair, Wing, George III, Mahogany, Gadroon Skirt, Claw & Ball Feet, 49 In. 1035.00
Chair, Wing, Georgian Style, Mahogany, Arched Back, Damask, Scrolled Arms, 48 In. ... 1320.00
Chair, Wing, Georgian, Mahogany, Serpentine Padded Back, Cabriole Legs, 49 In. 1650.00
Chair, Wing, Mahogany, Arched Crest, Square Legs, Scrolled Arms, 43 In. 165.00
Chair, Wing, Mahogany, Raked Rear Legs, Arched Crest Rail, Arms, 46 In. 784.00
Chair, Wing, Mahogany, Ring Turned Legs, Damask, c.1810 .... 2055.00
Chair, Wing, Mahogany, Tapered Front Legs, Scrolled Arms, 46 1/2 In. 3584.00
Chair, Wing, Queen Anne, Yellow Pine, Arched Back, Cabriole Legs, 48 In. 3300.00
Chair, Wing, Sheraton, Cherry, Barrel Back, Upholstered, 1835 .... 440.00
Chair, Wing, Sheraton, Mahogany, Crest Back, Serpentine Wings, 1810, 46 In. 3410.00
Chair, Wing, Toshiyuki Kita, Steel, Whimsical Shape, Upholstered, 1976, 41 In. 805.00
Chair, Wing, Wegner, Papa, Teakwood Legs, Wool, Cantilevered Arms, 33 In. 1265.00
Chair, Wing, William & Mary Style, Arched Back, Out-Scrolled Arms, 1880s, 51 In. 1150.00
Chair, Wing, William IV, Out-Curved Arms, Foliate Front, Tufted Leather, Pair 11500.00
Chair, Wrought Iron, Damask, Scrolled Arms, Italy, 1925, 90 In. 2185.00
Chair & Footstool, Louis XVI, Fluted Legs, Needlepoint Seat, 30 In. 2750.00
Chair & Ottoman, Bentwood, Fleece, Ekstrom, 1945 .... 550.00
Chair & Ottoman, Eames, Laminated Wood, Leather, 32 In. 1265.00
Chair & Ottoman, Saarinen, Grasshopper, Laminated Legs, Upholstered, 33 In. 3735.00
Chair & Ottoman, Saarinen, Womb, Chrome Legs, Upholstered, c.1948, 36 1/2 In. 1635.00
Chair & Ottoman, V. Kagan, Sculpted Back & Seat, X-Shaped Base, 1960s, 41 In. 865.00
Chair & Ottoman, W. Plattner, Bronze Wire Construction, Upholstered, 39 x 40 In. 915.00
Chair & Ottoman, Wegner, Steel Pipe Legs, 1960 .... 4600.00
Chair Set, Alpine, Arched Back, Cutouts, 36 x 16 x 16 In., 6 .... 1045.00
Chair Set, Arts & Crafts, Ladder Back, Leather Cushion, 37 In., 6 .... 1100.00
Chair Set, Arts & Crafts, Oak, 3 Horizontal Slats, Slip Seat, 1912, 5 .... 2185.00
Chair Set, Balloon Back, Pierced Crest, Fiberglass Splat, Plank Seat, 1850, 6 .... 1430.00
Chair Set, Balloon Back, Plank Seat, Overall Floral Reserves, 19th Century, 6 .... 770.00
Chair Set, Balloon Back, Stenciled, Green Paint, Pennsylvania, c.1840, 6 .... 1045.00
Chair Set, Baluster Splat, Red & Black Graining, Plank Seat, Pennsylvania, c.1835, 6 ... 6325.00
Chair Set, Bamboo Turning, 3 Horizontal Spindles, Rush Balloon Seat, 33 x 18 In., 6 .... 805.00
Chair Set, Baroque Style, Walnut, Carved, Cut Velvet, 1 Armchair, 6 .... 1980.00
Chair Set, Baroque, Walnut, Fretted Cartouche Crest Rail, Square Legs, 12 .... 862.00
Chair Set, Biedermeier, Feather Splat, Upholstered Seat, 19th Century, 35 3/4 In., 8 ..... 6612.00
Chair Set, Bird's-Eye Maple, Horizontal Back Splats, Saber Legs, 1830, 32 3/4 In., 4 .... 1680.00
Chair Set, Bird's-Eye Maple, Scrolled Back, Cane, c.1835, 34 x 17 In., 6 .... 1840.00
Chair Set, Cane Back, Upholstered Seat, Painted, France, 4 .... 275.00
Chair Set, Captain's, Gold Stripes, Gold Masonic Emblem On Crest, 30 3/4 In., 6 ...... 770.00
Chair Set, Charles II, Walnut, Carved Crest, Padded Seat, 45 x 49 In., 6 .... 8250.00
Chair Set, Cherry, Brocade Seat, 37 In., 1 Armchair, 6 .... 1540.00
Chair Set, Chippendale Style, Mahogany, Carved, Gothic Tracery Splat, 6 .... 1840.00
Chair Set, Chippendale Style, Mahogany, Tracery Splat, Shaped Crest Rail, 5 .... 545.00
Chair Set, Chippendale, Claw & Ball Feet, 1900, 6 .... 3850.00

Chair Set, Chippendale, Mahogany, Claw & Ball Feet, 2 Armchairs, 8 .... 1760.00
Chair Set, Chippendale, Mahogany, Pierced Splats, Trapezoidal Seat, 38 x 18 In., 3 ..... 5462.00
Chair Set, Chippendale, Mahogany, Strapwork Splats, Cabriole Legs, 2 Armchairs, 8 .... 1320.00
Chair Set, Chippendale, Pierced Splats, Upholstered Seat, Phila., 2 Armchairs, 8 .... 5280.00
Chair Set, Classical, Mahogany, Figured Crests, Saber Legs, 19th Century, 4 .... 935.00
Chair Set, Classical, Mahogany, Flame Grained Crests, Stylized Lyre Splats, 8 .... 880.00
Chair Set, Classical, Mahogany, Modified Lyre Back, Saber Legs, Damask, 8 .... 3850.00
Chair Set, Continuous Tubular Steel, Leather Sling Back, 6 .... 690.00
Chair Set, Curved Upholstered Back, Pierced Splats, Inventory Marks, c.1790, 3 .... 2845.00
Chair Set, Directoire, Cherry, Curved Rail, Woven Rush Seat, 2 Armchairs, 6 .... 1200.00
Chair Set, Directoire, Hardwood, Tapered Legs, Slip Seat, 34 In., 6 .... 600.00
Chair Set, Dutch Neoclassical, Elm, Feather Splat, Padded Seat, 34 3/4 In., 6 .... 4400.00
Chair Set, E. Wormley, Leather, Dunbar Tag, 31 In., 4 .... 2300.00
Chair Set, Eames, DCM, Chrome, Walnut Plywood Seat, 29 In., 4 .... 1100.00
Chair Set, Eames, Stacking, Turquoise, Right-Hand Fold-Up Tablet Arm, 12 .... 630.00
Chair Set, Eames, Wire, Black, Contoured Seat, Herman Miller, 31 1/2 In., 4 .... 385.00
Chair Set, Empire, Arched Vase-Form Splat, Drop-In Seat, 6 .... 8055.00
Chair Set, Empire, Horizontal Splat, Upholstered Seat, c.1835, 5 .... 4035.00
Chair Set, Empire, Plain Carved Crest Rail, Lyre Splat, Saber Legs, 5 .... 690.00
Chair Set, Faux Bamboo, Deep Rush Seat, 1830, 1 Armchair, 5 .... 1250.00
Chair Set, Federal, Mahogany, 3 Pierced Splats, Upholstered Seat, 1810, 4 .... 2310.00
Chair Set, Federal, Mahogany, Curved Crest Rails, Slip Seat, Saber Legs, Pa., 8 .... 5500.00
Chair Set, Federal, Mahogany, Open Back, Arched Scrolled Crest Rail, 4 .... 490.00
Chair Set, Fornasetti, Corinthian Column, Transfer Print, 1950s, 6 .... 8625.00
Chair Set, Fornasetti, Plastic Back & Seat, Black Designs, 31 In., 6 .... 1320.00
Chair Set, Frank Lloyd Wright, Mahogany, Upholstered Back & Seat, Label, 32 In., 4 ... 2970.00
Chair Set, Frank Lloyd Wright, Wood Dowel Frame, Greek Key Carving, 4 .... 2070.00
Chair Set, Frankl, Dark Mahogany, Upholstered Seat, 16 x 33 In., 6 .... 880.00
Chair Set, French Style, Overall Floral, Quilted Design, Upholstered Seat, 3 .... 104.00
Chair Set, G. Stickley, 3 Horizontal Slats, Red Decal, 4 .... 1650.00
Chair Set, G. Stickley, No. 1297, Leather Seat, 37 1/2 x 18 x 16 In., 4 .... 3410.00
Chair Set, G. Stickley, No. 3533, Oak, Slat Back, 9 1/4 In., 6 .... 2760.00
Chair Set, George II Style, Mahogany, Racquet Splat, Serpentine Seat, 4 .... 1495.00
Chair Set, George II Style, Walnut, Shell Carved Cabriole Legs, 2 Armchairs, 10 .... 19800.00
Chair Set, George III Style, Inlaid Mahogany, Open Back, 6 Splats, 1 Armchair, 6 ...... 920.00
Chair Set, George III, Mahogany, Anthemion, Bellflower Splat, 37 In., 4 .... 6037.00
Chair Set, George III, Mahogany, Carved, Open Back, Pierced Crossbar, 4 .... 1150.00
Chair Set, George III, Mahogany, Foliate Carved Crest Rail, Foliate Splat, 8 .... 10925.00
Chair Set, George III, Mahogany, Foliate Crest Rail, Pierced Splat, Scrolled Feet, 2 ..... 2760.00
Chair Set, George III, Mahogany, Shaped Crest, Vase-Form Splat, 6 .... 2415.00
Chair Set, George IV, Mahogany, Banister Back, Leather Seat, 12 .... 14300.00
Chair Set, George IV, Mahogany, Curved Crest Rail, Cane Seat, 35 In., 12 .... 5775.00
Chair Set, George IV, Mahogany, Shell & Fan Splat, Cushion, 2 Armchairs, 6 .... 7700.00
Chair Set, Gilt, Pierced Vertical Splat, Scarlet, Cabriole Legs, 37 1/4 In., 10 .... 3450.00
Chair Set, H. Bertoia, Painted Wire, Vinyl Seat Pad, 4 .... 1840.00
Chair Set, Half Spindle, Painted Grapes On Crest, Plank Bottom, J.W. Morrison, 6 ...... 1056.00
Chair Set, Half Spindle, Stenciled, Brown Ground, Pa., 19th Century, 6 .... 1540.00
Chair Set, Hepplewhite Style, Mahogany, Early 20th Century, 16 .... 4000.00
Chair Set, Heywood-Wakefield Co., Bentwood Oak, Maple, 2 Armchairs, 8 .... 2860.00
Chair Set, Heywood-Wakefield Co., Upholstered Seat, Eagle Shaped Mark, 6 .... 288.00
Chair Set, Hitchcock, Black, Natural Plank Seat, Gold Stencil, 20th Century, 4 .... 195.00
Chair Set, Hitchcock, Ebonized, Stencils, Rush Seat, Turned Crest, 34 In., 4 .... 310.00
Chair Set, Hitchcock, Painted, Floral Stencil, c.1835, 33 1/2 In., 6 .... 1667.00
Chair Set, Hitchcock, Sheraton, Rush Balloon Seat, 4 .... 385.00
Chair Set, Howe, Stenciling On Splat & Crest, Label, 33 1/4 In., 6 .... 990.00
Chair Set, Jacobsen, Plywood Back & Seat, 3 Tubular Steel Legs, 1952, 30 In., 4 .... 1380.00
Chair Set, Kitchen, Oak, 9 Spindles, Oak Leaf Design, 4 .... 290.00
Chair Set, L. & J.G. Stickley, 3 Slats, Plank Seat, 36 x 18 In., 4 .... 1650.00
Chair Set, L. & J.G. Stickley, 3 Vertical Slats, Rush Seat, 4 .... 3300.00
Chair Set, L. & J.G. Stickley, 8 Slats, Mahogany, 41 In., 8 .... 6600.00
Chair Set, L. & J.G. Stickley, Ladder Back, Vinyl Cushion, 37 In., 6 .... 3080.00
Chair Set, Ladder Back, 4 Slats, Hardwood, Delaware River Valley, 6 .... 3300.00
Chair Set, Ladder Back, Oak, Rush Seat, 1920-1950, 6 .... 2300.00

Chair Set, Ladder Back, Woven Seat, Lancaster County, 2 Armchairs, 10 . . . . 3960.00
Chair Set, Laminated Wood, String Seat & Back, Scandinavia, c.1952, 33 In., 4 . . . . 1150.00
Chair Set, Limbert, 3 Vertical Slats, Leather Seat, 1 Armchair, 6 . . . . 2640.00
Chair Set, Limbert, Ash, 2 Slats, Arched Top, 2 Armchairs, 8 . . . . 4125.00
Chair Set, Limbert, Vertical & Horizontal Slats, Branded Signature, 38 x 17 In., 4 . . . . . . 1980.00
Chair Set, Louis Philippe, Mahogany, Molded, Cane Seat, 37 1/2 In., 4 . . . . 2530.00
Chair Set, Louis XIV, Oak, Multicolored Woven Rush Seat, Block Legs, 37 In., 6 . . . . . . 805.00
Chair Set, Louis XV Style, Ladder Back, Woven Seat, Painted, 37 In., 6 . . . . 1320.00
Chair Set, Louis XV Style, Ribbon Carved Crests, Cabriole Legs, Green Paint, 9 . . . . 4400.00
Chair Set, Louis XV, Beechwood, Floral Carved Top Rail, Cane Back & Seat, 4 . . . . 2090.00
Chair Set, Louis XV, Oak, Needlework, Square Legs, 36 In., 6 . . . . 1601.00
Chair Set, Louis XV, Walnut, Molded Top Rail, Padded Back & Seat, 37 1/2 In., 4 . . . . . . 1610.00
Chair Set, Louis XVI Style, Mahogany, Cane Back, Tapered Legs, 4 . . . . 195.00
Chair Set, Louis XVI, Fruitwood, 3 Scalloped Splats, Woven Rush Seat, 40 In., 8 . . . . 862.00
Chair Set, Mahogany, Carved Splats, Bellflower, Line Inlay, 43 In., 10 . . . . 4125.00
Chair Set, Mahogany, Crest Rail Over X-Shaped Crossbar, Overhanging Crest, 6 . . . . 400.00
Chair Set, Mahogany, Ebonized, Stiles With Palmettes, Padded Seat, c.1820, 4 . . . . 8050.00
Chair Set, Mahogany, Rectangular Back, Pierced Sheaf Splat, Drop-In Seat, 7 . . . . 2300.00
Chair Set, Mahogany, Reeds & Shell Carved Splat, Upholstered Seat, 34 In., 6 . . . . 1840.00
Chair Set, Mahogany, Shaped Crest, Pierced Splat, Saddle Seat, 1830s, 7 . . . . 2070.00
Chair Set, Mahogany, Shieldback, Square Tapered Feet, 37 In., 2 Armchairs, 6 . . . . 2070.00
Chair Set, Neoclassical, Fruitwood, Plain Crest Rail, Saber Legs, Italy, 4 . . . . 1150.00
Chair Set, Neoclassical, Walnut, Intertwined Gilt Serpents On Seat, 34 In., 10 . . . . 4180.00
Chair Set, Oak, Chestnut, Ladder & Spindle Back, 19th Century, 3 Armchairs, 9 . . . . 5175.00
Chair Set, Oak, Elm, Solid Splat, Rush Seat, H-Stretcher, England, 19th Century, 4 . . . . . 565.00
Chair Set, Oak, Hardwood, Bentwood Back, 3 Spindles, 35 In., 6 . . . . 500.00
Chair Set, Oak, Twist Turned Posts, Padded Seat, 6 . . . . 630.00
Chair Set, Pennsylvania, Banding, Flowers, Gilt, Brown Paint, 1860-1880, 6 . . . . 390.00
Chair Set, Plexiglas, U Shape, Ultra Suede, 6 . . . . 460.00
Chair Set, Plywood, Molded, Modernist Design, c.1955, 32 In., 4 . . . . 195.00
Chair Set, Pub, Elm, Spindles, Splayed Legs, England, Armchairs, 6 . . . . 825.00
Chair Set, Queen Anne, Walnut, Cabriole Legs, Pad Feet, Upholstered, 4 . . . . 2530.00
Chair Set, Rectangular Concave Splat, 4 Spindles, Scrolled Seat, 33 x 18 In., 5 . . . . 860.00
Chair Set, Regency, Ebonized Wood, Round Saber Legs, Down-Swept Arms, 4 . . . . 3795.00
Chair Set, Regency, Faux Bamboo, Spindle Back, Rush Seat, 34 1/2 In., 3 . . . . 2600.00
Chair Set, Regency, Mahogany, Carved, Shaped Medial Rail, 1 Armchair, 5 . . . . 1100.00
Chair Set, Regency, Mahogany, Floral Carved Splat, Cane, Cushion, 6 . . . . 1955.00
Chair Set, Regency, Mahogany, Inlaid Top Rail, Shell Carved, 19th Century, 8 . . . . 4200.00
Chair Set, Regency, Mahogany, Reeded Top Rail, Carved Seat, Saber Legs, 8 . . . . 2875.00
Chair Set, Regency, Mahogany, Spiral Carved Crest, Pierced Splat, Saber Legs, 2 . . . . 980.00
Chair Set, Rococo, Laminated Oak, Open Shell & Serpent Carved Back, 6 . . . . 4850.00
Chair Set, Rococo, Walnut, Laminated, Carved, Pierced Scrolled Back, 8 . . . . 3520.00
Chair Set, Rod Back, Painted Floral Design, Centre County, Pa., 19th Century, 6 . . . . 2800.00
Chair Set, Rohde, Black Lacquer, Upholstered Arms, Back, Seat, 1930s, Armchairs, 6 . . . 3450.00
Chair Set, Rosewood, Curved Oval Back, Cane Panel & Seat, 8 . . . . 1800.00
Chair Set, Rosewood, Floral Carved Crests, Oval Back, Mid 19th Century, 4 . . . . 880.00
Chair Set, Rosewood, Horizontal Back Rails, Carved Seat, Saber Legs, 32 In., 6 . . . . 1650.00
Chair Set, Roycroft, Hourglass Back Slats, Leather Seat, 40 In., 6 . . . . 8800.00
Chair Set, Rush Seat, Painted, Scrolls, Fruit, Gilt, Red Ground, Mid 19th Century, 6 . . . . . 1980.00
Chair Set, Scalloped Back Slats, Red, Black Graining, Gilt, Rush Seat, 32 1/2 In., 4 . . . . . 335.00
Chair Set, Shaped Crest, Vase-Form Splat, Floral, Brown Reserves, Pa., c.1830, 6 . . . . . . 550.00
Chair Set, Sheraton, Maple, Thumb Back, Rush Seat, 33 In., 2 Armchairs, 8 . . . . 2640.00
Chair Set, Sheraton, Red & Black Graining, Rush Seat, Yellow Stripes, Floral, 6 . . . . 990.00
Chair Set, Sheraton, Rush Seat, Grape Cluster Design, Grain Painted, 6 . . . . 600.00
Chair Set, Sheraton, Yellow & Gold Stripes, Stenciled Fruit & Cornucopia, 6 . . . . 715.00
Chair Set, Spiral Turned Crest Rail, Horizontal Gilt Shell Splat, 1 Armchair, 6 . . . . 2100.00
Chair Set, Tiger Maple, Cane Seat, Peaked & Scalloped Back, 4 . . . . 355.00
Chair Set, Tiger Maple, Open Back, Curved Scrolled Crest Rail, Splayed Feet, 4 . . . . 1320.00
Chair Set, Tiger Maple, Saber Legs, Philadelphia, c.1830, 6 . . . . 2640.00
Chair Set, Van Der Rohe, Stainless Steel, Leather Back & Seat, 1926, 6 . . . .*Illus* 865.00
Chair Set, W. Plattner, Wire, Vertical Wire Basket Seat, 29 x 26 1/2 In., 4 . . . . 1840.00
Chair Set, Walnut, Backrest Over Cross Bar, Reeded Posts, Bun Feet, 12 . . . . 1900.00
Chair Set, Walnut, Burl Panels, Oval Crest, Top Knob Accents, Upholstered, 4 . . . . 510.00

Don't ship furniture from a hot to a cold climate or a wet to a dry climate, if it can be avoided. The wood will expand or contract, causing cracks and other damage.

Furniture, Chair Set, Van Der Rohe,
Stainless Steel, Leather Back & Seat, 1926, 6

Chair Set, Walnut, Burl Veneer, Upholstered, Victorian, 36 3/4 In., 4	330.00
Chair Set, Walnut, Floral Crest, Pierced Vase-Form Splat, Upholstered Seat, 6	2530.00
Chair Set, Walnut, Fruit Carved Crest, Upholstered Seat, Victorian, 6	660.00
Chair Set, Walnut, Needlepoint, 3-Slat Back, Cane Turned Front Legs, Spindles, 6	225.00
Chair Set, Walnut, Open Back, Bent Splat, Saddle-Shaped Seat, 4	650.00
Chair Set, Walnut, Padded Oval Back, Overstuffed Seat, 2 Armchairs, 12	1035.00
Chair Set, Walnut, Scroll & Leaf Crest, Shaped Seat, Pad Feet, Upholstered, 6	865.00
Chair Set, Walnut, Vase-Form Splat, Mother-Of-Pearl Inlay, Drop-In Seat, 1700, 4	4025.00
Chair Set, Walnut, Yoke Crest, Square Legs, H-Stretcher, Slip Seat, Pa., 39 In., 4	9900.00
Chair Set, William IV, Mahogany, Foliate Horizontal Back, Peg Feet, 32 1/2 In., 6	1150.00
Chair Set, William IV, Mahogany, Pierced Shaped Crest, Reeded Legs, 35 In., 8	8340.00
Chair Set, Windsor, Bamboo Turning, 5 Spindles, Shaped Crest, 2 Armchairs, 6	880.00
Chair Set, Windsor, Birdcage, 7 Spindles, Bamboo Turning, Painted, c.1810, 32 In., 4	1550.00
Chair Set, Windsor, Butterfly-Birdcage, Bamboo Turning, Pinstripes, Pa., 1830, 6	6325.00
Chair Set, Windsor, Cowed Crest, 7 Spindles, Saddle Seat, 34 1/2 In., 5	1430.00
Chair Set, Windsor, Phoenix Chair Co., Brace Back, 36 In., 4	495.00
Chair Set, Windsor, Plank Seat, Red Paint, Black Stripes, Child's, 4	330.00
Chair Set, Windsor, Rod Back, Scalloped Seat, Bamboo Turning, 4	660.00
Chair Set, Windsor, Stenciled Fruit & Leaves, New England, 1830-1840, 33 In., 6	3220.00
Chair Set, Windsor, Step-Down, 7 Spindles, Raked Stiles, Bamboo Turning, 33 In., 6	1150.00
Chair Set, Windsor, Yew Wood, Elm, Pierced Splat, Ring, Baluster Legs, 6	3450.00
Chair Set, Wing, George III, Mahogany, Square Legs, H-Stretcher, 2	1725.00
Chair-Library Steps, Mahogany, Metamorphic, Seat Opens To Treads	4830.00
Chair-Table, Pine, Birch, Lift Top Seat, Rectangular Arms, c.1840, 29 1/2 In.	1760.00
Chair-Table, Pine, Stretcher, Painted Base, Square Arms, Late 1700s, 29 x 42 In.	4025.00
Chaise Longue, Arched Back, Shaped Ottoman, Down-Scrolled Arms, 37 1/2 In.	1495.00
Chaise Longue, Bamboo, Neck Rest, Retractable Footrest, Ching Dynasty, 23 x 46 In.	490.00
Chaise Longue, Beechwood, Flower Heads Continuing To Armrests, 77 In.	9200.00
Chaise Longue, E. Wormley, No. 5525, Upholstered, 1 Arm, 78 In.	5750.00
Chaise Longue, Empire, Mahogany, Trapezoidal Seat, 34 x 18 x 16 In., Pair	1150.00
Chaise Longue, J. Hoffman, Tubular Steel, Oilcloth, 1939, 74 In.	1725.00
Chaise Longue, Jacobean, Oak, Pierce Carved Crest, Cane Back & Seat, 65 In.	575.00
Chaise Longue, Louis XV, Walnut, Cabriole Legs, Damask, 37 1/2 In.	575.00
Chaise Longue, Louis XVI, Giltwood, Swags On Top Rails, Balloon Seat, 32 In.	1840.00
Chaise Longue, Louis XVI, Walnut, 4 Cane Panels, Padded Armrests, 41 1/2 In.	3450.00
Chaise Longue, R. Schultz, Patio, Adjustable Wire, Cushion, 1961, 76 In.	3450.00
Chaise Longue, Rectangular Seat, Saber Legs, Upholstered, 33 In.	6900.00
Chaise Longue, Teakwood, Cane Back & Seat, Chinese, Late 1800s, 35 x 24 x 31 In.	460.00
Chaise Longue, Wicker, Brass Casters, Painted, Victorian, England	930.00
Chaise Longue & Ottoman, Walnut, Scroll Carved Rails, Upholstered, 31 In.	2070.00
Chest, 2 Over 4 Drawers, Beveled Oval Mirror, 68 x 34 1/4 In.	1344.00
Chest, 4 Drawers, Wood Pulls, Side Lock, Bun Feet, 15 x 9 3/4 x 14 In.	316.00
Chest, 4 Graduated Drawers, Pullout Shelf, Carved Leaf Handles, c.1840, 24 x 29 In.	695.00
Chest, 5 Dovetailed Drawers, Side Lock, Carved, Medallions, Victorian, 44 x 51 In.	1595.00
Chest, 6-Board, Lidded Till, Bootjack Ends, Grain Painted, 1800s, 20 x 41 x 16 In.	1725.00
Chest, 6-Board, Molded Base, Lock, Black Paint, 9 1/2 x 19 In.	230.00

Chest, Art Deco Style, Birch, Trapezoid, Rectangular Top, Acorn Pulls, 31 x 38 In. 805.00
Chest, Bachelor's, Mahogany, 4 Drawers, Bracket Feet, c.1795, 36 In. 2970.00
Chest, Bamboo, Faces Adorned With Foliage, Shells, Ebonized Ground, 30 In. 865.00
Chest, Baroque, Walnut, Rectangular Top, 3 Drawers, 19th Century, 40 x 58 x 26 In. 3000.00
Chest, Biedermeier, Mahogany, 4 Long Drawers, Block Feet, 43 1/2 In. 12650.00
Chest, Biedermeier, Mahogany, 7 Drawers, Stepped Rectangular Top, 52 In. 2875.00
Chest, Birch, 4 Drawers, Backboard, Scalloped Apron, c.1830, 44 x 19 x 43 In. 1210.00
Chest, Birch, Maple, Molded Edge, Turned Ball Feet, Red Paint, 39 x 43 x 19 In. 2415.00
Chest, Birch, Rectangular Top, 4 Thumb-Molded Drawers, Bracket Feet, 1800, 41 In. ... 1540.00
Chest, Bird's-Eye Maple, 4 Drawers, Overhanging Top, Ohio, c.1835, 43 x 41 x 20 In. .. 1955.00
Chest, Blanket, 4 Long Drawers, 2 Faux Drawers, New England, c.1820, 38 x 40 In. 1265.00
Chest, Blanket, 4-Board, Urn Front Panel, Red Paint, 1800 ....*Illus* 9350.00
Chest, Blanket, Batchelder, Stylized Daffodil Panel, 15 x 27 In. 9350.00
Chest, Blanket, Bird & Flowers, 2 Banded Inlay Panels, Ball Feet, 46 1/2 In. 3630.00
Chest, Blanket, Blue Paint, 7 1/2 x 11 x 6 1/2 In. ....*Illus* 1650.00
Chest, Blanket, Bracket Feet, Stipple Design, Green Trim, Initials H.W.M., 35 x 21 In. 2300.00
Chest, Blanket, Cherry, Poplar, Blue Grained, Turned Feet, 40 x 23 In. 1705.00
Chest, Blanket, Chippendale, Walnut, 2 Doors, Dovetailed Feet, 26 x 49 x 22 In. 615.00
Chest, Blanket, Chippendale, Walnut, 2 Drawers, Inlay, 1791 ....*Illus* 3500.00
Chest, Blanket, Chippendale, Walnut, Dovetailed, Fishtail Strap Hinges, 50 x 24 In. 1045.00
Chest, Blanket, Chippendale, Walnut, Drawers, Dovetailed, Bracket Feet, 48 x 23 In. 3300.00
Chest, Blanket, Chippendale, Walnut, Yellow Pine, 2 Dovetailed Drawers, 28 In. 2100.00
Chest, Blanket, Curly Maple, Turned Feet, 48 1/2 x 27 x 33 1/2 In. 2200.00
Chest, Blanket, Cutout Bracket Feet, Red Paint, New England, 21 x 39 x 15 In. 935.00
Chest, Blanket, Dovetailed Design, Blue Paint, Pa., 1800, 21 1/2 In. 1540.00
Chest, Blanket, George III, Mahogany, Molded Rectangular Top, Bracket Feet, 30 In. 1092.00
Chest, Blanket, Hinged Lift Top, Metal Handles, Till, Green Paint, Child's, 21 x 13 In. 275.00
Chest, Blanket, Lift Top, 2 Drawers, Red Paint, Early 19th Century, 41 x 38 In. 825.00
Chest, Blanket, Lift Top, 2 Drawers, Red Paint, New England, 1760, 40 x 47 In. 1320.00
Chest, Blanket, Lift Top, 2 Drawers, Red Stain, Varnished, 1876, Pa., 28 x 48 In. 825.00
Chest, Blanket, Lift Top, Pa., Mid 19th Century, 8 1/4 x 11 x 6 3/4 In. 550.00
Chest, Blanket, Lift Top, Pine, 2 Drawers, Snipe Hinges, 19th Century, 41 In. 440.00
Chest, Blanket, Lift Top, Pine, 2 Faux Over 2 Working Drawers, Black Paint, 37 In. 770.00
Chest, Blanket, Lift Top, Pine, Dovetailed, Center Heart, Grain Painted, Pa., 21 In. 550.00
Chest, Blanket, Lift Top, Pine, Poplar, 2 Drawers, Grain Painted, 1800, 26 x 48 In. 990.00
Chest, Blanket, Lift Top, Pine, Smoke Design, Black Trim, Pa., 1820, 25 x 43 In. 1760.00
Chest, Blanket, Lift Top, Poplar, Till, Stars & Tulips, Initials W.S. 1873, 23 x 41 In. 2200.00
Chest, Blanket, Lift Top, Straight Bracket Feet, Yellow Paint, 1840, 12 x 19 In. 600.00
Chest, Blanket, Lift Top, Till, Yellow & Ocher Sponge, Pa., 1820, 19 3/4 x 30 In. 3300.00
Chest, Blanket, Lift Top, Walnut, 2 Drawers, Dovetailed, 1790, Pa., 52 x 28 In. 1760.00
Chest, Blanket, Lift Top, Walnut, Spurred Ogee Bracket Feet, Pa., 1780, 9 1/2 In. 13200.00
Chest, Blanket, Oak, Hinged Top, Iron Lock, Trestle Base, England, 18 x 36 In. 385.00
Chest, Blanket, Pine, 2 Drawers, Crab Lock, Strap Hinges, Pennsylvania, 28 x 50 In. 1210.00
Chest, Blanket, Pine, 2 Drawers, Thumbnail Molding, 1800, 40 x 18 x 40 In. 985.00
Chest, Blanket, Pine, 2 Faux Over 1 Working Drawer, New England, 34 x 38 x 19 In. 1725.00
Chest, Blanket, Pine, 6-Board, Cotter Pin Hinges, Till, Blue Paint, 17 x 40 1/2 In. 430.00
Chest, Blanket, Pine, Bear Trap Lock, Painted, Pa. German, 23 x 50 x 21 In. 525.00
Chest, Blanket, Pine, Brown Vinegar Grain, Black, 50 x 20 3/4 x 24 In. 245.00
Chest, Blanket, Pine, Dovetailed, Till, Grain Painted, 44 x 22 x 25 In. 440.00
Chest, Blanket, Pine, Drop Front, White Metal Plaques, Korea, 19th Century, 33 In. 980.00

Furniture, Chest, Blanket,
4-Board, Urn Front Panel,
Red Paint, 1800

Furniture, Chest, Blanket, Blue
Paint, 7 1/2 x 11 x 6 1/2 In.

Furniture, Chest, Blanket,
Chippendale, Walnut,
2 Drawers, Inlay, 1791

Chest, Blanket, Pine, Folk Art Design, Straight Bracket Feet, 49 x 25 x 26 In. 770.00
Chest, Blanket, Pine, Orange Star & Circle, Green Ground, Pa., c.1825, 30 In. 4180.00
Chest, Blanket, Pine, Poplar, Hinged Cleated Top, 4 Feet, Red Paint, 1750, 36 In. 5462.00
Chest, Blanket, Pine, Poplar, Till, Red Graining, Yellow Ground, 47 x 21 x 24 In. 800.00
Chest, Blanket, Pine, Rectangular Top, Green Stippled Panels, Vermont, 1800, 27 In. 2090.00
Chest, Blanket, Pine, Rectangular, Molded Lid, Brown Wood Grain, Yellow, 22 3/4 In. 287.00
Chest, Blanket, Pine, Scalloped Skirt, Red & Ochre Grained, 1830, 7 1/2 x 10 1/2 In. 3850.00
Chest, Blanket, Pine, Strap Hinges, Till, Bracket Feet, 1760s, 49 In. 1002.00
Chest, Blanket, Pine, Till, Brown Comb Grained, 44 x 21 1/2 x 24 1/2 In. 440.00
Chest, Blanket, Pine, Till, Grain Painted, E.Z. Miley, 46 x 21 x 23 In. 440.00
Chest, Blanket, Poplar, 2 Drawers, Green & Red Paint, Pa., 1830, 26 1/2 In. 660.00
Chest, Blanket, Poplar, Bracket Feet, Blue Paint, Yellow Stripes, 28 In. 4400.00
Chest, Blanket, Poplar, Cherry Finish, Till, Breadboard Ends, 36 x 17 x 13 3/4 In. 300.00
Chest, Blanket, Poplar, Rectangular Molded Top, Molded Plinth Base, 22 x 24 In. 517.00
Chest, Blanket, Poplar, Walnut, Turned Feet, 19th Century, 22 x 40 x 18 In. 310.00
Chest, Blanket, Queen Anne, Oak, 2 Dovetailed Drawers, Block Cabriole Feet, 38 In. . . .   1320.00
Chest, Blanket, Shaker, Cherry, 2 Drawers, Dovetailed, Hinged Top, c.1840, 43 x 17 In. . .   1380.00
Chest, Blanket, Sheraton, Overall Yellow, Red Grain, Pa., 1840, 24 1/2 x 36 In. 770.00
Chest, Blanket, Sheraton, Pine, 3-Panel Front, Glove Box, Colorful Wash, 42 x 26 In. . . .   1870.00
Chest, Blanket, Snipe Hinges, Bootjack Ends, Red Paint, c.1860, 49 x 17 x 24 3/4 In. 143.00
Chest, Blanket, Softwood, Paneled, Tapered Legs, Mustard Paint, 28 x 18 x 21 In. 305.00
Chest, Blanket, Till, Turned Legs, Painted Interior, 24 x 37 x 20 In. 220.00
Chest, Blanket, Walnut, 2 Drawers, Rectangular Top, Turned Feet, Pa., 1810, 48 In. 2090.00
Chest, Blanket, Walnut, Ironwork, Figural Hinges, 17th Century, 22 In. 2800.00
Chest, Blanket, Walnut, Molded Top, Bracket Base, 19th Century, 26 3/4 In. 475.00
Chest, Blanket, Walnut, Rectangular Top, Till, 3 Drawers, 29 In. 2475.00
Chest, Blanket, Walnut, Scalloped Bracket Feet, Miniature, 7 1/2 x 13 x 7 1/2 In. 2860.00
Chest, Blanket, Walnut, Wrought Iron Hardware, Pa., 1780, 44 1/2 x 25 In. 715.00
Chest, Blanket, Walnut, Wrought Iron Strap Hinge & Handles, Pa., 22 In. 880.00
Chest, Blanket, White Pine, Dome Top, Iron Handles, Painted, 1856, 24 x 39 In. 280.00
Chest, Blanket, Yellow Pine, Till, Painted, Delaware, 1800, 32 x 20 In. 2750.00
Chest, Bowfront, Cherry, Poplar, 4 Graduated Drawers, Reeded Top, 41 1/2 In. 950.00
Chest, Bowfront, Mahogany, 3 Long Graduated Drawers, Rectangular Top, 41 3/4 In. 460.00
Chest, Bowfront, Mahogany, 4 Drawers, 1830s, 36 1/2 In. 1840.00
Chest, Bowfront, Mahogany, 4 Drawers, Flared French Feet, 1810, 38 1/2 In. 1650.00
Chest, Bowfront, Mahogany, Pine, 4 Graduated Drawers, 43 1/2 x 43 x 23 In. 450.00
Chest, Brass Medallion, Paneled Doors, Hinged Top, Chinese, 1800s, 25 x 30 x 20 In. . . .   460.00
Chest, Cabinet Maker's, Cherry, 3 Drawers, Lift Top, Paneled, 30 x 14 x 12 In. 400.00
Chest, Cabinet Maker's, Pine, Poplar, Painted Design, W.H. Walker, 24 x 16 x 14 In. 355.00
Chest, Campaign, Burl Walnut, Pigeonholes, Line Inlay, 1800-1830, 41 x 38 In. 7150.00
Chest, Campaign, Camphorwood, 2 Drawers Over 3 Graduated Drawers, 1850s, 49 In. 920.00
Chest, Campaign, Camphorwood, Brassbound, Compartments, Drawers, 41 x 36 In. 4025.00
Chest, Campaign, George IV, Mahogany, 2 Over 3 Drawers, Brass, 42 x 41 x 11 In. 3080.00
Chest, Campaign, Hardwood, Anglo-Indian, 19th Century, 41 x 35 In. 172.00
Chest, Campaign, Mahogany, 2 Long Drawers, Pigeonhole, Brass, 40 x 38 In. 715.00
Chest, Campaign, Mahogany, 3 Over 2 Drawers, Brass Handles, 38 x 36 x 18 In. 715.00
Chest, Campaign, Oriental Style, Brass Hardware, 20th Century, 20 x 39 x 18 In. 170.00
Chest, Campaign, Rosewood, Glazed Doors, East India Company, 70 In. 330.00
Chest, Campaign, Slant Front, Mahogany, 36 In. 3300.00
Chest, Campaign, Teakwood, Brass, Recessed Wood Handles, 40 1/2 In., 2 Piece 3630.00
Chest, Campaign, Yew Wood Veneer, 4 Drawers, Brass Fittings, Hekman, 14 1/2 In. 300.00
Chest, Charak, Federal, Bowfront, Mahogany, 5 Drawers, Rectangular Top, 45 In. 748.00
Chest, Charak, Federal, Mahogany, 4 Graduated Drawers, Rectangular Top, 34 In. 748.00
Chest, Charles II, Oak, 4 Drawers, Raised Geometric Panels, 37 1/4 x 43 In., 2 Piece 3080.00
Chest, Cherry, 3 Bird's-Eye Maple Veneer Drawers, c.1860, 39 x 19 1/2 x 37 1/2 In. 300.00
Chest, Cherry, 4 Curly Maple Graduated Drawers, c.1860, 37 x 18 1/2 x 46 In. 825.00
Chest, Cherry, 4 Drawers, Backsplash, Notched Tapered Legs, c.1845, 46 x 42 x 18 In. . . .   415.00
Chest, Cherry, 8 Drawers, Reeded Quarter Columns, Upper Drawers Lock, 60 In. 7500.00
Chest, Cherry, Rectangular Top, 3 Graduated Drawers, Ring Turned Legs, 17 x 8 In. 805.00
Chest, Cherry, String Inlay, 4 Graduated Drawers, Splayed French Feet, 36 3/4 In. 5750.00
Chest, Cherry, Walnut, Maple, 4 Dovetailed Drawers, 41 x 20 x 43 In. 600.00
Chest, Chinoiserie, Bowfront, Apple Green, 6 Drawers, 19th Century, 41 In. 3740.00
Chest, Chippendale Style, 2 Over 3 Drawers, Reeded Columns, 21 x 43 x 48 In. 1320.00

Furniture, Chest, Chippendale, Walnut,
4 Drawers, Philadelphia, 1780

Furniture, Chest, Federal, Cherry,
1800-1810, 36 x 37 x 19 In.

Chest, Chippendale Style, Mahogany, 3 Drawers, Block Front, Shells, 35 In. 2875.00
Chest, Chippendale, Applewood, 4 Drawers, New England, 1790s, 35 x 37 x 19 In. 2070.00
Chest, Chippendale, Birch, 4 Dovetailed Drawers, Serpentine, Mass., 22 x 38 In. 8800.00
Chest, Chippendale, Birch, 4 Graduated Drawers, c.1775, 34 x 36 x 17 In. 6785.00
Chest, Chippendale, Birch, Overhanging Top, 4 Beaded Drawers, c.1780, 36 x 18 In. 2645.00
Chest, Chippendale, Bowfront, Mahogany, Overhanging Top, Claw & Ball Feet, 34 In. . . . 5460.00
Chest, Chippendale, Bowfront, Maple, 4 Graduated Drawers, 36 x 39 x 34 In. 3080.00
Chest, Chippendale, Cherry, 2 Small Drawers Over 5 Drawers, 84 In. 37950.00
Chest, Chippendale, Cherry, 2 Thumb-Molded Drawers, Ogee Bracket Feet, 42 In. 2415.00
Chest, Chippendale, Cherry, 4 Graduated Drawers, Bracket Feet, 34 x 38 x 20 In. 2990.00
Chest, Chippendale, Cherry, 4 Graduated Drawers, Reeded Columns, 37 In. 5775.00
Chest, Chippendale, Cherry, 5 Thumb-Molded Graduated Drawers, 52 x 17 In. 4600.00
Chest, Chippendale, Cherry, 6 Graduated Drawers, Bracket Feet, c.1790, 55 x 35 In. 5175.00
Chest, Chippendale, Cherry, 7 Graduated Drawers, Bracket Feet, 62 x 37 In. 7475.00
Chest, Chippendale, Cherry, Maple, 5 Graduated Drawers, Bracket Feet, 49 In. 3100.00
Chest, Chippendale, Cherry, Rectangular Top, 4 Graduated Drawers, 34 x 41 In. 4140.00
Chest, Chippendale, Cherry, Rectangular Top, 4 Graduated Drawers, 35 x 20 In. 1265.00
Chest, Chippendale, Mahogany, 4 Dovetailed Drawers, Reverse Oxbow, 42 x 46 In. 7150.00
Chest, Chippendale, Mahogany, 4 Dovetailed Drawers, Serpentine, 31 In. 9900.00
Chest, Chippendale, Mahogany, 4 Drawers, Claw & Ball Feet, c.1770, 36 x 21 In. 9200.00
Chest, Chippendale, Mahogany, Fluted Quarter Columns, Pa., 1780, 35 x 40 In. 6325.00
Chest, Chippendale, Maple, 2 Graduated Short Drawers, Bracket Feet, 44 1/2 In. 4025.00
Chest, Chippendale, Maple, 2 Thumb-Molded Short Drawers, 1780, 53 In. 3450.00
Chest, Chippendale, Maple, 4 Graduated Thumb-Molded Drawers, 1780, 31 1/2 In. 2300.00
Chest, Chippendale, Maple, 4 Overlapping Drawers, Molded Top, 19 x 39 x 36 In. 1430.00
Chest, Chippendale, Maple, 5 Graduated Drawers, Rectangular Top, 1780, 41 In. 1610.00
Chest, Chippendale, Maple, 6 Graduated Drawers, Bracket Feet, 58 x 36 x 18 In. 6615.00
Chest, Chippendale, Maple, Birch, 5 Thumb-Molded Graduated Drawers, 50 In. 2875.00
Chest, Chippendale, Maple, Birch, Shaped Bracket Base, 1700s, 34 1/2 x 37 x 17 In. 2530.00
Chest, Chippendale, Maple, Overhanging Top, Bracket Feet, c.1800, 32 x 38 x 17 In. 2415.00
Chest, Chippendale, Pine, Maple, 5 Drawers, Goodale, Mass., 1700s, 46 x 37 x 18 In. . . . 3220.00
Chest, Chippendale, Sycamore, 6 Graduated Drawers, Cock-Beaded, c.1780, 56 In. 4310.00
Chest, Chippendale, Tiger Maple, 7 Thumb-Molded Drawers, c.1790, 57 x 36 x 18 In. . . . 5463.00
Chest, Chippendale, Walnut, 3 Over 5 Drawers, Ogee Bracket Feet, 69 In. 4315.00
Chest, Chippendale, Walnut, 4 Drawers, Ogee Molded Bracket Feet, 34 x 42 In. 4890.00
Chest, Chippendale, Walnut, 4 Drawers, Philadelphia, 1780 . . . . *Illus* 4950.00
Chest, Classical, Mahogany, 2 Over 2 Over 3 Drawers, New England, 46 1/2 In. 1980.00
Chest, Classical, Mahogany, Overhanging Drawer Over 3 Drawers, Carved, 33 In. 1045.00
Chest, Colonial Revival, Walnut, Lift Top, Sunflower, 1920, 40 x 48 In. 550.00
Chest, Curly Maple, Chippendale, 5 Overlapping Drawers, 45 1/2 In. 3575.00
Chest, Curly Maple, Empire, 4 Drawers, Burl Knobs, 49 x 42 1/2 In. 550.00
Chest, Document, Campaign, Calamander, 4 Drawers, John Wood & Sons, 12 In. 580.00
Chest, Dome Top, Leather Covered, Brass Tack Designs, S.B., 1836, 15 x 30 In. 1380.00
Chest, Dovetailed, New Mexico, Early 18th Century, 20 x 52 1/4 In. 825.00
Chest, Dower, 3 Drawers, Ogee Bracket Feet, Pa., Early 19th Century, 29 x 49 In. 3410.00

Chest, Dower, Chippendale, Walnut, 2 Drawers, Lift Top, 1787, 26 1/2 x 48 x 22 In. 2200.00
Chest, Dower, Heart-Shaped Crest, Pa., 1774, 50 x 27 x 24 In. 3900.00
Chest, Dower, Lift Top, 2 Arched Panels, Pinwheel Design, Pa., 1780, 26 x 51 In. 880.00
Chest, Dower, Lift Top, Dovetailed, Painted Tulips, Pa., 1800, 25 x 48 In. 3025.00
Chest, Dower, Pine, Central Elliptic Cartouche, Blue, Green Stippled Ground, 27 In. 3520.00
Chest, Dower, Pine, Poplar, Rectangular Top, Floral, Bracket Feet, 1778, 24 In. 2530.00
Chest, Dower, Poplar, Molded Lid, Pair Of Lovebirds Over Tulips, 1800, 20 3/4 In. 9200.00
Chest, Dower, Rectangular Lift Top, Blue & Red, Bracket Feet, 1790, 24 In. 2310.00
Chest, Dower, Red, Brown, White, Green Paint, Potted Flower Design, Pa., 24 In. 1320.00
Chest, Dowry, Iron Strapping, Wood Wheels, Colonial India, 37 x 44 x 25 In. 330.00
Chest, Duncan Phyfe, Mahogany, 2 Over 4 Drawers, Ring Turned Legs, c.1830, 47 In. 4675.00
Chest, Eastlake, 8 Drawers, Gallery, Carved Hatbox, 67 x 39 x 24 In. 4125.00
Chest, Empire, 2 Over 3 Drawers, Stepped, Brass Pulls, Miniature, 18 x 10 In. 385.00
Chest, Empire, Bowfront, Mahogany, 4 Drawers, Twisted Columns, 40 In. 1380.00
Chest, Empire, Cherry, 2 Over 3 Drawers, Bracket Feet, 50 1/2 x 42 x 16 1/4 In. 560.00
Chest, Empire, Cherry, 4 Dovetailed Drawers, Acanthus Carved Posts, 52 3/4 In. 550.00
Chest, Empire, Cherry, 4 Dovetailed Drawers, Turned Feet, 45 In. 660.00
Chest, Empire, Cherry, Bird's-Eye Maple, 6 Drawers, 3/4 Columns, 47 x 43 x 20 In. 440.00
Chest, Empire, Cherry, Bird's-Eye Maple, 7 Dovetailed Drawers, 58 1/2 In. 935.00
Chest, Empire, Cherry, Curly Maple Veneer, 4 Drawers, Half Pilasters, 42 x 45 In. 465.00
Chest, Empire, Mahogany, 3 Over 4 Drawers, Marble Top, 1840, 44 x 42 x 20 In. 440.00
Chest, Empire, Mahogany, 4 Drawers, Paw Feet, Marble, Green Paint, 51 x 38 In. 2530.00
Chest, Empire, Mixed Woods, Dovetailed Drawers, Square Nails, 15 In. 415.00
Chest, Empire, Poplar, 3 Graduated Drawers, Rectangular Top, Ball Feet, 45 In. 287.00
Chest, Empire, Satinwood, Embossed Brass Frieze, Marble Columns, 36 x 24 In. 3960.00
Chest, Empire, Walnut, 4 Drawers, Setback Lower Section, Pillars, Claw Feet, 45 In. 335.00
Chest, Empire, Walnut, 4 Graduated Drawers, Turned Feet, 41 1/2 x 42 x 20 In. 335.00
Chest, Federal, 4 Graduated Drawers, Serpentine, Inlay ....*Illus* 6500.00
Chest, Federal, Basswood, 4 Drawers, Painted Design, H. Davist, 1815, 41 x 19 In. 7475.00
Chest, Federal, Birch, 4 Graduated Drawers, Oval Brass Pulls, c.1800, 39 x 38 In. 1955.00
Chest, Federal, Birch, Mahogany Veneer, 4 Drawers, c.1820, 41 x 40 In. 1840.00
Chest, Federal, Bowfront, Cherry Veneer, 4 Drawers, Lunette, c.1820, 37 x 40 x 17 In. 3795.00
Chest, Federal, Bowfront, Cherry, 4 Graduated Drawers, Bracket Feet, 35 In. 8625.00
Chest, Federal, Bowfront, Inlaid Mahogany, 4 Drawers, Bracket Feet, 36 x 42 In. 3740.00
Chest, Federal, Bowfront, Mahogany Veneer, Lunette Inlay, c.1820, 37 x 40 x 18 In. 4900.00
Chest, Federal, Bowfront, Mahogany Veneer, Spiral Columns, Carved, 39 x 38 x 19 In. .. 1495.00
Chest, Federal, Bowfront, Mahogany, 4 Drawers, Cyma Skirt, c.1820, 33 x 41 x 19 In. 3335.00
Chest, Federal, Bowfront, Mahogany, 4 Drawers, Inlay, c.1810, 34 x 38 1/2 x 22 In. 2300.00
Chest, Federal, Bowfront, Mahogany, 4 Drawers, Tapered Round Legs, 1800, 40 In. 1725.00
Chest, Federal, Bowfront, Mahogany, 4 Graduated Drawers, Bracket Feet, 39 In. 3450.00
Chest, Federal, Bowfront, Mahogany, Bird's-Eye Maple, Curved Feet, 37 In. 9775.00
Chest, Federal, Bowfront, Mahogany, Inlaid Birch, Oblong Top, 1800, 38 x 42 In. 6900.00
Chest, Federal, Cherry, 1800-1810, 36 x 37 x 19 In. ....*Illus* 4600.00
Chest, Federal, Cherry, 3 Short Over 5 Graduated Drawers, Dart Inlay, 61 x 40 In. 3450.00
Chest, Federal, Cherry, 4 Drawers, Shaped Skirt, Tiger Maple Banding, 40 In. 1495.00
Chest, Federal, Cherry, 4 Graduated Drawers, French Feet, New England, 38 x 42 In. 2640.00
Chest, Federal, Cherry, Bird's-Eye Maple, 4 Drawers, Rectangular Top, 1840, 53 In. 1320.00
Chest, Federal, Cherry, Overhanging Rectangular Top, French Feet, 1810, 36 1/2 In. 4600.00

Furniture, Chest,
Federal, Mahogany,
New Hampshire,
37 x 40 x 22 In.

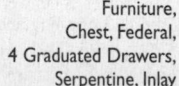

Furniture,
Chest, Federal,
4 Graduated Drawers,
Serpentine, Inlay

Furniture, Chest, G. Stickley, Strap
Hinges, Decal, 18 x 35 x 20 In.

**Don't wax a piece of furniture that has
not been cleaned in the past year.**

**Felt tops on card tables and desks
attract moths. Vacuum tops carefully at
least once a year.**

Chest, Federal, Cherry, Overhanging Top, Bracket Base, Mass., 1800s, 33 x 41 x 19 In. . . . 2415.00
Chest, Federal, Cherry, White Pine, 4 Drawers, Crossbanded Edge, 39 x 42 In. 575.00
Chest, Federal, Mahogany, 3 Drawers, Short Turned Feet, 1825, 12 x 13 1/4 In. 1870.00
Chest, Federal, Mahogany, 3 Graduated Drawers, Overhanging Rectangular Top, 39 In. . . . 488.00
Chest, Federal, Mahogany, 3 Over 3 Drawers, Serpentine Front, Inlay, 45 x 37 In. 4315.00
Chest, Federal, Mahogany, 4 Drawers, Ebony Stringing, 38 In. 1495.00
Chest, Federal, Mahogany, 4 Graduated Drawers, Rectangular Top, 1810, 40 In. 4140.00
Chest, Federal, Mahogany, 5 Drawers, Inlay, Splayed Bracket Feet, 40 x 36 In. 2070.00
Chest, Federal, Mahogany, Maple, Birch, 4 Long Drawers, 1810, 39 1/4 In. 8050.00
Chest, Federal, Mahogany, New Hampshire, 37 x 40 x 22 In. . . . .*Illus* 9775.00
Chest, Federal, Mahogany, Poplar, 2 Over 4 Graduated Drawers, 48 3/4 x 46 In. 1960.00
Chest, Federal, Overhanging Drawer Over 3 Drawers, Red Washed, 49 x 41 1/2 In. 770.00
Chest, Federal, Tiger Maple, 4 Drawers, Cyma Skirt, Mass., 1800s, 35 x 39 x 18 In. 3738.00
Chest, Federal, Wavy Birch, 4 Drawers, New Hampshire, Early 1800s, 38 x 39 x 18 In. . . . 1840.00
Chest, Folk Art, Geometric Marquetry, Wallpaper Interior, c.1900, 25 x 12 In. 2400.00
Chest, French Empire, Figured Veneer, 4 Drawers, Ebonized Trim, 36 x 17 x 31 In. 740.00
Chest, Fruitwood, 2 Drawers, Rectangular Top, Tapered Square Legs, 34 x 41 In. 550.00
Chest, Fruitwood, 2 Long Drawers, Rectangular, Continental, 19th Century, 36 In. . .: 2750.00
Chest, G. Stickley, 2 Over 2 Drawers, Mirror, Harvey Ellis Style, 66 x 48 In. 4125.00
Chest, G. Stickley, No. 906, Oak, 2 Short & 4 Long Drawers, 1912, 48 x 21 In. 13800.00
Chest, G. Stickley, Strap Hinges, Decal, 18 x 35 x 20 In. . . . .*Illus* 25300.00
Chest, George I, Burl Walnut, Divided Rectangular Top, Bracket Feet, 29 x 28 In. 2070.00
Chest, George II Style, Burl Walnut, 4 Over 2 Drawers, Bracket Feet, 33 1/2 In. 3100.00
Chest, George II Style, Oyster Veneer, 5 Drawers, Bracket Feet, 40 1/4 x 37 3/4 In. 3960.00
Chest, George II Style, Oyster Walnut, 2 Over 2 Drawers, Bracket Feet, 33 x 35 In. 440.00
Chest, George II Style, Walnut, Burl Walnut, 3 Drawers, 33 1/2 x 40 In. 1320.00
Chest, George II, Walnut, 2 Over 3 Drawers, Ebony Inlay, 36 1/4 x 37 1/2 In. 4400.00
Chest, George III Style, Burl Walnut, 5 Drawers, Compass Ray Inlay, 39 In. 3740.00
Chest, George III Style, Mahogany, 3 Drawers, Gilt Brass Pulls, 35 x 37 In. 2090.00
Chest, George III Style, Oyster Veneer, Banded Top, 2 Over 2 Drawers, 30 x 37 In. 3520.00
Chest, George III, Bowfront, Mahogany, 2 Over 3 Drawers, 36 3/4 x 41 1/2 In. 2300.00
Chest, George III, Bowfront, Mahogany, 2 Over 3 Drawers, 41 3/4 x 45 1/4 In. 3740.00
Chest, George III, Bowfront, Mahogany, 2 Over 3 Drawers, Bracket Feet, 41 In. 1320.00
Chest, George III, Bowfront, Mahogany, 3 Drawers, Overhanging Banded Top, 35 In. 1650.00
Chest, George III, Bowfront, Mahogany, 3 Graduated Drawers, Bracket Feet, 36 In. 3220.00
Chest, George III, Bowfront, Mahogany, 4 Graduated Cock-Beaded Drawers, 34 In. 6325.00
Chest, George III, Mahogany, 2 Over 3 Drawers, Bracket Feet, 37 1/2 x 20 x 32 In. 2300.00
Chest, George III, Mahogany, 3 Graduated Drawers, Rectangular Top, 40 1/2 In. 2950.00
Chest, George III, Mahogany, 4 Drawers, Serpentine, Satinwood Banding, 35 1/4 In. 3740.00
Chest, George III, Mahogany, 4 Graduated Drawers, Rectangular Top, 44 In. 1610.00
Chest, George III, Mahogany, 4 Graduated Drawers, Serpentine Front, 1770, 39 In. 12650.00
Chest, George III, Mahogany, 4 Graduated Drawers, Bracket Feet, 40 1/2 In. 630.00
Chest, George III, Oak, 3 Graduated Drawers, Rectangular Molded Top, 38 1/2 In. 805.00
Chest, Georgian, Bowfront, Mahogany Veneer, 2 Drawers, Crossbanded Top, 38 In. 605.00
Chest, Georgian, Bowfront, Mahogany Veneer, 5 Drawers, French Feet, 1790, 44 In. 660.00
Chest, Georgian, Japanned, Short Cabriole Legs, England, 44 x 38 In. 1870.00
Chest, Hardwood, 3 Dovetailed Drawers, Paint Traces, Continental, 14 x 8 x 8 In. 275.00
Chest, Hepplewhite, 2 Over 3 Drawers, Shaped Backsplash, Inlay, 15 1/4 x 19 In. 1075.00

Chest, Hepplewhite, Bowfront, 4 Graduated Drawers, 38 x 42 x 19 In. 1760.00
Chest, Hepplewhite, Bowfront, Cherry, 4 Dovetailed Drawers, Inlay, 38 x 43 In. 3300.00
Chest, Hepplewhite, Bowfront, Cherry, 4 Inlaid Drawers, 1800, 42 x 43 In. 4125.00
Chest, Hepplewhite, Bowfront, Mahogany Veneer, Scalloped Skirt, 1795, 39 In. 2310.00
Chest, Hepplewhite, Bowfront, Mahogany, 4 Graduated Drawers, 39 x 42 x 19 In. 2475.00
Chest, Hepplewhite, Bowfront, Mahogany, Veneers, 4 Drawers, 35 1/2 x 41 In. 3080.00
Chest, Hepplewhite, Cherry, 4 Beaded Edge Drawers, French Feet, 1810, 34 In. 3025.00
Chest, Hepplewhite, Cherry, 4 Drawers, Bath, Maine, 19 1/2 x 42 x 47 In. 1650.00
Chest, Hepplewhite, Cherry, 6 Dovetailed Beaded Drawers, 40 x 50 In. 1100.00
Chest, Hepplewhite, Mahogany, 4 Graduated Drawers, Dentil Molding, 35 x 36 In. 1120.00
Chest, Hepplewhite, Mahogany, Oak, 5 Bowed Drawers, Brass Terminations, 55 In. 1155.00
Chest, Hepplewhite, Pine, 3 Over 4 Lipped Drawers, 18th Century, 40 x 59 x 18 In. 1870.00
Chest, Hepplewhite, Pine, New England, 1810, 38 x 36 In. 990.00
Chest, Hepplewhite, Walnut, 4 Drawers, Oblong Reeded Edge Top, Pa., 1810, 37 In. 4125.00
Chest, Hinged Lid, 6-Board, Blue, Green Paint, New England, 25 x 50 x 19 In. 1725.00
Chest, Hinged Top, Bracket Feet, Painted, Early 19th Century, 24 1/2 x 48 In. 1150.00
Chest, Immigrant's, Pine, Dome Top, Iron Handles, Brown Paint, 20 In. 300.00
Chest, Immigrant's, Pine, Dovetailed Case, Domed Lid, Initials, 1834, 45 In. 300.00
Chest, Immigrant's, Pine, Iron Strapping, German Inscriptions, Label, 1854, 36 In. 165.00
Chest, Joined Oak, Hinged Lid, Paneled, England, Early 17th Century, 26 1/2 x 55 In. . . . 315.00
Chest, Limbert, Attached Mirror, 5 Graduated Drawers, Branded, 69 x 36 x 20 In. 2750.00
Chest, Liquor, Mahogany, Inlay, Hinged Top, Fitted Interior, c.1795, 8 x 11 x 7 In. 9200.00
Chest, Louis XVI, Amaranth, Parquetry Marble Top, Canted Stiles, 54 1/4 x 13 In. 575.00
Chest, Louis XVI, Mahogany, 6 Drawers, Brass Gallery, 54 x 34 x 17 In. 980.00
Chest, Mahogany, 3 Drawers, Marquetry Flower, France, 32 x 37 1/2 In. 1430.00
Chest, Mahogany, 3 Drawers, Rectangular Top, Turned Legs, Casters, Victorian, 23 In. . . . 690.00
Chest, Mahogany, 4 Cock-Beaded Drawers, Fruit Carved Capitals, 43 1/3 In. 1495.00
Chest, Mahogany, 4 Dovetailed Drawers, Side Lock, 16 x 11 3/4 x 18 1/2 In. 385.00
Chest, Mahogany, 4 Graduated Drawers, Bracket Feet, Continental, 42 1/2 In. 400.00
Chest, Mahogany, 6 Drawers, Scroll, Leaf Design, Victorian, 55 x 26 x 70 In. 290.00
Chest, Mahogany, 7 Drawers, Brass Hardware, Carved Bracket Feet, c.1930, 58 In. 400.00
Chest, Mahogany, Bachelor's, Fold Top, Late 19th Century, 34 1/4 x 41 3/4 In. 980.00
Chest, Mahogany, Camphorwood, 2 Short, 3 Long Drawers, Brassbound, 39 x 20 In. 4025.00
Chest, Mahogany, Empire, 2 Short Over 3 Long Drawers, 1830s, 41 1/2 In. 750.00
Chest, Mahogany, Poplar, 1 Large Over 3 Graduated Drawers, 1840, 47 x 43 In. 1905.00
Chest, Maple, 6 Drawers, Bracket Feet, Late 18th Century, 44 x 35 1/2 In. 1760.00
Chest, Mule, George II, Elm, Chestnut, 5 Drawers, Rectangular Hinged Top, 35 In. 4600.00
Chest, Mule, Hepplewhite, 2 Long Drawers, Lift Top, Scalloped, 39 x 44 In. 1760.00
Chest, Mule, Oak, Pine, 2 Dovetailed Drawers, 6 Faux Fronts, Hinged Lid, 21 x 50 In. . . . 2200.00
Chest, Mule, Pine, 2 Dovetailed Drawers, Hinged Top, Scrolled Apron, 37 3/4 In. 330.00
Chest, Mule, Pine, 2 Dovetailed Drawers, Lift Top, Dark Stain, 37 x 39 1/4 In. 605.00
Chest, Mule, Pine, 2 Overlapping Drawers, Hinged Lid, Lid On Till, 39 3/4 In. 357.00
Chest, Mule, Pine, Chestnut, Red Paint, Overlapping Drawer, 32 1/4 In. 1375.00
Chest, Mule, Poplar, 3 Overlapping Over Faux Drawer, Scrolled Apron, 45 In. 1000.00
Chest, Neoclassical, 3 Graduated Drawers, Rectangular Faux Marble Top, 36 In. 2530.00
Chest, Neoclassical, Mahogany, 5 Drawers, Canted Corners, Parquetry, Holland, 37 In. . . 3080.00
Chest, Neoclassical, Mahogany, Birch, Parcel Gilt, Marble Top, Spain, 43 1/2 In. 4180.00
Chest, Oak, Dome Top, Truncated Case, Iron Hardware, Continental, 47 x 25 x 28 In. . . . 220.00
Chest, Oak, Maple, Drawer, Frieze Over 3 Part Case, Pilgrim Century, 30 In. 6300.00
Chest, Oak, Panels, Rosette-Guilloche Banding, England, 17th Century, 47 In. 575.00
Chest, Painted, Blue, Green & Red Tulip & Heart Design, 19th Century, 14 x 31 In. 220.00
Chest, Pine, 2 Dove Tailed Drawers, 6-Board, Bracket Feet, 26 x 46 x 21 In. 600.00
Chest, Pine, 2 Faux & 2 Working Drawers, Molded Lift Top, 37 x 39 x 18 In. 1150.00
Chest, Pine, 2 Faux & 3 Working Drawers, Cutout Rear Feet, Gray, Brown, 49 In. 2415.00
Chest, Pine, 2 Paneled Doors, Backsplash, 19th Century, 51 x 42 x 17 1/2 In. 450.00
Chest, Pine, 2 Thumb-Molded Drawers, Red Paint, New England, 41 1/4 In. 1840.00
Chest, Pine, 4 Dovetailed Drawers, Red Brown Flame Graining, Cutout Feet, 37 In. 1155.00
Chest, Pine, 4 Drawers, Grain Painted, Mass., 1800, 36 In. 2310.00
Chest, Pine, 6-Board, Hinged Top, Bootjack Ends, Painted, 1700s, 25 x 51 x 17 In. 1610.00
Chest, Pine, 6-Board, Hinged Top, Dovetailed Case, 1830s, 28 1/2 x 45 In. 1840.00
Chest, Pine, 6-Board, Hinged Top, Red Paint, Mid 1800s, 24 x 48 x 21 In. 1093.00
Chest, Pine, 6-Board, Lift Top, Dovetailed, Floral Designs, 18th Century, 16 x 42 In. 2415.00
Chest, Pine, 6-Board, Wrought Iron Handles, Green Paint, 16 x 49 In. 460.00

Chest, Pine, 6-Board, Wrought Iron Handles, Red, Brown Paint, 16 x 48 In. 460.00
Chest, Pine, Bench, Molded Top Rail, Panels, Hinged, 19th Century, 48 x 73 x 21 In. 805.00
Chest, Pine, Lift Top, Working Drawer, Demilune Ends, Conn., 1700s, 33 x 39 x 18 In. .. 805.00
Chest, Pine, Lower Drawer, Front Ball Feet, Molded Base, 18th Century, 33 x 42 In. 4600.00
Chest, Pollard Wood, 7 Drawers, Serpentine Top, Cabriole Legs, 51 In. 2530.00
Chest, Poplar, 3 Drawers, Wavy Red Grained, Cutout Feet, 16 x 9 1/2 x 18 3/4 In. 2585.00
Chest, Poplar, 8 Drawers, Rectangular Top, Spiral Columns, Pa., 1800, 23 In. 8800.00
Chest, Queen Anne Style, Burl Walnut, 2 Over 3 Drawers, Bun Feet, 38 1/2 x 36 In. 2860.00
Chest, Queen Anne Style, Burl Walnut, 2 Over 3 Drawers, Compass Ray Inlay, 38 In. ... 3300.00
Chest, Queen Anne Style, Figured Walnut, 2 Over 3 Drawers, Bun Feet, 34 1/4 In. 2860.00
Chest, Queen Anne Style, Oyster Veneer, 2 Over 3 Drawers, Bun Feet, 36 x 39 In. 3740.00
Chest, Queen Anne Style, Pollard, Oak, 5 Drawers, Concave, Inlay, 31 x 39 In. 1870.00
Chest, Queen Anne Style, Walnut, Oyster Veneer, 2 Over 3 Drawers, 37 x 42 In. 1540.00
Chest, Queen Anne, 2 Over 3 Drawers, England, 18th Century .... *Illus* 5200.00
Chest, Queen Anne, 4 Drawers, Bonnet, Brass Finials, Ogee Bracket Feet, 33 In. 2575.00
Chest, Queen Anne, Burl Walnut, 3 Graduated Drawers, Rectangular Top, 40 3/4 In...... 3960.00
Chest, Queen Anne, Maple, 5 Over 3 Drawers, Cabriole Legs, c.1800, 63 x 36 x 20 In. ... 5750.00
Chest, Queen Anne, Maple, 8 Drawers, Falmouth, Maine, 62 x 37 x 19 1/2 In. 11000.00
Chest, Queen Anne, Poplar, Rectangular Hinged Molded Top, 45 x 35 x 17 In. 2070.00
Chest, Queen Anne, Walnut, 2 Narrow Drawers, Molded Top, 4 Legs, Bun Feet, 35 In. ... 8800.00
Chest, Queen Anne, Walnut, 2 Over 3 Drawers, Bracket Feet, String Inlay, 36 In. 3740.00
Chest, Queen Anne, Walnut, 2 Short Over 4 Drawers, Herringbone Bands, 44 x 36 In. ... 2300.00
Chest, Queen Anne, Walnut, 3 Graduated Drawers, Banded Rectangular Top, 33 In. 1845.00
Chest, Queen Anne, Walnut, 8 Drawers, Cabriole Legs, Trifid Feet, Pa., 1765, 72 In. 16500.00
Chest, Regency, Mahogany, 3 Cock-Beaded Drawers, Rectangular Top, 41 x 21 In. 1380.00
Chest, Regency, Pine, 5 Ogee Front Dovetailed Drawers, Wood Pulls, 59 In. 935.00
Chest, Restauration, Walnut, 4 Drawers, Black Marble Top, Bracket Feet, 34 x 40 In. 1760.00
Chest, Rococo, Burl Walnut, 3 Drawers, Serpentine, Canted Corners, Holland, 33 In. 5500.00
Chest, Rococo, Rosewood, 4 Drawers, Overhanging Marble Top, 32 1/2 In. 1540.00
Chest, Rococo, Walnut, 3 Long Concave & Convex Drawers, Carved Top, 34 In. 3220.00
Chest, Roycroft, 5 Graduated Drawers, Gallery .... *Illus* 15400.00
Chest, Semainier, Fruitwood, Serpentine Front, Cabriole Legs, Continental, 51 In. 2310.00
Chest, Shaker, 11 Drawers, Wood Pulls, Brown Stain, 44 x 20 x 71 1/2 In. 4950.00
Chest, Sheraton, Bowfront, 4 Graduated Drawers, Reeded Columns, 43 x 39 In. 1650.00
Chest, Sheraton, Bowfront, Cherry, Mahogany, 4 Drawers, 1800, 41 x 46 In. 2750.00
Chest, Sheraton, Cherry, 4 Beaded Drawers, Turned Legs, Maryland, 1820, 40 In. 880.00
Chest, Sheraton, Cherry, Curly Maple, Poplar, 4 Dovetailed Drawers, 40 x 42 In. 1650.00
Chest, Sheraton, Cherry, Walnut, 4 Dovetailed Drawers, Ohio, 41 1/2 In. 687.00
Chest, Sheraton, Cherry, Walnut, Graduated Drawers, 1830, 45 x 40 In. 2750.00
Chest, Sheraton, Mahogany Veneer, 2 Over 4 Drawers, Turned Columns, 47 x 42 In. 1045.00
Chest, Sheraton, Mahogany, Veneers, White Pine, Poplar, 5 Drawers, 38 1/2 In. 1010.00
Chest, Sheraton, Tiger Maple, Turret Corner Over 4 Drawers, 38 x 42 In. 715.00
Chest, Sheraton, Walnut, 4 Cock-Beaded Drawers, Turned Legs, c.1820, 39 1/2 In. 2310.00
Chest, Sheraton, Walnut, Maple, 7 Nailed Drawers, 30 1/4 x 26 x 28 1/4 In. 2090.00
Chest, Spice, Pine, 3 Dovetailed Overlapping Drawers, Bracket Feet, 16 In. 825.00
Chest, Spice, Pine, 6 Drawers, Round Wood Pulls, Red Paint, 12 3/4 In. 1840.00
Chest, Sugar Walnut, Drawer, Shenandoah Valley .... *Illus* 2000.00

Furniture, Chest,
Queen Anne,
2 Over 3 Drawers,
England, 18th Century

Furniture, Chest,
Roycroft, 5 Graduated
Drawers, Gallery

Animal-hide glue was usually used on furniture made before the 1900s. The glue was made by boiling animal heads—which explains the saying about taking the horse to the glue factory. The glue is strong but not water resistant. You can dissolve and remove the old glue with hot water, then reglue the joints. New glues will not work unless the wood is clean.

Furniture, Chest, Sugar Walnut,
Drawer, Shenandoah Valley

Chest, Sugar, Federal, Cherry, Flower Head Case, Splayed Bracket Feet, 20 In. 2875.00
Chest, Sugar, Opens To Well, Tapering Legs, Hinged Lid, 1830s, 28 In. 2090.00
Chest, Sugar, Queen Anne, Mixed Woods, Rose Nailheads, Painted, 1770, 30 x 24 In. . . . 4480.00
Chest, Tiger Maple, Convex Frieze Drawer, 3 Long Drawers, 43 x 41 In. 1035.00
Chest, Tiger Maple, Queen Anne, Cornice Molding, Cyma Skirt, 1700s, 70 x 35 x 17 In. . 16100.00
Chest, Walnut, 2 Short & 2 Long Drawers, Serpentine, Paneled Sides, c.1750, 32 In. 6900.00
Chest, Walnut, 2 Short & 3 Long Drawers, Gallery, Carved, Bonnet Door, 40 x 64 In. 2090.00
Chest, Walnut, 3 Drawers Victorian, 26 x 14 x 26 In. 748.00
Chest, Walnut, 3 Drawers, Reverse Serpentine Front Edge, Parquetry, 48 In. 7475.00
Chest, Walnut, 3 Figural Wood Drawer Fronts, Casters, Victorian, 38 x 18 x 41 In. 410.00
Chest, Walnut, 3 Over 3 Drawers, Scrolled Bracket Base, Pennsylvania, 36 In. 1430.00
Chest, Walnut, 4 Drawers, Scrolled Crest, Varnish, 13 x 7 1/2 x 12 1/4 In. 550.00
Chest, Walnut, 4 Drawers, Scrolled Legs, Paneled Ends, Brass Locks, 1860s, 45 In. 310.00
Chest, Walnut, 4 Graduated Drawers, Banded Top, Bracket Feet, Fan Inlay, 37 In. 2200.00
Chest, Walnut, 5 Dovetailed Drawers, Beveled Front, 8 1/4 x 5 3/4 x 9 3/8 In. 495.00
Chest, Walnut, Burl Walnut Veneer, 3 Drawers, Marble Top, 33 In. 375.00
Chest, Walnut, Burl Walnut Veneer, Glove Boxes, Swivel Mirror, 1800s, 74 x 40 In. 525.00
Chest, Walnut, Burl, 6 Graduated Drawers, Overhanging Corners, c.1865, 57 1/2 In. 1330.00
Chest, Walnut, Door Flanked By Panels, Iron Lock, Afghanistan, 16th Century, 33 In. . . . 1100.00
Chest, Walnut, Lift Top, Heraldic Crest, Paw Feet, Lion Carved Arms, 54 x 72 In. 3300.00
Chest, White Pine, 3 Drawers, Floral, Black Ground, Victorian, 31 1/2 x 42 x 21 In. 1010.00
Chest, Widdicomb, Mediterranean, 4 Drawers, Antique White, Faux Marble Top, 36 In. . . 770.00
Chest, William & Mary, Walnut, 2 Drawers Over 3 Graduated Drawers, 60 In. 1840.00
Chest, William & Mary, Walnut, Ball Feet, c.1730, 37 In. 2090.00
Chest, William & Mary, Walnut, Molded Top, Door, Pa., 1770, 28 x 14 In. 8250.00
Chest-On-Chest, Chippendale, Mahogany, Pine, 5 Drawers, 70 x 40 In. 3162.00
Chest-On-Chest, Chippendale, Walnut, 3 Over 7 Drawers, c.1750, 76 In. 8960.00
Chest-On-Chest, George II, Burl Walnut, 3 Graduated Drawers, 41 x 23 x 67 In. 6900.00
Chest-On-Chest, George III, Mahogany, 8 Drawers, 60 1/2 x 43 In. 4600.00
Chest-On-Chest, Hepplewhite, Walnut, 9 Drawers, Pa., 1790, 69 x 41 x 20 In. 7150.00
Chest-On-Chest, Tiger Maple, Yellow Pine, 4 Long Drawers, Flat Top, 1830, 72 In. 1790.00
Chest-On-Frame, Queen Anne, Mahogany, 4 Drawers, Inlay, Grand Rapids, 21 x 31 In. . . 550.00
Chest-On-Frame, William & Mary Top, Chippendale Base, Walnut, 69 In. 5500.00
Chest-On-Stand, Baroque, Ivory, Rectangular, 4 Baluster Turned Legs, 55 In. 2645.00
Chest-On-Stand, Chippendale, Inlaid Walnut, 4 Drawers, Cabriole Legs, 41 In. 3740.00
Chest-On-Stand, George I, Walnut, 3 Crossbanded Drawers, Cabriole Legs, 62 In. 2860.00
Chest-On-Stand, Queen Anne Style, Figured Walnut, 7 Drawers, 65 In. 2420.00
Chest-On-Stand, Queen Anne, Walnut, 5 Over 4 Drawers, Scalloped Apron, 62 1/2 In. . . . 3080.00
Chest-On-Stand, Walnut, 2 Short & 3 Long Drawers, 18th Century, 62 In. 3737.00
Chiffonier, Louis XV Style, 3 Drawers, Marquetry, Flowers, Cabriole Legs, 28 In. 1320.00
Chiffonier, Louis XV Style, Kingwood Parquetry, 2 Drawers, Marble Top, 33 In. 1870.00
Chiffonnier, Bird's-Eye Maple, 4 Drawers, Variegated Gray Marble Top, 55 In. 2070.00
Chiffonnier, Louis XV Style, Fruitwood, 6 Drawers, 1875-1900, 59 In. 2090.00
Chiffonnier, Louis XV, Kingwood, 6 Drawers, Rouge Marble Top, 46 x 14 x 10 In. 1540.00
Chiffonnier, William IV, Rosewood, 2 Shelves, Fabric Lined Doors, Bun Feet, 58 In. 1980.00

Coat Rack, 6 Arms, Revolving, 4-Arm Umbrella Holder, Paw Feet, Cast Iron, 71 In. 546.00
Coat Rack, Arts & Crafts, 2 Corseted Slats, 3 Shelves, Alligatored Finish, 67 In. 165.00
Coat Rack, Arts & Crafts, Cruciform Base, Hooks, 72 In. 110.00
Coat Rack, Eames, Hang It All, White Wire, Painted Wood, 1963, 19 3/4 In. 2760.00
Coat Rack, Stickley Brothers, 72 In. 990.00
Coat Rack, Walnut, Twig Hooks, Barley Twist Support, Brass Ball Feet, 84 In. 1320.00
Coffer, Colonial Revival, Hardwood, Wrought Iron, Portugal, c.1750, 29 x 38 1/2 In. 1100.00
Coffer, George III, Mahogany, Satinwood, Rectangular Top, Bracket Feet, 14 In. 1380.00
Coffer, Jacobean, Oak, Rectangular Hinged Top, Geometric Carved Front, 21 In. 805.00
Coffer, Oak, Hinged Lid, 3 Raised Fielded Panels, Beveled Molding, 30 1/2 In. 402.00
Coffer, Queen Anne, Oyster Veneer, Rectangular Hinged Top, Bun Feet, 33 In. 2300.00
Coffer, Rectangular Hinged Top, Tapered Square Legs, 19th Century, 58 1/2 In. 2070.00
Coffer, Regency, Bird's-Eye Maple, Bronze Lion's-Head Handles, 9 x 17 x 6 3/4 In. 862.00
Coffer, Renaissance Revival, Giltwood, Domed & Hinged Lid, Italy, 22 x 31 x 15 In. 3220.00
Coffer, Renaissance Revival, Walnut, Hinged Rectangular Lid, Paw Feet, 23 1/4 In. 1610.00
Coffer, Walnut, Birds & Trees, Internal Hinges, Continental, c.1650, 16 x 29 In. 1100.00
Commode, 3 Frieze Drawers Over 3 Paneled Doors, Marble Top, 34 x 60 In. 345.00
Commode, 3 Long Drawers, Variegated Gray Marble Top, Bracket Feet, 31 1/2 In. 990.00
Commode, Biedermeier, Birch, Rectangular Top, 3 Drawers, Block Feet, 30 In. 2185.00
Commode, Biedermeier, Fruitwood, Beveled Rectangular Top, 3 Drawers, 32 In. 2530.00
Commode, Biedermeier, Mahogany, 3 Long Drawers, Block Feet, 32 3/4 In. 1612.00
Commode, Biedermeier, Walnut Veneer, Drawers Over 2 Doors, 33 3/4 In. 1680.00
Commode, Bombe, Inlaid Walnut, Dressing Mirror, Holland, 18th Century, 63 In. 3740.00
Commode, Bombe, Inlay, Cabriole Legs, France, 1880, 11 1/2 x 12 1/2 x 7 In. 1850.00
Commode, Bombe, Kingwood, 2 Drawers, Marble Top, Trellis Parquetry, 34 In. 690.00
Commode, Charles X, Bird's-Eye Maple, White Marble Top, 30 In. 2200.00
Commode, Charles X, Rectangular Top, Rosettes On Top Of Drawers, 35 1/4 In. 4140.00
Commode, Dutch Neoclassical, Bowfront, Walnut, Tambour Doors, 35 x 56 In. 6050.00
Commode, Empire, Cherry, Mahogany, Rectangular Top, Square Sectioned Legs, 35 In. . . 865.00
Commode, Empire, Drawer, Square Marble Top, Doric Columns, 29 1/2 In. 690.00
Commode, Empire, Fruitwood, Ormolu, Variegated Marble Top, 35 1/2 x 42 In. 1980.00
Commode, Empire, Mahogany, 3 Graduated Drawers, Doric Columns, 83 In. 2245.00
Commode, Empire, Mahogany, 4 Drawers, Gilt Metal, Marble Top, France, 37 In. 3025.00
Commode, Empire, Mahogany, 4 Drawers, Gilt, Marble Top, France, 39 In. 3520.00
Commode, French Provincial, Carved Walnut, 3 Drawers, Rouge Marble, 40 In., Pair 2310.00
Commode, French Provincial, Walnut, 3 Drawers, Cabriole Legs, 27 In. 1150.00
Commode, Fruitwood, 3 Drawers, Marble Top, Bun Feet, Holland, 34 x 47 x 19 In. 3680.00
Commode, Fruitwood, Mottled Marble Rectangular Top, Italy, 33 In., Pair 3450.00
Commode, George III, Mahogany, 2 Cupboard Doors, 31 1/4 In., Pair 3450.00
Commode, George III, Mahogany, 2 Drawers, Lift Top, 3 Sections, 33 In. 4400.00
Commode, George III, Mahogany, Square Top, Incurved Stretcher, Dish Center, 31 In. . . . 690.00
Commode, George IV, Mahogany, Door, Pullout Seat, Square Legs, 30 In. 1430.00
Commode, Louis Philippe Style, Elm, Cherry, Marble Top, 32 1/4 In. 360.00
Commode, Louis Philippe, Amboyna, Walnut, Marble Top, 33 x 15 1/2 In. 600.00
Commode, Louis Philippe, Bird's-Eye Maple, Gray Variegated Marble Top, 30 In. 3300.00
Commode, Louis Philippe, Burl Walnut, Swirled Marble Top, 37 1/2 x 46 1/4 In. 1760.00
Commode, Louis Philippe, Fruitwood, Marble Top, Grillwork Doors, 35 x 47 In. 2100.00
Commode, Louis Philippe, Rosewood, Inset Dish Marble Top, 35 1/4 x 16 In. 1100.00
Commode, Louis XV Style, 4 Drawers, Parquetry, Mottled Marble Top, 48 x 35 In. 3520.00
Commode, Louis XV Style, Kingwood, 2 Drawers, Bombe, Marble Top, 36 x 50 In. 1980.00
Commode, Louis XV Style, Serpentine Top, 1850-1875, 32 1/2 x 41 In. 1980.00
Commode, Louis XV Style, Walnut, Bombe, Parquetry, Marble Top, 35 In. 345.00
Commode, Louis XV Style, Zebrawood, Bombe, Marble, Marquetry, 31 In. Pair 550.00
Commode, Louis XV Transitional, Oak, 2 Drawers, Doors, Cabriole Legs, 51 In. 2200.00
Commode, Louis XV, 2 Drawers, Rectangular Parquetry Top, 17 x 28 In., Pair 575.00
Commode, Louis XV, Burl, 3 Drawers, Green Marble Top, Curved Legs, 34 In. 575.00
Commode, Louis XV, Mahogany, Serpentine Marble Top, Cabriole Legs, 32 In., Pair 1320.00
Commode, Louis XV, Marble Top, Cabriole Legs, Bronze Sabots, 30 In., Pair 1840.00
Commode, Louis XV, Oak, 3 Long Fitted Drawers, Cabriole Feet, 34 1/2 x 24 In. 2990.00
Commode, Louis XV, Satinwood, Bombe, White Marble Top, Foliate, 35 In. 1380.00
Commode, Louis XV, Serpentine Marble Top, Oriental Scene, Black Lacquer, 31 In. 2530.00
Commode, Louis XV, Serpentine Molded Top, Scrolled Toes, Cabriole Legs, 33 In. 6037.00
Commode, Louis XV, Tulipwood, Serpentine Marble Top, Sabot Feet, 1900, 13 In. 750.00

Commode, Louis XVI Style, Inlaid Oak, 4 Drawers, Fluted Stiles, Continental, 37 In. 405.00
Commode, Louis XVI Style, Kingwood, 3 Drawers, Parquetry, Brass, 26 x 47 In. 5940.00
Commode, Louis XVI Style, Mahogany, 5 Drawers, Marble Top, Gilt Bronze, 36 In. 3735.00
Commode, Louis XVI Style, Mahogany, Ormolu, After Guillaume Benneman, 36 In. 2475.00
Commode, Louis XVI Style, Mahogany, Ormolu, Marble Top, Paw Feet, 36 x 60 In. 770.00
Commode, Louis XVI Style, Marble Top, Brass Inlay, Urn, Arabesques, 35 1/2 In. 2100.00
Commode, Louis XVI, 3 Frieze & 2 Long Drawers, Marble Top, 34 1/4 In. 4675.00
Commode, Louis XVI, 3 Long Drawers, Marble Top, Fluted Stiles, 31 1/4 In. 1760.00
Commode, Louis XVI, Beechwood, Pine Grain, 47 1/2 x 59 In. 2420.00
Commode, Louis XVI, Mahogany, 3 Drawers, Marble Top, Tapered Legs, 33 In. 1650.00
Commode, Louis XVI, Mahogany, Cream, Green Variegated Marble Top, 34 In. 2185.00
Commode, Mahogany, 2 Drawers Over 2 Doors, French Feet, c.1820, 28 1/2 In. 440.00
Commode, Mahogany, Bombe Frieze Drawer Over 3 Drawers, Continental, 41 In. 290.00
Commode, Mixed Wood, Bombe, Parquetry, Marble, France, 34 x 37 x 19 In., Pair 3300.00
Commode, Neoclassical Fruitwood, 2 Recessed Paneled Drawers, Italy, 31 In. 3450.00
Commode, Neoclassical Style, Fruitwood, 4 Drawers, Gray Marble Top, 38 1/2 In. 1045.00
Commode, Neoclassical, Burl Walnut, 2 Drawers, String Inlay, 30 In. 1870.00
Commode, Neoclassical, Inlaid Rosewood, 3 Over 3 Drawers, Continental, 42 In. 545.00
Commode, Neoclassical, Oak, Frieze Drawer Over 3 Long Drawers, 38 In. 2530.00
Commode, Neoclassical, Variegated Gray & White Marble Top, Cream Paint, 35 In. 2650.00
Commode, Neoclassical, Walnut, Ribbon Parquetry, Italy, 36 1/2 x 45 1/2 In. 3960.00
Commode, Pine, Poplar, Chamfered Corners, Zoar, Ohio, 34 3/4 In. 330.00
Commode, Pot, William IV, Mahogany, Round, Crotch Veneer Cupboard Door, 30 In. 880.00
Commode, Regency Style, 4 Drawers, Marble Top, Chinoiserie, 44 x 20 x 32 1/2 In. 4600.00
Commode, Regency, Kingwood, Walnut, 4 Drawers, Serpentine Top, 33 1/2 x 21 In. 2760.00
Commode, Renaissance Revival, Walnut, Marble Top, Marquetry Border, 28 In. 770.00
Commode, Restauration, Mahogany, 5 Drawers, Marble Top, France, 37 x 50 1/2 In. 1430.00
Commode, Rococo Style, Oak, Patinated, France, 1800-1810, 35 x 47 In. 4400.00
Commode, Rococo Style, Walnut, Bombe, Marble Top, Serpentine, Continental, 37 In. ... 1540.00
Commode, Rococo, 3 Graduated Drawers, Cabriole Legs, Gray, Blue Paint, 28 In., Pair .. 980.00
Commode, Rococo, Walnut, 3 Wavy Graduated Drawers, Molded Top, 32 x 21 In. 3450.00
Commode, Satinwood, Gilt, Gesso, White Marble Top, Victorian, 32 x 80 x 22 In. 5520.00
Commode, Walnut, 2 Drawers, Cube Parquetry, Italy, Late 18th Century, 32 x 51 In. 6900.00
Commode, Walnut, 3 Dovetailed Drawers, Victorian, 28 x 16 x 28 In. 275.00
Commode, Walnut, 3 Short Drawers, Molded Top, Late 18th Century, 44 In. 977.00
Commode, Walnut, 4 Drawers, Red Marble Top, France, 19th Century, 47 x 41 In. 2970.00
Commode, Walnut, Birch, 3 Drawers, Crossbanded Top, Burl Inlay, 32 1/4 In. 5750.00
Commode, Walnut, Carved, Marble Top, Overhanging Corners, c.1850, 28 In. 825.00
Commode, Walnut, Curly Maple Ends, Dovetailed Drawer, Ohio, 33 In. 250.00
Commode, William IV, Mahogany, Lift Top, Cupboard, Octagonal Base, 35 In. 2530.00
Commode, William IV, Rosewood, Round Molded Top, Plinth Base, 1835, 18 In. 230.00
Console, Andre Arbus, Marble, Wood Lacquer, Drawer, 1942, 25 3/4 In., Pair 4315.00
Console, Art Deco, Mahogany, 2 Short Drawers, Plinth Base, France, 29 x 19 In. 865.00
Console, Art Deco, Wrought Iron Support, Marble, France, 1925, 63 In. 4310.00
Console, Baroque, Beechwood, Serpentine White Marble Top, Fruit, Foliage, 37 In. 2750.00
Console, Biedermeier, Fruitwood, Drawer, Rectangular Ebonized Top, 31 In. 575.00
Console, Bird's-Eye Maple, Dark Orange, Black Diamonds, 3 Legs, W. Castle, 38 In. 6900.00
Console, D-Shaped Mirrored Top, Scrolled Frieze, Plinth Base, 61-In. Mirror, 30 In. 518.00
Console, Demilune, Gilt, Carved, Marble, 5 Scrolled Acanthus Legs, Italy, 47 x 24 In. ... 2185.00
Console, Empire Style, Walnut, Metal Mounted, Black Marble Top, 37 x 48 In. 935.00
Console, Empire, Fruitwood, Charcoal Gray Marble Top, Square Legs, 40 1/2 In. 1100.00
Console, Empire, Mahogany, Ormolu Mounts, Scrolled Legs, 36 x 50 x 19 In. 7975.00
Console, Empire, Mahogany, Rectangular Serpentine Top, Canted Corners, 36 In. 690.00
Console, French Provincial, Walnut, Gallery Top, Columnar Supports, 31 x 35 3/4 In. 1265.00
Console, French Revival, Round White Marble Top, Gold Swags, 1900, 27 In. 1495.00
Console, Giltwood, Marble Top, Cartouche Entwined Flowering Vines, 36 In. 5750.00
Console, Giltwood, Tropical Foliage, Cabriole Legs, Victorian, 30 3/4 x 38 x 14 In. 7425.00
Console, Hekman, Regency Style, Demilune Top, Drawer, Grille Front Door, 32 In. 290.00
Console, Louis Philippe, Mahogany, 3 Drawers, Rectangular Tan Marble Top, 36 In. 5060.00
Console, Louis XV Style, Wrought Iron, Gilt, Marble Top, 37 x 57 x 19 In. 7425.00
Console, Louis XV Style, Wrought Iron, Gilt, Marble, Scrolls, Flowers, 37 x 57 In. 5280.00
Console, Louis XV, Gilt, Serpentine Top, Cabriole Legs, 30 x 32 x 19 1/4 In. 1870.00
Console, Louis XV, Mahogany, Marble Top, Pierced Brass Gallery, 35 1/2 x 26 In. 4400.00

Console, Louis XV, Walnut, Serpentine Top, Scrolled Legs, Cartouche, 35 In., Pair 7150.00
Console, Louis XVI Style, Marble Top, Carved Frieze, Top-Shaped Feet, 31 x 40 In. 460.00
Console, Louis XVI, Fruitwood, Bowed Red Marble Top, 35 x 26 In. 4400.00
Console, Louis XVI, Walnut, Rectangular Rouge Marble Top, Floral Swags, 41 In. 920.00
Console, Louis XVI, Wood Demilune, Gray Marble Top, Scrolled Legs, 26 In., Pair 5175.00
Console, Neoclassical Style, Demilune, Gilt, Mermaids, Italy, 35 x 58 In., Pair 5500.00
Console, Neoclassical, Giltwood, Ebonized Marble Top, Figural Supports, 36 In. 4675.00
Console, Neoclassical, Giltwood, Rectangular Brown Fossilized Top, Italy, 30 In. 5750.00
Console, Neoclassical, Polychrome, Mottled Gray Marble Top, Italy, 37 In., Pair 6050.00
Console, Neoclassical, White Marble Top, Peg Feet, Green Paint, Italy, 34 x 19 In. 4025.00
Console, Paul Kiss, Wrought Iron, Marble, 1925, 34 x 24 1/2 In. 4140.00
Console, Regency Style, Marble Top, Serpentine, Late 19th Century, 74 x 32 In. 2970.00
Console, Regency, Black Marble D-Shaped Top, Grapevine Design, Paw Feet, 33 In. 1380.00
Console, Victorian Revival, Oak, Mirror, Cartouche, Putti, Griffins, 86 1/2 x 54 In. 8525.00
Console, William IV, Mahogany, Drawer, Rectangular Top, Ebony, 37 In. 3300.00
Cradle, Arched Paneled Hood, Cutout Handles, Rockers, c.1780, 29 x 44 In. 675.00
Cradle, Cutout Sides, Scalloped Rocker, Hood, c.1800, 14 x 17 In. 247.00
Cradle, French Provincial, Fruitwood, 1875-1900, 31 1/2 x 45 1/2 In. 550.00
Cradle, Gilt, Italian Garden Scenes, Venetian, 19th Century, 44 x 25 x 30 In. 1150.00
Cradle, Mahogany, Cutout Rockers, Dovetailed, Hood, Ex Ludlow, 44 In. 1210.00
Cradle, Mahogany, Heart Cutout Handles & Footboard, Hood, 1780, 41 In. 1800.00
Cradle, Pine, Baluster Turned Posts, Ball Finials, Red Over Black Paint, 32 1/4 In. 515.00
Cradle, Poplar, Scalloped Head & Footboard, c.1790, 20 In. 220.00
Cradle, Walnut, Dovetailed Case, Side Heart Cutouts, 19 x 41 In. 255.00
Cradle, Walnut, Heart-Shaped Handholds, Hood, Pa., c.1800, 50 In. 410.00
Cradle, Walnut, Paneled, Dovetailed, Red & Black Paint, 39 In. 275.00
Credenza, Classical Ruins, Floral, Marble, White Paint, 43 x 14 x 41 In. 385.00
Credenza, Florence Knoll, Rosewood, 5 Drawers, Marble Top, Steel Base, 38 In. 920.00
Credenza, Florence Knoll, Rosewood, Marble Top, 4 Doors, Steel Base, 1950s, 72 In. ... 2530.00
Credenza, Gothic Style, Oak, Iron Mounted Reticulated Doors, Victorian, 28 x 57 In. 550.00
Credenza, Oak, Keyed Tenons, Strap Hinges, N.V. Paerels, Amsterdam, 34 x 81 In. 2640.00
Credenza, Rococo, Rosewood, Serpentine Front, Marble Top, 34 x 67 In. 2860.00
Credenza, Walnut, Carved Eagle Crest, Victorian, 70 In., 2 Piece 3850.00
Credenza, Walnut, Drawer Over 2 Paneled Doors, Italy, 34 3/4 x 35 In. 3450.00
Credenza, Walnut, Marble Top, Grillwork Panel, Conforming Base, 1890s, 48 In. 485.00
Crib, Bentwood, Shell Shape, 1905, 76 In. 1380.00
Crib, Pierced & Carved Foliage Ends, Ribbon Bound Foliage, Hood, 1870s, 27 In. 5175.00
Cupboard, 12-Pane Door, Bracket Feet, 87 x 66 x 20 In. 3520.00
Cupboard, 2 Doors Over Shelf, 3 Drawers Over Paneled Doors, 67 x 87 In. 8525.00
Cupboard, Black Lacquer, Trompe L'Oeil Books On Door, Hong Kong, 47 In. 550.00
Cupboard, Blue & White Paint, Ireland, c.1840, 53 x 73 In. 3450.00
Cupboard, Cherry, 2 Doors, Painted Interior, Pa., 1820, 87 1/2 In. 2970.00
Cupboard, Cherry, Curly Maple, Paneled Doors, Turned Feet, 87 3/4 In. 7700.00
Cupboard, Cherry, Glass & Paneled Doors, 47 x 84 In., 2 Piece 3850.00
Cupboard, Cherry, Glazed Door, 4 Shelves, Divider Over 2 Doors, c.1825, 89 In. 9775.00
Cupboard, Chimney, Pine, Door, 3 Recessed Panels, Cutout Bracket Feet, 78 In. 1520.00
Cupboard, Chimney, Pine, Paneled Door, Cutout Feet, Blue Paint, 75 In. 525.00
Cupboard, Chippendale, 2 Doors, Dovetailed, Chamfered Corners, 32 x 19 x 15 In. 3080.00
Cupboard, Corner, 2 Doors, 8-Paned, Shelves, Stile Feet, White Paint, 85 In. 2185.00
Cupboard, Corner, 2 Doors, Black Molded Cornice, Yellow Paint, Pa., 1820, 76 In. 1430.00
Cupboard, Corner, Cherry, 2 Double Crotch Mahogany Doors, Shelves, 87 In. 6440.00
Cupboard, Corner, Cherry, 2 Long Doors, 3 Raised Panels, Bracket Base, 47 x 95 In. 2600.00
Cupboard, Corner, Cherry, 8-Pane Paneled Doors, 44 x 48 x 80 In. 2640.00
Cupboard, Corner, Cherry, 12-Pane Door, Scrolled Apron, Base Doors, 83 1/2 In. 6875.00
Cupboard, Corner, Cherry, Cornice Molded Case, Bracket Feet, 86 In. 4950.00
Cupboard, Corner, Cherry, Glazed Door, 12 Panes, 1830s, 83 1/2 In. 4368.00
Cupboard, Corner, Cherry, Glazed Door, Cavetto Cornice, 1800-1850, 83 x 48 In. 2415.00
Cupboard, Corner, Cherry, Poplar, 12-Pane Doors, Drawer, 54 x 83 In. 2640.00
Cupboard, Corner, Chippendale, Cherry, 12 Panes, Drawers, 2 Doors, 102 In. 9350.00
Cupboard, Corner, Chippendale, Mahogany, Paneled Doors, 90 In., 2 Piece 2420.00
Cupboard, Corner, Chippendale, Pine, Hinged Glazed Doors, 1780, 104 In. 5460.00
Cupboard, Corner, Chippendale, Walnut, Arched Door Over 2 Doors, 2 Piece ......*Illus* 6500.00
Cupboard, Corner, George III, Marble Top, Chinoiserie, 18th Century, 38 x 22 In. 1980.00

Furniture, Cupboard,
Corner, Chippendale,
Walnut, Arched Door
over 2 doors, 2 Piece

Furniture, Cupboard,
Corner, Walnut, 16 Panes,
Inlay, Shenandoah Valley

Cupboard, Corner, Hanging, Bleached Walnut, Door, Shenandoah Valley, 44 x 31 In. 1230.00
Cupboard, Corner, Hanging, Floral Design, 3 Butterfly-Shaped Shelves, 42 In. 1045.00
Cupboard, Corner, Hanging, Paneled Door, Fishtail Drop, Green Paint, 1800, 50 In. 5225.00
Cupboard, Corner, Hanging, Regency, Mahogany, 9 Glass Panes, 33 1/2 x 43 In. 935.00
Cupboard, Corner, Lid Cornice, 12-Pane Door, Raised Paneled Doors, Pa., 88 In. 3575.00
Cupboard, Corner, Mahogany, Upper Urn Finials, 3 Shaped Shelves, 93 In. 1380.00
Cupboard, Corner, Paneled Door, Molded Cornice, Cutout Bracket Feet, 87 In. 3960.00
Cupboard, Corner, Pine, 2 Doors, Molded Cornice, Early 19th Century, 89 In. 1725.00
Cupboard, Corner, Pine, 3 Shelves, Red, Brown Paint, 1780, 84 In. 7475.00
Cupboard, Corner, Pine, 9-Pane Door, 2 Raised Panels, Bracket Feet, 1810, 82 In. 2090.00
Cupboard, Corner, Pine, 10-Pane Glazed Doors, Bracket Feet, 1810, 86 1/2 In. 1760.00
Cupboard, Corner, Pine, Door, 4 Raised Panels, Yellow, Red Paint, 66 x 41 In. 3300.00
Cupboard, Corner, Pine, Glazed Door, Paneled Door, Side Panels, c.1800, 84 x 48 In. . . . 3450.00
Cupboard, Corner, Pine, Lower Paneled Door, Open Top, Red Paint, Pa., 79 In. 4270.00
Cupboard, Corner, Pine, Poplar, Scrolled Apron, 49 x 55 1/2 x 88 In. 4400.00
Cupboard, Corner, Poplar, 2 Doors, Painted Interior, Pa., 1825, 85 In. 4950.00
Cupboard, Corner, Poplar, Dark Red Finish, Bracket Feet, 84 1/2 In. 2750.00
Cupboard, Corner, Poplar, Doors, Stepped Raised Panels, Beveled Cornice, 84 In. 2860.00
Cupboard, Corner, Poplar, Split Paneled Door, Bracket Feet, Red Paint, 85 In. 3850.00
Cupboard, Corner, Red & Black Rosewood Grained, Pa., 1830, 78 x 43 In. 4290.00
Cupboard, Corner, Softwood, Cornice, Gray Paint, 1900, Child's, 57 3/4 x 25 In. 3080.00
Cupboard, Corner, Walnut, 3 Shelves, Red Paint, 1820, 82 x 54 In. 5175.00
Cupboard, Corner, Walnut, 16 Panes, Inlay, Shenandoah Valley . . . . *Illus* 4000.00
Cupboard, Corner, Walnut, Crest, Pane Door Over 2 Pressed Panels, Victorian, 79 In. 715.00
Cupboard, Corner, Walnut, Doors, Pierced Crest, Open Shelf, Moorish Arches, 75 In. 920.00
Cupboard, Corner, Walnut, Pine, 2 8-Pane Doors, Virginia, 19th Century, 82 In. 2520.00
Cupboard, Eastlake, Oak, 2 Doors, 19th Century, 82 1/2 x 41 x 18 In. 747.00
Cupboard, French Provincial, Oak, Rack, Pierced Spindles, 1800s, 30 x 35 x 16 In. 1035.00
Cupboard, French Provincial, Pine, Foliate Crest, Doors, Stile Legs, 88 x 53 In. 3740.00
Cupboard, French Provincial, Rectangular Top, 6 Drawers, Cabriole Legs, 75 In. 1006.00
Cupboard, Hanging, 2 Paneled Doors, Cove Cornice, Graining, Pa., 1850, 64 In. 880.00
Cupboard, Hanging, Corner, Oak, 2 Raised Paneled Doors, Continental, 47 1/2 In. 250.00
Cupboard, Hanging, Corner, Oak, Scrolled Crest, Vine, Berry Design, 1870, 39 In. 825.00
Cupboard, Hanging, Corner, Pine, Dentil Molded Cornice, Pa., 1800, 37 x 34 In. 935.00
Cupboard, Hanging, Pine, 2 Raised Paneled Doors Over 2 Drawers, Pa., 1835, 83 In. 660.00
Cupboard, Hanging, Pine, Door, Grain Painted, 19th Century, 30 1/2 x 22 In. 495.00
Cupboard, Hanging, Pine, Wood Turned Handle, Red Paint, Maine, 17 x 23 1/2 In. 1760.00
Cupboard, Hanging, Poplar, 3 Dovetailed Drawers, Brown Graining, 84 1/2 In. 1650.00
Cupboard, Hanging, Poplar, Brown Graining Over Red, Ohio, 91 In. 2100.00
Cupboard, Hanging, Step Back, Cherry, Poplar, 3 Dovetailed Drawers, Ohio, 81 In. 2970.00
Cupboard, Hanging, Step Back, Pine, Poplar, Red Flame Graining, Yellow, 84 In. 6875.00
Cupboard, Hanging, Wall, Pine, Red Paint, 33 x 24 x 9 In. 880.00
Cupboard, Hanging, Walnut, Double Doors, Leaded Glass Cornice, 30 3/4 In. 415.00
Cupboard, Hanging, Walnut, Poplar, 2 Glazed Doors, Recessed Bracket Feet, 87 In. 4400.00
Cupboard, Jacobean, Door, Turned Legs, England, 23 x 17 x 52 In. 550.00
Cupboard, Jelly, 2 Doors, 2 Drawers, Yellow Grain, Backsplash, Pa., 1840, 48 In. 715.00
Cupboard, Jelly, 2 Drawers Over 2 Doors, Backsplash, Grain Painted, 43 x 43 In. 630.00

Cupboard, Jelly, Cherry, 2 Drawers Over 2 Doors, Inner Shelves, 48 In. 860.00
Cupboard, Jelly, Pine, 2 Doors, Cutout Feet, Secret Compartment, 44 In. 910.00
Cupboard, Jelly, Pine, 2 Doors, Shaped Gallery, 2 Dovetailed Drawers, 52 In. 2200.00
Cupboard, Jelly, Pine, 2 Paneled Doors, 63 x 46 x 19 1/2 In. 415.00
Cupboard, Jelly, Pine, Poplar, 2 Drawers Over 2 Doors, Red Paint, Pa., 1830, 45 In. 1430.00
Cupboard, Jelly, Poplar, 2 Dovetailed Drawers, Yellow Paint, Pa., 58 In. 4400.00
Cupboard, Jelly, Poplar, 2 Drawers Over 2 Doors, Pa., 1830, 49 1/2 x 43 In. 935.00
Cupboard, Jelly, Walnut, 2 Panels In Each Door, Square Corner Posts, 51 In. 1650.00
Cupboard, Jelly, Yellow Pine, 2 Doors, Dowels, Mortise Design, 45 x 127 x 27 In. 335.00
Cupboard, Louis XV, Door, Serpentine Cornice, Drawer, Yellow, Venetian, 72 In. 865.00
Cupboard, Mahogany, 2 Doors, 15 Panes, Marble Top, 2 Drawers, Mirror, 91 In. 550.00
Cupboard, Maple, Pewter, 3 Open Shelves, Dark Red Paint, 81 In. 3300.00
Cupboard, Maple, Poplar, 3 Dovetailed Drawers, White Painted Interior, 88 In. 7425.00
Cupboard, Oak, Door, Turned Feet, Rope Pilasters, Continental, 20 x 35 x 59 In. 440.00
Cupboard, Open Shelves Over Hinged Door, Blue Paint, 79 x 42 x 14 In. 1100.00
Cupboard, Paneled Doors, Interior Shelves, Painted, Pa., c.1830, 84 In. 2530.00
Cupboard, Paneled Frieze, Gilt Carved Swags, Faux Marble Paint, 47 1/2 In. 1380.00
Cupboard, Pewter, Canted Back, Pine, 3 Open Shelves, Dark Finish, 1735, 74 x 49 In. ... 3190.00
Cupboard, Pewter, Hardwood, 2-Door Base, 3-Shelf Top, 36 x 16 x 81 In. 1430.00
Cupboard, Pewter, Poplar, Pine, Scalloped Top, Pa., Late 18th Century, 66 In. 7150.00
Cupboard, Pewter, Step Back, Spoon Rack, 2 Plate Racks, Red, 15 x 74 x 54 1/2 In. 600.00
Cupboard, Pine, 2 Doors Over 3 Short Drawers, Heart Design, 87 In. 2875.00
Cupboard, Pine, 2 Doors With 3 Panels, Molded Cornice, 1880s, 78 x 14 x 44 In. 1100.00
Cupboard, Pine, 2 Lower Doors, Shelf, 2 Drawers, Child's, 44 1/2 In. 600.00
Cupboard, Pine, 2 Paneled Doors, Cutout Bracket Feet, Red & Yellow Paint, 77 In. 4400.00
Cupboard, Pine, 2 Removable Doors, Red Lacquer, Chinese, 42 x 21 x 68 In. 440.00
Cupboard, Pine, 5 Spice & 1 Long Drawer, Blue Paint, 75 x 40 In. 5500.00
Cupboard, Pine, Door, Brown Graining, Chamfered Corners, Hanging, 15 x 21 In. 715.00
Cupboard, Pine, Door, Molded Cornice, 2 Cock-Beaded Shelves, 70 x 54 x 15 In. 920.00
Cupboard, Pine, Grain Painted, New England, Late 18th Century, 80 In., 2 Piece 1540.00
Cupboard, Pine, Paneled Door, Demilune, Bun Feet, England, 1850, 41 1/2 In. 2200.00
Cupboard, Pine, Paneled Door, Yellow & Salmon Graining, Pa., 1800, 31 In. 4125.00
Cupboard, Pine, Poplar, Horizontal Lower Doors, 4 Shelves, 1850s, 85 In. 960.00
Cupboard, Pine, Poplar, Paneled Door, Scrolled Apron, 22 x 19 1/2 x 33 In. 165.00
Cupboard, Poplar, 12 Pane Top, 2 Base Drawers, Brown Paint, 49 In. 880.00
Cupboard, Poplar, 12 Panes, 3 Drawers Over 2 Doors, c.1850, 84 x 54 In. 2420.00
Cupboard, Poplar, Overhanging Ogee Cornice, Canted Ends, 19th Century, 79 In. 315.00
Cupboard, Poplar, Rectangular Top, 2 Shelves, Black Paint, 1810, 42 In. 1955.00
Cupboard, Rectangular Top, 2 Doors, Block Feet, Continental, c.1850, 36 In., Pair 660.00
Cupboard, Renaissance Revival, Walnut, 2 Doors, 2 Drawers, Cornice, 59 x 104 In. 2475.00
Cupboard, Shaker, Pine, 2 Paneled Doors, Drawer, Hancock, 22 x 19 x 29 In. 825.00
Cupboard, Sheraton, Poplar, Paneled Doors, 15 Panes, Drawers, 86 In. 6325.00
Cupboard, Spice, George II, Walnut, Rectangular Molded Top, 3 Drawers, 1750, 37 In. .. 3220.00
Cupboard, Spice, Hanging, Ash, 6 Drawers, Pure Food & Spice, Cincinnati, Oh., 12 In. .. 577.00
Cupboard, Spice, Oak, Starburst Inlay, 10 Dovetailed Drawers, 13 x 19 In. 6875.00
Cupboard, Step Back, 4 Shelves, 2 Doors, Blue Paint, 82 x 48 In. 1045.00
Cupboard, Step Back, Ash, 2 Glass Doors, Pie Shelf, 83 x 44 1/2 In. 990.00
Cupboard, Step Back, Pine, 2 Doors Over 2 Drawers, Red Stain, 79 In. 4400.00
Cupboard, Step Back, Pine, 2 Plank Doors, 3 Open Shelves, Blue Paint, 67 1/2 In. 555.00
Cupboard, Step Back, Pine, Board & Batten Doors, Flame Graining, 76 In. 495.00
Cupboard, Step Back, Pine, Brown, Mustard, Green Over White, 92 x 42 x 22 In. 1680.00
Cupboard, Step Back, Pine, Paneled Door, 3 Shelves, Iron Hinges, 38 x 76 1/2 In. 3960.00
Cupboard, Step Back, Rectangular Top, 2 Short Drawers, Ball Feet, 44 x 98 In. 1610.00
Cupboard, Step Back, Walnut, 2 Glass, 2 Paneled Doors, Drawer, Child's, 31 x 18 In. ... 850.00
Cupboard, Step Back, Walnut, 2 Glazed Doors, Cutout Feet, 62 x 36 x 16 In. 2415.00
Cupboard, Step Back, Walnut, 3 Drawers, Gothic Door Panel, Child's, 13 x 9 x 19 In. ... 275.00
Cupboard, Step Back, White & Gray Paint, 1840, 71 In. 4300.00
Cupboard, Tiger Maple, Ogee Cornice, Cutout Feet, Painted, Pa., 1830, 80 In. 6600.00
Cupboard, Venetian Style, Polychrome, Scalloped, Serpentine Shelves, 74 In. 1320.00
Cupboard, Wallace Nutting, Pine, 1 Door Base, Open Scrolled Top ....*Illus* 4290.00
Cupboard, Walnut, 3 Shelves, Yellow & Orange, Mid-19th Century, 91 In. 7475.00
Cupboard, Walnut, Arched Paneled Doors, 3 Drawers, Pa., 88 1/2 x 54 In. 3300.00
Cupboard, Walnut, Beveled Glass Door Panes, 2 Paneled Drawers, 98 1/2 In. 990.00

Cupboard, Walnut, Cutout Feet, Brown Paint, Zoar, Ohio, 59 x 20 x 70 In. 6050.00
Cupboard, Willett, Hanging, Step Back, Cherry, 54 x 20 x 73 In., 2 Piece 825.00
Daybed, Beechwood, 2 Bolsters, 6 Cushions, Double Cane Ends, 35 1/2 In. 850.00
Daybed, Brass, Swan Finial, Cushion & Bolsters, France, 31 x 76 x 22 In. 760.00
Daybed, Directoire, Fruitwood, Padded Sides, Cushion, 1775-1800, 35 x 66 1/2 In. 2420.00
Daybed, E. Wormley, No. 3497, Mahogany, Upturned Arm, 29 In. 2875.00
Daybed, Elm, Scrolled Apron, Sword Legs, Inset Woven Mat, Chinese, 86 In. 330.00
Daybed, Empire, Rosewood, Scrolled Ends, Satinwood Stringing, 1830s, 78 In. 3740.00
Daybed, French Provincial, Free-Standing Columns, 37 1/2 x 70 1/2 In. 825.00
Daybed, G. Nelson, Birch, Brushed Chrome, Herman Miller, 28 In. 2970.00
Daybed, G. Stickley, No. 216, 5 Slats At Ends, Spring Seat, Cushion, 78 x 30 In. 3100.00
Daybed, Hairpin Legs, Removable Bolsters, Foam Rubber Mattress, 75 In. 2530.00
Daybed, L. & J.G. Stickley, Slant Back, Leather, 72 x 22 x 28 In. 1980.00
Daybed, Limbert, Oak, Curved Sideboards, Early 20th Century, 79 In. 865.00
Daybed, Limbert, Plank Head Board, Side Panels, Leather Cushion, 27 x 78 In. 1430.00
Daybed, Louis Philippe, Mahogany, Sleigh Shape, Classical Ormolu Mounts, 35 In. 2200.00
Daybed, Louis XV, Crackled Ivory Paint, Velvet Pillows, 67 x 27 x 35 In. 1495.00
Daybed, Mahogany, Paneled Sides, Carved Swan's Heads, 19th Century, 72 In. 140.00
Daybed, Maple, Ring Turned Crest Rail, Ball Finials, Late Empire, 78 1/2 In. 430.00
Daybed, Rounded Tops, Free-Standing Columns, Turret-Shaped Feet, c.1830, 70 1/2 In. . . 835.00
Daybed, Tiger Maple, Spindle Gallery Rails, Mid-19th Century, 74 1/2 In. 1150.00
Daybed, Van Der Rohe, Walnut, Leather Cushion, Bolster Pillow, 76 In. 6600.00
Daybed, Walnut, Baluster Ends, Paneled Head Board, 72 3/4 In. 725.00
Desk, Arne Vodder, Rosewood, 6 Locking Drawers, Book Shelf On Back, 56 1/2 In. 1540.00
Desk, Art Deco, Drop Front, Palisander, Parchment Veneer, 1925, France, 54 x 32 In. 1725.00
Desk, Art Deco, Oak, Center Drawer, 2 Drawers Each Side, France, 30 x 49 x 31 In. 865.00
Desk, Art Deco, Walnut, Cantilevered, U Shape, 1930s, 29 x 81 x 36 In. 3735.00
Desk, Arts & Crafts, Chalet, 3 Drawers, Trestle Sides, Scalloped Apron, 29 x 49 In. 385.00
Desk, Arts & Crafts, Copper Strap Hinges, Floral Design At Sides, Child's, 32 In. 440.00
Desk, Arts & Crafts, Double Pedestal, Slat Shelves, 30 x 43 1/2 In. 525.00
Desk, Arts & Crafts, Oak, Drawer, Wood Pulls, Rectangular Top, 1916, 29 In. 8005.00
Desk, Bent Willow Twig, Hinged Slope, X-Shaped Twig End & Supports, 33 In. 690.00
Desk, Biedermeier, Birch, Leather Lined Lift Top Writing Surface, 34 In. 3960.00
Desk, Biedermeier, Drop Front, Burl Olive Wood, 3 Fitted Drawers, 43 x 56 In. 1980.00
Desk, Birch Top, Pedestal, 4 Drawers, Bent Laminated U-Shaped Legs, 50 In. 2875.00
Desk, Birch, Table Top, Bi-Paneled Front, Interior Pigeonholes & Drawers, 26 1/2 In. 115.00
Desk, Burl, 5 Drawers, Leather Inset Top, Continental, Woman's, 30 In. 4800.00
Desk, Butler's, Drop Front, Tiger Maple, 5 Drawers, Ohio, 41 1/2 x 23 x 50 3/4 In. 1540.00
Desk, Butler's, Empire, Mahogany, Drop Front Drawer, Turned Feet, 43 x 45 In. 505.00
Desk, Butler's, Empire, Mahogany, Secretary Drawer, 3 Lower Drawers, 46 In. 1725.00
Desk, Butler's, Federal, 3 Drawers Over 4 Compartments, 1800, 44 In. 2530.00
Desk, Butler's, Federal, Mahogany, 6 Drawers, Molded Rectangular Top, 46 1/2 In. 546.00
Desk, Butler's, Federal, Mahogany, Overhanging Rectangular Top, 44 x 41 x 23 In. 920.00
Desk, Butler's, Sheraton, Mahogany, Fitted Tiger Maple Interior, 44 x 22 x 49 In. 2530.00
Desk, Carlton, Satinwood, Polychrome, Center Medallion, Victorian, 38 x 50 In. 10450.00
Desk, Carved Pillar, 2 Cupboard Doors, Continental, 53 x 28 In. 990.00
Desk, Charak, Federal, Mahogany, 4 Short Drawers, Tapered Legs, 30 In. 6900.00

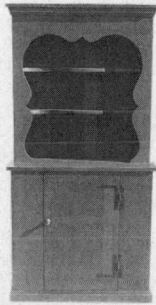

Furniture, Cupboard,
Wallace Nutting, Pine,
1 Door Base, Open
Scrolled Top

Furniture, Desk,
Chippendale, Slant Front,
Walnut, Cherry, 1780,
41 x 35 x 19 In.

Desk, Cherry, Compartments, Fold-Out Writing Surface, 1860, 65 x 36 x 23 In. 1210.00
Desk, Chippendale Style, Slant Front, Mahogany, 4 Drawers, Carved, c.1900, 39 In. 1650.00
Desk, Chippendale, Cherry, 2 Drawers, 4 Pigeonholes, Ogee Bracket Feet, 44 In. 4400.00
Desk, Chippendale, Slant Front, Birch, 3 Drawers, 2 Tiers, 42 1/2 x 39 1/2 x 19 In. 3738.00
Desk, Chippendale, Slant Front, Birch, 10 Interior Compartments, 1780, 44 In. 1955.00
Desk, Chippendale, Slant Front, Cherry, 4 Graduated Drawers, 40 x 34 x 18 In. 1870.00
Desk, Chippendale, Slant Front, Cherry, 4 Graduated Drawers, c.1780, 40 x 37 In. 3105.00
Desk, Chippendale, Slant Front, Cherry, 4 Graduated Thumb-Molded Drawers, 42 In. 2185.00
Desk, Chippendale, Slant Front, Cherry, 9 Drawers, Bracket Feet, 1770, 40 In. 6325.00
Desk, Chippendale, Slant Front, Cherry, Line Inlay, Pigeonholes, 41 x 39 x 22 In. 3300.00
Desk, Chippendale, Slant Front, Cherry, Molded Drawers, Fitted Interior, 41 In. 5390.00
Desk, Chippendale, Slant Front, Mahogany, 2 Drawers, Cabriole Legs, 1770, 45 In. 11500.00
Desk, Chippendale, Slant Front, Mahogany, 3 Concave Drawers, Bracket Feet, 42 In. 27600.00
Desk, Chippendale, Slant Front, Mahogany, 4 Drawers, Serpentine, Fitted, 36 x 42 In. ... 385.00
Desk, Chippendale, Slant Front, Mahogany, 4 Graduated Drawers, 41 x 21 x 33 In. 3300.00
Desk, Chippendale, Slant Front, Mahogany, 8 Drawers, Bracket Feet, 41 In. 2415.00
Desk, Chippendale, Slant Front, Mahogany, Flower Inlay, Leaves, Acanthus, 43 In. 730.00
Desk, Chippendale, Slant Front, Mahogany, Hinged Lid, 2 Drawers, 1770, 44 In. 4600.00
Desk, Chippendale, Slant Front, Mahogany, Reverse Serpentine, 1770, 43 x 42 In. 5500.00
Desk, Chippendale, Slant Front, Maple, 4 Graduated Drawers, Rectangular Top, 43 In. ... 3737.00
Desk, Chippendale, Slant Front, Maple, Curly Maple, 4 Drawers, 36 x 19 x 41 In. 2540.00
Desk, Chippendale, Slant Front, Maple, Curly Maple, 4 Drawers, 41 x 37 1/2 x 20 In. ... 3080.00
Desk, Chippendale, Slant Front, Rectangular Hinged Molded Top, Ogee Feet, 40 In. 9200.00
Desk, Chippendale, Slant Front, Tiger Maple, 4 Graduated Drawers, 44 In. 3737.00
Desk, Chippendale, Slant Front, Walnut, 4 Drawers, Reeded Pilasters, Pa., 44 In. 2200.00
Desk, Chippendale, Slant Front, Walnut, 4 Graduated Drawers, 1780, 42 x 45 In. 3025.00
Desk, Chippendale, Slant Front, Walnut, 4 Short Drawers, Bracket Feet, 42 In. 5750.00
Desk, Chippendale, Slant Front, Walnut, Cherry, 1780, 41 x 35 x 19 In. ....*Illus* 3737.00
Desk, Chippendale, Slant Front, Walnut, Mahogany, Poplar, Ogee Feet, 43 In. 8525.00
Desk, Chippendale, Slant Front, Wavy Birch, Late 18th Century, 42 1/2 x 36 x 17 In. 2070.00
Desk, Classical Revival, Slant Front, Mahogany, Grotesque & Foliate Carving, 42 In. 2420.00
Desk, Cylinder, Eastlake, Walnut, 4 Drawers In Each Pedestal, 51 x 55 In. 1430.00
Desk, Cylinder, Louis XVI Style, Mahogany, Chinoiserie Panel, Bronze, 42 In. 6900.00
Desk, Cylinder, Louis XVI Style, Mahogany, Gilt Bronze, Musical Trophy, 45 In. 11500.00
Desk, Cylinder, Oak, 3 Drawers, Door, Black Paint, 36 x 22 x 42 In. 220.00
Desk, Davenport, Eastlake, Lift Top, Pierced Gallery, 19th Century, 44 x 23 x 24 In. 1210.00
Desk, Davenport, Eastlake, Walnut, 4 Drawers, Shelves, Fitted Interior, 46 In. 460.00
Desk, Drawer, 4 Narrow Vertical Slats On Each Side, 28 x 36 x 22 1/2 In. 165.00
Desk, Drop Front, Mahogany, Drawer Over 2-Door Cupboard, Side Drawers, 55 In. 630.00
Desk, Drop Front, Mahogany, Fitted Interior, 3 Drawers, 41 x 34 In. 180.00
Desk, Drop Front, Walnut, Fitted Interior, Burl Door & Drawer Front, 1860s, 65 In. 4200.00
Desk, Drop Front, Walnut, Interior Prospect & Document Drawers, c.1840, 44 In. 1045.00
Desk, E. Wormley, Rosewood, Walnut, 3 Drawers, H-Stretcher Base, 74 In. 2300.00
Desk, Edwardian, Mahogany, Marquetry, Leather Lined Top, 42 In. 1430.00
Desk, Edwardian, Satinwood, Oval, Tooled Leather Top, Cabinet Doors, 31 In. 10725.00
Desk, Elm, 5 Drawers, Ching Dynasty, 50 x 23 x 33 In. 1035.00
Desk, Escritoire, Adams Revival, Satinwood, Brocade Surface, Woman's, 44 In. 2185.00
Desk, Escritoire, T. Brooks, Rosewood, Carved, Brooklyn, N.Y., Victorian, 74 In. 3740.00
Desk, Federal, Drop Front, Cherry, Interior Drawers, Over 4 Drawers, 44 x 39 In. 2185.00
Desk, Federal, Mahogany, 3 Dovetailed Drawers, Woman's, 40 x 22 x 57 In. 1925.00
Desk, Federal, Mahogany, 3 Inlaid Doors Over Upper Case, Inlaid Legs, 49 1/2 In. 690.00
Desk, Federal, Mahogany, Inlay, Hinged Lid, Felt Surface, c.1800, 47 x 41 In. 1725.00
Desk, Federal, Slant Front, Birch, 4 Graduated Drawers, 1800, 43 x 39 x 19 1/2 In. 2530.00
Desk, Federal, Slant Front, Mahogany, Birch, Oxbow, 1780, 43 1/2 x 40 In. ....*Illus* 4025.00
Desk, Federal, Slant Front, Mahogany, Fitted Interior Over 4 Drawers 42 x 22 In. 2240.00
Desk, Federal, Slant Front, Mahogany, Graduated Drawers, 44 x 42 In. 4600.00
Desk, Federal, Slant Front, Maple, 4 Drawers, New England, c.1820, 44 x 39 x 20 In. ... 4312.00
Desk, Floral & Landscape, Overall Gilt, 32 x 54 In. 920.00
Desk, G. Nakashima, Walnut, Pedestal ....*Illus* 7840.00
Desk, G. Nelson, Steel, White Laminate Top, Orange & Green Drawers, 42 In. 690.00
Desk, G. Nelson, Walnut Veneer, 2 Drawers, Chrome Pulls & Legs, 69 In. 660.00
Desk, G. Stickley, Chalet, Inside Gallery, Shoe Feet, Chamfered Back, 46 x 24 In. 2750.00
Desk, G. Stickley, Drop Front, 4 Drawers, Gallery Interior, Decal, 43 x 32 x 16 In. 1100.00

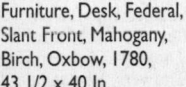

Furniture, Desk, Federal,
Slant Front, Mahogany,
Birch, Oxbow, 1780,
43 1/2 x 40 In.

Furniture, Desk, G. Nakashima,
Walnut, Pedestal

Desk, G. Stickley, Drop Front, Drawer, 2 Cabinet Doors, Gallery, c.1901, 38 In. 8250.00
Desk, G. Stickley, No. 650, Drawer, Rectangular Top, 1916, 30 In. 900.00
Desk, G. Stickley, No. 709, 5 Drawers, Copper Pulls, 29 x 42 In. 1100.00
Desk, G. Stickley, No. 729, 2 Half & 3 Full Drawers, Slab Sides, 37 x 15 x 45 In. 3850.00
Desk, George II, Standup, Oak, Lift Top, Hepplewhite Legs, 39 x 30 In. 660.00
Desk, George III, Mahogany, 2 Drawers, Rectangular Leather Inset Top, 30 In. 920.00
Desk, George III, Mahogany, Tambour Lid, 3 Hinged Compartments, 37 In. 8625.00
Desk, George III, Slant Front, Mahogany, Boxwood Inlay, 43 1/2 x 42 1/4 In. 1955.00
Desk, George III, Slant Front, Oak, Drawers, Fitted Interior, Pigeonholes, 42 In. 2420.00
Desk, George IV, Slant Front, Walnut, Ivory Escutcheon, Turned Legs, 35 x 34 In. 935.00
Desk, Golden Oak, Slant Front, Fitted, Stencil, Cabriole Front Legs, 1910, 31 x 42 In. . . .   275.00
Desk, Gothic Revival, Drop Front, Oak, Drawer, England, 39 x 33 In. 880.00
Desk, Hepplewhite, Mahogany, 3 Over 2 Drawers, Inlay, England, 51 x 24 In. 880.00
Desk, Hepplewhite, Slant Front, Cherry, 4 Graduated Drawers, 41 x 40 x 21 In. 1650.00
Desk, Hepplewhite, Slant Front, Crotch Mahogany Veneer, 4 Drawers, 36 x 45 In. 1760.00
Desk, Herman Miller, Cast Aluminum Legs, Laminated Top, Action Office, 49 In. 1380.00
Desk, Heywood-Wakefield, Drawer, Rectangular Top, Squat Oval Feet, 43 x 29 In. 288.00
Desk, Heywood-Wakefield, Drop Front, 3 Drawers, Open Shelves, 42 x 60 x 13 In. 440.00
Desk, Industrial Art, Lewis E. Myers & Co., Drop Front, Rectangular Legs, 43 In. 258.00
Desk, Kneehole, Arts & Crafts, Blind Center Drawer, 2 Side Drawers, 42 In. 660.00
Desk, Kneehole, Chinoiserie, Black Lacquer, Casters, 1850-1900, 31 1/2 x 46 In. 4600.00
Desk, Kneehole, Chippendale, Oak, 8 Drawers, Central Cabinet, England, 32 1/2 In. 990.00
Desk, Kneehole, Compartments Each Side, Sliding Lid, 29 x 66 1/2 In. 1495.00
Desk, Kneehole, George II Style, Black Lacquer, Chinoiserie, England, 50 In. 9200.00
Desk, Kneehole, George III, Parcel Gilt, Black Japanned, 2 Doors, 29 x 35 In. 2760.00
Desk, Kneehole, Mahogany, Leather, 20th Century, England, 35 x 29 In. 410.00
Desk, Kneehole, Poplar, 8 Drawers, Scrolled Base Apron, 26 x 54 In. 660.00
Desk, Kneehole, Rectangular Top, Pastoral Italian Scene, Frieze Of Putti, 29 x 28 In. 2200.00
Desk, Kneehole, Renaissance Revival, Walnut, Upper Gallery, 52 x 56 1/2 In. 1540.00
Desk, Kneehole, Walnut, Center Drawer, 2 Drawers, Flowering Vine Band, 40 In. 475.00
Desk, Kneehole, William & Mary, Walnut, Parquetry, Chevron Banding, 31 In. 5405.00
Desk, L. & J.G. Stickley, Drop Front, Mahogany, 2 Open Shelves, 35 In. 1840.00
Desk, L. & J.G. Stickley, Drop Front, Walnut, Handcraft, 39 1/2 x 29 1/2 x 17 In. 1430.00
Desk, L. & J.G. Stickley, Rectangular Top, 1912, 29 In. 520.00
Desk, Lap, 3 Inkwells, Pen Holder, Drawer, Compartment, Brass Handles, 12 In. 290.00
Desk, Lap, Black Lacquer, Abalone Inlay, Painted Castle Top, Velvet Surface, 21 In. 395.00
Desk, Lap, Black Lacquer, Fruit Sprays, Lakeshore Scene, Crane, 6 In. 315.00
Desk, Lap, Burl Elm, Brass Mounted, England, 18 In. 175.00
Desk, Lap, Folding, Mahogany, Brass Mounts, 4 1/4 x 14 x 9 1/2 In. 165.00
Desk, Lap, George II, Mahogany, Brassbound, 1800, 6 3/4 x 19 1/2 In. 330.00
Desk, Lap, Mahogany, Brass Bail Handles, 22 1/2 x 11 x 7 In. 165.00
Desk, Lap, Mahogany, Rectangular Top, Leather Interior, Victorian, 24 1/2 x 11 In. 1160.00
Desk, Lap, Rosewood, Bone Inlay, Ebony Bands, Keys, England, c.1855, 16 x 10 In. 1100.00
Desk, Lap, Slant Front, Sandalwood, Fitted For Implements, 16 1/2 In. 230.00
Desk, Lift Top, Black Lacquer, Well & Compartments, Velvet Interior, 29 x 24 In. 275.00
Desk, Limbert, Drop Front, Oak, Drawer, 34 1/2 x 18 1/4 In. 1210.00
Desk, Limbert, No. 718, 2 Drawers, Central Pen Tray, Mich., 1912, 38 x 36 x 20 In. 1090.00
Desk, Limbert, No. 727, Drawer, Drop Front, Gallery Top, Plank Legs, 40 x 33 In. 990.00

Desk, Lion & Dragon, Bone & Ivory Inlay, Japan, 52 x 45 In. 1870.00
Desk, Louis XV, Fruitwood, Inset Leather Top, Cabriole Legs, 31 In. 1265.00
Desk, Louis XVI, Marquetry, Bombe, Floral Garland, Woman's, 36 In. 1100.00
Desk, M. Breuer, Birch, 4 Drawers, Rectangular, Bryn Mawr, 50 x 29 In. 3300.00
Desk, Mahogany, Center Drawer, Banks Of Drawers, Leather, 19th Century, 49 In. 3100.00
Desk, Mahogany, Easel Top, Henry Walling, 1775-1800, 36 x 52 In. 19800.00
Desk, Mahogany, Henry IX Style Frieze, Leather Top, Double Pedestal, 31 x 63 In. 2420.00
Desk, Oak, Drawer, Rectangular Top, Domed Splat, Plinth Base, 30 x 45 In. 460.00
Desk, Oak, Stool, Divided Hinged Slope, Interior Over Cabinet Doors, 56 1/4 In. 2300.00
Desk, Partners, George III, Mahogany, 3 Drawers, Leather Top, 1785, 32 x 72 In. 7425.00
Desk, Partners, George III, Mahogany, Leather Top, 2 Doors, 30 In. 9200.00
Desk, Partners, George III, Mahogany, Rectangular Molded Top, 31 x 68 In. 8050.00
Desk, Partners, Georgian, Mahogany, 3 Drawers, Gadroon Edge, 32 3/4 In. 7150.00
Desk, Partners, Georgian, Mahogany, 4 Drawers, Rectangular Leather Top, 30 In. 3680.00
Desk, Partners, Limbert, 2 Letter Holders, Slat Stretcher, Trestle Legs, 39 x 38 In. 2090.00
Desk, Partners, Mahogany, 3 Drawers One Side, Door Other Side, Leather Top, 60 In. ... 4025.00
Desk, Partners, Mahogany, Inset Leather, Carved Pedestals, c.1870, 33 In. 455.00
Desk, Partners, Mahogany, Leather Lined Top, Victorian, 30 x 71 In. 4620.00
Desk, Partners, Oak Veneer, Oval, Ornate Carving, Claw Feet, 61 x 38 In. ....*Illus* 3575.00
Desk, Partners, Paine Furniture Co., 29 x 56 x 36 In. 1100.00
Desk, Partners, Regency, 5 Drawers, Rectangular Top, 20th Century, 31 x 45 In. 385.00
Desk, Partners, Renaissance Revival, Walnut, Burl Panels, 32 x 55 x 34 In. 4125.00
Desk, Partners, William IV, Mahogany, Tooled Leather Top, 29 3/4 In. 2990.00
Desk, Pedestal, George III, Mahogany, Drawer, Rectangular Leather Top, 30 x 72 In. 9775.00
Desk, Pedestal, Georgian Revival, Mahogany, Leather Lined Top, 30 x 47 In. 800.00
Desk, Pine, Dovetailed Lift Top, Fitted Interior, 48 1/2 x 18 1/2 In. 440.00
Desk, Plantation, Cherry, 2 Drawers Under Double Door, 1 Pane, 77 In. 495.00
Desk, Plantation, Poplar, 6 Panes, Beveled Cornice, 66 1/2 In. 550.00
Desk, Plantation, Slant Front, Turned Legs, Cross Stretcher, Painted, 39 x 39 In. 635.00
Desk, Post Office, Oak, Drawer, 34 Pigeonholes, 62 x 36 In. 400.00
Desk, Queen Anne, Cherry, 7 Drawers, 8 Pigeonholes, Bracket Feet, 1770, 43 In. 3080.00
Desk, Queen Anne, Slant Front, Mahogany, 3 Short Drawers, Hinged Lid, 42 In. 8625.00
Desk, Queen Anne, Slant Front, Maple, 1730-1750, 41 x 33 3/4 x 18 In. ....*Illus* 6325.00
Desk, Queen Anne, Slant Front, Maple, 2 Graduated Drawers, Child's, 20 x 19 x 11 In. .. 2530.00
Desk, Queen Anne, Slant Front, Walnut, 4 Graduated Drawers, Bracket Feet, 42 In. 7425.00
Desk, Queen Anne, Walnut, Table Top, 2 Drawers, Inkwell, Pa., 1760, 16 1/2 In. 2530.00
Desk, Regency Style, Oak, Shell & Flower, Cabriole Legs, 31 1/2 x 55 x 33 In. 2760.00
Desk, Regency, Mahogany, Gilt Metal Rail, Tooled Leather Writing Surface, 39 In. 1150.00
Desk, Regency, Mahogany, Interior Compartments, 21 x 18 In. 415.00
Desk, Rococo, Slant Front, Rosewood, Pierced Carved Crest, Woman's, 46 In. 2860.00
Desk, Roll Top, G. Nelson, Walnut Tambour Door Top, 49 x 32 x 29 In. 690.00
Desk, Roll Top, G. Nelson, Walnut, Filing System, 49 In. 2012.00
Desk, Roll Top, Mahogany, Rectangular Top, Fitted Interior, Victorian, 34 x 24 In. 1495.00
Desk, Roll Top, Oak, Dovetailed Drawers, Tambour Base Drawer, Fitted Interior, 47 In. .. 990.00
Desk, Roll Top, Oak, Rectangular Top, Drawer, Interior Compartments, 49 In. 575.00
Desk, Roll Top, Pedestal, Quartered Oak, Cabinet, Boston, Late 19th Century, 68 In. 2760.00
Desk, Roll Top, S Roll, Mahogany, Fitted, 2 Pedestal, 4 Drawers, Privacy Panel, 60 In. ... 2310.00
Desk, Rosewood, Central Cabinet, Urn Marquetry, Leather Inset, Work Basket, 42 In. 970.00

Furniture, Desk, Partners, Oak
Veneer, Oval, Ornate Carving, Claw
Feet, 61 x 38 In.

Furniture, Desk,
Queen Anne, Slant
Front, Maple, 1730-1750,
41 x 33 3/4 x 18 In.

Desk, Roycroft, Drop Front, Drawer, Strap Hardware, Mackmurdo Feet, 44 x 38 In. 8800.00
Desk, Satinwood, Leather Top, Center Drawer, 3 Graduated Drawers, 1900, 29 In. 3105.00
Desk, Schoolmaster's, Hinged Lid, Walnut, Turned Legs, 1830, 37 x 30 x 24 In. 605.00
Desk, Schoolmaster's, Lift Top, Pine, Pigeonholes, Mustard Paint, 45 x 27 In. 550.00
Desk, Schoolmaster's, Pine, Lift Top, Interior Pigeonholes, Drawers, c.1830, 35 In. 495.00
Desk, Schoolmaster's, Slant Front, Pine, Poplar, Dark Red Paint, 42 In. 660.00
Desk, Schoolmaster's, Slant Front, Yellow Pine, Tapered Legs, 34 x 31 1/2 x 20 In. 335.00
Desk, Schoolmaster's, Walnut, Gallery, Pigeonholes, 36 x 24 x 37 In. 275.00
Desk, Secretary, Hepplewhite, Tambour Door, 2 Inlaid Drawers, 44 x 36 In. 1100.00
Desk, Secretary, Molded Cornice, 2 Paneled Doors, Lancaster, 1790, 35 x 14 In. 7150.00
Desk, Secretary, Sheraton, Mahogany, 2 Mullioned Doors, 1810, 85 x 40 In. 6050.00
Desk, Shaker, Cherry, Drawer, Lift Top, Compartments, c.1830, 51 x 31 x 20 In. 2875.00
Desk, Slant Front, Cherry, Cutout Gallery, Red, Fitted, Dovetailed, 18 x 18 In. 415.00
Desk, Slant Front, Cherry, Fitted Interior, Cheney, Connecticut, 43 x 40 x 21 In. 2750.00
Desk, Slant Front, Cherry, Pigeonholed Interior, 4 Drawers, Ball Feet, 1790, 40 In. 1100.00
Desk, Slant Front, Cherry, Scalloped Ends, 1815, Child's, 32 x 24 In. 357.00
Desk, Slant Front, Drawer, Mass., Early 1800s, 36 1/2 x 38 1/2 x 18 In. 1265.00
Desk, Slant Front, Figured Maple, 6 Interior Pigeonholes & Drawers, 1780, 42 In. 7475.00
Desk, Slant Front, Mahogany, 4 Graduated Drawers, Bracket Feet, 42 1/4 In. 865.00
Desk, Slant Front, Mahogany, Copper Gallery, 3 Drawers, 1900, Woman's, 42 x 31 In. ... 415.00
Desk, Slant Front, Mahogany, Fitted Interior, 3 Drawers, Bracket Feet, c.1760, 29 In. 9200.00
Desk, Slant Front, Mahogany, Step-Down Interior, 4 Molded Drawers, 39 x 31 In. 2750.00
Desk, Slant Front, Maple, 4 Graduated Thumb-Molded Drawers, 1790, 47 1/2 In. 17250.00
Desk, Slant Front, Maple, Fitted Interior, 4 Graduated Drawers, c.1800, 39 x 35 In. 5225.00
Desk, Slant Front, Maple, Scalloped Apron, 4 Dovetailed Drawers, 43 1/2 In. 1615.00
Desk, Slant Front, Pine, Drawer, Pa., 1750, 38 1/2 x 24 In. 2200.00
Desk, Slant Front, Tiger Maple, 10 Interior Drawers Red Wash, 1790, 38 In. 3410.00
Desk, Slant Front, Tiger Maple, Fitted Interior, Bracket Feet, c.1770, 42 1/2 In. 4145.00
Desk, Slant Front, Tiger Maple, Maple, 10 Pigeonholes, 5 Drawers, 41 In. 3960.00
Desk, Slant Front, Tiger Maple, Stepped Interior, Document Drawers, 44 1/4 In. 6325.00
Desk, Slant Front, Walnut, Crossbanded Lip, Stepped Serpentine Interior, 39 In. 3300.00
Desk, Student's, Slant Front, Walnut, Plank Ends, 1830s, 26 x 47 1/2 In. 660.00
Desk, Tambour, Tiger Maple, Banded Inlay, Mass., 1800, 6 1/2 x 11 In. 935.00
Desk, Thonet, Tubular Steel, 3 Drawers Right Side, Painted Wood, 1930, 54 In. 2070.00
Desk, Twin Pedestal, Mahogany, Oak, Leather Inset Top, Victorian, 33 1/2 x 70 In. 2420.00
Desk, Walnut, 2 Arched, Glazed Doors, Serpentine Front, Bracket Feet, 1860, 87 In. 1100.00
Desk, Walnut, 4 Drawers, Pullout Writing Surface, Victorian, Woman's, 41 1/2 In. 390.00
Desk, Walnut, Clerk's, Slanted Writing Surface, Interior Storage, Pen Drawers, 46 In. 1380.00
Desk, Walnut, Poplar, 2 Drawers, Molded Top, 74 x 31 x 27 In. 920.00
Desk, Walnut, Relief Carved Allegorical Figures, England, c.1900, 59 x 31 In. 1495.00
Desk, William & Mary, Slant Front, Walnut Veneer, 4 Drawers, Turned Feet, 40 In. 5175.00
Desk, Wolverine, 5 Drawers, Inset Top, Slat Sides, Decal, 29 1/2 x 42 x 26 In. 385.00
Desk, Wooton, Burl Walnut Panels, Hinged Doors, Fitted, 1876-1880, 72 In. 11500.00
Desk-Bookcase, Drop Front, Walnut, 2-Door Top, Pigeonholes, Victorian, 84 x 48 In. 550.00
Desk-Bookcase, Federal, Cherry, Poplar, 6 Doors, Reeded Panels, c.1820, 80 x 39 In. 5175.00
Desk-Bookcase, Mahogany, 2 Glazed Doors, 3 Drawers, c.1825, 79 x 36 x 19 In. 2990.00
Desk-Bookcase, Queen Anne, Painted Oriental Scenes, Spain, 40 x 34 x 17 In. 895.00
Desk-Bookcase, Slant Front, Mahogany, Mullioned Doors, Fitted Interior, 86 In. 4312.00
Dinette Set, Chrome Plated, Laminated Leaf Design Top, 35 x 48 In., 5 Piece 175.00
Dinette Set, Maple, Plank Seat, Leaves, Step Back Chairs, 42 In., 5 Piece 345.00
Drawing Board, Adjustable, Shelf With Drawer, Washburn Shops, 33 In. 415.00
Dresser, Arts & Crafts, 2 Half Over 2 Full Drawers, Swivel Mirror, 70 In. 1045.00
Dresser, Classical, Mahogany, Rectangular Black Mirror, 1825, 63 In. 3000.00
Dresser, Empire, Mahogany, 3 Over 4 Drawers, Gilt Bronze, France, 82 In. 3300.00
Dresser, Empire, Mahogany, 4 Over 2 Drawers, Turned Columns, Mirror, 77 3/4 In. 1000.00
Dresser, Empire, Mahogany, 5 Drawers, Carved, Swing Mirror, 54 x 72 In. 545.00
Dresser, Federal, Mahogany, 4 Drawers, 2 Acanthus Leaf Columns, 1840, 42 In. 1000.00
Dresser, Frank Lloyd Wright, 11 Graduated Drawers, 62 x 28 In. 1760.00
Dresser, Gilt Design, Lyre Mirror, Inlaid Pulls, Azull, 37 In. 5700.00
Dresser, Gothic Revival, Mahogany, 2 Drawers, Marble, Mirror, 87 x 52 In. 1430.00
Dresser, Mahogany, 3 Drawers, Marble Top, Floral Marquetry, 43 x 36 x 22 In. 1650.00
Dresser, Mahogany, 4 Drawers, Brass Hardware, Carved Bracket Feet, c.1930, 38 In. 515.00
Dresser, Mahogany, 5 Veneer Drawers, Serpentine Marble Top, 81 x 21 1/2 In. 6612.00

Dresser, Mixed Woods, Walnut Stain, 3 Drawers, Child's, 37 x 22 In. 1200.00
Dresser, Neogrecque, Maple, Ebonized, Gilt, Marble Top, Mirror, 106 x 62 In. 4400.00
Dresser, Oak, Welsh, 3 Frieze Drawers, Square Feet, 18th Century, 81 In. 6900.00
Dresser, Regency, Burl Veneer, Mahogany, Serpentine, Marble Top, 90 x 48 In. 2350.00
Dresser, Renaissance Revival, Rosewood, Marble Topped Pedestals, 83 x 63 In. 4950.00
Dresser, Renaissance Revival, Walnut, Marble Top, Candle Shelves, Mirror, 92 In. 1120.00
Dresser, Stickley Brothers, 2 Over 2 Drawers, Attached Mirror, 68 x 43 x 22 In. 1925.00
Dresser, Stickley Brothers, 5 Drawers, Glasgow Rose, Mirror, 63 x 44 x 22 In. 6050.00
Dresser, Walnut Veneer, 4 Drawers, Ornate Top With Acanthus Leaves, 85 In. 1175.00
Dresser, Walnut, Marble Top, Carved Pulls, Handkerchief Drawers, Mirror, 73 In. 360.00
Dresser, Walnut, Marble Top, Handkerchief Drawer, Mirror, 84 In. 1760.00
Dresser, Welsh, Oak, 3 Aligned Drawers Rectangular Top, Bracket Feet, 39 In. 8050.00
Dry Sink, Down-Swept Supports, Shelf, Zinc Lined Sink, Paneled Doors, 47 In. 630.00
Dry Sink, High Back, 2 Lower Sunken Paneled Doors, Pa., 1850, 51 x 48 3/4 In. 600.00
Dry Sink, Hinged Lid, 2 Drawers, Squiggle Design To Panels, 1840, Pa., 35 In. 1815.00
Dry Sink, Hutch, Walnut, Poplar, Red & White Paint, 50 x 18 1/4 x 54 In. 770.00
Dry Sink, Oak, Drawer, 2 Doors, High Back With Shelf, Copper Liner, 47 x 19 In. 525.00
Dry Sink, Pine, 2 Drawers, Mustard Paint, Pa., 1860, 42 1/2 In. 605.00
Dry Sink, Pine, Drawer, 2-Door Base, Interior Yellow Paint, York County, 33 x 51 In. 660.00
Dry Sink, Pine, Hinged Lid, Drawer, Cupboard, 19th Century, 30 x 29 x 18 In. 385.00
Dry Sink, Pine, Hinged Lid, Paneled Cupboard Doors, 19th Century, 30 In. 275.00
Dry Sink, Pine, Paneled Doors, Copper Lined Top, 42 x 16 x 21 In. 660.00
Dry Sink, Pine, Well Over 2 Cupboard Doors, Red Paint, Pa., 1830, 34 In. 1045.00
Dry Sink, Pine, White Over Green Paint, Pa., 1840, 30 x 37 1/2 In. 550.00
Dry Sink, Poplar, Drawer Over 2 Recessed Paneled Doors, 1850, 33 x 43 In. 880.00
Dry Sink, Poplar, Drawer Over Well, 2 Doors, Pa., 19th Century, 47 x 44 In. 275.00
Dry Sink, Poplar, Lift Top, Scalloped Sides, 2 Doors, 81 x 47 x 20 In. 1065.00
Dry Sink, Poplar, Ocher Graining, Pa., 19th Century, 33 x 43 In. 550.00
Dumbwaiter, George III, Mahogany, Graduated Tiers, Pad Feet, 1780s, 41 In. 2875.00
Dumbwaiter, Mahogany, 3 Graduated Round Tiers, Turned Pedestal, c.1800, 41 In. 1760.00
Dumbwaiter, Mahogany, Drop Sides, 3 Splayed Legs, Brass Casters, 37 In. 460.00
Easel, Ebonized, Incised Portfolio, Ratchet Mechanism, Brass Mounted, 83 In. 1100.00
Easel, Forged Steel, Patinated Bronze, Pierced Foliate Scroll, 66 x 28 In. 520.00
Easel, Neogrecque, Ebonized, Brass Mounts, Griffins, Gold Brocade, 82 3/4 In. 2640.00
Easel, Oak, Brush Tray, Suspended Cabinet With 3 Swing Drawers, Cupboard, 80 In. 235.00
Easel, P. Evans, Steel, Gesso, 2 Feet, Tall Spine, 1970, 31 x 70 In. 2200.00
Easel, Regency, Faux Bamboo Standards, 66 In. 75.00
Easel, Rosewood, Carved, Inlay, Brass Center Track, Double, N.Y., c.1875, 86 In. 22000.00
Etagere, Black Forest, Winged Dragon, Mirror, Jardiniere, Plant Stand, 92 In. 3850.00
Etagere, Briar, Metal, Malabar, Ettore Sottsass, 1982, 94 x 100 In. 6900.00
Etagere, Eastlake, Walnut, 3 Drawers Over 3 Doors, Gilt, Ebonized Panels, 70 In. 3400.00
Etagere, Edwardian Style, Walnut, 2 Shelves, Baluster Supports, c.1900, 24 x 24 In. 550.00
Etagere, Edwardian, Bamboo, Black Lacquer, Turned Supports, Spiral Reeds, 36 In. 1600.00
Etagere, Egyptian Revival, Mahogany, Ivory Egyptian Women Facing Back, 98 In. 5175.00
Etagere, George III Style, Mahogany, 4 Tiers, 2 Drawers, Turned Posts, 58 In. 1380.00
Etagere, George IV, Mahogany, 4 Tiers, Pierced Gallery, Lower Drawer, 60 1/2 In. 5750.00
Etagere, Kingwood, 3 Shelves, Tulipwood Parquetry, 32 1/2 x 20 1/2 In. 6900.00
Etagere, Kingwood, Tiers, Bronze Molding, 2 Flaps, Inner Storage Wells, 26 1/2 In. 1200.00
Etagere, Louis Philippe, Mahogany, 2 Shelves, Marble Top, 42 x 24 x 16 In. 3900.00
Etagere, Mahogany, 3 Rectangular Tiers, Peg Feet, Casters, Victorian, 39 1/2 In. 4025.00
Etagere, Mahogany, Ebony, 5 Tiers, 2 Drawers, Bun Feet, 56 1/2 In. 3735.00
Etagere, Napoleon III, Burr Elm, 3 Tiers, Gallery, Bronze Inlay, Finials, 33 In. 630.00
Etagere, Oriental, Cherry, Center Mirror, Black Paint, c.1900, 69 x 38 1/2 In. 450.00
Etagere, Regency, Mahogany, 3 Tiers, Casters, 38 x 18 In. 1430.00
Etagere, Regency, Mahogany, 4 Tiers, 66 x 4 3/4 x 30 1/2 In. 6900.00
Etagere, Rosewood, 3 Rectangular Tiers, Brass Caps, Casters, 1850, 37 In. 5460.00
Etagere, Rosewood, 3 Tiers, Fretwork Gallery, Drawer, Casters, Victorian, 42 x 20 In. . . . 1650.00
Etagere, Teakwood, 3 Stepped Shelves, Drawer & Door, Chinese, 19th Century, 61 In. . . . 1375.00
Etagere, Walnut, 3 Shelves, Grape & Vine Pierced Crest, 1870, 88 x 48 In. 3300.00
Etagere, Walnut, Classical Maidens Holding Torches, 2 Doors, 1900, 67 x 13 In. 460.00
Etagere, Walnut, Gallery, 3 Conforming Drawers Over 3 Shelves, c.1870, 42 1/2 In. 1495.00
Etagere, William IV, Mahogany, 3 Tiers, 1840s, 41 1/2 In. 6900.00
Etagere, Wrought Iron, Twisted Rope, Tassel Finials, Gilt, 32 x 26 1/2 x 8 In. 230.00

Fainting Couch, Walnut, Tufted Back, Velvet, 70 In. 550.00
Footstool, Arts & Crafts, Inverted V Aprons, Upholstered Inset Top, 16 x 19 In. 330.00
Footstool, Arts & Crafts, Splayed Sides, Teardrop Cutouts, 26 x 17 In. 467.00
Footstool, Arts & Crafts, Stretchers, Leather Seat, 16 x 21 In. 195.00
Footstool, Arts & Crafts, Tapered Posts, Leather, 20 x 17 In. 140.00
Footstool, Classical, Mahogany, Foliate Apron, Needlepoint, 18 In. 1092.00
Footstool, Classical, Mahogany, Scrolled Legs, Upholstered, c.1835, 25 x 17 In. 1380.00
Footstool, Club, Jacobean Legs, Pillow Top, Leather, 21 x 16 x 16 In. 450.00
Footstool, G. Stickley, Mahogany, Turned Legs, Leather Seat, 15 x 21 x 17 In. 440.00
Footstool, G. Stickley, No. 301, Leather Over Straight Apron, 15 x 16 In. 605.00
Footstool, Giltwood, Faux Bamboo, Velvet, France, 8 x 40 x 9 1/2 In. 545.00
Footstool, Hardwood, Horseshoe Shape, Good Luck, Velvet, 13 x 13 In. 110.00
Footstool, Horn Legs, Hide, Western Style, 1920s, 10 In. 77.00
Footstool, L. & J.G. Stickley, 2-Board Stretchers, Brown Suede, Decal, 18 x 14 In. 210.00
Footstool, L. & J.G. Stickley, Mahogany, Arched Apron, Leather Seat, 15 x 19 In. 220.00
Footstool, L. & J.G. Stickley, No. 394, 15 x 19 x 15 In. 495.00
Footstool, Leather, Early 20th Century, 12 x 21 In. 395.00
Footstool, Limbert, Drawer, Leather Top, 13 x 18 x 12 In. 2200.00
Footstool, Louis XV Style, Painted Frieze, Flowers, Upholstered Top, 18 x 7 In. 370.00
Footstool, Mahogany, Scroll & Anthemion Carved Base, Needlepoint, 23 In. 550.00
Footstool, Mahogany, Sleigh Bed Shape, Scrolled Ends, Block Feet, c.1830 .... 545.00
Footstool, Pine, Curved Cutout Ends, 7 1/8 x 13 1/2 In. 110.00
Footstool, Pine, Salmon Graining, Light Ground, Cutout Feet, 7 x 13 x 7 1/2 In. 247.00
Footstool, Regency, Mahogany, Leopard Top, Beige Suede Canted Sides, 9 In., Pair 2760.00
Footstool, Rosewood, Convex Rails, Berlin-Work Padded Top, Victorian, 37 3/4 In. 345.00
Footstool, Roycroft, Inset Vinyl Seat, Orb & Cross Mark, 14 x 17 x 12 In. 990.00
Footstool, Sheraton, Hickory, Brass Tacks, Oval Needlepoint, 6 1/2 x 12 1/2 In. 305.00
Footstool, Walnut, Scrolled Apron, Cutout Feet, 7 x 16 1/2 x 7 In. 220.00
Frame, Art Nouveau, Giltwood, 12 3/4 x 9 1/4 In. 88.00
Frame, Empire, Rope Twisted Half Columns, 39 1/2 In. 80.00
Frame, Rococo, Giltwood, Scrolled Foliage, Gilt Surface, Italy, 1900, 48 1/2 In. 1265.00
Game Table, Anglo-Indian, Brass, Mother-Of-Pearl, Foldover Top, 40 x 27 3/4 In. 978.00
Hall Rack, Eagle Crest, Mirror, 8 Hooks, Umbrella Stand, Iron, Painted, 1880s, 75 In. ... 770.00
Hall Stand, Art Deco, Chrome, Center Mirror, Hat Shelf, Disk-Shaped Hooks, 72 In. 3740.00
Hall Stand, Art Deco, Wrought Iron, Mirror, 2 Umbrella Stands, France, 1925, 71 In. 2875.00
Hall Stand, Carved, Rouge Marble Top, Chinese, 19th Century, 32 x 12 x 17 In. . .230.00 to 470.00
Hall Stand, Colonial Revival, Golden Oak, Crest, Mirror, Bench, Hooks At Sides, 91 In. . 5040.00
Hall Stand, Jean Lucien, Streamline, Chrome Aluminum, Hat Pegs, 1935, 70 In. 805.00
Hall Stand, Mahogany, Lift Seat, Horizontal Beveled Mirror, Brass Hangers, 86 In. 985.00
Hall Stand, Mahogany, Lift Seat, Umbrellas, Hats & Coats, Beveled Mirror, 75 In. 410.00
Hall Stand, Oak, Hinged Seat, Mirror, 4 Coat Hooks, c.1900, 21 x 77 In. 375.00
Hall Stand, Oak, Lift Seat, Brass Fittings, Floral On Panels, Beveled Mirror, 80 In. 495.00
Hall Stand, Rococo, Iron, Umbrella Stand, Mirror, Painted, 77 1/2 In. ....*Illus* 990.00
Hall Stand, Walnut, Elaborate Pierced Back, Mid 19th Century, 87 x 35 1/2 In. 1210.00
Hall Stand, Walnut, Faux Bamboo Platform, Portugal, 95 In. 825.00
Hall Tree, Bear Climbing Tree, Cub On Top, Glass Eyes, Mirror, 32 x 83 In. 11550.00
Hall Tree, Eastlake, Walnut, Walnut Burl, Cast Iron Drip Pan, 1870s, 85 1/2 In. 1695.00

Furniture, Hall Stand,
Rococo, Iron, Umbrella
Stand, Mirror, Painted,
77 1/2 In.

Furniture, Hutch Table,
Hepplewhite, Gray Paint,
Smoke Design,
29 x 52 x 38 In.

Hall Tree, Iron, Naturalistic Trees, Shell-Shaped Drip Pan, 73 In., Pair 2175.00
Hall Tree, Limbert, No. 229, Branded, 71 1/2 In. 935.00
Hall Tree, Stickley Brothers, No. 175, 71 1/2 x 24 x 12 In. 470.00
High Chair, Ladder Back, Walnut, Mahogany, Rush Seat, 19th Century, 35 In. 385.00
High Chair, Maple, Chestnut, Arched Backrest, Plank Seat, 1730s, 35 3/4 .... 4315.00
High Chair, Windsor, Bamboo Turning, Black Paint, Varnish, Stencil, 21 1/2 x 33 In. 430.00
Highboy, Chippendale Style, Walnut, 11 Drawers, Bonnet Top, Cabriole Legs, 83 In. 4025.00
Highboy, Chippendale, Cherry, Brass, Connecticut, 42 1/4 In. 1380.00
Highboy, Chippendale, Walnut, 3 Over 2 Over 3 Drawers, Flat Top, 74 1/2 In. 11215.00
Highboy, Curly Maple, 4 Overlapping Lower Drawers, Duck Feet, 74 In. 6600.00
Highboy, Eldred Wheeler, Queen Anne Style, Cherry, 11 Drawers, Fan Carved, 71 In. 2200.00
Highboy, Mahogany, 3 Over 3 Drawers, Scrolled Top, 73 x 38 In. 1625.00
Highboy, Queen Anne, Mahogany, 2 Over 3 Long Drawers, Cabriole Legs, 61 x 33 In. ... 280.00
Highboy, Queen Anne, Mahogany, 2 Short Over 5 Long Drawers, 74 In. 690.00
Highboy, Queen Anne, Maple, 6 Over 3 Drawers, Flat Top, Cabriole Legs, 67 In. 5175.00
Highboy, Queen Anne, Tiger Maple, 10 Drawers, Flat Top, Cabriole Legs, 71 In. 4070.00
Highboy, Queen Anne, Walnut, 3 Graduated Drawers, Swan's Neck, 81 1/2 In. 3990.00
Highboy, William & Mary, 2 Over 3 Over 3 Drawers, Black & Red Paint, 61 In. 10450.00
Highboy, William & Mary, Burl, 2 Upper & 3 Long Drawers, 63 In. 2530.00
Highboy, William & Mary, Walnut, 5 Drawers, 6 Trumpet Legs, Ball Feet, 68 In. 5500.00
Hoosier Cabinet, Folding Work Table, Tinplate, Painted, 76 x 36 x 18 In. 2850.00
Hoosier Cabinet, Oak, 4 Drawer Bins, 45 x 25 x 70 In. 385.00
Hoosier Cabinet, Oak, Graniteware, 5 Blind Doors, 4 Drawers, Board, 71 x 40 In. 950.00
Huntboard, Mahogany, Sheraton, 2 Drawers, Brasses, 36 1/2 In. 3520.00
Hutch, Cherry, 6-Pane Astragal Doors, 3 Drawers, 1800-1850, 88 In. 6900.00
Hutch, Pine, Brown Stain, 60 x 38 1/2 x 30 In. 1320.00
Hutch, Pine, Maple, Round Overhanging Top, 4 Square Legs, 29 x 44 In. 800.00
Hutch, Pine, Poplar, Hardwood, 44 x 26 In. 1430.00
Hutch, Pine, Yellow & Brown Graining, Paneled Ends, Hinged Seat, 39 x 58 In. 1870.00
Hutch, Watch, Pine, Glazed, Lollipop-Shaped Backboard, Painted, 16 x 7 In. 3735.00
Hutch, Yellow Pine, Red Paint, 19th Century, 30 x 60 1/2 In. 1230.00
Hutch Table, Hepplewhite, Gray Paint, Smoke Design, 29 x 52 x 38 In. ....*Illus* 7150.00
Iron, Stand, Fishbowl, Gilt, Rope Twist Shaft, Square Base, Victorian 70.00
Iron, Stand, Plant, Circular Copper Basin, Black Paint, 3 Incurving Legs, 46 x 19 In. 2990.00
Kas, Pine, Heavily Chamfered Corners, Compass Rays On 2 Doors, c.1800, 58 In. 550.00
Kas, Pine, Molded Cornice, 2 Painted Doors, Chamfered Corners, 1800, 65 In. 660.00
Kneeling Bench, Prie-Dieu, Louis Philippe, Walnut, Ebonized, Brass Inlay, 36 In. 1980.00
Lectern, Arts & Crafts, Oak, Square Slant Front, Open Shelf, c.1920, 43 In. 345.00
Lectern, George III, Mahogany, Fluted Frieze, Paneled Front, Sides, 49 In. 1380.00
Lectern, Walnut, Architectonic Shape, Sloped Bookrest, Arched Panel, 43 x 40 In. 1030.00
Library Steps, George III, Mahogany, 1811, 36 In. 8625.00
Linen Press, Charles II Style, Oyster Veneer, 3 Drawers, Geometric Inlay, 77 In. 2310.00
Linen Press, Chippendale, Gumwood, 4 Drawers, Ogee Bracket Feet, 78 In. 6900.00
Linen Press, Dutch Rococo, Walnut, Bombe, Arched Cornice, Swelled Base, 96 In. 7150.00
Linen Press, Frieze Over Front, Bi-Paneled Doors, 6 Trays, Casters, 78 In. 4315.00
Linen Press, George III Style, Mahogany, 2 Over 2 Drawers, 2 Doors, 79 x 51 In. 5060.00
Linen Press, George III, Mahogany, 4 Drawers, Half Drawers Inside 2 Doors, 81 In. 2640.00
Linen Press, George III, Mahogany, 6 Drawers, Paneled Doors, 79 x 51 1/2 In. 3960.00
Linen Press, George III, Mahogany, Dentil Cornice, Fluted Frieze, 75 1/4 x 51 In. 7150.00
Linen Press, George III, Mahogany, Rectangular Dentil Cornice, 84 x 24 In. 6325.00
Linen Press, George IV, Mahogany, 2 Graduated Drawers, 85 x 22 1/2 In. 3680.00
Linen Press, Georgian, Mahogany, 2 Paneled Doors, 3 Graduated Drawers, 82 In. 1380.00
Linen Press, Hepplewhite, Cherry, Poplar, Molded Top, 2 Doors, 82 x 40 1/2 In. 1460.00
Linen Press, Hepplewhite, Mahogany, Flat Top, 2 Doors, French Feet, 1890, 45 In. 1345.00
Linen Press, L. & J.G. Stickley, Shelves, Open Bottom, Handcraft, 55 x 48 x 18 In. 3300.00
Linen Press, Mahogany, 2 Short & 1 Long Drawer, Recessed Doors, c.1780, 75 In. 3520.00
Linen Press, Mahogany, 3 Drawers, 2 Doors, String Inlay, Crossbanded, 86 In. 1570.00
Linen Press, Maple, Frieze Drawer, Wood Screw With Acorn Finial, 50 1/2 In. 287.00
Linen Press, Queen Anne Style, Oyster Veneer, 4 Drawers, 2 Doors, 79 x 45 In. 6325.00
Linen Press, Regency, Hardwood, Sunburst Doors, 4 Drawers, Anglo-Colonial, 83 In. ... 11550.00
Linen Press, Shaker, Pine, 6 Nailed Drawers, 2 Doors, Red Stain, 54 x 19 x 74 In. 3025.00
Linen Press, Triple-Paneled Doors, Inner Shelves, Quarter-Column Stiles, 71 In. 2070.00
Linen Tree, Limbert, Tapered Post, Brass Hooks, Dark Finish, 69 In. 470.00

Love Seat, Club, 2 Cushions, Leather, 56 x 31 x 31 In. 920.00
Love Seat, Floral, Down & Feather Pillows, 60 In. . . . . .690.00 to 920.00
Love Seat, George III, Rectangular Padded Back, Cushions, 56 In. 488.00
Love Seat, Heywood Bros. & Co., Wicker, Cushion, Victorian, 32 x 48 x 24 In. 2200.00
Love Seat, Rococo, Rosewood, Fruit Carved Crest, Upholstered, Arms, 42 x 64 In. 3410.00
Lowboy, George III, Oak, Drawers, Willow Brasses, Scalloped Apron, c.1780, 30 In. 2305.00
Lowboy, Queen Anne Style, Maple, 1 Over 3 Drawers, Fan Carving In Center, 30 In. 825.00
Lowboy, Queen Anne, Curly Maple, 2 Drawers, Slipper Feet, 35 3/4 x 37 3/4 In. 1760.00
Lowboy, Queen Anne, Inlaid Walnut, 3 Drawers, Shaped Skirt, Cabriole Legs, 28 In. 2200.00
Lowboy, Queen Anne, Walnut, 2 Drawers, Scroll Molded Skirt, Carved Shell, 29 In. 2990.00
Lowboy, Walnut, 1 Long, 3 Small Drawers, Chippendale Brasses, Phila., 32 x 31 In. 2970.00
Lowboy, William & Mary, Walnut, Drawer, Trumpet Legs, Ball Feet, 28 x 31 In. 1100.00
Mirror, Aesthetic Revival, Walnut, Stylized Flower Heads, c.1875, 23 x 29 In. 315.00
Mirror, Arched Crest Over Molded Amber Outer Frame, Venetian, 55 x 28 In., Pair 1380.00
Mirror, Art Deco, Everglades Scene, Flamingos, Flowers, American, 26 x 44 1/4 In. 230.00
Mirror, Art Deco, Light Mahogany, Molded Stepped Frame, France, 42 x 36 In. 145.00
Mirror, Art Deco, Wrought Iron, Diamond-Shaped Frame, Tendrils, Scrolls, 62 In. 1035.00
Mirror, Arts & Crafts, Wall, Oak Frame, Rectangular, Early 20th Century, 40 In. 172.00
Mirror, Baroque, Brass, Foliate Scrolled Crest, Canted Frame, Italy, 51 1/4 x 30 In. 2185.00
Mirror, Baroque, Foliate Carved Frame, Rectangular, 58 x 39 In. 1955.00
Mirror, Baroque, Giltwood, Rays Of Light Frame, Round, Italy, 23 1/2 In. 360.00
Mirror, Belle-Epoque, Giltwood, Gilt Gesso, Asymmetrical Cartouche Plate, 60 In. 3450.00
Mirror, Biedermeier, Stylized Fruitwood, Ebony Frame, 31 x 41 In. 1840.00
Mirror, Biedermeier, Walnut, Rectangular, Tapered Pilasters, 52 1/4 In. 1265.00
Mirror, Bird's-Eye Maple, Rectangular, Ogee Frame, Victorian, 25 x 27 In. 345.00
Mirror, Brass, Repousse, Foliate Molded Frame, 18th Century, 25 In. 175.00
Mirror, Bronze, Lily Pads & Frogs, 13 1/2 x 14 1/2 In. 145.00
Mirror, Carved Spread-Winged Eagle, 2 Cornucopia, Gold, 20th Century, 26 x 25 In. 415.00
Mirror, Charles X, Classical Medallions, Anthemia, Cream Paint, 66 1/2 x 37 In. 990.00
Mirror, Charles X, Giltwood, Ogee Frame, Classical Designs, 59 x 34 In. 825.00
Mirror, Cheval, Framed Plate, Trestle Base, 70 1/4 In. 1450.00
Mirror, Cheval, Mahogany, Columnar Supports, Ogee Frame, 19th Century, 71 In. 1540.00
Mirror, Cheval, Oval Plate, Gadroon Frame, Flowering Urn, Lotus Feet, 70 1/2 In. 990.00
Mirror, Cheval, Victorian Style, Brass, Balustrade, Splayed Legs, 77 1/2 In. 260.00
Mirror, Cheval, Walnut, Triple Arch, Candle Branches, Floral Marquetry, 83 1/2 In. 2645.00
Mirror, Chinese Chippendale, Bamboo, Phoenix Birds, 19th Century, 48 x 26 In. 670.00
Mirror, Chippendale Style, Walnut, Arched Fretted Crest, Eagle, 36 1/2 x 19 In. 230.00
Mirror, Chippendale, Curly Maple, Scroll, 30 1/2 x 16 3/4 In. 385.00
Mirror, Chippendale, Giltwood, Carved, Scrolling Leaves, Eagle, c.1850, 64 x 44 In. 3450.00
Mirror, Chippendale, Mahogany On Pine, Scroll, Gilt Phoenix, 26 x 14 1/2 In. 3575.00
Mirror, Chippendale, Mahogany Veneer, Fret Glass, Gilt Trim, 30 1/8 x 18 In. 590.00
Mirror, Chippendale, Mahogany Veneer, Scrolled Crest, 36 x 19 In. 1210.00
Mirror, Chippendale, Mahogany, Carved Phoenix Bird Over String Liner, 46 In. 2300.00
Mirror, Chippendale, Mahogany, Carved, Scrolled, Pierced, c.1790, 27 x 18 In. 635.00
Mirror, Chippendale, Mahogany, Gilt Gesso, Pierced Phoenix Crest, 37 x 18 In. 545.00
Mirror, Chippendale, Mahogany, Gilt Gesso, Pierced Crest, Phoenix Bird, 28 In. 460.00
Mirror, Chippendale, Mahogany, Gilt Gesso, Scrolled Frame, Gilt Eagle, 1800, 40 In. 1495.00
Mirror, Chippendale, Mahogany, Gilt Phoenix Bird, Gilt Liner, Gilt Gesso, 17 In. 260.00
Mirror, Chippendale, Mahogany, Giltwood, Carved Phoenix Bird, 1810, 33 In. 747.00
Mirror, Chippendale, Mahogany, Parcel Gilt, Gesso, c.1790, 29 x 14 1/2 In. 230.00
Mirror, Chippendale, Mahogany, Parcel Gilt, Plumes, c.1790, 34 x 17 1/2 In. 230.00
Mirror, Chippendale, Mahogany, Parcel Gilt, Scalloped, Gilt Edge, 1775, 51 In. 5750.00
Mirror, Chippendale, Mahogany, Pierced Gilt Phoenix, Late 18th Century, 56 In. 2185.00
Mirror, Chippendale, Mahogany, Rectangular, Beveled Glass, 35 1/2 x 20 In. 690.00
Mirror, Chippendale, Mahogany, Scalloped Crest & Ears, Pa., 1780, 32 In. 880.00
Mirror, Chippendale, Mahogany, Scroll Cut, 1790, 18 x 11 1/2 In. 330.00
Mirror, Chippendale, Mahogany, Scrolled Crest, Gilt Eagle, c.1790, 22 1/2 In. 275.00
Mirror, Chippendale, Mahogany, Scrolled Crest, Phila., 1780, 37 x 19 1/2 In. 4025.00
Mirror, Chippendale, Mahogany, Scrolled Frame, Bird Cutout, 24 x 15 In. 4890.00
Mirror, Chippendale, Mahogany, Scrolled Frame, Molded, 1810, 33 x 17 In. 2760.00
Mirror, Chippendale, Mahogany, Scrolled Fretwork, 18 1/2 x 11 1/2 In. 154.00
Mirror, Chippendale, Mahogany, Veneer, Scrolled Crest & Pediment, 40 In. 2415.00
Mirror, Chippendale, Mahogany, Winged Eagle Over Arched Crest, 1765, 42 In. 4180.00

Mirror, Chippendale, Walnut, Parcel Gilt, Gilt Incised Liner, 43 1/4 x 24 3/4 In. 2415.00
Mirror, Chippendale, Walnut, Rectangular, Fretted Crest, Skirt, 34 1/2 In. 230.00
Mirror, Chippendale, Walnut, Scrolled Frame, 19th Century, 43 x 21 1/2 In. 3105.00
Mirror, Classical Style, Giltwood, Shield Shape, Fleur-De-Lis, 36 x 24 In. 305.00
Mirror, Classical, Gilt Gesso, Eagle, Cornucopias, 26 x 25 In. 220.00
Mirror, Classical, Giltwood, Split Baluster Frame, Ebonized, 23 1/4 x 57 In. 330.00
Mirror, Classical, Mahogany, Convex Molded Frame, c.1830s, 44 x 23 In. 935.00
Mirror, Classical, Reeded Styles, Acanthus Leaf & Drape, Fruit Urn & Flowers, 46 In. 415.00
Mirror, Convex, Applied Composition Flags & Shield, Gold Paint, 24 x 18 In. 65.00
Mirror, Convex, Balls On Frame, Eagle Finial, 38 1/2 x 33 1/2 In. 385.00
Mirror, Convex, Gilt, Eagle Top, 32 1/2 x 18 1/2 In. 575.00
Mirror, Convex, Regency, Giltwood, Acanthus Plumes, Black Ground, 48 1/4 In. 3960.00
Mirror, Copper, Hammered, Green, Rectangular, Round Blue Ornament, 35 In. 1955.00
Mirror, Demilune, Cast Gray Metal, Putti & Man In Moon, 12 3/4 In. 110.00
Mirror, Dressing, Empire, Bowfront, Carved & Reeded Supports, 32 x 26 1/2 In. 1430.00
Mirror, Dressing, Empire, Mahogany, Ogee, Beveled Mirror, 69 x 33 In. 495.00
Mirror, Dressing, Federal, Inlaid Mahogany, Satinwood Banding, 31 x 24 In. 635.00
Mirror, Dressing, Federal, Mahogany, 1800, 24 x 16 x 11 3/4 In. 420.00
Mirror, Dressing, George III, Mahogany, Rectangular, Beveled Glass, 22 In. 345.00
Mirror, Dressing, George IV, Mahogany, Reeded Supports, Base Drawer, 24 x 27 In. 423.00
Mirror, Dressing, Hepplewhite Style, Mahogany, 2 Drawers, Brass Pulls, 20 x 20 In. 137.50
Mirror, Dressing, Hepplewhite, Bleached Mahogany, Bun Feet, 1800, 25 x 19 In. 395.00
Mirror, Dressing, Mahogany Veneer, 2 Drawers, Ogee Bracket Feet, American, 19 In. 440.00
Mirror, Dressing, Mahogany, Dolphin Supports, Paw Feet, 76 In. 5500.00
Mirror, Dressing, Mahogany, Rectangular, String Frame, 3 Short Drawers, 24 In. 258.00
Mirror, Dressing, Scarlet Japanned, Chinese Figures, c.1725, 22 x 16 3/4 In. 1035.00
Mirror, Dressing, Walnut Frame, Acanthus Carved Legs, France, c.1930, 74 In. 690.00
Mirror, Ebonized Walnut, Figural Putti, Birds, Leaves, Oval, 1875-1900, 65 x 48 In. 10350.00
Mirror, Edgar Brandt, Wrought Iron, Flower Heads, 2 Ball Feet, 1925, 12 In. 2587.00
Mirror, Embossed & Punched Tin, Black Frame, 69 3/4 x 30 1/2 In. 385.00
Mirror, Empire, 3 Sections, Acorn Drops, Half Columns, 27 x 67 In. 495.00
Mirror, Empire, Cornice & Acorn Pendants, Half Columns, 1835, 46 x 27 In. 935.00
Mirror, Empire, Floral, Scrolled Gilt Design, 37 x 49 In. 345.00
Mirror, Empire, Fruitwood, Cupid Presenting A Flower, Giltwood, 63 In. 1610.00
Mirror, Empire, Giltwood, 3 Sections, Half Columns, Corner Blocks, 47 In. 525.00
Mirror, Empire, Giltwood, Floral & Leaf Columns, Corner Rosettes, 31 x 21 In. 220.00
Mirror, Empire, Giltwood, Molded Cornice, Rope Twist Borders, 31 In. 1095.00
Mirror, Empire, Giltwood, Rectangular, Various Classical Designs, 66 In. 3080.00
Mirror, Empire, Mahogany, 2 Panels, Canal Scene Lithograph On 152 1/2 x 25 In. 143.00
Mirror, Empire, Mahogany, 2 Swing-Style Candle Arms, Giltwood Swag, 50 In. 1840.00
Mirror, Empire, Mahogany, Cherub Crest, Floral Volutes, 77 1/2 x 23 1/2 In. 2530.00
Mirror, Empire, Mahogany, Ogee Molded Frame, 32 1/4 x 24 1/4 In. 150.00
Mirror, Empire, Pine, Reverse Painted Houses, Fluted Frame, 21 x 13 In. 155.00
Mirror, Empire, Sheraton, Rosewood, Cornice, Reeded Capitals, 37 x 18 In. 275.00
Mirror, Federal Style, Giltwood, Eagle & Wheat Pediment, 50 x 28 In. 1320.00
Mirror, Federal Style, Mahogany, Parcel Gilt, Swan's-Neck Crest, Eagle, 46 In. 200.00
Mirror, Federal Style, Shield Shape, Wire & Composition Design, c.1930, 26 In. 260.00
Mirror, Federal, Architectural, Giltwood, Eglomise Reverse Painted Ship, 37 x 20 In. 440.00
Mirror, Federal, Architectural, Giltwood, Reverse Painted, Eglomise Flowers, 49 In. 660.00
Mirror, Federal, Eglomise Panel, Ship & House, 1810, 31 x 15 In. 220.00
Mirror, Federal, Eglomise Panel, Ships In Harbor, Reeded Pilasters, 37 x 19 In. 220.00
Mirror, Federal, Gilt Gesso, American Naval Battle Scene, 1820, 35 1/2 x 16 In. 1610.00
Mirror, Federal, Gilt Gesso, Carved Wood Eagle, Molded Frame, 1830, 33 In. 4480.00
Mirror, Federal, Gilt Gesso, Sailing Ship Panel, Applied Balls, 31 x 20 In. 1955.00
Mirror, Federal, Giltwood, Ebony, Convex, Spread-Winged Eagle, N.Y., 1815, 50 In. 6900.00
Mirror, Federal, Giltwood, Eglomise Panel, Harbor Scene, Boston, 48 x 28 In. 2090.00
Mirror, Federal, Giltwood, Figural Urn, Bird Crest, 53 x 33 In. 660.00
Mirror, Federal, Half Spindle, Rosette Corner, Black Paint, 1840, 27 x 18 1/2 In. 600.00
Mirror, Federal, Mahogany, Carved Turned Side Columns, Brass Rosettes, 38 x 22 In. 385.00
Mirror, Federal, Pine, Reverse-Painted Tablet Over Mirror, c.1820, 29 x 15 In. 230.00
Mirror, Federal, Spool Frame, Block, Rosette Corners, 1845, 41 x 28 3/4 In. 1320.00
Mirror, Federal, Urn Shape, Floral Swags, Scrolled Frame, 23 1/2 x 43 1/2 In. 430.00
Mirror, Floral & Urn Crest, Painted, Early 20th Century, 37 x 19 In. 50.00

Mirror, Frankl, Silver Leaf, Round, 1930, 46 In. 6325.00
Mirror, Fruitwood, Winged Griffin, Tail Curling At Bottom, 34 x 23 In. 400.00
Mirror, G. Nakashima, Holly Wood, Free-Edge Side Rails, 38 1/4 x 21 1/2 x 4 In. 1700.00
Mirror, G. Stickley, Rectangular, Angled Shoe Feet, 21 In. 690.00
Mirror, George II Style, Giltwood, Oval, Female Mask, Acanthus Leaves, 68 x 42 In. 7475.00
Mirror, George II Style, Mahogany, Parcel Gilt, Rocaille, Garlands, 51 x 28 In. 575.00
Mirror, George II, Mahogany, Rectangular, Pierce Carved Crest, 1765, 45 In. 1495.00
Mirror, George II, Mahogany, Scalloped Crest, Parcel Gilt, 42 x 25 In. 430.00
Mirror, George II, Walnut, Parcel Gilt, Prince Of Wales Feathers, 28 x 16 In. 1035.00
Mirror, George III Style, Giltwood, Oval, Scrolls, 1825-1850, 60 x 36 In. 3960.00
Mirror, George III, Gilt Gesso, Ho-Ho Bird Suspending Garlands, 63 x 33 In. 1265.00
Mirror, George III, Giltwood, Drapery Swag Looped Through Spiral Husks, 39 In. 345.00
Mirror, George III, Giltwood, Floral, Foliate Urn, Beveled Glass, 30 In., Pair 11500.00
Mirror, George III, Giltwood, Scroll & Floral, 19th Century, 70 x 50 In. 5520.00
Mirror, George III, Giltwood, Shell Scrolled Frame, Trailing Floral Vines, 81 1/2 In. 9775.00
Mirror, George III, Mahogany, Giltwood, Carved Crest, Gilt Leaves, 57 x 26 In. 715.00
Mirror, George III, Mahogany, Giltwood, Scrollwork, Phoenix, 30 1/2 x 17 3/4 In. 440.00
Mirror, George III, Medallion Crest, Oval, Parcel Gilt, Painted, 37 x 13 In., Pair 3165.00
Mirror, George III, Pine, Overhanging Crest, Carved Frame, 51 x 37 In. 1775.00
Mirror, George III, Pine, Overhanging Crest, Guilloche Frame, 51 x 31 In. 1150.00
Mirror, George Washington Crossing The Delaware, 1890, 32 3/4 x 19 In. 330.00
Mirror, Georgian Style, Giltwood, Festooned Urn, Beveled Glass, 54 x 33 In. 825.00
Mirror, Georgian, Giltwood, C-Scroll, Leaf Crest, Phoenix Birds, 63 x 40 In. 1760.00
Mirror, Gilt Gesso, Octagonal, Flowers, Putto, Victorian, 66 x 46 In. 1980.00
Mirror, Gilt Gesso, Openwork Crest, Corner Blocks, 1700-1800, 43 In. 605.00
Mirror, Gilt Gesso, Oval, Ornate Crest, Flying Birds, Scrollwork, 62 x 42 In. 2420.00
Mirror, Gilt Gesso, Scrolling Leaves, Beveled Glass, Late 19th Century, 45 In. 345.00
Mirror, Gilt Gesso, Shell Shape, Beaded Edge, 7-In. Wide Frame, 50 x 40 In. 1870.00
Mirror, Giltwood, Beaded, Reeded Frame, Ornate Carved Crest, France, 60 x 35 In. 575.00
Mirror, Giltwood, Beveled, Beaded, Scrolls, Continental, Victorian, 62 x 39 In. 460.00
Mirror, Giltwood, C-Scroll Frame, Floral Medallions, Italy, 20th Century, 72 In. 990.00
Mirror, Giltwood, Cartouche Shape, Cherubs, Italy, 19th Century, 20 x 26 In., Pair 1595.00
Mirror, Giltwood, Carved Leaf & Berry, Oil Painted Courting Scene, 46 x 48 In. 465.00
Mirror, Giltwood, Carved, Raised Flowers, Leaf Corners, c.1900, 23 x 15 In. 690.00
Mirror, Giltwood, Carved, Spread-Winged Eagle Finial, Convex Plate, c.1825, 42 In. 2875.00
Mirror, Giltwood, Cherub Head, Crest, Scrolls, Italy, 19th Century, 22 x 16 In., Pair 515.00
Mirror, Giltwood, Convex, Eagle Crest, Flanked, Pierced Border, c.1860, 52 In. 2300.00
Mirror, Giltwood, Floral Carved Corners, Pierced Leaves, Victorian, 25 x 22 In. 85.00
Mirror, Giltwood, Florentine Frame, 37 x 25 1/2 In., Pair 4125.00
Mirror, Giltwood, Flower & Leaf Swags, Carved, Mid 19th Century, 47 x 26 In. 2620.00
Mirror, Giltwood, Flower Frame, Rocaille Crest, Classical Figure, 49 x 37 1/2 In. 2590.00
Mirror, Giltwood, Leafy Scrolled Border, Flower Head Sides, 63 x 45 In. 9200.00
Mirror, Giltwood, Molded Beaded Flower Head Carved Frame, 43 3/4 x 31 1/2 In. 125.00
Mirror, Giltwood, Oval Profile Medallion, Foliate Swags, 1780s, 39 x 13 In. 5750.00
Mirror, Giltwood, Oval, Applied Carved Flower Heads, 24 x 20 1/2 In. 58.00
Mirror, Giltwood, Oval, Oak Leaves & Flower Heads, Victorian, 78 x 33 In. 230.00
Mirror, Giltwood, Painted Door, Iron Dial, Benjamin Morrill, 1830, 30 In. 5175.00
Mirror, Giltwood, Parcel Gilt, Neoclassical Panel At Top, 63 x 40 In. 1265.00
Mirror, Giltwood, Pierced Crest, Scroll & Florals, 19th Century, 61 In. 715.00
Mirror, Giltwood, Pink Marble, Rectangular, Beveled Glass, 30 In. 2070.00
Mirror, Giltwood, Rope Twist Border, Top Crest Rail, 40 x 31 In. 3335.00
Mirror, Giltwood, Scroll & Leaf Carving, 19th Century, 46 x 28 In. 1935.00
Mirror, Giltwood, Shaped Crest, Rocaille Design, Divided Plate, 53 x 25 In. 3450.00
Mirror, Giltwood, Shell Carved Frame, Italy, 1750s, 30 1/4 x 20 In. 2875.00
Mirror, Giltwood, Turned Columns, Adna Adams Treat, Troy, N.Y., 1827, 43 In. 770.00
Mirror, Girandole, Gilt Gesso, Spherules & Eagle On Rocky Perch, 1810, 32 In. 9200.00
Mirror, Girandole, Giltwood, Carved Eagle In Flight, Round Convex Glass, 39 In. 2645.00
Mirror, Girandole, Regency, Giltwood, Ebonized, 2 Scrolled Arms, Convex, 41 In. 3080.00
Mirror, Girandole, Regency, Giltwood, Ebonized, Convex, Bull's-Eye, Eagle, 37 In. 9240.00
Mirror, Gothic Revival, Giltwood, Spire Finials, Mantel, 65 1/2 In. 8625.00
Mirror, Hardwood, Carved Floral, Brass Liner, Beveled Glass, 27 x 41 In. 385.00
Mirror, Hepplewhite, Mahogany, Beaded Shaped Supports, Bracket Feet, 23 In. 490.00
Mirror, Iron, Arched Fame, Center Gilt Urn, Floral Bouquet, 36 x 21 In. 165.00

Mirror, Iron, Jenny Lind, Women In Gowns, American Flag On Base, 21 In. 1265.00
Mirror, Iron, Oval, Floral, Eagle Finial, Gold Paint, 15 1/2 x 11 1/4 In. 220.00
Mirror, John Elliott, Mahogany, Molded Frame, 1775, 13 1/2 x 14 In. 770.00
Mirror, John Elliott, Queen Anne, Mahogany, Shaped Crest, Wall, 1765, 47 In. 4255.00
Mirror, Louis Philippe, Giltwood, Gesso, Floral, Cream Paint, 38 1/2 x 20 1/2 In. 460.00
Mirror, Louis Philippe, Giltwood, Gesso, Incised Floral Borders, 54 In. 1725.00
Mirror, Louis XV Style, Giltwood, Bird & Basket Crest, 19th Century, 41 x 21 In. 4310.00
Mirror, Louis XV Style, Giltwood, Double-Bordered Frame, 60 x 38 In. 4310.00
Mirror, Louis XV Style, Rocaille Crest, Black, Parcel Gilt, Mantel, 65 x 41 In. 2640.00
Mirror, Louis XV, Brass, Molded Top, Gadroon Border, 27 x 15 In. 288.00
Mirror, Louis XV, Giltwood, Plume Carved Crest, Foliate Frame, 55 1/2 In. 747.00
Mirror, Louis XV, Walnut, Carved Panels Of Flowers, 93 In. 1650.00
Mirror, Louis XVI Style, Arched Frame, Floral Carving, 52 x 27 1/2 In., Pair 1045.00
Mirror, Louis XVI Style, Giltwood, Floral Urn On Crest, Painted, 30 x 19 In. 495.00
Mirror, Louis XVI Style, Giltwood, Trumeau, Urn, F. Pays, 1800s, 62 x 41 In. 840.00
Mirror, Louis XVI, Giltwood, Bay Leaves, 44 3/4 x 24 In. 1430.00
Mirror, Louis XVI, Giltwood, Floral & Ribbon Motifs, Carved Crest, 1700s, 21 In. 575.00
Mirror, Louis XVI, Giltwood, Foliage, Trailing Vines, Scrolled Leaves, 72 In., Pair 16600.00
Mirror, Louis XVI, Giltwood, Frame Carved With Calla Lilies, 19th Century, 72 In. 3530.00
Mirror, Louis XVI, Giltwood, Spread-Winged Bird Atop Trophies, 40 In. 1760.00
Mirror, Louis XVI, Mahogany, Brass Inset Fluted Columns, 87 x 49 x 5 In. 770.00
Mirror, Mahogany Veneer, Cove Cornice, Reverse Painted Panel, 1830, 30 x 16 In. 605.00
Mirror, Mahogany, Giltwood Eagle Finial, Scalloped Sides, 44 x 19 3/4 In. 375.00
Mirror, Mahogany, Ringed Half Columns, Rosettes, 1820, 23 In. 190.00
Mirror, Mahogany, Scrolled Crest, Pierced Top Medallion, 1780s, 36 1/2 In. 1840.00
Mirror, Mahogany, Swing Frame, 1880, 13 x 16 In. 195.00
Mirror, Molded Frame, Blue, Green, Ormolu, Red & Gold Paint, France, 52 x 32 In. 110.00
Mirror, Mother-Of-Pearl & Bone Inlay, Beveled Glass, Scrolled Toes, 81 1/2 In. 2737.00
Mirror, Napoleon III, Beechwood, White Paint, 84 x 54 In. 4180.00
Mirror, Napoleon III, Giltwood, Burnished, Geometric Design, 52 1/2 In. 1045.00
Mirror, Napoleon III, Giltwood, Pierced Cartouche Over Beaded Frame, 54 In. 1540.00
Mirror, Napoleon III, Giltwood, Rectangular, Molded Frame, Cream Border, 48 In. 920.00
Mirror, Napoleon III, Giltwood, Rectangular, Trailing Flowers, 63 x 44 In. 1380.00
Mirror, Napoleon III, Giltwood, Urn With Foliage, 90 1/2 x 17 1/2 In., Pair 7150.00
Mirror, Natural Wood, Carved Floral, 50 1/4 x 32 1/4 In. 770.00
Mirror, Neoclassical Style, Giltwood, 2 Doves, Urn With Flowers, 41 x 34 In. 1320.00
Mirror, Neoclassical Style, Giltwood, Oval, Ribbon Carving, Victorian, 41 In., Pair 3080.00
Mirror, Neoclassical Style, Mahogany, Giltwood, Griffins, Urn, 40 x 22 In., Pair 4620.00
Mirror, Neoclassical, Giltwood, Cupid's Bow & Quiver, Red Paint, 26 x 17 In. 460.00
Mirror, Neoclassical, Giltwood, Flowers & Leaves, 55 3/4 x 38 In. 495.00
Mirror, Neoclassical, Giltwood, Reeded Columns, Eagle Tablet, c.1810, 39 In. 1495.00
Mirror, Neoclassical, Giltwood, Ribbon, Foliate Pierced Crest, Italy, 48 x 26 In. 575.00
Mirror, Neoclassical, Giltwood, Round, Carved, Convex, 63 In. 26450.00
Mirror, Neoclassical, Giltwood, Swan & Wreath On Upper Panel, Painted, 76 In. 3080.00
Mirror, Neoclassical, Giltwood, Wreath Over Ribbon Frame, Convex, 1900, 22 In. 1840.00
Mirror, Neoclassical, Mahogany, Rectangular, Brass Border, 37 In. 4315.00
Mirror, Octagonal, Reverse Engraved Panel, 20th Century, 47 x 40 In. 770.00
Mirror, Ogee & Dentil Cornice Relief Carved Frame, 33 x 24 3/4 In. 880.00
Mirror, Ornate Painted Crest, Italy, 20th Century, 58 1/2 x 39 In. 412.00
Mirror, Oval Plate, 2 Love Birds At Top, Female Figures, 31 1/4 In., Pair 6900.00
Mirror, Oval, Beveled, Flower Heads, Ball Feet, Iron, Edgar Brandt, 1925, 12 In. 2585.00
Mirror, Papier-Mache, Shelf, Floral, England, 19 1/2 In. 460.00
Mirror, Pier, Eastlake, Walnut, Marble Shelf, Fan Skirt, 92 x 24 In. 505.00
Mirror, Pier, Empire, Mahogany, Carved, Cavetto Molded Cornice, 35 x 21 In. 230.00
Mirror, Pier, George III Style, Giltwood, Carved Pagoda, Scrolls, Birds, 52 x 41 In. 1320.00
Mirror, Pier, George III Style, Giltwood, Eagle Holding Vine In Beak, 64 x 32 In. 1100.00
Mirror, Pier, George III, Giltwood, Pierced Leaf & Scrolled Crest, 51 x 26 In., Pair 16500.00
Mirror, Pier, Giltwood, Rococo Pierced Shell, Scrolled Crest, Victorian, 113 x 32 In. 2640.00
Mirror, Pier, Giltwood, Wheat Sheaf & Cornucopia, 19th Century, 67 In. 4312.00
Mirror, Pier, Late Classical, Giltwood, Molded Frame, Beveled Glass, 52 x 38 In. 605.00
Mirror, Pier, Mahogany, Rectangular, 1850s, 33 x 25 In. 575.00
Mirror, Pier, Musical & Theatrical Trophies Crest, Painted, 92 x 40 In. 7475.00
Mirror, Pier, Neoclassical, Giltwood, Polychrome, Faux Marble, Italy, 76 x 50 In. 4400.00

Mirror, Pier, Neoclassical, Giltwood, Wreath, Musical Instruments, Italy, 79 x 37 In. 2420.00
Mirror, Pier, Neoclassical, Mahogany, Brass Putto, Sunburst, Germany, 77 x 29 In. 3300.00
Mirror, Pier, Pine, Carved Walnut Crest, 2 Angels, 108 x 30 In. 335.00
Mirror, Pier, Regency, Giltwood, Ebonized Wood, Key Design Frieze, 40 x 31 In. 3300.00
Mirror, Pier, Rococo Style, Giltwood, Flowering Woody Vine, 70 1/2 x 35 In. 1093.00
Mirror, Pier, Rococo Style, Pine, Stained, Parcel Gilt, Italy, 56 x 35 1/2 In., Pair 770.00
Mirror, Pier, Rococo, Giltwood, Scrolled Frame, Pierced Crest, Venetian, 76 x 35 In. 1725.00
Mirror, Pierced Crest, Center Urn Issuing Flowers Over Trophy, 60 In. 4887.00
Mirror, Pine, Entwined Branches, Pendant Shield, Oak Leaves, 33 x 20 In. 747.00
Mirror, Pine, Green Floral Decal, Salmon Paint, Pa., 19th Century, 21 x 13 In. 715.00
Mirror, Pine, Lyre Shape, Carved Foliage & Mask Frame, 92 x 51 In. 5175.00
Mirror, Pressed Metal, Rectangular, Floral, Scroll Design, 48 x 40 In. 345.00
Mirror, Queen Anne Style, Mahogany Veneer, Carved, Scroll, Gilt Garlands, 43 In. 495.00
Mirror, Queen Anne, Arched, Beveled Glass, Black Paint, 16 x 17 In. 690.00
Mirror, Queen Anne, Giltwood, Scrolled Crest, 23 1/2 x 13 3/4 In. 410.00
Mirror, Queen Anne, Mahogany Fretwork, Chamfered Corners, 51 1/2 In. 3640.00
Mirror, Queen Anne, Pine, Fret Carved Pediment, Gilt Eagle, 16 In. 546.00
Mirror, Queen Anne, Serpentine, Carved Rocaille Crest, 39 x 18 In. 460.00
Mirror, Queen Anne, Walnut Veneer On Pine, Gold Paint, 24 1/2 x 14 In. 550.00
Mirror, Queen Anne, Walnut Veneer, Applied Gilt Carvings, Ogee Frame, 31 In. 1870.00
Mirror, Queen Anne, Walnut Veneer, Beveled Bottom Section, 1962, 44 x 17 In. 2750.00
Mirror, Queen Anne, Walnut Veneer, Gilt Cartouche Crest, 18th Century, 38 x 15 In. 855.00
Mirror, Queen Anne, Walnut, Bird's-Head-Shaped Crest, 1735, 38 x 22 1/2 In. 605.00
Mirror, Queen Anne, Walnut, Ogee Molded Frame, 19th Century, 34 x 16 In. 865.00
Mirror, Queen Anne, Walnut, Scrolled Crest, Wall, 1740, 31 x 12 In. 2645.00
Mirror, Queen Anne, Walnut, Side Garlands, London, 1742, 37 1/2 x 19 1/4 In. 1100.00
Mirror, Rectangular, Beveled Glass, Grapevine Crest, Russia, 54 1/2 x 28 In. 1725.00
Mirror, Rectangular, Reverse Ogee Frame, Grain Painted, American, 1800s, 10 x 8 In. . . . 1380.00
Mirror, Regency Style, Giltwood, Carved, Arched Top, Acanthus Scrolls, 70 x 45 In. 3450.00
Mirror, Regency, Ebonized, Wingspread Eagle On Rocky Crag, Convex, 54 In. 5750.00
Mirror, Regency, Giltwood, 3 Mirror Plates Flanked By Columns, 30 3/4 In. 440.00
Mirror, Regency, Giltwood, Cavetto Frame, Oak Leaf Sprays, 26 1/2 In. 1870.00
Mirror, Regency, Giltwood, Eagle On Top Of Eglomise Panel, Egg, Dart Mold, 82 In. . . . 5060.00
Mirror, Regency, Giltwood, Ebonized Slip Frame, Trailing Foliage, Convex, 40 In. 7190.00
Mirror, Regency, Giltwood, Grissaille, Rosettes, 72 1/4 x 72 In. 3740.00
Mirror, Regency, Giltwood, Laurel Leaf Frame, Heroic Eagle On Top, 40 x 23 In. 4400.00
Mirror, Regency, Giltwood, Molded Spherule Frame, Convex, 47 1/4 In. 4600.00
Mirror, Regency, Giltwood, Ogee Molded Frame, Scrolls, 33 x 20 In. 745.00
Mirror, Regency, Giltwood, Plumed Crest, Dart Frame, Beveled Glass, 61 In. 2300.00
Mirror, Regency, Giltwood, Round Frame, Egg, Dart Design, Convex, 21 1/2 In. 800.00
Mirror, Regency, Giltwood, Swag Frieze, Acanthus Frame, 53 x 61 In. 3680.00
Mirror, Regency, Giltwood, Urn & Leaf Crest, Scrolled Openwork Corners, 51 x 32 In. . . 770.00
Mirror, Renaissance Revival, Giltwood, Mantel, 81 In. 3450.00
Mirror, Rococo Style, Giltwood, Polychrome, Eagles, Festoons, C-Scroll, 41 x 35 In. 1150.00
Mirror, Rococo Style, Parcel Gilt, Ebonized, Venetian, 1875-1900, 45 x 36 In. 550.00
Mirror, Rococo, Ear Shape, C-Scroll Crest, Foliate Borders, 15 x 12 In., Pair 880.00
Mirror, Rococo, Giltwood, Acanthus, Foliate Swags On Sides, 41 3/4 x 22 In. 575.00
Mirror, Rococo, Giltwood, Beveled Glass, Italy, 1900, 40 x 23 In. 977.00
Mirror, Rococo, Giltwood, Bird Nesting Amidst Floral Carving, 1900, 40 x 26 In. 805.00
Mirror, Rococo, Giltwood, Composition, Cherub In Shell, Mantel, 47 In. 1650.00
Mirror, Rococo, Giltwood, Floral Scrolled Crest & Frame, Italy, 27 1/4 In. 880.00
Mirror, Rococo, Giltwood, Foliate Crest, Leaf Design, Mantel, 73 x 55 In. 1045.00
Mirror, Rococo, Giltwood, Grape Clusters, Leaves, Mantel, 63 In. 5060.00
Mirror, Rococo, Giltwood, Leaf, Scrolled Sides, Leaf Pendant, 1900, Italy, 28 In., Pair . . . 431.00
Mirror, Rococo, Giltwood, Pierced Carved Frame, C-Scroll Birds, 41 In. 1610.00
Mirror, Rococo, Giltwood, Scrolled Crest, Acanthus, C-Scroll Frame, Italy, 47 In. 1265.00
Mirror, Rococo, Pinched Waist Shape, Scrolled Foliate Carving, Italy, 60 1/2 In. 1870.00
Mirror, Rococo, Reverse Engraved Flowers & Leaves, 19th Century, 38 x 18 In. 310.00
Mirror, Roycroft, 6 Hammered Hooks, Chains, 30 x 50 x 36 In. 2200.00
Mirror, Scrolled Frame, Cherub Each Side, Woman's Head, Dresden, 22 1/2 In. 1035.00
Mirror, Shaving, Biedermeier, Mahogany, 3 Inlaid Drawers, 1820, 26 x 19 In. 412.00
Mirror, Shaving, Bowfront, Mahogany, 3 Dovetailed Drawers, Oval, 21 x 8 x 25 In. 495.00
Mirror, Shaving, Bowfront, Mahogany, 3 Dovetailed Drawers, Oval, Inlaid, 17 x 24 In. . . . 275.00

Furniture, Parlor Set,
Mother-Of-Pearl, Copper,
Silver, Upholstered,
Victorian, 3 Piece

Mirror, Shaving, Federal, Inlaid Mahogany, 2 Drawers, Swing Frame, 17 1/2 In. 230.00
Mirror, Shaving, George III, Mahogany, Revolving, Bracket Feet, 1800, 30 In. 550.00
Mirror, Shaving, Hepplewhite, Mahogany, 3 Drawers, Serpentine, Oval, 17 x 23 In. 1320.00
Mirror, Shaving, Hepplewhite, Mahogany, 3 Drawers, Shield Shape, 17 3/4 In. 880.00
Mirror, Shaving, Mahogany Veneer, Rectangular, Bun Feet, 26 1/2 In. 110.00
Mirror, Shaving, Mahogany, Pierced Scrolled Supports, England, Victorian, 24 In. 140.00
Mirror, Shaving, Mahogany, Swing Frame, Scribed Posts, Bracket Feet, 17 1/2 In. 230.00
Mirror, Shaving, Poplar, Adjustable, Bun Back Feet, 19th Century, 29 In. 340.00
Mirror, Shaving, Sheraton Style, Bowfront, Cherry, 2 Dovetailed Drawers, 16 x 20 In. . . .   248.00
Mirror, Shaving, Sheraton, Curly & Bird's-Eye Maple, Mahogany Veneer, 16 1/2 In. 632.00
Mirror, Sheraton, Black & Gold, Reverse Painted Landscape, 24 x 12 In., 2 Piece 110.00
Mirror, Sheraton, Giltwood, Cornucopia, Turned Column, Ebonized, c.1820, 36 x 17 In. . .   880.00
Mirror, Sheraton, Giltwood, Reverse Painted Landscape Scene, 38 x 18 In., 2 Piece 193.00
Mirror, Sheraton, Mahogany, Eglomise Panel, Sailing Ship, Shore, 38 x 20 In. 495.00
Mirror, Sheraton, Reverse Painted House, Gold Turnings, 20 3/4 In. 245.00
Mirror, Sheraton, White Pine, Giltwood, Ships Over Mirror, Acanthus Top, 32 1/2 In. 560.00
Mirror, Stickley Brothers, No. 7577, Oak, Wrought Iron Hooks, 31 1/2 In. 1840.00
Mirror, Sue Et Mare, Giltwood, Oval, c.1925, 35 x 26 In. 3680.00
Mirror, Swan Neck Pediment, Oak Branch Swags, Phoenix Finial, 6 1/4 x 29 In. 672.00
Mirror, Tabernacle, Giltwood, Reverse Painted, Revolutionary War Design, 35 In. 1045.00
Mirror, Tabernacle, Sheraton, Giltwood, Reverse Painted Eagle, 33 x 20 In., 2 Piece 715.00
Mirror, Tortoiseshell, Ebonized Moldings, Giltwood, Flemish, c.1900, 40 x 33 In. 8525.00
Mirror, Tortoiseshell, Stamped Brass, Antwerp, 1775-1800, 26 1/2 x 23 In. 3080.00
Mirror, Vanity, Stepped Arch, Geometric Fittings, Reverse Painted, c.1925, 38 In. 460.00
Mirror, Walnut, Candleholders, Comb Box, 18 x 13 In. 90.00
Mirror, Walnut, Leaf Tip Border, Panel Of Bacchanalian Revelry, Birds, 55 x 37 In. 6325.00
Mirror, Walnut, Pierce Carved, Flower Heads & Medallions, 59 x 43 In. 1980.00
Mirror, Washington Memorial, Swag Frieze Over Panel, c.1800, 31 1/2 In. 8050.00
Ottoman, 4 Floral Leaf Panels, Tufted Velvet, Victorian, 24 In.   575.00
Ottoman, Empire, Rectangular, Bun Feet, Upholstered, 22 x 17 1/2 x 14 In. 58.00
Ottoman, Georgian Style, Cabriole Legs, Claw & Ball Feet, Upholstered, 30 x 17 In. 525.00
Ottoman, J. & J.W. Meeks, Inlaid Rosewood, Serpentine, New York, 43 In. 2875.00
Ottoman, Mahogany, Carved, Straight Rail, Bracket Feet, c.1835, 16 1/2 x 48 In. 1045.00
Ottoman, Van Der Rohe, Tufted Leather, Knoll, 24 x 23 x 15 In.   1100.00
Parlor Set, Art Nouveau, Walnut, Peacocks, Flowers, Scrolls, Italy, c.1900, 7 Piece 8625.00
Parlor Set, Eastlake, Walnut, Upholstered, Settee, Rocker, Armchair, c.1890, 3 Piece 500.00
Parlor Set, Harden, Oak, Slat Back & Sides, Settee, Armchair, Rocker, Paper Label 2695.00
Parlor Set, Louis XV Style, Giltwood, Cartouche-Shaped Back, 3 Piece 9775.00
Parlor Set, Louis XV Style, Walnut, Gilt, Sofa, Chairs, Padded Backs, c.1900, 3 Piece . . .   1540.00
Parlor Set, Mahogany, Bellflower, Mother-Of-Pearl Design, Cabriole Legs, 3 Piece 1150.00
Parlor Set, Mahogany, Lion Heads, Acanthus, Claw & Ball Feet, Victorian, 3 Piece 1680.00
Parlor Set, Mother-Of-Pearl Inlay, Upholstered, Victorian, 3 Piece 1100.00
Parlor Set, Mother-Of-Pearl, Copper, Silver, Upholstered, Victorian, 3 Piece . . . .*Illus*   1210.00
Parlor Set, P.E. Guerin, Second Empire, Mahogany, Gilt Ormolu Mounts, 3 Piece 4180.00
Parlor Set, Rococo Style, Giltwood, Scrolled Crests, Carved Back, 3 Piece 1185.00
Parlor Set, Wicker, Olive Green Paint, Black Trim, Rocker & Chair, Child's, 3 Piece 1895.00
Patio Set, Faux Wicker, 2 Tables, 8 Arm Chairs, Ottoman, 2 Serving Carts, 14 Piece 1845.00
Pedestal, Art Deco, Oak, 57 1/4 In., Pair 3450.00
Pedestal, Art Deco, Rosewood, Marble Top, Canted Corners, France, 48 x 18 x 18 In. . . .   1725.00

Furniture, Pie Safe, 12 Punched
Tin Panels, 2 Base Drawers

**Brown shoe polish is good to cover scuffs
and slight damage on furniture.**

**If you spill nail polish on furniture, try this
cure: Rub the spot with 0000-grade steel
wool dipped in liquid wax polish. Wipe, then
rewax with your usual furniture polish.**

Pedestal, Art Nouveau, Mahogany, Classical Maiden, c.1900, 37 1/2 In. 825.00
Pedestal, Arts & Crafts, Wood, 38 In. 275.00
Pedestal, Baroque, Green Marble Top, Foliate Column, Plinth Base, 42 In., Pair 1207.00
Pedestal, Black Marble, Fluted Column, Parcel Gilt Egg & Dart, 52 In., Pair 2420.00
Pedestal, Empire, Giltwood, Acanthus, Ferns, Onyx Top, 1800s, 40 x 20 In. 1795.00
Pedestal, George III, Mahogany, Corinthian Capitals Over Standard, 44 In., Pair 12650.00
Pedestal, George III, Mahogany, Rectangular Top, Rosettes At Corners, 42 In., Pair 3740.00
Pedestal, Gilt Lotus Molding, White Paint, 55 1/2 In., Pair 1100.00
Pedestal, Green Marble, Gilt Metal, 46 1/2 In., Pair 2100.00
Pedestal, Louis XVI, Mahogany, Square Marble Top, Cove Plinth, 1900, 45 In., Pair 3450.00
Pedestal, Mahogany, Checkered Oval Inlay, George III, 40 1/2 x 12 In. 1210.00
Pedestal, Marble, Alabaster, Round Top, Reeded Column, 20th Century, 36 In. . . .525.00 to 600.00
Pedestal, Marble, Alabaster, Round Top, Reeded Column, Octagon Base, 31 x 10 In. 286.00
Pedestal, Neoclassical Style, Obelisk, Marble Top, Gilt Brass, 42 3/4 In. 440.00
Pedestal, Neoclassical Style, Walnut, Square, Tapered, Reverse Ogee Capital, 40 In. 115.00
Pedestal, Neogrecque, Ebonized, Gilt Incised, Marble Top, Classical Column, 45 In. 2200.00
Pedestal, Neogrecque, Walnut, Marquetry, Ebonized, Gilt, 41 In. 2420.00
Pedestal, Oak, 8-Column Support, Carving Between Upper Sections, 15 3/4 x 43 In. 198.00
Pedestal, Oak, Maiden With Hands Over Head, Victorian, 25 1/2 In., Pair 880.00
Pedestal, Oak, Marble Top, Square Support, Plinth Base, France, 31 In. 220.00
Pedestal, Onyx, Gilt Bronze Fittings, Rotating Top Shelf, 11 x 11 x 41 In. 220.00
Pedestal, Onyx, Ormolu Mounts, Square, 40 x 10 In. 440.00
Pedestal, Onyx, Square Top & Base, Turned Column, 40 In. 725.00
Pedestal, Onyx, Square Top, 8-Sided Stepped Base, 48 x 14 In. 770.00
Pedestal, Rose Valley, King Arthur's Round Table, Carved, Swivels, 22 x 5 In. 2310.00
Pedestal, Round, Tapered Column, 2 Tiers, Painted, 1920, 14 x 36 In. 415.00
Pedestal, Steel, Brass Trim, Marble Top, Pakistan, 13 x 13 x 41 In., Pair 385.00
Pedestal, Steel, Marble Top, Open Columns, Sheet Metal Triangles, 54 In., Pair 3500.00
Pedestal, Tile Top, Latticework Sides, Flowering Vine, Twist Turned Legs, 38 In. 2875.00
Pedestal, Walnut, Figural, Blackamoor Acrobat Doing Handstand, Venice, 32 In. 4350.00
Pedestal, Yellow Panels, Stepped Molding, 63 x 21 x 31 In. 880.00
Pie Safe, 12 Punched Tin Panels, 2 Base Drawers . . . .*Illus* 1450.00
Pie Safe, Fruitwood, Zinc Panels, Drawer, Stile Legs, 1850-1900, 33 x 53 In. 750.00
Pie Safe, Pine, Drawer, Gallery Top, Green Paint, 1840, 56 x 39 1/2 In. 2200.00
Pie Safe, Pine, Poplar, 12 Punched Tin Panels, Porcelain Pulls, 24 1/2 In. 2530.00
Pie Safe, Pine, Poplar, 3 Punched Tin Panels Each Side, Drawer, 57 3/4 In. 605.00
Pie Safe, Pine, Punched Tin Panels, Geometric Designs, Red Paint, 57 1/2 In. 990.00
Pie Safe, Pine, Red, Punched Tin Panels, Circles & Stars, Hanging, 30 x 20 In. 935.00
Pie Safe, Poplar, 3 Punched Tin Panels, 2 Doors, Stars, Pa., 1840, 56 x 40 In. 1210.00
Pie Safe, Poplar, Double Doors, Red & Black Paint, 43 1/4 x 48 In. 4840.00
Pie Safe, Poplar, Punched Tin Panels, 2 Doors, Pa., 1840, 39 1/2 x 56 In. 550.00
Pie Safe, Poplar, Punched Tin Panels, Red Paint, Pa., 1840, 53 1/2 In. 1430.00
Pie Safe, Punched Tin Panels, Drawer Over 2 Doors, Painted, Virginia, 1820, 42 In. 2600.00
Pie Safe, Punched Tin Panels, Long Drawer Over 2 Doors, Stars, Green Paint, 52 In. 825.00

Pie Safe, Walnut, 2 Doors, Stile Legs, Rectangular Gallery Top, 1820, 47 x 18 In. 3300.00
Pie Safe, Walnut, 3 Punched Tin Panels, Tulips, Scrolled Feet, Pa., 1830, 57 In. 2200.00
Pie Safe, Walnut, 4 Doors, 2 Middle Drawers, Step Back, Blue Paint, 40 x 79 In. 2200.00
Pie Safe, Yellow Pine, Punched Tin Panels, 3 Doors, Tulips, 1820, 50 x 38 In. 3300.00
Pie Safe, Yellow Pine, Punched Tin Panels, Painted, Virginia, 1800s, 49 x 45 In. 1955.00
Pipe Rack, Ram's Horn, Horse Finial, Hinged Top & Well, 12 Rests, 11 x 17 In. 747.00
Plant Stand, Papier-Mache, Gilt Birds, Landscape, Chinese, Scroll Feet, 36 x 23 In. 430.00
Planter, Carved Wooden Bear Holding Palm Tree, 42 x 16 In. 15000.00
Porch Swing, Arts & Crafts, Horizontal Slats, Leather Cushion, 82 In. 2860.00
Porch Swing, Arts & Crafts, Vertical Slats, Hanging Hooks, 34 x 66 x 23 In. 385.00
Rack, Drying, Pine, 3 Bars, Shoe Feet, Mortise & Pin Construction, 53 x 49 In. 330.00
Rack, Drying, Pine, Black Finish, 2 Sections, 35 In. 120.00
Rack, Drying, Pine, Folding, 3 Sections, Zoar, Ohio, 42 1/2 x 48 In. 275.00
Rack, Magazine, Arts & Crafts, Slat Sides, 4 Shelves, 38 x 18 1/2 x 13 In. 140.00
Rack, Magazine, Beechwood, Looping & Overlapping Dowels, Kohn, 1900, 16 1/2 In. 2185.00
Rack, Magazine, L. & J.G. Stickley, 3 Vertical Slats, 4 Shelves, Oak, 42 x 21 x 12 In. 1870.00
Rack, Magazine, Mahogany, Cross Stretcher, 5 Sections, England, 36 x 15 x 33 In. 440.00
Rack, Magazine, Stickley Brothers, Oak, 5 Shelves, Slat Sides, 47 x 15 x 12 In. 1320.00
Rack, Quilt, Walnut, 30 x 26 In. 175.00
Rack, Rifle Storage, Ash, Butternut, Numbered Spaces, 48 x 63 In. 4200.00
Recamier, Empire, Mahogany, Down-Swept, Padded Back, Paw Feet, 77 In. 2415.00
Recamier, Empire, Mahogany, Ormolu Swan's Head On Padded Seat, 33 x 62 In. 1650.00
Recamier, Mahogany, Lion's-Paw Feet, Casters, Upholstered Back, 78 1/2 In. 977.00
Recamier, Walnut, Scrolled Back, Cabriole Legs, Damask, 77 In. 2300.00
Recamier, Walnut, Velvet, Nailheads, Italy, 82 x 27 x 25 In. 1610.00
Recamier, William IV, Mahogany, Scrolled Backrest, Carved, Arms, 73 x 30 In. 2450.00
Rocker, 4 Rectangular Concave Splats, Rush Seat, Green Paint, 44 1/2 x 16 In. 230.00
Rocker, Adirondack, Bentwood, Slat Back & Seat, Branch Posts, 39 In. 250.00
Rocker, Adirondack, Hickory Bark, Twigs, 24 1/2 x 16 1/2 In. 425.00
Rocker, Arts & Crafts, Back Panel, Leather Drop-In Seat, Corbel Arms, 37 In. 110.00
Rocker, Arts & Crafts, Mahogany, 5 Vertical Slats, Spring Seat, Cushion, 33 3/4 In. 375.00
Rocker, Arts & Crafts, Oak, 4 Crest Rails, Spring Seat, Leather Cushion, 1910, 35 In. . . . 230.00
Rocker, Arts & Crafts, Oak, 4 Vertical Slats, Spring Seat, Cushion, 1912, 39 In. 375.00
Rocker, Arts & Crafts, Oak, 5 Vertical Slats, Curved Crest Rail, Arms, c.1910, 38 In. 170.00
Rocker, Arts & Crafts, Oak, Slat Back, Bent & Shaped Arms, c.1910, 40 In. 2760.00
Rocker, Bamboo, Yellow Stripes, Stenciled Fruit & Foliage, Arms, 43 In. 440.00
Rocker, Bentwood, Ash, Cane, Cane Seat, 1900, 36 x 19 x 32 In. 170.00
Rocker, Bentwood, Rustic, Coiled Back, Splint Seat, Painted, 41 1/2 x 14 1/2 In. 920.00
Rocker, Conant-Ball, Spindle Back & Arms, Saddle Seat, 36 In. 110.00
Rocker, Eames, Ocher Molded Fiberglass Shell, Zinc Struts, 26 In. 825.00
Rocker, Eames, Wire Top, Bikini Pad, Black Struts, 28 In. 1045.00
Rocker, Eero Aarnio, White Molded Plastic, Gyro, 37 In. 1095.00
Rocker, G. Nakashima, Windsor, Hickory, Hand Hewn, Writing Arm, 33 1/2 In. 4000.00
Rocker, G. Stickley, 4 Vertical Slats, Leather Seat, 34 x 24 In. 550.00
Rocker, G. Stickley, High Back, 5 Vertical Slats Under Arms, 41 x 29 x 30 In. 1980.00
Rocker, G. Stickley, Oak, 5 Vertical Slats, 37 x 29 x 32 In. 2310.00
Rocker, G. Stickley, V-Back, Decal, Arms, 34 In. 880.00
Rocker, Harden, 4 Curved Vertical Slats, Leather Seat, 35 In. 2090.00
Rocker, Harden, Curved Crest Rail, Spring Seat, Cushion, 37 1/2 In. 690.00
Rocker, Harden, Oak, 4 Vertical Slats, Curved Crest Rail, 37 x 27 In. 517.00
Rocker, Harden, Slat Back & Sides, Upholstered Seat, 38 x 31 x 27 In. 935.00
Rocker, Harden, Vertical Slat Back & Sides, 2-Slat Crest Rail, 36 x 29 1/2 In. 1045.00
Rocker, Harden, Vertical Slat Back, Slats Under Arms, Spring Seat, 35 1/2 In. 525.00
Rocker, Heywood Bros. & Co., Wicker, Arms, Victorian, 40 x 22 In. 7150.00
Rocker, Hunzinger, Lollipop, Continuous Arms, Upholstered Seat 700.00
Rocker, Intertwined Over Solid Splat, Plank Seat, Dark Surface, Child's, 10 In. 230.00
Rocker, L. & J.G. Stickley, 6 Vertical Slats, Leather Seat, Arms, 38 1/2 In. 1980.00
Rocker, L. & J.G. Stickley, Ladder Back, Cushion, Arms, 32 x 27 In. 275.00
Rocker, L. & J.G. Stickley, No. 451, 6 Vertical Slats, Concave Crest Rail, 38 In. 1380.00
Rocker, L. & J.G. Stickley, Slat Back, Leather Seat, Open Arms, Handcraft, 38 x 28 In. . . 1155.00
Rocker, Ladder Back, Gold Stripes, Rush Seat, Arms, Father Freetowne, 1818, 39 In. 557.00
Rocker, Ladder Back, Red Brown Stain, Cane Seat, Arms, 44 1/4 In. 245.00
Rocker, Ladder Back, Walnut, 3 Slats, Scrolled Arms, 18th Century, Child's, 18 In. 440.00

Furniture, Rocker,
Maple, Natural,
Brocade, Arms,
Nat'l Chair Mfg.,
37 In.

Furniture,
Rocker, Platform,
Hardwood, Stain,
Upholstered,
Arms, Nat'l Chair
Mfg., 42 In.

**Glue weather stripping
to the bottom of a
chair rocker to protect
the floor.**

Rocker, Ladder Back, Woven Splint Seat, 39 1/2 In.	55.00
Rocker, Limbert, 4 Vertical Slats, Heart-Shaped Cutouts On Sides, 38 x 32 In.	550.00
Rocker, Limbert, 5 Vertical Slats, 3 Slats Under Arms, Upholstered Back, 42 In.	1650.00
Rocker, Limbert, Cushion, Branded, Arms, 31 x 31 x 33 In.	2035.00
Rocker, Limbert, No. 1646, Vertical Slat Back & Sides, Leatherette Seat, 36 In.	2200.00
Rocker, Limbert, Slats, Banded, Arms, 34 In.	770.00
Rocker, Maple, Natural, Brocade, Arms, Nat'l Chair Mfg., 37 In. ....*Illus*	83.00
Rocker, Morris, L. & J.G. Stickley, 6 Slats Under Arms, Adjustable Back, 39 In.	3300.00
Rocker, Oak Craft, Slat Back, Branded, Arms, 32 In.	220.00
Rocker, Pine, Balloon Back, Overall Fruit, Gilt Design, Pa., 1840, 44 x 24 In.	220.00
Rocker, Platform, Hardwood, Stain, Upholstered, Arms, Nat'l Chair Mfg., 42 In. ....*Illus*	83.00
Rocker, Platform, Mahogany, Carved Lion's-Head Arms & Crest, Velvet, 38 In.	220.00
Rocker, Platform, Oak, Allover Geometric Shapes, Drop-In Leather Seat, 40 3/4 In.	862.00
Rocker, Red & Black Graining, Floral, Yellow Stripes, 39 In.	245.00
Rocker, Roycroft, 5 Vertical Slats, Leather Seat, Open Arms, 36 In.	1870.00
Rocker, Sewing, Arts & Crafts, Oak, 3 Vertical Slats, Curved Crest Rail, 1912, 32 In.	115.00
Rocker, Sewing, Chestnut, Ash Splints, Woven Seat, 39 x 18 x 24 In.	65.00
Rocker, Sewing, G. Stickley, Ladder Back, Leather Cushion, 33 In.	220.00
Rocker, Sewing, G. Stickley, Ladder Back, Rush Seat, 30 x 16 x 23 In.	250.00
Rocker, Sewing, G. Stickley, Mahogany, Tall Spindle Back, Alligatored, Decal, 40 In.	2420.00
Rocker, Sewing, L. & J.G. Stickley, 5 Vertical Slats, Arched Rail, 33 1/4 In.	350.00
Rocker, Sewing, L. & J.G. Stickley, Vertical Slats, Drop-In Spring Seat, 35 In.	220.00
Rocker, Sewing, Roycroft, Mahogany, 5 Vertical Slats, Leather Seat, 33 In.	990.00
Rocker, Sewing, Shaker, Taped Seat, Mt. Lebanon, 34 1/4 In.	355.00
Rocker, Sewing, Stickley Brothers, Mahogany, Slat Back, 34 In.	55.00
Rocker, Shaker, 3 Slats, Shawl Bar, Shaped Arms, Mt. Lebanon, 41 In.	1045.00
Rocker, Shaker, Maple, Birch, 3 Arched Slats, Taped Seat, c.1840, 41 In.	805.00
Rocker, Shaker, Maple, Birch, 4 Slats, Rush Seat, Arms, c.1850, 43 In.	7475.00
Rocker, Shaker, Mushroom Caps, Rush Seat, Arms, Mt. Lebanon, 1880-1830, 41 1/2 In.	1495.00
Rocker, Shaker, No. 1, Taped Seat, Mt. Lebanon, Child's, 29 In.	935.00
Rocker, Shaker, No. 3, Red, Green Taped Seat, Arms, 1880, 33 1/2 x 14 In.	460.00
Rocker, Stickley & Brandt, 3 Vertical Slats, Drop-In Leather Cushion, Decal, 34 In.	1650.00
Rocker, Stickley Brothers, 4 Horizontal Slats, Leather Seat, Open Arms, 40 In.	330.00
Rocker, Stickley Brothers, 4 Slats, Cutout Arms, Paper Label, 41 x 20 In.	715.00
Rocker, Stickley Brothers, Tall Back, Vertical Slat Back & Arms, 38 1/4 In.	415.00
Rocker, Stripes & Stenciled Floral & Fruit, Angel Wing Crest, Green Paint, 42 1/2 In.	715.00
Rocker, Thonet, Bentwood, Cane Back & Seat, 39 1/2 In.	170.00
Rocker, Tub Style, Slats To Floor, Continuous Arm, 32 x 25 x 21 In.	3850.00
Rocker, Wicker, Bar Harbor Style, Continuous Arms, Child's	150.00
Rocker, Windsor, Arrow Back, Splayed Arms, Child's	138.00
Rocker, Windsor, Comb Back, 6 Spindles, Painted, Arms, c.1820, 44 1/4 In.	860.00
Rocker, Windsor, Painted, Stenciled Fruit & Foliage, Wm. H. Norris	400.00
Screen, 2-Panel, Door, Persian, 17th Century, 66 x 31 In.	1895.00
Screen, 2-Panel, Ivory, Mother-Of-Pearl, Birds & Flowering Trees, 70 x 33 In.	172.00
Screen, 3-Panel, Applied Flamingo At Water's Edge, Cattails, 60 x 60 In.	220.00
Screen, 3-Panel, Ebonized, Mirror, Inset Geometric Molding, 71 In.	770.00
Screen, 3-Panel, Faux Leather, Painted Scene, Casters, 69 1/4 In.	690.00

Screen, 3-Panel, G. Stickley, Stenciled Burlap, 63 x 68 In. 3275.00
Screen, 3-Panel, Giltwood, Tapestry, Carved Foliage, Landscape, 29 In. 1840.00
Screen, 3-Panel, Louis XVI Style, Arched Panel, Carved & Gilt Mullions, 63 In. 1100.00
Screen, 3-Panel, Painted Leather, Serpentine Top, Hunting Scene, 72 x 20 In. 3737.00
Screen, 4-Panel, Arched Leaf, Carved 3 Figures, Religious, 19th Century, 70 1/2 In. 747.00
Screen, 4-Panel, Courtyard Scene, Peacocks, Ducks, Doves, Italy, 67 x 16 In. 805.00
Screen, 4-Panel, Floral Landscape, Courtly Women, Flowers, 72 x 63 1/2 In. 200.00
Screen, 4-Panel, Flowering Tree & Bird Design, 78 In. 50.00
Screen, 4-Panel, Hayward, Oil On Canvas, Hand-Painted Cow Scenes, 42 x 84 In. 2090.00
Screen, 4-Panel, Lacquered, Arched Scenic Panels, 19th Century, 67 1/2 x 74 In. 1100.00
Screen, 4-Panel, Lacquered, Faux Ivory & Stone Inlay, Hong Kong, 64 x 72 In. 220.00
Screen, 4-Panel, Louis XV Style, Blue Floral Design, Green Ground, 67 x 93 In. 2860.00
Screen, 4-Panel, Oak, Stick & Ball, Woman Each Panel, 71 x 67 In. . . . . *Illus* 3630.00
Screen, 4-Panel, Oriental, Wood, Pierced Scroll & Leaf, 72 In. 245.00
Screen, 4-Panel, P. Fornasetti, Printed Wood Panels, Basketweave Reverse, 54 In. 5500.00
Screen, 4-Panel, Painted English Village Figures, Varnished, England, 76 x 70 In. 1400.00
Screen, 4-Panel, Painted Leather, Garden Scenes, 68 1/2 x 17 In. 1495.00
Screen, 4-Panel, Parcel Gilt On Paper, Painted Flowers, Brocade Trim, 36 x 18 In. 55.00
Screen, 4-Panel, Saatto, Ink & Color On Paper, Geese In Flight, 19th Century, 58 In. 400.00
Screen, 4-Panel, Silk Damask, Chinoiserie, Chinese Figures, Parasols, 36 x 114 In. 980.00
Screen, 4-Panel, Wood, Carved & Pierced Scroll & Leaf, 72 In. 245.00
Screen, 6-Panel, Eames, Ash Joined By Canvas Webbing, 67 In. 3680.00
Screen, 6-Panel, Eames, Lace Wood, Canvas Connectors, c.1946, 69 In. 9200.00
Screen, 6-Panel, Hard Stone, Birds, Branches, Reverse Intaglio Scenes, 72 1/4 In. 490.00
Screen, 6-Panel, Hard Stone, Black Lacquer, Reverse Painted Avian, 72 x 16 In. 520.00
Screen, 6-Panel, Reverse Painted Glass & Hardwood, Deities, Symbols, 96 x 16 In. 2990.00
Screen, 6-Panel, Silk, Carved Flower Crest, Paneled Base, 72 In. 3220.00
Screen, 6-Panel, Wallpaper, Pavilions, Mountains, Figures, Chinese Export, 94 x 21 In. . . 6900.00
Screen, Arts & Crafts, Horizontal & Vertical Panels, Red Poppy Band, 68 In. 990.00
Screen, Embroidered Silk Panel, Bed & Flower, Black Ground, Lion's Feet, 60 In. 2128.00
Screen, Flowers At Brick Wall, Hand Painted, 20th Century, 68 x 60 In. 840.00
Secretaire A Abattant, Art Deco, Rosewood, Rectangular Top, 51 x 21 In. 1725.00
Secretaire A Abattant, Biedermeier, Drop Front, Fruitwood, Fitted Interior, 78 In. 4187.00
Secretaire A Abattant, Biedermeier, Drop Front, Walnut, Fitted Interior, 60 1/2 In. 2400.00
Secretaire A Abattant, Brass Inlay, Metal Dolphin Mounts, Fitted Interior, 61 In. 2860.00
Secretaire A Abattant, Drop Front, Drawer, Marble Top, Leather Surface, 58 3/4 In. 6900.00
Secretaire A Abattant, Drop Front, Drawers, Fitted Compartment, 1850s, 60 In. 2070.00
Secretaire A Abattant, Empire Style, Drawer, Paneled Cupboard Doors, 54 1/2 In. 2705.00
Secretaire A Abattant, Empire, Mahogany, 3 Drawers, Marble Top, 26 In. 690.00
Secretaire A Abattant, Louis Philippe, Mahogany, Marble Top, Fitted, 59 x 38 In. 1610.00
Secretaire A Abattant, Mahogany, Drawer Over Witting Surface, Marble Top, 57 In. 3475.00
Secretary, Aesthetic Revival, Drop Front, Japonism, Floral Marquetry Panel, 52 In. 5775.00
Secretary, Arts & Crafts, 2 Drawers, 2 Leaded Glass Doors, Inlaid Front, 60 x 32 In. 2300.00
Secretary, Biedermeier, Birch, Pine, 3 Drawers, 4 Interior Drawers, 43 In. 1840.00

**A roll top on a roll top desk can
be repaired with window-shade
material. Glue the slats to the
material with white glue. Be
careful; this is not an easy repair
and slats must be spaced properly.**

Furniture, Screen, 4-Panel, Oak,
Stick & Ball, Woman Each Panel, 71 x 67 In.

Secretary, Charles X Style, Drop Front, Fruitwood, 3 Drawers, 61 1/2 x 41 1/4 In. 1760.00
Secretary, Chippendale, Cherry, Poplar, White Pine, 4 Dovetailed Drawers, 42 In. 1455.00
Secretary, Chippendale, Slant Front, Mahogany, 4 Drawers, 2 Doors, 91 In. 5775.00
Secretary, Drop Front, Mahogany, 10 Drawers, 2 Doors, Victorian, 52 x 43 x 20 In. 1045.00
Secretary, E. Bugatti, Mahogany, Pewter & Brass Inlay, Fitted Interior, 1900, 15 In. 4600.00
Secretary, Ebony, Brass Ormolu, 2 Shelves, 57 x 23 1/2 In. 3450.00
Secretary, Ebony, Ivory, Marble Top, 6 Lower Shelves, 1924, 58 In. 6900.00
Secretary, Empire, Cherry, Mahogany Veneer, 42 x 19 x 86 In., 2 Piece 1430.00
Secretary, Empire, Mahogany, 2 Doors, 2 Base Drawers ....*Illus* 3500.00
Secretary, Empire, Mahogany, 2 Drawers, 2 1-Pane Doors, Cornice, 72 x 42 In. 660.00
Secretary, Empire, Mahogany, Fold-Out Writing Surface, c.1840, 41 x 19 x 69 In. 1320.00
Secretary, Empire, Mahogany, Veneers, Flat Front, 3/4 Columns, 67 1/2 In. 2090.00
Secretary, Federal, Bird's-Eye Maple, Rosewood, 6 Drawers, Bracket Base, 89 In. 3450.00
Secretary, Federal, Mahogany, Crossbanded Drawers, Bookcase Top, 71 1/2 In. 3520.00
Secretary, Fruitwood, 2 Short Over 2 Short Drawers, Bun Feet, 61 In. 14950.00
Secretary, George II, Walnut, Leather Lined Desk Interior, 37 x 23 In. 3220.00
Secretary, Gothic Revival, Slant Front, Walnut, Molded Base, 63 1/2 x 36 x 20 In. 2415.00
Secretary, Hepplewhite, 4 Drawers, Blind Front, Flap Front, Line Inlay, 50 1/2 In. 2640.00
Secretary, Louis Philippe, Burl Elm, Drop Front, Marble Top, 38 x 53 In. 1760.00
Secretary, Louis Philippe, Drop Front, Mahogany, Marble Top, 60 1/2 x 39 In. 2200.00
Secretary, Louis Philippe, Drop Front, Mahogany, Recessed Cornice, 62 x 40 In. 3080.00
Secretary, Mahogany, 2 Flame Doors, Turned, Reeded Legs, 1800, Woman's, 51 In. 2200.00
Secretary, Oak, Adjustable Interior Shelves, Mid 19th Century, 86 In. 8500.00
Secretary, Oriental, Red Lacquer, Overall Flowers, 19th Century, 66 In. 365.00
Secretary, Rococo, Slant Front, Rosewood, Bombe Sides, Cabriole Legs, 83 In. 9200.00
Secretary, Sheraton, Mahogany, Blind Front, Stepped Upper Section, 52 x 41 In. 2000.00
Secretary, Sheraton, Mahogany, Flat Front, 3 Drawers, Astragal Glazed Doors, 63 In. 3080.00
Secretary, Slant Front, Mahogany, 4 Overlapping Drawers, Fitted Interior, 92 In. 6875.00
Secretary, Walnut, 2 Blind Doors Over Pullout Work Surface, 2 Doors, 60 In. 400.00
Secretary, William & Mary, Drop Front, Cedar, 9 Drawers, Ogee Feet, 62 In. 6900.00
Secretary-Bookcase, Chippendale, Cherry, 8 Short Drawers, 83 In. 9775.00
Secretary-Bookcase, Classical, Mahogany, Glazed Doors, Baltimore, 94 In., 2 Piece 6875.00
Secretary-Bookcase, Empire, Astragal Doors, Leather Writing Surface, 64 In. 1265.00
Secretary-Bookcase, Federal, Cherry, 13-Pane Astragal Doors, 89 1/4 x 47 In. 5465.00
Secretary-Bookcase, George III, Mahogany, 3 Astragal Doors, 79 x 60 In. 1265.00
Secretary-Bookcase, Georgian, Mahogany, Gilt Tooled Leather Top, 1790, 92 In. 6615.00
Secretary-Bookcase, Gothic Style, Walnut, Mahogany, Fold-Out Desk, 39 x 84 In. 1430.00
Secretary-Bookcase, Mahogany, 2 Doors Over 2 Drawers, 1835, 93 1/2 In. 9200.00
Secretary-Bookcase, Mahogany, 6-Pane Doors, 2 Shelves Over Drawers, 76 In. 860.00
Secretary-Bookcase, Mahogany, Interior Drawers, 2 Mirrored Doors, 87 1/2 In. 2130.00
Secretary-Bookcase, Mahogany, Mullioned Doors, Fitted Interior, 1870s, 81 In. 4315.00
Secretary-Bookcase, Mahogany, Regency, 12 Pane Doors, Fitted Interior, 103 In. 5775.00
Secretary-Bookcase, Rosewood, Arched Mirrored Doors, Victorian, 98 In. 6900.00
Secretary-Bookcase, Walnut, Drawer, Glazed Doors, Shelves, 1790, 102 In. 8050.00
Secretary-Bookcase, Walnut, Fold-Out Writing Surface, c.1840, 43 x 19 x 83 In. 1320.00
Server, Arts & Crafts, 2 Drawers, Lower Shelf, Backsplash, Slat Sides, 35 In. 550.00
Server, Arts & Crafts, Mahogany, Plate Rack, Lower Stretcher, 37 1/2 x 40 x 18 In. 470.00
Server, Arts & Crafts, Oak, Canted Shape, Long Mirror With Arch, 1915, 37 1/2 In. 1265.00
Server, Classical, Mahogany, Gallery Back, Corinthian Columns, Carved, 48 In. 1320.00
Server, Eastlake, Ebonized Finish, Turned Posts & Spindles, 62 1/4 x 56 In. 470.00
Server, Ebony, String Inlay, Bronze Ormolu, Porcelain Inset Doors, 39 x 66 In. 1210.00
Server, French Style, 2 Paneled Doors, Overall Fruit, Ribbon, Mask Design, 38 In. 150.00
Server, G. Stickley, 2 Drawers Over Linen Drawer, Plate Rack, 43 1/2 x 48 In. 2100.00
Server, G. Stickley, 3 Over 1 Drawer, Gallery Top, Harvey Ellis, 40 x 18 In. 22000.00
Server, G. Stickley, No. 818, 3 Drawers, Lower Shelf, Red Decal, 45 x 48 In. 4400.00
Server, Hepplewhite, Mahogany, 3 Drawers, Splayed Feet, 42 1/4 x 21 3/4 x 30 In. 468.00
Server, Hepplewhite, Mahogany, Veneer, 3 Drawers, Inlay, 54 In. 11000.00
Server, Jacobean, Oak, Drawer, Rectangular Top, 1890, 45 1/4 x 32 In. 330.00
Server, L. & J.G. Stickley, 2 Drawers, 2 Doors, Mirror, 49 x 48 x 20 In. 3025.00
Server, Louis XV Style, Walnut, 3 Drawers, 3 Doors, Carved, Marble Top, 57 x 50 In. ... 1210.00
Server, Mahogany Veneer, 5 Drawers, Marble Top Shelf, Scrolled Pulls, 34 3/4 In. 330.00
Server, Mahogany, Regency, 2 Shelves, Gallery Edge, 27 5/8 x 27 3/4 In. 935.00
Server, Oak, 2 Doors, 3 Drawers, Pressed & Applied Design, Mirrored Back, 62 In. 550.00

Furniture, Secretary,
Empire, Mahogany,
2 Doors,
2 Base Drawers

Furniture, Settee, Eastlake, Walnut,
Upholstered, Victorian, 46 1/2 In.

Server, Sheraton, Cherry, Poplar, Dovetailed Drawer, Turned Legs, 32 3/4 In. 852.00
Settee, Arrow Back, 3-Ring Symbols On Crest Rail, Leather Seat, 118 In. 1210.00
Settee, Arts & Crafts, Oak, 13 Slats, 4 Slat Sides, c.1910, 35 x 85 1/2 In. 4890.00
Settee, Baroque Revival, Walnut, Cabriole Legs, Needlepoint, Continental, 59 In. 2990.00
Settee, Baroque Style, Trefoil Arch Columns, Upholstered Back & Seat, 56 x 43 In. 790.00
Settee, Beechwood, Shaped Back, Foliate & Garland Carved Crest, Cushion, 74 In. 3220.00
Settee, Belter, Rosalie With Grapes, Serpentine Back, Floral Crest, 40 x 65 In. 5520.00
Settee, Bentwood, Beechwood, Cane Seat, J. Hoffman, 1905, 45 In. 3450.00
Settee, Biedermeier, Birch, Floral Arabesques, Padded Arms, 1820s, 73 1/2 In. 2530.00
Settee, Biedermeier, Walnut, Scrolled Down-Swept Arms, 1830, 79 In. 1380.00
Settee, Carved Scrolled Legs, Reeded & Carved Scrolled Arms, 56 In. 490.00
Settee, Cherry, Out-Curved Sides, Upholstered Back & Seat, 84 In. 4830.00
Settee, Chinese Chippendale, Fret Pierced Stretcher, 35 x 55 In. 825.00
Settee, Chippendale Style, Mahogany, 19th Century, 61 x 37 In. 1980.00
Settee, Chippendale, Shell At Knee, Scroll, Curved Arms, 19th Century, 44 x 41 In. 2520.00
Settee, Double Arched Foliate Crest, Foliate Carved Arms, 50 In. 885.00
Settee, Eastlake, Walnut, Upholstered, Victorian, 46 1/2 In. . . . . *Illus* 275.00
Settee, Edwardian, Inlaid Mahogany, Padded Back, Down-Swept Arms, 46 In., Pair 1610.00
Settee, Empire Style, Fruitwood, Carved, Upholstered, c.1900, 34 1/2 x 63 In. 1010.00
Settee, French Provincial, Walnut, Curved Slats, Square Legs, 1790, 34 In. 1650.00
Settee, Fruitwood, 4-Spindle Back, Rush Seat, Reeded Arms, 19th Century, 60 In. 518.00
Settee, G. Stickley, No. 165, Mahogany, Curved Slats, Mohair, 41 In. 18700.00
Settee, George III, Mahogany, Serpentine Back, Fret Carved Straight Legs, 42 In. 4687.00
Settee, Georgian, Mahogany, Bellflower Design, Upholstered, 53 In. 374.00
Settee, Georgian, Mahogany, Floral Design, Upholstered, Down Cushion, 65 In. 863.00
Settee, Half Spindle, Black Paint, Gold Stencil, 19th Century, Child's, 22 In. 440.00
Settee, Half Spindle, Pa., 1840, 35 x 70 In. 465.00
Settee, Half Spindle, Stencil Design, Green Ground, Pa., 1830, 82 In. 825.00
Settee, Haungli, Low Backrest, Oval Designs, Chinese, 19th Century, 60 x 31 In. 1350.00
Settee, Herter Bros., Rosewood, Marquetry Seat Rail, Casters, 36 x 53 1/2 In. 660.00
Settee, Italian Rococo, Walnut, Serpentine Cartouche Carved Back, 74 In. 4400.00
Settee, Louis XV, Beechwood, Shell Crest, Serpentine Seat, 40 In. 1540.00
Settee, Louis XV, Tapestry Seat, Cabriole Legs, 19th Century, 26 x 32 In. 390.00
Settee, Louis XV, Walnut, Arched Padded Back, Cushion, 40 In. 1980.00
Settee, Louis XVI, Carved, Cane Back & Seat, 20th Century, 46 In. 880.00
Settee, Louis XVI, Giltwood, Beaded, Turned Legs On Casters, 37 In. 2070.00
Settee, Mahogany, Finger Carved, Reupholstered, Victorian, 46 1/2 In. . . . . *Illus* 275.00
Settee, Mahogany, Scrolled Arms, Saber Legs, Upholstered Slip Seat, 42 In. 635.00
Settee, Mahogany, Serpentine Back, Straight Tapered Legs, 91 In. 1840.00
Settee, Neoclassical, Cane Seat, Tapered Square Legs, Green Paint, 64 1/2 In. 1495.00
Settee, Neoclassical, Mahogany, Exotic Birds, Upholstered Seat, 95 In. 4600.00
Settee, P. Evans, Textured Gesso, Plush Back & Seat, 64 In. 860.00
Settee, Padouk, Triple Cane Back, Serpentine, Cabriole Legs, 1860, India, 72 In. 660.00
Settee, Plank Seat, Scalloped Rail, Black Paint, Stenciled Fruit & Flowers, 81 In. 1320.00
Settee, Renaissance Revival, Walnut, 2-Section Back, Italy, 51 In. 375.00
Settee, Rococo, Walnut, Serpentine Top Rail, Double Cushion, Italy, 48 In. 7475.00

Settee, Rosewood, Carved Pierced Back, Hawthorn Flowers, Upholstered, 44 In. 635.00
Settee, Rosewood, Half-Spindle Back, Cupid Bow Crest, Arms, c.1840, 72 In. 2640.00
Settee, Steer Horn, Horn Legs, Upholstered Back & Seat, 19th Century 1925.00
Settee, Triple Back, Plank Seat, Scrolled Arms, Painted, 1840, 32 x 72 In. 605.00
Settee, Upholstered Back, Sides & Seat, Carved Wood Arms, 33 x 78 x 34 In. 1905.00
Settee, Walnut, 2 Vase-Form Splats, Shell Knees, Shepherd's-Crook Arms, 58 In. 3920.00
Settee, Walnut, 3 Seats, 3 Oval Upholstered Panels, Scrolled Arms, 72 1/2 In. 625.00
Settee, Walnut, Fruit, Leaf & Nut Crest, Medallion Back, Shaped Seat, Arms, 57 In. 345.00
Settee, Walnut, Padded Back, Carved Female Busts At Knees, Curved Arms, 44 In. 172.00
Settee, Windsor, Arrow Back, Poplar, Downward Scrolled Arms, 1825, 35 x 74 In. 2640.00
Settee, Windsor, Birdcage Back, Plank Seat, Bamboo Turning, 1810, 34 In. 1760.00
Settle, Arrow Back, Floral & Fruit On Crest, Wide Plank Seat, Painted, 60 In. 880.00
Settle, Arrow Back, Plank Seat, Arrow Spindles, Arms, 73 1/2 In. 962.00
Settle, Arts & Crafts, Broad Vertical Slats, Attributed To George Maher, 40 x 78 In. 2970.00
Settle, Arts & Crafts, Oak, 11 Vertical Slats, Flat Arms, 3 Arm Slats, c.1912, 81 In. 1092.00
Settle, Arts & Crafts, Paneled Back, Even Arm, 47 x 84 x 34 In. 2475.00
Settle, Elm, Pine, Paneled Back, Storage Compartment, England, 1900, 52 1/2 In. 825.00
Settle, G. Stickley, Horizontal Board Back, 5 Slats Under Arms, 78 In. 6875.00
Settle, G. Stickley, No. 205, 5 Wide Slats, Cushion, Even Arms, 30 In. 3737.00
Settle, G. Stickley, No. 210, Cushion, Knock-Down Even Arms, 36 x 84 In. 8750.00
Settle, G. Stickley, No. 222, Pencil Post, Leather, 36 x 79 In. 1540.00
Settle, J.M. Young, Slat Back, Leather Seat, Even Arm, 34 x 78 x 29 In. 5500.00
Settle, L. & J.G. Stickley, No. 281, Cube, Vertical Slats, Leather Spring Seat, 77 In. 8800.00
Settle, L. & J.G. Stickley, Quartersawn Oak, Carved Paneled Slats, 39 x 59 In. 9900.00
Settle, L. & J.G. Stickley, Slat Back, Even Arm, Label, 34 x 76 x 31 In. 8800.00
Settle, L. & J.G. Stickley, V Crest Rail, Sprig Seat, Open Arms, Red Decal, 38 x 76 In. . . . 3575.00
Settle, Limbert, No. 570, 3/4 Arms, 30 x 79 In. 4750.00
Settle, Limbert, Oak, Triple Back, Cane Sides, Back & Seat, 72 In. 2860.00
Settle, Limbert, Vertical Back Slats, Drop-In Seat, 2 Pillows, Open Arm, 74 In. 2200.00
Settle, Mission Oak, Curved Crest Rail, 13 Vertical Slats, Medium Brown, 38 In. 750.00
Settle, Plank Seat, Yellow & Orange Stripes, Floral Crest & Slat, 81 In. 880.00
Settle, Spindle Back, Turned Legs, Plank Seat, Painted, Scrolled Arms, Pa., 78 In. 275.00
Settle, Stickley & Brandt, Mahogany, Leather Cushion, Even Arms, 33 x 72 x 29 In. 3960.00
Settle, Stickley & Brandt, Vertical Slats, Leather Seat, Even Arms, 32 x 27 In. 3190.00
Settle, Turned Legs, Rungs, Posts & Spindles, Plank Seat, 71 In. 770.00
Settle, Windsor, Bamboo Turning, Yellow Stripes, 78 In. 1100.00
Shelf, Adam Style, Mahogany, Floral Garland, Bracket, 14 x 10 x 6 In., Pair 2530.00
Shelf, Corner, Hanging, 2 Serpentine Doors, Gilt, Japanned, 44 In. 345.00
Shelf, Corner, Hanging, George III, Mahogany, Bowfront, Cavetto Base, 42 1/2 In. 1955.00
Shelf, Corner, Hanging, Mahogany, Carved Scrolls, Beveled Glass, 1860s, 39 In. 900.00
Shelf, Hanging, 3 Graduated Shelves, 2 Vertical Back Supports, Brown Grain, 30 In. 1035.00
Shelf, Hanging, Birch, Wire Nail Construction, 41 In. 110.00
Shelf, Hanging, Georgian Style, Mahogany, Drawer, Carved, Pierced Sides, 34 In. 220.00
Shelf, Hanging, Gothic Revival, Oak, Carved Tracery, 27 1/2 x 13 1/2 In., Pair 2090.00
Shelf, Hanging, Green Paint, Fruit Filled Bowl, Continental, 36 x 37 In. 1320.00
Shelf, Hanging, Mahogany, 2 Dovetailed Drawers, 19th Century, 33 x 42 x 9 In. 2200.00
Shelf, Hanging, Napoleon III, Giltwood, Polychrome, Spiral Fluting, 9 x 12 In., Pair 1870.00
Shelf, Hanging, Neoclassical, Gilt, Pentagonal Stepped Bracket, Continental, 14 In. 1035.00

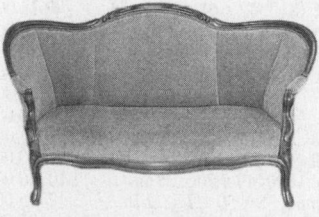

Furniture, Settee, Mahogany, Finger Carved,
Reupholstered, Victorian, 46 1/2 In.

Examine a piece of furniture and look for unexplained holes, stains, and fade marks. They may indicate a fake.

Furniture, Sideboard, Empire, Mahogany,
Brass Medallions, 6 Legs, 52 x 26 In.

Furniture, Sideboard, Federal, Mahogany, Inlay,
1800, 40 x 67 x 21 In.

Shelf, Hanging, Oak, 2 Shelves, Incised Floral Panels, Edge Carving, 24 1/2 x 14 In. 100.00
Shelf, Hanging, Pine, Brown Finish, 4 Shelves, Turned Corner Posts, 28 x 7 x 34 In. 1045.00
Shelf, Hanging, Pine, Molded Top, Paneled Door, Reeded Pillars, 28 x 38 In. 2035.00
Shelf, Hanging, Poplar, 24 Pigeonholes, Red Paint, New England, 56 x 24 x 9 In. 550.00
Shelf, Hanging, William IV, Giltwood, Grissaille, Egg & Dart Carving, 11 x 22 In. 880.00
Shelf, Hanging, Yellow Pine, Scalloped Sides, Flowing Flower Concave, 20 x 24 In. 225.00
Shelf, Neoclassical, Giltwood, Bowed, Leaf Scrolls, Bracket, 10 1/2 x 9 x 6 In., Pair 1150.00
Shelf, Oak, Dark Varnish, 3 Shelves, Victorian, 30 1/2 x 21 x 6 3/4 In. 165.00
Shelf, Oak, Pewter, Fluted Pilasters, 46 x 63 In. 1895.00
Shelf, Rococo Style, Giltwood, 5 Sides, Bracket, Italy, 18th Century, 18 x 25 In. 1100.00
Shelf, Silver Gilt, Mirrors, Fretwork, Flowers, Victorian, 14 1/2 x 82 1/2 In. 4400.00
Shelf, Walnut, 4 Graduated Shelves, Turned Posts, Finial, 30 x 9 3/4 x 34 1/2 In. 330.00
Shelf, Walnut, Carved, Dog's Head & Birds In Nest Relief, 1800s, 15 x 13 1/2 In........ 495.00
Sideboard, 2 Doors, Mirrored Top, Exotic Birds, Plinth Base, 72 In. 1265.00
Sideboard, 2 Short Drawers, Rectangular Top, Red & Gold Graining, 1840, 50 In. 1840.00
Sideboard, Aesthetic Revival, Walnut, Late 19th Century, 89 x 67 In. 345.00
Sideboard, Art & Crafts, Oak, 2 Half Drawers, 2 Doors Over Long Drawer, 55 In. 490.00
Sideboard, Art Deco, Mahogany, Macassar Ebony, Serpentine, 1930, 79 In. 2645.00
Sideboard, Arts & Crafts, Oak, 3 Drawers, Side Rolling Doors, Canopy, Mirror, 58 In. ... 920.00
Sideboard, Baroque, 2 Doors, Rectangular Top, Finials, Fluted Columns, 95 In. 2300.00
Sideboard, Chippendale, Mahogany, Serpentine Front, Arched Kneehole, 68 In. 6900.00
Sideboard, Classical, Mahogany, Carved, Brass Inlay, Molded Backsplash, 62 In. 3850.00
Sideboard, Eastlake, Walnut, Burl Veneer, Marble Top, Flowers, Mirror, 85 In. 1850.00
Sideboard, Empire, Cherry, Mahogany Burl, 2 Doors, Backsplash, 59 x 63 x 25 In. 1650.00
Sideboard, Empire, Figured Veneer, 5 Drawers, 5 Doors, France, 78 x 22 x 37 In. 935.00
Sideboard, Empire, Mahogany Veneer, 3 Drawers, 4 Doors, 71 x 24 x 51 In. 1650.00
Sideboard, Empire, Mahogany Veneer, Poplar, 2 Drawers, Reeded Feet, 49 In. 895.00
Sideboard, Empire, Mahogany, 3 Drawers, Carved, Ionic Columns, 45 x 73 In. 5750.00
Sideboard, Empire, Mahogany, 4 Doors, 4 Ionic Columns, Paw Feet, 1900, 40 In. 1045.00
Sideboard, Empire, Mahogany, Brass Medallions, 6 Legs, 52 x 26 In. ....*Illus* 1320.00
Sideboard, Empire, Mahogany, Swan's-Neck Pediment, Columns, 77 x 56 In......... 3450.00
Sideboard, Empire, Walnut, 2 Drawers, Beveled Doors, Paw Feet, 23 x 50 1/2 x 4 In. 1100.00
Sideboard, Empire, Walnut, Burl Veneer, 2 Drawers Over 3 Doors, 43 x 62 x 21 In. 355.00
Sideboard, Empire, Walnut, Curly Maple Veneer, 2 Top Decks, 73 1/2 x 24 x 59 In. 1650.00
Sideboard, Federal Style, Inlaid Mahogany, Serpentine Front, 40 x 65 1/4 In. 4600.00
Sideboard, Federal, Bowfront, Mahogany, 3 Frieze Drawers, 1810, 42 x 61 In. 8625.00
Sideboard, Federal, Bowfront, Mahogany, White Pine, Cherry, 39 1/2 In. 10350.00
Sideboard, Federal, Bowfront, Mahogany, White Pine, Rectangular Top, 52 In. 1955.00
Sideboard, Federal, Mahogany Veneer, 2 Side Doors, Turned Legs, 37 3/4 In. 310.00
Sideboard, Federal, Mahogany, Inlay, 1800, 40 x 67 x 21 In. ....*Illus* 11500.00
Sideboard, Federal, Mahogany, Inlay, 42 x 71 x 26 In. ....*Illus* 23000.00
Sideboard, Federal, Mahogany, Inlay, D Shape, 1810, 29 x 61 x 23 In. ....*Illus* 8625.00
Sideboard, Federal, Mahogany, Scalloped Gallery, Oblong Top, 1820, 47 In. 2640.00
Sideboard, Federal, Mahogany, Shaped Top, Inlay, Boston, c.1800, 40 x 70 x 28 In. 10350.00
Sideboard, French Empire Style, Marble Top, Ormolu Mounted, 38 x 50 1/2 x 22 In. 2415.00
Sideboard, French Style, Overall Polychrome, 3 Drawers, Cabriole Legs, 39 In. 127.00
Sideboard, G. Stickley, 4 Center Drawers, 2 Doors, Branded, 50 x 70 In. 8800.00
Sideboard, G. Stickley, Brass Mounted Oak, 3 Drawers, Cupboard, 1910, 60 In. 1380.00

Sideboard, George III Style, Mahogany, Sawtooth Inlay, Ribbons, Swags, 36 x 78 In. 7700.00
Sideboard, George III, Bowfront, Mahogany, 6 Square Legs, 36 In. 8337.00
Sideboard, George III, Bowfront, Mahogany, Center Drawer, Tapered Legs, 36 In. 862.00
Sideboard, George III, Inlaid Mahogany, Serpentine Front, 72 x 34 1/2 In. 3740.00
Sideboard, George III, Inlaid Mahogany, Turned Brass Gallery, 36 1/2 x 80 In. 4180.00
Sideboard, George III, Mahogany, 5 Drawers, Center Drawer Over Arch, 36 x 60 In. 16500.00
Sideboard, George III, Mahogany, 5 Drawers, Serpentine Top, Splayed Feet, 37 In. 7765.00
Sideboard, George III, Mahogany, Center Drawer, Deep Drawers, Inlay, 54 1/2 In. 1725.00
Sideboard, George III, Mahogany, Ebonized, Center Drawer, Side Drawers, 61 In. 4025.00
Sideboard, George III, Mahogany, Inlaid Drawers, D Shape, 1810, 36 1/4 In. 4675.00
Sideboard, George III, Mahogany, Rectangular Top, Tambour Front, 1790, 39 In. 7475.00
Sideboard, George III, Mahogany, Reeded Top Over Drawers, Paw Feet, 56 In. 4600.00
Sideboard, George IV, Mahogany, Bronze Mythological Mask Handles, 36 x 72 In. 7425.00
Sideboard, George IV, Mahogany, Overhanging Top, Reeded Legs, 36 x 60 In. 5775.00
Sideboard, Georgian, Inlaid Mahogany, Satinwood, Serpentine Front, 38 x 60 In. 6325.00
Sideboard, Georgian, Mahogany, Drawer, 4 Doors, Serpentine Top, 71 x 36 1/2 In. 3135.00
Sideboard, Georgian, Mahogany, Serpentine Rectangular Top, 59 x 22 1/2 x 35 In. 1093.00
Sideboard, Georgian, Rectangular Top, Crossbanded Edge, 59 x 22 1/2 x 35 In. 1840.00
Sideboard, Hepplewhite Style, Bowfront, Mahogany, Bellflower Inlay, 74 In. 2750.00
Sideboard, Hepplewhite Style, Bowfront, Mahogany, Marquetry, 64 x 24 x 37 In. 1760.00
Sideboard, Hepplewhite Style, Mahogany, 3 Conforming Drawers, 3 Doors, 71 In. 5500.00
Sideboard, Hepplewhite Style, Mahogany, Serpentine, Grand Rapids, 37 x 69 In. 1430.00
Sideboard, Hepplewhite, Brass Gallery, Shell Inlay, 49 x 66 x 22 In. 1150.00
Sideboard, Hepplewhite, Mahogany, Serpentine Center, Bowed Ends, 39 x 62 In. 5775.00
Sideboard, Hepplewhite, Mahogany, Veneers, Serpentine Front, Inlay, 41 x 75 In. 7975.00
Sideboard, Jacobean, 2 Doors, Arches & Crest, Crossed Swords Center, 33 x 62 In. 935.00
Sideboard, Jacobean, Oak, 2 Drawers, 2 Doors, Carved, High Gallery, 50 x 63 In. 1430.00
Sideboard, L. & J.G. Stickley, 2 Doors, 2 Drawers, Plate Rack, 45 x 60 x 22 In. 4125.00
Sideboard, L. & J.G. Stickley, 4 Middle Drawers, Plate Rack, Red Decal, 48 x 54 In. 4130.00
Sideboard, L. & J.G. Stickley, 6 Drawers, 2 Doors, Plate Rack, Decal, 48 x 54 In. 4675.00
Sideboard, Leon Jallott, Mahogany, Parchment, Chrome, 1937, 36 x 60 In. 6325.00
Sideboard, Lifetime, Veneer, Mirror, Signed, 50 x 54 x 21 In. 1155.00
Sideboard, Limbert, 3 Drawers & Doors, Backsplash, Corbels, Branded, 44 x 57 In. 3580.00
Sideboard, Limbert, No. 1013 1/4, 3 Drawers, 2 Doors, Arched Plate Rack, 45 In. 2860.00
Sideboard, Limbert, No. 1454, Mirrored Gallery, Branded, 54 x 54 x 20 In. 3300.00
Sideboard, Mahogany, 2 Drawers, 2 Doors, Fruitwood Inlay, 1920s, 72 x 39 In. 1495.00
Sideboard, Mahogany, 3 Drawers, 2 Doors, Faux Marble Top, Brass Gallery, 56 In. 935.00
Sideboard, Mahogany, 3 Front Drawers, Door, Hairy Paw Feet, 44 In. 1840.00
Sideboard, Mahogany, 4 Drawers, Recessed Center, 44 x 85 x 27 In. 4400.00
Sideboard, Mahogany, 7 Concave Drawers, Tassel Inlay, 33 x 81 1/2 In. 2587.00
Sideboard, Mahogany, Drawer Over Tambour Doors, 6 Legs, 37 1/2 In. 935.00
Sideboard, Mahogany, Gallery, Flame Grained, New York, 1810, 65 x 43 In. 3950.00
Sideboard, Mahogany, Wine & Cabinet Drawer, Serpentine Front, 77 1/2 In. 3248.00
Sideboard, Marble Top & Columns, Mirror-Backed Kneehole, Lobed Feet, 49 In. 9200.00
Sideboard, McCobb, Walnut, 3 Drawers, Brass Stretchers, Calvin, 66 x 36 In. 605.00
Sideboard, Oak, 3 Center Drawers, Serpentine Front, Beveled Mirror, 54 x 72 In. 505.00
Sideboard, Oak, 3 Drawers Over 2 Doors, Scalloped Top, Victorian, 81 x 46 In. 560.00
Sideboard, Oak, 4 Paneled Doors, Top Over Frieze, Molded Base, 32 x 82 In. 660.00
Sideboard, Oak, Gadroon Top, Ornate Skirt, Cabriole Legs, Continental, 47 1/2 In. 2090.00

Furniture, Sideboard, Federal, Mahogany,
Inlay, 42 x 71 x 26 In.

Furniture, Sideboard, Federal, Mahogany,
Inlay, D Shape, 1810, 29 x 61 x 23 In.

Sideboard, Open Shelves, Marble Top, Carved Fleur-De-Lis, c.1870, 81 x 47 x 24 In. ... 920.00
Sideboard, Pine, 3 Drawers Over 2 Paneled Doors, Tapered Legs, 25 x 46 1/2 In. 1760.00
Sideboard, Queen Anne, 3 Aligned Drawers, Rectangular Top, Buffalo, N.Y., 33 In. 1610.00
Sideboard, Regency, Mahogany, Utensil Drawer, Ball Feet, 40 1/2 x 71 x 21 In. 1540.00
Sideboard, Rococo, Chestnut, 2 Drawers, Marble Top, Fruit Carving, 87 In. 2070.00
Sideboard, Rosewood, Serpentine Base, Mirror, Victorian, 69 x 79 In. 1430.00
Sideboard, Stickley Brothers, 4 Drawers, 2 Doors, Plate Rack, 37 x 65 x 23 In. 2310.00
Sideboard, Walnut, 2 Drawers, 2 Doors, Marble Top, Carved, 19th Century, 41 In. 560.00
Sideboard, Walnut, 2 Drawers, Carved Sides, Marble Top, 19th Century, 38 1/2 In. 860.00
Sideboard, Walnut, Deep Drawer, Pullout Fitted Desk, c.1820, 38 3/4 In. 3360.00
Sideboard, Walnut, Drawers & Doors, Marble Top, Mirror, c.1875, 87 x 66 In. 2300.00
Sideboard, Walnut, Open With Shelf, Side Doors, Shell Frieze, 64 1/2 In. 1035.00
Sideboard, William IV, Mahogany, Pedestal Ends, Stepped Top, 51 x 78 1/4 In. 2090.00
Sideboard, William Leavens & Co., Oak, 2 Drawers, Copper Pulls, 60 x 48 x 21 In. 405.00
Sofa, Arched Back, Straight Seat, Ash Legs, Upholstered, 31 x 73 x 27 In. 747.00
Sofa, Arched Back, Straight Seat, Block Turned Legs, Blue Paint, 30 1/2 In. 1955.00
Sofa, Arched, Padded Back, Legs, c.1775, 76 In. 3750.00
Sofa, Baroque, Rectangular Back, Baluster Legs, X-Shaped Stretchers, 84 In. 805.00
Sofa, Beechwood, 3 Seats, Arched, Padded Back, Cushion, Down-Swept Arms, 72 In. ... 1380.00
Sofa, Beechwood, Triple Back, Flower Heads, Carved Knees, Padded Armrests, 76 In. ... 8050.00
Sofa, Belter, Rosewood, Rosalie, Cabriole Front Legs, 1860, 40 x 75 1/2 In. 8400.00
Sofa, Belter, Rosewood, Rosalie, Serpentine Back, Floral Crest, Upholstered, 43 In. 5060.00
Sofa, Biedermeier, Birch, Arched Crest, Early 19th Century, 77 x 32 1/2 In. 7700.00
Sofa, Burl, Asymmetrical Upholstered Back, Scrolled Arms, 92 In. 1725.00
Sofa, Button Tufted Back, Acanthus Foliage, Scrolled Arms, 65 In. 115.00
Sofa, C.J. & J.F. Whiter, Classical, Mahogany, Crest, Rolled Arms, 1825, 35 x 90 In. 2530.00
Sofa, Carved Beaded Borders, Tapered Fluted Legs, White Paint, 49 In. 1150.00
Sofa, Cherry, Walnut, Zoar, Ohio, Victorian, 79 In. 550.00
Sofa, Chippendale Style, Mahogany, Claw & Ball Feet, 3 Cushions, 78 In. 575.00
Sofa, Chippendale, Camelback, Straight Square Legs, 1770, 59 In. 1100.00
Sofa, Chippendale, Mahogany, Camelback, Serpentine Crest, Seat, 1780, 38 In. 6325.00
Sofa, Classical, Mahogany, Carved Crest, Casters, Scrolled Arms, 91 x 37 x 23 In. 2640.00
Sofa, Classical, Mahogany, Horizontal Paneled Crest, Animal Paw Feet, 14 In. 5175.00
Sofa, Classical, Mahogany, Paw Feet, Acanthus Carved Scrolled Arms, 38 x 91 In. 1540.00
Sofa, Classical, Mahogany, Rolled Crest, Scrolled Arms, Mass., c.1825, 35 x 89 In. 545.00
Sofa, D. Becker & Sons, 4 Seats, Upholstered, 28 1/2 x 152 In. 88.00
Sofa, Directoire, Fruitwood, Tapered Legs, Scrolled Arms, 41 x 70 In. 1650.00
Sofa, Duncan Phyfe Style, Mahogany, Reeded Legs, Carved, Pillows, Bolsters, 78 In. 1430.00
Sofa, E. Wormley, No. 4907, Linen, Down Filled, Brass Legs, Dunbar, 108 In. 4025.00
Sofa, Eames, Chrome Steel, Upholstered, 3 Sections, 72 x 29 In. 1100.00
Sofa, Empire, Animal-Paw Feet, Pa., Late 19th Century, 83 In. 715.00
Sofa, Empire, Figured Mahogany Veneer, Lyre, Acanthus Scroll, 92 In. 1265.00
Sofa, Empire, Mahogany Veneer, Camelback, Rolled Arms, Child's, 20 x 38 x 15 In. 800.00
Sofa, Empire, Mahogany, Scrolled Crest Rail & Legs, Arms, 86 1/2 In. 2300.00
Sofa, Empire, Mahogany, Sleigh, Rolling Pin Crest, Upholstered, Rolled Arms, 54 In. 355.00
Sofa, Federal Style, Scrolled Crest Rail, Carved Leaf Scroll, Crosshatch, 88 x 33 In. 1405.00
Sofa, Federal, Carved Walnut, Paw Feet, Damask, 74 In. 1430.00
Sofa, Federal, Mahogany, Hairy Paw Feet, Carved Arms, 1840, 34 x 97 x 27 In. 1870.00
Sofa, Federal, Mahogany, Reeded Flared Supports, Square Tapered Legs, 38 In. 3735.00
Sofa, Federal, Mahogany, Sloping Sides, Reeded Arms, c.1810, 37 x 78 x 25 In. 8625.00
Sofa, Federal, Mahogany, Turned Legs, Down-Scrolled Arms, 34 x 72 In. 2530.00
Sofa, Federal, Walnut, Turned Crest Rail, Claw Feet, Scrolled Arms, 89 In. 1265.00
Sofa, Finger Carved, Ribbed Back, Velvet, Victorian, 62 In. 355.00
Sofa, Florence Knoll, Tubular Steel, Upholstered, c.1954, 27 1/2 x 72 In. 1150.00
Sofa, French Provincial, Fruitwood, Rectilinear Back, 3 Legs, 37 x 54 In. 2640.00
Sofa, French Provincial, Oak, Serpentine, Upholstered, Arms, 19th Century, 55 In. 495.00
Sofa, Fruitwood, Scrolled, Carved Eagle Bust Terminals, 19th Century, 90 In. 2640.00
Sofa, George III Style, Hepplewhite Style, Mahogany, Square Tapered Legs, 75 In. 935.00
Sofa, George III, Giltwood, Cushion Leaf Capped Arms, Elbow Rests, 76 In. 4310.00
Sofa, George III, Mahogany, Padded Backrest, Rectangular Seat, 35 1/4 In. 5280.00
Sofa, George III, Mahogany, Serpentine Crest, Padded Back, Peg Feet, 72 In. 1495.00
Sofa, George III, Mahogany, Serpentine Molded & Padded Back, 37 x 62 In. 5500.00
Sofa, George III, Shaped Back, Square Legs, Upholstered, 58 In. 1540.00

Sofa, Hepplewhite Style, Mahogany, Inlay, Tapered Legs, Brocade, 79 In. 1870.00
Sofa, Hepplewhite, Mahogany, Splayed Feet, Upholstered Seat, 33 x 64 In. 550.00
Sofa, Herman Miller, Aluminum, Vinyl, 72 x 33 In. 2750.00
Sofa, Jacobsen, Fiberglass Shell, Aluminum Base, 3 Sections, 56 In. 3160.00
Sofa, Jeliff & Co., Walnut, Triple Back, Oval Center, Bust Arm Supports, 76 In. 2200.00
Sofa, L. & J.G. Stickley, No. 295, Mahogany, Spring Seat, Cushion, 1910, 22 In. 1150.00
Sofa, Louis Philippe, Mahogany, Reeded Arms, Floral Volutes, 41 1/2 x 70 In. 2760.00
Sofa, Louis XV Style, Walnut, Carved Crest, Open Arms, c.1900, 68 1/2 In. 1540.00
Sofa, Louis XV, Wood Back, Upholstered, Scrolled Arms, 87 In. 288.00
Sofa, Louis XVI, Giltwood, Napoleon III Aubusson Tapestry, 40 x 73 In. 3300.00
Sofa, Mahogany, Arched Back, Tapered Legs, Upholstered Arms, c.1810, 72 In. 495.00
Sofa, Mahogany, Carved Crest, Foliate Carving In Front, Paw Feet, c.1900, 62 In. 2095.00
Sofa, Mahogany, Carved Tubular Crest, Acanthus Terminals, Scrolled Arms, 70 In. 2110.00
Sofa, Mahogany, Cornucopia Carved Crest Rail, Cornucopia Arms, c.1820, 92 In. 2240.00
Sofa, Mahogany, Cylindrical Crest Rail, Upholstered, Scrolled Arms, 63 1/2 In. 2645.00
Sofa, Mahogany, Griffin Heads, Upholstered, 31 x 32 x 78 In. 990.00
Sofa, Mahogany, Rolled Crest Rail, Vase-Form Feet, Out-Curved Arms, 34 x 91 In. 935.00
Sofa, Mahogany, Slipper, Triple Back, Button Tufted, 1840s, 53 In. 522.00
Sofa, Mahogany, Upholstered Back, Rod-Shaped Rams, Leaf Carved Feet, 1815, 79 In. . . 7475.00
Sofa, McIntyre Style, Pine, Paw Feet, Acanthus Carving, Centennial, 36 x 80 In. 880.00
Sofa, Padded Hoop Back, Square Legs, Down Scrolled Arms To Seat, 84 In. 550.00
Sofa, Regency, Mahogany, Inlaid Crest Rail, Reeded Legs, 58 In. 880.00
Sofa, Restauration Style, Mahogany, Curved Crest Rail, Mid-19th Century, 84 In. 2090.00
Sofa, Rococo, Walnut, Out-Curved Arms, Padded Seat, 46 1/2 x 107 1/2 In. 6325.00
Sofa, Rosewood, Latticework Crest Rail, Grape & Scroll Supports, 39 x 79 In. 1760.00
Sofa, Rosewood, Shell & Scroll Crest, Tufted Seat, 1860s, 68 In., Pair 5750.00
Sofa, Sheraton, Mahogany, Poplar, Upholstered, 1820, 33 x 72 x 22 In. 2350.00
Sofa, Sheraton, Mahogany, Tufted Back, Cushion, 76 x 28 In. 330.00
Sofa, Walnut, 2 Carved Supports, Tufted, C-Shaped Arms, 1870, 67 In. 728.00
Sofa, Walnut, Carved Eagle Crest, Upholstered, 1870s, 71 In. 1850.00
Sofa, Walnut, Foliate Crest, Tapered Legs, Cushion, Continental, 74 In. 460.00
Sofa, Walnut, Grapevine, Bird's Nest Design, Upholstered, 72 In. 1955.00
Sofa, Walnut, Padded Back, Casters, Stuffed Seat, Rectangular Arms, 61 In. 1092.00
Sofa, Walnut, Pierced Scroll, 3-Section Back, Upholstered, 37 x 74 In. 425.00
Sofa, Walnut, Shaped Back, Gothic Arches, Spindle Turned Arms, Upholstered, 77 In. . . . 460.00
Sofa, Warren McArthur, Anodized Tubular Aluminum, 3 Seats, Armrest, 28 x 66 In. 5500.00
Spoon Rack, Carved, Oak, Georgian Era, 10 7/8 x 14 3/8 In. 235.00
Spoon Rack, Oak, Scroll, Flowers, England, 18th Century, 8 x 10 In. 950.00
Stand, 3 Tiers, Rosewood, Fretwork Backsplash & Sides, Columns, 44 x 21 x 15 In. 2640.00
Stand, 3 Tiers, White Onyx, Columnar Supports, Gilt Bronze Capitals, Feet, 34 1/2 In. . . . 850.00
Stand, 18th Century Style, Giltwood, Pierced, Grotesque Mask, Italy, 12 In., Pair 2645.00
Stand, Arts & Crafts, 2 Long Over 2 Small Drawers, Shelf, Wood Pulls, 28 x 18 In. 1210.00
Stand, Arts & Crafts, 4 Sided Column, Greene & Greene Style, 37 3/4 x 15 1/4 In. 1320.00
Stand, Arts & Crafts, Wrought Iron, 2 Tiers, Marble Top, Gallery, New Glass, 28 1/2 In. . . 715.00
Stand, Bamboo, Brass Tray, Joined By Stretchers, 38 In. 920.00
Stand, Birch, Drawer, Turned Legs, Brass Pulls, 28 x 22 x 17 1/2 In. 440.00
Stand, Book, Rococo, Giltwood, Extended Paw Feet, Umber Paint, Italy, 10 In. 977.00
Stand, Charles X, Fruitwood, Drawer Over Tambour Drawer, 28 In. 1100.00
Stand, Cherry, 2 Tiers, Beaded Drawer, Scalloped, Square, 27 x 27 In. 210.00
Stand, Cherry, Bird's-Eye Maple Veneer, Dovetailed Drawer, 27 In. 440.00
Stand, Cherry, Bird's-Eye Maple, Poplar, 2 Dovetailed Drawers, 28 In. 335.00
Stand, Cherry, Drawer, Sandwich Glass Pulls, 1830s, 30 x 20 In. 675.00
Stand, Cherry, Poplar, Dovetailed Drawer, Turned Legs, 27 3/4 In. 385.00
Stand, Cherry, Poplar, Tiger Maple Top, Beveled Drawer, Pa., Child's, 15 In. 605.00
Stand, Chestnut, Poplar, Round Top, Trifid Feet, Bucks County, Pa., 1750, 27 In. 3080.00
Stand, Chippendale, Mahogany, Drawer, Rectangular Top, 1780, 29 x 23 In. 3410.00
Stand, Drop Leaf, Bleached Mahogany, 2 Drawers, 29 x 19 x 24 In. 770.00
Stand, Drop Leaf, Federal, Cherry, 2 Drawers, Ring Turned Legs, Mass., 1800s, 29 In. . . . 575.00
Stand, Federal, Birch, Bird's-Eye Maple, Drawer, Overhanging Top, c.1810, 28 x 20 In. . . 1380.00
Stand, Federal, Cherry, Bird's-Eye Maple, Mahogany, Tapered Feet, 27 3/4 In. 690.00
Stand, Federal, Cherry, Dovetailed Drawer, 1-Board Top, Square, 18 In. 575.00
Stand, Federal, Cherry, Overhanging Square Top, 4 Square Tapered Legs, 26 1/2 In. 805.00
Stand, Federal, Cherry, String Inlay, Drawer, 1800, 28 x 19 x 18 In. 1380.00

Stand, Federal, Mahogany, 4 Square Supports, Tapered Legs, 30 x 16 x 15 3/4 In. 690.00
Stand, Federal, Mahogany, Cherry, Drawer, Serpentine, Tapered Legs, c.1800, 28 In. 2070.00
Stand, Fern, Belle Epoque, Cast Brass, Black Marble Top, Cabriole Legs, 32 1/2 In. 405.00
Stand, Fern, Cast Iron, 3 Elephant Heads, Round Top, 30 In. 1045.00
Stand, Fern, Mahogany, Round Top, Carved Flowers, Cabriole Legs, 1900, 36 x 15 In. 517.00
Stand, Figured Maple, Cherry, Drawer, 1830-1840, 28 x 21 x 19 In. 305.00
Stand, Folding, Red Lacquer, Cherry Blossom Design, 2 Sections, 54 In. 143.00
Stand, Frank Lloyd Wright, Drawer, 2 Open Shelves, Signed, 25 x 21 In. 1100.00
Stand, French Style, Urn Shape, 3 Tiers, Rectangular, 24 1/2 x 14 x 27 1/4 In. 155.00
Stand, G. Nakashima, Walnut, Square, X Base, Kornblut, 21 3/4 x 18 In. 12000.00
Stand, G. Stickley, Drawer, Round Wood Pull, 1912, 28 1/2 x 16 In. 575.00
Stand, G. Stickley, Round Top, Lower Shelf, Cross-Stretchers, 29 x 18 In. ......880.00 to 1045.00
Stand, Hepplewhite Style, Drawer, Round Top Corners, c.1830, 16 x 16 x 28 In. 220.00
Stand, Hepplewhite, Cherry, 2 Drawers, Glass Pulls, Square Tapered Legs, 29 In. 715.00
Stand, Hepplewhite, Drawer, Square Tapered Legs, 17 x 26 In. 247.00
Stand, Hepplewhite, Inlaid Mahogany, Drawer, Lower Shelf, 29 1/2 In. 360.00
Stand, Hepplewhite, Inlaid Mahogany, Rectangular Top, Cuffed Legs, 1800, 27 In. 4070.00
Stand, Hepplewhite, Mixed Woods, 4 Scalloped Stretchers, Square, 26 x 19 In. 165.00
Stand, Hepplewhite, Pine, Maple, Drawer, 25 x 19 x 28 1/2 In. 385.00
Stand, Hepplewhite, Tiger Maple, Drawer, 27 1/2 x 17 1/2 x 21 In. 2090.00
Stand, Hepplewhite, Walnut, Drawer, Square Tapered Legs, 29 x 30 x 19 In. 1650.00
Stand, Holloway, Reading, Cast Iron Base, Claw Feet, Casters, 30 In. 125.00
Stand, Inset Marble Top, Female Busts, Joined By Shelves, c.1900, 43 1/2 In., Pair 5750.00
Stand, L. & J.G. Stickley, Round Overhanging Top, Lower Shelf, 24 In. 1320.00
Stand, Limbert, Drawer, Door, Copper Pulls, 36 x 17 In. 1430.00
Stand, Louis XV, Walnut, Drawer, Cupid's Bow Gallery, 33 In. 1100.00
Stand, Luggage, Mahogany, Molded Slats, Bulbous Legs, Victorian, 19 x 30 1/2 In. 1320.00
Stand, Magazine, Arts & Crafts, 3 Shelves, Lakeside Craft Shop, 32 x 27 x 11 In. 495.00
Stand, Magazine, Arts & Crafts, 4 Shelves, Slat Sides, 40 1/2 x 21 1/2 In. 385.00
Stand, Magazine, Arts & Crafts, 5 Shelves, Cutout Sides, 50 x 17 x 11 In. 330.00
Stand, Magazine, Cushman, 5 Shelves, Square Top, 44 x 14 In. 660.00
Stand, Magazine, Ford & Johnson, 4 Shelves, Horizontal Slat At Sides, 18 x 42 In. 715.00
Stand, Magazine, G. Stickley, 3 Shelves, Ellis, Red Decal, 42 x 21 x 13 In. 4235.00
Stand, Magazine, G. Stickley, No, 547, 3 Shelves, Paneled, 35 x 15 In. 4950.00
Stand, Magazine, L. & J.G. Stickley, 4 Shelves, 3 Slats On Sides, 42 x 12 In. 2640.00
Stand, Magazine, L. & J.G. Stickley, 4 Shelves, Slats, Onondaga Shops, 42 x 21 In. 1430.00
Stand, Magazine, L. & J.G. Stickley, No. 40, Branded, 44 x 23 1/2 x 13 In. 2475.00
Stand, Magazine, Mahogany, Tree-Of-Life, Poppies, Inset Slag Glass, 1906, 43 In. 525.00
Stand, Magazine, Oak, Thistle & Floral Carved Sides, 4 Shelves, Tobey, 1910, 41 In. 862.00
Stand, Magazine, Pyrographic, 31 x 30 In. 800.00
Stand, Magazine, Roycroft, 3 Shelves, Dark Finish, Orb & Cross, 38 x 32 x 15 In. 8250.00
Stand, Magazine, Roycroft, No. 078, 37 In. 6050.00
Stand, Magazine, Roycroft, Slat Sides, 2 Shelves, Mackmurdo Feet, 15 In. 15400.00
Stand, Magazine, Roycroft, Tapered Sides, Rounded Top, 3 Shelves, Orb & Cross, 37 In. . 9350.00
Stand, Magazine, Stickley Brothers, 4 Shelves, 3 Slats Each Sides, Back, 36 In. 1210.00
Stand, Magazine, Stickley Brothers, Gallery Top, Spindle Sides, 31 In. 1045.00
Stand, Magazine, Stickley Brothers, No. 4804, Mahogany, 3 Side Slats, 36 In. 4400.00
Stand, Mahogany, 2 Drawers, Lift Top, Adjustable Surface, c.1810, 22 x 18 x 30 In. 880.00
Stand, Mahogany, Square Top, Glass Over Pierced Frieze, Square Legs, 16 In. 38.00
Stand, Marble Top, Shelf, Carved Apron, Straight Molded Legs, Chinese, 31 x 16 In. 165.00
Stand, McCobb, Maple, 2 Drawers, Tall Mirror, Tapered Legs, 46 In. 230.00
Stand, Music, Lyre Upper Section, Divided Rack, Open Shelf, 1870s, 54 1/2 In. 880.00
Stand, Music, Mahogany, Double Canted Top, Hinged Stops, Adjustable, 38 In. 2070.00
Stand, Music, Oak, Iron, Adjustable, c.1900, 39 1/2 In. 275.00
Stand, Music, Rosewood, Adjustable, Candle Arms, Tripod Base, c.1815, 46 In. 5462.00
Stand, Music, Soft Woods, Duet, Cast Foliate Support Brackets, 59 In. 675.00
Stand, Music, Walnut, Marquetry, C Spindler, c.1900, 47 In. 9975.00
Stand, Music, William IV, Mahogany, Concave Plinth, Bun Feet, 44 x 14 In. 6037.00
Stand, Pine, Poplar Turned Legs, Red Paint, 29 In. 440.00
Stand, Plant, Art Nouveau, Teakwood, Square Top, Shelf, c.1875, 51 x 10 In. 345.00
Stand, Plant, Arts & Crafts, Corseted Vertical Slats, Beveled Edge, 28 In., Pair 525.00
Stand, Plant, Carved Frieze, Claw & Ball Feet, 2 Tiers, 31 1/2 In. 150.00
Stand, Plant, Demilune, Blue-Green Paint, 20th Century, 33 x 51 In. 300.00

Stand, Plant, G. Stickley, Dark Mahogany, Square Tapered Posts, 28 x 12 In. 33.00
Stand, Plant, Giltwood, Fluted Column, Trifid Base, Scrolled Feet, 42 In. 403.00
Stand, Plant, Hardwood, Allover Pressed Floral Design, 18 x 20 x 28 In. 120.00
Stand, Plant, Hardwood, Porcelain Plaque, Bird In Fruit Tree, Chinese, 32 1/2 In. 405.00
Stand, Plant, Hardwood, Serpentine Edge, Marble Top, Pierced Frieze, Chinese, 30 In. . . . 430.00
Stand, Plant, Hunzinger, Painted, Gilt Highlights, N.Y., c.1875, 55 1/2 x 37 In. 2300.00
Stand, Plant, Iron, Onyx, c.1880, 13 x 31 In. 130.00
Stand, Plant, L. & J.G. Stickley, Clip Corners, Lower Shelf, Cross Stretchers, 29 In. 1100.00
Stand, Plant, Limbert, No. 238, Round Top, Lower Shelf, 26 x 15 3/4 In. 1760.00
Stand, Plant, Limbert, Splayed Legs, Base Shelf, Branded, 33 x 10 In. 770.00
Stand, Plant, Louis XVI Style, Onyx Top, Gilt Metal Mounts, Tapered Legs, 40 In. 240.00
Stand, Plant, Mahogany, 3 Carved Legs, 2 Medial Stretchers, 43 In., Pair 977.00
Stand, Plant, Oak, Grueby Tile Top, 4 Legs, Trumpeted Stretchers, c.1906, 22 In. 3075.00
Stand, Plant, Oriental, Rosewood, Inset Marble, Shelf, Heavily Carved, 6 Legs, 32 In. . . . 530.00
Stand, Plant, Pine, 3 Demilune Graduated Shelves, Painted, 1800s, 40 x 37 x 18 In. 518.00
Stand, Plant, Rosewood, Marble Top, Pierced Frieze, 1890s, 26 In. 460.00
Stand, Plant, Scalloped Top, Inset Marble, Prunus Blossom Stretcher, 28 In. 115.00
Stand, Plant, Square Tapered Pedestal, Scrolled Feet, Painted, 30 1/2 In. 145.00
Stand, Plant, Strouds, Regency, Wood, Floral Panels, Bamboo Legs, Painted, 36 In. 220.00
Stand, Plant, Teakwood, Pierce Carved, Inset Marble, 3 Legs, Chinese, 36 In. 209.00
Stand, Plant, Wrought Iron, Scrolling Vine, Stem Into Vine-Shaped Hook, 67 1/2 In. 440.00
Stand, Plant, Wrought Iron, Wirework, Arabesque Design, Tripod Base, 42 In., Pair 865.00
Stand, Planter, Cast Iron, Polychrome, Tripod Base, 19th Century, 59 1/2 In. 3450.00
Stand, Queen Anne, Cherry, Round Top, Cabriole Legs, Pad Feet, 26 1/2 x 18 In. 863.00
Stand, Regency Style, Mahogany, Brass, Baluster Turned Column, 23 1/2 In. 545.00
Stand, Regency, Mahogany, Door, 19th Century, 30 1/4 In. 550.00
Stand, Rosewood, Marble Top, Open Carved Apron, Victorian, 12-In. Legs 245.00
Stand, Round, Brass, Marble Top, Stylized Floral Wreaths, 4 Tubular Legs, 32 In. 460.00
Stand, Serving, Lacquer, Fitted, Ivory Trim, Chinese Export, 19th Century, 28 In. 190.00
Stand, Shaving, Drawer, Arched Mirror, 27 x 21 3/4 In. 145.00
Stand, Shaving, Federal, Mahogany, 2 Drawers, Bowed Front, 1830, 27 1/2 In. 1980.00
Stand, Shaving, Federal, Mahogany, 3 Drawers, Revolving Mirror, 1810, 25 In. 357.00
Stand, Shaving, Mahogany Veneer, Lift Top, 2 Tiers, Mirror, c.1830, 63 In. 1322.00
Stand, Shaving, Mahogany, 2 Drawers, Grecian Pediment, Tilting Mirror, 36 1/2 In. 392.00
Stand, Shaving, Mahogany, 3 Drawers, Swivel Mirror, 28 1/2 In. 220.00
Stand, Shaving, Quartersawn Oak, 3 Compartments, Shelf, Beveled Mirror, 69 In. 895.00
Stand, Sheraton, Birch, Drawer, 1-Board Top, 17 x 20 x 29 In. 410.00
Stand, Sheraton, Cherry, Dovetailed Drawer, 19 x 21 3/4 x 29 In. 302.00
Stand, Sheraton, Cherry, Drawer, Splayed Legs, Pennsylvania, c.1820, 30 1/2 In. 550.00
Stand, Sheraton, Mahogany, 2 Drawers, Rope Turned Legs, 27 1/2 x 18 In. 635.00
Stand, Sheraton, Mahogany, Drawer, Carved Edge, Ribbed & Turned Legs, 28 In. 770.00
Stand, Sheraton, Tiger Maple, Drawer, c.1820, 29 x 20 1/4 In. 995.00
Stand, Smoking, G. Stickley, Interior Drawer, Tenon Corners, 27 x 17 x 15 In. 6050.00
Stand, Smoking, Jacobean, Oak, Copper Lined, 15 1/2 x 28 1/2 In. 127.00
Stand, Smoking, Mahogany, Copper Lining, Cushman, 12 1/2 x 19 1/2 x 26 In. 50.00
Stand, Square, Cross Stretcher, Michigan Chair Co., 30 x 16 In. 330.00
Stand, Teakwood, Carved, Round Inset Pink Marble Top, China, 19th Century, 18 In. 400.00
Stand, Teakwood, Lion's-Head Legs, Claw & Ball Feet, Inset Soapstone, Chinese, 18 In. . 220.00
Stand, Teakwood, Marble Top, Mother-Of-Pearl Inlay, Chinese, 20 In. 200.00
Stand, Telephone, Arts & Crafts, Shelf, 33 x 18 x 15 In. 195.00
Stand, Telephone, G. Stickley, No. 605, Lower Shelf, 29 In. 1540.00
Stand, Tiger Maple, Square Top, Shaped Corners, 1815-1825, 28 1/2 x 16 x 16 In. 1265.00
Stand, Tilt Top, Ebonized, Floral Design, Mother-Of-Pearl Inlay, 27 x 19 In. 385.00
Stand, Twig, Wood, Polka Dot Design, 22 x 12 x 12 In. 65.00
Stand, Walnut, Oak, 2 Drawers, Turned Tapered Legs, 28 3/4 x 24 In. 280.00
Stand, Walnut, Poplar, 2 Graduated Drawers, Turned Legs, 29 x 24 x 20 In. 335.00
Stand, William IV, Mahogany, Ebonized, Hinged Handle, Everted Rim, 17 In. 977.00
Stand, Writing, Walnut, Satinwood, Domed Top, Fitted Interior, 1840s, 35 In. 2980.00
Stool, 4 Splayed Legs, Snake Feet, Upholstered Serpentine Seat, 18 1/2 In. 805.00
Stool, Aalto, 3 Laminated Birch Legs, Black Linoleum Top, 17 In. 230.00
Stool, Alexander Girard, Round, Herman Miller, 1963, 19 In. 1610.00
Stool, Arts & Crafts, Mahogany, Round Top, Arched Apron, 29 3/4 x 15 In. 165.00
Stool, Arts & Crafts, Turned Legs, Cross Stretchers, 17 x 17 1/2 x 12 In. 99.00

Stool, Carved Giltwood, Foliate & Wave Carved Apron, Scrolled Toes, 12 1/4 In. 1495.00
Stool, Chippendale, Mahogany, Carved Apron, Leaf Carved Cabriole Legs, 20 In. 172.00
Stool, Chippendale, Mahogany, Claw & Ball Feet, Upholstered, 1770, 19 In. 3190.00
Stool, Chippendale, Upholstered, Baker Co., 19 In. . . . . .260.00 to 315.00
Stool, Chrome, Red Stain, A. Lorenz, c.1930, 18 3/4 In. 1495.00
Stool, Drafting, Herman Miller, Leather Seat, Chrome Footrest, 41 In. 575.00
Stool, Eames, Walnut, Bulbous Middle, Herman Miller, 15 x 12 3/4 In. 605.00
Stool, Eames, Walnut, Corseted Mid-Section, Herman Miller, 13 x 15 In. 880.00
Stool, Edwardian, Round, Tufted Velvet, Late 19th Century, 20 x 15 In. 430.00
Stool, George II, Mahogany, Scrolled Apron, Cabriole Legs, 18 1/2 x 15 In., Pair 431.00
Stool, George III, Mahogany, Rectangular Seat, Block Feet, 21 x 16 In. 1265.00
Stool, George III, Mahogany, Round, Cabriole Legs, Needlepoint Seat, 17 x 14 In. 747.00
Stool, George III, Walnut, Fruit, Needlepoint Seat, 19 x 17 1/2 In. 1380.00
Stool, I. Noguchi, Walnut, Chrome Steel Legs, Rocking, c.1954, 16 1/2 In. 8050.00
Stool, Jacobean, Walnut, Turned Legs, Damask, 19 1/2 x 22 In., Pair 920.00
Stool, Louis XVI, Mahogany, Foliate Carved, Needlepoint Seat, 18 1/2 In. 1035.00
Stool, Napoleon III, Ebonized, Rope Twist Supports Ending In Tassel Feet, 16 In. 5175.00
Stool, Needlework, Velvet Sides, Victorian, 14 x 24 In. 1725.00
Stool, Nickel Steel, Upholstered Seat, 21 In. 515.00
Stool, Oak, Pierced Stop, Square Canted Legs, c.1820, 20 x 14 In. 518.00
Stool, Pad Feet, Leather Seat, Red Paint, Continental, 16 1/2 x 27 In. 3737.00
Stool, Piano, Adjustable, Shell-Shaped Cushion, Victorian, 27 3/4 In. 495.00
Stool, Piano, Cast Iron, Needlework, Portable Piano Stools, Briggs Patent, 21 In. 220.00
Stool, Piano, Double Seat, Ebonized, Carved, C.A. Schindlers, 1872 . . . . 715.00
Stool, Piano, Napoleon III, Mahogany, Rope Twist Legs, Knotted Feet, 19 In. 5750.00
Stool, Piano, Velveteen, 19th Century, Child's, 12 1/2 In. 63.00
Stool, Queen Anne, Mahogany, Cabriole Legs, Square Stuffed Seat, 19 In. 200.00
Stool, Rosewood, Dentil Carved Seat Rail, Brass Feet, 17 x 28 1/2 In., Pair 2530.00
Stool, Rosewood, Square Seat, Gilt Design On Cabriole Legs, Victorian, 14 In., Pair 1980.00
Stool, S. Yanagi, Rosewood Plywood, Butterfly, Brass Stretcher, Tags, 15 x 17 In. 2310.00
Stool, Saarinen, Round Seat, White Enamel Base, 14 x 16 In., Pair 440.00
Stool, Shaker, Woven Splint Seat, Red Paint, 12 3/4 x 12 3/4 x 18 In. 50.00
Stool, Vanity, Swivel Top, Upholstered, 24 In. 35.00
Stool, William IV, Mahogany, Lotus Clad Stem, Concave Plinth, Bun Feet, 19 In. 1265.00
Stool, Windsor, Round Seat, X Stretcher, Turned Splayed Legs, 23 1/2 In. 330.00
Stool, Wood, Mushroom Shape, Tree Trunk Pedestal, Child's, 9 x 7 1/2 In. 375.00
Stool Set, Bar, Black Iron, Chrome Arched Back, Swiveling, 1940-1950, 32 In., 10 . . . . . 920.00
Table, Altar, Hardwood, Dark Red Lacquer, Fretwork Panels, Chinese, 40 x 106 In. 550.00
Table, Altar, Hardwood, Pierced Legs, Pierced Scroll Frieze, Black Lacquer, 31 In. 430.00
Table, Altar, Hardwood, Pierced Legs, Pierced Scrolled Frieze, Black Lacquer, 31 In. 430.00
Table, Altar, Rectangular Top, Bird's Tail Ends, Coiled Dragons, 32 x 61 x 16 In. 2100.00
Table, Altar, Rosewood, Scrolled Frieze, End Supports, Open Panel Shape, 34 x 61 In. . . . 442.00
Table, Art Deco, Burl Walnut, 4 Wedge-Shaped Pullout Tables, 1930, 21 x 31 In. 6900.00
Table, Art Deco, Eglomise, Gilt Metal, Interlaced Apron, Cabriole Legs, 20 In. 2100.00
Table, Art Deco, Jacques Adnet, Inlaid Amboyna, Ebony, 2 Tiers, 1930, 32 x 29 In. 515.00
Table, Art Deco, Jacques Adnet, Rosewood, Chrome Plated, 2 Tiers, 1935, 21 x 25 In. . . . 2875.00
Table, Art Deco, Leon Jallott, Macassar Ebony, Sharkskin, Round, 1930, 28 In. 7475.00
Table, Art Deco, Macassar Ebony, Inverted U-Shaped Base, 1930, 20 x 59 x 23 In. 2100.00
Table, Art Deco, Macassar Ebony, Oval Glass Top, Shaped Plinth, 16 x 48 x 22 In. 1150.00
Table, Art Deco, Mahogany, Vellum, Rectangular Pattern, 1930, 16 x 21 In., Pair 2585.00
Table, Art Deco, Marble Top, Hexagonal, Birdcage, Trapezoidal Base, 30 x 20 In. 345.00
Table, Art Deco, Rosewood, Stepped Rectangular Top, Nickel Bronze, 21 x 25 In. 4600.00
Table, Art Deco, Wrought Iron, Round Marble Top, 1930, 27 1/4 x 44 In. 1840.00
Table, Arts & Crafts, Bungalow, Rectangular Top Over Lower Shelf, 35 x 30 In. 880.00
Table, Arts & Crafts, Copper Tacks On Legs, 17 x 29 In. 120.00
Table, Arts & Crafts, Round Tacked On Leather Top, Lower Shelf, 29 x 26 In. 1540.00
Table, Arts & Crafts, Square Top, Cross-Stretcher Base, 16 x 30 In. 410.00
Table, Arts & Crafts, Square Top, Cutout Apron, Flared Legs, 29 1/2 x 22 In. 470.00
Table, Arts & Crafts, Wicker, Round Top, Lower Shelf, Brown Finish, 27 x 26 In. 90.00
Table, Arts & Crafts, Wrought Iron, 15 Delft Tiles On Top, 17 x 21 x 13 In. 385.00
Table, Baroque Revival, Black Marble Oval Top, Early 20th Century, 30 x 22 In. 800.00
Table, Baroque, Elm, Pine, D-Shaped Top, Scroll Cut Legs, 29 x 51 In., Pair 6325.00
Table, Biedermeier, Cherry, Radiating Panels On Top, 1820s, 30 In. 9200.00

Furniture, Table, Card, Federal,
Mahogany, Inlay, 1790,
28 x 36 x 17 In.

Furniture, Table, Card, Federal,
Mahogany, Inlay,
Tapered Legs, 1700, 35 x 17 In.

Furniture, Table, Card, Federal,
Mahogany, Serpentine, 1800,
36 x 76 x 79 In.

Table, Biedermeier, Walnut, Rectangular Top, Block Feet, 30 x 12 1/2 In.	145.00
Table, Black Lacquer, Stepped Top, Open Shelves, Ridged Plinth, 26 1/2 In.	865.00
Table, Brass, 3 Tiers, Rectangular Glass Top, 4 Legs, Casters, 35 In.	4025.00
Table, Brass, Cast Iron, Rectangular Pink & Red Variegated Marble Top, 30 In.	5520.00
Table, Brass, Round Glass Inset Top, Continental, 26 1/2 In.	260.00
Table, Bronze Trimmed Marble Top, Cabriole Legs, 28 3/4 x 23 3/4 In.	750.00
Table, Burl Ash, Ebonized, Quadruped Pedestal, Victorian, 27 1/2 x 48 In.	1870.00
Table, Burl Veneer, Scalloped Top, 3 Legs, 1875, 29 x 20 In.	225.00
Table, Card, Beacon Hill, Chippendale, Mahogany, Turret Corners, 33 1/2 x 17 In.	825.00
Table, Card, Chippendale, Mahogany, Carved Top Edge, Claw & Ball Feet, 32 In.	770.00
Table, Card, Chippendale, Mahogany, Carved, Cock-Beaded, c.1780, 32 x 15 In.	5465.00
Table, Card, Chippendale, Mahogany, Molded Lip Drawer, Phila., 1770, 34 x 18 In.	4125.00
Table, Card, Classical, Mahogany Veneer, Rectangle, Boston, 1835, 29 x 17 x 36 In.	460.00
Table, Card, Empire, Mahogany, Convex Frieze, Acanthus Leaf Shaft, 29 x 18 In.	1045.00
Table, Card, Empire, Walnut, Turned Legs, Hinged Scalloped Top, 31 x 15 x 28 In.	495.00
Table, Card, Federal Style, Inlaid Mahogany, Foldover Top, D Shape, 35 1/2 x 29 In.	520.00
Table, Card, Federal, Cherry, Bowed Top, Veneer Frieze, c.1820, 29 x 37 x 17 In.	3105.00
Table, Card, Federal, Mahogany, 4 Square Tapered Legs, 1790, 30 x 35 x 17 In.	2875.00
Table, Card, Federal, Mahogany, Crossbanded Edge, Round, 29 In.	3565.00
Table, Card, Federal, Mahogany, Demilune, Tapered Reeded Legs, Peg Feet, 28 In.	3160.00
Table, Card, Federal, Mahogany, Flame Birch Veneer, Serpentine Top, 1800, 30 In.	7475.00
Table, Card, Federal, Mahogany, Foldover Top, Tapered Legs, c.1800, 28 x 36 In.	6325.00
Table, Card, Federal, Mahogany, Incised Beaded Edge, 4 Tapered Legs, 1800, 28 In.	1725.00
Table, Card, Federal, Mahogany, Inlay, 1790, 28 x 36 x 17 In. . . . . *Illus*	3565.00
Table, Card, Federal, Mahogany, Inlay, Tapered Legs, 1700, 35 x 17 In. . . . . *Illus*	2300.00
Table, Card, Federal, Mahogany, Rectangular Foldover Top, 4 Tapered Legs, 29 In.	1380.00
Table, Card, Federal, Mahogany, Rectangular Foldover Top, Tapered Legs, 29 x 18 In. . . .	1840.00
Table, Card, Federal, Mahogany, Satinwood, Inlay, Mass., c.1800, 28 x 35 x 18 In.	2185.00
Table, Card, Federal, Mahogany, Serpentine, 1800, 36 x 76 x 79 In. . . . . *Illus*	7475.00
Table, Card, Federal, Mahogany, Serpentine, Foldover Top, R.I., 1810, 29 In.	15400.00
Table, Card, Federal, Mahogany, Tiger Maple Inlay, Mass., c.1810, 29 x 37 x 17 In.	1840.00
Table, Card, Federal, Mahogany, Veneer, Acanthus Legs, 18 x 36 x 29 In.	1045.00
Table, Card, Federal, Tiger Maple, Foldover Top, 4 Square Tapered Legs, 28 1/2 In.	1840.00
Table, Card, Flower Print Foldover Top, 1940s, 27 In.	68.00
Table, Card, Hepplewhite Style, Mahogany, Band & Striped Inlay, Leaf, 36 x 17 In.	440.00
Table, Card, Hepplewhite, Demilune, Mahogany, Banded Inlay, Tapered Legs, 36 x 26 In.	2640.00
Table, Card, Hepplewhite, Mahogany, Demilune Top, Splayed Feet, 1790, 29 3/4 In.	3520.00
Table, Card, Hepplewhite, Mahogany, Inlay, c.1790, 30 x 36 x 17 1/2 In.	1200.00
Table, Card, Hepplewhite, Mahogany, Inlay, Square Swing Legs, W.P., 35 x 27 In.	3850.00
Table, Card, Hepplewhite, Mahogany, Pine, Demilune, Swing Leg, 1800, 35 In.	4200.00
Table, Card, Hepplewhite, Mahogany, Serpentine, Hinged Leaf, c.1800, 29 x 34 In.	2640.00
Table, Card, Hepplewhite, Mahogany, Shaped Top, Tapered Legs, c.1800, 28 x 34 In.	1430.00
Table, Card, J. Wilson, Hepplewhite, Mahogany, Inlay, Swing Leg, 36 x 18 In.	3025.00
Table, Card, Louis XV, Rectangular Top, Floral, Cabriole Legs, 30 x 23 In.	920.00
Table, Card, Mahogany, Inlaid Skirt, Drawer, 1800, 29 3/4 x 33 x 16 In.	1760.00
Table, Card, Mahogany, Louis Philippe, Inset Felt, Turned Feet, 29 In.	600.00
Table, Card, Mahogany, Maple, Inlay, Shaped Top, Mass., c.1814, 29 1/2 In.	1680.00

Table, Card, Mahogany, Rectangular Foldover Top, Turned Legs, 29 x 34 x 17 In. 546.00
Table, Card, Mahogany, Serpentine, Turned Legs, Ball Feet, Pa., 1820, 35 x 30 In. 825.00
Table, Card, Mahogany, Shaped Top, 4 Acanthus Legs, Brass Casters, 30 In., Pair 4675.00
Table, Card, Mahogany, Swivel Top, Leaf, Pedestal, 4 Legs, Casters, 36 x 18 In. 1680.00
Table, Card, Queen Anne, Mahogany, Foldover Top, Demilune, Storage Well, 28 In. 3450.00
Table, Card, Rectangular Foldover Top, Beaded Edge, Acanthus Leaf Scroll, 30 In. 4900.00
Table, Card, Sheraton, Mahogany, Cookie Corner Top, Reeded Legs, 1810, 29 In. 2860.00
Table, Card, Sheraton, Scalloped Front, Rope Turned Legs, 29 1/2 x 36 x 17 1/2 In. 990.00
Table, Carved, Inlay, Gallery, Pedestal, 4 Cabriole Legs, 27 x 29 In. 600.00
Table, Center, Aesthetic Revival, Mahogany, Round Overhanging Top, 29 In. 1840.00
Table, Center, Baroque Style, Patinated Bronze, Marble Top, 28 In. 3165.00
Table, Center, Baroque, Giltwood, Variegated Round Marble Top, 30 In. 1760.00
Table, Center, Baroque, Mahogany, Black Marble Top, 17 1/2 x 25 x 16 In. 290.00
Table, Center, Baroque, Oak, Plaint Top, Massive Baluster Legs, Bun Feet, 29 In. 1725.00
Table, Center, Biedermeier, Fruitwood, 3 Doric Columns, Block Feet, 30 x 31 In. 1650.00
Table, Center, Biedermeier, Pine, Round Marble Top, Scrolled Feet, 28 In. 630.00
Table, Center, Birch, Oak, Octagonal Top, Inset Bamboo, Victorian, 39 3/4 In. 1475.00
Table, Center, Charles X Style, Fruitwood, Inset Granite Top, Scrolls, 43 In. 1540.00
Table, Center, Charles X, Mahogany, Round Gray Marble Top, Pedestal, 29 x 38 In. 2090.00
Table, Center, Classical, Mahogany, Square Marble Top, c.1830, 29 x 37 In. 2420.00
Table, Center, Eastlake, Mahogany, White Marble Top, c.1850, 28 In., 2 Piece 520.00
Table, Center, Eastlake, Oak, Spoon Carving, Scrolled Legs, Porcelain Casters, 30 In. 170.00
Table, Center, Eastlake, Walnut, Burl Veneer, Marble Top, 21 x 31 1/4 x 30 1/2 In. 275.00
Table, Center, Eastlake, Walnut, Parcel Gilt, Marble Top, Round, 29 In. 1095.00
Table, Center, Edwardian, Satinwood, Octagonal, Ebonized Banding, 29 In. 825.00
Table, Center, Empire Style, Gilt Bronze, Marble Top & Stretcher, 33 1/2 In. 6900.00
Table, Center, Empire, Figured Mahogany Veneer, Pie Shape, 6 Legs, 55 x 31 In. 3575.00
Table, Center, Empire, Mahogany, 10 Sides, Scrolled Supports, 29 x 34 In. 1760.00
Table, Center, Empire, Mahogany, Carved Pedestal, 4 Claw Feet, Gadroon, 30 In. 520.00
Table, Center, Empire, Mahogany, Marble, Hexagonal Standard, 28 In. 2185.00
Table, Center, Empire, Mahogany, Octagonal Pedestal, Round, 37 x 29 In. 495.00
Table, Center, Empire, Mahogany, Round Dish Marble Top, France, 29 x 39 In. 3025.00
Table, Center, Empire, Mahogany, Round Onyx Top, Gilt, Bronze, Round Legs 29 In. ... 2875.00
Table, Center, Empire, Mahogany, Round Top, Round Pedestal, 26 x 33 In. 690.00
Table, Center, Empire, Mahogany, Sprays Of Laurel, Rectangular Legs, 29 x 32 In. 1150.00
Table, Center, George III Style, Mahogany, Serpentine Top, Victorian, 30 x 49 In. 3960.00
Table, Center, Georgian Style, Mahogany, Lion's-Head Frieze, Ireland, 75 x 32 In. 6050.00
Table, Center, Georgian Style, Mahogany, Round Top, Carved Shells, 37 x 30 In. 1025.00
Table, Center, Gilt Bronze, Champleve Enamel, Onyx Top, Shelf, Casters, 31 1/2 In. 9775.00
Table, Center, Jules Leleu, Mahogany, Round Top, 4 Down-Swept Feet, 29 In. 8050.00
Table, Center, Louis Philippe, Marble, Molded Border, Paw Feet, Round, 29 x 38 In. 2070.00
Table, Center, Louis XV Style, Walnut, Parquetry, Serpentine Edge, 30 1/2 In. 400.00
Table, Center, Louis XV, Onyx Top, Carved Frieze, Cabriole Legs, 31 x 36 x 25 In. 825.00
Table, Center, Louis XVI Style, Giltwood, Oval Marble, Trumpet Legs, 29 x 46 In. 1760.00
Table, Center, Louis XVI, Round Marble Top, Female Busts On Legs, 30 x 26 In. 690.00
Table, Center, Mahogany, Beveled Glass Tray Top, 4 Cabriole Legs, Victorian, 30 In. 1495.00
Table, Center, Mahogany, Brass Banding, Cartouche-Shaped Top, France, 43 In. 865.00
Table, Center, Neoclassical Style, Mahogany, Simulated Marquetry, 32 1/2 In. 935.00
Table, Center, Neoclassical, Ebonized, Round Top, 4 Reeded Supports, 29 In. 16100.00
Table, Center, Neoclassical, Mahogany, Gray Marble Top, Bulbous Stem, Italy, 30 In. 4840.00
Table, Center, Neoclassical, Mahogany, Tapered Ribbed Stem, Continental, 29 In. 2200.00
Table, Center, Neoclassical, Marble Top, Concentric Bands, Italy, 33 1/2 In. 8800.00
Table, Center, Neoclassical, Oak, Round Top, 3 Curved Legs, Russia, 29 In., Pair 6050.00
Table, Center, Neoclassical, Rectangular Marble Top, Gilt, Shaped Feet, 31 x 27 In. 6325.00
Table, Center, Neoclassical, Rosewood, Round, Brassbound Top, Russia, 30 1/2 In. 6050.00
Table, Center, Neogrecque, Marquetry, Gilt, Trumpet Legs, 30 1/2 x 49 In. 5500.00
Table, Center, Oval Marble Top, Scrolled Base, Victorian, 34 x 28 In. 690.00
Table, Center, Regency Style, Walnut, Marble Top, Serpentine Edge, Gilt, 30 In. 1150.00
Table, Center, Regency, Mahogany, Round Banded Top, Paw Feet, 29 In. 970.00
Table, Center, Renaissance Revival, Rosewood, Marble Top, 19 x 41 x 33 In. 2970.00
Table, Center, Renaissance Revival, Walnut, 6-Sided Top, Dragons, Italy, 29 x 59 In. 5060.00
Table, Center, Rococo, Rosewood, Marble Turtle-Shaped Top, Cabriole Legs, 39 In. 1760.00
Table, Center, Rococo, Rosewood, Rouge Brescia Marble Top, 29 x 28 1/2 In. 2760.00

Table, Center, Rococo, Rosewood, Tortoiseshell Top, Pierced Apron, 30 x 45 In. 11000.00
Table, Center, Rococo, Rosewood, Turtle-Shaped Marble Top, 29 x 37 In. 2200.00
Table, Center, Rosewood, Hinged Oval Top, Lotus Leaf Stem Base, 29 x 49 In. 5280.00
Table, Center, Rosewood, Rectangular Top, Brass Floral Design, Victorian, 32 In. 3450.00
Table, Center, Slate Top, Bird Inlay, Gilt Banana Tree & Dragon Base, 33 1/2 In. 8050.00
Table, Center, Spanish, Overall Floral Design, Central Iron Grate, Turned Legs, 30 In. . . . 230.00
Table, Center, Walnut, Burl Veneer, Marble, Taylorson & Sill, Victorian, 21 x 30 In. 355.00
Table, Center, Walnut, Oval Molded Edge, 4-Part Cutout Legs, 27 3/4 In. 220.00
Table, Center, Walnut, Round Black Marble Top, Bone Marquetry, 31 1/8 In. 12650.00
Table, Center, Walnut, Serpentine Marble, Lyre-Shaped Supports, Victorian, 30 In. 750.00
Table, Center, Walnut, Walnut Burl, Carved, Marble Top, Victorian, 24 x 32 x 29 In. 935.00
Table, Center, William IV, Coromandel, 4 Splayed Cabriole Legs, 54 In. 2875.00
Table, Center, William IV, Mahogany, Round Top, Faceted Base, 29 x 47 1/2 In. 1100.00
Table, Center, William IV, Mahogany, Round Top, Plain Frieze, Lotus Feet, 29 In. 2530.00
Table, Center, William IV, Pollard Oak, Triangular Concave Plinth, Bun Feet, 29 In. 14950.00
Table, Charles X, Mahogany, Round Variegated Gray Marble Top, 29 1/2 In. 1495.00
Table, Cherry, Dark Finish, 2 Dovetailed Drawers, Turned Legs, Zoar, Ohio, 29 In. 1045.00
Table, Cherry, Farmhouse, Drawer, Turned Legs, 1825-1850, 30 x 57 In. 1210.00
Table, Cherry, Farmhouse, Lift Top, Red Stain, 2 Large Drawers, c.1820, 87 In. 3190.00
Table, Cherry, Molded Top, Drawer, Splayed Legs, Pa., 28 1/2 x 16 1/2 In. 300.00
Table, Cherry, Notched Corner Top, Drawer, 29 x 20 In. 605.00
Table, Cherry, Rectangular Post, Triangular Platform, Gray Paint, 24 3/4 In. 50.00
Table, Cherry, Tiger Maple, Overhanging Drawer, Splayed Legs, 1815, 29 x 24 In. 3300.00
Table, Chippendale, 3 Revolving Round Graduated Shelves, 44 In. 4145.00
Table, Chippendale, Birch, Long Drawer, Painted, c.1790, 28 x 17 In. 5750.00
Table, Chippendale, Cherry, Marlboro Legs, New England, c.1780, 27 x 14 x 21 In. 2530.00
Table, Chippendale, Claw & Ball Feet, Cabriole Legs, 26 x 37 In. 300.00
Table, Chippendale, Glass Top, Yellow Finish, 20th Century, 73 x 44 In. 110.00
Table, Chippendale, Mahogany, Gadroon Border, Pad Feet, 31 In. 290.00
Table, Classical, Mahogany, Hinged Rectangular Leaves, Square Pedestal, Me., 28 In. . . . 690.00
Table, Classical, Mahogany, Round Marble Top, Scrolled Feet, c.1840, 29 x 36 In. 4025.00
Table, Classical, Mahogany, Scrolled Gallery, 2 Ring Turned Legs, 35 In. 750.00
Table, Classical, White, Gray Rectangular Mottled Top, Paw Feet, 1825, 38 In. 17250.00
Table, Coffee, Black Marble Top, Zodiac Design Inlay, Iron Base, 25 x 16 In. 145.00
Table, Coffee, E. Wormley, Black Lacquered Top, 2 Shelves, Wood, 53 In. 1035.00
Table, Coffee, E. Wormley, Pentagonal Walnut Top, Janus, 38 x 20 In. 4675.00
Table, Coffee, Frankl, Biomorphic Cork Top, Splayed Mahogany Legs, 14 In. 1320.00
Table, Coffee, G. Nelson, Drop Leaf, Walnut Veneer Top, Herman Miller, 16 In. 2310.00
Table, Coffee, Geo Ponti, Glass Top, Bronze, Marble Slab, 1950s, 31 3/8 In. 1150.00
Table, Coffee, H.S. Eskild, Tile Top, Bronzed, Tiles Form Organic Design, 38 In. 935.00
Table, Coffee, Irwin, Round Inset Glass Top, X-Base, 14 1/2 x 36 In. 660.00
Table, Coffee, Karl Springer, Faux Albino Snakeskin, 1970, 27 x 18 x 15 In. 715.00
Table, Coffee, La Barge, Brass, Lobed Glass Top, Cabriole Legs, 50 x 30 x 17 In. 1035.00
Table, Coffee, Louis XV Style, Fruitwood, Stippled Marble Top, 18 1/2 x 50 In. 1430.00
Table, Coffee, Louis XV, Rectangular Molded Marble Top, Beige, Rose, 19 x 16 In. 86.00
Table, Coffee, Louis XVI Style, Giltwood, Marble Top, Fluted Legs, 17 x 42 x 22 In. 460.00
Table, Coffee, Louis XVI, Satinwood, Amboyna, Round Top, Splayed Legs, 18 In. 495.00
Table, Coffee, Noguchi, Birch, Triangular Glass Top, Adjustable Base, 43 In. 3105.00
Table, Coffee, P. Evans, Steel & Gesso Stalagmite Base, Glass Top, 16 x 42 In. 1540.00
Table, Coffee, Paul Laszlo, Round Birch Top, Ebonized Legs, 48 x 14 In. 550.00
Table, Coffee, Saarinen, Round Walnut Veneer Top, White Enamel Base, 15 In. 330.00
Table, Coffee, Square Flamed Ash Top, Clear Lucite Base, 65 1/2 x 15 1/2 In. 115.00
Table, Coffee, Square, Beveled Glass Top, Scrolled X-Stretcher & Feet, 18 1/2 In. 1035.00
Table, Coffee, Tapio, Wirkkala, For Asko . . . . *Illus* 4480.00
Table, Conference, Eames, Rosewood Veneer Top, 72 x 29 In. 470.00
Table, Conference, Herman Miller, Art Moderne, Oak, 28 x 120 In. 80.00
Table, Console, Art Deco, Macassar Ebony, Molded Plinth, France, 30 x 42 x 16 In. 2300.00
Table, Console, Baroque Style, Giltwood, Onyx Top, Pierced Frieze, Italy, 35 x 59 In. . . . 1095.00
Table, Console, Edgar Brandt, Wrought Iron, Rectangular Marble Top, 47 x 38 In. 7475.00
Table, Console, Empire, Mahogany Veneer, Marble Top, Lyre Legs, Mirror, 36 In. 2640.00
Table, Console, Empire, Mahogany, Marble Top, Serpentine Front, Mirror, 52 In. 2530.00
Table, Console, Federal, Inlaid Mahogany, Demilune, Reeded Edge, 33 x 37 In. 1610.00
Table, Console, George II Style, Walnut, Granite Veneer Top, Carved, 55 x 22 x 30 In. . . . 690.00

Furniture, Table, Coffee, Tapio, Wirkkala, For Asko

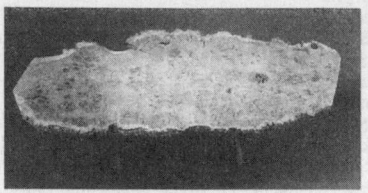

Furniture, Table, Dining, G. Nakashima, Burled Oak, Concoid, Free Edge

Table, Console, Giltwood, Canted Black Marble Top, Continental, 48 x 21 x 32 In. 880.00
Table, Console, Hardwood, Rectangular Top, Foliate Carved Frieze, 30 In., Pair 275.00
Table, Console, Lifetime, Bowfront, 6 Legs, Center Drawer, Paper Label, 31 x 67 In. 8250.00
Table, Console, Louis Philippe, Mahogany, Black & Rust Marble Top, 71 1/2 In. 2090.00
Table, Console, Louis XIV Style, Giltwood, Marble Top, Carved, Pierced, 33 x 43 In. . . .   3735.00
Table, Console, Louis XV Style, Beechwood, Serpentine Marble Top, 25 In. 920.00
Table, Console, Louis XVI Style, Marble Top, Urn Stretcher, Painted, 39 x 69 In. 6325.00
Table, Console, Pine, Carved Acanthus Leaves, Scrolled Feet, 19th Century, 52 In. 1265.00
Table, Console, Rococo, Giltwood, Marble Top, Winged Female Figures, 33 In. 7475.00
Table, Console, Rococo, Pine, Serpentine Marble Top, C-Scroll Legs, Italy, 34 In. 5175.00
Table, Console, Trestle, Regency, Walnut, Pink Marble Top, Drawer, 30 In. 1955.00
Table, Corner, Gilt, Salmon Marble Top, Foliate Cabriole Legs, Blue Paint, 31 In. 4312.00
Table, Corner, Louis XV, 2 Tiers, Shaped Backsplash, Cabriole Legs, 24 x 40 In. 86.00
Table, Corner, Mahogany, Lyre Support, Tricorner Base, Carved Feet, 31 x 29 In. 245.00
Table, Corner, Queen Anne, Walnut, Handkerchief, Scalloped Apron, 1749, 32 In. 4140.00
Table, Dinette, Eames, Metal, Aluminum Base, 1960s, 27 x 36 In. 285.00
Table, Dining, Art Deco, Mahogany, Stepped Top, Plinth Base, France, 32 x 67 x 40 In. . .   863.00
Table, Dining, Art Deco, Walnut, Pedestal, Molded Frieze, Plinth, 55 x 43 In. 430.00
Table, Dining, Arts & Crafts, Carved, Trestle, 30 x 71 1/2 x 35 3/4 In. 1320.00
Table, Dining, Biedermeier, Fruitwood, 3-Part Base, Paw Feet, 1830s, 41 1/4 In. 5750.00
Table, Dining, Charles X, Mahogany Extension, Round Divided Top, 29 In. 21850.00
Table, Dining, Classical, Mahogany, Carved, Lyre-Shaped Supports, c.1820, 50 In. 2990.00
Table, Dining, Donald Deskey, Black Lacquer, Asymmetrical Rectangular Top, 31 In. 2300.00
Table, Dining, Drop Leaf, Cherry, Oval, Center Leg, 4 Leaves, c.1860, 42 x 54 In. 715.00
Table, Dining, Drop Leaf, Cherry, Square Tapered Legs, 2 Leaves, 29 x 16 x 45 1/2 In. . .   440.00
Table, Dining, Drop Leaf, Chippendale, Mahogany, Angular Cabriole Legs, 27 In. 7475.00
Table, Dining, Drop Leaf, Chippendale, Mahogany, Carved, c.1770, 47 x 46 1/4 In. 4600.00
Table, Dining, Drop Leaf, Chippendale, Mahogany, Claw & Ball Feet, c.1770, 47 In. 2415.00
Table, Dining, Drop Leaf, Chippendale, Mahogany, Oblong Top, Cabriole Legs, 28 In. . . .   3450.00
Table, Dining, Drop Leaf, Chippendale, Walnut, Carved, Claw Feet, c.1780, 47 x 47 In. . .   2070.00
Table, Dining, Drop Leaf, Empire, Mahogany, Rectangular, Down-Swept Feet, 29 In. 545.00
Table, Dining, Drop Leaf, Federal, Cherry, Hinged, Straight Skirt, 1800s, 29 x 50 In. 1265.00
Table, Dining, Drop Leaf, Federal, Mahogany, Pedestal, Brass Paw Feet, 1820, 41 In. 770.00
Table, Dining, Drop Leaf, G. Nakashima, Walnut, Frenchman's Cove, 30 In. 21850.00
Table, Dining, Drop Leaf, George III Style, Mahogany, England, 29 1/2 x 92 In. 1610.00
Table, Dining, Drop Leaf, Golden Birch, Rectangular Top, X-Shaped Supports, 30 In. . . .   1380.00
Table, Dining, Drop Leaf, Hepplewhite, Mahogany, Inlaid Panels, 112 In. 2640.00
Table, Dining, Drop Leaf, Heywood-Wakefield Co., Maple, Wishbone Base, 59 In. 1150.00
Table, Dining, Drop Leaf, Mahogany, Ball Feet, c.1820, 29 x 118 In. 2750.00
Table, Dining, Drop Leaf, Queen Anne, Mahogany, England, 18th Century, 102 In. 4400.00
Table, Dining, Drop Leaf, Queen Anne, Walnut, Oblong, Cabriole Legs, 1750, 27 In. 2475.00
Table, Dining, Drop Leaf, Sheraton, Bowed Front, Wood Pulls, 28 1/2 x 19 x 50 In. 660.00
Table, Dining, Drop Leaf, Sheraton, Cherry, 39 x 14 x 28 In. 600.00
Table, Dining, Drop Leaf, Sheraton, Mahogany, 6 Turned Legs, Casters, 48 x 17 In. 330.00
Table, Dining, Drop Leaf, Sheraton, Mahogany, Turned Legs, 29 1/2 x 16 1/2 x 47 In. . . .   440.00
Table, Dining, Drop Leaf, Sheraton, Pa., 1840, 29 x 42 In. 165.00
Table, Dining, Dunbar, Burl Walnut, 2 18-In. Leaves, 66 x 42 x 29 In. 230.00
Table, Dining, Duncan Phyfe, Mahogany, Crossbanded Veneer, 2 Pedestals, 64 In. 990.00
Table, Dining, Duncan Phyfe, Mahogany, Veneer, Double Pedestal, 147 x 110 In. 3190.00
Table, Dining, Federal, Mahogany, Rectangular Top, Serpentine End Stretchers, 30 In. . . .   345.00
Table, Dining, Florence Knoll, Oval Walnut Top, Bronze, 78 x 48 x 29 In. 935.00

Table, Dining, Frank Lloyd Wright, Double V-Shaped Base, 18-In. Leaves, 64 In. 550.00
Table, Dining, Frank Lloyd Wright, Rectangular Top, 2 Leaves, 64 x 29 In. 1210.00
Table, Dining, Frankl, Rectangular Light Walnut Top, Square Legs, 52 x 29 In. 495.00
Table, Dining, G. Nakashima, Burled Oak, Concoid, Free Edge . . . .*Illus* 56000.00
Table, Dining, G. Nelson, White Laminate Top, Herman Miller, 29 In. 1880.00
Table, Dining, G. Stickley, No. 634, Mahogany, 4 Heavy Square Posts, 30 In. 11500.00
Table, Dining, George II Style, Walnut, Parcel Gilt, 19th Century, 140 In. Open 2875.00
Table, Dining, George III, Walnut, Mahogany, Brass Inlay, 2 Pedestal, 62 x 39 In. 4315.00
Table, Dining, Limbert, No. 1480-C-54, Pedestal, Leaves, 28 x 54 In. 3575.00
Table, Dining, Limbert, No. 419, Round, Branded, Casters, 4 Leaves, 31 x 48 In. 2860.00
Table, Dining, Limbert, Round Top, 4-Sided Pedestal Base, Leaf, 29 3/4 x 48 In. 3300.00
Table, Dining, Limbert, Round Top, Square Pedestal, Leaves, 45 In. 2200.00
Table, Dining, Louis XV, Rectangular Top, Shaped Skirt, Cabriole Legs, 30 In. 980.00
Table, Dining, Louis XV, Walnut, Rosewood, Crossbanding, Gilt, Cabriole Legs, 30 In. . .   865.00
Table, Dining, Louis XVI, Mahogany, Convex Brass Edge, Brass Top Feet, 30 In. 865.00
Table, Dining, Mahogany, 2 Pedestal Base, 2 Leaves, Thomasville, 44 1/2 x 66 In. 715.00
Table, Dining, Mahogany, Crossbanded Top, Trifid Base, 66 In. 920.00
Table, Dining, Mahogany, Gadroon Carved Border, Leaf Carved Support, 72 In. 1150.00
Table, Dining, Mahogany, Reeded Scimitar Legs, Brass Paws, Leaves, 45 x 71 In. 5775.00
Table, Dining, Mahogany, Ring Turned Legs, 4 Leaves, 102 3/4 In. 345.00
Table, Dining, Mahogany, Round Top, Cluster Column Split Pedestal, 29 1/2 In. 2990.00
Table, Dining, Mahogany, Round, 4 Curved Acanthus Legs, 55 In. 1430.00
Table, Dining, Mahogany, Round, Leaves, c.1900, 60 In. 4950.00
Table, Dining, McCobb, Round Dark Walnut Top, 6 Legs, Calvin, 44 x 29 In. 155.00
Table, Dining, Mission, Oak, Square, 49 x 43 x 30 In. 440.00
Table, Dining, Napoleon III, Brass Mounted, Ebony Extension, 30 x 72 x 44 In. 6900.00
Table, Dining, Oak, Frieze, Drawers, Baluster Legs, Late 1800s, 30 x 70 x 33 1/2 In. 1380.00
Table, Dining, Oak, Marquetry Top, Carved Pedestal Base, Griffins, 49 x 30 In. 2070.00
Table, Dining, Oak, Round Top Expanding To Banquet Size, Split Pedestal, 98 In. 3630.00
Table, Dining, P. Evans, Glass Top, Steel & Gesso Stalagmite Base, 54 In. 2090.00
Table, Dining, Quartered Oak, 2 Frieze Drawers, Chamfered Legs, 79 In. 1380.00
Table, Dining, Regency Style, Mahogany, 2 Leaves, 29 x 44 x 117 In. 3740.00
Table, Dining, Regency, Mahogany, Crossbanded, String Top, Down-Swept Legs, 28 In. . . .   5465.00
Table, Dining, Regency, Mahogany, Rectangular Reeded Top, 4 Splayed Legs, 28 In. 11500.00
Table, Dining, Regency, Plain Frieze, Triangular Pedestals, Scrolled Feet, 29 In. 4600.00
Table, Dining, Rosewood, Carved Fruit & Foliage, Square Cabriole Legs, 28 1/2 In. 550.00
Table, Dining, Roycroft, 2 Original Leaves, Marked, 30 x 48 In. 5250.00
Table, Dining, Roycroft, Square, 4 Leaves, Marked, 48 In. 5100.00
Table, Dining, Saarinen, Round White Enamel Top, White Enamel Base, 29 In. 660.00
Table, Dining, Saarinen, Round White Marble Top, Knoll, 54 x 29 In. 1210.00
Table, Dining, Stickley Brothers, Oak, Corbel Pedestal Base, 1916, 29 1/2 In. 4025.00
Table, Dining, Stickley Brothers, Round, Pedestal, Shoe Feet, Paper Label, 30 x 48 In. . . .   2200.00
Table, Dining, Vico Magistretti, Fiberglass, 4 Detachable Legs, 29 In. 230.00
Table, Dining, Walnut, Applied Apron Trim, Spool Legs, 4 Leaves, c.1870, 42 In. 275.00
Table, Dining, Walnut, Round, Lazy Susan Top, Turned Legs, 19th Century, 53 In. 1760.00
Table, Dining, William Heal & Son, Queen Anne Style, Burl Walnut, London, 111 In. 1100.00
Table, Dining, William Leavens & Co., 4 Leaves, Dark Finish, 30 In. 690.00
Table, Drawer, 2-Board Top, Stretcher Base, c.1800, 33 1/2 x 53 1/2 x 26 1/2 In. 440.00
Table, Dressing, Bird's-Eye & Tiger Maple, 2 Short Drawers, 4 Square Legs, 58 In. 1095.00
Table, Dressing, Chippendale, Walnut, Rectangular Top, Cabriole Legs, 31 In. 11000.00
Table, Dressing, Faux Rosewood Surface, Gallery, Long Drawer, c.1840, 36 1/3 In. 990.00
Table, Dressing, Federal, Cherry, Veneer, 5 Drawers, Lyre Post Mirror, 33 x 57 In. 1320.00
Table, Dressing, George II, Walnut, 3 Drawers, Cabriole Legs, Pad Feet, 26 1/2 In. 430.00
Table, Dressing, Louis XV, Bronze, Gilt, Frieze Drawer, Oval Mirror, 56 x 17 In. 800.00
Table, Dressing, Louis XVI, Walnut, Banded Top, Tapered Legs, Lift-Up Mirror, 28 In. . . .   2530.00
Table, Dressing, Mahogany, 2 Drawers, Mirror, S-Scroll Support, Phila., 1830, 56 In. 1760.00
Table, Dressing, Mahogany, 3 Drawers, Lift Top, Serpentine Case, Tilt Mirror, 31 In. 495.00
Table, Dressing, Mahogany, Charcoal Marble Top, Small Drawer, Apron, 66 In. 2420.00
Table, Dressing, Mahogany, Melon Feet, Rectilinear Mirror, 69 In. 3220.00
Table, Dressing, Mahogany, Recessed Drawers, Lyre-Shaped Support, Mirror, 77 In. 1540.00
Table, Dressing, Oak, Ormolu, 2 Hinged Side Mirrors, Spain, 63 x 32 In. 770.00
Table, Dressing, Pine, Scrolled Backsplash, 16 x 30 In. 230.00
Table, Dressing, Queen Anne, Walnut, 2 Short Drawers, Pa., 33 x 30 In. 3200.00

Furniture, Table, Drop Leaf, Federal,
Mahogany, 1790-1800, 28 x 20 x 30 In.

Look at the hinge on a tilt top table. The wear should show on both the top and the base if it is old.

Never wash lacquered wood. Just wipe it clean with a damp cloth. Water could seep into the base wood and cause damage.

Table, Dressing, Queen Anne, Walnut, 3 Molded Drawers, Cabriole Legs, 29 In. 14850.00
Table, Dressing, Queen Anne, Walnut, 4 Drawers, Rectangular Molded Top, 29 In. 9200.00
Table, Dressing, Queen Anne, Walnut, Swiveling, Lacquer, 33 3/4 In. 2750.00
Table, Dressing, Queen Anne, Walnut, Thumb-Molded Top, 4 Cabriole Legs, 30 In. 10350.00
Table, Dressing, Rosewood, Opening Panel, Mirror Storage Wells, 32 1/4 In. 700.00
Table, Dressing, Shaped Backsplash Over 2 Stepped Drawers, Long Drawer, 42 In. 4125.00
Table, Dressing, Sheraton, Cherry, Poplar, 2 Short Drawers, Oblong Top, 28 In. 1035.00
Table, Dressing, Sheraton, Mahogany, 2 Sections, Ivory Inlay, Mirror, 60 In. 880.00
Table, Dressing, Sheraton, Mahogany, 3 Gallery Drawers, Step Back, 32 x 17 x 39 In. . . . 770.00
Table, Dressing, Sheraton, Pine, Yellow Paint, Black Stripes, 35 x 16 x 42 In. 990.00
Table, Dressing, William & Mary, Walnut, 3 Drawers, Rectangular, Bell Legs, 30 In. 750.00
Table, Drop Leaf, 4 Leaves, c.1870, 30 1/4 x 41 1/2 In. 210.00
Table, Drop Leaf, Art Deco, Walnut, Rounded Corners, Plank Stretcher, 80 x 29 In. 1035.00
Table, Drop Leaf, Birch, Turned Legs, 2 15-In. Leaves, 29 x 41 1/2 x 18 1/2 In. 270.00
Table, Drop Leaf, Carved Pedestal & Feet, Drawer, Victorian, 29 x 39 In. 2200.00
Table, Drop Leaf, Cherry, 4 Turned Legs, Mid-19th Century, 29 x 41 x 22 In. 225.00
Table, Drop Leaf, Cherry, Double Ogee Convex Molded Skirt, Cabriole Legs, 30 In. 935.00
Table, Drop Leaf, Cherry, Ribbed & Chamfered Legs, 18th Century, 38 x 26 1/2 In. 770.00
Table, Drop Leaf, Cherry, Turned Legs, Early 19th Century, 47 1/4 x 19 1/2 In. 330.00
Table, Drop Leaf, Chippendale Style, Mahogany, Cabriole Legs, 49 In. 1725.00
Table, Drop Leaf, Chippendale, Cherry, Drawer, c.1780, 28 x 39 x 34 1/2 In. 715.00
Table, Drop Leaf, Chippendale, Mahogany, Oblong Top, Gold, Brown, 1780, 28 In. 8625.00
Table, Drop Leaf, Chippendale, Walnut, Drake Feet, 27 3/4 x 46 In. 1380.00
Table, Drop Leaf, Classical, Mahogany, Carved, Shaped, N.Y., c.1825, 29 x 38 x 23 In. . . 690.00
Table, Drop Leaf, Crossbanded, Inlay, Frieze Drawer, Tapered Legs, 28 x 30 x 19 In. 575.00
Table, Drop Leaf, Edwardian, Satinwood, Octagonal Top, Cupid Reserves, 28 In. 5175.00
Table, Drop Leaf, Empire Style, Mahogany, 2 Convex Drawers, Tripod Base, 28 In. 375.00
Table, Drop Leaf, Empire, Maple, Ogee Frieze, Octagonal Legs, 1840s, 47 In. 450.00
Table, Drop Leaf, Farmhouse, Drawer Ends, Turned Legs, Painted, 29 x 27 x 44 In. 880.00
Table, Drop Leaf, Federal, Mahogany, 1790-1800, 28 x 20 x 30 In. . . . . *Illus* 2300.00
Table, Drop Leaf, Federal, Mahogany, 2 Drawers, Reeded Legs, c.1820, 28 x 17 In. 495.00
Table, Drop Leaf, Federal, Mahogany, Carved, Hinged, Round Corners, 29 x 42 In. 920.00
Table, Drop Leaf, Federal, Mahogany, Drawer, 2-Board Top, 17 x 36 In. 550.00
Table, Drop Leaf, Federal, Mahogany, Drawer, 27 1/4 x 32 1/2 In. 1380.00
Table, Drop Leaf, Federal, Mahogany, Drawer, Pedestal, c.1860, 30 x 54 In. 3410.00
Table, Drop Leaf, Federal, Mahogany, Inlay, 57 1/4 In. 950.00
Table, Drop Leaf, Federal, Mahogany, Inlay, Drawer, Hinged Leaves, 29 x 36 x 22 In. . . . 460.00
Table, Drop Leaf, Federal, Mahogany, Line Inlay, Icicle, 29 In. 2875.00
Table, Drop Leaf, Federal, Mahogany, Molded Top, Tapered Legs, 29 x 41 In. 400.00
Table, Drop Leaf, Federal, Mahogany, Oak, White Pine, Tapered Legs, Md., 29 3/4 In. . . . 2760.00
Table, Drop Leaf, Federal, Mahogany, Reeded Tapered Legs, 1800s, 29 x 35 x 22 In. 460.00
Table, Drop Leaf, Federal, Mahogany, Rule-Jointed Leaves, Arched Frieze, 60 x 28 In. . . . 430.00
Table, Drop Leaf, Federal, Tiger Maple, Drawer, Tapered Legs, c.1805, 20 x 19 In. 4315.00
Table, Drop Leaf, Frank Lloyd Wright, Mahogany, Signed, 14 x 60 In. 1760.00
Table, Drop Leaf, G. Stickley, Through Tenon Base, Round, 30 x 32 In. 1870.00
Table, Drop Leaf, George II, Mahogany, Drawer, Tripod Base, Baluster, 29 In. 1265.00

Table, Drop Leaf, George III, Mahogany, Molded Top, Cabriole Legs, 28 1/2 In. 10925.00
Table, Drop Leaf, George III, Mahogany, Oval, Square Legs, 19 x 15 1/2 In. 1495.00
Table, Drop Leaf, Hepplewhite Style, Mahogany, Tooled Leather, Inlay, 28 x 41 In. 115.00
Table, Drop Leaf, Hepplewhite Style, Walnut, 19th Century, Child's, 18 x 24 In. 415.00
Table, Drop Leaf, Hepplewhite, Mahogany, Shell Inlay, 28 x 28 x 19 In., Pair 805.00
Table, Drop Leaf, Hepplewhite, Maple, Square Tapered Legs, 28 x 41 x 17 In. 550.00
Table, Drop Leaf, Hepplewhite, Mixed Woods, Drawer, 50 x 22 In. 300.00
Table, Drop Leaf, Hepplewhite, Pine, Grain Painted, 25 x 48 In. 410.00
Table, Drop Leaf, Hepplewhite, Rectangular, Plain Apron, Tapered Legs, 23 x 22 In. 1210.00
Table, Drop Leaf, Hepplewhite, Walnut, 30 x 46 x 61 In. 85.00
Table, Drop Leaf, Jacobean Style, Oak, Oval, Carved Border, 19th Century, 29 In. 230.00
Table, Drop Leaf, Mahogany, Drawer, Reeded Legs, 1820, 29 x 46 In. 550.00
Table, Drop Leaf, Mahogany, Rectangular Top, D-Shaped Leaves, Round Legs, 29 In. . . . 288.00
Table, Drop Leaf, Maple, Corner Detail, Square Tapered Legs, 2 Leaves, 27 x 43 In. 220.00
Table, Drop Leaf, Marquetry, Center Frieze Drawer, Holland, 1730s, 28 3/4 In. 3025.00
Table, Drop Leaf, Marquetry, Ormolu, Fluted Legs, Continental, 1800s, 20 In. 1320.00
Table, Drop Leaf, Pine Top, Birch Base, Farmhouse, 27 1/2 In. 3080.00
Table, Drop Leaf, Queen Anne, Cherry, Connecticut, 13 x 42 x 14 In. 2200.00
Table, Drop Leaf, Queen Anne, Mahogany, Duck Feet, Swing Legs, 28 In. 660.00
Table, Drop Leaf, Queen Anne, Mahogany, Oval Top, Cabriole Legs, 28 x 46 x 15 In. . . . 1870.00
Table, Drop Leaf, Queen Anne, Mahogany, Pine, Club Feet, 1720, 39 x 15 3/4 In. 3025.00
Table, Drop Leaf, Queen Anne, Mahogany, Recessed Frieze, Pad Feet, 28 x 50 In. 1092.00
Table, Drop Leaf, Queen Anne, Mahogany, Turned Cabriole Legs, Pad Feet, 35 In. 2070.00
Table, Drop Leaf, Queen Anne, Maple, 2 Swing Legs, Duck Feet, 11 x 41 In. 2420.00
Table, Drop Leaf, Queen Anne, Maple, Cabriole Legs, Pad Feet, Late 1700s, 27 x 54 In. . . 1150.00
Table, Drop Leaf, Queen Anne, Maple, Scrolls, Cabriole Legs, c.1750, 27 x 42 x 13 In. . . 4313.00
Table, Drop Leaf, Queen Anne, Walnut, 3-Board Top, Cabriole Legs, 16 x 43 x 29 In. . . . 1925.00
Table, Drop Leaf, Queen Anne, Walnut, Scalloped End Aprons, 6 Legs, 27 3/4 In. 550.00
Table, Drop Leaf, Rectangular Top, Reeded Edge, Hairy Paw Feet, 1825, 30 In. 2990.00
Table, Drop Leaf, Regency, Burl Walnut, Lyre Supports, Paw Feet, 19 1/2 x 19 In. 546.00
Table, Drop Leaf, Rosewood, Crossbanded Top, Drawer, Down-Swept Legs, 61 In. 4600.00
Table, Drop Leaf, Russel Wright, Maple Top, Folding Leaves, Gate Leg, 44 x 25 In. 460.00
Table, Drop Leaf, Shaker Style, Maple, 2 Drawers, 28 1/2 In. 330.00
Table, Drop Leaf, Sheraton, Cherry, 2-Board Top, Turned Legs, 18 x 36 In. 300.00
Table, Drop Leaf, Sheraton, Cherry, Maple, 6 Legs, Casters, 21 x 46 In. 440.00
Table, Drop Leaf, Sheraton, Curly Maple, Turned Legs, 17 1/2 x 39 In. 745.00
Table, Drop Leaf, Sheraton, Mahogany, Drawer, Carved Legs, Casters, 29 x 34 x 21 In. . . 470.00
Table, Drop Leaf, Sheraton, Mahogany, Drawer, Rope Turned Legs, 29 1/2 x 41 In. 550.00
Table, Drop Leaf, Sheraton, Mahogany, Ribbed Legs, 28 1/2 x 48 x 17 In. 470.00
Table, Drop Leaf, Sheraton, Mahogany, Rope Turned Legs, 30 In. 990.00
Table, Drop Leaf, Sheraton, Mahogany, Turned Legs, 1830, 29 In. 250.00
Table, Drop Leaf, Sheraton, Poplar, Turned Legs, Pa., 1830, 28 3/4 In. 165.00
Table, Drop Leaf, Walnut, 4 Turned Legs, Mid-19th Century, 28 1/2 x 38 x 18 In. 225.00
Table, Drop Leaf, Walnut, Cabriole Legs, Pennsylvania, c.1760, 57 x 41 1/2 In. 3250.00
Table, Drop Leaf, Walnut, Rectangular Top, Tapered Turned Legs, 33 x 15 x 29 In. 230.00
Table, Drop Leaf, Walnut, Round Corner Leaves, Turned Legs, 29 x 36 x 21 In. 335.00
Table, Drop Leaf, William & Mary, Oak, Rectangular Top, Twist Turn Legs, 40 1/2 In. . . . 287.00
Table, Drop Leaf, William IV, Mahogany, c.1825, 28 x 39 In. 500.00
Table, Drum, Edwardian, Satinwood, Central Floral Bouquet, 4 Reeded Legs, 27 In. 3910.00
Table, Drum, Mahogany Veneer, Swan Base, Gold Trim, 25 3/4 x 18 In. 355.00
Table, Drum, Mahogany, Revolving Tooled Leather Top, 1840, 30 In. 4315.00
Table, E. Wormley, Exotic Wood Veneer, 27 x 15 In. 825.00
Table, E. Wormley, Oak, Laminate Top, Half-Shelf, 6 Legs, Dunbar, 86 In. 605.00
Table, E. Wormley, Square Walnut Top, X-Stretchers, 20 In. 3300.00
Table, Eames, DTM, White Laminate Top, 39 x 29 In. 495.00
Table, Eames, Rectangular Walnut Top, 1950, 21 x 17 In. 1760.00
Table, Edwardian, Satinwood, Oval Top, Cupid Adorned With Garlands, 30 In. 1495.00
Table, Egyptian Revival, Burl Veneer, Gilt, 3 Hoof Feet, 1900s, Round, 28 x 30 In. 385.00
Table, Elm, Dark Lacquer, Chinese, 20 3/4 x 86 x 32 In. 385.00
Table, Elm, Red & Black Lacquer, Mortised, Chinese, 20 x 29 x 33 In., Pair 220.00
Table, Empire Style, Marble, Bronze, 3 Neoclassical Maiden Supports, 20 In. 3080.00
Table, Empire, Figured Mahogany Veneer, Marble, Swan Legs, France, 22 x 31 In. 4180.00
Table, Empire, Mahogany, Rosewood, Rectangular Crossbanded Top, 20 In., Pair 10925.00

Table, Empire, Walnut, Maple, Rectangular Top, 2 Drawers, Foliate Legs, 1830, 28 In. 1495.00
Table, F. Camp, Round Top, 4 Flat Legs, 1974, 15 1/2 x 33 In. 770.00
Table, Federal Style, Cherry, Round, Tripod Base, Baluster, Down-Swept Legs, 28 In. . . . 260.00
Table, Federal Style, Inlaid Mahogany, Serpentine, 3 Drawers, 60 x 35 In. 2185.00
Table, Federal Style, Molded Rectangular Top, Square Sectioned Legs, 28 In. 140.00
Table, Federal, Cherry, Bird's-Eye Maple, Drawer, 4 Swelled Legs, 28 x 19 In. 1495.00
Table, Federal, Cherry, Drawer, Serpentine Leaves, New England, 1800s, 28 x 36 In. 748.00
Table, Federal, Inlaid Walnut, D-Ends, 12 Tapered Legs, 30 x 90 In. 2185.00
Table, Federal, Mahogany Veneer, Rectangular Top, Beaded Skirt, 1810, 29 In. 865.00
Table, Federal, Mahogany, Birch, 4 Square Tapered Legs, 1800, 27 x 17 1/2 In. 2875.00
Table, Federal, Mahogany, Teardrop & Oval Inlay, Drawer, 29 x 21 1/2 x 31 1/2 In. 7475.00
Table, Federal, Maple, Canted Corners, Tripod Base, Baluster Turned Standard, 24 In. . . . 175.00
Table, Flame Mahogany, Ring & Spiral Turned Legs, Ball Feet, 90 1/4 In. 920.00
Table, Floral Pendants, 6 Sides, Painted, 1880s, 15 x 28 In. 465.00
Table, Folding, Hardwood, Foliate Border, Ivory Inlay, 27 x 30 x 20 In. 5175.00
Table, Folding, Mahogany, Flame Grain Veneer, 20th Century, 31 x 37 In. 880.00
Table, Folding, Trestle, Oak, Oilcloth, Shoe Feet, 39 1/2 In. 440.00
Table, Frank Lloyd Wright, Cypress, Triangular, Shelf, 1951, 35 1/2 In. 1100.00
Table, Frank Lloyd Wright, Hexagonal Top, Triple-Slab Base, Signed, 17 x 48 In. 1760.00
Table, Frank Lloyd Wright, Square Top, Recessed Handle, 26 x 23 In. 1540.00
Table, Frankl, Mahogany Base, Cork Top, Shelf, 21 x 30 In., Pair 1100.00
Table, French Provincial, Oak, Rectangular Plank Top, Turned Legs, 28 3/4 x 37 In. 1495.00
Table, French Style, Marble Top & Shelf, Brass Trim, Medallion, 12 x 10 x 30 In. 935.00
Table, Fruitwood, Carved Apron, Cabriole Legs With French Toes, 15 In. 8800.00
Table, G. Nakashima, Walnut, 4 Legs, 13 x 100 In., Pair 10350.00
Table, G. Nakashima, Walnut, 4 Short Drawers, 1979, 17 x 28 1/2 In. 2875.00
Table, G. Stickley, Arched Cross Stretchers, Round, 16 x 14 In. 600.00
Table, G. Stickley, Keyed Through Tenon Stretcher, Decal, 29 x 40 In. 1980.00
Table, G. Stickley, No. 410-L, Stack Stretcher, Red Decal, 30 x 48 In. 38500.00
Table, G. Stickley, No. 802, Harvey Ellis Design, Label, 39 x 42 In. 11550.00
Table, G. Stickley, Round Top, Arched Apron, Flared Plank Legs, 40 x 29 In. 4675.00
Table, Galle, Fruitwood, Marquetry, Leaves, 2 Tiers, 1900, 25 x 14 In. 1935.00
Table, Game, Art Deco, Rosewood, Galuchat, Sharkskin, Drawer, France, 1930, 27 In. . . . 5750.00
Table, Game, Arts & Crafts, Checkered Inlay, Pedestal, 30 x 33 In. 660.00
Table, Game, Baroque, Flip Top, Center Frieze Drawer, 4 Scrolled Feet, 32 x 14 In. 690.00
Table, Game, Cherry, Drawer, Reverse Painted Checkerboard, 26 x 18 x 18 In. 495.00
Table, Game, Cherry, String Inlay, Frieze Drawer, Brass Pulls, c.1800, 29 3/4 In. 4890.00
Table, Game, Classical, Mahogany, Rectangular Flip Top, Acanthus Legs, 28 In. 2300.00
Table, Game, Classical, Rosewood Verdigris, Rectangular Top, 1825, 30 In. 8050.00
Table, Game, Demilune Top, Sun Ray Design, Continental, 19th Century, 29 In. 1210.00
Table, Game, Drop Leaf, George III Style, Bowfront, Sliding Top, 28 1/2 x 42 In. 880.00
Table, Game, Drop Leaf, Straight Legs, Shelf, Upholstered, Continental, 29 x 26 In. 1035.00
Table, Game, Drop Leaf, Yew, William IV, Chessboard Inlay, 28 In. 4830.00
Table, Game, E. Wormley, Octagonal Walnut Top, 4 Legs, Brass Feet, 25 In. 2200.00
Table, Game, Edwardian, Inlaid Mahogany, Flip Top, Plinth Base, 29 1/2 In. 440.00
Table, Game, Empire, Mahogany, Flip Top, Rectangular Top, Ogee Frieze, 29 1/2 In. 315.00
Table, Game, Empire, Mahogany, Rectangular Swivel Top, Plinth Base, 29 In. 490.00
Table, Game, Empire, Mahogany, Satinwood, Scrolled Plinth Base, Casters, 28 In. 750.00
Table, Game, Federal, Mahogany, D-Shaped Top, Tapered Legs, Peg Feet, 1810, 29 In. . . . 4025.00
Table, Game, Federal, Mahogany, Oblong Top, Reeded Legs, Peg Feet, 30 x 36 In. 8050.00
Table, Game, Federal, Mahogany, Rectangular Top, 4 Down-Swept Legs, 30 In. 7475.00
Table, Game, Federal, Mahogany, Rectangular Top, Drawer, 34 1/2 x 30 In. 290.00
Table, Game, Federal, Mahogany, Rectangular Top, Square Tapered Legs, 1795, 29 In. . . . 3450.00
Table, Game, Federal, Mahogany, Rectangular Top, Tapered Legs, 28 1/2 In. 4310.00
Table, Game, Federal, Mahogany, Rosewood, 19th Century, 29 1/2 x 36 In. 1330.00
Table, Game, Federal, Mahogany, Shaped Inlaid Top, 4 Inlaid Legs, 1790, 29 In. 6900.00
Table, Game, Federal, Mahogany, Shaped Inlaid Top, Square Legs, 1795, 29 x 36 In. 6325.00
Table, Game, Federal, Mahogany, Tiger Maple Inlay, Square Legs, 1815, 29 In. 3735.00
Table, Game, Federal, Mahogany, Triple Elliptic Top, Reeded Legs, 30 In., Pair 19550.00
Table, Game, G. Stickley, Leather Top, Keyed-Through Stretcher, 38 In. 4950.00
Table, Game, Gateleg, Dutch Rococo, Serpentine Flip Top, Drawer, 29 1/2 In. 3300.00
Table, Game, Gateleg, George II, Mahogany, Flip Top, Cabriole Legs, 28 1/2 In. 1650.00
Table, Game, Gateleg, George III, Mahogany, Flip Top, 28 3/4 x 17 1/4 In. 1495.00

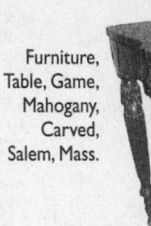

Furniture,
Table, Game,
Mahogany,
Carved,
Salem, Mass.

Furniture,
Table, Game,
Mahogany,
Turret Top,
Claw Footed

Table, Game, Gateleg, Walnut, Bead Molded Drawer, c.1750, 35 3/4 In.	3250.00
Table, Game, George III, Calamander Wood, Satinwood, Hinged D-Shaped Top, 29 In.	1540.00
Table, Game, George III, Flip Top, Mahogany, Ribbon Edge, 29 x 30 x 14 In.	2990.00
Table, Game, George III, Flip Top, Serpentine, Crossbanded, 29 x 36 x 18 In.	1320.00
Table, Game, George III, Mahogany, Banded Interior, Satinwood Shell, 28 1/4 In.	1955.00
Table, Game, George III, Mahogany, Rectangular Flip Top, Drawer, 28 In.	2200.00
Table, Game, George III, Satinwood, Mahogany, Baize Lined Surface, 30 In.	5280.00
Table, Game, George III, Satinwood, Serpentine Top, Foliate, Drawer, 28 1/2 In.	2760.00
Table, Game, George IV, Mahogany, D-Shaped Top, Ebony Geometric Inlay, 29 In.	605.00
Table, Game, Hunzinger, Oak, Mixed Woods, Felt Center, Round, 1894, 29 x 36 In.	505.00
Table, Game, Italian Rococo, Kingwood, Walnut, Flip Top, 1775-1800, 30 In.	3960.00
Table, Game, Louis Philippe, Mahogany, Square Flip Top, Baize Interior, 30 In.	550.00
Table, Game, Louis XIV, Tortoiseshell Marquetry, Brass, Flip Top, 29 x 35 x 18 In.	375.00
Table, Game, Louis XV Style, Walnut, Backgammon Board, 42 x 27 In.	690.00
Table, Game, Louis XV, Burl Elm, Lift-Out Gameboard, Inlay, Rectangular, 29 In.	1840.00
Table, Game, Louis XV, Walnut, Square Inset Top, Scrolled Feet, Needlework, 30 In.	1840.00
Table, Game, Louis XVI, Brass, Gilt, Rectangular Top, Top-Shaped Feet, 30 In.	1035.00
Table, Game, Mahogany Veneer, 4 Rope Twist Legs, 1840, 29 x 36 x 18 In.	1210.00
Table, Game, Mahogany, Beaded Drawer, Marlborough Feet, 1760, 29 1/4 In.	9200.00
Table, Game, Mahogany, Carved, Salem, Mass. ....*Illus*	1800.00
Table, Game, Mahogany, Crossbanded Flip Top, Tapered, 42 x 20 x 30 In.	460.00
Table, Game, Mahogany, Flip Top, Frieze Inlay, Down-Swept Legs, 1810, 29 In.	3450.00
Table, Game, Mahogany, Flip Top, Frieze On Ring Turned Legs, 1850s, 30 3/4 In.	575.00
Table, Game, Mahogany, Fruitwood, Leather Surface, Aperture For Lamp, 43 1/2 In.	8050.00
Table, Game, Mahogany, Turret Top, Claw Footed ....*Illus*	3750.00
Table, Game, Poplar, Checkerboard Design, 4 Drawers, 1825, 28 3/4 x 18 x 16 In.	1090.00
Table, Game, Queen Anne, Mahogany, Rectangular Flip Top, 29 x 32 x 15 In.	6325.00
Table, Game, Rattan Covered Valise Top, Chess & Backgammon, 4 Drawers, 42 In.	2875.00
Table, Game, Regency, Colonial Penwork, Ivory, Ribbed Bun Feet, 30 In.	4400.00
Table, Game, Regency, Mahogany, Demilune, Flip Top, 28 x 36 x 17 In.	1980.00
Table, Game, Rococo, Rosewood, Leather, Shaped Flip Top, 30 x 31 In.	2640.00
Table, Game, Rococo, Walnut, Cabriole Legs, Hoof Feet, 18th Century, 32 x 16 In.	10925.00
Table, Game, Rosewood, Flip Top, Foliate Carved Standard, Down-Swept Legs, 31 In.	3220.00
Table, Game, Sheraton Style, Mahogany, Flip Top, Mid-20th Century, 32 x 29 In.	375.00
Table, Game, Walnut, Accordion Action, Leather Surface, Scrolled Toes, 30 1/2 In.	3450.00
Table, Game, Walnut, Floral Mother-Of-Pearl Marquetry, Baize Surface, 29 In.	7475.00
Table, Game, William IV, Mahogany, Flip Top, Flared Pedestal, 29 x 36 In.	1980.00
Table, Gateleg, Charles II, Oak, Narrow Top, Hinged Leaves, Turned Legs, 28 In.	1265.00
Table, Gateleg, Chippendale, Mahogany, Pine, 1780, 22 x 48 In.	1680.00
Table, Gateleg, Federal, Mahogany, Swing Leg, 20 x 46 x 21 In.	1210.00
Table, Gateleg, George II, Mahogany, Cabriole Legs, Ball Feet, 28 In.	2070.00
Table, Gateleg, Hepplewhite, Mahogany, Floral & Shell Inlay, c.1820, 41 x 53 In.	1100.00
Table, Gateleg, Maple, Oval, Hinged, Drawer, Heavily Turned Base, 1700s, 29 x 13 In.	4830.00
Table, Gateleg, Queen Anne, Maple, Scrolled Aprons, 28 1/2 In.	1100.00
Table, Gateleg, Queen Anne, Maple, Swing Legs, 12 x 42 In.	3850.00
Table, Gateleg, Queen Anne, Maple, Tapered Legs, Leaves, 11 x 42 In.	2420.00
Table, Gateleg, Queen Anne, Maple, Wrought Iron Butterfly Hinge, 26 In.	2420.00
Table, Gateleg, Queen Anne, Walnut, Oval Top, Baluster Turned Legs, 43 x 27 In.	1380.00
Table, Gateleg, Sheraton, Mahogany, 6 Reeded Legs, 21 x 50 In.	1760.00

Table, Gateleg, William & Mary, Oak, 2 D-Shaped Leaves, 22 x 53 In. 935.00
Table, Gateleg, William & Mary, Walnut, Oval Top, 2 Drawers, 1730, 29 In. 16500.00
Table, George II, Mahogany, Hinged Top, Tripod Base, Cabriole Legs, 25 x 23 In. 990.00
Table, George III Style, Satinwood, Tambour Door, 32 x 18 1/4 In., Pair 1980.00
Table, George III, Hinged Lid, Drawer, Square Legs, 32 x 15 1/2 x 15 In. 805.00
Table, George III, Mahogany, Center Drawer, Carved Cabriole Legs, Ireland, 33 In. 13750.00
Table, George III, Mahogany, Oval Top, 8 Molded Square Legs, 29 1/2 x 72 In. 1092.00
Table, George III, Mahogany, Pierced Gallery, Pullout Drawer, 29 In. 2420.00
Table, George III, Mahogany, Rectangular Top, 3 Drawers, Peg Feet, 37 In. 6900.00
Table, George III, Mahogany, Vertical Tambour Door, Square Legs, 33 In. 750.00
Table, George IV, Mahogany, Molded Drawers, Ring Turned Legs, 1825, 34 In. 745.00
Table, Georgian, Mahogany, Octagonal Glass Lift Top, Scrolled Feet, 26 x 27 1/2 In. 175.00
Table, Giltwood, Onyx Top, Women's Heads On Legs, Arched Stretcher, 29 In. 1100.00
Table, Gueridon, Dorothy Draper, Art Deco, Mahogany, Round Top, 23 In., Pair 3450.00
Table, Gueridon, Empire Style, Round Marble Top, Ormolu Mounts, Caryatids, 33 In. . . . 1100.00
Table, Gueridon, Fruitwood, Marble Top, Mid-19th Century, 28 x 22 1/4 In. 2200.00
Table, Gueridon, Louis XV Style, Mahogany, Gilt Bronze, Inset Marble Top, 30 In. 3160.00
Table, Gueridon, Louis XV Style, Tulipwood, Marquetry, Gilt Bronze, c.1900, 29 In. 7475.00
Table, Gueridon, Louis XVI, Mahogany, Round Marble Top, Fluted Legs, 29 1/4 In. 977.00
Table, Gueridon, Mahogany, Gray, White Flecked Round Top, Bun Feet, 28 x 25 In. 1610.00
Table, Gueridon, Neoclassical Style, Cavorting Putti, Painted, 29 1/2 In., Pair 880.00
Table, Hardwood, Octagonal Top, Floral, Ivory Inlay, 2 Drawers, 24 1/2 In. 6900.00
Table, Hardwood, Oval Top, Inset Marble, Cabriole Legs, Chinese, 19 In. 140.00
Table, Hepplewhite Style, Drawer, Yellow Paint, c.1830, 35 3/4 x 24 x 29 In. 550.00
Table, Hepplewhite Style, Mahogany, Drawer, 19th Century, 35 x 43 In. 4840.00
Table, Hepplewhite, Cherry, 2-Board Top, Drawer, 24 x 30 x 28 In. 410.00
Table, Hepplewhite, Cherry, Inlay, 2-Board Top, Drawer, New England, 17 x 32 In. 770.00
Table, Hepplewhite, Cherry, Oblong Backboard, Square Tapered Legs, 1800, 37 In. 2640.00
Table, Hepplewhite, Line & Bellflower Inlay, Drawer, 1830, 31 In. 1815.00
Table, Hepplewhite, Mahogany, Round, Crossbanded Top, Banded Frieze, 26 x 26 In. . . . 230.00
Table, Hepplewhite, Mahogany, Scalloped Apron, Drawer, 28 3/4 In. 1870.00
Table, Hepplewhite, Pine, Scalloped Top, Drawer, 1810, 27 3/4 x 18 In. 467.00
Table, Hepplewhite, Square Top, Drawer, 1820, 28 x 16 In. 440.00
Table, Hepplewhite, Square, Checkerboard, Drawer, 18 x 25 In. . . . . *Illus* 715.00
Table, Hepplewhite, Walnut, Drawer, Square Tapered Legs, c.1810, 26 3/4 In. 825.00
Table, Hepplewhite, Walnut, Square Tapered Legs, Lower Shelf, 1820, 29 x 21 In. 3300.00
Table, I. Noguchi, Black Birch, Rudder, Aluminum, c.1946, 15 1/2 In. 5750.00
Table, Ice Cream, Art Nouveau, Iron, Pink Milk Glass Top, Round, 24 In. 165.00
Table, Ice Cream, Round Wood Top, Floral, Lion Design, Claw Feet, 29 In. 400.00
Table, Ico & Louisa Parisi, Glass Top, 4 Bentwood Legs, Brass Feet, 1950s, 49 In. 1150.00
Table, Iron, Marble Top, 3 Iron Foliate Panels, 4 Straight Legs, 41 x 23 3/4 In. 410.00
Table, Iron, Pink Marble Top, Grapes, Leaves & Vines Bottom, 31 x 56 In. 3410.00
Table, Kelvin Philip, Rectangular Top, Brass Patina, 17 x 19 In., Pair 1840.00
Table, L. & J.G. Stickley, Leather Top, Tacked Cross Stretcher, 30 x 42 In. 6600.00
Table, L. & J.G. Stickley, No. 574, Clip Corner, Branded, 29 x 18 In. 1100.00
Table, L. & J.G. Stickley, Round Top, Onondaga, 29 x 48 In. 305.00
Table, L. & J.G. Stickley, Round Top, Shelf, Arched Stretchers, 29 x 18 In. 470.00
Table, Laminated Glass, Triangular Top, Tripod Base, Turquoise, John Lewis, 31 In. 4600.00
Table, Library, Arts & Crafts, Drawer, Flat Stretcher, 4 Slats On Ends, 42 x 30 In. 280.00

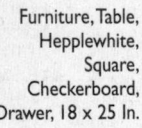

Furniture, Table,
Hepplewhite,
Square,
Checkerboard,
Drawer, 18 x 25 In.

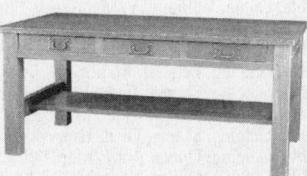

Furniture, Table, Library, G. Stickley,
3 Drawers, Shelf, Decal, 30 x 66 x 36 In.

Table, Library, Arts & Crafts, Oak, 2 Drawers Over Shelf, 30 1/2 x 48 In. 240.00
Table, Library, Arts & Crafts, Oak, 4 Vertical Slats, Median Shelf, 1912, 30 1/2 In. 805.00
Table, Library, Arts & Crafts, Raised Top, Molded Edge, Post Legs, 32 x 84 x 31 In. 385.00
Table, Library, Arts & Crafts, Reticulated Legs, 2 Hinged Storage Areas, 36 In. 385.00
Table, Library, Auglaize Furniture Co., Oak, Rectangular Top, Door, Oh., 30 In. 230.00
Table, Library, Baroque, Oak, 2 Drawers, Fruits & Flower Carved Supports, 35 In. 5225.00
Table, Library, Drawer, Rope Turned Legs, Acanthus Carved Apron, 39 1/4 In. 506.00
Table, Library, Federal, Mahogany, Rectangular Top, 2 Drawers, Arched Legs, 27 In. 290.00
Table, Library, G. Stickley, 2 Drawers, Shelf, Red Decal, 30 x 54 x 32 In. 1540.00
Table, Library, G. Stickley, 3 Drawers, Shelf, Decal, 30 x 66 x 36 In. . . . .*Illus* 27500.00
Table, Library, G. Stickley, Leather Top, 2 Drawers, Oval Hardware, 30 x 48 In. 2970.00
Table, Library, G. Stickley, No. 614, Oak, 2 Drawers, Shelf, c.1909, 41 3/4 In. 2070.00
Table, Library, George IV Style, Mahogany, Leather Top, 3 Drawers, 30 x 60 In. 2860.00
Table, Library, Gilt Tooled Leather Top, Paneled Frieze, Brass Caps, c.1880, 33 In. 4887.00
Table, Library, L. & J.G. Stickley, Bookcase Sides, Branded, 30 x 42 x 28 In. 1100.00
Table, Library, L. & J.G. Stickley, Leather Top, Shelf, Handcraft Decal, 29 x 36 In. 1595.00
Table, Library, L. & J.G. Stickley, Long Drawer, Branded, 42 In.   1430.00
Table, Library, L. & J.G. Stickley, No. 375, Open Sides, Onondaga Shops, 29 x 42 In. . . .   2090.00
Table, Library, L. & J.G. Stickley, No. 597, Overhanging Top, Shelf, Label, 40 x 28 In. . .   1760.00
Table, Library, Lifetime, No. 698, Drawer, 30 x 45 x 26 In. 990.00
Table, Library, Limbert, No. 153, Turtle-Shaped Top, Blind Drawer, Shelf, 29 x 48 In. . . . 10450.00
Table, Library, Limbert, Oak, Oval, Branded, 29 x 44 x 30 In. 5500.00
Table, Library, Limbert, Overhanging Top, 2 Drawers, Corbels, Branded, 29 x 48 In. 1430.00
Table, Library, Limbert, Triple Corbels, Oak, 29 1/4 x 49 3/4 x 28 In. 2860.00
Table, Library, Mahogany, 3 Short Drawers, Fretted Square Legs, 29 x 50 In. 9775.00
Table, Library, Mahogany, Burl Walnut Veneer, Carved Legs, 29 1/2 x 47 In. 495.00
Table, Library, Mahogany, Regency Style, 27 x 15 3/4 In. 690.00
Table, Library, Mahogany, Trefoil Leaves, Paneled Frieze, c.1810, 51 In. 2875.00
Table, Library, Mersman Bros., Drawer, Lower Shelf, Cutout Side Shelves, 48 In. 605.00
Table, Library, Michigan Chair Co., Center Drawer, Side Shelves, 29 x 42 x 26 In. 770.00
Table, Library, Roycroft, Drawer, Cutout Plank Sides, Orb & Cross Mark, 59 x 30 In. 8800.00
Table, Library, Roycroft, Mackmurdo Feet, Skinned Finish, 28 x 10 x 22 In. 4400.00
Table, Library, Stickley & Brandt, Slat Ends, Branded, 30 x 36 x 24 In. 440.00
Table, Library, Stickley Brothers, Rectangular Top, 2 Legs, Prairie Design, 39 In. 1870.00
Table, Library, Walnut, Drawer, Cabriole Legs, Animal Paw Feet, Italy, 35 x 47 In. 4675.00
Table, Library, Walnut, Removable Top, 2 Drawers, Dutch Pad Feet, 28 1/2 x 54 In. 9500.00
Table, Library, William IV, Rosewood, Carved, Brass Inlay, Leather, 51 In. 5175.00
Table, Lifetime, Round, Lower Shelf, Paper Label, 29 x 24 In. 1045.00
Table, Limbert, Gallery, Drawer, Branded, 41 x 40 x 17 In. 2200.00
Table, Limbert, No. 158, Double Oval, 48 x 36 x 29 In. 9900.00
Table, Limbert, No. 240, Square Top, Solid Base, 30 x 20 x 20 In. 7150.00
Table, Louis Philippe, Mahogany, Rectangular Top, 2 Drawers, 29 1/2 In. 4600.00
Table, Louis Philippe, Mahogany, Rosewood, Marble Top, Concave Base, 28 1/4 In. 2420.00
Table, Louis XV Style, 3 Drawers, Leather Top, Gilt, Ormolu, 33 In. 1760.00
Table, Louis XV Style, Giltwood, Carved, Marble Top, Pierced Base, 34 x 60 In. 5225.00
Table, Louis XV Style, Kingwood, Oval Marble Top, Brassbound, 20 x 25 In. 525.00
Table, Louis XV Style, Mahogany, Brass, Demilune, Hinged Top, Casters, 37 x 42 In. . . .   1210.00
Table, Louis XV Style, Mahogany, Kidney Top, Baluster Brass Gallery, 32 x 49 In. 1210.00
Table, Louis XV Style, Marquetry, Serpentine Top, Floral Inlay, 26 1/2 In. 880.00
Table, Louis XV Style, Satinwood, Floral Basket Inlay, Brass Gallery, 30 In. 520.00
Table, Louis XV, Inlay, Oval, France, 28 1/2 x 30 1/2 In. 330.00
Table, Louis XV, Kingwood, 3 Drawers, Rectangular Leather Top, 29 In. 1955.00
Table, Louis XV, Kingwood, 3 Frieze Drawers, Rectangular Top, 31 1/2 In. 977.00
Table, Louis XV, Mahogany, Oval Top, Cabriole Legs, 26 x 14 In. 201.00
Table, Louis XV, Rectangular Lipped Edge Top, Cabriole Legs, 27 x 17 x 28 In., Pair 35.00
Table, Louis XV, Rosewood, Round Gilt Metal Top, Cabriole Legs, 30 x 24 In., Pair 1265.00
Table, Louis XV, Round Inlaid Top, Bronze Cabriole Legs, 28 1/4 In. 345.00
Table, Louis XV, White Marble Top, 3 Long Drawers, 24 x 14 x 29 In. 316.00
Table, Louis XV, White Marble Top, Overall Floral & Shell, Geometric Design, 34 In. . . .   546.00
Table, Louis XVI Style, Giltwood, Marble Top, Guilloche Carved Frieze, 19 In. 1495.00
Table, Louis XVI Style, Kingwood, Parquetry, Leather, Drawers, 30 x 72 In. 6325.00
Table, Louis XVI Style, Marble Top, Carved Frieze, Tapered Legs, c.1880, 32 x 21 In. . . .   1150.00
Table, Louis XVI Style, Satinwood, Gilt, Bronze Paw Feet, 50 1/2 x 61 In. 315.00

Table, Louis XVI Style, Walnut, Inlay, Late 19th Century, 31 3/4 x 16 x 13 1/2 In. 690.00
Table, Louis XVI, Ebony, Rectangular Top, Ormolu Border, 17 1/4 x 5 x 36 In. 11500.00
Table, Louis XVI, Kingwood, Tulipwood, Drawer, Marble Shelf, 31 3/4 In. 2420.00
Table, Louis XVI, Mahogany, Oval White & Gray Marble Top, 31 In. 1495.00
Table, Louis XVI, Mahogany, Variegated Gray Marble Top, Top-Shaped Feet, 35 In. 2990.00
Table, Louis XVI, Walnut, Floral Inlay, 3 Drawers, 29 x 16 In. 1035.00
Table, Louis XVI, Walnut, Rectangular Brass Top, 2 Drawers, 4 Legs, 27 1/2 In. 1495.00
Table, Louis XVI, Wrought Iron, Marble Top, Scrolled & Foliate Base, 37 x 118 In. 1980.00
Table, M. Breuer, Tubular Chrome, White Laminate Top, 1960, 18 In. 175.00
Table, Mahogany, Baltic, Wedge Veneer, Round Plinth Base, 31 1/2 x 49 1/2 In. 2350.00
Table, Mahogany, Banded Table Top, Griffin Head, Cornucopia, Sprig, 53 In. 2090.00
Table, Mahogany, Carved Skirt, Birds & Flowers, Claw & Ball Feet, 16 x 18 In. 235.00
Table, Mahogany, Drawer, Pullout Side, England, 29 1/2 In. 546.00
Table, Mahogany, Hinged Top, 3 Carved Claw & Ball Feet, 28 x 33 1/2 In. 1540.00
Table, Mahogany, Hinged Top, Adjustable Slope, Shelf, Marlborough Feet, 41 In. 1495.00
Table, Mahogany, Marble Top, 3 Mounted Columnar Supports, Ball Feet, 28 In. 750.00
Table, Mahogany, Ormolu Mounts, Jules Leleu, 1935, 15 x 30 In. 7475.00
Table, Mahogany, Oval Top, Molded, Pierced Frieze, Scrolled Legs, Germany, 27 In. 920.00
Table, Mahogany, Rectangular Top, Crossbanded, 28 x 23 In. 546.00
Table, Mahogany, Rectangular Top, Drawer, Compass Rays, 1840, 29 x 39 In. 5775.00
Table, Mahogany, Rectangular Top, Flowering Urn, Tapered Legs, 30 In. 400.00
Table, Mahogany, Ripple Molding, Lyre-Shaped End Supports, 1830s, 35 1/2 In. 1380.00
Table, Mahogany, Square Top, 2 Drawers, Turned Reeded Legs, 1820, 29 In. 660.00
Table, Mahogany, Veneer, Inlay, Demilune Ends, England, 44 x 103 In. 2090.00
Table, Maple, Drawer, Stretcher Base, New England, c.1740, 29 x 32 In. 6900.00
Table, Maple, Pine, Breadboard Top, Lower Shelf, Square Legs, Painted, 47 x 44 In. 5175.00
Table, Marble Top, 2 Drawers, Pierced Gallery, 1880s, 28 1/2 In. 7475.00
Table, Marble Top, Reeded Brass Legs, Stretchers, Round, 29 x 24 In. 3740.00
Table, Marble, Mahogany, Serpentine Top, Brown Marble Inset, 19 x 28 x 18 In. 280.00
Table, McCobb, Brass, Inset White Glass Top, 14 x 20 In. 357.00
Table, McCobb, Walnut Top, 2 Recessed Drawers, Brass, 25 In., Pair 1725.00
Table, McCobb, Wood, Leather & Brass Banded Top, Lower Shelf, 20 In. 230.00
Table, Metal, Book Shape, Stack Of Volumes, Italy, 17 1/2 x 17 In. 2070.00
Table, Micro-Mosaic, Marble Top, Greek Key Border, 3 Incurved Supports, 31 In. 9775.00
Table, Napoleon III, Ebonized, Gilt Bronze, Tooled Leather Top, 30 1/2 In. 3160.00
Table, Napoleon III, Gilt Brass, Marble Top, Shelf, Round, 29 In. 2860.00
Table, Napoleon III, Mahogany, Ormolu, Round Marble Top, 30 In. 2860.00
Table, Neoclassical Style, Ebonized, Ormolu, Egyptian Marble Top, 25 x 19 In. 660.00
Table, Neoclassical Style, Mahogany, Parcel Gilt, Canted Corners, 29 x 40 In. 1980.00
Table, Neoclassical, Brass, Rectangular Mirrored Top, Square Fluted Legs, 17 x 28 In. ... 430.00
Table, Nesting, Federal, Mahogany, Pencil Inlay, 27 x 16 x 25 In., 4 Piece 173.00
Table, Nesting, George IV, Mahogany, Bamboo Turned Supports, 30 1/2 In., 3 Piece 1430.00
Table, Nesting, Oak, Turned Legs, 26 x 17 In., 4 Piece 195.00
Table, Nesting, Rectangular, Japanese Figural Landscape, Victorian, 29 In., 4 Piece 2300.00
Table, Oak, Elm, Slant Front, Inner Drawers, 1840s, 37 1/2 In. 905.00
Table, Oak, Marble Top, Serpentine Frieze, Carved Stretcher, Flower Heads, 34 In. 4000.00
Table, Octagonal Top, 8 Display Compartments, 4 Deer Legs & Hooves, 33 x 31 In. 1100.00
Table, Padouk, Molded Top, Splayed Legs, Stretcher, 24 In. 55.00
Table, Palisander, Mahogany, Square, Twisted Ropes, Balls, Gilt Metal Feet, 28 In. 8625.00
Table, Papier-Mache, Faux Bamboo, Black, Gilt Border, 28 x 23 In. 635.00
Table, Pembroke, Cherry, Square Tapered Legs, 2 Leaves, American, 29 x 32 x 18 In. 1155.00
Table, Pembroke, Chippendale, Cherry, Dovetailed Drawer, 20 x 34 In. 2300.00
Table, Pembroke, Chippendale, Mahogany, 2 Drawers, 1770, 26 In. 4400.00
Table, Pembroke, Chippendale, Mahogany, Rectangular Top, 1775, 32 x 27 In. 1870.00
Table, Pembroke, Duncan Phyfe, Mahogany, Elliptical Leaves, c.1815, 37 1/2 In. 9775.00
Table, Pembroke, Federal, Cherry, Drawer, Tapered Legs, c.1800, 37 x 33 In. 7475.00
Table, Pembroke, Federal, Cherry, Rectangular Top, Frieze Drawer, 28 In. 3740.00
Table, Pembroke, Federal, Mahogany, Drawer, Tapered Legs, 37 x 29 In. 3335.00
Table, Pembroke, Federal, Mahogany, Inlay, New Jersey, Early 1800s, 27 x 32 In. 3740.00
Table, Pembroke, Federal, Mahogany, Rectangular Top, 31 x 29 In. 1725.00
Table, Pembroke, Federal, Mahogany, Rectangular Top, Tapered Legs, 28 1/2 In. 1955.00
Table, Pembroke, George III, Mahogany, Banded Frieze, Square Legs, 27 1/2 In. 635.00
Table, Pembroke, George III, Mahogany, Cup Casters, 27 1/2 x 30 In. 1100.00

Table, Pembroke, George III, Mahogany, Hepplewhite Legs, 28 In. 6875.00
Table, Pembroke, George III, Mahogany, Square Tapered Legs, 27 In., Pair 1955.00
Table, Pembroke, Hepplewhite, Cherry, Drawer, 27 1/2 x 35 x 17 In. 550.00
Table, Pembroke, Hepplewhite, Inlay, Bowed Drawers, c.1820, 26 x 31 In. 3400.00
Table, Pembroke, Hepplewhite, Mahogany, Shaped Top, Casters, 31 1/2 In. 2090.00
Table, Pembroke, Hepplewhite, Mahogany, Shaped Top, Square Legs, 29 x 32 x 19 In. . . . 825.00
Table, Pembroke, Hepplewhite, Mahogany, Square Tapered Legs, 31 x 19 x 28 In. 660.00
Table, Pembroke, Mahogany, Crossbanded, Bowed Ends, Leaves, 28 1/4 In. 8050.00
Table, Pembroke, Mahogany, Drawer, Turned Legs, 1870, 29 x 20 In. 300.00
Table, Pembroke, Mahogany, Floral Marquetry, Frieze Drawer, Holland, 29 In. 2875.00
Table, Pembroke, Mahogany, Pierced Stretcher, c.1775, 27 In. 2300.00
Table, Pembroke, Mahogany, Rectangular Top, Faux Birch Drawers, 4 Legs, 28 In. 2300.00
Table, Pembroke, Sheraton, Cherry, Scalloped Top, Drawer, 1840, 28 In. 360.00
Table, Pembroke, Walnut, Drawer, Pa., 1800, 38 x 32 In. 880.00
Table, Pembroke, Walnut, Oblong Top, Drawer, Pa., 1800, 29 x 31 3/4 In. 715.00
Table, Pembroke, William IV, Mahogany, Rectangular Top, 2 Drawers, 28 In. 1495.00
Table, Phillipe Starck, Wooden Top, 3 Chrome Posts, c.1980, 20 x 16 In. 1840.00
Table, Pier, Brooks Household Art Co., Classical Revival, Mahogany, 43 In. 1540.00
Table, Pier, Classical, Mahogany, Marble Top, Turned Pilasters, Mirror, 39 x 43 In. 1540.00
Table, Pier, Classical, Mahogany, Marble, Ormolu Mount, Mirror, 1820, 38 x 42 In. 4950.00
Table, Pier, Empire, Mahogany, Marble Top, Mirror-Backed Base, 36 x 45 In. 3165.00
Table, Pier, Mahogany, Gilt Bronze Capitals, Platform Base, 1820s, 36 In. 8050.00
Table, Pier, Mahogany, Giltwood, White Marble Top, 4 Classical Columns, 38 In. 2300.00
Table, Pier, Mahogany, Molded Apron, Scrolled Feet, Mirrored Back, 1835, 37 x 41 In. . . 1650.00
Table, Pine, 2-Board Top, Tapered Legs, Ball Feet, Red Paint, 29 In. 9775.00
Table, Pine, Dovetailed Curved Corners, 1850, 24 x 24 In. 595.00
Table, Pine, Dovetailed Gallery, 2 Drawers, Turned Legs, 39 x 18 In. 1540.00
Table, Pine, Farmhouse, Breadboard Top, Dovetailed Drawer, Tapered Legs, 62 In. 825.00
Table, Pine, Farmhouse, Flat Feet, 19th Century, 29 x 72 1/2 x 28 In. 140.00
Table, Pine, Rectangular Top, 2 Drawers, Turned Legs, 32 x 20 In. 550.00
Table, Pine, Red Paint, New England, 18th Century, 26 1/2 x 42 x 43 1/4 In. 1380.00
Table, Queen Anne, Mahogany, Dish Top, Molded Edge, Mass., 1700s, 28 x 26 1/2 In. . . . 2310.00
Table, Queen Anne, Maple, Overhanging Top, 4 Tapered Legs, Pad Feet, 26 In. 3220.00
Table, Red Lacquer, Parcel Gilt, Orientals In Costumes, Chinese Export, 13 In. 7475.00
Table, Refectory, Chestnut, Rectangular Breadboard Top, Late 19th Century, 36 In. 3737.00
Table, Refectory, French Provincial, Cherry, X-Shaped Stretcher, 30 x 84 In. 1980.00
Table, Refectory, Gothic Revival Style, Oak, Late 19th Century, 53 3/4 In. 935.00
Table, Refectory, Gothic Revival, Fir Wood, Arches, Quatrefoils, Victorian, 30 x 72 In. . . . 1200.00
Table, Refectory, L. & J.G. Stickley, Pine, Rectangular, 1928, 144 x 27 In. 6900.00
Table, Refectory, Louis XIII, Oak, Rectangular Plank Top, Barley Twist Legs, 29 In. 2646.00
Table, Refectory, Oak, Grotesque Frieze, Cup & Cover Supports, 31 x 98 1/4 In. 2070.00
Table, Refectory, Oak, Overhanging Top, 2 Drawers, Spain, c.1780, 34 x 83 In. 5060.00
Table, Refectory, Renaissance Revival, Oak, Walnut, Parquetry, Spain, 30 x 74 In. 3740.00
Table, Refectory, Renaissance Revival, Walnut, Rectangular, Paw Feet, 29 x 84 In. 3300.00
Table, Refectory, Walnut, Stylized 4 Short Drawers, Late 17th Century, 32 x 85 In. 4600.00
Table, Regency Style, Mahogany, D-Shaped Top, 2 Leaves, 105 In., 2 Piece 3520.00
Table, Regency Style, Yew Wood, Mahogany, Pedestal, Round, 29 x 60 In. 2300.00
Table, Regency, Mahogany, 2 Drawers, Cup Casters, 28 1/2 x 31 In. 3300.00
Table, Regency, Mahogany, Rectangular Crossbanding, Ring & Block Stretcher, 27 In. . . . 1380.00
Table, Regency, Mahogany, Rectangular Leather Top, Down-Swept Legs, 29 In. 2530.00
Table, Regency, Mahogany, Rectangular Molded Top, Reeded Down-Swept Legs, 29 In. . . 635.00
Table, Regency, Mahogany, Rectangular Top, Paw Feet, 19 1/2 In. 86.00
Table, Regency, Mahogany, Round Banded Top, Brass Paw Feet, 30 In. 6325.00
Table, Regency, Rosewood, Round Top, Reeded Pedestal, 3 Feet, 17 x 18 In., Pair 1840.00
Table, Rene Drouet, Burl Walnut, Bronze Scrolled Supports, 28 In. 1380.00
Table, Robsjohn-Gibbings, Mahogany Veneer, Leaf, Widdicomb, 58 In. 3775.00
Table, Robsjohn-Gibbings, Rectangular Walnut Top, Curved Legs, 26 x 25 In. 360.00
Table, Rococo, Gilt, Faux Marble, Serpentine, Venetian, 16 x 32 1/2 x 33 In. 920.00
Table, Rococo, Giltwood, Inset Glass Top, Drawer, Italy, 28 In., Pair 1980.00
Table, Rococo, Giltwood, Rectangular Top, Cabriole Legs, Italy, 18 In. 800.00
Table, Rococo, Octagonal Floral Pietra Dora Marble Top, 21 x 21 In. 2100.00
Table, Rococo, Round Molded Top, Kneeling Blackamoor, 20th Century, 20 In. 2645.00
Table, Rosewood, Brass Inlay, Tilting Mechanism, Paw Feet, 49 1/2 In. 4620.00

Table, Rosewood, Brown Marble Top, Carved Faces, 4 Legs, 1900, 32 In. 575.00
Table, Rosewood, Gallery Shelf, Satinwood Inlay, c.1910, 28 x 29 3/4 In. 1210.00
Table, Rosewood, Ivory Inlay, Landscapes, Chinese, 19th Century, 29 In. 1075.00
Table, Rosewood, Marble Top, Leaf & Cornucopia Carved Paw Feet, c.1815, 37 In. 5175.00
Table, Rosewood, Marble Top, Variegated, Pierced Apron, 20 1/2 In. 800.00
Table, Rosewood, Paneled Top, Carved Flower Head Border, Oriental, 16 1/4 In. 60.00
Table, Russel Wright, Patio, Folding, White Tubular Steel, Metal Top, 1945, 29 In. 515.00
Table, Saarinen, Round White Laminate Top, Enamel Metal Base, 20 1/2 In. 242.00
Table, Sawbuck, Pine, 2-Board Top, 29 x 47 1/2 In. 660.00
Table, Sawbuck, Pine, Breadboard Top, 28 3/4 x 57 In. 962.00
Table, Sawbuck, Pine, Center Stretcher, Late 19th Century, 79 1/2 In. 715.00
Table, Sawbuck, Pine, Green & Blue Paint, 19th Century, 29 1/2 x 48 x 26 In. 615.00
Table, Sawbuck, Pine, Scrubbed 1-Board Top, Painted, 26 x 50 x 30 In. 550.00
Table, Sewing, 2-Board Top, Black & Red Sponging, Turned Legs, 27 x 32 x 20 In. 120.00
Table, Sewing, Biedermeier, Mahogany, Rectangular Lift Top, S-Scrolled Legs, 30 In. . . . 660.00
Table, Sewing, Biedermeier, Pale Birch, Ebony, Applied Decoupage, 29 x 29 1/4 In. 2100.00
Table, Sewing, Biedermeier, Rosewood, Serpentine Lift Top, Bobbin Stem, 29 In. 2420.00
Table, Sewing, Cherry, Rectangular Overhanging Top, 2 Drawers, 28 x 19 3/4 In. 460.00
Table, Sewing, Cherry, String Inlay, 3 Center Drawers, Storage Each Side, 29 In. 275.00
Table, Sewing, Chippendale, Walnut, 3 Dovetailed Drawers, Marlboro Legs, 30 In. 505.00
Table, Sewing, Classical, Mahogany, 2 Graduated Drawers, Beaded Legs, 1825, 29 In. . . . 1265.00
Table, Sewing, Classical, Mahogany, Carved, 3 Drawers, Gilt Stencil, New York, 29 In. . . . 5500.00
Table, Sewing, Classical, Mahogany, Hinged Checkerboard Top, 2 Drawers, 32 In. 2750.00
Table, Sewing, Classical, Mahogany, Trestle, 4 Ring Turned Posts, 30 In. 1150.00
Table, Sewing, Drop Leaf, Cherry, Bird's-Eye Maple, Frieze, Drawer, 28 3/4 In. 460.00
Table, Sewing, Drop Leaf, Empire, 2 Drawers, Mahogany, Pedestal Base, 29 In. 1430.00
Table, Sewing, Drop Leaf, Empire, Mahogany, 2 Ogee Molded Drawers, 29 In. 1035.00
Table, Sewing, Drop Leaf, Empire, Mahogany, Revolving Top, 2 Drawers, 29 In. 305.00
Table, Sewing, Drop Leaf, Federal, Butternut, 2 Drawers, Tapered Legs, Ball Feet, 29 In. . . 375.00
Table, Sewing, Drop Leaf, Late Classical, Mahogany, 2 Drawers, Basket, 29 x 18 In. 1870.00
Table, Sewing, Drop Leaf, Tiger Maple, 2 Walnut Faced Drawers, Peg Feet, 27 3/4 In. 2760.00
Table, Sewing, Empire, Inlaid Mahogany, 2 Drawers, Twist Legs, Casters, 30 In. 1035.00
Table, Sewing, Empire, Mahogany Veneer, 2 Drawers, 4 Scrolled Feet, 28 In. 275.00
Table, Sewing, Empire, Mahogany, 2 Drawers, Convex Work Boxes On Side, 29 In. 5175.00
Table, Sewing, Empire, Mahogany, 2 Mirrored Veneer Drawers, 29 x 24 3/4 In. 345.00
Table, Sewing, Empire, Mahogany, Rectangular Top, 2 Drawers, Plinth Base, 33 In. 920.00
Table, Sewing, Empire, Maple, Drawer, Twist Turned Legs, c.1880, 27 x 20 In. 1210.00
Table, Sewing, Federal, Mahogany Veneer, 2 Graduated Drawers, 28 x 18 x 15 In. 2070.00
Table, Sewing, Federal, Mahogany, 2 Drawers, Baluster Turned Legs, 30 x 21 1/2 In. 920.00
Table, Sewing, Federal, Mahogany, 2 Paneled Drawers, Ball Feet, 28 x 21 1/2 In. 520.00
Table, Sewing, Federal, Mahogany, 3 Graduated Drawers, Brass, 32 1/2 x 18 In. 2875.00
Table, Sewing, Federal, Mahogany, Oblong Top, 2 Graduated Drawers, 1815, 29 In. 7475.00
Table, Sewing, Federal, Mahogany, Overhanging Top, Tapered, Ring Legs, 30 In. 690.00
Table, Sewing, Federal, Mahogany, Rectangular Top, Reeded Legs, Peg Feet, 1810 . . . . . . 6325.00
Table, Sewing, Federal, Mahogany, Rectangular Top, Tapered Legs, Ball Feet, 29 In. 115.00
Table, Sewing, Federal, Maple, 2 Cock-Beaded Short Drawers, Leaf Swags, 29 In. 9200.00
Table, Sewing, Federal, Pine, Frieze Drawer, Ring Turned Legs, 29 x 23 x 19 3/4 In. 230.00
Table, Sewing, Federal, Tiger Maple, Mahogany, Bowfront, 2 Drawers, 27 x 18 In. 2415.00
Table, Sewing, George III, Mahogany, Rectangular Top, Ringed Turned Legs, 28 In. 1725.00
Table, Sewing, Hepplewhite, Birch, Pinned Apron, Red Paint, 28 x 41 1/2 x 28 In. 1210.00
Table, Sewing, Mahogany, 2 Drawers, Vase Turned Pedestal, Tripod Base, 30 In. 275.00
Table, Sewing, Mahogany, 3 Drawers, Grapevine Foliate, Brass Cuffs, c.1810, 31 In. 6900.00
Table, Sewing, Mahogany, Cookie Corners, 1 Side & 2 Front Drawers, 29 In. 825.00
Table, Sewing, Mahogany, Fitted Top Drawer Over 2 Drawers, 29 x 20 x 16 In. 1120.00
Table, Sewing, Mahogany, Flame, 2 Drawers, Turned Columns, Claw Feet, 30 x 21 In. 1210.00
Table, Sewing, Mahogany, Oblong Top, 2 Drawers, Rope Legs, Low Shelf, 1820, 21 In. . . 1045.00
Table, Sewing, Mahogany, Octagonal Box, Fitted, Reeded Base, 28 x 18 x 13 In. 605.00
Table, Sewing, Mahogany, Overhanging Frieze Drawer, Paneled Drawer, 28 In. 126.00
Table, Sewing, Mahogany, Pedestal Base, Paw Feet, Turned Column, 30 In. 330.00
Table, Sewing, Mahogany, Tilt Top, 2 Drawers, 30 x 25 In. 2200.00
Table, Sewing, Maple Top, Drawer, Turned Tapered Legs, 17 1/2 x 29 In. 260.00
Table, Sewing, Papier-Mache, Black Lacquer, Chinoiserie, 1825-1850, 29 In. 1210.00
Table, Sewing, Pine, 2 Drawers, Turned Pedestal, 3 Scrolled Legs, 27 1/2 In. 90.00

Table, Sewing, Poplar, Red Brown Finish, Drawer, Turned Legs, 29 x 48 In. 220.00
Table, Sewing, Regency, Rosewood, Beaded Rectangular Top, Brass Paw Feet, 30 In. 2200.00
Table, Sewing, Rosewood, Regency, Lift Top, 2 Drawers, Theorem Panel, Slide, 28 In. . . . 1725.00
Table, Sewing, Roycroft, 3 Drawers, Lift Top Bins On Sides, 29 3/4 x 16 1/2 In. 4400.00
Table, Sewing, Satinwood, Fitted Drawer, Pleated Silk Basket, Casters, 29 1/2 In. 2070.00
Table, Sewing, Satinwood, Frieze Drawer, Sliding Basket, Pineapple Finial, 27 In. 2760.00
Table, Sewing, Sheraton, Cherry, 2 Front Drawers, Turned Legs, 29 x 21 3/4 In. 410.00
Table, Sewing, Sheraton, Mahogany Veneer, 2 Drawers, 19th Century, 29 x 19 x 18 In. . . . 880.00
Table, Sewing, Sheraton, Mahogany, 2 Sectioned Drawers, Basket, 1820, 28 x 23 In. 1320.00
Table, Sewing, Sheraton, Poplar, Red Stain, Removable 1-Board Top, 18 x 32 x 29 In. . . . 245.00
Table, Sewing, Tiger & Bird's-Eye Maple, 2 Drawers, Brass Pulls, 1825, 28 In. 805.00
Table, Sewing, Tiger Maple, 2-Board Top, 30 x 53 x 32 In. 440.00
Table, Sewing, Walnut, 2 Dovetailed Drawers, Diamonds On Door, Zoar, Oh., 30 In. . . . 9350.00
Table, Sewing, Walnut, 3-Board Top, Drawer, Stretcher Base, 1780, 48 x 36 x 27 In. 1200.00
Table, Sewing, Walnut, D-Shaped Leaves, 2 Drawers, Tapered Carved Legs, 29 1/2 In. . . . 345.00
Table, Sewing, Walnut, Overlapping Drawer, Removable Top, Square Feet, 26 1/2 In. 3300.00
Table, Sewing, Walnut, Pencil Post Legs, 29 x 42 x 28 In. 357.00
Table, Sewing, Yellow Pine, Oak Legs, Mid-19th Century, 25 1/2 x 29 x 26 In. 125.00
Table, Shaker, Maple, Pine, Rectangular Top, 1 Drawer, 19th Century, 25 In. 460.00
Table, Sheraton, Cherry, 1-Board Top, Drawer, 19 x 21 x 29 In. 440.00
Table, Sheraton, Cherry, 4-Board Top, 2 Drawers, 21 x 24 x 27 In. 440.00
Table, Sheraton, Cherry, Curly Maple, Dovetailed Drawer, 28 3/4 In. 2200.00
Table, Sheraton, Mahogany, 2 Serpentine Front Ends, 1800, 31 x 72 In. 1210.00
Table, Sheraton, Mahogany, Bird's-Eye Maple, 2 Drawers, Brass, 29 x 17 x 22 In. 798.00
Table, Sheraton, Mahogany, Square Top, Spiral Legs, Conn., 1815, 31 x 20 1/2 In. 440.00
Table, Sheraton, Overhanging Rectangular Top, Red & Black Graining, 1835, 22 In. 10450.00
Table, Sheraton, Poplar, Drawer, Turned Legs, Pa., 1830, 28 x 19 In. 302.00
Table, Sheraton, Rectangular Top, Drawer, Red Paint, 1840, 32 1/2 x 30 In. 300.00
Table, Side, Anglo-Colonial, Hardwood, Fan Carved Backsplash, 52 x 57 In. 1760.00
Table, Side, Art Deco, Bronze, Black Glass Top, Semicircular Support, 20 x 26 In. 110.00
Table, Side, Cherry, Square Tapered Legs, Early 19th Century, 25 1/2 x 17 x 18 In. 330.00
Table, Side, Chippendale Style, Mahogany, Blind Fret Apron, Chinese, 26 x 19 In. 250.00
Table, Side, Classical, Mahogany, Serpentine White Marble Top, 29 x 23 1/2 In. 750.00
Table, Side, Drop Leaf, Empire, Maple, Frieze Drawer, Rule-Jointed Leaves, 43 In. 200.00
Table, Side, Edwardian, Mahogany, 2 Drawers, Grillwork, 60 In. 4400.00
Table, Side, Edwardian, Mahogany, Demilune, Splayed Feet, 35 In. 6040.00
Table, Side, Empire, Mahogany, Ogee Molded Drawer, Octagonal Pedestal, 29 In. 980.00
Table, Side, Empire, Round Top, Brass Greek Key Design, 3 Fluted Legs, 25 In. 115.00
Table, Side, Federal, Inlaid Cherry, 2 Drawers, Boxwood & Ebony Stringing, 33 In. 490.00
Table, Side, Federal, Pine, 2 Drawers, Square Section Tapered Legs, 28 1/4 In. 750.00
Table, Side, Federal, Pine, Oak, Overhanging Top, Frieze Drawer, Tapered Legs, 28 In. . . 375.00
Table, Side, George II Style, Giltwood, Shaped Marble Top, c.1900, 37 x 84 In. 6875.00
Table, Side, George II, Walnut, Rectangular Green Marble Top, Cabriole Legs, 30 In. 2415.00
Table, Side, George III, Demilune, Mahogany, Satinwood, Splayed Feet, 30 In., Pair 2300.00
Table, Side, George III, Mahogany, Bowed Banded Top, 3 Inlaid Drawers, 35 In. 2100.00
Table, Side, George III, Mahogany, Drawer, Splayed Feet, 28 3/4 x 14 1/2 In. 1840.00
Table, Side, George III, Mahogany, Fluted Frieze, Square Legs, 31 x 48 x 29 In. 4180.00
Table, Side, George III, Mahogany, Reeded Top, Drawer, 29 3/4 x 13 In. 1265.00
Table, Side, George III, Mahogany, Serpentine Top, Block Feet, 33 x 66 x 28 In. 2185.00
Table, Side, George III, Satinwood Panel, Rectangular Banded Top, 1900, 34 In. 1600.00
Table, Side, George III, Satinwood, Banded Top, Tapered Legs, Cuffed Feet, 31 In. 13225.00
Table, Side, Italian Provincial, Fruitwood, Red & Gray Marble Top, Carved, 32 In. 2420.00
Table, Side, Louis XV Style, Walnut, Marble Top, Cabriole Legs, c.1900, 29 1/2 In. 1540.00
Table, Side, Louis XV, Marquetry, Marble Top, Ormolu Mounts, 21 In. 440.00
Table, Side, Louis XV, Triangular Molded Top, Cabriole Legs, 21 x 33 In. 60.00
Table, Side, Louis XVI, Ebony, Rectangular Top, Square Tapered Legs, 17 In., Pair 4600.00
Table, Side, Louis XVI, Ebony, Rectangular Top, Square Tapered Legs, 26 In., Pair 17250.00
Table, Side, Louis XVI, Gallery Marble Top, Fluted Round Legs, 20 x 12 x 18 In. 835.00
Table, Side, Louis XVI, Mahogany, Removable Glass Top, 26 x 16 x 20 In. 35.00
Table, Side, Neoclassical Style, Mixed Metals, Greek Key Apron, Square, 21 In. 195.00
Table, Side, Regency, Mahogany, Oblong, Brass Inlay, 29 3/4 x 36 1/4 In. 2200.00
Table, Side, Rococo, Walnut, Tooled Leather Top, Rosewood Edging, Italy, 27 In. 2760.00
Table, Side, Saarinen, Round White Laminate Top, Metal Base, 20 1/2 In. 275.00

Table, Side, Sheraton, Mahogany, Veneers, Drawer, Brass Pulls, 28 x 23 In. 935.00
Table, Square, Cork Inlay, Hinged Corner Drawers, 28 In. 800.00
Table, Steel, Marble Top, 3 Incurved Iron Supports, Dragon Mask, 30 x 31 1/8 In. 4600.00
Table, Stickley Bros., No. 2504, Round Top, Cross-Stretcher Base, 24 x 30 In. 660.00
Table, Stickley Brothers, No. 2674, Square Overhanging Top, Dark Finish, 30 In. 935.00
Table, Tavern, 2 Drawers, Turned Legs, c.1790, 31 1/2 In. 550.00
Table, Tavern, 3-Board Pine Top, Scrolled Skirt, Early 18th Century, 29 x 57 In. 2310.00
Table, Tavern, Elm, 19th Century, 27 x 27 1/4 In. 345.00
Table, Tavern, Federal, Pine, Maple, Square Tapered Legs, Painted, c.1800, 46 x 28 In. . . . 2530.00
Table, Tavern, Hepplewhite, Pine, 2-Board Top, Red, Splayed Base, Pa., 22 x 26 In. 990.00
Table, Tavern, Maple, Pine, Ring Turned Legs, Button Feet, Blue Paint, 26 In. 1265.00
Table, Tavern, Maple, Pine, Thumb-Molded Drawer, Turned Feet, 28 1/2 x 44 In. 4315.00
Table, Tavern, Oak, Poplar, Drawer, Bulbous Legs, Pa., c.1760, 30 x 33 In. 1870.00
Table, Tavern, Oak, William & Mary, Frieze Drawer, Turned Supports, 28 x 32 1/2 In. . . . 690.00
Table, Tavern, Pine, Central Stretcher Base, Breadboard End, 26 x 28 x 45 In. 440.00
Table, Tavern, Pine, Cherry, Oblong Top, 2 Drawers, Turned Legs, Pa., 1790, 28 In. 1320.00
Table, Tavern, Pine, Overhanging Top, Drawer, Green Paint, 1760, 42 x 25 In. 1100.00
Table, Tavern, Pine, Triangular Apron, 3 Tapered Legs, Duck Feet, 30 1/2 In. 600.00
Table, Tavern, Poplar, Yellow Pine, Rectangular Top, 28 x 27 In. 5500.00
Table, Tavern, Walnut, Poplar, Battened Top, Baluster Legs, Virginia, 1770, 28 In. 2750.00
Table, Tavern, Walnut, Rectangular Batten Top, Scrolled Skirt, Pa., 1740, 29 In. 3740.00
Table, Tavern, William & Mary, Drawer, Block Turned Legs, 18th Century, 27 x 42 In. . . . 2990.00
Table, Tavern, William & Mary, Oak, Drawer, Ring Turned Legs, 27 x 36 In. 1330.00
Table, Tavern, William & Mary, Rectangular Overhanging Top, Turned Feet, 26 In. 2070.00
Table, Tavern, William & Mary, Walnut, Frieze Drawer, Ball Feet, 1730, 29 1/2 In. 4600.00
Table, Tavern, Yellow Pine, Overhanging Top, Drawer, Virginia, 27 x 34 x 24 In. 2695.00
Table, Tea, Biedermeier, Figured Maple, Foldover Top, Cabriole Legs, 30 1/2 In. 4890.00
Table, Tea, Cherry, Oval, Turned Legs, Block Vase Base, 18th Century, 27 x 39 In. 2300.00
Table, Tea, Chippendale, Mahogany, Dish Top, Birdcage, Down-Swept Legs, 29 In. 16100.00
Table, Tea, Chippendale, Mahogany, Dish Top, Urn-Shaped Pedestal, 1700s, 28 x 37 In. . . 2300.00
Table, Tea, Chippendale, Mahogany, Foldover Top, Frieze Drawer, 30 x 38 In. 2875.00
Table, Tea, Chippendale, Mahogany, Round Top, Tripod Base, Claw & Ball Feet, 29 In. . . 2415.00
Table, Tea, George III, Demilune, Foldover Top, Cock-Beaded Apron, 29 3/4 x 38 In. 980.00
Table, Tea, Hardwood, Foldover Top, Carved Sunburst, Square Down-Swept Legs, 31 In. . . 315.00
Table, Tea, L. & J.G. Stickley, No. 587, Square Top, 4 Post Legs, 1902, 27 In. 460.00
Table, Tea, Louis XVI, Walnut, Foldover Top, Demilune, Continental, 30 In. 2185.00
Table, Tea, Mahogany, 1-Board Top, Rectangular, Rhode Island, 1780, 30 x 19 In. 2240.00
Table, Tea, Mahogany, 3 Tiers, Dish Shelves, Tripod Base, Snake Feet, 1850s, 43 In. 1320.00
Table, Tea, Mahogany, Pie Crust Edge, Vase-Form Pedestal, Arched Legs, 34 1/2 In. 5500.00
Table, Tea, Mahogany, Pie Crust, Suppressed Ball Standard, Cabriole Legs, 27 In. 3740.00
Table, Tea, Mahogany, Removable Tray, Brass Handles, Early 1900s, 31 x 23 x 20 In. . . . 865.00
Table, Tea, Mahogany, Shell & Foliate Apron, Shell Cabriole Legs, Ireland, 29 In. 2185.00
Table, Tea, Maple, Pine, Oval Top, Turned Legs, Mass., Late 1700s, 27 x 31 x 24 In. 2875.00
Table, Tea, Poplar, Scrolled Base, Black Paint, 28 1/2 x 23 1/4 In. 1000.00
Table, Tea, Queen Anne, Maple, Oval Top, Turned Tapered Legs, 27 x 33 x 26 In. 5460.00
Table, Tea, Queen Anne, Maple, Pine, Rectangular Top, 4 Cabriole Legs, 27 In. 2875.00
Table, Tea, Roycroft, Deep Apron, Mackmurdo Feet, Orb & Cross Mark, 36 In. 4675.00
Table, Tea, Tilt Top, Chippendale, Applewood, Serpentine, 1700s, 27 1/4 x 35 x 34 In. . . . 460.00
Table, Tea, Tilt Top, Chippendale, Cherry, 2-Board Top, Tripod Base, 31 x 32 x 27 In. . . . 1000.00
Table, Tea, Tilt Top, Chippendale, Mahogany, 2-Board Top, Tripod Base, 34 x 29 In. 1000.00
Table, Tea, Tilt Top, Chippendale, Mahogany, Acanthus Legs, Hairy Claw Feet, 27 In. . . . 3450.00
Table, Tea, Tilt Top, Chippendale, Mahogany, Birdcage, Claw & Ball Feet, 1760, 28 In. . . 9200.00
Table, Tea, Tilt Top, Chippendale, Mahogany, Cabriole Legs, c.1780, 29 x 30 In. 1610.00
Table, Tea, Tilt Top, Chippendale, Mahogany, Tripod Base, England, 32 In. 885.00
Table, Tea, Tilt Top, Chippendale, Mahogany, Urn-Shaped Column, 29 In. 1035.00
Table, Tea, Tilt Top, Chippendale, Maple, Round, Tripod Base, 29 3/4 x 37 3/4 In. 460.00
Table, Tea, Tilt Top, Chippendale, Walnut, Turned Posts, Birdcage, 28 In. 4400.00
Table, Tea, Tilt Top, Empire, Mahogany, Reeded Saber Legs, Brass Paw Feet, 29 In. 805.00
Table, Tea, Tilt Top, Mahogany, Revolving Birdcage Base, Round, 29 In. 1400.00
Table, Tea, Tilt Top, Mahogany, Turned Column, Tripod Base, Pad Feet, 32 x 27 In. 885.00
Table, Tea, Tilt Top, Maple, Shaped Top, Turned Pedestal, Tripod Base, 27 In. 885.00
Table, Tea, Tilt Top, Queen Anne, Cherry, 3-Board Top, Pad Feet, Mass., 26 1/2 x 31 In. . . 1150.00
Table, Tea, Tilt Top, Queen Anne, Cherry, Maple, Pad Feet, Late 1700s, 25 x 30 In. 925.00

Table, Tea, Tilt Top, Queen Anne, Walnut, 3 Legs, Round, 28 1/2 x 28 In. 785.00
Table, Tea, Tilt Top, Queen Anne, Walnut, Massachusetts, 31 1/2 x 28 1/2 In. 1980.00
Table, Tea, Tilt Top, Walnut, Round Molded Top, Tripod Cabriole Legs, 29 x 19 In. 1955.00
Table, Tea, Tilt Top, Walnut, Round, Birdcage Support, Pa., 1775, 29 x 28 In. 825.00
Table, Tea, Walnut, Round Dish Top, Tripod Base, Pa., 1790, 23 x 32 1/2 In. 1200.00
Table, Telephone, Arts & Crafts, Square Top, 2 Side Stretchers, 18 1/2 In. 300.00
Table, Thonet, Orange Formica Top, Brushed Chrome Pedestal Base, 30 In. 55.00
Table, Thonet, Walnut, Intricately Bent Standard & Legs, c.1900, 29 3/4 In. 2760.00
Table, Tilt Top William IV, Mahogany, Round, Scrolled Feet, 30 x 52 In. 4840.00
Table, Tilt Top, Allegorical Scene, Hexagonal Stem, 31 1/4 In. 3450.00
Table, Tilt Top, Chippendale, Birdcage, Claw & Ball Feet, 29 In. 1100.00
Table, Tilt Top, Chippendale, Cherry, Round Tilt Top, Pad Feet, 1780, 28 In. 635.00
Table, Tilt Top, Chippendale, Mahogany, Birdcage, 27 3/4 In. 2185.00
Table, Tilt Top, Chippendale, Mahogany, Birdcage, Claw & Ball Feet, 34 1/2 x 26 In. 1650.00
Table, Tilt Top, Chippendale, Mahogany, Round Molded Top, Claw & Ball Feet, 30 In. . . 230.00
Table, Tilt Top, Chippendale, Mahogany, Round, Tripod Base, Baluster Standard, 27 In. . . 865.00
Table, Tilt Top, Chippendale, Santo Domingo Mahogany, Claw & Ball Feet, 33 In. 8250.00
Table, Tilt Top, Chippendale, Walnut, Baluster Standard, Tripod Base, 29 1/2 In. 635.00
Table, Tilt Top, Federal, Mahogany, Double Elliptic Top, 3 Flared Legs, 27 In. 1495.00
Table, Tilt Top, Federal, Mahogany, Rectangular Top, Tripod Base, 28 1/4 x 23 1/2 In. . . . 345.00
Table, Tilt Top, Federal, Maple, Tripod Base, Baluster Turned Standard, 29 x 23 In. 150.00
Table, Tilt Top, George II Style, Mahogany, Dish Top, Birdcage, Tripod Base, 34 In. 1035.00
Table, Tilt Top, George III, Mahogany, Round Desk Top, Cabriole Legs, 28 In. 2860.00
Table, Tilt Top, George III, Mahogany, Round Top, Pie Crust, Claw & Ball Feet, 26 In. . . 3910.00
Table, Tilt Top, Georgian, Mahogany, Round, 1770, 27 1/2 x 19 1/2 In. 445.00
Table, Tilt Top, Mahogany, 1-Board Top, Chinese Vase, Pad Feet, 19th Century, 33 In. . . . 670.00
Table, Tilt Top, Mahogany, Birdcage, Turned Baluster, Cabriole Legs, 12 x 9 In. 3500.00
Table, Tilt Top, Mahogany, Inlaid Center, Tripod Base, Mid 20th Century, 24 x 28 In. . . . 165.00
Table, Tilt Top, Mahogany, Piecrust Edge, Tripod Base, Carved Knees, 28 x 20 In. 315.00
Table, Tilt Top, Oak, Tripod Base, Crewelwork Top, Shell Carved Cabriole Legs, 28 In. . . 6900.00
Table, Tilt Top, Regency, Gilt, Octagonal Top, Apollo In Chariot, Tripod Base, 29 In. 7475.00
Table, Tilt Top, Regency, Mahogany, Rectangular, 4 Legs, 1830, 55 In. 4675.00
Table, Tilt Top, Regency, Mahogany, Turned Pedestal, 29 x 40 x 52 In. 3520.00
Table, Tilt Top, Sheraton, Mahogany, Quatrefoil, Tripod Base, c.1820, 28 1/2 In. 1210.00
Table, Tilt Top, Tiger Maple, Birdcage, Cut Corners, Tripod Base, 25 x 21 x 21 In. 1430.00
Table, Tilt Top, Walnut, Hunting Scenes & Foliage On Top, Tripod Base, 30 1/2 In. 1495.00
Table, Tree Trunk-Shaped Base, Fiberglass Top, 29 1/2 x 47 In. 775.00
Table, Trestle Louis Philippe, Rosewood, Marble Top, Oval, 30 1/2 x 46 In. 1650.00
Table, Trestle, Art Deco, Rosewood, Round Top, 1930, 21 In. 2300.00
Table, Trestle, Arts & Crafts, 2 Drawers, Rope Carved, 26 x 43 x 30 In. 825.00
Table, Trestle, Arts & Crafts, Oak, Medial Shelf, Pegged Tenons, 28 1/4 In. 2300.00
Table, Trestle, Arts & Crafts, Plank Top, Lower Shelf, Through Tenons, 31 x 95 In. 4125.00
Table, Trestle, G. Stickley, Keyed Through Tenon Lower Shelf, 48 In. 1650.00
Table, Trestle, Jacobean, Oak, Batten Top, Shoe Feet, 30 x 73 In. 885.00
Table, Trestle, L. & J.G. Stickley, Lower Shelf, Keyed Through Tenons, 48 In. 1870.00
Table, Trestle, L. & J.G. Stickley, No. 593, Branded, 54 x 36 In. 1980.00
Table, Trestle, Walnut, Rectangular Top, 2 End Drawers, 4 Square Legs, 1800, 29 In. 1760.00
Table, Tulipwood, Flower Basket, Trellis Parquetry, Writing Slide, 29 In. 7475.00
Table, Van Der Rohe, Chrome Plated Tubular Steel, Black Glass Top, c.1934, 24 In. 2070.00
Table, Van Der Rohe, Stainless Steel, Plate Glass Top, Knoll, 40 In. 1430.00
Table, Vitrine, Louis XVI Style, Mahogany, Oval Beveled Glass Top, 31 x 22 x 30 In. . . . 880.00
Table, W. Plattner, Round Marble Top, Chrome Wire Base, 24 x 18 In. 600.00
Table, Walnut, Brown Marble Top, Open 5 Column Pedestal, Victorian, 29 x 21 In. 165.00
Table, Walnut, Farmhouse, Battened Top, 3 Drawers, Button Feet, Pa., 1800, 71 In. 6600.00
Table, Walnut, Marble Top, Notched Corners, Pedestal Base, 28 x 20 In. 330.00
Table, Walnut, Marble Top, Serpentine Edges, Foliate Scrolled Feet, 1860s, 32 In. 600.00
Table, Walnut, Rectangular, Drawer, Tambour Door, Late 1800s, 29 1/2 x 26 x 12 In. 345.00
Table, Walnut, Tilt Top, Birdcage, Turned Pedestal, Tripod Base, 18th Century, 29 In. . . . 1100.00
Table, Walnut, Turned Legs, Scrubbed Top, Side Stretchers, c.1860, 24 x 19 x 29 In. 445.00
Table, Waterfall, Cut Glass, 4 Legs, Turquoise, Signed, John Lewis, 21 1/2 In. 8050.00
Table, William IV, Rosewood, Round Lozenge Plinth, Scrolled Feet, 28 1/2 In. 2530.00
Table, William IV, Rosewood, Tripod Base, Stationary Top, Beaded Molding, 29 In. 715.00
Table, Wine Tasting, French Provincial, Chestnut, Tile Top, Trestle, 29 x 38 In. 900.00

Table, Wine Tasting, Mahogany, Tripod Base, Down-Swept Legs, Pad Feet, 26 1/4 In. ... 90.00
Table, Wine Tasting, Pine, Round Plank Top, Trestle, 28 3/4 x 40 3/4 In. 1210.00
Table, Wine Tasting, Regency, Mahogany, Brass, Lotus Stem, Paw Feet, 29 3/4 In., Pair .. 2860.00
Table, Wine Tasting, Walnut, Oak, Hinged Round Top, Trestle, 26 x 42 In. 1540.00
Table, Wine Tasting, William IV, Mahogany, Demilune Molded Top, Reeded Legs, 28 In. .. 3335.00
Table, Wormley, Rosewood Veneer, 60 x 17 x 27 In. 1450.00
Table, Writing, Biedermeier, Elm, Fruitwood, Banded Rectangular Top, 31 1/2 In. 3450.00
Table, Writing, Bonheur Du Jour, Mahogany, Satinwood, Marble, Victorian, 54 In. 7475.00
Table, Writing, Charles X, Mahogany, Side Drawers, Curule-Shaped Legs, 30 x 43 In. ... 2750.00
Table, Writing, Chippendale, Pine, Serpentine Front, Felt Lined Top, 31 x 34 In. 750.00
Table, Writing, Federal, Yellow Pine, Rectangular Chamfered Top, Ball Feet, 28 In. 520.00
Table, Writing, G. Stickley, Mahogany, 4 Tapered Legs, 36 x 24 x 29 In. 1760.00
Table, Writing, George III, Satinwood, Kidney Shape, Storage Space, 29 3/4 In. 3000.00
Table, Writing, Louis XVI, Dark Wood, Drawer, Carved, Continental, 35 x 21 In. 665.00
Table, Writing, Mahogany, 3-Part Leather Top, Ratchet Center, 1830s, 29 x 36 In. 5465.00
Table, Writing, Mahogany, Drawers, Arched Backboard, Mirror, 41 In. 575.00
Table, Writing, Mahogany, Pine, 2 Dovetailed Drawers, 30 3/4 In. 1045.00
Table, Writing, Marcel Coard, Lacquered Rosewood, Leather, 1928, 41 In. 2100.00
Table, Writing, Queen Anne Style, Mahogany, 2 Drawers, England, 29 1/2 x 39 In. 635.00
Table, Writing, Roycroft, Mahogany, 2 Drawers, Slat Sides, Orb & Cross Mark, 30 In. ... 5500.00
Table, Wrought Iron, Gilt, Pierced Top, Twisted Legs, Tassel Feet, 17 x 20 x 16 In. 175.00
Table, Wrought Iron, Round Marble Top, 4 Scrolled Legs, 17 3/4 In. 550.00
Table-Bed, United Table Co., 31 x 54 In. 850.00
Tabouret, Arts & Crafts, Flush Round Top, Straight Cross-Stretchers, 21 x 18 In. 330.00
Tabouret, Arts & Crafts, Round Top, X Stretcher, 18 x 13 In. 55.00
Tabouret, Arts & Crafts, Square Top, Arched Stretchers, Mackmurdo Feet, 18 In. 110.00
Tabouret, Empire, Mahogany, Anthemion & Flower Heads, Paw Feet, 1900, 17 In. 1610.00
Tabouret, G. Stickley, Round Overhanging Top, Cloud-Lift Cross-Stretchers, 14 In. 1100.00
Tabouret, L. & J.G. Stickley, No. 558, Octagonal Top, Red, Yellow Decal, 1912, 17 In. .. 400.00
Tabouret, L. & J.G. Stickley, No. 559, Octagonal Top, Decal, 20 x 18 In. 2310.00
Tabouret, L. & J.G. Stickley, Tray Top, Octagonal Top, Mortised Shelf, 24 x 20 In. 1550.00
Tabouret, Louis XV Style, Cabriole Legs, Needlepoint, 19th Century, 16 x 19 1/2 In. 395.00
Tabouret, Regency, Painted, 20th Century, 20 x 23 x 13 1/2 In., Pair 290.00
Tabouret, Roycroft, Square Leather Overhanging Top, 21 x 15 In. 2300.00
Tabouret, Roycroft, Square Overhanging Top, Flared Legs, 19 x 12 In. 2400.00
Tabouret, Stickley Brothers, Square Top, Mackmurdo Feet, Label, 18 x 14 In. 410.00
Tabouret, Walnut, Molded Seat, Conforming Rails, Swirl Feet, 19th Century, 19 In. 115.00
Tea Cart, 2 Shelves, Drop Leaf, Combination Products Co., 30 x 30 x 16 In. 1000.00
Tea Cart, Art Deco, Burl, Drop Leaf, 1930s, 31 In. 980.00
Tea Cart, Art Deco, Chrome, Smoky Glass Top, Oval, Shelf, 26 x 31 1/2 x 18 In. 800.00
Tea Cart, Drop Leaf, Mahogany, 27 x 26 In. 45.00
Tea Cart, Federal, Inlaid Cherry, Drop Leaf, Serpentine Edge, 30 x 37 In. 2760.00
Tea Cart, Geo Ponti, Mahogany, Glass Top, Lower Shelf, Brass Casters, 29 In. 1200.00
Tea Cart, Mahogany, Brass Inlay, Glass Shelf, Doors, 1900s, 31 x 29 x 18 In. 1265.00
Tea Cart, Mahogany, Drop Leaf, Scrolled Standard & Legs, Casters, 30 In. 2070.00
Tea Cart, Stickley Brothers, Glass Tray, Lower Shelf, Slat Sides, Branded, 33 x 17 In. ... 1200.00
Teapoy, William IV, Mahogany, Carved, Sarcophagus, Hinged, Pedestal, 31 In. 1495.00
Teapoy, William IV, Rosewood, Hinged Top, Pair Of Covered Compartments, 32 In. 1725.00
Umbrella Stand, Arts & Crafts, Hammered Copper, Patina, 29 In. 935.00
Umbrella Stand, Arts & Crafts, Round, Slats, 28 In. 90.00
Umbrella Stand, G. Stickley, 2 Handles, Repousse Design, 24 In. 10000.00
Umbrella Stand, G. Stickley, Branded, 33 x 11 x 11 In. 445.00
Umbrella Stand, G. Stickley, Red Decal, 33 1/2 x 20 1/2 x 11 1/2 In. 885.00
Umbrella Stand, Hammered Brass, Cylindrical, Lions'-Head Ring Handles, 25 In. 65.00
Umbrella Stand, Lakeside Crafters, Cylindrical, Slats, Drip Pan, 26 In. 165.00
Umbrella Stand, Regency, Mahogany, Brass Bindings, Lion's-Head Handles, 24 In. 1320.00
Umbrella Stand, Thousand Butterfly, 3 Rows Of Butterfly Panels, Ribbed, 24 In. 1840.00
Vanity, G. Stickley, 2 Drawers, Tapered Legs, Mirror, Harvey Ellis, 54 x 36 In. 2475.00
Vanity, Teakwood, Marble Top, Swivel Mirror, c.1879, 60 1/2 x 28 1/2 x 21 3/4 In. 400.00
Vitrine, Art Deco, Rosewood, Rectangular Top, 2 Steel Supports, 63 In., Pair 2185.00
Vitrine, Baroque Style, Walnut, Geometric Glazed Door, Holland, 29 x 28 In. 300.00
Vitrine, Bowfront, Bronze Ormolu, Glass Panels, 2 Shelves, Mirrored, 26 x 60 In. 1430.00
Vitrine, Bowfront, Mahogany, Bronze Ormolu Trim, Glass Panels, Inlay, 25 x 56 In. 1430.00

Vitrine, Edwardian, Satinwood, Oval Hinged Top, Fabric Lined Interior, 28 In. 635.00
Vitrine, Louis XV Style, Walnut, Ormolu Mounts, Faux Tortoiseshell Panels, 68 In. 775.00
Vitrine, Louis XV, Kingwood, Marble Top, Bronze, Landscape Scenes, 71 In. 16100.00
Vitrine, Louis XV, Kingwood, Rectangular Gray Marble Top, Drawer, 75 In. 2760.00
Vitrine, Louis XVI Style, Kingwood, Marble Top, Glazed Doors, Bronze, 61 In. 10925.00
Vitrine, Louis XVI, Kingwood, 3-Quarter Pierced Gallery, Door, Gilt, 61 In. 12650.00
Vitrine, Louis XVI, Rectangular Top, Glazed Door, Floral Panel, 30 x 16 x 65 In. 405.00
Vitrine, Mahogany, 4 Cutout Panels, Splayed Feet, c.1940, 27 x 26 In. 750.00
Vitrine, Mahogany, Applied Brass Trim, Door, Frieze Inlay, 41 x 30 In. 525.00
Vitrine, Mahogany, Ormolu, Truncated Sides, Glass, France, 1900s, 10 x 14 x 40 In. 775.00
Vitrine, Napoleon III, Ebony, Center Beveled Glass Door, 51 In. 6050.00
Vitrine, Napoleon III, Serpentine Top, Lined Interior, 39 x 23 1/2 In. 3300.00
Vitrine, Red Lacquer, Domed Top, Astragal Glazed Door, Lower Drawer, 65 In. 935.00
Vitrine, Regency, Mahogany, Inset Glass, Square Legs, 29 1/2 x 27 x 16 In. 315.00
Vitrine, Rococo, Slant Front, Green Lacquer, Floral, Leafy Crest, 82 In. 6900.00
Vitrine, Rococo, Wood, Shelf Stretcher, Cabriole Legs, 40 x 15 In. 920.00
Vitrine, Teakwood, Glazed Cupboard Doors, Interior Shelves, Paneled Doors, 69 In. 400.00
Vitrine, Teakwood, Oval Door, Shaped Cornice, Holland, 19th Century, 73 x 36 In. 635.00
Vitrine, Viardot, Napoleon III, Dragon, Figural Panel, 65 In. 4600.00
Vitrine, Walnut, Marble Top, Frieze Drawer, Velvet Lined, 19th Century, 39 In. 1800.00
Wardrobe, Applewood, 2 Drawers, 2 Doors, Channel Islands, 79 x 60 In. 6325.00
Wardrobe, Arts & Crafts, Lower Drawer, Mirrored Door, Harrods Of London, 75 In. 335.00
Wardrobe, G. Stickley, Walnut, 2 Paneled Doors, 44 x 23 x 78 In. 7150.00
Wardrobe, Hardwood, Walnut Finish, Paneled Doors, Beveled Glass Panel, 90 In. 1980.00
Wardrobe, Pine, 2 Blind Doors, Grain Painted Panels, 46 x 60 x 17 In. 1485.00
Wardrobe, Pine, 2 Doors, Grain Painted, Salmon Ground, 48 x 54 x 86 In. 1320.00
Wardrobe, Pine, Framed Paneled Doors, Scrolled Finial, 79 x 36 In. 335.00
Wardrobe, Poplar, Center Door, Scalloped Cornice, Cutout Base, 87 x 41 x 21 In. 210.00
Wardrobe, Satinwood, 3 Doors, Victorian, 95 In. 4400.00
Wardrobe, Walnut, Butternut, Folk Art Inlay, 2 Doors, Victorian, 92 x 64 In. 5500.00
Wardrobe, Walnut, Paneled Door, Cutout Feet, Interior Shelf, 19 x 45 x 77 In. 1870.00
Washstand, Cherry, Dovetailed Drawer, Shelf, Backsplash, 19th Century, 38 In. 430.00
Washstand, Cherry, Drawer, Lower Shelf, Backsplash, Basin Cutout, c.1810, 38 In. 410.00
Washstand, Cherry, Drawer, Shelf, Gallery, Scalloped Back, 36 x 29 In. 465.00
Washstand, Cherry, Serpentine, Drawer, Scalloped Backsplash, 29 x 18 In. 415.00
Washstand, Corner, Hepplewhite, Mahogany, Drawer, Lower Shelf, 42 In. 600.00
Washstand, Corner, Mahogany, Reeded Legs, Scrolled Backsplash, 41 x 18 In. 385.00
Washstand, Eastlake, Walnut, Black Marble Top, 19th Century, 45 1/2 x 18 In. 290.00
Washstand, Eastlake, Walnut, Gray Marble Top, Late 19th Century, 37 x 28 x 15 In. 315.00
Washstand, Empire, Mahogany, Rectangular Top, Scrolled Pilaster Columns, 36 In. 400.00
Washstand, Federal, Mahogany, Crossbanded Frieze, Drawer, c.1800, 18 1/2 x 19 In. 200.00
Washstand, G. Stickley, Walnut, 2 Paneled Doors, Red Decal, 21 x 44 In. 4950.00
Washstand, Mahogany, Cabriole Legs, Pad Feet, 14 x 31 In. 230.00
Washstand, Mahogany, Charles X, Marble Top, Stretcher Shelf, c.1825, 32 In. 440.00
Washstand, Mahogany, Federal, Square Lift Top, Drawer, Paneled Door, 32 In. 440.00
Washstand, Mahogany, Hepplewhite, Corner, Drawer In Shelf, Inlay, 38 In. 330.00
Washstand, Mahogany, Lift Top, Drawer, Inlay, 1800, 31 3/4 x 16 In. 935.00
Washstand, Mahogany, Marble Top, Inset Marble On Stretcher, 3 Drawers, 51 In. 1210.00
Washstand, Pine, Drawer, Backsplash, Yellow Grain Painted Design, 34 In. 130.00
Washstand, Pine, Drawer, Lower Shelf, Turned Legs, 32 x 17 1/2 x 34 In. 330.00
Washstand, Pine, Drawer, Yellow, Crest On Gallery, Stripes, 16 x 14 x 30 In. 220.00
Washstand, Sheraton, Bird's-Eye Maple, Pine, Drawer, Turned Legs, 28 x 21 x 17 In. . . .   440.00
Washstand, Sheraton, Curly Maple, Dovetailed Drawer, Paneled Door, 31 In. 495.00
Washstand, Sheraton, Gallery Top, Turned Legs, Pa., 1820, 32 1/2 x 16 In. 440.00
Washstand, Sheraton, Mahogany, Drawer, Scalloped Backsplash, 38 In. 935.00
Washstand, Sheraton, Mahogany, Drawer, Shelf, Cutout Bowl, Towel Rack, 24 x 32 In. . .   300.00
Washstand, Walnut, Drawer, Bottom Shelf, 28 3/4 In. 175.00
Washstand, Walnut, Turned Legs, Mid-19th Century, 33 1/2 x 36 x 19 In. 170.00
Washstand, William IV, Mahogany, Serpentine Marble Top, Drawer, 41 In. 865.00
Wastebasket, Laugh-In, Tin Lithograph, Full Color Character Pictures, 1968 . . . .   65.00
Whatnot Shelf, Corner, Walnut, 6 Tiers, Spool Turnings, 19th Century, 69 In. 495.00
Whatnot Shelf, Mahogany, 3 Tiers, Spiral Turned Supports, Victorian, 31 x 18 In. 330.00
Whatnot Shelf, Rosewood, Shaped Shelves, Lower Drawer, c.1860, 49 In. 1840.00

Window Seat, Classical, Rectangular Seat, Square Legs, Scrolled Arms 30 In. 1150.00
Window Seat, Fruitwood, Scrolled Arms, Pierced Splats, Upholstered, 76 In. 2875.00
Window Seat, George III, Shield-Shaped Ends, Vase & Flowers, 34 1/2 In. 5750.00
Window Seat, Giltwood, Tapestry, Late 19th Century, 52 In. 4600.00
Window Seat, Louis XIV, Walnut, Needlepoint, 29 1/2 In. 315.00
Window Seat, Louis XVI, Mahogany, Turned & Fluted Legs, 25 x 45 In. 440.00
Window Seat, Neoclassical, Carved, Gilt, Italy, 36 1/2 In. 2970.00
Window Seat, Out-Curved Sides, Casters, 1760s, 51 In. 6900.00
Window Seat, Out-Curved Upholstered Sides, Parcel Gilt, Painted, 43 1/2 In. 5465.00
Window Seat, Rococo, Rosewood, Serpentine Crest Rail, Velvet, 48 In. 1760.00
Wine Cooler, Hexagonal, Loop Handles, Brassbound, Casters, c.1800, 24 x 21 In. 1955.00
Wine Cooler, Spindle Cage Center Pedestal, Carved Knees & Pad Feet, 27 In. 1045.00
Wine Safe, Sheraton, Cherry, Marble Top, Drawer, Turned Legs, 26 1/2 x 17 In. 303.00

G. ARGY-ROUSSEAU is the impressed mark used on a variety of objects in the Art Deco style. Gabriel Argy-Rousseau, born in 1885, was a French glass artist.

G-ARGY-ROUSSEAU

Bowl, Geometric, Brown Leaves, Pate-De-Verre, 1926, 3 1/8 In. 6900.00
Bowl, Geometric, Brown, Tan, Pate-De-Verre, 1926, 3 1/8 In. 5175.00
Bowl, Light Green Rabbits, Brown, Pate-De-Verre, 1932, 3 1/2 In. 13800.00
Box, Cover, Foliage, Purple, Central Red Flowers, Amber, Pate-De-Verre, 5 In. 4312.00
Lamp, Geometric, Tan, Dark Brown, Black, Pate-De-Verre, Iron Base, 11 1/2 In. 5750.00
Night-Light, Red Circle In Center, Pate-De-Verre, Wrought Iron, 7 In. 6900.00
Vase, Deer, Pate-De-Verre, 1928, 3 3/4 In. 11500.00

GALLE was a designer who made glass, pottery, furniture, and other Art Nouveau items. Emile Galle founded his factory in France in 1874. After Galle's death in 1904, the firm continued to make glass and furniture until 1931. The name *Galle* was used as a mark, but it was often hidden in the design of the object. Galle glass is listed here. Pottery is in the next section. His furniture is listed in the Furniture category.

Gallé

Atomizer, Brown Grapevine, 11 In. 920.00
Atomizer, Burgundy To Yellow, Flowers & Leaves, Cameo, 9 In. 1540.00
Bowl, Centerpiece, Brown Leaves, Orange Ground, Cameo, 1900, 15 In. 5175.00
Bowl, Flower, 4 Pulled Points, Pale Pink, Light Yellow Green, Amber, Cameo, 4 x 8 In. . . 690.00
Bowl, Green Fern Leaves, Yellow To Frost, Etched, Signed, Cameo, 5 x 7 1/2 In. 2200.00
Bowl, Pale Yellow, Lavender, Blue Flowering Myrtle Vines, Pinched, Cameo, 6 In. 805.00
Box, Cover, Leaves & Berries, Purple Etched To Frosted, 3 x 7 In. 2585.00
Box, Cover, Lotus & Dragonfly, Signed, Cameo, 1900, 2 3/4 x 7 In. 6325.00
Decanter, Iris, Deep Purple, Upturned Rim, Purple Ground, Conical Stopper, 10 In. 2530.00
Ewer, Orchid, Leaf Green, Floral Sprays, Maroon, Pink, Blue Mushrooms, 1880, 20 In. . . 5750.00
Lamp, Butterfly, Brown, Turquoise Ground, Cameo, Signed, 1900, 11 x 10 1/2 In. 16100.00
Lamp, Chrysanthemum Shade, Cameo, Bronze, Signed, 1900, 11 x 10 In. 17825.00
Lamp, Floriform Shade, Cameo, Bronze, Brown Patina, Signed, 1900, 20 1/2 x 12 In. . . . 31625.00
Lamp, Grand Swallows, Cameo, Signed, 1900, 12 x 11 In. 9775.00
Lamp, Oleander Shade, Cameo, Bronze, Signed, 28 x 17 In. 57500.00
Lamp, Prunus Shade, Cameo, Bronze, 1900, 11 1/4 In. 17250.00
Pitcher, Oriental Berry Vine Design, Dark Teal, Gold Enameled 1150.00
Plaque, Landscape, 4 Cows, 12 1/2 In. 805.00
Tazza, Clematis, Amber, Yellow, Maroon Clematis Vines, Cameo, 10 3/4 In. 1150.00
Tazza, Pink, Green Thistles, Leaves, Thistle Base, Amber, 1900, 5 1/8 In. 1380.00
Vase, 2-Tone Brown Orchids, Yellow, Brown Mottled Ground, Cameo, Signed, 7 In. 1100.00
Vase, 2-Tone Foliate, Peach To Gray Ground, Signed, 8 1/2 In. 1380.00
Vase, Amber Clematis, Yellow Ground, 9 1/2 In. 8525.00
Vase, Aspen, Pale Pink Layers, Green, Brown, Grass, Cameo, 8 In. 460.00
Vase, Berries & Branches, Yellow, Green Ground, Cameo, Signed, 5 1/2 x 2 x 1 In. 850.00
Vase, Berry, Pink Cased, Olive Green, Cameo, Bulbous, Signed, 3 1/2 In. 460.00
Vase, Berry, Purple Over Yellow Green, Blueberry Branches, Cameo, 6 1/4 In. 345.00
Vase, Berry, Sprays Of Cascading Berries, Olive, Brown, Cameo, France, 16 In. 546.00
Vase, Bleeding Heart Design, Diamond Shape, Signed, 7 1/2 In. 1512.00
Vase, Blossoms & Leaves, Cameo, Gray, Blue, Pink, Signed, 1900, 10 1/2 In. 5460.00
Vase, Blossoms & Leaves, Purple To Frost, Shaded To Amber, Yellow, Cameo, 13 In. 1595.00
Vase, Boat Shape, Applied Starfish & Plants, Multicolor, 5 x 11 x 7 In. 4255.00

Vase, Brown Berry & Vine, Clambroth Ground, Mounted As Lamp, 11 In. 460.00
Vase, Brown, Green Raspberries, Light Brown Ground, Cameo, Signed, 8 In. 1210.00
Vase, Bud, Hydrangeas, Purple, Green, Gray, Cameo, 1900, 6 3/4 In. 515.00
Vase, Burgundy To Brown To Green, Baluster, Footed, Cameo, 9 In. 1100.00
Vase, Cherries, Red, Opalescent Yellow Ground, Cameo, Signed, c.1900, 2 3/4 In. 750.00
Vase, Cherry Blossoms On Branch, Yellow, Pink, Double Overlay, Cameo, 14 In. 10065.00
Vase, Clematis, Gray, Yellow, Purple Blossoming Vine, Cameo, Trumpet Shape, 13 In. 977.00
Vase, Clusters Of Wildflowers, Yellow Layers, Cameo, Signed, 5 In. 575.00
Vase, Cobalt, Pink Bleeding Heart Branches, Gray, Quatrefoil Rim, Cameo, Signed, 5 In. .   2585.00
Vase, Columbine, Yellow, Pink, Mauve Layers, Cameo, France, 13 1/4 In. 1150.00
Vase, Cut Cranberry Wildflowers, Yellow Etched Ground, Tapered, Cameo, 5 7/8 In. 770.00
Vase, Cut Flower Buds & Leaves, Signed, c.1925, 2 1/8 In. 805.00
Vase, Cut Leaves & Berries On Vines, Crimped Top, Signed, 5 In. 770.00
Vase, Cut Leaves, Blossoms, Violet, Brown, Flared Top, Cameo, Signed, 5 1/2 In. 850.00
Vase, Daffodils In A Meadow, Yellow, Orange, Green Layers, Cameo, 4 3/4 In. 977.00
Vase, Etched Hydrangea Blossoms, Signed, Early 20th Century, 6 1/8 In. 460.00
Vase, Etched Landscape & Village Scene, Cameo, Signed, 9 3/4 In. 2530.00
Vase, Etched Landscape Scene, Cameo, Signed, 8 1/4 In. 1760.00
Vase, Etched, Acorns & Leaves, Cameo, Signed, 14 In. 2200.00
Vase, Fern, Leafy Green Over Amber, Cameo, 1904, 6 1/2 In. 517.00
Vase, Fern, Pink & Green, Signed, 9 1/4 In. 700.00
Vase, Floral Pod Clusters, Chartreuse Ground, Cameo, Signed, 7 In. 550.00
Vase, Floral, Brown To Light Green To Frost, Cameo, 8 1/4 In.   2145.00
Vase, Floral, Leaf Design, Amber, Cylindrical, Cameo, 1 1/2 x 4 In. 287.00
Vase, Flower, 5 Petals, Yellow, Russet, Narrow Neck, Foliate Rim, Cameo, 4 1/4 In. 1265.00
Vase, Flowers & Leaves, Burgundy To Brown Yellow, Flattened Oval, 7 In. 1100.00
Vase, Flowers & Leaves, Burgundy To Orange, Tapered Cylinder, 7 1/2 In. 1155.00
Vase, Flowers, Light Green, Dark Olive Green Base, Cameo, 1900, 29 In. 6325.00
Vase, Flowers, Pale Yellow Ground, Black Base, Cameo, 1900, 19 7/8 In. 11500.00
Vase, Flowers, Red, Yellow Citron Ground, Cameo, Signed, c.1900, 4 3/4 In. 690.00
Vase, Fruiting Grapevines, Light Brown, Peach Color, Opalescent, Cameo, 1900, 23 In. . .   4025.00
Vase, Fruiting Vine, Green & Gray Ground, Signed, 6 1/2 In. 860.00
Vase, Fuchsia, Light Orange, Cameo, 1925, 11 5/8 In. 8625.00
Vase, Gray With Green, Applied Flower Buds, Signed, c.1925, 5 1/2 In. 1150.00
Vase, Green & Rose Ground, Acorns, Cameo, Slender Neck, Bulbous Base, 1910, 6 In. . .   700.00
Vase, Green Flowers, Rose, White, Cameo, Signed, 2 3/4 In. 862.00
Vase, Green Leaves Cut To Pink, Frosted Ground, Signed, 23 1/2 In. 1760.00
Vase, Green Thistle, Pink & Frost Ground, Cameo, Signed, 17 1/4 In. 990.00
Vase, Hanging Blossom, Pink Streaks, Light Green Layers, 13 1/4 In. 575.00
Vase, Hydrangea, Pink, Periwinkle, Green, Etched, Cameo, Signed, 7 7/8 In. 747.00
Vase, Hydrangea, Shell Pink, White, Periwinkle, Green, Cameo, 6 1/2 In. 977.00
Vase, Iris Foliage Design, Crystalline, 7 In. 575.00
Vase, Iris, Orange To White, Cameo, Signed, 17 In. 1400.00
Vase, Landscape, Brown Trees, River, Cameo, Signed, 1900, 8 1/2 In. 5462.00
Vase, Landscape, Mountain, Gray, Green, Blue & Pink, Cameo, Baluster, 18 In. 7075.00
Vase, Landscape, Purple, Blue Trees On Lakeshore, Gray, Oblong, Cameo, 1900, 11 In. . .   4310.00
Vase, Landscape, River, Pink, White, Dark Rose, Cameo, 13 In.   2990.00
Vase, Landscape, Trees, Opalescent, Orange, Green, Brown, Cameo, Signed, c.1900, 6 In.   1150.00
Vase, Leaf Design, Orange To Frost, Ruffled Edge, Cameo, 10 In. 1375.00
Vase, Leafy Maple Branch, Amber, Light Green Layers, Cameo, Signed, 13 In. 920.00
Vase, Leaves, Berries, Yellow, Orange Ground, Cameo, Signed, 5 1/2 x 2 x 1 In. 850.00
Vase, Leaves, Pale Yellow Ground, 1900, 4 1/2 In. 5750.00
Vase, Light To Dark Green Leaves & Flowers, Pink Frosted Ground, Signed, 11 1/2 In. . .   1320.00
Vase, Lily, Gray, Amethyst Overlay, Cameo, Baluster, Star Mark, 6 1/2 In. 705.00
Vase, Lotus, Cameo, Signed, 1900, 10 1/4 In. 10925.00
Vase, Magnolia, Branches, Light Rose Pink, Swollen Disk Base, 23 In. 3450.00
Vase, Magnolia, Branches, White, Rose, Pink, Swollen Disk Base, 15 In. 690.00
Vase, Marine, Tan, Brown, Cameo, Signed, 1900, 14 In. 5750.00
Vase, Pastel Cornflower Blue, Lavender, Pink, Cameo, Signed, 4 3/4 In. 690.00
Vase, Pendant, Bleeding Heart Blossoms, Yellow, Ruby, Flared Lip, Cameo, 1900, 8 In. . .   1840.00
Vase, Pilgrim, Green Leaves, Pale Yellow, Cameo, 1900, 17 5/8 In. 10350.00
Vase, Pink Poppies, Yellow, Gray, Cylindrical Neck, Cameo, 1900, 13 1/4 In. 1610.00
Vase, Pink, Purple, Crocus In A Field, Cameo, Signed, 8 In. 1265.00

Vase, Plum, Pale Yellow Ground, Cameo, 1900, 15 5/8 In. 6900.00
Vase, Plum, Pale Yellow Ground, Cameo, 1925, 13 In. 14950.00
Vase, Purple & Blue Landscape, Mountains, Frosted Yellow Ground, Signed, 7 In. 440.00
Vase, Purple & Green Floral, Gray Ground, Signed, 8 1/4 In. 1380.00
Vase, Purple & Green Floral, Signed, 5 1/4 In. 860.00
Vase, Purple Flowers, Scrolled Vines, White, Gray, Bulbous Base, Cameo, 16 In. 4600.00
Vase, Purple To Green To Frost, Long Cylindrical Neck, Cameo, Bulbous Base, 8 1/2 In. . 1595.00
Vase, Purple Trumpet Flowers, Yellow, Gray, Petal Rim, Cameo, 1900, 5 In. 3160.00
Vase, Purple, Blue & Green Landscape, Frosted Ground, Signed, 5 In. 352.00
Vase, Red Floral, Leaf Design, Cylindrical, Cameo, 2 x 12 1/8 In. 258.00
Vase, Red Flowers, Yellow Ground, Signed, 7 In. 2415.00
Vase, Red To White, Floral, Fire Polished, Signed, 13 1/2 In. 1500.00
Vase, Ripening Apples On Branches, Lime Green, Deep Amber, Cameo, 1925, 11 5/8 In. . 9775.00
Vase, Starflower, Seed Pods, Leaves, Pink & Frosted, Cameo, Signed, 10 3/4 In. 880.00
Vase, Stick, Iris, Cameo, Depose, Fire Polished, Signed, 8 3/4 In. 750.00
Vase, Stick, Plum Feathers, Cameo, Signed, 9 1/2 In. 700.00
Vase, Stylized Flowers, Pink Streaks, Periwinkle, Green Layers, Gray Neck, Cameo, 8 In. 862.00
Vase, Tangerine Flowering Vine, Long Tapering Neck, Cupped Rim, Signed, 12 5/8 In. . . 1090.00
Vase, Thistle, Mauve, Green, Tapered Neck, Cameo, 1895, 7 In. 1265.00
Vase, Thistle, Pink, White, Green, Ruffled Edge, Foot Rim, Cylindrical, 1890, 7 7/8 In. . . 660.00
Vase, Topaz Grains Of Barley, Barrel, France, 1890, 8 1/2 In. 862.00
Vase, Woodland Orchids, Pale Yellow Case, Brown, Cameo, Signed, 6 3/4 In. 517.00
Vase, Yellow Dragonflies, Cameo, Signed, 1900, 18 In. 8050.00

GALLE POTTERY was made by Emile Galle, the famous French designer, after 1874. The pieces were marked with the initials *E. G.* impressed, *Em. Galle Faiencerie de Nancy*, or a version of his signature. Galle is best known for his glass, listed above.

Figurine, Cat, Seated, Blue Circle, Foliate, Heart Design, Yellow Ground, 13 In. 2415.00
Figurine, Cat, Seated, Overall Multicolored Floral, Ribbon, White, Yellow, 14 In. 5175.00

GAME collectors like all types of games. Of special interest are any board games or card games. Transogram and other company names are included in the description when known. Other games may be found listed under Card, Toy, or the name of the character or celebrity featured in the game.

12 O'Clock High, Ideal, Board, Box, 1965 . . . . 39.00
12 O'Clock High, Milton Bradley, Card, 1965 . . . . 35.00
20,000 Leagues Under The Sea, Sealed 75.00
A-Team, 1984 . . . . 8.00
Across The Channel, Wolverine Supply & Mfg., Co., Metal Board, 1920s 75.00
Addams Family, Ideal, Board, Box, 1964 . . . . 35.00
Adventures Of Rin-Tin-Tin, Transogram, TV Show, Box 50.00
Alee-Oop, Royal Toy Co., 1937 . . . . .25.00 to 80.00
Alien, Kenner, 1979 . . . . 100.00
All Star Baseball, Cadaco-Ellis, Board, 1969 . . . . 20.00
American Roll Game, Marx, Box, 1920s 210.00
Anagram Dice, The Embossing Co., Wooden Blocks, 1930s 15.00
Anagrams, Salem Edition, Parker Brothers, Card, Red Box, 1930s 15.00
Andy Bizzy Jr., Wolverine Supply & Mfg. Co., Folding Cardboard Box, 1918 . . . . 30.00
Around The World In 80 Days, Transogram, Michael Todd Co., Board, 1957 . . . . 30.00
As The World Turns, Parker Brothers, Board, 1966 . . . . 40.00
Assembly Line, Selchow & Righter, Board, 1953 . . . . 45.00
Authors, McLaughlin Brothers, Card, 1890s 20.00
Auto Race, Gotham Press Steel Corp., Metal Board, Roulette Type Game, 1930s 120.00
Babe Ruth's Official, Wooden Bat, Markers, Tin Pennant, Tin Strike Zone 325.00
Bagatelle, Paper On Wood, Chromolithographic, 2 Clowns, Pat. March 7, 1895, 13 In. . . . 290.00
Ball Toss, Philadelphia Toboggan Co., Kicking Mule, 84 x 54 In. 2875.00
Ball Toss, Punch The Clown, 1880s 3800.00
Baseball, Olsen's, Card, 1922 . . . . 68.00
Baseball, Parker Brothers, 1950 . . . . 25.00
Bat Masterson, NBC TV Show, Lowell, Box, 1958 . . . . .50.00 to 70.00
Battle Line, Ideal, Board, Box, 1964 . . . . 35.00

Bazooka Bagatelle, Marx, Tin, Plastic, Partial Box, 1950s, 6 1/4 x 12 3/4 In. 85.00
Beat The Clock, Lowell, Board, 1954 .... 25.00
Ben Casey MD, Transogram, Board, 1961 .... 30.00
Bermuda Triangle, Bradley, Board, Box, 1976 .... 28.00
Bewitched, Card ....150.00 to 195.00
Bewitched, Samantha & Endora Game, Box, 1965 .... 37.00
Bible Girls, Evangelical Pub. Co., 1905 .... 15.00
Bicycle Race, McLoughlin, Board, Box, 1890 .... 925.00
Bicycle Race, Wooden Box, France, 17 x 12 x 4 1/2 In. 6500.00
Big Business, Transogram, 1948 .... 10.00
Bild-A-Word Picture Puzzles, Educational Card & Game Corp., 1930s 25.00
Bing Crosby, Call Me Lucky, Parker Brothers, Board, 1954 .... 40.00
Bingo, Pressman Toy Corp., Metal Board, Tin Spinner, 1930s 15.00
Bizzy Andy Jr., Wolverine Supply & Mfg. Co., 1918 .... 30.00
Blondie Goes To Leisureland, Westinghouse Premium, K.S.F., Board, 1935 .... 75.00
Board, Black & Green M Painted Gold Border 1 Side, Other Game, 16 x 24 1/2 In. 1265.00
Board, Cribbage, Brass, Turned Legs, 10 In. 27.00
Board, Cribbage, Engraved Salmon, Walrus Ivory, Nome Alaska, Horn Shape, Pins, 9 In. . 330.00
Board, Faro, Folding, Hand Painted, c.1900 .... 1650.00
Board, Parcheesi, Red, White, Green Paint, Breadboard Ends, Maine, 16 x 24 In. 2310.00
Board, Parchesi, Red & Orange, Dark Green Ground, Framed, 17 1/2 x 17 1/2 In. 7475.00
Bobbsey Twins, On The Farm, Milton Bradley, Board, 1957 .... 75.00
Brady Bunch, Hex-A-Game, Larami, 1973 .... 40.00
Bridge Table Markers, Pencils, Golfer, Celluloid Figures, Goofy Heads, 4 1/4 In. 211.00
British & Foreign Birds, William Carton, Canvas Back Folding Board, London, 1820 ... 975.00
Burke's Law, Transogram, Box 30.00
Candyland, 1st Edition, Milton Bradley, Board, 1949 .... 32.00
Captain Video, Milton Bradley, Board, Box, 1952 .... 81.00
Casper, Friendly Ghost, Casper Figure, Box 60.00
Chain Of Events In English History, John Betts, c.1840 .... 725.00
Charlie Brown's All-Star Baseball, Parker Brothers, Board, 1968 .... 50.00
Charlie's Angels, Milton Bradley, Board, 1977 .... 5.00
Charlotte's Web, Hasbro, 1960s 35.00
Checkerboard, 2 Sides, Another Game On Reverse, Painted, 24 1/2 x 24 3/4 In. 990.00
Checkerboard, 2 Sides, Painted Game Other, 18 x 18 1/2 In. 605.00
Checkerboard, Gold, Black & White Paint, Round Frame, 19 5/8 In. Diam. 235.00
Checkerboard, Painted Cream, Red & Black, 2 Storage Compartments, 19 x 24 In. 3800.00
Checkerboard, Painted, Arched Top, Green & Yellow, 19 1/4 x 12 1/4 In. 275.00
Checkerboard, Painted, Geometric Pattern On Reverse, 1800s, 14 x 14 In. 7475.00
Checkerboard, Pine, 140 Squares, 17 x 24 In. 220.00
Checkerboard, Poplar, Blue & Maroon Paint, Black Gallery, 17 x 19 1/2 In. 110.00
Checkerboard, Red & White, 140 Squares, 20 x 32 In. 357.00
Checkerboard, Salmon & Black Paint, 19th Century 360.00
Checkerboard, Walnut & Maple, Inlay Borders, 20th Century, 38 x 27 In. 110.00
Chess, Rosewood Board, Ivory & Ebony Squares, Inlay Floral Borders, Complete 105.00
Chess Set, Box Converts To Board, Ivory 287.00
Chess Set, Carved Ivory, Tallest Piece 5 1/2 In. 350.00
Chess Set, Figures Set On Carved Puzzle Balls, Early 20th Century 402.00
Chess Set, Ivory, Playing Board On Case, Oriental, Mid 20th Century 145.00
Chess Set, Red & White, Ivory, Chinese, 19th Century, 3-In. King 330.00
Chessboard, Onyx, Black, Mottled Brown, Square, 14 In. 44.00
Chessboard, Slate, Brown Paint, Grooved Squares, Cut Corners, 15 1/4 In. 105.00
Ching Gong, Samuel Gabriel, Board, 1937 .... 65.00
CHiPs, Milton Bradley, Board, 1977 .... 28.00
Chiromagica, McLoughlin, Carry Case, Slide Cover, Question & Answer Sheets, c.1870 . 275.00
Chuck Aluck, Metal Dice Cage, Wooden Base, 17 In. 209.00
Chutes & Ladders, Milton Bradley, Board, 1956 .... 20.00
Civil War 1863, Parker Brothers, Board, 1961 ....40.00 to 65.00
Clue, Parker Brothers, 1949 .... 80.00
Combat, Ideal, Board, TV Show, Vic Morrow On Cover, 1963 .... 65.00
Cops & Robbers, Milton Bradley, Box, 1938 .... 40.00
Cottage Of Content, Wm. Spooner, Right Roads & Wrong Ways, London, 1848 .... 975.00
Countdown Space, Transogram, 1959 .... 85.00

Croquet Set, 7 Balls, 8 Mallets, Case 100.00
Crow Hunt, Parker Brothers, 1930 .... 60.00
Dart Board, Pabst Blue Ribbon Ale, Masonite, Drawings Of Hitler & Tojo, 18 x 18 In. .. 63.00
Detective, Bliss, Board, 1889 .... 4070.00
Dexterity Puzzle, Circus Seals, Tin Rim, Glass Front, U.S. Zone Germany, 1950s 28.00
Dexterity Puzzle, Horseshoes, Metal 35.00
Dexterity Puzzle, Monkey Face, Wagner's Home Bread, Tin Rim, Germany, 1930s 40.00
Dexterity Puzzle, Smiling Man's Face, Cigar, Tin Rim, Insert Mirror, Germany 58.00
Dice, Rhinestones, Blue Leather Case, 1 x 3/4 In., Pair. 33.00
Dick Van Dyke, Standard Toykraft, Board, Box, 1964 .... 60.00
Dominoes, Bone & Ebony, 12 Tiles, Wooden Case, Sliding Lid, 19th Century 145.00
Dominoes, Bone & Ebony, 18 Tiles, Wooden Case, Sliding Lid, 19th Century 300.00
Dominoes, Bone & Ivory, Box, Sliding Lid, Civil War Era 110.00
Dominoes, Ebony & Ivory, 28 Tiles, Box, Sliding Lid 250.00
Dominoes, Whalebone, Wooden Case, Sliding Lid, 19th Century, Complete 230.00
Easy Money, Milton Bradley, Board, 1936 ....15.00 to 20.00
Egg, Wooden Eggcups, Eggs & Paddles, Box, France, c.1900, 10 1/2 x 8 In. 200.00
Electric Horserace, Pressman Toy Co., 1950s ....90.00 to 95.00
Emergency, Milton Bradley, Board, 1974 ....10.00 to 20.00
Felix The Cat, Board, 1960 .... 45.00
Fibber McGee & Molly, Milton Bradley, Board, Wistful Vista Mystery, 1940 .... 15.00
Fireball XL5, Milton Bradley, Board, Box, 1964 .... 39.00
Flip-It, Flip Wilson's, Large Wheel, Gambling, Number 21 .... 50.00
Flipper Flips, Mattel, Board, Dolphin & Scuba Diver On Box, 1960s 26.00
Flivver, Milton Bradley, Board, Model T Ford Graphics, 1927 .... 325.00
Football, Electric, Tin, Pat. 1949, 16 x 26 In. 35.00
Fortune Teller, Milton Bradley, Board, 1906 .... 40.00
Frontierland, Walt Disney ....45.00 to 70.00
Funky Phantom, Milton Bradley, Board, 1971 .... 40.00
Game Of Authors, Russell Mfg. Co., Card, 1920s 40.00
Game Of High Spirits With Calvin & Colonel, Milton Bradley, 1962 .... 80.00
Game Of India, Milton Bradley, Camels & Pyramid On Front, 1940s, 11 1/4 In. 33.00
Game Of Mail Express Or Accommodation, Milton Bradley, 1930s, 22 x 14 3/4 In. 110.00
Game Of The States, Milton Bradley, 1940 .... 55.00
Gee-Wiz Horse Race, N.M.T., 1930s 175.00
Gee-Wiz Horse Race, Wolverine, Sandy Andy, Box, 1923 .... 475.00
Go To The Head Of The Class, Board, 1967 .... 13.00
Going To Jerusalem, Parker Brothers, Board, 1955 .... 100.00
Golf, Ferdinand Strauss Corp., Windup, Tin, Holes In Bowling Pin Pattern, 1920s 1790.00
Goose, Board, Mary D. Carol, Made By Charles Akerman, 1855, 20 In. 230.00
Grand Jeu Du Bebe Jumeau, Eiffel Tower, Dolls, Paper, Framed, 1889, 18 x 27 In. 1450.00
Grande Auto Race, Atkins & Co., Board, 1920 .... 65.00
Great American Game Baseball, Franz, Tin Lithograph, Original Markers 155.00
Green Acres, Standard Toykraft, Board, Box, 1960s 50.00
Have Gun Will Travel, Parker Brothers, Board, 1959 .... 59.00
Hit The Beach, Milton Bradley, Board, World War II, 1965 .... 36.00
Hocus Pocus, Transogram, Board, Magician's Delight, Box 100.00
Hokum, Parker Brothers, Card, 1927 .... 35.00
Hollywood Squares, Ideal, Box, TV Game, 1974 .... 20.00
Horse Racing, Metal, Drum Shape, Painted, Horse & Rider Figures 635.00
Horses, All Far, 1929 .... 55.00
I Dream Of Jeannie, Milton Bradley, Board, 1965 ....40.00 to 130.00
Illya Kuryakin, Milton Bradley, Card, 1966 .... 20.00
Indoor Golf, 5 Dice, Pigskin Golf Club Bag, Original Rules, 4 In. 23.00
Inventors, Parker Brothers, Board, 1974 .... 15.00
It's About Time, Ideal, Board, Box, 1966 .... 175.00
Jack & The Beanstalk, Transogram, Board, 1957 .... 20.00
Jackie Gleason, Transogram, Board, 1956 .... 128.00
James Bond 007 Assault, Victory, 1961 .... 55.00
Jigsaw Puzzle, 3 Stooges, Can, 1974 .... 60.00
Jigsaw Puzzle, Addams Family, Cleopatra's Flight, Box, 1965 .... 125.00
Jigsaw Puzzle, Blondie & Dagwood, Gaston Mfg. Co., Blocks, 20 Piece ....*Illus* 20.00
Jigsaw Puzzle, Bugs Bunny Licking Lollipop, 65 Pieces, 1960, 7 x 9 In. 20.00

Jigsaw Puzzle, Chicklets, Chicklet Shape 10.00
Jigsaw Puzzle, Chitty Chitty Bang Bang, Whitman, Frame Tray 25.00
Jigsaw Puzzle, Chopped Up Niggers, McLoughlin Brothers, Mid 19th Century 490.00
Jigsaw Puzzle, Dracula, Jaymar, 1960s 85.00
Jigsaw Puzzle, Dukes Of Hazzard, Box, 1981 ....15.00 to 25.00
Jigsaw Puzzle, Farrah Fawcett, With Famous Reclining Pose, 1977, 12 x 20 In. 24.00
Jigsaw Puzzle, Folger's Coffee, Can Shape 10.00
Jigsaw Puzzle, Frankenstein, Jaymar, 1960s 85.00
Jigsaw Puzzle, Godzilla, 1970s 50.00
Jigsaw Puzzle, Lifesaver's, Lifesaver Shape 10.00
Jigsaw Puzzle, Map, Indian Territory, School, Missing N. Hampshire, Wooden, 1880s 30.00
Jigsaw Puzzle, Mother Goose, Platt Munk, Box, Set Of 6 .... 45.00
Jigsaw Puzzle, New York World's Fair, Parker Brothers, Map, 32 Piece, Box, 1939 ...... 93.00
Jigsaw Puzzle, Prince & Princess, Maxwell Parrish, 250 Piece 185.00
Jigsaw Puzzle, Superboy With Dog, 1968, 11 x 14 In. 35.00
Jigsaw Puzzle, Wyatt Earp, Tray, 1958 .... 35.00
Jigsaw Puzzle Box, Walnut, Ivory Knob, Brass Bound, Civil War Era, 4 1/2 x 2 In. 88.00
Jimmy The Greek, Aurora, Board, 1974 .... 60.00
King Kong, Ideal, Board, 1976 .... 32.00
Life & Legend Of Wyatt Earp, Transogram, Box, 1958 .... 50.00
Little Firemen, McLoughlin, Board, 1897 .... 2870.00
Little Shoppers Game, Gibson Game Co., Board, Boston, 1915, 14 x 20 In. 20.00
Locomotive Game Of Railroad Adventures, Edward Wallis, London, 1840s 550.00
Mah-Jongg, 5-Drawer Cabinet, Bamboo Tiles, Bone Facing, 7 1/2 x 7 3/4 In. 70.00
Major League Baseball, Tin, 2 Darts, Box, 1920s, 13 1/2 x 17 1/2 In. 85.00
Marathon, Sports, Start Of Marathon, Box, Sports Game Company, 11 x 5 In. 20.00
Marble, Operation Moon Probe, Plastic, Tin, Wolverine Toy Works, 1960s, 13 x 23 In. ... 22.00
Marble, Windup, Elephant & Whirligig, Germany, 1950s 475.00
Mechanical Dice, Tin Lithograph, Marx, 1920s, 5 In. 210.00
Meet The Missus, Fitzpatrick Brothers, Board, 1937 .... 65.00
Men Into Space, Milton Bradley, Board, Box, 1960 .... 42.00
Miami Vice, Pepper Lane, Board, TV, 1984 .... 20.00
Michelin Dice, Plastic Carrier With 8 Plastic Dice, White, 3 1/2 x 2 1/2 In. 95.00
Mister Ed The Talking Horse, Parker Brothers, Board, Box, 1962 .... 42.00
Monopoly, Card Binder, Money Drawer, Wooden Case, Franklin Mint, 1991, 21 3/4 In. .. 400.00
Moon Blast-Off, Schaper, Board, 1970 .... 48.00
Movie Millions, Transogram, Board, 1938 .... 100.00
My Favorite Martian, Transogram, Board, 1963 .... 50.00
Mysto Magic Exhibition, No. 2001, Gilbert, Box, Instruction Booklet, 1930 .... 70.00
NBC-TV News Game With Chet Huntley, Box, 1960s 22.00
New Game Of Royal Mail, J. Jaques & Son, Railway Game, London, Victorian 575.00
Nightmare On Elm Street, Freddy Game, Cardinal, Box, 1989 .... 23.00
Nurses, Ideal, Board, 1963 .... 75.00
Old Maid, Built-Rite, Card 20.00
Our Tipple-Toppe, Box, 1930 .... 575.00

Organic chemicals like skin oil or
perspiration will eventually interact
with paper and cause damage. Never
trim a frayed piece of paper with
scissors you use to cut your hair or
to cut flowers in the garden.

Game, Jigsaw Puzzle, Blondie & Dagwood,
Gaston Mfg. Co., Blocks, 20 Piece

Overland Trail, Transogram, Board, 1960 .... 90.00
Parcheesi, Selchow & Righter, Scene Of Snake Charmer, Box, 16 x 8 In. 32.00
Parlor, Ball, 5 Wooden Balls, 10 x 22 In. 550.00
Pathfinder, Milton Bradley, Board, 1977 ....38.00 to 60.00
PDQ, Milton Bradley, Box, 19 x 9 In. 45.00
Pegboard, Pine, Handmade, Handle, Missing Pegs, 5 1/2 x 5 7/8 In. 60.00
Pinball, Stevens Mfg. Co., Play Ball, Tin, Plastic, 1964, 6 1/4 x 11 1/2 In. 45.00
Pinball, Zip, Court Jesters, Tin, Wooden Frame, 1940s-1950s, 11 x 18 In. 75.00
Pirate & Traveler, Milton Bradley, Board, 1936 .... 60.00
Poison Ivy, Ideal, 1969 .... 30.00
Pony Express, Polygon, Board, 1947 .... 165.00
Popeye, Blondie, Beetle Bailey, Card 35.00
Posse, Marc, Target, Tin Lithograph 65.00
Pro Football, Milton Bradley, Board, 1964 .... 35.00
Pumpkin Face, Ring, Box, Schecth Rubber Co., 1927 .... 390.00
Puzzle, Block, Germany, Box, 5 Piece 585.00
Quick Draw McGraw, Knickbocker, Board, 1960 .... 44.00
Quiz Kids Own Game Box, Parker Brothers, 1940 .... 20.00
Racing, Sandown Registered F.H. Ayres Ltd., Mahogany, England, 1900, 12 In. 465.00
Robin Hood, Parker Brothers, Board, 1973 .... 25.00
Rook, Parker Brothers, Card, 1913 .... 20.00
Rose Bowl Football, Leather Helmets, 1949 .... 25.00
Roulette Wheel, H.C. Evans, 9 Reverse Painted Mirrored Panels, Dice, 1920s, 60 In. 2300.00
Roulette Wheel, Jockey On Steed, Reverse Painted Mirrored Panels, Evans, 60 In. 3737.00
Roulette Wheel, Plywood, Old White, Red, Black & Green Paint, 41 Ft. Diam. 220.00
Route 66 Travel Game, Transogram, Board, Box, 1962 .... 72.00
Rummy, Milton Bradley, Card, 1914 .... 38.00
Santa Claus, Milton Bradley 410.00
Sea Hunt, Lloyd Brides On Cover, Lowell, 1960 .... 80.00
Sea Hunt, Lowell, Board, TV Game, 1960 .... 76.00
Seduction, Createk, Board, 1966 .... 20.00
Sir Peter Peppercorn, Parker Brothers, 1894 .... 20.00
Slide, Marble, Wooden, 13 x 25 In. 60.00
Snagglepuss, Transogram, Board, 1961 .... 45.00
Snooker Table, Regulation Size Table, Regulation Size 800.00
Spiderman, Ideal, Board, Web Spinning Action, 1979 .... 65.00
Spin A Roo, Wolverine Toy, Marbles, Plastic, Tin Base 22.00
Spinnette, Milton Bradley, 1924 .... 20.00
Spoof, Milton Bradley, 1918 .... 15.00
Sports Yesteryear, Skor-Mor, Board, 1977 .... 15.00
Squire Or Sir Peter Peppercorn, Parker Brothers, 1894 .... 20.00
Stage, C.M. Clark Publishing Co., Inc., Card, 1904 .... 65.00
Stagecoach West Adventure Game, Transogram, TV Show, Box, 1961 .... 38.00
Star Authors, McLoughlin, Card, 1887 .... 25.00
Starsky & Hutch, Milton Bradley, Board, Detective, 1977 .... 35.00
State Capitals, Parker Brothers, 1966 .... 10.00
Steeple Chase, McLoughlin, Board, Pieces, Instructions In Lid, 1889 .... 258.00
Steeple Chase, Spears Games, 1930s 40.00
Stop & Go, Whitman Publishing Co., 1939 .... 40.00
Strat-O-Matic Baseball, Board, 1988 .... 32.00
Stratego, Milton Bradley, Board, 1961 .... 20.00
Strategy, Corey Games, Board, 1945 .... 150.00
Strategy, Knights Jousting, Corey Games, Box, 18 x 12 In. 140.00
Strategy, Milton Bradley, 1962 .... 40.00
Sunken Treasure, Parker Brothers, Board, 1948 .... 18.00
Supercar To The Rescue, Milton Bradley, Board, Box, 1962 .... 80.00
Superstition, Milton Bradley, Board, 1977 .... 35.00
Sweeps, All Fair, 1940s 25.00
Swing Pin, Tudor Metal Products Corp., Metal Board, 9 Pins, 1930s 35.00
Syllable Game, Garrard Publishing Co., Card, 1948 .... 15.00
Table Tennis, Milton Bradley, 1935 .... 20.00
Tag, Milton Bradley, 1958 .... 10.00
Take It & Double, Frederick H. Beach, Board, 1941 .... 35.00

Tank Battle, Box, Milton Bradley, Board, 20 x 12 In. 45.00
Tank Battle, Milton Bradley, 1975 .... 20.00
Tantalizer, Northern Signal Co., Board, 1965 .... 75.00
Target, Black Man, Waist High, From Ball Toss Carnival Booth 2310.00
Target, Posse, Wyandotte, Windup 145.00
Target, World War I Marine, Waist High, From Ball Toss Carnival Booth 1760.00
Tarzan To The Rescue, Milton Bradley, Board, 1977 .... 20.00
Tattler Quiz, Parker Brothers, 1947 .... 10.00
Tenpins, Army Cadet, 1930s, Box 125.00
Three Little Kittens,, Milton Bradley, Board, 1938 .... 25.00
Tip Top Fish Pond, Pond, 2 Poles, Fish, 1940s, 9 In. 28.00
Tom & Jerry, Milton Bradley, Board, 1977 .... 20.00
Tom Hamilton's Football, Board, Instructions, Parts, Parker Brothers 57.00
Tournament Checkers Set, Wooden, Box, Early 1900s 15.00
Toy-Town Telegraph Office, Parker Brothers, Board, c.1910 .... 55.00
Trump Indicator, Ashtray, Bakelite, Celluloid Center Disc, England, 5 In. 61.00
Trump Indicator, Ashtray, Flapper, Porcelain, Missing Pointer, 2 1/2 In. 242.00
Trump Indicator, Ashtray, No Fume, Painted, Metal Base, Chrome Plated Top, 3 3/4 In. . 453.00
Trump Indicator, Brass Harp, Celluloid, Engraved, Unmarked, 3 In. 121.00
Trump Indicator, Celluloid, Whitehead & Hoag, Patented 1905, Photo, 3 1/8 In. 114.00
Trump Indicator, Chrome Plated, Celluloid Indictors, 3 In. 121.00
Trump Indicator, Cube, Tray, Tortoise, Brass Plated Cube Holder, 2 1/4 In. 242.00
Trump Indicator, Deco Lucite, 2 3/4 In. 121.00
Trump Indicator, Drum, Nickel Plated Brass, US Patent No., DRP, 1 3/4 In. 152.00
Trump Indicator, Horseshoe Harp, Nickel Plated, Celluloid, 4 1/4 In. 121.00
Trump Indicator, Lighthouse, Red Marble, Nickel Plated Brass Harp, Celluloid, 8 In. ... 440.00
Trump Indicator, Pad, Aluminum, Sliding Indicators, Pad, WMF, French, 2 1/2 x 8 In. 303.00
Trump Indicator, Porcelain Boy, Drum, Cardboard Dial, Marked 7533, 2 1/2 In. 469.00
Trump Indicator, Push Button, Nickel Plated Brass, 2-Sided Celluloid Dial, 4 In. 121.00
Trump Indicator, Souvenir, Sand Filled Tubes, Plastic Pointer, Isle Of Wight, 4 In. 429.00
Trump Indicator, Table Number, Original Box, Set Of Six, 2 1/2 In. 288.00
Trump Indicator, Windmill, Painted Wood, Replace Blade, 3 1/2 In. 388.00
Trump Indicator, Wire Frame, Gold Plated, Celluloid, Registration, England, 5 In. 97.00
Twister, Milton Bradley, Box 50.00
Wagon Train, Milton Bradley, Box, 1960, 16 x 8 In. 30.00
Wanted Dead Or Alive, Lowell, Board, 1959 .... 195.00
Welcome Back Kotter, Milton Bradley, Card, 1976 .... 30.00 to 40.00
Western Bulldogging, Kellogg's, Instructions, 1950s 75.00
Wheel, Carnival, Evans Of Chicago, 6 Ft. 3500.00
Wheel, Horse Race, Painted Panel Doors, 27 In. 2750.00
Wheel, Red, White & Blue, Advance Whip & Novelty Co., Inc., 30 In. Diam. 650.00
Whirly Bird Play Catch Game, Suction Cups, Metal Target, Warren Spahn On Box Lid .. 20.00
Whist Marker, Camden, Exotic Wood, Ivory Markers, England, 3 5/8 In. 112.00
Willy's Walk To See Grandmamma, Myers & Co., London, 1869 .... 400.00
Wizard Of Oz, Cadaco, Board, 1974 .... 12.00
Yogi Bear, Milton Bradley, Board, 1971 .... 22.00

GAME PLATES are plates of any make decorated with pictures of birds, animals, or fish. The game plates usually came in sets consisting of twelve dishes and a serving platter. These sets were most popular during the 1880s.

2 Ducks, Hand Painted, 10 In. 28.00
Bird, Hand Painted, Transfer, Garland Of Oak Leaves, Acorns, c.1892, 8 1/2 In. 55.00
Gilt Rim, Limoges, c.1906, 10 In. 125.00
Hand Painted, Lewis Straus, 1890s 138.00

GARDEN FURNISHINGS have been popular for centuries. The stone or metal statues, wire, iron, or rustic furniture, urns and fountains, sundials, and small figurines are included in this category. Many of the metal pieces have been made continuously for years.

Bench, Cast Iron, Fern-Shaped Design, 19th Century, 59 1/2 In. 2300.00
Bench, Double, Folding, Scrolled Arms, Cast Iron, 26 x 56 In. 715.00
Bench, Filigree Design, Cast Iron, Painted White, 44 In. 895.00

Bench, Fish Scale Design, Rococo Floral Trim, Kramer Bros. Fdy., Cast Iron, 43 In. 495.00
Bench, Floral & Vining Lattice, White Paint, Bird Arms, Cast Iron, 39 x 32 In. 990.00
Bench, Flower & Minerva Head, Cast Iron, Cream Repaint, 46 In. 220.00
Bench, Gothic Style, White, Cast Iron, Late 19th-Early 20th Century, 36 x 46 In., Pair . . . 1045.00
Bench, Grape Design, Open Seat, Cast Iron, Pair 385.00
Bench, Medallions In Foliage Scrolls, Cast Iron, 39 In. 247.00
Bench, Park, Wooden Seat & Back, 48 In., Cast Iron, Pair 415.00
Bench, Pierced Geometric & Leaf Scroll, White Paint, Cast Iron, Pat. 5-17-1895, 33 In. . . 600.00
Bench, Pierced Gilt, 6 Twisted Legs, Wrought Iron, 26 1/4 In. 460.00
Bench, Scrolled Crest Rail, Floral Splayed Seat, Scrolled Arms, Cast Iron, 45 In., Pair . . . 1725.00
Bench, Scrolling Splayed Legs, Cast Iron, c.1850, 79 1/2 In. 1025.00
Birdbath, 2 Doves, Fluted Standard, Pierced Design Of Roses Base, Cast Iron, 33 In. 330.00
Birdbath, Bird & Shell, Cast Iron, Victorian 520.00
Chair, Box Form, Crisscross Back, Painted Iron, 31 x 24 1/2 In., Pair 275.00
Dining Set, Patio, Metal, Glass Rectangular Top, Scroll Back Chairs, 5 Piece 110.00
Figure, Bearded Man, Standing In Tan Robe, Porcelain, Russia, 9 In. 977.00
Figure, Chinese Woman, Carved Stone, 50 In. 3162.00
Figure, Dog, Cement, Staffordshire Type, Black & White Paint, Green Base 185.00
Figure, Egyptian Pharaoh, Seated, Cast Lead, 52 In. 385.00
Figure, Flamingo Set, Cast Metal, 20th Century, 52-In. Largest, 3 Piece 1540.00
Figure, Four Seasons, Cast Stone, 46 1/2 In., 4 Piece 1210.00
Figure, Jester, With Lute, S.A. Salata, Bronze, 1887, 46 In. 1610.00
Figure, Lion, Recumbent, Patinated Bronze, 20 x 36 In., Pair 2170.00
Figure, Lion, Seated, Flowing Mane, Cast Stone, Neoclassical Style, 54 In., Pair 3740.00
Figure, Little Girl, Boy Reading Book, Bronze, M. Geiss, 19th Century, 40 In., Pair 5460.00
Figure, Nude Boy, After Nino Geraci, Patinated Bronze, 2-Part Marble Plinth, 26 1/2 In. . . 2090.00
Figure, Peasant Man, Seated, Drinking, Wearing White Tunic, Porcelain, Russia, 6 In. . . . 920.00
Figure, Rabbit, Full-Bodied, Iron, 10 3/4 In. 165.00
Figure, Rabbit, Sitting, Cast Iron, Full-Bodied, Worn White Repaint, 11 3/4 In. 275.00
Figure, Squirrel, Eating Nut, Lead, 11 In. 143.00
Fountain, 2 Putti, Playing Flutes, Flowers, Berries, Dolphin, Patinated Bronze, 39 In. 3450.00
Fountain, 2 Young Children Under An Umbrella Form, Girl Wearing Dress, Iron, 60 In. . . . 4125.00
Fountain, Birds, 5 Tiers, Carved Wood, Gold Paint, 1890-1910, 30 In. 1760.00
Fountain, Boy, Holding Goose, Mouth Plumbed For Water, Cast Iron, 32 In. 630.00
Fountain, Cranes & Cattails Base, Leaf Basin, Cast Iron, J.W. Fiske, 1800s, 47 x 26 In. . . . 2875.00
Fountain, Dolphin & Boy, Cast Iron, Zinc, 66 x 70 In. 4950.00
Fountain, Lion, Wall, Head Spout, Scroll & Leaf, Green Patina, Bronze, 40 x 26 In. 2070.00
Fountain, Pan, Playing Flute, Cast Zinc, 31 1/2 In. 467.50
Fountain, Putti, 2 Coquiform Tiers, Dolphin Base, Bronze, Verdigris Patina, 84 In. 4950.00
Fountain, Putti, Supporting Bowl, Cast Iron, Victorian, 45 In. 1045.00
Fountain, Putto Heads & Musicians, Baroque, Bronze, 2 Tiers, 79 1/2 In. 4025.00
Fountain, Putto, Amid Water Leaves, With Shell Basin, Limestone, 19th Century, 42 In. . . . 2070.00
Fountain, Seahorse, On Sandy Mound, Sea Creatures, Bronze, 36 1/2 In. 850.00
Fountain, Swan, Floating On Water, Outstretched Neck, 36 In., Pair 2070.00
Fountain, Wall, Lion's Head, Lobed Demilune Reservoir, Cast Iron, Black Paint, 51 In. . . . 805.00
Fountain, Wall, Louis XVI Style, Leaf, Lion Head, Fruit, Patinated Bronze, 39 In. 1455.00
Fountain, Wall, Shell Form, Scrolled Backplate, Lion Head & Putti, 60 In. 2000.00
Fountain, Winged Horse Over Mermaids, Cherub Masks, Dolphins, Bronze, 81 In. 1840.00
Fountain, Winged Putto Head, Bronze, 14 x 30 In. 575.00
Fountain, Winged Youth, Seated, Holding Bird Bath, 2 Birds, 36 In. 2185.00
Fountain, With Octagonal Aquarium, Scroll, Bird, Leaf Design, Iron, 1870, 72 x 44 In. . . . 7150.00
Fountain, Young Boy & Dolphin, Seaweed & Flowers, Bronze, 51 In. 1800.00
Fountain, Young Boy, Crane, Turtle & Fish On Base, Bronze, 55 In. 3335.00
Fountain, Youth, Holding Shell-Form Basin, Cast Iron, Octagonal Base, 81 1/2 In. 1095.00
Group, Man Standing At Table, Flanked By Seated Man, Porcelain, Russia, 5 In. 747.00
Group, Woman Assisting Drunk, With Child At Her Side, Porcelain, Russia, 6 In. 1495.00
Hitching Post, Classical Column, Horse Head Top, Cast Iron, White Paint, 19th Century . 275.00
Hitching Post, Horse Head Top, Ring Through Nose, Cast Iron, 13 In. 66.00
Hitching Post, Horse Head, Cast Iron, Blue Green Worn Paint, 70 1/4 In. 1100.00
Hitching Post, Jockey, Lawn, Cast Iron, Polychrome, 36 In. . . . . .165.00 to 330.00
Hitching Post, Man Holding Ring, Plinth, Cast Iron, 37 1/2 In. 175.00
Hitching Post, Sambo, Cast Iron, R. Wood & Co., Philadelphia, 48 In. . . . . *Illus* 2860.00
Hitching Post, Stable Boy, Jockey Clothes, Cast Iron, J.W. Fiske, 46 In. 7475.00

Garden, Hitching Post,
Sambo, Cast Iron,
R. Wood & Co.,
Philadelphia, 48 In.

Garden, Planter, Cast
Iron, Acanthus Leaves,
Cherubs' Heads,
Pedestal, Victorian, 48 In.

Hitching Post, Tree Stump Form, Cast Iron, Black Paint, 19th Century 110.00
Lamp, 4-Light, Over 4-Light Center Lantern, Fluted Standard, 118 In. 375.00
Ornament, Cherubs, Holding Cornucopia, Cast Iron, Pair 1540.00
Ornament, Sphinx, Egyptian Revival, Cast Stone, Continental, 21 1/2 In., Pair 1320.00
Ornament, Stag, Cement, Brown Paint, Green Marble Eyes, Pfaltzgraff 385.00
Ornament, Stag, Cement, Brown Paint, Red Marble Eye, Pfaltzgraff 220.00
Planter, Cast Iron, Acanthus Leaves, Cherubs' Heads, Pedestal, Victorian, 48 In. .... *Illus* 1570.00
Planter, Iron, Galvanized, Oak Leaf Running Pattern, 19th Century, 38 x 52 In., Pair 1680.00
Planter, Lily Pad Design, Cast Iron, Wreath Scroll Handles, Oval, 29 In. 374.00
Planter, Urn Shape, Cement, White Paint, Weathered, Pair 175.00
Plaque, Lion Face, Cast Iron, 1850, 14 In. Diam., Pair 1895.00
Porch Set, Metal, Swing Couch, Glass Top Coffee & Nesting Tables, Cushions, 6 Piece .. 110.00
Porch Set, Rattan, Upholstered Cushions, Sofa, 2 Chairs, 2 Tables, 5 Piece 275.00
Pump, Animal Head Spout Reservoir, Bouquet Of Flowers At Top, 1840s, 40 In. 1540.00
Sculpture, Celestial, Iron, Pedestal, 4-Footed, 1930s, 41 In. 3600.00
Sculpture, Putti, Concrete, Weathered, 25 In. 245.00
Seat, Barrel Form, Alternating Court Scenes, Floral, Rose Medallion, 18 In. 1725.00
Seat, Barrel Form, Floral & Geometric Border, Chinese Export, 19th Century, 19 In., Pair 3220.00
Seat, Majolica Style, Relief Exotic Birds, Pedestals, Vines, Continental, 20 3/4 In. 4025.00
Seat, Majolica, Molded Birds, Cattails, Dragonflies, Water Lilies, George Jones, 18 In. 9630.00
Seat, Pewter & Brass, Bird & Peony Design, Pierced Lattice Sides, 1860, 18 In. 165.00
Seat, St. Louis, Prunus & Stylized Chrysanthemums, Wedgwood, Signed, 17 5/8 In. 920.00
Seat, Vintage, Scroll Pierced Seat, Vine Shaped Legs, 28 x 38 In. 302.00
Settee, Floral Design, Open Latticework Back, Scrolled Legs, Iron, 44 1/2 In. 86.00
Settee & Chair Set, Fern Design, Cast Iron, White Paint, 55 x 33-In. Settee, 3 Piece 1430.00
Settee Set, Cast Iron, Vintage Pattern, 2 Chairs, Table, 4 Piece 385.00
Settee Set, Patio, Iron, Brass, White Paint, Weathered, Table, 2 Armchairs, 4 Piece 2640.00
Sprinkler, Little Girl With Umbrella & Flowers, 2 Sides, Tin & Metal, 51 In. 575.00
Stand, Fern, Wirework, 3 Baskets, Everted Rims, Scroll Feet, 19th Century, 57 In. 430.00
Sundial, Blue Numerals & Compass, Bronze Shade Caster, Stoneware, 5 5/8 In. 5500.00
Sundial, Boy With Golf Driver, 9 1/2 In. 165.00
Sundial, Bronze, Engraved, Roman Numerals, 19th Century, 9 In. 385.00
Sundial, Cast Iron, Griswold 350.00
Sundial, Stand, Terra-Cotta Base Form Of 3 Gargoyles, 34 In. 975.00
Table, Cast Iron, Marble Top, 2 Inset Planter Boxes, Rope Twist Legs, 1880s, 67 x 28 In. . 4800.00
Table, Cast Iron, Round Red & White Marble Top, 3 Cabriole Leg Base, White, 29 In. ... 220.00
Table, Cast Stone, 5 Figures Top, Gentlemen Various Pursuits, 7 x 23 1/2 In. 630.00
Table, Nesting, Lily Pad Form, Scrolling Base, 22 x 14 1/2 In., Pair 165.00
Urn, 4 Grotesque Faces On Bowl, Iron, J.W. Fiske, Patd. June 1, 1875, 17 x 16 In. 465.00
Urn, Angels, Garland, Neoclassical Style, Cast Iron, Waisted Stem, 39 In., Pair ...660.00 to 770.00
Urn, Campana Form, Marble, 18 In., Pair 1552.00
Urn, Campana Form, Pedestal, Louis XVI Style, Cast Iron, 42 3/4 In., Pair 1035.00
Urn, Cast Iron, Applied Frieze With Putti, 39 In., Pair 770.00
Urn, Cast Iron, Nickel Finish, Green Marble Plinth, 14 In., Pair 220.00
Urn, Cast Iron, Stork & Griffin Handles, Fiske 4070.00
Urn, Classical Figures On Sides, Lion Mask Handles, Winged Putti, 62 1/2 In., Pair 1265.00

Urn, Classical Figures, Pedestal, Leaf Capped Body, Loop Handles, Cast Iron, 37 In., Pair 1150.00
Urn, Cover, Baluster Shape, Angels, Symbolizing Day & Night, Cast Iron, 1880s, 71 In. . . 18315.00
Urn, Cover, Ram's Head Handles, Cast Stone, 36 x 20 In., Pair 1815.00
Urn, Devil Head Profile, Cover, Cast Iron, 31 In., Pair 1150.00
Urn, Gadrooned Body, Campana Form, Late 19th Century, 14 1/2 In., Pair 172.00
Urn, Green Repaint, Handles, Iron, 20 x 31 1/2 In. 355.00
Urn, Leaf Form Scrolled Handles, Cast Iron, 21 x 30 In., Pair 58.00
Urn, Marble, Inverted Bell Form, Everted Rim, Gadrooned Body, 28 1/2 In., Pair 2475.00
Urn, Stone, Carved, Marbled Green, Foo Dog, Ring Handles, Finials, Cover, 9 In., Pair . . 220.00
Wheelbarrow, Wooden, Red Paint, 67 In. 185.00

GARDNER Porcelain Works was founded in Verbiki, outside Moscow,
by the English-born Francis Gardner in 1766. The Gardner family
retained ownership of the factory until 1891 and produced porcelain
tablewares, figurines, and faience.

ГАРДНЕРЪ

Figurine, Cossack, Long Blue Tunic, Magenta Sash, Hat, Square Base, 1810, 8 1/2 In. . . . 2990.00
Figurine, Jewish Man, Long Gray Coat, Leaning On Umbrella, 19th Century, 8 3/4 In. . . . 3450.00
Plate, Star Of Imperial Order St. Vladimir, Late 18th Century, 9 In. 6900.00
Plate, Star, Imperial Order Of St. George, Late 18th Century, 9 3/4 In. 7475.00
Tea Set, Courting Couples, Landscapes, 18-In. Oval Tray, 1890, 15 Piece 2645.00

GAUDY DUTCH pottery was made in England for America from about
1810 to 1820. It is a white earthenware with Imari-style decorations of
red, blue, green, yellow, and black. Only sixteen patterns of Gaudy
Dutch were made: Butterfly, Carnation, Dahlia, Double Rose, Dove,
Grape, Leaf, Oyster, Primrose, Single Rose, Strawflower, Sunflower,
Urn, War Bonnet, Zinnia, and No Name. Other similar wares are called
Gaudy Ironstone and *Gaudy Welsh.*

Bowl, Double Rose, Bird Head Handles, 6 3/4 In. 4840.00
Creamer, Carnation, Handle, Signed, John Schuman, 3 3/4 x 5 1/2 x 2 3/4 In. 170.00
Cup & Saucer, Carnation, Handleless, 2 1/2 x 3 3/4 In. 392.00
Cup & Saucer, Carnation, Handleless, Signed, John Schuman, 2 1/2 x 3 3/4 In. . . .170.00 to 390.00
Cup & Saucer, Leaf, Handleless 3520.00
Cup & Saucer, Single Rose, Handleless . . . . .330.00 to 357.00
Plate, Butterfly, 8 3/8 In. 2310.00
Plate, Double Rose, 7 3/4 In. 550.00
Plate, Oyster, 8 In. 90.00
Plate, Primrose, 8 1/4 In. 1760.00
Plate, Single Rose, 7 1/2 In. 410.00
Plate, Strawberry, 12 Sides, 9 7/8 In., 4 Piece 1200.00
Plate, Strawflower, 10 In. 3410.00
Plate, War Bonnet, 8 In. 660.00
Plate, War Bonnet, Early 19th Century, 7 1/4 In. 605.00
Plate, Zinnia, 10 In. 2860.00
Plate, Zinnia, Riley, 10 In. 2200.00
Sugar, Carnation, Cover, 5 1/4 In. 728.00
Sugar, Carnation, Cover, Signed, John Schuman, 5 1/4 In. 730.00
Sugar, Cover, War Bonnet, 5 In. 440.00
Sugar, Single Rose 355.00
Teapot, Carnation, John Schuman, 6 In. 1680.00
Waste Bowl, Carnation, Signed, John Schuman, 2 3/4 x 5 3/4 In. 250.00
Waste Bowl, Single Rose, 6 1/4 In. 1650.00

GAUDY IRONSTONE is the collector's name for the ironstone wares
with the bright patterns similar to Gaudy Dutch. It was made in England for the American market. There may be other examples found in
the listing for Ironstone or under the name of the ceramic factory.

Cup, Handless 40.00
Cup Plate, Blue Floral Transfer, Spatter Border, Staffordshire, 4 Piece 330.00
Plate, Floral, Red & Green Enameling & Luster, 9 3/4 In. 440.00
Platter, Grape & Leaf, Blue Border, Blue Grape Bunch, Leaf In Center, 17 In. 250.00
Platter, Strawberry, Blue Vines, Green Leaves, Fruits, 15 1/2 x 12 In. 560.00
Platter, Underglaze, Blue & Polychrome Floral, 22 1/2 In. 495.00

Tureen, Oriental Design, Mulberry Transfer, Hicks & Meigh, 11 In. 770.00
Vase, Floral Design, Bulbous, Flared Opening, 10 In., Pair 1045.00

GAUDY WELSH is an Imari-decorated earthenware with red, blue, green, and gold decorations. Most Gaudy Welsh was made in England for the American market. It was made after 1820.

Biscuit Tray, Tulip, Gold, Handles, Signed, John Schuman 90.00
Bowl, Floral Design, Blue Underglaze, Red, Green Enamel Luster, Footed, 5 In. 165.00
Coffeepot, Branch Handles, Copper Pink Luster Trim, 5 1/4 x 4 In., 3 Piece 115.00
Cup & Saucer 40.00
Sugar, Cover, Pinwheel Pattern, 6 1/2 x 7 In. 425.00
Tea Set, 12 Handleless Cups, 11 Saucers, Porcelain 575.00
Tea Set, Child's, Oyster Teapot, Pink Luster Glaze, 5 1/4-In. Teapot, 22 Piece 450.00
Tea Set, Feather, Teapot, Sugar, Creamer, Cup & Saucer 795.00
Tea Set, Oyster, Pink Luster Trim, Child's, 22 Piece 448.00
Tea Set, Sudlow-Burslem, 4 Piece 100.00
Tea Set, Tulip, Teapot, 8 In., 29 Piece 390.00

GEISHA GIRL porcelain was made for export in the late nineteenth century in Japan. It was an inexpensive porcelain often sold in dime stores or used as free premiums. Pieces are sometimes marked with the name of a store. Japanese ladies in kimonos are pictured on the dishes. There are over 125 recorded patterns. Borders of red, blue, green, gold, brown, or several of these colors were used. Modern reproductions are being made.

Cup & Saucer, Demitasse, Brown Dragon, Girl Lithophane, Marked 40.00
Teapot, Sugar & Creamer, Covers, Footed 125.00
Vase, Moriage, Marked, 2 3/4 In. 5.00

GENE AUTRY was born in 1907. He began his career as the *Singing Cowboy* in 1928. His first movie appearance was in 1934, his last in 1958. His likeness and that of the Wonder Horse, Champion, were used on toys, books, lunch boxes, and advertisements.

Banner, Felt, Champ, Back In The Saddle 55.00
Bike, Monark, Rodeo Brown, 29 x 58 In. 2420.00
Book, Gene Autry & The Bad Men Of Broken Bow .... .25.00 to 45.00
Book, Hard Cover, Dust Jacket, Whitman 27.00
Boots, Brown Leather, Black Clasp Buckles, Child's 275.00
Boots, Little Gents, 3 Buckles, Box, 1950 .... 600.00
Cap Gun, Cast Iron, Design, 6 1/2 In. 375.00
Cap Gun, Cast Iron, Kenton, 1939, 8 3/8 In. 400.00
Coaster, Gene Autry Hotel, Palm Springs, Cal., Leather, 1980s, 3 1/4 In. 8.00
Guitar, Emenee, Tan Plastic, Cameo Cowboy Designs, Papers, Box 220.00
Luggage Tag, Gene Autry Hotel, Palm Springs, Cal., White Plastic, 4 1/2 x 2 1/2 In. 7.00
Poster, Man From Music Mountain, Republic, 1938, One Sheet 805.00
Poster, Movie, Sunset In Wyoming, Maris Wrixon, Smiley Burnette, 41 x 27 In. 370.00
Record, Album, Western Classics, 1947, 78 RPM 71.00
Record, Rudolph The Red Nose Reindeer, 45 RPM 15.00
Sheet Music, Red River Valley 11.00

GIBSON GIRL black-and-blue decorated plates were made in the early 1900s. Twenty-four different 10 1/2-inch plates were made by the Royal Doulton pottery at Lambeth, England. These pictured scenes from the book *A Widow and Her Friends* by Charles Dana Gibson. Another set of twelve 9-inch plates featuring pictures of the heads of Gibson Girls had all-blue decoration. Many other items also pictured the famous Gibson Girl.

Plate, Miss Babbles Brings A Copy Of Morning Paper, 10 1/2 In. 128.00
Plate, She Becomes A Trained Nurse, 10 1/2 In. .... .202.00 to 250.00
Plate, She Looks For Relief, 10 1/2 In. 133.00
Plate, They All Go Skating, 1901, 10 1/2 In. 80.00
Plate, They Go Fishing, 1908, 10 1/2 In. 127.00
Postcard, Why Do They Call Me A Gibson Girl, Postmark, 1923 .... 12.00

GIRL SCOUT collectors search for anything pertaining to the Girl Scouts, including uniforms, publications, and old cookie boxes. The Girl Scout movement started in 1912, two years after the Boy Scouts. It began under Juliette Gordon Low of Savannah, Georgia. The first Girl Scout cookies were sold in 1928.

Bookends, Trefoil Shape	250.00
Knife, Leather Grip, Brown Leather Sheath, Marbles, 7 1/2 In.	200.00
Knife, Pocket, Green Plastic Grips, Gilt Emblem, Kutmaster, 1940s-1950s	28.00
Lunch Box, Vinyl, Metal Thermos, 1960	225.00
Photograph, La Habra, Ca.'s, Corn Festival, Float, 1950s, 8 x 10 In.	15.00

GLASS-ART. Art glass means any of the many forms of glassware made during the late nineteenth or early twentieth century. These wares were expensive and production was limited. Art glass is not the typical commercial glass that was made in large quantities, and most of the art glass was produced by hand methods. Later twentieth-century glass is listed under Glass-Contemporary, Glass-Midcentury, or Glass-Venetian. Even more art glass may be found in categories such as Burmese, Cameo Glass, Tiffany, Venini, and other factory names.

Basket, Pink Over White, Silver Mica Flecks, Clear Rim, Handle, 7 x 8 1/2 In.	55.00
Basket, Yellow, Spiral Twist Form, 3 Lobed Feet, Handle, 8 1/2 In.	112.00
Biscuit Jar, Enameled Poppies, Satin, 8 In.	150.00
Bottle, Cranberry, Ribbed, Embossed, Pewter Stopper, 9 1/4 In.	175.00
Bowl, Amethyst, Wide Base, 11 1/4 x 5 1/2 In.	115.00
Bowl, Blue Iridescent, Green & Amber Design, Loetz Type, 7 3/4 In.	140.00
Bowl, Pink Opalescent, Squared Rim, Monot Stumpf, Pantin, 3 1/8 x 4 In.	110.00
Creamer, Reddish Brown, Marbleized, Gold Trim, White Opalescent Interior, 3 In.	135.00
Cruet, Blue, Enameled Flowers, Amber, Stopper, 9 1/2 In.	495.00
Decanter, Stretched Grape & Vine, Band Of Ribbing At Bottom, 11 In.	365.00
Epergne, Blue Overlay, 4 Trumpets, Serpent Design, 1890s, 11 x 21 In.	1200.00
Epergne, Cranberry To Clear, Funnel Shape Center, Ruffled Edges, 22 x 11 1/4 In.	590.00
Epergne, Light Blue Cased With White, 5 Trumpets, Ruffled Edges, 1880s, 21 In.	1200.00
Epergne, Lime Green To Clear, Lily Vase Center, Ruffled Edges, 17 x 10 In.	325.00
Ewer, Pink & White, Amber Thorn Handle, Applied Leaves, Hobbs Style, 10 In.	44.00
Figurine, Madonna, Satin, France, 9 1/2 In.	196.00
Jug, Claret, Green, Art Nouveau, Embossed Pewter Lid & Mount, 12 In.	225.00
Loving Cup, Engraved Floral, Handles, 7 3/8 In. ....*Illus*	66.00
Panel, Birds, Fish, Insects & Flowers, 36 x 48 In.	1550.00
Pitcher, Blue Enameled Flowers, Scrolling Vine Design, Rose Ground, 8 In.	92.00
Pitcher, Orchid, Yellow Mother-Of-Pearl, Gold Trim, Gourd Shape, Victorian, 7 In.	30.00
Rose Bowl, Green, Gold Trim, Ribbed, Crimped Edge, 2 In.	85.00
Salt, Blue, Embossed, Double Silver Plated Holder, 6 1/4 In.	115.00
Salt, Pink Opalescent, Gold Luster, Monot Stumpf, Pantin, Squared Top, 1 1/2 x 2 In.	70.00
Shade, Yellow Ground, Pulled Green & Yellow Trailings, Bell Shape, 6 In.	140.00
Teapot, Cover, Murrines, Royal Blue, Yellow, White Base, Handle, R. Marquis, 8 In.	9200.00
Vase, Aqua, Embossed Classical Scenes, G. De Feare, 5 1/2 In.	200.00
Vase, Ball, Clear Rigaree, Enameled Flowers & Butterflies, Footed, 4 3/4 x 3 3/4 In.	225.00
Vase, Beige Striated Glass, Blue, Gray, Mauve, Ocher, 5 In.	400.00
Vase, Birds On A Thistle, Deep Red, White Interior, Gilt, 10 1/4 In.	259.00
Vase, Blue Iridescent, Blue & Opaque Pulled Design, 11 1/2 In.	125.00
Vase, Blue Pulled Loop Design, White, Orange, Gold Interior Neck, 1925, 7 In.	230.00
Vase, Bud, Black, Flying Geese, Metal Base, 6 In.	110.00
Vase, Cobalt Blue, Branches, Leaves, White & Pink Flowers, Resilvered Base, 9 1/2 In.	395.00
Vase, Crocus Shape, White, Blue, Pink, Green Petals, Textured, 1900, 15 In.	1955.00
Vase, Gold Enameled Floral, Foliate & Beast Design, Blue Ground, Central Band, 8 In.	145.00
Vase, Green & Purple, Enameled Flame, Brouwer, 8 1/2 x 5 1/4 In.	1760.00
Vase, Internally Decorated Design, Etched, Maurice Marinot, 1925, 6 3/4 In.	4600.00
Vase, Large Iris Blossom, Leaves, Silver Rim, France, 9 3/4 In.	490.00
Vase, Mottled Blue & Orange, Bulbous, Small Mouth, France, c.1900, 7 x 12 In.	385.00
Vase, Olive Green, Iridescent Panels, Threaded Line Grid, 8 Ribs, Ruffled Edge, 4 In.	200.00
Vase, Pale Blue, White Edge, Handles, Footed, 10 In.	290.00
Vase, Pastoral Scene, Rectangular, Le Gras, 8 In.	495.00

Tired of scrubbing and scrubbing
glass to remove marks from
masking tape and labels? Get
commercial hand cleaner, pat
some on the stain, and let it stay
for 30 minutes. Then rub it off
with a cloth and wash the glass.

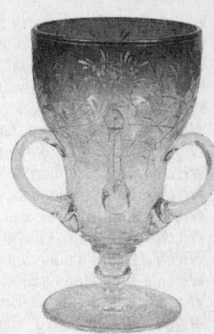

Glass-Art, Loving
Cup, Engraved
Floral, Handles,
7 3/8 In.

Vase, Pink, Blue, Creamy Yellow Over White, Ribbed, 13 In.	245.00
Vase, Pink, Frosted Swirl, Enameled Flowers, Butterfly, Ruffled Edge, 10 3/8 x 3 1/2 In.	195.00
Vase, Pulled Heart & Vine Design, Green, Gold Exterior Rising To Deep Blue, 9 In.	520.00
Vase, Sapphire Blue, White Enameled Lace Overall, Ormolu Stand, 5 5/8 In.	115.00
Vase, Shaded Pink Over White, Ruffled Edge, Handles, 6 7/8 In.	125.00
Vase, Smoke, Enameled Design, Pinched, 7 1/2 In.	50.00
Vase, Stylized Flowers, Leaves, Gold & Cobalt Blue Enameled, 8 5/8 In.	175.00
Vase, Trumpet, Cranberry Flashed, Ruffled Edge, Iron Stand, Victorian, 15 In.	230.00
Vase, Urn Shape, Amethyst, Rose Garlands, Etched, 10 x 8 1/4 In., Pair	475.00
Vase, Yellow & Orange, Bronze Ivy Holder & Base, France, 14 In.	350.00

GLASS-BLOWN was formed by forcing air through a rod into molten
glass. Early glass and some forms of art glass were hand blown. Other
types of glass were molded or pressed.

Beaker, 100th Anniversary 116th Infantry, 1913, 1/4 Liter	68.00
Bottle, Rolled Rim, Amber, 4 1/4 x 8 1/2 In.	522.00
Bottle, Toilet Water, Lavender Blue, Tam-O-Shanter Stopper, 1830s, 6 3/8 In.	242.00
Bowl, Enameled, Crimped, 19th Century, 10 In.	660.00
Celery Vase, Baluster, Footed, Flint, c.1840, 8 1/2 In.	210.00
Chalice, Masonic Symbols, George III, 1816 Sixpence In Hallow Stem, 9 In.	575.00
Compote, Cover, American, Mid 19th Century, 10 In.	165.00
Compote, Paneled, Coned Cover, Finial, Flint, 9 1/4 In.	10.00
Creamer, Sapphire Blue, Squat, Solid Handle, 3 1/8 In.	302.00
Decanter, 3-Piece Mold, Applied Rings, White, Blue Enamel, 9 1/2 In.	415.00
Decanter, 3-Piece Mold, Fluted Band, Pale Bluish Green, Club, Kent, 1840, 7 1/4 In.	1430.00
Decanter, 3-Piece Mold, Starburst Band, Stopper, Bulbous, 1840	210.00
Decanter, 3-Piece Mold, Starburst, Lip, Yellow Olive, Bulbous, Keene, 1820-1840	880.00
Decanter, Conical, Enameled, Silver, Mounted, Nephrite Stones, Russia, 12 In.	1150.00
Decanter, Sulfide Cherub Cameo, Octagonal Stopper, England, 10 1/2 In.	275.00
Decanter, Vertical Rib Design, Horizontal Ribs, Ribbed Stopper, 11 1/2 In.	85.00
Fly Trap, Etched Sprays Of Bamboo, Glass Bubble Stopper, 14 In.	2055.00
Hat, Aquamarine, Rolled Rim, Applied Treading, 3 x 9 In.	330.00
Hurricane Shade, Classical Border, Cylindrical, Rolled Bottom Rim, 21 In.	1092.00
Ice Pail, Geometric, Panels, Scalloped Handles, 19th Century, 5 1/2 x 8 In.	715.00
Inkwell, 3-Piece Mold, Diamond Band, Golden Amber, Olive Tone, Keene, 2 In.	135.00
Inkwell, 3-Piece Mold, Yellow Olive, Diamond Band, Coventry Glass Works	120.00
Jar, Apothecary, Lion & Unicorn, Reverse Gold, Victorian, 30 x 12 In.	1380.00
Jar, Tobacco, Tin Cover, Amber, Square, William S. Kimball & Co., Rochester, N.Y.	110.00
Jug, Rum, Arched Diamond Point	90.00
Lamp, Lace Maker's, Drip Pan, Spherical Font, Tin Drop Burner, Clear, 8 In.	522.00
Lamp, Spherical Font, Pewter Collar, Clear, 11 1/8 In.	385.00
Milk Pan, Aqua, Folded Top Rim, Pontil Scar, Early 19th Century, 6 1/4 In.	805.00
Pitcher, 4 Horizontal Ribs, 9 In.	165.00
Saltcellar, 12 Ribs Swirled To Right, Double Bowl, Flat Foot, Sapphire Blue, 3 x 2 In.	1430.00
Sugar, Cover, Bulbous Form, Galleried Rim, Chain Design, 1820s, 6 In.	1450.00
Tankard, Amethyst, Clear Handle, 13 1/2 In.	60.00
Tumbler, Flip, Molded, Engraved, Early 19th Century, 4 1/2 In.	99.00

Whimsy, Bell, Cranberry Swirl Pattern, Sheared Rim, 1840-1870, 12 In. 120.00
Whimsy, Bellows, Ice Blue, Rigaree, 1870, 10 In. 185.00
Whimsy, Egg, Milk Glass, Blue Spatter, 1870, 2 5/8 In. 175.00
Whimsy, Pipe, Ruby To Cranberry Shading, 1870, 16 1/2 In. 85.00
Whimsy, Pipe, Yellow Amber, Rigaree, 1870, 15 1/2 In. 120.00
Whimsy, Powder Horn, Golden Amber, Tooled Mouth, 1870, 13 In. 440.00
Wig Stand, Ribbed & Twisted Design, 7 1/2 In. 230.00
Witch's Ball, Cranberry, Amethyst Tint, Chain, 3 5/8 In. 120.00
Witch's Ball, Milk Glass, Brown, Blue, Teal Spatter, 1840-1870, 4 In. 330.00
Witch's Ball, Milk Glass, Red, Blue, Green Flecks, 1830-1870, 3 In. 85.00
Witch's Ball, Milk Glass, Red, Green, Pigeon Blood Spatter, 1870, 4 3/4 In. 66.00
Witch's Ball, Opaque Variegated Pink Rose, 1840-1860, 6 In. 200.00
Witch's Ball, Red & Blue Spatter, Internal Plaster Of Paris Coating, 4 In. 85.00
Witch's Ball, White & Blue Splatter, 1870, 4 In. 135.00
Witch's Ball, White & Clear Swirls, 5 In. 100.00
Witch's Ball, White Geometric Loopings, 1870, 4 1/2 In. 305.00
Witch's Ball, White Loopings, Opalescent, 1860, 4 1/2 In. Diam. 230.00

GLASS-BOHEMIAN Bohemian glass is an ornate overlay or flashed glass made during the Victorian era. It has been reproduced in Bohemia, which is now a part of the Czech Republic. Glass made from 1875 to 1900 is preferred by collectors.

Beaker, Medallions, Ruby Cut To Clear, Pedestal, Gold Trim, 6 In., Set Of 6 .... 60.00
Beaker, Ruby Cut To Clear, Building, Chiesa Della B.V. Della Salute, 5 In. 115.00
Bell, Christmas 1973, Enameled, 5 1/2 In. 11.00
Bowl, Centerpiece, Cut Female Portrait Medallion, Diamond Panels, 14 1/8 In. 745.00
Bowl, Ruby Cut To Clear, Allover Foliate, Geometric, Bird Design, 9 In. 69.00
Box, Cover, City View, Ruby Flashed, Etched, 4 1/2 x 3 1/2 In. 2070.00
Box, Ruby & White Cut To Clear, Gold Floral Scroll, Jeweled, 7 In. 750.00
Box, White Overlay, Flowers, Gold Trim, Enameled 44.00
Chalice, Engraved Stag & Deer In Woods, Silver Plate Lid, 9 3/4 In. 747.00
Compote, Cover, Rolled Rim, Circle Design, 12 In., Pair 440.00
Decanter, Dark Cranberry, Gold Design, Hexagonal, Stopper, 10 In. 175.00
Decanter, Elongated, Rudy Flashed, Etched Flowers, Oval Cuts, 16 1/2 In. 52.00
Decanter, Ruby Cut To Clear, Allover Vintage Design, Stopper, 14 In. 69.00
Epergne, Panels Of Colored Foliage, Cranberry & White, c.1900, 18 1/2 In. 1725.00
Ewer, Hinged Cover, Faceted, Ruby, Late 19th Century, 11 1/4 x 10 In. 2585.00
Eyewash Cup, Gilt, Figural Design 220.00
Goblet, Cobalt Blue, Iridescent Oil Spots, Czechoslovakia, 6 1/2 In. 375.00
Goblet, Engraved Floral Design, Ribbon Garland, Amethyst Rim, 6 3/4 In. 150.00
Goblet, Etched Snake Coiled Around Body, Amber, 5 3/4 In. 345.00
Jar, Cover, Clear Panels, Opaque Ground, Hand Painted Floral, 9 1/2 In. 125.00
Lustre, Cranberry, Bobeche, Beads, Gold Medallions, Round Foot, 12 In., Pair 316.00
Tazza, Gold Design, Ruby, Late 19th Century, 10 1/4 x 11 In., 3 Piece 8625.00
Vase, Alternating Reserves Of Raised Leaves, Emerald Green, 16 In., Pair 7475.00
Vase, Amber, Blue & Gold Leaves, 2 Handles, Bulbous, F. Heckert, 9 1/2 In. 115.00
Vase, Berries On Hawthorn Branches, Orange, Maroon Ground, 12 In. 345.00
Vase, Castle & Bird, Engraved, Ruby Stained, c.1890, 6 1/2 In., Pair 125.00
Vase, Enameled, Rustic Village, Sailing Ship, Castle, Baluster, 11 In. 385.00
Vase, Fish Design, Enameled, Bulbous, Flared Rim, Elephant Handles, 5 In. 345.00
Vase, Floral Scrolls, Bulbous, Long Slender Neck, Floral Scrolls, 13 In. 405.00
Vase, Geometric Design, White, Blue, Gilt, 16 1/2 In. 1150.00
Vase, Geometric Design, White, Blue, Gilt, Flared Neck, 16 In., Pair 2070.00
Vase, Gold Design, Ruby, Baluster, 1850, 11 In., Pair 5460.00
Vase, Green, Enameled Portrait Of Woman, Gold, Foliate Design, 15 1/2 In. 230.00
Vase, Green, Mauve & Yellow Iris, Etched, Gold, Tapered Oval, 8 3/4 In. 520.00
Vase, Medallions, Mother & Child, White Overlay, Ruby Flashed, 12 In., Pair 5465.00
Vase, Opaque White Cut To Cobalt Blue, Panels, Stylized Flowers, Gold, 5 In. 115.00
Vase, Overall Loosely Draped Purple Windings, Gourd Shape, c.1900, 5 1/4 In. 172.00
Vase, Pinched, Vine-Like Ribs, Ruffled Rim, Light Blue Luster, 6 3/4 In. 172.00
Vase, Scroll & Flower Decoration, Enameled, Ground Pontil, 22 1/2 In. 280.00
Vase, Shaded Pink, Flowers, Gold Leaves, Propeller Mark, Harrach, 8 1/4 In. 450.00
Vase, Stylized Flowers, Pale Amber, Dark Metal Mount, 9 3/4 In. 172.00

Vase, White Cut To Cranberry, Gilt, 13 In. 55.00
Vase, White Cut To Green, Flowers, Gothic Cut Rim, Chalice Shape, 14 In. 1130.00
Vase, White, Heavy Gold Overlay, Applied Floral & Jewels, 14 In. 90.00
Vase, Zigzag Textures, White Streaks, 20th Century, 9 1/2 In. 172.00
Wedding Beaker, Portrait Of Woman, Brass Center, Floral, Fritz Heckert, 7 In. 1155.00

GLASS-CONTEMPORARY includes pieces by glass artists working after
1975. Many of these pieces are free-form, one-of-a-kind sculptures.
Paperweights by contemporary artists are listed in the Paperweight
category. Earlier studio glass may be found listed under Glass-
Midcentury or Glass-Venetian.

Bottle, Moon, Oval, Small Mouth, Blue, Mauve, John Lewis, 1976, 4 1/2 In. 230.00
Bowl, Berry, Vine Overlay, Blue Satin, Geometric Cameo, John Byron, 10 In. 588.00
Bowl, Centerpiece, Yellow, Cobalt Foot, 6 3/4 In. 144.00
Bowl, Navaho Blanket, Bright Orange, Signed, Dale Chihuly, 5 In. 6900.00
Figurine, Cat, Satin, Sitting On Clear Crystal Rock, Hoya, 6 In. 145.00
Figurine, Penguin, 3 Sides, Cobalt Blue, Wooden Base, 17 In. 175.00
Figurine, Vase, Flared, Hoya, 11 In. 105.00
Sculpture, Loop, Dark Blue, Crystal Lines, Curved, H. Littleton, 15 In. 9200.00
Sculpture, Ruby Gem Mesa, Jose Chardiet, 1989, 21 In. 10925.00
Vase, Amethyst, Glass Fiber, Tapered Cylinder, Motzfeldt, c.1975, 6 In. 290.00
Vase, Cased Opal, Aqua, Blue Leaf, Vine, Iridized Silver, Lotton, 1991, 7 In. 336.00
Vase, Geometric Bird, Sand-Blasted, Teal, Signed, Dan Dailey, 11 In. 5175.00
Vase, Geometric, Sand-Blasted, Pale Yellow, Signed, Dan Dailey, 12 In. 6615.00
Vase, Hunting Scene, Dark Green, Cranberry, Blue, William Morris, 19 In. 13225.00
Vase, Jack In The Pulpit, Pulled Feathers, Iridescent, Lotton, 1988, 9 In. 252.00
Vase, Leaf & Vine, Silvered, Iridescent Blue, David Lotton, 1990, 7 In. 448.00
Vase, Oil Spots, Cobalt Blue, Iridescent, Brent Cox, 1989, 7 In. 112.00
Vase, Oil Spots, Iridescent, Brent Cox, 1991, 7 1/2 In. 224.00
Vase, Pink Clematis, Blue Vines, Paperweight Finish, Lotton, 10 1/2 In. 504.00
Vase, Pulled Drape, Iridescent, Blue, Gold, Purple, Lotton, 1975, 6 1/4 In. 252.00
Vase, Pulled Green Leaf, Blue Vine, Apricot, Paperweight, Lotton, 1990, 6 In. 937.00
Vase, Pulled Green Leaf, Blue Vine, Yellow Opal, Lotton, 1993, 8 1/2 In. 280.00
Vase, Pulled Zipper, Red, Purple, Green, Iridescent, Lotton, 1989, 6 1/4 In. 336.00
Vase, Red Floral, Green, Blue, Smoked Ground, Lotton, 1996, 8 In. 448.00
Vase, Reptilian Green, Red, Amber, Midnight Blue, Lotton, 1989, 7 In. 84.00
Vase, Space, Spiral, Suspended Sphere, Weighted Base, Berger, 1978, 20 In. 476.00
Vase, Star Wiggle, Fossil Series, Brent Kee Young, 1979, 8 1/4 In. 600.00
Vase, Swirl, Blue, Yellow, Bulbous, Slender Tapered Neck, 14 In. 72.00
Vase, Venetian, Red, Signed, Dale Chihuly, 17 1/2 In. 7475.00
Vase, White Flowers, Green Ground, Rolled Rim, Mark Peiser, 1971, 4 In. 375.00

GLASS-CUT, see Cut Glass category.

GLASS-DEPRESSION, see Depression Glass category.

GLASS-MIDCENTURY refers to art glass made from the 1950s to the
1980s. Some glass factories, such as Baccarat or Orrefors, are listed
under their own categories. Earlier glass may be listed in the Glass-Art
and Glass-Contemporary categories. Italian glass may be found under
Venini and Glass-Venetian.

Bookends, Rearing Horse, Red, L.E. Smith, 1950s 75.00
Bottle, Scent, Green, White Filigrana Wrapped Canes, Stopper, 1950, 9 In. 297.00
Bowl, Bubble Design, Clear, Opaque White, Flared Rim, Boda, 1963, 7 In. 290.00
Bowl, Magenta, Coquille Casing, Flygsfors, Paul Kedley, 1957, 4 1/4 x 9 1/2 In. 88.00
Bowl, Pale Blue, Flared, Triangular, Holmegaard, Per Lutken, 1960, 5 x 16 In. 77.00
Candy Dish, Bird, Cover, Medium Green, 12 In. 85.00
Champagne, Golf Ball, Ruby, Morgantown 15.00
Cordial, Golf Ball, Ruby, Morgantown 35.00
Dish, Pale Blue, Free Form, Holmegaard, Per Lutken, 1953, 2 x 6 In. 33.00
Figurine, Bird, Orange, Viking, 10 In. 45.00
Figurine, Bird, Teal, J-Form Body, A. Pianon, Vistosi, 1962, 11 3/4 In. 1725.00
Figurine, Robin On Stump, Haley Glass 25.00
Figurine, Thrush, Frosted, Haley Glass 30.00

Soap Dish, Swan, Missing Beads, Ice Beads, L.E. Smith, 8 1/2 In. 50.00
Tumbler, Whiskey, Big Shot, Morgantown, Green, 5 1/2 In. 25.00
Tumbler, Whiskey, Half Shot, Morgantown, Red, 3 1/2 In. 45.00
Tumbler, Whiskey, Little Shot, Morgantown, Green, 3 In. 35.00
Tumbler, Whiskey, Sure Shot, Morgantown, Green, 5 In. 30.00
Vase, Amethyst, Controlled Bubbles, Gunnel Nyman, c.1953, 5 1/4 In. 160.00
Vase, Black Internal Layer, Orange, Red, White Murrines, Toshi Iwata, 10 In. 22.00
Vase, Ebony, 2 Dancing Ladies, L.E. Smith, Pair 40.00
Vase, On Black Base, Signed, John Lewis, 1942, 21 In. 4025.00
Vase, Teal, Embossed Soldier, Square, Flared Rim, Blenko, 18 x 8 1/2 In. 121.00

GLASS-VENETIAN. Venetian glass has been made near Venice, Italy,
since the thirteenth century. Thin, colored glass with applied decoration is favored, although many other types have been made. Collectors
have recently become interested in the Art Deco and 1950s designs.
Glass was made on the Venetian island of Murano from 1291. The out-
put dwindled in the late seventeenth century but began to flourish
again in the 1850s. Some of the old techniques of glassmaking were
revived, and firms today make traditional designs and original modern
glass. Since 1981, the name *Murano* may only be used on glass made
on Murano Island. Other pieces of Italian glass may be found in the
Glass-Contemporary, Glass-Midcentury, and Venini categories of this
book.

Ashtray, Hot Pink Raspberry, Bubbles, Murano 28.00
Bottle, Light Green, Red, Green Circular Murrines, Cenedese, 1960, 5 In. 200.00
Bottle, Scent, Marbled, Silhouettes, Adventurine, Murano, c.1850, 2 1/2 In. 1265.00
Bottle, Scent, Swirled Red Canes, Gold Leaf, Archimede Seguso, 1950, 10 In. 286.00
Bottle, Triangular Body & Stopper, Incised Surface Lines, Venini, 1950s, 14 In. 1430.00
Bowl, Caramel Tiles, Black Outlines, Barovier E. Toso, 14 In. 1265.00
Bowl, Gray, White, Purple Bull's-Eye Murrines, Barovier & Toso, 1960 .... 3300.00
Bowl, Green & White Ribbons, 5 1/2 x 12 In. 185.00
Bowl, Internal Green Fenicio Veins, Tyra Lundgren, Venini, 1930s, 8 In. 715.00
Bowl, Millefiori, Red, Ivory, Gray, Green, Yellow, 3 In. 170.00
Bowl, Overall Confetti Design, Murrhina, Latticinio Canes, Martens, 7 x 2 In. 88.00
Bowl, Pink, Gold Swirled Ribbon, Round, 8 In. 104.00
Bowl, Purple, Pulled Canes, Gold Foil, 4 Raised Sides, Murano, 3 x 6 1/2 In. 55.00
Bowl, Swirling Confetti, Murrines & Latticinio Canes, Dino Martens, 7 x 2 In. 231.00
Bowl, White, Stone Finish, Cased Clear To Amethyst Inside, Murano, 7 1/4 In. 260.00
Candelabrum, 6-Light, Clear & Opaque, S-Shaped Arms, Electrified, 26 In. 460.00
Chandelier, 6 Curved Arms, Pearl, Pink Shades, Italy, 1960, 18 In. 747.00
Chandelier, 32 Branching Floral & Leaf Arms, White, Yellow, Italy, 29 In. 862.00
Chandelier, Amber & Pink Opalescent, Baluster Shaft, Flower Heads, 1950, 33 In. 1850.00
Clock, Blue, Green Inclusions, Signed, Venini, 1950s, 6 x 6 1/4 In. 402.00
Compote, Floral Design Stems, 6 x 6 In., Pair 385.00
Decanter, Pink Latticinio Stripes, Ball Stopper, Murano, 18 1/2 In. 172.00
Figurine, Bird On Perch, Turned Head, Amber, Murano, 7 1/8 In., Pair 115.00
Figurine, Clown, Holding Guitar, Murano, 12 In. 250.00
Figurine, Dove, Amber, Wings, Feathers, Tyra Lundgren, Venini, 1930s, 12 In. 467.00
Figurine, Fish, Red, Yellow, White, Murano, 13 x 10 In. 115.00
Figurine, Pelican, Turquoise, Silver Flecks, Murano 60.00
Figurine, Pheasant, Blue, Burgundy, Pedestal, Gold Leaf, Murano, 12 In., Pair 224.00
Figurine, Pheasant, Orange Cased In Clear, Gold Flecks, Murano, 15 1/2 In., Pair 200.00
Figurine, Seagull, Purple, Outstretched Wings, Gold, Murano, 10 In. 200.00
Figurine, Whale, Humpback, Aquamarine, Etched, Cenedese, Murano, 15 In. 575.00
Holder, Calling Card, Swan, Amber, Gold Flecks, Glass Eyes, 6 In., Pair 35.00
Humidor, Cover, Ruby Cut, Gilt Design, 10 Sides, 4 x 4 In. 137.00
Jar, Orange Cased In Clear, Gold Flecks, Regulated Air Inclusions, Murano, 9 In. 86.00
Lamp, Aquarium, 2 Orange Fish, Footed, Murano, Mid 20th Century, 13 In. 2070.00
Perfume Falcon, Pear Form, Twist-Turned Body, Green, Gold Flecks, 5 5/8 In. 121.00
Pitcher, Bulbous, Clear, Swirls, Blue Prunt & Rim, Domed Foot, 11 In. 200.00
Plate, Dessert, Opalescent, Gilt, Enameled, Late 18th Century, 7 In., 12 Piece 275.00
Salviati, Figurine, Gull, Amber, 4 1/2 x 14 In., Pair 33.00

Sconce, 2-Light, Mirrored Back, Floral & Foliate, 25 In., Pair 690.00
Sculpture, Emergence, Clear, Dichroic Pink & Orange, Labino, 1972, 7 In. 4890.00
Tray, Pale Blue, Red Fused Square Canes, Lino Tagliapietra, 1988, 16 x 12 In. 632.00
Urn, Cobalt Blue & Clear, Gilt Flecks, 2 Handles, Murano, 9 1/4 In., Pair 175.00
Vase, A Canne, Clear, Fused Multicolored Stripes, Conical, Venini, 1954, 9 In. 2875.00
Vase, Amber Internal Layer, Amethyst Spiral, Vetri D'Arte, 1960, 13 In. 495.00
Vase, Aventurine, Gilded Overlay Leaves & Vine, 5 1/2 In. 66.00
Vase, Black Glass, White Marble, Oval, Labino, Signed, 1967, 6 In. 385.00
Vase, Blue Swirls Cased To Ruby, Oval, Rolled Rim, 2 Handles, Labino, 6 3/4 In. 405.00
Vase, Bubbled, Randomly Placed Squares, Dino Martens, c.1953, 11 1/4 In. 1725.00
Vase, Clear, Blue Face, Maroon Bands, Aldo Bon, Ear Handles, Murano, 12 3/4 In. 1150.00
Vase, Cobalt Blue, White Enameled Palace, Flower Buds, Footed, Handles, 7 1/2 In. 145.00
Vase, Corroso & Battuto, Gray, Acid Stamp, 5 1/4 In. 770.00
Vase, Dark Cobalt Interior, Egg Shape, Timo Sarpaneva, 1987, 9 In. 805.00
Vase, Fasce Verticale, Fused Vertical Stripes, Cylindrical, Venini, 1952, 9 In. 7475.00
Vase, Filigrana, White & Clear, Flared, Paolo Venini, 10 x 6 In. 88.00
Vase, Flat Circular Body, Pale Pink Glass, Ruffled, Murano, 8 In. 121.00
Vase, Green, Amber Horizontal Patches, Aventurine Striations, 1950, 9 In. 4950.00
Vase, Handkerchief, Light Blue, Transparent Blue, Gold, Murano, 4 3/4 In. 230.00
Vase, Handkerchief, White Glass Exterior, Beige Interior, 12 1/2 In. 2875.00
Vase, Light Green, Ribbed Ball Stem, Vittorio Zecchin, 1920, 13 In. 1760.00
Vase, Opaque Red Wide Canes, Bright Blue Body, Bianconi, 1950, 11 In. 4125.00
Vase, Pale Blue Narrow Neck, 2 Cobalt Handles, Fratelli Toso, 11 In. 575.00
Vase, Red, Applied Clear Swan Handles, Round Foot, Square, 5 In. 100.00
Vase, Red, Green Vertical Canes, Fulvio Bianconi, 1950, 12 In. 5500.00
Vase, Soffiati, Light Blue Pillow, Ribbed Ball Stem, V. Zecchin, 1920, 10 In. 770.00
Vase, Soffiati, Light Green, Vertical Ribs, Handles, 1920, 5 1/2 In. 55.00
Vase, Sommerso, Green, Amber Internal Layers, Vetri D'Arte, 1950, 14 In. 440.00
Vase, Sommerso, Rose & Black Interior, Inlaid Foil, 10 1/2 x 6 1/2 In. 275.00
Vase, Transparent Vertical Stripes, Gray Band, Seguso, 1975, 13 In. 747.00
Vase, White Filigrana Canes, Amethyst Murrines, Barovier & Toso, 1951, 8 In. 7700.00

GLASSES for the eyes, or spectacles, were mentioned in a manuscript in
1289 and have been used ever since. The first eyeglasses with rigid
side pieces were made in London in 1727. Bifocals were invented by
Benjamin Franklin in 1785. Lorgnettes were popular in late Victorian
times. Opera glasses are listed in their own category.

Batwing, White & Silver Plastic, France, 1950s 450.00
Lorgnette, Black Onyx, Marcasite, France 895.00
Lorgnette, Faux Tortoiseshell, Pierced Handle, Swiveling Eye Piece, 8 In. 88.00
Lorgnette, Sterling Silver 75.00
Lorgnette, Tortoiseshell, Folding, Lever Opens Spectacle, 3 1/2 In. Closed 172.00
Pince-Nez, 2 Lenses, Leather Pocket Case 45.00
Spectacles, Amber Tint, Pinpoint Style Center Rings, Gold Tone Nose Bridge, 4 In. 25.00
Spectacles, Blue Tinted Lenses, Adjustable Metal Frames, Early 19th Century 46.00
Spectacles, Brass & Iron, Sliding Lid Case, Revolutionary War 295.00
Spectacles, Brass Frames, Telescoping Ear Pieces, 4 1/4 In. 20.00
Spectacles, Eye, Round Lenses, 12K Gold Filled Frames, Blue Fitted Snap Case, 1940 ... 26.00
Spectacles, Pince Nez, Sunglasses, Yellow Glass Lenses, 4 In. 20.00
Spectacles, Ring End, Tin Case, c.1725, 6 3/8 x 1 In. 210.00
Spectacles, Silver Tone, Yellow Tint, Metal Frames, 5 In. 20.00
Spectacles, Smokey Glass Lenses, Wire Frame, 4 1/2 In. 20.00
Spectacles, Steel, Brass Case, Engraved, Victorian 35.00
Spectacles, Woman's, Pince Nez, Silver Tone, Aluminum Case, 4 1/4 In. 30.00
Spectacles, Woman's, Sunglasses, Green Glass Lenses, Nose Clip, 4 In. 20.00
Wire Frame, Brass, Oval Lenses, Leatherette Case 25.00

GOEBEL is the mark used by W. Goebel Porzellanfabrik of Oeslau,
Germany, now Rodental, Germany. Many types of figurines and dishes
have been made. The firm is still working. The pieces marked *Goebel
Hummel* are listed under Hummel in this book.

Ashtray, Friar Tuck 50.00

Ashtray, Thumper, Disneyana, Full Bee	275.00
Bank, Child Depositing Coin, 5 1/4 In.	110.00
Candlestick, No. 314, Soldier, Crown Mark, Pair	105.00
Cookie Jar, Friar Tuck, 1957	800.00
Creamer, Cardinal, 3 In.	195.00
Decanter, Liquor, Young Man, Bois	250.00
Figurine, Camera Shy, No. 70, Marked Goebel, Germany	160.00
Figurine, Dog, Labrador Retriever, Yellow Brown	55.00
Figurine, Dog, Old English Sheep Dog, Marked Goebel, Germany	75.00
Figurine, Duck, Glass, 1978, 4 1/2 In.	20.00
Figurine, Our Lady Of Fatima	675.00
Group, 3 Dancers, Art Deco, 1930	7340.00
Pitcher, Friar Tuck, 6 1/2 In.	300.00
Pitcher, Harlequin, Black Collar, Stylized Bee	65.00
Salt & Pepper, Bear & Beehive, Full Bee	25.00
Salt & Pepper, Duck & Drake, Stylized Bee	25.00
Salt & Pepper, Dutch Boy & Breton Girl, Crown Mark	65.00
Salt & Pepper, Flower The Skunk, Foil Label, Full Bee	250.00
Salt & Pepper, Monks, Small	20.00
Sugar & Creamer, Underplate, Friar Tuck, 3 Piece	40.00
Tray, No. 28A, Golfer, Crown & Full Bee	50.00

GOLDSCHEIDER has made porcelains in three places. The family left Vienna in 1938 and started factories in England and in Trenton, New Jersey. The New Jersey factory started in 1940 as Goldscheider-U.S.A. In 1941 it became Goldscheider-Everlast Corporation. From 1947 to 1953 it was Goldcrest Ceramics Corporation. In 1950 the Vienna plant was returned to Mr. Goldscheider, and the company continues in business. The Trenton, New Jersey, business, now called *Goldscheider of Vienna*, imports all of the pieces.

Bust, Bali Head, 12 In.	115.00
Bust, Gloria, J. Riza, 9 1/2 In.	86.00
Bust, Madonna	135.00
Bust, Woman, Bonnet Over Shoulder, 6 1/2 In.	50.00
Bust, Woman, Holding Fan	50.00
Clock, Figural, The Creation, Earthenware, Glass Cabochon, Electrified, 37 In.	4310.00
Figurine, Girl With Wolfhound, Pink Dress, 16 x 12 In.	85.00
Figurine, Putto, Standing, Arms Filled With Painted Flowers, 1920s, 14 In.	1165.00
Figurine, White Christmas, Musical	135.00
Lamp, Maiden Reaching Up To Apple Tree, 38 x 16 In.	1380.00
Plaque, Double Headed Eagle, Man Sowing Seeds, Plow Horse, 17 x 9 In.	230.00
Plaque, Young Girl With Peacock Standing Under Apple Tree, 29 x 20 In.	1380.00

GOLF, see Sports category.

GONDER Ceramic Arts, Inc., was opened by Lawton Gonder in 1941 in Zanesville, Ohio. Gonder made high-grade pottery decorated with flambe, drip, gold crackle, and Chinese crackle glazes. The factory closed in 1957. From 1946 to 1954, Gonder also operated the Elgee Pottery, which made ceramic lamp bases.

Figurine, Coolie, Kneeling, Marbleized Yellow, 5 1/2 In.	25.00
Flower Holder, Swan, Golden Crackle	25.00
Head Vase, Doe, Turquoise, 9 3/4 In.	55.00
Vase, Pink Interior, Marbleized Green & Black Outside, 2 Handles, 9 In.	35.00

GOOFUS GLASS was made from about 1900 to 1920 by many American factories. It was originally painted gold, red, green, bronze, pink, purple, or other bright colors. Many pieces are found today with flaking paint, and this lowers the value.

Bowl, Strawberries, Gold, Red, Scalloped, 10 1/2 In.	50.00
Plate, Blue Bird, Red Strawberry, 12 In.	195.00
Plate, Grapes	15.00
Vase, Cabbage Roses, Repainted, 8 1/2 In.	20.00

GOUDA, Holland, has been a pottery center since the seventeenth century. Two firms, the Zenith pottery, established in the eighteenth century, and the Zuid-Hollandsche pottery made the brightly colored wares marked *Gouda* from 1880 to about 1940. Many pieces featured Art Nouveau or Art Deco designs.

Candlestick, Collier, Tapered, Loop Handle, Leaves, Scrolls, Zuid, c.1921, 8 3/4 In.	115.00
Candlestick, Massa, Tapered, Loop Handle, Panel Bands, Peacock Feathers, Zuid, 10 In.	110.00
Candlestick, Twisted, Ink Mark, 7 3/4 In., Pair	220.00
Clock, Stylized Iris, Leaves, Dark Blue, Green, Mauve, Rust, Yellow, Gilt Metal, 9 In.	805.00
Decanter, Tray, Madeleine, Flower & Leaf Design, Zuid, Estie & Co., c.1929, 10 3/4 In.	175.00
Ginger Jar, High Gloss, 5 In.	250.00
Lamp Base, Floral & Leaf Body, Linear & Dot Bands, 2-Socket, c.1937, 13 1/4 In.	545.00
Pitcher, Floral Painting, Petaled Flowers, Cascading Vine, 7 x 7 1/4 In.	250.00
Pitcher, Stylized Flowers, Yellow, Green, Purple, Ivory Ground, 5 1/2 In.	250.00
Vase, Abstract Design, Baluster Shape, Ivora, 1920s, 17 5/8 In.	400.00
Vase, Banded Design, Landscape Scene, Dutch Woman & Child, Pale Pink, 9 In.	195.00
Vase, Bottle Shape, Cows In Pastoral Scene, Ink Mark, 10 In.	415.00
Vase, Bottle Shape, Stylized Tulips, Yellow, Green, Purple, Cobalt Blue Ground, 7 In.	300.00
Vase, Bottle, Lavender, Pink & Brown Blossoms, Zuid, 1920s, 13 In.	430.00
Vase, Crocus Pattern, 8 In.	145.00
Vase, Flared, Polychrome Flowers, Green Interior, Ink Mark, 8 In.	140.00
Vase, Floral On Yellow Ground, 4 Strap Handles, Early 20th Century, 7 1/2 In.	265.00
Vase, Hand Painted Florals, Stylized Tulips, Raven Black High Glaze, Signed, 12 1/2 In.	880.00
Vase, Lobai, 2 Loop Handles, Scrollwork Band, Oval, Zuid, c.1924, 6 3/4 In.	160.00
Vase, Roma, Oval, Slender Neck, Floral Band, Scroll Borders, Zuid, c.1924, 8 1/2 In.	145.00
Vase, Swirl Of Green & Cream On Blue Ground, Drilled, Signed, c.1920, 11 1/2 In.	230.00
Vase, Westland, 4 Loop Handles, Leaves, Blue, Orange, Green, Cream, Zuid, 7 1/2 In.	230.00
Vase, Yellow Sunflowers, Green Leaves, Ivory Ground, Ink Mark, 12 In.	525.00

GRANITEWARE is an enameled tinware that has been used in the kitchen from the late nineteenth century to the present. Earlier graniteware was green or turquoise blue, with white spatters. The later ware was gray with white spatters. Reproductions are being made in all colors.

Ashtray, Red, Green & White Swirl, End-Of-Day, 4 3/4 In.	125.00
Baking Pan, Cobalt & White Swirl, Genuine Delft, Simmons Hardware, 8 x 10 In.	800.00
Basin, Baby's, Brown & White Swirl, 24 In.	325.00
Basin, Blue & White Speckle, 11 In.	40.00
Basin, Blue & White Swirl, 21 1/2 In.	110.00
Bedpan, Blue & White Swirl, Egg Shape, 17 In.	120.00
Bedpan-Urinal, Blue & White Mottled, Paddle Shape, 16 In.	75.00
Berry Bucket, Blue & White Swirl, Granite Cover, 4 1/2 In.	295.00
Biscuit Cutter, Blue & White Swirl, 2 1/4 In.	1950.00
Boiler, Coffee, Tin Cover, Mottled, Wooden Bail, 6 Qt.	75.00
Bowl, Blue & White, Lion Scene, Red Trim, Japy Email Anzin, 12 1/2 In.	75.00
Bucket, Blue & White Spatter, Wire Bail, Wood Handle, 10 Qt.	125.00
Bucket, Blue & White Swirl, Wood & Bail Handle, 12 Qt.	275.00
Bucket, Cover, Brick Red & Gray Mottled, Wire Handle, 1 Qt.	10.00
Bucket, Cream & Green Trim, Wood & Bail Handle, Emaillerie Parisienne, 12 Qt.	110.00
Cake Pan, Blue & White Swirl, 8 1/2 In.	20.00
Candleholder, Wee Willie, Green, England	18.00
Candlestick, Blue & White Mottled Swirl, 4 3/4 In.	120.00
Candlestick, Blue & White, Scalloped, 6 1/2 In.	35.00
Candlestick, Solid Blue, Scalloped, 6 In.	40.00
Candlestick, Solid Green, 5 In.	35.00
Candlestick, White & Blue Stripes, Star Mark, 5 1/2 In.	20.00
Canister Set, Solid Brick Red, Embossed, Graduated, 6 Piece	235.00
Canister Set, White & Red Veined, Graduated, 6 Piece	295.00
Chamber Pot, Blue & White Swirl, 9 1/2 In.	125.00
Coffee Biggin, Gray & White Spatter, Straight Neck, 10 In., 4 Piece	95.00
Coffee Biggin, Green & White Swirl, Gooseneck, 4 Piece	650.00
Coffee Biggin, Red & White Mottled Swirl, Gooseneck, 11 1/2 In.	395.00
Coffee Boiler, Brown & White Swirl, 11 1/4 In.	365.00

Coffee Carrier, Cover, Green & White Swirl, 9 In. 235.00
Coffeepot, Gray & White Spatter, Gooseneck, 7 In. 40.00
Coffeepot, Hinged Cover, Blue & White Mottled, Short Spout, 10 In. 75.00
Coffeepot, Mottled Dark Gray, El-An-Ge, L & G Mfg. Co., 8 1/2 In. ....155.00 to 175.00
Coffeepot, Orange & White Speckled, Gooseneck, 9 1/2 In. 95.00
Coffeepot, Red & White Spatter, Gooseneck, 8 1/2 In. 160.00
Colander, Brick Red, Gray Interior, Footed, 9 3/4 In. 65.00
Colander, Dark Red, Black & White Mottled, 8 In. 30.00
Colander, Gray, Miniature, 3 7/8 In. 800.00
Colander, Relish Pattern, 10 1/4 In. 75.00
Cream Can, Tin Cover, Blue & White Swirl, 7 1/2 In. 275.00
Cuspidor, Cobalt & White Swirl 300.00
Cuspidor, Hinged Cover, Light Blue, 4 1/4 In. 65.00
Dish, Refrigerator, Cream & Green, Square, 6 1/4 In. 30.00
Double Boiler, Blue & White Swirl, 6 1/2 In. 110.00
Double Boiler, Blue & White Swirl, 8 In. 75.00
Figure, Horse, Standing, White, Porcelain Finish, Brass Base 150.00
Flask, Olive Green, 8 In. 25.00
Foot Warmer, Cobalt Blue & White Swirl, Cast Iron, Godin & Cie, 9 In. 225.00
Funnel, Brick Red & Gray Spatter Interior, 5 3/4 In. 30.00
Funnel, Solid Cobalt Blue, White Interior, 5 In. 15.00
Gas Burner, Gray & White Spatter, Cast Iron, 8 3/4 In. 110.00
Grave Marker, White, Photographic, 7 In. 25.00
Griddle, Bacon, Blue & White Swirl 235.00
Inhalator, Gray & Blue Speckled, Logo Mark 65.00
Invalid Feeder, White & Black, Polar, Bear Logo, 4 In. 80.00
Irrigator, Blue & White Swirl, 10 1/2 In. 195.00
Irrigator, Dark Blue & White Swirl, 10 In. 160.00
Irrigator, Light Blue, Knight, Shield & Crown Mark, 10 1/2 In. 35.00
Irrigator, Pink, With Gold Pinstripes, 10 1/2 In. 40.00
Irrigator, White & Blue Pinstripes, 8 1/2 In. 35.00
Jar, Tin Cover, White, Wire Handle, Strainer Pump, 9 1/4 In. 120.00
Kettle, Chrysolite, Granite Cover, Dark Green & White Mottled, 5 5/8 x 7 5/8 In. 145.00
Kettle, Cover, Blue & White, Wire Bail Handle, 9 x 8 1/4 In. 65.00
Ladle, Brick Red & Gray White Spatter, 15 In. 20.00
Ladle, Straining, Blue & White Mottled, 13 3/4 In. 20.00
Ladle, Straining, Brick Red, Gray & White Spatter Interior, 16 In. 10.00
Ladle, Straining, Red, Light Green & White Spatter Interior, 14 1/2 In. 20.00
Ladle, Yellow & White, 14 In. 10.00
Lavabo Set, Cream & Green Shade, Stenciled Iris, 6 Qt., 2 Piece 100.00
Lavabo Set, Green, Pink & White Swirl, End Of Day, 2 Piece 795.00
Lavabo Set, Pink, Green & White Spatter Swirl, End-Of-Day, 2 Piece 245.00
Lunch Box, Green & White Spatter, Bail Handle, Aluminum Insert, 5 1/2 In. 65.00
Lunch Box, Green & White Speckled, Bail Handle, Aluminum Insert, 4 1/2 In. 30.00
Lunch Box, Light & Dark Green Shaded, Bail Handle, Aluminum Insert, 4 1/2 In. 40.00
Lunch Pail, Lid, Gray, Bail Handle, 7 1/2 In. 38.00
Lunch Pail, Wire Carry Handle, Gray Mottled Surface, 10 In. 50.00
Measure, Gray, 1/4 Quart 165.00
Measure, Gray, One-Gill, 1/8 Quart 500.00
Mixing Bowl, Cobalt Blue, White Vertical Stripe, 9 1/2 In. 80.00
Pail, Water, Chrysolite, Original Paper Label, 8 3/8 In. 600.00
Pan, Baking, Brick Red & Gray, Oval, 13 x 9 1/2 In. 25.00
Pan, Egg, Brick Red, Gray & White Spatter, 2 Handles, 8 3/4 In. 20.00
Pan, Fish, Blue & White Plaid, 17 3/4 In. 65.00
Pan, Milk, Red Swirl, 2 x 8 3/8 In. 700.00
Pan, Pudding, Blue & White Swirl, Deep, 10 1/4 In. 125.00
Pan, Roasting, Emerald Green, Vent Hole, 19 In. 198.00
Pie Plate, Blue & White Swirl, 9 1/2 In. 20.00
Pitcher, Blue & White Shaded Stripe, 15 In. 420.00
Pitcher, Blue & White Speckled, 15 1/2 In. 110.00
Pitcher, Green Shaded Molasses, 4 1/4 In. 60.00
Pitcher, Pink, Green & White Swirl, End-Of-Day, 15 In. 395.00

Plate, Brown Garden Transfer, 11 1/2 In. 60.00
Rack, Towel, Cream, Green Trim, 14 In. 120.00
Rack, Utensil, Blue & White Checked, BB Shield Mark 85.00
Rack, Utensil, Brick Red, Wreath, Shield & Crown Mark 65.00
Rack, Utensil, Red & White Plaid, White Bowl Ladle, Czech Mark, 2 Piece 125.00
Rack, Utensil, Red & White Shaded Stripe, Strainer, Ladle, 3 Piece 195.00
Roaster, Cobalt & White Swirl, 3 Piece, Miniature, 7 1/4 x 3 7/8 In. 1800.00
Roaster, Nesco, Oval, 18 In. 30.00
Salt & Pepper, Blue & White Swirl, 2 1/2 In. 900.00
Salt Box, Blue, Sel, Wall, 10 In. 75.00
Salt Box, Violet Blue & White Spatter, Art Deco Stencil, Sel, Wall, 9 In. 95.00
Saucepan, Cover, Blue & White Checker Swirl, 2 Handles, 1 Qt. 175.00
Saucepan, Cover, Brick Red & Gray Mottled, 2 Handles, 1 Cup 20.00
Saucepan Set, Cobalt Blue & White Plaid, Graduated, 4 Piece 145.00
Skillet, Gray & White, Wood Handle, 11 In. 20.00
Soap Dish, Blue & White Mottled 30.00
Soap Dish, Cobalt Blue & White Shaded, Gold Trim, Ruffled, 4 1/4 In. 60.00
Soap Tray, Green, Ivory Drainer, England 30.00
Strainer, Brick Red & Gray Mottled, 7 1/2 In. 30.00
Strainer, Sink, White, Black Trim, Triangular, 10 1/2 In. 55.00
Table, ABC, Calumet Baking Powder, Child's 215.00
Teakettle, Blue & White Shaded, Gooseneck, Bail Handle, 4 Qt. 95.00
Teakettle, Red & White Mottled, 3 Qt. 95.00
Teapot, Dark Blue, 4 1/2 In. 35.00
Teapot, Gray, Straight Spout, 4 1/4 In. 475.00
Teapot, Green, Pewter Top, Wooden Handle 250.00
Teapot, Turquoise, Red & White Swirl, End-Of-Day, Bulbous, No Cover, 6 1/4 In. 75.00
Tray, Blue & White Swirl, White Interior, Rectangular, 16 1/2 x 13 In. 120.00
Tray, White, Blue Trim, Boy's Portrait In Enamel, Grovic, 1938, 17 x 20 1/2 In. 2500.00
Trivet, Blue, Green Trim, Cast Iron, 7 In. 20.00
Trivet, Gray, Blue & White Speckled Spatter, End-Of-Day, Pierced, 8 1/2 In. 95.00
Trivet, Pink, Ravens In Tree, Art Deco Pierced, Cast Iron, Oval, 9 1/4 In. 95.00
Umbrella Stand, Light Blue, Cast Iron, Fancy Drip Pan, 10 1/2 x 7 1/2 In. 50.00
Umbrella Stand, White & Blue, Stencil, 20 1/2 In. 495.00
Vase, Violet, Gray & Blue, End-Of-Day, Cast Iron, 7 1/2 In. 70.00
Washbowl & Pitcher, Blue & White Swirl, 10 3/8-In. Bowl, 7 1/2-In. Pitcher 850.00

GREENTOWN glass was made by the Indiana Tumbler and Goblet
Company of Greentown, Indiana, from 1894 to 1903. In 1899, the factory became part of National Glass Company. A variety of pressed
glass was made. Additional pieces may be found in other categories,
such as Chocolate Glass, Holly Amber, Milk Glass, and Pressed Glass.

Brazen Shield, Tumbler, Cobalt Blue 60.00
Cat On Hamper, Dish, Cobalt Blue, Tall 420.00
Cord Drapery, Compote, Cobalt Blue, 4 In. 525.00
Cord Drapery, Goblet, Emerald 470.00
Cord Drapery, Mug, Footed, Cobalt Blue 325.00
Cord Drapery, Relish, Amber 160.00
Cord Drapery, Relish, Cobalt Blue 225.00
Dewey, Mug, Nile Green 180.00
Dewey, Pitcher, Emerald 150.00
Dewey, Tumbler, Canary 60.00
Diamond Prisms, Tumbler, Emerald 340.00
Diamond Prisms, Wine 250.00
Herringbone Buttress, Bowl, Amber, 5 3/4 In. 350.00
Herringbone Buttress, Cake Stand, Emerald 475.00
Herringbone Buttress, Cordial, Emerald 400.00
Herringbone Buttress, Punch Cup, Emerald 180.00
Outdoor Drinking Scene, Mug 155.00
Ruffled Eye, Pitcher, Amber 125.00
Shuttle, Cake Stand, 10 In. 150.00
Teardrop & Tassel, Relish, Nile Green 480.00

GRUEBY Faience Company of Boston, Massachusetts, was incorporated in 1897 by William H. Grueby. Garden statuary, art pottery, and architectural tiles were made until 1920. The company developed a matte green glaze that was so popular it was copied by many other factories making a less expensive type of pottery. This eventually led to the financial problems of the pottery.

Bookends, Tile, Landscape, The Pines, Hammered Copper Frames, 6 In.	8800.00
Bowl, Applied Leaves To Side, Matte Green, Light Blue Glaze, 5 In.	4390.00
Bowl, Applied Leaves, Tooled, Matte Green Glaze, Stamped Mark Ms, 1 3/4 x 5 In.	825.00
Bowl, Coupe Shape, Footed, Green Matte Glaze, Glossy Interior, 3 3/4 x 4 3/4 In.	550.00
Bowl, Glossy Dark Green Glaze, Impressed Mark, 6 1/4 In.	165.00
Bowl, Glossy Dark Green Glaze, Impressed Mark, 8 In.	275.00
Bowl, Glossy Light Green Glaze, Impressed Mark, 7 In.	275.00
Bowl, Green Matte Glaze, Bulbous, Wilhemina Post, 6 1/2 In.	2255.00
Bowl, Green Matte Glaze, Glossy Green Interior, Low, 7 In.	715.00
Bowl, Green Matte Glaze, Glossy Green Interior, Low, 8 In.	440.00
Bowl, Raised Leaf Design Sides, Yellow Matte Glaze, Signed, c.1905, 7 In.	4600.00
Candlestick, Tooled Leaves, Leathery Dark Blue Matte Glaze, 8 3/4 x 4 In.	1650.00
Fireplace Surround, 7 Rectangular Tiles, Landscape Frieze, 29 x 45 In.	24750.00
Frieze, Water Lilies, Green Leaves, Dark Green Ground, 3 Tiles, 6 x 18 In.	4675.00
Jardiniere, Curdled Green Matte Glaze, 5 3/4 x 8 3/4 In.	1760.00
Jardiniere, Mottled Green Matte Glaze, 5 x 3 1/2 In.	440.00
Lamp, Cobalt Blue Matte Leathery Glaze, Slag Glass Shade, 11 x 7 3/4 In.	9900.00
Lamp Base, Tooled Stylized Leaves, Cobalt & Charcoal Matte Glaze, Bulbous, 6 In.	660.00
Paperweight, Green Matte Glaze, Circular Grueby Mark On Base, 4 x 2 3/4 In.	517.00
Paperweight, Scarab, Green Matte Glaze, 4 x 2 In.	525.00
Paperweight, Scarab, Green Matte Glaze, Oatmeal Texture, Stamp, 2 1/2 In.	358.00
Tile, 4 Penguins On Iceberg, Brown, Blue, Green, Square, 4 In.	935.00
Tile, Burned Candle, Name, 6 x 4 1/2 In.	4000.00
Tile, Grapevine Cluster & Leaves, Tan Ground, Signed, Early 20th Century, 6 x 6 In.	747.00
Tile, Green & Brown Mottled Glaze, Square, 8 In.	65.00
Tile, Haystack In Landscape, Square, 5 1/2 In., 4 Piece	6600.00 to 7700.00
Tile, Molded Child With Balloons, Square, 6 In.	465.00
Tile, Oriole, White & Blue Floral Ground, Faience, Scalloped, c.1917, 8 1/2 x 13 In.	770.00
Tile, Purple Berries, Green Leaves, Blue Ground, 3 x 6 In., Pair	495.00
Tile, Tall Ship, Green Sea, Blue Sky, Leathery Glaze, Stamped, Square, 8 In.	990.00
Tile, Tulip, Mustard Yellow Blossom, Green Matte Glaze, Footed Copper Frame, 6 In.	1095.00
Tile, Water Lilies, Light Green, Yellow, Dark Green Ground, 6 In.	2420.00
Tile, Waves, Flying Seagulls, Sea Blue Ground, Arts & Crafts Frame, 6 In.	1540.00
Tile, White Horses, Blue Sky, Square, RE In Glaze, 1902, 6 In.	1870.00
Tile, White, Yellow Water Lilies, Green Lily Pads, Blue Ground, Oak Frame, 6 In.	1320.00
Vase, 3-Lobe Opening, Applied Leaves & Buds, Green Matte Glaze, Faience Stamp, 8 In.	1760.00
Vase, Applied & Tooled Leaves, Green Matte Glaze, Marie Seaman, 7 1/2 x 4 1/2 In.	3575.00
Vase, Applied Leaves & Flowers, Yellow Daffodils, Green Matte Glaze, 13 In.	11110.00
Vase, Applied Leaves At Bottom, Sculpted, Green Matte Glaze, 7 In.	2310.00
Vase, Applied Leaves, Curdled Ocher Glaze, Stamped, Ovoid, 10 x 6 In.	3850.00
Vase, Applied Leaves, Green Matte Glaze, 22 1/2 x 8 In.	13200.00
Vase, Applied Vertical Leaves, Green Matte Glaze, 7 1/2 In.	1320.00
Vase, Applied Vertical Leaves, Green Matte Glaze, 9 In.	4125.00
Vase, Applied Yellow Buds, Leaves, Green Matte Glaze, Stovepipe Neck, 23 In.	27500.00
Vase, Blue Matte Glaze, Broad Shoulder, 9 In.	1045.00
Vase, Blue-Green Matte Glaze, Tooled & Applied Leaves, Faience Stamp, 7 1/2 In.	1980.00
Vase, Bottle Shape, Feathery Green Matte Glaze, Stamped, 13 1/4 x 8 In.	4675.00
Vase, Buds & Leaves, Leathery Green Matte, Closed In Rim, Stamped, 11 3/4 In.	7150.00
Vase, Cabinet, Ribbed Base, Leathery Blue Glaze, 4 In.	465.00
Vase, Carved & Applied Leaves, Green Matte Glaze, Bottle Shape, 9 x 5 3/4 In.	1100.00
Vase, Carved & Tapered Leaves & Buds, Green Matte Glaze, Bulbous, Tapered, 6 In.	5500.00
Vase, Carved Leaves & Daffodils, Green Matte Glaze, Oval, Marie Seaman, 11 In.	7150.00
Vase, Curdled Green Matte Glaze, Bulbous, Impressed Mark, Paper Label, 3 x 3 In.	770.00
Vase, Curly Leaves, Tall Buds, Green Matte Glaze, Bottle Shape, 8 x 5 In.	1650.00
Vase, Feathered Spicy Brown Glaze, 6 Panels, Ruth Erickson, 11 1/2 x 5 In.	3575.00
Vase, Full-Length Leaves, Light Green Matte Glaze, Oval, Stamped, 5 1/2 x 4 In.	1540.00
Vase, Green Matte Glaze, Alternating Leaf, Bud Design, 1905, 7 1/2 In.	1955.00

Vase, Green Matte Glaze, Applied Leaves, Scroll Handles, Faience Mark, 11 1/2 In. 7925.00
Vase, Green Matte Glaze, Oval, Collared Rim, Shaved Base, MS, 5 1/2 x 4 In. 715.00
Vase, Leaf Shaped Panels, Green Matte Glaze, Bulbous, 7 1/2 x 4 1/2 In. 3080.00
Vase, Leathery Green Matte Glaze, Bulbous, 7 x 5 In. 1870.00
Vase, Leathery Green Matte Glaze, Squat Base, Cylindrical Neck, 6 1/2 x 4 1/2 In. 990.00
Vase, Mottled Light Blue Matte Glaze, Tapered, 4 In. 470.00
Vase, Organic Dark Blue Glaze, Vertical Ridges, 9 x 4 In. 2310.00
Vase, Ribbed Shoulder, Leathery Green Matte Glaze, Stamped Mark, Squat, 3 1/4 x 5 In. .. 990.00
Vase, Sculpted Leaves At Bottom, Tooled Stems, Buds At Top, Signed, 9 1/2 In. 4675.00
Vase, Stylized Leaves, Green Glaze, Tapered, 1900, 7 In. 1840.00
Vase, Stylized Leaves, Mottled Green Matte Glaze, Stamped, Squat, 7 1/4 x 8 1/4 In. 6050.00
Vase, Tobacco Yellow Matte Glaze, 9 1/2 In. 1540.00
Vase, Tooled & Applied Daffodil Blooms, Buds, Green Matte Glaze, 1904, 13 In. 10350.00
Vase, Tooled & Applied Daffodils, Yellow, Red Center, Green Matte Glaze, 11 In. 11000.00
Vase, Tooled & Applied Leaves, Green Matte Glaze, Scrolled Handles, 11 In. 2420.00
Vase, Tooled & Applied Leaves, Yellow Buds, Pulled Greem Matte Glaze, 11 In. 9350.00
Vase, Yellow Matte Glaze, Carved Vertical Leaves, 7 In. 2860.00

GUNDERSON glass was made at the Gunderson-Pairpoint Glass Works of New Bedford, Massachusetts, from 1952 to 1957. Gunderson Peachblow is especially famous.

Decanter, Peachblow, Pink, White, Rolled Rim, Mid-20th Century, 12 In., Pair 575.00
Pitcher, Peachblow, White Handle, 6 1/2 In. 180.00
Vase, Burmese, Pineapple, 3 1/2 In. ....200.00 to 210.00
Vase, Peachblow, Angular Body, Reeded Handles, Deep Raspberry Rim, 1940, 4 In. 460.00

GUNS that may be classed as toys, such as BB guns, air rifles, and cap guns, are listed in the Toy category.

GUSTAVSBERG ceramics factory was founded in 1827 near Stockholm, Sweden. It is best known to collectors for its twentieth-century art wares, especially a green stoneware with silver inlay called *Argenta*. **Gustafsberg**

Box, Cover, 2 Stylized Birds, Teal Matte Ground, Argenta, Square, 4 In. 195.00
Vase, Dark Green Leaves, Chartreuse Ground, Gourd Shape, 5 1/2 In. 250.00
Vase, Fish & Bubbles, Argenta, Wilhelm Kage, Mark, 5 x 4 1/4 In. 220.00

GUTTA-PERCHA was one of the first plastic materials. It was made from a mixture of resins from Malaysian trees. It was molded and used for daguerreotype cases, toilet articles, and picture frames in the nineteenth century.

Daguerreotype Case, The Country Life, 5 x 6 In. 275.00
Picture Frame, Crenellated Border, Inset Grapevine, Oval, 5 1/2 x 4 1/2 In. 220.00

HAEGER Potteries, Inc., Dundee, Illinois, started making commercial art wares in 1914. Early pieces were marked with the name *Haeger* written over an *H*. About 1938, the mark *Royal Haeger* was used. The firm is still making florist wares and lamp bases.

Ashtray, Gold Tweed, 8 In. 14.00
Bank, Owl 65.00
Dish, Spiral Plum 36.00
Figurine, Blue Dog 45.00
Figurine, Bucking Bronco, Amber, 1940s, 13 In. 165.00
Figurine, Putti Holding Bowl Over Head, 12 In. 14.00
Lamp, Dark Green Hollowed Arches, Floral & Leaves, Sticker, 22 1/2 In. 75.00
Pitcher, Ebony Cascade, Handles, 18 1/2 In. 40.00
Planter, Turtle 45.00
Plate, Leaf, Blue Agate, 16 x 16 In. 25.00
Vase, Gazelle, 14 In. 14.00
Vase, Morning Glory, 16 1/2 In. 45.00
Vase, Pitcher Shape, Brown, 18 In. 50.00
Vase, Purple & Blue Crackled Glaze, Bottle Shape, 10 In. 55.00
Vase, Stork, Baby Line 25.00

HALF-DOLL, see Pincushion Doll category.

HALL CHINA Company started in East Liverpool, Ohio, in 1903. The firm made many types of wares. Collectors search for the Hall teapots made from the 1920s to the 1950s. The dinnerwares of the same period, especially Autumn Leaf pattern, are also popular. The Hall China Company is still working. For more information, see *Kovels' Depression Glass & Dinnerware Price List.* Autumn Leaf pattern dishes are listed in their own category in this book.

HALL'S
SUPERIOR
QUALITY
KITCHENWARE

Blue Blossom, Cookie Jar, Sundial	295.00
Blue Garden, Jug, Batter	150.00
Crocus, Bean Pot, No. 782	225.00
Crocus, Salt & Pepper	95.00
Gold Dot, Bowl Set, Nested, 3 Piece	40.00
Meadow Flower, Casserole, Ivory	50.00
Old Crow, Punch Set, 11 Piece	175.00
Poppies, Bowl, 9 In.	35.00
Red Poppy, Platter, 13 In.	18.00
Red Poppy, Salt & Pepper, Handle	18.00
Red Poppy, Tumbler	20.00
Rose Parade, Jug, 7 1/2 In.	50.00
Saf-Handle, Cookie Jar, Red	325.00
Teapot, Airflow, Orange, 6 Cup	250.00
Teapot, Automobile, Green Luster, 6 Cup	650.00
Teapot, Birdcage, Canary, Yellow	300.00
Teapot, Boston, Maroon, Sugar & Creamer, 3 Piece	80.00
Teapot, Car, Green Glaze, c.1940, 9 1/4 In.	290.00
Teapot, Golden Glo, Sugar & Creamer, 3 Piece	50.00
Teapot, Hollywood, Green Gold Trim, 6 Cup	35.00
Teapot, Los Angeles, Canary Yellow, 6 Cup	75.00
Teapot, McCormick, Yellow, No Infuser	125.00
Teapot, Moderne, Ivory, Gold Trim	30.00
Teapot, New York, Cobalt Blue, Gold Trim, 4 Cup	50.00
Teapot, Newport, Cobalt Blue	40.00
Teapot, Ohio, Maroon	295.00
Teapot, Philadelphia, Yellow, With Sugar & Creamer, 3 Piece	80.00
Teapot, Star, Cobalt, 6 Cup	125.00 to 165.00
Teapot, Streamline, Chinese Red	170.00
Teapot, Surfside, Cadet, 6 Cup	275.00
Teapot, Twin Spout, Cobalt	100.00
Teapot, Twin-Tee, Yellow, Gold Decoration	95.00
Teapot, Windshield, Ivory, Gold Trim, 6 Cup	45.00
Teapot, Windshield, Maroon, Gold Trim, 6 Cup	35.00
Teapot, Windshield, Turquoise, Gold Trim, 6 Cup	65.00

HALLOWEEN is an ancient holiday that has changed in the last 200 years. The jack-o'-lantern, witches on broomsticks, and orange decorations seem to be twentieth-century creations. Collectors started to become serious about collecting Halloween-related items in the late 1970s. The papier-mache decorations, now replaced by plastic, and old costumes are in demand.

Bottle Opener, Black Cat, Playing Guitar, Metal	17.00
Candy Container, Clown, Hobo	385.00
Candy Container, Jack-O'-Lantern, Basket, Pressed Cardboard, 9 In.	385.00
Candy Container, Pumpkin Boy	395.00
Candy Container, Pumpkin, Glass, 1905	250.00
Candy Container, Roly Poly, Witch	475.00
Candy Container, Witch, Germany, 1920s	240.00
Costume, Alien, Box	135.00
Costume, Boss Hogg, Dukes Of Hazzard, Mask, Ben Cooper, 1982, Size 10	36.00
Costume, Fonz, Happy Days, Ben Cooper	50.00
Costume, Laura, Little House On The Prairie, Ben Cooper	30.00
Costume, Mickey Mouse, Walt Disney Productions	48.00
Costume, Spiderman, Mask, Ben Cooper, Box, 1976	45.00
Jack-O'-Lantern, Black, Germany, 1920s	225.00

Jack-O'-Lantern, Cardboard, Wire Handle 125.00
Jack-O'-Lantern, Red & Green, Original Paper, Germany 285.00
Lantern, Cat, Papier-Mache 45.00
Mask, Barnabas, Dark Shadows 60.00
Mask, Bride Of Frankenstein, Large 100.00
Mask, Froggy The Gremlin, 1948, 10 1/4 In. 50.00
Mask, Mummer's Head, Mardi Gras, Oliver Hardy, Papier-Mache, Bowl Cut Hair 895.00
Mask, Mummer's Head, Mardi Gras, Smiling German Man, Plastic, White Hair, 1930 ... 125.00
Mask, Pinocchio, Paper, Gillette Advertising On Back, Box 25.00
Mask, Smokey The Bear, 9 In. 38.00
Noisemaker, Pan Knocker, Tin, Chein, 1910 .... 400.00
Noisemaker, Witch Picture, Tin 20.00
Pen Wiper, Witch, Nut Head, Miss Hickory, c.1890 .... 95.00
Sparkler, Witch, Japan 135.00
Ticket, Spook Show, 1940s 15.00

HAMPSHIRE pottery was made in Keene, New Hampshire, between 1871 and 1923. Hampshire developed a line of colored glazed wares as early as 1883, including a Royal Worcester-type pink, olive green, blue, and mahogany. Pieces are marked with the printed mark or the impressed name *Hampshire Pottery* or *J.S.T. & Co., Keene, N.H.* Many pieces were marked with city names and sold as souvenirs.

Biscuit Jar, Cover, Cream, Painted Violets, Gold Trim, Melon Shape, 6 In. 80.00
Bowl, Flattened Spherical Form, Green Matte Glaze, C. Robertson, 5 1/2 In. 170.00
Bowl, Fruit, Embossed Grape Vine & Leaves, Cream, Gold Trim, 9 1/2 In. 165.00
Bowl, Green Matte Glaze, Impressed Mark, 2 1/2 In. 165.00
Bowl, On Stand, Embossed Leaf & Branch, Brown, Yellow, Green, Majolica, 10 In. 1320.00
Butter, Tan Glaze, Gold Flecks, Gold Twig Handle, Purple Mark, 8 1/2 In. 50.00
Candleholder, Green Matte Glaze, Handle, Hooded, Impressed Mark, 7 1/4 In. ...140.00 to 150.00
Candleholder, Green Matte Glaze, Handle, Impressed Mark, 5 3/4 In. ....165.00 to 205.00
Candleholder, Leaves, Olive Green Glaze, Handle, 2 1/2 In. 50.00
Candlestick, Green Matte Glaze, Aladdin Lamp Shape, 3 3/4 x 6 1/2 In. 245.00
Candy Dish, Old House Tavern, Sudbury, Mass., Cream, Gold Trim, 5 3/4 x 4 3/4 In. 45.00
Chocolate Pot, Floral Bands, Cream Glaze, Gold Trim, 7 In. 110.00
Chocolate Set, Cream Glaze, Brown, Lime Green, Gold & Black Trim, 11 Piece 275.00
Creamer, Leaves, High Green Glaze, Handle, Impressed Mark, 3 1/2 In. 28.00
Cuspidor, Light Blue To Cream Glaze, Gold Flecks & Trim, Ruffled, 7 1/4 In. 50.00
Ewer, Green Matte Glaze At Bottom, 9 x 9 1/2 In. 550.00
Hair Receiver, High Burnt Orange Glaze, Hand Painted Ferns, 1 1/2 In. 55.00
Inkwell, 3 Openings At Perimeter, Green Matte Glaze, Hollow Form, 3 x 4 In. 220.00
Inkwell, Cover, Beige Matte Glaze, Impressed Mark, 4 In. 220.00
Inkwell, Green Matte Glaze, Incised Mark, 2 3/4 In. 230.00
Jardiniere, Green Matte Glaze, Bulbous, 3-Footed, Unmarked, 6 1/2 In. 605.00
Lamp, Gourd Shape, Silk Lined Wicker Shade, Impressed Mark, 6 1/2 x 11 In. 1320.00
Lamp, Green Matte Glaze, Impressed Mark, 5 1/2 x 10 1/4 In. 175.00
Lamp, Tapered Standard, Molded Tendrils, Green Matte Glaze, c.1900, 24 In. 1495.00
Lamp, Water Lilies Design, Green Matte Glaze, Ceramic Base, 10 In. 3300.00
Lamp Base, Alternating Bud On Stem, Lotus Leaves, Cadmon Robertson, 19 In. 575.00
Lamp Base, Oil, Green Matte Glaze, 2 Ring Handles, Squat, Bulbous, 4 1/2 In. 935.00
Lamp Base, Short Neck, Cerulean Blue Matte Glaze, Signed, 18 1/2 In. 770.00
Pitcher, Berries On Branch Transfer, Yellow & Green Bands, Marked, 7 3/4 In. 120.00
Pitcher, Cream, Blue & Pink Flowers, Gold Trim, Ewer Shape, 6 In. 80.00
Pitcher, Cream, Pilgrims Landing, Transfer, Holly, Brown Bands, Reeded Handle, 7 In. .. 120.00
Pitcher, Dark Green Glaze, J.S.T. & Co., Large Ewer Shape, 10 1/2 In. 165.00
Pitcher, Embossed Leaves, Green Matte Glaze, Vine Handle, Melon Shape, 8 1/2 In. 935.00
Pitcher, Green Matte Glaze, Embossed Leaves, Impressed Mark, 7 1/2 x 4 In. 165.00
Pitcher, Green Matte Glaze, Handle, Pear Shape, Impressed Mark, 4 In. 305.00
Pitcher, Green Matte Glaze, J.S. Taft & Company, Large Ewer Shape, 9 1/4 In. 525.00
Pitcher, Hand Painted Purple Flowers & Green Leaves, Cream, Green Tint, 4 In. 100.00
Pitcher, Jackson House, Cream, Pink Tint, Gold Trim, Bulbous, Footed, 5 In. 110.00
Pitcher, Pedestal, Brown Painted Flowers, High Cocoa Glaze, Pear Shape, 6 3/4 In. 55.00
Pitcher, Watch Hill Life Station Transfer, White, Blue, Tan, Twig Handle, 3 1/2 In. 65.00
Planter, Green Matte Glaze, Handles, Squat, 3 In. 250.00

Stein, Embossed, Green Matte Glaze, Flip Handle, 8 1/2 In. 140.00
Stein, Memorial Park, Malone, NY, Cream, Gold Flecks, Peach Handle, 6 In. 55.00
Sugar, Leaves, High Dark Green Glaze, Unmarked, 2 1/2 In. 28.00
Sugar & Creamer, Embossed Flowers & Birds, Tan & White Glaze, Square, 4 In. 55.00
Sugar & Creamer, Oval Bulbous, Green & Cream, Painted Leaves, 4 In. 110.00
Tea Set, Hand Painted Flowers, Cream To Peach Glaze, Melon Shaped, 3 Piece 165.00
Teapot, Butterfly On Cover, Cream Matte Glaze, Blue Flecks, Squat, Oval, 4 3/4 In. 110.00
Teapot, Green Glaze, Twig Handle, Square Trivet, Raised Mark, 5 In. 55.00
Teapot, Hand Painted Flora, Black Borders, Insert, 4 1/2 x 8 In. 605.00
Toothpick, Embossed Shield, Tan Matte Glaze, Ribbed, Oval, 2 In. 45.00
Toothpick, Green Glaze, Conway, N.H., Oval, 2 In. 28.00
Tray, Dresser, Pink & Green Flowers, Gold Trim, Rectangular, 10 1/2 x 6 In. 65.00
Tumbler, High Green Glaze, Lakewood N.J., Gold Lettering, Impressed Mark, 4 1/2 In. .. 28.00
Umbrella Stand, Green Matte Glaze, Floral Band At Top, Fluted, 20 3/4 In. 155.00
Urn, Green Matte Glaze, Stamped, J.S.T. & Co., 2 Handles, Grecian Shape, 10 1/2 In. 415.00
Vase, Alternating Buds & Leaves, Leathery Blue Green Glaze, Oval, 6 1/2 In. 440.00
Vase, Band Of Swastikas, Embossed, Green Matte Glaze, Squat, 2 1/4 x 5 1/2 In. 200.00
Vase, Beige Glaze, Bulbous, 6 1/4 x 5 3/4 In. 190.00
Vase, Black, Semimatte Glaze, Bulbous, 2 Handles, 2 3/4 In. 90.00
Vase, Blue Matte Glaze, Floral, Bell Shaped Flowers, Bulbous, 5 1/2 In. 520.00
Vase, Blue Matte Glaze, Impressed Mark, Trumpet Neck, Broad Base, 9 1/2 In. 360.00
Vase, Blue Matte Glaze, Tapered, Incised Mark, 6 3/4 x 3 3/4 In. 330.00
Vase, Blue Matte Glaze, White On Shoulder, J.S. Taft & Co., Oval, 4 1/2 In. 660.00
Vase, Blue, Green Matte Glaze, Cabbage Shape, 4 1/4 In. 300.00
Vase, Blue, Green Matte Glaze, Stylized Flowers, 7 In. 770.00
Vase, Blue, Green Matte, Black, White Accents, Cylindrical, 12 In. 660.00
Vase, Bottle Neck, Green Matte Glaze, Red Mark, 6 In. 275.00
Vase, Broad Leaves, Blue Glaze, White Detail, Oval, 7 1/2 In. 550.00
Vase, Broad Leaves, Green & Blue Glaze, Closed-In Rim, Incised, 6 3/4 x 3 3/4 In. 825.00
Vase, Cabbage Leaves, Green & Brown Thick Matte Glaze, 2 3/4 In. 200.00
Vase, Cabbage Shape, Green Matte Glaze, No Mark, 2 1/2 x 4 1/4 In. 145.00
Vase, Debossed Flowers, Green Matte Glaze, Cone Shape, 6 1/2 In. 175.00
Vase, Embossed Cattails, Mustard Matte Glaze, Squat, 4 1/4 x 6 1/4 In. 340.00
Vase, Embossed Leaves & Buds, Green Matte Glaze, Bulbous, 2 1/4 In. 330.00
Vase, Embossed Leaves, Green, Vine Handle, Pitcher Shape, 8 1/4 In. 880.00
Vase, Embossed Sponge Design, Green Matte Glaze, Impressed Mark, 2 1/2 In. 185.00
Vase, Embossed Water Lily, Green Matte Glaze, Pear Shape, Impressed Mark, 7 In. 880.00
Vase, Floral Design At Top, Green Matte Glaze, 4 1/2 In. 220.00
Vase, Flowers, Buds, Green Matte Glaze, Bulbous, Mark, Label, 5 1/2 In. 340.00
Vase, Flowers, Green Matte Glaze, Squat, Raised Mark, 3 x 5 1/2 In. 300.00
Vase, Geometric Design, Green Matte Glaze, 2 1/2 x 5 1/2 In. 345.00
Vase, Gourd Shape, Lobed, Green Matte Glaze, 5 1/2 In. 770.00
Vase, Greek Key Design, Green Matte Glaze, Signed, 6 In. 286.00
Vase, Green & Brown Matte Glaze, Mottled, Oval Shape, Mark, 6 x 4 In. 330.00
Vase, Green Matte Glaze, 2 Spouts, 6 1/2 In. 175.00
Vase, Green Matte Glaze, 3 Handles, Stamped Mark, 4 3/4 In. 165.00
Vase, Green Matte Glaze, Blue Glaze, Flared Neck, 9 In. 1210.00
Vase, Green Matte Glaze, Bottle Shape, 5 x 3 3/4 In. 275.00
Vase, Green Matte Glaze, Bulbous, Incised Geometric Band, 4 x 4 3/4 In. 420.00
Vase, Green Matte Glaze, Cylindrical Neck, Handles, Squat Base, 4 1/2 In. 330.00
Vase, Green Matte Glaze, Dandelion Leaves, Cylindrical, 6 In. 1100.00
Vase, Green Matte Glaze, Melon Shape, Impressed Mark, 6 1/2 In. 770.00
Vase, Green Matte Glaze, Peacock Feathers, Spherical, 5 1/4 In. 550.00
Vase, Green Matte Glaze, Ribbon, Bag Shape, 11 In. 135.00
Vase, Green Matte Glaze, Spherical, 6 3/4 In. 165.00
Vase, Green Matte Glaze, Squat, Bulbous, Raised Mark, 5 1/2 In. 605.00
Vase, Green Matte Glaze, Tapered Cylindrical Form, C. Robertson, Signed, 7 1/2 In. 400.00
Vase, Incised Panels Rim To Base, Oatmeal To Mustard Yellow Glaze, 7 1/2 In. 715.00
Vase, Lavender Matte Glaze, Closed-In Rim, Cylindrical, 7 3/4 In. 465.00
Vase, Leafy Vines, Fruit, Blue, Green Matte Glaze, Early 20th Century, 4 In. 920.00
Vase, Molded Flowers At Shoulder, Gray Matte Glaze, Marked, 7 1/2 In. 550.00
Vase, Molded Leaf Design, Green Matte Glaze, 2 Open Handles, 8 In. 385.00
Vase, Molded Vertical Leaves Separated By Molded Stems, Buds, Green, 7 In. 715.00

Vase, Mottled Sections, Feathered Glaze, Steel To Navy Matte, Signed, 5 1/4 In. 660.00
Vase, Pink Veined Matte Glaze, 7 In. 88.00
Vase, Salmon Pink Matte Glaze, Mottling Throughout, Signed, 5 In. 440.00
Vase, Squat, Embossed, Swirls, Brown Matte Glaze, Kiln Kiss, 2 1/4 x 5 1/4 In. 253.00
Vase, Squat, Flared Neck, Green Matte Glaze, 4 3/4 In. 250.00
Vase, Taupe Mottled Glaze, Panel Design, Squat, 3 1/2 x 4 1/2 In. 330.00
Vase, Trillium, Taupe Matte Glaze, Bulbous, 7 1/2 x 6 In. 330.00
Vase, Turquoise Blue Matte Glaze, 2 Handles, Bulbous, 5 In. 330.00
Vase, Yellow Matte Glaze, Bulbous, J.C. Taft & Co., 3 1/2 In. 440.00

HANDEL glass was made by Philip Handel working in Meriden, Connecticut, from 1885 and in New York City from 1893 to 1933. The firm made art glass and other types of lamps. Handel shades were made not only of leaded glass in a style reminiscent of Tiffany but also of reverse painted glass. Handel also made vases and other glass objects.

Ashtray, Owl Perched On Branch, Leaves, Cigarette Rests, Circular, 4 3/4 In. 170.00
Chandelier, 6-Light, Mottled Slag Glass, 8-Panel, Brass Strapping, c.1900, 15 x 26 In. . . . 2200.00
Humidor, Green, Red, Cover, Pipe Form 660.00
Lamp, 3 Birds In Flight, Domed Shade, Iridescent Melon Sky, Bronze Base, 18 In. 7700.00
Lamp, 8 Painted Panels, Grape & Leaf Clusters, 4-Paneled Shade To Match, 18 In. 2350.00
Lamp, Aquarium, Underwater Scene, Bronzed Base, Signed Bedigie, 16 In. . . . . *Illus* 82500.00
Lamp, Birds In Flight, Domed, Ribbed, Vertical Lobes, Bronzed Urn Shaped Base, 18 In. . . 9350.00
Lamp, Blue Parrot Amid Branches, Pink Berries, Green, Painted Shade, 13 In. 3450.00
Lamp, Bronze Lily Pad Base, 2 Leaded Green Slag Glass Shades, Marked, 16 x 18 In. . . . 1870.00
Lamp, Bronze Metal Base, Green Etched Glass Shade, Pine Needle, 10 x 14 In. 1540.00
Lamp, Bronze Patina, Adjustable Arched Neck, Green Shade, Pine Needle, 11 In. 545.00
Lamp, Brown Chipped Ice Shade, Bronze Harp Base, 10 x 57 In. 2860.00
Lamp, Caramel, White Slag Glass Shade, Roses & Leaf Design, 18 x 24 In. 4950.00
Lamp, Chipped Ice Shade, Bronzed Metal Base, Signed, 57 In. 410.00
Lamp, Chipped Ice, Bell Flower Design, Painted Shade, Bronze Base, Signed, 24 In. 4675.00
Lamp, Continuous Band Of Trees, Pink Sky, Painted Shade, 24 x 17 1/4 In. 6325.00
Lamp, Daffodil, Painted Shade, Cone Shape, Bronzed Base, 18 In. 14300.00
Lamp, Domed Birch Trees & Woodlands Shade, Bronzed Base, 16 In. 3300.00
Lamp, Domed Rambling Book & Trees, Orange & Yellow Sky, PAL, 16 In. 3025.00
Lamp, Domed Woodland Scene, Artist P., 15 In. 5500.00
Lamp, Egg Shaped Bird In Flight Shade, Chinese Pierced Hardwood Stand, 7 1/2 In. 2585.00
Lamp, Elephantine Island, Domed Shade, Winged Griffin Base, No. 6691, 18 In. 8800.00
Lamp, Etched Medieval Knight On Horse, Handel Square Base 3300.00
Lamp, Evening Desert Scene Shade, Label, Signed, 15 In. 1800.00
Lamp, Floral Border, Painted Shade, Domed, Incised Fretwork Base, 23 x 16 In. 7700.00
Lamp, Floral Border, Yellow Painted Shade, No. 7169, 14 In. 900.00
Lamp, Floral, Green Slag Glass, Shade, 18 In. 3450.00
Lamp, Green Cased Shade, Cone Shape, Brass Base, 57 In. 935.00
Lamp, Green Glass Tile Shade, 5 Petal Flowers, White Border, 1905, 18 In. 2760.00
Lamp, Hanging, Lattice Pattern, Rose Lattice Border, 6 In. 770.00
Lamp, Jungle Bird, Macaws, Painted Metal Base, Japanese Style, Signed, 18 In. 17600.00
Lamp, Landscape, Green, Brown, Blue, Painted Shade, Flared, 1910, 13 In. 4312.00
Lamp, Lapped Petal Design, Amber, Cream Slag Glass, Domed Shade, 26 In. 3335.00
Lamp, Leaded Glass Domed Shade, Roses, Metal Urn Base, 1910, 42 In. 5750.00
Lamp, Leafless Trees, Snow, Yellow Sky, 8 In. 3850.00
Lamp, Leaves & Branches, Painted Shade, Cone Shape, Signed, 18 In. 8800.00
Lamp, Moorish Scene, Chipped Ice, Painted Shade, Bronze Base, Signed, 23 In. 6875.00
Lamp, Mountainous Landscape, Trees, Painted Shade, 13 In. 2300.00
Lamp, Multicolored Floral Design Border, Painted Shade, 23 1/2 In. 3850.00
Lamp, Mushroom Coiled Dragon Shade, Green Ground, Square Base, 12 In. 6050.00
Lamp, Obverse & Reverse Coralene, 8 Sides, Floral Shade, 18 In. 3162.00
Lamp, Orange Flowers, Painted, Chipped Ice Shade, Metal Base, Signed, 24 In. 4400.00
Lamp, Oriental Pheasant Shade, Metal Base, 18 In. . . . . *Illus* 23100.00
Lamp, Painted Yellow Opaline Bamboo Shade, Gilt Copper, Kerosene, 1904, 19 In. 690.00
Lamp, Parrots, Butterfly, Blossoming Peonies, Painted Shade, 18 In. 9900.00
Lamp, Parrots, Peonies, Black Ground, Green Glass Finial, Bronzed Metal Base, 18 In. . . 17600.00
Lamp, Patinated Brass, Flared Shade, Mottled Ivory & Green Panels, 16 3/4 In. 2860.00
Lamp, Peacock Feather Design, Brown, Green, Red, Ivory Slag Glass, 20 x 24 In. 8250.00

| Handel, Lamp, Aquarium, Underwater Scene, Bronzed Base, Signed Bedigie, 16 In. | Handel, Lamp, Oriental Pheasant Shade, Metal Base, 18 In. | Handel, Lamp, Treasure Island, Signed, 18 In. |

Lamp, Peacock Trail, Lavender, Brown Slag Glass Shade, Church & Trees, Bridge, 23 In.   1150.00
Lamp, Polychrome Leaded Slag Glass Shade, Bronze Flower Shape Base, 16 In. 1045.00
Lamp, Raspberry Flowers, Green Foliage Border, Domed Shade, Bronzed Base, 14 In. . . .   2035.00
Lamp, Red Thistles, Green Leaves, Painted Shade, Light Green Interior, 21 1/2 In. 88000.00
Lamp, Rose, Vine & Leaf, Painted Shade, Brass Base, Scalloped Edge, 14 1/2 In. 1610.00
Lamp, Scenic, Wooded Landscape, Tree, Waterfront, Painted Shade, 15 In. 1380.00
Lamp, Student, Bronze, Amber Glass Shade, Pine Needle, Cloth Label, 12 1/4 In. 1500.00
Lamp, Sunset Palm, Filigree Silhouettes, Oasis, Palm Trees, Amber, Red Tones, 16 1/2 In.   4675.00
Lamp, Sunset Palm, Multicolored, Bent Glass Panels, Filigree, 16 1/2 In. 3300.00
Lamp, Temple Of Karnac, Painted Shade, Domed, Amphora Base, 18 In. 10450.00
Lamp, Treasure Island, Signed, 18 In. . . . .*Illus*   9900.00
Lamp, Tropical Overlay, Shade, Curvilinear Slag Border, Bronze Base, 14 1/2 In. 2300.00
Lamp, Tropical Sunset, Painted Shade, Hexagonal, 1916, 14 1/2 In. 2585.00
Lamp, Umbrella Shaped Shade, Green Border, Leaded, Signed, 18 In. 3740.00
Lamp, Venetian Harbor, Simulated Chinese Carved, Hardwood Stand, 7 In. 6325.00
Lamp, Venetian Scene, Painted Shade, Domed, Enameled, 18 In. 11550.00
Lamp, Woodland Scene, Orange Moonlit Sky Shade 6600.00
Lamp, Yellow Tree Scene Shade, Cone Shape, 18 In. 6600.00
Lamp, Yellow Tulips, Green Leaves, Leaded, Metal Base, Unsigned, 22 In. 4400.00
Lantern, Hanging, Black Paint Over Copper, Signed, 32 In. 880.00
Light, Ball, Hanging, Reverse Painted Birds In Flight, Iridescent, 10 In. 4840.00
Shade, Bursting Fireworks, Amber, Etched, Domed, 1910, 14 In. 1035.00
Shade, Hanging, Caramel, White Striated Glass Tiles, Stylized Floral Border, 22 In. 1150.00
Shade, Hanging, Leaded Glass, Pink, Amber Flowers, Green Leafy Vines, 1905, 24 In. . . .   8625.00
Shade, Mosserine, Green, Signed, 10 In. 2100.00
Torchere, Long Stemmed Floral Design, Cylindrical Shade, Artist, 9 In., Pair 440.00
Torchere, Stemmed Yellow Flowers, Blue Ground, Cylindrical Shade, 18 In., Pair 3300.00
Vase, Teroma, Landscape, Lockraw, 4 3/4 In. 220.00
Vase, Teroma, Palm Trees, Frosted Ground, Sand Finished, Ruffled, Floriform, 14 In. 1650.00
Vase, Teroma, Scenic, Obverse Painted Grove Of Trees By A Lake, Green, Brown, 8 In. . .   1150.00
Vase, Teroma, Scenic, Obverse Painted Mountains, Birch Trees By Lake, 1925, 8 In. 920.00

HARDWARE, see Architectural category.

HARKER Pottery Company of East Liverpool, Ohio, was founded by
Benjamin Harker in 1840. The company made many types of pottery
but by the Civil War was making quantities of yellowware from native
clays. They also made Rockingham-type brown-glazed pottery and
whiteware. The plant was moved to Chester, West Virginia, in 1931.
Dinnerwares were made and sold nationally. In 1971 the company was
sold to Jeannette Glass Company and all operations ceased in 1972.
For more information, see *Kovels' Depression Glass & Dinnerware
Price List.*

Cameoware, Rolling Pin, Blue & White, 15 In. 35.00

Chesterton, Creamer 15.00
Chesterton, Cup & Saucer 11.00
Chesterton, Gravy Boat, Underplate 38.00
Chesterton, Plate, 10 1/4 In. 9.00
Chesterton, Plate, 6 1/4 In. 4.00
Chesterton, Plate, Gray, 9 In. 16.00
Cock O'Morn, Bowl, 5 1/2 In. 8.00
Cock O'Morn, Cup & Saucer 10.00
Corinthian, Creamer 16.00
Corinthian, Gravy Boat, Underplate, Teal 30.00
Corinthian, Plate, Tea 6 1/4 In. 5.00
Cottage, Teapot 90.00
Currier & Ives, Cake Server 35.00
Currier & Ives, Plate, 6 1/ 4 In. 9.00
Dane, Plate, Blue, 6 1/2 In. 10.00
Gadroon, Cup & Saucer, Blue 11.00
Ivy, Plate, 6 1/4 In. 6.00
Magnolia, Bowl, 8 In. 20.00

HARLEQUIN dinnerware was produced by the Homer Laughlin Company from 1938 to 1964, and sold without trademark by the F. W. Woolworth Co. It has a concentric ring design like Fiesta, but the rings are separated from the rim by a plain margin. Cup handles are triangular in shape. For more information, see *Kovels' Depression Glass & Dinnerware Price List.*

Chartreuse, Casserole, Cover 240.00
Chartreuse, Cup & Saucer 12.00
Chartreuse, Cup & Saucer, After Dinner 435.00
Chartreuse, Nappy, 9 In. 35.00
Chartreuse, Plate, 7 In. 8.00
Dark Green, Pitcher, Ball 125.00
Gray, Plate, 8 In. 35.00
Green, Ashtray, Basket Weave 50.00
Green, Nut Dish 110.00
Green, Sugar & Creamer 50.00
Maroon, Casserole, Cover 195.00
Maroon, Figurine, Penguin 285.00
Mauve, Cup & Saucer, After Dinner 100.00
Mauve, Eggcup, Double 60.00
Mauve, Figurine, Penguin 285.00
Mauve, Sugar, Cover 25.00
Mauve, Teapot, Cover 95.00
Medium Green, Bowl, 5 1/2 In. 30.00
Medium Green, Creamer 15.00
Medium Green, Plate, 9 In. 12.00
Medium Green, Platter, 11 In. 395.00
Red, Creamer 5.00
Red, Pitcher, Water, Service 135.00
Red, Platter, 10 In. 15.00
Red, Teapot 150.00
Rose, Gravy Boat 25.00
Rose, Marmalade 335.00
Rose, Nut Dish 95.00
Rose, Pitcher, 22 Oz. ....42.00 to 50.00
Rose, Sugar & Creamer 25.00
Rose, Teapot, Cover ....100.00 to 140.00
Rose, Tumbler 85.00
Spruce Green, Figurine, Donkey 325.00
Spruce Green, Sugar & Creamer, After Dinner 195.00
Spruce Green, Teapot, Cover 95.00
Turquoise, Ashtray, Basket Weave 25.00
Turquoise, Eggcup, Double 1.00
Yellow, Ashtray, Basket Weave 30.00

Yellow, Ashtray, Saucer 90.00
Yellow, Marmalade 535.00
Yellow, Sugar & Creamer 15.00
Yellow, Syrup, Drip Cut Top ....275.00 to 575.00

HATPIN collectors search for pins popular from 1860 to 1920. The long pin, often over four inches, was used to hold the hat in place on the hair. The tops of the pins were made of all materials, from solid gold and real gemstones to ceramics and glass. Be careful to buy original hatpins and not recent pieces made by altering old buttons.

Amethyst Faceted Crystal, 9 3/4 In. 45.00
Art Nouveau, Collet Set Amethyst, 14K Gold, Openwork 290.00
Art Nouveau, Enameled Green Dragonfly, 14K Gold, Hedges 1495.00
Art Nouveau, Woman's Face, 14K Gold, Gold Filled Stem 230.00
Balloon Form, Ribbed Plastic, Pearl Trim, 7 1/4 In. 27.00
Bar Wrapped With Gilt Rope, 8 1/2 In. 14.00
Black Faceted Crystal, 7 1/2 In. 7.00
Black Reverse Painted Glass Over Mother-Of-Pearl Top, 9 1/4 In. 165.00
Clear Rhinestone On Top, Held By Opalescent Stones, 6 1/4 In. 38.00
Cupid Heads, 2 Sides, Sterling Silver, 6 5/8 In. 60.00
Cupid Heads, 4 Sides, Sterling Silver, 6 3/4 In. 100.00
Domed Top, Brown Velvet, Held By Framework Of Dozens Of Rhinestones, 8 In. 155.00
Flowers, Blue Enamel, Ball, Gilt, 8 In. 70.00
Gilt, Red Cabochon Stone On Top, 7 In. 38.00
Gilt Initial E Inside 1/2 Circle, 8 In. 7.00
Gilt Open Framework, Bezel-Set Oval Green Stone, 10 In. 105.00
Head, Mercury Glass, Teardrop Shape, 4 In. 60.00
Indian Head, Gilt Framework, 7 1/8 In. 35.00
Maple Leaf, Enameled, Sterling Silver, 9 3/4 In. 18.00
Mosaic Top, Covered With Blue & White Flowers, 7 1/2 In. 198.00
Peacock Eye, Bezel Set, Gilt, 8 In. 175.00
Polished Black Jet, Soldered To Wire Frame, 9 1/8 In. 55.00
Polished Black Riveted Jet, Oval Head, Stones Soldered To Wire Frame, 9 3/4 In. 357.00
Porcelain Floral, 5 Pink Stones On Top, 5 3/4 In. 198.00
Profile, Bakelite, Celluloid, Marbled Butterscotch, Red, Yellow, Switzerland, 2 1/2 In. ... 210.00
Triangular Shape Pink Glass, 7 5/8 In. 38.00
Winged Dragon, Silver, Garnet Eye, White Rhinestone Mouth, 1 3/4 x 11 In. 150.00
Woman, Engraved, Clear Glass, 5 3/4 In. 45.00

HATPIN HOLDERS were needed when hatpins were fashionable from 1860 to 1920. The large, heavy hat required special long-shanked pins to hold it in place. The hatpin holder resembles a large saltshaker, but it often has no opening at the bottom as a shaker does. Hatpin holders were made of all types of ceramics and metal. Look for other pieces under the names of specific manufacturers.

Aqua, Green Trim, Roses & Bird, Banded, Pottery, Unmarked, 5 1/2 x 3 In. 75.00
Cameo On 2 Sides, White, Green & Pink Trim, 6 In. 175.00
Cobalt Blue, White & Floral Bands, Pottery, 5 x 2 1/2 In. 80.00
Gold Textured Overlay, Solid Bottom, Artist Signed, 4 7/8 In. 70.00
Lavender Floral, Flowers, Leaves, Gold Floral Band Bottom, 4 1/4 In. ....90.00 to 150.00
Oval Citrine, Openwork Sterling Silver Mount, Arts & Crafts, Kalo 575.00
Woman On Round Base, Hatpins Around Her 65.00
Woman Playing Harp, Pewter, Silver Plate 55.00

HAVILAND china has been made in Limoges, France, since 1842. The factory was started by the Haviland Brothers of New York City. Pieces are marked *H & Co.*, *Haviland & Co.*, or *Theodore Haviland*. It is possible to match existing sets of dishes through dealers who specialize in Haviland china. Other factories worked in the town of Limoges making a similar chinaware. These porcelains are listed in this book under Limoges.

HAVILAND & CO.

Bone Dish, Pink Tinged Roses, Gilt Rim, 1890-1910, 6 In., 12 Piece 140.00
Bowl, Apple Blossom, 8 In. 38.00

Haviland, Compote, Lobster, Red, Green,
Black, Marked

Haviland, Plaque, Veiled Prophet, St. Louis,
Oct. 2, 1894, 5 3/4 x 4 3/8 In.

Compote, Lobster, Red, Green, Black, Marked .... *Illus*   550.00
Creamer, Apple Blossom 8.00
Creamer, Clinton 25.00
Creamer, Yellow Leaves, Black Flowers, Green & Black Band, Circle, Gold Edge 28.00
Cup, Pink & Yellow Flowers, Gray Green Leaves 16.00
Cup & Saucer, Delaware 35.00
Cup & Saucer, Pale Pink Flowers, Lacy Green Foliage, Gold Trim, Demitasse 30.00
Cup & Saucer, Pink & Gray Roses, Violets, Lacy Foliage, Green & Maroon Border 22.00
Cup & Saucer, Pink Roses, Gray Leaves, Gold Trim 19.00
Dish, Red & Pink Roses, Scalloped Edge, Oval, Buxton, 7 1/4 In. 62.00
Gravy Boat, Apple Blossom 150.00
Gravy Boat, Underplate 65.00
Plaque, Veiled Prophet, St. Louis, Oct. 2, 1894, 5 3/4 x 4 3/8 In. .... *Illus*   230.00
Plate, Apple Blossom, 6 1/4 In. 27.00
Plate, Apple Blossom, 7 In. 30.00
Plate, Bird In Flight, President Hayes Service, 9 In. .... *Illus*   1100.00
Plate, Dark Turquoise Flowers, Green Leaves, Brown Lines, 7 1/2 In. 32.00
Plate, Delaware, 6 1/4 In. 10.00
Plate, Greek Key, 9 1/2 In. 60.00
Plate, Green Leaves & Ribbons, Red Lines & Dots, Gold Band, Gold Edge, 10 In. 25.00
Plate, Pink Roses, Gray Leaves, Gold Trim, 10 In. 20.00
Plate, Serving, Floral, Gilt, 10 In. 75.00
Plate, Yellow & Black Design, Gold Edge, 10 In. 20.00
Punch Bowl, Baltimore Rose, Footed, Scalloped, 7 1/4 x 14 1/2 In. .... *Illus*   1210.00
Ramekin, Green Leaves & Ribbons, Red Lines & Dots, Gold Band, Gold Edge 20.00
Soup, Cream, Underplate, Anjou, Gold Trim 35.00
Soup, Cream, Underplate, Pink Roses, Gray & Tan Chain On Black, Gold Edge 28.00
Sugar, Cover, Apple Blossom 75.00
Teapot, Duck Shape, 7 1/4 In. .... *Illus*   495.00
Teapot, Maiden, Basket Of Grapes, Molded Gilt Leaf Design, Floral Finial, 9 1/2 In. 155.00

Haviland, Plate,
Bird In Flight,
President Hayes
Service, 9 In.

Haviland, Punch Bowl, Baltimore Rose,
Footed, Scalloped, 7 1/4 x 14 1/2 In.

Haviland, Teapot,
Duck Shape,
7 1/4 In.

Haviland, Tureen, Oyster, Cover, Dammouse,
1876-1889

Tureen, Oyster, Cover, Dammouse, 1876-1889 ....*Illus* 1045.00
Vase, Flare, Mountain Lake Roundels, Cobalt & Gilt Handles, c.1875, 8 1/2 In., Pair 220.00

HAWKES cut glass was made by T. G. Hawkes & Company of Corning, New York, founded in 1880. The firm cut glass blanks made at other glassworks until 1962. Many pieces are marked with the trademark, a trefoil ring enclosing a fleur-de-lis and two hawks. Cut glass by other manufacturers is listed under either the factory name or in the general Cut Glass category.

Bottle, Rum, Brazilian, Strap Handle, 8 3/4 In. 300.00
Bowl, Centauri, Brilliant, 10 1/2 In. 450.00
Bowl, Floral & Vine, 13 1/2 In. 150.00
Bowl, Gladys, Signed, 3 x 10 In. 425.00
Bowl, Hobstar, Crosscut Diamond & Fan, Signed, 8 In. 170.00
Box, Handkerchief, Basket Of Flowers On Cover, 2 1/2 x 6 1/4 In. 425.00
Candlestick, Intaglio Berries & Leaves, Hollow Stem, 10 1/2 In. 350.00
Carafe, Brazilian, Strap Handle, 8 3/4 In. 300.00
Carafe, Russian, Thumbprint Neck, 8 In. 60.00
Nappy, Empire, Signed, 6 In. 160.00
Pitcher, Brunswick, Triple Notched Handle, Rayed Star Base, 7 1/2 x 6 In. 730.00
Pitcher, Champagne, Hobstar, Cane, Strawberry-Diamond & Fan, 11 In. 375.00
Pitcher, Devonshire, Signed, 11 In. 610.00
Pitcher, Milk, Chrysanthemum, Triple Notched Handle, Signed, 7 In. 525.00
Plate, Carnation Pattern, Gravic, 7 1/2 In. 225.00
Plate, Hobstars, Crosscut Tile, Strawberry-Diamond, 7 In. 300.00
Plate, Intaglio, Chain Of Hobstars, 7 In. 295.00
Punch Cup, Strawberry-Diamond & Fan, Signed, 4 In., 8 Piece 325.00
Rose Bowl, Allover Hobstar & Fan, Scalloped Base, Signed, 8 1/8 In. 305.00
Shaker, Martini, Checkerboard, Sterling Silver Lid, 12 In. 285.00
Shaker, Martini, Flower & Leaf Design, Silver Plated Lid, c.1915, 10 In. 195.00
Sugar & Creamer, Chrysanthemum, Double Thumbprint Handles 60.00
Vase, Fan, Floral, Green Foot, Signed, 10 1/2 In. 250.00
Vase, Fan, Sprays & Baskets Of Flowers, Signed, 20th Century, 7 1/2 In. 115.00
Vase, Garlands Of Trailing Flowers & Medallions, Signed, 8 In. 143.00
Vase, Oval, Amethyst Cut To Clear, Bird On Flowering Branch, 10 In. 290.00
Wine, Stars, Flared Bowl, 6 Piece 145.00

HEAD VASES, generally showing a woman from the shoulders up, were used by florists primarily in the 1950s and 1960s. Made in a variety of sizes and often decorated with imitation jewelry and other lifelike accessories, the vases were manufactured in Japan and the U.S.A. Less elaborate examples were made as early as the 1930s. Religious themes, babies, and animals are also common subjects. Other head vases are listed under manufacturers' names and can be located through the index at the back of this book.

African Man, Woman, Pair 450.00

Barbie 110.00
Becky ....95.00 to 120.00
Black Dress 120.00
Black Girl, Gold Basket On Head, 5 In. 35.00
Blue Hat, Pearl Earrings & Necklace, National Potteries, Japan, 5 3/4 In. 83.00
Blue Hat, Rose, Lashes, Blond Hair, Earrings, Napco, 4 3/4 In. 55.00
Coat & Hat, Hand On Upturned Collar, Napco, 5 1/2 In. 165.00
Conchita, Kreiss, 5 In. 45.00
Flora Belle, Betty Lou Nichols, 11 In. ...../...................................... 750.00
Glamour Girl 25.00
Glossy, Bonnet, Paper Label, Japan, 7 In. 75.00
Green Bow In Blond Hair, Label 150.00
Hair Comb, Pearl Earrings & Necklace, 1963, 10 In. 370.00
Lady, Open Eye, Bonnet, Pearl Earrings, Wales, 5 In. 45.00
Long Brown Hair, Flower, Jeweled, Lashes, 5 1/4 In. 88.00
Madonna, Blue, Gold Trim, Relpo 40.00
Madonna, Blue, Haeger 35.00
Pearl Earrings, Necklace, Brinnis, 7 In. 220.00
Sandy & Jean, Green Plaid, 7 In., Pair 60.00
Teenager, Brown Hair In Ponytails, Green Shirt, Inarco 75.00
Woman, Blue, Napco, 1958 .... 55.00
Yellow Bonnet 130.00

HEDI SCHOOP Art Creations, North Hollywood, California, started about 1945 and was working until 1954. Schoop made ceramic figurines, lamps, planters, and tablewares.

Hedi Schoop
S

Figurine, Fantasy Pair, Gold Speckles, Rose Accents, 11 1/2 In. ....185.00 to 250.00
Figurine, Owl, Sitting On Gnarled Branch, 6 x 6 In. 65.00
Figurine, Spanish Dancers, 10 & 9 In., Pair 325.00
Flower Holder, Tyrolean Girl, Holding Skirt, Marked, 11 In. 90.00
Planter, 12 3/4 In. 5500.00
Planter, Girl, Flowers, 9 In. 58.00
Planter, Horse, Marked, 7 In. 56.00

HEINTZ ART Metal Shop made jewelry, copper, silver, and brass in Buffalo, New York, from 1906 to 1935, when a new company name was taken and the mark became *Silvercrest*. The most popular items with collectors today are the copper desk sets and vases made with applied silver designs.

Ashtray, Matchbox Holder, Impressed Logo, 4 x 7 1/2 In. 220.00
Bookends, Floral, 3 1/2 x 3 In., Pair 135.00
Bowl, Daffodils, Silver On Bronze, Footed, Stamped, 5 1/2 x 11 In. 220.00
Bowl, Floral, Silver On Bronze, Signed, 8 In. 520.00
Bowl, Flowers, Silver On Bronze, Mottled, 1920, 9 In. 330.00
Bowl, Hummingbird & Branch, Silver On Bronze, 9 In. 140.00
Bowl, Silvercrest, Pinecone, Wide Rim, 2 1/2 x 6 In. 220.00
Box, Cigarette, Silver On Bronze, Impressed Logo, 2 1/2 x 9 x 4 In. 550.00
Box, Cover, Silver On Bronze, Original Patina, 1919, 10 x 6 In. 220.00
Box, Domed Cover, Curl Footed, 2 x 3 1/2 x 12 1/2 In. 120.00
Box, Double Lidded, Center Handle, Signed, 4 x 8 In. 330.00
Candlestick, 3-Light, Green Matte Glaze, Bronze, Signed, 8 In. 1980.00
Candlestick, Golf Scene, Original Silver Patina, 8 In. 295.00
Candlestick, Leaf Design, Silver On Bronze, Brown Patina, 8 1/4 x 4 1/2 In. 770.00
Candlestick, Silver On Bronze, Original Patina, 11 1/2 In., Pair 440.00
Desk Items, Silver Foliate, Metal, Copper, 5 1/2 x 9 In. 345.00
Humidor, Dog & Tree Scene, 6 In. 495.00
Humidor, Geometric, Cedar Lining, Silver On Bronze, Stamped, 8 1/2 x 3 1/2 In. 605.00
Humidor, Silver On Bronze, Mesh Panel, HAM Stamp, 3 x 10 In. 330.00
Humidor, Silvercrest, Signed, 2 1/2 x 9 x 3 1/2 In. 385.00
Humidor, Viking Ship Overlay, Silver On Bronze, Stamped, 3 x 10 x 6 In. 495.00
Inkwell, Geometric Design, Silver On Bronze, 4 In. 305.00
Inkwell, Silver On Bronze, Patent August 12, 1912, 4 In. 88.00
Lamp, Arts & Crafts Geometric Design, Silver On Bronze, 9 In. 935.00

Lamp, Boudoir, Acid Etched, Helmet Shade, Vertical Moorish, Mica, 10 In. 2420.00
Lamp, Desk, Acid Etched, Gold Dore, Dancing Maids, Pierced Shade, 12 In. 2860.00
Lamp, Floral, Silver On Bronze, Original Verdigris Patina, Cut Out Shade, 12 In. 2090.00
Lamp, Helmet, 10 1/2 In. 1925.00
Lamp, Silver On Bronze, Original Copper Patina, Mica Insert In Shade, 14 In. 4675.00
Lamp, Silver On Bronze, Round Base, Poppies, Cone Shape Shade, Mica, 10 In. 2200.00
Lamp, Silver Pinecone Design Base, Cutout Design Shade, 10 x 8 In. 2310.00
Letter Holder, Verdigris Bronze, Original Patina, Cutout Handle, 4 x 7 1/4 In. 90.00
Loving Cup, Handball Singles Tournament, Silver On Bronze, Handles, 1920, 11 In. 1100.00
Trophy, Silvercrest, Footed, Large Scroll Handles, Signed, 15 In. 165.00
Vase, 3 Orchids, Silver On Bronze, Cylindrical, 10 In. 275.00
Vase, Bird On Branch, Bronze Patina, Silver On Bronze, 5 3/4 x 3 3/4 In. 330.00
Vase, Bulbous, Mountain Laurel, Silver On Bronze, Brown Patina, 5 x 4 In. 550.00
Vase, Bulbous, Poppies, Silver On Bronze, Brown Patina, 11 1/4 x 5 1/2 In. 1210.00
Vase, Cabinet, Stylized Daisies, Silver On Bronze, Cleaned Patina, 4 In. 165.00
Vase, Cattail Design, Silver On Bronze, Impressed Mark, 6 In. 305.00
Vase, Cattail Design, Silver On Bronze, Original Verdigris Patina, 10 In. 1045.00
Vase, Classic, Silver On Bronze, Dancing Maidens Panels, Stamped, 12 1/2 In. 770.00
Vase, Cyclamen, Bronze Patina, Silver On Bronze, Cylindrical, 9 1/2 In. 440.00
Vase, Daffodils, Verdigris Patina, Silver On Bronze, Cylindrical, 12 In. 1100.00
Vase, Flaring Rolled Over Flanged Rim, Floral Spray On Front, 3 x 6 In. 75.00
Vase, Floral, Silver On Bronze, Brown Patina, 10 1/4 x 4 1/2 In. 660.00
Vase, Floral, Silver On Bronze, Original Patina, 12 1/2 In. 715.00
Vase, Floral, Silver On Bronze, Signed, 8 In. 440.00
Vase, Floral, Small Applied Buffalo, Silver On Bronze, 6 In. 715.00
Vase, Floral, Textured Ground, Sterling On Bronze, Silver Crest, Signed, 12 1/2 In. 467.00
Vase, Flower Overlay, Silver On Bronze, Verdigris Patina, 4 1/4 x 3 In. 429.00
Vase, Flowering Branches, Silver On Bronze, Cleaned Patina, 9 3/4 In. 220.00
Vase, Mountain Landscape, Silver On Bronze, Cylindrical, 11 1/2 x 5 1/4 In. 880.00
Vase, Open Rose, Trumpet, Silver On Bronze, 17 In. 850.00
Vase, Oval, Cattails, Silver On Bronze, Brown Patina, 7 3/4 x 3 1/2 In. 605.00
Vase, Overlay Of Daffodils & Leaves, Silver On Bronze, Cylindrical, 6 In. 330.00
Vase, Pine Boughs & Cones, Silver On Bronze, Brown Patina, 8 3/4 x 3 In. 275.00
Vase, Rose, Silver On Bronze, Dark Patina, Bulbous, 5 1/4 In. 305.00
Vase, Sterling Silver Rose, Green Patina Ground, Impressed Signature, 5 In. 495.00
Vase, Stylized Tree, Sterling On Bronze, Silver Crest, Signed, 6 In. 385.00
Vase, Tapered, Roses, Silver On Bronze, Brown Patina, 11 x 4 1/2 In. 770.00
Vase, Wild Flowers, Silver On Bronze, Original Bronze Patina, 6 x 3 In. 165.00

HEISEY glass was made from 1896 to 1957 in Newark, Ohio, by A. H. Heisey and Co., Inc. The Imperial Glass Company of Bellaire, Ohio, bought some of the molds and the rights to the trademark. Some Heisey patterns have been made by Imperial since 1960. After 1968, they stopped using the *H* trademark. Heisey used romantic names for colors, such as *Sahara*. Do not confuse color and pattern names. The Custard Glass and Ruby Glass categories may also include some Heisey pieces.

Animal, Colt, Kicking 175.00
Animal, Colt, Standing 90.00
Animal, Gazelle 1500.00
Animal, Goose, Wings Half ....75.00 to 95.00
Animal, Goose, Wings Up 85.00
Animal, Ringneck Pheasant 160.00
Athena, Bowl, 12 In. 50.00
Athena, Plate, Sandwich, 13 In. 50.00
Banded Flute, Claret, 3 Oz. 45.00
Banded Flute, Wine, 2 Oz. 27.00
Beaded Panel & Sunburst, Sauce, Gold Trim 12.00
Beehive, Plate, Moongleam, 8 In. 15.00
Bob White, Sherbet, Peacock Edge 10.00
Carcassone, Sherbet, 5 Oz. 3.00
Cascade, Candlestick, 3-Light, Pair 275.00
Charter Oak, Champagne, Flamingo 27.00

Chintz, Cordial, 1 Oz.	120.00
Colonial, Basket, Flower On Each Panel, 7 In.	250.00
Colonial, Bowl, Cover, Crushed Fruit, Inner Drip & Drain Rim, 9 1/2 In.	245.00
Colonial, Cup & Saucer	65.00
Colonial, Plate, 4 3/4 In.	5.00
Creole, Champagne, Alexandrite	150.00
Crystolite, Bowl, Round, 10 In.	43.00
Crystolite, Box, Cigarette, Cover	15.00
Crystolite, Nut Dish, Swan, Individual	20.00
Crystolite, Nut Set, Swan, Master, 13 In., 8 Piece	910.00
Double Rib & Panel, Mustard, Cover, Flamingo	63.00
Empress, Celery Dish, Sahara, 10 In.	35.00
Empress, Creamer, Dolphin Feet, Sahara	40.00
Empress, Cup & Saucer, Sahara	40.00
Empress, Lemon Dish, Oval, Etched Cover, Dolphin Finial, 6 1/2 In.	65.00
Empress, Plate, Alexandrite, 7 1/2 In.	90.00
Empress, Plate, Sahara, 6 In.	14.00
Empress, Plate, Sahara, 7 In.	15.00
Empress, Plate, Square, Tangerine, 8 1/2 In.	150.00
Empress, Sugar & Creamer, Individual, Sahara	70.00
Empress, Vase, Dolphin Feet, Sahara, 9 In.	185.00
Fairacre, Goblet, 10 Oz.	15.00
Fancy Loop, Cake Stand, 9 1/4 In.	125.00
Fancy Loop, Vase, 8 In.	37.00
Fancy Loop, Wine, Gold Trim	65.00
Fish, Candlestick, Pair	350.00
Greek Key, Pitcher, 1 Pt.	320.00
Greek Key, Relish, 2 Sections, 11 1/2 In.	90.00
Ipswich, Centerpiece, Footed, Prisms	95.00
Jack-Be-Nimble, Chamberstick	100.00
Lariat, Basket, Footed, 10 In.	225.00
Lariat, Basket, Sweet Meat, Handle, 7 In.	175.00
Lariat, Bowl, Silver Overlay, Oval, 12 In.	24.00
Lariat, Candlestick, 2-Light, Pair	55.00 to 60.00
Lariat, Cologne Bottle	75.00
Lariat, Cup & Saucer	22.00
Lariat, Plate, Floral Cutting, 14 In.	45.00
Mars, Candlestick, 4 In, Pair	35.00
Me You & Us, Cocktail Set, 3 Piece	75.00
Mercury, Candlestick, Moongleam, Pair	31.00
Mercury, Candlestick, Pair	21.00 to 35.00
Minuet, Champagne, 6 Oz.	30.00
Minuet, Goblet, 9 Oz.	45.00
Minuet, Plate, 8 In.	20.00
Minuet, Relish, 2 Sections	50.00
Minuet, Sugar & Creamer	80.00
New Era, Candlestick, 2-Light	40.00
New Era, Celery Dish, 13 In.	35.00
New Era, Claret, 4 Oz.	22.00 to 25.00
New Era, Cocktail, 3 Oz.	20.00
New Era, Cordial, 1 Oz.	45.00
New Era, Cup & Saucer	65.00
New Era, Nut Cup	60.00
New Era, Pilsner, 12 Oz.	60.00
New Era, Plate, 6 In.	35.00
New Era, Tumbler, Juice, Footed, 5 Oz.	23.00 to 25.00
Octagon, Basket, Moongleam, 5 In.	395.00
Octagon, Plate, Sandwich, Moongleam, 12 In.	265.00
Octagon, Sugar, Flamingo	10.00
Old Colony, Cup & Saucer, Sahara	40.00
Old Colony, Plate, Square, Sahara, 8 In.	22.00
Old Sandwich, Cruet, Sahara, 2 Oz.	30.00
Old Sandwich, Cup, Pink	60.00

Old Sandwich, Mug, Beer, Sahara, 12 Oz. 160.00
Old Williamsburg, Candelabrum, 3-Light, Short Base 275.00
Old Williamsburg, Candelabrum, Bobeches, Prisms, 11 In., Pair 195.00
Orchid Etch, Ashtray, 3 In. 22.00
Orchid Etch, Bottle, Oil, Stopper, Footed, 3 Oz. 200.00
Orchid Etch, Candlestick, 2-Light, Waverly, Pair 120.00
Orchid Etch, Candlestick, Mercury 33.00
Orchid Etch, Cigarette Holder, Cover, Seahorse Handles 150.00
Orchid Etch, Cocktail Shaker, 1 Pt. 295.00
Orchid Etch, Cocktail, 3 Oz. 40.00
Orchid Etch, Cocktail, Icer Insert 275.00
Orchid Etch, Creamer, Footed 40.00
Orchid Etch, Decanter, Sherry, Oval, 1 Pt. 300.00
Orchid Etch, Goblet, Low, 10 Oz. 36.00
Orchid Etch, Pitcher, Donna, 1/2 Gal. 625.00
Orchid Etch, Plate, 7 In. ....18.00 to 24.00
Orchid Etch, Sherbet 20.00
Orchid Etch, Sherry, 2 Oz. 120.00
Orchid Etch, Tumbler, Footed, 12 Oz., 7 3/4 In. 60.00
Parallel Quarter, Candlestick, Cutting, 3 1/4 In., Pair 45.00
Patrician, Candlestick, 9 In., Pair 52.00
Peerless, Pickle Jar, Cover 58.00
Pineapple & Fan, Salt & Pepper 73.00
Pineapple & Fan, Salt & Pepper, Bulbous Base 25.00
Plantation, Bottle, Oil, Stopper, 3 In. 130.00
Plantation, Bowl, Dressing, 3 Sections 31.00
Plantation, Bowl, Flared, 12 1/2 In. 145.00
Plantation, Butter, Ivy Etch, Round, 5 In. 160.00
Plantation, Candy Dish, Cover, 5 In. 195.00
Plantation, Relish, 4 Sections, 8 In. 70.00
Plantation, Syrup 150.00
Priscilla, Nappy, 4 1/2 In. 6.00
Provincial, Pitcher, Iced Tea, Limelight, 23 Oz. 73.00
Provincial, Plate, 7 In. 15.00
Puritan, Pitcher, 1 Pt. 140.00
Puritan, Salt & Pepper 13.00
Quator, Sugar & Creamer 80.00
Queen Ann, Bowl, Floral, 10 1/2 In. 37.00
Queen Ann, Bowl, Oval, Footed, 13 In. 15.00
Queen Ann, Candlestick, Prisms, 8 In., Pair 150.00
Queen Ann, Candy Dish, Footed, Handle, 5 1/2 In. 75.00
Recessed Panel, Basket, Side Handle, 8 In. 155.00
Recessed Panel, Candy Jar, Cover, Amethyst Flashed 80.00
Recessed Panel, Candy, 3 Lb. 250.00
Ridgeleigh, Ashtray, Original Box 75.00
Ridgeleigh, Bowl, Floral, Oval, Limelight, 11 In. 15.00
Ridgeleigh, Bowl, Swan Handles, Oval, 14 In. 75.00
Ridgeleigh, Decanter, Stopper 149.00
Ridgeleigh, Ice Tub 115.00
Ridgeleigh, Plate, 11 1/2 In. 40.00
Ridgeleigh, Relish, 2 Sections 10.00
Ridgeleigh, Sugar & Creamer 18.00
Ridgeleigh, Vase, 6 In. 49.00
Rose Etch, Bowl, 2 Sections, Oval 65.00
Rose Etch, Bowl, Dressing, 2 Sections, Oval, 6 1/2 In. 60.00
Rose Etch, Bowl, Gardenia, 13 In. 100.00
Rose Etch, Butter, Cover, 1/4 Lb. ....275.00 to 375.00
Rose Etch, Cake Plate, Footed 285.00
Rose Etch, Candy Dish, Cover, Seahorse Handles, Waverly 225.00
Rose Etch, Celery Dish, Oval, 12 In. 95.00
Rose Etch, Champagne, 6 Oz. 30.00
Rose Etch, Compote, 6 In. 65.00
Rose Etch, Cordial, 1 Oz. 175.00

Rose Etch, Cup & Saucer, Waverly	90.00
Rose Etch, Goblet, Water, 9 Oz.	35.00 to 42.00
Rose Etch, Plate, 8 1/2 In.	20.00
Rose Etch, Plate, Waverly, 7 In.	20.00
Rose Etch, Relish, 2 Sections	60.00
Rose Etch, Relish, 3 Sections, 11 In.	80.00
Rose Etch, Salt & Pepper, Waverly	75.00
Saturn, Cocktail, Oyster, Limelight	152.00
Saturn, Compote, Limelight, 7 In.	355.00
Saturn, Mustard, Cover	38.00
Saturn, Plate, Limelight, 8 In.	75.00
Savoy Plaza, Cordial, 1 Oz.	95.00
Stanhope, Cocktail, 3 Oz.	30.00
Sunburst, Punch Bowl, Base, 14 In.	325.00
Sunburst, Punch Cup	20.00
Tally Ho, Decanter, 1 Pt.	175.00
Town & Country, Bowl, Salad, Underplate, Limelight, 11 In.	142.00
Town & Country, Plate, Sandwich, Dawn	75.00
Trident, Candlestick, 2-Light, Sahara, Pair	295.00
Tudor, Goblet, 8 Oz.	52.00
Twentieth Century, Tumbler, Dawn, 12 Oz.	40.00
Twist, Bonbon	28.00
Twist, Bowl, Floral, Oval, Flamingo, 12 In.	7.00
Twist, Plate, Moongleam, 11 In.	10.00
Victorian, Ashtray, Match Holder	11.00
Warwick, Candlestick, 2-Light, Pair	135.00
Waverly, Cup & Saucer	20.00
Whirlpool, Bowl, Floral, 12 In.	20.00
Winged Scroll, Toothpick	115.00
Yeoman, Bowl, Cut Star Bottom, Engraved Floral Rim, 8 3/4 In., 12 Piece	165.00
Yeoman, Compote, Moongleam, 5 In.	35.00

HEREND, see Fischer category.

HEUBACH is the collector's name for Gebruder Heubach, a firm working in Lichten, Germany, from 1840 to 1925. It is best known for bisque dolls and doll heads, their principal products. They also manufactured bisque figurines, including piano babies, beginning in the 1880s, and glazed figurines in the 1900s. Piano babies are listed in their own category. Dolls are included in the Doll category under *Gebruder Heubach* and *Heubach*. Another factory, Ernst Heubach, working in Koppelsdorf, Germany, also made porcelain and dolls. These will also be found in the Doll category under Heubach Koppelsdorf.

Figurine, Baby, Removing Socks, Nightshirt, Cap, In Wicker Chair, 4 3/4 In.	250.00
Figurine, Boy & Girl, Each Leaning On Log, 6 In., Pair	55.00
Figurine, Dutch Boy, Sitting, Hat, Shoes & Scarf, 6 In.	235.00
Figurine, Dutch Girl, Sitting, Blue & White Dress, 6 1/2 In.	195.00 to 235.00
Figurine, Mother, Holding Baby In Arms, Signed, 11 1/2 In.	300.00
Figurine, Seashore, 12 In., Pair	1295.00
Group, A Dark Secret, Bisque, 10 In.	385.00

HIGBEE glass was made by the J. B. Higbee Company of Bridgeville, Pennsylvania, about 1900. Tablewares were made, and it is possible to assemble a full set of dishes and goblets in some Higbee patterns. Most of the glass was clear, not colored. Additional pieces may be found in the Pressed Glass category by pattern name.

Candy, Bijou, 1900, 7 1/2 In.	40.00
Compote, Era, Cover, 4 In.	35.00
Spooner, Thistle	40.00

HISTORIC BLUE, see factory names, such as Adams, Clews, Ridgway, and Staffordshire.

HOBNAIL glass is a style of glass with bumps all over. Dozens of hobnail patterns and variants have been made. Clear, colored, and opalescent hobnail have been made and are being reproduced. Other pieces of hobnail may also be listed in the Duncan & Miller and Fenton categories.

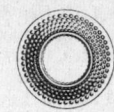

Berry Set, Cranberry Opalescent	200.00
Bottle, Milk Glass, Stopper, 6 In.	20.00
Bowl, Shaded Pink, Ruffled Edge, Brass Base, 7 3/4 In.	175.00
Candleholder, Amber, 5 1/2 x 1 In.	8.00
Cruet, Blue Opalescent	11.00
Pitcher, Water, Vaseline & Cranberry Opalescent, Handle, Bulbous, 8 In.	143.00
Rose Bowl, Cranberry Opalescent	30.00
Tumbler, Amber, Wide Rim	20.00
Vase, Blue Mother-Of-Pearl, Square Top, 5 In.	225.00
Vase, Whimsy, Vaseline Opalescent, Clear Vine With Leaves, Footed, 8 1/4 In.	175.00
Water Set, Cranberry To Clear, 6 Piece	275.00

HOLLY AMBER, or golden agate, glass was made by the Indiana Tumbler and Goblet Company of Greentown, Indiana, from January 1, 1903, to June 13, 1903. It is a pressed glass pattern featuring holly leaves in the amber-shaded glass. The glass was made with shadings that range from creamy opalescent to brown-amber.

Butter, Cover	1050.00
Plate, Round, 7 1/2 In.	775.00
Spooner	700.00 to 750.00
Toothpick	425.00 to 585.00
Tray, Round, 9 1/4 In.	1150.00

HOLT-HOWARD was an importer who started working in 1949 in Stamford, Connecticut. He sold many types of table accessories, such as condiment jars, decanters, spoon holders, and saltshakers. The figures shown on some of his pieces had a cartoon-like quality. The company was bought out by General Housewares Corporation in 1969. Holt-Howard pieces are often marked with the name and the year or *HH* and the year stamped in black. There was also a black and silver label.

Ashtray, Christmas Tree, 1960, 4 3/4 In.	*Illus*	5.00
Candy Dish, Santa Claus, Pop-Up		210.00

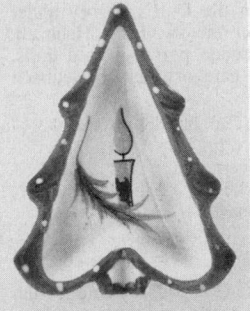

Holt-Howard, Ashtray, Christmas Tree, 1960, 4 3/4 In.

Holt-Howard, Jar, Instant Coffee, Pixie, Brown, Blond Hair, Sticker, 1958, 6 In.

Holt-Howard, Sugar & Creamer, Chickens, Saccharine Holder In Sugar

Cookie Jar, Winking Santa	85.00
Dish, Hors D'Oeuvre, Pixie	275.00
Jar, Instant Coffee, Pixie, Brown, Blond Hair, Sticker, 1958, 6 In. ....*Illus*	395.00
Letterholder, Kitten	55.00
Salt & Pepper, Daisy Dorable, Sticker	125.00
Salt & Pepper, Winking Cats	37.50
Shaker, Nutmeg, Winking Santa Claus, Label, 4 1/2 In.	35.00
String Holder, Cat's Head	50.00
Sugar & Creamer, Chickens, Saccharine Holder In Sugar ....*Illus*	45.00

HOPALONG CASSIDY was a character in a series of twenty-eight books written by Clarence E. Milford, first published in 1907. Movies and television shows were made based on the character. The best-known actor playing Hopalong Cassidy was William Lawrence Boyd. His first movie appearance was in 1919, but the first Hopalong Cassidy film was not until 1934. Sixty-six films were made. In 1948, William Boyd purchased the television rights to the movies, then later made fifty-two new programs. In the 1950s, Hopalong Cassidy and his horse, named *Topper*, were seen in comics, records, toys, and other products. Boyd died in 1972.

Badge, Bar 20, Portrait, Original Card, 1950	47.00
Badge, Star, Hoppy In Center, Gray Metal, 2 In.	38.00
Badge, Star, Hoppy, Eat Bond Bread, Silver & Black Plastic	22.00
Badge, Tab, Lithograph, Hoppy Image, Post Raisin Bran, 2 In.	35.00
Barrette, Hoppy, Metal	25.00
Book Cover, Butternut Bread Premium	17.00
Bottle Cap, Milk, Linton Dairy, Ohio, 1950, 1 5/8 In.	10.00
Brochure, Dr. Ross Dog Food, 4 Pages, 5 x 7 In.	75.00
Cap Gun, Holster, Belt, Wyandotte	500.00
Card, Greeting, Oversized, Inset Picture Of Hoppy	35.00
Coloring Book, Trouble Shooter, 1950	60.00
Compass, Wrist, 1 In.	85.00
Gloves, Leather	350.00
Gun & Holster, Double, Cuffs, Schmidt	1400.00
Knife, Pocket, Hoppy	.67.00 to 69.00
Lamp, Gun In Holster, Milk Glass	350.00
Lamp, Motion, Plastic, 1949	1250.00
Money Clip	55.00
Outfit, Plaid Shirt, Pants Chaps, Box	350.00
Record Album, Square Dance Holdup, Photograph, 33 1/3 RPM	40.00
Ring, Metal, Hoppy's Face In Horseshoe	95.00
Slide, Scarf, Ebony, Embossed Steer Horns, Plastic	100.00
Tin, Potato Chip	60.00
Toy, Hopalong & Topper, Action Arm, Ideal, Box, 1950s, 4 & 5 In.	280.00
Toy, Range Rider, Marx, Box	1250.00
Toy, Rocking Horse, Plastic, Wooden Legs, Aluminum Frame, Rich, 30 In.	320.00
Toy, Shooting Gallery, Key Wind	475.00
Wristwatch, Timex	100.00

HOWARD PIERCE has been working in Southern California since 1936. In 1945, he opened a pottery in Claremont. His contemporary-looking figurines are popular with collectors. Pieces are marked with his name. He stopped making pottery in 1991.

Howard Pierce

Figurine, Bulldog, U.S.M.C., 5 In.	200.00
Figurine, Chipmunks, Matte Finish, Brown Stripes, Marked, 3 In. & 5 In.	90.00
Figurine, Dog, Long Droopy Ears, Brown Matte, Marked, 8 1/4 In. & 6 In., Pair	160.00
Figurine, Native Couple, Marked, 7 1/4 In.	190.00
Figurine, Quail Family, Marked, 1950, 5 1/2 In.	95.00
Figurine, Quail, In Tree, Marked	100.00
Figurine, Road Runner, Brown Matte Glaze, Marked, 12 In.	125.00
Figurine, St. Francis, Holding Bird, Marked, 12 In.	195.00
Figurine, Water Bird, Cream, Brown Markings, Marked, 14 In.	80.00
Figurine, White Owl, Marked, 5 In.	60.00

Howdy Doody,
Doll,
Composition,
Wooden, Jointed,
12 1/2 In.

Check the supports on wall-hung
shelves once a year. Eventually a
heavy load will cause "creep."
The metal brackets will bend,
and the shelf will fall.

Flower Holder, Owls On Limbs Of Bare Tree, Marked, 7 1/2 In.	95.00
Vase, Bud, Gray Volcanic Matte Finish, Marked, 3 1/2 In.	45.00

HOWDY DOODY and Buffalo Bob were the main characters in a children's series televised from 1947 to 1960. Howdy was a redheaded puppet. The series became popular with college students in the late 1970s when Buffalo Bob began to lecture on campuses.

Book, Howdy Doody Fun Book, Unused, 1951	39.00
Book, Sticker Fun, Paste & Cut, 1951	125.00
Box, Ice Cream Cake Roll, 1950s, 4 In.	83.00
Box, TV Shaped, Tiny Pair Of Cowboy Boots Inside, Porcelain, 2 x 3 1/2 In.	25.00
Doll, Bisque Head & Hands, Resin Feet, Posable, Stand, Box, 16 In.	65.00
Doll, Composition, Wooden, Jointed, 12 1/2 In. *Illus*	660.00
Doll, Posable, Porcelain Head & Hands, Doll Stand, Stanton Arts, 16 In.	95.00
Doll, Sleep Eyes, Effanbee, Box, 1948, 23 In.	400.00
Figurine, Clarabel, Chalkware, Universal Statuary Corp, 1966, 24 In.	75.00
Game, Time Teacher, Package, 1960s, 10 x 20 In.	35.00
Lamp, Howdy, Sitting	45.00
Puppet, Flub-A-Dub, Push, Kohner, Box	365.00
Puppet, Princess Summerfall-Winterspring, Composition, Complete	365.00
Puzzle, Jigsaw, 1950s	95.00
Shelf Sitter, Howdy, Musical, Plays Memories, Box, 5 In.	45.00
Teaspoon, Says Howdy Doody, Marked Kagran, 1950s	40.00
Toy, Swing, Howdy Hanging From Bar, Box, Arnold	875.00
Wristwatch, Howdy's Face, Copyright Bob Smith, Switzerland	265.00
Wristwatch, Howdy's Face, Green & Tan Band, Patent Watch Co., 1954, 1 In.	85.00

HULL pottery was made in Crooksville, Ohio, from 1905. Addis E. Hull bought the Acme Pottery Company and started making ceramic wares. In 1917, A. E. Hull Pottery began making art pottery as well as the commercial wares. For a short time, 1921 to 1929, the firm also sold pottery imported from Europe. The dinnerwares of the 1940s, including the Little Red Riding Hood line, the high gloss artwares of the 1950s, and the matte wares of the 1940s, are all popular with collectors. The firm officially closed in March 1986.

Alpine Village, Tankard Set, 5 Piece	125.00
Apple, Cookie Jar	50.00
Bank, Pig, 8 In.	65.00
Blossom, Bowl, Kitchenware, 10 In.	55.00
Blossom, Grease Jar, Kitchenware, 5 3/4 In.	30.00
Blossom, Mixing Bowl, Kitchenware, 9 In.	55.00
Bow Knot, Basket, Pink & Blue, 10 1/2 In.	695.00
Bow Knot, Vase, Pink, 8 1/2 In.	275.00
Bow Knot, Wall Pocket, Iron, 6 1/4 In.	200.00
Cinderella, Teapot, 42 Oz.	45.00

Dogwood, Pitcher, Pink, Blue, 4 3/4 In. 100.00
Ebb Tide, Basket, Fish Handle, 16 In. 60.00
Figurine, Siamese Cat & Kitten, 5 3/4 In. 95.00
Floral, Cookie Jar, 8 3/4 In. 135.00
Gingerbread Man, Cookie Jar 150.00
Granada, Vase, Off-White, 9 In. 50.00
Happy Days Are Here Again, Mug, 4 1/2 In. 25.00
House 'n Garden, Coffeepot, Cover 20.00
House 'n Garden, Dish, Leaf, 12 In. 28.00
House 'n Garden, Plate 4.00
House 'n Garden, Salt & Pepper 8.00
House 'n Garden, Salt & Pepper, Mushroom 15.00
Little Red Riding Hood, Cookie Jar, Blue Trim 350.00
Little Red Riding Hood, Cookie Jar, Gold Bows 600.00
Little Red Riding Hood, Pitcher, Milk 300.00
Little Red Riding Hood, Sugar & Creamer, Crawling 300.00
Little Red Riding Hood, Teapot, Head Tilted, 8 In. ....195.00 to 325.00
Magnolia, Console Set, Gloss, 3 Piece 180.00
Magnolia, Vase, Gloss, 8 1/2 In. 125.00
Magnolia, Vase, Gloss, 12 1/2 In. 275.00
Magnolia, Vase, Matte, 5 In. 60.00
Magnolia, Vase, Matte, 6 1/2 In. 70.00
Magnolia, Vase, Matte, 8 1/2 In. 73.00
Parchment & Pine, Basket, 16 1/2 In. 130.00
Parchment & Pine, Candleholder, 5 In., Pair 45.00
Parchment & Pine, Console, 16 In. 130.00
Parchment & Pine, Ewer, 14 1/2 In. ....195.00 to 240.00
Planter, Kitten, With Spool 35.00
Planter, Telephone, 9 In. 60.00
Poppy, Basket, Pink & Cream, 12 In. 1100.00
Serenade, Bowl, Fruit, 7 In. 160.00
Water Lily, Cornucopia, Double, 12 In. 145.00
Water Lily, Vase, 6 In. 80.00
Water Lily, Vase, 11 In. 195.00
Whisk Broom, Wall Pocket, Blue, 8 In. 275.00
Wildflower, Console Set, Label, 3 Piece 575.00
Wildflower, Vase, 6 1/2 In. ....75.00 to 85.00
Wildflower, Vase, 10 1/2 In. ....150.00 to 225.00
Woodland, Cornucopia, 5 1/2 In. 30.00
Woodland, Cornucopia, 11 In. 95.00
Woodland, Vase, 12 1/2 In. 375.00

HUMMEL figurines, based on the drawings of the nun M.I. Hummel (Berta Hummel), are made by the W. Goebel Porzellanfabrik of Oeslau, Germany, now Rodenthal, Germany. They were first made in 1934. The *Crown* mark was used from 1935 to 1949. The company added the *bee* marks in 1950. The *full bee* with variations, was used from 1950 to 1959; *stylized bee,* 1960 to 1972; *three line mark,* 1968 to 1972; *last bee,* sometimes called *vee over gee,* 1972 to 1979. In 1979 the V bee symbol was removed from the mark. *U.S. Zone* was part of the mark from 1946 to 1948; *W. Germany,* was part of the mark from 1960 to 1990; The *Goebel, W. Germany* mark, called the *missing bee* mark, was used from 1979 to 1990; *Goebel, Germany* with the crown and WG, originally called the *new mark,* was used from 1990 through part of 1999. The newest version of the bee mark with the word *Goebel,* the *current mark,* was adopted in 2000. A special *Year 2000* backstamp was also introduced. Porcelain figures inspired by Berta Hummel's drawings were introduced in 1997. These are marked BH followed by a number. They are made in the Far East, not Germany. Other decorative items and plates that feature Hummel drawings have been made by Schmid Brothers, Inc., since 1971.

Ashtray, Singing Lesson 100.00

Bell, 1983, Christmas, Angelic Message 20.00
Bookends, No. 61A & No. 61B, Playmates, Chick Girl, Full Bee 300.00
Bust, No. HU1, Three Line Mark 800.00
Bust, No. HU2, Vee Over Gee . . . . .40.00 to 70.00
Bust, No. HU3, Box, Vee Over Gee 145.00
Candleholder, No. 37, Herald Angels, Stylized Bee 90.00
Candleholder, No. 192, Candlelight, Full Bee 400.00
Candleholder, No. 192, Candlelight, Vee Over Gee 135.00
Figurine, No. 7/I, Merry Wanderer, Stylized Bee 720.00
Figurine, No. 8, Book Worm, Full Bee 85.00
Figurine, No. 10/1, Flower Madonna, Blue Cloak, Full Bee 350.00
Figurine, No. 10/1, Flower Madonna, White Overglaze, Full Bee 150.00
Figurine, No. 10/III, Flower Madonna, Full Bee 192.00
Figurine, No. 12/2/0, Chimneysweep, Vee Over Gee 60.00
Figurine, No. 13/2/0, Meditation, Three Line Mark 135.00
Figurine, No. 15/0, Hear Ye, Hear Ye, Vee Over Gee 105.00
Figurine, No. 16, Little Hiker, Crown Mark 390.00
Figurine, No. 16/2/0, Little Hiker, Stylized Bee 195.00
Figurine, No. 16/I, Little Hiker, Full Bee 300.00
Figurine, No. 21, Heavenly Angel, Vee Over Gee 185.00
Figurine, No. 28/II, Wayside Devotion, Stylized Bee 240.00
Figurine, No. 49/0, To Market, Stylized Bee . . . . .45.00 to 235.00
Figurine, No. 49/I, To Market, New Mark 175.00
Figurine, No. 50/2/0, Volunteers, Full Bee 115.00
Figurine, No. 51/1/0, Village Boy, Vee Over Gee 70.00
Figurine, No. 51/3/0, Village Boy, Full Bee 45.00
Figurine, No. 55, St. George, Last Bee 220.00
Figurine, No. 56/B, Out Of Danger, Stylized Bee . . . . .150.00 to 175.00
Figurine, No. 57/0, Chick Girl, Stylized Bee 200.00
Figurine, No. 58/0, Playmates, Stylized Bee 55.00
Figurine, No. 63, Singing Lesson, Last Bee 100.00
Figurine, No. 64, Shepherd's Boy, Full Bee 90.00
Figurine, No. 67, Doll Mother, Full Bee 115.00
Figurine, No. 67, Doll Mother, Stylized Bee 150.00
Figurine, No. 68, Lost Sheep, Full Bee 300.00
Figurine, No. 69, Happy Pastime, Last Bee 145.00
Figurine, No. 74, Little Gardener, Missing Bee 125.00
Figurine, No. 80, Little Scholar, Full Bee 250.00
Figurine, No. 81/0, School Girl, Last Bee . . . . .80.00 to 175.00
Figurine, No. 81/0, School Girl, Stylized Bee 100.00
Figurine, No. 82/0, School Boy, Full Bee 350.00
Figurine, No. 82/0, School Boy, Last Bee 125.00
Figurine, No. 82/2/0, School Boy, Stylized Bee 55.00
Figurine, No. 89/I, Little Cellist, Crown Mark 250.00
Figurine, No. 110/0, Let's Sing, Vee Over Gee 70.00
Figurine, No. 111/I, Wayside Harmony, Full Bee 375.00
Figurine, No. 124/0, Hello, Full Bee 350.00
Figurine, No. 127, Doctor, Full Bee 100.00
Figurine, No. 131, Street Singer, Vee Over Gee 85.00
Figurine, No. 141/3/0, Apple Tree Girl, Last Bee . . . . .85.00 to 125.00
Figurine, No. 142/I, Apple Tree Boy, Full Bee 600.00
Figurine, No. 143/3/0, Apple Tree Boy, Last Bee 125.00
Figurine, No. 150/2/0, Happy Days, Full Bee 300.00
Figurine, No. 152/0A, Umbrella Boy, Last Bee 475.00
Figurine, No. 152/0B, Umbrella Girl, Last Bee 475.00
Figurine, No. 169, Bird Duet, Stylized Bee 55.00
Figurine, No. 174, She Loves Me, She Loves Me Not, Full Bee . . . . .90.00 to 275.00
Figurine, No. 174, She Loves Me, She Loves Me Not, Stylized Bee 70.00
Figurine, No. 175, Mother's Darling, Full Bee . . . . .80.00 to 235.00
Figurine, No. 175, Mother's Darling, Vee Over Gee 145.00
Figurine, No. 175, Mothers Darling, Stylized 145.00
Figurine, No. 176/0, Happy Birthday, Last Bee 185.00

Figurine, No. 178, Photographer, Three Line Mark 185.00
Figurine, No. 179, Coquettes, Stylized Bee ....175.00 to 325.00
Figurine, No. 182, Good Friends, Stylized Bee 225.00
Figurine, No. 188, Celestial Musician, Three Line Mark 150.00
Figurine, No. 195/2/0, Barnyard Hero, Three Line Mark 90.00
Figurine, No. 196/0, Telling Her Secret, Stylized Bee 325.00
Figurine, No. 198/2/0, Home From Market, Missing Bee 110.00
Figurine, No. 200/0, Little Goat Herder, Stylized Bee 225.00
Figurine, No. 201, Retreat To Safety, 5 In. 235.00
Figurine, No. 220, We Congratulate, Full Bee ....40.00 to 170.00
Figurine, No. 240, Little Drummer, Vee Over Gee 125.00
Figurine, No. 300, Bird Watcher, Vee Over Gee 115.00
Figurine, No. 306, Little Bookkeeper, Three Line Mark 300.00
Figurine, No. 307, Good Hunting, Stylized Bee 550.00
Figurine, No. 308, Little Tailor, Vee Over Gee 123.00
Figurine, No. 321, Wash Day, Last Bee 70.00
Figurine, No. 321, Wash Day, Three Line Mark 300.00
Figurine, No. 327, Run-A-Way, Full Bee 100.00
Figurine, No. 328, Carnival, Three Line Mark 240.00
Figurine, No. 336, Close Harmony, Three Line Mark 125.00
Figurine, No. 345, A Fair Measure, Vee Over Gee 155.00
Figurine, No. 346, Smart Little Sister, Three Line Mark 100.00
Figurine, No. 386, On Secret Path, Last Bee 240.00
Figurine, No. 396, Ride Into Christmas, Vee Over Gee 230.00
Figurine, No. 421, It's Cold, Missing Bee 145.00
Figurine, No. 422, What Now?, Missing Bee 150.00
Lamp, No. 229, Apple Tree Girl, Stylized Bee, 10 1/2 In. 175.00
Lamp, No. 230, Apple Tree Boy, Stylized Bee, 10 3/4 In. 175.00
Plaque, 60 Years, Box 225.00
Plaque, No. 125, Vacation Time, Crown Mark 300.00
Plaque, No. 168, Standing Boy, Full Bee 250.00
Plaque, No. 180, Tuneful Goodnight, Crown Mark 300.00
Plaque, No. 310, Searching Angel, Vee Over Gee 165.00
Plaque, No. 323, Merry Christmas, Vee Over Gee 165.00
Plaque, No. 690, Smiling Through, Vee Over Gee 75.00
Plaque, No. 767, Puppy Love, 60 Year Anniversary 190.00
Plate, Anniversary, 1975, Stormy Weather 200.00
Plate, Annual, 1971, Heavenly Angel, Box ....370.00 to 400.00
Plate, Annual, 1972, Hear Ye, Hear Ye 35.00
Plate, Annual, 1973, Globe Trotter, Box 45.00
Plate, Annual, 1975, Ride Into Christmas 80.00
Plate, Annual, 1976, Apple Tree Girl ....25.00 to 45.00
Plate, Annual, 1977, Apple Tree Boy, Box 45.00
Plate, Annual, 1978, Happy Pastime ....45.00 to 95.00
Plate, Annual, 1979, Singing Lesson, Box ....40.00 to 75.00

HUTSCHENREUTHER Porcelain Company of Selb, Germany, was established in 1814 and is still working. The company makes fine quality porcelain dinnerwares and figurines. The mark has changed through the years, but the name and the lion insignia appear in most versions.

Figurine, Dancer On Gold Ball, Signed, 8 1/2 In. 320.00
Figurine, Dancer, Polychrome, Signed, 9 In. 220.00
Figurine, Deer, Lying 265.00
Figurine, Doe 75.00
Figurine, Dog, Poodle, White ....175.00 to 185.00
Figurine, Girl Playing Flute 85.00
Figurine, Mephisto, Signed, 7 1/2 In. 330.00
Figurine, Nude Female, Feeding Deer, 20th Century, 9 1/2 In. 402.00
Figurine, Nude Figure, White, On Gold Ball, 1930 .... 400.00
Figurine, Nude Woman, Bisque, 13 In. 800.00
Pipe, Stag Scene, Twig Stem, 30 In. 50.00
Plaque, General Hoche, Green Jacket, Gilt Border, 3 1/4 In. 172.00

Plate, Cobalt & Gilt Scalloped Rim, 9 1/2 In., 15 Piece 345.00
Plate, Roses Of Redoute, Box, Certificate, 8 Piece 175.00
Stein, Tobacco Pouch, Porcelain, Inlaid Lid, 1/2 Liter 1072.00

ICONS, special, revered pictures of Jesus, Mary, or a saint, are usually
Russian or Byzantine. The small icons collected today are made of
wood and tin or precious metals. Many modern copies have been made
in the old style and are being sold to tourists in Russia and Europe.

Adoration Of Mother Of God, Gilded Silver Oklad, Moscow, 1856, 13 1/4 x 11 1/4 In. ... 4025.00
Alexi Man Of God, Aleksey Chelovek Bozhly Depicted As Holy Fool, 1900, 8 x 10 In. ... 784.00
All Seeing Eye Of God, Christ Emanuel In Center Circle, Faux Enamel Borders, 12 In. ... 1680.00
Anastasis, Metal Border, 1700, 16 3/4 x 16 3/4 In. 3450.00
Annunciation, Applied Metal Basma, 17 x 14 In. 4600.00
Annunciation, St. Nicholas Of Mojhaisk, Foliate Silver Basma, 12 1/2 x 10 1/2 In. 2587.00
Archangel Gabriel, Gold Leaf, Strapwork, Scrolled Foliage, Russia, c.1890, 18 x 10 In. .. 840.00
Archangel Michael, Russia, 1800, 20 x 42 In. .... Illus 12096.00
Birth Of Christ, 16th Century Style, Russia, 19th Century, 19 x 17 1/2 In. 3810.00
Blessing Of The Children, Christ At Center Surround By Children & Apostles, 14 In. 2240.00
Christ Appearing At Sea Of Tiberias, Russia, Late 18th Century, 20 1/2 x 18 In. 1035.00
Christ Enthroned, 19th Century, 20 x 17 In. 4887.00
Christ Flanked By Chosen Saints, Composition, Greece, 19th Century, 24 x 16 In. 4025.00
Christ The Pantokrater, With Book, Silver Gilt Riza, Russia, 19th Century, 6 3/4 In. 200.00
Convincing Of Holy Apostle Thomas, Resurrected Christ Amidst Apostles, 12 x 10 In. ... 2800.00
Council Of The Archangel Michael, Embroidered, Oval, Frame, Russia, 20 x 14 1/2 In. .. 1610.00
Cross, Patriarchal, Crucifixion Surrounded By Major Feast Days, Bronze, 16 x 9 In. 728.00
Crucifixion, Lord Sabbath & The Sun, Which Has Darkened, 12 1/4 x 10 1/2 In. 1120.00
Diptych, 9 Festivals & Elevation Of The Chalice, 2 Panels, Greece, 1700, 9 x 14 In. 4885.00
Doll, Infant Of Prague, Chalkware, Blue Satin & Silver Lace Gown, Italy 65.00
Dormition Of Holy Virgin, Silver Oklad Border, Russia, 1700, 12 x 10 In. 2585.00
Extended Deisis, Bronze, 19th Century, 5 x 4 In. 179.00
Feodorskaya Mother Of God, Byzantine Style, Russia, 19th Century, 10 1/2 x 8 3/4 In. ... 335.00
Fire-Appearing Mother Of God, Mary Depicted Without Child, 19th Century, 14 In. 1344.00
Florus & Laurus, Archangel Michael Holding Holy Napkin, 1890, 12 1/4 x 10 In. 1344.00
Holy Virgin Contemplating Crucified Christ, Greece, 18th Century, 11 3/4 x 9 In. 1150.00
Holy Virgin Key To Wisdom, Selected Saint Border, 19th Century, 12 x 10 In. 2300.00
Iverskaya Mother Of God, Mount Athos, Mary Pointing To Her Son Christ, 14 x 12 In. .. 1960.00
Kazan Mother Of God, Mary & Christ Delivering A Blessing, Gold Leaf, 12 x 10 In. 2688.00
Kazan Mother Of God, Repousse Silver Riza, Seed Pearls, 12 1/2 x 10 1/2 In. ...... Illus 4480.00
Kazan Mother Of God, Young Girl Matrona, Silver Gilt Repousse, Chased Riza, 12 In. .. 1680.00
King Of Kings, Christ Enthroned & Robed As Bishop, Mary At His Right, 12 x 14 In. ... 3472.00
Korsun Mother Of God, Mother & Child In Endearing Embrace, 19th Century, 12 In. ... 2800.00
Korsunskaya Efesskaya Mother Of God, Great Prince Vladimir On Black Sea, 12 In. 1904.00
Lord Almighty, Christ Delivering A Blessing, Holding Book Of Gospels, 12 1/4 x 10 In. . 1960.00

Icon, Archangel
Michael, Russia, 1800,
20 x 42 In.

Icon, Kazan Mother Of God,
Repousse Silver Riza, Seed
Pearls, 12 1/2 x 10 1/2 In.

Icon, Triptych, Saint, Micro-Mosaic,
Russia, 1855,
7 1/2 x 6 1/2 In.

Madonna & Child, Punched Tin, Mexico, 10 x 6 3/4 In. 67.00
Mary Of Egypt With Life Scenes, Mary Of Egypt, Actress & Prostitute, 11 x 9 In. 1960.00
Metrophan Bishop Of Voronezhskiy & Miracle Worker, 1850, 9 x 11 1/2 In. 1680.00
Mid Pentecost, Boy Christ Is Surrounded By Learned Men In Temple, 12 1/4 x 10 In. ... 1680.00
Mother Of God, Festival Celebrating Mary's Ascension Into Heaven, 14 x 12 In. 1904.00
Mother Of God, Life-Giving Wellspring, Mary Holding Infant Christ, 1800, 12 x 14 In. .. 1400.00
Mother Of God, Melter Of Hearts, Prophecy Of Simeon, 1800, 7 1/4 x 9 In. 616.00
Mother Of God, Soothe My Sorrow, Virgin Holding Infant Son Across Chest, 12 In. 896.00
Mother Of God & Child, Kneeling Saint, Silver Oklad, Russia, 12 1/2 x 10 1/2 In. 3740.00
Mother Of God Hodegitria, Early 18th Century, 11 3/4 x 9 1/2 In. 575.00
Mother Of God Of Iberia, Chased Oklad, Gilt Metal Frame, Russia, 19th Century, 3 In. .. 205.00
Mother Of God Of The Sign, 17th Century, 12 3/8 x 10 1/2 In. 3220.00
Nativity, Mary, Lying Before A Cave In A Hill, 1900, 12 1/4 x 10 1/2 In. 2352.00
Nativity Of Mother Of God, Early 19th Century, 17 1/4 x 14 1/2 In. 3162.00
New Testament Trinity, 3 Persons Of The Trinity Depicting Christ, 1890, 12 x 14 In. 1624.00
Old Testament Trinity, Abraham & Sara Waiting On 3 Angels Seated At Table, 12 In. ... 1344.00
Pendant, St. Nicholas, Carved Ivory, Russia, 19th-20th Century, 2 x 1 3/4 In. 290.00
Prophet Daniel, Holding Scroll In His Left Hand, 24 1/2 x 15 1/2 In. 7475.00
Prophet Noah, Holding Ark, Russia, 19th Century, 19 1/2 x 15 1/2 In. 5375.00
Prophet Zakharia, 1700, 19 1/4 x 16 1/4 In. 2070.00
Resurrection, Christ, Above His Tomb, 1900, 12 1/4 x 10 In. 3080.00
Resurrection With Feasts, Descent Into Hades, Faux Enameled Borders, 1890, 12 In. ... 1456.00
Selected Saints, Holy Martyr John, Venerable Mary Of Egypt, St. Nicholas, 9 x 7 In. 448.00
Smolensk Mother Of God, Virgin & Christ Child In Seed Pearls, Gemstones, 13 In. 6160.00
St. Alexander Nevsky, Gilded Silver Oklad, St. Petersburg, 1895, 10 x 8 1/2 In. 2530.00
St. Dmitrios, Greece, 18th Century, 9 x 7 In. 1150.00
St. Emogen Patriarch, Faux Border, Gilt Ground, Moscow, 1900, 3 1/2 x 2 In. 308.00
St. George, Atop His Horse Plunging A Lance Into Dragon, Gold Leaf, 12 In. 1400.00
St. George, Slaying The Dragon, Russia, 19th Century, 17 1/2 x 15 3/4 In. 2300.00
St. John The Baptist, Hagiographical, Early 19th Century, 17 1/2 x 14 1/2 In. 2300.00
St. John The Evangelist, 1800, 17 1/2 x 14 3/4 In. 2875.00
St. Nicholas, Bishop, Repousse & Chased Riza, Russia, 19th Century, 12 1/4 x 10 In. 560.00
St. Nicholas, Delivering A Blessing, Holding Gospels Open, Faux Enamel, 8 In. 1344.00
St. Nicholas, Depicted As A Bishop, Christ On Left Presenting Gospels, 11 In. 1232.00
St. Nicholas, Gilded Silver Oklad, Chased Strapwork, Foliage, 1875, 17 3/4 x 14 3/4 In. .. 2587.00
St. Nicholas, Hagiographical, 19th Century, 21 x 17 In. 2300.00
St. Nicholas, Silver Border Chased With Scrolling Leaves, Moscow, 1740, 12 x 10 In. ... 2070.00
St. Nicholas, Western Style, Red Cape, Russia, 19th Century, 12 1/4 x 10 1/2 In. 670.00
St. Nicholas, With Saints, Enamel, Bronze, 19th Century, 5 x 4 In. 196.00
St. Pantelemon, Faux Enameled Borders, Gilt Ground, 1900, 5 1/2 x 7 In. 392.00
St. Pantelemon, Russia, 19th Century, 11 x 8 3/4 In. 375.00
St. Seraphim Of Sarov, Seraphim In Midst Of Wilderness, Kneeling Before Icon, 14 In. ... 1120.00
Tikhvin Mother Of God, Gilded Silver Oklad, 1820, 19 1/2 x 15 3/4 In. 4025.00
Tolga Mother Of God, Russia, Early 18th Century, 12 1/2 x 11 In. 977.00
Triptych, Christ At Center Flanked By Mary & John, Bronze, 8 x 3 In. 252.00
Triptych, Christ Enthroned, Gilt Silver Oklad, Russia, 18th Century, 7 3/4 x 9 3/4 In. 3450.00
Triptych, Folding, Selected Saints, The Annunciation At Top, Bronze, 5 In. 140.00
Triptych, Saint, Micro-Mosaic, Russia, 1855, 7 1/2 x 6 1/2 In. ....*Illus* 19600.00
Unburnt Thornbush Mother Of God, Bronze, 19th Century, 3 1/4 x 3 1/4 In. 100.00
Virgin Kazanskaya, Silvered Brass Riza & Kiot, Russia, 1860s, 5 x 4 In. 200.00
Virgin Of Tenderness, Brass Riza, Russia, 12 1/4 x 10 3/4 In. 460.00
Virgin Of Tenderness, Embroidered, Painted Hands & Face, 8 3/8 x 6 1/2 In. 200.00
Virgin With 3 Hands, Gilded Silver Oklad, Seed Pearl Robes, 19th Century, 12 x 10 In. .. 3737.00
Vladimir Mother Of God, Mother & Child, Cheek-To-Cheek, Enamel Borders, 12 In. 2016.00

IMARI patterns are named for the Japanese ware characteristically decorated with orange, red, green, and blue stylized designs. The bamboo,
floral, and geometric patterns on the Japanese ware became so familiar that the name *Imari* has come to mean any patterns of this type. It
has been copied by Asian, European, and American factories since the
eighteenth century. It is still being made.

Bowl, Asymmetrical Floral Interior, Exterior Panels, Scalloped Mouth, 8 1/2 In. 546.00
Bowl, Chrysanthemum Form, Enamel Floral Center, Brocade, 1860, 9 5/8 In. 407.00

Bowl, Cover, Allover Red, Blue & Gold Floral, 18th Century, 4 x 5 1/2 In. 805.00
Bowl, Fan Form, Phoenix Design, 10 1/2 In. 385.00
Bowl, Floral Design, Iron Red, Cobalt, Gold Interior, 3 x 7 1/2 In. 488.00
Bowl, Floral Design, Shallow, 12 1/4 In. 575.00
Bowl, Floral Filled Panel, Hexagonal, 9 In. 375.00
Bowl, Floral Medallion, Shield-Shaped Panels, Flowers, Signed, 18th Century, 13 In. 345.00
Bowl, Floral Reserve Center, Gold Outlined, Scalloped Rim, Late 19th Century, 15 In. . . . 2250.00
Bowl, Kwannon Bosatsu, Blue Drip Rim, Cloud Ground, 19th Century, 6 In. 220.00
Bowl, Overall Fan Shaped Panels With Exotic Birds, Free-Form Leaf, Floral Design, 8 In. . . 632.00
Bowl, Prunus Boughs With Roosting Birds, Brocaded Fan Panels, 10 In. 805.00
Bowl, Red & Blue Chrysanthemums, Panels, Gate, Butterflies, Fukagawa Mark, 9 1/2 In. . . 140.00
Bowl, Scalloped Edge, Circular, 10 In. 213.00
Charger, Blue Center Design, Flowers, Butterflies In Various Shapes, 18 1/4 In. 505.00
Charger, Central Vase Of Floral Design, 18 1/4 In. 430.00
Charger, Floral Design, Late 19th Century, 13 1/4 In. 149.00
Charger, Floral Landscape, Birds, Late 19th Century, 15 3/4 In. 230.00
Charger, Foo Dogs, House Boats, Floral Design In Windows, Blue & Red Reverse, 18 In. . . 670.00
Charger, Landscape, Horse Filled, Prunus Center, Bird, Floral Cartouches, 18 In. 1045.00
Charger, Mandarin Duck Scene, Early 19th Century, 14 1/2 In. 247.00
Charger, Peony Flowers, 3 Panels, Foo Dogs, Fans, Cobalt Zigzag Border, 18 In. 445.00
Charger, Phoenix, Landscape, Floral & Foliate Design, 8 1/2 In. 1095.00
Charger, Pine Tree Design, Cobalt Bamboo, Deep Red, Green, Yellow, Gold Border, 3 In. . 632.00
Charger, Polychrome, Man On Boat, Heron, Panels, Red & Blue On Reverse, 18 1/2 In. . . . 365.00
Charger, Stand, 19 In. 440.00
Chop Plate, Blue & White, Japan, 12 1/4 In. 82.00
Chop Plate, Floral Design, 3 Panels, 2 Birds, Cobalt & Geometric Design, 14 1/2 In. 505.00
Cup & Saucer, Gilt, 1800-1825 . . . . 110.00
Dish, Scallop Shell, Painted Clumps Of Flowering Plants, 7 2/3 In., 6 Pair 2990.00
Ginger Jar, Arita Style, Blue & White, Floral, Dragons, Foo Dog Finial, 12 1/2 In. 225.00
Ginger Jar, Polychrome, Warrior On Horse, Panel Of Birds & Flowers, Ball Finial, 13 In. . . 225.00
Jar, Barrel Form, Flower Garden, Brocade Design, 1900, 7 In. 120.00
Jar, Cover, Bird, Floral & Foliate, Foo Dog Finial, 21 In. 1150.00
Jardiniere, Flowers, Bird, & Landscape, 14 x 19 In. 460.00
Jardiniere, Ormolu Mounted, Landscape, Dragon Form Handles, 14 In. 1495.00
Mug, Floral, Bulbous, 19th Century, 3 1/2 In. 220.00
Plate, Alternating Floral, Brocade, Garden Trellis, Blue, Gilt Floral Center, 13 In. 120.00
Plate, Floral Center, Floral Border, Scalloped Edge, 19th Century, 8 1/2 In. 135.00
Plate, Floral Spray, Butterfly, Floral Border With Swimming Carp, 1 1/2 x 11 3/8 In. 103.00
Plate, Flower Form, Brush & Floral Center, 8 1/2 In. 33.00
Plate, Flower Form, Peach Center, Porcelain, 19th Century, 9 1/2 In. 50.00
Plate, Flowers, Bird Border Reserves, 1850-1875, 9 5/8 In. 275.00
Plate, Hundred Butterflies, Allover Butterflies & Insects, Multicolored Enamels, 8 1/4 In. . 110.00
Plate, Nobleman Crossing Bridge, Flowering Foliage, 8 1/2 In., 6 Piece 920.00
Plate, Scalloped & Fluted, 13 1/2 In. 650.00
Platter, 2 Panels, Bird, Branch & Deer, Flowers, Cobalt, Red & Gold, 16 x 12 5/8 In. 250.00
Serving Dish, Leaves, Open Handles, Square, England, 1815, 7 In., Pair 650.00
Tray, Peony, Shishi, Dragon Design, Square, 10 1/4 In. 495.00
Tray, Polychrome, Scalloped Open Handles, Foo Dogs, Flowers, Vines, Gold Trim, 14 In. . 225.00
Umbrella Stand, 19th Century, 24 In. 135.00
Umbrella Stand, Cobalt Blue Design, Phoenix, Dragons, Medallions, Flowers, 24 In. 1430.00
Vase, 2 Men Play Music In Garden, 3 Children, Pink & Green Flowers, Black, 15 In. 55.00
Vase, Allover Floral, Tree, Peonies, Cobalt Border, Ruffled Rim, 18 1/2 x 8 In. 365.00
Vase, Arita Style, Blue & White, Raised Dragon On Both Sides, 12 x 6 1/2 In. 165.00
Vase, Bird, Insect & Floral, Spherical Base, 18 In. 690.00
Vase, Blue Floral Panels, Art Deco Brass Base, Late 19th Century, 9 1/4 x 6 In. 515.00
Vase, Blue, Red & Gilt Floral Panels, Exotic Birds, Creatures, Mounted As Lamp, 14 In. . . 1980.00
Vase, Cover, Baluster, Birds & Floral Sprays, Gilt, 19th Century, 24 In. 4025.00
Vase, Floral & Medallion, Bulbous, Narrow Tapering Neck, 6 1/2 In., Pair 440.00
Vase, Flower Panels, Ormolu Mounted, Dragon Form Handles, 6 Sides, 10 In., Pair 1610.00
Vase, Foliate Design, Reserves Of Birds, Female Mask Handles, Late 19th Century, 9 In. . . 405.00
Vase, Ormolu Mounted, 6 Sides, Japan, 10 3/4 In., Pair 1610.00
Vase, Overall Floral Brocading, Diapering Within Landscape Scene, 26 In. 862.00

IMPERIAL GLASS Corporation was founded in Bellaire, Ohio, in 1901. It became a subsidiary of Lenox, Inc., in 1973 and was sold to Arthur R. Lorch in 1981. It was sold again in 1982, and went bankrupt in 1984. In 1985, the molds and some assets were sold. The Imperial glass preferred by the collector is freehand art glass, carnival glass, slag glass, stretch glass, and other top-quality tablewares. Tablewares and animals are listed here. The others may be found in the appropriate sections.

Animal, Airedale, Caramel Slag	180.00
Art Glass, Vase, Gold Iridescent Exterior, 3 Holly Leaves Rising From Base, 10 In.	575.00
Art Glass, Vase, White Case, Cobalt Blue Exterior, Orange Iridescent Rim Interior, 9 In.	575.00
Candlewick, Ashtray, 5 In.	8.00
Candlewick, Bonbon, Heart Shape, Handle Turned To Center	20.00
Candlewick, Bowl, 10 1/2 In.	50.00
Candlewick, Bowl, 2 Handles, 9 In.	30.00
Candlewick, Bowl, 2 Sections, Oval, 11 In.	575.00
Candlewick, Bowl, 6 In.	12.00
Candlewick, Bowl, Blue, 5 In.	45.00
Candlewick, Bowl, Footed, 10 In.	205.00
Candlewick, Bowl, Heart Shape, 5 1/2 In.	25.00
Candlewick, Bowl, Oval, 14 In.	329.00
Candlewick, Bowl, Ribbed, Floral Cutting, Footed	120.00
Candlewick, Butter, Cover, 1/4 Lb.	40.00
Candlewick, Cake Knife	550.00
Candlewick, Cake Plate, Birthday, 72 Candleholders, 14 In.	500.00
Candlewick, Candlestick, 3 1/2 In., Pair	125.00
Candlewick, Cocktail, Seafood, Icer Insert	90.00
Candlewick, Compote, 5 In.	145.00
Candlewick, Condiment Set, 4 Piece	130.00
Candlewick, Cruet, 4 Oz.	48.00
Candlewick, Cruet, 6 Oz.	75.00
Candlewick, Cup & Saucer	15.00
Candlewick, Dish, Mayonnaise, 2 Sections, 3-Footed	85.00
Candlewick, Dish, Mayonnaise, Underplate	40.00
Candlewick, Fork & Spoon Set	30.00
Candlewick, Goblet, 10 Oz.	20.00 to 40.00
Candlewick, Lamp, Hurricane	165.00
Candlewick, Lemon Tray	47.00
Candlewick, Marmalade	110.00
Candlewick, Mustard, Cover	26.00
Candlewick, Nut Cup	12.00
Candlewick, Pitcher, 80 Oz.	195.00
Candlewick, Plate, 7 In.	10.00
Candlewick, Plate, 9 In.	45.00
Candlewick, Plate, Deviled Egg	150.00
Candlewick, Plate, Dinner, 10 In.	45.00
Candlewick, Platter, 16 In.	275.00
Candlewick, Powder Box, Cover	200.00
Candlewick, Punch Bowl, Cover, Ladle	850.00
Candlewick, Relish, 2 Sections, 6 In.	25.00
Candlewick, Relish, 2 Sections, 8 In.	30.00
Candlewick, Relish, 2 Sections, Handle, 7 1/2 In.	35.00
Candlewick, Relish, 3 Sections, 10 In.	75.00
Candlewick, Relish, 4 Sections, Rectangular, 12 In.	115.00
Candlewick, Relish, 5 Sections, 13 In.	80.00 to 130.00
Candlewick, Salt & Pepper	17.00
Candlewick, Soup, Cream	50.00 to 55.00
Candlewick, Sugar & Creamer	17.00
Candlewick, Tray, 3 Sections, 8 In.	50.00
Candlewick, Tray, Fruit, Center Handle, 10 1/2 In.	295.00
Candlewick, Tray, Pastry, Center Handle, Red, 11 1/2 In.	500.00
Candlewick, Tumbler, 12 Oz.	10.00

Candlewick, Vase, Bud, 7 In.	450.00
Candlewick, Vase, Bud, 8 1/2 In.	150.00
Candlewick, Vase, Ruffled Edge, 6 In.	75.00
Candlewick, Vase, Ruffled Edge, 8 In.	125.00
Cape Cod, Basket	350.00
Cape Cod, Bowl, 2 Sections, Oval, 11 In.	95.00
Cape Cod, Bowl, 10 In.	80.00
Cape Cod, Bowl, 12 1/2 In.	50.00
Cape Cod, Bowl, Heart Shape, 5 In.	15.00
Cape Cod, Cake Plate	75.00
Cape Cod, Cake Plate, 4-Footed	100.00
Cape Cod, Cake Stand, 10 In.	65.00
Cape Cod, Cake Stand, 11 In.	125.00
Cape Cod, Centerpiece	65.00
Cape Cod, Coaster	10.00
Cape Cod, Cocktail, Oyster	7.00
Cape Cod, Compote, Footed, 7 In.	65.00
Cape Cod, Condiment Set, 5 Piece	350.00
Cape Cod, Cordial, 1 1/2 Oz.	10.00
Cape Cod, Cordial, Red, 1 1/2 Oz.	35.00
Cape Cod, Creamer	15.00
Cape Cod, Cruet, 4 Oz.	20.00
Cape Cod, Cruet, 6 Oz.	48.00
Cape Cod, Decanter Set, Ruby, Stopper, 30 Oz., 5 Piece	500.00
Cape Cod, Decanter Set, Rye, Bourbon, Scotch, Raised Letters, Metal Stand	650.00
Cape Cod, Decanter, 24 Oz.	65.00
Cape Cod, Decanter, 30 Oz.	88.00
Cape Cod, Decanter, Stopper, Ruby, 30 Oz.	365.00
Cape Cod, Dish, Spider, Handle, 6 In.	38.00
Cape Cod, Eggcup	32.00
Cape Cod, Goblet, 11 Oz.	6.00
Cape Cod, Mustard, Cover	23.00 to 25.00
Cape Cod, Pepper Mill	30.00
Cape Cod, Pitcher, Ice Lip, 40 Oz.	85.00
Cape Cod, Pitcher, Milk, 1 Pt.	43.00 to 50.00
Cape Cod, Plate, 5 In.	12.00
Cape Cod, Plate, 6 1/2 In.	7.00
Cape Cod, Plate, 14 In.	30.00
Cape Cod, Punch Cup	7.00
Cape Cod, Salt Shaker	20.00
Cape Cod, Sherbet, Low, 6 Oz.	5.00 to 9.00
Cape Cod, Sherbet, Ruby	19.00
Cape Cod, Sugar & Creamer	35.00
Cape Cod, Tray, Square, 8 In.	300.00
Cape Cod, Tumbler, Footed, 10 Oz.	10.00
Cape Cod, Tumbler, Footed, 12 Oz.	10.00
Cape Cod, Vase, Bud, 6 3/4 In.	50.00
Cathay, Bookend, Lu-Tung	175.00
Cathay, Bowl, Flower, Junk Boat	85.00 to 95.00
Cathay, Pagoda, 3 Piece	650.00
Cut Glass, Centerpiece, Stretch, Green Iridescent, 12 1/2 x 5 In.	130.00
Frosted Block, Rose Bowl, White, 5 In.	25.00
Grape, Bowl, Ruby Slag, Ruffled Edge	75.00
Grape, Pitcher, Ruby Slag	95.00
Molly, Cup & Saucer, Pink	12.00
Molly, Plate, Pink, 8 In.	11.00
Molly, Sugar & Creamer, Pink	22.00
Owl, Sugar & Creamer, Purple Slag	75.00
Persian Medallion, Vase, Urn Shape, Vaseline, Opalescent, Fluted, 1970s	35.00
Ripple, Vase, Clambroth Carnival, 9 3/4 In.	55.00
Ripple, Vase, Green Carnival, 9 3/4 In.	65.00
Rose, Bowl, Red Slag, Ruffled Edge, 9 In.	45.00
Southern Lady, Bell, Sticker	40.00

INDIAN art from North America has attracted the collector for many years. Each tribe has its own distinctive designs and techniques. Baskets, jewelry, pottery, and leatherwork are of greatest collector interest. Eskimo art is listed in another category in this book.

Awl Case, Apache, Woman's, Beaded, Tin Cones, c.1890, 10 x 1 1/2 In.	990.00
Ax, Hohokam, Arizona, 5 5/8 In.	120.00
Ax, Midwest, Illinois, 3/4 Groove, 6 7/8 In.	165.00
Baby Carrier, Hupa, Basketry	440.00
Bag, Apache, Plains, Beaded, Rosette, 6 In.	605.00
Bag, Apache, Western, Beaded & Fringed, 15 In.	412.00
Bag, Bandolier, Sioux, Otter & Mirror, Beaded & Quill Panel, Ray Hawkins, 1961, 42 In.	440.00
Bag, Bandolier, Woodlands, Beaded Flowers, Leaves & Vines, Tassels, 1890s, 40 x 14 In.	1210.00
Bag, Medicine, Crow, Sinew Sewn, Tin Cones, Horsehair Suspensions, c.1880, 8 x 6 In.	605.00
Bag, Medicine, Navajo, Purple Velvet, Misc. Contents, 1930s, 10 1/2 x 12 1/2 In.	165.00
Bag, Micmac, Bilateral Floral Bead Work, Velvet, Silk, Mid 1800s, 4 1/2 In.	230.00
Bag, Nez Perce, Corn Husk, Rainbow Colored Yarn Design, 1950s-1960s, 10 x 8 In.	385.00
Bag, Nez Perce, Flat, Beaded Roses, Hide Back, 1940s-1950s, 13 1/2 x 10 1/2 In.	385.00
Bag, Northern Plains, Beaded Rosette, c.1900, Round, 4 1/2 In.	250.00
Bag, Northern Plains, Parfleche, Fringed, Buckskin, c.1890, 11 1/2 x 43 In.	3738.00
Bag, Northern Plains, Parfleche, Polychrome, Long Buckskin Fringe, c.1890	3737.50
Bag, Plains, Beaded & Fringed, 5 1/2 In.	143.00
Bag, Plains, Beads & Cones, Circular, 6 1/8 In.	770.00
Bag, Plains, Double Tab, Beaded, c.1890, 7 1/2 In.	105.00
Bag, Pouch, Leather, Beaded, Geometric, 2 Loops, Tourist Ware, 4 x 3 In.	95.00
Bag, Sioux, Beaded, Quilled, c.1880, 4 1/2 x 4 In.	330.00
Bag, Sioux, Pipe, Sinew Sewn, Alice Blackhorse, 33 In.	715.00
Bag, Tlingit, Octopus, Bilateral Floral, White, Yellow, Green, Blue, c.1890, 19 1/2 In.	1380.00
Bag, Woodland, Beaded, Floral, Cloth Handle, 6 1/2 x 6 In.	55.00
Bannerstone, Banded Slate, Tubular Type, Hole Drilled Vertically, 3 In.	160.00
Basket, Apache, Burden, Geometric Design, Hide Drops, Tin Cones, 1960s, 15 x 24 In.	495.00
Basket, Apache, Burden, Polychrome, 1900s-1920s, 14 1/2 x 16 In.	2750.00
Basket, Apache, Burden, Red Trade Cloth, Hide Bottom, Fringed, 1900s-1920s, 12 In.	1320.00
Basket, Apache, Burden, Tin Cones, 12 In., Pair	55.00
Basket, Apache, Pinion Pitch Covered, Horsehair Handles, 1920s, 12 x 8 In.	140.00
Basket, Apache, Polychrome, 1920s, 2 x 8 In.	770.00
Basket, Bowl, Apache, Coiled, Willow & Devil's Claw, 8 1/2 In.	1200.00
Basket, Bowl, Hupa, 1920, 7 1/2 x 4 In.	770.00
Basket, Bowl, Mission, Polychrome, Radiating Steps, Brown, Yellow, c.1900, 11 3/4 In.	1093.00
Basket, Bowl, Pima, Coiled, 3 1/2 x 12 In.	660.00
Basket, Bowl, Ute, Coiled, 4 x 14 In.	145.00
Basket, Bowl, Yokut, Coiled, Polychrome, Hour Glass Motif, Mid 1800s, 11 3/4 In.	2185.00
Basket, Bowl, Yokut, Polychrome Design, 1950s, 2 x 4 In.	220.00
Basket, Canoe, Maine, Woven Reed	2750.00
Basket, Chemehuevi, Tray, Polychrome, c.1940, 3 x 13 In.	2640.00
Basket, Cherokee, Splint, Red, Green, Blue, Herringbone, Twist Handles, 6 1/2 x 10 In.	140.00
Basket, Cherokee, Work, Handle, 8 1/2 In.	70.00
Basket, Choctaw, Chevron Design, Cover, 29 x 22 In.	545.00
Basket, Cover, Clemencia Flores, 1930s, 7 1/8 x 7 3/4 In.	90.00
Basket, Desert Cahuilla, Orange, Brown Woven Design, c.1905, 13 1/2 In.	1045.00
Basket, Havasupai, Polychrome, Natural & Analine Red Dye, 1920s-1930s, 5 x 8 In.	525.00
Basket, Havasupai, Twine, Varnished, 1920s, 8 x 13 In.	195.00
Basket, Hopi, 2nd Mesa, Crow Mother, Mud Heads, 1950s-1960s, 6 1/2 x 10 1/2 In.	470.00
Basket, Hopi, Coil, Eagle Design, 1960s, 14 In.	415.00
Basket, Jicarilla Apache, Polychrome, c.1920, 16 x 4 1/2 In.	230.00
Basket, Klamth, Gambling, 1900s, 16 1/2 In.	660.00
Basket, Klickitat, Berry, Geometric Design, c.1930, 4 x 4 1/2 In.	240.00
Basket, Klickitat, Polychrome, 1930, 8 x 3 In.	93.00
Basket, Mescalero, Tray, 2 1/2 x 14 In.	440.00
Basket, Mescalero, Tray, Flower Design, 1940s, 15 In.	415.00
Basket, Micmac, Birch Bark, Cover	2640.00
Basket, Miniature, Sweetgrass, Coil Construction, Signature Woven In, 1 1/2 x 3/4 In.	55.00
Basket, Mission, Flared Rim Juncus, c.1920, 5 1/2 x 3 1/2 In.	190.00

Basket, Mission, Flared Rim, 1920, 4 x 3 1/4 In.	385.00
Basket, Navajo, Flower Design, Sally Black, 1980s, 2 x 14 In.	440.00
Basket, Navajo, Wedding, 1950s, 3 x 12 In.	220.00
Basket, Navajo, Wedding, 1960s, 3 1/2 x 14 1/2 In.	165.00
Basket, Northeast, Splint Woven, Hickory Swing Handle, 11 x 12 In.	65.00
Basket, Northwest Coast, Canoe & Duck Design, 7 x 5 In.	72.00
Basket, Northwest, Makah, Duck Design, 1 1/2 x 3 1/2 In.	137.00
Basket, Papago, Double Rattlesnake, Spider, 1960s, 3 1/2 x 16 1/2 In.	605.00
Basket, Papago, Pictorial, Picking Cactus Apples, Julia Lewis, 1960s, 6 1/2 x 7 1/2 In.	250.00
Basket, Pawnee, Splintwork, Beaded, Butterfly Design, 5 1/8 In.	440.00
Basket, Penobscot, Ash Splint, 9 x 11 In.	65.00
Basket, Pima, Beaded Rim, 1920, 7 1/2 In.	550.00
Basket, Pima, Coiled, Human & Animal Figures, c.1920, 3/4 x 1/2 In.	143.00
Basket, Pima, Female Figures, 1930s, 3 x 9 In.	305.00
Basket, Pima, Figures, Father Kino Beads On Rim, 1900s, 5 x 10 In.	1100.00
Basket, Pima, Maze Pattern, Flared Sides, Early 1900s, 4 x 14 1/2 In.	1485.00
Basket, Pima, Olla, Willow & Devil's Claw, 8 x 9 1/2 In.	850.00
Basket, Pima, Woven, Tapered Sides, Braided Rim, 15 x 9 1/2 x 6 1/2 In.	275.00
Basket, Plains, Storage, Woven Grass, Vegetable Dyed Rings & Squares, 9 x 5 3/8 In.	110.00
Basket, Quinault, Berry, Woven Red, Brown, 1920, 5 x 5 In.	159.00
Basket, Tray, Papago, Geometric, 1930s, 3 x 14 In.	305.00
Basket, Wakashan, Trinket, Makah, Lid, Woven, Geometric Design, 2 x 4 In.	220.00
Basket, Washo, Grasshopper Stitch Bottom, 1920s, 2 1/2 x 6 1/2 In.	440.00
Belt, Beaded, Repeat Geometric Design, White Ground, Rawhide Strap, 32 1/4 In.	138.00
Belt, Central Plains, Childs, Harness Leather Strap, Metal Conchas, c.1900, 22 In.	173.00
Belt, Concha, Link Style, 12 Conchas & Buckle, Oscar Alexis, 1950s, 35 In.	125.00
Belt, Navajo, Concha, Diamond Slot Revival, Sand Cast Buckle, Leather, 1970s, 36 In.	880.00
Belt, Plains, Men's, Beaded, c.1880, 35 1/2 In.	120.00
Belt, Plains, With Pouch, Beaded, 27 1/2 In.	137.00
Belt, Sioux, Beaded With American Flag Design	247.00
Belt, Sioux, Beaded, Initialed SD, Dated 1904, 36 In.	395.00
Belt, Zuni, Concha, Sun Face, Turquoise, Mother-Of-Pearl, Coral, Shell, 1970s, 35 In.	495.00
Birdhouse, Tlingit, Long House, Cedar, Painted Design, 1940s, 22 x 16 x 19 In.	550.00
Blanket, Cayuse, Pendleton, 68 x 57 In.	295.00
Blanket, Navajo, Banded Pattern, Dyed & Natural Homespun Wool, 51 x 29 In.	201.00
Blanket, White Field, Red, Black, Orange Crosses, 1940s, 28 1/2 x 30 In.	305.00
Blouse, Navajo, Silver & Turquoise Buttons, Collar Tips, Pins, 1940s-1950s	330.00
Bolo Tie, Zuni, Mosaic Inlaid, Bent Rainbow Man, 1950s, 2 3/4 In.	110.00
Bolo Tie, Zuni, Silver, Fully Inlaid, Mud Head Kachina, c.1870, 2 x 2 In.	70.00
Bottle, Paiute, Beaded, White Ground, Blue & Green Design, 1950s, 10 In.	275.00
Bow, Cheyenne, Recurved With Original Sinew String, 1850s, 44 In.	550.00
Bow, Plains, Sinew Backed, Decorated, c.1870, 40 In.	960.00
Bow Case & Quiver, Lakota, Child's, Bar & Box Design, Hide, Late 1800s, 25 In.	3450.00
Bowl, Hopi, E. Poochico, c.1920, 4 1/2 In.	300.00
Bowl, Mississippi, Red, Double Handles, 7 1/2 In.	176.00
Bowl, San Ildefonso, Polished Blackware, Clara Martinez, 1980s, 3 x 4 1/2 In.	305.00
Bowl, San Ildefonso, Polished Blackware, Maria Poveka, 1970s, 3 1/2 x 4 1/2 In.	990.00
Bowl, San Ildefonso, Step Pattern, Pottery, Signed Marie, 3 1/2 x 8 1/2 In.	264.00
Bowl, Santa Clara, Blackware, Carved Water Serpent, Donna Tafoya, 6 x 6 In.	330.00
Bowl, Santa Clara, Carved Water Serpent Design, Phyllis Tayofa, 1960s, 4 x 7 In.	200.00
Bowl, Southwest, Terra Cotta, Wide Band Of Geometric Designs, 12 In.	415.00
Bowl, Zia, 1930s, 4 x 6 1/2 In.	275.00
Bowl, Zuni, Ceremonial, Polychrome Design, 4 x 9 In.	935.00
Bowl, Zuni, Orange, Brown Polychrome Design, 1890, 14 In.	2420.00
Box, Cree, Bride's, Cover, Square Nails, 19th Century, 9 1/2 x 23 3/4 In.	525.00
Box, Navajo, Peyote, Painted Design, 1950s, 6 x 19 1/2 In.	165.00
Box, Navajo, Silver, Overlaid Top, L. Long, 1970s, 6 1/2 x 4 In.	550.00
Box, Navajo, Silver, Stamped Design, Hinged Lid, 1960s, 2 x 4 x 5 1/2 In.	200.00
Box, Navajo, Silver, Stamped Design, Turquoise Stone, Susie James, 1970s, 3 x 5 In.	345.00
Box, Navajo, Silver, Sunburst Turquoise Design On Lid, 1970s-1980s, 7 x 4 1/2 In.	605.00
Box, Tlingit, Barrel Form, 3 In.	99.00
Bracelet, Navajo, Oval Turquoise Stone, Stamped Arrow Design, 1940s, 1 1/4 In.	195.00
Bracelet, Navajo, Shadow Box Style, 3 Turquoise Stones, 1970s, 2 In.	77.00

Bracelet, Navajo, Turquoise Stone, Stamped Crossed Arrows, Turtles, 1930s-1940s 110.00
Bracelet, Zuni, Inlaid Devil Dancer Center, c.1970, 6 In. 88.00
Bracelet, Zuni, Inlay Turquoise, Silver & Coral, 2 1/2 x 7 In. 170.00
Bracelet, Zuni, Mosaic, Inlaid Sun Face Design, 1970s, 2 In. 140.00
Breastplate, Hide, Shells, Horsehair, Trade Beads, c.1920, 21 x 9 In. 550.00
Breastplate, Nez Perce, Glass & Brass Beads, Bone Tubes, Silver Medallion, 11 In. 275.00
Buckle, Zuni, Inlaid, Effie Qualo, 3 x 4 In. 192.00
Buffalo Hide, Cheyenne, Tanned, Painted, Box & Border Design, c.1870-1880s, 7 x 6 Ft. . 3025.00
Cane, Iroquois, Incised Serpent, 36 In. 180.00
Canoe, Canada, Birchbark, 1920s, Miniature 2800.00
Canteen, Acoma, Bird Design, Leather Thong, c.1958, 7 x 8 1/2 In. 440.00
Canteen, Navajo, Silver, Turquoise, Stamped Star Design, Terry Martinez, 1960s, 7 In. .. 880.00
Canteen, Pueblo, Silver, Stamped Design, Oyster Shell Front, 1970s, 4 x 3 1/2 In. 110.00
Canteen, Zuni, Pottery, K. Pino, 5 x 5 In. 100.00
Card Case, Red Wool, Moose Hair Flowers, Late 18th Century, 3 3/4 x 2 1/2 In. 835.00
Case, Apache, Awl, Beaded Both Sides, Geometric Patterns, c.1920, 17 In. 935.00
Case, Sioux, Knife, Sinew Sewn Rawhide, 2 x 12 In. 88.00
Change Purse, Bird Design, Beaded, 1900, 4 3/4 In. 82.00
Club, Algonquin, Carved, Grotesque Mask, Creatures, c.1900, 31 In. 140.00
Club, Iroquois, Carved Wood, Face On Tip, 18 In. 260.00
Club, Penobscot, Carved Indian, 24 In. 412.00
Club, Penobscot, Moose, Eagle, Deer Face Carvings, 28 In. 632.00
Club, Plains, Buffalo Horn Head, Beaded Handle, Drop, 1880s, 24 x 7 1/2 In. 330.00
Club, Sioux, Stone Head, Beaded, Sinew Sewn Handle, c.1880, 25 In. 3385.00
Coat, Iroquois, Beaded, Over 1 Lb. Of Beads, 1890s 625.00
Cradle, Eastern Plains, Beaded On Canvas, Tacked Boards, 1940s-1950s, 33 x 10 In. 1100.00
Cradle Board, Apache, Wooden Frame, Muslin, 38 x 14 In. 750.00
Cradle Board, Paiute, Toy, Wicker, Cotton, Hide, 1920s, 6 1/2 In. 201.00
Cradle Cover, Cheyenne, Beaded Top, 1920s-1930s, 30 x 11 In. 880.00
Cuff, Cochiti, Silver, Bent Rainbow Man Design, Joe Quiatana, 2 1/4 In. 275.00
Dance Wand, Plains, Beaded & Hide Handle, Buffalo Horn, Flex Case, 25 1/2 In. 2750.00
Dance Wand, Plains, Horns On End 165.00
Doll, Beaded Hide, 19th Century, 18 In. 935.00
Doll, Cheyenne, Wooden, Incised, c.1890, 8 1/2 x 10 1/4 In. 550.00
Doll, Hopi, Tawa, Walter Howato, 1970s, 23 In. 550.00
Doll, Huron, Embroidered, Beaded, Cape With Cross In Center, Green Cloth, 1900s 77.00
Doll, Lakota, Hide & Muslin, Stepped Geometric Dress, Blue Beads, c.1900, 15 In. 345.00
Doll, Northwest Coast, Tourist, c.1930, 8 3/4 In., Pair 66.00
Doll, Sioux, Real Hair, Beaded Yoke, Belt, Knife Sheath, Awl Case, 1930s, 12 1/2 In. 550.00
Doll, Squaw, 2 Papooses On Back, Plastic, Jointed, Sleep Eyes, Vinyl Outfit, 11 1/2 In. 22.00
Doll, Yuma, Female, Breech Cloth, Headband, Signed, Mina Hills, 1950, 10 In. 82.00
Doll, Yuma, Male, Breech Cloth, Headband, 10 1/2 In. 82.00
Dress, Deerskin, Laced Sides, Fringed Pointed Hem, With Matching Leggings, 41 In. 360.00
Dress, Nez Perce, Beaded Yoke & Sleeves, Hide Fringe, Green Trade Cloth, 45 In. 330.00
Dress, Nez Perce, Large Beaded Floral, Purple Trade Cloth, c.1900, 44 x 38 In. 990.00
Drum, Iroquois, Double Headed, Polychrome Hollow Tree Trunk, 13 1/4 In. 440.00
Drum, Plains, Harvest, Painted Ear Of Corn, Bentwood Hull, 3 5/16 x 13 1/8 In. 385.00
Drum, Seminole, Rawhide & Bark, Florida, 20th Century, 3 x 5 1/2 In. 35.00
Drum, Tarahumare, Hide Heads, c.1900, 10 x 7 In. 160.00
Drum, Zuni, Painted Kachinas On Drum Heads, Duane Dishta, 1987, 18 x 11 In. 825.00
Earrings, Navajo, Turquoise & Silver Circle, Tobe Turpen Sr., c.1940, 2 1/2 x 3/4 In. 155.00
Fan, Pueblo, Peyote, Macaw Feathers, Beaded Handle, 1960s, 24 In. 220.00
Figurine, Acoma, Bird, Lucy Lewis, 1970s, 2 x 4 1/2 In. 605.00
Figurine, Cochiti, Story Teller, Pottery, Felecita Eustace, 1960s-1970s, 5 1/2 In. 360.00
Figurine, San Ildefonso, Turtle, Pottery, Tony Da, 1970s, 5 1/2 x 8 In. 6710.00
Fish Club, Northwest Coast, Carved Sea Lion Head, Yew, 23 In. 489.00
Gauntlets, Beaded Buffalo Design, Leather Fringe, 13 3/4 In. 430.00
Gauntlets, Beaded, Hand Sewn, Lining, 1900 .... 350.00
Gauntlets, Crow, Buckskin, Beaded Floral, Fringed, c.1940, 13 In. 247.00
Gloves, Nez Perce, Beaded Tops 44.00
Gloves, Nez Perce, Buckskin, Beaded 88.00
Hat, Hupa, Basketry, 3 x 7 In. 330.00
Hat, Hupa, Twine, Brown, Yellow, Stepped & Interlocking Geometric, c.1915, 7 In. 345.00

Hat, Osage, Wedding, Top Hat, Painted, Beaded Hat Band, 1880s, 7 x 12 In. 1760.00
Headband, Iroquois, Beaded American Flag, 31 In. 155.00
Headdress, Apache, Medicine Man's, 1865 . . . . 1650.00
Headstall, Navajo, Silver, Petit Point Turquoise & Stamped Design, 1960s 660.00
Headstall, Navajo, Silver, Turquoise In Brown Band & Naja, 1960s, 23 x 6 In. 495.00
Iroquois, House, Birch Bark, Small Mask Hung In Doorway, 26 x 20 In. 17.00
Jacket, Athabascan, Fringe, Appliqued, Bilateral Flora, Zigzag, c.1890 . . . . 1840.00
Jacket, Cree, Tanned Moose Hide, Fringed & Beaded Star Design, c.1920 . . . . 185.00
Jar, Acoma, Geometric Design, Black & White, 13 x 7 1/4 In. 2750.00
Jar, Acoma, Geometric Design, Signed, Debbie Brown, 6 In. 200.00
Jar, Acoma, Seed, Sarah Garcia, 1970s, 5 1/2 x 7 In. 250.00
Jar, Acoma, Shoulder Form, Geometric Medallions, Brown & Orange Slip, c.1930, 7 In. . . 431.00
Jar, Hopi, Polychrome Design, Fannie Nampeyo, 1950s-1960s, 7 1/2 In. 4290.00
Jar, Hopi, Seed, Stylized Bear Paw Design, Elva Nampeyo, 1970s, 4 x 6 1/2 In. 660.00
Jar, Hopi, Wedding, Erma Tawyesva, 1930s, 9 1/2 In. 467.00
Jar, Maricopa, Effigy, 3 Heads, Barbara Johnson, 1970s, 9 1/2 x 7 1/2 In. 550.00
Jar, San Ildefonso, Abstract Floral, Red, Orange-Red, Black Slip, Early 1900s, 8 3/4 In. . . 1265.00
Jar, Santa Clara, Blackware, Bulbous, Signed, Helen Shapla, 3 1/2 In. 145.00
Jar, Santa Clara, Blackware, Bulbous, Signed, Reyecita Chavarrio, 1 7/8 In. 45.00
Jar, Santa Clara, Blackware, Geometric Design, Bulbous, 3 5/8 In. 100.00
Jar, Santa Clara, Sharon Maranjo, 8 x 7 In. 520.00
Jar, Zuni, Butterflies, Polychrome, c.1920, 6 x 7 1/2 In. 715.00
Kachina, Hopi, All Silver, Mudhead, c.1970, 4 In. 155.00
Kachina, Hopi, Butterfly Maiden, Ivan Jackson, 1980s, 16 In. 195.00
Kachina, Hopi, Carved, Painted, 19th Century, 22 x 6 In. 6000.00
Kachina, Hopi, Clown, Walter Howato, 1970s, 27 In. 550.00
Kachina, Hopi, Eagle, Manuel P. Quavehema, 1960s, 12 In. 195.00
Kachina, Hopi, Koshare, Walter Howato, 1970s, 17 x 9 In. 330.00
Kachina, Hopi, Tony M. Espinosa, 1970s, 24 In. 330.00
Kilt, Dance, Hopi, Embroidered Design, 1960s-1970s, 32 x 50 In. 195.00
Knife, Inuit, Half Bone, Reindeer & Bushes Carved, 10 In. 195.00
Knife Sheath, Plains, Beaded, c.1900, 27 In. 520.00
Knife Sheath, Sioux, Beaded, c.1880, 10 3/8 In. 1760.00
Knife Sheath, Sioux, Beaded, Dentalium Drops, Leather Back, 1900s, 8 1/2 x 2 3/4 In. . . . 550.00
Leggings, Apache, Plains, Fringed, 35 3/8 In., Pair 495.00
Leggings, Arapaho, Beaded, Sinew Sewn 605.00
Leggings, Cheyenne, Child's, Lazy Stitch, White Field, Blue Edge, Early 1900s, 14 In. . . . 345.00
Leggings, Nez Perce, Geometric Beaded, Red Trade Cloth, c.1900, 31 In. 520.00
Leggings, Nez Perce, Red Felt & Beads, 16 In. 522.00
Leggings, Sioux, Beaded, c.1890-1910, 15 x 5 In. 935.00
Leggings, Sioux, Child's, Beaded, Pictograms, White, Green, Yellow, Red, Blue, 20 In. . . . 2420.00
Mask, Iroquois, Corn Husk, False Face Society, Ceremonial, 16 x 14 In. 300.00
Mask, Kwakiutl, Bear, Sam Johnson, 1970s, 10 x 18 x 8 In. 440.00
Mask, Kwakiutl, Dance, Red Cedar, Frank Nelson King, 1980s, 11 x 8 1/2 x 9 In. 385.00
Mittens, Cree, Moosehide, Floral Embroidery, Sealskin Strips, Blanket Lined, 13 In. 137.00
Moccasins, Apache, Child's, High Top, 6 x 6 1/2 In. 155.00
Moccasins, Arapaho, Beaded Buckskin, c.1890 . . . . 1840.00
Moccasins, Blackfoot, Beaded, Sinew Sewn, Buffalo Hide, c.1880, 10 1/2 In. 880.00
Moccasins, Cheyenne, Beaded Deerskin, Buffalo Hide Soles, 1875-1900 . . . . 7475.00
Moccasins, Cheyenne, Beaded, Turquoise, Red, Yellow, White, Hard Soles, 1950s, 10 In. . 195.00
Moccasins, Cheyenne, Child's, Beaded, Parfleche Soles, 1880s-1890s, 6 1/2 In. 690.00
Moccasins, Crow, Fully Beaded, Sinew Sewn, Rawhide Soles, c.1890 . . . . 880.00
Moccasins, Hopi, Kachina Dance, All Leather, 10 x 10 In. 2205.00
Moccasins, Kickapoo, Child's, Beaded Toe Fronts, 8 1/4 In. 99.00
Moccasins, Kiowa, Buckskin, Beaded, Fringed, c.1880 . . . . 6325.00
Moccasins, Kiowa, Stylized Geometric, Painted Yellow, c.1910, 9 1/2 In. 489.00
Moccasins, Lakota, Beaded Buffalo Hide, c.1880 . . . . 3737.50
Moccasins, Lakota, Buffalo Tracks, White Field, 1880s, 10 1/2 In. 1093.00
Moccasins, Lakota, Teepee, Cross, Buffalo Tracks, White Field, 1880s, 11 In. 3738.00
Moccasins, Nez Perce, Fully Beaded Hide, Floral, Geometric, c.1920, 11 In. 550.00
Moccasins, Nez Perce, Fully Beaded, Soft Soles, 5 1/2 x 11 In. 467.00
Moccasins, Plains, Beaded, Geometric, High Top, Red, Blue, Yellow & White 415.00
Moccasins, Plains, Child's, Beaded, Geometric, Green, Red, Yellow, Blue, White, 5 In. . . . 580.00

Moccasins, Plains, Child's, High Top, Beaded Sides, c.1880, 7 3/4 In. 320.00
Moccasins, Plains, Hightop, Geometric Design, Red, Blue, Yellow, White 415.00
Moccasins, Plains, Man's, Blue Beaded Ground, Red Trade Cloth Cuffs, 10 1/2 In. 550.00
Moccasins, Seneca, Puckered Toe, Hide, Beaded Toe & Cuffs, 9 In. 245.00
Moccasins, Sioux, Beaded Checkerboard Design, Parfleche Soles, 1900s, 10 In. 275.00
Moccasins, Sioux, Beaded Salt & Pepper Design, Parfleche Soles, 1920s, 10 In. 550.00
Moccasins, Sioux, Beaded, White, Green, Blue, Red, Parfleche Soles, c.1900, 10 In. 440.00
Moccasins, Sioux, Child's, Beaded, Quilled, 1890, 8 1/2 In. 1210.00
Moccasins, Sioux, Quilled, Beaded, Parfleche Soles, c.1890, 5 x 9 In. 715.00
Moccasins, Sioux, Salt & Pepper, Yellow Beaded Design, Parfleche Soles, 1890s, 11 In. ... 330.00
Moccasins, Woodlands, Beaded, Floral & Leaf Design 275.00
Necklace, Navajo, Coral & Silver Squash Blossom, 24 In. 275.00
Necklace, Navajo, Silver Dime, Squash Blossom, 22 In. 155.00
Necklace, Navajo, Squash Blossom, Box Bow, Natural Turquoise Stones, 1940s, 12 In. ... 605.00
Necklace, Pueblo, Coral Beads, Spider Web Turquoise Disc Spacers, 1960s, 13 1/2 In. ... 165.00
Necklace, Squash Blossom, Silver Dollar Blossoms, 1970s, 16 In. 250.00
Necklace, Zuni, 3 Oval Pendants, Inlaid Mountain Spirits, Turquoise, 1960s-1970s 220.00
Necklace, Zuni, Channel-Inlaid Face Design, Silver Fluted Beads, 1970s 165.00
Olla, Acoma, Fine Line Design, Lucy M. Lewis, 1960s, 4 In. 935.00
Olla, Acoma, Geometric Arcs Of Lozenges, 1900, 8 1/4 In. 2200.00
Olla, Apache, Willow, Devil's Claw, Radiating Borders, Early 1900s, 16 1/2 In. 3335.00
Olla, Laguna, Geometric Polychrome Design, 1900, 13 In. 3080.00
Olla, Southwest, Orange, Brown Polychrome Design, 5 1/2 In. 137.00
Paddle, Northwest Coast, Ceremonial, Carved, Painted, c.1880-1890, 36 In., Pair 1045.00
Pants, Crow, Hide, Beaded Flowers, c.1930, 42 x 18 In. 305.00
Pipe, Lakota, Carved Turtles, Stone T-Shaped Bowl, Carved Ash Stem, Early 1900s, 9 In. 374.00
Pipe, Plains, Catlinite, 4-Hole Keel, c.1880, 6 3/4 In. 220.00
Pipe, Plains, With Original Stem, Beaded, Inlaid Steatite, 16 1/2 In. 687.00
Pipe, Plains, Woman's, Pipestone, Stem & Bowl, 1890s, 6 In. 220.00
Pipe, Plains, Wooden, Twisted Stem, Rattlesnake & Lizard On Bowl, 1870s-1880s, 25 In. 1320.00
Pipe, Sioux, Hand Carved Eagle Claw & Stem, c.1880, 18 In. 1045.00
Pipe & Stem, Plains, Carved Twisted Stem, Pipestone, Bowl, c.1890, 32 In. 935.00
Pipe Bag, Central Plains, Beaded, Dyed Quill Work, Cowhide Fringe, c.1900, 27 In. 1100.00
Pipe Bag, Cheyenne, Beaded, Fringed, c.1870, 34 In. 13475.00
Pipe Bag, Sioux, Beaded Base, Woven Cotton, Fringed, 19th Century, 13 3/4 In. 845.00
Pipe Bag, Triangles, Crosses, Red, Yellow, Green, Blue, Field, Late 1800s, 36 In. 1380.00
Pipe-Tomahawk, Phase 1 Head, Hand Forged, 15 3/8 In. 1265.00
Pipe-Tomahawk, Plains, Original Brass Tacked Handle, 1850s-1870s, 25 In. 7700.00
Plaque, Northwest Coast, Fish, Carved, Wooden, Patty Fawn, 1970s, 12 In. 165.00
Plaque, Papago, Basketry, Martynia & Willow, c.1920, 9 In. 150.00
Plate, Hopi, Basketery, Kachina & Bird, Nampeyos, 1940s, 8 1/2 In. 330.00
Plate, Zia, Pottery, Polychrome, Helen Gachupin, 1970s, 4 1/2 In. 250.00
Pot, Acoma, Orange & Black Bird, Floral, c.1930, 10 x 13 In. 4675.00
Pot, San Ildefonso, Serrated Design, Pottery, Signed Marie, 5 x 7 1/2 In. 242.00
Pot, Zuni, Red Clay, Stylized Deer, Lightning Bolts, 13 In. 6120.00
Pouch, Apache, Hide, Beaded, Ball Drops, 1930s-1940s, 10 x 7 In. 195.00
Pouch, Belt, Crow, Beaded, Blue Field, Leaves, c.1890, 4 x 4 1/2 In. 330.00
Pouch, Cherokee, Hide, Geometric Designs, Tassels, 20th Century, 6 1/2 x 4 In. 125.00
Pouch, Plains, Beaded, Fringed, c.1880, 6 1/2 In. 88.00
Pouch, Sioux, Beaded, Quill, c.1890-1910, 10 x 7 In. 440.00
Powder Horn, Plains, Painted, 11 3/4 In. 50.00
Purse, Huron, Beaded, Teardrop Shape, 1840 .... 295.00
Quiver, Fringe, Shoulder Strap, 3 Arrows, No Feathers, 101 Ranch, 28 1/2 x 3 In. 565.00
Rattle, Northwest Coast, Shaman's, 7 x 8 In. 310.00
Rattle, Plains, Painted Hide, c.1880, 8 1/2 In. 50.00
Ring, Zuni, Mosaic Inlaid Bent Rainbow Man, 1940s-1950s, Size 10 1/2, 2 In. Long 83.00
Rope, Crow, Horsehair, Orange, Red, Black, White, 1940s 100.00
Rug, Burntwater, Vegetable Dyes, Marie Lester, 42 x 57 In. 5600.00
Rug, Navajo, 2 Facing Figures, White Bodies, Gray-Brown Field, Border, 33 x 49 In. 385.00
Rug, Navajo, 3 Vertical Panels, Stylized Stars, Spear Points, 58 x 32 In. 575.00
Rug, Navajo, 3 Yei, Red, Orange, Black, Brown & White, 56 x 51 In. 3190.00
Rug, Navajo, 5 Sawtooth Diamonds, Gray Ground, 62 x 40 In. 330.00
Rug, Navajo, Black & Red, Swastika Design, 34 x 32 1/2 In. 180.00

Rug, Navajo, Center Block, Block & Diamond Border, Repair, 1930, 73 x 46 In. 245.00
Rug, Navajo, Central Ivory Medallion, Within Sawtooth Border, 48 x 36 1/2 In. 300.00
Rug, Navajo, Central Serrated Medallion, Striped Bands, 53 x 25 In. 575.00
Rug, Navajo, Chinle, Banded Design, Vegetable Dyes, Earth Tones, 1950s, 45 x 38 In. . . .   195.00
Rug, Navajo, Cream & Black Geometric Design, Red Ground, 70 x 41 In. 1760.00
Rug, Navajo, Cream Geometric Design, Red Ground, 62 x 63 In. 2200.00
Rug, Navajo, Double Diamond Pattern, Tan, Brown, Red, Black, 60 x 29 In. 154.00
Rug, Navajo, Gray, White, Black & Red Geometric, 65 1/2 x 39 3/4 In. 468.00
Rug, Navajo, Klagetoh, Black, White, Gray, Red, 1960s, 44 1/2 x 31 In. 360.00
Rug, Navajo, Medallions, Diamonds, White Field, Red & Black Sides, 77 x 45 In. 440.00
Rug, Navajo, Red Border, White, Gray, Orange & Green, 1930s, 51 x 72 In. 2500.00
Rug, Navajo, Red, Brown, Tan Geometric Design, 1940, 35 x 61 1/2 In. 165.00
Rug, Navajo, Red, Brown, Tan, White Diamond Pattern, 46 x 64 1/2 In. 330.00
Rug, Navajo, Red, Gray & Black Zigzag Bands, Merino Wool, 1890s, 76 x 55 In. 740.00
Rug, Navajo, Star In Concentric Sawtooth Diamonds, Germantown, 84 x 61 In. 4600.00
Rug, Navajo, Storm Design, Swastika Center, 64 x 48 In. 495.00
Rug, Navajo, Teec Nos Pos, Earth Tones, Cecilia George, 1980s, 54 x 39 In. 1155.00
Rug, Navajo, Transitional, Banded Pattern, 1890s, 88 1/2 x 56 1/2 In. 635.00
Rug, Navajo, Triangle & Diamond Bands, Sawtooth Border, c.1930, 60 x 34 In. 690.00
Rug, Navajo, Two Gray Hills, Double Medallion, Spirit Line, c.1935, 50 x 32 In. 220.00
Rug, Navajo, Two Gray Hills, Natural, Black, Brown, Tan, White, 1970s, 32 x 25 In. 230.00
Rug, Navajo, Two Gray Hills, Vegetable Dyes, Helen Begay, 1960s, 40 x 30 In. 385.00
Rug, Navajo, Wide Ruins, Tan, Gray, White, Brown Field, Helen Kaye, 1970, 84 x 47 In. .   745.00
Rug, Navajo, Wide Ruins, Vegetable Dyed, Virginia Ambrose, 1970s, 84 x 53 In. 1210.00
Rug, Navajo, Yei, 7 Figures, Red Border, Hand Carded & Spun Wool, 28 x 38 In. 880.00
Rug, Navajo, Yei, Rainbow Colors, Gray Ground, 1970s, 34 x 48 In. 385.00
Rug, Navajo, Yei, Rainbow Colors, Tan Field, Gray & Brown Border, 1970s, 29 x 48 In. .   345.00
Rug, Navajo, Zigzag Design, Red, Tan, Black, Beige, Black Border, c.1940, 51 x 37 In. . .   690.00
Saddle Blanket, Navajo, 3rd Phase Variant, Natural Colors, c.1880, 53 x 31 In. 135.00
Saddle Blanket, Navajo, Double, Diamond Twill, Brown, Tan, White, 1950s, 52 x 30 In. . .   145.00
Saddle Blanket, Rio Grande, Natural Gray, Red, Black & White, 1920s, 48 x 72 In. 1400.00
Sash, Osage, Child's, Blue-Green, Maroon, Zigzag, Knotted Tassels, Late 1800s, 39 In. . .   345.00
Scraper, Plains, Horn, Brass Tack Design, 1920s, 13 1/2 x 4 1/2 In. 83.00
Serape, Saltillo, Stepped Geometric, Zigzag, 2 Joined Panels, Mexico, 82 x 41 In. 575.00
Shield, Plains, Buckskin Cover Over Buffalo Hide, Mineral Painted, 20 In. 660.00
Shirt, Ghost Dancer, Canvas, Leather Fringe, Horsehair Drops, Circle & Half Moon 1100.00
Shirt, Seminole, Appliqued, Patchwork, Shoulder Gathers, Cotton, Silk, Rickrack, 28 In. . 2070.00
Shirt, Seminole, Man's, Appliqued, Patchwork, Brightly Colored, 1920s, 47 In. 2300.00
Shoes, Iroquois, Corn Husk, Worn By Corn Husk Mask Dancers, 1940s, 10 In. 605.00
Shot Pouch, Cheyenne, Beaded, White Ground, Blue, Cut Metal, 1890-1900s, 4 1/2 In. . .   250.00
Skirt, Seminole, Patchwork, Appliqued, Cotton, 20th Century, 26 In. 236.00
Snowshoes, Trail, Wood Frames, Woven Rawhide Mesh, 38 In., Pair 79.00
Snuffbox, Zuni, Silver, 3 x 2 1/4 In. 176.00
Spoon, Central Plains, Lakota, Cow Horn, Carved, Roll Beaded Handle, 1890s, 11 1/2 In.   374.00
Spoon, Cheyenne, Buffalo Horn, Horse Effigy, Beaded Handle, Fringed, 12 In. 605.00
Spoon, Plateau, Horn, Beaded, c.1890, 11 In. 240.00
Spoon, Sioux, Horn, c.1870, 13 x 6 In. 305.00
Spoon, Woodlands, Carved Duck Head, Wood, 9 1/2 In. 110.00
Strike-A-Lite, Plains, Beaded, Cones, c.1880, 30 3/4 In. 300.00
Tomahawk, Catlinite, Incised Carved Head, 1896, 10 3/8 In. 297.00
Tomahawk, Plains, Handwrought Head, 20th Century, 21 In. 220.00
Totem Pole, Haida, Carved Argalite, Concave Back, Bear & Human Forms, 12 3/4 In. . . . 1093.00
Totem Pole, Haida, Polychrome, Cedar, Late 19th Century, 58 In. 6325.00
Totem Pole, Northwest Coast, Eagle At Top, Animals, 40 In. 337.00
Totem Pole, Northwest Coast, Painted Eagle, Raven, Hawk, Cedar, 1930, 32 In. 2600.00
Tray, Apache, Basketry, Dark Center, Radiating Checkerboard, Dogs, Early 1900s, 17 In. . 2415.00
Tray, Apache, Classic Star & Lightning Design, 4 x 13 In. 2200.00
Tray, Hopi, Lizard Design, 7 1/4 In., 2 Piece 104.00
Tray, Navajo, Wedding, Basketry, Coiled, Polychrome, Geometric, c.1900, 14 In. 460.00
Tray, Papago, Mary Pablo, Stanfield, Arizona, c.1920, 7 1/2 In. 55.00
Tray, Pima, Basketry, Coiled, Maze Pattern In Panels, Early 1900s, 16 In. 863.00
Tray, Washo, Winnowing, 1920, 12 x 11 In. 385.00
Tunic, Tlingit, Black Wool, Front Plaquette, Bilateral Abstract Design, c.1900, 40 In. 2530.00

Vase, Blackfoot, Pottery, Signed Nana, 1980s, 14 x 10 In. 140.00
Vase, Jemez, Squash Style, Stone Polished Red Neck, Juanita Fragua, 1970s, 6 In. 165.00
Vase, Maricopa, Black On Red, Long Neck, Ida Red Bird, 1960s, 9 In. 360.00
Vase, Santo Domingo, Wedding, Black On Red, 1960s, 12 x 9 In. 110.00
Vase, Santo Domingo, Wedding, Polychrome, 1920s, 5 x 5 1/2 In. 140.00
Vest, Crow, Floral Design, Beaded, White Buckskin, 24 x 21 In. 220.00
Vest, Lakota, Cloth, Beaded, Teepees, Yellow Field, 1930s, 19 In. 518.00
Vest, Sioux, Child's, Beaded, Pictograms, Blue, Yellow, Red, White Field, 12 1/2 In. 1320.00
Wall Pocket, Iroquois, Floral Beaded, Velvet, 8 In. 143.00
War Club, Plains, Hide On Handle, c.1880, 37 x 5 1/2 In. 165.00
Weaving, Navajo, Chief's Pattern, Striped Ground, 56 x 38 In. 4880.00
Weaving, Navajo, Dyed Wool, Stepped Diamond, Red, Brown, Gray, 86 x 43 In. 1380.00
Weaving, Navajo, Homespun Wool, Cream, Brown, Dark Brown, Gray Field, 80 x 51 In. . . 431.00
Weaving, Navajo, Sawtooth Design, Red, Black, White, Gray, 67 x 39 In. 302.00
Weaving, Third Phase Chief's, Terrace, 1880, 76 x 58 In. 1265.00

INDIAN TREE is a china pattern that was popular during the last half of the nineteenth century. It was copied from earlier Indian textile patterns that were very similar. The pattern includes the crooked branch of a tree and a partial landscape with exotic flowers and leaves. Green, blue, pink, and orange were the favored colors used in the design.

Bowl, Scalloped, Syracuse, 5 1/2 In. 27.00
Cheese Dish, Cover, Ironstone, Polychrome 55.00
Creamer, Green Greek Key, Johnson Brothers 42.00
Creamer, White, Johnson Brothers 26.00
Cup, White, Johnson Brothers 23.00
Cup & Saucer, Bouillon, Scalloped, Syracuse 27.00
Cup & Saucer, Greek Key, Scalloped, Coalport 80.00
Gravy Boat, Greek Key, Cream Ground, Johnson Brothers 64.00
Plate, Coalport, 9 In. 50.00
Plate, Johnson Brothers, 6 1/4 In. 10.00
Plate, Myott, 7 In. 25.00
Plate, Orange & Rust, Scalloped, Spode, 10 1/4 In. 50.00
Platter, Ironstone, Polychrome, 21 In. 250.00
Saucer, Wood & Sons 6.00
Service For 6, Syracuse 250.00
Sugar, Cover, Johnson Brothers 35.00
Tureen, Soup, Cover, Undertray, Ironstone, Polychrome, 14 In. 120.00

INKSTANDS were made to be placed on a desk. They held some type of container for ink, and possibly a sander, a pen tray, a pen, a holder for pounce, and even a candle to melt the sealing wax. Inkstands date to the eighteenth century and have been made of silver, copper, ceramics, and glass. Additional inkstands may be found in these and other related categories.

2 Tiers, Molded Glass Upper, Silver Plate Inkwells, Grooved Pen Rest Lower Part 1100.00
Brass, 2 Blown Glass Inserts, Scroll Design, 3 3/4 x 7 x 4 In. *Illus* 75.00
Brass, 2 Lift Tops, Pressed Glass Inkpots, Surmounted Clock, 6 x 9 In. 85.00
Brass, Art Nouveau Scroll, Butterfly On Lily-Of-The-Valley 90.00

Inkstand, Brass, 2 Blown Glass Inserts,
Scroll Design, 3 3/4 x 7 x 4 In.

**Clean brass with commercial
brass polish. Wear white
cotton gloves. The gloves
make the difference.**

Brass, Enamel, Hunter On Horse, Flowers, Persia, 19th Century, 9 x 5 1/4 x 3 In. 130.00
Brass, Mercury Flanking 2 Wells, Pen Tray, Engraved 1857, 8 x 13 In. 460.00
Brass, Rococo Style, Floral Borders, Soapstone, Crocodile Hide, c.1900, 9 x 6 In. 165.00
Bronze, 2 Stylized Griffins, Rectangular Marble Base, Foliage, France, 5 x 7 In. 173.00
Bronze, Chinoiserie Style, Seated Warrior Underneath Tree, 9 3/4 In. 1840.00
Bronze, Green Marble, 2 Fluted Wells, Gilt, Hinged Lids, Napoleon III, 4 x 12 5/8 In. . . . 715.00
Bronze, Painted Dogs, Looking Into Round Tray, Onyx, 3 x 6 In. 805.00
Bronze, Renaissance Style, Gilt, Hinged Lid, Onyx Base, 4 3/4 In. 275.00
Bronze, Vienna, Rococo Style, Center Urn, Blackamoors With Basket, c.1900, 7 In. 670.00
Cast Iron, 2 Pressed Glass Wells, Hinged Lids, Judd, Pat. 1879, 7 5/8 x 4 1/2 In. 150.00
Iron, Glass Ball Well, Patd. Dec. 11, 1855, 3 3/4 In. 300.00
Marble, Seated Pharaoh, 2 Wells, Hinged Lid, Marble, 4 Sphinx Feet, 10 x 20 In. 1475.00
Marble & Porcelain, Pierced Border, 2 Floral Wells, Rose Finial, French, 7 In. 545.00
Metal, 2 Pewter Leaves At Base, Acorn In Inkwell, Quill Hole, c.1910, 2 3/4 In. 82.00
Metal, Figural Sacre Coeur Cathedral, Pen Tray, 3 x 5 1/4 In. 45.00
Metal, Pen Tray, Slopes To 3 Wells, Ink Bottle, Windsor Mason Pen Point, 7 3/4 In. 185.00
Metal, Pierced Sand Holder, Cut Glass Well, Leaf Tip Bun Feet, 1840s, 6 x 12 1/2 In. . . . 2012.00
Porcelain, Floral, Gold Trim, Octagonal, 2 3/4 In. 135.00
Silver, 2 Bottles, Chamberstick, H. Chawner, J. Eames, London, 1797, 8 x 6 In. 2750.00
Silver, 2 Pen Trays, 3 Holders, 3 Cut Glass Bottles, J. Scofield, England, 1787, 10 In. . . . 6900.00
Silver, Oval Base, 2 Beehive Wells, Gypsy Dancer Candlestick, Continental, 6 1/2 In. . . . 525.00
Silver, Shell & Leaf Rim, William B. Meyers, c.1930, 10 3/4 In. 1380.00
Silver, Stylized Flowers, Pierced & Beaded Rim, 1 Inkwell, Gorham, 10 In. 230.00
Silver Metal, Hinged Top, Shagreen, 2 Small Drawers, Art Deco, 8 1/4 In., 2 Piece 3160.00
Silver Plate, Mythological Figure, Beast's Heads, Eagle & Serpent Finial, 10 In. 690.00
Tin, Postal Scale, Stenciled, 2 Drawers On Side, Inkwells Missing, 7 In. 11.00
Wooden, 2 Cut Glass Inkpots, Black Painted Highlights, Rectangular, 6 x 12 In. 144.00
Wooden, Mother-Of-Pearl Inlay, Gilt, Painted, 2 Crystal Wells, Victorian, 11 x 8 In. 88.00
Wooden, Neoclassical Marquetry, Gilt Bronze Mounts, Fitted & Slide Drawer, 27 In. 8825.00

INKWELLS, of course, held ink. Ready-made ink was first made about
1836 and was sold in bottles. The desk inkwell had a narrow hole so
the pen would not slip inside. Inkwells were made of many materials,
such as pottery, glass, pewter, and silver. Look in these categories for
more listings of inkwells.

Boat Form, 2 Dandies On Top, Lift Top, Porcelain Well & Sander, Staffordshire, 7 In. . . . 460.00
Brass, Hinged Cover, Nasturtiums On Ball Feet, Swirl Design, Vine, Flowers, 4 x 8 In. . . 140.00
Brass, Kidney Shape, Diamond Cut Wells, Gilt, 1900, 2 3/4 x 2 1/2 In. 69.00
Brass, Lady With Bonnet, 5 1/2 x 5 1/2 In. 185.00
Bronze, Cherub Standing On A Leaf, Gilt, Victorian, 1848, 4 3/4 In. 518.00
Bronze, Cover, Spaniel Pouncing On Stack Of Books, Early 19th Century, 5 1/2 In. 345.00
Bronze, Deer Finial, Cover, c.1880 . . . . 525.00
Bronze, Figural, 2 Muscular Nude Men, Michel F. Gustave, 1895, 6 1/2 In. 1725.00
Bronze, Fish, Japanese, 19th Century 85.00
Bronze, Owl, Yellow, Black Glass Eyes, Bradley & Hubbard, 4 x 9 1/2 x 5 7/8 In. 747.00
Bronze, Painted Parrot, Signed, G.F. Schutzt, 7 1/2 In., Pair 862.00
Bronze, Polychrome, Glass Insert, Tray, Cold Paint, 8-In. Tray, 3-In. Inkwell 138.00
Bronze, Tooled Ink Pots, Green Marble Base, Eagle Feet, 8 x 18 In. 1210.00
Bronze, Turk Playing Instrument, Painted Nodder Head, Spiral Swirl Glass Well, 3 In. . . . 517.00
Cast Iron, Deer Head, 7 1/2 In. 155.00
Coral Glaze, Gilt Rectangular Plinth, Paris, 3 1/2 x 6 x 2 In. 460.00
Cut Glass, Geometric, Silver, Edward Barnard & Sons, London, 1890, 2 1/2 In. 140.00
Cut Glass, Hobstar & Fan, 3 1/2 In. 130.00
Cut Glass, Sterling Silver Cover, Ball Feet, Square, England, 6 1/4 In. 310.00
Glass, Half Sphere, Hinged Metal Lid, Polished Pontil 120.00
Glass, Pyramid Shape, Hinged Brass Collar & Lid 165.00
Glass, Silver, Hinged Cover, Leafy Scrolls, Flower Heads, Gorham, 1 1/2 x 2 1/4 In. 345.00
Glass, Spherical, Molded Swirl, Brass Collar & Hinged Lid 185.00
Glass, Swirled, Brass Swirled Top, Square 145.00
Glass, Teakettle, Robin's-Egg Blue, Gold Trim, Brass Collar, Octagonal, 1860 . . . . 264.00
Lead, Indian In Headdress, 3 1/2 In. 61.00
Metal, Neoclassical Figures, Floral Garlands, Putto On Cover, Filigree Mounts, 4 In. 250.00
Milk Glass, Cobalt Blue Cased, Enameled Butterfly, Hinged Lid, 1900, 1 7/8 In. 45.00

Milk Glass, Inlaid Floral Medallion, Brass Fittings, Victorian, 4 In. 75.00
Onyx & Bronze, Modeled Masks, Foliage, Footed Base, 19th Century, 7 In. 402.00
Pewter, 4 Sides, New England, 1807, 1 1/4 In. 250.00
Pink Roses, Purple Morning Glories, Gold Trim, Gilt Arabesque Band, Paris, 3 In. 345.00
Pressed Glass, Pinwheel, Embossed Floral & Foliate, Silver Plated Cover, 6 1/4 In. 430.00
Silver, Arts & Crafts, England, c.1910, 3 1/4 x 1 3/4 In. 105.00
Silver, Collar, Hinged Cover, Engraved Crown, Bradbury, England, 1911, 2 1/2 In. 260.00
Silver, Cover, Gadrooned Rim, 2 Oval Wells, J.S. & S., England, 1909, 10 3/8 In. 431.00
Silver, Gadrooned Rim, Rounded Corners, Currier & Roby, N.Y., 1870, 9 x 5 In. 517.00
Silver Plate, 2 Glass Inserts, Hinged Lid, Center Compartment, Bun Feet, 10 x 13 In. 330.00
Tulips & Birds, Staffordshire, 3 In. 210.00
Wooden, Mold Blown Glass Well, Engine Turned Ligum Vitae, 2 3/4 In. 165.00
Wooden, Porcelain Insert, Fanciful Landscape, Incised, Painted, Russia, 5 1/2 In. 200.00
Wooden, Pyrography, Flower & Leaf Outline, Paint Tinted, Flemish Art, 1920s 30.00

INSULATORS of glass or pottery have been made for use on telegraph
or telephone poles since 1844. Thousands of different styles of insulators have been made. Most common are those of clear or aqua glass;
most desirable are the threadless types made from 1850 to 1870.

American Insurance Co., Green Aqua, Crude 18.00
American Telegraph & Telephone Co., No. 121, Blue Aqua 30.00
American Telephone, No. 110, Purple 22.00
Armstrong, Whitall Tatum, Salesman Sample, Clear 340.00
B.T. Co. Of Canada, Montreal, Clear 4.00
B.T. Co. Of Canada, No. 102, Royal Purple 40.00
Beehive, Aqua, Swirls, Chunk Of Milk Glass In Side, Montreal Telegraph 20.00
Beehive, Light Straw Color, Canada 6.00
Beehive Shape, Lime Green, Hemingray, Large 90.00
Bell System, New York, Cobalt Blue, Bell Shape 150.00
Blobs Inside, Flatdome, Aqua Blue, Bubbles & Swirls, Canada, 1860s, 3 1/2 In. 180.00
Brookfield, No. 100, Yellow Green 25.00
Brookfield, No. 133, Light Aqua 2.00
Cable, No. 2, Forest Green 23.00
Cable, No. 3, Emerald Green, Swirls 125.00
Cable, No. 3, Light Blue Aqua 70.00
Cable, No. 262, Green 20.00
California Electric Works, Clear 425.00
California Electric Works, Purple, Bubbles 20.00
California Electric Works, Sage 65.00
Canadian Pacific, No. 143, Light Green, Purple Swirls 3.50
Confederate Egg, Threadless, Lockport Green, 4 1/4 In. 260.00
Dominion 42, Golden Yellow Ember 60.00
Duquesne, Blue 38.00
E.C. & M., Emerald Green 2500.00
Flat Dome, Aqua Blue, Bubbles & Swirls, 1860s, 3 1/2 In. 180.00
Gayner, No. 620, Aqua 30.00
H.G. Co., Pat. May 2nd, Aqua 15.00
H.G. Co., Petticoat, Blue Aqua, Amber Wisp Front, 1893 . . . .   7.00
H.G. Co., Petticoat, Clear, Smooth Base 19.00
H.G. Co., Petticoat, Ice Blue, 1893 . . . .   18.00
Hemingray, Carnival 30.00
Hemingray, No. 9, Jade Green Milk, 1893 . . . .   13.00
Hemingray, No. 14, Clear 2.00
Hemingray, No. 21, Aqua 2.00
Hemingray, No. 23, Hemingray Blue 14.00
Hemingray, No. 45 . . . .   13.00
Hemingray, No. 62 . . . .   6.00
Hemingray, No. 75, Hemingray Blue 100.00
Hemingray, No. 80, Smooth Base, Blue 27.00
Hemingray, No. 95, Short, Clear 65.00
Hemingray, No. 120, Green 25.00
Hemingray, No. 125, Aqua 6.00
Hemingray, No. 154, Blue, Smooth Base 25.00

Hemingray, No. 219, Honey Olive Amber	17.00
Hemingray, No. 230, Gold Carnival	25.00
Hemingray, No. 510, Carnival	46.00
Imperial, White Porcelain	42.00
Jeffrey Mine, Original Pin	275.00
Kimble, No. 239, Light Straw	4.00
Lightning Rod, Unembossed, Orange Amber, 10 Flat Sides	140.00
Locke, No. 10, Italian Blue	45.00
Lynchburg, No. 20, Aqua	42.00
Lynchburg, No. 38, Yellow Green	13.00
Lynchburg, No. 44, Clear	30.00
Lynchburg, No. 44, RDP, Ginger Ale	15.00
Lynchburg, No. 154, Green	15.00
Maydwell, No. 106, SCA	7.50
Maydwell, No. 164, Milk Glass	8.00
McLaughlin, No. 16, RDP, Lime Apple	40.00
McLaughlin, No. 20, Dark 7-Up Green	25.00
McLaughlin, No. 42, Light Cornflower Blue	50.00
McLaughlin, No. 62, Blue Sage	4.00
McLaughlin, No. 100, Cornflower & Steel Blue	70.00
Mulford, Biddle, Aqua	500.00
Mushroom Type Top, Embossed Brookfield On Skirt, 3 1/2 In.	14.00
N.A.T. Co., No. 30, Deep Peacock Blue	975.00
National Battery Co., Embossed	25.00
New England Telegraph & Telephone, Light Medium Green	14.00
New England Telegraph & Telephone, No. 104, Aqua	5.00
Number 9 On Dome, Flared Skirt, Duquesne Glass Co., 1 In.	85.00
Oakman, Boston, Embossed Base, Aqua, Jumbo	375.00
Oakman, Cable, Embossed Base	55.00
Pyrex, No. 30, Carnival	37.00
Pyrex, No. 40, Carnival	37.00
Pyrex, No. 171, Carnival	78.00
Sombrero, Grand Coulee Dam, Dark Carnival	35.00
Star, No. 10, Aqua	110.00
Star, No. 260, Light Green, Amber Streaks Ears	225.00
Star, Pointed Dome, Yellow Green	15.00
Swirl Of Emerald In Side, Milk Flecks, Canada, c.1860, 3 1/2 In.	80.00
Threadless, Aqua Blue, Swirl Of Emerald On Side, Canada, 4 In.	140.00
Threadless, Round Dome, Teal, Canada, c.1860, 4 In.	430.00
Tillotson, Threadless, Deep Ice Blue	230.00
W. Brookfield, Cliff St., Green	150.00
W. Brookfield, No. 150, Apple Green	150.00
W.G.M. Co., Purple	30.00
Whitall Tatum, No. 1, Pink	12.00
Whitall Tatum, No. 4, Clear	4.00
Whitall Tatum, No. 5, Clear	5.00
Whitall Tatum, No. 9, Light Olive Green	16.00
Whitall Tatum, No. 14, Light Straw	6.00
Whitall Tatum, No. 154, Pink Tint	10.00
Whitall Tatum, No. 154, Purple	22.00
Whitall Tatum, No. 216, Amber	3.00

IRISH BELLEEK, see Belleek category.

IRON is a metal that has been used by man since prehistoric times. It is a popular metal for tools and decorative items like doorstops that need as much weight as possible. Items are listed here or under other appropriate headings, such as Bookends, Doorstop, Kitchen, Match Holder, or Tool. The tool that is used for ironing clothes, an iron, is listed in the Kitchen category under Iron and Sadiron.

Ankle Ball, Prisoner Or Slave, Ring On Top, 1/2-In. Hole In Side, 12 Lbs.	115.00
Ashtray, Fireman, Figural	50.00
Ashtray, Griswold, No. 00/5770, Iron, Pale Green Porcelain	105.00

Ashtray, Griswold, No. 33, Windproof ....20.00 to 50.00
Bed Warmer, Chased Cover & Hinge, Rattail Handle 295.00
Bit, Western, Engraved Diamond-Shaped Concha, Marked Fino, 1940s, 8 x 6 In. 250.00
Bit, Western, Silver Concha & Cheek Piece, Crockett, 1950s, 8 x 5 1/2 In. 110.00
Bit, Western, Spade Style, Silver Conchas On Side Plate, 1920s 415.00
Boot Scraper, Dachshund, Cast Iron, Repainted, 21 1/2 In. 120.00
Boot Scraper, Ram's-Horn Terminals, Heart Cutouts, 18th Century, Pair 1650.00
Bootjack, Beetle, Silver Paint, Marked Name & Address, France, 11 In. 16.00
Bootjack, Cow Head, 101 Ranch, Pat. Pend., Original 1st Type, 11 1/2 In. 254.00
Bootjack, Fish, Paw Feet At Base Of Lyre, 14 In. 95.00
Bootjack, Grasshopper, Black, Gold & Red Paint, Hubley 85.00
Bootjack, Naughty Nelly, 9 1/2 In. 45.00
Candle Bracket, 5 Jointed Arms Attached To Vertical Sliding Carrier, 25 In. 920.00
Candleholder, Hanging, 18th Century, 17 In. 395.00
Candlesnuffer, With Cutter 125.00
Candlestand, Tripod Base, Twisted Detail, Finial, 5 Segment Candle Arm, 56 In. 1375.00
Cigar Cutter, Figure Of Man, 12 1/2 In. 200.00
Cigar Cutter, Single Arm, Framed Paper Image, Manuel Lopez, c.1906, 9 x 9 In. 530.00
Cigar Cutter, Single Arm, Image Of Charles Denby, 1900, 9 x 8 1/2 In. 1072.00
Cigarette Dispenser, Elephant 395.00
Coal Hod, Embossed Lion, Flowers 220.00
Corn Drier, 18 In. 15.00
Cuspidor, Black Paint, 7 1/4 In. 220.00
Door Knocker, Basket Of Flowers, Polychrome, Cast Iron 50.00
Door Knocker, Grotesque Mask, Mid 19th Century, 15 x 9 In. 440.00
Doormat, Rows Of Shaped Hearts, Wire Rod Running Through Shoulders, 35 x 22 In. 258.00
Fern Stand, Intricate Scroll Work, Turned Center Post, 20th Century, Pair 385.00
Figurine, Boy With Dolphin, 6 1/4 In. 145.00
Figurine, Dappled Gray Horse, Painted, Leather Harness, 20th Century, 10 1/2 In. 130.00
Figurine, Eagle, Copper Paint, Spread Wings, 43 1/2-In. Wingspan, 23 In. 1540.00
Figurine, Eagle, Stepped Rectangular Base, Gilt, 19th Century, 5 3/4 In., Pair 172.00
Figurine, Golfer, Painted, Movable Head, 5 1/2 In. 110.00
Figurine, High Top Button Shoes, 6 1/2 In., Pair 130.00
Figurine, Male & Female Peacocks On Stump, 17 In. 100.00
Figurine, Tetsubin, Skirted Form, Stone Cast Surface, 19th Century, 9 3/4 In. 357.00
Firemark, Eagle Hose No. 2 .... 130.00
Flint Striker, Figural, Monster Serpent, 17th Century, 4 1/2 In. 450.00
Flint Striker, Pouncing Cat, Early 18th Century, 6 In. 895.00
Grisette, For Soaking Rush, Handle, 3 Short Feet, 10 x 12 In. 247.00
Handcuffs, Single Link Center, Nickeled Iron, H&R Arms Co., No Key 85.00
Hinge, Rattail Terminals, Mid 18th Century, Pa., Pair 935.00
Hinge, Stag Horn, Tulip, Leaf Shape, Mid 18th Century, Pair 1870.00
Hook, Beam Spike, For Fat Lamp, Liberty Cap Design, 18th Century 395.00
Hook, White Bird, Ornate Door Handle, Latch, 1800, Pair 770.00
Humidor, Allover Engraved, Pitcher & Goblets, Brass, England, 19th Century, 7 x 4 In. ... 315.00
Humidor, Allover Engraved, Sailing Ship, Brass, England, 4 1/8 x 2 3/4 x 5 3/4 In. 345.00
Jardiniere, Stepped, Edgar Brandt, 1925, 41 x 40 In. 18400.00
Mailbox, Griswold, Bail Paper Holder, Brown 55.00
Mailbox, Griswold, No. 4 .... 225.00
Mailbox, Griswold, No. 6, Selden 3300.00
Model, Cannon On Truck, 39 In. 880.00
Mold, Bookend, Galleon, On Board, 1930, 5 1/2 x 5 In., 24-In. Board 160.00
Mold, Bookend, Horse, On Board, 1930, 4 3/4 x 5 1/2 In., 24-In. Board 160.00
Obelisk, Tapered Column, Latticework, On 4 Spheres, Plinth, Patinated, 86 In., Pair 1870.00
Pipe Tongs, 21 In. 1155.00
Pitcher, Cover, Kendrick & Sons, c.1800 .... 850.00
Plant Cage, Wiltshire, England, 19th Century, 18 In. 265.00
Porringer, Hand Painted Pheasant, Round Pontil, 19th Century, 4 1/8 In. Diam. 85.00
Rushlight, Forged, Turned Wooden Base, 12 In. 155.00
Safe, Herring, Farrel & Sherman, Crenellated Skirt, Sphinx On Hoof Feet, 42 3/4 In. 3630.00
Sculpture, Classical Maiden With Torch, Bronze Patinated, Napoleon III, 99 1/2 In. 6600.00
Sculpture, Stag, Exaggerated Eyes, Antlers, Brown Paint, 1870s, Life Size, Pair 11000.00
Shoehorn, Sheet Iron, Heart Cutout, 9 1/2 In. 120.00

Smoker Set, Griswold, No. 771, 772 & 773, 3 Piece 180.00
Snow Eagle Bird, Bracket For Hanging, 6 x 6 1/2 In., Pair 65.00
Striker, Flint, Early Shape, 17th Century, 5 3/4 In. 295.00
Striker, Flint, Fox Form, Late 17th Century, 5 In. 725.00
Tsuba, Mokko Form, Calligraphic Design, 1800, 3 In. 137.00
Tsuba, Mokko Form, Gourd, Floral Design, Silver Inlaid, 1800, 3 In. 220.00
Tsuba, Naga-Maru-Gata, Bamboo Design, Signed, 18th Century, 3 In. 605.00
Tsuba, No Maru-Gata, Inlaid Bamboo Design, 17th Century, 2 1/2 In. 110.00
Tsuba, No Maru-Gata, Sukashi Design Of Grasses, Signed, Munetoshi, 3 In. 770.00
Tsuba, No Maru-Gata, Sukashi Lotus Design, 18th Century, 2 3/4 In. 110.00
Tsuba, No Maru-Gata, Sukashi Plum Blossom Design, Signed, Umetada, 3 1/4 In. 330.00
Tsuba, Shin No Maru-Gata, Butterfly Design, 18th Century, 3 1/4 In. 605.00
Tsuba, Shin No Maru-Gata, Gilded Tama Design, Pierced, Signed, 18th Century, 3 In. . . . 550.00
Tsuba, Shin No Maru-Gata, Sukashi Wave, Wine Jar Design, 18th Century, 3 1/4 In. 632.00
Tsuba, Water Wheel Form, Signed, Shoami, 17th Century, 3 1/4 In. 687.00
Vase, Black Enamel Holder, Citrine Blown Glass Insert, 11 In. 110.00
Windmill, Weight, Chicken Shape 715.00
Windmill Weight, Bobtail Horse, Dempster, 17 x 16 1/2 In. . . . . .150.00 to 180.00
Windmill Weight, Bull, Black, White Lettering, Fairbury, Neb., c.1900, 18 x 24 In. 920.00
Windmill Weight, Horse, Standing, Old White Paint, Early 20th Century, 16 1/2 x 17 In. . 920.00
Windmill Weight, Horse, Tin Base, Dempster Mfg., Beatrice, Neb., 16 1/2 x 17 1/2 In. . . 575.00
Windmill Weight, Rooster, Elgin Wind, Power & Pump Co., 1840, 13 In. 330.00
Windmill Weight, Rooster, Molded, Rectangle Base, Weathered, c.1900, 15 1/2 x 17 In. . . 1495.00
Windmill Weight, Rooster, Old Paint, Elgin Co., Late 19th Century, 15 x 19 In. 2185.00
Windmill Weight, Star Form, 5 Points, American, 19th Century, 15 x 15 In. . . . . .978.00 to 1035.00
Windmill Weight, W, Hexagon Serifs, Side Mount, Weathered, Early 1900s, 9 x 16 1/2 In. 546.00

IRONSTONE china was first made in 1813. It gained its greatest popularity during the mid-nineteenth century. The heavy, durable, off-white pottery was made in white or was decorated with any of hundreds of patterns. Much flow blue pottery was made of ironstone. Some of the decorations were raised. Many pieces of ironstone are unmarked, but some English and American factories included the word *Ironstone* in their marks. Additional pieces may be listed in other categories, such as Chelsea Grape, Flow Blue, Gaudy Ironstone, Moss Rose, Staffordshire, and Tea Leaf Ironstone.

Biscuit Jar, Flow Blue, Oriental Pattern, 7 In. 175.00
Box, Salt, Blue & White, Wooden Cover, 6 In. 104.00
Coffee Set, Wide Border Of Large Flower Blossoms, Scrolls, Geometric, 27 Piece 345.00
Compote, Overglaze Polychrome Floral, Blue Underglaze, 10 1/4 In. 100.00
Lamp, Geometric Transfer Green & Orange Design, 10 In. 57.00
Plate, Black Transfer 3 Rabbit & Frog Scene, 5 3/4 In., 6 Piece 495.00
Platter, Blue & White, Oval, Central Transfer, Leaf & Cloud Design, c.1846, 13 1/2 In. . . 69.00
Platter, Floral Design, Scalloped Edge, Marked, Coldren, England, 25 In. 990.00
Platter, Floral, Blue & White, Flat Back, 22 x 16 1/2 In. 255.00
Platter, Lake Scene, Floral Border, Scalloped, Blue, White, Colonial Pottery, 16 In. 55.00
Platter, Landscape, Shannon Pattern, Blue, White, 17 In. 265.00
Sugar & Creamer, Cover, White, Wheat Border, England 35.00
Teapot, Paneled, Purple Enamel, Jenny Lind, C.M. & S., 8 1/2 In. 110.00
Tureen, Cover, Blue & White Scenes Of Rural Life, 14 In. 275.00
Tureen, Cover, Molded Acanthus Handles, Figural Scenes, England, 16 1/2 In. 220.00
Tureen, Sauce, Stand, Transfer Landscape Scenes, Foliage, 6 x 7 1/2 In. 45.00
Tureen, Sauce, Wheat & Barley, W. Taylor, Ladle 65.00
Tureen, Vegetable, Cover, England, 19th Century, 11 3/4 In. 230.00

IVOREX plaques were made in England by Arthur Osborne in the beginning of the 1900s. The plaques, made of a material he called *sterine wax*, pictured buildings or room interiors modeled in three dimensions. After Osborne's death, his daughter Blanche ran the company. It was closed in 1965, then purchased by W. H. Bossons Ltd. in 1971. Production of the plaques started again in 1980.

"IVOREX"
OSBORNE-(COPYRIGHT.
MADE IN ENGLAND.

Plaque, Friendly Call, Osborne, 9 1/2 x 6 In. 20.00
Plaque, Old Folks At Home, Osborne, 9 1/2 x 6 In. 30.00

IVORY from the tusk of an elephant is thought by many to be the only true ivory. To most collectors, the term *ivory* also includes such natural materials as walrus, hippopotamus, or whale teeth or tusks, and some of the vegetable materials that are of similar texture and density. Other ivory items may be found in the Scrimshaw and Netsuke categories. Collectors should be aware of the recent laws limiting the buying and selling of elephant ivory and scrimshaw.

Basket, Rose, 4 In.	70.00
Boat, Cockerel Head Prow, 7 Figures, Base Carved To Depict Waves, 15 In.	1955.00
Box, Bald Man, With Earrings Caricature, Japan, 19th Century, 1 1/8 x 1 1/8 In.	280.00
Box, Cover, Portrait Of King Edward VII, 2 3/4 In.	420.00
Box, Powder, Dome Top, Ivory Puff Handle, Bailey Banks & Biddle, Continental, 1800s	431.00
Box, Small Circles & Dots, Dyed Red, 19th Century, 3 In.	172.00
Bust, Of Woman, Her Hair Drawn Up, Set With Leaves, Onyx Pedestal, 11 In.	862.00
Bust, Woman, African, Large Facial Features, Elaborate Hairstyle, 3 5/8 In.	115.00
Card Case, Carved, 19th Century, 4 1/2 x 3 In.	165.00
Card Case, Ebonized Geometric Designs, Anglo-Indian, 1875-1900, 4 x 3 In.	165.00
Card Case, Figures With Pavilions & Willow Trees, 3 3/8 x 1 3/4 In.	165.00
Card Case, Landscape, Early 19th Century, 3 1/4 In.	230.00
Card Case, Penwork Floral, Scroll Design, Mahogany Case, 4 1/2 x 3 1/2 In.	302.00
Carriage, Passengers, Driver, Oxen, Continental, Late 19th Century, 3 3/4 In.	374.00
Casket, Hinged Cover, Foliate Cartouche Surrounded By Butterflies, 5 3/4 In.	1150.00
Cigar Holder, Inlaid Wire, Gold Color, 3 1/2 In.	40.00
Cigarette Holder, Amber, Gold, Orlik, 20th Century, 4 In.	25.00
Cigarette Holder, Woman's, Carved Floral	65.00
Crucifix, Walnut Cross, Continental, 13 1/2 In.	345.00
Dagger Handle, Carved Ivory Sheath, 10 In.	60.00
Figurine, 2 Children, Holding Basket On Rockery Under Peach Tree, 7 In.	373.00
Figurine, 2 Figures & Deer Among Gnarled Trees, Hand Carved, 7 In.	77.00
Figurine, 3 Men Paddling Canoe, 3 x 8 1/2 In.	345.00
Figurine, Basket, Crabs & Water Plants, 12 In.	1380.00
Figurine, Bishop, Holding Staff & Chalice, Continental, 19th Century, 6 1/2 In.	825.00
Figurine, Boy Holding A Double Gourd Bottle, 4 1/4 In.	99.00
Figurine, Bridge, Figures & Pavilions, Pierced, 10 In.	192.00
Figurine, Buddha, Seated On Ornate Double Throne, Early 19th Century, 6 1/2 In.	690.00
Figurine, Chinese Sage, Horn, 19th Century, 5 1/2 In.	357.00
Figurine, Cupid Holding Bouquet Of Flowers, 5 3/4 In.	1092.00
Figurine, Daikoku Holding His Hammer In 1 Hand, Rat In Other Hand, 3 1/8 In.	88.00
Figurine, Deity, Many Hands Holding Instruments, Standing On Demon, India, 9 In.	440.00
Figurine, Dragon, Chasing Flaming Pearl, 5 1/2 In.	550.00
Figurine, Elephant, Trunk Up, 5 In.	224.00
Figurine, Emperor & Empress, Standing Holding A Ju-I Scepter & Sword, 8 In., Pair	247.00
Figurine, Farmer, With Hoe, Signed With 2 Character Mark, 6 1/2 In.	425.00
Figurine, Female Deity, Rides On Phoenix, Male Deity Rides On Dragon, 6 In., Pair	1320.00
Figurine, Fisherman, Catching Carp, Signed, 6 1/4 In.	115.00
Figurine, Fisherman, Sitting, Holding Catch, Signed, Chinese, 5 In.	230.00
Figurine, Fisherman, With Net, China, 7 In.	280.00
Figurine, Fukurokuju, Standing Beside Recumbent Ram, 2 In.	99.00
Figurine, Fukurokuju, Standing With Fan In One Hand, Tortoise In The Other, 3 In.	55.00
Figurine, Joss, Seated, Holding Double Gourd Bottle, 4 In.	88.00
Figurine, King, With Sword & Scepter, Continental, 19th Century, 7 1/4 In.	815.00
Figurine, Lohan, 10 3/4 In.	862.00
Figurine, Madonna & Child, Scepter, Flowing Robes, Child Holding Orb, 9 In.	2300.00
Figurine, Madonna, Glass Inset Eyes, Santos, 31 In.	690.00
Figurine, Man, Carrying Basket, Japan, 4 3/4 In.	89.00
Figurine, Man, Holding Blossoms, 5 In.	345.00
Figurine, Man, With Sword, Blowing Conch Shell, Polychrome, Signed, Chinese, 3 In.	405.00
Figurine, Marie De Bourgogne, Necklace, Fur Trimmed Robe, Holding Hawk, 12 In.	2645.00
Figurine, Minerva, Signed Bernoud, Gilt Bronze, Marble Base, 11 1/2 In.	3220.00
Figurine, Nude Bather, Clasped Towel At Waist, Arm Raised, Pedestal, 11 In.	2875.00
Figurine, Peasant, Carrying Broken Basket With Spill Peaches, 5 1/2 In.	220.00
Figurine, Pierrot, Standing, Pulling On Pants, Columnar Pedestal, 19th Century, 5 3/4 In.	525.00
Figurine, Qwannon, Holding Basket & Lotus Flower, Japan, 19th Century, 12 In.	550.00

Figurine, Sage, Seated On Rockery Holding His Bear, 1 Hand, Fan In Other, 3 In., Pair .. 357.00
Figurine, Samurai Warrior, 9 In. 400.00
Figurine, Seal Hunter, Fighting Bear, Walrus, 5 1/2 In. 920.00
Figurine, St. George, Slaying The Dragon, Continental, 4 In. 347.00
Figurine, St. Jerome, Glass Inset Eyes, Santos, 21 In. 460.00
Figurine, Viking, Draped Cloak, Leaning Against Shield, Ivory Base, 8 3/4 In. 1725.00
Figurine, Warrior In Full Dress With Sword, Incised, Signed, Teakwood Stand, 7 In. 600.00
Figurine, Woman, Holding Fan, Plate With Teapot & Peaches, Japan, 8 1/2 In. 635.00
Figurine, Woman, Holding Lute, Seated On Garden Seat, Rosewood Stand, 7 In. 460.00
Game Box, Hinged Cover, Battle Scenes, Signed, France, 1720, 3 3/8 In., 4 Piece 4885.00
Group, 2 Men With Musical Instruments, Incised, Polychrome, Signed, Chinese, 3 In. . . . 230.00
Group, 4 Figures, 2 Animals In Row Boat, Signed, 3 In. 500.00
Group, Antelope, Crocodile, Penguins, 7 In. 195.00
Group, Dog Sled, Walrus, 17 3/4 In. 2070.00
Group, Man, Sitting Near Table, Boy, Carrying Axe, 12 x 8 In. 175.00
Hair Clip, Oriental, 6 1/2 In. 16.00
Handle, Parasol, Carved Dog's Head, 8 3/4 In. 55.00
Humidor, Rectangular Hinged Cover, Shagreen, Fitted Interior, 6 x 13 1/4 x 10 1/4 In. . . . 7475.00
Mask, Africa, 1930s, 4 3/4 x 2 3/4 In. 250.00
Model, Steam Engine, Articulated, Gears & Beams, Wood Base, 12 3/4 In. 6900.00
Okimono, Bearded Sage 2750.00
Okimono, Fukurokuju Holding Inro & A Peach, Early 20th Century, 2 In. 121.00
Panel, Cavaliers, On Horseback, Soldiers, Curved, Walnut Frame, France, 5 x 15 In. 4715.00
Pipe Rest, Tavern Revelers Smoking Pipes, Continental, 7 1/2 In. 402.00
Plaque, Medieval Soldiers On Horseback Parading Through Village, 3 1/2 x 2 3/4 In. 402.00
Plaque, Roman Battle Scene, Emperor, Continental 2300.00
Portrait, Gentleman, Bust Length, Green Coat, Tie, Woven Hair Reverse, 1780, 3 x 3 In. . 550.00
Puzzle Ball, Figural Shaft, 19th Century, 2 1/4-In. Ball, 5 In. 230.00
Puzzle Ball, Floral & Geometric Design, Figural Pedestal, Japan, 8 3/4 In. 295.00
Puzzle Ball, Stand, 2 1/2 x 8 1/2 In. 70.00
Sphere, On Stand, Concentric Circles, African Tusk Ivory, Hong Kong, 9 In. 55.00
Tankard, Battle Scene On Sleeve, Chased Scrolled Foliage, Caryatid Handle, 12 In. 9200.00
Tankard, Medieval Battle, Silver Repousse Base & Lid, Nuremburg, 18th Century, 13 In. . 7425.00
Teapot, Floral & Foliate Design, Dragon Handle, Foo Lion Finial, Chinese, 6 In. 290.00
Tusk, Carved, 8 Immortals & Dragon, Japan, 19th Century, 17 1/2 In. 880.00
Tusk, Man & Woman, 10 In., Pair 175.00
Tusk, Village Scene In The Round, Carved, Africa, 11 1/2 In. 399.00
Vase, Figural & Animal Designs, Chinese, 5 3/4 In. 805.00
Walrus, Icon, Crucifixion, Leaf Beaded Border, 18th Century, 11 1/2 x 8 1/4 In. 1035.00
Wax Seal, Brass, Tapered Handle, Noble Crest, Motto, England, 1820-1830, 3 3/4 In. 88.00

JACK-IN-THE-PULPIT vases, oddly shaped like trumpets, resemble the
wild plant called jack-in-the-pulpit. The design originated in the late
Victorian years. Vases in the jack-in-the-pulpit shape were made of
ceramic or glass, and the complete list of page references can be found
in the index.

Vase, Amethyst, Silver, Blue Spots & Lines, Loetz, c.1900, 4 x 5 In. 975.00
Vase, Black Glass, 10 1/2 In. 125.00
Vase, Blue & Lavender Top & Stem, Fluted Crystal Base, 11 In. 65.00
Vase, Brown On Cream, Czechoslovakia, 7 In. 95.00
Vase, Olive & Amber Streaked, Art Glass, 8 In. 40.00
Vase, Pale Chartreuse Iridescent, Emerald Green Pulled Leaves, 8 1/2 In. 1800.00
Vase, Rubina Frost, Crimped, Pulled Rim, 10 1/2 In. 165.00
Vase, Stretch Glass, 17 In. 35.00
Vase, Vaseline Body, Blue Opalescent Top, Cranberry Edging, 5 1/4 In. 90.00
Vase, Yellow, White & Crystal, Art Glass, 8 3/4 In. 75.00

JADE is the name for two different minerals, nephrite and jadeite.
Nephrite is the mineral used for most early Oriental carvings. Jade is a
very tough stone that is found in many colors from dark green to pale
lavender. Jade carvings are still being made in the old styles, so collectors must be careful not to be fooled by recent pieces. Jade jewelry
is found in this book under Jewelry.

Box, Carved, Melon Form, Flowers & Vines, Bird On Top, Pale Green, 3 In. 345.00

Figurine, 3 Birds Among Flowering Cherry, Wooden Stand, 10 7/8 x 7 x 2 In. 85.00
Figurine, Basket Of Crabs, Pale Green, 6 In. 172.00
Figurine, Bird Perched On Fruited, Flowering Tree, 3 1/2 x 4 In. 230.00
Figurine, Buddha, Apple Green, 19th Century, 1 1/2 In. 125.00
Figurine, Dancing Buddha, Teakwood Base, 8 1/4 In. 895.00
Figurine, Foo Dog, Carved, Wooden Base, 4 In., Pair 259.00
Figurine, Goat, Carved, Fitted Case, Semi-Modern, Chinese, 5 In. 196.00
Figurine, Gorilla, Holding Its Young, Diamond Eyes, 2 3/4 In. 2300.00
Figurine, Horse, Celadon Striations, Deep Green, 5 1/2 In. 575.00
Figurine, Phoenix & Another Bird On Floral Branch, Teakwood Stand, Chinese, 8 In. 175.00
Figurine, Stallion, 14 In. 80.00
Group, 3 People Sailing Junk, Carved Wooden Base With Waves, 9 1/2 In. 650.00
Hook, Belt, 5 Dragon Hooks, 5 Archer Rings, Gray Jade Finial, Pipe Bowl, 12 Piece 1265.00
Scepter, 3 Panels, Gods Of Longevity, Deer, Pine Tree & Crane, 19th Century, 16 In. 1090.00
Vase, Ingrid Series, 3 Women Dancing In Vineyard, Deep Green, Schlevogt, 1935, 8 In. . . 345.00

JAPANESE WOODBLOCK PRINTS are listed in this book in the Print category under Japanese.

JASPERWARE can be made in different ways. Some pieces are made from a solid colored clay with applied raised designs of a contrasting colored clay. Other pieces are made entirely of one color clay with raised decorations that are glazed with a contrasting color. Additional pieces of jasperware may also be listed in the Wedgwood category or under various art potteries.

Cheese Dome, Stand, Dark Blue, White, Acorn Finial, 8 1/2 In. 305.00
Clock, Ansonia, Scrolled Case, Putti & Leaves, 6 1/4 In. 172.00
Ewer, Blue, White Basket Weave, Pewter Lid, Milan, 9 In. 440.00
Ewer, Lavender Glazed, Pewter Lid, Classical Figures, S. Alcock, c.1847, 11 In. 250.00
Hair Receiver, 3 Grecian Women At Sides, Jewels From Box, Birds On Cover, 4 In. 95.00
Hair Receiver, Grecian Women Around Sides, Holding Bird, Blue & White, 4 In. 110.00
Lamp, Blue, White, Bronze Lights, 29 In. 440.00
Pitcher, Scene, Green, White, Germany 85.00
Pitcher, Water, Classical Scene, Blue, White, 19th Century, 8 In. 220.00
Plaque, Free-Form, Scrolled Rim, White Animals & Female Figures, 1900, 12 In. 316.00
Sugar, Cover, Blue, White, Adams 110.00
Teapot, Cover, Dark Blue, White, Adams 165.00
Vase, Blue, White Classical Design, 10 1/2 In. 195.00

JEWELRY, whether made from gold and precious gems or plastic and colored glass, is popular with collectors. Values are determined by the intrinsic value of the stones and metal and by the skill of the craftsmen and designers. Victorian and older jewelry have been collected since the 1950s. More recent interests are Art Deco and Edwardian styles, Mexican and Danish silver jewelry, and beads of all kinds. Copies of almost all styles are being made. American Indian jewelry is listed in the Indian category.

Barrette, Open Rectangle, Collet Set Diamonds, Pearls, 14K Gold, Victorian 430.00
Belt, Concha, Sterling Silver, Oval Rosette, Swirled Rectangular Buckle, RR Mark 275.00
Belt Buckle, Jadeite, Pierce Carved Dragons, Dragon's Head Clasp, 3 1/2 In. 14300.00
Bracelet, 3 Rows Of Sapphires & Diamonds, Gebelein, 6 3/4 In. 9200.00
Bracelet, 4 Bead Set Diamonds, Onyx Line, Art Deco, 7 1/8 In. 4025.00
Bracelet, 7 Moonstones, 7 Pairs Of Sapphires, Tiffany & Co., c.1915, 7 1/2 In. 17250.00
Bracelet, 15 Round Cut Diamonds, 14K Rose Gold, Retro 3737.00
Bracelet, Agate, Alternating Carved Floral & Bar Links, Scotland, 7 In. 488.00
Bracelet, Aztec Design Rectangular Links, Rubies, Tiffany & Co., 7 1/4 In. 1840.00
Bracelet, Bakelite, Bangle, Apple Juice, Reverse Carved, Crosshatch, Red Paint 1760.00
Bracelet, Bakelite, Bangle, Bowties, Orange, 1 In. 3575.00
Bracelet, Bakelite, Bangle, Hinged, Green, Brown Wood Turtle 315.00
Bracelet, Bangle, 2 Concentric Pears Shape, Sterling Silver, Signed, Los Castillo, Taxco . 258.00
Bracelet, Bangle, 3 Sapphires, 2 Round Cut Diamonds, Victorian, Box, 1889 . . . . 3680.00
Bracelet, Bangle, Chased Foliate Design, Art Nouveau, 14K Yellow Gold 1035.00
Bracelet, Bangle, Crosillon, Yellow Gold, Green Enamel, Schlumberger, 5 3/4 In. 7475.00

Bracelet, Bangle, Diamonds, Black Enamel, 14K Gold, Victorian 980.00
Bracelet, Bangle, Green Splashes, White, 19th Century, 2 3/4 In., Pair 2750.00
Bracelet, Bangle, Inset With Opals, Diamonds, Filigree Top, 14K Gold, c.1970 .... 175.00
Bracelet, Bangle, Ivory, Carved Floral & Leaf 110.00
Bracelet, Bangle, Peridot & Pearls, 9K Yellow Gold, London, 1977 .... 260.00
Bracelet, Bangle, Tiger, Enamel, Red Stone Eyes, Gold 201.00
Bracelet, Blister Pearls, Gold Grape & Leaf Links, Baroque Pearl Drop, Arts & Crafts ... 405.00
Bracelet, Cameo, Classical Scenes, Dancing Maidens, Gilt Metal 750.00
Bracelet, Carved Carnelian Links, 18K Gold Links, Seaman Schepps, 7 1/2 In. 2875.00
Bracelet, Carved Stone, Leaf Design, 2 Carnellian Scarabs, 14K Gold, Edwardian 375.00
Bracelet, Centered By Horseshoe, Toggle Design, Victorian, 15K Gold 1725.00
Bracelet, Charm, 12 Discs, With Different Flower For Each Month, 14K Yellow Gold ... 862.00
Bracelet, Charm, 4 Heart Charms & Padlock, England 70.00
Bracelet, Chestnut, Links, Art Nouveau, 14K Gold, Rokesley, 7 1/4 x 1/2 In. 6000.00
Bracelet, Circular Gilt Clasp Center, Sterling Silver, 1900 .... 546.00
Bracelet, Copper, Enameled, Wide, Mattisse 42.00
Bracelet, Cuff, Aluminum, Seahorse 130.00
Bracelet, Cuff, Diamond Clusters, Abstract Textured 18K Gold, David Webb 3740.00
Bracelet, Cuff, Reeded Design, Diamonds In Greek Key Design, 18K Gold, Tiffany 2875.00
Bracelet, Daisy, Openwork, Yellow Gold, Schlumberger, 7 1/4 In. 4025.00
Bracelet, Diamonds, Platinum, Flexible Geometric Links, Art Deco, 6 3/4 In. 13225.00
Bracelet, Diamonds, Platinum, Geometric Plaques, Round Links, Art Deco, 7 1/2 In. 6040.00
Bracelet, Diamonds, Sapphires, Geometric Design, Platinum, Art Deco, 7 1/4 In. 5750.00
Bracelet, Emerald, Diamond Surround, Seed Pearls, Platinum, Belle Epoque, 7 3/4 In. ... 2185.00
Bracelet, Flexible Cuff, Movable Sections, 18K Gold, Stainless Steel, Bulgari 2645.00
Bracelet, Gold Filled Links, Cat Charm, Marcasite Collar, Judith Jack, 8 In. 115.00
Bracelet, Gold Knot, Beaded Box Link Chain, Blue Beads, Diamonds, Victorian, 7 In. ... 635.00
Bracelet, Gold Mesh Chain, Slide, Pearl Center, Beaded, Tracery Accents, Victorian 980.00
Bracelet, Gold Mesh, Fleur-De-Lis Engraved Plaque, Red & Green Stones, Georgian 1380.00
Bracelet, Gold Slide, Victorian, 18K Yellow Gold 2185.00
Bracelet, Gold Snake's Head, Sapphire Eyes, Snake Link Band, Diamond Tail, c.1890 ... 8625.00
Bracelet, Gold, Oval Openwork Links, Scroll Motif, 18th Century, 9 In. 1380.00
Bracelet, Hinged Bangle, Faceted Garnet Clusters, Gilt Mount, Victorian 260.00
Bracelet, Hinged Bangle, Gold, Oval Garnet, Blue Enamel, Repousse Scroll, Victorian ... 315.00
Bracelet, Hinged Bangle, Row Of Pearls, Rose Diamonds, Gold, Renaissance Revival ... 4600.00
Bracelet, Hinged Geometric Plaques, Diamonds, Platinum, Art Deco, 7 1/4 In. 12650.00
Bracelet, Hinged, Gold, Purple Marquise, Rhinestone Leaves, Monet 75.00
Bracelet, Hinged, Pearl Row, Blue Enamel, Renaissance Revival, 18K Gold 4600.00
Bracelet, Invisible Rubies, Baguette Diamonds, Platinum & Gold, 1945, 6 1/4 In. 7476.00
Bracelet, Link, Hinged Plaques, 18K Gold, Retro, 8 In. 980.00
Bracelet, Linked Letters, Spelling I Love You, 14K Yellow Gold 431.00
Bracelet, Love Token, Silver, 11 Foreign Suspended Coins, 6 Engraved With Names 60.00
Bracelet, Marquis Diamond, 3 Rows Of Box Set Diamonds, Emeralds, Art Deco, 7 In. ... 25300.00
Bracelet, Mesh, Central Knot, Pearls, Rose Cut Starburst Design, 14K Gold, Victorian ... 1150.00
Bracelet, Mesh, Seed Pearls, Platinum, Diamond Spacers, Edwardian, 7 3/4 In. 8625.00
Bracelet, Mesh, Shield Shaped Slide, Cloverleaf, Seed Pearls, 14K Gold, Victorian, Pair . 1265.00
Bracelet, Mother-Of-Pearl Butterfly, Sterling Silver, Mexico 25.00
Bracelet, Mutton Fat Jade, Carved Hound, Deer & Bat, 18th Century 230.00
Bracelet, Openwork Foliate Panels, 235 Diamonds, Pearls, Belle Epoque, 7 1/4 In. 13800.00
Bracelet, Oval Moonstones, Sapphires, Fancy Links, 14K Gold, Raymond Yard, 6 3/4 In. . 2300.00
Bracelet, Pearl, 6 Twisted Strands, Enamel & Gold Frog Pair Clasp, David Webb 1610.00
Bracelet, Pearls, Diamonds, Platinum Curb Link Chain, Edwardian, 7 In. 920.00
Bracelet, Purple Rhinestones, Eisenberg, 7 In. 143.00
Bracelet, Rhinestone, Aqua Rhinestone Flowers, Silver Metal, Eisenberg, 7 1/2 In. 132.00
Bracelet, Rhinestones, Safety Chain, Eisenberg, 7 1/4 In. 143.00
Bracelet, Round Cut Diamonds, Art Deco, 18K White Gold 109.00
Bracelet, Round Cut Diamonds, Emeralds, Art Deco 46.00
Bracelet, Round Onyx Links, Lapis Spacers, Silver Art Moderne, France, 7 3/4 In. 1725.00
Bracelet, Rubies, Diamonds, 14K Gold Rope Scroll Links, Tiffany & Co., Case 3220.00
Bracelet, Rubies, Round Ornament, Hinged, 18K White Gold, Mid 20th Century 460.00
Bracelet, Silver Gilt, Floral Paneled Sections, Chinese Export, 1840 .... 605.00
Bracelet, Silver, 8 Half-Dome Rectangular Segments, Pin Clasp, Los Castillo, 2 In. 172.00
Bracelet, Silver, Hinged Geometric Forms, Antonio Pineda, Mexico, 9 1/2 In. 575.00

Bracelet, Smoky Quartz, Citrine, Lalique, 1908, 8 1/4 In. 18400.00
Bracelet, Snake, Silver Mesh, Whiting & Davis 42.00
Bracelet, Sterling Link, S-Clasp, Livingston, 1 In. 190.00
Bracelet, Sterling Silver, Cuff Style, Etched Line, Georg Jensen, After 1945, 6 5/8 In. . . . 520.00
Bracelet, Sterling Silver, Floral, Turquoise, Southwest Native, Signed, Jeri Clark 85.00
Bracelet, Tennis, 14K White & Yellow Gold, 34 Sapphires, 34 Diamonds, 7 3/4 In. 440.00
Bracelet, Token, From 1 Dollar Gold Pieces, Re-Engraved Reverse, Pat. Feb. 18, '17 . . . . 415.00
Bracelet, Woman's, Black Enamel, Gold Arabic Numerals, Gold Foxtail Fringe, 1950 . . . 575.00
Bracelet & Earrings, Bakelite, Bangle, Hinged, Yellow, Carved Flowers 290.00
Bracelet Watch, Sapphire, Ruby, Snake Link Band, Gold Padlock, Platinum, Gold, 1945 . 7476.00
Buckle, Deer In Forest, Tree, Perched Birds On Clasp, Copper, 1947, 3 In. 2990.00
Buckle, Fish, Bakelite, 3 Buttons Of Carved Fish, Green Buckle, 4 1/2 x 2 In. 495.00
Buckle, Pearls, Rectangular, Silver, Arts & Crafts, 1 3/4 x 2 1/8 In. 395.00
Chatelaine, 8 Drops, Thread Winder, Pencil Ivory 875.00
Chatelaine, Aide Memoir, Waist Clip, Silver Plate, 6 x 2 1/2 In. 325.00
Chatelaine, Dagger, Scabbard, Gilt Metal, Amethysts & Turquoise, Waist Clip, 7 In. 500.00
Chatelaine, Gilt Base Metal, Amethysts, Pencil, Dance Tablet 495.00
Chatelaine, Mourning Fan, Black Metal, Long Chain, Egyptian Revival 285.00
Chatelaine, Mourning, Metal, Jet Stones, 4 Chains, Bottle, Stiletto, Needle Case, Box . . . 695.00
Chatelaine, Vinaigrette, Silver Gilt, Waist Clip, 19th Century 595.00
Chatelaine, Walnut Shape, Repousse, Gilt Interior, Art Nouveau, ... 575.00
Chatelaine, Wheat, Geometric Design, Sterling Silver, Art Nouveau 460.00
Cheroot Case, Tortoiseshell, Pique Work, Belle Epoque, c.1900, 5 1/2 x 3 In. 495.00
Cigarette Case, Buckhorn, 3 In. 20.00
Cigarette Case, Chrome, Evans 25.00
Cigarette Case, Domed Square Design, Monogram, 14K Gold, Tiffany & Co. . . . . \. . 545.00
Cigarette Case, Monogram Cover, Link Chain, 14K Gold, Alling & Co., Newark 230.00
Clip, Bakelite, Apple Juice, Carved, Multicolored Crystals, Gilt Metal, Chanel 195.00
Clip, Bird, Red, Green, Blue Enamel, Pave Rhinestones, Stamped, Trifari, 4 In. 253.00
Clip, Blue Rhinestones, Silver Metal, Stamped, Eisenberg, 3 In. 220.00
Clip, Bouquet, Fuchsia Rhinestones, Stamped, Eisenberg, 4 1/2 In. 550.00
Clip, Bouquet, Purple, Pink Rhinestones, Gilt Sterling, Eisenberg, 4 1/2 In. 770.00
Clip, Clam Shell, Light Green Rhinestone Center, Stamped, Rhinestone, 2 In. 242.00
Clip, Dancer, Pave Rhinestones, Stamped, Trifari, 2 1/2 In. 770.00
Clip, Dancer, Red Pearlized Enamel, Red Cabochons, Pave Rhinestones, Boucher, 2 In. . . 1100.00
Clip, Dress, Lily Pad, Silver Beads & Wirework, Sterling Silver, Mary Gage, 2 In. 287.00
Clip, Faux Pearls, Green Rhinestones, Eisenberg 495.00
Clip, Figural Bust, Purple Rhinestones, Stamped, Eisenberg, 3 1/2 In. 550.00
Clip, Fish, Pave Rhinestones, Cabochon Eye, Silver Metal, Trifari, 3 1/4 In. 605.00
Clip, Floral Cascade, Citrine, Purple, Red, Green, Blue Rhinestones, Eisenberg, 4 In. 715.00
Clip, Floral, Aqua, Crescent Rhinestones, Green, Brown Enamel, Stamped, Trifari, 3 In. . . 1320.00
Clip, Flower Bouquet, Purple, Topaz Pave Rhinestones, Silver Metal, Trifari, 2 In. 242.00
Clip, Fruit Salad, Carved Rhinestones, Silver Metal, Trifari, 1 1/2 In. 385.00
Clip, Fruit Salad, Floral Design, Carved Moonstones, Red Rhinestones, Trifari, 4 In. 1650.00
Clip, Fruit Salad, Pave Rhinestones, Silver Metal, Trifari, 3 1/4 In. 308.00
Clip, Fur, Sterling Silver, Tiara Shaped Top, Eisenberg, 2 x 2 1/2 In. 195.00
Clip, Fur, Tiara Shape, Rhinestone, Sterling Silver, Eisenberg, 2 x 2 1/2 In. 195.00
Clip, Green Enamel Leaves, Faux Pearls, Gilt Metal, Eisenberg, 4 In. 330.00
Clip, Leaf, Purple Crescent Rhinestones, Pave Rhinestones, Stamped, Trifari, 4 In. 1210.00
Clip, Pink Rhinestones, Floral Spray, Stamped, Eisenberg, 4 1/2 In. 209.00
Clip, Rhinestone Cascade, Stamped, Eisenberg, 3 1/4 In. 121.00
Clip, Rooster, Red, White, Blue Enamel, Stamped Staret, 2 1/2 In. 176.00
Clip, Sailboat, Blue Enamel, Diamonds, Platinum, Art Deco 520.00
Clip, Swiss Miss, Girl With Red, Black Enamel, Pave Rhinestones, Trifari, 2 1/2 In. 220.00
Clip, Topaz Rhinestones, Gilt Metal, Eisenberg, 2 1/2 In. 187.00
Clip & Earrings, Star Burst, Rhinestones, Gilt Sterling, Trifari, 2 1/2 x 1/4 In. 176.00
Clip & Earrings, Tree Pin, Blue, Topaz Crescent Rhinestones, Trifari, 3 x 1/4 In. 2288.00
Comb, Chased Wild Roses, Sapphires, 14K Gold, Tortoiseshell, Art Nouveau 290.00
Comb, Tortoiseshell, Chased Gold Leaves, C-Scrolls, Art Nouveau, 6 1/8 In. 260.00
Cuff Link & Stud Set, Mother-Of-Pearl Discs, Platinum, Pearls, Edwardian, 9 Piece 635.00
Cuff Links, 2 Ovals, 14K Gold, Green & Blue Enamel Stripes, Marti, c.1960, 3/4 In. 345.00
Cuff Links, Bird, Berry Design, Silver, Signed, Georg Jensen 374.00
Cuff Links, Chased & Engraved Floral Border, 14K Gold, Art Nouveau 230.00

Jewelry, Cuff Links, Indian Goddess Dancing In
Lotus, Metal, Under Lucite, 1 1/4 In.

Always make sure the repairs to jewelry are made with matching solder—gold on gold, platinum on platinum. Lead solder will lower the value of any piece of jewelry.

Cuff Links, Club Shaped Links, Gold Beads, Gold Chain, Schlumberger, Tiffany	1495.00
Cuff Links, Diamond Pave Top, 14K Gold, Twist, Textured, c.1960, 1 1/8 In.	145.00
Cuff Links, Female Bust, Depicting 4 Seasons, Gold, Art Nouveau, J.E. Caldwell, Box	750.00
Cuff Links, Female Profile In Relief, Onyx, 10K Gold, Victorian	290.00
Cuff Links, Floral Border, Art Nouveau, 14K Yellow Gold	230.00
Cuff Links, Indian Goddess Dancing In Lotus, Metal, Under Lucite, 1 1/4 In. ....*Illus*	35.00
Cuff Links, Jadeite, Navette Shape, 14K Gold, c.1920, 1 1/8 x 3/8 In.	290.00
Cuff Links, Nautilus, Circular Links, Sterling Silver, Signed, Georg Jensen	345.00
Cuff Links, Opossum Plaque, Sterling Silver, Unger Brothers	430.00
Cuff Links, Raised Whiplash, Stippled Surface, 14K Gold, Art Nouveau	125.00
Cuff Links, Snake, Green Plique-A-Jour Enamel, 18K Gold	1380.00
Cuff Links, Sterling Silver & Ebony, Lewittes	55.00
Cuff Links, Textured Gold Oval Outline, Oblong Link, 18K Gold, Mario Buccellati	2300.00
Cuff Links, Tortoiseshell, Silver Trim, Mexico	50.00
Dog Collar, Classical Busts On Diamond Shaped Plaques, Silver, Shiebler, 13 In.	750.00
Dress Set, Cuff Links, Shirt Studs, Coral, 14K Gold, Angelskin, Edwardian, 5 Piece	290.00
Earrings, 2 Ribbed Hearts, Bowknots Above, 14K Gold, Tiffany & Co., 7/8 In.	175.00
Earrings, 5-Pointed Star, 18K Yellow Gold, B.S.K.	575.00
Earrings, Arrow Top, Hammered Sterling Silver, Antonio, Mexico, 2 In.	440.00
Earrings, Beaded Oval, Silver, Georg Jensen, Denmark, 1 In.	287.00
Earrings, Bust Of Woman, Suspended From Floral Gold Cameo, 18K Yellow Gold	734.00
Earrings, Clover, 18K Yellow Gold, Clip-On, Signed, A. Cipullo Cartier	805.00
Earrings, Concave Rounded Discs, Sterling Silver, Signed, Georg Jensen, Pair	287.00
Earrings, Concentric Pear Shaped Drops, Gold, Foxtail Fringe, Victorian, 3 In.	920.00
Earrings, Coral, Mabe Pearl, White Gold Diamonds, 14K Yellow Gold	632.00
Earrings, Coral, Teardrop Shape, Coral Bead Top, Victorian, 18K Yellow Gold	575.00
Earrings, Diamond Tops, Elongated Pear Shaped Jade Drops, Link Chain, Art Deco	1265.00
Earrings, Directoire, Pear Shaped Drop, Blue, White Champleve, 18K Yellow Gold	431.00
Earrings, Dragon, Pewter, Brass, Clip-On, La Porte Bleure, Paris, 1910	45.00
Earrings, Drop, Fan Shaped Top, Diamonds, Open Pear Shaped Drop, Art Deco	5290.00
Earrings, Drop, Flower, Split Pearls, 18K Gold, Victorian, c.1865	1210.00
Earrings, Emerald & Ruby, East Indian, 22K Gold	330.00
Earrings, Etruscan Revival, Garnet Carbuncles, Enamel Accents, Gold Fringe	520.00
Earrings, Female Bust Within An Oval Frame, Agate, Seed Pearls, 18K Yellow Gold	690.00
Earrings, Flexible Bow & Ribbon, 14K Gold, Tiffany, 1985, 2 1/4 In.	520.00
Earrings, Flower, Leaves, Grape Clusters, 12K Gold, Black Hills, Clip-On	20.00
Earrings, Flowerhead, Rubies, Diamonds, Platinum, 14K Gold, Retro, Clip-On	2185.00
Earrings, Fluted Amethyst Teardrop, Platinum, Diamond Link Chain, Art Deco	2185.00
Earrings, Garnet Cabochon, Faceted Garnet Clusters, 3 Garnet Drops, 3 In.	690.00
Earrings, Girandole, Silver Paste, Engraved Closed Backs, c.1900, 3 In.	460.00
Earrings, Granite, Gray Triangular Tops, 2 Half Moons, Peach Granite, Silver	200.00
Earrings, Half-Hoop Design, 16 Diamonds, Ribbed, 18K Gold, Clip-On, Tiffany	1495.00
Earrings, Hoop, Bakelite, Butterscotch, 1 1/2 In.	30.00
Earrings, Hoop, Huggies Style, Pave Set Diamonds, Platinum	1955.00
Earrings, Lion's Head, Classical Revival, 18K White Gold, Mauboussin, Paris	805.00
Earrings, Mogul Style, Rose Cut Diamonds, Green Stones, Seed Pearl	690.00
Earrings, Moonstone Cabochons, Red Rhinestones, Trifari, 1 In.	121.00
Earrings, Onyx Ring, 3 Pyramid Shaped Frosted Crystals, 18K Gold, Cartier, A. Cipullo	2530.00
Earrings, Openwork Foliate, Circular Cut Diamonds, Textured Gold, M. Buccellati	3450.00
Earrings, Pearls, Baroque, Bead Set Rose Cut Diamonds, Gold Mount, Victorian	1495.00
Earrings, Pearls, Baroque, Diamonds, 18K Gold, David Webb	2185.00

SPECIAL MOMENTS, SPECIAL EVENTS, AND SPECIAL DAYS

YOU CHERISH Grandmother's sugar bowl, the Chatty Cathy doll saved from your childhood, and the oak chair you bought at an antiques shop years ago as much for the memories they evoke as for their look. Collecting is a way to remember the special moments of times past. Souvenirs of rocket launches and Niagara Falls, memorabilia from birthdays and holidays, and even family photographs all recall events of importance.

Vendors since ancient times have catered to the wishes of tourists and made souvenir items to be bought and taken home. The ancient Greeks offered small coins, medieval churches sold relics, and nineteenth-century gift shops and fairs sold specially decorated plates, needle cases and thimbles, handkerchiefs, dolls, tablecloths, cards, and knickknacks to those taking home a memory. Most of these mementos have remained low-priced and create an interesting area of collecting.

Today Christmas and Halloween are the most popular holidays for collectors, followed closely by Valentine's Day and the Fourth of July. Collectors look for anything connected with these holidays, even new pieces. World's Fair items, British royal family coronation and jubilee pieces, and political campaign collectibles are also popular. This year, look for a new collection of memories, still to be found at low prices.

SPECIAL DAYS THROUGHOUT THE YEAR

J A N U A R Y

The year 1930 could have started with a New Year's Eve noisemaker like this one decorated with a clown face. It was made by the U.S. Metal Toy Manufacturing Co. The 8-inch lithographed tin clacker is worth $7.

New Year's postcards and greeting cards were not very popular until the early 1900s. Although holly berries, snow, and birds are symbols often used on Christmas cards, they are also appropriate for a postcard that reads "A Happy New Year." Not as popular as Christmas postcards, this one is worth $5.

Cards and poetry have been part of the celebration of Valentine's Day since 1415, when Charles, Duc d'Orleans, sent a rhymed love letter from his cell in the Tower of London. The use of a Valentine card didn't became popular, however, until the nineteenth century. This 9 3/4-by-7 3/4-inch Valentine shows cupid, a dove, and other symbols of the holiday. It is signed on the back, "Emma's First Valentine from John, 1880." It was bought at a street fair last year for $25.

During the 1960s, florists delivered romantic Valentine's Day planters filled with flowers. This Valentine girl planter says, "Keep It Under Your Hat, I Love You." The 5 3/4-inch planter was made in Japan. It was purchased at a flea market for $15.

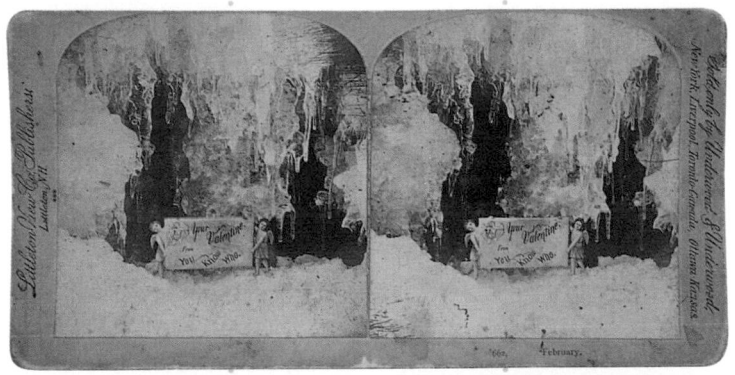

You could even get a stereo card to put in your viewer on Valentine's Day. This one says, "From You Know Who," and pictures cupids in an ice cave. Littleton View Company and Underwood & Underwood produced this card, made of the usual two photographs mounted on a curved 3 1/2-by-7-inch piece of cardboard. It sold for $10.

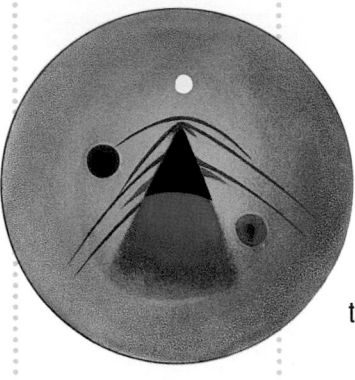

Sometimes a souvenir's meaning is lost in time. This 7 1/2-inch enameled plate is marked on the back "NBC-TV, Wide Wide World Program, February 17, 1957, George Air Force Base, California." A paper label says, "Made in California, B. Alexander." The abstract rocket design makes the enamel desirable and worth the $15 price.

Until 1971, the United States celebrated both George Washington's birthday on February 22 and Abraham Lincoln's on February 12. The separate holidays ended when President Richard Nixon set aside the third Monday of the month to honor all past presidents. Washington has been remembered in many ways. This pieced, appliqued, and printed quilt shows Martha and George Washington. It was made for the 1876 centennial celebration. It sold at auction in 1996 for $4,600.

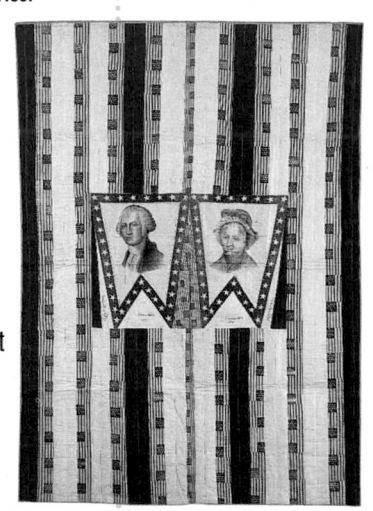

CHRISTIE'S, NEW YORK

M   A   R   C   H

George Washington was a hero to the country in a way not seen today. In 1889 the United States marked the centennial of the day Washington signed the Constitution as the first president, March 4, 1789. This jacquard-woven linen towel includes the words, "Independence of the United States of America Declared July 4th 1776, Washington Elected President of the Federal Union March 1789, E Pluribus Unum." The red-and-white towel is worth $100.

March 9 is the day Jews celebrate Purim in 2001. The holiday
festivities retell the story of the Jewish Queen Esther, who saved
Persian Jews from destruction by the king's chief minister, the wicked
Haman. This twentieth-century plate pictures a couple on their way to
a Purim celebration. The Hebrew text relates to Purim. At auction in
1999, this plate sold for $1,100.

A P R I L

April Fool's Day was celebrated by many
people as early as the eighteenth century.
This puzzle jug is an old form often used
as a joke in pubs. The decoration says,
"From Mother Earth I Took My Birth, I'm
Made a Joke for Man, And Now Am
Here Fill'd with Good Beer, Come Tate
[sic] It If You Can." The unwary
drinker will spill beer from the holes
in the neck of the English delft jug. The
knowing drinker will place his fingers over
the proper holes in the neck and use one spout
like a straw to sip the beer. Collectors today like
both delft and jokes, which makes this
13-inch puzzle worth $300.

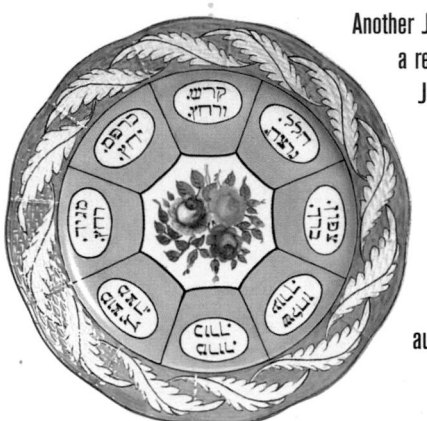

Another Jewish holiday is Passover, a remembrance of the exodus of the Jews from Egypt, celebrated in 2001 on April 8. At the Passover seder, celebrants serve symbols of the holiday on a special plate. The famous Herend factory made this early twentieth-century Hungarian seder plate. It sold at auction for $1,725 two years ago.

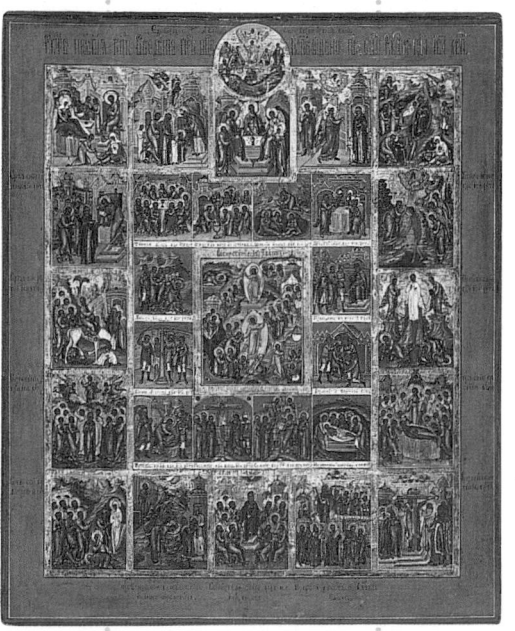

Easter, the feast commemorating the Resurrection of Christ, is celebrated with religious observances and family dinners. This Russian icon pictures the Anastasis (Resurrection), surrounded by twelve scenes of the Passion. The outer border shows sixteen feasts. This nineteenth-century icon, 21 1/2 by 17 1/4 inches, auctioned in 1999 for $4,600.

Easter also includes Easter egg hunts for children. This egg plate with chicks and eggshells is useful as a centerpiece filled with a dozen colored Easter eggs. Plates made to hold cold, hard-boiled eggs did not become popular until the 1930s, although some were made before that. The 10-inch plate is worth $30.

M A Y

Mother's Day, the second Sunday in May, was the brainchild of Julia Ward Howe in 1872. Mottoes like this one for Mother's Day have become popular collectibles. The text includes a poem titled "Mother of Mine." The motto is marked "Gibson Product, ©1927 G.A. Co." The price at a flea market: $6.

MOTHER of MINE

a SMILE,
Like the sun through the
clouds comes a-peeping,
a VOICE,
Like sweet music, two
dear eyes a-shine,
a HEART
That is filled with a
sweet understanding;
There's no one on earth like
THAT MOTHER
of MINE!
E.M. BRAINERD

5¢

FIRST FLIGHT NEW YORK TO PARIS MAY 20-21, 1927-33½ HOURS

Spirit
of St.Louis

LONG FILLER IMPORTED SUMATRA WRAPPER

MAZER-CRESSMAN
CIGAR CO. Inc.   SPIRIT OF ST. LOUIS   DETROIT. MICH

Charles Lindbergh flew his airplane, *The Spirit of St. Louis*, across the Atlantic Ocean on May 20 to 21, 1927. It was the world's first transatlantic flight, and was memorialized with all sorts of souvenirs, including a cigar label. The label, 7 3/4 by 6 5/8 inches, is valued at $25.

J U N E

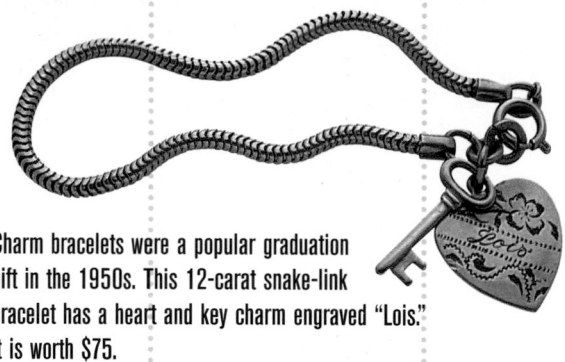

Charm bracelets were a popular graduation gift in the 1950s. This 12-carat snake-link bracelet has a heart and key charm engraved "Lois." It is worth $75.

The coronation of England's King George V and Queen Mary was held June 22, 1911. This 5-inch commemoration saucer was made by Tuscan China of England. It was just $7 at a flea market.

A Shriners' Convention was held at the Al Koran Temple in Cleveland, Ohio, June 23 to 25, 1896. This creamer, sold at the convention, is inscribed "22nd Annual Session, Gen. Moses Cleaveland, Founder of the City, 1796." The Shriner Emblem is on the back. The creamer was made by the Wellsville Pioneer Pottery Co. of Ohio. There are many collectors of fraternal memorabilia. Prices in this year's price book range from $3 to $1,760.

June is the traditional month for weddings. Many couples save wedding mementos, such as cake toppers, garters, engraved match covers, and ring pillows. This Victorian wedding pillow held the ring at a nineteenth-century ceremony and was saved for many years. A rarity today, a special example like this sells for $395.

TIMEWORN TREASURES, POUGHKEEPSIE, NEW YORK

Old bridal photos have become a new area of collecting. This picture of a bride, groom, bridesmaid, and best man was taken at the Beros Studio in Cleveland, Ohio. The dress suggests the wedding was held in the 1940s. The picture sold for $12 at a show.

J U L Y

The Fourth of July is a legal holiday celebrating the country's independence. The sesquicentennial year, 1926, gave the country a reason for a larger celebration. Printed on the tummy of this Liberty Belle doll are the words "150 Years of American Independence, 1776–1926." The doll looks surprisingly like Clara Bow, a famous movie star of the day. The 13-inch doll sold for $60 in 1999.

Paper is perishable, so paper collectibles can be hard to find. This Fourth of July paper tablecloth was made by Hallmark in 1976 for the bicentennial celebration. The 60-by-102-inch tablecloth, still wrapped in plastic and marked $1.50, the original price, is now worth $15.

A U G U S T

Important birthdays, like Ralph Kovel's, are celebrated in August. These birthday candles shaped like a boy and a girl were new in the 1950s. Today they sell for $20 a pair.

Colorful printed plastic trays have been popular souvenirs in Europe, but few were made for United States locations. This tray was one of a collection of 1970s souvenir trays purchased recently for $1 apiece. It shows a "Thatched Cottage" in Connemara, Ireland. Other trays in the collection pictured locations in England, Italy, and Spain.

Thatched Cottage, Connemara, Ireland.

For many girls, summer vacation includes a trip to Girl Scout camp. Both Scout collectors and hanky collectors would want this souvenir that says, "Girl Scouts Have Fun." The 11 1/2-inch square, made from 1950 to 1960, is worth $10.

Vacation souvenirs sometimes are made a long way from the vacation site they advertise. These shell people are made of painted wood, plastic leaves, and shells found far from Florida. Marked as souvenirs of Hollywood, Florida, they were made in Japan using Pacific Ocean shells. The 6-inch figures sold at a flea market for $20.

Butterfly-wing pictures have been popular souvenirs since the nineteenth century. This 4-by-8-inch framed view of the Bay of Naples is made of iridescent tropical butterfly wings. A souvenir from the 1930s, it is now worth $50.

Decorated china plates are the most popular of all souvenir items. Collectors usually buy either a favored location or favored maker. This 6-inch lace-edge plate sold for $15 in Ohio, but is probably worth half that much anywhere else. That's because it's a souvenir of Cedar Point, a well-known Ohio amusement park.

Even the Allegheny, Pennsylvania, post office was pictured on a souvenir. This miniature vase was made for McCrory's 5 & 10¢ Store to sell to Allegheny visitors. Its value today is under $5.

SEPTEMBER

September means the first day of school. This child's handkerchief set was boxed with rulers, crayons, and pencil to be ready for that big day. It sold recently for $10.

OCTOBER

DUNBAR GALLERY, MILFORD, MASSACHUSETTS

Halloween is a major holiday for collectors. This 8-inch cardboard accordion jack-o'-lantern was made in Germany in the 1920s. There are paper inserts in the eyes. Prices are high for pre-1940s decorations. This very rare jack-o'-lantern sold for $275 in 1993. It is worth about the same today.

Terry Kovel's birthday is in October, another important birthday month. Dress up the cake with this cake-decorating kit that includes plastic numbers and words. It was made in the 1950s by Harris & Cain Products, Pleasantville, New Jersey. The set is complete, and includes the box. This is one of many cooking collectibles attracting interest today. It's only $20, and it's useful, too.

Souvenir packages of needles are hard to find today, and few would be decorated with Veterans Day pictures. This needle pack pictures heroes of World War I, indicating it was made around 1920. Both military collectors and sewing collectors would buy this souvenir for $20.

A large platter for your Thanksgiving turkey would be handy on November 22, the day the holiday is celebrated in 2001. This platter by Bishop & Stonier came with six matching plates. It was made about 1900. The set is worth $350.

Hanukkah, the eight-day Jewish holiday called the Feast of Lights, commemorates the victory in 165 B.C. of the Maccabees over the Syrian army and the rededication of the Temple in Jerusalem.

This late 18th-century Polish menorah burns oil, not candles. It sold last year for $1,840. This year Hanukkah starts at sunset on December 21.

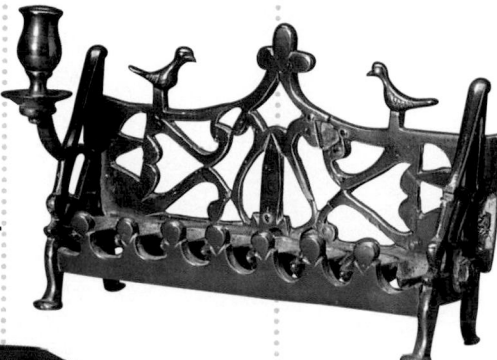

SKINNER, INC., BOSTON

Collectors of Christmas items want all kinds. This beehive tissue-paper Santa is only 3 3/4 inches high. It was made in Denmark for a Christmas in the 1960s and is worth $45.

Several sets of dishes made for Christmas have remained popular through the years. This Christmas Eve–pattern plate, made by Salem China Company of Salem, Ohio, was designed by the famous Viktor Schrekengost. Schrekengost is best known for his work at Cowan Pottery in Rocky River, Ohio. He also worked as an industrial designer. The 11-inch plate sells for $25.

S P E C I A L   M O M E N T S

Some special moments are lost in time and
all but ignored by most collectors.

A gold watch and a party are not the
only remembrances of a retirement.
A doctor was given this enamel
plate filled with symbols of his
life, past and future. The island
scene, medical symbols, key
(perhaps representing the Florida
Keys), dice, fish (perhaps for the
retiree's name), and blue cross all
related to David Fishman's retirement,
mentioned on the plate. It is signed "Betty
Jane, 1968." The plate sold for just $23 because the maker is unknown and because
collectors rarely want mementos of the lives of people who are not famous.

Almost any event can be worthy of a celebration. This is a retablo thanking the
Virgin of San Juan for helping a man survive his term in jail. This folk-art painting on
tin would have been displayed in church as a thank-you to God. The painting includes
a picture and a verse in Spanish about receiving protection while in jail.
The 7 1/4-by-10-inch painting is worth more than $150.

Earrings, Pearls, Cultured, Diamond, Gold, Retro, Pair 345.00
Earrings, Pendant, Onyx, Oval, Navette, Triangular Shapes, Pearl Accent, Victorian 345.00
Earrings, Prong Set Amethysts, Blue Zircons, Arts & Crafts 1265.00
Earrings, Rhinestone, Round Drop Type, Bogoff 40.00
Earrings, Rhinestone, Yellow Ground, Clip-On, Weiss 32.00
Earrings, Rhinestones, Gilt Metal, Stamped, Trifari, 1 In. 110.00
Earrings, Round Top, Turquoise, Enamel, Tapered Gold Pendants, Victorian, 2 3/4 In. ... 2300.00
Earrings, Shakudo, Mixed Metal, 18K Gold, Oval, Adell, 1988 .... 230.00
Earrings, Shield Shape, Filigree, Bead Set Round Diamonds, Platinum, Edwardian 1380.00
Earrings, Tortoiseshell, Silver Wings, William Spratling, Mexico, c.1947, 1 1/4 In., Pair .. 862.00
Earrings, Tourmaline, Leaves, Scroll, Gold, Gilbert Oakes, Arts & Crafts, 3/4 In. 1700.00
Fob, Gold, Amethyst, Mythological Figures, Chased & Repousse, Victorian 375.00
Hatpins are listed in this book in the Hatpin category.
Lavaliere, 21 Clear Stones, 1 Red Glass Stone, 14K Yellow Gold, Silver Top, Gold Chain . 465.00
Lavaliere, Bow, Foliate Spray, Fringed Tails, Diamonds, Platinum, Edwardian 1265.00
Lavaliere, Intertwined Snakes, Emeralds, Diamonds, Rubies, Gold, Art Nouveau, 11 In. ... 5175.00
Lavaliere, Pendant, European Cut Diamonds, White Gold Chain 340.00
Lavaliere, Sapphire & 3 Seed Pearls, Fresh Water, Gold Chain, c.1915 .... 135.00
Locket, Album, Book Form, 3 Fold-Out Frames Interior, Yellow Gold, 7/8 x 3/4 In. 330.00
Locket, Art Nouveau Woman's Profile, 14K Gold, Diamond In Star, Chain, Victorian 185.00
Locket, Black Onyx, Marcasite, Sterling Silver, Victorian 175.00
Locket, Heart, Repousse Lid, Female Bust, Art Nouveau, 10K Yellow Gold 460.00
Locket, Overall White, Blue Translucent Enamel, Wave Ground, Russia, 1917, 1/4 In. ... 224.00
Locket, Pendant, Enamel, Putto, Foliate Frame, Seed Pearls, Limoges, Victorian, 26 In. .. 575.00
Locket, Portrait, Painting, On Ivory, Frame, Henry Kensil, 2 1/4 x 2 In. 330.00
Locket, Shield Shape, Hinged Top Opens To Hidden Locket, 14K Yellow Gold 316.00
Locket Pendant, Saber Shape, Imperial Cipher, Russia, 1900, 2 In. 3910.00
Lorgnette, Platinum, Diamonds, France, Art Deco 2415.00
Lorgnette, Reverse Intaglio Dancer, Crystal, Diamonds, Platinum, Chain, Art Deco 8625.00
Money Clip, Aluminum, Gray, Natef, Zippo, 1992, Box 35.00
Money Clip, Vernon Lumber Co., Black Finish, Oval, 1930, 1 x 2 In. 20.00
Money Clip, Vintage Car, Base Metal, Gold Color, Anson, 1960, 1 x 2 In. 15.00
Necklace, 14K Gold Beads, Applied Wire Twist Design, Etruscan Revival, 18 In. 1095.00
Necklace, Alternating Bands, Plaques, Figure 8 Links, 14K Gold, Faro, Italy, 17 In. 315.00
Necklace, Amber Beads, Dark Cherry, Graduated, 40 In. 520.00
Necklace, Amethyst, Pear Shape, Silver Gilt Bezels, 15 3/4 In. 200.00
Necklace, Bakelite, Figural Mixed Vegetables, Cellulose Acetate, 16 1/4 In. 4400.00
Necklace, Bakelite, Pickle, Cream, Light Green, White Celluloid Chain, 15 x 2 In. 7150.00
Necklace, Bakelite, Reverse Medallions, Apple Juice With Radiating Center, 2 In. 121.00
Necklace, Cabochon Sapphires, 18K Gold, Entwined Ropes, Tiffany & Co., 14 1/2 In. ... 3680.00
Necklace, Central Oval Blue Chalcedony, Rope Twist Frame, 14K Yellow Gold 632.00
Necklace, Chain, 14K Gold Trace Links, Pearls, Graduated Baroque, Art Nouveau, 56 In. . 1150.00
Necklace, Chain, Art Nouveau, 18K Yellow Gold, 58 In. 1725.00
Necklace, Chain, Baroque Pearl Drops, Gold Foliate Caps, Art Nouveau, 38 In. 1725.00
Necklace, Chain, Diamonds, Platinum, Pendant, Navette Clasp, Edwardian, 17 1/4 In. ... 12650.00
Necklace, Chain, Double-Sided Flowers, Silver, Enamel, Bernard Cuzner, 57 In. 1840.00
Necklace, Chain, Memorial, Woven Gilt, Pale Blue Enamel, 15 3/4 In. 690.00
Necklace, Chain, Reeded Links, Victorian, 14K Yellow Gold 747.00
Necklace, Chain, Rhinestones, Simulated Baroque Pearls, Miriam Haskell, 30 In. 125.00
Necklace, Chain, Seed Pearl & Diamond Snow Flake, 2 Tassels, Platinum, c.1910, 26 In. . 9200.00
Necklace, Chain, Silver Plate, Female Profile Plaques, Circular, Art Nouveau, 42 1/2 In. .. 460.00
Necklace, Charm, Sailboat, Bucket, Corkscrew, Key, 14K Gold 115.00
Necklace, Choker, 3 Half-Moon Links, Turquoise Beads, Signed, Hans Hanson, Denmark 432.00
Necklace, Choker, 7 Indian Arrowheads, 14K Yellow Gold, Mignon Faget 2200.00
Necklace, Choker, Gold & Silver Plated Links, Faux Jewels, Trifari, 15 1/4 In. 165.00
Necklace, Choker, Turquoise Flower, Coral Hand Amulets, Silver Mesh Braid, Victorian . 1955.00
Necklace, Citrine, Collet Set Cabochon, Citrine Beads, Sterling Silver, Art Nouveau 1035.00
Necklace, Clear Rhinestones, Eisenberg, 16 1/2 In. 185.00
Necklace, Collar Style, 18K Gold, 80 Rubies On Ends, Signed Gucci 2590.00
Necklace, Copper, Graduated Hammered Disks, Beads, 23 In. 248.00
Necklace, Coral Beads, 14K Yellow Gold Clasp 690.00
Necklace, Coral Stones, Gold Plated Setting, Articulated Links, Trifari, 16 In. 70.00
Necklace, Egyptian Figures, Judith Lieber 500.00

Necklace, Faceted Pendant, Reverse Hair Locket, Yellow Gold Wire Links 977.00
Necklace, Faceted, Cherry Amber Beads, Graduated, Victorian, 19 1/2 In. 430.00
Necklace, Faux Pearls, Miriam Haskell 115.00
Necklace, Flat Curb Link Chain, Slide, Swivel Link, 14K Yellow Gold, 60 In. 345.00
Necklace, Floral Center, Seed Pearls, Bezel Set Garnet, 10K Gold, 15 1/2 In. 402.00
Necklace, Freshwater Pearls, 14K Yellow Gold, Art Nouveau 488.00
Necklace, Fringe, Gold Drops, Applied Wire Twist Flowers, Etruscan Revival, 18 In. 3565.00
Necklace, Gold Coin Pendant, 18K Gold, Flat Links, Diamonds, David Webb, 15 In. 1840.00
Necklace, Gold Coins, Images Of Buddha, Double Chains, Beads, 1970, 36 In. 375.00
Necklace, Gold Flower Each Link, Rhinestone Center, Topaz Rhinestones, Lisner, 16 In. . 65.00
Necklace, Jade Links, Coral Rondel Spacers, 2 Coral Beads, 1920, 30 In. 546.00
Necklace, Lapis Lazuli Beads, Gumps, 16 1/2 In. 1095.00
Necklace, Lapis Lazuli, 68 Beads, Graduated, 15 1/2 In. 80.00
Necklace, Lavaliere Style Pendant, Faux Pearl Chains, Coro, 26 In. 38.00
Necklace, Locket, 2 Hearts, 2 Diamonds In Star-Type Setting, Gold, c.1900 .... 405.00
Necklace, Mask, Alternating Leaves & Enamel Grapes, Gold, Classical Revival, 15 In. ... 8050.00
Necklace, Onyx, Rectangular Jade Plaque, Geometric Frame, Art Deco, 17 1/2 In. 2415.00
Necklace, Oval Rhodolite Garnet, Gilt Accents, 16 1/4 In. 546.00
Necklace, Panda Coin, 14K Yellow Gold Bezel, Yellow Gold Chain 57.00
Necklace, Pearls, Cultured, 3 Strands, Platinum, Diamond Clasp, Art Deco, 19 In. 1265.00
Necklace, Pearls, Cultured, Graduated, Platinum Clasp, Mikimoto, Box, 21 1/2 In. 920.00
Necklace, Pearls, Geometric, Paper Clip Chain, Arts & Crafts, 22 In. 350.00
Necklace, Pearls, Leaves, Shield Frame, Sterling Silver, Kalo Shop, Arts & Crafts, 18 In. . 4200.00
Necklace, Pendant, Amber Faceted, Brass, Cut Glass Bean, 2 In. 20.00
Necklace, Pendant, Beetle, Micromosaic, Oval Frame, Scroll Accents, 23 In. 345.00
Necklace, Pendant, Silver, Labradorite, Floral Chain Links, Fluted Beads, Peruzzi, 32 In. . 345.00
Necklace, Pendant, Sterling Silver, Signed, Hans Hansen 175.00
Necklace, Pin & Earrings, Carved Coral Rose Bouquet, Bar Links, Victorian 750.00
Necklace, Pink Coral & Black Onyx Beads, M. Buccellati, 32 In. 3450.00
Necklace, Prong Set Multicolored Gemstones, Dorrie Nossiter, England, 15 In. 11500.00
Necklace, Prong Set Rhinestone, Gold Finish, Hobe, 36 In. 20.00
Necklace, Purple Iridescent Pendant, Art Moderne 45.00
Necklace, Puzzle Links Of Gold, Bars Of Stainless Steel, Bulgari, 15 1/2 In. 3220.00
Necklace, Rhinestones, Safety Chain, Eisenberg, 13 1/4 In. 209.00
Necklace, Rhinestones, Scalloped, Silver Color, Coro 40.00
Necklace, Scrolled Spray, Red, Clear Rhinestones, Gilt Metal, Trifari, 16 In. 165.00
Necklace, Shield Form Pendant, Seed Pearls, Beaded Chain, 14K Yellow Gold 977.00
Necklace, Silver Gilt, Crescent Pendant, Garnets, Paper Clip Chain, Shaw, c.1911, 16 In. . 6900.00
Necklace, Snake Link Chain, 3 Diamond Cluster Sides, 14K Gold, Jabel, 15 In. 1840.00
Necklace, Snake, Turquoise, Gold Petal Links, 14K Yellow Gold, 15 In. 1265.00
Necklace, Squash Blossom, Turquoise, Silver, Southwest Native, 30 In. 345.00
Necklace, Stylized Sunburst Design, 11 Amethyst Cabochons, Sterling Silver 1150.00
Necklace, Turquoise Beads, Carved Floral Turquoise Pendant, 1923, 30 In. 690.00
Necklace, Turquoise, Silver, 4 Stones In Leaf Frames, Signed, Marie Herrera 286.00
Necklace, Twisted Copper Rope, Hammered Gold Plated Links, Les Bernard, 63 In. 112.00
Necklace & Earrings, Rhinestone Hearts, Pink Rhinestones, Stamped, Pennino, 18 In. ... 143.00
Necklace & Earrings, Silver Filigree, Turquoise Matrix Beads, 14 In. 172.00
Necktie, Rhinestones, Prong Mounted, 16-In. Rhinestone Chain 30.00
Pendant, 2 Lions Battling With Green Jadeite, Red, Sea Green, 3 In. 550.00
Pendant, Amber, Large Free Form, 14K Gold Chain 385.00
Pendant, Amethyst Glass, Wasps In Circle, Black Silk Cord, Lalique, 1920, 2 1/4 In. 690.00
Pendant, Ball, Pave Diamonds, Diamond Bail, Platinum Mount, Art Deco 5980.00
Pendant, Baroque Pearls, Collet Set, Gilt Mount, Austria 230.00
Pendant, Bearing Head Of Christ, Czarist Era, Silver, Oval, Russia 70.00
Pendant, Chain, Turtle, Enamel, Gold, White, Miriam Haskell 295.00
Pendant, Cherub With Harp, Oval Turquoise Frame, Bow Above, Victorian 345.00
Pendant, Clover, 3-Leaf Clover, 4 Collet Set Diamonds, 18K Yellow Gold 3335.00
Pendant, Flower In Circles, Enamel, Sapphires, Ruby, Diamond, Gold, Russia, c.1910 ... 1725.00
Pendant, Flowering Branch, Diamonds, Garnets, Russia, Art Nouveau, 1900, 2 5/8 In. ... 3450.00
Pendant, Gold Coin, French, 20 Francs, 14K Gold Setting, 1910, 1 1/8 In. 175.00
Pendant, Gold Coin, Liberty Head, Gold Reticulated Leaf Setting, 1909, 1 1/8 In. 345.00
Pendant, Ivory Disc In 18K Gold Wire Twist Frame, Cipullo, Cartier, 1972 .... 230.00
Pendant, Ivory, Carved & Pierced Rose, Floral & Leaf Border, 2 3/4 In. 85.00

Pendant, Ivory, Ornate Phoenix & Dragon, 2 3/4 In. 245.00
Pendant, Jade, Carved, Pierced, Green, White, 14K Gold Mount, Burma, c.1930, 2 In. . . . 150.00
Pendant, Locket, Cross Design, Black Enamel, Diamonds, 14K Gold, Victorian 315.00
Pendant, Negligee, Diamond Ribbon, 2 Emerald & Diamond Drops, Chain, Art Deco . . . 4600.00
Pendant, Persian Turquoise, Pearls, Diamond, Gold, Flower Design, Victorian 1380.00
Pendant, Portrait, 2 Children, Polychrome Enamel, Gilt Mount, Etruscan Revival 1725.00
Pendant, Portrait, Woman, White Dress, Painting On Ivory, Frame, 3 x 2 1/4 In. 520.00
Pendant, Scarab, Yellow, Orange, Brown, Black Glass, 1920, 1 3/4 In. 2015.00
Pendant, Shield, Rose, Diamond, Seed Pearls, 14K Gold, 20th Century, 1 3/4 In. 230.00
Pendant, St. Sergius Founder Of Holy Trinity Monastery, North Of Moscow, 4 In. 756.00
Pendant, Woman's Bust Framed By Rose Cut Diamonds, 18K Yellow Gold 2300.00
Pendant, Wreath, Platinum Grille, Diamonds, Seed Pearl Link Chain, Edwardian, 20 In. . 1495.00
Pin, 2 Amethyst Cabochons, Silver Stems, Leaves, Los Castillo, Taxco, Mexico, 5 In. 230.00
Pin, 2 Birds Perched On Green Enamel Branch, Green, Pink, Red Rhinestones, 2 In. 880.00
Pin, 2 Flowers, 14K Gold Petals, Rubies, Diamonds, Retro, Tiffany & Co. 1380.00
Pin, 2 Interlinked Ovals, Diamonds, Onyx Baguettes, Platinum, Art Deco 1840.00
Pin, 2 Joined Batons, Beaded Terminals, 18K Gold, Etruscan Revival, c.1880 . . . . 415.00
Pin, 3 Curved Bars Surrounding Geometric Form, Signed, Ed Wiener, 1950 . . . . 172.00
Pin, 3 Fruits, Lapis Lazuli, Pearls, Cultured, Gold Wire Surround, Schlumberger, Tiffany . 2070.00
Pin, 3 Large Garnets, Yellow Gold, c.1880, 1 x 2 In. 330.00
Pin, Agate, Diana, Goddess Of The Hunts, Within Scroll Frame, 18K Yellow Gold 1265.00
Pin, Agate, Landscape, Bezel Set, Rectangular Yellow Gold Frame, 1955, 18K Gold 920.00
Pin, American Indian, Pave Rhinestones, Silver Metal, Coro, 3 In. 357.00
Pin, Amethysts, Baroque Pearls, Diamond, Platinum Leaves, 14K Gold, Arts & Crafts . . . 4025.00
Pin, Aqua Rhinestone Cascade, Small Pink Rhinestones, Stamped, Pennino, 3 In. 1320.00
Pin, Art Deco Design, Sterling Silver, Marcasite, Judith Jack, 2 In. 460.00
Pin, Art Deco, Rubies & Circular Cut Diamonds, Tied Bow, Platinum, Tiffany, 1915 . . . . 8625.00
Pin, Artichoke, Carved Carnelian, 18K Gold, Seaman Schepps 1495.00
Pin, Asian Warrior, 14K Gold, Cabochon Jadeite 95.00
Pin, Bakelite, American Indian, Caramel, Black Feather, Brass Headband, 3 In. 2310.00
Pin, Bakelite, Bulldog, Butterscotch, 2 1/2 In. 1430.00
Pin, Bakelite, Charm, 5 Brown Olives, Green Olive Leaf, 3 1/2 In. 275.00
Pin, Bakelite, Charm, Carrots, 3 Carrots With 3 Green Stems, Black Oval, 3 1/2 In. 210.00
Pin, Bakelite, Chicken, Celluloid Beak, Brass Wings, Martha Sleeper, 2 1/4 In. 550.00
Pin, Bakelite, Currant Bunch, Carved Leaves, Brass Rings, 2 3/4 In. 330.00
Pin, Bakelite, Dog, Airedale, Green 45.00
Pin, Bakelite, Dog, Chained, Butterscotch, Brass Collar, 3 1/2 In. 880.00
Pin, Bakelite, Dog, Soldier, Pivoting, Marble Red, Pivoting Arm With Rifle, 3 In. 2860.00
Pin, Bakelite, English Bobby, Black, Ivory, Green, 4 In. 550.00
Pin, Bakelite, Flamingo, Green, Cream, Applied Eyes, 4 In. 770.00
Pin, Bakelite, Flower Spray, Frosted Glass, Brass Stems, Blumenthal, 4 1/2 In. 2200.00
Pin, Bakelite, Gold Scatter, Cream Golf Balls, Celluloid Chain, 4 In. 715.00
Pin, Bakelite, Harpo Marx, Articulated, Celluloid Cigar, Cotton Hair, 3 1/2 In. 3190.00
Pin, Bakelite, Hat, Black Lucite Brim, Red Band, Bow, 2 1/2 In. 176.00
Pin, Bakelite, Hat, Marbled Butterscotch, Brown Dots, Brown Rope Band, 2 1/2 In. 440.00
Pin, Bakelite, Hat, Marbled Butterscotch, Light Blue Band, Straw Flowers, 3 In. 550.00
Pin, Bakelite, Hat, Marbled Red, White Band, Navy Balls, 2 1/4 In. 660.00
Pin, Bakelite, Lobster, Resin Wash Overdyed, Gimp Antennae, Glass Eyes, 3 In. 880.00
Pin, Bakelite, Ruler, Suspended 2 Blue Pencils, Red Trimmed Slate 345.00
Pin, Bakelite, Sailboat, Butterscotch 45.00
Pin, Bakelite, Shield Form, Marbled Green Center, Red, Aqua Rhinestones, 3 1/4 In. 176.00
Pin, Bakelite, Shovel, Butterscotch, Black Strap At Handle, 3 1/2 In. 264.00
Pin, Bakelite, Totem Pole, Enameled . . . . *Illus* 2750.00
Pin, Bakelite, Uncle Sam, Cream, Navy, Celluloid Cane, Straw Beard, 3 1/2 In. 1210.00
Pin, Bakelite, Woman In Swimsuit, Palm Tree, Translucent Green, Painted, 2 1/2 In. 605.00
Pin, Ballerina, Blue Rhinestones, Gilt Sterling, Stamped, Eisenberg, 3 1/4 In. 660.00
Pin, Ballerina, Green Rhinestones, Gilt Sterling, Stamped, Eisenberg, 3 1/4 In. 715.00
Pin, Ballerina, Red Rhinestones, Stamped, Eisenberg, 3 1/4 In. 660.00
Pin, Bar, Aquamarine, Diamonds, Pearls, Gold, Victorian 390.00
Pin, Bar, Bakelite, Carved Red Foliage, 3 1/4 In. 110.00
Pin, Bar, Bow, Diamonds, Platinum, Tiffany & Co., Art Deco 2645.00
Pin, Bar, Diamond & Sapphire, Yellow Gold, Silver Top, 1920-1960 . . . . 800.00
Pin, Bar, Diamonds, Geometric Design, Platinum, Millegrain Accents, Art Deco 1380.00

Pin, Bar, Diamonds, Platinum, Crescent Shaped Arches, Fleur-De-Lis, Edwardian 1610.00
Pin, Bar, Diamonds, Synthetic Sapphire Accents, Pierced Platinum Mount, Art Deco 635.00
Pin, Bar, Engraved & Cutout Design, 14K Gold, Edwardian 115.00
Pin, Bar, Flowering Hawthorn Branch, Blue Glass, Gilt Metal, Lalique, 1912, 3 In. 460.00
Pin, Bar, Knot In Center, 14K Yellow & Rose Gold, Cartier 290.00
Pin, Bar, Lobed Terminals, Wire Twist Accents, 14K Gold, Victorian 230.00
Pin, Bar, Modified Lozenge, Openwork, Diamonds, Platinum, Belle Epoque 1150.00
Pin, Bar, Molded Glass, Floral Design, Blue Ground, Brass Mounted, Lalique 345.00
Pin, Bar, Octagonal, Mine Cut & Single Cut Diamond, Platinum, Art Deco 2420.00
Pin, Bar, Sapphires, Diamonds, Platinum Filigree, 14K Gold, Art Deco 805.00
Pin, Bar, Sapphires, Diamonds, Platinum Mount, Gold, Edwardian, D. De W. Brokaw ... 490.00
Pin, Beaded Accents, Hand Hammered, Sterling Silver, Signed, Georg Jensen 374.00
Pin, Bean Pod, Green, Yellow Pearlized Enamel, Pave Rhinestones, Boucher, 3 In. 770.00
Pin, Bearded Man, Brass, Joseph Hollywood 165.00
Pin, Bee, Gray South Sea Pearl, Bead Set Round Diamonds, 18K Yellow Gold 1150.00
Pin, Beetle, Gold, Cabochon Garnet, Jewels, Russia, 1910, 2 1/2 In. 2875.00
Pin, Beetle, Green Guilloche Enamel Wings, 14K Yellow Gold 1725.00
Pin, Bird In Wreath, Openwork Design, Silver, Malachite, Georg Jensen, 1915-1927 .... 460.00
Pin, Bird In Wreath, Silver, Georg Jensen, Denmark, 1 3/4 In. ....258.00 to 316.00
Pin, Bird Of Paradise, Sterling Silver, Carved Ivory, 1940s 430.00
Pin, Bird's Wing & Scroll, Abstract, Double Clip, 14K Gold, Retro, Larter 865.00
Pin, Bird, Blue, Green Pearlized Enamel, Stamped, Boucher, 4 1/4 In. 880.00
Pin, Bird, Blue, Purple Pearlized Enamel, Stamped, Boucher, 4 In. 1320.00
Pin, Bird, Gilt, Cranberry, Blue, Yellow, Green, Pave Rhinestones, Corocraft, 4 In. 176.00
Pin, Bird, Green Rhinestones, Purple, Green, Red Enamel, Stamped, Eisenberg, 2 In. 176.00
Pin, Bird, Large Blue Rhinestone, Stamped, Eisenberg, 3 1/2 In. 440.00
Pin, Bird, Pave Rhinestones, Silver Metal, Stamped, Trifari, 4 In. 176.00
Pin, Bird, Purple, Blue, Green Pearlized Enamel, Pave Rhinestones, Boucher, 5 In. 1760.00
Pin, Blossom, Cutout, Oval, Sterling Silver, Kalo Shop, Arts & Crafts, 1 3/4 x 2 3/8 In. .. 450.00
Pin, Blue & Green Enamel, Sterling Silver, Liberty & Co., Arts & Crafts, 3/4 x 1 1/4 In. . 295.00
Pin, Blueberry, Deep Purple, Fuchsia, Green Pearlized, Stamped, Boucher, 2 1/4 In. 715.00
Pin, Bouquet, Center Ruby, Flowers Of 8 Stickpins, Gem Stones, Pearls, 2 1/4 In. 605.00
Pin, Bow, Large Purple Rhinestones, Pave Rhinestones, Stamped, Eisenberg, 2 In. 275.00
Pin, Bow, Onyx, Pearls, Pave Diamond Accents, Engraved Platinum Mount, Art Deco ... 980.00
Pin, Bow, Purple Rhinestone Center, Stamped, Eisenberg, 2 1/4 In. 330.00
Pin, Bow, Red Rhinestones, Sterling, Stamped, Eisenberg, 2 1/2 In. 220.00
Pin, Branches, Stylized, 2 Round Green Stones, Arts & Crafts, 1 1/2 x 1 1/8 In. 230.00
Pin, Buckle Shape, Brass, Purple Glass Stone Center, 2 1/4 x 2 In. 20.00
Pin, Buckle, Openwork, Demontoid Garnets, Diamonds, Silver-Topped Gold, Edwardian . 1840.00
Pin, Buckle, Single Cut Diamonds, Gold Pin Stem, Platinum, Art Deco 805.00
Pin, Bug, Blue Cabochons, Pink Pave Rhinestones, Corocraft, 2 1/2 In. 357.00
Pin, Bug, Purple, Green, Red Cabochons, Topaz Rhinestone, Trifari, 1 1/2 In. 220.00
Pin, Bumblebee, Black, Yellow, Red Enamel, Rhinestones, Stamped, Trifari, 2 In. 230.00
Pin, Bust Of Woman In Bonnet, Gilt, Art Nouveau 1035.00
Pin, Butterfly, Amethyst Quartz Wings, Diamond Set Body, Platinum, Art Deco 4315.00
Pin, Butterfly, Gold On Sterling, Faux Moonstones, Rubies, Trifari 250.00
Pin, Butterfly, Golden Rhinestones, Gold Tone Metal, 2 x 2 In. 40.00
Pin, Butterfly, Movable Wings Set With Diamonds, 14K Yellow Gold, 1 3/4 In. 605.00
Pin, Cabochon Blue Stone, Gold Leaf Frame, 4 Emeralds, Renaissance Revival 805.00
Pin, Caliber Cut Onyx, Diamonds, Openwork Platinum Mount, Art Deco 3450.00
Pin, Calla Lily Blossom Design, Sterling Silver, Arts & Crafts, 2 3/4 x 1 1/2 In. 287.00
Pin, Cameo, Carved Shell, Flower Urn, Love Birds, Rectangular, Victorian, 2 In. 200.00
Pin, Cameo, Flapper, Silver Filigree Mount, Seed Pearls, Early 20th Century, 1 In. 46.00
Pin, Cameo, Gold Frame, Marked 12K Gold Filled 66.00
Pin, Cameo, Onyx, Female Bust Profile, 1866, 14K Yellow Gold 1380.00
Pin, Cameo, Shell, 14K Gold, Filigree, Victorian 165.00
Pin, Cameo, Shell, 2 Warrior's Profiles With Putto, 14K Yellow Gold 546.00
Pin, Cameo, Variegated Chalcedony, Diamond Border, 18K Gold, Victorian, Cebara 5465.00
Pin, Cameo, Victorian Lady, 14K White Gold, Filigree Setting, Oval, c.1930, 2 1/2 In. ... 175.00
Pin, Cameo, Woman In Elizabethan Dress, Seed Pearls, 14K Gold 1035.00
Pin, Cameo, Woman, Embossed Ceramic, Victorian, 2 In. 28.00
Pin, Cameo, Woman, Headdress Of Wings & Snakes, Shell, 14K Gold, Victorian 460.00
Pin, Cameo, Woman, Milk Glass, Black Onyx, Gilt Frame, Diamond Chip, 1 1/2 In. 56.00

Pin, Cameo, Woman, Sardonyx, Diamonds, Black Enamel Beads, Victorian, Oval 2070.00
Pin, Cameo, Yellow Gold Frame, Mid 19th Century 1150.00
Pin, Can-Can Dancer, Red Rhinestones, Stamped, Eisenberg, 3 1/4 In. 825.00
Pin, Carnelian Scarab, Plique-A-Jour Enamel, Marcasite, Silver, Egyptian Revival 490.00
Pin, Cat, Figural, Sterling Silver, Mexico, 2 1/4 In. 290.00
Pin, Central Purple Stone, Rope Twist Accents, Victorian 258.00
Pin, Chair, Gold, Rhinestone Tipped, Rows Of Rhinestones, A. Caviness, 1 1/2 In. 125.00
Pin, Cherries, Red, Green, Yellow Pearlized, Enamel, Pave Rhinestones, Boucher, 2 In. ... 385.00
Pin, Child, Pensive Looking At Daisy, Ivory, Seed Pearls Around Rim 1800.00
Pin, Christmas Candle, Gold Metal, Rhinestone Flame, Plastic, 2 In. .... *Illus* 25.00
Pin, Christmas Tree, Varicolored Rhinestones, 1 1/4 x 2 1/8 In. 10.00
Pin, Christmas Tree, White Enamel On Branches, Green On Trunk, 2 In. 14.00
Pin, Christmas Tree, White Enamel On Branches, Varicolored Rhinestones, 2 1/4 In. 18.00
Pin, Circle, Double Curb Links, 2-Color 14K Gold, Tiffany 345.00
Pin, Circular Knot, Rhinestone Highlights, Sterling, Pennino, 3 1/2 In. 121.00
Pin, Citrine, Diamonds, Rubies, 2-Color 14K Gold Scroll Design, Retro 1150.00
Pin, Clip, Openwork Shield Shape, Diamonds, Pearls, Onyx, Platinum, Art Deco 2185.00
Pin, Cockatoos, Carved Tourmaline & Black Onyx, Diamond Eyes, Gage, c.1990 .... 6900.00
Pin, Conch Shell, Yellow Gold, Blue Enamel, Schlumberger 3450.00
Pin, Coral Reef Branch, Textured Gold, Carved Nephrite Jade, Anthony Puccio, Box 290.00
Pin, Crane, Orange, Yellow Stones, Rose Cut Diamonds, Art Nouveau 2415.00
Pin, Crescent & Leaves, Diamonds, Platinum-Topped 14K Gold, Edwardian 1265.00
Pin, Crescent, Rose Cut Diamonds, Silver, Gold Mount, Victorian 920.00
Pin, Crescent, Sapphires, 10 Diamonds, Yellow Metal, Victorian 750.00
Pin, Deer, Brushed Body, Inset Ruby Eyes, 18K Gold, 1 1/2 In. 230.00
Pin, Diamond Leaves, Center Sapphire, Case, St. Petersburg, 1910, 1 1/2 In. 4310.00
Pin, Diamonds, Platinum, Foliate Design, Millegrain Accents, Tiffany, Art Deco 18400.00
Pin, Dog's Head, Pave Diamond Nose, Ruby Accents, 18K Gold, Tiffany & Co. 1495.00
Pin, Dog, Airedale, Hand Chased, Enamel Collar, Red Stone Eye, 14K Gold, Edwardian . 315.00
Pin, Dog, German Shepherd, White Gold Collar, 14K Yellow Gold 200.00
Pin, Dog, Poodle, Green, Blue Rhinestones, Gilt Metal, Stamped, Trifari, 1 1/4 In. 132.00
Pin, Double Bow, Blue Iridescent Pave Rhinestones, Large 35.00
Pin, Douglas Aircraft, Merit Award, Globe & Muscleman, Sterling Silver, 3/4 In. 22.00
Pin, Dove In Round Frame, Sterling Silver, No. 5014, Georg Jensen 260.00
Pin, Dove, Floral Ground, Sterling Silver, Georg Jensen, Denmark 230.00
Pin, Dragonfly, Prong, Collet Set Round Diamonds, 18K White Gold 1725.00
Pin, Duck, Topaz Rhinestones, Stamped, Eisenberg, 4 1/2 In. 1430.00
Pin, Edelweiss, Center Pearls, White Enamel Petals, 18K Gold, Tiffany, Art Nouveau 2645.00
Pin, Entwined Serpents, Gold, Faceted Sapphire, Diamonds, Bolin, 1890, 3/4 In. 4600.00
Pin, Faceted Oval Amethyst, Floral, Leaf Design, Sterling Silver, 2 1/2 x 3/4 In. 230.00
Pin, Family Mourning, Portrait Of Man At Center, Glass Lens, Oval, 1 1/2 In. 22.00
Pin, Faux Pearl & Pave Rhinestone, Eisenberg 200.00
Pin, Feather, Stylized, Rubies, Diamonds, Platinum-Topped 18K Gold, Retro 3450.00
Pin, Female In Profile, Pave Rhinestones, Blue Cabochons, Gilt, Corocraft, 3 In. 440.00
Pin, Figure Of Christ, Top Opens To Reveal Rosary With Cross, Silver 21.00
Pin, Fish, Amethyst Cabochon Eye, Sterling Silver, Sam Kramer, c.1948, 4 1/4 In. 1100.00
Pin, Fish, Faux Pearls, Rhinestones, Eisenberg, 2 1/2 In. 523.00
Pin, Fish, Green, Gold Enamel, Red Cabochon, Pearls, Rhinestones, Trifari 231.00
Pin, Fish, Large Pink Rhinestones, Gilt Metal, Stamped, Eisenberg, 3 In. 1430.00
Pin, Fish, Red Rhinestones, Black Enamel, Stamped, Eisenberg, 3 1/4 In. 990.00
Pin, Floral Design, Red Rhinestones, Moonstone Cabochon Center, Trifari, 4 In. 143.00
Pin, Floral Design, Silver Metal, Rhinestones, Trifari, 3 In. 88.00
Pin, Floral Spray, Black Opals, Pave Diamond Petals, 18K Gold, W.T. Ltd. 2415.00
Pin, Floral Spray, Colored Rhinestones, Haskell 65.00
Pin, Floral Spray, Lilac, Yellow, Pink, Green, Dorrie Nossiter, Arts & Crafts 2760.00
Pin, Floral Spray, Marquise Cut Diamonds, Platinum Mount, Tiffany, France 4830.00
Pin, Floral, Carved Red Petals, Pave Rhinestones, Tamped, Trifari, 3 In. 385.00
Pin, Flower & Leaf Design, Oval, Sterling Silver, Georg Jensen, Denmark, 1 1/4 In. 172.00
Pin, Flower Basket, Enamel, Diamonds, Pearls, Platinum Over 14K Gold, Edwardian 635.00
Pin, Flower Blossom, Stylized, Sterling Silver, Denmark, 1 1/4 In. 316.00
Pin, Flower Bud, Rubies, Diamond, 18K Gold, Cartier 1150.00
Pin, Flower Head, Stylized, Sterling Silver, Stamped 925, No. 86, Georg Jensen 145.00
Pin, Flower Shape, Diamonds, Pearl, Cultured, Gold, Retro 405.00

Jewelry, Pin,
Bakelite, Totem
Pole, Enameled

Jewelry, Pin, Christmas Candle,
Gold Metal, Rhinestone Flame,
Plastic, 2 In.

Jewelry, Pin, Owl, Rhinestones,
Gold Metal, Coro,
1 1/2 In.

Pin, Flower Spray, 9 Green Tourmalines, 2-Color 14K Gold, Tiffany & Co., Retro 920.00
Pin, Flower Sprig, Gold, Sapphires, Diamonds, Retro, Van Cleef & Arpels 2185.00
Pin, Flower, 5 Petal, Pierced, Sterling Silver, Arts & Crafts, Kalo Shop, 1 3/4 In. 425.00
Pin, Flower, Blue Corundum Petals, Diamonds, 18K Gold, Retro, Oscar Heyman Bros. ... 8625.00
Pin, Flower, Carved Crystal Petals, Cabochon Ruby, Diamonds, White Gold, Art Deco ... 430.00
Pin, Flower, Citrine, Moonstone Petals, 14K Gold, Tiffany & Co., Retro 805.00
Pin, Flower, Coral, Light Blue, Blue, Green & Red Cabochons, Eisenberg, 3 In. 176.00
Pin, Flower, Detachable Vine Of Diamond Set Leaves, Diamonds, Gold, 1865 .... 4600.00
Pin, Flower, Diamond Stem, Cabochon Turquoise, Diamond Stem, David Webb 6900.00
Pin, Flower, Emerald Cabochon Center, Diamond Stamens, 14K Gold, 1943 .... 805.00
Pin, Flower, Fuchsia, Green Pearlized Enamel, Rhinestones, Stamped, 3 1/2 In. 357.00
Pin, Flower, Red Rhinestones, Yellow, Green, Red Enamel, Coro, 3 In. 120.00
Pin, Flower, Symmetrical, Coral, Diamonds, France 4500.00
Pin, Flower, Textured & Layered Gold Petals, Diamond Melee, Hammerman Bros. 1035.00
Pin, Flowers & Leaves, Dot Design, Sterling Silver, Georg Jensen, Denmark, 1 3/8 In. 345.00
Pin, Fox, Garnet Eyes, 14K Yellow Gold 316.00
Pin, Fox, Gold, Pave Diamond Ears, Emerald Eyes, 18K Gold, Van Cleef & Arpels 2990.00
Pin, Fox, Swirl Design, Plastic, Lea Stein, Paris, 1950s 285.00
Pin, Frog On Ladder, Plastic, Lea Stein 85.00
Pin, Garnet Carbuncle, Enamel & Beaded Accents, 14K Gold, Victorian Revival 520.00
Pin, Giraffe, Maroon Guilloche Enamel Body, Gold Wire Accents, Tiffany & Co., Italy .. 405.00
Pin, Girasol, Demantoid Garnets, Turquoise, 18K Gold, Schlumberger, Tiffany 13800.00
Pin, Gold Star, Wing Style Rays, Platinum, Cluster Of 58 Diamonds, Schlumberger 9775.00
Pin, Golden Angel, Sparkling Halo, Dangling Star Or Rhinestones, H. Carnegie, 1 In. 105.00
Pin, Grasshopper, Green, Yellow, Brown Enamel, Silver Metal, Stamped, Coro, 3 In. 467.00
Pin, Green Enamel Oval, Dove In Flight, Seed Pearls, Gold Filled, Victorian, 2 1/4 In. ... 460.00
Pin, Green Rhinestones, Fuchsia, Green, Purple, Black Enamel, Eisenberg, 2 In. 176.00
Pin, Green Tourmalines, Freshwater Pearls, Diamond Corners, Silver, Arts & Crafts 2070.00
Pin, Greyhound Lines, 20 Years Service, Dog, 10K Gold, Plastic Case, 3/4 In. 38.00
Pin, Griffin, Whiplash Tail, Seed Pearl Accent, 14K Gold, Art Nouveau 430.00
Pin, Grouse Foot, Sterling Silver, Amethyst 50.00
Pin, Hammered Silver Disc, Center Boss, Beaded Accents, J. Despres, Art Moderne 3738.00
Pin, Hawaiian Flower, Rubies, Sapphire & Diamonds, Van Cleef & Arpels, 6 3/4 In. 9430.00
Pin, Heart & Fleur-De-Lis, Silver, Enamel, Cobalt Blue & Orange, 1902 .... 173.00
Pin, Heart Shape, Painted Courting Couple Scene, Porcelain, Victorian 155.00
Pin, Heart Shaped Leaves, Oval, Sterling Silver, Arts & Crafts, 1 1/2 x 2 In. 125.00
Pin, Holly Leaves, Red Berries, Silver Color, 1 3/4 In. 16.00
Pin, Horse & Coach, Coro, 2 In. 35.00
Pin, Horse & Whip In Horseshoe, Red, White, Brown Enamel, Trifari, 3 In. 1320.00
Pin, Horseshoe, 33 Diamonds, Platinum, Black, Starr & Frost 3450.00
Pin, Hummingbird, Enamel, Cabochon Ruby Eye, 18K Gold, Cooper, 2 1/4 In. 200.00
Pin, Initial, Mod Bead Set, Caliber Sapphire Frame, Platinum, Art Deco 575.00
Pin, Jade Leaf, Carved Nephrite Leaf, Pearls, Cultured, 14K Yellow Gold 230.00
Pin, Jade, Leaves & Vines, Oval, Sterling Silver, Arts & Crafts, 1 1/2 x 2 1/8 In. 365.00

Pin, Kingfisher, Perched On A Leafy Branch, Sterling Silver, Denmark, 1 3/4 In. 460.00
Pin, Large Sapphire, Diamonds, Openwork Foliate Design, Platinum, Edwardian 7475.00
Pin, Leaf & Bead Design, Silver, Oval, Georg Jensen, Denmark, 1 3/4 In. 316.00
Pin, Leaf Form, Diamonds, 14K Gold, Corleto, 2 1/2 In. 1540.00
Pin, Leaf Shape, Gold Vermeil Over Sterling, Danecraft, 2 1/4 In. 38.00
Pin, Leaf, Pave Rhinestones, Silver Metal, Stamped, Trifari, 2 1/2 In. 100.00
Pin, Leaf, Rock Crystal, Diamonds, Platinum-Topped 14K Gold, Tiffany & Co. 2070.00
Pin, Leaf, Scroll, Bead, 14K Gold, Gilbert Oakes, Arts & Crafts, 1 1/4 x 1 5/8 In. 3000.00
Pin, Leaves, Scrolls, Sterling Silver, Gold, Moonstone, Round, E. Oakes, 1920s, 2 In. 4200.00
Pin, Lily Of The Valley, Sterling Silver, Panis Gallery, Arts & Crafts, 3 3/8 x 1 3/4 In. . . . 150.00
Pin, Lily, Sterling Silver, Panis Gallery, Arts & Crafts, 3 x 2 1/8 In. 150.00
Pin, Locket, Floral Seed Pearls, Blue Guilloche Enamel, Silver, Gold, Victorian 375.00
Pin, Mabe Pearl, Bright Cut Gold Mount, Inscribed, Late 19th Century, 2 1/4 In. 200.00
Pin, Mermaid, Large Aqua Rhinestone, Aqua Glass Stones, Gilt Sterling, 3 In. 1430.00
Pin, Mermaid, Large Green Rhinestones, Green Glass Stones, Eisenberg, 3 In. 1870.00
Pin, Mexican Boy With Donkey, Taxco 65.00
Pin, Micromosaic, Round, Shepherd & Lambs, Wire Twist Gold Frame, Victorian 805.00
Pin, Micromosaic, Vatican, Malachite, Gold Wire Twist & Scalloped Frame, Victorian . . . 2300.00
Pin, Mine Cut Diamond, Demantoid Garnet Stripe, Ruby Eyes, c.1900 . . . . 5750.00
Pin, Moon Face, Joseph Of Hollywood 250.00
Pin, Moonstones, Bead & Scroll, Sterling Silver, Arts & Crafts, 2 3/8 In. 425.00
Pin, Mosaic Floral Design, Multicolored, 1 1/2 In. 20.00
Pin, Opal Doublet, Openwork Leaves, Tendrils, Bead Accents, 14K Gold, Arts & Crafts . . 1130.00
Pin, Open Crescent, Diamonds, Pearls, Platinum-Topped 14K Gold, Edwardian 635.00
Pin, Open Square, 2 Dolphins, Vine, Sterling Silver, No. 251, Georg Jensen, 1969 . . . . . . 260.00
Pin, Openwork Silver Leaf, Bead Accents, Round Gilt Border, Arts & Crafts 460.00
Pin, Outer Circle, Center Scroll Design, 14K Gold, Diamonds, Rubies, Retro 690.00
Pin, Oval Jade Plaque, Carved Leafy Design, Enamel, Diamonds, White Gold, Art Deco . 1380.00
Pin, Owl, Rhinestones, Gold Metal, Coro, 1 1/2 In. . . . .*Illus* 60.00
Pin, Pansy Blossom & Leaves, Sterling Silver, 2 7/8 x 1 7/8 In. 230.00
Pin, Pansy, Round Turquoise Stone, Beaded Setting, Sterling Silver, Mary Gage, 1 In. . . . 230.00
Pin, Parrot, Plastic, Lea Stein 95.00
Pin, Partridge, Green Rhinestones, Red Enamel, Gilt Sterling, Eisenberg, 3 In. 440.00
Pin, Peacock Feather, 14K White Gold, Opal & Diamonds, 1930s, 1 1/2 In. 975.00
Pin, Peacock, Diamond Feathers, Citrine Beak, Ruby Crest, c.1910 . . . . 7820.00
Pin, Pearl Drop In Foliate Design Frame, Diamonds, Platinum, Gold, Edwardian 4600.00
Pin, Pearls, Gray, Cream, Silver Foliate Accents, 1950 . . . . 1725.00
Pin, Pendant & Earrings, Scroll Design, Sapphire, Diamonds, Pearls, 1903 . . . . 7765.00
Pin, Pendant & Ring, Cameo, Woman, Coral, Gold Filled Mount, Victorian, 1 3/4 In. 635.00
Pin, Pendant, Cameo, Agate, Split Pearls, Rose & Yellow Gold Frame, Victorian 750.00
Pin, Pendant, Cameo, Woman, Coral, 14K Gold, Whiplash Frame, Art Nouveau 750.00
Pin, Pendant, Clover, 3 Pear Shaped Amethysts, Diamond Accent, 14K Gold, Victorian . . 375.00
Pin, Pendant, Colored Pearls, Enamel Leaves, Gold Vines, Art Nouveau, Krementz & Co. 750.00
Pin, Pendant, Emerald, Rubies, Gold Filigree, Bead & Wire Twist Accents, Georgian 1725.00
Pin, Pendant, Pearls, 1 Mine Cut Diamond, 14K Rose Gold, Victorian 220.00
Pin, Pendant, Wreath, Suspended From Bow, Diamonds, Platinum, Edwardian 4890.00
Pin, Pietra Dura, 2 Birds On Floral Branch, 10K Gold Frame, Victorian 750.00
Pin, Pietra Dura, Oval Hardstone, Red & White Flower, Gold Wirework Frame, Victorian 375.00
Pin, Pink Glass, V Shape, Saw Pierced, Geometric, Arts & Crafts, 2 3/4 In. 185.00
Pin, Plaque, Micromosaic, Flower Basket, Gilt Silver Frame, 1880s, 1 3/4 x 1 5/8 In. 2185.00
Pin, Portrait, Woman In Hat, Hand Painted, Porcelain, Silvered Frame, 2 3/4 In. 84.00
Pin, Portrait, Woman, Frame, Hand Painted, Frame, Art Nouveau, 2 1/4 In. 28.00
Pin, Portrait, Woman, Hand Painted, Ivory, Silver Frame, 800 Mark, 19th Century, 2 In. . . 168.00
Pin, Portrait, Woman, Ringlets, Necklace, Painting, On Ivory, Gold Frame, 2 1/2 In. 230.00
Pin, Portrait, Young Woman, White, Flowing Scarf, Porcelain, Oval 95.00
Pin, Prong Set Faceted Amethyst, Split Pearls, Dorrie Nossiter, England 1092.50
Pin, Prong Set Oval Amethyst Cabochon, Seed Pearls, Dorrie Nossiter, England 3680.00
Pin, Pussy Willow & Sea Grass, Natural Shell, Pearl, 14K Gold, Victorian 805.00
Pin, Question Mark, Stylized, Yellow Gold, Schlumberger 920.00
Pin, Rectangular, Diamond, 3 Pave Set Diamond Plaques, White Gold, Art Deco 6900.00
Pin, Ribbon, Blue Rhinestones, Turquoise Glass Stones, Pave Rhinestones, 2 1/4 In. 66.00
Pin, Ribbon, Tied, Rose Cut Diamond, Laurel, Platinum & Gold, c.1905 . . . . 6325.00
Pin, Rooster, Green, Blue Rhinestones, Gilt Metal, Stamped Trifari, 2 1/4 In. 143.00

Pin, Rose, Textured Leaves, 18K Yellow & White Gold, Tiffany & Co. 290.00
Pin, Sailboat, Red Enamel Stripe, 14K Gold 1035.00
Pin, Sapphire & Diamond, Center Oval Sapphire, Bezel Set, c.1930 . . . .   1725.00
Pin, Scarf, Butterfly, Openwork, Seed Pearls, 14K Yellow Gold 230.00
Pin, Scepter, Red, Green Cabochons, Rhinestones, Gilt Metal, Stamped, Trifari, 3 In. 110.00
Pin, Scroll Filigree, 39 Diamonds, Platinum, Rectangular, c.1920, 1 1/2 In. 345.00
Pin, Scroll, Cabochon Turquoise, Sapphires, Diamonds, 18K Gold, David Webb 2990.00
Pin, Sea Horse, Sterling Silver, 2 3/4 In., Pair 106.00
Pin, Sea Urchin, Gold, Sapphire & Ruby Flower Accent, Tiffany & Co. 1840.00
Pin, Setting Sun, Figures At Stream, Painting, On Abalone, Gold Frame, 2 x 2 1/2 In. 1070.00
Pin, Silver Body & Wings, Tortoiseshell Wings, W. Spratling, Mexico, 1931, 2 In., Pair . .   1150.00
Pin, Silver Lapel, Hairwork Scene With A Bull On 1 Side, Art Nouveau 805.00
Pin, Silver, St. Peter With Gate Keys, Los Castillo, Mexico, 3 In.   200.00
Pin, Spades, Black Enamel, Peal, Agate, 18K Yellow Gold, 1872 . . . .   2185.00
Pin, Spanish Woman & Boy, Enamel, Rhinestones, Corocraft, 2 3/4 In. 330.00
Pin, Spray Of Water, Fish Form, Hammered, Sterling Silver, Denmark, 1 1/4 In. 431.00
Pin, Squirrel, Faux Pearls, Pave Rhinestones, Boucher, 3 In. 231.00
Pin, Star Burst, Blue Rhinestones, Silver Metal, Stamped, Trifari, 2 1/2 In. 66.00
Pin, Star On Circle, Turquoise Beads, 18K Gold, Hand Chased, Victorian 575.00
Pin, Starfish, Carved Sandalwood, Mabe Pearls, 18K Gold Accents, Seaman Schepps 1265.00
Pin, Stylized Flowers, Brass, Acid Etched, Carence Crafters, Arts & Crafts, 3 x 3 1/2 In. .   395.00
Pin, Sun Face, Joseph Of Hollywood 295.00
Pin, Sunburst, Large Rhinestones, Weiss, c.1940 . . . .   55.00
Pin, Sword Jabot, Bead Set With Round Diamonds In Silver, 14K Gold 632.00
Pin, Treble Clef, Metal, Bakelite Guitar, Banjo & Violin Drops, 2 1/2 In. 360.00
Pin, Tree With Crescent Moonstones, Red Rhinestones, Trifari, 2 In. 286.00
Pin, Tree, Pearls, Cultured, 14K Gold, Mikimoto 240.00
Pin, Trefoil Shape, 3 Leaves, Cabochon Garnet, 14K Gold, Victorian, 1 1/2 In. 115.00
Pin, Turquoise Cabochon, Brass, Arts & Crafts, 1 3/4 x 2 3/4 In.   175.00
Pin, Turtle, Red Rhinestones, Plastic Turquoise Stones, c.1965, 2 1/8 In. 90.00
Pin, Winged Design, Blue Rhinestones, Gilt Metal, Stamped, Eisenberg, 2 1/2 In. 187.00
Pin, Woman's Head, Opens 2 Spaces, Sterling Silver, WH Co. 40.00
Pin, Woman's Head, Veiled, Plumed Hat, Sterling Silver, Art Nouveau, 2 3/8 In. 920.00
Pin, Yachting Pennant Flag, Diamonds, Sapphires, Rubies, Gold, England, c.1978 . . . . . .   1610.00
Pin, Zebra, Rhinestones, Red, Black Enamel, Stamped, Eisenberg, 3 1/4 In. 990.00
Pin & Earrings, Amethyst, Gold, Scrolled Design, Flower In Center, Victorian 575.00
Pin & Earrings, Bee, Red Stone Eyes, 14K Gold, Tiffany & Co. 805.00
Pin & Earrings, Bug, Large Purple, Red Rhinestones, Reja, 1 3/4 In. 121.00
Pin & Earrings, Camelia, Enameled, Sarah Coventry 48.00
Pin & Earrings, Crown, Rhinestones, Gilt Metal, Stamped, Trifari, 1 1/2 x 1 In. 247.00
Pin & Earrings, Curved Teardrop Shape, Sterling Silver, Both Signed, Georg Jensen 374.00
Pin & Earrings, Fruit Salad, Carved Rhinestones, Trifari, 1/2 In. 286.00
Pin & Earrings, Goose, Pave Rhinestones, Stamped, Trifari, 3 1/4 In. 880.00
Pin & Earrings, Pyramid Shape, Teardrops, Malachite, 14K Gold, Victorian 920.00
Pin & Earrings, Shield Shape, Faceted Garnet Clusters, Retractable Bail 375.00
Pin & Earrings, Textured Gold Center, Enamel Tracery, Chain, 3 Gold Drops, Victorian . .   805.00
Pin Bar, Moonstone, Leaf, Scroll, Bead, Gold, E.E. Oakes, Arts & Crafts, 5/8 x 2 1/4 In. .   2900.00
Ring, 2 Cabochon Shaped Moonstones, Floral Design, 14K Gold, Arts & Crafts 230.00
Ring, 2 Diamonds, Engraved Platinum Mount, Edwardian 10925.00
Ring, 3 Diamonds, Lozenge Border, 21 Smaller Diamonds, Platinum, Belle Epoque 4600.00
Ring, 3 Diamonds, Pierced Platinum & Diamond Mount, Art Deco 14950.00
Ring, 4 Diamonds, 8 Smaller Diamonds, Platinum Openwork Mount, Belle Epoque 1725.00
Ring, 19 Rubies In 2 Lines, Diamonds, 18K Gold, Oscar Heyman Brothers, Size 6 . . . . . .   2300.00
Ring, Bakelite, Random Dot, Yellow, Cream Dots, 1 In. 265.00
Ring, Band Of Marcasites, Sterling Silver, Heavy, Victorian 150.00
Ring, Band, Carved Ruby Cabochons, Millegrain Design, Platinum, Art Deco, Size 6 . . . .   2645.00
Ring, Berden, Yellow Beryl, 18K Gold Wire Surround, Schlumberger, Size 5 1/2 . . . .   4370.00
Ring, Blister Pearl, 4 Round Diamonds, Art Deco 517.00
Ring, Citrine, Diamonds, Platinum Mount, Art Deco 690.00
Ring, Class, Blue Stone, School Crest, 10K Gold, Dieges & Clust, 1964, Size 6 1/2 . . . . .   78.00
Ring, Class, North Marion High School, 10K Gold, Red Stone, Balfour, 1968 . . . .   60.00
Ring, Class, Pasadena City College, White Gold, Gray Stone, Nursing Emblem 60.00
Ring, Class, Windsor Teacher's College, 10K Gold, Red Stone, 1967, Size 4 . . . .   65.00

Ring, Cluster, Prong Set Oval Sapphire, 8 Prong Set Aquamarines, Dorrie Nossiter 2415.00
Ring, Cobalt Blue Enamel, Rose Cut Diamonds, 14K Yellow Gold 2500.00
Ring, Cobalt Blue, Powder Blue, Yellow Enamel, Seed Pearl Accents 172.00
Ring, Cocktail, Emerald, Mine Cut Diamond, 18K Gold 5750.00
Ring, Diamond Solitaire, 6 Smaller Diamonds, Platinum Basket Mount, Art Deco 1380.00
Ring, Diamond, 2 White & Black Pearls, 18K Gold, Victorian 2185.00
Ring, Diamonds In Geometric Design, 12 Blue Stones, Platinum Mount, Art Deco 865.00
Ring, Diamonds, Sapphires, Platinum-Topped 18K Gold, Edwardian, Size 4 1/4 .... 1150.00
Ring, Elongated Turquoise, 14K Gold, Arts & Crafts, Arizona Turquoise Mines Co. 230.00
Ring, Emerald, Diamond, Foliate Openwork Platinum Mount, Art Deco, Size 6 1/2 ...... 490.00
Ring, Emerald, Square Cut, Diamond Surround, 18K White Gold, Amsterdam & Sauer ... 3105.00
Ring, Engagement, Square Diamond, Diamond Surround, Platinum, Art Deco 14950.00
Ring, Eternity Band, Brilliant Cut Diamonds, 14K Yellow Gold 690.00
Ring, European Cut Diamond, Pierced Platinum Mount, Diamond Accents, Art Deco 2990.00
Ring, Eye, Pink Tourmaline, Textured 18K Gold, Schlumberger, Tiffany, Size 5 1/2 ..... 1150.00
Ring, Filigree Dome, Sapphires, Emeralds, Diamonds, 18K Gold, Van Cleef & Arpels ... 1840.00
Ring, Geometric Design, Platinum, Art Deco 690.00
Ring, Golden Sapphire, 2 Brilliant Diamonds, Platinum 1150.00
Ring, Green Chrysoprase, Textured 18K Gold, David Webb, Size 9 1/2 .... 1380.00
Ring, Green Tourmaline, Rectangular, Signed, Georg Jensen, 7 3/4 In. 1610.00
Ring, Heart Shaped Iolite, Bead Set Round Brilliant Diamonds, 18K Yellow Gold 1092.00
Ring, Indian Chief, Eagles On Sides, Plated Brass, Copper, Mexico, Size 6 1/4 .... 20.00
Ring, Jade Cabochon, Dragon Grasping Stone In Jaws, 18K Yellow Gold 635.00
Ring, Lapis Lazuli Cabochon, 18K Gold Wire Surround, Schlumberger, Tiffany & Co. 635.00
Ring, Lozenge Shape, Diamonds, Platinum, Millegrain Accents, Art Deco, Size 7 .... 1610.00
Ring, Mine & European Cut Diamond, Openwork Frame, Platinum & Gold 8625.00
Ring, Moonstone, Bezel Oval, Signed, Georg Jensen, 18K Yellow Gold 865.00
Ring, Navette, Emeralds, Diamonds, 18K Gold, Pierced Gallery, Victorian 1150.00
Ring, Navette, Rubies, Diamonds, 18K Yellow Gold, Pierced Gallery, Victorian 1840.00
Ring, Opal, Demantoids, Diamond Shoulders, 18K White Gold, Art Deco, France 2185.00
Ring, Opals, Floral & Bead Accents, 18K Gold Openwork, Arts & Crafts, Size 7 .... 635.00
Ring, Open Heart Design, Bead Set Round Diamonds, Peretti Spain, Tiffany & Co. 345.00
Ring, Oval Blue Star Sapphire, 12 Diamonds, Platinum, Art Deco, c.1920 .... 920.00
Ring, Oval Cabochon Amethyst, 18K Gold, No. 1046A, Georg Jensen 920.00
Ring, Oval Cabochon Jade, 8 Diamonds, 14K Silver-Topped Gold, Victorian 460.00
Ring, Oval Sapphire, Diamonds, Platinum, Tiffany & Co., Art Deco 8625.00
Ring, Peridot, Gypsy Set, Cheminee, Textured 18K Gold, Schlumberger, Tiffany 1955.00
Ring, Poison, Sterling Silver, Hinged Lid, Garnet On Top, Filigree, Hook, Size 10 1/2 .... 20.00
Ring, Purple Amethyst, 22 Rose Cut Diamonds, 18K Gold, Victorian 445.00
Ring, Rose Gold Florals, 1 Carat Champagne Diamond Solitaire, Silver, Tiffany 1200.00
Ring, Round Sapphire, Diamonds, Pierced Platinum Mount, Art Deco 1095.00
Ring, Sapphire, 13 Diamonds, Platinum Mount, 14K White Gold Shank, Art Deco 4830.00
Ring, Sapphire, Diamonds, Platinum, Engraved, Art Deco 4715.00
Ring, Sapphire, Pierced Gallery, Engraved Platinum Shank, Art Deco, 1929 .... 2070.00
Ring, Silver, 2 Moonstones, Flower Shoulders, Georg Jensen, Pilstrup 690.00
Ring, Snake, 2 Snakes Entwined In Sinuous Loops, 18K White, Yellow Gold 290.00
Ring, Snake, Tapering Coil, Cabochon Sapphire, 22K Yellow Gold 460.00
Ring, Star Sapphire, Diamonds, Platinum, J.E.C. & Co., For Caldwell, Art Deco 1380.00
Ring, Star, Baguette Cut Diamond, Sapphire, Art Deco 1200.00
Ring, Step Cut Citrine, Quatrefoil Mount, 14K Rose Gold, Retro, Size 8 .... 1725.00
Ring, Synthetic Blue Sapphire, 30 Diamonds Surround, Platinum, c.1930 .... 630.00
Ring, Trellis, Bombe Design, Diamonds, Sapphires, Yellow Gold, Schlumberger, Size 3 .. 1610.00
Ring, Yellow Center Diamond, Diamonds & Sapphires In Swirl, Platinum, c.1940 .... 8625.00
Sautoir, Seed Pearls, 10 Strands, Diamonds, Platinum Topped Gold, Belle Epoque, 27 In. 8625.00
Shoe Buckle, Polished Steel, Whitesmith, 18th Century, Pair 195.00
Stickpin, 14K Gold, Cameo, Scene, Victorian 85.00
Stickpin, Cameo, Man, Coral, Gold Stem, Victorian 575.00
Stickpin, Emerald, Diamonds, Pierced Platinum Millegrain Mount, Art Deco 1495.00
Stickpin, Enamel, Shield Shape, Sterling Silver, Rokesley Shop, Arts & Crafts, 3/4 In. ... 395.00
Stickpin, Moonstone Face, 4 Prong Set, 14K Yellow Gold 865.00
Stickpin, Oval Moonstone, Channel Set Emeralds, 14K Yellow Gold 345.00
Stickpin, Pear Shaped Sapphire, Bezel Set, 14K Gold, Tiffany & Co., Edwardian 980.00
Stickpin, Reverse Painted Crystal, Horse's Head, 14K Gold, J.E. Caldwell Co. 290.00

Stickpin, Reversible, Sapphires & Diamonds In Rings, Art Deco, Cartier Paris Londres ..	4140.00
Stickpin, Scarab, Opal, Carved, Modified Fleur-De-Lis Prongs, 14K Gold, Edwardian ...	635.00
Stickpin, Shield Shape, Channel Set Rubies, Sapphires, 18K Yellow Gold	287.00
Stickpin, Sparrow, Pearl & Ruby, Russia	45.00
Stickpin, Tourmaline, 18K Gold	90.00
Tie Bar, Gold Club, Pearl, Cultured, 14K Gold	165.00
Watches are listed in their own category.	
Watch Chain, 14K Gold, British Gold Coin Fob	100.00
Watch Chain, 14K Rose Gold Slide, Fleur-De-Lis & Enameled Trim	305.00
Watch Chain, 4-Sided Flower Design Links, Mixed Metal, Victorian, 51 In.	2185.00
Watch Chain, Platinum, Pearls, Paperclip Links, Edwardian, 22 In..................	805.00
Watch Chain, Rope Twist, 14K Gold, Slide & Lodge Fob	120.00
Watch Chain, Rose & White Gold, c.1900, 14 1/2 In.	110.00
Wristwatches are listed in their own category.	

JOHN ROGERS statues were made from 1859 to 1892. The originals were bronze, but the thousands of copies made by the Rogers factory were of painted plaster. Eighty different figures were created. Similar painted plaster figures were produced by some other factories. Rights to the figures were sold in 1893 and they were manufactured for several more years by the Rogers Statuette Co. Never repaint a Rogers figure because this lowers the value to collectors.

Group, Coming To The Parson, 22 x 16 In.	175.00
Group, Tap On The Window, 19 1/2 x 15 In.	143.00
Group, Traveling Magician, 22 1/3 x 15 In.	2530.00
Group, Wounded To The Rear, One More Shot, 20 In.	1955.00

JOSEF ORIGINALS ceramics were designed by Muriel Joseph George. The first pieces were made in California from 1945 to 1962. They were then manufactured in Japan. The company was sold to George Good in 1982 and he continued to make Josef Originals until 1985. The company was then sold to Southland Corporation. The name is now owned by Applause.

Doll Of The Month, March, 3 In.	60.00
Doll Of The Month, October, 3 In.	35.00
Figurine, Birthday Girl, February, 4 In.	15.00
Figurine, Birthstone Doll, December, 3 1/2 In.	25.00
Figurine, Bridal Shower, 4 1/2 In.	55.00
Figurine, Christmas, Angel, 4 In.	65.00
Figurine, France, Little International Series, 3 1/2 In.	45.00
Figurine, Jacques, 5 1/2 In.	65.00
Figurine, January, 3 1/2 In.	20.00
Figurine, Lady With Mirror, Colonial Days Series, 8 In.	165.00
Figurine, Little Tutu, Yellow, 3 1/2 In.	50.00
Figurine, Mrs. Claus With Cake	25.00
Figurine, Pennies From Heaven	40.00
Figurine, Penny, Rose Dress, 4 In.	55.00
Figurine, Pin Box, Girl, Purple, 2 1/2 In.	50.00
Figurine, Ring Bearer, 3 In.	40.00
Figurine, Rose Garden, Brown Eyes, 5 In.	85.00
Figurine, Roses, Flower Girl Series, 5 1/2 In.	45.00
Figurine, Spoon Holder, Pink	65.00
Figurine, Wednesday, Days Of The Week Series	85.00
Figurine, Wee Japanese Kabuti, Shakuhachi	40.00
Figurine, Wee Ling, 5 In.	42.00
Figurine, Wu Fu, 10 In.	125.00
Lipstick Holder, Mermaid Blue	45.00
Music Box, Humoresque, Girl At Piano, Candles, Paper Label	75.00
Music Box, Love Is A Many Splintered Thing	75.00
Music Box, Recital, Fascination, 4 1/2 In.	100.00
Music Box, Spring Bouquet, 7 1/2 In.	50.00
Salt & Pepper, Mary & Lamb	45.00
Salt & Pepper, Miss Muffet & Spider	45.00
Salt & Pepper, Peter, Peter & Wife	45.00

JUDAICA is any memorabilia that refers to the Jews or the Jewish religion. Interests range from newspaper clippings that mention eighteenth- and nineteenth-century Jewish Americans to religious objects, such as menorahs or spice boxes. Age, condition, and the intrinsic value of the material, as well as the historic and artistic importance, determine the value.

Box, Charity, Building Form, Coin Slot, Metal, Palestine, 13 In.	2875.00
Box, Charity, Building Form, Slot On Roof, Sterling Silver, Israel, Lavaton, 9 In.	3105.00
Box, Charity, Wire Handle Ring, Slot On Top, Map Of Palestine, 6 7/8 In.	92.00
Breast Plate, Festival Plaque, Columns, Tulips, Foliate Border, Silver Plate, 11 In.	575.00
Breast Plate, Torah, Cartouche Form, Floral, Scroll Work, Hebrew Text, 1870, 14 In.	632.00
Breast Plate, Torah, Crown Above Candelabra, Tulips, Grape Clusters, Silver, 9 In.	2530.00
Breast Plate, Torah, Names Of 12 Tribes Of Moses, Brass, Stone, 8 In.	460.00
Candelabrum, Sabbath, 7-Light, Temple Menorah Form, Brass, 15 1/2 x 8 In.	175.00
Candlestick, Sabbath, Bobeche Over Baluster, Leaves, Silver, Poland, 8 In., Pair	2070.00
Candlestick, Sabbath, Chased With Lions, Star Of David, Silver, Poland, 13 In., Pair	805.00
Candlestick, Turned Form, Domed Round Foot, North Africa, 13 In., Pair	460.00
Card, Greeting, New Year, Steamer At Sea, American Flag, Statue Of Liberty, 12 x 9 In.	230.00
Coaster, Star Of David, Sterling Silver, Set Of 6	225.00
Container, Etrog, Domed Hinged Lid, Leaf Design, Cast Feet, Silver, 1890, 6 1/2 In.	345.00
Container, Etrog, Hinged Lid, Fruit Form, Hebrew Text, Palestine, 7 In.	287.00
Cookbook, Art Of Jewish Cooking, Random House, N.Y., 1958	115.00
Cookbook, Tempting Kosher Dishes, Prepared From Manischewitz's Matzo, 1930	115.00
Cover, Matzo, Silk, Leaf Design, Satin Hebrew Text, Magenta Ground, 1906, 18 In.	287.00
Crown, Torah, Berry, Leaf Finial, Star Of David, Silver, Gilt, Continental, 4 In.	805.00
Cup, Kiddush, Crown & Tablet Design, Baroque, Flared, Silver, Circular Foot, 5 In.	3220.00
Cup, Kiddush, Floral Designs, Bands, Rampant Lion, Hebrew Text, Flared Rim, 3 In.	460.00
Cup, Kiddush, Leaf Design, Baroque, Silver, Gilt, 3 Ball Feet, 4 In.	1725.00
Cup, Kiddush, Star Of David, Hebrew Text Relating To Elija, Silver, Round, 6 In.	400.00
Cup, Kiddush, Tapered Bowl, Spreading Round Foot, Ruby Flashed, 4 In.	172.00
Finials, Torah, Foliate, Animal Design, Deer & Bells, Hebrew Text, Silver, 12 In., Pair	805.00
Finials, Torah, Leaf, Berry Finial Over Reeded Ball, Stylized Arches, Bells, Silver, 16 In.	805.00
Group, Judgment Of King Solomon, Silver Metal, Marble, Wooden Base, 11 In.	115.00
Knife, Circumcision, Double-Edged Steel Blade, Silver, Agate Handle, 6 1/2 In.	977.00
Knife, Shabbat, Mother-Of-Pearl, Hebrew Inscription, Metal, Marked, Karlsbad, 5 In.	287.00
Lamp, Hanukkah, Allover Foliate Design, Oil Font Base, Plain Feet, Bronze, 6 In.	632.00
Lamp, Hanukkah, Bronze, Double Headed Eagle, Row Of 8 Oil Fonts, 11 In.	345.00
Lamp, Hanukkah, Lions Holding Candelabra, Silver, Brass, Poland, 9 1/2 In.	460.00
Lamp, Hanukkah, Stylized Leaves, Birds, Oil Font Base, Circular Feet, Bronze, 6 In.	1840.00
Lamp, Sabbath, Hanging, Attached Drip Pan, Bulbous Stem, Brass, Germany, 20 In.	402.00
Menorah, Brass, Round, 6 Candleholders, 1 Raised In Center, 8 1/2 x 4 1/2 In.	160.00
Menorah, Hanukkah, Lamp, Birds Among Branches, Round Domed Feet, Silver, 5 In.	632.00
Menorah, Hanukkah, Sterling Silver, 1920s, 9 1/2 In.	345.00
Menorah, Hebrew Inscription On Stem, Sterling Silver, Germany, 12 In.	1400.00
Mezuzah, Hinged Cover, Leaves & Cherubs, Adam & Eve, Silver, 3 1/2 In.	977.00
Noisemaker, Purim, Black Design Of Characters, Hebrew & English Text, 4 In.	402.00
Noisemaker, Purim, Walnut, Continental, Early 20th Century, 6 3/4 In.	374.00
Plaque, Woman, Weeping, Terra-Cotta Relief, Hebrew Text, Bezalel, 1914, 9 x 12 In.	3450.00
Plate, Purim, Hebrew Text Relating To Purim, Oval, Continental, 13 1/4 In.	1092.00
Plate, Seder, Divided Compartments For Seder Implements, Green Rim, Round, 10 In.	489.00
Plate, Seder, Man Carrying Child, Star Of David Rim, Hebrew Porcelain, c.1885, 10 In.	510.00
Plate, Seder, Reserves With Hebrew Text, Leaves Design, Leaf Rim, Pale Green, 10 In.	1725.00
Pointer, Torah, Curved To Terminate In Hand As Pointed Index Finger, Silver, 8 In.	977.00
Pointer, Torah, Floral Designs, Metal Chain, Sterling Silver, 9 3/4 In.	210.00
Pointer, Torah, Rampant Lion With Shield, Star Of David, Silver, 12 In.	460.00
Postcard, New Year's, Pop-Up Temple, Rabbi Reciting From Book, 10 x 8 7/8 In.	460.00
Poster, Jewish National Fund, Ben Uri, On Linen, Grafica, Jerusalem, 1936, 20 In.	690.00
Scroll, Esther, Applied Bands Of Foliage, Handwritten Ink On Calfskin, 9 1/4 In.	431.00
Scroll, Esther, Fruitwood Rollers, Handwritten Ink On Calfskin, 17 1/2 In.	345.00
Scroll, Esther, Silver Crown With Green Stones, Jerusalem, Bezalel, 1940, 12 In.	7475.00
Scroll, Esther, Silver Filigree, Turned Handle, Jerusalem, 1940, 4 In.	1150.00
Sign, Synagogue, Blue Hebrew Lettering, White Ground, Metal, Palestine, 13 In.	402.00
Spice Box, Floral Scrollwork Cone, Silver Filigree, Domed Foot, Bezalel, 5 In.	920.00

Spice Box, Hinged Reticulated Lid, Silver, Continental, 2 1/2 In. 345.00
Spice Box, Pendant Flag Over Tapered Spire, Silver Filigree, Germany, 11 In. 862.00
Spice Box, Pierced Sides, Hebrew Letters, Leaf Capped Feet, Sterling Silver, 2 1/2 In. ... 110.00
Spice Box, Rachel's Tomb, Blessing Spices, Brass, Palestine, 4 In. 460.00
Spice Box, Removable Lid, Incised Leaf Design, Silver, Post-1953, 10 In. 1265.00
Spice Box, Round Hinged Lid, Chased Foliate Design, Bird Finial, Silver, 5 In. 805.00
Spice Box, Sabbath Candelabra Finial Above Octagonal Body, Ivory, 11 In. 8050.00
Spice Box, Tower, Central Spire & Turrets, Leaves, Silver, Germany, 6 In. 1265.00
Spice Box, Tower, Hinged Door, Pendant Flag Above Onion Form Spire, Silver, 14 In. ... 2300.00
Spice Box, Tower, Pendant Flags, Rectangular, Silver, 5 1/2 In. 805.00
Spice Container, Hour Glass Shape, Tower, Central Door, Silver, Russia, 1880, 10 In. ... 400.00
Tefilin Bag, Blue Silk, Leaf Design, Hebrew Text, Late 19th Century, 8 In. 230.00
Tray, Seder, 6 Bowls For Implements Of Seder, Plate, Order Of Seder, 15 3/4 In. 115.00
Tray, Seder, 6 Cups To Hold Ritual Items, Round Dish, Bone China, 15 In. 345.00
Vase, Circle Depicting Rachel's Tomb, Bombe Of Rachel, Hebrew Text, Bezalel, 7 In. ... 460.00
Wine, Engraved Star Of David, Sterling Silver, 4 1/8 In., 4 Piece 88.00

JUGTOWN Pottery refers to pottery made in North Carolina as far back as the 1750s. In 1915, Juliana and Jacques Busbee set up a training and sales organization for what they named *Jugtown Pottery*. In 1921, they built a shop at Jugtown, North Carolina, and hired Ben Owen as a potter in 1923. The Busbees moved the village store where the pottery was sold to New York City. Juliana Busbee sold the New York store in 1926 and moved into a log cabin near the Jugtown Pottery. The pottery closed in 1959. It reopened in 1960 and is still working near Seagrove, North Carolina.

Bowl, Chinese Blue Glaze, Flat Rim, Circular Stamp, 4 1/2 x 7 1/4 In. 825.00
Bowl, Ruffled Rim, Green & Gray Mottled Glaze, Marked, 8 In. 77.00
Figurine, Chicken, Glossy Caramel Feldspathic Glaze, 1986, 8 1/8 x 11 1/2 In. 165.00
Figurine, Chicken, Glossy Mustard Feldspathic Glaze, Claw Feet, 1984, 8 1/4 x 7 3/4 In. . 110.00
Jar, Salt Glaze, Stoneware, 4 x 3 3/4 In. 33.00
Jug, Spouted, Stoneware, Applied Handle, Orange Peel Highlights, 1983, 10 3/8 In. 110.00
Pitcher, Frogskin, Green, 4 1/4 In. 55.00
Urn, Chinese Blue & Red Glaze, 2 Handles, Stamped Mark, 7 x 5 1/2 In. 990.00
Vase, Chinese Blue Glaze, Circular Stamp, 4 x 3 In. 825.00
Vase, Chinese Blue Glaze, Ovoid, Circular Stamp, 5 1/4 x 4 In. 770.00
Vase, Embossed Medallions, Mottled White Semimatte Glaze, 14 1/2 x 6 In. 1100.00
Vase, Matte White Glaze, Raised Rim, Signed, 5 3/4 In. 172.00
Vase, Mirrored Black Glaze, Impressed Mark, 7 x 7 In. 550.00
Vase, White Semimatte Glaze, Brown Clay, Egg Shape, Circular Stamp, 6 1/2 In. 495.00

JUKEBOXES play records. The first coin-operated phonograph was demonstrated in 1889. In 1906 the *Automatic Entertainer* appeared, the first coin-operated phonograph to offer several different selections of music. The first electrically powered jukebox was introduced in 1927. Collectors search for jukeboxes of all ages, especially those with flashing lights and unusual design and graphics.

Pla-Mor, Packard Mfg. Co., Remote Selector, 7 1/2 x 11 1/2 In. 145.00
Rock-Ola, Plays 45s, Chrome Trim, 1956 .... 2200.00
Seeburg, 100 Select-O-Matic, Chrome & Mirrored Front, 54 In. 1725.00
Seeburg, 100 Series, Table Top, 1950s 275.00
Seeburg, 200 Select-O-Matic 3910.00
Wurlitzer, Model 616 .... 1430.00
Wurlitzer, Model 750E, Electric Keyboard, c.1941 .... 5175.00
Wurlitzer, No. 1400 .... 850.00

KATE GREENAWAY, who was a famous illustrator of children's books, drew pictures of children in high-waisted Empire dresses. She lived from 1846 to 1901. Her designs appear on china, glass, and other pieces. Figural napkin rings depicting the Greenaway children may also be found in the Napkin Ring category under Figural.

Book, Birthday 50.00
Clock, Figural, Children Playing On Slide, Meriden & Co., 5 3/4 x 5 In. 258.00
Figurine, Amy, White & Blue, No. 2958 .... 250.00

Kay Finch,
Figurine, Choir
Boy, Kneeling,
No. 211, 5 1/2 In.

Kay Finch,
Figurine, Choir
Boy, Standing,
No. 210,
7 1/2 In.

**When ordering
antiques by mail, do
not send cash; send
a check or charge
them. Keep a copy of
your order.**

Figurine, Carrie, Turquoise, No. 2800 .... 325.00
Figurine, Sophia, Red & Green, No. 2833 .... 325.00
Figurine, Tom, Blue & Yellow, No. 2864 .... 475.00
Salt & Pepper, Boy, Girl 55.00

KAY FINCH Ceramics were made in Corona Del Mar, California, from
1935 to 1963. The hand-decorated pieces often depicted whimsical
animals and people. Pastel colors were used.

*Kay Finch
CALIFORNIA*

Figurine, Baby Rabbit, Cottontail, Pink, White, No. 152 .... 85.00
Figurine, Choir Boy, Kneeling, No. 211, 5 1/2 In ....*Illus* 100.00
Figurine, Choir Boy, Standing, No. 210, 7 1/2 In. ....*Illus* 125.00
Figurine, Hoot Owl, No. 187 .... 150.00
Figurine, Lion, Lying, 1953, No. 811 .... 350.00
Godey Man, Pink, Blue, No. 160, 7 1/2 In. 85.00
Planter, Baby's Block, Bear 125.00
Planter, Bear, No. 4908 .... 120.00

KAYSERZINN, see Pewter category.

KELVA glassware was made by the C. F. Monroe Company of Meriden,
Connecticut, about 1904. It is a pale, pastel-painted glass decorated
with flowers, designs, or scenes. Kelva resembles Nakara and Wave
Crest, two other glasswares made by the same company.

KELVA

Dish, Sweetmeat, Pink Floral, 6 Sides, Silver Plate Lid & Bail, Signed, 4 In. 600.00
Humidor, Labeled Cigars, Enameled, Allover Floral, Gray Ground, 5 3/4 In. 375.00
Jewelry Box, Ink Floral, Green, Square, 4 In. 650.00
Powder Box, Oval, Signed, 5 x 3 1/2 In. 468.00

KEMPLE glass was made by John Kemple of East Palestine, Ohio, and
Kenova, West Virginia, from 1945 to 1970. The glass was made from
old molds. Many designs and colors were made. Kemple pieces are
usually marked with a *K* on the bottom. Many milk glass pieces were
made with or without the mark.

Box, Trinket, Milk Glass, 4 x 6 In. 25.00
Compote, Milk Glass, 1940s, 6 1/2 x 5 1/2 In. 20.00
Dish, Chicken On Basket Cover, Amber, 6 In. 30.00
Dish, Fox On Basket Cover, 6 In. 80.00
Relish, Milk Glass, 10 1/2 In. 18.00

KENTON HILLS Pottery in Erlanger, Kentucky, made art wares, including vases and figurines that resembled Rookwood, probably because
so many of the original artists and workmen had worked at the Rookwood plant. Kenton Hills opened in 1939 and closed during World
War II.

Bowl, Heavy Layered Glaze, Floral Interior, Unica, Alza Stratton, 8 In. 3000.00
Figurine, Sigrid, David Seyler, 6 1/4 In. 192.00
Lamp Base, Leaping Stage, Jewel Porcelain Mint Green Glaze, Hentschel, 9 In. 297.00
Vase, Unica, Crossed Leaf Design, Alza Stratton, c.1939, 5 1/4 In. 660.00

KEW BLAS is the name used by the Union Glass Company of Somerville, Massachusetts. The name refers to an iridescent golden glass made from the 1890s to 1924. The iridescent glass was reminiscent of the Tiffany glass of the period.

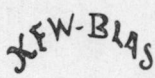

Paperweight, Scarab, 1920s	950.00
Tumbler, Pinched Bottom, Marked, 3 1/2 In.	350.00
Vase, Trumpet Form, Amber Iridescent, Gold Iridescent Interior, Disk Foot, 12 In.	865.00
Vase, White & Gold, Gold Interior, Signed, 8 In.	900.00

KEWPIES, designed by Rose O'Neill, were first pictured in the *Ladies' Home Journal*. The figures, which are similar to pixies, were a success, and Kewpie dolls and figurines started appearing in 1911. Kewpie pictures and other items soon followed. Collectors search for all items that picture the little winged people.

Advertising Card, Hendler's Ice Cream, Rose O'Neill, 1920s, 4 x 10 In.	15.00
Bisque, Googly Eyes, Smile, Side Curls, Blue Wings, O'Neill, c.1910, 12 In.	1500.00
Bisque, Handwerck, Black Side Glancing Googly Eyes, Forelock Curls, 1910, 9 In.	440.00
Bisque, Seated, Arm Clasping Bisque Basket, Paper Label, 4 In.	525.00
Bisque, Sitting, Playing Mandolin, 4 In. ....*Illus*	475.00
Bisque, Traveler, Umbrella, Suitcase, Rose O'Neill, Incised, 3 1/2 In.	224.00
Bookmark, Pink Silk Ribbon, Through Gold Toned Loop Top, Floral, 1930	159.00
Candy Container, Glass, George Borgfeldt, No. 3 Size	85.00
Candy Container, Standing By Cup, Glass, 3 x 3 1/4 In.	67.00
Celluloid, Soldier, 2 1/2 In.	48.00
Composition, All-In-One Body & Legs, Jointed At Shoulders, Paper Label, 1919, 12 In.	175.00
Composition, Molded Hair, Cameo Doll, Rex Doll & Mutual Doll Co., 1930s, 11 In.	230.00
Dish, Rose O'Neill, 5 1/4 In.	110.00
Googly, Costumed As Bunny, Rose O'Neill, Germany, c.1910, 7 1/2 In.	650.00
Plaster, 12 In.	40.00
Plastic, Painted, Jointed Arms & Legs, Cameo, 1966, 26 In.	230.00
Plate, Rose O'Neill, 1910	125.00
Print, Ice Cream Kewpie, Color, Rose O'Neill, 1920s, 8 1/2 x 11 In., Pair	32.00
Salt & Pepper, Rose O'Neill Label, 2 1/4 In.	550.00
Scootles, Black, Cameo	995.00
Scootles, Tousled Curls, Watermelon Smile, Dimpled Cheeks, Cameo, c.1935, 21 In.	1100.00
Toothpick Holder, Standing Next To Holder	160.00
Uncle Sam, Ribbon Says Maine, Original Hat & Hair, 11 In.	1850.00
Vase, Playing Guitar, With Doodledog, 4 1/4 In. ....*Illus*	2600.00
Vinyl, Fully Jointed, Cameo, Box	95.00
Vinyl, Jesco, Box, 24 In.	250.00
Vinyl, Jointed, Cameo, Canister Box, 9 In.	95.00

KIMBALL, see Cluthra category.

KING'S ROSE, see Soft Paste category.

Kewpie, Bisque, Sitting,
Playing Mandolin, 4 In.

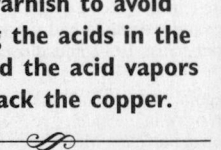

Kewpie, Vase, Playing Guitar,
With Doodledog, 4 1/4 In.

KITCHEN utensils of all types, from eggbeaters to bowls, are collected today. Handmade wooden and metal items, like ladles and apple peelers, were made in the early nineteenth century. Mass-produced pieces, like iron apple peelers and graniteware, were made in the nineteenth century. Other kitchen wares are listed under manufacturers' names or under Advertising, Iron, Tool, or Wooden.

Ashtray, Griswold, No. 00	30.00
Baker's Table, Chapman & Smith Co., Top Slides For Storage, 1880s	4850.00
Baker's Table, Double Possum Belly, Sheet Metal Drawers, Cutting Boards, Pine, 1880s .	575.00
Basket, Picnic, Wooden, Plaid, Metal Handles, Indian Label, 11 x 12 x 18 In.	45.00
Batter Beater, Metal, Marked A & J, Batter Beater Curved To Fit The Bowl, 11 1/2 In. . .	5.00
Bean Pot, Marcrest, Impressed, 6 x 5 1/2 In.	25.00
Beater, Rug, Loop, Wooden Handle	17.00
Beater, Wooden Handle, Metal Wheel, Pat. Oct. 9-1923, Made In USA, 10 1/2 In.	10.00
Blender, Osterizer Deluxe, White Enamel Base, Glass Top, 1950s, 16 In.	81.00
Bowl, Burl Ash, 16 1/4 x 5 3/4 In.	1265.00
Bowl, Cover, Crisscross, 5 1/4 In.	150.00
Bowl, Patty, Griswold, No. 72, Deep . . . . .40.00 to 60.00
Bowl, Scotch, Griswold, No. 2, Erie	75.00
Box, Knife, Square Nail Construction, Hanging, Red Paint, 18 1/2 x 10 In.	575.00
Box, Pantry, Lentils Inscribed On Lid, Late 18th Century, 10 In.	850.00
Box, Salt, Oak, Hanging, Hinged Lid, Shaped Crest, Pine Bottom, 16 x 7 1/4 In.	440.00
Box, Salt, Wall, Mahogany, Hinged Slant Front, Shaped Crest, 8 x 6 1/2 x 10 In.	440.00
Box, Salt, Wall, Walnut, Hinged Lid, 8 1/4 x 6 x 7 7/8 In.	275.00
Box, Storage, Bread & Cake, Words On Box, Bold Top	140.00
Bread Maker, Table Clamp, Universal, Gold Medal Winner, St. Louis Exposition, 1904 . .	235.00
Bread Maker, Universal No. 4, Awarded Gold Medal-St. Louis Expo., 1904	95.00
Broiler, Fish, Wire Wrapped Iron Rod, C.E. Paris, 19th Century, 28 In.	575.00
Broiler, Whirling, Heart Cutout Handle, 33 x 17 In.	340.00
Bucket, Mop, Metal, Wooden Rollers, Red Trim	25.00
Butcher Block, Wooden, Iron Ring, Iron Blade, Horn Handle, 19th Century, 24 In.	490.00
Butter, Crisscross, Blue, 1/4 Lb.	150.00
Butter, Wooden, Revolving Table, Churns Water Out	250.00
Butter Kneader, Wooden, Scrubbed, Wormholes, 1750, 12 1/8 x 3 3/8 In.	185.00
Butter Mold, look under Mold, Butter in this category.	
Butter Paddle, Burl, Horse Head Handle, 9 1/4 In.	825.00
Butter Stamp, Acorns & Leaves, Threaded Handle, 4 7/16 In.	95.00
Butter Stamp, Boxwood, Maltese Cross, 3 1/2 In.	210.00
Butter Stamp, Chicken & House, Hinged Sides, 4 1/2 x 10 In.	190.00
Butter Stamp, Chicken, Grass On Either Side, Carved Wood, Round	120.00
Butter Stamp, Cow & Tree, 1 Piece, Turned Handle, 4 1/2 In.	165.00
Butter Stamp, Eagle, Screw-In Handle, 3 1/4 In.	110.00
Butter Stamp, Geometric, Hex Sign, 4 1/2 In.	330.00
Butter Stamp, Man On Horseback, Date 1684, Basket Of Flowers, 5 x 5 1/2 In.	742.00
Butter Stamp, Pineapple, Carved Wood, Pat'd. April 17, 1866, Round	60.00
Butter Stamp, Pineapple, Fern Leaf Design	60.00
Butter Stamp, Sheaf Of Wheat	44.00
Butter Stamp, Star Flower, Inserted Handle, 4 7/8 In.	357.00
Butter Stamp, Strawberry, Pat'd. April 17, 1866	85.00
Butter Stamp, Stylized Tulip, 1 Piece, Turned Handle, 3 1/4 In.	357.00
Butter Stamp, Stylized Tulip, Round, 4 In.	220.00
Butter Stamp, Swan, Round, 3 1/2 In.	120.00
Butter Stamp, Tulip & Heart, 7 1/2 In.	680.00
Butter Stamp, Tulip & Round Wreath, Pennsylvania German	165.00
Butter Worker, Hooks To Bowl Edge	30.00
Cabbage Cutter, Ash, Heart Cutout, 1855, 22 x 8 1/2 In.	247.00
Cabbage Cutter, Hand Crank, Zoar, Ohio	150.00
Cabbage Cutter, Walnut & Hardwood, Heart Shaped Cutout In Handle, 22 In.	440.00
Cabinet, Bread Storage, Walnut, Paneled Door, 4 Spindles, 28 x 35 1/2 x 18 In.	3910.00
Cabinet, Maple, Blind Door, 2 Tilt-Out Base Drawers, McDougall, 1899	985.00
Cake Board, 2 Sides, Deer, Bear, 19 x 13 1/2 In.	99.00
Cake Board, Soldier With Sword, On Horseback, Walnut, Square, c.1820, 11 In.	1850.00
Cake Board, Steam Locomotive, Oval Border, c.1830, 8 1/4 x 14 1/2 In.	3740.00

Cake Saver, Tin, Green, Round, 7 x 12 In. 35.00
Can Opener, Dazey, Heavy Duty, Ace 80.00
Canister, Coffee, Round, Delphite, 40 Oz. 450.00
Canister, Sugar, Round, Delphite, 40 Oz. 475.00
Canister, Tea, Round, Delphite, 20 Oz. 275.00
Canister Set, Aluminum, Pink, Black Lids & Design 20.00
Cheese Cutter, Self-Gauging 700.00
Cheese Keeper, Maple & Glass, 6 Sides, 26 x 13 In. 430.00
Cheese Press, Hardwoods, Hand Forged, Wooden Cheese Hoop, Mid 1800s, 31 In. 160.00
Cherry Pitter, Cast Iron, Side Crank, 1890s 90.00
Cherry Pitter, Enterprise, No. 16, Iron 60.00
Chocolate Shaver & Bean Frencher, Worn Red Paint, 1900, 2 Piece 135.00
Chopper, Herb, Cast Iron, Boat Shape, Wooden Handle, 6-In. Disk, 18 In. 275.00
Churn, Dasher, Cover, Strap Handles, Tin, 33 1/2 x 9 1/8 In. 55.00
Churn, Dazey, 1 Qt. 2200.00
Churn, Dazey, No. 4 . . . . 125.00
Churn, Gifford's Improved, Cast Iron, Yellow Paint, Sawhorse Stand 500.00
Churn, Orchid Design, Whites', Utica, N.Y., c.1865, 4 Gal. 1210.00
Churn, Parrot & Plume, F.B. Norton & Co., Worcester, Mass., c.1875, 4 Gal. 3080.00
Churn, Red Clay, Green Amber Glaze, Applied Handles, Galena Pottery, 4 1/2 In. 1430.00
Churn, Stave Constructed, Red Paint, Black Bands, Penna., 27 1/2 In. 330.00
Churn, Sunflower Design, J. Burger, Rochester, N.Y., 19th Century, 3 Gal. 550.00
Churn, Universal, Landers, Frary & Clark, Table, 14 x 6 1/2 In. 185.00
Churn, Wooden, Drum Shape, Interior Paddles, Metal & Wood Handle, 17 In. 78.00
Cleaver, Crudely Forged, Stamped Designs On Both Sides, 18th Century, 6 1/8 In. 130.00
Cleaver, Iron, Bird Shape Handle, France, 19th Century 56.00
Cocktail Shaker, Bell Shape, Nickel Plated Striker, Wooden Handle, 1940 . . . . 75.00
Coffee Grinders are listed in their own category.
Coffee Machine, Sintrax, Gerhard Marcks, c.1930, 12 1/4 In. 805.00
Coffee Service, Catalin, Handle, Electrical 125.00
Coffeepot, Autumn Leaves, Porcelier, 6 Cup 55.00
Coffeepot, Drip, Porcelier, Children In Garden 65.00
Coffeepot, Drip, Silver Seal, Griswold, Complete 35.00
Coffeepot, Dutch Windmill, Porcelier, 6 Cup 55.00
Coffeepot, Enamel, Hinged Cover, Yellow, Blue, 10 In. 28.00
Coffeepot, Enamel, White, Black, Bail Handle, 12 1/2 In. 28.00
Colander, Redware, Red Glaze Interior, Green Glaze Exterior, 2 Twisted Handles 40.00
Cookie Board, 12 Segments, Fruit & Birds, Pewter, 7 1/2 In. 165.00
Cookie Board, 12 Segments, Occupations, Pewter, 8 In. 192.00
Cookie Board, Full-Length Man, Gun On Side, Woman, Basket Of Flowers, 26 1/2 In. . . . 1017.00
Cookie Board, Indian In Circle, Rifle, Tomahawk, Pineapple In Circle Reverse, 8 In. 825.00
Cookie Board, Indian With Gun, Pineapple On Reverse, Pine, 5 x 8 In. 825.00
Cookie Board, Man On 1 Side, Woman On Other, Wooden, 17 x 5 3/4 In. 173.00
Cookie Cutter, Abraham Lincoln, Beard, 3/4 View, Tin, 4 1/4 x 5 In. 105.00
Cookie Cutter, Angel, Raised Hand, 3 Fingers, 4 Holes In Back, Tin, 3 7/16 x 6 In. 130.00
Cookie Cutter, Eagle, Crimped Tail, Applied Arched Handle, Tin, 3 7/8 x 4 In. 85.00
Cookie Cutter, Elephant, Standing, Arched Handle, Tin, 4 x 2 1/4 In. 100.00
Cookie Cutter, Horse, Standing, Folk Art Type, 8 x 9 1/2 In. 525.00
Cookie Cutter, Horse, Tin, 8 x 8 1/2 In. 40.00
Cookie Cutter, Indian, Feather On Head, Tomahawk In Hand, Tin, 5 x 7 1/2 In. 625.00
Cookie Cutter, Man Jumping, Hat, Hands In Pocket, 7 1/2 In. 300.00
Cookie Cutter, Man Riding Pig, 3-Hole Back, Tin, 4 x 5 In. 575.00
Cookie Cutter, Man With Hat, Tin, 9 In. 44.00
Cookie Cutter, Man, Profile, Pewter, Teapot, Smith & Co., 1835, 7 1/2 In. 200.00
Cookie Cutter, Moose, Large Antlers, 2-Hole Back, Tin, 4 5/8 x 5 7/8 In. 270.00
Cookie Cutter, Peacock, Crimped Tail, Pierced Back, 4-Hole Back, Tin, 8 x 7 In. 1550.00
Cookie Cutter, Sheaf Of Wheat, Glass, McKee, 1875-1885 . . . . 275.00
Cookie Cutter, Woman, Folded Arms & Apron, 8 1/2 In. 285.00
Cookie Sheet, Griswold, No. 18 . . . . 105.00
Corer, Apple, Bone, Presentation, To Dear Aunt Jane, 1821 . . . . 210.00
Corn Popper, Galvanized Tin, Wooden Handle, Rectangular 35.00
Corn Stick, Griswold, No. 2073, Hammered 375.00
Cup, Handi Measure, McKee, Custard 50.00

Cup, Pine, Carved, Handless, 3 In. 45.00
Damper, Stove, Iron, Griswold, 6 In. 10.00
Damper, Stove, Iron, Griswold, No. 5-9 .... 45.00
Dipper, Maple, Carved, 19th Century, 1 1/2-In. Handle, 2 3/4 In. 2100.00
Dish, Au Gratin, Griswold, No. 76, Yellow & Gray Porcelain Over Iron, Pair 30.00
Dish, Baby's Feeding, Gingham Dog, Calico Cat, 3 Sections, Metal Base, Excell 68.00
Double Broiler, Griswold, No. 875/876 .... 275.00
Dough Board, Breadboard Ends, Scalloped Crest, Square Nails, c.1800, 23 In. 225.00
Dough Box, Pine, Poplar, Canted Sides, Splayed Base, Turned Legs, Pa., 29 In. 660.00
Dough Box, Pine, Red, Chip Carved, Amish, 12 x 27 x 11 In. 270.00
Dough Box, Pine, Splayed Square Tapered Legs, 28 x 35 x 16 In. 330.00
Dough Box, Poplar, Dovetailed Case, 1-Board Top, 28 1/2 x 40 In. 469.00
Dough Box, Poplar, Pine Graining, 50 1/2 x 19 3/4 x 29 1/2 In. 825.00
Doughnut Cutter, Rumford 12.00
Doughnut Maker, Ace Cloverleaf, Iron 120.00
Dutch Oven, Griswold, No. 6, Black Porcelain Lining 245.00
Dutch Oven, Griswold, No. 6, Tite-Top 260.00
Dutch Oven, Griswold, No. 8, Glass Cover 35.00
Dutch Oven, Griswold, No. 8, Iron Mountain 40.00
Dutch Oven, Griswold, No. 8, Tite-Top, Chrome, No Cover 40.00
Dutch Oven, Griswold, No. 9, Tite-Top, With Trivet 145.00
Dutch Oven, Griswold, No. 10, Chuck Wagon ....150.00 to 200.00
Dutch Oven, Griswold, No. 10, Cover 130.00
Dutch Oven, Griswold, No. 11, Tite-Top, Raised Letters 315.00
Dutch Oven, Griswold, No. 12, Tite-Top 550.00
Egg Cutter, Figural, Rooster, Gilt, G. Peres, Germany 35.00
Egg Timer, Bellhop, Figural 75.00
Egg Timer, Black Chef, Figural 115.00
Egg Timer, Colonial Woman, Figural 90.00
Egg Timer, Prayer Lady ....95.00 to 98.00
Eggbeater, Keystone, Heavy Glass, 5 1/4 In. 18.00
Eggbeater, Taplin 12.00
Fish Set, Stainless Steel, Celluloid Handles, Presentation Box, England 140.00
Flatware Set, Red Bakelite, 8 Piece 20.00
Flue Cover, 2 Women In Garden, Painting Vase & Watching 105.00
Flue Cover, Country Scene 35.00
Fluter, Cast Iron & Brass, Moreenwood & Co., 9 1/2 In. 110.00
Fluter, Fixed Handle, Erie 750.00
Food Chopper, Griswold, No. 1113 .... 135.00
Food Mill, Metal, Plastic Knob, Foley Food Mill, Foley, Mpls., 5 1/4 In. 5.00
Fork, Forged, Double Heart Handle, 2 Tines, Iron, 14 1/2 In. 105.00
Fork, Rattail End, Twisted Shaft, Swirls, 3 Tines, Iron, 18th Century, 20 1/2 x 3 3/4 In. 231.00
Fork, Wrought Iron, Sawtooth Design, Pa., 1803 .... 247.00
Fryer, Chicken, Cover, Iron Mountain, No. 8 .... 35.00
Fryer, Chicken, Cover, Wagner, No. 1400, Square 110.00
Fryer, Chicken, Wagner, Iron, Square, 2 Piece 85.00
Frying Pan, Griswold, 11 In. 25.00
Frying Pan, Wagner, No. 3 .... 25.00
Grater, Copper, Ash, 17 1/2 x 38 1/2 In. 265.00
Grater, Iron & Red Oak, Wrought Nails, 18th Century, 19 In. 245.00
Grater, Metal, Mouli, 7 1/2 In. 5.00
Grater, Nutmeg, Formed As Hinged Nut, Revealing A Grater, Silver, 2 In. 172.00
Griddle, Griswold, 3 Independent Flop Pans, 1883 .... 350.00
Griddle, Griswold, 7 Round Molds, Drip Spout, Iron 28.00
Griddle, Griswold, No. 0, Handle 900.00
Griddle, Griswold, No. 10, Bail Handle, Block Erie, Pa., U.S.A. 85.00
Griddle, Wagner Ware, Sidney, O., No. 9 .... 30.00
Grill, Forged Iron, Shaped Handle, Rectangular, 28 1/2 In. 85.00
Grill, Tote, Griswold, Box 45.00
Grinder, Meat, Wooden, With Bench Mount 125.00
Grinder, Nut, Green Metal, Lorraine Metal Co., Cast Iron 50.00
Grinder, Nut, Table Clamp, Iron Frame, Wooden Handle, Lorraine Metal Co., Iron 45.00
Grinder, Spice, Maple, 18th Century, 5 1/4 In. 285.00

Hair Dryer, Star-Rite, Chrome, 1930s 55.00
Holder, Skewer, Iron, Blacksmith-Made, American, 18th Century 250.00
Hot Pot, Cover, Wagner, No. 1368 .... 85.00
Ice Bucket, Lid, West Bend, Penguins, Chrome, Bakelite Handles, Insulated, 7 In. 20.00
Ice Crusher, Dazey, Rocket Shape, White Metal Top, Red Plastic Base, Bracket 45.00
Ice Shave, Griswold, No. 1 .... 95.00
Ice Tongs, Cast Iron 14.00
Ice Tongs, Iron 12.00
Ice-O-Mat, Bucketeer, Rival Stainless 35.00
Icebox, Chestnut, Gallery, Brass Spigot, Victorian, 58 x 36 x 20 In. 3135.00
Icebox, Oak, Cold Storage, Eau Clair, Wis., 2 Raised Panels Doors, Tall 995.00
Icebox, Top Loader, Pressed Wood, c.1905 .... 895.00
Infuser, Tea, Electroplated Brass, Christian Dell, c.1940, 5 1/8 In. 2990.00
Iron, Charcoal, Brass 230.00
Iron, Fluter, Cast Iron, Brass 195.00
Iron, Pressing, Blacksmith Made, Twist Handle, Ending In Curl, 18th Century, 6 In. 195.00
Iron, Slug, Wrought Iron, 1720 .... 7990.00
Iron, Wafer, Baccellieri Bros. Mfg. Co., Phila., Pa., Diamond, 23 In. 40.00
Iron, Wafer, Word Fa-Str, Swags Below, 1840, 33 In. 50.00
Iron, With Iron Rest, Brass, Pierced, Ball Feet, England, 1780s 385.00
Jagging Wheel, Ivory, Scrolling Serpent, Fluted Wheel, 6 1/2 In. 1380.00
Juicer, Lemon, TZA, Iron, Large 90.00
Kettle, Apple Butter, Copper, Dovetailed, Large 220.00
Kettle, Apple Butter, Wrought Iron Handle, Pennsylvania, 18th Century 357.00
Kettle, Brass, Birds On Fruiting Branch, 11 1/4 x 8 1/4 x 8 In. 165.00
Kettle, Cast Iron, Brass Spout, Kendrick, 16 In. 66.00
Kettle, Cover, Raised On 3 Claw Feet, Ceramic Handle, Copper & Brass, 14 In. 63.00
Kettle, Wagner, Open 12.00
Kettle Shelf, Wrought Iron, Turned Wooden Handled, Pierced Brass Shelf, 7 x 13 In. 330.00
Knife, Stonex, Amber Light 350.00
Knife & Fork Set, Keen Kutter, Oak Box, Service For 6 .... 25.00
Knife Rack, Hanging, Pine, Red Painted Surface, Carved Crest, c.1770, 18 1/2 In. 350.00
Knife Sharpener, Delta Porter Cable, PC Hardware & Machinery Co. 24.00
Knife Sharpener, Pheasant's Inc., Mitchell, S.D., Celluloid, 2 3/16 In. 18.00
Lazy Susan, Bird's Eye Maple, Dish Top, 15 3/4 x 3 1/2 In. 165.00
Martini Shaker, Enameled Glass, Carriage Scene, Late 1950s 45.00
Match Holders can be found in their own category.
Match Safes can be found in their own category.
Match Strike, Man With Sharpening Block, Die Cut, Tin, An Plow Co., 7 x 2 3/4 In. 615.00
Measure, Pine, Stave, Brass, Peck & Half, 19th Century, 12 3/4 x 11 In. 60.00
Measuring Cup, 2-Spout, Seville, Yellow 275.00
Measuring Cup, 3-Spout, Opalescent 110.00
Measuring Cup, Delphite, 1 Cup 110.00
Measuring Cup, Glass, Guernsey 17.00
Meat Grinder, Countertop, Tin Plated Steel, Keen Kutter, 8 x 6 In. 20.00
Meat Grinder, White Metal Hand Crank, Tin Finish, Enterprise Mfg. Co., Philadelphia ... 22.00
Meat Tenderizer, Stenciled Wildflowers, Pottery, Salt Glaze, Blue, White, 3 3/4 In. 250.00
Mixer, Dormeyer, Silver Chef, Model 4300, Chrome, Tabletop, 12 x 11 In. 25.00
Mixer, Electric, Vidrio, Cobalt Blue 125.00
Mixer, Hamilton Beach, Blue Porcelain 165.00
Mixer, Hamilton Beach, Single Head, Stainless Steel, Cream Enamel, 1941 .... 60.00
Mixer, Malt, Eskimo 40.00
Mixer, Malt, Gilcrist 115.00
Mixer, Milkshake, Hamilton Beach, Green Porcelain, Chrome, 2 Speeds, Canister 165.00
Mixer, Milkshake, Hand Crank, Floor Model, 48 In. 2012.00
Mixing Bowl, Pyrex, 4 Colors, Original Box, 1950s, 4 Piece 50.00
Mixing Bowl Set, Tulip, Set Of 3 .... 95.00
Molds may also be found in the Pewter and Tinware categories.
Mold, Butter, Acorn & Fern Design, Geometric Floral, Zipper Border, 4 In., Pair 115.00
Mold, Butter, Acorn & Leaves, 1 Lb. 66.00
Mold, Butter, Block Type, Made From Prune Advertising Box 30.00
Mold, Butter, Floral, Almond Shape, Hardwood, 9 3/4 In., 2 Piece 245.00
Mold, Butter, Leaf At Left, Ridge Form Border, Handle, 4 1/8 x 3 1/8 In. 115.00

Mold, Butter, Maple, Flower & Leaf Design, 1/2 Lb. Size 56.00
Mold, Butter, Pineapple & Leaves, Floral Spray, Geometric Border, 4 3/4 In., Pair 115.00
Mold, Butter, Pomegranate, Leaves, Pat. Apr. 17, 1866, 4 3/4 In. 135.00
Mold, Butter, Sheath Of Wheat & Ferns, Wood Grain, 4 3/4 In., Pair 170.00
Mold, Cake, Rabbit, Griswold, Iron, Box 260.00
Mold, Cake, Santa Claus, Griswold, Aluminum 950.00
Mold, Candle, see Tinware category.
Mold, Cheese, Pine, Dovetailed, Rosehead Nails, 1762 .... 395.00
Mold, Chocolate, Rabbit, Half, Tin, 17 3/4 In. 100.00
Mold, Chocolate, Rabbit, Leaping, Large 295.00
Mold, Chocolate, Rabbit, Tin, 18 In. 145.00
Mold, Cookie, Sleigh Full Of Toys, Cast Iron, 7 x 15 1/4 In. 145.00
Mold, Corn Stick, Cast Iron, 10 1/2 x 5 1/4 In. 35.00
Mold, Fish, Redware 650.00
Mold, Food, Bear, John J. Burke 175.00
Mold, Food, Fluted Interior, Redware, Brown Sponging On Orange Ground, 4 1/4 In. 110.00
Mold, Food, Spiral, Rockingham, 9 3/4 x 3 1/4 In. 65.00
Mold, Griswold, No. 252, Crispy Corn, Cast Iron, 8 1/2 x 4 In. 65.00
Mold, Heart & Star, Griswold, No. 100 .... 900.00
Mold, Ice Cream, see Pewter category.
Mold, Patty, Biscola, Straight Handle 25.00
Mold, Patty, Bowl With Timbales, Griswold, No. 72, Boston Store, Box 25.00
Mold, Patty, Griswold, No. 3, Box 120.00
Mold, Pudding, Swirl, Copper, Temple & Crook, 5 1/2 In. 85.00
Mold, Redware, Flower Form, Black Glaze, 10 1/2 In. 65.00
Mold, Santa, Griswold, Iron, Mark On Bag, With Recipe 650.00
Mold, Shortbread, Strolling Gentleman, Wriggle Work Jacket, Carved Oak, 37 In. 200.00
Mold, Turk's Head, Griswold, No. 14 .... 1150.00
Mold, Turk's Head, Redware, Amber Glaze, Brown Exterior Splotches, 9 In. 55.00
Mold, Turk's Head, Redware, Dark Brown, 2 1/4 x 7 1/2 In. 65.00
Mold, Vegetable, Ivory, Calif. USA 236 Oven Proof, 8 1/2 In. 22.00
Mold, Wedding Cake, Heart Shape, 19th Century, 17 In. 695.00
Mold Cheese, Carved Form Of Dog & Rider, 15 1/4 In. 145.00
Mortar & Pestle, Blue Green Paint, Wooden, 7 In. 302.00
Muffineer, Pottery, Roses & Bird, 5 1/2 In. 145.00
Napkin Holder, Doll, Wooden, Sweden, 10 In. 22.00
Napkin Holder, Paramount, Pink 550.00
Napkin Holder, Prayer Lady, Pink 25.00
Noodle Cutter, Cast Iron, Crank, Wooden Board, Geschutzt, Germany, 1900 .... 350.00
Oven, Chuck Wagon, Cover, Griswold, No. 10 .... 200.00
Paddle, Laundry, Figural Form, Carved Stars & Initial S, 19th Century, 28 In. 85.00
Pan, Apple Cake, Griswold, No. 32 .... 40.00
Pan, Au Gratin, Griswold, No. 81, Oblong, Red & Cream 35.00
Pan, Bundt, Frank Hay, Griswold 375.00
Pan, Cake, Apple, Griswold, No. 32 .... 40.00
Pan, Cake, Sheet Iron, Heart Form, 19th Century, 17 1/4 In. 195.00
Pan, Chicken, Cover, Griswold, Block Erie, Pa., Deep 50.00
Pan, Chicken, Cover, Square, Wagnerware, No. 1400 .... 135.00
Pan, Copper, Cast Iron Handle, J.L. Chand, Washington, D.C., 7 1/2 x 12 3/4 In. 302.00
Pan, Corn Bread, Griswold, No. 24 .... 300.00
Pan, Corn Stick, Griswold, No. 273, Erie ....35.00 to 95.00
Pan, Corn Stick, Griswold, No. 931 .... 150.00
Pan, Little Slam Bridge, Wagner Ware, Cast Iron 140.00
Pan, Loaf, Griswold, No. 877, Nickel Plated 210.00
Pan, Loaf, Redware, Coggled Rim, Combware Design, 15 1/2 In. 550.00
Pan, Loaf, Redware, Multicolored Slip Design, Notched Rim, Oblong, 1830, 10 In. 6900.00
Pan, Loaf, Redware, Yellow Slip, Coggled Rim, 14 1/4 In. 770.00
Pan, Muffin Gem, Griswold, No. 5, Variation No. 1 .... 50.00
Pan, Muffin Gem, Griswold, No. 8 .... 35.00
Pan, Muffin Gem, Turk's Head, Wagner Ware, 11 Cup 80.00
Pan, Muffin Gem, Waterman, No. 4 .... 50.00
Pan, Muffin, H Type, Wagner Ware, Iron 350.00
Pan, Muffin, N. Waterman, Boston, Patented April 5, 1839 .... 40.00

Pan, Muffin, Turk's Head, Griswold, 12 Cup 120.00
Pan, Omelet, Wagner Ware, Sidney, O., No. 820 .... 28.00
Pan, Popover, Griswold, No. 10 .... 100.00
Pan, Popover, Griswold, No. 18, 6 Cup ....45.00 to 65.00
Pan, Popover, Wagner Ware, No. 1323 .... 30.00
Pan, Sauce, Cover, Swain, Iron Handle, Cloverleaf, No. 7, 8 Pt. 25.00
Pan, Vienna Roll, Griswold, No. 2, Var. 2 .... 950.00
Pan, Vienna Roll, Griswold, No. 6, Raised Letters Inside Cups 175.00
Pan, Wheat & Corn Stick, Griswold, Best Maid 65.00
Pastry Wheel, White Smithed Steel, 18th Century, 8 1/2 In. 225.00
Peel, Forged Iron, Ram's Horn Handle, 43 In. 70.00
Peel, Iron, Ram's Horn Handle, 23 1/2 In. 120.00
Peel, Wrought Iron, Inlaid Brass, Handle, Engraved Initials & 1827, 21 5/8 In. 110.00
Peeler, Apple, Bonanza 70.00
Peeler, Apple, Reading, Cast Iron 120.00
Peeler, Apple, Square Nails, New England, Early 19th Century 95.00
Percolator, Blown Glass, WTCo., Sun-Colored Amethyst, 14 In. 58.00
Pie Bird, Bathing Beauty, Nude, Bisque, Germany, 3 In. 225.00
Pie Bird, Benny Baker ....75.00 to 135.00
Pie Bird, Black Girl, Outstretched Arms, Blue Apron 155.00
Pie Bird, Blackbird, Yellow Beak 27.00
Pie Plate, Mrs. Wagner's Pies Impressed On Bottom, 9 1/2 In. 10.00
Pitcher, Plastic Top, Liberty Bell 1776 In Raised Relief, Anchor Hocking, 7 1/2 In. 10.00
Pitcher, Syrup, Green, Metal Top, Hazel Atlas, 6 In. 65.00
Pitcher, Water, Griswold, Aluminum Bail Handle 330.00
Platter, Sizzling Steak, Wagner Ware, Aluminum 10.00
Platter, Tree, Griswold, No. 61, Metal Alloy 70.00
Posset, Bell Metal, Footed, 1650, Pair 595.00
Pot, Griswold, No. 84, Gray Porcelain Over Iron, Handle 40.00
Potato Masher, Stainless Steel, Red & Cream Handle, A & J, 10 1/2 In. 10.00
Potato Slicer, Mechanical, Clamp-On, Cast Iron, Eagle Engineering Co., 1918 .... 75.00
Potholder, Crocheted, 2 Cherries, Folds To Form Mitt, 8 1/2 In. ....*Illus* 8.00
Potholder, Crocheted, Hat, Flowers, Satin Ribbon, 5 3/4 In. ....*Illus* 5.00
Press, Lard, Wooden Screw, Wooden Wedges, Large 80.00
Press, Meat Juice, Columbia, Iron, Landers, Frary & Clark 25.00
Press, Queen City, Shepard's, Orange Red, Pat. June 26, 1888, 2 Qt. 55.00
Pressure Cooker, Marmite Lilor No. 2, Paris, Brick Red, 6 Qt. 160.00
Rack, Drying, Walnut, Penna., 1840, 32 x 24 In. 825.00
Reamers are listed in their own category.
Refrigerator Dish, Crisscross, Blue, 3 1/2 x 5 3/4 In. 175.00
Refrigerator Dish, Crisscross, Blue, 4 x 4 In. 65.00
Roaster, Bird, Adjustable Hood, Sheet Iron, Late 18th Century 395.00
Roaster, Cover, Mi-Pet, No. 4, Oval 80.00
Roaster, Griswold, No. 5, With Trivet, Oval 495.00
Roaster, Guardian Ware, 12 In. 35.00
Roaster, Montgomery Ward & Co., Oval 110.00
Roaster, Wagner, No. 3, Cover, Drip-Drop, Oval 95.00
Rolling Pin, Blown Glass, Julia Of Wells, Milk Glass, Painted Ship, 1870, 14 In. 88.00

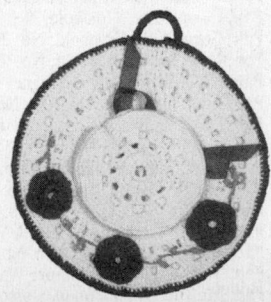

Kitchen, Potholder,
Crocheted, Hat,
Flowers, Satin
Ribbon, 5 3/4 In.

Kitchen, Potholder, Crocheted, 2 Cherries,
Folds To Form Mitt, 8 1/2 In.

Rolling Pin, Blown Glass, Present For A Friend Forget Me Not, Blue, Red, 1880, 14 In. ... 99.00
Rolling Pin, Blown Glass, Present For Brother, Sapphire Blue, Painted Flowers, 15 In. 99.00
Rolling Pin, Blown Glass, Robin's-Egg Blue, Opalescent, 1870, 15 In. 66.00
Rolling Pin, Flowers, Wooden Handles, China, 16 In. 215.00
Rolling Pin, Glass, Blue Green, Seed Bubbles, Saratoga, 1885, 17 1/2 In. 355.00
Rolling Pin, Opalescent Glass, Open On Pontil End, 13 1/2 In. 50.00
Rolling Pin, Pastry, Butter Mold, 1850s, 15 In. 425.00
Rolling Pin, Stenciled Wildflowers, Pottery, Salt Glaze, Blue, White, 15 In. 360.00
Rolling Pin, Tiger Maple, Ends Cut Into Tulips, Early 19th Century, 36 In. 995.00
Rolling Pin, Wildflower, A. & H. Bounds Dry Goods & Groceries, Blue & White 895.00
Sadiron, Handle, Griswold, 4 Lb. 125.00
Sadiron Heater, Griswold, No. 1313, Round Classic Style 90.00
Salt & Pepper Shakers are listed in their own category.
Sausage Stuffer, Hand Crank, 28 x 11 In. 145.00
Scoop, Cranberry, 19th Century 55.00
Scoop, Cranberry, Cape Cod, 19th Century ....110.00 to 340.00
Scoop, Cranberry, Wooden, Makepeace & Co., 17 In. 230.00
Scoop, Ice Cream, Dover Springless, Size 20 .... 90.00
Scoop, Ice Cream, Dover, No. 20, Sickle Shaped Lever, Pat'd Feb. 1924, 11 In. 230.00
Scoop, Ice Cream, Erie, Conical Bowl, Size 24 .... 95.00
Scoop, Ice Cream, Gilchrist, No. 31 .... 80.00
Scoop, Ice Cream, Gilchrist, No. 34, Banana Split 675.00
Scoop, Ice Cream, H.S. Geer, Size 16 .... 400.00
Scoop, Ice Cream, Hamilton Beach, No. 50 .... 30.00
Scoop, Ice Cream, Indestructo, Size 24 .... 90.00
Scoop, Ice Cream, Kingery 125.00
Scoop, Ice Cream, Metal, Turn Key To Release Ice Cream, Cone Shape, 8 In. 45.00
Scoop, Ice Cream, Mosteller, No. 77, Flat Plate 350.00
Scoop, Ice Cream, No-Pak 31, Pat. No. 1861655, Metal, Wooden Handle, 9 3/4 In. 75.00
Scoop, Ice Cream, Tin, Key Operated 23.00
Shaker, Nutmeg, Painted Flowers & Fruit, Raised Relief, Japan, 3 1/4 In. 20.00
Shaker, Paprika, Round, Delphite 185.00
Shaker, Paprika, Tulips, Marked, 4 In. 10.00
Sharpener, Knife, Dazey 40.00
Shredder, Coconut, Rodent Form, Teeth Project From Mouth, Glass Eyes, Hand Held ... 495.00
Sieve, Canted Sides, Narrow Slats, Wooden, Pine, 23 x 24 1/2 In. 110.00
Sieve, Cheese, Heart Shape, 3 Ring Feet, Tin, 5 3/4 x 6 1/2 In. 203.00
Sieve, Wood & Leather, 18th Century, 23 In. 302.00
Sifter, Flour, Sifting Blades Inside, Hunter's, Wood & Cast Iron, 30 In. 330.00
Sifter, Metal, Screen, Sifting Mechanism In Handle, Impressed 2 Cups, 3 x 3 1/2 In. 10.00
Skillet, Favorite Piqua Ware, No. 3 .... 20.00
Skillet, Favorite, No. 8 .... 25.00
Skillet, Griswold, No. 3, Cliff Cornell 325.00
Skillet, Griswold, No. 4, Smooth, Lid 625.00
Skillet, Griswold, No. 5 .... 300.00
Skillet, Griswold, No. 6, Erie, Smoke Ring 50.00
Skillet, Griswold, No. 7, Erie, Heat Ring 60.00
Skillet, Griswold, No. 8, 3-Hole, Shallow, Slant Erie 135.00
Skillet, Griswold, No. 8, Mt. Man, Cover 75.00
Skillet, Griswold, No. 9, Heat Ring 70.00
Skillet, Griswold, No. 10, Chrome 55.00
Skillet, Griswold, No. 11, Large Block 120.00
Skillet, Griswold, No. 12, Heat Ring 75.00
Skillet, Griswold, No. 13, Slant, Heat Ring 1050.00
Skillet, Griswold, No. 15, Fish, Oval 275.00
Skillet, Griswold, No. 666, Breakfast, Colonial 40.00
Skillet, Griswold, No. 1008, All-In-One 375.00
Skillet, Griswold, Utility, Square, 9 x 9 In. 45.00
Skillet, Iron, Forged Handle, Straps, 28 1/2 In. 60.00
Skillet, Spider, Erie No. 8, Seldon & Griswold, Web Mark, Pre-1890 .... 1800.00
Skillet, Superior Cleveland, No. 10 .... 50.00
Skillet, Wagner Ware, Double, Sidney, O., No. 1401 .... 135.00
Skillet, Wagner Ware, No. 2, Iron ....80.00 to 125.00

Skillet, Wagner Ware, No. 4B, Smoke Ring	26.00
Skillet, Wagner Ware, Sidney, O., Magnalite, With Trivet	27.00
Skillet Cover, Wagner Ware, No. 7, Black	44.00
Skillet Set, Griswold, No. 2 To 13, Erie	3200.00
Skillet Set, Victor, No. 5 To 9, 5 Piece	1175.00
Skimmer, Wrought Iron, Brass, 4 Inlaid Hearts On Handle, Penna., 1820, 24 1/2 In.	385.00
Slicer, Part Label, Cabbage Cutter, Spencer, Bartlett, 15 1/2 x 6 In.	50.00
Snack Tray, Walnut, Cheese Tile & Knife, Marked, Georges Briard	30.00
Spice Box, Lidded Compartments, Brass, 18th Century	325.00
Spice Box, Pine, Sliding Lid, 6 Part Interior, 4 7/8 x 9 5/8 In.	165.00
Spice Box, Punched Design, Ring Feet & Handle, Tin, Center Grater, 8 In.	110.00
Spice Cabinet, Inlaid Oak, Queen Anne, Miniature	3162.00
Spice Chest, 11 Drawers, Spice Names On Drawers, Porcelain Knobs, Hanging	240.00
Spice Chest, 3 Rows Of 4 Drawers, Turned Wooden Knobs, Cutout Base, 13 x 24 In.	400.00
Spice Chest, 8 Drawers, Central Door, Walnut & Maple, 20 x 19 In.	990.00
Spice Jar, Treenware, Red Paint, 18th Century, 4 3/4 In.	310.00
Spice Safe, Named Queen Safe, Canisters, Painted Tin	2400.00
Spice Set, Wooden, 7 Stenciled Boxes, In 8-In. Round Holder	175.00
Spoon, Wooden, Carved, Whale's Tail Handle, 1800, 6 1/8 In.	85.00
Spoon Rest, 3 Bananas, Painted, Glazed, Japan Stamped, 6 1/2 x 3 1/2 In.	10.00
Spoon Rest, Celery Shape, 10 In.	10.00
Sprinkler Bottle, Elephant	85.00
Sprinkler Bottle, Mammy	65.00
Stand, Muffin, Oak, Rope Turned Frame, 1900, 35 1/2 x 11 In.	151.00
Stepstool, 2 Steps, Griswold On Riser	70.00
Stepstool, Chrome, Griswold	45.00
Stove & Counter Mat, Metal, Cardboard Back, Ballonoff, Cleveland, Ohio, 14 x 17 In.	5.00
Strainer, Handle, Redware, 16 x 8 1/2 In.	90.00
Strainer, Tea, Metal, Green Handle, 7 In.	20.00
String Holder, Bird	55.00
String Holder, Boy Fishes Through Whale's Mouth, F & F	40.00
String Holder, Campbell Kid	95.00
String Holder, Cat, F & F	50.00
String Holder, Chef's Head, 8 In.	50.00
String Holder, Dome, Cast Iron, 5 x 6 In.	30.00
String Holder, Hanging, One Cone, 7 Hooks, 9 1/2 In.	330.00
String Holder, I Hate Housework	100.00
String Holder, Puppy's Head, Ceramic, 5 1/4 In.	75.00
Swizzle Stick, Pink Flamingo, Wooden, Large	12.00
Syrup, Aunt Jemima, F & F Mold	65.00
Tankard, Wooden, Carved From 1 Piece, Oval, 4 x 2 1/4 In.	70.00
Teakettle, Cast Iron, Wrought Iron Handles, J. & J. Siddons, 10 In.	110.00
Teakettle, Copper, Brass On Brass Stand, 21 2/3 In.	137.00
Teakettle, Raised Boss Design, Cast Iron, 18th Century, 7 1/2 In.	132.00
Teapot, Cast Iron, Favorite Ware, White Porcelain Knob	590.00
Teapot, Copper, Bird, Floral Design, Bamboo Form, Meiji Period	319.00
Teapot, Handle, Iron, Penna., Late 18th Century, 5 In.	250.00
Teapot, Iron, Nubby Texture, Floral Finial, Japan, 8 x 7 In.	250.00
Teapot, Yellow Lattice, Porcelier, 4 Cup	55.00
Tester, Cheese, Forged, 6 In.	25.00
Toaster, 4-Slice, Art Deco, 4 Flipper Panels, Round, Germany, 8 x 10 In.	94.00
Toaster, Hotpoint, 2-Slice, Wooden Knobs, Edison, 7 1/2 x 8 x 5 1/2 In.	22.00
Toaster, Marion Grand, Flip-Flop, Rutenber Electric Co., Marion, Ind.	50.00
Toaster, Rowenta, 2-Slice, Tin Plated, Flip-Down Panels, Germany, 8 x 4 x 7 In.	42.00
Toaster, Sunbeam, Model T-20, 2-Slice, Lighter-Darker Control Knob	42.00
Toaster, Sunbeam, Model T-9, Art Deco, Chrome Plated, 1940s-1950s, 9 x 8 x 4 In.	31.00
Toaster, Super Lectric, Art Deco	45.00
Toaster, Thermax, Landers, Frary & Clark	65.00
Toaster, Toastmaster, Model A-1, 1-Slice, Electric, Chrome, 10 x 5 x 7 1/2 In.	42.00
Trammel, Wrought Iron, Sawtooth, 40 In.	165.00
Trammel, Wrought, Iron, Early 19th Century, 36 x 33 In.	460.00
Tray, Cutlery, Cherry, Rectangular	920.00
Tray, Cutlery, Mahogany, 2 Sections, 13 1/2 x 9 1/2 In.	88.00

Tray, Dough, Yellow Pine, Wooden, Wythe County, Va., 9 x 43 x 21 1/2 In. 310.00
Trencher, Maple, Yellow Paint Traces, Wedge Shape Repair, 12 5/8 x 4 7/8 In. 190.00
Trivet, Iron, Black Paint, 12 x 12 x 10 1/2 In. 33.00
Wafer Iron, Harp In Center Surrounded By Horns, Floral, 28 1/2 In. 95.00
Wafer Iron, Hearts & Face Design, Iron, 1741 . . . . 350.00
Wafer Iron, Wagner, No. 1450 . . . . 95.00
Wafer Iron, Wrought Iron, Hex Sign & Star Design Plates, 1875, 29 In. 55.00
Waffle Iron, 2 Long Handles, Rectangular Press, France, 1821 . . . . 372.00
Waffle Iron, Griswold, Black Iron, Square 500.00
Waffle Iron, Griswold, Heart & Star, 1920 . . . . 88.00
Waffle Iron, Griswold, No. 0 . . . . 2950.00
Waffle Iron, Griswold, No. 2, Base 750.00
Waffle Iron, Griswold, No. 11, Stand, Marked American 44.00
Waffle Iron, Rey-O-Noc, No. 8, Wire Handles 42.00
Waffle Iron, Wagner, Cast Iron, 1910, Salesman Sample 395.00
Waffle Iron, Wagner, Twin, 1910 . . . . 375.00
Waffle Iron, Wrought & Cast Iron, Forged Handles, 19th Century, 23 In. 60.00
Wall Pocket, Apple On Branch, Pottery, 7 In. 55.00
Washboard, 16 Horizontal Rows On Scrub Side, Wooden Frame, 12 x 8 x 1 1/2 In. 115.00
Washboard, Family Size, Carolina Washboard Co., Glass 58.00
Washing Machine, Coffield Copper Tub 300.00
Washing Machine, Copper, Nickel Plated, 1911 . . . . 600.00
Washing Machine, Maytag, Wringer, 1940s 40.00
Washing Machine, Wooden, Hand Crank, Hand Pump, Paddles, Stenciled Name 250.00

KNIFE collectors usually specialize in a single type. In the 1960s, the United States government passed a law that required knife manufacturers to mark their knives with the country of origin. This seemed to encourage the collectors, and knife collecting became an interest of a large group of people. All types of knives are collected, from top quality twentieth-century examples to old bone- or pearl-handled knives in excellent condition.

Astronaut, M-1, NASA, 25th Anniversary 1958-1983, Case, Plastic Handle, 16 1/2 In. . . . 77.00
Bayonet, Brass Handle, Engraved, Scabbard, 1870, 27 1/2 In. 55.00
Blade, Flint Ridge, Dovetail, Ashland Co., Ohio, 2 7/8 In. 242.00
Bouka, Folding, Iron, Scabbard, Sweden, 3-In. Blade 225.00
Bowie, Buck, Black Molded Grip, Aluminum Pommel Cap, Black Sheath, 5 1/2-In. Blade 20.00
Bowie, Confederate, Brass Handle, Brass Pin, Double Hand Guard, 8 1/2-In. Blade 488.00
Bowie, CSA On Handle, Walnut Stand, 14 1/2 In. 55.00
Bowie, Handmade, Wooden Grip, Brass Guard, Indian Wars Era, 10 3/8-In. Blade 235.00
Bowie, Sheffield, 1835, 16 In. 1950.00
Bowie, Stag Grip, Kingman & Hassam, Boston, 14 In. 4760.00
Bowie, Stag Grip, Stag Crown As Guard, Early 19th Century 750.00
Brass Lining, Nickel Silver Bolster & Cap, Etched Blade, Pyralin Handle, Striped, 5 In. . . 30.00
Buck Skinner, Black Plastic Handle, Aluminum Ends, Cross Guard, Box, 8 In. 20.00
Clasp, Hand Forged Iron Handle, Crude Rivets, 18th Century, 5 3/8-In. Blade 110.00
Cooper's, Chamfer 60.00
Dagger, Antler Handle, Medial Ridge On Double Edge Blade, 12 1/4 In. 250.00
Dagger, Arm, Boa Skin & Leather, c.1880 . . . . 1200.00
Dagger, Brass Ricasso & Ferrule, Bone Handle, Leather Sheath, Asia, 6 3/4-In. Blade 31.00
Dirk, Brass, Wooden Hilt, Basket Weave Design, Scottish Highland, 17 1/2 In. 3100.00
Dirk, Navel, Brass Mounted, Eagle Head Pommel, Bone Grip, Early 19th Century 950.00
Fishing, Hans Anderson, Denmark, Steel Blade, Wooden Handle, Leather Scabbard, 9 In. . 20.00
Flax Scutching, Wooden 10.00
Flint, Ridge, Fairfield Co., Ohio, 3 7/8 In. 253.00
Folding, Fruit, Ivory Tone Celluloid Handle, John Morrell & Co., 4 1/4-In. Blade 35.00
Hunting, Blade Marked Marbles, Leather Belt Case, Staghorn Mounts 800.00
Hunting, Remington, 175th Anniversary, Leather Handle, 4 1/2-In. Blade, Box 110.00
Machete, Brass Eagle Head Haft, Bone Handle, Mexico, c.1920, 30 In. 110.00
Naval, Confederate, 13 1/2 In. 968.00
Nickel Silver Bolster & Cap, Glazed & Etched Blade, Brass Lining, 5 In. 25.00
Pen, Mother-Of-Pearl, Q.T.E.V., Queen Of Bermuda, Enameled, 3 Stacker 75.00
Poacher's, Staghorn Handle, 19th Century, 9 In. 168.00

Pocket, Brown Shoe, Germany, 1 7/8 In. 30.00
Pocket, Cork Screw, Bottle Shape, Fur Jedentisch, F.W. Jordan, Wald Soungen, 2 1/2 In. . 65.00
Pocket, Keen Kutter, Black Bone Grips, 1 1/4-In. Blade, 2 1/4 In. 25.00
Pocket, Keen Kutter, White Celluloid Handle, 2-In. Blade, 3 1/2 In. 20.00
Pocket, Kensington Knife Co., Hound Shape, Papier-Mache, c.1920, 3 1/4 In. 29.00
Pocket, Key Work Clothes, 2 Blades, Red, White, Blue, Imperial, 3 In. 25.00
Pocket, Lighthouse, In/Out Button, Souvenir, Germany, Rotesand Leuchtiurm, 3 1/4 In. .. 20.00
Pocket, Marilyn Monroe, Color Nude Photo Of Marilyn Monroe On Handle, 1 Blade 150.00
Pocket, Quincey Brewing Co., Compliments Dick & Bros., 3 1/4 In. 120.00
Pocket, Zippo, Rinker Oil Corp., Tiger Head, Brushed Finish, Blade, Nail File, 2 x 1 In. . 30.00
Pressed Horn Hilt, German Silver Figure, Hunter & Hounds, Chasing Stag, 9 3/4 In. 300.00
Pushbutton, Folding Cross Guards, Griffen, Starburst Bone Handles, Blade 5-In., Italy .. 75.00
Pushbutton, Italian Style, White Plastic Grips, 4-In. Blade 70.00
Pushbutton, Stiletto Style, White Handle, 4-In. Blade 85.00
Skinning, Steel Blade, Stag Handle, Wostenholm & Son Co., 10 In. 22.00
Spear Pointed, Hickory Handle, 10 In. 175.00
Stonex, Dark Amber, Box 375.00
Stonex, Opalescent, Milk Glass 400.00
Trench, Springfield Armory, Scabbard Hanger, Wateruliet Arsenal, World War I, 13 In. ... 440.00
Trench, World War I, 1917-1918 .... 250.00

KNOWLES, TAYLOR & KNOWLES items may be found in the KTK and Lotus Ware categories.

KOREAN WARE, see Sumida.

KOSTA, the oldest Swedish glass factory, was founded in 1742. During the 1920s through the 1950s, many pieces of original design were made at the factory. The firm is still working.

KOSTA

Bowl, Internal Blue To Red Swags, Footed, Warff, 5 In. 120.00
Bowl, Mottled Exterior, Signed, Foil Label, 6 1/2 x 9 1/2 In. 110.00
Bowl, Rainbow, 6 x 8 In. 60.00
Figurine, Fish, Controlled Bubbles, Vicke Lindstrand, No. 91623, 2 x 8 In. 88.00
Porringer, Rooster's Head Form, Etched Eyes, Signed, 10 1/2 In. 115.00
Vase, Dark Blue, Asymmetrical Opening, Nils Landberg, 7 In. 210.00
Vase, Fishnet, Purple Blue Stripes, Black Base, Warff, 8 In. 350.00
Vase, Garnet To Clear, Asymmetrical Opening, Elliptical, Vicke Lindstrand, 8 In. 143.00
Vase, Green Patches Cut Through Oval Windows, Vicke Lindstrand, 8 1/2 In. 770.00
Vase, Green, Blue & Amber, Clear Cased, Nils Landberg, 6 In. 187.00
Vase, Internal Threads, Clear Cased, Vicke Lindstrand, 8 In. 770.00
Vase, Spiral, Aubergine Lines, Vicke Lindstrand, 1955, 5 1/2 In. 460.00

KPM refers to Berlin porcelain, but the same initials were used alone and in combination with other symbols by several German porcelain makers. They include the Konigliche Porzellan Manufaktur of Berlin, initials used in mark, 1823–1847; Meissen, 1723–1724 only; Krister Porzellan Manufaktur in Waldenburg, after 1831; Kranichfelder Porzellan Manufaktur in Kranichfeld, after 1903; and the Kister Porzellan Manufaktur in Scheibe, after 1838.

Basket, Fruit, Enameled Floral, Pierced Rim, Pink Ground, Late 19th Century, 8 In. 287.00
Basket, Reticulated, 2 Handles, Flower & Leaf Design, Monochrome, 11 3/4 In. 315.00
Charger, Temple Of Athena & Temple Of Jupiter, 12 1/2 In., Pair 747.00
Charger, Trio Of 2 Cherubs & Putti Amid Clouds, Signed, 15 3/4 In., Pair 3024.00
Coffeepot, Pear Shape, Doves, Leafy Branches, Scroll Handle, Gilt, 11 1/2 In. 230.00
Dish, Floral Sprays, 2 Leaf-Form Sections, Entwined Handle, Porcelain, 13 3/4 In. 172.00
Dish, Lobster, Gilded, Floral, 2 Sections, Marked 90.00
Figurine, Elephant, 13 1/2 In. 690.00
Inkwell, Removable Covered Ink Pot, Sander, 8 1/2 In. 250.00
Jardiniere, Wilderness Scene, Moon Overhead On 1 Side, Tiger In Wilderness, 9 In. 5175.00
Lithophane, see also Lithophane category.
Plaque, Boy Smoking, Enamel, Giltwood Frame, O. Liebmann 747.00
Plaque, Empress Louise, Descending Staircase, Signed, 13 x 7 3/4 In. 2800.00
Plaque, Eve, Porcelain, Gilded Rococo Frame, Signed L. Sibinzel 4675.00
Plaque, Girl With Floral Bouquet, Gilt Frame 1595.00

Plaque, Herd Boy, Oval, Painted, 9 x 6 1/2 In. 1150.00
Plaque, Leda & Swan, Frame, Signed, 9 1/4 x 6 1/2 In. 2000.00
Plaque, Lithophane, Mother & Child, Leaded Glass Border, Sword Mark, 13 In. 300.00
Plaque, Madonna, Child & Angel Scene, Gilt Frame, Oval, 10 3/4 In. 900.00
Plaque, Maiden With Daisies In Hair, Wagner, Oval, Gesso Frame, 8 1/2 x 6 1/2 In. 4480.00
Plaque, Maiden With Goat In Forest, Signed O.M., Frame, 9 1/4 x 6 1/4 In. 1150.00
Plaque, Man & Woman Dancing, Signed, 7 x 8 In. 238.00
Plaque, Mary Being Carried Heavenward On Shoulders Of Angels & Cherubs, 10 In. 1980.00
Plaque, Mary Magdalene Gazing Upward, Scepter Mark, Frame, 8 x 6 1/2 In. 1355.00
Plaque, Monks At Midday Meal, Framed, Edward Grutzner, 18 1/4 x 16 In. 5500.00
Plaque, Portrait, Clementine, Late 19th Century, 9 1/2 x 7 In. 9200.00
Plaque, Portrait, Seated Woman, Holding Oil Lamp, Incised, Gilt Frame, 11 x 8 1/2 In. .. 3300.00
Plaque, Portrait, Young Woman, Wm. C.W.M. Walthen, 11 x 9 1/2 In. 5175.00
Plaque, Ruth, After Charles Zacharie Landelle, Wide Gilt Frame, Rectangular, 7 x 5 In. .. 2910.00
Plaque, Three Fates, Frame, Signed, 9 1/4 x 6 1/2 In. 1800.00
Plaque, Victorian Woman, Oval, Late 19th Century, 13 In. 546.00
Plaque, Woman In Oriental Costume, Before Well, Signed, Late 19th Century, 13 In. 7475.00
Plaque, Woman Nude, Semi-Profile, Oval, Gilt Designed Frame, 14 x 11 In. 12000.00
Plate, Multicolored Floral Center Medallion, Pierced Latticework Rim, 8 1/2 In., Pair ... 55.00
Platter, Floral & Butterfly, Molded Basket Weave Border, 12 In. 172.00
Platter, Floral Still Life, Borders With Swags, 19th Century, 22 1/2 In. 1035.00
Vase, Hand Painted Pansies & Apple Blossoms, Foliage Around Neck, Signed, 6 In. 425.00

KTK are the initials of the Knowles, Taylor & Knowles Company of East Liverpool, Ohio, founded by Isaac W. Knowles in 1853. The company made many types of utilitarian wares, hotel china, and dinnerwares. They made the fine bone china known as Lotus Ware from 1891 to 1896. The company merged with American Ceramic Corporation in 1928. It closed in 1934. Lotus Ware is listed in its own category in this book.

K.T.&K.
CHINA

Creamer 20.00
Gravy Boat 30.00
Pitcher, Milk, Gold Design, 1872, 5 1/4 In. 50.00
Plate, 6 1/4 In. 10.00
Punch Set, Roses, 14- x 9-In. Bowl, 9 Piece 165.00
Soup, Dish, Ivory 20.00

KU KLUX KLAN items are now collected because of their historic importance. Literature, robes, and memorabilia are available. The Klan was outlawed in 1869 and reemerged in 1915. It is still in existence, so new material is found.

Belt Buckle, Hood & Cross, Realm Of Georgia, 1916 .... 400.00
Belt Buckle, Image Of Klansman In Robe Holding Bible, Dark Gray, Pewter 20.00
Belt Buckle, Image Of Klansman With U.S. Flag, Bible, Enamel, 3 In. 20.00
Belt Buckle, KKK In Relief, Dark Bronze, Oval, 1926, 3 1/4 x 2 1/4 In. 245.00
Belt Buckle, Realm Of Georgia, Hood & Cross, 1916 .... 400.00
Book, The Clansman, Thomas Dixon Jr., 1905, 374 Pages 40.00
Bumper Plate, Auto, Enameled Brass, Logo, Wing Nut, 75 mm 190.00
Hood, Pointed Hat, Stiffener, Neck Cape, Brown Tassel, Pre-World War II 255.00
Photograph, Pennsylvania Klan Reunion, Gettysburg, 1925, 10 x 42 In. 340.00
Pin, Klansman On Horse, Litho, Herring & Corpe, Chicago, Round, 13/16 In. 91.00
Record, Kajun Ku Klux Klan, Looking For A Handout, Reb Rebel, 1960s 29.00
Tie Tack, AKIA, Brass, Gold Letters, Red Enamel Ground, Triangular, 1923, 3/8 In. 41.00

KUTANI ware is a Japanese porcelain made after the mid-seventeenth century. Most of the pieces found today are nineteenth-century. Collectors often use the term *kutani* to refer to just the later, colorful pieces decorated with red, gold, and black pictures of warriors, animals, and birds.

九
谷

Bowl, Stylized Design, White Slip Floral, 7 3/4 In. 460.00
Censor, Cover, Figural & Bird Cartouches, Figure Of Man, Pierced Lower Band, 15 In. ... 630.00
Charger, Figures In Mountainous Landscape, Meiji Period, Verso Inscription, 18 In. 160.00
Figurine, Geisha On Elephant Back, 7 1/2 In. 258.00

Figurine, Hotei, Holding Fan, Lucky Bag, Small Child, Early 20th Century, 12 1/2 In. 345.00
Figurine, Owl, Perched On Tree Stump, Hawthorn Tree, Gilded Eyes & Beak, 11 In. 345.00
Jar, Domed Lid, Samurai Finial, Side Panels, Samurai, Women, Birds, 13 In., Pair 1320.00
Plate, 7 Gods Of Good Fortune, Early 20th Century, 8 1/2 In. 49.00
Plate, White Slip Floral Design, 4 3/4 In. 172.00
Tea Set, Art Deco, 15 Piece 120.00
Tray, Landscape Design, Gilt, Floral, Handles, 10 x 14 1/4 In. 230.00
Vase, 2 Oval Reserves, Enamel Brocade, Calligraphy Interior, Signed, 2 1/8 In. 505.00
Vase, Double Gourd Form, Floral Design, Rust Red, Meiji Period, 9 1/2 In. 110.00

L.G. WRIGHT Glass Company of New Martinsville, West Virginia, started selling glassware in 1937. Founder "Si" Wright contracted with Ohio and West Virginia glass factories to reproduce popular pressed glass patterns, like Rose & Snow, Baltimore Pear, and Three Face, and opalescent patterns, like Daisy & Fern and Swirl. Collectors can tell the difference between the original glasswares and L.G. Wright reproductions because of colors and differences in production techniques. Some L.G. Wright items are marked with an underlined W in a circle. Items that were made from old Northwood molds have an altered Northwood mark—an angled line was added to the N to make it look like a W. Collectors refer to this mark as "the wobbly W."

Bride's Basket, Mauve, 10 In. 180.00
Candy Container, Union Pacific Railroad, 2 x 5 In. 10.00
Canoe, Candy Dish, Blue, 10 1/4 In. 10.00
Cherry, Pitcher, 8 Tumblers, Marked, 8 In. 50.00
Daisy & Button, Shoe, Cat's Head, Blue 20.00
Daisy & Fern, Lamp, Gone With The Wind, Cranberry Opalescent ....175.00 to 375.00
Daisy & Fern, Lamp, Vaseline Opalescent, 20 1/2 In. ....135.00 to 250.00
Daisy & Fern, Rose Bowl, 4 1/4 x 5 3/4 In. 125.00
Dot, Lamp, Gone With The Wind, Cranberry Opalescent, Miniature 235.00
Dot, Sugar Shaker, Blue Opalescent 95.00
Green Slag, Creamer, Ivory Interior 35.00
Green Slag, Sugar 38.00
Magnolia, Vase, Milk Glass, Outlined Petals, 13 In. 127.00
Moon & Star, Compote, Cover, 11 1/2 In. 95.00
Moon & Star, Epergne, Amber, 2 Piece 85.00
Moon & Star, Relish, Canoe 165.00
Pump & Trough, Sugar & Creamer, 4 In. 20.00

LACQUER is a type of varnish. Collectors are most interested in the Chinese and Japanese lacquer wares made from the Japanese varnish tree. Lacquer wares are made from wood with many coats of lacquer. Sometimes the piece is carved or decorated with ivory or metal inlay.

Basket, Red, Ching Dynasty, Handle, 11 x 11 x 18 In. 75.00
Bowl Set, Japan, 7 Piece 95.00
Box, Cover, Troika Flying In The Sky, Multicolored Black Ground, Gilt Borders, 6 In. ... 126.00
Box, Painted Courtyard Scene, Red, Fir, Ching Dynasty, 13 x 13 x 10 In. 173.00
Box, Tea, Bird Decoration, Chinese, 19th Century, 8 x 11 x 8 In. 88.00
Cabinet, Sewing, Oriental Figures, Flowers, Regency, 1800-1825, 10 x 11 1/2 In. 1430.00
Canister, Hinged, Eagle, Dancing Bear Plaque, Russia, 10 In. 85.00
Card Case, Figural Landscape Design, Nashiji Interior, Black, Gold, 4 1/4 In. 55.00
Cigarette Case, Eggshell, Black, White Spots, Red, Jean Dunand, 1925, 4 1/2 In. 3795.00
Game Set, Gold, Floral Sprays, Mother-Of-Pearl Loo Counters, Cards, c.1820, 10 In. 880.00
Inro, Oni Hiding Under Fan, Shoki's Hat & Sword On Reverse, 4 Case 357.00
Jewelry Casket, Chinoiserie, Mirror, Tray, Chinese, 19th Century, 5 1/2 x 8 1/4 In. 770.00
Lap Desk & Letter Box, Mother-Of-Pearl, Hand Painted Floral Interior, 8 x 10 In. 355.00
Pen Box, Chinoiserie, Cartouche, Floral Ground, Chinese, 19th Century, 11 1/2 In. 1070.00
Puzzle Box, Traveling, Ivory, Scroll Shape, Chinese, 1840, 16 3/4 x 10 1/4 In. 1870.00
Smoking Set, Cigarette Box, Matchbox Holder, Black, Brass, Coral Flower, 2 Piece 250.00
Stand, Flower & Fern Design, Nashiji Ground, Black, Gold, 9 In. 275.00
Tray, Daruma In Red Robes, Gold Trim, Signed, Shibata Zeshin, 14 1/2 x 6 In. 1540.00
Tray, Floral, Seashell Stencil Design, Rectangular, 19th Century, 22 x 30 In. 715.00
Tray, Pagoda & Sailing Ship, Oblong, Early 19th Century, 28 x 21 In. 550.00

Tray, Peasant Couple Scene, Man, Holding Scythe, Wearing Birch Shoes, 1890, 6 In. 145.00
Tray-On-Stand, Black, Gilt Leaves, Flowers, Faux Bamboo Stand, Victorian, 22 1/2 In. .. 3960.00
Urn, Diaper, Domed Lid, Black Lacquer, Twin Scroll Handles, 30 x 18 1/2 In., Pair 575.00
Vase, Eggshell, Burnt Orange, White, Jean Dunand, 1925, 7 1/2 In. 11500.00
Water Basket, Swan Shape, Red, Chinese, 19th Century, 24 In., Pair 290.00

LADY HEAD VASE, see Head Vase.

LALIQUE glass was made by Rene Lalique in Paris, France, between
the 1890s and his death in 1945. The glass was molded, pressed, and
engraved in Art Nouveau and Art Deco styles. Pieces were marked   *LALIQUE*
with the signature *R. Lalique.* Lalique glass is still being made. Pieces
made after 1945 bear the mark *Lalique.* Jewelry made by Rene Lalique
is listed in the Jewelry category.

Ashtray, Dindon, Molded Turkey, Smoky Brown, Circular, 1925, 3 In. 690.00
Bookends, Libellule, Dragonfly, With Upright Wings, Signed, France, 8 In., Pair 4945.00
Bowl, Cyprins, Intaglio Fish, Spiraling Out From Center Of Bubbles, 1931, 10 In. 402.00
Bowl, Honfleur, Nasturtium Leaf Border, Signed, 10 1/2 In. 165.00
Bowl, Marguerites Daisies, 13 In. 747.00
Bowl, Montigny, Serrated-Edge Leaves, Pyramidal Feet, 1928, 12 In. 575.00
Bowl, Nonnettes, Birds In Flight, Opalescent On Clear, 8 5/8 In. 290.00
Bowl, Perruches, Parakeets, Marked, 9 1/2 In. 600.00
Bowl, Plumes De Paon, Overlapping Peacock Feathers, Opalescent, 1932, 12 In. 1265.00
Bowl, Saint-Denis, Stylized Berries, Thorny Vines, Black Accents, Circular, 7 In. 1495.00
Bowl, Vernon, Overlapping Sunflowers, Frosted, Signed, 1941, 10 1/2 In. 575.00
Bowl, Volubilis, Convolvulus Flowers, Opalescent, 8 1/2 In. 575.00
Box, Cover, Dresser, Epines, Thorny Brambles, Sepia Patina, 3 In. 345.00
Box, Cover, Pomade Coquilles, 8 Radial Shell Panels, Signed, 1930s, 2 13/16 In. 345.00
Box, Cover, Quatre Papillons, 4 Butterflies, Flowers, Round, 3 1/8 In. 575.00
Box, Cover, Roger, Scrolling Grapevines & Pheasants, Round, 1926, 5 1/4 In. 805.00
Box, Cover, Six Dahlias, Leaves, Round, 1922, 8 In. 1265.00
Box, Cover, Tokio, Large Chrysanthemum On Cover, Opalescent, Round, 7 In. 745.00
Ceiling Light, Dahlias, Dahlia Blossoms, Leaves, Glass Cap, Signed, 12 In. 2587.00
Chandelier, Boule De Gui, Mistletoe, Ball Shape, Gray Glass, 1922, 19 3/4 In. 13800.00
Chandelier, Perles, Pearls, 3 Tiers, Gray Glass, Chromed Metal, 1931, 32 In. 13800.00
Clock, Deux Figurines, 2 Figurines In Frosted Glass Surrounding Clock, 1926, 13 In. 6900.00
Clock, Mantel, Moineaux, Sparrows, Flower Relief, Gray Patina, Signed, 1924, 6 1/8 In. . 1495.00
Dish, Volubilis, 3 Convolvulus Blossoms, Blue Patina, Raised On 3 Feet, 1921, 4 In. 3450.00
Figurine, Aigle, Eagle, Standing, Signed, Label, 9 1/2 In. 286.00
Figurine, Chat Couche, Crouching Cat, 8 3/4 In. ....690.00 to 952.00
Figurine, Cygne Tete Baissee, Swan, Head Tucked, Signed, 2 1/2 In. 103.00
Figurine, Danseuse, Frosted, 1942, 9 1/4 In. 545.00
Figurine, Danseuse, Nude, Clear Frosted, Paper Label, c.1960, 9 1/4 In. 375.00
Figurine, Gregoire, Toad, Frosted, Polished, Mid 20th Century, 3 1/8 In. 230.00
Figurine, Leda, Nude With Swan, Molded Acid Finish, Marked, 4 1/2 In. 202.00
Figurine, Tete De Cheval, Horse's Head, 1950s, 16 1/2 In. 5850.00
Figurine, Thais, Nude Woman, Holding Drapery, Opalescent, 8 1/4 In. 5175.00
Figurine, Vierge Mains Jointes, Madonna, Praying, Pleated Robe, Signed, 9 1/2 In. 172.00
Hood Ornament, Comete, Comet, c.1928 .... 5175.00
Hood Ornament, Epsom, Glass Car, Horse's Head With Mouth Open, Ears Back, 5 In. .. 4025.00
Hood Ornament, Libellule, Stylized Dragonfly, 1928, 8 1/4 In. 3450.00
Hood Ornament, Longchamp, Horse Head Shape, Frosted, 1929, 5 In. ....2530.00 to 3530.00
Hood Ornament, Tete De Paon, Peacock Head, Black Glass, 1928, 8 In. 6325.00
Jardiniere, St. Hubert, Gazelle Leaping, Gray Patina, Handle, Signed, 18 5/8 In. 2185.00
Match Holder, Smyrne, Frosted Swirl Pattern, 2 3/4 In. 176.00
Medallion, Louis Pasteur, 1822-1922, Profile, Presentation Box, 4 In. 588.00
Paperweight, Antilope, Antelope, 3 3/4 In. 316.00
Paperweight, Cheval, Horse, 3 5/8 In. 316.00
Paperweight, Chrysis, Female Nude On Her Knees, Leaning Back, 1931, 5 In. 1610.00
Paperweight, Chrysis, Nude, Kneeling, Stretching Backwards, Frosted, 1932, 5 1/4 In. 4025.00
Paperweight, Levrier, Greyhound, Running, Intaglio Form, 1928, 7 3/4 In. 1725.00
Paperweight, Moineau Fier, Sparrow, Signed, 3 1/4 In. 287.00
Paperweight, Moineau Sournois, Sparrow, Clear Frosted, Signed, 5 x 2 1/2 In. 145.00
Paperweight, Tang, Horse, Pinned Ears, Short Tail, Signed, 4 In. 86.00

Paperweight, Tete De Coq, Rooster Head, Signed, 20th Century, 7 In.	290.00
Perfume Bottle, Ambre D'Orsay, D'Orsay, Draped Women, Purple, 1911, 5 1/8 In.	1725.00
Perfume Bottle, Au Coeur Des Calices, Coty, Blue, Molded, Stopper, 1913, 2 1/2 In.	2875.00
Perfume Bottle, Habanita Molinard, Opposing Nude Females, Floral Top, 4 1/2 In.	1265.00
Perfume Bottle, Muguet, Lily-Of-The-Valley Stopper	187.00
Perfume Bottle, Panier De Roses, Pale Green, Frosted, 3 7/8 In.	948.00
Perfume Bottle, Replique, Raphael, Molded Strawberry, Signed, 2 In.	85.00
Pin, Plique-A-Jour, Winged Sphinx, Gold, Enamel, 1905, 1 3/4 In.	25875.00
Plate, Actinia, Sea Anemone, Opalescent, Acid Stamped, 11 In.	290.00
Plate, Algues, Algae, Aquatic Plant Design, Black Satin, Mark Lalique, 8 In., 10 Piece	632.00
Powder Box, Cover, Le Lys, Flowers, D'Orsay, Signed, 4 1/2 In.	275.00
Powder Box, Cover, Trois Figurines, 3 Nudes, Embossed, Acid Finish, D'Orsay, 4 In.	168.00
Smoking Set, Tete De Leon, Lion's Head, Urn, Lighter & Ashtray	495.00
Table, Metal, Cactus, Molded, 1947, 28 1/4 In.	34500.00
Tumbler, Chene, 4 Frosted Oak Leaves, Signed, 4 3/4 In.	103.00
Tumbler, Napsbury, Small Daisies Etched Around Body, Signed, 4 In.	40.00
Vase, Amorique, Overlapping Leaves, Opalescent, 1927, 8 5/8 In.	4887.00
Vase, Aras, Birds & Branches, Wintergreen, Original White Patina, 1924, 9 1/2 In.	11500.00
Vase, Archers, Nude Male Figures, Shooting Bows & Arrows, Gray, 1913, 10 In.	12650.00
Vase, Bacchantes, Continuous Scene Of Nudes, 20th Century, 9 3/4 In.	1495.00
Vase, Bagatelle, Overall 12 Birds Nesting Amid Leaves, Signed, 1950s, 6 3/4 In.	575.00
Vase, Biskra, 8 Long Narrow Leaves, Melon Form, Amber Glass, 11 1/2 In.	5405.00
Vase, Camargue, 4 Cartouches, Horse In Rearing Position, Mauve Patina, 11 1/4 In.	3450.00
Vase, Cerises, Opalescent, Stems Of Cherries, Flared, 1930, 7 7/8 In.	1610.00
Vase, Damiers, Spiraling Rectangles, Enameled, 1936, 9 1/8 In.	7475.00
Vase, Domremy, Thistle Relief, Signed, 1926, 8 1/2 In.	1495.00
Vase, Druides, Frosted Berries, c.1932, 7 x 7 In.	605.00
Vase, Espalion, Frosted, Ferns, 7 In.	605.00
Vase, Ferrieres, 5 Rows Of Flowers, Leafy Stems, Molded & Frosted, 1929, 6 3/8 In.	1090.00
Vase, Fontaines, Flames Pattern, Blue Frosted, Egg Shape, 1912, 5 3/4 In.	1090.00
Vase, Formose, Allover Molded Goldfish, Gray, R. Lalique, 7 In.	1380.00 to 3450.00
Vase, Gui, Dense Small Leaves, Berries, Tapered, 1920, 6 3/4 In.	4600.00
Vase, Guirlandes, Overlapping Crimped Bands, Dished Lip, Tapered, 8 1/4 In.	2300.00
Vase, Malesherbes, Opalescent, Pointed Leaves, Teardrop Form, Everted Rim, 1927, 9 In.	1495.00
Vase, Malesherbes, Pointed Leaves, Teardrop Form, Everted Rim, 1927, 9 1/8 In.	660.00
Vase, Moissac, Overlapping Leaves, Opalescent, Molded, Blue Patina Traces, 5 In.	1380.00
Vase, Orleans, Scrolling Floral Vine Around Flared Rim, 1930, 7 7/8 In.	2875.00
Vase, Perruches, Parakeets, Amber, Dark Red, 1919, 9 7/8 In.	9775.00
Vase, Poivre, Pepper Berries, Deep Charcoal Gray, 1921, 9 1/2 In.	5750.00
Vase, Quatre Groupes De Lezards, 4 Bands Of Lizards, Flared Lip, 1912, 12 3/8 In.	3450.00
Vase, Raisins, Grapes, Scrolling Vines, Molded & Frosted, 1928, 6 1/4 In.	690.00
Vase, Renoncules, Buttercups, Clear Frosted, Blue Patina, Bulbous, 6 In.	635.00
Vase, Ronces, Brambles, Emerald, Green, Thorny Branches, Egg Shape, 1921, 9 1/2 In.	6325.00
Vase, Saint-Francois, Chickadees Perched On Leafy Stems, Molded & Frosted, 7 In.	1090.00
Vase, Tourterelles, Turtle Doves, Pale Brown Patina, 1925, 11 3/8 In.	5175.00

LAMPS of every type, from the early oil-burning Betty and Phoebe lamps to the recent electric lamps with glass or beaded shades, interest collectors. Fuels used in lamps changed through the years; whale oil (1800–1840), camphene (1828), Argand (1830), lard (1833–1863), turpentine and alcohol (1840s), gas (1850–1879), kerosene (1860), and electricity (1879) are the most common. Other lamps are listed by manufacturer or type of material.

Airplane Design, Streamline, Silver, Nickel Plated Wings, Tail, Base, 1935, 8 x 11 In.	373.00
Aladdin, B-13, Beehive, Ruby, Red Shade	585.00
Aladdin, B-25, Victoria, Gold Bands	675.00
Aladdin, B-26, Simplicity, Alacite, Decalmania, Burner	300.00 to 450.00
Aladdin, B-75, Tall Lincoln Drape, Alacite	175.00
Aladdin, B-77, Tall Lincoln Drape, Red Drape, Burner	750.00
Aladdin, B-80, Beehive, Clear, Burner	80.00 to 100.00
Aladdin, B-83, Beehive, Ruby	567.00
Aladdin, B-87, Vertique, Rose Moonstone	600.00
Aladdin, B-88, Vertique, Yellow Moonstone	540.00

Aladdin, B-93, Vertique, White Moonstone 1075.00
Aladdin, B-96, Queen, White Moonstone, Burner 300.00
Aladdin, B-103, Venetian, Rose 230.00
Aladdin, B-106, Colonial, Amber 200.00
Aladdin, B-110, Cathedral, White Moonstone 375.00
Aladdin, B-112, Cathedral, Rose Moonstone 375.00
Aladdin, B-120, Majestic, White 400.00
Aladdin, B-122, Majestic, Green Moonstone 550.00
Aladdin, B-130, Orientale, Ivory 200.00
Aladdin, E-304, Vogue, Red 525.00
Aladdin, G-130, Lady & Cape, Wreath Finial 3700.00
Aladdin, G-163, Double Nudes, Shade, Finial 1850.00
Aladdin, G-186, Alacite, Precision Finial 55.00
Aladdin, G-232A, Alacite, Closed Urn 295.00
Aladdin, G-378C, Hopping Bullet 400.00
Alcohol, Sterling Silver Overlay, 3 1/2 In. 155.00
Argand, Bronze, Acanthus Standard, Gadrooned Edge Plinth, Floral Swag, 24 In., Pair ... 2300.00
Argand, Double Arm, Etched Shades, Messenger & Sons, Early 19th Century, 20 In., Pair 2105.00
Argand, Etched Glass Shades, Louis Veron & Co., Philadelphia, 16 In., Pair 1870.00
Argand, Hand Cut Shades, Prisms, Mans Head With Hat Prism Rings, c.1830, Pair 4500.00
Argand, Single Arm, Bronze, Clear Shade, Folded Rim, 16 In., Pair 920.00
Argand Style, Relief Rococo Scrolling, Garland, Head, France, 15 1/2 In., Pair 825.00
Astral, Bennington Flint Base, Engraved Glass Shade, Prisms, 21 1/4 In. 5060.00
Astral, Cobalt & Milk Glass Standard, Frosted Clear Shade, Dietz, 25 In. 2070.00
Astral, Engraved Font, Brass Fittings, Flint, Bennington Base 4400.00
Astral, Frosted & Cut Glass Shade, Prisms, 28 In. 977.00
Astral, Soldered Shade Frame, Brass Stem, 20 3/4 In. 357.00
Astral, Star Cut To Clear Stem, Prisms, Frosted & Cut Glass Shade, Brass, 20 3/4 In. 430.00
Astral, Turnip Shape Cut Crystal Shade, Grape Cluster, Prisms, 18 In. 140.00
Astral, Wheel Cut Frosted Shade, Brass Standard, Square Marble Base, Prisms, 19 3/4 In. 1035.00
Bacterium Print, Metal Fixtures, Fluorescent Tubes, Sottsass, 1979, 98 In. 4025.00
Betty, Adjustable, Sheet Metal, Copper & Iron, Arrow Feet, 26 In. 715.00
Betty, Clarke-Hess, L & R Boker, Hanger, 1830 .... 265.00
Betty, Copper, Complete, Late 18th Century 325.00
Betty, Cover & Hanger, 18th Century, 5 1/2 In. 250.00
Betty, Peter Derr, Wick Support, Chain, Hook 2400.00
Betty, Silver Paint, Tin, Portsmouth, N.H., 6 In. 165.00
Betty, Tin, Dish Foot, Cylindrical Font, Cover, 7 In. Diam., 10 In. 198.00
Betty, Wrought Iron, Hanging Spike, Double Well, Marked M. Lomb, 6 1/2 In. 230.00
Bouillotte, 2 S-Scroll Arms, 2 Female Terms, Footed, Silver Plate, Late 1800s, 16 In. 633.00
Bouillotte, 2-Light, Empire Style, Gilt Bronze, Pierced Dish Base, Tole Shade, 30 In. 1320.00
Bouillotte, 3-Light, Patina, Gilt Bronze, Green Tole Shade, Empire Style, 39 In., Pair 2860.00
Bouillotte, Brass, Tole Shade, Rectangular Stem, Serpentine Foot, 25 x 14 In. 2760.00
Bradley & Hubbard lamps are included in the Bradley & Hubbard category.
Candelabrum, 3-Light, Crest, Gadroon Borders, Sheffield, 19th Century, 17 In. 2530.00
Candelabrum, 3-Light, Female Terminal, Leopards Eating Grapes, 21 In., Pair 5750.00
Candelabrum, 3-Light, Putti Holding Spray Of Lilies, Gilt Bronze, 19 In. 430.00
Candelabrum, 3-Light, Ram's Head Terminals, Hoofed Feet, 1800s, 26 In., Pair 5462.00
Candelabrum, 4-Light, Draped Bead Chain, 19th Century, 20 1/2 In. 550.00
Candelabrum, 4-Light, Hanging Prisms, 20 1/2 In., Pair 247.00
Candelabrum, 4-Light, Leaf Tip Stem, Central Reeded Stem, 24 1/2 In. 3450.00
Candelabrum, 4-Light, Rose Bouquet, White Marble & Bronze, c.1890, 19 In. 2420.00
Candelabrum, 5-Light, Gilt Bronze & Basalt, Scrolled Arms, Foliate & Mask Base 430.00
Candelabrum, 7-Light, Scrolling Arms, Sienna Marble Base, c.1830, 21 x 9 1/2 In. 2410.00
Candelabrum, Spiraling Bands, Vasiform Nozzle, Curved Branches, 1820s, 16 In., Pair .. 4887.00
Candle, Jeweler's, Amber Glass, Patent Sep. 14th, 1880, 7 In. 155.00
Candle, Jeweler's, Cobalt Blue, Miniature 135.00
Candle, Lace Maker's, Freeblown, Cobalt Blue Base, Knopf Stem, 1810-1830, 7 1/4 In. ... 7700.00
Candle, Lace Maker's, Spherical Font, Hollow Stem, Drip Pan Wafer, 8 1/2 In. 357.00
Chandelier, 3-Light, Bronze, 3 Flying Bats, Brass Foliate Fixtures, 21 1/2 In. 7190.00
Chandelier, 3-Light, Bronze, Figure Of Youth Upholding Torches, 24 x 12 In. 2760.00
Chandelier, 3-Light, Cascade Of Luster Ropes, Prismatic Drops, Cut Glass, 41 In. 425.00
Chandelier, 3-Light, Etched Globes, Brass, Victorian, c.1900, 30 In. 650.00

Chandelier, 3-Light, Napoleon III, Gilt Brass, Green Shade, Scroll Rope, Electrified 1380.00
Chandelier, 3-Light, Porcelier, Flowers, Gold Trim 40.00
Chandelier, 3-Light, Wedgwood, Jasper Dip, Brass, Blue, White Bowl & Font, 19 1/4 In. . 1093.00
Chandelier, 4 Chains Attached To Ceiling Plate, Light Deflector Panels, 54 x 40 In. 6000.00
Chandelier, 4 Leaded Glass Shades, Brass Rods, Prairie School, 28 In. 2310.00
Chandelier, 4-Light, Blue Bearded, Crystal, Blue Teardrop Prisms, Electrified, 28 In. 1870.00
Chandelier, 4-Light, Brass, Laurel Leaf, 4 Leaf Fronds, Early 20th Century, 29 x 24 In. . . 1380.00
Chandelier, 4-Light, Candle, Maple & Chestnut, Tin Sockets & Pans, 30 1/2 In. 1760.00
Chandelier, 4-Light, Clear & Celadon Glass, Beaded Chains, Prisms, Electrified, 28 In. . . 2090.00
Chandelier, 4-Light, Empire Style, Gilt Bronze, Cut Glass, Prisms, Electrified, 42 In. 2200.00
Chandelier, 4-Light, Gondolier, Balloon Overlay, Italy, 19th Century, 18 x 36 In. 1955.00
Chandelier, 5-Light, Bronze & Abalone Shell, Bronze Rods, c.1900, 33 1/2 In. 4887.00
Chandelier, 5-Light, Continental, Scalloped Corona Issuing Flower Heads, 34 x 19 In. . . . 977.00
Chandelier, 5-Light, Cut Crystal, Drop Ball Base, Prisms, 26 x 22 In. 465.00
Chandelier, 5-Light, Floral Design, Brass Fixture, Arts & Crafts, 19 x 41 In. 880.00
Chandelier, 5-Light, Foliate Form Shades, Venetian, c.1930, 22 x 34 In. 690.00
Chandelier, 5-Light, Renaissance Style, Giltwood, Leaves, Corded Sockets, 1900s, 26 In. . 980.00
Chandelier, 6-Light, Art Deco, Painted Iron, Foliate & Scrolls, Glass Bowl, 24 1/2 In. . . . 825.00
Chandelier, 6-Light, Black Patinated Brass, Broad Teardrop Prisms, 29 x 20 1/2 In. 467.00
Chandelier, 6-Light, Bunch Of Grapes & Wheat Ears, Sky Blue Opaque Glass, 25 1/2 In. . . 690.00
Chandelier, 6-Light, Cage Shape, Metal, Clear & Rose Glass, Chains, Prisms, 30 In. 3080.00
Chandelier, 6-Light, Domed Alabaster Shade, Curved Stepped Candle Arms, 32 In. 1035.00
Chandelier, 6-Light, Empire, Overall Berry Vines, 24 x 29 In. 575.00
Chandelier, 6-Light, Figural, Floral Reserves, Light Blue Ground, Knop Standard, 22 In. . 1265.00
Chandelier, 6-Light, Foliate Scrolls, Stylized Beasts, Knight's Heads, Electrified, 22 In. . . 460.00
Chandelier, 6-Light, French Provincial, Iron, Arched Frame, Squirrels, 20 x 35 In. 1650.00
Chandelier, 6-Light, Garland Of Glass, Brass, Venetian, 18th Century, 34 In., Pair 9200.00
Chandelier, 6-Light, Giltwood, Circular Support, Pinecone Finial, Electrified, 15 1/2 In. . . 550.00
Chandelier, 6-Light, Giltwood, Painted, Tassels, Garlands, Italy, c.1900, 52 In. 5775.00
Chandelier, 6-Light, Glass & Gilt Brass, Baluster Form Shaft, Pendants, 23 1/2 In. 660.00
Chandelier, 6-Light, Glass, Gilt Bronze, Molded Flowers, Foliate Corona, 27 In. 1100.00
Chandelier, 6-Light, Greek Key Border, White Mottled Glass Tiles, Gilt Bronze, 20 In. . . 3200.00
Chandelier, 6-Light, Hanging, Bellflower, Swag Design, Brae Burn, 1904, 21 x 37 In. . . . 259.00
Chandelier, 6-Light, Hanging, Heraldic Relief Design, Brae Burn, 1904, 22 x 17 In. 489.00
Chandelier, 6-Light, Hanging, Heraldic Relief Design, Brae Burn, 1904, 37 In. 230.00
Chandelier, 6-Light, Harp & Cherub On Swing Design, Bronze, Crystal Prism, 20 In. 287.00
Chandelier, 6-Light, Louis XVI, Wrought Iron, Shield Shape, Clock Dial, 40 In. 1210.00
Chandelier, 6-Light, Napoleon III, Bronze Dore, Crystal, Crystal Swags, 45 x 33 In. 3450.00
Chandelier, 6-Light, Neoclassical Style, Gilt Bronze, Tole, Anthemion & Lions, 28 In. . . . 770.00
Chandelier, 6-Light, Neoclassical Style, Giltwood, Glass Chains, Italy, 1900, 44 1/2 In. . . 7425.00
Chandelier, 6-Light, Pewter, Bulbous Sphere, Continental, 24 In. 550.00
Chandelier, 6-Light, Pricket, Giltwood, Gilt Metal, Glass, Continental, c.1900, 46 In. 5775.00
Chandelier, 6-Light, Rococo Style, Brass, Glass Chains, Prisms, Electrified, 38 In. 2200.00
Chandelier, 6-Light, Rococo Style, Gilt Tole, Swirling Leaves, Prisms, Glass Ball, 46 In. . 2860.00
Chandelier, 6-Light, Rococo, Scrolled Candle Arms, Knop Standard, 34 In. 1610.00
Chandelier, 6-Light, Venetian Glass, Tendrils & Arms Separate Pieces, 30 x 26 In. 1500.00
Chandelier, 6-Light, Wrought Iron, Hot Air Balloon Suspending Pierced Basket, 37 In. . . . 1840.00
Chandelier, 8-Light, Black Iron Cage, Colorless Glass Baluster, Prisms, 36 In. 2300.00
Chandelier, 8-Light, Brass, Plumed Leaves Corona, Glass Rosettes, 28 x 26 In. 2200.00
Chandelier, 8-Light, Corona Suspending Greek Strapwork, 37 1/2 x 26 In. 1725.00
Chandelier, 8-Light, Louis XV Style, Bronze Cage Frame Shape, 44 In. 3450.00
Chandelier, 8-Light, Louis XVI, Bronze, 2 Arms, Cut Glass Prisms, 40 x 28 In. 4025.00
Chandelier, 8-Light, Neoclassical Style, Glass, Gilt Metal, Prisms, c.1900, 28 x 24 In. . . . 2860.00
Chandelier, 8-Light, Neoclassical, Beaded Corona Hung, Spear Prisms, 1900, 30 In. 3680.00
Chandelier, 8-Light, Porcelain & Gilt Brass, Figural Vignettes, Chains, 23 In. 1035.00
Chandelier, 8-Light, Scrolled Corona, Arms With Cut Glass Spires, 48 x 28 In. 3220.00
Chandelier, 8-Light, Scrolled Leaves, Pink, Yellow, Blue Flowers, 46 In. 3162.00
Chandelier, 9-Light, Gilt Bronze, Glass, Bucks & Steers With Lanterns In Mouths, 25 In. . 965.00
Chandelier, 9-Light, Regency, Female Masks, Foliate Arabesques, 24 x 22 In. 632.00
Chandelier, 11-Light, Glass, Brass, Scrolls, Stars, Prisms, Late 19th Century, 40 In. 4400.00
Chandelier, 12-Light, Baroque, Brass, S-Scroll Candle Arms, 1900, 48 x 38 1/2 In. 3450.00
Chandelier, 12-Light, Brass, Cage Form, Amber Opalescent Glass, Chain, 60 x 34 In. 11212.00
Chandelier, 12-Light, Brass, Dutch Colonial Style, Baluster Standard, Sphere, 28 In. 995.00

Chandelier, 12-Light, Central Baluster Standard, Prisms, Gilt Bronze, 35 x 22 In. 3220.00
Chandelier, 12-Light, Central Faceted Spine Standard, Prisms, 37 1/2 In. 920.00
Chandelier, 12-Light, Drip Pan, Scrolling Arms, Brass Ring, Electrified, 27 1/2 In. 2760.00
Chandelier, 12-Light, Empire Style, Gilt Bronze, Prisms, Acanthus Corona, 27 In. 1100.00
Chandelier, 12-Light, Gilt Metal, Glass, Scrolled Arms, Teardrop Prisms, 51 In. 4675.00
Chandelier, 12-Light, Glass & Rock Crystal, Different Shapes Of Lustres, Chains, 40 In. . 2912.00
Chandelier, 12-Light, Molesworth, Wrought Iron, Indians Pursuing Buffalo, 60 In. 21850.00
Chandelier, 12-Light, Napoleon III, Gilt Bronze, Dancing Faun, Bamboo Rods, 30 In. . . . 1540.00
Chandelier, 12-Light, Rococo Style, Black Patinated & Gilt Brass, c.1920, 22 x 28 In. . . . 550.00
Chandelier, 12-Light, Rococo Style, Glass, Gilt Bronze, Glass, 30 In. 660.00
Chandelier, 12-Light, Rococo, Knop Central Support, Scroll Arms, Electrified, 24 In. 1430.00
Chandelier, 12-Light, William IV, Gilt, Bronze, Circular Frame Garland Swags, 45 In. . . . 17050.00
Chandelier, 15-Light, Neoclassical Style, Brass, Glass Bead Chains, 56 In. 3740.00
Chandelier, 15-Light, Rococo Revival Style, Gilt Bronze, Prisms, Openwork, 31 In. 1650.00
Chandelier, 16-Light, Brass, 2 Tiers Of Scrolled Arms, Mid 20th Century, 36 In. 920.00
Chandelier, 16-Light, Gilt Bronze & Cut Crystal, 36 In. 605.00
Chandelier, 18-Light, Gilt Brass, Glass Prisms, Chains, Continental, 1875-1900, 48 In. . . . 3520.00
Chandelier, 18-Light, Louis XV Style, Bronze, Patinated Iron, Glass, Electrified, 42 In. . . 2420.00
Chandelier, 18-Light, Neoclassical Style, Gilt Bronze, Glass, Italy, c.1900, 50 1/2 In. 7260.00
Chandelier, 24-Light, Leaf Capped Downswept Branches, 2 Tiers, Drip Pans, 25 1/2 In. . . 546.00
Chandelier, 36-Light, Rococo Style, Gilt Bronze, Prisms, Victorian, 76 In. 4400.00
Chandelier, Art Deco, Pendant Circular Center Section, Reeded Column, 24 In. 6325.00
Chandelier, Art Deco, Spreading Circular Shade, Pale Amber Glass, 1930, 18 In. 1265.00
Chandelier, Art Deco, Twisted Supports, Wild Animals Scene, White Fabric, 1925, 54 In. . 2070.00
Chandelier, Arts & Crafts, Mica Panels, Tennis Scene, 5 1/2 x 18 x 12 In., Pair 935.00
Chandelier, Brass, Lion, Crest, Dutch, 1880, 23 x 20 In. 1550.00
Chandelier, Bronze Scroll Arms, Candle Cups Hung With Prisms, Cut Crystal, 36 In. 1540.00
Chandelier, Conical Shade, Pale Pink Glass, Rose Border Centering A Star, 1925, 48 In. . . 1265.00
Chandelier, Continental, Cut Glass, Round Corona, Waterfall Crystals, Chains, 26 In. 2420.00
Chandelier, Edgar Brand, Central Domed Shade, Gray, Orange, Purple, 1925, 26 In. 6610.00
Chandelier, Empire Style, Gilt Bronze, Glass, 25 In. 385.00
Chandelier, Globe, Caramel Bent Glass Panels, Floral Border, c.1920, 20 In. 345.00
Chandelier, Hanging Lantern, Onondaga, Cutout Top, Ring Support, Chain, Iron, 48 In. . . 3300.00
Chandelier, Hanging, Slag Glass Palmettes, Fleur-De-Lis Inserts, 22 In. 275.00
Chandelier, Italian Rococo Style, Cut Glass, Brass, 2 Tiers, Scrolls, Bead Chains, 26 In. . . 1540.00
Chandelier, Leaded Glass, Arts & Crafts Design, Green & White, 32 x 24 In. 4950.00
Chandelier, Leafy Fronds Arms Hung With Pendants, Gilt, Bronze, 26 In. 2070.00
Chandelier, Louis XVI Style, Gilt Brass, Glass, Drops, Swags, C-Scrolls, c.1900, 27 In. . . 1045.00
Chandelier, Pierced, Cast Fleur-De-Lis & Scroll Design, Bronze, c.1935, 12 x 20 In. 2990.00
Chandelier, Porcelain, 2 Tiers, Foliate Branches, Electrified, Continental, 35 In. 805.00
Duffner & Kimberly, Leaded Glass Shade, 20 In. 4950.00
Electic, Sweet Cuba, Tin Lithograph, Shade, 30 In. 105.00
Electric, 2 Shades, Caramel Slag Panels, Arts & Crafts, Desk, 21 x 21 In. 245.00
Electric, 2 Women With Lotus Blossoms, Rose Quartz, Green Jade, 22 In. 525.00
Electric, 2-Light, Oriental Figures Carrying Box On Base, 20 In. 125.00
Electric, 3 Bronze Cherubs, White Marble, Ormolu, Worn Silk Shade, 37 In. 1100.00
Electric, 3-Light, Bouillotte, Adjustable Tole Shade, Pierced Base, 24 In. 3162.00
Electric, 4 Seasons, Green Glass, Green Cased Shade, Patent 1868 . . . . 121.00
Electric, 5 Branching Arms, Metal & Lucite, Plastic Globe Shade, 1960s, 72 In., Pair 165.00
Electric, 6 Seashells On Shade, Hammered Copper Base, Elizabeth Burton, 13 In. 5500.00
Electric, 6 Striated Caramel, White Panels, Mistletoe Base, Light Blue, Bent, 21 x 16 In. . 431.00
Electric, Akari, Isamu Nouguchi, Signed, 32 In. 258.00
Electric, Albert Paley, Fabricated Steel, 1992, 41 1/2 In. 13800.00
Electric, Aluminum, Hammered, Curled End Stand, Rectangular Polished Shade, Desk . . 235.00
Electric, Angle, 4 Gloves, Brass, Embossed, Angle Lamp Co., 36 In. 825.00
Electric, Arbor Surrounding A Maiden Drawing Water Over Pond, White, Metal, 31 In. . . 920.00
Electric, Arne Bang, Gourd Shape, White Crystalline Glaze, 10 1/2 In. 165.00
Electric, Arne Jacobsen, Black Painted Aluminum, Domed Shade, 19 1/2 In. 175.00
Electric, Art Deco, Metal Dancing Nude Figure On Top, Amber Glass Globe, 18 In. 303.00
Electric, Art Deco, Nude, Standing, Arms Up, Holding Leaded Glass Fan, 9 x 10 In. 185.00
Electric, Art Deco, Satin Glass, Apricot, 9 1/2 In, Pair 200.00
Electric, Art Deco, Stylized Woman, Pottery, Pink Marble Base, 1920s, GD., Pair 995.00
Electric, Art Deco, Triangular Brass Base, Floral, 17 x 6 1/2 x 7 In. 210.00

Electric, Art Deco, Tubular Shade, Pivoting On Angular Arm, Chrome, Desk, 15 In. 1035.00
Electric, Art Nouveau Girl, Metal Overlay, Parker, 18 x 26 In. 1840.00
Electric, Art Nouveau, Alabaster Top, Figural Woman, 3 Columns, 19 1/2 In. 550.00
Electric, Art Nouveau, Leaded Glass Shade, Bronzed Base, Flowers, 15 In. 1195.00
Electric, Arts & Craft, Hammered Brass, Square Base, 27 1/2 x 10 In. 440.00
Electric, Arts & Crafts, Chocolate Glass, Hanging, Nickel Plated Frame, 6 Sides, 32 In. . . 245.00
Electric, Arts & Crafts, Fluted Bronze Base, 6-Sided Shade, Green Slag Panels, 25 In. . . . 660.00
Electric, Arts & Crafts, Glass Bowl, 4 Chains, Hanging, C In Diamond, 20 x 12 1/2 In. . . 715.00
Electric, Arts & Crafts, Iron, Mica, Black Paint, 66 In. 330.00
Electric, Arts & Crafts, Iron, Painted Acanthus Leaf, Open Scroll Base, 5-Light, Floor . . . 210.00
Electric, Arts & Crafts, Silvercrest, Bronze, Silver Overlay, Helmet Shade, 12 x 7 In. 825.00
Electric, Arts & Crafts, Wicker, Domed Shade, 25 x 17 In. 440.00
Electric, Bellflower, Scalloped Base, Flint, c.1850 . . . . 290.00
Electric, Bent Panel, Gold, Green Textured Glass, White Metal Base, Art Nouveau, 22 In. . 575.00
Electric, Bigelow & Kennard, Green Glass, Leaded, 24 In. 5500.00
Electric, Bigelow & Kennard, Leaded Glass, Bronze, Brown Patina, 1915, 59 In. 32200.00
Electric, Black Enameled & Nickel Metal, Adjustable, c.1930, 61 In. 4600.00
Electric, Black Marble Cutout Corner Base, Pierced Metal Surrounds, Floor 245.00
Electric, Blackamoor, Holding 7-Light Candelabrum, Floor, Pair 925.00
Electric, Bouillotte, Fluted, Leaf C-Scroll Candle Branches, Green Tole Shade, Charles X . 748.00
Electric, Brass Grille At Base, Cobalt Blue Ground, Pink Roses, 13 3/4 In., Pair 30.00
Electric, Brass, Green Striated Glass, Knop Standard, Lion's Paw Feet, 73 In. 2070.00
Electric, Brass, Pierced Shade, Cylindrical Base, Middle East, 20th Century, 73 In. 335.00
Electric, Brass, Pierced, Arabesque Design, Amber Beaded Fringe Shade, Syria, 76 In. . . . 740.00
Electric, Brass, Secessionist Style, 3 Claw Feet, Applied Jewels, 18 x 10 In. 660.00
Electric, Bronze, 3-Light, Glass Mosaic Shards, Dragonfly, Flower Filigree, Squat, 12 In. . 154.00
Electric, Bronze, Boy With Smiling Father Time, Girl With Surprised Father Time, Pair . . 373.00
Electric, Bronze, Bronze Peacock, Mother-Of-Pearl Shade, Floral Base, 1900, 71 In. 2587.00
Electric, Bronze, Green & Mixed Colored Landscape, Pedestal, 21 In. 330.00
Electric, Bronze, Man On Elephant, Light From Tower Window, Marble Base, Austria . . . 4070.00
Electric, Bronze, Samurai With Bowl, Wooden Stand, Signed, Japan, 25 1/2 In. 375.00
Electric, Camille Faure, Curlicued Iron Base, Geometric Mushroom Shape Shade, 14 In. . 3190.00
Electric, Candle, Brass & Tole, Green, Cream Color Interior, F.W. Walker, 15 x 5 3/8 In. . 185.00
Electric, Candle, Bronze, Winged Gargoyle On Marble, Hexagonal Glass Shade, 9 1/2 In. 172.00
Electric, Candle, Gilt, Pricket Stick Top, Bulb & C-Scroll Base, Putti, 31 In., Pair 1210.00
Electric, Candle, Pressed, Jack-O'-Lantern Shape, 3 In. 159.00
Electric, Candle, Regency, Silver Plate, Pebbled Square Base, Glass Shade, 19 In. 690.00
Electric, Carved Dragon Tropical Wood, Dark Finish, China, No Shade, 55 1/2 In. 300.00
Electric, Carved Masks & Foliage, Pricket Stick, 26 In., Pair 862.00
Electric, Ceiling, Richard Winkelmayer, Paper, Nickeled Brass, c.1931, 85 In. 2300.00
Electric, Ceiling, Scrolled Leaves & Flower Frame, Gold Iridescent Glass, 9 x 10 In. 935.00
Electric, Ceramic Jar Base, Lavender Iris, Green & Black Ground, Shade, 31 In., Pair . . . 300.00
Electric, Ceramic, Vase Form, Faience Lovers & Landscape Scene, Signed, 14 In. 264.00
Electric, Champleve, Enamel Bands, Women & Birds, 2-Light, Slag Glass Shade, 68 In. . . 440.00
Electric, Charles Disderot, Wooden, Black Enamel, Laminated, 1965, 63 In., Pair 5750.00
Electric, Christian Dell, Chromed Metal & Wood, Idell, Adjustable, c.1933, 18 1/2 In. . . . 690.00
Electric, Christian Dell, Chromed Metal, Idell, Adjustable, c.1933, 17 1/2 In. 805.00
Electric, Chrome, Round Base, Tube Shaft, 8 Globe Lights In 2 Tiers, 26 x 14 In. 55.00
Electric, Classical, Green Glass Font, Metal Open Pedestal, 4 Masks, Marble Base, 27 In. . 145.00
Electric, Cobalt Cut To Clear, Brass Column, Stepped Marble Base, c.1860, 22 In. 1430.00
Electric, Columnar, Brass, Stepped Marble Base, Snowflake Prisms, Cut Shade, 19 In. . . . 1030.00
Electric, Colza, Regency, Bronze, Urn Font Above 2 Lights, Glass Shades, 18 In., Pair . . . 4370.00
Electric, Continental, Landscape Scene, Reserves Of Cupids, Porcelain, Lavender, 20 In. . 1725.00
Electric, Copper, Cloisonne, Engraved Design, Bulbous Turned Stand, Oriental, Floor . . . 413.00
Electric, Copper, Hammered, Mica Conical Shade, Carved Base, Dirk Van Erp, 15 In. . . . 1380.00
Electric, Cornelius & Baker, Crimped Frosted Glass Shade, c.1845, 24 In., Pair 3300.00
Electric, Cornelius & Baker, Rococo Revival, Brass, Flowers, Tripod Base, 25 In. 605.00
Electric, Cornelius & Co., Brass, Corinthian Column, Marble Base, Pat. 1845, 20 In. 660.00
Electric, Cranberry Glass Shade, Iron Base, Brass Font, 13 x 9 In. 330.00
Electric, Cranberry Glass, Clear Grape & Leaf Design, Marble & Metal Base, Table 85.00
Electric, Cut Glass, Mushroom Silver Plated Frame Shade, Prisms, 19 x 11 In. 1265.00
Electric, Deer Hoof Base, Black Silk Shade, 23 In. 415.00
Electric, Dirk Van Erp, Bean Pot Form, Box, c.1920, 11 x 10 3/4 In. 9775.00

Electric, Dirk Van Erp, Copper, Hammered, 1 Socket, 3-Paneled Shade, Mica, 11 x 11 In.   6050.00
Electric, Domed Floral Shade, Bronze Classical Base, 18 In. 6600.00
Electric, Domed Shade, Stylized Border, Olive Green, Bronze Base, 6 In. 1650.00
Electric, Duffner & Kimberly, Domed Shade, Geometric Green Slag Glass, 23 In. 2185.00
Electric, Duffner & Kimberly, Leaded Glass, Bronze, c.1910, 24 1/2 In. 7475.00
Electric, Elizabeth Burton, Copper, Hammered Base, 5 Seashells Emit Light, 9 In. 3080.00
Electric, Elizabeth Burton, Copper, Hammered, Slag Glass, 23 In. 2420.00
Electric, Emeralite & Brass, Adjustable, Green Cased Shade, c.1909, 29 In. 660.00
Electric, Emeralite, M.G. McFaddin, Double Knuckle, Green Glass Shade, 1916 . . . .   250.00
Electric, Emeralite, Metal Base, Green Glass Shade, Desk, 19th Century 220.00
Electric, George Nakashima, Burlwood, Cylindrical Parchment Shade, Desk, 19 x 10 In. . .   4000.00
Electric, George Nakashima, Cylindrical Parchment Shade, Burlwood, Desk, 19 1/2 In. . . .   4400.00
Electric, Gilt Fittings, 3 Caryatids On Urn Stem, Green Onyx Insert, Shade, 27 In. 300.00
Electric, Gilt Metal, Bronze, Diamond, Fan Standard, Trio Of Seated Putti, 17 In., Pair . . .   2300.00
Electric, Gilt Metal, Classical, Round Alabaster Base & Trim, Floor 385.00
Electric, Glass, Raymond Subes, Wrought Iron, 1925, 24 1/2 In. 14950.00
Electric, GLS Co., Metal Base, Green Stone Top, Adjustable Shade, 12 1/2 In. 55.00
Electric, Golfer, Nickeled Brass, Round Shade, Glass Ball Top, Art Deco, 12 In. 60.00
Electric, Gone With The Wind, Brass, Milk Glass, Wild Rose Design 120.00
Electric, Green Emeralite Shade, Adjustable Bronze Base, Arts & Crafts, 22 In. 132.00
Electric, Green Slag Glass Shade, Enameled Metal, Arts & Crafts, 22 x 12 In. 770.00
Electric, Greta Grossman, Grasshopper, Tripod Base, Shade On Gooseneck, 48 x 24 In. . .   550.00
Electric, Gustav Stickley, Copper, Hammered, Baluster, 3 Sockets, Marked, 20 x 7 In. . . .   2860.00
Electric, Gustav Stickley, Copper, Hammered, Wicker Shade, 23 In. 3025.00
Electric, H.G. Cleveland, Copper, Embossed, Mica Shade, Leather Lacing, 18 1/2 In. 2200.00
Electric, Hampshire Base, Incised Water Lily, Handel Shade, Bradley & Hubbard, 16 In. .   4125.00
Electric, Hanging, Leaded Glass Squares, Red, Orange, Green, Yellow, 8 x 16 1/2 In. 62.00
Electric, Harvard, Student, Double, New Pink Cased Glass Shades, 1920s 1980.00
Electric, Hawaiian Woman, Hands Down, Shade, 1940s 1200.00
Electric, Ingo Mauer, Light Bulb Form, Chromed Base, Label, c.1980, 1 In. 345.00
Electric, International Silver Co., Lacquered, Glass Emerald Shade, 1847, 20 x 10 In. 40.00
Electric, Island Woman, Jug On Shoulder, Red, Chalkware, Shade, 1950s, Pair 350.00
Electric, Jefferson, Conical Gladiolas & Green Leaf Border Shade, Orange Sky, 18 In. . . .   4950.00
Electric, Jefferson, Reverse Painted Domed Shade, Landscape, Metal Base, 1910, 22 In. .   2300.00
Electric, Jefferson, Reverse Painted Landscape Shade, Ice Glass Base, 18 In. 4600.00
Electric, Jefferson, Reverse Painted Landscape, Geometric Band, Bronze Finish 3575.00
Electric, Jefferson, Reverse Painted Shade, Purple Flowers, Green Leaves, 22 In. 1870.00
Electric, Jenny Lind Style, Acid Etched Flowers On Shade 88.00
Electric, Karl Trabert, Metal & Steel, Adjustable, Painted Black, c.1932, 18 In. 2300.00
Electric, Lacquered, Spiral Band On Upper Section, 1847, 32 x 6 In., Pair 115.00
Electric, Le Gras, Etched Glass, Sailboats At Dusk, Etched Signature, 7 1/2 x 5 In. 468.00
Electric, Limbert, 4-Panel Mica Shade, Copper Frame, Leaf Cutouts, 19 x 24 In. 20900.00
Electric, Limbert, No. 507, 22 x 23 In. 5335.00
Electric, Lithophane Sides, Landscape Scenes, Star Punched Brass Frame, 5 1/4 In. 195.00
Electric, Louis XVI Style, Porcelain Urn, Gilt Bronze, Swan's Neck Handles, 20 In., Pair   5460.00
Electric, Marble, Brass, 3 Tiers, Square Top, Ornate Brass Fittings, 34 1/2 In. 1035.00
Electric, Mermaid, 23 1/2 In. 149.00
Electric, Metal, Bronze, Butterfly, Nude Figures, Blue Leaded Glass Wings, 1930, 9 In. . .   373.00
Electric, Metal, Domed Shade, Chartreuse, Pale Orange Interior, Green Landscape, 18 In.   920.00
Electric, Metal, Reverse Painted Shade, Russet Interior, Leaves, Pittsburgh Glass, 25 In. . .   2875.00
Electric, Metal, White, Boy Blowing Bubble, Iridescent Bubble Shade, 8 x 8 In. 258.00
Electric, Metallic Baluster Standard, Tripod, Shell Feet, Floor 175.00
Electric, Miller, Paneled Shade, 18 In. 935.00
Electric, Moe-Bridges, Exotic Birds Shade, 18 In. 7700.00
Electric, Moe-Bridges, Reverse Painted Shade, River & Landscape Design, 21 In. 2185.00
Electric, Moe-Bridges, Reverse Painted Shade, Springtime, Trees At Base, 23 In. 3640.00
Electric, Moe-Bridges, Reverse Painted, Greek Ruins, Domed, Signed On Rim, 18 In. 4400.00
Electric, Moe-Bridges, Reverse Painted, Trees, Water Scene, Brown, Blue, Yellow, 16 In. .   1815.00
Electric, Monkey, Sitting, Holding Sphere, Terra-Cotta, Unpainted, 1920s, 7 1/2 In. 135.00
Electric, Mood, Molded Turquoise Shade, Square Pattern, 3-Footed Base, 1960s, 13 In. . .   39.00
Electric, Morgan, Trailing Grapevines, Purple, Red, Tree Form Base, Grape, 64 In. 23000.00
Electric, Motion, Locomotive, Econolite, 1956 . . . .   135.00
Electric, Motion, Mountains 95.00

Electric, Motion, Statue Of Liberty 65.00
Electric, Mushroom, Brilliant Cut Glass Shade, Prisms, 19 x 12 In. 1870.00
Electric, Mushroom, Hand Painted Flowers, Pottery, 1950, 18 In. 373.00
Electric, Neoclassical Style, Medici Urn Shape, Variegated Brown Alabaster, Italy, 20 In. . 250.00
Electric, Night-Light, Ball Shape, Brass Base, Candle Inside Globe, 5 1/2 In. 165.00
Electric, Night-Light, Cabbage Patch Doll 45.00
Electric, Nude Female On Marble Base, Bronze, Glass Shade, Signed, 20 1/2 In. 1495.00
Electric, Nude Woman, Metal, Green Patina, Glass Panel, Marble Base, Fayral, 16 In. ... 2300.00
Electric, Oak & Copper, Mica Panel Shade, 26 x 15 x 15 In. 1265.00
Electric, Oak, Carmel Slag Glass Shade, Rectangular Base, Prairie School, 18 x 27 In. ... 1650.00
Electric, Oak, Copper, Hammered, Wood Base, Gustav Stickley, 10 1/2 x 14 In. 6050.00
Electric, Oak, Glass & Metal Ball & Claw Footed, 24-Square Contoured Top 325.00
Electric, Oriental, Marble, Mahogany, Round Top, Brown Marble Inset, 4 Cabriole Legs . 560.00
Electric, Oscar Bach, Bronze, Ring Turned Oval Standard, 4 Stylized Lions, 1925, 14 In. . 3450.00
Electric, Partially Nude Female Figure Standing Under A Canopy, Bronze, 16 In. 440.00
Electric, Partner's, Green Glass Shades, Brass, c.1900, 13 x 18 In. 1250.00
Electric, Patinated Metal, Candlestick Shape, Tripod Base, Black Silk Shade, 33 In. 165.00
Electric, Peacock Shape, Czechoslovakia, 16 In. 1760.00
Electric, Phoenix, Conical Woodland Scene Shade, 16 In. 1375.00
Electric, Phoenix, Orange, Yellow & Brown Water Scene Shade, 16 In. 1650.00
Electric, Pittsburgh, Call Of The Wild, Trees, Teepee, Domed, Bronze Owl Base, 18 In. ... 5500.00
Electric, Pittsburgh, Domed Winter Woodland Shade, 14 In. 1650.00
Electric, Pittsburgh, Reverse Painted Landscape Shade, Indian Metal Base, 18 In. 1150.00
Electric, Pittsburgh, Reverse Painted Shade, Autumn Leaf, Domed, 18 In. 3575.00
Electric, Pittsburgh, Reverse Painted Shade, Indian Motifs, Base Illuminates, 18 In. 6600.00
Electric, Pittsburgh, Reverse Painted, Landscape Scene On Shade, Bronze Base, 25 In. ... 4887.00
Electric, Poll-Parrot Shoes, Electric, Plastic Shade, Metal Base, 19 1/2 In. 83.00
Electric, Porcelain, Blue Ground, Oval Reserves, England, 16 In., Pair 430.00
Electric, Porcelain, Painted, Romantic 18th Century Couples, Brass, 30 In., Pair 415.00
Electric, Porcelain, Rococo Style, Floral Design, Germany, 32 In. 460.00
Electric, Porcelain, Seated Monkey, Naturalistic, Germany, 8 In. 782.00
Electric, Prairie School, Green, Red, Caramel Linear Designs, 15 x 20 In. 880.00
Electric, Prairie School, Mahogany, Octagonal Shade, Hammered Panes, 70 x 27 In. 1650.00
Electric, Prairie School, Square Shade, 23 x 5 x 18 1/2 In. 4400.00
Electric, Rabbto, Brass, Indian Man & Woman, Stained Glass, 21 x 14 x 11 In. 3164.00
Electric, Reading, Stylized Tulip Design Amber Leaded Glass Shade, 53 In. 545.00
Electric, Reverse Painted Shade, Colorful Landscape, Peacock In Foreground, 17-In. Shade 1650.00
Electric, Reverse Painted Shade, Open Field, Directoire Style Base, Art Deco, 14 In. Diam. 523.00
Electric, Reverse Painted, Peacock On Fence, 22 In. 1800.00
Electric, Rock Crystal, Giltwood, Beaded Border, Shaped Square Base, 22 1/2 In., Pair .. 10350.00
Electric, Samuel Yellin, Wrought Iron, 3-Footed, Shade, 68 1/2 In. ....*Illus* 24750.00
Electric, Schlitz Beer, Figural, Woman Holding Globe, 1976, 48 In. 185.00
Electric, Shagreen, Silver Gilt, Hexagonal Stem, Vellum Shade, 1930, 72 In. 8625.00
Electric, Slag Glass, Brown, Light Blue-Red Blossoms, Orange Border, Miller, 58 1/2 In. . 1150.00
Electric, Slag Glass, Garden Scene, 6 Panels, Lighted Base, 20-In. Shade ....*Illus* 3410.00

Chandeliers can be cleaned in place with a new spray cleaner made for that purpose. Cover the floor with paper or cloth to catch the drips. Then spray the chandelier. It will clean and drip dry.

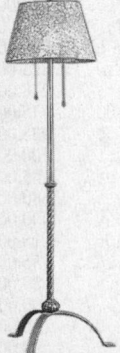

Lamp, Electric, Samuel Yellin, Wrought
Iron, 3-Footed, Shade, 68 1/2 In.

Lamp, Electric, Slag Glass,
Garden Scene, 6 Panels,
Lighted Base, 20-In. Shade

Electric, Slag Glass, Green Panels, Mission, Black Metal Base, Miller, 17 In. 520.00
Electric, Slag Glass, Green, 4-Panel, Young & Co., Philadelphia, Early 20th Century 302.00
Electric, Slag Glass, Green, Domed Shade, 6 Multicolored Panels, 22 In. 805.00
Electric, Slag Glass, Green, Oak, Octagonal Shade, 25 x 18 In. 715.00
Electric, Slag Glass, Green, White Interior, 2-Tierd Oak Base, Arts & Crafts, 20 x 11 In. . 460.00
Electric, Slag Glass, Green, Windmill, House, Trees Scene, 22 1/2 In. 258.00
Electric, Slag Glass, Multicolored, 6-Panel Shade, Adjustable Height, 16 In. 750.00
Electric, Slag Glass, Pink, Brown, Conical Shade, Green Patina, 25 In. 3737.00
Electric, Slag Glass, Turquoise, Domed Shade, Fleur-De-Lis, Duffner & Kimberly, 22 In. . 9775.00
Electric, Slag Glass, White, Brown, Brass, Hammered, Arts & Crafts, 18 x 25 In. 715.00
Electric, Stilnovo, Black, Brass Cantilevered Support Arm, Black Aluminum Shade 1265.00
Electric, Student, 2-Light, Brass, Green Glass Shades, 24 In. 520.00
Electric, Student, 2-Light, Opaque White Shades, 24 In. 200.00
Electric, Student, Brass, Nickel Plated, Etched Cut Glass Font, Glass Shade, 20 In. 275.00
Electric, Student, Brass, Opal Glass Shade, 20 3/4 In. 530.00
Electric, Student, G.H. Covell, Brass, Ribbed Yellow Amber Shade, 21 In. 330.00
Electric, Student, Gilt Metal, Columnar Standard, Frosted Floral Shade, 23 1/2 In. 488.00
Electric, Stylized Poppy Border, Floral, Bronze Metal Base, Arts & Crafts, 20 x 22 In. . . . 1210.00
Electric, Suess, Stylized Flowers, Leaded, 18 In. 4675.00
Electric, Turned & Fluted Walnut Base, Leaded Glass Floral Shade, 68 1/2 In. 385.00
Electric, Victorian Man On 1, Woman On Other, Blue, Porcelain, Table, Pair 140.00
Electric, Wall, Schlitz, 7 Oz. Bottle, Lighted Base, Long-Neck Bottle, 1959, 16 x 9 In. . . . 100.00
Electric, Wicker, Flared Base, Celadon Paint, Arts & Crafts, 67 In. 250.00
Electric, Wilkenson, Leaded Glass, Floral, Bronze Base, 24 In. 6325.00
Electric, Wrought Iron, Gilt, Cage Form, Scroll Arms, Feet & Candle Cups, 75 x 21 In. . . 978.00
Fairy, 3 Arms, Brass Standard, Burmese, Clarke's Cricklite 770.00
Fairy, Figural, Owl, Glass Eyes, White Feathers, Gray, Lilac Base 375.00
Fat, Iron, Pick & Hammer Handle, Heart Center, Chicken Finial 355.00
Fluid, 3 Printie Blocks, Brass Collar, Free-Blown Shade, Etched Floral, 1840s, 15 In. 220.00
Fluid, Blown Glass, Opaque Blue Base, Cobalt Blue Font, Brass Collar, 12 In, Pair 358.00
Fluid, Blown, Globular Font, Trapped Bubble Baluster Form Stem, 9 1/2 In. 143.00
Fluid, Blue Thumbprint Font, Electrified 93.00
Fluid, Brass, Glass, Etched Font, Painted Milk Glass Pedestal, 19th Century, 16 In. 88.00
Fluid, Cranberry Glass Shade, Veritas Clockworks, Late 19th Century, 20 In. 373.00
Fluid, Diamond Cut Font, Silver Plate, 28 In., Pair 1380.00
Fluid, Freeblown Font, Cut Flutes, Hexagonal Standard, 1830s, 8 5/8 In. 55.00
Fluid, Hammered Copper, Shade, B & H 165.00
Fluid, Lace, Ruffled Shade, Bulb Form, Free-Blown Cut Punty, Yellow, 19 1/4 In., Pair . . 805.00
Fluid, Opalescent Blue Coin Spot, Pear Shape Font, Milk Glass Standard, 13 1/2 In., Pair . 375.00
Fluid, Paneled Font With Wafer, Flint, Pewter Collard, 10 In., Pair 220.00
Fluid, Pressed Glass, Bull's-Eye With Fleur-De-Lis, 9 1/2 In., Pair 185.00
Fluid, Pressed Glass, Horn-Of-Plenty, 6-Sided Base, 10 1/2 In., Pair 420.00
Fluid, Tin, Painted, Cone Shape, Chamber Stick Base, Hinged Mica Lens, 4 In. 121.00
Gas, Enameled Opaline Glass, Flowering Branches, Brass Mount, Electrified, 18 In., Pair . 175.00
Gasolier, 5-Light, Tulip Form Shaft, Swagged Chains, Electrified, 31 x 28 In. 3960.00
Gasolier, 6-Light, Cut Glass Shade, Electrified, 42 x 30 In. 3235.00
Grease, Hanging, Open Pan, Hanger, 17 In. 192.00
Grease, Pan, Wrought Iron, Rattail Hooked Top, Continental, 18th Century, 19 1/2 In. . . . 410.00
Grease, Strap Handle, Pottery, Wheel Thrown Pottery, 4 1/4 In. 165.00
Grease, Tin, On Saucer Base, Sam Davis, Original Dark Japanning, Stenciled Label 121.00
Handel lamps are included in the Handel category.
Hanging, Arts & Crafts, Green Slag Glass Panels, Leaded Glass, 9 1/2 x 9 3/4 In. 115.00
Hanging, Arts & Crafts, Red Tulip, Green, Tan Rectangular Panels, 8 1/2 x 4 5/8 In. 143.00
Hurricane, Brass, Floral Shade, Porcelain, Early 20th Century 104.00
Kerosene, 8-Paneled Stem, Flattened Diamond Font, Flint, Pewter Collar, 7 1/2 In., Pair . . 165.00
Kerosene, Banquet, Amber Swirled Globe, Brass, Ceramic Foot 137.00
Kerosene, Banquet, Brass, Glass, Prisms, England, 26 In. 2415.00
Kerosene, Banquet, Cupids, 31 In. 600.00
Kerosene, Banquet, Cut Glass, Russian Pattern, 26 In. 150.00
Kerosene, Banquet, Delft Windmill Design, 30 In. 895.00
Kerosene, Banquet, Onyx Stem, Embossed Lily Shade 310.00
Kerosene, Banquet, Porcelain, Enameled Milk Glass Shade, Cartier, Baccarat, 35 In. .*Illus* 1650.00
Kerosene, Black Marble Globe, Reeded Metal Post, 3 Gilt Winged Lions, Tripod, Floor . . . 550.00

Lamp, Kerosene, Banquet,
Porcelain, Enameled Milk Glass
Shade, Cartier, Baccarat, 35 In.

Lamp, Kerosene, Parlor, Blue Satin
Opalescent, Quilted Diamond,
Prisms, Hanging

Kerosene, Brass Base, Eagles, Red Glass Globe Shade, Clear Drops, 1930s-1940s, 29 In.	495.00
Kerosene, Brass Column, Mounted As Table Lamp, 31 In.	220.00
Kerosene, Brass Font, 3-Footed Brass Base, White Shade, Aladdin Burner, 69 In.	250.00
Kerosene, Brass, Victorian, Cranberry To Clear Frosted, Handle, Hanging	2295.00
Kerosene, Candle, Hanging, Blue Jewels In Split Metal Filigree, Chains, 20 x 5 In.	95.00
Kerosene, Candlestick, Fan & Diamond Cut, Hurricane Shades, 17 In., Pair	615.00
Kerosene, Coach, Beveled Glass Panels, Nickel, Copper, Silver, Reflectors, 27 In., Pair	2300.00
Kerosene, Dog Form Base, Pierced Shade, Bronze, c.1875, 22 In.	2420.00
Kerosene, Floral Glass Shade, Brass Trim, Smoke Bell, Prisms, Hanging	375.00
Kerosene, Glass, 3 Rows Of Punties, 1 Row Of Ovals, Brass Collar, Marble Base, 14 In.	373.00
Kerosene, Gone With The Wind, Pink, Roses, 28 In.	990.00
Kerosene, Kettle, On Stand, Tin, Removable Font, Saucer Base, Chain, 6 1/2 In.	135.00
Kerosene, Loop, New England, c.1850, 11 In.	795.00
Kerosene, Opaque White Cut To Red, Prisms, Stepped Marble & Brass Base, 23 1/2 In.	2200.00
Kerosene, Parlor, Blue Satin Opalescent, Quilted Diamond, Prisms, Hanging *Illus*	4480.00
Kerosene, Parlor, Cherub, Standing, Spelter, Brass Font, Etched Cranberry Shade, 27 In.	245.00
Kerosene, Parlor, Cut Glass, Harvard Band & Daisy, Brilliant, Prisms, 22 In.	1850.00
Kerosene, Parlor, Hobnail Amber Shade, Pendants, Brass, Electrified, Victorian, 28 In.	336.00
Kerosene, Piano, White Glass Shade With Lion Design, Wrought Iron & Brass, 67 In.	172.00
Kerosene, Pressed Glass Font, Brass & Marble Base, Drilled, Electrified, 11 In.	88.00
Kerosene, Pressed, Berry, Clambroth Base, Blue Font, Brass Connector, Collar, 9 In.	275.00
Kerosene, Rayo, Nickel Plated, Milk Glass Shade	55.00
Kerosene, Rayo, Squatty, Bulbous Font, Milk Glass Shade, Electrified, Pair	220.00
Kerosene, Rayo, Worn Chrome, 12 5/8 In.	55.00
Kerosene, Student, Green Cased Shade, Nickel On Brass, c.1870	850.00
Kerosene, Swirl, White Metal Base, Columnar Stem, 29 1/2 x 6 3/8 In.	30.00
Kerosene, Tin, Brass Burner, Clear Chimney, 10 1/4 In.	192.00
Kerosene, Tin, Cylindrical Font, Tubular Ring Burner, Green Japanning, 1856, 7 1/8 In.	220.00
Kerosene, Wedgwood, Rosso Antico, Enamel, Flowers, Marked, Mid 19th Century, 5 In.	517.00
Kerosene, White Onyx, Frosted Spherical Shade, Electrified, 1885, 29 In.	2450.00
Kerosene, White Opaque Glass, Molded Cherub Faces, Victorian, 26 In.	250.00
Lard, Cylindrical Font, Double Wick, Saucer Base, 7 In.	120.00
Lard, Kinnear, Cast Iron Base, Pat. Feb. 4, 1850, 8 1/4 In.	165.00
Lard, Tin, Rectangular Font, Old Deep Yellow Paint, 8 1/4 In.	330.00
Lard, Tin, Saucer Base, Handle, 7 1/2 In.	110.00
Oil, 4 Convex Lithophane Sides, Landscapes Scenes, Pierced Gallery, 5 In.	300.00
Oil, 8-Sided Baluster Stem, Square Foot, 4-Printie Font, 12 1/4 In.	135.00
Oil, Acanthus Capped Handle, Issuing A Boar's Head, Electrified, 10 In.	1380.00
Oil, Amber Glass, 4-Part Mold, No Burner, 8 3/4 In.	35.00
Oil, Amber, Melon Ribbed, Round, 9 1/4 In.	45.00
Oil, Amberina, Shaded, Footed, Miniature	1900.00
Oil, Art Nouveau Floral Design, Patinated Metal, Glass, Painted Wood, 31 In.	58.00
Oil, Banquet, Blue Delft Windmill Base, Miniature	1250.00
Oil, Banquet, Floral Embossed, Milk Glass Shade, Brass, Miniature	675.00
Oil, Banquet, Monkey, Squatting, Holding Coconut, Electrified, Repainted, 1880	885.00
Oil, Banquet, Orange Peel Font, Brass, Miniature	625.00

Oil, Beehive, Glass, 1880, Miniature 75.00
Oil, Blue Draped Column, Black Figure Of Girl With Gold Basket, Glass Font, 14 In. 55.00
Oil, Blue Satin Glass, Melon Font, Floral Shade, Brass Burner, Miniature, 6 3/4 In. 275.00
Oil, Brass Column, Glass Globe, Prisms, Marble Mounted, Electrified, 26 In. 690.00
Oil, Brass Connector, Round Crystal Font, Blue Stem, No Burner, 11 In. 80.00
Oil, Brass Coupling, Amber Stem, Light Blue Font, Square Base, No Burner, 12 In. 85.00
Oil, Brass Standard, Marble Base, Blue Satin Glass, 12 1/2 In. 160.00
Oil, Brass, Baluster Stem, Campana Form Oil Receptacle, 1850, 11 3/4 In., Pair 230.00
Oil, Brass, Tags, Property Of Wells Fargo & Co. Express, San Francisco Division, 26 In. . 660.00
Oil, Brass, Tapered Shaft, Socle Base, Oil Receptacle, Victorian, 21 1/2 In. 230.00
Oil, Bronze Glass, Angels Frolicking In The Heavens, Sevres Champleve's, 10 In. 517.00
Oil, Bronze, Grand Tour, 2 Spouts, Pedestal Base, Acanthus Handle, 9 x 5 In. 110.00
Oil, Bronze, Kneeling Silenus Holding Tazza, Scrolled, Leaf Handle, Electrified, 18 In. .. 1840.00
Oil, Bronze, Patinated, Grand Tour, Dragon Handle, Gilt Salamander, Italy, 11 In. 1980.00
Oil, Cased Blue Satin, White Glass, Ornate Brass Base, Ribbed Stem, No Burner, 11 In. .. 140.00
Oil, Chain Hung With Snuffer, Circular Stepped Base, Scroll Loop Handle, 25 1/4 In. 5520.00
Oil, Chased With Bands Of Foliage, Fluted, Garlands, Harp Form Handle, Italy, 43 In. 4370.00
Oil, Chrysanthemum, Pink Flowers, Green Swirl, Miniature 400.00
Oil, Coin Spot, Opaque, White Scalloped Base, Threaded Stem, Cranberry Font, 9 In. 90.00
Oil, Cranberry, Green Fluted Shade, Footed Base, 8 x 6 1/2 In. 287.00
Oil, Crusie, Cruciform, Cloverleaf Handle, Wrought Iron, 3 1/4 In. 175.00
Oil, Crusie, Double, Iron, 11 3/4 In. 220.00
Oil, Crusie, Double, Scrollwork, Hanging Glass Holders, 10 1/2 In. 175.00
Oil, Crusie, Stand, Penny Feet, Elongated Pan With Spout, Wrought Iron, 8 In. 467.00
Oil, Cut Glass Font, Brass Columnar Standard, Square Foot, 17 In. 143.00
Oil, Dalzell, Gilmore & Leighton, Sweetheart, Clear, Frosted Hearts, Miniature 260.00
Oil, Enameled Glass, Ovoid Body, Painted Flowers On Red Ground, 18 In. 65.00
Oil, Finger, Torpedo, 1890 .... 95.00
Oil, Green Diamond Quilted Fount, Acid Cut Ruffled Shade, Marble & Metal Base, 24 In. 425.00
Oil, Handle, Oil Guard, Sept. 20, 1870 .... 85.00
Oil, Hanging, Bird Form, Chinese, Bronze, Late 19th Century, 9 In. 125.00
Oil, Hanging, Country Store, Brass Font, Tin Shade, Milk Glass Smoke Bell 132.00
Oil, Hanging, Gargoyles Holding Rings At Mouths, Foliate Stem, 23 x 20 In. 7475.00
Oil, Hanging, Harp Design, Adjustable Brass Band, White Paint, 31 1/2 In. 90.00
Oil, Hanging, Leaded Glass, Caramel, Grape Edge Design, Early 1900s 495.00
Oil, Hanging, Repousse Foliage, Diamond Shape Chain Links, Silver, Italy, 5 In. 1265.00
Oil, Hanging, Tin Shade, Harp Design, Ribbed Band, White Paint, 30 In. 100.00
Oil, Hanging, White Metal Shade, Label, Hans Wegner, L. Poulsen, Label, 14 x 20 In. 550.00
Oil, Hollow Blue Stem, Star On Bottom, Embossed, Crystal Font, 11 1/4 In. 65.00
Oil, Irises, Victorian, 22 In. 250.00
Oil, J.C. Webb, Marble, Brass, Oct. 14, 1851, Milk Glass Shade, 13 1/4 In. 110.00
Oil, Kenmar, Aladdin Type, Green Luster, Silver Springs, Japan 75.00
Oil, Kinnear, Tin, Wrought Iron Shovel Pick, 7 In. 165.00
Oil, McCormick & Co., Little Puck, Perfumery, Glass, Tin, Baltimore, Box, 4 In. 248.00
Oil, Milk Glass, Dolphin Base, Hexagonal, 9 In., Pair 175.00
Oil, Milk Glass, Pink Ground, Blue Pansies, Miniature 475.00
Oil, Milk Glass, Swirl, Gilt Trim, 9 In. 375.00
Oil, Milk Glass, Threaded Stem, Flowers, Vines, White Scalloped Base, 10 In. 55.00
Oil, Miller, Embossed Nickel Plate Font, Electrified, Victorian, 9 In. 39.00
Oil, Miller, Hanging, Cranberry Hobnail Shade, Victorian, 1912 .... 1155.00
Oil, Miller, Juno, Green Over White Chrysanthemum, Chimney, 24 1/4 In. 420.00
Oil, Miner's, Cast Iron, Chicken Finial, 7 1/2 In. 165.00
Oil, Morey & Ober Of Boston, Hand, Pewter, Early 19th Century, 5 In. 175.00
Oil, Opaque Pink To White Well, Etched Glass Shade, Electrified, 34 In. 200.00
Oil, Painted Flowers On Red Ground, Foliate Border, Stepped Foot, 18 In. 65.00
Oil, Peg, Apricot, Engraved Shade, Swirl, Brass Base, 25 In. 450.00
Oil, Peg, Brass, Design On Glass, Electrified, 14 1/2 In. 295.00
Oil, Peg, Frosted, Green To Clear, Purple Violets, Leaves, Petal Edge, Metal Base, 13 In. . 325.00
Oil, Pierced Floral Font, Putto & Foliate Base, Onyx & Silvered, 22 In. 105.00
Oil, Sanctuary, Bronze, Rim Of Winged Angels, 34 In. 308.00
Oil, Sandwich Style, Cased White To Cranberry, Milk Glass Pedestal, 19th Century, 12 In. 140.00
Oil, Sapphire Blue Glass, Ruffled Shade, Marble Column, Chimney, 17 In. 395.00
Oil, Sinumbra, Brass & Marble, 2-Step Foot 4197.00

Oil, Sinumbra, Columnar, Cut & Etched Shade, 19th Century, 12 1/2 In. 2540.00
Oil, Smocking Pattern, Yellow Font, Clear Foot, Brass Collar, 9 1/4 In. 165.00
Oil, Solar, Frosted Glass Shade, Pendants, Electrified, Mid 19th Century 1900.00
Oil, Tin, Red, White, Blue, Yellow, Gold, Signed, 1792, 18 1/2 x 32 x 10 In. 450.00
Oil, Upside Down Cup & Saucer, Amber, Miniature 370.00
Oil, Vaseline, Pressed Glass, Blown Nailsea Swirled Font, 10 In. 1900.00
Oil, Wall Sconce, Tin, 19th Century, 14 x 8 3/4 In. 980.00
Oil, Yellow, Blown Mold, Eye & Scale Pattern, Hexagonal Base, 9 1/2 In., Pair 880.00
Olive Oil, Adjustable, 3 Wicks, Flat Base, Attached Wick Pick, 23 In. 92.00
Opium, Clear Dome, Cut Panels, Brass Pipe, Bamboo Stem, 7 In. 137.00
Overall Embossed Nubs, Cobalt Glaze, Made In Sweden, 12 In. 220.00
Pairpoint lamps are in the Pairpoint category.
Rush, Spike, 18th Century 395.00
Sconce, 1-Light, Gilt Metal, Flower & Leaf Design, Teardrop Prisms, Electrified, Pair . . . 110.00
Sconce, 1-Light, Rococo Revival, Bronze, Leaping Gargoyle, Electrified, 15 x 6 In., Pair . 1650.00
Sconce, 2-Light, 2 Quezal Bell Form Shades, Gilt Bronze, Shades Signed, 14 1/2 In. 1092.00
Sconce, 2-Light, Blackamoor, Holding Torches, Ebonized, Painted, Gilt, Italy, 28 In., Pair 3080.00
Sconce, 2-Light, Brass, Adam Style, Classical Maiden In Oval Medallion, 13 In, Pair 115.00
Sconce, 2-Light, Brass, Birds With Rings In Beaks, 8 In. 205.00
Sconce, 2-Light, Brass, Gilt Gesso, Mirrored Cartouche, Stylized Flower, 17 In., Pair 520.00
Sconce, 2-Light, Brass, Rococo Style, Detachable, Floral Backplate, 5 1/2 x 14 In., Pair . . 66.00
Sconce, 2-Light, C-Shaped Arms, 2 Candle Nozzles, 9 In., Pair 345.00
Sconce, 2-Light, Candle, Cast Metal, Bronze Finish, Jewels, Mirror, Prisms, 21 In., Pair . . 465.00
Sconce, 2-Light, Continental, Ribbon Tied, Foliate Standard, Cut Glass, Electrified, Pair . . 1150.00
Sconce, 2-Light, Eagle, Carved Giltwood, 14 1/2 x 27 1/2 In. 285.00
Sconce, 2-Light, Fluted Column Supporting Basket Of Fruit Backplate, 9 In., Pair 545.00
Sconce, 2-Light, Gilt Bronze, Queen Seated Beneath Baldachin, Regency, 12 In., Pair . . . 2090.00
Sconce, 2-Light, Giltwood, Cartouche Mirrors, Continental, 19th Century, 39 In., Pair . . . 5335.00
Sconce, 2-Light, Louis XVI Style, Gilt Bronze, Drapery Backplate, 21 In., 4 Piece 8625.00
Sconce, 2-Light, Louis XVI, Gilt Metal, Looped Tassels From Candelabrums, 25 In., Pair 1390.00
Sconce, 2-Light, Tin, Beveled Mirror Backlight, Pressed Leaves, Continental, 17 In., Pair . 345.00
Sconce, 2-Light, Wood, Foliate Design, Continental, 38 In., Pair 517.00
Sconce, 3-Light, Acorn & Leaf Backplate, Trumpet Shape Arms, 36 In., Pair 990.00
Sconce, 3-Light, Baroque Style, Giltwood, Cartouche, Winged Putti, Venetian, 18 In., Pair 2760.00
Sconce, 3-Light, Brass, Arched Mirror, 1882 . . . . 120.00
Sconce, 3-Light, Brass, Beveled Mirror, Masque & Scroll Design, Pair 195.00
Sconce, 3-Light, Brass, France, 1860 . . . . 1375.00
Sconce, 3-Light, Charles X, Gilt Bronze, Ring Mounted On Rosette, 7 1/2 In., Pair 2640.00
Sconce, 3-Light, Gilt Bronze, Flowers, Leaves, Cabochon, Electrified, 31 In., 4 Piece 4600.00
Sconce, 3-Light, Gilt Metal, Stylized Flowers, Foliage, Standard Cast, 15 3/4 In., 4 Piece . 1380.00
Sconce, 3-Light, Gold, Turtleback, Marble, Inlay, Glass Supports, Pair . . . . *Illus* 23000.00
Sconce, 3-Light, Louis XVI Style, Giltwood, Lyre Backplate, Laurel Leaves, 27 In., Pair . 6900.00
Sconce, 3-Light, Regency Style, Gilt Bronze, Crowned Putti, Urn, c.1900, 16 In., Pair . . . 2875.00
Sconce, 3-Light, Scrolled Arms, Masks & Swags Backplate, 20 In., Pair 1725.00
Sconce, 4-Light, Empire, Gilt Bronze, Lion's Head Plaque, Goose Heads, 15 In., Pair 2615.00
Sconce, 4-Light, Louis XVI, Musical Instruments & Laurel Wreaths, 34 In., Pair 2070.00
Sconce, 5-Light, Louis XVI Style, Gilt Metal, Glass Beaded Chains, 44 In., Pair 3735.00
Sconce, 5-Light, Rococo Style, Bronze Dore, Scrolled Foliate Design, 25 In., Pair 1650.00
Sconce, 5-Light, Vine Form Candle Arms, Pricket Candleholders, 10 In., Pair 575.00
Sconce, 7-Light, Scrolling Arms, Prisms, Tole Painted, 23 In., Pair 460.00
Sconce, 9-Light, Giltwood, Central Foliate Standard, Continental, 49 x 22 In. 747.00
Sconce, Albert Cheuret, Alabaster, Stork, Bronze, 1925, 15 1/2 In., Pair 12460.00
Sconce, Art Deco, Saucer Form Shade, Metal, Curved Mount, 21 1/4 In., Pair 1035.00
Sconce, Bronze Dore, Inset Sevres Style Plaque, Prisms, Scroll Arms, 14 In. 275.00
Sconce, Bronze, Flying Bat, Brass Foliate Fixture Hangs From Mouth, 21 In., Pair 5175.00
Sconce, California Art Tile Co., 13 1/2 In., Pair 990.00
Sconce, Candle Arm Form Of Grotesque Man, Oval Backplate, 19th Century, Pair 630.00
Sconce, Candle, Crimped Crest, Rounded Crest, 11 1/2 In, Pair 385.00
Sconce, Candle, Mirror Back, Crimped Drip Pan, 9 1/4 In. 192.00
Sconce, Candle, Wire, Metal & Wood, Worn Gilt, Italy, 44 In., Pair 410.00
Sconce, Cartouche Backplate, 3 Hinged Glass Arms, 15 x 16 In. 300.00
Sconce, Center Shield, Lion & Mask, Acanthus Arms, 19th Century 745.00
Sconce, Ceramic & Glass, Bathroom, 1930s 125.00

Sconce, Copper, Hammered, Painted Glass Shade, Gustav Stickley, 10 x 8 1/2 In. 1760.00
Sconce, Enameled Floral Bouquet Back, Monster Head At Bottom, c.1780, 8 1/4 In., Pair . 7475.00
Sconce, Figural, Griffin, Carved, Incised Back, Italy, 29 In., Pair 1980.00
Sconce, Giltwood, Georgian, Prisms, 33 x 13 In., Pair 495.00
Sconce, Gothic Revival, Iron, Black Paint, Pierced Crown Over Flowers, 25 In., Pair 2875.00
Sconce, Grotto, Giltwood, Putto Holding A Basket, 25 x 19 In., Pair 1955.00
Sconce, Gustav Stickley, Candle, Copper, Hammered, 10 1/2 In., Pair 1980.00
Sconce, Leaf Cast Backplate, 2 Branches, Foliate Drip Pan, 18 3/4 In., Pair 5750.00
Sconce, Mirrored, Concave Back, 19th Century, 9 1/2 x 6 1/2 In., Pair 215.00
Sconce, Neoclassical, Bronze, Gilt, S-Scroll Arm, Foliate Backplate, 15 x 29 1/2 In., Pair . 1725.00
Sconce, Paul Evans, Steel Cylinders, Pierced Design, 30 x 45 In., Pair 3575.00
Sconce, Perzel, Bronze, Demilune Shape, Stepped Glass Support, 1935, 9 In., Pair 3162.00
Sconce, Perzel, Frosted Glass Brick, Z-Shape Brass Bracket, 1930, 16 In., Pair 1610.00
Sconce, Pine Blackamoor, Holding Fruit Cornucopia, Brass, c.1920, 17 In., Pair 1430.00
Sconce, Pressed Tin, Round Reflector, Crimped Drip Pan 155.00
Sconce, Satyr's Mask Over Drapery Backplate, 3 Candle Arms, Leafy Drip Pans, 22 In. . . 2530.00
Sconce, Winged Figure Of Liberty, Holding Pair Of Candle Cups, 16 In., Pair 3105.00
Shade, Bigelow & Kennard, Overall Yellow Trailings, Amber Rippled Roses, 22 In. 14950.00
Shade, Conical, Dark Amber Glass, Enameled Geometric Diamonds, Art Deco, 14 In. 2645.00
Shade, Hanging, Duffner & Kimberly, Brown Cattails, White Water Lilies, Amber, 24 In. . 2185.00
Shade, Hanging, Pink, Green, Red Roses, Clusters Of Grapes On Vines, 1905, 24 In. 1725.00
Shade, Hanging, Wisteria, Leaded Glass, Purple, Blue, Green, 1915, 14 In. 2300.00
Shade, Head Of Woman Form, Cylindrical Base, Chrome Metal, Art Deco, 10 In. .172.00 to 230.00
Shade, Jefferson, Scenic, Reverse Painted Lakeside Landscape, Summer Trees, 21 In. . . . 1265.00
Shade, Loetz Type, Globe Shape, 6 1/2 x 6 In. 264.00
Shade, Mica, Sunflower, Stylized Flowers, Metal Plate, Claw Feet, 76 In., Pair 6900.00
Shade, Parasol, Multicolored Flowering Vine, Green, Olive Trellis, Lead Glass, 28 In. 4887.00
Shade, Roses, Brown Patina, Leaded Glass, 1915, 23 x 19 In. 7475.00
Skater's, Blue Chimney, Miniature 475.00
Skater's, Emerald Green Globe, Brass, Tin, 7 In. 465.00
Skater's, Jewel, Finger, Candle Lantern 220.00
Skater's, Pressed Globe, Brass, Tin Bottom, 7 In. 82.00
Spelter, Arabian Woman In Tent, Man, Donkey, Palm Tree In Background, Cold Painted . 715.00
Tiffany lamps are listed in the Tiffany category.
Torchere, 2-Light, Giltwood, Adjustable Round Top, 19th Century, Italy, 69 In. 865.00
Torchere, 3 Scroll Supports, Carved Foliage, Giltwood, 44 In., Pair 1320.00
Torchere, 4-Light, Gilt Metal, Electrified, Iberian, 60 In. 330.00
Torchere, Alabaster Bowl, Reeded & Pierced Shaft, Pierced Base, 71 In., Pair 2925.00
Torchere, Alabaster, Classical Column, Palmetto & Acanthus Leaves, Italy, c.1900, 77 In. 2640.00
Torchere, Art Deco, Brass Washed, Faceted Base, Etched Alabaster Shade, France, 66 In. . 195.00
Torchere, Art Deco, Chromed Metal Shade, Gray Glass Cup, Circular Base, 1935, 66 In. . 3335.00
Torchere, Art Deco, Dished Shade, Chrome, Mahogany, Circular Base, 1935, 71 In. 2070.00
Torchere, Art Deco, Wrought Iron, Square Stepped Shade, Gray, 1925, 67 In. 3450.00
Torchere, Arts & Crafts, Bronze & Iron, Hammered Texture, 67 1/4 In. 935.00
Torchere, Copper, Applied Flowers, 49 In. 55.00
Torchere, Empire Style, Winged Lions, Black Paint, Parcel Gilt, France, 79 In., Pair 3080.00
Torchere, Giltwood, Carved, Pierced Standard, Hanging Garlands, Paw Feet, 71 In., Pair. . 8250.00
Torchere, Iberian Style, Cast Iron, Amber Glass Shade, 46 In. 140.00
Torchere, Louis XVI Style, Giltwood, Round Top, Tripod Support, 64 In., Pair 7475.00

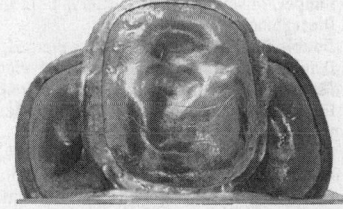

Lamp, Sconce, 3-Light, Gold, Turtleback,
Marble, Inlay, Glass Supports

Torchere, Neoclassical Style, Gilt Metal, Alabaster, Milk Glass Shade, Electrified, 60 In. .   165.00
Torchere, Neoclassical, 3 Fluted Columns, Surrounded By Female Bust, 79 In., Pair 6900.00
Torchere, Oscar Bach, Bronze, 6-Panel Mica Shade, Galleon Ship, 71 1/2 In., Pair 1350.00
Torchere, R. Wright, Reverse Taping Wood Standard, Aluminum Shade 920.00
Torchere, Reverse Painted, Trees On Orange Field, 13 1/2 In., Pair 373.00
Torchere, Tin Body, Paneled Geometric Framing, 6 Glass Panels, 19th Century 575.00
Torchere, Tole, Gilt, 40 In., Pair 275.00
Whale Oil, Milk Glass, Ribbed Tapered Conical Font, Pedestal Base, 8 1/2 In. 295.00
Whale Oil, Ostrander & Norris, Pewter, Saucer Base, American, 1848-1850, 5 In. 385.00
Whale Oil, Peg, Petticoat, 3 Tubes, Japanning, 4 1/2 In. 60.00
Whale Oil, Peg, Spherical, Pewter Collar, Tin, 4 1/2 In. 143.00
Whale Oil, Pewter, Turned Baluster Standards, Saucer Bases, Mid 1800s, 10 1/2 In., Pair .   518.00
Whale Oil, Replacement Burner, Paneled Font, Sandwich Glass, 11 x 4 1/2 In. 135.00
Whale Oil, Tin, Acorn Font, Whale Oil Burner, Old Black Paint, 5 1/4 In. 110.00
Whale Oil, White Opaque, Lotus Flower Stem, Brass Collar, 8 1/2 In. 990.00

LANTERNS are a special type of lighting device. They have a light
source, usually a candle, totally hidden inside the walls of the lantern.
Light is seen through holes or glass sections.

Barn, Hardwood, Dark Finish, Wooden Nuts, Posts, Handle, 10 1/4 In. 330.00
Barn, Pine, Natural, Tin, Glass, Wire Handle, 12 In. 275.00
Barn, Tin, Painted, Glass Panels, Wire & Wood Handle, Hanging Loop, Triangular, 19 In.   345.00
Brass, 4 Sides, Hinged Font, Whale Oil Burner, 9 1/4 In. 110.00
Brass, Female Heads & Medallions Joined By Beads, Tassels, Regency, 27 x 17 In. 2300.00
Brass, George III, Brass, Smoke Bell, Bead Hung Corona, 32 In., Pair 2760.00
Brass, Multi-Piece Construction, Vented Top, Marked, Made In U.S.A., 12 In. 120.00
Brass, Original Mica Windows, Ring, 19th Century, 6 3/4 In. 295.00
Brass Bezel, Ventilator & Fixtures, Smoke Bell, c.1830, 14 x 9 1/2 In. 1098.00
Candle, Crystal Pressed Glass, Removable Base, Candle Socket, 11 In. 275.00
Candle, Folding, Brown Japanning, Mica Windows, Folding, Jan. 21, 1865, 5 In. 110.00
Candle, Greek Key Band Above Anthemion, Floral, Leaf Design, Gilt, Bronze, 9 In. 935.00
Candle, Hanging, Copper & Glass, Octagonal, Open Crown Top, Ring Handle, 18 In. 175.00
Candle, Hanging, Tin, Conical Top, Loop Handle, 3 Glass Panels, 19th Century, 15 In. . . .   373.00
Candle, Nozzles Over Hexagonal Body, Faceted Glass Panels, Metal, 1870s, 41 In. 6900.00
Candle, Tin Cage, Square, 12 3/4 In. 230.00
Candle, Tin, 4 Glass Sides, Pyramidal Top, Gold Japanning Traces, Ring, 12 In. 135.00
Carriage, Sheet Iron, Beveled Glass Door, Black Paint, 19th Century, 20 In., Pair 880.00
Christopher Collins Mfg., Iron, Candle, 8 Glass Panels, Folding, Birmingham 145.00
Coach, Brass, 2-Tiered Canopies, Eagle On Top, Pair 55.00
Coleman, Chrome Fuel Tank & Lid, Micah Lens, Bail Handle, 14 In. 120.00
Coleman, Enameled Top, Chrome Base, Pyrex Globe, Dark Green, 1929 . . . .   65.00
Coleman, Hanging, Clear Globe, Green Painted Top, 15 In. 55.00
Coleman, Kerosene, Fuel Tank Base, Stainless, 14 x 6 In. . . . . .70.00 to 180.00
Coleman, Model 200A, Red, Metal, Wire & Wood Handle, Glass Globe, 12 In. . . . .90.00 to 120.00
Coleman, Model 228E, Steel, Green Painted Tank & Lid, Pyrex Globe, 15 In. 39.00
Coleman, Model No. 220F, Hanging, Enameled Top 29.00
Coleman, Single Burner, Glass, Metal, Red, Removable Handle, Sticker, 12 1/2 In. 65.00
Coleman, Standard, Green Metal Base, Porcelain Top, Bail Handle, 1959 . . . .   49.00
Colored Glass Cutouts, Glass & Metal, 30 1/4 In., Pair 557.00
Copper, Hanging, Hammered, Cutout Hearts, Milk Glass Shade, Gustav Stickley, 9 In. . . .   2530.00
Copper, Japan, Late 19th Century, 4 1/2 In. 88.00
Dietz, Skating, Dietz Wonder Jr. 95.00
Double Candle, Flowers, Circles, Pierced, Domed, Glass Panels, Tin, 15 x 11 x 5 1/2 In. .   546.00
Driving, Side Brackets, Headlight, Beveled Glass, Red Lens, 10 1/2 In., Pair 40.00
Ferguson, Sportsman's, Tin, Nickel Plated Brass, Leather Strap, Patent 1848, 8 1/2 In. . . .   55.00
G.E. Smith, Hand, Brass, Glass, Round Handle, 19th Century, 13 In. 470.00
Garden, Baroque, Wrought Iron, 96 In. 3300.00
Gilt Bronze, Regency, Cast Foliate Scroll Frame, Octagonal, 32 1/2 x 17 In. 1255.00
Gilt Metal, 4 Arched Supports, Bowed Glass Panels, Leaf Tip Molding, 30 In. 3450.00
Gustav Stickley, Hanging, Copper, Hammered, 4 Yellow Panels, Ceiling Plate, 7 In. 2530.00
Gustav Stickley, Iron, Heart Cutouts, Yellow Glass, Hanging, 13 In. 1925.00
H. & J. Sangster, Tin, Pierced, Vertical Ribbed Globe, Patent June 1851, 10 In. 690.00
Hall, Amber Glass, Smoke Bell, Pressed Metal Collar, Griffin Hooks, 14 x 10 1/2 In. 825.00

Hall, Cut Glass, Cylindrical, Prisms, Floral Corona, Electrified, 1875-1900, 36 In. 880.00
Hall, Patinated Metal, Floral Etched Glass Shade, Clear Smoke Bell, 10 x 9 1/2 In. 495.00
Hall, Pierced Rim, 4 Ram's Heads Suspended By Link Chain, Brass Mounted, 30 In. 2640.00
Hall, Tin, Glass Panes, 8 Sides, Hanging, 32 In., Pair 1650.00
Hall, Tole Peinte, Compressed Shape, Leafy Scroll Brackets, Electrified, 27 In. 605.00
Hand, Window Shield, Riveted Cowl, Sheet Brass, 1750s, 6 3/4 In. 1800.00
Hanging, 4-Light, Louis XV Style, Gilt Bronze, Glass Panels, Round, 34 In. 8625.00
Hanging, 6 Sides, Giltwood, Dragon Heads, Silk Panels On Glass, China, c.1900, 32 In. ... 1540.00
Hanging, Arts & Crafts, 4-Sides, Yellow & White Slag Glass Panels, 13 x 8 In. 880.00
Hanging, Brass, Louis XVI, 4 Glass Panels, Foliate Scrolled Supports, 29 In., Pair 5060.00
Hanging, Bronze, Napoleon III, Gilt, Goats' Heads Suspending Garlands, 26 In. 3680.00
Hanging, Glass, Edwardian, Bronze Mounted, Leaf Form Bracket Frame, 24 In., Pair 4140.00
Holmes, Booth & Haydens, Tin, Barrel Globe, Conical Top, Ring Handle, 3 1/2 In. 345.00
N.E. Glass Co., Tin, Punched Star & Diamond, Paneled Glass Globe, Ring, 13 In. 355.00
P.M. More, Punched Tin Revere Type, Star & Diamond, Ring Handle, 13 1/4 In. 632.00
Pierced Corona, Grapevine & Wheat Sheaths, Pinecone Finial, Metal, 42 1/2 In. 2300.00
Port, Copper, Brass, 20 In. 1430.00
Pyard, Candle, Brass, Narrow Cylindrical Glass, Pierced Frame, Paris, 12 1/2 In., Pair ... 210.00
Shoulder, Glass Lens, Angled Construction, Conforming Base, Tin, Wire Handles, 6 In. .. 230.00
Tin, 4 Trapezoid Glass Sides, Square Base, Hinged Handle, Oil Well, 13 In. 175.00
Tin, Candle, 4 Glass Panels, Handle, 13 In. 130.00
Tin, Candle, 6 Glass Panes, Conical Top, Air Vents, Ring Handle, 9 1/4 In. 300.00
Tin, Candle, Carrying Handle, Leaf Form Vent Smoke Deflector, 9 1/2 In. 240.00
Tin, Candle, Wire Cage, Rectangular, Match Safe Attached Back, 11 In. 175.00
Tin, Fluid, Filigreed, Hanging, 8 In. 75.00
Tin, Onion, Bulbous Glass Shade, Star & Diamond Pierced, Loop Handle, 12 In. 630.00
Tin, Pale Amethyst Glass Shade, 22 In. 125.00
Tin, Pierced, Beehive Pear Shaped Globe, Brass Top, Painted, Ring Handle, 11 1/2 In. 460.00
Tin, Pierced, Bulging Lighthouse Form, Glass Globe, Paint, Handle, 19th Century, 11 In. . 575.00
Tin, Pierced, Conical Top, Loop Handle, Hinged Door, Hasp, 17 In. 145.00
Tin, Pierced, Onion Globe, Ring Handle, Mid 19th Century, 14 In. 635.00
Tin, Pierced, Red Ribbed Swirl Globe, Ring Handle, Painted, 12 In. 175.00
Tin, Punched, Coned Top, Loop Handle, Cylindrical, 13 In. 275.00
Wrought Iron, Arts & Crafts, Cone Top, Riveted, No Glass, 10 In. 25.00

LE VERRE FRANCAIS is one of the many types of cameo glass made in
France. The glass was made by the C. Schneider factory in Epinay-sur-
Seine from 1920 to 1933. It is a mottled glass, usually decorated with
floral designs, and bears the incised signature *Le Verre Francais*.

Bowl, Pendant Berries, Rectangular Flowers, Yellow, Orange, Cameo, 11 In. 1380.00
Night-Light, Stylized Fuchsia Blossoms, White, Blue, Gray, 1925, 6 In. 920.00
Pitcher, Overlapping Grapes, Yellow, Orange, Angular Loop Handle, 15 In. 1380.00
Pitcher, Stylized Blossoms, Fan Shape Leaves, Strap Handle, 8 In. 1150.00
Vase, 3 Orchids, Red Orange, Purple, Brown, Gray, Cameo, 1927, 15 In. 1725.00
Vase, 3 Stylized Leaves, Yellow, Pink, Purple, Gray, 1925, 14 In. 805.00
Vase, 4 Pendant Clusters Of Leaves, Berries, Purple, Lavender, Gray, 17 In. 1725.00
Vase, Baluster, Smoky Topaz, Etched Leaf Band, c.1925, 14 In. 980.00
Vase, Butterflies Above Honeycomb Border, Turquoise, Gray, 11 In. 1380.00
Vase, Clusters Of Berries On Vines, Red, Yellow, Purple, Brown, 17 In. 2070.00
Vase, Clusters Of Flower Heads, Stylized Leaf Border, White, Light Blue, 10 In. 1380.00
Vase, Clusters Of Stylized Leafy Flowers, 2 Loop Handles, Red, Yellow, 15 In. 2185.00
Vase, Cobalt, Orange Fuchsia, Leaf Border, Turquoise, Yellow, Gray, 5 In. 690.00
Vase, Concentric Arches, Purple Foot, Squat, Cameo, 1930, 9 In. 1150.00
Vase, Etched Stylized Flowers, Blue Ground, Signed, 11 1/4 In. 1100.00
Vase, Flying Geese, Grassy Field, Brown, Cobalt, Yellow, Cameo, 11 In. 1610.00
Vase, Geometric Arches, Arcs, Blue, Purple, Cameo, 1930, 12 In. 7760.00
Vase, Pink Roses, Green Leaves, Cameo, 5 1/2 In. 500.00
Vase, Purple Festoons, Purple Flared Lip, Yellow, Green, 1925, 10 1/2 In. 1035.00
Vase, Stylized Clusters Of Flower Heads, Brickwork Border, 1931, 6 In. 1090.00
Vase, Stylized Clusters Of Flower Heads, Purple, White, Light Blue, 15 In. 1380.00
Vase, Stylized Flowers, Tendrils Of Berries, Brickwork Border, 1925, 19 In. 2185.00
Vase, Stylized Palm Trees, Gray Mottled, Pale Yellow, Blue, Orange, 25 In. 4600.00
Vase, Stylized Poppies, Orange, Purple Spots, Yellow Glass, 1925, 20 In. 2300.00

Vase, Stylized Vines, Dark Purple Circular Foot, 1925, 11 1/4 In.	805.00
Vase, Tortoise Colored Floral, Yellow & Orange Ground, 14 3/4 In.	1265.00
Vase, Tulip Shape, Art Deco Pattern, 18 In.	1300.00
Vase, Twisted Ribbons, Honeycomb Border, Purple, Gray, 15 In.	2300.00
Vase, Twisted Ribbons, Honeycomb Border, White, Gray, 11 In.	1150.00

LEATHER is tanned animal hide and it has been used to make decorative and useful objects for centuries. Leather objects must be carefully preserved with proper humidity and oiling or the leather will deteriorate and crack. This damage cannot be repaired.

Album, Photograph, Swiss, 3-In. Cylinder	11.00
Belt, Hand Tooled, Western, With Holster, 1940s, 43 In.	429.00
Boots, Blue, Aqua Feather Fan, Silk Handle, Green Lidded Box, 1875, 2 1/2 In.	660.00
Case, Scissors, Stamped Floral & Name I. Hewod, Continental, 5 In.	140.00
Casket, Brass Tacking, 19th Century	330.00
Ewer, Blackjack, Original Tar Lining Remnants, England, 1750, 14 1/2 In.	185.00
Gauntlets, Cowgirl, Beaded, Fringed, Flower Lining, 101 Ranch, Worn, 10 1/2 In.	424.00
Gauntlets, Doc Carver, Red Stars On Forehand, Fringe, Given To Charles Nordine, 1927 .	3390.00
Gauntlets, Flower & Fruit Motif, Glass Beads, Fringe, Lining, 7 1/2 x 14 In.	452.00
Gauntlets, Glass Beads, Flower Motif, Fringe, Lining, 7 x 14 1/2 In.	452.00
Gauntlets, Horseshoe Design, Embroidered, Fringe, Metal Buttons, Very Large	339.00
Holster, Gun, Heavy Brown Leather, Narrow Flap, Large Belt Loop, 1878	115.00
Holster, Hand Made, Open Top Pouch, 12 1/8 In., Pair	385.00
Humidor, Cigar, Cedar Lined, Brass Buckle, 9 1/2 x 8 x 3 3/4 In.	325.00
Rayeta, Western, Rawhide, 3-Plat Braided, 1940s	55.00
Rifle Case, Model 70-Type Rifle, Brass Strap Holders, H.H. Heiser, Colo. 839, 47 In.	220.00
Saddle, Cavalry, Spanish American War, Black, 1896	1450.00
Saddle, McClellan, Black, 1896	1450.00
Saddle, Parade, Western, Nickel & Brass Studs, 1940s	605.00
Saddle, Tooled, Floral Design, S.D. Myres, El Paso Tex., 3-In. Saddle Horn	1413.00
Saddle, Western, Black, Miles City Saddlery Co., Miles City, Mont., 1900s-1920s	385.00
Saddle, Western, Tooled, Whirling Log Design, 1930s-1940s	550.00
Saddle, Western, Tooled, Whirling Log Design, 1930s-1940s, 15-In. Seat	250.00
Saddle Bags, McClellan, Dyed Black	450.00
Tie Holder, Taft, Cal., Shield Design, Poem, Metal Holder, 1930s, Wall, 11 x 3 1/2 In.	18.00
Vest, Bow Tie, Dot Lind's, Fringe, Leather Strap Buttons, 18 x 15 1/2 In.	339.00
Writing Kit, Pressed Board, 3 Quill Pens, Ink Bottle, Marbled Paper, 1750	950.00

LEEDS pottery was made at Leeds, Yorkshire, England, from 1774 to 1878. Most Leeds ware was not marked. Early Leeds pieces had distinctive twisted handles with a greenish glaze on part of the creamy ware. Later ware often had blue borders on the creamy pottery. A Chicago company named Leeds made many Disney-inspired figurines. They are listed in the Disneyana category.

LEEDS POTTERY.

Basket, Undertray, Cobalt Blue Design, Basket Weave To Bottom, 8 1/4 x 10 In.	1200.00
Bowl, Soft Paste, Grape Cluster Band Design, 8 1/2 In.	240.00
Charger, Allover Floral & Leaf, Scalloped Blue Border, 13 1/2 In.	1320.00
Charger, Peafowl, Blue Sky, Scalloped Blue Border, 13 1/4 In.	1980.00
Coffeepot, Dome Lid, Blue Floral Sprays, White Ribbed, Border, Baluster, 10 In.	935.00
Coffeepot, Sprays Of Flowers Within Looped Swags Of Laurel, c.1780, 9 1/2 In.	2875.00
Cup & Saucer, Flower Basket	385.00
Cup & Saucer, Peafowl, Handleless, Blue & Yellow Rim	605.00
Cup & Saucer, Yellow & Orange Floral	165.00
Cup Plate, Floral, 3 In.	275.00
Mug, Yellow, Orange & Blue Floral Sprays, 6 In.	415.00
Pitcher, Allover Floral & Green Vine, Yellow Rim, 19th Century, 19th Century, 9 In.	990.00
Pitcher, Blue Band, Ocher & Blue Leaves, 5 In.	305.00
Pitcher, Trailing Orange & Blue Flowers, Green Leaves, 5 3/4 In.	605.00
Pitcher, Yellow Border, Blue, Green & Orange Sprigs, 6 In.	385.00
Plate, Brown, Yellow, Orange Sprigs, Scrolled Border, 7 In., 6 Piece	355.00
Plate, Double Pansy, Green Fishscale Border, 8 In.	550.00
Plate, Eagle & Shield, Green Feathered Edge, Scalloped, 8 In.	770.00
Plate, Eagle, Blue Scalloped Border, 6 1/4 In.	1210.00

Plate, Eagle, Blue Scalloped Border, 10 In. 1980.00
Plate, Floral, 10 In. 825.00
Plate, Oriental House & Green Trees, 10 In. 275.00
Plate, Peafowl, Blue Border, Octagonal, 9 In. 935.00
Plate, Peafowl, Feather Edge, 8 In. 795.00
Plate, Peafowl, Green Branch, 9 1/2 In. 1320.00
Plate, Peafowl, Green Scalloped Border, 8 In. 715.00
Plate, Pineapple, Green Border, 6 1/4 In. 385.00
Sugar, Cover, Blue & Orange Swags & Leaves, 4 1/2 In. 495.00
Sugar, Cover, Blue Swags, Orange Leaves, 4 1/2 In. 330.00
Sugar, Cover, Peafowl, 4 1/2 In. 495.00
Sugar, Peafowl, Blue Feather Edges, 6 1/2 In. 1595.00
Tea Set, Miniature, 3 Piece 2750.00
Teapot, Allover Orange Floral Sprays, Round, Scalloped Rim, 6 1/4 In. 660.00

LEFTON is a mark found on pottery, porcelain, glass, and other wares imported by the Geo. Zoltan Lefton Company. The company began in 1940 and is still in business. The company mark has changed through the years; but because marks have been used for long periods of time, they are of little help in dating an object.

Ashtray, No. 616 .... 2.00
Bank, All American Football Player 65.00
Bank, Hubert The Lion 25.00
Bowl, Holly, Oval, Footed, 9 In. 42.00
Bust, Brahms, No. 1161 .... 25.00
Coffeepot, Eastern Star, Cover 75.00
Cookie Jar, Miss Priss, No. 1502 .... 85.00
Cookie Jar, Mr. Toodles 325.00
Cookie Jar, Rustic Daisy 60.00
Creamer, Cow 32.00
Cup & Saucer, Pink Roses, Green Ground, 3-Footed Cup, 1964 .... 30.00
Dish, Shell, No. 6 .... 25.00
Egg, Musical, Hand Painted, 3 Cherubs, Wind Beneath My Wings, 5 3/4 In. 25.00
Eggcup, Bluebird, No. 282 .... 35.00
Figurine, Angel, Musical Instrument, No. 8192 .... 20.00
Figurine, Bride & Groom, Christopher Collection, 1982, Pair 20.00
Figurine, Golfer, Kneeling On Base, 6 In. 48.00
Figurine, Guardian Angel & Children, Box, 1985, 6 3/4 In. ....35.00 to 40.00
Figurine, Madonna, No. 433 .... 30.00
Figurine, Napoleon, On Horse, No. 4908, 11 In. 300.00
Figurine, Owl, No. 121, 4 1/2 In. 20.00
Gravy Boat, No. 5649 .... 30.00
Head Vase, Green Checkered Hat, Bow, 5 In. 50.00
Jam Jar, Applied Fruit, 5 In. 30.00
Mug, White Holly, No. 6066, 6 Piece 40.00
Pincushion, Mouse, No. 542, 3 1/2 In. 15.00
Planter, Dancing Leaves, No. 7884 .... 20.00
Planter, Lady, No. 10 .... 30.00
Plaque, Floral, 7 In. 50.00
Plaque, Four Seasons, No. 4927, 4 Piece 50.00
Relish, Holly, 3 Sections, Triangular 30.00
Relish, Violets 18.00
Ring Holder, Hand 12.00
Shaker, Owl, No. 30145, 3 1/2 In. 20.00
Tidbit, Holly, Candy Cane Edge 25.00
Wall Pocket, Dainty Miss, No. 6767 .... 45.00
Wall Pocket, Honey Bee, No. 1527 .... 35.00

LEGRAS was founded in 1864 by Auguste Legras at St. Denis, France. It is best known for cameo glass and enamel-decorated glass with Art Nouveau designs. Legras merged with Pantin in 1920 and became the Verreries et Cristalleries de St. Denis et de Pantin Reunies.

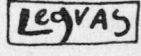

Basket, French Tigre, Mosaic, Cranberry, Cream, Gold Spatter, Ruffled Edge, 7 1/2 In. .. 185.00

Bowl, Swag & Drapery, Olive Green, Etched, 1925, 3 3/4 x 10 In. 805.00
Lamp, Desk, Winter Scene Shade, Brass, Signed, 20 In. 700.00
Lamp, Winter Scene At Sunset, Pierced Wood Base, Signed, 13 1/2 In., Pair 1495.00
Rose Bowl, Blackberry & Leaves, Enameled, Red Over Honey, 6 1/2 In. 168.00
Vase, Apple Blossoms, Gray, Citrine Over Powder Blue, Signed, 13 3/4 In. 2016.00
Vase, Birds In A Forest, Deep Red Over Blue, 7 In. 546.00
Vase, Dark Fuchsia Ivy, Pinched, Waisted, 1920, 5 5/8 In. 345.00
Vase, Enameled Leaves, Baluster, Gray Infused With Yellow, Signed, 14 1/2 In. 460.00
Vase, Flower Stem, Leaves, Mauve Over Frost, Cameo, 12 1/2 In. 1155.00
Vase, Green & Brown Oak Leaves, Thistles, Internal Facets, Signed, c.1900, 7 1/4 In. 460.00
Vase, Landscape, Tree & Lake, Cameo, Marked, 8 1/2 In. 500.00
Vase, Landscape, Trees Along River, Enameled, Signed, 4 In. 440.00
Vase, Leaves & Spidery Flower, Amber Handles, Cameo, 11 In. 990.00
Vase, Winter Scene At Sunset, Inverted Ruffled Edge, Signed, 5 1/2 In. 488.00
Vase, Winter Scene, Bare Trees In Snow At Sunset, Yellow, Orange, Brown, 5 In. 405.00

LENOX is the name of a porcelain maker. Walter Scott Lenox and Jonathan Cox founded the Ceramic Art Company in Trenton, New Jersey, in 1889. In 1906, Lenox left and started his own company called *Lenox*. The company makes a porcelain that is similar to Irish Belleek. The marks used by the firm have changed through the years and collectors prefer the earlier examples. Related pieces may also be listed in the Ceramic Art Co. category.

Cigarette Set, Container & 2 Ashtrays, White, Leaf Finial, Green Mark, 3 Piece 65.00
Lamp, Art Deco Style, Gilt White Base, Brass Feet, Laced Vellum Shade, 31 In., Pair 66.00
Lamp Base, Griffin & Urn, White & Blue Glazes, 11 In, Pair 165.00
Paperweight, Bust Of Young Woman, Bisque, Art Deco, Green Decal, 4 1/2 x 4 In. 121.00
Pitcher, White, 1906 .... 225.00
Plate, Lace Gold On Rose Design, 10 1/2 In., 11 Piece 603.00
Stein, Golf, 1/2 Liter 1540.00
Sugar & Creamer, Cover, Molded Leaves & Gold Marks, c.1960, 6 In. 115.00
Toby Jug, William Penn 250.00
Vase, Bud, Ivory, Sculptured Roses, Gold Trim, 7 1/2 In. 30.00
Vase, Sky Blue, White Interior, Alternating Vine & Ribbed Panels, Green Mark, 7 In. 125.00
Vase, White, Gold Bands, 9 In. 50.00

LETTER OPENERS have been used since the eighteenth century. Ivory and silver were favored by the well-to-do. In the late nineteenth century, the letter opener was popular as an advertising giveaway and many were made of metal or celluloid. Brass openers with figural handles were also popular.

Alligator, Double Handle 18.00
Alligator, Ivory 30.00
Aluminum Cooking Co., Wearever 8.00
Art Nouveau Woman, Celluloid, Applied Brass, 1900s, 6 1/2 In. 70.00
Bust Of Lady With Hat, Brass, Pedestal 44.00
Caduceus, Nickel Plated, 9 In. 2.00
Electrolux, Enamel On Chrome, 3 3/4 In. 65.00
Little Rock Bottling, Co., Silver, 7 1/2 In. 247.00
Mother-Of-Pearl, Sterling Silver Handle, 5 1/4 In. 20.00
Napoleon, Bust, Round Handle, Ruler Markings On Blade, Nickel, Italy, 9 In. 28.00
Nude, On Tiptoes, Ace Plastics, Akron, Ohio, 1940s, 11 In., Pair 24.00
Pinup Girl, Nude Woman, Plastic, Hanlon-Snitz & Co., Mo., 8 1/2 In. 46.00
Sleeping Luzern Lion On Handle, Flowers On Reverse, Ivory, 12 In. 190.00
Sterling Salt Co., Cow's Head Moves 5.00
Sword, Sterling Silver, Edinburgh, 1890, 6 In. 575.00
Universal Steamship Co., Detroit, Mi., Brass 7.00
Victor, Metal 5.00
Whale Shape Handle, Brass, Engraved, 9 In. 45.00
Whalebone, 10 1/2 In. 60.00
Wisconsin Lumber, Red Plastic, Magnifying Glass Center 5.00

Spray a glass flower vase with nonstick food spray. It will keep the water from staining the glass.

Libbey, Vase, Harvard, Amethyst To Clear, 20 In.

LIBBEY Glass Company has made many types of glass since 1888, including the cut glass and tablewares that are collected today. The stemwares of the 1930s and 1940s are once again in style. The Toledo, Ohio, firm was purchased by Owens-Illinois in 1935 and is still working under the name *Libbey* as a division of that company. Additional pieces may be listed under Amberina, Cut Glass, and Maize.

Basket, 4 Intaglio Cut Flowers, Leaves, Bull's-Eye Separators, Signed, 12 1/2 x 8 In.	995.00
Basket, Amberina, Marked, 8 In.	1600.00
Bowl, Amberina, 3-Footed, Marked, 6 In.	400.00
Bowl, Amberina, Footed, Marked, 3 1/2 x 7 1/2 In.	350.00
Bowl, Amberina, Low, Marked, 7 In., Pair	325.00
Bowl, Amberina, Rolled Rim, Footed, Marked, 8 1/2 In.	900.00
Bowl, Diamond & Fine Cut, Signed, 9 In.	180.00
Bowl, Ellsmere, 4 x 9 In.	1500.00
Bowl, Glenda, Signed, 8 In.	450.00
Bowl, Kenmore, Signed, 8 In.	250.00
Bread Tray, Anita, 8 x 12 In.	535.00
Candlestick, 24-Point Rayed Base, Teardrop Stem, 8 In.	185.00
Celery, Wedgemere, Rolled Rim, 5 1/2 x 11 1/2 In.	960.00
Cocktail, Crow, Pair	15.00
Compote, Colona, Footed, 8 x 7 In.	195.00
Console Set, Shallow Bowl, Art Deco, 3 3/4 In., 5 Piece	287.00
Nappy, Glenda, 5 In.	250.00
Perfume Bottle, Amberina, Signed	2300.00
Plate, Ellsmere, Signed, 7 In.	650.00
Plate, Kenmore, 7 In.	500.00
Punch Bowl, Colonna, Signed, 14 In.	2450.00
Sherbet, Underplate, Amberina, Signed, 8 1/2-In. Plate	975.00
Tray, Harvard, 8 1/2 x 13 1/2 In.	395.00
Tray, Spillane, Signed, 12 In.	1295.00
Vase, Amberina, Engraved Floral, Notched Neck, Marked, 16 In.	2600.00
Vase, Amberina, Mushroom Top, Marked, 4 x 6 In.	600.00
Vase, Amberina, Pinched Neck, Marked, 6 In.	500.00
Vase, Flower, Amberina, Marked, 7 1/2 In.	900.00
Vase, Harvard, Amethyst To Clear, 20 In. . . . . *Illus*	3400.00
Vase, Lily, Amberina, Marked, 11 1/2 In.	550.00
Vase, Trumpet, Amberina, Marked, 11 In.	1400.00
Water Set, Flute, 1906-1923 Mark, 9-In. Pitcher, 5 Piece	775.00

LIGHTERS for cigarettes and cigars are collectible. Cigarettes became popular in the late nineteenth century, and with the cigarette came matches and cigarette lighters. All types of lighters are collected, from solid gold to the first of the recent disposable lighters. Most examples found were made after 1940. Some lighters may be found in the Jewelry category in this book.

13th Air Force Patch Design, Brushed Nickel Finish, Korean War	20.00
Alaskan Command, Engraved Mountains, Silver, 1961	21.00

Aluminum, Lift Arm, Engraved, Cairo, Egypt, Palm Trees, Pyramids, Souvenir, 2 In. 20.00
Anson, Engraved Leaves At Lower Right, Silvertone, 1 1/4 In. 234.00
ATC, Letter Opener Shape, Brown Leather Wrapped Handle, 9 1/2 x 5 1/2 In. 35.00
Atlantic Imperial Oil Co., Key Wind Music Box, Cream Panel, Brass 20.00
Barcroft, Brushed Finish, Plain Case, Black Felt Pad, 1979, 3 1/4 In. 82.00
Beattie, Jet, Nickel Plated, 2 1/4 In. 25.00
Beer Can, Budweiser, Red, White, Blue, Steel, 6 In. 21.00
Bowers, Missouri, Silver Disc, Japan 60.00
Bowers, Wind Pocket, Brass Cylinder, Trench Style, 2 3/4 In. 43.00
Camel, Cool! Mild!, 1940s Pinup Girl 35.00
Chrome Lift Arm, Textured Side Panels, England, 1 3/4 x 1 1/4 In. 22.00
Cigar, Bust Of Victorian Woman, Pewter, Marble Base, Patent 1873, 12 In. 650.00
Cigar, Domed Center Font, 2 Copper Tubes, Brass, Metal Base, Square, 4 3/4 In. 120.00
Cigar, Dragon, Long Tail, Silver, Horn, W & H, England, 19th Century, 21 1/2 In. 1380.00
Cigar, Duralectric, Tin Base, Porcelain Connector At Back, 40 Watt, 10 x 5 In. 137.00
Cigar, E.L. Gelmelo Cigars, With Nipper, Cast Metal, 19th Century, 6 x 5 x 11 In. 920.00
Cigar, Eisenlohr's Cigars, 15 x 7 In. 2195.00
Cigar, Eldred Mfg. Co., Wireless, No. 12, Brass Swing Arm, Wooden Case, 15 In. 250.00
Cigar, Flor De Melba, Cigar Supreme, Reverse Glass, 3 3/4 In. 500.00
Cigar, Jester, Cigar In Mouth, Brass, Wall Mount, 19th Century, 10 x 5 In. 230.00
Cigar, Lamp, Blue Globe, 2 Wicks, Brass, 11 1/2 In. 750.00
Cigar, Locomotive Shape, Early 19th Century, 8 3/4 x 7 1/2 In. 115.00
Cigar, Man, Hand In Vest, Figural, Pot Metal, Black Paint, 19th Century, 4 1/2 In. 520.00
Cigar, Midland, Jump Spark, Push Handle To Ignite Wick, 15 x 7 1/2 In. 395.00
Cigar, Woodward Cahoone Mfg., Punch Type, Pot Metal, 19th Century, 4 1/4 In. 290.00
Clearfloat, Golfer In Sand Trap, Acrylic Base, Brass Insert, 3 3/4 In. 35.00
Consolidated Razor Blade Co., Aluminum, Blue Metallic Paint, Zippo Style, 1940s 41.00
Derringer Shape, Gas, White Metal, Japan, Box, 6 In., 3 Piece 22.00
Desilu 1960, Golf Tournament Giveaway, Zippo Style, Brushed Finish, Japan, 1960 . . . . .   60.00
Diplomat, Chromed Brass Lift Arm, M.E. Bernhardt Co., N.Y., 2 x 1/2 In. 35.00
Dunhill, Engine Turned Design, Gold Outer Jacket, 14K Gold 350.00
Dunhill, Rolalite Style, Silver, Engraved Dragon, Shanghai 50.00
Dunhill, Sterling Silver, Engine Turned Line Design, Red, Black Box, 2 In. 275.00
Dunhill, Sterling Silver, Engine Turned Vertical Design, Switzerland, 2 1/16 In. 418.00
Dupont, Gas, Gold Plated, Brushed Finish, France 75.00
Electro Match Korex Co., Black, Gold Trim, Battery Operated 35.00
Elgin, Engine Turned Line Design, Sterling Silver 45.00
Elgin, Goldtone, 3 Mother Of Pearl Panels, Box, 2 1/4 In. 20.00
Elizabeth Ames Of N.Y., Gold, Mother-Of-Pearl, Inlaid Sides, Leatherette Case, 2 In. 45.00
Engraved Map Of Newfoundland On Side, Towns Highlighted, 3 x 2 3/4 x 1 In. 32.00
Evans, Art Deco Design, Blue French Enamel Paint, Case, 1930, 4 1/2 x 2 1/2 In. 52.00
Evans, Black, White, Red Vinyl Wrap, Brass, 1/2 In. 30.00
Evans, Cornucopia, Brass Tone, Felt Pad On Base, Table, Box, 5 1/4 In. 20.00
Evans, Table, Mobilgas Pegasus Logo, Clear Acrylic Base, 3 1/4 In. 60.00
Evans, Watch In Cover, Engine Turned Line Design, 1940, 6 3/4 x 3 1/4 In. 125.00
Eveready, Chromed Flat Trench Style, 2 1/2 In. 25.00
Fire Fly Lighter, Original Box, 1940, 9 1/2 In. 330.00
Fireplace, Arts & Crafts, Brass, Hammered, Starter & Tray, Pat. May 2nd, 1916 . . . .   340.00
Flambeau, Bullet Shape, Tip Lifting, Red Enamel Painted Lines, Baron, 3 3/4 In. 25.00
Franklin, Aluminum, 1954, 3 1/2 x 2 1/4 In. 32.00
Gulf-Smith Oil Service, 2 In. 85.00
Hand Tooled Design, 800 Silver Case . . . . .36.00 to 60.00
Hand Tooled Design, Sterling Silver, Case, Mexico 52.00
Husky, Slimline, Japan, 2 In. 95.00
Ibelo, Engraved Map Of Germany With Cities Highlighted, West Germany, 1 3/4 In. 28.00
Imperial, Borden's Logo, Elsie The Borden's Cow, Flat, Polished Finish, Japan 55.00
Kraemer, Relief Elk Head & Clock, Nickel On Brass, Pat. Sept. 20, 1910 . . . .   55.00
Kreisler, Polished Top, Brushed Finish, 1 1/2 In. 22.00
Lift Arm, Muenchen, Kindl Figure, Nickel, Leatherette Wrap, Souvenir, 3 1/2 In. 25.00
Marathon, Nickel Lift Arm, Black, Rose, Green Enamel, 2 In. 28.00
Mother-Of-Pearl Inlay, Chrome On Brass Body, 2 x 1/2 In. 31.00
Motorcycle Boot Shape, Pot Metal, Tin Plated, Occupied Japan, 4 In. 30.00
Oasis Filter Cigarettes, Polished Finish, Blue, White Pack Logo, Oasis Filter On Sides . .   20.00

P & B Brand, Tobacco Can Shape, Nickel, 2 x 1/2 In. 25.00
Pacton, Sports, Brass Push-Together Ignition System, Brass 21.00
Park, West Vaco 1955 No-Accident 4 Year Award, Red, White, Green Enamel, Box 22.00
Park Sherman, World War II, Black Crinkle Paint 20.00
Playboy, Nickel Finish, White Lacquer Body, Black Bunny Head, 1960 .... 25.00
Regel, Nickel Lift Arm, Streamlined Cowling Design Over Lift Arm, Nickel, 2 x 1 1/2 In. 28.00
Regens, Squeeze Lever, Stainless Steel, Vertical Line Design, Instructions, Box 20.00
Reliable Pocket Lamp, Philadelphia, Nickel, Silver Plated Brass, Pat. 1890, 2 1/4 In. 135.00
Ronson, Accessory Kit, Brown, Gold Anodized Finish, Original Box 22.00
Ronson, Case, Brown Tortoise Enamel Painted Panels, Maroon Ronson Box, 4 x 2 In. ... 80.00
Ronson, Case, Brown Tortoise Enamel Painted Panels, Purple Pouch, 4 x 3 In. 69.00
Ronson, De-Light, Nickel Plate, Oval Monogram Shield, 1920 .... 30.00
Ronson, Decanter, Silver Plated, Felt On Base, Table, Gray Pouch, 4 1/2 In. 35.00
Ronson, Lady-Pact, Iris Flowers On Cover, Ivory Panels, Dureum Case, 1940, 3 1/4 In. ... 235.00
Ronson, Mastercase, Chrome, Art Deco 20.00
Ronson, Penciliter, 14K Gold Filled, Display Box, Cardboard Box, 1950s, 5 1/4 In. 40.00
Ronson, Penciliter, Mechanical Pencil, Original Case, 5 1/4 In. 41.00
Ronson, Pinup, Swimsuit Clad Pinup Girls On Sides, Penguin, Japan 20.00
Ronson, Queen Anne, Table Type 95.00
Ronson, Smart Set, Engraved RD, Black, White Enamel Polished Case 65.00
Ronson, Standard, Brown Alligator Style Leather Wrap 25.00
Ronson, Superlighter, Oldsmobile Logo, Polished Case, Brown Panel Wrap 25.00
Ronson, Table, Green Felt Pad On Base, Silver Plate, 1950, 3 1/4 In. 23.00
Ronson, Tortoise Enamel Painted Panels, 2-Tone Brown, 1930, 6 x 3 1/4 In. 70.00
Ronson, Venus, Frosted Brass Color, Silver Line Design, Cork Base, 3 x 2 In. 20.00
Ronson, Whirlwind Imperial, Crests Design On Side, World's Greatest Lighter Case 22.00
Ronson, Whirlwind, Helmet & Scroll, Wind Shield 20.00
Ronson, Windlite, Oldsmobile Rocket V-8 Emblem, Brushed Finish, 2 1/4 In. 21.00
Royal Case Lite, With Cigarette Case, Crisscross Design On Side Panels, 4 1/2 x 3 In. 26.00
Royal Crown Shape, RC Royal Crown Cola, Plastic, 2 3/4 In. 29.00
Sankei, TSS Festivale, Ocean Liner Shape, Red, Cream Enamel Paint, Original Box, 3 In. 34.00
Sarome Blue Bird, Automobile Shape, Gray, Cream Enamel, Metal, Japan 65.00
Scripto, Boston, Sailboats, Boston Cityscape 4.50
Scripto, Butane, Brass, Black Body, White Metal, Copper Floral Designs, Box, 2 1/4 In. . 20.00
Scripto, San Francisco, Cable Car 4.50
Scripto, Texas, Animated Chili Pepper Street Band 4.50
Scripto, Vu-Lighter, Football Players, Clear Body, 6 Black Bands, Chrome Lid 28.00
Scripto, Vu-Lighter, Poker Hand, Clear Plastic Body, Polished Lid, Blue Plastic Band ... 26.00
Scripto, Vu-Lighter, Wonderful K-Box Radio, Dallas, Black, White, 2 1/2 In. 27.00
Scripto, Washington, D.C., Jet Flies Past Capitol Building 4.50
St. George Slaying Dragon, Brass, 1 1/4 x 2 3/4 In. 87.00
Striker Pouch, Brass, Steel & Leather, Asia, Late 19th Century, 5 x 3 1/4 In. 105.00
Thailand, Relief Design, Native Dancers, Gods, Temples, Sterling Silver, Zippo Insert ... 25.00
Thorens, Automatic, Polished Finish, Multiple-Cylinder Base, 4 In. 45.00
Thorens, Engraved Flowers, Nickel Finish 53.00
Trench, AAF Winged Prop Device Affixed To Side, Brass Shell Casings, 3 1/2 In. 62.00
Trench, From World War II, English Half-Penny Affixed To Front & Back, Brass 40.00
Trench, Striking Wheel Affixed To Side, Brass, Cylinder, 2 In. 26.00
Vulcan, CSG Casting Sales Co., Blue Springs, Mo., Brushed Finish, Original Box 22.00
Wellington Windproof Cigarette Lighter, Original Plastic Case, 1955, 9 In. 132.00
Windy, Black Crackle Finish, The All Weather Lighter, Original Red, White Box 85.00
Winston Cigarettes Pack, Flat, Looking Like Winston Cigarettes, Red, White, 2 In. 20.00
World War I French Soldier Peeping Through Key Hole, Nude Woman, Brass 87.00
Zaima Cord, Tainan Taiwan NCO Open Mess, Brushed & Polished Finish, Box 20.00
Zippo, 106th Bombardment Wing, Red, Blue, Turquoise, White Enamel, 1955 .... 44.00
Zippo, 306th Bomb Group Headquarters, Red, Yellow, Blue Enamel, 1981 .... 30.00
Zippo, 1776, Bicentennial Scenes, Polished Finish, White & Gold Box 75.00
Zippo, Aircraft Carrier, USS Ranger CVA-61, Brushed Finish, 1973 .... 50.00
Zippo, Alfredo's '60, Brushed Finish, Red, White Enamel Paint, 1974 .... 30.00
Zippo, American LaFrance, Eagle, Brushed Finish, 1975 .... 47.00
Zippo, Amoco Ammar Oil Co., Marietta, Ohio, Red, White Enamel Paint, 1953 .... 28.00
Zippo, Archway, Brushed Finish, Red Enamel Engraved Logo, 1978 .... 35.00
Zippo, Army Air Corps Emblem Affixed, Steel Case, Brushed Finish, 1941 .... 280.00

Zippo, Bankers Trust Co., Blue Enamel Paint, Polished Finish, Slim, 1973 .... 40.00
Zippo, Barcroft, 2nd Model, Plain Case, Polished Finish, 1947, 4 1/4 In. .... .230.00 to 250.00
Zippo, Barcroft, 4th Model, Buick Foundry Housekeeping Award, Table, 3 1/4 In. 160.00
Zippo, Barcroft, 4th Model, USG, United States Gypsum, Safety 1965 .... 80.00
Zippo, Barcroft, U.S.S. Mattaponi, Ship, Southeast Asia Map, Brushed Steel 121.00
Zippo, Barry Goldwater, Box 65.00
Zippo, Black Crackle Finish, Steel Case, 3-Barrel Hinge, 1943-1945 ....155.00 to 210.00
Zippo, Black Matte Finish, Pot Metal 20.00
Zippo, Black, Red Enamel, Brushed Finish, 1964 ....,........ 30.00
Zippo, Blanchard Lumber Co., Walpole, Mass., Brushed Finish, 1969 .... 20.00
Zippo, BMA Affixed To 1 Side, White, Gold Slim Box, 1974 .... 28.00
Zippo, British Coins Affixed To Each Side, Polished Finish, 3-Barrel Hinge, 1945 ...... 125.00
Zippo, Brushed Finish, 3-Barrel Hinge, 1947 .... 54.00
Zippo, Camfield Logo, Brushed Finish, Blue Enamel, Box 70.00
Zippo, Circle Key Life Insurance Co., Tiger Of The Week, Brushed Finish, Box, 1969 ... 50.00
Zippo, Corinthian, Chalice, Turquoise, Ceramic, Polished Lid, Table, 1966, 4 In. 155.00
Zippo, Corvette, Red Enameled Car On Front, Silver Finish, Plastic Box 24.00
Zippo, Darby Builders, Polished Finish, 1961 .... 30.00
Zippo, Delivery Truck On Front, Friend Tire Service Inc., Red, Black, Turquoise Enamel . 25.00
Zippo, Diagonal Line Design, Brass Finish, Slim, Brass Finish, 1991 .... 20.00
Zippo, Diamond Reo, Red, Gray, Gold Enamel Paint, 1969 .... 30.00
Zippo, Dodge, Brushed Finish, 3-Barrel Hinge, Late 1940s 65.00
Zippo, Dog Sled Team, Alaska Beneath Team, Brushed Finish, 1972 .... 21.00
Zippo, Dr Pepper, Polished Finish, Red Enamel Logo, Slim, 1976 .... 120.00
Zippo, Duck Hunter, Brushed Finish, Enamel Paint, Striped Repair Box, 1959 .... 62.00
Zippo, Dumont, TV Set, Brushed Finish, Steel Case, Striped Box, 1953 .... 146.00
Zippo, Electronic Associates Incorporated On Side, Blue Enamel, Brushed Finish 38.00
Zippo, Engine Turned Line Design, Polished Finish, Striped Box, 1962 .... 40.00
Zippo, Engraved Face Of Man, Brushed Finish, 1950 .... 21.00
Zippo, Engraved Figure Of Man Trout Fishing, Brown, Blue, White, Pink Enamel, 1959 .. 28.00
Zippo, Engraved Man Figure Golfing, 6-Color Finish, Brushed Finish, 1988 .... 23.00
Zippo, Engraved Map Of Korea With Cities Highlighted, Korea 21.00
Zippo, Engraved Map Of USA & Train Engine, River Barge, Brushed Finish, 1967 ...... 30.00
Zippo, Enjoy Grapette Soda, Imitation Grape Flavor, Brushed Finish, 1962 .... 28.00
Zippo, ET East Texas Pulp & Paper Co., Green, Black Enamel, Brushed Finish, 1964 .... 21.00
Zippo, Fairbanks-Morse, Brushed Finish, Blue Logo, 1951 .... 80.00
Zippo, First National Bank, Kansas City Missouri, U.S. Eagle, Brushed Finish, 1973 .... 40.00
Zippo, Flo Air Ferrying Modifications Avionics, Wichita, Kansas, 67209, 1969 .... 30.00
Zippo, For Best Results Use Zippo Flints & Fluid, Engraved Yacht Club Flag, 1956 ..... 22.00
Zippo, Fort Greely, Kodiak, Alaska, 3/15/42, Brushed Finish, 4-Barrel Hinge 150.00
Zippo, France A Subsidiary Of Garlock, Blue, Black Enamel, Brushed Finish 28.00
Zippo, Galion Miles Ahead, Black, Gold Enamel Paint, Polished Finish, 1971 .... 42.00
Zippo, Gemini, May 22-June 21, Polished Finish, Slim, 1974 .... 35.00
Zippo, Goodall Rubber Co., 4-Leaf Clover Shape, Polished Finish, Slim, Box, 1962 .... 50.00
Zippo, Great Southern Life Ins Co. Founded 1909, Red, Black Enamel, Polished Finish .. 22.00
Zippo, Green Turtle At Lower Right Corner, Blue Denim Vinyl Side Panels, 1977 .... 45.00
Zippo, Grumman Intruder, Airplane, Engraved, Polished Finish, 1963 .... 39.00
Zippo, Gulf Research Center 1957, Brushed Finish, 1957 .... 40.00
Zippo, Hickory Charcoal Pellets, Brushed Finish, Steel Case, Striped Box, 1953 .... 60.00
Zippo, Honoring 100 Years Of Singer Sewing Machines, Brushed Finish, Box, 1950 ..... 88.00
Zippo, Into Whatsoever House I Shall Enter, Caduceus, Mortar & Pestle, 1962 .... 60.00
Zippo, John Deer Tractor, Green, Yellow Black, Polished Finish, 1963 .... 140.00
Zippo, Kansas-Nebraska Natural Gas Co., Brushed Finish, 1959 .... 70.00
Zippo, Kennecott Copper, Logo, Copper, Polished Finish, White & Gold Box, 1971 ..... 692.00
Zippo, Korean War, 1st Marine Division, Brushed Steel 25.00
Zippo, L & M Cigarettes, Looking Like L & M Cigarettes, White, Red, Japan 20.00
Zippo, Lady Bradford, Plain Case, Polished Finish, Table, 1950, 3 3/4 In. 200.00
Zippo, Liberty National Life Insurance Co., Statue Of Liberty, Brushed Finish, 1962 ..... 32.00
Zippo, Lighted Display Tower, Black Marbleized Plastic, Holds 20 Lighters, 23 In. 125.00
Zippo, Louis Frahm Pontiac Inc., Goldtone Logo, Polished Finish, 1963 .... 65.00
Zippo, Lowe's Of Winston-Salem 767-4950, Brushed Finish, 1976 .... 45.00
Zippo, Mack Trucks Bulldog, Brushed Finish, Box, 1972 .... 130.00
Zippo, Man In Hard Hat Setting Off Explosive Charge, Gold, Brushed Finish, White Box . 55.00

Zippo, Man Smoking, I'd Walk A Mile For A Camel Logo, Black Case, Plastic Box 36.00
Zippo, Mario De Santis, Brushed Finish, 4-Barrel Hinge, 1939 .... 158.00
Zippo, Marlboro, Steer Head On Star Emblem, Gilt Tone, Box 35.00
Zippo, Master Technician Conference, Chrysler Corp., Robot, Brushed Finish, 1958 ..... 85.00
Zippo, Mobil Oil, Red Winged Horse On White Circle, Plastic Box 39.00
Zippo, Monsanto, Engraved Orange & Black Logo, Brushed Finish, 1966 .... 35.00
Zippo, NASA, Quito, Ecuador, STDN Cotopaxi, Brushed Finish, 1977 .... 75.00
Zippo, National Water Main Cleaning Company, Steel Case, Brushed Finish, 1953 ...... 41.00
Zippo, Nickel Finish, 3-Barrel Hinge, Original Box, 1947 .... 115.00
Zippo, Outstanding Cadet 4th Sqd. 3d Plt Co. C, Steel Case, Brushed Finish, 1952 ...... 25.00
Zippo, Philadelphia Life Insurance Co., Brushed Finish, White & Gold Box, 1966 ...... 70.00
Zippo, Philip Hano Co., Blue, Red Enamel, Brushed Finish, Holyoke, Mass., 1950 ...... 58.00
Zippo, Photo Of Woman, Polished Finish, Slim, 1970 .... 160.00
Zippo, Picture Of Aircraft, Gates Aviation Corp., Blue, Black, Polished Finish 23.00
Zippo, Picture Of Devil Smoking, Red, White, Yellow, Black Enamel, Polished Finish ... 85.00
Zippo, Plain Case, Brushed Finish, 3-Barrel Hinge, Late 1940s 46.00
Zippo, Plain Case, Brushed Finish, 5-Barrel Hinge, 1941 .... 58.00
Zippo, Plain Case, Brushed Finish, Price Sticker, Red & White Striped Box, 1958 .... 55.00
Zippo, Plain Steel Case, Black Crackle Finish, 1943-1945 .... 245.00
Zippo, Plane Case, Brushed Finish, Red & White Striped Box, 1961 .... 40.00
Zippo, Prairie Maid Meats Lincoln, Nebr., Brushed Finish, Red Enamel, 1968 .... 35.00
Zippo, Purina Kitten Chow, Brushed Finish, Box, 1975 .... 68.00
Zippo, Raised Medallion Cat On Key, 14K Gold, Inscription Dated 1954 .... 415.00
Zippo, Range Instrumentation Ship U.S.N.S. Vandenberg, Polished Finish, Box, 1981 .... 40.00
Zippo, RCA Dog Nipper, RCA His Master's Voice On Other Side, Red, White Enamel ... 57.00
Zippo, Reddy Kilowatt, Polished Finish, Red Enamel, Reddy Kilowatt On Side, 1974 .... 66.00
Zippo, Replica Of 1932 Lighter, Brushed Finish, Gray Collector Case, 1988, 2 1/2 In. ... 165.00
Zippo, Ruttman Mini-Bike, Engraved, Brushed Finish, Box, 1970 .... 45.00
Zippo, Santa Fe All The Way, Indian, Santa Fe Railroad Logo, Polished Finish, 1981 .... 22.00
Zippo, Scandinavian Airlines Logo, Polished Finish, 1950 .... 30.00
Zippo, Shakespeare Reel, Logo, Brushed Stainless Steel, Box, 1963 .... 130.00
Zippo, Silvertone, Brushed Finish, Black Felt Pad Base, 1985, 13 1/4 In. 100.00
Zippo, Singer Comfortmaker Heating & Cooling, Brushed Silver Finish, Box, 1972 ..... 95.00
Zippo, Smith-Lee Co., Specialists In Dairy Packaging, Red, Black, Yellow Enamel, 1959 . 24.00
Zippo, Spooroco, Inc., Selinsgrove, Pa., South Hill, Va., Brushed Finish, 1978 .... 30.00
Zippo, Sun Kachina, Engraved Enamel, Polished Finish, Slim, 1978 .... 32.00
Zippo, Sunoco DX, Table, Box, 3 5/8 In. 90.00
Zippo, Tree Oil Co., Brushed Finish, Red & Yellow Paint, 1975 .... 40.00
Zippo, Trout Fisherman, Brushed Finish, Aqua & Tan Enamel, 1981 .... 36.00
Zippo, U.S. Naval Station, Midway Island, Engraved Gooney Bird, 1960 .... 21.00
Zippo, U.S. Navy Officer Cap Eagle Affixed To Side, Brushed Finish, 1953-1957 .... 40.00
Zippo, Uniroyal, Brushed Finish, 1978 .... 45.00
Zippo, USAF Strategic Air Command, Brushed Finish, 1959 .... 25.00
Zippo, USCGC Unimak WHEC 379, Coast Guard Ship, Polished Finish, Box, 1966 ..... 27.00
Zippo, USS Forrestal, First In Defense, Polished Finish, Slim, White, Gold Box, 1969 ... 40.00
Zippo, USS McKee AS-41, Nickel Case, Slim, 1974 .... 23.00
Zippo, Vertical Line Engraving, Monogram, 10K Gold Filled, Gold Finish, Slim, 1957 ... 40.00
Zippo, Vinyl Blue Denim Panels, Bumble Bee, Polished Finish, Box, 1975 .... 75.00
Zippo, W.B.B. Child & Co., Insurance Since 1892, Brushed Finish, 1969 .... 36.00
Zippo, Warwick Unions Logo, Blue, White Enamel, Brushed Finish 31.00
Zippo, Whalen Erecting Co., Inc., Polished Finish, Slim, White & Black Box, 1980 ..... 35.00
Zippo, Whalen Erecting Co., Inc., Steel Erectors, Polished Finish, Slim, Box, 1980 ...... 25.00
Zippo, White Mustang Power, Dalby White Truck, Inc., Horse, Brushed Finish, 1957 .... 48.00
Zippo, Winston, Polished Finish, Red & Gold Logo, 1983 .... 45.00
Zippo, Yacht Club Pennant Affixed To Side, Green Enamel, Brushed Finish, 1969 ...... 20.00

LIGHTNING RODS and lightning rod balls are collected. The glass balls
were at the center of the rod that was attached to the roof of a house or
barn to avoid lightning damage.

Arrow & Star Banner Directional, Star & Crescent Glass Ball, c.1900, 54 In. 316.00
Cow, Gilt Sunburst Finial, Turquoise Blue Glass Ball, c.1900, 69 x 22 1/2 In. 230.00
Milk Glass, Ribbed, 3 Rows Of Circles, 5 In. 65.00
Painted Shaft, Etched Ruby Flash Panel, White Glass Ball, c.1900, 48 In. 518.00

Trotting Horse, 5-Prong Finial, White Glass Ball, Gilt, Cretzer, c.1900, 69 In. 316.00
Trotting Horse, Celadon Green Molded Glass Ball, Zinc, c.1900, 54 x 28 In. 345.00
Trotting Horse, Sunburst Finial, Amethyst Glass Ball, Miller, c.1900, 68 In. 316.00

LIMOGES porcelain has been made in Limoges, France, since the mid-nineteenth century. Fine porcelains were made by many factories, including Haviland, Ahrenfeldt, Guerin, Pouyat, Elite, and others. Modern porcelains are being made at Limoges and the word *Limoges* as part of the mark is not an indication of age. Haviland, one of the Limoges factories, is listed as a separate category in this book.

Asparagus Server, Cream, Green, Cabbage Rose Bouquets, Gilt Edge, c.1915, 12 1/2 In. .. 130.00
Bone Dish, Pink Flowers, Gold Trim, Haviland, France 85.00
Box, Cover, Alternating Gilt Borders, Gilt, Squat Baluster, 4 In. 65.00
Box, Heart, Floral, 1987, 3 1/4 In. 550.00
Candy Dish, Roses, Scene On Cover Of Boy Playing With Dog, 7 x 3 3/4 In. 105.00
Charger, Center Parrot On Perch, Open Handles, Yellow Ground, 14 3/4 In. 260.00
Charger, Cockerel & Hens, Scalloped, Signed, Barbarin, 15 In. 230.00
Charger, Gentleman Helping Lady Over Puddle, Scalloped Rim, 13 1/4 In. 165.00
Charger, Green & Purple Grape Bunches, Vines, Signed, 1898, 12 1/2 In. 115.00
Cup & Saucer, Mustache, Forget-Me-Nots On White, 1893 .... 200.00
Dish, Cover, Raised Beaded Borders, Circular, 3 1/4 x 7 In. 103.00
Dish, Serving, Orchids, Scalloped Rim, Gilt, Rectangular, 15 7/8 In. 115.00
Dish, Sweetmeat, Roses, Gold Trim, Handle, 9 In. 110.00
Dish, Violets, Hand Painted, Open Handles, Footed, Marked, 4 1/2 In. ....*Illus* 80.00
Fish Set, Blue & Yellow Floral, 8 In., 6 Piece 305.00
Fish Set, Fish Scenes, Yellow & Gilt Vine Borders, 4 Piece 120.00
Fish Set, Scalloped Rim, Polychrome Fish, 16 1/2-In. Platter, 13 Piece 460.00
Jardiniere, Baluster, Claw-Footed Pedestal, Roses On Stems, 19th Century, 10 1/2 In. ... 550.00
Oyster Plate, Flowers, Gilt, Marked, 9 In., 6 Piece 405.00
Oyster Plate, Whiteware Mark, 1900-1941, 9 In. 295.00
Pancake Server, Floral Around Rim, Handle 310.00
Pancake Warmer, Plate & Lid, 9 In. 90.00
Pitcher, Cidercorn Painted On Outside, W.G. & Company, 6 1/2 In. 325.00
Pitcher, Cows 90.00
Pitcher, Gilt Floral, Lavender Ground, 19th Century, 6 3/4 In. 325.00
Pitcher, Gilt Leaf Design, Ivory Ground, 11 In. 103.00
Plaque, Cottages & Trees Near Water, Blue, Brown Glaze, 7 5/8 x 5 5/8 In. 1035.00
Plaque, Falconer, Red Velvet Frame, Foliate Border, 20 1/2 In. 4600.00
Plaque, River Scene, Frame, 9 1/2 x 11 In. 330.00
Plate, Bird, Hand Painted, Gold Trim, Signed Conderl, 11 1/2 In. 66.00
Plate, Cabinet, Floral Cartouches, Scene Of Lovers In Wooded Setting, 1900, 9 In. 175.00
Plate, Dessert, Flower, Scalloped Beaded Edge, Early 20th Century, 8 3/4 In., 12 Piece .. 360.00
Plate, Floral, Gilt, Marked, 10 In., 16 Piece 275.00
Plate, Game, Wild Boars, Tradeis, Coronet, 10 1/2 In. 105.00
Plate, Hanging Pheasant, Blakeman & Henderson, Signed, Baomy, 12 1/2 In. 110.00
Plate, Portrait, Transfer, Over Paint, Coronet, 9 1/2 In. 44.00
Plate, Rabbits, Hand Painted, Hanging, 10 In. 55.00
Plate, Rose Design, Beaded Gilt Border, 8 3/4 In., 12 Piece 345.00
Punch Bowl, Gilt Floral, Puce Ground, 14 1/2 In. 350.00

Maroon and yellowish chrome-green were never used to decorate porcelain during the eighteenth century. Almost all the eighteenth-century figures had brown eyes.

Limoges, Dish, Violets, Hand Painted, Open Handles, Footed, Marked, 4 1/2 In.

Punch Bowl, Overall Gray Clusters & Vines, Gold Rim, White Ground, c.1890, 16 In. . . . 1800.00
Sugar & Creamer, Violets, Gold Trim, Creamer, 3 1/2 In. 110.00
Tankard, Ears Of Corn, Gilt Figural Dragon Handle, Marked J.P.L. France, 15 In. 335.00
Tea Set, Art Deco, Floral, W. Guerin, 3 Piece 135.00
Tray, Dresser, Floral Design, 11 x 16 In. 66.00
Tureen, Undertray, Small Floral Sprays, Handles, Oval, 15 5/8 In. 57.00
Vase, Enamel Scene, Female Picking Flowers, Handles, c.1900, 15 In. 632.00
Vase, Foil Under Opalescent White, Copper, Gold, Black, Art Deco, C. Faure, 9 In. 3450.00
Vase, Multiple Nudes, Cummins, 13 In. 1300.00
Vase, Red, Pink Roses, Hand Painted, 8 1/4 In. 67.00

LINDBERGH was a national hero. In 1927, Charles Lindbergh, the aviator, became the first man to make a nonstop solo flight across the Atlantic Ocean. In 1932, his son was kidnapped and murdered, and Lindbergh was again the center of public interest. He died in 1974. All types of Lindbergh memorabilia are collected.

Candy Container, Spirit Of St. Louis, Pink Glass, Original Tin 550.00
Card, Playing, Pictures Plane, Clouds, Searchlight, Blue & White 16.00
Label, Cigar, USA Bird, Lone Eagle Hero, Good Will Flyer, 1927, 7 x 9 In. 12.00
Mirror, Statue Of Liberty, Eiffel Tower, Lindy In Center, Oval, 2 3/4 x 1 7/8 In. 695.00
Photograph, Lindbergh Gazing Skyward, Signed, Art Deco Frame 2660.00
Ribbon & Medal, Lindbergh-Herrick, Reception Committee, August 1, 1927 . . . . 120.00
Stereo Card, Our Ambassador Of The Air, Spirit Of St. Louis, Keystone, 1930 . . . . 22.00
Table Runner, Lindy, Plane, New York & Paris Skylines, Cloth, 60 x 18 In. 47.00

LITHOPHANES are porcelain pictures made by casting clay in layers of various thicknesses. When a piece is held to the light, a picture of light and shadow is seen through it. Most lithophanes date from the 1825–1875 period. A few are still being made. Many lithophanes sold today were originally panels for lampshades.

Country Scene, Girl Seated On Bench, Belleek, c.1985, 6 1/2 x 8 In. 150.00
Stein, Bavaria Monument, Munich Child, Porcelain Lid, 1/3 Liter 330.00
Stein, Clock Tower Form, Onion Dome, Pewter Mounts, Martin Pauson, 13 In. 420.00
Stein, Limbach, Transfer & Enamel, Brown, Pewter Lid, 1/2 Liter 140.00

LIVERPOOL, England, was the site of several pottery and porcelain factories from 1716 to 1785. Some earthenware was made with transfer decorations. Sadler and Green made print-decorated wares from 1756. Many of the pieces were made for the American market and feature patriotic emblems, such as eagles, flags, and other special-interest motifs. Liverpool pitchers are always called Liverpool jugs by collectors.

Bowl, Abolitionist, Woman Slave Holding Child, 8 1/2 In. 373.00
Bowl, Black Transfer, Ships, Sailor & Wife, Verse, 8 3/4 In. 715.00
Creamer, Verse, Where Brittons Rush On, Black Transfer, 4 1/2 In. 55.00
Jug, Benjamin Franklin, Transfer, 10 In. 5750.00
Jug, Brig Polly, Arms Of Appleton, 9 1/2 In. 245.00
Jug, Captain Jacob Jones, Black Transfer, Yellow Ground, England, 1800s, 6 3/4 In. 1725.00
Jug, Courting Couple, Children, At Waterside, 6 3/4 In. 120.00
Jug, English Coat Of Arms, Medallion Bust Of Wellington, Black Transfer, 9 In. 880.00
Jug, Fanny's Farewell, Warships, U.S. Great Seal, England, Early 1800s, 10 1/8 In. 1380.00
Jug, In Memory Of Washington & Patriots, Blank Transfer, England, 1800s, 8 In. 2300.00
Jug, Massacre Of The French King, Jan'y 20th 1793, Black Transfer, 7 3/4 In. 3220.00
Jug, Military Scene, Conquering Hero, Band Of Grapes & Flowers, 10 In. 690.00
Jug, Milk, Queen's Ware, Black Transfer, Lafayette & Benjamin Franklin, 5 In. 605.00
Jug, Portrait Medallions Of Samuel Adams, John Hancock, 10 3/4 In. 3450.00
Jug, President Thomas Jefferson, Transfer Apollo The God Of Music, 8 1/2 In. 16100.00
Jug, Success To Trade Of Rhode Island, Black Transfer, Buff, England, 1800s, 6 1/4 In. . . . 1610.00
Jug, Susan's Farewell, Nicholas Taylor, Black Transfer, 11 In. 935.00
Jug, Transfer Of Ship, Masonic Emblem On Reverse, Jefferson Quote, 11 In. 4025.00
Jug, Transfer, Washington Apotheosis, 2 Brothers Sailing Ship, 10 1/4 In., Pair 33350.00
Jug, U.S. Frigate Guerriere, Reverse 1818 Battle Stonington Harbor, 9 In. . . . . *Illus* 15400.00
Jug, Washington In Glory, America In Tears, Herculaneum Pottery, c.1800, 9 In. 2070.00

A matte glazed pottery piece can be rubbed with olive oil, then wiped clean.

The word "trademark" was used on English wares after 1855, but most of the pieces with the letters "LTD," the abbreviation for "Limited," were made after 1880.

Liverpool, Jug, U.S. Frigate Guerriere, Reverse 1818 Battle Stonington Harbor, 9 In.

Plate, Polychrome Floral, White Ground, Scalloped Rim, 9 In. 275.00
Teapot, Blue Floral Sprays, c.1770, 8 In. 1250.00

LLADRO is a Spanish porcelain. Juan, Jose, and Vicente Lladro opened a ceramics workshop in Almacera in 1951. They soon began making figurines in a distinctive, elongated style. In 1958 the factory moved to Tabernes Blanques, Spain. The company makes stoneware and porcelain figurines and vases in limited and unlimited editions. Dates given are first and last years of production.

LLADRÓ°

Bell, Autumn, No. 7615, Collectors Club, 1993 .... 35.00
Bell, Christmas, No. 5524, 1988 .... 40.00
Bell, Summer, No. 7614, Collectors Club, 1992 .... 35.00
Figurine, A Swimming Lesson, No. 6470, 1997 .... 180.00
Figurine, Aggressive Duck, No. 1288, Duck Chasing Girl, 1974-1995 ....200.00 to 450.00
Figurine, All Aboard, No. 7619, Collectors Club, 1992-1993 .... 450.00
Figurine, Angel With Lyre, No. 1321, Tall Angel Holding Lyre, 1976-1985 .... 450.00
Figurine, Anticipation, No. 5650, 1990-1993 .... 230.00
Figurine, At The Circus, No. 5052, 1979-1985, 13 In. 1300.00
Figurine, Basket Of Love, No. 7622, Collectors Club, 1994-1995 .... 425.00
Figurine, Belinda With Her Doll, No. 5045, Child Standing With Doll, 1980-1995 ...... 230.00
Figurine, Best Friend, No. 7620, Collectors Club, 1993-1994 .... 340.00
Figurine, Billy Soccer Player, No. 5135, 1982-1983 .... 615.00
Figurine, Bird Watcher, No. 4730, Boy Sitting With Bird On Toe, 1970-1985 .... 380.00
Figurine, Boy Pottery Seller, No. 5080, Boy Surrounded By Pots, 1980-1985 .... 850.00
Figurine, Boy With Book, No. 1024, 1969-1971 .... 400.00
Figurine, Boy With Yacht, 1972-19989 In. 105.00
Figurine, Can I Play, No. 7610, Collectors Club, 1990-1991 ....250.00 to 530.00
Figurine, Cat Girl, No. 5164, 1982-1985 .... 600.00
Figurine, Christmas Carols, No. 1239, 1973-1981 .... 800.00
Figurine, Christmas Melodies, No. 6128, 1994-1997, 10 1/2 In. 230.00
Figurine, Clean Up Time, No. 4838, 1973-1993 .... 250.00
Figurine, Clown's Head, No. 5129, 1982, 12 1/2 In. 258.00
Figurine, Daddy's Girl, No. 5584, Box, 1989-1996 .... 155.00
Figurine, Dentist, No. 6450, Box, 1997, 12 In. 230.00
Figurine, Discoveries, Columbus & Sailors, No. 3024, 1990-1994, 21 x 13 In. 2015.00
Figurine, Doctor, No. 4602.3, 1993, 13 1/4 In. 138.00
Figurine, Don Quixote, No. 1030, 1969 .... 603.00
Figurine, Doncel With Roses, No. 4757, 1971-1979 .... 800.00
Figurine, Donkey In Love, No. 4524, Donkey With Petals Of Flowers, 1969-1985, 5 In. ... 500.00
Figurine, Dove, No. 1016, 1969-1995 .... 200.00
Figurine, Dressmaker, No. 4700, 1970-1993, Box 450.00
Figurine, Ducks Flapping, No. 4759, 1971-1981 .... 750.00
Figurine, Eskimo Boy & Girl, No. 2038.3, 1971-1994 .... 455.00
Figurine, Flapper, Box, No. 5175, Box, 1982-1995 .... 140.00

Figurine, Flower Harmony, No. 1418, Box, 1982-1995 .... 130.00
Figurine, Flower Peddler, No. 5029, Cart Full Of Flowers, 1979-1985 ....1270.00 to 1500.00
Figurine, Flower Song, No. 7607, Collectors Club, 1988-1989 ....350.00 to 650.00
Figurine, Flowers In Pot, No. 5028, Girl Kneeling With Flowers, 1980-1985 .... 600.00
Figurine, From This Day Forward, No. 5885, Box, 1992, 7 3/4 In................... 230.00
Figurine, Garden Classic, No. 7617, Collectors Society, Limited Edition, 1991 .... 600.00
Figurine, Garden Dance, No. 6580, Special Edition, Retired 1999 .... 240.00
Figurine, Girl & Sparrow, No. 4758, 1971-1979 .... 800.00
Figurine, Girl Walking, No. 5040, Girl With Rose On Base, 1979-1981 .... 550.00
Figurine, Girl With Bonnet, No. 1147, Seated Girl Wearing Bonnet, 1971-1985 .... 350.00
Figurine, Girl With Dice, No. 1176, Clown Girl Sitting On Dice, 1971-1981 .... 250.00
Figurine, Girl With Doll, No. 1083, Applying Lipstick To Doll, 1969-1985 .... 300.00
Figurine, Girl With Lamb, No. 1010, Little Girl Holding Lamb, 1969-1993 .... 375.00
Figurine, Girl With Pig, No. 1011, 1969, 7 In.................................... 143.00
Figurine, Golfer, No. 4824, 1972, 10 1/2 In. ....115.00 to 132.00
Figurine, Good Bear, No. 1205, Seated, Two Paws Up, 1972-1989 .... 85.00
Figurine, Hamlet, No. 4729, Seated Holding Skull In Hand, 1970-1980 .... 800.00
Figurine, Hebrew Student, No. 4684, Boy Studying, 1970-1985, 11 1/2 In. ....300.00 to 800.00
Figurine, Hello, Flowers, No. 5543, Girl, Flowers, Limited Edition, 1989-1993, 7 1/2 In. . 650.00
Figurine, Hi There, No. 5672, Box, 1990-1996 .... 260.00
Figurine, I Love You Truly, No. 1528, Box, 1987 .... 315.00
Figurine, I've Got It, No. 5827, Black Figure With Baseball Equipment, 1991-1995 ..... 200.00
Figurine, In The Gondola, No. 1350, Caped Venetian Man, 3 Foreign Passengers, 1978 .. 2070.00
Figurine, It Wasn't Me, No. 7672, Limited Edition, 1998 Lladro Society 270.00
Figurine, Jazz Duo, No. 5930, 1992 .... 550.00
Figurine, Kissing Doves, No. 1169, 1971 .... 90.00
Figurine, Little Bo-Peep, No. 1312, Girl Feeding Sheep, 1974-1985 .... 450.00
Figurine, Little Girl With Cat, No. 1187, Girl With Cat At Base 400.00
Figurine, Little Shepherd & Sheep, No. 4817, Sitting With Sheep 400.00
Figurine, Love Birds, No. 3404D 165.00
Figurine, Love Letter, No. RL400, Norman Rockwell Series 1100.00
Figurine, Matrimony, No. 1404, 1982-1998 ....230.00 to 585.00
Figurine, Mother's Day, No. 5596, Box, 1989-1999 .... 230.00
Figurine, My Buddy, No. 7609, Collectors Club, 1989-1990 ....220.00 to 900.00
Figurine, My Goodness, No. 1285, Box, 1974-1995 .... 150.00
Figurine, My Little Pet, No. 4994, Girl Standing With Dog, 1978-1985 .... 250.00
Figurine, Nature's Bounty, No. 1417, Box, 1982-1995 .... 230.00
Figurine, Nostalgia, No. 5071, Box, 1980-1993 .... 98.00
Figurine, Nuns, No. 4611, Box, 1969 .... 69.00
Figurine, Once Upon A Time, No. 5721, Box, 1990-1997 .... 315.00
Figurine, Pekingese Sitting, No. 4641, Sitting At Attention, 1969-1985 .... 420.00
Figurine, Penguin, No. 5248, 1984-1988 .... 300.00
Figurine, Pensive Clown, Box, No. 5130, 1982 .... 185.00
Figurine, Pick Of The Litter, No. 7621, Limited Edition, 1993 .... 400.00
Figurine, Picking Flowers, No. 1287, Box, 1974-1998 .... 345.00
Figurine, Picture Perfect, No. 7612, Collectors Club, 1991 .... 650.00
Figurine, Pocket Full Of Wishes, No. 7650, 1997-1998 .... 320.00
Figurine, Pondering, No. 5173, Girl Basket Of Flowers, 1982-1993 .... 650.00
Figurine, Pottery Seller, No. 5079, Girl Painting Vases, 1980-1985 .... 800.00
Figurine, Ride In The Country, No. 5354, Two Children On Donkey, 1986-1993 .... 550.00
Figurine, Romeo & Juliet, No. 4750, 1971 .... 690.00
Figurine, School Days, No. 7604, Limited Edition, 1988-1989, 8 1/4 In. ....300.00 to 368.00
Figurine, Sea Gull, No. 1009, 1969-1970 ....350.00 to 400.00
Figurine, Seabreeze, Windblown Girl, No. 4922, Box, 1974 .... 150.00
Figurine, Serenading Colombina, No. 6322, 1996-1998, 10 In. 276.00
Figurine, Sorrowful Mother, No. 5849, Limited Edition 900.00
Figurine, Spring Bouquets, No. 7603, Box, Collectors Club, 1987-1988 ....600.00 to 1050.00
Figurine, Summer Stroll, No. 7611, Collectors Club, 1991-1992 .... 600.00
Figurine, Tailor Made ....140.00 to 180.00
Figurine, The Barrister, No. 4908, 1974-1985 .... 425.00
Figurine, The Debutante, No. 1431, Box, 1982-1998 .... 115.00
Figurine, Veterinarian, No. 4825, Matte, 1972-1985 .... 600.00
Figurine, Walk In Versailles, No. 5004, Man & Woman, 1978-1981, 15 3/4 In. 875.00

Figurine, Wedding Day, No. 5274, 1985 .... 325.00
Flowers Of The Season, Base, No. 1454, Box, 1983 .... 1725.00
Plate, Christmas, 1971, No. 7006, Caroling 250.00
Plate, Miniature, No. 7501, Exclusive For Franklin Mint 55.00

LOETZ glass was made in many varieties. Johann Loetz bought a glassworks in Austria in 1840. He died in 1848 and his widow ran the company; then in 1879, his grandson took over. Most collectors recognize the iridescent gold glass similar to Tiffany, but many other types were made. The firm closed during World War II.

Loetz Austria

Bowl, Gold Iridescent, Rolled Rim, Marked, 8 In. 200.00
Bowl, Green Iridescent, Handle, Footed, 8 x 4 1/2 In. 316.00
Bowl, Green Iridescent, Red Applied Design, Free Form, 8 In. 315.00
Bowl, Green Iridescent, Ruffled Edge, 6 1/4 In. 220.00
Bowl, Mica Flecks Interior, Amber Vertical Lines, Emerald Green, 4 1/4 In. 500.00
Bowl, Papillon, Amber, Iridescent, Bronze Mount, Snakes, Tulips, 1900, 6 x 9 In. 1725.00
Bride's Bowl, Amberina, Bronze Art Deco Frame, 10 x 10 In. 1700.00
Dish, Cranberry, Gold Interior, 2 1/2 In. 230.00
Ewer, Papillon, Blue, Silver Overlay Grapes & Vines, Flared Cylinder, 10 1/2 In. ... 8050.00
Humidor, Embossed Brass Cover, White, Lavender Iridescent, Freeform Threads, 7 In. 250.00
Jardiniere, Textured Green, Lily Pad Bronze Holder, Signed, c.1900, 8 1/4 In. 1450.00
Lamp, Crown & Jewel, Foliate Band, Red Glass Beads, Wreath Swags, 28 x 17 In. 8050.00
Lamp, Desk, Gold, White Iridescent Shade, Bronze, Signed, C. Rane, 14 1/2 x 8 In. 1610.00
Lamp, Desk, Raised Festoon, Gold Iridescent, Linen Fold Shade, Brass Base, 17 In. 1495.00
Lamp, Gold Iridescent Shade, Bronze, 20 x 12 In. 2185.00
Lamp, Hanging, Foliate Swags, Wheat, Greek Key Center, Amber Tiers, Bronze, 32 In. .. 3162.00
Lamp, Hanging, Textured Iridescent Shade, Bronze, 28 In. 920.00
Perfume Bottle, Green, Stopper, 6 1/2 In. 195.00
Shade, Papillon, Amber, Iridescent Gold Oil Spots, Bell Shape, Scalloped Rim, 6 In., Pair ... 805.00
Vase, Amber, Iridescent, 3 Dimples, Rolled Trefoil Rim, Loop Footed, 1900, 5 1/2 In. ... 4310.00
Vase, Amethyst Iridescent, Signed, 8 In. 200.00
Vase, Amethyst, Freeform Threading, 9 In. 125.00
Vase, Blue Iridescent, Oil Spots, Pulled Handles, Signed, 8 1/2 In. 4600.00
Vase, Blue Iridescent, Silver Overlay, 1900, 8 1/2 In. 4485.00
Vase, Bud, Crimson Iridescent, Pulled Trailings, Ruffled Edge, 1900, 9 1/2 In. 2760.00
Vase, Citrine, Cranberry Mottling, Pulled Green Leaves, Iridescent, 11 1/2 In. 1232.00
Vase, Clovers, Green, Silver-Blue Oil Spots, Silver Overlay, c.1900, 4 1/2 In. 805.00
Vase, Cobalt Blue Iridescent, Oil Spots, 6 1/4 In. 750.00
Vase, Cobalt Blue Iridescent, Silver Overlay, Irises & Leaves, Squat, 1900, 7 In. 1955.00
Vase, Crackling, Smooth Inside, 7 3/4 In. 175.00
Vase, Cranberry, Gray, Blue, 5 In. 287.00
Vase, Drape, Pinched, Amber, Gold Threading, Blue Luster, 1900, 5 In. 575.00
Vase, Enameled Thistle, Green Iridescent, 4 Handles, 10 In., Pair 500.00
Vase, Gold Iridescent Trailings, Pale Pink Glass, 4 Dimpled Sides, 1900, 8 In. 345.00
Vase, Gold Iridescent, Textured, Tricornered, Marked, 10 In. 1000.00
Vase, Gray Iridescent, Amber Oil Spots, Egg Shape, 1900, 5 1/2 In. 1955.00
Vase, Gray Iridescent, Oil Spot, Rolled Trefoil Rim, Egg Shape, 1900, 15 In. 1495.00
Vase, Gray Over Yellow, Geometric, Cameo, Josef Hoffmann, 1912, 10 1/4 In. 9200.00
Vase, Green Iridescent, Mottled, Irregular Rim, 13 1/2 In. ....*Illus* 440.00
Vase, Green, Applied Handles, 5 In. 258.00
Vase, Iridescent, Oil Spots, Turquoise Jewels, Silver Overlay Web, 1900, 5 1/8 In. 860.00
Vase, Jack-In-The-Pulpit, Green Iridescent, Crooked Neck, Early 20th Century, 10 1/2 In. .. 770.00
Vase, Marigold, Blue Iridescent Wavy Bands, Ground Pontil, 7 1/2 In. 252.00
Vase, Mottled Green, Irregular Rim, 13 1/2 In. 440.00
Vase, Oil Spot, Applied Rosettes, Cobalt, 3 Curved Handles, 1900, 6 In. 575.00
Vase, Oil Spot, Silver, Blue, Ruffled Edge, 8 x 4 1/2 In. 920.00
Vase, Papillon, Blue, Gold Iridescent, Dimpled Body, 8 3/4 In. 522.00
Vase, Papillon, Iridescent, Clear Over Olive Green, Oval, Applied Rim, 1900, 8 In. 1265.00
Vase, Papillon, Light Blue, Stylized Iris, Silver Overlay, 1900, 7 In. 1725.00
Vase, Papillon, Pinched, Gold Over Pale Green, Polished Pontil, 6 In. 287.00
Vase, Pearlized White, Lavender Heart & Vine Threaded, 9 In. 250.00
Vase, Pink Iridescent, Pulled Hearts And Vines, Amber Glass, 1900, 6 3/4 In. 1610.00
Vase, Pulled Handles, Pulled Lava Lines, 10 1/2 In. 3200.00

To test the age of engraving on glass, place a
white handkerchief on the inside. If the
engraving is old, the lines will usually show up
darker than the rest of the glass. New engraving
has a bright, powder-like surface.

Loetz, Vase, Green
Iridescent, Mottled,
Irregular Rim, 13 1/2 In.

Vase, Red & Green Iridescent, 5 1/2 In.	50.00
Vase, Sea Monster In Pond, Lotus Flowers, Amber, Oil Spots, 3 Lobes Shape, 7 In.	1025.00
Vase, Serpent Coiled Around Neck, Amber Iridescent, Bottle Shape, 1900, 7 1/8 In.	920.00
Vase, Silver Blue Oil Spots, c.1915, 9 1/4 In., Pair	575.00
Vase, Silver Deposit, c.1900, 6 In.	3750.00
Vase, Silver Flowers On Whiplash Vines, Peach, Cobalt Trailings, Gray Ground, 6 In.	2587.00
Vase, Stick, Red & Green Iridescent, 12 In.	200.00
Vase, Swirl, Green Iridescent, Stylized Silver Overlay, 1905, 6 1/2 In.	747.00
Vase, Swirl, Orange, Pale Yellow, Royal Blue, Red, 1900, 8 5/8 In.	7475.00
Vase, Thumbprint, Red & Green Iridescent, Pinched Sides, 12 In.	250.00
Vase, Triptych, Green Iridescent, Twisted & Braided Handles, 5 1/2 x 6 In.	603.00
Vase, Water Sprinkler Form, Citrine Mottling & Iridescent Oil Spot Finish, 13 1/2 In.	672.00
Vase, Yellow Iridescent Trailings, Oil Spots, Floral Silver Overlay, 1900, 5 In.	4025.00

LONE RANGER, a fictional character, was introduced on the radio in
1932. Over three thousand shows were produced before the series
ended in 1954. In 1938, the first Lone Ranger movie was made. Television shows were started in 1949 and are still seen on some stations.
The Lone Ranger appears on many products and was even the name of
a restaurant chain for several years.

Badge, With Secret Compartment	40.00
Blackout Kit, Lone Ranger Volunteers Patch, Mail Envelope, 1942	145.00
Book, Big Little Book, 1968	40.00
Book, Grosset & Dunlap, 1936	12.00
Boots, Lone Ranger & Tonto, Child's Size 10	110.00
Doll, Lone Ranger & Tonto, Faux Buckskin & Suede Clothes, 20 In., Pair	635.00
Figure, Lone Ranger & Tonto, Gabriel, 2 Piece	75.00
Game, Lone Ranger Game, Metal Horses, Parker Brothers, 1938	40.00 to 125.00
Guitar, Box	73.00
Gun, Squirt	20.00
Holder, Toothbrush, Lone Ranger On Rearing Horse, 1938	125.00
Movie Viewer, Rides Again, Box, 1939	25.00
Mutoscope Card, Lone Ranger, Inc., USA, 3 1/4 x 5 1/4 In.	18.00
Mystery Ranch, 1938	20.00
Pattern, Clothes	25.00
Pinback Button, Cabakco Safety Club, The Lone Ranger, Metal, Blue & Gold, 1 In.	55.00
Pinback Button, Lone Ranger, Sun Herald & Examiner, Tin Lithograph, 1 1/8 In.	60.00
Pinback Button, Trigger, Tin Lithograph, Multicolored, 1 In.	20.00
Poster, Lone Ranger & Tonto, Clayton Moore & Jay Silverheels Signed, 24 x 29 In.	925.00
Record, Lone Ranger He Finds Silver, 78 RPM, 1951	65.00
Record, Lone Ranger Meets The Stranger From The East, 78 RPM, 1953	65.00
Ring, Embossed Face Seal, 1940s	90.00
Sheet Music, The Lone Ranger Song, c.1939	85.00
Teepee, Box	35.00
Toy, Lone Ranger, On Silver, Twirling Lasso, Windup, Marx, 1938	375.00 to 595.00
Toy, Unmasked, 20 In.	687.00

LONGWY Workshop of Longwy, France, first made ceramic wares in 1798. The workshop is still in business. Most of the ceramic pieces found today are glazed with many colors to resemble cloisonne or other enameled metal. Many pieces were made with stylized figures and Art Deco designs. The factory used a variety of marks.

Figurine, Dutch Shoe, Polychrome Flowers, Enamel, 3 x 6 In., Pair	137.00
Vase, Broad Band Of Cranes & Palms, Dragon Handles, Turquoise Ground, 15 In., Pair	1955.00
Vase, Faience, Stylized Teal & Pink Berries, Crackled Ivory Ground, 1925, 22 In.	2300.00
Vase, Flowers, Polychrome Enamel, Brass Mount, 9 1/2 In.	176.00
Vase, Stand, Scrolled Foliage, Stand With Elephant Head, Crackle Ground, 13 In., Pair	1725.00

LOTUS WARE was made by the Knowles, Taylor & Knowles Company of East Liverpool, Ohio, from 1890 to 1900. Lotus Ware, a thin porcelain which resembles Belleek, was sometimes decorated outside the factory. Other types of ceramics that were made by the Knowles, Taylor & Knowles Company are listed under KTK.

Rose Bowl, KTK Co., 4 1/2 In. 25.00

LOW art tiles were made by the J. and J. G. Low Art Tile Works of Chelsea, Massachusetts, from 1877 to 1902. A variety of art and other tiles were made. Some of the tiles were made by a process called *natural*, some were hand modeled, and some were made mechanically.

Tile, Floral Design, Green Glossy Glaze, In Copper Trivet, Verdigris Patina, 3 In.	77.00
Tile Frieze, Banner, Motto, Tempus Fugit, 4 Cherubs, Frame, 1883, 7 3/8 x 31 3/4 In.	1092.00

LOY-NEL-ART, see McCoy category.

LUNCH BOXES and lunch pails have been used to carry lunches to school or work since the nineteenth century. Today, most collectors want either early tobacco advertising boxes or children's lunch boxes made since the 1930s. These boxes are made of metal or plastic. Boxes listed here include the original Thermos bottle inside the box unless otherwise indicated. Movie, television, and cartoon characters may be found in their own categories.

LUNCH BOX, 6 Million Dollar Man, Metal, Aladdin, 1975	17.00
Addams Family, Metal, King Seeley Thermos, 1974	85.00
Archies, Metal, Aladdin, 1969	20.00
Astronaut, Futuristic Space Men, Dome, Metal, King Seeley Thermos, 1960	300.00
Astronauts, Armstrong Walking On Moon, Metal, Aladdin, 1969	70.00
Banana Splits, King Seeley Thermos, 1969	500.00
Barbie & Midge, Metal, Dome, King Seeley Thermos, 1964	125.00 to 395.00
Bobby Sherman, Metal, King Seeley Thermos, 1972	75.00
Brady Bunch, Metal, King Seeley Thermos, 1970	75.00
Cable Car, Metal, Dome, Aladdin, 1962	40.00
Charlie's Angels, Metal, Aladdin, 1978	40.00
Curiosity Shop, Metal, King Seeley Thermos, 1972	55.00
Decoupage, Magazine Clippings, 10 1/4 In.	*Illus* 20.00

Install locks on all garage doors and windows.

Lunch Box, Decoupage Magazine Clippings, 10 1/4 In.

Dr. Seuss, Metal, Aladdin, 1970 .... 175.00
E.T., Metal, Aladdin, 1982 .... 125.00
Fall Guy, Metal, No Thermos, Aladdin, 1981 .... 110.00
Green Hornet, Metal, King Seeley Thermos, 1967 .... 435.00
Gunsmoke, Metal, Aladdin, 1959 .... 150.00
Gunsmoke, Metal, Aladdin, 1972 .... 110.00
Hardy Boys, Metal, King Seeley Thermos, 1977 .... 44.00
Heathcliff, Metal, Aladdin, 1982 .... 85.00
How The West Was Won, Metal, King Seeley Thermos, 1979 .... 35.00
Huckleberry Hound, Metal, Aladdin, 1961 .... 175.00
It's About Time, Metal, Dome, Aladdin, 1967 .... 200.00
Joe Palooka, Tin, 2 Handles, Continental Can Co., 1949 .... 175.00
Jr. Miss, Big Hat, Metal, Aladdin, 1970 .... 30.00
Kroft Supershow, Metal, Aladdin, 1976 .... 66.00
Land Of The Giants, Metal, Aladdin, 1969 .... 130.00
Land Of The Lost, Metal, Aladdin, 1976 .... 62.00
Liddle Kiddles, Vinyl, King Seeley Thermos, 1969 .... 125.00
Lost In Space, Metal, Dome, King Seeley Thermos, 1967 .... 450.00
McDonald's Sheriff, Metal, Aladdin 95.00
Munsters, Metal, King Seeley Thermos, 1965 .... 495.00
NFL Quarterback, Metal, Aladdin, 1964 .... 190.00
Osmonds, Metal, Aladdin, 1973 .... 50.00
Penny Post Cut Plug, Burley Tobacco Company, Brass Clasp 220.00
Pink Panther, Metal, Okay Industries, 1974 .... 44.00
Porky's Lunch Wagon, American Thermos, 1959 .... 160.00
Rat Patrol, Metal, Aladdin, 1967 .... 150.00
Red Barn, Open Doors, Metal, Dome, King Seeley Thermos, 1958 .... 75.00
Scooby Doo, No Thermos, King Seeley Thermos, 1973 .... 90.00
Sesame Street, Metal, King Seeley Thermos, 1980 .... 15.00
Space Explorer, Metal, Aladdin, 1960 .... 330.00
Space:1999, Scenes & Characters From Show, Metal, King Seeley Thermos, 1976 ...... 80.00
Star Trek, Metal, Dome, Aladdin, 1968 .... 680.00
Star Trek, Metal, King Seeley Thermos, 1979 .... 35.00
Submarine, Metal, King Seeley Thermos, 1960 .... 105.00
Tiger Tobacco, Red Basket Weave, Tiger, 10 x 7 In. 30.00
Tom Corbett Space Cadet, Aladdin, 1954 .... 220.00
Tropicana Swim Club, Vinyl, 1980 .... 90.00
Twiggy, Lavender, Zipper Top, Vinyl, Aladdin, 1967 .... 145.00
UFO, Space Scenes, Metal, King Seeley Thermos, 1973 .... 26.00
Universal's Movie Monsters, Metal, Aladdin, 1980 .... 50.00
Wagon Train, King Seeley Thermos, 1964 .... 225.00
Waltons, Aladdin, 1973 .... 40.00
Welcome Back Kotter, Metal, Aladdin, 1976 .... 450.00
Wild Wild West, Aladdin, 1969 .... 230.00
Wonder Woman, Yellow, Vinyl, Aladdin, 1978 .... 250.00
Zorro, Fencing, Metal, Aladdin, 1958 .... 250.00
LUNCH BOX THERMOS, Bonanza, Aladdin, 1965 .... 50.00
Bullwinkle, Telstar Satellite, Ohio Art, 1962 .... 56.00
Have Gun Will Travel, Aladdin, 1960 .... 65.00
Jet Patrol, Aladdin, 1957 .... 140.00
Man From Uncle, King Seeley Thermos, 1966 .... 50.00
Monkee's, King Seeley Thermos, 1967 .... 50.00
Osmonds, Plastic, Aladdin, 1973 .... 20.00
Voyage To Bottom Of Sea, Aladdin, 1967 .... 100.00
Wild Bill Hickock, Aladdin, 1956 .... 85.00

LUNEVILLE, a French faience factory, was established about 1730 by Jacques Chambrette. It is best known for its fine biscuit figures and groups and for large faience dogs and lions. The early pieces were unmarked. The firm was acquired by Keller and Guerin and is still working.

Bowl, White & Blue, 9 In. 220.00
Jardiniere, Art Nouveau Fish, Shells, Kelp, Nacreous Green, Yellow, Mauve, 9 In. 165.00

Oyster Bowl, Flowers, Blue & White, 6 In. 88.00
Pitcher, Flow Blue, 8 1/2 In. 325.00

LUSTER glaze was meant to resemble copper, silver, or gold. It has
been used since the sixteenth century. Some of the luster found today
was made during the nineteenth century. The metallic glazes are
applied on pottery. The finished color depends on the combination of
the clay color and the glaze. Blue, orange, gold, and pearlized luster
decorations were used by Japanese and German firms in the early
1900s. Tea Leaf pieces have their own category.

Copper, Figurine, Dog, 7 1/2 In. 450.00
Copper, Gravy Boat, Ironstone 40.00
Copper, Pitcher, Classical Scenes, Blue & White Band, 4 1/4 In. 165.00
Copper, Pitcher, Dancers Both Sides, c.1880, 5 1/2 In. 58.00
Copper, Pitcher, Embossed Grapes & Leaves, 8 1/2 In. 35.00
Copper, Pitcher, Painted Design, Blue Band, Molded Neck 130.00
Copper, Pitcher, Pink & Purple Flowers, Leaves, England, 3 In. 45.00
Copper, Pitcher, Relief Polychrome Design, Blue Bands, Small 65.00
Copper, Pitcher, Zebulon Pike Portrait, Be Always Ready To Die For..., 7 1/4 In. 8625.00
Copper, Platter, Ironstone 45.00
Fairyland luster is included in the Wedgwood category.
Pink, Cup & Saucer, Floral 60.00
Pink, Mug, Faith, c.1830 .... 200.00
Pink, Mug, Frog, Nested Within Nautical Compass, 3 3/4 In. 115.00
Pink, Mug, Sailor's Farewell On 1 Side, Sailor's Prayer On Reverse Side, 5 5/8 In. 600.00
Pink, Pitcher, Floral, Small 75.00
Pink, Pitcher, Hunters & Dogs, Relief Mold 275.00
Pink, Pitcher, Yellow Floral, Gray's Pottery 130.00
Pink, Plate, House Decoration, 10 In, Pair 165.00
Pink, Sugar, Cover, Floral 225.00
Pink, Vase, 6 In. 18.00
Silver, Pitcher, Bird & Stag, Small 120.00
Silver, Pitcher, Canary Yellow, Black Transfer, Captain Jones & Ship Macedonian, 8 In. ... 1725.00
Silver, Pitcher, No Design, Large 90.00
Silver, Pitcher, Yellow, Landscape Scenes, United States Seal Under Spout, 7 3/4 In. 4025.00
Silver, Teapot, Scroll Handle, England, 9 1/2 In. 105.00
Sunderland luster pieces are listed in the Sunderland category.
Tea Leaf luster pieces are listed in the Tea Leaf Ironstone category.

LUSTRE ART GLASS Company was founded in Long Island, New York,
in 1920 by Conrad Vahlsing and Paul Frank. The company made lampshades and globes that are almost indistinguishable from those made
by Quezal. Most of the shades made by the company were unmarked.

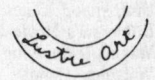

Floral & Garland, Ruby, Bohemian, Albert Prisms, 11 In. 485.00

LUSTRES are mantel decorations or pedestal vases with many hanging
glass prisms. The name really refers to the prisms, and it is proper to
refer to a single glass prism as a lustre. Either spelling, luster or lustre,
is correct.

Allover Flowers & Leaves, Prisms, Ruby, Fitted As Lamp, Bohemia, 19th Century, Pair .. 172.00
Blue Opaline, Gilt Tracery, Cut Glass Prisms, England, 19th Century, 10 1/4 In., Pair 460.00
Clear, Alternating Medallions, Maidens & Floral Sprays, Prisms, 12 In., Pair 3165.00
Crown Top Over Gilt & Floral Design, Hanging Prisms, Bristol, 15 In. 200.00
Enameled Floral & Jewel Design, Red & Gilt Ground, Shade, Bohemian, 24 In., Pair 690.00
Enameled Glass, Alternating Portraits & Floral, Allover Gilt Foliate, 13 3/4 In. 977.00
Mid Drip Pan, Faceted Prisms, Faceted Foot, 10 In., Pair 517.00
Ruby Etched To Clear, Bohemian, Flowers & Leaves, Hurricane Shade, 21 In., Pair 545.00

MAASTRICHT, Holland, was the city where Petrus Regout established
the De Sphinx pottery in 1836. The firm was noted for its transfer-
printed earthenware. Many factories in Maastricht are still making
ceramics.

Bowl, Abbey, 9 In. 33.00

Cup & Saucer, Oriental, c.1929, 4 3/4 In. 22.00
Cup & Saucer, Willow, Flow Blue Band 42.00
Plate, Oriental Blue, Scene Of Geisha Girls & Man, 8 1/2 In. 40.00
Platter, Holland Farm Scene, Windmills, 15 1/4 In. 65.00

MAIZE glass was made by W.L. Libbey & Son Company of Toledo, Ohio, after 1889. The glass resembled an ear of corn. The leaves were usually green, but some pieces were made with blue or red leaves. The kernels of corn were light yellow, white, or light green.

Butter, Cover, Blue Leaves, Edged In Gold 650.00
Celery Vase, Gold Leaves, 6 1/2 In. 225.00
Sugar Shaker, Opaque Mauve Barrel, Custard Leaves, Metal Lid, 5 5/8 In. 435.00
Tumbler, Green Leaves, Yellow Brown Tips, 4 In. 88.00

MAJOLICA is a general term for any pottery glazed with an opaque tin enamel that conceals the color of the clay body. It has been made since the fourteenth century. Today's collector is most likely to find Victorian majolica. The heavy, colorful ware is rarely marked. Some famous makers include Minton; Griffen, Smith and Hill (marked *Etruscan*); and Chesapeake Pottery (marked *Avalon* or *Clifton*). Majolica made by Wedgwood is listed in the Wedgwood category.

Asparagus Service, White Asparagus, Dark Green Ground, France, 13 Piece 1840.00
Basket, Twisted Twig Handle, Twig Rim, Pink Interior, Etruscan, 6 In. 440.00
Bowl, 3 Wood Nymphs Supporting Bowl, Continental, 19th Century, 16 In. 635.00
Bowl, Basket Weave & Laurel Swags, 2 Cherubs, Minton, c.1873, 10 1/2 In. 2585.00
Bowl, Crowned Woman, Fish In Border, 2 Handles, Late 19th Century, Spain, 14 1/4 In. . . . 275.00
Bowl, Embossed Leaf Design, 3 Light Blue Water Lilies, Dark Green, Green, 3 x 9 In. 85.00
Bowl, Scrolling Grape Vines, Winged Female Interior, Vine Handles, 7 1/4 In. 522.00
Bowl, Shell & Seaweed, Etruscan, 8 In. 137.00
Bowl, Shell & Seaweed, Pink, Brown, Blue-Gray, Green, Griffen, Smith & Hill, 8 3/8 In. . . 316.00
Box, Asparagus, France, 4 In. 255.00
Box, Cover, Flowers & Quail, Polychrome, 5 1/2 In. 385.00
Box, Cushion Tied With Yellow Ribbon, 5 Wells, G. Jones, 1870s, 10 5/8 In. 4312.00
Box, Sardine, Lily, White Lilies, Green Leaves, Yellow Ground, Etruscan, 9 In. 687.00
Box, Sardine, Pointed Leaves, Etruscan, 9 In. 412.00
Bread Tray, Oak Leaf, Acorns & Vine Handle, 12 In. 60.00
Butter, Branch Handle, Daisies On Cobalt Blue Ground, 7 3/4 In. 448.00
Butter Chip, Begonia Leaf, Etruscan, 3 In., Pair 66.00
Butter Chip, Geranium Leaf, Etruscan, 3 In., Pair 110.00
Butter Chip, Pansy, Etruscan, 3 In. 66.00
Butter Chip, Wire & Metal Frame Basket, Handle 275.00
Cachepot, Leaves, Wooden Staves, Rams With Horn Handle, 1800s, 8 x 9 In., Pair 875.00
Cachepot, Lions & Cubs With Blackamoor Masks, Late 19th Century, 11 In., Pair 2875.00
Cachepot, Snake, Lizard, Frogs, Man With Bagpipes, Marked, F. Mosin, 1880, 12 In. 1610.00
Cachepot, Winged Serpent Handles, 2 Acanthus Capped Columns, 10 1/4 In. 357.00
Cake Plate, Pond Lily, Brown, Green, Lavender, 12 In. 170.00
Cake Stand, Brown, Green Berries, Footed, 5 1/4 x 8 1/2 In. 110.00
Cake Stand, Dark Green, Etruscan 450.00
Cake Stand, Maple Leaves, Pink Ground, Etruscan 275.00
Cake Stand, White Ground, Etruscan 275.00
Candy Dish, Leaves & Pansy Shape, Green, Italy 58.00
Casket, Cover, Lizard Design, Snake, Palissy Style, 6 1/2 In. 1840.00
Centerpiece, 2 Mermen Supporting Shell, Children, Seaweed, Minton, 1865, 21 In. 8235.00
Centerpiece, 3 Tiers, Blue, Green, Mauve, Yellow, Winged Griffins 2750.00
Charger, Story Of Aurora & Cephalus, 12 1/4 In. 247.00
Cheese Keeper, Cover, George Jones 6600.00
Coffeepot, Shell & Seaweed, Etruscan, 6 In. 550.00
Compote, Dandy On Pedestal, Tree Trunk, Oval Bowl, 28 1/4 In. 92.00
Compote, Lily Pad, 3-Bird Base, 10 In. 440.00
Compote, Maple Leaf, Etruscan, 9 x 7 In. 302.00
Compote, Shell & Seaweed, Etruscan, 9 x 6 In. 385.00
Compote, Twisting Leaf, Vine Border, Green Glaze, 4 x 10 In. 93.00
Creamer, Blackberry, Mottled Green, 4 In. 30.00

Majolica, Garden Seat, Birds,
Floral, George Jones, 18 In.

Majolica, Pitcher,
Leaf & Floral, Minton, 8 In.

Majolica, Pitcher, Owl,
George Morley

Creamer, Cauliflower, Etruscan	70.00
Creamer, Corn, Etruscan, Signed, 3 7/8 In.	185.00
Creamer, Hawthorn, Etruscan, 4 1/4 In.	225.00
Cup & Saucer, Mustache, Shell & Seaweed, Etruscan	100.00 to 125.00
Cup & Saucer, Shell & Seaweed, Etruscan, 3-In. Cup, 6-In. Saucer	110.00
Cuspidor, Shell & Seaweed, Etruscan, 6 In.	275.00
Dish, Amorial, Lizard, Frog, Snake, Palissy Style, Oval, 1873, 11 x 8 In.	4600.00
Dish, Butter, Cover, Butterfly, Blue, Yellow Checkerboard Design, Etruscan, 8 In.	220.00
Dish, Butter, Cover, Shell & Seaweed, Etruscan, 4 In.	275.00
Dish, Cottage Scene, Oval, 1880, 11 3/4 x 7 3/4 In.	745.00
Dish, Fish & Shells, Palissy Style, Oval, 1885, 24 1/2 x 16 1/2 In.	1380.00
Dish, Fish In Center, Lizards, Green Leaves, Foliage, Palissy Style, 16 In., Pair	5750.00
Dish, Fish, Eel, Shells, Palissy Style, Green Leafage, Circular, Marked, Caldas, 16 In.	1265.00
Dish, Fish, Eels, Frog, Lizard, Shells, Palissy Style, Oval, 1880, 17 1/2 In.	3735.00
Dish, Fish, Shells, Eel, Palissy Style, Green Leaves, Foliage, Circular, 9 1/2 In.	1265.00
Dish, Fish, Shells, Foliage, Palissy Style, Oval, 1880, 12 In.	745.00
Dish, Flowering Branch, Bird Perched On Edge, Blue, Matching Slotted Spoon, 10 In.	1240.00
Dish, Frog & Butterfly, Circular, Marked, Jose A. Cunha, 5 3/4 In.	2185.00
Dish, Game Pie, Cover & Liner, Dead Partridge On Ferns, Signed, Jones, c.1865, 11 In.	3737.00
Dish, Game Pie, Dead Birds Rim, Fox Crouching Near Dead Bird, Jones, 1875, 11 In.	6900.00
Dish, Game, Dead Game On Cover, Twig Handle, Insert, Minton, 1867, 13 In.	1540.00
Dish, Grape Leaf, Phoenixville, Mid 19th Century, 9 In., Pair	220.00
Dish, Leaf, Begonia, Green Begonia Leaf, Yellow Butterfly Perched In Center, 6 In.	247.00
Dish, Lizard & Foliage, Palissy Style, Oval, 1870, 15 1/4 In.	2875.00
Dish, Lizard Fighting Snake, Insects, Butterfly, Circular, Da Rainha, 11 In.	865.00 to 1265.00
Dish, Lizards, Fighting, Frogs, Shells, Palissy Style, Silver, 1890, 19 x 14 In.	2185.00
Dish, Lizards, Mussels, Foliage, Silver, Palissy Style, Rectangular, 1888, 18 x 14 In.	3735.00
Dish, Lobster Amidst Cabbage Leaves, Circular, 1896, 17 In.	3450.00
Dish, Pickle, Begonia, Etruscan	120.00
Dish, Shells & Foliage, Palissy Style, Oval, 16 3/4 x 10 3/4 In., Pair	6325.00
Dish, Shells, Lizards, Frogs, Palissy Style, Silver, Oval, 1880, Pair	2875.00
Dish, Snake, Fish, Frogs, Foliage, Palissy Style, Oval, 1880, 21 x 14 In.	1380.00
Dish, Snake, Lizard, Lobster, Frog, Palissy Style, Oval, F. Maurice, 16 1/2 x 11 In.	2990.00
Dish, Snake, Toad, Lizard, Butterfly, Palissy Style, Circular, Marked, Jose A. Cunha	1955.00
Ewer, Continuous Frieze Of Animals, Landscape, 12 1/2 In.	230.00
Ewer, Flamingo, In Cattails, Head Handle, 22 In.	190.00
Ewer, Floral, Child & Scrolls, Blue Lining, Impressed, W.S. & S., 15 In.	660.00
Fern Stand, Green, Brown, Heron With Wings, On Pedestal, 37 1/2 x 20 In.	316.00
Figurine, Heron, Bold Colors, Minton, England, c.1870, 21 3/4 In.	3600.00
Figurine, Native Woman, Playing Cymbals, Natural Base, Continental, 19 1/2 In.	575.00
Figurine, Parrot, Perch On Branch, 12 In.	258.00
Figurine, Victorian Woman, On Bench With Cat	235.00
Figurine, Wading Bird, On Water Lilies, Blue, Continental, c.1870, 11 In., Pair	1840.00
Garden Seat, 3 Winged Lion Masks Supports, Continental, c.1880, 20 In.	2300.00
Garden Seat, Birds, Floral, George Jones, 18 In. Illus	9632.00

Humidor, Man With Mustache, Large Hat, 8 1/2 In. 385.00
Humidor, Monk Head 395.00
Humidor, Pipe Tobacco 95.00
Humidor, Shell & Seaweed, Etruscan 130.00
Inkstand, Circular Form Well, Masks Relief, Dolphin Base, Italy, 6 1/2 In. 290.00
Jar, Cover, Figural, Seated Indian Smoking Pipe, Continental, 10 In. 200.00
Jar, Druggist's, Handles, Mounted As Table Lamp, c.1920, 18 1/2 In. 250.00
Jardiniere, Fish & Seaweed, Green, Pink, Tan, Stand, 1920, 39 In. 287.00
Jardiniere, Medallions, Female Heads, America & Africa, Minton, c.1870, 19 1/2 In. 4600.00
Jardiniere, Mythological Figures, Pedestal, 19th Century, 57 1/2 x 16 x 16 In. 3360.00
Jardiniere, Pedestal, Herons & Birds Among Lotus Flowers, Relief, England, 40 In. 1955.00
Jardiniere, Peony Flowers, Oriental Ducks, Relief, Minton, c.1877, 10 1/2 In. 1265.00
Jardiniere, Stand Greek Border, Swooping Swallows, Holdcroft, 1870, 13 3/4 In. 977.00
Jardiniere, Stand, Classical Dancing Maidens, Tortoiseshell Glaze, 40 In. 1540.00
Jardiniere, Stand, Cobalt Blue, Turquoise, Brown & Tan Scrolls, 1875-1900, 44 1/2 In. . . 1320.00
Jardiniere, Stand, Vertical Foliate, 2 Hands Of Geometric Design, Brown, Beige, 27 In. . . 575.00
Jug, Baseball & Soccer Players, Pink Glaze Interior, Etruscan, 7 In. 1870.00
Jug, Flamingo, Neck Handle, Bulbous, 7 In. 280.00
Jug, Sunflower, Dimpled, Blue, Enamel, Etruscan, Griffen, Smith & Hill, 1800s, 7 5/8 In. . 430.00
Match Pot, Open Bamboo Stem, 2 Monkeys, Relief, Minton, c.1872, 7 1/2 In. 2587.00
Mug, Pineapple, Etruscan 325.00
Mug, Water Lily, Etruscan . . . . .25.00 to 50.00
Oyster Plate, 6 Shells, Vine Design 750.00
Oyster Plate, Shell Design, Scalloped Edge, Lavender, Green, Ivory Glaze, 8 1/2 In. 1320.00
Pedestal, Fruit-Filled Swags, Acanthus, Oak Leaves, Acorns, Minton, c.1880, 37 In. 1725.00
Pedestal, Molded Thistles, Austria, 36 In. 175.00
Pitcher, Basket Weave, Floral, George Jones, 1878, 8 3/4 In. 825.00
Pitcher, Cream, Albino Coral, Etruscan, 3 In. 66.00
Pitcher, Drinking Scene, Gargoyle Spout, France 175.00
Pitcher, Fern, Etruscan, 6 In. 176.00
Pitcher, Fern, Etruscan, 8 In. 600.00
Pitcher, Fish Form, Mouth Agape, Tail Forms Handle, Late 19th Century, 10 5/16 In. 200.00
Pitcher, Floral Design, Lily Pad, White Ground, 7 In. 250.00
Pitcher, Green Leaf, Embossed Flowers, Twig Handle, Minton, 8 In. 650.00
Pitcher, Hummingbird Body, Cobalt Blue, Yellow Caned Base, 8 1/4 In. 275.00
Pitcher, Leaf & Floral, Minton, 8 In. . . . .*Illus* 715.00
Pitcher, Owl, George Morley . . . .*Illus* 225.00
Pitcher, Peach Tree Design, 8 In. 275.00
Pitcher, Pink Leaf, Green, Pink Top Leaves, 8 In. 165.00
Pitcher, Shell & Seaweed, Etruscan, 6 1/2 In. 200.00
Pitcher, Shell & Seaweed, Etruscan, 8 In. 890.00
Pitcher, Syrup, Albino Sunflower, Etruscan, 8 In. 192.00
Pitcher, Syrup, Coral, Etruscan, 6 In. 165.00
Pitcher, Wild Rose, Butterfly Spout, Etruscan, 8 In. 225.00
Pitcher, Woven Fence, Leaves Growing Through Fence, Pink Interior, 8 In. 50.00
Planter, Basket Weave, 3 Tiers, Avian, Oak Branch, Leaf, Acorn Design, 10 1/2 In. 172.00
Planter, Mythical Figures, Pedestal, 1850 . . . . 1150.00
Plaque, Snake, Frog, Beetle, Butterfly, Caterpillars, Brown Mottled Glaze, 3 x 9 In. 977.00
Plaque, Snake, Lizard, Butterfly, Centipede, Beetle On Musgo Ground, 3 x 9 1/2 In. 1265.00
Plate, Begonia Leaf, Etruscan, 12 In. 110.00
Plate, Cauliflower, Etruscan, 8 In. . . . . .250.00 to 375.00
Plate, Cauliflower, Etruscan, 9 In. 275.00
Plate, Dandelions, Zell, 1907-1928, 7 1/4 In. 35.00
Plate, Escargot, 6 Shells, 8 1/4 In., 4 Piece 115.00
Plate, Hen, Fluted Rim, France, 9 In. 485.00
Plate, Leaf, 8 1/2 In. 100.00
Plate, Leaf, Green, Blue, White, 8 In. 65.00
Plate, Maple Leaves, Pink, Etruscan, 8 In. 275.00
Plate, Pond Lily, 5 In. 100.00
Plate, Rooster, Fluted Rim, France, 9 In. 325.00
Platter, Asparagus, Brown Basket, Asparagus Form Handle, 17 In. 200.00
Platter, Banana Leaves, Yellow & Green, 12 In. 140.00
Platter, Center Lobster, Frog, Lizard & Foliage Ground, T.V. Sergent, c.1880, 11 In. 4887.00

Platter, Central Lobster, Border Of Shell Fish, Jose A. Cunha, c.1900, 13 In. 6325.00
Platter, Dog & Doghouse, 10 1/2 In. 195.00
Platter, Geranium, Etruscan, 12 In. 192.00
Platter, Glazed Fish & Lobster, Frogs In Ground, Goras & Cie, 1891, 18 3/4 In. 3455.00
Platter, Oval Fan & Butterfly, Blue Ground, Shield Mark, 13 1/4 x 9 1/2 In. 185.00
Platter, Palissy Style, Shells, Lizards, Frogs, 15 x 12 In. 3000.00
Platter, Wheat, Eat Thy Bread, 12 1/2 In. 165.00
Platter, Wild Rose Design, Turquoise Ground, 13 In. 285.00
Punch Bowl, Lotus Blossoms, Cloud Design, Holdcroft, Late 19th Century, 15 In. 920.00
Salver, Grape Leaf Cluster, Strawberries, Dark Green, 2 1/2 x 8 1/2 In., Pair 90.00
Sauce, Daisy, Etruscan, 8 In. 275.00
Smoking, Stand, Black Boy With Pipe, Polychrome, 4 5/8 In. 302.00
Strawberry Dish, Spoon, Strawberry Plants, Figural Bird, George Jones, 11 In. 1725.00
Strawberry Set, Leaves & Blossoms, Heart Shape Tray, Creamer & Sugar, c.1870 . . . . . . 1150.00
Sugar, Fern & Bamboo, Wardie, Brown & Green 112.00
Syrup, Shell & Seaweed, Pair 605.00
Syrup, Sunflower 665.00
Teapot, Shell & Seaweed, Etruscan, 6 1/2 In. 465.00
Tile, Moor Geometric, Floral Design, Square, France, 10 1/2 In. 92.00
Tile, Roman Maiden Carrying Urn, Red, Sherwin & Cotton, 18 x 6 In., Pair 440.00
Tobacco Jar, Head Of Indian Chief 258.00
Tray, Biscuit, Deer & Dog, Scalloped, 11 In. 165.00
Tray, Leaf Shape, Begonia Leaf, Tan, Pink, Green, Etruscan, 9 x 6 3/4 In. 125.00
Tureen, Fish & Game, George Jones 8250.00
Umbrella Stand, Pierced Canopy Top, Green To Blue Glaze, 26 1/2 In. 690.00
Umbrella Stand, Tree Trunk Form, Stork & Ostrich, Turquoise Ground, 23 In. 345.00
Urn, Classical Figures, Landscape, Architecture, Satyr Faces, Snake Handles, 25 In., Pair . 2530.00
Urn, Cover, Winged Cherub Handles, Fruit Swags, Hugo Lonitz, c.1880, 28 In. 5175.00
Urn, Medieval Knights Jousting, Pastoral Landscape, Italy, 26 In. 550.00
Vase, Butterfly, Shells, Snails, Flowers, Alligator Handles, Palissy Style, 11 1/2 In. 600.00
Vase, Cherubs & Scrolled Foliage, Armorial Oval Reserve, 16 In. 747.00
Vase, Cherubs Reserve, Scrolled Snake Handles, Blue, Green Foliate Ground, 22 In. 690.00
Vase, Double Gourd, Lizard Design, 1906, 12 1/2 In., Pair 6900.00
Vase, Floral, Mottled Brown Ground, Belgium, 10 3/4 In. 58.00
Vase, Flower Blossoms, 18th Century Gentleman & Woman, c.1890, 12 In., Pair 145.00
Vase, Indian Woman, Holding Water Jug, Flower Forms Vase, 17 1/2 In. 330.00
Vase, Lizards, Frogs, Snakes, Handles, Baluster, 10 3/4 In., Pair 3740.00
Vase, Lizards, Frogs, Snakes, Handles, Baluster, 14 1/2 In., Pair 4600.00
Vase, Mask Of Medusa, 2 Handles, Achille Barbizet, 20 3/4 In., Pair 7475.00
Vase, Neptune & Wife, Tritons Surround, Satyr Masks, 19th Century, 16 In., Pair 770.00
Vase, Reptiles, Snakes, 2 Handles On Neck, 1870, 18 1/4 In., Pair 4600.00
Vase, Shield Shape, 2 Handles, Relief Children Playing, c.1880, 17 3/4 In., Pair 1725.00
Vase, Tree Branches, Green, Baluster, 1900, 14 1/2 In. 490.00
Wall Pocket, Butterfly, Cattails, Ferns, Yellow, Palissy Style, 11 1/2 In. 900.00
Wall Pocket, Crab & Snail, Palissy Style 175.00
Wall Pocket, Monkey Suspended By Arm, Gnarled Tree Trunk, c.1880, 18 In., Pair 4887.00
Window Box, Bamboo & Bird, Hampshire, 13 1/4 In. 110.00

MALACHITE is a green stone with unusual layers or rings of darker
green shades. It is often polished and used for decorative objects. Most
malachite comes from Siberia or Australia.

Ashtray, Green Glass, With Spites, Omela, Czech Republic, 7 3/4 In. 27.00
Box, Quatrefoil Shape, Foliage Mounts, Velvet Lined Interior, 7 In. 2185.00
Jewelry Box, Veneered, Silk Lining, Russia, Late 19th Century, 12 In. 3160.00
Vase, Green Glass, Molded Roses & Cut Panels, Omela, Czech Republic, 9 1/2 In. 55.00

MAPS of all types have been collected for centuries. The earliest known
printed maps were made in 1478. The first printed street map showed
London in 1559. The first road maps for use by drivers of automobiles
were made in 1901. Collectors buy maps that were pages of old books,
as well as the multifolded road maps popular in this century.

Albany, N.Y., 1851, 17 x 13 In. 71.00
America, G. Delisle, Engraving, Hand Colored, Covens & Mortimer, 1774, 21 x 24 In. . . . 1870.00

Anguar Island, Palua Group, Lt. Commander M.M. Champlin, 17 x 23 In. 165.00
Atlanta, Gulf Road, Color Picture Of Atlanta City Hall, 1972 .... 7.00
Brabant, Guillaume De L'Isle, Amsterdam, 18th Century, 26 x 27 In. 445.00
Cinquieme Plan De La Ville De Paris, Jucherau St. Denis, c.1703, 17 1/8 x 20 3/4 In. ... 2740.00
Connecticut, Comic Pictures, Yale, Mills, Hats, Sports, 1937, 12 x 9 In. 35.00
Connecticut, Hand Colored, Colton, 1855, 13 x 16 In. 75.00
Delaware, Industries, Chemicals, Fishing, Apple Growing Pictures, 1937, 9 x 12 In. 35.00
England, Counties, Waterways, Floral Wreath, Embroidered, Silk, Frame, 22 In. 488.00
Globe, Celestial & Terrestrial, Fruitwood Stand, W. & J.H. Bardin, London, 26 In., Pair .. 11500.00
Globe, Half-Meridian, Ebonized Stand, Dr. A. Krause, Germany, c.1930, 27 In. 860.00
Globe, John Betts, Queen's Royal Letters, 19th Century, Wooden Box, 14 In. 715.00
Globe, Joslin's Solar Telluric, Terrestrial, Brass Engraved Meridian Ring & Base 1650.00
Globe, Mahogany Standard, Pad Feet, Circular Compass, c.1800, 24 In. 3450.00
Globe, Owens-Illinois, Teardrop, Art Deco Aluminum 3-Footed Stand, 1931, 23 In. 515.00
Globe, Slate Surface, Ebonized Base, Jan Felkl & Son, Prague, c.1900, 21 1/2 In. 920.00
Globe, Terrestrial, Cast Iron Base, Leaf Tip Feet, H. Schedler, 1880s, 12 In. 805.00
Globe, Terrestrial, Cherry Stand, Josiah Loring, 1838 .... 2090.00
Globe, Terrestrial, Ebonized Wood Foot & Shaft Supports, Bastien, 21 1/2 In. 345.00
Globe, Terrestrial, Full Meridian, Stand, Downswept Legs, George F. Cram, 35 In. 1265.00
Globe, Terrestrial, Parchment Meridian & Chapter Ring, 1787, 19 x 12 1/2 In. 4312.00
Globe, Terrestrial, Raised On Ebonized Base, Jan Felkl & Son, 1921, 18 x 8 In. 490.00
Globe, Terrestrial, Reticulated Patinated Metal Base, Early To Mid 20th Century, 20 In. .. 130.00
Globe, Terrestrial, Victorian, Mahogany Stand, W. & D.K. Johnston, 1900, 43 x 25 In. ... 6325.00
Globe, Terrestrial, Wrought Iron Base, Ellen E. Fitz, Ginn & Heath, c.1870, 16 In. 1595.00
Globe, Traveler's On Voyages & Cruises, Sharkskin Case, Newton, 2 1/2 In. 8000.00
Great Salt Lake & Surrounding Country, Weller, 1858, 16 7/8 x 12 In. 115.00
Illinois & Missouri Roads, Tanner's Traveling Map, Canals, Railroads, 28 In. 220.00
Invasions Of England & Ireland, Hand Colored, Engraved, Speed, 15 x 20 1/2 In. 546.00
Jackson, California's Golden Chain, Mother Lode Highway, 1949, 22 x 17 In. 19.00
Jerome, Montgomery County, Texas, Folded, Late 19th Century, 20 x 16 In. 85.00
Kentucky, Ohio Falls Insert, Ornate, Matted, 1850, 11 x 14 In. 95.00
L'Amerique, Hand Colored, Framed, Paris, 21 1/4 x 28 1/2 In. 1705.00
London, Windsor, Hampton Court, Kensington Vignettes, Frame, Germany, 20 x 23 In. ... 385.00
Long Island, State Parks, 1939, 12 Pages, 4 x 9 In. 15.00
Louisiana, Blacks & Creole Pictures, 1937, 9 x 12 In. 25.00
Maine, Hand Colored, Ornate, Colton, 1855, 12 x 16 In. 90.00
Massachusetts, Cyclist's Road, 1891 .... 270.00
Minnesota, Motor Trails, Frye Drop Gasoline, 1928, 4 x 9 In. 230.00
Minnesota, Shell, 3 Panels, 1929, 12 x 9 In. 150.00
Minnesota & North Dakota, White Eagle Oil & Refining Co., 1929, 11 7/8 x 9 In. 60.00
Missouri & Arkansas, Map Of The States, S.A. Mitchell, 1844, 21 x 17 1/4 In. 203.00
New Map Of The Western Rivers Or Traveler's Guide, 1845, 12 x 24 In. 165.00
New Mexico, Indians, Cowboys, Mexican Border Residents Picture, 1937, 9 x 12 In. 35.00
New World, Northeast Coast Of Canada & America, Ottens, 1855, 19 3/4 x 24 In. 495.00
New York, Texaco Petroleum Products, 3 Panels, 1924, 4 x 9 In. 70.00
Norman's Plan Of New Orleans & Environs, Shields & Hammond, 1845, 18 x 24 In. 385.00
North & South Carolina, Henry Mouzon, 1775, 35 5/8 x 55 7/8 In. 5500.00
North Carolina, Hand Colored, Ornate Border, Colton, Matted, 1855, 12 x 16 In. 100.00
North Carolina, Matted, Framed, Samuel Lewis, 17 3/4 x 25 In. 440.00
North Part Of Great Britain Called Scotland, Herman Moll, Frame, 23 x 39 In. 440.00
Pennsylvania, Virginia, Delaware & Maryland, Johnston's, 18 x 26 1/4 In. 35.00
San Francisco, Exposition City, A Bird's Eye View, Lithograph, Frame, 14 1/2 x 22 In. ... 185.00
Scots Settlement In America, Called New Caledonia, Moll, 1710, 10 1/8 x 8 1/4 In. 172.00
Sketch Of Pontchartrain Harbour & Breakwater, c.1853, 7 3/4 x 35 3/4 In. 365.00
Smith's New Map Of Philadelphia & Vicinity, J.L. Smith, 1890, 22 1/2 x 28 1/2 In. 38.00
South Dakota, State Highway, Mt. Rushmore As Work In Progress, 1938 .... 11.00
Tennessee, Hand Colored, Nashville & Knoxville Inserts, Matted, 1850, 11 x 15 In. 100.00
Terra Australia, Captain Flinders, Surveyor, 1849, 27 x 39 In. 135.00
Thames & Medway, Tombleson's Panoramic Map, Frame, 49 x 10 In. 275.00
Turkey In Europe, New & Accurate Map, E. Bowen, 14 1/8 x 17 In. 115.00
U.S. & Eastern Canada, Atlas, Rand McNally, 1933, 97 Page, 14 x 10 In. 25.00
United States, Paper On Linen, Rod At Top & Bottom For Rolling, 1904, 64 x 84 In. ... 198.00
United States, Textile, Frame, G.W. Boynton, 1841, 28 1/2 x 26 1/2 In. 385.00

United States, Welling & Gray, 1871	165.00
Utah, Travel Utah With Conoco, Conoco Travel Bureau, 1933	18.00
Virginia & Maryland, New & Accurate Map, 1752, 13 1/8 x 9 1/4 In.	345.00
Western New World, Silk Embroidered, Garland Of Flowers, c.1800, 16 3/4 x 15 In.	345.00
World, Pen & Ink, By Emily Ellis, Shefford Academy, 1840, 11 1/4 x 17 1/4 In.	575.00

MARBLE collectors pay highest prices for glass and sulphide marbles. The game of marbles has been popular since the days of the ancient Romans. American children were able to buy marbles by the mid-eighteenth century. Dutch glazed clay marbles were least expensive. Glazed pottery marbles, attributed to the Bennington potteries in Vermont, were of a better quality. Marbles made of pink marble were also available by the 1830s. Glass marbles seem to have been made later. By 1880, Samuel C. Dyke of South Akron, Ohio, was making clay marbles and The National Onyx Marble Company was making marbles of onyx. The Navarre Glass Marble Company of Navarre, Ohio, and M. B. Mishler of Ravenna, Ohio, made the glass marbles. Ohio remained the center of the marble industry, and the Akron-made Akro Agate brand became nationally known. Other pieces made by Akro Agate are listed in this book in the Akro Agate category. Sulphides are glass marbles with frosted white figures in the center.

Bag, Master Made Marbles, Indian Head Design, White Leather, 5 1/4 x 3 1/2 In.	190.00
Clear, Mica Flakes, Pink & White Core, 1 7/16 In.	875.00
Latticinio, Orange & White, 5/8 In.	110.00
Latticinio, Red, Orange & White, 7/8 In.	225.00
Latticinio, White, 22 3/8 In.	310.00
Latticinio, Yellow & White, 1 13/16 In.	200.00
Lutz, 2 Gold Bands, 4 Brown Bands, 1 15/32 In.	475.00
Lutz, 4 Blue, 2 Gold Bands, 1 11/32 In.	175.00
Lutz, Onionskin, 2 1/32 In.	275.00
Lutz, Shooter, 2 Gold, 4 Orange Bands, 26/32 In.	140.00
Onionskin, Pee Wee, 3/4 In.	150.00
Onionskin, Red, Blue & White, Mica Flakes, 1 1/2 In.	525.00
Onionskin, Shooter, Mica, 26/32 In.	115.00
Sulphide, Andy, Comic, 5/8 In.	60.00
Sulphide, Bimbo, Comic, 11/16 In.	75.00
Sulphide, Boar, 1 1/2 In.	75.00
Sulphide, Hen Sitting On Nest, 1 18 1/2 In.	125.00
Sulphide, Husky Dog, 1 11/32 In.	90.00
Sulphide, Lion, 1 1/2 In.	65.00
Sulphide, Neanderthal Man, 1 1/2 In.	450.00
Sulphide, Punch 1 Side & Judy Other, 1 3/4 In.	1550.00
Sulphide, Siamese Kitten Laying Down, Gibson, 1 1/2 In.	35.00
Sulphide, Smitty, Comic, 5/8 In.	75.00
Swirl, Clear, 4 Colored Ribbons, White Threads, 1 1/2 In.	140.00

MARBLE CARVINGS, such as large or small figurines, groups of people or animals, and architectural decorations, have been a special art form since the time of the ancient Greeks. Reproductions, especially of large Victorian groups, are being made of a mixture using marble dust. These are very difficult to detect and collectors should be careful. Other carvings are listed under Alabaster.

Buddah Head, Asian, 17 1/2 In.	545.00
Bust, 2 Girls, Playing Peek-A-Boo, Italy, 19th Century, 23 1/2 In.	1380.00
Bust, Alexander The Great, Pedestal, Late 19th-Early 20th Century, 22 1/4 In.	9775.00
Bust, Apollo & Diana, Italy, 12 x 15 x 9 In., Pair	14850.00
Bust, Apollo, Carved Features & Tunic, Carrara Marble, P. Barzanti, 25 In.	2300.00
Bust, Bacchante, 31 In.	9775.00
Bust, Beauty With A Rose, Spiral Fluted Stem, Alabaster Pedestal, 20 In.	2645.00
Bust, Boy, Gold & Brown Cape On Mottled Base	190.00
Bust, Classical Maiden, C.A. Rossi, 1875, 23 x 16 In.	2660.00
Bust, Classical Male Portrait, Waldo Story, 21 In., 36-In. Pedestal	6900.00

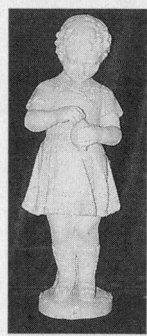

Marble Carving,
Statue, Girl,
Depositing Coin
In Bank, Antonio
Frilli, 31 In.

Marble is porous and will absorb water vapors into the stone up to 6 inches deep. Airborne pollutants will also be absorbed, and eventually, when the marble dries, the dirt will erode or stain the surface of the marble. Avoid humidity.

Bust, Dante, Socle Base, Italy, 25 In.	880.00
Bust, Harem Girl, A. Frille, Italy, 19th Century, 17 1/2 x 19 In.	2230.00
Bust, Male Figure, Ermes, 16 1/2 In.	715.00
Bust, Marie Antoinette, Draped Shoulders, Stepped Socle, 19th Century, 29 In.	4312.00
Bust, Milton, On Square Pedestal, L. Bentusi, 26 1/2 In., 49-In. Pedestal	2070.00
Bust, Moliere, On Mottled Pedestal, 22 In., 49 1/2-In. Pedestal	5750.00
Bust, Nell Gwinn, On Pedestal, Waldo Story, 39 In., 18-In. Pedestal	8625.00
Bust, Nero, Rose & White Veined Socle, Late 19th Century, 32 1/2 In.	7475.00
Bust, Roman Statesman, Coral Colored Cloak, Black Socle, 19th Century, 28 In.	4885.00
Bust, Roman Statesman, Veined Marble Robe, Socle, Late 19th Century, 32 3/4 In.	9775.00
Bust, Sappho, Laurel Wreath, Lyre, Plinth Base, R. Moulini, France, 16 In.	1100.00
Bust, Venus De Milo, Sculpted Marble Toro, Original Socle, Italy, 22 x 14 In.	2420.00
Bust, Woman, Bronze Toga, Green Base, Continental, 19th Century, 11 In.	1380.00
Bust, Woman, Deeply Carved Hair & Clothing, Round Footed Plinth, 24 In.	896.00
Bust, Woman, Gray Veined Marble Shawl, Gray Marble Base, 14 x 12 In.	660.00
Bust, Young Beauty, Rusticated Red Marble, Fluted Socle, Italy, 1900, 25 In.	2645.00
Bust, Young Girl, Yellow & Black Pedestal, F. Vichi, 27 In., 52-In. Pedestal	4885.00
Bust, Young Woman, Braided Hair, Pedestal, A. Gambacciani, c.1900, 29 1/4 In.	8050.00
Bust, Young Woman, Pious, Lace, Floral Bodice, Marble Socle, Italy, 6 In.	7475.00
Column, Green, Black Marble Base, 25 1/2 In., Pair	1650.00
Eskimo & Walrus, Dark Green, Canada, 7 x 13 In.	770.00
Ewer, Bacchanalian Mask, Leaf Design, Ram's Head Spout, 35 In., Pair	4600.00
Parian Figure, Rebecca At The Well, 21 In.	660.00
Pedestal, Antico Verde, Late 19th Century, 41 In.	1725.00
Pedestal, Column, 30 In., Pair	550.00
Pedestal, Faux Marble, Circular Columns, Square Plinth Base, 45 In., Pair	1265.00
Pedestal, Louis XVI, Green, Bronze Mounts, Tapered, 49 In., Pair	1650.00
Pedestal, Round Column, Square Base, Pair	5280.00
Pedestal, White, Gray Marble, Gadrooned Stem, Octagonal, 31 In.	460.00
Plaque, Crucifixion, Relief, Continental, 1876, 7 3/4 x 8 In.	336.00
Plaque, Profile Of Victorian Woman, Oval, Wood Frame, 20 x 15 1/2 In.	220.00
Polar Bear, Standing On Hind Legs, Bare Teeth, Green, Canada, 13 In.	740.00
Portrait Of Young Lady, Bronze, Ivory, George Van Der Straeten, 15 In.	2495.00
Statue, Cupid, Head On Quiver, Holding Bow, 19th Century, 13 x 22 In.	3630.00
Statue, Eagle, On Rocky Crag, Dead Lion Cub In Talons, 30 In.	1100.00
Statue, Girl, Depositing Coin In Bank, Antonio Frilli, 31 In. ....*Illus*	7150.00
Statue, Little Mischief Makers, G. Gambogi, 17 3/4 In.	3450.00
Statue, Musk Ox, Dark Green, Bone Horns, Canada, 13 x 16 In.	660.00
Statue, Ode To A Grecian Urn, Louis Carrier, 21 x 23 In.	7150.00
Statue, Poodle, Continental, 9 1/2 In.	430.00
Statue, Praying Madonna, Pink, Art Moderne, 27 In.	165.00
Statue, Roman Woman, Standing, Toga, Hair Pulled Back, c.1890, 39 In.	1840.00
Statue, Seated Angel Holding Butterfly, 20 In.	1210.00
Statue, Seminude Classical Female, Late 19th-Early 20th Century, 42 1/2 In.	6325.00
Statue, Shepherdess, Continental, 25 In.	460.00
Statue, St. Francis, Standing, Holding Christ Child, 40 1/2 In.	4600.00

Statue, Water Carrier, Standing By Fountain, 19th Century, Italy, 35 1/2 In. 4600.00
Tazza, Neoclassical, Waisted Stem, Stepped Black Marble Base, 8 In. 1380.00
Tazza, Scrolled Handles, Marble Bronze Base, 13 In., Pair 4025.00
Urn, Amphora Shape, Square Foot, Victorian, 1875-1900, 14 In., Pair 935.00
Urn, Bobbin Turned, Round Foot, Victorian, 1875-1900, 11 In., Pair 440.00
Urn, Bulbous, Round Foot, Victorian, 1875-1900, 12 In., Pair 770.00
Urn, Gilt Bronze, Rams' Heads, Guilloche Banding, Napoleon III, 19 In. 935.00
Urn, Louis XVI Style, Gilt Bronze Cover, Satyr's Mask Supports, 20 1/2 In., Pair 5175.00
Urn, Marble Tazza, Pedestal, Gray Veining Throughout, 43 In., Pair 402.00
Urn, Regency Style, Red, Gadrooned, Bronze Mounts, F. Barbedienne, 13 In. 9200.00
Vase, Louis XVI, Brass Stiff Leaves, Loop Handles, Wreath Foot, 15 In., Pair 2300.00
Walrus, Dark Green, Inserted Bone Tusks, Canada, 9 x 15 In. 630.00

MARBLEHEAD Pottery was founded in 1905 by Dr. J. Hall as a rehabilitative program for the patients of a Marblehead, Massachusetts, sanitarium. Two years later it was separated from the sanitarium and it continued operations until 1936. Many of the pieces were decorated with marine motifs.

Bookends, Embossed Green & Orange Ship, Blue Ground, Ship Stamp, 5 1/2 In. 880.00
Bookends, Painted & Carved Ships At Sea, Signed, Paper Label, Square, 5 In. 3575.00
Bookends, Triptych, Embossed, Blue Ground, 5 1/2 x 5 1/2 In., Pair 1045.00
Bowl, Blue Matte Glaze, Closed Form, 6 1/2 In. 285.00
Bowl, Blue Matte Glaze, Low, 6 In. 240.00
Bowl, Dark Cobalt Blue Matte Glaze, Closed-In Rim, Impressed Mark, 3 In. 375.00
Bowl, Flared, Lotus Design, Embossed, Light Blue Semimatte Interior, 4 x 8 In. 358.00
Bowl, Green & Charcoal Matte Glaze, Squat, Winged M Mark, 3 x 4 1/4 In. 440.00
Bowl, Green Matte Glaze, Impressed Mark, 7 1/2 In. 285.00
Bowl, Painted Geometric Design, Black Against Green Ground, Marked, 8 In. 2310.00
Bowl, Stylized Design, Dark Brown Against Oatmeal Ground, Marked, 7 In. 5500.00
Candlestick, Blue Matte Glaze, 6 1/2 In., Pair 440.00
Chamberstick, Rounded Handle, Green Matte Glaze, Impressed Mark, 8 1/2 In. 550.00
Pitcher, Blue Matte Glaze, 4 In. 285.00
Pitcher, Ship Picture, Impressed Logo, 5 In. 575.00
Tile, Ship, Sails Outlined In Blue, Clouds, Teal Green Ocean, 4 1/2 In. 357.00
Tile, White Ship, Blue Ground, Frame, 4 3/4 x 4 3/4 In. 330.00
Vase, 2-Tone Flowers & Stems, Gray Ground, Marked, 6 1/2 In.   550.00
Vase, 3-Color Grapes & Leaves, Lavender Ground, Blue Border, Marked, 5 In. 605.00
Vase, 4-Color Painted Fruit, Blue & Gay Ground, Hanna Tutt, 4 1/2 In. 1485.00
Vase, 8 Repeating Panels, Stylized Rose, Incised Outline, Marked, 6 7/8 In. 13750.00
Vase, Allover 2-Tone Brown Matte Glaze, Marked, 4 1/2 x 5 1/2 In. 410.00
Vase, Allover Lavender Matte Glaze, Marked, 6 1/2 In. 550.00
Vase, Blue Matte Glaze, Impressed Mark, 8 1/2 In. 1100.00
Vase, Blue Matte Glaze, Oval, Ship Mark, Paper Label, 3 1/2 In.   305.00
Vase, Blue Matte Glaze, Tapering Form, Marked, 8 In. 990.00
Vase, Brown Matte Glaze, Tapered, 6 In. 275.00
Vase, Brown Panthers, Windows, Light Green Ground, Hannah Tutt, 7 In. 18700.00
Vase, Brown Specked Matte Glaze, Beaker Shape, Impressed Mark, 6 In. 715.00
Vase, Brown Stylized Trees, Speckled Green Ground, Impressed Mark, 6 x 4 In. 3575.00
Vase, Carved & Painted Floral, Black, Green Matte Ground, Marked, 9 1/2 In. 1650.00
Vase, Dark Blue Matte Glaze, Bud, 5 3/4 In. 220.00
Vase, Dark Blue Matte Glaze, Flared Rim, Early 20th Century, 7 3/4 In. 805.00
Vase, Dark Blue Matte Glaze, Flared, Ship Mark, 5 1/2 x 5 In. 525.00
Vase, Dark Blue Speckled Matte Glaze, 9 x 4 In. 935.00
Vase, Dove Gray With Blue Speckling, Green Interior, Matte Finish, 3 3/4 In. 245.00
Vase, Embossed Fruit & Leaves, Brown & Blue, Gray Ground, Impressed Mark, 5 In. 1430.00
Vase, Geometric Design, Green Against Blue Ground, Arthur Baggs, 4 1/2 In. 1045.00
Vase, Gray Matte Glaze, Tapered Form, Marked, 6 In. 660.00
Vase, Green & Brown Matte Glaze, Marked, 4 In. 410.00
Vase, Green Matte Glaze, Incised Ribs, Checkered Bands, Corseted, A. Baggs, 8 In. 36300.00
Vase, Incised Dark Brown Flowers, Light Brown Ground, Bulbous, 6 x 5 In. 9350.00
Vase, Incised Geometric Design, Dark Blue, Green, Dark Green Matte Glaze, 9 In. 6050.00
Vase, Lavender Gray Matte Glaze, Cylindrical, Ship Mark, 9 x 4 In. 880.00

Vase, Lavender Matte Glaze, Marked, Label, 4 1/2 In. 470.00
Vase, Mustard Matte Glaze, Spherical, 5 1/4 In. 467.00
Vase, Speckled Brown Matte Glaze, Corseted, Ship Mark, 4 1/2 x 2 In. 275.00
Vase, Speckled Green Matte Glaze, Ovoid, Stamped MP Ship Mark, 8 In. 1100.00
Vase, Straight Sides, Red Stylized Flowers, Leaves, Blue Ground, Marked, 4 x 3 In. 1980.00
Vase, Stylized Square Leaves, Clumps Of Berries, Blue Ground, 7 In. 4950.00
Vase, Stylized Tree Design, Charcoal, Blue, Green Ground, 7 In. 6600.00
Vase, Stylized Trees, Black Trunks, Blue Leaves, Gray Ground, Bulbous, 4 In. 2415.00
Vase, Stylized Trees, Olive Green, Dark Blue Ground, Stamped Ship, 7 x 4 In. 3575.00
Vase, Swollen Form, Repeating Raised Flower On Rim, Blue, Red, Tan, 4 3/4 In. 1610.00
Vase, Teal Blue Matte Glaze, Black Underglaze Rim, Bulbous, 1910, 2 3/4 In. 375.00
Vase, Tear Shape, Gray Mottled Glaze, 5 1/2 In. 522.00
Vase, Trumpet Style Body, Sky Blue Glaze, Marked, 6 1/2 x 5 1/4 In. 245.00
Vase, Yellow Matte Glaze, Paper Label, 6 In. 253.00
Vase, Yellow To Brown Matte Glaze, Marked, 3 1/2 x 5 1/2 In. 715.00
Wall Pocket, Blue Matte Glaze, Turquoise Lined, Logo, 5 1/4 In. 330.00

MARTIN BROTHERS of Middlesex, England, made Martinware, a salt-
glazed stoneware, between 1873 and 1915. Many figural jugs and
vases were made by the three brothers. Of special interest are the fanciful birds, usually made with removable heads.

Bird Vessel, Green, Light Blue, Black Feathers, 1897, 10 x 8 In. 13530.00
Dish, Gargoyle, Unglazed, Incised, 1894, 2 3/4 x 5 1/2 In. 1870.00
Ewer, Stylized Cobalt Leaves, Gray, Amber Ground, 1870s, 10 x 5 1/2 In. 440.00
Humidor, Bird Shape, Fire Crack, Incised Mark, 11 1/2 x 5 1/2 In. 10450.00
Humidor, Bird, Figural, Hand Carved, Blue, Brown, Ivory Glaze, 1912, 6 In. 4400.00
Jar, Creature With Brown Scales, Stoneware, 5 1/2 x 3 1/2 In. 7150.00
Jug, Incised, Shell Medallions, Fish Handle, Oval, Buff Ground, 1874, 7 1/2 In. 1310.00
Jug, Sea Reptiles, Indigo, Amber, 9 3/4 x 5 In. 1760.00
Lamp, Oil, Chalice Form, Blue, Brown, Green, Panels, Flowers, 1886, 13 1/2 In. 2910.00
Mug, 2 Faces, Commemorative Inscription, Gray Glaze, c.1932, 4 1/2 In. 510.00
Mug, Tapered, Scroll Handle, Incised, Cream & Brown, 1888, 5 1/2 In. 945.00
Pitcher, Bulbous, Swirled Ribs, Gunmetal Brown Glaze, 1897, 8 x 4 In. 770.00
Pitcher, Cabinet, Incised With Brown Fish, Brown, Gray Ground, 1886, 2 x 3 In. 550.00
Pitcher, Grotesque Fish, 4 Sides, Signed, 1903, 9 In. 1100.00
Pitcher, Gunmetal Brown, Caramel Glaze, Embossed, 4 1/2 x 4 In. 2860.00
Spoon Warmer, Grotesque Creature, London & Soulhall, 5 3/4 In. .... *Illus* 650.00
Vase, Baluster, Allover Flowers, Brown Tones, Incised, 1884, 10 x 6 In. 1045.00
Vase, Bottle Shape, Birds In Chestnut Tree, Green, Brown, Ivory, 1890, 10 In. 770.00
Vase, Carved, Parent Storks & Young, Brown & Ivory, 1884, 9 1/2 In. 4675.00
Vase, Incised 4 Brown Fish, Green Ground, 1904, 2 1/4 x 1 3/4 In. 550.00
Vase, Incised With Green, Cobalt, Fish, Gray Ground, 4 Sides, 1913, 6 x 2 In. 715.00
Vase, Organic Bulbous, Blue & Ivory Glaze, Incised Wavy Lines, 10 In. 2420.00

**If the name "England" (or that of
some other country) appears, the
dish was probably made after 1891,
but it may have been made as early
as 1887. The words "made in England"
(or some other country) indicate the
piece was made after 1914.**

Martin Brothers, Spoon Warmer, Grotesque
Creature, London & Soulhall, 5 3/4 In.

MARY GREGORY is the name used for a type of glass that is easily identified. White figures were painted on clear or colored glass as the decoration. The figures chosen were usually children at play. The first glass known as Mary Gregory was made about 1870. Similar glass is made even today. The traditional story has been that the glass was made at the Sandwich Glass works in Boston by a woman named Mary Gregory. Recent research suggests that it is possible that none was made at Sandwich. In general, all-white figures were used in the United States, tinted faces were probably used in Bohemia, France, Italy, Germany, Switzerland, and England. Children standing, not playing, were pictured after the 1950s.

Beaker, Purple Portrait, Enameled, Purple, 6 In.	195.00
Bottle, Barber, Amethyst, 9 In.	350.00
Bottle, Barber, Girl, Rolled Lip, 8 In.	275.00
Bottle, Barber, Woman's Portrait, Thumbprint, Stopper	415.00
Bottle, Cologne, Girl, All White, Clear Bubble Stopper, Amber, 8 In.	185.00
Bottle, Girl, All White, Sapphire Blue, 8 1/2 In.	195.00
Bottle, Girl, Cut Stopper, While Enamel, Sapphire Blue, 8 1/2 In.	195.00
Box, Children Having Funeral For Bird, Black Glass, 12 1/2 In.	290.00
Decanter, Wine, Girl, Bag, All White, Amber Stopper, Amber, 11 In.	265.00
Jewelry Box, Hinged Cover, Boy Holding Bird, White, 3 x 3 1/2 In.	225.00
Tankard, Woman Watering Garden, Enameled, Amber Glass, 13 In.	140.00
Tumbler, Girl Holding Flower, White, Sapphire Blue, 6 1/2 In.	95.00
Vase, Boy & Girl, Coralene Beaded Clothes, Emerald Green, 8 In., Pair	595.00
Vase, Boy Running, Butterfly, Black Amethyst, 7 In.	135.00
Vase, Boy With Tray Of Flowers, All White, Green, 11 1/8 In.	225.00
Vase, Cranberry, 10 In., Pair	295.00

MASON'S IRONSTONE was made by the English pottery of Charles J. Mason after 1813. Mason, of Lane Delph, was given a patent for this improved earthenware. He usually called it "Mason's Patent Ironstone China." It resisted chipping and breaking so it became popular for dinnerwares and other table service dishes. Vases and other decorative pieces were also made. The ironstone was decorated with orange, blue, gold, and other colors, often in Japanese inspired designs. The firm had financial difficulties but the molds and the name Mason were used by many owners through the years, including Francis Morley, Taylor Ashworth, George L. Ashworth, and John Shaw. Mason's joined the Wedgwood group in 1973 and the name is still found on dinnerwares.

Compote, Imari, Patent, 11 x 6 5/8 In.	245.00
Foot Bath, c.1815	3200.00
Pitcher, Dragon, Patterned Handle, Octagonal, 6 1/4 In.	195.00
Pitcher, Oriental Design, Blue & White, Snake Handle, 7 In.	120.00
Pitcher, Overall Landscape, Floral, Figural, Branch Form Handle, 6 In.	403.00
Pitcher & Bowl, Floral, Gold, Blue, Rust, 12-In. Pitcher, 17-In. Bowl	525.00
Plate, Floral Transfer, Green, Gold Rim, 10 1/4 In., 9 Piece	245.00
Plate, Floral, Gaudy Design, 9 1/4 In., 6 Piece	550.00

MASONIC, see Fraternal category.

MASSIER, a French art pottery, was made by brothers Jerome, Delphin, and Clement Massier in Vallauris and Golfe-Juan, France, in the late nineteenth and early twentieth centuries. It has an iridescent metallic luster glaze that resembles the Weller Sicardo pottery glaze. Most pieces are marked *J. Massier*.

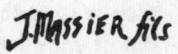

Dish, Cover, Thistle, Glossy Brown Ground, 4 1/2 x 8 In.	220.00
Jardiniere, Birds, Amphibians On Rim, c.1890, 23 1/2 In.	3450.00
Pitcher, Tapered Oval, Modeled Satyr, Draped Nude Handle, Green, Gold, 10 In.	1495.00
Planter, Brick Chimney Pot Form, 7 House Martins, c.1890, 13 In.	3450.00
Vase, 2 Incised Galleons At Sea, Umber & Teal, Mottled White, 2 Handles, 6 In.	99.00
Vase, Cabinet, Nacreous Flowers, Silver Overlay Leaves On Rim, Oval, 2 1/4 In.	143.00
Vase, Lily Of The Valley, Green Ground, Bulbous, 6 1/2 In.	220.00
Vase, Renaissance, Fish, Birds, Putti, Ruffled Rim, Bulbous, Jerome Massier Fils, 10 In.	275.00

Vase, Seaside Scene, Umber, Pink, Ivory Ground, 4 1/2 In. 99.00
Vase, Wheat Stalks, Green & Red Pearl, Tapering, Delphin Massier, 10 1/2 In. 770.00
Vase, Yellow Thistle, Brown, Black, Ivory Flambe Ground, 6 In. 165.00

MATCH HOLDERS were made to hold the large wooden matches that
were used in the nineteenth and twentieth centuries for a variety of pur-
poses. The kitchen stove and the fireplace or furnace had to be lit reg-
ularly. One type of match holder was made to hang on the wall, another
was designed to be kept on a tabletop. Of special interest today are
match holders that have advertisements as part of the design.

Aluminum, Palmer-Smith 17.00
Andes Stoves & Ranges, Use Andes Stoves & Ranges, Best In The World, 6 In. 165.00
Ashtray At Back, Pipe Rest Front, Bronzed, 5 3/4 In. 55.00
Bartholomay's Brewing Co., Yellow Kid, Match Me If Ye Can, Leather, 2 x 5 In. 330.00
Boots, Cast Iron, Black & Gold, Square Base, 3 1/2 x 3 3/8 In. 90.00
Ceresota Flour, Boy Sitting On Barrel, Die Cut, Tin, 5 1/2 x 2 1/2 In. 305.00
Ceresota Flour, Boy Sitting On Bench, Barrel, Tin Lithograph, 5 1/4 In. . . . . .66.00 to 83.00
De Laval Cream Separator, Die Cut, Tin, 6 3/8 x 4 In. . . . . .110.00 to 385.00
Elverso, Lady's Face, Brass, Elverso Cigars, San Felice Cigars, 1920, 8 1/4 In. 175.00
Eve Type Figure On Oval, Tin, Oval, 5 1/2 In. 55.00
Figure Holding Candle, Go To Bed, Cast Iron, 4 In. 225.00
Flower, Cigarettes & Matches Design, Standard Glaze, Elizabeth Lincoln, 2 In. 275.00
Fly Shape, Cast Iron, Painted, Simpson Iron Co., Col., O., 4 3/4 In. 235.00
Graniteware, Blue, Pitcher Shape, 10 1/2 In. 80.00
Graniteware, Gray & White Spatter, 5 In. 75.00
Graniteware, Gray Spatter, Pitcher Shape, 9 1/2 In. 65.00
Graniteware, Light Green, Pitcher Shape, 8 In. 55.00
Graniteware, Mottled, Twin Packet, Wall, 5 In. 125.00
Juicy Fruit, The Man, Tin Lithograph, 4 3/4 In. 77.00
Keeley Stove, Tin Lithograph, Ginna Mark, 7 In. 72.00
Log Cabin, Cast Iron, 2 3/4 In. 220.00
Man, 2 Barrels, Large For Cigars, Pot Metal, 6 1/2 In. 290.00
Man Playing Accordion, Basket 1 Side, Barrel Other, Majolica 120.00
Milk Glass, Basket Shape, Rabbit & Chick, Pierced, Hanging, Eagle Glass 125.00
Mother's Worm Syrup, Woman Giving Dose To Children, 2 1/4 x 6 3/4 In. 1045.00
Old Judson, Tin Lithograph, 5 In. . . . . .100.00 to 105.00
Omar Cigarettes, Metal 32.00
Safe Home, Matchbox Holder, Hand Striking Match, Tin, Black, 6 x 4 x 3 In. 28.00
Sharples Separators, Tin Lithograph, 6 1/2 In. 143.00
Shoe, Woman's, Polychrome, Cast Iron, 5 3/8 In. 100.00
Skull, Striker, Majolica, 2 1/2 In. 82.00
Solarine, Wise Wives Work Wonders, Tin Lithograph, 4 3/4 In. 120.00

MATCH SAFES were designed to be carried in the pocket. Early matches
were made with phosphorus and could ignite unexpectedly. The
matches were safely stored in the tightly closed container. Match safes
were made in sterling silver, plated silver, or other metals. The English
call these *vesta boxes.*

Admiral Cafe, Meriden, Conn., Young Woman, Nickel Finish 115.00
Alvarez Toledo, Gilt Steel, Quatrefoils, 1 7/8 x 1/2 In. 92.00
Animal Scene, Metal, 1900s 70.00
Chased Honeycomb Pattern, Sterling Silver, Sapphire, Ruby & Diamond Bee 575.00
Compliments Of Pabst Brewing Co., c.1890, 3 x 1 1/2 In. 66.00
Creel Shape, Rod & Line On Side, Tin, Wall 385.00
Deck Of Cards Design, Ivory, Continental, 2 3/8 In. 103.00
Dolphins, Shell, Shield, Gryphons, Sterling Silver, Gilt Interior, 2 3/4 x 1 3/4 In. 395.00
Eagle & Shield Design, With Lighter, 19th Century, 2 3/4 x 2 In. 230.00
Elephant, 2 In. 340.00
Engine Turned, Rounded Corners, Rectangular, R. Blackington & Co., 14K Gold 345.00
Evacuation Of Ft. Ontario, Whiskey Giveaway, Tin Lithograph Lid, 2 In. 17.00
High Wheel Bicycle, Sterling Silver 300.00
Hunter Baltimore Rye, Steeplechase Jumper, Whiskey Bottle, Nickel, Celluloid . .115.00 to 120.00
Indianapolis Brewing Co., Hinged Lid, 1 1/2 x 3 In. 61.00

John Hauck, King On Top Of World, Embossed, Hinged Lid, 1 1/2 x 3 In. 55.00
Lion & Unicorn Crest, Brass, Alex R. Stocker, New Vesta Match, England, 2 x 1 In. 39.00
National Lead Co., Cincinnati Branch, Tin, Cream & Black Celluloid, 2 3/4 In. 83.00
Nut Lined, Hinged, Carrying Ring, Shettelwood, Silver, 1886, 2 In. 93.00
Phoenix Brewery, St. Louis, Embossed, Hinged Lid, 1 3/4 x 3 In. 240.00
Pope Paul VI, Book Shape, Brass, Silver Plated, Souvenir, 2 x 2 3/8 In. 20.00
Scroll & Fleur-De-Lis, Dore Bronze, Stamped France, 4 1/2 In. 130.00
Sterling Silver, Birmingham, 1922, 1 7/8 x 1 3/8 In. 650.00
Westcott & Parker, Dealers In Coal & Wood, Utica, N.Y., Salt Glaze, 3 In. 275.00
Wiedemann Brewing Co., Plated Brass, 1 1/2 x 3 In. 55.00

MATSU-NO-KE was a type of applied decoration for glass patented by
Frederick Carder in 1922. There is clear evidence that pieces were
made before that date at the Steuben glassworks. Stevens & Williams
of England also made an applied decoration by the same name.

Candlestick, Steuben 495.00

MATT MORGAN, an English artist, was making pottery in Cincinnati,
Ohio, by 1883. His pieces were decorated to resemble Moorish wares.
Incised designs and colors were applied to raised panels on the pottery.
Shiny or matte glazes were used. The company lasted less than two
years.

Vase, Painted Floral Design, Signed, 3 1/2 In. 121.00

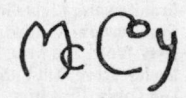

MCCOY pottery was made in Roseville, Ohio. Nelson McCoy and J.W.
McCoy established the Nelson McCoy Sanitary and Stoneware Company in Roseville, Ohio, in 1910. The firm made art pottery after 1926.
In 1933 it became the Nelson McCoy Pottery Company. Pieces marked
McCoy were made by the Nelson McCoy Pottery Company. Cookie
jars were made from about 1940 until December 1990, when the
McCoy factory closed. In 1990 the McCoy mark was put back on pottery by a firm unrelated to the original company. Because there was a
company named Brush-McCoy, there is great confusion between Brush
and Nelson McCoy pieces. See Brush category for more information.

Ashtray, Gray, Matte Glaze, Marked, 9 x 6 1/2 In. 20.00
Baby Shoe, Mary Ann, Pink, 5 In. 10.00
Bank, Hung-Over Dog, 6 x 8 In. 45.00
Bank, Seaman's, Sailor, White, Hand Painted, 5 3/4 In. 90.00
Bean Pot, Brown, Cover 25.00
Beverage Set, Pink & Black, 3 Piece 75.00
Bowl, El Rancho Sombrero, Hat On Bowl, 1960, 12 x 13 In. 450.00
Candleholder, Floraline, Oval 30.00
Casserole, Brown Drip Ware, Individual, 5 In. 8.00
Casserole, Cover, Textured Glaze, 5 x 10 In. 24.00
Cookie Jar, Apple 40.00
Cookie Jar, Boy On Baseball 295.00
Cookie Jar, Chairman Of The Board ....500.00 to 600.00
Cookie Jar, Chilly Willy 75.00
Cookie Jar, Chinese Lantern, Fortune Cookie 75.00
Cookie Jar, Chipmunk 115.00
Cookie Jar, Christmas Tree 720.00
Cookie Jar, Clown In Barrel, Pink 200.00
Cookie Jar, Coffee Grinder 60.00
Cookie Jar, Colonial Fireplace 100.00
Cookie Jar, Cook Stove, White ....30.00 to 40.00
Cookie Jar, Cookie Kettle 27.00
Cookie Jar, Corn, Upright Cob 115.00
Cookie Jar, Covered Wagon 120.00
Cookie Jar, Frontier Family 55.00
Cookie Jar, Fruit Festival, Tilt 23.00
Cookie Jar, Globe 375.00
Cookie Jar, Harley Hog, 1984 .... 155.00
Cookie Jar, Hobby Horse 150.00

Cookie Jar, Honey Bear 100.00
Cookie Jar, Indian .... 200.00 to 325.00
Cookie Jar, Keebler, Tree 17.00
Cookie Jar, Kerchief, White Dress .... 60.00 to 135.00
Cookie Jar, Kookie Kettle, Black 40.00
Cookie Jar, Kookie Kettle, White With Rose 250.00
Cookie Jar, Lunch Bucket 40.00
Cookie Jar, Mammy With Cauliflowers .... 975.00 to 1100.00
Cookie Jar, Mammy, Dem Cookies Sho Gots Dat Vitamin A, Yellow .... 400.00 to 465.00
Cookie Jar, Monk 45.00
Cookie Jar, Mouse On Clock 11.00
Cookie Jar, Oaken Bucket 20.00
Cookie Jar, Pepper, Green 60.00
Cookie Jar, Pineapple, Modern 110.00
Cookie Jar, Spaceship, Friendship 7 .... 180.00 to 225.00
Cookie Jar, Stagecoach 75.00
Cookie Jar, Teakettle 35.00
Cookie Jar, Teepee, Slant Top .... 300.00 to 365.00
Cookie Jar, Teepee, Straight Cover 295.00
Cookie Jar, Thinking Puppy, Tan .... 20.00 to 25.00
Creamer, Daisy 20.00
Dog Dish, 7 In. 75.00
Figurine, Bird, Wren, 4 1/4 In. 80.00
Figurine, Goose Pulling Oxcart, Green, 1940s 35.00
Flower Dish, White, 1940s, 9 1/2 In. 50.00
Flower Holder, Swan, White, 6 In. 38.00
Flower Holder, Swan, Yellow, 6 In. 45.00
Flowerpot & Saucer, Dragonfly, Pink, 5 In. 60.00
Hanging Basket, Aqua, 1940s, 3 1/2 In. 50.00
Jardiniere, Hobnail, White, 1940s, 3 1/2 In. 30.00
Jardiniere, Hobnail, White, 7 1/2 In. .... 35.00 to 50.00
Lamp, Cowboy Boots, Brown, 1956, 7 In. .... 100.00 to 130.00
Lamp, Panther, Lime Green 60.00
Mug, Grapes, Green 30.00
Mug, Suburbia, Brown 7.00
Mug, Willow Ware, Green 45.00
Music Jug, Onyx, Brown, 9 1/2 x 6 1/2 In. 125.00
Pitcher, Angel Fish, Aqua, 32 Oz. 50.00
Pitcher, Water Lily & Fish, Green, 7 In. 75.00
Pitcher, Water Lily & Fish, Tan, 7 In. 47.00
Pitcher, Windmill & Bush, Blues & Browns 100.00
Pitcher & Bowl, Grapes & Leaves, Green 45.00
Planter, Alligator, Green, 1950, 9 3/4 In. 85.00
Planter, Baseball Glove, 1957, 6 x 6 In. 175.00
Planter, Bird Dog, Pheasant, 8 13 In 150.00
Planter, Clown On Pig, 1951, 8 1/2 In. 150.00
Planter, Conch Shell, Green Spray, 7 In. 50.00
Planter, Doe & Fawn, White, 1940s, 7 In. 90.00
Planter, Fawn, Looking Back, White, 4 1/2 In. 75.00
Planter, Frog, With Leaf, Green, 1951, 7 1/2 In. 55.00
Planter, Goat, Standing, Aqua, 1940s, 5 1/4 In. 85.00
Planter, Hands Of Friendship, White, 4 In. 70.00
Planter, Happy Face, 5 In. 25.00
Planter, Lion, Blue, 1940s, 8 3/4 In. .... 95.00 to 100.00
Planter, Log, 1950s, 8 1/2 In. 30.00
Planter, Pussy At The Well, 1955, 8 1/4 In. 165.00
Planter, Quail, 1955, 9 In. .... 75.00 to 95.00
Planter, Rabbit, White, 7 1/4 In. 125.00
Planter, Rooster, On Wheelbarrow, White, Black, 10 1/2 In. 115.00
Planter, Turtle, Green, 1950, 8 In. 70.00
Planter, Wishing Well, 1949, 7 In. .... 20.00 to 45.00
Pot, Owl, Hanging, 7 3/4 In. 50.00
Snack Dish, Rustic, 3 Section, 1952, 11 x 8 In. 50.00

Sugar & Creamer, Daisy 35.00
Sugar & Creamer, Elmer & Elsie 45.00
Tankard, Buccaneer, Brown, 1926, 5 In. 35.00
Tanker, Willow Ware, Green Basket Weave, 9 In. ....75.00 to 100.00
Tray, Hands, Aqua, 1940s, 8 1/2 In. 150.00
Vase, Blossomtime, Handles, White, 6 1/4 In. 45.00
Vase, Blossomtime, Urn, Yellow, 6 1/2 In. 55.00
Vase, Bud, Lily, Blue, 1940s, 6 1/2 In. 60.00
Vase, Bud, Lily, White, 1940s, 8 In. 40.00
Vase, Butterfly, Blue, 7 In. 45.00
Vase, Butterfly, Lavender, 8 In. 125.00
Vase, Butterfly, Yellow, Double Handle, 10 In. 225.00
Vase, Cascade, Pearlescent White, Modern Shape, 1961, 9 In. 60.00
Vase, Cat, Black, 1959, 14 In. 250.00
Vase, Cherries, Yellow, Square, 10 In. 65.00
Vase, Chrysanthemum, Yellow, 1950, 8 In. 150.00
Vase, Cornucopia, Blue, 4 x 3 1/4 In. 36.00
Vase, Grape, 1951, 9 In. ....75.00 to 95.00
Vase, Hand, Yellow, 1943, 7 In. 150.00
Vase, Heart, White, 1940s, 7 1/2 In. ....50.00 to 80.00
Vase, Loy-Nel-Art, 6 In. 300.00
Vase, Loy-Nel-Art, 11 In. 325.00
Vase, Pony, Yellow, 1940s, 7 In. 100.00
Vase, Swan, Onyx, 1946, 9 In. 35.00
Wall Pocket, Fan, Gold, 1950s, 8 1/2 In. 85.00
Wall Pocket, Flower With Bird, Pink & Blue, 6 1/2 In. 75.00
Wall Pocket, Grape Leaf Green & Yellow, 7 In. 45.00
Wall Pocket, Lily Bud, Blue, 1940s, 8 In. 45.00

MCKEE is a name associated with various glass enterprises in the
United States since 1836, including J. & F. McKee (1850), Bryce,
McKee & Co. (1850 to 1854), McKee and Brothers (1865), and
National Glass Co. (1899). In 1903, the McKee Glass Company was
formed in Jeannette, Pennsylvania. It became McKee Division of the
Thatcher Glass Co. in 1951 and was bought out by the Jeannette Corporation in 1961. Pressed glass, kitchenwares, and tablewares were
produced. Jeannette Corporation closed in the early 1980s. Additional
pieces may be included in the Custard Glass category.

Bowl, Red Ships, 5 x 3 1/2 In. 35.00
Butter, Cover, Prize, Ruby Flashed 90.00
Butter, Cover, Red Ships, 1 Lb. 60.00
Canister, Cover, Custard, Medium 115.00
Compote, Rock Crystal Flower, Amber, 11 1/2 In. 65.00
Jug, Batter, Red 175.00
Pitcher, Cover, Water, Pink 350.00
Tumbler, Bottoms-Up, Carmel, Crystal Tray 145.00
Tumbler, Bottoms-Up, Nude, Caramel 85.00
Tumbler, Pink, Footed, 7 Oz. 25.00
Whimsy, Straw Hat, Milk Glass, 4 In. 55.00

MECHANICAL BANKS are listed in the Bank category.

MEDICAL office furniture, operating tools, microscopes, thermometers,
and other paraphernalia used by doctors are included in this category.
Medicine bottles are listed in the Bottle category. There are related collectibles listed under Dental.

Apothecary Set, Doctor's, Cherry, 2 Cobalt Blue Poison Bottles, 10 Bottles 330.00
Bleeder, Brass, Scrolled Foliate Design, 1773, 2 In. 316.00
Bleeder, Physician's, Penknife Blade, Brass Handle, Civil War Era, 3 1/4 In. 51.00
Book, Practitioner's Encyclopaedia Of Medicine & Surgery, Murphy, 1912 .... 20.00
Book, United States Pharmacopoeia, 1965 .... 27.00
Bottle, Hot Water, Kuddle Kitty, Figural, Rexall Drug Co., 8 3/4 In. ....*Illus* 15.00
Bottle, Hot Water, Red Riding Hood, Figural, Painted Face, 12 1/4 In. ....*Illus* 50.00

Bowl, Bleeding, Teardrop Shape, Silver Plate, France, 19th Century, 8 x 12 In. 140.00
Breast Pump, Glass, Trumpet Shape, Rubber Bulb 16.00
Cabinet, Apothecary, Lettering, Early 20th Century, 16 x 16 1/2 x 9 1/2 In. 305.00
Cabinet, Apothecary, Mahogany, 2 Upper Glazed Doors, 2 Shelves, 69 1/4 In. 1495.00
Cabinet, Apothecary, Pine, 18 Overlapping Drawers, Locks, 24 x 45 In. 825.00
Cabinet, Apothecary, Pine, Elm, Red Traces, 16 Drawers, China, 36 x 22 x 43 In. 990.00
Cabinet, Apothecary, Pine, Rectangular, 4 Drawers, Square Legs, 19 In. 185.00
Cabinet, Apothecary, Poplar, 54 Drawers, Porcelain Pulls, Wire Nails, 37 In. 1210.00
Cabinet, Apothecary, Southern Heart Pine, c.1800, 83 x 43 x 21 In., 2 Piece 2640.00
Cabinet, Apothecary, Stepped Graduated Rows, 6 Over 5, Over 2, 16 1/2 x 27 1/2 In. 805.00
Cabinet, Apothecary, Walnut, 13 Small Drawers, Late 18th Century, 12 1/4 In. 2530.00
Cabinet, Apothecary, Walnut, 20 Drawers, Molded Base, 26 x 42 x 9 In. 935.00
Cabinet, Veterinary, Tin, Dr. Daniels 5060.00
Chest, Apothecary, Pine, 15 Dovetailed Drawers, Porcelain Knobs, 24 1/2 x 23 In. 520.00
Corn Pads, J.R. Watkins, Sealed 16.00
Cup, Bleeding, Rolled Lip, Late 19th Century, 1 In. 30.00
Cup, Libation, Rhinoceros Horn, Phoenix & Vines Exterior, Lotus Interior, 3 1/2 In. 2300.00
Cysto-Urethroscope, Mahogany Box, 1920s, 13 In. 270.00
Diaphragm Kit, Ortho Coil Spring 16.00
Ear Scoop, Tongue Scraper Other End, Silvered Brass 295.00
Feeding Cup, Infant, England, Late 18th Century 195.00
Fleam, Case, Marked I-X-L, Pre-Civil War 145.00
Fleam, Veterinarian, Brass Frame, Reay & Robinson, Civil War, 1 x 4 1/4 In. 230.00
Fleam, William Achson, Sheffield Steel, Horn Handle, 1890s, 3 Blades 130.00
Funnel, Moody, Pre-1916, 8 1/2 In. 14.00
Glass, Medico-Chirurgical Hospital, Philadelphia, Pa., Flint, 1900, 5 1/2 In. 20.00
Hearing Aid, Harper Electronic Oriphone, Boston, Box 175.00
Inhaler, Ceramic, Stenciled, Cork Stopper, Boots Chemists, Dr. Nelson's, 6 In. 50.00
Instrument Kit, Box, 1900s, 10 Piece 60.00
Invalid Feeder, White Porcelain, W.T. & Co., 1900, 7 1/2 In. 40.00
Kit, 7 Probes, 3 Handles, Leather Covered Box, G.T. Craven & Co., 14 In. 137.00
Kit, Field Surgeon's, Feick Bros., Arnold & Son On Some Instruments 440.00
Lancets, Bone Handle, Marked Rogers Cutlers To Her Majesty, Double Edge, 6 1/2 In. .. 60.00
Machine, Jones Electric Basal Metabolism, Wooden, Porcelain, 1930-1940, 36 In. 6.00
Mask, Esmarach's Ether, Nickel-Plated Brass Wire, Hand Welded, 1920s 33.00
Medal, Hamburg Cholera Epidemic, 1892, 2 Men Battling Snakes, 71 mm. 210.00
Mirror, Doctor's Magnifying, Mother-Of-Pearl Fish Shaped Handle 30.00
Mold, Suppository, Brass, For Pearl Suppository Machine, Round, Makes 1 Piece 40.00
Mold, Suppository, Brass, For Whitall Tatum No. 3 Supp, Machine, Makes 3 Piece 36.00
Mold, Suppository, Brass, Handles, Late 19th Century, 8 In. 220.00
Mold, Suppository, Ef.J. Stokes Machine Co., Phila., Brass, 19th Century, 14 1/2 In. 100.00

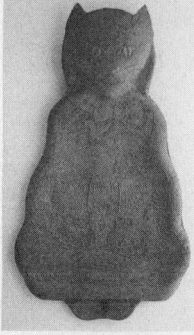

Medical, Bottle, Hot
Water, Kuddle Kitty,
Figural, Rexall Drug Co.,
8 3/4 In.

Be very careful when handling old bottles or medical equipment. The remains of old drugs, even toxic materials, may still cling to the surface. A broken bit of glass or a sliver could let these toxic materials reach your bloodstream.

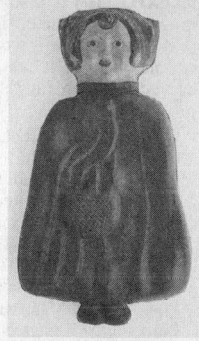

Medical, Bottle, Hot
Water, Red Riding Hood,
Figural, Painted Face,
12 1/4 In.

Mold, Suppository, For Applebaum Suppository Machine, 3-Part, Rectal, 12 Piece	40.00
Mortar & Pestle, Bell Metal, Floral Band, Whitechapel Foundry, London, 1700	495.00
Mortar & Pestle, Dark Wood, 9 In.	85.00
Mortar & Pestle, Porcelain, Glass Pestle, 2 1/2 x 4 1/2 In.	14.00
Mortar & Pestle, Schering Commemorative, 150th Anniversary Of USP, 1970	16.00
Mortar & Pestle, Schering, Pedanios Dioscorides, Commemorative, Metal, 1973, 4 In. ...	35.00
Mortar & Pestle, Standard Trenton, Wooden, Porcelain, 3 x 4 1/2 In.	55.00
Mortar & Pestle, Steel, 8 1/2 x 7 In.	77.00
Mortar & Pestle, Turned Wood, 7 In.	50.00
Mortar & Pestle, Wooden, Red Wash Trace	60.00
Pill Roller, Brass, Walnut, 1890s, 30 Pipes	355.00
Pill Roller, Mahogany, Brass, Sliding Tray, 7 3/4 x 13 In.	245.00
Pill Roller, Walnut, 1860, 4 1/4 x 10 7/8-In. Tray	190.00
Pill Roller, Wooden, Brass, 2 Piece	50.00
Quack Device, Boyd's Battery, 12 Metal Disks Around Copper Rosette, 1898	45.00
Quack Machine, Marvel Violet Ray, Case, Attachment, Document, Unused, 1930s	38.00
Quack Machine, Wappler, Electric, Wood Box, Attachment, 1920s	8.00
Rectal Dilators, Dr. Young's Improved, Hard Black Rubber, Box, Set Of 4	60.00
Sacrificator, Blood Letting, Brass, Octagonal, 10 Blades	395.00
Saw, Surgeon's, Horn Handle, 17th Century, 17 In.	928.00
Saw, Surgeon's, Mahogany Handle, 1860s, 15 1/2-In. Blade	65.00
Scale, Doctor's, Buffalo Scale Co., Iron, Black Paint, Gold Striping, 58 In.	55.00
Scalpel, Blackwood Handle, Savigny, 19th Century	60.00
Scalpel, Mathieu, Sliding Button Lock, Tortoiseshell Handle, Broad Blade, 5 In.	165.00
Scalpel, Surgeon's, Folding, Pocket, Bone Handle, NEFF, Early 1800s, 4 In.	145.00
Scarifier, 6-Blade, Nickel Plate, Cylindrical, 1910s	135.00
Sign, American National Red Cross, Porcelain, Flange, 14 x 11 In.	90.00
Sketch, Surgical Procedure, Split Graft Transfer From Abdomen, Melleoz, 1940	120.00
Slice, Bargebuilder's, Original Handle, Iron Ferrule, 18th Century, 2 7/8 In.	70.00
Slice, Shipwrights, H.H. Daye, Galton, Canada, 4-In. Slice, 24-In. Long	97.00
Slice, W. Butcher, Socketed, Octagonal Ash Handle, 1821-1825, 2 In.	115.00
Sterilizer, Electric Needle, Porcelain, Stainless Steel, No Cord, 1930-1940	18.00
Syringe, Brass & Nickel Plate, Wooden Pipe, Late 19th Century, 13 In.	55.00
Syringe Set, B-D, Hypodermoclysis, Dr. A. Harris, 30 cc To 50 cc., Box, 5 Piece	28.00
Thermometer, Animal, Case, Large	20.00
Thermometer, Nurse's, Round Bakelite Pocket Case, 1920s	20.00
Tool Set, For Making Artificial Limbs, 8 Piece	100.00
Tweezers, Lady's Leg Shape, Stocking & Garters, Embossed, Metal, 3 In.	20.00
Urinal, Man's, Glasco, 1930s, 32 Oz.	13.00
Urinal, Woman's, Glasco, 1930s, 32 Oz.	15.00
Urinometer, Glass Hydrometer Jar, Wooden Case, 1890	40.00

MEERSCHAUM is a soft white, gray, or cream-colored mineral named magnesium silicate. The name comes from the German word for seafoam, because it was sometimes found floating in the Black Sea and people thought it was petrified seafoam. Pipes and other pieces of carved meerschaum listed here date from the nineteenth century to the present.

Cigar Holder, Cheroot, Stag & Tree, Amber Tip, Fitted Case	40.00
Pipe, 2 Prancing Horses, Amber, 19th Century, 4 1/2 In.	65.00
Pipe, Allover Carved War Symbols, 18th Century, 4 1/2 In.	345.00
Pipe, Amber Stem, Red Velvet Lined Fitted Case, 5 x 2 In.	36.00
Pipe, American Indian, Feather Headdress, Case	172.00
Pipe, Bearded Man, Horn Form Stand, 6 1/2 In.	45.00
Pipe, Bearded Turk, Turban, Fitted Case	95.00
Pipe, Edwardian Woman's Head, Amber, F.A. Mitchell Tobacconist Case, 4 In.	70.00
Pipe, Figural, Man, Mustache, Seated, Brass Lid, 19th Century, 4 x 11 In.	115.00
Pipe, Form Of Eagle's Claw Holding Bowl, 19th Century, 5 3/4 In.	145.00
Pipe, Gentleman, Reclining, Amber Stem, Red Velvet Lined Fitted Case, 3 x 4 In.	30.00
Pipe, Hand With Cuff, Holding Bowl, Fitted Case, 19th Century, 4 1/4 In.	130.00
Pipe, Helmeted Warrior, Mother-Of-Pearl Design, 19th Century, 26 1/2 In.	750.00
Pipe, Horsehead, Case	200.00
Pipe, Nubian Head, Glass Eyes, Ivory Colored Teeth, 19th Century, 2 In.	345.00

Pipe, Running Stag Bowl, Brass Mounts, 10 1/2 In. 120.00
Pipe, Silver & Wood Mounted 70.00
Pipe, Silver & Wood Mounted, Napoleon Carving 288.00
Pipe, Silver Mounts, Over Sized, Austro-Hungarian, 19th Century, 13 1/4 In. 145.00
Pipe, Simple Form, No Design, Silver Lid, 19th Century, 12 1/2 In. 40.00
Pipe, Turk's Head, Long Stem, Case 55.00
Pipe, U-Shaped Bowl, Cherry, Ebony Fittings, 19th Century 200.00

MEISSEN is a town in Germany where porcelain has been made since 1710. Any china made in the town can be called Meissen, although the famous Meissen factory made the finest porcelains of the area. The crossed swords mark of the great Meissen factory has been copied by many other firms in Germany and other parts of the world. Pieces of Meissen dinnerware in the Onion pattern are listed in their own category in this book.

Basket, Raised Rococo Style Design, Gilt Metal Swing Handle, 12 In., Pair 430.00
Basket, Shaped Oval, Pierced Sides, Applied Flowers, Twig Handles, 1850-1900, 21 In. ... 3450.00
Basket, Winged Beast, Bird & Insects, Loop Mask Below Handles, 1740, 10 1/4 In. 1495.00
Beaker & Saucer, Ships Approaching Quayside, Gilt Rim, Signed, c.1735, 3 In. 2070.00
Bowl, Cover, Applied Floret Design, Female Blackamoor, Oval Base, Germany, 7 In. 686.00
Bowl, Gold Leaf Highlights, Embossed Leaf, 11 In. 50.00
Bowl, Insects, Attached Stand, 3 Lug Handles At Rim, 3 Scroll Feet, c.1740, 8 1/8 In. 1380.00
Bowl, Reticulated, Rococo Style, Gilt & White, 12 3/4 In. 175.00
Box, Cover, Lozenge Form, Floral, Gilt Design, 6 1/2 In. 231.00
Box, Hinged Cover, Bronze Trim, Romantic Scene, Blue, Gilt Design, 1 x 2 In. 110.00
Box, Painted Oval Fruit, Twig Knop Issuing 3 Leaves, Cover, c.1760, 4 1/2 In. 1380.00
Box, Rose Shape Finial, Domed Cover, Polychrome, 2 1/2 In. 230.00
Candelabra, 3-Light, Flowers & Leaves On Stem, Signed, c.1750, 12 3/8 In., Pair 8050.00
Candlestick, Cherubs & Flowers, Signed, 13 1/2 In., Pair 3080.00
Candlestick, Cobalt Blue, White, Leaves, 19th Century, 11 1/2 In., Pair 1035.00
Candy Dish, Woven Basket Form, Enameled Floral Well, Late 19th Century, 6 In. 257.00
Charger, Molded Rim & Border, Raised Gilding, Cobalt Blue Band, 12 1/4 In. 173.00
Chocolate Pot, Reverse Harbor Painted Scenes, Pink Ground, Silver Lid 8960.00
Clock, Allegorical, Floral Around Face, Figures Of Four Seasons, 18 3/4 In. 3915.00
Clock, Applied Flowers, Exotic Birds, Scroll-Molded Base, 1850-1900, 12 1/2 In. 5175.00
Clock Case, 4 Putti, Four Seasons, Flower Encrusted, Signed, 1870s.18 In. 4600.00
Coffee & Tea Set, Green Dragon, Acanthus Handle & Spout, Rose Bud Finials, 4 Piece .. 920.00
Coffeepot, Painted Oriental Figures, Birds & Insect On Back, c.1800, 7 3/8 In. 460.00
Coffeepot, Ships Docked Beside Cliffs, Flower At Spout, Signed, c.1735, 8 3/8 In. 2875.00
Compote, Blue Floral, Insects, Reticulated, Shell Base, Crossed Swords, 22 In. 2420.00
Compote, Figural, Boy & Girl, Around Tree Stump, Reticulated Bowl, 15 1/2 In., Pair ... 2970.00
Cup & Saucer, Demitasse, Painted, Multicolored Foliage, Box, 6 Sets 862.00
Cup & Saucer, Dragon 200.00
Cup & Saucer, Portrait, Pierre Boehmer, Biography, Marcolini Period 1150.00
Dish, 2 Overlapping Leaves, Scattered Sprays & Sprigs, Signed, c.1750, 14 3/4 In. 698.00
Dish, Sweetmeat, Figural, 18th Century Couple, Seated, Holding Dish, 12 In., Pair 2645.00
Epergne, 2 Tiers, Reticulated Plates, 18th Century Man With Bouquet, Red, 17 In. 1840.00
Ewer, Allegorical, Water, Seahorses, Mermaid, Neptune, 1850-1900, 25 3/4 In. 5175.00
Figurine, 2 Cherubs, Floral Wreaths, Pedestal, 4 In. 275.00
Figurine, 2 Putti Brick Layers, Building Wall, 4 In. 700.00
Figurine, 3 Hounds Attacking Bull, Rocky Base, c.1750, 6 3/4 In. 3220.00
Figurine, Bacchus, Wave Molded Circular Base, 8 3/4 In. 690.00
Figurine, Boreas & Oreithyia, 7 3/8 In. 750.00
Figurine, Boy With A Dog, On Square Base, 3 3/4 In. 635.00
Figurine, Cat, Seated, Green Eyes, c.1750, 2 1/4 In. 1380.00
Figurine, Cherub, Gilt, Crossed Swords, 7 3/8 & 7 5/8 In., Pair 1100.00
Figurine, Chocolate Maker, Putto By Brazier, 4 1/4 In. 517.00
Figurine, Cupid, Holding Heart, 1 With Love Bird, Late 19th Century, 11 1/2 In., Pair ... 345.00
Figurine, Eagle Perched On Rocky Outcrop, White, 10 1/2 In. 460.00
Figurine, Europa & Bull, Attended By 2 Women, Rococo Style Base, 8 1/2 x 8 In. 1840.00
Figurine, Female, Card Player, On Circular Base, 6 1/4 In. 1380.00
Figurine, Gardener, Leaning On A Shovel & Holding Flowers, 7 1/2 In. 575.00
Figurine, Girl Harvesting Grapes, 18th Century, 4 1/2 In. 165.00

**Floodlights facing toward the house
are better protection than
floodlights facing away from the
house. Moving figures and shadows
can be seen more easily.**

Meissen, Figurine,
Neptune, Blue Crossed
Swords, 6 In.

Figurine, Girl, Arms Support Bundle Of Pea Pods, Marked, c.1770, 5 3/8 In.		1092.00
Figurine, Lady, Seated In Armchair, Holding A Religious Book, 6 3/8 In.		1090.00
Figurine, Man & Woman, Crossed Swords, 2 1/4 In.		330.00
Figurine, Man With Bouquet, Woman Carrying Flowers, Marked, 19 1/2 In., Pair		4840.00
Figurine, Man With Crown Holding Woman Over Head, Marked, 7 1/4 x 5 In.		310.00
Figurine, Man With Walking Staff, Woman With Basket Of Flowers, 6 x 4 In., Pair		560.00
Figurine, Man, Yellow Jacket, Sweetheart, White Blouse, c.1755, 4 1/3 In.		1725.00
Figurine, Monkey Musician, Cellist, Late 19th Century, 4 1/2 In.		690.00
Figurine, Musical, Man Playing Flute, Woman Feeding Infant, c.1745, 5 3/4 In.		3737.00
Figurine, Neptune, Blue Crossed Swords, 6 In.	*Illus*	375.00
Figurine, Pagoda, Seated, Flowered Robe, Hand On Knee, 1729, 4 3/8 In.		8050.00
Figurine, Parrot, On Stump, Rocky Base, Red, Yellow, Blue, 1850-1900, 13 3/8 In.		1495.00
Figurine, Parrot, Perched On Stump, Head Turned Over Shoulder, c.1745, 7 5/8 In.		5520.00
Figurine, Pug, Seated, Head Turned, Left Leg Raised, c.1750, 2 In.		3680.00
Figurine, Putti Gardener, Leaning Into Shovel, c.1900, 4 3/8 In.		700.00
Figurine, Shepherd, Sheep, Pastel Colors, Signed, 12 3/4 x 17 1/4 In.		412.00
Figurine, Spinstress, Spindle In Hand, Pink Jacket, Yellow Skirt, 1750, 8 3/4 In.		1725.00
Figurine, Spring, Allegory Of Seasons, Blue Crossed Swords, 19th Century, 11 In.		1725.00
Figurine, Tailor On Goat, Rectangular Base, 9 1/4 In.		1840.00
Figurine, Violinist, Beribboned Hat, Lavender Coat, c.1755, 4 15/16 In.		4312.00
Figurine, Winter, Allegorical Man In Ermine Coat, Putto, 19th Century, 11 In.		1725.00
Figurine, Woman, Basket Of Flowers, Chicken On Nest, c.1900, 5 1/2 In.		365.00
Figurine, Woman, Exotic Dancer, Outstretched Hands, Holding Cape, 10 3/4 In.		2185.00
Figurine, Woman, Sitting, Eating Fruit, Gilt Trim, 5 1/4 In.		440.00
Fruit Knife, Porcelain Handle, Floral Sprigs, Gilt, 6 1/4 In., 6 Piece		140.00
Group, 18th Century Couple & Boy, She Plays Guitar, He Holds Flowers, 10 3/4 In.		2585.00
Group, 3 Hounds In Pursuit Of A Stag, Blue Underglaze, 19th Century, 9 In.		1495.00
Group, 4 Figures Playing Musical Instruments, Circular Base, 10 In.		2185.00
Group, 5 Children In Varying Poses, With Small Animals, Flowers, 6 1/2 In.		3680.00
Group, 5 Children Playing Musical Instruments, In Varying Poses, 6 1/2 In.		3450.00
Group, Allegorical Figure Of Africa, Female Figure Seated On Camel, 7 In.		690.00
Group, Allegorical, Water, Woman On Shell Chariot, Mermaids, 1850-1900, 9 In.		3735.00
Group, Animals Among Male & Female Lovers, Late 19th Century, 8 In.		1725.00
Group, Apple Pickers, One Boy On Ladder, 1850-1900, 11 3/8 In.		1725.00
Group, Bacchanalian, Astride Cask, Woman Behind Him, Cavorting Cherubs, 15 In.		575.00
Group, Bacchus, Seated On Wine Barrel Surrounded By Children, Women, 10 In.		1495.00
Group, Cupid Playing Horn & Cupid With Music Book In His Lap, 5 1/2 In.		1380.00
Group, Drunken Bacchus On Donkey, Attendant, Maiden, Putto, 1850-1900, 8 In.		1610.00
Group, Europa & The Bull, Handmaiden Drapes Flowers, 1850-1900, 8 5/8 In.		3735.00
Group, Female Figure With Servant Tending To Bird, Gilt, Enamel, 5 3/4 In.		1035.00
Group, Jacob & Rachel At The Well, Sheep, Rocky Base, 1850-1900, 9 3/4 In.		2300.00
Group, Man & Woman, 2 Boys, Apple Tree, Crossed Swords Mark, 11 In.		1800.00
Group, Musician's Scene, On Oval Base, Late 19th Century, 7 1/4 In.		865.00
Group, Shepherd & Nymph At Well, 11 In.		1265.00
Group, Tailor's Wife, Mother & Baby On Goat, Late 19th Century, 7 In.		2145.00
Nodder, Chinoiserie, Tongue & Hands		14950.00
Plaque, Iron Cross, 1914, 9 1/2 In.		275.00

Plate, Beethoven, Dated 1971, 10 In. 40.00
Plate, Cabinet, Cupid & Female, Wooded Landscape Scene, Pink, Burgundy, 10 In. 490.00
Plate, Dessert, Teal Banded, c.1885, 7 In., 6 Piece 105.00
Plate, Equestrian Center, Floral Boarder, Signed, 9 1/2 In. 187.00
Plate, Floral, Wide Grapevine Border, Scalloped, Late 19th Century, 10 1/4 In. 315.00
Plate, Oriental Flowering Plants, Lobed Rim, Signed, 1930s, 9 3/4 In., 10 Piece 230.00
Platter, Scalloped Edge, Couldon, England, B.W.M. & Co., 16 x 11 3/4 In. 105.00
Saucer, Oriental Gentleman, Seated Under Palm Tree, Steaming Kettle, c.1725, 5 In. 1150.00
Serving Dish, Scalloped, Pink Rose Design, Polychrome, 10 In.   230.00
Sugar Box, Painted Battle Scene On Cover, Ignaz Preissler, c.1713, 4 3/4 In. 5175.00
Sugar Sifter, Horizontal Ribs, Scattered Flowers, Gilt Edged Rim, c.1750, 3 1/8 In. 517.00
Tea Canister, Landscape, Shell & Scroll Border, Open Flower Knop, Signed, 5 In. 1150.00
Tea Service, Floral Design, Hand Painted, White Ground, Gilt, 13 Piece 1155.00
Teabowl & Saucer, 2 Mounted Huntsmen & Dogs, Pursuing Fox, c.1725, 5 In. 1150.00
Teapot, Chinese Woman Riding On Back Of Rooster, 9 x 7 In. 2300.00
Teapot, Cover, Flowering Spout, Grinning Mask, Loop Handle, 1730, 5 1/8 In. 6900.00
Teapot, Purple Deutsche Blumen, Bud Knop, Branch Spout, Globular, 18th Century 335.00
Teapot, Rooster, Enamel Design, Germany, Early 20th Century, 6 In. 575.00
Tureen, Partridge, Seated On Nest, Signed, c.1750, 5 5/8 In. 5750.00
Urn, Colorful Tulips, Roses, Butterflies On Neck, Snake Form Handles, 19 In. 3220.00
Urn, Rococo Style, Portrait, King Albert Of Saxony, Cherubs, Trumpeting Angel, 34 In. . . .   7475.00
Urn, Serpent Handles, Painted Fruit, White Ground, Mounted As Lamp, 15 In. 560.00
Vase, Angel With Trumpet, Putto, Cornucopia, Pate-Sur-Pate, Gilt, 14 In. 5750.00
Vase, Green & White, Green Leaf Band, 5 1/2 In. 145.00
Vase, Peony Bushes & Bamboo, Sprigs, Signed, 1749, 11 1/4 In. 2875.00
Vase, Pink Rose Design, Polychrome, 5 1/4 In. 200.00
Vase, Polychrome Floral Bouquet, 4 Feet, Circular Plinth, 5 1/2 In. 230.00
Vase, Silver Floral Design, Gold Trim, Scrolled Snake Handles, Germany, 15 1/2 In. 2300.00
Vase, Trumpet, Blue & Gold Borders, 6 7/16 In. 225.00
Vase, Trumpet, Floral Bouquets, Insects, White Ground, 20th Century, 9 3/16 In. 287.00
Vase, Woman, Stooping Forward, Lifting Apron, Basket On Back, c.1765, 10 1/2 In. 1265.00

MERCURY GLASS, or silvered glass, was first made in the 1850s. It lost
favor for a while but became popular again about 1910. It looks like a
piece of silver.

Communion Set, Amber, Bud-Shaped Hinged Cover, Bird, Branches, 10 In., 6 Piece 385.00
Compote, Enameled Birds & Flowers, Flared, Footed, 1875-1900, 7 In. 330.00
Figurine, Stag, Rectangular Base, 6 In. 165.00
Vase, Amber, Flared Rim, Tapered Body, Footed Base, 10 1/2 In. 195.00
Vase, Enameled, Footed, 7 In. 300.00
Vase, Flowers, Peach & Yellow, Baluster Shape, 1875-1900, 9 In. 140.00

MERRIMAC POTTERY Company was founded by Thomas Nickerson in
Newburyport, Massachusetts, in 1902. The company made art pottery,
garden pottery, and reproductions of Roman pottery. The pottery
burned to the ground in 1908.

Bowl, Carved Design, 5 x 9 In. 750.00
Bowl, Green Matte Glaze, Glossy Brown Interior, Scalloped Rim, 7 In. 495.00
Bowl, Green Matte Glaze, Squat, Impressed Mark, 4 x 9 In. 1320.00
Jar, Cover, Glossy Speckled Brown Glaze, Label, 5 1/4 x 3 1/4 In. 495.00
Umbrella Stand, Leathery Green Matte Glaze, Applied Leaves, 22 3/4 x 8 1/2 In. 4135.00
Vase, Broad Shoulder, Green Matte Glaze, Signed, 9 1/2 In. 2090.00
Vase, Green, Signed, 10 1/2 In. 715.00
Vase, Mirror Black Glaze, Green, Bulbous Base, Cylindrical Neck, 10 x 5 In. 1650.00
Vase, Speckled Green & Black Semimatte Glaze, 2 Handles, 3 1/4 In. 415.00
Vase, Trumpet Neck, Jade & Hunter Green Curdled Glaze, Signed, 4 x 3 1/2 In. 440.00

METTLACH, Germany, is a city where the Villeroy and Boch factories
worked. Steins from the firm are marked with the word *Mettlach* or the
castle mark. They date from about 1842. *PUG* means painted under
glaze. The steins can be dated from the marks on the bottom, which
include a date-number code. Other pieces may be listed in the Villeroy
& Boch category.

Beaker, 3 Men Bearing Large Barrel, Foliate Banding, 1850s, 7 1/2 In. 60.00

Beaker, No. 2327, 1/4 Liter, Frankfurt, 1908 .... 207.00
Beaker, No. 2327-1024, 1/4 Liter, Man Playing Flute 45.00
Beaker, No. 2327-1050, 1/4 Liter, Woman With Large Jug 110.00
Beaker, No. 2327-1052, 1/4 Liter, Woman With Tray ....115.00 to 121.00
Beaker, No. 2327-1137, 1/4 Liter, Couple Toasting 180.00
Beaker, No. 2327-1139, 1/4 Liter, Man Playing Violin 115.00
Beaker, No. 2327-1189, 1/4 Liter, Woman On Beach 90.00
Beaker, No. 2368-1032, 1/4 Liter, Gnomes Drinking 110.00
Beaker, No. 2368-1091, 1/4 Liter, Waiter Serving Wine 80.00
Beaker, No. 2368-1096, 1/4 Liter, Cavalier Pouring Wine 105.00
Beaker, No. 2954-1194, 1/4 Liter, Cupids, PUG 80.00
Biscuit Jar, No. 1208, Barrel Shape, Relief Design, Silver Plated Rim, Handle, 4 In. 210.00
Jug, Baluster Form, Serpent Handle, Stylized Floral, Pewter Mounts, 11 3/4 In. 460.00
Pitcher, No. 2486, The 5 Swans, Etched, Otto Eckmann, 1897, 8 In. 1155.00
Pitcher, No. 2863, Blue, Repeating Design, Etched, Glazed, 5 1/4 In. 175.00
Pitcher, No. 7022, Musicians & Dancing On Either Side, Phanolith Stahl, 16 In. 935.00
Plaque, Birds At Lake, Water Flowers Around Perimeter, 15 In. 935.00
Plaque, Deer In Forest, Art Nouveau Border, 15 In. 1870.00
Plaque, Mother's Day, 1978 .... 70.00
Plaque, No. 1044-148, Neuschwanstein, PUG, 14 In. 415.00
Plaque, No. 1044-168, Dresden Bruhlsohe Terrasse, PUG, 12 In. 210.00
Plaque, No. 1044-221, Munchen, PUG, 14 In. 355.00
Plaque, No. 1044-246, Rathaus, Rothenburg A.D. Tauber, PUG, 12 In. 345.00
Plaque, No. 1044-991, Gnome Picking Grapes, PUG, H. Schlitt, 7 1/2 In. 410.00
Plaque, No. 1044-1024, Flute Player, PUG, 8 1/2 In. 230.00
Plaque, No. 1044-1099, Young Girl, 2 Young Boys, Gold Rim, PUG, Reiss, 17 1/2 In. ... 925.00
Plaque, No. 1044-1100, Young Girl & Boy, PUG, F. Reiss, 17 1/2 In. 580.00
Plaque, No. 1108, Castle Scene, Etched, 17 In. ....*Illus* 500.00
Plaque, No. 1168, Bearded Man With Fancy Hat, Warth, 16 In. ....*Illus* 580.00
Plaque, No. 1385, Knight Carrying Weapon, Etched, Schultz, 1910, 14 1/2 In. 805.00
Plaque, No. 1411, Woman With Fancy Hat, Etched, Glazed, 17 In. 525.00
Plaque, No. 1548, Art Nouveau Girl, 18 1/4 In. ....*Illus* 660.00
Plaque, No. 1696, Woman, With Butterfly Wings, Branch, Relief, Blue, 16 1/2 In. 750.00
Plaque, No. 2078, 2 Soldiers On Horseback, Etched, Stocke, 15 In. ....800.00 to 1925.00
Plaque, No. 2081, 4 Husaren On Horseback, Etched, Stocke, 15 In. 880.00
Plaque, No. 2113, Gnome In Tree, Drinking From Mug, Etched, Schlitt, 16 In. .....*Illus* 1100.00
Plaque, No. 2142, Bismarck On Horseback, Etched, 15 In. 1155.00
Plaque, No. 2147, Artillery Men Moving Cannons, Stocke, Etched, 15 1/4 In. 1400.00
Plaque, No. 2148, Snow White & Seven Dwarfs, Etched, Schlitt, 16 In. ....*Illus* 1000.00
Plaque, No. 2196, Castle On Cliff, Etched, Stolzenfels, 17 1/2 In. 475.00
Plaque, No. 2361A, Wartburg Castle, Etched, 17 1/2 In. 775.00
Plaque, No. 2362, Heidelberg Castle, Etched, 17 1/2 In. 825.00
Plaque, No. 2518, Town Scene Of Meissen, Etched, 17 1/2 In. 1100.00
Plaque, No. 2534, Drachenfels Castle, Etched, 17 1/2 In. 575.00
Plaque, No. 2698, Gnome Reading Book, Toadstools, Etched, H. Schlitt, 17 In. 6600.00
Plaque, No. 2795, Words Of Love, Serenade Scene, Cameo, 17 1/2 In. 575.00

Mettlach, Plaque, No. 1108, Castle Scene, Etched, 17 In.

Mettlach, Plaque, No. 1168, Bearded Man With Fancy Hat, Warth, 16 In.

Mettlach, Plaque, No. 1548, Art Nouveau Girl, 18 1/4 In.

Mettlach, Plaque, No. 2113,
Gnome In Tree, Drinking From
Mug, Etched, Schlitt, 16 In.

Mettlach, Plaque, No. 2148, Snow
White & Seven Dwarfs, Etched,
Schlitt, 16 In.

Mettlach, Plaque, No. 2898, Young
Girl, Flowers, Spring Scene,
Etched, Gradl, 17 In.

Plaque, No. 2875, Figures, Woman Holding Banner, Etched, Cameo18 In. 550.00
Plaque, No. 2898, Young Girl, Flowers, Spring Scene, Etched, Gradl, 17 In. . . . . *Illus* 2475.00
Plaque, No. 7032, Woman's Profiles, Cameo Oval, Phanolith, 1900, 7 12 In. 325.00
Plaque, No. 7079, Man & Woman Sitting In Field, Sheep, Phanolith, 8 x 6 In. 575.00
Plate, No. 2960 II, Art Nouveau, Petal Design, Etched, 12 In. 475.00
Punch Bowl, No. 3088, 6 Liters, Noah Leading Animals Onto Ark, Etched, H. Schlitt 3830.00
Stein, No. 6, 2 1/2 Liter, Woman With Shield, Sword, 3panels, Relief, Inlaid Lid 155.00
Stein, No. 280, 1/2 Liter, Student Society, Hand Painted, Pewter Lid 715.00
Stein, No. 280F, 1/2 Liter, Student Society, Hand Painted, Relief, Pewter Lid 575.00
Stein, No. 409, 2 1/2 Liter, Drinking Scene, 4 Panels, Relief, Inlaid Lid 390.00
Stein, No. 580, 1/2 Liter, Hunter Smoking, PUG, Inlaid Lid 410.00
Stein, No. 591, 1/2 Liter, Lovers, PUG, Pewter Lid 175.00
Stein, No. 598, 1 Liter, Marksman, PUG, Pewter Lid 335.00
Stein, No. 676, 1/2 Liter, Man & Woman, Large Umbrella, PUG, Pewter Lid 520.00
Stein, No. 715, 1/2 Liter, Drunken Revelers, PUG, Pewter Lid 215.00
Stein, No. 726, 1/2 Liter, Steins Being Filled, PUG, Pewter Lid, H. Schlitt 580.00
Stein, No. 727, 1/2 Liter, Gnomes Bowling, PUG, Pewter Lid 330.00
Stein, No. 825, 1/2 Liter, Infantry Regiment, Crossed Weapons, Flag, PUG, Handle 555.00
Stein, No. 941, 1/2 Liter, Tavern, Beer Barometer, PUG, Pewter Lid 220.00
Stein, No. 943, 1/2 Liter, Knight Breaking Open Beer Barrel, Pewter Lid 320.00
Stein, No. 955, 3 1/3 Liter, Tavern Scene, PUG, Pewter Lid 605.00
Stein, No. 960, 1/4 Liter, Jester Playing Mandolin, PUG, Pewter Lid 165.00
Stein, No. 967, 1/3 Liter, Gnomes Drinking, Inlaid Lid, Schlitt 385.00
Stein, No. 1014, 4 1/4 Liter, Munich Child Over Globe, PUG, Pewter Lid 1485.00
Stein, No. 1038, 1/2 Liter, Frogs Drinking, PUG, Pewter Lid, Schlitt . . . . .550.00 to 850.00
Stein, No. 1042, 1/2 Liter, Man & Woman, Large Key, PUG, Pewter Lid 460.00
Stein, No. 1055, 1/2 Liter, Drunken Cavaliers, PUG, Pewter Lid 300.00
Stein, No. 1078, 1/2 Liter, Cavalier, PUG, Schlitt, Pewter Lid 150.00
Stein, No. 1110, 1 Liter, Drinking Scene, With Barmaid, PUG, Pewter Lid, H. Schlitt 360.00
Stein, No. 1110, 1/2 Liter, Soldiers Drinking Scene, Pewter Lid 330.00
Stein, No. 1128, 4 4/5 Liter, Fat Man & Barmaid, PUG, Pewter Lid 715.00
Stein, No. 1132, 1/2 Liter, Man Fiddling, Alligator, Pyramids, Etched, Inlaid Lid 810.00
Stein, No. 1143, 2 1/4 Liter, Cavaliers Drinking, PUG, Pewter Lid, Schlitt 520.00
Stein, No. 1162, 1/2 Liter, Dancing Scene, 3 Panels, Etched, Inlaid Lid, Signed, Warth . . . 460.00
Stein, No. 1176, 1/2 Liter, Games, Pewter Lid 410.00
Stein, No. 1177, 1/2 Liter, Music, PUG, Pewter Lid 310.00
Stein, No. 1200, 3 1/4 Liter, Prussian Eagle, PUG, Pewter Lid 460.00
Stein, No. 1212, 1/2 Liter, Bowling, Crest, PUG, Pewter Lid 200.00
Stein, No. 1219, 1/2 Liter, Students Drinking & Smoking, PUG, Pewter Lid 275.00
Stein, No. 1266, 1/4 Liter, Drinking Scenes, 3 Panels, Blue, Inlaid Lid, Relief 155.00
Stein, No. 1271, 1/2 Liter, Drunken Man In Wheelbarrow, PUG, Pewter Lid 465.00
Stein, No. 1273, 1/2 Liter, Drunken Man With Monkey On Back, PUG, Pewter Lid 385.00
Stein, No. 1280, 1/2 Liter, Dancing Scene, PUG, Inlaid Lid, Round 330.00
Stein, No. 1395, 1/2 Liter, French Cards, Inlaid Lid, Etched 465.00
Stein, No. 1396, 1/2 Liter, Nymph Drinking From Stein, Etched, Brass Lid, Warth 175.00

Stein, No. 1508, 1/2 Liter, Tavern Scene, Etched, Inlaid Lid 465.00
Stein, No. 1526, 1/2 Liter, 400 Year Anniversary, City Of Annaberg, Pewter Lid ...140.00 to 340.00
Stein, No. 1526, 1/2 Liter, Student Society, Hand Painted, Pewter Lid 880.00
Stein, No. 1593, 1/2, Liter, Jester, Etched, Pewter Lid 1870.00
Stein, No. 1642, 1 Liter, Man Drinking, Tapestry, Pewter Lid, 9 1/2 In. 290.00
Stein, No. 1654, 1/2 Liter, Geometric Design, Mosaic, Pewter Lid 250.00
Stein, No. 1655, 1/2 Liter, Dancing Scene, Etched, Inlaid Lid 455.00
Stein, No. 1725, 1/2 Liter, Man & Woman Toasting, Etched, Inlaid Lid 415.00
Stein, No. 1733, 1/2 Liter, Jockeys With Horses, Etched, Jockey Cap Inlaid Lid, Warth ... 1320.00
Stein, No. 1781, 1 1/2 Liter, Fleur-De-Lis Design, Mosaic, Glazed, Pewter Lid 880.00
Stein, No. 1795, 1/2 Liter, City Of Freiburg, Inlaid Lid, Warth ....605.00 to 825.00
Stein, No. 1797, 1/2 Liter, 4 Cards, Etched, Gold Coins, Inlaid Lid 740.00
Stein, No. 1809, 1 Liter, 5 Panels, Figure In Each, Etched, Relief, Inlaid Lid 1375.00
Stein, No. 1861, 1/2 Liter, Gambrinus Rex, Etched, PUG, Pewter Lid 410.00
Stein, No. 1864, 4 1/2 Liter, Hipp Hipp Hurrah, Oarsmen, Etched, Pewter Lid 4070.00
Stein, No. 1909, 1/2 Liter, Bartholomay's, Rochester, PUG, Winged Wheel, Pewter Lid .. 260.00
Stein, No. 1909, 1/4 Liter, Imported Humbser Beer, N.Y., Pewter Lid 190.00
Stein, No. 1932, 1/2 Liter, Cavaliers Drinking, Etched, Inlaid Lid, Warth 470.00
Stein, No. 1946, 1/2 Liter, Courting Scene, Etched, Love Birds On Inlaid Lid 440.00
Stein, No. 1947, 1/2 Liter, Man Sitting In Vines, Inlaid Lid 275.00
Stein, No. 1972, 1/2 Liter, 4 Seasons, Etched, Inlaid Lid 825.00
Stein, No. 1972, 1/4 Liter, 4 Seasons, Etched, Inlaid Lid 412.00
Stein, No. 1987, 1/2 Liter, Wild Rose Design, Etched, Pewter Lid, Hein 173.00
Stein, No. 2001C, 1/2 Liter, Scholars, Glazed, Hand Painted, Inlaid Lid 610.00
Stein, No. 2001F, 1/2 Liter, Architecture, Glazed, Hand Painted, Relief, Inlaid Lid 910.00
Stein, No. 2001H, 1/2 Liter, Forestry, Glazed, Hand Painted, Inlaid Lid 1375.00
Stein, No. 2001I, 1/2 Liter, Theology, Glazed, Hand Painted, Inlaid Lid 1880.00
Stein, No. 2002, 1/2 Liter, Munchen Skyline, Verse, Etched, Inlaid Lid ....460.00 to 880.00
Stein, No. 2007, 1/2 Liter, Black Cat, Etched, Inlaid Lid, Stuck 605.00
Stein, No. 2009, 1/2 Liter, Werner & Margarete Dancing, Etched, Inlaid Lid, Stuck 290.00
Stein, No. 2028, 1 Liter, Tavern Keeper Filling Steins, Etched, Pewter Lid 375.00
Stein, No. 2031, 1/2 Liter, Officers & Soldiers, Etched, Inlaid Lid 880.00
Stein, No. 2069, 1/2 Liter, Monkey Holding Fish, Inlaid Lid, Stoneware 4950.00
Stein, No. 2075, 1/2 Liter, Telegrapher, Eagle, Etched, Glazed, Inlaid Lid 1695.00
Stein, No. 2076, 1 1/3 Liters, Coat Of Arms, Inlaid Lid, 13 In. 125.00
Stein, No. 2082, 1/2 Liter, William Tell Shooting Apple, Etched, Inlaid Lid 880.00
Stein, No. 2083, 1/2 Liter, Boar Hunting Scene, Etched, Inlaid Lid 1210.00
Stein, No. 2086, 1/2 Liter, Dancing Scene, Relief, Inlaid Lid 305.00
Stein, No. 2090, 1/2 Liter, Man Sitting At Table Smoking Pipe, Etched, Inlaid Lid .250.00 to 465.00
Stein, No. 2092, 1/2 Liter, Gnomes Adjusting Clock, Etched, Inlaid Lid 780.00
Stein, No. 2100, 1/3 Liter, Prosit, Knight With Stein, Man In Fur, Etched, Inlaid Lid 605.00
Stein, No. 2106, 1/4 Liter, Monkeys In Cage, Monkey Handle, Etched, Relief, Inlaid Lid . 4950.00
Stein, No. 2122, 3/4 Liter, Crusader Drinking, Monk, Inlaid Lid, Schlitt 4400.00
Stein, No. 2131, 1/2 Liter, Barroom Characters, Relief, Inlaid Lid 308.00
Stein, No. 2134, 1/3 Liter, Gnome Sitting In Nest, Etched, Inlaid Lid, Schlitt 1265.00
Stein, No. 2191, 1/2 Liter, Military Joke, Inlaid Lid, Etruscan Style, Schlitt ......412.00 to 715.00
Stein, No. 2204, 1 Liter, Prussian Eagle, Relief, Inlaid Lid 1155.00
Stein, No. 2204, 1/2 Liter, Prussian Eagle, Etched, Relief, Inlaid Lid 695.00
Stein, No. 2219, 3 1/8 Liter, Dancing & Musician Scene, 3 Panels, Relief, Inlaid Lid 605.00
Stein, No. 2276, 1/2 Liter, Nurnberg Goose Boy, Etched, Inlaid Lid 685.00
Stein, No. 2277, 1/3 Liter, Heidelberg, Etched, Inlaid Lid ....300.00 to 325.00
Stein, No. 2382, 1 Liter, Thirsty Rider, Etched, Inlaid Lid, Schlitt 605.00
Stein, No. 2382, 1/2 Liter, Thirsty Rider, Etched, Inlaid Lid ....680.00 to 685.00
Stein, No. 2391, 1 Liter, Lohengrin Wedding Scene, Etched, Inlaid Lid 1905.00
Stein, No. 2520, 1/2 Liter, Student & Barmaid, Etched, Inlaid Lid, Schlitt ......605.00 to 935.00
Stein, No. 2532, 1/2 Liter, Drunken Scene, Etched, Inlaid Lid, Quidenus 620.00
Stein, No. 2580, 1/2 Liter, Die Kannenburg, Knight, Castle, Inlaid Lid, Schlitt ....700.00 to 850.00
Stein, No. 2582, 1 Liter, Jester Performing, Etched, Inlaid Lid, Schlitt 715.00
Stein, No. 2583, 1/2 Egyptian Scene, Man Eating, Etched, Inlaid Lid, Quidenus 960.00
Stein, No. 2632, 1/2 Liter, Bowling & Tavern Scene, Etched, Pewter Lid 230.00
Stein, No. 2640, 1/2 Liter, Cavalier & Barmaid, Etched, Pewter Lid, Quidenus 695.00
Stein, No. 2662, 1/2 Liter, Student Counting White Mice, Etched, Inlaid Lid 2655.00
Stein, No. 2693, 1/2 Liter, Tavern Scene, Barmaid & Drinker, Etched, Inlaid Lid 640.00

Stein, No. 2715, 1/2 Liter, Musical, Dancing & Drinking, Cameo, Pewter Lid 580.00
Stein, No. 2717, 1/2 Liter, Venus Target, Etched, Glazed, Inlaid Lid 3740.00
Stein, No. 2720, 1/2 Liter, Tailor Occupation, Etched, Glazed, Inlaid Lid 970.00
Stein, No. 2765, 1 Liter, Knight On White Horse, Etched, Inlaid Lid, Turret, Schlitt 2640.00
Stein, No. 2765, 1/2 Liter, Knight On White Horse, Etched, Inlaid Lid, Turret, Schlitt 1870.00
Stein, No. 2776, 1/2 Liter, Keeper Of Wine Cellar, Etched, Inlaid Lid 925.00
Stein, No. 2778, 1/2 Liter, Carnival Scene, Etched, Inlaid Lid, Schlitt 1485.00
Stein, No. 2801, 2 1/8 Liter, Art Nouveau Design, Etched, Inlaid Lid 975.00
Stein, No. 2807, 1/2 Liter, Tavern Scene, Etched, Inlaid Lid 695.00
Stein, No. 2809, 1/2 Liter, Faithful Eckhart, Etched, Inlaid Lid, Quidenus 770.00
Stein, No. 2823, 1 Liter, Girl With Rifle, Tapestry, Pewter Lid 695.00
Stein, No. 2823, 1/2 Liter, Girl With Rifle, Tapestry, Pewter Lid 435.00
Stein, No. 2833A, 1/2 Liter, Man In Red Cape, Brown Hat, Etched, Inlaid Lid 420.00
Stein, No. 2833D, 1/2 Liter, Man & Woman Holding Hands, Etched, Inlaid Lid 420.00
Stein, No. 2833D, 1/3 Liter, Man & Woman Holding Hands, Etched, Inlaid Lid 265.00
Stein, No. 2871, 1 Liter, Cornell University, Building & Song, Etched, Inlaid Lid 850.00
Stein, No. 2878, 1/2 Liter, Tyrolean Girls, Tapestry, Pewter Lid 345.00
Stein, No. 2880, 1/2 Liter, Tavern Scene, Etched, Inlaid Lid 695.00
Stein, No. 2903, 1/2 Liter, Art Nouveau, Etched, Inlaid Lid 495.00
Stein, No. 2917, 1 Liter, Munich Child, Lion & Shield, Inlaid Lid, Hein 1100.00
Stein, No. 2922, 1/4 Liter, Hunter Drinking, Etched, Inlaid Lid 265.00
Stein, No. 2936, 1/2 Liter, Elk's Club, Etched, Inlaid Lid . . . . .330.00 to 450.00
Stein, No. 2938, 1/2 Liter, Hunter With Dog, Etched, Inlaid Lid 770.00
Stein, No. 3001, 1/2 Liter, Man Walking, Etched, Pewter Lid 660.00
Stein, No. 3089, 1 Liter, Diogenes In Barrel, Etched, Inlaid Lid, Schlitt 1270.00
Stein, No. 3092, 1/2 Liter, Whiskey Man, Etched, Inlaid Lid, Schlitt 825.00
Stein, No. 3138, 2 2/5 Liter, Art Nouveau, Red & White, Etched, Inlaid Lid 825.00
Stein, No. 3191, 1/2 Liter, Man Drinking, Yellow Glaze, Inlaid Lid, Ringer 960.00
Stein, No. 3193, 1/2 Liter, Man With Jug, Red Glaze, Inlaid Lid, Ringer 690.00
Stein, No. 3236, 1/2, Liter, Art Nouveau, Blue & White, Etched, Inlaid Lid 500.00
Stein, No. 3251, 1/2 Liter, Hunter & Young Girl, Etched, Inlaid Lid 430.00
Stein, No. 3350, 1/2 Liter, Playing Finger Game, Etched, Inlaid Lid 1265.00
Stein, No. 5016, 1.1/3 Liter, Angels, Faience, Pewter Lid 1045.00
Stein, No. 5188, 1/2 Liter, Man Drinking At Table, Delft, Pewter Lid 470.00
Urn, Maidens At Toilette & Dancing, 2 Handles, Stoneware, 1896, 7 1/4 In., Pair 550.00
Vase, 3 Women On Either Side, Stahl, 14 3/4 In. 1100.00
Vase, No. 1317, Etched, Glazed, Floral Design, 3 1/2 In. 160.00
Vase, No. 2175, Woman, Etruscan, Handles, Etched, c.1900, 7 1/2 In., Pair 220.00
Vase, No. 2209, Scenes From Lohengrin, Siegfried, Figural Handles, Etched, 17 In. 2750.00
Vase, No. 2279, Wedding Scene, Etruscan Style, Etched, 13 1/2 In. 520.00
Vase, No. 2416, Art Nouveau, Flowers, 6 Handles At Top, Etched, 16 In. 715.00
Vase, No. 2453, Woman Dancing, Etruscan, Etched, 15 1/2 In. 1030.00
Vase, No. 2866, Geometric Design, Glazed, Terra-Cotta, Blue, Mosaic, 6 In. 140.00

MILK GLASS

MILK GLASS was named for its milky white color. It was first made in
England during the 1700s. The height of its popularity in the United
States was from 1870 to 1880. It is now correct to refer to some colored glass as blue milk glass, black milk glass, etc. Reproductions of
milk glass are being made and sold in many stores. Related pieces may
be listed in the Cosmos, Vallerysthal, and Westmoreland categories.

Biscuit Jar, David Lynch Co. 50.00
Bottle, Dresser, Gold Trim, Victorian, 10 In., Pair 60.00
Bowl, Acanthus Leaf, 10 x 4 1/2 In. 75.00
Butter, Cover, Blackberry 75.00
Butter, Ribs, Blue 55.00
Butter, Star & Fan, Cover 45.00
Compote, Atlas, Atterbury 125.00
Compote, Atlas, Open Edge, Atterbury, 8 1/4 x 8 1/4 In. 45.00
Creamer, Cord & Tassel, Holly 110.00
Creamer, Prism Arc 37.00
Dish, Chick & Eggs Cover, Pierced Edge Base, Late 19th Century, 6 3/4 In. 255.00
Dish, Cover, Hand & Dove, Pat. 1889, 8 1/4 In. 65.00
Dish, Fox Cover, Lacy Base, 7 1/2 In. 100.00

Old milk glass is slightly opalescent at the edge when held up to a strong light. New glass is not.

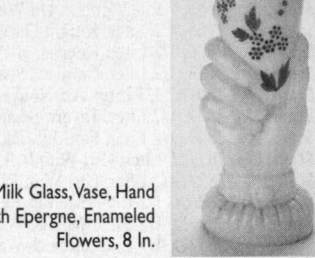

Milk Glass, Vase, Hand
With Epergne, Enameled
Flowers, 8 In.

Dish, Hen Cover, White Head, Blue, 5 1/2 In.		50.00
Dish, Hen On Nest Cover, Atterbury		195.00
Humidor, Brass Cover, 3 Shell Feet, Victorian, 4 x 8 In.		175.00
Inkwell, Bulldog's Head		750.00
Jar, Cover, Owl, Red Eyes, 6 3/4 In.		65.00
Jar, Dresser, Cover, Versailles, 3 x 3 1/2 In.		65.00
Lamp, Oil, Acanthus Leaf, Green & Gold Trim, Miniature		143.00
Match Safe, Pipe		35.00
Mug, Swan & Cattails		45.00
Mustard, Bull's Head, Atterbury		250.00
Pitcher, Opaque Scroll		125.00
Plaque, Lincoln, Brown Wash, 8 1/4 In.		80.00
Plate, Columbus, Club Border		40.00
Plate, Fern, Circle Border, Atterbury, 8 In.		30.00
Plate, Forget-Me-Not, Challinor, 7 In.		40.00
Plate, Pinwheel Border, Low Foot, Enameled Center, 11 In.		50.00
Salt & Pepper, Heron & Lighthouse, Original Top		95.00
Salt Shaker, Cone, Pink		45.00
Sugar, Cover, Roman Cross		65.00
Syrup, Enameled Flowers, Leaves, Pewter Top, 8 1/2 In.		115.00
Syrup, Scroll		75.00
Syrup, Tree Of Life, Pale Green, Copper Cover		350.00
Tankard Set, Scroll, Challinor, Taylor & Co., 1880s, 5 Piece		245.00
Toothpick, Bunch Of Cigars		25.00
Vase, Clear Ruffled Rim, 1930s, 7 In.		45.00
Vase, Floral, Hand Painted, Gold Trim, 5 In.		25.00
Vase, Green Floral, Avian Design, 8 1/4 In.		2875.00
Vase, Hand Holding Cornucopia, Ruffled, 8 1/2 In.		90.00
Vase, Hand With Epergne, Enameled Flowers, 8 In.	*Illus*	75.00

MILLEFIORI means, literally, a thousand flowers. Many small pieces of glass resembling flowers are grouped together to form a design. It is a type of glasswork popular in paperweights and some are listed in that category.

Figurine, Swan, 5 1/2 In.	60.00
Lamp, 19 1/2 In.	590.00
Perfume Bottle, c.1910, 4 1/2 In.	275.00
Pitcher, Pinched Body, 1930, 8 1/2 In.	375.00
Pitcher, Red Threaded Glass, Polished Pontil, 1930, 8 1/2 In.	375.00
Vase, Blue, 2 Handles, 5 In.	125.00
Vase, Burnt Orange Interior, Exterior Green, 8 1/4 In.	375.00

MINTON china has been made in the Staffordshire region of England from 1793 to the present. The firm became part of the Royal Doulton Tableware Group in 1968, but the wares continued to be marked *Minton*. Many marks have been used. The one shown dates from about 1873 to 1891, when the word *England* was added.

Bowl, Blue Willow, Stylized Twig Handles, Cobalt Blue, Gold, 1876, 4 x 11 In.	120.00

Bowl, Majolica, Staved Basket Form, Rope Handles, Painted, 2 Putti, c.1865, 11 In. 4800.00
Compote, 3 Puttis, 1 With Fish, 2 With Dead Game & Hunting Dog, 8 In. 650.00
Dish, Christmas Rose, Mistletoe, Cherubs, Crystal Palace Art Union, c.1859, 15 1/2 In. .. 3160.00
Dish, Gray Goose Standing At Water's Edge, Green Flower Sprays, Sprigs, 11 In. 690.00
Dish, Venus & Cupid Center, 8 Rim Wells, Satyr & Angel Masks, 1875, 19 1/2 In. 3450.00
Figurine, Greek Goddess Ariadne, 1864, 14 x 11 3/4 In. 2650.00
Figurine, Parrot, Majolica, Perched On Leafy Base, Green Glaze, 1890s, 8 1/4 In. 260.00
Garden Seat, Bamboo, Yellow, Turquoise Ribbon & Bow, 18 1/2 In. 1000.00
Jardiniere, Straps Set With Lion's Mask & Ring Handles, Paw Feet, Signed, 14 1/4 In. ... 2645.00
Jardiniere, Swags Of Fruit & Nuts Suspended, From Lion's Masks, c.1855, 14 In. 4600.00
Jug, Oak Leaf & Acorn, Snail Handle, 4 1/2 In. 375.00
Jug, Oak Leaf & Acorn, Snail Handle, 5 1/2 In. 450.00
Jug, Oak Leaf & Acorn, Snail Handle, 6 1/2 In. 350.00
Jug, Tower, 4 Dancing Figures, Pewter Mounted Cover, Jester's Head Knop, 13 In. 1610.00
Oyster Plate, Fish, Salt Glaze, 10 3/4 In. 200.00
Pitcher, Dark Green Ground, Cobalt Highlights, 8 In. 700.00
Pitcher, Mask Spout, Cobalt, 9 In. 225.00
Pitcher, Pineapple, Dark Green Handle, Spout, 6 1/2 In. 700.00
Pitcher, Tower, Dark Green, Spout, 9 1/2 In. 600.00
Plate, Bird Designs, Gold Border, Artist Signed, 8 3/4 In., 12 Pieces 1320.00
Plate, Dessert, Child In Center Panel, Gilt Scroll Border, c.1883, 9 1/2 In., 8 Piece 4025.00
Plate, Dessert, Poppy Border, c.1920, 9 In., 10 Piece 825.00
Plate, Flower Encrusted, Center Flowers & Fruit, Signed, c.1830, 9 In. 1955.00
Plate, Gilt Floral, Magenta & White Ground, Signed, 8 1/2 In., 8 Piece 365.00
Plate, Ruby Red Rim, Gilt Overlay, Ivory Ground, 10 1/2 In., 11 Piece 125.00
Platter, Anemone, Blue, 17 x 21 In. 305.00
Platter, Imari Poonah Pattern, 1840s-1850s, 17 x 21 1/2 In. 1650.00
Punch Bowl, Japan, Alternating Prunus & Peony Plants, Gilt Rim, 1810, 11 In. 3105.00
Soup, Dish, Ardmore, Foliate Rim, Center Rose, 8 Piece 55.00
Teapot, Fish Form, Seaweed Handle, Spout Protruding From Mouth, Signed, 7 3/8 In. ... 1495.00
Tray, Fish, Dark Green, Dark Brown Tail, 10 In. 650.00
Vase, Earthenware, Triple Gourd Form, Glazed Finish, Early 1900s, 6 1/2 In. 115.00
Vase, Pompadour Pink, Neoclassical Pate-Sur-Pate Figures, Oval Cartouches, 15 In. 1320.00
Vase, Secessionist Style, Art Nouveau, 13 In., Pair 450.00
Vase, Squeezebag, Stylized Plants, Bottle Shape, Stamped, 10 x 5 In. 1100.00
Vase, Squeezebag, Stylized Plants, Swags, Cylindrical, Handles, Marked, 11 3/4 In. 1045.00
Vase, Stenciled Flowers, Teal, Brown Glazes, Oval, Arts & Crafts, 9 1/2 In. 230.00
Vase, Stylized Peacock Feathers, Green, Lavender, 13 x 5 1/2 In. 2090.00

MIRRORS are listed in the Furniture category under Mirror.

MOCHA pottery is an English-made product that was sold in America
during the early 1800s. It is a heavy pottery with pale coffee-and-
cream coloring. Designs of blue, brown, green, orange, black, or white
were added to the pottery and given fanciful names, such as *Tree*, *Snail
Trail*, or *Moss*.

Bowl, Agate Design, 6 In. 340.00
Bowl, Balloons, Brown Ground, White Stripes, Handles, 3 x 4 In. 1760.00
Bowl, Black Band, White Wavy Lines, Stripes, 9 3/4 In. 715.00
Bowl, Cat's-Eye, Ocher, Brown, White, Blue Ground, White Waves & Leaf, 5 x 12 In. 4025.00
Bowl, Earthworm, 5 1/2 In. 440.00
Bowl, Earthworm, Blue, White, Brown, Orange Ground, Dark Brown Bands, 4 x 7 1/4 In. 230.00
Bowl, Seaweed, Blue & White Band, 8 1/2 In. 385.00
Bowl, Seaweed, White Band, Blue Stripes, 5 x 11 1/2 In. 265.00
Chamber Pot, Earthworm, Light Blue, Olive Bands, 9 In. 1980.00
Creamer, Cobalt Blue & White Band, Yellow Ground, 3 3/4 In. 630.00
Jar, Seaweed, Blue & White Bands, 8 1/2 In. 495.00
Mug, Banded, 6 In. 275.00
Mug, Blue & Green Seaweed, Light Blue Band, Incised Bands, 3 3/4 x 2 3/4 In. 975.00
Mug, Cream Dot, Blue Bands, Dark Brown Wavy Design, Cream Handle, 4 3/4 In. 1150.00
Mug, Earthworm, Blue Central Bands, Blue & White, 5 In. 575.00
Mug, Earthworm, Blue, Brown, Ocher, Light Blue Stripes, White Handle, 4 3/4 In. 2415.00
Mug, Earthworm, Green Band, Dark Brown Stripes, White Handle, 5 7/8 In. 2760.00

Mug, Earthworm, Orange & Yellow Stripe, Green Glaze, Impressed Band, 5 3/4 In. 2760.00
Mug, Geometrics, Brown, Dark Brown Yellow Stripes, White Handle 316.00
Mug, Geometrics, Dark Brown, Pumpkin, Dark Brown, Cream Stripes, 5 In. 632.00
Mug, Green Bands, Tan Stripes, Wide White Band, 5 1/2 In. 1485.00
Mug, Marbleized, Tan, Light Brown Band, 5 In. 2530.00
Mug, Open Chain, Upper & Lower Dark Brown Bands, White Handle, 5 3/8 x 6 In. 1955.00
Mug, Seaweed, Blue, White Band, Blue Border, Signed, McAllister, 3 1/8 x 3 In. 170.00
Mug, Seaweed, Cream Colored Ground, Handle, White & Brown Strips, 4 5/8 In. 1100.00
Mug, Seaweed, Green, White Band, Blue Stripes, 2 7/8 In. 395.00
Mug, Seaweed, Mustard Yellow Ground, 19th Century, 6 In. 470.00
Pepper Pot, Cat's Eye, Dark Brown, Blue, Cinnamon Stripes, 4 3/8 In. 920.00
Pepper Pot, Domed Cover, Cat's Eye, Cream, Celadon Stripes, 4 3/4 In. 1092.00
Pepper Pot, Domed Cover, Earthworm, Cinnamon, Dark Brown Stripe, Baluster, 5 In. ... 805.00
Pepper Pot, Plain Domed Cover, Tobacco Leaf, Dark Brown, Ginger, Cream, 4 3/8 In. .. 1955.00
Pitcher, 2 Black Bands, Stylized Flowers, Blue & Brown Stripes, 7 In. 430.00
Pitcher, Blue Bands, Black Stripes, White Ground, 7 5/8 In. 165.00
Pitcher, Brown & White Banding, Yellowware, 7 3/4 x 6 In. 745.00
Pitcher, Cat's Eye & Earthworm, Thin Brown Bands, Brown, 6 1/2 In. 3000.00
Pitcher, Cat's Eye & Waves, Blue, Brown, White, Yellow, Brown Bands, 8 x 5 1/8 In. ... 1265.00
Pitcher, Cat's Eye, Blue, White, Brown, Tan Ground, Blue & Brown Bands, 6 x 4 1/2 In. . 230.00
Pitcher, Cat's Eye, Brown, Green Leaf Design, Light Blue, Cream Stripes, 7 1/4 In. 3795.00
Pitcher, Cat's Eye, Ocher, Blue Band, Dark Brown, White Stripes, White Handle, 6 In. .. 1495.00
Pitcher, Cat's Eye, Orange Ground, Brown, Blue Bands, 6 1/4 x 4 1/2 In. 863.00
Pitcher, Earthworm, Blue & White, Aqua Ground, Brown, White Bands, 7 1/2 x 5 In. ... 805.00
Pitcher, Earthworm, Blue, White Ground, Bright Blue & Dark Brown Bands, 7 x 5 In. ... 230.00
Pitcher, Earthworm, Brown, Blue, Dark Brown, White Stripes, White Handle, 5 x 4 In. .. 1380.00
Pitcher, Earthworm, Brown, Green Band, Dark Brown, White Stripes, 6 x 4 In. 1380.00
Pitcher, Earthworm, Gray Ground, Blue, White Bands, Impressed Leaf, 8 1/4 x 5 In. ... 345.00
Pitcher, Earthworm, Green Bands, Brown, White Stripes, White Handle, 6 x 4 In. 1035.00
Pitcher, Earthworm, Light Green Bands, Light Blue Stripes, White Handle, 8 x 5 In. 2530.00
Pitcher, Geometrics, Dark Brown, Thin Dark Brown Stripes, White Handle, 7 In. 920.00
Pitcher, Marbleized, Blue, Brown, Black, White, Blue Band, White Handle, 7 3/4 In. 2415.00
Pitcher, Seaweed, Black, Blue Bands, Green Ground, 6 In. 440.00
Pitcher, Seaweed, Black, Blue Green Ground, Blue Stripes, White Handle, 8 3/4 x 6 In. .. 173.00
Pitcher, Seaweed, Blue On Orange Band, Black & White Stripes, Barrel Form, 5 In. 1870.00
Pitcher, Stylized Stars, Blue Ground, Brown, Aqua, White Bands, 6 1/2 x 4 In. 230.00
Pitcher, White Wavy Band, Ocher Ground, White, Brown, Blue Bands, 6 3/4 x 4 3/8 In. . 633.00

MONMOUTH Pottery Company started working in Monmouth, Illinois, in 1892. The pottery made a variety of utilitarian wares. It became part of Western Stoneware Company in 1906. The maple leaf mark was used until 1930. If *Co.* appears as part of the mark, the piece was made before 1906.

Pitcher, Blue Green Glaze, 1930s, 6 In. 22.50
Plate, 2 Handles, 10 In. 35.00
Salt & Pepper, Speckled Brown, 4 In. 6.00
Vase, Cobalt, Embossed Leaf Border, 17 7/8 In. 229.00

MONT JOYE, see Mt. Joye category.

MOORCROFT pottery was first made in Burslem, England, in 1913. William Moorcroft had managed the art pottery department for James MacIntyre & Company of England from 1898 to 1913. The Moorcroft pottery continues today, although William Moorcroft died in 1945. The earlier wares are similar to the modern ones, but color and marking will help indicate the age.

Berry Bowl, Footed, 5 1/2 In. 225.00
Bowl, Anemone Pattern, Flared, Signed, c.1925, 10 In. 415.00
Bowl, Flambe, Inverted Rim, 3 Fish Swimming, Sea Plants, c.1932, 12 1/4 In. 2475.00
Bowl, Squeezebag, Waving Corn, Celadon Ground, Stamped, 4 x 9 In. 715.00
Bowl, Wisteria, Flowers & Leaves Inside & Out, Mottled Blue, c.1922, 25 In. 470.00
Box, Pomegranate On Cover, c.1930, 4 x 6 In. 575.00
Candlestick, Orange Luster, Columnar Form, c.1922, 10 In., Pair 230.00

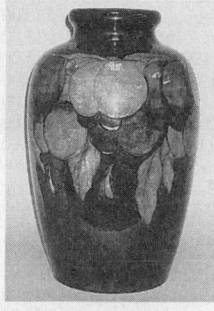

Moorcroft, Vase, Wisteria,
Flambe, 1929, 18 1/4 In.

Compote, Wisteria, Cobalt Blue Ground, Signed, c.1925, 11 In. 546.00
Ginger Jar, Pomegranate, Domed Cover, Fruit, Blue-Brown Ground, c.1925, 7 1/2 In. 1310.00
Jar, Pansy, Cover, 2 Handles, Oval, Flowers, Blue On Blue Ground, c.1922, 6 1/2 In. 870.00
Jardiniere, Yellow & Blue Swirling Medallions, Green Ground, 10 In., Pair 880.00
Lamp, 2-Light, Cascading Grapes & Pomegranates, Blue Ground, 20 1/2 In. 977.00
Lamp, Cornflower, Flambe, Cylinder, Impressed Mark, c.1930, 8 1/4 In. 1020.00
Perfume Bottle, Pansies, Cobalt Blue Ground, Silver Cap, 2 x 1 3/4 In. 660.00
Plate, Grape & Leaf, Painted, Flambe Tones, Circular Form, c.1925, 9 In. 725.00
Plate, Poppy, Flowers, Leaves, Blue Ground, Impressed Mark, c.1925, 8 3/4 In. 450.00
Sugar & Creamer, Florian, Flowers, Leaves, Greens & Blues, Macintyre, c.1902, 3 In. 400.00
Vase, 2 Pink To Burgundy Flowers, Green To Blue Field, 3 1/2 In. 154.00
Vase, Anemone, Mid 20th Century, Signed, 3 3/4 In. 200.00
Vase, Blue, Red Flowers, Green Leaves, Green To Dark Blue Ground, Signed, 5 1/4 In. .. 230.00
Vase, Cabinet, Grapes & Leaves, Green, Blue Ground, 4 1/4 In. 330.00
Vase, Cobalt Blue, Floral, Bulbous, 4 In. 220.00
Vase, Coral Hibiscus, Green Ground, Bulbous, 5 In. 247.00
Vase, Cornflower, Blue Flowers, Green Slip Outline, Speckled Ground, c.1925, 3 In. 1745.00
Vase, Cornflower, Flowers & Leaves, Red, Purple, Ocher, Blue, Brown, 12 1/4 In. 1890.00
Vase, Flamminian, 3 Foliate Roundels, Red & Blue Tones, Macintyre, c.1910, 6 1/4 In. .. 690.00
Vase, Floral Body, Blue, Flared Rim, Impressed, 6 In. 440.00
Vase, Floral, Red, Flared Rim, Impressed, 10 In. 770.00
Vase, Floral, Signed, 4 In. 110.00
Vase, Floral, Signed, 7 1/2 In. 425.00
Vase, Florian Ware, Blue Poppies, Leaves, White Glaze, Macintyre Stamp, 6 1/2 x 3 In. .. 1650.00
Vase, Florian Ware, Squeezebag, Jonquils, Blue Ground, Ink Mark, 6 3/4 x 3 In. 1980.00
Vase, Florian Ware, Violets, Yellow, Blue & Celadon, Signed, 9 x 3 3/4 In. 880.00
Vase, Florian, Pyriform, Daisies, Leaves, 3 Blue Tones, Macintyre, c.1902, 8 3/4 In. 870.00
Vase, Hibiscus Blossoms At Side, Label, c.1950, 4 3/8 In. 200.00
Vase, Landscape Scene, 9 1/2 x 6 In. 825.00
Vase, Moonlit Blue, Mounted As Lamp, 12 3/4 In. 1035.00
Vase, Orchid, Blue, Green, Yellow, Rose, Pale Blue, Green Ground, 4 In. 280.00
Vase, Orchid, Glossy Glaze, Painted Initials, 4 x 6 In. 230.00
Vase, Orchid, Tapered Oval Form, Flared Rim, Signed, 5 3/4 In. 373.00
Vase, Orchids, Oval, Purple, Red, Blue, White, Green, Blue Ground, c.1930, 10 In. 1525.00
Vase, Painted Signature, William Moorcroft, 8 1/8 In. 770.00
Vase, Palm Trees & Flowers, Water & Rocks, Signed, 14 3/8 In. 690.00
Vase, Pansy, Flowers, Leaves, Baluster Form, Blue Ground, c.1925, 12 1/8 In. 725.00
Vase, Pansy, Oval, Wide Mouth, Flowers & Leaves, Green Ground, c.1917, 20 1/4 In. 1455.00
Vase, Pink & Green Leaves, Red Berries, Cobalt Ground, Bulbous, Signed, 5 In. 605.00
Vase, Pomegranate, Fruit & Leaves, Red, Purple, Blue, Green, c.1915, 4 1/8 In. 580.00
Vase, Pomegranate, Rose, Blue, Green, Brown, Purple, Cobalt Ground, 9 In. 1375.00
Vase, Pomegranates, Amid Birds, Signed, c.1930, 13 In. 977.00
Vase, Poppies, Raised Petal Edges, White Ground, Signed, 8 1/2 In. 935.00
Vase, Poppy, Purple, Rose, Green, Cobalt Ground, 11 In. 1760.00

Vase, Ribbon Tied Garlands, Roses, Gilt, Red, Cream, Blue, Macintyre, c.1907, 7 In.	580.00
Vase, Squeezebag, Ivory Mushrooms, Blue, Gray & Green Ground, 12 x 7 In.	550.00
Vase, Stylized Red Roses, Blue Flowers, White Ground, Macintyre, 1 3/4 x 2 In.	935.00
Vase, Tudor Rose, Tapered, Stylized Flowers, Red, Cream, Green, Blue, c.1904, 7 1/2 In. .	1455.00
Vase, Wisteria, Bulbous, Blossoms, Leaves, Blue Ground, c.1925, 7 5/8 In.	365.00
Vase, Wisteria, Flambe, 1929, 18 1/4 In. . . . .*Illus*	6913.00
Vase, Wisteria, Oval, Puce, Yellow & Red Flowers, Blue Ground, 1929, 15 In.	2070.00
Vase, Wisteria, Ruby Flambe Glaze, Stamped, Script Signature, 14 1/4 x 6 In.	4675.00

MORIAGE is a special type of raised decoration used on some Japanese pottery. Sometimes pieces of clay were shaped by hand and applied to the item; sometimes the clay was squeezed from a tube in the way we apply cake frosting.

Bowl, Hand Painted Landscape, Marked, 2 x 7 In.	125.00
Bowl, Scenic, Swan, Teal, Orange, Yellow, Handle, Nippon, 10 In.	235.00
Bowl, Shell, 3 Sections, Nippon, 10 In.	350.00
Chocolate Pot, Nippon, 8 In.	525.00
Cup & Saucer, After Dinner, Medallions Of Man Playing Lute For Woman	95.00
Cup & Saucer, Blue Rim, Scrolled Gold, Floral, 5 1/2 In.	38.00
Cup & Saucer, Enameled Flowers, 1920s	30.00
Dish, Coin Purse Form, Luster Glaze, 3 1/2 x 2 1/4 In.	12.00
Ewer, Orchids, Green Ground, Black & White Trim, Nippon	650.00
Mug, Handle, Dutch Scene, Nippon	155.00
Plate, Flowers & Roses Center, 12 In.	200.00
Plate, Mountain & Surrounding Area, Pink Bushes, 9 /12 In.	36.00
Rooster, Holes For Hanging, 10 1/4 In.	18.00
Sugar, Orchids, Green Ground, Black & White Trim, Nippon	325.00
Sugar Shaker, Pink Flowers, Dot Trim, Cork Stopper, 4 1/2 In.	95.00
Teapot, Kutuni Mountain, Dragon Mouth Spout, Gold Trim	20.00
Urn, Cover, Handles, 7 In.	695.00
Vase, Applied Dragons, 2 1/2 In.	6.00
Vase, Bird Sitting In Tree, Overlooking Flower, 1890s, 12 In.	195.00
Vase, Ocean Scene With Bird, 13 In.	795.00
Vase, Raised Paint Design, Marked, 3 3/4 In.	10.00
Vase, Roses, 4 In.	100.00
Vase, Surreal Scene, Handles, Nippon, 7 In.	120.00
Wall Pocket, Center Pretty Woman On Front, Gold Beading, 3 1/4 x 5 1/2 In.	28.00

MOSAIC TILE COMPANY of Zanesville, Ohio, was started by Karl Langerbeck and Herman Mueller in 1894. Many types of plain and ornamental tiles were made until 1959. The company closed in 1967. The company also made some ashtrays, bookends, and related gift-wares. Most pieces are marked with the entwined *MTC* monogram.

Figurine, Bear, Standing, Open Mouth, Early 20th Century, 10 1/4 In.	172.00
Tile, Girl In Garden, M.R. Thompson, 5 3/4 In.	77.00
Tile, Spanish Galleon, Brown, Wavy Yellow Sea, Green Ground, 6 In.	360.00

MOSER glass is made by Ludwig Moser und Sohne, a Bohemian (Czech) glasshouse founded in 1857. Art Nouveau-type glassware and iridescent glassware were made. The most famous Moser glass is decorated with heavy enameling in gold and bright colors. The firm, Moser Glassworks, is still working in Karlsbad, West Czech Republic. Few pieces of Moser glass are marked.

Biscuit Jar, Applied Acorn Leaves, Cased Cream, 7 In.	450.00
Biscuit Jar, White, Enameled Floral, Brass Base, Lid & Bail, 9 In.	700.00
Bottle, Amethyst Cut To Clear, Gold Tracing, Steeple Stopper, Marked, 27 In., Pair	900.00
Bottle, Cranberry, Porcelain Portrait, Marked, 7 1/4 In., Pair	550.00
Bottle, Peach, Gold Trim, Floral, Steeple Stopper, 28 In., Pair	400.00
Bowl, Gold Bows & Ribbon, 5 x 7 In.	75.00
Bowl, Hand Painted Stagecoach Scene, Blue, 8 1/2 In.	40.00
Bowl, Multicolored & Gold Floral, Ruby, Rolled Edge, 10 In.	1955.00
Bowl, Multicolored Floral, Amethyst, Gold Rim, 12 1/2 x 5 1/2 In.	460.00

Box, Dresser, Mythological Figures Frieze, Cobalt Blue, 4 Ball Feet, 5 1/2 In. 172.00
Box, Egg Shape, Enameled, Hinged, Brass Base, 9 In. 300.00
Box, White Enameled Floral, Gold, Birds On Blue Ground, 4 Paw Feet, 4 1/4 In. 632.00
Candlestick, Dark Green, Raised Gold Band, Signed, 10 In. 25.00
Chalice, Intaglio Stag & Fawn Scene, Ruby Flashed, 9 1/2 In. 170.00
Compote, Amber, Raised Gold, 3 1/2 x 6 In. 60.00
Compote, Gold Enameled Chariot Scene, Green Glass, Satin Rim, 4 1/2 x 11 1/2 In. 373.00
Cordial Set, Oval Cuts, Pink Amber, Decanter, 6 Cordials, Signed, 10 3/4 In. 285.00
Cup, Pale Olive Green, 2 Applied Acorns, Paris 350.00
Cup & Saucer, Lavender, Clover Shape 50.00
Decanter, Enameled Gold & Fleur-De-Lis, Amber, Signed, 9 1/2 In. 225.00
Decanter Set, Green Cut To Clear, Intaglio Floral, 12-In. Decanter, 7 Piece 550.00
Dresser Set, Lavender Cut To Clear, Art Deco, Atomizer, Box, Signed, 4 Piece 400.00
Finger Bowl, Underplate, Cranberry, Floral Enameled 175.00
Goblet, Blue Panels, Gold Stencil, 7 3/4 In. 175.00
Lamp, Gone With The Wind, Enameled Birds & Flowers, Blue Glass, Electrified, 20 In. ... 1035.00
Lamp, Oil, Cranberry, Applied Salamander, Quilted & Ruffled Shade, 25 In. 1000.00
Lock Box, Dark Amethyst, Enameled Floral, Brass Handles & Fittings, 4 1/2 In. 500.00
Punch Set, Gold Enameled Stag & Fawn Scene, Olive Green, 9 1/2-In. Bowl, 5 Piece ... 250.00
Rose Bowl, Smoke, Acid Etched, Deer In Garden, c.1920, 5 1/2 In. 405.00
Sugar & Creamer, Band Of Amber Concave Ovals, Gold Enameled 340.00
Tumbler, Juice, Blue, Bugs & Grape Leaves, Applied Grapes 395.00
Tumbler, Juice, Blue, Enameled Leaves, Engraved John 80.00
Vase, Alexandrite, Honeycomb, Signed, 8 In. 300.00
Vase, Amber, Fighting Roman Soldiers In Gold Band, 14 In. 200.00
Vase, Amberina, Enameled, 8 1/2 In., Pair 475.00
Vase, Amberina, Swirl, Applied Amber Rigaree, 11 In., Pair 425.00
Vase, Amethyst, Greek Mythological Scene On Gold Band, Carlsbad, 8 In. 175.00
Vase, Applied Acorns, Birds, Pale Blue Ground, 4 x 12 In. 2070.00
Vase, Applied Amber Salamander, Floral Enameled, Dolphin Feet, 9 1/2 In. 1700.00
Vase, Applied Eagle On Branch, Enameled Leaves, Amethyst, 9 1/2 In. 2000.00
Vase, Aqua, Enameled Pattern, Gold Center, Corset, Signed, 17 In. 250.00
Vase, Blue, Enameled Peacock On Branch, 9 1/2 In. 435.00
Vase, Cranberry, Enameled Chrysanthemum, Applied Bees, 11 3/4 In. 325.00
Vase, Cranberry, Gold Man & Woman Scene, 5 In. 125.00
Vase, Dark Amber, Art Deco, 11 3/4 In. 150.00
Vase, Elephants Under Palm Tree, Inverted Baluster, Cameo, c.1925, 8 In. 1720.00
Vase, Enameled Floral, Cranberry, Footed, Applied Rim, 6 x 12 x 5 In. 300.00
Vase, Enameled Pansies, Aqua, Gold Rim, 13 1/2 In. 950.00
Vase, Geometric, Floral, Amethyst, Scroll Handles, 4 x 11 In. 920.00
Vase, Intaglio, Ruby Cut To Clear, Poppy Design, 10 In. 425.00
Vase, Lavender, Gold Enameled, 12 In. 80.00
Vase, Multicolored & Gold Floral, Cobalt Blue Ground, Handles, 9 In. 977.00
Vase, Multicolored Acorns, Salamander, Pale Blue Ground, 8 In. 2070.00
Vase, Multicolored Floral, Geometric, Pale Green, 4 Paw Feet, 7 In. 862.00
Vase, Multicolored Floral, Pale Green Ground, 5 x 11 In., Pair 402.00
Vase, Multicolored Floral, Ruby Ground, Gold Rim, 4 In. 805.00
Vase, Pillow, Pink, Enameled Floral, 6 In. 550.00
Vase, Pillow, Ruby, Engraved Floral & Bird, Footed, 5 In. 350.00
Vase, Tropical Fish, Sea Horses, Waterscape Cutting, Signed, 1930s, 8 1/2 In. 2012.00
Vase, Trumpet, Pink Camphor, Meriden Silver Plate Holder, 15 In. 350.00
Vase, Trumpet, Rubena Verde, Scroll & Trellis, Gold Enameled, Fluted Foot, 18 In. 360.00
Wine, Green, Red Jewels, 8 In. 80.00
Wine, Olive, Enameled Leaves, 7 1/4 In. 300.00

MOSS ROSE china was made by many firms from 1808 to 1900. It has
a typical moss rose pictured as the design. The plant is not as popular
now as it was in Victorian gardens, so the fuzz-covered bud is unfa-
miliar to most collectors. The dishes were usually decorated with pink
and green flowers.

Plate, Rose Color Border, Hand Painted, 10 In. 25.00
Teapot 55.00

MOTHER-OF-PEARL GLASS, or pearl satin glass, was first made in the 1850s in England and in Massachusetts. It was a special type of mold-blown satin glass with air bubbles in the glass, giving it a pearlized color. It has been reproduced. Mother-of-pearl shell objects are listed under Pearl.

Box, Art Deco, Grasshopper, Antennae, Brass-Inlaid Bakelite, France, 3 In.	201.00
Card Case, Diamond-Quilted, England, 19th Century, 4 x 3 In.	700.00
Jar, Herringbone, Pink To White, Cover, 7 In.	176.00
Pitcher, Herringbone, Blue, 7 1/2 In.	300.00
Pitcher, Water, Diamond-Quilted, Pink, Applied Rib Handle, 9 In.	80.00
Sugar & Creamer, Herringbone	5060.00
Vase, Blue, Herringbone, Melon Ribbed, Square, 5 1/4 In.	252.00
Vase, Cased, Zipper, Ruffled Edge, 5 In.	121.00
Vase, Diamond-Quilted, Pink Satin, 8 In.	345.00
Vase, Diamond-Quilted, Tangerine, 8 In.	60.00
Vase, Diamond-Quilted, White Interior, Satin Ruffled Edge, 5 In.	245.00
Vase, Herringbone, Yellow, 14 1/2 In.	155.00

MOTORCYCLES and motorcycle accessories of all types are being collected today. Examples can be found that date back to the early years of the twentieth century. Toy motorcycles are listed in the Toy category.

Belt, Harley-Davidson, Black Leather, Winged Logo, 3 Buckles, 7 In. Wide, Size 34	40.00
Belt, Kidney, Triple Belt Fastener, Brown Leather, 33 x 6 1/2 In.	25.00
Cap, Harley-Davidson, Black Twill Crown, White Patent Brim, 1950s, Size 7 1/8	150.00
Cap, Skull, White Cotton, Orange, Black, Gray, Emblem Sewn On Front	41.00
Helmet, Police, Bridgeport, Conn., Gold & Black Paint, Patent Leather Visor	45.00
Helmet, White Fiberglass Shell, Black Bill, Zip-On Leather Ear Flaps, 1950s	29.00
Jacket, American Motorcycle Association, Black Wool, Yellow Leather Sleeves	61.00
Jacket, Black Leather, Quilted Lining, Talon Zipper, Belted Waist, Schott, Size 44	145.00
Jacket, Cowhide, Black, Metal Stars On Epaulets, Talon Zipper, Size 36	203.00
Jacket, Leather, Black, 2 Zipper Pockets, Harley-Davidson, Medium	79.00
Jacket, Leather, Black, 2 Zipper Pockets, Hein Gericke, Size 42	26.00
Jacket, Leather, Black, Epaulets, Zipper Front, Quilted Lining, Size 40	32.00
Jacket, Leather, Black, Red Quilted Lining, Montgomery Ward	85.00
Jacket, Leather, Black, Zipper Pockets, 1960, Size 40	40.00
Jacket, Leather, Brown, Fleece Collar, Lining, Kurland, 1940, Medium	100.00
Jacket, Leather, Tan, Black Satin Lining, Talon Zipper, Snaps, 1950s, Size 42	330.00
Jacket, Leather, Waist Belt, Buckle, Quilted Lining, Sears Roebuck, 1950s	285.00
Jacket, Pigskin Leather, 4 Pockets, Zipper Front, Large	32.00
License Plate, Pennsylvania, 1915, 4 1/2 x 8 1/4 In.	70.00
Motorcycle, AJS, Handlebar Levers, Carburetor, Serial No. K7/L6672, 1929	6900.00
Motorcycle, AJS, Pilgrim Oil Pump, New Handlebar Levers, 1927	9200.00
Motorcycle, Ariel, Black Paint, Square Four 1000cc, 1955	9200.00
Motorcycle, Bradbury, Original Front Brake, Speedometer, 1911	8050.00
Motorcycle, Harley-Davidson, Cafe Racer, Black Paint, 1977	9200.00
Motorcycle, Marusho, 4-Speed Gearbox, Rear Shaft Drive, Chrome, 1965	3450.00
Motorcycle, Moto Morini, Corsaro, 125cc, Red Paint, 1974	2530.00
Motorcycle, Raleigh, Sturmey Archer, Front Brakes, 1925	4600.00
Motorcycle, Triumph, Ricardo Engine, 4 Valves, Black, Gray, Green Paint, 1922	9775.00
Motorcycle, Triumph, Trophy, Speedometer, Tank, Silver, Blue Paint, 1957	8050.00
Motorcycle, Whizzer, Black, Cream, Red Accents, Flyer Frame	2185.00
Motorcycle, Whizzer, Pacemaker, Maroon, White Stripping, 1951	4600.00
Motorcycle, Whizzer, Pacemaker, Telescopic Front Fork, Fishtail Exhaust	8625.00
Motorcycle, Whizzer, Schwinn Spring Fork, Black, Red Accents, Chrome Fenders	2100.00
Oil Can, Harley-Davidson Genuine Oil, 1 Qt.	150.00
Oil Can, Harley-Davidson Pre-Luxe Motorcycle, Contents, 1 Qt.	100.00
Patch, Harley-Davidson At Dodge City Races, 1956, 5 x 2 3/4 In.	85.00
Poster, Harley-Davidson, Dirt Bike, Paper, 34 3/4 x 7 In.	35.00
Poster, Motorcycle Race, Lithograph, Color, 1928, 12 x 20 In.	16.00
Program, Race, Unused, 1936, 8 x 10 In.	12.00
Scarf, Harley-Davidson, Black, Multicolored Eagle & Flag, Square, 20 In.	20.00

Spark Plug, Harley-Davidson, Red Celluloid Wrap, Box 65.00
Ticket, Hill Climb, All Different, 1937, 4 Piece 8.00
Tie Clasp, Harley-Davidson, Motorcycle Shape, Gilt, 1950s, 2 1/4 In. 45.00
Vest, Harley-Davidson Patch, Black Leather, Brass Snap Front 43.00
Wrench, Pocket, Indian Motorcycle, 7 In. 100.00

MOUNT WASHINGTON, see Mt. Washington category.

MOVIE memorabilia of all types is collected. Animation cels, games, sheet music, toys, and some celebrity items are listed in their own section. Listed here are costumes and paper collectibles. A lobby card is 11 by 14 inches. A set of lobby cards includes seven scene cards and one title card. A one sheet, the standard movie poster, is 27 by 41 inches. A three sheet is 81 by 40 inches. A half sheet is 22 by 28 inches. A window card, made of cardboard, is 14 by 22 inches. An insert is 14 by 36 inches. A herald is a promotional item handed out to patrons. A press book was sent to newspapers and magazines to promote a picture. Press books and/or press kits (with photos) were sent to the media to promote a movie.

Ad Picture, The Caddy, Dean Martin & Jerry Lewis, Matted, 6 1/4 x 10 In. 20.00
Autograph, Bing Crosby, Letter, 1941 .... 230.00
Autograph, Frank Sinatra, Photograph, Leaning On Airplane, 10 x 8 In. 60.00
Autograph, Frank Sinatra, Postcard, Microphone & Stools With Hat 105.00
Autograph, Frank Sinatra, Poster, AT&T National Fitness Foundation Benefit, 1984 ..... 195.00
Autograph, Frank Sinatra, Sinatra In Concert, With Pete Barbutti, Carnegie Hall, Frame .. 195.00
Autograph, Fred Astaire & Gene Kelly, Dancing, Photograph, Black & White, 8 x 10 In. .. 380.00
Autograph, Gina Lollobrigida, Sitting On Bed, Photograph, Glossy, 8 x 10 In. 57.00
Autograph, Henry Winkler, Sally Field, Photograph, Black & White, Frame 125.00
Autograph, Ingrid Bergman, Photograph, Dated 1947, 6 1/2 x 8 1/2 In. 255.00
Autograph, Julie Christie, Photograph, Color, 8 x 10 In. 27.00
Autograph, Mae West, Photograph, Full Length, Front Of 4 Spotlights, 8 x 10 In. 130.00
Autograph, Mary Pickford, Straw Hat, Poster, 1920s, 28 x 22 In. 400.00
Autograph, Sean Connery, Dennis Quaid, Dragonheart, Photograph, Color, Frame 160.00
Autograph, Sean Connery, The Rock, Photograph, Glossy, Silver Ink, 8 x 10 In. 86.00
Autograph, Shirley MacLaine, Fishnet Stockings, Photograph, Glossy, 8 x 10 In. 40.00
Book, Gone With The Wind, Movie Edition, Paperback, 1939 .... 45.00
Costume, 20000 Leagues Under The Sea, Pants, Nautilus Crew, Blue, Red Pockets 430.00
Costume, Caftan, Ben Hur, Worn By Charlton Heston, Letter Of Authenticity 4310.00
Costume, Close Encounters Of The Third Kind, Alien Outfit & Head, 1977 .... 4890.00
Costume, Dune, Fireman Jacket 520.00
Costume, Funny Lady, Straw Hat, Worn By Barbra Streisand, White, Black With Netting . 1380.00
Costume, Logan's Run, Sandman Outfit, 1976 .... 1095.00
Costume, Planet Of The Apes, Gorilla Guard Outfit, 1968 .... 635.00
Costume, Smokey & The Bandit, Shirt, Worn By Burt Reynolds, Letter Of Authenticity .. 1035.00
Costume, Staying Alive, Tights, Shirt, Leggings, Headband, Signed By Travolta 4890.00
Costume, Tuxedo, Cannonball Run, Worn By Roger Moore 1670.00
Dress, Babes In Toyland, Worn By Annette Funicello, Letter Of Authenticity 3740.00
Dress, Cocktail, Marilyn Monroe, Red Chiffon 3815.00
Dress, Marilyn Monroe, Black Chiffon, Sequins, Studio Tag, Letter Of Authenticity 10350.00
Herald, Clockwork Orange, Kubrick, 8 Pages, 1972 .... 12.00
Herald, Wild Bunch, Sam Peckinpah, 1969, 3 Page Fold-Out 24.50
Herald, Wild Bunch, Sam Peckinpah, 2 Sides, 3 Pages, 1969 .... 25.00
Lobby Card, Abilene Trail, Whip Wilson, Monogram, 1951 .... 90.00
Lobby Card, Above & Beyond, Robert Taylor, MGM, 1953 .... 85.00
Lobby Card, Across The Wide Missouri, Kirk Douglas, MGM, 1951 .... 125.00
Lobby Card, Action In The North Atlantic, Bogart, Warner Bros., 1943 .... 125.00
Lobby Card, Adventures Of Huck Finn, Tony Randall, MGM, 1960 .... 45.00
Lobby Card, Alligator People, Beverly Garland, Fox, 1959 .... 185.00
Lobby Card, Amazing Dr. Clitterhouse, Edward G. Robinson, Warner Bros., 1938 ...... 430.00
Lobby Card, Ambush At Cimarron Pass, Clint Eastwood, 1958 .... 125.00
Lobby Card, Ambush Bay, Mickey Rooney, UA, 1966 .... 45.00
Lobby Card, Angels With Dirty Faces, Cagney, O'Brien, Bogart, Warner Bros., 1938 .... 1555.00
Lobby Card, Battle At Apache Pass, Jeff Chandler, Universal, 1952 .... 45.00

Lobby Card, Battle At Bloody Beach, Audie Murphy, Fox, 1961 .... 50.00
Lobby Card, Battle Flame, Robert Blake, 1959 .... 35.00
Lobby Card, Beach Party, Frankie & Annette, AIP, 1963 .... 150.00
Lobby Card, Before Winter Comes, David Niven, Columbia, 1969 .... 35.00
Lobby Card, Behold A Pale Horse, Gregory Peck, Columbia, 1964 .... 50.00
Lobby Card, Big Heat, Glenn Ford, Columbia, 1957 .... 325.00
Lobby Card, Big Land, Virginia Mayo, Warner Bros., 1957 .... 70.00
Lobby Card, Big Mouth, Jerry Lewis, Columbia, 1967 .... 70.00
Lobby Card, Big Operator, Mamie Van Doren, MGM, 1959 .... 80.00
Lobby Card, Big Red, Walter Pidgeon, Disney, 1962 .... 50.00
Lobby Card, Big Sky, Kirk Douglas, RKO, 1952 .... 160.00
Lobby Card, Black Dakotas, Gary Merrill, Columbia, 1954 .... 60.00
Lobby Card, Black Gold, Philip Carey, Warner Bros., 1963 .... 35.00
Lobby Card, Black Orchid, Sophia Loren, Paramount, 1958 .... 60.00
Lobby Card, Black Patch, George Montgomery, Warner Bros., 1957 .... 45.00
Lobby Card, Black Spurs, Rory Calhoun, Paramount, 1965 .... 45.00
Lobby Card, Blind Husbands, Universal, 1919 .... 805.00
Lobby Card, Blood & Sand, Rudolph Valentino, Paramount, 1922 .... 345.00
Lobby Card, Bringing Up Baby, 1938, 11 x 14 In. 690.00
Lobby Card, Casablanca, Bogart, Greenstreet, Warner Bros., 1942 .... 2070.00
Lobby Card, Citizen Kane, Orson Welles, RKO, 1940 .... 575.00
Lobby Card, Dishonored, Marlene Dietrich, Paramount, 1931 .... 517.00
Lobby Card, Ex-Lady, Bette Davis, Gene Raymond, 1933 .... 1610.00
Lobby Card, Fair & Muddy, Our Gang, MGM, 1928 .... 290.00
Lobby Card, Fistfull Of Dollars, United Artists, 1967, Set 220.00
Lobby Card, Ghost Of Frankenstein, Universal, 1942 .... 1035.00
Lobby Card, Gone With The Wind, Clark Gable, Selznick/MGM, 1939 .... 862.00 to 1380.00
Lobby Card, High Sierra, Ida Lupino, Humphrey Bogart, Warner Bros., 1941 .... 490.00
Lobby Card, Horse Feathers, Paramount, 1932 .... 1092.00
Lobby Card, Iron Mask, Douglas Fairbanks Sr., United Artists, 1929 .... 230.00
Lobby Card, It Happened One Night, Clark Gable & Claudette Colbert, 1934 .... 2530.00
Lobby Card, Jezebel, Bette Davis, Warner, 1938 .... 3162.00
Lobby Card, Kid Galahad, Edward G. Robinson, Warner Bros., 1937 .... 1265.00
Lobby Card, Love Parade, Paramount, 1929 .... 517.00
Lobby Card, Love With The Proper Stranger, Natalie Wood 150.00
Lobby Card, Man Who Knew Too Much, Hitchcock, Gaumont-British 1035.00
Lobby Card, Marked Woman, Bette Davis, Humphrey Bogart, Warner Bros., 1937 ...... 1495.00
Lobby Card, Mighty Joe Young, Terry Moore, 1949 .... 230.00
Lobby Card, Mummy, Boris Karloff, Universal, 1932 .... 12650.00
Lobby Card, Mummy, Peter Cushing, Christopher Lee, Universal, 1959, Set 430.00
Lobby Card, Road To Utopia, Crosby, Hope, Lamour, Paramount, 1945, Set 460.00
Lobby Card, Saturday Night Kid, Clara Bow, Paramount, 1929 .... 290.00
Lobby Card, Shanghai Express, Marlene Dietrich, Clive Brook, Paramount, 1932 .... 660.00
Lobby Card, Spider Woman, Sherlock Holmes, Rathbone, Universal, 1944 .... 220.00
Lobby Card, Stagecoach, Claire Trevor, 1939 .... 575.00
Lobby Card, The Ghost Of Frankenstein, Universal, 1942 .... 2875.00
Lobby Card, The Phantom Of The Opera, Lon Chaney, Title Card, 1925 .... 920.00
Lobby Card, Top Hat, Fred Astaire, Ginger Rogers, RKO, 1935 .... 460.00
Lobby Card, Wedding Present, Joan Bennett, Cary Grant, Paramount, 1936 .... 300.00
Lobby Card, You Were Never Lovelier, Fred Astaire, Rita Hayworth, Columbia, 1942 ... 275.00
Lobby Card Set, Three Musketeers, Gene Kelly, Lana Turner, MGM, 1948 .... 335.00
Model, Alien Creature, Alien, Molded Rubber, Outstretched Arms, 7 Ft. 1000.00
Photograph, Elizabeth Taylor, 13 Years Old, 8 x 10 In. 500.00
Photograph, Harrison Ford, Star Wars, Color, Signed, 8 x 10 In. 86.00
Photograph, Magnificent 7, Autographed By 5 Cast Members, 8 x 10 In. 80.00
Photograph, Walt Disney, Signed, 8 x 10 In. 1085.00
Postcard, Margaret O'Brien, Child, Ribbons In Hair, Photograph, 3 1/2 x 5 1/2 In. 8.00
Postcard Book, John Travolta, 23 Color Photos, 1978 .... 12.00
Poster, 2001: A Space Odyssey, The Ultimate Trip, MGM, 1969, One Sheet 6325.00
Poster, A Place In The Sun, Montgomery Clift, Elizabeth Taylor, 1951, Six Sheet 2300.00
Poster, Abraham Lincoln, Walter Huston, One Sheet 150.00
Poster, Adventures Of Kitty O'Day, Jean Parker, 1944, 14 x 36 In., Insert 40.00
Poster, Adventures Of Robin Hood, Errol Flynn, Warner Bros., 1938, One Sheet 7475.00

Poster, American Venus, Paramount, 1926, Linen Backed, One Sheet 835.00
Poster, An American In Paris, Gene Kelly, MGM, Linen Backed, 1951, One Sheet 575.00
Poster, An American In Paris, MGM, 1951, Six Sheet 4312.00
Poster, Angel Face, Mona Freeman, Herbert Marshall, 1952, Three Sheet 977.00
Poster, Angels With Dirty Faces, J. Cagney, P. O'Brien, Warner Bros., 1935, Half Sheet .. 1495.00
Poster, Annie Hall, United Artists, 1977, One Sheet 115.00
Poster, Attack Of The 50 Ft. Woman, Allison Hayes, 1958, One Sheet 4600.00
Poster, Attack Of The Crab Monsters, Richard Garland, 1957, One Sheet 2070.00
Poster, Babe Ruth Story, Allied Artists, 1948, Three Sheet 1150.00
Poster, Babe Ruth Story, Spalding Sports Show, 1948 .... 150.00
Poster, Babes In Bagdad, Edgar Ulmer, 1952, 14 x 36 In. 30.00
Poster, Back To Bataan, John Wayne, RKO, 1945, One Sheet 660.00
Poster, Bambi, Walt Disney, 1942 .... 2875.00
Poster, Band Wagon, Fred Astaire, MGM, 1953, One Sheet 920.00
Poster, Barnsdale's Moving Pictures, Hobo, Independent, Linen Backed, 1904, One Sheet 575.00
Poster, Batman, Adam West, Burt Ward, 1966, One Sheet 258.00
Poster, Blazing Saddles, Mel Brooks, Director, 1974, 14 x 36 In. 125.00
Poster, Blue Dahlia, Alan Ladd, Paramount, 1946, One Sheet 4600.00
Poster, Bonnie & Clyde, Warner Bros., 1967, One Sheet 175.00
Poster, Boston Blackie, Fox, 1923, One Sheet 345.00
Poster, Breakfast At Tiffany's, Paramount, 1961, 14 x 36 In., Insert 1840.00
Poster, Broadway Bill, Warner Baxter, Myrna Loy, Columbia, 1934 .... 920.00
Poster, Bus Stop, Marilyn Monroe, 20th Century, 1956, 28 x 22 In., Half Sheet 373.00
Poster, Bye, Bye Birdie, 1963, 14 x 36 In. 125.00
Poster, Call Northside 777, 20th Century, Linen Backed, 1948, 27 x 41 In., One Sheet ... 460.00
Poster, Call Of The Jungle, Ann Corio, 1944, 14 x 36 In. 60.00
Poster, City For Conquest, James Cagney, Ann Sheridan, Warner Bros., One Sheet 805.00
Poster, City Streets, Gary Cooper, Paramount, 1931, One Sheet 4600.00
Poster, Cleopatra, Taylor, Burton, Harrison, 20th Century Fox, 1962, Six Sheet 3335.00
Poster, Clown, Red Skelton, Jane Greer, MGM, 1953, 14 x 17 In. 42.00
Poster, Cody Of The Pony Express, Chapter 12, Columbia Serial, 1950, One Sheet 56.00
Poster, Creature From The Black Lagoon, Richard Carlson, 1954, Half Sheet 4600.00
Poster, Creature From The Black Lagoon, Richard Carlson, 1954, One Sheet 6900.00
Poster, Crossfire, RKO, 1947, One Sheet 287.00
Poster, Cry Danger, RKO, 1950, Three Sheet 460.00
Poster, Dangerous, Bette Davis, Warner Bros., 1936, One Sheet 8625.00
Poster, Dawn Patrol, Errol Flynn, Warner Bros., 1938, One Sheet 1380.00
Poster, Day The Earth Stood Still, 20th Century Fox, 1951, Linen, Six Sheet 9490.00
Poster, Day The Earth Stood Still, Michael Rennie, 1951, One Sheet 6325.00
Poster, Designing Woman, Kapralik Artwork, Universal, 1957, One Sheet 115.00
Poster, Devil Girl From Mars, Adrienne Corri, 1955, 14 x 36 In. 600.00
Poster, Devil Is Driving, Richard Dix, 1937, 14 x 36 In. 100.00
Poster, Dial M For Murder, Alfred Hitchcock, 1954, 14 x 36 In. 750.00
Poster, Dirty Harry, Clint Eastwood, Warner Bros., 1971, Linen, One Sheet ...... 285.00 to 320.00
Poster, Don Q, Son Of Zorro, Douglas Fairbanks Sr., 1929 .... 6325.00
Poster, Don't Bother To Knock, Marilyn Monroe, 20th Century Fox, 1952, Insert 545.00
Poster, Dragonwyck, Gene Tierney, 20th Century Fox, 1945, Linen Backed, One Sheet .. 345.00
Poster, Easy Rider, Columbia, 1969, 27 x 41 In., One Sheet 460.00
Poster, Expensive Women, Dolores Costello, Warner Bros., 1931, One Sheet 1035.00
Poster, Far Country, James Stewart, Universal, 1955, Insert 375.00
Poster, Father Of The Bride, Tracy, Bennett, Taylor, MGM, 1950, One Sheet 290.00
Poster, Five Branded Women, Vera Miles, Van Heflin, Paramount, 1960, 14 x 36 In. 20.00
Poster, Flying Leathernecks, John Wayne, 1951, Window Card 3500.00
Poster, For Whom The Bell Tolls, Paramount, 28 x 22 In. 460.00
Poster, Forbidden Planet, Walter Pidgeon, MGM, 1956, One Sheet 5460.00
Poster, Fort Apache, John Wayne, Henry Fonda, Argosy, 1948, One Sheet 1035.00
Poster, French Connection II, Gene Hackman, 1975, 14 x 36 In. 60.00
Poster, From Russia With Love, Sean Connery, United Artists, Linen, 1964, Three Sheet . 460.00
Poster, Fun & Fancy Free, Edgar Bergen, Dinah Shore, Disney, 1947, Six Sheet 3737.00
Poster, Garden Of Eden, Corinne Griffith, 1928, 14 x 36 In. 500.00
Poster, General Crack, John Barrymore, 1930, 14 x 36 In. 1500.00
Poster, Gentlemen Prefer Blondes, Jane Russell, Marilyn Monroe, 1953, One Sheet 4312.00
Poster, Ghost Breakers, Bob Hope, Paulette Goddard, Paramount, 1940, One Sheet 980.00

Poster, Gone With The Wind, MGM, Linen Backed, 1939-1940, One Sheet 4600.00
Poster, Great Escape, McQueen, Garner, United Artists, 1963, Linen Backed, One Sheet . 320.00
Poster, Great Race, Tony Curtis, 1965, 14 x 36 In. 75.00
Poster, Gunfight At The OK Corral, Lancaster, Douglas, Paramount, 1957, One Sheet . . . 230.00
Poster, Gunga Din, Cary Grant, Doug Fairbanks Jr., 1939, One Sheet 6900.00
Poster, Hamlet, Laurence Olivier, Rank, 1949, One Sheet 747.00
Poster, Hammer Film Fest, Barbican Cinemas, London, Horror Films, Aug. 2-29, 1996 . . 100.00
Poster, High Noon, Gary Cooper, Stanley Kramer, 1952, Half Sheet 805.00
Poster, His Girl Friday, Cary Grant, Columbia, 1939, Half Sheet 1035.00
Poster, Hook, Line & Sinker, Jerry Lewis & Peter Lawford, 1969, 27 x 41 In. 30.00
Poster, House Of Dracula, Lon Chaney, Universal, 1945, Half Sheet 2300.00
Poster, I Walk Alone, Burt Lancaster, Paramount, 1948, One Sheet 230.00
Poster, In Harm's Way, John Wayne, Paramount, 1965, 27 x 41 In., One Sheet 115.00
Poster, Inherit The Wind, Spencer Tracy, 1960, 14 x 36 In. 100.00
Poster, Innocents, Deborah Kerr, 1961, 14 x 36 In. 75.00
Poster, Invasion Of The Body Snatchers, Kevin McCarthy, 1956, One Sheet 1495.00
Poster, It's A Wonderful Life, James Stewart, Donna Reed, Liberty, 1946, One Sheet 7475.00
Poster, Jackie Robinson Story, Jackie & Ruby Dee, 1950, 27 x 41 In. 2955.00
Poster, Jezebel, South's Greatest Romance, Bette Davis, Warner Bros., 1938, One Sheet . 9775.00
Poster, Julius Caesar, Marlon Brando, Louis Calhern, MGM, 1953, One Sheet 265.00
Poster, Killers, Burt Lancaster, Ava Gardner, Universal, 1956, One Sheet 1495.00
Poster, King Kong, Fay Wray, Bruce Cabot, 1933, Window Card 4310.00
Poster, King Of The Underworld, Bogart, Warner Bros., Linen, 1939, One Sheet 1555.00
Poster, Kiss Of Death, Victor Mature, 20th Century Fox, 1947, Three Sheet 2300.00
Poster, Lawrence Of Arabia, Peter O'Toole, Columbia, 1962, One Sheet 8050.00
Poster, Little Foxes, Bette Davis, Samuel Goldwyn, 1941, Half Sheet 690.00
Poster, Little Foxes, Bette Davis, Warner Bros., 1939, Linen Backed, One Sheet 1495.00
Poster, Lost Horizon, Frank Capra, Columbia, 1937, Half Sheet 1035.00
Poster, Macbeth, Orson Welles, Republic, 1948, One Sheet 1265.00
Poster, Mark Of Zorro, Tyrone Power, 1940, Window Card 1035.00
Poster, Marnie, Hitchcock, Universal, 1964, One Sheet 287.00
Poster, Meet John Doe, Frank Capra, Gary Cooper, Warner Bros., 1941, One Sheet 1035.00
Poster, Midnight, Claudette Colbert, Don Ameche, 1939, One Sheet 1955.00
Poster, Miracle On 34th Street, Maureen O'Hara, 20th Century Fox, Six Sheet 2070.00
Poster, Mogambo, Clark Gable, Ava Gardner, MGM, 1953, Three Sheet 1150.00
Poster, My Darling Clementine, Henry Fonda, 20th Century Fox, 1946, One Sheet 2875.00
Poster, Niagara, Marilyn Monroe, 20th Century Fox, 1953, Linen Backed, One Sheet 1035.00
Poster, Niagara, Marilyn Monroe, Joseph Cotten, 20th Century Fox, 1952, One Sheet . . . 1840.00
Poster, Niagara, Marilyn Monroe, Niagara Falls Scene Over 4 Photos, 22 x 28 In. 555.00
Poster, Night Of The Hunter, Lillian Gish, Robert Mitchum, 1955, One Sheet 1265.00
Poster, North By Northwest, Hitchcock, MGM, 1959, One Sheet 690.00
Poster, Notorious, Cary Grant, Ingrid Bergman, 1946, Six Sheet 3737.00
Poster, Oklahoma Kid, Warner Bros., 1939, 14 x 36 In. 1150.00
Poster, On The Town, Gene Kelly, Frank Sinatra, Frame, 41 x 27 In. 275.00
Poster, Outlaw, Jane Russell, 1946, One Sheet 1725.00
Poster, Postman Always Rings Twice, Lana Turner, 1946, One Sheet 3162.00
Poster, Private Lives Of Elizabeth & Essex, Bette Davis, Warner Bros., 1939, One Sheet . 1840.00
Poster, Psycho, Hitchcock, Anthony Perkins, 1960, One Sheet 1035.00
Poster, Rear Window, James Stewart, Grace Kelly, Paramount, 1954, Half Sheet 1380.00
Poster, Rebecca, Laurence Olivier, Selznick, 1940, Window Card 920.00
Poster, Rebecca, Selznick, France, Linen Back, 1940, 24 x 31 In., One Sheet 575.00
Poster, Reckless, Jean Harlow, William Powell, MGM, Linen Backed, 1935, One Sheet . . 1265.00
Poster, Road To Morocco, Crosby, Hope, Lamour, Paramount, 1942, One Sheet 575.00
Poster, Road To Singapore, Crosby, Lamour, Hope, Paramount, 1940, One Sheet 460.00
Poster, Roaring Twenties, James Cagney, Priscilla Lane, Warner Bros., 1939, Window Card 1495.00
Poster, Robin & Marion, Sean Connery, Audrey Hepburn, Columbia Pictures, 1976 . . . . . 40.00
Poster, Rocky, S. Stallone, United Artists, 1977, One Sheet 230.00
Poster, Romance Of The Rockies, B-Western, Monogram Pictures, 1930s, One Sheet 150.00
Poster, Safe At Home, William Frawley, Columbia, 1962, Half Sheet 1955.00
Poster, Sea Hawk, Errol Flynn, 1940, One Sheet 3737.00
Poster, Sergeant York, Gary Cooper, Warner Bros., Linen Backed, 1941, One Sheet 835.00
Poster, Seven Year Itch, Marilyn Monroe, Tom Ewell, 1955, Three Sheet 9200.00
Poster, She Wore A Yellow Ribbon, John Ford, John Wayne, 1949, One Sheet 2185.00

Poster, Six Shooter, Ken Maynard, B-Western, Grand National, 1936, One Sheet 509.00
Poster, Sleeping Beauty, Disney, 1959, UK Quad 546.00
Poster, Some Like It Hot, Marilyn Monroe, Tony Curtis, Mirisch, 1959, One Sheet 2587.00
Poster, Sons Of The Desert, Laurel & Hardy, MGM, 1933, Half Sheet 12075.00
Poster, Star Trek III, Search For Spock, Paramount, 1984, 41 x 27 In................. 54.00
Poster, Strangers On A Train, Ruth Roman, Warner Bros., 1957, One Sheet 1725.00
Poster, Sun Valley Serenade, Sonja Henie, 20th Century Fox, 1941, One Sheet 230.00
Poster, Swing Time, Fred Astaire, Ginger Rogers, 1936, One Sheet 5750.00
Poster, Taxi Driver, Robert De Niro, 1976, One Sheet 3737.00
Poster, Texans, Joan Bennett, May Robson, Randolph Scott, 1938, One Sheet 1035.00
Poster, The Clutching Hand, Jack Mulhall, Ruth Mix, Craig Kennedy Thriller, 1934 ..... 805.00
Poster, The Fighting Heart, 1926, Window Card 373.00
Poster, The Pinch Hitter, Charles Ray, Triangle, 1917, One Sheet 5175.00
Poster, The Pride Of The Yankees, Gary Cooper, 1949, One Sheet 3162.00
Poster, They Died With Their Boots On, Errol Flynn, 1941, Three Sheet 1610.00
Poster, This Gun For Hire, Veronica Lake, Alan Ladd, Paramount, 1942, One Sheet 1610.00
Poster, This Island Earth, Jeff Morrow, Universal, 1954, One Sheet 1035.00
Poster, Thomas Crown Affair, Steve McQueen, United Artists, 1968, One Sheet 201.00
Poster, Titanic, Barbara Stanwyck, Clifton Webb, 1953, One Sheet 230.00
Poster, To Catch A Thief, Cary Grant, Grace Kelly, Paramount, 1955, Six Sheet 2875.00
Poster, Tobor The Great, Charles Drake, Karin Booth, Republic, 1954, One Sheet 1495.00
Poster, Topaz, John Barrymore, Myrna Loy, RKO, Linen Backed, 1933, One Sheet 1325.00
Poster, Treasure Of The Sierra Madre, Bogart, 1948, One Sheet 3162.00
Poster, Vertigo, Hitchcock, James Stewart, Kim Novak, 1958, Half Sheet 1840.00
Poster, Vertigo, James Stewart, Paramount, 1958, One Sheet 1610.00
Poster, Virginia City, Errol Flynn, Miriam Hopkins, Warner Bros., 1940, One Sheet 1955.00
Poster, Virginian, Gary Cooper, Walter Huston, 1929, Window Card 805.00
Poster, Viva Zapata!, Marlon Brando, 20th Century Fox, 1952, One Sheet 1035.00
Poster, War Of The Worlds, H.G. Wells, Paramount, 1953, One Sheet 2587.00
Poster, West Of Rainbow's End, B-Western, Tim McCoy, Monogram, 1938, One Sheet .. 490.00
Poster, Westerner, Gary Cooper, Samuel Goldwyn, 1940, One Sheet 1840.00
Poster, Westward Ho, John Wayne, Republic, 1936, One Sheet 1495.00
Poster, Woman In Red, Barbara Stanwyck, Warner Bros., 1935, One Sheet 2587.00
Poster, You Only Live Twice, James Bond-007, Sean Connery, 1967, One Sheet 460.00
Poster, Young Frankenstein, Mel Brooks, Gene Wilder, 1974, One Sheet 150.00
Press Book, 200 Motels, Frank Zappa, 1971, Uncut, 4 Pages 11.00
Press Book, Producers, Mel Brooks, 1968, Uncut, 6 Pages 14.50
Press Kit, 48 Hours, Nick Nolte & Eddie Murphy, 9 Photographs, 1982 .... 22.00
Press Kit, Jeremiah Johnson, Robert Redford, 1972, 12 Photos 45.00
Program, Stairway To Heaven, David Niven, 1946, 4 Pages 9.00
Program, Taxi Driver, Robert De Niro, 1976 .... 15.00
Prop, Back To The Future II, 1950-2000 Sports Almanac 1440.00
Prop, Cleopatra, Shield 490.00
Prop, V, Shuttle, Mounting Rod On Side, 24 In.............................. 2185.00
Sheriff's Badge, Andy Griffith Show, Prop 2185.00
Spoon, Billie Burke, Silver Plate 20.00
Stickpin, Marilyn Monroe, Bathing Suit, 1953 .... 6.00
Toy, Airplane, Test Pilot, Tracy, Gable, Mecavion, 2 Engines, Box, 1938 .... 1800.00
Window Card, Island Of Lost Souls, Charles Laughton, Paramount, 1932 .... 1840.00

MT. JOYE is an enameled cameo glass made in the late nineteenth and twentieth centuries by Saint-Hilaire Touvier de Varraux and Co. of Pantin, France. This same company made De Vez glass. Pieces were usually decorated with enameling. Most pieces are not marked.

Bowl, Enameled Chestnuts On Leafy Branches, Ocher, Olive Green, 8 In. 517.00
Bowl, Flower & Leaf, Pink Rim, Footed, 4 In. 440.00
Globe, Lavender Rose, Gold Enameled, 12 In.................................. 500.00
Pitcher, Iris, Brass Handle & Spout, 9 In. 725.00
Rose Bowl, Green Ivy, Cameo, 4 1/2 In.................................... 300.00
Vase, Enameled Leaves, Top Border, Satin Ground, 6 1/2 In. 375.00
Vase, Enameled Spider Mums, Gold, Chipped Ice, Textured, Cameo, 7 3/4 In. 560.00
Vase, Fading Chrysanthemums, Gold Foliage, Spiked Border, c.1900, 7 1/2 In. 373.00
Vase, Gold Enameled Thistle, Corset, Cameo, Marked, 15 1/2 In. 1000.00

Vase, Green Thistle, Cameo, 8 In. 400.00
Vase, Jack-In-The-Pulpit, Lavender, Enameled Chrysanthemums, 14 In. 450.00
Vase, Lavender, Enameled Iris, 10 In. 400.00
Vase, Lavender, Gold Enameled Iris, Pulled Ears, Cameo, Square, 9 1/2 In. 450.00
Vase, Poppy, Green Textured Ground, Gold Rim, Cameo, 9 3/4 In. 350.00
Vase, Trumpet, White, Purple Enameled Floral, Cameo, 15 3/4 In. 450.00
Vase, Violets, 4 Handles, Cameo, 8 In. 500.00

MT. WASHINGTON Glass Works started in 1837 in South Boston, Massachusetts. In 1870 the company moved to New Bedford, Massachusetts. Many types of art glass were made there until 1894, when the company merged with Pairpoint Manufacturing Co. Amberina, Burmese, Crown Milano, Cut Glass, Peachblow, and Royal Flemish are each listed in their own category.

Biscuit Jar, Pink Enameled Floral, White, 7 1/2 In. 300.00
Biscuit Jar, White, Brown Overlay, Enameled Apple Blossom, 7 In. 750.00
Biscuit Jar, White, Enamel Floral, 8 1/2 In. 200.00
Biscuit Jar, White, Enameled Leaves, Melon Ribbed, 7 In. 200.00
Bowl, Duberry Pink Lion Griffins, Urns, Floral Garlands, Pink, 3 x 9 In. 467.00
Bride's Bowl, Hobnail, Yellow, Meriden Silver Plated Holder, 9 1/2 In. 225.00
Cracker Jar, Metal Cover, Melon Ribbed, Enameled Flowers 295.00
Creamer, Chicago's Columbia Exposition, 2 1/2 In. 500.00
Cruet, Inverted Thumbprint, Trefoil Spout, 5 1/2 In. 385.00
Finger Bowl, Underplate, Blush Pink, Ruffled Edge 310.00
Lamp, Cream, Pink Floral, Melon Ribbed, 17 In. 1000.00
Muffineer, Tomato Shape, Opaque, Enameled Flowers, Cover 258.00
Salt & Pepper, 1 Blue, 1 Peach, 2 In. 145.00
Salt & Pepper, Leaf Shape, White, Floral Design 70.00
Salt & Pepper, Melon Ribbed 40.00
Saltshaker, Egg In Blossom 200.00
Saltshaker, Egg Shape, Pinecone, White 60.00
Saltshaker, Tomato Shape, Blue, Floral 40.00
Sugar Shaker, Leaf & Enameled Berries 300.00
Vase, Club Form, Enameled, Branch & Fruit, Opalescent, 10 3/4 In. 165.00
Vase, Egyptian Desert Scene, Pyramids, Ibis In Flight, Gold Enameled, 11 1/2 In. 2530.00

MULBERRY ware was made in the Staffordshire district of England from about 1850 to 1860. The dishes were decorated with a reddish brown transfer design, now called *mulberry*. Many of the patterns are similar to those used for flow blue and other Staffordshire transfer wares.

Plate, Blue Center Armorial Design, Spatter Border, 9 In. 55.00
Platter, Corean, Octagonal, 19th Century, 10 In. 120.00
Platter, Corean, Octagonal, 19th Century, 16 In. 220.00
Platter, Corean, Octagonal, 19th Century, 17 In. 220.00
Platter, Corean, Octagonal, 19th Century, 18 In. 140.00
Soup, Dish, Bokhara, 19th Century, 7 1/4 In., 3 Piece 44.00
Wash Set, Corean, Ironstone, Podmore, Walker, 3 Piece 975.00

MULLER FRERES, French for Muller Brothers, made cameo and other glass from about 1895 to 1933. Their factory was first located in Luneville, then in nearby Croismare, France. Pieces were usually marked with the company name.

Lamp, Gray, Swans, Frosted, Domed Shade, Globular, 3 Arm Iron Mount, 15 In. 2300.00
Lamp Shade, Gray, Bullet Shape, Wrought Iron Base, 1925, 16 In. 1725.00
Vase, 2 Cranes Wading Amidst Aquatic Grasses, Flowers, Cranberry, White, 5 In. 1725.00
Vase, Cameo, Trees, Dark Green, Gray, Globular, 5 In. 770.00
Vase, Fish, 7 In. 3700.00
Vase, Fruit Blossoms, Vines, Gray, Purple, Green, Pillow Form, 10 In. 2128.00
Vase, Landscape, River Scene, Birch Trees, Cameo, Signed, 1900, 8 1/4 In. 4885.00
Vase, Overlapping Leaves, Pale Orange, Cameo, Signed, 1925, 17 In. 7475.00
Vase, Stylized Flower Heads Enclosed By 4 Reserves, Orange, Brown, 17 In. 805.00

Vase, Tapered Oval, Frosted, Mottled Cobalt, Orange & Yellow, 11 1/4 In. 635.00
Vase, White Floral Cut To Red, Cameo, Marked, 14 In. 150.00

MUNCIE Clay Products Company was established by Charles Benham in Muncie, Indiana, in 1922. The company made pottery for the florist and giftshop trade. The company closed by 1939. Pieces are marked with the name *Muncie* or just with a system of numbers and letters, like *1A*.

Vase, Corset Form, Purple Over Pink Matte Glaze, 12 1/4 In. 330.00
Vase, Embossed Grasshoppers On Grass Stems, Signed, 5 7/8 In. 330.00
Vase, Green Matte Glaze, 4 Openings, 3 Handles, 5 1/2 In. 220.00

MURANO, see Glass-Venetian category.

MUSIC boxes and musical instruments are listed here. Phonograph records, jukeboxes, phonographs, and sheet music are listed in other categories in this book.

Accordion, Jupiter, Wood Construction, Metal Valves, Hand Strap 55.00
Accordion, Rani, Chrome, Mother-Of-Pearl, Red 305.00
Accordion, Schubert, Inlaid Wood, Glass Button & Celluloid Keys 110.00
Accordion, Tanzabar, Note Push-Up, Restored 995.00
Band Organ, Wurlitzer, No. 103, 6 Rolls 6500.00
Banjo, TBC Sterlim, Sultry Woman On Drum Body, 17 Frets 44.00
Bow, Violin, Marked Theodore Olofson, 31 In. 302.00
Bow, Violin, Sterling Silver Frog, Decorated, France 920.00
Box, Amberola, Edison, Floor Model, 65 Glass Cylinders, Mahogany, 19 x 41 In. 1095.00
Box, Burl, Inlay, 8 Tunes, Swiss, 1880, 16-In. Cylinder, 14 1/2 x 29 In. 4950.00
Box, Burl, Mother-Of-Pearl & Silver Design, 10 x 7 1/4 x 2 7/8 In. 285.00
Box, Cigarette, Singing Bird, Hinged Sides, Enclosed Movement, Silver, 4 3/4 In. 3565.00
Box, Criterion, Oak, 12 9-In. Discs, Late 19th Century, 8 x 12 In. 605.00
Box, Cylinder, 3 Bells, 8 Tunes, Swiss, Late 19th Century, 6 In. 1430.00
Box, Cylinder, Burl Elm, Cased, 6 Tunes, Continental, 10 1/2 In. 315.00
Box, Cylinder, Drum & Bells, Enamel Butterflies, Swiss, c.1880, 18 x 8 1/2 In. 1150.00
Box, Cylinder, Inlaid Oval Reserve, Fruitwood, 6 Tunes, Swiss, 27 x 12 In. 5175.00
Box, Cylinder, Mahogany, Musical Instrument Inlay, Ratchet Wind, 1860s, 27 x 10 In. ... 895.00
Box, Cylinder, Stop/Start, Change/Repeat Levers, Swiss, Late 19th Century, 22 1/2 In. ... 2300.00
Box, H. Gautsch & Sons, Walnut, 8 Tunes, 16 3/4 In. 575.00
Box, Kalliope, 12 Bells, c.1896, 20 1/2 In. 8500.00
Box, Lyon & Healy, Empress, 30 12-In. Discs, c.1890, 17 x 11 In. 2990.00
Box, Mandolin, 8 Tunes, Swiss, c.1880, 17 x 5 1/2 In. 1150.00
Box, Mermod Freres, Mira, Console, c.1900, 18 1/2 In. 11500.00
Box, Musical Trio, Woman Pianist, Man Violinist, Girl Dancer, Key Wind, 12 3/4 In. 3105.00
Box, Oak, Cylinder, Swiss, 1890, 9 x 29 1/2 x 11 In. 1610.00

If you have an old piano, beware of moths. They sometimes infest the interior fabrics.

Music, Box, Polyphon, No. 104, Duplex
Comb, Coin-Operated, 19 5/8 In.

Box, Olympia, Mahogany, Embossed, 15 3/4-In. Disc 3190.00
Box, Piano, Beveled Crystal Lid, Floral Design, Velvet Lining, 1950, 4 x 6 In. 103.00
Box, Polyphon, Mahogany, Stop/Start Lever, Crank At Side, Germany, 1900, 81 In. 8050.00
Box, Polyphon, No. 104, Duplex Comb, Coin-Operated, 19 5/8 In. ....*Illus* 8222.00
Box, Polyphon, Walnut, 12 Bells, 14-In. Disc 5500.00
Box, Regina, On Stand, Cover, Mahogany, Late 19th Century 4950.00
Box, Regina, Orchestral Corona, Duplex Comb, 20-In. Disc, 1900, 28 1/2 x 23 1/2 In. ... 5750.00
Box, Regina, Orchestral, 27-In. Disc, Folding Top, 1896, 32 1/2 In. 9200.00
Box, Regina, Polyphon, Model No. 38631, Mahogany, 22 1/2 x 12 In. 2875.00
Box, Rosewood, 1 Drawer Base, Turned Octagonal Shaped Legs, 38 x 40 x 26 In. 6270.00
Box, Rosewood, Ebonized Thumb Molded Top, Early 20th Century, 4 1/2 x 11 3/4 In. ... 330.00
Box, Rosewood, Inlay, 6 Tunes, Swiss, 4 1/2 x 11 3/4 In. 355.00
Box, Rosewood, Zither Inlay, 8 Tunes, Replaced Movement, Swiss, 4 1/2-In. Cylinder ... 305.00
Box, Singing Bird, 2 Feathered Birds, Birdcage, Gilt Metal Cage, 22 In. ....1840.00 to 3740.00
Box, Singing Bird, Enamel, Moving Neck, Wings, Perch, 3 3/4-In. Cylinder 6325.00
Box, Singing Bird, Leaf, Geometric, Alpine Scene, Key Wind, Swiss, 3 7/8-In. Cylinger .. 3162.00
Box, Singing Bird, Moving Perch, Wings, Metal Beak, Griesbaum, 4 1/4-In. Cylinder 1840.00
Box, Singing Bird, Silver Case, Putti, Foliage, Moving Wings, Perch, 4-In. Cylinder 1092.00
Box, Singing Bird, Wattesque Scenes, Pierced Sides, Moving Perch, Wings, Beak, 6 In. .. 1495.00
Box, Stella, Carved Foliate, Mahogany, 63 Discs & Booklets, 38 1/2 x 29 In. 6612.00
Box, Stella, Mahogany, 17-In. Disc, Duplex Comb, 1900, 13 x 28 In. 5175.00
Box, Stella, No. 54845, Mahogany, 15 1/2-In. Disc 4125.00
Box, Sublime Harmonie, Walnut, 18-In. Cylinder, Stop/Play Lever, 16 x 36 In. 6900.00
Box, Symphonion, Burled Walnut, 13 5/8-In. Disc 3750.00
Box, Symphonion, Oak, Original Paper Label, 6 Discs, 6 7/8 x 7 7/8 In. 825.00
Box, Thorens, 31 Discs, 6 1/4 In. 230.00
Box, Walnut Veneered Case, Floral Inlay, 12 Tunes, 6 1/2 x 24 In. 880.00
Box, Walnut, 6 6-In. Cylinders, 36 Tunes, Tune Card, Swiss, 19 3/4 In. 1150.00
Box, Woman Surrounded By Cherubs Playing Music Under Lid, 55 x 63 In. 2545.00
Box, Wurlitzer, Mahogany, 18 Disks, 9 x 19 3/4 In. 3135.00
Cabinet, French Style, Bronzed Ormolu & Painted Decoration, 22 3/4 x 38 1/2 In. 660.00
Clarinet, Reso-Tone, Case 125.00
Drum, Marching Band, 9th Regiment U.S. Infantry, Eames Drum Co., 17 x 19 In. 110.00
Drum, Snare, Wood Frame, Brass Sides, 12-In. Head 20.00
Drum, Tension, Silvered Tin, Embossed Band Players, Sticks, Pre-Civil War, Child's 445.00
Drumstick, Hickory, Sewn Leather Head, 18th Century, 13 1/2 In. 165.00
Figure, Nipper, Papier-Mache, 17 1/2 In. 632.00
Flute, Fitted Case, Civil War Period, 11 3/4 In. 215.00
Guitar, C.P. Martin, Mahogany, Spruce, Mother-Of-Pearl, Ebony Fingerboard, 1932 ..... 2200.00
Guitar, C.P. Martin, Style 18, Wooden Case 800.00
Guitar, F.H. Griffith, Phila., 6 Strings, Irving College, Case, 1896 .... 195.00
Guitar, Fender Squire Stratocaster, Signed By Neil Young 865.00
Guitar, Fender, Electric, Squire, Stratocaster, Signed By Bruce Springsteen 1725.00
Guitar, Kay, Signed By Johnny Cash 1265.00
Guitar Strings, Gretsch Mfg. Co., Box, 12 Piece 60.00
Harmonica, Hohner, 64 Chromonica, Wooden Case, Professional Model 35.00
Harmonica, Horner, 151, Marine Band Tremolo, Partial Box, 6 3/4 In. 21.00
Harmonica, Mahogany, Open Glass Vessels, Rectangular Hinged Top, 34 x 23 1/4 In. 2300.00
Harmonica, Rolmonica, Autoplay, Bakelite, 4 Song Rolls, Germany, 1930s, 4 In. 125.00
Harp, Erard, Figural & Architectural Designs, Giltwood, 70 In. 5750.00
Harpsichord, Kingwood Veneer, Wooden Black & White Keys, 55 1/2 In. 862.00
Jewelry Box, Singing Bird, Verse, Champleve & Stones, Moving Parts, 4 3/8 In. 1840.00
Mandolin, Neopolitan, Mother-Of-Pearl Inlay, Leather Case 185.00
Melodia, Elbow, Rosewood, Tiger Maple, 5 Octaves, Ivory Keys, D.B. Bartlett, 7 x 28 In. 862.00
Metronome, Electric, Bakelite, Swirl 165.00
Metronome, Electric, Marbleized Plastic Case 120.00
Nickelodeon, Howard, A-Roll, Stained Glass 3500.00
Nickelodeon, Peerless, Beveled Glass Front, 1902 .... 4500.00
Nickelodeon, Seeburg, Dog Racing Scene, Oak Case, Glass Panel 9900.00
Nickelodeon, Seeburg, Upright, Beveled Glass Front, Coin Operated 4500.00
Nickelodeon, Seeburg, Upright, Stained Glass Panel, Electric 6000.00
Nickelodeon, Wurlitzer, Flute Pipes, Stained Glass, 1912 .... 7500.00

Organ, Barrel, Molinari, 20 Key, c.1890 .... 4800.00
Organ, Barrel, Molinari, Flute & Violin Pipes, c.1890 .... 9500.00
Organ, Mandolina, Walnut Case, Paper Label, Playing Instructions, 14 1/4 x 15 1/2 In. 440.00
Organ, Packard, Cherry, Eastlake Style, Fold Down Candleholders, c.1890, 53 x 46 In. 225.00
Organ, Roller, Ehrlich, Ebonized, Paper Disk, France, 11 x 6 3/4 In. 190.00
Organ, Rolmonica, Autoplay, Bakelite, 4 Song Rolls, Germany, 1930s, 4 In. 100.00
Organette, Autophon, Gem Roller, Front Crank, Wood Valves, Box Of Rolls 300.00
Organette, Bellows, Revival Style, Console Top, Cabriole Legs, c.1900 .... 525.00
Piano, Baby Grand, Baldwin, Bench, Hinged Top 6900.00
Piano, Baby Grand, Chickering, Walnut, 12 Ampico Rolls, 5 Ft. 4 In. 5500.00
Piano, Baby Grand, Kranich & Bach, Mahogany, Rococo Style, Patent 1889 .... 3300.00
Piano, Baby Grand, Mahogany Veneer, Art-O-Tone, Alaska Union Pacific Expo 935.00
Piano, Baby Grand, Sohmer & Co., Mahogany, 60 In. 6380.00
Piano, Baby Grand, Steinway, No. J262/273991 .... 1150.00
Piano, C.F.L. Albrecht, Mahogany, Foliate, Ring Turned Legs On Castors, 1825, 35 In. .. 345.00
Piano, Grand, A. & J. Keough, Inlaid Rosewood, Painted Cityscapes, Victorian, 79 In. ... 3165.00
Piano, Grand, Chappel & Co., London, Black Lacquer, Brass Casters, 42 x 57 x 60 In. ... 5500.00
Piano, Grand, Chicago Organ & Piano Co., Painted, Matching Bench 3080.00
Piano, Grand, John Broadwood & Sons, Black, Trumpet Legs, Bench, 39 In. 6325.00
Piano, Grand, Lester, Philadelphia, 1920s 3000.00
Piano, Grand, Steinway & Sons, Rosewood, 19th Century, 8 Ft. 4 In. 19550.00
Piano, Grand, Steinway & Sons, Rosewood, Floral Harp, Bench, Spade Feet, 38 In. 8912.00
Piano, Grand, Steinway, Rosewood, Square, 1873 .... 5500.00
Piano, Player, Baby Grand, Chickering, Walnut, Bench 3136.00
Piano, Player, Grand, Chickering, Mahogany, c.1925 .... 4600.00
Piano, Player, Push-Up, Seeburg, 65 Note 2195.00
Piano, Reproducing, Steinway, Duo-Art 4200.00
Piano, Upright, Steinway, Rosewood 6950.00
Pianoforte, T. Gibson, Mahogany, Rosewood, Carved, Stencils, 34 1/2 x 67 1/2 x 28 In. .. 1380.00
Pitch Pipe, Inlaid Satinwood Scale, Mahogany, 1759, 15 In. 285.00
Player, Reproducing, Baby Grand, Aeolian, Duo Art 2000.00
Saxophone, Buescher, Academy Case 40.00
Tableaux, Automaton, Alpine Scene, Moving Grain, Manfielle, 11 1/2 In. 632.00
Ukelin, Oscar Schmidt International Corp., 1920s, 27 x 8 In. 28.00
Ukulele, Banjo, Vega, Bird's-Eye Maple, Ebony Keyboard, Mother-Of-Pearl Star 187.00
Ukulele, Le Domino, Lithographed Dominos Around Sound Hole, Case, 22 In. 46.00
Violin, E.J. Albert, Philadelphia Case, Pat. Nov. 10, 1885 .... 385.00
Violin, John Johnson, 2-Piece Top, Grafted Scroll, Case, London, 1759 .... 2760.00
Violin, Nicolous Vasich, Spruce, Maple, Bow, Case, Mid 1900s 1265.00
Whistle, Military, Brass, Chain, Horstmann, Phila., 19th Century 350.00
Zither, Columbian, Pat. May 29, 1894, 14 x 20 In. 325.00

MUSTACHE CUPS were popular from 1850 to 1900 when the large,
flowing mustache was in style. A ledge of china or silver held the hair
out of the liquid in the cup. This kept the mustache tidy and also kept
the mustache wax from melting. Left-handed mustache cups are rare
but are being reproduced.

American Indian Chief, White Ground, Large, Saucer 82.00
Blue Flowers, Pink Ground, 6 Sides 40.00
Blue Rim, Roses, 3 1/2 In. 55.00
Ducks In Flight, Saucer, Gilt Trim, c.1939 .... 60.00
Fan Handle, Saucer, Victorian 60.00
Fire Helmet, Ax, Trumpet, 1890 KFD, 1879 .... 35.00
Flowers, Saucer, Swirl Around Top Of Cup & Saucer 68.00
Fruit, Green Leaf, Saucer, 2 7/8 In. 85.00
Gold Trim On Cup Rim, 2 Leaves, Twig Handle, Saucer, 3 In. 85.00
Orange & Maroon Flowers, Saucer, Gaudy Welsh, 1850s 75.00
Present, Pink Luster, Saucer, c.1910 .... 75.00
Purple Flowers Interior & Exterior, Saucer, Limoges, c.1900 .... 235.00
Rustic Scene, Saucer, Nippon, Marked 215.00
Scrolled Handle, Footed, Saucer, Silver Plate, 1893 .... 95.00
Violets, Saucer, Limoges, c.1894 .... 235.00

MZ AUSTRIA is the wording on a mark used by Moritz Zdekauer on porcelains made at his works in Altrolau, Austria, from 1884 to 1909. The mark was changed to MZ Altrolau in 1909, when the firm was purchased by C.M. Hutschenreuther. The firm operated under the name Altrolau Porcelain Factories from 1909 to 1945. It was nationalized after World War II. The pieces were decorated with lavish floral patterns and overglaze gold decoration. Full sets of dishes were made as well as vases, toilet sets, and other wares.

MZ Austria

Bowl, Ruffled Edge, c.1909, 9 In.	200.00
Candy Dish, Seafoam Green, Peach Roses, 6 1/2 In.	80.00
Cup & Saucer, Interior Hand Painted Flowers, c.1900	50.00
Mayonnaise Set	35.00
Plate, Pink Roses, Gold Floral Trim, c.1909, 9 1/2 In.	65.00
Sugar & Creamer	75.00

NAILSEA glass was made in the Bristol district in England from 1788 to 1873. It was made by many different factories, not just the Nailsea Glass House. Many pieces were made with loopings of either white or colored glass as decoration.

Flask, Canteen Shape, Blue, White Loopings, 1840s, 6 1/8 In.	275.00
Powder Horn, Cranberry Loopings, Blue Stripes, Pontil Scar, 1870, 13 1/2 In.	440.00
Rolling Pin, Aqua, Ruby Loopings, 1870, 14 3/4 In.	275.00
Rolling Pin, Clear, Pink & White Loopings, 17 In.	440.00
Rolling Pin, Medium Greenish Aqua, White Loopings, 1870, 13 3/4 In.	230.00
Rolling Pin, Milk Glass, Pink Loopings, Knot Handles, 15 7/8 In.	412.00
Rolling Pin, Pink, White & Blue Loopings, 1870, 16 1/2 In.	255.00
Rolling Pin, Red Loopings, Knot Handles, 14 1/2 In.	143.00
Rolling Pin, Sapphire Blue & Milk Glass Loopings, 1850-1880, 15 In.	120.00
Rolling Pin, Sapphire Blue Loopings, Knot Handles, 1860s, 16 In.	120.00 to 265.00
Rolling Pin, White & Robin's-Egg Blue Loopings, 1860s, 16 3/8 In.	357.00
Whimsy, Pipe, Cranberry, Tight White Loopings, 1870, 17 In.	230.00
Whimsy, Pipe, Milk Glass, Rose Loopings, 1870, 23 In.	305.00

NAKARA is a trade name for a white glassware made about 1900 by the C. F. Monroe Company of Meriden, Connecticut. It was decorated in pastel colors. The glass was very similar to another glass made by the company called *Wave Crest*. The company closed in 1916. Boxes for use on a dressing table are the most commonly found Nakara pieces. The mark is not found on every piece.

NAKARA

Jewelry Box, Hinged, Blue, Enameled Beads, Floral, Brass Base, 4 In.	325.00
Jewelry Box, Portrait Of Queen Louise, Pink & Cream, Square, 5 1/2 In.	800.00
Powder Box, Floral, Blue Ground, Milk Glass	440.00

NANKING is a type of blue-and-white porcelain made in Canton, China, since the late eighteenth century. It is very similar to Canton, which is listed under its own name in this book. Both Nanking and Canton are part of a larger group now called *Chinese Export* porcelain. Nanking has a spear-and-post border and may have-gold decoration.

Bidet, Elongated Waisted Shape, Diapered Edge, Flowers, c.1790, 6 x 23 x 12 In.	1430.00
Bowl, Cut Corner, 19th Century, 5 x 9 1/2 x 9 In.	545.00 to 860.00
Bowl, Petal, Scalloped Rim, Central Reserve, Landscape, Ribbed, Footed, 5 x 10 1/4 In.	1035.00
Bowl, Scalloped Edge, 19th Century, 9 1/4 x 10 1/4 In., Pair	635.00
Bowl, Square, 9 3/4 In.	200.00
Bowl, Vegetable, Gilt Edge, Finials, Rectangular, 6 x 11 x 10 In., Pair	635.00
Charger, Woman & Child Spear Fishing, Willow Tree, Lappet Border, c.1780, 16 1/4 In.	1540.00
Cider Jug, Blue & White	1455.00
Dish, Lake Scene, Sailboat, Pavilion, 8 Sides, c.1780, 9 7/8 x 6 3/4 In.	305.00
Dish, Leaf Shape, 19th Century, 6 1/2 x 5 In.	155.00
Dish, Pavilions Along Waterway, Sailboats, 8 Sides, c.1780, 11 1/2 x 9 1/4 In.	385.00
Dish, Serving, Nested, Oval, 19th Century, 9 x 7 In., 10 x 8 In. & 11 x 9 In., 3 Piece	495.00
Dish, Watery Landscape, Buildings, Bridge, 2 People, 8 Sides, c.1780, 11 3/8 x 9 In.	440.00
Gravy Boat, 2 Handles, 19th Century, 8 1/2 x 7 In.	220.00
Group, Plate, Floral Sprays, Dagger Border, Blue, White, 10 In., 3 Piece	287.00

Pitcher, Cover, Foo Finial, Entwined Twig Strap Handle, 11 In. 1265.00
Plate, 19th Century, 8 1/2 In., 6 Piece 250.00
Plate, Dinner, 19th Century, 10 In., 12 Piece 605.00
Platter, Chinese Pavilions, c.1810, 14 1/2 In. 147.00
Platter, Flower Sprays, Complex Lappet Border, 8 Sides, c.1780, 12 x 9 3/4 In. 470.00
Platter, Gilt Highlights, Oval, 19th Century, 20 x 17 In. 145.00
Platter, Landscape, Oval, 19th Century, 17 1/4 In. 440.00
Platter, Oval, 19th Century, 15 x 11 1/2 In. 345.00
Platter, Pavilion On Promontory, Rocky Coast, 8 Sides, c.1780, 15 7/8 x 13 In. 935.00
Platter, Pierced Insert, Gilt Highlights, Oval, 19th Century, 16 x 13 In. 745.00
Platter, Pierced Insert, Oval, 19th Century, 15 1/4 x 13 In. 745.00
Platter, Shrine On Hilly Island, Tall Trees, c.1780, 11 1/4 x 14 1/4 In. 605.00
Platter, Willow Tree, Flowers, Lappet Edge, Oval, Late 18th Century, 12 x 15 1/2 In. . . . 495.00
Relish, Lozenge Shape, 19th Century, 8 1/2 x 5 1/2 In. 230.00
Sauceboat, Leaf Shape, Fitzhugh Style Border, 8 In. 230.00
Sauceboat, Leaf Shape, Handle, 19th Century, 7 x 3 1/2 In. 110.00
Tureen, Sauce, Oval, 19th Century, 5 3/4 x 8 1/2 x 5 1/4 In., Pair 345.00
Tureen, Soup, Oval, 19th Century, 10 1/2 x 15 x 10 1/2 In. 1610.00

NAPKIN RINGS were in fashion from 1869 to about 1900. They were
made of silver, porcelain, wood, and other materials. They are still
being made today. The most popular rings with collectors are the silver
plated figural examples. Small, realistic figures were made to hold the
ring. Good and poor reproductions of the more expensive rings are
now being made and collectors must be very careful.

2 Cadets, On Either Sides, Pushing Ring, Signed 375.00
Applied Letter E, Kalo Shop, Silver, 3 3/4 In. 95.00
Applied Letter E, Rectangular, Lebolt & Co., Silver, 3 x 7/8 In. 85.00
Applied Letter E, Rectangular, Marshall Field Craft Shop, Silver, 3 1/8 In. 85.00
Applied Letter G, Rectangular, Lebolt & Co., Silver, 2 1/4 x 5/8 In. 65.00
Applied Letter T, Kalo Shop, Silver, 3 3/4 In. 95.00
Applied Monogram FED, TC Craft Shop, Silver, 2 1/2 x 5/8 In. 70.00
Castor Stand, Salt Cellar, Pepper Castor, Glass Cruet, Silver Plate, 8 In. 605.00
Chased With Foliage, Gilt Interior, Silver, Ivan Khlebnikov, St. Petersburg, 1 In. 56.00
Elephants, Ivory, India, Early 10th Century, 6 Piece 245.00
Figural, Castor Stand, Boy, Outstretched Arms, Silver Plate, Cromwell Plate Co., 7 In. . . . 3740.00
Figural, Chinaman, New Haven Silverplate Co., 3 1/2 x 4 3/4 In. 977.00
Figural, Conquistador, Silver Plate, Toronto Silverplate Co., 3 1/2 In. 1540.00
Figural, Dapper Lad & Lass, Silver Plate, Late 19th Century, 3 3/4 In., Pair 4840.00
Figural, Giraffe, Silver Plate, Racine Silver Co., Late 19th Century, 4 1/4 In. 360.00
Figural, Man Carrying Barrel, Silver Plate, Simpson, Hall, Miller, 4 1/4 In. 1760.00
Figural, Samurai With Trained Dog, Silver Plate, Simpson, Hall, Miller, 4 1/2 In. 1320.00
Figural, Wolf, Barbour, 3 1/2 In. 950.00
Gilt, Overall Enamel, Oval, Silver, Grigory Spitnev, Russia, 1908, 2 1/4 In. 196.00
Graniteware, White, 2 In. 25.00
Rope Edge Border, Silver, Mexico, 8 Piece 130.00
Silver, Continuous Figural Scene, Chinese, 19th Century, Pair 230.00
Silver, Engraved, Germany 510.00
Silver, Overall Scrolled Foliage, Enameled, Oval, Gilt, Russia, 2 1/4 In. 224.00
Wood, Mauchline Ware, Various Scenes, 14 Piece 110.00

NASH glass was made in Corona, New York, from about 1928 to 1931.
A. Douglas Nash bought the Corona glassworks from Louis C. Tiffany
in 1928 and founded the A. Douglas Nash Corporation with support
from his father, Arthur J. Nash. Arthur had worked at the Webb factory
in England and for the Tiffany Glassworks in Corona.

NASH

Frame, Flowing Leaves & Vine, Blue Iridescent, 1911, 9 x 7 1/2 In. 1840.00
Vase, Blue Base, Gold Iridescent, Amethyst Rim, 7 1/4 In. 880.00
Vase, Chintz, Pale Gold Stripes, Red, Short Flared Lip, 1930, 11 In. 545.00
Vase, Chintz, Zipper, Brown, Yellow, Rust, Caramel Interior, 6 In. 230.00
Vase, Trumpet, Gold Iridescent, 6 In. 495.00
Vase, White Amethyst, Calyx Leaves, Gold Iridescent Stretch Rim, 5 1/4 In. 935.00

NAUTICAL antiques are listed in this category. Any of the many objects that were made or used by the seafaring trade, including ship parts, models, and tools, are included. Other pieces may be found listed under Scrimshaw.

Anchor, Double Fluke, Iron, 19th Century, 8 Ft. 6 In.	385.00
Bag, Seaman's, Hand Stitched, Sail Cloth, Lettered In Blue, H.S. Taylor, 19th Century	310.00
Bell, Brass, Name Cygonie, Repaired Clapper, 8 1/2 In.	355.00
Bell, Ship's, Brass, Hanging Bracket, Flange, 8 In. Diam.	65.00
Bell, Ship's, Brass, Shott's NCB, 19th Century, 6 In.	120.00
Binnacle, Brass, Kerosene Side Light, 18 1/2 x 14 In.	385.00
Binnacle, Brass, Side Light, 9 1/2 In.	100.00
Binnacle, Brass, With Lamps, 19th Century, 26 1/2 In.	850.00
Binnacle, Oak, Brass Cover, 10 1/2 In.	605.00
Binnacle, U.S. Maritime Commission, Compass, Copper, W.M. Welch, 4 In.	195.00
Binnacle, U.S. Maritime Commission, Compass, Copper, W.M. Welch, 9 1/2 In.	330.00
Binoculars, Ship's, Brass, Liverpool, 5 x 5 In.	60.00
Block, Wooden, 4-Sheave, No Sheave, 19th Century, 14 1/2 x 15 x 12 In., Pair	530.00
Box, Instrument, Gedney King & Son, Mahogany, Label, 23 In.	33.00
Box, Lift Top, Wooden, Painted Compass Rose Top, 25 x 15 In.	145.00
Box, Storage, Chip Carved Designs, Wax Inlays, 11 1/2 In.	5225.00
Candy Dish, Heart Shape, Swedish American Lines, Silver Plate	44.00
Cannon, Brass, On Wooden Truck, 9 1/2 x 3 1/4 In., Pair	200.00
Canoe, Grand Lake, Kenneth Wheaton, Grand Lake Stream, Me., Square Stern, 19 Ft.	1650.00
Canoe, Old Town Canoe Co., Painted, 2 Caned Seats, Red & Green Exterior, 201 In.	3105.00
Chart, A General Chart Of Western Ocean, Tower Hill, London, Frame, 20 x 24 In.	165.00
Chart Kit, Brass & Ivory Instruments, 7 In.	495.00
Chest, Sea, Blue Paint, Knot Work Handles, Brass Hinges, 42 x 17 x 18 In.	715.00
Chest, Sea, Camphorwood, Brass Handles & Fittings, 33 x 16 x 14 In.	440.00
Chest, Sea, Elm, Lift Top, 37 x 17 In.	440.00
Chest, Sea, Lift Top, Gray Paint, Ditty Box, Snipe Hinges, 17 x 46 x 18 In.	55.00
Chest, Sea, Lift Top, Green Paint, Ditty Box Interior, Strap Hinges, 19th Century	190.00
Chest, Sea, Pine, Lift Top, Ship Picture, Green Paint, 17 1/2 x 17 x 18 In.	715.00
Chest, Sea, Pine, Painted, 17 x 37 x 16 In.	1430.00
Chest, Sea, Wooden, Victorian Women Pictures Interior	395.00
Chronometer, Marine, 56-Hour, Brass, Russia	660.00
Chronometer, Marine, 56-Hour, Thomas Mercer Ltd., St. Albans, England	1045.00
Chronometer, Model 21, U.S. Navy, Wooden Outer Carrying Case	2495.00
Chronometer, Parkinson & Frodsham, Mahogany, Ivory, Brass Dial	1750.00
Chronometer, Thomas Mercer Ltd., St. Albans, England, U.S. Army, 5 In.	550.00
Clock, Chelsea Clock Co., Boston, U.S. Maritime Commission, Brass, Key, 7 1/2 In.	415.00
Clock, Chelsea Clock Co., U.S. Navy, Brass, Mounted On Wooden Shield, 5-In. Face	330.00
Clock, Chinese Calligraphy On Face, Brass, 7 1/4 In.	195.00
Clock, Marine, Salem, 8-Day, Brass Wheel, Silvered Metal Face, Ship's Bell Jewel, 8 In.	242.00
Clock, Marine, Seth Thomas, Brass Frame, Silvered Metal Face	154.00
Clock, Salem, 8-Day, Ship's Bell, Brass Ship's Wheel, Silvered Metal Face, Jewel, 8 In.	154.00
Clock, Seth Thomas, Brass Plated Rim, Black Painted Metal Base	99.00
Clock, Ship's Bell, Chelsea, Ball Feet, Metal Face, Applied Numerals, Brass Frame	550.00
Clock, Ship's, 8-Day, Seth Thomas, Mahogany, Wheel, Domed Glass, 21 x 15 In.	1155.00
Clock, Ship's, Chelsea Clock Co., U.S. Government, Metal, Black Paint, 6 In.	195.00
Clock, Ship's, Chelsea Clock Co., U.S. Navy, 24-Hour, 1940s, 10 In.	415.00
Clock, Ship's, Schatz, Brass, Bell, Germany, 4 In. Diam.	220.00
Clock, Ship's, Seth Thomas, Brass, Outside Bell, 5 1/2 In.	245.00
Clock, Ship's, Seth Thomas, U.S. Maritime Commission, Plastic, 8 In.	165.00
Clock, Submarine, Seth Thomas, U.S. Navy, 1944, 6 1/2 In.	495.00
Comb, Coffin Case, Convex Mirror, Horn, Sailor Made, 3 7/16 In.	240.00
Compass, Brass, Mahogany, 6 1/2 In.	310.00
Compass, Brinton, Brass, 1914, Pocket, 2 x 3 In.	90.00
Compass, C.C. Hutchinson, Cased, Box, 3 x 4 1/2 In.	55.00
Compass, Dry Card, Brass, Gimbal, Paper Dial, 4 1/2 In.	90.00
Compass, Dry Card, Brass, Gimbal, Wooden Box, Sliding Cover, 4 In.	75.00
Compass, Thos. Loughlin, Portland, Me., Cased	35.00
Compass, W.M. Welch Co., U.S. Maritime Commission, Copper, Brass, 1940s, 8 In.	145.00

Compass, Wilcox Crittendon, Brass, Gimbal, Dovetailed, 4 In. 100.00
Creamer, Missouri Pacific Lines, Silver Plate 60.00
Cup & Saucer, Clyde Mallory Steamship 130.00
Desk, Captain's, Scrimshaw, Abalone Star Top, 15 x 9 In. 880.00
Diorama, U.S. Ship Thusa, Lighthouse, Wooden, Shadow Box, Victorian, 28 x 38 In. 1210.00
Diorama, Yacht, American Flag, Pennant, Painted Sky, Molded Sea, 26 x 27 x 5 In. 3850.00
Distance Log, Negus Improved Patent Log, Measures Distance Traveled, Box 80.00
Ditty Box, Bone, Prisoner Of War, 6 In. 355.00
Epaulet, Gold Braid, Pair 75.00
Figure, Sea Captain, Holding Sextant, Wooden, Painted, Chapman, 24 In. 990.00
Flare Gun, Metal, Bell Muzzle, 1940s 65.00
Fog Horn, Bellows, Brass Trumpet, 36 1/2 In. 145.00
Fog Horn, Fishing Boat, New England, 19th Century, 36 In. 95.00
Fog Horn, Lothrop's, Wooden Case, Red Paint 330.00
Frame, 7 Picture Openings, Oval Hemp Border, 19th Century, 19 1/2 x 15 1/2 In. 1200.00
Half-Model, Gloucester Schooner, 1920, 5 3/4 x 42 In. 1545.00
Half-Model, John McKeon, Schooner, 8 x 33 In. 495.00
Half-Model, Red & Black Paint, Mounted, 8 1/2 x 28 In. 120.00
Half-Model, Thomas D. Conlon, 1868 New York Pilot Boat, Phantom, 11 x 48 In. 770.00
Half-Model, Thomas D. Conlon, Schooner Yacht, America, 8 x 34 In. 385.00
Half-Model, Yacht, Genesta, 1885 America's Cup, Planked, 8 x 29 In. 440.00
Harpoon, Double Fluke, Iron, 37 In. 935.00
Harpoon, Toggle, For Use With Darting Gun, Stamped LB & Cal, 1842 .... 990.00
Harpoon, Walrus Tusk, Stone Point, 10 1/4 In. 465.00
Helmet, Deep Sea Diver's, Brass, Copper 880.00
Jacket, Sailor's, Canvas, From Thomas W. Lawson's Yacht Dreamer, Built 1899 .... 100.00
Jug, Water, Knot Work Cover, 12 x 22 In. 120.00
Knife, Ivory, Ebony Bands, 9 1/2 In. 220.00
Knife, Shucking, Brass Guard, Stag Handle 100.00
Knife, U.S. Coast Guard, Wooden Handle 55.00
Ladder, Boat, Teak, 2 Steps, Brass Binding, 34 x 15 In. 66.00
Lamp, Brass Burner, Keystone, 6 x 12 In. 165.00
Lamp, Brass, Gimbal, Smoke Bell, Teak Plaque, 19th Century, 15 x 4 1/2 In. 110.00
Lamp, Gimbal, Kerosene, Brass, 19th Century, 5 1/2 In., Pair 215.00
Lamp, Perko, Brass, 180 Clear Ribbed Lens, 12 In. 110.00
Lamp, Port & Starboard, Wooden, 7 x 17 x 8 In., Pair 130.00
Lamp, Signal, Brass, For Sending Morse Code, Handle, 14 In. 245.00
Lantern, Beaded Double Bull's-Eye Globe, Pierced Tin, 6 Sides, Ring Handle, 12 In. 2300.00
Lantern, H. & J. Sangster, Pierced Brass, Wire Guards, June 1851 Patent, 13 1/2 In. 635.00
Lantern, Onion Globe, Pierced Bronze, Tie Down Rings, 19th Century, 11 In. 635.00
Lantern, Ship's, Meteorlite, 14 In. 220.00
Lantern, Ship's, Schiffslairennenwerk, 360 Degree Lens, 23 1/2 In. 55.00
Lantern, Stamped Wm. Porter Maker, Fixed Globe, Pierced Brass, Rings, Handle, 13 In. .. 515.00
Lantern, Wilcox Crittenden, Masthead, Metal, Brass, Red, Blue Lenses, Electric, 9 In. 120.00
Life Jacket, SS United States, Orange Twill, White Web Straps, 1962 .... 24.00
Light, Port & Starboard, Tin, Gold Paint, Electric, 9 x 13 In., Pair 170.00
Light, Ship's Anchor Type, Copper, 14 In. 75.00
Mallet, Lignum Vitae, Turned, 1880, 10 3/4 In. 55.00
Model, 3-Masted Ship, Brown Finish, Sailor Made, 50 x 36 In. 715.00
Model, 3-Masted Ship, White Paint, On Board, 19th Century, 24 x 30 In. 495.00
Model, Amerigo Vespucci, Wood With Brass & White Metal Fittings, 30 In. 550.00
Model, Boxer, M. Costagliola, Brig, 2-Masted, Exposed Starboard Side, Case, 32 In. 8625.00
Model, Buckeye State, Ohio River Stern Wheeler, 48 x 41 x 15 1/2 In. 660.00
Model, Canoe, Mad River, Pine, Gray Paint, With 11-In. Paddles, 36 In. 220.00
Model, Clipper, Floor-Standing Case, 43 In., 62 x 49-In. Case 3850.00
Model, Clipper, Flying Cloud, Fully Rigged, Glass Case, American, 29 x 42 In. 2185.00
Model, Clipper, Mary, Salem, Mass., Fully Rigged, Wooden Cradle, 31 x 46 In. 990.00
Model, Clipper, Sea Witch, H. Meyer, Fully Rigged, On Wooden Table, 25 In. 4025.00
Model, Corsair I, Steam Yacht, Mahogany & Glass Case, 15 x 27 1/2 x 9 In. 1540.00
Model, Diorama, In Bottle, 4-Masted Bark, Town & Trees, 10 1/2 In. 100.00
Model, Excaliber, Tramp Steamer, Brass Trimmed Case, Mahogany Base, 13 x 32 In. 2860.00
Model, Flagship, Star-Kist, Folding Paper, 8 x 19 x 5 In. 16.00
Model, Freighter, Gray, Black & Red, Sailor Made, 20th Century, 16 x 29 In. 165.00

Model, French Frigate LaBelle Poole, Cased, Appraisal, 50 x 17 x 35 In. 4400.00
Model, H.M.S. Prince, Plank On Bulkhead, Brass & Metal Fittings, 42 x 44 In. 650.00
Model, Ketch, Full Sail, Pine, Brass & Steel, Early 20th Century, 35 x 41 In. 230.00
Model, Nicole, Match Sticks & String, 3-Masted Schooner, Glass Case, 22 1/4 In. 275.00
Model, Orkin Nevada, Dreadnought, Steel, Clockwork, 22 In. 1540.00
Model, Pond Sloop, Green & Red Paint, No Rigging, 19th Century, 12 x 51 In. 440.00
Model, Prince De Neufchatel, John Sotham, 2-Masted, 22 Cannon, Lifeboat, 22 In. 3450.00
Model, Prisoner Of War, 3-Masted, Fully Rigged, Wooden Base, Ivory, 15 1/2 In. 2995.00
Model, Sailboat, Pond Yacht, Wooden, Worn Paint, Canvas, 64 x 80 In. 88.00
Model, Sailboat, Tin, France, Late 1800s, 45 x 34 1/2 In. 660.00
Model, Schooner, Frigatta Espinol, Wooden, Fabric Masts, 20th Century, 41 x 31 In. 750.00
Model, Shadowbox, Ship Approaching Lighthouse, Early 20th Century, 18 x 24 In. 770.00
Model, Ship, Sail & Steam, Fold Art Style 2800.00
Model, Speedboat, Wooden, 2 Electric Motors, Black, Red Trim 165.00
Model, Star Yacht, Wooden, Orange & Blue Cloth Sails, Birkenhead, England, 16 In. 125.00
Model, Wanderer, New Bedford, Whaling Ship, 1920s, 31 x 24 x 10 In. 2250.00
Model, Whaleboat, New England, Harpoons, Glass Case, 9 x 23 x 9 In. 770.00
Model, Whaleship, Wanderer, Late 19th-Early 20th Century, 27 In. 550.00
Model, Yacht, Defender, 1899 America's Cup, Rigged, Full Sails, 71 x 70 In. 2200.00
Model, Yacht, Schooner, America, Rigged, Full Sails, Copper Sheathed Hull, 29 x 36 In. . 3740.00
Model, Yacht, Schooner, Atlantic, Planked Mahogany Deck, Rigged Sails, 48 x 60 In. . . . 2420.00
Model, Yacht, Wm. Hitchcock, Mayflower, America's Cup, Glass Case, 29 x 32 In. 1980.00
Octant, Ebony, Ivory & Brass, Step Case 525.00
Octant, Ivory Scale, Brass Arm & Shades, 14 In. Radius 373.00
Octant, Spencer, Browning & Rust, Brass, Ivory Scale, 19th Century 330.00
Octant, Spencer, Browning & Rust, Ivory Scales, Mahogany Case 1100.00
Pass Keys, Captain's, Steamship, City Of Brocton, Brass 130.00
Photograph, Carboat Race, Frame, Early 20th Century, 17 x 21 In. 350.00
Photograph, Whaling Bark, Albert Cook Church, New Bedford, Ma., Frame, 15 x 19 In. . . 230.00
Picture, 3-Masted Warship, Chasing Brig, Watercolor, Pastel, 1887, Frame, 17 x 24 In. . . 880.00
Picture, Blackball Liner, Montezuma, W.M. Birchall, Frame, 1930, 9 x 11 In. 1100.00
Quadrant, Ebony, Ivory Scales, Brass Mounts, 17 In. 525.00
Quadrant, J. Harrison, Brass, Mahogany, Silver Scale, 2 Eyepieces, 19th Century 575.00
Quadrant, Spencer, Browning & Rust, Brass, Ebony, 1785 . . . . 1320.00
Rattle, S.B. Tallman, Providence, R.I., Watchman's, Wooden, 19th Century, 8 1/2 In. 90.00
Sailboat, Pond, Mahogany, Racing Hull, 1900s, 60 x 90 In. 2090.00
Sailboat, Pond, Original Sails, 1925, 36 In. 660.00
Sailor's Valentine, Double, 9 In. 3300.00
Sailor's Valentine, Shellwork, Octagon, Double Hinge, Forget-Me-Not, 9 x 9 In. 2990.00
Sextant, Bendix Aviation Corp., U.S. Navy, Bureau Of Ships, Brass, Wooden Case 385.00
Sextant, Brass, Black Frame, Silvered Gauge, Fitted Mahogany Case, 19th Century 355.00
Sextant, Duren & Costigan, No. 20 Burling Slip, New York, Brass, Box 470.00
Sextant, Kueffer & Esser, U.S. Navy, Box, Small 660.00
Sextant, Spencer Barrett Co., Ebony & Brass, Label, Case 660.00
Sextant, Wilson & Gillie Quay North Shields, 4 Eyepieces, Brass, Silver Scales 910.00
Ship In Bottle, 4-Masted Bark & Sloop, Town Ground, Late 19th Century, 11 1/2 In. 120.00
Ship In Bottle, Fully Rigged, Late 19th Century, 10 In. 230.00
Ship In Bottle, Karla, 4-Masted Bark, Scandinavian, Harbor Scene, 1920, 9 3/4 In. 410.00
Ship Model, see Nautical, Model.
Sign, Andrew J. Morse, Diving Apparatus, Wooden, Gold & Red Letters, 22 x 36 In. 355.00
Sign, Brig Pallas, Caleb Clark Norfolk, Sailing Ship Scene, 1900, 43 x 29 In. 220.00
Sign, Do Not Disturb, Pacific Far East Line, Vinyl, Doorknob Hanger, 8 x 3 In. 4.50
Sign, Flag Shape, Iron, Painted P.T.C., Green & White, 35 x 34 In. 410.00
Spear, Blackfish, Wrought Iron, Handle, 61 In. 175.00
Spear, Eel, 5-Prong, Wooden Handle, 19th Century, 34 In. 55.00
Spear, Eel, 7-Prong, Wooden Handle, 19th Century, 12 In. 100.00
Stadimeter, U.S. Navy Mark V, Case 355.00
Sticker, Baggage, New York & Porto Rico Steamship Co., Unused, 1921, 4 x 6 In. 18.00
Tankard, Pewter, Shanghai Spring Regatta 1875 8-Oar Race, England 165.00
Telescope, Brass, 3-Draw, Leather Sleeve, Brass End Caps, 23 3/4 In. 165.00
Telescope, Brass, Leather, 3-Draw, 19th Century, Opens To 28 1/2 In. 100.00
Telescope, Child's, Brass, 18th Century 175.00
Telescope, French Inscription, Wooden Case, Silver, November 1861, 24 1/2 In. 2070.00

Telescope, U.S. Navy, 16 Power Mark, 1941, 31 In. 242.00
Tellurian, W.& S. Jones, London, Bronze Base, 18th Century, 10 In. Diam. 1100.00
Whaler's Flenser, Blubber Spade, Double Edged, 17 3/8 In. 230.00
Wheel, Ship's, Brass Rim Stars, From Square Rigger, 19th Century, 62 In. Diam. 1100.00
Wheel, Ship's, Brass, Wooden Handles, 19th Century, 52 In. 1020.00
Wheel, Wooden, Brass Hub & Band, 19th Century, 33 In. 575.00
Wheel, Yacht's, Brass Hub, Plastic & Nickel Plated Spokes, 22 In. Diam. 75.00
Whistle, Bosun's, American Navy, Mid 1800s, 6 7/16 In. 155.00
Whistle, Bosun's, J.H. Rowe General Agents, Brass, 10 1/4 In. 235.00

NETSUKES are small ivory, wood, metal, or porcelain pieces used as
toggles on the end of the cord that held a Japanese money pouch. The
earliest date from the sixteenth century. Many are miniature, carved
works of art.

Boar's Tusk, Carving Of Bat, Inlaid Eyes, Mitsunobu 880.00
Bone, Puppy, Seated, 19th Century 154.00
Boxwood, Coiled Snake, Black 150.00
Copper, Kagamibuta, Woman's Head With Gilt Details, 19th Century 165.00
Ebony, Hippopotamus, Inlaid Eyes, Sosui 1430.00
Ivory, 2 Karakos, 1 Wearing Shishi Mask, Other Playing Drum, Meiji Period 247.00
Ivory, 2 Men Riding On Carp, Incised, Polychrome, 2 In. 175.00
Ivory, 2 Rakans Bathing In Large Beggar's Bowl, Signed, 20th Century 412.00
Ivory, 2 Sages Riding In A Boat While Playing Go, Signed, Kozan 220.00
Ivory, 4 Men Climbing On Basket, Incised, Monochrome, Signed, 2 In. 345.00
Ivory, Bearded Man, Sitting, Incised, Monochrome, Signed, 2 1/4 In. 290.00
Ivory, Blind Man Walking With Cane 110.00
Ivory, Coiled Dragon, Gold Eyes Holding Pearl, Meigyokusai 2310.00
Ivory, Crayfish, Inlaid Eyes 275.00
Ivory, Dog, Ball Under Paw, Signed, 1 1/2 In. 132.00
Ivory, Dog, With Monkey On Back, 1 1/2 In. 40.00
Ivory, Elephant, Meiji Period 105.00
Ivory, Emperor & Empress, On Throne, 6 1/4 In. 630.00
Ivory, Figure Holding Slabs, Signed 140.00
Ivory, Fishmonger, Revolving Face 85.00
Ivory, Foo Dog, With Puppies, 1 1/2 In. 20.00
Ivory, Horse Being Groomed, Meigyoku 517.00
Ivory, Hotei, Child Writing On His Belly, Signed 172.00
Ivory, Hotei, Holding Scepter, Robes, Inlaid Boxwood, Signed 115.00
Ivory, Hotei, Holding Sword Behind Back, 1 7/8 In. 220.00
Ivory, Hotei, Seated On Treasure Sack, Drinking Sake, Masatoshi 3740.00
Ivory, Immortal With Toad, Inlaid Eyes, Tadayoshi 172.00
Ivory, Man Carrying A Drinking Vessel & Hatchet 33.00
Ivory, Man Carrying Bag, 1 3/4 In. 70.00
Ivory, Man Carrying Dragon Mask, Incised, Polychrome, Signed, 1 3/4 In. 460.00
Ivory, Man On His Horse, With Servant, Incised & Polychromed, Signed, 2 In. 350.00
Ivory, Man Seated, With Hat, Signed, Meiji Period 92.00
Ivory, Man Standing Beside Tree Stump Smoking Pipe, 3 In. 88.00
Ivory, Man Standing, Holding Basket, Seated Boy, Signed, 2 1/4 In. 300.00
Ivory, Man With Birdcage, Incised, Polychrome, 2 In. 460.00
Ivory, Man With Fan 50.00
Ivory, Man With Leaves, Signed 195.00
Ivory, Monkey, With Fruit, 1 1/2 In. 25.00
Ivory, Mouse With Watermelon, Incised, Polychrome, Signed, 1 3/4 In. 690.00
Ivory, Nursing Woman & Child, Tortoise At Feet 3410.00
Ivory, Okame Hinding Under Wine Cup, 4 Characters, Signed 200.00
Ivory, Old Man, Smiling, With Fan & Bag 44.00
Ivory, Oval, Female Mask One Side, Male Mask On Reverse, Signed, 2 In. 275.00
Ivory, Rat Gnawing On Sandal, Masaka 2640.00
Ivory, Reclining Tiger, Scratching Ear, Inlaid Horn Eyes 5500.00
Ivory, Seated Elephant, Meigyokusai 1035.00
Ivory, Skeleton Holding Masks, Monochrome, Signed, 2 In. 230.00
Ivory, Sleeping Bear 345.00
Ivory, Squirrel Eating A Nut, Signed, 2 In. 115.00

Ivory, Study Of Mare & Foal, Meigyoku 862.00
Ivory, Toad Atop Leaf, Masakazu 285.00
Ivory, Wandering, Priest, Playing Reed Flute, Ichiro 1045.00
Ivory, Woman With 2 Children, Holding Mask, Meiji Period 375.00
Porcelain, Man, Lotus Leaf For Hat, Turquoise, 19th Century, 3 In. 431.00
Porcelain, Monkey In Courtier Outfit, Movable Tongue & Head, 19th Century, 3 In. 172.00
Porcelain, Monkey, Seated 770.00
Porcelain, Shishi, Celadon Green Glaze, Masakazu 797.00
Porcelain, Tiger With Underglaze Blue Stripes 287.00
Staghorn, Calligraphic Scroll, On Well Basket, Leaves & Vines 357.00
Staghorn, Sage Riding Horse, Opens To Small Knife, 6 3/4 In. 3080.00
Wood, Ashinaga Fisherman, Holding Octopus In Arms, Inlaid Eyes 1760.00
Wood, Badger Dressed In Lotus Leaf Robe, Horn & Amber Eyes, Church 2640.00
Wood, Boar, Resting, Signed, 19th Century 110.00
Wood, Dancer's Gigaka Mask, Carved Interior, 2 In. 115.00
Wood, Farmer With Hoe, 19th Century 172.00
Wood, Floral Trellises, Cinnabar Lacquer, 1 3/4 In. 172.00
Wood, Group Of Masks, Signed, 19th Century 460.00
Wood, Hotei Seated With Treasure Sack, Signed, Sansho, 1800 .... 412.00
Wood, Man Fending Off Frog With Umbrella, Mitsukuni 1650.00
Wood, Manju With Cinnabar Lacquer, Floral Trellises, 1 1/4 In. 143.00
Wood, Monkey, Inlaid Eyes, Seated On Tortoise, 19th Century 115.00
Wood, Sarumawashi Entertainer, Offering Peach To Monkey On Shoulder, Sosei 3080.00
Wood, Shrouded Daruma & Man In Kimono, Ivory & Coral Inlay 172.00

NEW HALL Porcelain Manufactory was started at Newhall, Shelton, Staffordshire, England, in 1782. Simple decorated wares were made. Between 1810 and 1825, the factory made a glassy bone porcelain sometimes marked with the factory name. Do not confuse New Hall porcelain with the pieces made by the New Hall Pottery Company, Ltd., a twentieth-century firm.

New Hall

Cup & Saucer, Flowers, c.1800 .... 185.00
Cup & Saucer, Japanese Style, c.1805 .... 195.00
Cup & Saucer, Mandarin Scene, 1800-1820 .... 245.00
Cup & Saucer, Queen's Rose, Pearlware, Pink Diaper Pattern Border, 1800-1820 .... 170.00

NEW MARTINSVILLE Glass Manufacturing Company was established in 1901 in New Martinsville, West Virginia. It was bought and renamed the Viking Glass Company in 1944. In 1987 Kenneth Dalzell, former president of Fostoria Glass Company, purchased the factory and renamed it Dalzell-Viking. Production ceased in 1998.

Berry Set, Carnation, 9 1/2-In. Bowl, 7 Piece 55.00
Clipper Ship, Bookends 60.00
Eagle, Bookends 40.00
Elephant, Bookends 125.00
Figurine, Baby Seal, 4 1/2 In. 65.00
Figurine, Chick, 1 In., Pair 45.00
Figurine, Hen, 5 In. 75.00
Figurine, Horse, Head Up, 8 In. 85.00
Figurine, Hunter, Woodsman, 7 3/8 In. 95.00
Figurine, Mama Bear, 4 x 6 In. ....145.00 to 225.00
Figurine, Papa Bear, 4 x 6 1/2 In. ....165.00 to 225.00
Figurine, Pelican, 8 In. 65.00
Figurine, Police Dog, German Shepherd, 5 In. 55.00
Figurine, Rooster, 7 1/2 In. 60.00
Figurine, Squirrel, 4 1/2 In. 35.00
Figurine, Squirrel, On Base, 5 1/2 In. 45.00
Figurine, Tiger, Head Up, 6 1/2 In. 150.00
Figurine, Wolfhound, 7 In. ....65.00 to 85.00
Gazelle, Bookends, Leaping 100.00
Janice, Basket 56.00
Janice, Bowl, Swan, 10 In. 48.00
Janice, Plate, Center Handle, Silver Overlay, 12 In. 50.00

Moondrops, Berry Bowl, Ruby, 5 1/4 In. 30.00
Moondrops, Bowl, 3-Toed, Amber, 8 In. 22.00
Moondrops, Butter, Cover, Cobalt Blue 550.00
Moondrops, Cocktail Shaker, Handle, Ruby 80.00
Moondrops, Cordial, Amber, 2 7/8 In. 25.00
Moondrops, Cup & Saucer, Amber 10.00
Moondrops, Cup & Saucer, Footed, Ruby 20.00
Moondrops, Plate, Amber, 6 1/8 In. 4.00
Moondrops, Plate, Amber, 8 1/2 In. 8.00
Moondrops, Plate, Ruby, 9 1/2 In. 430.00
Moondrops, Sherbet, Ruby, 4 1/2 In. 27.00
Moondrops, Soup, Dish, Ruby, 6 3/4 In. 115.00
Moondrops, Sugar, Amber 10.00
Moondrops, Sugar, Ruby, 2 3/4 In. 13.00
Moondrops, Tumbler, 5 Oz. 24.00
Moondrops, Tumbler, Handle, Pink, 9 Oz., 4 7/8 In. 13.00
Moondrops, Tumbler, Juice, Footed, Amber, 3 Oz., 3 1/4 In. 8.00
Moondrops, Tumbler, Juice, Footed, Ruby, 3 Oz., 3 1/4 In. 14.00
Moondrops, Tumbler, Whiskey, Dark Green, 2 Oz., 2 3/4 In. 8.00
Moondrops, Tumbler, Whiskey, Ruby, 2 Oz., 2 3/4 In. 14.00
Moondrops, Vase, Bud, Rocket, Light Green, 8 1/2 In. 250.00
Moondrops, Wine, Ruby, 4 Oz., 4 In. 22.00
Nautilus, Bookend ....22.00 to 25.00
No. 2, Waffle Set, 2 Pitchers, Covers, Tray, Cobalt Blue 300.00
Radiance, Bowl, Ruffled Edge, Ruby, 10 In. 95.00
Radiance, Cover, Ice Blue, 6 In. 275.00
Radiance, Decanter Set, Silver Overlay, Ruby, Stopper, 7 Piece 325.00
Radiance, Pitcher, Ruby, Silver Trim, 64 Oz. 270.00
Radiance, Plate, Ice Blue, 8 In. 18.00
Radiance, Punch Bowl Set, Light Blue, 9 Pieces 320.00
Radiance, Punch Cup, Ice Blue 12.00
Radiance, Relish, 2 Sections 27.00
Radiance, Relish, Handles, 3 Sections, Ruby, 8 1/2 In. 50.00
Radiance, Sugar, Pink 20.00
Radiance, Vase, Crimped, Cobalt Blue, 12 In. 295.00
Roly Poly, Decanter, Handle, Ruby 145.00
Scroll, Bookends 75.00

NEWCOMB Pottery was founded by Ellsworth and William Woodward at Sophie Newcomb College, New Orleans, Louisiana, in 1895. The work continued through the 1940s. Pieces of this art pottery are marked with the printed letters *NC* and often have the incised initials of the artist as well. Most pieces have a matte glaze and incised decoration.

Bowl, Blue Crocus, Denim Blue Ground, Henrietta Bailey, 1916, 3 1/4 x 6 In. 1430.00
Bowl, Dogwoods In Low Relief, Blue Matte Glaze, Henrietta Bailey, 4 x 5 1/2 In. 1320.00
Bowl, Flower Frog, Flowers, Blue Ground, A.F. Simpson, 4 x 11 1/4 In. 1760.00
Bowl, Flowers, Blue Matte Glaze, A.F. Simpson, 2 1/4 In. 665.00
Bowl, Flowers, Sadie Irvine, 1912, 5 In. 1540.00
Bowl, Painted Flowers, Rose Matte Glaze, A.F. Simpson, 10 1/2 In. 1430.00
Bowl, Stylized Flowers, Purple Overglaze, Squat, A.F. Simpson, 19815, 3 x 5 In. 1320.00
Candlestick, Pink Spiderwort, Blue Ground, Sadie Irving, 1923, 7 1/4 In., Pair 1870.00
Candlestick, White, Yellow Flowers, Green Leaves, A.F. Simpson, 1917, 7 x 5 In. 2760.00
Inkwell, Incised Tulips, Blue, Green, Lid, Knob Finial, Harriet C. Joor, 1906, 4 In. 2200.00
Jar, Cover, Incised Landscape, Stylized Trees, Harriet Joor, 1906, 6 1/4 x 4 3/4 In. 7700.00
Lamp, Poppy, White Flowers, Leafy Stems, Blue Semimatte Glaze, J. Meyer, 7 1/2 In. ... 8800.00
Letter Holder, 2 Sections, Wading Birds, Flowers, Mary G. Sheerer, c.1898, 7 In. 2860.00
Mug, Floral Cobalt Blue Band, Denim Blue Base, S.E. Wells, 1911, 4 x 3 In. 1650.00
Mug, High Glaze, 5 1/8 In. 4125.00
Pitcher, Black, Cream Flowers, Pale Yellow Ground, Amelie Roman, 1913, 7 In. 8800.00
Pitcher, Lake Pontchartrain Sunset, Low Relief, S. Irvine, J. Meyer, 1918, 4 1/2 In. 4180.00
Pitcher, Milk, Ivory Flowers, Green Leaves, Cobalt Band, Mazie Ryan, 1904, 8 In. 9350.00
Pitcher, Stylized Floral, Alice R. Urquhart, 1905, 3 1/2 In. 3850.00

Pitcher, Stylized Green Leaves, Dark Blue Ground, Sadie Irvine, 4 x 4 In. 1320.00
Pitcher, White, Blue, Green Ground, Sadie Irvine, 1909, 7 1/2 x 5 1/2 In. 4400.00
Pitcher, Yellow Roses, Blue Green, Henrietta Bailey, 1903, 2 1/2 x 3 1/4 In. 1760.00
Plaque, Flowers, A.F. Simpson, 1928, 4 In. 550.00
Plaque, Oak Tree, Spanish Moss, Riverbank, A.F. Simpson, Frame, 1915, 6 x 9 In. 7150.00
Plaque, Vellum, Snow Scene, Birches At Dawn, Sallie Coyne, 10 x 7 In. 4675.00
Plate, Daisy Border On Yellow Band, Signed MC/12-20-16, 8 1/4 In. 110.00
Plate, Incised Stylized Tulip & Leaf Border, Light Blue, Green, L. Nicholson, 9 In. 1840.00
Shade, Metal Cut Pine Trees, Striated Slag Glass, Signed, 22 1/2 x 18 In. 6050.00
Tea Set, Stylized Flowers, Green, Gold, Cobalt, Ivory, H. Bailey, 1907, 3 Piece 15400.00
Teapot, Cover, Daisies, Blue Matte Glaze, Magenta Ground, A.F. Simpson, 1919, 3 In. ... 690.00
Teapot, Pinecone Design, Blue Matte Glaze, Handle, H. Bailey, 1930, 5 x 5 1/2 In. 805.00
Tile, Bamboo & Lilies, Blue & Green Matte Glaze, Corinne M. Chalaron, 4 x 4 In. 120.00
Tile, Red Cross, Marked, Leona Nicholson, 1925, 3 1/4 In. 660.00
Trivet, Live Oak Draped In Spanish Moss, A.F. Simpson, 5 7/8 In. 3145.00
Trivet, Pink Flowers, Green Leaves, Blue Ground, A.F. Simpson, 5 1/2 In. 1110.00
Trivet, Stylized Blossom Wreath, Ivory Ground, Mary Butler, 1905, 6 In. Diam. 1540.00
Vase, Band Of Stylized Blossoms, Leaf Blades, Blue Ground, Sadie Irvine, 1920, 4 In. ... 2090.00
Vase, Black Matte Glaze, 4 In. 440.00
Vase, Blue Green Irises, Blue Ground, Sadie Irvine, 1913, 12 x 5 1/2 In. 3300.00
Vase, Bud, Oxblood Glaze, 1910, 6 In. 1210.00
Vase, Butterflies, Cotton Blossoms, Bulbous, Sadie Irvine, 1926, 7 x 6 1/4 In. 8800.00
Vase, Corn Stalks, Green, Cobalt Blue Glossy Ground, Roberta Kennon, 1902, 9 x 4 In. ... 4400.00
Vase, Crocus, Green & Blue Ground, Signed, Marie Hoa LeBlanc, 4 In. 8250.00
Vase, Dark Green Matte Glaze Over Light Green, Cylindrical, 12 1/2 In. 747.00
Vase, Dark Green Matte Glaze, Cobalt Blue Ground, Joseph Myers, 6 1/2 x 4 In. 2200.00
Vase, Dogwood Blossoms, Blue Green Ground, Cynthia Littlejohn, 1914, 5 1/2 In. 1760.00
Vase, Espanol Pattern, Sadie Irvine, 1927, 2 1/2 x 2 3/4 In. 1540.00
Vase, Espanol, Flared Rim, Cylindrical, Sadie Irvine, 1926, 9 1/2 x 4 1/2 In. 7150.00
Vase, Flowers, A.F. Simpson, 1922, 8 x 2 1/2 In. 1430.00
Vase, Flowers, Alma Mason, 1911, 4 1/2 In. 2640.00
Vase, Flowers, Pink Blossoms, Dark Blue Ground, A.F. Simpson, 6 In. 1870.00
Vase, Flowers, Red Matte Glaze Over Blue Matte Glaze, Sadie Irvine, 6 In. 3850.00
Vase, Green, Blue Trees, Joseph Meyer, 3 In. 2420.00
Vase, Incised Cats In Silhouette, Landscape, Cobalt Blue & White, Kennon, 1902, 7 In. ... 19800.00
Vase, Incised Design At Bottom & Lid, Rose To Yellow Glaze, Sadie Irvine, 7 In. 1100.00
Vase, Iris & Leaves, Blue Semimatte Glaze, A.F. Simpson, 1918, 7 x 6 In. 4600.00
Vase, Ivory, Amber Stylized Dog's Heads, Sabina Wells, 1902, 4 3/4 x 2 3/4 In. 3850.00
Vase, Landscape, Carved Trees, Hanging Moss, Moon Through Trees, Signed, 7 In. 3850.00
Vase, Landscape, Moss Trees, Palmettos, A.F. Simpson, 11 In. 14300.00
Vase, Live Oaks, Spanish Moss, A.F. Simpson, 1922, 8 1/4 x 5 In. 3850.00
Vase, Live Oaks, Spanish Moss, A.F. Simpson, 1928, 4 3/4 x 3 3/4 In. 4950.00
Vase, Live Oaks, Spanish Moss, Full Moon, Blue, Henrietta Bailey, 5 In. 605.00
Vase, Live Oaks, Spanish Moss, Full Moon, Sadie Irvine, Joseph Meyer, 1932, 9 In. 2640.00
Vase, Moon & Moss, Incised Base, Francis Ford, 4 3/4 x 5 In. 1870.00
Vase, Moonlight Scene, Oak Trees, Restored Hole, Sadie Irvine, 1925, 11 1/4 In. 4130.00
Vase, Moonlit Landscape, Tall Oaks With Spanish Moss, A.F. Simpson, 8 In. 5500.00
Vase, Narcissus, Pale Blue Ground, Corset, A.F. Simpson, 1924, 8 1/2 In. 3580.00
Vase, Oak Trees, Spanish Moss, Beige Ground, A.F. Simpson, 1918, 5 1/4 x 3 In. 1650.00
Vase, Oak Trees, Spanish Moss, Blue & Green Matte Glaze, H. Bailey, 6 3/4 x 8 1/2 In. ... 6050.00
Vase, Oak Trees, Spanish Moss, Dark Blue Ground, Oval, Sadie Irvine, 5 1/2 x 3 In. 1980.00
Vase, Oak Trees, Spanish Moss, Full Moon, Carved, A.F. Simpson, 1928, 5 x 4 In. 3575.00
Vase, Oak Trees, Spanish Moss, Ovoid, A.F. Simpson, 1926, 7 1/2 x 4 In. 8250.00
Vase, Pink Flowers, Green Leaves, Dark Blue Ground, A.F. Simpson, 1928, 8 1/2 In. 3580.00
Vase, Semimatte Raspberry Glaze, Blue Interior, Stamped NC, 5 1/4 x 4 1/2 In. 440.00
Vase, Slender, Transitional, Oak Trees, Spanish Moss, Henrietta Bailey, 1915, 6 x 2 In. ... 1540.00
Vase, Squat, Flowers, Raspberry & Blue Matte Glaze, Sadie Irvine, 1918, 1 x 4 In. 1100.00
Vase, Squat, White Daffodils, Green Leaves, Blue Ground, Sadie Irvine, 1920, 5 In. 1650.00
Vase, Stylized Cactus Plants, Large Yellow Blossoms, Marie Ross, 1903, 5 In. 13200.00
Vase, Stylized Flower & Leaf, Blue Ground, Sadie Irvine, 1921, 4 x 6 In. 880.00
Vase, Stylized Mushrooms, Incised & Painted High Glaze, Sabina Wells, 6 In. 3850.00
Vase, Stylized Tulip, White Clay Body, c.1907, 5 3/4 In. 6955.00
Vase, Stylized White Narcissus, Light Blue Ground, Irene B. Keep, 1903, 10 3/4 In. 4950.00

Vase, Stylized White Narcissus, Long Green Leaves, A.F. Simpson, 1914, 9 x 4 In. 4125.00
Vase, Tall Pines, Pink Sky, Sadie Irving, 1916, 4 x 3 1/2 In. 880.00
Vase, Tapered, White Gladiola, Green Leaves, Blue, A.F. Simpson, 1919, 8 1/2 In. 3850.00
Vase, Tobacco Leaves, White & Yellow Flowers, Flared, Sadie Irvine, 1923, 7 In. 935.00
Vase, Transitional, Jonquils, Blue Ground, Henrietta Bailey, 1910, 7 In. 990.00
Vase, Wheat Design Repeating Around Top, Joseph Meyer, 11 In. 4400.00
Vase, White Flowers, Blue Green Ground, Bulbous, May Morel, 1913, 5 x 5 In. 1733.00
Vase, White Flowers, Multitone Blue Matte Ground, A.F. Simpson, 6 In. 1430.00
Vase, White Gladiola, Green Stems, Blue Ground, Sadie Irvine, 1926, 4 1/4 x 5 In. 2640.00
Vase, White Jonquils, Yellow Centers, A.F. Simpson, 4 In. 1045.00
Vase, White, Yellow Flowers, Dark Blue, Blue Green Ground, A.F. Simpson, 5 In. 2310.00
Vase, Wild Roses, Pink & Cream Centers, Green Leaves, Sadie Irvine, 8 In. 4400.00
Wall Pocket, Stylized Trees, Cobalt Blue, Green, Leona Nicholson, 1904, 11 x 4 In. 9350.00

NILOAK Pottery (Kaolin spelled backward) was made at the Hyten
Brothers Pottery in Benton, Arkansas, between 1909 and 1947.
Although the factory did make cast and molded wares, collectors are
most interested in the marbleized art pottery line made of colored
swirls of clay. It was called *Mission Ware.* By 1931 the company made
castware, and many of these pieces were marked with the name
Hywood.

Figurine, Woman, Seated 80.00
Humidor, Marbleized, Brown, Bulbous, Stamped, 5 x 5 1/4 In. 465.00
Planter, Camel 65.00
Planter, Kangaroo 65.00
Planter, Polar Bear 65.00
Vase, Bud, Marbleized, Brown, Tan, Cream, 6 In. 175.00
Vase, Dusty Pink, Base Handles, Signed, 7 In., Pair 165.00
Vase, Marbleized, Blue, Buff & Brown, Bulbous, Impressed Mark, 6 1/2 x 4 In. 110.00
Vase, Marbleized, Blue, Buff & Brown, Bulbous, Impressed Mark, 8 1/2 x 5 In. 165.00
Vase, Marbleized, Blue, Buff, Terra-Cotta & Brown, Bulbous, 6 1/2 x 4 In. 165.00
Vase, Marbleized, Blue, Swirl Design, Brown, Red, Bulbous, 5 In. 230.00
Vase, Marbleized, Brick Red, Tan, Brown, Blue, Cream Swirl Design, 2 Handles, 17 In. . . 2750.00
Vase, Marbleized, Brown, Beige & Terra-Cotta, Corseted, 6 In. 88.00
Vase, Marbleized, Brown, Blue & Tan Clays, Bulbous, 8 x 4 In. 231.00
Vase, Marbleized, Brown, Blue, Cream, 18 In. 2310.00
Vase, Marbleized, Brown, Blue, Tan, Stamped, 4 1/4 In. 88.00
Vase, Marbleized, Brown, Blue, Terra-Cotta, Corseted, 10 x 4 In. 275.00
Vase, Marbleized, Brown, Blue, Terra-Cotta, Sand, Egg Shape, Paper Label, 8 In. 220.00
Vase, Marbleized, Brown, Ivory & Terra-Cotta, Oval, Marked, 12 x 7 In. 490.00
Vase, Marbleized, Brown, Tan, Cream, 4 1/2 In. 120.00
Vase, Marbleized, Brown, Tan, Cream, 7 1/2 In. 190.00
Vase, Marbleized, Brown, Tan, Cream, 8 1/2 In. . . . . .220.00 to 285.00
Vase, Marbleized, Brown, Tan, Cream, 10 1/2 In. 230.00
Vase, Marbleized, Brown, Tan, Cream, Original Paper Label, 3 In. 155.00
Vase, Marbleized, Brown, Tan, Flared Neck, 9 In. 275.00
Vase, Marbleized, Multicolored, Rolled Rim, Stamped, 10 x 5 1/2 In. 275.00
Vase, Marbleized, Oval, Brown, Ivory, Terra-Cotta, Marked, 12 x 7 In. 490.00
Vase, Marbleized, Shouldered, Paper Label, 8 In. 195.00
Vase, Marbleized, Signed, 16 In. 2090.00

NIPPON porcelain was made in Japan from 1891 to 1921. *Nippon* is the
Japanese word for *Japan.* A few firms continued to use the word
Nippon on ceramics after 1921 as a part of the company name more
than as an identification of the country of origin. More pieces marked
Nippon will be found in the Moriage and Noritake categories.

Ashtray, Swan, 3 Rests, Green Crown Mark 35.00
Biscuit Jar, Flowers, Gold Trim, Wide Cobalt Bands, Cover, Mark, 7 In. 392.00
Biscuit Jar, House In Meadow, Hand Painted, Cover, Green M In Wreath, 7 In. 168.00
Bowl, Jeweled Border, Flowers, Footed, 7 In. 85.00
Bread Tray, Blue Center, Pink & Yellow Roses, Gold Border, 11 1/2 In. 200.00
Butter Chip, Old Geisha Girl, 3 1/4 In. 10.00
Candlestick, Floral, White Ground, Green Wreath, 6 1/4 In., Pair 225.00

Nippon, Vase, Roses, Cobalt
Blue Ground, 24 In.

**If you take the glass out of a picture frame
to clean it, wipe the glass horizontally on
one side, vertically on the other. Then you
can tell which side is streaked.**

Chocolate Set, Poppies, Brown Mottled Ground, Gilt Handle & Finial, 13 Piece	515.00
Cracker Jar, 2 Handles, Overall Turquoise Beading, Gold Ground	335.00
Creamer, Basket Of Roses, White & Gold, 8-Footed	35.00
Creamer, White & Gold, Leaf Mark, 3-Footed	35.00
Dish Set, Silhouette, Children's, 14 Piece	70.00
Hatpin, Pink Florals, Raised Gold Design, Jewels, Mark	135.00
Inkwell, Brown & Black, Raised Gold, 4 In.	575.00
Jardiniere, Flowers, Butterflies, Bird In Border, Yellow Background, 13 x 16 In.	132.00
Nut Set, Oval Serving Dish, 6 Miniature Bowls, Swan Design, 12 3/4 In., 7 Piece	120.00
Plaque, Asian Boy, Bisque Socket Head, Enamel Glass Eyes, Closed Mouth, 12 In.	605.00
Plate, Lake, Trees, House, Gold Trim, Ears, Nagoya SNB Mark, 9 In.	45.00
Plate, Yellow, Green Apples, 8 In.	48.00
Sugar & Creamer, Floral Bands	78.00
Tea Set, Girls, Holding Basket, Rising Sun, Child's, 7 Piece	145.00
Vase, 6 Different Scenic Panels, 7 1/2 In.	1140.00
Vase, Carnation Design, Soft Colors, 8 In.	145.00
Vase, Cherry Blossom, Gilt, Double Ribbon Shaped Handles, Green M In Wreath, 11 In. .	715.00
Vase, Coralene, Water Lilies, Brown Ground, Gilt, 2 Handles, Kinran Mark, 7 In., Pair . . .	860.00
Vase, Flowers, Green, Red Ground, Crow's-Foot Base, 2 Handles, 11 1/2 In.	112.00
Vase, Flowers, House & Meadow, Gilt, 2 Handles, Green M In Wreath, 6 In.	170.00
Vase, Flowers, Ruffled, 15 In.	465.00
Vase, Grapevine, Gilt Design, 12 1/4 In.	115.00
Vase, House & Meadow, Swans, Scroll Handle, Blue M In Wreath, 11 In.	390.00
Vase, Landscape, Hand Painted, 5 In., Pair	27.00
Vase, Man On Camel, Gilt Trim, Beading, 2 Handles, Green M In Wreath, 6 1/2 In.	145.00
Vase, Oval, Flowers, Gilt Enamel, 2 Handles, 3-Footed, Blue Maple Leaf Mark, 9 1/2 In. .	335.00
Vase, Overall Gilt Enamel Scrolling, 4 Floral Medallions, 3 Handles, 5 1/2 In.	225.00
Vase, Poppies, Cobalt & Gilt, Handle, 9 In.	165.00
Vase, Red Rose, Green, 8 1/2 In.	75.00
Vase, Reserve With Scene, Gilt, 10 1/2 In.	85.00
Vase, Roses, Cobalt Blue Ground, 24 In. . . . . *Illus*	8000.00
Vase, Seashore Scene, Mother-Of-Pearl Band, 1920s, 11 In.	150.00
Vase, White Lilies, Gilt Enamel, 2 Handles, Blue Mum Mark, 9 1/2 In.	145.00

NODDERS, also called nodding figures or pagods, are figures with
heads and hands that are attached to wires. Any slight movement
causes the parts to move up and down. They were made in many countries during the eighteenth, nineteenth, and twentieth centuries. A few
Art Deco designs are also known. Copies are being made. A more
recent type of nodder is made of papier-mache or plastic. These often
represent sports figures or comic characters. Sports nodders are listed
in the Sports category.

Baby, Pulling Sock Off Foot, Bisque, Head Nods, 4 1/2 In.	225.00
Beetle Bailey, 1960s	175.00
Ben Casey	185.00
Braying Donkey, Seated, Hair	30.00
Bulldog, Papier-Mache, On Wheels, 1900s, Full Size	1800.00

Cat, Mouse In Mouth, Head & Tail, Papier-Mache, 21 1/2 In., Pair 805.00
Chinese Gentleman, Floral Robe, Chinoiserie, Meissen, 12 x 13 In. 14950.00
Colonel Sanders, Plastic, Painted, Paramount RP, 1960s, 7 In. 150.00
Colonial Man, Standing, Holding Pipe, Composition, Wood, 7 1/2 In. 450.00
Donkey, Braying, With Hair, Sitting, Ceramic, 5 In. 25.00
Duck, Suit, Tie, Easter, Composition, Germany 95.00
Elephant, Jumbo, Cast Iron, Wheeled Platform, Gilt, 5 1/4 x 3 7/8 In. 355.00
Foxy Grandpa, Ashtray, Austria, 1920s 145.00
Hold That Tiger, Jeweled Eyes, Head Moves Back & Forth, Box, 3 1/2 x 8 In. 48.00
Lt. Fuzz, 1960s 250.00
Mandarin, Seated, Flowered Robe, Potschappel, Early 20th Century, 10 In., Pair 6035.00
Martian, Plastic, 4 In. 32.00
Maude The Mule, Germany, Papier-Mache, 6 In. 440.00
Mr. Wicker, Bisque, Germany 375.00
Oriental Potentates, Porcelain, Jacob Petit, Paris, 14 3/8 In. 3740.00
Phantom Of The Opera, Ghoulish Style, Universal Studios California, 1960s 225.00
Salt And Pepper shakers are listed in the Salt & Pepper category.
Sgt. Snorkel, 1960s 140.00
Skeezix, Bisque, Germany 185.00
Uncle Walt, Bisque, Germany 185.00

NORITAKE porcelain was made in Japan after 1904 by Nippon Toki
Kaisha. The best-known Noritake pieces are marked with the M in a
wreath for the Morimura Brothers, a New York City distributing company. This mark was used until 1941. There may be some helpful price
information in the Nippon category, since prices are comparable. Noritake Azalea is listed in the Azalea category in this book.

Bowl, Vegetable, Lyric, No. 519 ....   20.00
Cake Plate, Tree In Meadow, Open Handles 35.00
Candy Dish, Tree In Meadow, Octagonal, 8 In. 365.00
Cheese Dish, Tree In Meadow, Cover 95.00
Coffeepot, Tree In Meadow, Demitasse 225.00
Creamer, Tree In Meadow 23.00
Cruet Set, Oil & Vinegar, Tree In Meadow, Conjoined 295.00
Cup & Saucer, Laureate Pattern, Demitasse 15.00
Cup & Saucer, Tree In Meadow 19.00
Gravy Boat, Lyric 20.00
Hatpin Holder, Bands & Panels Around Top, Stylized Blossoms, 2 1/4 x 4 1/8 In. 65.00
Lamp Base, Green, Pink & White Floral Medallion Urn, Square Base, 24 In. 55.00
Platter, Tree In Meadow, 14 In. 60.00
Relish, Willowbrook, 9722 ....   56.00
Sauce, Gordona, Signed 20.00
Soup, Dish, Tree In Meadow, 7 1/2 In. 33.00
Sugar, Cover, Blue, White, Key Design Rimmed Bottom 12.00
Sugar & Creamer, Orange, Peacock Eyes, Art Deco 48.00
Sugar & Creamer, Scenic, Brown Bead Trim 120.00
Tea Set, Tree In Meadow, 17 Piece 285.00
Toast Rack, Figural Bird, 4-Slice, Luster, Hand Painted ....85.00 to 100.00

NORTH DAKOTA SCHOOL OF MINES was established in 1892 at the
University of North Dakota. A ceramic course was included and pieces
were made from the clays found in the region. Students at the university made pieces from 1909 to 1949. Although very early pieces were
marked *U.N.D.*, most pieces were stamped with the full name of the
university.

Coaster, Deer Design, Dark Green, Brown, 4 In. 165.00
Figurine, Cowboy, Bentonite, Glaze, J. Mattson, 1913, 4 In. 715.00
Lamp Base, Plum Sung Glaze, Footed, Mark, 10 3/4 In. 176.00
Lamp Base, Tobacco Brown Matte Glaze, 1926, 13 In. 880.00
Vase, American Birds, Armstrong, 1948, 4 x 4 3/4 In. 990.00
Vase, Band Of Oxen & Covered Wagons, Brown Glaze, 6 x 7 In. 1430.00
Vase, Blossoms, Incised Stylized Turquoise, 7 x 3 1/2 In. 1430.00
Vase, Blue Matte Glaze, Squat, 1930, 3 3/4 In. 165.00

Vase, Bronco Riders, Matte Glaze, J. Mattson, 6 3/4 x 4 In. 2310.00
Vase, Buffalo, Blue, Gray, Julia Mattson, 4 x 4 1/2 In. 1870.00
Vase, Cowboy Scene, Brown Glaze, Flora Huckfield, 7 1/4 In. 1650.00
Vase, Coyote Silhouettes, Cobalt & Ivory, Ink Stamp, 3 1/2 In. 1320.00
Vase, Daffodils, Carved, Matte Glaze, McCosh, 1948, 8 x 5 In. 1210.00
Vase, Flowers, Matte Glaze, Buff Clay Body, M. Cable, 3 1/4 In. 330.00
Vase, Green To Beige Matte Glaze, Julia Mattson, 2 x 4 In. 192.00
Vase, Lattice, Cobalt Blue, Ivory Ground, Egg Shape, 6 1/2 In. 440.00
Vase, Leaves, Incised, Outlined In Brown, J. Mattson, 7 In. 605.00
Vase, Meadowlark Birds, Chartreuse Matte Glaze, 3 x 5 In. 660.00
Vase, Narcissus, Carved, Dark Brown, F. Cunningham, 1950, 9 In. 1100.00
Vase, Prairie Rose, Carved Flowers, Margaret Cable, Marked, 5 In. 990.00
Vase, Prairie Roses, Green Crystalline, Huckfield & Steen, 5 In. 1320.00
Vase, Red Matte Glaze, Ribbed Top, Flora Huckfield, 5 x 3 In. 275.00
Vase, Sheaves Of Wheat, Purple Brown Matte Glaze, 10 In. 1430.00
Vase, Speckled Turquoise Glaze, Flora Huckfield, 3 x 5 In. 412.00
Vase, Stylized Leaves, Shaded Blue Ground, Oval, 3 3/4 In. 220.00
Vase, Umber Bands, Beige, Celadon, Cylindrical, 5 In. 220.00
Vase, Viking Ship, Blue, Green, Julia Mattson, 5 x 4 3/4 In. 1650.00
Vase, Yellow Lanterns, Charcoal Blue, Round Mark, 5 1/2 In. 5500.00

NORTHWOOD Glass Company was founded by Harry Northwood, a glassmaker who worked for Hobbs, Brockunier and Company, La Belle Glass Company, and Buckeye Glass Company before founding his own firm. He opened one factory in Indiana, Pennsylvania, in 1896, and another in Wheeling, West Virginia, in 1902. Northwood closed when Mr. Northwood died in 1923. Many types of glass were made, including carnival, custard, goofus, and pressed. The underlined N mark was used on some pieces.

Beaded Drapes, Bowl, Blue, c.1905, 8 3/4 In. 65.00
Blue Opalescent, Vase, 8 In. 80.00
Blue Scroll & Acantha, Pitcher, White Opalescent Trim At Top, 4 3/4 In. 55.00
Button Panels, Bowl, Green, c.1902, 3 1/8 x 7 1/2 In. 75.00
Cherry & Cable, Tumbler, Gold Trim Rim, 1909, 4 Piece 300.00
Cherry Lattice, Tumbler 45.00
Chinese Coral, Console Set, c.1924, 8 3/4 In., Pair 300.00
Chrysanthemum Sprig, Compote, 5 In. 75.00
Chrysanthemum Spring, Tumbler, Starburst Bottom, 1899, 3 3/4 In., 5 Piece ... 200.00
Daisy & Plume, Bowl, Piecrust, 3 1/2 x 9 In. 90.00
Flower Decorated, Tumbler, Green, Enameled, Flared 15.00
Fluted Scrolls, Candy Dish, 7 1/2 In. 70.00
Fluted Scrolls, Table Set, Vaseline, 4 Piece 400.00
Grape & Cable, Bowl, Large 80.00
Grape & Cable, Compote 45.00
Grape & Cable, Fernery, Iridescent Custard 4000.00
Grape & Cable, Relish 20.00
Grape & Cable, Spooner 65.00
Hobnail, Creamer, Vaseline Opalescent, Scalloped Edge 100.00
Hobnail, Dish, Rectangular, 4 x 7 In. 45.00
Jackson, Bowl, 3 1/2 x 7 1/2 In. 134.00
Leaf Medallion, Cruet, Emerald Green, Gold 300.00
Louis XV, Pitcher 230.00
Nearcut, Goblet 50.00
Ribbed Pillar, Pitcher, Red Spatter, Star, Ruffled Edge, 9 In. 90.00
Royal Art, Basket, Thorn Twist Handle, 8 In. 100.00
Royal Oak, Sugar Shaker, Frosted Rubina 195.00
Shell & Wild Rose, Bowl, 3 x 7 In. 58.00
Sir Lancelot, Butter, Cover, Opalescent Rim 135.00
Vaseline Stretch, Compote, 4 3/4 In. 83.00
Waterlily & Cattails, Tumbler, C, 1905, 4 1/4 In. 45.00
Wide Panel, Epergne, Green Opalescent, 4-Lily 1050.00

NU-ART see Imperial category.

NUTCRACKERS of many types have been used through the centuries. At first the nutcracker was probably strong teeth or a hammer. But by the nineteenth century, many elaborate and ingenious types were made. Levers, screws, and hammer adaptations were the most popular. Because nutcrackers are still useful, they are still being made, some in the old styles.

Alligator, Iron, 13 1/4 In.	82.00
Brass, England, Early 18th Century	150.00
Crocodile, Wooden Base, R. Frisbies Patent, J. & E. Stevens	70.00
Dog, Tail Lever, Cast Iron, 11 In.	60.00
Dog, Wooden Base, Cast Iron, 11 In.	38.00
Elephant, Red & Black Paint, Cast Iron, 4 1/2 In.	275.00
Elf On Whale Tail, Articulated Mouth, Black Forest, c.1900, 10 1/2 In.	120.00
German Military Head, Beard, Wooden, Carved, Wiesheiden, 12 Aug., 1897	145.00
Pierced Thumbscrew, Brass, Late 17th Century, 3 3/4 In.	150.00
Pinocchio, Figural, Wooden, Box	150.00
Squirrel, Cast Iron, Patented May 28, 1879, 8 1/2 In.	415.00
Squirrel, Full-Bodied, Hinged Tail, Iron, American, Early 20th Century, 7 1/2 In.	690.00
Squirrel, Hinged Tail, Brown Paint, Green Step Base, Iron, 1900s, 7 x 6 In.	400.00
Squirrel, Hinged Tail, Walnut Base, Silver Paint, Iron, Late 1800s, 8 x 7 In.	460.00
Squirrel, Iron, Patented May 28, 1879, 8 1/2 In.	410.00

NYMPHENBURG, see Royal Nymphenburg.

OCCUPIED JAPAN was printed on pottery, porcelain, toys, and other goods made during the American occupation of Japan after World War II, from 1945 to 1952. Collectors now search for these pieces. The items were made for export.

Candy Dish, Flower Shape, Painted Flower In Center, 3 1/2 In.	24.00
Clock, Figural, Colonial Couple, Teapot, Flowers, Marked Ardalt, 11 1/2 x 10 In.	950.00
Cup & Saucer, Dragon, Blue & White	20.00
Figurine, Cherub, Shell-Shaped Basket On Back, 5 1/2 In.	17.00
Figurine, Clown, Seated On Pig, 5 x 4 3/8 In.	100.00
Figurine, Comic Frog, 4 In.	25.00
Figurine, Comic Frog, 4 In., Pair	125.00
Figurine, High Fashion Woman, Marked In Red, 5 3/4 x 2 1/2 In.	15.00
Figurine, Little Girl Fiddler & Duck, Marked, 2 3/4 x 2 1/4 In.	8.00
Figurine, Mud Man, 4 In.	18.00
Figurine, Oriental Woman, Flower Basket, Marked, 3 3/4 x 2 1/4 In.	12.50
Incense Burner, Figural, Oriental Man, Marked In Red, 4 1/4 x 2 1/2 In.	20.00
Lamp, Figural, Colonial Man & Woman, Bisque, Painted, No Shade, 10 In.	44.00
Match Holder, Hanging, Figural, Colonial Man & Woman, Baskets, Bisque	35.00
Mug, Indian Character	20.00
Necklace, Pearl, 3 Strands, Paper Label	35.00
Pin, Scotty, Double, Celluloid	10.00
Planter, Black Girl	20.00
Planter, Puppy, Black Horseshoe Mark	13.50
Planter, Woman, Holding Skirt	20.00
Salt & Pepper, Colonial Man & Woman, Holder, 3 x 3 In., 3 Piece	42.50
Sugar & Creamer, Tomato, Signed	25.00
Tape Measure, Pig, Blue, Celluloid	45.00
Teapot, Cottageware	65.00
Teapot, Lusterware, Dark Brown, Painted Flowers, 6 1/2 In.	22.00
Wall Hanger, Dutch Boy & Girl, Folk Costume, Pottery, 6 In., Pair	28.00
Wall Pocket, Log Cabin	15.00
Wall Pocket, Woman, Full Skirt, 6 In.	35.00

OFFICE TECHNOLOGY includes office equipment and related products, such as adding machines, calculators, and check-writing machines. Typewriters are in their own category in this book.

Arithmometer, Odhner No. 1, Russia, 1886 ....*Illus*	5060.00
Arithmometer, Seidel & Naumann, Dresden, Step-Drum, 1906 ....*Illus*	4427.00
Calculator, Wolverine, Tin, Red & Blue, Sliding Slots, No Pegs, 1930s	15.00

Office, Arithmometer, Seidel &
Naumann, Dresden, Step-Drum, 1906

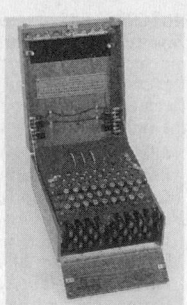

Office, Cipher
Machine, Enigma
Type A, 1940s

Office, Arithmometer, Odhner
No. 1, Russia, 1886

Cipher Machine, Enigma Type A, 1940s .... *Illus*	36000.00
Cipher Machine, Hagelin Cryptos, 1929	3670.00
Letterpress, Label, Thomas Lund, Letter Copying Machines, c.1775, 5 x 11 x 15 In.	4600.00
Paper Fastener, Hole Punch, Bump Paper Fastener Co., 1920-1940, 4 In.	20.00
Stamp Pad, Bell System, No. 00, Logo, Rectangular, 3 x 1 3/4 In.	2.00
Stamp Pad, Carter, No. 1, Rectangular, 4 1/4 x 2 3/4 In.	4.00
Stamp Pad, Eberhard Faber, No. 1, Black & Cream, Rectangular, 4 1/4 x 2 3/4 In.	5.00
Stamp Pad, Jiffy Mohaw, Rectangular, 5 1/4 x 3 1/4 In.	5.00
Stamp Pad, Sanford's, No. 0, Light Blue, Rectangular, 2 1/4 x 3 1/2 In.	3.00
Stamp Pad, Superior Solid Rubber, Rectangular, 2 1/2 x 3 1/2 In.	4.00
Stock Ticker, Edison	9655.00
Telegraph, Key Speedx	15.00

OHR pottery was made in Biloxi, Mississippi, from 1883 to 1918 by
George E. Ohr, a true eccentric. The pottery was made of very thin clay
that was twisted, folded, and dented into odd, graceful shapes. Some
pieces were lifelike models of hats, animal heads, or even a potato.
Others were decorated with folded clay *snakes*. Reproductions and
reworked pieces are appearing on the market. These have been
reglazed, or snakes and other embellishments have been added.

Ashtray, Pipe Knocker In Center, Moss Green, Brown, Marked, Biloxi, Miss., 2 x 4 In. ..	440.00
Bottle, Dark Brown Glaze, 14 3/4 x 7 3/4 In.	4125.00
Bowl, Asymmetrically Crimped, Brown, Green Mirrored, Amber Glaze, 3 3/4 x 7 1/4 In. .	1650.00
Bowl, Bisque, Pinched & Folded, Dendrite Pattern, Script Mark, 5 x 7 1/2 In.	5500.00
Bowl, Copper Dust Glaze, Raised Finial, Signed, 4 1/2 In.	550.00
Bowl, Folded Sides, Mottled Glazed Interior, Burgundy Exterior, 2 7/8 In.	6620.00
Bowl, Mirror Black Speckle Glaze, Dimples & Pinched, 4-Lobe Opening, 3 x 4 1/2 In. ...	3850.00
Bowl, Purple & Green Glaze, Dimpled, Pinched 3 Sides, Stamped, 3 x 4 1/4 In.	5500.00
Chamberstick, Bisque, Twisted Shaft, G.E. Ohr In Script, 4 3/4 In.	1265.00
Chamberstick, Green, Brown Glaze, Pinched Handle, Signed, 3 In.	460.00
Chamberstick, Gunmetal Glaze, Dimpled, Bulbous, Incised, 5 x 3 3/4 In.	1650.00
Cup, Ribbed Body, Exterior Mirror Finish, Ocher Interior, Signed, 3 1/3 In.	385.00
Eggcup, Sheer Teal Green Speckled Glaze, Serrated Edge, 1 1/4 x 1 3/4 In.	495.00
Inkwell, Cabin Shape, Glossy Green Glaze, Stamped, 3 x 4 1/2 In.	2310.00
Inkwell, Mountain Lion Head, Shimmering Green Glaze, Stamped, 3 1/2 x 4 1/2 In.	1320.00
Inkwell, Ocher, Gunmetal Glaze, Folded Rim, 1 1/2 x 4 In.	467.00
Jug, Cadogan, Embossed Twig Design, Green & Umber Glossy Glaze, 6 1/4 x 4 1/4 In. ..	330.00
Mug, Applied Snake, Gunmetal Brown Mottled Glaze, Ribbed Top, Signed, 5 In.	3575.00
Mug, Black, Orange, Green, Red, Brown Glaze, Handle, 3 5/8 In.	1045.00
Mug, Gunmetal Glaze, Fluted Body, Bulbous, Signed, 4 3/4 x 5 1/2 In.	360.00
Mug, Olive Green Glaze, Pierced Rim, Handle, Signed, 3 1/2 In.	270.00
Mug, Puzzle, Mottled Gunmetal & Green Glaze, 3 1/2 x 5 1/4 In.	1320.00
Mug, Stylized Rabbit Form Handle, Brown Glaze, Reticulated Rim, 3 1/2 In.	1150.00
Palette, Green Luster Glaze, Marked G.E. Ohr, 2 x 6 1/2 x 5 1/2 In.	4125.00
Pitcher, Cobalt Blue Glaze, 4 1/2 x 4 3/4 In.	10450.00
Pitcher, Cobalt Blue Mottled Glaze, Pinched & Cutout Handle, 4 x 5 1/2 In.	1980.00
Pitcher, Cobalt, Gunmetal Exterior, Green, Red Interior, 2 1/2 x 8 In.	7700.00
Pitcher, Marbleized Clay, Pinched, 3 3/4 x 5 In.	6050.00

Pitcher, Scalloped Rim, Pink Exterior Glaze, Charcoal Interior, 4 1/2 In. 6900.00
Pitcher, Sponged Umber & Green Bands, Clear Glaze, Stamped, 8 3/4 x 4 In. 5500.00
Teapot, Chartreuse Volcanic Glaze, 6 x 8 1/2 In. 13200.00
Teapot, Cover, Brown, Black, Green, Orange Glaze, Handle, 3 7/8 x 6 1/2 In. 7425.00
Teapot, Cover, Green Mirrored Glaze, Beige Clay, 4 x 7 1/2 In. 14300.00
Teapot, Incised Bands, Speckled Brown Glaze, Stamped Mark, 4 1/4 x 7 1/4 In. 825.00
Vase, Asymmetrical, Deeply Folded & Pinched Rim, Gunmetal Black Glaze, 3 3/4 In. . . . 1980.00
Vase, Bisque, 4 Indentations, Signed, 5 1/2 In. 660.00
Vase, Bisque, Folded & Dimpled, Script Mark, 5 1/2 x 4 In. 1320.00
Vase, Bisque, Swirling Brown & Terra-Cotta Clay, Signed, 5 1/2 In. 605.00
Vase, Bisque, Whimsical Face, Folded Rim, Signed, 5 x 5 3/4 In. 7150.00
Vase, Black Glaze, Crimped Rim, Cylindrical, Signed, 4 3/4 In. 1380.00
Vase, Bright Pink, Blue, Green Sponge Glaze, 2 1/2 x 4 1/2 In. 4675.00
Vase, Brown Glaze, Red Thumbprint Base, Circular, 2 1/2 In. 1150.00
Vase, Brown, Gray Sponge Matte Glaze, Cobalt Band At Neck, 5 x 4 1/2 In. 6050.00
Vase, Brown, Green Glaze, Red Spots, 4 1/4 x 6 1/2 In. 12100.00
Vase, Bulbous, Gunmetal Glaze, Script Signature, 7 In. 550.00
Vase, Cabinet, Gray, Green Glaze, Twisted Rim, 2 x 3 In. 2310.00
Vase, Charcoal, Light Green Speckled Glaze, Light Red Clay, 5 In. 2310.00
Vase, Cobalt Glossy Glaze, Cupped Rim, Twisted Body, 3 1/2 x 3 3/4 In. 3575.00
Vase, Cobalt, Red, Green Sponged Glaze, Ear Handles, 1896, 4 x 6 In. 3300.00
Vase, Crimped Form, Cutout Handle, Matte To High Glaze, Signed, 4 In. 4125.00
Vase, Dark Green Glaze, Bulbous, Folded Rim, Stamped, 4 x 2 3/4 In. 1650.00
Vase, Double Gourd Form, Tortured Top, High Glaze, Signed, 9 1/2 In. 495.00
Vase, Doughnut Shape, Folded Sides, Palette, Poem On Base, Biloxi Welcome, 2 x 7 In. . . . 990.00
Vase, Flared Rim, Mottled Dark Blue & Gray Glaze, Stamped Mark, 4 x 2 In. 770.00
Vase, Folded Rim, Green & Amber Speckled Semimatte Glaze, Footed, 3 3/4 x 2 1/2 In. . . 1870.00
Vase, Glossy Raspberry Glaze, Deep In-Body Twist, Stamped Mark, 5 1/2 x 3 1/4 In. 6600.00
Vase, Green & Brown Speckled Mirrored Glaze, Labial Rim, Pinched Side, 4 1/2 In. 3850.00
Vase, Green & Gunmetal Mottled Glaze, Bottle Shape, Script Mark, 7 x 4 In. 2970.00
Vase, Green Flecked Glaze, Gourd Form, c.1895, 3 3/4 In. 4370.00
Vase, Gunmetal Glaze, Bulbous, Cupped Rim, In-Body Twist, 5 x 2 1/4 In. 1540.00
Vase, Gunmetal, Green & Raspberry Glaze, Asymetrical Ribbon Handles, 4 x 5 In. 7700.00
Vase, Gunmetal, Raspberry & Green Frothy Glaze, Bottle Shape, Squat Base, 4 In. 3300.00
Vase, Leathery Black Glaze, Tapering, Bulbous Base, G.E. Ohr In Script, 4 In. 688.00
Vase, Marbleized Clay, 1907, 4 x 7 In. 2530.00
Vase, Mirrored Brown Mottled Glaze, Ruffled, Stamped, 6 1/4 x 5 3/4 In. 6600.00
Vase, Mirrored Gunmetal Glaze, Flared, Asymmetrical Ruffled Neck, Squat Base, 4 In. . . 2640.00
Vase, Mottled Gunmetal & Green Matte Glaze, Irregular Dimples, Oval, 4 3/4 In. 1870.00
Vase, Mottled Red, Green, Blue & Amber Glaze, Pinched & Folded Rim, 6 1/2 In. 5225.00
Vase, Orange, White Swirlware Design, Signed, 1900, 4 1/4 In. 275.00
Vase, Pink & Green Mottled Glaze, Bottle Shape, Ruffled, Stamped, JHP, 7 x 3 1/4 In. . . . 4400.00
Vase, Pink Volcanic Glaze, Green, Black, White Sponge Glaze, Spherical, 5 x 5 In. 5500.00
Vase, Purple & Green Leathery Matte Glaze, 5 1/2 In. 6050.00
Vase, Red, Gunmetal Sponge Glaze, 3 3/4 x 3 3/4 In. 1650.00
Vase, Ribbed Form, Handle, Green & Brown High Glaze, Signed, 7 In. 3850.00
Vase, Speckled Olive Green & Orange Glaze, In-Body Twist, Folded Rim, Bulbous, 4 In. . . 4675.00
Vase, Speckled Olive Green Glaze, Triangular 3-Lobed Top, Bulbous, 4 1/2 x 3 In. 2420.00
Vase, Speckled Olive Green Matte Glaze, Marked, Biloxi, Miss., 4 1/4 x 3 1/4 In. 660.00
Vase, Squat, Pink, Purple, Red, Green Sponge Glaze, 1899, 2 3/4 x 3 3/4 In. 1870.00
Vase, Tiger-Eye, Brown Flambe Glaze, Row Of Dimples, 4 3/4 x 4 In. 3850.00
Vase, Tortured Waist & Top, Green & Purple High Glaze, Signed, 5 In. 990.00
Vase, Twist Design, Curdled Yellow Glaze, Matte Cobalt Blue, Signed, 5 x 4 In. 5500.00

OLD IVORY china was made by the Ohme Porcelain Works in Silesia,
Germany, a factory working from 1882 to 1928. The china had an
ivory matte background and was usually decorated with flowers or
fruit. Dinner sets, fish sets, mustache cups, and souvenir pieces were
also made. Pieces were marked with a crown, the cipher OH, and the
word *Silesia*. Some pieces are also marked with the words *Old Ivory*.
The pattern numbers appear on the base of many pieces.

OLDIVORY
84

Biscuit Jar, Chantilly, Pink, Yellow Roses, Gold, Handles, Signed 145.00
Bowl, Clarion, No. 11, 10 In. 73.00

Cup & Saucer, Elysee, No. 4	50.00
Dish, No. 29, Oval, 6 3/4 x 4 3/4 In.	55.00
Plate, 6 1/2 In.	48.00
Sugar & Creamer, No. 16, Regal	140.00

OLD PARIS, see Paris category.

OLD SLEEPY EYE, see Sleepy Eye category.

OLYMPIC, see Souvenir category.

ONION PATTERN, originally named *bulb pattern,* is a white ware decorated with cobalt blue or pink. Although it is commonly associated with Meissen, other companies made the pattern in the late nineteenth and the twentieth centuries. A rare type is called *red bud* because there are added red accents on the blue-and-white dishes.

Barrel, Spice, Cloves	45.00
Barrel, Spice, Ginger	45.00
Bowl, Meissen, 13 3/4 In.	200.00
Canister Set, Dutch Scene, Stamped C.A.W. Germany, Inge, 15 Piece	210.00
Platter, Meissen, 13 3/4 In.	145.00
Platter, Meissen, 15 3/8 x 11 1/4 In.	75.00
Platter, Meissen, 19 In.	405.00
Platter, Oval, Scalloped, Meissen, 20th Century, 17 1/4 In.	120.00
Platter, Scalloped Rim, Blue, White, Meissen, 19th Century, 21 In.	495.00
Rolling Pin, Blue	145.00
Soup Ladle, Blue	90.00
Tazza, Meissen, 13 In.	345.00
Tureen, Cover, Rectangular, Meissen, 11 1/4 In.	175.00 to 230.00

OPALESCENT GLASS is translucent glass that has the tones of the opal gemstone. It originated in England in the 1870s and is often found in pressed glassware made in Victorian times. Opalescent glass was first made in America in 1897 at the Northwood glassworks in Indiana, Pennsylvania. Some dealers use the terms *opaline* and *opalescent* for any of these translucent wares. More opalescent pieces may be listed in Hobnail, Northwood, Pressed Glass, and other glass categories.

Alaska, Berry Bowl, White	225.00
Alaska, Butter, Cover, Vaseline	335.00
Alaska, Creamer, Blue	85.00
Alaska, Saltshaker, Blue	75.00
Alaska, Sauce, Blue	50.00 to 65.00
Alaska, Sauce, White	60.00
Alaska, Spooner, Blue	75.00 to 85.00
Alaska, Spooner, White	85.00
Alaska, Sugar, Cover, Blue	225.00
Alaska, Sugar, Cover, Vaseline	250.00
Alaska, Tumbler, Blue	150.00
Beatty Rib, Cracker Jar, Cover, Blue	495.00
Bubble Lattice, Sugar Shaker, Blue	175.00
Chippendale, Dish, Ice Cream, Vaseline, 6 In.	65.00
Christmas Snowflake, Pitcher, Ribbed, Cranberry	1995.00
Coinspot, Pitcher, 8 1/2 In.	150.00
Coinspot & Swirl, Syrup, Blue, 6 1/2 In.	120.00
Criss-Cross, Berry Set, Cranberry, 5 Piece	395.00
Daisy & Fern, Cruet, Cranberry	795.00
Daisy & Fern, Pitcher Set, Cranberry, 3 Piece	250.00
Daisy & Fern, Tumbler, Blue	30.00
Daisy & Fern, Tumbler, Cranberry	110.00
Diamond Spearhead, Toothpick, Vaseline	40.00
Drapery, Tumbler, Blue	35.00
Everglades, Pitcher, Water, Blue	495.00
Everglades, Spooner, Blue, Gold Trim	375.00
Fern, Sugar Shaker, Cranberry	695.00
Fluted Scroll, Bowl, Tricornered, Blue	65.00

Fluted Scroll, Salt & Pepper, White 125.00
Hilltop Vines, Compote, Jelly, White 35.00
Hobnail, Sugar & Creamer, Vaseline 70.00
Honeycomb, Sugar Shaker, Cranberry 165.00
Intaglio, Compote, Jelly, Blue ....35.00 to 65.00
Jewel & Flower, Butter, Cover, Blue 495.00
Lattice Medallions, Sugar Shaker, Vaseline 375.00
Maple Leaf, Jelly, Blue 40.00
Pearl Flowers, Bowl, Green, Footed, 9 1/2 In. 45.00
Regal, Butter, Cover, Green 375.00
Regal, Sugar, Green 95.00
Ribbed Opal Lattice, Berry Set, Cranberry 135.00
Scroll With Acanthus, Tumbler, Blue 75.00
Seaweed, Pitcher, Square Mouth, Cranberry, 8 3/8 In. 950.00
Seaweed, Water Set, Blue, 7 Piece 895.00
Stripe, Tumbler, Cranberry 85.00
Swirl, Pitcher, Clear Handle, 9 1/4 In. 690.00
Swirl, Sugar Shaker, Blue ....130.00 to 200.00
Toothpicks are listed in the Toothpick category.

OPALINE, or opal glass, was made in white, green, and other colors. The glass had a matte surface and a lack of transparency. It was often gilded or painted. It was a popular mid-nineteenth-century European glassware.

Box, Dresser, Green, 8 Sides, Brass Mounted, 9 x 5 1/2 x 3 In. 550.00
Box, Dresser, Green, 8 Sides, Brass Mounted, Hinged Cover, 2 3/4 x 4 3/8 In. 525.00
Perfume Bottle, Reverse Painted Medallion, Green, Floral & Foliate Mounts, 8 In. 345.00
Tazza, Ormolu Mount, Openwork Base, Acanthus, Flowers, France, 19th Century, 5 In. .. 316.00
Vase, Bud, White, Blue Foot, Enameled Church & Flowers, France, 8 In. 73.00
Vase, Flattened Spherical Form, Cherubs In Clouds On Neck, Gilt, 8 1/2 In. 345.00
Vase, Ribbed Gourd Form, Pale Amber Surface, Pale Pink Top, Enamel, 8 In. 690.00
Vase, White, Embossed Floral, Handles, Trim, 12 In. 150.00

OPERA GLASSES are needed because the stage is a long way from some of the seats at a play or an opera. Mother-of-pearl was a popular decoration on many French glasses.

A.M. Wentworth, Mother-Of-Pearl Paneled Body, c.1890 .... 115.00
Chevalier, Mother-Of-Pearl, Pewter Finish, Hunting Scene, Pair 201.00
Lemaire, Mother-Of-Pearl, Brass, Fitted Case, Paris, Early 20th Century, 2 3/4 In. 88.00
Lemaire, Mother-Of-Pearl, Brass, Gold, Original Fitted Case, Paris, Pair 90.00
Lemaire, Mother-Of-Pearl, Brass, Leather Case, Marked, Paris, 1900, 3 1/2 In. 137.00
Lemaire, Mother-Of-Pearl, Telescoping Handle 217.00
Mother-Of-Pearl, Brass, France, Pair 85.00
Mother-Of-Pearl, Brass, Gold, Handle, Fitted Case, France, 4 1/2 In. 98.00
Mother-Of-Pearl, Teal Blue Guilloche Enamel, Gold 345.00

ORPHAN ANNIE first appeared in the comics in 1924. The redheaded girl and her friends have been on the radio and are still on the comic pages. A Broadway musical show and a movie in the 1980s made Annie popular again and many toys, dishes, and other memorabilia are being made.

Badge, Radio Orphan Annie's Secret Society, Bronze, 1934, 1 In. 31.00
Bank ....*Illus* 370.00
Book, Little Orphan Annie In The Circus, Hard Cover, 1937 .... 75.00
Coloring Book, Colored, Signed Harold Gray, 1930 .... 55.00
Doll, Annie, Composition, Jointed, Arms, Cloth Legs, 14 In. ....*Illus* 231.00
Doll, Annie, Fabric Clothes, World Of Annie, Knickerbocker, On Card, 1982, 6 In. 27.00
Doll, Daddy Warbucks, World Of Annie, Knickerbocker, On Card, 1982, 6 In. 25.00
Foto Reel, Original Film, c.1938 .... 110.00
Game, Annie, The Movie Game, Board, Parker Bros., 1981 .... 20.00
Game, Treasure Hunt, Ovaltine Premium, 1933, 11 x 16 1/2 In. 45.00
Lamp, Annie & Dog, Metal & Plastic 49.00
Map, Simmons Corners, Radio, Mailer, 1937, 23 1/2 x 19 In. 37.00

Orphan Annie, Bank

Orphan Annie, Doll, Annie,
Composition, Jointed, Arms,
Cloth Legs, 14 In.

Marble, Sandy Picture, 11/16 In.	120.00
Mug, Orphan Annie With Mug Of Ovaltine, 1932	75.00
Paper Dolls, Daddy Warbucks, Annie, Sandy, Hinges, In Envelope, 1944	48.00
Pin, Orphan Annie Loves Red Cross Macaroni, Celluloid, 1 1/4 In.	50.00
Salt & Pepper, Annie & Sandy	38.00
Shake-Up Mug, Ovaltine, Teal, Red Cap, Beetleware Plastic, 1940	50.00
Sheet Music, Ovaltine, 1931	65.00
Sundial Compass	85.00
Toy, Sandy Chases Ball, Windup, 1930s	350.00

ORREFORS Glassworks, located in the Swedish province of Smaaland, was established in 1898. The company is still making glass for use on the table or as decorations. There is renewed interest in the glass made in the modern styles of the 1940s and 1950s. Most vases and decorative pieces are signed with the etched name.

Orrefors

Bowl, Allover Controlled Bubbles, Signed, 4 x 6 In.	550.00
Bowl, Ariel, Celadon Stripes, Controlled Bubbles, Ohrstrom, No. 1281E, 3 x 4 1/2 In.	187.00
Bowl, Ariel, Cobalt Yellow, Spaced Vertical Linear Air Inclusions, E. Ohrstrom, 5 In.	250.00
Bowl, Ariel, Garnet Stripes, Submerged Bubbles, Ohrstrom, No. 1711E, 1 1/2 x 8 In.	165.00
Bowl, Blue & White Swirls, Corseted, 7 1/4 x 3 1/4 In.	88.00
Bowl, Checkered, Triangular, Signed, 5 1/2 x 6 1/2 In.	1430.00
Bowl, Cherub, Satin, Oval, 9 In., Pair	330.00
Bowl, Fish Graal, Fish & Seaweed, Umber, Celadon, Edward Hald, 1956, 1 3/4 x 7 In.	143.00
Bowl, Graal, Blue, Loops, Blue Interior, Disk Foot, Edvard Hald, 2 1/4 x 6 In.	1380.00
Bowl, Mottled Cobalt, Garnet, Clear, Sven Palmquist, No. 4122-530, 3 1/2 x 7 In.	132.00
Bowl, Ravenna, Blue Windows, 3 1/2 x 2 In.	308.00
Bowl, Satin Bands, 3 x 11 In.	132.00
Bowl, Swirl, Amethyst, Footed, Oval, 9 1/4 x 3 1/4 In.	330.00
Candlestick, Flower Form, 1 1/8 In., Pair	86.00
Vase, Cobalt Blue, Clear Cased, Etched, 7 In.	230.00
Vase, Fish Graal, Fish Among Seaweed, Deep Green, Edvard Hald, 1940, 4 3/4 In.	747.00
Vase, Fish, Internal Swimming Fish, Aquatic Plants, Signed, c.1950, 5 In.	488.00
Vase, Green Interior, 4-Sided Sommerso, Signed, 10 In.	220.00
Vase, Indian Chief, Standing, Headdress, Engraved, Textured Ground, Oval, 1937, 13 In.	2300.00
Vase, Kraka, Blue, Green Internal Swags, Teardrop, Sven Palmquist, 1955, 5 In.	715.00
Vase, Nude Dancer, Engraved, Vicke Lindstrand, c.1933, 8 1/2 In.	1430.00
Vase, Oriental Princess, Profile, Florals, Dove Within Frame, 1937, 8 In.	4025.00
Vase, Pearl Divers, Nude Men, Engraved, 1932, 8 In.	4025.00
Vase, Shark Killer, Diving Nude Man, Knife, Engraved, Vicke Lindstrand, 12 1/2 In.	9200.00
Vase, Tulpenglazer, Goblet Shape, Amber Interior, Nils Landberg, c.1958, 20 In.	2640.00
Vase, Underwater Scene, Graal, Lobster & Crab, Edvin Hald, 1940, 6 1/2 x 7 In.	1200.00
Vase, Young Girl Looking At Moon, Engraved, Signed, Orrefors 2769, 6 1/2 In.	67.00

OTT & BREWER Company operated the Etruria Pottery at Trenton, New Jersey, from 1863 to 1893. They started making belleek in 1882. The firm used a variety of marks that incorporated the initials *O & B.*

Biscuit Jar, Acorn, Flow Blue On White, Gilt, 2 Handles, Stamp, 8 In	132.00

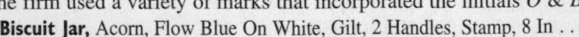

Plate, Hummingbird Flying Over Orchid, Square, 3 x 8 In. 990.00
Vase, Duck Flying Over Dandelions, Coral Ground, Gold, 10 1/4 x 7 In. 20900.00

OVERBECK pottery was made by four sisters named Overbeck at a pottery in Cambridge City, Indiana. They started in 1911. They made all types of vases, each one-of-a-kind. Small, hand-modeled figurines are the most popular pieces with today's collectors. The factory continued until 1955, when the last of the four sisters died.

Bowl, High Purple Glaze, Tan Glaze Interior, 6 1/4 x 2 1/2 In. 4000.00
Figurine, Black-Capped Chickadee 525.00
Figurine, Cat, Stalking, Yellow, Brown & Black Striped, 5 In. 1300.00
Figurine, Choir Director, 4 In. 175.00
Figurine, Colonial Woman, Pink & Blue Striped Dress, Incised OBK, 5 In. 341.00
Figurine, Dog, Standing, Geometric Bull's-Eye Design, 3 x 3 3/7 In. . . . . .1000.00 to 1550.00
Figurine, Farmer's Wife, Holding Vegetables Both Hands, 4 In. 900.00
Figurine, Farmer, Holding Apple In 1 Hand, Ears Of Corn Other, 4 1/2 In. 850.00
Figurine, Fisherman With Fish, 5 1/8 In. 1450.00
Figurine, Girl, Chased By Goose, 4 1/2 In. 4000.00
Figurine, Girl, Seated On Pottery Rug 3500.00
Figurine, Lady In 19th Century Dress, Pink, Purple, White Glazes, OBK, 4 In. 319.00
Figurine, Lady, Wearing Period Gown, Carrying Parasol, 4 In. 495.00
Figurine, Man, Playing Guitar, 4 In. 450.00
Figurine, Robin, Feeding 4 Babies In Nest, Reglued Heads, 3 1/2 x 5 1/4 In. 1450.00
Figurine, Singer, White Shirt, Blue Pants, Holding Songbook, 3 7/8 In. 550.00
Figurine, Skunk, 3 In. 400.00
Figurine, Southern Belle, 4 In. . . . . .400.00 to 450.00
Figurine, Violin Player, Yellow & White Clothes, 4 1/4 In. 500.00
Figurine, Winged Insect, 1 3/8 In. 450.00
Vase, Aqua Green, High Gloss, 2 Handles, 1916 . . . . 1100.00
Vase, Bud, Young Woman, Matte Glaze, Clay Body, E. & M.F. Overbeck, 2 5/8 In. 770.00
Vase, Cutback, 15 Birds In 3 Panels, Dull, Signed, 5 1/2 In. 1210.00
Vase, Floral Design, Cream, Light Green, Olive, 6 In. 3575.00
Vase, Tan Glaze, Incised Flower Over Leaves Pattern, E & H, 6 1/4 x 7 1/2 In. 3300.00

OWENS Pottery was made in Zanesville, Ohio, from 1891 to 1928. The first art pottery was made after 1896. Utopian Ware, Cyrano, Navarre, Feroza, and Henri Deux were made. Pieces were usually marked with a form of the name *Owens*. About 1907, the firm began to make tile and discontinued the art pottery wares.

Candlestick, Green, Signed, 11 In. 495.00
Cruet, Cream & Gray, 4 3/4 In. 165.00
Humidor, Lid, Incised & Painted Designs, Glazed Interior, 4 3/8 In. 330.00
Jardiniere, Virginia Creeper, 8 7/8 In. 550.00
Lamp Vase, Lasa, Scene, John Lessell, 14 1/4 In. 1760.00
Tankard, Spray Of Daisies, Glossy Glaze, Flaring Spout, Signed, 12 1/2 In. 115.00
Vase, Aborigine, Squat, Beige, Black, Brown Ground, Incised, 5 1/2 x 6 In. 138.00

Owens, Vase, Utopian, Sioux Indian,
Jack Red Cloud, Anna F. Best, 17 In.

Vase, Alpine, Cherries, Matte Glaze, Slip Decorated, Stamped, 10 x 5 1/4 In. 770.00
Vase, Art Nouveau Floral, 9 7/8 In. 1650.00
Vase, Chief White Man, Standard Glaze, 10 3/4 In. 980.00
Vase, Clover Blossoms, Leaves, Dark Brown Ground, Cylindrical, 12 In. 66.00
Vase, Clover Design, Harry Larzelere, 13 5/8 In. 330.00
Vase, Electroplated Copper Deposit, Handles, 4 5/8 In. 660.00
Vase, Flowers, Art Nouveau, 11 7/8 In. 660.00
Vase, Grapes, Charles Chilcote, 12 1/2 In. 550.00
Vase, Greek Key, Green Matte Smooth Glaze, Flared Rim, 4 Buttressed Feet, 9 In. 330.00
Vase, Leaves, Embossed, Rose Matte Glaze, Tear Shape, 6 1/2 x 4 1/4 .... 330.00
Vase, Lotus, Red & Purple Berries, Shaded Gray Ground, 14 x 5 1/4 In. 440.00
Vase, Tulips, Leaves, Peach, Cream, Blue, Signed, 7 In. 440.00
Vase, Twisted, Apple Blossoms, Orange & Green Ground, Stamped, 4 1/2 In. 165.00
Vase, Utopian, Bottle Shaped, Wild Roses, Shaded Brown To Blue Ground, 8 In. 352.00
Vase, Utopian, Clover Blossoms, Leaves, Brown & Orange Ground, Stamped, 15 In. 135.00
Vase, Utopian, Coralene, Opalescent, Twisted, Gooseberries, Textured Ground, 5 x 4 In. ... 137.00
Vase, Utopian, Pansies, Green & Gold Coralene Ground, 4 Sides, 5 3/4 x 2 1/4 In. 193.00
Vase, Utopian, Sioux Indian, Jack Red Cloud, Anna F. Best, 17 In. ....*Illus* 5040.00
Vase, Utopian, Wild Roses, Shaded Brown Ground, Die Stamped, 13 In. 352.00

OYSTER PLATES were popular from the 1880s. Each course at dinner was served in a special dish. The oyster plate had indentations shaped like oysters. Usually six oysters were held on a plate. There is no greater value to a plate with more oysters, although that myth continues to haunt antiques dealers. There are other plates for shellfish, including cockle plates and whelk plates. The appropriately shaped indentations are part of the design of these dishes.

5 Wells, Haviland, Set Of 4 ....*Illus* 412.00
6 Wells, Groups Of Shells & Seaweed, Signed, 1863, 9 1/2 In. 3450.00
6 Wells, Star Shape, Haviland, Set Of 8 ....*Illus* 770.00
Allover Multicolor, Ships In Wells, 8 1/2 In. 395.00
Animals In Wells, Fan Shape, 9 1/2 In. 550.00
Blue Ground, Lattice, Pink & Brown, 9 5/8 In. 92.00
Brown, Gilt, Porcelain, Continental, 6 Piece 403.00
Brown, Porcelain, Continental, 6 Piece 575.00
Brown, Yellow Ground, Porcelain, Continental, 8 3/8 In. 86.00
Crescent Shape, Pink, Green Seaweed, Brown Ground, 10 In. 550.00
Floral, Sprays, Gilt Border, Porcelain, Continental, 8 1/2 In., 5 Piece 403.00
Gilt, Scalloped Rim, Porcelain, Continental, 8 1/4 In., 4 Piece 345.00
Leaf Form, Leaf-Form Sections, Earthenware, Bohemia, 10 In. 115.00
Majolica, Cream, Violet & Cobalt Center, 10 In. 575.00
Multicolored Design, C. Tielsch & Co., 9 In., 10 Piece 975.00
Rose & Ribbon Bow, 6 Piece 304.00
Scalloped Shape, Rococo Scroll Handle, Painted Floral Swags, KPM, 10 In. 875.00
Thistle, Gilt Rim, 3 Plates Yellow, 1 Purple, Limoges, 9 In., 4 Piece 451.00
Trellis Work Of Foliage Border, 6 Blue, 6 Pink, 20th Century, 10 In., 12 Piece 920.00
Turquoise, Minton 450.00

Oyster Plate,
5 Wells, Haviland,
Set Of 4

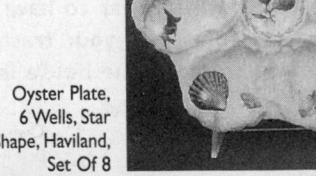

Oyster Plate,
6 Wells, Star
Shape, Haviland,
Set Of 8

PADEN CITY Glass Manufacturing Company was established in 1916 at Paden City, West Virginia. The company made more than seventy different colors of glass. The firm closed in 1951.

Ardith, Bowl, Yellow, Footed, 11 In.	60.00
Ardith, Cake Plate, Yellow, Footed, 11 In.	145.00
Ardith, Gravy Boat, Green	80.00
Black Forest, Bowl, Pink, Rolled Rim, 11 3/4 In.	250.00
Black Forest, Cake Stand, Low, Pink	110.00
Black Forest, Cup, Red	120.00
Black Forest, Sugar & Creamer	100.00
Black Forest, Tray, Center Handle, Green	80.00
Crow's Foot, Compote, Cobalt, 6 1/2 In.	75.00
Crow's Foot, Cup & Saucer, Red	15.00
Crow's Foot, Gravy Boat	70.00
Crow's Foot, Tumbler	100.00
Crow's Foot, Vase, Red, Flared, 8 In.	150.00
Cupid, Bowl, Pink, Rolled Rim, 11 In.	400.00
Cupid, Candlestick, Pink	175.00
Cupid, Compote, Pink	325.00
Cupid, Tray, Oval, Pink	375.00
Cupid, Tumbler, Iced Tea, Green	325.00
Figurine, Bird, Blue, 5 In.	165.00
Figurine, Chanticleer, Blue, Frosted, 9 1/2 In.	175.00
Figurine, Chinese Pheasant, Blue, 13 3/4 In.	125.00 to 175.00
Figurine, Dragon Swan, Blue, 9 3/4 In.	750.00
Figurine, Goose, Blue, 5 In.	165.00
Figurine, Pheasant, Head Turned, Blue, 12 In.	175.00
Figurine, Rooster, Head Down, Blue, 8 3/4 In.	225.00
Gazebo, Cake Salver	125.00
Gazebo, Plate, 11 In.	50.00
Gazebo, Relish, 3 Sections	25.00
Party, Tumbler, Soda, Green, 6 3/4 In.	18.00
Peacock & Wild Rose, Candlestick, Pink, 5 In., Pair	80.00
Peacock & Wild Rose, Console, Pink, 14 In.	195.00
Peacock & Wild Rose, Vase, Regina, Black, 6 1/2 In.	150.00
Penny, Sherbet, Red	8.00
Pouter Pigeon, Bookends	150.00 to 175.00
Rena, Dish, Banana Split, Green	20.00
Roosters, Bookends, Head Down	140.00

PAINTINGS listed in this book are not works by major artists but rather decorative paintings on ivory, board, or glass that would be of interest to the average collector. Watercolors on paper are listed under Picture. To learn the value of an oil painting by a listed artist you must contact an expert in that area.

Acrylic On Canvas, Autumn Nests, Giuliano Crivelli, 1983, 27 1/4 x 31 1/2 In.	230.00
Acrylic On Masonite, Houses By A River, Van Crews Jr., 1967, 13 3/4 x 27 1/2 In.	200.00
Ink On Paper, 2 Sages Conversing In Landscape, 19th Century, 57 x 15 3/4 In.	200.00
Oil On Board, Farmstead At Sunset, River, Frame, 1890, 7 x 10 1/4 In.	200.00
Oil On Board, Forest Fire, Frame, 12 x 18 In.	465.00
Oil On Board, Haystack Landscape, Ornate Gold Frame, 18 x 24 In.	165.00
Oil On Board, Hunter, Dogs With Fowl, Frame, 1870, 12 1/8 x 16 3/4 In.	355.00
Oil On Board, Landscape With Sunset, W. Rouzee, Frame, 1884, 5 1/4 x 7 1/4 In.	975.00
Oil On Board, Landscape, 2 Men In Boat, Framed, 13 1/4 x 9 1/4 In.	60.00
Oil On Board, Landscape, America, Frame, 19th Century, 19 x 13 In.	155.00
Oil On Board, Landscape, Cows Near Stream, Frame, Thos. B. Craig, '79, 9 x 17 In.	1320.00
Oil On Board, Landscape, Farm, Ben Marcune, 24 x 36 In.	220.00
Oil On Board, Landscape, Mountain Scene, Rustic, Frame, 1920, 29 1/4 x 47 1/2 In.	1495.00
Oil On Board, Mother Cow & Calf, Frame, 12 1/2 x 9 1/4 In.	140.00
Oil On Board, Mountain Scene, Man, Boy, Frame, 19th Century, 5 3/8 x 7 3/8 In.	175.00
Oil On Board, Mountains & Lake Scene, Harry Farlow, 19 x 23 1/2 In.	165.00
Oil On Board, Mountains, Tree Foreground, Frame, 15 1/2 x 13 1/2 In.	330.00
Oil On Board, New England Lighthouse, H.F. Simpson, 11 1/2 x 15 1/2 In.	130.00

Oil On Board, Northeast Woodlands Scene, Frame, 13 1/8 x 6 7/8 In., Pair 200.00
Oil On Board, Old Witch Hazel Mill & Brook, July 1952, I.R. Doerfler, 15 x 19 In. 110.00
Oil On Board, Over Photograph, Portrait, Noah Zane, Frame, 16 x 14 In. 358.00
Oil On Board, Pasture With Sheep, Gilt Frame, 22 3/4 x 16 3/4 In. 245.00
Oil On Board, Ruwenzori Mountains, Africa, E.M.C. Hawkins, 22 1/4 x 30 In. 290.00
Oil On Board, Seacoast, E. Taylor Baker, Frame, 4 1/2 x 9 In. 1540.00
Oil On Board, Ships In Harbor, C. Conner, Frame, 5 x 11 In. 825.00
Oil On Board, Still Life, Apples, Grapes, Pear, Frame, 9 x 12 In. 550.00
Oil On Board, Villagers Watching Cock Fight, M.G. Carrera, 10 5/8 x 14 5/8 In. 345.00
Oil On Board, White Hills, Walter E. Baum, Ornate Frame, 3 x 6 In. 1870.00
Oil On Board, Winter Children, Sledding, Skating, Ornate Frame, 1881, 11 x 17 In. 100.00
Oil On Board, Woman Bust, European Clothes, 19th Century, 24 1/4 x 18 1/4 In. 505.00
Oil On Canvas, 19th Century Type Hunt Scene, Gilt Frame, 20th Century, 24 x 35 In. 550.00
Oil On Canvas, 2 Children, White Dresses, Gilt Frame, 45 3/4 x 36 In. 330.00
Oil On Canvas, 2 Women, Dim Lighted Room, Bart Weise, 20th Century, 27 x 39 In. 315.00
Oil On Canvas, 3 Children, Hen & Chicks, On Masonite, Frame, 22 1/2 x 24 1/2 In. 245.00
Oil On Canvas, 3-Masted Bark Under Sail, Frame, 16 x 25 In. 825.00
Oil On Canvas, Anglers In Birchbark Canoe, Frame, 1920s, 12 x 18 In. 605.00
Oil On Canvas, Arrival Of Newborn Child, Frame, 19th Century, 28 x 35 1/2 In. 785.00
Oil On Canvas, At The Well, D'Grau, 18 x 12 In. 175.00
Oil On Canvas, Autumn Landscape With Stream & Trees, Hal Robinson, 16 x 24 In. 935.00
Oil On Canvas, Barge & Castle River Scene, E. Lancaster Hooper, 23 1/2 x 35 In. 495.00
Oil On Canvas, Barnyard Scene, Chickens & Doves, Gilt Frame, 26 3/4 x 30 3/4 In. 245.00
Oil On Canvas, Bavarian Man With Pipe, Ernst Lang, Frame, 1922, 14 x 17 1/2 In. 935.00
Oil On Canvas, Bear & Cub, P. Hammond, 14 x 10 In. 230.00
Oil On Canvas, Birches, Greenwood, South Carolina, Mrs. Samuel Landon, 7 x 21 In. . . . 200.00
Oil On Canvas, Blond Child, Red Dress, With Hammer, Frame, 30 x 25 In. 1650.00
Oil On Canvas, Boats On A Canal, A. DeMazade, Gilded Frame, c.1870, 9 1/2 x 14 In. 468.00
Oil On Canvas, Brampton Manor Farm, J. Squires, 19th Century, 14 1/4 x 12 In. 460.00
Oil On Canvas, By The Lake, Jean Vollet, 20th Century, 10 3/4 x 16 1/2 In. 633.00
Oil On Canvas, Call Of The Hills, Jonas Joseph La Valley, 25 x 30 In. 2070.00
Oil On Canvas, Capri, Federico, 11 x 14 In. 115.00
Oil On Canvas, Card Game, 18th Century Room, Gold Leaf Frame, 20 x 28 In. 715.00
Oil On Canvas, Chateau De Vasgoeuil, Andre Bouquet, 18 1/8 x 21 3/4 In. 345.00
Oil On Canvas, Child, Basket Of Fruit, 15 3/4 x 13 1/4 In. 330.00
Oil On Canvas, Child, M.J. Whipples, Oval, 27 x 22 In. 750.00
Oil On Canvas, Children On The Beach, S. Hodgson, 20 x 32 In. 1100.00
Oil On Canvas, City Canal, Signed, G. Mascart, 18 x 24 In. 825.00
Oil On Canvas, Clipper Ship Scene, Henri Miloch, 1936, 7 1/2 x 10 3/4 In. 330.00
Oil On Canvas, Coastal Scene, V. De V. Bonfield, 12 1/2 x 20 3/4 In. 880.00
Oil On Canvas, Colorful Flowers & Vases, Martin Rettig, Frame, 22 x 28 In. 880.00
Oil On Canvas, Contemporary, Child, Blue Dress, With Ball, Gilt Frame, 16 x 12 In. 330.00
Oil On Canvas, Cypress Tree At Ousley's Landing, William Ousley, 22 1/4 x 15 3/4 In. . . . 1045.00
Oil On Canvas, Danish Cottage, Mary Elisa Bonfils, 1909, 15 1/2 x 21 3/8 In. 490.00
Oil On Canvas, Daphne & Cupid, L. Bierman, 19th Century, 14 x 11 In. 489.00
Oil On Canvas, Death Of Virgin, Renaissance Style, 19th Century, 15 x 21 In. 560.00
Oil On Canvas, Deux Soeurs, Alfred Boisseau, 1890, 24 3/4 x 18 1/2 In. 920.00
Oil On Canvas, Dining Room At Wick House, Elizabethan, Frame, 12 x 15 1/2 In. 355.00
Oil On Canvas, Discussion Among The Cardinals, Rudolph Klingsbogel, 27 x 21 3/4 In. . . . 1980.00
Oil On Canvas, Dutch Scene, 2 Mothers & 2 Children, P. Doering, Frame, 24 In. 330.00
Oil On Canvas, Elegant Lady, Austria-Hungary, 18th Century, 16 x 12 3/4 In. 290.00
Oil On Canvas, English Fortune Teller & Girl, Robert Smirke, Frame, 19 x 15 In. 385.00
Oil On Canvas, English Hunt Scene, Cleaned, Gilt Frame, 30 x 36 In. 885.00
Oil On Canvas, English Military Scene, Tents, Horses, Crazed, Frame, 18 x 14 1/4 In. 550.00
Oil On Canvas, Estes Park Scene In Colorado, Matt Daly, Frame, 24 x 20 In. 1540.00
Oil On Canvas, Fence, Girl, Folk Art, Frame, Hudson River School, 1870, 24 x 30 In. . . . 2200.00
Oil On Canvas, Figure In Landscape, Rollet, 19 1/4 x 25 1/2 In. 345.00
Oil On Canvas, Fisherman, Passiac Falls, M.H. Mason, 1888, 34 x 28 In. 635.00
Oil On Canvas, Flirtation, J. Zermett, 17 1/2 x 22 1/2 In. 1725.00
Oil On Canvas, Flowering Trees, Gilt Frame, Robert Decker, 8 1/2 x 17 1/4 In. 385.00
Oil On Canvas, Flowers In A Vase, M.S. Joffe, 33 x 25 In. 230.00
Oil On Canvas, Flowers In Basket, Recessed Frame, 19th Century, 27 x 43 In. 335.00
Oil On Canvas, French Interior With Chess Game, Ornate Gilt Frame, 32 x 26 In. 520.00

Oil On Canvas, Fruit Still Life, Continental, Late 19th Century, Oval, 17 x 14 In. 605.00
Oil On Canvas, Fuji, Hayashi Nobui, 12 1/2 x 16 1/4 In. 230.00
Oil On Canvas, Gentleman, Gilt Frame, Mid 19th Century, 24 x 19 In. 245.00
Oil On Canvas, Gentleman, Large Moustache, 1890, 20 x 16 In. 495.00
Oil On Canvas, Girl With Pear, Lotti, 24 x 20 In. 27.00
Oil On Canvas, Harbor Scene, At Harbor, Venice, Framed, Carl Schmidt, 30 x 24 In. 2750.00
Oil On Canvas, Harbor Scene, Steamers At Quay At Night, 10 3/4 x 14 In. 135.00
Oil On Canvas, Haystacks, Albert Insley, 14 x 20 In. 2875.00
Oil On Canvas, Herder At Rest, 19th Century, 20 x 14 In. 40.00
Oil On Canvas, Herder With Livestock Wooded Road, J.W.A. Scott, Frame, 36 In. 2300.00
Oil On Canvas, Hetsteiger Rotterdam, The Quay, Chris Soer, 24 x 40 In. 1210.00
Oil On Canvas, His Last Will, F. W. Palmer, 1902, 18 1/4 x 10 In. 260.00
Oil On Canvas, Horse Portrait, England, Frame, 19th Century, 20 x 26 In. 525.00
Oil On Canvas, Hudson River, Lake, Mountains, Frame, 16 x 24 In. 550.00
Oil On Canvas, Hunting Dog Scene, Gilt Frame, 26 x 39 In. 825.00
Oil On Canvas, In The Beech Woods, Thomas Mower Martin, 14 x 21 1/2 In. 375.00
Oil On Canvas, In The Wye Valley, G. Weston, 19th Century, 12 x 18 In. 635.00
Oil On Canvas, Italian Clipper, Barque Payta, 1892, 9 1/2 x 11 3/4 In. 315.00
Oil On Canvas, Knights On Horseback, Louis Dunki, 23 1/2 x 28 5/8 In. 690.00
Oil On Canvas, L'Orpheon, Jean Fous, 22 x 26 In. 165.00
Oil On Canvas, Lady, Richard Shepard, 10 x 8 In. 58.00
Oil On Canvas, Landscape & Castles, Signed E. Michel, 1800s, 39 1/2 x 58 In. 1265.00
Oil On Canvas, Landscape In Snowstorm, John Lillie, Frame, 18 x 24 In. 90.00
Oil On Canvas, Landscape With Abbey Ruins, 19th Century, 12 x 16 In. 145.00
Oil On Canvas, Landscape With Creek, Daniel Charles Grose, 1867, 8 x 12 In. 140.00
Oil On Canvas, Landscape With Haystack, Enrico Donati, Frame, 6 x 12 In. 210.00
Oil On Canvas, Landscape With Lake, H.W. Kemper, Frame, 13 x 18 In. 1430.00
Oil On Canvas, Landscape, Cottage By Bridge, 19th Century, 10 x 12 In. 165.00
Oil On Canvas, Landscape, House & Barn, McCollister, Frame, 8 1/4 x 11 1/4 In. 302.00
Oil On Canvas, Landscape, John Fox, 12 x 8 In. 550.00
Oil On Canvas, Landscape, Mountains, Mary Cable Butler, 20 x 28 In. 775.00
Oil On Canvas, Landscape, Water Mill, People, R.E. Casey, Frame, 24 x 36 In. 330.00
Oil On Canvas, Los Volcanenos, Noe Canjura, 21 1/4 x 19 In. 316.00
Oil On Canvas, Man & Woman, Mounted On Masonite Board, 22 x 17 In., Pair 400.00
Oil On Canvas, Man & Woman, Sitting, Modern Gilt Frame, 42 x 35 In., Pair 1540.00
Oil On Canvas, Man, Chin Whiskers, S. Brewer Label Back, 1848, 16 x 12 In. 55.00
Oil On Canvas, Man, Period Gilt Frame, Mid 19th Century, 29 x 24 In. 495.00
Oil On Canvas, Martyrdom Of Peter Martyr, Frame, 15 3/4 x 21 1/4 In. 1150.00
Oil On Canvas, Modern Scene, LR Bernard, 19th Century Style, Frame, 25 x 35 In. 465.00
Oil On Canvas, Monk Repairing His Umbrella, Frame, 12 3/8 x 10 In. 1495.00
Oil On Canvas, Mountain Landscape, Boy, Continental, 20th Century, 23 3/4 x 12 In. 370.00
Oil On Canvas, Mountain River Settlement, Frame, Hudson River School, 22 x 27 In. 275.00
Oil On Canvas, Neapolitan Street Scene, Carlo Ciappa, 27 1/2 x 19 5/8 In. 545.00
Oil On Canvas, New England Coastal Cliff, G.W. Picknell, 28 x 23 7/8 In. 690.00
Oil On Canvas, Night Scene, Figures, Stream, Restored, 19th Century, 26 3/4 x 36 In. 785.00
Oil On Canvas, On Cliffs By Sea, A De Breanski, Frame, 6 x 9 In. 575.00
Oil On Canvas, Orthodox Jew With Tefillin, S. Seeberger, 16 1/8 x 13 In. 165.00
Oil On Canvas, Parisian Street Scene, Jean Remy, 20 x 24 In. 220.00
Oil On Canvas, Persian Kitten Beau Brummel, May Palmer Hawkins, 30 x 23 In. 575.00
Oil On Canvas, Portrait, Thomas Paine, Frame, 30 x 26 In. 2750.00
Oil On Canvas, Rabbi, K. Szewecznko, 20 x 16 In. 285.00
Oil On Canvas, Rat Terrier Litter, In Barn, 19th Century, 9 1/2 x 15 3/4 In. 195.00
Oil On Canvas, Rest On Flight Into Egypt, Frame, 17 x 23 1/2 In. 690.00
Oil On Canvas, Returning With The Duck, M.B. McIlhany, England, 12 x 9 In. 715.00
Oil On Canvas, Rochelle, Robert Phillip, 10 1/8 x 8 In. 460.00
Oil On Canvas, Sailing Ship At Night, James G. Tyler, 30 x 25 In. 470.00
Oil On Canvas, Sailing Ship, Story Seas, 20th Century, 22 x 14 In. 110.00
Oil On Canvas, Saint Paul, Frame, 28 1/4 x 24 3/4 In. 2990.00
Oil On Canvas, Schooner At Twilight, Warren Sheppard, Frame, 14 x 22 1/2 In. 1760.00
Oil On Canvas, Seascape, E. Johnson, 15 3/4 x 27 1/4 In. 30.00
Oil On Canvas, Seashore Scene, 19th Century, 14 x 17 1/2 In. 110.00
Oil On Canvas, Seaside Buildings, Wharves, Ruth O. Huestis, Frame, 14 1/2 x 16 In. 192.00
Oil On Canvas, Serenity, Trees, Yellows & Greens, M.E. Cohs, 19 x 23 In. 245.00

Oil On Canvas, Serving Girl, With Tray, Frame, 27 3/4 x 18 1/2 In. 990.00
Oil On Canvas, Ships In Moonlit Harbor, Gilt Frame, 19th Century, 18 1/2 x 14 1/2 In. . . . 350.00
Oil On Canvas, Sleeping On Porch Bench, Faundree, Frame, 16 x 16 In. 110.00
Oil On Canvas, Sowing Seeds, Henry Bacon, Frame, 1879, 20 x 28 1/2 In. 1430.00
Oil On Canvas, Spinning Yarn, F. Peddicord, 1892, 13 3/4 x 19 In. 105.00
Oil On Canvas, St. Peter Healing Tabitha, Continental, 18th Century, 44 x 52 1/2 In. 5225.00
Oil On Canvas, Standing Nude Among Cattails, Oswald Grill, Frame, 43 x 31 In. 2090.00
Oil On Canvas, Still Life, Cut Glass Pitcher, Elise Ford, 19 1/2 x 15 1/2 In. 305.00
Oil On Canvas, Still Life, Fruit, P. Serra, 1907, 12 x 17 In. 415.00
Oil On Canvas, Still Life, Peaches, C.P. Ream, Gilt Frame, 1897, 26 x 32 In. 2200.00
Oil On Canvas, Still Life, Plums, Richard F. Maynard, 1910, 11 1/2 x 16 1/2 In. 880.00
Oil On Canvas, Still Life, Roses, American, Frame, 19th Century, 11 x 16 In. 145.00
Oil On Canvas, Summer Landscape, Fence, Wildflowers, G. Harvey, Frame, 24 x 16 In. . . 286.00
Oil On Canvas, Swiss Alpine Scene, Village Of Zermat, Frame, 32 x 24 In. 180.00
Oil On Canvas, The Curious Dog, American School, 19th-20th Century, 14 x 20 In. 518.00
Oil On Canvas, The Procession, Wagner, 19th Century, 25 x 30 5/8 In. 2875.00
Oil On Canvas, The Shepherdess, L. Bieman, 19th Century, 14 x 11 In. 430.00
Oil On Canvas, Three Fates, 32 1/2 x 24 1/4 In. 2760.00
Oil On Canvas, Traffic In The Channel, James Wilson Carmichael, 1850, 20 x 29 In. 9775.00
Oil On Canvas, Vase Of Flowers, Gabriel Buy, 1964, 36 1/8 x 23 5/8 In. 115.00
Oil On Canvas, Vase Of Mixed Flowers, 28 1/2 x 23 1/4 In. 165.00
Oil On Canvas, Venetian Scene, Continental, Early 20th Century, 20 x 20 In. 880.00
Oil On Canvas, Venice Scene, Signed, Jean Kline, France, 20th Century, 23 1/2 x 21 In. . . 460.00
Oil On Canvas, Venice, Nicolas Briganti, 17 5/8 x 13 5/8 In. 1495.00
Oil On Canvas, Vermouth Bottle, Yarnell Abbot, '33, Frame, 22 3/4 x 27 3/4 In. 110.00
Oil On Canvas, Westminster Bridge & Hall, Joseph Paul, 24 1/8 x 36 1/8 In. 3335.00
Oil On Canvas, Winter Farm Scene, John Hare, Frame, 20 x 26 In. 660.00
Oil On Canvas, Winter Landscape, Cottages & Stream, Gilded Frame, 14 1/2 In. 190.00
Oil On Canvas, Winter Landscape, P. Woimann, 20 x 28 In. 690.00
Oil On Canvas, Winter Stream Scene, Frame, 19 3/4 x 27 1/2 In. 55.00
Oil On Canvas, Woman By Stream, Continental, Frame, 19th Century, 53 x 35 In. 2970.00
Oil On Canvas, Woman In Flower Garden, Edmund Garrett, Frame, 32 x 28 In. 5775.00
Oil On Canvas, Woman Reading, Gary Shankman, 20 x 14 In. 230.00
Oil On Canvas, Woman Riding Donkey, Henry Bacon, Frame, 13 1/4 x 16 In. 770.00
Oil On Canvas, Woman, Red Chair, Window, R. Street, Gilt Frame, 1847, 30 x 25 In. 1760.00
Oil On Canvas, Wooded Landscape, 2 Swans, Modern Frame, 20 x 14 In. 80.00
Oil On Canvas, Woodland Scene, Deer Forest, Gilt Frame, Artist Wood, 15 x 19 1/2 In. . . 165.00
Oil On Canvas, Young Girl, Purdy, '61, 16 x 20 In. 220.00
Oil On Canvas, Young Girl, Seated, American, c.1830, 12 x 10 In. 405.00
Oil On Canvas, Young Woman, Mary Spencer, 1892, 20 x 16 In. 247.00
Oil On Canvasboard, Pirate With Earrings, B.E. Jamieson, Black Frame, 25 1/4 x 20 In. . . 27.00
Oil On Cardboard, Landscape With Figure, Eugene Leroy, France, 9 1/4 x 12 3/4 In. 489.00
Oil On Masonite, Landscape From Akero, Pine, Reinhold Von Rosen, 1929, 14 x 21 In. . . 135.00
Oil On Panel, Barnyard Scene, Chickens, H. Prumm, 10 1/2 x 13 In. 85.00
Oil On Panel, Country Lane, Wagon & Farm House, Giovanni, 14 3/4 x 22 In. 105.00
Oil On Panel, Elegant Ladies With Whippet, Florent Willems, 24 3/4 x 19 In. 5750.00
Oil On Panel, Figures At Rest In Landscape, Flemish, 17th-18th Century, 10 x 13 In. 1035.00
Oil On Panel, Garden Party, France, Late 19th Century, 28 x 24 In. 1760.00
Oil On Panel, Gentleman With Pipe, Hedwig Oehring, 10 1/2 x 8 1/4 In. 880.00
Oil On Panel, Market Stall, Ele Bemindi, 12 1/2 x 9 1/2 In. 1150.00
Oil On Panel, Mill Scene, Arched Type, 12 3/4 x 5 In. 90.00
Oil On Panel, Mountain Landscape, Figure Boating On Lake, R. Munel, 7 x 12 1/2 In. . . . 405.00
Oil On Panel, Musketeer's Life, T. Fuchs, 10 1/4 x 8 1/8 In. 230.00
Oil On Panel, Oak Lined Pathway, Carl C. Brenner, 1887, 10 x 6 7/8 In. 1095.00
Oil On Panel, Peasants Resting In Mountainous Setting, J. A. Knip, 9 1/2 x 12 In. 1320.00
Oil On Panel, Pennsylvania Autumn Farm, 13 1/2 x 17 1/2 In. 130.00
Oil On Panel, Savage, Tugboat, In Baltimore Harbor Area, 20th Century, 16 x 22 In. 275.00
Oil On Panel, Sunshine, Orange Street, H.H. Sutton, 8 x 10 In. 81.00
Oil On Panel, Symbols Of Music, Other Symbols Of Gardening, 61 x 15 In, Pair 575.00
Oil On Panel, The Stepping Stones, Frederick R. Lee, 15 x 27 In. 605.00
Oil On Panel, Town Scene, Horse & Buggies, Adolph Gerhard, 7 1/2 x 12 In. 330.00
Oil On Paper, Abstract Figure, Alexander Gore, 10 3/4 x 7 3/4 In. 121.00
Oil On Paper, Abstract, Toward Final Good, Littlefield, Frame, 1960, 9 1/2 x 24 In. 130.00

Oil On Paper, Harbor Scene, Jan Evert Moll, Frame, 9 3/4 x 13 7/8 In. 880.00
Oil On Silk, Mother & Child, Edna Hibel, 28 x 25 In. 1210.00
Oil On Tin, Priest In Victorian Chair, Frame, 16 1/2 x 12 5/8 In. 115.00
Oil On Wood, European Landscape, Gondola, Buildings, W.M. Hull, Frame, 17 In. 165.00
Oil Wash On Board, Sunset Bayou Scene, Alexander J. Drysdale, 14 1/2 x 19 1/2 In. . . . 1760.00
On Celluloid, Woman, Dressed In 18th Century Costume, 3 x 3 5/8 In. 27.00
On Fabric, Signed Mr. Harumitsu Utagawa, Japan, 15 1/2 x 10 In. 65.00
On Ivory, Architectural Ruins & Tower, Circular, Gilt Metal, 3 x 4 1/2 In. 460.00
On Ivory, Aristocratic Woman, Roses In Hair, Gutta-Percha Frame, c.1850, 2 x 1 In. 345.00
On Ivory, Baby, Blue Eyes, White Dress, Blond Hair In Back, Colored Case, 2 3/4 In. . . . 220.00
On Ivory, Boy, With Dog, 3 1/4 In. 325.00
On Ivory, Catherine Of Russia, Bowknot, Easel Back, Brun, 19th Century, 1 3/4 In. 315.00
On Ivory, Child Holding Flower, Oval, 19th Century, 3 1/4 x 2 1/4 In. 935.00
On Ivory, Child, Seated On Red Cushion, Wooden Frame, 2 1/4 x 2 In. 1035.00
On Ivory, Duchess Of Devonshire, Gilt Metal Frame, 2 x 2 In. 285.00
On Ivory, Elderly Woman, Fitted Box, C.P. Newell, 1914, 31 1/2 In. 230.00
On Ivory, Elegantly Dressed Woman, Tortoiseshell Frame, 5 x 5 3/4 In. 275.00
On Ivory, Gentleman, F.R., London, 1798, 2 3/4 x 2 1/4 In. 1275.00
On Ivory, Gentleman, Formal Clothes, Allyn Williams, Frame, 1899, 4 In. 135.00
On Ivory, Gentleman, Gold Memoriam Frame, Lock Of Hair In Back, 1830s, 3 In. 1035.00
On Ivory, Gentleman, Wearing Medal, Brass Oval Frame, 3 x 2 1/2 In. 135.00
On Ivory, Girl, Fancy Dress, 3 1/4 In. 325.00
On Ivory, Indian Nobleman, Ornamental Dress, Gutta-Percha Frame, 4 x 3 3/4 In. 170.00
On Ivory, Lady, Gilt Metal Frame, 19th Century, 3 1/2 x 2 3/4 In. 430.00
On Ivory, Lady, Guiding A Group Of Children Carrying Flags, 3 3/4 x 4 In. 540.00
On Ivory, Man & Boys Feeding Bird, Interior, Shadowbox Frame, 4 3/4 x 4 In. 330.00
On Ivory, Man, Stern Face, Black Coat, Modern Frame, 6 5/8 x 5 1/2 In. 300.00
On Ivory, Marie Louise, Wooden Frame, 1 3/16 In. 280.00
On Ivory, Mother & Child, Seated, Front Of Red Drape, Frame, 3 3/4 x 3 In. 190.00
On Ivory, Parents, 2 Children, Before A Table, Rosewood Frame, 1809, 2 In. 2300.00
On Ivory, Portrait, Marie Antoinette & Louis XVI, 4 In., Pair 400.00
On Ivory, Portrait, Mrs. Caley, Gentleman, Shadowbox Frame, 1775, 1 3/4 In., Pair 715.00
On Ivory, Robespierre, Blue Jacket, Gilt Metal Frame, Late 19th Century, 4 In. 290.00
On Ivory, Roman Goddess, Holding Urn, Red Cape, 3 x 2 1/2 In. 120.00
On Ivory, Shepherdess & Sheep, Floral Design On Reverse, 3 3/4 In. 275.00
On Ivory, Susanna Niles Thayer, Child, Red Dress, Holding Book, 3 1/2 In. 2750.00
On Ivory, Taj Mahal, Carved & Floral Frame, 17 1/8 In. 130.00
On Ivory, William Henry Harrison, Seated, Leather Case, 19th Century, 4 x 3 1/2 In. 920.00
On Ivory, Woman, Blue Hat, Encasing Cologne Bottle, Brass Frame, 1 3/16 In. 245.00
On Ivory, Woman, Coral Necklace, Red, White Dress, Wooden Frame, 1830, 2 1/2 In. . . . 345.00
On Ivory, Woman, Curled Hair, Black Dress, Locket Within Frame, 2 1/2 x 2 In. 460.00
On Ivory, Woman, Decollete Dress, Landscape Ground, Gilt Metal Frame, 2 In. 520.00
On Ivory, Woman, In Blue, Brass Frame, Circle Of 33 Stones, 1 1/2 In. 250.00
On Ivory, Woman, Jewel & Feather Hair Piece, Gilt Brass Frame, 4 1/8 x 6 3/4 In. 400.00
On Ivory, Woman, Jeweled & Feathered Hat, Lace Collar, Ormolu Frame, 5 3/8 In. 405.00
On Ivory, Woman, Pearl Earrings, Necklace, Brooch, Shawl Over Shoulder, 3 7/8 In. 345.00
On Ivory, Woman, Pompadour, Morin, Brass Frame, 2 In. 285.00
On Ivory, Woman, Wearing Diadem, Augustin, Jeweled Brass Frame, 3 1/2 In. 330.00
On Ivory, Woman, White Dress, Velvet Lined Oval Case, c.1820, 3 1/4 x 2 3/4 In. 460.00
On Ivory, Young Girl Wearing A White Dress, Pink Sash, Carrying Basket, 4 x 3 In. 575.00
On Ivory, Young Girl, Long Hair, Leatherized Case, Brocade Interior, 3 1/4 In. 440.00
On Ivory, Young Man, Black & White Coat, Early 19th Century, 2 1/2 In. 520.00
On Ivory, Young Woman, Roadway & House, Plumed Hat, Gilt Frame, 6 3/8 In. 687.00
On Ivory, Young Woman, Top Curls, Ruffled Collar, Black Eglomise, Mat, 2 1/2 In. 415.00
On Masonite, Sailing Ship, Joseph Conrad, J.D. Poty, 18 x 28 In. 275.00
On Paper, 2 Red Birds, Branches, Watercolor, Frame, Amish, 1860, 6 1/4 x 8 In. 660.00
On Porcelain, Girl, Large Black Bonnet, Gilt Oval Frame, 4 1/8 In. 185.00
On Porcelain, Woman, Carved Frame, Oval, 4 1/2 In. 275.00
On Porcelain, Young Boy, Blond Hair, Frame, 3 5/16 In. 160.00
On Silk, Oriental Scene, Japan, 25 x 38 In., Pair 3300.00
On Velvet, 3-Masted Sailing Ship, American Flag, Wm. Rank, Frame, 21 1/2 x 23 In. . . . 140.00
Reverse On Glass, Basket Of Fruit, Mahogany Veneer Frame, 9 1/2 x 11 1/2 In. 690.00
Reverse On Glass, Bird, Black Frame, 8 1/2 x 7 1/2 In. 70.00

Reverse On Glass, Child Fishing, Oriental, Frame, 20 1/2 x 14 1/4 In. 165.00
Reverse On Glass, Chinese Palace Scene, Figures, 22 1/2 x 32 1/2 In., Pair 1550.00
Reverse On Glass, Figures In Courtyard, 3 Figures Drinking Tea, Key Border, 25 In. 5750.00
Reverse On Glass, Gentleman, Gilt Frame, 16 1/2 x 13 1/2 In. 880.00
Reverse On Glass, George & Martha Washington, Frame, 22 x 20 In., Pair 2425.00
Reverse On Glass, Memorial, Mother Mourning Loss Of Children, 2 1/2 x 2 In. 1725.00
Reverse On Glass, Napoleon, Round, White Ground, Matted, Frame, 11 x 9 In. 220.00
Reverse On Glass, Pungdrugterin, Woman, Turban, Frame, 12 3/4 x 9 3/4 In. 240.00
Reverse On Glass, Silhouette, Gentleman, Bronze Frame, 2 3/4 In. 60.00
Reverse On Glass, Sinking Of The Titanic, Frame, Early 20th Century, 13 1/2 x 29 In. . . . 165.00
Reverse On Glass, Woman, Ornate Dress & Hat, Frame, 12 x 9 1/2 In. 135.00
Reverse On Glass, Woman, Yellow Dress, Gilt Frame, 10 7/8 x 8 1/2 In. 220.00
Scroll, Chinese Male Ancestor Portrait, Laid On Board, 43 1/4 x 24 1/4 In. 575.00

PAIRPOINT Manufacturing Company started in 1880 in New Bedford, Massachusetts. It soon joined with the glassworks nearby and made glass, silver-plated pieces, and lamps. Reverse-painted glass shades and molded shades known as *puffies* were part of the production until the 1930s. The company reorganized and changed its name several times but is still working today. Items listed here are glass or glass and metal. Silver-plated pieces are listed under Silver Plate.

Biscuit Jar, Blue Flowering Branches, Bulbous, Silvered Rim, Signed, 7 In. 345.00
Bowl, Daisies & Butterfly, Bishop's Hat, Hobstar Base, 15 In. 625.00
Box, Cover, Romantic Scene On Cover, Floral Swag, Silver Plate, 3 x 4 In. 143.00
Candlestick, Brass, Cast Floral, Square Bobeche, Prisms, 15 1/2 In. 145.00
Candlestick, Geometric Band, Hexagonal, Metal, Stem, 8 In., Pair 285.00
Compote, Cranberry, Cut To Clear, Floral, 8 1/2 x 8 In., Pair 330.00
Console Set, Canary, Cut To Clear, Prisms On Candlesticks, 12 In., 3 Piece 575.00
Cup & Saucer, Panels Of Exotic Flora, c.1885, 5 1/2 In. 25.00
Lamp, 2 Peacocks On Garden Wall Shade, Silver Plated Base, Carlisle, 18 In. 5500.00
Lamp, 4 Seasons Panels Shade, 16 In. 4350.00
Lamp, 4 Seasons Panels, Mahogany Base, 20 In. 5500.00
Lamp, Berkely Shade, Floral Border, Signed Base, 16 In. 3575.00
Lamp, Butterfly, Blue, Pink Floral, 22 In. 2300.00
Lamp, Candle, Enameled Shade, Leafy Birch Trees, Metal Mounts, 9 In., Pair 402.00
Lamp, Candle, Flared Shade, Birch Trees, Yellow Interior, Metal Mounts, 21 1/2 In. 805.00
Lamp, Candy Stripe Shade, Polished Brass Base, 13 In. 3575.00
Lamp, Carlisle Shade, Floral Border, Signed Base, 18 In. 2585.00
Lamp, Cavetto Shade, Garlands, Cornucopia, Creatures, 22 1/2 In. 2640.00
Lamp, Chesterfield Shade, Garden Of Allah, Ribbed, Signed, 16 In. 16500.00
Lamp, Chesterfield Shade, Oriental Carpet, 21 In. 1610.00
Lamp, Chrysanthemum & Hummingbird Shade, Signed, 14 In. 7700.00
Lamp, Danver Shade, Peach Blossom, 20 x 14 In. 1380.00
Lamp, Danver Shade, Stylized Floral, 8 In. 935.00
Lamp, Directoire Shade, Scenic Woodland Shade, Signed, 16 In. 3300.00
Lamp, Directoire Shade, Tapestry Panels, Hexagonal, Signed Base 2750.00
Lamp, Directoire Shade, Vibrant Flowers, Metal Pairpoint Base 6600.00

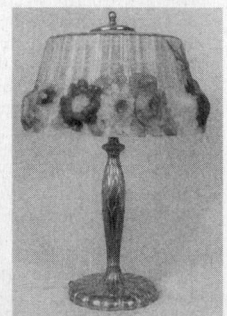
Pairpoint, Lamp, Puffy,
Hummingbird &
Roses, Silver Plated
Base, 21 1/2 In.

Lamp, Domed Shade, Autumn Leaf Trees Amidst Grass, Flowers, 10 In. 1265.00
Lamp, Exeter Shade, Floral, Stylized Flowers & Birds, 17 In. 2310.00
Lamp, Exeter Shade, Pastoral Trees, Yellow Band, 23 In. 2990.00
Lamp, Harbor Scene, Rowboat, 5 Men, 22 In. 4370.00
Lamp, Landscape Between Paneled Borders, 1910, 27 In. 7475.00
Lamp, Nautical Scene, Matching Base, 20 In. 8250.00
Lamp, New Bedford Harbor Scene, Moonlit Sky, Bombay Shape, Signed, 20 In. 7150.00
Lamp, Oil, Banquet, White, Floral, Gold Trim, Night-Light, 18 In. 1500.00
Lamp, Pastoral Scene Of Trees, Grassy Hillside, 22 x 17 In. 2070.00
Lamp, Pink Shade, White Flowers, Leaves, Jar Shape Base, Flowers, Vines, 21 In. 2560.00
Lamp, Puffy, Apple Tree, Green Mottled Patina, 1907, 23 In. 40250.00
Lamp, Puffy, Begonia, Green, Red, Cream, Round Base, 4 Scrolled Feet, 20 In. 8580.00
Lamp, Puffy, Dogwood, Yellow Highlights, Green Ground, Signed, 5 In. 4730.00
Lamp, Puffy, Floral, Butterflies & Roses, Square Base, 8 In. 3575.00
Lamp, Puffy, Grape, Deep Green Ground, Signed, 5 In. 3850.00
Lamp, Puffy, Hummingbird & Roses, 14-In. Shade 4000.00
Lamp, Puffy, Hummingbird & Roses, Silver Plated Base, 21 1/2 In. . . . .*Illus* 8800.00
Lamp, Puffy, Lotus, Yellow, Pink Highlights, Signed Base, 12 In. 17600.00
Lamp, Puffy, Malta Shade, Brass Base, Signed, 13 In. 5750.00
Lamp, Puffy, Pansy, Yellow, Raspberry, Antique Brass Urn Base, Signed, 5 In. 4675.00
Lamp, Puffy, Papillion Butterflies & Roses Shade, Pink Ground, Signed, 8 In. 5225.00
Lamp, Puffy, Papillion Butterflies & Roses, Closed Top, 8 In. 8800.00
Lamp, Puffy, Portsmouth Floral Shade, 5 In. 3850.00
Lamp, Puffy, Reverse Painted, Rose, Lily Pad Base, 1920s, 21 In. 4025.00
Lamp, Puffy, Stratford Shade, Floral Border, Lattice, Signed, Pat. Applied 1907, 8 In. 2750.00
Lamp, Puffy, Stratford Shade, Gladioli, Lilac, Orange, Yellow, Signed Base, 14 In. 13200.00
Lamp, Puffy, Stratford Shade, Hummingbirds & Roses, White Ground, 14 In. 8250.00
Lamp, Puffy, Torino Shade, Peonies, Dots Ground, Original Base, Signed, 10 In. 9900.00
Lamp, Quatrefoil Shade, 4 Roses, Pink, Yellow, 1910, 11 In. 5175.00
Lamp, Reverse Painted, Bombay Shade, Trees & Orange Sky, Signed, 16 In. 3025.00
Lamp, Reverse Painted, Roses, Pale Yellow, White Ground, 14 In. 2070.00
Lamp, Scene Of Trees & Lake Shade, Signed, 24 In. 4000.00
Lamp, Scrolled Floral Vines, Dotted Borders, Green, 17 In. 1495.00
Lamp, Sea Gull Shade, Signed, Fisher, 20 In. 6900.00
Lamp, Seville Shade, Exotic Birds, Branches, Signed, 16 In. 4950.00
Lamp, Seville Shade, Flowers, Acanthus, 3-Candle Base, 24 In. 1792.00
Lamp, Sheep Grazing In Field, Purple, Green, Brown, 14 In. 1725.00
Lamp, Ship Scene, Triple Dolphin Base, F. Chadd, 16 In. 7700.00
Lamp, Single Red Poppy, Frosted Ground, 7 In. 1430.00
Lamp, Slag Glass Shade, Silver Plated, Owl Base, Signed, 16 In. 1495.00
Lamp, Stratford Shade, Hummingbird & Roses, Silver Plated Base, 14 In. 8250.00
Lamp, Torino Shade, Venetian, Sailing Vessels On The Bay, Signed Base, 14 In. 9900.00
Lamp, Touraine Shade, Windmills, Signed, A. Schultz, 18 In. 2585.00
Lamp, Vienna Shade, Seascape & Village, Planter, Signed, 14 In. 4950.00
Lamp, Vienna Shade, Stylized Flowers & Leaves, Closed Top, 14 In. 1650.00
Paperweight, Scattered Floral Canes, Pedestal Of Leaves & Flowers, 3 1/2 In. 275.00
Paperweight Perfume, Swan Finial, 1930, 5 3/4 x 2 1/4 In. 46.00
Punch Ladle, Crosscut Diamond Handle, Silver Plated Dipper 350.00
Shade, Pansies, Purple, Red, Yellow, Brown Stems, Aqua Ground, 5 In., Pair 2990.00
Vase, Adelaide, Cobalt Blue, Trumpet, Controlled Bubble, Ball Connector, 13 In., Pair . . . 2530.00
Vase, Buckingham, Onyx Paw Footed Base, Baluster, 15 In., Pair 1840.00
Vase, Tavern, Floral, Enameled, 1920, 8 1/2 In. 290.00
Wine, Rouge Flambeau, 6 Piece 1000.00

PALMER COX, BROWNIES, see Brownies category.

PAPER collectibles, including almanacs, catalogs, children's books, some greeting cards, stock certificates, and other paper ephemera, are listed here. Paper calendars are listed separately in the Calendar category. Paper items may be found in many other sections, such as Christmas and Movie.

Banner, Flagstaff, Ariz., San Francisco Peaks, 3 1/2 x 7 1/2 In. 6.00
Banner, North Dakota, Indian Picture, Red Ground, 1939, 2 3/4 x 7 1/4 In. 6.00

Blotter, Maryland Casualty Co., Man Juggling Numbers, Baltimore, 3 1/2 x 6 1/4 In. 3.00
Book, Big Little Book, $1000 Reward, McNeal, 1938, 392 Pages 30.00
Book, Big Little Book, Barney Baxter, In The Air With The Eagle Squadron, 1938 . . . . . . 37.00
Book, Big Little Book, Bronc Peeler The Lone Cowboy, 1937 . . . . 40.00
Book, Big Little Book, Bugs Bunny In Double Trouble, 1967 . . . . 20.00
Book, Big Little Book, G-Man, Breaking The Gambling Ring, 1938, 426 Pages 20.00
Book, Big Little Book, Guns In The Roaring West, 1937 . . . . 40.00
Book, Big Little Book, Kayo & Moon Mullins, 1939 . . . . 30.00
Book, Big Little Book, Red Ryder 20.00
Book, Big Little Book, Snow White & Seven Dwarfs, 1938 . . . . 75.00
Book, Big Little Book, Tim McCoy, 1939 . . . . 35.00
Book, Little Golden Book, Captain Kangaroo, 1956 . . . . 20.00
Booklet, Ex-Lax, Strange As It Seems, John Hix Radio Show, 22 Page, 1936, 6 x 9 In. . . . 15.00
Booklet, Tourist, Hawaii U.S.A., Women In Leis, 1942, 20 Pages 38.00
Catalog, Aldens, 1958, Christmas 80.00
Catalog, Aldens, 1959, Christmas 100.00
Catalog, Aldens, 1963, Christmas, Barbie, Ken & Midge On Cover 50.00
Catalog, Arnold Schwinn & Co., Bicycles & Accessories, 1966, 36 Pages 35.00
Catalog, C.M. Mossman & Brother, 1890, For Horse Owners, Illustrated, 15 x 11 In. 147.00
Catalog, Creek Chub, 1925, Fishing, 47 Pages 605.00
Catalog, Cybis Art Studio, 1979, Commemorative, 121 Pages 25.00
Catalog, Dayton's, 1978, Christmas, 48 Pages 15.00
Catalog, Edward Von Hofe, 1931, Fishing, 171 Pages 295.00
Catalog, F.A.O. Schwartz, 1965, Christmas 75.00
Catalog, F.A.O. Schwartz, 1982, Fall & Winter, 36 Pages 25.00
Catalog, Fisher-Price, 1956, Dealers, 16 Pages 100.00
Catalog, General Motors Corporation, 1949, Detroit, Michigan, 32 Pages 35.00
Catalog, Higbee's, Cleveland, 1970, Christmas, 32 Pages 25.00
Catalog, Hudson's, 1983, Christmas, 69 Pages 15.00
Catalog, JCPenney, 1965, Christmas 100.00
Catalog, JCPenney, 1986, Christmas 30.00
Catalog, Jefferson College, 1850, Canonsburg, Pa., Rules, Faculty, History Of School 65.00
Catalog, Lowe Campbell Sports, 1958, Fall & World Series, Braves At Yankees 65.00
Catalog, Maas & Steffen, 1927, Furbearers, 26 Pages 60.00
Catalog, Margarete Steiff's Realistic Toy Animals, 1957, Germany, 15 Pages 51.00
Catalog, Marshall Field Co., Chicago, 1946, Christmas, 24 Pages 25.00
Catalog, Montgomery Ward, 1917, Spring & Summer 65.00
Catalog, Montgomery Ward, 1933, Christmas 125.00
Catalog, Montgomery Ward, 1966, Christmas 80.00
Catalog, Oliver Plows & Cultivators, 1910, 16 Pages 10.00
Catalog, R.H. Macy & Co., 1906, Christmas, 48 Pages 100.00
Catalog, S & H Green Stamp Redemption, 1956 . . . . 25.00
Catalog, Samuel Sloan & Co., 1926, Plumbing & Heating Supplies, No. 5, 360 Pages 20.00
Catalog, Sears Roebuck, 1901, Price One Dollar, Hard Cover, 1200 Pages 94.00
Catalog, Sears Roebuck, 1927, Fall & Winter 120.00
Catalog, Sears Roebuck, 1956, Christmas 125.00
Catalog, Sears Roebuck, 1971, Christmas 70.00
Catalog, Sears Roebuck, 1975, Fall & Winter, 1491 Pages 22.00
Catalog, Sears Roebuck, 1978, Toy 40.00
Catalog, Sears Roebuck, 1982, Christmas 45.00
Catalog, Sotheby's, 1983-1984, Art At Auction, Ayers, 416 Pages 25.00
Catalog, Spiegel's, 1942, Christmas 100.00
Catalog, Spiegel's, 1977, Christmas 50.00
Catalog, Stanley Hardware, No. 15, 1930, 265 Pages, 8 x 11 In. 30.00
Catalog, True Value Hardware, 1972, Christmas, 48 Pages 25.00
Catalog, Villeroy & Boch, 1900, Spiral Bound, F.L. Berninger, Frankfort, 50 Plus Pages . . 65.00
Catalog, Walgreen Agency Drug Stores, 1960, Christmas, 244 Pages 100.00
Catalog, Ward's, 1958, Christmas 50.00
Catalog, Western Auto Stores, 1964, Christmas, 56 Pages 30.00
Coloring Book, Apollo 11, Saalfield, 1969 . . . . 20.00
Coloring Book, Bat Masterson, 1959 . . . . 25.00
Coloring Book, Fat Albert, 1978 . . . . 35.00
Coloring Book, Fonzie, Happy Days, 1976 . . . . 10.00

Coloring Book, My Favorite Martian, No. 1148, Whitman, 1964, 128 Pages 52.00
Coloring Book, Roger Ramjet, 120 Pages, Whitman, 1966 .... 45.00
Coloring Book, Terry & The Pirates, Unused, 1946 .... 50.00
Decal, Boys Town, 1 Boy Carrying Another, He Ain't Heavy, He's M'Brother, 1940, 4 In.   6.00
Deed, 2 Wax Seals, Watertown, Province Of Massachusetts, 1697, 16 x 17 In. 440.00
Deed, Pen & Ink, Property, Watertown, Prov. Of Mass., 1697, Frame, 11 1/4 x 12 1/2 In. . 440.00
Document, Signature, Andrew Jackson, T. Scott As Land Office Registrar Office, 1829 .. 523.00
Document, Signature, James F. Wade, On U.S. Army Recruiting Poster 440.00
Document, Signature, William McKinley, Commission For James F. Wade, 1898 .... 770.00
Envelope, C.O.D., Wells, Fargo & Co. Express, Steam Train, 1880s 39.00
Fraktur, 2 Rows Women & Men, Buds On Tulip Branch, Angels, France, 13 x 17 In. 275.00
Fraktur, Alphabets, Numbers, Yellow, Green, Black, Pa. German, Frame, 10 x 12 In. 660.00
Fraktur, Anna Geeyer, Whitehall Township, Dec. 27, 1807, Watercolor, Ink, 13 x 16 In. .. 9900.00
Fraktur, Baptism, Friedrich Spreyer, Taufschein, Born 1790, Baptized 1807, Birds 5390.00
Fraktur, Bird, Hans George Petry, 1759, Cutwork, Watercolor, Ink, Round, 12 1/2 In. 3300.00
Fraktur, Bird, Sarah Ann Kaufman, 1845, Tulip Plants, Vines, 12 1/2 x 16 In. 2750.00
Fraktur, Birds, Flower Urn, Daniel Peterman, Shrewsbury, Dec. 12, 1845, 13 x 16 In. ... 7040.00
Fraktur, Birth & Baptismal, Benjamin Gantz, Watercolor, 1815, 12 1/2 x 7 3/4 In. 1045.00
Fraktur, Birth Record, Yellow, Brown, Black, Green, Pa. German, Grained Frame, 1771 .. 1210.00
Fraktur, Birth, Frederick Haffel, Nov. 5, 1798, Heart, Stars, Hand Colored, 13 x 16 In. .. 2310.00
Fraktur, Birth, Magdalena Schreiner, Floral Wreath, Frame, 1775, 12 5/8 x 16 3/4 In. 1155.00
Fraktur, Birth, Martin Brechall, Stylized Floral, Beveled Poplar Frame, 1845, 13 In. 2090.00
Fraktur, Birth, Michael Hummel, Penns Township, Watercolor, Ink, Frame, 13 x 15 In. .. 4290.00
Fraktur, Birth, Suzanna Schlegel, Blowsy Angel, Watercolor, 1808, 12 x 15 In. 1650.00
Fraktur, Christian Bamberger, 3 Tulip Pots, Doves, Colored, 1824, 11 1/2 x 13 1/4 In. ... 7700.00
Fraktur, Daniel Otto, Tulips, Watercolor, Frame, 9 3/4 x 8 In. 7700.00
Fraktur, Daniel Peterman, December 12, 1845, Birds, Flower Spray, 13 x 16 In. 7040.00
Fraktur, Elizabeth Gehrhard, 1808, Watercolor, Ink, Frame, 12 1/2 x 8 1/4 In. 2530.00
Fraktur, Flowers, Verse In Ovals, Sophia Wannenmacher, 13 3/4 x 16 3/4 In. 770.00
Fraktur, Friederich Kuster, 1800, Heart, Eagles, Watercolor, Ink, Frame, 13 x 16 In. 1760.00
Fraktur, Geburts Und Taufschein, Birth In Lebanon County, Colored Birds, 17 x 13 In. .. 467.00
Fraktur, Georg Friederich Speyer, Watercolor, Ink, 1788, Frame, 13 x 16 In. 4675.00
Fraktur, God Is Great, Balance Scale, Potted Plants, Bill Rank, 13 x 18 1/2 In. 300.00
Fraktur, Heinrich Frantz, Den 31 Fen Merz 1818, Watercolor, Ink, Frame, 7 x 12 In. 2200.00
Fraktur, Henry Young, Profile Of Couple, Watercolor, Ink, Frame, 1860, 12 x 8 In. 4400.00
Fraktur, Inscription In Heart, Pennsylvania German, Frame, 9 1/2 x 8 1/2 In. 200.00
Fraktur, Jacob Kimbal, Vorschrift, Watercolor, Ink, 8 x 13 In. 2090.00
Fraktur, Jacob Zigler, Heidleburg Township, Oct. 16, 1811, Watercolor, Ink, 13 x 16 In. .. 3300.00
Fraktur, Katherinn Kessle, Annville Township, 1820, Watercolor, Ink, 13 x 16 In. 7700.00
Fraktur, Levi Atland Birth, Aug. 31, 1862, Birds & Flowers, Daniel Peterman 4510.00
Fraktur, Magdalena Schansten, 1792, Heart, Script, Watercolor, Ink, 9 1/2 x 8 In. 2090.00
Fraktur, Maria German, Script, Mermaid, Watercolor & Ink, 1804, 3 x 5 3/4 In 2420.00
Fraktur, Painted Lithograph, E.B. Ebner, Child Samuel Nocolir, Frame, 13 1/4 x 16 In. .. 240.00
Fraktur, Ribbon & Holly Ivy, Angels, German Inscription, Bill Rank, 7 1/2 x 9 1/2 In. 75.00
Fraktur, Rooster, Potted Plants, Black, Green, Yellow, Red, G.B. French, 17 x 16 In. 355.00
Fraktur, Samuel Bossard, Bern Township, 1821, Watercolor, Ink, 7 1/2 x 11 In. 6600.00
Fraktur, Sussana & Johanes Drinkelberger, 1818, Watercolor, Ink, Frame, 13 x 16 In. 5500.00
Fraktur, Watercolor, I Have Gone Astray Like A Lost Sheep, Pa. German, 1761, 9 3/4 In. . 385.00
Handbill, Star-Spangled Banner, 91st Anniversary, Jamaica, N.Y., 1867, 4 1/2 x 10 In. ... 45.00
Invoice, Gustav Stickley, List Of Purchased Items, Frame, 1914, 13 1/2 x 6 1/2 In. 440.00
Ledger, Griswold Family, Bartered Goods, Recipes, Guilford, Connecticut, 1772 .... 1450.00
Magazine, Cottage Hearth, August 1877, Home Arts & Home Leisure 25.00
Magazine, Life, On The Moon, Aug. 8, 1969 .... 25.00
Magazine, The Autocar, October 21, 1927, England, 150 Pages 40.00
Magazine, TV Guide, Lucy's $50 Million Baby, Minneapolis-St. Paul, April 3-9, 1953 ... 400.00
Magazine, USGA Golf Magazine, Woman Golfer, Feb. 1898, Vol. II, No. 2, 66 Pages 745.00
Menu, Berstein's Fish Grotto, San Francisco, Cal., Boat, Mermaid, 1930s, 10 x 13 In. 20.00
Menu, El Mirador Hotel, Palm Springs, Cal., Night Scene, Color, 1954, 8 x 10 In. 33.00
Menu, Hotel Oakland, Japanese Hotel Men's Delegation, 1929, 5 x 8 In. 19.00
Menu, Los Angeles Turf Club, Santa Anita Tour Luncheon, March 1, 1941, 7 x 10 In. 27.00
Menu, United States, Capitol At Colonial Williamsburg, Map On Back, 1962, 8 x 11 In. .. 15.00
Program, 35th Annual Cheyenne Frontier Days, Black & White Photos, 1931, 11 x 8 In. . 186.00
Program, 101 Ranch Wild West Show, 13 1/2 x 10 In. 186.00

Program, Annie Oakley, Young Buffalo Wild West Show, Charleston, Il., 1914, 9 1/2 In. . . 294.00
Program, Chalfonte-Haddon Hall, March Musicals, Atlantic City, N.J., 1926, 4 Pages 10.00
Program, Hippodrome, New York, Lithograph, Andrew Kellogg Co., 1906, 12 x 8 1/4 In. 107.00
Program, Playbill, Sweet Bird Of Youth, Paul Newman, Martin Beck Theatre, 1959 . . . . . 20.00
Program, Sutro Baths, San Francisco, Aquatic & Musical Schedule, 1899, 9 x 12 In. . . . 30.00
Program, Wyoming Bill's Wild West Show, NYC & Lancaster, PA, 10 3/4 x 7 3/4 In. 266.00
Receipt, Department Of The Interior, United States Indian Service, 1906, 10 1/2 x 8 In. . . 25.00
Receipt, Vault & Embellishments, St. Vincent De Paul Cemetery, New Orleans, 1873 . . . . 55.00
Songbook, Hank Williams, Signed, 1956 . . . . 35.00
Stock Certificate, Deadwood Gold Mining Co., Nevada, California, 1870s 25.00
Stock Certificate, Kaiser-Frazer Corporation, Blue, Redeemed, 1945 . . . . 27.00
Stock Certificate, Lone Star & Crescent Oil Co. Of New Orleans, 1901 & 1902, Pair 165.00
Stock Certificate, Scadden Flat Gold Mining Co., California, 50 Shares, 1879 . . . . 30.00
Tautschein, Birth & Baptism, Johann Peter Hammer, Dec. 1803, Angels, 12 x 15 In. 4950.00
Ticket, Sacramento Aircraft Show, 25 Cents, May 25-27, 1929, Square, 2 1/2 In. 35.00

PAPER DOLLS were probably inspired by the pantins, or jumping jacks, made in eighteenth-century Europe. By the 1880s, sheets of printed paper dolls and clothes were being made. The first paper doll books were made in the 1920s. Collectors prefer uncut sheets or books or boxed sets of paper dolls. Prices are about half as much if the pages have been cut.

Buffy, 1968, 10 x 13 In. 60.00
Chatty Baby, 1963, Cut 20.00
Dolly Dingle, Sheet 30.00
Dotties Dressed, Uncut 55.00
Down On The Farm, 1940s, Uncut 38.00
Fashion Flatsy, Whitman, 1971, Uncut 30.00
Fred & Wilma Flintstone, Barney & Betty Rubble, Cut Clothes 20.00
Girl Pilots Of Ferr Command, Merill, 1943, Uncut 75.00
Kewpie, Woman's Home Companion, 6 Pages 100.00
Laugh-In, 1969, 6 Dolls, Uncut 150.00
Page, Gody's Ladies Book, October, 1959 . . . . 100.00
Princess Diana, 1985, Uncut 80.00
Put Together Dolls, Embossed Sheet, 1920s, 16 x 12 In. 270.00
Raggedy Ann & Andy, 1974, Uncut 25.00
Rub-A-Dub Dolly, Whitman, 1941, Uncut 20.00
School Days, Gabriel & Sons 45.00
School Mate, Gabriel & Sons 35.00
Twiggy, Carry-Pockets, Whitman, 1967, Uncut 95.00

PAPERWEIGHTS must have first appeared along with paper in ancient Egypt. Today's collectors search for every type, from the very expensive French weights of the nineteenth century to the modern artist weights or advertising pieces. The glass tops of the paperweights sometimes have been nicked or scratched, and this type of damage can be removed by polishing. Some serious collectors think this type of repair is an alteration and will not buy a repolished weight; others think it is an acceptable technique of restoration that does not change the value. Baccarat paperweights are listed separately under Baccarat.

Advertising, Babcock, Submarine, On Base, Cast Metal 75.00
Advertising, Bausch & Lomb, Medal, 2 Busts, 75 Anniversary, 81 mm. 30.00
Advertising, Bergfels Hinge Saddle, Rectangular, Cast Metal 50.00
Advertising, Bucki Carbons Ribbons, Dog, Gold Painted, 1 3/4 x 1 In. 40.00
Advertising, Champion Blower & Forge Co. 175.00
Advertising, Chesterfield, Smoking Pipe 275.00
Advertising, Crane & Breed, Scotty Dog 75.00
Advertising, Dickenson Pine Tree, Cast Iron 120.00
Advertising, F.G. Davis & Co., Wholesale Grocers, Lewiston, Maine, Glass, 1915 . . . . . . 45.00
Advertising, Germer Stove Co. 180.00
Advertising, Hetherington Co., Cast Iron 95.00
Advertising, Karg Bros. Pigskin Leather Gloves, Boar Standing, Cast Metal 115.00
Advertising, Kendalville Foundry Inc., Man Pouring Iron, Cast Iron 65.00
Advertising, Libby's Boneless Beef, Bull, On Base, Cast Metal 65.00

Advertising, Merchant's Motor Freight, Celluloid, 2 Sides, 3 1/2 In. 95.00
Advertising, Monarch Faucets, Globe, On Base, Cast Metal 60.00
Advertising, National Lead Company, Dutch Boy, Lead, 1930s 35.00
Advertising, Oil Well Supply Co., Oil Derrick 115.00
Advertising, Reliance Shirts, Stack Of Shirts 175.00
Advertising, Rouse Co. Apple Juice & Cider, Tanker Truck, On Base, Cast Metal 115.00
Advertising, Toledo Scale 265.00
Advertising, Young's, Tanker Truck, On Base, Cast Metal 115.00
Agnew Associates, In Circle, Marble Type, Enameled, 1 1/2 In. 20.00
Applied Multicolored Fruit, Raspberries, Gray Kalgan Jasper Base, 1870, 6 In. 2990.00
Ayotte, Blue Bird, Perched On Magnolia Branch, 1988, 2 1/4 In. 285.00
Bacchus, Millefiori, Feather Canes, Ruffle, Cog & Star Canes, 3 9/16 In. 9000.00
Banford, Cabbage Rose Bouquet, Pink, Green Leaves, White Ground, 2 1/2 In. 345.00
Bronze, Hand Holding Flower, Black Marble Plinth, Continental, 4 In. 70.00
Calla Lilies, Lavender, Bubbles, Monte Dunlavy, 3 1/4 x 4 In. 30.00
Cameo, 2 Twined Carp & Waves, Blue & Gray Ground, University City, 2 1/2 In. 990.00
Clichy, Chequer, Roses, Pastry Mold, Cog, Prairie & Bull's-Eye Canes, 2 7/8 In. 2250.00
Clichy, Clematis, Lavender, Cobalt Blue, Pink, White, Millefiori Centers, 3 1/8 In. 14000.00
Clichy, Concentric Millefiori, Piedouche, Blue & White Pedestal, 2 13/16 In. 3500.00
Clichy, Millefiori, Magnum Spaced, Roses, Cog, Edelweiss, Star Canes, 3 13/16 In. 8000.00
Clichy, Spaced Millefiori, Rose, Cog, Moss, Star & Bull's-Eye Canes, 2 7/8 In. 1200.00
Jack-In-The-Pulpit, Cobalt Blue, Wilkerson, Marked, 3 In. 35.00
Kaziun, Millefiori, Gold & Amethyst Ground 675.00
Kaziun, Pansy, Gold Bee, Blue Ground 700.00
Lampwork Black Flower, Bubbles, Multicolored Ground, Continental, 3 In. 100.00
New England Glass Co., Scrambled, Cog Canes, Twists, Lace Filigree, 2 1/2 In. 350.00
New England Glass Co., Scrambled, Twisted Ribbon, Filigree, 2 1/2 In. 180.00
Perthshire, Christmas, Portrait Canes, Santa, Reindeer, Millefiori, 1981, 2 7/8 In. 550.00
Perthshire, Crown, Twisted Ribbons, Filigree Spokes, Millefiori, 1969, 2 15/16 In. 800.00
Perthshire, Floral Bouquet, Dragonfly, Crosshatched Base, c.1974, 3 In. 405.00
Perthshire, Tudor Rose, Spaced Garland, Cog, Star & Quatrefoil Canes, 1975, 3 In. 650.00
Sea Serpent, Bronze, 3 7/8 x 3 1/8 In. 95.00
Snowdome, Bullwinkle & Rocky 48.00
Snowdome, Deer 75.00
Snowdome, Rabbit 75.00
Snowdome, Snowman 75.00
St. Clair, Pear, Yellow 40.00
St. Louis, Carpet Ground, Millefiori, Dancing Woman, Dog, Camel, 2 1/2 In. 8000.00
St. Louis, Concentric Millefiori, Piedouche, Star & Cog Canes, Latticinio, 2 11/16 In. 2500.00
St. Louis, Fruits In Latticinio Base Basket, 3 In. 1150.00
St. Louis, Latticinio Filigree, Scrambled, Complex Canes, 3 1/16 In. 1000.00
St. Louis, Latticinio, Pompom, Red Swirl, Dated 1975, 2 1/4 In. 440.00
St. Louis, Lion, Pressed, Frosted, Ribbed Glass Base, 2 11/16 x 5 5/8 In. 650.00
St. Louis, Millefiori, Hawaiian, Complex Quatrefoil Canes, 1975, 3 1/16 In. 750.00
St. Louis, Sulphide, American Eagle, Deep Blue Ground, 1976 .... 175.00
Stankard, Pineland Pickerel-Weed Botanical, Spirit, Bee, Ant, Square, 2 In. 2300.00
Studio Ahus, Submerged White Chevron, Teardrop Shape, Sweden, 5 1/2 x 4 1/2 In. 99.00
Tarsitano, 3 Multipetaled Flowers, Leaves, Pods, Berries, 3 1/4 In. 865.00
Tarsitano, Pansy, Purple, White Center, Star Cut Base, 3 1/4 In. 545.00
Tarsitano, Strawberry, 2 Blossoms, Berry, Leaves, Star Cut Base, 2 1/4 In. 635.00
Water Pump, Cast Metal 55.00
Whitefriars-Type, Concentric Millefiori, Cog & Quatrefoil Canes, 2 11/16 In. 425.00

PAPIER-MACHE is made from paper mixed with glue, chalk, and other ingredients, then molded and baked. It becomes very hard and can be painted. Boxes, trays, and furniture were made of papier-mache. Some of the nineteenth-century pieces were decorated with mother-of-pearl. Furniture made of papier-mache is listed in the Furniture category.

Box, Cutlery, Lacquered, Chinoiserie Design, Gilt 45.00
Box, Desk, Mandarin Family, Black, Chinoiserie, England, 1900, 7 x 6 In. 110.00
Box, Figures Racing 3-Horse Cart, Black Lacquer, Red Interior, 13 In. 1035.00
Box, Pencil, Figures In Interior, Gilt On Black Ground, 11 3/4 In. 110.00
Box, Tobacco, La Fille De Village, Child & Dog At Play, Signed, 3 1/2 In. 120.00

Box, Writing, Applied Gilt-Brass Corners, Portrait Medallion, 1 1/2 x 2 5/8 In. 115.00
Dish, Entwined Serpent Handles, Painted Oriental Scenes, 8 3/4 In. 85.00
Doll, Man & Woman, Wooden, Shell Dressed, 1820-1830, 5 1/2 In., Pair 1200.00
Dust Pan & Brush, Figures In Landscape, Mother-Of-Pearl Inlay, 12 In. 175.00
Egg, 1 Side With Resurrection, Other Side With View Of Kremlin, Red, 1880, 6 In. 2300.00
Figure, St. John The Baptist, Holding Lamb, Wood Plinth, Mexico, 18 1/4 In. 405.00
Lap Desk, Mother-Of-Pearl & Enamel Castle, 13 1/2 In. 345.00
Snuffbox, Hinged Lid, Oval, c.1820, 2 1/2 In. 80.00
Tea Box, Gilt Scenic Medallion, Lead Liner, Chinese, 6 In. 290.00
Tray, Bamboo Stand, Victorian, Black Lacquer, c.1860, 30 In 980.00
Tray, Central Floral Bouquet, Mother-Of-Pearl Highlights, 31 1/2 In. 520.00
Tray, Faux Bamboo Stand, Oval Mother-Pearl, Oval, Medial Shelf, 23 In. 1150.00
Tray, Floral, Leaves Medallion, Black Lacquer, Jennings & Bettridge, 21 In. 1955.00
Tray, Oval, Bamboo Folding Stand, Grapes & Gilt Grape Leaves, 1880s, 20 In. 2070.00
Tray, Painted Gilt Sailing Vase, 17 1/4 In. 160.00
Tray, Painted, Sacrifice Of Abraham, England, 19th Century, 25 1/2 In. 290.00
Tray, Stand, Black Lacquer, Painted Landscape, c.1820, 27 1/2 In. 3220.00
Tray, Stand, Lacquer, Polychrome, Fountain, Peacocks, Flowers, Victorian, 24 In. 3080.00
Tray, Stand, Regency, Black Lacquer, Chinoiserie Figures In Landscape 10350.00

PARASOL, see Umbrella category.

PARIAN is a fine-grained, hard-paste porcelain named for the marble it resembles. It was first made in England in 1846 and gained in favor in the United States about 1860. Figures, tea sets, vases, and other items were made of Parian at many English and American factories.

Bust, Jenny Lind, Mid 19th Century, 12 3/8 In. 78.00
Bust, May Queen, J. Durham & Co., 1868, 13 1/4 In. 80.00
Bust, Milton, 16 1/4 In. 275.00
Bust, Napoleon, Marble Pedestal, Octagonal Base, Paw Feet, 13 x 5 In. 3450.00
Figurine, Classical Female, Reclining Against Pillar, 13 1/2 In. 170.00
Figurine, Female Nude, Riding Lion, 14 3/4 In. 520.00
Nodder, Nobleman, Movable Head & Hands, 6 In. 275.00
Pitcher, Grapevine, Fluted Borders, Campbell & Co., 7 1/4 In. 65.00
Urn, Neoclassical Style, Mermaids, Mermen & Cherubs In Relief, 21 1/2 In. 2420.00

PARIS, Vieux Paris, or Old Paris, is porcelain ware that is known to have been made in Paris in the eighteenth or early nineteenth century. These porcelains have no identifying mark but can be recognized by the whiteness of the porcelain and the lines and decorations. Gold decoration is often used.

Basket, Above Tapered Stem, Square Plinth, 8 1/2 In. 605.00
Basket, Elliptical, Palmetto & Water Leaves, 2-Tone Border, 4 Paw Feet, 12 x 13 x 7 In. . . 6325.00
Basket, Everted Rim, Rosette Matte Wickerwork, Still Leaf Border, 14 In., Pair 4830.00
Basket, Faux Marble Frieze, Deep, Blue Matte Border, Paw Feet, 6 1/2 In. 1100.00
Basket, Gilt Bowl & Stem, Marbleized Square Base, Round, 1825-1850, 10 In. 990.00
Basket, Gilt, Pierced, Gilt Banded Foot, 1825-1850, 8 1/4 x 9 1/2 In. 825.00
Basket, Gilt, Pierced, Pale Green Ground, Round, 8 3/4 x 9 In. 1380.00
Basket, Reticulated, Salmon, White, Twig Shaped Double Loop Handles, 10 In., Pair 770.00
Basket, Vintage Banding, Tapered Stem, Square Plinth, 9 1/2 In., Pair 2090.00
Bowl, Ducks & Birds Of Paradise, Gilt Loop Handle, Mid 19th Century, 10 1/2 In. 2760.00
Cachepot, Band Of Pink Roses, Cornflowers, Gilt Lion Mask Handles, 6 In. 488.00
Cachepot, Gilt Vines, Floral Bouquets, Garland, Bands Of Gold, 7 x 10 In. 747.00
Canister, Cover, Red Key, Black Vine, Gold Bands, 6 1/2 x 5 In. 230.00
Clock, Figural, Falconer With Prey & Dog, Floral Cartouche, Leaf Design, 19 In. 1265.00
Coffeepot, Gilded Lid, Handle With Anthemion Pendant, Bird Head Spout, 10 x 9 In. 345.00
Coffeepot, Well-Formed Roses & Foliage, Gilt Spout, 7 x 4 1/2 In. 287.00
Cologne Bottle, Colorful Flowers, Alternating Leaf Borders, Stopper, 6 1/2 In. 201.00
Cologne Bottle, Green Ground Panels, Black Leaves, Gold Flowers, Stopper, 8 In., Pair . . . 690.00
Cologne Bottle, Green, Brown Cabochons, Gold Trim, Birds & Insects, Stopper, 9 In. 115.00
Cologne Bottle, Mandarin Hat Form, Gilt Vines, Beads, Purple, Burnt Orange, 7 1/2 In. . . . 287.00
Creamer, Figure Of Demure Provincial Beauty, Peach Body, Gilt Border, 8 In. 770.00
Creamer, Flowering Vine, Tapered Body, Gilt, 7 In. 1100.00
Creamer, Hand Painted Seashells, Swans & Mythical Fish, 3 1/2 x 4 1/2 In. 385.00

Cup, Flared, Winter Scene, Chateau, Puce Ground, 19th Century, 3 1/2 In. 170.00
Cup, Front Painted View Of Couple, Landscape, Gilt Bands On Verso, 4 1/4 In. 135.00
Cup, Tapered Cylinder, Hunt Scene, Puce Ground, Empire Style, 19th Century, 3 1/4 In. ... 175.00
Cup & Saucer, Bread & Milk, Bird & Fruit Reserves, Magenta Ground, Gilt Interior 220.00
Cup & Saucer, Cabinet, Dolphin Tails, Serpent Heads, Bifurcated Handle, 4 1/2 In. 316.00
Cup & Saucer, Cabinet, Everted Rim, Nude Couple Embracing By Stream, Gilt, 6 In. 1092.00
Cup & Saucer, Cabinet, Greek Honeysuckle, Basket Of Roses, Trailing Vines, 4 1/2 In. ... 402.00
Cup & Saucer, Cabinet, Rosettes Design, Band Of Vines, Cobalt Blue Ground, 4 3/4 In. ... 230.00
Cup & Saucer, Cafe Au Lait, Green Diamonds, Gold Border, Peach Ground, 3 1/2 In. 230.00
Cup & Saucer, Gilt Everted Rim, Scroll Handle, Beaded Medallion Border, Puce, 6 In. ... 373.00
Cup & Saucer, Landscape, Black Garlands, Rose Pompadour Grounds, 3 x 5 In. 575.00
Figurine, Lass & Lassie, 18th Century Costume, Standing, Flowering Trees, 10 In., Pair .. 550.00
Garniture, Corbeilles, Figural Centerpiece, Kneeling Putti, Gilt, Copper Liners, 5 Piece .. 1650.00
Garniture, Table, Center Bowl, Corbeilles, Reticulated, Flowers, Scrollwork, 3 Piece 2200.00
Inkwell, Continuous Rustic Landscape, Buildings & Mountains, Paw Feet, 5 x 3 In. 1035.00
Jar, Apothecary, Extr. Glycyr. G., In Oval, Winged Eagle, 1850-1875, 10 1/2 In. 165.00
Jardiniere, Base, Allover Flowers, White & Black Lappets, Blue Border, Gilt, 7 1/2 In. 440.00
Jardiniere, Rustic Landscape, 2-Tone Gilt Allegorical Scene, Floral Border, 8 1/4 In. 1650.00
Jardiniere, Sprigs & Gilt Leaves, Gilt Twin Handles, Lobed Foot, 5 1/2 In. 2990.00
Lamp Base, Column, Spiral Flower Design, Square Base, 20 In. 660.00
Night-Light, Veilleuse, 4-Part, Tower Form Base, Lidded Teapot, Dragon Spout, 9 1/4 In. .. 330.00
Night-Light, Veilleuse, Sultana Holding Ewer, Torso As Teapot, 13 In. 605.00
Pitcher, Gilt & Floral Design, 9 In. 230.00
Plate, 1 Village With Moat, 1 Tavern Scene, With Men Drinking, Blue, 9 In., Pair 575.00
Plate, Center Map Of Petersburg, 4 Trophies, Rosette Medallions, c.1810, 9 1/4 In. 747.00
Plate, Gilt Band, Key Border, Shell & Ducks, 9 In., Pair 862.00
Plate, Harlequin, Gothic Tracery, Darte, 1800-1825, 9 1/4 In., 4 Piece 880.00
Plate, Iroquois Chief, Ceremonial Dress, Gilded Border, Denuelle, c.1820, 9 1/2 In., Pair . 6270.00
Plate, Service, Concentric Bands, Floral Garlands, Gilt Leaves, 3 Busts, 10 In., 12 Piece . 2070.00
Plate, Wreath, Rosette, Grecian Honeysuckle, Orange Glaze, Gilt Border, 9 In. 1035.00
Potpourri, Domed Lid, Flared Rim, Leaves, Floral Reserves, Hippocampi, 11 In., Pair ... 2420.00
Salt Cellar, Shell Form, Colorful Roses, Gold Outlined Exterior, 4 1/2 In. 345.00
Sauceboat, Tray, Gold Butterscotch Border, Gilt Rim, Shell Handle, 8 1/2 In. 488.00
Saucer, Round Cover, Classical Busts On Stepped Plinth, Ring Handle, 8 3/4 In. 715.00
Scent Bottle, Alternating Floral, Puce & Gilt Panels, Stopper, 19th Century, 7 In., Pair .. 910.00
Scent Bottle, Figural, Jeanette, By Tree Trunk, With Lantern, 1825-1850, 5 3/4 In. 360.00
Stand, Sweetmeat, 2 Tiers, Polychrome Floral, 11 1/2 In. 302.00
Stand, Sweetmeat, 3 Tiers, White Ground, Lion Paw Feet, 16 x 9 1/2 In. 1045.00
Syrup, Figural, Italian Gentleman & Consort, 1825-1850, 12 In., Pair 770.00
Syrup, Joan D'Arc, Hand On Flask, Green, Red, 10 1/2 In. 165.00
Tea & Coffee Set, Romantic & Family Vignettes, Amber, Gilt Banding, 11 Piece 2200.00
Tea Service, Floral Panels, Rocailled Border, Peach Ground, 6 5/8-In. Teapot 1650.00
Teapot, Cover, Gilt Vine, Scroll Handle, Burnt Orange Arcade Border, 6 x 7 x 4 In. 402.00
Teapot, Floral Design, Cobalt Bordered Panels Of Garden Flowers, 7 In. 288.00
Teapot, Greek Key Border Within Gold Bands, Eagle's Head Spout, 7 1/2 In. 402.00
Teapot, Leaf Medallion, Lavender, Green Leaves, Sprig Border, Loop Handle, 7 x 8 In. .. 402.00
Tray, Continuous Floral Vine, Scrolled Bands, Empire Blue Border, Gilt Rim, 11 In. 172.00
Tray, Dessert, 3 Tiers, Blue Border, Gilt Bands, Ring Handle, 19th Century, 16 x 9 In. 550.00
Tray, Polychrome Flowers, Gilt Leaf Tips, 2 Sections, Gilt Handle, 6 x 9 In. 431.00
Tureen, Cover, Rosette Ended Handles, Oval Foot, 13 x 14 x 10 In. 935.00
Tureen, Domed Lid, Leaf Tip Finial, Gilt Leopard's Head Handles, 10 1/2 In. 1955.00
Urn, 2 Girls With Dog On Front, Floral Sprays On Verso, Loop Handles, 11 In., Pair 1150.00
Urn, Campana, Classical Profiles, Gilt, Green Ground, Greek Key Border, 13 1/2 In. 495.00
Urn, Campana, Cobalt Blue, Pastoral Scenes, Gilt Classical Designs, 6 1/2 In., Pair 715.00
Urn, Campana, Figural Cartouche, Blue Ground, Gilt Handles With Mask, 11 In. 545.00
Urn, Gold Concentric Bands, Peach Border, 16 1/2 x 10 In., Pair 16675.00
Urn, Harbor Scene, c.1840, 11 In., Pair 3000.00
Urn, Napoleon, Gilt Handles, Pair ....*Illus* 2100.00
Vase, Allegory Of Fawn, Mountainous Landscape, Swan Neck Handles, 13 In., Pair 3680.00
Vase, Baluster, Applied Gilt Handles, Chinoiserie Figures, Bird, Moth, Flowers, 21 1/2 In. 1165.00
Vase, Baluster, Garden Landscapes, Mint Green Ground, Late 19th Century, 14 In., Pair .. 440.00
Vase, Burnished Cornucopia, Blue Body, Gilt Borders, Winged Female Handles, 13 In. ... 2420.00
Vase, Campana, Italian Landscape, Reserve, Green Ground, Twin Handles, 14 In., Pair ... 3080.00

Paris, Urn,
Napoleon, Gilt
Handles, Pair

When removing a stain from fabrics or marble or any other surface, apply the stain cleaner from the edge to the center to avoid spreading the stain.

Vase, Cluster Of Water Lilies, Snails, Green, Brown, Handles, Leaf Feet, 10 In., Pair	1725.00
Vase, Cornucopia, Floral Design, Mounted As Lamb, 9 In., Pair	373.00
Vase, Figural, Floral Cartouches, Gilt Leaf Frame, Blue Ground, 14 In., Pair	2645.00
Vase, Floral Friezes, Blue Ground Border, White Ground, 19th Century, 9 1/4 In., Pair	1035.00
Vase, Floral Reserve, Gilt Bird Within Scrolling Vines, Green Ground, Scroll Feet, 14 In.	1380.00
Vase, Floral Sprays, Latticework, Flowers On Black Ground, Leaf Scroll Feet, 14 In., Pair	1265.00
Vase, Flowers, Classical Modeled Plinth, Paw Feet, 7 3/4 In.	1760.00
Vase, Gilt Panel Of Flowers Front, Pierced Rocaille Foot, c.1840, 15 1/2 In., Pair	546.00
Vase, Hand Form, Holding Cornucopia, 5 1/2 In.	185.00
Vase, Inswept Sides, Elephant's Mask Handles, Late 19th Century, 24 In., Pair	4600.00
Vase, Landscape Scene & Figures Of Courting Couple, Italy, 10 1/4 In., Pair	805.00
Vase, Medallion Of Woman Being Crowned, Fuchsia Ground, Pierced Rim, 19 1/2 In.	460.00
Vase, Oriental Boys At Play, Colorful Bouquet On Other Side, 15 In., Pair	6600.00
Vase, Portrait Medallion, Gilt Ground, Floriform Handles, 9 3/8 In., Pair	575.00
Vase, Romantic Couple Reclining By A Tree, Gilt Rim, Green Ground, Oval, 8 1/2 In.	230.00
Vase, Rural Landscape & Harbor Scene, Everted Rim, Inverted Neck, 13 1/2 In., Pair	2185.00
Vase, Shell & Swag Design, Salmon Ground, Raised Gold Arabesques, 16 1/5 In., Pair	4400.00
Vase, Woman & Young Girl, Molded Leaf Design, Blue, Gilt, White, 26 In., Pair	2760.00

PATE-DE-VERRE is an ancient technique in which glass is made by blending and refining powdered glass of different colors into molds. The process was revived by French glassmakers, especially Galle, around the end of the nineteenth century.

Bowl, Dark Purple Interior, Lappet Design Around Rim, 1910, 5 3/8 In.	1380.00
Bowl, Scalloped Autumn Vines, Red Berries Clusters, Green, Plum Glaze, 6 In.	3190.00
Box, Cover, Orange, Pale Yellow, 1923, 3 3/8 In.	8625.00
Dish, Butterfly, With Pine Needles, Yellow, Green, Brown, 1920, 6 7/8 In.	2070.00
Figurine, Parrot, On Perch, Squared Base, Signed, 11 1/4 In.	805.00
Moth, Red Amber, Black Head, Yellow, Red Eyes, 2 1/2 x 1 3/4 In.	1430.00
Plate, 4 Seasons, Mythical Figures, Signed, 1669, 10 1/2 In., 4 Piece	9920.00
Vase, 2 Snakes Coiled Among Leaves, c.1965, 11 3/4 In.	833.00
Vase, Flute Mold, Vetruvian Scrolls, Amber, Purple, Gray Glass, 1925, 7 In.	1955.00
Vase, Gray, Lavender, Green Vertical Highlights, Signed, 5 1/2 In.	5500.00

PATE-SUR-PATE means paste on paste. The design was made by painting layers of slip on the ceramic piece until a relief decoration was formed. The method was developed at the Sevres factory in France about 1850. It became even more famous at the English Minton factory about 1870. It has since been used by many potters to make both pottery and porcelain wares.

Charger, Maidens In Wooded Landscape, Signed Schenk, c.1880, 12 In.	1265.00
Lamp, Fluid, Gilt Metal Mounted, Floral Shade & Globe, 24 1/2 In., Pair	2070.00
Pitcher, Baluster, Man Seated On Bench, Pale Green, Brown Ground, 7 1/2 In.	633.00
Plaque, Battle Scene, Warrior Over Fallen Soldier, Frame, Signed, 28 1/2 In.	2645.00
Stein, Cavalier At Table With Older Man, Marble, Figural Porcelain Lid, 1/2 Liter	522.00
Vase, Angel, Feet Bound By Chain & Hall, Signed, c.1865, 7 3/8 In.	517.00
Vase, Maple Leaves, White Berries, Bisque, University City, 1913, 7 In.	4125.00

Vase, Scenes Of Diana Assisting Cupid Firing Arrow, c.1900, 7 1/2 In 5175.00
Vase, Stylized Leaves Design, Square Form Handles, Scrolled Ends, 10 In. 5175.00
Vase, Woman, Bordered By Silver Overlay, 4 1/2 In. 385.00

PAUL REVERE POTTERY was made at several locations in and around
Boston, Massachusetts, between 1906 and 1942. The pottery was operated as a settlement house program for teenage girls. Many pieces were
signed *S.E.G.* for Saturday Evening Girls. The artists concentrated on
children's dishes and tiles. Decorations were outlined in black and
filled with color.

Bookends, Blue, Green Mosaic Ground, 1921, 4 1/4 x 5 In., Pair 495.00
Bowl, Band Of White Orchids, Blue & Beige, S.E.G., 3 x 8 In.   2200.00
Bowl, Blue & Ivory Ground, S.E.G., Ink Mark, 1 3/4 x 6 In. 165.00
Bowl, Cereal, Black, Yellow Ground, 1916, 2 1/2 x 5 1/2 In. 247.00
Bowl, Cereal, Blue Trees, Ivory Sky, Blue Green Ground, 5 In. 1100.00
Bowl, Flared Rim, White, Painted Green Leaves, Blue Band, 4 1/4 x 10 3/4 In. 880.00
Bowl, Geometric Border, Sage Green Glaze, Blue Ground, S.E.G., 1911, 4 In. 550.00
Bowl, Green Trees, Moss Green Matte Ground, S.E.G., 3 x 7 In. 2970.00
Bowl, Landscape, Green, Blue, Black, Ivory Ground, Signed, 4 1/2 In. 715.00
Bowl, Lotus Blossoms, Speckled Green Ground, 6 1/4 In. 385.00
Bowl, Stylized Arrowheads, Celadon, Blue Ground, S.E.G., 4 x 10 In. 525.00
Bowl, Trees On Band Interior, Blue Ground, 2 x 6 1/4 In. 770.00
Bowl, Whimsical Rabbits, Brown & White, S.E.G., 2 x 5 In. 2310.00
Bowl, White Geese, Blue, Gray Ground, 1917, 2 1/4 x 5 1/2 In.   770.00
Breakfast Set, Yellow, Chicks & Rabbits, Ellen-Louisa, PRP Ink Mark, 1941, 4 Piece . . .   1540.00
Cup & Saucer, Dark Blue Rims, Yellow Floral Border, Cream Ground, 1912, 2 In. 575.00
Inkwell, Trees, Landscape, Square, Ink Mark, Label, 2 x 2 1/2 x 2 3/4 In. 935.00
Mug, Landscape Medallion, Blue, Brown, Yellow, 3 1/2 In. 286.00
Paperweight, Octagonal, Tree, Green Grass, Blue Sky, S.E.G., 2 1/2 In. 440.00
Paperweight, Pilgrim Portrait In Center, 2 1/2 In. 195.00
Pitcher, Milk, Blue, White Tortoise & Hare, Slow But Sure, S.E.G., Ink Mark, 4 In. 1650.00
Teacup, Stylized Flower Band, Blue Matte Ground, 1911, 2 1/2 In. 220.00
Tile, Geometric Design, Arts & Crafts Oak Frame, Square, 6 In. 825.00
Vase, Black & Blue High Glaze, Signed, 13 In. 495.00
Vase, Blue Green Mottled Glaze, Stamped Mark, 4 1/4 In. 121.00
Vase, Blue Semigloss Glaze, 1929, 6 1/4 x 3 1/4 In. 165.00
Vase, Blue, Landscape, Stamped Mark, 1925, 4 x 3 3/4 In. 935.00
Vase, Closed-In Rim, Stylized Flowers, Blue Ground, S.E.G., 4 x 6 In. 4125.00
Vase, Cobalt Blue Glaze, Cylindrical, 3 7/8 In. 145.00
Vase, Cover, Painted 4 Colors Ship At Sea, Label, Signed, 4 In. 495.00
Vase, Cover, Painted Floral, Cream Ground, 5 In. 440.00
Vase, Deep Blue, Signed, 4 In. 120.00
Vase, Geometric Top, Black, Light Green Ground, Signed, 4 In. 605.00
Vase, Greek Key, Brown, Blue, Green Ground, Ink, 4 1/2 x 2 1/4 In. 825.00
Vase, Iced White Glaze, Bulbous, Flared Rim, 5 In. 155.00
Vase, Landscape, Band Of Trees, Blue Matte Ground, 19097, 10 1/4 x 5 In. 4400.00
Vase, Mint Green Dripping Glaze, 1938, 8 In. 250.00
Vase, Speckled Dark Blue Glaze, Bulbous Base, Early 20th Century, 7 1/8 In. 345.00
Vase, Teal Green Matte Glaze, 1922, 13 1/2 x 8 1/2 In. 715.00
Vase, Tulip Band, Cobalt Blue Ground, Glaze Drip Rim, Bulbous, 4 3/4 x 4 In. 550.00
Vase, Yellow Flowers, Green Geometric Design, Black, White, Peach, 4 x 5 In. 935.00
Vase, Yellow Matte Glaze, Classical Shape, 6 1/2 x 5 In. 220.00

PEACHBLOW glass was made by several factories beginning in the
1880s. New England peachblow is a one-layer glass shading from red
to white. Mt. Washington peachblow shades from pink to bluish-white.
Hobbs, Brockunier and Company of Wheeling, West Virginia, made
coral glass that they marketed as Peach Blow. It shades from yellow
to peach and is lined with white glass. Reproductions of all types
of peachblow have been made. Related pieces may be listed under
Gunderson and Webb Peachblow.

Biscuit Jar, Enameled Yellow Roses, Satin, 7 In. 448.00
Cruet, Satin, Handle, Stopper, 7 1/2 In. 336.00

Epergne, Lily, Enameled Flowers, Ruffled Edge, 18 1/2 In. 795.00
Mustard, Glossy, Silvered Mount Handle, Thumblift Cover, Wheeling, 2 1/2 In. 476.00
Pitcher, Bulbous Body, Amber Handle, Wheeling, Late 19th Century, 5 1/4 In. 373.00
Pitcher, Drape, Reeded Handle, Late 19th Century, 6 1/2 In. 460.00
Punch Cup, Wheeling 70.00
Punch Cup, White Handle 30.00
Toothpick, Wheeling 1265.00
Tumbler, Wheeling, 3 3/4 In. 258.00
Vase, Applied Flowers, Wheeling, 10 1/4 In. 187.00
Vase, Applied Gold Apple, Wheeling, 9 In. 187.00
Vase, Bird & Floral, 6 Footed, 6 1/2 In. 100.00
Vase, Blue Floral, Ruffled Edge, 6 In. 150.00
Vase, Daisy, 2 Handles, 6 In. 110.00
Vase, Design, Kimble & Duncan, 8 3/4 In. 150.00
Vase, Design, Kimble & Duncan, 9 In., Pair 350.00
Vase, Design, Kimble & Duncan, 11 In. 175.00
Vase, Mother-Of-Pearl, Enameled Floral & Dragonfly, Footed, 12 In. 425.00
Vase, Stick, Gold Rim, Wheeling, 9 In. 230.00
Vase, Stick, Satin, Wheeling, 8 1/2 In. 392.00
Vase, Stick, Tapered Oval Base, Wheeling, 13 3/4 In. 545.00

PEANUTS is the title of a comic strip created by cartoonist Charles M.
Schulz (1922-2000). The strip, drawn by Schulz from 1950 to 2000,
features a group of children, including Charlie Brown and his sister
Sally, Lucy Van Pelt and her brother Linus, Peppermint Patty, and Pig
Pen, and an imaginative and independent beagle named Snoopy. The
Peanuts gang has also been featured in books, television shows, and a
Broadway musical.

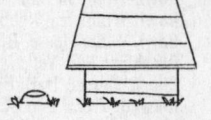

Bank, Snoopy, Silver Plate, Metal, 1960s 75.00
Banner, Lucy, I'm Frustrated, Red Felt, United Features, 1967, 33 In. 36.00
Banner, Snoopy, I Think I'm Allergic To Mornings, Pink Wool, 32 In. 28.00
Banner, Snoopy, I've Got To Start Acting Sensible...Tomorrow, 32 In. 35.00
Birdhouse, Woodstock Wild Bird Home, Snoopy, Doghouse, Plastic, Box, 5 x 7 x 6 In. . . 37.00
Bottle, Charlie Brown, Shampoo, Red Baseball Hat, Plastic, Avon, Box, 1968, 4 Oz. 32.00
Bottle, Linus, Shampoo, White Plastic, Avon, 1968 . . . . 31.00
Bottle, Lucy, Shampoo, Red Cap, Avon, 1970 . . . . 22.00
Bottle, Snoopy Flyer, Bubble Bath, Avon, Unused, Box, 1973 . . . . 45.00
Dog Feeder, Automatic, Snoopy Snack Attack, Doghouse, Plastic, Gabriel, 11 x 7 In. 21.00
Magazine, Life, Charlie Brown & Snoopy On Cover, March 17, 1967 . . . . 46.00
Music Box, Peanuts & Red Baron In Airplane, Wooden, Schmid 225.00
Night-Light, Snoopy, Soft Molded Plastic, Painted Details, 6 In. 42.00
Pin, Charlie Brown, Celluloid, United Features, 1 1/4 In. 20.00
Pin, Snoopy, Celluloid, United Features, 1 1/4 In. 20.00
Plate, '76, Bicentennial, Snoopy On Liberty Bell, Box, Schmid, 8 In. 21.00
Roller Skates, Snoopy, Plastic, Adjustable, Nash Mfg. Co., c.1966 . . . . 27.00
Snowdome, Peanuts, Snoopy & Woodstock Roasting Marshmallows, 4 In. 23.00
Telephone, Snoopy & Woodstock, American Telecommunications Company, 1976, 13 In. . . 140.00
Telephone, Snoopy & Woodstock, Hard Plastic, Rotary Dial, 14 In. 88.00
Telephone, Snoopy, Joe Cool, Woodstock, Touch Tone, Box, Seika Corp., 11 x 8 1/2 In. . . 105.00
Telephone, Snoopy, Push Button Dial On Back, United Syndicate, Box, 7 In. 45.00
Toy, Charlie Brown, Plastic, Red Shirt, Black Pants, Pocket Doll, 1960s, 7 In. . . . . . . 37.00 to 52.00
Toy, Charlie Brown, Vinyl, Painted, First Style, Hungerford, 1958, 7 1/2 In. 75.00
Toy, Linus, Molded Plastic, United Features Syndicate, 1950s, 8 1/2 In. 75.00
Toy, Linus, Molded Vinyl, Plastic, Fabric Clothes, Pocket Dolls, 1960s, 7 In. 42.00
Toy, Linus, Molded Vinyl, Plastic, Hungerford, 1958, 7 In. 76.00
Toy, Lucy, First Edition, Molded Vinyl, Hungerford, United Features, 1958, 7 In. . . . 75.00 to 80.00
Toy, Music Box, Snoopy As WWI Flying Ace, Doghouse, Yellow, Green, Rotates, 8 x 5 In. 62.00
Toy, Snoopy, Molded Plastic, Painted Ears & Tail, Movable Limbs, KTC, 1970s, 9 In. . . . 45.00
Toy, Snoopy, Molded Plastic, Plush Ears, Tail, Posable, Determined Productions, 8 In. . . . 28.00
Toy, Snoopy, Stuffed, Beanie Arms & Feet, Hallmark, 1966, 7 In. 21.00
Toy, Snoopy, Vinyl, Denim Jeans & Jacket, 9 In. 100.00
Toy, Snoopy, Vinyl, Denim Jeans, Jacket, Snoopy Patch, Determined Products, 1970, 8 In. 40.00
Toy, Snoopy, Vinyl, Painted, Squeeker, Hungerford, 1950s, 7 1/4 In. 130.00

Toy, Snoopy, Walker, Windup, Hard Plastic, Hong Kong, Box, 3 In. 22.00
Toy, Snoopy, WWI Flying Ace, White Vinyl, Brown Suede Flight Helmet, 7 In. 51.00
Wastebasket, Charlie Brown, Lucy, Snoopy, Movie Director, Metal, 13 In. 24.00

PEARL items listed here are made of the natural mother-of-pearl from
shells. Such natural pearl has been used to decorate furniture and small
utilitarian objects for centuries. The glassware known as mother-of-
pearl is listed by that name. Opera glasses made with natural pearl
shell are listed under Opera Glasses.

Dessert Service, Oak Case, 6 Forks, 6 Knives, 1900, 12 Piece 230.00
Fish Service, Mahogany Case, 6 Forks, 6 Scrolled Knives, 1920, 12 Piece 316.00
Penholder, Brass, 5 1/2 In. 35.00
Wall Pocket, Carved Horn, Philippine Scenes Inlay, Pair 28.00

PEARLWARE is an earthenware made by Josiah Wedgwood in 1779. It
was copied by other potters in England. Pearlware is only slightly
different in color from creamware and for many years collectors have
confused the terms. Wedgwood pieces are listed in the Wedgwood category in this book.

Pearl

Bidet, Scenes Of Ducks Interior, Birds On Branches, Fence Rails, c.1883, 18 1/2 In. 172.00
Bowl, Gaudy Design, Large Bloom Sunflower, 12 1/2 x 4 In. 385.00
Bowl, Polychrome Enamel, Oriental Design, 10 3/8 In. 440.00
Bust, John Wesley, 1820, 11 In. 850.00
Creamer, Pigeon Beak, Leeds Type Design, c.1800, 3 1/4 In. 300.00
Cup & Saucer, Brown Willow Transfer, Orange Edge, 5 3/4 In., Set Of 6 .... 465.00
Cup & Saucer, Handleless, Black Transfer, Horse Drawn Chariot, Putti, Set Of 6 ...... 525.00
Cup & Saucer, King's Rose, Solid Pink Border 137.00
Cup & Saucer, Peafowl, Red, 4 1/2 In. 230.00
Cup Plate, Flower, Orange & Yellow 55.00
Cup Plate, Molded Floral Border, Brown Transfer, Present For Martha, 4 5/8 In. 220.00
Figurine, Cleopatra & Anthony, England, 10 In., Pair 2990.00
Figurine, Horse & Groom, Sponged Racehorse Wearing Ocher Blanket, 11 In. 16100.00
Inkwell, Lion, 19th Century, 4 x 5 x 2 3/4 In. 1265.00
Mug, Franklin's Maxims, Staffordshire, 2 1/2 In. 130.00
Mug, To Washington The Patriot Of America, American Eagles, Child's 345.00
Pitcher, Flowers & Birds, Silver Luster, 5 1/2 In. 357.00
Pitcher, Milk, Floral, 5 Colors, Elmer Webster, 4 7/8 In. 660.00
Plaque, Woman On Hillside, Oval Black Transfer, Inscription, 6 1/2 x 8 1/2 In. 430.00
Plate, Blue Chinoiserie Design, Blue Feather Edge Rim, 9 1/2 In., Pair 520.00
Plate, Massacre Of The Innocents, Molded Floral Border, 8 1/2 In. 145.00
Plate, Red Flower, Molded Border, Red Band, Crazed, 7 In. 95.00
Platter, Chinoiserie Scene, Blue & White, 18 1/2 In. 258.00
Platter, Meat, Blue Border, Central Circle, England, 19th Century, 13 x 11 In. 23.00
Salt & Pepper, Medium Blue Transfer, House, People, Deer, c.1795, 3 1/2 In. 895.00
Sugar, Cover, England, 4 1/4 x 5 3/8 In. 325.00
Sugar, Peacock In Sponged Tree, Leaf Ends On Handle, 4 1/2 In. 110.00
Teapot, Leaves & Swag, 10 1/2 In. 58.00
Teapot, Leeds Type Floral, 5 Colors, 6 In. 220.00
Tray, Egg, 6 Holders, Central Salt Cellar, Flowers, Gilt Trim, 1830s, 10 1/2 In. 1265.00

PEKING GLASS is a Chinese cameo glass first made popular in the
eighteenth century. The Chinese have continued to make this layered
glass in the old manner, and many new pieces are now available that
could confuse the average buyer.

Bowl, Cover, Landscape, 4 5/8 In. 715.00
Bowl, Deer, Crane, Pines & Flowers, Ruby Red, 6 In. 1150.00
Bowl, Lotus Form, Seed Pod Interior, Pink, Lotus Leaf Foot, 5 1/8 In. 2420.00
Bowl, Quatrefoil Form, Green, Late 19th Century, 8 In. 360.00
Bowl, Ribbing & Foliate Edge, Deep Purple, 13 In. 290.00
Jar, Cover, Overall Peaches & Bats, Green To White, 7 1/2 In. 400.00
Jar, Flowering Peony Plants, Carved Butterflies On Cover, 6 1/2 In. 345.00
Snuff Bottle, Chinese Blue, Clock On 2 Sides, Flanked By Flowers, 2 In. 345.00
Teapot, Landscape, Flowering Vines, Globular, 18th Century, 7 1/2 In. 1320.00
Vase, 12 Sides, Club Form, Yellow, 19th Century, 8 1/2 In. 1320.00

Vase, Birds & Fruiting Branches, Blue Cut To Clear, 10 1/4 In., Pair 345.00
Vase, Butterflies & Flowers, Early 20th Century, 8 3/4 In. 85.00
Vase, Clouds & Phoenix Roundels, Green To White, Marked, 20th Century 1380.00
Vase, Double Gourd Form, Cobalt Blue, 19th Century, 8 1/2 In. 1375.00
Vase, Flower Design, 4 1/2 x 5 1/2 In. 45.00
Vase, Geometric Designs Of Floral Panels, 20th Century, 5 1/2 In. 805.00

PELOTON glass is a European glass with small threads of colored glass rolled onto the surface of clear or colored glass. It is sometimes called spaghetti, or shredded coconut, glass. Most pieces found today were made in the nineteenth century.

Tumbler, Colored Threads, 19th Century, 3 3/4 In. 195.00
Vase, Multicolored Strings Of Glass, 7 In. 145.00
Vase, Red, Kralik, 7 In. 200.00

PENS replaced hand-cut quills as writing instruments in 1780 when the first steel pen point was made in England. But it was 100 years before the commercial pen was a common item. The fountain pen was invented in the 1830s but was not made in quantity until the 1880s. All types of old pens are collected.

PEN, Conklin, Crescent Filler, Gold Filled Filigree 185.00
Eclipse, Fountain, Celluloid, Black & Olive Green, 1923, 5 1/4 In. 25.00
Eversharp, Gulf Oil 30.00
Eversharp, Manifold, Marbleized 40.00
Eversharp, Wahl, Fountain, Black Plastic Body, 14K Gold Nib, 1930 .... 30.00
Eversharp, Wahl, Fountain, Gold Seal, Green, Filler Lever, 14K Gold Plated Nib, 5 In. 25.00
Eversharp, Wahl, Fountain, Pyrite, Orange, Gold Filled Accents, 14K Gold Nib, 5 In. 35.00
Eversharp, Wahl, Fountain, Rose Colored, 14K Gold Nib, 4 1/2 In. 30.00
Float About, Alfred Hitchcock, 6 Different Portraits, Twist & Click 5.00
Float About, Circus World, Children, On Tiger, 1982 .... 3.00
Float About, Curious George, Yellow Hat, Twist & Click 5.00
Float About, Studebaker, From Speedway, 1852-1966, Red Champion Convertible 4.00
Float About, Washington, Classic Style, Glitter, Twist & Click 5.00
Moore, Fountain, Loyal Order Of The Red Men, Black, 14K Gold Junior 4 Nib, 5 In. 25.00
National, Lincoln Pen, Fountain, Celluloid, Black & Green Marbleized Design, 5 1/4 In. . 25.00
Parker, Duofold, Jr., Black, Tan, Light Green Marbleized, Lucky Curve, 4 1/2 In. 80.00
Parker, Fountain, Black Hard Rubber, Gold Overlay With Cap, 4 In. 140.00
Parker, Fountain, Celluloid, Oriental Dragons, Rust Colored, 14K Gold Nib, 5 In. 95.00
Parker, Fountain, Duofold, Green Body, Parker Duofold Rib, 5 In. 50.00
Sheaffer, Fountain, Courtesy, 1956 .... 115.00
Sheaffer, Fountain, Green, Black Striped Body, 5 In. 30.00
Sheaffer, Fountain, Lifetime, Black Pearl Radite, 5 1/4 In. 100.00
Sheaffer, Fountain, Lifetime, Triumph, Woman's 30.00
Traveler, Tan Celluloid, 14K Gold Nib, 5 In. 30.00
Vacuum-Fil, Fountain, Green & Black Marbleized Design, 5 In. 25.00
Wahl, Fountain, Gray, Brown, Filler Lever, Pat. 1904, 5 1/4 In. 20.00
Waterman, Sterling Silver Filigree, Pat. 1884 .... 35.00
Waterman Ideal, Patent 1899 & 1903 .... 125.00
PEN & PENCIL, Eversharp, Skyline, 14K Gold, Set 450.00
Eversharp, Wahl, Gold Tone, 14K Nib, 1920 .... 175.00
Eversharp, Wahl, Green Fountain Pen, 14K Gold, 4 1/2-In. Pen 75.00

PENCILS were invented, so it is said, in 1565. The eraser was not added to the pencil until 1858. The automatic pencil was invented in 1863. Collectors today want advertising pencils or automatic pencils of unusual design. Boxes and sharpeners for pencils are also collected.

PENCIL, Cross, Purse Size, 10K Gold, 3 1/2 In. 20.00
Lead, San Antonio, Tex., 1950, 8 1/2 In. 247.00
Mechanical, Auto-Lite Spark Plugs, Secretary Pen Company, 5 1/2 In. 23.00
Mechanical, Central Fire Truck Corporation, 1920s Truck, Celluloid, 5 1/4 In. 22.00
Mechanical, Cities Service, Black, Cream, Celluloid, 5 1/2 In. 20.00
Mechanical, J.W. McComas, You Can Whip Our Cream, Milk Truck, 6 In. 42.00
Mechanical, Parker, Black, Light Lime Marble Body, Brass Ends, 5 1/4 In. 90.00
Mechanical, Parker, Parkette, Ruby, Marbleized, 4 3/4 In. 35.00

Mechanical, Pencraft, Black, Yellow Highlights, Marble Look, 5 1/8 In. 20.00
Mechanical, R. Loeb & Co. Inc., Pearlized, 3 Lead Colors, 5 1/2 In. 29.00
Mechanical, Richfield Products, Perpetual Calendar, 1940s Eagle Logo, 5 In. 60.00
Mechanical, S. Mordan & Co., Tri-Color Gold, Relief Flowers, Amethyst, 3 1/2 In. 290.00
Mechanical, Sheaffer's, Ball & V Design, Metal, Pair 20.00
Mechanical, Shur-Rite, Gold Filled, Designed To Hang From Chain Or Necklace, 4 In. . . . 20.00
Mechanical, Standard Oil Company Golden Jubilee, Red, Cream, Celluloid, 5 1/4 In. 20.00
Mechanical, Tiona Petroleum Co., Tiopet Indian, Perpetual Calendar, 5 1/2 In. 60.00
Mechanical, Waterman's, Sterling Case, 5 1/2 In. 80.00
Sheaffer, Skyboy, Brown Marbleized 35.00
Wahl Eversharp, Gold Filled 20.00
PENCIL SHARPENER, Climax, Shavings Drawer, Pat. 1900-1906, 8 x 5 1/2 In. 175.00
Climax, Steel, Shavings Drawer, Pat. 1900-1906, 8 x 5 1/2 In. 175.00
Empire State Building, 3 1/2 In. 18.00
Joe Carioke, Bakelite, 1940s 50.00
Motorcycle, Plastic, Sharpener In Seat, Germany, 3 1/2 In. 25.00
Sword, c.1830 . . . . 2970.00

PENNSBURY Pottery worked in Morrisville, Pennsylvania, from 1950
to 1971. Full sets of dinnerware as well as many decorative items were
made. Pieces are marked with the name of the factory.

Pennsbury Pottery

Amish Farm Family, Chop Plate, 11 In. 70.00
Amish Farm Scene, Pitcher, Milk, 6 1/2 In. 175.00
Baltimore & Ohio Railroad, Plaque, Retired Workers, 5 3/4 x 7 3/4 In. 65.00
Doylestown Trust Company, Coaster 25.00
Fairless Works Steel Mill, Ashtray, 7 x 5 In. 45.00
Heads, Cruet, Oil & Vinegar 85.00
Rooster, Casserole, Cover, 8 1/4 In. 55.00
Rooster, Sugar & Creamer, Marked, 4 In. 28.00
Rooster, Tip Tray, 6 x 8 In. 50.00
Yellow Rooster, Creamer, 4 1/2 In. 45.00
Yellow Rooster, Pitcher, Milk, 7 1/2 In. 150.00

PEPSI-COLA, the drink and the name, was invented in 1898 but was not
trademarked until 1903. The logo was changed from an elaborate
script to the modern block letters on the 1970 Pepsi label. Several different logos have been used. Until 1951, the words *Pepsi* and *Cola* were
separated by 2 dashes. These bottles are called *double dash*. In 1951 the
modern logo with a single hyphen was introduced. All types of advertising memorabilia are collected, and reproductions are being made.

Bank, Cooler, Composition, 4 In. 116.00
Bank, Jukebox, Musical 20.00
Bottle, 1972, 32 Oz. 5.00
Bottle, New York, N.Y., 1954, 12 Oz. 10.00
Bottle, NKC, Mo., 1948, 12 Oz. 15.75
Bottle, Swirl, 4 3/8 In. 15.00
Bottle Opener, New York, N.Y., 1920-1930 . . . . 25.00
Calendar, 1944, Our America, Family Scene In Kitchen, Dark Brown, 22 x 17 In. 35.00
Carrier, 6-Pack, Wooden, 1940 . . . . 95.00
Carrier, 6-Pack, Wooden, Cutout Handle Top 155.00
Clock, Be Sociable, Have A Pepsi, Pale Yellow Ground, 1950, 8 x 8 1/2 In. 2057.00
Clock, Fiberboard Case, Red, White & Blue, 1940s 545.00
Clock, Reverse Painted, Woman, With Glass, Battery Operated, Frame, 13 x 25 In. 50.00
Clock, Round, Light-Up 275.00
Clock, Say Pepsi Please, Pepsi-Cola, Pale Yellow Ground, 1950, 8 1/2 x 9 In. 1210.00
Glass, Goofy, Early 1980s 100.00
Glass, Grumpy, Snow White & Seven Dwarfs, Blue 16.00
Glass, Happy Birthday Mickey, Donald 5.00
Glass, Happy Birthday Mickey, Goofy 8.00
Glass, Slow Poke Rodriguez, 1973, 16 Oz. 50.00
Glass, Sneezy, Snow White & Seven Dwarfs, Green 14.00
Glass, Speedy Gonzales, Tim Horton, 1978 . . . . 20.00
Glass, Tasmanian Devil, 1973, 16 Oz. . . . . .15.00 to 20.00

Kick Plate, Bottle Bursting Through Paper, 1940, 14 x 36 In. 6980.00
Lighter, Cigarette, Zippo Style 4.00
Pen, Fountain, Red Lettering, 1940, 6 In. 40.00
Pin, Driver's, Lapel, 1940 .... 6.00
Radio, Pepsi-Cola Bottle, Bakelite, 23 In. 1045.00
Salt & Pepper, Swirl Shape, Plastic Cover, 4 3/8 In. 30.00
Sign, Bottle Over Valley, 28 x 32 In. 110.00
Sign, Bottle With Sailboat, 22 x 29 In. 22.00
Sign, Couple In Surf On Rocks, 9 1/2 In. 275.00
Sign, Couple On Rocks At Beach, 22 x 29 In. 86.00
Sign, Girl At Rail With Camera, 20 x 28 In. 385.00
Sign, Girl Holding Bottle, 20 x 28 In. 38.00
Sign, Girl In Green Skirt, 22 x 29 In. 33.00
Sign, Girl In Polka Dot Dress, 22 x 29 In. 33.00
Sign, Girl On Mountain Top, 21 x 28 In. ....55.00 to 82.00
Sign, Girl With 2 Bottles, 25 x 29 In. 11.00
Sign, Sold Here, Pepsi-Cola, 5 Cents, Bigger-Better, Red Lettering, Black, 28 x 20 In. 360.00
Sign, Tin, Bottle Cap Die Cut, Lithograph, Double Dot, 13 In. 358.00
Sign, With Babbling Brook, 20 x 28 In. 110.00
Thermometer, Double Dot, Tin Litho, Glass, 27 In. 798.00
Thermometer, More Bounce To The Ounce, White Ground, 27 x 8 In. 275.00
Thermometer, Pepsi Logo, White Ground, Tin, 28 x 7 In. 50.00
Thermometer, The Light Refreshment, Light Green Ground, Metal, 27 x 7 1/2 In. 105.00
Toy, Truck, Delivery, White Ground, Ny-Lint, Original Box, 1960, 8 x 8 1/2 In. 412.00
Tray, Pepsi-Cola Bigger & Better, Tin, Black Paint, Floral Design, 14 x 10 1/2 In. 27.00

PERFUME BOTTLES are made of cut glass, pressed glass, art glass, silver, metal, enamel, and even plastic or porcelain. Although the small bottle to hold perfume was first made before the time of ancient Egypt, it is the nineteenth- and twentieth-century examples that interest today's collector. DeVilbiss Company has made atomizers of all types since 1888 but no longer makes the perfume bottle tops so popular with collectors. These were made from 1920 to 1968. The glass bottle may be by any of many manufacturers even if the atomizer is marked *DeVilbiss*. The word *factice*, which often appears in ads, refers to store display bottles. Glass or porcelain examples may be found under the appropriate name such as Lalique, Czechoslovakia, Glass-Bohemian, etc.

Agate, Sterling Silver, Gilt Floral Repousse Lid, Gorham, 1880, 2 3/4 In. 440.00
Amber, Green & Amber Celluloid Stopper, Brass Neck, 1930s, 7 In. 65.00
Art Glass, Geometric, 7 In. 50.00
Atomizer, Trumpet Enameled, Pinecones, Branches, France, Signed PAC 125.00
Baccarat, Dolphins, 6 1/4 In. 369.00
Blown Glass, Bird Interior, English Sterling Silver Holder, 19th Century 175.00
Blue Iridescent, Green, Purple Accents, Floral Stopper, Carder, 4 In. 862.00
Bourjois, Evening In Paris, Blue, New York, 2 In. 20.00
Brass, Mother-Of-Pearl, Inlaid Checkerboard Design, 2 1/2 In. 130.00
Cameo Glass, Berry Design, Atomizer, G. Raspiller, 7 In. 175.00
Cameo Glass, Duck Bill, Thomas Webb & Sons 7700.00
Caron, Nuit De Noel, Black Glass, Foil Label, Sealed But Evaporated, 3 In. 35.00
Cartier, Oval, Blue-Black Glass, Acid Etched Geometric, Art Deco, 4 1/4 In. 430.00
Chanel, Mademoiselle Chanel, 31 Rue Cambon, Paris, Stopper 660.00
Charbert, Amber, 1940s 40.00
Christian Dior, J'Appartiens A Miss Dior, Dog Shape, Frosted, Stopper 12100.00
Christian Dior, Urn Shape, 3 3/4 In. 125.00
Cologne, Gold Mica Spangles, Crystal Foot, Crystal Stopper, Italy, 4 In., Pair 90.00
Cologne, Light Green, Sheared Lip, Open Pontil, 2 7/8 In. 35.00
Cranberry, Fine & Heavy Gold Bands, Stars, Clear Bubble Stopper, 7 3/4 In. 165.00
Cranberry Overlay, Cameo Cut Flowers, Cristal-Nancy, France, 6 1/2 In. 130.00
Cut Glass, Amber, Flowers On Top 85.00
Cut Glass, Renaissance Pattern, Stopper, Dorflinger, 3 1/4 In. 125.00
Cut Glass, Triple Miter, Amberina Overlay, Stopper, 6 1/2 In. ....*Illus* 10000.00
Daniel Lotton, Atomizer, Coral & Blue Pulled Feather, 1988 .... 170.00

Delettrez, Le Parfum XXIII, Pearl Shape, Necklace, Box, 1923, 13 Piece 9350.00
Deroc, Gai Montmartre, Moulin Rouge Windmill Shape, 1925 . . . . 90.00
DeVilbiss, Atomizer, Hand Blown 95.00
Display, Shalimar, Contents, 14 In. 875.00
Dream Girl, Toilet Water, Box, No. 2159 . . . . 90.00
Falcon, Silver Overlay, Squat Baluster, Flowers, Leaves, Cartouche, 4 1/4 In. 315.00
Figural, Woman Holding Bottle, Porcelain, Germany 175.00
Figural, Woman, Porcelain, Separates At Waist & Elbows, S & Crown, 4 In. 100.00
Floral, Central Band Of Horizontal Reeding, Dominick & Haff, 9 In. 805.00
Frosted, Embossed Woman & Cupid, Lalique Style, 8 In., Pair 75.00
Fuller Frog, Solid 40.00
Gloria Vanderbilt, Pen, Box 55.00
Gold & Jade Color, Flared Lip, Open Pontil, 6 1/4 In. 155.00
Hattie Carnegie, Carnegie Blue, Box 1210.00
Houbigant, Subtilite, Figural Buddah, Baccarat, Shrine Shaped Box 605.00
Interior Red-Orange Bubble, Flattened Round Form, Stopper, 5 1/2 In. 410.00
J.R. Watkins Co., Mimosa, Cork Lined Stopper 30.00
J.R. Watkins Medical Co., White Rose, Box 25.00
Jean Patou, Joy, Cut Glass, Diamond Cut, Baccarat 170.00
Laird Perfumer, New York, Milk Glass 12.00
Lapis Lazuli, Coral Cap, Silver, Katherine Pratt, 3 1/2 In. 920.00
Lazell, Jockey Club, Milk Glass, Reverse Glass Label, Pat'd Apr. 2, 1889, 7 1/4 In. 225.00
Les Parfums De Muray, Notturno, Black, Gold Enameled Stopper, 4 1/4 In. 485.00
Lubin, Magda, Clear, Frosted Woman's Head, Flowers In Hair Stopper 7050.00
Lucien Lelong, Jabot, 1940s 48.00
Lucretia Vanderbilt, Blue Over White Glass, Elegant Tassel Box 935.00
Lundberg, Rosa Pink Neck, Blue Feather Body, Gold Teardrop Stopper, 8 3/4 In. 175.00
Malachite, Czechoslovakia, 5 1/2 In. 5225.00
Malachite, Globe Shape, Elephant With Upturned Trunk Stopper 5225.00
Mary Chess, Yram, 1930s-1940s 30.00
Mary Gregory, Falcon, Enamel, Girl, Basket, Dragonflies, Square, Stopper, 4 In. 201.00
Max Factor, Tender Teddy, Solid Type 30.00
Melon Ribbed, Celeste Blue Flame Stopper, Carder, 4 In. 402.00
Melon Ribbed, Gold Iridescent, Aurene, Ball Top Stopper, Steuben, 1910, 7 In. 635.00
Oval, White Classical Figures, Solid Pale Blue Jasper, 1880s, 3 1/4 In. 460.00
Paperweight, 5 Pink Trumpet Flowers, White Spatter, Global Stopper, 4 In. 35.00
Paperweight Stopper & Base, Millefiori, Continental, 6 1/2 In. 525.00
Pink Cut, Mother-Of-Pearl, Diamond Quilted, Gold Floral, Atomizer 250.00
Portraits Of Frederick I, Richard Molesworth, Silver Lid, Wedgwood, 2 3/8 In. 1380.00
Prince Matchabelli, Stradivari, Crown Type, Box 50.00
Quilted, Satin Glass, Ground Bud Top Stopper, 5 In. 35.00
Reeded Double Bottle, Mounted At Neck With Scrolling Leaves, 4 3/4 In. 115.00
Ribbed Pansy Design, Ribbed Stopper, Signed, 2 3/4 In. 150.00
Ring, Baroque Pearl, Solid 35.00
Rosaline, Teardrop Shape, Pink, Alabaster Glass Foot, Steuben, 1925, 6 In., Pair 430.00
Rose Color, Art Glass, 5 1/2 In. 50.00
Royall Spyce, Amber, Embossed, Leaves, Crown Lid, Royall Lyme Ltd., 5 1/2 In. 15.00
Sapphire Blue, Cut Panels, Cut Stopper, 6 3/4 In. 95.00

**Never display bottles with labels
in a sunny window. The labels
will fade.**

Perfume Bottle, Cut
Glass, Triple Miter,
Amberina Overlay,
Stopper, 6 1/2 In.

Scent, Coquilla Nut, Carved Music Instruments, Floral, 2 1/2 In.	460.00
Schiaparelli, Bust, With Ribbon, Contents, 2 In.	125.00
Schiaparelli, Le Roy Soleil, Clear, Inner Stopper, Sunburst Overcap	4400.00
Schiaparelli, Snuff, Pipe Shape, Box	275.00
Schiaparelli, Torso, Half Casket Box, Miniature	70.00
Silver, Mermaid Shape, 2 1/2 In.	55.00
Silver Sterling Overlay, Engraved Floral, Stopper, Monogram, 1906	250.00
St. Clair, Atomizer	30.00
Toilet Water, Cobalt Blue, Flared, 2 Neck Rings, Ribbed, Open Pontil, 1820s	275.00
Venetian Glass, Black, White Spots, Gold Foil, Spring Top, 19th Century, 4 In.	185.00
Venini, Thick Rib, Gold Mica, 8 1/2 In.	200.00
Viard, Marche Nuptiale, Flask, Clear & Frosted, Marques De Elorza	4675.00
Weil, Bamboo, Clear, Red Opaque Glass Topper	1430.00
Woman, Butterfly Wings, Red, Frosted, Lily Stopper, Czechoslovakia, 10 In.	750.00
Yellow, Art Glass, 4 1/2 In.	50.00
Yellow, Red, Art Glass, Contemporary, Paperweight	25.00

PETERS & REED Pottery Company of Zanesville, Ohio, was founded by John D. Peters and Adam Reed in 1897. Chromal, Landsun, Montene, Pereco, and Persian are some of the art lines that were made. The company, which became Zane Pottery in 1920 and Gonder Pottery in 1941, closed in 1957. Peters & Reed pottery was unmarked.

Basket, Hanging, Cosmos, Green Matte Glaze, 3 3/4 x 8 In.	165.00
Bowl, Embossed, Branches & Berries, Blue Semimatte Glaze, 3 1/2 x 8 In.	90.00
Bowl, Laurel Branch, Green Matte Glaze, 3 3/4 x 8 1/2 In.	190.00
Flower Frog, Brown Brush Disc, 3 1/2 In.	20.00
Flower Frog, Brown, 3 1/2 In.	25.00
Mug, Moss Aztec, Grape Clusters, Signed Ferrel, 6 In.	66.00
Planter, Abstract Pattern, 3 1/2 x 4 3/4 In.	75.00
Planter, Moss Aztec, Grape & Leaf Band, 5 x 6 In.	85.00
Umbrella Stand, Moss Aztec, Band Of Celtic Knots, Grape Clusters, 23 x 10 In.	330.00
Umbrella Stand, Moss Aztec, Grape Clusters, Corseted, Frank Ferrell, 22 1/2 In.	350.00
Vase, Black Drips On Ocher Ground, Oval, 10 1/4 In.	265.00
Vase, Chromal, Classically Shaped, 6 1/4 In.	120.00
Vase, Chromal, Squat, 4 x 4 In.	220.00
Vase, Floral Design, Red Clay, Green Matte Ground, 6 In.	120.00
Vase, Landsun, Blue, Green, Yellow Glaze, Cylindrical, 5 3/4 x 4 In.	275.00
Vase, Landsun, Olive Green, Purple Ground, 10 In.	135.00
Vase, Molded Leaves, Grapes In Grape Vine, Cream, Brown Glaze, 12 In.	230.00
Vase, Moss Aztec, Floral On Red Ground, 12 In.	360.00
Vase, Moss Aztec, Zinnias, Cylindrical, 8 In.	55.00
Vase, Moss Rose, 10 In.	135.00
Vase, Oval, Flame, Blue, Green & Beige Matte Glaze, 9 3/4 In.	195.00
Vase, Pereco, Blue Glossy Glaze, Pinched Waist, Mark, 8 1/4 In.	110.00
Vase, Raised Flowers, Green Over Red Clay, 6 In.	200.00
Vase, Sprigged-On Leaf, 2 Handles, Standard Glaze, 16 x 6 In.	135.00
Wall Pocket, 1 Beige, 1 Green Matte Glaze, 8 In., Pair	330.00
Wall Pocket, Blue, Green Matte Glaze, Fluted, 8 1/2 In.	110.00
Wall Pocket, Ibis, Green, 8 In.	165.00

PETRUS REGOUT, see Maastricht category.

PEWABIC POTTERY was founded by Mary Chase Perry Stratton in 1903 in Detroit, Michigan. The company made many types of art pottery, including pieces with matte green glaze and an iridescent crystalline glaze. The company continued working until the death of Mary Stratton in 1961. It was reactivated by Michigan State University in 1968.

Box, Lid, Bird Finial, Blue Glossy Glaze, Rectangular, 3 In.	165.00
Candlestick, Matte Glaze, Signed, 6 In.	385.00
Candlestick, Orange & Yellow Matte Glaze, Signed, 9 In.	253.00
Goblet, Raspberry, Beige Crystalline & Turquoise Flambe Glaze, 2 3/4 In.	220.00
Plate, Dragonflies, Blue Slip, White Crackled Ground, Stamped, 10 3/4 In.	1100.00
Tile, Brown Cat In Center, Turquoise Ground, Square, Signed, 3 1/4 In.	220.00
Tile, Cat, Sitting, Signed, Square, 3 1/4 In.	220.00

Vase, Brown, Green & Blue, Drip Matte Glaze, Sloped Shoulder, Stamped, 7 x 5 1/4 In. . . . 660.00
Vase, Celadon & Lavender Luster Glaze, 2 1/4 x 2 1/2 In. 365.00
Vase, Celadon & Oxblood Luster Glaze, Stamped Mark, 2 1/2 x 2 In. 385.00
Vase, Celadon & Purple Luster Glaze, Stamped Cylindrical Mark, 4 3/4 x 4 In. 550.00
Vase, Cobalt, Light Blue Luster Glaze, Squat, 2 3/4 x 4 1/2 In. 1025.00
Vase, Copper & Gold Luster Glaze, 18 In. 935.00
Vase, Gold & Mauve Luster Glaze, Round Stamp, 4 3/4 x 3 1/2 In. 715.00
Vase, Gold Drip Glaze, Glossy Blue Ground, Bulbous, Round Stamp, 4 3/4 x 4 In. 1210.00
Vase, Green, Red Luster Glaze, 2 1/4 x 1 1/2 In. 550.00
Vase, Gunmetal, Turquoise Luster Glaze, Squat, 2 1/4 x 3 1/2 In. 1320.00
Vase, Mauve, Gold Drip Matte Glaze, Squat, 3 x 4 In. 415.00
Vase, Persian Blue Test Crackled Glaze, Round Stamp, 2 x 2 1/2 In. 245.00
Vase, Pink, Gold, Blue Drip Glaze, Round Stamp, 2 1/2 x 2 3/4 In. 1320.00
Vase, Pink, Gray, Gold Luster Glaze, Spherical, 5 x 4 1/2 In. 1540.00
Vase, Platinum & Purple Metallic Glaze, 4 In. 355.00
Vase, Squat, Blue, Green & Mauve Semimatte Glaze, Stamped, Paper Label, 3 3/4 In. 660.00
Vase, Teal Crystalline Glaze, Bulbous, Stamped Mark, 4 1/2 In. 360.00
Vase, Thick Blue Drip Glaze Over Mustard Base, 2 1/2 In. 305.00
Vase, Turquoise Drip, Purple Luster Glaze, Bulbous, Circle Stamp, 3 3/4 In. 660.00
Vase, Turquoise Glaze Over Gold Ground, 4 1/2 x 2 1/2 In. 1340.00
Vase, Turquoise, Green & Blue Drip Glaze, Round Stamp, 2 1/2 x 2 In. 465.00
Vase, Volcanic Cobalt Blue, Celadon Glaze, Squat, 4 3/4 x 9 1/4 In. 5225.00
Vase, Yellow, Copper Luster Glaze, Squat, 2 x 2 1/2 In. 880.00

PEWTER is a metal alloy of tin and lead. Some of the pewter made after 1840 has a slightly different composition and is called *Britannia metal*. This later type of pewter was worked by machine; the earlier pieces were made by hand. In the 1920s pewter came back into fashion and pieces were often marked *Genuine Pewter*. Eighteenth-, nineteenth-, and twentieth-century examples are listed here.

Ashtray, Matchbox Holder, Kayserzinn, 6 x 6 In. 165.00
Basin, Compton, London, 3 1/2 x 14 In. 425.00
Basin, Engraved Lydia Quick 1799, 6 1/4 In. 750.00
Basin, Gershom Jones, 7 3/4 In. 275.00
Basin, Townsend & Compton, 9 1/8 In. 165.00
Basin, Townsend & Compton, 11 3/4 x 3 In. 385.00
Bowl, Allover Repousse Work, c.1720, 12 In. 295.00
Bowl, Federal, Molded Lid, Beaded Rim, Circular Domed Foot, Phil., 1800, 4 x 5 In. 6900.00
Bowl, G. Lightner, 1806, 13 1/4 In. 990.00
Bowl, KWH, Brass Trim, 3 x 13 1/2 In. 55.00
Box, Desk, 2 Sections, Hemispherical Feet, Isaac Dupee, Boston, Aug. 1833 . . . . 192.00
Box, Hinged Cover, Liberty, Inset Enameled Seascape, Wooden Lined, 1 1/2 x 3 3/4 In. . . . 465.00
Box, Liberty, Inset Turquoise, Signed, Square, 3 1/2 In. 715.00
Candlestick, Nekrasoff, Arts & Crafts, Hammered, 2 Handles, 2 x 6 In., Pair 55.00
Candlestick, Pushup, 9 3/4 In. 300.00
Chalice, Circular Foot, 8 1/2 In. 110.00
Charger, B & Co., Wide Flanged Rim, Raised Edge, Marked, 16 5/8 In. 170.00
Charger, Cartouche, Plain Wide Flanged Rim, 16 1/2 In. 170.00
Charger, City Of Exeter Arms, England, 17th Century, 17 1/2 In. 1900.00
Charger, Crown & Rose Touchmark, Continental, 12 1/4 In. 190.00
Charger, CTM Mark, Continental, 1800, 20 In. 825.00
Charger, Kayserzinn, Embossed Stylized Flowers & Leaves, 8 1/2 In. 110.00
Charger, Wide Flanged Rim, Crown Over Triangle, 16 1/2 In. 195.00
Coffee Urn, Wooden Feet & Finials, 17 3/4 In. 190.00
Coffeepot, Cover, Sellew & Co., Cincinnati, 9 In. 140.00
Coffeepot, Domed Lid, Pear Shape, Incised Bands, 12 1/4 In. 245.00
Coffeepot, Lighthouse, P. Wayne & Son., Philada., 9 1/2 In. 415.00
Coffeepot, Lighthouse, W. Calder, Knopped Finial, Multiple Rings, 11 1/4 In. 1150.00
Coffeepot, Porter, Westbrooke, Maine, c.1830, 12 In. 650.00
Coffeepot, Rogers Smith & Co., Hartford, Ct., 13 In. 155.00
Coffeepot, Smith & Bellmay, Albany, 1830 . . . . 525.00
Coffeepot, Smith & Co., Handle, 10 In. 165.00
Creamer, Boardman & Hart, Crooked Handle, 6 1/2 In. 110.00

Cup, Pedestal, Hallmark, RWP In Circle, 7 x 3 1/2 In. 35.00
Decanter, James Powell & Sons, Stylized Berries, Green Glass Liner, Tudric, 12 In. 5225.00
Dish, Kayserzinn, Footed, Lid With Finial, Embossed Leaves & Berries, 10 In. 140.00
Dish, Kayserzinn, Leaf Shape, Stem Handle, Embossed Lily-Of-The-Valley, 9 In. 88.00
Flagon, Baluster Turned Thumblatch, Monogram, Continental, Early 19th Century 305.00
Flagon, George Friedrich Schwager, Domed Cover, Recurved Handle, 1815, 10 In. 110.00
Flagon, Smith & Feltman, Domed Cover, Recurved Handle, Albany, N.Y., 11 1/2 x 7 In. . . 505.00
Food Warmer, James Dixon & Sons, 1850, 9 5/16 x 1 7/16 In. 140.00
Humidor, Domed Top, Figural Scenes, Octagonal, England, 19th Century, 5 x 7 In. 230.00
Ice Cream, Lobster, c.1920 . . . . 205.00
Inkwell, Hinged Lid, Acorn Finial, Continental, 5 1/2 x 4 3/4 In. 40.00
Jam Pot, Sir George Alderson, London, Early 19th Century, Large 295.00
Jar, Snuff, Arms Of Curtiss Of Mayfield, 18th Century, 5 In. 395.00
Knife Rest, Puma, Kayserzinn, Pair 250.00
Lamp, Chamber, Fluid Burner, Snuffer Caps, 3 7/8 In. 110.00
Lamp, Grease, Open Pan, Mid Drip Pan, Handle With Wick Pick On Chain, 11 1/4 In. . . . 275.00
Lamp, Oil, Coste Animes, Square Base, Paw Feet, 19th Century, 12 In. 230.00
Lamp, Whale Oil, Roswell Gleason, Chamber, Brass Collar, 1 Spout, 4 In. 385.00
Measure, Bulls Head Strand Green, 18th Century, England, 8 1/2 In. 605.00
Measure, England, 1 1/2 To 6 7/8 In., 6 Piece 885.00
Measuring Set, Eagle With Spread Wings, Flat Square Handles, 7 Piece 195.00
Measuring Set, England, 1830-1845, Gill, 1/2 Gill, 3 Piece 155.00
Measuring Set, England, 19th Century, Two 1/2 Pt., One 1/2 Gill, 3 Piece 90.00
Mug, Edgar Curtis, c.1800, 4 7/8 In. 220.00
Mug, Flat Cover, Handle, Thumblifts, 4 x 3 1/3 In. 44.00
Mug, Flat Cover, Handle, Thumblifts, 6 1/4 x 3 1/4 In. 44.00
Mug, Joseph Danforth, Middletown, Conn., 1780-1788, 1 Qt. 2860.00
Mug, Tavern, Alexander Bain, Engraved Name, Edinburgh, 1 Qt. 495.00
Napkin Ring, Book Shape, Boy Reading, Silver Plate 45.00
Pan, Pudding, 18th Century, 14 1/2 In. 185.00
Pitcher, H.I. Sun Romford, England, 1800, 11 1/4 In. 825.00
Pitcher, Karl Kipp, Incised Design On Side, Handle, 8 In. 110.00
Pitcher, Water, F. Porter, Westbrook, 7 In. 300.00
Pitcher, Water, Handle, Portland, Me., 6 1/2 In. 220.00
Plate, Bailey & Putnam, 14 7/8 In. 265.00
Plate, Broad Rim, Square, Continental, 17th Century, 16 In. 550.00
Plate, Deep, A.H., 9 1/2 In. 145.00
Plate, Johannes Schmerrer, Engraved Bear Holding Flag, 1705, 9 In. 90.00
Plate, Love, 7 3/4 In. 300.00
Plate, Milton & Alexander, Signed, 19th Century, 9 1/2 In., 4 Piece 75.00
Plate, Rolled Edge, 10 In. 45.00
Plate, S. Kilbourn, Eagle, Baltimore, Md., 1839, 7 3/4 In. 220.00
Plate, Thomas Badger, 15 In. 130.00
Plate, Townsend & Compton, England, 1801-1811, 8 3/4 In. 130.00
Platter, 2-Headed Eagle, Crown Heads, Double Border, 19th Century, 1 5/16 x 19 In. . . . 80.00
Platter, Thomas Compton, Oval, London, 26 x 20 In. 1550.00
Porringer, Crown Handle, 19th Century, 6 1/4 In. 35.00
Porringer, Frederick Bassett, Shell Handle, 18th Century, 4 1/2 In. 140.00
Porringer, Heart Cutout Handle, 4 3/4 In., Pair 110.00
Porringer, Pierced & Heart Cutout Handle, 6 1/4 In. 130.00
Porringer, Pierced Handle, Heart Design, Early 19th Century, 4 3/4 In., Pair 45.00
Porringer, Samuel Hamlin, Openwork Handle, Providence, R.I., 19th Century, 8 In. 140.00
Porringer, Tab Handle, Scratch Engraved 1848, 5 1/4 In. 110.00
Pot, Pear Shape, Wooden Feet, 10 1/4 In. 140.00
Pot, Tall, Eagle Touch, 10 3/4 In. 465.00
Pot, Tall, Homan & Co., Floral Finial, 11 In. 110.00
Salt, Double, Hinged Covers, Footed 50.00
Salt, Footed, England, 1720 . . . . 185.00
Salt, Gadrooned Design, England, 17th Century, 2 Sizes, Pair 495.00
Salver, London Hallmarks, England, c.1800, 16 3/4 In. 220.00
Spoon, Rattail, Portrait Of George II At Top, c.1720, 7 1/4 In. 150.00
Sugar, Robert Palethorpe, Jr., Philadelphia, 1817, 8 1/8 In. 220.00
Sugar & Creamer, James Dixon & Sons, Octagonal, 7 In. 100.00

Sundial, Samuel Melville, Newport, R.I., Late 18th Century, 4 1/2 In. 770.00
Syrup, Homan & Co., Cincinnati, 6 3/4 In. 55.00
Syrup Set, Tray, American, 5 1/2 x 7 3/8-In. Tray, 4 In., 3 Piece 190.00
Tankard, Cylindrical Body, Shaped Spout, Switzerland, Dated 1605, 8 1/4 In. 750.00
Tankard, Hinged Cover, Inside Initials, England, 7 In. 550.00
Tankard, Initials, Baluster, Dated 1775, 13 1/2 In. 715.00
Tea Set, Sellew & Co., Acorn Finials, 4 Piece 360.00
Tea Set, Stylized Floral, Turquoise, Green, Wicker Handle, England, 9 In., 3 Piece 275.00
Teapot, Allen Porter, Elongated Pear Form, Bone Finial, 12 In. 280.00
Teapot, Britannia Metal, R. Dunham, 19th Century, 8 3/4 In. 55.00
Teapot, Cusp Lid, Petal Topped Urn Finial, Handle, Footed, Bulbous, 10 x 6 3/4 In. 110.00
Teapot, Dixon & Sons, Round Base, Wooden Handle & Finial, 8 In. 100.00
Teapot, Flower Finial, Octagonal, Wooden Handle, 7 1/2 In. 65.00
Teapot, G. Lewis, Wooden Finial, 8 In. 40.00
Teapot, J. Danforth, Lid Finial, 6 1/2 In. 165.00
Teapot, James H. Putnam, Cusp Lid, Curved Handle, Thumblift, 7 3/4 x 5 1/2 In. 125.00
Teapot, Katherine Ebert, Black Painted Handle, Footed, Bulbous, 7 3/4 x 6 In. 125.00
Teapot, Morey & Ober, Straight-Sided, Boston, 8 In. 300.00
Teapot, Roswell Gleason, Cover, Recurved Wooden Handle, 4 Ornate Feet, 8 x 5 In. 80.00
Teapot, Wrigglework, Inscribed 1709, Dutch 1100.00
Tray, Fish, Kayserzinn, 24 x 11 In. 440.00
Tray, Kayserzinn, Horseshoe Design, 6 In. 55.00
Tray, Woman, Flowing Hair, Orivit 150.00
Tureen, Leaf Handles, 10 In. 495.00
Tureen, With Ladle, England, 18th Century, 13 In. 290.00
Urn, Cover, Acorn Finial, Shaped Loop Handles, England, c.1870, 13 In. 675.00
Vase, Archibald Knox, Bullet, 3 Buttresses, Embossed, Stylized Rose, Tudric, 7 In., Pair . 2860.00
Vase, Hammered, Buttresses, England, 7 1/2 In. 550.00
Vase, Kayserzinn, 5 Fish, Open Handles, 6 1/2 In. 200.00
Vase, Kayserzinn, Butterflies, Stylized Floral, Running Length Of Vase, Signed, 8 In. 285.00
Vase, Liberty, Hammered, Shell Casing, Tudric, 7 1/4 In. 330.00
Vase, Liberty, Open Handles, Motto, For Ole Times Sake, Signed, 8 In. 715.00
Water Pot, Flagg & Homan, Cover, Pear Shape, Recurved Handle, 10 1/2 x 5 In. 145.00
Wine Measure, Double Volute Thumbpiece, England, 1750-1750, Gill 395.00

PHOENIX BIRD, or Flying Phoenix, is the name given to a blue-and-white kitchenware popular between 1900 and World War II. A variant is known as Flying Turkey. Most of this dinnerware was made in Japan for sale in the dime stores in America. It is still being made.

Cup & Saucer, Thin 10.00
Salt & Pepper, 2 1/4 In. 28.00
Tea Strainer, 2 Piece 110.00

PHOENIX GLASS Company was founded in 1880 in Pennsylvania. The firm made commercial products, such as lampshades, bottles, and glassware. Collectors today are interested in the "Sculptured Artware" made by the company from the 1930s until the mid-1950s. Some pieces of Phoenix glass are very similar to those made by the Consolidated Lamp and Glass Company. Phoenix made Reuben Blue, lavender, and yellow pieces. These colors were not used by Consolidated. In 1970 Phoenix became a division of Anchor Hocking, then was sold to the Newell Group in 1987. The company is still working.

Cake Salver, Jewel & Dewdrop, Blue, White Ground, 11 1/2 In. 145.00
Vase, Bluebells, White On Blue, 7 In. 45.00
Vase, Bluebells, White On Ivory, 7 In. 105.00
Vase, Chickadee, White On Blue 225.00
Vase, Daisy, Pearl On Light Green, 1930s 395.00
Vase, Dancing Nymphs, Cobalt Blue, 12 In. 460.00
Vase, Dogwood, Blue, 10 3/4 In. 425.00
Vase, Dragonflies & Cattails, Pearlized, White, 6 In. 385.00
Vase, Fern, Blue, 7 1/4 In. 295.00
Vase, Foxglove, Orange, 10 1/2 In. 245.00
Vase, Freesia, White On Blue, 8 1/4 In. 175.00

Treat vintage photographs with care. Keep them out of direct sunlight, and don't touch them with your fingertips. Don't use tape or glue to mount your photos. Mount and mat photos on 100 percent cotton-rag acid-free museum board and display them under Plexiglas rather than regular glass. Be sure the photo does not touch the Plexiglas.

Phonograph, Capitol, Mod. EA, 1919

Vase, Love Birds, Gold On White 165.00
Vase, Love Birds, Peach On White, 6 1/2 In. 35.00
Vase, Wild Rose, White Burgundy, 1930s, 10 1/2 In. 175.00

PHONOGRAPHS, invented by Thomas Edison in 1877, have been made by many firms. This category also includes other items associated with the phonograph. Jukeboxes and records are listed in their own categories.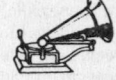
Bell, Horizontal Soundbox, Ratchet Wind Motor, Internal Horn, Metal Case 172.00
Capitol, Mod. EA, 1919 ....*Illus* 3795.00
Case, Packing, Victrola Morning Glory Horn, Wooden Strips Form 395.00
Edison, 16 Cylinders, Blue Blossom Horn 1325.00
Edison, Black & Brass Outside Horn, Rolls 1200.00
Edison, Floor Model, Brass Arm & Turntable, Fretwork Grill, Records 410.00
Edison, Horn, No. 87784, Oak Case, 18 x 14 In. 1575.00
Edison, Mahogany Veneer, No. 18, 19 Records, No. 18, 42 3/4 In. 275.00
Edison Diamond, Disc, Adapter, Plays 78 Records, 33 x 19 x 20 In. 900.00
Fern-O-Grand, Baby Grand Piano Shape 2200.00
Graphanola, Oil, Hinged Lid, Turn Crack, 1900, 13 1/2 x 18 1/2 In. 350.00
Graphophone, Columbia Phonograph Co., Oak, Brass Horn 380.00
Japanned, Oriental Scene, Brass Hardware 1500.00
RCA, Model VV4-3-40510, 20 x 19 In. 725.00
RCA Victrola, Golden Oak 395.00
RCA Victrola, Walnut 350.00
Reginaphone, No. 240, Metal Discs & Records 9800.00
Silvertone Tru-Phonic, Wooden Console, Windup 185.00
Sonora, Mahogany, Floor Model, Fretwork Grill, Drawer, 1916 .... 275.00
Traveling, Wooden, Leatherized Cloth Covering, Handle, 4 1/4 x 4 x 6 1/4 In. 275.00
Victor II, Golden Oak, Speakers Behind Top Doors, Slanted Record Shelves, 1917 ...... 495.00
Victor IV, Table Top 350.00
Victor Monarch, Wooden, Brass, Windup, 1902 .... 3200.00
Victor Talking Machine, 1930s 275.00
Victrola, Victor Talking Machine Co., Camden, N.J., Records ....120.00 to 230.00
Victrola, Wooden, Cabriole Legs, Floor Model 160.00

PHOTOGRAPHY items are listed here. The first photograph was a view from a window in France taken in 1826. The commercially successful photograph started with the daguerreotype introduced in 1839. Today all sorts of photographs and photographic equipment are collected. Albums were popular in Victorian times. Cartes de visite, popular after 1854, were mounted on 2 1/2-by-4-inch cardboard. Cabinet cards were introduced in 1866. These were mounted on 4 1/4-by-6 1/2-inch cards. Stereo views are listed under Stereo Card. The cases for daguerreotypes are listed in the Gutta-Percha category. Stereoscopes are listed in their own section.

Album, 105 Far East Views, Captions, Folio, 1890s 2300.00

Album, 23 Cartes De Visite, Erotica, Japan, Mori, 1882 .... 3900.00
Album, Col. Makins, Chimborazo Cruise, 1890, 267 Views, Italy, Greece, Turkey 1495.00
Album, Harvard College, Class Of 1861, Morocco Folio 5525.00
Album, India & Far East, Portraits, Street Life, Bourne, Scowen, 1880s 4370.00
Album, Jamaica, Countryside, Workers, James Valentine, Folio, 1880s 8625.00
Album, Middle East Views, Louis-Desire Blanquart-Evrard, Du Camp, 1852 .... 4830.00
Album, New Caledonia, Natives, Habitat, E. Robin, 1860s 4370.00
Album, Panoramas, Sydney & New South Wales, Fold Out, Morocco Folio 25300.00
Album, Philadelphia Photographic Society, 85 Images, 1874-1886 .... 6900.00
Album, Southern United States, Blacks, 42 Various Locales, 1860s 1265.00
Album, Travel, English Colonies In Pacific & Indian Oceans, 117 Views, 1889 .... 1850.00
Albumen, Cathedral Spires, Yosemite, 1872, 21 x 16 1/2 In. 1495.00
Albumen, Civil War, Confederate Prisoners, Board Mount, 6 3/4 x 9 1/4 In. 2200.00
Albumen, Field Telegraph Wagon, Alexander Gardner, Civil War, 9 x 7 In. 385.00
Albumen, Infantry Officer, Frock Coat, Sword, E.J. Jacobs, Frame, 14 x 16 In. 415.00
Albumen, Japan, Hand Colored, 38 Prints, 1870s To 1905 .... 1725.00
Albumen, Male Nude Studies, Von Gloeden, Pluschow, 1890s, 6 Piece 4830.00
Albumen, President Lincoln & Son Thaddeus, 1865, 8 1/2 x 6 1/4 In. 2760.00
Albumen, Surprised Young Man, Von Gloeden, c.1900, 9 x 6 3/4 In. 2070.00
Albumen, Thomas Edison & Early Phonograph, c.1877, 5 1/4 x 4 1/4 In. 225.00
Albumen, Voluptuous Angel, 1880s, 10 1/2 x 7 1/4 In. 805.00
Ambrotype, Abraham Lincoln, Portrait, Geometric Union Case, 1/2 Plate 515.00
Ambrotype, Alabama Slave & Baby, W.H. Frear, Full Case, 1/6 Plate 1350.00
Ambrotype, Black Man, Sitting With Box Of Handrolled Cigars, 1/6 Plate 630.00
Ambrotype, Black Woman, Hat On Lap, Leather Case, 2 x 2 1/2 In. 190.00
Ambrotype, Brother & Sister, Ruby Glass, Half Case, 1/6 Plate 125.00
Ambrotype, Carpenter, Stonington, Connecticut, Man With Hammer, 1/6 Plate 125.00
Ambrotype, Cavalryman, With Dog, 1/6 Plate 1290.00
Ambrotype, Civil War Soldier, Standing, Pistols, Musket & Bayonet, 1/6 Plate 465.00
Ambrotype, Family At Niagara Falls, Canadian Side, Wooden Frame, Full Plate 115.00
Ambrotype, Family Reunion Of 10 People, Leather Case, 1/2 Plate 230.00
Ambrotype, Fireman, Holding Trumpet, 1/4 Plate 805.00
Ambrotype, Fireman, Standing, Posed With Arm On Column, 1/6 Plate 630.00
Ambrotype, Hound & Sweet Girl, Flowers, Hand Tinted, Case, 1860s, 1/6 Plate 805.00
Ambrotype, Hunter With Rifle, Myron Shew, Phila., Oval Matted, 1/4 Plate 500.00
Ambrotype, Little Soldier Boy, Pack On Back, Full Case, 1/6 Plate 70.00
Ambrotype, Man Holding His Dog, Union Forever, Berg, Ruby Glass, 1/9 Plate 295.00
Ambrotype, Niagara Falls Scene, 5 People On Vacation, Full Plate 1780.00
Ambrotype, Niagara Falls, Man, 2 Women, Case, Full Plate 2090.00
Ambrotype, Soldier, Standing With Musket, 1/2 Plate 460.00
Ambrotype, Soldier, Standing, Arm On Table, 1/6 Plate 2415.00
Ambrotype, Union Officer, Holding Kepi 240.00
Ambrotype, Washington Monument, Mother & Child, 1/2 Plate 345.00
Ambrotype, Wheelwright, Geometric Union Case, 1/4 Plate 345.00
Ambrotype, White Dog Smoking Pipe, Half Leather Case, 1/6 Plate 2760.00
Ambrotype, Young Couple, Playing Dominoes, Leatherette Case, 1/2 Plate 460.00
Cabinet Card, Advertising, Lady, Atlantic Mills, Woman, Banner, Umbrella 215.00
Cabinet Card, Annie Oakley, Rifle, Baker's Art Gallery, 1880s, 5 1/2 x 4 In. 4370.00
Cabinet Card, Baby, Long Dress, Marengo, Iowa, C.A. Cartwright, 1890 .... 9.00
Cabinet Card, Banjoettes, Lillie & Me Playing Banjoes, Holyoke, Mass. 215.00
Cabinet Card, Bearded Man, W.A. Faze, Charleston, Ind., 1885 .... 25.00
Cabinet Card, Buffalo Bill, Stacy, Brooklyn 500.00
Cabinet Card, Child, Long Dress, Belle Plaine, Iowa, Keyser & Brinkley, 1885 .... 10.00
Cabinet Card, Clint Montgomery, Territorial Expo 1888, Prescott, 6 1/2 x 4 In. 790.00
Cabinet Card, Cowgirl, Mexican Western Outfit, Norgauer, Muenchen, 1911 .... 140.00
Cabinet Card, Crow, Northern Pacific R.R. Golden Spike Ceremony, 1883, 7 x 10 In. ... 1100.00
Cabinet Card, Edwin Booth, J. Notman, Boston 70.00
Cabinet Card, Elizabeth Cady Stanton 454.00
Cabinet Card, Geronimo Chief Of Apache Indians, Overstreet Studio, 1880s 1380.00
Cabinet Card, Indian, Na-Hu-Da, War Bonnet, Ross Fork Reservation, Idaho, 8 In. 90.00
Cabinet Card, Knife Throwing Act 110.00
Cabinet Card, Louie Sitting Bull, D.F. Barry, Bismarck, 6 1/2 x 4 1/2 In. 173.00
Cabinet Card, Mexican Performer In Pawnee Bill Show, Gifford, 7 x 5 1/4 In. 170.00

Cabinet Card, Mrs. James K. Polk, Signed Both Sides, Nashville Imprint 2200.00
Cabinet Card, Pittsburgh Cowboy, Dude In Fringe Leather Shirt, Holding Rifle 206.00
Cabinet Card, Prairie Flower Show, Wenona Or Lillian Smith, 6 1/2 x 4 1/2 In. 209.00
Cabinet Card, Roller Rink Personnel & Dog, Curtis, Lewiston 650.00
Cabinet Card, Rutherford B. Hayes, Geo. R. Elliott & Co., Columbus, Ohio, 1876 ...... 100.00
Cabinet Card, Son Of Kit Carson, Williams & Hansman, Label, 19th Century 905.00
Cabinet Card, Susan B. Anthony 575.00
Cabinet Card, Ute Chief, Ouray, W.H. Jackson, Early 1870s 1150.00
Cabinet Card, Ute, Chief Buckskin Charlie & Band Of Indians 595.00
Cabinet Card, Woman Wild West Performer, Sepia, Johnson, Danforth 245.00
Cabinet Card, Young Boy, White Dress, O.E. Flaten, Artistic Photographer, 1880s 35.00
Cabinet Card, Young Man, F.J. Williams Artist Photographer On Back, 1880s 20.00
Cabinet Card, Young Man, Frank A. Rankin, Eugene City, Oregon, 1880s 20.00
Camera, 210 Polaroid, Automatic, Original Black Case, Light Bulb Attachment 21.00
Camera, Altura, Contessa-Nettel, Folding, Leather Case, 1921 .... 30.00
Camera, Ansco, Cadet, Plastic, Metal Front, Flash Attachment, 5 Bulbs, 2 x 3 x 5 In. 23.00
Camera, Ansco, Clipper, Telescoping Lens, Metal, Plastic, Box, 1940s 20.00
Camera, Argus, 35mm, Brown Leather Case 22.00
Camera, Argus, 35mm, Chrome, Black Leatherette, Art Deco, 5 x 3 x 2 In. 21.00
Camera, Argus, 35mm, Metal Body, Partial Leather Case, 2 x 3 x 5 In. 30.00
Camera, Argus, C-3, Range Finder, Metal, Black Leatherette, Strap, Leather Case 40.00
Camera, Bell & Howell Foton, 35 mm., Case 700.00
Camera, Blair Camera Co., Lucidograph No. 3, Folding Plate, c.1886 .... 1610.00
Camera, Brownie, Flash Six-20, Black Leatherette, Flash Attachment, 3 x 4 In. 25.00
Camera, Camera, Field, E. & H.T. Anthony & Co., Focus Novelette, Folding, 1891 ..... 400.00
Camera, Canon Pelix, 35 mm, 1965-1966 .... 175.00
Camera, Canon, A-1, 35mm, Single Lens Reflex, Polycarbonate Body, c.1978 .... 230.00
Camera, E. & H.T. Anthony & Co., Marlborough, Folding Plate, c.1900 .... 920.00
Camera, Emil Wunsche, Tailboard, Folding, Mahogany Body, Tripod, 1890s 545.00
Camera, Field, Century Camera Co., No. 2, Folding, Mahogany Body, c.1905 .... 160.00
Camera, Field, Kodak, Eastman View No. 1, Folding, Mahogany Body, 1920s 200.00
Camera, Franke & Heidecke, Heidoscop Stereo Reflex, Metal Body, c.1924 .... 400.00
Camera, Franke & Heidecke, Rollei 35, Leiss Tessar Lens, Case, Booklet, c.1968 .... 345.00
Camera, Grundlach, 2 Film Holders, Cherry, c.1910, 5 x 7 In. 490.00
Camera, Kodak Baby Brownie, New York World's Fair Faceplate, 1940 .... 250.00
Camera, Kodak, Brownie, Hawkeye, Plastic, Flash Attachment, 12 Bulbs 20.00
Camera, Kodak, Duaflex II, Bakelite, Brushed Aluminum Trim, 1950s, 3 x 4 In. 20.00
Camera, Kodak, Ektra 35mm Rangefinder, Leather-Covered Metal, Early 1940s 860.00
Camera, Kodak, Folding, Black Leatherette, Original Box, 6 1/2 x 3 1/2 x 1 In. 33.00
Camera, Kodak, No. 1A, Pocket Junior 50.00
Camera, Kodak, No. 3-A, Folding Bellows Style, 4 3/4 x 9 1/2 In. Closed ....37.00 to 68.00
Camera, Kodak, No. 4 Jr., Roll-Film, Leather-Covered Wood, c.1890 .... 430.00
Camera, Kodak, Rainbow Hawkeye, No. 2, Model C, Blue Leatherette, Box 35.00
Camera, Lens, Nikon, Fish-Eye-Nikkor 8mm, Filter Wheel, Leather Case, c.1962 .... 975.00
Camera, Magazine, Drop Plate, Leather-Covered Wood, Germany, c.1900 .... 115.00
Camera, Minolta Super A, 35 mm, 1957 .... 55.00
Camera, Minolta-16MG, Accessories, Leatherette Case, Hinged Lid, 1960s, 4 In. 93.00
Camera, Minox, Spy, Brown Leather Case, Leather Box, West Germany 199.00
Camera, Movie, Argus, Model 810 Super Eight, Metal Body, Japan, 3 x 5 x 6 In. 23.00
Camera, Movie, Bauer 88B, Cloth Case, Instruction Book, Germany, Early 1950s 100.00
Camera, Movie, Fairchild, Cinephonic 8mm, Sound Recording, 3 Lenses 30.00
Camera, Nikon, F2A 35mm Single Lens Reflex, MD-2 Motor Drive, Late 1970s 490.00
Camera, Pacemaker Crown Graphic Press, 4 x 5 In. 250.00
Camera, Pignons Alpa 11E, Black Crackle Finish, Switzerland, Early 1970s 1035.00
Camera, Polaroid, Automatic 100 Land, Flash, Carry Case, 1974, 7 1/2 x 5 In. 50.00
Camera, Polaroid, Model 220, Flash Attachment, Luggage Style Case 21.00
Camera, Polaroid, SX-70 Sonar, Electric Eye Focusing, Instruction Sheet, Box 40.00
Camera, Seneca View, Wooden Tripod, Film Holders, c.1910, 7 x 5 In., 4 .... 465.00
Camera, Spy, Pocket Watch Form, 1904 .... 150.00
Camera, Stereo, Kiner Co., Kin-Dar 35mm, Black Leather, 2 Lenses, Box, c.1954 ...... 200.00
Camera, Voigtlander Avus 125.00
Camera, Zeiss Ikon Maximar 80.00

Camera, Zeiss Ikon Prontors, Bellows, Metal, Leatherette, Leather Case, 5 In. 95.00
Camera, Zeiss Ikon, Aetna Tele Rokuna 200mm Lens, Light Meters, Case 115.00
Carte De Visite, Abner Doubleday, Brigadier General, Seated 495.00
Carte De Visite, Abolitionist John Brown, McAllister & Brother, Philadelphia 90.00
Carte De Visite, Alexander Stephens, Vice President Of Confederacy 140.00
Carte De Visite, Black Youth, Full Standing, Hand On Studio Urn 120.00
Carte De Visite, Boot Salesman, Standing, Carrying 3 Pairs Of Boots, 1869 .... 121.00
Carte De Visite, Brigadier General Abner Doubleday, Seated, Brady 495.00
Carte De Visite, Brigadier General George Armstrong Custer, Brady, 1864 .... 2070.00
Carte De Visite, Brigadier General William Whipple, Wendroth & Taylor 220.00
Carte De Visite, Buffalo, 9 Soldiers, Identifying People, Brady, 10/66 .... 450.00
Carte De Visite, Castle Thunder, Robert E Lee, Salt Print, Mounted, 1860s 1150.00
Carte De Visite, Corporal Calvin Bates, 20th Maine Infantry 1760.00
Carte De Visite, Corporal John January, 14th Illinois Cavalry 1375.00
Carte De Visite, Dr. W.L. Atlee, Uniform, Medical Sword, J. Cremer & Co. 110.00
Carte De Visite, Fitzhugh Lee, Confederate General, Standing, Civilian Clothes 578.00
Carte De Visite, Gen. A.A. Humphreys, Bust View Of General, 1860 .... 132.00
Carte De Visite, General A.A. Humphreys, Seated, Brady 275.00
Carte De Visite, General George Armstrong Custer, 1863 .... 440.00
Carte De Visite, General George Gordon Meade, Uniform, Wenderoth & Taylor 100.00
Carte De Visite, General George McClellan, In Uniform, Next To Wife, 1860 .... 66.00
Carte De Visite, General Grant, Seated 187.00
Carte De Visite, General Philip Sheridan, Seated 193.00
Carte De Visite, General Samuel Heintzelman, J. Gurney & Son, New York 60.00
Carte De Visite, General U.S. Grant, Uniform, Gurney & Son 155.00
Carte De Visite, General William Duncan, Civilian Clothes, J. Cremer & Co. 40.00
Carte De Visite, Girl, Bustle Type Dress, Mrs. C.H. Levi, Photographic Artist, 1880 ..... 15.00
Carte De Visite, Johann Strauss, Composer & Waltz King, Gurney, 1870s 45.00
Carte De Visite, John Wilkes Booth, Knees Up, Imprinted Name 185.00
Carte De Visite, Joining Union Pacific & Central Pacific, 1869 .... 7700.00
Carte De Visite, Lambertson Importer & Mfg., Of Human Hair, Phila., 1880 .... 38.00
Carte De Visite, N.P. Willis, New York Writer, Rockwood 80.00
Carte De Visite, Native American Warrior, Chief Of Gull Lake, Seated, 1862 .... 550.00
Carte De Visite, Native American Warrior, Wind Comes Home, 1862 .... 550.00
Carte De Visite, North Western Indian Commission, D. Hinkle, 1866 .... 1900.00
Carte De Visite, Parakeet On Perch 50.00
Carte De Visite, Pennsylvania, Volunteer Infantry, Phila., 1860 .... 440.00
Carte De Visite, Portrait, Adm. D.G. Farragut, Standing, Wearing Uniform, 1860 .... 88.00
Carte De Visite, Portrait, Albert Bierstadt, Landscape Artist Of Am. West, 1860 .... 247.00
Carte De Visite, Portrait, Confederate Col. R.M. Gano, Seated, 1913 .... 220.00
Carte De Visite, Private Benjamin Daugherty, 31st Illinois Infantry 795.00
Carte De Visite, Rembrandt Peale, Wearing Dark Clothes, 1860 .... 100.00
Carte De Visite, Rosa Bonheur, French Realist Painter, 1870 .... 33.00
Carte De Visite, Scene, Frederick Church, American Landscape Artist, 1860 .... 165.00
Carte De Visite, Wm. Sidney Mount, American Painter, Signed, 1860 .... 38.00
Carte De Visite, Women Ice Skaters, Same Women In 2 Poses, 1860 .... 88.00
Cyanotype, Providence Rhode Island, Aerial View, 1890s, 6 3/4 x 8 1/2 In. 1265.00
Daguerreotype, 2 Children Standing, Full Leather Case, 1/2 Plate 4370.00
Daguerreotype, 2 Gentlemen, Mathew Brady, Leather Case, 1850s, 1/4 Plate 862.00
Daguerreotype, 2 Houses Nestled In The Woods, Full Leather Case, 1/6 Plate 690.00
Daguerreotype, 2 Sisters, Mascher's Case, Full Leather, 1/4 Plate 255.00
Daguerreotype, Asa Stanton Portrait, John V. Parker, Matted, 1853, 1/6 Plate 977.00
Daguerreotype, Black Man, Fence, Richmond Va., Frame, 1865, 4 1/4 In. 275.00
Daguerreotype, Canine, Lying On Oriental Rug, Leather Case, 1/6 Plate 4830.00
Daguerreotype, Carpenter, Top Hat, Holding Hammer, Block Plane, Case, 1/6 Plate 1705.00
Daguerreotype, Child In Yellow Dress, Tinted, Scalloped, 1/6 Plate 315.00
Daguerreotype, Child Sleeping, Oval Matted, 1/6 Plate 300.00
Daguerreotype, Child With Doll, Lying Down, Geometric Union Case, 1/6 Plate 115.00
Daguerreotype, Child With Doll, Standing, Full Leather Case, 1/6 Plate 635.00
Daguerreotype, Civil War Figure, Uniform, Gutta Percha Case, c.1865, 3 x 2 In. 340.00
Daguerreotype, Classical Woman, Cloak Draped Around Her, W. Root, 1/6 Plate 1850.00
Daguerreotype, Early Marriage, Double Matted, Full Case, 1/6 Plate 145.00

Daguerreotype, English Gentleman Smoking Cigar, Tinted, 1/9 Plate 265.00
Daguerreotype, Family Grouping, 4 Persons, 1844, 3/4 Plate 1155.00
Daguerreotype, Fireman, Parade Hat & Horn, Mid 19th Century 825.00
Daguerreotype, Gallery Token, Eagle, Brass, N.Y., 1 In. 66.00
Daguerreotype, Gallery Token, Eagle, Brass, St. Louis, 1 In. 91.00
Daguerreotype, Gentleman Astride Horse, Hand Colored, Case, 1860s, 1/6 Plate 1265.00
Daguerreotype, Gentleman Seated In Chair, Mounted, Frame, 1850s 1955.00
Daguerreotype, Gentleman, Dog On Sofa, Mounted, Frame, 1850s, 1/4 Plate 2185.00
Daguerreotype, Gentleman, High Collar Shirt, Vest, Thermoplastic Frame, 5 In. 247.00
Daguerreotype, Gentleman, Seated, Holding Cane, Leatherette Case, 1/4 Plate 85.00
Daguerreotype, Girl & Doll, Striped Floral Dress, 1/6 Plate 355.00
Daguerreotype, Girl With Apron, Striped Stockings, Chair, Full Case, 1/6 Plate 90.00
Daguerreotype, Girl, With Medical Condition, Full Leather Case, 1/6 Plate 345.00
Daguerreotype, Harness Maker, 1/4 Plate 3575.00
Daguerreotype, Harness Maker, Split Leather Case, 1/6 Plate 6610.00
Daguerreotype, Importer's Token, Eagle, Brass, N.Y., 1 In. 63.00
Daguerreotype, Josiah Quincy, 1/4 Plate, 4 5/8 x 3 6/8 In. 575.00
Daguerreotype, Man & Woman, Holding Parasol, 1/2 Plate 240.00
Daguerreotype, Man & Woman, Seated, 1/6 Plate 82.00
Daguerreotype, Man & Woman, Seated, Leatherette Case, 1/2 Plate 275.00
Daguerreotype, Man, Riding Horse & Carriage, With Dog, 1/4 Plate 460.00
Daguerreotype, Margaret Cardeza, Seated, Full Plate 2640.00
Daguerreotype, Military Officer, Seated, 1/6 Plate 907.00
Daguerreotype, Miner, Blousey Shirt, Eagle Belt Buckle, 1850s, 1/6 Plate 2185.00
Daguerreotype, Mother & Father Mourn Loss Of Daughter, 1/6 Plate 5225.00
Daguerreotype, New York Winter Scene, Split Leather Case, 1/2 Plate 230.00
Daguerreotype, Old Man Wearing Masonic Uniform, 1/6 Plate 1150.00
Daguerreotype, Old Woman, Boston School, 1/6 Plate 3680.00
Daguerreotype, Philadelphia Gent, Top Hat, W.B. Swift, 1/6 Plate 135.00
Daguerreotype, Photographer's Assistant, Jacket, High Boots 900.00
Daguerreotype, Stern Man In Torn Coat, 1/6 Plate 30.00
Daguerreotype, Street Scene, City Shoe Store, 1/2 Plate 145.00
Daguerreotype, Woman & Flowers, Woman Holding Book, 1/6 Plate 123.00
Daguerreotype, Woman & Girl, W. & F. Langenheim, Case, 1/4 Plate 415.00
Daguerreotype, Woman In Bonnet & Fishnet Shawl, Blue, 1840, 1/6 Plate 83.00
Daguerreotype, Woman Reading Book, Full Leather Case, 1/6 Plate 1955.00
Daguerreotype, Woman, Black Gown, Cape, Full Leather Case, 1850s, 1/4 Plate 747.00
Daguerreotype, Woman, Seated, Bonnet, 1850, 1/6 Plate 220.00
Daguerreotype, Woman, Seated, Bonnet, Phila., 1840, 1/6 Plate 121.00
Daguerreotype, Woman, Seated, Holding Portrait, 1850, 1/6 Plate 100.00
Daguerreotype, Woman, Seated, Leatherette Case, 1840, 1/9 Plate 110.00
Daguerreotype, Woman, Seated, Period Dress, 1/6 Plate, Pair 385.00
Daguerreotype, Woman, Seated, Wearing Blue Tinted Dress, 1/4 Plate 2645.00
Daguerreotype, Young Boy Standing By Table, Case, c.1860, 2 x 2 1/2 In. 65.00
Daguerreotype, Young Gentleman, Full Leather Case, 1/2 Plate 1035.00
Daguerreotype, Young Girl, Fat Rabbit, Leather Case, 1850s, 1/6 Plate 4140.00
Daguerreotype, Young Girl, Standing, Leatherette Case, 1850, 1/6 Plate 121.00
Daguerreotype, Young Man In Sports Tunic, 1/6 Plate 514.00
Daguerreotype, Young Music Master, Holds Violin & Bow, 1/2 Case, 1/6 Plate 3500.00
Daguerreotype, Young Sisters, Hand Colored, Leather Case, 1850s, 1/2 Plate 1150.00
Film Canister, Kodak, 1952 Helsinki Logo, 2 In. ....*Illus*   5.00
Magic Lantern, American Scout, Glass Slides & Film 160.00
Magic Lantern, Ernst Planck, Germany, 18 Glass Slides, Box 130.00
Magic Lantern, Large Front Lens, 2 Lamps, Schoenner, Child's, 10 In. 184.00
Magic Lantern, Tin, Brass Fittings, Wooden, Gloria EP, Laterna Magica, 13 In. 100.00
Photograph, 3 Nude Women, Vincenzo Galdi, c.1900, 8 3/4 x 6 1/2 In. 747.00
Photograph, 76th Infantry, 12 German Soldiers With Beer Steins, 1909, 14 In. 115.00
Photograph, Abraham Lincoln, Hesler, Ayres, 1860, 9 1/2 x 7 1/4 In. 2185.00
Photograph, Abraham Lincoln, Portrait, Moses P. Rice, 1863, 13 x 10 In. 1840.00
Photograph, Aviatrix With Plane & Dog, 3 1/2 x 4 1/4 In. 150.00
Photograph, Baltimore, U.S. Naval Academy, Fischer & Bros., 4 Views, 1860 .... 1150.00
Photograph, Buffalo Bill, C. Vandyk, c.1900, 10 1/2 x 6 1/2 In. 2530.00
Photograph, Buffalo Bill, Courier Co., Buffalo, Frame, 21 1/2 x 15 1/2 In. 396.00

Photograph, California Joe, Scout To Custer, D.F. Barry, 6 1/2 x 11 In. 230.00
Photograph, Carousel Horses, Israel Bidermanas, 1940s, 9 1/2 x 11 1/4 In. 1150.00
Photograph, Chief Black Bird, Rinehart, Matted, c.1900, 9 1/4 x 7 1/3 In. 1300.00
Photograph, Chief Black Bird, Warrior, Horseback, Toned, Silver, 10 x 7 3/4 In. 747.00
Photograph, Chief Goes To War, No. 762, Signed, Frank Rinehart, 1898, 9 x 7 In. 575.00
Photograph, Child, Arthur In Coffin, Hand Tinted, Matted, 6 x 8 1/4 In. 75.00
Photograph, Children Singing In Rain, 1950, 13 5/8 x 17 1/2 In. 485.00
Photograph, Chinese Family, San Francisco's Chinatown, 1920s, 8 x 10 In. 37.00
Photograph, Darien Expedition, Moran, Sullivan, 26 Image, 1870 . . . . 27600.00
Photograph, Egyptian Ruins, John Bulkley Greene, 1850s, 9 1/4 x 11 1/4 In. 2300.00
Photograph, First Lieutenant James Jackson Lowell, Crutches, 1861, 7 x 6 In. 1725.00
Photograph, Fishermen, Jerry's Bait & Tackle Shop, San Fran., 1930s, 8 x 10 In. 45.00
Photograph, French Circus Performers, 1870s, 15 x 11 In. 632.00
Photograph, Furnace Creek Camp, Death Valley, Stetson Hindes, 1930s, 5 x 7 In. 38.00
Photograph, Giant Sequoias, Redwood National Forest, Sepia, Frame, 18 In. 77.00
Photograph, Himalayans From Nepal & Bhutan, A. Hefferan, 1890s 1265.00
Photograph, Horse-Drawn Wagon In Front Of Leather Shop, Matted, 5 x 7 In. 25.00
Photograph, Josephine Earp, Diaphanous Sheath, 1880s, 20 1/2 x 8 3/4 In. 1840.00
Photograph, Knitting By The Seaside, Frank Meadow Sutcliffe, 1880s, 8 x 6 In. 1150.00
Photograph, Leaping In The Blender, 1965, 17 1/2 x 13 5/8 In. 488.00
Photograph, Little Bird, Arapahoe, Rinehart, Matted, c.1898, 9 1/4 x 7 1/2 In. 1350.00
Photograph, Lumberjack, Tree Grove, Sepia Toned, J.D. Cress, 1800s, 30 x 20 In. 198.00
Photograph, Maison Carree, France, Salt Print, 1850s, 7 1/2 x 10 In. 862.00
Photograph, Mariposa Big Tree Grove Calif., H.C. Tibbits, c.1899, 16 x 21 In. 198.00
Photograph, Masted Clipper At Sea, Charles E. Bolles, 1900, 21 x 16 1/2 In. 2070.00
Photograph, Monument To War, 1959, 8 3/4 x 6 1/4 In. 1920.00
Photograph, New York, Street, River Scenes, Loeffler Studio, 12 Views, 1880s 3450.00
Photograph, On Summit Of Pike's Peak, July 19, 1891, Harlan & Clew, 8 x 5 In. 45.00
Photograph, Orotone, Chief Joseph, Nez Perce, Edward Curtis, 13 x 10 In. 38500.00
Photograph, Orotone, Road, Trees, Spanish Moss, R.H. Le Sesne, Frame, 12 x 9 In. 355.00
Photograph, Panorama, 101 Ranch, Cowboy Old Timers, 1921, 7 1/2 x 46 In. 424.00
Photograph, Panorama, 101 Ranch, Washington, D.C., 1925, Russell, 8 x 33 In. 960.00
Photograph, Panorama, Constantinople, Pris De La Tour De Galata, 1870s 2760.00
Photograph, Panorama, Jess Willard's Wild West Show, 1917, 11 x 41 In. 1073.00
Photograph, Panorama, New York, 5 Part Brooklyn Bridge, 1876 . . . . 4140.00
Photograph, Parade-Apsaroke, Sepia, Rice Paper, Frame, 1908, 12 x 14 In. 341.00
Photograph, Picasso, At La Victorine Studio, Andre Villers, 1955, 11 x 14 In. 800.00
Photograph, Platinum, Guner Working Up To Fowl, Peter H. Emerson, 1888 . . . . 3220.00
Photograph, Platinum, Major General Joseph Hooker, Frame, 1860s, 14 x 17 In. 517.00
Photograph, Platinum, Schooner John Speckles, 1905, 18 x 24 In. 55.00
Photograph, Platinum, Sioux & Omaha Images, Frank A. Rinehart, 1898 . . . . 920.00
Photograph, Point Barrow, Alaska, Eskimos, Building, 1920, 3 x 5 1/2 In. 15.00
Photograph, Pretty Girl, Bow In Hair, Evans, Oval Mount, 1905 . . . . 11.00
Photograph, Quincey Market & Beacon Hill Reservoir, Salt Print, 1850s 3450.00
Photograph, Red Wing, First Public Flight In America, 1908, 4 7/8 x 7 In. 160.00
Photograph, Republican Rally, Springfield, Ill., 1880, 9 1/2 x 13 In. 2530.00

Photography, Film
Canister, Kodak,
1952 Helsinki
Logo, 2 In.

Photography, Photograph, Wedding Party Scene,
Ohio, 1930s, 9 1/4 x 7 1/2 In.

Photograph, Sojourner Truth, I Sell The Shadow To Support The Substance	660.00
Photograph, Son Of The Sun, Kiowa Chief, Indian, Cavalry Jacket, 5 1/2 x 4 In.	546.00
Photograph, Steam Engine & Baler In Hay Field, Matted, 5 x 7 In.	25.00
Photograph, Storefronts, Horse Drawn Wagon, Early Autos, Matted, 5 x 7 In.	25.00
Photograph, Sue Lewen, Maxfield Parrish's Model, Matted, 7 3/4 x 5 3/4 In.	415.00
Photograph, Swiss Chateau, Adolophe Braun, 1880s, 14 1/2 x 18 3/4 In.	1150.00
Photograph, Terminus Of Hoosac Tunnel Route, Stebbins, Frame, 16 x 27 In.	175.00
Photograph, The Dirty Monk, Julia Margaret Cameron, 1869, 10 1/4 x 8 In.	5290.00
Photograph, Tom Mix, William Fox Studios, Mailing Envelope, 9 1/2 x 7 1/2 In.	119.00
Photograph, View From Algonquin Hotel, Ilse Bing, 1936, 8 1/2 x 11 In.	3450.00
Photograph, Wedding Party Scene, Ohio, 1930s, 9 1/4 x 7 1/2 In. . . . . *Illus*	17.00
Photograph, Western Rock Formations, Andrew J. Russell, 4 Views, 1860s	2530.00
Photograph, Wild Bill Hickok, Original Mount, c.1872	1380.00
Photograph, Woman In Profile, Julia Margaret Cameron, 1860s, 10 x 8 In.	2300.00
Photograph, Woman, Leaves, Julia Margaret Cameron, 1870s, 14 x 10 In.	3910.00
Photograph, Women, Nude, Pierre Louys, 1890s, 3 1/2 x 3 1/2 In.	2070.00
Photograph, Workshop, Women Working At Tables, Matted, c.1900, 8 x 6 In.	50.00
Photograph, Young Woman, Oval, Matted, Emerson's Studio, 1900	10.00
Photograph, Zack Miller, Autograph, 101 Ranch, 1937, 19 1/2 x 16 1/2 In.	226.00
Photogravure, Aubrey Beardsley, Frederick H. Evans, Sepia Toned, 1899	1150.00
Photogravure, Quail Shooting, Covey, A. Lassell Ripley, Frame, 13 x 8 In.	27.00
Slide, Glass, Abraham Lincoln, Holley Process	60.00
Tintype, 2 Union Soldiers, Holding Muskets, 1/6 Plate	975.00
Tintype, 2 Women, Plains, Sitting, 1 Holding Papoose, 19th Century, 3 3/4 In.	215.00
Tintype, 3 Soldiers, Standing, Split Leather Case, 1/4 Plate	920.00
Tintype, Bearded Man In Civil War Uniform, Case, 3 x 2 1/2 In.	165.00
Tintype, Captain Thayer, Kalamazoo, Michigan, Paper Frame	100.00
Tintype, Carpenter & Saw, Hand Tinted, Adirondack Leaf Frame, 1870s	1265.00
Tintype, Cherokee Man With Headdress, Woman In Victorian Dress, c.1860	358.00
Tintype, Civil War Captain, Holding Officer Sword, Seated, 1/4 Plate	1380.00
Tintype, Civil War Private, Seated, Union Case, 1/6 Plate	745.00
Tintype, Civil War Soldier, Forage Cap, Seated, Leatherette Case, 1/4 Plate	195.00
Tintype, Civil War Soldier, Holding Springfield Rifle With Bayonet	138.00
Tintype, Civil War Soldier, Standing, Octagonal Union Case, 1/6 Plate	2590.00
Tintype, Civil War Soldiers, 1 Standing, 1 Seated, Union Case, 1/9 Plate, Pair	4600.00
Tintype, Civil War Soldiers, Seated, Split Leather Case, 1/9 Plate, Pair	575.00
Tintype, Cross Dresser, Man, Standing, Card Frame, 2 x 3 1/2 In.	67.00
Tintype, Dandy Dan & His Black Troupe, White Man In Suit, 1/6 Plate	137.00
Tintype, Dashing Young Gents, Standing By Tree, 3 1/2 x 2 1/4 In.	55.00
Tintype, Ella, Cattle Kate Watson & James Averell, Uncased, 1885, 1/9 Plate	1495.00
Tintype, Fireman, Belt, Bib Shirt, Union Geometric Case, 1/9 Plate	154.00
Tintype, German Soldier, Standing, Overpainted, Victorian Frame, Full Plate	415.00
Tintype, Hunter With Shotgun & 3 Ducks, 1/6 Plate	169.00
Tintype, Indian Scout, Long Rifle, Bowie Knives, 1/6 Plate	110.00
Tintype, John Wilkes Booth, Pewter Frame, 19th Century, 4 1/4 x 6 1/2 In.	185.00
Tintype, Kate Brigolt, Actress, Silsbee, Case	50.00
Tintype, Post Mortem, Child, Purple Ruffled Blouse, Case, 1/6 Plate	415.00
Tintype, Private William Noll, Zouaves, Overpainted, 1861, 8 1/2 x 6 1/2 In.	2070.00
Tintype, Soldier Atop His Horse, Split Leather Case, 1/4 Plate	1440.00
Tintype, Young Ojibwa Woman, Authentic Garb, Beaded Bag, 1880s, 1/6 Plate	465.00
Tintype, Young Soldier, Standing Next To Mantel, Full Case, 1/6 Plate	330.00
Tray, Graniteware, Inserted Cover, Green & White, 12 3/4 x 10 In.	80.00
Tray, Graniteware, White, Blue Trim, Cesco, Columbia Eagle Mark, 8 x 5 3/4 In.	30.00

PIANO BABY is a collector's term. About 1880, the well-decorated home had a shawl on the piano. Bisque figures of babies were designed to help hold the shawl in place. They range in size from 6 to 18 inches. Most of the figures were made in Germany. Reproductions are being made. Other piano babies may be listed under manufacturers' names.

In Shoe, Sunburst Mark, Gebruder Heubach, 11 3/4 In. . . . .*Illus*	1900.00
Sitting, Blue Pleated Dress, Bonnet, Gebruder Heubach, 6 In. . . . .*Illus*	600.00
Sitting, Holding Cup, Girl, Bisque, 12 In.	175.00
Sitting, Ruffled Baby Dress, Gebruder Heubach, 10 In. . . . .*Illus*	550.00

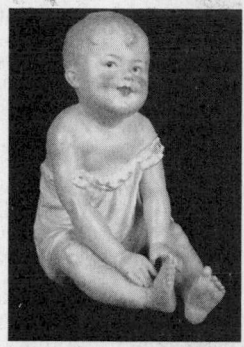

Piano Baby, In Shoe, Sunburst
Mark, Gebruder Heubach,
11 3/4 In.

Piano Baby, Sitting, Blue Pleated
Dress, Bonnet, Gebruder
Heubach, 6 In.

Piano Baby, Sitting, Ruffled
Baby Dress, Gebruder
Heubach, 10 In

PICKARD China Company was started in 1898 by Wilder Pickard. Hand-painted designs were used on china purchased from other sources. In the 1930s, the company began to make its own china wares in Chicago, Illinois. The company now makes many types of porcelains, including a successful line of limited edition collector plates.

Bonbon, Gold Floral, Basket Style Handle	45.00
Celery Dish, Gold Design	30.00
Pitcher, Iris, Hand Painted, Gilt, Frederick J. Linder, 1900s, 6 1/8 In.	465.00
Pitcher, Morning Glories, Gilt Band, Mark, 1912-1918, 6 1/2 In.	110.00
Pitcher, Poppy Design, Silver, Gold Finish, Gilt Handle, Hexagonal, 10 In.	185.00
Plate, Trumpeter Swan, Lockhart, 10 In.	200.00
Relish, China Gold, Geometric Floral, Divided, 6 1/2 In.	30.00
Vase, Oval, 2 Handles, Gilt, 6 In.	105.00

PICTURE FRAMES are listed in this book in the Furniture category under Frame.

PICTURES, silhouettes, and other small decorative objects framed to hang on the wall are listed here. Sandpaper pictures are black and white charcoal drawings done on a special sanded paper. Some other types of pictures are listed in the Print and Painting categories.

Calligraphy, Alphabet, Rustic Style, I.F. Mountz, 12 x 15 In.	50.00
Calligraphy, Ink On Paper, Running Deer, Frame, 14 x 19 1/2 In.	546.00
Calligraphy, Record, Maulfair Family, Lion, Frame, 1850, 13 x 10 In.	1100.00
Calligraphy, Spread-Winged Eagle, Above Fish, Birds, 19th Century, 14 x 19 In.	1100.00
Calligraphy, Stag, Swan, Dove Corners, S.R. Crounauer, 1890, 19 x 24 In.	1650.00
Charcoal, On Paper, Large House, Frame, 21 3/4 x 30 In.	575.00
Cut Paper, Eagle & Snake, Potted Flowers, France, 1989, 9 1/2 x 5 1/2 In.	90.00
Diorama, 2-Masted Ship, Choppy Seas, 22 3/4 x 29 x 5 1/2 In.	330.00
Diorama, Essex, 3-Masted Ship, Painted Ground, 21 1/2 x 30 3/4 x 5 3/4 In.	1100.00
Diorama, Farmers Working In Field, Church, Shadowbox Frame, 7 1/4 x 9 1/4 In.	1150.00
Diorama, Ship & Lighthouse, Wooden, Painted, Putty, Black Frame, 17 1/2 x 24 x 4 In. ..	880.00
Engraving, Battle Of Gettysburg, James Walker, 14 1/4 x 35 In.	95.00
Engraving, Botanical Implements, Ferrari, Germany, c.1638, 7 3/4 x 5 3/4 In.	990.00
Engraving, Courting Scene, R. Gaillard, 17 x 14 In., Pair	195.00
Engraving, Jakob, Portrait, German Inscription, Gilt, Colored, Frame, 4 1/4 x 3 In.	60.00
Engraving, Juvenile Retirement, Early 19th Century Clothes, J. Ward, 18 1/2 x 15 In.	85.00
Engraving, Portland Harbor Panorama, Frame, 30 x 47 In.	175.00
Etching, St. Michael's, Charleston, Alfred Heber Hutty, 1928, 10 1/4 x 8 1/2 In.	825.00
Etching, Stagehand, Arcadia, Ark., Santa Anita Race Track, Matted, 1938, 7 x 8 In.	95.00
Gouache, 3 Pool Players, Lang, Frame, 20 x 28 1/2 In.	770.00
Gouache, Coastal Views, J. Preston, 7 3/4 x 14 5/8 In., Pair	290.00
Gouache, Figures On Pathway, Bay Of Naples, Italy, 19th Century, 14 1/2 x 20 1/2 In. ...	920.00

Gouache, Landscape With Tall Trees, Florence Este, Frame, 23 1/2 x 18 In. 935.00
Gouache, Silhouette, Gentleman, Top Hat, Cane, Gilt Matte, Ebonized Frame, 11 x 7 In. . 275.00
Gouache, U.S. Lighthouse Society Ship, Maple, Signed Selby, Frame, 11 1/2 x 19 In. 850.00
Gouache On Silk, Figures On Patio, 19th Century, Frame, Chinese, 22 x 34 In. 145.00
Graphite, Reclining Gentleman, After Egon Schiele, 13 1/2 x 10 1/2 In. 275.00
Grease Pencil, Ink, Crayon & Watercolor, Juggler, B. Browne, 1952, 12 1/2 x 10 In. 100.00
Indian, Mission Squaw, Pastels On Birchbark, 1900-1910, Frame, 17 x 12 In. 120.00
Ink, Old Man, Beard, Skull Cap, 8 3/4 x 6 1/2 In. 55.00
Ink Wash, Glenfiddoch Shooting Lodge, John Scott, 1870, 11 x 19 1/2 In. 605.00
Marquetry, Classical Woman, Holding Staff, Frame, 1800s, 27 x 21 In. 385.00
Motto, Mother Of Mine, Crocuses, Frame, Gibson, 1927, 8 5/8 x 5 1/4 In. ....*Illus* 6.00
Motto, Mother, Children, Frame, Gibson, 1926, 10 5/8 x 6 5/8 In. ....*Illus* 12.00
Needlepoint, American Flag, Animal & Floral Surround, 1880, 21 1/2 x 20 1/2 In. 605.00
Needlepoint, Aubusson Pattern, Green & Tan Border, Corner Medallions, 9 x 12 In. 880.00
Needlepoint, George Washington, Valley Forge, Minnie Golber, 1936, 34 x 43 In. 880.00
Needlepoint, Wool, Giving Alms, Mary Anne Donnelly, Frame, England, 29 x 28 In. 1155.00
Needlework, Angel Feeding Saint, Reverse Painted Glass, Frame, c.1830, 14 x 17 In. 410.00
Needlework, Embroidered, Wool On Linen, Tree, Frame, 35 x 27 In. 465.00
Needlework, Embroidery On Silk, Oriental Floral Basket, Frame, 1875, 20 x 17 In. 25.00
Needlework, England & Wales Map, Oval, Gilt Frame, 20 1/2 x 16 1/2 In. 385.00
Needlework, Federal House Scene, Shrubs, Trees, Birds, Sawtooth Border, 13 x 17 In. ... 1495.00
Needlework, Flowering Wreath Beneath Alphabet Panels, Birds, Trees, 1822, 22 In. 860.00
Needlework, Metal Stitched, Orange Ground, Center Picture, Oriental, 49 x 21 In. 110.00
Needlework, Moravian Silk & Gauze, Flowers, Pa., 1830, 15 1/2 x 12 1/2 In. 1760.00
Needlework, On Paper, Bird, Flowing Tree, Label, March 13th 1781, Frame, 10 x 8 In. .. 260.00
Needlework, Pompeiian Fresco, Italy, 19th Century, 65 1/4 x 24 3/4 In. ....920.00 to 1035.00
Needlework, Silk On Linen, Youth Sowing Seeds, Gilt Frame, 12 x 9 1/4 In. 605.00
Needlework, Silk On Silk, 2 Classical Women, Sitting, On Wall, England, 21 x 11 In. 465.00
Needlework, Silk, Jesus, As Gardener, Mary Magdalene, Matted, Frame, 18 In. 575.00
Needlework, Silk, Memorial, Watercolor, Child, Woman, Frame, 1820, 22 x 20 In. 8050.00
Needlework, Silk, Rebecca At The Well, Chenille Threads, Silk Ground, 14 x 14 In. 805.00
Needlework, Silk, Young Lady Playing A Harp, Seated Beside Urn, 14 1/2 x 18 In. 805.00
Needlework, Stitched, Oriental Figure, Flowers, Brown, 20th Century, 40 x 27 In. 170.00
Needlework, Swans, Water Lilies, Cattails, Silk, Painted, Gilt Shadowbox, 50 x 31 In. ... 440.00
Pastel, Caprice Morning, Walter Shirlaw, N.A., 20 3/4 x 23 3/4 In. 715.00
Pastel, Old Woman, Blue Eyes, Shawl & Bonnet, Gilt Frame, England, 11 1/8 x 9 In. 385.00
Pastel, On Buff Paper, Tree & Field Landscape, A.C. Goodwin, 17 1/4 x 23 1/2 In. 1320.00
Pastel, On Canvas, Retriever, Woodcock In Mouth, M. Martin, Frame, 14 x 20 In. 110.00
Pastel, On Paper, Winter Scene, Mill & Houses, H.H. Coots, 12 1/2 x 18 1/2 In. 55.00
Pastel, Portrait Of A Lady, Unsigned, France, Late 1800s, 24 1/4 x 20 In. 575.00
Pastel, Trees In Forest, Will Henry Stevens, 15 3/4 x 13 3/4 In. 2640.00
Pastel, Tugboat, Herman Atkins Macneil, N.A., 10 x 12 1/2 In. 288.00
Pastel & Pencil, Rose Lucy & Godfrey Beckett Hodgson, Frame, 1865, 9 x 7 7/8 In. 2200.00
Pastel On Board, Profile Portrait Of Woman, 27 1/2 x 20 7/8 In. 290.00
Pastel On Paper, 2 Fish, Light Purple, William Hentschel, Signed, 1934, 14 1/2 In. 550.00
Pen & Ink, On Paper, Friendship, Spencerian, E.A. Brown, Frame, 5 1/2 x 7 1/2 In. 165.00
Pen & Ink On Paper, Cowboy, On Horse, Watercolor, Olaf Carl Wieghorst, 9 x 7 In. 3000.00
Pencil, Victorian House, 1890, 14 x 18 In. 110.00
Pencil, Watercolor, Gouache, Coronation Platform, Nicholas II, 13 1/4 x 16 1/2 In. 450.00
Silhouette, 2 Women, 2 Children Playing, Hollow Cut, Frame, 11 1/2 x 17 In. 520.00
Silhouette, Apollo & Diana In Chariots, Hollow Cut, Matted, Frame, 3 3/4 In., Pair 200.00
Silhouette, Charles Burrall Hoffman, Frame, 1837, 11 x 8 In. 1265.00
Silhouette, Child In Dress, Full Length, Oval Brass Frame, 5 1/2 x 4 1/2 In. 440.00
Silhouette, Dr. Franklin, Bust, Signed S. Moore, Mahogany Frame, 9 1/8 x 8 1/8 In. ... 195.00
Silhouette, Gentleman, Hollow Cut, Daguerreotype Gutta-Percha Case, 4 x 3 1/2 In. 110.00
Silhouette, Ink On Paper, Boy With Hoop, 5 x 4 In. 230.00
Silhouette, Johnathan Morgan Esq., Peg Leg, Black Cloth On Paper, Frame, 8 x 6 In. ... 180.00
Silhouette, Tree, Birds, Stag & Rabbit, Frame, Ralph Lindsay, 6 3/4 x 8 3/4 In. 135.00
Silhouette, Woman, Flower Portrait, Full-Length, Augustin Edouart, 1825, 9 1/2 x 7 In. .. 515.00
Silhouette, Woman, Hollow Cat, Mary Amber, Mahogany Veneer Frame, 10 x 9 In. 245.00
Silhouette, Woman, Low-Cut Dress, Jewelry, Signed Dowa, Gilt Frame, 9 x 8 In. 70.00
Silhouette, Young Man, Gold Frame, 1886, 8 1/2 x 6 3/4 In. 45.00
Theorem, Basket Of Flowers, Watercolor, 12 x 14 1/4 In. 575.00

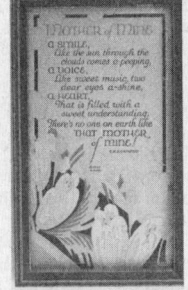

Picture, Motto,
Mother Of Mine,
Crocuses, Frame,
Gibson, 1927,
8 5/8 x 5 1/4 In.

Picture, Motto,
Mother, Children,
Frame, Gibson, 1926,
10 5/8 x 6 5/8 In.

Theorem, Bird, Cherries On Branch, Watercolor, Mahogany Frame, 1864, 2 3/4 x 4 In. 415.00
Theorem, Fruit In Blue Basket, Maple Frame, Early 19th Century, 5 x 5 1/2 In. 825.00
Theorem, Fruit Surrounded By Birds & Butterflies, Elizabeth Robinson, 1810, 21 In. 1610.00
Theorem, Fruit, Watercolor On Paper, Frame, 19th Century, 7 x 9 In. 550.00
Theorem, On Velvet, Bee Skep, Flowers, Terrence Graham, Frame, 21 x 20 1/2 In. 520.00
Theorem, On Velvet, Bird, With Fruit & Flowers, Watercolor, 19th Century, 18 x 20 In. . . 550.00
Theorem, On Velvet, Bowl Of Fruit, Melon & Grapes, Watercolor, Frame, 19 x 24 In. . . . 385.00
Theorem, On Velvet, Yellow & White Striped Cat On Rug, Bill Rank, Frame, 16 x 15 In. . . 465.00
Theorem, Roses, Cherries, Watercolor, G.W. Champion, Frame, 1866, 22 x 26 In. 305.00
Theorem, Roses, Pansies & Leaves, Mahogany Veneer Frame, 17 1/2 x 12 3/8 In. 70.00
Theorem, Watermelon, Grapes & Peaches, Mid 19th Century, 18 x 23 In. 1550.00
Wallpaper, Castle Garden, Hand Printed, White, Yellow & Brown, Frame, 15 x 15 In. . . . 110.00
Watercolor, 3-Masted Schooner, Cutter-Type Bow, Frame, England, 1880, 10 x 15 In. . . . 330.00
Watercolor, Autumn River Landscape, Hugo Fisher, 11 x 22 3/4 In. 165.00
Watercolor, Banff To Windimun Road, British Columbia, Frame, 10 1/2 x 7 In. 225.00
Watercolor, Beach Scene, Pier & Horses, William Spring, Matted, Frame, 14 x 27 In. . . . 55.00
Watercolor, Bird On Green Branch, Frame, 19th Century, 9 x 7 In. 2530.00
Watercolor, Birds In Marshy Landscape, Agnes A. Abbot, 21 1/8 x 30 In. 200.00
Watercolor, Bluebills Flying Over Marsh, Joseph Day Knap, Frame, 13 x 20 In. 385.00
Watercolor, Boat Yard Scene, Frame, L.E. Smith, 18 1/2 x 22 1/2 In. 165.00
Watercolor, Cat, Sitting, Foujita, Matted, Frame, 1947, 11 3/4 x 8 5/8 In. 530.00
Watercolor, Church On A River, Anna Richards Brewster, Monogram, 1897, 15 x 11 In. . . 275.00
Watercolor, Cottage Scene, Mother & Child, Frame, 31 1/2 x 25 In. 250.00
Watercolor, Cowboy, Sitting On Wagon Wheel, Cigarette, Oval, Frame, 16 x 20 In. 395.00
Watercolor, Duck Hunter In Boat, Ed Walatis, Frame, 20 1/4 x 27 1/2 In. 300.00
Watercolor, Dutch Waterways, Windmills, Sailboats, Frame, M. Stoughton, 14 x 17 In. . . 10.00
Watercolor, Family Tree, R. Robertson & Jane House, 1916, 29 x 21 In. 1710.00
Watercolor, Figure In Landscape, Castle, Europe, 19th Century, 8 3/8 x 11 1/4 In. 175.00
Watercolor, Fishing Boats Off Shore, S.A. Mulholland, 16 1/2 x 26 5/8 In. 220.00
Watercolor, Floral Still Life, G.B. French, Frame, 11 1/2 x 15 1/2 In. 200.00
Watercolor, Gentleman, Top Hat, Umbrella, Joshua Dighton, Matted, Frame, 11 x 7 In. . . 275.00
Watercolor, Girl, Harriete Hallaron, Born 1843, Died 1911, Frame, 6 x 5 3/8 In. 495.00
Watercolor, Graphite, Sailing, A.E.H., 1901, 8 x 11 In. 690.00
Watercolor, Gypsy Woman, Continental School, 19th Century, 9 x 5 In. 315.00
Watercolor, Horse Auction, Chauncey F. Ryder, 15 1/2 x 19 3/4 In. 2185.00
Watercolor, Landscape At Sunset, Gilt Frame, C.R. Raymond, 10 x 13 In. 110.00
Watercolor, Landscape With Pond, George Overbury Pop Hart, 15 1/2 x 22 In. 220.00
Watercolor, Landscape, Shoreline, Edmund Darch Lewis, 1881, 17 x 28 In. 770.00
Watercolor, Last Supper, American, Frame, 19th Century, 3 1/2 x 7 In. 200.00
Watercolor, Lithograph, Clipper Yacht American. Currier, 14 x 18 In. 975.00
Watercolor, Lumber Schooner Frenchman's Bay, Franz Lesshafft, Frame, 14 x 10 In. 385.00
Watercolor, Man Profile, Black Frock Coat, Mahogany Frame, 6 3/8 x 4 5/8 In. 385.00
Watercolor, Man, Ascot, Woman, White Dress, 19th Century, 6 1/4 x 4 3/4 In., Pair 275.00
Watercolor, Man, Bust Portrait, American, Frame, 19th Century, 2 x 1 3/4 In. 176.00
Watercolor, Man, With Sword, Standing, Ponytail, Black & Gray, Frame, 7 x 5 In. 160.00
Watercolor, Matronly Woman, Brown Dress, Hat, Rosewood Frame, 10 3/8 x 9 In. 55.00
Watercolor, Mother, Baby & Boy, P. Fyfe, July-August, 1844, Matted, Frame, 18 x 7 In. . 220.00
Watercolor, Mourning, 3 Girls, Monument, Willow Tree, 8 3/4 x 12 3/4 In. 1100.00

Watercolor, Musician, Oriental, Rice Paper, Early 20th Century, 52 1/2 x 29 In. 880.00
Watercolor, Nassau Cottages, Bahamas, Elmer Joseph Read, 1904, 10 1/4 x 14 3/4 In. . . . 660.00
Watercolor, New England Winter Scene, Inn, People, L.C. Hickman, 1958, 15 x 21 In. . . 35.00
Watercolor, Off To Work, Peter Kraemer, Frame, 8 x 6 3/8 In. 690.00
Watercolor, Old Woman, Black Dress, White Bonnet, Rosewood Frame, 7 1/2 x 6 In. . . . 330.00
Watercolor, Oriental Figures & Buildings, Silk Border, Frame, 25 x 29 In. 50.00
Watercolor, Oriental Man, With Children, 19th Century, 34 x 20 3/4 In. 110.00
Watercolor, Parisian Street Scene, Booksellers, William Wing Howard, 22 x 31 In. 275.00
Watercolor, Parrot, Bird Of Paradise & Squirrel, Frame, 12 x 15 3/4 In. 850.00
Watercolor, Peasant Couple, In Kitchen, C.A. Shimmin, Frame, 19 x 26 In. 165.00
Watercolor, Pencil & Inkpot Of Stylized Tulips, Frame, 7 1/2 x 6 1/4 In. 110.00
Watercolor, People On Village Road, Frame, 5 x 7 In. 250.00
Watercolor, Pilgrim On Shore, Looking To Sea, Sepia Tone, 23 1/4 x 15 1/2 In. 165.00
Watercolor, Pont Neuf, L. Ducuing, France, 20th Century, 11 x 15 In. 200.00
Watercolor, Quebec Docks, Henry Ward Ranger, Matted, Frame, 1885, 17 x 22 In. 1540.00
Watercolor, River Landscape, Robert Gallon, 12 1/2 x 20 1/2 In. 135.00
Watercolor, Rooftops, William Joseph Eastman, Matted, Frame, 10 1/2 x 14 In. 20.00
Watercolor, Seated Dutch Man With Pipe, H. Van Steenwyck, 13 x 9 In. 140.00
Watercolor, Ship In Full Sail, Rocky Shoal, Signed E.G. Good II, 18 x 27 1/2 In. 15.00
Watercolor, Sleigh & Snow Scene, Hattie K. Bruner, 10 1/2 x 14 1/2 In. 1210.00
Watercolor, Soldier, Johann Christian Jochinke, With Note, 1789, 9 1/2 x 7 1/2 In. 495.00
Watercolor, Stormy Landscape, House In Field, H. Gasser, 14 x 19 In. 275.00
Watercolor, Stream In Winter, Agnes A. Abbot, 15 x 21 1/2 In. 105.00
Watercolor, Stylish Man, Blue Frock Coat, Grained Frame, 5 x 4 1/4 In. 410.00
Watercolor, Surf At Boothbay Shores, Norman Merritt, 15 1/8 x 22 1/2 In. 175.00
Watercolor, The Haircut, Continental, Late 19th-Early 20th Century, 8 7/8 x 6 3/4 In. 175.00
Watercolor, Trees By River, Dodge MacKnight, Matted, 14 x 21 In. 770.00
Watercolor, Tropical Motif, Elsa V. Shaw, Frame, 29 1/2 x 37 In. 330.00
Watercolor, True Love Knot, Frame, WC 1830, 9 1/2 x 8 In. 2860.00
Watercolor, Tugboats In Harbor, Frame, John Whorf, 21 x 29 1/4 In. 8625.00
Watercolor, View Of Nazareth, Ch. F. Kluge, 7 x 9 1/2 In. 1650.00
Watercolor, View Of The Lake, Clarence Kerr Chatterton, 11 1/4 x 15 1/2 In. 85.00
Watercolor, Villager With Mule, George Overbury Hart, 12 1/2 x 9 3/4 In. 125.00
Watercolor, Waterfront Village, Florence Robinson, 11 x 15 In. 265.00
Watercolor, Winter Afternoon, Birch Trees, Valley, Wuermer, Frame, 25 x 30 In. 3575.00
Watercolor, Winter Scene, Railroad Station Near Water, Ship, H. Gasser, 14 x 21 In. 1540.00
Watercolor, Woman & Dog Outdoor Scene, Velvet, 17 1/2 x 21 3/4 In. 1840.00
Watercolor, Woman, 19th Century Dress, Bonnet, Black Frame, 3 1/2 x 4 1/2 In. 20.00
Watercolor, Woman, Black Dress, Rosewood Veneer Frame, 13 1/2 x 10 1/4 In. 495.00
Watercolor, Young Man, Seated, Black Frock Coat, Frame, 8 x 6 1/4 In. 355.00
Watercolor, Young Woman, Reeded Frame, Henry Walton, 5 3/8 x 4 5/8 In. 550.00
Watercolor & Ink, House, School, Alice J. Wise, Ezer Lamborn, 19th Century, 7 x 9 In. . . . 3850.00
Watercolor & Pencil, Family Record, John & Mary Morton Married 19th Decr 1799 . . . . 545.00
Watercolor & Pencil, Flower For The Lady, France, 19th Century, 9 1/4 x 7 1/2 In. 195.00
Watercolor & Pencil, Geo. Washington, Horse, Frame, 1880s, 17 x 14 In. 1800.00
Watercolor & Pencil, Memorial, Sally McFarland, August 1807, Frame, 12 x 11 In. 1380.00
Watercolor & Pencil, Seascape, Crashing Surf, Sailboats, S.A. Mulholland, 11 x 23 In. . . 330.00
Watercolor On Board, Low Tide, Edward F. Ertz, Signed, Frame, 14 7/8 x 10 1/8 In. 200.00
Watercolor On Ivory, Gentleman, Wooden Frame, Gilded Liner, 5 1/4 In. 248.00
Watercolor On Paper, Hay Wagon, Woman Spinning, J.S. March, 1876, 16 x 19 In. 155.00
Wax Portrait, Benjamin Franklin, Shadowbox Frame, 6 x 5 5/8 In. 880.00
Wax Portrait, Gentleman, Curly Hair, Black Cloak, Frame, 2 1/2 In. 170.00
Wax Portrait, Gentleman, Early 19th Century, 3 1/4 In. 430.00
Wax Portrait, Woman, Relief, Shadow Box Frame, 19th Century, 5 3/4 x 4 1/4 In. 345.00
Wax Relief, Man's Profile, Period Costume, Frame, Leslie Ray, London, 5 x 5 1/2 In. 520.00

PIERCE, see Howard Pierce category.

PIGEON FORGE Pottery was started in Pigeon Forge, Tennessee, in 1946. Red clay found near the pottery was used to make the pieces. Molded or thrown pottery with matte glaze and slip decoration was made. The pottery is still working.

Pitcher Set, Khaki Color, Blue Slip Interior, 5 1/2-In. Pitcher, 5 Piece 75.00

Vase, Dogwood, 3 1/2 In. 22.00
Vase, Double, Dogwood, 8 In. 45.00

PILKINGTON Tile and Pottery Company was established in 1892 in
England. The company made small pottery wares, like buttons and hatpins, but soon started decorating vases purchased from other potteries.
By 1903, the company had discovered an opalescent glaze that became
popular on the Lancastrian pottery line. The manufacture of pottery
ended in 1937. Pilkington's Tiles Ltd. has worked from 1938 to the
present.

Bowl, Centerpiece, Royal Lancastrian, Flowers, Persian Design, 5 x 10 In. 1210.00
Vase, Cover, Royal Lancastrian, 4 Galleons At Sea, Borders, c.1908, 7 1/2 In. 3490.00
Vase, Fish & Seaweed, Sang-De-Boeuf Glaze, Stamped, 7 3/4 x 5 In. 1540.00
Vase, Royal Lancastrian, Baluster From, Tulips, Persian Style Flowers, c.1913, 9 In. 2765.00
Vase, Sunstone Glaze, Bottle Shape, Animal Logo, 5 3/4 x 3 1/2 In. 825.00

PINCUSHION DOLLS are not really dolls and often were not even pincushions. Some collectors use the term *half-doll*. The top half of each
doll was made of porcelain. The edge of the half-doll was made with
several small holes for thread, and the doll was stitched to a fabric
body with a voluminous skirt. The finished figure was used to cover a
hot pot of tea, powder box, pincushion, whisk broom, or lamp. They
were made in sizes from less than an inch to over 9 inches high. Most
date from the early 1900s to the 1950s. Collectors often find just the
porcelain doll without the fabric skirt.

Holding Fan, To Chest, Pleated Skirt Holds 5 Powder Puffs, 1920s, 2 1/2 In. 175.00
Holding Parrot On Arm, 3 In. 850.00
Old Woman, Eyes Shut, Bisque Head, Original Dress, Germany, c.1910, 6 In. 100.00
Porcelain, 1 Arm On Waist & Other Near Face, Germany, 3 1/2 In. 15.00
Porcelain, Colonial Lady, On Powder Puff, 4 In. 85.00

PINK SLAG pieces are listed in this book in the Slag Glass category.

PIPES have been popular since tobacco was introduced to Europe by
Sir Walter Raleigh. Carved wooden, porcelain, ivory, and glass pipes
may be listed here. Meerschaum pipes are listed under Meerschaum.

Amber Bakelite, Stem With Black Bowl, 5 In. 44.00
Blown Glass, Light Aqua, Kentucky Glass Works, 1840s, 26 In. 120.00
Brass, Opium, Twisted Rib Bowl, 11 1/2 In. 80.00
Briar, Bowl Has Hinged Metal Lid, Brown Wooden Stem 27.00
Burlwood, Brass Cape, Serpent Closure, 19th Century, 19 x 9 In.   465.00
Calabash, Cast Iron, 6 In. 25.00
Carved Wood, Bavarian Peasant Head, Hat, Painted, 19th Century, 11 x 5 In. 345.00
Carved Wood, Bearded Man's Head, Silver Mounted, Continental, 19th Century, 30 In. . .   260.00
Carved Wood, Black Man, Wearing Cap, 19th Century, 5 1/2 x 2 3/4 In. 260.00
Carved Wood, Draped Woman, Seated Near Urn, Chain, 19th Century, 10 1/2 In. 460.00
Carved Wood, Dutch Figures, Standing, Large Hats, 19th Century, 12 In. 1440.00
Carved Wood, Horn, Silver Top, Crocodile & Lion In Battle, Denmark, 8-In. Bowl 595.00
Carved Wood, Hunter, Dead Stag, Silver Color Lidded Top, 19th Century, 21 In. 260.00
Carved Wood, Man, Tricornered Hat, Original Paint, 19th Century, 8 1/2 In. 345.00
Carved Wood, Opium, Man In Relief, Pewter Top, 7 1/4 In. 175.00
Carved Wood, Silver Mount, Eagle, Basket Of Flowers, 19th Century, 11 1/2 In. 460.00
Carved Wood, Tavern Scene, 7 Men, 19th Century, 19 In. 460.00
Catlinite Bowl, Face, Civil War Era 165.00
Clay, Political, Protection For American Labor, 19th Century, 5 1/4 In. 115.00
Clay Bowl, Black, Silver Wire, 19th Century, Far East, 20 In. 30.00
Iron, Opium, Brass Bowl & Stem, 5 1/2 In. 18.00
Ivory & Wood, Crowned Head, Glass Eyes, 19th Century, 26 In. 545.00
Porcelain, 2 Horses, Metal Hinged Lid, Abguss, Bavarian Type, 9 In. 40.00
Porcelain, Figural, Buffalo Head, Glass Eyes, Debossed Gruyere Garantie 44.00
Porcelain, Humorous Man On Knees, Polishing Woman's Shoes, 19th Century, 5 1/4 In. . .   75.00
Porcelain, Humorous One-Eyed Man, Mustache, 19th Century, 10 1/4 In. 545.00
Porcelain, Knights In Armor, Monk, Wallensteins Lager, 19th Century, 12 1/2 In. 30.00
Porcelain, Man, Hunter, Dog, No Lid, 19th Century, 15 1/2 In. 60.00

Porcelain, Regimental, 8 Foot Artillery, Diedenhofen, 1910-1911, 57 In. 475.00
Porcelain, Wood & Stag Horn, Painted 3 Busts Within Leaves, Marked Res. Frick II 230.00
Porcelain, Wood & Stag Horn, Painted Soldiers, Verse, Germany 200.00
Porcelain, Wood & Stag Horn, Soldiers, Inscription, Germany 80.00
Porcelain, Y-Shaped Bowl, Wilhelm JM Hoff, Cassel, 19th Century, 11 3/4 In. 260.00
Pottery, Man's Head Coming Out Of Shoe, Stamped J.G., 19th Century, 12 5/8 In. 405.00
Sapling, Civil War, GAR, Post 271, 17 In. 125.00
Silver, Sultan's Head, Cigarillo, 4 1/2 In. 290.00
Stag Horn Shaft, Ornate, Tin Bowl, Germany, 8 In. 30.00
Wood, Buffalo Head, Glass Eyes, Gruyere Garantie 45.00
Wood, Domed Pierced Silver Lid, 19th Century, 11 In. 175.00
Wood, Ribbed, Ribbed Cap, Early 19th Century, 16 1/2 In. 45.00

PISGAH FOREST pottery was made in North Carolina beginning in
1926. The pottery was started by Walter R. Stephen in 1914, and after
his death in 1961, the pottery continued in operation. The most famous
kinds of Pisgah Forest ware are the cameo type with designs made of
raised glaze and the turquoise crackle glaze wares.

Bowl, Interior Matte Ivory, Opaque Violet Plum Glaze Base, 1934, 8 In. 110.00
Lamp, Indian Scene, 1942 . . . . 2900.00
Pitcher, Glossy Turquoise Glaze Exterior, Rose Interior, Handle, 1950, 6 In. 77.00
Pitcher, Mottled Green & Teal Glossy Glaze, Raised Mark, 8 In. 165.00
Tea Set, Cameo Ware, Covered Wagon, Dark Green Matte Glaze, 1943, 3 Piece 770.00
Vase, Amber Flambe Glaze, Celadon Crystals, Stephen Mark, 3 3/4 x 4 1/2 In. 305.00
Vase, Amber Glaze, Gray Crystals, Potter's Mark, 6 1/2 x 4 1/2 In. 415.00
Vase, Amber Glaze, White & Blue Crystals, Bulbous, Potter's Mark, 5 1/4 In. 305.00
Vase, Amber Glaze, White & Blue Crystals, Stephen Mark, 1947, 5 x 5 3/4 In. 385.00
Vase, Blue Crystalline Over Glossy Ivory Glaze, Bulbous, 1949, 5 1/4 In. 305.00
Vase, Blue, Cream Glaze, 4 1/2 In. 22.00
Vase, Blue, Green & White Crystalline Glaze, Raised Mark, 1949, 7 3/4 x 4 In. 495.00
Vase, Bottle Shape, White Glaze, White Crystals, Mark, 8 x 5 1/4 In. 715.00
Vase, Brown & Amber Flambe Glaze, Blue Clusters, Embossed Mark, 7 In. 605.00
Vase, Classic, Amber Glaze, White & Blue Crystals, 1940, 6 1/2 x 4 In. 660.00
Vase, Classic, Amber Glaze, White & Blue Crystals, 1949, 7 3/4 x 4 3/4 In. 770.00
Vase, Cobalt Blue Double Dip, 1933, 7 1/8 In. 3960.00
Vase, Covered Wagon Scene, Bulbous, Green Matte, Turquoise, 7 In. 495.00
Vase, Cutouts On Sides, Transparent Turquoise Glaze, Signed, After 1961, 5 In. 57.00
Vase, Glossy Mint Aqua Glaze, Rose Interior, 2 3/4 x 4 In. 77.00
Vase, Glossy Mint Green Exterior, Pale Green, 9 1/4 In. 275.00
Vase, Glossy Turquoise Glaze Exterior, 1952, 9 1/4 In. 247.00
Vase, Glossy Turquoise Glaze, Pale Rose Interior, Handle, 1953, 8 1/8 In. 121.00
Vase, Green Crystalline Glaze, Caramel Ground, 5 In. 330.00
Vase, Multitone Blue, Green, Red Highlights, 1939, 5 1/2 In. 99.00
Vase, Musicians, Couples Dancing, Green Ground, Cameo, 1950s, 8 1/2 In. 1210.00
Vase, People On Horseback Trailing Wagon Pulled By Oxen, 10 In. 935.00
Vase, Purple Glaze, 5 In. 100.00
Vase, Turquoise Mottled Glaze, 2 Handles, 4 In. 192.00
Vase, Turquoise, Bulbous, 1938, 4 1/2 In. 95.00
Vase, White & Blue Crystalline Glaze, Squat, Raised Mark, 1948, 4 x 5 1/2 In. 605.00
Vase, White Crystalline Glaze, Squat, Raised Mark, 1942, 4 1/2 x 6 In. 330.00
Vase, White Over Sky Blue Crystalline Glaze, 1952, 5 In. 330.00

PLANTERS PEANUTS memorabilia is collected. Planters Nut and
Chocolate Company was started in Wilkes-Barre, Pennsylvania, in
1906. The Mr. Peanut figure was adopted as a trademark in 1916.
National advertising for Planters Peanuts started in 1918. The company was acquired by Standard Brands, Inc., in 1961. Standard Brands
merged with Nabisco in 1981. Some of the Mr. Peanut jars and other
memorabilia have been reproduced and, of course, new items are being
made.

Ashtray, Mr. Peanut In Center 10.00
Bag, Marble, Mr. Peanut, Contents, 1950s 7.00
Bag, Paper, Mr. Peanut, Blue & Yellow, 3 Lb. 5.00

Blotter, Mr. Peanut, Old Truck, 1930 ....10.00 to 15.00
Booklet, Histories Of President Through Hoover 35.00
Box, Planters Salted Nuts, Fresh Roaster To You, Black Lettering, 1950 .... 11.00
Box, Planters Spanish Peanuts, Cardboard, 8 Oz. 2145.00
Box, Red-Skin Planters Salted Peanuts, Cardboard, 5 Oz. 2200.00
Butter Maker, Mr. Peanut, Plastic Figure Standing, Hand Crank, 12 In. 28.00
Can, Original Lid, Turquoise Ground, Top Red Border, 10 Lb. 55.00
Coloring Book, Presidents 20.00
Dispenser, Mr. Peanut, Black Lettering, White, Porcelain, Germany, 16 In. 385.00
Display, Planters Peanut Specialties, 3 Varieties, Z-Shaped Rack 2090.00
Figure, Mr. Peanut, Black Body, Turquoise Hat, Wooden, 8 1/2 In. 120.00
Figure, Mr. Peanut, Stand-Up, 1940, 7 In. 8.00
Figure, Mr. Peanut, Walking, Green, 8 1/2 In. 412.00
Fishbowl, Cover, Original Decal, Red Lettering, 10 In. ....175.00 to 240.00
Glass, Cocktail, Mr. Peanuts Stem 550.00
Jar, 1940 Leap Year, Rectangular, Glass, Embossed Front, Tin Lithograph, 8 1/2 In. 110.00
Jar, Barrel, Cover, Embossed With Figures, Red Lettering, 5 In. 577.00
Jar, Cover, Square, 5 In. 60.00
Jar, Fishbowl, Peanut Finial Cover 55.00
Jar, Football, Peanut Finial Cover 250.00
Jar, Glass, Peanut Finial 110.00
Jar, Nut Finial, Square, Glass, Embossed, 9 In. 88.00
Jar, Peanut Top, Square 62.00
Mr. Peanut Peanut Butter Maker, Emenee, Crank, 1960 .... 25.00
Pail, Planters High Grade Peanut Butter, Red, 25 Lb. 798.00
Paint Book, Planters Peanuts Seeing The USA, 1950 .... 10.00
Pen, Float About, Mr. Peanut, Peanut Ground 4.00
Pencil, Mechanical, Mr. Peanut, Plastic, Ritepoint, 6 In. 21.00
Pocket Protector, Plastic, 1960s 25.00
Scale, Penny, Mr. Peanut, Figural, Cast Iron, 46 In. 12100.00
Spoon, Bar 55.00
Statue, Plastic, Light-Up, 1950s 930.00
Tin, Mother's Brand, The Planters Salted Peanuts, Mother & Child, 10 Lb. 12430.00
Tin, Pennant Brand, Lithograph, Store Bin, 10 1/2 In. 165.00
Tin, Planters Peanut Salted Peanuts, Large 17.00
Tin, Planters Pennant Brand Salted Peanuts, Sample, 2 1/2 x 2 3/8 In. 8580.00
Tin, Salted Peanut, Mr. Peanut, Red Banner, 10 Lb. 65.00
Tin, Suffolk Brand, Round, 10 Lb. 7370.00
Tray, Pennant Fresh Roasted Peanuts, Mr. Peanut, 15 5/8 x 11 1/8 In. 18.00

PLASTIC objects of all types are being collected. Some pieces are listed
in other categories; gutta-percha cases are listed in photography, celluloid in its own category.

Dresser Set, Glass, Frame, Jar, Mirror, Shoehorn & Corm, Box, 5 Piece 65.00
Figure, Dachshund, Bakelite, Caramel Colored, Carved, 1930s, 3 1/2 In. 20.00
Mug, Fred Flintstone, Hanna-Barbera, 1968, 3 1/4 In. ....*Illus* 7.50
Mug, Rin Tin Tin, Yellow & Blue, 1956 .... 70.00
Mug, Yogi Bear, Hanna-Barbera, c.1964, 6 1/2 In. ....*Illus* 7.50

Plastic, Mug,
Fred Flintstone,
Hanna-Barbera,
1968, 3 1/4 In.

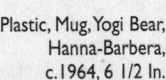

Plastic, Mug, Yogi Bear,
Hanna-Barbera,
c.1964, 6 1/2 In.

Powder Box, Knob On Puff, Pink Satin, Tubular, 2 1/2 x 2 In. 120.00
Sugar & Creamer, Butter, Lilac, Melmac, 3 Piece 25.00

PLATED AMBERINA was patented June 15, 1886, by Joseph Locke and made by the New England Glass Company. It is similar in color to amberina, but is characterized by a cream colored or chartreuse lining (never white) and small ridges or ribs on the outside.
Pitcher, Late 19th Century, 4 In. 370.00

PLIQUE-A-JOUR is an enameling process. The enamel is laid between thin raised metal lines and heated. The finished piece has transparent enamel held between the thin metal wires. It is different from cloisonne because it is translucent.
Spoon, Sugar Bell Shape, Blue, Yellow, Red, Green, Flowers At End Of Handle 85.00
Tea Strainer, Turquoise Flowers, Bands, Flowers On Edge, 5 x 3 In. 495.00

POLITICAL memorabilia of all types, from buttons to banners, is collected. Items related to presidential candidates are the most popular, but collectors also search for material related to state and local offices. Many reproductions have been made. A jugate is a button with photographs of both the presidential and vice presidential candidates. In this list a button is round, usually with a straight pin or metal tab to secure it to a shirt. A pin is brass, often figural, sometimes attached to a ribbon.

Apron, Campaign, Lincoln, Hamlin, 31-Star Flag, 1860, 24 3/4 x 23 1/4 In. 9200.00
Ashtray, Elephant & Donkey Fighting, Ceramic, Green, We Have Choice, 1952, 6 In. 18.00
Autograph, President Jimmy Carter, Governor Of Georgia, 11 x 14 In. 100.00
Badge, Assistant Sergeant At Arms, Republican National Convention, 1920 .... 62.00
Badge, Blaine Logan, Hard Rubber, 1884 .... 12.00
Badge, GAR, Scenes Of Saratoga, Celluloid 57.00
Badge, Harrison, Morton Inaugural, 1889 .... 78.00
Badge, McKinley, Des Moines Convention, 1899, 2 Sides, 1 3/4 In. 48.00
Badge, McKinley, Hobart, Tin Shell, 1896, 2 1/2 In. 40.00
Badge, Uncle Joe Cannon, Picture 15.00
Ballot, General Election, Pink Paper, Nov. 5, 1940, 19 x 30 In. 40.00
Bandana, Benjamin Harrison, Levi Morton, 1889, 23 x 24 In. 275.00
Bandana, Grover Cleveland, Floral Design, 26 x 21 1/2 In. 1265.00
Bandana, Roosevelt & Fairbanks, Right Men In The Right Place, 1904, 17 In. 125.00
Bandana, Win With Ike For President, Portrait, Red Ground 60.00
Bank, Barrel, New Deal, Happy Days, Tin, Black, Brown, 4 In. 12.00
Bank, Elephant, GOP, Art Deco, Cast Iron, 4 3/8 In. ....275.00 to 385.00
Bank, Elephant, McKinley-Roosevelt, Cast Iron, U.S., 1900, 2 1/2 In. 550.00
Bank, John F. Kennedy, 1917-1963, Bronze Finish, Slot Base, Banthrico, 5 1/2 In. 35.00
Bank, Past Presidents Up To Nixon Pictures, Tube Shape, Cardboard, 8 In. 12.00
Banner, Red White & Blue, Silver Bullion Thread & Fringe, Chester Arthur Medal, 1881 . 385.00
Banner, Welcome Socialists, Lily Dale, New York, c.1916 .... 22.00
Banner, Win With Franklin D. Roosevelt, Red, White & Blue, 9 x 12 In. 45.00
Bookmark, FDR Bust, The People's Friend, Aluminum 20.00
Bottle Opener, George Bush For President, Corkscrew, Blade, Plastic Handle, 4 Piece ... 20.00
Box, McGovern Cigarettes, Each Cigarette Says McGovern, 3 x 3 1/2 In. 20.00
Brochure, Ted Kennedy For President, Autographed, 1980, 3 1/2 x 8 In. 18.00
Bumper Sticker, George Wallace For President, Autographed, 1968 .... 24.00
Bumper Sticker, Mondale & Ferraro, Autographed, 1984, 3 x 12 In. 45.00
Bust, Wilson, Plaster, Color, 6 In. 30.00
Button, All The Way With L.B.J., Tree Center, Blue & White, 1 1/4 In. 15.00
Button, Better A Third Termer Than A Third Rater, 1 1/4 In. 5.00
Button, Boycott Grapes, Hot Pink, 1/4 In. 23.00
Button, Boycott Non-Union Lettuce, Red, Black, White, UFW Eagle, 1/4 In. 11.00
Button, Bryan, Stevenson Pictures, Draped Flag, 1 1/4 In. 90.00
Button, Bryan, Stevenson, Portraits, 2 In. 75.00
Button, Buy Only UFWOC AFL-CIO Lettuce, Red, Black On White, 1 1/4 In. 7.00
Button, Campaign Manager, La Guardia, 1 In. 7.00
Button, Central Jewish Relief Committee, Liberty Welcoming Refugees, 1 1/4 In. 33.00

Button, Chisholm, Unbought, Unbossed, 1 In. 10.00
Button, CIO For Willkie, 1 In. 25.00
Button, CIO, Win The War Fund, Red, White, Blue, Green Duck, 5/8 In. 27.00
Button, Coal Miners Dig Reagan Bush '84, Black & White, 1 3/4 In. 20.00
Button, Coolidge, Dawes, 1 In. 7.00
Button, Delano, Grapes Of Wrath, Light Purple, 1 1/4 In. 14.00
Button, Dewey In 1948, Elephant, 2 1/4 In. 58.00
Button, Dick & Pat Nixon, For President, For First Lady, Picture, 1 3/4 In. 24.00
Button, Don't Eat Grapes, Green, Black Ground, 1/4 In. 6.00
Button, Eisenhower Photograph, Color, 2 1/4 In. 15.00
Button, Elect Nixon & Lodge, White, Blue Letters, 3 In. 70.00
Button, Feliz Navidad, Green, White Ground, 1/4 In. 11.00
Button, Fight Fraud, Vote No On 22, White, Black, 1 1/4 In. 30.00
Button, Ford For Vice-President, Yellow, Black Letters, 1960, 1 3/4 In. 55.00
Button, Ford, Dole, '76, Texas Design, 1 3/4 In. 17.00
Button, Franklin D. Roosevelt, Don't Be A Third Term-Ite, 1/2 In. 15.00
Button, Franklin Roosevelt, No Fourth Term Either, 1/2 In 12.00
Button, Goldwater For President, Photograph, 7 In. 20.00
Button, Goldwater, Miller, Photographs, 1 1/4 In. 5.00
Button, Harris '76, 1 In. 2.00
Button, Herbert Hoover, For President, Picture, 1 In. 30.00
Button, Hispanics For Bush, Quayle, '88, 2 In. 2.00
Button, Hold On Muskie, Blue, Green, Stick Figure Animal, Holding On Tail, 1 1/2 In. . . 6.00
Button, I Like Ike, 1 In. 5.00
Button, I'm A Democrat, Don't Bug Me, Bug Caricature Center, 1 1/2 In. 15.00
Button, I'm A Friend Of Jimmy Hoffa, 2 In. 49.00
Button, Ike, Dick Flasher, Peace, Progress, Prosperity, 2 In. 30.00
Button, Jackson Means Jobs, 1 1/2 In. 7.00
Button, Just For Farm Workers, Vote No On 22, Black, Orange, 1/4 In. 7.00
Button, Keep Prosperity With Roosevelt, 1 1/4 In. 5.00
Button, Labor Likes Ike, 1 In. 5.00
Button, Landon, Knox, Elephant Center, 3/4 In. 10.00
Button, Lehman For Governor, 1 In. 4.00
Button, Liberty Bell, Vote Reagan To Keep It, Brown, White, 1 1/4 In. 5.00
Button, Lincoln Centennial, Celluloid, Bust Of Lincoln, Ohio Badge Co., 1909, 1 1/4 In. . 29.00
Button, Lyndon B. Johnson, Inauguration, Jan. 20, 1965, 1 3/4 In. 5.00
Button, Make Jobs, Return Actors To Theaters, Red, White, Blue, 8 In. 33.00
Button, McKinley Picture, Stars & Stripes In Border, 1 1/4 In. 20.00
Button, Mondale, Labor Unity Candidate, 3 In. 6.00
Button, My First Presidential Vote For Willkie, 1 1/4 In. 65.00
Button, Nixon Eats Lettuce, Black, Green, Eagle On Bottom, 1 1/4 In. 19.00
Button, Nixon, Agnew, 2 In. 5.00
Button, Nixon, Agnew, Picture, 1 In. 10.00
Button, Nixon, Kissinger, Border, 1 1/4 In. 10.00
Button, Nixon, Progress For All, 2 In. 6.00
Button, No Beer No Work, Anti-Prohibition, Celluloid, Black & White, 1 1/4 In. 14.00
Button, Our First Third Term President, Franklin D. Roosevelt, Portrait, 3 In. 47.00
Button, Our Next President, Wendell Lewis Willkie, Photo, 1 1/4 In. 15.00
Button, Papa I Want To Be A Captain Too, 1 1/4 In. 5.00
Button, Re-Elect Dick Nixon In '72, Red, White, Blue, 1 1/4 In. 5.00
Button, Re-Elect Muskie For Senator, 1 In. 7.00
Button, Reagan, Bush, '84, 3/4 In. 1.00
Button, Reappoint Ford To Congress In '76, 1 1/4 In. 12.00
Button, Rockefeller, He's Done A Lot, He'll Do More, 1/2 In. 3.00
Button, Roosevelt Recruits, Oval, 1 In. 22.00
Button, Roosevelt, 1 In. 6.00
Button, Shirley Chisholm For President, Catalyst For Change, 2 In. 4.00
Button, Spiro Our Hero, Mickey Mouse Head, 1 1/4 In. 5.00
Button, Stevenson For President, Picture, 1960, 1 1/4 In. 4.00
Button, Students For Kennedy, Picture, 1 1/4 In. 10.00
Button, Students For Reagan, 1 In. 4.00
Button, The Game's Not Over Till The Last Man Is Out, Watergate, 1 1/4 In. 5.00
Button, The Watergate Gang, Nixon In Center, 2 In. 43.00

Button, Thomas Eagleton For President, 1/2 In. 14.50
Button, Truman For Ex-President, 1 In. 25.00
Button, Turn On LBJ, 1 In. 6.00
Button, Two Good Terms Deserve A Rest, Red, White, 1 1/4 In. 5.00
Button, UFW-Endorsement, Eagle With Scales, Black, White, Red Ground, 2 1/4 In. 57.00
Button, Viva LaHuelga-Zapata, Brown, Cream, 1/4 In. 11.00
Button, Vote Carter, Remember The Bugging, 1 1/4 In. 7.00
Button, Vote Stevenson, 1/2 In. 11.00
Button, Wallace For President, Picture, 1 In. 4.00
Button, We Want Teddy For President, 1 In. 17.00
Button, William Jennings Bryan Picture, Oval Brass Frame, 1 1/4 In. 30.00
Button, Winning Team For Indiana, Bush, Mutz, Racer Pictured, Oval, 2 1/4 In. 5.00
Button, Wm. J. Bryan For President, Celluloid, Sepia, 2 1/4 In. 65.00
Button, Woodruff, Lieutenant Governor Candidate, Sepia, 1 3/4 In. 50.00
Button, Write-In For President, Mario Cuomo, 1 3/4 In. 3.00
Calendar, John F. Kennedy, Blue Celluloid, 1952 .... 235.00
Cap, Baseball Type, Willkie & McNary, Eagle, Elephants, Red, White & Blue, 6 3/4 In. .. 85.00
Card, John F. Kennedy Campaign, 1st Election To House, 1946 .... 300.00
Card, Playing, Help Draft Senator Barry Goldwater, Air Force Uniform, Double Deck 38.00
Card, Playing, Kennedy Kards, Caricatures, Unopened, Cellophane 25.00
Card, Ronald Reagan, Color Photograph, Signed, 8 x 10 In. 225.00
Charm, Admiral Dewey 15.00
Cigar, FDR Cigar Band, Box, 8 1/2 In. 65.00
Cigar Box, Henry Clay, Fabrica De Tabacos, Habana, Wooden, Inside Label 45.00
Cigar Box, James G. Blaine, Greatest Statesman, Wooden, Label 60.00
Cigar Box, John Hay, Secretary Of State, Pres. Hopeful, Wooden, Inside Label 45.00
Clock, Alarm, George Wallace, Plastic Face 40.00
Clock, LFB Top, Past Presidents Around Clock Face, White House Center, Tin, 10 In. 25.00
Coloring Book, John F. Kennedy, Cartoon & Caricatures, Unused 15.00
Cuff Links, White Metal, Brass Luster, Elephant Wearing Eyeglasses 35.00
Cup, FDR & Churchill, Flags, Statue Of Liberty, Champions Of Democracy, 3 In. 40.00
Decal, Window, Wendell Willkie, The Hope Of Our Country, Colorful 31.00
Document, John Quincy Adams, Pennsylvania Land Grant, 26th Day Of July, 1825 ..... 460.00
Ferrotype, John C. Fremont, Cochrane On Reverse, 1864 .... 1650.00
Flyer, Samuel J. Tilden For Governor Of N.Y., 1874 .... 8.00
Frame, Harrison, Engraved Eagle, Log Cabin, American Flag, Tortoise Shell, 11 In. 3735.00
Game, Al Smith To The White House, State Names On Wooden Blocks, Box, 5 1/2 In. 55.00
Glass, Good Luck, Mamie & Ike, Golfing, Fishing, Barbecue Scene, 5 1/2 In. 20.00
Glass, Roosevelt & Churchill, Hands Across The Sea, Red, White & Blue, 4 1/2 In. 32.00
Glass, Vote To Win In 1960 With Jack Kennedy, Lyndon Johnson, Blue Lettering 75.00
Glass, Wendell Willkie, Acceptance Speech, Aug. 17, 1940, Elwood, Ind., 4 1/2 In. 25.00
Hat, Campaign, Nixon, Lodge, Heavy Paper, 1960 .... 18.00
Invitation, White House Reception, President & Mrs. Coolidge, December 1926 ...... 35.00
Jar, Mustard, McKinley Picture, Handle, No Cover, 3 1/2 In. 30.00
Key Chain, Nixon The One, Gold Color 10.00
Leaflet, Rally Round Reagan, Illinois, GOP Convention, Full Color, 15 x 18 In. 15.00
License Plate, Al Smith, Red & White 35.00
License Plate, All The Way With L.B.J. 30.00
License Plate, Goldwater 14.00
License Plate, Hoover, Blue & White, Metal 55.00
License Plate, I Like Ike, Ike Picture In Military Cap, Yellow Ground 38.00
License Plate, Official, G.O.P. National Convention, Land Of Lincoln, 1960 .... 35.00
License Plate, Veteran World War II, Red On Front 30.00
License Plate, W-567, Presidential Inauguration, Reagan, Metal, 1981 .... 52.00
License Plate, Win With Roosevelt, Rectangular 50.00
License Plate Attachment, Tulip Shape, Roosevelt & Wallace 50.00
Lighter, Nixon 10.00
Mug, EMK & Jimmy Carter On Donkey, Cartoon, Saying, 1979, 3 1/4 In. 10.00
Necktie, Landon For President 50.00
Paddle, Ping-Pong, Chairman Mao & Richard Nixon 50.00
Pamphlet, Ed Muskie For President, Autographed, 1972 .... 25.00
Paper Money, Great Society Funny Money, Cartoon, Anti-LBJ, 1964, 3 x 6 In. 15.00

Paperweight, I Croak For The Jackson Wagon, Frog, Cast Iron, 6 In. ....: 145.00
Paperweight, McKinley & Teddy Roosevelt, Sepia Picture Side By Side 60.00
Pen, White House, Presidential Seal, Facsimile Johnson Signed, Box 30.00
Pencil, Anti-FDR, No Third Term, Wooden 47.00
Pencil, Franklin Delano Roosevelt, 1933-1945, Your Favorite President, On Card 25.00
Pencil, Stevenson For President, Red, Wooden 40.00
Pencil, Thomas F. Dewey, Portrait, Wooden 59.00
Pencil Box, Hoover & Curtis, Chief Commanders, Gold & Dark Green, Child's 30.00
Pennant, Felt, Vote For Barry M. Goldwater For President, 28 In. 28.00
Photograph, Calvin Coolidge, Autographed, Matted, Frame, 13 x 16 1/2 In. 285.00
Photograph, Gerald Ford, Color, 8 x 10 In. 50.00
Photograph, James Garfield, Poem About Vaseline On Reverse, 1880, 4 x 6 1/2 In. 42.00
Photograph, President George Bush, Autographed, With Best Wishes, 8 x 10 In. 90.00
Photograph, Richard Nixon, 80th Birthday, With Grandchildren, 5 x 7 In. 225.00
Pin, Campaign, McKinley & Hobart, Gold Standard Protection, Celluloid, 1 In. 43.00
Pin, Grover Cleveland, Brass, 1 1/2 In. 45.00
Pin, San Francisco Chinatown Tong Politics, Eagle, Metal, 1910, 1 x 1/4 In. 33.00
Pin, Wings For Willkie America, Red, White & Blue, Airplane, 1 1/8 In. 2.00
Pin, Youth For Kennedy, 2 1/4 In. 995.00
Pin Dish, Gerald R. Ford, VP Of US, April 27, 1974, Tulsa, Ok., Gold, Smoky Back 35.00
Pin Dish, Willkie, Preparedness, Peace, Prosperity, Milk Glass 25.00
Place Mat, Pictures Of JFK, Johnson, Nixon, Lodge, Paper, 1960s, 13 x 10 In. 20.00
Plate, Admiral George Dewey, Milk Glass, Green & Brown Picture, Scalloped, 7 1/4 In. . 50.00
Plate, Alf Landon Silhouette, 9 In. 75.00
Plate, For Pres. James A. Garfield, Ironstone, Blue & White, Gold Rim, 9 In. 40.00
Plate, Gen. MacArthur, Brown Picture, Allied Nations Flags Surround, 10 3/4 In. 30.00
Plate, Gerald R. Ford, 38th President, Gold Trim, 9 In. 8.00
Plate, John F. Kennedy, Blue & Gold Trim, Laurelton China, 10 In. 15.00
Plate, Lincoln & Eisenhower, 1854-1954 Republican Centennial, Gold, 9 In. 22.00
Plate, McKinley, Inside Shield, Protection & Plenty, Glass, 7 1/4 In. 35.00
Plate, Plains, Georgia, Home Of President Jimmy Carter, 10 In. 18.00
Plate, President & Mrs. John F. Kennedy Picture, Gold Trim, 9 1/4 In. 10.00
Plate, President Kennedy Holding Caroline's Hand, Jackie With John Jr., 9 In. 100.00
Plate, State Of Liberty, Roosevelt & Churchill, Champions Of Democracy, 8 In. 35.00
Plate, Taft & Sherman Picture, Eagle & Flags, Gold Rim, 7 1/4 In. 20.00
Postcard, Anti-Axis, Cartoon Of American Soldier Bayoneting Tojo, 1942 .... 18.00
Postcard, Campaign, I'm For Nixon Are You?, Handwritten 375.00
Postcard, Gerald Ford, Autographed, 1980s 80.00
Postcard, John F. Kennedy, Commemorative, Color, Germany 1020.00
Postcard, Nixon With Indiana Congressman Dick Roudebush, Slogan, 1972 .... 15.00
Postcard, Our Choice, Picture Of Bob Dole, Hopeful States Of America, Autographed ... 25.00
Postcard, Pledge, Garner For President Committee, 1940 .... 15.00
Postcard, Presidential Campaign, Hoover & Curtis Portraits Inset, Jugate 18.00
Postcard, Taft's Vice President James Sherman, Slogan, Our Jim Is It, 1908 .... 18.00
Postcard, Teddy Roosevelt Cartoon, Roughrider On Front, Slogan, 1907 .... 28.00
Postcard, Wallace For President, Pictured At Top, Slogan, Outline Of Ohio, 1968 ...... 20.00
Postcard, We Miss Ike, We Even Miss Harry, Anti-JFK, 1961 .... 15.00
Poster, Apostle Of Prosperity, Roosevelt Campaign, Matted, Frame, 32 x 23 In. 1200.00
Poster, Dwight D. Eisenhower, Republican, For President, Photo, 1952, 11 x 14 In. 25.00
Poster, For President, Franklin D. Roosevelt, Labor's Non-Partisan League, 8 x 10 In. ... 25.00
Poster, Franklin D. Roosevelt, America Above All, 10 x 13 In. 25.00
Poster, George McGovern, One World McGovern, Shriver, 1972, 18 x 24 In. 25.00
Poster, Johnson, Humphrey For USA, Black, White, Paper, 14 x 22 In. 20.00
Poster, Labor Committee For Stevenson & Sparkmen, Full Color, 1952, 22 x 28 In. 3000.00
Poster, Nixon's The One, Color Photo, Cardboard, 1972, 14 x 22 In. 30.00
Poster, Pres. Cleveland, Buffalo Bill, Hoffman House Hotel, 36 x 30 In. 1265.00
Poster, Pres. Cleveland, Wm. McKinley, Jr., Hoffman House Cigar, 1912, 36 x 30 In. 1610.00
Poster, Vote The Straight Democratic Ticket, Truman, Ky. Candidates, 1948, 22 In. 250.00
Program, Bifold, Reception For Adlai Stevenson, Balboa Park, 5 x 9 In. 17.00
Program, Presidential Inaugural, 1953 .... 10.00
Program, Willkie Pictures As Featured Speaker, Reunion Sons Of Indiana Of N.Y. 18.00
Puzzle, Franklin D. Roosevelt, Mass., Box, Unused, 1933, 3 1/2 x 6 1/2 In. 50.00

Puzzle, GOP, Elephant, Elect Nixon, Lodge On Reverse, Paper, With String, 5 1/2 In.	20.00
Rain Cap, Goldwater In 64	12.00
Record, Adlai E. Stevenson Accpetance Speech, DNC, 78 RPM, Red Color, 1952	25.00
Record, Franklin D. Roosevelt, 78 RPM, 1945, Part 1 & 2	35.00
Record, Stevenson & Kefauver, Let's Go With Adlai Stevenson, 45 RPM, 1956	40.00
Ribbon, A Martyr For Ireland, Green, White, Yellow, San Francisco, 1 1/4 In.	82.00
Ribbon, Benjamin Harrison, Tippecanoe Club, Hand Painted Eagle, Cabin, Indian	225.00
Ribbon, Kennedy For Vice President, Black, White Lettering, 1956	187.00
Ribbon, McKinley, Log Rolling, Black & White, 1 1/4 In.	413.00
Ribbon, Pres. Truman Picture, Red, White & Blue Ribbon, With Donkey	65.00
Ribbon, Republican Congressional Convention, Red, Gold Lettering, 1908	22.00
Ribbon, Welcome James G. Blaine, New York City, Bust Of Blaine, 1888, 9 x 3 In.	37.00
Ribbon Badge, Silver Republican Convention, July 4, 1900	170.00
Ring, Al Smith	20.00
Ring, Hoover	20.00
Sheet Music, Al Smith For President, Sidewalks Of New York, 1928	28.00
Sheet Music, Campaign, Greeley's, Log Cabin, Map On Cover	27.00
Sheet Music, Don't Forget 'Twas Votes For Women, Helped Win Victory, Too, 1916	17.00
Sheet Music, Hubert Humphrey March, 1960	12.00
Sheet Music, McKinley, 1896	15.00
Sheet Music, Nixon Is The One	4.00
Sheet Music, On With Roosevelt, Red, White & Blue, 1936	25.00
Spoon, Brave Clutching Tomahawk, Sterling Silver, After Dinner, 6 Piece	78.00
Stereoview, Cleveland & Stevenson Campaign Banner, 1892	355.00
Sticker, Lapel, Proxmire Worker, Bill Proxmire For Senator, 1960s, 3 In.	15.00
Stickpin, Death To Rum, Hatchet Form	52.00
Stickpin, Harding, Brown Tone	40.00
Stickpin, Harrison	20.00
Stickpin, Taft	17.00
Stickpin, Teddy Roosevelt, 1/2 In.	28.00
Streetcar Card, Edith Roosevelt Article, Red & Black	30.00
Stud, Anti Bryan, 1/8 In.	40.00
Stud, Cleveland, Shield, Enameled	35.00
Stud, McKinley & Hobart, Enameled, Elephant, Blue, Gilt Ground, 3/4 In.	30.00
Sunglasses, Stars & Stripes Rims, 2 Dangling Portraits Of Ford	132.00
T-Shirt, Goldwater Black Picture, Unwashed, Large	20.00
Tab Button, Adlai, Estes	5.00
Tab Button, Connally	10.00
Tab Button, Donkey Form, Vote Democratic	8.00
Tab Button, Eisenhower, Nixon	5.00
Tab Button, Hoover, Embossed	10.00
Tab Button, Ike	4.00
Tab Button, Kefauver For President	8.00
Tab Button, Paulsen	3.00
Tab Button, Watch Willkie Win	9.00
Thimble, With Truman	75.00
Tie, Roosevelt Repeated Design	60.00
Tie, Willkie Picture	28.00
Tie Clasp, Roosevelt, Script	28.00
Torch, Campaign, 2 Spouts, Brass, 9 3/4 In.	770.00
Tray, Columbia Flanked By William Jennings Bryan, Adlai Stevenson, 12 In.	275.00
Tray, White House & Franklin D. Roosevelt Upper Corner, Tin, 10 1/2 x 13 1/2 In.	35.00
Umbrella, Carter Picture, Double Print, White, 1976, Full Size	40.00
Walking Stick, Bust Of McKinley, Protection 1896, 33 1/4 In.	148.00
Watch Fob, Bryan, Kern, Brass, 1908	35.00
Watch Fob, Franklin Roosevelt	45.00
Watch Fob, Harding, Coolidge, Brass Shell, 1920	80.00
Watch Fob, Parker, Davis, 1904, 3/4 x 3/4 In.	35.00
Watch Fob, Taft Picture	50.00
Watch Fob, Taft, Enamel On Brass, Black	40.00
Watch Fob, Taft, Sherman, Pictures White House	45.00
Watch Fob, Teddy Roosevelt, For President, Leather Strap, C.F. Mfg. Co.	31.00

POMONA glass is a clear glass with a soft amber border decorated with pale blue or rose-colored flowers and leaves. The colors are very, very pale. The background of the glass is covered with a network of fine lines. It was made from 1885 to 1888 by the New England Glass Company. First grind was made from April 1885 to June 1886. It was made by cutting a wax surface on the glass, then dipping it in acid. Second grind was a less expensive method of acid etching that was developed later.

Lemonade, Diamond-Quilted, Pale Blue Cornflower, Amber Leaves, 5 3/4 In. 110.00
Pitcher, Inverted Thumbprint, Pale Amber, Handle, 6 In. 60.00
Tumbler, Blue Cornflower, Amber Leaves, 2nd Grind, 3 5/8 In. ....115.00 to 165.00

PONTYPOOL, see Tole category.

POPEYE was introduced to the Thimble Theater comic strip in 1929. The character became a favorite of readers. In 1932, an animated cartoon featuring Popeye was made by Paramount Studios. The cartoon series continued and became even more popular when it was shown on television starting in the 1950s. The full-length movie with Robin Williams as Popeye was made in 1980.

Bank, Dime Register, Popeye Has Upside-Down Pipe, Lithographed Characters 115.00
Bank, Dime Register, Tin 60.00
Bank, Register, Daily Quarter Bank, Tin, Hubley, 1930, 4 11/16 In. 175.00
Book, Big Little Book, Ghost Ship To Treasure Island, 1967 .... 20.00
Book, Big Little Book, Popeye & Queen Olive Oyl, 1973 .... 20.00
Box, Coffee, Cartoon Picture, 1 Lb. 12.00
Card, Playing, Olive Oyl & Popeye 30.00
Chalkboard 20.00
Cookie Jar, Popeye, American Bisque 500.00
Doll, Composition & Wood, King Features, 14 In. ....*Illus* 880.00
Drawing, Popeye & Wimpy, Ahoy, Where's Th' Fire?, Bela Zaboly, 1950, 10 In. 280.00
Flashlight, Figural, Plastic Head, Tin Lithograph, 1930s, 2 1/4 In. 38.00
Game, Popeye The Juggler, 1929 .... 150.00
Game, Popeye's Bingo, Box, 1929 .... 150.00
Lantern, Linemar 595.00
Lunch Box, Popeye, No Thermos, King Seeley Thermos, 1964 .... 225.00
Marble Set, Akro Agate, Popeye Characters, King Features, Box, Bag, 1929, 15 Piece ... 2100.00
Mask Set, Party, Popeye & Wimpy, 2 Piece 65.00
Night-Light, Popeye, Vinyl, 1959, 8 1/2 In. 175.00
Purse, Change 34.00
Submarine, Plastic, Rubber Band-Powered, On Card, King Features, 1973, 8 x 5 In. 45.00
Toothbrush, Electric, Box, 1983 .... 445.00
Toy, Eugene The Jeep, Composition Figure, Yellow, Red, King Features Label, 12 In. 690.00
Toy, Express, Riding Through Tunnels & Bridge, Tin, Louis Marx, 10 In. 235.00
Toy, On Roller Skates, Tin, Windup, Linemar, 6 In. 220.00
Toy, Parrot Cage In Each Hand, Windup, Walking 400.00
Toy, Pilot, Flying Plane, Red, Blue, Disc Wheels, Yellow, White, Marx, 8 In. ....785.00 to 1100.00
Toy, Popeye & Olive Oyl Handcar, Windup, Marx, 1930s 675.00

Keep a "mystery disaster" box. If you find a piece of veneer, an old screw, or even a porcelain rose bud, put it into the box until you are able to make the necessary repairs.

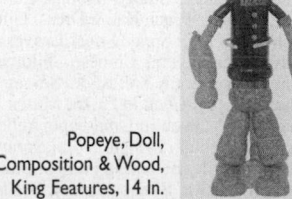

Popeye, Doll,
Composition & Wood,
King Features, 14 In.

Toy, Popeye & Olive Oyl Rooftop Jigger, Windup 1050.00
Toy, Popeye Carrying Parrot Cages, 2 Parrots, Cages, Tin, Lithograph, Chein, 8 1/2 In. 340.00
Toy, Popeye Dancing On Roof, Windup, Marx, 1930s 850.00
Toy, Popeye In Barrel, Walks, Windup, Chein, 1930s 550.00
Toy, Popeye In Rowboat, Tinplate, Battery Operated, Remote Controlled, Linemar 9200.00
Toy, Popeye On Unicycle, Linemar 1200.00
Toy, Popeye Riding Spinach Cycle, Cast Iron, 1930s 850.00
Toy, Popeye Spinach Can, Mattel 200.00
Toy, Popeye Standing With Drum Sticks In Hand, Tin, Chein, 7 In. 1330.00
Toy, Popeye The Pilot, Tin Lithograph, Windup 715.00
Toy, Popeye The Sailor Seated In Rowboat, Pressed Steel, Hoge Mfg., 1935, 14 In. 510.00
Toy, Popeye With Parrots, Windup, Tin, Marx, 1935, 8 1/2 In. ....345.00 to 440.00
Toy, Puncher, Windup, Chein 4400.00
Toy, Pushing Trunk On Wheel Barrow With Parrot On Lid, Tin, Louis Marx, 8 In. 785.00
Toy, Roller Skater, Popeye Carrying Plate Of Spinach, Tin, Japan, 6 3/4 In. 365.00
Toy, Spinach Eater, Fisher-Price 725.00
Toy, With Celluloid Punching Bag, On Stand, Tin Lithograph, Chein, 7 In. 845.00

PORCELAIN factories that are well known are listed in this book under
the factory name. This category lists pieces made by the less well-
known factories.

Basket, Leaves, Gilded Handle, Early 20th Century, 10 In. 143.00
Beaker, Peter The Great, Alexander I, Nicholas II, Ribbon Of Imperial Order, 1910, 4 In. .. 2070.00
Berry Set, Red & Yellow Roses, Gilt Enamel, Elaborate Moldings, Germany, 5 Piece 140.00
Biscuit, Tan & Green, Floral, Bonn Style, England, 7 In. 80.00
Biscuit Jar, Cottage & Boat Scenes, Green & Yellow, 6 In. 100.00
Biscuit Jar, Painted Transfer, Floral Bands, Black Ground, Gilt, 8 In. 55.00
Bowl, Bell Form, Flower Garden Design, 1900, 3 1/2 In. 38.00
Bowl, Bulb, Clair De Lune, 10 1/2 In. 357.00
Bowl, Center Shells, Flowers & Garlands, Reticulated Sides, Germany, 12 1/4 In. 82.00
Bowl, Continental, Rustic Lover Scene, Cartouche Shape, In Shadow Box, 16 In. 230.00
Bowl, Disconnected Landscapes & Building In Center, Blue, Green, Gilt, 9 In., Pair 220.00
Bowl, Dragon & Phoenix, Mount Fuji, Japan, Late 19th Century, 11 In. 242.00
Bowl, Flared Lip, Floral Panels, Central Rosette, Gilt, Continental, 12 In. 195.00
Bowl, Floral, Landscape Filled Medallion, Japan, 9 1/2 In. 149.00
Bowl, Frolicking Figures In Silhouette, Red Ground, Leighton Pottery, 9 In. 110.00
Bowl, Gold Fish Interior, Oval, 10 3/4 x 8 3/4 In. 137.00
Bowl, Hand Painted Roses, Gilt Trim, Swan Head Handles, Oval, 14 1/4 In. 265.00
Bowl, Oriental Enameled Dancers, Cartouche Mark, 12 7/8 x 5 1/2 In. 190.00
Bowl, Painted Carp Interior, Seaweed, Tan Glaze Exterior, Blue, White, 4 In., Pair 345.00
Bowl, Polychrome Enameled Oriental Scenes, Orange Peel Glaze, 10 1/2 In. 1540.00
Bowl, Putti On Cover With Cornucopia, 3 Babies, Ring Handles, Continental, 8 In. 200.00
Bowl, Sgraffito Flowers, White & Gold Interior, Waylande Gregory, 1940, 7 1/2 In. 66.00
Bowl, Tray, Domed Lid, Knop Finial, Animals & Birds, Gilt, Continental, 6 x 19 In. 287.00
Bowl, Trumpet Form, Flower Garden Design, 19th Century, 3 1/2 In. 27.00
Bowl, White, Recessed Dry Bottom Rim, Seltmann Weiden Bavaria, 6 3/4 In. 10.00
Bowl, Woman Transfer, Green Rim, Gilt, Crown Mark, Austria, 10 1/2 In. 70.00
Box, Cover, 12 Sides, Pale Blue Glaze, Incised Dragon, Korea 1980.00
Box, Dresser, Sevres Style, Colonial Couple In Country, Brass Frame, 12 x 9 In. 605.00
Box, Elephant Form, Chinese, 19th Century, 7 3/4 x 6 1/4 In. 80.00
Box, Floral Sprigs, White Ground, Green Borders, Gilt, Oval, 4 3/4 x 3 3/4 In. 175.00
Box, Sevres Style, Woman, Blue, Gilt, Brass, Hinged Lid, Luce, 3 3/4 x 1 3/4 In. 525.00
Brush Pot, Crackle Glaze, Chinese, 19th Century, 3 1/2 In. 38.00
Bust, Woman, L. Strauss & Sons, Germany, 16 1/2 In. 315.00
Bust, Woman, Peach Hat & Dress, Gilt Floral Design, Germany, 18 In. 230.00
Cachepot, Floral Spray, Silver Leaves & Mounts, Germany, 3 1/8 In., Pair 490.00
Centerpiece, Figural, Chinese Children With Basket, Meissen Style, 13 3/4 x 12 In. 1100.00
Centerpiece, Louis XVI Style, Sevres Style, Gilt Bronze Bands, Garlands, 16 In. 6325.00
Character Jug, Cook In Parka, Mittens, Binoculars, Germany, 4 3/8 In. 50.00
Charger, 3 Women In Landscape, Yellow Ground, Japan, 20th Century, 18 In. 230.00
Charger, Bamboo Design, Floral Sprays With Fans Border, Blue, White, 14 In. 1320.00
Charger, Birds, Blooming Prunus, Bamboo Fence, Japan, 19th Century, 21 1/2 In. 560.00
Charger, Central Blossom Spray, Scalloped Rim, Blue, White, 14 In. 825.00

Charger, Figures & Flowers, Blue & White, Japan, 18 1/4 In. 230.00
Charger, Figures In Landscape, Floral Border, Japan, 20 In. 230.00
Charger, Floral Design, Floral Relief Molding, IPF Germany, 13 In. 85.00
Chocolate Pot, Cobalt Blue, Gilt & Enamel Foliate Design, Continental, 10 In. 90.00
Compote, Applied Floral, Palmetto Shaft, 3 Molded Putto, Floral, Sitzendorf, 16 In. 345.00
Compote, Floral Center, Pink Borders, White Ground, England, 4 1/2 In. 105.00
Compote, Flowers Over Figure In Bocage, Floral Round Base, 12 In., Pair 316.00
Compote, Footed Base, Cherubs, Polychrome Flowers, Von Schierholz, 8 In. 195.00
Compote, Putti, Flowers, Pierced Bowl, Polychrome, c.1900, 14 1/2 In. 165.00
Compote, Vase Shape, Pedestal, Circular Foot, Green Banding, England, 7 In. 80.00
Compote, Woman & Putto, Reticulated Base, Applied Flowers, 18 1/2 In. 315.00
Creamer, Blue Underglaze, Shell Molded Body, England, 18th Century, 3 1/4 In. 316.00
Creamer, Rose Medallion, Octagonal, 19th Century, 5 1/2 In. 523.00
Cup, Undertray, Shell Shape, Flowers, Gilt, Coral Handle, Jacob Petit, 4 x 7 In. 1430.00
Cup & Saucer, Eagle's Head Handle, Gold Medallion Of Fruit, 19th Century 1210.00
Decanter, Robj-Style, Russian Cossack, White Glaze, Silver Luster, 1930, 10 3/4 In. 115.00
Dish, Fruit, Applied Enamel Fruit Design, Foliate Rim, Early 19th Century, 11 In. 115.00
Dish, Handles, Gilt, Hand Painted, Leaves & Berries, Monbijou, Germany, 11 x 7 1/2 In. .. 155.00
Dish, Melon Form, Relief Of Birds, Vines, Blue, White, 5 1/2 In. 374.00
Dish, Orchard Gold, Oval, Aynsley Crest, England, 8 x 5 1/4 In. 75.00
Dish, Orchard Gold, Oval, Aynsley Crest, England, 10 x 8 3/4 In. 145.00
Dish, Shou Design, Yellow Ground, 7 In., Pair 165.00
Egg, Blooming Clematis, Cyrillic Inscription, Russia, 19th Century, 4 1/4 In. 310.00
Egg, Blooming Flowers, Sky Blue Field, Russia, 19th Century, 3 1/2 In. 196.00
Egg, Blooming Tulips, Mist Green Ground, Russia, 19th Century, 4 1/4 In. 170.00
Egg, Kristos Voskrese!, Blooming Mums, Russia, 19th Century, 3 In. 168.00
Egg, Wheat & Blooming Flowers, Yellow Field, Russia, 19th Century, 4 1/2 In. 335.00
Figurine, Allegorical, 4 Continents, Late 19th Century, 10 3/4 In., 4 Piece 2070.00
Figurine, Deity, Seated, On Rocky Plinth, Japan, 13 1/4 In. 345.00
Figurine, Geisha, Holding Dog, Japan, Late 19th Century, 25 In. 1150.00
Figurine, Girl, With Flowers, Gilt, Continental Crossed Swords, 5 5/8 In. 55.00
Figurine, Jalousie & Architecture, M.W. Claus & Bourdois & Bloch, 8 1/2 In. 485.00
Figurine, Knight On Horseback, Continental, 12 1/2 In. 405.00
Figurine, Male & Female In Classical Attire, Gilt, Off-White, 14 1/4 In., Pair 35.00
Figurine, Man & Woman In 17th Century Dress, Blue Polychrome, 13 In., Pair 115.00
Figurine, Oriental Woman, Parrot, Wings Outstretched, Ludwigsburg, c.1770, 6 In. 690.00
Figurine, Pheasant Girl, Wearing Flowered Blue Apron, St. Petersburg, 13 1/2 In. 4600.00
Figurine, Pheasant, Sitzendorf, 13 1/2 x 14 In. 405.00
Figurine, Quanyin, Goddess Of Mercy, Seated, Fruit In Proper Hand, 8 In. 165.00
Figurine, Woman, Long Dress, Holding Jardiniere, Austria, 17 In. 495.00
Figurine, Woman, Red Gown, Long Hair, Gold Gilt Frame, Painted, 3 In. 330.00
Figurine, Young Woman Carrying Basket, 17 1/2 In. 220.00
Fish Bowl, Floral & Lappets Exterior, Carp Swimming Interior, Blue, White 1650.00
Ginger Jar, Cover, Allover Floral Design, Chinese, Late 19th Century, 17 1/2 In. 220.00
Group, 18th Century Couple, Man With Rose, Sleeping Woman, 11 1/4 In. 715.00
Group, Man & Woman, Reclining Against Pillows, H. Meisel, Dated 1922, 11 In. 4235.00
Group, Neptune In Shell Chariot, Maiden, Putti, Naples, Late 19th Century, 16 1/8 In. 3735.00
Humidor, Cover, Young Man, 5 In. 450.00
Incense Burner, Blue, White, Cylinder, 17th Century, 6 In. 1925.00
Incense Burner, Crackleware, 3 Stump Feet, 1900, 3 3/4 In. 55.00
Jar, Blossoms & Scrolls, Blue & White, Foo Dog Finial, Handles, 19th Century, 8 In. 288.00
Jar, Capo-Di-Monte Style, Bacchanalian Frieze, Woman & Putto On Lid, 12 In. 635.00
Jar, Cover, Figures, Horse & Cart, Famille-Verte, Signed, Chinese, 10 1/4 In. 230.00
Jar, Cover, Owl Shape, Enamel, Gilt, 9 1/8 In. 220.00
Jar, Derr & Landscape Design, Blue, White, Chinese, 2 3/4 In. 82.00
Jar, Dragon Design, Red, Blue Underglaze, 7 3/4 In. 605.00
Jardiniere, Bird & Floral Transfer Design, Blue & White, Japan, 15 In. 145.00
Jardiniere, Fruit Garland Design, Ram's Head Handles, Germany, 7 In. 385.00
Jardiniere, Gilt Bronze, Polychrome Fruit & Insects, Continental, 11 x 15 In., Pair 3410.00
Jardiniere, Water Lilies, Bird, Fish, Navy Blue, Oriental, 14 1/2 In. 165.00
Jug, Cider, Flowers, Foo Dog Finial, Blue & White, Chinese, 11 In. 1840.00
Lamp, Vase Shape, Enameled French Man In Garden, Ormolu, Shade, 33 In. 220.00
Lobed Jar, Cover, Overall Floral, Leafage, Mythological Winged Creatures, 9 In. 1870.00

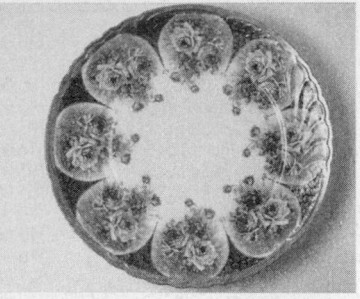

Porcelain, Platter, Roses, Hand Painted,
Gold Border, 13 1/2 In.

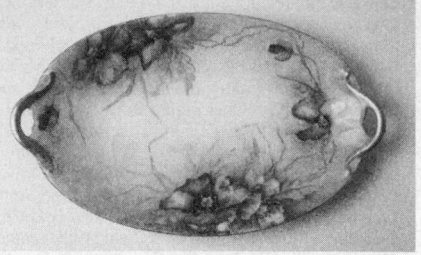

Porcelain, Relish, Poppies, Hand Painted, Handles,
GDA, France, 9 1/4 In.

Mug, Red & Gold Leaf Design, Hand Painted, J.P.L., France, 1/2 Liter	75.00
Neoclassical, Couple Embracing, Floral & Geometric Designs, Gilt, 13 In.	1430.00
Night-Light Veilleuse, Napoleonic Emblems, Gilt, Empire Style, Continental, 8 3/4 In.	275.00
Pin Dish, Fluted, Crimped Edge, Flower Cluster Pattern, Rosina, England, 4 1/8 In. .	20.00
Pitcher, Sunflower, Cobalt & Green Design, Applied Strap Handle, England, 4 In.	120.00
Pitcher, Yellow Bird & Rosebud, Tucker	6720.00
Plaque, 4 Baby Figures With Curly Tresses, Seated, Enjoying Grapes, 11 x 14 In.	3680.00
Plaque, Gypsy Girl, Wooded Landscape Standing By Tree, Giltwood Frame, 9 In.	1840.00
Plaque, Lady, Flowers In Her Hair, Hand Painted, Oval, 4 x 5 In.	275.00
Plaque, Madonna & Child, Ebonized Wooden Frame, 19th Century, 13 x 10 In.	2875.00
Plaque, Men, Herding Cows & Goats, Hand Painted, H. Desprez, 14 x 11 In.	400.00
Plaque, Mythical Figures In Relief, 5-Star Crown, 1860, 17 In.	373.00
Plaque, Napoleon, Red Moire, Giltwood Frame, Signed, Wanthy, 1900, 8 x 7 In.	316.00
Plaque, Noblewoman, 18th Century Dress, Giltwood Frame, 3 1/4 In.	230.00
Plaque, Psyche On Sea, Shadowbox Frame, 7 x 5 In.	3160.00
Plaque, Queen Louise, Crystals Surround, Oval, AMW, 5 1/2 In.	1150.00
Plaque, Ruth, Holding Stalks Of Wheat, Paper Label, Gilt Frame, 1880s	770.00
Plaque, Taxile Doat, Bacchus, Flowers, Arabesques, Pate-Sur-Pate, 1889, 13 1/4 In.	3850.00
Plaque, Woman Portrait, Daisies, Hand Painted, Oval, 3 In.	300.00
Plate, Camellia Design, Blue, White, Japan, Late 19th Century, 7 1/2 In., Pair	357.00
Plate, Center Figural Scene, Blue & Floral Edge, Japan, 8 1/2 In., 8 Piece	125.00
Plate, Imperial Eagle, Leaves, Gilt, Imperial Porcelain Mfg., 9 1/2 In., Pair	4885.00
Plate, Kirin In Cloud Design, 8 1/2 In., Pair	187.00
Plate, Place, Flowers, Green & Cream Borders, Tirschenreuther, 11 In., 8 Piece	275.00
Plate, Portrait Of Central Woman, Gilt Border, Burgundy Ground, 9 In.	1955.00
Plate, Putto, Raised Gilt Ribbons & Vines, Tounai, 9 1/4 In., Pair	1150.00
Platter, Allover Floral Design, Hand Painted, Oval, Early 18th Century, 13 In.	412.00
Platter, Rose Pattern, Gilt Rim, 2 Open Heart Handles, Square, Bavaria, 12 1/2 In.	65.00
Platter, Roses, Hand Painted, Gold Border, 13 1/2 In. . . . .*Illus*	145.00
Potpourri, Domed Lid, Satiric Dinner Scenes, Gilt Bronze, Continental, 20 In.	4025.00
Powder Box, Colonial Lady, Pink Dress, 6 1/4 In.	65.00
Powder Box, Purple & Green Lid, Roses, Germany, 1920s, Round, 3 In.	95.00
Relish, Poppies, Hand Painted, Handles, GDA, France, 9 1/4 In. . . . .*Illus*	80.00
Serving Dish, 4 Shell-Shaped Sections, Grapevine Design, Gilt, Germany, 14 In.	100.00
Soup, Coupe, Domed Lid, Sevres Style, Enamel, Gilt, Loop Handles, 6 1/4 In., Pair	605.00
Sugar, Cover, Abolitionist, Foliate Loop Handles, Slave Holding Child, 6 1/2 In.	3450.00
Sugar & Creamer, Cover, Tiny Yellow Flowers, Purple Asters, 6 x 6 1/2 In.	115.00
Tankard, Blue, Landscape Pattern, Underglaze, England, 18th Century, 3 3/4 In.	489.00
Tea & Coffee Service, Coral Branch Design, Gilt Scrolls, France, 39 Piece	8625.00
Tea Bowl, Everted Rim, Lotus Blossoms Radiating Tendrils, Blue, White, 4 In., Pair	115.00
Tea Service, Polychrome & Gilt Grapevine Design, Black Ground, 19 Piece	375.00
Tea Set, Hand Painted Roses, 24K Gold, Retsch & Co., Wunsiedel, c.1953	175.00
Tea Set, White, Gilt, Hammersley, England, c.1960, 3 Piece	58.00
Teapot, Elephant Form, Tusks, Rider, Rattan Handle, 1930s, 8 In.	95.00
Teapot, Oriental, Green Leaves, Polychrome Butterflies, Flowers, 7 1/2 In.	385.00
Teapot On Stand, Monk Shape, Arm & Glass Form Spout, Continental, 12 In., Pair	375.00

Tobacco Jar, Pewter Cover & Handle, Marque Possee, Continental, 6 x 5 In. 75.00
Tray, Fox Delivering Her Kill To Cubs, Scrolling Gilt Rococo Border, Germany, 15 In. . . . 145.00
Tray, Sailing Ships, Putty, Gilt, Lion & Unicorn Mark, 11 1/2 In. 150.00
Tray, Toothbrush, Classical Figures, Key Border, 1875-1900, 5 x 8 5/8 In. 110.00
Tureen, Vegetable, Cover, White, Gilt & Blue Garland, England, c.1900, 10 1/2 In. 155.00
Umbrella Stand, Flowering Tree Design, Japan, 24 In. 200.00
Umbrella Stand, Warriors, Horseback, Famille Noir, Chinese, Late 19th Century, 24 In. . . 374.00
Urn, Allover Gilt Design, Purple Ground, Ram's Head Handles, Germany, 33 In. 345.00
Urn, Black Ground, Gold Trim, Maroon Handles, Chariot, Figures, Cherubs, 20 In. 770.00
Urn, Capo-Di-Monte Style, Neoclassical, Bacchic Dancers, Mounted As Lamp, 35 In. . . . 770.00
Urn, Cover, Enameled Boy Portrait, Gilt Metal Frame, Artist, 14 In. 300.00
Urn, Cover, Enameled Floral Bands, Bronze Square Base, Vase Shape, 12 In., Pair 3575.00
Urn, Cover, Schneballen, Applied Flowers, Germany, 20 In., Pair 3450.00
Urn, Cover, Square Base, Mythological Reserves, Austria, c.1930, 14 1/2 In., Pair 1495.00
Urn, Cover, White & Lavender, Floral, 14 1/2 In. 60.00
Urn, Cover, Young Gentleman, Ormolu, Leafy S-Scroll Handles, Germany, 11 In. 403.00
Urn, Harbor Scene, Ram's Head Handles, Augustus Rex Mark, Continental, Pair 3335.00
Urn, Marble Base, Bronze Floral Enamel Pedestal, Squat, Hand Painted, 9 In. 2530.00
Urn, Moorish Town Scene, Hand Painted, Pedestal, Silver, Gilt, France, 14 In., Pair 3630.00
Urn, Ribbed Body, Figural Cartouches, Laurel Wreath, Bird Finial, 17 1/2 In., Pair 4888.00
Urn, Sevres Style, Cherubs Among Clouds, Biscuit, Gilt Bronze Mount, 24 1/2 In. 4840.00
Urn, Sevres Style, Nobleman, Chateau, Gilt Bronze Base, Eron, 19th Century, 11 In. 225.00
Urn, Sevres Style, Pastoral Scenes, Cloisonne Neck, Base, Alabaster Base, 17 In. 605.00
Vase, Allover Flowering Prune Branches, Blue, White, 30 In. 316.00
Vase, Allover Lotus Flowers Amidst Floating Scrolls, Blue, White, 20 In., Pair 4400.00
Vase, Allover Swirling Leaves Design, Blue & White, 19th Century, 14 In., Pair 630.00
Vase, Amphora Shape, Poppies, Ernst Wahliss, Alexandra Porcelain Works, 8 In. 58.00
Vase, Applied Design, Young Girl Picking Grapes, Art Nouveau, Silvered, 9 1/4 In. 92.00
Vase, Art Deco, Geometric Star, 1 Blue, Other Green, Mougin, 10 1/2 In., Pair 2300.00
Vase, Berry Sprigs, Sangue-De-Boeuf & Ivory Glaze, Bulbous, England, 3 1/4 In. 55.00
Vase, Blanc-De-Chine, Baluster Shape, Square Sides, Scholars, Trees, 16 1/2 In. 260.00
Vase, Bottle Shape, Flambe, Flowering Tree Design, Red Ground, Japan, 13 1/2 In. 315.00
Vase, Butter-Yellow Matte Glaze, Saxbo Stentos, 15 1/4 In. 275.00
Vase, Butterscotch Flambe Glaze, Adelaide Robineau, 1904, 2 1/2 x 2 In. 2300.00
Vase, Cobalt Blue Crystalline Glaze, Adelaide Robineau, 3 3/4 x 4 1/4 In. 6600.00
Vase, Continental, Rustic Maiden, Lavender Luster Ground, Wooden Base, 15 In., Pair . . . 5462.00
Vase, Cover, Baluster, Hawthorn, Blue & White, Chinese, 26 In. 3735.00
Vase, Cover, Enamel Figures, Landscapes, Gilt, Cobalt Blue Ground, 13 In., Pair 2300.00
Vase, Cover, Lily, Dragon Handles, Finial, Cobalt Blue Ground, 14 In., Pair 550.00
Vase, Cover, Water Landscape, Floral Border, Blue, White, 8 1/2 In., Pair 7425.00
Vase, Figural Panels, Flowers, Allover Floral Medallions, Japan, 22 In., Pair 690.00
Vase, Floral Design, Blue, White, Korea, 8 3/4 In. 4290.00
Vase, Floral Design, Green Ground, Japan, 9 In. 161.00
Vase, Gold & Blue Luster, Sisters Of Notre Dame, Bavaria, 11 1/2 In. 75.00
Vase, Gunmetal, Green Drip, Blue Glaze, Bulbous, Losanti, 3 1/2 x 3 1/4 In. 715.00
Vase, Inverted Pear Shape, Bird & Peony Design, Turquoise Ground, 6 In. 100.00
Vase, Inverted Pear Shape, Pink Coral Glaze, Elongated Neck, 4 1/2 In. 165.00
Vase, Linear, Floral Black Design Exterior, Gilt, Sidney T. Callowhill, 11 1/4 In. 110.00
Vase, Lovers In A Landscape Design, Cobalt Blue, Gilt, Leafy Scroll Handles, 9 In. 35.00
Vase, Marble Base, Bronze Floral Enamel Pedestal, Hand Painted, 7 1/2 In., Pair 715.00
Vase, Molded Dragons, Blue & White, Blue Floral Ground, Japan, 18 In., Pair 200.00
Vase, Neoclassical, Grisaille Romantic Landscape, Loop Handles, 13 In. 690.00
Vase, Orange Ground, Enamel Highlights, Japan, c.1900, 13 In. 46.00
Vase, Ornamental Gilt Arabesque, Twin Bamboo Handles, Royal Blue, 17 In., Pair 690.00
Vase, Oxblood Glaze, Oval, Script Mark, Serber, 5 1/2 In. 77.00
Vase, Painted Leaves, Black & White Photograph Of Girl, Moon Shape, 9 In. 632.00
Vase, Pair Of Birds, Butterflies, Oriental Flowers, Pale Seafoam Ground, 17 In. 172.00
Vase, Parakeets, Black Field, Flared Rim, Gibson & Sons, 7 1/2 x 5 In. 101.00
Vase, Passion Flower Design, Blue, White, 5 3/8 In. 440.00
Vase, Pastel Flowers, Gilt, Oval, Split Neck, Serpent Handles, Continental, 10 In. 173.00
Vase, Peacock, Floral Band, Inscription, Pichard, H & Co., Bavaria, 1920, 11 7/8 In. 550.00
Vase, Potschappel, Historical Edifice, Angel Handles, Carl Thieme, 17 In., Pair 2640.00
Vase, Prunus Branch Design, Blue, White, Korea, 5 In. 1650.00

Vase, Quail, Painted, Kozan, Japan, 5 3/4 In. 920.00
Vase, Seed Form, Wisteria Design, Makazu Kozan, Japan, Late 19th Century, 8 In. 2530.00
Vase, Spanish Maidens Within Gilt Arabesque Border, Pale Lavender, 15 In., Pair 575.00
Vase, Teardrop Form, Robin's-Egg Blue, Early 19th Century, 7 In. 220.00
Vase, Trumpet Mouth, Landscape Cartouches, Brocade Ground, Baluster, 24 In. 1100.00
Wall Pocket, Greens, Browns, Reds, Oranges, Pinks, Japan, 8 1/2 x 3 1/2 In., Pair 120.00
Washing Bowl, Pair Of Entwined Carp Interior, Scroll Rim, Blue, White, 3 3/4 In. 258.00
Wine Cistern, Oval Celeste Blue Body, Helmet Coat Of Arms In Center, 9 In. 4140.00
Wine Cooler, Figure In River Landscape, Ozier Border, Ludwigsburg, c.1770, 5 In., Pair . 3220.00

POSTCARDS were first legally permitted in Austria on October 1, 1869.
The United States passed postal regulations allowing the card in 1872.
Most of the picture postcards collected today date after 1910. The
amount of postage can help to date a card. The rates are: 1872 (1 cent),
1917 (2 cents), 1919 (1 cent), 1925 (2 cents), 1928 (1 cent), 1952 (2
cents), 1959 (3 cents), 1963 (4 cents), 1968 (5 cents), 1973 (8 cents),
1975 (7 cents), 1976 (9 cents), 1978 (10 cents), 1981 (12 cents), 1981
(13 cents), 1985 (14 cents), 1988 (15 cents), 1991 (19 cents), 1995 (20
cents).

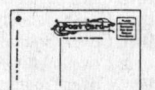

American Steel & Wire Co., Office Bldg. With Smoky Sky Overview, Donora, Pa. 259.00
Anheuser-Busch Packing House & Delivery Trucks, 1900s 20.00
Antler's Hotel, 1930s Cars, Taylorville, Ill., 1944 .... 6.00
Atomic Bomb Explosion, Yucca Flats, Nev., Mushroom Cloud, Chrome, 1950s 15.00
Biggest Little City In The World, Reno, Nev., Black & White, 1948 .... 12.00
Boulder Bay, Big Bear Lake, Ca., Pier & Cabins, Royal, 1950s 9.00
Budweiser II, Land Cruiser Picture, Anheuser-Busch, St. Louis, Mo., 1920s 12.00
Bullet Shape, Complete 1919 Calendar, 10 1/2 In. 55.00
Busch Yeast, St. Louis, Mo., 1920s 18.00
Cataba River Scene, Morganton, N.C., Burke Drug Co., Germany 3.50
Christ Episcopal Church, Alameda, Ark., 1907 .... 5.00
Coastal Highway Rt. 17, Clementia Tourist Camp, Cabins, Filling Station, Penna., 1930 .. 5.00
Commemorating Airship Flight, Russia, 1934 .... 35.00
Date Palms, Palm Springs, Orchard, Royal, 1950s 6.00
Dill's Balm Of Life, Dill Medicine Co., Wise Mother Using Dill's Balm Of Life 193.00
Dorothy Healey & Communist Farm Organizers, Sacramento, Ca., 1934 .... 273.00
Early Aviatrix, Woman At Controls, 2-Seater Biplane At Daytona Beach, 3 x 9 In. 213.00
El Mirador Hotel, Palm Springs, Cal., 1950s 9.00
Elsie The Cow & Her Brand New Twins, 1957 .... 9.00
Fanny Brice, Baby Snooks CBS Radio Show, Post Toasties, Postmarked 1944 .... 16.00
Father's Day, Love To Daddy, Glitter Trim 5.00
Flagstaff, Ariz., Indians, Cowboys, History On Back, 1940s 7.50
Ford Assembly Plant, Richmond, Cal., Parked Cars, 1945 .... 6.00
Forest Home Christian Conference Grounds, Cal. Photograph, Frasher, 1950 .... 6.00
Ft. Smith, Ark., Country Club, Snow, 1908 .... 7.00
Gangsters' Armored Car, Big Bullet Holes In Sides, Home Made, 1927 .... 115.00
Glacier National Park, Folder, 18 Views, Color, 1930s 11.00
Governor's Square, Tree Lined Area, Topeka, Kansas, Germany, 1908 .... 9.00
Grand Canyon, El Tovar Hotel, Linen, Fred Harvey, 1940s 6.00
Halloween, S. Birdman, 1913 .... 15.00
Harrah's Lake Tahoe, Stateline, Color, 1950s 7.50
Hearst Ranch, West's Largest Most Popular Dude Ranch, Pleasanton, Cal., Zan, 1930 ... 16.00
Indians, Tribal Clothes, Williams, Ariz., Chrome, 1950s 3.50
La Quinta Hotel, Swimming Pool, Cal., Frasher, Photograph, 1940s 10.00
Lick Observatory, Mt. Hamilton, Cal., Color, 1907 .... 3.50
Memorial Day, Divided Back, Embossed, 1909 .... 6.00
Mill Creek, San Bernardino Mts., Snow-Covered Lodge, Royal, 1950s 9.00
Narragansett Beer Wagon, Narragansett Brewing Co., Providence, R.I. 165.00
New Cornelia Copper Co., Ajo, Arizona, Plant & Mill, 1930s 10.00
New Year's Day, Nash, 1912 .... 2.00
Parker, Ariz., Main Street, Merle Porter, 1950s 3.50
Phoenix, Ariz., Looking West On Adams, History On Back, Linen, 1940s 5.00
Polomar Mountains, Ca., Highway To The Stars, Poster Design, Frasher, 1950s 9.00
Post Office Force, Brecksville, Oh., 3 White Mail Wagons, July, 1912 .... 67.00

Presbyterian Church, Perry, N.Y., Photograph, 1920 .... 3.50
Promenade, Laurel Beach, Conn., Cottages, People, Boardwalk, 1907 .... 5.00
Railroad Depot, Las Vegas, Nev., Art Deco Station Design, Royal, 1948 .... 13.00
Red Cross Malt Tonic, Denver, Co., Capitol Building Reverse, 1900s 12.00
Rehoboth Beach, Hotel Carlton, Delaware, Parking Lot, With Cars, 1940s 6.00
Ritter Midgets, Performing Troupe Of 10, Leo Hoffmann, Berlin, 1920 .... 44.00
Ruins Of Mission San Luis Rey, Cal., Photograph, 1940s 6.00
Scene At Amana, Iowa, Ox Yoke Inn, July 31, 1948 .... 10.00
Skyland Lodge, Crestline, Ca., Patio In Large Trees, Frasher, Poster Design, 1950s 9.00
Southern Textile Strikers, Picket Line Ready For Duty, Mill In Background 221.00
SS Mariposa & SS Monterey Pacific Far East Line, 6 x 8 In., 4 Pages 5.00
Suds Pioneer Bar, Crowley, La., Bar With Cattle Brands, Linen, 1940 .... 6.00
Sunset On Lake Gregory, Pine Tree, Royal, 1950s 12.00
Thanksgiving, S. Garre, 1909 .... 8.00
Tombstone, Ariz., Boothill Cemetery, Bill Clinton Shot, 1881, Photograph, Frasher 9.00
Troy Normal School, Troy, Ala., Front View 5.00
Union Pacific Sign, Train Station, Las Vegas, Nevada, 1948 .... 10.00
Valentine's Day, Silk Heart Insert 15.00
Washington's Birthday, Whitney, 1916 .... 10.00
Zuni Pottery, Indian Ceremonial, Linen, Gallup, N.M. 9.00

POSTERS have informed the public about news and entertainment events since ancient times. Nineteenth-century advertising or theatrical posters and twentieth-century movie and war posters are of special interest today. The price is determined by the artist, the condition, and the rarity. Other posters may be listed under Movie, Political, and World War I and II.

2 Chinese Beauties, Shanghai, 1920-1930, 29 1/2 x 19 1/2 In. 405.00
American Pie, Zippo Lighter & Home Made Apple Pie, By Zippo Employees, 23 In. 28.00
And They Thought We Couldn't Fight, Clyde Forsythe, 1917, 40 x 30 In. 175.00
Avec Vous Le Souirire, Jules-Alexander Grun, 1900, 48 1/2 x 34 In. 1330.00
B.B. King, Moby Grape, Steve Miller Band, 1967, 4 1/4 x 7 1/2 In. 11.00
Barnum & Bailey Desperado's Leap, Lithograph, 17 x 12 In. 123.00
Big Brother & Holding Co., Richie Haven, Sly & Family Stone, 1968, 7 In. 71.00
Bring Down The Air War, New Haven Air War Collective, 1972, 11 x 17 In. 85.00
Buffalo Bill Program, 17th Season, Official Program From Harrisburg, Pa., 7 x 9 In. 454.00
Buffalo Bill's Wild West Show, Color, Frame, 1905, 30 x 40 In. 9240.00
Buffalo Ranch Real Wild West, Vignettes Of Cowboy Equestrian Football, 56 In. 3300.00
Calendar Girl, Shanghai, 1920s, 29 x 19 3/4 In. 115.00
Chinese Girl With Boizoi, Shanghai, 1920-1930, 29 x 18 1/2 In. 400.00
Chinese Girl With Her Pekinese, Shanghai, 1920-1930, 27 3/4 x 19 1/2 In. 400.00
Chinese Girl With Horse, Shanghai, 1920-1930, 29 x 19 3/4 In. 400.00
Chinese Girl With Violin, Shanghai, 1920-1930, 29 x 19 3/4 In. 575.00
Christmas Eve, Maxfield Parrish, 1947, 16 1/2 x 13 1/2 In. 330.00
Cigarette Girl, Shanghai, 1920-1930, 29 1/2 x 19 1/2 In. 400.00
Circus, Great Coleman's & Kit Carson Himself, 28 x 10 1/2 In. 339.00
Colonel Tim McCoy Wild West Show, 1916, 36 x 29 In. 2750.00
Cora Hiard, Leon-Louis Oury, 1894, 47 1/2 x 35 In. 605.00
Country Joe & Fish, Incredible String Band, 1968, 4 1/2 x 7 In. 11.00
Cow Brand Girl, Shanghai, 1920-1930, 28 1/2 x 19 3/4 In. 375.00
Crusader, Knight Holding Flag, Tobacco, 1890, 7 x 13 In. 24.00
Empire Needs Men, Enlist Now, Arthur Wardle, 20 x 29 5/8 In. 92.00
Exhibition At The Musee Du Petit Palais, James Ensor, Frame, 72 x 50 In. 374.00
Father Of Our Country & Heroes Of 1776, Washington, Frame, 43 x 36 In. 165.00
Foggs Ferry Show, Man With Woman Trouble, 1910, 20 x 30 In. 38.00
Geronimo As Prisoner Of War At Ft. Sill, Baker & Bros., Lawton, Ok., 5 x 7 In. 67.00
Geronimo!, Chiricahua Apache Chief On Mountain In Albuquerque, N.M., 7 x 10 In. 445.00
Get The Pentagon Off Our Backs, Anti-War Demo At Madison Square Garden, 23 In. 33.00
Girl With Cherry Blossoms, Shanghai, 1920-1930, 28 1/2 x 20 1/2 In. 460.00
Golden Gate Peace Rally, San Francisco Golden Gate Park, 1972, 14 x 19 1/2 In. 55.00
Great Eastern Dispensary Ltd., Shanghai, 1920-1930, 28 1/2 x 19 1/2 In. 400.00
Higher Per Capita, Steps To Higher Per Capita, Sales Development, 1940, 22 x 34 In. 165.00
I.W. Baird's Famous Minstrels, Stone Lithograph, 1890s, 25 x 33 In. 750.00

International Student Strike, Stop Drafts, End Racial Oppression, 1968, 17 x 22 In. 91.00
Jefferson Airplane-Great Society, Bill Graham Fillmore Gig, June, 1966, 5 x 7 In. 11.00
Jinfan Girl, Shanghai, 1920-1930, 28 1/2 x 19 1/4 In. 380.00
Join The Navy, Sailor Riding Torpedo, 40 x 28 In. 60.00
Join The Noisy Majority, Local Anti-War Events In Wake Of Bombing Of Hanoi, 17 In. . .   59.00
Juanita De Frezia, 19th Century, 49 x 34 1/2 In. 905.00
Katamen, Cigarette Girl, Shanghai, 1920-1930, 26 1/2 x 18 1/4 In. 400.00
Lost In Space, Silk Screen, April, 1998, 6-Color, Mark Arminski, 25 x 13 In. 25.00
Majestic, World's Largest Ship, White Star Line, c.1932, 29 1/2 x 29 1/2 In. 690.00
March On Washington, Moratorium, Arlington Cemetery To Capitol, 1969, 25 In. 112.00
Palace Theatre, West Salem, Ill., Clark Gable, Norma Shearer, Roy Rogers, 14 x 22 In. . .   24.00
Panel Of Dolls, French Text, Henri Loyer, c.1918, 45 x 30 1/2 In. 230.00
Phil. Street Carmen's Union Pres., Peter Driscoll, Union Pres., Division 477, 15 In. 34.00
Piano Player With Singer, Shanghai, 1920-1930, 28 x 18 In. 345.00
Pittsburg Glass Blowers, Image Of Blowers At Work, Portland, Me., 1906, 10 x 12 In. . .   34.00
Red Riding Hood Show, Pinup Girl, Lecherous Wolf, 1929, 20 x 30 In. 18.00
Regenerez Vous Par Le Sirop Vincent, Jules Cheret, 1893, 48 x 34 In. 2300.00
Ringling Bros. Shows, Clowns, Frame, 16 1/2 x 12 1/2 In. 110.00
Scribner's Magazine, Butler Carrying Christmas Pudding, 1897, 30 x 21 3/4 In. 990.00
Sinbad The Sailor, Color Graphics, 1930's, 20 x 30 In. 26.00
Steppenwolf, Creedence, Butterfield, 10 Years After, 1968, 4 1/2 x 7 In. 71.00
Strike Leader, C.O. Pratt, Philadelphia Street Car Strike, Brown Ink, 1910, 10 x 20 In. . . .   27.00
Tarzan Escapes, Signed, Johnny Weissmuller, 1954, 22 x 28 In.   70.00
Teens!, Make The Scene At Dick Clark's TV Celebrity Party!, 1963, 12 x 18 1/2 In. 100.00
The Doors, Concert, Vancouver Coliseum, June 6, 1970, 23 x 14 1/2 In. 920.00
The Turtles, Oxford Circle, 1 Night Only!!, July 6, Wed., Black Ground, 1966, 5 x 7 In. . .   11.00
Tim McCoy Wild West, Indian Village Scene, Full Color, Lithograph, 20 1/2 x 27 In. 1921.00
Toilet Soap Girl, Shanghai, 1920s, 28 1/4 x 21 In. 315.00
Tom Mooney Molders' Defense Commander, 2 Sides, 1935, 28 x 34 In. 82.00
Uncle Sam, Die Cut Cardboard, Dressed In Red, White & Blue, 38 x 25 1/2 In. 135.00
Vallauris Pottery Exposition, Black & Mustard, Frame, Picasso, 24 x 16 In. 3000.00
Virginia Peanut Field, 1920, 20 x 32 In. 605.00
Vocal & Instrumental Concert, Mr. & Mrs. J.H. Butler, Nov. 2, 1876, 19 x 7 1/2 In. 25.00
Voodoo Tiger, Signed, Johnny Weissmuller, Columbia, 1952, 14 x 36 In. 85.00
West Va. Coal Miners, Portrait Of Miners Outside Mine Entrance, W. Va., 3 x 8 In. 22.00
Winnebago Chiefs, 1 Holding Large Pipe, 2 With Bows & Arrows, St. Paul, 10 x 12 In. . .   359.00
Woodstock, An Aquarian Exposition, Original Design, Walkill, New York, 13 x 22 In. . . .   460.00
Your Navy Victor In War, Guardian In Peace, October 27, 1950s, 28 x 39 In. 22.00

POTLIDS are just that, lids for pots. Transfer-printed potlids had their
heyday from the 1840s to the early 1900s. The English Staffordshire
potteries made ceramic containers with decorative lids for bear's
grease, shrimp or meat paste, cold cream, and toothpaste. Printed
advertising and pictures of historical events, portraits of famous people, or scenic views were designed in black and white or color. Reproductions have been made.

Bear's Grease, 3 In. 550.00
Cherry Toothpaste Patronized By Queen, 3 In. 44.00
New St. Thomas Hospital, Multicolored Transfer, England, 1870, 4 1/4 In. 145.00
Pegwell Bay, Established 1760, Multicolored Transfer, England, 1870, 4 In. 130.00
Residence Of Anne Hathaway, Multicolored Transfer, England, 1870, 4 1/8 In. 110.00
Transplanting Rice, Multicolored Transfer, Wooden Box Frame, England, 4 In. 160.00
Uncle Toby, Multicolored Transfer, England, 1850, 4 1/4 In. 165.00
Uncle Toby, Pratt, On Mahogany, 4 1/8 In. 155.00
Village Wedding, Pratt, Frame 165.00

**If you are using glue to fix an antique, work in a room that is about
70° F. Glue will not work well if it's too hot or too cold.**

POTTERY and porcelain are different. Pottery is opaque; you can't see through it. Porcelain is translucent. If you hold a porcelain dish in front of a strong light, you will see the light through the dish. Porcelain is colder to the touch. Pottery is softer and easier to break and will stain more easily because it is porous. Porcelain is thinner, lighter, and more durable. Majolica, faience, and stoneware are all pottery. Additional pieces of pottery are listed in this book in the Art Pottery category and under the factory name. For information about pottery makers and marks, see *Kovels' Dictionary of Marks—Pottery & Porcelain: 1650–1850* and *Kovels' New Dictionary of Marks—Pottery & Porcelain: 1850 to the Present.*

Ashtray, Blue Swirled To Shades Of Green Glaze, John B. Taylor, 7 1/2 In.	75.00
Basket, Blue & Gold Flambe Glaze, Greber, 5 1/2 In.	110.00
Batter Pail, Dark Brown Albany Slip, Bail Handle, c.1870, 1 Gal., 10 In.	99.00
Beaker, Drinking Elves, Bristol Glaze, Tooled Relief Beading, Whites Utica, 5 In.	305.00
Bean Pot, Boston Baked Beans, Children Eating, Bristol Glaze, Whites Utica, 8 1/2 In.	470.00
Bowl, Brown, Green & Blue Dripping Crystalline Glaze, Denbuc, 9 1/4 In.	33.00
Bowl, Celadon Matte Glaze, Vivika & Otto Heino, 20th Century, 3 1/4 x 4 1/2 In.	165.00
Bowl, Cream Feldspathic Glaze, Light Rose Color Design, 1960, 2 7/8 x 6 1/2 In.	495.00
Bowl, Cubist Form, High Glaze, Blue & Black Ground, M. Fantoni, 1950s, 8 In., Pair	230.00
Bowl, Dark Tan, Handles, Thomas D. Chollar, Homer, c.1830, 11 In.	305.00
Bowl, Figure Of Woman, Birds Within Rings, Stoneware, Scheier, 14 1/2 In.	140.00
Bowl, Flower Frog, Ducks Taking Flight, 11 3/4 x 8 1/4 In., 2 Piece ....*Illus*	58.00
Bowl, Folded Semispherical, Mustard Volcanic Glaze, Beatrice Wood, 6 1/2 In.	1210.00
Bowl, Frothy Hare's Fur Glaze, Paper Tag, Natzler, 4 x 5 In.	2530.00
Bowl, Gray, Green Interior, Chocolate Brown Exterior, Charles Abbot, 8 x 1 In.	230.00
Bowl, Green, Blue Drip Glaze, Brown Body, Signed, Koseki, 19th Century, 4 In.	247.00
Bowl, Hare's Fur Glaze, Natzler, Signed, 5 1/2 In.	5500.00
Bowl, Leathery Dark Blue Glaze, Squat, W.J. Walley, 4 1/2 x 6 1/2 In.	220.00
Bowl, Light Blue Volcanic Glaze, Footed, Beatrice Wood, 3 3/14 x 7 1/2 In.	1210.00
Bowl, Monteith, White Tin Glaze, Tan, 15 1/2 In.	220.00
Bowl, Stag In Center, Gold, Black, Red, Waylande Gregory, 1940s, 7 1/2 In.	66.00
Bowl, Stylized Basket, Broad Oval, 4 Peaked Handles, Opal Blue Over Camel, 13 In.	200.00
Bowl, Turquoise, Blue Glaze, Circular, Austria, 2 3/8 x 7 7/8 In.	172.00
Bowl Set, Graduated, Scrolled Bands, Yellow, Green, 5 1/2 To 9 3/4 In., 5 Piece	290.00
Bust, Walrus, Blue, Green Ground, Signed, Walters, 1932, 18 In.	35.00
Candlestick, Chinese White Glaze, Ben Owen, 1962, 6 1/8 In., Pair	121.00
Canister, Leaf Form, Green, Signed, Raku, Late 19th Century, 7 3/4 In.	137.00
Chalice, White Sheer Glaze, Incised Signature, Harding, Black, 6 1/2 x 6 In.	88.00
Charger, Hand Painted Fruits, Sculpted Rim, A. Luccha, Italy, 22 1/2 In.	150.00
Charger, Ring Of Nude Maidens, Turquoise Glaze, Eugene Froment, 1900, 16 In.	575.00
Charger, Tulip Design, Octagonal, Lester Breininger, 1977	95.00
Coaster, Adam & Eve, Piero Fornasetti, Box, 1950s, 4 In., 16 Piece	1725.00
Compote, Cover, Cabbage & Rabbits, Camphor Footed, 10 In.	335.00
Cream Pot, Dotted Bird, Binghamton, N.Y., c.1860, 7 In., 1 Gal.	2035.00
Cream Pot, Triple Tornado Design, Lyons, c.1860, 2 Gal.	470.00
Creamer, Left-Handed, Russell Henry, 1975	145.00
Cup & Saucer, Vue Dune Chaumiere, French Scene, Black Transfer, Canary, P & H	210.00
Cuspidor, Relief Shell Pattern, Bennington Type	85.00
Dish, Volcanic Turquoise Glaze, Natzler, 5 1/2 In.	1100.00
Ewer, Exotic Bird Perched On Branch, Gray Blue, Cream, Royal Jubilee, 12 In.	172.00
Ewer, Mauve Mottled, Verdigris Glaze, Richard Uhlemeyer, Germany, 1935, 10 In.	115.00
Figurine, Amish Couple, Polychrome Glaze, Stoneware, Mary Scheier, 1940, 4 In., Pair	135.00
Figurine, Bride & Groom, Pink, Gold Leaf, Waylande Gregory, c.1940, 10 1/2 In.	100.00
Figurine, Canine, Basket In Mouth, Glossy Green & Ivory, Billy Ray Hussey, 6 1/2 In.	358.00
Figurine, Devil With Snake, Mottled Green & Red Glaze, Billy Ray Hussey, 8 1/4 In.	209.00
Figurine, Double Figure, Cubist Figures, Signed, Marcello Fantoni, 1957, 27 1/4 In.	4887.00
Figurine, Dove, Gilded, White Glossy Ground, Waylande Gregory, c.1940, 4 1/2 x 7 In.	66.00
Figurine, Eel, Coffee Bean Eyes, Lustered Glaze, Beatrice Wood, 14 In.	1760.00
Figurine, Fish, Swimming, Dark Pink, Black Trim, California, 8 1/2 x 11 In.	40.00
Figurine, Flower Frog, Glossy Royal Blue Glaze, E.H. Pinewood, N.C., 1944, 3 3/4 In.	220.00
Figurine, Frog, Green & Copper Glaze, Thomasch Sierndorf, Austria, c.1930, 8 In.	345.00
Figurine, Horse, Blue Matte Glaze, Waylande Gregory, c.1940, 8 1/2 In.	110.00

Pottery, Figurine, Putto, Playing
Flute, Michael Powolny

Pottery, Bowl, Flower Frog,
Ducks Taking Flight, 11 3/4 x 8 1/4 In.,
2 Piece

Pottery, Plate, Salesman Samples,
Emblems & Fraternal Signs Rim,
Shenango, 9 In.

Figurine, Lion, On Base, Pink Clay, Green & White Traces, 7 1/2 x 9 1/2 In. 165.00
Figurine, Lion, Unglazed Buff Clay, Brown Highlights, 9 1/4 In. 110.00
Figurine, Lohan, Holding Staff & Peach, Glazed, Chinese, 32 In. 145.00
Figurine, Man In Middle Eastern Clothes, Terra-Cotta, Continental, 41 In. 1840.00
Figurine, Mermaid, Celadon Green, Brown, O. Wilhelmson, Strommen, 1966, 20 In. 520.00
Figurine, Pikin' Frog, Frog Strumming Banjo, Green Glaze, W.A. Flowers, 10 1/2 In. 66.00
Figurine, Putto, Playing Flute, Michael Powolny . . . . *Illus* 20160.00
Figurine, Rooster, Silver Leaf, White Ground, Waylande Gregory, c.1940, 14 x 13 In. 245.00
Figurine, Seated Cat On Blue Pillow, Thelma Frazier Winter, Signed Base, c.1940, 7 In. . . . 280.00
Figurine, Stylized Bird, Orange, Brown Glaze, Braytons-Laguna, 20th Century, 9 1/2 In. . . 44.00
Figurine, Woman In Cape, Headpiece, Bird & Deer Design, Lenci, 1937, 11 1/2 In. 460.00
Foot Warmer, Bristol Glaze, Threaded Stopper, c.1880, 5 1/2 x 9 In. 22.00
Hat, Scroddleware, W. Dawson Preston, 1889, 4 x 6 In. 375.00
Honey Pot, Slipware, Handle, England, 18th Century, 6 1/2 In. 550.00
Humidor, Hunting Dog, Relief, Salt Glaze, Whites Utica, 6 1/2 In. 165.00
Humidor, Lead, Dog Finial Top, Domestic Scene, Octagonal, England, 5 x 3 3/4 In. 70.00
Humidor, Lead, Man & Bagpipe Finial, Man Smoking & Drinking, England, 10 3/4 In. . . 200.00
Humidor, Lead, Man Smoking Pipe, Octagonal, England, 5 1/4 x 4 x 5 1/2 In. 115.00
Jar, Canning, Blue Leaf Designs, Shenandoah Valley, c.1860, 1 Qt., 6 3/4 In. 275.00
Jar, Canning, Cortland, Double Tulip, c.1860, 9 In., 1 Gal. 385.00
Jar, Canning, Cowden & Wilcox, Harrisburg, Pa., Drooping Hops Design, 1 Gal. 385.00
Jar, Canning, Double Flowers, c.1850, 1/2 Gal., 8 1/2 In. 120.00
Jar, Canning, Wm. Hare, Wilmington, Del., Brown Accents, Stopper, c.1860, 1 Qt. 120.00
Jar, Confit, Part Mustard Glaze, France, 19th Century, 10 1/2 x 10 In. 1265.00
Jar, Confit, Terra-Cotta, Loop Handles, Partial Tan Glaze, 19th Century, 9 In. 88.00
Jar, Cover, Glossy, Orange, Red Glaze, Ben Owen, 1930, 3 1/2 In. 192.00
Jar, Olive, Terra-Cotta, Bulbous, Partly Glazed Rolled Rim, French Provincial, 31 In. 470.00
Jar, Oliver McGurrin, 30 St. & 8th Aves. N.Y., Bird, Ellenville Pottery, c.1880, 5 Gal. . . . 495.00
Jar, Thompson Williams & Co., Morgantown, W.Va., c.1875, 3 Gal., 13 1/2 In. 330.00
Jardiniere, Dragon & Bamboo Design, Green, Yellow Glaze, Oval, 48 x 24 In. 385.00
Jardiniere, H. Loundes Manufacturer, Petersburg, Va., Flowers, c.1840, 6 Gal. 5390.00
Jardiniere, Vertical Ribs, Floral, Peach & Green Matte Glaze, 8 1/2 In. 120.00
Jug, Bird On Tree Stump, New York State, c.1870, 18 In., 5 Gal. 935.00
Jug, Bird, Blue, J. & E. Norton, Bennington, Vt., c.1855, 11 1/2 In., 1 Gal. 745.00
Jug, Brushed Blue Spitting Flower Design, E.W. Farrington Co., Elmira, N.Y., 2 Gal. 415.00
Jug, Cowden & Wilcox, Harrisburg, Pa., Brushed Plume Design, c.1870, 10 1/2 In. 305.00
Jug, Crossed & Dotted Birds, Y-Shaped Tree, Whites Binghamton, N.Y., 1860, 3 Gal. 1705.00
Jug, Dotted Snowflake Design, 1853, I.H. Wands, Olean, N.Y., 2 Gal. 1045.00
Jug, Musical, Katzenjammer Kids, Blondie, Andy Gump, Stopper, 1900s 495.00
Lamp Base, Wax Resist, Abstract Pattern, White Satin Finish, Italy, 15 In. 250.00
Milk Pan, Cowden & Wilcox, Harrisburg, Pa., Man-In-The-Moon Design, 2 Gal. 4510.00
Mixing Bowl, Pouring Spout, Light Ocher Interior, France, c.1900, 10 x 21 5/8 In. 135.00
Mug, Buffalo, Tavern, Bristol Glaze, Whites Utica, 4 1/4 In. 22.00
Mug, Harbard Decennial, 90, Richard Briggs, Co., Boston, Bristol Glaze, 5 3/4 In. 220.00

Mug, Smiley Face, Yellow, 3 3/4 In.	25.00
Pie Plate, I. Stahl, 1939, 9 In.	115.00
Pie Plate, Slipware, Sgraffito, 7 In.	135.00
Pie Plate, Slipware, Sgraffito, 8 In.	150.00
Pitcher, Glossy Blue, Green, Dark Emerald Glaze, Handle, 1940, Walter Owen, 7 3/4 In. .	99.00
Pitcher, Glossy Orange, Green Spotted, Red Glaze, Ben Owen, 1920, 7 3/8 In.	330.00
Pitcher, Glossy Orange, Red Glaze, Handle, Ben Owen, 1930, 9 1/4 In.	192.00
Pitcher, Left-Handed, Floral Design, Russell Henry, 1975	215.00
Pitcher, Vine & Flowers, Brushed Blue Accents, c.1850, 10 1/4 In., 1 Gal.	800.00
Plate, 2 Native Indians Doing Polka, Polka-Hontus, England, 19th Century	495.00
Plate, Center Flower, German Script, Slip Design, 8 1/2 In.	60.00
Plate, Palissy Ware, Relief Butterfly, Shells, Ivy Garland, France, c.1860, 8 1/2 In.	1035.00
Plate, Picasso, Bull Under Tree, Terre De Faience, 1952, 7 3/4 In.	1265.00
Plate, Picasso, Picador, Terre De Faience, 1952, 7 1/2 In.	1380.00
Plate, Salesman Samples, Emblems & Fraternal Signs Rim, Shenango, 9 In. ......*Illus*	100.00
Plate, Sgraffito, Stars, Spread-Winged Bird, Yellow Glaze, 1830, 9 3/4 In.	3190.00
Plate, Slipware, Feather & Comb Slip, Red Ground, Coggled Edge, 9 3/4 In.	605.00
Plate, Soup, Strawberry Leaf, Central Floral Bouquet, Scattered Sprigs, Longton Hall ...	635.00
Platter, Palissy Ware, Serpent On Leaves, Fish, France, Late 19th Century, 18 1/2 In.	4600.00
Porringer, Slipware, Child's, Dutch, Late 17th Century	350.00
Punch Set, Cover, Pedestal, Castles, Cobalt Blue Ground, 6 Cups, Germany	800.00
Rocker, Scroddleware, Dated 1896, 8 In.	350.00
Serving Bowl, Crimped Edge, Green Glaze, France, 4 1/2 x 11 In.	230.00
Serving Bowl, Starburst, Mottled Blue Glossy Ground, Glidden, 20th Century, 12 In.	77.00
Serving Bowl, Terra-Cotta, Green Glaze, Mottled Finish, 12 In., 4 Piece	360.00
Soap Dish, Flower Cluster, Fish, Walled Edge, Salt Glaze, Blue, White, 5 In.	66.00
Stirrup Cup, Head Of A Dog, Black Spotted Face, The Other As A Fox, 4 x 4 In., Pair ...	575.00
Sugar, Melon Shape, Molded Flowers, Salt Glaze, England, 19th Century, 5 In.	6.00
Sugar & Creamer, Cover, Brown & Blue, Germany, 5 3/8 In.	80.00
Tea Set, Blue, Green, Yellow & White, Germany, 14 Piece	170.00
Tea Set, Red & Blue Tulips, Painted, Germany, c.1930, 15 Piece	58.00
Teapot, Cover, Glossy Tobacco Spit Red Glaze, Ben Owen, 1920, 6 1/2 x 10 1/2 In.	275.00
Teapot, Figural, Crouching Black Man, Snake, Afonso Angelico, Portugal, 10 1/4 In.	2875.00
Teapot, Silver-Resist Dragon Design, Green Glaze, Globular	143.00
Umbrella Stand, Alligator, Butterflies, Relief, Cattails, Salt Glaze, Whites Utica, 20 In. . .	825.00
Umbrella Stand, Pique-Assiette, White Daisies, Gold Enamel Grout, c.1910, 20 1/2 In. ..	660.00
Urn, Bulbous, Handles, Green, Blue & Red Fish, Ivory Ground, Barum, c.1900, 7 In.	440.00
Urn, Chinese Style, Dragon, Crimson, Gilt, 36 x 17 In.	110.00
Urn, Incised Band, Terra-Cotta, 15 3/4 In.	140.00
Urn, Satyr's Mask Handles, Gadrooned Rims, Cream Glaze, Continental, 30 In., Pair	2875.00
Urn, Wax-Resist Cowboys On Horses, Dark Blue Glaze, R. Crook, 1892, 16 1/2 In.	4130.00
Urn, Wooden Cover, Cafe-Au-Lait Glaze, Fan, Fruit Lozenge Cartouches, Stand, 24 In. ..	357.00
Vase, 2 Handles, Glossy White Glaze, Trenton Art Pottery, Ink Mark, 8 In.	44.00
Vase, 3 Handles, White & Celadon Mottled Glaze, North State, 6 1/2 In.	88.00
Vase, 4 Open Buttresses, Salmon Matte Glaze, 6 1/2 In.	120.00
Vase, Banded Design, Black Glaze, Signed, Maria Popovi, 5 1/2 x 4 1/4 In.	200.00
Vase, Blue & Brown, Kahler, 7 x 6 In. ....*Illus*	295.00
Vase, Blue Crystalline Glaze, Catalina Island, 10 1/2 In.	415.00

Pottery, Vase, Blue &
Brown, Kahler, 7 x 6 In.

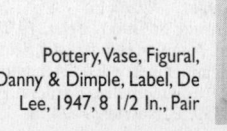

Pottery, Vase, Figural,
Danny & Dimple, Label, De
Lee, 1947, 8 1/2 In., Pair

Pottery, Vase,
Sgraffito Floral,
Blue, Kahler,
1915, 6 1/2 In.

Pottery, Vase,
Trumpet, Tendrils,
Cream, Kahler,
1920, 6 In.

Vase, Blue Matte Glaze, Inverted Rim, Per Lindemann Schmidt, 1912, 9 5/8 In. 747.00
Vase, Brown Splotches, Floral, Yellow Green Ground, Tuckware, 8 In. 45.00
Vase, Brown, Blue, Green Glaze, Closed Rim, Vivika, O. Heino, 1940s, 3 1/2 x 5 In. 220.00
Vase, Charlotte Rhead, Ribbed, Dragons, Squeezebag, Green Glaze, 7 In. 525.00
Vase, Chester Co., Black Matte Glaze, 8 x 7 In. 40.00
Vase, Chinese Blue Glaze, Violet, Red Glaze, Ben Owen, 1930, 5 In. 770.00
Vase, Chinese Blue Glaze, Violet, Red, Ben Owen, 1930, 3 3/4 In. 495.00
Vase, Chrysanthemums & Leaves, Blue Ground, Bulbous, John Bennett, 6 1/2 In. 660.00
Vase, Classic Shape, Brown & Gold Crystalline Glaze, Guerin, 12 x 7 1/2 In. 330.00
Vase, Copperdust Crystalline, Flambe Interior, Bulbous, Delaherche, 6 x 6 In. 825.00
Vase, Crackle Glaze Neck, Ruse Mottled Over Green Glaze, 20th Century, 13 In. 172.00
Vase, Cream Crackle Ground, Pink & Gilt Orchid Sprays, 1925, 9 1/2 In., Pair 77.00
Vase, Crosshatched Shoulder, Mottled Glaze, Artist's Initials, 12 x 7 1/2 In. 33.00
Vase, Cubist Figures, High Glaze Blue & Black Ground, M. Fantoni, 1950s, 12 1/2 In. 400.00
Vase, Cylindrical Form, Multicolored Cubist Forms, Marcello Fantoni, 1950s, 9 In. 345.00
Vase, Cylindrical, Flowers, Blue Bands, Cream Ground, E. La Chenal, 13 1/2 In. 520.00
Vase, Dark Blue Mottled, Black Glaze, Gray, Green, Patrick Nordstrom, 1922, 3 In. 690.00
Vase, Dark Blue Mottled, Black Glaze, Per Lindemann Schmidt, 1912, 6 3/4 In. 575.00
Vase, Dark Green Abstract, Blue, Maija Grotell, Cranbrook Art School, Mich., 9 1/2 In. .. 518.00
Vase, Double Gourd Shape, Flambe Glaze, 7 1/2 In. 50.00
Vase, Double Gourd Shape, Mottled Green Matte Glaze, Luxemburg, 8 In. 110.00
Vase, Egyptian Revival, Terra-Cotta, Black & Gilt Egyptian Design, c.1920, 20 In. 1210.00
Vase, Fan, Chinese Blue, Turquoise Glaze, Signed, Walter Owen, 1930, 3 1/4 x 5 In. 110.00
Vase, Figural, Danny & Dimple, Label, De Lee, 1947, 8 1/2 In., Pair .... *Illus* 75.00
Vase, Glossy Black, Green Glaze, Jonah Owens, 1926, 5 1/2 In. 385.00
Vase, Glossy Chrome Red, Black, Signed, Colonial Pottery, 5 1/2 In. 715.00
Vase, Glossy Chrome Red, Buff Glaze, Jonah Owens, 1925, 6 1/4 In. 357.00
Vase, Green & Rose, Fluted, Catalina Pottery, 5 x 5 1/2 In. 50.00
Vase, Log Cabin & Pines, Brown, Blue, Tan Ground, Hilton, N. Carolina, 6 In. 250.00
Vase, Molded Figural Panels, Vine & Phoenix Design, Foo Lion Heads, Japan, 14 In. 1100.00
Vase, Multicolored Cubist Figures, Signed, Marcello Fantoni, 1950s, 12 1/2 In. 400.00
Vase, Oval, Blades Of Grass On Brown Ground, Squeezebag, Max Lauger, 8 1/2 In. 385.00
Vase, Oval, Dancing Maiden & Satyr In Relief, Aqua, Pink, Yellow, France, 13 In. 865.00
Vase, Oxblood High Glaze, Catalina Island, 10 1/2 In. 415.00
Vase, Random Gunmetal Brush Strokes, White Ground, Vivka & Otto Heino, 11 In. 770.00
Vase, Red Chrome, Handles, Sunset Mountain, 1930, 8 1/4 In. 143.00
Vase, Salt Glaze, 2 Handles, Green Glaze, Ben Owen, 1920, 5 1/2 In. 935.00
Vase, Sgraffito Floral, Blue, Kahler, 1915, 6 1/2 In. .... *Illus* 250.00
Vase, Spill, Greek Warrior, Shield At Feet, Terra-Cotta, Enamel, England, 5 In. 99.00
Vase, Stippled Turquoise Glaze, Dark Brown Ground, Primavera, France, 10 In. 517.00
Vase, Sunburst Design, Blue Matte Ground, 5 1/4 In. 58.00
Vase, Trumpet, Tendrils, Cream, Kahler, 1920, 6 In. .... *Illus* 150.00
Vase, Turquoise Glaze, Signed, Gertrude & Otto Natzler, 1950s, 8 In. 4600.00
Vase, Turquoise, Brown Drip Glaze, Angular Handles, Christopher Dresser, 20 In. 2070.00
Vase, Urn Shape, Scalloped Rim Hearts, Cherry, Mid-Atlantic, 1900, 10 1/4 In. 140.00
Vase, Urn Shape, Stylized Exotic Birds, Geometric Borders, 19 7/8 In. 488.00
Vessel, Tear Shape, Semi-Volcanic Glaze, Natzler, 9 3/4 In. 12100.00

Wall Pocket, Bird, Multicolor Glazed & Painted, 1950s, 6 In.	28.00
Wall Pocket, Black & Gold Fish, With Bubbles, Green Bow, West Pottery	25.00
Wall Pocket, Molded, Old Woman With Child & Basket On Back, Continental, 15 In.	58.00
Wall Pocket, Parrot On Branch, Japan	20.00
Water Cooler, Deer In Woods, Relief, Salt Glaze, Blue, Cream, 11 In.	525.00

POWDER FLASKS AND POWDER HORNS were made to hold the gunpowder used in antique firearms. The early examples were made of horn or wood; later ones were of copper or brass.

POWDER FLASK, Blown Glass, White Loops, Applied Neck Rings & Lip, Pontil, c.1835	200.00
Brass, 2 Quail, 6 1/2 In.	45.00
Brass, Middle East	17.00
Copper, Embossed Eagle, Shield, Stars, E. Pluribus Unum, Brass Trim, 4 1/2 In.	100.00
Copper, Floral Design, Brass Trim, 6 1/2 In.	50.00
Copper, Hunter & Dog, Water's Edge, Brass Trim, 6 1/4 In.	40.00
Horn, Brass Top, 8 1/4 In.	61.00
POWDER HORN, Bone, Wood & Brass, 1820	110.00
Carved American Map I Side, 1760	6050.00
Horn Screw Cap, Coarse Grained Gunpowder, England, 18th Century	250.00
Inscribed, Buildings, Trees, Leaves, Vines, David Noble, American, 1776, 7 3/4 In.	1380.00
Lead Inlay, Bag, Patch Knife Sheath Sewed In, Attached Beaded Strap	908.00
Metal, End Cap & Plug, 13 1/4 In.	66.00
Roses & Tulips Design, England, 17th Century	750.00
Safety-First Powder Glass, Composition, 13 x 5 3/4 In.	275.00
Ship Under Full Sail, Shield, Success To American Eagle, G. Swartnout, 9 In.	1265.00
Sioux, S. Dakota, Some Red Paint, Early 1800s, 9 In.	330.00
Wooden End Cap, Spring-Loaded Nozzle, Early	55.00
Wooden End Cap, Star On End Cap & Horn	110.00

PRATT ware means two different things. It was an early Staffordshire pottery, cream-colored with colored decorations, made by Felix Pratt during the late eighteenth century. There was also Pratt ware made with transfer designs during the mid-nineteenth century in Fenton, England. Reproductions of the transfer-printed Pratt are being made.

PRATT FENTON

Jar, Deer At Watering Hole Transfer, Crazing, Fenton, England, 4 3/4 In.	60.00
Jar, Lid, New St. Thomas Hospital	80.00
Jar, Snuff, Blue Design, c.1800, 4 In.	325.00
Jug, Sportive Innocence On 1 Side, Mischievous Sport On Reverse Side, 5 7/8 In.	316.00
Lid, Pegwell Bay Established 1760, Frame	45.00
Lid, Room In Which Shakespeare Was Born 1564, Stratford On Avon, Frame	120.00
Lid, The Wolf & The Lamb, Frame	100.00
Lid, Village Wedding, Tenierspinx, Registry Mark, Jan. 11, 1857, Frame	100.00
Pitcher, Acanthus Leaves & Peacocks, Pearlware, 8 3/4 In.	1430.00
Pitcher, Cottage, Cottage Doors & Windows, Berry Garland, Green Handle, 6 In.	275.00
Pitcher, Portrait Medallions, Polychrome, 19th Century, 7 1/4 In.	230.00
Potlid, Allied Generals F.M. Lord Raglan, Gen. Canrobert, Frame, Registry Mark, 1854	120.00
Potlid, Portrait, Hand Painted, 10 In.	195.00
Stirrup Cup, Band Of Short Blue Lines, Brown Edged Rim, 6 1/8 x 5 In., Pair	920.00
Stirrup Cup, Leaf Sprigs, Bands Of Green, Blue, Brown, 1800, 6 1/2 In.	1150.00

PRESSED GLASS was first made in the United States in the 1820s after the invention of glass pressing machines. Hundreds of patterns of pressed glass were made in complete table settings. Although the Boston and Sandwich Works was the most famous of the pressed glass factories, there were about sixteen other factories making pressed glass from 1830 to 1850, and still more from 1850 to 1900, when pressed glass reached its greatest popularity. It is now being widely reproduced. The pattern names used in this listing are based on the information in the book *Pressed Glass in America* by John and Elizabeth Welker. A number of very rare pieces sold for high prices this year and are listed. There may be pieces of pressed glass listed in this book in other categories, such as Lamp, Ruby, Sandwich, and Souvenir.

1000-Eye pattern is listed here as Thousand Eye.

Pressed Glass,
Actress

Pressed Glass,
Beaded Grape Medallion

Pressed Glass,
Bellflower

Acorn Medallion pattern with beading is listed here as Beaded Acorn Medallion.

Actress, Cheese Dish, Cover, Two Dromios, Frosted	250.00
Actress, Platter, Pinafore	125.00
Actress, Relish, Kate Claxton	70.00
Ada, Saltshaker	30.00
Alaska, Cruet, Green, Enameled Elephant Ears, Forget-Me-Nots	225.00
Alaska, Saucer, Vaseline	60.00
Alligator, Goblet, Deer & Dog Etch	100.00
Amazon, Creamer, Child's	35.00
Amberette, Table Set, 4 Piece	400.00
Arched Grape, Goblet	50.00
Argus, Goblet, Flint	125.00
Art, Celery Vase	55.00
Ashburton, Bottle, Bitters, Stopper, Flint	85.00
Ashburton, Champagne	65.00
Ashburton, Goblet	45.00 to 50.00
Ashburton, Sugar, Flint	45.00
Ashburton, Tumbler, Water	75.00
Ashburton, Wine	40.00
Atlanta, Goblet	30.00
Atlas, Goblet	35.00 to 45.00
Atlas, Tumbler	25.00
Austrian, Creamer, Footed, 4 1/4 In.	65.00
Austrian, Goblet	60.00
Aztec, Goblet	40.00

Baby Thumbprint pattern is listed here as Dakota.
Balder pattern is listed here as Pennsylvania.
Balky Mule pattern is listed here as Currier & Ives.

Ball & Swirl, Compote, Jelly, Cover, Milk Glass	55.00
Bamboo, Plate, 10 In.	30.00
Banded Portland, Goblet	45.00

Bar & Diamond pattern is listed here as Kokomo.

Barberry, Creamer	35.00
Barberry, Wine	30.00
Barley, Bread Tray	65.00
Barley, Cake Stand, 9 3/4 In.	45.00

Barley & Oats pattern is listed here as Wheat & Barley.
Barley & Wheat pattern is listed here as Wheat & Barley.

Barred Forget-Me-Not, Plate, Vaseline, Handle, 9 In.	95.00

Barrel Honeycomb, see also the related pattern Honeycomb.

Barrel Thumbprint, Compote, Cover, 7 In.	17.00
Barrel Thumbprint, Goblet, Flint	25.00

Barreled Block pattern is listed here as Red Block.

Basket Weave, Pitcher, Blue	85.00
Basket Weave, Tray, Water	65.00
Beaded Acorn Medallion, Goblet	10.00

Beaded Dewdrop pattern is listed here as Wisconsin.

Beaded Grape, Cake Stand, Emerald, 8 In.	145.00
Beaded Grape, Celery Dish	25.00
Beaded Grape, Compote, Jelly, Green	65.00
Beaded Grape, Pitcher, 10 In.	145.00
Beaded Grape, Salt & Pepper	90.00
Beaded Grape Medallion, Goblet	40.00

Bearded Head pattern is listed here as Viking.

Beatty Honeycomb, Mug, White Opalescent	45.00
Beautiful Lady, Plate, Square, 7 In.	45.00
Beaver Band, Goblet	850.00
Beehive, Wine	65.00
Belcher Loop, Goblet	25.00
Bellflower, Champagne	135.00
Bellflower, Compote, Flint, 10 In.	475.00
Bellflower, Decanter, Cut Ovals On Neck, Stopper, 11 3/4 In., 1 Pt.	690.00
Bellflower, Goblet	75.00
Bellflower, Lamp, Brass Collar, Iron Base, 8 1/2 In.	155.00
Bellflower, Pitcher, Water	625.00
Bellflower Double Vine, Pitcher, Water	625.00

Bent Buckle pattern is listed here as New Hampshire.

Big Button, Tumbler, Water, Ruby Stain	55.00
Birch Leaf, Spooner, Milk Glass	45.00
Bird & Strawberry, Bowl, Flared, 10 In.	115.00
Bird & Strawberry, Butter, Cover	165.00 to 175.00
Bird & Strawberry, Compote, 7 1/2 In.	145.00
Bird & Strawberry, Compote, Cover, 6 In.	150.00
Bird & Strawberry, Compote, Ruffled Edge, 7 In.	145.00
Bird & Strawberry, Punch Cup	115.00
Bird & Strawberry, Tumbler	40.00
Bleeding Heart, Cake Stand, 9 1/2 In.	60.00 to 85.00
Bleeding Heart, Mug	45.00
Bleeding Heart, Mug, Milk Glass	125.00

Block & Fan pattern is listed here as Romeo.
Block & Fine Cut pattern is listed here as Fine Cut & Block.
Block & Lattice pattern is listed here as Big Button.
Block & Star pattern is listed here as Valencia Waffle.

Block & Thumbprint, Goblet, Flint	55.00

Bluebird pattern is listed here as Bird & Strawberry.

Bohemian, Goblet	30.00
Bohemian Grape, Tumbler, Juice, Ruby Stain	35.00
Bowtie, Bowl, 8 In.	40.00
Broken Column, Celery Vase	80.00
Broken Column, Compote, Jelly, 5 In.	65.00
Broken Column, Compote, Notched Cover, 8 In.	350.00
Broken Column, Compote, Ruby Stain, Flared, 8 In.	350.00

Pressed Glass,
Bird & Strawberry

Pressed Glass,
Bull's Eye & Fan

**Stains on crystal stemware
can sometimes be removed
by rubbing the stain with
a cut lemon or a cloth
dipped in turpentine.**

Broken Column, Honey Dish 45.00
Broken Column, Pitcher, Water 170.00
Broughton pattern is listed here as Pattee Cross.
Bucket pattern is listed here as Oaken Bucket.
Buckle, Wine 30.00
Bull's-Eye, Goblet, Flint, Knop Stem 85.00
Bull's-Eye & Daisy, Goblet, Amethyst Stain 25.00
Bull's-Eye & Daisy, Goblet, Green 35.00
Bull's-Eye & Fan, Berry Set, Gold Trim, 7 Piece 65.00
Bull's-Eye & Fan, Goblet 30.00
Bull's-Eye & Fan, Mug, Iced Tea, Handle 40.00
Bull's-Eye & Fan, Vase, 10 1/2 In. 45.00
Bull's-Eye & Fleur-De-Lis, Bottle, Flint, 8 In. 253.00
Bull's-Eye & Fleur-De-Lis, Compote, Flint, 6 3/4 x 4 In. 363.00
Bull's-Eye & Fleur-De-Lis, Pitcher, Flint, 9 1/2 In. 132.00
Bull's-Eye & Fleur-De-Lis, Pitcher, Water, Flint, 9 1/2 In. 330.00
Bull's-Eye & Fleur-De-Lis, Sugar, Cover, Flint, 9 In. 77.00
Bull's-Eye & Fleur-De-Lis, Sugar, Flint 60.00
Bull's-Eye & Prism, Decanter, Cut Panel Neck, Stopper, 11 1/2 In. 28.00
Bull's-Eye With Diamond Point, Goblet, 6 7/8 In. 130.00
Buzz Star, Goblet 30.00
Cabbage Rose, Goblet 30.00
Cabbage Rose, Pitcher, 1/2 Gal. 100.00
Cabbage Rose, Tumbler 25.00
California pattern is listed here as Beaded Grape.
Candlewick as a pressed glass pattern is properly named *Banded Raindrop*. There is also a pattern called *Candlewick*, which has been made by Imperial Glass Corporation since 1936. It is listed in this book in the Imperial Glass category.
Cane Horseshoe, Goblet, Gold Trim 30.00
Cannon Ball Pinwheel, Goblet 25.00
Capital Building, Goblet 30.00
Capital Building, Wine 23.00
Carmen pattern is listed here as Paneled Diamond & Finecut.
Carolina, Compote, Domed Cover, 13 1/2 x 8 1/2 In. 55.00
Casco, Goblet 15.00
Cathedral, Wine 28.00
Celtic Cross, Goblet 45.00
Centennial, see also the related patterns Liberty Bell, Philadelphia Centennial, Viking, and Washington Centennial.
Chain & Star, Goblet 30.00
Chain With Diamonds pattern is listed here as Washington Centennial.
Chandelier, Butter, Cover 95.00
Chandelier, Creamer 65.00
Checkerboard, Goblet 45.00
Cherry, Goblet 75.00
Cherry Thumbprints, Butter, Domed Cover 35.00
Chrysanthemum Leaf, Tumbler, Gold Trim 50.00
Coarse Zigzag, Saltshaker 30.00
Coin Spot pattern is listed in this book in its own category.
Colorado, Salt & Pepper, Blue, Gold Trim 395.00
Colorado, Sherbet, Green, Gold 20.00
Colorado, Toothpick, Green, Enameled Floral, Gold 40.00
Colorado, Toothpick, Green, Gold 35.00
Columbian Exposition, Goblet, 1893 .... 50.00
Comet, Goblet 145.00
Comet, Goblet, Flint 200.00
Comet, Tumbler, Water 165.00
Connecticut, Cracker Jar, Enameled Flowers 165.00
Conventional Band, Goblet, Etched 35.00
Cord Drapery, Creamer 60.00
Cordova, Syrup 55.00
Cosmos pattern is listed in this book as its own category.
Crane pattern is listed here as Stork.

Croesus, Compote, Jelly, Green, Gold Trim 245.00
Croesus, Creamer, Amethyst, Gold Trim 185.00
Croesus, Sauce, Green, Gold Trim 45.00
Croesus, Spooner, Green, Gold Trim 90.00
Croesus, Sugar, Cover, Amethyst, Gold Trim 225.00
Croesus, Table Set, Green, Gold Trim 450.00
Croesus, Tray, Condiment, Green, Gold Trim 125.00
Cromwell, Punch Cup, Pink Stain, Gold Trim 10.00
Crowfoot, Pitcher, Water 75.00
Crown Jewels is a name used for two different patterns listed here as Chandelier or Queen's Necklace.
Crystal Wedding, Banana Stand 135.00
Crystalina, Relish, Green, Gold Trim, 6 x 4 In. 7.00
Cube, Cup, Green 9.00
Cupid & Venus, Celery Vase 85.00
Cupid & Venus, Compote, Cover, 6 In. 55.00
Cupid & Venus, Compote, Cover, 8 In. 225.00
Cupid & Venus, Creamer 65.00
Cupid & Venus, Relish, Oval, 7 In. 35.00
Currant, Cake Stand, 11 In. 95.00
Currier & Ives, Compote, Amber, 7 In. 85.00
Currier & Ives, Tumbler, Milk Glass 10.00
Curtain Tieback, Goblet 35.00
Cut Log, Goblet 55.00
Cut Log, Mustard, Cover 65.00
Cut Log, Tankard 135.00
Daisies In Oval Panels pattern is listed here as Bull's-Eye & Fan.
Daisy & Button, Bottle, Ink, Amber, Glass Lid, 1 3/4 In. 185.00
Daisy & Button, Celery Boat, Silver Plated Holder, Swordfish Handle, 12 In. ... 575.00
Daisy & Button, Goblet, Blue 30.00
Daisy & Button With Thin Bars, Goblet 40.00
Dakota, Butter, Ruffled Base, Cover 65.00
Dakota, Goblet ....20.00 to 30.00
Dakota, Goblet, Leaf & Berry Etch 35.00
Deer & Oak Tree, Pitcher, Water 150.00
Deer & Pine Tree, Goblet 40.00
Delaware, Tankard Set, Rose, Gold Trim, 8 Piece 425.00
Delaware, Tankard, Green, Gold Trim 85.00
Delaware, Vase, Green, Gold Trim, 8 In. 80.00
Delaware, Water Set, Green, 7 Piece 450.00
Dewdrop, Goblet 25.00
Dewey, Mug, Amber 75.00
Dewey, Pitcher, Gridley, 9 1/4 In. 165.00
Dewey, Pitcher, Water, 9 1/8 In. 75.00
Dewey, Plate, 6 In. 15.00
Dewey, Relish, Amber 65.00
Dewey, Tray, Amber` 65.00

Pressed Glass,
Dakota

Pressed Glass,
Dragon

Pressed Glass,
Fine Cut & Block

Dewey, Tumbler, Canary	80.00
Diamond & Bull's-Eye Band, Compote, Jelly	50.00
Diamond & Button With Crossbar, Bowl, Blue, 6 x 2 In.	15.00
Diamond & Sunburst, Goblet	35.00
Diamond Medallion pattern is listed here as Grand.	
Diamond Point, Cake Stand, 9 1/2 In.	48.00
Diamond Point, Compote, Scalloped Rim, Flint, 6 1/4 x 8 In.	140.00
Diamond Point Band, Cake Stand	65.00
Diamond Point Band, Mug, Green	40.00
Diamond Quilted, Compote, Large	40.00
Diamond Ridge, Goblet, Gold	60.00
Diamond Sunburst Variant, Tumbler, Ruby Stain	35.00
Diamond Thumbprint, Celery Vase, Flint, Pair	450.00
Diamond Thumbprint, Compote, Scalloped Rim & Foot, Flint, 8 In.	125.00
Diamond Thumbprint, Goblet	650.00
Diamonds & Crossbars, Goblet	35.00
Doric pattern is listed here as Feather.	
Double Daisy pattern is listed here as Rosette Band.	
Double Leaf, Saltshaker, Blue Opaque	75.00
Double Vine pattern is listed here as Bellflower Double Vine.	
Doyle's Honeycomb, Butter	120.00
Dragon, Goblet	1600.00
Drape, Pitcher	160.00
Eastern Star, Goblet	30.00
Egg In Sand, Pitcher, Water	30.00
Egyptian, Bowl, Footed, 6 In.	45.00
Egyptian, Bread Tray	80.00
Egyptian, Compote, Cover	365.00
Egyptian, Water Set, 7 Piece	185.00
Elaine, Plate, Frosted, Leaf Handles	85.00
Empire, Pitcher, Green, Gold Trim, 7 In.	135.00
English Hobnail, Salt, Open	15.00
English Hobnail Cross pattern is listed here as Amberette.	
Esther, Celery Dish	65.00
Esther, Cruet, Green, Gold	66.00
Esther, Tumbler, Amber Stain	60.00
Etched Dakota pattern is listed here as Dakota.	
Etta, Goblet	40.00
Excelsior, Carafe, Bar Lip	125.00
Eyewinker, Cake Stand, 9 In.	295.00
Fan With Diamond pattern is listed here as Shell.	
Fancy Arches, Saltshaker	30.00
Feather, Cruet, Green	225.00
Feather Duster, Tumbler, Green	20.00
Fern Burst, Goblet	35.00
Festoon, Cake Stand	95.00
Festoon, Tumbler, Water	24.00
Fine Cut & Block, Pitcher, Water	165.00
Fine Cut & Block, Sugar & Creamer, Pair	210.00
Fine Cut & Feather pattern is listed here as Feather.	
Fine Cut & Panel, Goblet	30.00
Fine Cut & Panel, Wine, Vaseline	35.00
Fishscale, Tray, Water	75.00
Flamingo Habitat, Goblet, Etched	50.00
Fleur-De-Lis, Celery Vase, Handle	65.00
Fleur-De-Lis, Toothpick	50.00
Flora, Table Set, Green, Gold Trim, 4 Piece	345.00
Floral Oval, Goblet	50.00
Florodora pattern is listed here as Bohemian.	
Flower Flange pattern is listed here as Dewey.	
Flute, Goblet, Flint	35.00
Forget-Me-Not, Saltshaker	40.00
Frosted patterns may also be listed under name of main pattern.	

Frosted Block, Butter, Cover 95.00
Frosted Block, Spooner 65.00
Frosted Circle, Cake Stand, 9 1/2 In. 85.00
Frosted Circle, Compote, 6 In. 17.00
Frosted Crane pattern is listed here as Frosted Stork.
Frosted Dog, Compote, Cover, 8 x 14 In. 185.00
Frosted Eagle, Cake Stand, 8 In. 265.00
Frosted Eagle, Compote, 7 In. 185.00
Frosted Eagle, Salt & Pepper 80.00
Frosted Eagle, Sugar, Cover, Frosted Eagle Finial 305.00
Frosted Stork, Waste Bowl 135.00
Frosted Waffle pattern is listed here as Hidalgo.
Galloway, Saltshaker 30.00
Galloway, Vase, Flower 28.00
Garden Of Eden, Bread Tray 45.00
Garfield Drape, Bread Tray, Frosted 75.00
Garfield Drape, Goblet 90.00
Garfield Drape, Pitcher, Water 135.00
Garfield Memorial, Plate, Frosted Center 47.00
Geneva, Bowl, Green, Gold Trim, Oval, 6 1/2 In. 55.00
Good Luck pattern is listed here as Horseshoe.
Graduated Diamonds, Goblet 35.00
Grand, Cake Stand 35.00
Grant Memorial, Plate, Amber 65.00
Grape, see also the related patterns Beaded Grape and Beaded Grape Medallion.
Grape, Bread Tray 50.00
Grape & Cable pattern is listed in this book in the Northwood category.
Grasshopper, Sugar, Cover, Etched 85.00
Grogan, Goblet 30.00
Halley's Comet, Celery Vase 45.00
Hamilton, Goblet, Flint 60.00
Harp, Coaster 3.00
Harp, Sandwich Server 28.00
Hawaiian Lei, Sugar & Creamer, Cover 80.00
Heart With Thumbprint, Goblet, Ruby Stain 2500.00
Heart With Thumbprint, Pitcher, Water 2450.00
Heart With Thumbprint, Tumbler, Gold 295.00
Heart With Thumbprint, Wine, Gold Trim 85.00
Herringbone Band, Goblet 25.00
Hidalgo, Dish, Cover, Enameled Roses, 7 1/2 x 12 In. 175.00
Hobnail pattern is in this book as its own category.
Honeycomb, Carafe 85.00
Honeycomb & Diamonds, Goblet 35.00
Horn Of Plenty, Compote, Scalloped Edge, Flint, 8 In. 185.00
Horn Of Plenty, Decanter, Diamond-Point Stopper, Flint, Qt. 175.00
Horn Of Plenty, Decanter, Flint, 8 1/2 In. 165.00
Horn Of Plenty, Goblet 90.00

Pressed Glass,
Lion, Frosted

Pressed Glass,
Heart With Thumbprint

Pressed Glass,
Hildalgo

Pressed Glass,
Horseshoe

Pressed Glass,
Inverted
Thumbprint

Pressed Glass, Liberty Bell

Horn Of Plenty, Sugar, Flint	50.00
Horn Of Plenty, Tumbler, Water	110.00
Horn Of Plenty, Wine, Flint	140.00
Horseshoe, Goblet	22.00
Horseshoe, Relish	45.00
Horseshoe, Salt, Wheelbarrow	145.00
Hourglass, Wine	20.00
Huckle pattern is listed here as Feather Duster.	
Illinois, Berry Bowl, Flared, 9 1/2 In.	295.00
Indiana Swirl pattern is listed here as Feather.	
Intaglio, Custard, Green, Gold Trim, 7 In.	395.00
Inverted Eye, Compote, Cover, 7 In.	145.00
Inverted Thumbprint, Goblet, Amber	38.00
Iowa, Wine, Gold Trim	30.00
Iris With Meander, Spooner, Green, Gilt Trim	75.00
Ivy Band, Goblet	125.00
Ivy In Snow, Toothpick, Frosted Cracquell	225.00
Jacob's Ladder, Cake Stand, 10 1/2 In.	125.00 to 145.00
Jacob's Ladder, Celery Vase	85.00
Jacob's Ladder, Compote, Dolphin Stem	425.00
Jacob's Ladder, Creamer	35.00
Jacob's Ladder, Goblet	65.00
Jacob's Ladder, Relish	18.00
Jersey, Salt, Light Green	316.00
Jewel, Pitcher, Tumble-Up, Clear To Cranberry	110.00
Jewel & Dewdrop, Bread Tray	55.00
Jewel & Dewdrop, Cake Plate, 8 In.	35.00
Jewel & Dewdrop, Goblet	60.00
Jewel & Dewdrop, Spooner	85.00
Jewel & Dewdrop, Toothpick	55.00
Jewel Band, Bread Tray	25.00
Jeweled Moon & Star pattern is listed here as Moon & Star.	
Job's Tears pattern is listed here as Art.	
Josephine's Fan, Saltshaker	30.00
Kallbach, Goblet	10.00
Kamoni pattern is listed here as Pennsylvania.	
Kansas pattern is listed here as Jewel & Dewdrop.	
King's 500, Tumbler, Frosted	36.00
King's Crown, see also the related pattern Ruby Thumbprint.	
King's Crown, Goblet	10.00
Klondike pattern is listed here as Amberette.	
Knobby Bull's-Eye, Sugar & Creamer, Amethyst, Gold Trim, Large	125.00
Knurled Band, Goblet	25.00
Kokomo, Goblet	35.00
Lacy Daisy, Berry Set, 7 Piece	105.00
Lacy Medallion, see also the related pattern Princess Feather.	
Lacy Medallion, Saltshaker, Green	40.00
Ladder With Diamond, Goblet, Gold Trim	30.00
Ladder With Diamond, Spooner, Gold Trim	12.00

Leaf & Dart, Goblet	10.00
Leaf In Oval, Creamer, Gold Trim	10.00
Liberty Bell, Goblet	15.00
Liberty Bell, Goblet, Knop Stem	70.00
Liberty Bell, Platter, Signers	125.00
Lily-Of-The-Valley, Goblet, Etched	35.00
Lily-Of-The-Valley, Relish, Scoop	22.00
Lincoln Drape, Eggcup	65.00
Lincoln Drape, Goblet	135.00
Lion, Compote, Cover, 8 In.	130.00
Lion, Frosted, Compote, Cover, 13 x 8 In.	44.00
Lion, Frosted, Goblet	135.00
Lion, Frosted, Pitcher, Milk, Applied Handle	5100.00
Lion, Frosted, Platter, 13 In.	95.00
Lion, Sauce, Footed	20.00
Lion's Leg pattern is listed here as Alaska.	
Locket On Chain, Compote, 8 In.	195.00
Locket On Chain, Spooner	95.00
Long Tidy, Goblet	10.00
Loop, see also the related pattern Seneca Loop.	
Loop & Dart With Diamond Ornaments, Goblet	35.00
Loops & Drops pattern is listed here as New Jersey.	
Maine, Compote, 5 In.	20.00
Maltese Cross In Circles, Bread Tray	55.00
Manhattan, Salt & Pepper	40.00
Maple Leaf Band, Goblet	60.00
Maryland, Goblet	35.00
Mascotte, Creamer, Etched	45.00
Mascotte, Jar, Store, 3 Tiers	1000.00
Massachusetts, Sherry	125.00
Medallion Sunburst, Celery Vase	85.00
Melrose, Compote, Jelly	45.00
Memphis, Sugar, Cover, Green, Gold Trim	45.00
Memphis, Tumbler, Green, Gold Trim	25.00
Michigan, Goblet	35.00
Michigan, Tumbler	25.00
Michigan, Water Set, 6 Piece	90.00
Mikado, Goblet	40.00
Minnesota, Goblet	30.00
Minnesota, Mug, Gold Trim	25.00
Mioton, Goblet	10.00
Missouri is listed here as Palm & Scroll.	
Mitchell, Goblet, Engraved Grapes, Flint	40.00
Moon & Star, Butter, Amber, Round	65.00
Moon & Star, Compote, 8 In.	42.50
Moon & Star, Compote, Cover	395.00
Morning Glory, Compote	525.00

Pressed Glass,
Lily-Of-The-Valley

Pressed Glass,
Ostrich Stork & Heron

Pressed Glass,
Oval Miter

Morning Glory, Goblet 1850.00
Mount Vernon, Salt, Black Olive, 1 3/4 x 2 7/8 x 2 In. 805.00
Nailhead, Bread Tray 25.00
New England Centennial, Goblet 250.00
New England Pineapple, Compote, Flint, 8 1/2 x 6 In. 385.00
New Hampshire, Tumbler, Water 15.00
New Jersey, Dish, Pickle, Arapahoe Furniture Co., Denver 18.00
New Jersey, Tumbler, Water 22.00
New Jersey, Vase, Swung, 12 In. 55.00
Niagara, Goblet, Gold Trim 15.00
Oaken Bucket, Creamer 60.00
Odd Fellows, Goblet 110.00
Old Abe pattern is listed here as Frosted Eagle.
Old State House, Bread Tray 55.00
Omnibus, Goblet, Gold 25.00
Oregon, Saltshaker 50.00
Oriental, Creamer 75.00
Oriental, Sugar, Cover 125.00
Orion pattern is listed here as Cathedral.
Ostrich Stork & Heron, Goblet 1500.00
Oval Miter, Goblet 40.00
Oval Star, Table Set, 4 Piece 145.00
Owl pattern is listed here as Bull's-Eye With Diamond Point.
Palm & Scroll, Cake Stand, 9 In. 75.00
Palm Leaf Fan, Goblet 90.00
Palmette, Plate, Amber, 2 Handles, 10 1/2 In. 58.00
Paneled Diamond & Finecut, Compote, Jelly, Amber Stain 55.00
Paneled Diamonds & Flowers, Goblet 60.00
Paneled Dogwood, Banana Bowl, Green, Gold Trim 26.00
Paneled Dogwood, Berry Bowl, Green, Gold Trim, Oval, Master 75.00
Paneled Forget-Me-Not, Cake Stand 60.00
Paneled Strawberry, Sugar, Ruby Stain, Gold Trim, 2 Handles 25.00
Pattee Cross, Berry Bowl, Plain Petal, Individual 15.00
Pattee Cross, Goblet 35.00
Pavonia, Celery Vase, Bird & Oak Leaf Etch 125.00
Pavonia, Celery Vase, Maple Leaf Etch 75.00
Peacock Feathers, Cake Stand 30.00
Peacock Feathers, Cruet 25.00
Peacock's Eye pattern is listed here as Peacock Feathers.
Pennsylvania, Goblet, Gold Trim 16.00
Pennsylvania, Plate, Enameled Scene, Knight, Elkin & Co., 10 1/4 In. 110.00
Pennsylvania, Sugar & Creamer, Cover 150.00
Pennsylvania, Wine 25.00
Petticoat, Sauce, Vaseline, Gold Trim 48.00
Petticoat, Toothpick, Hat 45.00
Philadelphia Centennial, Goblet 45.00
Pinafore pattern is listed here as Actress.
Plain Sunburst, Goblet 30.00
Pleat & Panel, Bowl, Rectangular, 9 In. 29.00
Pleat & Panel, Pitcher, Milk 165.00
Polar Bear, Pitcher, Water 1050.00
Portland, Cake Stand, 11 In. 125.00
Portland Tree Of Life, Goblet 95.00
Portland Tree Of Life, Sugar, Cover, Silver Plate Holder 110.00
Portland With Diamond Point Band pattern is listed here as Banded Portland.
Portrait, Goblet, Father 1000.00
Prayer Rug pattern is listed here as Horseshoe.
Princess Feather, Compote, Cover, 8 1/4 x 7 In. 85.00
Princess Feather, Pitcher, Water 110.00
Princess Feather, Plate, 6 In. 20.00
Princess Feather, Spooner 45.00
Printed Hobnail, Goblet 25.00
Queen's Necklace, Compote, 8 In. 85.00

Rail Fence Band, Goblet 10.00
Rebecca At The Well, Candlestick, Frosted, Pair 150.00
Recessed Ovals, Goblet 10.00
Red Block, Goblet 48.00
Red Block, Wine 40.00
Reverse Torpedo pattern is listed here as Diamond & Bull's-Eye Band.
Ribbed Ivy, Tumbler, Whiskey 100.00
Richmond, Goblet 40.00
Ring & Block, Tumbler, Ruby Stained 45.00
Roanoke Star, Goblet 25.00
Rochelle pattern is listed here as Princess Feather.
Rock Of Ages, Bread Tray 35.00
Rock Of Ages, Bread Tray, Milk Glass Insert 350.00
Romeo, Saltshaker 35.00
Rooster, Creamer 225.00
Rose In Snow, Butter, Cover, Square 95.00
Rose Sprig, Relish, Amber 35.00
Rose Sprig, Relish, Blue, Boat Shape 40.00
Rosette & Palms, Goblet 45.00
Rosette Band, Pitcher, Water, Etched 275.00
Rosette Band, Water Set, 6 Piece 295.00
Rosette Medallion pattern is listed here as Feather Duster.
Royal Ivy, Butter, Cover 375.00
Royal Ivy, Creamer 290.00
Royal Ivy, Cruet, Clear To Cranberry ....380.00 to 690.00
Royal Ivy, Marmalade, Silver Plated Holder 325.00
Royal Ivy, Pitcher, Clear To Cranberry, Frosted 550.00
Royal Ivy, Pitcher, Water 550.00
Royal Ivy, Rose Bowl 125.00
Royal Ivy, Sugar Shaker 270.00
Royal Oak, Table Set, Clear To Cranberry, 5 Piece 400.00
Ruby Thumbprint, see also the related pattern King's Crown.
Ruby Thumbprint, Pitcher, Etched 325.00
Ruby Thumbprint, Saltshaker, Etched 30.00
S-Repeat, Celery Vase, Blue 17.00
Sandwich Star, Goblet 1950.00
Sawtooth, Butter, Cover, Acorn Finial 125.00
Sawtooth, Compote, Cover, Acorn Finial, 8 In. 125.00
Sawtooth Band pattern is listed here as Amazon.
Sawtooth Circle, Salt, Footed 30.00
Saxon, Goblet 30.00
Scalloped Swirl, Compote, Ruby Stain, 8 In. 250.00
Scalloped Tape pattern is listed here as Jewel Band.
Scroll & Shell, Tumbler, Green, Gold Trim, Geneva 25.00
Seed Pod, Butter, Cover, Green, Gold Trim 175.00
Seneca Loop, Spooner 45.00
Shell, Goblet 30.00
Shell & Tassel, Mug, Cobalt Blue, 2 In. 145.00
Shell & Tassel, Tumbler, Blue 15.00
Shields, Goblet 40.00
Six Panel Finecut, Berry Bowl, 8 In. 35.00
Six Panel Finecut, Tumbler, Amber Stain, Etched 65.00
Snow Band, Goblet 30.00
Star, Water Set 65.00
Star & Buckle, Syrup, Applied Handle, Metal Hinged Cap, 6 1/2 In. .. 185.00
Star & Punty pattern is listed here as Moon & Star.
Star Rosetted, Goblet 35.00
Stars & Stripes, Cake Stand 65.00
Stippled Forget-Me-Not, Cake Stand 50.00
Stippled Ivy, Goblet 40.00
Stippled Paneled Flower pattern is listed here as Mainc.
Stork, Goblet 85.00
Strawberry & Fan Variant, Tumbler 55.00

Pressed Glass,
Stork

Pressed Glass,
Three Face

Pressed Glass,
Thumbprint

Sylvan, Berry Bowl, Gold Trim	10.00
Tape Measure pattern is listed here as Shields.	
Tappan, Creamer, Child's	30.00
Teardrop & Tassel, Pitcher, Tankard	65.00
Texas, Creamer	20.00
Texas, Tankard, Water	225.00
Texas, Toothpick, Gold Trim	20.00
Thousand Eye, Bowl, Vaseline, 10 In.	110.00
Thousand Eye, Cake Stand, 8 1/2 In.	75.00
Thousand Eye, Tumbler, Amber	25.00 to 35.00
Thousand Eye Band, Goblet	45.00
Three Face, Champagne, Hollow Stem	4600.00
Three Graces, see also the related pattern Three Face.	
Three Panel, Sugar, Cover, Vaseline	55.00
Three Sisters pattern is listed here as Three Face.	
Thumbelina, Butter	40.00
Thumbprint, Compote, Cover	3600.00
Thumbprint, Wine	38.00
Torpedo, Goblet	60.00
Tropical Villa, Celery Vase	40.00
Tulip With Sawtooth, Compote, 8 In.	48.00
Twin Snowshoes, Goblet, Gold Trim	16.00
Valencia Waffle, Goblet	35.00
Venetian, Tumbler, Cranberry	35.00
Vermont, Vase, Custard, 6 1/2 In.	135.00
Viking, Celery Dish	50.00
Viking, Eggcup	70.00
Wabash, Butter	50.00
Wabash, Punch Bowl	50.00
Washington, Tumbler, Juice	25.00
Washington Centennial, Platter, Frosted Head Center, Dated Handles	95.00
Westward Ho, Compote, Cover, 5 In.	475.00 to 495.00
Westward Ho, Pitcher, Milk	700.00
Wheat & Barley, Tumbler, Water	35.00
Whirligig pattern is listed here as Buzz Star.	
Wildflower, Tumbler, Water, Blue	45.00
Willow Oak, Sauce, Footed, Blue, 4 In.	35.00
Willow Oak, Spooner, Amber	35.00
Willow Oak, Tumbler, Water	45.00
Windflower, Wine	40.00
Winged Scroll, Tumbler, Green, Gold Trim	40.00
Wisconsin, Compote, Cover, 7 In.	65.00
Wisconsin, Saltshaker	25.00
Wooden Pail pattern is listed here as Oaken Bucket.	
Yale pattern is listed here as Crowfoot.	
Yoked Loop, Goblet, Flint	35.00

PRINT, in this listing, means any of many printed images produced on paper by one of the more common methods, such as lithography. The prints listed here are of interest primarily to the antiques collector, not the fine arts collector. Many of these prints were originally part of books. Other prints will be found in the Advertising, Currier & Ives, Movie, and Poster categories.

3 Children, 18th Century Clothes, 1915, 16 1/2 x 13 1/4 In.	305.00
Anheuser-Busch, Steamboat Robert E. Lee Being Loaded With Beer, 41 x 18 In.	85.00

Audubon bird prints were originally issued as part of books printed from 1826 to 1854. They were issued in two sizes, 26 1/2 inches by 39 1/2 inches and 11 inches by 7 inches. The quadrupeds were issued in 28-by-22-inch prints. Later editions of the Audubon books were done in many sizes, and reprints of the books in the original size were also made. The bird pictures have been so popular they have been copied in myriad sizes by both old and new printing methods. This list includes originals and later copies because Audubon prints of all ages are sold in antiques shops.

J.W.Audubon

Audubon, Belted Kingfisher, 3 1/4 x 25 3/8 In.	400.00
Audubon, Blue-Headed Pigeon, 1833, 25 x 38 In.	550.00
Audubon, Blue-Winged Teal, 18 11/16 x 23 1/16 In.	1210.00
Audubon, Boat-Tailed Grackle, Large Folio, Frame, 34 1/2 x 23 In.	550.00
Audubon, Brown Pelican, Leipzig Edition, 1970s, 36 1/2 x 25 In.	990.00
Audubon, Buff-Breasted Sandpiper, Chromolithograph, Matted, Frame, 11 1/2 x 18 In. . . .	80.00
Audubon, Canada Jay, R. Havell, 1831, 25 3/4 x 20 1/2 In.	3520.00
Audubon, Canvas-Backed Duck, View Of Baltimore, 27 1/4 x 40 In.	1610.00
Audubon, Carolina Turtle Dove, R. Havell, 1830, 25 3/4 x 20 1/2 In.	2750.00
Audubon, Florida Jay, R. Havell, 1830, 25 3/4 x 20 1/2 In.	1430.00
Audubon, Glossy Ibis, 1860, 26 5/8 x 35 3/8 In.	920.00
Audubon, Jumping Mouse, 18 1/2 x 25 1/2 In.	247.00
Audubon, Little Sandpiper, Colored By R. Havell, 1836, 14 3/4 x 21 1/2 In.	275.00
Audubon, Northern Meadow-Mouse, 1848, 18 1/2 x 25 1/2 In.	190.00
Audubon, Orchard Oriole, R. Havell, London, 1828, 31 1/4 x 25 1/2 In.	715.00
Audubon, Passenger Pigeon, Audubon Society, Abbeville Press, 1985, 30 1/2 x 22 1/2 In. .	440.00
Audubon, Pectoral Sandpiper, Chromolithograph, Matted, Frame, 1860, 10 x 18 In.	121.00
Audubon, Red-Breasted Merganser, 25 x 38 In.	190.00
Audubon, Sparrow Hawk, Leipzig Edition, 1970s, 27 x 20 In.	495.00
Audubon, Ursus Maritimes, 1846, 21 5/8 x 27 1/2 In.	1725.00
Audubon, White Heron, Audubon Society, Abbeville Press, c.1985, 25 x 37 In.	990.00
Audubon, Whooping Crane, G. Schut & Zonen, 1970s, 36 3/4 x 25 1/2 In.	990.00
Audubon, Yellow-Breasted Chat, Amsterdam Edition, 1972, 27 1/2 x 20 1/2 In.	605.00
Bellows, George, Arrangement, Emma In A Room, 1923, 7 3/8 x 5 3/4 In.	745.00
Bierstadt, Albert, The Rocky Mountains, 1866, 16 3/4 x 28 1/4 In.	5290.00
Brouet, Auguste, Les Danseuses, 1900, 10 1/4 x 7 7/8 In.	1955.00
Buhot, Felix, Debarquement En Angleterre, 1879, 11 3/4 x 7 1/8 In.	1955.00
Buhot, Felix, L'Hiver A Paris, 1879, 9 3/8 x 13 3/4 In.	545.00
Chagall, Marc, Am Grabstein Der Mutter, Man Kneeling, Signed, 1922, 4 3/4 x 3 In.	3680.00
Congdon, C.H., Hickory Dickory Dock, 3 Scenes, Frame, 1917, 27 x 58 1/2 In.	275.00
Cross, Henri Edmond, Les Champs-Elysees, 1898, 8 1/8 x 10 1/2 In.	920.00
Currier & Ives, View On Long Island N.Y., Lithograph, Matted, Frame, 15 x 20 In.	286.00
Dehn, Adolf Arthur, Fishing In Colorado, 10 x 13 1/2 In.	20.00
Denis, Maurice, Tendresse, Couple Embracing, 1893, 12 x 10 In.	2760.00
Destruction Of San Francisco By Earthquake & Fire, Frame, 1906, 31 In.	305.00
Fox, R. Atkinson, English Thatched Roof Cottage, Garden, Frame, 20 3/4 x 32 1/2 In. . . .	110.00
Fox, R. Atkinson, Girl In Landscape, Frame, 19 3/4 x 15 3/4 In.	110.00
Gould, Common Curlew, Lithograph, Colored, Hallmandel, Frame, 14 x 20 1/2 In.	275.00
Gould, Statue Of Liberty, Harbor, Frame, 16 x 24 In.	145.00
Gutmann, Baby, Double Print, Frame, 11 1/2 x 30 In.	200.00
Gutmann, Lorelei, 18 x 14 In. . . . . *Illus*	1430.00
Haden, Francis, Seymour, Fruit Scene, Signed, 1870, 7 3/4 x 16 1/2 In.	575.00
Hamilton, Classical Figures, Lithograph, Frame, Late 19th Century, 10 x 16 In.	220.00
Haskell & Allen, Trotting Cracks On Brighton Road, Lithograph, Frame, 22 x 28 In.	190.00
Hyde, Sam, Large Windblown Tree, Signed, Matted, Arts & Crafts Oak Frame, 10 x 8 In. .	715.00

Don't frame a good print in a clip frame. There should be air space between the paper and the glass. Don't write on the back of a print with either pencil or ink. Eventually the writing will bleed through to the front.

Print, Gutmann,
Lorelei, 18 x 14 In.

Icart prints were made by Louis Icart, who worked in Paris from 1907 as an employee of a postcard company. He then started printing magazines and fashion brochures. About 1910 he created a series of etchings of fashionably dressed women and he continued to make similar etchings until he died in 1950. He is well known as a printmaker, painter, and illustrator. Original etchings are much more expensive than the latter photographic copies.

Icart, Attic Room, Signed, 14 3/8 x 16 1/2 In.	2300.00
Icart, Before The Raid, Signed, 17 1/4 x 21 1/4 In.	2530.00
Icart, Chestnut Vendor, Signed, 18 7/8 x 14 In.	1150.00
Icart, Coursing II, 1929, 15 7/8 x 25 7/8 In.	1380.00
Icart, Don Juan, Signed, 20 1/2 x 13 1/4 In.	1150.00
Icart, Grapes, 1920, 16 x 11 1/4 In.	805.00
Icart, Gust Of Wind, Signed, 1925, 21 1/8 x 17 5/8 In.	1725.00
Icart, Human Grenade, Signed, 17 3/8 x 12 In.	1495.00
Icart, Intimacy, Matted, Frame, Signed, 1928, 15 x 17 3/4 In.	1150.00
Icart, Joy Of Life, Signed, 23 3/8 x 15 1/8 In.	3450.00
Icart, Lady In Long Robe, Matted, Frame, Signed, 17 x 12 1/2 In.	690.00
Icart, Lady Of The Camelias, Matted, Frame, Signed, 1927, 17 1/2 x 22 3/4 In.	1265.00
Icart, Masked Swordsman With Damsel, Etched, Aquatint, 1928, 21 x 14 In.	770.00
Icart, Masks, Matted, Frame, 1925, 18 1/2 x 14 1/2 In.	1380.00
Icart, Mealtime, Signed, 1927, 17 1/2 x 13 In.	1380.00
Icart, Mockery, Etched, Signed, 1928, 15 1/4 x 18 1/4 In.	1380.00
Icart, Modern Eve, Signed, 21 1/4 x 16 1/2 In.	2760.00
Icart, Scared, Etched, Signed, 11 x 14 7/8 In.	1495.00
Icart, Sleeping Beauty, Hand Colored Etching, Aquatint, 1927, 15 1/4 x 19 In.	920.00
Icart, Smoke, Etched, Signed, 1926, 14 1/8 x 19 3/8 In.	1610.00
Icart, Speed, Etched, Signed, 1927, 24 7/8 x 14 3/4 In.	2300.00
Icart, Spilled Milk, Frame, Signed, 16 1/4 x 20 3/4 In.	1380.00
Icart, The Cat, Signed, 11 1/4 x 7 1/4 In.	975.00
Icart, The Poem, Etched, Matted, Frame, 1928, 18 x 21 1/2 In.	1840.00
Icart, Winged Victory, Signed, 21 1/4 x 14 7/8 In.	2185.00
Icart, Winsome, Etched, Signed, 17 x 15 1/4 In.	1265.00
Icart, Winter Bouquet, 1924, 17 5/8 x 12 5/8 In.	805.00
Icart, Wisteria, Signed, 17 1/4 x 21 In.	1840.00
Icart, Woman In Evening Dress Sitting Near Pond, Etched	4950.00
Icart, Young Woman & Carriage, Etched	2145.00

Jacoulet prints were designed by Paul Jacoulet (1902-1960), a Frenchman who spent most of his life in Japan. He was a master of Japanese woodblock print technique. Subjects included life in Japan, the South Seas, Korea, and China. His prints were sold by subscription and issued in series. Each series had a distinctive seal, such as a sparrow or butterfly.

Jacoulet, Betelnut Boy, Boat Seal, 1940	1100.00
Jacoulet, Bride, Owl Seal, 1948	660.00
Jacoulet, Butterflies Of The Tropics, Boat Seal, Frame, 1939	1155.00
Jacoulet, Chinese Gamblers, Seal Of Carver, 1941	330.00

Jacoulet, Chinese Puppets, Mandarin Duck Seal, 1935 .... 1210.00
Jacoulet, Crab, Double Gourd Seal, Signed, 1935 .... 2420.00
Jacoulet, Dead Parakeet, Ivy Seal, 1948 .... 1210.00
Jacoulet, Evening Flowers, Sparrow Seal, 1941 .... 1430.00
Jacoulet, First Love, Good Luck Hammer Seal, 1937 .... 3080.00
Jacoulet, In The Private Gardens Of Palace, Sparrow Seal, 1947 .... 990.00
Jacoulet, Jade Lady, Boat Seal, 1940 .... 1320.00
Jacoulet, Joruri Singer, Double Gourd Seal, 1936, 14 1/4 x 9 1/2 In. 1760.00
Jacoulet, Kaikoku, Dieu De La Richesse, 1952, 15 3/8 x 11 7/8 In. 690.00
Jacoulet, Korean Baby In Ceremonial Costume, Fan Seal, Signed, 1934 .... 880.00
Jacoulet, Man Of Yap, Mandarin Duck Seal, 1935 .... 1100.00
Jacoulet, Mandarin With Glasses, Mandarin Duck Seal, 1950 .... 880.00
Jacoulet, Master Potter, Butterfly Seal, 1940 .... 825.00
Jacoulet, Minado Man & Mangosteen, Fan Seal, 1935 .... 1540.00
Jacoulet, Nest, Sparrow Seal, 1941 .... 1650.00
Jacoulet, Old Aino Woman, Owl Seal, 1950 .... 440.00
Jacoulet, Old Carp Seller, Seal Of Carver, Kentaro Maeda 550.00
Jacoulet, Old Salt Seller, Good Luck Hammer Seal, 1936 .... 1100.00
Jacoulet, Parisian Lady, Fan Seal, Signed, 1934 .... 5500.00
Jacoulet, Sawara Fisherman, Mandarin Duck Seal, 1936 .... 385.00
Jacoulet, Star Of Gobi, Owl Seal, 1951 .... 1925.00
Jacoulet, Three Koreans, Mandarin Duck Seal, 1935 .... 715.00
Jacoulet, Under Banana Trees, Seal Of Carver 825.00
Jacoulet, Woodcut, Vendeuse Des Mangues, 1939, 15 3/8 x 11 3/4 In. 285.00
Jacoulet, Young Boy Of Saipan Holding Shells, Fan Seal, 1934 .... 1430.00
Jacoulet, Young Girl Of Fiji, Fan Seal, 1935 .... 1320.00
Jacoulet, Young Girl Of Polowat, Peach Seal, 1948 .... 3410.00

Japanese woodblock prints are listed as follows: Print, Japanese, name
of artist, title or description, type, and size. Dealers use the following
terms: Tate-e is a vertical composition. Yoko-e is a horizontal composition. The words Aiban (13 by 9 inches), Chuban (10 by 7 1/2 inches),
Hosoban (12 by 6 inches), Oban (15 by 10 inches), and Koban (7 by 4
inches) denote size. Modern versions of some of these prints have been
made.

Japanese, Chikanobu, Woman In Western Dress, Man In Uniform, c.1890 .... 165.00
Japanese, Chikanobu, Women Relaxing, Waterfalls, Bridges 192.00
Japanese, Eizan, Beauty With Young Child, Matted, Frame, 9 1/4 x 14 In. 400.00
Japanese, Hasui, Mountain Landscape Seen From Room, Matted, Frame, 10 x 14 In. 935.00
Japanese, Hiroshi Yoshida, Cherry Tree In Kawagae, Matted, Frame, 9 1/2 x 14 3/4 In. .. 495.00
Japanese, Hiroshi Yoshida, In Temple Yard, Matted, Frame, 9 1/2 x 14 3/4 In. 495.00
Japanese, Hiroshi Yoshida, Pagoda Reflected, Pond, Matted, Frame, 9 1/2 x 14 3/4 In. ... 770.00
Japanese, Hiroshige, Ando, Mannen Bridge, Fukagawa, 1857 .... 515.00
Japanese, Hiroshige, Ando, Oban Tate-e, Coastal Outcropping 515.00
Japanese, Hiroshige, Bird, Kinkeicho, Trimmed, 15 x 5 In. 55.00
Japanese, Hiroshige, Catalpa Tree With Entwined Branches Azuma Grove 170.00
Japanese, Hiroshige, Clear Weather After Snow At Kameyama, Framed, Oban Yoko-e ... 440.00
Japanese, Hiroshige, Drapery Lane, Odemma Street 150.00
Japanese, Hiroshige, Ferry Boat At Rokugo Near Kawasaki, Frame, Oban Yoko-e 360.00
Japanese, Hiroshige, Figures Having A Picnic Under Cherry Trees, Frame 75.00
Japanese, Hiroshige, Hauling Canal Boats, Yotsugi Road 230.00
Japanese, Hiroshige, Mt. Kurawa By Moonlight, Matted, Frame, 4 x 6 In. 140.00
Japanese, Hiroshige, Portage Across The River Within View Of Fuji 290.00
Japanese, Hiroshige, Rice Field Near The River, 8 3/4 x 13 3/4 In. 110.00
Japanese, Hiroshige, Suruga Bank Of Oi River Near Shimada, Frame, Oban Yoko-e 300.00
Japanese, Hiroshige, Utagawa, Figures On Bridge 90.00
Japanese, Hokkei, Totoya, Family Of Four, At Seashore 220.00
Japanese, Hokuba, Figures Crossing Nihon Bashi, Frame, Oban Yoko-e 880.00
Japanese, Hokuba, Figures Under Trees At Ferry Landing, Frame 330.00
Japanese, Hokusai, Katsushika, Puppeteer Holding Puppet, Go Board, Frame, Surimono . 385.00
Japanese, Kiyoshi Saito, Bust Portrait, Signed, 1960, 14 1/4 x 8 1/2 In. 2070.00
Japanese, Kiyoshi Saito, Clay Image, Signed, 1952, 20 1/8 x 12 1/4 In. 2070.00
Japanese, Koson, 2 Carp Swim Among Water Lilies, Oban Tate-e 495.00

Japanese, Koson, 2 Cranes In Marsh Under Rain, Hosoban 355.00
Japanese, Koson, 5 White Egrets In A Snowstorm, Oban Tate-e 495.00
Japanese, Koson, Hawk Chasing Rabbit Through Snow Filled Field, Hosoban 245.00
Japanese, Koson, Hen & Drake Pheasant In Grasses, Hosoban 220.00
Japanese, Koson, Raven On Snow Covered Branch, Aiban 440.00
Japanese, Koson, Willow Bridge, 2 Figures Crossing Snow Covered Bridge 880.00
Japanese, Kunichika, Toyohara, Ghost With Pruning Knife, Frame 120.00
Japanese, Kuninao, Woman In Floral Designed Kimono On Hillside Path, Frame 75.00
Japanese, Kuniyoshi, Utagawa, Man & Woman, Intimate Posture 302.00
Japanese, Kuniyoshi, Utagawa, Nobleman & Attendants, Observe Waterfall, c.1840 ..... 275.00
Japanese, Kuniyoshi, Utagawa, Woman Reads From Book With Carp On Cover, Frame .. 65.00
Japanese, Kuniyoshi, Utagawa, Woman Sits Beside Koto, Frame, Oban Tate-e 65.00
Japanese, Shuncho, Katsukawa, Acot Shikara Danjuro C In Role 400.00
Japanese, Sumo Wrestlers, Matted, Frame, 19th Century, 16 x 7 1/2 In............... 260.00
Japanese, Tadashi Asoma, Red Sky, 27 7/8 x 27 In. 230.00
Japanese, Toshikata, Courtesan & Her Child, c.1940, 12 x 8 In. 85.00
Japanese, Toyokuni III, Man With Large Axe Fights With Woman Holding Tree Branch .. 100.00
Japanese, Toyokuni III, Woman Wearing Blue Kimono Standing In Front Of Mt. Fuji 80.00
Japanese, Trees Reflected In River, Matted, Rosewood Frame, 9 1/2 x 14 3/4 In. 330.00
Japanese, Vision Of Masked Figures, 1870 .... 860.00
Japanese, Yoshichika, Tattooed Man Holding Censer, Oban Tate-e 100.00
Japanese, Yoshida, Hiroshi, Plum Gateway 370.00
Japanese, Yoshida, Toshi, From Ryogyoku Bridge, Signed, Chuban 165.00
Japanese, Yoshida, Toshi, Tenryu River, Signed, Chuban 120.00
Japanese, Yoshimune, Kohama Beach By Moonlight, 7 x 10 In. 170.00
Kent, Woman On Doorstep, Wood Engraving, Signed, 1940s-1950s, 7 x 5 In. 850.00
Leetthausser, Northern Shore, Signed, 1977, 9 x 11 7/8 In. 110.00
Legrand, Louis, Fleur De Lit, Windmill Scene, 1890, 10 1/4 x 6 5/8 In. 690.00
McKenney & Hall, Encampment Of The Piekann Indians, Lithograph, 13 x 18 1/4 In. 1760.00
McKenney & Hall, Mohongo, F.W. Greenough, Lithograph, 1841, 17 x 12 In. 770.00
McNulty, John, Racing Ahead, Signed, 17 1/2 x 23 1/2 In. 385.00

Nutting prints are now popular with collectors. Wallace Nutting is known for his pictures, furniture, and books. Nutting *prints* are actually hand-colored photographs issued from 1900 to 1941. There are *Wallace Nutting* over 10,000 different titles. Wallace Nutting furniture is listed in the Furniture category.

Nutting, A Chair For John, 4 1/2 x 6 3/4 In. 90.00
Nutting, A Lane In Sorrento 880.00
Nutting, A Rug Pattern 670.00
Nutting, Between The Gates 800.00
Nutting, Christmas Welcome Home 1100.00
Nutting, Floral Arrangement, Pencil Signed, Frame, 9 1/2 x 7 1/2 In. 155.00
Nutting, Lakeside Cottages 745.00
Nutting, Maple Sugar Cupboard, 19 In. 220.00
Nutting, Old Homestead 880.00
Nutting, Old Tune Revisited, Signed 295.00
Nutting, Rapid Transit, Stagecoach Scene ....1540.00 to 1650.00
Nutting, To Meet The Rector 990.00
Nutting, Tranquility Farm 880.00
Palmer, Samuel, Christmas, Folding The Last Sheep, Signed, 1850, 5 x 4 1/8 In. 2530.00
Palmer, Samuel, Cypress Grove, Woman Working In Grove, 1880, 5 x 7 3/8 In. 1725.00

Parrish prints are wanted by collectors. Maxfield Frederick Parrish was an illustrator who lived from 1870 to 1966. He is best known as a *Maxfield Parrish* designer of magazine covers, posters, calendars, and advertisements.

Parrish, Air Castles, Boy Blowing Bubbles, Frame, 1905, 17 1/4 x 13 1/4 In. 330.00
Parrish, Brazen Boatmen, Prince Descending Steps, Frame, 1907, 12 x 10 In. 275.00
Parrish, Circe's Place, 10 1/2 x 12 1/2 In. 115.00
Parrish, Cleopatra, Egyptian Queen, Frame, 17 1/2 x 19 12 In. 935.00
Parrish, Daybreak, Oak Frame, 1920s, 14 1/2 x 17 1/2 In. 175.00
Parrish, Dinkey Bird, Frame, 12 1/4 x 16 In. 170.00
Parrish, Dreaming, Woman, Under Tree, Frame, 22 x 33 1/2 In. 1320.00

Parrish, Errant Pan 500.00
Parrish, Eventide, House, Snowy Knoll, Matted, 1944, 13 1/4 x 17 1/4 In. 330.00
Parrish, Garden Of Allah, Frame, 12 x 21 In. 185.00
Parrish, Gardener, Artist Proof, 1906, 16 x 12 In. 800.00
Parrish, Hilltop, 2 Girls, Frame, 32 x 20 1/2 In. 1980.00
Parrish, Jason & The Talking Oak, Frame, 15 x 11 3/4 In. 550.00
Parrish, Moonlight, Printers Proof, 1934, 19 1/8 x 8 1/2 In. 880.00
Parrish, Morning & Evening, 11 x 7 In., Pair 715.00
Parrish, Old Glen Mill, Matted, Frame, 1954, 22 x 18 In. 800.00
Parrish, Page, Red Feathered Hat, Purple Cape, Frame, 11 1/2 x 13 1/2 In. ....185.00 to 255.00
Parrish, Pied Piper, Leading Children Into Hills, Frame, 9 1/2 x 23 5/8 In. 1155.00
Parrish, Pierrot, Frame, 12 1/4 x 14 In. 310.00
Parrish, Poster, Jack Sprat, Swift's Premium Ham 3410.00
Parrish, Prince, Frame, 11 x 13 1/2 In. 575.00
Parrish, Reveries, Frame, 17 x 24 1/2 In. 460.00
Parrish, Romance, Frame, 26 x 16 1/2 In. 1090.00
Parrish, Royal Gorge Of Colorado, Frame, 1925, 22 x 18 In. 385.00
Parrish, Rubaiyat, Frame, 31 1/4 x 9 1/4 In. 368.00
Parrish, Sing A Song Of Six Pence 2420.00
Parrish, Stars, Octagon Shape Frame, 7 1/2 x 11 In. 435.00
Parrish, Sugar Plum Tree 600.00
Parrish, Templed Hills, 2 Trees, Frame, 1942, 13 1/2 x 10 1/2 In. 175.00
Parrish, Triptych, Prince, Romance & Page, Frame, 16 1/2 x 44 3/4 In. 1375.00
Parrish, When Day Is Dawning, Frame, 13 x 15 1/2 In. 355.00
Parrish, White Birch 95.00
Parrish, With Trumpet & Drum, Children, Flags, Frame, 1905, 17 3/4 x 13 In. 2420.00
Parrish, Wynken, Blinken & Nod, 3 Boys, Oak Frame, 1905, 19 x 14 In. 550.00
Petitot, Enneamond-Alexandre, Masquerade A La Grecque, 1771, 10 7/8 x 7 3/8 In. ... 3450.00
Reich, Jacques, Portrait Of Whistler, 1916, 23 x 13 1/8 In. 690.00
Rossi, Woman & Swan, Silk, Frame, 31 In. 400.00
Rossi, Woman, With Blossoms, Silk, Frame, 31 In. 375.00
Sadler, Golfer Cleaning Clubs, Frame, 15 x 11 In. 80.00
Sandzen, Birger, Linoleum Cut, Willow & Cottonwood, Edition Of 100, 8 x 12 In. 450.00
Seligmann, Kurt, The Childhood Of Oedipus, Signed, 1944, 17 3/4 x 11 3/4 In. 1035.00
Seligmann, Kurt, The Sphinx 1, Signed, 1944, 18 x 11 7/8 In. 920.00
Spruamce, Benton M., Prelude To Rest, Signed, 1935, 8 7/8 x 13 In. 7475.00
Wilson, Sydney E., Benevolent Sportsman & Sportsman's Return, 16 3/4 x 21 In., Pair 385.00
Woodblock, Black, Gray, Silver Clouds, Green Ground, Arts & Crafts, Frame, 5 x 6 In. .. 285.00
Woodblock, Chase, Waldo, Before The White Man, Matted, Signed, 1930, 17 x 12 In. 1100.00
Woodblock, Chase, Waldo, Nomad, Ship At Sunset, Frame, 1932, 12 x 7 In. 825.00
Woodblock, Cockatoo, Arts & Crafts, Matted, Frame, Signed, 12 x 16 In. 310.00
Woodblock, Floral, Arts & Crafts, Matted, Frame, 8 1/2 x 8 In. 110.00
Woodblock, Gardiner, Eliza D., Feed The Pigeons, Mother & Child, Matted, 10 x 8 In. 165.00
Woodblock, Gardiner, Eliza D., Fig Market, Mother & Child, Matted, 8 x 7 In. 330.00
Woodblock, Gray Birds, Leaves, Coral, Deep Green, Arts & Crafts, Oak Frame, 5 x 6 In. . 230.00
Woodblock, Hall, Norma Bassett, Mt. Hood, Oregon Scene, Oak Frame, 8 x 10 1/2 In. ... 880.00
Woodblock, Harbor Scene, Blue, Gray, Brown, Green, Germany, Frame, 9 1/2 x 13 In. 195.00
Woodblock, Heinrichs, Joseph, Compote, Signed, 15 In. 220.00
Woodblock, Hurley, E.T., Tall Buildings, People, 11 1/2 x 9 1/2 In. 190.00
Woodblock, Hyde, Helen, Chinese People, Walking Alongside River, Oak Frame, 20 In. .. 2110.00
Woodblock, Hyde, Helen, Young Girl & Geese, Rame, Signed, 3 1/2 x 8 1/2 In. 935.00
Woodblock, Irvine, Sadie, Sailboat At Night, Stars In Sky, Frame, Signed, 7 x 9 1/2 In. .. 1540.00
Woodblock, Kunst, Wolf, Cottage Scene, Arts & Crafts, Frame, 7 x 6 In. 110.00
Woodblock, Lemos, Pedro, 4 Birds On Branch, Title, Sleepyheads, Signed, Frame, 11 In. . 935.00
Woodblock, Mirin, Georges, Springfield, Mass., Night Landscape, Frame, 6 x 4 1/2 In. .. 275.00
Woodblock, Mountain Behind Evergreens, Arts & Crafts, Matted, Frame, 10 x 16 In. 385.00
Woodblock, Norton, Elizabeth, Avignon, Matted, Signed, 1926, 6 1/2 x 6 In. 440.00
Woodblock, Patterson, Margaret, City Building Scene, Arts & Crafts, Frame, 7 x 10 In. .. 440.00
Woodblock, Pelican Scene, Arts & Crafts, Matted, Frame, Signed, 18 x 19 In. 360.00
Woodblock, Play, Chu-Shin-Gura, Triplet Paper, Matted, Frame, 13 x 27 In. 225.00
Woodblock, Rice, William, Alaska Peaks, Matted, Frame, Signed, 6 x 5 1/4 In. 880.00
Woodblock, Rice, William, Wind-Blown Poplars, Matted, Frame, Signed, 12 x 9 In. 2090.00
Woodblock, Rice, Wm. S., Eucalypti Sunset, Tree Silhouette, Matted, Frame, 7 x 9 In. 2200.00

Woodblock, Ship At Sea, Arts & Crafts, Matted, Frame, Signed, 3 1/2 x 4 In. 165.00
Woodblock, Ship In Full Sail, Arts & Crafts, Matted, Frame, Signed, 3 x 4 In. 165.00
Woodblock, Watson, Eva A., Gulls, Blue, Gray & Green, Matted, Frame, 11 In. 165.00
Woodblock, Windmill, Watercolor, Margaret Patterson, Signed, 1910, 8 x 5 1/2 In. 990.00
Woodblock, Woolard, Dorothy, Dutch Market Scene, Matted, Frame, 9 1/2 x 8 1/2 In. . . . 65.00
Woodcut, Abromovitz, Abraham, Wuxtry, Signed, c.1938, 14 1/2 x 10 In. 2990.00
Woodcut, Branell, B., Little Sarah & Her Bird, Philadelphia, Colored, Frame, 9 x 6 In. . . 55.00
Woodcut, Drewes, Werner, Cathedral Of Redwoods, 1957, 31 x 16 In. 200.00
Woodcut, Keith, Elizabeth, Ying Lin Monastery, Signed, c.1925, 15 1/2 x 10 7/8 In. 745.00
Woodcut, Kollwitz, Kathe, Das Letzte, Signed, 1925, 12 x 5 In. 1725.00
Woodcut, Lum, Bertha, Courtyard View From Doorway, Matted, Frame, 14 x 8 1/2 In. . . 1650.00
Woodcut, Summers, Carol, Magic Mountain, Signed, c.1956, 12 5/8 x 16 3/4 In. 747.00
Woodcut, Summers, Carol, Palazzo Malatesta, Rimini, Signed, c.1980, 36 x 36 5/8 In. . . . 690.00
Yard Long, Meditation Girl 200.00
Yard Long, Pompeian Beauty 200.00
Young Girl & Dog, Chromolithograph, Frame, 19th Century, America, 26 x 20 In. 90.00
Zorn, Anders, Berserk, Partially Naked Woman, Dressing, 1914, 9 7/8 x 7 1/8 In. 1035.00
Zorn, Anders, Dal River, Naked Woman Wiping Hands On Towel, 1919, 7 x 4 In. 1090.00
Zorn, Anders, The Cabin, 2 Naked Women Going Down Stairs, 1917, 11 5/8 x 7 5/8 In. . . 1840.00
Zorn, Anders, The Two, Man Playing Lute, 1916, 7 5/8 x 5 3/4 In. 860.00
Zorn, Anders, Vicke, Naked Man & Woman Standing, 1918, 7 7/8 x 11 5/8 In. 920.00

PURINTON POTTERY COMPANY was incorporated in Wellsville, Ohio, in 1936. The company moved to Shippenville, Pennsylvania, in 1941 and made a variety of hand-painted ceramic wares. By the 1950s Purinton was making dinnerware, souvenirs, cookie jars, and florist wares. The pottery closed in 1959.

Apple, Ashtray, Metal Stand, 5 1/2 In. 45.00
Apple, Basket, Candy, Ring Handle 50.00
Apple, Bottle, Water 70.00
Apple, Bowl, Spaghetti, 14 1/2 In. 150.00
Apple, Butter, 6 1/2 In. 185.00
Apple, Coffeepot, 8 Cup 80.00
Apple, Console, 11 In. 500.00
Apple, Cruet, Oil, Round 85.00
Apple, Cup & Saucer 13.00
Apple, Mug, Beer, 16 Oz. 80.00
Apple, Planter, Rum Jug, 6 1/2 In. 35.00
Apple, Salt & Pepper, Range, 4 In. 35.00
Apple, Sugar, Cover 25.00
Apple, Sugar, Shake & Pour, 4 1/2 In. 85.00
Blue Pansy, Basket, Planter, 6 1/4 In. 55.00
Blue Pansy, Cruet, 5 In. 30.00
Cookie Jar, Humpty Dumpty 160.00
Cookie Jar, Normandy Plaid, Wide Oval 45.00
Cookie Jar, Rooster 60.00
Daisy, Jug, Rebecca, 7 1/2 In. 60.00
Fruit, Night Bottle, 1 Qt. 27.00
Fruit, Pitcher, Milk, 1 Pt. 65.00
Intaglio, Butter, Brown 25.00
Intaglio, Chop Plate, Brown, 12 In. 85.00
Intaglio, Teapot, Brown, 6 Cup 30.00
Liberty Blue, Bowl, Vegetable, Round 45.00
Maywood, Bowl, Vegetable, 8 1/2 In. 12.00
Maywood, Grill Plate, 12 In. 45.00
Maywood, Relish, 3 Sections, 10 In. 35.00
Mountain Rose, Bowl, Fruit, 12 In. 160.00
Mountain Rose, Teapot, Individual 38.00
Normandy Plaid, Bowl, Cereal, 5 1/4 In. 10.00
Normandy Plaid, Salt & Pepper, Range 32.00
Palm Tree, Plate, 10 In. 450.00
Provincial Fruit, Jam & Jelly Dish, 2 Sections 90.00
Saraband, Chop Plate, 12 In. 110.00

Saraband, Jam & Jelly Dish 60.00
Tea Rose, Cup, Coffee 57.00

PURSES have been recognizable since the eighteenth century, when leather and needlework purses were preferred. Beaded purses became popular in the nineteenth century, went out of style, but are again in use. Mesh purses date from the 1880s and are still being made. How to carry a handkerchief and lipstick is a problem today for every woman, including the Queen of England.

Alligator, Brown, Paris 75.00
Alligator, Red, Paris 50.00
Alumesk, White Mesh, Plastic Cream Trim, Link Chain Handle, Whiting Davis 45.00
Bag, Flint, Leather, Low Edge Steel Striker, Silver Tacks, Beads, Persia, 4 1/2 x 2 1/2 In. . 110.00
Basket Form, Nantucket, Whaling Scene, Ivory Pin, Knob & Latch, 1950s, 11 1/4 In. ... 1035.00
Beaded, 3 Butterflies, Turtle 350.00
Beaded, Amber, Envelope, Italy, 8 1/2 x 6 In. 55.00
Beaded, Bird Design, Enamel Frame, Deco, 6 x 5 In. 175.00
Beaded, Cobalt Blue, Drawstring 75.00
Beaded, Design On Both Sides, White, Red, Green, Blue & Gold, Penn., 6 x 5 In. 250.00
Beaded, Double Hinged, Brass Frame, c.1930, 6 x 6 In. 75.00
Beaded, Drawstring, Cobalt Beads 75.00
Beaded, Fringed, Copper Colored 95.00
Beaded, Gold Floral, Filigree, Chain, Fringe, 1900-1920, 8 x 5 In. 385.00
Beaded, Gold Steel, Turquoise Cabochons Frame, Rhinestones, No Lining, 4 x 3 1/2 In. ... 170.00
Beaded, Lady Under Glass Center, France 185.00
Beaded, Maroon, Pouch, Silk Lining, Beaded Tassel, 1920s, 7 x 5 In. 160.00
Beaded, Multicolored Floral, Detachable Handle, Valance, Hand Made, France, 9 x 6 In. . 95.00
Beaded, Owl's Eye, Judith Leiber 610.00
Beaded, Venetian Canal Scene, Micromosaic Frame, Italy, 13 x 8 In. 60.00
Beadlite, Mesh, Silver Plated Floral Frame, Whiting Davis, 7 x 3 1/4 In. 245.00
Cloth, Chatelaine, Sterling Silver Frame & Waist Clip, Steel Beads, Fringe, W & D 395.00
Crochet Cotton, Celluloid, Cameo Swivels Opens, Silk Lining, 5 In. 165.00
Embroidered, Clutch, Evening, Floral Panels, Crystals, Chain, Judith Leiber ...... *Illus* 920.00
Embroidered, On Net, Celluloid Frame, Egyptian Type, Wooden Catch, France, 5 1/2 In. . 250.00
Embroidered, Silver & Gold On Ivory Damask, Silk Lining, 17th Century 1350.00
Embroidered, Trapunto, Metallic Threads, Ornate Jeweled Frame, Chain Handle 155.00
Flame Stitch, Made For Peter Levigood, 1768, 8 In. 1100.00
Flame Stitch, Needlepoint Case, Marked M.L., 1800, 4 x 7 In. 1870.00
German Silver, Coin, Courting Scene Each Side, Moire Interior, 2 3/4 In. 200.00
Gold Mesh, Cathedral Frame, Engraved Leaves, Seed Pearl Tassel, Sapphires, Art Deco .. 805.00
Gold Trace-Links, Freshwater Pearls, Floral Silk Bag, Telescoping Neck, Edwardian 690.00
Goldstone Steel Beads, Chatelaine, Openwork Frame, Waist Clip, 8 1/2 In. 300.00
Inro, 5 Sages, 1 Compartment, Cinnabar Lacquer, 19th Century, 3 1/2 In. 545.00
Inro, Gold Stylized Chrysanthemum & Peony, Melon Form, 19th Century 290.00
Jet Bead, Elephant, Clutch, Saks Fifth Avenue, 1940s 595.00
Knit Material, Brown, Pouch, Allover Cut Steel Designs, 1900s, 11 x 7 In. 245.00

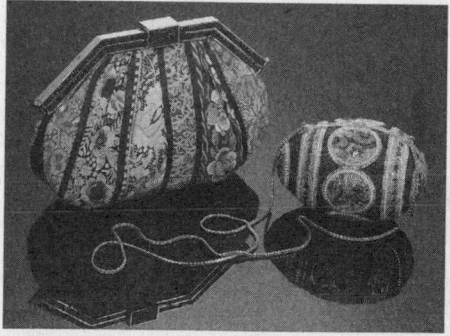

Purse, Embroidered, Clutch, Evening, Floral Panels, Crystals, Chain, Judith Leiber; Purse, Mosaic Egg, Faberge Type, Pave Crystals, Ruby, Floral, Chain, Judith Leiber

Knitted, Drawstring, 19th Century, Miniature 80.00
Leather, Black, Bakelite Closing, Deco Design 85.00
Leather, Brown, Clutch, Art Deco, Bakelite Frame & Clasp, 6 1/2 x 6 1/2 In. 45.00
Leather, Embossed 55 Chevy, Amusement Park, India, 13 x 14 In. .... *Illus* 20.00
Linen, Metalwork Clasp, Monogram, 10 1/2 x 10 1/2 In. 358.00
Lizard, Black, Foldover, Fan Applique, Shoulder Strap, Judith Leiber 920.00
Lucite, Pearlized Gray, Keystone Shape, 1940s 125.00
Mesh, Art Deco Design, Silver Plated Frame, Whiting Davis, 7 1/2 x 3 1/4 In. 275.00
Mesh, Beaded, Black, Blue & Gold, Mandalian, 7 In. 350.00
Mesh, Beaded, Floral, Black Ground, Turquoise Band, Fringe, 10 In. 550.00
Mesh, Beaded, Multiblue, Gold Frame, Mandalian, 6 3/4 In. 325.00
Mesh, Beaded, Peacocks & Roses, Silver Embossed Frame, 12 In. 525.00
Mesh, Beaded, Pouch, Celluloid Frame, 1920s, 9 x 6 1/2 In. 295.00
Mesh, Beaded, Roses, Navy Ground, Metal Frame, Turquoise Stones, 12 In. 650.00
Mesh, Coin, Garnets, Simons Brother Of Philadelphia, 3 x 2 1/2 In. 295.00
Mesh, Coin, Interwoven Faceted Beads, 18K Gold 230.00
Mesh, Design, Gold Ground, Dangles, Mandalian, 6 3/4 x 3 1/2 In. 385.00
Mesh, Evening, Ivory & Gold, Whiting Davis 25.00
Mesh, Floral Pattern, Silver Plated Frame, Manalian, 7 In. 165.00
Mesh, Gold Color, Compartments, Enameled Stones 160.00
Mesh, Gold Tone Filigree Frame, Turquoise Glass Stones, White Ground, 7 1/2 x 5 In. ... 350.00
Mesh, Gold Tone Frame, Fringe, Mandalian, 8 x 4 In. 320.00
Mesh, Gold, Chain Handle, Whiting Davis, Small 60.00
Mesh, Gold, Envelope, Jeweled Snap Closure, Accessories, Whiting Davis 75.00
Mesh, Ivory, Black & Orange Design, Silver Tone Frame, Whiting Davis, 5 1/2 x 3 In. ... 150.00
Mesh, Ivory, Hot Pink & Lime Green, Silver Floral Frame, Whiting Davis, 7 x 4 In. 220.00
Mesh, Mandalian, 3 Colors 125.00
Mesh, Silver Plated Floral Frame, Spider Web, Fringe, Mandalian, 8 1/2 x 4 In. 395.00
Mesh, Silver, Birmingham, England, 1937 .... 110.00
Mesh, Silver, Chain Link Handle, Floral Frame, Wanamaker Box, 5 1/2 x 7 In. 225.00
Mesh, Silver, Marked German Silver 35.00
Mesh, Silver, Whiting & Davis, Sapphire Clasp, Fringe, 1913 .... 250.00
Metal, Coin & Stamp, Cabochon Garnet Top 70.00
Mosaic Egg, Faberge Type, Pave Crystals, Ruby, Floral, Chain, Judith Leiber .... *Illus* 4700.00
Needlework, Flame Stitch, West Norriton, Pa., 1763, 3 3/4 x 7 In. 5500.00
Papillon, Crystal Cabochon Butterfly Shape, Gilt Sides, Judith Leiber 3450.00
Patent Leather, Clutch, Shirred, Gilt Frame, Lizardskin Shoulder Strap, Judith Leiber ... 515.00
Persian Lamb, Black, Muff Combo 45.00
Petit Point, Amber Frame 35.00
Petit Point, Scene, Ornate Carnelian & Marcasites Set Frame 290.00
Plastic, Black, Football Shape, White Stripes, Team, 1960s 255.00
Plastic, Gray, Marbleized, Carved Flower On Lid 75.00
Red Leather, Kamera Pak Style, Chrome, Cigarettes, Lipstick 125.00
Satin, Cafe-Au-Lait, Clutch, Filigree Frame, Crystal, Judith Leiber 745.00
Silk, Pouch, Floral, Celluloid Frame, Handle, 6 In. 165.00
Silk Brocade, Containing Gold Lacquer Comb, Floral Bronze Mirror 50.00
Silk Moire, Clutch, Black, Ivory, Gray Squares, Cartier, 18K Yellow Gold Clasp 2070.00
Silver Lame & Snakeskin, Pleated, Square Handles, Crystal, Judith Leiber 4140.00
Silver Plate, Chatelaine, Steel Beads, Pie Shape, Fringe, Repousse Frame & Clip 245.00

Purse, Leather,
Embossed
55 Chevy,
Amusement
Park, India,
13 x 14 In.

Purse, Woven Pineapple, Natural,
6 1/2 x 11 In.

Snakeskin, Clutch, Paneled Ecru, 4 Staghorn Appliques, Shoulder Strap, Judith Leiber ... 515.00
Sterling Silver, Billfold, Compact & Coin Purse, c.1900 .... 225.00
Sterling Silver, Chatelaine, Victorian 195.00
Sterling Silver, Elaborate Finger Ring Chain, Victorian 115.00
Sterling Silver, Pattern, William Kerr, Chain 260.00
Sterling Silver, Unger Bros. ....250.00 to 325.00
Suede, Black, Enamel Flowers, Rhinestones, Beads, Martha Klien 110.00
Tapestry, Brass Frame, Green Jewel Fastener 125.00
Topaz Crystal, Gilt Frame, Pave Set Swan Catch, 2 Handles, Judith Leiber 6325.00
Tortoiseshell, Coin, Vacant Gold Cartouche, Divided Interior, Metal Frame, 2 3/4 In. 230.00
Tortoiseshell, Gold Inlaid, Book Page, Star Design, Oval, 3 1/4 In. 360.00
Velvet, Black, Chatelaine, Sterling Silver Frame, Waist Clip 395.00
Velvet, Gray, Chatelaine, Sterling Silver Acorn Frame, Steel Bead Waist Clip 250.00
Woven Pineapple, Natural, 6 1/2 x 11 In. ....*Illus* 25.00

QUEZAL glass was made from 1901 to 1924 by Martin Bach, Sr., in Queens, New York. Other glassware by other firms, such as Loetz, Steuben, and Tiffany, resembles this gold-colored iridescent glass. Martin Bach died in 1921. His son-in-law, Conrad Vahlsing, Jr., went to work at the Lustre Art Company about 1920 and his son, Martin Bach, Jr., worked at the Durand Art Glass division of the Vineland Flint Glass Works after 1924.

Quezal

Bowl, Gold Iridescent, Marked, 7 In. 425.00
Bowl, Gold Iridescent, Spreading Foot, 7 1/2 In. 660.00
Cup & Saucer, Band Of Pulled Feathers, Amber Saucer, Iridescent, 1900, 4 In. 805.00
Globe, Acorn Shape, 5 Gold Iridescent Leaves, Signed, c.1910, 10 1/2 In. 1495.00
Lamp, Desk, Bronze, 5 Broad Pulled Feathers, Gold Iridescent Shade, 19 In. 1725.00
Lamp, Desk, Curved Reeded Arm, Domed Base, Signed, Early 20th Century, 12 1/4 In. .. 402.00
Lamp, Lily Shade, Woman With Plant, Bronze, Kip Mo Cau, 36 In. 500.00
Shade, Amber, Gold Iridescent, Signed, c.1910, 7 Piece 805.00
Shade, Gold Iridescent, Ribbed, Signed, Pair 250.00
Shade, Gold Iridescent, Signed, 5 1/2 In., Pair 440.00
Vase, Blue & Silver Swirls, Orange, Signed, 6 In. 1100.00
Vase, Blue, Green Pulled Feathers & Swirls, Gold Glass, Signed, 4 In. 770.00
Vase, Gold Iridescent, Amber, Ribbed, Bulbous Base, 3 In. 690.00
Vase, Gold Luster, 6 Flared Rim, Bulbous Base, Ground Pontil, Signature, 12 3/4 In. 1568.00
Vase, Gold Stretch Border, Bold Green Leaves Exterior, Ruffled Edge, 6 1/2 In. 1870.00
Vase, Green, Silver Swirl Iridescent, 3 In. 350.00
Vase, Pulled Green & Gold Feathers, Signed, 7 3/8 In. 3262.00
Vase, Pulled Leaves, Gold Luster Iridescent, Gold Neck, 9 In. 4600.00
Vase, Pulled Spider Web, Bronze & Silver, Signed, 4 In. 1250.00

QUILTS have been made since the seventeenth century. Early textiles were very precious and every scrap was saved to be reused. A quilt is a combination of fabrics joined to a filler and a backing by small stitched designs known as quilting. An appliqued quilt has pieces stitched to the top of a large piece of background fabric. A patchwork, or pieced, quilt is made of many small pieces stitched together. Embroidery can be added to either type.

Amish, 3 Purple Bars, Blue, Meandering Border, Green Calico Back, 47 x 49 In. 1650.00
Amish, 9 Patch, Crib, 39 1/2 x 47 3/4 In. 440.00
Amish, Center Medallion, Cotton & Sateen, Scrolled Leaf Border, Stars, 69 x 85 1/2 In. .. 275.00
Amish, Patchwork, 9 Patch, Dark Blue Ground, Blue, Gray, Mauve, 77 x 63 In. 465.00
Amish, Patchwork, Grandmother's Flower Garden, White Ground, 109 x 119 In. 330.00
Amish, Patchwork, Pinwheel, Black & Salmon Wool, Red Calico Back, 82 x 82 In. 355.00
Amish, Patchwork, Tree Of Life, Meandering Vine Outline, Cotton, 38 x 56 In. 1150.00
Amish, Sunshine & Shadow, Wool, Crepe Corner Blocks, Vine Border, 82 x 82 In. 2035.00
Appliqued, 3 Concentric Red Stars, 4 Eagles Surround, 19th Century, 82 x 32 In. 1320.00
Appliqued, 4 Oak Leaf Pinwheels, Meandering Floral Border, 74 x 74 In. 440.00
Appliqued, 9 Blocks, Oak Leaf & Berry, Sawtooth Border, Pa., 77 x 79 In. 825.00
Appliqued, 9 Medallions, Stylized Tulips, Pencil Pattern, 64 x 104 In. 550.00
Appliqued, 12 Medallions With Stylized Tulips, Ivory, Pa., 19th Century, 67 x 87 In. 440.00
Appliqued, 12 Sunbonnet Babies, Red & White Border, Child's, 42 x 70 In. 110.00

Appliqued, 16 Blocks, Green Wreaths, 4 Red Roses, Pa., 19th Century, 77 x 77 In. 550.00
Appliqued, 16 Blocks, Oak Leaf, Swag Border, Frances Wenger, 1848, 88 x 89 3/4 In. ... 3575.00
Appliqued, 16 Blocks, Sunflowers, Border, Allover Feather Quilting, 1880, 98 x 102 In. ... 1210.00
Appliqued, 16 Floral Wreaths, Vining Border, 84 x 84 In. 330.00
Appliqued, 16 Squares, 8-Pointed Heart, Green, Red Paint, White Ground, 80 In. 770.00
Appliqued, 20 Lyres, Green & Goldenrod, Knit Binding, 82 x 86 In. 715.00
Appliqued, 65 Embroidered Squares, Floral Bursts, Wool, 1899, 76 x 66 In. 2760.00
Appliqued, Album, 16 Squares, Stars, Baskets Of Flowers, 1853, 76 x 76 In. 5462.00
Appliqued, Album, 30 Squares, Floral & Bird, 77 x 91 In. 4950.00
Appliqued, Alternating Squares Of Black, Burgundy, Floral, 75 x 68 In. 1455.00
Appliqued, Center Star, 4 Small Surround Stars, White Ground, 1928, 80 x 81 In. 1210.00
Appliqued, Concentric Leafy Vines, Flower Filled Urn, Crewel Embroidery, 75 x 86 In. .. 2645.00
Appliqued, Fan, Silk, Small Squares Border, Art Deco, 74 x 96 In. 165.00
Appliqued, Floral & Swag, Stars & Swags, Center Wreath, 1896, 78 x 70 In. 805.00
Appliqued, Floral, Multicolored Bouquet, White Ground, Scalloped, 1940s, 74 x 87 In. .. 240.00
Appliqued, Floral, Red & Green, Vine Border 3 Sides, 1870s, 92 x 78 In. 880.00
Appliqued, Flower Basket, Birds, Oak Leaves, Red & White, Cotton, 79 x 66 1/2 In. 402.00
Appliqued, Kerchief, George Washington, Eagles, Flags, Cotton, 1876, 101 x 92 In. 9200.00
Appliqued, Lone Star, Blue Print, White, Machine Sewn Binding, 72 x 84 In. 300.00
Appliqued, Lone Star, Intertwined Red & Yellow Sawtooth Border, Pa., 96 x 84 In. 605.00
Appliqued, Lone Star, Multicolored Calico, Pink Calico Ground, Crib, 39 x 52 In. 275.00
Appliqued, Pineapple & Tulip, Dark Green Band & White Border, 81 x 92 In. 230.00
Appliqued, Pineapple Variation, White, Lavender Chintz, L.F. Bealen, 87 x 86 In. 305.00
Appliqued, Poppy Medallions, Vine Border, 90 x 92 In. 605.00
Appliqued, Princess Feather, Red & Green Feather Medallions, Pink Ground, 90 x 90 In. .. 220.00
Appliqued, Red & Yellow Stylized Flowers, Feather Variation, Swag Border, 89 x 78 In. . 460.00
Appliqued, Red, Yellow & Tan Flowers, Pa., 19th Century, 20 1/4 x 20 1/4 In. 605.00
Appliqued, Rose Wreaths, Goldenrod Flower Centers, 72 x 75 In. 247.00
Appliqued, Stylized Floral, Green, Beige, Blue, Yellow, Vine Border, 84 x 90 In. 550.00
Appliqued, Tulips, Red & Gold, Green Stems, Banded Green Border, 76 x 76 In. 795.00
Appliqued, Victory, Portrait Of Stalin & Churchill, Yellow, Green Cotton, 1945, 96 In. ... 4885.00
Appliqued, Wreath Of Pansies Center, Pansies Scalloped Border, 1950s, 78 x 92 In. 110.00
Crazy, Bird, Heart Design, Embroidered Flannel & Velvet, 61 x 76 1/2 In. 125.00
Crazy, Embroidered, Center Rectangular Block, Different Fabrics, 60 x 75 In. 160.00
Crazy, Embroidered, Silk, Taffeta, Velvet, Cotton, Border, 60 x 59 In. 200.00
Diamond In Square, Doll's, 20th Century, 15 3/4 x 15 3/4 In. 275.00
Patchwork, 4 Patch, Brown, Gold Calico, Tan Calico Ground, 46 3/4 x 38 In. 345.00
Patchwork, 6 Star Medallions, Goldenrod & White, 72 x 89 In. 350.00
Patchwork, 6-Pointed Star, Red Sawtooth Border, 79 x 84 In. 220.00
Patchwork, 9 Sunburst Star Medallions, White Ground, Border, 94 x 96 In. 1100.00
Patchwork, 12 Floral Baskets, Pink, Green, Maroon, Gray, 78 x 94 In. 825.00
Patchwork, 12 Stylized Floral Medallions, Gray, Red, Vine Floral Border, 82 x 98 In. ... 357.00
Patchwork, 16 Blocks, Pinwheel, Multicolored, Wide Pink Border, 70 x 70 In. 176.00
Patchwork, 16 Blocks, Windmill, Sawtooth Border, Penna., 19th Century, 78 x 78 In. ... 715.00
Patchwork, 16 Stars, Yellow, Pink Calico, Green Calico Ground, 82 x 82 In. 550.00
Patchwork, 20 Diamond Medallions, Stars, Calico Ground, Striped Border, 73 x 91 In. ... 715.00
Patchwork, 20 Star Medallions, Multicolored, White Ground, 74 x 91 In. 935.00
Patchwork, 30 Crosses, Calico, Pink Grid, Brown Borders, 74 x 82 In. 550.00
Patchwork, 35 Baskets, White Alternating With Blue Print, 60 x 72 In. 247.00
Patchwork, Album, 36 Squares, Urns & Bouquets, Embroidered, White Field, c.1850 ... 3450.00
Patchwork, Album, Signed By Smith Family, Early 19th Century, 66 x 84 In. 2500.00
Patchwork, Allover Diamond In Square, Pa., 19th Century, 82 x 86 In. 355.00
Patchwork, American Flag, Civil War Central Medallion, Red, White, Blue, 88 In. 12650.00
Patchwork, American Flag, Counter Striped Borders, White Cotton Field, 76 In. 2185.00
Patchwork, Basket, Red, Brown & Green, White Ground, 91 x 100 In. 355.00
Patchwork, Blue, White Calico, White Homespun Back, 66 x 70 In. 577.00
Patchwork, Buggy, Blue, Red, Cream, Yellow, c.1890, 68 1/2 x 56 In. 210.00
Patchwork, Buggy, Corduroy & Velvet, Merino Wool, c.1890, 68 1/2 x 56 In. 110.00
Patchwork, Butterfly, Blue Bands, c.1930, 88 x 70 In. 245.00
Patchwork, Center Lone Star Pattern, Red Border, Allover Feather Quilting, 78 x 78 In. .. 935.00
Patchwork, Century Of Progress, George Washington & Abe Lincoln, 1945, 80 x 66 In. ... 5460.00
Patchwork, Courthouse Steps, Silk, 1917 .... 3900.00
Patchwork, Delectable Mountains, Red, Yellow & Green Calico, Print Back, 76 x 80 In. . 880.00

Patchwork, Diagonal Stripe, Multicolored Prints & Solids, 68 x 78 In. 2585.00
Patchwork, Diamond & Chain, Calico Binding, Mennonite, 85 x 85 In. 825.00
Patchwork, Diamond & Sawtooth, Blue, Black, Red, Wool, 102 x 100 In. 745.00
Patchwork, Diamond In Square Medallions, Calico Ground, Mennonite, 70 x 86 In. 550.00
Patchwork, Dresden Plate, Royal Blue Sashing, 81 x 80 In. 145.00
Patchwork, Drunkard's Path, Blue Print, 70 x 74 In. 192.00
Patchwork, Drunkard's Path, Red, Green Calico, Sawtooth Border, 84 x 84 In. 610.00
Patchwork, Embroidered, Scalloped Border, Grid Framing, 20th Century, 102 x 110 In. ... 415.00
Patchwork, Fan, Printed Cloth, Art Deco, 1920s, 78 x 71 In. 195.00
Patchwork, Flower Garden, Blue, Green, Purple, Pink, Cream, 1930s, 95 x 78 In. 173.00
Patchwork, Flower, Blue Border, Anna McCartney, 1920s, 82 x 78 1/2 In. 375.00
Patchwork, Flowerpot, Green & Red, White Ground, Heavily Quilted, 84 x 84 In. 264.00
Patchwork, Friendship, Signed Patches, Brown & Blue Chintz, Floral, 98 x 98 In. 550.00
Patchwork, Grandmother's Flower Garden, 20th Century, 118 x 126 In. 688.00
Patchwork, Grandmother's Flower Garden, Black Sashing, 78 x 76 In. 1375.00
Patchwork, Irish Chain Ground, Stylized Floral Medallions, 87 x 99 In. 852.00
Patchwork, Irish Chain, Navy Blue Print, White, 66 x 74 In. 410.00
Patchwork, Irish Chain, Quilted Star Flowers, 71 x 82 In. 330.00
Patchwork, Irish Chain, Red & Green Calico, Cotton Homespun, Ohio, 82 x 97 In. 715.00
Patchwork, Log Cabin, Concentric Black Diamonds, Multicolored Prints, 82 x 84 In. 660.00
Patchwork, Log Cabin, Multicolored, 75 x 75 In. 605.00
Patchwork, Log Cabin, Pinwheel Variation, Chevron Border, Wool, 70 x 74 In. 355.00
Patchwork, Lone Star, Multicolored, 73 x 88 In. 357.00
Patchwork, Mariner's Compass, Yellow & Blue On Muslin, 78 x 78 In. 230.00
Patchwork, Monkey Wrench, Calico, Homespun Back, Mennonite, 68 x 82 In. 468.00
Patchwork, Mosaic Diamond, Running Diamond & Chevron Quilting, 58 x 62 In. 1265.00
Patchwork, Pinwheels, Mary Viets For Thomas Jenkins Birth, 1927, 70 x 83 In. 275.00
Patchwork, Red Squares, Green 3 Leaf Clovers, White Ground, Scalloped, 68 x 84 In. 550.00
Patchwork, Red, Green Flower Basket, Flowering Vine Border, 83 x 81 In. 400.00
Patchwork, Red, White & Blue, Spread-Winged Eagle, Union, Cotton, 1915, 76 x 76 In. .. 8050.00
Patchwork, Red, White, Crib, 35 x 39 In. 357.00
Patchwork, Sawtooth, Red & White, 80 x 80 In. 895.00
Patchwork, Schoolhouse, 79 x 73 In. 2850.00
Patchwork, Star In Solid Colors, White Ground, Yellow Back, 70 x 86 In. 440.00
Patchwork, Star Medallions, Multicolored Prints, Calico Border, Mennonite, 70 x 82 In. . 495.00
Patchwork, Star Of Bethlehem, Stars In Corners, Pa., c.1890, 76 x 76 In. 880.00
Patchwork, Star, Blue Prints On White, Early 1900s, 70 x 84 In. 495.00
Patchwork, Stars, Suns & Rising Suns, Calico, Floral Print, 101 x 101 In. 2310.00
Patchwork, Triangular Medallions, Blue & Gray Print, Plaid Flannel Back, 72 x 80 In. 245.00
Patchwork, Tulip, Le Moyne Star Border, Red, Green, Orange, Cotton, 80 x 80 In. 488.00
Patchwork, Wedding Ring, Multicolored Prints, Scalloped Border, 80 x 92 In. 330.00
Patchwork & Appliqued, Triangles, Bird & Tree Border, Ohio, 82 x 97 In. 520.00
Puffed Pennies, Cotton, 22 Squares, No Backing, 66 x 107 In. 165.00
Trapunto, Floral, Basket Center, Handmade Fringe, 84 x 86 In. 302.00
Trapunto, Floral, Woven Fringe, 82 x 86 In. 2530.00
Trapunto, Pinwheel Flower Medallion, Stylized Floral, 88 x 88 In. 962.00
Trapunto, Silk, Rose, Scalloped, New England, 19th Century, 78 x 63 In. 250.00

QUIMPER pottery has a long history. Tin-glazed, hand-painted pottery has been made in Quimper, France, since the late seventeenth century. The earliest firm, founded in 1685 by Jean Baptiste Bousquet, was known as HB Quimper. Another firm, founded in 1772 by Francois Eloury, was known as Porquier. The third firm, founded by Guillaume Dumaine in 1778, was known as HR or Henriot Quimper. All three firms made similar pottery decorated with designs of Breton peasants and sea and flower motifs. The Eloury (Porquier) and Dumaine (Henriot) firms merged in 1913. Bousquet (HB) merged with the others in 1968. The group was sold to a United States family in 1984. The American holding company is Quimper Faience Inc., located in Stonington, Connecticut. The French firm has been called Societe Nouvelle des Faienceries de Quimper HB Henriot since March 1984.

HR.
Quimper

Bookends, Figural, Frenchman Sitting, Making Basket, 6 In., Pair 190.00
Bowl, 2 Men With Bagpipes, Almond Shape, Marked, 14 In. 550.00

Bowl, Cloth Bag With Drawstring Shape, Woman, H.R. Quimper, 5 1/2 In. 385.00
Bowl, Figure Of Woman, Scalloped & Fluted, 10 3/4 In. 170.00
Bowl, Mush, Figure Of Woman, 6 In. 110.00
Bowl, Peasants, Yellow & Blue Bands, Flat Tab Handle, 5 1/4 In., 6 Piece 135.00
Bowl, Pipe Playing Figure, Scrolled Foliage Border, Handles, 13 7/8 In. 518.00
Bowl, Swan Shape, Signed, 7 In., Pair 77.00
Butter, Man & Woman, Floral, H.B., 7 1/2 In. 110.00
Candlestick, Horse, Yellow, Pair 239.00
Charger, Bird In Nest, Flowers, Orange Sponged Rim, Crazing, H. Quimper, 12 3/8 In. . . . 190.00
Coffeepot, 6 Sides, Peasant Woman With Bouquet, Flowers, Crosshatching, 9 In. 90.00
Cup & Saucer, Trefoil, Henriot, Pair 200.00
Dish, Cover, Hat Shape, Man, Seated, Henriot Quimper, 5 3/4 In. 190.00
Egg Holder, With 6 Eggcups, Swan Shape, Restored, 1885-1890, 16 In. 910.00
Figurine, Dancing Couple, Signed, c.1930, 9 x 7 In. 595.00
Figurine, Goose, De La Hubaudiere Faiencerie, 1885, 8 In. 960.00
Figurine, Man, With Bagpipe, Yann, H. Quimper, 3 3/4 In. 330.00
Inkwell, Cover, Flowers & Boy, Insert, Henriot Quimper, 3 3/4 x 3 3/4 In. 275.00
Jardiniere, Duck, 1940s, 7 1/4 In., Pair 550.00
Jug, Cider, Orange Sponged Handles & Spout 325.00
Pitcher, Modern Movement, Artist, 1930, 8 1/2 In. 185.00
Pitcher, Woman, Henriot Quimper, 7 5/8 In. 165.00
Planter, Swan, With Lady, Henriot Quimper, 1935, 7 x 8 x 3 1/2 In. 495.00
Plate, Breton Peasant, 6 In. 62.00
Plate, Breton Woman, 9 1/8 In. 375.00
Plate, Convolvulus With Insect, Botanique Series, Marked, 9 1/4 In. 880.00
Plate, Different Occupation Scene, Porquier-Beau Mark, 9 3/8 In., 4 Piece 990.00
Plate, Scenes De Bretonnes, Porquier-Beau, 1875-1880, 9 1/4 In. 1245.00
Plate, Woman, Headdress, 8 1/2 In. 82.00
Platter, 3 Young Bretons, Native Dress, 17 3/8 In. 3600.00
Platter, Floral, Oval, c.1930, 16 x 11 In. 495.00
Platter, Malicorne, Tavern Scene, PBX Mark, 1890, 20 In. 2390.00
Porringer, Peasant, Blue Pantaloons, Green Jacket, Blue Handles, Signed, 5 3/4 In. 95.00
Snuff Bottle, Floral Shape, Breton With Stick On Reverse, HR, 1890, 3 1/2 In. 335.00
Snuff Bottle, Pocketwatch Shape, 3 1/4 In. 440.00
Tea Set, 6 Sides, Pink Flowers, Crosshatching, 5 3/4-In. Teapot, 4 Piece 112.00
Tureen, Cover, Pink, 9 3/4 In. 77.00
Vase, Odetta, Marked, 1920s, 12 1/2 In. 1160.00
Vase, Woman & Man, Tassel Shaped Handles, c.1925, 8 1/2 In., Pair 1250.00
Wall Pocket, Bagpipe Shape, Quimper & Odet River, Marked, 1895, 17 1/4 In., Pair 3960.00
Wall Pocket, Breton Man, 1930s, 9 1/4 In. 210.00
Wine Set, Oval Barrel, 6 Cups, Wooden Stand, Peasant Man, Flowers, 8 Pieces 123.00

RADFORD pottery was made by Alfred Radford in Broadway, Virginia, Tiffin and Zanesville, Ohio, and Clarksburg, West Virginia, from 1891 until 1912. Jasperware, Ruko, Thera, Radura, and Velvety Art Ware were made. The jasperware resembles the famous Wedgwood ware of the same name.

RADURA.

Umbrella Stand, Spray Of Yellow, Red Tulips, Green, Brown Ground, 23 In. 517.00
Vase, Floral, White Matte Glaze, Red & Yellow Flowers, 9 In. 75.00

RADIO broadcast receiving sets were first sold in New York City in 1910. They were used to pick up the experimental broadcasts of the day. The first commercial radios were made by Westinghouse Company for listeners of the experimental shows on KDKA Pittsburgh in 1920. Collectors today are interested in all early radios, especially those made of Bakelite plastic or decorated with blue mirrors. Figural advertising radios and transistor radios are also collected.

A-C Dayton, Model XL-20, Battery Operated, 3-Dial Panel, Lift Top, 1926 . . . . 120.00
A-C Dayton, Model XL-25, Battery Operated, 5 Tubes, 2-Dial Panel, Wooden Case, 1926 . 110.00
Advertising, Dr Pepper, Cooler, Wooden, White Paint, 1940, 7 In. 990.00
Advertising, Raisin Man, AM, Plastic, Bendable Arms, Legs, Chinese, 1988, 7 In. 40.00
Advertising, Tropicana Pure Premium Orange, Plastic, AM-FM, 2 AA Batteries, 1980s . . . 28.00
Arvin, Model 62R48, Transistor, AM, Black Leather, Metal Trim, 1962, 6 1/4 x 3 In. 27.00

Radio, Emerson,
Model BT-245,
Louvered
Tombstone, Blue,
Catalin, 1938, 10 In.

Radio, Garod, Model 126, 3 Ring, Maroon
Body, Yellow Grille, Catalin, 1940, 8 In.

Atwater Kent, Model 10A, Battery Operated, Breadboard Mounted, 1923 . . . .   900.00
Atwater Kent, Model 20, Big Box, Battery Operated, 1924, Table Model 80.00
Atwater Kent, Model 40, Metal, Lift-Off Top, 1928, Table Model 60.00
Atwater Kent, Model 60, Kiel Table Model, 1929 . . . .   375.00
Automatic Radio, Model TT 600, Tom Thumb, Transistor, Red Case, 1955 . . . .   210.00
Bulova, Model 290, Transistor, White Plastic, Box, 1958, 2 x 3 x 5 In. 66.00
Catalin Sentinel, Model 248NI, Yellow Body, Amber Grill, 1940s, Table Model 1280.00
Character Doll, General Electric, Drum Major, Jointed Arms & Legs, 1930s, 19 In. 1150.00
Clarion, Model AC-85, Cathedral, AC Powered, Wooden Base 475.00
Crosley, Model 10-138, Plastic, AC/DC Power, 1950, Table Model 120.00
Crystal, Baby Grand, 1925, 2 x 4 In. 475.00
Crystal, Champion, Wooden Case, 1924 . . . .   150.00
Doll, RCA, Jointed Arms & Legs, Wooden, Radio-Tube Hat, 1930, 16 In. 1210.00
Emerson, Model BT-245, Louvered Tombstone, Blue, Catalin, 1938, 10 In. . . . . *Illus*   6600.00
Emerson, Patriot, Red, White & Blue, Bakelite, 1940, Table Model 1320.00
Fada, Catalin, Model 652, Temple, Broadcast Channels, AC/DC, 1946, Table Model 500.00
Fada, Catalin, Model 1000, Bullet, Bakelite, Red & Orange, 1946, Table Model 1400.00
Freed-Eisemann, Model NR-5, Mahogany, 5 Tubes, 1923, Table 75.00
Garod, Model 126, 3 Ring, Maroon Body, Yellow Grille, Catalin, 1940, 8 In. . . . . . . *Illus* 11000.00
Garod, Model RAF, Battery Operated, 5 Tubes, Mahogany, 1923, Table Model 200.00
General Electric, Model 400, AM, Bakelite, Brown, Table Model 25.00
General Electric, Model A63, Tombstone, Walnut Veneer, Art Deco, 1935 . . . .   105.00
General Electric, Model H600, AM, Bakelite, Brown, Table Model 45.00
General Electric, Model H621, 6 Tubes, Bakelite, 1939, Table Model 60.00
Greenville Piano Co., Decal, Wooden, Original Finish, 1924 . . . .   60.00
Headset, Ear Phone, Microphone On/Off Switch, Leatherette Case, Gem Earphone Co. . .   22.00
Kennedy, Model V, Battery Operated, 3 Exposed Tubes, 1923, Table Model 270.00
Kolster Marshall, No. 5, Battery Powered, Built-In Speaker, 1925 . . . .   300.00
Majestic, Model 130, Portable, Battery Powered, Red Leatherette Cover, 1939 . . . .   160.00
Melco Supreme, Battery Powered, 1920s 250.00
Motorola, Model 51X, Yellow Body, Green Grille, Catalin, 1941, 7 In. . . . . *Illus*   4125.00
Nurse, Zenith, Metal Guardian Ear, Isamu Moguchi, c.1937, 8 1/8 In. 2530.00

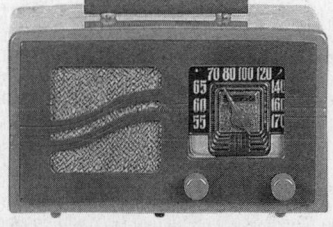

Radio, Motorola, Model 51X, Yellow Body,
Green Grille, Catalin, 1941, 7 In.

**Restoring and reusing old things is
the purest form of recycling.**

Philco, Model 38-3, Console, Cloth Grill, Dial, Standard & Shortwave, 1938 .... 65.00
Philco, Model 71, Cathedral, 2-Tone Wooden Case, 1932 .... 300.00
Philco, Model 80, Junior Cathedral, 2-Tone Wood, 1933 .... 100.00
Philco, Model 90, Console, Lowboy, 2 Doors, 1931 .... 375.00
Philmore, Model 2001, Crystal, Original Box 70.00
Radiola, Electrola, Radio & Phonograph, Legs, 1929 .... 100.00
RCA Victor, Model R-32, Victor Lowboy, Console, 1929 .... 85.00
Sparton, Junior Model 410, Window Dial, Cutout Grill, Arched Top, 1930, Table Model . 270.00
Splitdorf, Model RV-695, 6 Tubes, Battery Powered, 2-Tone Wooden Case 125.00
Tele-Tone, Model 100, Slide Rule Dial, 5 Tubes, 1946, Table Model 10.00
Transistor, Atlantic Model, Black Vinyl Cover, Strap, White Plastic Case, Earphone 20.00
Transistor, Portable, Black Plastic, Screen Front, Brass Stand, Viscount 7, 2 1/4 x 4 In. .. 20.00
Transistor, Portable, Brown Leather Case, Handle, Airline 10, 4 x 7 x 11 In. 21.00
Tube, Arcturus 30, Blue 20.00
Tube, DeForest 20, Open Fil 5.00
Tube, Moorehead, Brass Base Tipped, Open 15.00
Tube, WE, 101M, Box 70.00
Westinghouse, Aeriola Senior, Battery Operated, 1 Exposed Tube, 1922 .... 180.00
Westinghouse, Art Deco, Clock, Pedestal, Wired Remote Control, 1932 .... 374.00
Westinghouse, Model H-126, Little Jewel, Portable, Ivory, 1945 .... 90.00
Westinghouse, Model H-902P6GPA, Transistor, Plastic, Blue, Leather Case, 1965 ...... 25.00
Zenith, Model 5-S-119, Broadcast & Short Wave Bands, 5 Tubes, Wooden Case, 1936 ... 190.00
Zenith, Model 7-5-449, Chairside, Wood, Broadcast & Short Wave Bands, 1939 .... 165.00
Zenith, Model G-500, Transoceanic .... 32.00 to 55.00

RAILROAD enthusiasts collect any train memorabilia. Everything is wanted, from oilcans to whole train cars. The Chessie system has a store that sells many reproductions of their old dinnerware and uniforms.

Bell, Horse-Drawn Streetcar, Bushwick Railroad, Brass, Iron Clapper 350.00
Bell, MPRR, Cast Metal, 7 1/4 In. 525.00
Bench, Station, Oak 585.00
Blanket, Salmon Wool, Pullman Co., Size 58 x 86 In. 65.00
Book, Maintenance Manual, Model 567A Engines, GM Electro-Motive Division, 1944 ... 22.00
Book, Official Guide Of Railways & Steam Navigation Lines, 1942, 1504 Pages 30.00
Book, One Hundred Years Of American Railroading, Photos, 1929, 336 Pages 68.00
Bottle Opener, B & O Railroad, 3 3/8 x 1 1/2 In. 23.00
Brochure, North Pacific Dude Ranch Vacations, 1952 .... 20.00
Card, Playing, Chicago & North Western Railway, Yellow, Green Diesel Engine 35.00
Coat, Engineer, Striped Denim, Grand Trunk Railroad, Long 225.00
Dish, Ice Cream, Shell Shape, Santa Fe, California Poppy 125.00
Express Box, Ticket Agent's, Gray, Green, Carry Handle, Clasp, Wood, 12 x 9 x 9 In. 50.00
Headlight, Frisco Railroad, Metal Mount, Lighted Numbers On Side 1400.00
Jacket, Conway Scenic Railroad, Sanforized, Lee, Man's, Size 40 .... 225.00
Lamp, Drawbridge, New Haven, Middletown & Willimantic RR 1150.00
Lantern, BR Railroad, Red Glass Globe, Black Toned Metal, Bail Handle, 9 In. 61.00
Lantern, BR Railroad, Red Glass Globe, Gray Toned Metal, Bail Handle, 10 In. 67.00
Lantern, Burlington Route, Red Glass Globe, Wire Ring Base, Bail Handle, 10 1/2 In. ... 75.00
Lantern, Chicago, Milwaukee & St. Paul Railway, Glass Globe, Wire Ring Base, 11 In. .. 75.00
Lantern, Concord Railroad, Red Globe, 11 1/4 In. 635.00
Lantern, Dietz, Ideal Inspector Lamp, 11 1/2 In. 100.00
Lantern, E.A. Haynes, Dane Westlake & Co., Nickel, 1865 .... 750.00
Lantern, Missouri Pacific, Glass Globe, Bell-Shaped Base, Bail Handle, 11 In. 65.00
Lantern, New York Central System, Adlake, Red Globe 65.00
Lantern, NYLE & WRR, Embossed Globe, 5 3/8 In. .... 475.00 to 495.00
Lantern, NYNH & H, Dietz Vesta, Kerosene, Tin Plated, Bail Handle, 11 In. 43.00
Lantern, NYO & W, Dietz Vesta, Clear, 11 In. 150.00
Lantern, P & LERR, Dietz, Steel Framed, Handle, 1904, 7 x 11 In. 65.00
Lantern, Penna., Presentation, F.A. Denning, Ring Handle, May 7, 1855, 12 1/2 In. 7040.00
Lantern, Pennsylvania, Presentation 6400.00
Lantern, PRR, Keystone, Red Etched 135.00
Lantern, Pullman Co., Iron Name Plate, Bail Wire Hanger, 10 In. 150.00

Lantern, Star Headlight & Lantern Company 165.00
Lantern, Switchman, Great Northern Railway, Clear Globe, 5 3/8 In. ....175.00 to 200.00
Lantern, Union Pacific, Adlake Kero, Red Glass Globe, Wire Ring Base, 9 1/2 In. 38.00
Level, Pennsylvania Railroad 500.00
Lock, Switch, Chain, Key, Union Pacific Railroad, Brass, 4 In. 100.00
Lock, Switch, Rock Island, Pat Date 1915, 1936 .... 22.00
Menu, City Of Denver, Union Pacific 15.00
Oil Can, New York, New Haven & Hartford, Galvanized Metal, 9 1/2 In. 26.00
Padlock & Key, Santa Fe, Brass Key, Steel Adlake, 3 1/2 In. 45.00
Padlock & Key, Santa Fe, Steel, AT & SF RY, Fraim, 3 In. 40.00
Paper Roll Holder, Union Pacific Railroad, 6 In. 75.00
Paperweight, Railroad Spike, U.S. Steel 35.00
Pin, Brotherhood Of Locomotive Firemen & Engineers, 40 Years Membership, 1/2 In. ... 23.00
Pin, Lapel, Brotherhood Of Locomotive Engineers, Steam Engine, 1900s, 1 In. 36.00
Pin, Lapel, Missouri Pacific, Red & Black Enamel, Round, 1/2 In. 25.00
Pin, Oregon Short Line, Safety First, Union Pacific Shield, Whitehead & Hoag, 1 In. 38.00
Pin, Western Maryland Railways Co., Safety Record, Green & White, 3/4 In. 27.00
Plate, Child's, Union Pacific Railroad, Clown, 8 In. 140.00
Plate, Salad, Western Pacific Railroad 95.00
Relish, Canadian National RR, Hotel Vancouver, Royal Doulton 150.00
Shirt, Boston & Main RR, Serge, Olive Drab, Long Sleeves, Brass Buttons, Large 55.00
Sign, Boston & Maine Railroad, Reverse Painted 165.00
Signal, NYLE & WRR, Red Cast Globe 475.00
Step Box, Pullman 300.00
Stepstool, Canadian National Railroad, Stenciled Metal, Rubber Top, 10 1/2 In. 110.00
Stock Certificate, Cape Cod Central RR Co., Handkerchief, 1861, 6 3/4 x 9 3/4 In. 44.00
Stock Certificate, New York Central Railroad Co., 100 Shares, Redeemed, 1967 .... 27.00
Stock Certificate, Pennsylvania Railroad Co., 100 Shares, 1955 .... 27.00

RAZORS were used in ancient Egypt and subsequently wherever shaving was in fashion. The metal razor used in America until about 1870 was made in Sheffield, England. After 1870, machine-made hollow-ground razors were made in Germany or America. Plastic or bone handles were popular. The razor was often sold in a set of seven, one for each day of the week. The set was often kept by the barber who shaved the well-to-do man each day in the shop.

Acme, Straight, Engraved Blade 80.00
Freidmann & Lautrijung's Electric Razor, Vogel Bros., Pre-1901, Tin, 6 1/2 In. 33.00
Gillette, Gold Tech, Box 20.00
Gillette, Short Handle, Velvet Box 24.00
Gillette, With Case 35.00
Straight, Strop, White Celluloid Handle, Wade & Butcher Corp. 28.00
Weller Tree, Straight, Box, 2 Pieces 33.00
Wilkinson, Empire Model, 7 Day Set, By Appointment To Late King George V, Box 65.00
Yale Safety Razor, Double Edge, Blade Sharpening Holder, Black Leatherette Case 20.00

REAMERS, or juice squeezers, have been known since 1767, although most of those collected today date from the twentieth century. Figural reamers are among the most prized.

Cambridge, Green 200.00
Crisscross, Blue ....300.00 to 375.00
Crisscross, Pink ....275.00 to 325.00
Duck, Small 75.00
Erie, Cast Iron 110.00
Fenton, Black, 2 Pieces 1700.00
Fleur-De-Lis, Red 750.00
Fleur-De-Lis, Yellow, Orange 650.00
Fry, Amber 375.00
Fry, Emerald Green, Ruffled 650.00
Hazel Atlas, 2-Cup Pitcher Set, Yellow 475.00
Jadite, Grapefruit 400.00
Jeannette, Blue 125.00

Jeannette, Delphite ....80.00 to 125.00
Jeannette, Pink 175.00
McBeth-Evans 185.00
Saunders, Black 2500.00
Stover Mfg. Co., Cast Iron 50.00
Sunkist, Black ....600.00 to 800.00
Sunkist, Caramel 375.00
Sunkist, Crown Tuscan 375.00
Sunkist, Custard 65.00
Sunkist, Jadite 95.00
Sunkist, Opalescent 200.00
Sunkist, Opalescent White 45.00
Sunkist, White 38.00
Valencia, Green 225.00
Wagner Ware, Aluminum 70.00

RECORDS have changed size and shape through the years. The cylinder-shaped phonograph record for use with the early Edison models was made about 1889. Disc records were first made by 1894, the double-sided disc by 1904. High-fidelity records were first issued in 1944, the first vinyl disc in 1946, the first stereo record in 1958. The 78 RPM became the standard in 1926 but was discontinued in 1957. In 1932, the first 33 1/3 RPM was made but was not sold commercially until 1948. In 1949, the 45 RPM was introduced. Compact discs became available in the U.S. in 1982 and many companies began phasing out the production of phonograph records.

Album, Forbidden Planet, Image Of Robby The Robot, 33 RPM, 1970s 65.00
Album, More Of The Monkees, 1966 .... 21.00
Album, Oklahoma, 6 Records, Decca, 78 RPM, 1943 .... 20.00
Album, The Archies, 33 RPM, 1968 .... 15.00
Bee Gees, Idea, Atco, LP 26.00
Charlie Daniels, American Farmer, Epic, 45 RPM, 1980s 2.00
Chevrolet, SS 396, Camaro, Columbia Special Products, 45 RPM 22.00
Diana Ross, All The Great Hits, Motown, 33 RPM 6.00
Frank Sinatra, It Was A Very Good Year, Autographed, Reprise, 33 RPM, 1965 .... 675.00
Jimmy Dean, Big Bad John, One Hell Of A Man Version, Columbia, 1961 .... 20.00
Johnny Mathis, Right From The Heart, Columbia, 45 RPM, 1980s 2.00
Marvin Gaye, It's Madness, Columbia, 45 RPM, 1980s 2.00
Planet Of The Apes, 4 Stories, Power Records, LP 32.00
Ricky Nelson, Songs By Ricky, EP, Imperial Records, 1960s 46.00
Righteous Brothers, Go Ahead & Cry, Verve, 33 RPM 6.00
Smothers Brothers, It Must Have Been Something I Said, Mercury Records, 1960s 35.00
Teddy Pendergrass, Somewhere I Belong, Asylum, 45 RPM, 1985 .... 2.00
Washboard Trio, Washboard Rag, Paramount, 78 RPM 150.00

RED WING Pottery of Red Wing, Minnesota, was a firm started in 1878. The company first made utilitarian pottery. In the 1920s art pottery was made. Many dinner sets and vases were made before the company closed in 1967. Rumrill pottery was made for George Rumrill by the Red Wing Pottery and other firms. It was sold in the 1930s. For more information, see *Kovels' Depression Glass & Dinnerware Price List.*

Advertising, Beater Jar, Blue & White, Kiln Line Interior 175.00
Advertising, Pitcher, N. Frudden & Son, Lumbermen Since 1889, Saffron, 6 1/2 In. 100.00
Art Pottery, Figurine, Gopher On Football 200.00
Bob White, Bread Tray, 24 In. 115.00
Bob White, Butter, Cover 75.00
Bob White, Hors D'Oeuvre, Bird 65.00
Bob White, Sugar, Notched Cover, 5 1/2 In. ....*Illus* .. 22.00
Cherry Band, Pitcher, Advertising, Pour Spout 170.00
Churn, White Glaze, Red & Blue Screened Label, 3 Wing, 14 In. 135.00
Cookie Jar, Katrina, Dutch Girl, Blue ....75.00 to 95.00
Cookie Jar, Katrina, Dutch Girl, Yellow 135.00
Cookie Jar, King Of Tarts, Multicolored 1150.00

You might be able to remove the warp from a 78 RPM record. Put it between two pieces of glass in a sunny window for a day. Let it cool. This should straighten the record.

Red Wing, Bob White, Sugar, Notched Cover, 5 1/2 In.

Cookie Jar, Pierre, Chef	135.00
Gourd, Salt & Pepper, Rum Rill	125.00
Lamp, Handle, Mustard Yellow, 2 Pull Ribbon, 23 1/2 In.	225.00
Lions, Vase, Beige, Green Mottled Glaze, 7 1/2 In.	305.00
Midnight Rose, Platter, 13 In.	25.00
Minnesota Centennial, Trivet, 1858-1958, Yellow & Brown	75.00
Morning Glory, Plate, Handle, 5 In.	10.00
Random Harvest, Cup & Saucer	6.00
Random Harvest, Plate, 6 3/4 In.	5.50
Random Harvest, Plate, 8 1/2 In.	8.00
Random Harvest, Plate, 10 3/4 In.	12.00
Random Harvest, Soup, Dish	10.00
Random Harvest, Vegetable, Oval	22.00
Scroll, Butter, Blue & Yellow, With Bail, No. 1	300.00
Shoe Shape, Planter, Celadon Glaze Exterior, Pair	110.00
Spongeware, Bowl, 6 In.	120.00
Stoneware, Churn, Bail Handles, Dasher, Cover, 18 In., 6 Gal.	140.00
Stoneware, Crock, Bread, Sheaves Of Wheat	1950.00
Stoneware, Crock, Large Wing, 1 Gal.	175.00
Stoneware, Jug, Old Rose, Blue & White, 1/2 Gal.	110.00
Stoneware, Jug, Winged, Beehive, 5 Gal.	350.00
Town & County, Creamer, Metallic Brown	25.00
Town & County, Marmite, Rust	45.00
Town & County, Relish, Metallic Brown, 9 In.	25.00
Town & County, Salt & Pepper, Shmoo, Zeisel	115.00
Vase, Green, Brown Matte Mottle Glaze, Bulbous, 8 1/2 In.	138.00

REDWARE is a hard, red stoneware that originated in the late 1600s and continues to be made. The term is also used to describe any common clay pottery that is reddish in color.

Bank, Clock Form, White Face, Raised Handles, 4 1/4 In.	2650.00
Bank, Jug Shape, Manganese Slip, Egg Shape, Penna., 1840, 6 In.	935.00
Bank, Pear Form, Bird, Yellow & Brown Swirl Glaze, Slip Date, 1880, 9 In.	375.00
Basket, Green Splotches, 9 1/2 In.	305.00
Bedpan, Orange Glaze, Black Manganese Splotches, 13 1/2 In.	70.00
Bowl, Black Glaze, Flared Lip, 11 1/2 x 4 3/4 In.	185.00
Bowl, Black Manganese Striping, Slip Squiggle Border, Pa., 2 1/2 x 8 1/2 In.	650.00
Bowl, Daisy Design, 1975, 14 x 10 In.	70.00
Bowl, Incised Band, Orange Brown Glaze, Dark Brown Manganese, 3 x 6 In.	345.00
Bowl, Manganese Splotches, Solomon Miller, Oct. 22, 1879, 5 1/2 x 3 1/8 In.	3525.00
Bowl, Milk, Stripe On Rim, 5 1/4 x 11 7/8 In.	50.00
Bowl, Orange Glazed, 19th Century, 3 7/8 In.	355.00
Bowl, Raised Floral Design, 14 In.	175.00
Bowl, Rim Handles, Pouring Spout, 2-Tone Glaze, 6 1/2 x 9 3/4 In.	50.00
Bowl, Yellow Slip Chicken, Jugtown Ware, 13 In.	165.00
Bowl, Yellow Slip Design, 3 x 14 In.	295.00
Charger, 2 Men On Horseback, Sgraffito, Yellow Ground, Breininger, 1972, 12 3/4 In.	135.00

Charger, Flowers, German Verse, Signed Verso, Breininger Pottery, 17 1/4 In. 385.00
Charger, Overall Orange Glazing, Trailing Slip, Early 19th Century, 14 3/4 In. 2525.00
Charger, Stylized Floral, Sgraffito Inscription, Yellow, Breininger, 1980, 20 In. 245.00
Charger, Tulip Design, No. 1, Octagonal, 1977 . . . . 95.00
Colander, 2 Parts, Brown Mottled Glaze, 2 Handles, 4 1/2 x 11 1/4 In. 375.00
Colander, Brown Glaze, Black Streaks, 2 Handles, Pierced Base, 10 1/4 x 2 1/2 In. 165.00
Crock, Black Underglaze Brush Stroke, 11 In. 165.00
Crock, Incised Line, Black Underglaze Design, Egg Shape, 11 In. 310.00
Crock, John Bell, Waynesboro, Manganese Flower, Applied Handles, 13 In. 880.00
Crock, Oval, Loop Handles, 19th Century, 9 1/4 In. 99.00
Crock, Ring Incised Design, Manganese Splotches, 2 Handles, 19th Century, 10 In. 165.00
Cup, Manganese Splotches, York Co., Pa., 3 x 4 In. 165.00
Cup & Saucer 225.00
Dish, Green Slip Floral Design, 19th Century, 3 3/4 In. 345.00
Dish, Loaf, 4-Line Yellow Slip, Coggled Rim, 17 1/2 In. 440.00
Dish, Loaf, Green Slip Design, Vertical Bands, Orange, Brown Ground, 10 1/2 In. 7475.00
Dish, Slip Design, Rectangular, 19th Century, 14 1/2 x 9 3/4 In. 450.00
Dish, Stylized Bird Within A Compass, Brown, Green, White Slip Design, 15 In. 6325.00
Dish, Stylized Yellow, Green Plumes, Dots, Green Pinwheel Slip Design, 10 In. 6900.00
Dish, Tulip Blossoms, Yellow Buds, Green Slip, Orange Brown Ground, 9 In. 18400.00
Dish, Tulips, Sgrafitto & Slip Design, 1800, 13 In. 3300.00
Dish, White Slip Design, Dark Brown Glaze, 14 1/2 x 11 x 2 1/2 In. 220.00
Dish, Yellow Slip, Sgraffito Flowers, Green Splotches, Scalloped Edge, 1979, 11 In. 40.00
Dish, Yellow, Glaze, Green, Orange Slip Design, Tulip Tree Sgraffito Design, 13 3/8 In. . . . 6050.00
Eggcup, Black Sponging, 3 In. 470.00
Eggcup, Shenandoah, White Slip, Green Pebble Glaze, 3 In. 495.00
Figurine, Bear, Standing On 4 Legs, Red, Brown Glaze, 3 1/2 x 7 1/4 In. 2000.00
Figurine, Cat, Seated, Streaked Glaze, 19th Century, 5 3/4 In. 200.00
Figurine, Frog, Green, 8 In. 55.00
Figurine, Hen, Sitting, France, 20 In. 295.00
Figurine, Lion, Peach, Brown Glaze, 7 In. 250.00
Figurine, Lion, Spaghetti Mane, Yellow Slip, 1982, 9 1/4 In. 495.00
Figurine, Owl, Perched, 1 3/4 In. 30.00
Figurine, Rooster, France, 27 In. 350.00
Flask, Orange, Brown Slip Glaze, Round, Pocket, 1847, 5 1/2 In. 4300.00
Flowerpot, Attached Saucer, 3-Line Brown Slip, 7 In. 165.00
Flowerpot, Attached Saucer, Tooled Lines, Mottled Orange, Cream & Brown, 5 In. 360.00
Flowerpot, Coggled Line, Cylindrical, Allover White & Green Glazed, 1820, 6 3/4 In. 775.00
Flowerpot, Orange Glaze, Black Manganese Design, Pa. 220.00
Flowerpot, Yellow Slip, 1864 & Wavy Lines, Impressed Mark, H. Brooks, 5 x 5 3/8 In. . . . 1265.00
Jar, Applied Grape & Leaf, Brown Glaze, J.S. Stahl, Aug. 27, 1947, 6 7/8 In. 550.00
Jar, Dark Glaze, Oval, John Bell, Waynesboro, 7 1/2 In. 275.00
Jar, Domed Cover, Orange, Brown, Yellow Glaze, Manganese Zigzags, 1830, 13 In. 2300.00
Jar, Green Glaze, Orange Spots, Strap Handle, 8 3/4 In. 220.00
Jar, Light Brown Glaze, Dark Brown Slip, 8 1/2 In. 345.00
Jar, Storage, Cover, Black Brush Stroke Underglaze Design, 10 In. 175.00
Jar, Storage, Glossy Orange, Brown, Red Glaze, Black, Brown Highlights, 7 1/2 In. 65.00
Jar, Tooled Ribs, Shoulder Handles, Egg Shape, 8 1/2 In. 100.00
Jar, White Slip, Amber, Brown, Green, Applied Shoulder Handles, 7 3/4 In. 660.00
Jar, Yellow Slip Glaze, Dark Brown, Dark Green, Cylindrical, 7 1/4 In. 575.00
Jar, Yellow Slip, Brown Glaze Design, 2 Strap Handles, 7 In. 200.00
Jug, Amber & Brown Spots, Brown & Green Glaze, Strap Handle, 9 1/4 In. 600.00
Jug, Applied Top Handle With Spout & Airhole, 10 1/2 In. 140.00
Jug, Brown Flecks On Metallic Amber Ground, Egg Shape, 7 1/4 In. 192.00
Jug, Brown, Green Glaze, 6 In. 880.00
Jug, Brown, Green Glaze, 9 1/2 In. 2310.00
Jug, Deep Olive Green Glaze, Dots Of Orange, Dark Brown, Angular, 9 In. 515.00
Jug, Face, Stylized Head Of Man, Jug Ears, Open Mouth, Dark Brown Glaze, 6 In. 1380.00
Jug, Grotesque Face, Allover Brown Glaze, Blue Slip Design, W.A. Flowers, 8 In. 200.00
Jug, Grotesque Face, Nose & Cigar, Olive Amber Glaze, 8 In. 165.00
Jug, Grotesque, Black Glaze, Georgia, 6 1/2 In. 440.00
Jug, Handle, Oval, Olive Green Glaze, Brown & Orange Mottled, 9 1/2 In. 700.00
Jug, Manganese Glaze, Applied Strap Handle & Pouring Spout, 9 In. 40.00

Jug, Manganese Splash Glaze, Handle, Mid 19th Century, 13 In. 70.00
Jug, Milk, Gray Green Glaze, Orange Mottling, 5 3/4 In. 1495.00
Jug, Orange, Green Glaze, 8 In. 250.00
Jug, Red, Brown Glaze, 7 In. 220.00
Jug, Yellow Glaze, Brown Spots, Curved Handle At Neck, Massachusetts, 10 In. 6050.00
Loaf Pan, Slip Design, Coggled Edge, Pa., 1830, 15 1/2 x 11 1/2 In. 2200.00
Loaf Pan, Slip Design, Pennsylvania 2200.00
Mug, Orange, Brown Slip Glaze, Dots & Linear Wavy Green, White Stripes, 5 In. 1265.00
Pan, White, Brown, Green Slip Design, Orange, Brown Ground, 3 x 13 In. 6900.00
Pie Plate, 3-Line Yellow Slip, Pa., 10 1/4 In. 440.00
Pie Plate, 3-Line Yellow Slip, Squiggles & Dot Design, 10 x 8 1/2 In. 495.00
Pie Plate, Bird, Tulip Tree Sgraffito Design, Pa., 8 3/4 In. 660.00
Pie Plate, Black Manganese Slip Design, Pa., 1887, 8 1/2 In. 385.00
Pie Plate, Coggled Rim, 4-Line Yellow Slip, 1-Line Wavy Brown Bands, 9 5/8 In. 440.00
Pie Plate, Coggled Rim, ABC Yellow Slip, Breininger, 1981, 10 1/2 In. 65.00
Pie Plate, Yellow Slip Design, Pa., 8 3/4 In. 660.00
Pie Plate, Yellow Slip Linear Comb Trailings, Orange, Brown Ground, 11 In. 4600.00
Pie Plate, Yellow, Black Slip Design, Pa., 7 3/4 In. 1045.00
Pie Plate, Yellow, Green Slip Tulip Design, Pa., 9 In. 3960.00
Pitcher, Brown Splotches & Flecks, Ribbed Strap Handle, 6 3/4 In. 220.00
Pitcher, Cover, Brown Mottled Glaze, Offset Handle, 5 1/4 In. 460.00
Pitcher, Dark Brown Glaze, Yellow, White, Black, Pulled Strap Handle, 5 In. 460.00
Pitcher, Hunting Scene, Stags & Hounds, Tree Limb Handle, Dark Brown, 1850, 8 In. 4025.00
Pitcher, Mask Form Spout, Signed, 19th Century, 8 In. 385.00
Pitcher, Milk, Manganese Splotching, York Co., Penna., 6 1/2 In. 685.00
Pitcher, Molded Lip, Strap Handle, Brown Splotches On Orange Ground, 11 In. 493.00
Pitcher, Orange, Brown Slip Glaze, Applied Strap Handle, Baluster, 7 In. 2875.00
Pitcher, Pitted Light Green Glaze, Applied Strap Handle, Baluster, 5 1/4 In. 5175.00
Pitcher, Tobacco Spit Glaze, Applied Handle, N.C., 11 1/2 In. 670.00
Pitcher, Tree Stump, Yellow, Orange, Brown Slip, Spurred Strap Handle, 7 In. 9200.00
Pitcher, Water, Black Underglaze Sponged, Strap Handle, 9 1/2 In. 165.00
Pitcher, Yellow Glaze, Dark Brown, Applied Strap Handle, 5 1/2 In. 2587.00
Plate, 4-Line Slip Design, Pa., Early 19th Century, 8 1/4 In. 660.00
Plate, Flower & Leaf, Cream & Green Line Borders, 18th Century, 17 3/4 In. 1760.00
Plate, Polychrome & Sgraffito, Crimped Edge, Green, Brown, Leaf & Berry, 11 1/2 In. .. 8625.00
Plate, Slip Design, 4 Stylized Leaves, Crimped Edge, 19th Century, 9 3/4 In. 490.00
Plate, Yellow Slip, 4-Line Squiggle Bands, Crisscrossing, 8 1/2 In. 230.00
Platter, Tooled Band, Marbleized, White Slip Interior, 8 1/8 In. 550.00
Platter, Zigzag & Yellow Serpentine Designs, Oval, 19th Century, 13 1/2 In. 517.00
Pot, Fitted Cover, Orange, Brown Glaze, Black, Yellow, Loop Handle, 7 In., 3 Piece 8050.00
Pot, Knife-Sharpening Rim, 8 1/2 In. 55.00
Roach Trap, Pennsylvania, 6 1/2 In. 135.00
Salt, Brown Glaze, Dated 1801 .... 495.00
Shaving Bowl, The Sun Inn, Sun On Bottom, 1977, 8 In. 35.00
Sugar, Cover, Rope Twist Handles, York Co., Pennsylvania 715.00
Teapot, Green Glaze, Orange Spots, 7 1/2 In. 385.00
Teapot, Whimsical Design, Cat's Head Finial, 7 In. 357.00
Tobacco Jar, No. 86, Inner Jar, Pierced Outer Jar, 1991 .... 95.00
Tray, Cutlery, Orange, Black Manganese Glaze, Heart Cutout Handle, Pa., 2 1/2 In. 660.00
Tray, Yellow Slip, 3 Bands, 3 Wavy Center Lines, Orange Red Glaze, 17 1/2 x 12 In. ... 313.00
Umbrella Stand, Tree Trunk Shape, Bird & Vine, Allover Ivory Glazed, 1890, 22 In. 1100.00
Urn, Cover, J.S. Stahl, Floral, Leaves, Brown, Green & Yellow Glaze, 2 Handles, 9 In. ... 1870.00
Vase, Cream, Yellow Slip Glaze, Dark Green, Brown, Elongated Neck, 8 1/2 In. 4600.00
Vase, Fan, Landscape, Fisherman, Branch Handles, Sponged Interior, F. Delgas, 6 1/2 In. .. 125.00
Vase, Yellow Sponge Decoration, 8 3/4 In. 220.00
Vase, Yellow, Brown Glaze, Variegated Green, Molded Lip, Baluster, 7 1/4 In. 3160.00
Vase, Yellow, Brown Green Glaze, Dark Brown Speckled Interior, 8 1/2 In. 3160.00
Wall Pocket, Incised Bird & Floral Design, Yellow, Green, Brown, 7 1/4 In. 3737.00
Whistle, Bird, 19th Century, 10 In. 330.00
Whistle, Bird, Brown, Yellow Glaze, 19th Century, 6 3/4 In. 357.00
Whistle, Vase Shape, Dark Brown Glaze, Unglazed Spout, 3 3/4 In. 490.00

REGOUT, see Maastricht category.

Ridgway, Plate, Cow Center,
Flow Blue, 4 Piece

Ridgway, Platter, Turkey, Flow Blue,
With 6 Plates, 7 Piece

RICHARD was the mark used on acid-etched cameo glass vases, bowls, night-lights, and lamps made by the Austrian company Loetz after 1918. The pieces were very similar to the other French cameo glasswares made by Daum, Galle, and others.

Richard

Vase, Building, Palm Trees, Yellow, Orange & Brown, Cameo, 14 In.	3025.00
Vase, Plant Design, Cameo, 6 3/4 In.	350.00
Vase, Ruins, Farm By Lake, Brown, Pink To Green, Etched Cameo, 8 1/4 x 4 1/2 In.	695.00
Vase, Stylized Flowers & Leaves, Blue, Tan, Cameo, Signed, 21 3/4 In.	2090.00

RIDGWAY pottery has been made in the Staffordshire district in England since 1808 by a series of companies with the name Ridgway. The transfer-design dinner sets are the most widely known product. They are still being made. Other pieces of Ridgway are listed under Flow Blue.

Bowl, Fantasia, Cobalt Blue, Red, Green, Gilt Veining, Handle, 1820, 5 3/4 x 10 In.	550.00
Creamer, Osborne	95.00
Cup & Saucer, Litchfield Pattern, Flow Blue	45.00
Dish, Gilt Urns On Border, Scrolling Leaves, 1840s, 11 1/8 In.	220.00
Pitcher, Dueling Knight Design, Salt Glaze, Mustard Yellow, 9 In.	155.00
Plate, Apple Blossom, Polychrome Transfer, 9 In., 8 Piece	415.00
Plate, City Hall New York, Blue, 9 7/8 In.	175.00
Plate, Cow Center, Flow Blue, 4 Piece ....*Illus*	350.00
Plate, Library, Philadelphia, Beauty Of America, 8 In.	285.00
Plate, Octagon Church, Boston, Blue & White, 10 In.	345.00
Plate, Turkey Center, Floral Border, Scalloped, Flow Blue, England, 10 In., Set Of 6	660.00
Platter, Oriental, Light Blue Transfer, 60 In.	88.00
Platter, Pennsylvania Hospital, Blue & White, 20 In.	4885.00
Platter, Pennsylvania, Hospital, Philadelphia, Blue, 18 3/4 In.	1210.00
Platter, St. Paul's Church, Boston, Hanley, 9 1/2 x 6 1/2 In.	865.00
Platter, Turkey, Flow Blue, With 6 Plates, 7 Piece ....*Illus*	475.00
Platter, Well & Tree, Blue & White, Ironstone, 19 1/4 In.	460.00
Platter, Well & Tree, Flow Blue, Simlay	625.00
Punch Bowl, Corey Hill, Flow Blue, Light Blue Glaze, 6 1/2 x 15 3/8 In.	420.00
Tureen, Vegetable, Cover, Josephine, Flow Blue, 12 In.	550.00

RIFLES that are firearms are not listed in this book. BB guns and air rifles are listed in the Toy category.

RIVIERA dinnerware was made by the Homer Laughlin Co. of Newell, West Virginia, from 1938 to 1950. The pattern was similar in coloring and in mood to Fiesta and Harlequin. The Riviera plates and cup handles were square. For more information, see *Kovels' Depression Glass & Dinnerware Price List.*

Dark Blue, Plate, 7 In.	75.00
Green, Butter, Cover, 1/4 Lb.	170.00
Green, Casserole, Cover	95.00
Green, Jug, Batter, Cover	80.00

Green, Salt & Pepper 12.00
Green, Teapot 185.00
Ivory, Bowl, Oatmeal, 6 In. 95.00
Ivory, Cup & Saucer, After Dinner 115.00
Ivory, Plate, Deep 45.00
Mauve, Bowl, Baker, Oval, 9 In. 12.00
Mauve, Casserole, Cover 110.00
Mauve, Platter, 13 1/4 In. 10.00
Mauve, Tumbler, Juice 30.00
Red, Butter, Cover, 1/2 Lb. 185.00
Red, Salt & Pepper 10.00
Red, Sugar & Creamer 10.00
Red, Sugar, Cover 13.00
Red, Syrup, Cover 200.00
Red, Tray, Tidbit, 2 Tiers 17.00
Yellow, Casserole, Cover 50.00
Yellow, Platter, 11 1/4 In. 12.00

ROBLIN Art Pottery was founded in 1898 by Alexander W. Robertson and Linna Irelan in San Francisco, California. The pottery closed in 1906. The firm made faience with green, tan, dull blue, or gray glazes. Decorations were usually animal shapes. Some red clay pieces were made.

Vase, Blue, Gray, Green Crackled Glaze, 4 1/2 x 3 In. 300.00
Vase, Redware, Embossed Shoulders, Incised J.D.P., 3 3/4 x 2 1/4 In. 305.00

ROCKINGHAM, in the United States, is a pottery with a brown glaze that resembles tortoiseshell. It was made from 1840 to 1900 by many American potteries. Mottled brown Rockingham wares were first made in England at the Rockingham factory. Other types of ceramics were also made by the English firm. Related pieces may be listed in the Bennington category.

Box, Toby, Cover, Dark Brown Glaze, 4 1/4 In. 260.00
Creamer, Cow, 7 x 5 1/4 In. 220.00
Cuspidor, Shell Shape, 8 1/4 x 3 3/4 In. 55.00
Doorstop, Dog, 11 In. 185.00
Figurine, Dog, Seated, 10 3/8 In. 357.00
Figurine, Lion, Rectangular Base, 9 1/4 In. 495.00
Flask, Book Shape, 5 1/2 x 7 3/4 In. 220.00
Flask, Camel, 4 3/4 In. 120.00
Flask, Standing Fish Shape, 9 In. 285.00
Inkwell, Dog Shape, Lying, 4 1/2 x 2 1/2 In. 440.00
Jug, Toby, Duke Of Wellington, Brown Mottled Glaze, 8 In. 195.00
Mug, Novelty, Frog In Base, Drippy Brown Over Blue & Green Glaze, 4 1/2 In. 105.00
Pitcher, Berries, 6 In. 175.00
Pitcher, Embossed Design, Glazed, c.1880, Large 325.00
Pitcher, Game Design, 7 1/2 In. 88.00
Pitcher, Game Design, 8 1/2 In. ....120.00 to 200.00
Pitcher, Gothic Design, 8 1/4 In. 100.00
Pitcher, Hunt Scene, Hanging Game, 9 In. 110.00
Pitcher, Raised Game Design, Hound Form Handle, 9 In. 120.00
Stirrup Cup, Dog, 1840, 5 In. 1000.00
Sugar, Scalloped Panels, 8 3/4 In. 93.00
Toby Jug, Duke Of Wellington, Born 1st May 1769, Died 1859, Thompson, 8 In. 190.00

ROGERS, see John Rogers category.

ROOKWOOD pottery was made in Cincinnati, Ohio, from 1880 to 1960. All of this art pottery is marked, most with the famous flame mark. The R is reversed and placed back to back with the letter P. Flames surround the letters. After 1900, a Roman numeral was added to the mark to indicate the year. The name and some of the molds were purchased in 1984. A few new pieces were made, but these were glazed in colors not used by the original company.

Ashtray, Blue, Huenfeld Co., Cincinnati, Oh., 1947 .... 57.00

Ashtray, Mauve High Glaze, Krueger & Hudepohl, Inc., Cincinnati, Oh., 1955, 4 In. 44.00
Ashtray, With Clown & Puppy, Sallie Toohey, 1930, 4 In. 495.00
Basket, Pink Matte Glaze, Incised Band At Rim, 1922, 6 In. 195.00
Bookends, Dog, Persian Red Glaze 55.00
Bookends, Elephant, Ivory Matte Glaze, 1920, 4 3/4 In. 230.00
Bookends, Flowering Branches & Rooks, Green Matte Mottled, 1924, 6 In. 1150.00
Bookends, Giraffe, Brown Matte Glaze, 1948, 4 3/4 In. 2090.00
Bookends, Horse Heads, Gunmetal Matte Glaze, 1927, 6 In. 715.00
Bookends, Jay, Oak Leaves, Cream Matte Glaze Acorns, 1929, 5 3/8 In. 316.00
Bookends, Kingfisher, Gray Matte Glaze, William P. McDonald, 5 1/2 In. 165.00
Bookends, Lady, Seated In Full Skirt With Fan, 1943, 7 In. 55.00
Bookends, Owl Standing On Book, Green Matte Glaze, W. McDonald, 5 In. 275.00
Bookends, Peacock, Yellow Matte Glaze, McDermott, 1918, 4 x 5 In. 275.00
Bookends, Rook, White Matte Glaze, W. McDonald, 1938, 5 x 5 1/4 In. 250.00
Bookends, Rooks With Berries, Green Crystalline Glaze, 1930, 5 1/4 In. 605.00
Bookends, Sailing Ships, Cream Matte Glaze, W. McDonald, 1943, 5 1/2 In. 200.00
Bookends, Saint Francis Kneeling With Fox & Bird, Brown, Gray, Black, 7 In. 300.00
Bookends, Ships Sailing, Umber, Charcoal Matte Glaze, McDonald, 5 In. 140.00
Bookends, Sleeping Girl, Turquoise Matte Glaze, 5 In. 231.00
Bookends, Woodpecker, Naturalistic Perch, c.1922, 5 1/2 In. 403.00
Bottle, Limoges Style, Butterflies, Albert Valentien, 1885, 17 1/2 In. 1540.00
Bottle, Orange Chrysanthemums, Black, Rose Ground, E. Lincoln, 1926, 16 x 7 In. 4125.00
Bowl, Berries, Orange, Green To Orange Ground, Standard Glaze, 1899, 6 In. 220.00
Bowl, Blackberries, Leaves, 3 Handles, Standard Glaze, Toohey, 4 In. 467.00
Bowl, Cherry Blossoms, Scalloped Rim, Sallie Toohey, 1888, 6 1/2 In. 357.00
Bowl, Clover, Standard Glaze, 3 Feet, M. Perkins, 1887, 9 In. 165.00
Bowl, Dogwood, Scalloped Rim, Mary Nourse, 1894, 6 1/2 In. 440.00
Bowl, Flowers, Brown Leaves, Tan Matte Glaze, William Hentschel, 1928, 9 In. 495.00
Bowl, Garland Of Green Tulips, Blue Leaves, William Hentschel, 1910, 3 x 5 In. 1000.00
Bowl, Green High Glaze Interior, Ivory Exterior, 1928, 7 In. 120.00
Bowl, Leaves, Molded, Pink Matte Glaze, 1917, 2 1/4 In. 55.00
Bowl, Lobed Form, Blue, Tan, Green, Gray High Glaze, 1932, 8 In. 165.00
Bowl, Orange High Glaze, 1954, 7 1/2 In. 66.00
Bowl, Stylized Flowers At Rim, Charles Todd, 1920, 9 In. 1045.00
Bowl, Stylized Flowers, Geometric Design, Wm. E. Hentschel, 1921, 6 In. 440.00
Bowl, Stylized Leaves, Molded, Green, Maroon Matte Glaze, 1921, 6 1/2 In. 240.00
Bowl, Water Bird, Limoges Glaze, Scalloped Rim, Martin Rettig, 1882, 6 In. 120.00
Box, Oriental Design, Turquoise High Glaze, 1955, 3 1/4 In. 175.00
Butter, Blue Ship, 6 1/2 In., 12 Piece 360.00
Candleholder, Apple Blossoms, Dark Brown Ground, Standard Glaze, 1890, 5 In. 165.00
Candleholder, English Roses, Blue Matte Glaze, Sallie Toohey, 1919, 8 1/2 In. 880.00
Candlestick, Dolphin Heads, Twisted, Green Glossy Glaze, 1922, 12 In. 175.00
Candlestick, Double, Yellow Matte Glaze, 1940, 4 1/2 In., Pair 220.00
Candlestick, Flowers, Broad Leaf Design, Brown Matte Glaze, 1920, 7 In. 330.00
Candlestick, Flowers, Turquoise Matte Glaze, 1921, 1 1/4 In. 88.00
Candlestick, Stylized Design, Pink Matte Glaze, Flame Mark, 1921, 10 In. 99.00
Candlestick, Twisted Column, Dolphin Heads At Base, Rich Blue High Glaze, 11 In. 220.00
Centerpiece, Geometric Design, Violet Matte Glaze, Walter Henschel, 1914, 7 In. 770.00
Chalice, Llamas, Ivory, Brown, Cobalt Butterfat Ground, Jens Jensen, 1933, 6 x 3 In. 2310.00
Chamberstick, Flowers, Standard Glaze, 1900, 8 In. 345.00
Chamberstick, Flowers, Yellow Matte Glaze, 1921, 5 x 1 1/2 In. 110.00
Chamberstick, Golden Trefoils, Standard Glaze, S. Markland, 1894, 3 x 8 In. 330.00
Compote, Yellow & Metallic Gunmetal Glaze, 1922, 6 x 10 1/4 In. 154.00
Console, Celadon Green Glaze, 1950, 12 1/2 x 4 In. 66.00
Creamer, Flowers, Standard Glaze, E.P. Cranch, 1894, 5 In. 220.00
Creamer, Flowers, Standard Glaze, L.N. Lincoln, 1893, 5 In. 120.00
Cup & Saucer, Blue Ship, 2 1/2 In., 14 Piece 550.00
Cup & Saucer, Flowers, Painted & Incised, Light Standard Glaze, 1886, 2 1/4 In. 275.00
Dish, Almond Shape, Floral Interior, Bisque Exterior, 1899, 6 In. 159.00
Dish, Mice, Scalloped Rim, Light Standard Glaze, 1886, 7 In. 275.00
Dish, Shield Form, Pink Matte Greek Letters In Raised Block Design, 1920, 6 In. 55.00
Ewer, Berries & Holly, Standard Glaze, Elizabeth Lincoln, 1901, 5 1/2 In. 410.00
Ewer, Berries & Leaves, Standard Glaze, Anna Marie Valentien, 1894, 10 1/2 In. 385.00

Rookwood, Ewer, Flowers, Yellow, Overlay, Harriet R. Strafer, 1892, 10 1/2 In.

Rookwood, Mug, Goblin On Mushroom, Overlay, Harriet E. Wilcox, 1892, 5 In.

Rookwood, Pitcher, Black Iris Glaze, Overlay, Shirayamadani, 1900, 9 In.

Ewer, Bird Flying Amongst Reeds, A.M. Bookprinter, 1886, 8 1/2 In.	880.00
Ewer, Blossoms, Pink, Celadon, Bulbous, Cameo Ware, H. Wilcox, 1889, 6 1/4 In.	600.00
Ewer, Cherry Blossoms, Laura Fry, 1883, 10 1/2 In.	990.00
Ewer, Daffodils, Standard Glaze, Matt Daly, 1891, 9 1/2 In.	285.00
Ewer, Delicate Flowers, Standard Glaze, Sadie Markland, 1892, 6 1/2 In.	410.00
Ewer, Dogwood, Standard Glaze, C.J. Dibowski, 1895, 5 1/2 In.	357.00
Ewer, Dragon, Brown, Celadon Ground, Sea Green, Matt Daly, 1897, 9 In.	4675.00
Ewer, Flowers, Painted, Leaves, A.R. Valentien, 1886, 19 In.	1210.00
Ewer, Flowers, Standard Glaze, Anna Marie Valentien, 1898, 7 1/2 In.	550.00
Ewer, Flowers, Standard Glaze, Josephine Zettel, 1898, 7 In.	465.00
Ewer, Flowers, Yellow, Overlay, Harriet R. Strafer, 1892, 10 1/2 In. ....*Illus*	2420.00
Ewer, Iris, Standard Glaze, Sallie Toohey, 1896, 12 In.	140.00
Ewer, Iris, Wild Roses, Blue Ground, A.R. Valentien, 1894, 5 1/2 In.	2200.00
Ewer, Mums, Yellow, Mahogany Glaze, Sallie Toohey, 1890, 7 In.	465.00
Ewer, Oak Leaf & Acorn, Silver Overlay, Standard Glaze, Asbury, 10 In.	1760.00
Ewer, Pansies, Green, Brown Ground, Standard Glaze, J. Zettel, 1894, 7 x 4 In.	2310.00
Ewer, Robin's-Egg Blue, Peach Glaze, Flower Branches, A.R. Valentien, 1889, 9 In.	315.00
Ewer, Trumpet Flowers On Red Clay, Mahogany Glaze, Matt Daly, 1889, 12 In.	550.00
Ewer, Wild Roses, Standard Glaze, L.N. Lincoln, 1897, 5 1/2 In.	220.00
Figurine, Camel, Seated, Caramel Matte Glaze, Louise Abel, 1930, 6 1/2 In.	120.00
Figurine, Cardinal, Dark Red, Polychrome, 1946, 7 In.	440.00
Figurine, Donkey, Cream Matte Glaze, William McDonald, 1932, 6 In.	520.00
Figurine, Honey Bear, Gold High Glaze, 1990, 4 In.	77.00
Flower Frog, Nude, Mushroom, Tan, Gold, Blue Matte Glaze, 1921, 6 1/2 In.	462.00
Flower Frog, Satyr With Turtle, Ivory Semimatte Glaze, 6 3/4 In.	143.00
Flower Frog, Woodpecker, Cream Matte Glaze, 1925, 5 In.	110.00
Humidor, Ferns Around Base, Green Matte Glaze, A. Pons, 1908, 8 x 6 In.	770.00
Humidor, Pipe, Matches, Cigar Design, Standard Glaze, Lenore Asbury, 1898, 6 In.	990.00
Humidor, Portrait, American Indian Brave, Painted, Standard Glaze, 1900, 5 In.	3575.00
Inkwell, Dark Blue Matte Glaze, 1917, 7 x 10 In.	660.00
Inkwell, Interior Cover, Blue Matte Glaze, 1926, 4 In.	297.00
Jar, Band Of Pink Cherry Blossoms, Cobalt Ground, Lorinda Epply, 1919, 3 In.	220.00
Jar, Cover, Brown, Green Mottled Matte Glaze, Footed, Shirayamadani, 1910, 6 In.	440.00
Jar, Potpourri, Birds In Flight, Shaded Blue & Bisque, Daly, 1896, 10 In.	1430.00
Jar, Potpourri, Blue Flower Clusters, Butterfat Ground, Louise Abel, 1925, 4 In.	880.00
Jug, Bats, Flying Against Moon, Handle, A.R. Valentien, 1882, 4 1/2 In.	605.00
Jug, Bird In Tree On 1 Side, Comical Fish, Handle, E.P. Cranch, 1894, 7 In.	1210.00
Jug, Dragon, Incised In Front Of Swirling Waves, H. Wilcox, 1893, 8 In.	8250.00
Jug, Dragon, Standard Glaze, Silver Overlay, Wilcox	8250.00
Jug, Ear Of Corn, Silver Overlay Leaves & Hops, W.P. McDonald, 7 In.	3850.00
Jug, Ear Of Corn, Standard Glaze, Sallie Coyne, 1899, 7 In.	310.00
Jug, Grapes, Standard Glaze, Clara Lindeman, 1907, 6 In.	330.00
Jug, Leaves, Incised & Carved, Harriet Wenderoth, 1883, 5 In.	360.00
Jug, Water, Bird, Black, Gray, Flying From Pine Branch, Matt Daly, 1886, 9 x 7 In.	1100.00

Lamp, Storks, Flying Above Water Lilies, Incised, Sea Green Glaze, 1901, 15 In. 33000.00
Letter Holder, Blue Matte Glaze, 1924, 4 In. 308.00
Lighter, Painted Purple Butterflies, Light Purple, Jane Sacksteder, 1946, 4 In. 285.00
Loving Cup, Underwater Scenes, Seaweed, Shirayamadani, 1897, 8 In. 3300.00
Mug, American Indian, Green To Amber Ground, Artus Van Briggle, 1897, 5 In. 715.00
Mug, Apple Blossom Branch, Asymmetric Handle, Green Standard Glaze, 4 In. 460.00
Mug, Chinese Peasant, Standard Glaze, Cylindrical, A. Valentien, 1890, 6 In. 415.00
Mug, Goblin On Mushroom, Overlay, Harriet E. Wilcox, 1892, 5 In. . . . . *Illus* 5500.00
Mug, Japanese Man In Kimono, Playing Flute, Albert Valentien, 1887, 5 7/8 In. 1870.00
Nut Dish, Green High Glaze, 1951, 5 1/2 In. 209.00
Paperweight, Bird, Cobalt Blue, Semimatte Glaze, Production, 1916, 2 1/4 x 4 In. 385.00
Paperweight, Dog, Ivory Matte Glaze, 1928, 5 In. 275.00
Paperweight, Elephant & Clown, Clowns Flank Elephant's Head, 1923, 3 In. 465.00
Paperweight, Penguin On Rock With Seashells, Rust, Green Matte Glaze, 1927, 5 In. . . . 467.00
Paperweight, Polar Bear, Ivory Matte Glaze, Louise Abel, 1949, 4 In. 578.00
Paperweight, Squirrel, Tan, Green Lavender Matte Glaze, Sallie Toohey, 1928, 4 In. 550.00
Picture, Wisteria, Flowering, Green, Purple, Black, Frame, 1900, 10 1/2 x 15 In. 460.00
Pin Tray, Clown, Blue Matte Glaze, Sallie Toohey, 1943, 4 In. 440.00
Pitcher, Berries, Red, Green, Orange Leaves, Standard Glaze, C.J. Dibowski, 5 In. 4292.00
Pitcher, Bird Soaring Over Tree Branch, Gold Accents, 1885, 7 In. 176.00
Pitcher, Black Iris Glaze, Overlay, Shirayamadani, 1900, 9 In. . . . . *Illus* 13200.00
Pitcher, Brown, Red, Tan, Green, Beige, Tricornered, 20th Century, 4 1/2 In. 402.00
Pitcher, Butterflies, Black & White, Bamboo, Gray, White Ground, 1883, 6 In. 660.00
Pitcher, Daisies, Shaded Orange & Brown, Standard Glaze, Asbury, 1900, 10 In. 495.00
Pitcher, Flowers, Yellow, Gold, Brown Ground, Standard Glaze, Zettel, 7 x 4 In. 2310.00
Pitcher, Geese, Bamboo, By Lake, Smear Glaze, Bulbous, Valentien, 7 In. 550.00
Pitcher, Limoges Type, Dated 1883, E.C. Winslow, 6 1/4 In. 2800.00
Pitcher, Pansies, Brown, Shaded Gold, Brown Ground, Standard Glaze, 9 In. 330.00
Pitcher, Stylized Jellyfish, Green, Brown Ground, Matt Daly, 1886, 8 1/2 x 10 In. 825.00
Pitcher, Tricornered, Poppies, Shaded Black To Brown, C. Steinle, 1907, 5 x 5 In. 305.00
Pitcher, Wax Matte, Roses, Yellow Butterfat Ground, K. Jones, 6 1/2 In. 688.00
Planter, Flowers, Blue, Blue Green Butterfat Ground, L. Abel, 1925, 6 x 6 1/2 In. 770.00
Plaque, Autumn Landscape, Mountains, Trees, E.T. Hurley, 1946, 9 1/2 x 12 In. 8250.00
Plaque, Birches Along Lake, Landscape, Purple Mountains, Hurley, 16 In. 18700.00
Plaque, Birches Along River Bank, Landscape, E.T. Hurley, 1940, 12 In. 10450.00
Plaque, Cincinnati, River & Boats, Matted, Frame, Hurley, 12 1/2 In. 495.00
Plaque, Dogwood, Pink, White, Vellum Glaze, E.T. Hurley, 1942, 6 1/2 In. 2200.00
Plaque, Geese Along Road & House In Background, Sallie Toohey, 9 In. 3190.00
Plaque, Harbor Scene, 5 Boats At Sea Reflected In Water, C. Schmidt, 8 In. 4125.00
Plaque, Horse Drawn Carriage, Matted, Frame, Hurley, 1915, 9 1/2 x 12 In. 4675.00
Plaque, Hummingbird, Painted, Feeding On Flowers, Bruce Horsfall, 7 x 10 In. 1100.00
Plaque, Landscape Scene Along Riverbank, Frame, Ed Diers, 9 x 8 In. 770.00
Plaque, Landscape Scene, Dark Trees In Front, Carl Schmidt, 1917, 8 In. 2860.00
Plaque, Mountain Landscape, Green, Dark Mauve Matte Glaze, S. Toohey, 1902, 11 In. . . 7700.00
Plaque, Mt. Adams Street Scene, Showing Vintage Cars, Frame, Hurley, 12 In. 880.00
Plaque, Portrait Of European Gentleman, Frame, Grace Young, 1902, 7 x 9 In. 5500.00
Plaque, Scenic, Birch Trees By River, Vellum, E.T. Hurley, 1912, 11 x 9 In. 7700.00
Plaque, Snow Covered Ground Along Stream, Landscape, Oak Frame, Rettig, 9 In. 770.00
Plaque, Snow Covered Ground, Landscape, Red Sky, E.F. McDermott, 1818, 9 In. 3850.00
Plaque, Spanish Galleons, Blue Clouds, Fred Rothenbusch, 1926, 12 x 9 In. 7700.00
Plaque, Summer Sunset, Sailboats, Carl Schmidt, Frame, 1914, 5 x 9 1/8 In. 4887.00
Plaque, Trees Along Stream, Landscape, Vellum Glaze, Ed Diers, 1921, 8 x 6 In. 4125.00
Plate, Turtle Swimming Through Waves & Vegetation, Painted & Incised, 6 In. 550.00
Plate, Wasp Hovering Over Foliage, Painted & Incised, 1885, 6 In. 330.00
Ring Tray, Clown Figure, Seated, Yellow, Black, Sallie Toohey, 1929, 4 In. 352.00
Stein, Ears Of Corn, Embossed, Z-Line, Green Matte Glaze, J.D. Wareham, 1902, 5 In. . . 248.00
Stein, Monkey, Standard Glaze, Silver Overlay, Horsfall 4750.00
Stein, Silver Lid, Primate Dressed In Orange Pants Carrying Bottle, 1895, 7 In. 3850.00
Sugar, Cover, Greek Key Collar, Blue Over Green Matte Glaze, 5 1/4 In. 330.00
Sugar & Creamer, Blue Matte Glaze, 1928, 3 1/2-In. Creamer, 3-In. Sugar 165.00
Sugar & Creamer, Roses, Shaded Brown & Yellow Ground, Standard Glaze, 5 In. 330.00
Tankard, Grapes, Wild Oats, Thistles, Poppies, 4 Panels, Rats On Handle, 1887, 8 In. 2530.00
Teapot, Cover, Green Glaze Clover, Gold Highlights, Pink Matte Glaze, 1884, 4 In. 230.00

Teapot, Tan Matte Glaze, Braided Twig Handle, Angel Feet, 1919, 4 1/2 In. 165.00
Tile, Cockatoo, Square, 1930, 5 1/2 In. 220.00
Tile, Dutch Figures, Landscape, Cuenca, Polychrome, 1930, 5 1/2 In. 165.00
Tile, Geometric Design, Ivory, Blue Matte Glaze, Square, 8 In. 286.00
Tile, Iris Glaze, Pink, Dusty Rose Crocuses On Ground, Josephine Zettel, 1902, 6 In. 825.00
Tile, Landscape, Trees Along Riverbank With Mountains, Oak Frame, 12 In. 4950.00
Tile, Large Landscape, Trees Along Riverbank With Mountains, Oak Frame, 12 In. 2200.00
Tile, Molded Geometric Fern, Green Glaze Over White, Square, 5 3/4 In. 110.00
Tile, Sailing Ship At Sea, Arts & Crafts Oak Frame, 8 x 12 In. 3080.00
Tile, Ship Sailing At Sea, Matte Glaze, Arts & Crafts Oak Frame, 1905, 5 1/2 In. 522.00
Tile, Woman Holding Parasol, 1928, 5 1/2 In. 287.00
Tray, Brown High Glaze, 1960, 4 In. 40.00
Tray, Mums, Standard Glaze, E.D. Foertmeyer, 1894, 11 In. 276.00
Tray, Mushrooms & Tree Branch, Copper Overlay, Iris Glaze, 1901, 7 In. 2090.00
Tray, Orchid On 1 End Of Large Leaf, Deeply Carved, A.M. Valentien, 1904, 14 In. 1980.00
Tray, Purple Mottled High Glaze, 1964, 7 1/2 In. 310.00
Tray, Rook, Tan Mottled High Glaze, 1950, 5 1/2 In. 165.00
Tray, With Flower Frog, Blue Matte Glaze, 1928, 5 1/2 In. 220.00
Tray, Yellow Matte Glaze, Corners Hold Greek Letter In Blue Matte, 1908, 3 x 1 In. ... 120.00
Trivet, Flower Basket, Butterflies, Pastel Colors, Gilt Accents, 1927, 7 1/2 In. 250.00
Trivet, Grapevine, 1919, 6 In. 360.00
Trivet, Green Molded Design, William McDonald, 1920, 4 1/2 In. 220.00
Trivet, Parrot, 1925, 6 x 6 In. 209.00
Trivet, Pirate Ship, Blue Matte Glaze, 1914, 5 In. 210.00
Trivet, Seagulls, White, Blue & Green Waves, Round, 1919, 5 3/4 In. 360.00
Urn, Flowers & Rabbits, Molded, Arthur Conant, 1920, 14 In. 1045.00
Urn, Stylized Floral Sprays At Handle, Purple Glaze Interior, Sara Sax, 1928, 12 In. ... 2530.00
Urn, Young Man, Shaded Green To Brown, Standard Glaze, M. Daly, 1891, 9 In. 2200.00
Vase, Abstract Design, Dark Green, Indigo Red Glaze, Wm. Hentschel, 1912, 5 x 3 In. ... 715.00
Vase, Abstract Flowers & Leaves, Green Butterfat Ground, Jens Jensen, 1930, 9 In. 1540.00
Vase, Abstract Flowers, Raspberry, Elizabeth Barrett, 1924, 7 1/2 In. 660.00
Vase, Apple Blossom Branches, Dark Blue Glaze, Light Blue Cream, 1885, 11 In. 920.00
Vase, Apple Blossoms, Iris Glaze, Shaded Gray To Pink, Diers, 1905, 7 In. 1430.00
Vase, Apple Blossoms, Yellow, Standard Glaze, Bottle Shape, E. Lincoln, 8 1/4 In. 550.00
Vase, Apple Branches, Pink, Green Ground, Vellum, Ed Diers, 1908, 9 x 7 In. 850.00
Vase, Art Deco Flowers, Purple, Blue, Ivory Ground, Bulbous, Lorinda Epply, 1933, 6 In. 990.00
Vase, Asian Figures & Rabbit With Snow Laden Trees, M.L. Nichols, 1882, 7 In. 2970.00
Vase, Band Of Berries, Leaves Near Rim, Mauve, Brown, Yellow, Todd, 1919, 9 In. 1150.00
Vase, Band Of Parrots, Branches, Vellum, Sarah Sax, 1913, 9 1/4 x 4 1/2 In. 1000.00
Vase, Band Of Pink Flowers, Molded, Yellow Centers, Todd, 1915, 7 In. 635.00
Vase, Beautiful Flowers, Multicolored Ground, Shirayamadani, 4 1/2 In. 1210.00
Vase, Bees Feeding On Clover, Iris Glaze, Carl Schmidt, 1900, 7 In. 2640.00
Vase, Berries, Red, Green Leaves, Yellow Butterfat Ground, Sallie Coyne, 1925, 8 In. ... 1320.00
Vase, Billowy Clouds Behind Trees, Landscape, Fred Rothenbusch, 1909, 14 In. 4400.00
Vase, Birch Trees Along Riverbank, Landscape, Vellum Glaze, E.T. Hurley, 5 1/2 In. 2420.00
Vase, Birch Trees, Landscape, Colorful Sky, Vellum Glaze, E.T. Hurley, 7 In. 935.00
Vase, Birch Trees, Pastel Sky, Top & Base, Shirayamadani, 1911, 9 In. 400.00
Vase, Birches By Lake, Vellum, Drill Hole, Diers, 1920, 18 x 7 1/4 In. 3300.00
Vase, Bird Amongst Finely Painted Foliage, A.R. Valentien, 1884, 12 1/2 In. 1200.00
Vase, Bird In Flight, Oriental Grasses, M. Rettig, 1885, 2 7/8 In. 315.00
Vase, Bird, Painted & Incised, Brilliant Gold Crystals, Matt Daly, 1899, 8 1/2 In. 6600.00
Vase, Birds Flying Through Tree, Kate Curry, 1917, 8 5/8 In. 2200.00
Vase, Birds Soaring Above Foliage, Gold Accents, Matt Daly, 1885, 13 In. 715.00
Vase, Bleeding Heart Band, Ivory, Teal Ground, Oval, Sallie Coyne, 1915, 7 3/4 In. 578.00
Vase, Blossom, Orange, Caramel, Standard Glaze, Mary Nourse, 1903, 13 In. 5500.00
Vase, Blossoms, Pink, Yellow, Blue, Pink Butterfat Ground, McDonald, 1930, 6 In. 770.00
Vase, Blossoms, Yellow, Olive Green, Yellow Interior, Sara Sax, 1923, 5 In. 1495.00
Vase, Blue & Pink Flowers, Lime Green Matte Glaze, Wm. E. Hentschel, 10 In. 825.00
Vase, Blue Gray Glaze, White Roses, Velum, Elizabeth McDermott, 1915, 4 1/4 In. 715.00
Vase, Bluebird On Pine Branch, Gray Ground, Shirayamadani, 1888, 6 3/4 x 6 In. 1760.00
Vase, Blues & Greens, Vellum, Louise Abel, 1921, 9 1/2 In. 525.00
Vase, Bone, Brown Swirl Design, Cobalt Ground, Jens Jensen, 1933, 5 3/4 x 5 In. 1760.00
Vase, Brown Glaze Shading To Olive Green, 1905, Clara C. Lindeman, 5 5/8 In. 110.00

Vase, Bud, Cherry Blossoms, Rose Ground, Jewel Porcelain, Ed Diers, 1923, 7 x 2 In. 520.00
Vase, Bud, Pink & Green Shaded Matte Glaze, 1928, 7 1/2 In. 165.00
Vase, Canadian Geese Soaring Above Trees, Shirayamadani, 1911, 9 In. 7700.00
Vase, Carnations, Blue, Blue & Claret Ground, Wax Matte, Oval, 1925, 7 1/2 In. 1200.00
Vase, Carnations, Vellum Glaze, Ed Diers, 1902, 9 In. 1320.00
Vase, Carnations, White & Lavender, Iris Glaze, Albert Valentien, 1904, 11 3/8 In. 6600.00
Vase, Carp, Painted & Incised, Mahogany Glaze, Shirayamadani, 8 In. 3086.00
Vase, Carved Flowers At Collar & Shoulder, William Hentschel, 1915, 9 In. 3300.00
Vase, Cherry Blossoms, Ivory, Green, Pink Ground, E.T. Hurley, 1918, 8 In. 660.00
Vase, Cherry Blossoms, Pink Ground, Vellum, Sara Sax, 1911, 7 1/4 In. 605.00
Vase, Cherry Blossoms, Ribbed Form, E.D. Foertmeyer, 1891, 5 1/2 In. 880.00
Vase, Cherry Blossoms, Vellum Glaze, E.T. Hurley, 1927, 5 1/2 In. 990.00
Vase, Cherry Blossoms, Vellum, Blue, Bulbous, F. Rothenbusch, 1925, 5 1/2 In. 1210.00
Vase, Cherry Blossoms, Vellum, Peach Ground, E.T. Hurley, 1912, 9 3/4 In. 440.00
Vase, Chrysanthemums, Butterflies, Purple Interior, Lenore Asbury, 1920, 8 In. 7425.00
Vase, Chrysanthemums, White, Blue Ground, Vellum, Busch, 1925, 5 1/2 x 6 In. 1760.00
Vase, Circular Design, Multi Blue Tone, John D. Wareham, 1952, 6 1/2 In. 880.00
Vase, Clover Blossoms, Shaded Brown Ground, Standard Glaze, Squat Base, 12 In. 330.00
Vase, Clover, Iris Glaze, White, Blue Tone, Clara Lindeman, 1907, 5 1/2 In. 385.00
Vase, Clover, Standard Glaze, Clara Lindeman, 1904, 7 1/2 In. 360.00
Vase, Columbine, Purple, Blue, Pink Ground, Vellum, Ed Diers, 1931, 8 x 4 1/2 In. 1320.00
Vase, Coromandel Glaze, Charcoal, Mahogany Flambe Ground, Hentschel, 1933, 8 In. 1650.00
Vase, Crab, Shellfish, Tiger Eye, 1885, 8 1/2 In. 935.00
Vase, Crane Flying Over Brown, Black Reeds, Gold Accents, Daly, 12 In. 3850.00
Vase, Cranes In Tall Grasses, Sturgis Laurence, 1902, 13 7/8 In. 9900.00
Vase, Crocus & Stems, Black Iris Glaze, Matt Daly, 1900, 4 In. 4675.00
Vase, Crocus, Purple, Purple Ground, Vellum, Carolyn Steinle, 1912, 5 In. 330.00
Vase, Crocus, Yellow, Surrounded By Clouds, Leaves, Mary Nourse, 8 In. 2860.00
Vase, Crocuses, Pink, Dusty Rose, Iris Glaze, Josephine Zettel, 1902, 6 In. 825.00
Vase, Curling Leaves, Brown, Yellow Bands, Blue Ground, Barrett, 8 In. 770.00
Vase, Cyclamen, Red, Deep Green, Dark Yellow Ground, Harriet Wilcox, 1901, 9 In. 825.00
Vase, Daffodils, Incised, Buds, Leaves, Shirayamadani, 1904, 9 1/4 In. 7150.00
Vase, Daffodils, Iris Glaze, White & Gray Ground, Sarah Sax, 1899, 7 1/4 In. 2090.00
Vase, Daffodils, Standard Glaze, Mary Nourse, 1899, 10 In. 522.00
Vase, Daffodils, Yellow, Tan Ground, Spherical, A.R. Valentien, 1901, 4 1/2 In. 1650.00
Vase, Daisies, Shaded Brown Ground, Standard Glaze, Caroline Steinle, 4 In. 305.00
Vase, Daisies, Yellow, Blue Ground, Vellum, Bulbous, Ed Diers, 1921, 5 x 3 1/2 In. 1210.00
Vase, Deer & Foliage, Molded, Blue High Glaze, Wm. E. Hentschel, 11 In. 550.00
Vase, Deer, Leaping, Flowers, Base Circles, William Hentschel, 1927, 16 5/8 In. 2750.00
Vase, Detailed Trees Around Lake, Landscape, Vellum Glaze, Diers, 10 In. 2970.00
Vase, Dogwood Blossoms, Blue Green Butterfat Ground, L. Abel, 1927, 7 1/2 In. 1430.00
Vase, Dogwood Blossoms, Green, Orange Ground, Standard Glaze, Altman, 6 In. 550.00
Vase, Dogwood Blossoms, Mottled Taupe Ground, Bulbous, Sara Sax, 1927, 9 In. 3300.00
Vase, Dogwood Blossoms, Silver Gray Ground, Spherical, Hurley, 1900, 6 In. 4675.00
Vase, Dogwood Blossoms, Standard Glaze, Bulbous, C. Steinle, 1901, 5 1/4 In. 330.00
Vase, Dogwood, Vellum Glaze, Mary Grace Denzler, 1913, 5 In. 495.00
Vase, Dogwood, White, Iris Glaze, Lenore Asbury, 1905, 8 In. 1760.00
Vase, Dogwood, White, Lavender Ground, Vellum, Edith Noonan, 1908, 6 x 3 In. 1210.00
Vase, Dogwood, Yellow, Surrounded By Silver Overlay, K. Hickman, 1899, 7 In. 3190.00
Vase, Ducks, Flock, Marsh Landscape, Vellum, Shirayamadani, 1909, 9 In. 1100.00
Vase, Dutch Gentleman Wearing A Wide-Brimmed Hat, Pillow, Daly, 1894, 8 In. 1380.00
Vase, Exotic Bird Above Branches, Leaves & Berries, Vellum Glaze, Sax, 11 In. 1320.00
Vase, Fan, White Flower, Green Leaves, White Ground, Jens Jensen, 1946, 7 3/4 In. 440.00
Vase, Fern, Burnt Orange Matte Glaze, Wm. E. Hentschel, 1927, 7 1/2 In. 2310.00
Vase, Fish, Foliage, Jens Jensen, 1944, 7 In. 990.00
Vase, Fish, Molded, Green Interior, Black High Glaze, Shirayamadani, 6 1/4 In. 440.00
Vase, Fish, Swimming, Green Watery Ground, Vellum, Lenore Asbury, 1919, 7 In. 1210.00
Vase, Fishing Boats, Blue, Vellum, Flared, Carl Schmidt, 1925, 8 3/4 x 4 3/4 In. 6050.00
Vase, Flower Band Circles Top, Brown Matte, Charles S. Todd, c.1926, 8 1/4 In. 465.00
Vase, Flowering Trees & 3 Peacocks Below Rim, Sara Sax, 1915, 15 3/8 In. 6875.00
Vase, Flowers & Birds, Butterfat Glaze, Lorinda Epply, 1927, 12 In. 4950.00
Vase, Flowers & Branches, Standard Glaze, Shirayamadani, 1890, 14 In. 4675.00
Vase, Flowers & Leaves, Iris Glaze, Matt Daly, 1900, 14 In. 3850.00

Vase, Flowers At Top & Bottom, Vellum Glaze, M.G. Denzler, 1914, 6 In. 412.00
Vase, Flowers At Top, Dark Green, Cobalt, Katherine Jones, 1925, 8 In. 297.00
Vase, Flowers At Top, Pale Yellow Matte Glaze, Shirayamadani, 5 1/2 In. 1210.00
Vase, Flowers At Top, Vellum Glaze, M.H. McDonald, 1914, 7 In. 412.00
Vase, Flowers On Bottom, Charles Todd, 1919, 8 1/2 In. 825.00
Vase, Flowers, Bamboo, Tall Grasses, Tiger Eye, H.E. Wilcox, 1894, 8 1/4 In. 1210.00
Vase, Flowers, Brown, Green, Yellow, Green Mottled Ground, M.H. McDonald, 7 In. 360.00
Vase, Flowers, Drip Design At Top, Vellum Glaze, M.G. Denzler, 1916, 5 In. 770.00
Vase, Flowers, Incised, Early High Glaze, Anna Marie Bookprinter, 1885, 9 1/2 In. 467.00
Vase, Flowers, Incised, Standard Glaze, Harriet Wilcox, 1898, 4 1/2 In. 770.00
Vase, Flowers, Incised, William Hentschel, 1914, 11 In. 825.00
Vase, Flowers, Leaves, Blue & Green Matte Glaze, Arthur Ponds, 1907, 2 1/2 In. 360.00
Vase, Flowers, Multicolored, Arthur Conant, 1917, 7 1/2 In. 2640.00
Vase, Flowers, Multicolored, Lorinda Epply, 1927, 13 1/2 In. 880.00
Vase, Flowers, Purple, Green Leaves, Cream Matte Ground, L. Asbury, 1916, 8 In. 990.00
Vase, Flowers, Purple, Loretta Holtkamp, 1952, 12 1/2 In. 825.00
Vase, Flowers, Red, Green Butterfat Ground, Bulbous, Anna Marie Valentien, 4 1/4 In. ... 853.00
Vase, Flowers, Standard Glaze, Constance Baker, 1898, 5 In. 357.00
Vase, Flowers, Tiger Eye, Anna Marie Valentien, 1889, 6 In. 935.00
Vase, Flowers, Turquoise Matte Glaze, Sallie Coyne, 1929, 7 1/2 In. 412.00
Vase, Flowers, Vellum Glaze, Lenore Asbury, 1923, 6 In. 825.00
Vase, Flowers, Yellow & Green, Standard Glaze, S. Laurence, 1902, 11 In. 5225.00
Vase, Flowers, Yellow, Dark Brown, Bottle Shape, Adeliza Sehon, 1902, 7 In. 440.00
Vase, Flowers, Yellow, Green Leaves & Stems, Early Standard Glaze, Laura Fry, 8 In. ... 605.00
Vase, Flowers, Yellow, Orange, Silver Overlay, Standard Glaze, 1892, 5 1/2 In. 3300.00
Vase, Flowers, Yellow, Red, Blue Ground, C.S. Todd, 1914, 7 1/2 x 2 3/4 In. 825.00
Vase, Forest Landscape, Fall Foliage, Vellum, Flame Mark, E.T. Hurley, 1908, 9 In. 4950.00
Vase, Fruit On Limbs, Brown Stems, Squeezebag, Elizabeth Barret, 10 In. 1540.00
Vase, Geese, Flying, Goldstone Glaze, Shirayamadani, 1939, 6 1/2 In. 715.00
Vase, Geometric Design At Shoulder, Molded, Green Matte Glaze, 1913, 7 x 4 In. 770.00
Vase, Geometric Design, Green, Lavender, Blue Drip, Wm. E. Hentschel, 1915, 5 In. 467.00
Vase, Geometric Design, Molded, Blue, Green, Brown Matte, J.D. Wareham, 9 In. 770.00
Vase, Geometric Foliage Design, Slip, William Hentschel, 1930, 5 1/2 In. 935.00
Vase, Geometric, Foliage Design, Blue, Black, Blue Ground, Sara Sax, 1928, 6 In. 805.00
Vase, Gingko Leaves & Nuts, Green, Brown, Tooled, Shirayamadani, 1901, 12 In. 25300.00
Vase, Grapes, Leaves & Vines, Vellum Glaze, M.H. McDonald, 1912, 8 In. 825.00
Vase, Grapevine, Iris Glaze, Lenore Asbury, 1907, 7 1/2 In. 1760.00
Vase, Grapevine, Leaves & Vines, Standard Glaze, V. Demarest, 1901, 8 In. 415.00
Vase, Grapevine, Standard Glaze, Lenore Asbury, 1900, 8 In. 990.00
Vase, Green Flowers, Silver, Standard Glaze, Adeliza Sehon, 1894, 6 1/4 In. 2750.00
Vase, Hanging Vegetation, A.B. Sprague, 1901, 6 1/2 In. 1320.00
Vase, Hollyhocks, Orange, Green To Orange Ground, Sturgis Laurence, 1901, 14 In. 3080.00
Vase, Honeysuckle Branches, Brown Shaded Ground, Shirayamadani, 1903, 11 In. 2200.00
Vase, Horizontal Lines, Squeezebag, Elizabeth Barret, 1928, 12 1/2 In. 1210.00
Vase, Horizontal Ribs, Multitone Brown High Glaze, 1885, 6 In. 415.00
Vase, Hummingbirds, Flowers, Green Ground, Arthur P. Conant, c.1921, 6 1/2 In. 2070.00
Vase, Hyacinths, Purple, Edward George Diers, c.1914, 9 1/2 In. 1595.00
Vase, Hydrangea, White, Encircle Vase, Iris Glaze, Albert Valentien, 14 3/8 In. 6600.00
Vase, Hydrangea, White, Gray & Cobalt Ground, Iris Glaze, Edith Noonan, 1905, 5 In. .. 605.00
Vase, Incised, Flowers, Gold Highlights, Anna Marie Valentien, 1887, 6 In. 319.00
Vase, Iris Buds, Leaves, Sea Green, Matthew Daly, 1897, 9 1/2 x 3 3/4 In. 715.00
Vase, Iris, 2-Tone Blue Blooms, Sage Green Matte Glaze, Vellum, Duell, 1908, 7 In. 805.00
Vase, Iris, Black To Ivory Ground, Bulbous, Lenore Asbury, 1907, 10 In. 2860.00
Vase, Iris, Black, Pink Apple Blossoms, Black Ground, Rothenbush, 1900, 5 In. 1430.00
Vase, Iris, Blue Green Butterfat Ground, Wax Matte, Jens Jensen, 1929, 11 In. 2420.00
Vase, Iris, Gray To Celadon Ground, Sallie E. Coyne, 1905, 11 1/4 In. 2860.00
Vase, Iris, Shaded Gray Ground, Sallie E. Coyne, 1907, 10 3/4 In. 1980.00
Vase, Iris, Standard Glaze, Carl Schmidt, 1900, 9 In. 990.00
Vase, Iris, Yellow Clay, Standard Glaze, Marie Rauchfuss, 1890, 9 1/2 In. 715.00
Vase, Irises, Black Iris Glaze, Carl Schmidt, 1909, 11 In. 13200.00
Vase, Irises, Blue, Standard Glaze, Sturgis Lawrence, Paper Label, 1902, 17 x 6 In. 3575.00
Vase, Jonquils, Yellow, Green Leaves, Brown, C.A. Baker, 1901, 10 x 5 In. 4950.00
Vase, Landscape, Cream & Crimson Ground, Katherine Van Horne, c.1917, 7 3/8 In. 1840.00

Vase, Landscape, Vellum, Cylindrical, Frederick Rothenbusch, 1933, 8 3/4 In. 2585.00
Vase, Leaf, Blossoms, Deep Pink, Green, McDonald, 1926, 8 3/4 In. 690.00
Vase, Leafy Branches, Soft Brown, Green, Red Berry Clusters, Sara Sax, 7 3/8 In. 1495.00
Vase, Leathery Blue Green Glaze, Bulbous, Lorinda Epply, 1906, 4 1/2 x 4 In. 330.00
Vase, Leaves & Berries, Standard Glaze, E.T. Hurley, 1900, 12 In. 715.00
Vase, Leaves & Flowers, Vellum Glaze, M.H. McDonald, 1923, 5 In. 660.00
Vase, Leaves, Blue, Green Matte Glaze, Wm. E. Hentschel, 1913, 6 1/2 In. 1430.00
Vase, Light Blue, Green, Ivory High Glaze, Rueben E. Menzel, 1954, 7 In. 230.00
Vase, Lilac & Rose Poppies, Brown Ground, Trumpet, Sallie E. Coyne, 1923, 8 1/2 In. 1380.00
Vase, Lily Of The Valley, Gray Ground, Iris Glaze, Laura E. Lindeman, 1903, 6 x 3 In. 1320.00
Vase, Lily Of The Valley, Vellum Glaze, Caroline Steinle, 1912, 7 In. 525.00
Vase, Magnolia Blossoms, Sturgis Laurence, 1901, 10 5/8 In. 6875.00
Vase, Magnolia, Jens Jensen, 1946, 8 In. 550.00
Vase, Magnolia, Light Green Tint, Iris Glaze, Harriet Wilcox, 1900, 6 1/2 In. 4950.00
Vase, Magnolia, Standard Glaze, Albert Valentien, 1898, 11 In. 990.00
Vase, Magnolias, Pink & White, Blue Ground, Lenore Asbury, 1930, 12 1/2 In. 7150.00
Vase, Magnolias, Vellum Glaze, L.N. Lincoln, 1906, 5 1/2 In. 660.00
Vase, Maple Leaf, Margaret H. McDonald, 1943, 12 In. 660.00
Vase, Maple Leaves, Pink, Pods, Purple Ground, O.G. Reed, 1905, 10 1/2 In. 4950.00
Vase, Mistletoe, Standard Glaze, Grace Hall, 1904, 4 1/4 In. 175.00
Vase, Misty Landscape, Vellum, Banded, Lenore Asbury, 1923, 11 In. 2750.00
Vase, Morning Glories & Leaves, Vellum Glaze, Sara Sax, 1908, 9 In. 1045.00
Vase, Morning Glories, Standard Glaze, Albert Valentien, 1889, 8 In. 440.00
Vase, Morning Glory, Cobalt Ground, Vellum, Oval, M.H. McDonald, 1917, 8 In. 990.00
Vase, Mountain Laurel, Shaded Green & Orange, Standard Glaze, 1893, 11 In. 770.00
Vase, Mountainous Site, Landscape, Grassy Plains, Lenore Asbury, 1921, 9 In. 1680.00
Vase, Mushroom, Standard Glaze, Carl Schmidt, 1898, 6 In. 1870.00
Vase, Narcissus, Pink, Purple Ground, Bulbous, Shirayamadani, 1944, 9 In. 2640.00
Vase, Nasturtium, Purple, Blue, Pumpkin Butterfat Ground, Sallie Coyne, 1925, 8 In. 1650.00
Vase, Nasturtium, Yellow, Iris Glaze, Black To Gray Ground, S. Coyne, 1904, 7 In. 3575.00
Vase, Nasturtiums, Standard Glaze, A.D. Sehon, 1900, 7 In. 525.00
Vase, Oak Leaf & Acorn, Standard Glaze, Elizabeth Lincoln, 1904, 8 In. 415.00
Vase, Oak Leaves, Purple, Green Ground, Carved Matte, Sallie Toohey, 1904, 7 In. 2530.00
Vase, Oak Trees In A Meadow, Vellum, Ed Diers, 1917, 10 1/4 x 7 1/4 In. 4125.00
Vase, Orchids, Green Leaves, Green Ground, Wax Matte, Jens Jensen, 1929, 9 In. 1540.00
Vase, Pansies, Brown Ground, Standard Glaze, Squat, E.T. Hurley, 1898, 5 x 8 In. 660.00
Vase, Pansies, Standard Glaze, Caroline Steinle, 1896, 4 In. 385.00
Vase, Peacock Feather, Tiger Eye Glaze, A.R. Valentien, 1898, 15 In. 3282.00
Vase, Peacock Feathers, Teal Microcrystalline Glaze, 1926, 7 1/4 In. 385.00
Vase, Peacock, Vellum, Based Drilled, Cylindrical, Sara Sax, 1915, 15 1/2 In. 4310.00
Vase, Peonies, Incised, E.T. Hurley, 1944, 6 1/2 In. 1980.00
Vase, Pinecones & Pine Boughs, 2 Handled Form, L.N. Lincoln, 1928, 6 In. 550.00
Vase, Pinecones, Vermilion Butterfat Ground, Elizabeth Lincoln, 1927, 9 1/2 In. 1210.00
Vase, Pink Matte Glaze, Band Of Embossed Triangles, Oval, 1926, 7 In. 165.00
Vase, Pink, Blue, Purple Drip, Multitone Brown High Glaze, 1932, 3 1/4 In. 415.00
Vase, Pink, Green Matte Glaze, Flame Mark, 7 1/2 x 3 In. 165.00
Vase, Poppies, 4-Sided Top, Sea Green Glaze, Sallie Coyne, 1901, 8 In. 3790.00
Vase, Poppies, Bending, Spattered Interior, Shirayamadani, 1944, 9 In. 3575.00
Vase, Poppies, Dark Brown, Standard Glaze, HPL, 1892, 8 In. 275.00
Vase, Poppies, Orange, Brown & Yellow Ground, A.M. Valentien, 1899, 14 x 5 In. 1980.00
Vase, Poppies, Pink, Blue, Gray Ground, Vellum, E. Lincoln, 1918, 5 1/2 x 7 In. 1760.00
Vase, Poppies, Red, Silver Overlay, Standard Glaze, L.N. Lincoln, 1903, 10 In. 2860.00
Vase, Poppy, Shaded Pink Ground, Vellum, Sarah Sax, 1904, 6 x 3 In. 1210.00
Vase, Portrait Of Native American, Standard Glaze, Grace Young, 1900, 9 In. 770.00
Vase, Portrait, European Old Master, Standard Glaze, Artus Van Briggle, 9 In. 2200.00
Vase, Primate In Tree Covered With Gold Flecks, Tiger Eye Glaze, Daly, 1894, 8 In. 2860.00
Vase, Purple, Brown Glaze, Dark Blue Drip Band, C.S. Todd, 1917, 9 In. 1760.00
Vase, Purple, Brown, Blue Crystalline Glaze, John D. Wareham, 1924, 10 1/2 In. 385.00
Vase, Rooster, Cattails & Mushrooms, Gray Ground, Flame Mark, 1919, 13 1/2 In. 1430.00
Vase, Rose, Leaves & Flowers, Iris Glaze, Sallie Coyne, 1907, 9 1/2 In. 2640.00
Vase, Rose, Orange, Green Leaves, Purple Ground, Matte, Olga Reed, 1907, 7 In. 2860.00
Vase, Roses, Beige, Standard Glaze, Oval, Caroline Steinle, 1907, 7 3/4 In. 550.00
Vase, Roses, Red, Green Leaves, Dark Blue Ground, Catherine Crabtree, 1923, 9 x 4 In. ... 1540.00

Rookwood, Vase, Vellum, Ed Deirs, 1926, 13 1/2 In.

The less you handle an antique or collectible the better. Always pick up an antique with two hands.

Vase, Roses, Shaded Blue & Tan Ground, Oval, C.S. Todd, 1920, 5 1/2 In. 485.00
Vase, Roses, Yellow, Standard Glaze, Bottle Shape, Mattie Fogleson, 1897, 7 In. 605.00
Vase, Roses, Yellow, Standard Glaze, Harriette Strafer, 1893, 6 1/2 In. 550.00
Vase, Sailing Ships On Turbulent Sea, Vellum Glaze, Lorinda Epply, 1908, 7 In. 1980.00
Vase, Scenic, Repeating Border, Fred Rothenbusch, 1924, 12 3/4 In. 8150.00
Vase, Seascape Scene, Painted Boats At Sea, Green Vellum Glaze. L. Asbury, 9 In. 605.00
Vase, Sheep On Grassy Slope, Blue Landscape, Amelia Sprague, 1895, 7 3/8 In. 5500.00
Vase, Snow Covered Ground Along Icy Water, Landscape, E.F. McDermott, 8 In. 990.00
Vase, Snow Covered Ground, Landscape, Purple Tree Line, Sallie Coyne, 11 In. 7700.00
Vase, Snow Scene, Yellow Sky, Vellum, F. Rothenbusch, 1912, 8 1/4 In. 1650.00
Vase, Stark Trees Along Water, Landscape, Vellum Glaze, Sallie Coyne, 1914, 8 In. 1650.00
Vase, Sumac Flowers, Iris Glaze, Bottom Leaves, John Dee Wareham, 1900, 15 In. 8250.00
Vase, Tall Barren Trees, Landscape, Vellum Glaze, E.F. McDermott, 1916, 7 In. 1100.00
Vase, Tall Pines, Winter Landscape, Vellum, Sallie Coyne, 1918, 9 In. 3080.00
Vase, Tall Trees In Front Of Rose Sky, Landscape, Vellum Glaze, E.T. Hurley, 11 In. 825.00
Vase, Tall, Thin Trees Along Riverbank, Vellum Glaze, Shirayamadani, 9 1/2 In. 2000.00
Vase, Tiger Lily, Tulip, Molded, Green, Blue Matte, Shirayamadani, 11 In. 880.00
Vase, Tree, Molded, Maroon, Green Matte, Shirayamadani, 7 In. 385.00
Vase, Trees & Houses, Landscape, Jens Jensen, 1944, 6 In. 2300.00
Vase, Trees & Lake Against Pastel Sky, Vellum, E.T. Hurley, 1939, 16 x 7 In. 7150.00
Vase, Trees Along Lake, Landscape, Vellum Glaze, Carl Schmidt, 1915, 11 In. 4620.00
Vase, Trees Around Lake, Landscape, Vellum Glaze, Ed Deirs, 1918, 7 In. 1870.00
Vase, Trees In Dark Green, Vellum, Fred Rothenbush, 1912, 5 3/4 x 3 1/2 In. 715.00
Vase, Trees Surrounding Body Of Water, C.J. McLaughlin, 1915, 7 In. 4950.00
Vase, Trees, Blue & Green, Landscape, Jewel Porcelain, M.H. McDonald, 1940, 11 In. ... 3190.00
Vase, Trees, Finely Detailed, Landscape, Vellum Glaze, Ed Deirs, 1922, 6 In. 1760.00
Vase, Trees, River, Houses, Landscape, Fred Rothenbusch, 1926, 14 1/2 In. 10450.00
Vase, Trillium, Blue & Green Ground, Vellum, Carl Schmidt, 1915, 9 x 4 1/4 In. 880.00
Vase, Trumpet Flowers, White, Eggplant Ground, Harriet Wilcox, 1927, 11 x 5 In. 4675.00
Vase, Tulip & Leaves, A.R. Valentien, 1896, 15 In. 990.00
Vase, Tulips, French, Orange & Brown, Standard Glaze, Sturgis Lawrence, 1902, 13 In. .. 1980.00
Vase, Tulips, Molded, Paneled, Blue Matte, Shirayamadani, 1924, 10 In. 605.00
Vase, Tulips, Porcelain, E.T. Hurley, 1944, 6 1/2 In. 770.00
Vase, Tulips, Red, Blue Leaves, Elizabeth Lincoln, Flame Mark, 1919, 7 x 3 3/4 In. 935.00
Vase, Tulips, Yellow, Bands Of Silver Overlay, Standard Glaze, 7 In. 2420.00
Vase, Tulips, Yellow, Green To Orange Ground, Constance Baker, 1902, 10 3/4 In. 1100.00
Vase, Tulips, Yellow, Teal To Amber Ground, Oval, Kate Van Horn, 1908, 6 1/2 In. 1320.00
Vase, Vegetation, Margaret H. McDonald, 1928, 8 1/2 In. 880.00
Vase, Vellum, Ed Deirs, 1926, 13 1/2 In. ....*Illus* 4480.00
Vase, Vertical Eucalyptus Branches, Heavy Slip, William Hentschel, 1930, 12 In. 1210.00
Vase, Vertical Leaves On 3 Panels, Molded, Blue Matte Glaze, 1910, 6 In. 275.00
Vase, Vertical Leaves, Molded, Multitone Blue Matte Glaze, Munson, 1919, 11 In. 550.00
Vase, Violets, Iris Glaze, Fred Rothenbusch, 1902, 7 In. 1650.00
Vase, Water Bird, Incised, Gold Streaks, Mahogany & Tiger Eye Glaze, 1896, 7 In. 3410.00
Vase, Water Lilies, Pink, Shaded Ground, Carved Vellum, L. Epply, 1907, 8 x 4 1/2 In. 1210.00
Vase, Water Lily, Black Opal Glaze, Harriet E. Wilcox, 1926, 16 In. 8800.00
Vase, Wheat, Handles, Margaret H. McDonald, 1936, 7 1/2 In. 470.00

Vase, White, Brown, Red Matte, Squeezebag, Jens Jensen, 1943, 4 1/2 x 5 1/2 In. 410.00
Vase, Wild Rose, Detailed Leaves, Kate Matchette, 1892, 5 1/2 In. 470.00
Vase, Wild Rose, Iris Glaze, Marianne Mitchell, 1902, 6 1/2 In.   990.00
Vase, Wild Roses, Green & Ivory Butterfat Ground, C. Steinle, 1923, 7 x 3 3/4 In. 880.00
Vase, Wild Roses, Vellum Glaze, Fred Rothenbusch, 1914, 8 In. 990.00
Vase, Wild Roses, White, Pink, Vellum Glaze, F. Rothenbusch, 1908, 10 In. 550.00
Vase, Wild Violets, Swirling Leaves & Stems, Ed Diers, 1930, 7 7/8 In. 4620.00
Vase, Winter, Snow Covered Landscape, Brown Trees, Diers, 9 In. 1430.00
Vase, Wisteria, Blue, Purple, Vellum Glaze, 1926, E.T. Hurley, 14 In. 7700.00
Vase, Wisteria, Iris Glaze, Lenore Asbury, 1906, 9 In. 1540.00
Vase, Women Amidst Foliage, Tan Matte Glaze, Wm. Hentschel, 1920, 19 In. 2530.00
Vase, Yellow, Brown Matte Glaze, Dark Blue Top, Wm. E. Hentschel, 1915, 5 In. 470.00
Vase, Yellow, Green Drip, Multitone Pink Ground, 1932, 7 In.   255.00
Wall Pocket, Purple Matte Glaze, 1925, 7 1/2 In. 253.00

RORSTRAND was established near Stockholm, Sweden, in 1726. By the nineteenth century they were making English-style earthenware, bone china, porcelain, ironstone china, and majolica. The company is still working. The three crown mark has been used since 1884.

Bowl, Blue Transfer, Ship With Cows In Foreground, Flower Border, 6 In. 65.00
Charger, Concentric Circles, Gray & White, Sarek, Signed, 14 In. 247.00
Pitcher, Ribbed Body, Striated Blue-Green To Brown Matte Glaze, 11 In. 550.00
Vase, Embossed Nasturtium & Leaves, White Ground, 5 1/4 x 3 1/4 In. 355.00
Vase, Stoneware, Diamond Pattern, Teal, Brown Matte Glaze, Nylund, 8 1/2 x 3 In. 77.00

ROSALINE, see Steuben category.

ROSE BOWLS were popular during the 1880s. Rose petals were kept in the open bowl to add fragrance to a room, a popular idea in a time of limited personal hygiene. The glass bowls were made with crimped tops, which kept the petals inside. Many types of Victorian art glass were made into rose bowls.

Diamond-Quilted, Mother-Of-Pearl, 5 1/2 In. 400.00
Jefferson, 1890, 5 In. 115.00
Sterling Silver, Floral Repousse, Claw Footed, 5 x 3 3/4 In. 200.00
Vaseline Glass, Wreath & Shell, Opalescent 100.00

ROSE CANTON china is similar to Rose Medallion, except no people or birds are pictured in the decoration. It was made in China during the nineteenth and twentieth centuries in greens, pinks, and other colors.

Bowl, Gilt Bronze Mounted, Pierced Rim, Double Greek Key Handles, 13 In. 1650.00
Butter Chip, 2 1/2 In., 12 Piece 170.00
Vase, Baluster Body, Blossom Shaped Lip, Mid 19th Century, 11 1/2 In., Pair 935.00

ROSE MANDARIN china is similar to Rose Medallion. If the panels in the design picture only people and not birds, it is called Rose Mandarin.

Bowl, Vegetable, 9 x 8 In., Pair 880.00
Brush Box, 7 3/4 In. 690.00
Charger, 16 1/2 In. 1840.00
Creamer, 3 1/2 In. 260.00
Dish, 6 1/4 In. 140.00
Dish, Hot Water, Cover, Oval, 14 In. 1495.00
Dish, Hot Water, Cover, Oval, 15 In. 2300.00
Jug, Cider, Foo Dog Finial, 11 In. 2070.00
Pitcher, Paneled, 7 1/4 In. 385.00
Plate, 8 In. 575.00
Plate, Dinner, 9 7/8 In., Pair . . . . .460.00 to 920.00
Platter, 13 3/8 In. 1035.00
Platter, 17 1/8 In. . . . . .1725.00 to 1840.00
Platter, 19th Century, 18 1/4 x 15 1/4 In. 1092.00
Platter, Butterfly, Rose Border, 1850, 11 In. 165.00
Platter, Deep, 14 In. 1095.00

Platter, Oval, 19 In.	2415.00
Platter, Oval, 19th Century, 18 1/4 x 14 1/4 In.	1610.00
Platter, Oval, 20 x 17 In.	1100.00
Platter & Mazarine, 17 1/2 In.	2415.00
Soup, Dish, 9 7/8 In., 3 Piece	545.00
Soup, Dish, 9 7/8 In., Pair	430.00 to 750.00
Tureen, Soup, Cover, 19th Century, 10 1/2 x 14 1/2 x 9 In.	3450.00
Urn, Cover, Baluster Shape, 12 1/2 In.	1610.00
Vase, Bottle Shape, 12 In., Pair	1725.00
Vase, Foo Dog & Kylin Design, Scalloped Rim, 19th Century, 17 In.	1495.00
Vase, Nobles At Literary Pursuits, Exotic Birds & Butterflies, 18 In., Pair	4600.00

ROSE MEDALLION china was made in China during the nineteenth and twentieth centuries. It is a distinctive design with four or more panels of decoration around a central medallion that includes a bird or a peony. The panels show birds and people. The background is a design of tree peonies and leaves. Pieces are colored in greens, pinks, and other colors. It is similar to Rose Canton.

Basin, 16 1/4 In.	750.00
Basket, Alternating Panels, Reticulated, Birds, Fruit, Foliage, 11 In.	920.00
Basket, Fruit, Tray, Reticulated, 19th Century, 14 1/4 In.	1610.00
Basket, Fruit, Undertray, Oval, 1910, 8 3/4 & 9 1/4 In., 2 Piece	285.00
Bough Pot, Cover, Squire Form, Berries, Squirrels Scene, Cut Corner, 9 In.	865.00
Bowl, 11 1/4 x 5 In.	374.00
Bowl, 19th Century, 4 1/2 x 10 1/4 In.	520.00
Bowl, 19th Century, 11 1/2 In.	990.00
Bowl, 19th Century, 13 In.	1320.00
Bowl, 9 1/2 In.	440.00
Bowl, Alternating Panels Of Nobles Beneath Pavilions, 9 5/8 In.	935.00
Bowl, Foliate Cast Rim, 2 Handles, 4-Footed, 10 1/4 In.	230.00
Bowl, Gilt Brass Mounted, 19th Century, 10 3/4 In.	1320.00
Bowl, Ormolu Mounts, 19th Century, 8 x 10 In.	770.00
Bowl, Panels Depict Nobles At Outdoor Pursuits, Floral, Bird, 5 1/8 In.	880.00
Bowl, Pod Finial Cover, Butterfly & Flower, Orange Peel Glaze, 8 3/4 In.	340.00
Bowl, Scalloped Edges, 9 x 2 1/4 In.	460.00
Brush Pot, Cylindrical, 19th Century, 4 3/4 In.	143.00
Brush Pot, Cylindrical, 9 1/4 In.	285.00
Butter, Double Flower Finial Cover, Ice Insert	210.00
Candlestick, 8 3/4 In.	440.00
Candlestick, Molded Kylin Design, 7 1/2 In., Pair	490.00
Charger, 19th Century, 19 In.	488.00
Charger, Alternating China Life Scenes, Bird, Butterfly, Rose Panels, 16 In.	412.00
Chocolate Pot, Late 19th Century, 9 1/2 In.	385.00
Chop Plate, 19th Century, 12 In.	330.00
Coffee Service, Cylindrical Teapot, Tea Canister, 23 Piece	550.00
Coffeepot, Slightly Ribbed Body, 10 In.	490.00
Compote, 19th Century, 3 1/2 x 9 1/2 In.	287.00
Compote, Diamond Shape, 19th Century, 3 x 14 x 11 In.	747.00
Dish, Footed, Shaped, 13 7/8 In.	290.00
Dish, Oval, Court Figures, Tree Peonies, Early 20th Century, 8 3/4 x 10 5/8 In.	88.00
Dish, Oval, Scalloped, 10 3/4 In.	175.00
Dish, Rectangular, 19th Century, 8 1/2 x 7 1/2 In.	286.00
Dish, Shrimp, 10 1/2 In.	175.00 to 430.00
Dish, Shrimp, 19th Century, 9 3/4 x 10 1/2 In.	345.00
Dish, Shrimp, Floral Flange, 19th Century, 9 1/2 x 10 In.	460.00
Dish, Soap, Cover, Perforated Insert, Rectangular, 19th Century, 3 In.	260.00
Garden Seat, 18 In., Pair	316.00
Garden Seat, 6 Sides, 19th Century, 19 x 12 x 10 In.	2185.00
Jar, Cover, Foo Dog Finial, Brass Strapwork, Baluster, 17 1/2 In.	1725.00
Jar, Domed Flanged Cover, Court Figures Within Pavilions, 23 In.	2200.00
Plate, 1860, 9 1/2 In.	100.00
Plate, 19th Century, 8 In., 8 Piece	220.00
Plate, 3-Lobed Form, 19th Century, 10 In.	345.00

Plate, 8 Sides, 6 1/2 In., 6 Piece 155.00
Plate, 9 1/2 In. 28.00
Plate, Alternating Panels Of Nobles, Flowers, Reticulated Rim, 7 In., 15 Piece 460.00
Platter, 11 In. 155.00
Platter, 18 In. 770.00
Platter, 19th Century, 11 x 9 In. 145.00
Platter, Late 19th Century, 14 x 17 1/2 In. 675.00
Platter, Mandarin Scenes, 16 1/2 In. 580.00
Platter, Oval, 12 In. ....130.00 to 193.00
Platter, Oval, 19th Century, 11 3/4 x 14 3/8 In. ....259.00 to 345.00
Platter, Oval, 6 Figural & Foliate Reserves, Late 19th Century, 14 1/2 In. 345.00
Punch Bowl, 16 In. 1980.00
Punch Bowl, 1910, 13 1/2 In. 495.00
Punch Bowl, 1920s, 6 1/2 x 14 In. 550.00
Punch Bowl, 19th Century, 5 3/4 x 13 3/4 In. 1380.00
Punch Bowl, 19th Century, 6 x 13 1/2 In. 1320.00
Punch Bowl, 19th Century, 6 1/2 x 15 3/4 In. 2070.00
Punch Bowl, 19th Century, 13 1/2 In. 825.00
Punch Bowl, 19th Century, 16 In. ....920.00 to 1980.00
Punch Bowl, Alternating China Life Scenes, Bird, Butterfly, Rose Panels, 12 In. 440.00
Punch Bowl, Alternating Mandarin Floral, Avian Reserves, 4 x 11 In. 258.00
Punch Bowl, Alternating Panels Of Flowers & Court Figures, Gilt, 10 In. 1035.00
Punch Bowl, Alternating Panels, Nobles, Birds, Fruiting Trees, 15 1/2 In. 1430.00
Sauceboat, Undertray, Lobed Shape, 2 Side Handles, Spoon, 8 x 9 3/4 In. 550.00
Serving Dish, Lozenge Form, 19th Century, 20 1/2 x 9 In. 385.00
Soap Dish, 5 1/2 In. 405.00
Tazza, 19th Century, 4 x 8 In. 303.00
Tazza, 19th Century, 4 1/2 x 10 1/2 In. 545.00
Tea Set, Teapot, Drum Form, 2 Cups, Wicker Case, 19th Century, 4 Piece ....195.00 to 250.00
Teapot, Cover, Landscape, Birds, Butterflies, Blossoms, Handle, 9 x 7 In. 315.00
Teapot, Cylindrical, Entwined Strap Handle, 19th Century, 5 In. 230.00
Teapot, Domed Lid, 19th Century, 8 1/2 In. ....316.00 to 495.00
Teapot, Drum Form, 19th Century, 5 1/2 In. 193.00
Teapot, Drum Form, 19th Century, 5 3/4 In. 77.00
Teapot, Peach Shape, 6 1/2 In. 430.00
Teapot, Woven Straw Basket Caddy, Chintz Liner 275.00
Tray, Fluted, Square, 9 In. 245.00
Tureen, Cover, 2 Handles, 19th Century, 6 1/2 x 9 In. 660.00
Tureen, Cover, Bombe Shape, People, Birds, Gilt Handles, c.1840, 14 In. 1150.00
Tureen, Cover, Traditional Design, Oval, 19th Century, 11 1/4 In. 550.00
Tureen, Sauce, Cover, 19th Century, 6 In., Pair 2645.00
Tureen, Soup, Cover, 11 In. 1430.00
Tureen, Soup, Figural Scenes, Branch Handles, 1875, 15 In. 2530.00
Undertray, Leaf Shape, 8 1/2 In. 240.00
Urn, Cover, Molded Foo Lion & Ring Faux Handles, 16 In. 805.00
Vase, Alternating Nobles Within Pavilions, Floral Panels, 18 In. 522.00
Vase, Alternating Panels Of Court Pursuits, Exotic Birds, 18 x 8 In., Pair 3910.00
Vase, Alternating Panels Of Exotic Birds & Flowering Shrubs, 24 In., Pair 2185.00
Vase, Alternating Panels Of Notables, Birds With Flowers, 18 In., Pair 1760.00
Vase, Applied Foo Dog Handles, Baluster, 13 In. 245.00
Vase, Baluster Shape, 19th Century, 13 x 6 1/2 In. 1380.00
Vase, Baluster Shape, Alternating Panels, c.1870, 12 In., Pair 1045.00
Vase, Baluster Shape, Domed Lid, Dog Finial, Early 20th Century, 24 In., Pair 2420.00
Vase, Baluster Shape, Molded Foo Lions Neck, 19th Century, 24 In., Pair 2990.00
Vase, Baluster, 19th Century, 12 In., Pair 440.00
Vase, Bottle Form, 19th Century, 13 1/2 x 8 In. 1150.00
Vase, Club Form, Foo Lion Handles, Chih Lung Dragon At Shoulder, 10 In. 195.00
Vase, Court Scene Of Birds & Butterflies Amidst Flowers, 18 In., Pair 1955.00
Vase, Court Scene Panels, Gilt Salamanders, 14 x 7 3/4 In., Pair 2760.00
Vase, Court Scenes & Figures Surrounded By Floral Design, 17 In., Pair 575.00
Vase, Court Scenes, Butterflies, Applied Gilt Salamanders, 17 5/8 In., Pair 1540.00
Vase, Cover, Alternating Panels Of Flowers, Birds, 14 x 6 In. 1870.00
Vase, Gilt Foo Dogs & Kylins, 19th Century, 25 In., Pair 2990.00

Vase, Hexagonal, Relief Foo Lions, 19th Century, 9 In.	358.00
Vase, Ku Form, 20th Century, 13 3/4 x 8 3/4 In.	430.00
Vase, Kylin Handles, Baluster Form, 10 In., Pair	495.00
Vase, Molded Dragons, Figural, Floral Reserves, Animal Handles, 19 1/2 In.	920.00
Vase, Nobles Within Pavilions, Exotic Birds Amidst Flowers, 14 In., Pair	1725.00
Vase, Nobles, Pavilions, Flower & Butterfly Panels, Foo Dog On Lid, 12 3/8 In.	495.00

ROSE O'NEILL, see Kewpie category.

ROSE TAPESTRY porcelain was made by the Royal Bayreuth factory of Tettau, Germany, during the late nineteenth century. The surface of the porcelain was pressed against a coarse fabric while it was still damp, and the impressions remained on the finished porcelain. It looks and feels like a textured cloth. Very skillful reproductions are being made that even include a variation of the Royal Bayreuth mark, so be careful when buying.

Creamer	300.00
Powder Jar, Courting Scene On Domed Cover, Signed, 3 1/2 In.	170.00
Ring Holder, Scalloped Edge, Center Ring Support, Signed, 3 1/4 In.	345.00
Shoe, Woman's Lace Up, Roses, Signed, 3 3/4 In.	515.00
Vase, Bud, 4 7/8 In.	330.00
Vase, Cherub & Woman Harvesting, Pompedeur, 8 1/2 In.	235.00

ROSEMEADE Pottery of Wahpeton, North Dakota, worked from 1940 to 1961. The pottery was operated by Laura A. Taylor and her husband, R.I. Hughes. The company was also known as the Wahpeton Pottery Company. Art pottery and commercial wares were made.

Figurine, Cat, White Tail Up	80.00
Paperweight, Buffalo, Small	150.00
Planter, Doe, 4 In.	40.00
Salt & Pepper, Cattle & Blockhouse, Purple	1400.00
Salt & Pepper, Corn	40.00
Salt & Pepper, Mallard	90.00
Salt & Pepper, Peace Garden	325.00
Salt & Pepper, Pheasants, Tail Down	100.00
Salt & Pepper, Pheasants, Tail Up	60.00
Salt & Pepper, Trout	300.00
Salt & Pepper, Turkey	.65.00 to 90.00
Spoon Rest, Pheasant	75.00
Sugar & Creamer, Turkey	180.00

ROSENTHAL porcelain was made at the factory established in Selb, Bavaria, in 1880. The factory is still making fine-quality tablewares and figurines. A series of Christmas plates was made from 1910. Other limited edition plates have been made since 1971.

Bowl, Vegetable, Cover	22.00
Cup & Saucer, Donatello, Hand Painted, AG, Selb, Artist Marked, 1929	99.95
Cup & Saucer, Donatello, White & Fired Gold, Celb Bavaria, 4 3/4 In.	25.00
Cup & Saucer, Maria, Raised Flower Design, Demitasse	18.00
Cup & Saucer, Monbijou, 2446 Shape, Relief Mold, Woman At Lakeside	150.00
Figurine, Bulldog, 6 x 4 In.	595.00
Figurine, Classical Girl, 14 In.	143.00
Figurine, Crouching Female, Bisque Finish, Signed, 17 In.	385.00
Figurine, Dachshund, Sitting On Back Legs	225.00
Figurine, Dog, Borzoi, Lying On Side, 20th Century, 5 1/2 x 3 1/2 In.	475.00
Figurine, Foal, Lying, White	455.00
Figurine, Fox, Brown, Gray & White, U.S. Zone, 11 1/2 In.	135.00
Figurine, Fox, M.H. Fritz, 9 7/8 In.	525.00
Figurine, German Short Hair Pointer, Signed, 10 1/2 x 6 In.	595.00
Figurine, Hound, 20th Century, 10 In.	532.00
Figurine, Penguin, 3 In.	135.00
Figurine, Poodle, Standing, Tongue Out, 8 1/4 x 8 In.	495.00
Figurine, Scotch Terrier, White, Black Nose & Head, 5 1/2 x 6 1/4 In.	295.00

Luncheon Set,	Starburst On White Ground, Decal, Service For 12	520.00
Plaque,	Flowers, Giltwood Frame, 9 1/4 x 7 1/4 In.	402.00
Plate,	Center Female Portraits, c.1900, 10 In., 3 Piece	287.00
Plate,	Central Floral Medallion, Gilt Lace Surround, 10 3/4 In., 12 Piece	175.00
Plate,	Figural Gilt Rim, Green Border, Ivory Ground, 11 In., 12 Piece	632.00
Vase,	Stylized Tree, 5 In.	51.00

ROSEVILLE Pottery Company was organized in Roseville, Ohio, in 1890. Another plant was opened in Zanesville, Ohio, in 1898. Many types of pottery were made until 1954. Early wares include Sgraffito, Olympic, and Rozane. Later lines were often made with molded decorations, especially flowers and fruit. Most pieces are marked *Roseville*. Many reproductions made in China have been offered for sale the past few years.

Roseville
U.S.A.

Apple Blossom,	Basket, Blue, Handle, 10 In.	285.00
Apple Blossom,	Basket, Green, Handle, 8 In.	150.00
Apple Blossom,	Basket, Green, Handle, 10 In.	350.00
Apple Blossom,	Basket, Green, Hanging, 5 In.	170.00
Apple Blossom,	Basket, Pink, Handle, 8 In. . . . . .250.00 to 300.00
Apple Blossom,	Bookends, Green	195.00
Apple Blossom,	Bowl, Green, 6 In.	78.00
Apple Blossom,	Bowl, Green, 8 In.	105.00
Apple Blossom,	Bowl, Green, Flat Handles, 6 1/2 x 2 1/2 In.	145.00
Apple Blossom,	Candlestick, Blue, 4 1/2 In., Pair	350.00
Apple Blossom,	Candlestick, Pink, 2 In., Pair	100.00
Apple Blossom,	Console, Blue, 12 In.	195.00
Apple Blossom,	Console, Green, 14 In.	200.00
Apple Blossom,	Console, Pink, 10 In.	195.00
Apple Blossom,	Console, Pink, 12 In.	175.00
Apple Blossom,	Cornucopia, Blue, 6 In.	60.00
Apple Blossom,	Cornucopia, Green, 6 In. . . . . .65.00 to 70.00
Apple Blossom,	Flowerpot, Pink, Saucer, 5 In.	170.00
Apple Blossom,	Jardiniere, Pedestal, Green & Brown, 24 2/4 In.	935.00
Apple Blossom,	Jardiniere, Pedestal, Pink, 31 In.	1250.00
Apple Blossom,	Planter, Blue, 4 In.	135.00
Apple Blossom,	Planter, Green, 4 In.	135.00
Apple Blossom,	Tea Set, Blue, Teapot, Creamer & Sugar, Raised Mark, 3 Piece	440.00
Apple Blossom,	Teapot, Cover, Pink	256.00
Apple Blossom,	Vase, Blue, 2 Handles, 7 In.	200.00
Apple Blossom,	Vase, Blue, 2 Handles, 10 In.	195.00
Apple Blossom,	Vase, Blue, 2 Handles, Footed, Raised Mark, 10 In.	190.00
Apple Blossom,	Vase, Blue, 2 Handles, Raised Mark, 6 In. . . . . .135.00 to 165.00
Apple Blossom,	Vase, Green, 2 Handles, 6 In.	70.00
Apple Blossom,	Vase, Green, 2 Handles, 8 In.	170.00
Apple Blossom,	Vase, Green, 7 In.	135.00
Apple Blossom,	Vase, Pink, 7 In.	100.00
Apple Blossom,	Vase, Pink, Base Handle, 12 In.	295.00
Apple Blossom,	Wall Pocket, Blue, Handle, 8 In.	215.00
Apple Blossom,	Wall Pocket, Brown, Handle, 8 In.	190.00
Apple Blossom,	Wall Pocket, Green, Handle, 8 In.	250.00
Apple Blossom,	Window Box, Blue, 2 Handles, 2 1/2 x 10 1/2 In.	120.00
Apple Blossom,	Window Box, Green, 12 In.	160.00
Artwood,	Vase, Green, 10 In.	135.00
Aztec,	Vase, Blue & Orange, Blue Ground, Tapered	330.00
Baneda,	Candlestick, Pink, 4 1/2 In., Pair	575.00
Baneda,	Candlestick, Pink, 5 In., Pair	750.00
Baneda,	Console, Green, 6 Sides, Handle From Base, 12 In.	525.00
Baneda,	Console, Pink, 10 In.	395.00
Baneda,	Jardiniere, Green, 2 Handles, 4 In.	385.00
Baneda,	Jardiniere, Green, 2 Handles, 7 In.	1540.00
Baneda,	Jardiniere, Pedestal, Green, 28 In.	4290.00
Baneda,	Jardiniere, Pink, 8 In.	1870.00
Baneda,	Vase, Green, 2 Handles, Original Black Paper Label, 6 In.	500.00

Baneda, Vase, Green, 4 In. 450.00
Baneda, Vase, Green, 7 In. 795.00
Baneda, Vase, Green, Handles From Base, 7 In. 400.00
Baneda, Vase, Green, Orange Fruit, Blue Band, 2 Handles, 9 In. 1110.00
Baneda, Vase, Green, Short Collared Neck, 9 In. 795.00
Baneda, Vase, Green, Squat, Unmarked, 4 1/4 In. 578.00
Baneda, Vase, Pink, 2 Handles, 4 In. 220.00
Baneda, Vase, Pink, 2 Handles, 6 In. . . . . .450.00 to 550.00
Baneda, Vase, Pink, 2 Handles, 9 In. 825.00
Baneda, Vase, Pink, Cylindrical, 9 In. 825.00
Baneda, Vase, Pink, Foil Label, 7 In. 465.00
Baneda, Vase, Pink, Oval, 2 Handles, 12 In. 770.00
Baneda, Vase, Pink, Trumpet Shape, 7 In. 700.00
Bittersweet, Bowl, Green, 8 In. 225.00
Bittersweet, Candlestick, Green, Handles, 3 In., Pair 98.00
Bittersweet, Console, Yellow, 14 In. 175.00
Bittersweet, Jardiniere, Pedestal, Green, 24 In. 1295.00
Bittersweet, Jardiniere, Pink, 8 In. 165.00
Bittersweet, Vase, Green, 10 In. 165.00
Bittersweet, Vase, Green, Bud, Double, 6 In. 235.00
Bittersweet, Vase, Yellow, Raised Marks, 16 In. 880.00
Blackberry, Bowl, 8 In. 385.00
Blackberry, Console, 3 1/2 x 13 In. 451.00
Blackberry, Jardiniere, 9 In. 1430.00
Blackberry, Jardiniere, Green, 4 x 5 1/2 In. 495.00
Blackberry, Vase, Corseted, 5 In. . . . . .467.00 to 522.00
Blackberry, Vase, Green, 2 Small Handles At Neck, 6 x 5 1/2 In. 522.00
Blackberry, Vase, Handles, Label, 8 x 6 In. 525.00
Blackberry, Vase, Squat, 2 Handles, 4 In. 506.00
Bleeding Heart, Basket, Pink, Raised Mark, 10 In. 245.00
Bleeding Heart, Bookends, Book Shape, Pink, Raised Mark, 5 1/2 In. 385.00
Bleeding Heart, Candlestick, Pink, 2 In., Pair 175.00
Bleeding Heart, Jardiniere, Pink, Raised Mark, 8 In. 1045.00
Bleeding Heart, Vase, Green, 2 Angular Handles, 7 In. 165.00
Bleeding Heart, Vase, Green, 6 In. 121.00
Bleeding Heart, Vase, Pink, Dark Green Base, Handles, 9 In. 412.00
Burmese, Bookends, Green 350.00
Bushberry, Compote, Orange, 6 In. 200.00
Bushberry, Pitcher, Blue, Raised Handle, 8 1/4 In. 440.00
Bushberry, Vase, Blue, Flared Rim, Impressed Mark, 18 In. 550.00
Bushberry, Vase, Blue, Manufacturer's Mark, 12 1/2 In. 258.00
Bushberry, Vase, Green, Pink, 8 1/4 In. 165.00
Bushberry, Vase, Green, Raised Mark, 18 In. 880.00
Carnelian, Bowl, Pink, 3 x 8 x 3 In. 220.00
Carnelian, Vase, Mottled Purple, 8 In. 305.00
Carnelian I, Vase, Blue Matte, 10 In. 175.00
Carnelian I, Vase, Blue, Pink Matte, Angular Handles, Black Label, 10 1/4 In. 415.00
Carnelian I, Vase, Blue, Pink Matte, Scrolled Handles, RV Ink Mark, 12 In. 440.00
Carnelian II, Bowl, Mottled Pink & Green Glaze, 14 In. 550.00
Carnelian II, Jardiniere, Rose, Mauve, Green, Buttressed Handles, 12 x 7 3/4 In. 1650.00
Carnelian II, Vase, Mottled Pink, Yellow & Green Glaze, Scrolled Handles, 9 3/4 In. 770.00
Carnelian II, Vase, Pink & Green Glaze, Scrolled Handles, 7 1/4 In. 275.00
Cherry Blossom, Jardiniere, Brown, 7 In. 550.00
Cherry Blossom, Jardiniere, Green With Pink, 2 Handles, 5 1/4 In. 345.00
Cherry Blossom, Jardiniere, Pink, 5 1/4 x 7 In. 605.00
Cherry Blossom, Vase, Terra-Cotta Matte Glaze, 2 Handles, 8 In. 660.00
Cherry Blossom, Vase, Terra-Cotta, 2 Handles, 10 In. 715.00
Chloron, Wall Pocket, Green Matte Glaze, Embossed Leaves 660.00
Clematis, Basket, Green, Hanging, 7 In. 95.00
Clematis, Basket, Orange & Tan, Yellow Flowers, Molded Handle, 7 1/4 In. 225.00
Clematis, Bookends, Green, 5 1/4 In. 190.00
Clematis, Bowl, Green, Handle, 10 In. 120.00
Clematis, Candlestick, Green, 4 1/4 In., Pair 75.00

Clematis, Console, Blue, 14 In. 100.00
Clematis, Ewer, Blue, 10 In. 195.00
Clematis, Flower Frog, Blue, 4 In. 39.00
Clematis, Flowerpot, Green, 5 In. 55.00
Clematis, Vase, Blue, 7 In. 77.00
Clematis, Vase, Brown, 6 In. 85.00
Clematis, Vase, Green, 8 In. ....90.00 to 144.00
Clematis, Vase, Green, 12 In. 325.00
Clematis, Vase, Green, Floral, 2 Handles, 10 In. 55.00
Clematis, Wall Pocket, Blue, 8 In. 170.00
Clemena, Vase, Green, 2 Handles, 7 In. 450.00
Columbine, Basket, Blue, 7 In. 260.00
Columbine, Bowl, Blue, 6 In. 67.00
Columbine, Ewer, Blue, 7 In. 180.00
Columbine, Jardiniere, Blue, Raised Mark, 10 In. 413.00
Columbine, Vase, Blue, 10 In. ....295.00 to 320.00
Columbine, Vase, Brown, Buttressed Base, 14 In. 440.00
Columbine, Vase, Corseted, Blue, Raised Mark, 7 In. 110.00
Cosmos, Console, Blue, 9 In. 154.00
Creamware, Juvenile, Creamer, Chick, Side-Pour, 4 In. 140.00
Creamware, Juvenile, Plate, Rolled Edge, Rabbits, 8 In. 120.00
Creamware, Juvenile, Plate, Rolled Edge, Sunbonnet Babies, Ink Mark, 7 1/2 In. 165.00
Cremona, Vase, Green, Blue, Tan, Cream, 8 In. 165.00
Cremona, Vase, Green, Flared Rim, 10 x 5 1/2 In. 193.00
Cremona, Vase, Pillow, Pink & Yellow Mottled Glaze, 6 In. 66.00
Crystalis, Vase, Celadon, Ocher Glaze, 13 1/4 x 3 3/4 In. 1100.00
Crystalis, Vase, Olive & Blue Glaze, 3 Monks' Heads, 15 x 4 1/2 In. 2090.00
Dahlrose, Console, Frog, Oval, 10 In. 185.00
Dahlrose, Jardiniere, 6 In. 195.00
Dahlrose, Jardiniere, Pedestal, 20 1/2 In. 770.00
Dahlrose, Vase, Floral, 2 Handles, 8 In. ....245.00 to 440.00
Dawn, Vase, Yellow, Buttressed Handles, Impressed Mark, 10 In. 358.00
Della Robbia, Pitcher, Signed F.S., 7 1/2 x 8 1/2 In. 2420.00
Della Robbia, Vase, Carved Poppies In 5 Panels, Peach, Deep Green, 17 In. 12100.00
Dogwood I, Jardiniere, 8 1/2 x 12 In. 303.00
Dogwood I, Planter, 11 x 6 x 6 1/2 In. 195.00
Dogwood I, Vase, Oval, Ink Mark, 6 1/4 x 5 1/4 In. 88.00
Dogwood II, Basket, 6 In. ....250.00 to 285.00
Dogwood II, Jardiniere, 11 x 12 In. 165.00
Dogwood II, Umbrella Stand, Signed, 20 In. 770.00
Dogwood II, Vase, 8 In. ....110.00 to 295.00
Donatello, Ashtray, 4 1/2 In. 110.00
Donatello, Jardiniere, 7 In. ....145.00 to 150.00
Donatello, Jardiniere, 8 1/2 x 11 1/2 In., Pair 275.00
Donatello, Jardiniere, 10 In. 77.00
Donatello, Jardiniere, Bulbous, 10 x 14 In. 85.00
Donatello, Powder Jar 275.00
Donatello, Umbrella Stand, Green, 21 x 10 In. 413.00
Donatello, Vase, Gray, 11 3/4 In. 144.00
Donatello, Window Box, Cherubs Exterior Scene, 16 In. 165.00
Earlam, Vase, Orange, Green, Blue Matte Glaze, Bulbous, 2 Handles, 7 1/4 x 7 In. 413.00
Egypto, Bowl, Green Matte Glaze, 3 Handles, 8 1/2 In. 66.00
Egypto, Pitcher, Green Matte Glaze, 7 1/2 In. 550.00
Egypto, Vase, Green Matte Glaze, 3 Handles, 3 Footed, 7 x 4 In. 175.00
Falline, Vase, Brown, Bulbous, 6 1/2 x 8 In. 660.00
Falline, Vase, Green, 2 Handles, Stepped In Neck, 7 In. 770.00
Falline, Vase, Green, Bulbous, 2 Handles, 7 x 7 In. 605.00
Ferella, Bowl, Brown, Flower Frog, 10 In. 550.00
Ferella, Vase, Brown, 2 Handles, 5 In. 605.00
Ferella, Vase, Green & Cream, Silver Sticker, 9 1/4 In. 1045.00
Ferella, Vase, Red, Handles, 5 In. 440.00
Florentine, Jardiniere, Pink, 9 x 11 In. 165.00
Florentine, Pedestal, Blond, 17 In. 110.00

Florentine, Sand Jar, Blond, 14 In. 395.00
Foxglove, Basket, Pink, Impressed Mark, 12 In. 330.00
Foxglove, Bowl, Blue, 3 x 13 x 7 In. 110.00
Foxglove, Candlestick, Pink, Raised Mark, 5 In., Pair 190.00
Foxglove, Pitcher, Blue, 7 In. 195.00
Foxglove, Rose Bowl, Pink, 6 In. 260.00
Foxglove, Vase, Blue, 4 In. 85.00
Foxglove, Vase, Blue, Fan, Buttressed Base, Impressed Mark, 8 In. 110.00
Foxglove, Vase, Green, Bulbous, Raised Mark, 15 In. 385.00
Foxglove, Vase, Green, Handles, 8 In. 165.00
Foxglove, Vase, Pink, Footed, 7 In. 138.00
Foxglove, Vase, Pink, Raised Mark, Initials H.B., 18 In. 715.00
Freesia, Basket, Handle, Tropical Green, 10 In. 310.00
Freesia, Basket, Hanging, 5 x 8 In. 180.00
Freesia, Bookend, Delft Blue, 10 In. 75.00
Freesia, Bookends, Delft Blue, 10 In., Pair 205.00
Freesia, Bowl, Tangerine, 4 In. 84.00
Freesia, Candlestick, Tangerine, 5 In., Pair 135.00
Freesia, Cookie Jar, Delft Blue, 8 In. 450.00
Freesia, Ewer, Tangerine, 15 In. 450.00
Freesia, Tea Set, Tropical, Green, Teapot, 8 In., 3 Piece 330.00
Freesia, Vase, Delft Blue, 2 Handles, 12 In. 245.00
Freesia, Vase, Delft Blue, 6 In. 165.00
Freesia, Vase, Delft Blue, Raised Mark, 18 In. 495.00
Freesia, Vase, Green, 15 1/2 In. 415.00
Freesia, Vase, Green, 9 In. 110.00
Freesia, Vase, Green, Handles, 10 1/2 In. 130.00
Freesia, Vase, Green, Handles, 15 In. 357.00
Freesia, Vase, Tangerine, 7 In. 88.00
Freesia, Vase, Tangerine, 8 3/4 In. 120.00
Freesia, Wall Pocket, Green, 8 1/4 In. 155.00
Fuchsia, Bowl, Terra-Cotta, 2 Handles, 8 In. 100.00
Fuchsia, Ewer, Green, 10 In. 220.00
Fuchsia, Flowerpot, Bluc, 5 In. 275.00
Fuchsia, Jardiniere, Green, Impressed Mark, 6 In. 275.00
Fuchsia, Vase, Terra-Cotta, 10 In. 430.00
Fuchsia, Vase, Terra-Cotta, Impressed Mark, 6 In. 165.00
Futura, Jardiniere, Burnt-Orange, Yellow, Green, Blue, Lavender, 6 x 8 1/2 In. 248.00
Futura, Jardiniere, Purple, Pink, Purple Leaves, Protruding Shoulder, 9 x 13 In. 275.00
Futura, Jardiniere, Rose, Green, Polychrome Leaves, 6 x 9 In. 330.00
Futura, Planter, Blue Green, Orange Glaze, Oval, Footed, 7 1/2 x 5 In. 385.00
Futura, Vase, Beehive Shape, Blue Green Matte Glaze, Buttressed Corners, 8 In. 523.00
Futura, Vase, Blue Ground, Blue, Green, Spherical, Pentagon Base, 8 x 5 1/4 In. 495.00
Futura, Vase, Blue, 9 1/2 In. 660.00
Futura, Vase, Green, Brown, Orange, Squat, Bottle Shape, 8 1/2 In. 1320.00
Futura, Vase, Green, Gray Glaze, Stepped Neck, Buttressed Handles, 9 1/4 x 5 In. 660.00
Futura, Vase, Green, Pink Glaze, Spherical Base, Stepped Neck, 8 1/4 x 5 In. 495.00
Futura, Vase, Orange, Blue, Green Matte Glaze, Buttressed Corners, 8 x 3 3/4 In. 413.00
Futura, Vase, Orange, Blue, Green, 4 Sides, Flared, Buttressed Corners, 5 1/4 x 4 1/4 In. . . 193.00
Futura, Vase, Orange, Gray & Green, Polygon-Shaped, Flared, 4 In. 660.00
Futura, Vase, Orange, Green Chevron, Flared, Buttresses, Semispherical, 12 1/4 x 5 In. . . . 1045.00
Futura, Vase, Pink, 9 1/2 In. 660.00
Futura, Vase, Pink Matte Glaze, Embossed Twigs, Fan, Buttressed, 4 x 6 1/2 In. 385.00
Futura, Vase, Pink, Green Glaze, 4 Sides, Buttressed Handles, Pillow, 8 1/2 x 6 1/4 In. . . . 770.00
Futura, Vase, Reddish Brown To Brown, 2 Handles, Embossed Mark, 10 1/4 In. 56.00
Futura, Vase, Sailboat, Floral Design, Ocher Interior, Drip Glaze, 12 x 5 x 3 In. 470.00
Futura, Vase, Turquoise & Green Glaze, 4 Sides, Squat, 9 3/4 In. 465.00
Futura, Vase, White Overglaze, Orange, Brown, Square Base, 12 x 4 1/2 In. 1430.00
Gardenia, Basket, Seafoam Green, Raised Mark, 8 In. 209.00
Gardenia, Bookends, Seafoam Green 235.00
Gardenia, Bowl, Seafoam Green, Squat, 5 1/4 In. 173.00
Gardenia, Candlestick, Silver Haze Gray, Pair 75.00
Gardenia, Flowerpot, Golden Tan, 3 In. 67.00

Gardenia, Vase, Golden Tan, 2 Handles, 8 In. 125.00
Gardenia, Window Box, Silver Haze Gray, 12 In. 170.00
Gardenia, Window Box, Silver Haze Gray, 2 Handles, 8 In. 125.00
Hexagon, Bowl, Dark Green Matte Glaze, 2 Angled Handles, Zanesville, Oh., 2 In. 86.00
Imperial I, Basket, 6 In. 121.00
Imperial II, Jardiniere, Green Glaze, Sky Blue Base, Gourd Shape, 5 1/2 x 8 In. 660.00
Imperial II, Vase, Cobalt Blue, White Raised Border, 9 3/4 x 5 1/2 In. 1540.00
Iris, Bowl, Blue, 2 Handles, Impressed Mark, 6 In. 165.00
Iris, Jardiniere, Pink, Raised Mark, 10 In. 605.00
Iris, Vase, Blue, Bulbous, 9 In. 358.00
Iris, Vase, Brown, 8 In. 185.00
Iris, Vase, Brown, Footed, Pillow, Raised Mark, 8 In. 187.00
Iris, Vase, Coral To Green, 8 In. 140.00
Iris, Vase, Coral To Green, 10 In. 180.00
Iris, Vase, Coral, 2 Handles At Neck, 8 In. 385.00
Iris, Vase, Coral, 6 In. 50.00
Ivory, Vase, Chalice Shape, Branch Handles, Tree-Trunk Stem, 9 1/4 x 6 1/4 In. 275.00
Ivory, Vase, Tuscany Mold, 9 In. 85.00
Ixia, Lamp, Pink, Bulbous, Foil Label, 7 3/4 In. 825.00
Ixia, Vase, Coral, Tapered, Impressed Mark, 12 In. 385.00
Ixia, Vase, Yellow, Buttressed, Impressed Mark, 8 In. 220.00
Jonquil, Jardiniere, 8 x 10 In. 275.00
Jonquil, Vase, 2 Handles, 4 In. 330.00
Jonquil, Vase, 2 Handles, 6 1/2 x 7 1/2 In. .... .295.00 to 413.00
Jonquil, Vase, 2 Handles, 8 In. 660.00
Jonquil, Vase, Tapered, 2 Handles, 4 x 4 1/2 In. 110.00
Lamp Base, Golden Brown Mottled Glossy Glaze, Factory, Tuscany Style, 8 1/4 In. 242.00
Laurel, Jardiniere, Green, Bulbous, Silver Foil Label, 7 1/2 In. 578.00
Laurel, Vase, Green, 14 1/4 x 8 In. 880.00
Laurel, Vase, Orange Matte Glaze, 2 Open Handles, 7 In. 330.00
Luffa, Bowl, Brown, 4 x 10 x 6 In. 330.00
Luffa, Vase, Brown, 6 1/4 In. 303.00
Luffa, Vase, Green, 7 3/4 In. 275.00
Lustre, Candlestick, 1915, 10 In., Pair 425.00
Magnolia, Bowl, Green, 10 In. 99.00
Magnolia, Console Set, Blue, 14-In. Bowl, 3 Piece 375.00
Magnolia, Cookie Jar, Brown, 8 In. 225.00
Magnolia, Ewer, Blue, Mark, 15 In. 341.00
Magnolia, Green, 2 Handles At Neck, 15 In. 275.00
Magnolia, Jardiniere, Green, 8 1/4 In. 135.00
Magnolia, Tea Set, Blue, 3 Piece 220.00
Magnolia, Tea Set, Green, 3 Piece 340.00
Magnolia, Vase, Brown, 16 In. 247.00
Magnolia, Vase, Brown, 2 Handles, 9 In. 95.00
Magnolia, Vase, Brown, 2 Handles, Raised Mark, 7 In. 75.00
Mayfair, Basket, Cocoa Brown, 10 In. 110.00
Ming Tree, Basket, Jade Green, 12 In. 77.00
Ming Tree, Basket, Rose, Brown, Branch Handle, 8 1/2 In. 125.00
Mock Orange, Cornucopia, Yellow, 6 In. 65.00
Mock Orange, Pedestal, Yellow, 17 In. 286.00
Monticello, Basket, Aqua, 6 1/4 In. 355.00
Monticello, Bowl, Flower Frog, Tan, 6 Sides, 2 Handles, 13 In. 275.00
Monticello, Jardiniere, Brown, Bulbous, Mark, 5 In. 264.00
Monticello, Lamp, Tan, Handles, 1931 .... 360.00
Monticello, Planter, Tan, Squat, Oblong, Flower Frog, Paper Label, 3 x 13 In. 440.00
Monticello, Vase, Tan, Corseted, Black Paper Label, 4 1/4 x 5 1/2 In. 358.00
Morning Glory, Jardiniere, Green, Squat, Bulbous, Foil Label, 6 1/4 x 7 1/2 In. 440.00
Morning Glory, Vase, Green, Squat, 2 Handles, Foil Label, 4 1/4 In. 468.00
Morning Glory, Vase, White, 7 In. 525.00
Moss, Vase, Pink, Flared, Footed, Raised Mark, 5 In. 198.00
Mostique, Flower Block, Tan, 2 1/2 In. 220.00
Mostique, Vase, Gray, Green, Yellow, Blue, Tan, Geometric Design, 15 In. .... .660.00 to 715.00
Mostique, Vase, Gray, Tan, 10 In. 220.00

Mostique, Vase, Tan, Floral Design, 6 In. 275.00
Normandy, Jardiniere, Black Foil Label, 8 In. 275.00
Normandy, Jardiniere, Unmarked, 8 x 10 In. 165.00
Orion, Vase, Red, Green Interior, Spherical, 2 Handles, No Mark, 6 1/2 x 9 In. 220.00
Orion, Vase, Turquoise, Taupe Interior, Footed, No Mark, 10 1/2 In. ....230.00 to 253.00
Panel, Candlestick, Green, RV Ink Mark, 8 1/2 In. 110.00
Panel, Vase, Nude, Brown, RV Ink Mark, 8 1/4 x 5 1/2 In. 440.00
Panel, Vase, Nude, Green, Footed, Flared, RV Ink Mark, 11 1/2 x 5 1/4 In. 1980.00
Peony, Basket, Sienna Brown, Hanging, Original Chains, 7 In. 88.00
Peony, Ewer, Nile Green, 14 In. 110.00
Peony, Jardiniere, Nile Green, 3 In. 35.00
Peony, Vase, Coral, 15 In. 495.00
Peony, Vase, Coral, Green, 2 Handles, 7 In. 73.00
Peony, Vase, Coral, Green, 2 Handles, 10 In. 190.00
Peony, Vase, Green Matte Glaze, Crimped Petals, Signed, 18 1/2 In. 550.00
Peony, Vase, Nile Green, 15 In. 275.00
Peony, Vase, Nile Green, 18 In. 550.00
Peony, Vase, Nile Green, 2 Handles, 6 In. 84.00
Peony, Vase, Nile Green, Small Handles At Neck, 7 1/4 In. 275.00
Peony, Vase, Sienna Brown, 8 In. 385.00
Persian, Jardiniere, Ivory, No Mark, 5 x 6 1/2 In. 165.00
Pine Cone, Ashtray, Brown, Signed, 7 In. 410.00
Pine Cone, Bowl, Blue, Signed, 1931, 6 1/2 In. 258.00
Pine Cone, Bowl, Green, Twig Handles, 4 x 6 1/2 In. 110.00
Pine Cone, Candlestick, Blue, Purple Edge Base, 4 In., Pair 385.00
Pine Cone, Ewer, Brown, Impressed Mark, 15 In. 1045.00
Pine Cone, Jardiniere, Brown, 6 x 7 In. 286.00
Pine Cone, Jardiniere, Green, Spherical, 5 In. 165.00
Pine Cone, Jardiniere, Pedestal, Brown, 10 In. 1540.00
Pine Cone, Jardiniere, Pedestal, Brown, 28 5/8 In. 1430.00
Pine Cone, Jardiniere, Pedestal, Brown, No Mark, 8 In. 1760.00
Pine Cone, Pitcher, Blue, Gold Foil Label, 9 1/4 In. 1870.00
Pine Cone, Pitcher, Blue, Impressed Mark, 10 In. 770.00
Pine Cone, Pitcher, Green, Brown Matte Glaze, Branch Handle, 8 In. 315.00
Pine Cone, Umbrella Stand, Blue, Impressed Mark, 20 In. 3166.00
Pine Cone, Vase, Blue, 2 Handles, 8 In. 495.00
Pine Cone, Vase, Blue, 2 Handles, Cutout Rim, Impressed Mark, 10 In. 825.00
Pine Cone, Vase, Blue, 7 1/4 In. 75.00
Pine Cone, Vase, Blue, Corseted, Impressed Mark, 12 In. 660.00
Pine Cone, Vase, Blue, Green Interior, Branch Handles, 7 3/8 x 5 In. 95.00
Pine Cone, Vase, Brown, 10 In. ....385.00 to 475.00
Pine Cone, Vase, Brown, Bud, Double, Raised Mark, 8 1/4 In. 305.00
Pine Cone, Vase, Brown, Footed, Pillow, Impressed Mark, 7 In. 248.00
Pine Cone, Vase, Brown, Triple Bud, Foil Label, 8 1/4 In. 415.00
Pine Cone, Vase, Fan, Green, 6 In. 275.00
Pine Cone, Vase, Green, 8 In. 225.00
Pine Cone, Vase, Green, Twig Handles, 12 In. 245.00
Pine Cone, Wall Pocket, Brown, Triple, Impressed Mark, 8 1/4 In. 605.00
Pine Cone, Window Box, Brown Base, Pine Branch Handle With Needles, 3 x 8 3/4 In. ... 95.00
Poppy, Jardiniere, Pink, 6 In. 193.00
Poppy, Vase, Green, Bulbous, Impressed Mark, 9 In. 303.00
Primrose, Umbrella Stand, Tan, Raised Mark, 21 x 11 In. 1320.00
Primrose, Vase, Pink, 2 Angular Handles, 6 In. 192.00
Primrose, Wall Pocket, Tan, 8 In. 660.00
Raymor, Serving Set, Wire, Rattan Stand, Ivory, Brown Mottled Glaze, 24 x 5 In. 357.00
Rosecraft, Vintage, Vase, Brown, RV Ink Mark, 12 1/2 In. 715.00
Rosecraft Hexagon, Vase, Green, RV Ink Mark, 8 x 4 1/2 In. 385.00
Rozane, Vase, Brown, Yellow & Orange Blossoms, Leaves, c.1900, 5 In. 200.00
Rozane, Vase, Cream, Molded Flowers, Pastel, Footed, c.1917, 10 In. 173.00
Rozane, Vase, Overlaid Silver Flowers, Signed, c.1900, 4 1/4 In. 287.00
Rozane, Vase, Pink, Oval, Roses, W. Meyers, 14 In. 190.00
Rozane Royal, Vase, Green, Yellow Roses, Leaves, Shaded Brown, Orange, 19 In. 1925.00
Russco, Vase, Cream, Green Crystalline Glaze, 2 Buttresses, 8 1/2 In. 220.00

Russco, Vase, Cream, Green Crystalline Glaze, Flared, Gold Foil Label, 7 1/4 In. 275.00
Russco, Vase, Gold, Caramel Crystalline Glaze, 2 Handles At Shoulder, 7 1/2 In. 230.00
Russco, Vase, Gold, Caramel Crystalline Glaze, 2 Handles, 8 In. 275.00
Silhouette, Box, Cigarette, 1952 .... 165.00
Silhouette, Vase, Pink, Embossed Leaf Panel, Raised Mark, 9 In. 121.00
Snowberry, Basket, Hanging, 2 Handles, Dusty Rose, 5 1/2 In. 60.00
Snowberry, Bookends, Blue, 5 In. ....73.00 to 140.00
Snowberry, Console, Rose Matte Glaze, 8 In. 110.00
Snowberry, Tea Set, Blue, Teapot, Creamer, Sugar, Raised Mark, 3 Piece 305.00
Snowberry, Tea Set, Rose, 3 Piece 385.00
Snowberry, Vase, Blue Matte Glaze, 6 In. 85.00
Snowberry, Vase, Blue, Raised Mark, 18 In. ....440.00 to 523.00
Snowberry, Vase, Bud, Blue, 7 In. 140.00
Snowberry, Vase, Green, 9 In. 150.00
Snowberry, Vase, Green, 15 In. ....193.00 to 245.00
Snowberry, Vase, Rose Matte Glaze, 7 In. 95.00
Snowberry, Vase, Rose Matte Glaze, 9 In. 85.00
Snowberry, Vase, Rose, Raised Mark, 18 In. 330.00
Snowberry, Wall Pocket, Rose, 8 In. 285.00
Sunflower, Basket, Hanging, 5 1/4 x 8 In. 935.00
Sunflower, Jardiniere, Bulbous, 2 Handles, 8 1/4 In. ....825.00 to 1100.00
Sunflower, Vase, 2 Handles, 4 1/4 In. 625.00
Sunflower, Vase, 2 Handles, 5 1/2 In. ....550.00 to 660.00
Sunflower, Vase, 7 1/2 x 9 1/2 In. 990.00
Sunflower, Vase, 8 In. 725.00
Sunflower, Vase, Bulbous, 2 Handles, 9 1/4 x 7 In. 1210.00
Sunflower, Vase, Corseted, Flared Rim, 7 1/4 In. 990.00
Sunflower, Vase, Egg Shape, 10 1/2 In. 1100.00
Sunflower, Vase, Spherical, 2 Handles, Black Foil Label, 4 In. 525.00
Sunflower, Vase, Spherical, 7 1/4 x 8 In. ....1320.00 to 1540.00
Sunflower, Wall Pocket, 7 In. 415.00
Teasel, Vase, Blue, Footed, Impressed Mark, 6 In. 165.00
Teasel, Vase, Pale Blue, Footed, 9 In. 137.00
Teasel, Vase, White, 15 In. 275.00
Thorn Apple, Flowerpot, Blue, Saucer, 5 In. 220.00
Thorn Apple, Vase, Brown, Corseted, Impressed Mark, 12 In. 413.00
Thorn Apple, Vase, Torpedo Shape, Blue, 1930 .... 275.00
Tourmaline, Vase, Blue & Yellow, Laurel Mold, 8 In. 145.00
Tuscany, Lamp, Pink Semimatte Glaze, 8 1/4 x 7 In. 220.00
Velmoss II, Candlestick, Triple, Rose, 5 1/2 In., Pair 275.00
Velmoss II, Vase, Blue, Bulbous, Foil Label, 5 1/4 x 5 3/4 In. 220.00
Velmoss Scroll, Wall Pocket, 10 1/2 x 4 In. 165.00
Vista, Jardiniere, Signed, 8 1/4 In. 770.00
Vista, Vase, Bulbous, Faint Ink Stamp, 12 x 4 3/4 In. 825.00
Vista, Vase, Buttressed Handles, Faint Ink Stamp, 12 x 6 In. 1045.00
Vista, Vase, Cylinder Shape, 14 1/2 x 5 In. ....770.00 to 1045.00
Vista, Vase, Landscape, Handle, 9 In. 660.00
Vista, Vase, Molded Landscape, 9 1/2 x 10 1/2 In. 550.00
Vista, Vase, Molded Landscape, Multicolored, 8 1/2 In. 357.00
Vista, Vase, Oval, No Mark, 12 x 5 1/4 In. 660.00
Water Lily, Conch Shell, Blue, 8 In. 210.00
Water Lily, Cookie Jar, Pink, Purple, 6 In. 440.00
Water Lily, Cornucopia, Tan, Brown, Yellow Lily, 6 In. 62.00
Water Lily, Vase, Brown, Impressed Mark, 15 In. 413.00
Water Lily, Vase, Pink, Raised Mark, 14 In. 303.00
Water Lily, Vase, Purple, Green, 2 Handles, Cutouts, Oval, 18 1/2 In. 127.00
White Rose, Cornucopia, Green, 8 In. 175.00
White Rose, Pitcher, Green, Pink, 7 In. 56.00
White Rose, Vase, Blue, Pink, 19 In. 330.00
White Rose, Vase, Brown, Footed, Pillow, Impressed Mark, 8 In. 248.00
Wild Rose, Platter, Blue, 13 In. 500.00
Wincraft, Basket, Embossed Berries, Blue, 12 In. 165.00
Wincraft, Bookends, Embossed Flowers, Yellow, Brown, 6 In., Pair 100.00

Wincraft, Cornucopia, Green, 8 In.	95.00
Wincraft, Planter, Boat Shape, Embossed Flowers, Yellow, Brown, 10 In.	45.00
Windsor, Vase, Burnt-Orange, Green, Flared, 2 Handles, 7 1/2 x 4 1/4 In.	330.00
Windsor, Vase, Green, Yellow, Geometric Squares, Rectangles, 6 1/4 x 4 1/2 In.	440.00
Wisteria, Jardiniere, Brown, Sphere Shape, Closed In Rim, 6 1/2 x 9 In.	798.00
Wisteria, Jardiniere, Pedestal, Brown, 1933, 24 1/2 In.	3575.00
Wisteria, Vase, Brown, Bulbous, 4 In.	385.00
Wisteria, Vase, Brown, Tapered, Buttressed Base, Foil Label, 8 1/4 In.	468.00
Wisteria, Vase, Bulbous, Blue, 7 In.	908.00
Wisteria, Vase, Purple, 8 1/2 In.	220.00
Wisteria, Vase, Purple, Green Leaves, 2 Handles, 9 In.	1210.00
Woodland, Vase, Bisque, Amber Poppies, Bulbous, 7 1/2 In.	880.00
Woodland, Vase, Bisque, Orange & Green, Tapered, 10 1/2 x 4 In.	385.00
Zephyr, Wall Pocket, Sienna, 8 In.	95.00
Zephyr Lily, Basket, Blue, Hanging, 5 1/2 x 7 1/2 In.	110.00
Zephyr Lily, Bookends, Green, 5 1/4 In., Pair	190.00
Zephyr Lily, Bowl, Boat Shape, Green, 16 3/4 In.	80.00
Zephyr Lily, Bowl, Green, 14 In.	95.00 to 110.00
Zephyr Lily, Candlestick, Brown, 2 In., Pair	110.00
Zephyr Lily, Console Set, Green, 10-In. Bowl, 2-In. Candlesticks	85.00
Zephyr Lily, Cookie Jar, Brown, 8 In.	330.00
Zephyr Lily, Vase, Blue, 12 In.	220.00 to 325.00
Zephyr Lily, Vase, Blue, 18 1/2 In.	550.00 to 770.00
Zephyr Lily, Vase, Brown, Impressed Mark, 10 In.	77.00
Zephyr Lily, Vase, Green, 7 1/2 In.	90.00
Zephyr Lily, Vase, Green, 10 3/8 In.	110.00
Zephyr Lily, Vase, Green, 12 1/2 In.	135.00 to 165.00
Zephyr Lily, Vase, Orange, 9 In.	135.00

ROWLAND & MARSELLUS Company is part of a mark that appears on historical Staffordshire dating from the late nineteenth and early twentieth centuries. Rowland & Marsellus is the mark used by an American importing company in New York City. The company worked from 1893 to about 1937. Some of the pieces may have been made by the British Anchor Pottery Co. of Longton, England, for export to a New York firm. Many American views were made. Of special interest to collectors are the plates with rolled edges, usually blue and white.

Tumbler, Views Of Washington, D.C., 3 Views, 4 In.	160.00

ROY ROGERS was born in 1911 in Cincinnati, Ohio. In the 1930s, he made a living as a singer; in 1935, his group started work at a Los Angeles radio station. He appeared in his first movie in 1937. From 1952 to 1957, he made 101 television shows. The other stars in the show were his wife, Dale Evans, his horse, Trigger, and his dog, Bullet. Roy Rogers memorabilia is collected, including items from the Roy Rogers restaurants.

Bank, Boot Shape, Bronze, 1960s	48.00
Bank, Horseshoe	250.00
Book, Hardcover, Dust Jacket, Whitman, 1955	28.00
Camera, Unused Fan Club Application, c.1950	250.00
Card Set, Gum, 1950s, Complete	165.00
Coloring Book, Trigger & Bullet, Whitman, 1956, 30 Pages	27.00
Comic Book, Happy Trails, No. 80, Signed, 1954	105.00
Comic Book, Queen Of The West, Dale Evans, Dell, No. 479	230.00
Comic Book, Western Roundup, Roy Rogers, Gene Autry, Dale, Dell, 1952	350.00
Crayon Set, 39 Crayons, Picture, Stencils, Box, 10 x 15 In.	90.00
Figure, Roy & Dale, Plastic, 4 In., Pair	64.00
Harmonica, Original Box	50.00
Holster Set, Leather, Tan, Black Holsters, Metal Studs, Conchos, 1950s	140.00
Lamp, Chalkware, Figural, Roy On Trigger Base, Shade, 1950s	425.00 to 595.00
Lantern, Lithograph	80.00
Lunch Box, Metal, 1953	125.00
Mug, Plastic, Painted, 1950s, 4 1/2 In.	55.00

Necktie, Roy Rogers & Trigger, Child's, 1950s	135.00
Outfit, Brown Shirt, Tan Chaps, Cowboy Hat, Child's, 1950s-1960s	55.00
Paint Book, Roy Rogers & Dale Evans, 25 Pages, 1950, 10 x 15 In.	40.00
Photograph, Cowboy Clothes, Inscription, Black & White, 1940s, 10 x 8 In.	195.00
Portrait, Paint By Number, Roy & Dale Evans, 8 x 10 In., Pair	125.00
Postcard, Apple Valley, Swimming Pool, Unused	4.00
Poster, Heart Of The Golden West, Republic, 1942, One Sheet	660.00
Poster, Young Buffalo Bill, Republic, 1940, One Sheet	865.00
Scarf, King Of The Cowboys, Red & Yellow, 24 In.	22.00
T-Shirt, Roy Rogers & Trigger, Store Paper Label, 1950s, Child's	165.00
Thermos, For Lunch Box	65.00 to 80.00
Watch, Roy Rogers & Dale Evans	500.00
Watch, Trigger, Stop Watch Action, 2 In.	302.00
Yo-Yo, Roy Picture, 1950s	13.00
Yo-Yo, With Trigger, 1940s	15.00

ROYAL BAYREUTH is the name of a factory that was founded in Tettau, Bavaria, in 1794. It has continued to modern times. The marks have changed through the years. A stylized crest, the name *Royal Bayreuth*, and the word *Bavaria* appear in slightly different forms from 1870 to about 1919. Later dishes may include the words *U.S. Zone*, the year of the issue, or the word *Germany* instead of *Bavaria*. Related pieces may be found listed in the Rose Tapestry, Snow Babies, and Sunbonnet Babies categories.

ROYAL BAYREUTH
BAVARIA

Bowl, Grape, Iridescent White, Blue Mark, 5 1/2 In.	45.00
Bowl, Peacock, Shell & Leaf Design, 10 1/2 In.	950.00
Bowl, Tapestry, Pink American Beauty Roses, Shell & Leaf Design, 10 1/2 In.	110.00
Cake Plate, Poppy, White Satin, Gold & Pink Center, 10 In.	73.00
Candleholder, Boy With Donkeys, 5 In.	170.00
Chocolate Cup, Poppy, Yellow, 3 In.	1100.00
Creamer, 2 Cavaliers, Drinking At Table, 3 3/4 In.	55.00
Creamer, Arab On Horse, 3 1/2 In.	50.00
Creamer, Black Cat, 4 3/4 In.	300.00
Creamer, Coachman, 4 1/2 In.	195.00
Creamer, Elk, 3 1/2 In.	120.00 to 130.00
Creamer, Fish Head, 4 In.	250.00
Creamer, Geranium, 4 In.	595.00
Creamer, Parakeet, Aqua & Yellow, 3 3/4 In.	425.00
Creamer, Peasant Musicians, Playing Bass & Mandolin, 3 1/2 In.	55.00
Creamer, Pelican, 3 1/2 In.	350.00
Creamer, Poppy, White Satin, Gold Trim, 3 1/2 In.	265.00
Creamer, Santa Claus, 4 1/4 In.	4290.00
Creamer, Seal, 4 1/2 In.	250.00
Creamer, Shell, Lobster Handle, 2 1/2 In.	135.00
Creamer, Strawberry, Marked, 4 In.	135.00
Cup, Goose Girl, 2 Handles, 2 1/4 In.	110.00
Cup, Snow Babies, Children On Sled, Child's, 2 1/4 In.	192.00
Cup & Saucer, Tomato, Demitasse, 2 In.	80.00
Dresser Tray, 2 Deer In Meadow, 11 x 7 3/4 In.	195.00
Flowerpot, Tapestry, White Rose, 2 3/4 In.	100.00
Gravy Boat, Poppy	225.00
Hair Receiver, Sand Babies, 3 Feet, Gilt Accents, 3 1/2 x 4 In.	195.00
Hatpin Holder, Dachshund, Figural, Brown, 4 1/2 In.	475.00
Hatpin Holder, Poppy, Figural, 4 In.	335.00
Hatpin Holder, Tapestry, Bathers, Castle, Reticulated Base, 4 1/2 In.	310.00
Jam Jar, Grape, 4 In.	350.00
Nappy, Lettuce Leaf, 5 1/2 In.	22.00
Pitcher, Cards, Devil Handle, 7 1/4 In.	510.00 to 535.00
Pitcher, Cockatoo, 5 In.	750.00
Pitcher, Little Boy Blue, Child's, 3 3/4 In.	105.00
Pitcher, Sheep Scene, Reticulated Neck, 2 1/2 In.	40.00
Pitcher, Water Buffalo Scene, Blue Mark, 5 In.	150.00
Pitcher, Watermelon, 5 In.	550.00

Plate, Girl With Dog, 7 In.	120.00
Plate, Highland Sheep, 6 In.	39.00
Plate, Little Boy Blue, Marked, 6 In.	135.00
Plate, Man With 2 Turkeys, 8 In.	68.00
Salt & Pepper, Plum, Blue, Figural, 3 1/4 In.	100.00
Sugar & Creamer, Cover, Tomato Shape, 3 1/2 & 3 In.	225.00
Sugar & Creamer, Grape, Purple, 3 1/4 & 4 In.	395.00
Sugar & Creamer, Spiky Shell, Creamer 2 1/2 In.	145.00
Teapot, Roses, Cream Ground, Footed, Blue Mark, 4 x 4 In.	85.00
Teapot, Spiky Shell, White Satin, Shell Finial, 3 1/2 In.	115.00
Toothpick, Cavalier Musicians, Knob Handles	135.00
Vase, 2 Arabs & Mule, Blue Overglaze Mark, 8 In.	250.00
Vase, 2 Swans On Lake, 3 3/4 In.	50.00
Vase, Arab On Brown Horse, 2 Handles, 3 In.	85.00
Vase, Birch Trees, Goats, Marked	125.00
Vase, Cavalier Musicians, 2 Handles, 3 1/4 In.	30.00
Vase, Couple Hunting With Horses, Dogs, 2 Handles, 3 1/4 In.	870.00
Vase, Fox Hunt, Footed, 2 Handles, 3 In.	35.00
Vase, Goose Girl, 2 3/4 In.	55.00
Vase, Goose Girl, 4 1/4 In.	60.00
Vase, Musician Scene, Bulbous, 3-Footed, 3 In.	55.00
Vase, Stag & Fawn, 2 Handles, 3 In.	45.00
Vase, Tapestry, Bathers, Castle, Bulbous, Stick Spout, 4 In.	280.00
Vase, Tapestry, Toaster Cavalier, Glass Extended, Bulbous, 3 1/2 In.	130.00

ROYAL BONN is the nineteenth- and twentieth-century trade name for the Bonn China Manufactory. It was established in 1755 in Bonn, Germany. A general line of porcelain was made. Many marks were used, most including the name *Bonn*, the initials *FM*, and a crown.

Bowl, Hand Painted, Metal Rim, Marked, c.1888, 4 In.	150.00
Clock, Floral, White Ground, Gilt, C-Scroll Design, Ansonia Clock Company, 16 1/2 In.	1265.00
Clock, Poppy, Yellow & Blue, Mantel, 14 1/2 In.	550.00
Clock, White & Green, Lilac Design, Open Escapement, Mantel, 14 In.	450.00
Ewer, Flower Decoration, Gold Trim, Hand Painted, 12 1/2 In.	154.00
Tile, Windmill Scene, Frame, Delft, Signed, 7 1/2 x 7 3/4 In.	40.00
Urn, Painted Allover Floral, Foliate Handles, Figure Of Putti, Pan Finial, 19 In.	250.00
Vase, Birds Amid Chrysanthemums, Reticulated & Gilded Handles, 24 1/2 In.	1430.00
Vase, Cherries Clustered In Stages Of Maturity, Flowers, Signed, 7 3/4 In.	290.00
Vase, Continuous Scene, Aphrodite Emerging From Sea, c.1900, 23 In.	1265.00
Vase, Cylindrical, Polychrome Floral Design, Hand Painted, 3 Handles, Marked, 7 In.	220.00
Vase, Enamel Floral Garden Design, Ivory Ground, 2 Handles, 11 1/2 In.	115.00
Vase, Young Woman Seated On Rock, Landscape, Line Borders, c.1900, 22 3/4 In.	1380.00

ROYAL COPENHAGEN porcelain and pottery have been made in Denmark since 1772. The Christmas plate series started in 1908. The figurines with pale blue and gray glazes have remained popular in this century and are still being made. Many other old and new style porcelains are made today.

Ashtray & Cigarette Holder, Flowers, Crackle Glaze, 3 1/3 In. ....*Illus*	75.00
Basket, Fruit, Flora Danica, Reticulated, Trellis Work Sides, 10 In.	4312.00
Bowl, 2 Ducks On Rim, Water Lily Pattern, 1930s	145.00
Bust, Girl's Head, Turquoise, Faience, 1969, 13 In. ....*Illus*	600.00
Decanter, Herring Egeskov Castle	50.00
Decanter, Kronborg Castle, #4454, KHX, Stopper, 9 3/4 In.	75.00
Dish, Flora Danica, 9 1/8 In.	862.00
Dish, Pickle, Flora Danica, Flowering Vetch, Serrated Rim, 8 3/4 In., Pair	2300.00
Figurine, Boy Combing Cat, 6 In.	155.00
Figurine, Girl With Calf, No. 779	185.00
Figurine, Girl With Trumpet	550.00
Figurine, Goose Girl, No. 527, 7 In.	275.00
Figurine, Mercury, Holding Flute & Sword, 3 Wavy Lines, 1870, 19 In.	690.00
Figurine, Tiger, Reclining, 12 In.	155.00
Figurine, Venus, Bertel Thorwaldsen, Biscuit, c.1865, 12 In.	330.00

Royal Copenhagen, Ashtray & Cigarette Holder, Flowers, Crackle Glaze, 3 1/3 In.

Royal Copenhagen, Bust, Girl's Head, Turquoise, Faience, 1969, 13 In.

Group, Peasant Couple, Harvesting Wheat, No. 1352, 17 In.	690.00
Plaque, Snowy Landscape, Farm, Trees, Valley, Round, 1924, 16 In.	475.00
Plate, Christmas, 1909, Danish Landscape	275.00
Plate, Christmas, 1919, In The Park	150.00
Plate, Christmas, 1941, Danish Village Church	375.00
Plate, Christmas, 1942, Bell Tower, Old Church In Jutland	495.00
Plate, Christmas, 1952, Christmas In The Forest	195.00
Plate, Christmas, 1963, Hojsager Mill	50.00 to 75.00
Plate, Christmas, 1970, Christmas Rose & Cat	55.00
Plate, Christmas, 1974, Winter Twilight	27.00
Plate, Christmas, 1988, Christmas Eve In Copenhagen	65.00
Plate, Christmas, 1999, Sleigh Ride	58.00
Plate, Emperor Napoleon & Empress Josephine, c.1920, 10 1/2 In., Pair	165.00
Plate, Flora Danica, 8 1/8 In.	690.00
Plate, Leaf Shape, 8 In.	100.00
Platter, Flora Danica, Flowering Bramble, Serrated Rim, 16 In.	1495.00
Sauceboat, Flora Danica, 6 1/4 In.	287.00
Teapot, Half Lace	270.00
Vase, Female, Nude, Sitting On Rock, Sailboats, Seagull On Reverse, Langelinie	125.00
Vase, Gourd Shape, Crystalline Glaze, Axel Salto, Marked, 9 x 6 In.	7700.00
Vase, Incised Crosshatched, Crystalline Glaze, Gerd Bogelund, 11 In.	660.00
Vase, Mottled Matte Glaze, Notched Neck, Marked, 12 x 9 1/2 In.	680.00

ROYAL COPLEY china was made by the Spaulding China Company of Sebring, Ohio, from 1939 to 1960. The figural planters and the small figurines, especially those with Art Deco designs, are of great collector interest.

Bank, Pig, Blue Bow	65.00
Figurine, Dog, Raised Paw	90.00
Figurine, Dog, With Suitcase	45.00
Figurine, Island Lady	180.00
Head Vase, Old Man, 8 In.	65.00
Head Vase, Old Woman, 8 In.	65.00
Planter, Jumping Salmon	93.00
Tidbit, Fish, Blue	30.00
Tidbit, Rooster, Yellow	30.00
Vase, Green, Yellow Flowers, Blue Green Leaves, Mark, Stamped, 8 In.	15.00
Vase, Yellow Flowers, Blue & Green Leaves, Shaped Green Ground, Marked, 8 In.	15.00
Wall Pocket, Blackamoor	90.00

ROYAL CROWN DERBY Company, Ltd., was established in England in 1890. There is a complex family tree that includes the Derby, Crown Derby, and Royal Crown Derby porcelains. The Royal Crown Derby mark includes the name and a crown. The words *Made in England* were used after 1921. The company is now a part of Royal Doulton Tableware Ltd.

Cup & Saucer, Imari	79.00
Cup & Saucer, Imari, 1927, 6 Piece	450.00
Cup & Saucer, Imari, Demitasse, 6 Piece	200.00

Figurine, Blue Tit, c.1967, 5 1/2 In. 70.00
Figurine, Cockatoo, c.1952, 7 In. 70.00
Tea Set, Old Avesbury Pattern, 7-In. Teapot, 3 Piece 220.00
Toothpick, Red, Gold & Cobalt Blue, c.1920 .... 85.00
Vase, Gilt Floral Sprays, Blue Ground, Egg Shape, Narrow Neck, 7 3/8 In. 345.00

ROYAL DOULTON is the name used on Doulton and Company pottery made from 1902 to the present. Doulton and Company of England was founded in 1853. Pieces made before 1902 are listed in this book under Doulton. Royal Doulton collectors search for the out-of-production figurines, character jugs, vases, and series wares. Some vases and animal figurines were made with a special red glaze called flambe. Sung and Chang glazed pieces are rare. The multicolored glaze is very thick and looks as if it were dropped on the clay.

Animal, Cat, Dinner Time, DA 229, 2 1/2 In. 49.00
Animal, Cat, Lucky, K 12, 2 3/4 In. 200.00
Animal, Cat, With Bandaged Paw, DA 195, 3 1/4 In. 49.00
Animal, Dog With Ball, HN 1103, 2 1/2 In. 95.00
Animal, Dog, Airedale Terrier, Ch. Cotsford Topsail, HN 1022 .... 750.00
Animal, Dog, Bulldog, HN 1044, 3 1/4 In. 350.00
Animal, Dog, Bulldog, HN 1047, 3 1/4 In. 85.00
Animal, Dog, Bulldog, Union Jack With Trinity Cap, D 6183, 2 3/4 In. 215.00
Animal, Dog, Cairn Terrier, K 11, 2 1/2 In. 200.00
Animal, Dog, Character, Bone In Mouth, HN 1159 .... 200.00
Animal, Dog, Character, Eating From Plate, HN 1158 .... 200.00
Animal, Dog, Cocker Spaniel, HN 1002, 6 1/2 In. 450.00
Animal, Dog, Cocker Spaniel, HN 1021, 3 1/2 In. 85.00
Animal, Dog, English Setter, HN 1050, 5 1/2 In. 150.00
Animal, Dog, Foxhound, K 7, 2 1/2 In. 200.00
Animal, Dog, French Poodle, HN 1631 .... 135.00
Animal, Dog, Give Me A Home, DA 196, 5 3/4 In. 93.00
Animal, Dog, Irish Setter, HN 1054, 7 1/2 In. 700.00
Animal, Dog, Pekinese, HN 1012, 3 In. 135.00
Animal, Dog, Scottish Terrier, K 10, 2 1/2 In. 200.00
Animal, Dog, Sheepdog & Pup, DA 176, 4 1/2 In. 98.00
Animal, Dog, Spaniel & Pup, Golden, DA 174G, 5 1/2 In. 98.00
Animal, Dog, St. Bernard, Lying, K 19, 2 1/2 In. 45.00
Animal, Dog, Welsh Corgi, K 16, 2 1/2 In. 200.00
Animal, Dragon, Flambe, 7 1/2 In. 1050.00
Animal, Duck, Drake, Flambe, 6 1/2 In. ....145.00 to 210.00
Animal, Elephant, Fighter, HN 2640, 12 x 9 In. 1090.00
Animal, Elephant, Trunk In Salute, Flambe, 5 1/2 In. 198.00
Animal, Fox, Huntsman, D 6448, 4 1/2 In. 95.00
Animal, Fox, Seated, Flambe, 4 1/2 In. 175.00
Animal, Guinea Fowl, Flambe, 5 1/2 In. 145.00
Animal, Guinea Fowl, HN 125, 3 1/2 In. 595.00
Animal, Rabbit, Reclining, Flambe, 4 1/4 In. 92.00
Animal, Swallowtail Butterfly, HN 2606 .... 600.00
Animal, Tiger, On Rock, HN 2639, 12 In. 1500.00
Ashtray, John Barleycorn, D 5602 .... 150.00
Biscuit Jar, Shakespeare, Juliet Scene, 7 In. 175.00
Bottle, Gourd Shape, Gold Luster, Sang-De-Boeuf & Black Flambe Glaze, 5 In. 195.00
Bowl, Cereal, Bunnykins, Mr. Piggly 45.00
Bowl, Dickens, Town Scene, Transfer, 9 x 4 In. 154.00
Bowl, Salad, Tree & Lake Scene, Brown, Pedestal, 7 x 12 In. 200.00
Bowl, Sugar, Tony Weller, D 6103, 2 1/2 In. 750.00
Celery Dish, Old English Coaching Scenes 90.00

Royal Doulton character jugs depict the head and shoulders of the subject. They are made in four sizes: large, 5 1/4 to 7 inches; small, 3 1/4 to 4 inches; miniature, 2 1/4 to 2 1/2 inches; and tiny, 1 1/4 inches. Toby jugs portray a seated, full figure.

Character Jug, 'Arriet, Large 250.00

Character Jug, 'Arriet, Small 125.00
Character Jug, 'Arry, Tiny .... .50.00 to 225.00
Character Jug, Anne Boleyn, Large .... .80.00 to 180.00
Character Jug, Antique Dealer, Large 145.00
Character Jug, Apothecary, Large 175.00
Character Jug, Apothecary, Miniature 100.00
Character Jug, Artful Dodger, Tiny 50.00
Character Jug, Athos, Large 130.00
Character Jug, Auld Mac, Tiny 65.00
Character Jug, Bacchus, Large 86.00
Character Jug, Beefeater, Miniature .... .30.00 to 115.00
Character Jug, Beefeater, Red, Large .... .75.00 to 145.00
Character Jug, Beefeater, Small .... .58.00 to 100.00
Character Jug, Blacksmith, Miniature 80.00
Character Jug, Buzfuz, Small 135.00
Character Jug, Capt. Henry Morgan, Large 135.00
Character Jug, Capt. Henry Morgan, Small 60.00
Character Jug, Captain Hook, Crocodile & Clock Handle, Large 605.00
Character Jug, Captain Hook, Silver Hook & Crocodile Handle, Large 300.00
Character Jug, Cardinal, Large 195.00
Character Jug, Cardinal, Small 25.00
Character Jug, Cardinal, Tiny .... .80.00 to 125.00
Character Jug, Charles Dickens, Small 115.00
Character Jug, Count Dracula, Large 135.00
Character Jug, Cyrano De Bergerac, Large 130.00
Character Jug, Dick Turpin, Large 135.00
Character Jug, Don Quixote, Miniature 75.00
Character Jug, Don Quixote, Small 80.00
Character Jug, Elephant Trainer, Large 275.00
Character Jug, Fagin, Tiny 85.00
Character Jug, Falconer, Small 75.00
Character Jug, Falstaff, Large 150.00
Character Jug, Farmer John, Large 65.00
Character Jug, Farmer John, Small 120.00
Character Jug, Fat Boy, Tiny 80.00
Character Jug, Gardener, Large 175.00
Character Jug, Genie, Large 425.00
Character Jug, George Washington, Large 200.00
Character Jug, Gladiator, Large 605.00
Character Jug, Gladiator, Miniature 525.00
Character Jug, Gladiator, Tiny 650.00
Character Jug, Gondolier, Large 660.00
Character Jug, Granny, One Tooth Showing, Miniature 70.00
Character Jug, Granny, One Tooth Showing, Small 55.00
Character Jug, Granny, Toothless, Large 880.00
Character Jug, Groucho Marx, Large 200.00
Character Jug, Hamlet, Large 175.00
Character Jug, Izaak Walton, Large 55.00
Character Jug, John Barleycorn, Large 225.00
Character Jug, John Doulton, Small 35.00
Character Jug, John Peel, Black & Orange Handle, Small 30.00
Character Jug, John Peel, Gray Handle, Tiny 115.00
Character Jug, John Peel, Large 135.00
Character Jug, Lobster Man, Large 100.00
Character Jug, Mark Twain, Large 175.00
Character Jug, Mikado, Large 322.00
Character Jug, Mine Host, Small 80.00
Character Jug, Mr. Micawber, Miniature 110.00
Character Jug, Mr. Pickwick, Miniature 80.00
Character Jug, Mr. Pickwick, Tiny 80.00
Character Jug, Mrs. Bardell, Tiny 55.00
Character Jug, Night Watchman, Large 155.00
Character Jug, North American Indian, Small 65.00

Character Jug, Old Charley, Large 78.00
Character Jug, Old Charley, Miniature 60.00
Character Jug, Old King Cole, Tiny 175.00
Character Jug, Old Salt, Small 60.00
Character Jug, Parson Brown, Large 110.00
Character Jug, Pearly King, Large 200.00
Character Jug, Poacher, Large ....110.00 to 135.00
Character Jug, Punch & Judy Man, Small 175.00
Character Jug, Queen Victoria, Large 250.00
Character Jug, Regency Beau, Large 880.00
Character Jug, Robin Hood, Large 150.00
Character Jug, Robin Hood, Miniature 75.00
Character Jug, Robin Hood, Small 40.00
Character Jug, Robinson Crusoe, Small 75.00
Character Jug, Sairey Gamp, Small, 1935-1986 .... 65.00
Character Jug, Sairey Gamp, Tiny ....110.00 to 125.00
Character Jug, Sam Johnson, Large ....375.00 to 425.00
Character Jug, Sam Weller, Large 400.00
Character Jug, Sam Weller, Small 125.00
Character Jug, Samson & Delilah, Large 120.00
Character Jug, Sancho Panca, Large 145.00
Character Jug, Sancho Panca, Small 90.00
Character Jug, Santa Claus, Doll & Drum Handle, Large ....55.00 to 300.00
Character Jug, Santa Claus, Plain Handle, Tiny ....70.00 to 125.00
Character Jug, Santa Claus, Sack Of Toys, Handle, Tiny 70.00
Character Jug, Scaramouche, Guitar, Comedy & Tragedy Masks Handle, Large 936.00
Character Jug, Simon The Cellarer, Large 135.00
Character Jug, Sir Henry Doulton, Small.................................... 200.00
Character Jug, Sleuth, Miniature 80.00
Character Jug, Snake Charmer, Large 265.00
Character Jug, St. George, Small ....175.00 to 250.00
Character Jug, Tony Weller, Miniature ....65.00 to 75.00
Character Jug, Touchstone, Large 350.00
Character Jug, Town Crier, Small 58.00
Character Jug, Trapper, Small 30.00
Character Jug, Ugly Duchess, Large 110.00
Character Jug, Viking, Large 125.00
Character Jug, Walrus & Carpenter, Large 200.00
Character Jug, Walrus & Carpenter, Small................................... 150.00
Character Jug, Witch, Large ....325.00 to 450.00
Character Jug, Yachtsman, Large 175.00
Charger, Painted, Woman's Head, Matte Polychrome Glaze, 1877, 14 In. 286.00
Charger, Yellow Chrysanthemums, 16 In. ....135.00 to 145.00
Creamer, Fireglow ....29.00 to 72.00
Creamer, Rural England, Country Garden, Milkmaid, Red Dress 950.00
Cup, Bunnykins, 2 Handles, 3 In. 30.00
Cup & Saucer, Fireglow ....20.00 to 40.00
Ewer, Cobalt Blue Neck, Brown Textured, Floral, 14 In. 200.00
Figurine, Affection, HN 2236 .... 70.00
Figurine, Afternoon Tea, HN 1747 ....260.00 to 650.00
Figurine, Alison, HN 3264 .... 200.00
Figurine, Amy, HN 3316 .... 950.00
Figurine, Animal, Dog, French Poodle, HN 2631, 5 1/4 In. 115.00
Figurine, Anna, HN 2802 .... 150.00
Figurine, Annabel, HN 3273 .... 225.00
Figurine, Annabella, HN 1872 .... 1400.00
Figurine, Antoinette, HN 2236 .... 175.00
Figurine, Ascot, HN 2356 ....110.00 to 155.00
Figurine, At Ease, HN 2473 ....100.00 to 350.00
Figurine, Autumn Breezes, HN 1911 .... 175.00
Figurine, Autumn Breezes, HN 1934 ....175.00 to 300.00
Figurine, Autumn Breezes, HN 2147 .... 475.00
Figurine, Autumntime, HN 3231 .... 250.00

Figurine, Babie, HN 1679 .... 75.00
Figurine, Bachelor, HN 2319 .... 245.00
Figurine, Ballerina, HN 2116 .... 235.00
Figurine, Balloon Man, HN 1954 ....130.00 to 345.00
Figurine, Basket Weaver, HN 2245 .... 225.00
Figurine, Bedtime Story, HN 2059 .... 495.00
Figurine, Bedtime, HN 1978 .... 58.00
Figurine, Biddy Penny Farthing, HN 1843 .... 225.00
Figurine, Biddy, HN 1500 .... 1000.00
Figurine, Blacksmith Of Williamsburg, HN 2240 .... 145.00
Figurine, Blithe Morning, HN 2021 .... 350.00
Figurine, Bo-Peep, HN 1811 .... 175.00
Figurine, Boatman, HN 2417 .... 175.00
Figurine, Boudoir, HN 2542 .... 625.00
Figurine, Bridget, HN 2070 .... 270.00
Figurine, Bunny's Bedtime, HN 3370 .... 210.00
Figurine, Bunnykins, Drum Major, Oompah Band, DB 27 .... 100.00
Figurine, Bunnykins, Sousaphone, Oompah Band, DB 23 .... 100.00
Figurine, Bunnykins, Trumpeter, Oompah Band, DB 24 .... 100.00
Figurine, Camellias, HN 3701 .... 350.00
Figurine, Camille, HN 1648 .... 1750.00
Figurine, Captain, HN 2260 ....127.00 to 190.00
Figurine, Carpet Seller, Hand Closed, HN 1464, 9 1/4 In. 215.00
Figurine, Cavalier, HN 2716 ....115.00 to 190.00
Figurine, Centurion, HN 2726 .... 175.00
Figurine, Chloe, M 9 .... 190.00
Figurine, Christmas Morn, HN1992 ....260.00 to 270.00
Figurine, Christmas Time, HN 2110 .... 625.00
Figurine, Clarinda, HN 2724 .... 155.00
Figurine, Clarissa, HN 2345 .... 155.00
Figurine, Clockmaker, HN 2279 .... 450.00
Figurine, Clown, HN 2980 ....190.00 to 350.00
Figurine, Cobbler, HN 1706 .... 115.00
Figurine, Colonel Fairfax, HN 2903 .... 315.00
Figurine, Coppelia, HN 2115 .... 875.00
Figurine, Country Lass, HN 1991 .... 155.00
Figurine, Cup Of Tea, HN 2322 .... 100.00
Figurine, Curly Knob, HN 1627 .... 1500.00
Figurine, Daffy Down Dilly, HN 1712 ....170.00 to 500.00
Figurine, Darby, HN 1427 .... 205.00
Figurine, Darby, HN 2024 .... 250.00
Figurine, Darling, HN 1319 .... 275.00
Figurine, Debbie, HN 2385 .... 90.00
Figurine, Debbie, HN 2400 .... 165.00
Figurine, Dick Turpin, HN 3272 .... 525.00
Figurine, Doctor, HN 2858 .... 195.00
Figurine, Dorcas, HN 1558, Purple, 6 3/4 In. 450.00
Figurine, Drummer Boy, HN 2679 .... 375.00
Figurine, Elsie Maynard, HN 2902 .... 300.00
Figurine, Ermine Coat, HN 1981 ....345.00 to 425.00
Figurine, Erminie, M 40, 4 In. 1325.00
Figurine, Esmeralda, HN 2168 .... 600.00
Figurine, Eventide, HN 2814 ....100.00 to 165.00
Figurine, Falstaff, HN 2054 .... 165.00
Figurine, Family Album, HN 2321 .... 550.00
Figurine, Fiddler, HN 2171 .... 1300.00
Figurine, Fiona, HN 2694 .... 200.00
Figurine, First Steps, HN 2242 .... 325.00
Figurine, Flower Seller's Children, HN 1342 ....265.00 to 800.00
Figurine, Foaming Quart, HN 2162 ....165.00 to 175.00
Figurine, Forty Winks, HN 1974 .... 325.00
Figurine, Fragrance, HN 2334 .... 143.00
Figurine, Francine, HN 2422 ....155.00 to 175.00

Figurine, Friar Tuck, HN 2143 . . . . 260.00
Figurine, Gay Morning, HN 2135 . . . . 245.00
Figurine, Geisha, HN 3229 . . . . .200.00 to 350.00
Figurine, Geraldine, HN 2348 . . . . .110.00 to 200.00
Figurine, Good King Wenceslas, HN 2118 . . . . 550.00
Figurine, Gossips, HN 1429 . . . . 1300.00
Figurine, Gossips, HN 2015 . . . . 700.00
Figurine, Grand Manner, HN 2723 . . . . 225.00
Figurine, Grandma, Brown Shawl, HN 2052A 600.00
Figurine, Granny's Heritage, HN 2031 . . . . 775.00
Figurine, Gwynneth, HN 1980, Harradine 525.00
Figurine, Gypsy Dance, HN 2230 . . . . 230.00
Figurine, Hannah, HN 3649 . . . . 140.00
Figurine, Henrietta Maria, HN 2005 . . . . .245.00 to 850.00
Figurine, Her Ladyship, HN 1977 . . . . .270.00 to 500.00
Figurine, Hilary, HN 2335 . . . . 225.00
Figurine, Honourable Frances Duncombe, Gainsborough Ladies, HN 3009 . . . . 700.00
Figurine, Invitation, HN 2170 . . . . 120.00
Figurine, Jack Point, HN 2080 . . . . 1265.00
Figurine, Jacqueline, HN 2001 . . . . 800.00
Figurine, Janine, HN 2461 . . . . 190.00
Figurine, Jean, HN 2032 . . . . 375.00
Figurine, Julia, HN 2705 . . . . 120.00
Figurine, June, HN 1690 . . . . 1200.00
Figurine, Just One More, HN 2980 . . . . 200.00
Figurine, Karen, HN 1994 . . . . 750.00
Figurine, Lady April, HN 1958 . . . . 200.00
Figurine, Lady Betty, HN 1967 . . . . 650.00
Figurine, Lady Charmian, HN 1948 . . . . 185.00
Figurine, Lady Pamela, HN 2718 . . . . 200.00
Figurine, Laird, HN 2361 . . . . 155.00
Figurine, Lambing Time, HN 1890 . . . . .115.00 to 325.00
Figurine, Leisure Hour, HN 2055 . . . . 335.00
Figurine, Lido Lady, HN 1220 . . . . 3000.00
Figurine, Lisa, HN 2310 . . . . .121.00 to 190.00
Figurine, Little Nell, HN 540 . . . . 65.00
Figurine, Lobster Man, HN 2317 . . . . 110.00
Figurine, Lobster Man, HN 2323 . . . . 190.00
Figurine, Lorraine, HN 2118 . . . . 300.00
Figurine, Lunchtime, HN 2485 . . . . 175.00
Figurine, Lynne, HN 2329 . . . . 104.00
Figurine, Maisie, HN 1619 . . . . 175.00
Figurine, Margaret Of Anjou, HN 2012 . . . . 290.00
Figurine, Marie, HN 1370 . . . . 150.00
Figurine, Mask Seller, HN 2103 . . . . 175.00
Figurine, Masque, HN 2554 . . . . 200.00
Figurine, Meg, HN 2743 . . . . 225.00
Figurine, Melanie, HN 2271 . . . . 165.00
Figurine, Milkmaid, HN 2057 . . . . 155.00
Figurine, Miss Demure, HN 1402 . . . . 325.00
Figurine, Nana, HN 1767 . . . . 195.00
Figurine, Nina, HN 2347 . . . . .132.00 to 200.00
Figurine, Old Balloon Seller, HN 1315 . . . . 145.00
Figurine, Old Mother Hubbard, HN 2314 . . . . 500.00
Figurine, Olivia, HN 1995 . . . . 115.00
Figurine, Omar Khayyam, HN 2247 . . . . 170.00
Figurine, Orange Lady, HN 1759 . . . . 220.00
Figurine, Orange Lady, HN 1953 . . . . .88.00 to 375.00
Figurine, Owd Willum, HN 2042 . . . . 200.00
Figurine, Paisley Shawl, HN 1914 . . . . 175.00
Figurine, Paisley Shawl, HN 1988 . . . . 235.00
Figurine, Paisley Shawl, M 26 . . . . 190.00
Figurine, Pantalettes, HN 1362 . . . . 345.00

Figurine, Patricia, HN 1414 .... 1250.00
Figurine, Paula, HN 2906 .... 300.00
Figurine, Pecksniff, HN 1891 .... 420.00
Figurine, Penelope, HN 1901 .... 400.00
Figurine, Piper, HN 2907 .... 225.00
Figurine, Pirate King, HN 2901 .... 300.00
Figurine, Pride & Joy, HN 2945 .... 350.00
Figurine, Priscilla, HN 1337 .... 850.00
Figurine, Priscilla, HN 1340 .... 175.00
Figurine, Priscilla, M 24 .... 190.00
Figurine, Prized Possessions, HN 2942 ....400.00 to 750.00
Figurine, Professor, HN 2281 ....165.00 to 275.00
Figurine, Punch & Judy Man, HN 2765 ....225.00 to 285.00
Figurine, Rag Doll, HN 2142 .... 185.00
Figurine, Reverie, HN 2306 .... 225.00
Figurine, Rosemary, HN 3143 .... 275.00
Figurine, Royal Governor's Cook, HN 2233 ....375.00 to 500.00
Figurine, Sabbath Morn, HN 1982 .... 400.00
Figurine, Schoolmarm, HN 2223 .... 350.00
Figurine, Sharon, HN 3603 .... 250.00
Figurine, Shore Leave, HN 2254 .... 100.00
Figurine, Silks & Ribbons, HN 2017 .... 155.00
Figurine, Silversmith Of Williamsburg, HN 2208 .... 250.00
Figurine, Sleepy Darling, HN 2953 .... 275.00
Figurine, Soiree, HN 2312 .... 170.00
Figurine, Southern Belle, HN 2229 ....330.00 to 370.00
Figurine, Southern Belle, HN 3174 .... 125.00
Figurine, St. George, HN 2051 .... 490.00
Figurine, Stephanie, HN 2807 .... 155.00
Figurine, Stitch In Time, HN 2352 ....88.00 to 180.00
Figurine, Stop Press, HN 2683 ....150.00 to 175.00
Figurine, Summertime, HN 3478 .... 270.00
Figurine, Sunday Best, HN 2698 .... 225.00
Figurine, Sunday Morning, HN 2184 .... 175.00
Figurine, Suzette, HN 2026 .... 245.00
Figurine, Sweet Anne, M 5 .... 85.00
Figurine, Sweet Anne, M 27 .... 180.00
Figurine, Sweet Dreams, HN 2380 .... 175.00
Figurine, Teatime, HN 2255 .... 300.00
Figurine, Tete-A-Tete, HN 0799 .... 4000.00
Figurine, Time For Bed, HN 3762 .... 145.00
Figurine, Tinsmith, HN 2146 .... 490.00
Figurine, Top O' The Hill, HN 1834 .... 260.00
Figurine, Top O' The Hill, HN 1849 .... 175.00
Figurine, Top O' The Hill, HN 3499 .... 140.00
Figurine, Toymaker, HN 2250 .... 375.00
Figurine, Tuppence A Bag, HN 2320 .... 175.00
Figurine, Valerie, HN 2107 .... 145.00
Figurine, Veneta, HN 2722 .... 155.00
Figurine, Veronica, HN 1517 .... 175.00
Figurine, Victorian Lady, Green & Purple, HN 1345 .... 1100.00
Figurine, Victorian Lady, M 2 .... 190.00
Figurine, Votes For Women, HN 2816 ....175.00 to 325.00
Figurine, Wedding Vows, HN 2750 .... 275.00
Figurine, Wigmaker Of Williamsburg, HN 2239 .... 200.00
Figurine, Winston S. Churchill, HN 3433 .... 325.00
Figurine, Wizard, HN 2877 .... 175.00
Figurine, Wood Nymph, HN 2192 .... 450.00
Figurine, Yeoman Of The Guard, HN 2122 .... 1300.00
Figurine, Young Love, HN 2735 .... 490.00
Figurine, Young Miss Nightingale, HN 2010 .... 375.00
Figurine, Yum-Yum, HN 2899 .... 300.00
Inkwell, Dogs & Game, Dog, Pheasant In Mouth, 7 x 8 1/4 In. 395.00

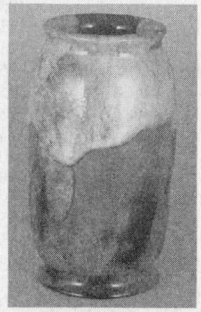  

Royal Doulton, Vase, Chang, Glazed, D.J. Noke & H. Nixon, 1930, 7 3/4 In.

Royal Doulton, Vase, Dancing Girls, Vines, Morrisian, 1900, 22 3/4 In.

Royal Doulton, Vase, Sung, Wild Turkey, Purple Ground, Noke & Eaton, 1930, 5 3/4 In.

Jardiniere, Footed, 3 Handles, Textured Gold, Banded Rim, 8 x 9 In.	385.00
Jug, Coaching Days, Stagecoach & Passengers, 7 1/2 In.	110.00
Jug, Gallant Fishers, Commemorative Scene, Izaak Walton, 8 In.	99.00
Jug, Mr. Pickwick, 8 In.	100.00
Jug, Oliver Twist, Oliver Asking For More	275.00
Jug, Puzzle, Motto, Signed, c.1890, 9 In.	192.00
Lamp, Mask Seller	500.00
Lighter, Lawyer	225.00
Lighter, Mr. Pickwick	375.00
Lighter, Poacher	175.00
Liquor Container, Captain Cook, Small	125.00
Liquor Container, Falstaff, Small	150.00
Liquor Container, Mr. Pickwick, Small	100.00
Liquor Container, Poacher, 4 In.	95.00 to 150.00
Liquor Container, Poacher, Small	150.00
Liquor Container, Uncle Sam, Small	200.00
Liquor Container, William Grant, Large	500.00
Liquor Decanter, Town Crier Of Eatanswill, Small	150.00
Pitcher, Cartouche, Lamplighter In Front Of Tavern, Porcelain, 7 1/2 In.	120.00
Plate, Aeronautical Scenes	750.00
Plate, Bill Sykes, Dickens, 6 In.	68.00
Plate, Charles Dickens Bust In Center, Characters Surround	150.00
Plate, Christmas, Annual, Winter Fun, 1977	85.00
Plate, Durham Cathedral, J.H. Plant, 10 1/2 In.	100.00
Plate, Falconry, 10 1/2 In.	125.00
Plate, Fireglow, 6 1/4 In.	9.00
Plate, Fireglow, 10 1/4 In.	40.00
Plate, Gallant Fishers, Of Recreation There Is None So Free, 10 1/2 In.	187.00
Plate, Nursery Rhymes, Goosey, Goosey Gander, 6 In.	45.00
Plate, Roger Salem El Cobler, Cobbler, D 6302, 10 1/4 In.	33.00
Plate, Under The Greenwood Tree, Robin Hood & Friar Tuck, Signed, 7 1/2 In.	85.00
Sugar, Cover, Fireglow	30.00 to 88.00
Toby Jug, Cap'n Cuttle, Small	70.00
Toby Jug, Mr. Micawber, Small	80.00
Toby Jug, Mr. Pickwick, Small	80.00
Toby Jug, Winston Churchill, Small	40.00
Tray, Flambe, Woodcut, Round, Sloped Sides, Landscape, 4 1/2 In.	40.00
Vase, Aventurine Glaze, Stamped Mark, 5 1/4 x 3 In.	770.00
Vase, Chang, Glazed, D.J. Noke & H. Nixon, 1930, 7 3/4 In. *Illus*	509.00
Vase, Dancing Girls, Vines, Morrisian, 1900, 22 3/4 In. *Illus*	1091.00
Vase, Flambe, Black Scenic Decoration, 5 In.	99.00
Vase, Floriform, Yellow, Daisy & Mixed Flowers, Green Crown Mark, 11 In.	275.00
Vase, Fruiting Vines, Brown & Green, Blue Mottled Ground, c.1920, 5 1/2 In.	160.00
Vase, Romantic Lake Scene, Gilt Line Border, Oval, Charles Hart, c.1929, 8 In.	190.00

Vase, Stylized Roses, Tall Stems, Cobalt & Ivory Ground, Egg Shape, 8 In.	305.00
Vase, Sung, Baluster Form, Darkened Base, Veined, No. 1605, 8 1/2 In.	115.00
Vase, Sung, Flambe, Globular, Upright Neck, Black Glaze, No. 1605, 4 1/4 In.	105.00
Vase, Sung, Globular, Upright Neck, Veined, Green, Yellow, No. 1606, 4 In.	86.00
Vase, Sung, Veined, No. 1617, 13 In.	345.00
Vase, Sung, Wild Turkey, Purple Ground, Noke & Eaton, 1930, 5 3/4 In. ....*Illus*	1528.00
Vase, Sung, Woodcut, Veined, Oval, Green To Yellow, No. 1613, 6 1/2 In.	115.00
Vase, Swirls, Yellow & Red Flowers, Stamped Mark, 9 In.	220.00
Vase, Titanian, Swan, Green & Blue Ground, Stamp, 2 1/2 x 2 In.	440.00
Vase, Woman, White Goose, Landscape Either Side, Lambeth, c.1912, 8 1/2 In.	750.00
Vase, Woodcut, Flambe, Baluster Shape, Landscape, No. 1603, 7 In.	145.00
Vase, Woodcut, Flambe, Baluster, Black Landscape Base, No. 1614, 4 In.	115.00
Vase, Woodcut, Flambe, Oval, Red Neck, Black Base, No. 1613, 6 1/2 In.	175.00

ROYAL DUX is the more common name for the Duxer Porzellanmanu-faktur, which was founded by E. Eichler in Dux, Bohemia, in 1860. By the turn of the century, the firm specialized in porcelain statuary and busts of Art Nouveau–style maidens, large porcelain figures, and ornate vases with three-dimensional figures climbing on the sides. The firm is still in business.

Bowl, Shell Shape, Woman Filling Water Jug, 9 In.	140.00
Centerpiece, 4 Maidens In Relief, Branches, Large Leaves, Buff Glaze, 18 In.	750.00
Centerpiece, Maiden Holding Open Net, Shell Form Bowls, Naturalistic Base, 16 In.	1380.00
Centerpiece, Woman Holding Dish, Art Nouveau, 16 In.	900.00
Dealer's Plaque, Relief, White, Gilt Design, 5 1/2 In.	73.00
Figurine, 2 Hunting Dogs, Pink Mark, Base Crack, 14 In.	22.00
Figurine, Boy With Setter, Enamel & Gilt, Early 20th Century, 13 1/4 In. ....220.00 to 287.00
Figurine, Boy, Carrying Basket & Fruit, 15 In.	375.00
Figurine, Cockatoo, 8 In.	85.00
Figurine, Girl, With Fishnet, Pastel, Wooden Dowel Pole, Marked, 20 In.	165.00
Figurine, Good Soldier Schwejk, Gray, Brown, Czechoslovakia, 7 In.	45.00
Figurine, Lady, With Fan, Signed, 7 In.	275.00
Figurine, Lion Cub, 3 In.	25.00
Figurine, Male Wood Nymph, Blowing Shell Horn, Gold Gilt Trim, 15 In.	1100.00
Figurine, Man, Reading Scroll, 13 In.	300.00
Figurine, Nude Woman, Blue Drape, Art Nouveau, 9 3/4 In.	220.00
Figurine, Nude Woman, With Butterfly, 8 In.	140.00
Figurine, Peasant Couple, Signed, Late 19th Century, 21 In., Pair	632.00
Figurine, Pedestal Shell, Woman Seated, Instrument, 15 x 12 In.	900.00
Figurine, Poacher, Deer & Dog, Signed, 22 In.	185.00
Figurine, Polar Bear, White, 10 In. ....385.00 to 550.00
Figurine, Woman, On Rocky Ledge, 15 1/2 In.	575.00
Figurine, Woman, Sitting On Shell, 11 In.	500.00
Figurine, Woman, Waist Up, On Floral Wall Pedestal, Shell, Art Nouveau, 6 1/2 In.	425.00
Figurine, Young Nude, Polychrome, Marked Royal Dux Czech Republic, 8 1/2 In.	179.00
Group, Camel, Rider, Attendant, Landscaped, Gilt, 1920s, 24 In.	725.00
Group, Lovers, 22 1/2 In.	850.00
Group, Woman In Royal Coach, 2 Attendants, Cobalt Blue, White, Gilt, 15 In. ....460.00 to 670.00
Group, Young & Older Woman Dancing, Pastel, Marked, 19 1/2 In.	165.00
Lamp, Man & Woman, Figural, 30 In.	650.00
Vase, 2 Ducks Chasing Frog Near Tree, 19 In.	900.00
Vase, Cobalt & White Floral, 2 Handles, 31 In., Pair	230.00
Vase, Dutch Woman, Carrying Basket, Tree, 17 In.	450.00
Vase, Milkmaid With Cow, Tree Trunk Form, Signed, c.1900, 15 x 15 In.	400.00
Vase, Molded Poppies, Painted Stems, Baluster Form, c.1900, 13 In.	470.00
Vase, Pastel Floral, Gilt, Marked, 13 3/4 In.	80.00
Vase, Woman, Brown Dress, Sitting On Yellow Vase, 7 1/2 x 9 In.	150.00

ROYAL FLEMISH glass was made during the late 1880s in New Bedford, Massachusetts, by the Mt. Washington Glass Works. It is a colored satin glass decorated with dark colors and raised gold designs. The glass was patented in 1894. It was supposed to resemble stained glass windows.

Ewer, Lion Crest, Shield, Scrolls, Gold Segments, 10 In.	1400.00

Vase, 4 Rayed Suns, Gold Tracery, 6 1/2 In.	2200.00
Vase, Allover Rose Trailing, Enameled, Pink, Green, 1894, 9 In.	3335.00
Vase, Cherub Fighting Griffin & Serpent, Scrolls, Eagles Crest, 13 1/2 In., Pair	8600.00
Vase, Owl, Gold Decoration, 9 In.	715.00
Vase, Raised Gold Design, Floral, Squat, 5 In.	2400.00
Vase, Stick, Raised Gold Design, Medallions Around Neck, 11 1/2 In.	2100.00

ROYAL IVY pieces are listed in the Pressed Glass category by that pattern name.

ROYAL NYMPHENBURG is the modern name for the Nymphenburg porcelain factory, which was established at Neudeck-ob-der-Au, Germany, in 1753 and moved to Nymphenburg in 1761. The company is still in existence. Marks include a checkered shield topped by a crown, a crowned *CT* with the year, and a contemporary shield mark on reproductions of eighteenth-century porcelain.

Bowl, Fruit, Reticulated Cobalt Blue & Gilt Edge, c.1900, 8 1/2 In., 7 Piece	275.00
Figurine, Comedic Character, Blanc De Chine, 7 In.	154.00
Figurine, Dwarf, Baby In Basket, Flowing Beard, 1850s, 3 1/2 In.	2185.00
Figurine, Julia In A Kneeling Position, Blanc De Chine, 6 In.	143.00
Figurine, Mounted Rider, Officer Des Bayer, 12 1/8 In.	420.00
Figurine, Rabbit, 8 In.	125.00
Figurine, Scholar, Blanc De Chine, 1900, 8 1/2 In.	154.00
Jar, Gilt Striped White Ground, Enameled Bouquets, c.1900, 13 1/4 In.	575.00
Urn, Neoclassical Portrait, Male Masks Handles, Signed, 9 1/4 In.	258.00

ROYAL OAK pieces are listed in the Pressed Glass category by that pattern name.

ROYAL RUDOLSTADT, see Rudolstadt category.

ROYAL VIENNA, see Beehive category.

ROYAL WORCESTER is a name used by collectors. Worcester porcelains were made in Worcester, England, from about 1751. The firm went through many different periods and name changes. It became the Worcester Royal Porcelain Company, Ltd., in 1862. Today collectors call the porcelains made after 1862 *Royal Worcester*. In 1976, the firm merged with W. T. Copeland to become Royal Worcester Spode. Some early products of the factory are listed under Worcester.

Biscuit Jar, Allover Gilt Foliate, 6 1/2 In.	100.00
Bowl, Basket Weave Outside, Open Handles, Multicolored Flowers, 8 In.	295.00
Bowl, Shell Shape, Rolled Handle, Polychrome Flowers, Gilt Trim, 9 1/2 In.	225.00
Ewer, Allover Red, Blue Raised Flowers, Demon Mask, Gilt, Handle, 8 In., Pair	2415.00
Ewer, Dragon Form Handle, 11 1/2 In.	172.00
Ewer, Enamel Floral & Foliate, Marked, c.1889, 9 1/2 In.	115.00
Ewer, Florals Outlined In Gold, Scalloped, Pedestal, 9 In.	298.00
Ewer, Fruit Blossom Designs, Gilt Trim, 7 In.	140.00
Ewer, Powder Horn Form, Gilded Foliage, 8 1/2 In.	258.00
Figurine, February, Child Wearing Green Coat, Freda Doughty, c.1952, 6 1/4 In.	100.00
Figurine, Mother Machree, Tartan Shawl, Freda Doughty, 1940s, 6 In.	135.00
Figurine, Wren, Burnet Rose, Cock, Hen, Dorothy Doughty, c.1964, 7 In., Pair	580.00
Flask, Moon, Landscape Scenes Within Medallions, Blue, 11 In., Pair	4600.00
Jar, Cover, Lobed Body, Pierced Panels, Gilt Trim, Signed, c.1891, 5 In.	495.00
Jar, Potpourri, Cover, Fruit, Pierced Lappets, Freeman, Post-1955, 13 1/2 In., Pair	4600.00
Jardiniere, Goats Mask Handles, Pedestal, Peacocks, Gilt Border, 1907, 17 In.	4000.00
Jug, Enamel & Gilt Floral, Dragon Handle, 1883, 10 3/4 In.	373.00
Jug, Goldware, Boughs Of Fruit, Flowers, Leaves, Gilt, c.1887, 7 In.	175.00
Jug, Mask Spout, Gilt & Enamel Floral, 9 1/2 In.	546.00
Nut Dish, Yellow Flowers, 4 1/2 In.	6.50
Pitcher, 2 Gnomes, Tree, Hand Painted, Tapered, Twig Handle, 10 1/4 In.	415.00
Pitcher, Bird & Fern, Hummingbird, Serpent Handle, Squat, Marked, 8 In.	330.00
Pitcher, Cherry Blossom, Hand Painted, Gilt Leaf Band, Marked, 8 1/2 In.	120.00
Pitcher, Floral, Cream Ground, Gilt Handle, Marked, 7 3/4 In.	275.00
Pitcher, Morning Glory, Cherry Blossom, Dogwood, Bamboo Style Handle, 10 In.	132.00
Pitcher, Staghorn Type Handle, Gold Decoration, 9 1/2 In.	88.00
Pitcher, Thistle & Flower, Gilt Decoration, 5 In.	132.00

Pitcher, Thistle & Flower, Gold Handle, 7 1/2 In. 99.00
Plate, Still Life, Raised & Burnished Gilt Borders, c.1940, 9 1/4 In., Pair 320.00
Plate, Varying Still Life, 20th Century, 10 5/8 In., 12 Piece 5175.00
Stand, Open Bamboo Canes, Majolica, Turquoise Interior, c.1875, 27 In. 6610.00
Tankard, Embossed Apple Blossom Design, Bound Reed Style Handle 66.00
Tea Service, Bird, Flowering Leaves & Borders, c.1940, 6 Piece 255.00
Teapot, Flowers, Blue & Ivory, C-Scroll Handle, Purple Crown Mark, 9 1/2 In. 415.00
Teapot, Polychrome & Gilt Design, Off-White Ground, Reticulated, 9 1/2 In. 245.00
Tray, 6-Lobed Edge, Blue Floral Rim, 19 1/4 In. 258.00
Vase, Bamboo Style Gilt Trim, 6 1/2 In. 77.00
Vase, Bud, Reticulated Leaf, Hand Painted, Gilt, Triangular Handle, Marked, 3 In. 65.00
Vase, Carafe Shape, Flower & Gold Decoration, 10 In. 110.00
Vase, Cover, Highland Cattle At River, Mountains, Gilt, c.1929, 12 1/4 In. 1125.00
Vase, Cover, Pierced Flowers & Leaves, Sprays Of Fern, 19 1/4 In. 3250.00
Vase, Cylindrical, Aesthetic Style, Bird On Prunus Tree, Relief, c.1876, 12 1/2 In. 920.00
Vase, Enamel & Gilt Floral, Ivory Ground, c.1884, 12 1/2 In., Pair 230.00
Vase, Floral, Butterflies, Hand Painted, 10 1/4 In. 420.00
Vase, Flowers, Gilt, Yellow Ground, Reticulated Rim, 4 Scrolled Feet, 9 In. 250.00
Vase, Highland Cattle, Landscape, 2 Handles, Harry Stinton, c.1911, 10 3/8 In., Pair 1265.00
Vase, Highland Cattle, Landscape, 2 Handles, John Stinton, c.1910, 12 5/8 In. 2875.00
Vase, Oval, Sheep In Landscape, 2 Handles, Harry Davis, c.1912, 10 In., Pair 7475.00
Vase, Painted Orchids, 2 Angular Handles With Flowers, 9 1/2 In. 137.00
Vase, Spill, Squirrel, Green Stump, Majolica, Turquoise Interior, c.1870, 7 3/4 In. 1380.00
Vase, Thistle Shaped Urn, Oval Townscape, 2 Handles, c.1875, 12 1/4 In., Pair 5460.00

ROYCROFT products were made by the Roycrofter community of East
Aurora, New York, in the late nineteenth and early twentieth centuries.
The community was founded by Elbert Hubbard, famous philosopher,
writer, and artist. The workshops owned by the community made furniture, metalware, leatherwork, embroidery, and jewelry. A printshop
produced many signs, books, and the magazines that promoted the sayings of Elbert Hubbard. Furniture by the Roycroft community is listed
in the Furniture category.

Andirons, Wrought Iron, Vine Scrolled Feet & Base, 25 x 12 3/4 x 27 In. 2860.00
Appointment Set, Copper, Hammered, Base Holds Items, 2 1/2 x 11 1/4 In., 5 Pieces ... 451.00
Ashtray, Copper, Hammered, Original Patina, Impressed Mark, 4 In. ....55.00 to 90.00
Ashtray, Match Holder, Marked, 3 3/4 x 3 In. 60.00
Bean Bag, Clownie, Paper Tag, 6 In. 165.00
Bell, Copper, Hammered, Cone Shape, 3 x 1 1/4 In. 770.00
Bell, Dinner, Copper, Hammered, Orb & Cross Mark, 3 x 1 3/4 In. 495.00
Bookends, Brass, Hammered, Verdigris Medallion, 5 In. 330.00
Bookends, Copper, Hammered, Embossed Flower, 8 1/4 x 5 3/4 In. 220.00
Bookends, Copper, Hammered, Embossed Peacock Design, Brass Washed, 4 In. 165.00
Bookends, Copper, Hammered, Embossed Ship Medallion, Brass Washed, 5 In. ....165.00 to 220.00
Bookends, Copper, Hammered, Flowers, Pyramid Shape, 4 1/2 x 4 1/2 In. 121.00
Bookends, Copper, Hammered, Incised With Owls, 4 x 6 1/2 In. 220.00
Bookends, Copper, Hammered, Mottled Green Patina, Applied Brass, Marked, 4 1/2 In. ... 770.00
Bookends, Copper, Hammered, Orb Mark, 3 x 3 In. 165.00
Bookends, Copper, Hammered, Original Patina, 3 1/4 x 4 1/4 In. 272.00
Bookends, Copper, Hammered, Owl In Leather Medallion, Marked, 4 1/2 x 4 In. 330.00
Bookends, Copper, Hammered, Poppy, 5 3/4 x 5 1/4 In. 715.00
Bookends, Copper, Hammered, Quatrefoils, Border Bands, 4 1/2 x 5 In. 605.00
Bookends, Copper, Hammered, Ring Center, Orb Mark, 5 x 4 In. 770.00
Bookends, Copper, Hammered, Spade Shape, Stylized Flowers, 5 x 3 1/2 In. 415.00
Bookends, Copper, Hammered, Stylized Dogwood, Orb & Cross Mark, 4 1/2 x 5 In. 330.00
Bookends, Copper, Hammered, Stylized Floral, Original Patina, Original Box, 3 x 2 In. ... 660.00
Bookends, Copper, Hammered, Tooled Design, 8 1/2 In. 412.00
Bookends, Copper, Hammered, Tooled Floral Design, 3 In. 198.00
Bookends, Copper, Hammered, Tree, Dark Patina, Early Orb & Cross Mark, 6 1/2 x 4 In. . 8250.00
Bookends, Copper, Hammered, Triangular Form, Sailing Ship, Dark Patina, 5 In. 287.00
Bookends, Copper, Hammered, Trillium, Original Patina, 5 x 3 1/2 In. 330.00
Bookends, Peacock, Marked, c.1925, 4 1/4 x 6 1/8 In. 205.00
Bookends, Pinecone Design, Tooled Leather, Square, 5 1/2 In. 550.00

Bookends, Poppy, Marked, 5 1/2 x 5 In. 550.00
Bookends, Sailboats, 5 x 5 1/2 In. 172.00
Bookrack, Little Journeys, Cutout Trefoil Sides, 7 x 24 In. ....275.00 to 330.00
Bowl, 3-Footed, Original Patina, Orb & Cross Mark, 3 x 7 In. 341.00
Bowl, Copper, Hammered, Closed-In Rim, Squat, Orb & Cross Mark, 3 x 10 1/2 In. 495.00
Bowl, Copper, Hammered, Flared, Original Patina, 5 In. 165.00
Bowl, Copper, Hammered, Footed, Orb Mark, 4 In. 330.00
Bowl, Copper, Hammered, Incised Lotus Design, Orb & Cross Mark, 3 x 3 3/4 In. 385.00
Bowl, Copper, Ribbed, Round Footed, Marked, 5 x 12 In. 330.00
Bowl, Cover, Copper, Hammered, Dark Patina, 2 1/2 x 6 In. 394.00
Bowl, Lobed, Copper, Hammered, 4 3/4 In. 220.00
Bowl, Lotus, Copper, Hammered, Old Cleaned Patina, 4 In. 360.00
Box, Goodie, Mahogany, Footed, Strap Hardware, Mildred Hopper, 10 1/2 x 24 In. 990.00
Box, Letter, Oak, Carved Orb & Cross Mark, 3 1/4 x 10 x 13 In. 1320.00
Box, Mahogany, Copper Hinges & Handles, Orb & Cross Mark, 9 1/2 x 23 x 12 In. 1210.00
Calendar, Copper, Hammered, Orb Mark, 3 1/2 x 4 1/4 In. 110.00
Candelabra, 3-Light, Copper, Hammered, Brass Wash, Orb & Cross Mark, 20 In., Pair ... 1430.00
Candlestick, Copper, Hammered, Brass Wash, Orb & Cross Mark, 13 x 5 In. 715.00
Candlestick, Copper, Hammered, Round Base, Flared Bobeche, 6 1/2 x 3 In., Pair 825.00
Candlestick, Copper, Hammered, Square Bobeche, Tulip Shape Top, 15 In., Pair 3080.00
Candlestick, Copper, Hammered, Twisted Stems, Orb & Cross Mark, 12 In. 1100.00
Candlestick, Copper, Hammered, Victor Toothaker, 20 1/2 In., Pair 3300.00
Candlestick, Metal, Acid Etched, Footed, Orb Mark, 3 In., Pair 330.00
Candlestick, Princess, Marked, 7 1/2 In., Pair 880.00
Candy Dish, Copper, Hammered, Trefoil & Starburst, 4 1/2 x 5 1/2 In. 385.00
Chamberstick, 1 With Glass Chimney, Overcoated Finish, Pair 110.00
Chamberstick, Copper, Hammered, 3 1/4 x 4 1/2 In. 220.00
Chamberstick, Copper, Hammered, Riveted Handle, 2 1/4 x 3 1/2 In., Pair 360.00
Chandelier, 5 Shades, Wrought Iron, Marked Ceiling Plate, 25 In. 9350.00
Clock, Mantel, Tooled Leather Case, Stylized Floral, Orb & Cross Mark, 4 1/2 x 6 In. 8250.00
Crate, Shipping, Selected Writings Of Elbert Hubbard, Wooden, 7 x 21 x 10 In. 165.00
Crumb Scraper Set, Copper, Hammered Foliate Design, Marked, 8 1/4 In. 172.00
Desk Blotter, Copper, Hammered, Brass Washed Corners, Ivy Design, 14 x 20 In. 110.00
Desk Organizer, Copper, Hammered, Glass Inkwell, 2 Stamp Boxes, 10 x 2 In. 660.00
Desk Set, Copper, Hammered, Indian Design, Orb & Cross Mark, 7 Piece 2420.00
Desk Set, Copper, Hammered, Original Patina, Scalloped Edge Design, 9 Piece 660.00
Dish, Copper, Hammered, Embossed Geometric Band, Original Patina, 5 3/4 In. 195.00
Dish, Copper, Hammered, Original Patina, 5 1/2 In. 90.00
Doorknocker, Copper, Hammered, Box, 3 1/2 x 1 1/2 In. 440.00
Frame, Leather, Tooled Daisy, Orb & Cross Mark, 9 x 6 1/2 In. 1650.00
Frame, Leather, Tooled, Glasgow Roses, Orb & Cross Mark, 8 x 5 1/2 In. 1430.00
Frame, Oak, 11 x 15 In. 440.00
Frame, Picture Of Embossed Cherries, Motto, Copper, 9 1/2 x 7 1/2 In. 176.00
Frame, The Adman's Philosophy, Matted, Marked Hubbard, c.1915, 33 1/2 x 24 In. 660.00
Hatpin, Copper, Hammered, Circular Finial, Brass Pin, 10 x 1 1/2 In. 330.00
Hatpin, Copper, Hammered, Orb & Cross Mark, 1 1/2-In. Square Head 825.00
Holder, Plant, Floral Type Top, 9 In., Pair 195.00
Humidor, Copper, Hammered, Riveted Handle, Dark Patina, Circular, 3 x 5 In. 825.00
Humidor, Cover, Copper, Hammered, 4-Pointed Arrow, Orb & Cross Mark, 4 1/2 In. 1210.00
Humidor & Pipe Stand, Copper, Hammered, Brushed Patina, Round, 6 In. 250.00
Inkwell, 2 Leaded Glass Wells, Pen Tray, Orb & Cross Mark, 2 1/2 x 15 In. 660.00
Inkwell, Copper, Hammered, Embossed Quatrefoil Design, Glass Liner, 2 1/4 In. ..195.00 to 495.00
Inkwell, Splayed Riveted Base, Glass Insert, Hinged Lid, 2 1/4 x 4 1/4 In. 220.00
Jardiniere, Marked, c.1915, 10 7/8 In. 6750.00
Lamp, Boudoir, Green Bubble Glass, Silk Shade, 16 In. 1540.00
Lamp, Boudoir, Leaded Slag Glass Shade, Orb & Cross Mark, 14 3/4 In. 5225.00
Lamp, Boudoir, Silver Washed Base, Steuben Glass, Orb & Cross Mark, 15 In. 660.00
Lamp, Desk, Copper, Hammered, Mica Panels, Orb & Cross Mark, 14 x 10 In. 2860.00
Lamp, Helmet, Copper, Hammered, Medium Patina, 1919, 14 1/4 In. 1840.00
Lamp, Helmet, Copper, Original Patina, Marked, 13 1/2 x 6 In. 2035.00
Lamp, Rawhide Shade, Copper, Hammered, 20 x 14 In. 1650.00
Lamp Base, Copper, Hammered, Original Patina, Orb & Cross Mark, 10 In. 374.00
Letter Opener & Pen Tray, Copper, Hammered, Orb & Cross Mark, 9 & 8 In., 2 Piece ... 220.00

Mat, Table, Leather, Tooled Trillium & Celtic Rose, Orb & Cross Mark, 12 1/2 In. 3300.00
Mouse Trap, Better Mouse Trap, Unused, 8 3/4 x 1 3/4 In. 140.00
Nut Bowl, Copper, Hammered, Closed-In Rim, Footed, Orb & Cross Mark, 2 1/4 x 10 In. 440.00
Nut Bowl, Copper, Hammered, Closed-In Rim, Orb & Cross Mark, 2 1/2 x 6 In. 605.00
Nut Bowl, Copper, Hammered, Overcoated Original Finish, 9 1/2 In. 195.00
Nut Set, Copper, Hammered, Funnel Holds 6 Picks, Orb & Cross Mark, 4 x 8-In. Bowl . . 465.00
Paperweight, Hat, Doughboy, Copper, Original Patina, 1 1/2 x 3 In. 396.00
Pen Tray, Copper, Hammered, Orb Mark, 9 1/2 x 2 1/2 In. 120.00
Penholder, Copper, Hammered, Stylized Owl Medallion, Brass Washed, 7 1/4 In. 55.00
Poker Chip Rack, Copper, Hammered, Orb & Cross Mark, 6 1/2 x 4 3/4 In. 660.00
Punch Set, Brown Glaze, Marked, 10 3/8-In. Bowl, 7 Piece 310.00
Purse, Tooled Leather, Day Lily, Orb & Cross Mark, 3 x 3 1/4 In. 770.00
Purse, Woman's, Tooled Leather, Embossed Floral Design, Orb & Cross Mark, 7 x 6 In. . 660.00
Sconce, Brass, Hammered, Original Patina, Impressed Mark, 10 1/2 In. 165.00
Sconce, Copper, Hammered, Faceted, Orb & Cross Mark, 7 3/4 In. 99.00
Sign, Carved Ash Motto, Old Things Are Best, Orb & Cross Mark, 10 x 42 In. 7150.00
Spoon, Nut, Scrolling Handle, Marked, c.1920, 7 3/4 In., Pair 287.00
Tray, Card, Copper, Hammered, Brass Washed, Embossed, 9 3/4 In. 65.00
Tray, Card, Copper, Hammered, Embossed Trefoils, Verdigris Medallions, 10 In. 415.00
Tray, Card, Copper, Hammered, Silver Washed, Walter Jennings, Orb & Cross Mark, 7 In. 415.00
Tray, Copper, Hammered, 3 Trefoils, Round, 9 3/4 In. 360.00
Tray, Copper, Hammered, Original Patina, 2 Handles, Impressed Mark, 18 1/2 In. 550.00
Tray, Copper, Hammered, Oval, Stylized Medallions, Patina, 21 1/2 In. 407.00
Tray, Copper, Hammered, Riveted Handles, Round, 16 In. 415.00
Tray, Copper, Hammered, Twin Handles, Early 20th Century, 17 1/4 In. 345.00
Tray, Fruit, Copper, Hammered, Stylized Rim Design, 9 3/4 In. 520.00
Urn, Copper, Hammered, Flared, Rolled Rim, Medium Patina, 3 3/4 x 5 1/4 In. 121.00
Vase, American Beauty, Marked, c.1915, 21 3/8 In. . . . . .2300.00 to 2750.00
Vase, Bud, Copper, Hammered, Dogwood, Glass Liner, Square, Orb & Cross Mark, 8 In. . 385.00
Vase, Bud, Copper, Hammered, Wood Grain, Silver, 4 Riveted Buttresses, 8 In. 5500.00
Vase, Bud, Hanging, Embossed Stylized Flower, Glass Insert, Patina, 9 In. 143.00
Vase, Copper, Hammered, Applied Nickel Design, Original Patina, 6 1/2 In. 825.00
Vase, Copper, Hammered, Brass Wash, 7 In. 150.00
Vase, Copper, Hammered, Brass Wash, Embossed Quatrefoils, Mark, 7 In. 1540.00
Vase, Copper, Hammered, Brass Wash, Footed, Scalloped Rim, 5 1/4 In. 165.00
Vase, Copper, Hammered, Bulbous, Closed-In Rim, Orb & Cross Mark, 5 x 4 1/2 In. 358.00
Vase, Copper, Hammered, Buttressed Handles, Monterey Mission Orb, 7 x 4 1/2 In. 6600.00
Vase, Copper, Hammered, Closed-In Rim, Bulbous, Orb & Cross Mark, 5 x 4 1/2 In. 525.00
Vase, Copper, Hammered, Curled Rim, Flowers, 9 1/4 x 3 3/4 In. 1100.00
Vase, Copper, Hammered, Cylindrical, Flowers, Orb & Cross Mark, 9 1/4 x 3 3/4 In. 550.00
Vase, Copper, Hammered, Cylindrical, Orb Mark, 10 x 3 In. 1925.00
Vase, Copper, Hammered, Cylindrical, Ruffled, Orb Mark, 10 In. 2475.00
Vase, Copper, Hammered, Diamond Band Pattern, 12 x 4 1/4 In. 1210.00
Vase, Copper, Hammered, Original Patina, Bulbous, 4 1/2 In. 385.00
Vase, Copper, Hammered, Original Patina, Spherical, 3 In. 165.00
Vase, Copper, Hammered, Oval, 8 1/4 x 4 In. 550.00
Vase, Copper, Hammered, Riveted Base, Cylindrical, Orb & Cross Mark, 10 1/2 x 6 In. . . 5230.00
Vase, Copper, Hammered, Silver Bands, Secessionist Design, Closed-In Rim, 6 In. 1320.00
Vase, Copper, Hammered, Squat, Flared Neck, Dark Patina, Orb & Cross Mark, 4 x 6 In. . 880.00
Vase, Copper, Hammered, Steuben Glass Insert, 6 In. 230.00
Vase, Copper, Hammered, Stylized Diamond Shaped Flowers, Green Triangles, 7 In. 920.00
Vase, Copper, Hammered, Stylized Floral Design, Cylindrical, 10 x 3 In. 1650.00
Vase, Copper, Hammered, Tapered, Closed-In Rim, Orb & Cross Mark, 5 1/4 x 2 1/2 In. . 308.00
Vase, Copper, Hammered, Tapered, Geometric Band, Flaring Rim, 4 3/4 x 3 3/4 In. 341.00
Vase, Copper, Hammered, Tooled Floral Design, 10 In. 770.00
Vase, Flared, Scalloped Edge, 3 1/4 In. 345.00
Vase, Stylized Verdigris Flowers, Polychrome, Copper, Cylindrical, 7 In. 2255.00

ROZANE, see Roseville category.

ROZENBURG worked at The Hague, Holland, from 1890 to 1914. The most important pieces were earthenware made in the early twentieth century with pale-colored Art Nouveau designs.

    Inkwell, Stylized Iris & Roosters, Green, Olive Ground, 3 In. 550.00

Pitcher, Stylized Flowers, Magenta, Purple, White, Green, Brown Ground, 6 In. 440.00
Vase, Eggshell, Exotic Flowers In Square Section, Leafy Stems, c.1902, 6 1/2 In. 510.00
Vase, Iris & Scroll Polychrome Throughout, 16 In. 345.00
Vase, Rooster Within A Cartouche, Cobalt, Turquoise, Yellow, Brown, 1900, 10 In. 405.00

RRP is the mark used by the firm of Robinson-Ransbottom. It is not a
mark of the more famous Roseville Pottery. The Ransbottom brothers
started a pottery in 1900 in Ironspot, Ohio. In 1920, they merged with
the Robinson Clay Product Company of Akron, Ohio, to become
Robinson-Ransbottom. The factory is still working.

Bowl, Brown Sponge, Yellowware, Incised, Stamped RRPC, 6 1/2 In. 50.00
Figurine, Boston Pug, Standing, Glass Eyes, Late 1930s 1950.00
Pitcher, Brown Band Top, Cream Bottom, Impressed Mark R.R.P.Co. U.S.A., 4 1/2 In. . .   12.00
Pitcher, Brown Band, Cream Bottom, Impressed Mark, 4 1/2 In.   45.00

RS GERMANY is part of the wording in marks used by the Tillowitz,
Germany, factory of Reinhold Schlegelmilch from 1914 until about
1945. The porcelain was sold decorated and undecorated. The
Schlegelmilch families made porcelains marked in many ways. See
also ES Germany, RS Poland, RS Prussia, and RS Silesia.

Basket, Art Deco, Pheasants, Yellow Ground, Green Mark, 5 In.   250.00
Bowl, Art Deco Mold, 2 Handles, Green R.S.G. Mark, 8 1/2 In. 56.00
Bowl, Bluebird On Cherry Tree, Pierced Sides, 6 In. 73.00
Bowl, Flowers, Green Ground, Gilt, Scalloped Edge, 2 Pierced Handles, 7 1/2 In. 39.00
Bowl, Large White Flower, Art Deco Mold, 2 Handles, Green Mark, 7 In. 50.00
Bowl, Pink & Yellow Roses, Art Deco Shape, 2 Handles, Green Mark, 10 In. 95.00
Bowl, White Roses, Gilt Accents, Square, 2 Handles, Blue Mark, 8 1/2 In. 56.00
Chocolate Set, Pink Tulips, Gold Leaves, Art Deco Mold, 10 In., 10 Piece 365.00
Coffeepot, Red Roses, Gilt Trim, Blue Mark, 8 1/2 In. 90.00
Condensed Milk Holder, Lid, White Roses, Gilt Accents, Blue Mark, 4 3/4 In. 100.00
Cup, White Flowers, Green & White Pearlized Ground, Swirl Blown-Out Shape, 3 1/2 In.   39.00
Ewer, Floral Design, Mold 640, Green Mark, 5 In. 170.00
Fernery, Footed, Floral Design, Red Steeple Mark, 6 1/2 x 3 1/2 In. 180.00
Hatpin Holder, Floral Design, Mold 656, Green Mark, 4 1/2 In.   90.00
Hatpin Holder, Pink Roses, Green Mark 125.00
Hatpin Holder, Roses, Mold 77, Blue Mark, 4 3/4 In. 130.00
Mustache Cup & Saucer, Floral Design, Mold 26, Green Mark 90.00
Nappy, Large White Flowers, 2 Pierced Handles, Blue Mark, 7 1/2 In. 28.00
Nappy, Molded Parrot, Floral Design, 1 Handle, Black Mark, 6 1/2 In. 110.00
Night-Light, Owl, 5 In. . . . . *Illus*   896.00
Pin Box, Snow Drops, Art Deco 275.00
Pin Tray, Roses In Center, Pearlized Finish, Mold 327, Green Mark, 5 1/2 In. 39.00
Pitcher, Milk, Rose Design, 5 1/2 In. 140.00
Plate, Portrait, Flossie, Mold 256, Steeple Mark, 8 1/2 In. 280.00
Ring Tree, Pointed Scallops, Gilt Highlights, Green Mark, 4 3/8 In. 45.00
Sauce, Footed, Polychrome Flowers, Blue Luster Panels, Handles, 6 1/4 In. 39.00
Sauceboat, Undertray, Painted Flowers, Blue Mark, Small 75.00

**If you discover a cache of very dirty
antiques and you are not dressed in
work clothes, make yourself a temporary
cover-up from a plastic garbage bag.**

RS Germany,
Night-Light,
Owl, 5 In.

Sugar, Ornate Design, Gilt, Blue Mark 110.00
Sugar, Satin, Hand Painted Roses, Artist 375.00
Tankard, Pink Roses, White Ground, Mold 584, 10 In. 280.00
Teapot, Yellow Roses, Locking Lid, Blue Mark, Red Script, 5 1/2 In. 73.00
Toothpick, Footed, Rose Design, 3 Handles, Mold 362, Green Mark, 2 In. 90.00
Toothpick, Lily, Green Mark, 2 1/4 In. 78.00

RS POLAND (German) is a mark used by the Reinhold Schlegelmilch
factory at Tillowitz from about 1946 to 1956. After 1956, the factory
made porcelain marked PT Poland. This is one of many of the RS
marks used. See also ES Germany, RS Germany, RS Prussia, and RS
Silesia.

Bowl, Centerpiece, Blown-Out Panels, Garlands Of Roses, Marked 675.00
Mayonnaise Set, Saucer, Hand Painted Hydrangeas, Double Mark 175.00

RS PRUSSIA appears in several marks used on porcelain before 1917.
Reinhold Schlegelmilch started his porcelain works in Suhl, Germany,
in 1869. See also ES Germany, RS Germany, RS Poland, and RS
Silesia.

Biscuit Jar, Footed, Leaf Design, Gilt Accents, Mold 878, Red Mark, 5 1/2 In. 260.00
Biscuit Jar, White Rose Design, Flared Lid, Signed, 6 1/2 In. 125.00
Bowl, Basket Of Roses, Mold 7, Oval, Red Mark, 12 1/2 In. 140.00
Bowl, Flora Portrait, Stenciled Designs, 10 In. 1600.00
Bowl, Flower Bouquet In Center, Purple & Green Luster, 11 In. 200.00
Bowl, Flowers, Satin, Mold 254, 10 In. 110.00
Bowl, Painted Roses, Arch Design, Gilt, Red Star, 10 3/4 In. 260.00
Bowl, Pastel Roses, Molded Flowers, Pleated Panels, Gesetzlich Geschutzt, 9 3/4 In. 336.00
Bowl, Pink & White Wild Roses, 8 Lobes, 4-Footed, Signed, 9 In. 285.00
Bowl, Rose & White Lilacs, Pierced Handles, Mold 404, Red Mark, 10 In. 101.00
Bowl, Rose Centered Design, Scalloped Mold, 10 In. 170.00
Bowl, Roses & Daisies, Beaded Edge, 12 Scallops, Mold 182, 8 1/2 In. 56.00
Bowl, Roses & Daisies, Luster Design, Mold 91, 10 1/2 In. 140.00
Bowl, Scalloped Floral Center, Scalloped Border, Mold 211, 10 In. 170.00
Bowl, Snowbird, Satin, 11 In. 750.00
Bowl, Spray Of Roses, Ruffled Edge, Red Mark, 9 In. 85.00
Bowl, Turkeys, Ducks & Swallows In 3 Scenes, Mold 77 Variant, Red Mark, 11 In. 1570.00
Bowl, Turkeys, Pheasants, Swans, Swallows, 4 Scenes, Mold 304, 10 In. 450.00
Bowl, White Flowers, Green Foliage, Evergreens, Gilt Trim, 10 1/4 In. 143.00
Bread Tray, Cotton Plant Design, Pierced Handles, Red Mark With Script, 11 In. 195.00
Cake Plate, Pink & Yellow Ground, Flowers, Leaves, Gold Trim, 9 3/4 In. 225.00
Cake Plate, Water Lilies Reflection, Handles, 10 1/4 In. 250.00
Celery Dish, Painted Roses, Purple, Lavender, Mold 16, RSP Mark, 12 1/2 In. 146.00
Chocolate Pot, White Flowers, White Ground, Mold 509A, 9 In. 170.00
Compote, Center Floral Design, Green Swag, Beaded Jewels, Mold 157, 4 1/2 In. 180.00
Creamer, Upper Medallions, Yellow Roses Transfer, 19th Century, 4 1/2 In. 58.00
Cup & Saucer, Pink & White Daisy, Demitasse 65.00
Muffineer, Roses, 2 Handles, Mold 781, Red Mark, 5 In. 280.00
Mustard, Blue & Multicolored Roses, White 150.00
Pitcher, Water, Carnation Mold, 8 3/4 In. 660.00
Plate, Flower, White Satin, Mold 31, Red R.S.P. Mark, 11 In. 90.00
Plate, Flowers, Satin, Pierced Handles, Mold 301, 9 1/2 In. 130.00
Plate, Melon Eaters, Mold 300, 10 1/2 In. 670.00
Plate, Mill Scene, Mold 300, Brown Mark, 8 1/2 In. 420.00
Plate, Poppies & Roses, Mold 277, Red Mark, 9 1/2 In. 90.00
Plate, Red Roses, Gilt, Mold 156, Red Mark, 8 1/2 In. 140.00
Plate, Violets, Water Lily, Red R.S.P. Mark, 6 In., Pair 67.00
Shaving Mug, 3 1/16 In. 225.00
Sugar, Cover, Roses, 2 Handles 80.00
Sugar & Creamer, Labrun Portrait On Sugar, Recamier On Creamer 2500.00
Sugar & Creamer, Pink Flowers, Tan, Green Border 40.00
Sugar & Creamer, Pink Rose, Square 70.00
Syrup, Lid, Swans Swimming, Pearlized Finish, Mold 577, Red Mark, 5 1/2 In. 235.00
Tankard, Allover Pink Poppies, 11 In. 1100.00

Tankard, Red Poppies, Cream Ground, Mold 586, 11 1/2 In. 560.00
Teapot, Pink & Yellow Roses, Yellow To Blue Ground, 9 In. 220.00
Teapot, White Wild Rose, Watered Silk Finish, Molded Base, Red Mark, 5 1/2 In. 170.00
Toothpick, Flowers, Gold Trim, Marked, 2 1/2 In. 50.00
Vase, Kitten Examining Boot, 4 In. 88.00
Vase, Oranges, White Flowers, Marked, Handles, 17 In. 1500.00

RS SILESIA appears on porcelain made at the Reinhold Schlegelmilch factory in Tillowitz, Germany, from the 1920s to the 1940s. The Schlegelmilch families made porcelains marked in many ways. See also ES Germany, RS Germany, RS Poland, and RS Prussia.

Bowl, Floral, c.1910, 7 1/2 In. 65.00
Pin Dish, Violets, Marked, c.1910, 5 1/4 In. 35.00

RUBENA is a glassware that shades from red to clear. It was first made by George Duncan and Sons of Pittsburgh, Pennsylvania, about 1885. This coloring was used on many types of glassware. The pressed glass patterns of Royal Ivy and Royal Oak are listed under Pressed Glass.

Basket, Honeycomb, Ruffled Edge, Square Handle, 9 x 5 1/2 In. 175.00
Compote, Diamond Quilted, Silver Plated Base, 6 3/4 In. 195.00
Creamer 240.00
Pitcher, Opalescent Swirls, Ruffled Square Mouth, Clear Handle, 8 1/2 In. 135.00
Sugar, Cover 280.00
Vase, Trumpet, Satin, Flowers On Gold Branch, Brass Stand, 16 1/2 In. 225.00

RUBENA VERDE is a Victorian glassware that was shaded from red to green. It was first made by Hobbs, Brockunier and Company of Wheeling, West Virginia, about 1890.

Butter, Cover, Vaseline Underplate, Inverted Thumbprint, Daisy & Button 550.00
Centerpiece, Maiden Reading Letter, Silver Plated Base, 15 In. 575.00
Compote, Figural Base, Cranberry To Pale Green Opal Points, Art Nouveau 595.00
Pitcher, Hobnail, 7 3/4 In. 165.00

RUBY GLASS is the dark red color of the precious gemstone known as a *ruby*. It was a popular Victorian color that never went completely out of style. The glass was shaped by many different processes to make many different types of ruby glass. There was a revival of interest in the 1940s when modern-shaped ruby table glassware became fashionable. Sometimes the red color is added to clear glass by a process called flashing or staining. Flashed glass is clear glass dipped in a colored glass, then pressed or cut. Stained glass has color painted on a clear glass. Then it is refired so the stain fuses with the glass. Pieces of glass colored in this way are indicated by the word *stained* in the description. Related items may be found in other categories, such as Cranberry Glass, Pressed Glass, and Souvenir.

Basket, Entwined With Vines & Bird, 19th Century, 14 In. 6900.00
Cordial, Gold Stem & Medallions, 18th Century Courtesans, 5 In. 65.00
Jar, Cover, Gold Filigree & Trim, Ball Feet, Finial, 5 1/2 In. 165.00
Tea Set, Floral, Gilt Trim, 8-In. Pot, 9 Piece 165.00

RUDOLSTADT was a faience factory in the Thuringia region of Germany from 1720 to about 1791. In 1854, Ernst Bohne began working in the area. From about 1887 to 1918, the New York and Rudolstadt Pottery made decorated porcelain marked with the RW and crown familiar to collectors. This porcelain was imported by Lewis Straus and Sons of New York, which later became Nathan Straus and Sons. The word *Royal* was included in their import mark. Collectors often call it *Royal Rudolstadt*. Most pieces found today were made in the late nineteenth or early twentieth century. Additional pieces may be listed in the Kewpie category.

Bowl, Openwork, Ram's Heads & Dolphin Standard, 11 1/2 In. 345.00
Bust, Woman, Fan In Hand, Head Covering, 15 In. 935.00
Clock, Mantel, Putti With Anvil, Floral, 8-Day, New Haven Clock Co., 17 In. 405.00
Pitcher, Hand Painted, Embossed, Fancy Gilt Handle, 6 In. 44.00

Urn, Floral Design, Hand Painted, Gilt Handles, Lemon Yellow, Peach Base, 22 In. 30.00
Vase, Trumpet Form, Maiden & Cupid Within Gilt Border, Magenta Ground, 10 In. 86.00

RUGS have been used in the American home since the seventeenth century. The oriental rug of that time was often used on a table, not on the floor. Rag rugs, hooked rugs, and braided rugs were made by housewives from scraps of material.

Afghan, Geometric, Brown, Black, Red, 1950s, 3 Ft. 6 In. x 6 Ft. 6 In. 110.00
Afghan Bokhara, Gul Design, 9 Ft. 4 In. x 12 Ft. 10 In. 550.00
Afghan Ersari, Floral Diamond, Stepped Border, 1920, 7 Ft. x 9 Ft. 7 In. 5230.00
Afshar, Flowers, Star, Red Ground, Blue Border, Wool, 13 Ft. 3 In. x 9 Ft. 4 In. 1625.00
Afshar, Square Medallion, 2 Squares, Blue Field, Red Border, 5 Ft. 4 In. x 4 Ft. 2 In. 1265.00
Alexander Calder, Geometric Design, Orange, Gold, Red, 1963, 6 Ft. 10 In. x 5 Ft. 7 In. . 3737.00
Art Deco, Animal Scene, Tan Ground, 1930, 10 Ft. 7 In. x 8 Ft. 5 In. 11500.00
Art Deco, Bird & Branch, Burgundy & Blue Borders, Wool, Chinese, 10 Ft. x 13 Ft. 2 In. 990.00
Aubusson, Floral Design, Central Medallion, Light Rose Flowers, 8 Ft. 2 In. x 9 Ft. 2 In. . 7187.00
Aubusson, Floral Medallion Center, Ivory Field, 18-In. Border, 12 x 20 Ft. 440.00
Aubusson, Needlepoint, Allover Floral Design, Rose, Green, Gray, 8 x 10 Ft. 115.00
Azerbaijani, Allover Floral, Geometric Design, Red Field, 3 Ft. 7 In. x 10 Ft. 5 In. 980.00
Bakhtiari, Floral Medallion, Crimson Ground, Double Border, 13 Ft. x 10 Ft. 5 In. 1430.00
Bakhtiari, Geometric Floral, Navy & Red Field, Persia, 5 Ft. 8 In. x 11 Ft. 8 In. 800.00
Baluchi, Diagonal Rows Of Small Boteh, Camel Field, 5 Ft. 4 In. x 3 Ft. 4 In. 635.00
Baluchi, Paired Leaf Design, Red, Rose, Navy Blue, Camel Field, 4 Ft. 4 In. x 2 Ft. 575.00
Baluchi, Prayer, Midnight Blue, Tree Of Life, Camel Field, 5 Ft. 5 In. x 2 Ft. 10 In. 635.00
Baluchi, Staggered Rows Of Hooked Diamonds, Camel Field, 4 Ft. 9 In. x 3 Ft. 2 In. 690.00
Baluchi, Tribal Mat, 2 Medallions, Geometric, Brown Field, 3 Ft. 6 In. x 6 Ft. 8 In. 165.00
Baluchi, Tribal, 3 Angular Medallions, Brown, Indigo, Rose, 3 Ft. 6 In. x 6 Ft. 5 In. 360.00
Beshir Torba, Geometric, Brick Red Field, Fringe Long Side, 3 Ft. 9 In. x 1 Ft. 9 In. 165.00
Bibibaff, Dark Blue Ground, Red Border, c.1925, 8 Ft. 11 In. x 11 Ft. 6 In. 2750.00
Bibibaff, Off-White Field, Floral, Multicolored Border, 8 Ft. 3 In. x 11 Ft. 5 In. 1150.00
Bidjar, Blue Field, Red Border, 6 Ft. 2 In. x 9 Ft. 2 In. 3300.00
Bidjar, Runner, Spandrels, Blue Border, Red Ground, Runner, 2 Ft. 9 In. x 11 Ft. 4 In. ... 245.00
Bokhara, Bird Design, Ivory Field, Maroon Border, 4 Ft. 3 In. x 3 Ft. 1 In. 605.00
Bokhara, Repeating Geometric, Wine Field, 1920, 6 Ft. 7 In. x 4 Ft. 3 In. 495.00
Bokhara, Repeating Red Octagons, Rust Borders, 20th Century, 9 Ft. 2 In. x 6 Ft. 3 In. .. 330.00
Braided, Wool, Linen Thread, Alternating Colors, Split At End, 18 Ft. 8 In. x 14 Ft. 5 In. . 550.00
Caucasian, 16 Medallions, Brown Ground, 6 Ft. 4 In. x 3 Ft. 11 In. 440.00
Caucasian, Floral, Beige Field, 6 Ft. 10 In. x 4 Ft. 8 In. 1045.00
Caucasian, Geometric, Prayer Niche, Rust, Blue, Beige Ground, 3 Ft. 9 In. x 5 Ft. 9 In. .. 575.00
Caucasian, Herati Design, Midnight Blue Field, Red Border, 11 Ft. 4 In. x 5 Ft. 9 In. 1150.00
Caucasian Bidjar, Animals & People, Late 19th Century, 3 Ft. 4 In. x 5 Ft. 3 In. 4070.00
Caucasian Kazak, Brick Red Field, Geometric Border, 4 Ft. 2 In. x 9 Ft. 9 In. 330.00
Caucasian Lesghi, Medallions, Blue Ground, Borders, 1900, 6 Ft. 10 In. x 12 Ft. 9 In. 4290.00
Caucasian Shirvan, Geometric, Rust Field, Border, 19th Century, 4 Ft. 5 In. x 3 Ft. 8 In. . 715.00
Chi Chi, Hooked Polygons & Octagons, Blue Field, Black Border, 5 Ft. x 3 Ft. 6 In. 1495.00
Chinese, 5 Vases Of Flowering Plants, 6 Floral Groups, 1920s, 11 Ft. 8 In. x 9 Ft. 2415.00
Chinese, Art Deco, Floral, c.1920, 5 x 3 Ft. 150.00
Chinese, Bamboo Design, Deep Green Field, 4 Ft. 6 In. x 7 Ft. 460.00
Chinese, Central Medallion, Geometric Corner & Border, 13 Ft. 5 In. x 10 Ft. 10 In. 11500.00
Chinese, Dragons, Floral Sprays, Vases, Deep Blue Field, Runner, 11 Ft. 6 In. x 2 Ft. 7 In. 1380.00
Chinese, Floral & Birds, Dark Gray Ground, Burgundy Border, 9 Ft. 2 In. x 11 Ft. 8 In. .. 465.00
Chinese, Flowering Vine, Powder Blue Ground, Light Blue Border, 13 Ft. 6 In. x 11 Ft. .. 575.00
Dhurrie, Red, Blue Vertical Bands, Stylized Vines & Flowers, 8 Ft. 2 In x 9 Ft. 8 In. 121.00
Drugget, Floral Design, Blue, Oatmeal Ground, Maroon Border, 9 Ft. 3 In. x 14. Ft. 3 In.. 286.00
Drugget, Gustav Stickley, 8 Ft. x 9 Ft. 9 In. 1375.00
Drugget, Tan Center, Rickrack Border, Gustav Stickley, 9 Ft. 8 In. x 6 Ft. 2 In. 440.00
Embroidered, 3 Borders Center, Oriental, 20th Century, 2 Ft. 6 In. x 1 Ft. 4 In. 90.00
Ersari, 3 Columns, 8 Guls, Apricot, Ivory, Blue, Red Field, 9 Ft. 7 In. x 6 Ft. 7 In. 745.00
Feraghan, Center Medallions, Rust Ground, Borders, 4 Ft. 1 In. x 6 Ft. 9 In. 5225.00
Feraghan, Medallion, Peacocks, Tree Border, 19th Century, 7 Ft. x 4 Ft. 7 In. 2420.00
Feraghan, Medallions, Allover Floral, Rust Ground, 6 Ft. 6 In. x 4 Ft. 6 In. 1320.00
Gashgai, Floral, Tan Border, Late 19th Century, Runner, 7 Ft. 11 In. x 3 Ft. 5 In. 495.00
Gashgai, Geometric Medallion, Blue, Wool, 20th Century, 8 Ft. 2 In. x 5 Ft. 4 In. 690.00

Gorevan, Center Medallion, Dark Blue Border, c.1940, 8 Ft. 6 In. x 11 Ft. 3 In. 3080.00
Gorevan, Red, Black, Blue & Green, c.1950, 11 Ft. 9 In. x 9 Ft. 5 In. 880.00
Grenfell, Mat, Sled Dogs, Stylized Trees, 11 x 22 In. 695.00
Grenfell, Polar Bear On Ice Floe Center, 20 x 32 In. 1650.00
Hamadan, Allover Geometric Design, Red Field, 2 Ft. 7 In. x 8 Ft. 3 In. 430.00
Hamadan, Expanded Herati, Deep Red Field, Iran, c.1960, 2 x 3 Ft. 33.00
Hamadan, Geometric, Floral, Avian Design, Red Field, Runner, 3 Ft. 5 In. x 9 Ft. 8 In. 258.00
Hamadan, Hexagonal Medallion, Diamonds, Camel Field, 3 Borders, 11 Ft. x 3 Ft. 2 In. .. 920.00
Hamadan, Mat, Allover Geometric, Tan Ground, 4 Ft. 10 In. x 3 Ft. 9 In. 110.00
Hamadan, Mat, Rust Ground, 4 Ft. 11 x 3 Ft. 4 In. 245.00
Hamadan, Persian, Geometric, Red, Brown, Green, 4 Ft. 2 In. x 8 Ft. 4 In. 224.00
Hamadan, Stylized Designs, Salmon Field, 1950, 11 Ft. 4 In. x 8 Ft. 3 In. 990.00
Heriz, 3 Medallions, Indigo Field, Rust Border, 6 Ft. x 4 Ft. 5 In. 1760.00
Heriz, Allover Floral, Indigo Field, Red & Blue Borders, 7 Ft. 1 In. x 4 Ft. 10 In. 880.00
Heriz, Angular Medallion, Stylized Floral Vinery, Rose, Border, 9 Ft. 9 In. x 12 Ft. 5 In. . 1430.00
Heriz, Burgundy Field, Red, Burgundy, Blue, Low Knot Count, 11 Ft. 10 In. x 8 Ft. 5 In. . 1570.00
Heriz, Center Medallion, Rust Ground, Mid 20th Century, 13 Ft. 10 In. x 9 Ft. 8 In. 3410.00
Heriz, Contemporary, Spandrels, Red Ground, Blue Border, Runner, 3 Ft. x 5 Ft. 2 In. ... 300.00
Heriz, Diamond Medallion Center, 14-In. Border, Red & Navy, 9 Ft. x 6 Ft. 9 In. 550.00
Heriz, Gabled Medallion, Floral, Terra-Cotta Field, Blue Border, 10 Ft. 4 In. x 8 Ft. 10 In. 4025.00
Heriz, Geometric Figures, Geometric, 3 Borders, Runner, 14 Ft. 2 In. x 3 Ft. 6 In. 1010.00
Heriz, Geometric Medallion, Borders, Blue Ground, 1940, Persia, 11 Ft. 5 In. x 8 Ft. 3 In. 1120.00
Heriz, Ivory Spandrels, Midnight Blue Border, Red Ground, 9 Ft. 6 In. x 17 Ft. 9 In. 4125.00
Heriz, Red Ground, 1920, 4 Ft. 5 In. x 6 Ft. 3 In. 330.00
Heriz, Shield Medallion, Florals, Terra-Cotta Red Field, Spandrels, 10 Ft. x 8 Ft. 10 In. .. 4255.00
Heriz, Square Medallion, Flowing Vines, Rust Field, Tan Border, 11 Ft. 8 In. x 9 Ft. 2530.00
Heriz, Stylized Stars, Center Medallion, Allover Red & Blue, 20th Century, 9 x 7 Ft. 895.00
Hooked, 15 Squares, 8 Geometric & 8 Pictures, 53 x 33 In. 120.00
Hooked, 2 Cats, 28 x 40 In. 2090.00
Hooked, 2 Lions, Floral & Leaf Surround, Striped Border, 20th Century, 30 x 61 In. 1045.00
Hooked, 2-Masted Yacht, Rigged Fore & Aft, 53 x 30 In. 305.00
Hooked, Bird In Flight, Floral Surround, Josephine Baril, 18 1/2 x 35 In. 305.00
Hooked, Blue & Brown Dog, Rainbow Corners, Mounted, 21 x 35 In. 385.00
Hooked, Brown Dog & Flowers, Brown Leaf Border, Wool, 66 x 39 In. 690.00
Hooked, Center Cartouche, Wool, 1848, 99 1/2 x 129 1/2 In. 5462.00
Hooked, Covered Bridge, Trees, Reds, Greens & Blues, Mounted, 26 x 44 In. 165.00
Hooked, Dog Lying Down, 30 x 58 In. 1210.00
Hooked, Floral, Blue, Gray, Red & White, Mounted, 33 x 22 In. 275.00
Hooked, Geometric Design, Shades Of Green, Blue, White & Yellow, 27 x 60 In. 330.00
Hooked, Geometric Medallion, 50 x 59 In. 935.00
Hooked, Geometric, Brown, Blue, Black & Gray, 27 x 43 In. 495.00
Hooked, Geometric, Faux Persian, Cranberry, Blue & Tan, 20 x 46 In. 325.00
Hooked, Geometric, Multicolored Rectangles, Black Border, 9 x 12 In. 330.00
Hooked, Heart Center, Braided Rag, 24 x 30 In. 795.00
Hooked, Heron With Butterfly Standing Among Cattails, 27 x 52 1/2 In. 290.00
Hooked, Horse, Blue On Gray Ground, 25 x 39 In. 395.00
Hooked, Jeweled Diamond Pattern, Blue Border, Wool, 23 x 45 In. 120.00
Hooked, Lion In Foreground, Smaller In Background, Late 19th Century, 33 x 60 In. 1610.00
Hooked, Lions In Forest, Ebenezer Ross, Burlap Backing, 33 x 63 In. 1430.00
Hooked, Lions Paused In Exotic Foliage, Green, Beige Rope Border, 1920, 63 In. 3160.00
Hooked, Man In Buggy Scene, 41 x 26 In. 75.00
Hooked, Multicolored Floral, Tan Field, Wool On Linen, 1930, 67 x 97 In. 280.00
Hooked, Musical Notes, Grays, Reds & Blues, 20 x 46 In. 325.00
Hooked, Noah's Ark, Glad They Were To Be Ashore, Blue, Brown, Green, 54 x 30 In. 1380.00
Hooked, Noah's Ark, Noah Seated With His Scroll, I Hope He Don't Miss Any, 52 x 33 In. 1380.00
Hooked, Pictorial, 2 Horses, Central Medallion, 1930s, 18 x 35 1/2 In. 1035.00
Hooked, Pictorial, Spread-Winged Eagle, Sailing Ship, Late 19th Century, 34 x 56 In. ... 1092.00
Hooked, Purple Horse, Oval Landscape, Leaf Design Surround, 22 x 36 In. 525.00
Hooked, Rag, Black Carriage, Horse & Driver, Beige Striped Ground, 24 x 45 In. 275.00
Hooked, Rag, Home Sweet Home, Floral Design Corners, Border, 28 x 40 In. 155.00
Hooked, Rag, House Snow Scene, Blue, Green, Brown, Rebacked, 24 x 34 In. 220.00
Hooked, Rag, Roses, Large Comic Message In Corner, Blue Border, 21 x 35 In. 1015.00
Hooked, Rag, Stag In Winter, Owl In Tree, White, Gray, Black, Tan, Yellow, 34 x 36 In. . 1165.00

Hooked, Rag, Stylized Deer & White Birch Scene, 26 x 39 In. 300.00
Hooked, Rag, Stylized Dog & 2 Fawns Scene, 19 x 40 In. 245.00
Hooked, Roses & Petunias Center, Border, Maine, 1920, 24 x 36 In. 295.00
Hooked, Signed S.C.D., 1876, 28 x 42 In. 6500.00
Hooked, Skunk In A Landscape, 33 x 20 In. 920.00
Hooked, Sleeping Blue Cat, Multicolored Ground, Salmon Border, Mounted, 22 x 32 In. . . 385.00
Hooked, St. Bernard, Green, Mustard & Rust, 36 x 57 In. 1800.00
Hooked, Village Winter Scene, Signed Q.E.T., 39 x 58 In. 175.00
Hooked, Welcome, Red Flowers, Black Ground, Mounted, 24 x 40 In. 220.00
Hooked, Winter Landscape, Sled Team & Drivers, Brown, Blue, Red, Green, 1920, 38 In. 4600.00
Indo-Tabriz, Center Medallion, Allover Floral, Ivory Ground, 6 Ft. 4 In. x 4 Ft. 2640.00
Isfahan, Red Medallion, Multiple Borders, 13 Ft. 2 In. x 9 Ft. 4 In. 505.00
Karabagh, Allover Feather & Floral, Indigo Field, Border, Runner, 3 Ft. x 16 Ft. 3 In. . . . 3410.00
Karabagh, Dark Ground, Borders, Some Fringe Loss, 1900, 6 Ft. 5 In. x 4 Ft. 1 In. 385.00
Karabagh, Octagonal Medallions, Cloud Bands, Rust, Blue Border, 6 Ft. 5 In. x 4 Ft. 975.00
Karaja, Geometric Medallions, Cinnabar Ground, Floral Borders, 11 Ft. 5 In. x 3 Ft. 3 In. . . 715.00
Karaja, Salmon Spandrels, Midnight Blue Border, 12 Ft. 3 In. x 15 Ft. 10 In. 11550.00
Kashan, Center Medallion, Multiple Borders, 20th Century, 6 x 9 Ft. 280.00
Kashan, Flower Vase, Bird & Vine, Navy Ground, Red Border, 14 Ft. x 10 Ft. 5 In. 8625.00
Kashan, Prayer, Stylized Flowers, 3 Borders, Wool, 6 Ft. 5 In. x 4 Ft. 2 In. 505.00
Kasvin, Red Field, Reds & Blues, c.1940, 17 Ft. 10 In. x 9 Ft. 10 In. 2860.00
Kazak, 3 Octagonal Medallions, Blue Field, 4 Ft. 8 In. x 8 Ft. 10 In. 880.00
Kazak, Geometric, Cocoa Field, Multiple Borders, 5 Ft. 10 In. x 7 Ft. 10 In. 605.00
Kazak, Octagonal Medallions, Cloud Bands, Red Field, Ivory Border, 8 Ft. 6 In, x 4 Ft. .. 1840.00
Kazak, Stylized Medallions, Blue Field, Southwest Caucasus, 8 Ft. 1 In. x 3 Ft. 9 In. 175.00
Kazak, Turkoman Style Medallions, Red Field, Ivory Border, 7 Ft. x 5 Ft. 4 In. 2300.00
Kerman, Central Floral Medallion, Tree Design, Rose Ground, 9 Ft. 9 In. x 15 Ft. 5 In. .. 4675.00
Kerman, Ivory Field, Light Blues, c.1950, 8 Ft. 2 In. x 2 Ft. 6 In. 440.00
Kerman, Medallion, Open Blue Field, Reds & Ivory, c.1940, 14 Ft. 2 In. x 11 Ft. 8 In. ... 3025.00
Kerman, Pale Green Floral Border, Ivory Ground, 8 Ft. 6 In. x 12 Ft. 495.00
Kerman, Stylized Floral Medallion, Ivory Field, 1930, 6 Ft. 1 In. x 9 Ft. 1 In. 525.00
Khorasan, Spandrels, Red Ground, Blue Border, 10 Ft. 1 In. x 13 Ft. 5 In. 440.00
Kilim, Sunflowers & Grape Clusters, c.1910, 4 x 6 Ft. 2640.00
Kuba, Ivory, Red Ground, Multicolored Borders, 3 Ft. 6 In. x 11 Ft. 2 In. 1870.00
Kurd, 5 Diamond Medallions, Red Field, Multicolored Border, 12 Ft. x 3 Ft. 6 In. 745.00
Kurd, Filigree Style Boteh, Red Field, Ivory Border, 8 Ft. 9 In. x 4 Ft. 10 In. 635.00
Kurd, Geometric, Abstract Design, Red Ground, 20th Century, 7 Ft. 8 In. x 4 Ft. 8 In. 335.00
Kurdish, Hamadan, Midnight Blue Ground, Borders, Runner, 4 Ft. 2 In. x 10 Ft. 5 In. 990.00
Kurdish, Stylized Floral, Blue Ground, Runner, 19th Century, 9 Ft. 10 In. x 3 Ft. 9 In. ... 825.00
Kurdish, Stylized Medallions, Salmon Field, Northwest Persia, 1930, 6 Ft. 8 In. x 4 Ft. .. 440.00
Kurdish Kazak, Midnight Blue, Salmon Ground, Ivory Borders, 5 Ft. 11 In. x 6 Ft. 8 In. .. 440.00
Lillihan, Central Flower Medallion, Rose Color Field, Floral Sprays, c.1930, 40 x 60 In. . . 209.00
Lillihan, Floral, Navy, Ivory, Dark Red Ground, Borders, 4 Ft. 11 In. x 2 Ft. 9 In. 460.00
Lillihan, Medallion, Field Of Trees Surround, Blue, 14 Ft. 4 In. x 10 Ft. 4 In. 2015.00
Malayer, Overall Herati Design, Blue Field, Ivory Border, 6 Ft. 4 In. x 4 Ft. 4 In. 805.00
Malayer, Stepped Hexagonal Medallions, Early 20th Century, 4 Ft. 9 In. x 3 Ft. 5 In. 632.00
Mashad, Vines, Flowers, Palmettes, Magenta Field, c.1920, 10 Ft. 6 In. x 17 Ft. 1980.00
Mongolian, Floral, Medallion Design, Deep Blue Field, 2 Ft. 3 In. x 4 Ft. 1 In. 345.00
Mosul, Geometric, Navy Field, Multiple Borders, Runner, 3 Ft. 5 In. x 13 Ft. 5 In. 495.00
Mosul, Medallion, Allover Geometric, Terra-Cotta Field, Borders, 4 Ft. 9 In. x 7 Ft. 5 In. . . 440.00
Needlepoint, 25 Octagonal Figural, Animal Panels, Russia, 1850, 9 Ft. 5 In. 14950.00
Needlepoint, Blossoming Plants, Ivory Field, 4 Narrow Borders, 9 x 8 Ft. 632.00
Oushak, Lozenge Medallions, Pendants, Pale Blue Field, 4 Ft. 11 In. x 11 Ft. 11 In. 825.00
Pakistani, Green Field, 3 Octagonal Designs, 6 Ft. 5 In. x 4 Ft. 935.00
Penny, Appliqued Circles, Blue & Black On Red & Green Ground, 28 x 46 In. 440.00
Penny, Beige, Elongated Hexagon, Medallions, American, Early 1900s, 59 1/2 x 20 In. 316.00
Penny, Hearts, Stars, Sailing Ships, Ducks, 62 In. 885.00
Penny, Hexagonal, Wool, Brown Ground, 45 x 50 In. 337.00
Perpedil, Blue Birds, Flowers, Blue Field, Border Designs, 3 Ft. 2 In. x 4 Ft. 3 In. 1650.00
Persian, Floral, Indigo Field, 3 Borders, 5 Ft. 1 In. x 4 Ft. 3 In. 1100.00
Persian, Overall Herati, Medallion Design, Floral Border, 4 Ft. 9 In. x 7 Ft. 6 In. 115.00
Persian, Overall Leafy Flowering Plants, Navy, Sky Blue, 10 Ft. 8 In. x 7 Ft. 6 In. 1610.00
Prayer, Caucasian, Ivory, Orange & Blue, 3 Ft. 7 In. x 3 Ft. 2 In. 195.00

Qum, Floral Medallion, Vines, White & Rose Ground, Silk, 6 Ft. 2 In. x 4 Ft. 7 In. 1725.00
Rag, 4 Strips Sewn Together, Stripes, 150 x 180 In. 247.00
Rag, Crocheted, Pink & Gray, Black & White, Ohio In Center, 27 x 56 In. 220.00
Rag, Yellow, Mauve, Blue & Yellow Stripes, Pennsylvania, 102 x 114 In. 330.00
Sarouk, Allover Floral, Red Field, Mid 20th Century, 11 Ft. 9 In. x 8 Ft. 10 In. 3520.00
Sarouk, Blue Design, Red Ground, Runner, c.1930, 2 Ft. 2 In. x 6 Ft. 5 In. 1760.00
Sarouk, Blue Floral, Red Field, 15 Ft. 6 In. x 8 Ft. 11 In. 4400.00
Sarouk, Blue Floral, Red Ground, Burgundy Border, 12 Ft. 2 In. x 9 Ft. 1210.00
Sarouk, Center Medallion, Allover Floral, Crimson, 1930s, 10 Ft. 3 In. x 14 Ft. 5 In. 2860.00
Sarouk, Center Medallion, Floral, Wine Field, 5 Borders, 10 Ft. 5 In. x 7 Ft. 8 In. 3850.00
Sarouk, Floral Medallion, Midnight Blue Field, 1920, 12 Ft. 1 In. x 8 Ft. 11 In. 8800.00
Sarouk, Floral Sprays, Red Field, Blue, Floral Scroll Border, 14 Ft. 9 In. x 11 Ft. 10 In. ... 2970.00
Sarouk, Floral, Blue Field, 6-In. Border, Mat, 3 x 3 Ft. 605.00
Sarouk, Floral, Purple Ground, 3 Floral Borders, c.1920, 10 Ft. 4 In. x 13 Ft. 7 In. 2530.00
Sarouk, Medallion, Flowers & Vine Surround, Borders, 12 x 9 Ft. 3 In. 3360.00
Sarouk, Spandrels & Blossoming Vines, Blue Border, 6 Ft. 6 In. x 4 Ft. 632.00
Sarouk, Spandrels, Burgundy Ground, Midnight Blue Border, 7 Ft. 11 In. x 10 Ft. 2200.00
Sarouk, Stylized Floral & Vines, Burgundy Field, 1930, 4 Ft. 2 In. x 2 Ft. 320.00
Seichour, Arabesque Leaf, Florals, Brown Field, Blue Border, 5 Ft. 10 In. x 3 Ft. 10 In. ... 575.00
Sennah, Running Geometric, Blue Ground, Persia, 20th Century, 9 Ft. 9 In. x 5 Ft. 730.00
Shashavan, Repeating Diamond, Brown Ground, Runner, 3 Ft. 8 In. x 11 Ft. 9 In. 1320.00
Shirvan, 3 Medallion Field, 3 Ft. 3 In. x 4 Ft. 10 In. 880.00
Shirvan, Floral Medallions, Blue Ground, 4 Ft. 3 In. x 6 Ft. 1 In. 495.00
Shirvan, Hexagonal Medallions, Geometric Design, Blue Field, 5 Ft. 5 In. x 3 Ft. 8 In. 1495.00
Shirvan, Prayer, Blue Mihrab, Flowers, Palmettes, Vines, Cypress, c.1920, 33 1/2 x 53 In. 770.00
Soumak, 3 Medallions, Allover Geometric, Multiple Borders, 10 Ft. 2 In. x 7 Ft. 5 In. ... 550.00
Soumak, Allover Geometric Design, Blue Field, Floral Border, 4 Ft. 8 In. x 8 Ft. 4 In. 315.00
Soumak, Allover Geometric, Floral, Green, Blue, 20th Century, 9 x 6 Ft. 280.00
Tabriz, Birds & Flower Urns, Beige Ground, Borders, 6 x 9 Ft. 520.00
Tabriz, Center Medallion, Blue Ground, Persia, 20th Century, 9 Ft. 10 In. x 6 Ft. 6 In. ... 560.00
Tabriz, Medallion, Allover Stylized Floral, Navy Field, Borders, Persia, 9 Ft. x 12 Ft. 4 In. 1320.00
Tabriz, Multicolor Central Medallion, Red Field, 11 Ft. 1 In. x 12 Ft. 11 In. 2960.00
Tabriz, Multicolored Floral, Animals In Ground, 8 Ft. 2 In. x 11 Ft. 7 In. 3575.00
Tabriz, Multicolored Floral, Arabesque Panels, Salmon Border, 9 Ft. 9 In. x 13 Ft. 3300.00
Tabriz, Prayer, Ivory Ground, Blue Border, c.1920, 8 Ft. 8 In. x 11 Ft. 4 In. 3520.00
Tabriz, Stylized Flowers, Red Ground, 3 Borders, Geometric, 11 Ft. 5 In. x 17 Ft. 1400.00
Tekke Engsi, Rust Garden, Plants, Blue, Ivory, Apricot, Border, 4 Ft. 8 In. x 4 Ft. 2 In. ... 430.00
Turkish, Center Medallion, Floral Surround, Tan Field, Silk, 8 Ft. 6 In. x 6 In. 1210.00
Turkish, Prayer, Camel & Olive Border, Slat Blue Spandrels, Red Ground, Silk, 4 x 6 Ft. . 135.00
Turkoman, Midnight Blue Ground, Red Border, Contemporary, 3 Ft. 8 In. x 7 Ft. 220.00
Ushak, Stylized Palmettes, Foliage, Rose Color Field, c.1920, 10 Ft. 6 In. x 13 Ft. 8 In. .. 2860.00
Verner Panton, Geometric Circles & Squares, 1960s, 11 Ft. 1 In. x 8 Ft. 1092.00
Yastik, 3 Medallions, Multiple Borders, Brown, Red, Turkey, Mat, 2 Ft. 8 In. x 1 Ft. 8 In. 60.00
Yastik, Geometric, Mustard Field, Fringe Loss, Mat, 3 x 2 Ft. 1430.00

RUMRILL Pottery was designed by George Rumrill of Little Rock, Arkansas. From 1933 to 1938, it was produced by the Red Wing Pottery of Red Wing, Minnesota. In 1938, production was transferred to the Shawnee Pottery in Zanesville, Ohio. Production ceased in the 1940s.

RumRill

Ewer, Green, Brown Mottled, Stamped, 10 In. 45.00
Jug, Mottled Orange, No Stopper 65.00
Pitcher, Orange, Ice Lip 85.00
Vase, Black, Swan Handles, 10 In. 125.00
Vase, Renaissance Pattern, Orange, 8 In. 85.00

RUSSEL WRIGHT designed dinnerwares in modern shapes for many companies. Iroquois China Company, Harker China Company, Steubenville Pottery, and Justin Tharaud and Sons made dishes marked *Russel Wright.* The Steubenville wares, first made in 1938, are the most common today. Wright was a designer of domestic and industrial wares, including furniture, aluminum, radios, interiors, and glassware. Dinnerwares and other pieces by Wright are listed here. For more information, see *Kovels' Depression Glass & Dinnerware Price List.*

Russel Wright
MFG. BY
STEUBENVILLE

American Modern, Bowl, Vegetable, 2 Sections, Coral 85.00

American Modern, Bowl, Vegetable, 2 Sections, Granite Gray 85.00
American Modern, Bowl, Vegetable, 2 Sections, White 100.00
American Modern, Bowl, Vegetable, Cover, Black Chutney, 12 In. 70.00
American Modern, Bowl, Vegetable, Cover, Seafoam, 12 In. 70.00
American Modern, Bowl, Vegetable, Granite Gray 20.00
American Modern, Casserole, Cover, Bean Brown, 2 Qt. 75.00
American Modern, Celery Dish, Granite Gray, 13 In. 25.00
American Modern, Chop Plate, Cedar Green, 14 In. 35.00
American Modern, Coaster, Seafoam 15.00
American Modern, Coffeepot, Coral, After Dinner 110.00
American Modern, Creamer, Bean Brown 18.00
American Modern, Creamer, White 18.00
American Modern, Cup & Saucer, Black Chutney, After Dinner 25.00
American Modern, Cup & Saucer, Coral, After Dinner 25.00
American Modern, Cup & Saucer, Granite Gray, After Dinner 25.00
American Modern, Gravy Boat, Coral 20.00
American Modern, Hostess Plate, With Cup, Black Chutney 80.00
American Modern, Hostess Plate, With Cup, Chartreuse 80.00
American Modern, Hostess Plate, With Cup, Granite Gray 85.00
American Modern, Pitcher, Water, Black Chutney 110.00
American Modern, Pitcher, Water, Chartreuse .... .90.00 to 150.00
American Modern, Pitcher, Water, Seafoam 110.00
American Modern, Plate, Bean Brown, 10 In. 15.00
American Modern, Plate, Chartreuse, Child's 50.00
American Modern, Plate, White, 10 In. 25.00
American Modern, Platter, Coral, 13 1/4 In. 25.00
American Modern, Ramekin, Cover, Granite Gray 175.00
American Modern, Relish, Rosette, Coral 150.00
American Modern, Sugar, Bean Brown 18.00
American Modern, Sugar, Coral 50.00
American Modern, Sugar, White 18.00
American Modern, Teapot, Chartreuse 100.00
Spun Aluminum, Appetizer Server, Round, Domed Cover, Wooden Handle, 13 In. 405.00
Spun Aluminum, Bun Warmer, Pivoting Top, Bamboo Handle, 9 In. 260.00
Spun Aluminum, Serving Tray, Circular Form Cane Wrapped Handles, 15 In. 145.00
Spun Aluminum, Spaghetti Set, Pot With Lid, Cheese Shaker, Cane Accents, 8 In. 1725.00
Theme Formal, Cordial, 3 Oz. 210.00

SABINO glass was made in the 1920s and 1930s in Paris, France. Founded by Marius-Ernest Sabino (1878–1961), the firm was noted for Art Deco lamps, vases, figurines, and animals in clear, colored, and opalescent glass. Production stopped during World War II but resumed in the 1960s with the manufacture of nude figurines and small opalescent glass animals. The new pieces are a slightly different color and can be recognized.

Sabino
France

Figurine, Bird, Opalescent, Signed, 5 1/2 In. 172.00
Figurine, Idole, Young Woman With Long Hair Seated On Cushion, Opalescent, 6 In. 1150.00
Perfume Bottle, Pinecone Shape, 5 1/2 In. 100.00
Plaque, Advertising, Sabino Of France, Crossed Flags & Shield, 3 1/2 x 6 In. 115.00
Plaque, Nymphs, Dancing, Frieze Of Figures In Classical Dress, Light Blue, 12 x 7 In. ... 230.00
Vase, Bacchanalia, Band Of Overlapping Oval Sections, Satin, 1925, 8 In. 287.00

SALOPIAN ware was made by the Caughley factory of England during the eighteenth century. The early pieces were blue and white with some colored decorations. Another ware referred to as *Salopian* is a late nineteenth-century tableware decorated with color transfers.

Salopian

Bowl, Oriental Scene, 5 1/2 In. 120.00
Candlestick, Flint Glaze, 7 In., Pair 495.00
Cup & Saucer, Girl Milking Cow 255.00
Cup & Saucer, People Landscape 285.00
Pitcher, Cabbage Leaf Mold, Blue, White, 1770, 9 1/4 In. 302.00
Plate, Bird Center, 7 In. 200.00

SALT AND PEPPER SHAKERS in matched sets were first used in the nineteenth century. Collectors are primarily interested in figural examples made after World War I. *Huggers* are pairs of shakers that appear to embrace each other. Many salt and pepper shakers are listed in other categories and can be located through the index at the back of this book.

Amish Girl & Boy, Metal, 2 1/2 In.	13.00
Art Deco Style, Lusterware, Hand Painted, Japan, 4 In.	28.00
Aunt Jemima & Uncle Remus, Celluloid, F & F Mold & Die Works, 3 1/2 In.	43.00
Ball Mason Jar, Glass, Box	24.00
Bavarian Man & Woman, Germany, 2 3/4 In.	25.00
Beer Stein, Japan, 2 In.	12.00
Black Couple In Chefs' Hats, Holding Fruit Plates, Japan, 4 In.	35.00
Boots, Cowboy, Texas, Metal, 2 1/4 In.	19.00
California Fruit, 2 Different, Plaster, 3 In.	13.00
Campbell's Soup Can	15.00
Cardinal, 2 1/2 In.	10.00
Cat, Black, Gold Bows, Shafford, 5 1/2 In.	25.00
Cat, With Yarn Ball, Japan, 3 3/4 In.	15.00
Cherokee Rose	15.00
Corn, Large & Small, Stanford	26.00
Dog & Cat, F & F	12.00
Dr Pepper, Glass	25.00
Duck, Dressed Going To Town, Holder, Japan, 4 1/4 x 3 1/2 In.	27.00
Duck, Lusterware, Japan, 3 In.	16.00
Dutch Girl, Plaster, Hand Painted, 3 1/2 In.	15.00
Dutch Man & Woman, Japan, 3 1/4 In.	20.00
Dutch Man & Woman, Van Tellingen	50.00
Eisenhower Picture, Teardrop Shape, Glass, Blue Ground, 1 7/8 In.	30.00
Elephant, Blue, Germany, 2 1/4 In.	15.00
Ernie, Keebler Elf, Green Jacket	8.00
Fish, Catalina, Gladding McBean	32.00
Frog, Looking For Flies, Japan, 2 1/2 In.	12.00
Gas Pump, Co-Op, Box, 2 3/4 In.	125.00
Gingham Dog, Calico Cat, Brayton	85.00
Golf Ball On Green, On Tees, 18th Hole Flag Handle On Base, Japan	21.00
Goose, Golden Egg	10.00
Hillbilly Man & Woman, Holder, Plastic, 5 1/2 x 3 In., 3 Piece	35.00
Humpty Dumpty, White	7.00
Humpty Dumpty & Girl	10.00
Indian Chief, Forest Ground, Holder, Japan, 4 x 3 3/4 In.	37.00
Indian Teepee, 3 In.	13.50
Jar, Handle, Bull Holder, 5 1/4 x 4 In., 3 Piece	20.00
JFK Saltshaker, Sits In Pepper Shaker Rocker, Ceramic	32.00
John & Jackie Kennedy, Gold Trim	335.00
Ladybug	7.00
Laurel & Hardy	230.00
Little Miss Muffet & Spider	35.00
Little Riding Hood, Brown Fox	22.00
Lusterware, Handled Holder, Japan, 3 x 3 1/2 In.	25.00
Lyndon & Mrs. Johnson	35.00
MacArthur, General Douglas, Pipe & Hat	75.00
Mammy, Black & White Checked Dress, 4 In.	95.00
Mammy & Chef, Pearl China	200.00
Man & Horse, 4 In.	15.00
Mary & Little Lamb	22.00 to 25.00
Mickey McGuire, Occupied Japan	85.00
Mother Chicken & Chick Coming Out Of Egg, Holder, Japan, 4 1/4 x 3 1/4 In.	37.00
Niagara Falls, Mug Shape, Souvenir, Japan, 2 1/4 x 2 1/2 In.	12.50
Noah & Ark, Brown	30.00
Old King Cole, On Chair	25.00
Old MacDonald, Wife, Regal	60.00
Old Mother Hubbard, Dog, Japan	28.00

Paul Bunyan & Babe, Blue 18.00
Pebbles & Bamm Bamm, Flintstones 45.00
Penguins, Kool Cigarettes 28.00
Pepsi-Cola, Plastic, Original Box, 1950, 9 In. 66.00
Pig, Male & Female, Dressed For The Evening, Japan, 3 In. 14.00
Potato Head, Mr. & Mrs. 16.00
Prayer Lady, Pink, Enesco ....20.00 to 25.00
Race Horse, Lexington, Kentucky, Metal, 2 1/4 x 2 In. 30.00
Railroad Lantern, Metal & Glass, 3 In. ....15.00 to 17.00
Red Hen On Nest, Rooster, Metlox 40.00
Robot, 5 In. 16.00
Rub-A-Dub-Dub, 3 Men In Tub 58.00
Salty & Peppy, Pearl China, 4 In. ....155.00 to 235.00
Santa, Mrs. Claus, Hallmark, 3 1/2 In. 16.50
Swan, 2 1/2 x 2 1/2 In. 18.00
Teapot Shape, Comical Black Face, Pottery, Wire Handle, Japan, 3 In. . 22.00
Tee & Eff, Tasty Freeze Characters, 3 1/2 In. 35.00
Turtle & Hare, Brown 15.00
Vase, Side Handle, Floral, Japan, 3 In. 8.50
Woman In Rocking Chair, Iron 15.00

SALT GLAZE has a grayish white surface with a texture like an orange
peel. It is a method of decoration that has been used since the eighteenth century. Salt-glazed pieces are still being made.

Churn, Cobalt Blue Snake Design, 1 1/2 Gal. 175.00
Crock, Blue Floral, Handle, 4 Gal. 145.00
Crock, Blue Floral, Marked Olean, N.Y., Handle, 4 Gal. 220.00
Crock, Churn, Blue Design, 2 Gal. 275.00
Crock, Cobalt Blue 4 & Underlines, 4 Gal. 85.00
Crock, Cobalt Blue Apple, 2 Gal. 130.00
Crock, Cobalt Blue Stylized Starburst, 3 Gal. 70.00
Crock, E. & L.P. Norton, Bennington, Vermont, Blue Floral, Strap Handle, 2 Gal. 525.00
Crock, Storage, Orange Peel Rim & Interior, Late 19th Century, 10 1/4 In. 44.00
Figurine, Woman, Bead Necklace, Watteau Panel At Back, Punchwork 3 3/4 In. 805.00
Jar, Cobalt Blue Stencil Around Gallon Number, 3 Gal. 120.00
Jar, Gray & Brown, Buff Clay, Solomon Bell, Strasburg, Va., 10 7/8 In. 165.00
Jug, J.F. Field, Utica, Gray, Cobalt Blue Flower, Handle, Oval, 13 5/8 In. 385.00
Pitcher, Cobalt Blue Flower, Dark Green Leaf, Lula Belle Owens Bolick, 1970, 3 1/4 In. . 22.00
Pitcher, Raised Form Design, Medium Green, 8 In. 50.00
Pot, Molded Classic Design, Applied Figures, England, 9 5/8 In. 300.00
Sauceboat, Stand, Leaf Shape, Gnarled Stem, Staffordshire, 1755, 10 1/8 In. 6325.00

SAMPLERS were made in America from the early 1700s. The best
examples were made from 1790 to 1840. Long, narrow samplers are
usually older than square ones. Early samplers just had stitching or
alphabets. The later examples had numerals, borders, and pictorial decorations. Those with mottoes are mid-Victorian. A revival of interest in
the 1930s produced simpler samplers, usually with mottoes.

ABCDE

Adam, Eve, Tree Of Life, Border, Judith Shutt, 1813, Silk On Linen, Frame, 21 x 20 In. ... 1100.00
Adam & Eve, Angels, Strawberry Border, Alice Waddicor, 1834, 21 x 16 In. 495.00
Almira Gilbert, Born 1798, Silk On Linen, Frame, 12 3/4 x 12 In. 220.00
Alphabet, Adam & Eve, Entwined Serpent, Flowers, Flowering Vine Border, 16 x 16 In. . 345.00
Alphabet, Adam & Eve, Unicorn, Mary Ogleed 1694, Silk On Linen, Frame, 10 x 10 In. . 5775.00
Alphabet, Dancing Figures, Me Rebekah Hancock Aged 8 Years 1698, Frame, 35 x 8 In. . 8050.00
Alphabet, Elizabeth Cochran, Frame, Early 19th Century, 14 x 12 1/2 In. 470.00
Alphabet, Emma Nunns Aged July 18, 1837, Frame, 7 7/8 x 12 1/2 In. 60.00
Alphabet, Flowers, Bird, Dorothy Perason, Aged 11, 19th Century, 13 x 11 In. 187.00
Alphabet, Flowers, Mary McLeren Crieff, 1776, Frame, 17 x 8 1/2 In. 635.00
Alphabet, Maria Horne, August 19, 1782, Frame, 10 3/8 x 8 7/8 In. 112.00
Alphabet, Numerals, Verse, Sarah Elizabeth Thurman, 1814, Frame, 19 x 15 In. 805.00
Alphabet, Phebe French, In 14th Year Of Her Age 1776, Canvas, Frame, 6 x 6 In. 525.00
Alphabet, Signed, Mora, Wool, Mid 19th Century, 14 x 22 In. 550.00
Alphabet, Stars, Tree, 2 Roosters, Pa., Silk On Linen, 19th Century, 13 x 11 In. 1045.00

Alphabet, Trailing Vines, Hearts, Tulip Trees, 1847, Silk On Gauze, 12 x 12 In. 660.00
Alphabet, Tulips Surrounded By Butterflies, Sally Armstrong, 1803, 15 x 14 In. 4950.00
Alphabet, Verse, Bird & Flowering Bush, Sarah C. Case, Sept. 28, 1831, 16 x 17 In. 523.00
Alphabet & Numbers, Harriet Peeks, Brookfield, June 20th, 1820, 5 1/2 x 11 In. 385.00
Alphabet & Numbers, Josephine Onderdonk, November, 1844, 13 1/4 x 13 3/4 In. 990.00
Alphabet & Numbers, Maria Onderdonk, 8th Year, 1840, 12 3/4 x 17 1/2 In. 990.00
Alphabets, Adam & Eve, Religious Symbols, Wreath, Frame, 18th Century, 41 x 10 In. . . .   805.00
Alphabets, Band Of Birds, Mary Gillette, Aged 10, 1857, 15 x 16 1/2 In. 605.00
Alphabets, Birds, Dogs, Theresa Sachet, 1833, Frame, 10 x 8 In. 850.00
Alphabets, Birds, Flowers, Verse, Mary Ann Lloyd, 11 Years, Frame, 19 x 19 In. 1100.00
Alphabets, Blue, Brown, Green, Tan, Silk On Linen Homespun, 12 x 8 3/4 In. 440.00
Alphabets, Elizabeth Lamb, Silk On Linen Homespun, Blue, Olive, Frame, 1825, 18 In. . . .   110.00
Alphabets, Flowering Plants, Floral Borders, Sarah Hodge, 1806, 12 x 9 1/2 In. 935.00
Alphabets, Girl, Dog, Mary Fisher, Wrought In The 12th Year Of Her Life, 18 x 16 In. . . .   440.00
Alphabets, House, Mary J. Keely, 1811, Aug. 29, Aged 16, Ohio, Silk On Linen, 19 In. . . .   3740.00
Alphabets, Mary Elizabeth Beatty Aged 8 Years, Silk On Linen, Frame, 20 x 20 In. 495.00
Alphabets, Numbers, Anna Maria Reitzel, Feb. 2nd, 1838, 8 1/4 x 17 3/4 In. 2040.00
Alphabets, Red, White, Marie Rodsczinsky, Cotton, Frame, 1852, 16 In. 495.00
Alphabets, Shepherdess, Tree, J. Melross, 1825, Silk On Linen, Frame, 18 x 18 In. 880.00
Alphabets, Sophie Bailly, Mackinac, Janvier 21, 1828, Silk On Linen, 13 x 10 7/8 In. 8335.00
Alphabets, Stylized Floral, Margaret, 1843, 12 x 12 In. 355.00
Alphabets, Stylized Flowers, 2 People, Silk On Linen, Initials, Frame, 14 1/4 x 25 In. . . .   525.00
Alphabets, Weston Family Genealogy, Trees, Frame, 19th Century, 16 x 14 In. 980.00
Anne Hosmer, 8th Year, Cross-Stitch On Linen, c.1796, 8 x 7 In. 330.00
Anne Reesor, April 6, 1845, Vine Border, Cotton Homespun, Frame, 19 x 16 In. 330.00
Bands Of Alphabets, Stylized Florals, Mary H. Morrison, 1827, 16 x 17 In. 3162.00
Baskets Of Flowers, Jane Dunn's Work, 1794, Linen, Gilt Frame, 23 x 20 In. 4250.00
Birds, Butterflies, Windmill, Floral Border, Mary Ann Jones, 1826, 18 3/4 x 15 In. 990.00
Birds, Flower Basket, Diamond Border, Sarah Clark, Aged 12, 1824, 15 x 15 1/2 In. 920.00
Charlotte Dyer Married Edmand Bidwell, 1834, E. Tuller Preceptress, 13 x 11 In. 770.00
Churchyard, Birds, Mary Ann Pritchard, 1803, 11 1/2 x 17 1/2 In. 495.00
Deer, Trees, Birds, Strawberry Border, M. Stepney, 1830, Silk On Linen, 16 x 13 In. 440.00
Elizabeth Warding, Born September 19, 1823, Silk On Linen, 13 x 13 1/4 In. 990.00
Family Register, Mayberry Family, Windham, Me., Frame, 10 1/2 x 15 In. 1430.00
Family Register, Polly Grant, Nov. 6, 1786, Falmouth, Me., Matted, Frame, 8 x 6 In. 1650.00
Flowers, Animal, Trees, Verse, Charlotte Neal, May 22nd 1819, Frame, 15 x 13 1/2 In. 770.00
Flowers, Animals, Initialed SS, Linen, Frame, 15 1/2 x 8 1/2 In.   308.00
Flowers, Cartouche, Catrina Elizabeth, 1755, 17 x 16 1/2 In. 862.00
Flowers, Hearts, Birds, Crowns, Ann Wood, 1840, Gilt Frame, 15 x 10 3/4 In. 1760.00
Flowers, Home, Birds, Trees, Angaela Nicholas, 9 Years, 1835, Frame, 17 x 19 In. 445.00
Flowers, Large Brick Building Flanked By Flowering Trees, Jane Padbury, 6 x 7 In. 977.00
Flowers, Trees, Birds, Stylized Tulip Border, Mary Snealus, 1794, Silk, 16 x 11 In. 2090.00
Hannah Schell, 1818, Silk On Linen, 9 3/4 x 7 1/2 In. 550.00
Happy Man, Tree Of Life, Adam & Eve, Mary Caeside, 1846, Silk On Linen, 27 x 24 In. . .   1100.00
Harriet Reed, Aged 12, 1837, 14 3/4 x 17 In. 1980.00
House, Tree, Green Lawn, Pa., 1822, Silk, 16 1/4 x 12 1/2 In. 220.00
Inscribed Mary Brown, Finished Work December 8th, 1834, 8 Years, 13 x 15 In. 1575.00
Legend, Mary Whipple, 9 Years, 19th Century, 8 1/2 x 16 1/2 In.   385.00
Letters, Crowns, Candlesticks, Isabella Walker, 18 x 20 In. 500.00
Louisa Garris, Aged 7, Silk On Linen, Early 19th Century, 10 x 8 In. 247.00
Maria Tooke Livick, Aged 11, 1773, 16 1/2 x 12 In. 750.00
Masonic Symbols, In God We Trust, Sarah Ann Hagerty, Frame, 27 3/4 In. 4400.00
Mottoes, Sayings, Cornelia Grace, November 11th, 1812, 13 x 13 In. 575.00
Numerals, Birds On Pedestal, Melinda Turner, AD 1812, 11 1/2 x 11 1/2 In. 1035.00
Pious Verse, Sarah P. Crane, Flanked By Animals, 1849, 24 1/2 x 29 In. 4025.00
Punch Pattern, Old Oaken Bucket, Not Embroidered, 10 1/2 x 23 In. 28.00
Running Deer & Couple Holding Grapes, Stylized Floral Border, 1756, 15 x 14 In. 550.00
Ship, Scottish Flag, Margaret Sayer, Rothesay, Isle Of Bute, 1789, 15 x 12 5/8 In. 2450.00
Soldiers, Birds, Ann Summerfield, Aged 12, 1833, Silk On Linen Homespun, 14 1/2 In. . . .   412.00
Standing Deer, Stylized Floral Border, Flowers, Mary Ann Garnett, Silk, 25 x 25 In. 880.00
Trees & Parrots Perched On Branches, Strawberry Border, Ann Sargent, 13 x 13 In. 935.00
Verse, 5 Alphabet Panels, Rows Of Geometric Design, Ocean Wave Border, 17 x 17 In. . . .   1092.00
Verse, Birds & Trees, Vine Floral Border, Eliza Andrews, 1832, Frame, 25 x 21 In. 1320.00

Verse, Boy Chasing Dog, Eliza J. Shafer, 1841, Linen Homespun, Frame, 16 x 16 In. 550.00
Verse, Flower Baskets, Mary Ann Bartlett, 1817, Linen, 16 1/2 x 12 In. 517.00
Verse, House, Men, Urns, Ships, Dorothy Smith, 1828, Aged 9, 15 x 14 In. 525.00
Verse, Mary D. Buckingham, Worked In 11th Year, 1826, Silk On Linen, Frame, 14 In. .. 467.00
Verse, Rosela F. Murray's, 1821, 15 x 19 In. 1870.00
Verse, Signed Emma Camm, 1852, 15 x 16 In. 286.00
Verse, Tulip Border, Loretta D. Bleyler, January 9, 1824, Linen, 16 x 17 In. 7150.00
Verse In Wreath, Flower Baskets, Betsey J. Conklin, August 9th, 1835, 17 x 16 In. 1840.00
View Of Grand Suspension Bridge, Wales, Anne Jones, 1839, 16 x 24 In. 920.00

SAMSON and Company, a French firm specializing in the reproduction of collectible wares of many countries and periods, was founded in Paris in the early nineteenth century. Chelsea, Meissen, Famille Verte, and Chinese Export porcelain are some of the wares that have been reproduced by the company. The firm uses a variety of marks on the reproductions. It is still in operation.

Figurine, Bocage, Gold Anchor Mark, 10 In., Pair 825.00
Figurine, Putti Standing Over Baby Dragon, 7 3/4 In. 70.00
Figurine, Woman, Eyes Downcast, Warrior, Hands Together, 19th Century, 27 1/2 In. 3680.00
Figurine, Young Woman, Classical Clothes, Standing By Plinth, Gilt, 11 In. 450.00
Group, Country Lady Seated On A Rocky Base With Bird In Hand, 6 3/8 In. 173.00
Group, Maiden, Arm Over Face, Holding Vessel, Late 19th Century, 13 1/4 In. 860.00
Plate, Hand Painted Design, Signed, 10 In., 6 Piece 650.00
Punch Bowl, Polychrome Floral, Bianco Sopora Bianco, Late 19th Century, 14 In. 747.00
Vase, Cover, Green Dragons, Peony Vines, Cover, Famille Verte, 14 1/4 In., Pair 2070.00
Vase, Cover, Hunting Scenes On 1 Side, Scattered Flower Bouquets, 31 In., Pair 7475.00
Vase, Exotic Bird, Flowering Branches, Gilt Base, Mounted As Lamps, 20 In., Pair 10350.00
Vase, Floral Bouquets & Lattice Work, Pierced Border Supporting Vase, 8 1/8 In. 122.00

SANDWICH GLASS is any of the myriad types of glass made by the Boston and Sandwich Glass Works in Sandwich, Massachusetts, between 1825 and 1888. It is often very difficult to be sure whether a piece was really made at the Sandwich factory because so many types were made there and similar pieces were made at other glass factories. Additional pieces may be listed under Pressed Glass and in related categories.

Bowl, Princess Feather, 7 1/4 In. 160.00
Bowl, Princess Feather, 10 In. 375.00
Bowl, Rayed Peacock Eye, Clambroth, 6 1/2 In. 175.00
Candlestick, Amethyst, 3 In., Pair 650.00
Candlestick, Dolphin, Clambroth Base, Electric Blue Top, 10 In., Pair 2090.00
Candlestick, Milk Glass, 3 1/2 In., Pair 100.00
Cup Plate, Harrison Cabin, Flag 65.00
Curtain Tieback, Flower, Green, Pewter Stem, 3 1/2 In. 75.00
Decanter, 3-Piece Mold, Starburst, 3 Neck Rings, Bulbous, 1840 .... 185.00
Hat, Cobalt Blue, 3-Piece Mold, Rolled Rim, Pontil, 2 In. 715.00
Hat, Flared Rim, Cylindrical Body, 3-Piece Mold, Pontil, c.1830, 2 1/2 In. 143.00
Lamp, Cranberry Cut To Clear, Brass Column, Marble Base, Electrified, 17 In. 495.00
Lamp, Latticinio Swirl, Brass Column, Marble Base, 9 3/4 In. 2000.00
Lamp, Light Emerald Green Cut To Clear, Stepped Marble Base, 12 3/4 In. 1150.00
Mustard, Cover, Underplate, Peacock Eye 225.00
Paperweight, Fruit Basket 685.00
Salt, Chariot Race, Opaque Blue, 1 5/8 x 2 7/8 x 2 In. 345.00
Salt, Chariot, Blue 690.00
Salt, Eagle, Lacy, Dark Amber 2070.00
Salt, Oval, Lacy, Opalescent 748.00
Scent Bottle, Lime Green, Elongated Loop, Polished Pontil 750.00
Scent Bottle, Star & Punty, Vaseline 550.00

SARREGUEMINES is the name of a French town that is used as part of a china mark. Utzschneider and Company, a porcelain factory, made ceramics in Sarreguemines, Lorraine, France, from about 1775. Trans-fer-printed wares and majolica were made in the nineteenth century. The

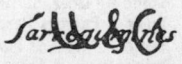

nineteenth-century pieces, most often found today, usually have colorful
transfer-printed decorations showing peasants in local costumes.

Bowl, Fruit, Allover Green Enameled, 5 x 12 x 7 In.	140.00
Candlestick, Figural, Monkey On Darwin Book, Majolica, 1870s, 7 1/2 In.	1380.00
Jug, Face, Man With Sideburns, 7 1/2 In.	150.00
Jug, Face, Puck, 7 1/2 In.	125.00
Oyster Plate, Turquoise, 9 1/2 In.	100.00
Pitcher, Face, The English, 9 1/2 In.	150.00
Pitcher, Figural, Monkey, Brown, 9 1/2 In.	375.00
Plate, Majolica, Medallion, Berry Border, Turquoise, Marked D., 8 In., Pair	115.00
Sauce, Playful Winged Cherubs, Handle, c.1800, 3 1/4 In.	105.00
Stein, 1 Liter, City Crest Of Darmstadt, Pewter Lid	1265.00
Stein, 1/2 Liter, Dachshund Finial, Pewter Lid	742.00
Stein, 1/2 Liter, Repeating Design, Silver Lid	297.00
Stein, 3/4 Liter, Children, Transfer, Pottery, Pewter Hinge	385.00
Stein, Mother & Baby Deer, Air Brushed, Hand Painted, Pewter Lid, 1 Liter	320.00
Stein, No. 2668, 1 Liter, Fish & Sausages, Figural Cat Handle, Pewter Lid	742.00
Stein, No. 2783, 1 Liter, Stag, Figural Fox Handle, Pewter Lid	1072.00
Stein, No. 2784, 1 Liter, Munich Child, Pewter Lid	1265.00
Stein, No. 2888, 1 Liter, Drunken Man Walking Past Lightpost	1980.00
Stein, No. 2889, 1/2 Liter, Man At Table With Baby, Pewter Lid	797.00
Tray, Strawberry Decoration, Majolica, 12 1/2 x 9 In.	275.00
Vase, Figural, Monkey, Playing Organ, Glazed, Impressed Mark, 8 In.	630.00
Vase, Trumpet Form, Wide Gilt Band Of Leaves, Green Ground, 11 In., Pair	345.00

SASCHA BRASTOFF made decorative accessories, ceramics, enamels on
copper, and plastics of his own design. He headed a factory, Sascha
Brastoff of California, Inc., in West Los Angeles, from 1953 until
about 1973. He died in 1993. Pieces signed with the signature *Sascha*
Brastoff were his work and are the most expensive. Other pieces
marked *Sascha B.* or with a stamped mark were made by others in his
company. Pieces made by Matt Adams after he left the factory are
listed here with his name.

Ashtray, Abstract, Free-Form, 8 In.	40.00
Ashtray, Abstract, Hooded, Rooster Mark, Marked	45.00
Ashtray, Americana, Floral, Enamel On Copper, 5 In.	30.00
Ashtray, Fruit, 8 3/4 In.	45.00
Ashtray, Poodle, Square, Ceramic, 8 In.	70.00
Ashtray, Rooftops, Enamel On Copper, 8 1/2 In.	30.00
Bowl, Abstract, Blues & Golds, Rooster Mark	55.00
Box, Minos, 9 In.	195.00
Box, Mosaic, Dog Finial, Square, 5 1/2 In.	165.00
Bride's Basket, Lavender To Orange, Berries & Leaves At Top, 9 In.	198.00
Cachepot, Ruffled Top, Light & Dark Greens	65.00
Cachepot, Scalloped Top, 4 1/2 x 6 In.	70.00
Dish, Shell, Gold & White Drip Accents, Marked	65.00
Figurine, Polar Bear, 9 In.	195.00
Lamp, Marked	695.00
Tobacco Jar, Abstract, Stainless Steel Lid, 6 1/2 In.	65.00
Tray, Free-Form, 24K Gold Trim, c.1950, 11 In.	45.00
Vase, Gold & White Rings, Marked, 12 In.	125.00
Vase, Painted Elk, Marked, 8 In.	75.00
Vase, Speckled Yellow Ground, Gold Leaves, Rooster Mark, 9 In., Pair	265.00
Vase, Walrus, Marked, 8 In.	75.00

SATIN GLASS is a late nineteenth-century art glass. It has a dull finish
that is caused by hydrofluoric acid vapor treatment. Satin glass was
made in many colors and sometimes has applied decorations. Satin
glass is also listed by factory name, such as Webb, or in the Mother-of-
Pearl category in this book.

Compote, Dragonflies, Flowers, Ruffled Edge, Silver, C-Scroll Base, 7 In.	220.00
Jar, Sweetmeat, Pink, Resilvered Cover & Handle, 6 x 5 1/4 In.	475.00
Pitcher, Diamond-Quilted, Blue, 8 In.	70.00

Pitcher, Peach, Diamond-Quilted, Pinched, Reeded Handle, 19th Century, 9 In. 260.00
Pitcher, Water, Diamond-Quilted, Pink, 7 In., Pair 125.00
Powder Jar, Pink, Dog Handle, Diamond Shaped, 6 x 4 1/2 In. 30.00
Rose Bowl, 4 Crimped Corners, Bird, Blue, 3 x 3 In. 65.00
Rose Bowl, White To Pink, Leafy Branch, Rolled Ruffled Rim, 19th Century, 5 1/2 In. . . .   115.00
Tumble-Up, Diamond-Quilted, Pink, 8 In. 60.00
Vase, Diamond-Quilted, Pink, 7 1/2 In. 90.00
Vase, Floral, Pink Overlay, Enameled Flowers, Gold Leaves, 10 In., Pair 175.00
Vase, Green Over Custard, Enameled Apple Branches, Fruit, England, 8 1/2 In. 168.00
Vase, Milk Glass, Blue, White & Gold Enamel, Green Ruffled Edge, Bulbous, 11 In. 140.00
Vase, Peach To Pink To White, Enameled Daisies, 10 1/4 In., Pair 224.00
Vase, Shaded Pink, Ribbed, 8 1/2 In. 100.00
Vase, Stick, Diamond-Quilted, Yellow, 7 In. 25.00
Vase, Zigzag, Blue, 9 1/2 In. 70.00

SATSUMA is a Japanese pottery with a distinctive creamy beige crackled glaze. Most of the pieces were decorated with blue, red, green, orange, or gold. Almost all Satsuma found today was made after 1860. During World War I, Americans could not buy undecorated European porcelains. Women who liked to make hand painted porcelains at home began to decorate plain Satsuma. These pieces are known today as *American Satsuma*.

Biscuit Jar, Cover, Center Band Floral Design, A.A. Frazer 825.00
Bowl, Cover, Women & Warriors In Scrolls, Medallions, Interior Warriors, 4 In. 200.00
Bowl, Duck, Flowering Branch, 5 In. 143.00
Bowl, Figures Under Cherry Trees In Interior, 6 In. 2860.00
Bowl, Flower Form, Raised Figural Scenes, Brocade Ground, Signed, 12 1/4 In. 6050.00
Bowl, Interior Peacock & Peahen In Garden, Floral Border, Kanzan, 12 In. 862.00
Bowl, Mountain, River, Figural Scene, Floral Panel, Greek Key Border, 6 In. 165.00
Bowl, Raised Figural Scenes, Brocade Ground, Gold Lacquer Signed, Kinkozan, 12 In. . .   6050.00
Bowl, Shishi Design, 4 x 2 1/2 In. 577.00
Box, Cover, Flower Blossom Form, Weeping Cherry Tree Design, 3 In. 143.00
Box, Multicolored Flowers, Gold Ground, 19th Century, 1 x 3 In. 275.00
Charger, Hunt Scene, 3 Warriors & Stag, Seal, Signed, 18 In. 1035.00
Charger, One Thousand Flowers, Allover Flowers, Red & Gold Border, Signed, 18 In. . . .   445.00
Figurine, Elephant, Mounted By Sages Holding Scrolls, 19th Century, 12 In., Pair 3220.00
Incense Burner, Small Boy & Frog, Brocade Patterns, Late 19h Century, 7 In. 230.00
Jar, Cover, Floral, Butterfly Design, Gilt Highlights, 1 1/2 x 2 In. 460.00
Jar, Cover, Inverted Pear Shape, Dragons Above Curling Waves, Gosu Blue, 12 In. 4950.00
Jar, Domed Cover, Gods Of Good Fortune Scene, Gosu Blue, Gilt, 9 1/2 In. 4400.00
Jar, Rose, Raised Floral Design, Dark Green Ground, c.1900, 6 In. 27.00
Jar, Silver Cover, Phoenix Design, Globular, c.1800, 4 3/4 In. 2420.00
Koro, Incense Burner, Cover, 4 Panels, Calligraphy, Signed, 1850s, 7 1/4 x 9 In. 3155.00
Lamp, Silk Shade, Electrified, 33 In. 1250.00
Lamp, Warriors, 4 Scholars On Reverse, Vase Shape Base, Double Sockets, 31 In., Pair . .   390.00
Plate, 2 Dragons, 1 Gold, 1 White, Clouds, Brocade Borders, Signed, 1880, 9 3/4 In. 575.00
Tea Set, Figures, Black Ground, Molded Dragon Design, 15 Piece 175.00
Teapot, Bridge, Pagoda & River, 6 In. 92.00
Teapot, Garden Scenes, Figures, Flowers, Beaded, Gilt Ground, Flower Form, 17 In. 252.00
Urn, Cover, Black & White Peony, Birds, Red-Orange Glaze, 3 Mask Feet On Pedestal . .   132.00
Vase, 2 Women, Tan Band, Floral Enameling, Green Glaze, 15 In. 95.00
Vase, Baluster Shape, Beauties, Children, Reticulated Canework Design, 6 1/2 In. 690.00
Vase, Buddha Riding Elephant, Figures Projecting Out On Sides, Signed, 12 In. 700.00
Vase, Butterflies On Orange Ground, Brocade Border, Tanzan, c.1900, 12 In. 345.00
Vase, Cherry Blossoms, White Reserve, Late 19th Century, 22 1/4 In., Pair 275.00
Vase, Cobalt Glaze, Figural Design, Reverse With Flowers, Serpent Handles, 14 In. 50.00
Vase, Figures Around, Shimazu, 20 In. 2530.00
Vase, Figures, Early 20th Century, 10 1/4 In., Pair 316.00
Vase, Floral Design, Japan, 8 In. 138.00
Vase, Gilt Brocade Framing Reserves Of Woman & Children, Kinkozan, 15 In., Pair 1150.00
Vase, Gilt Phoenixes, Heart Shape Surrounded By Women, Children, 1870s, 6 In. 2645.00
Vase, Hundred Cranes, Gilt Scrolling, Taizan, 1 3/4 In. 632.00
Vase, Inverted Pear Shape, Figural Landscape Panels, Floral, 5 1/4 In. 1100.00

Vase, Landscape Cartouche On 1 Face, Peacock, Flower On Other Side, 1900, 16 In. 880.00
Vase, Mirror Image Reserves, Birds & Flowers, Court Scenes, c.1880, 8 1/2 In., Pair 5462.00
Vase, Monks & Animals, Figures Projecting Out Of Sides, 12 In.   700.00
Vase, Procession At Nijo Shrine, Cloisonne Borders, Kuntoin, c.1880, 6 1/2 In 1265.00
Vase, Procession Of Various Insects, Elephant Head Handles, 1880s, 12 1/2 In. 172.00
Vase, Reserves Of People In Garden, Fan Forms, Floral Border, Signed, 5 1/4 In. 172.00
Vase, Reserves Of Women & Children, Floral Borders, Signed, 3 1/2 In. 402.00
Vase, Stand, Enamel & Gilt Figural Courtyard Scenes, Foo Lion Finial, 44 1/2 In. 345.00
Vase, Teal & Gold Floral, 18 1/2 In. 172.00
Vase, Trumpet Form, Figural Design, Blue Ground, Gilt Signature, 7 1/4 In. 357.00
Vase, Trumpet Form, Figural Design, c.1900, 5 In. 247.00
Vase, Wall, Polychrome Immortals, Gilt Dragon, c.1900, 8 1/4 In., Pair 550.00

SATURDAY EVENING GIRLS, see Paul Revere Pottery category.

SCALES have been made to weigh everything from babies to gold. Collectors search for all types. Most popular are small gold dust scales and special grocery scales.

1 Cent, Birth Month, Readout In Pounds, Enameled Body, American Scale, 1938, 61 In. . .   460.00
Analytical Balance, Henry Troemner, Mahogany, Glass Case, Brass, 16 In. 360.00
Assay, No. 5A, Wooden Case, All Weights 195.00
Balance, Becker's & Sons, Rotterdam, Mahogany, Ivory Knobs, Drawer, Weights, 17 In. .   220.00
Balance, Brass Scoop & Arm, Numbered 0 To 8, Black Iron, 9 x 11 In. 150.00
Balance, Carved Marble, Brass Pans, 22 In. 275.00
Balance, Cast Iron, Brass, Wooden, Pans, 5 Weights, 1880s, 10 1/4 In. 44.00
Balance, Hanging Pans, Figural Knight, Brass, 1920s-1930s 22.00
Balance, Henry Broemner, Brass Pan, Cast Iron & Brass, 26 In. 165.00
Balance, Henry Trommer, Oak, Marble, 13 In. . . . . *Illus*   144.00
Balance, Pans, Weights, Mahogany Base With Drawer, 1 Lb., 13 3/4 In. 143.00
Balance, Pratt & Son, Brass, Floral Mosaic Base, 9 1/2 x 6 x 6 In.   465.00
Balance, Savage, Mahogany, Weights, 21 In. . . . . *Illus*   575.00
Butter, Hand Held 70.00
Calculating, Toledo, Glass Pan, 21 In. 28.00
Candy, Toledo Scale Company, Style 405CA, White Enamel, 1917, 14 1/2 x 7 In. 85.00
Coin-Operated, Jennings, Correct Weight, No. 2761, 70 In. . . . . *Illus*   288.00
Computing, 30 Lb. Capacity, 31 1/2 In. 413.00
Computing, National, Ceramic, Brass Pan, 34 In. 120.00
Computing, Standard, Blue, 24 Lb. Capacity, Brass Marquee, 32 In. 55.00
Computing Scale Co., Dayton, Oh., 12 In. . . . . *Illus*   173.00
Countertop, Dayton, 2-Sided Scales, Pan, 2 Lbs. 172.00
Dayton, No. 144 . . . .   700.00
Double Balance, Eastman Kodak Co., Studio Scale, Wood Base, 6 Counterweights, 9 In. . .   60.00
Egg, Jiffy Way, Box 40.00
Egg, Reliable Egg Scale, Speed Accuracy, Steel, Lead Weights, 1915 . . . .   65.00
Eine, Cast Iron Suspension Bridge, Calibrated Weight, Hooks, Chains, 19th Century 3750.00
Feed-Grain, Carvens, Green Paint, 1935 . . . .   100.00

Scale, Balance, Henry Trommer, Oak, Marble, 13 In.

Scale, Balance, Savage, Mahogany, Weights, 21 In.

Scale, Coin-Operated,
Jennings, Correct
Weight, No. 2761,
70 In.

Scale, Weighing,
Rosenfield Reliance,
Penny, Cast Iron

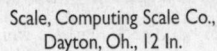

Scale, Computing Scale Co.,
Dayton, Oh., 12 In.

Gold, Brass, 4 Weights	70.00
Gold, Phillip Harris, 1900s	195.00
Gold, Triumph, Box	70.00
Laboratory, Rexo, No. L-665, Metal, Gray Enamel Paint, Pelouze Co., Box, 9 x 4 In.	70.00
Landers, Frary & Clark, Tin Lithograph, Porcelain Pan, 22 In.	99.00
Mahogany, Brass Tray, On Rectangular Inlaid Box, 16 1/4 In.	115.00
Micrometer, Dodge Mfg., Cast Metal & Marble Base, 11 1/8 In.	88.00
Milk, Chatillon's Improved Circular Spring Balance, Brass, 12 In.	25.00
Penny, Lollipop, Did You Weigh Yourself Today, Porcelain, 69 x 19 In.	515.00
Platform, Peerless, Brass, Mirrored Marquee, 1 Cent, 73 In.	632.00
Postage, Brass & Mahogany, England, 4 x 9 In.	50.00
Postage, Mahogany, Brass, England, 19th Century, 11 In.	402.00
Precision, Ainsworth & Sons, Glaze Metal Case	200.00
Set, Oak Case, Eastlake Carving, Brown Marble Top, 8 1/4 x 21 1/4 x 9 3/4 In.	250.00
Shopkeeper's, Brass, Marble, Scroll Support, 19th Century, 28 x 12 x 27 In.	305.00
Torsion Balance Co., Chrome, Glass, 1950s	24.75
Weighing, Rosenfield Reliance, Penny, Cast Iron ....*Illus*	10925.00
Weighing, Uncle Sam, Arcade Type, 1900s	2645.00
Weighing, Universal Landers, Frary & Clark Family Scale, Glass, Brass, Conn., 8 In.	45.00
Weight Set, Apothecary, Brass, Hole Drilled Center, 10 Piece	275.00
Wrigley's Candy, Decals, Brass Dial & Pan, Tin Construction, 8 In.	385.00

SCHAFER & VATER, makers of small ceramic items, are best known for their amusing figurals. The factory was located in Volkstedt-Rudolstadt, Germany, from 1890 to 1962. Some pieces are marked with the crown and R mark, but many are unmarked.

Creamer, Clown Playing Mandolin, 3 1/2 In.	110.00
Figurine, 2 Googly-Eyed Children, Rabbits, Doves, 3 3/4 In.	145.00
Figurine, Man, Top Hat, Stick Legs, Bald Head, Carrying Bouquet, 7 3/4 In.	165.00
Hatpin Holder, Egyptian Head, Gray & Green Jasper Ware, Pink Face, 5 In.	325.00
Humidor, Lavender, Man With Pipe	525.00
Match Holder, Striker, Scratch Your Match On My Patch, 3 3/4 x 2 1/4 In.	165.00
Pitcher, Elongated Man Handle, Pink & Green	145.00
Toothpick, Green Medallion, Pink, 3 Footed	68.00
Vase, Jeweled, 4 1/2 In.	110.99
Vase, Swan With Beautiful Maiden, Bisque, Germany, 6 x 8 In., Pair	126.00

SCHNEIDER Glassworks was founded in 1913 at Epinay-sur-Seine, France, by Charles and Ernest Schneider. Art glass was made between 1913 and 1930. The company still produces clear crystal glass.

Centerpiece, Blue, Turquoise, Tangerine, Burgundy, Tapered, Rolled Rim, 15 In.	1495.00
Chandelier, 3-Light, Orange To Alabaster Domed Base, Floral Cast Iron Frame, 21 In.	1380.00
Dish, Dark Blue Flecks, Metal Leaf Mounts, Signed, 3 1/2 In.	143.00
Shade, Hanging, Orange, Brown, White, Bronzed Metal Collars, 13 In., Pair	550.00
Tazza, White, Amethyst, Rolled Blue Rim, Double Bulbed Stem, Disc Foot, 8 In.	862.00
Vase, 3 Clusters Of Red Grapes, Yellow, 1925, 3 5/8 In.	575.00

Vase, 3 Etched Squares, 2 Rectangles, Tangerine Base, 1928, 14 In. 1725.00
Vase, 3 Prunts, Mottled Gourd, Signed, c.1925, 8 In. 862.00
Vase, Gourd Form, Dark Purple Vertical Dashes, Yellow Dots, White, Purple, 11 In. 920.00
Vase, Purple, Burgundy, Pink, Cherries, Iron Base, 1910, 17 In., Pair 3000.00
Vase, Purple, Deep Purple Circular Foot, Etched, 1925, 11 1/4 In. 575.00
Vase, Red, Purple, Green, Orange Glass, Vertical Stems Holding Thorns, 16 1/2 In. 1100.00
Vase, Ribbed, Lemon Yellow, Gray Glass, Circular Dark Purple Glass Foot, 8 In. 1265.00
Vase, Stylized Foxglove, Pedestal Base, Signed, 20 1/4 In. 2300.00
Vase, Stylized Interlaced Ropes, Dark Purple Circular Foot, Purple, 1925, 9 In. 402.00
Vase, Trumpet, Yellow Interior, Cobalt, Russet, Cylindrical, Cushion Foot, 16 In. 1035.00
Vase, Yellow Spatters, Shaded Pale Rose To Deep Magenta, Flared Lip, 1915-1925, 8 In. .. 660.00

SCIENTIFIC INSTRUMENTS of all kinds are included in this category.
Other categories such as Barometer, Binoculars, Dental, Nautical,
Medical, and Thermometer may also price scientific apparatus.

Calipers, Brass, 18th Century 110.00
Chronometer, Model 22, Arabic Numerals, Mahogany Case, 6 In. 747.00
Chronometer, Seconds & Wind Dial, Case, Webster, Cornhill 690.00
Compass, Dry, Bywater, Dawson & Co., Wooden, 7 In. 185.00
Compass, Marbles Brand, Brass, Glass Face, Thumb Holder, Pin Mount 75.00
Compass, N.Y. Case, S. Thaxter & Son, Boston, 1825 .... 330.00
Compass, Nickel, Brass, Brinton, C.S.A., Stanley, London, Brassbound Box 350.00
Compass, Plated Brass, Usanite, Taylor, Rochester, N.Y., 1918, 1 1/2 In. 80.00
Compass, Surveyor's, Wooden Case, 20th Century, W. & L.E. Gurley, N.Y. 95.00
Electrostatic Generator, 2 Leyden Jars, Brass Gimbals, 15 1/2 In. 460.00
Magnifier, Tabletop, Adjusts Up, Down, Sideways, Angles, 1887, 10 In. 230.00
Magnifying Glass, Brass, Handle Made From Fire Tool, 9 1/2 In. 77.00
Micrometer, L. Schopper, Circular Scale, Gauge & Cast Iron Stand 345.00
Microscope, 3 Section, Brass Body, Under Stage Mirror, 1880s 1210.00
Microscope, Bausch & Lomb, Brass, Case ....165.00 to 357.00
Microscope, Brass, Mahogany Case, Drawer, 19th Century, Miniature 265.00
Microscope, Brass, Metal, Early 20th Century, 12 In. 82.00
Microscope, Carl Ziess, Wooden Case, 14 3/4 x 6 3/4 In. 215.00
Microscope, George Adams, London, Improved Double, 1780 ....*Illus* 4111.00
Microscope, Klonne & Muller, Berlin, 1900 ....*Illus* 7590.00
Microscope, Leitz, Micrometer Focusing, Accessories, 1888, 11 In. 488.00
Microscope, Monolux, With Dissecting Kit, Original Case 35.00
Microscope, Pocket, Louisiana Purchase Exposition 200.00
Microscope, Spence, No. 5, 3-Power Turret, 1914 .... 85.00
Microscope, T.J. Young, Accessories, Mahogany Case, 11 In. 862.00
Microscope, Universal, R. & J. Beck, London, 1865 ....*Illus* 3289.00
Microscope, White, With Slides, Case 935.00
Microscope, Zeiss/Hughes-Owens, Black & Chrome, 12 1/2 In. 115.00

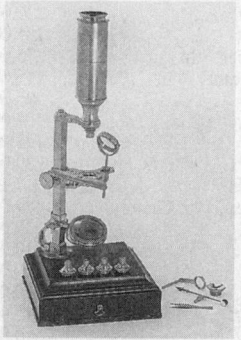

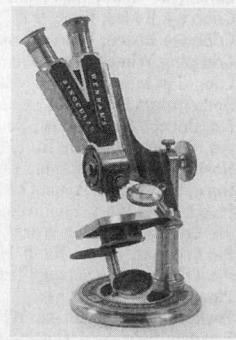

Scientific Instrument,
Microscope, George Adams,
London, Improved Double, 1780

Scientific Instrument,
Microscope, Klonne & Muller,
Berlin, 1900

Scientific Instrument,
Microscope, Universal,
R. & J. Beck, London, 1865

Microscope, Zentmayer, Dissecting, Jointed Lens, Case, 4 1/2 In. 430.00
Octant, Mahogany, Brass, Ivory Scale, Elpalet Loring Name Plaque, 17 In. 600.00
Parallel Rule, Ebony, Brass, 18 In., Pair....................................... 99.00
Planetarium, Tellurium, 1880 .... 2750.00
Semicircumferentor, Mahogany Case, Late 18th Century, 3 x 6 In. 690.00
Star & Planet Finder, Barritt-Serviss, Square, 1906, 15 In. 143.00
Sundial-Compass, Rollin Co., Brass, Egyptian Designs Back, 1 1/2 In. 70.00
Telescope, 3 Draw, Brass, 19th Century, Extends To 16 1/2 In. 65.00
Telescope, 3 Draw, Brass, Fitted Case, 13 1/2 In. Extended 120.00
Telescope, 3 Draw, Brass, Sun Sleeve, American, 1850, 32 In. 275.00
Telescope, 4 Draw, Leather Covered, 1 In. Diam., 16 1/2 In. 154.00
Telescope, 6 Draw, Lens Covers, Sunshade, Silver Plated 675.00
Telescope, Bardou & Son, Paris, Brass, Tripod Base, 19th Century, 38 In. 2090.00
Telescope, Crichton & Sons, Surveyor's, Brass, Mahogany, 33 In............\...... 1265.00
Telescope, J.P. Cutts, Brass 120.00
Telescope, Osborne, London, 3 Draw, Brass, Leather, 21 In. 90.00
Telescope, Pocket, 3 Draw, Fitted Case, 22 1/2 In. Extended 120.00
Telescope, Single Draw, Brass, Leather Barrel Cover, 37 1/2 In. Extended 185.00
Telescope, Stanley, London, Brass, Box, 1885, Opens To 16 In. 200.00
Telescope, W.Y. McAllister, 3 Draw, Brass, Philadelphia, 19th Century 145.00
Telescope, Widdifield, Single Draw, Wooden, Boston, 33 In. 465.00
Telescope, Wooden, Brass Stand, 35 In. 1705.00
Telescopic Lens, Blunt & Son, London, Ivory, Leather Case, Signed, 2 In. 402.00
Tellurium, Gears, Compass, Brass Base, Trippensee, c.1930, 14 x 20 In. 2070.00
Ticker Tape Machine, Excelsior, Metal Frame, Beveled Glass Sides, 8 In. 138.00
Transit, Surveyor's, Keveel & Easser, Great Northern Railway, Box, 20 In........... 500.00
Transit, W. & L.E. Gurley, Brass, Fitted Case, c.1880 .... 770.00
Tube Checker, Burton Rogers, Type B, Bakelite, 1929, 7 x 5 x 2 In. 30.00
Tube Tester, Jackson, Model 648, Dynamic, Carry Case, 1960s, 16 In. 83.00
Weather Gauge, Hygrometer, Thermometer, Wooden, Brass, 16 In.................. 185.00
Weather Guide Meteorological Standard, Metal, Plastic, 1940s, 10 In. 20.00

SCRIMSHAW is bone or ivory or whale's teeth carved by sailors and others for entertainment during the sailing-ship days. Some scrimshaw was carved as early as 1800. There are modern scrimshanders making pieces today on bone, ivory, or plastic. Other pieces may be found in the Ivory and Nautical categories.

Bodkin, Bone, Sewing Punch, 4 In. 11.00
Box, Checkerboard Design, Baleen & Ivory, Fitted Tray, 3 3/4 x 5 x 10 In. 1870.00
Box, Ditty, Whalebone 5500.00
Box, Ivory, Engraved, Whaling Scene, Compass Positions, Early 1900s, 2 x 2 1/4 In. 259.00
Buggy Whip, Whalebone Handle 30.00
Busk, Whalebone, Sunburst, Eagle, Shield & Fan, Geometric, 11 3/4 In. 431.00
Caricature Head, Whale Ear Bone, Portrait, Painted, c.1930, 5 In., Pair 680.00
Cribbage Board, Bone, 9 1/2 x 2 1/4 In. 220.00
Cribbage Board, Walrus Tusk, Brass Cap, 19th Century, 14 In. 165.00
Crimping Wheel, Whalebone, Offset, Fish 1 Side, Mary Gendron Other, 7 In. 375.00
Cup, Man Making Chest, Man & Woman On Pathway, Horn, 19th Century, 6 In. 115.00
Doll, Walrus Ivory, 4 In. 395.00
Fid, Bone, Clenched Fist, Red, White & Blue Twist Carved, Cambria, 7 1/2 In. 495.00
Fid, Whalebone, 7 1/2 In. 175.00
Horn, Buffalo Bill Roping Cow, Flowers On Base, Stand, c.1894, 12 x 18 x 10 In. 339.00
Horn, Carving Of Annie Oakley & Johnny Baker, W.O.H., 1899, 17 In. 1017.00
Match Safe, Ivory, Engraved, Whale, 6-Point Star & Arrows, American, 19th Century ... 489.00
Pie Crimper, Jagging Wheel, Ivory, Ebony Inlaid Dots, 6 In. 330.00
Pie Crimper, Whale Tooth, Hand Shaped Handle, Mid 19th Century 2310.00
Pie Crimper, Whalebone, Teardrop Handle, 8 1/2 In. 220.00
Pipe, Walrus Shape, 7 In. 440.00
Pocketbook, Whalebone, Whaling Scene, Signed Arroyo, Swing Handle, 4 x 7 In. 1815.00
Powder Horn, Seal, Castles, Figures, Deer, England, 9 In........................ 355.00
Rolling Pin, Whale, Wooden Handles 575.00
Rule, Island Wood, Diamond Center & End, 14 In. 330.00
Ship, 2-Masted, Bone, American Flag, Stained Top, 4 1/2 x 4 1/8 In. 330.00

Snuffbox, Architectural & Marine, Date AD 1853, William Sandilands, 5 In. 1095.00
Swift, Whalebone, With Case, Circular Wooden Stand, 18 3/4 x 22 1/2 In. 2645.00
Tooth, Whale, 2 Full-Rigged Ships Engaged In Battle, 7 1/2 In. 1955.00
Tooth, Whale, Arctic Whaling Scene, 5 3/8 In. 440.00
Tooth, Whale, Bald Eagle, American Shield, 4 1/4 In. 322.00
Tooth, Whale, Cherub, With Wings, Releasing Pigeons, 8 In. 660.00
Tooth, Whale, Dragon, Pearl Eyes, 1900, 4 3/4 In. 440.00
Tooth, Whale, Engraved, Portrait, Captain Charles M. Scammon, Inscription, 6 In. 400.00
Tooth, Whale, Full-Rigged Ship, Rebecca, Holding Book, 19th Century, 7 In. 1045.00
Tooth, Whale, Lady Liberty, Justice, Sailing Ships, Polychrome, 4 1/2 In., Pair 6325.00
Tooth, Whale, Mermaid, Sailing Ship, Signed Lee 77, 6 x 3 In. 415.00
Tooth, Whale, Monks' Chicken Fighting, Holding Whips, 19th Century, 5 In. 550.00
Tooth, Whale, Sailor, Anchor, American Flag, Polychrome, 6 1/2 In. 795.00
Tooth, Whale, Ship Design, Woman Resting On An Anchor Holding Flag, 4 3/8 In. 690.00
Tooth, Whale, Ships In Line Etching, 4 3/4 In. 200.00
Tooth, Whale, Sperm Whale, 6 1/2 In. 245.00
Tooth, Whale, U.S. Ranger vs. H.M.S. Drake, K. Newman, 1960s, 7 1/2 In. 465.00
Tooth, Whale, Whales, Vessels, Forts, Flowers, 19th Century, 6 In., Pair 2800.00
Tooth, Whale, Whaling Ship, Progress N.B., 1852, 4 1/2 In. 465.00
Tooth, Whale, Woman Holding A Broom Pointing A Finger, 4 3/4 In. 1725.00
Tooth, Whale, Woman's Portrait, 19th Century, 6 In. 660.00
Tusk, Walrus, 2 Eagles, Lady, Indian, Vulture, 18 7/8 In. 1840.00
Tusk, Walrus, Carved, 2 Children Embracing, Man Wearing Hat, Flag, 10 In. 315.00
Tusk, Walrus, With Cribbage Board, 19th Century, 18 In. 220.00
Watch Holder, Prisoner-Of-War, Whalebone, Ivory, Ebonized Wood Frame, 14 In. 4025.00
Yarn Swift, Whalebone, Flowers, Expanding Frame, Table Clamp, 9 1/2 x 14 In. 1725.00
Yarn Swift, Whalebone, Ribbon Bows, Sealing Wax Decoration, 1800s, 22 In. 1035.00

SEBASTIAN MINIATURES were first made by Prescott W. Baston in
1938 in Marblehead, Massachusetts. More than 400 different designs
have been made, and collectors search for the out-of-production models. The mark may say *Copr. P. W. Baston U.S.A.,* or *P. W. Baston,*
U.S.A., or *Prescott W. Baston.* Sometimes a paper label was used.

George Washington, Mason, 1951, 3 5/8 In. 45.00
Paul Bunyon, 1944 . . . . 85.00
Plate, Grand Canyon, Preston W. Baston, 1979, 8 3/4 In. 225.00

SEG, see Paul Revere Pottery category.

SEVRES porcelain has been made in Sevres, France, since 1769. Many
copies of the famous ware have been made. The name originally
referred to the works of the Royal Porcelain factory. The name now
includes any of the wares made in the town of Sevres, France. The
entwined lines with a center letter used as the mark is one of the most
forged marks in antiques. Be very careful to identify Sevres by quality,
not just by mark.

Beaker, 2 Floral Sprays, Gilt Borders, Bellflower Garland, Scrolled Toes, 1760s, 5 In. . . . 1495.00
Bowl, Center, Cartouche Courting Couples, Period Dress, Ormolu Handles, 14 1/2 In. 1840.00
Bowl, Cover, Classical Scenes, Cobalt Blue Ground, Bronze Mounts, 5 3/4 In. 920.00
Bowl, Cover, Figural & Landscape Reserves, Cobalt Blue Ground, Gilt, 7 1/4 In. 632.00
Bowl, Footed, Gilt Butterflies, Lily Leaves, Cobalt Blue Ground, 1915, 18 In. 5175.00
Box, Cartouche Of Figure In Landscape, Gilt Foliate, Cobalt Blue Ground, 5 3/4 In. 230.00
Bust, Jules Grevy, Biscuit, Cobalt Blue, 16 1/4 In. 632.00
Bust, Marie Antoinette, Socle, Garland, Monogram, Bisque, Gilt Highlights, 1800s, 13 In. 748.00
Butter Tub, Attached Stand, Upright Lug Handles, Floral Groups, Hoop Knop, 1776 . . . . 7475.00
Candelabrum, Porcelain Urn, Figure In Landscape, Handles With Putto & Floral, 30 In. . . 6035.00
Centerpiece, Putti & Goat, Landscape, Puce Ground, Bronze Mounts, Oval, 16 In. 2300.00
Centerpiece, Women & Musician In Landscape, Cartouches, Ormolu Mounts, 16 In. 1725.00
Charger, Louis XVI & His Courtiers, Pink Ground, Gilt, 1875, 20 In. 880.00
Clock & Candelabra, 3-Light, Figures, Ormolu, Bisque, Garland, Hoof Feet, Late 1800s . . 1610.00
Coffee Cann & Saucer, Pink Drapery Swags, Laurel Wreath On Saucer, 1766, 1 7/8 In. . . . 1150.00
Coffee Cann & Saucer, River Landscape, Gilt Foliate Band At Rim, 1767, 2 3/8 In. 2645.00
Cup, Tulip Shape, Everted Gilt Rim, Puce, Green, Gilt Trim, 3 1/4 In. 76.00
Cup & Saucer, Cobalt Blue, Gilt Accents, Hand Painted, Man With Guitar, 3 1/2 In. 130.00

Cup & Saucer, Groups Of Flowers, Dentil-Edged Rim, Foliate Handle, 1756 . . . . 4025.00
Cup & Saucer, Royal Portraits Within Red Jewels, Coat Of Arms Saucer, 1870s 2587.00
Dish, Bird Perched On Leafy Branch, Gilt Bands, Shell Shape, 1786, 9 In. 1725.00
Dish, Dessert, Center Arabesques Within Border, Gilt Rim, Triangular, 1790s, 8 1/2 In. . . . 920.00
Dish, Feuille De Choux, Cabbage Leaf, 1781, 10 3/4 In. 747.00
Dish, Flower Sprays, Porcelain Flower Heads, c.1760, 13 1/2 In. 2300.00
Figurine, Madonna & Child, Signed On Base, 10 1/2 In. 73.00
Figurine, Maiden On Classical Throne, Biscuit, Raymond Sudre, 1908, 14 1/4 In. 920.00
Figurine, Marley Horse, Rearing, Nude Male Figure On Base, 21 1/2 In. 330.00
Garniture, Female In Greek Toga, Charger Resting On Head, c.1867, 3 Piece, 30 In. 4675.00
Ginger Jar, Blue Flambe, Ormolu, Pair 2300.00
Gravy Boat, Pale Blue, Gilt Anthemia Band Of Vines, Scroll Handle, 1859, 6 3/4 In. 690.00
Group, Boy With Fawn, Draped Over Boy's Neck & Shoulders, Bisque, 15 In. 805.00
Group, Diane Au Bain, Ormolu Base, Bisque, Impressed Mark, Mid 1800s, 18 In. 3450.00
Jar, Cover, Coiled Cobras Handles, Lime Green, Bronze, 1943, 25 5/8 In. 36800.00
Lamp, Oil, Campana Form, Maiden Head Handles, Medallion Of Mother, Child, 18 In. . . 1090.00
Lamp, Painted Courting Couples, Foliate Sprays, 19th Century, 17 In., Pair 977.00
Lamp Base, Ormolu Mounts, Removable Fount, Hand Painted Scenes, 22 3/4 In. 825.00
Pedestal, Gilt Acanthus, Green Enameled Ground, Onyx Top & Base 2587.00
Plaque, Portrait, Napoleon III & Empress Eugenie, Biscuit, Jules Peyre, 7 In., Pair 360.00
Plate, Transfer Scene Of Amorous Couple, Cobalt Rim, Metal Stand, 8 1/2 In. 172.00
Platter, Arrival Of Louis XIV At Dunkerque, Jeweled Bands, 1850-1900, 13 1/4 In. 2585.00
Potpourri, Domed Cover, Figures, Landscape, Pierced Rim, Gilt Bronze, Tonet, 22 In. 13800.00
Sauceboat, Undertray, Swan Form, 6 1/4 In. 160.00
Sugar, Cover, Panels Of Flowers, Bands Of Foliate Scrolls, Floral Knop, c.1760, 3 In. . . . 1610.00
Tazza, Ormolu Mounts, Floral Border, S-Scroll Supports, 3-Part Base, 1847, 5 In. 415.00
Urn, Cherubs With Tambourines, Bronze Female Figures, Garlands, Bronze Base, 36 In. . 2860.00
Urn, Dover, Art Nouveau Woman, Scroll Sides, Footed . . . . .Illus 3300.00
Urn, Maiden & Cherub Design, Cobalt Blue Ground, Ormolu Mounts, 16 In., Pair 1955.00
Urn, Oval, Reclining Woman, Cupid With Scroll, Domed Lid, 20th Century, 19 In. 1035.00
Urn, Porcelain, Woman With Jeweled Crown, Flowers, Blue Background, Gilt, 30 In. 3300.00
Urn, Powder Blue, Bronze Mounts, 14 1/2 In. 430.00
Urn, Turquoise Glaze, Classical Male On Side, Female On Other, Ribbon Handle, 10 In. . 350.00
Urn, Vase Shape, Gilt Bronze Mounts, Artichoke Finial, Eagle's Head Supports, 33 In. . . . 4885.00
Vase, Courting Couple, Elegantly Dressed, Gilt Borders, Cobalt, Brass Foot, 11 In. 259.00
Vase, Cover, Baluster, Gentleman With Seated Lady, Gilt Bronze Mask Handles, 19 In. . . 1540.00
Vase, Cover, Cherubs Within Stylized Floral Designs, 1900, 38 In. 6900.00
Vase, Cover, Gilt Overall Floral & Foliate Swags, Gilt Metal Handles & Knop, 23 In. 3737.00
Vase, Oval, Slender Neck, Red Glaze, Blue Mottled Streaks, c.1920, 12 1/4 In. 160.00
Vase, Painted Cupid & Maiden, Gilt Metal Mounted, 12 In. 460.00
Vase, Salon, 18th Century People In Garden, Dore Bronze Mounts, 22 In., Pair 5175.00
Vase, Sprays Of Summer Flowers, White Ground, Foliate Handles, Paris, 1880, 5 In. 3450.00
Vase, Tapered Oval, Glossy Dark Red, Silver Stepped & Beaded Base & Rim, 6 In. 805.00
Vase, Thistle, White Ground, Classic, Stamp Mark, 1907, 9 1/4 x 4 3/4 In. 1760.00
Vase, Turquoise & Green Crystalline Glaze, Bottle Shape, 5 1/4 x 3 In. 935.00

Sevres, Urn, Dover, Art
Nouveau Woman, Scroll
Sides, Footed

Do not display silver on unsealed wood, felt, wool, or velvet. They all contain sulfides that will tarnish the silver.

Don't display silver pieces near horn or tortoiseshell. They cause tarnish.

Vase, Venus, Chariot, Angles, Maidens, Angelica Kaufmann, 10 1/4 In. 385.00
Vase, Young Girl In Landscape, Verso Flowers, Square Handles, Signed, 12 In., Pair 3220.00

SEWER TILE figures were made by workers at the sewer tile and pipe
factories in the Ohio area during the late nineteenth and early twentieth centuries. Figurines, small vases, and cemetery vases were favored.
Often the finished vase was a piece of the original pipe with added decorations and markings. All types of sewer tile work are now considered
folk art by collectors.

Ashtray, Lion Head, Carl Vera, 4 In. 120.00
Bank, Dog, Seated, 10 1/4 In. 154.00
Figurine, Dog, Seated, Amber Glaze, 4 1/2 In. 198.00
Figurine, Dog, Seated, Superior Clay Co., Walter Smith, 12 1/2 In. 330.00
Figurine, Dog, Seated, Tooled Scalloped Base, 10 1/2 In. 135.00
Figurine, Lion, Molded & Tooled, Repaired, Mar. 7-27, KAR, Ohio, 15 In. 300.00
Figurine, Lion, R.L.W., Ohio, Early 20th Century, 8 x 12 In. 550.00
Figurine, Lion, Rectangular Base, Ohio, 5 In. 385.00
Figurine, Lion, Scalloped Edge Base, Antonini, 10 1/2 In. 412.00
Figurine, Lion, Wadsworth, Ohio, Unglazed, 8 1/2 In. 220.00
Figurine, Shoe, Laced With Old Green Ribbon, 5 In. 137.00
Figurine, Squirrel, Eating Nut, 6 3/4 In. . . . . .215.00 to 220.00
Figurine, Train Engine, Walter Smith, Superior Clay Corp, Uhrichsville, Ohio, 19 1/4 In. .   660.00
Pitcher, Akron Clay Products, 5 In. 82.00
Pitcher, Tooled Bark, Tooled Face On Spout, Jamie Stasser, 6 1/2 In. 148.00
Pitcher, Tooled Tree Bark, Knots, 7 3/4 In. 120.00
Planter, Center Cylinder With 4 Branches, Tooled Bark, Unglazed Red Clay, 22 In. 50.00
Planter, Tree Stump, Vines, Interior Signed, 14 In. 143.00
Plaque, Stag, Doe, Flowers, Trees, Allover Manganese Glaze, Reverse Basalt, 14 In. 355.00

SEWING equipment of all types is collected, from sewing birds that
held the cloth to tape measures, needle books, and old wooden spools.
Sewing machines are included here. Needlework pictures are listed in
the Picture category.

Basket, 6 Sections, No Handle, 5 x 12 In. 175.00
Bird, 2 On Egg Base, Wooden, Carved, Velvet Pincushion, 1913, 4 x 5 In. 85.00
Bird, 2 Pincushions 200.00
Bird, Silver, Brass, 2 Pincushions, Victorian, 5 In. 170.00
Box, Black Lacquer, Fitted Interior, Lift-Out Tray, Compartments, 11 x 16 In. 950.00
Box, Cover, Fitted Interior, Walnut, Diamond Shape Mother-Of-Pearl Inlay, 12 In. 172.00
Box, Diamond, Mother-Of-Pearl, Purple Velvet Lined Interior, Bun Feet, 3 x 6 In. 357.00
Box, Etched Ivory & Sandalwood, Fitted Interior, Lower Drawer, 19th Century, 12 In. 2415.00
Box, Hinged Cover, Landscape, 2 Buildings, Trees, Red, Black Paint, 2 x 6 In. 5175.00
Box, Hinged Cover, Mother-Of-Pearl Sides, Floral Sprays, Fabric Liner, 8 1/4 In. 315.00
Box, Hinged Cover, Serpentine Form, Floral, 4 Ball Feet, Tunbridgeware, 6 In. 260.00
Box, Lacquer, Gilt Design, Dragon & Figural, Fitted Compartments, Handles, 7 In. 1725.00
Box, Lacquer, Octagonal, With Ivory Pieces, 1 Missing Handle, 6 x 14 x 10 In. 660.00
Box, Marquetry, Exotic Wood, Mother-Of-Pearl, Lift-Out Tray, 11 x 7 x 5 In. 475.00
Box, On Box, Wood, Thread Holes, Hinged, Painted, Inscription, 19th Century, 8 x 11 In. . .   920.00
Box, Pincushion Top, 3 Tiers, Initialed R.S., 1892, 13 1/2 In. 4025.00
Box, Pine, Wallpaper Covered, Pincushion Lid, Mirror, 5 1/2 x 8 x 5 1/2 In. 825.00
Box, Serpentine Case, Lift Top, 2 Doors, Fitted Interior, Brass Stamp Box, 10 x 9 In. 805.00
Box, Spool Holder, Poplar, Doors, Interior Shelves, 2 Drawers, 1930s, 20 3/4 In. 305.00
Box, Stacked, Dark Brown Finish, 4 Graduated Overlapping Drawers, 15 In. 660.00
Box, Stylized Bird On Cover, Gilded Leaf Swags, Steel, 1830, 5 In. 2300.00
Box, Tambour Front, Ebony Pinstriping, Marquetry, 18th Century 695.00
Box, Tools, Dorman, Miniature 2100.00
Box, Wooden, Incised Design, Wooden Hinge, Side Lacing, Oval 450.00
Box, Zebrawood, Lift-Out Interior Tray, Fitted, Multiple Inlays, 5 x 14 1/2 In. 275.00
Cabinet, Spool, see Advertising category under Cabinet, Spool.
Caddy, Maple, Walnut, Rotary Top Spool Holder, Round, Victorian, 30 In. 715.00
Caddy, Peaseware, J.C. Brown, 1930, Signed, 6 In. 275.00
Case, Ivory, Gilt Silver Scissors, Thimble, France, 19th Century, 7/8 x 4 x 2 1/4 In. 374.00
Case, Ivory, Silver Thimble, Gilt Scissors, Thread Pull, 3/4 x 2 1/2 x 1 1/2 In. 316.00

Sewing, Machine, Clark's, Foliage, 1859   Sewing, Machine, Shaw & Clark, 1864

Case, Thimble, Mt. Washington Summit On Cover 195.00
Case, Thimble, Stork, Silver Plate & Bakelite 195.00
Chatelaine, Sewing, 7 Drops, Ribbon Threader, Ivory 785.00
Darner, Blown Glass, Brick Red, Tooled Mouth, 1870-1920, 6 3/4 In. 88.00
Darner, Blown Glass, Electric Blue, 1870-1920, 6 1/2 In. 120.00
Darner, Blown Glass, Gold Iridescent Art Glass, 1920, 6 In. 440.00
Darner, Blown Glass, Iridescent Blue Art Glass, 1920, 7 In. Long. 605.00
Darner, Blown Glass, Milk Glass, Yellow, Blue, Green, Pink, Orange, 1920, 5 1/2 In. 130.00
Darner, Iridescent Gold Art Glass, 1880s, 5 1/4 In. 187.00
Darner, Milk Glass, Red, Pink & Blue Cased, 1870s, 7 In. 143.00
Darner, Milk Glass, Shades Of Green, Blue, Pink & Purple Cased, 6 1/8 In. 65.00
Darner, Milk Glass, Turquoise, Orange, Blue, Teal & Pink Cased, 1890s, 6 3/4 In. 198.00
Dressmaker Form, Wooden Base, Pewter Top, Dress & Riding Coat, Child's, 42 In. 310.00
Jagging Wheel, 2-Twined Crimper, Baleen Spacer, Sea Serpent Handle, Ivory, 5 1/4 In. ... 1725.00
Loom, Weaving, Barn Type, Large 10.00
Machine, Atlas, Jack, 1914 .... 22.00
Machine, Clamp-On, Marked Soeze, 1901 .... 2500.00
Machine, Clark's, Foliage, 1859 ....*Illus* 4745.00
Machine, Muller, No. 20 .... 750.00
Machine, Shaw & Clark, 1864 ....*Illus* 6958.00
Machine, Singer, Featherweight, Attachments, Case 395.00
Machine, Singer, Featherweight, Freearm, Zigzag, Buttonholer, Case 1050.00
Machine, Singer, Featherweight, Tools, Book, Box 350.00
Needle Case, Bean Pod Form, Ivory, 1900, 3 3/4 In. 66.00
Needle Case, Ornate Butterfly, Ivory, 3 1/4 In. 55.00
Needle Case, Tape Measure Top, Bone & French Ivory, 4 In. 44.00
Needle Case, Woman Figure, Horn & Ivory, 17th Century, 3 1/2 In. 345.00
Pattern, Barbie, McCall, No. 7840 .... 10.00
Pattern, Barbie, Simplicity, No. 6208 .... 10.00
Pincushion, Bird, Embroidered, 18th Century, Rectangular 295.00
Pincushion, Bulldog, Metal, Velvet, 2 x 2 1/2 In. 45.00
Pincushion, Donkey, Figural, Sterling, 2 In. 150.00
Pincushion, Dutch Shoe, 2 1/4 In. 58.00
Pincushion, Footstool, Victorian, 2 In. 55.00
Pincushion, Green Velvet, Wallpaper Covered Pine Box, Interior Mirror, 4 x 7 x 4 In. 345.00
Pincushion, Indian Beadwork 110.00
Pincushion, Lion, Brass, c.1890, 5 In. 98.00
Pincushion, Mahogany, Round Box, 19th Century, 7 1/4 In. 66.00
Pincushion, Shoe, Leather, Beadwork, Stacked Reed, 4 1/2 In. 38.50
Pincushion, Shoe, Victorian, 3 1/2 In. 48.00
Pincushion, Tinkerbell, Original Box 45.00
Pincushion, Urn, Carved, French Ivory, Velvet Insert, 2 1/4 In. 27.50
Pincushion Dolls are listed in their own category.
Rug Hooker, Wooden, 1881 .... 35.00
Scissors, Embroidery, Scrolled Ends, Forged Iron, 5 In. 125.00
Scissors, Embroidery, Steel, 2 1/2 x 1 1/2 In. 17.00
Scissors, Embroidery, Sterling Silver Handles, 5 1/4 In. 11.00

Scissors, Pierced Handles, Floral Design, Silver, Dutch, 11 In.	50.00
Shuttle, Tatting, Engraved Birds Both Sides, Pakton, Late 18th Century	235.00
Spool Cabinets are in the Advertising category under Cabinet, Spool.	
Spool Holder, Hardwood, Varnish, Pincushion, 3 Tiers, 5 3/4 In.	70.00
Spool Holder, Pine, Hinged Ends, Horizontal Rods, Blue, 19th Century, 7 x 6 x 3 In.	545.00
Spool Holder, Tin, Wooden, 3 Tiers, Candle Insert On Lift Lid	65.00
Swift, Carved, Ivory Whalebone, Red, Sealing Wax Inlay, 19th Century, 14 In.	1495.00
Tape Measure, Cat, Pull Tail, Metal	85.00
Tape Measure, Daisy, Sterling	150.00
Tape Measure, Jester, Celluloid, 2 1/4 In.	400.00
Tape Measure, Kangaroo, Brown, Celluloid, Japan	90.00
Tape Measure, Pig, Blue Plastic, Red Hat	75.00
Tape Measure, Pig, Cedar Rapids, Iowa	40.00
Tape Measure, Sailing Ship, Celluloid, 1920s, 2 In.	85.00
Tape Measure, Ship, Figural, Red, Celluloid, Japan, 1940s	90.00
Tape Measure, Sprinkling Can, Brass, Germany, 1900s	125.00
Thimble, 10K Gold	55.00
Thimble, Greek Key, Gold	85.00
Thread Waxer, Black Frozen Charlotte, Attached To Beeswax Heart, Needle	115.00
Tool, Dressmaker's, Computing Wheel For Yardage, Rotating Scale, Boxwood, 24 In.	85.00
Yarn Holder, Brown, Sommer	40.00
Yarn Holder, Chalkware, Red, Sommer	40.00
Yarn Winder, Wool, Old Red Wash	185.00

SHAKER items are characterized by simplicity, functionalism, and orderliness. There were many Shaker communities in America from the eighteenth century to the present day. The religious order made furniture, small wooden pieces, and packaged medicines, herbs, and jellies to sell to *outsiders*. Other useful objects were made for use by members of the community. Shaker furniture is listed in this book in the Furniture category.

Almanac, 1886, Mt. Lebanon, N.Y., 32 Pages	58.00
Basket, Berry, Flaring Form, Late 19th Century, 4 1/2 In.	80.00
Basket, Sewing, 3-Finger, Oval, Satin Lined, Lid, Swing Handle, 4 x 12 x 8 1/2 In.	460.00
Basket, Splint, Looped Handles, Upright Cut Off & Turned Down On Outside, 14 1/2 In.	2990.00
Box, 1-Finger, Polished Copper Tacks, Oval, Refinished, 6 1/8 In.	190.00
Box, 3-Finger Base, Red Paint, Oval, 4 1/4 x 11 x 7 1/2 In.	375.00
Box, 4-Finger, Copper Tacks, Late 19th Century, 11 1/2 In.	715.00
Box, 9-Finger, Oval, Maple, Pine, 19th Century, 19 3/4 x 15 1/4 x 10 3/4 In.	745.00
Box, Bentwood, Finger Construction, Copper Tacks, Refinished, Round, 9 3/4 x 5 In.	165.00
Box, Bonnet, Single Lap, Bail Handle, Square Wooden Pegs, 8 1/4 x 10 1/4 In.	230.00
Box, Cover, Oval, 5 In. Diam.	235.00
Box, Curly Maple, Mortised Stretchers & Apron, Copper Tacks, Carved Lid, 10 1/2 In.	340.00
Box, Pantry, New Ipswich, 3 3/8 In.	890.00
Carrier, Copper Tacks, Bentwood Handle, 9 1/2 x 13 In.	192.00
Pail, Ears & Bail Handle, 4 Scribe Lines, Number 43, Black Trim, 12 x 8 1/2 In.	1380.00
Pail, Painted & Stenciled, Pine Staves, Iron Hoops, Coffin Shape Bail, 7 x 8 3/4 In.	977.00
Peeler, Apple, With Hand Held Knife, Child's, 14 1/2 In.	395.00
Rack, Harness, 6 Pegs, Blue Paint, 4 1/2 x 62 In.	1150.00
Watering Can, Tin	550.00

SHAVING MUGS were popular from 1860 to 1900. Many types were made, including occupational mugs featuring pictures of men's jobs. There were scuttle mugs, silver-plated mugs, glass-lined mugs, and others.

Fraternal, Foresters Of America, G. Alerich, 4 In.	88.00
Fraternal, Order Of United American Mechanics	93.00
Medallion, Flower Border, Blue, Yellow, Green, Indented Rim, Portugal, 3 5/8 In.	115.00
Occupational, Artist, Eisermann	175.00
Occupational, Bar Room Scene, John Basse, Flowers On Sides, 1925, 3 7/8 In.	330.00
Occupational, Baseball Player, Mike J. Barry, 3 3/4 In.	1015.00
Occupational, Blacksmith	165.00
Occupational, Blacksmith, James Babb, 3 7/8 In.	550.00

Occupational, Blacksmith, W.W. Parks, Gilt, Porcelain, 3 5/8 In. 300.00
Occupational, Butcher, Winged Logo, Side Florals 130.00
Occupational, Carpenter, Gold Trim, Name 88.00
Occupational, Electric Trolley, John T. Sullivan, T & V Limoges, 3 5/8 In. 495.00
Occupational, Engineer, Limoges 143.00
Occupational, Farmer, Limoges 100.00
Occupational, Farrier, G.B. Crosley, 3 7/8 In. 5720.00
Occupational, Fisherman 215.00
Occupational, Funeral Director 93.00
Occupational, Groceries & Meats, Chris A. Heil, Flowers, Wagon, 3 5/8 In. 355.00
Occupational, Horse Trainer, J.K. Potter 687.00
Occupational, Junk Dealer, George Palangio, 3 3/4 In. 660.00
Occupational, Livestock Dealer, Kirt Baumgaarner, 3 3/4 In. 880.00
Occupational, Mailman, Horse Drawn Wagon, R. Shotwell, 1925, 4 In. 965.00
Occupational, Man At Bar, J.D. Rosensted, Porcelain, Gilt, Austria, 3 1/2 In. 190.00
Occupational, Mortar & Pestle, B.M. Slocum, T & V Limoges, 1925, 3 5/8 In. 165.00
Occupational, Musician, Clarinet, E.F. Hebner, Wreath Of Flowers, 3 1/2 In. 120.00
Occupational, Paper Hanger, E.F. Kennedy, 4 In. 132.00
Occupational, Railroad Man, Alex Smirlis, 3 5/8 In. 467.00
Occupational, Red Caboose, Tom C. Donovan, Gilt, 1925, 3 5/8 In. 210.00
Occupational, Standing Steer, A.J. Luedke, 3 5/8 In. 255.00
Occupational, Tailor At Bench, Jack J. McGuire, Leonard Vienna, 3 7/8 In. 825.00
Occupational, World Our Field Koken St. Louis, P.O. Weller, Limoges, 3 7/8 In. 4510.00

SHAWNEE POTTERY was started in Zanesville, Ohio, in 1937. The
company made vases, novelty ware, flowerpots, planters, lamps, and
cookie jars. Three dinnerware lines were made: Corn, Lobster Ware,
and Valencia (a solid color line). White Corn pattern utility pieces were
made in 1945. Corn King was made from 1946 to 1954; Corn Queen,
with darker green leaves and lighter colored corn, from 1954 to 1961.
Shawnee produced pottery for George Rumrill during the late 1930s.
The company closed in 1961.

Casserole, Corn King, Cover 85.00
Cookie Jar, Dutch Boy, Blue Pants 165.00
Cookie Jar, Dutch Girl, Tulip 25.00
Cookie Jar, Elephant, Decals, Gold Trim 280.00
Cookie Jar, Happy 50th Birthday 400.00
Cookie Jar, Puss 'n Boots 125.00
Cookie Jar, Smiley Pig, With Shamrock 185.00
Creamer, Chanticleer 80.00
Mug, Corn King 35.00
Planter, Bear & Wagon, Green 95.00
Planter, Blackie Cat 25.00
Planter, Clown, With Pot 35.00
Planter, Coal Car, Yellow 35.00
Planter, Deer 35.00
Planter, Dog, On Button Shoe 35.00
Planter, Elf, On Shoe, Green 35.00
Planter, Hound Dog 35.00
Planter, Parakeet 18.00
Planter, Piano 35.00
Planter, Rooster 40.00
Planter, White Pony 40.00
Planter, Wishing Well, Dutch Boy & Girl, Gold 42.00
Range Set, Smiley & Winnie, Drip Jar, 3 Piece 150.00
Salt & Pepper, Bo Peep & Sailor 20.00
Salt & Pepper, Corn King, Large . . . . .38.00 to 50.00
Salt & Pepper, Muggsy 85.00
Shaker, Corn King 45.00
Sugar, Corn Queen 30.00
Teapot, Fern, 2 Cup 60.00
Teapot, Granny Ann, Peach Apron 125.00
Teapot, Granny Ann, Purple Apron 230.00

Vase, Elephant Leaf	100.00
Wall Pocket, Telephone	35.00

SHEARWATER pottery is a family business started by Mr. and Mrs. G. W. Anderson, Sr., and their three sons. The local Ocean Springs, Mississippi, clays were used to make the wares in the 1930s. The company is still in business.

Figurine, Androcles & Lion, Walter Anderson, 5 1/2 In.	300.00
Vase, Flaring Form, Multitone Blue Drip Over Green, Marked, 9 1/2 In.	285.00

SHEET MUSIC from the past centuries is now collected. The favorites are examples with covers featuring artistic or historic pictures. Early sheet music covers were lithographed, but by the 1900s photographic reproductions were used. The early music was larger than more recent sheets, and you must watch out for examples that were trimmed to fit in a twentieth-century piano bench.

Alabama Jigger, Black Man Dancing Cover, 1913	70.00
All The Way With LBJ, Photograph On Front, 1964	30.00
Andy Gump, Smoking Cigar, Dixon-Lane Music Company, 1940s	12.00
Away Down East In Maine, Rustic Cottage Cover, 1922	11.00
Banjo Picker, 1936	10.00
Black Hills Of Dakota, Calamity Jane Movie, Doris Day, 1953	16.00
Blowin' In The Wind, Bob Dylan, Autographed	635.00
Buttons & Bows, From The Movie, The Paleface, Bob Hope, Jane Russell, 1948	20.00
Christy's Minstrels, My Old Kentucky Home, Stephen Foster, 1840s	225.00
Custer's Last Charge, John Philip Sousa, 1922	50.00
Dance With A Dolly With A Hole In Her Stockin', 1944	3.00
Dark Town Cabaret, Fancy Black Folks Dancing Cover, 1913	38.00
Das Star Spangled Banner, Black Troubadour, Ethiopian Cherubs, 10 In.	27.00
Do I Love Her, Cole Porter, 1943	3.00
Don't Give Up The Ship, Shipmates Forever, Dick Powell, Ruby Keeler, 1935	20.00
Down Souf In Alabama, Black Man Strutting With Cane Cover, 1898	39.00
Dragnet, Jack Webb Photo, 1953	40.00
Drummer Boy Of Shiloh, Drummer Boy Praying As Soldier Weeps, 1863, 13 In.	38.00
Help Me Make It Through The Night, Kris Kristofferson, 1970	6.00
Home On The Range, Art Deco Design, 1932	7.00
Hot Off The Griddle, Black Couple Cake Walking Cover, 1915	12.00
I Don't Like No Cheap Man, McIntyre & Heath In Blackface Cover, 1897	20.00
Kinky Kids Parade, Gus Kahn & Walter Donaldson, 1925	50.00
Klondike Annie, Mae West On Cover, 1936	135.00
Koontown Koffee Klatsch, 3 Black Women Klatsching On Cover, 1904	55.00
Lavender Blue, Cartoon Characters, Walt Disney	15.00
Midnight Fire Alarm, 3 Horses Pulling Tanker, 6 Pages, 1918	28.00
My Sweetheart Went Down With The Ship, Titanic On Cover, 1912	35.00
Not A Coon Came Out The Way He Went In, Blacks Escaping On Cover, 1898	143.00
Oh Peter You're So Nice, Glen Oswald's Serenaders, 1924	11.00
Oh! My Pa-Pa, Shapiro, Eddie Fisher, 1953	3.00
On The Avenue, Leeds, Strolling Couple, Hearts, 1947	3.00
Rose Of The Rio Grande, Girl Picture, 1922	12.00
She Wore A Yellow Ribbon	37.00
Songs Cowboy Copas Sings, 1949, 48 Page, 9 x 12 In.	15.00
Southern Jollifications, Blacks Playing & Dancing On The Levee On Cover, 1890	30.00
Teddy Bears' Picnic, Witmark, 1947	5.00
That's Amore, The Caddy Movie, Dean Martin & Jerry Lewis	22.00
That's Why Darkies Were Born, George White's Scandals, 1939	20.00
The Charlie Chaplin Walk, Charlie On Front, New Fox Trot, 1915	75.00
The Smiler, Black Man Stealing Watermelon Cover, 1907	7.00
There'll Be A Hot Time In The Town Of Berlin, World War II, 1943	40.00
Tropical Magic, Week-End In Havana, Carmen Miranda, 1941	18.00
Uncle Tom's Cabin Rag, Topsy Dancing To Uncle Tom's Banjo Playing Cover, 1911	80.00
Wild West, A Cowboy Indian Intermezzo, 1908	22.00
Zambesi Dance, White Woman Looking At Colorful African Native Cover, 1912	3.00

SHEFFIELD items are listed in the Silver-English and Silver Plate categories.

SHELLEY first appeared on English ceramics about 1912. The Foley China Works started in England in 1860. Joseph Ball Shelley joined the company in 1862 and became a partner in 1872. Percy Shelley joined the firm in 1881. The company went through a series of name changes, and in 1910 the then Foley China Company became Shelley China. In 1929 it became Shelley Potteries. The company was acquired in 1966 by Allied English Potteries, then merged with the Doulton group in 1971. The name *Shelley* was put into use again in 1980. A trio is the name for a cup, saucer, and cake plate set.

Butter, Maytime, Cover, Rectangular	375.00
Butter Chip, English Charm	75.00
Cake Plate, Gladiola, Tall Queen Anne, c.1932	80.00
Cake Plate, Melody, Center Handle	165.00
Coffeepot, Posie Spray, 5 In.	375.00
Coffeepot, Rock Garden, Spout, Pale Green Handle & Finial, 7 1/2 In.	775.00
Condiment Set, Melody, Salt, Pepper, Mustard & Tray	475.00
Cup & Saucer, Blue Spray, Henley	55.00
Cup & Saucer, Blue, Dainty	85.00
Cup & Saucer, Chintz, Gold Trim, Blue	80.00
Cup & Saucer, Cottage, Queen Anne, c.1928, Demitasse	165.00
Cup & Saucer, Gainsborough Shape, Green, Pattern 13290	85.00
Cup & Saucer, Green, Daisy	135.00
Cup & Saucer, Indian Peony, Gainsborough	75.00
Cup & Saucer, Ludlow, Demitasse	42.00
Cup & Saucer, Melody	150.00
Cup & Saucer, Posie Spray	50.00
Cup & Saucer, Regency, Dainty, Demitasse	38.00
Cup & Saucer, Rose Pansy Forget-Me-Not	35.00
Eggcup, Bridal Rose	110.00
Maytime, Pin Tray, Chintz, 4 1/2 In.	70.00
Nut Dish, Flowers, 3 Piece	75.00
Pin Dish, Bittersweet Trim, Tab Handles, 4 x 5 1/4 In.	55.00
Pin Dish, Hibiscus, Round, Fluted, 4 1/4 In.	68.00
Pin Dish, Hollyhocks & Bridge	58.00
Pin Dish, Rosebud, Tab Handles, Dainty	65.00
Plate, Blue Rock, 8 In.	80.00
Plate, Blue, Dainty, 10 1/4 In.	90.00
Plate, Rock Garden, 8 In.	80.00 to 110.00
Snack Set, Bridal Rose, Round	80.00
Soup, Cream, Bridal Rose, Underplate	45.00
Sugar & Creamer, Blue Rock	100.00
Sugar & Creamer, Posie Spray	125.00
Sugar & Creamer, Stocks, Dainty	80.00
Tea Set, Vogue Sun Ray, Art Deco	3900.00
Teapot, Blue, Dainty, 8 Cup	540.00
Teapot, Evening Star, 6 1/2 In.	325.00
Teapot, Melody, 7 In.	850.00
Teapot, Wildflowers, 5 In.	275.00
Tray, Sandwich, Lily Of The Valley	240.00
Trio, Blue, Daisy	175.00
Trio, Bridal Rose, Dainty	90.00 to 110.00
Trio, Daffodil Time	90.00
Trio, Regency, Dainty	72.00
Trio, Stocks, Dainty	105.00 to 120.00
Vase, Garden Flowers, Leaves, Black Cracked Ice Ground, c.1915, 5 In.	205.00

SHIRLEY TEMPLE, the famous movie star, was born in 1928. She made her first movie in 1932. Thousands of items picturing Shirley have been and still are being made. Shirley Temple dolls were first made in 1934 by Ideal Toy Company. Millions of Shirley Temple cobalt blue glass dishes were made by Hazel Atlas Glass Company and U.S. Glass Company from 1934 to 1942. They were given away as premiums for Wheaties and Bisquick. A bowl, mug, and pitcher were made as a

breakfast set. Some pieces were decorated with the picture of a very young Shirley, others used a picture of Shirley in her 1936 *Captain January* costume. Although collectors refer to a cobalt creamer, it is actually the 4 1/2-inch-high milk pitcher from the breakfast set. Many of these items are being reproduced today.

Book, Child Star	20.00
Doll, Composition, Stuffed Torso, Sleep Eyes, Plaid Coat, 1930s, 26 In.	87.00
Doll, Ideal, 4 Teeth, Blond Wig, Green Tagged Costume, c.1935, 13 In.	1600.00
Doll, Ideal, Composition, Jointed, Sleep Eyes, Trunk Of Cloths, c.1936, 13 In.	690.00
Doll, Ideal, Composition, Music Note Dress, 20 In.	550.00
Doll, Ideal, Composition, Open Mouth, 4 Teeth, Mohair, Box, 20 In.	775.00
Doll, Ideal, Composition, Sleep Eyes, 6 Teeth, 5-Piece Body, 18 In.	475.00 to 650.00
Doll, Ideal, Open Mouth, Pink Pleated Costume, c.1935, 17 In.	1300.00
Doll, Ideal, Original Dress & Hat, 16 In.	395.00
Doll, Ideal, Vinyl, Sleep Eyes, 6 Teeth, Rooted Hair, Box, 1962, 15 In.	275.00
Lobby Card, Captain January, 5 Piece	460.00
Lobby Card, Little Miss Broadway, 20th Century Fox, 1938	460.00
Lobby Card, Littlest Rebel, 4 Piece	345.00
Mirror, Pocket	2.00
Mug, Cobalt Blue	32.00
Paper Doll, 1976, Uncut	20.00
Pattern, Doll Dress, McCall, Made For Schools, Envelope, 5 x 3 3/4 In.	55.00
Photograph, Teenager, Matte Finish, Autograph, 5 x 7 In.	145.00
Photograph, Young, Autograph, Sepia, 8 x 10 In.	745.00
Pitcher, Cobalt Blue, 4 1/2 In.	22.00 to 95.00
Poster, The Little Colonel, 20th Century Fox, 1935, Linen, One Sheet	1670.00
Scrapbook	95.00
Soap, Round, Box, 1930s	65.00

SHRINER, see Fraternal category.

SILVER DEPOSIT glass was first made during the late nineteenth century. Solid sterling silver is applied to the glass by a chemical method so that a cutout design of silver metal appears against a clear or colored glass. It is sometimes called silver overlay.

Bowl, Floral, 11 1/2 In.	70.00
Bowl, Green, Ground Bottom, 11 3/8 In.	35.00
Bowl & Double Candleholders, 4 1/2 x 9 In.	425.00
Cake Dish, Floral, 30 In.	45.00
Candy Dish, Ruffled Rim, 3 Legs, 7 1/2 In.	38.00
Coaster, 25th Anniversary, Mercury Glass Overlay, Heart Center, 6 Piece	25.00
Cookie Jar, Flowers, Black	90.00
Cruet, Cranberry, c.1900, 10 In.	2530.00
Decanter, Marked, Heisey Logo, 5 In.	105.00
Dish, Pale Green Crystal, 6 2/3 In.	22.00
Dish, Swan, Pall Mall, Crystal, 5 3/4 x 7 3/4 In., Pair	115.00
Perfume Bottle, 2 In.	8.00
Perfume Bottle, Overlay Design, Green, 4 1/2 In.	660.00

Never use lemon-scented dishwashing detergent to clean silver. It will leave spots.

Silver Deposit, Vase, Trumpet, Cranberry, 15 In.

Plate, Sandwich, 14 In.	125.00
Tray, 25th Anniversary, Crystal, 13 In.	15.00
Vase, Art Nouveau, Bohemia, 9 1/2 In.	2450.00
Vase, Black Amethyst, Trophy, Handle, Scalloped Edge, 8 In.	70.00
Vase, Fan, Floral Design, Geometric, Opaque, Black, Signed, Rockwell, 8 In.	259.00
Vase, Green Glass, Marked, c.1910, 10 In.	2090.00
Vase, Green Glass, Marked, c.1910, 12 In.	2200.00
Vase, Rose, 10 1/2 In.	35.00
Vase, Swirled Red & Black, Beads & Stone Each Panel, 12 In.	145.00
Vase, Trumpet, Cranberry, 15 In.	*Illus* 1320.00

SILVER FLATWARE includes many of the current and out-of-production silver and silver-plated flatware patterns made in the past eighty years. Other silver is listed under Silver-American, Silver-English, etc. Most silver flatware sets that are missing a few pieces can be completed through the help of one of the many silver matching services that advertise in many of the national publications.

SILVER FLATWARE PLATED, Antique, Creamer, Wallace, 1926, 5 In.	190.00
Canterbury, Cream Soup Spoon, Towle, 12 Piece	99.00
Columbia, Gravy Ladle, Rogers	20.00
Evening Star, Butter Knife, Oneida	10.00
Floral, Berry Spoon, Wallace, 1902	40.00
Fontana, Sugar Spoon, Towle	14.00
Fontana, Teaspoon, Towle	11.00
King, Asparagus Server, Mappin & Webb	410.00
LaVigne, Meat Fork, Rogers	30.00
Old Lace, Pickle Fork, Towle	15.00
Old Lace, Sugar Spoon, Towle	12.00
Old Lace, Teaspoon, Towle	10.00
Old Master, Salad Fork, Towle	25.00
Orange Blossom, Gravy Ladle, International	35.00
Paul Revere, Pie Server, Towle	25.00
Queen Elizabeth, Iced Tea Spoon, Towle	29.00
Queen Elizabeth, Lasagna Server, Towle	31.00
Rambler Rose, Jelly Spoon, Towle	15.00
Rose Solitaire, Teaspoon, Towle	10.00
RSVP, Bonbon Spoon, Towle	12.00
RSVP, Teaspoon, Towle	10.00
Sculptured Rose, Cosmetic Brush, Towle	14.00
Silver Plumes, Sugar Spoon, Towle	32.00
Silver Plumes, Tablespoon, Towle	56.00
SILVER FLATWARE STERLING, 1810, Demitasse Spoon, International	15.00
1810, Ice Cream Fork, International	25.00
Aegean Weave, Gravy Ladle, Wallace	37.00
Aegean Weave, Sugar Spoon, Wallace	25.00
American Beauty, Fork, Manchester, 1 In.	50.00
American Beauty, Salad Fork, Manchester	19.00
American Classic, Baked Potato Server, Easterling	23.00
American Classic, Gravy Ladle, Easterling	28.00
American Classic, Luncheon Fork, Easterling	16.00
American Classic, Sugar Spoon, Easterling	11.00
American Classic, Teaspoon, Easterling	9.00
Ancestry, Poultry Shears, Weidlich	37.00
Angelique, Baked Potato Server, International	28.00
Angelique, Ice Cream Fork, International	13.00
Angelique, Sugar, International	9.00
Antique Lily, Teaspoon, Whiting, 6 Piece	35.00
Ashmont, Cold Meat Fork, Reed & Barton	70.00
Ashmont, Tablespoon, Pierced, Reed & Barton	65.00
Asparagus Server, Flowers, Danish Style, Julius O. Randahl, 10 In.	525.00
Autumn Leaves, Sugar, Reed & Barton	18.00
Autumn Leaves, Teaspoon, Reed & Barton	11.00
Avalon, Cucumber Server, International	*Illus* 195.00

Avalon, Dessert Spoon, International 35.00
Avalon, Fork, International, 6 3/4 In. 30.00
Baby Spoon, Chased Line Around Edge, Arthur J. Stone, 4 1/4 In. 125.00
Bamboo, Fork, Tiffany 50.00
Bel Chateau, Salad Fork, Lunt 28.00
Botticelli, Sugar & Creamer, Whiting 20.00
Bridal Rose, Salad Set, Alvin, 9 1/8 In. 600.00
Bridal Rose, Sardine Fork, Alvin, 5 1/4 In. 150.00
Brocade, Fork, International, 7 1/4 In. 20.00
Brocade, Knife, International, 9 1/8 In. 20.00
Burgundy, Pasta Scoop, Reed & Barton 25.00
Burgundy, Salt Spoon, Reed & Barton 15.00
Burgundy, Steak Knife, Reed & Barton 30.00
Camellia, Dinner Fork, Gorham 19.00
Camellia, Luncheon Fork, Gorham 17.00
Camellia, Teaspoon, Gorham 9.00
Caribbean, Cheese Server, Wallace 22.00
Caribbean, Soup Ladle, Wallace 30.00
Carthage, Bouillon Spoon, Wallace 12.00
Carthage, Dinner Fork, Wallace 18.00
Castle Rose, Stuffing Spoon, Royal Crest 50.00
Celeste, Teaspoon, Gorham 11.00
Cellini, Sugar Spoon, Engraved, Reed & Barton 15.00
Chantilly, Cheese Scoop, Gorham, American 231.00
Chantilly, Luncheon Service For 8, Gorham, 48 Piece 632.00
Chapel Rose, Luncheon Knife, Gorham 13.00
Chateau Rose, Teaspoon, Alvin 12.00
Chippendale, Bouillon Spoon, Monogram, Gorham, 12 Piece 143.00
Chippendale, Cake Server, Reed & Barton 25.00
Chippendale, Salad Fork, Reed & Barton 25.00
Chippendale, Tablespoon, Reed & Barton 60.00
Chrysanthemum, Berry Spoon, Durgin, 9 1/2 In. 450.00
Chrysanthemum, Cracker Scoop, Durgin, 8 1/2 In. 650.00
Chrysanthemum, Serving Fork, Tiffany 330.00
Cinderella, Cream Soup Spoon, Gorham 18.00
Cinderella, Iced Tea Spoon, Gorham 18.00
Cinderella, Salad Fork, Gorham 20.00
Classic Rose, Dessert Spoon, Reed & Barton 26.00
Cluny, Knife & Fork, Gorham, Child's 143.00
Cluny, Soup Ladle, Gorham, 7 1/2 In. 505.00
Colfax, Teaspoon, Durgin 7.00
Coligni, Soup Ladle, Gold Washed Bowl, Monogram, Gorham 385.00
Colonial, Lettuce Fork, Monogram, Whiting 75.00
Colonial Fiddle, Tablespoon, Pierced, Tuttle 55.00
Colonial Manor, Cream Soup Spoon, Lunt 10.00
Columbia, Dinner Fork, Lunt 25.00
Columbia, Salad Fork, Lunt 21.00
Columbia, Teaspoon, Lunt 15.00
Commonwealth, Butter Pick, Porter Blanchard, 5 1/4 In. 65.00
Commonwealth, Butter Spreader, Porter Blanchard, 5 7/8 In. 55.00
Commonwealth, Dessert Spoon, Porter Blanchard, 6 1/2 In. 75.00
Commonwealth, Dinner Fork, Porter Blanchard, 7 1/4 In. 85.00
Commonwealth, Mustard Spoon, Porter Blanchard, 4 In. 45.00
Commonwealth, Teaspoon, Porter Blanchard, 6 In. 65.00
Continental, Gravy Ladle, Tuttle 70.00
Continental, Lemon Fork, Tuttle 15.00
Corsage, Fork, Stieff, 7 In. 20.00
Da Vinci, Teaspoon, Engraved, Reed & Barton 15.00
Damask Rose, Fork, Oneida, 7 5/8 In. 16.00
Dauphin, Serving Spoon, Durgin 550.00
Dawn Star, Place Setting, Wallace, 4 Piece 88.00
Delicacy, Spoon, Lunt 23.00
Dimension, Pickle Fork, Reed & Barton 15.00

Early American, Cold Meat Fork, Lunt	48.00
Early American, Dinner Fork, Engraved, Lunt	28.00
Early American, Gravy Ladle, Lunt	52.00
Early Colonial, Cold Meat Fork, Lunt	38.00
Early Colonial, Gravy Ladle, Lunt	41.00
Early Colonial, Sugar Spoon, Lunt	19.00
Eighteenth Century, Cream Soup Spoon, Reed & Barton	15.00
Eighteenth Century, Iced Tea Spoon, Reed & Barton	25.00
Eighteenth Century, Salad Fork, Reed & Barton	30.00
El Grandee, Sugar Spoon, Towle	18.00
El Grandee, Teaspoon, Towle	16.00
Elegante, Cold Meat Fork, Reed & Barton	35.00
Eloquence, Soup Spoon, Oval, Lunt	27.00
Empire, Pie Server, Gilt, Monogram, Whiting	170.00
Empire, Preserve Spoon, Gilt, Monogram, Whiting	95.00
Evening Rose, Place Setting, Lunt, 4 Piece	52.00
Fairfax, Iced Tea Spoon, Gorham	24.00
Fiddle, Sauce Ladle, Clemens Friedell, 6 1/2 In.	215.00
Fiddle, Serving Fork, Engraved G, George C. Erickson, 8 In.	125.00
Florence, Egg Spoon, Wallace	12.00
Florence, Salad Set, Wallace, Large	150.00
Florentine Lace, Gravy Ladle, Reed & Barton	55.00 to 60.00
Florentine Lace, Ice Cream Fork, Reed & Barton	38.00
Fontaine, Luncheon Fork, International	25.00
Fontainebleau, Soup Ladle, Gorham	440.00
Francis I, Cold Meat Fork, Reed & Barton	55.00
Francis I, Sugar Tongs, Reed & Barton	38.00
Frontenac, Dessert Spoon, Monogram, International	30.00
Frontenac, Fork, International, 7 1/8 In.	25.00
Frontenac, Salad Fork, International	65.00
Frontenac, Sugar Tongs, International	65.00
George II, Butter Spreader, Watson	14.00
Georgian Maid, Dinner Fork, International	15.00
Georgian Maid, Luncheon Fork, International	14.00
Georgian Rose, Tablespoon, Reed & Barton	55.00
Georgian Rose, Teaspoon, Reed & Barton	15.00
Grande Renaissance, Cream Soup Spoon, Reed & Barton	23.00
Grande Renaissance, Iced Tea Spoon, Reed & Barton	23.00
Grande Renaissance, Tablespoon, Pierced, Reed & Barton	60.00
Greenbriar, Butter Knife, Individual, Gorham	10.00
Heraldic, Asparagus Fork, Monogram, Whiting	475.00
Heraldic, Dessert Spoon, Monogram, Whiting	45.00
Heraldic, Fork, Monogram, Whiting, 7 1/2 In.	45.00
Honeysuckle, Mustard Ladle, Monogram, Whiting	95.00
Hunt Club, Cocktail Fork, Gorham	11.00
Imperial Chrysanthemum, Fish Serving Fork, Gorham, 8 1/2 In.	310.00
Imperial Queen, Butter Pick, Whiting	95.00
Imperial Queen, Butter Spreader, Whiting, 5 3/8 In.	30.00
Imperial Queen, Gravy Ladle, Whiting	115.00
Imperial Queen, Strawberry Fork, 2 Tines, Whiting	45.00
Irving, Teaspoon, Wallace	9.00
Ivy, Sugar Tongs, Gorham, 6 1/2 In.	135.00
Japanese, Serving Spoon, Exotic Bird, Whiting, 9 In.	415.00
Josephine, Punch Ladle, Double Lip, Monogram, Whiting	175.00
King, Fork, Dominick & Haff, 7 1/2 In.	29.00
King, Sugar Spoon, Dominick & Haff	24.00
King, Teaspoon, Dominick & Haff	32.00
King Christian, Knife, Wallace	15.00
King Christian, Salad Fork, Wallace	13.00
King Edward, Sauce Ladle, Monogram, Whiting	115.00
King Edward, Serving Spoon, Whiting	115.00
King Edward, Teaspoon, Whiting	20.00
Lafayette, Spoon, Pierced, Monogram, Towle	90.00

Lancaster, Cucumber Server, Gorham 145.00
Laureate, Soup Ladle, Whiting 200.00
Les Six Fleurs, Cream Soup Spoon, Reed & Barton 35.00
Lily, Berry Spoon, Whiting 330.00
Lily, Butter Knife, Gorham 80.00
Lily, Cold Meat Fork, Monogram, Whiting 225.00
Lily, Fork, Monogram, Whiting 72.00
Lily, Fried Oyster Server, Gorham, 7 1/8 In. 105.00
Lily, Gravy Ladle, Whiting, 7 5/8 In. ....170.00 to 180.00
Lily, Ice Cream Fork, Whiting, 5 1/8 In. 100.00
Lily, Knife, Whiting, 8 7/8 In. 60.00
Lily, Macaroni Server, Whiting, 9 3/8 In. 150.00
Lily, Pie Server, Whiting 65.00
Lily, Salad Fork, Whiting 100.00
Lily, Salad Set, Whiting, 2 Pieces 633.00
Lily, Sugar Shell Spoon, Whiting 80.00
Lily, Tablespoon, Pierced, Gorham, 8 1/2 In. 160.00
Lily, Tablespoon, Whiting, 8 1/4 In. ....120.00 to 160.00
Lily, Teaspoon, Gorham, 5 7/8 In. 43.00
Lily, Teaspoon, Monogram, Whiting, 5 3/8 In. 28.00
Lily, Teaspoon, Whiting ....20.00 to 47.00
Lily, Wedding Cake Knife, Gorham, 12 1/2 In. 140.00
Lily Of The Valley, Dinner Fork, Whiting, 8 1/4 In. 100.00
Lily Of The Valley, Fish Fork, Whiting, 7 In. 170.00
Lily Of The Valley, Soup Spoon, Whiting, 5 1/8 In. 80.00
Lily Of The Valley, Teaspoon, Whiting 45.00
Louis XIV, Old Style, Asparagus Server, Bigelow, Kennard, 9 3/8 In. ... 258.00
Louis XV, Cucumber Server, Whiting 149.00
Love Disarmed, Cake Slice, Reed & Barton 103.00
Love Disarmed, Salad Serving Set, Parcel Gilt, Reed & Barton, 2 Piece .. 1210.00
Lyric, Sugar Spoon, Gorham 13.00
Madam Jumel, Cold Meat Fork, Monogram, Whiting 55.00
Madam Jumel, Salad Fork, Monogram, Whiting 25.00
Madrigal, Cake Server, Lunt 40.00
Madrigal, Tablespoon, Pierced, Lunt 58.00
Maryland, Soup Spoon, Gorham, 6 1/2 In., 6 Piece 99.00
Meadow, Punch Ladle, Curved Handle, Wildflowers, Gorham, 13 In. ... 220.00
Meadow Song, Place Setting, Towle, 4 Piece 64.00
Meadow Song, Sugar Spoon, Towle 16.00
Medallion, Jug, Milk, 4 Medallions, Foliate Thumbpiece, Gorham, 1895 .. 175.00
Narcissus, Berry Spoon, Gilt Bowl, Unger, 9 1/4 In. 350.00
Old Baronial, Serving Spoon, Engraved Crest, Gorham 165.00
Old Colonial, Cream Ladle, Towle, 5 3/4 In. 95.00
Old English, Punch Ladle, Dominick & Haff, 1913, 12 In. 335.00
Old English, Salt Spoon, Hyams & Hyams, London, 1874, Pair 155.00
Old Newbury, Butter Spreader, Flat Handle, Towle 25.00
Old Newbury, Cheese Knife, Stainless Steel Blade, Towle 38.00
Old Newbury, Cocktail Fork, Towle 17.00
Old Newbury, Fork, Towle 50.00
Old Newbury, Iced Tea Spoon, Towle 45.00
Old Newbury, Salad Fork, Towle 44.00
Old Newbury, Soup Spoon, Towle 42.00
Old Newbury, Sugar Tongs, Towle 35.00
Old Newbury, Teaspoon, Towle 20.00
Oval Twist, Butter Knife, Master, Whiting 50.00
Oval Twist, Cream Ladle, Whiting 60.00
Oval Twist, Sugar Tongs, Whiting 55.00
Paramount, Sugar Spoon, Kirk 18.00
Paris, Fish Serving Fork, Gorham, 8 3/8 In. 375.00
Prelude, Cream Soup Spoon, International 20.00
Prelude, Fork, Child's, International 17.00
Prelude, Gravy Ladle, International 40.00
Prelude, Teaspoon, International 12.00

Princess Ingrid, Carving Fork, Stainless Prongs, Whiting, 11 5/8 In. 60.00
Princess Ingrid, Carving Set, Whiting, 2 Piece 120.00
Princess Ingrid, Demitasse Spoon, Whiting, 4 1/4 In. 22.00
Princess Ingrid, Iced Tea Spoon, Whiting, 7 3/8 In. 36.00
Princess Ingrid, Poultry Shears, Whiting, 11 1/2 In. ....140.00 to 160.00
Princess Ingrid, Soup Spoon, Whiting, 6 1/4 In. 36.00
Princess Ingrid, Teaspoon, Whiting 24.00
Princess Mary, Dinner Fork, Wallace 20.00
Processional, Butter, Master, International 12.00
Processional, Cream Soup Spoon, International 15.00
Queen's Lace, Lemon Fork, International 17.00
Queen's Lace, Teaspoon, International 10.00
Quintessence, Dinner Fork, Lunt 29.00
Quintessence, Fish Serving Fork, Lunt 44.00
Raphael, Butter Knife, Master, Alvin, 7 1/4 In. 285.00
Raphael, Lettuce Fork, Alvin, 8 7/8 In. 595.00
Raphael, Sugar Spoon, Alvin 195.00
Regent, Serving Fork, Durgin 275.00
Renaissance, Serving Fork, Tiffany 468.00
Repousse, Butter Knife, S. Kirk & Sons, 2 Piece 46.00
Repousse, Carving Set, Bailey Banks & Biddle, 5 Piece 286.00
Revere, Croquette Spoon, International 185.00
Rhythm, Dinner Fork, Wallace 18.00
Rhythm, Teaspoon, Wallace 9.00
Rococo, Fork, Dominick & Haff, 6 3/4 In. 18.00
Rococo, Fork, Dominick & Haff, 7 1/2 In. 25.00
Rococo, Ice Cream Slice, Bigelow, Kennard & Co., 12 1/4 In. 316.00
Rose, Baby Fork, Stieff 21.00
Rose, Fruit Spoon, Stieff 21.00
Rose, Jelly Server, Stieff 20.00
Rose, Luncheon Knife, Wallace 20.00
Rose, Sugar Spoon, Stieff 19.00
Rose Point, Butter Knife, Hollow Handle, Wallace 15.00
Rose Point, Place Knife, Wallace 20.00
Rouen, Serving Spoon, Gorham 315.00
Royal Danish, Cocktail Fork, International 15.00
Royal Danish, Fork, International, 7 1/8 In. 20.00
Royal Danish, Sugar Spoon, International 20.00
Sculptured Rose, Sugar Spoon, Towle 11.00
St. Cloud, Punch Ladle, Broad Shell Handle, Gorham, 1885, 13 1/2 In. 655.00
Stardust, Teaspoon, Gorham 13.00
Symphony, Chased, Tablespoon, Towle 26.00
Trianon, Berry Spoon, International, 8 5/8 In. 100.00
Trianon, Candlesnuffer, International 60.00
Trianon, Cocktail Fork, International 30.00
Trianon, Cold Meat Fork, International, 1921, 8 3/4 In. 65.00
Trianon, Ice Cream Scoop, Tuttle 25.00
Versailles, Ladle, Floral Sprays, Scrolls, Gorham, 4 In. 575.00
Villa Norfolk, Tomato Server, Gorham 125.00
Violet, Butter Knife, Master, Whiting 50.00
Violet, Gravy Ladle, Monogram, Whiting 160.00
Virginia Carvel, Bouillon Spoon, Towle 13.00
Virginia Carvel, Salad Fork, Towle 23.00
Virginia Carvel, Teaspoon, Towle 10.00
Wild Rose, Place Setting, International, 4 Piece 112.00

SILVER PLATE is not solid silver. It is a ware made of a metal, such as
nickel or copper, that is covered with a thin coating of silver. The letters *EPNS* are often found on American and English silver-plated
wares. Sheffield is a term with two meanings. Sometimes it refers to
sterling silver made in the town of Sheffield, England. In this section,
Sheffield refers to a type of silver plate, usually English.

 Basket, Ruby Glass Liner, Swing Handle, Scroll & Floral Feet, Victorian, 5 In. 85.00

Basket, Sweetmeat, Openwork Sides, Hats & Flowers On Front, 7 1/8 In. 175.00
Biscuit Barrel, Staves Pattern, Frosted, c.1900, 7 x 5 1/2 In. 75.00
Biscuit Box, Cover, Hinged, Geometric, Vintage Etched Border, 7 x 8 In. 185.00
Bowl, Center, Chased, Repousse Edge, Floral Design, International Silver Co., 2 In. 40.00
Bowl, Montieth, Drop Ring Handles, England, 14 1/2 In. 1725.00
Bowl, Nut, Oak Leaf Bottom, Twig Form Handle & Legs, Meriden Brittania Co......... 345.00
Bowl, Nut, Squirrel On Side, Victorian 155.00
Bowl, Overall Ribbed Body, Ram's Head, Loose Ring Handles, Oval, 8 1/2 In. 604.00
Bowl, Presentation, Stylized Cast Handles, Spreading Circular Foot, 13 In. 201.00
Bowl, Vegetable, Cover, C-Scroll & Leaf Border, Rectangular, Stamped 16, 11 x 9 In. 130.00
Bowl, Vegetable, Cover, Gadroon Borders, Shell & Leaf, Removable Handle, 12 x 9 In. .. 95.00
Bowl, Vegetable, Cover, Pineapple Finial On Cover, Circular, 1880, Pair 5750.00
Box, Letter, Flowers, Leather, Bombe Cover, Plated Openwork, 11 1/4 x 9 1/4 In. 747.00
Bread Basket, Embossed Flowers & Acanthus Leaves, Swing Handle 195.00
Bun Warmer, Chased Flowers, Beaded Rim, Lineer & Maazzarine, 12 1/2 In. 315.00
Bun Warmer, Cover Chased With Flowers, 4 Paw Feet, Elkington & Co., 13 In. 431.00
Butter, Egg-&-Dart Border, Goat Finial, Lion Masks Handles, 6 In. 690.00
Butter, Triple Plate, Domed Lid, Rockford, Racine S.P. Co., Victorian 175.00
Cake Basket, Georgian Style, Gadroon Edge, England, Late 19th Century, 10 In. 88.00
Candelabrum is listed in its own category.
Candlesticks are listed in their own category.
Centerpiece, Art Nouveau Woman, Standing On Ball, Vines, Victorian, Vienna 1800.00
Centerpiece, Undulating Rim, Inscribed, Joseph Heinrichs, 13 x 7 3/4 In. 44.00
Chafing Dish, Art Deco, Lurelle Guild, International Silver, c.1930 .... 1200.00
Chafing Dish, Staghorn Handles, 3-Leg Frame, Empress New York, 1895, 12 In........ 28.00
Cigar Cutter, Horse Head Form, 5 3/4 In. 143.00
Cigar Holder, 3 Hexagonal Cups, 6 Holes Each, Sheffield, 19th Century, 9 In. 115.00
Cocktail Shaker, Milk Pail Shape, Reed & Barton, 10 In. 100.00
Coffee & Tea Set, Footed Tray, Towle, 7 Piece 355.00
Coffee Set, Dirilyte, Open Sugar, 3 Piece 575.00
Coffee Set, Footed, Ornate Curved Handle, Sheets, R.S. Co., 7 Piece 110.00
Coffee Urn, Ornate Floral & C-Scroll, Eagle Head Spout, Claw Footed, 21 In. 495.00
Compote, Mayflower Plaque, Floral, Rope Border, 4-Footed, 1885, 8 1/4 x 3 In. 245.00
Compote, Oval, Reticulated, Swag & Floral Design, Ellis Barker, 4 x 13 x 10 In. 275.00
Cover, Meat, Acanthus Handle, Sheffield, 18 1/2 In. 255.00
Cup, Demon Mask Handles, Circular, Meriden Britannia Co., 6 1/4 In. 35.00
Desk Set, Floral, Birds, 4 Hinged Sections, Candle Socket, Rogers Smith, 8 x 11 In. 495.00
Dish, Cover, Entree, Beaded Rim, Beaded Band, 2 Scroll Handles, With Liner, Pair 345.00
Dish, Entree, Gadrooned Rim, Shell, Leaves At Intervals, Scroll Handle, 11 In., Pair 690.00
Dish, Entree, Lid, Warming Compartment, Sheffield, 1825-1850, 9 x 13 1/2 In. 195.00
Dish, Entree, Warming Compartments, Removable Trays, Sheffield, 8 x 15 In., Pair 195.00
Dish Cross, Georgian Style, Pierced Stylized Shell Supports, England, 12 1/2 In. 385.00
Dish Cross, Stylized Flower Form Feet, 19th Century, 13 1/2 In., Pair 143.00
Egg Set, 4 Cups, Footed Holder, Handle, England 140.00
Epergne, Birds & Flowers, Original Silk Lined Wooden Case, 1910, 11 1/2 In. 112.00
Epergne, Egyptian Revival, Sphinxes, Cut Glass Vase, Frosted, England, 21 In. 1980.00
Epergne, Foliate, Rose Base, 4 Scrolled Arms, Early 20th Century, 15 In............. 1870.00
Epergne, Lyre Form, Oval Wirework Base, Early 20th Century, 17 3/4 In. 1265.00
Fish Serving Knife & Fork, Bull Rush Design, Fitted Case, Christofle & Cie, France 165.00
Fish Serving Set, Reeded Ivory Handles, Fitted Satin Lined Case, 13 3/4-In. Knife 431.00
Flower Holder, Cupid, Holding Crystal Vase, Frolicking Cupids, Meriden, 8 In. 245.00
Frame, Repousse, Dragons, Berry & Leaf Border, 11 1/2 x 8 3/4 In. 145.00
Hot Water Dish, Detachable Cover, Ivory Handle, Round, England, c.1860, 7 In. 63.00
Hot Water Urn, Burner, Lid, Wooden Finial, Knob, International Silver Co., 18 In. 140.00
Hot Water Urn, Domed Cover, Ivory Pineapple Finial, Ring Handles, 22 In. 2587.00
Hot Water Urn, Lamp, Meridian Britannia, 19 In. 845.00
Hot Water Urn, Quadripartite Base, 4 Wooden Ball Feet, 2 Loop Handles, 21 In. 690.00
Jardiniere, Leaves, Flower Heads, 2 Detachable Liners, Cardeillac, 15 In., Pair 6900.00
Jug, Milk, Egyptian Style Handle, 8 1/2 In. 65.00
Kettle, Stand, Chased Hinged Cover, Floral & Leaf On Body, 11 1/2 In. 85.00
Lamp, Candlestick, 2 Curved Arms 745.00
Lazy Susan, Cover, 6 Compartments, Glass Liners, Scrolled Leaves, Flowers, 19 1/2 In. .. 110.00
Liquor Set, 3 Cut Glass Decanters, Beaded Edge Tray, Chased Swags, French Feet 525.00

Martini Shaker, Rangely Lakes, Maine, C.C.B. Co. Tournament, 1929, 15 In. 300.00
Mirror Plateau, Scrolls, Flowers & Acanthus, Reed & Barton, 14 In. 400.00
Mirror Plateau, Shaped Oval, Scrolls, Shells, Garlands, France, 24 1/2 In. 1725.00
Napkin Rings are listed in their own category.
Perpetual Fountain, Rotating Spheres, Cranberry Glass Bowl, J.W. Tufts, 20 In. 5500.00
Pitcher, Band Of Anthemion Trim, 20th Century, 7 3/4 In. 30.00
Pitcher, Chased Design, Ice Lip, Anston, 7 1/2 In. 130.00
Pitcher, Water, May 1890, 2 Drilled Holes In Base, 11 In. 55.00
Pitcher, Water, Raised Floral Design, Meriden & Co. 82.50
Pitcher, Water, Tilter Type, Eastlake, 1880s, 18 In. 410.00
Plaque, Goddess On Chaise, Attendants, 3-D, Electroplated, Elkington, 19 1/2 In. 880.00
Plate, C-Scroll, Birds, Floral Garlands, Baskets, 6 1/2 In., Set Of 4 . . . . 45.00
Plate, Serpentine Edge, Foliate Center Border, Continental, 13 In., 12 Piece 805.00
Plateau, Ornate, Foliate Scrolled Frame, 4 Cast Female Heads, 1900, 4 x 17 In. 1437.00
Platter, Well & Tree, Grapevine At Interval Border, Oval, 29 In. 172.00
Punch Bowl, Double Lip Ladle, Scrolling Leaves & Flowers, Rogers, 2 Piece 175.00
Punch Bowl, Floral Foliate Scrolling, 4 Cartouches, 14 3/4 In. 430.00
Punch Bowl, Ladle, Putti Playing Instrument, Glass Liner, Figural Finial, 25 In. 1510.00
Punch Bowl, Rococo Revival Style, Chased & Repousse Flowers, 14 3/4 In. 415.00
Punch Set, Bowl, Tray, 12 Cups, Ladle, Vintage, 9 x 13 In., 15 Piece 330.00
Reliquary, 6 Rotary Compartments, Repousse, Animals, Flowers, Round, 15 In. 260.00
Salt & Pepper, Victorian Style, Kingsway Silver Plate From England 95.00
Salt Cellar, Boat Shape, Snakes, Serpent Handles, Well On Pedestal, 4 x 6 In. 220.00
Salt Cellar, Cranberry Glass Liner, Pierced Sides, Ball Feet, c.1890, 1 1/2 In., Pair 90.00
Salver, Round, Geometric & Floral Border, Quadruple Plate, Pairpoint, 10 3/8 In. 10.00
Samovar, Fluted Body, Circular Base, Wooden Handles, Vase Form, 20 In 460.00
Samovar, Inverted Pear Shape, Lobed Body, 4-Footed, Wooden Handles, Russia, 16 In. . . 750.00
Sauceboat, Double Lipped, Graceful Loop Handles On Side, France, 5 1/2 In. 330.00
Sauceboat, Floral Rococo Design, 9 x 5 1/4 In. 55.00
Server, Domed, Double Hinged Lid, Beaded Edge, Loop Handle, 4-Footed Stand, 10 In. . . 275.00
Serving Dish, Revolving, Dome, Engraved Fern Wreaths, England, 14 1/2 In. 260.00
Silent Butler, Copper, Hammered, Monogram, Dirk Van Erp, 11 x 7 1/2 In. 495.00
Spoon, Souvenir, see Souvenir category.
Spoon Warmer, Bright Cut Design, c.1870, 4 1/2 x 6 1/2 In. 450.00
Sugar & Creamer, Engraved Leaves, Scroll Handles, Sheffield, 4 3/4 In. 50.00
Tazza, Secessionist Pattern Base, Floriform Glass Plate, WMF, c.1905, 12 In. 275.00
Tea & Coffee Set, Acorn Finials, Leafy Spouts, Footed Tray, Wallace, 5 Piece 230.00
Tea & Coffee Set, Ivory Handles, Gadrooned Lower Half, Germany, 6 Piece 880.00
Tea & Coffee Set, Meriden Britannia Co., 4 Piece 77.00
Tea & Coffee Set, Rococo Style, Gadrooned Body, Reed & Barton, 1938, 6 Piece 690.00
Tea Service, Paneled Shape, Squared Ebony Handles, Chase Floral, Wallace, England . . . 65.00
Tea Urn, Canted Corners, 4 Scroll Feet, 2 Scroll Handles, 16 In. 776.00
Tea Urn, Cover, Paneled Spout, 2 Circular Pendant Handles, 16 3/4 In. 402.00
Tea Urn, Engraved Flowers, Shoulder Reeded Band, Loop Handles, 18 1/2 In. 460.00
Tea Urn, Finial Cover, Sheffield . . . .*Illus* 1400.00
Tea Urn, Interior Heating Element, Scroll Crest, Mappin & Webb, 19 In. 522.00
Tea Urn, Vase Shape, Square Base, 4 Ball Feet, C-Scroll Handles, 15 In. 190.00

Be sure to rinse a piece of silver until all of the polish is removed. If some remains in the crevices, it will continue to react and may lead to corrosion. A toothpick or toothbrush will help you get the polish out of crevices.

Silver Plate, Tea Urn,
Finial Cover, Sheffield

Teakettle, Stand, With Burner, Repousse Dragon, Oriental, 20th Century, 14 In. 460.00
Teapot, Dimension, Reed & Barton, c.1960, 6 1/2 x 10 In. 225.00
Teapot, Neoclassical, Engraved, Ivory Trim, England, 6 In. 190.00
Teapot, Reeded, Paneled, Ebony Finial & Handle, Inserted Burner, 15 1/2 In. 165.00
Teapot, Repousse Dragon, Bamboo Style Handle, Canton, Early 20th Century 230.00
Teapot, Ribbed, Fruit Finial, Philip Ashberry & Sons, 8 In. 190.00
Teapot, Tilting, Stand, James W. Tufts, Victorian, 12 1/2 In. 50.00
Teapot, Warming Stand, Classical, Caned Handle, Beaded Edges, Sheffield, 15 In. 165.00
Teaspoon Caddy, Handle Bell Ringer, Rogers Bros., Victorian, 12 In. 146.00
Tray, Applied Grapevine At Intervals, 2 Handles, Rectangular, 29 In. 431.00
Tray, Border, Sheffield, W & H Set In Flag, K 52304 A1, 10 In. 95.00
Tray, Chased Floral Design, Grapevine Border, Handles, Rectangular, 14 3/4 In. 143.00
Tray, Chased With Lotus Flowers, Gadrooned Rim, Circular, 19 1/2 In. 103.00
Tray, Engraved Scrolls, Engraved Flowers & Leaves, Vacant Cartouche, 25 1/2 In. 1035.00
Tray, Floral, Leaf & Thistle, Pierced Lip, Avian, Floral & Acorn, 18 1/4 x 25 In. 575.00
Tray, Gadroon Border, Floral, Copper, Octagonal, England, 29 1/2 x 18 In. 715.00
Tray, Gallery, Engraved Leaf, 4 Scroll Feet, Sheffield, 24 x 18 In. 500.00
Tray, Gallery, Pierced Rows Of Geometric Design, Cased Border, 4 x 24 x 17 In. 546.00
Tray, Ornate Scroll Design, Deer & Hunting Dog, Egg-&-Dart Border, Oval, 30 In. 410.00
Tray, Pierced Gallery, Open Handles, Griffins Within Leaf Border, 24 x 18 In. 605.00
Tray, Plain Rim, 2 Bifurcated Handles, Monogram, England, 25 1/2 In. 175.00
Tray, Raised Grape & Leaf Border, Scroll & Floral Engraving, 28 In. 275.00
Tray, Reticulated Rim, Monogram, England, 24 3/4 In. 410.00
Tray, Rococo, Footed, 1900, 28 1/2 x 19 3/4 In. 30.00
Tray, Scroll, Seashell Design, 2 Handles, Oval, 20 3/4 x 13 1/2 In. 46.00
Tray, Serving, 2 Handles, Scroll & Floral Engraving, England, 30 In. 385.00
Tray, Serving, Chased Floral & Scroll Center, Reeded Edges, Ornate Loop Handles 880.00
Tray, Serving, Georgian Style, Ellis-Barker Silver Co., England, 18 x 30 In. 305.00
Tray, Serving, Serpentine Pierced Gallery, Acanthus Handles, 6 x 31 1/2 In. 632.00
Tray, Shell Floral & Foliate, Center Vacant Cartouche, Handles, 26 1/2 In. 125.00
Trophy Cup, Scroll, Leaves Chasing, Camel-Form Handles, Silva, Sheffield, 9 3/4 In. 173.00
Tureen, Cover, Cast Spear Finial, C-Scroll Legs, Late 19th Century, 22 x 18 In. 1650.00
Tureen, Domed Cover, C-Scroll Legs Lower Part, Fitted Sheet Iron Liner, 21 In. 1540.00
Tyg, Stylized Lilies, Swirling Flowers, 3 Handles, E.G. Webster & Son, 1900, 12 In. 805.00
Urn, Anthemion Leaf & Grape Cluster, Spigot, Burner, Late 19th Century, 17 In. 355.00
Urn, Cover, Georgian Style, Cobalt Glass Liner, Ellis Barker, England, 10 In., Pair 1265.00
Vase, Bottle Form, Aquatic Flowers, 2 Mermaids, Lobster, Snail, 1900, 23 In. 1725.00
Waiter, Applied Vintage Design, Pierced Border, 29 In. 66.00
Wine Chariot, c.1860, 8 x 14 In. 1695.00
Wine Coaster, Gadrooned Rim, Turned Wooden Bottom, 2 x 6 1/4 In., Pair 247.00
Wine Coaster, Reticulated, Mahogany Base, Early 20th Century, 5 1/2 In., 3 Piece 250.00
Wine Coaster, Scrolled Leaf Design, Treen Interior, Sheffield, c.1825, 7 1/4 In. 290.00
Wine Cooler, Fluted Campana Form, Foliate Shell Handles, 6 1/2 In. 230.00
Wine Cooler, Upright Acanthus Cast Handles, Sheffield Silver Co., 9 x 8 In., Pair 546.00

SILVER, SHEFFIELD, see Silver Plate; Silver-English categories.

SILVER-AMERICAN. American silver is listed here. Coin and sterling silver are included. Most of the sterling silver listed in this book is subdivided by country. There are also other pieces of silver and silver plate listed under special categories, such as Candelabrum, Napkin Ring, Silver Flatware, Silver Plate, Silver-Sterling, and Tiffany Silver. For information about makers and marks, see *Kovels' American Silver Marks: 1650 to the Present.*

SILVER-AMERICAN, Basket, Art Deco, Hand Hammered, Wallace, 1910, 6 x 9 1/2 In. 850.00
Basket, Piecrust & Pierced Rim, Henckle, Fixed Handle, 10 3/4 In. 110.00
Basket, Pinched Sides, Parrots On Wirework Handle, Gorham, 1872, 10 In. 1495.00
Basket, Serving, Repousse, Floral Repousse, Jenkins & Jenkins, 13 In. 805.00
Basket, Sweetmeat, Scalloped Top, Hinged Handle, George III, 1815, 4 x 6 In. 1100.00
Beaker, Flared Lip, Bowed Tapering Sides, Paul Revere Jr., 1800, 3 3/4 In. 8050.00
Beaker, Hunters On Horses, Chasing Stags, c.1880-1900, 5 1/2 In. 330.00
Beaker, Molded Rims, Coin, Anthony Rasch, Pa., 1807, 3 x 3 In. 488.00
Beaker, W. Thompson, c.1831, 5 3/4 In. 785.00

Bowl, 3 Floral Sprays, Hammered, Watsoncraft, 10 3/4 In.	275.00
Bowl, 4-Sided Flower Shape, Rolled Rim, Hammered, Randahl, 7 In.	195.00
Bowl, 5 Petals, Inverted Rim, Presentation Inscription, Kalo, Round, 9 In.	405.00
Bowl, 7-Sided Rolled Rim, Flared Footed Base, Hammered, Kalo, 9 In.	345.00
Bowl, Applied Ivy Leaves, Scroll Rim, Oval, International Silver Co., 10 5/8 In.	230.00
Bowl, Arts & Crafts, Karl F. Leinonen, 1 3/4 x 5 3/4 In.	350.00
Bowl, Beaded Rim, Gilt Interior, Whiting, 8 1/4 In.	115.00
Bowl, Bucket Shape, Allover Repousse, Flowers, Jacobi & Jenkins, 3 3/4 In.	260.00
Bowl, Center, Quilt Style Pattern, Monogram, Frank W. Smith Co., 14 In.	1840.00
Bowl, Centerpiece, Shaped Floral Rim, Whiting Co., 2 3/4 x 10 1/2 In.	220.00
Bowl, Central Tooled Flower, Dot, Line Border, Circular, Herbert A. Taylor, 8 In.	1150.00
Bowl, Chased Foliate, Arthur Stone, 2 x 4 1/4 In.	1150.00
Bowl, Chased With Foliate Garlands, 2 Angular Handles, Coin, 1810, 7 1/4 In.	488.00
Bowl, Cover, Band Of Stylized Leaves, Leaf Tips, Osmon Reed, c.1840, 7 In.	287.00
Bowl, Flared Rim, Hoof Feet, Baldwin, Miller Co., 8 1/4 In.	200.00
Bowl, Flared, Flutes, Arts & Crafts, James T. Woolley, 2 1/4 x 4 1/2 In.	325.00
Bowl, Flared, Rolled Rim, Stepped Base, Signed, Arthur Stone, c.1935, 6 3/8 In.	402.00
Bowl, Flower Repousse, 4 Foliate Feet, S. Kirk & Son, 6 1/2 In.	1725.00
Bowl, Flower Shape, 5 Petal Panels, Hammered, Kalo Shop, 7 In.	405.00
Bowl, Flower Shape, 5 Petal Panels, Scalloped Rim, Katherine Pratt, 4 In.	200.00
Bowl, Fluted, Scalloped Rim, Hammered, Arts & Crafts, Gyllenberg, 2 1/4 In.	450.00
Bowl, Footed, Francis I, Reed & Barton, 8 In.	250.00
Bowl, Fruit, Chrysanthemums, Daisies, Dominick & Haff, 12 1/2 In.	1150.00
Bowl, Fruit, Poppy Blossom Form, 4 Petals, Hammered, Fiedell, 12 3/4 In.	2688.00
Bowl, Fruit, Stylized Leaves & Berries, Randahl Sterling, 9 In., Pair	190.00
Bowl, Hammered Finish, Flared Rim, Engraved Initials, Gyllenberg, 6 In.	145.00
Bowl, Hammered Surface, Notched Intervals, Katherine Pratt, 5 3/4 In.	287.00
Bowl, Hammered, Band Of Turquoise, White Grapevine, Mary Knight, 4 Oz.	4025.00
Bowl, Hammered, Flared, Footed, Kalo, 4 1/2 In.	440.00
Bowl, Leaf Spray, Reeded Edge, Monogram, The Sweetser Co., 10 In.	230.00
Bowl, Lobed Interior, Center Foliage, Durgin, 14 1/4 In.	385.00
Bowl, Lobed Rectangular, Paw Footed, Gorham, 12 In.	185.00
Bowl, Lobed Sides, Foliate Scrolls & Buds, Frank Smith, 20th Century, 16 In.	863.00
Bowl, Marie Antoinette, Repousse Border, Garlands, Bellflowers, Gorham, 10 In.	275.00
Bowl, Pierced & Chased Foliate, Arthur Stone, 12 In.	546.00
Bowl, Repousse Rim, Monogram MBS, S. Kirk & Son, 11 In., Pair	1210.00
Bowl, Repousse, Flowers, Leaves, Round Foot, Jacobi & Jenkins, 9 In.	2185.00
Bowl, Reticulated Floral Rim, Chester Billings & Co., 11 x 4 1/2 In.	605.00
Bowl, Reticulated, Chased, Footed, Whiting, 9 In.	495.00
Bowl, Revere, Impressed Wallace Sterling B405, 6 In.	45.00
Bowl, Ribbed Sides, Escalopped Rim, Whiting Mfg. Co., 3 1/2 In., Pair	2585.00
Bowl, Ribbed, Oval, 4 Claw Feet, Reed & Barton, 13 x 9 In.	355.00
Bowl, Scroll Design, Scalloped Border, Gorham, 8 1/4 In.	550.00
Bowl, Swan Shape, Gorham, 8 In.	330.00
Bowl, Vegetable, Cover, Engraved C-Scrolls, Reed & Barton, 4 x 10 1/2 In.	355.00
Bowl, Vegetable, Shallow Cover, Flat Leaf Handle, Monogram, Gorham, 11 In.	575.00
Bowl, Wide Band Of Swags & Scrolls, Foliate Scroll Feet, Whiting, 11 3/4 In.	1980.00
Box, Apple Shape, Cover, Arts & Crafts, 1 3/4 In.	175.00
Box, Cigar, Hinged Cover, Cedar Lining, Humidor Fitting, Kalo Shop, 55 Oz.	1725.00
Box, Cigar, Inscribed, Treen Interior, 3 Sections, Andrew A. Taylor, 9 x 6 In.	175.00
Box, Desk, Copper & Gold Inlay, 3 Hot Air Balloons, Cartier, Round, 2 1/4 In.	990.00
Box, Trinket, Napoleon & Josephine As Romans, Whiting, c.1890, 2 x 3 In.	715.00
Bread Basket, Oval, Fluted, Reeded Rim, Gorham, Bigelow, Kennard & Co., 12 In.	160.00
Bread Tray, Raised Floral Design, Gorham, 15 In.	360.00
Bread Tray, Repousse Border, Leaves, Flowers, Jacobi & Jenkins, Oval, 10 In.	345.00
Brush & Mirror, Beaded Edge, Scrolled Monogram, International, 9 1/2 In.	44.00
Butter, Hammered, Fluted Edge, Arts & Crafts, Porter Blanchard, 6 In.	235.00
Butter, Raised Border, Round, Arts & Crafts, Theodore Hanford Pond, 6 In.	395.00
Butter, Scallop Shell Shape, 3 Ball Feet, Early 20th Century, 7 In.	250.00
Butter Knife, Cast Recumbent Cow, Foliate Scroll, Ball, Black & Co., 8 In., Pair	1725.00
Butter Knife, Engraved Monogram, Arthur J. Stone, c.1913, 7 1/8 In., 6 Piece	350.00
Butter Knife, Monogram E, Arthur J. Stone, 6 3/8 In.	85.00
Butter Spreader, Hammered, Lebolt & Co., 5 3/4 In.	375.00

Caddy Spoon, Stone Associates Mark, Arthur J. Stone 125.00
Cake Basket, Reticulated, Swing Handle, Reeded Rim, Gorham, 1908, 12 In. 373.00
Cake Server, Harbor Scene On Blade, Engine Turned Ground, Coin, 9 In. 201.00
Candelabrum is listed in its own category.
Candlesnuffer, Arts & Crafts, Randahl Of Chicago 143.00
Candlesticks are listed in their own category.
Candy Dish, Hammered, Trumpet Base, Kalo Shop, 5 3/4 x 5 1/2 In. 990.00
Card Box, Thai Design, Cover, 5 1/4 x 4 1/4 In. 66.00
Card Case, Garden Fountain, H.L.Webster & Company, 1800s, 2 1/2 x 3 1/2 In. 202.00
Card Case, Monogram Medallion, Leaves, Whiting, Fitted Box, 3 3/4 In. 200.00
Card Case, Scrolled Leafy Sprays, Wood & Hughes, c.1850, 3 1/2 x 2 1/2 In. 94.00
Carving Set, Applied Gothic Monogram, Shreve & Co., 2 Piece 195.00
Carving Set, Art Deco, Richard Blanchard, 2 Piece 295.00
Carving Set, Monogram, R. Wallace, 3 Piece 11.00
Child's Set, Hammered, Frank W Smith Silver Co., 3 3/4 In., 3 Piece 225.00
Cider Strainer, Star, Coin, 18th Century, 1.5 Oz. 330.00
Cigar Lighter, Handle, Thomas Bradbury & Sons, 1885, 2 1/2 x 5 x 3 In. 880.00
Cigarette Case, Caddy Carrying Bag Of Clubs, Unger Bros., c.1900, 3 1/4 In. 775.00
Cocktail Shaker, Threaded Rims & Borders, Crighton & Co., 10 1/4 In. 545.00
Coffee & Tea Set, Creamer, Gold Interior, Dunkirk Silversmiths Inc., 5 Piece 920.00
Coffee & Tea Set, Globular, Leaves, Arts & Crafts, Arthur J. Stone, 7 Piece 17000.00
Coffee & Tea Set, Oval Form, Flowers, Repousse, Engraving, R & W Wilson, Phila. 6050.00
Coffee & Tea Set, Plymouth Pattern, Gorham, 6 Piece 2200.00
Coffee & Tea Set, Repousse, S. Kirk, 5 Piece 5775.00
Coffee & Tea Set, Repousse, Whitney, 5 Piece 3300.00
Coffee Set, Classic, Monogram, Arts & Crafts, Arthur J. Stone, 3 Piece 3200.00
Coffee Set, Contour Pattern, Plastic Tray, With Silver Rim, Towle, 4 Piece 1650.00
Coffee Set, Demitasse, Georgian Style, International Silver Co., 4 Piece 220.00
Coffee Set, Hand Hammered Surface, Monogram, Arts & Crafts, 4 Piece 632.00
Coffee Set, Monogram, Arts & Crafts, Lebolt & Co., 4 Piece 2700.00
Coffee Set, Nesting, 2 Angled Wooden Handles, Lebkuecher & Co., 3 Piece 375.00
Coffee Set, Revival, Angular Handles, Gorham, 18 1/2-In. Coffeepot, 7 Piece 9200.00
Coffee Set, Ribbed, Ebony Handle, Arts & Crafts, Whiting Mfg. Co., 3 Piece 2100.00
Coffeepot, Embossed, Flowers, Serpentine Handle, Frank W. Smith, 9 In. 402.00
Coffeepot, Engraved Name & Date, Oval Reserves, G. Sharp, 1860, 12 1/2 In. 825.00
Coffeepot, Floral Domed Cover, Exotic Chinoiserie Hillside Village, 14 In. 3105.00
Coffeepot, Monogram, Lincoln & Reed, Boston, 1845, 11 1/2 In. 468.00
Coffeepot, Repousse Floral Pattern, S. Kirk & Son, 8 In. 900.00
Coffeepot, Repousse Flowers On Lower Half, S. Kirk & Son, 8 In. 900.00
Coffeepot, Urn Shape, Fluted, Joseph Richardson Jr. 8960.00
Compote, Circular Stem & Foot, Kalo, 5 In. 287.00
Compote, Classical Man Holding Grapes, Bigelow, Kennard & Co., 4 In. 690.00
Compote, Diamond, Applied Scroll Rim, Black, Starr & Frost, 7 3/4 In., Pair 690.00
Compote, Everted Chased Rim, Leaf Center, Dominick & Haff, 12 In. 880.00
Compote, Flat Top, Pierced Floral Rims, Howard & Co., 1930, 3 1/4 In., Pair 700.00
Compote, Flower & Leaf Repousse, Shaped Foot, S. Kirk & Son, 9 In. 545.00
Compote, Footed, Francis I, Reed & Barton, 11 In. 855.00
Compote, Footed, H. Lewis, Phila., Coin, 1820, 6 x 7 1/4 In. 605.00
Compote, Georg Jensen Style, Conical Bowl, Stylized Flowers, Leaves, 6 In. 275.00
Compote, Hammered Stem & Foot, Kalo, Signed, 4 1/4 In. 315.00
Compote, Repousse Floral & Leaf, Footed, S. Kirk & Son, 4 1/4 x 11 1/2 In. 825.00
Compote, Rose Design, Lunt, 5 1/2 In., Pair 45.00
Cordial, Flowers & Leaves, Monogram Cartouche, Baldwin, Miller, 12 Piece 150.00
Creamer, Antique, Wallace, 1926, 5 In. 190.00
Creamer, Applied Decoration, Monogram, Marked, Coin, 1821, 7 In. 358.00
Creamer, Engraved Wreath, Ribbon, Initials, C.G., 4 1/2 In. 660.00
Creamer, Helmet Form, Beaded Edge, Strap Handle, J. Shoemaker, c.1800 .... 1430.00
Creamer, Monogram In Laurel Wreath, Robert Fairchild, c.1790 .... 160.00
Creamer, Pear Shape, Lyre Handle, Scroll Feet, Ball, Black & Co., 5 Oz. 180.00
Creamer, Scrolled Handle, Swirled Rim Base, Daniel Van Voorhis, 1785, 5 In. 1210.00
Crumber, Scrolling Leaves & Flowers, Scalloped Edge, W. Gale & Son 150.00
Cup, Baby's, Engraved Monogram, Arts & Crafts, Arthur J. Stone, 2 x 4 In. 445.00
Cup, Child's, Beaded Borders, Handle, Towle, 2 1/4 x 2 3/4 In. 1015.00

Cup, Cover, Urn Form, Beaded Rim, Joseph Lownes, Philadelphia, c.1785, 10 In. 1870.00
Cup, Exotic Edifices, Charters, Cann & Dunn, N.Y., Coin, c.1850, 4 3/4 In. 440.00
Cup, Mask Handles, Scroll Frieze On Rim, Pedestal Base, 8 1/2 In. 500.00
Cup, Medallion, Engraved Midsection, Inscribed, J. Westervelt, 3 In. 88.00
Cup, Molded Band, Monogram, Harris Stanwood & Co., Coin, 3 1/2 In. 175.00
Cup, Reeded Band On Rim, Marked, I. Mullin, Coin, 3 1/4 In. 316.00
Cup, Trumpet Form Body, 3-Leaf Clover, Blossoms, Gorham, c.1905, 15 In. 6900.00
Demitasse Set, Allover Dense Design, Vines, The Sweetser Co., 3 Piece 488.00
Dinner Fork, Gaylord Craft, 7 1/2 In., 6 Piece 395.00
Dinner Fork, Monogram, Arthur J. Stone, c.1913, 7 3/4 In., 6 Piece 395.00
Dinner Knife, Engraved G, Stainless Steel Blade, Arthur J. Stone, 9 1/2 In. 88.00
Dinner Knife, Gaylord Craft, 9 3/4 In. 65.00
Dish, Engraved Base, Alma June Bleicher, Arthur Stone, 1941, 7 7/8 In. 630.00
Dish, Entree, Flower & Leaf Repousse, Schoffield, 10 1/2 In. 805.00
Dish, Francis I Patter, Reed & Barton, 12 In. 715.00
Dish, Gadrooned Rim, Strawberry Handles, Coin, Eoff & Shepherd, 6 In. 430.00
Dish, Geranium, 3 Overlapping Leaves, Reed & Barton, 1940, 7 In. 165.00
Dish, Open Clam Shell, Arts & Crafts, 3 1/4 In., Pair 95.00
Dish, Oyster Shell Form, Monogram, Wood & Hughes, 1870s, 6 3/4 In. 690.00
Dish, Pierced, Raised Scroll, Monogram, Wise & Son, Oval, 14 In. 415.00
Dish, Poppies, Scrolled Rim, Gorham, 9 3/4 x 12 3/4 In. 355.00
Dish, Rectangular, Fluted Ends, International Silver Co., 12 In. 77.00
Dish, Repousse, Flowers, Leaves, Fixed Handle, S. Kirk & Son, 1907, 8 In. 1265.00
Dish, Scallop Form, 3 Grape Cluster Feet, Reed & Barton, 20 Troy Oz. 523.00
Dish, Shell Form, Scalloped, 2 Ball Feet, Gorham, 1957, 9 1/2 In. 258.00
Dish, Shell Form, Scalloped, 2 Ball Supports, Gorham, 20th Century, 6 In., Pair 316.00
Dish, Trefoil, Cluster Of Grapes On Vine, Mario Buccellati, 18 1/2 x 17 In. 8625.00
Divider, Engraved Case, Coin, 3 1/4 In. 115.00
Ewer, Globular Shape, Leaves, Scrolls, Diapers & Flowers, 1828, 15 1/4 In. 400.00
Ewer, Grape & Vine, Handle, Peter L. Krider Co., PA, B.H. Stieff Jewelry, 15 In. 1650.00
Ewer, Wine, Helmet Lid, Philadelphia Contribution, J. Howell, 1797, 54 Oz. 7560.00
Feeder, Invalid, Curved Spout, Sarah Wistar To Sarah H. Morris, 1859 . . . . 840.00
Finger Bowl, Repousse, Baltimore Sterling Silver Co., 4 1/2 In. 220.00
Fish Knife, Gothic, Coin, Gale & Hayden, 1849, 10 3/4 In. 1500.00
Fish Server, Pierced Dolphin, Monogram, Bailey & Company 223.00
Fish Server, Scrolls, Leaves, Fish, Tiffany, Young & Ellis, 1848-1852 . . . . 315.00
Fish Set, Stylized Flowers, Danish Style, Julius O. Randahl, 10 1/2 In., 2 Piece 795.00
Fish Slice, George P. Blanchard, 9 3/4 In. 225.00
Flask, Hip, Allover Flowering Leaves, Bailey, Banks & Biddle, 6 1/4 In. 460.00
Flask, Reeded Design, Hinged Cover, Monogram, Blackinton, 7 3/4 In. 275.00
Flower Basket, Handle, Ribbon, Floral Swags, Gorham, 1916, 16 In. 575.00
Flower Basket, Scroll Border, Swing Handle, Shreve, Crump & Low, 16 In. 747.00
Fork, Child's, Bunny Handle, Stone Associates Mark, Arthur J. Stone, 4 In. 295.00
Fork, Child's, Squirrel Handle, Arthur J. Stone, 4 In. 325.00
Frame, Frank In Block Letters, Arts & Crafts, Lebolt & Co., 12 1/2 x 10 In. 795.00
Frame, Hammered, Geometrical Design, Scharling, 11 1/2 x 8 1/2 In. 400.00
Glass, Sherry, Round Foot, Bailey, Banks & Biddle, 4 In., 8 Piece 175.00
Goblet, Beaded Rim & Foot, T & W, Presentation Monogram, 1843, 5 In. 200.00
Goblet, Flared Rim, Gilt Interior, Monogram, Gorham, 6 3/4 In., 5 Piece 170.00
Goblet, Floral Branches, Coin, Adolphe Himmel, New Orleans, 1861-1877, 6 In. 880.00
Goblet, Flowers & Leaves On Stippled Ground, Kirk, 6 3/4 In. 172.00
Goblet, Presentation, Beaded Shoulder, Border, Domed Foot, 1857, 6 In., Pair 920.00
Goblet, Water, Plain Pedestal Base, Wallace, 7 In., 8 Piece 550.00
Goblet, Wine, Floral At Base, International Sterling, 6 Piece 170.00
Grape Scissors, Grape Design, Sterling Silver, 7 In. 67.00
Grape Shears, Twig-Shaped Handles, Whiting Mfg. Co., c.1890, 7 In. 140.00
Hair Brush, New King, Dominick & Haff, 9 1/8 In. 165.00
Hairpin, Woman's, Unger Bros., 5 In. 90.00
Honey Pot, Fine Silver, Honey Bee Form 175.00
Ice Cream Slice, Medallion, Classical Style, George W. Shiebler & Co., 10 In. 4025.00
Jug, Cream, Applied Rim, Strap Handle, Coin, Joseph Foster, 4 In. 488.00
Jug, Twining Grapes, Grape Vines, Draw Handle, Alvin Mfg. Co., 9 In. 1380.00
Julep Cup, Applied Band To Rim, Base, Coin, Henderson & Gaines, 3 In. 431.00

Julep Cup, Molded Rim & Base, Fisher, 3 3/4 In., Pair 290.00
Julep Cup, Reeded Band, International Sterling Co., 3 3/4 In., Pair 260.00
Knife, Child's, Bunny Handle, Stone Associates Mark, Arthur J. Stone, 5 1/4 In. 295.00
Ladle, Cream, Hall & Elton, Coin 45.00
Ladle, Engraved M, Mary Knight, 6 In. 495.00
Ladle, Feather Edge, Round End Handle, R. Humphreys, Late 1700s, 14 3/4 In. 633.00
Ladle, Fiddle Thread Design, Shoulders, R.T. & Co., Coin, 1800-1850, 14 3/4 In. 305.00
Ladle, Marked L. Hollard, Littleton Holland, Baltimore Md, Coin, 1770-1847 .... 248.00
Ladle, Monogram, John Burger, c.1800, 14 1/2 In. 715.00
Ladle, Notched Handle, Hammered, Kalo Shop, Early 20th Century, 8 1/8 In. 259.00
Ladle, Round End Handle, Initials, Impressed J.B., Early 1800s, 14 x 6 1/2 In. 460.00
Ladle, Turned Wood Handle, Monogram, Mid 18th Century 137.00
Ladle & Bowl, Palmer & Ramsey, c.1847, 12 3/4-In. Bowl 2215.00
Letter Knife, 4-Leaf Clover On Handle, Leonore Doskow, 7 In. 65.00
Letter Opener, Putto & Dragons Handle, George Shiebler, c.1900, 14 1/4 In. 632.00
Loving Cup, Grape Repousse, 3 Handles, Gorham, 1907 Mark 925.00
Lozenge & Leaf Order, Lundt, 9 1/2 In. 100.00
Luncheon Fork, Engraved GP, Arthur J. Stone, c.1913 .... 65.00
Luncheon Fork, Monogram E, Arthur J. Stone, 7 1/8 In. 85.00
Luncheon Fork, Monogram, Arthur J. Stone, c.1913, 7 In., 6 Piece 395.00
Martini Spoon, Hammered, Kalo, 13 1/2 In. 220.00
Match Safe, Repousse, Monogram, #8 3803, Gorham, 1 3/4 x 2 3/4 In. 39.00
Mirror & Brush, Repousse, Acanthus, Cartouche, Webster Co., 14 In. 29.00
Mug, Beaded Rim, Angular Handle, Bigelow & Kennard & Co., 1869, 7 Oz. 460.00
Mug, Greek Key Border, Scroll Handle, Cylindrical, John L. Westervelt, 4 In. 201.00
Mug, Presentation, Rococo Cartouche On Front, Ear Handle, Boston, 4 In. 172.00
Napkin Rings are listed in their own category.
Nut Dish, Rose In Center, Round, Arts & Crafts, Arthur J. Stone, 3 1/2 In. 625.00
Nut Service, Repousse Shell, Swirling Roses, R. & W. Wallace, 1900, 3 1/2 In. 143.00
Olive Spoon, Gaylord Craft, 6 In. 85.00
Pastry Server, Monogram, Duhme & Co., Cincinnati, Oh, c.1830, 3.2 Troy Oz. 336.00
Pie Server, Pierced, Foliate Scrolls, New York, Coin, 1840s-1850s, 10 1/2 In. 140.00
Pill Box, Oval, Domed Cover, Arts & Crafts, Arthur J. Stone, 3/4 x 2 1/4 In. 595.00
Pin Tray, Ornate Pierced Border, Gilt, Schreiber, 5 x 4 3/4 In. 165.00
Pitcher, Bird & Floral, S. Kirk & Son, c.1880, 8 In. 2640.00
Pitcher, Bulbous Body, Hammered, Ear Handle, Gorham, Signed, 7 3/4 In. 485.00
Pitcher, Center Repousse, Cartouche, Coin, Haddock, Lincoln & Foss, 9 In. 160.00
Pitcher, Chased, Repousse, Overall Flowering Trees, S. Kirk & Son, 6 1/2 In. 1540.00
Pitcher, Floral Relief Border, C-Scroll Handle, 4 Floral Feet, Poole, 9 In. 440.00
Pitcher, Floral Repousse, Chased Design, 1888, 7 In. 1155.00
Pitcher, Gadroon Borders, Leaf Handle, William Gale, 19th Century, 12 In. 1815.00
Pitcher, Hand Hammered Surface, Ear Handle, Arts & Crafts, 1915, 7 In. 575.00
Pitcher, Leaf Band On Shoulder, Angular Handle, International, 9 In. 345.00
Pitcher, Loop Handle, Plain Bombe, Allan Adler, 8 In. 545.00
Pitcher, Louis XIV, Towle, 10 In. 550.00
Pitcher, Martini, Strainer Spout, Angular Handle, Lebolt, 9 1/2 x 7 In. 660.00
Pitcher, Repousse, Chased Design, Scroll Handle, Coin, Wm. Tenney, 11 In. 1150.00
Pitcher, Scroll Handle, Gorham, 8 3/4 In. 200.00
Pitcher, Scroll Handle, Graff, Washbourne & Dunn, 1950, 9 In. 160.00
Pitcher, Scroll Handle, Wire At Neck, Wallace, 8 1/2 In. 400.00
Pitcher, Vase Shape, Scroll & Floral, Watson & Co., 11 In. 1028.00
Pitcher, Water, Classical Shape, Royal Danish, 9 In. 495.00
Pitcher, Water, Federal, Pear Shape, S-Scroll Handle, Fisher, 9 1/2 In. 690.00
Pitcher, Water, Grecian Shape, Arts & Crafts, Arthur J. Stone, 7 1/2 x 8 3/4 In. 2400.00
Pitcher, Water, Ribs, Panels, Arts & Crafts, Julius O. Randahl, 9 x 8 1/4 In. 2600.00
Pitcher, Water, Royal Danish, 8 1/4 In. 495.00
Pitcher, Water, Serpentine Handle, Monogram, Watson Co., 8 3/8 In. 373.00
Pitcher, Water, Sinuous, Loop Handle, Arts & Crafts, Kalo Shop, 9 3/4 x 8 In. 2750.00
Pitcher, Water, Wallace, 8 5/8 In. 500.00
Pitcher Spoon, Porter Blanchard, 11 1/4 In. 175.00
Plate, Molded Rim, Monogram, Watson, 6 1/2 In., 8 Piece 125.00
Plate, Place, Double Beaded Rims, Norbert Mfg. Co., 12 In., 24 Piece 11500.00
Plate, Place, Serpentine Edge, Flowers, J.E. Caldwell, 11 1/4 In., 12 Piece 9350.00

Plate, Scalloped Borders, John Angell, 1825, 34 Oz., Pair 770.00
Plate, Scrolled Flower & Leaf Design, Handicraft Shop, 1904, 9 3/4 In. 430.00
Plate, Scrolling Rim, International, 6 In., 12 Piece 460.00
Plate, Service, Randahl Sterling, 10 1/2 In. 134.00
Plate, Woman With Flowing Tresses, Art Nouveau, Gorham, 1883, 7 1/4 In. 1150.00
Platter, Meat, Oval, Reeded Edges, Laurel Clusters, Reed & Barton, 1934, 10 In. 450.00
Platter, Serving, Applied Foliate Scrolls, Monogram, Gorham, 16 In., Pair 747.00
Porringer, Baby's, Scene Of Bears Playing & Eating, 1907, 6 1/2 In. 805.00
Porringer, Bombe Sides, Keyhole Handle, E. Pelletreau, c.1760, 7 Oz. 5175.00
Porringer, Hammered, Arts & Crafts, Kalo Shop, 2 x 8 In. 595.00
Porringer, Pierced Designed Handle, Inscription, Dominick & Haff, 5 In. 110.00
Porringer, Pierced Handles, Stamped F.G.B., 14 In. 110.00
Porringer, Round Flat Openwork Handle, Dominick & Haff, 5 1/4 In. 115.00
Porringer, Round Flat Pierced Handle, Monogram, Reed & Barton, 4 3/4 In. 45.00
Porringer, Stylized Pineapple, Pierced Handle, Arthur J. Stone, 7 1/2 In. 546.00
Punch Ladle, Classical Revival, Warrior's Head Medallion, W & H, 15 In. 905.00
Punch Ladle, Double Lip, Terminal Repousse, Flowers, S. Kirk & Son, 14 In. 315.00
Punch Ladle, Heraldic, Fluted Bowl, Whiting, 13 In. 358.00
Punch Ladle, Wrigglework, Coin, John McMullin, Phila., 1790-1815, 14 1/2 In. 825.00
Salad Set, Kalo Shop, 8 3/4 In., 2 Piece 495.00
Salt, Greek Key, Spoons, Arts & Crafts, Marcus & Co., 1 x 1 3/4 In., Pair 165.00
Salt, Open, Allover Floral, 3 Scrolled Shell Feet, Stieff, 1 3/4 In., Pair 258.00
Salt, Open, Gold Interior, Cobalt Blue Glass Liner, Ball, Black & Co., 3 In., Pair 143.00
Salt & Pepper, Chased, Repousse, Roses, Leaves, 1900-1910, 5 3/4 In., Pair 330.00
Salt Cellar, Cranberry Glass, Satyr Playing Pipes, Gorham, 1901, 3 In., Pair 1650.00
Salt Cellar, Krater Form, Animal Head Handles, Coin, Wood & Hughes, 3 In. 402.00
Salt Dip, Abraham Carlisle, 1791, Pair 180.00
Salad Fork, Monogram E, Arthur J. Stone, 6 3/4 In. 85.00
Salver, Allover Circular Design, Central Laurel, Monogram, Krider & Biddle 345.00
Salver, Field Of Flowers, Leaves, Scrolls, Vacant Cartouche, Kirk, 14 In. 1035.00
Salver, Floral Bouquets & Garland, Gadrooned Edging, International, 11 In. 120.00
Salver, Hammered Finish, Kalo, 11 In. 287.00
Salver, Lobed Rim, Kalo, 13 7/8 In. 690.00
Salver, Reticulated, Pierced Scroll & Floral, Theodore B. Starr, 10 In. 247.00
Salver, Round, Pinched Upright Rim, Randahl, 1950, 14 In. 350.00
Salver, Scrolls With Small Rocaille Shells, Theodore B. Starr, 7 x 7 1/8 In., Pair 373.00
Sardine Fork, Trident Prongs, Arthur J. Stone, 5 1/4 In. 325.00
Sauce Ladle, Arthur J. Stone, 5 1/2 In. 80.00
Sauceboat, Fluted Bowl, Scrolled Handle, Bird, Coin, Wood & Hughes, 8 1/4 In. 1000.00
Sauceboat, Gilt, Scroll Figural Handle, Coin, 1871, 8 1/4 x 4 1/2 In. 1000.00
Serving Bowl, Aesthetic Movement, Mixed Metal, Whiting, 2 3/4 x 10 In. 4312.00
Serving Bowl, Arts & Crafts, Fluted Interior, Shreve & Co., 10 1/2 In. 88.00
Serving Bowl, Floral, Foliate Scrolls On Sides, Repousse, Joseph Armiger, 2 In. 258.00
Serving Fork, Old Newbury Crafters, 8 3/4 In. 185.00
Serving Spoon, Arthur J. Stone, 9 1/8 In. 185.00
Serving Spoon, Floral & Leaf, Gold Wash Floral Bowl, Gorham 465.00
Serving Spoon, Hammered, Engraved Letter N, Lebolt & Co. 145.00
Serving Spoon, Stone Associates Mark, Arthur J. Stone, 9 1/2 In. 225.00
Shaker, Cocktail, 6 Shot Glasses, Ahrendt & Taylor Co., Inc., 6 1/2 In. 360.00
Shaker, Martini, Hammered, Diamond Shaped Applique, Gorham, 10 x 4 In. 220.00
Small Ladle, George C. Gebelein, 2 3/4 In. 90.00
Soup Ladle, Fiddle Thread, Inscription, Jones Ball & Poor, Boston, c.1840 .... 220.00
Soup Ladle, Fiddle Thread, Monogram, John B. Ginochio, c.1837 .... 330.00
Soup Ladle, Justice & Arminger, Baltimore, Md., c.1891-1893 .... 140.00
Soup Ladle, Oval Pointed Handle, Beaded Edge, Bailey & Co., 1861 .... 190.00
Soup Spoon, Engraved GP, Arthur J. Stone, c.1913 .... 75.00
Spoon, Arthur J. Stone, 7 In. 175.00
Spoon, Enamel Grape Design, Mary Knight, 1906, 6 In. 290.00
Spoon, Newell Harding & Co., Coin, 1860, 8 Piece 140.00
Spoon, Stirring, Hammered Finish, Kalo, Signed, 13 1/2 In. 345.00
Spoon, Terminal With Flowers, Leaves, Monogram On Back, G.B. Sharp 287.00
Spoon & Fork, Christening, Vermeil, Leather Case, Gorge W. Adams, 8 1/4 In. 300.00
Spoon & Knife, Child's, Hammered, Karl F. Leinonen, 5 1/4 In. & 4 3/4 In. 250.00

Spurs, Man's, Eddy Hulbert, Montana, 19th Century 7700.00
Spurs, Woman's, Eddy Hulbert 4620.00
Sugar, Chased Scroll & Leaves, Sing Handle, 4 In. 225.00
Sugar, Cover, Bombe Form, Pedestal Base, Engraved, Harvey Lewis, 6 1/2 x 8 In. 415.00
Sugar, Cover, Francis I, Repousse, Foliate Scrolls, Reed & Barton, 1929, 5 3/4 In. 880.00
Sugar, Foliate Rim Cover, Scrolling Leaves, Angular Handles, Schofield, 7 In. 80.00
Sugar & Creamer, Aesthetic Movement, Mixed Metal, Gorham, 1882, 3 In. 1840.00
Sugar & Creamer, Baluster Form, Scalloped Rim, Monogram, Gorham 75.00
Sugar & Creamer, Gorham, 2 3/4 In. 55.00
Sugar & Creamer, Lobed Urn Form, Blossoms At Neck, Codman & Codman 1265.00
Sugar & Creamer, Urn Shape, Swirled Finial, Jones Ball, c.1852 .... 550.00
Sugar Shovel, Aesthetic Movement, Whiting Mfg. Co., 5 3/4 In. 70.00
Sugar Shovel, Coin, D.B. Hempsted 40.00
Sugar Shovel, Gaylord Craft, 6 In. 75.00
Sugar Tongs, John Proctor Trott, 1805, 5 1/8 In. 150.00
Sugar Tongs, Pierced & Engraved, Anthemia Terminals, Marked D.V. 165.00
Sugar Tongs, Stylized Tulip Bud, Arthur J. Stone, 3 In. 125.00
Sugar Tongs, Wide Bow Form, Plain Oblong Terminals, Coins, 19th Century 77.00
Sugar Urn, Cover, Beaded Rim, Armorial Base, J. Richardson Jr., 1795, 10 In. 2640.00
Sugar Urn, Cover, Joseph Richardson Jr. 6600.00
Sugar Urn, Galleried Top, Joseph Richardson Jr., 18th Century, 10 1/4 In. 8800.00
Syrup, Cover, Beaded Rim, Scrolled Handle, N.Y., 4 In. 121.00
Tablespoon, Coin, I. Fales, 18th Century, 4 Piece 175.00
Tablespoon, Coin, W. Kendrick, Louisville 50.00
Tablespoon, Embossed Scalloped Shell, Coin, Samuel Edwards, 1762, 8 In. 632.00
Tablespoon, Engraved Greek Key Edging, E. Lownes, 1817, 6 Piece 402.00
Tankard, Tapered Cylindrical Form, Domed Cover, Engraved, c.1730, 8 In. 6600.00
Tankard, Urn & Flame Finial, Hollow Handle, Benjamin Burr, 9 In. 1475.00
Tazza, Floral Cornucopia Stem, Domed Weighted Foot, 5 5/8 In., Pair 345.00
Tazza, Gold Wash Interior, Stepped Weighted Base, Watson Co., 9 In., Pair 258.00
Tazza, Quilt Style Pattern, Monogram, Frank W. Smith Co., 4 In., Pair 2415.00
Tazza, Reticulated Band, Applied Scroll Rim, Howard & Co., 1898, 2 In., Pair 690.00
Tazza, Rocaille Scrolls, Domed Reticulated Foot, Howard & Co., 3 In., Pair 1150.00
Tazza, Round, Art Deco Style, Alvin Silver Co., 5 x 12 In. 305.00
Tazza, Scroll, Floral Reticulated Foot, Monogram, Howard & Co., 3 1/2 In. 575.00
Tazza, Scrolling Leaf Rim, 3 Center Cartouches, Bailey, Banks & Biddle, 8 In. 488.00
Tea & Coffee Set, Allover Repousse, Flowers, Dominick & Haff, 5 Piece 3450.00
Tea & Coffee Set, Baluster Shape, Reed & Barton, 4 Piece 430.00
Tea & Coffee Set, Flowers, Leaves, Berries, Bailey, Banks & Biddle, 6 Piece 6160.00
Tea & Coffee Set, Foliate Scroll Handles, Serpentine Spouts, Towle, 5 Piece 2070.00
Tea & Coffee Set, Foliate Sprays, Cartouches, Gorham, 6 Piece 4025.00
Tea & Coffee Set, Pear Form, Pad Feet, Graff, Washburn & Dunn, 8 In., 4 Piece 468.00
Tea & Coffee Set, Plymouth, Gorham, 5 Piece 1500.00
Tea & Coffee Set, Prelude, International, 5 Piece ....605.00 to 2300.00
Tea & Coffee Set, R & W Wilson, 6 Piece 6720.00
Tea & Coffee Set, Sinuous Loop Handles, 20th Century, Towle, 5 Piece 1725.00
Tea & Coffee Set, Vase Form Bodies, Monogram, Gorham, 1904, 6 Piece 4312.00
Tea & Coffee Set, With Tray, Louis XIV Pattern, Towle, 7 Piece 4620.00
Tea Set, 6 Sides, Beaded Rim, Wooden Handle, Bigelow, Kennard & Co., 4 Piece 345.00
Tea Set, Baluster Shape, Flower Finial, Coin, Davis Palmer & Co., 3 Piece 805.00
Tea Set, Dimension, John Prip, Reed & Barton, 4 Piece 475.00
Tea Set, Domed Hinged Covers, Baluster Finials, Reed & Barton, 3 Piece 375.00
Tea Set, Floral Band, Palmettes Rim, Center Mask, Harvey Lewis, 3 Piece 1610.00
Tea Set, Floral Repousse, S. Kirk & Son, 4 Piece 1760.00
Tea Set, Grape Vine & Floral Band, Coin, John Crawford, 3 Piece 2875.00
Tea Set, Oval, Lobed Body, Domed Cover, Coin, Joseph Lownes, c.1804, 4 Piece 3105.00
Tea Set, Reed & Barton Tray, Monogram, Lunt, 6 Piece 2775.00
Tea Strainer, Lunt, 1 1/2 In. 50.00
Tea Strainer, Lunt, 5 In. 50.00
Tea Strainer, Pierced Handles, Katherine Pratt, 6 In. 258.00
Tea Strainer, Spout, Watrous, c.1920, 2 1/2 In. 55.00
Teapot, Baluster Form, Lobed Body, Beaded Rim, Galt & Brothers, 8 In. 550.00
Teapot, Baluster Shape, Hinged Cover, Scroll Handle, Reed & Barton, 8 3/4 In. 175.00

Silver-American, Teapot, Mayflower Pattern,
Blackson Silver Co., 5 3/4 In.

> You might be able to remove salt spots from your silver-plated saltshakers with olive oil. Rub it on the spots, let stand a few days, then wipe it off.

Teapot, Domed Cover, Overall Grapes & Grape Vine, Pear Shape, 9 In. 920.00
Teapot, Flat Hinged Cover, Flowers, Leaves, Basketry Handle, Gorham, 1882, 7 In. 143.00
Teapot, Mayflower Pattern, Blackson Silver Co., 5 3/4 In. ....*Illus* 65.00
Teaspoon, Applied Letter R, Lebolt & Co., 6 Piece 375.00
Teaspoon, Coin, Harris & Stanwood 12.00
Teaspoon, Five-O'Clock, Poppy On Handle, Arthur J. Stone, 5 In. 250.00
Teaspoon, Full Figure, Indian Handle, Paye & Baker, c.1890, 6 Piece 600.00
Teaspoon, Hammered, Applied Letter R, Lebolt & Co. 68.00
Teaspoon, Oval Handle, Joseph Richardson, Jr., 1785, 6 Piece 172.00
Teaspoon, Scallop, AGK Engraved Vertically, Arthur J. Stone, 6 In., 6 Piece 480.00
Teaspoon, Wheat Sheaf, Arthur J. Stone, 5 1/2 In., 6 Piece 675.00
Tray, Applied Guilloche Border, Leaves, Scrolls, Wood & Hughes, 14 In. 488.00
Tray, Arts & Crafts, Oval, Hand Hammered, McAuliffe & Hadley, 17 x 12 In. 660.00
Tray, Baltimore Rose, Scrolls, Flowers At Intervals, Schofield Co., 10 In. 632.00
Tray, Border Repousse, Diaper Pattern, Jacobi & Jenkins, Square, 6 1/4 In. 405.00
Tray, Classical Revival Band, Floral Swag Border, Whiting, 22 x 15 In. 865.00
Tray, Classical Revival Floral Swags, Octagonal, Wm. B. Durgin Co., 12 In. 402.00
Tray, Embossed Border, Coat Of Arms In Center, S. Kirk & Sons, 20 In. 1495.00
Tray, Fenestrated & Chased Design, Round, 11 In. 175.00
Tray, Fluting, Monogram, Oval, Arts & Crafts, Kalo Shop, 14 x 7 1/2 In. 1750.00
Tray, Francis I, Hand Chased, Reed & Barton, 30 1/2 x 23 In. 10500.00
Tray, Gadrooned Border, Rectangular, Reed & Barton, 12 3/4 x 8 3/4 In. 175.00
Tray, Molded Border, Gadrooned Rim, Graff, Washbourne & Dunn, 15 In. 805.00
Tray, Pin, Art Nouveau, Repousse Clover Border, Hammered, Wm. Kerr, 11 In. 200.00
Tray, Raised Border, Oval Depression, Arts & Crafts, Mulholland Bros., 9 In. 65.00
Tray, Rectangle, Galleried Border, 2 Handles, Dominick & Haff, 1895, 22 x 15 In. 4180.00
Tureen, Soup, Cover, Flowers & Fruit, Basketwork Rim, Gorham, 14 In. 5750.00
Vase, 2 Large Engraved Roses On Each Side, Matthews Co., N.J., 8 1/4 In. 862.00
Vase, Baluster, Flared Mouth, Handles, Flowers, Scrolls, Gorham, 14 1/2 In. 3575.00
Vase, Bud, Flower Shape, Fluted Body, J.E. Caldwell, Redlich & Co., 12 In. 345.00
Vase, Flared, Art Deco Style, Alvin Silver Co., 9 1/2 In., Pair 660.00
Vase, Flowers, Leaves, Glass Liner, Trumpet Foot, I.N. Deitsch, 11 1/4 In. 690.00
Waiter, Border Repousse, Rutter & Sullivan, For S. Janovitz & Son, 6 In. 175.00
Wine Cooler, Bands Of Scrolls, Stag's Head Handles, Gorham Mfg. Co., Pair 8050.00
Wine Cooler, Greek Key Base & Bands, Stag's Head Handles, Gorham, 12 In. 3737.00
SILVER-AUSTRIAN, Centerpiece, Figural, Hunter With Horn, Crossbow, 10-Point Stag, 9 In. . 4600.00
Coffee Set, Floral & Foliate Cartouche, Shell Finials, c.1865, 3 Piece 545.00
Figurine, Stag, Baying, Removable Head, Marble Base, 1920s, 18 In. 5750.00
Salt, Vienna, 18th Century, Master, Pair 395.00
SILVER-BELGIAN, Coffeepot, Scrolls, Shells & Foliate Sprays, J.J. Brichaut, 1769, 13 3/4 In. 9200.00
SILVER-CANADIAN, Bowl, Arched Handle, Blossom End, Leafage On Foot, c.1940, 7 1/2 In. 402.00
Porringer, Openwork Handle, Birks, 5 3/4 In. 80.00
SILVER-CHINESE, Bowl, Centerpiece, Marked WH, 1860-1880 .... 4885.00
Bowl, Floral, Zeewo, Chinese, 19th Century, 7 1/2 In. 905.00
Box, Cover, Landscape & Dragon Design, Jadeite Finial, 19th Century, 4 3/4 In. 575.00

Box, Repousse Phoenix, Flower & Shou Design, Gilt, 19th Century, 6 1/8 In. 990.00
Cake Basket, 8 Panels, Dragon, Flowering Branch & Grapevine, KHS, 10 In. 1150.00
Card Case, Chased Figural Landscape, 1840, 3 3/4 x 2 1/2 In. 685.00
Card Case, Chased Figural Landscape, WS, Late 19th Century, 4 1/4 In. 330.00
Card Case, Elephant & Animals, Monogram, 1840, 3 1/2 x 2 In. 190.00
Card Case, Figures At Leisure, c.1850, 3 3/4 x 2 3/8 In. 550.00
Cigarette Case, Bamboo, Calligraphic & Urn Design, 3 1/2 x 2 1/2 In. 410.00
Cigarette Case, Bowed Square, Figures At Leisure, 3 1/4 x 3 1/8 In. 330.00
Cigarette Case, Chased Dragon Design, Gilt, Inscription, 1945, 5 1/2 In. 45.00
Cigarette Case, Chased Dragons, Clouds & Figures, 1840, 5 1/4 x 3 In. 505.00
Cocktail Set, Shaker, Tray, 6 Glasses, Marked Tuokchang 1575.00
Cup, 2 Handles, 19th Century, 19 In. 4310.00
Cup, 2 Handles, Signed, Early 20th Century, 5 In., Pair 77.00
Cup, Cover, Handles, Marked CW, Hong Kong, 1880-1900 . . . . 4025.00
Dish, Bamboo Border, Round, 1840, 11 1/2 In. 660.00
Figure, Box Shape, Foo Dog Finial, 1840, 2 1/4 In. 220.00
Fish Set, Figural Landscapes, Mother-Of-Pearl, 19th Century, Box, 2 Piece 715.00
Flask, Coral & Turquoise Accents, Jade Medallions, Dragon Form Handles 690.00
Mirror, Hand, Jade, Enameled 355.00
Punch Bowl, Lee Yee Hing, Hong Kong, Large 4025.00
Shoehorn, Floral, 8 1/2 In. 90.00
Sugar & Creamer, Raised Floral, 2 1/2 In. 385.00
Vase, Cover, Landscape Scene, 2 Dragon Handles, Tuck Chang, 1830, 11 In. 2640.00
SILVER-CONTINENTAL, Asparagus Server, Standing Figure, Floral Basket, Handles, 11 In. . . 230.00
Basket, Figural Lion Feet, 3 1/2 In. 335.00
Beaker, Broad Matted Band, J.F. Theurer, 1660s, 3 1/2 In. 2990.00
Bowl, Center, Putti Playing Ring Around The Rosey, Foliate Rim, 16 In. 690.00
Bowl, Circle, Repousse, Scrolled Leaves & Flowers, Scalloped Edge, 6 In. 460.00
Bowl, Filigree Lattice Work, Scroll, Geometric Design, Beaded Edge, 11 In. 467.00
Bowl, Shagreen, Pierced Band Of Masks, 8 Leaf Supports, 1840, 14 In. 7475.00
Bowl, Shaped Circle, Openwork, Leaf & Flower Design, Cherubs, 5 In. 375.00
Bowl, Shaped Circle, Pierced Scrolled Leaves, Bird, Garland, 9 In. 520.00
Bowl, Swags, Scroll, Bird, 8 x 9 In. 135.00
Box, 18th Century Courting Couple, Enamel, 20th Century, 2 x 3 In. 460.00
Box, Cigar, Hinged Cover, Flower Scrolled Leaves, 20th Century, 7 In. 920.00
Box, Cigarette, Hinged Cover, Chased With Flowers, Reeded Sides, 1 x 5 In. 230.00
Box, Dresser, Oval, Flower Basket On Lid, 2 x 3 3/4 x 5 In. 77.00
Box, Gleaners On Cover, Foliate Border, Mirror Interior, c.1900, 4 1/4 In. 245.00
Box, Hinged Blue Glass Cover, Floral, Leather Case, 6 1/4 In. 1150.00
Box, Lapis Lazuli Cover, Scrolled Silver Border, Gold Interior, 3 In. 287.00
Box, Raised Rococo Design, 18th Century, 4 1/4 In. 230.00
Box, Trinket, Silver Inlaid Flowers, Animals, Slide Top, 19th Century, 3 In. 60.00
Cake Basket, Scene Of Dancers In 18th Century Dress, Oval, 3 x 18 In. 990.00
Castor, Repousse Cherubs, Scrolls, Dolphin Finial, c.1900, 8 In., Pair 605.00
Chalice, Chased With Coat Of Arms In Wreath, Gold Interior, 9 In. 1150.00
Cigarette Case, Reeded, Sapphire Thumbpiece, 5 Sections, 1920, 3 1/2 In. 690.00
Coffeepot, Scrolled Leaves Band, Fluted Domed Lid, 1850s, 7 In. 287.00
Condiment Caddy, Twist Standard, 2 Footed Cups, Scroll & Lattice, 10 In. 250.00
Condiment Jar, Hinged Cover, Cobalt Glass Liner, 4 3/4 In. 373.00
Dish, Reticulated, Profile Of Frederick Augustus, Duke Of Saxony, 7 In. 115.00
Dish, Scrolled Leaves, Pierced Putti, 5 Sections, Glass Liners, 8 In. 460.00
Frame, Niello, Floral Border, Gilt & White Insignia, c.1900, 15 x 11 In., Pair 990.00
Handle, Cane, Hippo Form, Band, Blue Enamel Stones, 5 3/4 In. 2530.00
Jardiniere, Flowers, Bowtie Garlands, 2 Bow Form Handles, 12 In., Pair 4745.00
Jewelry Box, Leafy Scroll Cover, Bombe Form, 4 Scroll Feet, 7 1/4 x 2 In. 345.00
Ladle, Silver Stem, Turned Wooden Handle, 19th Century, 15 1/2 In. 172.00
Mirror, Silver On Copper, Heart Form, Beasts, Birds, Flowers, 13 1/2 x 10 In. 258.00
Mustard, Pierced Body, Floral Garlands, Putti Figural Medallion, Liner 115.00
Mustard, Spoon, Beaded Rim, Cobalt Blue Liner, 3 1/4 In. 315.00
Pitcher, Shaped Rectangle, Scroll Handle, Monogram Cartouche, 7 In. 345.00
Punch Ladle, Conch Shell Shape, Twisted Ivory Handle, 1850-1900 . . . . 450.00
Salt, Shell, On Wheels, Cherub Driving, 2 Cherubs Pulling, 3 1/2 In. 385.00
Serving Spoon, Pierced, Reticulated Bowl, Classical Designs, c.1900, 8 In. 77.00

Snuffbox, Cartouche With Birds On Cover, Foliate Garland, 3 In. 260.00
Snuffbox, Cat, Hanging, Mice, Engraved Names, 19th Century, 2 5/8 In. 520.00
Snuffbox, Laurel Wreath Hinged Cover, Foliate Band, Gold Interior, 3 In. 431.00
Strainer, Wine, Loop Handles, Twin Handled, 14 1/4 In. 588.00
Sugar, Cover, Engraved Wreath Design, Gilt Interior, c.1900, 5 1/2 In. 66.00
Tankard, Continuous Repousse Battle Scene, Herm Handle, 7 1/4 In. 1265.00
Tazza, Shaped Circle, Pierced, Flowers, Putti, Glass Liner, 9 1/2 In. 1035.00
Tea Set, Gadrooned Baluster Form, Scrolled Handles, Fruit Finials, 3 Piece 395.00
Waiter, Fluted, Floral & Leaf Border, 19 1/2 In. 415.00
Wedding Cup, Beaded Figure With Chased Skirt, 19th Century, 9 In. 1955.00
SILVER-DANISH, Bowl, Fruit, Applied Fruit, Loop Handles, Georg Jensen, 1926, 14 In. 8625.00
Bowl, Hemispherical, Flared Rim, Georg Jensen, 1925, 35 Oz. 10350.00
Bowl, No. 584 C, Gustave Pedersen, Post 1945, 6 7/8 x 9 In. 6750.00
Bowl, Openwork Stylized Plant, Flared Rim, Georg Jensen, 40 Oz. 9775.00
Bowl, Scrolled Vines, Clusters, Flared Rim, Oval, Georg Jensen, 1944, 61 Oz. 17250.00
Bowl, Vegetable, Blossom, Fixed Divider, Circular, Georg Jensen, 40 Oz. 5175.00
Coffee Service, Blossom, Creamer, Sugar Bowl, Georg Jensen, 1944, 3 Piece 4890.00
Coffeepot, Vertical Banding, Embossed Flowers, & Rocaille, Swing Handle, 7 In. 545.00
Compote, Grape, No. 264 Z, Georg Jensen, 1918, 10 3/4 In. 9200.00
Condiment Set, Mustard Pot, Mustard Spoon, Georg Jensen, 3 Piece 1380.00
Demitasse Spoon, Pierced Terminals, Georg Jensen, 1909-1914, 6 Piece 175.00
Dinner Service, Acorn, Georg Jensen, 1944, 113 Piece 9775.00
Dinner Set, Flatware, Acanthus, Georg Jensen, 73 Piece 4600.00
Gravy Boat, Blossom, Georg Jensen, No. 180, 1945, 9 In. 2875.00
Gravy Boat, Grape, Georg Jensen, Signed, c.1930, 4 1/2 x 6 3/4 In. 3737.00
Ladle, Grape, Peterson, 7 3/4 In. 170.00
Ladle, Handle, Flower Blossom, Leaf Design, Hammered, Denmark, 1942, 5 In. 144.00
Pitcher, Water, Stylized Floral Terminal To Top, Wooden Handle, Sterling, 10 In. 747.00
Place Setting, Caravel, Georg Jensen, 1945, 19 Piece 4310.00
Salad Server, Pyramid Pattern, Georg Jensen, 9 3/4 In., Pair 550.00
Soup, Coupe, Reticulated Leaf & Berry Base, William De Matteo, 4 1/2 x 5 In. 525.00
Spoon, Leaf & Berry, Curved Handle, Georg Jensen, 5 1/2 In. 190.00
Spoon, Scrolled Flower Handle, Georg Jensen, 6 In. 99.00
Stuffing Spoon, Catherine Fines, 1884 .... 150.00
Sugar & Creamer, No. 43, Johan Rohde, 1908 .... 5520.00
Sugar Tongs, Cactus, Georg Jensen, Early 20th Century, 1 Troy Oz., Pair 115.00
Tea & Coffee Service, Pear Shape, Beaded Rims, Georg Jensen, 1929, 6 Piece 18400.00
SILVER-DUTCH, Bowl, Embossed Country Scenes, 2 Pierced Handles With Putto, 14 1/4 In. .. 460.00
Bowl, Reed Rim, Paneled Bowl, Foliate Scrolls, Octagonal, 19th Century, 4 In. 402.00
Box, Hinged Cover, Classical Battle Scene, Square, Late 19th Century, 2 3/4 In. 402.00
Box, Tobacco, Floral, Brass, Slide Has Scenes, 5 1/8 x 2 1/4 In. 3365.00
Fish Server, Reticulated, Embossed Fishing Port, Angel, Indian, Dog, 14 3/4 In. 231.00
Jug, Claret, Spiral Ribbing, Human Mask Below Spout, 19th Century, 12 1/2 In. 1610.00
Salt & Pepper, Figural, Girl & Boy Form, 3 In. 165.00
Tea Caddy, Slip-On Domed Cap, Urn Finial, Daniel Jeffrey, 1745, 4 1/8 In. 2875.00
Teapot, Pearl Shape, Floral Finial, Engraved Motto, c.1890, 6 In. 330.00
SILVER-ECUADORIAN, Platter, Round, Scrolled Rim With Leaves, 17 In. 545.00
SILVER-EGYPTIAN, Tray, Shell & Scrolling Rim, 22 1/2 In. 330.00

SILVER-ENGLISH. English sterling silver is marked with a series of four
or five small hallmarks. The standing lion mark is the most commonly
seen sterling quality mark. The other marks indicate the city of origin,
the maker, and the year of manufacture. These dates can be verified in
many good books on silver.

SILVER-ENGLISH, Asparagus Server, Reeded Rim, William Eley & William Fearn, 1824 .... 920.00
 Asparagus Tongs, Sheffield, George III 605.00
 Asparagus Tongs, Shell & Thread, Medial Shell Arms, George III, 1780, 10 In. 805.00
 Asparagus Tongs, Shell Design, Heraldic Crest, Pierced Blades, 9 3/4 In., Pair 920.00
 Basket, Oval, Scrolled & Beaded Feet, Laurel Swags, 1884, 5 3/4 In. 400.00
 Basket, Scalloped, Bamboo Design, Birmingham, 1911-1912, 9 x 11 1/2 In. 450.00
 Basket, Scrolls & Flower Heads, Pierced Body, W. Comys, 1891, 11 1/2 In. 1150.00
 Beaker, Horizontal Leaf Band Top To Bottom, Floral Swag, George III, 4 In., Pair 1265.00

Berry Spoon, In Fitted Box, Jane Lambe, London, 1728, Pair 316.00
Bowl, Center, Lobed Body, 2 Scroll, Acanthus Handles, Robert Garrard, 5 In. 4312.00
Bowl, Cover, Reeded Rim, Handles, Octagonal Finial, Crichton, 1909, 10 In. 575.00
Bowl, Lobed Sides, Round, 1940-1941, 2 1/2 x 5 In. 1000.00
Bowl, Reeded Body, Flared Rim, Reeded Foot, Jas. Deakins & Sons, 1903, 5 In. 287.00
Bowl, Shield Shape Panels, Hammered, W. Comyns & Sons, 1902, 11 x 5 In. 431.00
Bowl, Vegetable, Cover, Serrated Rim, Mappin & Webb, 1977, 11 In., Pair 2070.00
Box, Cigar, Bearskin Form, W. Comyns, 1913, 14 3/8 In. 6900.00
Box, Keepsake, Ivory Letter, Mid 19th Century, 2 1/4 x 6 3/4 x 4 1/2 In. 2090.00
Bread Basket, Sprays Of Wheat, Floral Swags, Swing Handle, E. Romer, 1769 .... 4887.00
Bread Basket, Wirework, Gadroon Border, Swing Handle, Oval, 1800, 9 In. 135.00
Cake Basket, Boat Form, Beaded Rim, Laurel Festoons, C.S. Harris, 1894, 14 In. 5462.00
Cake Basket, Openwork Foliate Apron, 4 Scroll Feet, Wm. Plummer, 14 In. 4600.00
Cake Basket, Openwork Twisted Ribbon Design, Swing Handle, c.1810, 13 In. 295.00
Cake Basket, Pierced With Scrolls, Rope Twists Handles, George II, 1758, 4 In. 1400.00
Cake Basket, Wirework, Gadroon Border, Swing Handle, Sheffield, 10 In. 465.00
Candelabrum is listed in its own category.
Candle Cup, Applied Molded Band, Ear Shape Handles, Wastell, 1704, 6 In. 2990.00
Candlesticks are listed in their own category.
Cann, S-Scroll Handle, Edmund Pearce, 1728, 3/4 In. 165.00
Card Case, Allover Leafy Scrolls, Name On Front, N. Mills, 1843, 3 1/2 In. 345.00
Card Holder, Swordsmen & Helmets, 1 1/2 In., 6 Piece 410.00
Carving Set, Steel, Stag Handles, Birks, Birmingham, c.1900, 3 Piece 110.00
Castor, Beaded Rims, Pierced Cover, Flame Finial, George III, 1775, 5 3/4 In. 325.00
Castor, Domed Cover, Pear Shape, Stepped Base, Joseph Ward, 7 In., Pair 4600.00
Castor, Pierced Lid, Turned Body, 8 In. 110.00
Centerpiece, Plated Flower Grid, Rectangular, Frost, Wakely & Wheeler, 1965 .... 2645.00
Chafing Dish, Cover, Bud Finial, Paul Storr, 1811, 11 1/4 In. 6900.00
Chalice, Circle, Lappet, Band Of Leaves, W. Hutton & Sons, Edward VIII, 4 In. 345.00
Charger, Gadrooned, Shell Border, Rebecca Emes, 1826, 12 In. 1380.00
Cigar Case, Interior Strap, Push Button Release, 1913, 5 1/2 x 3 1/2 In. 400.00
Cigarette Coffer, Wood Interior, Birmingham, Art Deco, 1932, 2 1/2 x 6 1/2 In. 110.00
Claret Jug, Hinged Cover, Scrolled Acanthus Border, Gilt Interior, 9 1/2 In. 504.00
Coaster, Token Center, Ten-Pence, Edward VII, Birmingham, 1904, 5 In., Pair 115.00
Coffeepot, Chased With Flower Heads, Gadrooned Rim, Wooden Scroll Handle 3450.00
Coffeepot, Domed Cover, Scroll Spout, Wooden Scroll Handle, 1730, 9 In. 2760.00
Coffeepot, Domed Hinged Cover, Serpentine Spout, George III, 1767, 14 In. 5750.00
Coffeepot, Gadroon Borders, Writhen Finial, F. Crump, 1769, 10 1/2 In. 3105.00
Coffeepot, Leaf Capped Spout, Urn Finial, Walter Brind, 1781, 12 1/2 In. 2990.00
Coffeepot, Pear Form, Charles Wright, George III, 1769, 11 3/8 In. 2070.00
Coffeepot, Pineapple Finial, Original Pearwood Handle, Sheffield 715.00
Coffeepot, Reeded Cover, Fruitwood Loop Handle, George III, 1806, 8 7/8 In. 745.00
Coffeepot, Urn Form, Band Of Leaves At Shoulder, Wreath Of Leaves, 11 In. 1380.00
Compote, Panther's Heads On 4 Sides, Band Of Laurel Leaves, 9 In., Pair 3680.00
Condiment Stand, Goat Supporting Glass Mustard Pot, 5 1/2 In., Pair 4315.00
Creamer, Bead Below Short Spout, T. Mann, George I, 1722, 3 1/8 In. 2415.00
Creamer, Beaded Edge, Floral Engraving, Peter & Ann Bateman, 1791, 6 In. 995.00
Creamer, Chased Foliate & Floral Band, Reeded Loop Handle, George III, 6 In. 400.00
Creamer, Cow Form, Bee On Hinged Cover, George Fox, 1867, 4 1/4 In. 6325.00
Creamer, Floral Swag, Fluted Body, George III, 1796, 4 In. 200.00
Creamer, Helmet Shape, Square Foot, Bright Cut Leaf Design, London, c.1796 .... 315.00
Creamer, Pear Form, Leaf Cap, Double Scroll Handle, 3 Hoof Feet, 1741 .... 695.00
Creamer, Scroll Handle, Monogram, Paul Storr, William IV, 1831, 3 In. 287.00
Cruet, 2 Cut Glass Bottles, Engraved Crest, B. Godfrey, 1732, 6 3/4 In. 2070.00
Cruet, Egg, 6 Cups, Gilded Interior, Sheffield, Oval, c.1810, 6 x 8 In. 485.00
Cruet Set, Engraved Arms, Rococo Ring Finial, Cinquefoil Frame, S. Wood, 1760 ..... 7187.00
Cruet Set, Foliate Scrolls, Acanthus Legs, 4 Paw Feet, George III, 1817, 9 In. 1725.00
Cruet Stand, Floral Border, Lion's Paw Feet, 1830, 10 In. 880.00
Crumber, Stag Hunt, George Adams, 1848, 13 In. 1150.00
Cup, 2 Handles, Baluster, George III, 1801, 5 5/8 In. 490.00
Cup, Alternate Grotesque Mask & Bellflower, T. Ley, 1726, 5 In. 2530.00
Cup, Caudle, Cartouche Of Arms, Leaf Bands, Richard Green, 1703, 4 1/4 In. 1840.00

Cup, Caudle, Fluted Body, Monogram, Richard Green, 1709, 4 1/4 In. 1500.00
Cup, Caudle, Silver Footed Tray, 1799 . . . . 770.00
Cup, Caudle, Strapwork Handles, Scroll Chasing, Samuel Wood, 1766, 7 In. 990.00
Cup, Domed Cover, Vase Shaped, Leaf Scroll Handle, 1752, 13 In. 3450.00
Cup, Lower Foliate Flutes, Thistle & Rose Band, Alwyn Carr, 1920, 6 1/2 In. 1495.00
Cup, Presentation, Applied Band Of Grapes, Grape Leaves, George III, 9 In. 1610.00
Decanter, Gadroon, Shell Border, Turned Wooden Base, Sheffield, 7 In., Pair 605.00
Dish, 3 Sections, 2 Crests On Cover, C.H. Townley & J.W. Thomas, 1909, 17 In. 1840.00
Dish, Alternating Shells In Cartouches, 4 Bracket Feet, George II, 9 In. 14950.00
Dish, Domed Fluted Cover, Reeded Side Handles, 4 Scroll Feet, 11 In. 5750.00
Dish, Entree, Cover, Gadrooned, Shell Rim, Leaf, Shell Handle, George IV, 12 In. 1725.00
Dish, Entree, Cover, Scrolled Leaves, Detachable Handle, Sheffield, 12 In. 345.00
Dish, Entree, Domed Cover, Detachable Twig Handles, T. Robins, 12 In., Pair 3335.00
Dish, Meat, Molded Wavy Rim, Beaded Border, Robert Hennell, 24 In., Pair 8050.00
Dish, Shell Form, Mollusk Border, 3 Dolphin Feet, Edward VII, 1902, 6 In., Pair 2530.00
Dish, Souffle, Liner With Grips, Earl's Coronet, Paul Storr, 1836, 10 3/8 In. 4600.00
Dish, Sweetmeat, Scalloped, Swans, Snake Handles, FW, c.1665, 4 1/4 In. 8050.00
Dish, Sweetmeat, Scroll Handles, Fruit & Leaves, IG, 1633, 7 In. 345.00
Dish, Sweetmeat, Shell Form Handles, Leaves, William Maddox, 1632, 7 In. 4025.00
Dish, Victorian, Roses, Ribbons & Scrolls, Rose Sprays, W. Comyns, 1890, 8 1/4 In. 485.00
Dish Cross, Plate Supports, Burner With Gadrooned Rim, George III, 12 In. 1265.00
Dish Warmer, Venison, Leaves, Gadrooned Rim, Scroll Handles, Sheffield 1035.00
Dresser Set, Cobalt Blue Foil Enameled, 3 Piece 145.00
Egg Spoon, Tipped Fiddle, Ducal Crest On Handle, Paul Storr, 1813, 12 Piece 1150.00
Epergne, Scroll, Shell Border, Scrolled Arms, 1913, 11 3/4 In. 6325.00
Ewer, Chased With Overall Swirling Waves, Rocaille, Leaves, 1853, 17 In. 5780.00
Ewer, River God's Mask, Leaf Capped Double Scrolled Handle, 1831, 14 In. 13800.00
Figurine, Swan, Gilt Eyes & Beak, Removable Grids, C.J. Vander, 1997, 11 In. 9775.00
Fish Server, Scrolled Leaf Blade, Gadroon Edge Handle, 1770, 11 1/4 In. 1092.00
Fish Service, Coral & Vegetation, Porcelain, George Jones & Sons, 15 Piece 3910.00
Fish Slice, Crescents, Chased Foilage, Duncan Urquhart & Napthali Hart, 1803 . . . . 115.00
Fish Slice, Fiddle, Reticulated Blade, Robert Makepeace, 1810 . . . . 275.00
Fish Slice, Pierced Blade, Monogram, WE, 1843 . . . . 175.00
Fish Slice, Shell & Laurel King's, Engraved Handle, 2 1/2 In. 1150.00
Flask, Pocket, Gilt Line Cup, Hallmarks 77.00
Fork & Knife Set, Queen Anne, Agate Handle, James Bernardo, 1710, 8 Piece 1250.00
Frame, Egg Cup, 6 Egg Cups, Reeded Handle, 4 Ball Feet, Henry Nutting, 1800 . . . . 546.00
Frame, Picture, Navy Velvet, Double, Easel Back, 7 x 8 1/2 In. 3385.00
Funnel, Reeded Rim, Detachable Liner, Peter, Ann & William Bateman, 1804, 6 In. 980.00
Goblet, Beaded Collar, Beaded Trumpet Foot, 1775, 6 1/2 In., Pair 1955.00
Goblet, Engraved Crest, Thomas Chawner, George III, 6 1/2 In., Pair 1955.00
Goblet, Floral & Scroll Bowl, Monogram, MLF, 1865 . . . . 235.00
Goblet, Gadrooned, Beaded Bands, Gilt Interior, C. Wright, 1769, 6 In., Pair 3450.00
Goblet, Octagonal Panel, Ribbed Trumpet Foot, 1801, 7 In., Pair 1150.00
Grater, Nutmeg, Engraved Coronet, Hinged Side Opening, TT, 1834, 3 1/2 In. 748.00
Gravy Spoon, Fiddle Pattern, William Ely, William Fearn, 1805, 12 In. 175.00
Humidor, Wood Lined, Carry Handle, W. Comyns & Sons, London, 1909, 5 x 10 In. 415.00
Jug, Allover Repousse Design, Satyrs, Putti, Grapevines, London, 1883, 5 3/4 In. 1320.00
Jug, Beer, Pear Form, Double Scroll Handle, P. & A. Bateman, 1796, 8 In. 4600.00
Jug, Claret, Acanthus, Berry Mounts, Gilt, John Grinsell & Sons, 1897 . . . . 4310.00
Jug, Cream, Acanthus, Flower Heads, Oriental Figures Amid Landscape, 5 In. 920.00
Jug, Cream, Wooden Handle, Faceted Spout, Robert Makepeace, 3 3/8 In. 6900.00
Jug, Pear Shape, Serpentine Scroll Handle, Wm. Shaw & Wm. Priest, 8 In. 4315.00
Kettle, Hot Water, Applied Design, Swing Handle, McAuliff & Hadley, 8 3/4 In. 303.00
Knife, Silver Pistol Grip Handle, England, c.1760, 3 Piece 295.00
Ladle, Engraved Heraldic Symbol, London, 1824-1825, 13 1/4 In. 105.00
Ladle, Profile Medallion Of A Classical Woman, Velvet Lined Case, 12 1/2 In. 1150.00
Ladle, Shell, Ducal Crest On Handle, Paul Storr, 1813, 12 3/4 In., Pair 2070.00
Ladle, Stem & Shell Bowl, Monogram, T. & W. Chawner, 1768, 13 1/4 In. 632.00
Ladle, Toddy, Oval Bowl, 13 1/2 In. 110.00
Ladle, Toddy, Reeding Floral Husk Swags, Motto On Rim, Handle, 13 1/4 In. 115.00
Ladle, Twist-Turned Horn Handle, EM, George III, 1805 . . . . 165.00
Marrow Scoop, George Smith, William Fearn, George III, 1792, 8 1/4 In. 200.00

Marrow Scoop, London, George III, 1789, 1 Oz. 258.00
Marrow Scoop, Sterling Silver, Peter & William Bateman, London, 1801 .... 220.00
Marrow Spoon, Randall Chatterton, London, 1792 .... 275.00
Meat Cover, Gadroon Banding, Shell Handle, George III, 1776, 9 1/2 In. 2000.00
Meat Skewer, Loop Handle, Shell Ornament, George III, London, 1762, 14 In. 330.00
Mirror, Scrolls, Flowers, Curved Top, London, 1887, 14 1/4 In. 977.00
Muffineer, Cover, Twisted Banding, Domed Foot, Charles S. Harris, 7 In. 290.00
Muffineer, Tapered Cover, Tiered Foot, Charles S. Harris, 1899, 8 1/2 In. 805.00
Mug, Gilt Interior, Cylindrical, Gerald Benney, 5 1/4 In., Pair 1610.00
Mug, Shaving, Trefoil Thumbpiece, Folding Brush Bracket, G.Y. & Co., 1898, 4 In. 430.00
Mug, Tapered, Molded Rim, Coin, Scroll Handle, Asprey & A.C. Ltd., 1936, 4 3/4 In. ... 490.00
Mustard, Hinged Lid, Reeded Strap Handle, Crystal Liner, 1811 .... 247.00
Napkin Rings are listed in their own category.
Nips, Pair 44.00
Open Salt, Bombe Shape, Gadrooned Edges, Cabriole Legs, 1770, 2 In. 500.00
Pepper Castor, Baluster Form, Crispin Fuller, 1795, 6 In. 330.00
Pie Server, Oval, Pierced, Engraved Geometric Design, Charles Chesterman, 1788 ...... 115.00
Pill Box, Winged Putto, Scrolled Acanthus, Monogram, 1800s, 2 In. 28.00
Pitcher, Milk, Urn Form, Henry Vincent, 1800, 3 3/4 In. 198.00
Pitcher, Square Base, London, George III, 1814, 5 In. 275.00
Plate, Domed Meat Cover, Shell Border, Fruit Handle, Sheffield, 11 1/2 In. 3450.00
Plateau For Wine Cooler, Sheffield, c.1840 .... 3650.00
Punch Bowl, Gadroon & Dimple Banding, Charles S. Harris, London, 1898, 13 In. 1760.00
Punch Bowl, Repousse C-Scroll & Flowers, Martin Hall & Co., Sheffield, 7 In. 990.00
Punch Bowl, Swirled Lobes, Digby Scott & Benjamin Smith, 1805, 14 1/4 In. 5175.00
Punch Ladle, Down Turned Tip, Lion Crest, Hester Bateman, 14 In. 825.00
Punch Ladle, Downturned Tip, Engraved Crest, H. Bateman, 1778, 13 In. 825.00
Punch Ladle, Engraved Lion Crest, H. Bateman, 14 In. 825.00
Punch Ladle, Feather Edge Handle, Hester Bateman, 13 In. 825.00
Punch Ladle, R.S., London, 1900-1901 .... 145.00
Punch Ladle, Upturned Handle Tip, Shell Bowl, Ebenezer Coler, 1753, 13 In. 520.00
Rattle, Coral Teething End, Missing Bells, Birmingham, 5 1/2 In. 110.00
Salt, Contemporary Crests, 3 Scroll Feet, P. Storr, 1819, 3 1/4 In., 3 Piece 4887.00
Salt, Leaves Issuing From 3 Hoof Feet, Hester Bateman, 1780, 2 1/2 In., Pair 1495.00
Salt, Open, 3 Bands Of Horizontal Reeding, 2 Reeded Drop Handles, 1 In., Pair 402.00
Salt, Open, 3 Shell Feet, Scroll Legs With Flowering Vines, Gadroon Rim, 3 In. 259.00
Salt, Open, 3 Shell-Form Legs, Hoof Feet, George II, 1767, 1 3/4 In. 230.00
Salt, Scrolls & Paterae On Ground, Gold Washed Interior, R. & D. Hennell, Pair 690.00
Salt Spoon, Fiddle, Engraved Crest, William Chawner, London, 1829, Pair 98.00
Salt Spoon, Fiddle, Monogram, Hands & Son, London, 1855, 2 Piece 52.00
Salt Spoon, Fiddle, Monogram, Jacab Wintle, London, 1848, Pair 86.00
Salt Spoon, Fiddle, Monogram, James Beebe, London, George IV, 1825, 2 Piece 40.00
Salt Spoon, Master, Edward Edwards, London, 1951, Pair 175.00
Salt Spoon, Old English, Monogram, Samuel Hennell, London, 1805, Pair 29.00
Salver, 4 Scroll Leaf Feet, Molded Shell Rim, Coat Of Arms, George II, 13 In. 2185.00
Salver, Beaded Rim, 3 Tapered Supports, Hester Bateman, 1787, 12 In. 3450.00
Salver, Beaded Rim, Engraved Arms Center, Richard Rugg, 1776, 14 5/8 In. 4887.00
Salver, Beaded Rim, Monogram, Ball, Claw Feet, George III, 1780, 10 In. 4840.00
Salver, Beaded, Ribbed Border, Beaded, Ribbed Feet, 1813, 16 In. 3740.00
Salver, Bright Cut Border, Beaded Rim, 4 Bracket Feet, James Young, 19 In. 5520.00
Salver, Chased Design, Shell Border, Padded Hoof Feet, 1765, 13 In. 1485.00
Salver, Chippendale Rim, Scroll Supports, 18th Century Arms, T. Farren, 1735 .... 5460.00
Salver, Crest Design, Beaded Rim, 4 Bracket Feet, J. Bateman, 1790, 12 In. 3910.00
Salver, Engraved Coat Of Arms In Cartouche, Richard Rugg, 1759, 7 1/2 In. 632.00
Salver, Engraved Coat Of Arms, Beaded Rim, J. & T. Hannam, 1773, 14 In. 1725.00
Salver, Fruit Filled Roundels, Scalloped Rim, 3 Claw Feet, 1904, 12 1/4 In. 483.00
Salver, Gadroon Border Rim, Stylized Pad Feet, 1770s, 13 In., Pair 3450.00
Salver, Gadrooned Border, 4 Ball, Claw Feet, Footed, Edward VII, 1904, 8 In. 489.00
Salver, Hairy Ball, Claw Feet, Reeded Scroll, Shell Border, George III, 12 In. 2070.00
Salver, Masks & Shells Border, Coat Of Arms, William Burwash, 1821, 14 In. 2760.00
Salver, Piecrust Border, Circular, 3 Scrolled Feet, London, 1936, 6 In. 103.00
Salver, Piecrust Border, Scrolls & Shells, W. & R. Peaston, 1758, 9 1/2 In. 400.00
Salver, Piecrust Edge, Scroll Feet, Coat Of Arms, George II, 1733, 2 x 14 In. 3200.00

Salver, Piecrust Rim, 3 Foliate Feet, Wakely & Wheeler, 1979, 8 1/4 In. 345.00
Salver, Shaped Molded Border, 4 Scroll Feet, George II, 6 In., Pair 4025.00
Salver, Wide Band Of Florals, Fruits, Shells, Footed, 1750, 23 In. 4315.00
Sauce Ladle, Coburg, Paul Storr, 1804, 7 In., Pair 1840.00
Sauce Ladle, Crest On Terminal, George Sutton, George III, 1788 . . . .   170.00
Sauce Ladle, Onslow, Shell Bowl, W. & R. Peaston, George III, 1762, Pair 920.00
Sauceboat, 3 Hoof Feet Topped With Shells, Scroll Handle, George III, 8 In. 546.00
Sauceboat, Bombe Shape, Scalloped Edge, Scroll Handle, 1776, 3 1/2 In. 350.00
Sauceboat, Gadrooned Rim, Leaf Capped Flying Scroll Handle, I.F. & Sons, 1936 . . . . . .   315.00
Sauceboat, Oval, Gadrooned Rim Hoof Feet, William IV, 1835, 6 1/2 In. 313.00
Sauceboat, Raised On 3 Shell & Scroll Supports, R. Piercy, 1774, 7 3/4 In., Pair 4370.00
Sauceboat, Sides Chased With Spiral Flutes, Handle, 1843, 9 In., Pair 16100.00
Sauceboat, Snake Handle, Silver Gilt Stand, Rawlings & Summers, 10 In. 10350.00
Serving Bowl, Repousse, Open Rim, 1895, 2 x 10 1/4 In. 355.00
Serving Dish, Cover, Flat Leaves, Acanthus, Lion Herm Handles, 8 x 10 1/2 In. 805.00
Serving Spoon, Apostle, W. Hutton & Sons, Presentation Case, 1895, Pair 195.00
Serving Spoon, Engraved Crest, William Eley & William Fearn, 1818, 11 3/4 In. 200.00
Serving Spoon, Scrolled Leaves, William Bateman, Daniel Ball, 1840, 11 1/2 In. 200.00
Shaving Mug, Reeded Rim, Ivory Handle, Hinged Cover, Engraved Crest, 4 In. 400.00
Soup, Dish, Gadroon Rims, Double Shells, Robert Garrard, 1842, 10 In., 8 Piece 3450.00
Soup Ladle, Dart Handle, Sheffield, 1905, 12 Oz. 100.00
Soup Ladle, Fiddle Thread Pattern, Crest, George Angel, London, 1863 . . . .   220.00
Soup Spoon, Peter, Ann & William Bateman, George III, 1803, Pair 200.00
Spice Box, Cherub, Holding Flower, Motto, Thomas Tysoe, c.1690, 1 5/8 In. 1840.00
Spoon, Fluted Bowl, Demitasse, John Wren, George III, 5 In., 6 Piece 258.00
Spoon Set, Demitasse, Leather Case, Liberty, 6 Piece 220.00
Stand, Dessert, Flowers, Leaves & Buds On Base, B. Smith III, 9 5/8 In. 5462.00
Stuffing Spoon, Engraved Crest, John Beldon, George III, 1804 . . . .   230.00
Stuffing Spoon, Fiddle Handle, 1850 . . . .   275.00
Stuffing Spoon, George Wintle, George III, 1802, 12 In. 172.00
Stuffing Spoon, Matched Heraldic Crest, Thomas Dealtry, 11 3/8 & 12 In., Pair 373.00
Stuffing Spoon, Monogram, George III, 1809, 4 Oz. 230.00
Stuffing Spoon, Old English, George III, 1817, 12 In. 302.00
Stuffing Spoon, Shell, Ducal Crest, Handle, Paul Storr, 1813, 12 1/2 In., 4 Piece 3680.00
Sugar, Ribbon Tied Floral Sprays, Beaded Rim, Spiral Loop Handles, 5 In. 345.00
Sugar, Ribbon Tied Floral Sprays, Swags, Beaded Rim, George III, 1769, 8 In. 405.00
Sugar & Creamer, Reeded Lower Section, Angular Handles, George III, 4 In. 316.00
Sugar Box, Chinamen Picking Tea Leaves, Thomas Heming, 1753, 5 In. 4887.00
Sugar Castor, Flowers & Leaves, Ball Finial, 1897, 7 1/4 In. 375.00
Sugar Spoon, Beaded Rim, Peter & Anne Bateman, London, 1791 . . . .   120.00
Sugar Tongs, Bright Cut Design, Monogram, Hester Bateman, George III 430.00
Sugar Tongs, Bright Cut Design, Monogram, Hester Bateman, London, c.1780 . . . .   260.00
Sugar Tongs, Bright Cut Zigzag Design, Stephen Adams, London, 1800 . . . .   105.00
Sugar Tongs, Engraved Design, Acorn Bowl, London, 1803 . . . .   95.00
Sugar Tongs, Outstretched Monkey Form, Crabstock Handles, 1884, 5 In., Pair 920.00
Sugar Tongs, Plain Fiddle Bow, Thomas Sewell, Newcastle, 1873 . . . .   71.00
Tablespoon, Fiddle, Monogram, William Eley, George IV, 1826, 8 3/4 In., Pair 201.00
Tablespoon, Stag's Head Crest, TL, London, 1784, Pair 295.00
Tablespoon, T & W Chawner, c.1769, Pair 287.00
Tankard, Cartouche Body, Gadrooned Foot Rim, Serpentine Handle, 7 In. 1265.00
Tankard, Crest, Heart Terminal Handle, T. Whipham & C. Wright, 1758, 7 1/4 In. 2645.00
Tankard, Domed Cover, Handle, Alice & George Burrows, 1813, 8 1/4 In. 3105.00
Tankard, Vacant Cartouche, Birds On Branches, Gabriel Sleath, 1748, 8 1/4 In. 2300.00
Taperstick, Paneled Stem, Stepped Base, George II, 1737, 4 1/4 In., Pair 1035.00
Tea & Coffee Service, Domed Cover, Angular Handles, George V, 4 Piece 460.00
Tea & Coffee Service, Plain Wreath To 1 Side, John Emes, 1802, 3 Piece 1955.00
Tea & Coffee Service, Scroll Handles, Stepped Lids, George V, 1911, 4 Piece 1380.00
Tea & Coffee Service, Scroll, Shell Lozenges, Shell Feet, London, 1862, 6 Piece 4312.00
Tea & Coffee Set, Band Of Aesthetic Movement Style Scroll Vines, 3 Piece 575.00
Tea & Coffee Set, Ear Handles, Flat Leaves, Manchester Silver Co., 5 Piece 1092.00
Tea & Coffee Set, Floral Swags, Crest, Paneled, Hexagonal, Victorian, 5 Piece 1650.00
Tea & Coffee Set, Melon Form, Silver Handle, 1829, 4 Piece 2420.00
Tea & Coffee Set, Wooden Handles, Scroll Feet, George VI, 1948, 4 Piece 5460.00

Tea Caddy, Floral Rim, Swags, Flower Finial, Ayme Videau, 1753, 6 In., Pair 2990.00
Tea Caddy, Hinged Cover, Beaded Design, Urn Finial, 4 1/4 In. 300.00
Tea Caddy, Oval Plaque With Bat's Wing Fluting, Crichton Bros., 1911, 4 3/4 In. 575.00
Tea Service, Convex Horizontal Band With Florals, Hannah Northcote, 6 In. 1380.00
Tea Service, Ebonized Finials, Peter, Ann & Wm. Bateman, 1800, 3 Piece 2420.00
Tea Service, Pear Shape, Ivory Loop Handle, Monogram, George V, 10 In. 862.00
Tea Service, Rococo Style, Bird Finial, Martin Hall & Co., Ltd., c.1885, 5 Piece 895.00
Tea Set, Engraved Family Crest, Alexander Field, George III, 3 Piece 3000.00
Tea Set, Family Crest, Scroll Handles, Alexander Field, 3 Piece 3000.00
Tea Set, Floral Finial, Panel Design, Acanthus Scroll Feet, Marked BP, 4 Piece 3200.00
Tea Set, Partial Vertical Lobing, Angular Handle, Wm. Bateman, 1800, 3 Piece 1495.00
Tea Urn, 2 Lion's Masks, Ring Handles, 4 Ball Feet, John Robins, 1788, 17 In. 2300.00
Tea Urn, Floral Swags, Beaded Loop Handles, 4 Ball Feet, 1778, 15 In. 2070.00
Tea Urn, Ivory Spigot, Beaded Rims, Circular Foot, C. Wright, 1781, 19 In. 3450.00
Teakettle, Floor Stand, Swan's Neck Spout, L.A. Crichton, 1912, 37 1/4 In. 2300.00
Teapot, Bands Of Chased Diamond, Stag Armorial Reserves, George III, 7 In. 1210.00
Teapot, Bullet Form, Engraved Scrolls, Ivory Handles, 1884, 5 In. 650.00
Teapot, Chased Diamond Design, Stag Armorial Reserve, George III, 1800, 7 In. 825.00
Teapot, Cover, Serpentine Spout, Scroll Ear Handle, William IV, 1837, 5 In. 488.00
Teapot, Domed Cover, Bright Cut Rim, Ear Handle, George III, 1798, 6 In. 865.00
Teapot, Flat Cover, Bullet Shape, Wooden Handle, George I, Joseph Clare, 4 In. 6900.00
Teapot, Flowers, Fruit & Rococo Leaves, Sheffield, 9 1/4 In. 1045.00
Teapot, Fluted Oval Body, Floral Border, Peter & Ann Bateman, 1798, 6 1/2 In. 1760.00
Teapot, Overall Leaf & Scroll, Hands & Son, 1868, 5 1/2 In. 460.00
Teapot, Scrolls, Cartouches, Paneled Serpentine Spout, Handle, 1843, 6 In. 546.00
Teapot, Serpentine Handle, Male Figure Serpentine Spout, J.E. Terry, 1832, 7 In. 1265.00
Teapot, Tied Floral Spray, Shield & Crest, Robert Hennell, 1785, 6 1/2 In. 920.00
Teapot Stand, 4 Ball & Claw Feet, Oval, George III, 1809, 6 1/2 In. 172.00
Toast Rack, Ball Feet, London, 5 In. 165.00
Toast Rack, Central Handles, Rectangular, George III, 1793, 6 1/2 In. 546.00
Toast Rack, Joseph Craddock & William Reid, George III, 1783, 6 1/2 In. 460.00
Toby Mug, Strap Handle, James Goodwin, 1714, 2 In. 1265.00
Tray, Alternating With Rococo Cartouches, 4 Ball Feet, Oval, 30 1/2 In. 4600.00
Tray, Beaded Border, Lion Guarding Castle Feet, John Sheffield, 1780, 18 In. 3450.00
Tray, Circular Piecrust Top, 4 Feet, London, 1738, 10 In. 880.00
Tray, Engraved Scrolls & Grapes, Shell Rim, F. Kandler, 1756, 13 1/2 In. 2070.00
Tray, Gadroon Border, Handles, Oval, Robert Garrard, George III, 17 3/4 In. 3220.00
Tray, Gadrooned Edge, Stylized Feathers On Handles, George III, 1817, 25 In. 2415.00
Tray, Handles From Leaves, Scrolling Leaves, Crouch & Hannam, 27 In. 6900.00
Tray, Leaf & Scroll Intervals, Arms, Ebenezer Coker, 1768, 12 3/4 In. 2830.00
Tray, Molded Wavy Rim, Openwork Scrolls, Scroll Handles, 1878, 31 In. 6900.00
Tray, Openwork Grape Clusters, Bacchic Masks, Crichton Bros., 1911, 30 In. 6900.00
Tray, Oval, Engraved Flowers, Double Handles, c.1950, 15 x 25 In. 300.00
Tray, Oval, Engraved Flowers, Scrolls In Wheel, Double Handle, 1950, 15 In. 350.00
Tray, Pierced Rim, Shell & Leaf Borders, Hoop Handles, Maxfield, 29 In. 5175.00
Tray, Reeded Molded Border, Reeded Side Handles, 4-Footed, 27 In. 3680.00
Tumbler, Engraved Coat Of Arms, Richard Bayley, 1717, 2 5/8 In. 2530.00
Tureen, Sauce, Cover, Boat Shaped Body, Ribbed, Monogram, George III, Pair 2760.00
Tureen, Sauce, Cover, Bombe Form, Leaves, Flowers, 2 Handles, 8 In., Pair 5520.00
Tureen, Sauce, Hinged Ring Handles, Foliate Ring Finials, P. Podio, 1802, 6 In. 3737.00
Tureen, Soup, Shell, Acanthus Leaves, Acanthus Handles, 1819, 14 1/2 In. 7475.00
Vase, Bowtie Leaf Garlands, 2 Handles, Wm. Jackson & W. Chase, 1881, 6 In. 230.00
Vase, Trumpet, Acanthus Leaves, Lions' Masks, Fruit, Heming, 1908, 15 In., Pair 9775.00
Vase, Trumpet, Floral Form Pierced Lip, George V, 1919, 11 1/4 In. 350.00
Waiter, Piecrust Border, 3 Hoof Feet, John Robinson, 1741, 6 1/2 In. 632.00
Waiter, Serpentine Shell, Center Flowers, W.M. Easton, 1749, 7 In. 715.00
Waiter, Tray, Chased Line Design, Stag Head, George III, 1800, 6 In. 660.00
Water Jug, Floral & Fruit Band, Center Vacant Cartouche, Elkington, 14 In. 1955.00
Wine Coaster, Gadroon Rim, Turned Hardwood Base, 1810, Pair 605.00
Wine Coaster, Pierced Latticework Sides, 5 In., Pair 550.00
Wine Cooler, Gadrooned & Leaf Band, Coat Of Arms, Reeded Handles, 9 In. 460.00
Wine Cooler, Leaf Scrollwork, Noble Crest On Front & Back, 9 x 11 In., Pair 1650.00
Wine Funnel, Banded Design, Charles Chesterman II, George III, 1813, 6 In. 880.00

Wine Funnel, Gadrooned Edge, Feather Design, George III, 1817, 5 In. 550.00
SILVER-FRENCH, Bowl, Empire, Cut Glass, Mounted, Scroll Handles, Cover, c.1819, 8 1/2 In. 1380.00
  Cigarette Case, Alternating Bands Of Red, Yellow Gold, 2-Tone Gold, 1930 .... 4025.00
  Coffee & Tea Set, Ribbed Baluster, Wooden Handles, Late 19th Century, 4 Piece 2185.00
  Coffeepot, Domed Cover, Foliate Swags, Sprays, Wreaths, Louis XVI, 8 1/2 In. 1150.00
  Coffeepot, Domed Cover, Pear Shape, Serpentine Handle, 9 1/4 In. 460.00
  Coffeepot, Domed Hinged Cover, Pear Shape, Wooden Handle, Louis XVI, 8 In. 1725.00
  Coffeepot, Domed Stepped Cover, Wooden Handle, 1938, 7 1/2 In. 1092.00
  Condiment Set, Wire Work Bodies, Baluster Handles, 1836, Pair 6325.00
  Dish, Cover, Crayfish, Snip Shape, Twig Shaped Handles, Turquet, 11 In., Pair 9775.00
  Dish, Cover, Liner, Loop Handles, Seated Boy Finial, A. Aucoc, 12 3/4 In. 2090.00
  Dish, Sweetmeat, Shell Form, Putto, Standing, Poised As Neptune, 5 In., Pair 2070.00
  Mustard, Idiot, Kneeling Woman Form, Applied Nuts & Bolts, 1920s, 5 In. 6612.00
  Mustard, Palmette Band At Foot & Rim, Loop Handle, Cobalt Liner, 6 In., Pair 630.00
  Pepper Mill, Baluster Form, Swirled Panels, 4 3/4 In., Pair 325.00
  Pitcher, Basin, Churn Shape, Spot-Hammered, G. Keller, 1890, 13 In. & 10 In. 4600.00
  Platter, Fish Serving, Reeded Rim, Monogram, Oval, 1838, 27 3/4 In. 1265.00
  Platter, Fish, Berried Laurel Rim, Interrupted By Acanthus, 23 1/2 In., Pair 2070.00
  Platter, Louis XV, Arms On Rim, Signed, Guillaume Hannier, 1738, 15 In. 3105.00
  Platter, Meat, Tetard Freres, Laurel Rim, Leaves At Intervals, 23 3/4 In., Pair 2875.00
  Punch Cup & Saucer, Engraved Foliate, c.1870, 6 Sets 430.00
  Punch Ladle, Long Curved Handle, Shallow Bowl, 18th Century, 14 In. 140.00
  Saucepan, Bands Of Roses, Ivory Handle, 1880 .... 4890.00
  Serving Dish, Vertical Reeded Border, 2 Shell Handles, Oval, 2 1/4 In. 488.00
  Snuffbox, Beaded Cover, Center Monogram, Keller, 3 1/4 In. 230.00
  Snuffbox, Engine Turned, Berried Leaves On Lid, c.1880, 3 In. 315.00
  Stand, Pierced Border, Putti, Cartouches, Paw Feet, Cardeilhac, 6 In., Pair 865.00
  Tea Set, Monogram, Louis Philippe, Mid 19th Century, 4 Piece 1380.00
  Teapot, Serpentine Spout, Wooden Handle, Fruit Sprig Finial, 1850s, 11 3/4 In. 230.00
  Tray, Hammered, Glass Bottom, Handle, LeBolt, 10 x 5 In. 230.00
  Tray, Stepped Molded Borders, Plain Panels Corners, Ghiso, 1940, 16 In., Pair 3737.00
  Tumbler, Picasso Style, Gold Interior, 3 1/2 In. 175.00
  Tureen, Flat Leaf Cover, Reeded Shoulder, Angular Handles, 12 3/4 In. 1840.00
  Urn, Caviar, Domed Cover, Parrot Finial, Spoon Holder, 11 1/4 In. 690.00
  Wine Cooler, Berried Laurel Swags On Body, Laurel Rims, 20th Century, 9 In. 1495.00
  Wine Taster, Inset 18th Century Style Coin, Louis XVI On Handle, 3 1/2 In. 495.00
  Wine Taster, Raised Boss Bottom, Smaller Domes, Mid 19th Century, 2 3/4 In. 440.00
  Wine Taster, Swirl & Inverted Dome Border, 1903, 3 In. 275.00
SILVER-GERMAN, Basket, Latticework, Open Berried Border, Acanthus Ends, 14 1/2 In. 690.00
  Basket, Pierced Paneled Sides, Flowers, Garlands, 4 Vacant Cartouches, 14 In. 175.00
  Beaker, Sides Chased With Floral Swags, Shell, Scroll Cartouches, 5 In., Pair 19550.00
  Beaker, Underplate, Cartouches, Courting Couples, Gold Interior, 6 In., Pair 375.00
  Book Cover, Spine Chased With Rocaille, Figure Of Faith On Back, 1750, 7 In. 1840.00
  Bowl, Courting Couple Scene, Reticulated, Foliate Swags, Leaves, 10 1/2 In. 431.00

Silver-German, Salt & Pepper,
Swan Finial, Base, Engraved,
19th Century, 6 In.

**Do not display or store silver on
shelves painted with latex paint.
It encourages tarnish.**

Bowl, Repousse Figures, Acanthus Leaves, c.1900, 6 1/2 In. 58.00
Bowl, Repousse, Chased With Panels Of Bunches Of Fruit, Footed, 3 In., Pair 402.00
Chain, Black Grosgrain Ribbon, Sterling Silver 230.00
Cigarette Case, Engine Turned, c.1925, 4 x 2 3/4 In. 110.00
Creamer, Figural, Cow, Standing Heifer, Upturned Tail As Handle, 1924, 7 In. 2760.00
Cup, Cover, Vase Shape, Putto At Country Scene, Lavender Ground, 3 In. 4025.00
Cup, Presentation, Urn Shape, Art Nouveau, Elk Finial, 1930, 21 x 8 In. 1540.00
Dish, Sweetmeat, 4 Figures Playing Game, Hans Jacob Baur III, 6 3/8 In. 1035.00
Figure, Pheasant, Movable Wings, 17 1/2 & 14 1/2 In., Pair 2465.00
Inkstand, Fruit & Leaf Swags, 2 Sand & Ink Vessels, Frey, c.1700, 11 In. 3450.00
Match Safe, Envelope Shape, Blue Cabochon Stone, 2 x 2 1/4 In. 105.00
Ornament, Pheasant, Male & Female, Articulated Wings, 1910s, 18 In., Pair 2645.00
Prayer Cup, Shaped Handle, Chain, 9 1/4 In. 770.00
Salt & Pepper, Swan Finial, Base, Engraved, 19th Century, 6 In. ....*Illus* 125.00
Serving Bowl, 9 Panels, Cupid & Companions, Glass Liner, 1870s, 7 x 9 In. 710.00
Serving Dish, Trefoil Shape, 3 Handles, Repousse Leaf Buds & Lines, 12 In. 1150.00
Ship Model, Neresheimer, Spanish Arms, Sailors, Cannon, 1906, 21 1/2 In. 7475.00
Tea & Coffee Service, Baluster Form, Leaf Handles, 80 Oz., 5 Piece 805.00
Teapot, Leaf Tip Borders, Swan's Head Spout, G.L. Howaldt, c.1825, 6 1/4 In. 4025.00
Teapot, Vase Form, Flared Spout, Silver & Wood Finial, J.F. Wiese, 1737, 4 In. 6037.00
Tray, Dogwood Panels Border, 15 In. Diam. 465.00
Tray, Fluted, Scalloped Border, Scroll Footed, 12 In. Diam. 245.00
Wine Cooler, Race Prize, Entwined Vine Branch Handles, 1830, 11 In. 6900.00
Punch Ladle, Handle, Gold Washed Bowl, Sterling Silver, 1888, 13 3/4 In. 56.00
SILVER-INDIAN, Bowl, Center, 9 Panels, Peasants, Short Stem, Round Foot, Calcutta, 9 In. ... 140.00
SILVER-IRISH, Cake Basket, Openwork Rim Linked By Shells, Ovals, JL, c.1770, 14 In. 6900.00
Caudal Cup, Cover, Single Molded Band, Crabstock Handle, 7 1/4 In., Pair 5175.00
Cup, Leaf Capped Double Scroll Handles, Thomas Walker, 4 1/2 x 6 7/8 In., Pair 6000.00
Fish Server, Engraved Dolphin, Richard Garde, Leroy Williams, 1821, 11 In. 330.00
Gravy Boat, Lion Mask, Paw Feet, Scroll Handle, John Williams, c.1770, 8 In. 1150.00
Salver, Heraldic Crest In Center, Scrolled Legs, 3 Pad Feet, George II, Dublin, 6 In. 1092.00
Sauceboat, Trailing Flowers, 3 Shell & Hoof Feet, G. Hill, c.1760, 8 1/4 In., Pair 4312.00
Sugar Basket, Boat Shape, Swing Handle, Thomas Jones, 1791, 5 1/2 In. 1265.00
Teapot, Cartouche On Sides, Leaf Ear Handle, Serpentine Spout, J. Le Bass, 6 1/8 In. ... 805.00
Teapot, Panels Of Foliate Scrolls, Vine Scroll Spout, J. LeBass, 1841, 6 1/4 In. 1955.00
Tray, Snuffer, Octagonal Boat Shape, Heraldic Crest, William Doyle, Dublin, 10 In. 690.00
SILVER-ITALIAN, Basket, Centerpiece, Fruit Cluster Cover, Twig Handle, M. Buccellati, 9 In. 8050.00
Bowl, 6 Nautilus Shells, Ring Of Clam Shells, Buccellati, 79 Oz. 9775.00
Bowl, Centerpiece, Cabbage Form, Hollow Interior, Buccellati, 10 In. 3220.00
Jardiniere, Metal, Turned Ring Handles, Flat Bun Feet, 14 7/8 x 20 1/2 In., Pair 10350.00
Lamp, Oil, 3 Spouts, Lions' Masks, Snuffers, Tweezers, 26 In. 8050.00
Pepper Mill, Artichoke Form, 7 1/4 In., 4 Piece 7475.00
Salt Cellar, Figural, Shell Supported By Boy On Dolphin, 6 1/4 In., Pair 990.00
Tea & Coffee Set, With Tray, Swirl Pattern, Pear Shape, Buccellati, 7 Piece 10230.00
SILVER-JAPANESE, Berry Spoon, Strawberry, Clam Shell Bowl, 9 In. 1200.00
Bowl, 9 1/4 x 14 1/2 In. 7475.00
Punch Bowl, Late 19th Century 4600.00
Saltshaker, Fan Shape, Parcel Gilt, 2 3/4 In. 55.00
Tea Caddy, Hand Hammered, Vacant Cartouche Center, Octagonal, 4 1/2 In. 115.00
Tray, Arthur & Bond, Yokohama, Round, 18 In. 1955.00
Vase, Engraved Pagoda, Trees & Mountains, 10 In. 518.00
SILVER-MEXICAN, Ashtray, Dot Design, Holders At Top, 3 Ball Feet, Spratling, 2 1/4 In. ... 410.00
Bowl, Acanthus, Sanborns Mexico Sterling, Footed, 5 In., 13 Oz., Pair 84.00
Bowl, Revere Style, Conquistador Mexico 925/1000, 9 1/2 In., 28 Oz. 134.00
Bowl, Scalloped Edge, Shaped Feet, Handles, Silver Beads, 19 1/4 In. 172.00
Bowl, Scrolled Acanthus, Sterling 930, 6 In., 10 Oz. 34.00
Box, Ornate Repousse Border, Hechden, 4 x 8 In. 165.00
Cake Knife, Rosewood Handle, William Spratling, c.1947, 6 1/2 In. 143.00
Candleholder, William Spratling, Taxco, 1931-1945 .... 2750.00
Coffee Set, William Spratling, c.1967, 8 3/4 In. 2530.00
Cribbage Set, Rosewood Case, Los Castillo, c.1950, 7 5/8 In. 1150.00
Dish, Sectional, Round, 6 Sections, Embossed Scrolls, 1940, 22 1/4 In. 300.00
Dish, Shell, Scroll Footed, Sanborns Sterling, 8 1/2 x 5 In., Pair 440.00

Ice Bucket, Scrolled Acanthus, Eagle Mark, 5 In, 24 Oz. 364.00
Letter Opener, Stylized Beaver On Handle, William Spratling, c.1950, 7 1/2 In. 1380.00
Pitcher, Bands At Neck, Hammered, Ebony Handle, Spratling, 1950s, 6 In. 4125.00
Pitcher, Leaf Capped Scroll Handle, Colorado Silver Company, 10 1/4 In. 125.00
Pitcher, Parrot Form Handle, Malachite Green Trim, 12 In. 275.00
Pitcher, Scrolled Acanthus, Eagle Mark, 930 Silver, 12 1/2 In., 43 Oz. 504.00
Plate, Service, Scalloped Edge, Molded Rim, 25 Oz. 89.00
Punch Bowl, Scrolled Acanthus, Molded, Carved, Crown 925, 9 x 14 In. 840.00
Punch Ladle, Rope Design, Connecting To Mahogany Handle, Signed, 12 In. 550.00
Salt & Pepper, Pierced Leaf Overlay, 3 In. 70.00
Sugar & Creamer, Scrolled Acanthus, Crown 925, Cover, 7 In., 45 Oz. 364.00
Sugar & Creamer, Tray, C-Scroll Borders, Serpentine Handles, 11-In. Tray 175.00
Tea & Coffee Set, Double-Handled Tray, Taxco, Late 20th Century, 6 Piece 2300.00
Tea & Coffee Set, Scrolled Feet, Monogram, Signed, 6 Piece 920.00
Tea Set, Rose Decoration, 4 Piece 770.00
Tea Set, Scrolling Leaf Design At Base, 8 Piece 3450.00
Tray, Acanthus, Handles, Caral 925, 28 In., 80 Oz. 952.00
Tray, Acanthus, Sterling, Mexico, Caral, Crown, 19 1/2 In., 45 Oz. 280.00
Tray, Molded Border, Pierced Handles, Maciel Sterling, 20 In., 45 Oz. 252.00
Tray, Scalloped Blown-Out Rim, Acanthus, 925, 23 In., 104 Oz. 896.00
Tray, Scalloped Rim, Pierced Handles 333.00
Tray, Serving, Scrolled Acanthus Border, Handles, Sterling Silver, 50 Oz. 308.00
Tray, Twisted Handles, Hammered, Oval, Spratling, 13 1/2 In. 4950.00
SILVER-NORWEGIAN, Spoon, Squirrel, Acorn Design On Handle, Th. Marthinsen, 9 In. 374.00
SILVER-PERSIAN, Sprinkler, Rosewater, Removable Spire, Dangling Ornaments, 13 In. 405.00
SILVER-PERUVIAN, Aquamenile, Crowned Lion Shape, 19th Century, 10 x 9 In. 605.00
Bowl, Scroll & Flower Designs, 13 1/2 In. 230.00
Sauceboat, Attached Undertray, Shaped Oval, Scrolls & Flowers, 9 1/2 In. 115.00
SILVER-POLISH, Pomander, 5 Compartments Top, 18th Century, 3 3/8 In. 3162.00
Sugar Box, Foliate Body, Hinged Cover, Chased Geometric Design, 5 In. 115.00
SILVER-PORTUGUESE, Dish, Pierced Rim With Cartouches, Flower Head Design, 14 1/4 In. . 980.00
Ewer, Paneled & Chased Body, Baroque Cartouches, c.1760, 9 1/2 In. 4600.00

SILVER-RUSSIAN. Russian silver is marked with the Cyrillic, or Russian, alphabet. The numbers 84, 88, or 91 indicate the silver content. Russian silver may be higher or lower than sterling standard. Other marks indicate maker, assayer, or city of manufacture. Many pieces of silver made in Russia are decorated with enamel. Faberge pieces are listed in their own category.

SILVER-RUSSIAN, Altar, Crucified Christ On Front, Crosses, Moscow, 1917, 10 1/2 In. 672.00
Basket, Enameled Leaf Reserves, Moscow, 1900, 3 1/8 x 4 In. 1495.00
Basket, Enameled Scalework, Gilt, Nemirov-Kolodkin, 1895, 6 In. 2875.00
Basket, Fruit, Wreath Of Cherries Interior, Bail Handle, Moscow, 1889, 11 In. 560.00
Beaker, Chased Wide Band Of Birds, Moscow, 1775, 3 1/4 In. 1495.00
Beaker, Niello, Ship At Port & Peter The Great, Moscow, 1840, 2 1/4 In. 728.00
Beaker, Pair Of Lovebirds & Swags, Cylindrical, Moscow, 1793, 3 In. 336.00
Beaker, Repousse, Eagles, Leaves, Cyrillic A.V. Mark, Moscow, 1798, 3 1/4 In. 196.00
Beaker, Scrolled Flowering Leaves, Bear & Elk Lower Border, 1890, 9 In. 7475.00

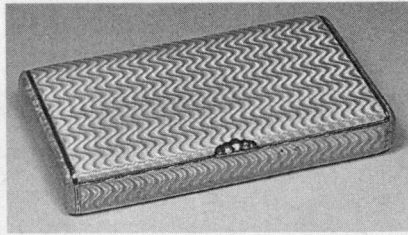

Silver-Russian, Cigarette Case, Guilloche Enamel,
Andre Goreanov, 3 1/2 In.

Silver-Russian, Kovsh, Blue, Floral,
Artel, 1908-1917, 11 In.

To copy a silver hallmark, try this. Hold a candle under the mark so the candle soot covers the mark. After the silver cools, put a piece of transparent tape over the mark and push it down. Remove the tape and put it on a piece of paper. You should have a copy of the mark.

Silver-Russian, Pot, Cover,
Shaded Enamel, 3 1/2 In.

Beaker, Vodka, Gilt Interior, Niello, 1855-1870, 3 In., Pair	260.00
Bell Push, Figure Of An Elephant Standing On Enameled Mat, Moscow, 1900, 2 In.	3162.00
Belt, Niello, Cyrillic L.K. Mark, Kiev, Child's, 1890, 24 In.	280.00
Bowl, Caviar, Slip-On Cover, Stand, Hoops, M. Ivanov, 1896, 18 Oz.	1150.00
Bowl, Cover, Flowering Plants, Gilt Stippled, A. Kuzmichev, 4 3/4 In.	1380.00
Bowl, Cover, Stand, Fruit Shape, Repousse, Twig Handles, Sazikov, 1878, 7 In.	1380.00
Bowl, Enameled Floral, Peacock Interior, M. Semyonova, 1900, 4 In.	4600.00
Bowl, Tongs, Landscape Scene With Pond Lilies, Moscow, 1908, 4 In.	336.00
Box, Cigar, Trompe L'Oeil, Wood Grain Bands, Andeiev, St. Petersburg, 1891	14950.00
Box, Egyptian Motifs, Enameled, Moscow, 1908, 1 1/4 In.	56.00
Box, Niello Design On Cover, 1867, 2 3/4 x 4 1/2 In.	460.00
Box, Niello, Cityscape, Trompe L'Oeil Engraving, Geometric Design, 1877, 4 In.	390.00
Box, Niello, Gilt Cartouche, Geometric Designs, Nikolai Ivanov, 1869, 3 x 2 In.	280.00
Buckle, Silver Filigree, Tiflis, 1908, 3 1/2 In.	84.00
Cake Basket, Basket Weave, Napkin, Rope Handles, Khlebnikov, 1881, 15 In.	2875.00
Cake Basket, Swing Handle, Gilt Interior, St. Petersburg, 1885, 10 7/8 In.	1725.00
Chalice, Acanthus Leaves, Bundle Of Wheat Stem, Domed Base, Gilt, 10 In.	1400.00
Chalice, Repousse Domed Base With 4 Evangelists, Moscow, 1892, 9 In.	2128.00
Cigarette Case, Alternating Yellow, Red Gold, 2-Tone Gold, St. Petersburg, 1910	5750.00
Cigarette Case, Cover, Cast Leaves, Blossoms, Rose Cut Diamond, 3 3/4 In.	5175.00
Cigarette Case, Cover, Vesta Compartment, Moscow, 1917	2875.00
Cigarette Case, Enameled Kremlin, Mosaic Base, Khlebnikov, 1875, 4 1/4 In.	5520.00
Cigarette Case, Enameled, Varied Reeds, Gold Monogram, Moscow, 1908	1380.00
Cigarette Case, Gold Enamel Over Central Sunburst, Rectangular, 1890, 3 In.	8050.00
Cigarette Case, Guilloche Enamel, Andre Goreanov, 3 1/2 In. *Illus*	5600.00
Cigarette Case, Hinged Cover, Gold, Tsar Nicholas II Diamond Frame, 4 In.	3920.00
Cigarette Case, Hinged Cover, Translucent Blue, Diamond, Wave Ground, 3 In.	2016.00
Cigarette Case, Hinged Match Compartment, Rectangular, 1890, 4 x 2 In.	431.00
Cigarette Case, Lapis Lazuli Thumbpiece, Rectangular, St. Petersburg, 1890, 3 In.	460.00
Cigarette Case, Oyster, Diamond Set Thumbpiece, Fitted Wooden Case, 1910, 3 In.	4600.00
Cigarette Case, Psyche & Cupid, Sterling Silver, 4 x 3 In.	355.00
Cigarette Case, Reeded, Gold Monogram, Moscow, 1880	490.00
Cigarette Case, Ribbon Tied Palmette Band, Rose Cut Diamonds, 3 1/2 In.	9200.00
Cross, Baptismal, Moscow, 1896, 2 x 1/4 In.	100.00
Cross, Priestal, Crucified Christ, Gilt, Cipher Of Tsar Paved 1 On Reverse, 26 In.	1008.00
Cross, Priestal, Marked, Kiev, 1908, 27 In.	448.00
Crucifix, Enameled Plaque, Ovchinnikov, 1900, 19 In.	4600.00
Cup, Toasting, 2 Winged Cherubs Blowing Trumpets, Floral, Moscow, 5 In.	336.00
Cup & Saucer, Flowering Leaves, Gilt Stippled, Openwork Handle, 1900, 5 In.	4887.00
Cup & Saucer, Multicolored Flowers, Cream, Blue Ground, Moscow, 1900, 5 In.	2587.00
Dish, Salt, Strapwork & Scales, Moscow, 1854, 3 In.	196.00
Egg, Christ Has Risen!, Gilt Interior, Moscow, 1908, 3 In.	672.00
Egg, Engraved Cross, Christ Has Risen!, 2 Sections, Moscow, 1899, 2 3/4 In.	252.00
Egg, Engraved Roosters, 2 Sections, Cyrillic P.T. Mark, Moscow, 1908, 2 1/2 In.	224.00
Egg, Hand Painted With Flowers, Lavender Ground, Gilt, 2 1/4 In.	168.00

Egg, Lacquered, Cityscape, Hinged, Amber Glass Egg Within, Hallmark, 2 3/4 In. 224.00
Egg, Reverse Side Has Swallows, Pink Ground, 19th Century, 3 In. 448.00
Holder, Matchbox, Colorful Swan Surrounded By Blooming Florals, 2 1/2 In. 504.00
Holder, Tea Glass, Birch Basket, Heavy Handle, Moscow, 1890, 3 1/2 In. 196.00
Holder, Tea Glass, Blank Cartouche, Moscow, 1892, 3 1/2 In. 196.00
Holder, Tea Glass, Champleve, Gilt Hoops, Sazikov, 1875, 2 3/4 In. 460.00
Holder, Tea Glass, Enameled, Gilt Stippled, Handle, Khlebnikov, 1910, 3 3/4 In. 2300.00
Holder, Tea Glass, Pierced Body, Art Nouveau Handle, 4 1/4 In. 196.00
Holder, Tea Glass, Pierced Rim, Moscow, 1917, 4 In. 196.00
Holder, Tea Glass, Stylized Leaves, Gilt Tippled, Gustav Klingert, 1888, 3 3/4 In. 920.00
Jug, Cream, Cover, Milk Can Form, Gilt Interior, St. Petersburg, 1885, 4 1/2 In. 448.00
Kovsh, Blue, Floral, Artel, 1908-1917, 11 In. ....*Illus* 7000.00
Kovsh, Canary Yellow Enameled Interior, Handle, Ring Foot, 1900, 5 1/4 In. 4600.00
Kovsh, Cloisonne Enamel, Nikolay Vasilevich Alexeyev, c.1896 .... 715.00
Kovsh, Enamel Leaves, Hook Handle, Ring Foot, F. Ruckert, 1900, 4 3/4 In. 2530.00
Kovsh, Enamel, Boyarina, Holding Bread & Salt, Kurlukov, 1910, 10 3/4 In. 9200.00
Kovsh, Enamel, Gustav Klingert, c.1900, 8 In. 4480.00
Kovsh, Enamel, Multicolored Leaves, Peach Ground, Hook Handle, 1910, 4 In. 1725.00
Kovsh, Enamel, Pan Slavic Design, Hook Handle, 1917, 3 In. 1344.00
Kovsh, Enamel, Pan Slavic Design, Hook Handle, Cream Ground, 1917, 6 In. 2800.00
Kovsh, Enamel, Scrolled Leaves, Floral Buds On Raised Repousse, Cream, 6 In. 1792.00
Kovsh, Enamel, Scrolled Leaves, Red, Gilt Interior, IR In Shield Mark, 5 In. 1380.00
Kovsh, Gilt, Enamel, Flowers, Green Ground, Handle, 1900, 8 3/4 In. 7475.00
Kovsh, Gilt, Enamel, Leaf Interior, Hook Handle, Khlebnikov, 1910, 4 In. 1840.00
Kovsh, Multicolored Flowering Leaves, Enamel, Cream Ground, Moscow, 3 In. 1840.00
Kovsh, Multicolored Leaves, Sea Green Ground, Handle, 1894, 4 3/4 In. 3737.00
Kovsh, Overall Plique-A-Jour Enamel, Hallmark 88, Makers Mark, 6 In. 1960.00
Kovsh, Plain Silver Body, Flat Handle, Oval Base, A. Bragin, 1917, 10 1/4 In. 1960.00
Kovsh, Plique-A-Jour Enameled Leaves, Border, Foot, Ovchinnikov, 1900, 6 In. 2585.00
Kovsh, Rose Pink Enameled Interior, Handle, Ring Foot, 1900, 5 1/4 In. 2875.00
Kovsh, Scrolled Leaves, Beaded Silver Droplets, 1908, 6 In. 2576.00
Kovsh, Scrolled Leaves, Enameled, Gilt Stippled, Hook Handle, 1900, 5 In. 2300.00
Kovsh, Stylized Leaves, Cutout Handle, White Beaded Border, 1900, 6 3/4 In. 7475.00
Kovsh, Stylized Leaves, Flat Handle, Moscow, 1876, 7 In. 5175.00
Kovsh, Swirl Fluted Body, Flowering Leaves, Hook Handle, Stippled, 11 In. 7000.00
Ladle, Ninello, Bird Above Fruiting Vine, Handle, Gold Interior, 1862, 16 In. 635.00
Ladle, Scrolled Leaves, Vacant Cartouches, Ivory Stopper, 1858, 11 1/2 In. 290.00
Letter Opener, Bear Climbing Tree Handle, Agate, 1908, 7 1/2 In. 1495.00
Liqueur Set, Engraved Leaves, Inscription, Gilt, Moscow, 1890, 8 Piece 1265.00
Perfume Bottle, Lavaliere, Niello, Suspended Cap, Button Clip, 800 Mark, 4 In. 252.00
Pitcher, Baluster Shape, Reeded Gilt Body, Putti, Sazikov, 1850, 6 3/4 In. 6900.00
Plate, Stylized Leaves, Champleve Enamel, Oyster, 1910, 10 7/8 In., Pair 10350.00
Plate, Stylized Leaves, Champleve Enamel, Pale Blue, 1910, 10 7/8 In., Pair 8625.00
Plate, Stylized Leaves, Champleve Enamel, Sky Blue, 1910, 10 7/8 In., Pair 14950.00
Plate, Stylized Leaves, Champleve Enamel, Turquoise, 1910, 10 7/8 In., Pair 11500.00
Pot, Cover, Shaded Enamel, 3 1/2 In. ....*Illus* 2240.00
Powder Box, Geometric, Enameled, Cover, Mark, Moscow, 1889, 2 x 2 3/4 In. 672.00
Punch Ladle, Enameled Bird Hook Handle, Feodor Ruckert, 1890, 8 1/2 In. 2875.00
Punch Ladle, Gilt, Niello, Fruiting Vines, Rosette, Alexander II, 1862, 16 1/2 In. 1210.00
Punch Set, Bucket Type, Engraved, Part Gilt, Tray, B.T. Sokolov, 1900, 7 Piece 1495.00
Purse, Evening, Gilt, Flower Engraving, Green Cabochon, Mark, 1899, 5 x 4 In. 140.00
Reliquary, Cross, Receptacles, Hinged Lid, 20th Century, 4 x 3 1/2 In. 308.00
Salt, Baroque, Carl Magnus Stahle, St. Petersburg, 1841, 3 1/2 In. 140.00
Samovar, Engraved, Baluster, Bamboo Handles, Mamontov, 1876, 17 In. 6900.00
Serving Spoon, Butterfly Attached To Twisted Handle, Moscow, 1888, 7 In. 1400.00
Serving Spoon, Enameled, Handle, Crown Finial, 5 1/4 In. 196.00
Serving Spoon, Floral Design, Niello, Moscow, 1833, 6 1/4 In. 868.00
Sherbet Cup, Enameled Oyster, Champleve Enamel Border, 1910, 7 In., Pair 11500.00
Sherbet Cup, Enameled Pale Blue, Plique-A-Jour Border, 1910, 7 1/2 In., Pair 16100.00
Sherbet Cup, Enameled Sky Blue, Plique-A-Jour Border, 1910, 7 1/2 In., Pair 13800.00
Sherbet Cup, Enameled Turquoise, Plique-A-Jour Border, 1910, 7 1/2 In., Pair 11500.00
Snuffbox, Hinged Lid, Architectural Scene, Geometric, Rectangular, Niello, 1872 .... 287.00
Snuffbox, Niello, Scrolled Leaves, Architectural, Boat At Sea, Gilt, 3 1/4 In. 375.00

Snuffbox, Suitcase Design, Trompe-L'Oeil, Henrik Lassas, 1870, 3 x 2 1/4 In.	365.00
Snuffbox, Trompe L'Oeil, Woven Bag, Straps, Henrik Lassas, 1870, 3 x 2 1/4 In.	448.00
Spoon, Champleve, Portrait Of Young Woman In Russian Dress, 1886, 9 In.	1495.00
Spoon, Cream, Twisted Handle, Engraved Bowl, Cyrillic Mark, 1875, 7 1/2 In.	56.00
Spoon, Filigree, Enamel, Blue, Turquoise, White, Twist Handle, c.1890, 5 1/2 In.	173.00
Spoon, Marked, Cipher, 1880, 7 x 5 In., 3 Piece	112.00
Spoon, Niello, Gilt, Antip Kuzmichev, Moscow, 1881, Pair	336.00
Spoon, Twisted Stem, Blue, White Enamel, Early 20th Century, 6 1/2 In.	115.00
Standish, Bell, Silver-Mounted Glass Inkwell, St. Petersburg, c.1825, 8 In.	1380.00
Stein, Figural Silver Lid, City Scene With River & Bridge, 1/3 Liter	2420.00
Stein, Silver Lid, Character Barrel Design, Footed, 1851, 1/2 Liter	3520.00
Sugar, Detachable Cover, Scroll Capped Handles, J.A., St. Petersburg, 7 In.	345.00
Sugar, Flowers & Leaves, Monogram, Swing Handle, 3 In.	225.00
Sugar & Creamer, Melon Shape, Champleve Enamel, Gilt, Moscow, 1893, 3 Piece	672.00
Sugar Basket, Gilt, Enameled Peacocks, Swing Handle, 1900, 5 3/4 In.	3450.00
Sugar Sifter, Champleve Enamel, Twisted Handle, Cyrillic Mark, 1899, 6 In.	224.00
Sugar Sifter, Scrolled Leaves, Handle, Enamel, Moscow, 6 1/2 In.	1008.00
Sugar Tongs, Cyrillic N.G. Mark, Moscow, 1898, 6 In.	84.00
Tankard, Barrel, Dancing Peasants, Hinged Handle, M. Ivanov, 1874, 6 In.	2300.00
Tankard, Barrel, St. Petersburg, 1858, 1/2 Liter	3520.00
Tankard, Cover, Geometric, Foliate Sprays With Birds Perching, 1894, 8 In.	865.00
Tazza, Square, Lobed Sides, Applied Band, Leaves, Fruits, Acorns, 1832, 7 In.	750.00
Tea & Coffee Set, Coat Of Arms, Scroll Handles, Sazikov, 1850, 6 Piece	9200.00
Tea & Coffee Set, Gilt, Niello, Cathedral Scenes, Semyonov, 1870, 4 Piece	1725.00
Tea Set, Champleve, Sprays Of Roses, Spoon & Tongs, 1882, 6 Piece	8625.00
Teakettle, Lampstand, Monogram & Coronet, Swing Handle, Lokin, 12 In.	1955.00
Tray, Blue Cabochon Interior, Half Ball Feet, Moscow, 1917, 13 In.	196.00
Tray, Cucumber, Applied Geometric Border, Cylindrical Handle, 11 In.	201.00
Tray, Lacquer, Peasant Family Gathered Around Samovar Having Tea, 5 x 7 In.	212.00
Tray, Pierced Border, 2 Cutout Handles, St. Petersburg, 1808, 25 1/4 In.	3450.00
Vase, Engraved, Scrolling Leaves, St. Petersburg, G.O. Mark, 1855, 6 1/2 In.	420.00
SILVER-SCANDINAVIAN, Bowl, Scrolled Edge, c.1950, 9 3/8 In.	495.00
SILVER-SCOTTISH, Dessert Set, Hardstone Handle, 1877, Pair	2750.00
Goblet, Ceremonial, Aesthetic Movement, Engraved Leaf Spray, 1876, 7 1/2 In.	110.00
Ladle, Hot Toddy, Twisted Horn Handle, Robert Keay, c.1810	180.00
Ladle, James Hewitt, Edinburgh, 1780	175.00
Plate, Meat, Oval, Domed Cover, Gadrooning Rim, Hamilton & Inches, 22 In.	1600.00
Punch Ladle, Twisted Baleen Handle, Edinburgh, 1820, 14 1/2 In.	145.00
Quaich, Agates, Celetric Cross, Birmingham, 1906, 3 1/2 In.	650.00
Quaich, Celtic Design On Handle, Edinburgh, 1973, 3 1/2 In.	225.00
Quaich, Handles, Edinburgh, 1923, 7 In.	475.00
Quaich, Mirror, Regency, Eagle Finial, 41 In.	550.00
Sauceboat, Gadrooned Rim, Scroll Handle, Hamilton & Inches, 1905, 7 In.	390.00
Saucepan, Brandy, Round, Ebonized Handle, H. & I., Edinburgh, 1855, 5 3/4 In.	220.00
Snuff Mull, Curled Horn, Chased Thistle, Jeweled, 1836, 3 3/4 x 2 1/2 In.	950.00
Teapot, Ball, Leaf Design, Wooden Handle, Scrolled Spout, George II, 1735	2750.00
Tureen, Soup, Boat Form, Artichoke Finial, W. & P. Cunninghamn, 1802, 13 In.	8050.00

SILVER-STERLING. Sterling silver is made with 925 parts silver out of 1,000 parts of metal. The word *sterling* is a quality guarantee used in the United States after about 1860. The word was used much earlier in England and Ireland. Pieces listed here are not identified by country. Other pieces of sterling quality silver are listed under Silver-American, Silver-English, etc.

SILVER-STERLING, Basket, Fenestrated, Molded Handles & Feet, 13 1/2 In.	415.00
Basket, Reeded Swing Handle, Chased Floral, Pedestal, 12 1/2 In.	355.00
Bowl, Applied Acorn, Oak Leaf Design, Hexagonal, 1901, 11 In.	1705.00
Bowl, Black, Star & Frost Design, 3 Handles Form Feet, Monogram, 10 In.	220.00
Bowl, Chased & Pierced Decoration, S&E Mark, 15.4 Troy Oz., 10 In.	121.00
Bowl, Footed, Gadrooned, 11 1/2 x 3 In.	130.00
Bowl, Fruit, Overall Putti Design, Repousse Floral, Leaf Sides, 14 3/4 In.	1725.00
Bowl, Gilt Washed Interior, Monogram, 7 3/4 In.	50.00
Bowl, Lattice Pierced Sides, Ornate Scroll Border, 4 Leaf Feet, 11 In.	495.00

Bowl, Repousse Floral, Scroll Border, Reticulated, Circular, 11 x 5 In. 460.00
Bowl, Repousse, Allover With Flowers, Leaves, Stippled Ground, 1890, 11 In. 3162.00
Bowl, Scroll Design, Floral Ornate Border, Reeded Sides, 8 In. 385.00
Box, Desk, Tortoiseshell, 1897, 2 1/4 x 7 1/2 x 4 In. 935.00
Box, Gold Wash, Woman's Face, Flowers, Garnet Cabochon, Art Nouveau 750.00
Box, Shell, Hinged Tortoiseshell Cover, Wreath, Bows, Silk Lined Interior, 3 In. 364.00
Box, Stamp, Fleur-De-Lis Emblem 20.00
Box, Trinket, 2 Portrait Medallions, Crown, Bellflower Border, Hinged, 3 In. 155.00
Bread Tray, Oval, Scrolled Edge, Monogram, 13 In. 110.00
Bread Tray, Prelude, 11 In. 35.00
Buckle, Oval 25.00
Cake Plate, Fontainebleau, Floral Spray Rim, Gorham, 1927, 11 In. 345.00
Candelabrum is listed in its own category.
Candlesticks are listed in their own category.
Candy Dish, Leaf Form Base, Oval, Cellini, 5 1/2 In. 290.00
Candy Dish, Reticulated, Ruffled, Basket Weave, Monogram, 6 3/4 x 1 1/2 In. 120.00
Card Case, Chased Leaf Border, Gilt, Mirror, Coin Holder, Victorian, 3 1/2 In. 28.00
Card Case, Inscribed, From Joe To His Mother, Chased Design, 2 1/2 x 3 3/4 In. 101.00
Chalice, Edwardian, Chased With Ginko Leaves, Beaded Rim, 1902, 9 1/2 In. 258.00
Chalice, Inset Semiprecious Stones & Cross Around Base, Pedestal . . . . .Illus 5750.00
Chalice, Thorn, Wheat & Grapes, Applied Cross, Gold Finish, 9 In. 373.00
Cigar Case, Engraved Decoration, Gilt Interior, Monogram, 2.6 Troy Oz. . . . . .248.00 to 300.00
Cigar Case, Engraved Decoration, Inscription, England, Hallmark, 1875 . . . . 330.00
Cigarette Case, Engine Turned Line Design, Engraved Name, 4 1/4 x 3 In. 53.00
Cigarette Case, Reeded Design, Rectangular, 3 x 4 1/2 In. 58.00
Cigarette Case, Repousse, Figure & Horses, Scroll Design, Gilt Interior, 3 1/4 In. 230.00
Coasters, Glass, Cobalt Cut To Clear, 12 Piece 110.00
Cocktail Shaker, Scroll Handle, Manchester, 10 1/4 In. 258.00
Coffee Set, Tuttle, Scroll Handles, Individual, Monogram, 3 Piece 260.00
Coffee Set, Unger Bros., Demitasse, 3 Piece 875.00
Coffeepot, Leaf Design On Spout, Scrolled Handle, Mid 18th Century 715.00
Compote, Gold Washed, Allover Repousse Floral Design, 19th Century, 5 3/4 In. 825.00
Compote, Pierced & Chased Design, Repousse Sunflower Bands, 8 In., 4 Piece 1540.00
Cover, Meat, Engraved Family Crest, Vine Form Handle, 10 x 18 3/4 In. 143.00
Creamer, Lion's Head Feet, Monogram, 4 1/4 x 4 1/2 In. 123.00
Crown, Jeweled, Pierced Filigree Sphere At Top, Red, Blue Jewels, 6 x 5 In. 300.00
Dish, Children, Cherub Decoration, Chased, Reticulated, 9 In. 143.00
Dish, Oyster, Single, Matching Crab-Handles Spoon, 4.2 Troy Oz. 468.00
Dish, Repousse Flower & Leaf Border, 13 In. 770.00
Dresser Set, Art Nouveau Floral, 3 Piece 80.00
Dresser Set, Engraved Caliphs Of Cairo, Hand Mirror, Hairbrush & Comb, 1940 . . . . 110.00
Dresser Set, Reeded Design, Scrolled Leaves, Flowers, La Pierre Mfg. Co., 5 Piece 58.00
Dresser Set, Repousse Bellflower Swags, Hand Mirror, Brush, 10 3/4 In., 2 Piece 75.00
Fork, Cat & Fiddle, Child's, 4 In. 15.00
Frame, Navy Velvet, Easel Back, Double, 7 x 8 1/2 In. 385.00
Fruit Set, Mother Of-Pearl Handles, 12 Knives, 12 Forks 260.00
Grape Scissors, Calla Lilies On Handle, Late 19th Century 150.00
Grape Scissors, Presentation Box, Hallmarked WH & S 250.00
Gravy Boat, Chased, Repousse Form, Architectural Vistas, Curved Legs, 2 In. 920.00
Handle, Parasol, Allover Floral, Monogram On Knob, 1896, 9 1/2 In. 172.00
Jar, Dresser, Cut Glass, Floral Repousse Silver Cover, Monogram, 5 In. 330.00
Jewelry Box, Allover Equestrian Design, Lined Interior, Oval, 6 x 5 In. 1035.00
Jewelry Box, Bamboo, 3 Latches, 3 Velvet Lined Tiers, 4 x 4 3/4 x 3 1/2 In. 195.00
Jewelry Box, Flower & Leaf Repousse, Chased Pastoral Scene, Oval, 7 In. 690.00
Jewelry Box, Rectangle, Cut Corners, Flowers & Scrolls, 4 x 11 3/4 x 7 1/2 In. 3300.00
Kettle, Water, Squat Body, Scroll Ivory Handle, Gooseneck, 1880, 13 In. 750.00
Key Chain, Golf Club 45.00
Letter Opener, Ancestry, Weidlich 23.00
Match Case, Chased Knights Helmet & Shield, Acanthus, 1 3/4 x 2 3/4 In. 78.00
Match Case, Repousse, Flowers, Victorian, 2 1/2 In. 78.00
Match Case, Roses, Lattice, Repousse, Monogram, Victorian, 2 1/2 In. 62.00
Match Case, Scrolled Acanthus, Repousse, Victorian, 2 1/2 In. 22.00
Match Safe, Repousse Iris, Monogram, Victorian, 1 1/2 x 2 3/4 In. 101.00

Silver-Sterling,
Chalice, Inset
Semiprecious Stones
& Cross Around
Base, Pedestal

Silver-Sterling, Vase,
Floral Repousse,
Ruffled Edge, Green
Glass Insert, 10 In.

**Use your silver often and
wash it to keep it clean.
Polish it as seldom as
possible. Silver polish
removes a small bit of
silver each time it is used.**

Mirror, Hand, Art Nouveau	535.00
Mug, Chased With Ribboned Floral Swag, Victorian, 3 1/2 In.	143.00
Napkin Rings are listed in their own category.	
Note Clip, Embossed Putti Medallion	155.00
Nut Set, Almond Shape, Reticulated, 11 Individual Dishes, 12 Piece	220.00
Pencil Holder, Original Pencil, Monogram, 3 1/4 In.	6.00
Pitcher, Baluster Body, Beaded Border, Foliate Capped Handle, 16 1/4 In.	57.00
Pitcher, Carlo Scarpa, c.1987, 8 3/4 In.	3680.00
Pitcher, Water, Monogram, 4 1/2 Pt., 8 In.	605.00
Placecard Holder, 1 3/4 In., 4 Piece	30.00
Placecard Holder, Putti, Supporting Garland Crest, 2 1/2 In., 6 Piece	440.00
Plate, Place, Shaped Circle, Scrolled Leaf Border, 12 In., 10 Piece	2070.00
Platter, Shaped Circle, Scrolled Leaf Border, Camuso, 16 In.	575.00
Powder Box, Cover, Coral, White, Pink Roses, Enamel, 3 In.	140.00
Punch Ladle, Chased Floral, Monogram, Canfield Bro. & Co., 1850s	125.00
Salt & Pepper, Boat Form, Wooden Box	99.00
Salt & Pepper, Crown Sterling Weighted, 3 1/4 In, 2 Pair	34.00
Salver, Chippendale, Scalloped, Chamfered Corners, Ball Footed, 10 1/2 In.	220.00
Sauceboat, Acanthus Leaf Scrolled Handle, George III, 1774, 4 In., Pair	1430.00
Sauceboat, Cylindrical Form, S-Scroll Handle, Claw Feet, 1920, 3 In.	125.00
Sauceboat, Gadrooned Edge, S-Loop Handle, George III, 6 x 7 x 3 In., Pair	2760.00
Sherbet, Iris Design, Flowers & Butterflies, Porcelain Bowl, Handles, 5 In.	357.00
Snuffbox, Bright Cut Decoration, Hinged Lip, Flowers, 18th Century, 3 1/2 In.	253.00
Spoon, Souvenir, see Souvenir category.	
Sugar & Creamer, Embossed Floral, Gilt Interior, W.H., 1795, 5 & 4 1/4 In.	465.00
Sugar Tongs, Scissor Form, Shell Shaped Terminations, George III, 4 In.	275.00
Tantalus, 2 Glass Bottles, Engraved Landscape & Bird Design, 13 In.	415.00
Tazza, Applied With Foliate Over Beaded Band Rim, 10 1/2 In.	252.00
Tea & Coffee Set, Queen Anne, 4 Piece	504.00
Tea & Coffee Set, Reeded Waists, Gooseneck Spouts, Ebony Tray, 5 Piece	450.00
Tea & Coffee Set, Serpentine Handles, Spouts, 11-In. Coffeepot, 5 Piece	632.00
Tea Caddy, Gadrooned Upper Edge, Ivory Pineapple Finial, c.1930, 4 In.	105.00
Tea Set, Preisner, C-Scroll Handles, Pedestal Bases, 4 Piece	550.00
Tea Set, Repousse, Putti, Scrolls, Shells, Garland, 19th Century, 4 Piece	978.00
Tea Set, Rococo Revival, Vineyard Design, Tray, Late 19th Century, 4 Piece	1960.00
Tea Strainer, Art Nouveau Floral, Scrolled Edge, 5 1/4 In.	110.00
Tea Strainer, Floral Repousse, Warner, 19th Century	165.00
Tea Strainer, Flowers, Engraved R.F.B., Porter Blanchard, 6 1/2 In.	350.00
Teapot, Bands Of Chased Design, Straight Spout, Scrolled Wooden Handle, 5 In.	302.00
Tray, Hand Chased Floral, Gadrooned Border, Handles, 20 x 32 1/2 In.	3910.00
Tray, Rectangular, 2 D-Shaped Handles, 26 3/4 x 14 1/2 In.	860.00
Tray, Reticulated Border, Gadrooned Rim, Arrowsmith, 10 1/2 In.	55.00
Tray, Serving, Sprays Of Garden Blossoms, Gadrooned Rim, 15 x 5 In.	230.00
Tray, Vacant Cartouches, Scrolling Leaves, 15 In.	467.00
Tumbler, Landscape & Animals, Elephant, Tiger, Stag, 5 In.	247.00
Urn, Repousse Lion Head & Wreath Handles, Footed, 19 In.	5775.00
Vanity Set, Monogram, 5 Brushes, 7 Piece	85.00
Vase, Floral Repousse, Ruffled Edge, Green Glass Insert, 10 In. ....*Illus*	605.00

Vase, Inverted Pear Shape, Gilt, Box, 20th Century, 12 1/2 In. 1980.00
Vase, Tapered, Engraved Stylized Floral Design, 13 1/4 In. 855.00
Wedding Beaker, Bearded Man's Head With Crown, 1880, 18 1/4 In. 3630.00
Wine Funnel, With Internal Strainer, 5 x 3 1/2 In. 316.00
SILVER-SWEDISH, Box, Cigarette , Wooden Interior, 7 1/2 x 5 1/4 In. 625.00
Goblet, Gilt Interior, 3 1/2 In. 63.00
SILVER-SWISS, Frame, Dagobert Pesche, Wiener, Werkstatte, Zurich, Square, 5 1/2 In. 14300.00

SINCLAIRE cut glass was made by H.P. Sinclaire and Company of Corning, New York, between 1905 and 1929. He cut glass made at other factories until 1920. Pieces were made of crystal as well as amber, blue, green, or ruby glass. Only a small percentage of Sinclaire glass is marked with the S in a wreath.

Compote, Dorcas, 5 1/8 x 3 1/2 In. 215.00
Flowerpot, Cut Glass, 3 1/2 x 3 In. 225.00
Sugar & Creamer, Hobstar & Floral, Signed 100.00
Vase, Engraved Stylized Hollyhocks, Signed, Early 20th Century, 12 In. 488.00
Vase, Poppy, Colorless, Ovoid, 12 1/2 In. 100.00

SKIING, see Sports category.

SLAG GLASS resembles a marble cake. It can be streaked with different colors. There were many types made from about 1880. Caramel slag is the incorrect name for Chocolate glass. Pink slag was an American Victorian product made by Harry Barstow and Thomas E.A. Dugan at Indiana, Pennsylvania. Purple and blue slag were made in American and English factories. Red slag is a very late Victorian and twentieth-century glass. Other colors are known but are of less importance to the collector. New versions of chocolate glass and colored slag glass are being made.

Amethyst, Pitcher, Grapes & Floral, 9 1/2 In. 57.00
Amethyst, Sugar 38.00
Amethyst, Tumbler, Grapes & Floral, 4 Piece 445.00
Caramel slag is listed in the Chocolate Glass category.
Green, Box, Filigree Vine Design, Beaded Edges, 6 1/2 In. 545.00
Pink, Cruet, Inverted Feather & Fan 1475.00
Pink, Cruet, Stopper, Handle, 6 3/4 In. 1950.00
Pink, Toothpick, Inverted Feather & Fan 990.00

SLEEPY EYE collectors look for anything bearing the image of the nineteenth-century Indian chief with the drooping eyelid. The Sleepy Eye Milling Co., Sleepy Eye, Minnesota, used his portrait in advertising from 1883 to 1921. It offered many premiums, including stoneware and pottery steins, crocks, bowls, mugs, and pitchers, all decorated with the famous profile of the Indian. The popular pottery was made by Western Stoneware, Weir Pottery Company, and other companies long after the flour mill went out of business in 1921. Reproductions of the pitchers are being made today. The original pitchers came in only five sizes: 4 inches, 5 1/4 inches, 6 1/2 inches, 8 inches, and 9 inches. The Sleepy Eye image was also used by companies unrelated to the flour mill.

Bowl, Sugar, Blue & Yellow 950.00
Box, Cigar 575.00
Butter Jar, 1903 .... 1200.00
Label, Barrel, Chief 150.00
Mug, Blue & White, 4 1/4 In. ....150.00 to 200.00
Mug, Blue & White, Blue Bands, 4 1/4 In. 250.00
Mug, Blue & White, Brackets & White Handle, 4 1/4 In. 6500.00
Mug, Blue & Yellow, 4 1/4 In. 1100.00
Mug, Brush McCoy ....120.00 to 300.00
Mug, Tan, Sleepy Eye Handle 250.00
Pillow Top, Monroe ....675.00 to 800.00
Pillow Top, Trademark Indian Head 1450.00

Pitcher, No. 1, Blue & Gray, Circle Mark 550.00
Pitcher, No. 1, Blue & White, 4 In. 350.00
Pitcher, No. 1, Blue & Yellow, 4 In. 450.00
Pitcher, No. 1, Blue Rim, 4 In. 155.00
Pitcher, No. 2, Blue & Gray, 5 1/4 In. ....300.00 to 400.00
Pitcher, No. 3, Blue & White, 6 1/2 In. ....275.00 to 850.00
Pitcher, No. 4, Blue & White, 7 7/8 In. 130.00
Pitcher, No. 4, Blue Rim, 7 7/8 In. ....175.00 to 275.00
Pitcher, No. 4, Blue Rim, Weir Mark, 7 7/8 In. 850.00
Pitcher, No. 4, Brown & Yellow 1600.00
Pitcher, No. 4, Light Blue, 8 In. 825.00
Pitcher, No. 5, Blue & Gray, 8 7/8 In. ....450.00 to 625.00
Pitcher, No. 5, Blue & White, 8 7/8 In. 200.00
Postcard 35.00
Salt, Stoneware 300.00
Spoon, Demitasse ....100.00 to 120.00
Stein, 1952, Chestnut ....200.00 to 450.00
Stein, Blue & White ....280.00 to 550.00
Stein, Brown 1500.00
Trivet, Blue & White 1125.00
Vase, Cattail, Blue & Gray, 8 1/2 In. ....300.00 to 420.00
Vase, Cattail, Blue & White ....450.00 to 575.00
Vase, Cattail, Blue & White, 9 In. ....190.00 to 240.00
Vase, Cattail, Brown & Yellow 1300.00
Vase, Cattail, Green & White 1050.00

SLOT MACHINES are included in the Coin-Operated Machine category.

SMITH BROTHERS glass was made after 1878. Alfred and Harry Smith had worked for the Mt. Washington Glass Company in New Bedford, Massachusetts, for seven years before going into their own shop. They made many pieces with enamel decoration.

Smith Bros. Co.

Biscuit Jar, Floral, Blue & White, 7 In. 650.00
Biscuit Jar, Ivy, Melon Shape, Silver Plated Lid & Bail 500.00
Rose Bowl, Enameled Prunus, Gold Beaded, Cream Satin, Melon, 2 3/8 x 4 In. 250.00
Vase, Chrysanthemum Blooms, Leaves, Cream, Green, 8 1/2 In. 1150.00
Vase, Hand Painted Chrysanthemum Blooms, Yellow, Pink, Brown, 8 In. 460.00
Vase, Leaf & Ginkgo Tree Branches, Enameled White Dots, 19th Century, 5 In. 172.00

SNOW BABIES, made from bisque and spattered with glitter sand, were first manufactured in 1864 by Hertwig and Company of Thuringia. Other German and Japanese companies copied the Hertwig designs. Originally, Snow Babies were made of candy and used as Christmas decorations. There are also Snow Babies tablewares made by Royal Bayreuth. Copies of the small Snow Babies figurines are being made today and can easily confuse the collector.

Figurine, Black, Germany 10.00
Figurine, Fishing For Dreams 28.00
Figurine, Is That For Me 30.00
Figurine, This Is Where We Live 70.00
Figurine, Waiting For Christmas 40.00
Figurine, Winken, Blinken & Nod 65.00
Plate, 2 Babies On Skates 285.00

SNUFF BOTTLES are listed in the Bottle category.

SNUFFBOXES held snuff. Taking snuff was popular long before cigarettes became available. The gentleman or lady would take a small pinch of the ground tobacco or snuff in the fingers, then sniff it and sneeze. Snuffboxes were made of many materials, including gold, silver, enameled metal, and wood. Most snuffboxes date from the late eighteenth or early nineteenth centuries.

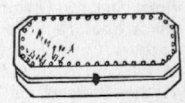

Antler, Silver Plate Top, Inscribed Initials L.B., Continental, 2 1/2 x 2 1/4 In. 85.00
Antler, Silver Plate Top, Inscribed Initials W.H., Continental, 1 5/8 x 1 1/2 In. 115.00

Bone, Courting Scene, Floral Surround, Continental, 18th Century, 3 3/4 x 1 5/8 In. 690.00
Bone, Figures Top & Sides, Floral Front & Back, Continental, 18th Century, 3 3/4 In. 290.00
Boxwood, Maria Conceta, Wax Inlay, Brass Hinge, Continental, 18th Century, 4 In. 980.00
Boxwood, Portly Man Shape, Ivory Buttons, Eyes, England, 19th Century, 2 3/4 In. 805.00
Brass, 4 Death Heads & Bones, Witch, Beggar, King, Beauty 495.00
Brass, Boat Shape, 3-Door Construction, Paul Pry, 19th Century, 2 1/8 In. 85.00
Brass, Boat Shape, Perpetual Calendar Lid, 19th Century, 3 x 1 1/2 In. 40.00
Brass, Copper, Garden Repose Top, Gilt Base, Continental, 19th Century, 3 1/4 x 2 In. . . . 200.00
Brass, Engraved Thomas Waldie, March 20th, 1836 Dalkeith Lid, 2 7/8 x 1 1/8 In. 90.00
Brass, Hoof, Tin Lining, England, 19th Century, 4 7/8 In. 60.00
Brass, Shell Shape, Isaac Brigg's Engraved Name, 19th Century, 3 1/4 In. 40.00
Brass, Stamped City Of Koln View, Germany, 19th Century, 3 1/4 In. 65.00
Brass, Stamped Portrait Charles James Fox, England, 19th Century, 3 In. 85.00
Brass, Stamped Portrait M. Stowe Lid, 19th Century, 2 5/8 x 2 In. 30.00
Brass, Tintype Of Owner Lid, Engraved Surround, England, 1864, 3 1/4 x 2 1/4 In. 230.00
Burl, Carved Tavern Scene, Figures, England, 18th Century, 4 3/4 x 2 3/4 In. 750.00
Burl, Landscape, Cows & Goats, Greek Rival Design, Tortoiseshell Lined, 4 x 2 In. 375.00
Burl, Natural, Penwork, Exotic Dancing Figures, Angels, 19th Century, 4 1/2 In. 975.00
Burl, Pewter, Bearded Man Shape 1 Side, Woman Other, England, 18th Century, 3 In. . . . 520.00
Burl, Telescoping, Crossed Pipes Design, England, 19th Century, 4 1/2 x 2 In. 60.00
Burl, Tortoiseshell, 3 Human Skulls, Pressed, Inscription, 3 1/8 In. 345.00
Coquilla Nut, Carved Figural & Floral Egyptian Scene, 3 1/2 x 2 In. 690.00
Coquilla Nut, Carved Figural & Floral, 19th Century, 3 1/2 x 1 3/4 In. 575.00
Coquilla Nut, Carved Figural & Floral, Soldier, 19th Century, 3 1/2 x 2 In. 185.00
Coquilla Nut, Carved Historical Scene, Animal Faces Ends, 19th Century, 3 1/2 In. 805.00
Coquilla Nut, Figural & Floral, Winged Angel Top, 19th Century, 3 1/2 x 2 In. 690.00
Enamel, Black Transfer Printed, White Ground, 1765, England, 3 3/8 In. 3200.00
Faux Malachite Enamel, Cushion Form, 3 In. 315.00
Gold, 2-Tone, Green, Gold Acorn, Leaf Border, Rectangular, 1817, 3 In. 2530.00
Gold, Animal & Leaf Cover, Scroll, Shell Border, France, 1726, 2 3/4 In. 6325.00
Gold, Cover, Allegorical Reserve, Enameled Royal Blue, 1800, 2 7/8 In. 3737.00
Gold, Cover, Portrait Of Lady Against Glazed Panel, Oval, 1809, 3 3/4 In. 1380.00
Gold, Cut Corner, Opalescent, Rectangular, 1800, 2 3/8 In. 2990.00
Gold, Enameled, Cover, Engine-Turned Panels, Blue Foliate Border, 1810, 3 In. 8625.00
Gold, Enameled, Cover, Floral Panels, Turquoise, Pink Ground, 1830, 4 In. 12650.00
Gold, Enameled, Cover, Garlands, Stiff Leaf Border, Oval, Continental, 3 In. 8625.00
Gold, Enameled, Cover, Harbor Scenes, Gold Leaves, Green Border, Oval, 4 In. 17250.00
Gold, Enameled, Cover, Harbor Scenes, Pale Green, Gold Border, 1830, 3 In. 12650.00
Gold, Enameled, Hardstone Cover, Bands Of Bright Cut Gold, 1800, 3 3/8 In. 3680.00
Gold, Enameled, Hinged Cover, Portrait Of Napoleon, 1820, 2 1/2 In. 9200.00
Gold, Hinged Cover, Applied Gold Courting Couple, Gold Scroll Border, 2 1/2 In. 6325.00
Gold, Hinged Cover, Chased With Altar Of Love, Leaf Tip Border, Oval, 1774, 2 1/2 In. . . 4025.00
Gold, Hinged Cover, Courting Couple In Garden, Translucent Royal Blue, 3 In. 6325.00
Gold, Hinged Cover, Floral Thumbpiece, Rectangular, England, 1819, 2 3/4 In. 3162.00
Gold, Leaves, Enameled Plaque, Alpine Lake Scene, Geneva, 1810, 3 1/2 In. 9200.00
Gold, Varicolored, Hinged Cover, 4 Oval Sections, Continental, 1840, 2 1/2 In. 6950.00
Hardwood, Horn, Unusual Multiple Top, Continental, 18th Century, 3 1/4 x 2 In. 230.00
Hardwood, Mother-Of-Pearl, Puzzle, Ship In Cradle Shape, 18th Century, 7 1/4 In. 2070.00
Horn, Cow, Silver Mounts, Applied Thistle Leaf, Hinged Horn Cover, c.1890, 10 x 3 In. . . 975.00
Horn, Eye Of God Lid, Saint On Base, S. Antoni, Continental, 19th Century, 2 3/4 In. . . . 115.00
Horn, Green & Red Wax Inlay, Late 18th Century, 3 3/4 x 2 1/2 In. 345.00
Horn, Hinged Silver Lid, Thistle Design, Monogram Shield, Scotland, 3 In. 715.00
Horn, Incised Flowers, Inscription Side, Continental, 19th Century, 2 x 1 1/2 In. 175.00
Horn, Measuring Mechanism Top, England, 19th Century, 4 1/8 In. 115.00
Horn, Silver Hinge, Monogram Cartouche, 3 In. 220.00
Horn, Stamped Oratorio Judith, Flowers, England, 18th Century, 3 In. 290.00
Horse Hoof, Horn Composition, Hinged Silver Lid, Horseshoe Design, 3 In. 300.00
Lacquer, Cover, Louis XV, Miniature Of A Lady, 18th Century, 3 In. 1150.00
Metal, Gilt, Musical, Engine-Turned Panels, Foliate Border, Rectangular, 4 In. 14950.00
Mother-Of-Pearl, Gilt Metal, Continental, Early 19th Century, 3 In. 316.00
Mull, Horn, Brass Mount, Scotland, 4 1/2 In. 145.00
Mull, Horn, Carved Animal Head, Inlaid Eyes, Silver Collar, Scotland, 3 3/4 In. 805.00
Mull, Horn, Carved Animal Head, Inlaid Eyes, Silver Mount, Scotland, 4 1/2 In. 750.00

Mull, Horn, Carved Animal Head, Ivory Teeth, Silver Top, Agate, Scotland, 5 3/4 In. 1210.00
Mull, Horn, Pewter Hinged Lid, Early 19th Century, 11 x 6 In. 545.00
Mull, Horn, Silver Collar & Top, Thistle & Crown, Scotland, 1815, 5 3/4 In. 430.00
Mull, Horn, Silver Mount, Owners Initials, 19th Century, 3 In. 230.00
Mull, Horn, Silver Mount, Plaque, Initials, Scotland, 5 1/4 In. 460.00
Mull, Horn, Silver Top, Thistle Design, Inset Cut Crystal, Scotland, 4 1/2 In. 980.00
Mull, Horn, Silver Top, Thistle, Coat Of Arms, Crystal, Scotland, 3 3/4 In. 460.00
Papier-Mache, 3 Men In Tavern, Drinking, Painted, England, 19th Century, 4 1/2 In. 200.00
Papier-Mache, 4 Men In Tavern Painted, Continental, 19th Century, 3 3/4 x 2 In. 200.00
Papier-Mache, Bataille De Leuipsie En 1813 Transfer, France, 3 1/2 In. 30.00
Papier-Mache, Black Lacquer, Hinged Lid, America, 1770, 2 1/4 In. 140.00
Papier-Mache, Brass, Perpetual Calendar Transfer, France, 19th Century, 3 1/2 In. 535.00
Papier-Mache, Carolina Queen Of Great Britain, England, 19th Century, 3 1/2 In. 460.00
Papier-Mache, Dog, Carrying Rabbit, England, 19th Century, 2 1/2 x 1 1/4 In. 120.00
Papier-Mache, Figures, Bird & Floral Transfer, Continental, 19th Century, 3 5/8 In. 60.00
Papier-Mache, French Inscription, Scientific Experiment, 19th Century, 3 3/8 In. 405.00
Papier-Mache, Grinning Match, Gold Ring Transfer, England, 19th Century, 2 7/8 In. 100.00
Papier-Mache, James J. Mapes Celebrated Snuff & Tobacco, Transfer, 3 3/8 In. 520.00
Papier-Mache, Man & Woman Fishing Transfer, France, 19th Century, 3 1/2 In. 50.00
Papier-Mache, Man & Women, Landscape, Continental, 19th Century, 3 1/4 In. 345.00
Papier-Mache, Painted Men Using Snuff, German Inscription, 19th Century, 5 In. 520.00
Papier-Mache, Painted Skulls, Continental, 19th Century, 4 In. 805.00
Papier-Mache, Reversible Silhouettes Transfer, Continental, 19th Century, 3 3/8 In. 75.00
Papier-Mache, Riverboat, Ship Transfer, Continental, 19th Century, 1 3/4 In. 145.00
Papier-Mache, Scene Of Hunters' Farewell, 3 In. 137.00
Papier-Mache, Shoe Form, 3 In. 28.50
Papier-Mache, Snuff Sold By J. Durno, Albany, N.Y. Transfer, 2 1/4 In. 40.00
Papier-Mache, Tam O Shanter Penwork, Continental, 19th Century, 3 1/4 x 2 In. 200.00
Pewter, Birds In Leaves Top, England, 2 3/4 x 1 1/2 In. 60.00
Pewter, Boat Shape, Allover Floral, England, 19th Century, 3 1/4 x 1 7/8 In. 145.00
Pewter, Dog, Leaves Surround, England, 19th Century, 2 x 1 1/4 In. 110.00
Pewter, Flowers, England, 2 7/8 x 1 1/2 In. 115.00
Pewter, Hinged Lid, Oval, 3 5/8 In. 137.00
Pewter, Hunter On Elephant, Lion, England, 19th Century, 2 3/4 x 1 1/4 In. 175.00
Pewter, Leaves, England, 19th Century, 3 1/8 x 1 1/2 In. 145.00
Pewter, Reeded Top, Molded Sides, England, 19th Century, 3 1/2 x 1 1/2 In. 140.00
Pewter, Right Honorable Lord Byron Portrait, Round, England, 3 1/8 In. 230.00
Pewter, Rose & Thistle, Initials R.L., England, 19th Century, 2 7/8 x 1 3/4 In. 115.00
Pewter, Steamboat Cover, England, 19th Century, 2 3/4 x 1 7/8 In. 405.00
Pewter, With Dispensing Mechanism, Floral, England, 3 3/4 x 1 5/8 In. 175.00
Porcelain, 8 Sides, Floral Spray, Powder Blue Ground, Gilt, Le Gallec, Paris, 3 1/2 In. 130.00
Porcelain, Birds & Prunus Blossoms, Stippled Ground, Chinese Export, Luen Wo, 2 In. ... 115.00
Porcelain, Flower Sprays, Foliate Cartouche, Oriental Inside Lid, 1765, 3 1/8 In. 6900.00
Porcelain, Kidney Shape, Floral Spray, Puce Ground, Gilt, Le Gallec, Paris, 3 3/4 In. 115.00
Porcelain, Kidney Shape, Floral Sprig, Dark Green, Gilt, Le Gallec, Paris, 4 In. 165.00
Porcelain, Man On Horseback, Floral Surround, England, 19th Century, 3 1/8 x 2 In. 85.00
Pressed Wood, Napoleon Cartoon, Continental, 19th Century, 3 5/8 x 2 1/4 In. 260.00
Shell & Floral, Owner's Name, Silver, Continental, 19th Century, 2 3/4 In. 85.00
Shell & Pewter, Continental, 19th Century, 3 1/4 In. 230.00
Silver, Continental, Repousse, Tavern Scene, Scrolls, .930 Fine, 3 1/8 In. 201.00
Silver, Copper & Brass Inlay On Lid, Boat Pounded By Waves, 1912, 3 In. 588.00
Silver, Domed Lid, Cavaliers, C-Scroll Border, Round, 2 In. 120.00
Silver, Engraved Flower Basket, Continental, 19th Century, 2 7/8 x 1 3/4 In. 60.00
Silver, Engraved Smokers Scenes, England, 19th Century, 1 3/8 x 1 5/8 In. 315.00
Silver, Engraved, Pique Inlay, 2 Angles, Trumpetson Lid, France, 1780s, 3 In. 1200.00
Silver, Figural Design, Chinese Export, 19th Century, 2 1/4 In. 120.00
Silver, Floral Swag & Shell, Urn Shaped, Ocean Liner, Germany, 1903, 2 1/2 x 2 In. 385.00
Silver, Mosaic Panel Of A Spaniel, Ormolu Frame, Rectangular, Italy, 3 In. 5175.00
Silver, Raised Ropes & Leafage, White Ground, A. Leschaudel, Paris, 1750, 3 In. 3450.00
Silver, Repousse, Medieval Warriors Shaking Hands, 1352, 19th Century, 2 In. 120.00
Silver, Shell, Engraved C.H. Lid, Continental, 18th Century, 3 In. 290.00
Silver, Wm. Wiggett, Norwich, 3 x 2 In. 220.00
Tin, Black Boy, Motto, England, 19th Century, 2 3/4 x 2 In. 460.00

Wood, Dog Shape, Carved, Hinged Back, Green, 18th Century, 4 3/4 x 2 3/4 In. 1555.00
Wood, Golden Horse Of 46 Guns, England, 19th Century, 3 1/2 In. 40.00
Wood, Horn, Coat Of Arms, Motto, Initialed R.K., 3 3/4 x 3 1/4 In. 1780.00
Wood, Made From Ship Royal George, Sunk 1782, 3 7/8 x 2 In. 35.00
Wood, Penwork Hunting Scene Lid, Continental, 19th Century, 3 3/8 x 2 In. 60.00
Wood, Portrait, Friedrich Wilhelm Kronprinz V Preusse, 19th Century, 4 In. 200.00

SOAPSTONE is a mineral that was used for foot warmers or griddles because of its heat-retaining properties. Soapstone was carved into figurines and bowls in many countries in the nineteenth and twentieth centuries. Most of the soapstone seen today is from China or Japan. It is still being carved in the old styles.

Candlestick, Turned, Petal Rim, Square Base, 8 1/2 In., Pair 82.50
Carving, Landscape, Dwellings, Trees, Mountains, People's Republic Of China, 16 In. ... 82.50
Figurine, Kuang Hsu, Enthroned Ming Emperor, c.1900, 8 1/2 In. 45.00
Figurine, Scarab, Hieroglyph Inscription, 3 1/2 In. 50.00
Figurine, Shou Lao With Deer & Attendant, 8 In. 121.00
Figurine, Sow & Piglets, 12 In. 1200.00
Figurine, Stele Of Goddess, Flanked By Attendants, 10 In. 373.00
Lamp, Figures & Animals, Gilt Metal Base 88.00
Shrine, 9 Stories, Openwork Fence, 17 In. 120.00
Teapot, Bird Finial, 3 3/4 In. 76.00
Vase, Carved Branch & Flower, 12 1/2 In. 132.00
Vase, Cover, Bird Shape, Flowering Prunus Branches, 22 In., Pair 1092.00

SOFT PASTE is a name for a type of pottery. Although it looks very much like porcelain, it is a chemically different material. Most of the soft-paste wares were made in the early nineteenth century. Other pieces may be listed under Gaudy Dutch or Leeds.

Cradle, Yellow Glaze, Early 19th Century, 4 3/4 In. 55.00
Creamer, Eagle & Shield, 4 1/2 In. 357.00
Cup & Saucer, King's Rose, Handleless 330.00
Jug, 2 Sides, Silver Luster, 5 In. 385.00
Mug, Chinese Landscape, Green & Brown Luster Design, 4 1/2 In. 275.00
Mug, Crown & Laurel Wreath Design, 5 In. 80.00
Mug, Franklin's Maxims, 3 1/4 In. 60.00
Mug, Leap Frog & Cricket, 2 1/2 In. 137.00
Mug, Ship Design, Pearlware, Pink Luster, 4 1/2 In. 400.00
Mug, Success To The Plow 60.00
Mug, The Young Sportsman & My Pretty Sheep, 2 1/4 In. 159.00
Pitcher, Gilt & Blue Glaze Design, 9 In. 122.00
Plate, Bird Design, England, 7 1/2 In. 120.00
Plate, Cat & The Fiddle, Handley, 7 In. 120.00
Plate, Indian Temple Pattern, Oriental, 19th Century, 8 1/2 In., 5 Piece 110.00
Plate, Satirical, Liars, 8 Sides, 5 1/2 In. 80.00
Teapot, Floral, Gaudy, 11 x 7 In. 250.00
Teapot, Leaf Design, Ornate Molded, Scalloped Foot, Handle, Green, Purple, 6 In. 55.00
Teapot, Twined Handle, 5 1/2 In. 192.00
Vase, Brooks, Monument, Hand Painted Scenes, 23 In. 215.00

SOUVENIRS of a trip—what could be more fun? Our ancestors enjoyed the same thing and souvenirs were made for almost every location. Most of the souvenir pottery and porcelain pieces of the nineteenth century were made in England or Germany, even if the picture showed a North American scene. In the twentieth century, the souvenir china business seems to have gone to the manufacturers in Japan, Taiwan, Hong Kong, England, and America. Another popular souvenir item is the souvenir spoon, made of sterling or silver plate. These are usually made in the country pictured on the spoon. Related pieces may be found in the Coronation and World's Fair categories.

Ashtray, Alaska, Land Of Midnight Sun, Embossed, Metal, 7 x 5 In. 24.00
Ashtray, Atlantic City, Coney Island, Embossed, Metal, 1940s, 5 1/2 x 3 1/2 In. 65.00
Ashtray, Diamond Head, Hawaii, Pottery, Japan, 1960s, 12 In. 57.00

Souvenir,
Figurine,
Eiffel Tower,
2 1/2 In.

Souvenir, Figurine,
Statue Of Liberty,
2 1/2 In.

Souvenir, Figurine,
Empire State Building,
2 1/2 In.

Ashtray, Florida, Alligator, Red Clay, Glazed, Japan, 5 x 3 1/2 In.	20.00
Ashtray, Florida, Panama City Beach, 4 In.	5.00
Ashtray, Kentucky, Red Cardinal, Pink Flowers, Stoneware, 4 1/2 In.	10.00
Bank, Asbury Park, Lobster, Ceramic, 3 In.	22.00
Bank, Barrel, White, Small Painted Flowers, Scranton, Pa., Ceramic, 3 In.	66.00
Booklet, Olympic, 1928, Amsterdam, Runner, 45 Pages	30.00
Booklet, Olympic, 1936, Berlin, Olympic Rings, Brandenburg Gate, 19 Pages	30.00
Box, Paper, Burgundy Velvet Cover, Souvenirs In Brass Ormolu, 1800s	90.00
Building, Miniature, Cadet Chapel, USAF, White Metal	99.00
Bust, Hula Bust, Black Coral	55.00
Card, Buffalo Bill Cody, Wild West Show, Marked Sitting Bull, 1884	341.00
Charm, Apollo 11, Revolving Bubble, 1969	15.00
Cigarette Case, Southern Africa Map, Engraved, Chrome, 1950s, 5 x 3 1/4 In.	20.00
Doll, Vietnamese, Composition, Silk Face, Ceremonial Dress, Lacquer Base, 13 In.	20.00
Figurine, Eiffel Tower, 2 1/2 In. ....*Illus*	6.00
Figurine, Empire State Building, 2 1/2 In. ....*Illus*	10.00
Figurine, Statue Of Liberty, 2 1/2 In. ....*Illus*	12.00
Matches, Stork Club, Unused, 1940s	50.00
Mug, Highland Light, Cape Cod Mass., Germany, I.L. Rosenthal, 5 In.	88.00
Mug, Pawnee Bill, Presentation To Black Cowboy, Stained Glass, 1910, 4 In.	283.00
Mug, Ruby Flash, Engraved, Galena Fair 1906 Buck, 2 3/4 In., Pair	17.00
Music Box, Hawaiian, Girl & Boy	65.00
Napkin Holder, California Midwinter Fair, 1894, 1 5/8 In.	7.00
Nut Dish, Hawaiian, Treasure Craft, 1962	18.00
Pendant, 1900 Paris Medical Congress, Goddess, Silver Plate, F. Vernon, 1 1/2 In.	20.00
Pennant, Gatlinburg, Tenn., Mt. Le Conte, Felt, 11 3/4 In. ....*Illus*	10.00
Pennant, West Virginia, Frontiersman, Orange Felt, 7 3/4 In. ....*Illus*	9.00
Pillow Cover, Goose Bay, Labrador, Red Edge, 14 x 14 In. ....*Illus*	5.00
Pillow Cover, Norfolk, Va. Scenes, Pink, Fringe, 14 x 14 In. ....*Illus*	5.00
Pin, Byrd Arctic Expedition, Guernsey Born 1933, Cow, Celluloid, 1 1/4 In.	25.00
Pin, Mardi Gras, Amphictyons, Goddess Diana, Quiver, Clouds, Round, 1908	215.00
Pin, Mardi Gras, Atlanteans, Let Wurra Worry, Gnome, In Clover, Gold Ball	193.00
Pin, Mardi Gras, Elves Of Oberon, Fan Shape, Billowing Clouds	150.00
Pin, Mardi Gras, Falstaffians, Round, Winged Fairy Holds Wand, 1909	120.00
Pin, Mardi Gras, Knights Of Momus, Link Choker, Sterling Silver, 1929	90.00

Souvenir, Pennant, Gatlinburg, Tenn.,
Mt. Le Conte, Felt, 11 3/4 In.

Souvenir, Pennant, West Virginia,
Frontiersman, Orange Felt, 7 3/4 In.

Souvenir, Pillow
Cover, Goose Bay,
Labrador, Red Edge,
14 x 14 In.

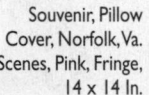

Souvenir, Pillow
Cover, Norfolk, Va.
Scenes, Pink, Fringe,
14 x 14 In.

Pin, Mardi Gras, Knights Of Momus, Maiden's Face, Tresses Border, 1902	90.00
Pin, Mardi Gras, Mithras, Cartouche, Repousse Fairy, 2 Phoenixes, 1921	90.00
Pin, Mardi Gras, Nereus, Serpents Around Pitch Fork, Gilt Metal, Enamel	112.00
Pin, Mardi Gras, Othras, Letter M, King Of Clubs, Hearts, Diamonds, 1913	120.00
Pin, Mardi Gras, Rex, Large Green Serpent, Gilt Scales, 1891	385.00
Pin, Niagara Falls, Celluloid, Pinback, 1896, 1 In.	7.00
Pin, Philadelphia My City, Celluloid, Pinback, 3/4 In.	5.00
Pitcher, Space Age & Rocket Center, Huntsville, Alabama, Grapes, 3 In.	10.00
Plate, 1972, Olympics, Munich, White, Blue Graphics, Porcelain, 12 In.	53.00
Plate, Colgate University, Sterling Silver, 1975	85.00
Plate, Dog's, Luana, Iowa	50.00
Program, Life Of Tom Mix, Sells-Fluto Circus, Illustrations, 10 1/4 x 6 3/4 In.	147.00
Program, Pawnee Bill Buffalo Ranch, Buffalo Head, 1911, 9 1/2 x 7 1/2 In.	339.00
Ring, Flicker, Apollo 11, 1969	30.00
Scarf, Niagara Falls, Silk, Square, Japan, 28 3/4 In. . . . .*Illus*	35.00
Spoon, Sterling Silver, Admiral Dewey Bust On Handle, New York In Bowl	40.00
Spoon, Sterling Silver, Arizona Grand Canyon	10.00
Spoon, Sterling Silver, Arkansas, State House	18.00
Spoon, Sterling Silver, Bennett House, North Carolina	22.00
Spoon, Sterling Silver, Buffalo, N.Y., Buffalo In Bowl	14.00
Spoon, Sterling Silver, California, 5 1/2 In. . . . .*Illus*	12.00
Spoon, Sterling Silver, Courthouse, Cairo, Illinois	55.00
Spoon, Sterling Silver, Epping Forest Rifle Club, Tree On Handle	30.00
Spoon, Sterling Silver, Figural, Santa Rosa, Cal., Woman On Handle, 1806	22.00
Spoon, Sterling Silver, Fort Dearborn, In Bowl	12.00
Spoon, Sterling Silver, King George & Queen Mary, Jubilee, 1935	25.00
Spoon, Sterling Silver, Library, Akron, Ohio	45.00
Spoon, Sterling Silver, McKinley Bust, White House In Bowl	35.00
Spoon, Sterling Silver, Michigan State	18.00
Spoon, Sterling Silver, Montreal, Enameled Maple Leaf, Shield Handle	35.00
Spoon, Sterling Silver, Springfield Il., Lincoln Handle, Capital In Bowl	18.00

Souvenir, Spoon, Sterling Silver,
California, 5 1/2 In.

Souvenir, Scarf, Niagara Falls,
Silk, Square, Japan, 28 3/4 In.

Spoon, Sterling Silver, Victoria, B.C., Etched Parliament Building Bowl 35.00
Spoon, Sterling Silver, Yellowstone Park, Deer 38.00
Thermometer, Florida, Flamingo, Ceramic, Japan, 6 x 3 In. 35.00
Torch, Olympic, Barcelona, 1992, 26 In. 4600.00
Torch, Olympic, Los Angeles, 1984, 23 In. 3220.00
Torch, Olympic, Montreal, XXI Olympiad, 26 In. 2760.00
Toy, Hula Dancer, Ukulele, Musical, Plays Blue Hawaii, Battery, 13 In. 24.00
Tray, My Home Town, Capscowood, Washington, D.C., Capitol, Wood, 9 1/4 In. 30.00
Tray, My Home Town, Titusville, Pa., Oil Centennial, 1859-1959, 6 1/2 x 4 1/2 In. 10.00
Tray, Yellowstone National Park, Metal, 11 In. 7.00
Vase, Colorado State Fair, Coors Beer, Brown & Teal, 1939, 7 1/4 In. 44.00
Wine, Algona Fair, 1906, Ruby Stain 48.00

SPATTER GLASS is a multicolored glass made from many small pieces
of different colored glass. It is sometimes called *End-of-Day* glass. It
is still being made.

Centerpiece, Pink, White, 10 In. 70.00
Cruet, Clear Handle & Stopper, Flattened Form, 4 1/4 In. 135.00
Cruet, Enameled Flowers, Clear Applied Handle & Stopper, 5 1/2 x 3 3/4 In. 265.00
Jar, Cover, Red, Green Rainbow, 8 1/4 In. 165.00
Pitcher, 5 Colors, Scalloped Edge, Scrolled Handle, Ribbed Body, 6 1/8 In. 7150.00

SPATTERWARE is the creamware or soft paste dinnerware decorated
with colored spatter designs. The earliest pieces were made in the late
eighteenth century, but most of the spatterware found today was made
from about 1800 to 1850, or it is a form of kitchen crockery with added
spatter designs, made in the late nineteenth and twentieth centuries. The
early spatterware was made in the Staffordshire district of England for
sale in America. The later kitchen type is an American product.

Bowl, Blue & Green Rainbow, Wide Rim, 1 3/8 x 9 1/2 In. 475.00
Bowl, Brown Border, Yellow Ground, 7 1/2 x 2 1/2 In. 546.00
Bowl, Morning Glory, Blue, Sprigs, Green, 5 3/4 In. 2090.00
Bowl, Stick, Red, Green, Brown & Blue Vertical Bands, 4 1/2 x 2 3/4 In. 200.00
Bowl, Tulip, Yellow Border, 4 1/2 In. 4070.00
Chamber Pot, Blue & White Allover, 8 3/4 In. 80.00
Coffeepot, Peafowl, Blue Ground, 1830, 9 In. 550.00
Creamer, 8-Paneled Sides, Narrow Blue Band Top, Floral Design, 5 x 3 In. 340.00
Creamer, Carnation Red, Black Border, 4 1/4 In. 605.00
Creamer, Clipper Ship, Blue Border, 5 5/8 In. 4840.00
Creamer, Fort, Blue, Black, Red, Gray, Green Border, 4 1/4 In. .... 440.00 to 495.00
Creamer, Holly Berry, Red, Green & Black Border, 4 In. 660.00
Creamer, Peafowl, Green Border, 3 3/4 In. 275.00
Creamer, Peafowl, Red, 4 1/2 In. 110.00
Creamer, Peafowl, Red, Blue, Yellow, Green Body, Handle, 3 3/4 x 4 In. 335.00
Creamer, Purple Allover, 4 In. 185.00
Creamer, Red & Green, Rainbow, 4 In. 525.00
Creamer, School House, Red, Grass & Trees, Green, Blue Border, 19th Century 3300.00
Creamer, Strawberry, Peafowl, Red, Green & Blue Border, 4 In. 5170.00
Cup, Purple & Blue Allover, Flower Inside, Red 120.00
Cup, Purple & Blue Rainbow, Blue Inner Border, Handleless, 3 3/4 x 2 1/2 In. 250.00
Cup, Thistle, 2-Tone, Blue Border, Handleless, 3 7/8 x 2 3/4 In. 195.00
Cup, Thistle, 2-Tone, Yellow & Red Rainbow, Handleless, 4 x 2 1/2 In. 615.00
Cup & Saucer, Blue Allover, Handleless 60.00
Cup & Saucer, Blue, Red Rainbow, Handleless, 2 1/2 x 4 1/4 In. 390.00
Cup & Saucer, Blue, Red Rainbow, Handleless, 2 3/8 x 3 3/4 In. 475.00
Cup & Saucer, Cannonball, Red, Green Border 3190.00
Cup & Saucer, Fort, Blue, Black, Red, Yellow, Green Border 550.00
Cup & Saucer, Lafayette At Franklin's Tomb, Blue 285.00
Cup & Saucer, Peafowl, Blue, Dark Red Saucer, Handleless, 2 1/2 x 4 In. 420.00
Cup & Saucer, Peafowl, Blue, Green, Yellow, Red Border, Handleless, 2 3/8 x 4 In. 225.00
Cup & Saucer, Peafowl, Blue, Red, Blue Border, Handleless, 2 1/4 x 3 7/8 In. 390.00
Cup & Saucer, Peafowl, Green, Blue, Green, Red Border, Handleless, 2 1/2 x 4 In. 475.00
Cup & Saucer, Peafowl, Green, Red, Blue Saucer, Handleless, 2 1/2 x 4 In. 450.00

Cup & Saucer, Peafowl, Red, Blue, Yellow, Green Border, Handleless, 2 x 3 7/8 In. 785.00
Cup & Saucer, Peafowl, Red, Yellow, Red Saucer, Handleless, 2 1/2 x 4 In. 450.00
Cup & Saucer, Pomegranate, Blue, Handleless, 2 5/8 x 4 In. 1065.00
Cup & Saucer, Purple Allover, 3 3/4 In. 155.00
Cup & Saucer, Purple, Dot 550.00
Cup & Saucer, Red, Dot, Miniature 165.00
Cup & Saucer, Rooster, Blue, Handleless 1320.00
Cup & Saucer, Rooster, Red 1430.00
Cup & Saucer, School House, Red, Green Border, Handleless 3190.00
Cup & Saucer, Star In Sunburst, Red, Blue & Green Border 605.00
Cup & Saucer, Sunburst, Green 660.00
Cup & Saucer, Swag & Tassel, Yellow, Green & Red Rainbow, Handleless 4070.00
Cup & Saucer, Thistle, Blue 165.00
Cup & Saucer, Thistle, Red 495.00
Cup & Saucer, Tulip, Blue, Handleless 525.00
Cup & Saucer, Tulip, Blue, Red & Blue Border, Handleless, 2 1/2 x 4 In. 420.00
Cup & Saucer, Tulip, Red, Blue, Light Blue Border, Handleless, 2 5/8 x 3 7/8 In. 195.00
Cup & Saucer, Tulip, Red, Yellow Border, Handleless 1430.00
Cup & Saucer, Windmill, Red, Blue, Yellow, Black Border, Handleless 2310.00
Cup & Saucer, Yellow, Red & Green Bands, Black Stripes, Miniature, Handleless 55.00
Mug, Present For A Good Boy, Canary 495.00
Pitcher, Acorn, Yellow, Green Branch, Purple Border, Early 19th Century, 7 1/2 In. 4400.00
Pitcher, Blue & White Allover 100.00
Pitcher, Blue, Red, Green Rainbow, Black Swirled Vertical Stripes, Handle, 7 In. 6720.00
Pitcher, Eagle & Shield, Blue Transfer, Red Border, 6 1/2 In. 467.00
Pitcher, Milk, 5 Colors, Vertical Bands, 6 In. 2310.00
Pitcher, Milk, Red & Blue Allover, 5 3/4 In. 110.00
Pitcher, Red, Blue Rainbow, 14 3/8 x 11 In. 840.00
Pitcher, Rose, Yellow, Red, Blue Rainbow, Blue On Handle, 9 x 6 In. 950.00
Plate, Acorn, Brown, Blue Border, Paneled, Early 19th Century, 9 In. 990.00
Plate, Acorn, Yellow, Purple Border, Paneled, 9 In. 1320.00
Plate, Blue Cockscomb Center, 9 1/2 In. 305.00
Plate, Blue, Red, Rainbow, 9 1/2 In. 390.00
Plate, Fort, Blue, Black, Red, Gray, Green, Brown, 9 1/2 In. 715.00
Plate, Green, Red Rainbow, 9 1/2 In. ....280.00 to 335.00
Plate, Peafowl, Blue, Red Border, 8 1/2 In. 990.00
Plate, Peafowl, Blue, Yellow & Green, Red Border, Early 19th Century, 9 In. 715.00
Plate, Peafowl, Green, Red, Red Border, 8 3/8 In. 840.00
Plate, Peafowl, Red, Blue, Green, Red Rainbow, 9 3/8 In. 505.00
Plate, Red Allover, 8 3/4 In. 55.00
Plate, Rose, Blue, 3-Tone Rainbow, 9 3/4 In. ....225.00 to 310.00
Plate, School House, Blue, 4-Tone Rainbow, 8 1/4 In. 2800.00
Plate, School House, Multicolored, Blue Border, 8 1/4 In. 2800.00
Plate, School House, Red, Blue Border, J. Goodwin, 19th Century 1650.00
Plate, School House, Tree, Red, Green Border, 9 1/4 In. 522.00
Plate, Star In Sunburst, Blue Border, 19th Century, 8 1/2 In. 355.00
Plate, Star, Red & Blue, Rainbow, 8 In. 825.00
Plate, Starflower, Blue, 4-Tone Rainbow, 8 1/2 In. 670.00
Plate, Thistle, Blue, Leaf, 4-Tone Rainbow, 8 1/2 In. 365.00
Plate, Toddy, Purple & Black Rainbow, Early 19th Century, 5 In. 770.00
Plate, Tulip, Green Leaf, Blue Border, 19th Century, 9 1/4 In. 550.00
Plate, Tulip, Green Leaf, Rainbow, 7 In. 1760.00
Plate, Tulip, Red, Blue Border, 8 1/4 In. 505.00
Platter, Blueberries, Leaves, Blue Border, England, 19 1/2 x 16 In. 650.00
Platter, Bull's-Eye, Red, Green Rainbow, 17 3/4 In. 3190.00
Platter, Flower, Purple Snowflake Border, 12 1/4 In. 330.00
Platter, Gooney Bird, Red, Green, Blue Border, 13 1/2 x 10 1/4 In. 1870.00
Platter, Peafowl, Blue, Red, Green Border, Paneled, 15 1/2 x 12 In. 3080.00
Platter, Red & Green Rainbow, 18 In. 3300.00
Platter, Red & Green, Rainbow, Octagonal 3190.00
Platter, Red, Blue Rainbow, Octagonal, 14 3/8 x 11 In. 840.00
Ramekin, Peafowl, Blue Border, 5 In. 550.00
Saucer, Blue Flower, Brown Border 495.00

Saucer, Red, Green, Yellow, Rainbow, Pair 1760.00
Saucer, Thistle, Green, Red & Black, Brown Rainbow 550.00
Sugar, Cover, Flowers, Blue, Red Border 245.00
Sugar, Cover, Windmill, Pink Border, 19th Century 825.00
Sugar, Rooster, Yellow, Blue, Red & Black Rainbow, 4 1/4 In. 880.00
Sugar & Creamer, Green & Purple Panels, 8 1/2 & 5 1/4 In. 230.00
Teapot, Cover, Red, Blue Rainbow, Blue Spout, Handle, 6 x 5 In. 3920.00
Teapot, Cover, Thistle, Blue Spout, Handle, 6 In. 3920.00
Teapot, Dove, Green Sprigs, Purple Border, 6 In. 1045.00
Teapot, Peafowl, Red Border, Paneled, 8 1/2 In. 1540.00
Teapot, School House, Red, Red Border, 7 In. 1210.00
Teapot, Tree, Green & Black, Purple Border, 6 In. 1980.00
Washbowl & Pitcher, Blue & White Allover, 11 3/4-In. Bowl, 9-In Pitcher 110.00
Waste Bowl, Fort, Blue, Black, Red, Yellow, Green Rainbow, 4 1/4 In. 495.00

SPELTER is a synonym for a zinc alloy. Figurines, candlesticks, and other pieces were made of spelter and given a bronze or painted finish. The metal has been used since about the 1860s to make statues, tablewares, and lamps that resemble bronze. Spelter is soft and breaks easily. To test for spelter, scratch the base of the piece. Bronze is solid; spelter will show a silvery scratch.

Bookends, Great Dane, Red Marble Base, 1920s, 8 1/2 In. 300.00
Figurine, Bear, Brown To Copper Patina, HB On Paw, c.1900, 3 1/2 In. 160.00
Figurine, Don Juan, 20 1/2 In. 305.00
Figurine, Le Calme, Patinated, Marble Base, Luca Madrassi, 31 3/4 In. 690.00
Figurine, Mercury, Running On Wind, Marble Base, 28 In. 1540.00
Figurine, Minerva, Holding Wreath, Atop Globe, Green Marble Base, 29 In. 805.00
Figurine, Warrior On Horseback, 7 x 8 In. 80.00
Figurine, Woman, Holding Flower, Fleur De Mai, A. De Ranieri, 1900, 27 1/2 In. .. 465.00
Inkstand, Lion, Continental, 10 1/2 In. 92.00
Lamp, Banquet, Putto Holding Orb, Green Glass Shade, 22 In. 300.00
Lamp, County Maid, Chickens, Premiere, After Bruchon, France, c.1900, 28 In. ... 330.00
Lamp, Figures, Rembrandt & Rubens, Black Patina, 1900, 17 1/2 In., Pair 170.00
Lamp, Maiden On Leaf Base, Gold Dore Patina, 24 x 13 In. 1380.00
Lamp, Woman Standing With Chalice, 29 1/4 In. 375.00
Match Holder, Monkey, With Quill, Books, Victorian, 5 3/4 In. 95.00
Urn, Cover, Putti, Berry Laurel, Acanthus Handle, 20 1/4 In., Pair 1955.00
Urn, Red To Olive Green, Bronze Mounts, Scrolled Leaf Handle, 19 In. 86.00

SPINNING WHEELS in the corner have been symbols of earlier times for the past 100 years. Although spinning wheels date back to medieval days, the ones found today are rarely more than 200 years old. Because the style of the spinning wheel changed very little, it is often impossible to place an exact date on a wheel.

Cherry, Signed, Joseph P. Piggon, 19th Century, 41 1/2 x 19 x 43 In. 310.00
Child's, Ivory Decoration, Europe, 1860, 12-In. Wheel, 26 In. 560.00
Flax, Mustard Paint 295.00
Flax Wheel, Hardwood, Bone Trim, Continental, 28 In. 165.00
Flax Wheel, Hardwood, Red Finish, Painted Design, Continental, 35 In. 190.00
Horseshoe Spinner 295.00
Maple, Salmon Paint Traces, Penna., J. Fox, Late 18th Century, 49 In. 470.00
Oak, Orange Highlights, 18th Century 135.00
Upright, 2 Bobbins, Hardwood, 42 1/2 In. 77.00

SPODE pottery, porcelain, and bone china were made by the Stoke-on-Trent factory of England founded by Josiah Spode about 1770. The firm became Copeland and Garrett from 1833 to 1847, then W.T. Copeland or W.T. Copeland and Sons until 1976. It then became Royal Worcester Spode Ltd. The word *Spode* appears on many pieces made by the factories. Most collectors include all the wares under the more familiar name of Spode. Porcelains are listed in this book by the name that appears on the piece. Related pieces are listed under Copeland and Copeland Spode.

Ashtray, Christmas Tree 22.00

Bowl, Christmas Tree, 9 In.	50.00
Bowl, Fruit, Summer Palace	50.00
Butter Chip, Blue Tower	24.00
Compote, Flowers, Apple Green Rim, Gold Trim, Gadrooned Foot, c.1860, 9 In., Pair	460.00
Creamer, Summer Palace	20.00
Cup & Saucer, Summer Palace	25.00
Dinner Service, Central Bow Knotted Bouquet Of Flowers, Japan, 1830, 28 Piece	4600.00
Pitcher, Assyrian, Bulbous, 9 In.	55.00
Pitcher, Water, Classical Figure, Serpent Handle, Greek Key Border, 8 In.	143.00
Plate, Buttercup, 12 In.	60.00
Plate, New Stone, c.1805, 9 1/2 In.	125.00
Plate, Peacock, 8 1/2 In., 8 Piece	1380.00
Plate, Two Temples, Blue Willow Variant, 1810	100.00
Punch Bowl, Imari, Floral, Blue Transfer Border, Gold Trim, c.1815-1830, 11 1/4 In.	1250.00

SPONGEWARE is very similar to spatterware in appearance. The designs were applied to the ceramics by daubing the color on with a sponge or cloth. Many collectors do not differentiate between spongeware and spatterware and use the names interchangeably. Modern pottery is being made to resemble the old spongeware, but careful examination will show it is new.

Bank, Pig, Blue & Brown, 4 In.	40.00
Bean Pot, Handle, Blue, White, Incised 2 Qt., 6 1/2 In.	175.00
Bowl, 2 Brown Bands, Impressed Squares On Outside, 8 In.	150.00
Bowl, Blue & White, Flared Sides, 11 x 7 In.	100.00
Bowl, Blue & White, Molded Arch & Pillar, 10 In.	120.00
Bowl, Blue & White, Molded Exterior, 12 1/4 x 5 7/8 In.	385.00
Bowl, Blue, Brown, Late 19th Century, 9 x 6 1/4 In.	137.00
Bowl, Blue, Molded Design, 8 1/2 In.	40.00
Bowl, Blue, White, Blue Banded Accents In Middle, 11 1/4 In.	130.00
Bowl, White Band, Blue Border, Signed, Kevin McConnell, 1890	100.00
Chamber Pot, Blue, White, Molded Vine, Bail Handle, 5 1/4 x 11 In.	110.00
Creamer, Blue, White, C Handle, White Part In Front, 4 x 3 1/4 In.	190.00
Crock, Butter, Cover, Blue, White, Molded Letters, 5 1/4 x 7 1/2 In.	175.00
Crock, Butter, Stenciled, Blue & White, 3 3/4 x 6 In. ....*Illus*	143.00
Cuspidor, Blue, White, Brass Cover, 4 x 10 1/4 In.	120.00
Dish, Blue & White, 1 1/4 x 10 1/4 In.	188.00
Ewer, Blue Bands, Small	135.00
Honey Pot, Cover, Blue, White, Bail Handle, 4 1/2 In.	525.00
Jug, Grandmother's Maple Syrup, Blue & White, Bail Handle, 8 In. ....*Illus*	1155.00
Mixing Bowl, Blue & Brown, Rite Hdwe. Co., 6 1/2 In. ....*Illus*	125.00
Nappy, Blue, White, 3 x 9 1/4 In.	165.00
Pitcher, 2 Narrow Blue Stripes, 6 5/8 x 7 1/4 x 5 3/8 In.	125.00
Pitcher, Blue & White, 7 1/2 In.	495.00
Pitcher, Blue & White, 8 In.	330.00

Spongeware, Crock, Butter,
Stenciled, Blue & White,
3 3/4 x 6 In.

Spongeware, Jug,
Grandmother's Maple Syrup,
Blue & White, Bail Handle, 8 In.

Spongeware, Mixing Bowl,
Blue & Brown, Rite Hdwe. Co.,
6 1/2 In.

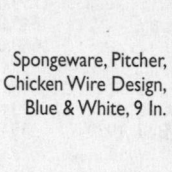

Spongeware, Pitcher,
Chicken Wire Design,
Blue & White, 9 In.

Spongeware, Pitcher,
Wild Rose, Blue,
Salt Glaze, 9 In.

Spongeware, Soap Dish, Blue &
White, Cutout Sides, 5 1/4 In.

Spongeware,
Teapot, Blue &
White, 5 1/2 In.

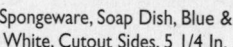

Pitcher, Blue & White, 9 In.	210.00 to 495.00
Pitcher, Blue & White, Blue Band At Top & Base, Bulbous, 8 1/2 In.	165.00
Pitcher, Blue & White, Bulbous, 9 1/2 In.	910.00
Pitcher, Blue & White, Molded Ribbons & Bows, Bulbous, 11 1/2 In.	990.00
Pitcher, Blue Accent Band On Top, Blue & White, 6 3/4 In.	210.00
Pitcher, Chain Link, Blue & White, 9 In.	415.00
Pitcher, Chain Link, Dark Blue & White, 8 3/4 In.	305.00
Pitcher, Chicken Wire Design, Blue & White, 9 In. .... *Illus*	523.00
Pitcher, Cover, Blue Flowers, Blue & White, 1850, 9 x 7 x 6 In.	175.00
Pitcher, Water, Blue Accent Bands, Blue & White, 12 In.	210.00
Pitcher, Wild Rose, Blue, Salt Glaze, 9 In. .... *Illus*	248.00
Plate, Blue & White, 7 In.	130.00
Plate, Blue & White, Scalloped Edge, 9 1/4 In.	115.00 to 145.00
Plate, Blue & White, Scalloped, Molded Edge, 10 1/4 In.	88.00
Plate, Rabbit Border, Flowers, Leaves & Frogs In Center, 9 1/4 In.	250.00
Plate, Rabbits In Center, Leaf & Flower Border, 9 1/4 In.	250.00
Platter, Blue & White, Serving, Oval, 13 In.	130.00
Platter, Blue, Oval, 11 1/2 In.	100.00
Salt, Cover, Chicken Wire Sponging, Blue, White, 5 3/4 In.	275.00
Salt, Relief Indian Good Luck Sign, Wooden Lid, Blue, White, 5 3/4 In.	165.00
Soap Dish, Blue & White, Cutout Sides, 5 1/4 In. .... *Illus*	154.00
Soap Dish, Dark Blue Bands, Blue Stars, 3 Piece	625.00
Teapot, Blue & White, 5 1/2 In. .... *Illus*	880.00
Vase, Cone Shape, Blue, White, Yellow, Flared Rim, 7 1/4 x 5 In.	80.00
Water Cooler, Filter, Blue & White, 1 Gal.	125.00

SPORTS equipment, sporting goods, brochures, and related items are
listed here. Items are listed by sport. Other categories of interest are
Bicycle, Card, Fishing, Sword, Toy, and Trap.

Archery, Bow & Arrow Set, Wooden Box, c.1890, 22 x 4 1/4 x 15 In.	81.00
Auto Racing, Scarf, Indy 500, Silk, Square, 30 In.	10.00
Baseball, Badge, Ebbets Field Employee, Silver, Green Center, 1940s, 2 In.	2130.00

Baseball, Ball, 1923 World Series Game 2090.00
Baseball, Ball, A.G. Chandler, 2nd Commissioner 83.00
Baseball, Ball, Autographed, American League, Babe Ruth & 2 Others 546.00
Baseball, Ball, Autographed, Babe Ruth, World's Home Run Record, 1919 .... 1150.00
Baseball, Ball, Autographed, Boston Red Sox, 1938 .... 345.00
Baseball, Ball, Autographed, Brooklyn Dodgers, 1955 .... 2660.00
Baseball, Ball, Autographed, Chicago White Sox, 24 Players, 1970 ....32.00 to 55.00
Baseball, Ball, Autographed, Don Newcombe, With Certificate, Box 48.00
Baseball, Ball, Autographed, Joe DiMaggio, American League, Rawlings, Box 170.00
Baseball, Ball, Autographed, Joe DiMaggio, Bobby Brown American League Ball, 1939 . 345.00
Baseball, Ball, Autographed, Lou Dials, Negro League, 1930s 23.00
Baseball, Ball, Autographed, Mickey Mantle 308.00
Baseball, Ball, Autographed, New York Yankees, DiMaggio & Mantle 2980.00
Baseball, Ball, Autographed, Nolan Ryan..................................... 35.00
Baseball, Ball, Autographed, Satchel Paige, Aug. 22, 1935 .... 1140.00
Baseball, Ball, Autographed, Ty Cobb, Little League, Green Ink, May 21, 1961 .... 2530.00
Baseball, Ball, Autographed, Willie Mays, Say Hey 103.00
Baseball, Ball, Cleveland Buckeyes Negro League Championship, 1949 .... 460.00
Baseball, Ball, Display Box, Standard Baseballs, Wooden 3410.00
Baseball, Ball, Mickey Mantle, Autographed In Blue Ink 90.00
Baseball, Bat, Autographed, Early Wynn, World Series, 1959 .... 2190.00
Baseball, Bat, Autographed, Mark McGwire, Rawlings, 1988, 34 1/2 In. 1835.00
Baseball, Bat, Autographed, Mickey Mantle, 536 Lifetime Home Runs, 1985 .... 1380.00
Baseball, Bat, Autographed, Ted Williams Limited Edition, No. 406 .... 1760.00
Baseball, Bat, Draper & Maynard, Lucky Dog, Converse Shoes 135.00
Baseball, Bat, Roger Maris Semipro Model, Wood, Dark, Regent Sports Co., 31 In. 110.00
Baseball, Button, Babe Ruth Club, Ivory Colored, Smiling Image, Greenduck Co., 1920s . 385.00
Baseball, Button, Bruce Sutter, Picture, Pitcher ERA, Fun Foods, 1984 .... 21.00
Baseball, Button, Dizzy Dean Winners Club, Baseball Shape, Copper, 1 In............. 30.00
Baseball, Button, Dizzy Dean Winners Club, Brass, 1930s, 1 In. 36.00
Baseball, Button, Ted Williams, Attached Ribbon, Chain, Ball & Glove, 1950, 1 1/4 In. .. 95.00
Baseball, Button, Willie Mays, Say Hey, Newspaper, Celluloid, 1970s, 3 1/2 In. 25.00
Baseball, Cap, Autographed, Brooklyn Dodgers, 1950s 350.00
Baseball, Cap, Autographed, Reggie Jackson, Hall Of Fame Election, 1993 .... 1070.00
Baseball, Cap, Game Worn, Montreal Royals, Navy, White Velvet Over Visor, 1940s 1035.00
Baseball, Cap, Kansas City Black Royals, 1920s 925.00
Baseball, Catcher's Helmet, Carlton Fisk, Boston, Red & Black, Size 7 1/4 .... 1080.00
Baseball, Catcher's Mitt, Bill Freehan Model, Wilson, 1950s 32.00
Baseball, Catcher's Mitt, Brass Eyelets, Old-Style Closure, 1930s 70.00
Baseball, Catcher's Mitt, Leather, Draper & Maynard, Box, 1930 .... 375.00
Baseball, Catcher's Mitt, Roy Campanella, Dodgers, Wilson, 2 Letters, 1950s 6110.00
Baseball, Catcher's Mitt, Winchester, Label, 9 In. 137.00
Baseball, Chair, Mickey Mantle, Restaurant, Wooden, 1950s 675.00
Baseball, Cigar Box, Home Run Stogies, Tin 1485.00
Baseball, Coin, Mickey Mantle, 1964 All Stars, Stamped Metal, Topps 25.00
Baseball, Figure, Ernie Banks At Bat, Chicago Cubs, Molded Plastic, Hartland, 7 In. 165.00
Baseball, Glass, Tom Henke, Toronto Blue Jays 9.00
Baseball, Glove, Stan Musial Model, Rawlings, 1940s 40.00
Baseball, Glove, Willie Puddin' Head Jones Model, Rawlings, 1940s 40.00
Baseball, Jacket, Billy Loes, Brooklyn Dodgers 1910.00
Baseball, Jacket, Gene Conley, Milwaukee Braves, No. 39, 1955 .... 2085.00
Baseball, Jersey, Giants, Souvenir, Barry Bonds 25 On Back, White, Size XXL 28.00
Baseball, Jersey, Joe DiMaggio, New York Yankees, 1939 .... 483.00
Baseball, Jersey, Pittsburgh Pirates, Souvenir, No. 8, Yellow, Wilson, Size 42 .... 45.00
Baseball, Jersey, Seattle Mariners, Souvenir, No. 19, White, Wilson, 1979, Size 42 ...... 36.00
Baseball, Medallion, Robert A. O'Farrel, Most Valuable Player, National League, 1926 .. 1320.00
Baseball, Nodder, Atlanta Braves, Ceramic, Decals, Green Base, 7 1/2 In. 38.00
Baseball, Nodder, Cincinnati Reds, Green Base, 1960s 300.00
Baseball, Nodder, Detroit Tigers, Green Base, 1960s 200.00
Baseball, Nodder, Mickey Mantle, New York Yankees, 1961-1962, 7 In. 735.00
Baseball, Nodder, Milwaukee Brewers, Ceramic, Decals, Green Base, 7 1/2 In. 38.00
Baseball, Nodder, Whitey Ford, Ceramic, Decals, Sam's, Box, 7 1/2 In. 28.00
Baseball, Nodder, Yogi Berra, Ceramic, Decals, Sam's, Box, 7 1/2 In. 24.00

Baseball, Pen & Pencil, Jimmy Foxx, Boston Red Sox, Bat Shape, Box, 1930s	290.00
Baseball, Pen, Babe Ruth Facsimile Autograph, Celluloid, R. Esterbrook Co., 5 1/4 In. . . .	86.00
Baseball, Pen, Float About, 2 Players, In Red, Runs Bases, Crowd	3.25
Baseball, Pencil Box, Civil War Era Players Artwork, 1860s, 1 1/4 x 2 x 8 In.	905.00
Baseball, Pencil Sharpener, Mickey Mantle	2.00
Baseball, Pennant, Brooklyn Dodgers, Championship, Red, Ebbets Field, 1949, 26 In. . . .	560.00
Baseball, Photograph, 4 New York Yankees, Centerfielders, 38-Year Span, 1980s	765.00
Baseball, Photograph, Babe Ruth & Lou Gehrig, Batting Cages, 1927	6875.00
Baseball, Photograph, Babe Ruth, Autographed, 1927, 7 x 9 In.	7930.00
Baseball, Photograph, Babe Ruth, Autographed, 8 x 10 In.	2875.00
Baseball, Photograph, Bob Feller, Autographed, Large	1705.00
Baseball, Photograph, Don Drysdale, Autographed, Inscription To Jack Lang	420.00
Baseball, Photograph, Goose Goslin, Autographed	322.00
Baseball, Photograph, Infielder, 1910, 6 1/2 x 8 1/2 In.	115.00
Baseball, Photograph, Johnny Bench, Autographed, In Buffalo Uniform, 8 x 10 In.	28.00
Baseball, Photograph, Mickey Mantle & Roger Maris, Autographed, Color, 8 x 10 In.	190.00
Baseball, Photograph, Philadelphia Athletics Team, Panoramic, 1929	5500.00
Baseball, Picture, Comic, Brooklyn Dodgers, Christmas, 1955, Hubenthal, 14 x 23 In. . . .	575.00
Baseball, Pocket Mirror, A.A. Baseball Team Photograph, 1913	26.00
Baseball, Popcorn Box, Megaphone Shape, N.Y. Yankees, 1960, 10 In.	8.00
Baseball, Postcard, Ty Cobb, Detroit Tigers, Sepia, Message On Back, 1910	345.00
Baseball, Program, Boston Red Sox vs. Philadelphia Phillies, Blue Tone, 1949	20.00
Baseball, Program, Boston Red Sox vs. St. Louis Cardinals, Blue Tone, 1950	35.00
Baseball, Program, Brooklyn Dodgers vs. Boston Red Sox, 1946	40.00
Baseball, Program, Cincinnati Reds vs. Brooklyn Dodgers, Blue Tone, 1956	40.00
Baseball, Program, Joe DiMaggio's Last Home Run, Blue, Red, White, 1951	260.00
Baseball, Program, New York Yankees vs. Chicago White Sox, 1951	50.00
Baseball, Program, Washington Senators, Last Game Of Season, 1971	315.00
Baseball, Program, World Series, 1950, Yankees vs. Phillies, 50 Pages	60.00
Baseball, Program, World Series, 1951, Yankees vs. Giants, 50 Pages	66.00
Baseball, Program, World Series, New York Yankees vs. Brooklyn Dodgers, 1955	200.00
Baseball, Program, World Series, Washington Senators vs. Pittsburgh Pirates, 1925	220.00
Baseball, Program, World Series, Yankees vs. Giants, 1921	798.00
Baseball, Scarf, Brooklyn Dodgers, World Series, Silk, 1955, 34 x 34 In.	740.00
Baseball, Scorebook, John Lang's, 1950 Dodgers Season	575.00
Baseball, Season Pass, Autographed, Joe McGinnity, 1910	1930.00
Baseball, Seat, Tiger Stadium, Green, Wood Slats, Oak Base, Set Of 3	630.00
Baseball, Seat, Yankee Stadium, Red Paint, Restored	1350.00
Baseball, Shoes, Black Leather, Steel Frame-Style Cleats, 1940s, Size 8	22.00
Baseball, Ticket Stub, Hank Aaron's 715th Home Run, Atlanta Stadium, April 8, 1974 . . .	175.00
Baseball, Ticket, World Series, Chicago Cubs, 1945	35.00
Baseball, Trophy, Tom Pitts, New York, Silver Plate, 1930s, 32 In.	2090.00
Baseball, Yearbook, New York Yankees, 1953	7.00
Basketball, Ball, Autographed, NBA, Dream Team, Molten, 1992	1265.00
Basketball, Ball, Miniature, Autographed, Bob Pettit, Brown Rubber, Spalding, 5 In.	41.00
Basketball, Ball, Miniature, Autographed, George Mikan, 5 In.	45.00
Basketball, Jacket, Larry Bird, Boston Celtics, Autographed, Mid 1980s	3050.00
Basketball, Jersey, Larry Costello, No. 7, Syracuse Nationals, Wilson, 1960	690.00
Basketball, Jersey, Michael Jordan, Autographed, Box, 1992	2645.00
Basketball, Photograph, Michael Jordan, Autographed, 8 x 10 In.	495.00
Basketball, Ticket, Milwaukee Bucks vs. Atlanta Hawks, Preseason, 10-15-1986	10.00
Billiard, Table, Victorian Style, Oak, Leather Pockets, Balls, Cues, 30 x 87 x 46 In.	330.00
Boxing, Figurine, Rocky Marciano, Art Of Sport, Porcelain, Suede Base	120.00
Boxing, Gloves, Autographed, Muhammad Ali, Painted Portrait, Everlast	485.00
Boxing, Jacket, Black Nylon, Team DeLaHoya, Hood, Extra Large	50.00
Boxing, Menu, Bal Masque, Miami Beach, Autographed, Sugar Ray & Jackie Robinson . .	345.00
Boxing, Photograph, Emile Griffith, Signed, 1950s, 8 x 10 In.	22.00
Boxing, Photograph, Gene Tunney & Jack Dempsey, Action, 1926	25.00
Boxing, Photograph, Gene Tunney, Black, White, Inscription, Dec. 12, 1926, 11 x 14 In. . .	350.00
Boxing, Photograph, Harry Greb & Gene Tunney, Black & White, 7 x 8 3/4 In.	30.00
Boxing, Photograph, James Corbett & Bob Fitzsimmons, Black, Frame, 8 x 10 In.	15.00
Boxing, Postcard, Dempsey & Carpentier, Underwood & Underwood, No. 460, 1921	25.00
Boxing, Robe, Muhammad Ali, World Champion, Terry Cloth	9775.00

Boxing, Sign, Block Letters, 19th Century, 4 x 20 1/2 In. 150.00
Football, Ball, Tampa Bay Storm Championship, 1933 . . . . 60.00
Football, Glass, New England Patriots, 4 Piece 20.00
Football, Helmet, Black & Red Leather, Felt Lining, 1940s, Child's 30.00
Football, Jacket, Official's, Black & White Stripes, Cotton, Rawlings, Large 37.00
Football, Jersey & Helmet, Tony Nathan, Autographed, Miami Dolphins, 1987 . . . . 965.00
Football, Jersey, Don Maynard, New York Jets, 1970s 4130.00
Football, Nodder, North Carolina, Tar Heels, Porcelain, BPI Collectibles, Box, 8 1/2 In. . . 24.00
Football, Nodder, St. Louis Cardinals, NFL, 1960 . . . . 70.00
Football, Shoes, Dan Marino, Autographed, Size 11 1/2 . . . . 3275.00
Football, Shoulder Pads, Leather, Spalding, 1916 . . . . 285.00
Golf, Bag, Woods, Palmer, Rodrigues & More, Autographed, Red, White, 19 x 10 In. 1070.00
Golf, Ball, Leather Cover Over Packed Feathers, Excavated, England, 18th Century 750.00
Golf, Display Ad, Scoreze Golf, 2 Golfers, Standup, 1949, 10 x 13 In. 16.00
Golf, Money Clip, Golf Ball, Royal Brand Logo, 1965, Round, 1 5/8 In. 50.00
Golf, Pen, Float About, Golf Club, Golfer, Bag, Ball Rolls From Club Across Grass 3.75
Golf, Picture, Comic, Ben Hogan & Sam Snead, 53-Year Duel, 9 x 14 In. 350.00
Hockey, Banner, New York Islanders, Team Autographed, 1980s, 4 x 6 Ft. 605.00
Hockey, Doll, Wayne Gretsky, Painted Blond Hair, Oilers Accessories 75.00
Hockey, Jersey, Giles Gilbert, Boston Bruins, Wilson, 1974-1975 . . . . 575.00
Hockey, Stick, Autographed, Ray Bourque, Boston Bruins 230.00
Horse Racing, Glass, Belmont, 1966 . . . . 60.00
Horse Racing, Glass, Belmont, 1993 . . . . 10.00
Horse Racing, Glass, Breeders' Cup, 1988 . . . . .5.00 to 8.00
Horse Racing, Glass, Kentucky Derby, 1948 . . . .*Illus* 165.00
Horse Racing, Glass, Kentucky Derby, 1953 . . . . .95.00 to 135.00
Horse Racing, Glass, Kentucky Derby, 1958 . . . . 115.00
Horse Racing, Glass, Kentucky Derby, 1960 . . . . 50.00
Horse Racing, Glass, Kentucky Derby, 1961 . . . . 65.00
Horse Racing, Glass, Kentucky Derby, 1964 . . . . .25.00 to 45.00
Horse Racing, Glass, Kentucky Derby, 1972 . . . . 10.00
Horse Racing, Glass, Kentucky Derby, 1976 . . . . 5.00
Horse Racing, Glass, Kentucky Derby, 1983 . . . . 5.00
Horse Racing, Glass, L.A. Downs, 1985 . . . . .15.00 to 20.00
Horse Racing, Glass, Preakness, 1975 . . . . 55.00
Horse Racing, Glass, Preakness, 1979 . . . . 35.00
Horse Racing, Photograph, Kentucky Derby, Rosebud, Frame, 8 1/2 x 11 In. 25.00
Horse Racing, Poster, Willie Shoemaker, The Shoe Wants You, Santa Anita, 36 x 26 In. . . 580.00
Horse Racing, Ribbon, Annual P.C.W.H.A., Pomona, Calif., Red Rosette, 1977 . . . . 6.00
Horse Racing, Tumbler, Kentucky Derby, 1940, Aluminum . . . . .500.00 to 800.00
Horseback Riding, Crop, Carved Ivory Horsehead Handle, France, Pedouin 460.00
Horseback Riding, Spurs, Parade, Metal, 6 Copper Stars, 101 Ranch, 9 1/2 x 5 In. 565.00
Hunting, Camouflage Suit, Brown & Green Cotton, Reversible, 1960s, L-XL 100.00
Hunting, Crow Call, Hoosier Call & Decoy Co., Box, 1920s 70.00
Hunting, Duck Call, Broadbill, H.C. Hansen, Dark Green, 1930s, 5 1/4 In. 85.00
Hunting, Duck Call, Broadbill, Zimmerman, Box 50.00
Hunting, Jacket, Duck, Canvas, Brown & Gold, Button Front, Bill, Large 21.00
Hunting, License Tag, Nationwide, For Male Wolf, Shield Shape, Fiber, 1945, 1 1/2 In. . . 24.00

**The most valuable autographed baseballs are signed by
one player on the "sweet spot," the narrow space
without printing between the stitches. There's a sweet
spot for autographs on bats, too, between the trademark at about the middle of the bat and the burned-
in name or other information near the end of the bat.**

Sports, Horse Racing, Glass,
Kentucky Derby, 1948

Hunting, License, Wisconsin, Celluloid, 1932, 1 1/2 In. 25.00
Hunting, Tie Bar, Working Bear Trap, Salesman's Sample, 2 1/2 In. 135.00
Hunting & Fishing, License, West Virginia, Celluloid, 1937, 1 3/4 In. 21.00
Ice Skating, Speed Skates, Black Leather, Steel Blades, Alfred Johnson, 1918, Size 9 . . . . 21.00
Pool, Table, Flaring Column Supports, Arts & Crafts, c.1920, 38 x 111 In. 9775.00
Skating, Skates, Wood, Iron, Curled Tip, 12 1/2 In. 165.00
Skiing, Brochure, Cannon Mountain, Franconia, N.H., Trail Map, 1940s 10.00
Skiing, Brochure, Haystack Mountain Resort, Vermont, Trail Map 3.00
Skiing, Brochure, Pigeon Mountain, Trans-Canada Highway, Fold-Out 6.00
Skiing, Brochure, Ski Thunder Mountain, Charlemont, Mass., 21 Trails 5.00
Skiing, Map, Ski Canada, Ontario, National Survey, 1973 . . . . 3.00
Snooker, Table, Walnut, Inlay, Brunswick 5009.00
Snowmobiling, Map, Eastern U.S. Trails, Maine To Penna., National Survey, Vt., 1974 . . . 3.00
Snowmobiling, Map, Wisconsin, Michigan & Minnesota, 1973 . . . . 3.00
Snowshoes, Bear-Paw Style, Faber, Made In Canada, 26 In., Pair 75.00
Snowshoes, Bentwood Frame, Rawhide & Leather Fittings, Snocraft Inc., Maine, 56 In. . . 110.00
Snowshoes, Thick Hide, Rawhide Thongs, Rosehead Nails, 19th Century, 14 1/2 x 34 In. . . 175.00
Soccer, Pen, Float About, Player, Moves Ball Across Field 3.25
Tennis, Racket, Maureen Connolly, 1950s 40.00

STAFFORDSHIRE, England, has been a district making pottery and porcelain since the 1700s. Hundreds of kilns are still working in the area. Thousands of types of pottery and porcelain have been made in the many factories that worked and still work in the area. Some of the most famous factories have been listed separately, such as Adams, Davenport, Ridgway, Rowland & Marsellus, Royal Doulton, Royal Worcester, Spode, Wedgwood, and others. Some Staffordshire pieces are listed under categories like Fairing, Flow Blue, Mulberry, Shaving Mug, etc.

Basket, On Tray, Marked Sewel, Creamware, Reticulated, c.1820 . . . . 1250.00
Bowl, Bread, Yellow Strapwork, Brown Ground, Slipware, 18th Century, 16 In. 316.00
Bowl, Vegetable, Arms Of Massachusetts, Blue, Thomas Mayer, 8 x 7 In. 1265.00
Bowl, Vegetable, Blue Transfer, Oval, Enoch Wood & Sons, 2 x 7 In. 3335.00
Bowl, Vegetable, Cover, Quebec, Blue Transfer, Enoch Wood & Sons, 10 In. 1090.00
Bowl, Vegetable, Erith On The Thames, Blue, Enoch Wood, 11 1/2 x 8 1/2 In. 660.00
Bowl, Vegetable, Florentine, Light Blue Transfer, T.J. & J. Mayer, 8 1/4 x 6 1/2 In. 45.00
Bowl, Washington Standing At His Tomb, Blue, Enoch Wood, 6 3/4 In. 230.00
Box, Castle Shape, Brown, Green, 3 x 2 1/2 In. 55.00
Bust, George Washington, Glazed, Impressed, Enoch Wood, 1813, 8 1/2 In. 1380.00
Bust, Voltaire, Blue Coat, Black Base, 1820, 6 In. 1000.00
Cake Stand, Wild Rose, Blue Transfer, Mid 19th Century, 12 In. 402.00
Cake Stand, Wild Rose, Landscape Center, Blue, 9 1/2 In. 305.00
Castor, Figural, Man Holding Mug, 5 3/4 In. 160.00
Coffee Set, Dome Lid, Floral, Mask Handles, Urn Shape, 3 Piece 2970.00
Coffeepot, Dome Lid, Bird Design, 11 1/2 In. 3300.00
Coffeepot, Dome Lid, Blue Floral Transfer, 11 In. 550.00
Coffeepot, Dome Lid, Strawberry, 11 1/4 In. 7425.00
Coffeepot, Lafayette At Franklin's Tomb, 11 1/2 In. 4887.00
Coffeepot, Spread Eagle, Blue, 11 1/2 In. 3300.00
Compote, European Scenery, Brown Transfer, Open Handles At Base, 11 In. 605.00
Compote, Valentine, Blue, Wilkie 2090.00
Creamer, Fourth Street Bridge, Waterloo, Iowa, Weimar Germany, 3 1/2 In. 28.00
Creamer, Lafayette At Franklin's Tomb, Blue, Enoch Wood 525.00
Cup & Saucer, Handleless, Peafowl, Red, Yellow, Blue 520.00
Cup & Saucer, Wadsworth Tower, Shell Border, Blue, Handleless, Enoch Wood . . .145.00 to 220.00
Dish, Boston Hospital Against Sea Wall, Blue, White, 10 1/2 In. 172.00
Dish, Hen On Nest Cover, Polychrome, 9 1/2 In. 465.00
Dish, Hen On Nest Cover, Yellow, Red, White & Black, Green Base, 5 1/2 In. . . . .110.00 to 165.00
Dish, Highlands, Hudson River, Blue Transfer, Enoch Wood, 9 1/2 x 8 In. 3335.00
Dish, West Point Military Academy, Blue Transfer, Enoch Wood, 9 1/2 x 7 3/4 In. 3735.00
Figurine, Androcles & Lion, 1860, 8 In. 425.00
Figurine, Bear Baiting, Jug, Seated On Grassy Base, Spotted Dog, 1820, 12 In. 4600.00
Figurine, Beesums, Man, Hat, Mule With Vegetables, 10 1/4 In. 575.00

Figurine, Bonnie Prince Charles, Horse, Plumed Hat, Gold Traces, 11 In. 185.00
Figurine, Boy & Girl In Arbor, Painted Face, Gold Traces, 14 1/2 In. 120.00
Figurine, Boy, With Rabbits, 1850, 4 3/4 In. 650.00
Figurine, Castle, Drummer Boy 1 Side, 9 1/4 In. 275.00
Figurine, Cat, On Pillow, 7 1/4 In., Pair 365.00
Figurine, Cats, Black & White, Pink & Gold Trim, 20th Century, 5 1/2 In., Pair 250.00
Figurine, Cherub, With Flower Basket, Garland In Hair, 1840, 5 In., Pair 230.00
Figurine, Child, In Cradle, Yellow, Blue, 4 In. 275.00
Figurine, Cottage, 7 1/4 x 5 1/2 In. 496.00
Figurine, Cottage, Floral Design, Crazed, 4 In. 330.00
Figurine, Cow & Milkmaid, With Pail, 7 x 9 In. 330.00
Figurine, Cow, Red & White, 1840, 3 x 3 In. 950.00
Figurine, David Garrick As Richard III, Seated In Arched Cave, 1840, 8 In. 170.00
Figurine, Dog, Dalmatian, 19th Century, 8 x 7 In., Pair 715.00
Figurine, Dog, Greyhound With Rabbit, 6 3/4 In. 300.00
Figurine, Dog, Greyhound, Seated, Dead Rabbit, Salmon Color, 8 1/2 In. 275.00
Figurine, Dog, Hound, Game At Feet, Early 19th Century, 4 In. 75.00
Figurine, Dog, King Charles Spaniel, 7 3/4 In., Pair 385.00
Figurine, Dog, King Charles Spaniel, 12 1/2 In., Pair 290.00
Figurine, Dog, King Charles Spaniel, 13 In., Pair . . . . .410.00 to 525.00
Figurine, Dog, King Charles Spaniel, Luster, 10 In. 145.00
Figurine, Dog, Poodle, Bird In Mouth, 4 In., Pair 1295.00
Figurine, Dog, Poodle, Brown & Black, 3 3/4 In. 100.00
Figurine, Dog, Poodle, Painted Face, Gilt Collar, Chain, 10 In. 175.00
Figurine, Dog, Poodle, White, Textured Fur, Yellow Eyes, 6 In., Pair 190.00
Figurine, Dog, Pug, White, Black Snout, Yellow Eyes, 19th Century, 13 In., Pair 290.00
Figurine, Dog, Seated, Brown & Gray, Gilt Collar, Glass Eyes, 13 1/2 In. 355.00
Figurine, Dog, Seated, Glass Eyes, 12 1/2 In., Pair 575.00
Figurine, Dog, Seated, White, Gold Trim, 9 1/4 In. 190.00
Figurine, Dog, Spaniel, Caramel & White, 12 1/2 In., Pair 370.00
Figurine, Dog, Spaniel, Gold Trimmed Collar, Locket, 4 1/2 In. 135.00
Figurine, Dog, Spaniel, Lying Recumbent On Pillow, Red & White, 5 1/2 In. 925.00
Figurine, Dog, Spaniel, Orange-Red, Gold Collars, Yellow Eyes, 12 3/4 In., Pair 850.00
Figurine, Dog, Spaniel, Reclining, White, Gilt Highlights, 5 1/2 x 10 In., Pair 200.00
Figurine, Dog, Spaniel, Sanded Design, Pink Luster Collar & Lock, 7 In., Pair 275.00
Figurine, Dog, Spaniel, Seated, Brown, White, 19th Century, 10 1/4 In., Pair 520.00
Figurine, Dog, Spaniel, Seated, Copper Luster, Green Accents, 1900, 11 In., Pair 345.00
Figurine, Dog, Spaniel, White Glaze, Gilt To Collar Chain, 13 In., Pair 230.00
Figurine, Dog, Spaniels, White, Black Fur, Pink Nose, 13 In., Pair 300.00
Figurine, Dog, Tan, White, Black Trim, Glass Eyes, 15 In. 275.00
Figurine, Dog, Whippet, 1865, 8 1/4 In. 435.00
Figurine, Dog, Whippet, 19th Century, 4 In. 165.00
Figurine, Dog, White Sanded Coat, Black, Gold & Peach, 20th Century, 8 In. 190.00
Figurine, Dog, White With Black Spots, Seated, Blue Base, 4 In. 200.00
Figurine, English Boy, Standing By Horse, Painted Face & Clothes, 9 In. 200.00
Figurine, Equestrian Scotsman, White, 14 1/2 In. 190.00
Figurine, Girl, Riding Goat, 5 1/2 In. . . . . .115.00 to 123.00
Figurine, Girl, Riding Goat, Pink Blouse, Yellow Hat, c.1840, 6 In. 230.00
Figurine, Hamlet, With Yorick Skull, 1860, 8 In. 450.00
Figurine, Hare, Recumbent, Black Spots, Long Ears Behind Head, 9 1/2 In., Pair 8050.00
Figurine, Highlander, Drum, Cannon Near Feet, 10 In. 95.00
Figurine, Highlander, Seated On Horse With Stag, 14 In. 121.00
Figurine, Lamb, With Spill Vase, Orange Stamp Mark, c.1900, 5 In., Pair 405.00
Figurine, Lion Slayer, 16 5/8 In. 308.00
Figurine, Lion, Green Base, Front Paw On Ball, 6 x 6 In., Pair 633.00
Figurine, Little Red Riding Hood, 9 1/8 In. 392.00
Figurine, Little Red Riding Hood, Basket, Wolf, 7 In. 250.00
Figurine, Little Red Riding Hood, Seated With Wolf, c.1835, 10 In. 275.00
Figurine, Little Red Riding Hood, With Wolf, 6 7/8 In. 315.00
Figurine, Man In Tent, 10 In. 165.00
Figurine, Milkmaid & Cow, 9 1/2 x 8 3/4 In. 300.00
Figurine, Napoleon & Catalogue Of Napoleonic Relics, 7 In. 330.00
Figurine, Organ Grinder, 14 3/4 In. 460.00

Staffordshire,
Figurine, St. Paul,
Ralph Wood,
14 1/2 In.

Staffordshire,
Figurine, St. Peter,
Ralph Wood,
14 1/2 In.

Staffordshire,
Figurine, St. Philip,
Ralph Wood,
14 In.

Figurine, Scotsman, Pottery, 19th Century, 14 In.	460.00
Figurine, Shepherd With Goat, Scrolled Base, 1860, 6 In., Pair	650.00
Figurine, St. Paul, Ralph Wood, 14 1/2 In. ....*Illus*	1300.00
Figurine, St. Peter, Ralph Wood, 14 1/2 In. ....*Illus*	750.00
Figurine, St. Philip, Ralph Wood, 14 In. ....*Illus*	1050.00
Figurine, Tam O'Shanter, Seated In Chair, 8 1/2 In.	86.00
Figurine, Watch Tower, Floral Design, 5 1/4 In.	165.00
Figurine, Woman, Dolphin, Shells At Base, 10 In.	400.00
Figurine, Woman, With Basket, Crazed, 14 In.	110.00
Group, 2 Lambs & Stylized Tree, Late 19th Century, 5 1/2 In.	66.00
Group, Courting Couple, With Pug Dog, Under Arbor, 19th Century, 14 In.	290.00
Group, Dog Tray, 12 5/8 In.	135.00
Group, Equestrian, Highland Hunter Astride His Horse, Carrying A Stag, 14 In.	488.00
Group, Horse, Rider & Dog, 7 3/8 In.	110.00
Group, Lad & Lass, 12 In.	155.00
Group, Man & Woman, Holding Their Dogs, 9 1/4 In., Pair	165.00
Group, Man Carrying Water, Woman Carrying Wood, 13 In.	66.00
Group, Prince Of Wales, Princess Alexandria, Denmark, 16 x 9 In.	165.00
Group, Sailor & Woman, Highland Saluting, 11 1/4 In., Pair	310.00
Group, Scotsman & Woman, Kilt & Bagpipes, Floral Dress, 13 In.	165.00
Group, Scotsman, Companion, Deer, Female Gardener Holding Donkey, 17 x 7 In.	430.00
Group, Scotsman, On Horseback, 2 Doves, 20th Century, 14 In.	300.00
Group, Scottish Lad & Lassie, Clock & Urn Of Flowers, 12 In.	275.00
Group, Scottish Lovers In Bower, 14 In. ....120.00 to	190.00
Group, Sheep, Ram, Lamb, Walton, Marked, 6 3/4 In., Pair	1430.00
Group, Tam O'Shanter & Jooter Johnny, Crazed, 13 In.	190.00
Group, Young Women Resting Under Bower, Polychrome, 4 x 3 1/2 In.	340.00
Jar, Melon Shape, Yellow & Green Stripes, Leaf Cover, 18th Century, 2 1/4 In.	4300.00
Jug, Admiral Nelson, Figural, Cobalt Blue Jacket, Black Hat, 11 1/2 In.	220.00
Jug, Puzzle, Figures Of Man & Woman, Latticework Center, 11 1/2 In.	2350.00
Jug, Puzzle, Sun Face Within Pierced Roundel, Figural Handle, 3 Spouts, c.1840	460.00
Jug, Tortoiseshell Glaze, Pear Form On 3 Lion Mask & Paw Feet, c.1770, 5 In.	258.00
Loving Cup, Flowers, 3 Relief Frogs, 2 Handles, Early 19th Century, 9 1/2 In.	110.00
Loving Cup, Landscape Scene, The Rejected & The Accepted, 5 In.	460.00
Mug, 3 Men Drinking On Front & Back, Frog In Bottom, Scotland, 5 1/4 In.	225.00
Mug, 3-Story Building, 2 Towered Structures, Blue & White Transfer, 6 In.	2300.00
Mug, Deer Stalking, Child's	250.00
Mug, French & English Tug Of War, Child's	175.00
Mug, Getting Ready For A Walk, Child's	200.00
Mug, Hunting With Dog & Gun, Child's	225.00
Mug, Verse, Black Transfer, Silver Luster Trim, Yellow Glaze, 3 1/2 x 3 1/2 In.	430.00
Mustard Pot, Cover, Catskill Mountains, Hudson River, Enoch Wood, 2 x 3 In.	920.00
Pastille Burner, Cottage, Mid 19th Century, 7 x 5 In.	225.00
Pastille Burner, Tudor Cottage, 2-Part, 1860, 3 3/8 In.	425.00
Pen Holder, Dogs & Spill Vase, Stippled, c.1900, 5 In.	58.00
Pen Holder, Whippet, 4 In.	185.00
Pitcher, American Naval Heroes, Blue Transfer, 1830s, 8 In.	745.00

Pitcher, Boston Commons & State House, Blue, Rogers, 7 1/2 In. 660.00
Pitcher, City Hall, New York, Blue, White Transfer, 1829, 7 In. 690.00
Pitcher, Classical Figures, Signed, Richard Evans, 1824, 6 In. 115.00
Pitcher, English Landscape Scene, Blue, Early 19th Century, 6 1/2 In. 400.00
Pitcher, Erie Canal, Utica Tribute, Blue, 5 In. 825.00
Pitcher, Irish Piper, Off-White Glaze, 6 3/8 In. 85.00
Pitcher, Lafayette At Franklin's Tomb, Blue, Wood, 5 1/4 In. 825.00
Pitcher, Lake, Swan Cartouche, Porcelain, 9 3/4 In. 86.00
Pitcher, Political Cartoon, Ensnaring Preston Cock, Backyard Scene, 4 1/4 In. 460.00
Pitcher, Table, Flowers, Coral & Cobalt Blue, Gilt, Pewter Lid, 7 In. 110.00
Pitcher, Table, Geometric Spatter Design In Panels, White Ironstone, 9 1/2 In. 280.00
Pitcher, Welcome Lafayette, The Nation's Guest & Our Country's Glory, 7 In. 1955.00
Pitcher, Wellington Portrait, Upside-Down Napoleon On Reverse, 6 1/4 In. 1725.00
Pitcher, Woman Potter With Vase, Charlotte Rhead, c.1970, 9 In. 35.00
Plate, Almshouse, New York, Andrew Stevenson, Blue & White, 10 In. 630.00
Plate, Arms Of New York, Thomas Mayer, Stoke, Blue & White, 10 In. . . . . .660.00 to 1150.00
Plate, Arms Of Rhode Island, Thomas Mayer, Stoke, Blue & White, 9 In. 575.00
Plate, Baltimore & Ohio Railroad, Dark Blue, Shell Border, Wood, 10 1/8 In. 935.00
Plate, Baltimore & Ohio Railroad, Incline, Blue, Shell Border, Wood, 9 In. 605.00
Plate, Bank Of The United States, Philadelphia, Blue & White, Stubbs, 10 In. 630.00
Plate, Black Transfer, Oberwessel On Rhine, Wood & Sons, 10 1/2 In. 220.00
Plate, Boston State House, Blue Transfer, 8 1/2 In. 110.00
Plate, Cadmus, Blue, 9 In. 495.00
Plate, Chief Justice Marshall, Troy, Enoch Wood & Sons, Blue & White, 10 In. 865.00
Plate, City Hall, New York, Medium Blue, 9 3/4 In. 190.00
Plate, City Hotel, New York, Blue, White Transfer, Stevens & Williams, 8 In. 690.00
Plate, Commodore MacDonnough's Victory, Blue, Wood, 7 1/2 In. 355.00
Plate, Crimeanware Commemorative, 1854 . . . . 175.00
Plate, Cupid Imprisoned, Blue, Wood, 9 In. 210.00
Plate, Dam & Waterworks Near Philadelphia, Blue, Henschall, 10 In. 385.00
Plate, East View Of LaGrange, Blue, Wood & Son, 9 1/4 In. 300.00
Plate, Erie Canal, De Witt Clinton Eulogy, Blue, 7 1/2 In. 220.00
Plate, Fair Mount Near Philadelphia, Blue, Stubbs, 10 1/4 In. . . . . .190.00 to 255.00
Plate, Game Birds, House & Floral Border, Blue, 10 In. 130.00
Plate, Hoboken, In New Jersey, Blue, White Transfer, 1829, 7 1/2 & 7 In. 690.00
Plate, Hospital Boston, Blue, White Transfer, 9 In. 460.00
Plate, Lafayette At Washington's Tomb, Blue, 10 In. 525.00
Plate, LaGrange The Residence Of Marquis Lafayette, Blue, Enoch Wood, 10 In. 275.00
Plate, Landing Of The Fathers, Blue, Wood, 10 In. 130.00
Plate, Landscape, Raised Floral Border, Queensware, 7 1/4 In. 55.00
Plate, Moulin Sur La Mame A Charenton, Dark Blue, Wood, 9 1/8 In. . . . . .145.00 to 165.00
Plate, Nahunt Hotel, Near Boston, Blue, Stubbs, 8 1/2 In. 415.00
Plate, New York From Brooklyn Heights, A. Stevenson, Blue & White, 10 In. 745.00
Plate, New York State Seal, Border Of Fruits & Flowers, 9 7/8 In. 920.00
Plate, Patrick Henry Addressing Virginia Assembly, St. John's Church, 10 In. 75.00
Plate, Quebec, Blue, Impressed Heart Back, 9 In. 300.00
Plate, Seashell Center, Trefoil Border, Stubbs, 8 3/4 In. 200.00
Plate, Select Views, Pains Hill, Blue, R. Hall, 10 In. 145.00
Plate, Sheltered Peasants, Fruit & Fruit Border, Blue, Hall, 8 1/2 In. 120.00
Plate, Steamboat, Diorama, Blue, 10 3/8 In. 440.00
Plate, Table Rock, Niagara, Enoch Wood & Sons, Blue & White Transfer, 10 In. 690.00
Plate, Upper Ferry Bridge Over River Schuylkill, Blue, Stubbs, 8 1/2 In. . . . . .275.00 to 295.00
Plate, View On The Road To Lake George, Andrew Stevenson, Blue & White, 9 In. 1150.00
Plate, Whitby, Dark Blue, Shell Border, Wood, 9 1/4 In. 385.00
Plate, Wild Rose, Blue Transferware, S & Co., 9 1/2 In. 11.00
Plate, Zebras & Ostrich Pattern, Scroll & Floral Border, Blue, 8 3/8 In. 255.00
Platter, Abbey Friar, Fishing Pole, Horse, Blue Transfer, 10 1/2 x 8 1/2 In. 240.00
Platter, Agricultural Vase, Light Blue & White, R.M.W. & Co., 15 In. 165.00
Platter, Almshouse, Boston, Ralph Stevenson, Blue & White, 6 1/4 x 13 In. 975.00
Platter, Blue, Hunt Scene, 3 Hunters, 2 Tigers, Incised Wood, 15 x 19 In. 525.00
Platter, Boston State House, Blue, Stubbs, 14 1/2 x 12 In. 550.00
Platter, Brooklyn Ferry, Ralph Stevenson, Blue & White, 8 x 10 In. 2300.00
Platter, Cape Coast Castle On Gold Coast Africa, E. Wood, 16 1/2 x 13 In. . . . .1870.00 to 2415.00

The blue Staffordshire patterns were the earliest, with both black and blue transfer designs used during the eighteenth century. Pink, green, or brown transfer designs were used about 1820, and the combination of several colors began about 1820.

Staffordshire, Platter, Lake George,
State Of New York, Wood, 18 3/4 In.

Platter, Castle Garden Battery, New York, Enoch Wood, Blue & White, 18 1/2 In.	2760.00
Platter, Castle Ruin Scene, Blue, White, 18 1/2 In.	522.00
Platter, Chase, Bird In Border, Blue, 14 x 11 3/4 In.	990.00
Platter, Christianburg, Danish Settlement, Enoch Wood & Sons, 20 1/2 x 16 In.	3735.00
Platter, Cows In Stream, Ruined Castle, Coysh, 16 x 12 In.	525.00
Platter, Dark Blue Transfer, Flowers & Fruit, Stubbs, 20 1/2 In.	1265.00
Platter, Detroit, Blue & White Transfer, 18 1/2 x 14 1/2 In.	3220.00
Platter, Fisherman, Blue Transfer, 16 In.	385.00
Platter, Fox Hunting, The Death, Blue, 18 1/4 x 15 In.	1540.00
Platter, Fruit, Floral, Blue, White, 14 1/2 In.	550.00
Platter, Lake George, State Of New York, Wood, 18 3/4 In. ....*Illus*	2090.00
Platter, Mendenhall Ferry, Joseph Stubbs, Burslem, Blue & White, 16 x 13 In.	1495.00
Platter, New York From The Heights Near Brooklyn, A. Stevenson, 16 1/2 In.	1840.00
Platter, Niagara Falls From American Side, Enoch Wood & Sons, 14 x 11 In. ..2010.00 to	2300.00
Platter, Oriental Ruins Scene, 2 Figures, Blue Transfer, 18 1/4 In.	355.00
Platter, Oriental Scene, Blue & White, 16 3/4 In.	395.00
Platter, Oriental Scene, Lion, Blue Transfer, Crazed, 17 In.	245.00
Platter, R. Hall's Select Views, Conway Castle, Carnarvonshire Wales, 15 1/4 In.	805.00
Platter, R. Hall's Select Views, St. Charles Church, Polytechnic School, 19 In.	1092.00
Platter, Sandusky, Floral Border, Blue, 16 1/2 x 13 In.	4950.00
Platter, Seashells, Blue, Stubbs, 14 1/2 x 11 3/4 In.	880.00
Platter, Sheep & Cows In Front, Ruins In Back, Blue, White Transfer, 19 In.	575.00
Platter, St. Paul's Church Yard, London, Blue, 13 x 10 3/4 In.	320.00
Platter, St. Paul's Church Yard, London, Blue, 18 x 14 1/4 In.	470.00
Platter, States, 14 1/2 In.	1400.00
Platter, Turkey, Brown Transfer, 21 1/2 In.	250.00
Platter, Turkey, Brown Transfer, Scalloped Panels, 21 In.	295.00
Platter, U.S. Capitol, Gentlemen & Lady Riders In Foreground, Blue, White, 12 In.	143.00
Platter, Upper Ferry Bridge Over River Schuylkill, Joseph Stubbs, 19 In.	1495.00
Platter, Valentine, Blue, Wilkie, 15 x 11 1/2 In.	990.00
Platter, Well & Tree, Hop Pickers, Second Quarter 19th Century, 19 In.	575.00
Platter, Well & Tree, Wallington Priory, Stevenson, 10 In.	880.00
Platter, Woodlawns Near Phila., Blue, White Transfer, 1829, 10 1/2 In.	975.00
Punch Bowl, Portland, Puce & Ocher Greek Design, Furnivals, c.1890, 16 In.	2200.00
Sauceboat, Footed, Blue & White, Floral Design, Landscape Interior, Pair	550.00
Saucer, Sheep & Shepherd, Church, Blue, Wood, 5 3/4 In.	45.00
Soup, Dish, Capitol, Washington, Blue, Stevenson, 8 1/2 In.	120.00
Soup, Dish, Figures In Landscape, Fruit & Leaf Border, Blue, White, 10 In., Pair	430.00
Soup, Dish, Strawberry Basket, 8 In.	1650.00
Spill Holder, 2 Swans, Coleslaw, 4 1/2 In.	250.00
Spill Holder, Cottage, Couple In Front Of Tree, 7 1/4 In.	110.00
Spill Holder, Lovers Sleeping, Watching Bird, 5 3/4 In.	245.00
Spill Holder, Robin Hood, Figure With Dog, 16 In.	77.00
Stirrup Cup, Dog, Tally-Ho, 1900, 5 In.	950.00
Stirrup Cup, Fox Head, Black Spotted Coat, Pink Luster Collar, 5 1/4 In., Pair	315.00
Stirrup Cup, Greyhound Head, Pale Mustard Coat, Black Edged Rim, 1825, 7 In.	1310.00

Sugar, English Peasant Scene, Blue, 6 In.	355.00
Tazza, Figural Scene, Blue, White, 11 1/2 In., Pair	172.00
Tea Set, Brown & White, Canova, T. Mayer, 36 Pieces	885.00
Tea Set, Creamer, Cup & Saucer, Brown, White Design, 19th Century	330.00
Tea Set, Strawberry, 19th Century, 3 Piece	2860.00
Teapot, Boston Harbor, Eagle On Shield, 8 In.	880.00
Teapot, Cover, 3-Story Mansion, White Salt Glaze, Loop Handle, 1750, 5 In.	865.00
Teapot, Diorama Series, Train Steam Engine & Coat	1100.00
Teapot, Fisherman, Walking, Lake, Blue, 8 In.	385.00
Teapot, Lafayette At Franklin's Tomb, Blue, Wood, 7 1/2 In.	605.00
Teapot, Landscape Design, Pagoda, Blue, White, 6 In.	402.00
Teapot, Mt. Vernon, Blue, White, 19th Century	2530.00
Teapot, Seated Man, Legs Forming Handle & Spout, 7 1/2 x 10 1/4 In.	80.00
Teapot, Sheep Herder, Sheep, Church Ruins, Blue, Wood	550.00
Teapot, Strawberry, 5 1/2 In.	825.00
Toby Jugs are listed in their own category.	
Tray, Dresser, Dubarry, Overall Multicolored Floral, Off-White Ground, 8 7/8 In.	52.00
Tray, Greek Ruins, Blue, White, Rogers, 10 1/2 In.	175.00
Tray, Playing Cards Design, Pierced Sides, Oval, 1775-1800, 3 x 4 x 1 1/4 In.	250.00
Tureen, Reticulated Finial, Meigh & Johnson, 1822, 7 x 11 1/2 In., Pair	1100.00
Tureen, Soup, Arms Of Maryland, Blue, Mayer, Arman, No Cover, 11 1/2 In.	2970.00
Vase, Blue, White Transfer, 14 3/4 In., Pair	1092.00
Waste Bowl, Strawberry, Pink Band, 19th Century, 6 3/8 In.	550.00
Waste Bowl, Wadsworth Tower, Shell Border, Blue, 6 1/2 In.	285.00
Whistle, Spaniel	45.00

STANGL Pottery traces its history back to the Fulper Pottery of New Jersey. In 1910, Johann Martin Stangl started working at Fulper. He bought into the firm in 1913, became president in 1926, and in 1929 changed the company name to Stangl Pottery. The pottery made dinnerwares and a line of bird figurines. The company went out of business in 1978. The numbers used by Stangl for the bird figures indicate two birds in one figure by adding the letter *D,* for double.

Americana, Platter, 15 In.	48.00
Americana, Soup, Cream	40.00
Apple Delight, Pitcher, Apple In Center, Green Band On Bottom, Ivory Ground, 6 In.	44.00
Bird, Blue Jay, Double, No. 3717D, 13 In.	2338.00
Bird, Blue Jay, No. 3715, Stamp Mark, Paper Label, 10 x 10 In.	605.00
Bird, Blue Jay, No. 3716, Maple Leaf, 10 1/2 x 7 In.	500.00 to 550.00
Bird, Bluebird, No. 3815, 6 1/2 In.	319.00
Bird, Broadtail Hummingbird, No. 3626	150.00
Bird, Cardinal, No. 3444	75.00
Bird, Chickadee, 3-On-A-Branch, No. 3581, 6 x 8 In.	99.00
Bird, Cock, Pheasant, No. 3492, 6 1/2 x 10 In.	121.00
Bird, Cockatoo, No. 3584, Stamp Mark, 12 1/2 In.	165.00
Bird, Cockatoo, White, No. 3580, 9 In.	429.00
Bird, Double Oriole, No. 3402D	125.00
Bird, Double, White Wing Crossbills, No. 3754D, Stamp Mark, 8 1/2 In.	451.00
Bird, Flying Duck, No. 3443, 10 x 13 In.	154.00 to 209.00
Bird, Flying Duck, No. 3443, Impressed Mark, 9 x 13 In.	198.00
Bird, Hen, Pheasant, No. 3491, 6 x 8 1/2 In., Pair	242.00
Bird, Hummingbird, Double, No. 3599D	350.00
Bird, Key West Quail Dove, No. 3454, 9 1/4 x 10 1/2 In.	176.00
Bird, Magpie Jay Bird, No. 3758, 10 1/2 In.	853.00
Bird, Owl, No. 3407, 4 1/2 In.	385.00
Bird, Parrot With Worm, No. 3449	170.00
Bird, Penguin, No. 3274, 5 In.	231.00
Bird, Prothonotary Warbler, No. 3447, 5 In.	75.00
Bird, Redstarts, No. 3490D, 9 In.	250.00
Bird, Riefers Hummingbird, No. 3628	150.00
Bird, Rufous Hummingbird, No. 3585	75.00
Bird, Scissor-Tailed Flycatcher, No. 3757, 11 In.	605.00
Bird, Shoveler Duck, No. 3455, Stamped, 12 x 15 In.	1238.00

Bird, Turkey, No. 3275 .... 450.00
Bird, Western Tanager, Double, No. 3750D, 8 x 7 In. 308.00
Bird, White-Crowned Pigeons, Double, No. 3518D, 7 1/2 x 12 1/4 In. 440.00
Bird, Wilson Warbler, No. 3597 .... 60.00
Dish, Display, Hand Painted, 22k Gold, Original Sticker, Daisy Flower Shaped, 1960s ... 65.00
Double Apple, Bowl, Gray, Green, 9 1/2 In. 21.00
Peter Rabbit, Plate, Child's, 9 In. 165.00
Ranger, Charger, Cowboy, Cactus, Green & Yellow Matte Glaze, 12 In. 330.00
Rooster, Plate, 8 In. 25.00
Tulip, Flowerpot 45.00
Vase, Rainbow, Oval, 3 Handles, 6 1/4 In. 195.00
Vase, Sunflower, Brown, 11 x 11 In. 135.00

STAR TREK AND STAR WARS collectibles are included here. The television series *Star Trek* ran from 1966 through 1969. The TV show *Next Generation,* a sequel, ran from 1987 to 1994. The first Star Trek movie was released in 1979 and 8 others followed, the most recent in 1999. The movie *Star Wars* opened in 1977 and sequels and prequels were released in 1980, 1983, and 1999. Other science fiction and fantasy collectibles can be found under Batman, Buck Rogers, Captain Marvel, Flash Gordon, Superman, Movie, and Toy.

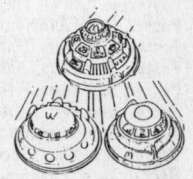

STAR TREK, Card, Trading, Star Trek, Next Generation, Series I, 1991, Set 25.00
Figure, Generations, Applause, Package, 6 All Different, 1994, 10 In. 60.00
Figure, Generations, Captain Kirk Meets Picard, Box, 1995 .... 40.00
Figure, Mr. Scott, Series 1, On Card, 8 In. 175.00
Game, Milton Bradley, Board, 1979 .... 65.00
Game, Star Trek, Board, Cards, Ideal, Box, 1967 .... 67.00
Game, Star Trek, Milton Bradley, Board, 1979 .... 50.00
Greeting Card, Captain Kirk, Punch-Out, 1976 .... 8.00
Greeting Card, Spock, Punch-Out, 1976 .... 8.00
Medallion, Star Trek III, Search For Spock, 1984 .... 12.00
Model, USS Enterprise, Plastic, Battery Operated, Milton Bradley, 10 x 20 In. 150.00
Mr. Spock, Standup, Die Cut Cardboard, 6 Ft. 64.00
Original Costume, Space Seed, Gold Mesh Sleep Outfit 4315.00
Ornament, Christmas, Captain Kirk, Hallmark 12.00
Ornament, Christmas, Star Trek, Shuttlecraft Galileo, Talking Display 45.00
Pin, 20 Years, 1966-1986 .... 15.00
Puzzle, Star Trek, Series II, Characters & Scenes From Show, 1970s 45.00
Toy, USS Enterprise Action Playset, 3 Figures, Mego, 1975, 16 In. 160.00
STAR WARS, Bed Sheet, Star Wars, Characters & Scenes, 1977, Twin Size, Pair 20.00
Belt Buckle, TIE Fighter & X-Wing, Gilt White Metal, 1977, 3 In. 21.00
Candle, Chewbacca, On Card, Wilton, 1980 .... 4.50
Candle, R2-D2, On Card, Wilton, 1980 .... 4.50
Card, Trading, Return Of The Jedi, Box, 1983, Set 20.00
Card, Trading, Vehicles, Box 40.00
Cookie Jar, C-3PO, Bust, 15 In. 200.00
Cookie Jar, Darth Vader 1 Side, C-3PO & R2-D2 Other Side, Box, 1977 ....125.00 to 175.00
Cookie Jar, Princess Leia, Bust, 15 In. 200.00
Cookie Jar, R2-D2, Roman Ceramics, 20th Century Fox Film Corp., 1977 ....185.00 to 225.00
Doll, Star Wars, Ewok, Leenie, Return Of The Jedi, 1983 .... 20.00
Figure, C-3PO, 3 3/4 In. 10.00
Figure, Chewbacca, Box, 1977, 15 In. ....165.00 to 180.00
Figure, Darth Vader, 3 3/4 In. 14.00
Figure, Darth Vader, Ceramic, Plastic Light Saber, Lights Up, 12 In. 150.00
Figure, Empire Strikes Back, Bespin Guard, Black, On Card, 1980 .... 100.00
Figure, Empire Strikes Back, Han Solo, Bespin Outfit, 1980 .... 21.00
Figure, Jawa, Vinyl Cape, On Card, 1977, 3 3/4 In. 3750.00
Figure, Return Of The Jedi, Emperor, Kenner, On Card, 1983 .... 21.00
Figure, Snaggletooth 19.00
Figure, Star Wars, Storm Trooper, On Card, 1977 .... 250.00
Game, Escape From Death Star, Kenner, General Mills, Box, 1977 .... 20.00
Game, Yoda, The Master Game, Kenner, 1981 .... 40.00
Glass, Star Wars, Burger King, 1977 .... 8.00

Lunch Box, Return Of The Jedi, Metal, King Seeley Thermos, 1983 .... 22.00
Mask, Return Of Jedi, Wickett W. Warrick, Don Post, 1983 .... 85.00
Model, Return Of The Jedi, AT-AT, MPC, Wrapped Box 21.00
Model Kit, Return Of The Jedi, R2-D2, Movable Dome, MPC, Box, 1983, 6 In. 25.00
Poster, Empire Strikes Back, 20th Century Fox, 1980, 30 x 40 In. 230.00
Poster, Empire Strikes Back, 20th Century Fox, 1980, Half Sheet 170.00
Poster, Empire Strikes Back, 20th Century Fox, 1980, One Sheet ....375.00 to 690.00
Poster, Empire Strikes Back, Advance Style A, Darth Vader's Face, One Sheet 545.00
Poster, Empire Strikes Back, NPR, Frame, 1982, 17 x 28 In. 2530.00
Poster, Guerre Stellari, 20th Century Fox, Italy, 1977 .... 400.00
Poster, La Guerre Des Etoiles, 20th Century Fox, France, 1977 .... 200.00
Poster, Return Of The Jedi, Character Montage, 1983, One Sheet 315.00
Poster, Return Of The Jedi, Hands Raising Lightsaber, 1983, One Sheet 175.00
Poster, Star Wars Symphonic Suite, Concert, John Williams, 1978, 24 1/4 x 37 In. 3735.00
Poster, Star Wars, 10th Anniversary, 20th Century Fox, 1987, One Sheet ....316.00 to 805.00
Poster, Star Wars, 20th Century Fox, 1977, 40 x 60 In. 287.00
Poster, Star Wars, First Advance, Mylar, 20th Century Fox, Frame, 1976 .... 2530.00
Poster, Star Wars, Luke Skywalker, Chaykin Art, Signed, 1976, 20 x 29 In. 2300.00
Poster, Star Wars, Radio Drama, NPR, 1981, 17 x 29 In. 402.00
Poster, Star Wars, Second Advance, 20th Century Fox, 1976, One Sheet 977.00
Record Tote, Fiberboard, Plastic Handle, 1982 .... 12.00
Ring, C-3PO Head, Brass-Toned Metal, Adjustable, Size 6 1/2 .... 20.00
T-Shirt, Darth Vader Lives, Dark Yellow 22.00
Toy, Empire Strikes Back, Vehicle Maintenance Energizer, Kenner, 1982 .... 22.00
Toy, Return Of The Jedi, Ewok, Caravan Of Courage 75.00
Toy, Return Of The Jedi, Sy Snootles & The Rebo Band, Kenner, On Card, 1983 ..150.00 to 500.00
Toy, Yoda The Jedi Master, Fortune Teller, 1981 .... 55.00

STEINS have been used by beer and ale drinkers for over 500 years. They have been made of ivory, porcelain, stoneware, faience, silver, pewter, wood, or glass in sizes up to nine gallons. Although some were made by Mettlach, Meissen, Capo-di-Monte, and other famous factories, most were made by less important German potteries. The words *Geschutz* or *Musterschutz* on a stein are the German words for *patented* or *registered design*, not company names. Steins are still being made in the old styles. Lithophane steins may be found in the Lithophane category.

Adolf Hitler, Third Reich, Porcelain, 1/2 Liter 880.00
Alpine Jager, Porcelain, Chamois Thumblift, Inlaid Lid, 1/2 Liter 632.00
Anheuser-Busch, Bevo Fox, Thewalt, 1/2 Liter 195.00
Anheuser-Busch, Budweiser Printed On Wagon, Ceramarte, 1/2 Liter 182.00
Anheuser-Busch, Busch Gardens, Ceramarte, 1/2 Liter 231.00
Anheuser-Busch, City Series, Hamburg, Ceramarte, 1/2 Liter 270.00
Anheuser-Busch, Grant's Farm, St. Louis Printed On Bottom, Ceramarte, 1/2 Liter 161.00
Anheuser-Busch, United States Of America, 200 Years, 1/2 Liter 308.00
Animals Running Through Forest, Fox Handle, Pottery, Inlaid Lid, 1/3 Liter 55.00
Antisemitic, Stoneware, Inlaid Lid, Dumler & Breiden, 1/2 Liter ....907.00 to 1100.00
Applied Blue Glass Bands Around Top Of Body, Silver Plated Brass Base, 1 Liter 715.00
Art Nouveau, Leaf Design, Pewter Lid, 1/2 Liter 825.00
Art Nouveau, Verse, Engraved, Blue Salt Glaze, Stoneware, Pewter Lid, Gerz, 1/2 Liter .. 245.00
Auerhahn, Fluted, Color Enamel, Glass, Clear, Blown, Pewter Lid, 1/2 Liter 160.00
Augustiner-Brau, Munchen, Etched, Black & Pink, Pottery, Relief Pewter Lid, 2/5 Liter .. 230.00
Bavaria Zither Club, Lithophane Bottom, Porcelain, 12 In. 135.00
Bavarian Couple, Transfer & Enamel, Porcelain, Pewter Lid, 1 Liter 130.00
Bicycle Form, 2-Sided Scene, Woman With Children In Center, Pewter Lid, 1/2 Liter 316.00
Bicycle Form, 3 Bicycle Scenes Including Standard, High Wheel, Pewter Lid, 1/2 Liter .. 330.00
Bicycle Form, Eagle With 2 Men Riding Standard Bicycles, Pewter Lid, 11 3/4 In. 550.00
Bicycle Form, Man Riding High Wheel Bicycle, Enameled, Pewter Lid, 1/2 Liter 687.00
Bicycle Form, Man Riding Standard Bicycle, Pottery, 2 Liter 231.00
Bicycle Form, Man Riding Standard Bicycle, White, Enameled, Pewter Lid, 1/2 Liter 632.00
Bicycle Form, Woman Riding Standard Bicycle, Amber, Glass, Pewter Lid, 1/2 Liter 660.00
Birch Trunk, Stag & Deer, Pottery, Hunter On Lid, 2 1/4 Liter 330.00
Bird, Floral Design, Pewter Lid, Westerwald, 1800, 2 Liter 1650.00

Bird, With Sausage Standing On Beer Stein, Pewter Lid, 1/2 Liter 825.00
Bird Scene, Floral Design, Gold, Red Accents, Porcelain, Inlaid Lid, 1 Liter 1072.00
Black, Brown Glaze, Art Nouveau Pewter Lid, 2 Liter 1815.00
Blue, Ribbed Body, Glass, Blown, Pewter Lid, 2 Liter 120.00
Bowling Scene, Bowling Ball & Pins, Relief, Tan, Brown, Green, Inlaid Lid, 2 Liter 460.00
Brewery Scene, Enameled, Stoneware, Pewter Lid, 1/2 Liter 330.00
Budweiser, Babe Ruth Sports Legend, Babe Pointing To Outfield, Germany, 8 In. 67.00
Budweiser, Bud Man, Stoneware, Ceramarte, 1/2 Liter 150.00
Building Scene, Floral Design, Dwarf Thumblift, Glass Prism Inlaid Lid, 1/2 Liter 770.00
Building Scene, Floral, Leaf Design, Gold Outline, Pewter Lid, 1/2 Liter 385.00
Butcher, 2 Scenes, Transfer & Enamel, Stoneware, Pewter Lid, 1/2 Liter 345.00
Caroline, Porcelain, Porcelain Lid, Schierholz, 1/2 Liter 795.00
Castle Stolzenfel Scene, Yellow Glass Inlaid Lid, 1850, 4 In. 385.00
Cavaliers, Eating & Drinking, Amber, Enameled, Glass, 1/2 Liter 360.00
Cavalry Scene, Brewmaster Holding Stein, Enameled, Pewter Lid, 1 Liter 440.00
Child With City Scene, Enameled, Pewter Lid, 1 Liter 330.00
Cleopatra, Pottery Lid, 1/2 Liter 660.00
Clown, Blue, Purple Salt Glaze, Stoneware, Lid, 1/2 Liter 962.00
Club Hubertus, Bavarian Schutzen Verband, Glass, Pewter Lid, 1/2 Liter 340.00
Coblenz, Transfer & Enamel, Porcelain, Pewter, Lid, 1/3 Liter 85.00
Combed Body, 4-Horse Thumblift, Pewter Base Ring, 1890, 1 Liter 632.00
Cornell College, Junior Smoker, Red Transfer, Pottery, 1903, 1/2 Liter 100.00
Couple Reading, Blue Design, Stoneware, 16 1/2 In. 70.00
Courting Scene, Relief, Salt Glaze, Lid, White's, Utica, 12 3/4 In. 605.00
Creussen, Stoneware, c.1680, 1 Liter 9625.00
Cut Circle, Yellow, Pink Stain, Glass Inlaid Lid, 1850, 1/2 Liter 495.00
Dancing Scene, Etched, Pottery, Pewter Lid, Hauber & Reuther, 1/2 Liter 250.00
Dancing Scene, Relief, Transfer & Enamel, Pottery, Pewter Lid, 1/2 Liter 95.00
Devil, Porcelain, Inlaid Lid, E. Bohne & Sohne, 1/2 Liter 635.00
Diagonal Ribbed Body, Deep Cobalt Blue Glaze, Pewter Lid, 18th Century, 2 Liter 797.00
Diamond Cut Design, Milk Glass, Silver Lid, 1/2 Liter 495.00
Diana & Hunter, Etched, Pottery, Inlaid Lid, Gerz, 1/2 Liter 145.00
Dog's Heads, Elves, Oak Leaf Design, Salt Glaze, Pour Spout, Lid, White's, Utica, 11 In. .. 470.00
Drinker Seated On Barrel, Drinking Phrase, Stoneware, Pewter Cover, 7 1/2 In. 33.00
Drinking Scenes, Figural Finial, Stoneware, Germany, 17 3/4 In. 220.00
Drunken Man Paying Barmaid, Pottery, Inlaid Lid, JWR, 1/4 Liter 121.00
Eagle, Deutsches Museum, Munchen, Engraved, Blue Glaze, Relief Pewter Lid, 1 Liter .. 175.00
Eisenbahn, Porcelain, Pewter Lid, 1960, 1/2 Liter 84.00
Enameled Flowers, Butterfly, Cobalt Blue, Horsehead Thumblift, Glass, 1/2 Liter 467.00
Enameled Heart, Flame, Flowers, Glass, Clear, Pewter Lid, 1/2 Liter 100.00
Faience, King Holding Infant, Pink, Blue Diamond, Pewter Lid, 1920, 3 Liter 1265.00
Faience, Pewter Base Ring, Early 18th Century, 3/4 Liter 880.00
Falstaff, Pewter Lid, Regensburg, 1860, 1 Liter 106.00
Falstaff, Pottery, Relief, Pewter Lid, Music Box Base, 1/2 Liter 105.00
Figural, Man & Woman In 19th Century Dress, Pewter Rim & Thumb Lift, c.1960, 10 In. . 85.00
Figural, Man, Foliate Mustache & Beard, Landscape Cartouche On Belly, Faience, 13 In. .. 440.00
Floral Design, Amber, Monkey Form Thumb Press, Pewter Mounted, Glass, 10 In. 115.00
Floral Design, Enameled, Milk Glass, Pewter Lid, 1800, 1 Liter 1100.00
Floral Design, Gold Verse, Pewter Lid, 1832, 1 Liter 742.00
Floral Design, Milk Glass, Pewter Lid, 1/2 Liter 550.00
Fountain Form, Staircase On Both Sides, Inlaid Lid, 1/4 Liter 330.00
Fox, Wearing Smoking Jacket, Holding Pipe, Beer Stein, Stoneware, Inlaid Lid, 1/2 Liter . 560.00
Gasthaus, Transfer, Painted, Threading, Pewter Lid, Hauber & Reuther, 1/2 Liter 330.00
German Warrior & Horse On Boat, Etched, Pottery, Inlaid Lid, Gerz, 1 Liter 380.00
Germania, Sword, Shield, Transfer & Enamel, Glass, Porcelain Inlaid Lid, 1/2 Liter 160.00
Glass, Cut, Silver Plated Brass Lid, Dwarf Finial, 1/2 Liter 235.00
Golf Scene, Man Swinging Golf Club, Sterling Silver Lid, 1/2 Liter 1540.00
Green Teardrops, Engraved Wheat, Glass, Clear, Pewter Lid, 1/2 Liter 155.00
Hops Lady, Porcelain, Inlaid Lid, Schierholz, 1/2 Liter 685.00
Horizontal Lines Around Top & Bottom Of Body, Stoneware, Germany, 2 1/2 Liter ... 3300.00
Hunter Sleeping, Porcelain Lid, Bauer, 1/2 Liter 440.00
Hunting Dog & Deer, Relief, Pottery, Pewter Lid, c.1960, 1/2 Liter 170.00
Indianapolis Motor Speedway, Marked Germany 75.00

Ivory, Deer Hunting, Man Blowing Horn & Riding Horse Relief, Brass Handle & Lid ... 2860.00
Joe Camel, Octoberfest, Ceramic, Lid 150.00
John F. Kennedy, Limited Edition, Porcelain, Lid, Gerz, 1 Liter 135.00
Large Bird Thumblift, Blown Glass, Cut Design, Pewter Lid, 1/2 Liter 115.00
Little Boy With Wooden Feet, Stoneware, Metal Lid, 1/2 Liter 110.00
Lovers, Blue Salt Glaze, Relief, Stoneware, Pewter Lid 345.00
Man & Woman, Enameled, Pewter Lid, 1/2 Liter 91.00
Man & Woman Kissing, Copper Wheel, Glass Inlaid Lid, 1/2 Liter 495.00
Man & Woman Reading, German Verse, Salt Glaze, Pewter Lid, 14 1/2 In. 1210.00
Man & Woman Speaking At River, Inlaid Lid, Marked, JWR, 1/3 Liter 138.00
Man Dancing, 2 Women, Flowers, Relief, Pewter, Pewter Lid, 1/2 Liter 110.00
Man Kissing Barmaid, Pottery, Inlaid Lid, 1/2 Liter 139.00
Man Looking Into Empty Stein, Transfer & Enamel, Stoneware, Pewter Lid, 1 Liter 180.00
Man On Horse, Blowing Trumpet, Porcelain, Pewter Lid, 8 3/4 In. 145.00
Man Playing Guitar, Enameled, Pewter Lid, 1/2 Liter 93.00
Man's Face, Tan, Brown, Black, Pottery, 1/2 Liter 104.00
Men Drinking, Relief, Tan, Brown, Green, Pottery, Acorns On Lid, 1/2 Liter 110.00
Men Drinking At Table, Etched, Pottery, Pewter Lid, Hauber & Reuther, 1/2 Liter 280.00
Men Playing Chess, Pottery, Inlaid Lid, JWR, 1 Liter 254.00
Mettlach steins are listed in the Mettlach category.
Military, Soldiers Marching With Flags, Enameled, Pewter Lid, 1915, 1 Liter 404.00
Military, Third Reich, Man Wearing Uniform, Flat Pewter Lid, 1935, 1/2 Liter ....165.00 to 385.00
Monk, Blue Salt Glaze, Stoneware, Inlaid Lid, 1/2 Liter 165.00
Monk, Blue, Purple Salt Glaze, Inlaid Lid, 1/2 Liter 217.00
Monkey, White Fur, Inlaid Lid, E. Bohne & Sohne, 1/2 Liter 3080.00
Monks, Tan, Green, Brown, Inlaid Lid, 1/4 Liter 165.00
Mother & Baby Deer, Enameled, Glass, Pewter Lid, 1/2 Liter 962.00
Munich Child, Bavaria Monument, Lithophane, Porcelain, Inlaid Lid, 1/3 Liter 264.00
Munich Child, City Scenes, Relief, Pewter Lid, 1 Liter 165.00
Munich Child, Enameled, Stoneware, Pewter Lid, 1/2 Liter 715.00
Munich Child, Porcelain, Inlaid Lid, 4 1/4 In. 687.00
Munich Child, Pottery, Inlaid Lid, 1/2 Liter 522.00
Munich Child, Pottery, Relief, Pewter Lid, 1/2 Liter ....110.00 to 198.00
Munich Child With Beer Stein, Enameled, Stoneware, Pewter Lid, 1/2 Liter 357.00
Musician Frogs & Elves, Etched, Pottery, Hauber & Reuter, No. 519, 1 Liter 650.00
Musicians Crossing Bridge, Etched, Pottery, Inlaid Lid, Marzi & Remy, 1/2 Liter 200.00
Nurnberg Tower, City Skyline On Front, Set-On Lid, 1897, 10 1/2 In. 1210.00
Nurnburg Tower, Tan, Pewter Lid, 1/2 Liter 89.00
Occupational, 3 Men, Shields With Tools, Glass, 1900, 2 Liter 2200.00
Occupational, Baker, Crest, Baking Scenes, Lithophane, Porcelain, Pewter Lid, 1/2 Liter . 460.00
Occupational, Beer Wagon Driver, Lithophane, Porcelain, Pewter Lid, 1/2 Liter 460.00
Occupational, Blacksmith, Fitting Shoe On Horse, Porcelain, Pewter Lid, 1/2 Liter 500.00
Occupational, Carpenter, Lithophane, Porcelain, Pewter Lid, 1/2 Liter 660.00
Occupational, Miller, Transfer, Enamel, Lithophane, Porcelain, Pewter Lid, 1/2 Liter 425.00
Occupational, Shoemaker Workshop, Pewter Lid, Stoneware, 1/2 Liter 467.00
Peasant Men, Stoneware, Pewter-Rimmed Lid, Simon Peter Gerz, c.1920, 6 3/4 In. 125.00
People, Flowers, Relief, Brown Pottery, Pewter Base Ring, Lid, Creussen, c.1900, 1 Liter 460.00
People Drinking Outdoors, Pewter Lid, Marked, JWR, 1/2 Liter 277.00
People Embracing, Winged Wheel Thumblift, Pewter Lid, 1/2 Liter 935.00
Pig, Porcelain, Inlaid Lid, E. Bohne & Sohne, 1/2 Liter 1705.00
Pig, Singing, Porcelain, Inlaid Lid, Schierholz, 1/2 Liter 440.00
Pig, Smoking, Porcelain, Inlaid Lid, Schierholz, 1/2 Liter 510.00
Portrait Of Man & Woman, Glass Prism Inlaid Lid, Porcelain, 1/2 Liter 880.00
Potato Head, Porcelain Lid, Schierholz, 1/2 Liter 264.00
Prima Beer, Glass, Porcelain Insert Lid, 1900s, 8 In. 55.00
Prosit, Sunflowers, Relief, Spout, Bristol Glaze, Blue Accents, White's, Utica, 10 In. 110.00
Rear Admiral Wm. T. Sampson, U.S.N., Relief, Pottery, Pewter Lid, 1/2 Liter 380.00
Red, White, Gold, Yellow, White Paint, Glass, 1850, 1/2 Liter 470.00
Regimental, 2-Sided Scene, 2nd Garde Ulan, Berlin, Eagle Thumblift, 1907, 1/2 Liter ... 690.00
Regimental, 2-Sided Scene, 5th Dragoner, Eagle Thumblift, Porcelain, 1/2 Liter 695.00
Regimental, 2-Sided Scene, 10 Names On Roster, Pottery, Eagle Thumblift, 1/2 Liter 880.00
Regimental, 2-Sided Scene, 23rd Garde Dragoon Darmstadt, Porcelain, 1900, 1/2 Liter ... 385.00
Regimental, 2-Sided Scene, 117th Infantry, Porcelain, Lion Thumblift, 1906, 1/2 Liter ... 460.00

Regimental, 2-Sided Scene, 120th Infantry, 1/2 Liter 468.00
Regimental, 2-Sided Scene, Bavarian Foot Artillery, Lion Thumblift, Stanhope, 1/2 Liter . 635.00
Regimental, 2-Sided Scene, Foot Artillery, Lion Thumblift, Stanhope, 1/2 Liter 535.00
Regimental, 2-Sided Scene, Pottery, Floral Thumbprint, Eagle Finial, 1 Liter 1270.00
Regimental, 2-Sided Scene, Roster, Lion Thumblift, Glass Prism Inlaid Lid, 1/2 Liter 880.00
Regimental, 2-Sided Scene, Roster, Sachsen Thumblift, Pewter Lid, 1/2 Liter 550.00
Regimental, 2-Sided Scene, S.M.S. Ostfriesland, Marine, Eagle Thumblift, 1913, 1 Liter . 1155.00
Regimental, 4-Sided Scene, 2nd Field Artillery, Lion Thumblift, Cannon Finial, 1/2 Liter . 620.00
Regimental, 4-Sided Scene, 3rd Jager Zu Pferde Colmar, 1912, Eagle Thumblift, 1 Liter . 1155.00
Regimental, 4-Sided Scene, 10th Infantry, Ingolstadt, Lion Thumblift, 1/2 Liter 520.00
Regimental, 4-Sided Scene, 23rd Bavarian Infantry, Lion Thumblift, Stanhope, 1/2 Liter . 635.00
Regimental, 4-Sided Scene, 112th Infantry, Porcelain, Griffin Thumblift, 1/2 Liter 530.00
Regimental, 4-Sided Scene, Infantry, Lion Thumblift, Pewter Lion Head, 1/2 Liter 805.00
Regimental, 4-Sided Scene, Infantry, Wurtemberg Thumblift, Pewter Lion, 1/2 Liter 575.00
Regimental, 4-Sided Scene, Lion Thumblift, Porcelain, 1/2 Liter 1155.00
Regimental, 4-Sided Scene, Roster, Lion Thumblift, Porcelain, 1/2 Liter .... .410.00 to 440.00
Regimental, 4-Sided Scene, Soldier Kneeling, Shooting On Lid Finial, 1/2 Liter 880.00
Regimental, Medic, Large Red Cross, Porcelain, Inlaid Lid, 1/2 Liter 880.00
Regimental, Navy, Porcelain, Pewter Lid, 1/2 Liter 80.00
Regimental, Roster, Eagle Thumblift, Porcelain, 1/2 Liter 467.00
Regimental, Ships Off Shore Near Lighthouse, Pewter Lid, 2 Liter 440.00
Regimental, Skull, Porcelain, Inlaid Lid, 1/2 Liter 2200.00
Repeating Bat Design, Inlaid Lid, Pottery, 1/2 Liter 880.00
Roly Poly Barmaid, Pottery, Inlaid Lid, 1/2 Liter 605.00
Sachsen Crest, Crown, Flowers & Leaves, Milk Glass, Lid, c.1850, 1/2 Liter 275.00
Sailor, Ship Name On Hat, Hamburg, Pottery Lid, 1/2 Liter 440.00
Santa Claus, In Blimp Dropping Presents To Children, Pewter Lid, 1/8 Liter 330.00
Scene Of Men Loading Ceramic Pipe Onto Truck, Pewter Lid, Glass, 1/2 Liter 630.00
Shooting Festival, Man Shooting Rifle, Enameled, Pewter Lid, 1906, 1/2 Liter 360.00
Skull, On Book, Porcelain, Inlaid Lid, E. Bohne & Sohne, 1/3 Liter 575.00
Soccer Ball, Pottery, Inlaid Lid, 1/2 Liter 1017.00
Spatenbrau, Munchen, Transfer & Enamel, Pewter Lid, 1892, 1/2 Liter 310.00
Spiral Air Pocket Design, Cut Panels On Exterior, Pewter Lid, 1/2 Liter 1100.00
St. George Slaying Dragon, Etched, Pottery, Inlaid Lid, Gerz, 1/2 Liter ....·. 345.00
Star & Floral Designs, Pewter Lid, 1820, 3/4 Liter 880.00
Student Society, Man Dressed As Warrior With Cape, Sword, Pewter Lid, 1 Liter 1980.00
Student Study, Turner Design, Handle, Stoneware, Pewter Lid, 1905, 1 Liter 800.00
Stuttgarter Hofbrau, Transfer & Enamel, Stoneware, Engraved Pewter Lid, 1/2 Liter ... 115.00
Trumpeter Of Sackingen, Black, Green, Tan, Pottery, Pewter Lid, 1 Liter .... .139.00 to 165.00
Vulture, Sitting Over Dead Stag, Blown Glass, Cobalt Blue, 1850, 1/2 Liter 1595.00
White & Purple Overlay, Set-On Lid, Glass, 1850, 1/2 Liter 660.00
Windmill, Harbor Scene, Windmill Shaped Porcelain Lid, Hand Painted, 1/2 Liter 340.00
Woman, Pottery, Inlaid Lid, Diesinger, 1/2 Liter 440.00
Woman, With Newspaper, Porcelain Lid, Schierholz, 1/2 Liter 265.00

STEREO CARDS that were made for stereoscope viewers became popular after 1840. Two almost identical pictures were mounted on a stiff
cardboard backing so that, when viewed through a stereoscope, a
three-dimensional picture could be seen. Value is determined by maker
and by subject. These cards were made in quantity through the 1930s.

Allegheny Mountains Resort, Cresson, Pa., 2 Views 84.00
Balley & Co. Jewelry Store, Phil., Langenheim, 1858 .... 127.00
Beach At Petoskey, Michigan, A.B. McBride 55.00
Calumet Copper Miners, Calumet, Mi., Miners Pushing Ore Carts 22.00
Chicago, Before & After Fire, Clark St. Bridge, Copelin & Hine 60.00
Civil War, Brady & Wagon At Chain Bridge, Washington, Anthony 505.00
Civil War, Wounded At Fredericksburg, Brady, Anthony Label 180.00
Coney Island, A Heavy Sea, Bathers, Sepia, Wm. H. Rau Publ., 1890 .... 20.00
Coney Island, Miss Ward, Greatest Woman Diver, Underwood & Underwood, 1889 ..... 45.00
Dallas City Landing On Columbia River, F. Jay Haynes, 1880 .... 27.00
Danver's Wizard Office, Newspaper Print Shop With Owner & 5 Workers, 1868 .... 33.00
Devil's Gate Bridge, Union Pacific Railroad Construction, Jackson 250.00
Grapery At Mr. Lovering's, Philadelphia, Gothic Greenhouse, Langenheim 45.00

Harbor, Mackinac Island, Children & Fishermen, L. Black & Co., John R. Bailier	100.00
Hawaii, Group, Eating Poi, Grass Hut, Sepia, Strohmeyer & Wyman, 1896	30.00
Indian Buffalo Hunt In Wild West Show, 101 Ranch, Meadville, Pa., 3 1/2 x 7 In.	260.00
Intoxicated Man, Cornucopia Urn, Pictorial Flask, Demijohn	55.00
Lincoln's Funeral In New York City, Anthony	100.00
Loading Mississippi Steamer, Waiting Blacks, New Orleans, 1925	15.00
Mayan Ruins, Sculptured Columns, Copan, Honduras	360.00
Me-Shaw-Ke-Ke-Shick, Chippewa Brave, Charles A. Zimmerman	300.00
Mother & Child, Before Window, Leather Case, Claudet	2800.00
N.Y. Canal Boat & Malt House, R.R. Abbott	33.00
People Walking Beach, Old Orchard Beach, Maine, J.O. Drugan, 1876	40.00
Philadelphia Street Scene, St. Mark's Episcopal Church, 1858	33.00
School Lessons, Children With Books Open	50.00
Steamer Horicon, Lake George, N.Y., Yellow Mount, 1870s	65.00
Steamer Richmond, Docked At St. Louis, Boehl & Koenig	95.00
Steamship Pearl, At Wharf, Cleveland, Ohio	33.00
William McKinley & Wife, Canton, Ohio, Sepia, Underwood, Floral Frame, 1896	18.00
Women's Rights, Woman Practices Speech, Man Does Laundry, 1875	60.00
Workman At Self-Feeding Presses, U.S. Bureau Of Printing, Keystone View Co.	32.00
World's Fair, Philadelphia, 1876, Centennial Photographic Co., 3 Piece	27.00

STEREOSCOPES were used for viewing stereo cards. The hand viewer was invented by Oliver Wendell Holmes, although more complicated table models were used before his was produced in 1859. Do not confuse the stereoscope with the stereopticon, a magic lantern that used glass slides.

Focusing Eye Piece, Hinged Top, Mahogany, Brewster	115.00
Keystone Eye Comfort & Depth Perception Series, 14 Cards	86.00
Perpecscope, Bird's-Eye Maple, Pat. 1896	80.00
Underwood & Underwood, Wood & Metal, Card Holder Bar, Pat. 1901, 13 In.	45.00
Walnut, Folding Handles, With Cards, Pat. June 4, 1881, 19 Cards	90.00

STERLING SILVER, see Silver-Sterling category.

STEUBEN glass was made at the Steuben Glass Works of Corning, New York. The factory, founded by Frederick Carder and T.G. Hawkes, Sr., was purchased by the Corning Glass Company. They continued to make glass called *Steuben.* Many types of art glass were made at Steuben. The firm is still making exceptional quality glass but it is clear, modern-style glass. Additional pieces may be found in the Aurene, Cluthra, and perfume bottle categories.

Bell, Air-Twist Handle, Signed, 6 In.	200.00
Bowl, Aurene Over Calcite, 5 1/2 In.	785.00
Bowl, Blown, 7 1/8 x 4 3/4 In.	135.00
Bowl, Dark Blue, Grape Etched, 17 In.	195.00
Bowl, Ivory, 2-Line Pillar, Domed Foot, Carder, 1930, 6 1/2 In.	431.00
Bowl, Ivory, Scalloped, Ruffled Edge, 6 1/2 x 11 3/4 x 6 3/4 In.	225.00
Bowl, Oriental Tree, Jade Acid Etched To Opalescent, 7 In.	825.00
Candlestick, Alabaster Stem, Green Foot, Signed, c.1920, 11 7/8 In., Pair	1610.00
Candlestick, Amber Glass, Twisted Stem, Signed, c.1925, 10 In., Pair	862.00
Candlestick, Amber Glass, Wide Disc Foot, Carder, 1925, 12 In., Pair	690.00
Candlestick, Amethyst, Half Twist Stem, Signed, Fleur-De-Lis, 12 In.	385.00
Candlestick, Pomona Green, Turned Stem, Clear Knop, Marked, 4 In., Pair	300.00
Candlestick, Rope Twist, 8 In., 4 Piece	1035.00
Candlestick, Shirley Cutting, Signed, Frederick Carder, 1920, 4 In., Pair	450.00
Candlestick, Wisteria, Pillar, Signed, Fleur-De-Lis, 8 In., Pair	1035.00
Centerpiece, Celeste Blue, Swirled Optic, Rolled Rim, Fluted Foot, Carder, 4 In.	405.00
Compote, Amber & Blue, Applied Disks, 8 In.	175.00
Compote, Band Of Red Threading, Domed Foot, Carder, 1925, 7 x 7 In.	315.00
Compote, Pomona Green Bowl & Foot, Twisted Yellow Stem, Paneled, 9 In.	550.00
Compote, Topaz Bowl, Paneled, Pomona Green Stem, Signed, 8 x 8 In.	550.00
Cruet, Needlenose, Crystal	1000.00

Decanter, Cocktail, Double Lipped, Tear Drop Stopper, Signed, 8 3/4 In. 225.00
Decanter, Ships, 32 Oz. 370.00
Figurine, Apple, Signed, Angus McDougal, 1940, 3 3/4 In. 345.00
Figurine, Dolphin, Leaping, Signed, George Thompson, 1940, 5 3/4 In. 230.00
Figurine, Eagle On Ball, 12 In. 495.00
Figurine, Elephant, 5 1/2 In. 280.00
Figurine, Excalibur, Sword In Stone, Box, 8 In. 2100.00
Figurine, Owl, Signed, 5 1/8 In. 400.00
Figurine, Penguin, Adult & Offspring, Signed, 6 3/8 In. 400.00
Figurine, Quail, Signed, Paul Schulze, 5 1/2 In. 290.00
Figurine, Rooster, No. 8074, 1955, 9 1/2 In. 990.00
Finger Bowl, Wisteria, Pillar, Marked, Fleur-De-Lis, 2 3/4 In. 750.00
Goblet, Celeste Blue, Light Ribbing, Flared, Carder, 1932, 6 x 4 1/2 In., 15 Piece 575.00
Lamp, Acanthus Leaf, Swirled Purple, Blue, Red Moss Agate, Urn, Carder, 10 In. 2415.00
Lamp, Belgrade, Plum Jade, Urn, Gold Metal Fittings, Carder, 12 In. 2415.00
Lamp, Grapes, Alabaster, Silver Metal Fittings, Carder, 1925, 14 In. 1150.00
Lamp, Green Jade, Applied Spiral Alabaster Threading, Rosettes, Carder, 11 In. 805.00
Lamp, Plum Jade, Double Gourd, 3 Scroll Arms, Carder, 28 In. 1840.00
Parfait, Rosaline, Cone Shape, Alabaster Foot, 2 1/2 x 4 3/4 In. 165.00
Perfume Bottle, Wolff Freres' Crisance, Presentation Box, 1948 .... 2200.00
Pitcher, Spanish Green, Ribbed Oval, Angled Handle, Signed, Fleur-De-Lis, 9 In. 460.00
Plate, Beadwork, Leaves, Signed, c.1920, 8 1/2 In., Pair 230.00
Plate, Bristol Yellow, Optic Ribbing, Rolled Rim, Carder, 1925, 14 In. 200.00
Plate, Flowers, Hearts, Applied Cobalt Blue Border, Signed Fleur-De-Lis, 8 Pieces 413.00
Plate, Ram's Head 295.00
Shade, Green & Gold, Pulled Feather Design Over Calcite, 5 1/2 x 7 In. 275.00
Shade, Trumpet, Iridescent, Amber, Blue Highlights, 5 In., Pair 518.00
Vase, 4 Scrolls Above Round Foot, Signed, c.1940, 8 1/4 In. 400.00
Vase, Amethyst, Gold Iridescent, 6 In. 605.00
Vase, Cased Pink Swirl, 8 1/2 x 7 1/2 In. 1650.00
Vase, Fan, Blue Ribbed Body, Knop Stem, Signed, Fleur-De-Lis, 8 1/2 In. 605.00
Vase, Fan, Bristol Yellow, Footed, Signed, 8 1/2 In. 500.00
Vase, Fan, Pomona Green, Pinched Sides, Footed, Signed, Fleur-De-Lis, 8 In. 400.00
Vase, Fan, Topaz, Pomona Green Foot, Signed, Fleur-De-Lis, 8 1/4 In. 400.00
Vase, Grape Clusters, Leaves, Vertical Ribbed, Conical Foot, 11 1/2 x 5 In. 155.00
Vase, Grasses & Stars, Disk Base, Walter Teague, 10 1/2 In. 575.00
Vase, Green Jade, Flared Neck, Alabaster M Handles, Carder, 1929, 10 In. 1092.00
Vase, Green Jade, Signed, Fleur-De-Lis, 10 In. 715.00
Vase, Green Swirl, Flared, Signed, 7 x 6 3/4 In. 175.00
Vase, Grotesque, Amethyst, Disc Foot, Carder, 1930, 9 In. 517.00
Vase, Ivory, Gourd, Waisted Neck, 5 In. 247.00
Vase, Ivrene, Ribbed, Fan, Signed, c.1920, 9 5/8 In. 805.00
Vase, Ivrene, Ribbed, Horn Shape, Signed, 1920s, 6 In., Pair 1035.00
Vase, Oriental Poppy, Green Foot, Signed, c.1920, 6 3/8 In. 862.00
Vase, Rose Threading, Diamond Optic, Flared, Ruffled Edge, Signed, 4 In. 135.00
Vase, Stick, Gold Aurene, Bulbous, 5 3/4 In. 1000.00
Vase, Strawberry Mansion, Raised On Square Plinth, 2 M Handles, Carder, 12 In. 1035.00
Vase, Trumpet, Prunts, George Thompson, 20th Century, 6 In. 230.00
Whimsey, Darning Egg, Blue Aurene, 7 In. 308.00

STEVENGRAPHS are woven pictures made like fancy ribbons. They
were manufactured by Thomas Stevens of Coventry, England, and
became popular in 1862. Most are marked *Woven in silk by Thomas
Stevens* or were mounted on a cardboard that tells the story of the Ste-
vengraph. Other similar ribbon pictures have been made in England
and Germany.

Bookmark, Home Sweet Home 45.00
Bookmark, T. Stevens, Coventry, 8 3/4 x 2 1/2 In. 70.00
Bookmark, Tassel, Signed, 1860, 9 In. 75.00
Bookmark, Woven Silk, Honour Thy Father & Thy Mother, T. Stevens, Coventry 30.00
Picture, Mail Coach, Frame, 2 1/2 x 13 In. 94.00

STEVENS & WILLIAMS of Stourbridge, England, made many types of glass, including layered, etched, cameo, and art glass, between the 1830s and 1930s. Some pieces are signed *S & W*. Many pieces are decorated with flowers, leaves, and other designs based on nature.

Basket, Pink & Vaseline, Thorn-Twist Handle, 9 In.	200.00
Basket, White, Blue Interior, Enameled Floral, Pulled Sides, Footed, 13 In.	900.00
Biscuit Jar, Cased White, Applied Amber Hooks, Leaves, 7 In.	275.00
Ewer, Cranberry, Ribbed, Cased, Handle, 7 1/2 In.	80.00
Pitcher, Peachblow, Amber Thorn Handle, 6 In.	100.00
Pitcher, Pink, Controlled Bubbles, Ribbed, Handle, 10 In.	325.00
Rose Bowl, Blue & White Stripe, Ruffled Edge, 2 In.	95.00
Tray, Card, Amber Over Cranberry Glass, c.1885, 7 In.	160.00
Vase, Deep Cranberry, Cased, 6 1/2 In.	50.00
Vase, Jack-In-The-Pulpit, White Over Pink, Amber Feet, 10 In., Pair	250.00
Vase, Orange, Swirled, Mother-Of-Pearl, Satin, Cased, 12 1/2 In.	952.00
Vase, Pink Threading, Raspberry Prunts, Rigaree Rim, 5 3/4 In.	150.00
Vase, Pink, Applied Cherry Blossoms & Cherries, Cased, 14 In., Pair	4250.00
Vase, Stick, Apple, Cameo, 6 3/4 In.	200.00
Vase, White, Floral, Applied Amber Handles, 9 In.	100.00
Vase, Yellow Over Blue, Controlled Bubbles, Applied Foot, 4 1/2 In.	225.00
Vase, Yellow, Applied Blue Feet, Floral, 10 In.	10.00

STIEGEL TYPE glass is listed here. It is almost impossible to be sure a piece was actually made by Stiegel, so the knowing collector refers to this glass as *Stiegel type*. Henry William Stiegel, a colorful immigrant to the colonies, started his first factory in Pennsylvania in 1763. He remained in business until 1774. Glassware was made in a style popular in Europe at that time and was similar to the glass of many other makers. It was made of clear or colored glass and was decorated with enamel colors, mold blown designs, or etching.

Bottle, Enameled Birds, Hearts & Flowers, c.1800, 7 In.	440.00
Cologne, 13 Diamonds, Medium Green, Blown Stopper, 1770s, 7 1/4 In.	495.00
Creamer, Cobalt Blue, Honeycomb, Footed, 3 1/4 In.	385.00
Mug, Enameled Floral Wreath, German Prose, 6 1/2 In.	375.00
Sugar, Expanded Diamond, Swirled Rib Finial Cover, 1763, 6 In.	2640.00

STONEWARE is a coarse, glazed, and fired potter's ceramic that is used to make crocks, jugs, bowls, etc. It is often decorated with cobalt blue decorations. In the nineteenth and early twentieth centuries, potters often decorated crocks with blue numbers indicating the size of the container. A "2" meant 2 gallons. Stoneware is still being made.

Ashtray, Hand Painted Flowers, Matte Glaze, Made In Brazil, 7 x 7 In.	15.00
Barrel, Brandy	35.00
Batter Jar, Blue Floral, Cowden & Wilcox, c.1869, 9 In.	1320.00
Batter Jar, Blue, Wire & Wooden Handle, Penna., 19th Century, 10 In.	3300.00
Batter Jar, E.W. Farrington, Albany Glaze, Bail Handle	70.00
Batter Jar, Lid, Wildflower, Blue & White	300.00
Batter Pail, Floral, Bail Handle, Cowden & Wilcox, 1 1/2 Gal.	1540.00
Bean Pot, Tenth Reunion, Sons & Daughters Of Vermont, 1883, 11 1/2 In.	3300.00
Beater Jar, Blue & White, Western Stoneware	200.00
Beater Jar, Colonial, Blue & White	425.00
Bottle, Blue Initials JL, 10 1/2 In.	85.00
Bottle, Hon & Winner, West Nanticoke, Pa., 1 Qt.	165.00
Bottle, Incised Hatch Marks, Semimatte Glaze, Pond Farm, 7 In.	220.00
Bottle, Taupe & Mauve Matte Glaze, Squat, Hoganas, Sweden, 6 1/2 x 6 In.	88.00
Bowl, Aqua Glaze, Nils Kahler, 1960, 1 3/4 x 4 In. *Illus*	75.00
Bowl, Bent, Glossy Olive Alkaline Glaze, Signed, Cheever Meaders, 1951, 2 x 7 In.	440.00
Bowl, Blue Interior, Bail Handle, Stamped Twentieth Century-Acid Proof-German	35.00
Bowl, L. Stanek, Ely, Iowa, All White, Blue Base	85.00
Bowl, Milk, Brushed Flowers Around Rim, Number 1 In Circle, 11 1/2 In.	440.00
Bowl, Pedestal, Cover, Gray, Korea, 6 In.	66.00
Canteen, Wooden Bail Handle, Cobalt Blue Design, 11 1/2 In.	650.00

Outdoor stonework and statues, even if made of granite, can be damaged by acid rain, frost, and plants like ivy. Put garden statues on stands to keep the moisture from the grass away from the statue. Wash with a hose and a soft brush.

Stoneware, Bowl, Aqua Glaze, Nils Kahler, 1960, 1 3/4 x 4 In.

Chamber Pot, Cover, Wildflower Bowtie, Blue & White	110.00
Churn, 4 Shoulder Handles, A.P. Donaghho, Parkersburg, W. Va., 16 In.	110.00
Churn, Bird On Branch, Quill Work, 4 Shoulder Handles, Hart Bros., 16 1/4 In.	165.00
Churn, Blue Decoration, Salt Glaze, Signed F. Young, 6 Gal.	99.00
Churn, Blue Leaf, Salt Glaze, Handles, Replaced Plunger, 4 Gal.	99.00
Churn, Blue Parrot, F.E. Norton & Co., Worcester, Mass., 1875, 4 Gal.	3080.00
Churn, Cobalt Blue Flowers 4, Oval, 16 1/4 In.	355.00
Churn, Cobalt Blue Scroll Design, 3 On Front, 9 3/4 In.	55.00
Churn, Double Hand Crank, Wooden, Cast Iron, c.1860, 29 x 14 x 14 In.	110.00
Churn, Folk Art Deer, West Troy Pottery, 6 Gal.	6600.00
Cream Pot, Binghamton, N.Y., Dotted Bird, 1860, 1 Gal.	2035.00
Cream Pot, Man In The Moon, Cowden & Wilcox, Harrisburg, Pa., c.1870, 1 1/2 Gal.	5390.00
Creamer, Castle, All Blue	124.00
Crock, Apricot, Honeycomb, Blue, White, Salt Glaze, 7 x 4 In.	170.00
Crock, Bird On Plume Design, West Troy Pottery, N.Y., c.1880, 9 1/2 In., 2 Gal.	415.00
Crock, Bird On Tree Stump, E. & L.P. Norton, Bennington, Vt., c.1880, 5 Gal.	2145.00
Crock, Bird On Twig, White's, Utica, N.Y., c.1865, 1 Gal.	715.00
Crock, Bird, S.L. Pewtress & Co., Fairhaven, Conn., c.1880, 10 In., 3 Gal.	470.00
Crock, Blue Bird Design, 2 Handles, 1840, 5 Gal.	465.00
Crock, Blue Bird, 2 Gal.	220.00
Crock, Blue Design, I.P. Wiands, 19th Century, 4 Gal.	190.00
Crock, Blue Duck, Cowden & Wilcox, Harrisburg, Pa., 2 Gal.	2200.00
Crock, Blue Feather, 2 Handles, 1840, 3 Gal.	165.00
Crock, Blue Flowers, 1 1/2 Gal.	450.00
Crock, Blue Flowers, 2 Handles, Evan R. Jones, Pittston, Pa., 1840, 4 Gal.	465.00
Crock, Blue Leaf, John Magee, 1874, 13 In.	835.00
Crock, Blue Leaves, Salt Glaze, Handles, 3 Gal.	121.00
Crock, Blue Oxide Top Line, Gray Body, Bautetourt Co., 1880s, 9 1/2 In.	135.00
Crock, Blue Parrot, F.B. Norton, 4 Gal.	950.00
Crock, Blue Stencil Design, H. Crowden, 10 In., Gal.	220.00
Crock, Braman & Gormly, Rochester, N.Y., Blue Stylized Design, c.1880, 4 Gal.	130.00
Crock, Butter, Cobalt Blue Design, 12 x 8 In.	155.00
Crock, Butter, Cover, Bail Handle, Indians, Dead Deer, Teepee, Salt Glaze, 4 x 6 In.	1020.00
Crock, Butter, Cow & Fence Design, Relief, Salt Glaze, Blue, White, No Lid, 4 x 7 In.	88.00
Crock, Butter, Cow Stencil, Thos. Johnston Manu'fr Of Stoneware, c.1870, 2 Gal.	2145.00
Crock, Butter, Daisy & Waffle, Relief, Salt Glaze, Navy Blue, Cream, 4 x 5 3/4 In.	100.00
Crock, Butter, Fall Harvest, Barn, Cows, Relief, Salt Glaze, Blue, White, 4 x 6 1/2 In.	165.00
Crock, Butter, Indians & Slain Deer, Blue & White, 4 1/4 x 5 3/4 In.	1015.00
Crock, Chicken Pecking Corn, New York State, c.1880, 4 Gal.	525.00
Crock, Chicken Pecking Corn, Straight Sides, 3 Gal.	550.00
Crock, Cobalt Blue Bird, Branch, Handles, 2 Gal.	305.00
Crock, Cobalt Blue Bird, Straight Sides, F.B. Norton, 1 Gal.	242.00
Crock, Cobalt Blue Design, Graham & Hower, Doylestown, 6 Gal.	800.00
Crock, Cobalt Blue Design, Oval, 2 Gal.	195.00
Crock, Cobalt Blue Design, Salt Glaze, J. & E. Norton, 1840, 9 1/4 In., 2 Gal.	5462.00
Crock, Cobalt Blue Feather Design, 9 1/2 In.	78.00
Crock, Cobalt Blue Floral Garland, 2 Handles, Salt Glazed, Incised 3, 13 In.	305.00
Crock, Cobalt Blue Flowers, 2 Applied Handles, G.T. Cook, Brooklyn, Mich., 2 Gal.	355.00
Crock, Cobalt Blue Flowers, 5 1/4 In.	120.00

Crock, Cobalt Blue Flowers, Applied Handles, No. 3, 11 In. 220.00
Crock, Cobalt Blue Flowers, Chas Schaffer, No. 215 Market St., Philadelphia, 10 In. 248.00
Crock, Cobalt Blue Flowers, Gray, Closed Handles, Brayton & Kellogg, Utica, 1 Gal. 525.00
Crock, Cobalt Blue Flowers, Salt Glaze, 2 Applied Handles, 4 Gal. 275.00
Crock, Cobalt Blue Flowers, Straight Sides, John Bell, Waynesboro, 1 Gal. 415.00
Crock, Cobalt Blue Leaf Design, F.B. Norton & Co., Worcester, Mass., c.1870, 2 Gal. . . . 385.00
Crock, Cobalt Blue Leaf, 2 Applied Handles, E.Woodworth, Burlington, Vt., 9 In. 275.00
Crock, Cobalt Blue Quill Flowers, Underwood & Tenney, 9 1/2 In. 275.00
Crock, Cobalt Blue Tree, Handles, Ovoid, Salt Glazed, Wide Mouth, 10 1/2 In. 85.00
Crock, Cobalt Blue Tulips, 2 Handles, Bulbous, 1840, 10 3/4 In. 300.00
Crock, Cover, Leathers & Bro., Howard, Pa., 1 1/4 Gal. 85.00
Crock, Cover, Love Birds, Relief, Salt Glaze, Blue, White, 7 1/2 In. 360.00
Crock, Dotted Winged Bird, Oval, Lug Handles, Cowden & Wilcox, 5 Gal. 1320.00
Crock, Dragonfly, 3, Quill Work, Handles, J. Fisher, 10 1/4 In. 412.00
Crock, Drooping Flowers, H.B. Pfaltzgraff, 3 Gal. 355.00
Crock, Ear, Loop Handle, E.L. Stork, 3 Gal., 14 1/2 In. 90.00
Crock, F.B. Norton & Co., Worcester, Mass., 3 Gal. 195.00
Crock, Floral Spray, H.B. Pfaltzgraff, 3 Gal. 385.00
Crock, Flower & Vine Design, White's, Utica, N.Y., c.1865, 4 Gal. 250.00
Crock, Flower, Accents At Handles, Clark & Fox, Athens, N.Y., Squat, 2 Gal. 385.00
Crock, Flower, Hamilton & Sons, New Geneva, Pa., Mid 19th Century, 9 1/2 In. 90.00
Crock, Flower, Handles, Ovoid, White's, Utica, 2 Gal. 440.00
Crock, J. Stadden, Summit Country, 1 Gal. 195.00
Crock, J.M. Pruden, Elizabeth, N.J., 2 Gal. 120.00
Crock, Jar Shape, Cobalt Blue Flowers, 2 Handles, Salt Glazed, 3 Gal. 550.00
Crock, Paddle-Tail Bird, Blue, N.A. White & Son, Utica, c.1870, 6 Gal. 825.00
Crock, Shoulder Line, Exotic Bird, Floral Spray, W. Roberts, Salt Glazed, 4 Gal. 1092.00
Crock, Stenciled Eagle & Shield, 2 Gal. 330.00
Crock, Stylized Swag & Leaf Design, Cobalt Blue Salt Glaze, 2 Handles, 13 In. 345.00
Crock, Thos. Johnston Manu'fr. Of Stoneware, Apollo, Armstrong Co., 1870, 2 Gal. 2145.00
Crock, Waddell, Gray & Brown, Mid 19th Century, 10 In. 230.00
Crock, Weyman & Brothers, c.1870, 10 In. 375.00
Cup, Pouring, Cobalt Blue Accents, Albany Slip Interior, c.1860, 4 In. 550.00
Cup, Thumbprint Band, Black Stripes, Ribbed Handle, 3 7/8 In. 357.00
Figurine, Dog, Glossy Cream, Brown Feldspathic Glaze, Signed, M. Rogers, 3 1/8 In. . . . 11.00
Figurine, Rooster, Glossy Celadon, Green Alkaline Glaze, Cobalt Blue Edge, 15 In. 1320.00
Flask, Molded Acorns & Oak Leaves, Tan Glaze, 3 In. 110.00
Flower Turtle, Barrel Shape, Freundschraft Stamm, Jackson Square Pottery, 7 In. 2310.00
Flowerpot, Repeated Leaf Design, Cobalt Salt Glaze, Attached Saucer, 7 x 8 In. 290.00
Foot Warmer, Blue & White, Henderson 110.00
Foot Warmer, Floral, White & Brown Glaze, Knob Top, Denby Bourne, 9 1/2 x 6 In. 60.00
Fountain, Gunmetal Brown Albany Slip Glaze, Brown, Gray Clay, 11 1/8 In. 165.00
Inkwell, Old Woman, Bonnet, Tan Glaze, 2 1/4 In. 275.00
Jar, 2 In Laurel Wreath, Shoulder Handles, Burger Bros., 12 In. 175.00
Jar, Advertising, Sibb J. Beighei, Blue Stenciled Grapes, Apples, c.1860, 2 Gal. 770.00
Jar, Apple Butter, F.H. Cowden, Harrisburg, 6 3/4 In. 27.00
Jar, Blue Brushed Design, 2, Shoulder Handles, Sipe & Sons, 10 In. 330.00
Jar, Blue Owl, Egg Shape, Double Ear Handles, 17 3/4 In. 880.00
Jar, Brushed & Stenciled Stylized Flowers, Shoulder Handles, J.A. Franze, 23 1/2 In. 3410.00
Jar, Canning, Brown Interior, Light Gray Glaze Exterior, Cupped Handles, 13 In. 590.00
Jar, Canning, Brushed Stripes & Floral, Offord & Federer, 10 1/2 In. 605.00
Jar, Canning, Chandler, Celadon Alkaline Glaze, 2 Handles, Signed, 20 x 51 In. 6600.00
Jar, Canning, Cherries Stencil, Hamilton & Jones, Greensboro, Pa., 1870, 1/2 Gal. 850.00
Jar, Canning, Cobalt Blue Commas, S. Bell & Son, Strasberg, Pa., 9 3/4 In. 245.00
Jar, Canning, Cobalt Blue Label, Handlan Ratcliff & Co., No. 2, 12 In. 220.00
Jar, Canning, Cobalt Blue Stenciled Design, Medium Brown, Handles, 5 Gal. 505.00
Jar, Canning, Cobalt Blue Straight & Wavy Lines, 7 7/8 In. 155.00
Jar, Canning, Cobalt Fig, Thick Dark Brown Glaze Over Center Of 1 Fig, 10 x 6 In. 100.00
Jar, Canning, Cover, Blue Stork, Samuel Bell, Strasburg, Va., 1850, 1/2 Gal. 2640.00
Jar, Canning, Glossy Chocolate Feldspathic Glaze, 2 Handles, 16 1/4 In. 88.00
Jar, Canning, Gray, 3 Blue Horizontal Stripes, 6 1/2 x 4 1/2 In. 145.00
Jar, Canning, Green, Black Glaze, Alkaline Glaze Handle, Brown Clay, 13 3/4 In. 99.00
Jar, Canning, Hamilton & Jones, Greensboro, Pa., c.1860, 10 In., 1 Gal. 200.00

Jar, Canning, J. Eberly & Strasburg, Va., 7 In. 192.00
Jar, Canning, Jas. Hamilton & Jones, Greensboro, Pa., Ferns, c.1870, 8 In., 1/2 Gal. 250.00
Jar, Canning, Khaki Alkaline Glaze, 2 Handles, 1850, 12 In. 770.00
Jar, Canning, Medium Green Alkaline Glaze, Jordan Style Handle, 12 1/2 In. 412.00
Jar, Canning, Stenciled Flowers, Jas. Hamilton, 2, 11 In. 2247.00
Jar, Canning, Striped & Dotted Band, c.1860, 12 1/2 In., 1 Gal. 635.00
Jar, Canning, Stripes & Dots, c.1850, 6 1/2 In., 1 Qt. 715.00
Jar, Canning, Tan Interior, Blue Accents At Handle Corners, Cupped Handles, 2 Gal. 140.00
Jar, Canning, Wax Seal, Eagle, A.P. Donaghho, Parkersburg, W.V., 1870, 1 Gal. 1070.00
Jar, Cobalt Blue Bird, Tan Ground, Brown Interior, Cup Handles, 2 Gal. 280.00
Jar, Cobalt Blue Brushed Floral & 4, Shoulder Handles, Hamilton, 15 In. 330.00
Jar, Cobalt Blue Clover Sprays, 3, Cup Handles, Cylindrical, 3 Gal. 185.00
Jar, Cobalt Blue Design, William Hastage, c.1865, 17 1/2 In. 975.00
Jar, Cobalt Blue Flowers, Applied Handles, Impressed Lyons, 10 In., 2 Gal. 140.00
Jar, Cobalt Blue Leaves, Cylindrical, Salt Glazed, Wide Mouth, 10 1/2 In. 110.00
Jar, Cobalt Blue Stripes & 2, Oval, 11 3/4 In. 165.00
Jar, Cobalt Blue, 10, Shoulder Handles, R.T. Williams, New Geneva, Pa., 20 1/2 In. 275.00
Jar, Cobalt Blue, Prussian Soldier Design, C. Haidle & Co., Newark, N.J., 1/2 Gal. 6600.00
Jar, Dark Brown Albany Slip Glaze, Wm. Hare, Wilmington, De., 9 1/2 In. 28.00
Jar, Flowers, H. Loundes Manufactor, Petersburg, Va., Oval, 1840, 6 Gal. 5390.00
Jar, Free-Form Cobalt Flower, Red Curlicue, Tapered, American, 19th Century, 13 In. ... 489.00
Jar, Glossy Medium Green, Brown Clay Body, Lug Style Handles, 11 x 33 In. 330.00
Jar, Green, Brown Glaze, Loop Handles, 19th Century, 9 1/2 In. 66.00
Jar, Preserve, Brush Blue Tulip Design, c.1860, 2 Gal., 11 1/2 In. 550.00
Jar, Salt Glaze, Handles, 19th Century, 8 In. 287.00
Jar, Star Face Design, T. Harrington, Lyons, New York, c.1850, 11 1/2 In., 2 Gal. 2420.00
Jar, Stenciled & Freehand Hamilton & Jones, Oval, 16 3/4 In. 660.00
Jar, Stenciled & Freehand Label, Stars, Vining Leaves, Hamilton & Jones, 16 In. 935.00
Jar, Tan, Brown Interior, Daisy Design, 5, Applied Cup Handles, 5 Gal. 155.00
Jar, Tan, Flowers, 4, Applied Cup Handles, 4 Gal. 250.00
Jar, Tobacco, Barrel, Head Finial, Says Tobacco, 7 In. 145.00
Jar, Tobacco, McGregor, Late 19th Century 115.00
Jar, Tulip Design, Cobalt Blue, Applied Shoulder Handles, 14 In. 605.00
Jar, White's, Utica, Blue Flowers, 2 Gal. 430.00
Jug, 2 Birds, Flowers, White's, Utica, 1865, 3 Gal. 2090.00
Jug, A. Hatke & Co., Distillers Of Fine Whiskeys, Brown, White, 1 Gal. 160.00
Jug, Abstract Circle, Triangle, Cobalt Blue, Beehive Shape, Albany, 1800s, 13 In., 2 Gal. .. 690.00
Jug, All White, Weeks, 1/2 Gal. 60.00
Jug, Bardwell's Root Beer, Wood & Wire Carrying Handle, 4 3/4 x 10 In. 845.00
Jug, Bellflower Pinwheel, Harrisburg, Pa., Cowden & Wilcox, 4 Gal. 1100.00
Jug, Benj Dawson, New Bedford, Mass., 19th Century, 2 Gal., 14 In. 80.00
Jug, Bird & Grape Cluster, Cobalt Blue Glaze, Looped Handles, Boston, 1800s, 13 In. 1725.00
Jug, Bird On Leaf Scroll, Applied Handle, Lack & Van Arsdale, 14 In. 385.00
Jug, Bird On Twig, Blue, J. Norton & Co., Bennington, Vt., c.1880, 14 In., 2 Gal. 525.00
Jug, Blue Bird, Ft. Edward Pottery, 19th Century, 1 1/2 Gal. 595.00
Jug, Blue Clamshell Design, Handle, Commeraws Stoneware, Oval, 1805, 2 Gal. 825.00
Jug, Blue Flowers, 2 Handles, Egg Shape, 1830, 3 Gal. 660.00
Jug, Blue Flowers, D.P. Shenfelder, 19th Century, 11 In. 355.00
Jug, Blue Stencil, Weeks Pottery, 1/2 Gal. 200.00
Jug, Blue Tulip, Ovoid, T. Reed 2, 14 1/4 In. 1870.00
Jug, Brady & Craft, Ellenville, N.Y., Impressed, Spout, 2 Gal. 250.00
Jug, Bright Blue Glaze, Glossy Cobalt Blue, Incised Eyebrows, Handle, 11 In. 275.00
Jug, Brown Speckled Glaze, 3, Mid 19th Century, 15 In. 45.00
Jug, Charlestown 2, Blue Bird On Flower Branch, Label, Strap Handle, 14 1/2 In. 545.00
Jug, Cobalt Blue Arrows, Salt Glaze, Oval, Handles 99.00
Jug, Cobalt Blue Bird On Branch, D. McCauley, Springfield, Mass., 3 Gal. 855.00
Jug, Cobalt Blue Bird, 2 Gal. 275.00
Jug, Cobalt Blue Bird, Flack & Van Arsdale, Cornwall, Ont. Stamped, 3 Gal. 415.00
Jug, Cobalt Blue Bird, Ft. Edward, N.Y., New York Stoneware Co., 2 Gal. 275.00
Jug, Cobalt Blue Butterfly, 2 Gal. 385.00
Jug, Cobalt Blue Decoration, Brown Salt Glaze, 3 Gal. 77.00
Jug, Cobalt Blue Design, St. John's, 3 Gal. 220.00
Jug, Cobalt Blue Floral, Salt Glaze, S.T. Brewer, Havana, 2 Gal. 220.00

Jug, Cobalt Blue Flower, J.A. & C.W. Underwood, Fort Edward, N.Y., 2 Gal. 140.00
Jug, Cobalt Blue Flower, J.E. Norton, Bennington, Vt., 2 Gal. 412.00
Jug, Cobalt Blue Flower, Salt Glaze, E. & LP Norton, Bennington, Vt., 2 Gal. 190.00
Jug, Cobalt Blue Flowers, Beehive Shape, Salt Glazed, Mark, 19th Century, 14 In. 173.00
Jug, Cobalt Blue Flowers, Cowden & Wilcox, Harrisburg, 1 Gal. 220.00
Jug, Cobalt Blue Flowers, Lyons, Strap Handle, Ovoid, 14 1/4 In. 247.00
Jug, Cobalt Blue Flowers, Somerset Potter's Works, 19th Century, 5 Gal. 360.00
Jug, Cobalt Blue Glaze, Gray, Tan, Applied Handle, Oval, C. Crolius, 14 In. 440.00
Jug, Cobalt Blue Stencil, 2, Williams & Reppert, Greensboro, Pa., 14 In. 330.00
Jug, Cobalt Blue Swirl, Dot Design On Shoulder, Handle, 8 1/2 In. 402.00
Jug, Cobalt Blue, Leaf Decoration, Somerset, Handles, 2 Gal., 15 In. 88.00
Jug, Codfish, Cobalt Blue, Jonathan Fenton, Boxton, 1800, 15 1/2 In. 1495.00
Jug, Cream Pale Salt Glaze, Semiflat Handle, Early 20th Century, 11 In. 33.00
Jug, Cream, Cobalt Blue Slip Floral, I. Seymour Troy Factory, Oval, 2 Gal. 255.00
Jug, Creature With Open Mouth, Dark Brown, Blue Glaze, R.W. Martin, 1880, 5 In. 1760.00
Jug, Crest, Lion, Gargoyles, Blue Salt Glaze, Metal Stopper, Cork, Bartman, 6 In. 115.00
Jug, Dark Brown Salt Glaze At Neck, 1 Handle At Neck & Shoulder, Boston, 15 In. 170.00
Jug, Dark Green Alkaline Glaze, Flat Tapered Handle, 12 1/4 In. 121.00
Jug, Dark Moss Green Alkaline Glaze, Rounded Top Handle, 8 1/2 In. 55.00
Jug, Dark, Light Blue Glaze, Bright Yellow Snake On Blue Jug, Signed, M. Rogers, 8 In. . . 99.00
Jug, Devil Face, Dark Brown Albany Slip Glaze, Flat Style Handle, 5 1/4 In. 66.00
Jug, Devil Face, Glossy Black, Brown Albany Slip Glaze, Flat Style Handle, 10 In. 303.00
Jug, Devil Face, Glossy Black, Brown, Thumb Grove Handle, 9 1/2 In. 110.00
Jug, Devil Face, Glossy Brown, Black Albany Slip Glaze, Flat Style Handle, 11 In. 1045.00
Jug, Devil Face, Khaki Alkaline Glaze, Dark Blue Incised Beard, White Clay, 11 In. 99.00
Jug, Distillery, Salt Glaze, Orange Peel Surface, Handle, Late 19th Century, 11 In. 33.00
Jug, Dotted Bird, On Log, J. Burger, Jr., Rochester, N.Y., 1885, 4 1/2 Gal. 1750.00
Jug, Double Handles, 2 Squiggle Lines Over Face, China Teeth, B. Craig, 15 In. 185.00
Jug, Drury & Jams, Groceries, Baltimore, Md., Incised Script, 8 In. 495.00
Jug, E & LP Norton, Bennington, Vt., Salt Glaze, 2 Gal. 430.00
Jug, E.J. Heffernan Wholesale Liquors, Brown, Cobalt Blue Letters, 1 Gal. 165.00
Jug, Engraved Design, Pewter Lid, Closed Hinge, Westerwald, c.1870, 1 Liter 175.00
Jug, Face, Gray, White Feldspathic Glaze, Haunting Smiling Expression, 11 1/2 In. 55.00
Jug, Face, Lime Green Matte Alkaline Glaze, White Eyes, 1900, 9 3/4 In. 77.00
Jug, Floral, Cowken & Wilcox, 14 3/4 In. 275.00
Jug, Flowers & Leaf, Cobalt Blue Glaze, Tan Ground, Tapered, Oval, 19th Century, 12 In. 547.00
Jug, Flowers In Vase, W. Roberts, Binghamton, N.Y., c.1860, 14 In., 2 Gal. 330.00
Jug, Flowers, Pfaltzgraff, 1 Gal. 385.00
Jug, Flowers, Wm. Moyer, Mid 19th Century, 14 1/2 In. 710.00
Jug, Glossy Straw Green Alkaline Glaze, Handle, Late 19th Century, 12 1/4 In. 192.00
Jug, Gray, Cobalt Blue Flower, Salt Glaze, Signed Lyons, 12 In. 77.00
Jug, Gray, Cobalt Blue Flowers, Salt Glaze, Oval, 2 Gal. 275.00
Jug, Gray, Cobalt Blue Impression, 3, Ottoman Bros. & Co., Fort Edward, N.Y., 3 Gal. 65.00
Jug, Gray, Cobalt Blue Slip Design, J.H. Farington, Saratoga Springs, 1 Gal. 265.00
Jug, Gray, Cobalt Blue, Fred Bellen, Glens Falls, Mid 19th Century, 15 In. 185.00
Jug, H. Free & Co., Fine Wines & Liquors, White Glaze, 1/2 Gal. 200.00
Jug, Horn Of Plenty, New York Stoneware Co., c.1880, 16 In., 3 Gal. 330.00
Jug, I.H. Wand, Olean, N.Y., Dotted Snowflake Design, 1853, 2 Gal. 1045.00
Jug, Incised Cobalt Blue Fish, 5 Rings, Jonathan Fenton, Boston, 1765, 8 In. 1000.00
Jug, John Downey, Groceries, Wines & Liquors, Gray Stamped, 8 1/2 In. 285.00
Jug, Kauffman Lattimer Co., Druggists, Albany, Sgraffito Inscription, Slip, 13 In. 105.00
Jug, Kauffman Lattimer Co., Wholesale Druggist, Albany Slip Glaze, 10 3/4 In. 80.00
Jug, L. Iorton, Oval, 1 Gal., c.1830 .... 495.00
Jug, Large Fantail Bird On Plume, E. & L.P. Norton, Bennington, Vt., c.1880, 4 Gal. 990.00
Jug, Leaves, Strap Handle, Oval, G. Heiser, 14 In. 440.00
Jug, Light Brown Glaze On Handle, Dark Brown Glaze On Shoulder, 5 Gal. 250.00
Jug, Light Tan Glaze, Mauve, Applied Handle From Neck To Shoulder, 1 Gal. 65.00
Jug, Long-Tailed Bird, New York Stoneware Co., Fort Edward, N.Y., c.1880, 2 Gal. 800.00
Jug, Milk, Large Cobalt Blue Bird & Branches, Joseph McGown, Mass., 11 x 7 In. 1495.00
Jug, Paddle-Tail Bird, Floral Spray, N.A. White & Son, Utica, N.Y., c.1870, 2 Gal. 1155.00
Jug, Pheasant On Stump, J. & E. Norton, Bennington, Vt., c.1855, 17 1/2 In., 4 Gal. 990.00
Jug, Poppy Design, Blue, White's, Binghamton, c.1860, 11 In., 1 Gal. 330.00
Jug, Rubbed Fern Design, H.M. Whitman, Havana, N.Y., c.1860, 3 Gal. 305.00

Jug, Rust, Black Rock Alkaline Glaze, Handle, 19th Century, 14 3/8 In. 165.00
Jug, Salt Glaze, Dark Gray, Handle, Signed, J.W. Welborn, 10 3/4 In. 99.00
Jug, Salt Glaze, Handle, Signed, E.S. Craven, 1850, 12 In. 825.00
Jug, Satterlee & Mory, 3 Gal. 425.00
Jug, Stackard, Chocolate Albany Slip, Flat Style Handle, Early 20th Century, 13 In. 66.00
Jug, Stag, Standing, J.C. Waelde, North Bay, 3 Gal. 3960.00
Jug, Strap Handle, Brushed Design, Cobalt Blue, 14 3/4 In. 220.00
Jug, Strap Handle, Cobalt Blue Quill Work, Frank B. Norton, 13 1/2 In. 220.00
Jug, Strap Handle, Incised Figure Of Woman With Crosshatched Dress, 13 In. 357.00
Jug, Strap Handle, West Troy Pottery, 14 In. 165.00
Jug, Strap Handles, Reeded Neck, Charlestown With G, Gray Salt Glaze, 11 1/2 In. 440.00
Jug, Tan Glaze On Lower Section, Handle, 14 1/2 x 11 1/2 In. 115.00
Jug, Whittmore, Mid 19th Century, 3 Gal. 190.00
Jug, Wine, Third Reich, Swastika, 1/2 Liter 173.00
Meat Tenderizer, Wildflower, 3 3/4 In. 245.00
Milk Pan, Man In Moon, Cowden & Wilcox, Harrisburg, Pa., 1 1/2 Gal. 4510.00
Mug, Blue & White, Robinson Windy City 125.00
Mug, Bottlers' Union, Compliment Of Bottlers' Lo. Union No. 183, Gold Trim 69.00
Mug, Grape & Shield, Green & Cream 10.00
Mug, Grape Cluster, Shield, Yellow & Green, 4 Piece 200.00
Mug, Raised Relief Windmill, Sailor On Reverse, Burley & Winter, 4 3/4 In. 65.00
Mug, Tavern Scene, Blue Buffalo 100.00
Pitcher, Allover Blue Flower & Ring, Presentation, Richard Remmey, 1870, 9 In. 2640.00
Pitcher, American Beauty Rose, Relief, Salt Glaze, Blue, White, 9 In. 305.00
Pitcher, Angled Spout & Ears, Wooden Handle, Brushed Design, E.B. Jones, 10 In. 467.00
Pitcher, Apricot Design, Relief, Salt Glaze, Blue, White, 8 In. 110.00
Pitcher, Apricot, Blue, White, Salt Glass, 8 x 5 In. 170.00
Pitcher, Band & Rivets, Blue & White, Seattle Extract Company, Chicago, Ill., 10 In. . . . 250.00
Pitcher, Bark, Benjamin Franklin, Fife & Drum Soldiers, Bristol Glaze, 8 1/4 In. 250.00
Pitcher, Bark, Man & Woman Reading, Roses, Salt Glaze, Whites Utica, 8 In. 55.00
Pitcher, Batter, Cover, Stenciled Flowers, Blue Lines 250.00
Pitcher, Blue Stencil Design, F.H. Cowden, Mid 19th Century, 11 In. 600.00
Pitcher, Blue, Green Exterior Glaze, Green Interior, Marked, Zark, 9 3/4 In. 330.00
Pitcher, Brushed Blue Flower, c.1860, 10 1/2 In., 2 Gal. 360.00
Pitcher, Brushed Leaf & Flower Design, 2 In Circle, c.1850, 13 In., 2 Gal. 330.00
Pitcher, Butterfly In Circle, Relief, Salt Glaze, Blue, White, 8 1/4 In. 175.00
Pitcher, Cattail, Blue & White, Bulbous, 7 In. 225.00
Pitcher, Cherries Band, Blue & White, 8 1/2 In. . . . . .100.00 to 125.00
Pitcher, Cherry Cluster Design, Relief, Flared Lip, Salt Glaze, Blue, White, 8 In. 385.00
Pitcher, Cobalt Blue Floral Design, c.1850, 1/2 Gal., 9 In. 715.00
Pitcher, Cow, Green & Cream, 7 1/2 In. 95.00
Pitcher, Daisy, Deep Blues, Bulbous, 10 In. 700.00
Pitcher, Dark Brown Albany Slip, Incised Lines, 10 1/2 In. 55.00
Pitcher, Diamond & Dot Tooled Design, Blue Stripes, Salt Glaze, White's, Utica, 9 In. . . . 88.00
Pitcher, Doe & Fawn, Relief, Salt Glaze, Blue, White, 8 1/4 In. 77.00
Pitcher, Drinking Scenes, Bristol Glaze, White's, Utica, 9 1/2 In. 55.00
Pitcher, Dutch Boy & Girl, Kissing, Embossed, Salt Glaze, Blue, White, 6 1/2 In. 77.00
Pitcher, Eagle, Blue, White, Salt Glaze, 8 x 5 In. 475.00
Pitcher, Eagle, Dotted Ground, Rope Design, 8 1/4 In. 412.00
Pitcher, Eagle, Relief, Rope Design, Dotted Ground, Salt Glaze, Blue, White, 8 1/4 In. . . 415.00
Pitcher, Floral In Brushed Cobalt Blue, Peter Hermann, 13 3/4 In. 440.00
Pitcher, Flower & Vine Design, Blue Accents, c.1860, 7 In., 1 Qt. 525.00
Pitcher, Flower, Relief, Salt Glaze, Blue, White, 8 1/2 In. 175.00
Pitcher, Flying Birds, 2 Birds On Twig, Relief, Salt Glaze, Blue, White, 8 In. 470.00
Pitcher, Glossy Blue Spongeware, White Feldspathic Glaze, Signed, W.J. Gordy, 8 In. . . . 110.00
Pitcher, Glossy Blue, Green Feldspathic Glaze, Handle, 1960, 3 In. 88.00
Pitcher, Glossy Bright Green Over Khaki Feldspathic Glaze, Walter Owen, 1927, 7 In. . . . 192.00
Pitcher, Glossy Dark Green Glaze, Double Grape Cluster, David Meaders, 10 1/4 In. 99.00
Pitcher, Glossy Opaque Feldspathic Glaze, Flowers, Signed, C. Meaders, 4 In. 99.00
Pitcher, Grape & Shield, Green & Cream, 8 In. 100.00
Pitcher, Grape Cluster On Basket Weave Design, Relief, Salt Glaze, Blue, White, 9 In. . . 165.00
Pitcher, Grape Cluster, Shield, Yellow & Green, 8 5/8 In. 100.00
Pitcher, Grapes & Leaves, Raised Relief, Ivory, 1/8 Cup Raised On Bottom, 2 In. 10.00

Pitcher, Gray Salt Glaze, Applied Ribbed Handle, 10 1/2 In. 220.00
Pitcher, Gray White Glaze, Blue Sponging Around Shoulder, 8 1/4 In. 120.00
Pitcher, Grazing Cows, Relief, Salt Glaze, Navy Blue, White, 8 In. 120.00
Pitcher, Grazing Cows, Yellow & Green, 7 3/8 In. 210.00
Pitcher, Green Drip Glaze, Cream Crackle Ground, 1910, 5 In. 27.00
Pitcher, Green Sponge Spatter, Blue Stripes On White Ground, 6 3/4 In. 165.00
Pitcher, Green, Stag Scene, Hound Handle, 13 In. 375.00
Pitcher, Hunt & Kitchen Scenes, Relief, Bristol Glaze, 7 1/2 In. 77.00
Pitcher, Impressed Face, Allover Green Glaze, 19th Century, 8 In. 1540.00
Pitcher, Indian Good Luck Design, Relief, Salt Glaze, Blue, White, 8 In. 110.00
Pitcher, Indian In War Bonnet, Relief, Salt Glaze, Blue, White, 8 In. 145.00
Pitcher, Indian Peace Sign, Blue & White, 10 In. 110.00
Pitcher, Iris, Salt Glaze, Blue, White, 8 1/2 In. 250.00
Pitcher, Leaping Deer, Relief, Salt Glaze, Blue, White, 8 In. 185.00
Pitcher, Lilies & Flowers, Cobalt Blue, 6 1/2 In. 145.00
Pitcher, Love Birds, Relief, Salt Glaze, Blue, White, 8 In. 155.00
Pitcher, Lovebirds, Blue & White, 10 In. 260.00
Pitcher, Memphis, Blue & White, Large 100.00
Pitcher, Monastery & Fish Scale, Blue & White, 9 In. 135.00
Pitcher, Multiple Flowers, Blue Swag Design On Rim, c.1860, 13 1/2 In., 2 Gal. 825.00
Pitcher, Pewter Lid, Bulbous, Carl Wengender, 1850, 12 3/4 In. 330.00
Pitcher, Pewter Lid, Man Astride Beer Barrel, Leaves, Late 19th Century, 13 In. 520.00
Pitcher, Pinecone, Blue & White, 9 In. 175.00
Pitcher, Poinsettia, Relief, Basket Weave Ground, Salt Glaze, Blue, White, 6 1/2 In. 130.00
Pitcher, Profile Of Woman In Bonnet, Relief, Salt Glaze, Blue, White, 8 1/4 In. 110.00
Pitcher, Pumpkin Shape, Mottled Brown & Blue Matte Glaze, Germany, 6 1/2 In. 55.00
Pitcher, Rose On Trellis Design, Relief, Salt Glaze, Blue, White, 8 1/2 In. 155.00
Pitcher, Salt Glaze, Green, Cat-O'-Nine-Tails Design, England, 19th Century, 6 1/2 In. .. 77.00
Pitcher, Satin Celadon, Green Alkaline Glaze, Signed, Cheever Meaders, 1960, 4 In. 357.00
Pitcher, Sgraffito Band & Banner, N.H. Barber, 8 3/4 In. 165.00
Pitcher, Singing Bird, Dots & Lines, New York State, c.1870, 1 Gal. 635.00
Pitcher, Solomon Bell, Cobalt Blue Stamped, Tulips, 1 Gal. 575.00
Pitcher, Stenciled Dutch Scene, Salt Glaze, Blue, White, 7 In. 99.00
Pitcher, Swan, Relief, Salt Glaze, Blue, White, 8 In. 220.00
Pitcher, T.F. Reppert, Greensboro, Pa., Blue Stencil, Geometric, 1880, 1 Gal. 1430.00
Pitcher, Table, Glossy Green, Black Glaze, Flat Style Handle, 7 1/2 In. 220.00
Pitcher, Table, Glossy Straw, Green Alkaline Glaze, Flat Style Handle, 1970, 7 In. 220.00
Pitcher, Table, Glossy Straw, Green Alkaline Glaze, Floral Design, 10 1/4 In. 88.00
Pitcher, White's, Utica, Pewter Lid, 1890, 12 In. 1095.00
Pitcher, Whitehall, Light Blue, 6 1/2 In. 135.00
Pitcher, Windmill & Bush, Blue & White 110.00
Pitcher & Bowl, Rose & Fish Scale, Blue & White 275.00
Planter, Tree Trunk, Vines In Relief Around Trunk, Brown Glaze, 12 3/8 In. 373.00
Platter, Wood Fired, Signed, Peter Voulkos, 1924, 22 In. 4885.00
Pot, Canning, Glossy Dark Green Alkaline Glaze, Handle, 10 5/8 In. 77.00
Pot, Cover, Salt Glaze, Cobalt Blue Design, Orange Peel Texture, 1930, 4 1/4 In. 88.00

Stoneware, Vase, Aqua
Glaze, Nils Kahler,
1950s-1960s, 5 1/2 In.

**If you are moving, be sure to get
special insurance coverage for damage
to your antiques. You may want
valuable pieces covered by your
insurance, not by the mover's policy.**

Rolling Pin, Wildflower, 15 In. 357.00
Salt, Hanging, Cover, Butterfly Design, Relief, Salt Glaze, Blue, White, 6 In. 250.00
Salt, Hanging, Cover, Stenciled Scroll Design, Salt Glaze, Blue, White, 6 1/4 In. 130.00
Salt Box, Oak Leaf, Blue & White 75.00
Tankard, Wildflower, Blue & White, Square Handle 85.00
Tea Set, Gray, Cobalt Blue, Ben Owen, 1964, 7-In. Teapot, 11 Piece 530.00
Teapot, Castleford Type, Seal Of The U.S., Classical Figure, Oval, 6 1/2 x 9 1/2 In. 490.00
Tureen, Cover, Floral Design, Blue & White, 15 1/2 In. 460.00
Urn, Frieze Of Cherubs, Floral Garlands, Gadrooning, Continental, 38 In. 1840.00
Vase, Aqua Glaze, Nils Kahler, 1950s-1960s, 5 1/2 In. ....*Illus* 95.00
Vase, Baluster Shape, Celestial Dragon, Red, Japan, c.1880, 12 1/2 In., Pair 99.00
Vase, Bell Shape, Chinese Blue Glaze, Ben Owen, 1930, 3 1/2 x 5 In. 550.00
Vase, Black Metallic Matte Glaze, Signed, W.J. Gordy, 3 7/8 In. 66.00
Vase, Brown, Gray Matte Glaze, Eva Staehr-Nielsen, Saxbo, 8 1/2 x 5 1/2 In. 220.00
Vase, Bud, Mottled Blue & Ivory Matte Glaze, Hjorth, Denmark, 6 1/4 x 2 3/4 In. 110.00
Vase, Chinese White Glaze, Signed, Ben Owen, 1930, 5 1/4 In. 195.00
Vase, Chocolate Albany Slip Glaze, Signed, 1930, 6 1/2 In. 135.00
Vase, Crosshatched, Small Opening, Brown Glaze, Signed, Smith, 1964, 23 In. 330.00
Vase, Flowers Under Multitoned Green Matte Glaze, Chicago Crucible, 9 In. 440.00
Vase, Glossy Celadon Green Alkaline Glaze, 2 Handles, 9 In. 1595.00
Vase, Glossy Celadon Green Alkaline Glaze, Double Grape Cluster, 1970, 7 In. 412.00
Vase, Glossy Dark Green Alkaline Glaze, 1980, 7 1/2 In. 220.00
Vase, Glossy Dark Green Alkaline Glaze, Double Grape Cluster, 9 1/2 In. 121.00
Vase, Glossy Dark Green Alkaline Glaze, Grape Cluster Design, 2 Handles, 10 In. 55.00
Vase, Glossy Medium Green Alkaline Glaze, Rose Design, 1974, 13 1/8 In. 3850.00
Vase, Glossy Streaked Dark Green Alkaline Glaze, Grape Clusters, 2 Handles, 19 In. 220.00
Water Cooler, Cover, Molded, Polar Bears, Flowers, Ice Insert, 6 Gal. 1210.00
Water Cooler, Grotesque Mask, Mouth Forms Spigot Hole, 1880s, 13 In. 605.00
Water Cooler, Polar Bear, White's, Utica, 1 Gal. 3100.00
Water Cooler, Rebecca At The Well, Spigot 550.00
Water Cooler, Salt Glaze, Blue, Gray, Flowers, 15 In. 260.00
Water Cooler, White Glaze, Blue Stripes, Nickel Plated Spigot & Lid, 12 1/2 In. 60.00

STORE fixtures, cases, cutters, and other items that have no advertising
as part of the decoration are listed here. Most items found in an old
store are listed in the Advertising category in this book.

Bin, Grain, Slant Front, Lift Top, Scalloped Skirt, Old Red Paint, 31 x 26 In. 220.00
Box, Seed, Vegetable & Flower, Wooden, Label Under Lid 150.00
Cabinet, Card File, Druggist, Tiger Oak, Recipe Cards, 1900-1930 .... 66.00
Cabinet, Display, 2 Shelf, Glass, Wooden, Sliding Rear Doors, Refinished, 20 In. 275.00
Candy Jar, Glass, Footed, Frame Type Stopper, 1880-1900, 18 1/2 In. 195.00
Case, Bread, Oak, With Glass 650.00
Case, Cheese, Countertop 500.00
Case, Counter, Bean, 31 Drawers, Country, 15 Ft. 9 In. 6500.00
Cigar Cutter, Reverse On Glass, Match Striker, Key Wind, Las Amantes, 1930, 8 In. 630.00
Coffee Grinders are listed in their own category.
Coin Changer, Automatic Countertop, Cast Iron & Chrome, 25 Cent, 1940s, 19 1/2 In. ... 50.00
Cutter, Paper & String Holder, Wooden, Ornate Cast Iron, 3 Rolls 82.00
Cutter, Paper, Iron, Wooden, 15 In. 25.00
Cutter, Paper, Star Knife Holder, 2 Tiers, Wooden, Cast Iron, Square, Pat. 1911 .... 38.00
Display, Cigar, Electric Pull-Down Lighter On Front, Tin Lithograph, 9 x 7 In. 35.00
Display, Countertop, Glass, Oak, Sliding Rear Doors, Mirror, Sun Mfg., 31 1/2 In. 275.00
Display, Ice Cream Cones, 5 Cents, 1970, 9 1/2 In., 4 Piece 550.00
Display, Postcard Carousel, Ferris Wheel Shape, Manual Turn, Embossed, Tin, 36 In. 468.00
Display Case, Pipe, Glass Door, Opens To Different Velvet Panels, 48 Pipes, 28 x 39 In. ... 575.00
Display Case, Pull-Down Mirrored Doors, Wooden, 47 1/2 In. 385.00
Display Case, Tiered, Curved Front, Oak, 45 In. 385.00
Display Case, Wooden, Slant Front, 130 Trout Fly Patterns, Green Felt, 20 x 20 In. 330.00
Display Rack, Countertop, Mahogany, For Seed Packets, Inlay, Brass Trim 100.00
Figure, Stork, Composition, 48 1/2 In. 230.00
Figure, Tack Shop, Horse, On Hind Legs, Wooden, Carved, 1930 .... 900.00
Frame, Hemp, 8 Bands Of Rope Around Frame, 40 1/2 x 33 1/2 In. 40.00
Hat Stretcher, Gold Finish, Size 6, 7 & 8 .... 50.00

Holder, Bag, Countertop, Homemade, Assortment Of Printed Bags, 15 In. 110.00
Holder, Bag, Wooden, Cutout, Curved 1450.00
Holder, Wrapping Paper, With String Dispenser 150.00
Mannequin, Articulated Arms, 19th Century 2800.00
Mannequin, Selina, Woman, Bust Type, 1930s, 28 1/2 In. 1900.00
Mannequin, Wooden, Used As Dress Form, Articulated Arms, Folk Type, 19 In. 3575.00
Shelves, Display, Oak, Step Back, 5 Tiers, 1880s, 37 x 71 In. 200.00
Shoeshine Stand, Ornate Wood, Marble 5000.00
Showcase, Double Cathedral, Walnut, Curved Glass Front, 8 Ft.   6500.00
Showcase, Mahogany, Ball & Claw Feet, Ornate, 8 Ft. 700.00
Showcase, Oak, Slant Front, Glass Sides, Old Refinish, New Glass Top, 5 x 2 Ft. 400.00
Showcase, Quartersawn Oak, Glass Panels All Sides, Swivel Base, 5 Ft. 4 In. 2800.00
Sign, Emporium, Copper, England, 1885, 42 x 7 In. 1700.00
Sign, Figural, Key, 19 In. 1495.00
Sign, Pawn Shop, 3 Gilt Balls, Copper, Iron Bracket, American, Late 1800s 2415.00

STOVES have been used in America for heating since the eighteenth
century and for cooking since the nineteenth century. Most types of
wood, coal, gas, kerosene, and even some electric stoves are collected.

Camp, Coleman, With Burner Unit At Top, Stainless Steel, 8 1/2 In. 70.00
Coal, Deville Paillette Forest, No. 17, Bronze Plaque, Pineapple Medallion, Iron, 36 In. . .   335.00
Coal Burning, Garland, Model 25, Cast Iron, Patent September 15, 1876 . . . .   4000.00
Cook, Gas, Arcade, White Paint, Silver Trim On Doors, Black Grill Top, Cast Iron, 6 In. . .   210.00
Cook, Monarch, Blue & Chrome 1900.00
Cook, U.S. Cook Stove Drier, Wood, Wire Mesh, Galvanized, 8 Drawers, 27 In. 247.00
Detroit, Jewel Gas, White, Black & Blue, 1930s 475.00
Globe Glow, Maid, Yellow Enamel 895.00
Heating, Cast Iron, Zoar, Ohio, 43 In. 137.00
Heating, Child's, Dolly's Favorite, Black, Silver Paint, Piqua, Ohio, Cast Iron, 23 In. 1705.00
Heating, Child's, Empire, Aqua Enamel, Nickel Plated, Electric, 20 x 9 1/4 x 16 3/4 In. . .   247.00
Heating, Franklin, Bed Chamber Insert, Hartshorn & Ames, Nashua, c.1850, 24 In. 170.00
Heating, Franklin, Cast Iron, Brass Ball Finials, 19th Century, 32 1/2 x 31 x 24 In. 220.00
Heating, Parlor, Coal Burning, Garland, No. 25, Patent 1876 . . . .   4000.00
Heating, Parlor, Detroit Stove Works, Griffin Each Side, Cast Iron & Steel, 38 In. 1500.00
Heating, Parlor, Stove & Range Co., Cast Iron, 28 In. 165.00
Heating, Potbelly, Sligo No. 18, Top Rack For 3 Irons, Cast Iron, 48 In. 55.00
Kerosene, Silber Light Co., Sphinxes & Owls, Aerotherm, Majolica, 28 x 12 1/2 In. 2500.00
Laundry, Union Stove Works, Flat Irons, 28 In. 2000.00

SUMIDA, or Sumida Gawa, is a Japanese pottery. The pieces collected
by that name today were made about 1895 to 1970. There has been
much confusion about the name of this ware, and it is often called
Korean Pottery. Most pieces have a very heavy orange-red, blue, or
green glaze, with raised three-dimensional figures as decorations.

Teapot, Gray, 7 1/2 In. 75.00
Teapot, Tigers 650.00
Vase, Applied Children & Wisteria Flowers, Black Ground, 16 In. . . . .*Illus*   1980.00

**Small nicks and scratches in decorative ironware
can be covered with black crayon. Wipe off the
excess with paper. Don't do this on pots and
pans you may use for cooking.**

Sumida, Vase, Applied
Children & Wisteria
Flowers, Black Ground, 16 In.

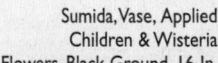

SUNBONNET BABIES were first introduced in 1900 in the book *The Sunbonnet Babies*. The stories were by Eulalie Osgood Grover, illustrated by Bertha Corbett. The children's faces were completely hidden by the sunbonnets. The children had been pictured in black and white before this time, but the color pictures in the book were immediately successful. The Royal Bayreuth China Company made a full line of children's dishes decorated with the Sunbonnet Babies. Some Sunbonnet Babies plates have been reproduced, but are clearly marked.

Pitcher, Wash Day, 3 1/2 In.	110.00
Postcard Set, 7 Days Of Week	60.00
Saucer, Sewing, 5 1/2 In.	105.00

SUNDERLAND luster is a name given to a special type of pink luster made by Leeds, Newcastle, and other English firms during the nineteenth century. The luster glaze is metallic and glossy and appears to have bubbles in it. Other pieces of luster are listed in the Luster category.

Pitcher, Black Transfer, Masonic Design & Verse, Charlotte Todd, 1825, 9 In.	770.00
Pitcher, Water, Lifeboat Scene, Motto, Susan & William Pictured, 7 1/4 In.	415.00
Plaque, Motto, Thou God See'st Me, Psalm, Angel, Flower Transfer, England, 8 x 9 In.	259.00

SUPERMAN was created by two seventeen-year-olds in 1938. The first issue of *Action* comics had the strip. Superman remains popular and became the hero of a radio show in 1940, cartoons in the 1940s, a television series, and several major movies.

Bank, Figural, Plastic	65.00
Bank, Register, Superman, Painted, Tin, Dime, 2 1/2 In.	231.00
Button, Club, 1966, 3 1/2 In.	50.00
Card, Trading, Movie, Complete Set, In Celluloid, 1978	50.00
Card, Trading, Set, Superman Scenes, Gum Inc., 1940, 72 Piece	1810.00
Card, Valentine, Away From You I'm Helpless, 1939-1940	85.00
Case, Pencil, 1940	150.00
Comic Book, Superman Action, Cover Image Fighting Nazi Tank, April, 1943	264.00
Display, Marionette, Motorized, 1978, 30 x 12 In.	200.00
Doll, Supergirl, Ideal	3000.00
Figure, Plastic, Painted, Hook & Loop On Front, Transogram Co., 1954, 12 In.	21.00
Game, Superman II, Milton Bradley, 1961	20.00
Game, Superman III, Parker Bros., 1982	20.00
Glass, Superman Breaking Chains On Front, Name On Reverse, 5 1/2 In.	20.00
Lunch Box, 1964	65.00
Magazine, TV Guide, No. 26, George Reeves, Man & Superman, 1953	820.00
Ornament, Hallmark, 1993	50.00
Pillow Case, 1978, 29 1/2 x 19 1/2 In.	335.00
Puzzle, Frame, 1979	10.00
Scissors, Figural, On Card, Symak, Canada, 1978	20.00
Soaky	100.00
Telephone, Plastic, Rotary Dial, Allied Telecommunications, c.1981, 17 In.	1000.00
Transfer, Emblem, Iron-On For T-Shirt, Rat's Hole, 1968, Small	20.00

SUSIE COOPER began as a designer in 1925 working for the English firm A.E. Gray & Company. In 1932 she formed Susie Cooper Pottery, Ltd. In 1950 it became Susie Cooper China, Ltd., and the company made china and earthenware. In 1966 it was acquired by Josiah Wedgwood & Sons, Ltd. The name Susie Cooper appears with the company names on many pieces of ceramics.

Charger, April, Stylized Flowers, Leaves, Feather Border, 1930s, 16 1/8 In.	230.00
Charger, Stylized Leaves, Scrolling Stems, Brown Bands, 1930s, 16 1/4 In.	245.00
Coffee Set, Tyrol, Brown Bands, Green Crosslets, Pot & 6 Cups & Saucers, 7 1/2 In.	465.00
Jam Jar, Cover, Stylized Leaves, Linear Border, Cream Ground, 1930s, 3 1/4 In.	205.00
Pitcher, Incised Design, Stylized Charging Rams, Signed, 8 1/2 In.	690.00
Pitcher, Molded Border, Ribbed Neck, Scroll Handle, Cream Glaze, 1930s, 14 In.	365.00
Vase, Foxes & Trees, Dark Blue Glaze, Signed, c.1933, 6 1/4 In.	287.00

SWANKYSWIGS are small drinking glasses. In 1933, the Kraft Food Company began to market cheese spreads in these decorated, reusable glass tumblers. They were discontinued from 1941 to 1946, then made again from 1947 to 1958. Then plain glasses were used for most of the cheese, although a few special decorated Swankyswigs have been made since that time. A complete list of prices can be found in *Kovels' Depression Glass & Dinnerware Price List.*

Antique, Blue, 3 3/4 In.	5.00
Band No. 1, Red, 3 3/8 In.	3.00
Band No. 2, Red & Black, 3 3/8 In.	4.00 to 5.00
Bustling Betsy, Blue, 3 3/4 In.	5.00
Bustling Betsy, Green, 3 3/4 In.	5.00
Bustling Betsy, Orange, 3 3/4 In.	5.00
Bustling Betsy, Red, 3 3/4 In.	5.00
Bustling Betsy, Yellow, 3 3/4 In.	5.00
Checkerboard, Red & White, 3 1/2 In.	27.00
Circles & Dots, Green, 3 1/2 In.	5.00
Cornflower No. 1, Light Blue, 3 1/2 In.	4.50
Cornflower No. 2, Dark Blue, 3 1/2 In.	4.00
Cornflower No. 2, Light Blue, 3 1/2 In.	4.00
Cornflower No. 2, Red, 3 1/2 In.	4.00
Cornflower No. 2, Yellow, 3 1/2 In.	4.00
Daisy, Red, White & Green, 3 3/4 In.	4.00 to 20.00
Forget-Me-Not, Blue, 3 1/2 In.	4.00
Forget-Me-Not, Red, 3 1/2 In.	4.00
Kiddie Kup, Bird & Elephant, Red, 3 3/4 In.	5.00
Kiddie Kup, Cat & Rabbit, Green, 3 3/4 In.	5.00
Kiddie Kup, Duck & Horse, Black, 3 3/4 In.	5.00 to 9.00
Kiddie Kup, Pig & Bear, Light Blue, 3 3/4 In.	5.00
Kiddie Kup, Squirrel & Deer, Brown, 3 3/4 In.	5.00
Sailboat, Red, 3 1/2 In.	9.00
Stars, Black, 3 1/2 In.	4.00
Tulip No. 1, Black, 3 1/2 In.	4.00
Tulip No. 1, Blue, 3 1/2 In.	4.00
Tulip No. 1, Green, 3 1/2 In.	4.00
Tulip No. 1, Red, 3 1/2 In.	4.00
Tulip No. 3, Dark Blue, 3 3/4 In.	4.00
Tulip No. 3, Red, 3 3/4 In.	4.00
Tulip No. 3, Yellow, 3 3/4 In.	4.00

SWORDS of all types that are of interest to collectors are listed here. The military dress sword with elaborate handle is probably the most wanted. Be sure to display swords in a safe way, out of reach of children.

Artillery, Brass Fish Scale Handle, Eagle, 1832, 18 3/4-In. Blade	345.00
Artillery, Brass Hilt, Lion's Head Pommel, 30 1/2 In.	192.00
Artillery, Confederate, Fish Scale Handle, Dark Patina, 1841	575.00
Artillery, Foot, Leather & Brass Scabbard, Model 1832, Short, 1847	1150.00
Artillery, Germany, Engraved Blade, Lion's Head Pommel Hilt	200.00
Artillery, U.S. & N.J., Cast Brass Hilt, Eagles, Dated 1855, 25 In.	440.00
Battlefield, Iron Grip Backstrap, Wooden Handle, 1890, 25 3/4 In.	460.00
British Royal Marines Band, Cruciform Hilt, Victorian, 19-In. Blade	225.00
Cane, Wooden Cane & Handle, Locking Catch, Release Button, 19th Century, 38 In.	130.00
Cavalry, Germany, Blued Iron Bowl Guard, 1900, 35 1/4-In. Straight Blade	210.00
Ceremonial, Exploits Of Samurai, Ivory, Scabbard, c.1900, 28 In.	2300.00
Commander's, Scrimshaw Ribbons & Leaves, Henderson Ames Co., 29 5/8-In. Blade	172.00
Concealed In Riding Crop Handle, Mother-Of-Pearl Inlay	132.00
Double, Japan, Steel Blades, Ivory Handles, Lacquer Scabbard, 19th Century, 32 In.	920.00
Dress, Overall Floral, Scroll Blade, Brass Handle, W.K. & Company, 30 In.	287.00
Hunting, Germany, Etched Trophies, Stagson Blade, Brass Mounts, Staghorn Handle	250.00
Hunting, Straight Blade, Etched Boar, Stags, Trophies, Nickel Hilt, Staghorn Grip	230.00
Japanese, Armor Piercing Tanto, 2 Mekugi-Ana, 1 Mumei, 5 3/4-In. Blade	747.00
Japanese, Katana Shin-Gunto Mounts, Leather Battle Wrap, 25 1/4-In. Blade, Signed	517.00

Japanese, Pierced Cast Iron Tsuba, Bronze Dragon Mounts, Scabbard, c.1940, 31 In. 750.00
Japanese, Shinto Ko-Katana, Copper Of Dragon In Clouds, 20 3/8-In. Blade, Signed 345.00
Japanese, Shinto Wakizashi, 3-In. Crane Over Sages, Signed, S. Hiro, 18-In. Blade 460.00
Japanese, Shinto Wakizashi, Shinoji Zukuri On Blade, Signed, 19 1/8-In. Blade 230.00
Japanese, Tanto In Shira Saya, Wooden Shira Saya, Signed, 9 3/4-In. Blade 402.00
Japanese, Wakizashi In Shira Saya Shinto, Suguha With Undulations, 15 1/2-In. Blade ... 546.00
Machete Blade, Silver Cap, Checkered Horn Grips, Leather Scabbard, 27 5/8-In. Blade .. 115.00
Officer's, Field & Staff, Sharkskin Grip, Tapered Blade, 38 3/4 In. 373.00
Officer's, Field, Model 1860, Steel Sheath, 34 In. 440.00
Officer's, Foot, Confederate, Floral Etching, Laurel Leaf Pommel, Leather Grip, Brass ... 3300.00
Officer's, Germany, Dress, Eagle Form Handle, Plated Curved Blade, Nazi Army 57.00
Officer's, Germany, Nazi Eagle Langet, WW II, Overall Oak Leaf Handle, Curved Blade . 747.00
Officer's, Infantry, England, Brass Gothic Hilt, Victorian, 32-In. Broad Blade 325.00
Officer's, Militia, Ivory Grip, Spreadeagle Crossguard, A.W. Spies, 1820, 38 In. 1782.00
Officer's, Naval, Nickel Narrow Blade, Black Leather Scabbard, SWD, 1912 .... 172.00
Officer's, Naval, Pearl Harbor Attack Assoc., Oak, Leaf, Acorn, Blue Leather Wrap, SWD 805.00
Officer's, Navel, Japan, Wire Wrapped Bone Grip, Brass Hilt, c.1940, 29 In. 260.00
Officer's, Rapier, Bronze Pommel, Wooden Handle, 18th Century, 30 3/4-In. Blade 340.00
Officer's, Revolutionary War, Steel, 29 1/2-In. Triangular Blade 325.00
Officer's, U.S. Cavalry, c.1860, 4 x 36 In. 330.00
Presentation, Floral Brass Hand Guard, Leather Handle, 1842, 30-In. Blade 1665.00
Saber, Brass Hilt, Wooden Handle, 33 3/4 In. 110.00
Saber, British, M, Scroll On Blade, Leather Sheath, England, 41 In. 200.00
Saber, Cavalry, 3-Branch Brass Hand Guard, Leather, Twisted Wire Handle, Civil War ... 316.00
Saber, Cavalry, 3-Branch Knuckle Guard, Leather Handle, 35 1/4-In. Blade, 1862 ...... 517.00
Saber, Cavalry, Henry Boker, Scabbard, Brass Hilt & Hanger, Leather Grip, 1860, 34 In. . 550.00
Saber, Checkered Design, Walnut, Metal Grip, Metal Hilt, Early 20th Century, 30 In. 253.00
Saber, Confederate Officer's, Marked CS, Leaves On Guard 1750.00
Saber, Double-Twisted Wire Wraps, Leather Handle, Pommel, Civil War, 36-In. Blade ... 488.00
Saber, Lion's Head Pommel & Scabbard, Embossed Wreath, Wire Wrap, 32 In. 165.00
Saber, Painted Scabbard, Ribbed Handle, Civil War, 1862, 31 1/2-In. Blade 149.00
Saber, Patton, Model 1913, Springfield Armory, 1918 .... 715.00
Saber, Scabbard, Brass Hilt, Stamped CSN & 1862, 26 1/2 In. Blade 330.00
Scimitar, Steel, 30 1/2 In. 220.00
Shamshir, 19th Century, 31-In. Blade 255.00
Trooper's, British Cavalry, 3-Bar Iron Hilt, 1827, 35 1/2-In. Blade 450.00
Turkish, Ivory Handle, Engraved Blade, Wooden Scabbard, 1927, 30 In. 145.00

SYRACUSE is a trademark used by the Onondaga Pottery of Syracuse, New York. The company was established in 1871. It is still working. The name became the Syracuse China Company in 1966. It is known for fine dinnerware and restaurant china.

Athena, Cup & Saucer 33.00
Athena, Plate, Dinner 43.00
Diane, Coffeepot, Cobalt Trim 304.00
Indian Tree, Bowl, Cereal, Pink, Scalloped 27.00
Nocturne, Bowl, Vegetable 101.00
Nocturne, Plate, Dinner 50.00
Santa Rosa, Gravy Boat 50.00
Suzanne, Cup & Saucer, Flowers, Gold Trim 42.00
Suzanne, Plate, Salad, Flowers, Gold Trim 24.00
Tom & Jerry, Eggnog Set, 6 Piece 40.00
Wayne, Platter, Maroon, Medium 88.00

TAPESTRY, PORCELAIN, see Rose Tapestry category.

TEA CADDY is the name for a small box made to hold tea leaves. In the eighteenth century, tea was very expensive and it was stored under lock and key. The first tea caddies were made with locks. By the nineteenth century, tea was more plentiful and the tea caddy was larger. Often there were two sections, one for green tea, one for black tea.

Aluminum, Tudric, For N.C. Joseph Ltd., Stylized Flowers, Leaves, 4 1/2 In. 99.00
Antler, Ivory & Sandalwood, Sarcophagus Form, Fitted Interior, 14 In. 3335.00
Biblical Scene, Slumbering Apostles, Lion Knop, Ogee Shape, 18th Century, 5 In. 928.00

Bird's-Eye Maple, Paneled Top, Fitted Interior, Ring Handles, 9 x 13 In. 488.00
Black Lacquer, Mahogany Lined Interior, Chinoiserie, Mid 19th Century, 7 x 9 1/2 In. . . 415.00
Brass Bale, Mahogany Veneer, 3 Interior Compartments, 9 3/4 In. 275.00
Brass Handle & Trim, Rosewood, 3 Compartments, Hidden Drawer, 6 1/2 In. 1085.00
Burl Walnut, Limewood & Satinwood Inlay, George III Style, Hexagonal, 5 x 6 In. 1265.00
Burnt Wood, Polychrome, Rural Winter Scene, Russia, c.1900, 7 1/2 In. 225.00
Cherry, Mahogany Banding, Chippendale, 3 Compartments, Brass Bale, 10 In. 2750.00
Crossbanded, Neoclassical & Floral, Painted, 3 Compartments, 5 3/4 x 12 In. 1092.00
Faux Tortoiseshell, Silver Mounted, England, 9 In. 600.00
Fruitwood, 2 Lidded Compartments, Ivory Handles, Key Escutcheon, 6 x 10 In. 365.00
Fruitwood, Pear Form, 18th Century, 6 1/2 In. 1380.00
Fruitwood, Pear Form, Regency, Stem & Escutcheon, England, 6 1/2 In. 1650.00
Fruitwood, Pear Form, Turned, England, 18th Century, 6 1/4 In. 5750.00
Gilt Floral, Brown Lacquer Ground, Pewter Inner Box, 13 1/4 In. 245.00
Hinged Cover, Black Lacquer, Gold Figures In Reserves, W. & F. Beakin, 5 x 8 In. 690.00
Ivory, Double, Landscape Cartouches, Floral Ground, Chinese, 5 x 9 1/4 In. 4290.00
Mahogany, 3 Tin Canisters, Brass Handle, England, 1770, 5 1/2 x 9 In. 660.00
Mahogany, Checkered Inlay, Stepped Top, Fitted Interior, 9 1/3 In. 345.00
Mahogany, George II, Hinged Lid, Fitted & Covered Interior, Brass Handles, 7 In. 300.00
Mahogany, George III, Ivory String Inlaid, Brass Ball & Claw Feet, 7 In. 425.00
Mahogany, George IV, Satinwood Border, Divided Interior, 4 1/2 x 7 1/4 In. 373.00
Mahogany, Hepplewhite, Banded Inlay, Replaced Interior, 7 5/8 In. 300.00
Mahogany, Herringbone Inlays, Ball Feet, 6 1/2 x 9 3/4 In. 385.00
Mahogany, Line Inlays, 5 1/2 x 9 1/4 In. 605.00
Mahogany, Shell Inlay, Georgian, 1790 . . . . 495.00
Mahogany, Sideboard Form, 3 Inner Compartments, c.1830, 8 In. 977.00
Mahogany Veneer, Inlay, Brass Ring Handles, 2 Compartments, 8 3/4 In. 468.00
Maple, Federal, Conch Shell Inlay, Green Ovals, 1800, 4 3/4 x 7 1/2 In. 935.00
Mother-Of-Pearl, Diamond, Fitted With Pair Of Matching Lids, 4 1/2 x 6 x 3 In. 440.00
Mother-Of-Pearl, Pair Of Lidded Compartments Interior, William IV, 6 In. 2860.00
Pine, Black Chagreen, Brass Fittings, Green Velvet Lining, 13 x 5 1/4 x 7 1/4 In. 1265.00
Porcelain, Imari, Royal Crown Derby, 5 1/4 In. 55.00
Porcelain, Landscape Scenes, Florals, Fitted Pewter Canister, Chinese Export, 4 x 7 In. . . . 517.00
Porcelain, Painted, Quatrefoil Shape, Sprigs Of Foliage, Samson, 4 1/2 In. 115.00
Quillwork, Hexagonal, Mahogany Frames, Floral & Leaf Designs, MC 1804, 5 x 8 In. . . . 2750.00
Rattan, Brass Handles, Brass Fish Motif Clasp, Oval, 9 x 6 x 6 In. 115.00
Rosewood, Bead, Reeded Design, 2 Lidded Compartments, Turned Feet, 7 x 12 In. 335.00
Rosewood, Brass Mounted, Banded, Lion Mask Handles, George IV, 6 1/2 x 12 In. 330.00
Rosewood, Federal, Brass Ring Handles, 2 Interior Compartments, 12 x 6 x 7 In. 990.00
Rosewood, Parquetry Inlaid Trim, 12 In. 275.00
Rosewood, Sarcophagus Form, Fitted Interior, Winged Scroll Feet, 8 x 12 x 6 In. 275.00
Russian Lacquer, Cover, With Horse Drawn Cart, Hound Following, 4 x 2 1/2 In. 179.00
Satinwood, George III, Hinged Rosewood Domed Top, Paper Lining, 5 x 7 1/4 In. 1150.00
Satinwood, Regency Style, 2 Hinged Compartments, Glass Bowl, 5 1/2 x 12 In. 550.00
Satinwood, Regency, Octagonal, Floral, 4 7/8 x 4 7/8 x 3 1/2 In. 745.00
Satinwood, Regency, Sarcophagus Form, Polychrome, Paw Feet, 8 x 12 x 6 In. 1035.00
Sheet Iron, Regency, Domed Cover, Black, Early 19th Century, 6 x 5 1/2 x 4 In. 137.00
Silver, Diamond Escutcheon, Apple Form, Foil Lined, 5 1/2 In. 632.00
Silver, Navette Shape, Repousse Figures, Dutch Second Standard, 19th Century, 3 In. 195.00
Silver, Repousse, Putti, Scrolled Foliage & Flowers, Detachable Cover, 4 In. 290.00
Silver, Waisted, Repousse 16th Century Scenes, Continental, 19th Century, 3 In. 220.00
Silver Plated, Cylindrical, Floral & Scroll Design, 2 Compartments, 4 Ball Feet, 6 In. . . . 145.00
Spatterware, Blue & White, 19th Century, 4 1/2 In. 130.00
Sterling Silver, Beaded Edge Cover, Foliate Scrolls, Cartouches, France, 5 In. 316.00
Sterling Silver, Mixed Metal, Basket Shape, Copper & Silver Poppies, 1875-1885 . . . . . . 1650.00
Tin, Squared Apple, 4-Footed, Divided, 19th Century, 7 In. 330.00
Tortoiseshell, Ball Finial, 2 Lidded Compartments, c.1820, 6 1/2 x 7 In. 2530.00
Tortoiseshell, Cover, Sarcophagus Form, Paktong Lining Interior, 5 7/8 x 5 In. 2640.00
Tortoiseshell, Domed Cover, Glass Beaker, Brass Ball Feet, 4 5/8 x 10 x 4 5/8 In. 2090.00
Tortoiseshell, Domed Lid, Bowfront, Ivory Ball Feet, George III, 6 x 7 x 5 In. 2420.00
Tortoiseshell, Domed Lid, Octagonal Case, Ivory Finial, 5 x 3 1/2 x 2 1/2 In. 1955.00
Tortoiseshell, Domed Lid, Pewter Strung, Single Division Case, Regency, 4 3/4 In. 2070.00
Tortoiseshell, Hinged Domed Cover, George III, Silver Strung, Ball Feet, 5 x 6 x 3 In. . . . 2760.00

Tortoiseshell, Ivory Banded, Divided Interior, Paktong Lining, 4 3/4 x 3 3/4 In. 1870.00
Tortoiseshell, Mother-Of-Pearl Floral Inlay, Georgian, c.1900, 5 3/4 x 6 1/2 In. 1980.00
Tortoiseshell, Regency, Ivory Faced, Lion Head Handles, Brass Paw Feet, 7 x 12 In. 4830.00
Tortoiseshell, Regency, Ivory Mounted, Oval, Divided Interior, 4 1/2 x 5 1/2 In. 1610.00
Tortoiseshell, Rounded Corners, Rectangular, 19th Century, 5 x 7 1/4 x 4 In. 2420.00
Tortoiseshell, Rounded Cover, Black Lacquer Ball Feet, George III, 6 x 6 1/2 In. 2640.00
Tortoiseshell, Sarcophagus Form, Hipped Lip, Ball Feet, Regency, 5 3/4 x 5 x 3 In. 1725.00
Tortoiseshell, Serpentine Sides, Velvet-Lined Interior, 8 3/4 In. 1610.00
Tortoiseshell Veneer, 2 Compartments, Bronze Ball Feet, Silver Lock Plate, 6 In. 660.00
Walnut, George III, Needlepoint Top, String Inlay, 1 Drawer, 6 x 8 x 5 1/2 In. 750.00
Walnut, Pagoda Top, Foil Lined, Crossbanded Throughout, 8 In. 402.00
Wood, Conforming Case, Crossbanded Edges, Inlaid Base, Ball Feet, 1790s, 7 x 10 In. . . . 1380.00
Wood, String Inlay, Ivory Escutcheon, 4 Paw, Fitted Interior, Bowl, 10 1/2 In. 805.00
Wood, Tunbridge Wells, Geometric Marquetry, 2 Lidded Compartments, 5 1/2 x 9 In. 632.00

TEA LEAF IRONSTONE dishes are named for their decorations. There
was a superstition that it was lucky if a whole tea leaf unfolded at the
bottom of your cup. This idea was translated into the pattern of dishes
known as *tea leaf*. By 1850, at least twelve English factories were
making this pattern, and by the 1870s, it was a popular pattern in many
countries. The tea leaf was always a luster glaze on early wares,
although now some pieces are made with a brown tea leaf.

Baker, Square, 8 In. 38.00
Bowl, Alfred Meakin, 5 x 14 3/4 In. 60.00
Bowl, Cover, Oval, Adams, 9 3/4 In. 157.00
Bowl, Leaf Center, Adams, 6 5/8 In. 20.00
Bowl, Vegetable, Cover, Gold Leaf Center, Red Cliff, Rectangular 180.00
Bowl, Vegetable, Cover, Oval, Adams 230.00
Bowl, Vegetable, Cover, Rectangular, Powell Bishop, 9 1/2 x 6 In. 135.00
Bowl, Vegetable, Gold Leaf Center, Red Cliff, Rectangular 180.00
Bowl, Vegetable, Oval, Flintridge, 9 7/8 In. 95.00
Bread Plate, Copper Trim, Wedgwood, 6 3/4 In. 25.00
Bread Plate, Gold Leaf Center, Red Cliff 24.00
Bread Plate, Red Cliff, 6 1/2 In. 22.00
Butter Chip, Gold Center Leaf, Red Cliff, 2 7/8 In. 12.00
Butter Chip, Meakin, 2 5/8 In. 30.00
Chamber Pot, Lion's Head, Mellor Taylor 175.00
Coffeepot, Cover, Leaf Center, Adams 164.00
Coffeepot, Gold Leaf Center, Red Cliff . . . . .163.00 to 180.00
Compote, Gold Leaf Center, Red Cliff, 4 1/4 In. 90.00
Creamer, Child's, Clementson . . . . *Illus* 525.00
Creamer, Flintridge 70.00
Creamer, Meakin . . . . *Illus* 195.00
Creamer, Teaberry, Clementson, Square 450.00
Cup & Saucer, Adams 40.00
Cup & Saucer, Footed, Flintridge 60.00
Cup & Saucer, Gold Leaf Center, Red Cliff . . . . .43.00 to 45.00
Cup & Saucer, Gold Luster, Flintridge 50.00
Cup & Saucer, Red Cliff, 2 7/8 In. 45.00
Cup & Saucer, White Flowers On Branch, Flintridge, 2 1/4 In. 48.00
Eggcup, Boston, Meakin 375.00
Gravy Boat, Meakin . . . . .143.00 to 190.00
Gravy Boat, Underplate, Adams 150.00
Gravy Boat, Underplate, Gold Leaf Center, Red Cliff . . . . .145.00 to 160.00
Nappy, Red Cliff 15.00
Nappy, Wedgwood, 4 3/8 In. . . . . .36.00 to 40.00
Pitcher, Adams, 5 1/4 In. 72.00
Pitcher, Alfred Meakin, 9 1/4 In. 60.00
Pitcher, Fishhook, Meakin 225.00
Pitcher, Gold Leaf Center, Red Cliff, 64 Oz., 8 1/4 In. 120.00
Pitcher, Meakin . . . . *Illus* 225.00
Pitcher, Milk, Adams 75.00
Pitcher & Bowl, Meakin 150.00

Tea Leaf Ironstone,
Creamer, Meakin;
Tea Leaf Ironstone, Creamer,
Child's, Clementson;
Tea Leaf Ironstone,
Teapot, Shaw;
Tea Leaf Ironstone, Vase,
Brush, Clementson;
Tea Leaf Ironstone,
Pitcher, Meakin

Plate, Adams, 10 1/8 In.	45.00
Plate, Gold Leaf Center, Red Cliff, 6 1/2 In.	14.00
Plate, Gold Leaf Center, Red Cliff, 8 3/8 In.	24.00
Plate, Gold Leaf Center, Red Cliff, 10 In.	45.00
Plate, Gold Luster, Flintridge, 8 3/8 In.	15.00
Plate, Leaf Center, Adams, 6 1/4 In.	13.00
Plate, Leaf Center, Adams, 7 3/4 In.	18.00
Plate, Leaf Center, Adams, 10 1/8 In.	38.00
Plate, Meakin, 7 7/8 In.	34.00
Plate, Meakin, 8 3/4 In.	40.00
Plate, Meakin, 10 In.	90.00
Plate, Wedgwood, 6 3/4 In.	26.00
Plate, Wedgwood, 8 3/4 In.	56.00
Platter, Empress, Adams, 13 1/2 In.	94.00
Platter, Empress, Oval, Adams	198.00
Platter, Gold Leaf Center, Red Cliff, 11 3/8 In.	125.00 to 140.00
Platter, Meakin, 10 In.	90.00 to 123.00
Platter, Oval, Gold Luster, Flintridge, 14 In.	75.00
Platter, Oval, Leaf Center, Adams, 11 1/2 In.	110.00
Platter, Oval, Leaf Center, Adams, 13 1/2 In.	92.00
Platter, Oval, Wedgwood, 16 3/8 In.	260.00 to 280.00
Platter, Powell Bishop, 16 x 11 3/4 In.	115.00
Platter, Rectangular, Meakin, 12 In.	135.00 to 150.00
Platter, Rectangular, Meakin, 15 7/8 In.	190.00 to 200.00
Platter, Rectangular, Wedgwood, 12 1/4 In.	200.00
Relish, Handle, Powell Bishop, 7 1/4 x 4 1/2 In.	30.00
Relish, Teaberry, Quartered Rose Style, J. Furnival	675.00
Saltshaker, Flintridge	26.00 to 36.00
Shaving Mug, Chinese Shape, Shaw	80.00
Soap Dish, Embossed Lily-Of-The-Valley, Shaw	525.00
Soap Dish, Ridged, Square, Wedgwood, 3 Piece	130.00
Soup, Dish, Adams	45.00
Soup, Dish, Rim, Leaf Center, Adams, 8 In.	28.00
Soup, Dish, Tea Leaf Center, Wedgwood, 9 In.	60.00
Sugar, Bamboo Shape, Meakin	65.00
Sugar, Cover, Powell Bishop	85.00
Sugar, Pagoda Shape, Burgess	85.00
Sugar & Creamer, Adams	90.00
Teapot, Cover, Leaf, Adams	160.00
Teapot, Embossed Hanging Leaves, Shaw	600.00
Teapot, Niagara Shape, Walley	700.00
Teapot, Shaw	*Illus* 400.00
Tureen, Cover, Wedgwood	409.00
Tureen, Sauce, Stand & Ladle, Red Cliff	175.00
Tureen, Wedgwood	450.00
Vase, Brush, Clementson	*Illus* 350.00

TECO is the mark used on the art pottery line made by the American Terra Cotta and Ceramic Company of Terra Cotta and Chicago, Illinois. The company was an offshoot of the firm founded by William D. Gates in 1881. The Teco line was first made in 1885 but was not sold commercially until 1902. It continued in production until 1922. Over 500 designs were made in a variety of colors, shapes, and glazes. The company closed in 1930.

Bowl, Green Matte Glaze, 4 1/2 In.	143.00
Bowl, Green Matte Glaze, Floral Design At Top, 9 1/2 In.	385.00
Jardiniere, Green Matte Glaze, Rounded Form, 4 Flared Feet, 16 x 21 In.	1650.00
Jardiniere, Hemispheric, Green Matte Glaze, 4 Buttressed Legs, 7 x 11 In.	6600.00
Pitcher, Green Matte Glaze, Wishbone Handle, 9 x 3 1/2 In.	1100.00
Planter, Applied Floral, Unglazed, 17 x 27 In., Pair	1100.00
Vase, Allover Beige To Pink Matte Glaze, Open Handles, 5 1/2 In.	520.00
Vase, Allover Green Matte Glaze, 2 Handles, Signed, 11 1/2 In.	1100.00
Vase, Allover Green Matte Glaze, 3 Sides, Signed, 8 In.	1045.00
Vase, Allover Green Matte Glaze, Open Handles, Signed, 4 In.	660.00
Vase, Architectural Form, Open Handles, Green Matte Glaze, Signed, 8 In.	1980.00
Vase, Beaker Shape, Buttressed Handles, Smooth Green Matte Glaze, Stamped, 8 x 5 In.	2640.00
Vase, Bottle Shape, Aventurine, Black, Gold & Amber Crystalline Flambe, 10 1/2 In.	2970.00
Vase, Brown Matte Glaze, 2 Closed Handles At Shoulder, 6 In.	1210.00
Vase, Brown Matte Glaze, Shouldered Form, 4 1/2 In.	495.00
Vase, Brown Matte Glaze, Tapered, 4 In.	400.00
Vase, Buttressed Tulip Shape, Green Matte Glaze, F. Moreau, 12 x 5 In.	4125.00
Vase, Embossed Tulip, 4 Vertical Buttresses, Green Matte Glaze, Signed, 11 1/2 In.	2530.00
Vase, Embossed, Leaf Blades, Flared Rim, Green Matte Glaze, Stamped, 12 x 4 In.	11000.00
Vase, Embossed, Lotuses, Green Matte Glaze, Stamped, 11 1/2 x 5 1/2 In.	7425.00
Vase, Flaring Lip Over 4 Vertical Buttresses, Heavy Charcoaling, Signed, 10 1/2 In.	2420.00
Vase, Gourd Shape, Buttressed Handles, Oriental Floral, Green Matte Glaze, 6 1/2 In.	2420.00
Vase, Gray Matte Glaze, Cylindrical Neck, 13 1/4 x 5 1/4 In.	1650.00
Vase, Gray Matte Glaze, Cylindrical, 6 In.	412.00
Vase, Green & Charcoal Green & Charcoal Matte Glaze, Squat Base, Stamped, 16 In.	1320.00
Vase, Green Matte Glaze, 2 Buttresses, 6 1/2 In.	495.00
Vase, Green Matte Glaze, 4 1/2 In.	385.00
Vase, Green Matte Glaze, 4 Curled Leaves At Rim, 6 x 9 1/2 In.	2640.00
Vase, Green Matte Glaze, 4 Lobes, Oval, Stamped, 5 1/2 x 3 1/2 In.	990.00
Vase, Green Matte Glaze, Bulbous, 4 1/2 In.	415.00
Vase, Green Matte Glaze, Charcoal Accents, 2 Handles, 9 In.	1320.00
Vase, Green Matte Glaze, Charcoal Accents, Split & Open Handle, 8 1/2 In.	3850.00
Vase, Green Matte Glaze, Charcoal Glaze, Leaves On Foot, Stamped, 18 x 16 In. . . . . *Illus*	66000.00
Vase, Green Matte Glaze, Impressed Signature, 16 1/2 In.	825.00
Vase, Green Matte Glaze, Open Handles At Top, Fritz Albert, 14 1/2 In.	18700.00
Vase, Green Matte Glaze, Spherical, 4 Flared Buttressed Feet, Stamped, 6 1/2 x 5 1/2 In.	7700.00
Vase, Green Matte Glaze, Tapered, 9 In.	825.00
Vase, Green Matte Glaze, Uneven Top, Bulbous Bottom, Signed, 5 In.	605.00
Vase, Green Smooth Glaze, Dimpled Sides, Spherical, 2 3/4 In.	275.00

Never use chlorine bleach on ironstone dishes. It will cause the glaze to flake off.

Teco, Vase, Green Matte Glaze, Charcoal Glaze, Leaves On Foot, Stamped, 18 x 16 In.

Vase, Green, Charcoal Matte Glaze, Dimpled, 3 3/4 x 3 1/4 In. 605.00
Vase, Pale Green Matte Glaze, Oval, 4 1/2 x 3 3/4 In. 440.00
Vase, Pink To Lavender Matte Glaze, 4 Cutout Handles At Top, Signed, 11 In. 6050.00
Vase, Rocket Ship, Green Matte Glaze, 8 1/2 x 3 3/4 In. 4125.00
Vase, Rocket Ship, Mauve Matte Glaze, 4 Swag Legs, 9 x 4 In. 7700.00
Vase, Seafoam Green Glaze, 4 Angular Handles, Beaker Shape, 1910, 7 5/16 In. 1840.00
Vase, Tulip Design, Green Matte Glaze, Charcoal, William Dodd, 11 In. 3575.00
Vase, Tulip, Green Matte Glaze, 4 Buttresses, 12 1/4 x 5 In. 4950.00
Wall Pocket, Stylized Leaves, Green Matte Glaze, Stamped, 16 3/4 x 6 1/2 In. 2145.00

TEDDY BEARS were named for a president of the United States. The
first teddy bear was a cuddly toy said to be inspired by a hunting trip
made by Teddy Roosevelt in 1902. Morris and Rose Michtom started
selling their stuffed bears as *teddy bears* and the name stayed. The
Michtoms founded the Ideal Novelty and Toy Company. The German
version of the teddy bear was made about the same time by the Steiff
Company. There are many types of teddy bears and all are collected.
The old ones are being reproduced. Other bears are listed in the Toy
section.

Bing, Mohair, Excelsior Stuffing, Long Arms, Jointed, c.1907, 16 In. 2300.00
Columbia, Laughing Roosevelt, Mohair, Yellow, 2 Teeth, Jointed, 1907, 18 In. 1265.00
Gebruder Sussenguth, Peter, Mohair, Teeth, Composition, Papers, Jointed, 13 In. 1725.00
Ideal, Blond Mohair, Excelsior Stuffing, Jointed, Glass Eyes, 12 In. 632.00
Ideal, Mohair, Gold, Excelsior Stuffing, Jointed, Glass Eyes, c.1919, 23 In. 230.00
Ideal, Mohair, Yellow, Excelsior Stuffing, Jointed, 21 In. 230.00
Knickerbocker, Polar, Plush, White, Movable Limbs, Plastic Eyes, 1940s, 18 In. 250.00
Lee, Plush, Brown, Blue Denim Jeans, Red Shirt, 12 In. 31.00
Lee, Plush, Light Brown, Blue Denim Bib Overalls, 12 In. 31.00
Lee, Plush, Tan, Wearing Lee Brand Indigo Denim Bib Overalls, 14 In. 21.00
Mohair, Blond Bristle, Hump, Pronounced Snout, Replaced Eyes, 21 In. 440.00
Mohair, Blond, Excelsior Stuffing, Jointed, Steel Eyes, c.1906, 10 In. 175.00
Mohair, Blond, Teeth, Jointed, Steel Eyes, c.1908, 11 In. 748.00
Mohair, Cream, Embroidered, Jointed, Excelsior Stuffing, Steel Eyes, 13 1/2 In. 175.00
Mohair, Ginger, Felt Pads, Excelsior Stuffing, Jointed, Steel Eyes, c.1919, 16 1/2 In. 805.00
Mohair, Gold, Clipped Muzzle, Swivel Head, 24 In. 172.00
Mohair, Gold, Felt Paw Pads, Embroidered Nose, Articulated, Glass Eyes, 21 In. 275.00
Mohair, Gold, Horizontally Stitched Nose, c.1910, 7 In. 690.00
Mohair, Gold, Straw Stuffed, Pointed Snout, Hump Back, Swivel Head, 10 1/2 In. 341.00
Mohair, Golden Brown, Embroidered, Jointed, Glass Eyes, 1920s, 24 In. 345.00
Mohair, Long, Yellow, Embroidered, Excelsior Stuffing, Jointed, England, 13 In. 260.00
Schuco, Mohair, Beige, Yes/No, Embroidered, Felt Pads, 1950s, 21 In. 805.00
Schuco, Mohair, Gold, Musical, Yes/No, Germany, 16 In. 2000.00
Schuco, Mohair, On Roller Skates, Windup, Embroidered, Overalls, Germany, 8 In. 490.00
Schuco, Mohair, Yellow, Bellhop, Yes/No, Excelsior Stuffing, Jointed, c.1923, 15 In. 1725.00
Schuco, Mohair, Yellow, Embroidered, Felt Pads, Jointed, Glass Eyes, 1920s, 12 In. 345.00
Schuco, Mohair, Yellow, Fully Jointed, Steel Eyes, Yes-No, Excelsior Stuffing, 12 In. 460.00
Smokey, Bendie, Brown, Yellow Hat, Blue Jeans, Advertising Council, 1987, 5 In. 25.00
Smokey, Plush, Brown, Blue Denim Jeans, Smokey Belt, Hat, 13 In. 40.00
Steiff, Beige, Button & Tag, 13 In. 895.00
Steiff, Cinnamon Plush, Humped Back, Excelsior, Swivel Joints, 1910, 17 In. 2875.00
Steiff, Embroidered, Excelsior Stuffing, Gold, Jointed, Steel Eyes, c.1906, 13 In. 2185.00
Steiff, Groaner, Leather Collar, On Wheels, Hump, c.1940, 14 In. 575.00
Steiff, Growler, Golden, Ear Button, 1905, 17 In. 3160.00
Steiff, Mohair, Blond, Excelsior Stuffing, Jointed, Shoebutton Eyes, c.1906, 11 In. 375.00
Steiff, Mohair, Cream, Embroidered, Felt Pads, Jointed, Steel Eyes, c.1906, 13 In. 1035.00
Steiff, Mohair, Felt Pads, Excelsior Stuffing, Jointed, c.1951, 11 1/2 In. 200.00
Steiff, Mohair, Ginger, Embroidered, Jointed, Steel Eyes, c.1905, 10 In. 1150.00
Steiff, Mohair, Gold, Flesh Felt Pads, Hump, Hinged Arms & Legs, 1950s, 12 In. 5170.00
Steiff, Mohair, Gold, Voice Box, Ear Button, Articulated Limbs, Glass Eyes, 29 In. 935.00
Steiff, Mohair, Golden Tan, Beige Felt Paw Pads, Button, Label, 16 In. 247.00
Steiff, Mohair, Tan, Embroidered, Excelsior Stuffing, Jointed, Ear Button, 13 1/2 In. 230.00
Steiff, Mohair, Tan, Plush, Swivel Head, Shoebutton Eyes, 10 In. 650.00

Steiff, Molly Bear, Seated, Labels, 14 In. 220.00
Steiff, Mother & Baby, Signed, 1981 .... 550.00
Steiff, Tan, Stitched Claws, Flossed Nose, Shoebutton Eyes, 9 1/2 In. 3495.00
Steiff, Zotty, Long Fur, Open Mouth, Fully Jointed, 1950s, 11 In. 86.00
Tara, Mohair, Gold, Open/Close Mouth, Jointed, Plastic Eyes, Ireland, 1950s, 16 In. 175.00
Yellow Long Hair, Jointed, Glass Eyes, 16 In. 350.00

TELEPHONES are wanted by collectors if the phones are old enough or unusual enough. The first telephone may have been made in Havana, Cuba, in 1849, but it was not patented. The first publicly demonstrated phone was used in Frankfurt, Germany, in 1860. The phone made by Alexander Graham Bell was shown at the Centennial Exhibition in Philadelphia in 1876, but it was not until 1877 that the first private phones were installed. Collectors today want all types of old phones, phone parts, and advertising. Even recent figural phones are popular.

101 Dalmatians 75.00
Almanac, Bell Telephone, 1924, 36 Pages 27.00
Alvin Chipmunk ....40.00 to 75.00
Booth, Survived Bombing Of London, Dark Brown, 101 x 36 x 36 1/2 In. 2200.00
Booth, Walnut, Seat, Light, Fan, Folding Glass Door 1200.00
Bozo The Clown, Kash N' Gold Ltd., 1988 .... 30.00
Buzz Lightyear, Brooktel, 1996 .... 80.00
Cabbage Patch Girl, Coleco Mfg., 1984 ....85.00 to 130.00
Charlie Tuna, Hong Kong, 1987 ....55.00 to 80.00
French, Rotary Dial, Painted, Converted To Modern Use, c.1920 .... 172.00
Garfield, Tyco Industries, 1978 .... 40.00
Gumby, 1980s 85.00
Kellogg, Wall, Oak, Magneto 150.00
Kellogg, Wooden Subset, Magneto 35.00
KISS, Neon, Black Plastic, Figures Light Up & Play Music, Box 98.00
Manhattan, Wall, Oak, Steerhorn Hook, Small 150.00
Northern Electric & Mfg. Co. Ltd., Stick, Brass 90.00
Paperweight, American Telephone & Telegraph Cable 35.00
Paperweight, C & P Telephone 175.00
Paperweight, New York Telephone Co. 85.00
Paperweight, Yellow Pages 90.00
Poster, The Telephone Story, 100th Year, 1876-1976, 24 x 28 In. 25.00
Sign, AT&T Bell System, White Lettering, Black Bell, Square, 1940, 11 In. 38.00
Sign, Bell System, Public Telephone, Porcelain, Round, 7 In. 60.00
Sign, Bell Telephone Co., Stop Accidents, Porcelain, Round, 5 5/8 In. 200.00
Sign, Bell Telephone Company Of Canada, Porcelain, Flange, 6 x 10 In. 155.00
Sign, Bell Telephone, Porcelain, 2 Sides, 12 1/4 In. 165.00
Sign, Illinois Bell Telephone Co., Porcelain, 2 Sides, Bracket, 19 1/2 x 21 1/2 In. 415.00
Sign, Independent, Telephone Pay Station, Porcelain, Flange, 18 x 8 In. 440.00
Sign, New England Telephone & Telegraph Co., Flange, 2 Sides, Blue, 16 x 16 In. 295.00
Sign, Public Telephone Sign, 5 1/2 x 12 1/2 In. 65.00
Sign, Public, Across Top Of Sign, Flange, 2 Sides, Blue, 20 x 20 In. 350.00
Toy, Truck, Bell Telephone, 1950s, 7 In. 60.00
Toy, Truck, Bell Telephone, Cast Iron, Hubley 1475.00
Toy, Truck, Bell Telephone, Pole Trailer & Auger, Cast Iron, Hubley, 10 In. ......750.00 to 798.00
Toy, Truck, Telephone Maintenance, Buddy L, No. 450, Green, Ladder, 2 Poles, Box 345.00
Toy, Truck, Telephone Repair, Friction, Lupor, Box, 11 In. 395.00
Toy, Truck, Telephone Service, Marx, 19 In. 200.00
Tray, Telephone Pioneers Of America, 1875-1911, Metal, Applied Enamel Medallion 12.50
Western Electric, Candlestick, 4-Line Intercom, c.1910 .... 275.00
Western Electric, Candlestick, Brass Plated, Bakelite Mouthpiece, 1910s, 13 In. 110.00
Western Electric, Candlestick, Pay, Coin Box, Brass, Black, Bakelite Receiver, c.1904 .. 275.00
Western Electric, Loudspeaking, 24-Volt Terminals, Mounted To Horn, 31 In. 375.00
Western Electric, Pink Princess, Transformer, With Bell Box, 1962 .... 50.00
Western Electric, Subscriber, Coin Collector, Nickel 600.00
Western Electric, Wall, No. 354, Hotel, Metal Dial, F-1 Handset, 1950s ....45.00 to 100.00
White Princess, Rotary, 1959 .... 7.00

TELEVISION sets are twentieth-century collectibles. Although the first television transmission took place in England in 1925, collectors find few sets which pre-date 1946. The first sets had only five channels, but by 1949 the additional UHF channels were included. The first color television set became available in 1951.

Kays Halbert M921, Wooden Body, Plexiglas Knobs, 11-In. Screen, 38 x 20 x 29 In.	500.00
Pilot Radio, No. 4095, 1939, 3-In. Screen	375.00
RCA, Model TRU, Push Button Radio, Wooden Body, 6-In. Screen, 43 x 28 x 20 In.	800.00

TEPLITZ refers to art pottery manufactured by a number of companies in the Teplitz-Turn area of Bohemia during the late nineteenth and early twentieth centuries. The Amphora Porcelain Works and the Alexandra Works were two of these companies.

Bowl, Flowers Molded Rim, 8 In.	28.00
Ewer, Lilies, Ivory To Green, Gilt, Handle, Turntemitz, Bohemia, Amphora, 13 3/4 In. . . .	75.00
Figurine, Hunting Owl, On Craggy Branch, Mossy Green, Marked, Amphora, 12 In.	1035.00
Figurine, Woman Holding 2 Baskets, Pale Green Dress, Marked, Amphora, 15 1/2 In. . . .	315.00
Plate, Russian Czar, Polychrome, Marked, Amphora, 8 1/4 In.	165.00
Statue, Peasant Girl, Wooden Shoes, Marked, Amphora, 24 In.	440.00
Vase, Applied Berries & Leaves, Blue Ground, Cream, Marked, Amphora, 9 1/4 In.	460.00
Vase, Applied Berries & Leaves, Blue Ground, Cream, Marked, Amphora, 12 1/8 In.	520.00
Vase, Art Nouveau Woman's Face, Bohemia, Marked, Amphora, 8 In.	1540.00
Vase, Art Nouveau Woman's Face, Marked, Amphora, 6 In.	1210.00
Vase, Blue & Ivory Crystalline Glaze, Buff, Bronze Mount, Handles, 1900, 18 1/2 In.	1150.00
Vase, Dragon Encircling Vessel, Crab Grasping Dragon's Tail, Marked, 1910s, 21 1/2 In. .	2185.00
Vase, Enameled Mary & Baby Jesus, Gray Sponged Luster Ground, Stellmacher, 8 In. . . .	245.00
Vase, Flower Buds At Rim, Trailing Vine Handles, Early 20th Century, 7 1/4 In.	172.00
Vase, Flower Extended In Hand, Handkerchief In Other, Gold Gilt, 12 In.	325.00
Vase, Golden Brown Tree Limbs, Deep Brown, Marked, Amphora, 10 In.	231.00
Vase, Green & Blue Glaze, Textured, Shouldered Form, Gilt, Amphora, 10 In.	580.00
Vase, Maiden Portrait, Footed, Egg Shape, Marked, Amphora, 1900, 10 1/2 In., Pair	6900.00
Vase, Molded With Leaves, Green Lilies, Cream, Open Handles, Amphora, 13 In., Pair . . .	402.00
Vase, Mottled Blue, Green, Rose, Columns, Baluster, Marked, Amphora, 1900, 14 In.	1610.00
Vase, Painted, Woman Against A Forest Glade, 4 Sides, Art Nouveau, Stamped, 8 1/2 In. .	1320.00
Vase, Pink Poppies, Green Leaves, Brown, Beige, Handles, Marked, Amphora, 16 In.	247.00
Vase, Sea Life, Octopus Capturing Crab, Blue, Yellow, Marked, Amphora, 19 In., Pair . . .	2875.00
Vase, Spider Web Top, Jewels, Bees & Butterflies Bottom, Marked, 7 1/2 In.	935.00
Vase, Stylized Arts & Crafts Landscape, Polychrome, Gold, Gourd Shape, Marked, 7 In. .	143.00
Vase, Urn Shape, Floral Center, Hand Painted, Textured Neck, 2 Handles, Marked, 14 In. .	275.00
Vase, Woman Portrait, Bottle Shape, Marked, Amphora, 5 1/2 x 3 3/4 In.	440.00
Vase, Woman's Bust, Applied Bosses, Egg Shape, Marked, Amphora, 1900, 6 1/2 In.	1840.00
Vase, Woman's Bust, Frosted Eagle Head, Egg Shape, Marked, Amphora, 1900, 10 3/4 In.	3160.00
Vase, Woman's Head, Flowing Hair, Blossoms, Ocher, Art Nouveau, Handles, 13 In.	440.00
Vase, Yellow Flowers, Olive Ground, Tear Shape, Handles, 17 x 12 1/2 In.	1760.00

TERRA-COTTA is a special type of pottery. It ranges from pale orange to dark reddish-brown in color. The color comes from the clay, which is fired but not always glazed in the finished piece.

Bowl, Serving, Blue, Green Glaze, France, 4 x 12 1/2 In., 5 Piece	316.00
Bust, Donatello, Bronze Patina, 19th Century, 15 1/2 x 16 x 10 In.	1200.00
Bust, Of A Maiden, Adorned With Poppies At Her Chest, Julien Causse, 17 1/2 In.	575.00
Bust, Smiling Chinese Coolie, Marked, Jean Mich, 20th Century, 15 3/4 In.	690.00
Figurine, Bulldog, Bemused Look, Sitting On Hind Legs, Continental, 20 In., Pair	3738.00
Figurine, Chinese Figure, Opal Set In Headdress, Wooden Base, 13 1/2 In.	22.00
Figurine, Dog, Lying Down, 26 In.	3000.00
Figurine, Dwarf Holding Bottle & Cup, 22 1/2 In.	1540.00
Figurine, Infant Jesus, Nativity Manger, Italian, 3 In.	1265.00
Figurine, Model Of Hebes, Holding Ewer & Bowl, Circular Plinth, 32 3/4 In.	7530.00
Figurine, Putti, Seated On Rock, 13 1/2 In., Pair	258.00
Figurine, Robed Classical Maiden, P. Ipsen Kiobenn, 10 1/4 In.	330.00
Jar, Confit, Handles, c.1890, 14 1/2 x 9 In.	135.00
Jar, Etruscan Style, Classical Borders With Allegories, Italy, 9 3/4 In., Pair	3080.00

Jar, Hunt Scene, Transfer Design, 19th Century, 4 1/4 In., Pair 57.00
Jardiniere, Raised Procession Of Bacchantes, Lion Head Handles, Italy, 15 In. 1495.00
Planter, Beaded Design, Italy, 14 x 17 x 11 3/4 In. 200.00
Planter, Bird, Animal & Floral Design, Italy, 8 x 13 1/2 x 8 1/8 In. 200.00
Planter, Bird, Animal & Floral Design, Italy, 9 3/8 In. 85.00
Planter, Classical Design, Italy, 10 1/2 x 15 x 10 1/2 In. 85.00
Planter, Face & Swag Design, Italy, 7 1/2 x 17 1/2 x 8 3/4 In. 200.00
Planter, Face & Swag Design, Italy, 8 3/4 x 18 1/4 x 11 1/4 In. 145.00
Planter, Floral Medallions & Beaded Swag, Trapezoidal, Italy, 14 x 18 x 15 In. 260.00
Plaque, Allegorical Scene, Venus Attended By Amorini, Floral Border, 24 In. 373.00
Plaque, Morning & Evening, Brick Red Ground, Circular, 5 1/4 In., Pair 605.00
Plaque, Raised Allegorical Figures, Brick Red Ground, 9 x 8 3/4 & 7 x 18 In., Pair 1320.00
Sculpture, Art Deco Woman, Sirkka Ahlskog, 24 In. 410.00
Tile, Mediterranean Design, Blues, White Glaze, Incised Espana, 8 In. 10.00
Urn, Garden, Female Faces As Handles, Baluster, Italy, 28 3/4 In., Pair 690.00

TEXTILES listed here include many types of printed fabrics and table
and household linens. Some other textiles will be found under Clothing, Coverlet, Quilt, Rug, etc.

Banner, Side Show, Snake & Contortionist, Man Killer, 15 x 10 Ft. 2070.00
Banquet Cloth, Crocheted, Ecru, Provenance, 90 x 144 In. 350.00
Bed Cloth, Floral, Chintz, 104 x 126 In. 1430.00
Bed Cloth, Palm Trees, Chintz, 78 x 97 In. 550.00
Bedspread, Candlewick, Pot Of Flowers, Tied Lace Fringe, White On White, 96 In. 440.00
Bedspread, Crocheted, Diamond Block, 1966, Full Size 110.00
Bedspread, Crocheted, Round Pillow Cover, Ivory Color 137.00
Bedspread, Palm & Pheasant, Quilted Chintz, Twill Binding, Early 19th Century, 110 In. .. 2070.00
Bell Pull, Aubusson, Fruiting Foliage, Silk Back, 73 In. 172.00
Blanket, Geometric Design, Pendleton, c.1920, 42 x 72 In. 65.00
Blanket, Glacier Park, Pendleton, c.1920, 60 x 84 In. 100.00
Blanket, Homespun, Star Center, Women Surrounded By Pine Trees, 99 x 63 In. 335.00
Blanket, Linsey-Woolsey, Indigo, Light Blue Back, Clam Shell Borders, 88 x 99 In. 3080.00
Blanket, Saddle, Military, Cavalry, Dark Blue, Yellow Trim, Yellow Star, 32 x 23 In. 1430.00
Blanket, Trapper Point, Wool, Red, Black Stripe Near Ends, Full Size 75.00
Blanket, Wool, Green & Black Plaid, Fringe, Pendleton, 36 x 60 In. 21.00
Buggy Robe, Chase, Foxhead Design 85.00
Cloth, Ceremonial, Hand Woven, Sumbawa 288.00
Cushion, Aubusson Tapestry Fragment, Trelliswork, Birds, France, 1900, 24 In., Pair 1150.00
Cushion, Beauvais Tapestry Fragment, 18th Century Style, Silk Fringe, 17 In., Pair 1150.00
Drapes, Geometric Shapes, Chartreuse, Violet, Peach, Salmon Ground, Lined, 1950s 140.00
Flag, American, 15 Stars, Cotton Stars, Hand Sewn, Wool, Grommets, 30 x 60 In. 2990.00
Flag, American, 16 Stars, Double-Faced 6 Point Stars, Grommets, c.1800, 37 x 66 In. 4600.00
Flag, American, 20 Stars, Double-Faced Stars And Grommets, 38 1/2 x 53 1/2 In. 4312.00
Flag, American, 36 Stars, Annin & Company, N.Y., 1865, 23 x 37 In. 259.00
Flag, American, 46 Stars, Silk 100.00
Flag, Center Star, Both Sides, Civil War, Woven Linen, 18 3/4 x 24 1/2 In. 260.00
Flag, Confederate, Louisiana Artillery, New Orleans, Red Silk, 25 1/2 x 19 1/2 In. 990.00
Flag, Parade, 29 Stars, 1848 .... 1650.00
Flag, Signal, Cheesecloth, Red & White, Germany, 1930s, On 3-Ft. Pole, 10 x 16 In. 50.00
Fragment, The Apotheosis Of Franklin, Brown, Cotton Ground, Frame, 27 x 16 In. 170.00
Handkerchief, Buffalo Bill Show, Indian Motif, Silk, 1910s, 27 x 28 1/2 In. 367.00
Handkerchief, Souvenir Of France, Lace & Silk, Embroidered 1919 .... 25.00
Hanging, Bed, Tree Of Life, Birds, Flowers On Linen, Cotton Weave, Crewelwork, 87 In. 2645.00
Mat, Hooked, Winter Village Scene, 10 x 12 In. 77.00
Needlework, 3 Children & Dog By Pond, Walnut Veneer Frame, 28 x 27 In. 225.00
Needlework, Embroidery, Bouquet, Silk, Gilt Frame, 18th Century, 10 x 12 In. 66.00
Needlework, Roman Warrior Leaving Family, Silk, Frame, 18th Century, 19 x 22 In. 550.00
Needlework, Silk Panel, House, Figures, Flower Border, Ogee Frame, 16 1/2 x 27 1/2 In. .. 1265.00
Needlework, Silk, Memorial Picture, Miss Olive Moors, Early 1800s, 17 1/2 x 17 1/2 In. .. 2300.00
Panel, Canvas, Painted, Woman On Throne, Monkeys, 86 x 51 In. 3735.00
Panel, Needlepoint, Petit Point, Cavalier, Drumming Boy, Victorian, Frame, 38 x 31 In. .. 1210.00
Panel, Noble Figures Within A Garden, Fruit Trees, Silk, Matted, Frame, 40 x 60 In. 7475.00
Panel, Schumacher Polychrome, Apple Blossom, Silk Ball Tassel, 44 x 82 In., Pair 25.00

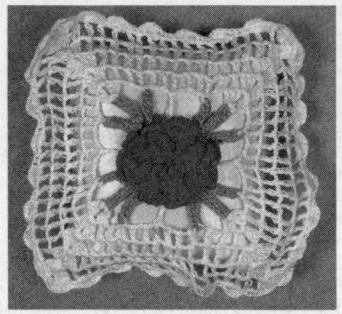

Textile, Sachet Pillow, Crocheted,
Heart, Yellow, Ribbons, 4 x 3 1/4 In.

Textile, Sachet Pillow, Crocheted, Red
Rose, Satin Back, 4 3/4 In.

Panel, Silk Damask, Allover Adam Design, Putti, Celadon, Fringe, 30 x 118 In., Pair	520.00
Panel, Silk, Embroidered, Birds On Cherry Blossom Branch, Chinese, Frame, 27 x 19 In.	63.00
Panel, Tapestry, Aubusson, Cream Ground, Flowers, 99 x 83 In., Pair	6875.00
Panel, Toile, Putti, Classical Urn, Ribbon & Garland Cartouche, 62 x 80 In., Pair	85.00
Pillow, Blue Floral, Embroidered, Linen, 20 x 12 In.	220.00
Pillow, Dragonflies & Water Lilies, Painted & Embroidered, Linen, 20 x 15 In.	770.00
Pillow, Linen, Embroidered Floral, Arts & Crafts Style, 17 x 21 In.	770.00
Pillow, Peach, Striped, Silk, Applied Velvet Crest, Embroidery, Gold Tassels, 17 x 16 In.	460.00
Pillow, Petit Point, Floral Sprays, Scroll Border, Pale Pink Fringe, 17 In., 3 Piece	3450.00
Pillow, Petit Point, Rosette In Center, Imperial Fritilaria, 19th Century, 21 x 20 In.	1840.00
Pillow, Velour, Embroidery, Flowers, Semiprecious Gems, Indo-Persia, Round, 19 In.	280.00
Pillow, Velvet, Damask, Tapestry, Applied Rosette Needlework, 26 x 18 1/2 In., Set Of 3	1840.00
Pillow Cover, Mohair, Red, Embroidered, Water Lilies, Arts & Crafts Style, 18 x 24 In.	330.00
Potholder, Crocheted, Large Star Center, Square	150.00
Runner, Embroidered, Butterflies, Macrame & Beadwork Trim, Linen, 17 x 58 In.	385.00
Runner, Embroidered, Stylized Leaves, Geometric Border, Arts & Crafts, 48 In.	220.00
Runner, Embroidery & Macrame, Heavy Linen, 88 x 23 In.	770.00
Runner, Needlepoint, Bouquets, Scrolls, Beige Field, Turquoise Border, 105 x 50 1/2 In.	1100.00
Sachet Pillow, Crocheted, Heart, Yellow, Ribbons, 4 x 3 1/4 In. *Illus*	11.00
Sachet Pillow, Crocheted, Red Rose, Satin Back, 4 3/4 In. *Illus*	6.00
Sash, Needlework, 2 Birds In Tree, Oriental, Matted, Frame, 41 x 18 In.	110.00
Seat Cover, Aubusson, Pastoral Panel, Louis XV Style, Silk, Wool, France, 61 x 12 In.	690.00
Sleeping Bag, Dukes Of Hazzard, Warner Bros., American Bag Corp. Lt., 1980	25.00
Table Mat, Embroidered, Painted, Daisies, Crocheted Edge, Arts & Crafts, Round, 8 In.	140.00
Tablecloth, Cotton, Embroidered, Roses, Red & Green On Black, Round, 24 In.	220.00
Tablecloth, Crocheted, White Medallions Of Gray Flowers, Ecru, 63 x 107 In.	93.00
Tablecloth, Cutwork, Embroidered, Lace, White, Linen, 24 Napkins	245.00
Tablecloth, Homespun, Red, White, Blue, 44 x 80 In.	275.00
Tablecloth, Jacquard Woven, Floral Pattern, Burgundy, Knotted Fringe, 54 x 56 In.	245.00
Tablecloth, Linen, Cutwork & Lace Embroidery, Italy, 108 x 69 In.	385.00
Tablecloth, Linen, Cutwork Flowers, Machine Stitched Embroidery, White, 106 In.	105.00
Tablecloth, Linen, Embroidered Poppies & Bees, Oval, 28 x 40 In.	550.00
Tablecloth, Linen, Embroidered Scarabs, Crocheted Lace Edge, Arts & Crafts, 30 In.	193.00
Tablecloth, Linen, Embroidered Water Lilies, Round, Arts & Crafts Style, 40 In.	330.00
Tablecloth, Linen, Floral & Bow Pattern, Organdy, Ireland, c.1960, 68 x 106 In.	92.00
Tablecloth, Linen, Painted & Embroidered, Poppies, 25 In.	550.00
Tablecloth, Linen, Painted & Embroidered, Yellow Poppies, Lace Trim, Round, 24 In.	220.00
Tablecloth, Linen, Red & White, Fern & Leaf Border, 62 x 83 In.	38.00
Tablecloth, Linen, Scroll Pattern, Damask, Ireland, c.1960, 68 x 104 In.	69.00
Tablecloth, Napkins, Linen, Lace, Cutwork, Embroidered, Ecru, 65 x 101 In., 13 Piece	355.00
Tablecloth, Napoleon III, American Indian Hunting Buffaloes, Fringe, 64 x 64 In.	175.00
Tablecloth, Silk, Gold, Red, Fuchsia, Blue, Green Sari Fragments, 96 x 108 In.	5175.00
Tablecloth, Silk, Green, Gold, Silver, Red, Fuchsia Sari Fragments, 84 x 10 In.	5465.00
Tablecloth, Silk, Maroon, Fuchsia, Silver Sari Fragments, 75 x 53 In.	4315.00

Tapestry, Aubusson, Couple In Central Wreath Medallion, 18th Century, 101x 61 In. 6900.00
Tapestry, Aubusson, General On Horseback, Trumpeting Angel, Floral Border, 110 In. ... 4887.00
Tapestry, Aubusson, Trumpeting Angel, General On Horse, 17th Century, 112 x 55 In. ... 4885.00
Tapestry, Bolton Abbey, Under Glass, Oak Frame, 20th Century, 25 x 33 In. 140.00
Tapestry, Fighting Dragons, American Flags, Eagles, Silk, Chinese, 19th Century, 43 In. . 220.00
Tapestry, Figures & Sheep In Landscape Scene, 39 x 59 In. 80.00
Tapestry, Figures In Courtyard, 63 1/2 x 76 In. 230.00
Tapestry, Figures In Landscape, Foliate Border, Wool, 39 3/4 x 58 3/4 In. 862.00
Tapestry, Flowers, Fruit & Birds, Fruits & Floral Border, Drapery Swags, 62 x 100 In. ... 5750.00
Tapestry, King & Religious Men, Floral Borders, Belgium, 152 x 192 In. 20900.00
Tapestry, Landscape, Castle In Background, Belgium, 19th Century, 102 x 78 In. 5750.00
Tapestry, Landscape, Thick Weave, Signed A. Caler, 1975, 96 x 73 In. 8625.00
Tapestry, Man & Woman Harvesting Grain, Needlework, 72 x 48 In. 100.00
Tapestry, Medieval Scene Of Men On Horseback, Woman On Ground, 30 x 54 In. 107.00
Tapestry, Mill & Water Wheel Scene, Hanging Rod, 32 x 62 In. 330.00
Tapestry, Needlepoint, Aubusson Style, Urn With Flowers, Leafy Border, 54 x 48 In. 690.00
Tapestry, Royal Feast, Multicolored, Taupe Border, 180 x 124 In. 23000.00
Tapestry, Scene, Hand Woven, Linen, Wool, 19th Century, 58 x 76 In. 1200.00
Wall Hanging, Amoebas, Boomerangs, Block Printed, Tekushan, 1950s, 48 x 38 In. 84.00
Wall Hanging, Hand Painted, Birds, Blossoming Trees, 98 x 33 1/2 In., Pair 2500.00
Wall Hanging, Jacquard, Japanese Style, Chrysanthemums, Arts & Crafts, 68 In........ 250.00
Wall Hanging, Mohair, Red, Arts & Crafts Design, 52 x 63 In. 330.00
Wall Hanging, Woven, Floral, Butterfly, Border, Scalloped, 102 x 50 In. 690.00
Window Surround, Aubusson, Pastoral Scenes, France, 1900, 120 x 78 In., Pair 5750.00

THERMOMETER is a name that comes from the Greek word for heat.
The thermometer was invented in 1731 to measure the temperature of
either water or air. All kinds of thermometers are collected, but those
with advertising messages are the most popular.

3-Oil Co., Campbell & Fletcher, Plastic, Box, 6 3/4 In. 175.00
7-Up, Quality Drink, Reverse On Glass, Dial, 10 In. 245.00
7-Up, The Uncola, Round, 1970s, 12 In. 70.00
Alta Crest Farms, Celluloid, Box 55.00
Arbuckle's Coffee, Tin, 19 In. 65.00
Bireley's, Orange Bottle, White Ground, 26 x 10 In. 75.00
Bireley's Orange Drink, Tin, 4 1/2 x 15 3/4 In. 220.00
Bireley's Orange Soda, Bottle, Young Thirsts Deserve The Best 295.00
Brass, Beehive Shape, Hanging 60.00
Buick, Bishop Buick Co., White Letters, Black Ground, Porcelain, 27 x 7 In. 495.00
Camels, Have A Real Cigarette, Metal, 6 x 14 In. 70.00
Casite, Guarantees, Dial Type, Round, 12 In. 110.00
Champale Malt Liquor, Tin Over Cardboard, 1960s, 8 1/2 x 8 1/2 In. ....5.00 to 20.00
Cheer Up, Enjoy, A Delightful Drink, Red Circle, 1940 .... 755.00
Chesterfield, More Than Ever They Satisfy, Metal, 3-D Cigarette Pack, 13 In. 37.00
Chevrolet, Pole, Plastic, 2 1/2 x 6 5/8 In. 170.00
Chew Mail Pouch, Treat Yourself To The Best, Black Ground, Metal, 39 x 8 In. 125.00
Conco, Plastic Pole, Box, 2 1/2 x 7 In. 150.00
Delco Dry Charge Batteries, Dial, Round, 12 In. 130.00
Desk, Inlaid Base, Carved Walrus Tusk, 1860 .... 450.00
Doan's Pill, Porcelain, 1940s, 6 x 22 In. 145.00
Dr Pepper, Bottle Cap Shape, Plastic, 11 In. 110.00
Dr Pepper, Drink A Bit To Eat At 10, 2 & 4, Aqua Highlights, 1930, 4 1/2 x 13 In. 2541.00
Dr Pepper, Hot Or Cold, Dial, 18 In. 120.00
Dr Pepper, Hot Or Cold, Tin, V Chevron Logo, 6 1/2 x 16 1/4 In. 120.00
Dr Pepper, Small Clock At Top, Pale Yellow Ground, 1940, 8 3/4 In. 1694.00
Drink Frostie Root Beer, Santa With Mittens, Tin, 8 x 36 In. 160.00
Drink Royal Crown Cola, Tin, 1950s, 25 In. 88.00
Ex-Lax, The Chocolated Laxative, Porcelain, 8 x 36 x 1 1/4 In. 355.00
Guinness Stout, Celluloid, Metal Gauge Insert, Round, 8 1/2 In. 32.00
Gulf, Plastic Pole, 7 In. 45.00
Hires Root Beer, Die Cut, Convex Tin Lithograph, Glass, 28 1/4 In. 198.00
Joe Camel, Holding Pack, Tin, Die Cut 65.00
Kendall Motor Oils, Porcelain, 9 1/4 x 27 1/4 In. 415.00

Kool Cigarettes, Come Up To Kool, Metal, 12 x 3 1/2 In. 42.00
Kuebler Beer, Barometer, Mirror, Frame, 1940s, 17 x 25 In. 40.00
Liberty Beer, Franklin D. Roosevelt & NRA Symbol, Plastic, Chain, 4 x 6 In. 55.00
Mail Pouch, Outdoor, Wooden Framing, 1920s, 74 x 19 In. 660.00
Mail Pouch Tobacco, Porcelain, 8 x 39 In. 330.00
Marlboro & Philip Morris Cigarettes, Packs, Metal, 13 1/2 x 5 3/4 In. 39.00
Marlboro Man, Plastic Cowboy Figure, 11 x 16 In. 25.00
Marvel's Cigarette, The Cigarette Of Quality, Black Ground, Tin, 12 x 4 In. 145.00
Michigan Propellers, Yellow Propeller In Center, Blue, Tin Face, 12 In. 385.00
Mission Orange, Bottle, White Ground, Tin, 17 x 5 In. 65.00
Mission Orange, Embossed Tin Lithograph, 16 3/4 In. 286.00
Mobil Car Care, At All Temperatures, Black Lettering, Tin Face, 11 3/4 In. 325.00
Nature's Remedy, 1920s, 27 x 7 In. 430.00
Nesbitt's, Made From Real Oranges, Porcelain, 7 1/2 x 27 In. 95.00
NR Nature's Remedy, Porcelain, 7 x 27 In. 90.00
Nu-Grape, A Flavor You Can't Forget, 6 Bottles Showing, Tin, 16 x 6 3/4 In. 100.00
Old Grand Dad, Reverse Glass, 1970s, 8 1/2 x 19 In. 45.00
Ort's Bread, Tin Lithograph, 13 1/4 In. 33.00
Pabst, Pam Clock Company 88.00
Peter's Weatherbird Shoes, Bird Sitting On Top, Light Green, White, 27 x 7 In. 175.00
Phillips 66, Plastic Pole, 2 1/2 x 7 In. 35.00
Prestone Antifreeze, Stamped Metal, 8 x 36 In. 85.00
Prestone Antifreeze, You're Set Safe Sure, Porcelain, 36 x 9 In. 175.00
Ramon Pills, Trademark, 27 1/2 In. 180.00
RCA Victor Radio, Porcelain, Woman Picture 2250.00
Red Crown Gasoline, Polarine Motor Oil, Porcelain, 72 In. 1800.00
Red Fox Beer, Barometer, Red, Logo, 1940s, 15 x 23 In. 290.00
Red Goose Shoes, Porcelain, 27 In. 715.00
Red Goose Shoes, Wooden, 21 In. 330.00
Red Seal Batteries, Porcelain, 7 x 27 In. 200.00
Royal Crown Cola, Better Taste Calls For RC, 25 1/2 In. 30.00
Royal Crown Cola, Embossed Tin Lithograph, Glass, 13 1/2 In. . . . . .205.00 to 220.00
S. Henry & Sons Havana Cigars, Tin Bulb Protector, Decal, Wooden, 24 x 6 In. 185.00
Seagram's Whiskey, Metal, Spanish Writing, Para Todos, 1970s, 8 1/2 x 24 In. 20.00
Signal Products, Plastic Pole, 2 1/2 x 7 In. 535.00
Silvered Scale, John Temple, Sliding Trunk, 38 In. 1495.00
Sohio, Guaranteed Starting, 6 1/2 In. 9.00
Squirt, Embossed Tin Lithograph, Glass, 13 1/2 In. 187.00
Sterling Oils, Orange, Black Ground, Round, Porcelain, 12 3/4 x 9 1/2 In. 1100.00
Sunbeam Bread, Glass Front, Square, c.1970, 12 In. 515.00
Taste Orange Crush, Round, 12 In. 73.00
Texaco, Tin Pole, 2 5/8 x 6 1/4 In. 390.00
Thermo Royal, Round Thermometer In Middle, Tin, 17 5/8 x 12 In. 275.00
Trico Wiper Blades, Dial Type, 15 x 9 1/2 In. 145.00
Tums, Red, White & Blue, 27 1/2 In. 80.00
Tums, Tin Lithograph, Glass, 9 In. 132.00
Winston Cigarette, Winston Tastes Good Like A Cigarette Should, Tin, 13 In. 45.00
Winston Filter Cigarettes, Winston Tastes Good, Pressed Steel, 13 1/2 x 6 In. 33.00
Wright Co., Jewelers, Opticians, Wooden, 3 1/2 x 5 1/2 In. 75.00

TIFFANY is a name that appears on items made by Louis Comfort
Tiffany, the American glass designer who worked from about 1879 to
1933. His work included iridescent glass, Art Nouveau styles of
design, and original contemporary styles. He was also noted for
stained glass windows, unusual lamps, bronze work, pottery, and silver. Other types of Tiffany are listed under Tiffany Glass, Tiffany
Gold, Tiffany Pottery, or Tiffany Silver. The famous Tiffany lamps are
listed in this section. Tiffany jewelry is listed in the jewelry and wristwatch categories. Reproductions of some types of Tiffany are being
made.

Louis C. Tiffany

Ashtray, Gold Dore, 2 Handles, Bronze, Signed, 4 In. 135.00
Ashtray, Gold Dore, Bronze Insert, Signed, 3 1/2 x 3 1/4 In. 400.00
Ashtray, Matchbox Holder, Spanish, Flame & Urn, Octagonal, 7 In. Diam. 550.00

Ashtray, Spanish Pattern, Bronze, Octagonal, Signed, 6 3/8 In. 220.00
Ashtray, Zodiac, Raised Outer Edge, Bronze, Gold Dore, 4 x 3 In. 135.00
Ashtray & Match Safe, Grapevine, Bronze Tray, Green Slag Glass, Signed, 4 1/2 In. 550.00
Blotter Ends, Grapevine, Gold Dore, 19 x 2 In. 300.00
Blotter Ends, Grapevine, Gold Dore, 4-Corner, 6 x 6 x 8 In. 300.00
Blotter Ends, Heraldic, Green Enamel, Signed, 12 1/4 x 2 In. 250.00
Blotter Ends, Heraldic, Green Enamel, Signed, 19 3/4 x 2 1/4 In. 350.00
Blotter Ends, Louis XVI, Floral Wreath, Border, Signed, 12 1/4 x 1 1/4 In. 350.00
Book Rack, Grapevine, Amber Slag Glass, Bronze, Extends, 6 x 5 3/4 x 23 In. 1800.00
Book Rack, Grapevine, Green Slag Glass, Bronze, 14 x 23 In. 2000.00
Bookends, Bronze, Gold Dore, Raised Leaves & Raised Bird Perched, 4 1/2 x 6 In. 1200.00
Bookends, Columns, Raised Leaves & Birds, Urns, Bronze, Enamel, 4 1/2 x 6 In. 1200.00
Bookends, Pine Needle, Amber Slag Glass, Gold Dore, 6 In. 1500.00
Bookends, Spanish Pattern, 3-Dimensional Sculpture, Bronze, Gold Dore Finish, 6 In. ... 1800.00
Bookends, Venetian, Bronze, Signed, 6 x 5 In. 1200.00
Bookends, Zodiac, Bronze, Brown Patina, 6 In. 690.00
Bookstand, Adjustable Rectangular Base, Brown Slag Glass, Bronze 2070.00
Bowl, Brass, Gold Dore, Mottled, Scroll Handles, Marked, 7 1/2 In. 130.00
Bowl, Embossed Geometric Border, Bronze, Gold Dore, Red, No. 1759, 1 1/4 x 8 3/4 In. . 115.00
Box, Bookmark, Bronze, Gold Dore, Signed, 5 x 1 1/4 In. 650.00
Box, Cover, Nautical, Bronze, Gold Dore, Round, 3 1/2 x 3 In. 275.00
Box, Glove, Grapevine, Green Slag Glass, Bronze Bottom, Ball Feet, 13 1/4 In. .1000.00 to 2700.00
Box, Grapevine, Amber Slag Glass, Bronze, Gold Dore, 4 Ball Feet, 4 x 2 x 1 In. 400.00
Box, Hinged Cover, Abalone, Leaf & Flowers, Tray, Bronze, 6 1/2 x 4 1/2 In. 1500.00
Box, Hinged Cover, Abalone, Leaf, Bronze, Gold Dore, 5 1/2 x 3 1/2 x 1 1/4 In. 750.00
Box, Hinged Cover, Adam, Bronze, Gold Dore, 5 In. ....750.00 to 950.00
Box, Hinged Cover, Zodiac, Multicolored Medallions, Bronze, Gold Dore, 2 1/2 In. 1610.00
Box, Jewel, Grapevine, Amber Slag Glass, Velvet Tray, Bronze, Signed, 9 x 7 In. 2000.00
Box, Pine Needle, Amber Slag Glass, Bronze, Ball Feet, 6 1/2 x 4 In. 650.00
Box, Pine Needle, Amber Slag Glass, Bronze, Gold Dore, 4 Ball Feet, 8 x 2 1/2 In. 1500.00
Box, Stamp, Abalone, Tray, 3 Sections, Bronze, Signed 550.00
Box, Stamp, Hinged Cover, Zodiac, 3 3/4 x 2 1/4 In. 400.00
Box, Stamp, Venetian, Signed, Tiffany Studios, 2 x 5 In. 485.00
Box, Twine, Hinged Cover, Bookmark, Hexagonal, Bronze, 3 In. 1500.00
Box, Venetian, Bronze, Gold Dore, 6 x 3 3/4 In. 1800.00
Box, Zodiac, Enameled, Bronze, Gold Dore, 2 x 4 1/2 x 3 1/2 In. 900.00
Calendar, Pine Needle, Green Slag Glass, Bronze, Etched, Signed, 7 x 6 In. 750.00
Candelabrum, 2-Light, Bronze, Trumpet Shape Snuffer, 3-Footed, 9 In. 1495.00
Candelabrum, 4-Light, Bronze, Gold Dore, Favrile Glass, 1918, 12 3/4 In., Pair 6210.00
Candelabrum, 4-Light, Bronze, Gold Dore, Green Glass, Favrile, 12 1/8 In., Pair 4310.00
Candle Lamp, Amber Iridescent, Spiral Stem, Ruffled Edge, Favrile, 1918, 14 In. 1495.00
Candle Lamp, Cylindrical Bronze Stem, Gold Iridescent Shade, Signed, 21 In. 1155.00
Candleholder, Purple Enamel, Bronze, Gold Dore, 3 1/2 In., Pair 1500.00
Candlestick, Beading & Reeding On Shafts, Bronze, c.1910, 8 In., Pair 825.00
Candlestick, Bronze, 7 Green & Gold Jewels, Brown, Green Patina, Favrile, 10 In. 1610.00
Candlestick, Bronze, Bud Shape Cup, Green Glass, Favrile, 17 3/4 In. 690.00
Candlestick, Bronze, Queen Anne's Lace On Foot, Corseted, Green Glass, 21 In. 4125.00
Chandelier, 4-Light, Lily, Bronze, Brown Green Patina, Favrile Glass, 1920, 32 In. 13225.00
Chandelier, 7-Light, Lily, Bronze, Brown Patina, Favrile Glass, 12 x 30 In. 18400.00
Clock, Brass, Beveled Glass Sides & Door, Samuel Marti, c.1900, 6 x 9 1/2 In. 635.00
Clock, Carriage, Repeater, Quarter Hour, Signed 1650.00
Clock, Desk, Zodiac, Bronze, Tiffany & Co., 4 x 4 1/4 x 2 In. 1500.00
Clock, Lion Heads, Eagles, Porcelain Numerals, Bronze, Gold Dore, Signed, 29 In. 1980.00
Compote, Abalone, Curved Leaves, Bronze, 3 1/4 x 3 1/2 In. 400.00
Compote, Bronze, Abalone Inlay, 7 1/2 In. 112.00
Compote, Bronze, Gold Dore, Etched, 1925, 4 1/4 In. 230.00
Compote, Spun Metal, Bronze, Peacock Eyes & Trailings, Signed, 8 In. Diam. 400.00
Compote, Spun Metal, Bronze, Variegated Green Finish, Signed, 7 3/4 In. 265.00
Cup, Thistle, For Engineers Club, December 9, 1907, Bronze, Gold Dore, 7 1/2 In. 895.00
Desk Set, Abalone, Bronze, 9 Piece 2585.00
Desk Set, Abalone, Bronze, Gold Dore, 3 Piece 1035.00
Desk Set, Bronze, Serpent, Bamboo Border, 1890s, 8 Piece 2035.00
Desk Set, Grapevine Green Slag Glass, Bronze, 5 Piece 1540.00

Desk Set, Pine Needle, Green Slag Glass, Bronze, Green Patina, 11 Piece 4400.00
Desk Set, Zodiac, Bronze, Signed, 7 Piece 1870.00
Frame, Abalone, Bronze, Signed, 10 x 7 /12 In. 3595.00
Frame, Abalone, Leaf & Floral, Bronze, Gold Dore, Oval Opening, 7 1/4 x 10 In. 2800.00
Frame, Bronze, Zigzag Border, Gilt, 1928, 10 x 7 1/4 x 9 1/4 In. 750.00
Frame, Double, Grapevine, Green Slag Glass, Beaded Edge, Bronze, Signed, 7 x 10 In. ... 3000.00
Frame, Grapevine, Green Slag Glass, Bronze, Brown Patina, Easel Back, 9 x 7 1/2 In. ... 2000.00
Frame, Pine Needle, Green Slag Glass, Bronze, Signed, 8 x 9 1/2 In. 2310.00
Hand Blotter, Adam, Knob Handle, Signed, 5 In. 200.00
Hand Blotter, Heraldic, Green Enamel, 5 1/4 x 2 3/4 In. 300.00
Hand Blotter, Louis XVI, Knob Handle, 5 1/4 x 2 3/4 In. 450.00
Index, Zodiac, Alphabetical Indicators, Bronze, Gold Dore, Side Knob, 3 x 4 1/2 In. ... 2500.00
Inkstand, Bronze, Opaque Green Glass Insert, Signed, 4 x 7 In. 2750.00
Inkwell, Abalone, Octagonal, Bronze, Gold Dore, 3 1/2 x 3 1/2 In. 750.00
Inkwell, Bronze, Domed Cover, Pale Green Insert, Rolled Rim, Favrile, 4 In. 2000.00
Inkwell, Bronze, Open Star Design, 7 x 3 1/2 In. 2000.00
Inkwell, Bronze, Spider Web, Brown Slag Glass Insert, Ball Feet, 4 In. 190.00
Inkwell, Byzantine, Coral Jewels, Beading, Bronze, Gold Dore, Round, 2 3/4 In. 2500.00
Inkwell, Chainlink & Mink, Bronze, 2 1/2 x 5 In. 750.00
Inkwell, Hinged Cover, Bookmark, Octagonal, Glass Insert, 2 1/2 In. 705.00
Inkwell, Hinged Cover, Grapevine, Green Slag Glass Insert, Bronze, Signed, 7 In. 1800.00
Inkwell, Hinged Cover, Heraldic, Silver Plated, Oxidized, Bronze, 3 1/2 x 3 In. 650.00
Inkwell, Hinged Cover, Louis XVI, Bronze, Gold Dore, Leaf Swag & Feet, 3 x 4 In. 1200.00
Inkwell, Hinged Cover, Nautical, Dolphin Corners, Bronze, Gold Dore, Signed, 5 In. 800.00
Inkwell, Hinged Cover, Ninth Century, Glass Jewels In Corners, Signed, 2 3/4 In. 550.00
Inkwell, Hinged Cover, Zodiac, Bronze, Gold Dore, 10 3/4 In. 1200.00
Inkwell, Pine Needle, Beading, Ball Feet, Green Slag Glass, Bronze, Signed, 4 x 4 In. ... 750.00
Inkwell, Turtleback, Jewel, Rounded, 3 Curved Feet, Bronze, Gold Dore, 4 In. 2500.00
Lamp, 3-Light, Amber Iridescent Lily Shades, Bronze Foliate Arms, Cushion Foot, 13 In. . 5175.00
Lamp, 3-Light, Gold Favrile Lily Shades, Bronze, 21 In. 3737.00
Lamp, 3-Light, Lily, Intaglio, Bronze, Gold Dore, Knop Stem, 16 1/4 In. 3165.00
Lamp, 3-Light, Opalescent Favrile Shades, Bronze, 12 1/2 In. 4140.00
Lamp, 3-Light, Pale Green Lily Shades, Bronze, Scrolled, Foliate Arms, 8 In. 4887.00
Lamp, 18-Light, Favrile Lily Shades, Favrile, Bronze, Gold Dore, 1920, 22 3/4 In. 40250.00
Lamp, Abalone, Bronze, 9 In. 4000.00
Lamp, Acorn, Amber, Domed Shade, 6 Arms, Hanging, Signed, 20 In. 22000.00
Lamp, Acorn, Domed Shade, Glass Tiles, Bronze, 21 1/2 In. 9775.00
Lamp, Acorn, Favrile, Bronze, Brown Patina, 1920, 22 x 16 In. 11500.00
Lamp, Acorn, Green, Yellow, Brown Ground, Bronze, Gold Dore, 20 In. 10450.00
Lamp, Blue Shade, Favrile, Bronze Bamboo Base, Signed, 14 1/2 In. 3450.00
Lamp, Bookmark, Angular Scrolls, Adjustable, Bronze, 13 In. 1035.00
Lamp, Bridge, Bronze, Harp Arms, Tripod Base, 54 3/4 In. 1265.00
Lamp, Bronze, Fluted Base, Glass Cabochons, Yellow, Green Glass Shade, 24 In. 14300.00
Lamp, Bronze, Partial Textured Gold Dore, 4-Panel Mica Shade, 64 In. 1380.00
Lamp, Bronze, Pine Needle, Etched Metal & Shade, Green Slag Glass, Signed, 18 In. 4000.00
Lamp, Chinese Pattern, Octagonal, Amber Slag Glass, Bronze, Brown Patina, 17 x 12 In. . 6000.00
Lamp, Colonial, Domed Shade, Pale Green Opalescent Rows, Circular Foot 6325.00
Lamp, Cypriote, Blue, Vase Shape, Bronze, Gold Dore, 21 1/2 In. 1380.00
Lamp, Damascene Domed Shade, Pink, Gold Iridescent, Intaglio Finish, 20 In. 3740.00
Lamp, Damascene, Favrile, Bronze, Brown Patina, 1920, 15 x 7 In. 4600.00
Lamp, Domed Shade, Gold Iridescent, Green Intaglio Leaves, Favrile, 15 In. 9775.00
Lamp, Domed Shell Shade, Bronze, Scalloped Circular Foot, 55 1/2 In. 2645.00
Lamp, Dragonfly, Favrile, Bronze, Brown Patina, 1920, 21 1/2 In. 16100.00
Lamp, Geometric Domed Shade, Bronze, Gold Dore, 9 1/2 In. 1610.00
Lamp, Greek Key, Green Colonial Shade, Bronze, Signed, 15 1/2 x 11 In. 12650.00
Lamp, Green Conical Shade, Vertical Geometric Design, Bronze, 23 In. 5175.00
Lamp, Green Feather Shade, Favrile, Bronze Base, 20 x 12 In. 2875.00
Lamp, Iridescent Green Feathers, Shade, Ball Feet, Bronze, Signed, 12 3/4 In. 2415.00
Lamp, Jonquil, Golden Amber, Mottled Green Leaves, Bronze Floral Stem Base, 14 In. ... 34100.00
Lamp, Linenfold, Bronze, Gold Dore, Signed, 12 In. ....*Illus* 24750.00
Lamp, Linenfold, Favrile, Bronze, Gold Dore, 1928, 23 1/2 x 19 In. 23000.00
Lamp, Linenfold, Favrile, Bronze, Greenish Brown Patina, 1920, 23 x 18 In. 13800.00
Lamp, Linenfold, Gold, Amber Glass, Bronze, Gold Dore, 14 In., Pair 24150.00

Tiffany, Lamp, Linenfold, Bronze, Gold Dore, Signed, 12 In.

Tiffany Glass, Shade, Acorn, Domed, Hanging, Marked, 20 In.

Lamp, Lotus, Bell Shade, Stylized Green Mottled Leaves, Bronze Base, Signed, 15 In. 16500.00
Lamp, Lotus, Bell, Favrile Shade, Bronze, Brownish Green Patina, 1920, 20 1/2 In. 32200.00
Lamp, Magnolia Blossoms, Leaded Domed Shade, Bronze, Tree Trunk Base, 29 In. 2070.00
Lamp, Mosque, Green Pulled Feathers, Bulbous, Bronze Finial, Signed, 8 1/2 In. 2800.00
Lamp, Mosque, Octagonal Shade, Bronze, Signed, 8 1/2 In. 2800.00
Lamp, Mushroom Shape, Amber Iridescent, Swirled, Favrile, 11 1/2 In. 1725.00
Lamp, Nautilus Shell, 5 Ball Feet, Bronze, Signed, 14 In. 2925.00
Lamp, Pine Needle, Domed Shade, Favrile, Bronze, 21 In. 6325.00
Lamp, Pulled Green Feathers, Gold Outlined, Bronze, 16 In. 1870.00
Lamp, Pulled Petals, Caramel, Gold, Bronze, Favrile, Gold Dore, 8 In. 1150.00
Lamp, Raised Scallop Design, Favrile, Bronze, Gold Dore, 19 1/2 In. 5000.00
Lamp, Ruffled Shade, Gold, Twisted Ribbed Body, Flange Top, Favrile, 12 In., Pair 3500.00
Lamp, Sconce, 2-Light, Favrile, Bronze, Brown Patina, 1920, 16 In. 8050.00
Lamp, Sconce, Favrile, Bronze, Green, 15 In., 4 Piece 11500.00
Lamp, Spanish Pattern, Urns On Post, Adjustable, Bronze, Signed, 14 In. 4500.00
Lamp, Stalactite Bullet Shape, Pulled Feathers, Hanging, 15 1/2 In. 5225.00
Lamp, Student, Favrile, 2 Arms, Bronze, Brown Green Patina, 26 x 10 In. 13800.00
Lamp, Student, Green Domed Shade, Bronze Overlay, Signed, 10 In. 7975.00
Lamp, Swirled Gold Iridescent Base, Blue Luster, Blue Shade, Favrile, 12 In. 1265.00
Lamp, Swirling Leaves, Favrile, Bronze, Gold Dore, 1920, 21 3/4 x 18 In. 14375.00
Lamp, Trumpet Shade, Amber, Pulled Green Trailings, Favrile, 17 In. 1150.00
Lamp, Tulip, Favrile, Bronze, Dark Brown Patina, 1920, 21 1/4 x 14 In. 27600.00
Lamp, Turtleback, Amber Iridescent Tiles, Cabochons, 5 Ball Feet, Bronze, 14 In. 6325.00
Lamp, Turtleback, Favrile, Bronze, Brown Black Patina, 24 x 18 In. 24150.00
Lamp, Turtleback, Oval Base, Adjustable, Bronze, Gold Dore, 7 1/2 x 8 x 4 1/2 In. 4500.00
Lamp, Turtleback, Purple & Blue Glass, Jewels, 14 In. 9200.00
Lamp, Weight-Balance, Adjustable Arm, Bronze, Pierced Tin Shade, 13 1/2 In. 2185.00
Lamp, Weight-Balance, Bronze, Patina, Adjustable Double-Scroll Arm, 55 In. 2875.00
Lamp, Weight-Balance, Bronze, Undulating Shade, Round Base, 56 In. 2960.00
Lamp, Weight-Balance, Favrile Bell Shade, Curved Arm, Ball, Bronze, 14 In. 5000.00
Lamp, White Shade, Pulled Gold Iridescent Feathers, Bronze, Gold Dore, 19 In. 1380.00
Lamp, Woodbine, Favrile, Bronze, Brown Patina, 1920, 21 1/4 In. 26450.00
Lamp, Zodiac, Amber Iridescent, Turtleback Tile, Bronze, 14 In. 6325.00
Lamp, Zodiac, Bronze, Gold Dore, 14 In. 880.00
Letter Holder, Bookmark, Bronze, Gold Dore, 5 1/4 x 9 x 2 1/4 In. 500.00
Letter Holder, Byzantine, Coral Inserts & Jewels, Raised Beads, Bronze, 6 x 4 1/2 In. . . . 950.00
Letter Holder, Grapevine, Amber Slag Glass, Ball Feet, Bronze, 4 x 6 In. 750.00
Letter Holder, Pine Needle, Center Divider, Green Slag Glass, Bronze, 4 1/2 x 6 1/4 In. . . 950.00
Letter Opener, Abalone, 10 In. 300.00
Letter Opener, Adam, Bronze, Gold Dore, Signed, 10 In. 250.00
Letter Opener, Bronze, Brown Patina, Scroll Handle, 1910, 8 1/2 In. 115.00
Letter Opener, Enameled Graduating Squares On Handle, Signed, 6 1/2 In. 575.00
Letter Opener, Zodiac, Signed, 10 1/4 In. 250.00
Letter Rack, Bookmark, Bronze, 13 x 8 In. 850.00
Letter Rack, Heraldic, Bronze, Green Enamel, 9 1/2 x 6 x 2 1/2 In. 750.00
Letter Rack, Paperweight, Pine Needle, Green Slag Glass, Signed, 3 1/2 In. Diam. 750.00
Letter Rack, Zodiac, Bronze, Gold Dore, 6 1/2 x 9 1/2 In. 750.00
Magnifying Glass, Bookmark, Bronze, Gold Dore, Signed, 8 3/4 x 4 In. 1500.00

Magnifying Glass, Graduate, Bronze, Gold Dore, Signed, 8 3/4 x 4 In. . . . . .1200.00 to 1500.00
Magnifying Glass, Venetian, Bronze, Gold Dore, Signed, 9 x 4 In. 1200.00
Magnifying Glass, Zodiac, Beaded Edge, 8 1/4 x 4 In. 1200.00
Medallion, Patrick Cardinal Hayes, Bronze, April 30, 1924, Presentation Box, 2 1/2 In. . . . 56.00
Memoranda Pad, Cover, Zodiac, Bronze, Brown Patina, Signed, 6 x 4 x 2 In. 850.00
Mirror, Hand, Grapevine, Amber Slag Glass, Bronze, Signed, 7 1/2 In. 1800.00
Model, Clipper Ship, Spanish, Wood, Canvas, On Cradle, Signed, c.1890, 41 x 36 In. 1955.00
Money Clip, Eagle & U.S. Flag, St. Louis World's Fair, 1904, 1 x 2 In. 285.00
Note Pad Holder, Hinged Cover, Grapevine, 7 1/4 x 4 1/2 In. 300.00
Nut Dish, 8 Ribs, Gold Iridescent, Ruffled Edge, 1 1/4 x 4 1/8 In. 375.00
Paper Clip, Abalone, Bronze, Signed, 2 3/4 In. 550.00
Paper Clip, American Indian, Bronze, Gold Dore, Signed, 2 3/4 x 4 In. 350.00
Paper Clip, Byzantine, Coral Inserts, Beading, Bronze, 3 1/4 x 2 1/4 In. 650.00
Paper Clip, Zodiac, Bronze, Gold Dore 350.00
Paper Rack, Bronze, Geometric Border, Red, Blue, Green, Rectangular, 8 In. 259.00
Paperweight, Abalone, Bronze, Square, Signed, 3 3/4 In. 800.00
Paperweight, Bronze, Green Swirls, Blue Iridescent, 3 1/2 x 2 3/4 In. 2800.00
Paperweight, Bulldog, Bronze, Signed, 1 1/2 x 2 3/4 In. 475.00
Paperweight, Bulldog, Sitting, Bronze, Brown Patina, Signed, 2 1/4 x 1 1/2 In. 475.00
Paperweight, Bulldog, Standing, Bronze, Gold Dore, 3 3/4 x 2 1/2 x 2 In. 1200.00
Paperweight, Byzantine, Beading, Coral Jewels, Knob Handle, Bronze, 3 3/4 In. 650.00
Paperweight, Green, 4 Prunts, Signed, 8 x 6 In. 230.00
Paperweight, Lioness, Reclining, Bronze, Gold Dore, Signed, 5 x 1 1/2 x 1 1/2 In. 700.00
Paperweight, Owl, Bronze, Brown Patina, 3 x 1 1/4 In. 850.00
Paperweight, Scarab, Beetle, Ridged Body, Opaque Black, 4 1/2 In. 550.00
Paperweight, Sphinx, Bronze, Signed, 1 1/2 x 2 1/4 In. 305.00
Pen Tray, Heraldic, 3 Compartments, Shield In Center, Signed 250.00
Pen Tray, Leaf Shape, Bronze, Brown Patina, 11 5/8 In. 1380.00
Pen Tray, Louis XVI, Ribbed Handle, Oval, Bronze, Signed, 8 1/4 x 3 1/3 In. 450.00
Pen Tray, Spanish Pattern, Raised Border, Signed, 9 3/4 In. 450.00
Pen Tray, Zodiac, Medallions On Each End, Bronze, Brown Patina, 10 In. 175.00
Planter, Bronze, Gold Dore, 11 In. 825.00
Planter, Gold Iridescent, 10 Small Feet, Brown Patina, Bronze, 6 1/2 x 1 1/4 In. 2800.00
Planter, Pine Needle, Green Slag Glass, Bronze, Brown Patina, 10 1/2 Diam. 2000.00
Roundel, Raised Central Flower Blossom, Green Petals, Leaves, Gold Dore, 13 In. 2300.00
Scale, Postage, Grapevine, Green Slag Glass, Meter In Front, Signed, 5 1/4 In. 3500.00
Scissors, Line Design, Bronze, Gold Dore, Marked, 9 In. 750.00
Sconce, Turtleback Tile, Bronze, Green Patina, Favrile, 1918, 32 In. 57500.00
Screen, Tea, 3-Panel, Filigree, Green & Slag Glass, Bronze, Favrile, 7 x 4 In. 1150.00
Smoking Stand, Attached Matchholder, Enameled Rim & Foot, Bronze, 31 1/2 In. 660.00
Smoking Stand, Bronze, Overlapping Leaf Design, Signed, 25 In. 1500.00
Smoking Stand, Enameled Floral & Vine, Fitted, Bronze, Signed, 11 1/4 In. 920.00
Smoking Stand, Overlapping Leaves, Scrolls, Bronze, Signed, 25 In. 1500.00
Tazza, Greek Key, Stylized Foliate Design, Green Enamel Insets, Oval, 2 x 7 1/4 In. 690.00
Thermometer, Glass, Grapevine, Beaded Border, Green Slag Glass, Green Patina, 9 In. . . . 1495.00
Thermometer, Pine Needle, 2 Rows Of Beading, Green Slag Glass, Bronze, 8 1/2 In. 1500.00
Thermometer, Zodiac, Bronze, Signed, 8 x 4 1/2 In. 1500.00
Tray, 2 Handles, Bronze, Gold Dore, Signed, 5 1/2 In. 155.00
Tray, Bronze, Geometric Line Design Rim, Raised Florets, Red Enamel Centers, 1 1/2 In. . . 550.00
Tray, Geometric Design On Rim, Bronze, Signed, 12 In. 300.00
Tray, Gilt Bronze, Stylized Flower Corners, Dot & Dash Border, Enameled, 4 x 2 In. 290.00
Tray, Hammered Surface, Raised Edge, Plain Rim, Bronze, 14 1/4 In. 2185.00
Tray, Pink Flowers, Green Leaves, Bronze, Gold Dore, 8 1/4 In. 550.00
Tray, Raised Rim, Bronze, Gold Dore, Signed, 14 In. 250.00
Tray, Random Fire Polish, Rolled Rim, Bronze, Gold Dore, 14 3/4 In. 980.00
Trivet, Aqua, Cypriote, Glass, Lattice & Stars, Bronze, Tiffany Furnaces, Square, 6 In. . . . 1725.00
Vase, Bronze Scrolled Case, Gold Iridescent, Favrile, 13 3/4 In. 1265.00
Vase, Long Green Leaves, Cylindrical, Bronze Holder, Gold Dore, Favrile, 13 1/2 In. 1495.00
Vase, Trumpet, Amber Iridescent, Bronze Holder, Favrile, 1920, 14 In. 1150.00
Vase, Trumpet, Gold Iridescent Feathers, Bronze Holder, Gold Dore, Favrile, 15 In. 1800.00
Vase, Trumpet, Green Pulled Feathers, Brass Holder, 14 1/2 In. 1350.00
Vase, Trumpet, Green Teardrop Enamel, Bronze Holder, Favrile, 16 3/16 In. 3160.00
TIFFANY GLASS, Bottle, Tel El Amarna, Green, Pulled Feathers, Gold Iridescent, 8 In. . . . 1870.00

Bowl, 8 Trailing Prunts, Gold Iridescent, Pulled Rim, 2 x 4 1/2 In. 575.00
Bowl, Amber Body, Double Bulb, 8 Ribs, Petal Rim, Favrile, 1910, 5 In. 500.00
Bowl, Blue, Optic Design Of Laurel Leaves At Bottom, Signed, 6 1/4 In. 950.00
Bowl, Cut Grape Leaves, Signed, 8 In. 1550.00
Bowl, Intaglio, Leaf, Vine Border, Gold, Ruffled Edge, Favrile, 2 3/4 x 6 1/4 In. 635.00
Bowl, Iridescent Blue, Ribbed, Scalloped, Rolled Rim, Signed, 7 In. 725.00
Bowl, Laurel Leaves, Electric Blue Upper Band, Pastel, 6 1/4 In. 950.00
Bowl, Leaves, Pastel Blue, Turquoise Blue Rim, Favrile, 4 x 10 1/4 In. 865.00
Bowl, Opalescent Optic, Laurel Leaves, Signed, 6 1/4 In. 950.00
Bowl, Ruffled, Gold Iridescent, Red, Blue Highlights, 2 x 4 In., Pair 750.00
Bowl, Stretched Gold Iridescent, Rainbow Highlights, Favrile, No. 1848, 12 In. 4850.00
Bowl, Vines, Leaves, Gold Iridescent, Low, Favrile, 12 1/2 In. 1000.00
Candlestick, Green Pulled Leaves Design, Amber, Favrile, 14 In., Pair 2070.00
Candlestick, Silver, Blue Rim, Gold Iridescent, Violet, Red Highlights, 4 In., Pair 2100.00
Candlestick, Stretched, Gold Iridescent, Favrile, 4 x 4 In., Pair 2100.00
Carafe, Ambergris, Gold, Pinched, Beaded Stopper, Favrile, 11 In. 1035.00
Cocktail, Conical Bowl, 4 1/8 In., 6 Piece 345.00
Compote, 2 Butterflies, Gold Iridescent, 4 In. 1150.00
Compote, Blue Luster, Cobalt, Rolled Rim, Signed, Favrile, 9 x 3 In. 805.00
Compote, Diamond Optic, Gold Iridescent, Pink, Favrile, 2 In. 1500.00
Compote, Flower-Form, Cobalt Iridescent, Favrile, 7 In. 1955.00
Compote, Gold Iridescent, Favrile, c.1910, 11 1/2 In. 1495.00
Compote, Gold Iridescent, Ribbed, Scalloped Rim, Favrile, 3 3/4 x 4 In. 750.00
Compote, Intaglio Leaf & Vine, Gold Iridescent, Favrile, 1911, 7 1/2 x 6 In. 795.00
Compote, Opalescent Leaf Design, Pastel Blue Onion Skin Texture, 6 1/2 In. 430.00
Compote, Quilted, Cobalt Iridescent, Stretched Rim, Favrile, 12 In. 1725.00
Compote, Quilted, Opalescent, Silvery Gold Iridescent, c.1892, 8 In. 490.00
Cup, Applied Pods, Trailing Vines, Gold Iridescent, Red Highlights, Favrile, 3 In. 750.00
Cuspidor, White Opaque, Vase Shape, 2 Handles, 1 1/2 In. 400.00
Decanter, Pinched Body & Stopper, Signed, 10 In. 2000.00
Goblet, Amber Opalescent, Pulled Feathers, Turned Amber Stem, Signed, 5 1/2 In. 385.00
Goblet, Engraved Band Of Grape Clusters, Leaves, Favrile, 1920s, 8 Piece 7200.00
Goblet, Light Gold Iridescent, Signed L.C.T., 8 1/4 In. 200.00
Inkwell, Grapevine, Amber Slag Glass, Insert, Bronze, 4 x 3 1/2 In. 750.00
Nut Dish, Gold Iridescent, 4 Stump Feet, Signed, 2 In. 145.00
Pen Tray, Grapevine, Bronze, 4 Ball Feet, 11 1/2 x 3 In. 250.00
Pitcher, Amber Iridescent, Ear Handle, Waisted, Favrile, 8 In. 805.00
Plate, White Radiating Stripes, Pink Opalescent, Favrile, 11 In. 745.00
Punch Cup, Applied Pods & Trailing Vines, Signed, 2 1/2 In. 750.00
Rose Bowl, Cobalt Blue, Ruffled Edge, 10-Ribs, Favrile, 1915, 3 3/4 In. 865.00
Rose Bowl, Green, Swirled Reds, Gold, Rust 5500.00
Salt, Blue & Violet, Raised Swirling Twists, 1 1/4 x 2 In. 375.00
Salt, Blue Iridescent, 8 Pulled Prunts, Favrile, 2 1/8 In. 805.00
Salt, Elephant, Diagonal Curled Ribs, Signed, 2 1/2 In. 1200.00
Salt, Flower-Form, Gold Iridescent, Signed, L.C.T., Favrile, 2 1/2 In. 196.00
Salt, Gold Iridescent, Blue, Green, Violet Highlights, Favrile, 1 1/2 x 2 In. 350.00
Salt, Gold Iridescent, Footed, 2 1/4 In., Pair 300.00
Salt, Ribbed Body, Gold Iridescent, Blue, Silver Highlights, Favrile, 1 x 2 1/4 In. 350.00
Salt, Swirling Pulled Trailings, Favrile, Signed, 2 In. 330.00
Scarab, Favrile Glass, Red Iridescent Glass, 3/4 In. 150.00
Shade, Acorn, Domed, Hanging, Marked, 20 In. . . . . *Illus* 22000.00
Shade, Damascene, Gold Iridescent Wavy Design, Yellow Opalescent, 10 In. 3735.00
Shade, Domed, Favrile, Green Optic, Trailing Gold Iridescent Ribbons, 10 Ribs, 7 In. . . . 3737.00
Shade, Green Pulled Swirls, Gold Iridescent, 7 In., Pair 1495.00
Tray, Card, Enameled Emerald Green, Zigzag & Linear Border, Favrile, Handles 2500.00
Tumbler, Juice, Gold Barrel, Threading, 3 3/4 In. 550.00
Tumbler, Threading, Amber Iridescent, Favrile, 4 In., 6 Piece 1265.00
Tumbler, Whiskey, Gold Iridescent, Blue, Silver, Pinched, Favrile, 1 1/2 In. 235.00
Vase, Amber Iridescent, 2 Scrolled Handles, Egg Shape, Favrile, 1910, 8 In. 1150.00
Vase, Amber Iridescent, Pulled Hearts, Baluster, Favrile, 1913, 8 3/4 In. 3735.00
Vase, Amber Iridescent, Pulled Hearts, Rolled Rim, Favrile, 1925, 9 In. 1725.00
Vase, Amber, Iridescent, Pulled Feathers, Oval, 8 1/2 In. 1035.00
Vase, Amber, Ribbed Trumpet Form, Rolled Rim, Bronze Holder, Favrile, 11 In. 800.00

Vase, Amber, Ribbed, Flared, Round Spreading Foot, Favrile, 1919, 11 3/4 In. 1035.00
Vase, Ambergris Neck, Blue Iridescent Pulled Feathers, Favrile, 20 In. 2760.00
Vase, Applied, Trailing Prunt, Gold Luster, 4 In. 230.00
Vase, Aquamarine, Favrile, Signed, c.1927, 6 3/8 In. 4025.00
Vase, Blue & Green Pulled Feathers, Amber Foot, Bulbous, 1892, 12 In. 880.00
Vase, Blue Iridescent, Gourd, 10 Ribs, Ruffled Edge, Favrile, 10 1/4 In. 1495.00
Vase, Blue Iridescent, Ribbed Baluster, Favrile, 1906-1912, 3 1/4 In. 470.00
Vase, Blue Iridescent, Shading Up To Gold, 2 7/8 In. 520.00
Vase, Bud, 6 Green Leaves, Gold Iridescent, Bronze Holder, Favrile, 16 In. 1035.00
Vase, Bud, Amber Iridescent, Green Leaf Base, Favrile, 1915, 12 In. 1150.00
Vase, Bud, Amber Iridescent, Waisted, Favrile, 1918, 10 In. 805.00
Vase, Bud, Enameled Green & Gold Band Base, Signed, 13 x 3 1/4 In. 990.00
Vase, Bud, Gray Opalescent, Pulled Feathers, Bronze Holder, Favrile, 13 In. 1035.00
Vase, Bud, Green Pulled Leaves, Amber Iridescent, Favrile, 14 In. 1035.00
Vase, Chain, Prunts, Gold Iridescent, Red, Blue Highlights, Favrile, 7 x 3 1/2 In. 1500.00
Vase, Cobalt Blue, Iridescent, Ribbed, Baluster, Favrile, 1916, 14 3/4 In. 1150.00
Vase, Cobalt Blue, Iridescent, Scalloped Rolled Rim, Favrile, 1905, 4 In. 1150.00
Vase, Cobalt Iridescent, Trumpet Neck, Bulbous Base, Favrile, 10 In. 1495.00
Vase, Cranberry, Yellow Band At Top, Favrile, 1915, 4 1/8 In. 17250.00
Vase, Crimson & Blue Striations, Favrile, Signed, 1899, 3 1/4 In.   690.00
Vase, Emerald & Ivory, Pulled Feathers, Iridescent, Favrile, 13 3/4 In. 1380.00
Vase, Favrile, Peacock Blue, Dore Bronze Holder, 17 In. 5500.00
Vase, Favrile, Ribbed Body, Gold Iridescent, Pink, Violet Highlights, 3 x 2 In. 650.00
Vase, Favrile, Silver, Blue Gold Swirl Design, Red Iridescent, 1 1/2 In. 2500.00
Vase, Flower-Form, Amber, Yellow & Red Striations, 8 1/2 In. 6325.00
Vase, Flower-Form, Blue Iridescent, Waisted Body, Ribbed Base, 15 1/4 In. 3630.00
Vase, Flower-Form, Blue, Ruffled Edge, Cobalt, Disk Foot, Favrile, 5 1/2 In. 980.00
Vase, Flower-Form, Citron Opalescent Body, Pulled Leaves, Yellow, 11 In. 4510.00
Vase, Flower-Form, Green Pulled Leaves, Gold Iridescent, Favrile, 1907, 5 In. 1380.00
Vase, Flower-Form, Opalescent, Pulled Green Leaves, Favrile, 1904, 13 In. 1035.00
Vase, Flower-Form, Peach Opal Petal, Pale Amber Stem, 9 1/2 In. 1955.00
Vase, Flower-Form, Ruffled Broad Blossom Rim, Gold Iridescent, 1910, 4 1/4 In. 1265.00
Vase, Gold Iridescent, Bulbous, Prunts, Tapered Neck, Favrile, 7 In. 1500.00
Vase, Gold Iridescent, Footed, Favrile, Signed, 6 In. 700.00
Vase, Gold Iridescent, Red Highlights, Pinched Neck, Favrile, 2 1/2 In. 650.00
Vase, Gold Iridescent, Scrolling Shell Handles, Signed, 4 1/2 In.   5465.00
Vase, Gold Iridescent, Tapered, Signed, L.C.T., 8 3/4 In. 1840.00
Vase, Gold Iridescent, Threaded, Marked, 3 In. 175.00
Vase, Gold Iridescent, Urn, Rolled Rim, Label, Favrile, 9 1/2 In.   1705.00
Vase, Gold Millefiori, 25 White Cane Blossoms, Amber Stems, Favrile, 5 In. 2415.00
Vase, Gold Pulled Zipper, Opaque White Ground, 10 1/2 In. 3250.00
Vase, Gold, Bulbous Base, Pinched, Tapered Neck, Favrile, 12 In.   1150.00
Vase, Gold, Purple, Blue Iridescent, Gourd, Cylindrical Neck, 3 3/8 In. 690.00
Vase, Gourd Shape, Amber Iridescent, Scarab Seal, Favrile, 6 In.   745.00
Vase, Gray, Swirled Stripes, Bubbles, Tapered Neck, Favrile, 1925, 8 1/8 In. 1380.00
Vase, Green Body, Gold Iridescent, 5 Amber Pulled, Coiled Leaves, Favrile, 4 3/4 In. 2415.00
Vase, Green Pulled Feathers, Gold Iridescent Interior, Favrile, 1919, 10 In. 1380.00
Vase, Green Pulled Leaves & Trailing Vines, Signed, 6 1/2 In. 1800.00
Vase, Green Pulled Leaves, Amber Iridescent Interior, Favrile, 1909, 8 In. 1955.00
Vase, Green Translucent Feathers, Gold Iridescent Interior, Favrile, 10 In. 290.00
Vase, Jack-In-The-Pulpit, Amber Iridescent, Favrile, 1920, 18 1/2 In. 17250.00
Vase, Jack-In-The-Pulpit, Pink Optic Interior, Amber Gold Iridescent, 17 In. 14950.00
Vase, Lava, Cobalt Blue Over Amber, 3 Handles, 5 1/2 In. 2875.00
Vase, Light Green, Bulbous, Signed, Favrile, 16 1/4 In. 1740.00
Vase, Magenta, Cobalt, Tangerine Iridescent, Hexagonal Rim, Favrile, 16 In. 1265.00
Vase, Paperweight, Amber, Garlic Shape, Favrile, 5 1/2 In. 1840.00
Vase, Paperweight, Ivory Morning Glory Blossoms, Green Leaf Vines, 5 In. 3450.00
Vase, Paperweight, Pale Aqua, Yellow, Red Millefiori Flowers, Favrile, 7 In. 6900.00
Vase, Paperweight, Tan, Amber, Favrile, 1909, 8 5/8 In. 11500.00
Vase, Paperweight, Trailing Ivy Leaves, Ocher, Red, Light Green, Favrile, 5 In. 6900.00
Vase, Paperweight, White Millefiori Flowers, Green Pulled Hearts & Vines, 4 In. 3450.00
Vase, Pulled Gold Iridescent Neck, Ribbed, Pinched Amber Body, 3 In. 430.00
Vase, Pulled Green Leaves, Gold Iridescent, Amber, Oval, 4 1/2 In. 635.00

Vase, Pulled Heart & Vine, Cobalt Blue, Purple Iridescent, Favrile, 6 1/4 In. 2185.00
Vase, Pulled Hearts & Vines, Amber, Disc Foot, 9 In. 1840.00
Vase, Pulled Leaf, Opalescent, Green, Silver, Gold, Blue, Favrile 9835, 2 In. 1568.00
Vase, Pulled Light Blue Ruffled Edge, 10 Ribs, Deep Blue Luster, Favrile, 1915, 5 In. . . . 1035.00
Vase, Pulled Tendrils, Cranberry, Yellow Band At Top, Favrile, 1905, 5 In. 23000.00
Vase, Silver, Blue Swirls, Bulbous, Favrile, 1921, 4 1/4 In. 575.00
Vase, Silver, Gold Iridescent, Favrile, 3 1/4 In. 650.00
Vase, Silvery Green Pulled Hearts, Silver Trailings, Cobalt, 1915, 9 In. 2875.00
Vase, Stick, Gold Pulled Feathers, Opaque White Ground, 11 3/4 In. 200.00
Vase, Tel El Amarna, Favrile, c.1912, 7 3/8 In. 4600.00
Vase, Trumpet, Amber, Ribbed, Flared, Short Stem, Favrile, 1919, 16 In. 1610.00
Vase, Tulip-Form, Amber Iridescent Pulled Leaves, Favrile, 12 In. 1035.00
Vase, Variegated Emerald Green Pulled Leaves, Onion Shape, Favrile, 13 In. 3960.00
Vase, Yellow, Wavy Trailings, Barbell Shape, Favrile, 1894, 9 1/4 In. 1955.00
Window, Confetti Glass, Spring Flowers, 1900s, 10 1/4 x 13 1/2 In. 13200.00
Wine, Blue & White Opaque, Signed, 8 In. 525.00
Wine, Gold Iridescent, 7 1/2 In. 275.00
Wine, Opalescent Bowls, Iridescent Stems, Signed, 7 1/2 In., Pair 1500.00
Wine Set, Amber Iridescent, Grapevine, Footed Decanter, Favrile, 5 3/4 In., 8 Piece 5750.00
TIFFANY GOLD, Cuff Links, Onyx, Hematite, 18K Gold, T & Co. 575.00
Cup, Cover, Gadrooned Borders, Saratoga Special, 14K Gold, c.1950, 7 5/8 In. 3450.00
Vanity Case, Enameled Muse With Harp, Diamonds, 1918, 3 1/4 x 2 1/4 In. 10925.00
TIFFANY POTTERY, Bowl, Cobalt, Green Matte Glaze, Squat, 6 1/4 x 10 3/4 In. 1100.00
Bowl, Fish & Shell, Fish & Waves, Green Interior, 8 In. 2000.00
Jar, Cover, Raised Leaves & Vines, Knop Finial, Signed, 9 In. 3500.00
Urn, 3 Handles, Frothy Celadon Crystalline Glaze, Favrile, 12 In. 8800.00
Vase, Black Over Purple, Textured, 4 1/2 In. 1500.00
Vase, Blossoms & Trailing Vines, Green Interior, Signed, 13 1/4 In. 1800.00
Vase, Dark Amber, Favrile, Signed, 1914, 5 1/2 x 14 1/2 In., Pair 4315.00
Vase, Fern Tendrils, Crackle Green Glaze, Signed, 10 In. 3500.00
Vase, Gourd Shape, Amber, Gunmetal & Ivory Glaze, Signed, L.C.T., 5 In. 2090.00
Vase, Green & Ivory Flambe Glaze, Rim, Favrile, 15 x 7 1/2 In. 880.00
Vase, Light Green, Favrile, Signed, 1914, 12 1/2 In. 3740.00
Vase, Mushrooms, Green Mottled Glaze, Favrile, Signed, L.C.T., 3 x 2 In. 1760.00
Vase, Oak Leaves, Old Ivory Matte Glaze, Signed, L.C.T., 9 3/4 x 3 1/2 In. 3850.00
Vase, Reticulated, White, Favrile, Signed, 7 3/4 In. 7475.00
Vase, Stylized Leaves & Berries, Mottled Green, Cobalt Blue Glaze, 1910, 6 In. 3450.00
Vase, White Bisque, Unglazed, Signed, L.C.T., 20 x 10 1/2 In. 550.00
Vase, Wisteria Pods, Apple Green & Turquoise Semimatte Glaze, 6 1/2 x 4 In. 990.00
TIFFANY SILVER, Bonbon, Still Life, Foliage, Pierced Sides, Flared Rim, 5 In. 265.00
Bowl, 2 Bands At Rim, Flared Rim, Deep Center, 11 In. 415.00
Bowl, Chased Flowers, Leaves, Fern Rim, Footed, 1902, 4 1/4 In. 1610.00
Bowl, Cupped Rim, Lapped Leaf Copper Inlay, 7 3/4 In. 635.00
Bowl, Diagonal Arch-Shaped Rim, 9 3/4 In. 440.00
Bowl, Enameled, Squares & Stylized Flowers Interior, c.1925, 8 1/8 In. 690.00
Bowl, Japanese Style, Gold Washed Turtles, Sea Plants, Undulating Rim, 5 In. 1525.00
Bowl, Pierced Clover Border, c.1891, 7 1/4 In. 695.00
Bowl, Reticulated Floral & C-Scroll, Ruffled Edge, Square, Marked, 9 x 3 1/4 In. 880.00
Bowl, Round, Threaded Rim, Monogram, 1907-1938, 8 1/2 In. 230.00
Bowl, Scalloped Edge, 10 3/4 In. 385.00
Bowl, Stylized Foliate Rim, Rolled & Lobed Border, 1907, 10 1/2 In. 920.00
Bowl, Sweetmeat, Oblong, Pierced, Ball Feet, Early 20th Century, 4 1/8 In., Pair 165.00
Box, Cigar, 1 3/4 x 5 3/4 In. 287.00
Box, Repousse, Flowers & Leaves, Detachable Cover, Monogram, Round, 3 1/2 In. 920.00
Box, Toilet, Rounded Corners, Pierced Circles, Sterling, c.1910, 3 3/8 x 2 1/2 In. 200.00
Cake Plate, Arcade & Fleur-De-Lis, Reeded Rim, Monogram, Low Foot, 17 Troy Oz. 375.00
Cake Stand, Reticulated Edge & Base, Fluted Border, 5 x 13 In. 2900.00
Candelabrum, 3-Light, Leaf Cornucopia, Shell Edge, Floral Repousse Foot, 12 In. 1150.00
Cann, Monogram IH, 4 1/2 In., 6 Piece 1210.00
Castor, Sugar, Pierced Cover, Ball Finial, 5 1/2 In. 460.00
Cigarette Case, Engraved, Hinged, Gilt Interior, Chain, 1917, 3 1/4 In. 165.00
Cocktail Shaker, Reeded Band, Detachable Cover, Strainer, Cap, 12 In. 1380.00
Coffee & Tea Service, Paneled Sides, Wooden Handles, Sterling, 7 Piece 7500.00

Coffee Set, Squat Spout, Hinged Cover, Egg Shape Finial, Wooden Handle, 3 Piece 1035.00
Compact, Hinged Lid, Enameled, Gilt, Engine-Turned Surface, 1920-1930, 2 1/2 In. 140.00
Compote, Cover, Squared Handles, Ivy Design, Blackamoor Head Finial, 7 In. 770.00
Compote, Vermeil Interior, Lobsters, Oval, Handles, 1870-1875, 13 x 6 In. 6260.00
Compote, Vermeil Interior, Oval, Handles, Marked, 13 x 6 In. 6880.00
Cup, Presentation, Beaded Rim, Midrib & Foot, Cherub Frieze, 1876, 3 7/8 In. 1460.00
Dish, Applied Foliage & Scrolls Rim, 1875, 7 1/2 In. 285.00
Dish, Chased With Flowers Within Scrolls, Paw Feet, Oblong, 2 1/2 In. 488.00
Dish, Gilt, Pierced Border, Stylized Foliage, Pineapple, 1900, 9 1/4 In., Pair 2760.00
Dish, Mint, Leaf Shape, 1925-1950, 3 1/4 In., 3 Piece 195.00
Dish, Shell, Monogram, Dated April 26, '48, Signed, 6 Piece 145.00
Fish Knife, Leaves, Flowers, Dolphin Terminals, 11 1/2 In. 335.00
Fork, Floral & Foliate, Monogram Both Sides, 19th Century, 4 Piece 135.00
Frame, Signed, 1920s, 10 x 7 1/2 In. 220.00
Grape Scissors, Pierced Handles, Flowers & Leaves, Trellis, Monogram 690.00
Jar, Cover, Stylized Urn, Fluted Sides, Ball Finial, 1902, 3 In. 250.00
Jar, Fluted, Engraved Body & Lid, Gold Washed Interior, 1871, 4 1/2 In. 575.00
Jewelry Box, Engine Turned Monogram, Velvet Lines, 1 1/4 x 5 3/8 In. 430.00
Ladle, Renaissance, Monogram On Handle, 1907, 10 1/2 In. 920.00
Ladle, Soup, Richelieu, Monogrammed 575.00
Mirror, Easel Back, Octagonal, c.1907, 18 x 13 1/2 In. 2000.00
Muffineer, Domed Cover, Urn Form Body, Stylized Leaf Banding, 7 1/2 In. 635.00
Mug, Young & Ellis, Repousse Flowers, 1851, 3 1/2 In. 488.00
Pie Server, Gold Washed Blade, Strawberry Handle, Early 20th Century, 11 In. 920.00
Pitcher, Foliate Band At Waist, Loop Handle, Monogram, 1875, 8 1/4 In. 1495.00
Pitcher, Foliate Garlands Upper Body, Paneled Lower Body, 1907, 8 1/4 In. 4025.00
Pitcher, Reeded Shoulder Band, Scroll Capped Handle, Monogram, 7 In. 460.00
Pitcher, Repousse, Flowers, Leaves, Waisted Baluster Form, 1902, 8 1/2 In. 3220.00
Pitcher, Water, Leafy Garlands, Waisted Band, Reeded Foot, Angular Handle 4025.00
Salt, Footed, Signed, L.C.T. 88.00
Salt, Master, Repousse Floral Design, 2 Ring Handles, No Liner, 3 x 2 1/4 In. 200.00
Salver, Stylized Shell Design, Scalloped Border, Footed, 1902, 7 In. 250.00
Saucepan, Angular Ebonized Handle, 1854-1870, 6 x 5 In. 605.00
Saucepan, Presentation, Brandy, Wooden Handle, 1857, 3 3/4 In. 345.00
Serving Spoon, Fruit, Parcel Gilt, Strawberry Handle, Early 20th Century, 9 1/2 In. 935.00
Serving Spoon, Olympian, c.1902-1907, 9 1/2 In. ....100.00 to 290.00
Shoehorn, Sterling, 8 In. 75.00
Spoon, Coffee, English King, 4 5/8 In., 3 Piece 100.00
Stuffing Spoon, Chrysanthemum, Sterling, Monogram, 12 1/2 In. 750.00
Tazza, Chased, Scalloped, Cornucopias, E.C. Moore, c.1873-1891, 9 1/4 In. 3740.00
Tazza, Scroll & Floral, c.1920, 4 1/2 x 6 In. 1045.00
Tea Service, Cast Rocaille Feet, Beaded Rim, Monogram, 1902, 4 Piece 2070.00
Tea Set, Urn Finials, Molded Borders, Tray, 12 In. 2875.00
Teakettle, Stand, Renaissance Style, E.C. Moore, 1854-1870, 14 In. 6050.00
Teaspoon, St. James, Monogram, 12 Piece 345.00
Tray, Monogram BWD, Footed, 3 x 9 In., Pair 600.00
Tray, Round, Beaded Band, Monogram, Inscriptions, 11 1/2 In. 290.00
Tray, Scrolled Rim, 18 1/2 In. 2200.00
Vase, Bud, Amphora, Circular Base, S-Form Handles, 10 1/2 In. 800.00
Vase, Scrolled Loop Handles, Ruffled Edge, 7 x 4 1/2 In. 865.00
Vase, Trumpet, Monogram, EHF, 14 In. 660.00

TIFFIN Glass Company of Tiffin, Ohio, was a subsidiary of the United
States Glass Co. of Pittsburgh, Pennsylvania, in 1892. The U.S. Glass
Co. went bankrupt in 1963, and the Tiffin plant employees purchased
the building and the inventory. They continued running it from 1963 to
1966, when it was sold to Continental Can Company. In 1969, it was
sold to Interpace, and in 1980, it was closed. The black satin glass,
made from 1923 to 1926, and the stemware of the last twenty years are
the best-known products.

Black Satin, Vase, Silver Overlay, 11 In. 275.00
Bulldog, Doorstop, Black Satin, Red Eyes, Brass Collar, 7 In. 275.00
Byzantine, Cocktail, Yellow, 3 1/2 Oz. 15.00

Byzantine, Decanter, Yellow 600.00
Byzantine, Plate, 8 1/2 In. 4.50
Byzantine, Plate, Yellow, 7 1/2 In. 15.00
Byzantine, Tumbler, Juice, Footed, 5 Oz. .... 16.00 to 18.00
Byzantine, Wine, 3 1/2 Oz. 18.00
Cadena, Cordial, Topaz, 3/4 Oz. 80.00
Cadena, Decanter, Squat, Yellow 450.00
Cadena, Sherbet, Low, Topaz, 5 Oz. 15.00
Cadena, Wine, Topaz, 3 1/2 Oz. 35.00
Cherokee Rose, Candlestick, 2-Light, Pair 85.00
Cherokee Rose, Goblet, 9 Oz. .... 28.00 to 32.00
Cherokee Rose, Sherbet, 5 1/2 Oz. 20.00
Cherokee Rose, Sherry, 2 Oz. 40.00
Classic, Decanter, Yellow 550.00
Classic, Tumbler, Whiskey, Footed, 2 1/2 Oz. 40.00
Classic, Vase, Bud, 10 1/2 In. 65.00
Classic, Wine, 3 Oz. 32.00
Cordelia, Cocktail, 3 1/2 Oz. 10.00
Cordelia, Sherbet, 5 Oz. 8.00
Figurine, Cat, Milk Glass, 11 In. 350.00
Figurine, Pheasant, Female, Head Down, No. 6042, Blue, 7 1/2 x 16 In. 450.00
Flanders, Champagne, 5 1/2 Oz. 14.75
Flanders, Cup & Saucer 45.00
Flanders, Decanter Set, Pink, 10 1/4 In., 5 Piece 165.00
Flanders, Decanter, Squat, Stopper, Yellow 600.00
Flanders, Decanter, Tall, Footed, Pink 450.00
Flanders, Goblet, Pink, 9 Oz. 75.00
Flanders, Pitcher, Footed, Pink, 65 Oz. 495.00
Flanders, Wine, Pink, 3 1/2 Oz. 90.00
Fuchsia, Champagne, 5 Oz. 18.00
Fuchsia, Cordial, 1 Oz. 35.00
Fuchsia, Goblet, 9 Oz. 80.00
June Night, Cordial, 1 Oz. .... 35.00 to 60.00
June Night, Tumbler, Juice, 5 Oz. 26.00
Persian Pheasant, Cordial, 1 Oz. .... 45.00 to 60.00
Swedish Optic, Vase, Floral Carving, 12 3/4 In. 100.00
Tea Rose, Cocktail, 4 Oz. 35.00
Tumble Up, Candlestick, Twist, Blue, 10 In., Pair 75.00

TILES have been used in most countries of the world as a sturdy building material for floors, roofs, fireplace surrounds, and surface toppings. Many of the American tiles are listed in this book under the factory name.

Arts & Crafts, Red, Green Matte Glaze, Oak Frame, Square, 6 In. 275.00
Bust, Woman Profile, 1 Girl With Umbrella Riding Donkey, 11 x 7 In., Pair 57.00
California Courtyard, Fountain, Arts & Crafts Frame, Impressed Mark, 8 x 12 In. 1760.00
Classical Maiden, Brown Glaze, 1870s, 18 1/2 x 6 In., 3 Piece 316.00
Covered Wagon, Going West, Faience, Pastel Glazes, Claycraft, Frame, 7 x 15 In. 2750.00
Horse & Rider, Persian, 12 x 8 In. 110.00
Incised Viking Ship, Polychrome, Franklin, Frame, 6 In. 195.00
Landscape, Mediterranean Houses, 5 Panels, Arts & Crafts Frame, Marked, 13 x 35 In. .. 2640.00
Landscape, Raised Tree, Sky, Body Of Water, Claycraft, Arts & Crafts Frame, 7 1/2 In. .. 1540.00
Landscape, Waterfall, Trees On Hillside, Rising Sun, Claycraft, Frame, 15 In. 2640.00
Mermaids, Ocean, Matisse Style, 6 Panels, Frame, 1950s, 11 1/2 x 17 3/4 In. 250.00
Peacock, California Art Tile Co., 1930s, 10 1/2 x 5 In. 750.00
Portrait, Longfellow, Umber Glaze, U.S. Encaustic, Square, 6 In. 55.00
Rampant Lions, 1598, 3 3/4 x 5 3/4 In., Pair 425.00
Road Through Mountains, Signed, Claycraft, Arts & Crafts Frame, 3 1/2 x 11 1/2 In. ... 1760.00
Scarab, Molded, Arts & Crafts, Blue High Glaze, Brick Red Matte Ground, 4 In. 295.00
Tropical Women, Palms, Cubist Style, Polychrome, 9 Panels, Frame, 1950s, 18 In. 440.00
Water Lilies, Green Lily Pads, Arts & Crafts, Ivory, Pink, Oak Frame, 20 x 4 In., Pair ... 715.00
Woman, Seated, Hovering Cranes, Polychrome, Matted, Frame, 9 Panels, 1950s, 18 In. ... 360.00

TINWARE containers for household use have been made in America since the seventeenth century. The first tin utensils were brought from Europe, but by 1798, tin plate was imported and local tinsmiths made the wares. Painted tin is called tole and is listed separately. Some tin kitchen items may be found listed under Kitchen. The lithographed tin containers used to hold food and tobacco are listed in the Advertising category under Tin.

Bread Basket, Painted Foliage & Fruit, Half Moon Style, 19th Century	615.00
Bread Tray, Foliate Design, Red Paint, Sloping Ends, Rectangular, 12 3/4 x 8 In.	575.00
Cage, Squirrel, Wire Bars, Punched Design Other Side, Air Holes, 23 In.	412.00
Canister, Cover, Worn Yellow Paint, 18 x 32 In.	165.00
Canister, Red Cherries, Green Leaves, White Border, Yellow Stylized Leaves, 6 In.	402.00
Carrier, Water, Hired Man's, Cup Holder Brackets	475.00
Coaster Set, Ruppert Knickerbocher, Lithograph, 1960s, 4 Piece	30.00
Coffeepot, Domed Cover, Lighthouse Form, Stylized Leaves, Floral, 10 In.	745.00
Coffeepot, Gooseneck Spout, Floral, Tinsmith Made	275.00
Coffeepot, Pewter Knob, 9 1/2 In.	247.00
Coffeepot, Tapered, Applied Handle & Spout, Hinged Lid, Brass Knopf Finial, 9 3/4 In.	330.00
Cuspidor, Stenciled, 7 1/2 In.	44.00
Dish Set, Child's, Geese Skiing, France, 1900	195.00
Floodlight, Theater, Tin, Kerosene, Curved Reflector, Paris, 1850, 15 5/8 In.	265.00
Flytrap, Hanging, Mesh, 9 In.	38.00
Foot Warmer, Punched, Curly Maple Frame, 5 3/4 x 8 x 8 1/2 In.	465.00
Horn, Fishmonger's, Red Paint Traces, 14 3/4 In.	77.00
Mold, Candle, 4 Tube, Inverted Funnel Base, Handle, Wide Ear, 12 1/2 x 6 1/2 In.	170.00
Mold, Candle, 8 Tube	45.00
Mold, Candle, 12 Tube, 2 Handles	88.00
Mold, Candle, 12 Tube, Ear Handle, 11 1/2 In.	302.00
Mold, Candle, 12 Tube, Fixed Handle	65.00
Mold, Candle, 12 Tube, Handle	50.00
Mold, Candle, 24 Tube, Ear Handles, 10 In.	275.00
Muffineer, Handle, 3 3/4 & 4 1/8 In., 2 Piece	80.00
Rattle, Baby's, Whistle End	115.00
Tinderbox, Flint Inside, 4 1/2 In.	357.00
Tray, John Mitchell, Miner At Left & Wife & Child, Gold, Red Border, Oval, 13 x 16 In.	275.00
Tray, Still Life, Painted, Gilt Leaf, Vine Border, 26 x 19 In.	190.00

TOBACCO CUTTERS may be listed in either the Advertising or Store categories.

TOBACCO JAR collectors search for those made in odd shapes and colors. Because tobacco needs special conditions of humidity and air, it has been stored in special containers since the eighteenth century.

Black Boy, Red Bowtie, 4 1/2 In.	302.00
Black Girl, Bandanna, 4 1/2 In.	220.00
Black Sailor, 6 1/4 In.	495.00
Blue Boar, Pottery, Coach & Inn Transfer, 6 x 5 7/8 In.	70.00
Carved Floral, Chinese Export, 5 5/8 In.	130.00
Chesapeake, 7 1/2 In.	145.00
Clown On Pig, 7 In.	165.00
Coach Form, 2-Cushion Seats, Caned Basket, Hinged Rear Luggage, 6 x 9 In.	7475.00
Cupid's Bow Apron, Lamb's Tongue, Brass, Late 18th Century, 6 In.	465.00
Frog With Mandolin, 6 1/2 In.	275.00
Indian Chief, 7 3/4 In.	160.00
Ivory Banding, Chest Of Drawers Form, 6 Drawers Over Cupboard, 12 1/2 In.	962.00
Lignum Vitae Wood, 18th Century	295.00
Man Helping Woman With Corset, Humorous, Pottery, 9 1/2 x 8 In.	520.00
Monkey Eating Fruit, Set-On Lid Porcelain, E. Bohne Sohne, 6 In.	1210.00
Monkey With Pipe, 4 3/4 In.	55.00
Pig With Fez, 6 In.	145.00
Pig With Umbrella, 7 In.	145.00
Railroad Coal Car Form, 2 Interior Sections, Striker, Match Holder, 13 In.	4312.00
Tabac, Relief, Stoneware, Set On Lid, Hubert Krameich-Remy, 5 1/2 In.	135.00
Woman With Umbrella, 7 In.	145.00

TOBY JUG is the name of a very special form of pitcher. It is shaped like the full figure of a man or woman. A pitcher that shows just the top half of a person is not correctly called a toby. More examples of toby jugs can be found under Royal Doulton and other factory names.

Admiral Nelson, Staffordshire, Early 19th Century, 11 1/2 In.	180.00
Black Hat & Jacket, Lilac Breeches, Staffordshire, 9 1/2 In.	290.00
Court Jester, Brick & Black, Scalloped Top, England, c.1820, 9 1/2 In.	225.00
Gentleman, Seated, Holding Pitcher, Blue, Red & Black, 8 1/2 In.	575.00
Man, Seated, Jug Of Flowers, Flowers Inside Lip, Empire Works, England	150.00
Man, Seated, With Mug & Pitcher, Runny Brown, Blue, & Yellow, 10 3/4 In.	35.00
Man, Sitting, Rockingham Glaze, Large	115.00
Man, Smoking Pipe, Holding Mug, 19th Century, 10 In.	330.00
Man, Wearing Tricorn Hat, Holding Mug & Pitcher, England, c.1850, 11 1/4 In.	975.00
Night Watchman, Staffordshire, 1860, 9 1/4 In.	700.00
Snuff Taker, Allerton, 7 In.	125.00
Squire, Sylvac, 4 In.	55.00
Uncle Sam, Royal Winton, 5 1/2 In.	89.00
Woman, Holding Beer Glass, c.1840-1860, 9 1/4 In.	750.00
Woodrow Wilson, Wilkinson, 10 1/2 In.	860.00

TOLE is painted tin. It is sometimes called *japanned ware*, *pontypool*, or *toleware*. Most nineteenth-century tole is painted with an orange-red or black background and multicolored decorations. Many recent versions of toleware are made and sold. Related items may be listed in the Tinware category.

Basin, Leaf Design, Salmon Ground, 2 Handles, France, 1870, 16 In.	440.00
Basket, Painted Floral Decoration, Footed, 19th Century, 3 1/2 x 19 x 14 In.	110.00
Box, Deed, Dome Top, Flowers, Worn Brown Japanning, 9 3/4 x 6 1/2 x 7 1/2 In.	245.00
Box, Document, Cover, Red, Yellow Flowers, Stevens Plains, Maine, 8 3/4 x 4 3/4 x 5 In.	2200.00
Box, Document, Dome Lid, Green, Red Trailing Vines & Flowers, Black Ground, 7 In.	330.00
Box, Document, Dome Lid, Swags, 19th Century, 5 1/2 x 8 1/2 In.	330.00
Box, Document, Handle Top, Flowers, 1840	575.00
Box, Document, Red & Yellow Design, Black Ground, 1830, 4 1/2 x 8 1/8 In.	220.00
Box, Dome Top, Decorated, Assorted Contents, 8 In.	132.00
Box, Dome Top, Flowers, Spiral Design On Lid, 9 x 4 3/4 x 5 1/4 In.	440.00
Bread Tray, Flowers, Brown Japanning, 8 x 14 1/4 In.	440.00
Bread Tray, Red Flowers, Green Foliage, Leafy Border, 13 1/2 In.	880.00
Cachepot, 18th Century Scenes, Reticulated Border, Lion Handles, Iron Base, 16 x 12 In.	1100.00
Candelabra, 3-Light, Blown Glass Shades, 19th Century, 27 1/2 In.	355.00
Candlesnuffer, Pair	395.00
Canister, Black Paint, Lion, Unicorn Crest, 18 In.	154.00
Canister, Tea, Polychrome, Leaf Tracery, Chinese Calligraphic Label, c.1860, 17 In.	550.00
Cellarette, Gilt Scrollwork, Gilt Cast Iron Base, Stags' Heads, 26 1/2 In.	1430.00
Coffeepot, Dome Lid, Green Leaves, Black Ground, 1825, 10 3/4 In.	1320.00
Coffeepot, Flowers, Leaf Design, Gold Accents, Black Surface, Tin, 19th Century, 10 In.	1100.00
Coffeepot, Polychrome Flowers, 10 1/2 In.	522.00
Coffeepot, Red & Yellow Flowers, Dark Brown Ground, 10 3/4 In.	330.00
Container, Hinged Cover, Flowers, Black Ground, Wire Handle, 1830, 6 x 9 In.	245.00
Creamer, Red, Green & Yellow Flowers, Brown Japanning, 4 3/8 In.	82.00
Jar, Wooden Lid, 3 3/4 x 4 1/2 In.	1150.00
Jardiniere, Flowers, Apple Green Ground, Shaped Gilt Lip, 19th Century, 5 x 10 1/2 In.	470.00
Jardiniere, Pagodas & Exotic Birds, Mountainous Setting, 11 1/4 In., Pair	2300.00
Lamp, Lard, Gray Paint, Gold Trim, Brass & Copper Burner, 6 In.	110.00
Lantern, Central Candle Nozzle, Mirrored Back, Foliate Corner Scrolls, Red, 41 In.	1380.00
Mug, Flowers, Dark Ground, 5 3/4 In.	330.00
Mug, Flowers, White Band, Brown Japanning, 4 1/2 In.	660.00
Sconce, Swan's Neck Sides, Acorn Finial, Glass Shades, c.1820, 12 In., Pair	4312.00
Shelf, Lighting, Star Design, 15 x 14 In.	495.00
Spice Box, 2 Lids & 3 Sections Each Side, Gold Stenciled Labels, Black, 9 1/2 In.	110.00
Spice Box, 5 Compartments, Landscape Design, Black Paint, Tin, 13 x 24 In.	1650.00
Spice Box, Brass Handle, England, 19th Century, Round	395.00
Tea Caddy, Flowers, Black Ground, 8 1/8 In.	55.00

Teapot, Lighthouse, 9 3/4 In. 440.00
Torch, Parade, Ritter's Old Method Keystone Copper-Steel, 4 Burners, 12 In. 95.00
Tray, Admiral Dewey, 5 5/8 In. 70.00
Tray, Allegorical Ottoman Scene, Faux Bamboo, Regency, 21 x 29 x 23 In. 770.00
Tray, Black Lacquer, Gilt Edge, Leaves & Flowers, Bamboo Stand, 21 1/4 x 30 x 23 In. . .   460.00
Tray, Black Lacquer, Oriental Landscapes, Faux Bamboo Stand, 20 3/4 x 22 1/2 x 18 In. .   1840.00
Tray, Black Lacquer, Oriental Scenes, Architecture, Faux Bamboo Stand, 21 x 29 In. 6325.00
Tray, Center Spaniel's Head, Papier-Mache, Faux Bamboo Stand, c.1860, 21 In. 825.00
Tray, Center Tulips, Yellow Leaves, Black Ground, 8 Sides, 12 x 17 In. 440.00
Tray, Central Floral Bouquet, Scrolled Gilt Border, Oval, Late 19th Century, 26 In. 288.00
Tray, Central Red Shell & Leaf, Black Ground, Greek Key Borders, c.1820, 28 x 21 In. . .   725.00
Tray, Cutout Handles, Fruiting Vines, Scene Of Kremlin, 20 1/2 In. 2875.00
Tray, Cutout Handles, Smoked Black, Gold & Bronze Paint, Flowers & Vase, 28 In. 750.00
Tray, Death Of General Wolfe, Pierced Oval, Carrying Handles, 22 x 28 In. 2537.00
Tray, Faux Bamboo Ebonized Gilt Stand, X-Frame Stretcher, c.1880, 24 x 33 In. 1495.00
Tray, Figural Gilt Oriental Landscape, Black Lacquer, Bamboo Stand, Gilt Accents, 21 In.   1955.00
Tray, Floral Urn Surrounded By Vines, 22 x 30 In. 715.00
Tray, Flowers, Black Faux Bamboo Stand, Circular, 19 3/4 x 26 1/2 In. 1725.00
Tray, Flowers, Black Lacquer, Parcel Gilt, Bamboo Stand, 21 1/2 x 21 In. 2070.00
Tray, Flowers, Black, Bamboo Stand, Gilt, 20 3/4 x 25 x 19 3/4 In. 1610.00
Tray, Fruit & Basket Design, 19th Century, 28 x 20 1/2 In. 88.00
Tray, Oriental & Landscape Scene, Pair Of Gilt Chinamen Seated By Table, 39 x 22 In. . .   1495.00
Tray, Oriental Design, Late 19th Century, 30 1/4 In. 110.00
Tray, Oriental Landscape, Black Lacquer Rectangular Top, Bamboo Stand, 21 x 19 In. . . .   1380.00
Tray, Oriental Riverscape, Rectangular Top, Bamboo Stand, 22 x 21 x 17 In. 1495.00
Tray, Pastoral Landscape Scene, Maidens & Couples, Deep Tan Ground, Stand, 21 In. . . .   1840.00
Tray, Polychrome Harbor Scene, Copper Rim, Faux Bamboo Stand, Victorian, 21 x 25 In.   990.00
Tray, Recumbent Stag Decoration, 19th Century, 20 x 28 In. 99.00
Tray, Red, White, Blue Flowers On Sides, Mixed Fruit, Dark Green, 16 x 19 3/4 In. 100.00
Tray, Sewing, Garden Scene, 2 Women At Fountain, 19th Century, 18 1/2 x 30 3/4 In. . . .   132.00
Tray, Stand, Center Sporting Dog, Woodland Setting, Faux Bamboo Stand, c.1880, 30 In. .   3737.00
Tray, Stand, Flowers Within Ribboned Floral Border, Bamboo Turned Legs, 27 In. 3737.00
Tray, Stand, Hunt Scene, Pierced Gallery Rail, Polished Brass Base, 20 x 17 In. 1035.00
Tray, Stand, Mythological Scene, Guilt Foliage, Pierced Handholds, 19th Century, 25 In. .   2070.00
Tray, Stand, Painted Visitors At Thames Tunnel, Foliate Border, Victorian, 24 x 17 In. . . .   230.00
Tray, Star & Pinwheels, Black Ground, 22 x 27 1/2 In. 220.00
Tray, Stenciled Scene Of Youth & Maiden In Garden, Floral Border, 18 x 24 1/4 In. 82.00
Tray, Young Girl Decorating A Statue, Gilt, Octagonal, 26 In. 154.00
Tub, Flowers, Cut Corners, Shelf, Soap Holder, Child's 627.00
Umbrella Stand, 2 Sections, Copper Color, Landscape Reserves, Gilt Highlights, 26 In. . .   385.00
Urn, Flower Sprays, Birds, Gilt Leaf Borders, 2 Handles, 19th Century, Pair 575.00
Urn, Gilt Floral, Birds, Butterflies, Slender Stem, 19th Century, 13 1/4 In., Pair 1725.00
Warmer, Leaves & Flowers, Cylindrical, Handles, With Cup & Burner, 1860, 9 1/4 In. . . .   525.00

TOM MIX was born in 1880 and died in 1940. He was the hero of over
100 silent movies from 1910 to 1929, and 25 sound films from 1929
to 1935. There was a Ralston Tom Mix radio show from 1933 to 1950,
but the original Tom Mix was not in the show. Tom Mix comics were
published from 1942 to 1953.

Badge, Decoder, 1941 . . . .   80.00
Badge, Dobie County 50.00
Badge, Straight Shooter 115.00
Bandanna, Best Wishes, Cloth, Early 1920s, 15 3/4 x 17 In. 95.00
Bottle, Coca-Cola, 1985 . . . .   20.00
Compass 60.00
Hat, Stetson, Black, Mel Tillis Autograph, Teners', Oklahoma City, Size 7 . . . .   452.00
Hat, Stetson, Felt, 2-In. Hat Band, Grant Boys Co., Costa Mesa, 7 1/2 x 14 In. 2034.00
Lasso, Red, White & Blue Nylon, Red Wooden Grip, Ralston Cereal Premium 48.00
Patch, Bar Diamond Brand, Felt, Ralston Premium, 1945, 2 1/2 In. 31.00
Poster, Miracle Rider, Universal, 1934, Linen, Three Sheet 2875.00
Saddle, Trick Riding, 1st Place Presentation, Leather, George Hall Saddle Maker 848.00
Telescope, 1937 . . . .   65.00

TOOLS of all sorts are listed here, but most are related to industry. Other tools may be found listed under Iron, Kitchen, Tinware, and Wooden.

Adze, Chairmaker's, Hollowing, England, 19th Century, 5 In.	82.00
Adze, Cooper's, No. 3, Greaves	35.00
Adze, Shipwright's	35.00
Air Gauge, Brass, 7 3/4 In.	60.00
Anvil, Blacksmith's, 1930s, Large	225.00
Anvil, Blacksmith's, Vulcan, Cast Iron, American, 1930s, Small	75.00
Auger, Bung Rasp, Cooper's, Goldenberg, France	115.00
Ax, Full Groove, Huron Co., Ohio, 2 5/8 In.	99.00
Ax, Groove, Newbo Hill, Illinois, 5 1/2 In.	660.00
Ax, Groove, Pike Co., Ill., 3 3/4 In.	104.00
Ax, Groove, Portland, Ind., 6 3/4 In.	330.00
Ax, Head, Side, The American Axe Company, U.S.A., 4 1/2 In.	45.00
Ax, Hohokam, Maricopa Co., Ar., 10 1/4 In.	467.00
Ax, Iron, Hand Forged, Wooden Handle, Signed	150.00
Ax, Marbles No. 6, Safety Guard, Polished Wooden Handle	190.00
Ax, Side, Robert Sorby, 18-In. Head, 8-In. Edge	248.00
Ax, Sugar, Ebony Handle	62.00
Ax, Timber Marking, Hachette De Forester, 19th Century	160.00
Bevel, Archaic, Franklin Co., Ohio, 2 1/2 In.	66.00
Blasting Machine, Metal, Leather Strap, Wooden Knob, Hercules Powder Co., 5 In.	95.00
Borer Mortise, For Post & Beam Constructions, Wooden, 2-Handle Crank	55.00
Box, 7 Drawers, Felt Lining, Machinist's, Leatherette, Gerstner, c.1930	150.00
Box, Conestoga Wagon, Fleur-De-Lis Hinges & Hasp, Rivet Design, 1800, 24 x 17 In.	880.00
Box, Conestoga Wagon, Ram's Horn Hasp, Mounted On New Backboard, 1800, 16 In.	605.00
Box, Machinist's, H. Gerstner & Sons, Dayton, Oh., Quartersawn Oak, 16 x 26 x 9 In.	425.00
Brace, Alfred Ridge, Metallic, Brass Frame, Inlaid Ebony, Rosewood Rotating Handle	416.00
Brace & Bit, Woodworker's, c.1870	60.00
Cabinet, Blacksmith's, Wooden, 4 Small & 1 Large Drawer, 1830, Large	285.00
Caliper, Dial, Stainless Steel, Measures 0-6 1/2 In., Shockproof, Case	37.00
Caliper, Inside, Starrett, 4 In.	15.00
Caliper, Inside-Outside, Opens To 13 In., 12 1/4 In.	110.00
Caliper, Wheelwright's, Late 18th Century, 15 1/2 In.	62.00
Carry-All, Blacksmith's, On Wheels, Pine, 14 x 12 x 15 In.	110.00
Chain Tightener, Harley-Davidson, Chrome	35.00
Chest, 4 Small Drawers, Shelves, Hanging, 1849-1892, 10 x 14 x 24 In.	585.00
Chest, Carpenter's, Pine, Lift Top, 19th Century, 14 x 41 x 16 In.	45.00
Chest, Carpenter's, Red Brown Paint, Wooden Planes, 14 1/2 x 32 x 16 In., 37 Piece	815.00
Chest, Lift Top, Hinged Lid, Black Cast Iron Handles, 33 x 21 x 20 In.	110.00
Chisel, Atco Tool Works, 2 In.	25.00
Chisel, Cabinetmaker's, Hickory Handles, Stanley Everlasting, Original Roll, 9 Piece	1785.00
Chisel, Mortise, Buck & Hickman, 1 In.	44.00
Chisel, Turning, Buck Bros., 4 Piece	70.00
Chisel Set, Tyzack, Bevel Edge, Ash Handle, 1/2 In., Set Of 8	97.00
Cobbler's Bench, Blue Paint, 2 Drawers	522.00
Cobbler's Bench, Pine, 4 Drawers, Posts Made To Hold Leather Vise, 35 1/2 x 43 In.	550.00
Cobbler's Bench, Pine, 9 Compartments, Drawer, 19th Century, 41 1/2 x 50 In.	225.00
Cobbler's Bench, Pine, 9 Small & 2 Large Drawers, Mass., 30 x 44 x 19 In.	1100.00
Cobbler's Bench, Poplar, Pencil Post Legs, 2 Drawers, 18 1/2 x 53 1/2 x 27 In.	467.00
Cobbler's Bench, Shelf Fitted With Tools, Gilt Stencil Work, 18 1/4 x 43 In.	80.00
Comb, Curry, Iron, Brass Design, Turned Wooden Handle, Penn. Dutch, 7 3/4 In.	110.00
Corn Sheller, Wooden, Weathered Paint, Hocking Valley	90.00
Cutting Machine, Gesetzl, Teschutzt, Iron, 3 Blades, Salesman's Sample, 12 In.	330.00
Draw Knife, Gentleman's, Thomas Ibbotson, Pear Shaped Boxwood Handles, 7 In.	21.00
Draw Knife, Steel Blade, No. 11, Wooden Handles, 17 x 6 In.	75.00
Drill, Belmont Co., Ohio, 4 1/2 In.	132.00
Edge Marker, A.R. Jacobs, Walnut, 2 x 6 1/2 In. Closed	60.00
Flashlight, Bell System C, Bright Star, Angle Head, Black Bakelite, 7 1/2 In.	21.00
Flashlight, Bond Electric Co., Angle Head, Corrugated Rubber Grip, 10 In.	20.00
Gauge, Balloon Tire Pressure, Schrader, Pat. Date 1923	65.00
Gauge, Bit Depth, Stanley, No. 49	22.00

Gauge, Butt & Rabbet, Stanley Rule & Level Co., No. 92, Pat. Aug. 23, 1892 .... 150.00
Gauge, Stanley, No. 49, Bit New In Box, c.1950 .... 35.00
Gauge, Stanley, No. 77, c.1875 .... 45.00
Gauge, Stanley, No. 89, Clapboard, c.1890 .... 60.00
Gauge, Surface, Lufkin, Spindle & Scribe 31.00
Gunpowder Tester, Brass, Continental, 18th Century 1100.00
Hammer, Sugar, Brass & Steel, Curly Maple Handle, 8 In. 1155.00
Handcuffs, H&R Arms Company, Steel, 2-Link Chain, Key 90.00
Handcuffs, Key, Mattatuck Mfg. Co., Waterbury, Conn., Nickel Finish, Key 120.00
Handcuffs, Marlin Firearm Co., New Haven, Conn., Nickel Finish, Key 380.00
Handcuffs, Nickeled Iron, Push Button, Patent 1884 .... 100.00
Handcuffs, Peerless Handcuff Co., Springfield, Mass., Steel, 2-Link Chain, Key, 9 In. 40.00
Hatchet, Pennsylvania, Date 1774 Both Sides 110.00
Hatchet, Shingling, Winchester, Original Handle 100.00
Hay Fork, Split Hickory, Orange Highlights, Child's, Inscribed With 1907, 35 1/2 In. 770.00
Jack, Conestoga Wagon, Wooden Handle, Red Paint, 1842 .... 190.00
Jointer, Chip Carved, Worm Holes, 1787, 33 In. 885.00
Jointer, Fruitwood, Chip Carved, 1816, 29 In. 1098.00
Kit, Bezel, Jewel, Watchmaker's, Case, French, 4 3/16 x 7/8 In. 110.00
Kit, Peres Solingen, Germany, Leather Case, Pocket Knife Type Handle, 5 x 6 In. 65.00
Knife, Chamfer, Cooper's, Marked 35.00
Last, Shoemaker's, Wooden, Size 8, Pair 60.00
Lawn Mower, Charter Mfg. Co., Cast Iron, Salmon Paint, 1875, 58 In. 1525.00
Leg Cuffs, American Munitions Co., Chicago, Ill., Prisoner, Steel, Key 61.00
Leg Irons, Nickeled Steel, 2 Keys, H.R. Arms, Worcester, Mass. 115.00
Level, Stanley, No. 31, Pocket, Hexagonal, c.1900 .... 35.00
Level, Stanley, No. 36, Cast Iron, c.1900 ....38.00 to 50.00
Level, Starrett, Cast Iron, Filigree, 24 In. 80.00
Level, Starrett, Inclinometer, 10 In. 60.00
Level, Surveying, Buff & Buff Mfg. Co., Lacquered Brass, Tripod Mount, 17 3/4 In. 295.00
Lifter, Hatbox, Thoroughbred Hats, Harris-Polk Hat Co., Saint Louis, Pat. 1901, 36 In. 55.00
Lock, Barrel, Key & Chain Keeper, Wrought Iron, 5 1/2 In. 250.00
Loom, Rag Rug, Early 19th Century, 30 In. 750.00
Miter Box, Pressed Steel Frame, Maple Board, Carton, c.1950 .... 50.00
Monkey Wrench, Acme, 21 In. 300.00
Nautical, Sailmaker's, Smoothing Sail Seams, Lignum Vitae, 2 Handles, 17 In. 165.00
Pipe Tongs, Wrought Steel, 22 3/4 In. 660.00
Pivot & Bushing Kit, C & E Marshall Co., Mahogany Case, 155 Piece 110.00
Plane, A. Mathieson, Steel Panel, Dovetailed, Inlaid Rosewood, 16 1/2 In. 868.00
Plane, Chamfer, C. Nurse & Co., Beech Box 88.00
Plane, Circular, Stanley Victor, No. 20, Logo On Blade 265.00
Plane, Dado, Stanley, No. 39 3/8 .... 132.00
Plane, Dovetail, A. Mathieson, Snicker Iron, Original Brass Skate 159.00
Plane, Jack, Stanley, No. 5 1/4, Logo, c.1925 .... 70.00
Plane, Jointer, Norris A-1, Dovetail Body, 28 1/2 In. 6958.00
Plane, Jointer, Sargent No. 722C 200.00
Plane, Miter, A. Mathieson, Improved Pattern, Steel, Dovetailed, Inlaid Rosewood 708.00
Plane, Molding, Complex, Griffiths, Norwich, 2 3/4 In. 185.00
Plane, Molding, MacGurie & Jago, Iron, 4 Piece 1384.00
Plane, Plow, D.R. Barton, Ivory Tips 300.00
Plane, Plow, Ohio Tool Co., Ebony, Ivory Tips 500.00
Plane, Rabbet & Block, Stanley, No. 140 .... 130.00
Plane, Smooth, Stanley, No. 4 1/2, Lever Cap 73.00
Plane Block, Stanley, No. 15 1/2, Squirrel Tailed, 1880 .... 250.00
Plane Block, Stanley, No. 95, Edge Trimming 162.00
Plumb Bob, Brass, String Attached, 4 1/4 In. 20.00
Plumb Square, Heart Shape Plumb Bob, Brass Fittings, 20 In. 600.00
Press, Soap, New England, Late 19th Century 375.00
Rake, Maple, Bent Wood Reinforcer, 19th Century, 71 x 27 In. 85.00
Router, Coachmaker's, E. Preston, Beech, Brass & Steel Fittings 81.00
Rule, Folding Pocket, Brass & Ivory, 18th Century 275.00
Rule, Folding, Stanley, No. 88, Ivory, 1920 .... 300.00
Rule, Rabone, No. 1119, Brass Hinges, Warranted Boxwood, 3 Ft. Folded, 1 1/2 x 9 In. .. 80.00

Rule, Rolling, Stanley, Brass, 12 1/4 In. 150.00
Rule & Level, Stanley, No. 41, Brass Top, Pat. June 23, 1896, 3 In. 65.00
Saw, Band, F.H. Clement Co., 1896, 28 In. 1050.00
Saw, Crosscut, 2-Man 17.00
Saw, Finger, Fine Teeth, Brass Frame, Walnut Handle, Initial F, 7 1/2 In. 115.00
Saw, Ice 37.00
Saw, Pit, Wooden Frame, 7 Ft. 900.00
Saw, Plow Type, Marks Blocks Of Pond Ice For Sawing, Horse Drawn 75.00
Scissors, Keen Kutter 25.00
Scissors Sharpener, Steel, Wooden, Bakelite Handle, Professional Imported, 10 x 7 In. . . . 24.00
Scraper, Veneer, Stanley, No. 12 . . . . 72.00
Screwdriver, Gunsmith's, Turned Ebony Handle, Brass Ferrule & Cap, 5 In. 45.00
Sheller, Corn, Wooden, Cast Iron, 1840 . . . . 500.00
Shovel, Curd, Wooden, 1 Piece 100.00
Slide Rule, Dated 1900 . . . . 25.00
Slide Rule, Otis King, Leather Pouch, Instructions 170.00
Slide Rule, Wood & Brass, Wooden Case, 17 x 21 In. 515.00
Spokeshave, Bailey, No. 2 . . . . 95.00
Spokeshave, Stanley, No. 67, Steel, Wooden Handles, 5 1/2 x 5 1/2 In. 67.00
Stretcher, Glove, Metal 15.00
Surveyor's Instrument, Brass, Metal, G.I. Berger & Sons, Instructions, Case, 9 x 19 In. . . . 250.00
Table, Laboratory, Rock Maple, Tiger Oak, Refinished, 20 Drawers, 6 Ft. 825.00
Telegraph Key, Vibroplex, Heavy Nickeled Metal, Red Plastic Finger Pads 75.00
Tongs, Blacksmith, Handmade, 1920s 20.00
Tongs, Pipe, Blacksmith Made, Iron, 18th Century, 19 In. 1250.00
Travisher, Chairmaker's, Hornbeam, 13 In. 128.00
Treadmill, Dog's, For Churning Butter Or Washing Machine, Red Paint 100.00
Vise, Blacksmith, Iron, 1920 . . . . 110.00
Vise, Weaver's, Stitching, For Broom, Handwrought Fittings, Attached Stool 60.00
Watchmaker's, G.B. Corp, Softwood, Pedal Operated, 3 Drawers, Fittings & Crystals . . . 105.00
Watchmaker's, Press, Screw Type, 3 3/4 In. 20.00
Weaner, Calf 35.00
Whaling, Blubber Gaff, Forged Iron, Oak Shaft, 35 3/4 In. 210.00
Wigmaker's, Dolls, Tools In Trunk, Iron Straps, Wooden Head Form, Mid 19th Century . . 1000.00
Wrench, Alexander 190.00
Wrench, Brass, Heart, 2 3/4 In. 38.00
Wrench, Buggy, Adjustable, Patent Applied For 210.00
Wrench, Cutout, Planet Jr. 1800.00
Wrench, Implement, Planet, Jr. No. 312 . . . . 1800.00
Wrench, John Deere, King Corn Silo 500.00
Wrench, Nut, Deere & Co., Wooden Handle 70.00
Wrench, Rope Bed, For 3/8-In. Bolt, 1840s, 6 3/4 In. 80.00
Wrench, Wagon 30.00
Yoke, Goat, Wooden 65.00
Yoke, Shoulder, Pine, Carved, 39 In. 39.00

TOOTHPICK HOLDERS are sometimes called *toothpicks* by collectors.
The variously shaped containers used to hold small wooden toothpicks
are made of glass, china, or metal. Most of the toothpick holders are
Victorian. Additional items may be found in other categories, such as
Bisque, Silver Plate, Slag Glass, etc.

Amberina, Square, New England 200.00
Beaded Swag, Ruby 55.00
Bisque, Black Boy, At Tree Stump 60.00
Boy Standing, Pewter, Silver Plated, Ruby Glass Insert 45.00
Bull's-Eye & Fan, Crystal 25.00
Centennial, St. Clair 35.00
Chick, Wishbone, Silver Plate 36.00
Connecticut, Flowers 95.00
Cornucopia, Milk Glass 35.00
Croesus, Green, Gold 50.00
Cut Glass, Vertical Prism, Serrated 65.00
Daisy & Button 15.00

Daisy & Button, Amber	20.00
Flute, Purple Carnival	65.00
Hand, Fan, Milk	25.00
Heart Band, Ruby Stained	50.00
Maine, Pressed Glass, Red & Blue Stain	625.00
One-O-One, Dark Green Opaque	60.00
Orinda, Milk Glass	30.00
Petticoat Hat, Vaseline, Gold	110.00
Pig, Blue, Gold Trim, Germany	50.00
Pineapple, Green	85.00
Prayer Lady, Blue	20.00
Ribbed Lattice, Cranberry Opal	265.00
Ribbed Spiral, Blue Opalescent	80.00
Rising Sun, Sun Colored Amethyst	25.00
Sheath Of Wheat, Nile Green	605.00
Souvenir, St. Mary's Hospital, Rochester, Minnesota, Custard	75.00
Thousand Eye, Blue	50.00
Thousand Eye, Vaseline	35.00
White Iridescent, St. Clair	47.00
X-Ray, Green	40.00
Zippered Swirl & Diamond, Crystal	35.00

TORQUAY is the name given to ceramics by several potteries working near Torquay, England, from 1870 until 1962. Until about 1900, the potteries used local red clay to make classical-style art pottery vases and figurines. Then they turned to making souvenir wares. Items were dipped in colored slip and decorated with painted slip and sgraffito designs. They often had mottoes or proverbs, and scenes of cottages, ships, birds, or flowers. The *Scandy* design was a symmetrical arrangement of brushstrokes and spots done in colored slips. Potteries included Watcombe Pottery (1870–1962); Torquay Terra-Cotta Company (1875–1905); Aller Vale (1881–1924); Torquay Pottery (1908–1940); and Longpark (1883–1957).

TORQUAY

Biscuit Jar, Cobalt Blue	595.00
Butter, Cottage, Motto Ware, Help Yourself Don't Be Shy, Cover, 3 1/2 x 4 1/4 In.	70.00
Candleholder, Motto Ware, Guid Nicht & Joy Be Wi Ye, Longpark	28.00
Chamberstick, Motto Ware, Boat, Men In Sailboat, 3 1/2 x 3 1/4 In.	85.00
Chamberstick, Motto Ware, Dinna Licht Yer Can'le At Bouith Ends, 5 1/4 In.	95.00
Chamberstick, Motto Ware, Guid Nicht An Joy Be Wi Ye, Ship, 4 1/4 In.	85.00
Creamer, Coreopsis	125.00
Creamer, Seagull, Blue, 1 3/4 In.	55.00
Cup & Saucer, Motto Ware, Have Another Cup Full, 3-In. Cup	75.00
Eggcup, Laid To Day, Footed, 3 1/4 In.	45.00
Hatpin Holder, Redware, Motto Ware, Long Park, Early 20th Century, 6 In.	60.00
Mustard, Few Words Are Best, Cover, Soon, 2 1/2 In.	55.00
Mustard, Motto Ware, Lands End On Front, I Improve Everything On Back, 2 3/4 In.	55.00
Mustard, Motto Ware, Soft Words Win Hard Hearts, 3 In.	55.00
Pitcher, Cottage, Motto Ware, Help Yourself Don't Be Shy, 5 1/4 In.	100.00
Pitcher, Original Top, Hand Painted Yellow Stripes	150.00
Sugar, Black Cockerel, Motto Ware, Be Aisy With Tha Sugar, 1 3/4 In.	65.00
Teapot, Cottage, Motto Ware	110.00
Tile, Tea, Cottage, Motto Ware, 5 1/2 In.	55.00
Vase, Cottage, Gather The Roses While Ye May & Old Time Is Still A Flying, 3 3/4 In.	95.00

TORTOISESHELL is the shell of the tortoise. It has been used as inlay and to make small decorative objects since the seventeenth century. Some species of tortoise are now on the endangered species list, and old and new objects made from these shells cannot be sold legally.

Box, Applied Pierced Bone Bands With Flowers, Bone Border, Rectangular	403.00
Box, Bonbon, Brass Lining, 20th Century, 3/4 x 1 1/2 In.	96.00
Box, Cover, 5 Divisions Interior, 4 Ball Supports, Rectangular, 1890, 11 In.	1840.00
Box, Cover, Allover Landscapes, Round, Chinese, 19th Century, 4 1/4 In.	1380.00
Box, Domed Hinged Lid, 3 Compartments, Flop Handle, 2 1/2 x 2 x 2 1/4 In.	230.00

Box, Hinged Cover, Rosewood, Red, Rectangular, 2 1/2 x 4 x 3 In. 302.00
Box, Ivory Paw Feet 750.00
Box, Sewing, Hinged Cover, Blond, Silver Plaques, Georgian, 4 x 10 x 7 In. 1840.00
Box, Stamp, Hinged Cover, Early 20th Century, 1 x 2 1/2 x 1 1/2 In. 66.00
Box, Storage, Mother-Of-Pearl Landscape Lid, Floral, Red Lacquer, 16 1/2 In. 1092.00
Box, Storage, Telescopes Over Bottom, Red Lacquer Edge, Red, Circular, 4 1/4 In. 8625.00
Card Case, Bone, Florentine Paper, England, 19th Century, 4 1/3 x 3 In. 430.00
Card Case, Cover, Mother-Of-Pearl, Ivory, 4 3/8 x 3 In. 165.00
Card Case, Cover, Sprays Of Thistles & Flowers, Mother-Of-Pearl, 4 In. 747.00
Card Case, Cover, Tooled, Leather, 3 3/4 x 2 5/8 In. 137.00
Card Case, Dark Brown, Ivory, 19th Century, 4 x 3 In. 192.00
Card Case, Elliptical, Silver Mounted, 19th Century, 3 3/4 x 2 In. 460.00
Card Case, Glass Panel With William Shakespeare's Home, 4 x 3 In. 302.00
Card Case, Hinged Cover, Ivory, Flowering Vine Border, 4 1/8 x 3 In. 247.00
Card Case, Ivory, 3 1/2 x 2 In. 96.00
Card Case, Ivory, Late 19th Century, 4 1/4 x 3 In. 247.00
Card Case, Ivory, Marked, Canton, 4 x 2 1/2 In. 192.00
Card Case, Mother-Of-Pearl Inlay 225.00
Card Case, Mother-Of-Pearl Inlay, Large Flower Design, Continental, 3 3/8 x 2 In. 414.00
Card Case, Mother-Of-Pearl, Flower Filled Urns, 4 1/4 x 3 1/4 In. 385.00
Card Case, Mother-Of-Pearl, Stylized Floral Design, Ivory, 4 x 2 5/8 In. 165.00
Card Case, Spatter, Mother-Of-Pearl Diamonds, Ivory, 4 x 3 1/8 In. 192.00
Casket, Low Domed Cover, Flowerhead Front, Brass Mounted, 6 x 13 x 10 In. 2640.00
Cigar Holder, Gold, Mother-Of-Pearl, Striker 685.00
Cigarette Case, Domed Oval, Applied Central Carved Monogram, 4 1/4 In. 374.00
Diary, Silver, Gold Inlay, Fleur-De-Lis, Floral Swag, Clasp, France, 4 1/2 x 3 1/8 In. 466.00
Jewelry Box, Octagonal, Bone Bun Feet, England, 2 x 6 x 3 In. 515.00
Lady's Set, Carte-De-Ball, Ivory, Rose Gold Fill, Monogram, Late 1800s, 4 x 2 7/8 In. 920.00
Loving Cup, Applied Bowl, Tapering Gadroons, S-Scroll Handles, 14 x 13 In. 4830.00
Mirror, Flemish Baroque Style, Molded Frame, Pierced Brass Mount, 13 x 11 In. 1610.00
Page Turner, Figures Of 18th Century Children On Handle, Sterling Silver, 16 In. 660.00
Picture Frame, Fitted With 2 Oval Apertures, Sterling Silver, 1971, 5 x 7 In. 715.00
Picture Frame, Green Tint, Beveled Form, Rectangular, 12 1/4 x 10 In. 275.00
Pocket Watch Case, Cover, Silk Lid Interior, Rectangular, 1 x 5 x 3 1/2 In. 385.00
Snuffbox, Burl, Historical Scene, Champ De Waterloo Le Juin 1815, 3 1/4 In. 200.00
Snuffbox, Burl, Trade Tools, Atelier De Tonnerier, Stamped, 3 3/4 In. 115.00
Snuffbox, Hinged Lid, 19th Century, 3 1/4 In. 285.00
Snuffbox, Man With Wife & Child On Lid, 1860s, 3 1/4 In. 175.00
Snuffbox, Men On Bicycles, Geometric, Continental, 19th Century, 3 In. 230.00
Snuffbox, Men, Bicycle, Geometric Design Base, Continental, 19th Century, 3 In. 315.00
Snuffbox, Sarcophagus, Hinged Lid, J. Holland Cartouche, 2 1/4 x 1 1/2 In. 110.00
Spectacles Case, Penwork Ivory Floral, Scroll, Silver, 1900, 5 3/4 In. 715.00
Tea Caddy, George III, Domed Segmented Lid, 2 Compartments, Ball Feet, 6 x 3 In. 2875.00
Tea Caddy, Regency, Sarcophagus Shape, Mother-Of-Pearl, 5 1/2 x 7 1/2 x 5 In. 4140.00

TOY collectors have special clubs, magazines, and shows. Toys are
designed to entice children, and today they have attracted new interest
among adults who are still children at heart. All types of toys are collected. Tin toys, iron toys, battery operated toys, and many others are
collected by specialists. Dolls, Games, Teddy Bears, and Bicycles are
listed in their own categories. Other toys may be found under company
or celebrity names.

Acrobats, Articulated, Overhead Bar, Wooden, Iron Base, 1880, 21 In. 990.00
Action Jackson, Box, 1971, 7 In. 75.00
Activity Album, Planet Of The Apes, Stand-Up Figures, Puzzles, Ape Mask, 1974 ...16.00 to 20.00
Advocate, Woman, Wearing Cloth Suit, Begins To Raise Arms When Activated, 9 In. 1150.00
Aerial Acrobats, 3 Acrobats, Marx, 1920 .... 400.00
Aero Speeders, Plane-Go-Round, Buffalo Toy, 10 In. 170.00
Airplane, Air Ford, Cast Iron, Hubley 200.00
Airplane, Air France, Paris-New York, Lockwork, Lithograph, 6 Motors, J.M.L. 2800.00
Airplane, Air Mail, Double Doors, Clicker, Nickel Propeller, Keystone, 1920s, 24 In. 1265.00
Airplane, Beechcraft, Spin Prop To Start, Tin, Japan, TN Co., 13-In. Wingspan 325.00
Airplane, Bell Airacuda, Die Cast, White Rubber Tires, Hubley, 1940s, 10-In. Wingspan .. 190.00

Airplane, Biplane, American Flyer Tri-Motor, No. 567, 24-In. Wingspan 2255.00
Airplane, Biplane, Army Bomber, Marx, 1932, 26-In. Wingspan 1695.00
Airplane, Boeing Twin Engine, Low Wings, Die Cast, Erie, 4-In. Wingspan 29.00
Airplane, Bomber, 4 Engines, Tin, Wooden Bombs, Marx, 14 3/4-In. Wingspan 110.00
Airplane, Bomber, Bremen Junkers, Hubley, c.1933 . . . . 3850.00
Airplane, Fighter, U.S. Air Force, Fold-Up Wings, Hubley, 10 In. 115.00
Airplane, Flying Fortress, Lithograph, Clockwork, Camouflage, Marx, 1930s-1940s 575.00
Airplane, Flying Tiger Cargo, Swing Tail, Japan, Box, 15 In. 585.00
Airplane, Hawker Hurricane, Die Cast Metal, Plastic, Camouflage, Dinky Toys, 6 x 8 In. . 44.00
Airplane, Hydro, Metal DC Motor, Tin, Box 495.00
Airplane, Jet Fighter, Delta Wing, Friction, Tin, Blue, Red Wings, Japan, 3 1/2 In. 20.00
Airplane, Jet, Friction Powered, Japan, 3 1/2 In. 25.00
Airplane, Jolly, Battery Operated, Green, Blue, TPS, Box, 1960s 250.00
Airplane, Lockheed Sirius, Decals, Parachute Doll, Pressed Steel, 21 In. 1650.00
Airplane, Lockheed Sirius, Old Repaint, Steelcraft 885.00
Airplane, Loop The Loop, Tin, Windup, C.K. Co. 230.00
Airplane, Looping, Pilot, Battery Operated, Remote Control, Box 195.00
Airplane, Looping, Tin, Windup, Marx, 5 In. 225.00
Airplane, Military, Flying Boxcar, 3 Vehicles, Gray Plastic, 1950s, 8 1/2 x 10 1/2 In. 50.00
Airplane, Military, Tin, Windup, Marx, Box, 18 1/2-In. Wingspan 725.00
Airplane, Monoplane, Chein, 6 1/4 In. 350.00
Airplane, Pilot, Primitive Plane, Propeller In Back, Windup, Gunthermann, 1910, 5 In. . . . 475.00
Airplane, Ride-On, Air Mail, Opening Door, Propeller, Decals, Keystone, 24 In. 517.00
Airplane, Rocket Shooting Fighter, 10 1/2 In. 165.00
Airplane, Scout, Army, Orange & Green Paint, Steelcraft, 22 In. 187.00
Airplane, Seaplane, Dewoitine, JEP F260, Red Lithograph, Clockwork Key, 1 Engine 5000.00
Airplane, Seaplane, Hot Job, Windup, Tin Lithograph, Ohio Art, 10-In. Wingspan 41.00
Airplane, Seaplane, Richfield, American Flyer, LaRosa, 20-In. Wingspan 1350.00
Airplane, Sky Cruiser, Friction, Marx, 18 3/4-In. Wingspan 220.00
Airplane, Sky Hawk, 2 Planes On Rod, Fly Around Tower, Windup, Lithograph, Marx . . . 275.00
Airplane, Spiral, Upwards, Green, Maroon Paint, Tin, 6 1/2 In. 395.00
Airplane, Stream Corporate Jet, Aluminum, Desk Model, 21 In. 125.00
Airplane, Tri-Motor, Cast Iron, Kilgore, 13 1/2 In. 2420.00
Airplane, Tri-Motor, Propellers To Wheels, Propellers Whirl, Hubley, c.1930, 17 In. 5737.00
Airplane, TWA, DC-3, Die Cast, Orange & Silver, Tootsietoy, 5 1/4-In. Wingspan 84.00
Airplane, U.S. Army, Machine Guns On Wings, Clockwork, Marx, 1940s 575.00
Airplane, United Airliner, 4 Engines, Blue, Wyandotte 500.00
Airplane & Donkey Cart, France, 1911 . . . . 11500.00
Alabama Coon Jigger, Tombo, Moving Erratically, Tin, Ferdinand Strauss, 10 In. . .120.00 to 510.00
Ambulance, Army, Tin, Friction, Japan, 1950s, 5 In. 65.00
Ambulance, Emergency, Beam, 16 In. 450.00
Ambulance, Military, No. 626, Army Green, Dinky Toys, 1956 . . . . 70.00
Ambulance, Military, Olive Drab, Black Rubber, Dinky Toys, Box, 1 3/4 x 4 1/2 In. 60.00
Ambulance, Red Cross Emblem On Roof & Doors, Canvas Sides, Tin, 11 In. 970.00
Amphibian, Silver Streak, 1967 . . . . 1000.00
Antiaircraft, Die Cast, Adjustment Knobs, Olive Drab, Britains 43.00
Apothecary Shop, Drawers, Metal Scales, 40 Miniature Bottles 1650.00
Attache Case, James Bond, Business Cards, Play Money, Gun, Scopes, 1965 . . . . 785.00
Baby In Walker, Windup, Soft Plastic, Fabric Clothes, Japan, 7 In. 73.00
Baby Snookums, Windup, 1900, 6 1/2 In. 650.00
Banjo, Tortoiseshell & Mother-Of-Pearl, 5 In. 50.00
Barnacle Bill, Standing, Wearing Colorful Uniform, Tin Lithograph, Chein, 6 In. 305.00
Barney Google, Rides Spark Plug, Tin, Windup, Nifty, Germany, 1920s 1275.00
Barney Rubble, Flintstones, Soft Rubber, Hanna-Barbera Prod., 1960, 10 In. 31.00
Barney Rubble, Pip-Squeak, 1960, Large 50.00
Barney Rubble, Tin, Windup, Box, Marx 450.00
Barrel Man, Suited Man Rolling 2 Barrels, Tin Lithograph Barrels, 7 1/4 In. 1450.00
Baseball, Ramp, Windup, Japan, 1930s 485.00
Baseball Player, Gold Uniform, Red Stockings, Cast Iron, A.C. Williams, 5 3/4 In. 460.00
Battleship, Japanese, 6 Flags, Penny, 4 1/2 In. 800.00
Battleship, Red Guns, Die Cast, Tootsietoy, 6 1/2 In. 25.00
Battleship, Texas, Gray Metal, Hollow Cast, 2 1/4 x 5 In. 27.00
Battlestar Galactica, Cylon, Raindeer, Box 100.00

Bears are also listed in the Teddy Bears category.

Bear, Blowing Bubbles, Windup, Papier-Mache, Fur, Roullet Et Decamps, c.1900, 17 In. . .	4800.00
Bear, Cubby Reading, Tin Book, Tin Pages, Turns Pages, Windup, Box	120.00
Bear, Golfer, Windup, Box	295.00
Bear, Growling, Pull Toy, Brown Mohair, Leather Muzzle, Glass Eyes, Wheels, 12 x 8 In.	220.00
Bear, Harry Skaters, Mechanical, TPS, Box	650.00
Bear, In Hoop, Windup, Synthetic Fur, Double Metal Hoops, Key, Japan, 7 In.	115.00
Bear, Ironing, Windup, Tin, Black Plush, Metal Ironing Board, Japan, 6 In.	66.00
Bear, Mohair, Orange, Tips Cardboard Top Hat, Windup, Germany, 7 1/4 In.	290.00
Bear, On Wheels, Mohair, Ginger, Steel Frame, Spoke Wheels, Steiff, c.1910, 11 1/4 In. . .	430.00
Bear, Picnic, Metal, Plush Cover, Battery Operated, Alp, Japan, Box, 11 In.	280.00
Bear, Smokey, Plastic, Campaign Hat, Shovel, R. Dakin & Co., 1970s, 8 In.	91.00
Bear, Smoking Papa, Battery Operated, San, Japan, Box, 1950s	175.00
Bear, Sneezing, Kleenex, Battery Operated, Linemar	345.00
Bear, Somersaulting, Windup, Key, Celluloid, 8 In.	85.00
Bear, The Three Bears, Bisque, Painted, Colorful Outfits, Box, 1910, 4 3/4 In., 3 Piece . . .	230.00
Bed, Doll's, Cast Iron, Scrollwork & Birds, White & Blue Repaint, 16 1/2 x 22 x 12 In. . .	220.00
Bed, Doll's, Cast Iron, Spindle Ends, Fall Finials	45.00
Bed, Doll's, Curly Maple, Turned Posts, Mattress, Bed Rug, 1840	375.00
Bed, Doll's, Mahogany, Pegged & Screwed, 8 5/8 In.	155.00
Bed, Doll's, Maple, Turned Posts, Feather Mattress, Blue Ticking, 11 x 15 x 11 In.	58.00
Bed, Doll's, Walnut, Victorian, 22 x 16 1/2 In.	190.00
Bed Warmer, Doll's, Brass Hinged-Lid Pan, Wooden Handle, France, c.1890, 9 In.	275.00
Beetle, Crawling, Penny Toy	150.00
Beetlejuice, Talking, Plastic, Striped Fabric Suit, Kenner, Box, 1989, 16 1/2 In. . . . . .20.00 to 30.00
Bell Ringer, Balancing Bear, Heart-Shaped Spokes, Tilts From Side To Side, 7 x 6 In. . . .	750.00
Bell Ringer, Raccoon & Man, At Log, As Pulled One Goes In, Other Out, c.1890, 9 In. . .	6325.00
Bicycle, New Century Cycle, Lehmann	550.00

Bicycles that are large enough to ride are listed in their own category.

Black Boy, White Horse, Wooden, Pull Toy, Hustler Toy Corp., 1920s, 11 In.	245.00
Black Boy On Tricycle, Japan, 1960s, 4 In.	350.00
Black Man, Carrying Bananas, Colorful Suit, Tin, Distler, 7 In.	1575.00
Blacksmiths, Hit Carriage Wheel With Hammers, Musical, Windup, Painted	950.00
Blocks, Blondie & Dagwood, Interchangeable, Box, 1951	85.00
Blocks, Nursery Rhyme, 18 Piece	70.00
Blocks, Three Little Kittens, Cobb House, McLaughlin, Box	165.00
Boat, Aircraft Carrier, Airplanes, Launching Helicopters, Marx, Box, 20 In.	600.00
Boat, Alaska Marine Ferry, Battery Operated, Box, 13 3/4 In.	40.00
Boat, Battleship, Texas, Paper On Wood, Chromo-Lithographic, Anchors & Guns, 14 In. .	490.00
Boat, Boattail Racer, Emmett Racer, Orange & Yellow, Wire Wheels, 20 In.	1780.00
Boat, Cabin Cruiser, Clockwork, Lindstrom, 1930s, 7 1/2 In.	110.00
Boat, Cabin Cruiser, Outboard Motor, With Trailer, Windup, Tin, Japan, 1960s, 8 In.	105.00
Boat, Cabin Cruiser, Tin Lithograph, Ohio Art, 1950s, 14 1/2 In.	175.00
Boat, Cabin Cruiser, Tin, Windup, Box, Chein, 16 In.	235.00
Boat, Chris-Craft Pleasure Cruiser, Kilgore, 11 In.	4070.00
Boat, Coast Guard, Canadian, Tin, Friction, Japan, 1950s, 11 In.	195.00
Boat, Destroyer, Friction, Tin, Rubber Wheels, Sparking Guns, Japan, 9 x 2 In.	45.00
Boat, Gunboat, 2 Stacks, Clockwork Motor, Fleischman, 11 In.	495.00
Boat, Harbor, Tin, Japan, 1950s	95.00
Boat, Hydroplane Racer, Gas Powered, 27 In.	700.00
Boat, Hydroplane, Mercury Outboard, Battery Operated, Purple Metallic, Fleetline, 10 In.	225.00
Boat, Kayo, Visible Engine, Battery Operated, Japan, 11 1/2 In.	695.00
Boat, Ocean Liner, Tin, Cannons & Lifeboats, Shoner, 30 In.	8050.00
Boat, Paddlewheel, Great Swanee, Friction, Whistle Mechanism, Box, TN, 10 1/4 In.	173.00
Boat, River, Betsy Green, Tin, Windup, Buffalo Toy, 26 In.	695.00
Boat, River, Bing, 1910, 16 In.	4800.00
Boat, Runabout, Electric Magnet Impulse Outboard Motor, Lindstrom, 1922, 20 In.	750.00
Boat, SeaMaster Race, Battery Operated, Bandai, 15 In.	750.00
Boat, Speedboat, Seated Driver, White Paint, Red Stripes, Meier, Germany	425.00
Boat, Speedboat, Tin, Driver, Hornby, 9 1/2 In.	525.00
Boat, Submarine, Flashing Light, Battery Operated, Remco, 1960s, 36 In.	140.00
Boat, Submarine, Nautilus, Working Light, Battery Operated, 1950s	395.00
Boat, Tugboat, Battery Operated, Malusan, 1950s	155.00

Boat, Tugboat, Tin Plate, Smoking Mechanism, Battery Operated, Box, San, 12 1/2 In. . . . 200.00
Boat, Windup, Chein, 8 1/2 In. 85.00
Book, Musical, Music Maker Book, Clementine, Mattel, 1952 . . . . 125.00
Bop Bag, V, Alien Graphics, Inflatable, 1984, 42 In. 31.00
Boxers, Slugger Champions, Tin, Clockwork, Rubber Band, Biller, 3 1/2 In. 325.00
Boy, Holding Baby Bottle, Smarty Pants, Pants Fall Down, Windup, Lithograph, Box 175.00
Boy, On Bike, Windup, Celluloid, Tin Lithograph, Japan, Box Lid, 1960s, 4 x 4 In. 55.00
Boy, On Horse, Pull Toy, Wooden, Toy Tinkers, Evanston 95.00
Boy, Riding Toboggan, Tin Lithograph, 4 Wheels, Penn, 3 1/2 In. 300.00
Boy, With Accordion, Tin, Windup 165.00
Boy's Express, Wagon & 2 Horses, Pratt & Letchworth, 1893, 17 1/2 In. 3800.00
Buckboard, Driver, Horse Drawn, Stevens & Brown, 1877 . . . . 2420.00
Buffalo, Jointed, Carved Mane, Wooden, Schoenhut, 8 In. 230.00
Bus, Canadian, Tin, Friction, Japan, 1950s, 5 In. 175.00
Bus, Cast Iron, Painted, Arcade, 4 3/4 In. 110.00
Bus, Cast Iron, Painted, Arcade, 11 In. 1870.00
Bus, Cast Iron, Painted, Kenton, 9 In. 285.00
Bus, Cast Metal, Plastic Wheels, Metal Masters Company, 1940s, 6 3/4 In. 38.00
Bus, Century Of Progress, Chicago World's Fair, Cast Iron, Arcade, 5 1/2 In. 688.00
Bus, Coast-To-Coast, Driver, Black On Gray, Cast Iron, Dent, 10 In. 517.00
Bus, Coast-To-Coast, Pressed Steel, Riding, Keystone 8250.00
Bus, Cross Country, Embossed On Sides, Rubber Tires, Arcade, 1937, 7 1/2 In. 120.00
Bus, Deluxe, Driver, Blue, Green Paint, White, Blue Trim, Tin, Strauss, 13 1/2 In. 715.00
Bus, Double-Decker, Driver, Penny Toy, Germany 650.00
Bus, Double-Decker, Green, Chicago Motor Coach Embossed On Sides, Cast Iron, 8 In. . . . 1210.00
Bus, Double-Decker, Meier, Penny Toy 1210.00
Bus, Double-Decker, Mobil & Shell Lithographs, Friction, 8 In. 75.00
Bus, Double-Decker, Omnibus, No. 116, Driver, Early 1900s, 6 In. 275.00
Bus, Double-Decker, Rear Stairway Leading To Upper Deck, Spoke Wheels, Tin, 8 In. 1150.00
Bus, Double-Decker, Rubber Wheels, Red & Green, Gold Trim, Kenton, c.1939, 9 1/2 In. 862.00
Bus, Double-Decker, Strauss, c.1920, 10 In. 605.00
Bus, Double-Decker, Tin, Friction, Japan, 7 1/2 In. 175.00
Bus, Double-Decker, Upper Deck Stairway, Yellow Body, Tin Lithograph, Distler 365.00
Bus, Electric Omnibus Company, Penny, Tin Lithograph, 3 1/2 In. 1760.00
Bus, Fageol, Arcade, 8 In. 725.00
Bus, General Autobus, Penny Toy, Fischer 295.00
Bus, Greyhound, Battery Operated, KKK 325.00
Bus, Greyhound, Blue, White, Nickeled Grills, Cast Iron, Arcade, 8 3/4 In. 540.00
Bus, Greyhound, Clockwork, Blue, Keystone, 18 In. 335.00
Bus, Greyhound, Tootsietoy 75.00
Bus, Inter-City Bus, Li'l Jim, Maroon, Steelcraft, 24 In. 775.00
Bus, Interstate, Double-Decker, Brown, Tin, Strauss, Box, 1920s, 10 1/4 In. . . . . .850.00 to 1330.00
Bus, Interstate, Green, Yellow Paint, Open Upper Deck, Tin, Strauss, 10 1/4 In. 665.00
Bus, Jitney, Driver, Green Body, Yellow, Metal Wheels, Ferdinand Strauss, 9 In. 1815.00
Bus, Los Angeles, Red, Steelcraft, 24 In. 795.00
Bus, Mack, Arcade, 13 In. 4070.00
Bus, National Trailways, Red, Yellow, Nickeled Grills, Cast Iron, Arcade, 9 1/8 In. 1030.00
Bus, Pullman, Penny, Embossed Tin Lithograph 1430.00
Bus, Red, Green Stripes, Original Tires, Kenton, 6 1/2 In. 1250.00
Bus, Streamlined, Dinky, Original Green Paint 250.00
Bus, Volkswagen, Driver, Hard Plastic, 4 1/4 In. 125.00
Bus, Volkswagen, Micro, Die Cast Metal, Yellow Paint, Matchbox, England, 2 1/4 In. 30.00
Busy Lizzie, Windup, c.1900, 7 In. 990.00
Butcher, In Cart, Pig, Windup, Painted, Stocke 850.00
Buzzy Bee, Fisher-Price 15.00
Cabinet, Doll's, Kitchen, Metal, Open Top, 2 Door Base, Wolverine, 1930s 35.00
Cabinet, Doll's, Mirror, Wooden, 8 x 12 In. 125.00
Cabinet, Doll's, Strawberry Shortcake, Hanging, 11 x 9 In. 75.00
Cable Car, Rigi, Battery Operated, Lehmann, Box, 1950s 185.00
Camel, 1 Hump, Schoenhut 260.00
Cannon, Artillery, Die Cast, Olive Drab, Working Mechanism, Britains, 2 x 5 In. 63.00
Cannon, Artillery, World War I Style, Die Cast, Olive Drab, Working Mechanism, 5 In. . . 36.00
Cannon, Big Bang 60 mm, Cast Iron, Rubber Tires, Conestoga Co., Inc., Box, 9 In. 21.00

Cannon, Coast Artillery, White Metal, Camouflage Paint, Spring In Barrel, 5 In. 22.00
Cannon, Die Cast, Movable Barrel, Rubber Tires, Barclay, 4 In. 46.00
Cannon, Field, Cast Iron, Adjustable Barrel, Marklin, 13 In. 115.00
Cannon, Long Range, Slush Mold Metal, Silver Paint, Wooden Tires, Barclay, 8 In. 22.00
Cannon, Metal, Dark Green, Fires Caps, Britains Ltd., 5 In. 55.00
Cannon, Napoleonic 12-Pounder, Cast Iron, Cast Bronze Barrel, 7 In. 20.00
Cannon, Slush, Movable Wheels, 19th Century Type, Painted, 2 1/2 In. 21.00
Cannon, Tin, Olive Drab, Spring Loaded, Marx, 8 In. 21.00
Cannon, Tin, Shooting Spring, Movable Wheels, Gray, 1910s, 1 x 3 In. 21.00
Canteen, Official Rin Tin Tin 101st Cavalry, Screen Gems, 1957 .... 24.00
Cap Gun, Billy The Kid, Cast Iron, Auto Stevens, 1938, 6 3/4 In. 140.00
Cap Gun, Border Patrol, Cast Iron, Kilgore 70.00
Cap Gun, Champ, Cast Iron, Hubley, 5 In. 70.00
Cap Gun, Cisko Kid, Box, Pair 750.00
Cap Gun, Colt, Patent 6/17/1890 .... 90.00
Cap Gun, Distintegrater, Hubley 375.00
Cap Gun, Eagle, Kilgore 40.00
Cap Gun, Flintlock, Hubley 35.00
Cap Gun, Hardcastle & McCormick, Daisy 18.00
Cap Gun, Iron, Sambo & Bear, Painted, 13 x 4 5/8 In. 690.00
Cap Gun, Longboy, Cast Iron, Kilgore, 1922, 11 In. 185.00
Cap Gun, National, Iron, 1915, 3 3/4 In. 60.00
Cap Gun, Nichols 41-40, 1958, 10 In. 325.00
Cap Gun, Pluck, 3 1/2 In. 55.00
Cap Gun, Rifleman, Lever Action, Hubley, 32 In. 100.00
Cap Gun, Rin Tin Tin 150.00
Cap Gun, Space, Sparking 30.00
Cap Gun, Stallion, Nichols 45, Chrome Finish, Plastic Grips, 1940-1944, 11 3/4 In. 315.00
Cap Gun, Star, Cast Iron, Stevens, 1890, 6 7/8 In. 160.00
Cap Gun, Texas, Cast Iron, Kenton, 1923, 6 7/8 In. 90.00
Captain Kangaroo, Squeeze Toy, Vinyl, Captain With Bunny In Pocket 100.00
Captain Kidd, Standing Next To Tree, Wearing Uniform, Cast Iron, 5 5/8 In. 120.00
Car, 1954 Model, Ford Hardtop, Marusan 295.00
Car, Agent 012, Friction, Tin Litho, Vinyl Head, Marx, 1966, 4 x 2 1/4 x 3 1/2 In. 75.00
Car, Airport Service, Pan-Am, Friction, Plymouth, 1964, 10 In. 200.00
Car, Alpha Romeo, Bandai, 7 1/2 In. 550.00
Car, Ambulance, Ford, Bandai, 1957, 12 In. 485.00
Car, Ambulance, Model A Ford, 1930 Model, Friction, Band Japan, 6 3/4 In. 175.00
Car, Ambulance, Opening Hood, Engine, Tinplate Lithograph, Friction, Box 325.00
Car, Andy Gump 348 Roadster, Arcade, 1920s 4070.00
Car, Austin Coupe, Orange, Barclay, 1931, 1 1/2 In. 27.00
Car, Batmobile, Battery Operated, Tin, Graphic Box 275.00
Car, BMW, Roadster, Goldeneye, James Bond 50.00
Car, Brinks, Armored, Battery Operated, Andy Gard, Box 450.00
Car, Bugatti, 1937 Model, Yellow & Red, Whitewall Tires, Hot Wheels, No. 28 .... 45.00
Car, Buick, Electric Mobile, Blue, Battery Operated, Box, 11 In. 1200.00
Car, Cadillac Convertible, Battery Operated, Box, Bandai, 1960s, 12 In. 225.00
Car, Carousel, Gunthermann, 1920s, 9 In. 4400.00
Car, Chevette, High Wheel, Yellow, Red Trim, Hot Wheels, 2 In. 5.00
Car, Chevrolet, 1954 Model, Linemar, 11 In. 2800.00
Car, Chevy Hardtop, Friction Power, Yellow, Ashahi Toy, Japan, 1955, 6 1/2 In. 130.00
Car, Chevy Roadster, Rumble Seat, Hubley, 1930s, 4 1/2 In. 300.00
Car, Chevy Wagon, Friction Power, Tin, Red, White Top, Bandai, Japan, 1956, 9 In. 320.00
Car, CHiPs, Highway Patrol Chase Car, Figure, Box, 1981 .... 40.00
Car, Chrysler, 1920s Model, Tin, Windup, Girard, 9 In. 685.00
Car, Citroen, DS 19, 2-Tone Blue, Bandai, Box, 8 In. 295.00
Car, Clark Hillclimber, 1905 Model, Touring, Green, Gold, 10 1/2 In. 495.00
Car, Clockwork, Woman Driver, Cast Iron Wheels & Driver, 9 In. 575.00
Car, Convertible Sedan, Friction, Japan, 1950s, 11 In. 250.00
Car, Convertible, Gear Changing, Distler 495.00
Car, Corvair Coupe, 1960s Model, Red, ATC, Box, 10 In. 625.00
Car, Corvette, 1980 Model, Blue, Hot Wheels, No. 30 .... 300.00
Car, Corvette, Light Over Dark Pink, Ertl, 1984, 12 x 5 In. 25.00

Car, Coupe, Red Paint, Decal, Arcade, 6 3/4 In. 850.00
Car, Coupe, Windup, Electric Lights, Tin, Marx, 8 In. 70.00
Car, Crazy, College Car, Windup, Tin Lithograph, Marx, 4 x 5 x 6 In. 160.00
Car, Crazy, Tin, Celluloid Driver, Windup, Japan, 1930s, 5 In. 395.00
Car, Crazy, Uncle Wiggily, Seated At Wheel, Tin, Distler, 9 1/2 In. 390.00
Car, Crazy, Uncle Wiggily, Seated, Peering From Seat, Tin, 1935, 8 In. 850.00
Car, Crazy, Uncle Wiggily, Tin, Lithographed Characters, c.1936, 6 1/2 In. 400.00
Car, Driver, Light Green Body, Tin, Lehmann, Germany, 4 In. 725.00
Car, Driver, Tin Lithograph, Battery, Nomura Toys, Japan, Box, 9 3/4 x 5 x 8 3/4 In. 250.00
Car, Duesenberg, Hubley Kit, 2-Tone Green, Cream 100.00
Car, Elekto Ingenico, Battery Operated, Schuco, Box 450.00
Car, Fire Chief, Courtland, 7 In. 70.00
Car, Fire Chief, Red Body, Yellow Lettering On Hood, Rubber Tires, Pressed Steel, 14 In. 1150.00
Car, Fire Department, Friction, Tin, Wiper Blades Work, AHI Brand Toys, Japan, 6 1/4 In. 44.00
Car, Flaminia, Lavender, Lancia, Box, 8 In. 675.00
Car, Ford Cortina, Rally, Metal, White Paint, Spotlight, Meccano, Dinky Toy, Box, 4 In. .. 30.00
Car, Ford, 1959 Model, Friction, Japan, 11 In. 295.00
Car, Ford, Convertible, 1957 Model, Friction, Haji, Japan 145.00
Car, Ford, Convertible, Friction, Bandai, 10 1/2 In. 695.00
Car, Ford, Coupe, Light Blue, Metal, Friction, 6 In. 40.00
Car, Ford, Custom, Battery Operated, A.M.T., Box, 8 In. 145.00
Car, Ford, Model A, 1930 Model, Tin, Touring, Abe Lincoln Driving, Japan, 6 1/4 In. 175.00
Car, Ford, Model A, 1930 Model, Touring, White, Blue & Black, Bandai, 6 1/4 In. 95.00
Car, Ford, Model A, Apple Green, Open Top, Tonka, 6 1/2 In. 6.00
Car, Ford, Model A, Sedan, Arcade, 4 In. 295.00
Car, Ford, Model A, Sedan, Green, Tootsie, 4 In. 25.00
Car, Ford, Model A, Sedan, Kilgore, 3 1/4 In. 190.00
Car, Ford, Model T, Coupe, Driver At Wheel, Black Paint, Spoke Wheels, 6 In. 395.00
Car, Ford, Model T, Flivver, Buddy L, 1920s, 11 In. 6050.00
Car, Ford, Model T, Roadster, Driver, Simulated Soft Top, Spoke Wheels, Tin, 6 In. 365.00
Car, Ford, Model T, Sedan, Black Paint, Spoke Wheels, Tin, Bing, Germany, 6 1/2 In. ... 240.00
Car, Ford, Model T, Touring, Black, Arcade, 6 1/4 In. 465.00
Car, Ford, Model T, Touring, Driver At Wheel, Black, Spoke Metal Wheels, 6 In. 665.00
Car, Ford, Mustang, Convertible, 1965 Model, White, Hot Wheels, No. 26 .... 160.00
Car, Ford, Phantom Sedan, Friction Power, Red, Black, Cream, Bandai, Japan, 1932, 6 In. 65.00
Car, Ford, Thunderbird Coupe, Friction Power, 2-Tone Cream, Bandai, Japan, 1963, 8 In. . 99.00
Car, Ford, Thunderbird, Model 1956, Battery Operated, Red & White, 11 In. 275.00
Car, Ford, Thunderbird, Remote Control, Box, Cragston, 11 1/2 In. 395.00
Car, Ford, Thunderbird, Tin Lithograph, Friction, Bandai, 1963, 8 1/8 In. 85.00
Car, Ford, Thunderbird, Tin, Red, Ichico, 1968, 10 1/2 In. 95.00
Car, Ford, Transit Van, Police Emergency, White, Dinky, 5 In. 16.00
Car, Funny Flivver, Driver, Dog & Suitcase On Sides, Tin, Louis Marx, 7 In. 1150.00
Car, Futura, Red, Friction, Replaced Antenna, 11 In. 2100.00
Car, G-Man Pursuit, Marx 1450.00
Car, Gangbusters, Marx 1750.00
Car, Girl With Wobbly Head, Marx, 6 1/2 In. 275.00
Car, Hi-Way Henry, Tin Figures Seated Inside, Curved Roof, Tin, Fischer, 10 In. 3390.00
Car, Hudson, 1956 Model, Blue, Package, Japan, 4 In. 125.00
Car, Indian Crash, Side Car, Twin Patrol, 3 Wheeler, Cast Iron, Hubley 2970.00
Car, Jaguar, Model XK-120, Roadster, Green, 1959, 3 In. 15.00
Car, Jiggs Jazz, Seated In Open Car, Tin, Nifty, Germany, 1924, 6 3/8 In. 1330.00
Car, Joke, Tin, Windup, Japan, Prewar, 3 3/4 In. 375.00
Car, Joy Rider, Clown, Seated In Open Car, Tin, Louis Marx, 7 1/4 In. 385.00
Car, Karl Bub Sedan, 12 In. 2600.00
Car, Komikal Kop, Beat It Cop Seated At Wheel, Tin Lithograph, Louis Marx, 7 1/4 In. .. 545.00
Car, Leaping Lena, Driver, Erratic Action, Windup, Strauss 285.00
Car, Limousine, Clockwork, Lehmann, 7 In. 1450.00
Car, Limousine, Driver, Luggage Rack, Hill Climber, Penny Toy, 4 In. 275.00
Car, Limousine, Flivver, Bottom Decal, Buddy L 1127.50
Car, Limousine, Opening Hood & Doors, Working Pistons, Windup, Tin, Moko, 9 1/2 In. .. 935.00
Car, Limousine, Roof Rack, Headlights, Opening Doors, Carette, 8 1/2 In. 1150.00
Car, Lincoln, Futura, Black 1750.00
Car, Lincoln, Sedan, Painted Red, Pressed Steel, 27 In. 6600.00

Car, Lolo Auto, Open Cab, Tin Lithograph, Lehmann, Germany, 3 3/4 In. 785.00
Car, Lotus, Elan Coupe, Model 319-A1, Die Cast, Hood Opens, Corgi, 1967, 1/43 Scale . . 50.00
Car, Lotus, Elan GT Sports Car, Friction Power, Tin Litho, Bandai, Japan, Box, 8 1/2 In. . 125.00
Car, Major Pack Racing Transporter, BP, Green, Red Wheels, Matchbox, 5 In. 40.00
Car, Mazda, Savannah, RX-7, Retractable Head Lamps, Nakada, Box, 11 1/2 In. 275.00
Car, Mercedes-Benz 230, Friction, Tin Plate, Red, Ichiko, Japan, 1960s, 10 In. 110.00
Car, Mercedes-Benz, Nickel Plated, 5 1/2 In. 220.00
Car, Mercedes-Benz, Sport Coupe, 2-Door, Tin Plate, Red, Chiko, Japan, Box, 24 In. 190.00
Car, Milton Berle, Seated In Open Car, Tin, Louis Marx, 6 In. . . . . .460.00 to 550.00
Car, Monkey, Driving In Open Seat, Tipping Hat, Spoke Wheels, Tin, Germany, 6 In. 905.00
Car, Mortimer Snerd, Driving Open Seat Car, Tin, Louis Marx, 7 1/4 In. 510.00
Car, Mortimer Snerd, Tricky Car, Windup Motor, Marx, Box, 8 In. 845.00
Car, Moxie, Horse, Standing In Open Touring Car, Disc Wheels, Die Cut, 1918, 9 In. 180.00
Car, Mr. Magoo At Wheel, Battery Operated, 9 1/2 In. 295.00
Car, Mr. Magoo At Wheel, Battery Operated, Box, 9 1/2 In. 595.00
Car, Naughty Boy, Driver & Boy Seated In Car, Tin, Lehmann, Germany, 5 In. . . .845.00 to 1015.00
Car, Oho Automobile, Driver, Light Green Body, Tin, Lehmann, Germany, 5 In. 845.00
Car, Oldsmobile, 1958 Model, Friction, Tin, 5 1/2 In. 55.00
Car, Oldsmobile, Convertible, 1988 Model, Friction, TN, Japan 165.00
Car, Oldsmobile, Red Rubber, Black Tires, Auburn Rubber Corp., 6 In. 22.00
Car, Oldsmobile, Red, Black Wheels, 4 Doors, Auburn Rubber, 5 In. 25.00
Car, Oldsmobile, Visdex, Pale Blue, Nickel Plated Wheels 1265.00
Car, Orange, Cast Iron, Hubley, 8 In. 330.00
Car, Packard, Landaulet, Red, 1962 Model Of Yesteryear, Matchbox 25.00
Car, Packard, Suitcase In Rear, JNF, Box 2100.00
Car, Panel, Balloon Tires, Dark Blue, National Products Co., 1930s, 12 In. 1320.00
Car, Plastic Girl Driver, Nodder, Marx, 6 3/4 In. 110.00
Car, Plymouth, Cast Metal, Yellow, White Balloon Tires, Arcade, 1933 . . . . 295.00
Car, Police, Dragnet, Plastic, Turn Crank To Talk, Playset Accessories, Box, 1955, 15 In. . 250.00
Car, Police, Edsel, Tin, Friction, Japan, 7 1/2 In. 245.00
Car, Police, Oldsmobile, 1959 Model, Siren, Battery Operated Light, Ichiko, 13 In. 425.00
Car, Police, Radio, Slush Mold, Barclay, 1930s, 3 3/4 In. 65.00
Car, Police, Squad, Friction, Lupor, Box, 11 In. 325.00
Car, Pontiac, Roadster, Cast Iron, Kilgore, 10 1/2 In. 11265.00
Car, Porsche, Gesha, Windup, Red, 1960s, 9 In. 595.00
Car, Racing Set, Thunderbolt III, Cars, Track, Transformer, Strombecker, 1968 . . . . . 43.00
Car, Racing, 2 Drivers, Boat Tail, Slush Mold, Orange, White Rubber Tires, 3 In. 28.00
Car, Racing, Animated Exhaust, Cast Iron, Painted, Hubley, 10 3/4 In. . . . . .2250.00 to 2950.00
Car, Racing, Austin, Green, 4 In. 295.00
Car, Racing, Blue Bird Air Flow, Sky Blue, Red Wheels, Buffalo Toy Works, Box, 22 In. . 520.00
Car, Racing, Boat Tail, Green, Silver Trim, Rubber, 1936, 7 1/2 In. 75.00
Car, Racing, Boat Tail, Metal, A.C. Williams, 1930s, 6 1/2 In. 325.00
Car, Racing, BRM, Model 152 A# S, Green, Union Jack, Corgi, 1961, 1/43 Scale 37.00
Car, Racing, Driver, Gray, Red, Engine Cover, Die Cast Metal, Rubber Tires, 8 In. 40.00
Car, Racing, Driver, Red Disc Wheels, Tin Lithograph, 4 3/4 In. 910.00
Car, Racing, Driver, Tin, Windup, Budwill, 8 In. 225.00
Car, Racing, Ferrari, Aluminum, Italy, 22 In. 6500.00
Car, Racing, Ford, 1957 Model, Micro, Schuco, Box, 1950s 185.00
Car, Racing, Gas Powered, Ohlson & Rice 660.00
Car, Racing, Indy Style, Remote Control, Battery Powered, Tin, Plastic, Bandai, 11 In. . . . 45.00
Car, Racing, Ingap Alfa, Chromed Tin, Composition Driver, Friction, 1949-1950, 9 In. . . . 570.00
Car, Racing, Ingap Ferrari F 1, Chromed Tin, Co, Driver, Friction, 1951-1952, 6 1/2 In. . . 400.00
Car, Racing, Lotus, No. 12, Aluminum, Tootsie, 2 1/4 In. 5.00
Car, Racing, Mercedes-Benz, W196, Friction, Silver, Japan, 4 In. 20.00
Car, Racing, Metal, Orange, Tootsietoy, 3 In. 10.00
Car, Racing, Micro Racer 1041, Windup, Metal, Rubber Tires, Schuco, Partial Box, 3 In. . 115.00
Car, Racing, Midget Champion, Tayonzawa, 7 In. 2450.00
Car, Racing, NSU Record Racer, Friction Power, Sparker, Tin Lithograph, Japan, 11 In. . . 340.00
Car, Racing, Orange, Animated Exhaust Stacks, Steel Wheels, Hubley, 10 In. 1750.00
Car, Racing, Pressed Steel, Wooden Wheels, 8 3/4 In., Pair 110.00
Car, Racing, Red, Hubley, 4 1/4 In. 190.00
Car, Racing, Red, Silver Trim, Driver, Auburn Rubber, 6 x 2 In. 65.00
Car, Racing, Shark, 1961 Model, Battery Operated, Box, Remco, 19 In. 125.00

Car, Racing, Sparking Hot Rod, Friction Power, Plastic, Red, White, Marx, 1930s, 7 In.   . .   100.00
Car, Radio, Schuco, No. 4012, U.S. Zone, Instructions, Key, Box 685.00
Car, Roadster, Bearcat, Windshield, Simulated Top Folded, Pressed Steel, Structo, 15 In.   .   910.00
Car, Roadster, Black, Battery Operated, Japan, 1918   . . . .   22.00
Car, Roadster, Flivver, Black, Rear Slant Down Trunk, Pressed Steel, Buddy L, 11 In.   . . .   115.00
Car, Roadster, Open Seat, Lady Driver, Spoke Wheels, Tin, Gundka, Germany, 5 1/2 In.   . .   715.00
Car, Roadster, Pressed Steel, Friction, Yellow & Black, 18 1/4 In. 255.00
Car, Roll-Over, Tin, Windup, Box, Marx 145.00
Car, Ruck-Ruck, Driver, Green Paint, 3 Spoke Wheels, Tin, Geppert & Kelch, 6 In. 785.00
Car, Run-A-Bout, Flywheel, Clark, 1902, 7 1/2 In. 475.00
Car, Rusher Z-28 Camero, Battery Operated, Metal, Rubber Tires, Taiwan, Box, 10 In.   . . .   31.00
Car, Sedan, Cast Iron, Painted, Dent, 5 In. 175.00
Car, Sedan, Clockwork, Gunthermann, 9 1/2 In. 1800.00
Car, Sedan, Red Body, Black Roof, Tin Lithograph, Ito, 6 1/2 In. 665.00
Car, Sedan, Scarab, Windup, Red, Buddy L, c.1930, 10 In. 230.00
Car, Sedan, Seated Lady Driver, Black, Tin, Bing, Germany, 8 1/2 In. 395.00
Car, Sedan, Valiant, Friction, White, Red Roof, Japan, 1960s, 9 In. 115.00
Car, Sedan, Windup, Tin Lithograph, Japan, 1930s, 6 1/2 In. 290.00
Car, Space Patrol, Tin Lithograph, Battery Operated, TN 500.00
Car, Speedway, Jr., Windup, Box 150.00
Car, Sports, Cunningham Convertible, Visible Engine, Friction, Tin, Yellow, Japan, 7 In. . .   180.00
Car, Stanley Steamer, Faux Canvas Roof, Spoke Wheels, Hood Opens, Lou Rac, 24 In.   . .   1150.00
Car, Station Wagon, Ford, 1962 Model, Black, ATC, 12 In. 1400.00
Car, Station Wagon, Ford, Model A, 1930 Model, Tin, Friction, Band Japan, 6 3/4 In. 75.00
Car, Station Wagon, Red, Silver Trim, Auburn Rubber, 4 1/2 In. 20.00
Car, Studebaker, Promotional, Yellow Paint, Spare Tire On Back, Rubber Tires, 12 In.   . . .   1000.00
Car, Stutz Blackhawk, 1928 Model, Speedster, Franklin Mint, Model, 1988, 1/24 Scale . . .   41.00
Car, Titania Sedan, Red & Blue, Lights, Lehmann, 10 In. 945.00
Car, Touring, Clockwork Mechanism, Tin Driver, Richter & Co., 8 In. 1330.00
Car, Touring, Garage, Penny Toy, 3 In. 395.00
Car, Toyota, James Bond, Sealed Secret Instructions, 1960s 475.00
Car, Traffic Police, Key, Minic, 1938, 5 In. 215.00
Car, Tucker, 1948 Model, Die Cast Metal, Dark Blue, Solido, Box, 1/43 Scale 35.00
Car, Turbo Jet Racer, Plastic, Battery Operated, Case & Cord, Hong Kong, Box, 7 In. 60.00
Car, Tut-Tut, Car & Driver, Blowing Horn, White Body, Gray Wheels, Tin, 6 1/2 In. 420.00
Car, Volkswagen, 1967 Model, Beetle, Road Legends, Blue, Metal, 9 In. 35.00
Car, Volkswagen, Sedan, Bandai, Box 295.00
Car, Whoopie, Model No. 150, Lithographed, Marx, Box, 1930s, 7 In. 750.00
Car, Woman Driver, Windup, Tin, Germany, Pre-World War I, 7 x 4 x 3 In. 185.00
Car & Boat Trailer, Blue Ford Convertible, Speedo Boat, Friction, Box, Haji, 8 In. 405.00
Cardinal, Pip-Squeak, Papier-Mache, Cloth-Covered Silent Bellows, 7 In. 125.00
Carousel, Airship, Blimps & Boats, Driven By Dolls, Music Plays, c.1910, 20 In. 4887.00
Carousel, Gunthermann, 1920s, 9 In. 4400.00
Carousel, Jazz Drum, France, 1940, 10 In. 265.00
Carpenter, Tinplate Workbench, Windup, Planes Wood, Martin, c.1910, 6 In. 2875.00
Carpet Ball, Pottery, Black Plaid 130.00
Carpet Ball, Pottery, Brown & White Pattern, Glazed 100.00
Carpet Ball, Pottery, Pink & White Pattern, Glazed 120.00
Carpet Ball, Pottery, Purple & Pink Plaid 120.00
Carriage, Doll's, Wicker, Wood, Wire Spoke Wheels, 1900, 27 x 15 x 24 In. 100.00
Carriage, Doll's, Wooden Wheels & Handle, Stenciled, Sun Shade, c.1869, 26 x 36 In.   . . .   315.00
Carriage, Horse Drawn, Seated Driver, Open Coach With Steps, Red Spoke Wheels, 5 In.   270.00
Carrying Case, World's Greatest Super Heroes, Vinyl, 1973   . . . .   50.00
Cart, Africa, Ostrich Mail, Black Driver In Open Cart Pulled By Ostrich, Tin, 7 1/2 In.   . .   510.00
Cart, Balky Mule, Comical Clown, Seated On Open Cart, Pulled By Donkey, Tin, 8 In.   . .   850.00
Cart, Boy Pulling Open Stake Cart With Girl Seated In Seat, Tin, 7 In. 425.00
Cart, Coal, Mule, Black Driver, Dent, 1906, 13 1/2 In. 1250.00
Cart, Doll's, Pine, Iron, 3 Wheels, Victorian, 24 x 15 In. 155.00
Cart, Figure, Orange, Back Peddles, Pushes Cart, Martin, c.1910, 7 In. 805.00
Cart, Goat Drawn, Young Girl Seated In Open Cart, Red Cart, Spoke Wheels, Tin, 4 In.   . .   365.00
Cart, Goat, Yellow Kid, Cast Iron, 7 1/2 In. 1200.00
Cart, Horse, Dandy, Converse, 12 In. 195.00
Cart, Knife Sharpener, Man, With Knife On Sharpening Stone, Spoke Wheels, 6 In. 1060.00

Cart, Milk, Sheffield Farms, Wood, White Articulated Horse, 21 In. 1495.00
Cart, Pak-Pak, Duck Pulling Her Ducklings Seated In Cart, Tin Lithograph, 7 In. 485.00
Cart, Vendor, Boy, Pushing Hot Food Cart, With Canopy, Tin, Rico, Spain, 5 In. 365.00
Cart, Vendor, Courtland Ice Cream, 6 1/2 In. 137.00
Cart, Zigzag, Seated Figures On Open Cart With Large Spoke Wheels, Red, Tin, 5 In. ... 945.00
Cart, Zulu, Black Driver Wearing Blue Uniform, Pulled By Brown Ostrich, Tin, 7 In. 2420.00
Cash Register, Hubley, 3 3/8 In. 50.00
Cash Register, Tom Thumb, Box 80.00
Cat, Felix, On Scooter, Germany, 1920s 635.00
Cat, Felix, Plastic, 3 In. 28.00
Cat, In Milk Bucket, Musical, Windup, Roullet Et Decamps, c.1910, 9 In. 2100.00
Cat, Knitting, Rocking Chair, 2 Needles, Moves Hands As If Knitting, Windup, Box 120.00
Cat, Knitting, Windup, Japan 165.00
Cat, Puss In Boots, Windup, Tin Lithograph, Plastic Boots, Ges Gesch, Germany, 5 In. ... 96.00
Cat, Roll Over, Tin, Windup, Marx, Box 165.00
Cat, Squeak, Gray & Black, Composition, Germany, 3 1/2 In. 295.00
Cat, Tabby, Plush, Gray, Black, Glass Eyes, Button, Tag, Steiff, U.S. Zone Germany, 7 In. 185.00
Cat, Tail-Spin Tabby, Fisher-Price, No. 600, 1947 .... 145.00
Chain Saw, No. 905, Ertl, Box, 15 In. 60.00
Chair, Boardwalk Rollo-Chain, Black Figure In White Suit Pushing Chair, 7 In. 970.00
Chair, Doll's, Folding, Embroidered Upholstery, Curved Arms, c.1860, 10 In. 100.00
Chair, Doll's, Sedan, Leather, Wood, Silk Lined, Handles, Hinged Door, c.1885, 13 In. 500.00
Chair, Lyre Back, Red Paint, Gold & White Designs, 16 1/2 In. 825.00
Chair, Rocker, Doll's, Ladder Back, Shaped Crest, Splint Seat, 10 1/2 In. 195.00
Chaise, Doll's, Oak, Floral Velvet Upholstery 75.00
Charles The Chimp, Hula Expert, Windup, Cardboard & Metal, Japan, Box, 9 In. 46.00
Charlie Chaplin, Composition & Cloth, Clockwork Motor, Walking Action, 12 In. 220.00
Charlie Weaver, Bartender, Battery Operated 45.00
Chatelaine, Doll's, 5 Chains, 1 With Perfume Bottle 145.00
Chatelaine, Doll's, Finger Ring, 3 Chains, Charms & Coins 100.00
Chatelaine, Doll's, Perfume Bottle, Waist Clip 195.00
Chatelaine, Doll's, Purse, Leather, With Finger Ring 65.00
Chatelaine, Doll's, Purse, Silver Mesh, Finger Ring 90.00
Chatelaine, Doll's, Thimble, Swan Scissors & Wax Emery 300.00
Chemistry Set, For Boys, No. 1, A.C. Gilbert, Box, 1940s 27.00
Chest, Empire, Ocher, Cream Paint, Wooden, 1840, 15 In. 935.00
Chicken Snatcher, Suited Figure With Chicken In Hand, Tin, Louis Marx, 8 1/2 In. 1150.00
Children On Sled, Slush Mold, Barclay, 1 1/2 In. 22.00
Chinese Man, With Colorful Tin Umbrella, Distler 545.00
Circus, Super, Marx, Box 475.00
Circus Set, Animals & People, Painted, Ringmaster, Schoenhut, 9 Piece 350.00
Circus Set, Humpty Dumpty, Canvas Tent, Wooden Base, Flags, Schoenhut, 18 x 24 In. ... 500.00
Circus Set, Humpty Dumpty, Clown, Jointed Elephants, Wooden, Schoenhut, 11 x 15 In. . 220.00
Circus Set, Humpty Dumpty, Schoenhut, 24 x 34-In. Tent, People & Animals, 27 Piece ... 6820.00
Circus Set, Humpty Dumpty, Schoenhut, Animals, Clowns, Chairs, 18 Piece 1210.00
Circus Truck, Overland, Cage, Driver, Kenton, 1930s, 7 1/2 In. 1095.00
Circus Truck & Trailer, With Animals, Nylint 125.00
Circus Wagon, Cast Iron, Kenton, Box 385.00
Circus Wagon, Horse Drawn, 1 Driver With 2 Bears, Cast Iron, 1900, 16 In. 825.00
Circus Wagon, Lion & Lion Tamer Inside Body, Seated Driver, Ferdinand Strauss, 9 In. ... 970.00
Circus Wagon, Lion, Folk Art, 13 3/4 x 14 In. 500.00
Circus Wagon, Overland Circus, 2 Horses, 2 Musicians & Driver, Cast Iron, 16 In. 385.00
Circus Wagon, Overland Circus, Cast Iron, Yellow Paint, Kenton, 9 x 6 In. 1025.00
Circus Wagon, Overland Circus, Gray Horse, Driver, Cast Iron, 7 1/2 In. 175.00
Circus Wagon, Wooden, Original Lion Bank, Arcade, 1923 .... 875.00
Clown, Drum, Windup, Japan, 6 1/2 In. ....*Illus* 50.00
Clown, Gymnast, Keyword, Accessories, 1920, 10 In., 16 Piece 805.00
Clown, Handstand, Windup, Chein 125.00
Clown, In Barrel, Clown's Head & Feet Protruding From Barrel, Stock & Co., 2 3/4 In. .. 270.00
Clown, Jointed, Painted Eyes, Leather Ears, Schoenhut, 9 In. 1155.00
Clown, Magician, Battery Operated, Box 550.00
Clown, On Skates, White Face, T.P.S., Box 695.00
Clown, Puncher, Chein 675.00

Toy, Clown, Drum,
Windup, Japan, 6 1/2 In.

**Restoration of an old dollhouse
should be restrained. Wash it, repair
the structural problems, repaint as
little as possible, and redecorate
with appropriate old wallpaper
fabrics and paint colors.**

Clown, Roller Skating, Windup, Tin, 1950s, 5 3/4 In.	175.00
Clown, Roly Poly, 2-Part Face, Large Ball, Jointed, Schoenhut, 6 1/2 In.	575.00
Clown, Roly Poly, Composition, 10 In.	290.00
Clown, Roly Poly, Composition, Felt Suit, Battery Operated, 8 In.	290.00
Clown, Roly Poly, Red Hat, Yellow, Green, Blue Suit, Schoenhut, 20th Century, 9 7/8 In.	115.00
Clown, Smilin' Sam, Windup, Tin, Cloth, 1940s, 10 In.	295.00
Clown, Smilin' Sam, Windup, Tin, Cloth, TPS, 1950s, 10 In.	275.00
Clown, Smiling, On Head, Spins In Circles, Girl Doll On Cart, c.1880	2300.00
Clown, Trick Poodle On Wheeled Platform, Windup, Painted, Gunthermann	475.00
Clown, Tumbling, Windup, Shuco	225.00
Coal Wagon, Horse Drawn, Black Driver, Cast Iron, 12 In.	605.00
Coffee Grinder, Doll's, Toleware, Cast Iron Handle, Meirklin, c.1910, 4 1/2 In.	300.00
Coffee Set, Doll's, Silver Plated, Gooseneck Spout, c.1875, 7-In. Tray, 10 Piece	425.00
Colorforms, Play Set, Green Hornet, Box, 1966	39.00
Colorforms, Play Set, Gremlins, Box, 1984	26.00
Colorforms, Shrinky Dinks, Box	22.00
Comical Clara, Mechanical, Box	595.00 to 650.00
Construction Set, Matador, Wood, Korbuly's	75.00
Costume, Robin, Action Boy, Box	1200.00
Costume, Western Boy Cowboy, R & S Toy Mfg. Co., Box, 1940s	110.00
Couch, Fainting, Maple, Muslin Cover, 1870, 19 1/2 x 37 In.	125.00
Cow, Brown & White, Glass Eyes, Composition, Red Wooden Base, 6 In.	155.00
Cow, Flat Tin, Bellows, 9 1/2 In.	295.00
Cow, Painted, With Wooden Manger, Schoenhut, 5 1/4 x 8 1/2 In., 3 1/4-In. Manger	315.00
Cowboy, Dangerous Dan, Flocked Hair, Accessories, Canada, Marx, 1967, 12 In.	350.00
Cowboy, Johnny West, On Horse, With Accessories, Plastic, Marx, Late 1960s, 12 In.	55.00
Cowboy, On Bucking Horse, Windup, Wood, Stamped Metal, Painted, 8 In.	26.00
Cowboy, On Horse, Shooting Pistol, Gray Metal, Painted, 4 In.	21.00
Cowboy, On Horse, Tin, Windup, Overhead Lariat, Box, 7 In.	273.00
Cowboy, On Rearing Horse, Composition, Painted, 1930s, 4 1/2 In.	25.00
Cradle, Doll's, Rocking, Blue Paint, Late 19th Century, 17 x 22 In.	475.00
Cradle With Indian Doll, Wooden Frame, Cloth Cover, c.1920, 5 1/2 x 2 In.	250.00
Crane, 20-Ton Lorry Mounted, Die Cast, Dinky Supertoys, Meccano Ltd., Box, 9 1/2 In.	160.00
Crocodile, Snapping, Tin Lithograph, Lehmann, c.1905	350.00
Croquet Set, Painted, Box, Early 20th Century	55.00
Cup & Saucer, Doll's, Chauffeur With Lady, Pink Luster	40.00
Cyclist, Celluloid Figure, Tin Lithographed Cycle, Lines Bros., Box, 7 x 8 In.	435.00
Cyclist, Girl, Tin, Friction, Japan, Box, 1950s	145.00
Cyclist, Kiddy, Windup, Unique Art, Box	295.00
Cyclist, Monkey, Tin, Lever Action, Marx, Box	245.00 to 285.00
Cyclist, Trixo The Wonder, Marx, 1930s	175.00
Dancer, African, Pango-Pango, Clockwork Motor, Dancing Action, Box, 6 In.	200.00
Dancer, Tap, Tin Dancer On Green Base, Tin Lithograph, Distler	330.00
Dancing Couple, Ballroom Attire, Mechanism In Woman's Skirt, Martin, c.1910, 7 In.	1265.00
Dancing Jigger, Clockwork, Fisher-Price, 6 1/2 In.	1200.00

Dancing Kittens, Cat Playing Fiddle, Shadowbox, Windup, Musical, c.1875, 8 x 10 In. ... 1400.00
Dancing Sam, Wooden, Box, 1930s, 10 In. 215.00
Dapper Dan, With Bar On Base, Wearing Plaid Jacket, Tin, Louis Marx, Box, 10 1/2 In. . 970.00
Digger, Buckeye, Chains, Buckets & Chute, Cast Iron, Kenton, 13 In. 1900.00
Dinner Set, Doll's, Amedeus, Brown, 19 Piece 155.00
Dinner Set, Doll's, Plates, Bowls, Tureen, Porcelain, Box, Late 19th Century, 19 Piece ... 425.00
Dog, Boxer, Gold Hair, Ear Button, Steiff, 5 In. 60.00
Dog, Chasing Boy, Being Bitten On Seat By Dog, Tin Lithograph, Germany, 6 1/4 In. ... 665.00
Dog, Collie, Mohair, Orange Felt Tongue, Button In Ear, Steiff, 8 1/2 In. 44.00
Dog, German Shepherd, Arco, Brown & Black, Red Collar, Paper Tag, Steiff, 1950s, 4 In. 60.00
Dog, Growler, Papier-Mache, Pull Chain, Growls, Jaw Opens, France, 19 In. 3200.00
Dog, Metal Wheels, Fabric Covered, Composition, Leather Collar, c.1890, 6 x 6 In. 145.00
Dog, Poodle, Wooden, Jointed, Painted, Pom-Pom Tail, 5 x 7 3/4 In. 145.00
Dog, Pull Toy, Mechanical, Head Moves, Ives, 1883 .... 1050.00
Dog, Ride-On, Mohair, St. Bernard, Steel Frame, Rubber Tires, 1930s, 18 x 22 In. 45.00
Dog, Sharik, Russian Comic Character, Gold Mohair, Jointed, 16 In. 155.00
Dog, Wee Scottie, Windup, Tin Lithograph, Black Rubber Ears, Tail, Marx, 5 In. 31.00
Dolls are listed in their own category.
Doll Cart, With Top, Wooden, Original Paint 55.00
Dollhouse, 2 Story, Fenced In Front Garden, Simulated Grass, Fountains, 28 3/4 In. 440.00
Dollhouse, 2 Story, Stucco Wood, Balcony, Lithographed Floor, Schoenhut, 19 In. 1150.00
Dollhouse, 2 Story, Wooden, Lithograph Paper, Front Porch, Bliss, 19 In. 1200.00
Dollhouse, 2 Story, Wooden, Lithograph Paper, Real Windows, Blue Roof, Bliss, 13 In. .. 900.00
Dollhouse, 2 Story, Wooden, Lithograph Paper, Some Paper Curtains, Bliss, 14 In. 575.00
Dollhouse, 3 Story, Painted To Represent Red Brick, Outside Flags & Bunting, Wooden .. 6550.00
Dollhouse, Bungalow, Wood & Board, Painted, Wall Covering, c.1920, 11 x 12 In. 290.00
Dollhouse, Cottage, 1 1/2 Story, Pine, Worn Red Paint, White Trim, 20 x 30 x 23 In. 660.00
Dollhouse, Mushroom House, All Felt, Gable Windows, Cloth, c.1930 .... 450.00
Dollhouse, Paper On Wood, Hinged Door, Porch, Lattice Work, Dormer, Bliss, 16 1/2 In. . 1725.00
Dollhouse, Printed Paper On Wood, Metal Trim, Gosetzlich Geschytz, 13 1/4 In. 247.00
Dollhouse, Victorian Style, 3 Story, Gables, Porches, Turret, Furniture, 44 x 36 In. 850.00
Dollhouse, Victorian, Green Yellow Paint, Mansard Roof, Hinged Front, 27 x 27 In. 600.00
Dollhouse, Victorian, Lithographed Paper On Wood, Blue Roof, Gottschalk, c.1870 ..... 4315.00
Dollhouse Furniture, Bathroom, Tub, Toilet & Sink, Marklin 1750.00
Dollhouse Furniture, Bed, Young Decorator, Ideal, 1951 .... 15.00
Dollhouse Furniture, Birdcage, Brass, Dutch, 7 In. 27.00
Dollhouse Furniture, Birdcage, Gilded, 2 In. 105.00
Dollhouse Furniture, Cabinet, China, Young Decorator, Ideal, 1951 .... 20.00
Dollhouse Furniture, Candelabra, 5-Light, Pewter, German, Pair 22.00
Dollhouse Furniture, Carpet Sweeper, Cast Iron, Kilgore 70.00
Dollhouse Furniture, China Cabinet, Plastic, Ideal, 1950s 20.00
Dollhouse Furniture, Clock, Tall Case, Ideal 12.00
Dollhouse Furniture, Copper Kitchen Utensils, 57 Piece 3125.00
Dollhouse Furniture, Dining Room, Marx, 7 Piece 25.00
Dollhouse Furniture, Fireplace, Blue Tile Inserts, 6 1/2 x 4 1/4 In. 110.00
Dollhouse Furniture, Garden, Plastic, Ideal, Box, 1950s, 11 Piece 700.00
Dollhouse Furniture, High Chair, Young Decorator, Ideal, 1951 .... 25.00
Dollhouse Furniture, Icebox, Alaska, White, Cast Iron, Arcade 455.00
Dollhouse Furniture, Kitchen Table, 2 Benches, Cast Iron, Arcade 485.00
Dollhouse Furniture, Lamp, Sconce, Pewter, 1 1/2 In., Pair 33.00
Dollhouse Furniture, Living Room, Tootsietoy, Box, 1930s, 7 Piece 270.00
Dollhouse Furniture, Mirror, Chevelle, Pewter, White 38.00
Dollhouse Furniture, Ornate Pewter, Brown & Gold, 8 Piece 5900.00
Dollhouse Furniture, Pram, Umbrella, Painted Yellow, Pewter 275.00
Dollhouse Furniture, Punch Bowl, Pewter, German 50.00
Dollhouse Furniture, Refrigerator, Plastic, Ideal, 1950s 25.00
Dollhouse Furniture, Screen, 3-Panel, Oil Painting, Brass 130.00
Dollhouse Furniture, Sewing Machine, Singer, Painted Tin, Gold Lettering, 4 3/4 In. 190.00
Dollhouse Furniture, Sofa & 6 Chairs, Painted, Wooden 7375.00
Dollhouse Furniture, Sofa, End Section, Young Decorator, Ideal, 1951 .... 15.00
Dollhouse Furniture, Stand, Fern, Gilded, 2 1/4 In. 170.00
Dollhouse Furniture, Table, Dining, Young Decorator, Ideal, 1951 .... 15.00
Dollhouse Furniture, Table, Marble Top, 4 3/4 In. 27.00

Dollhouse Furniture, Tea Set, Tray, Limoges, 7 Piece 70.00
Dollhouse Furniture, Toilet, Tootsietoy, No. 517, 1925 . . . . 165.00
Dolly Washing Machine, Ohio Art, Box 495.00
Donkey, Decal Eyes, Barrels, Pedestals & Chair, Schoenhut, Small 100.00
Donkey, Narrow Nose, Glass Eyes, Leather Ears, Schoenhut, 6 In. 55.00
Donkey, Pull Toy, Jack The Kicking Donkey, Wood & Metal, 1926 . . . . 104.00
Dopey, Moving Eyes, Snow White Sways, Tin, Windup, Marx, 1938, 8 1/2 In. 550.00
Dr. Evil, Captain Action Series, Ideal, Box, 1967 . . . . 1200.00
Dresser, Doll's, Cast Iron, Red Paint, 3 Drawers, Perforations, 5 x 3 3/8 x 6 1/2 In. 195.00
Drum, Carousel Horses, Children, Fern Bisel Peat Design, Ohio Art, 11 In. 315.00
Drum, Clown Picture, Tin Lithograph, Ohio Art 25.00
Drum, Merry-Go-Round, Fern Bisel Peat Design, Ohio Art 300.00
Drum, Picture Biplanes & Zepplins, Tin, 11 In. 295.00
Drum, Playtime, Tin Lithograph, Chein, 8 1/2 In. 145.00
Drum, Tin, Wooden Bands, American Flags, Gold Japanning, 1 Stick, 12 In. 355.00
Drummer, Celluloid & Wood, Mechanical, Prewar Japan 200.00
Drummer, Mortimer Snerd, In Parade Dress, Wheeling Drum, Tin, 8 1/2 In. 670.00
Drunkard, Tin Figure, Holding Bottle, Cup, In Drinking Motion, Tin, 8 1/2 In. 305.00
Duck, Cast Iron, Pull Toy, Hubley 2650.00
Duck, On Tricycle, Quacking, Tin, Windup, Japan, K Co. 225.00
Duck, On Tub, White Duck, Standing On Red Tub, Wearing Black Hat, Cast Iron, 5 In. . . 240.00
Duck, Penny Toy, Meier, 2 1/2 In. 295.00
Duck, Waddling, Windup, Tin Lithograph, J. Chein & Co., 3 1/2 In. 30.00
Duckling, Tin Lithograph, Friction Power, Lehmann, West Germany, 3 In. 35.00
Dustpan, Tin Lithograph, 1890s, 7 1/2 In. 90.00
E.T. The Extraterrestrial, Brown Vinyl, Stuffed, Paper Tag, Kamar, 9 In. 20.00
E.T. The Extraterrestrial, Talking, Plastic, Box In English & French, 7 In. 20.00
Easy Bake Oven, Pans, Kenner, Box, 1970 . . . . .48.00 to 50.00
Elephant, Circus, Sitting, Cast Iron, Hubley, 3 7/8 In. 365.00
Elephant, Jumbo, Gray Mohair, Airbrush Markings, Bell, Steiff, Paper Tag, 9 In. 110.00
Elephant, Windup, Tin Litho, Rubber Wheels, Flaps Ears, T.P.S., Japan, 4 x 2 x 1 1/2 In. . . 61.00
Elephant & Clowns, Celluloid, Windup, C.K. Japan, Box 750.00
Erector Set, Carousel 165.00
Erector Set, Gilbert, No. 7 1/2, Engineer's Set, Steel Chest 62.00
Erector Set, Meccano, Sheet Metal Rails, Gears, DC Electric Motor, Wooden Chest 80.00
Erector Set, No. 3 1/2, A.C. Gilbert, Box, 31 In. 31.00
Erector Set, No. 6 1/2, 100 Toys In One, A.C. Gilbert, Box, 1959 . . . . 20.00
Eskimo Girl, Turns In Circle, Windup, Lithograph, 1930s 175.00
Fan, Electric, Tin, Windup, C.K., Japan, Box 225.00
Farm Set, 16 Animals, Britains, 1940s, 18 x 12 In. 395.00
Farm Wagon, 2 Horses, Driver, Cast Iron, 10 1/2 In. 55.00
Farmyard, House, Barn, Fencing, Trees, Figures, Animals, Elastolin, Germany, 29 In. 1150.00
Father Francis' Pigs, Man, With Staff In Hand, Walking With 2 Pigs, Tin, 7 1/2 In. 1935.00
Fawn, Lying Down, Steiff, 12 In. 150.00
Ferris Wheel, 6 Gondolas, Tin Lithograph, Chein Co., Box, 17 In. 485.00
Ferris Wheel, Bisque Passengers, Hankotte & Klansman 2250.00
Ferris Wheel, Cast Iron, Brass, Tin, Hubley, 17 In. 4125.00
Ferris Wheel, Hercules, Tin, Windup, Chein, 17 In. . . . .*Illus* 330.00
Ferris Wheel, Mounted On Truck Bed, Box, 8 1/2 In. 225.00
Figaro, Friction, Linemar 85.00
Fire Patrol, Phoenix, 6 Riders, 1 Driver, Horse Drawn, Ives, 1893, 20 1/2 In. 2450.00
Fire Pumper, 2 Horses, Dent, 1910, 22 In. 2800.00
Fire Pumper, 2 Horses, Driver, Fireman, Cent, 1920, 22 In. 2800.00
Fire Pumper, Buddy L, Red Disc Wheels, Aluminum Tires, Pressed Steel 2060.00
Fire Pumper, Doepke, Box, 1952, 19 In. 750.00
Fire Pumper, Live Steam, Schoenner, 1890s 4800.00
Fire Pumper, Neptune, Clockwork, Painted & Stenciled, Box 7150.00
Fire Pumper, Rubber, Red, Yellow Wheels, Open Cab, Auburn Rubber Corp., 7 1/4 In. . . 25.00
Fire Pumper, Steam, 2 Black & 1 White Horse, Yellow Frame, Cast Iron, 21 In. 690.00
Fire Pumper, Tonka, 1955 . . . . 325.00
Fire Rescue Truck, Red, Steel, White Plastic Trim, Marx, 1968, 7 In. 63.00
Fire Truck, Aerial Ladder, Child's Seat, Pressed Steel, Keystone, 30 1/2 In. 2420.00
Fire Truck, Aerial Ladder, Doepke, Box, 1952, 54 In. 650.00

Fire Truck, Arcade, 1936, 7 In. 350.00
Fire Truck, Bump & Go, Battery Operated, Japan, Box 175.00
Fire Truck, Hook & Ladder, Rider, 3 Horses, Gong, Wilkins, 1911 .... 1695.00
Fire Truck, Hook & Ladder, Windup, Wilkins, 1950s, 13 In. 1495.00
Fire Truck, Horse Drawn, 3 Horses, Driver, Pumper, Cast Iron, 1900, 15 In. 330.00
Fire Truck, Horse Drawn, Cast Iron, 2 Horses, Driver, Water Tank, 9 1/2 In. 36.00
Fire Truck, Ladder, Cast Iron, Kenton, 1930, 22 1/4 In. 1595.00
Fire Truck, Ladder, Clockwork, Bumps Front, Ladder Extends, Kingsbury, 23 In. 400.00
Fire Truck, Lookie, Fisher-Price, No. 7 ....60.00 to 70.00
Fire Truck, Merry Weather, Kent Fire Brigade, Red, Gray Ladder, Matchbox King Size .. 20.00
Fire Truck, Nickel Wheels, c.1920, 5 In. 165.00
Fire Truck, Patrol, Gold Highlights, Eagle At Side, 2 Firemen, Cast Iron, 12 In. 385.00
Fire Truck, Pink, White Wheels, Silver Trim, Auburn Rubber, 6 In. 14.00
Fire Truck, Pumper, Metal, Red, Gold Accents, Turner, Early 20th Century, 19 1/2 In. 460.00
Fire Truck, Tin Lithograph, Rubber Tires, 3 Firemen, 2-Piece Ladder, Japan, 3 x 8 In. 40.00
Fire Truck, Water Tower, Packard, Real Pump, Brass Bell, Keystone, c.1926, 11 x 30 In. .. 310.00
Fire Wagon, 3 Horses, 2 Men, Original Paint, Cast Iron, 1900, 31 In. 500.00
Fire Wagon, Hook & Ladder, 3 Horses, Fireman, 1906, 15 In. 625.00
Fire Wagon, Hook & Ladder, Bell, Hubley, 1906, 24 In. 575.00
Fire Wagon, Ladder, 2 Horses, 2 Men, Kenton, 31 In. 995.00
Fisherman, Pivots At Hips, Kicks Up Legs, Pulling In Catch, Martin, c.1908, 8 In. 1725.00
Fishing Polar Bear, Battery Operated, Cragstan, Box, 1950s 315.00
Flight Helmet, Steve Canyon USAF, Plastic, Ideal, Box, Late 1950s 115.00
Flying Jeep, Space, Tin, Friction, MAR, 1950s, 7 In. 275.00
Flying Saucer, UFO XO5, Battery Operated, Plastic, Tin Litho, Masudaya, Box, 1960s ... 230.00
Football Player, With Football Tucked Under Arm, Gold, Cast Iron, A.C. Williams, 6 In. .. 580.00
Foxy Grandpa, Silver, Red Tie, Cast Iron, Wing, 5 1/2 In. 365.00
Frankenstein, Blushing, Battery Operated, Box 225.00
Fred Flintstone, Bedrock Band, Fred Playing Drums, Battery Operated, Box 800.00
Freddy Krueger, Nightmare On Elm Street, Talking, Plastic, Box, 18 In. 50.00
Freddy Krueger, With Accessories, Matchbox, Box, Unopened, 9 In. 76.00
G-Man Gun, Battery Operated, Marx, Box 595.00
G.I. Joe, Action Soldier, Green Beret 250.00
G.I. Joe, Adventure Team, Blond, Beard, Box ....*Illus* 145.00
G.I. Joe, Adventurer, Talking, 1970s ....135.00 to 140.00
G.I. Joe, Air Cadet, Painted Head 595.00
G.I. Joe, Arctic Stormtrooper, 5 In. 20.00
G.I. Joe, Astronaut, Space Capsule & Spacesuit, Box 240.00
G.I. Joe, Canadian Mountie, Figure 495.00
G.I. Joe, Case, Combat Equipment, 16 x 12 In. 27.00
G.I. Joe, Crash Crew, Navy Attache, Figure, Accessories 495.00
G.I. Joe, Deep Sea Diver, Accessories, Figure 550.00
G.I. Joe, Drawing Set, Electric, Lakeside Toys, 1965 .... 95.00
G.I. Joe, Fatigues, Ridgeway Hat, Brown Boots, FM 75-00, Dog Tag, Box, 12 In. 165.00
G.I. Joe, Foot Locker, Filled With Equipment, Box, 5 x 6 1/2 In. 50.00

Toy, Ferris Wheel,
Hercules,
Tin, Windup,
Chein, 17 In.

Toy, G.I. Joe,
Adventure Team,
Blond, Beard, Box

G.I. Joe, Green Beret, Accessories, Figure 495.00
G.I. Joe, Jouncing Jeep, Soldier, Open Car, Tin, Unique Art, Box, 1945, 7 1/4 In. . .305.00 to 325.00
G.I. Joe, Jungle Fighter, 1st Pattern, USMC Pocket Tag, Machete, Flame Thrower, 1964 . . 300.00
G.I. Joe, K-9 Cages, Unique Art 175.00
G.I. Joe, Leatherneck, Jointed, Color ID File Card Cutout, 4 In. 35.00
G.I. Joe, Marine Jungle Fighter 850.00
G.I. Joe, Marine, Commemorative Collection, Green Fatigues, 1964 .... 45.00
G.I. Joe, Mission Splashdown 130.00
G.I. Joe, Orange Jumpsuit, Life Vest, Shoulder Holster, Utility Pouch, Flashlight, 12 In. . . 62.00
G.I. Joe, Racing Car Driver 345.00
G.I. Joe, Sea Sled & Frogman, Box 165.00
G.I. Joe, Sea Sled, Frogman, Accessories 995.00
G.I. Joe, Shore Patrol, Duffel Bag, Sailor Cap, 1964 .... 200.00
G.I. Joe, State Trooper, Accessories, Figure 1495.00
G.I. Joe, West Point Cadet, Painted Head 550.00
G.I. Joe, With Army Manual, 1964 .... 95.00
Games are listed in their own category.
Garage, 2 Tin Windup Cars, Bing 880.00
Garage, Car, Hudson Sedan, Penny Toy, Tipp, 2 Piece 450.00
Garage, With 2 Cars, Bing, 3 Piece 1150.00
Gas Pump Set, Marx 475.00
Gas Station, Schuco, Box 195.00
Gas Station, Wood, Pressboard, Plastic, Keystone Mfg. Co., Box, 22 x 14 In. 120.00
General Grant, Smoker, Sitting On Chair, Ives 10350.00
George, Drummer Boy, Windup, Tin Litho, Stationary Eyes, Marx, 1930s, 9 x 3 In. 120.00
Ghost Trap, Real Ghostbusters, Plastic, Kenner, Box, 1986 .... 25.00
Giraffe, Ball Playing, Windup, Alps 275.00
Giraffe, Yellow Paint, Red Polka Dots, Wooden, 47 In. 935.00
Girl, Feeding Rooster, Penny, Embossed Tin Lithograph, 4 Wheels 410.00
Girl, Playing Xylophone, Windup, Tin, 1950s 1125.00
Girl, Strutting My Fair Dancer, Sailor Girl, Dancing On Drum, Battery Operated, Box . . 195.00
Gizmo, Gremlins, In Pink Corvette, Die Cast Metal, Plastic, Ertl, 1984, 12 In. .....86.00 to 100.00
Gizmo, Gremlins, Plush, Plastic Features, Label, 10 In. 23.00
Glider, Air Commanders, Sling Powered 25.00
Goat, Rocking, Wooden, Polychrome, Contemporary, 48 In. 252.00
Godzilla, Windup, Tin, Linemar 450.00
Golliwog, Figure, Standing, Red Pants, Cast Iron, John Harper, Ltd., 6 1/4 In. 665.00
Gorilla, Wooden, 2-Part Head, Composition Face, Painted, Schoenhut, 8 In. 3400.00
Graf Zeppelin, Silver, Steelcraft, 1929, Large 795.00
Grow Chart, Dr. Seuss Cat In The Hat, Box, 1978 .... 38.00
Guinea Pig, Swinny, Plush, White, Black, Tan, Button, Tag, Steiff, 7 1/2 In. 54.00
Guitar, Captain Kangaroo, 1968 .... 78.00
Guitar, Yogi Bear, Mattel, 1954 .... 65.00
Gun, Air Rifle, Saxby Palmer, Pump & Literature, Box 165.00
Gun, Atomic Rifle, Tom Corbett Space Cadet, Plastic, Marx Toys, Box, 1950s, 23 In. 81.00
Gun, BB, Daisy, Model 94, Red Ryder Carbine 33.00
Gun, Pistol, Pellet, Crosman 150, C02 Powered, Blue Steel, Plastic Grips, 9 1/4 In. 23.00
Gun, Pompom, U.S. Navy, Plastic, Aluminum Barrels, Remco, Box, Early 1960s, 18 In. . . 50.00
Gun, Pump, Daisy, Model 25, Blue Pressed Metal, Plastic, Crosshair Scope 40.00
Gun, Rubber, Occupied Japan, 1940s, 4 1/2 In. 30.00
Gun, Space, Friction, 9 In. 85.00
Gun, Space, Sparking Action, Tin Lithograph, Japan 35.00
Gun, Space, Tom Corbett, Marx, Box 895.00
Gun, Squirt, Tin, Jungle Liquid Pistol, Made In USA 303.00
Gun, Squirt-O-Matic, Daisy, No. 72, Plymouth, Mich., Combination 88.00
Gun, Super Nu-Matic Paper Buster Jr., Die Cast, On Card, Langson Mfg., 1949 .... 110.00
Gun, Tom Corbett, Space Cadet, Tin Lithograph, Clicker 200.00
Gun, Tommy, Combat, Molded Plastic, Sei-Mur Productions, On Card, 1963, 23 In. 64.00
Gun, Tommy, Olive Drab, Makes Sound, Marx, 1960-1979, 8 x 19 In. 43.00
Gun, Tommy, Untouchables, Battery Powered, Plastic, Marx, 23 In. 41.00
Gun, Water, Nickel Plated, Wizard, Dated 1896 .... 145.00
Ham & Sam, Minstrel Team, Piano Player, Banjo Player, Ferdinand Strauss, Tin, 6 In. ... 905.00
Handcar, Kayo, Lithographed Characters Pumping, Tin, Windup, Marx, 6 In. 688.00

Handcuffs, Junior Police, With Whistle, On Card, Japan, 1940s, 8 x 7 In. 80.00
Hangar, 3 Monocoupe Planes, Buddy L, 1920s, 20 1/2 In. 2750.00
Hangar, Catapult, Airplane, Lever Opens Doors, Pressed Steel, Buddy L, 1931, 12 In. 3960.00
Hangar, Monoplane, Catapult Airplane, Buddy L, 1931 .... 3960.00
Hansom Cab, Horse Drawn, Rider, Pratt & Letchworth, 1892, 13 In. 1950.00
Hansom Cab, With Driver, Penny Toy, Meier, 3 1/2 In. 495.00
Happy Hooligan, In Cart, Mule, Cast Iron, Kenton, 1900 .... 475.00
Happy Hooligan, Sitting In Wagon, Legs Move Up & Down, Wooden 125.00
Happy Jack Minstrel, Figure Standing On Edge Of Base, Tin Lithograph, 6 1/4 In. 785.00
Happy The Violinist, Mechanical, TPS, Box, 9 In. ....475.00 to 495.00
Hat Box, Doll's, Black & White, 4 1/2 To 8 In., 3 Piece 20.00
Hat Stand, Doll's Head, Composition, Wig, Felt Hat, Wooden, 10 1/2 In. 60.00
Hat Stand, Girl, With Cat, Wooden, Flat Back, Painted, 8 1/2 In. 105.00
Hauler, 3 Cars, Nickel Wheels, Arcade, 12 In. 385.00
Hedgehog, Joggi, Plush, Button, Tag, Steiff, Austria, 4 1/2 In. 39.00
Helicopter, A-Team, 1983, 17 In. 60.00
Helicopter, Flies Around Satellite, Brussels World's Fair, Germany, Box, 1958 .... 95.00
Helicopter, Flies When Plunger Pushed, Germany, 1950s, 11 In. 250.00
Helicopter, Forest Ranger, Cast Iron, Hubley, 12 In. 225.00
Helicopter, Rescue, Marasan, Box 295.00
Helicopter, Tin Lithograph, Plastic Blades, Battery Operated, Linemar, 1950s 225.00
Helicopter, U.S.A.F., Yellow, Hubley, 9 In. 75.00
Helmet, WWI Style, Stamped Steel, Olive Drab, Felt Inner Pad, Elastic Strap, 1940s 20.00
Hen, Cackling, No. 120, Fisher-Price 60.00
Hen, Perched On Nest, Pip-Squeak, Composition, Germany, 19th Century, 8 1/4 In. 1870.00
Hen & Rooster, Pip-Squeak, Wooden Case, Germany, 7 1/2 In. 145.00
Hit & Miss, Kohmer Products, No. 121, Box, 1930s 95.00
Hobo, 2-Part Head, Original, Schoenhut, 8 In. 385.00
Hobo, Wooden, Jointed, Painted, Shirt, Coat, Pants, Schoenhut, 8 In. 195.00
Hoisting Tower, 3 Telescoping Chutes, Buddy L, 38 In. 2320.00
Hoosier Cabinet, Doll's, Full Contents 300.00
Horse, Black Felt Over Wood & Papier-Mache, Fiber Tail, Glass Eyes, 7 In. 88.00
Horse, Bucking Bronco, Cowboy, Windup, Lehmann 650.00
Horse, Galloping Pony, Mechanical, Ride, 10 Cent, 1940s 1100.00
Horse, Hide Cover Over Wood, Harness, Tack Eyes, No Mane, Pull Toy, 10 3/4 In. 27.00
Horse, Hide Covering, Glass Eyes, Iron Wheels, Horsehair Tail & Mane, 31 1/2 In. 385.00
Horse, Mechanical, Tin Platform, Metal White Horse, Leather Harness, Windup, 6 1/2 In. 2000.00
Horse, On Wheels, Wood & Papier-Mache, Dapple Gray Paint, Pull Toy, 7 1/2 In. 192.00
Horse, Pine, Pull Toy, New England, 19th Century, 22 In. 950.00
Horse, Rocking, Carved & Painted, Leatherette Fitting, 19th Century 1840.00
Horse, Rocking, Cutout Silhouette, Seat Between, Original Design, 37 1/4 In. 82.00
Horse, Rocking, Dapple Gray, Glass Eyes, Saddle, Harness & Tail, 36 In. 550.00
Horse, Rocking, Dapple Gray, Saddle, Red Painted Stand, 33 x 45 1/2 x 14 In. 575.00
Horse, Rocking, Leather & Velvet Saddle, Horsehair Tail & Mane, Victorian, 32 x 27 In. . 505.00
Horse, Rocking, Platform, Dapple-Gray Paint, Hair Mane & Tail, Leather Saddle, 40 In. . 805.00
Horse, Rocking, Stylized, Bentwood Ply, Dowel Handle, Creative Playthings, 25 In. 195.00
Horse, Rocking, White, Leather Bridle & Saddle, 18th Century, 20 x 33 In. 355.00
Horse, Rocking, White, Original Saddle, Ears, Red, Green Frame, Wood, 28 x 35 x 12 In. 360.00
Horse, Rocking, Wooden, Painted Bashful-Looking Face & Black Mane & Tail, 1960s ... 25.00
Horse, Rocking, Wooden, Spindle Back Seat, Platform, Red, White Striping 525.00
Horse, Straw Stuffed, Bridle, 12 In. 95.00
Horse, Tin, Pull Toy, 1880s, 4 1/2 In. 245.00
Horse, Trick, Circus, Performing Bob, Paper Lithograph, Gibbs 248.00
Horse, Wild West Bucking Bronco, Windup, Tin, Lehmann, Box 1375.00
Horse & Wagon, 2 Horses, Nickel Driver, Kenton, 11 In. 165.00
Horse & Wagon, 2 Horses, Transfer, Open Body, Yellow Wheels, Cast Iron, 16 In. 230.00
Horse & Wagon, Contractor's Dump, 2 Horses, Driver, Cast Iron, Painted, 13 In. 305.00
Horse & Wagon, Driver, Penny Toy, 5 In. 385.00
Horse & Wagon, Express, Driver, Kenton, 1950s, 11 In. 325.00
Horse & Wagon, Farm, 2 Horses, Driver, Cast Iron, Painted, Kenton, 14 1/4 In. 260.00
Horse & Wagon, Ice, Driver, Cast Iron, Nickel Plated, Hubley, 8 1/2 In. 220.00
Horse & Wagon, Ice, With Driver, Original Paint, Cast Iron, 1900, 19 In. 550.00
Horse & Wagon, Man In Seat, Red, 2 Tan Horses, Auburn Rubber 20.00

Horse & Wagon, Medical, Germany, 8 x 10 In. 245.00
Horse & Wagon, Sealtest, Pull Toy, 1950s 550.00
Horse & Wagon, Stake, Driver, Green Undercarriage, Kenton, c.1900 .... 350.00
Horse & Wagon, Teamster's, 2 Horses, Yarn Manes & Tails, 20th Century, 14 In. 115.00
Horse & Wagon, U.S. Mail, 1900s, 6 In. 295.00
Horseless Carriage, Cast Iron, Kenton, c.1897, 5 1/2 In. 253.00
Hot Pot, Cover, Wagner Ware Toy Cookware, Cast Iron 85.00
Howitzer, Die Cast, Plastic Tires, Olive Drab Green, Tootsietoy, 4 In. 25.00
Howitzer, World War I Style, Cast Iron, David N. Carlin, 15 x 5 x 7 In. 130.00
Hula-Hoop Girl, West Germany, Box 350.00
Hurry-Gurdy, Monkey, Windup, Gorman 160.00
Hutch, Doll's, 4-Drawer Top Over 3 Drawers, 2 Doors, Wooden, 30 In. 175.00
Ice Cream Scooter, Windup, Courtland 375.00
Indian, Chief Cherokee, Molded Plastic, Accessories, Marx, 11 In. 65.00
Indian, With Tomahawk, Brown, Red, Gold Highlights, Cast Iron, Hubley, 5 7/8 In. 485.00
Iron, Little Mary Proctor, Box, 1960s 35.00
Iron, Wolverine 65.00
Jazzbo Jim, Dancer On Roof, Tin, Windup, Playing Banjo, Cabin, 10 x 5 In. 555.00
Jazzbo Jim, Windup, Tin Lithograph, Unique Art, c.1921, 5 x 3 1/2 x 10 In. 265.00
Jeep, Amphibious, USMC, Tin, Friction, Japan, Box, 1950s, 6 In. 145.00
Jeep, Army, Die Cast, Olive Drab, Rubber Tires, Metal Masters, 1940s, 6 In. 35.00
Jeep, Army, Die Cast, Olive Drab, Rubber Tires, Tootsietoy, 1950s, 4 1/2 In. 42.00
Jeep, Army, Green Rubber, Molded-In Driver, Plastic Tires, Auburn, 1950s, 4 In. 26.00
Jeep, Army, Olive, 1950, 3 In. 12.00
Jeep, Daisy, Dukes Of Hazzard, Tan, Die Cast, Ertl, Box, 6 1/4 In. 35.00
Jeep, Farm, Friction, Tin, Gray, Rubber Tires, Japan, 3 x 4 x 8 In. 90.00
Jeep, Jouncing, Tin, Windup, Unique 295.00
Jeep, U.S. Army, Die Cast, Dinky Toys, England, 3 1/4 In. 50.00
Jeep, U.S. Army, Plastic, Rubber Tires, Gas Engine, Cox, 12 In. 100.00
Jeep, U.S. Army, Tin, Friction, Japan, 1950s, 5 In. 45.00
Joe Penner, Duck, Wearing White, Black Checked Jacket, Tin, Louis Marx, 1934, 8 In. ... 665.00
Jolly Bambino, Eating Monkey, In High Chair, Battery Powered, Flare Toy, Box 595.00
Juice Machine, Sizzlers, Mattel, Box, 1970s 25.00
Junior Aircraft Warning Service Kit, ID Chart, Observers Handbook, Envelope 30.00
Kaleidoscope, Spyglass Shape, Turned Walnut Base, 19th Century, 10 In. 880.00
Kangaroo, Metal Eyes, Black Mouth, Pouch For Baby, 1920s, 25 In. 375.00
Kangaroo, Mohair, Jointed, Glass Eyes, Velveteen Baby Joey, Steiff, 1960s, 21 In. 375.00
Kettle, Iron, Griswold, No. 2, 3 Legs 110.00
Kiddie Car, Riding, Wooden, 3 Wheels, Decal, H.G. White 50.00
Kitchen Range, Chrome & Enameled, Gas, Lionel, No. 455, 1930s, Miniature 880.00
Kite, Gayla Space Craft 35.00
Ko-Ko, Sandwich Man, Windup, Japan, Box ....215.00 to 250.00
Lace-Making Set, Child's, Lace Roll, Bobbins, Tools, France, Box, c.1910, 11 x 14 In. ... 1300.00
Lantern, With Morse Code, Battery Operated, Signaling Flags, Box, 1950s 165.00
Launcher, With 3 Boxes Of Blades, Tinkertoy 125.00
Lawn Mower, Copper Frame, Revolving Blades, Cast Iron, Arcade, 4 In. 270.00
Lawn Mower, Red & Green, Cast Iron, Arcade, 22 x 8 In. 295.00
Leopard, Plush, Glass Eyes, Brass Button, Steiff, U.S. Zone Germany, 4 In. 110.00
Li'l Abner Dogpatch Band, All Around A Piano, Tin, Unique Art, Box, 1945, 5 x 9 In. ... 905.00
Li'l Abner Dogpatch Band, Windup, Tin Lithograph, Unique Art, c.1945, 10 x 6 x 8 In. ... 330.00
Limousine, Chrome Trim, Opening Hood, 6 Cylinder Engine, Tin, Distler, 9 3/4 In. 455.00
Limousine, Seated Chauffeur, Gray Paint, Brown Trim, Tin, Georg Fischer, 5 In. 240.00
Limping Lizzie, Tin Lithograph, Windup, Marx, Box 295.00
Lincoln Logs, Deluxe Set, Figures, Box 650.00
Lincoln Logs, Og Son Of Fire, 4 Humans, 2 Animals, Libby Premium, 1930s, Set Of 6 ... 124.00
Lincoln Tunnel, Windup, Lithograph, Unique Art 275.00
Lion, Windup, Marx, 9 In. 95.00
Loader, Automatic Tailgate, Ride-On Pull Toy, Rubber Tires, Buddy L, 25 In. 275.00
Locomotive, Ride-On, Bell & Lever, Pressed Steel, Keystone, No. 6400, 26 In. 258.00
Locomotive, Steam, Riding, Keystone 375.00
Looping Space Tank, Battery Operated, Tin, Plastic Dome, Daiya, Japan, Box, 8 x 4 In. ... 850.00
Lorry, Covered, Driver, Penny Toy, Distle 295.00
Maggie & Jiggs, Lithographed Tinplate, Clockwork Reversing Motor, Fighting, 7 1/2 In. ... 920.00

Maggie & Jiggs, Tin, He Has Cane, She Has Rolling Pin, Windup, Illfelder, 1920s 1800.00
Magic Slate, Fess Parker, 1964 . . . . 40.00
Maid, Chasing Rat, Wearing White Cloth Dress, 10 In. 1935.00
Man, Butter & Egg, Walking With Duck In Hand & Suitcase, Tin Lithograph, 8 In. 845.00
Man, Circus, Black Dude, Painted, Top Hat, White Shirt, Schoenhut, 8 In. 425.00
Man, Hard Hat, Green Shirt, Brown Pants, Fisher-Price, 3 1/2 In. 3.00
Man, Holding Violin In Hand, Gay Violinist, Painted Tin Head, Box, 7 1/2 In. 1110.00
Man, Plays Bass Fiddle, Bear Moves In Circle, Painted, Windup 950.00
Man, Top Hat, Ambles Forward, Lifts Arm, Cigar To Lips, Martin, c.1902, 8 1/2 In. 805.00
Man, Walking With Suitcases In Hand, Tin Lithograph, Distler, 7 In. 910.00
Mary & Little Lamb, Mary, Standing Next To Lamb, White, Cast Iron, 4 3/8 In. 485.00
Mary's Little Lamb, Windup, Tin, Pink Fleece, Alps, Japan, Box, 2 x 4 In. 52.00
Merry-Go-Round, 5 Tin Horses, 4 Tin Airplanes, Wolverine, 12 1/2 In. 358.00
Merry-Go-Round, Wyandotte, Box 395.00
Merrymakers Band, Mice, Marx, 5 1/2 x 9 In. 70.00
Merrymakers Band, Seated Mouse Violinist, Seated Drummer, Tin, Marx . . . . . . .905.00 to 970.00
Michelin Man, Holding A Michelin Man Doll, Wearing Blue Bib, 7 x 4 3/4 In. 140.00
Microscope, Gilbert, Accessories, Metal Box, 1960 . . . . 20.00
Microscope Set, Gilbert, Box, 1938 . . . . 45.00
Missile Defense Fort, Keystone, Box 495.00
Missile Launcher, Metal, Spring Launch, Olive Drab, Meccano Ltd., England, 7 In. 41.00
Missile Launching Platform, Exploding Unloader, Lionel, Box 160.00
Model Kit, Airplane, 1932 Boeing Gee Bee Racer, Hawk, Box, 1960 . . . . 25.00
Model Kit, Airplane, B-17G Flying Fortress, Plastic, Monogram, Box, 1/48 Scale 31.00
Model Kit, Airplane, Japanese M6A1, ABK, Shrink Wrapped Box, 1/72 Scale 35.00
Model Kit, Airplane, Lockheed C-130E Hercules, Airfix Productions, 1977, 1/72 Scale . . 31.00
Model Kit, Airplane, Macchi M.C. 72 Racing, Plastic, Artiplast, Box, 1960s, 1/50 Scale . . 23.00
Model Kit, Aliens, Alien Warrior, Plastic, Halcyon, Box, 1/9 Scale 23.00
Model Kit, Boat, USS Saipan Amphibious Assault, Revell, Box, 1970s, 1/720 Scale 25.00
Model Kit, Car, Johnny Toymaker Jaguar XKE Mold, Topper Toys, Box, 1968 . . . . 30.00
Model Kit, Car, Model SJ Duesenberg Town Car, Metal, Plastic, Hubley, Box, 1/18 Scale . 29.00
Model Kit, Car, Predicta, Based On 1957 Thunderbird, Monogram, Box, 1964 . . . . 28.00
Model Kit, Creature From Black Lagoon 175.00
Model Kit, Dukes Of Hazzard, Boss Hogg's Hauler Van, MPC, Box, 1980 . . . . 30.00
Model Kit, Dukes Of Hazzard, Sheriff Rosco's Police Car, MPC, Box, 1982 . . . . 30.00
Model Kit, Focke-Wulf 200C Condor, Revell, Sealed Box, 1965 . . . . 23.00
Model Kit, Lockheed T-33A, Plastic, Hawk, Box, 1966 . . . . 25.00
Model Kit, Outer Limits, Resin Monster 75.00
Model Kit, Pie Wagon, Decals, Instructions, Monogram, Box, 1/24 Scale 32.00
Model Kit, Pilgrim Observer Space Station, On Card, 1970 . . . . 28.00
Model Kit, Planet Of The Apes, Dr. Zira, Plastic, Addar Products, Box, 1974 . . . . 25.00
Model Kit, PZKW-IV Heuschrecke Grasshopper, Motorized, Bandai, Box, 1/30 Scale 100.00
Model Kit, Six Million Dollar Man, Fight For Survival, Fundimension, Box, 9 1/2 x 6 In. . 25.00
Monkey, Artist, Paints Picture, Windup, Tin Litho, Composite, Rubber, Japan, 6 x 3 In. . . . 76.00
Monkey, Black & Red Felt, Aqua Buttons, Tan Mohair, Composition Head, Schuco, 3 In. . 60.00
Monkey, Brown & White Mohair, Glass Eyes, Button, Label, Steiff, 13 In. 77.00
Monkey, Champion Weight Lifter, Battery Operated, Box 145.00
Monkey, Climbing Ladder, Tin, Penny Toy, 1920 . . . . 295.00
Monkey, Fishing, On Whale, T.P.S., Box 375.00
Monkey, Ironing, Windup, Cardboard, Plush Covered, Tin Litho Base, Japan, Box, 7 In. . . 86.00
Monkey, Riding Car, Windup, Tin, U.S Zone, 4 In. 75.00
Monkey, Rock'n Roll, Guitar, Battery Operated, Tin Litho, Plush, Alps, Japan, Box, 11 In. 420.00
Monkey, Roll Over, Tin Lithograph, Windup, 6 1/2 In. 175.00
Monkey, Satin, Muslin, Rubber Head, 1930s 165.00
Monkey, Traveler With Camera, Windup, Tin Body, Booklet, Box, Japan, 7 In. 155.00
Monkey, White Face, Felt Clown Costume, Baton & Chair, Schoenhut 525.00
Monkey, Windup, Combs Hair, Schuco, 5 In. 98.00
Monorail, Rocket Express, Battery Operated, Box 695.00
Moon Explorer, Crank Centrifugal Force 650.00
Motor Scooter, Vespa, Bandai 175.00
Motorcycle, Arcade, Large 440.00
Motorcycle, BMW 500, Tinplate, Black & Chrome, c.1952 . . . . 1119.00
Motorcycle, Cop Rider, Tin Lithograph, Windup, Marx 220.00

To keep tin toys from rusting further, try this: Rinse the metal, scrub, dry, then coat with a thin layer of Vaseline.

Toy, Motorcycle, Man & Passenger, Tin,
Tipp & Co., 1935, 12 In.

Motorcycle, Cop, Battery Operated, Headlight, Cast Iron, Champion, 6 1/4 In.	1485.00
Motorcycle, Driver, Cast Iron, Hubley, 12 In.	3630.00
Motorcycle, Echo, Man, Riding Cycle, Side Wheels, Tin Lithograph, 8 1/2 In.	790.00
Motorcycle, Electric Headlight, Cast Iron, Hubley, 7 In.	412.00
Motorcycle, Evel Knievel, Stunt	175.00
Motorcycle, Expert, Battery Operated, Modern Toys, Japan, 12 In.	770.00
Motorcycle, Green, Headlight, Sparking, Arnold, 7 1/2 In.	750.00
Motorcycle, Harley-Davidson, Sidecar, Passenger, Red Plastic, Thomas Toy, 3 x 4 In.	50.00
Motorcycle, Japanese Patrol, Box, 5 1/2 In.	425.00
Motorcycle, License Plate, Harley-Davidson, Box, 1959, 9 In.	1200.00
Motorcycle, License Plate, Harley-Davidson, Venus, Box, 1960	650.00
Motorcycle, Mac, Arnold, Key, Box	1100.00
Motorcycle, Man & Passenger, Tin, Tipp & Co., 1935, 12 In. . . . . *Illus*	15180.00
Motorcycle, Man, Riding, Leaning Forward Peddling Along, Spoke Wheels, Tin, 9 In. . . .	4840.00
Motorcycle, Parcel Post, Hubley, Replaced Rider	2150.00
Motorcycle, Penny Toy, Kellerman	415.00
Motorcycle, Police 55, 1950s, 5 In.	240.00
Motorcycle, Police, Harley-Davidson, Nickel Wheels, Cast Iron, 5 1/2 In.	115.00
Motorcycle, Police, Sidecar & Siren, Marx, 1930s	700.00
Motorcycle, Policeman, Orange, Cast Iron, Hubley	2200.00
Motorcycle, Racer, Technofix, No. 15, 7 In. . . . . .650.00 to 750.00
Motorcycle, Red Flame & Hood, White Wheels, Rider, Buddy L, 1980, 4 In.	10.00
Motorcycle, Rico Boy On Whizzer, Germany	6500.00
Motorcycle, Rider, Friction, Tin Litho, Rubber Wheels, Linemar, Marx, Japan, 2 x 3 In. . .	51.00
Motorcycle, Rider, Tippco, 7 In.	575.00
Motorcycle, Side Car, Running, Gutterman, c.1910, 6 In.	1430.00
Motorcycle, Socius, Tinplate Lithograph, Clockwork, Kellerman, 1938	1535.00
Motorcycle, Sparking Headlights, Arnold, 7 1/2 In.	1200.00
Motorcycle, Trooper, Japan	1350.00
Motorcycle, Venus, Black, 1960 License Plate, TN, 9 In.	450.00
Motorcycle, Young Man Peddling Along, Spoke Wheels, Tin Lithograph, 8 In.	3390.00
Mouse, Fiep, Gray Fur, 3 Tags, Steiff, West Germany, 5 In.	35.00
Mr. Dan, Coffee Drinking Man, Mechanical, Box	165.00
Mug, Grape & Festoon With Shield, Sun Purpled Glass, 1 3/4 x 2 3/8 In.	15.00
Mug, Grapevine With Ovals, Glass, 2 In.	25.00
Mule, Balky Mule, Tin, Strauss, 1920	415.00
Mule, Hee Haw, Plush, With Clothes, 16 In.	35.00
Music Box, Crank On Top, Tin Lithograph, Children Playing, Ohio Art Co., 6 In.	20.00
My Merry Dolly's Hostess Closet, Cardboard Box With Party Items, 1958, 7 x 10 In.	88.00
My Merry Toy Closet, Cardboard Box With Games, Chalk, Paint, 1960, 8 x 7 In.	32.00
Mysto Magic Exhibition Set, Gilbert, No. 2001, Instruction Booklet, Box, 1930	66.00
Native, Big Lips, Earrings, Rolling Eyes, Stamped Tin, Pull String, 2 1/2 x 3 In.	45.00
Naughty Boy, Father & Son, Horseless Carriage, Windup, Lehmann	750.00
Naugies, Stuffed 3 Naugahyde Forms In Shape Of Monster	405.00
New York, City Buildings Circle By Locomotive & Airplane, Tin, Louis Marx, 9 In.	1575.00
Noah's Ark, 40 Animals, 2 People, 7 x 12 In.	900.00
Owl, Arctic, Noah's Ark, Schuco, Box	125.00

Paddy & Pig, Tin Lithograph, Windup 495.00
Pail, Boy, Puppy, Beach Ball, Plaid Design, Ohio Art, 1950s, 3 In. 65.00
Pail, Circus Theme, Performing Animals, Chein, 1960s, 5 In. 125.00
Pail, Circus Theme, Ringmaster, Lion, Clown, Tiger 65.00
Pail, Comic Farmer, Strumming Banjo For Cows, Pigs, Ohio Art, 1970s, 5 In. 55.00
Pail, Coney Island Steeplechase, Chein, 1940s, 8 In. 145.00
Pail, Country & City Mouse, Fern Bisel Peat Design, Ohio Art, 5 1/2 In. 310.00
Pail, Drum Majorette, Boy Pumping Weights, Elaine Ends Hileman, Ohio Art, 1950s 95.00
Pail, Easter Bunny Scenes On Boardwalk, 7 1/2 In. 175.00
Pail, Fishing, Boys, Boat, Riding Large Fish, Red Plastic, Shield Logo, Chein, 1950s 65.00
Pail, Flipper, Children, Trick-Performing Dolphin, World's Best Toys, Ohio Art, 1960s .. 95.00
Pail, Garden, Boy, Girl Playing In Wheelbarrow, World's Best Toys, Ohio Art, 1960s 125.00
Pail, Humpty Dumpty, Ohio Art 43.00
Pail, Kids At Beach, Boy & Girl Playing Under Beach Umbrella, Chein, 1950s, 8 In. 65.00
Pail, Kids In Boat, Anchor Border, Ohio Art, 1950s 150.00
Pail, Kids On Carousel, Designed By Elaine Ends Hileman, No. 117, Ohio Art, 1950s ... 150.00
Pail, Nursery Candies, Lithograph, Hinged Lid, Bail Handle, Cartoon, 6 In. 220.00
Pail, Peter Rabbit, Cartoons, Tin Lithograph, Bail Handle, Deco Mark, 4 1/2 In. 138.00
Pail, Road Signs & Patch Pockets On Denim Ground, Ohio Art, 1970s, 8 In. 45.00
Pail, Robot Sandman 1150.00
Pail, Shirt Tales, Tyg & Pammy, Ohio Art, 1981 .... 25.00
Pail, Shovel, Children Playing At Beach, Fern Bisel Peat Design, Ohio Art, 8 x 8 In. 175.00
Pail, Story Of Peter Rabbit, Written Around Sides, Blue & Pink Ground, Chein, 1960 .... 145.00
Pail, Tiger Cubs Playing In Grass, Ohio Art, 1970s, 5 In. 65.00
Paint Box, Tin, Black Children, Boat, Elephant & Monkey, Western Germany, 6 3/4 In. .. 45.00
Pan Set, Wagner, Black Iron, 6 Piece 450.00
Parakeet, Hansi, Felt, Green, Yellow, Airbrushed, Plastic Eyes, Tag, Steiff, 6 1/2 In. 115.00
Parrot, Pip-Squeak, Papier-Mache, Sponged Paint, Cloth Covered Bellows, 7 In. 245.00
Pastry Set, Little Helper, Box, c.1950 .... 82.00
Pecking Chicken, Wooden, Red & Black, Pennsylvania, 19th Century, 2 1/2 x 4 In. 330.00
Pedal Car, Airplane, Murray 1150.00
Pedal Car, American National Liberty, All Original 4950.00
Pedal Car, Boat, Outboard Motor, Murray, 47 In. 825.00
Pedal Car, Bugatti, Gas Powered, 74 In. 2970.00
Pedal Car, Buick, Hood Ornament, Spot Lights, Horn, License Plate, Steelcraft, 38 In. ... 9200.00
Pedal Car, Chrysler, 1941, Headlights, Bumper, Hood Ornament, Murray 852.00
Pedal Car, Cord, White 2750.00
Pedal Car, Delivery Truck, Coca-Cola, Wooden Cases, 66 In. 2860.00
Pedal Car, Duesenberg, Restored, 65 In. 1610.00
Pedal Car, Dump Truck, Tail Gate, Jet Flow Drive, Hood Ornament, Murray, 48 In. 632.00
Pedal Car, Fire Chief's, Hood-Mounted Bell, Gendron 4400.00
Pedal Car, Ford, Mustang Sport GT, AMF 295.00
Pedal Car, Ford, Mustang, 1964, Plastic Trim, Pressed Steel, 39 In. 715.00
Pedal Car, Ford, Mustang, White Leather Seat, Stick Shift, Metal Steering Wheel 1000.00
Pedal Car, Gendron, Fire Chief, License Plate, Hand Brake, Bell, Gauges, 44 In. 4840.00
Pedal Car, Gendron, King, 1914 .... 4840.00
Pedal Car, Hot Rod, Gendron 1000.00
Pedal Car, Hot Rod, Lime Green, Garton, 1953 ....*Illus* 990.00
Pedal Car, Hudson, Painted Wood & Steel 3520.00
Pedal Car, Jeep, Metal Body, Rubber Tires, 15 x 21 x 39 In. 230.00
Pedal Car, LaSalle, 1937 Model 4200.00
Pedal Car, Lizzy, Fenders, Headlights, Windshield, Garton, 34 In. 852.00
Pedal Car, Locomotive, Keystone Kids, Red, No. 3000 ....200.00 to 250.00
Pedal Car, Marmon, Wasp, Yellow, Indianapolis 500 Racer 1210.00
Pedal Car, Metal Body Front, Red Rubber Tires, Red, Stegar, 22 x 18 x 43 In. 145.00
Pedal Car, Oscar Mayer Wienermobile, Fiberglass & Plastic, Bird, 1960s-1970s 200.00
Pedal Car, Racer, Boat Tail, Aluminum, Miller Style, 41 In. 3740.00
Pedal Car, Steger, Deluxe, 1948 .... 1200.00
Pedal Car, Tanker Truck, Shell, Packard Style Cab, King Kraft, 38 In. 2750.00
Pedal Car, Tractor, Allis Chalmers D-14 .... 900.00
Pedal Car, Tractor, Case International 200.00
Pedal Car, Tractor, John Deere, 1953 .... 2400.00
Pedal Car, Tractor, John Deere, 720, Original Canopy 850.00

Pedal Car, Tractor, Red Paint, International Harvester, Ertl 900.00
Periscope, Cardboard, Mirrors, Morton Salt Premium, 1930s-1940s, 18 In. Extended 30.00
Physics Set, Gilbert, 70 Pieces, No Manual, Box, 1960s 49.00
Piano, Grand, Doll's, Black Finish, 15 1/2 In. 50.00
Piano, Upright, Mahogany Finish, Schoenhut, Early 20th Century, 17 3//8 x 19 3/8 In. 258.00
Pickwick Nite Coach, Embossed Letters, Rear Spare Tire, Kenton, 10 In. 3740.00
Pigeon, Clockwork, Painted Tin, 7 In. 395.00
Pin, Red Ryder Victory Patrol, Metal, 1 1/4 In. 55.00
Pinocchio, Tin Lithograph, Windup, Marx, 1939 .... 250.00
Plate, Girl With Tray, Tin Lithograph, Ohio Art, 4 1/4 In. 9.00
Plate, Peter Rabbit's Radio Party, Tin Lithograph, 8 In. 264.00
Play Set, 10 Cars, Accessories, Racetrack, Midgetoy, Sealed Box, 1950s, 16 x 14 In. 225.00
Play Set, Fighting Knights, Case Folds Out For Playing Field, 12 3/4 x 19 In. 55.00
Play Set, Flintstones, Fuzzy Felt, Standard Toykrafts, Box, 1961 .... 20.00
Play Set, Moon City, Cragstan, 1970 .... 275.00
Play Set, Pee-Wee's Playhouse, Pee-Wee Herman, Unopened Box, 20 x 28 x 7 1/2 In. ... 30.00
Play Set, Rodeo, Wrangler, All Accessories, Metal, No. 3626, Ertl, 20 In. 420.00
Play Set, Service Station, Gulf, Accessories, Cardboard, My Merry, 1960, 7 x 8 In. 50.00
Pogo Stick, Hoppy The Hopparoo From The Flintstones, 1965 .... 285.00
Policeman, Mulligan, Wearing Blue Uniform, Cast Iron, A.C. Williams, 5 3/4 In. . .340.00 to 390.00
Policeman, Wearing Blue Buttoned Uniform, Cast Iron, Arcade, 5 1/2 In. 305.00
Porter, B.Z., Battery Operated, Modern Toys, Box, 8 In. 325.00
Porter, Red Cap, Colorful Uniform Carrying Suitcases, Tin, Louis Marx, 8 In. 485.00
Porter, Red Cap, With Bags, Slush Mold, Barclay, 3 In. 20.00
Porter, Rollo Chair, Boardwalk, Atlantic City, Clockwork Motor, 8 In. 1380.00
Porter, Wearing Colorful Suit, Pushing Cart, Cart Containing Tin Suitcase, 6 In. 790.00
Porter, With Baggage, Porter Pushing Cart Carrying Trunk, Georg Fischer, 3 In. 455.00
Porter, With Suitcase, Windup, Occupied Japan 250.00
Powerful Katrinka, Jimmy, Nifty Toy, 1923 .... 895.00
Powerful Katrinka, Tin, Windup, From Fontaine Fox's Comic Strip, 1913 .... 1600.00
Presto Slate, Stylus, Curious George Takes A Balloon Ride, 1969 .... 10.00
Prince, Silhouette, Wooden, Painted, Russia, c.1915, 7 1/2 In. 195.00
Punch Bowl Set, Cambridge Wheat Sheaf, Bowl, 6 Cups, 3 1/2-In. Bowl 55.00
Punch Bowl Set, Thumbelina, Flattened Diamond, 6 Cups, 4 1/4-In. Bowl 55.00
Purse, Doll's, Coin, Velvet 60.00
Puzzle, Godzilla, 1970s 35.00
Pygmyphone, Bing, Box 595.00
Rabbit, Easter Bunny, On Delivery Cycle, Push Toy, Wyandotte, 1930s 275.00
Rabbit, Reading, Windup, Tin Lithograph, Plush, Japan, 1950s, 8 In. 96.00
Race Chase, Speed Track, Matchbox, Box 45.00
Radio Rex, Small Dog Rushing Out Of Dog House, Battery Operated, Tin, Box, 5 1/2 In. .. 120.00
Rattle, Easter Rabbit, Plastic, 1950s 14.00
Rattle, Thistle Handle, Brass, c.1700 .... 1100.00
Rattle, Whistle, Engraved Mouthpiece, Pink Coral Handle, 18th Century 245.00
Rattle, Whistle, Sterling Silver, Ivory Handle, 6 1/4 In. 143.00
Ride A Rocket, Chein 695.00

Toy, Pedal Car, Hot Rod,
Lime Green, Garton, 1953

Toy, Robot, Robert, Remote Control,
Ideal, Box, 1959

Ring, Flicker, Green Hornet, Ideal, 1967 .... 5500.00
Ring, Flicker, Man From U.N.C.L.E., 1960s 25.00
Ring, Scooby Doo, Brass, Adjustable, Premium 20.00
Road Grader, No. 1760, Marx, Box, 17 In. 700.00
Road Roller, Hubley, 1930s, 8 In. 695.00
Robot, Astronaut, Battery Operated, 14 In. 2000.00
Robot, Blinking Top, Tin, Plastic, Battery Operated, KO In Diamond Mark, Japan, 12 In. . 1180.00
Robot, Bulldozer, Battery Operated, Tin, KO, Japan, Box, 7 x 4 x 5 In. 890.00
Robot, Chest Lights Up, Tin, Plastic, Battery Operated, Early 1960s 65.00
Robot, Chest Opens, Weapons Pop Out, Tin, Battery Operated, Japan, 12 In. 450.00
Robot, Dog, Battery Operated, Plastic, Hong Kong, 9 1/2 x 4 In. 22.00
Robot, Drumming, Walking, Battery Operated, TN, Japan, 1950s, 8 1/4 In. 1320.00
Robot, Hook, Friction, Skirted Head Moves When Pushed, 7 In. 2200.00
Robot, Killer, Battery Operated, Pink & Yellow, Plastic, Hong Kong, Large 475.00
Robot, Lilliput, Windup, Litho, Japan, 1940s 2860.00
Robot, Marvelous Mike, On Tractor, Saunders, Box 325.00
Robot, Mr. Battery, Compartment, Cragstan 1155.00
Robot, Mr. Hustler, Dark Gray, Red Feet, Battery Operated, Horikawa 325.00
Robot, On Tractor, Rubber Treads, Light-Up Eyes, Battery Operated, Japan, 6 In. 365.00
Robot, Pop Eyed, Windup, Tin Lithograph, Walks, 3 1/2 In. 91.00
Robot, Push Puppet, Hard Plastic, Orange, Hong Kong, 5 In. 75.00
Robot, Robby, Bill Blastoff, Store Display, Box, 1969 .... 750.00
Robot, Robert, 475, Plastic, Red & Gray, Battery Operated, Ideal 363.00
Robot, Robert, Remote Control, Ideal, Box, 1959 .... *Illus* 265.00
Robot, Rosko, Astronaut, Blue 1975.00
Robot, Silver Gray, Red Arms, Clear Head, Tin, Battery Operated, Cragstan, 10 In. 1725.00
Robot, Spaceman, Television, Battery Operated, Box & Insert, Alps 975.00
Robot, Sparking Mechanism In Chest, Windup, Walks, Tin Lithograph, 6 In. 110.00
Robot, Spinning Prop Top, Windup, Walks, Lithograph, 1970s, 6 In. 110.00
Robot, Tulip Head, Nomura, Box 1980.00
Robot, TV Chest, Shoes, Walks, Antenna Spins, Tin, Plastic Battery Case, Japan, 12 In. .. 400.00
Robot, Venus, Tin, Plastic, Japan, Box, 5 In. 395.00
Robot, Winkie, Clockwork, Metallic Silvery Blue, Tin, Missing Arm, 1960s, 9 In 636.00
Rocket, Space Ship X5, Japan, 12 In. 375.00
Rocket, Twirly Whirly, Battery Operated, Alps, Box 975.00
Rocket Launcher, Captain Video & His Video Rangers, Plastic, Rubber, Box, 1950s 75.00
Roller Coaster, Tin, Windup, 2 Cars, Chein, 19 In. .... *Illus* 302.00
Rollerskates, Blue Suede, White Trim, Nike, 1970, 10 1/2 In. 120.00
Rolling Pin, Lignum Vitae, 3 1/2 In. 10.00
Rooster, Felt & Feathers, Pip-Squeak, Wooden Cage, Drawer In Base, Germany, 6 x 7 In. . 275.00
Rooster, On Stump, Composition, Pip-Squeak, Bellows Base, Germany, 6 In. 165.00
Rooster, Pip-Squeak, Papier-Mache, Polychrome, 19th Century, 7 1/4 x 2 1/2 x 5 1/4 In. . 430.00
Rubber Stamps, Wild West, 4 Stamps, Ink Pad, Box, 4 1/4 x 4 x 1 In. 33.00
Rumpelstiltskin, Gold, Wearing Red Hat, Cast Iron, 1910, 6 In. 365.00
Sailor, Wearing Blue Scarf, Saluting, Silver, Cast Iron, Hubley, 5 1/4 In. 340.00
Sam, The City Gardner, Pushes Cart, Tools, Windup, Marx, Box .... 375.00 to 425.00
Sambo, Pull Toy, Hustler Toy Corp., 1920s 250.00
Sammy, Wong The Tea Totaler, Rosko Toy, Box 350.00

Toy, Roller Coaster, Tin, Windup, 2 Cars,
Chein, 19 In.

**Try cleaning 1920s celluloid with
a paste of vinegar and flour.
Rub, wait a few minutes, then
rinse and dry. If this doesn't
work, try dishwasher detergent
and warm water.**

Sand Loader, Aerial, Enameled Finish, Tonka, 25 x 19 In. 60.00
Sand Loader, Buddy L, No. 230 . . . . 375.00
Sand Sifter, Tin, Children In Water, Ohio Art 45.00
Satellite, Freedom, Tin Lithograph, Aluminum Rod, Marx, Japan, Early 1960s, 2 In. 26.00
Satellite Launcher, Battery Operated, 15 In. 650.00
Sawmill, Tableaux, Wooden, Tin Windmill, Painted, Electric Motor, 31 x 36 x 40 In. 1000.00
Schoolboy, Windup, c.1890, 7 1/2 In. 2300.00
Sea Sled, Frogman, Accessories, Box 895.00
Seal, Sleeping, Tan Mohair, Airbrushed Markings, Steiff, 15 In. 100.00
Seal, Tin, Celluloid Ball, Windup, Japan, Pre-1940s 95.00
Seesaw, Mobile, Mounted On Truck Bed, Cragston, 8 In. 225.00
Seesaw, Wanamaker's 15 Cent Price Tag, 21 In. 550.00
Seesaw, Yellow Painted Tower, Giabbus, 14 1/2 In. 165.00
Sewing Machine, Kay An Ee Sew Master, Manual, Red, Pressed Steel 28.00
Sewing Machine, Little Lady 190.00
Sewing Machine, Midget, Cast Iron, Black Paint, F & W. Mfg., Chicago, 1900 . . . . 465.00
Sewing Machine, Muller, No. 4, Pressed Steel, Painted 130.00
Sewing Machine, Sewhandy, No. 20, Singer, Box 200.00
Sewing Machine, Singer, Brass Name Plate, Metal, Tan Paint 75.00
Sewing Machine, Singer, Light Brown Paint, Metal, 6 In. 61.00
Sewing Machine, Singer, Original Case 450.00
Sewing Machine, Singer, Table Model, Cast Iron, Nickeled Steel, 6 3/4 In. 145.00
Sewing Machine, Stitch Mistress, Metal, Red Paint, Steel Hand Mechanism . . . . . . .75.00 to 100.00
Sewing Machine, Tan, Blue & White Case, Cast Metal, Works, Singer 50.00
Sharecropper, Standing, Hat, Dark Green Pants, Cast Iron, 5 1/4 In. . . . . .240.00 to 390.00
Sheep, Set, Wooden, Gesso, Painted, White Wooly Flannel, Germany, 2 1/4 In, 8 Piece . . . 245.00
Shepherdess, Lamb, Bisque Head, Wood, Pull Toy, Zinner & Sohne, c.1890, 12 In. 3200.00
Shoes, Doll's, Buckles, Black Leather, Jumeau, 2 1/4 In. 135.00
Six Million Dollar Man, Bionic Man, Box, 12 In. 56.00
Skateboard, Zipees Sidewalk Surf Board, Manning Mfg. Corp., 1960s, 19 x 5 In. . .65.00 to 125.00
Skillet, Aluminum, Griswold, No. 2 . . . . 210.00
Skip Rope Animals, Windup, Japan 350.00
Sky Rangers, Zeppelin & Prop Plane, Naval Tower Lighthouse, Unique Art, 1930s 390.00
Slate, Wooden Frame, 8 x 6 In. 50.00
Sled, Black Transfer Of Horse, Wrought Iron Rails, Wooden, Label PMC, 37 1/4 In. 360.00
Sled, Crusoe, Red, Green & Yellow Design, 19th Century, 29 In. 360.00
Sled, Hickory & Iron, Davos Center Splat, 32 In. 110.00
Sled, Stenciled Sailboat, Wood & Iron Runners, Child's 675.00
Sled, Swan's Head Finial, Steel Frame, Painted Landscape On Top, 30 In. 300.00
Sled, White Striping, Landscape Painting, Wooden, 31 In. 465.00
Sled, Wood, Iron, Black Painted Sides, 19th Century, 60 In. 55.00
Sled, Wood, Metal, Village, Gold Scrolling, Child's Name, c.1880, 26 x 6 1/2 In. 215.00
Sleigh, 4 Seats, Horse Drawn 2100.00
Sleigh, Push, Flowers, Blue Button Upholstery, Removable Handle, 48 In. 750.00
Sleigh, Push, Gold Vine Stenciling 715.00
Sleigh, Stenciled, Upholstered, Child's 330.00
Smoky The Pipe Smoking Bear, Battery Operated, SAN, 1950s, 9 In. 200.00
Sneaky Pete's Magic Show Set, 1950s 55.00
Soldier, 2 Stretcher Bearers With Stretcher, Metal, Canvas & Wood Stretcher, Barclay . . . 46.00
Soldier, 5th Royal Inniskilling Dragoon Guards, 30 Men, Britains, Set 2087, c.1950 . . . . . 165.00
Soldier, Arabs On Horses, 10 Men, Britains, Box, c.1950 . . . . 143.00
Soldier, Artillery Officer, Marching, Saluting, Composition, Elastolin, 3 In. 25.00
Soldier, Artillery Troops, Flat Metal, Wood Box, Switzerland, 1 1/2 In., 23 Piece 72.00
Soldier, Boxer, Metal, Manoil, 3 In. 88.00
Soldier, British Infantry, Gas Masks, Britains, 1952, 21 Piece 175.00
Soldier, British Sailors, Types' Box, Britains, 8 Piece 140.00
Soldier, Crawling, Rifle, Windup, Celluloid, Occupied Japan 150.00
Soldier, Dispatch Rider, No. 1791, Britains 110.00
Soldier, Drumming, Beating Bass Drum, Playing Cymbals, Spoke Wheels, Tin, 3 3/4 In. . . 1090.00
Soldier, Equestrian, Cast Lead, Painted, Orange Hat, Jacket, Blue Pants, c.1900, 3 x 3 In. . 20.00
Soldier, Foreign Legion, Britains, 80 Piece . . . . .Illus 412.00
Soldier, Grenadier Guards, Firing, Britains, 11 Piece 287.00
Soldier, Highland Light Infantry, Britains, c.1930, 8 Piece 290.00

Toy, Soldier, Foreign Legion, Britains, 80 Piece

Soldier, Imperial Russian Cossacks, 7 Men, Britains, Set 136, Box, c.1950	132.00
Soldier, Indian Army Service Corps, Regiments' Box, Britains	150.00
Soldier, King's Troop, Royal Horse Artillery, Britains, Box, 11 Piece	400.00
Soldier, Mignot Knight, Carrying Axe & Shield, Lead, Painted, France, 2 In.	22.00
Soldier, Mounted, White Horse, Composite, Painted, Lineol, 4 1/2 In.	51.00
Soldier, Officer, Marching, Cast Iron, Manoil, 3 In.	26.00
Soldier, On Horseback, Lead, Display Toy Tray, Eureka Metal Co., c.1898, 3 In., 6 Piece .	405.00
Soldier, On Horseback, Penny Toy	295.00
Soldier, Parade, 5th Version, Manoil, 3 Piece	29.00
Soldier, Princess Patricia's Canadian Light Infantry, 45 Men, No. 1633, Britains, c.1950 . .	220.00
Soldier, Prone Machine Gunner, Hollow Mold, Barclay, 3 1/4 In.	21.00
Soldier, Red Army Guard Infantry, Winter Coats, 70 Men, Set 2027, Britains, 1950	198.00
Soldier, Red Army Infantry, 63 Men, Set 2032, Britains, Box, c.1950	210.00
Soldier, Scots Guards, Regiments' Box, Britains, 7 Piece	315.00
Soldier, Scottish Highlander, Elastolin, Germany, 1920, 18 Piece	245.00
Soldier, Stretcher Carriers, With Stretcher, World War I, Slush Metal, 3 In., Pair	57.00
Soldier, Warwickshire Infantry, 37 Men, Set 206, Britains, c.1950	198.00
Soldier, World War I Officer On Horse, Hard Rubber, Painted, Auburn, 4 In.	25.00
Soldier, World War I, Kneeling, With Phone, Tin Helmet, Barclay	20.00
Soldier, Zouave Infantry, 24 Men, Britains, c.1950	110.00
Space Capsule, Astronaut Inside, Rotates, 9 1/2 In.	250.00
Space Capsule, Battery Operated, Japan, Box	275.00
Space Capsule, Friendship, Japan, Friction, 7 In.	135.00
Space Gun, Tom Corbett	495.00
Space Jeep, Tin, Friction, 1950s, 5 In.	65.00
Space Ship, Friction, Gyro, Plastic Canopy, Japan, 1960s, 6 1/2 In.	25.00
Space Tank, Tin, Friction, MAR, 1950s, 5 In.	75.00
Space Top Set, Battery Operated Spinner, Apollo, Marx, On Card, 1970	90.00
Speedy Gonzales, Vinyl, Dakin, 1970, 7 In.	35.00
Spic, Coon Drummer, Figure Seated On Bass Drum, Tin, Louis Marx, 8 3/4 In.	1450.00
Spic & Span, 2 Figures On Base, 1 Seated Playing Drums, Tin, Marx, 10 In.	2300.00
Squirrel, Brown Mohair, Velvet Nut, Steiff, 8 In.	95.00
Stable, 4 Stalls, Converse, 7 x 12 In.	195.00
Stable, Red Shingle Roof, Wooden, Lithograph Paper, Papier-Mache Horse, Bliss, 14 In. .	900.00
Stagecoach, Overland Stagecoach, Battery Operated, Cragston, Box, 18 In.	225.00
Steam Dredge, Metal, Alcohol Burning, American, 1930, 17 x 25 x 9 1/2 In.	395.00
Steam Engine, Vertical, With 3 Accessories, Marx, Box, 1950	245.00
Steam Shovel, Buddy L, Pressed Steel, Decals, 23 x 13 1/2 In.	935.00
Steam Shovel, Marion, Painted, Decals, Steelcraft, 1930	450.00
Stool, Piano, Doll's, Swivels From 5 1/2 To 7 In.	25.00
Stove, Acme, 7 Burners, 2 Ovens, Acme, Cast Iron, 11 In.	316.00
Stove, Copper Utensils, 7 x 6 In.	75.00
Stove, Crescent	250.00
Stove, Empire, Electric, 1927	95.00
Stove, Girard, 10 In.	40.00
Stove, Jewel Range Jr., Cast Iron, 6 Circular Lids, Detroit Stove Works, Miniature, 18 In. .	520.00
Stove, Little Eva, Twin Side Ovens, 4 Range Tops, Chimney, N.S. Cate	747.00
Stove, Royal, Cast Iron	30.00
Stove, Stainless Steel & Nickel Trim, 5 Pans, Germany, 1920, 15 x 11 x 9 In.	1150.00
Streetcar, Horse Drawn, Cast Iron, 1895, 14 In.	1395.00

Submarine, Battery Operated, Japan, 16 In.	650.00
Sunny Andy Kidde Kampers, Tin Lithograph, 14 In.	400.00
Supermarket, Counter, Folding Sides, Tin Lithograph, Miniature Boxes Of Groceries	220.00
Table, Doll's, Console, Sheraton Style, D Shape, Mahogany Veneers, 16 In.	115.00
Table Set, Wild Rose, Matte Silver & Red Paint, 4 Pieces	220.00
Tank, Army, Reproduced Tracks, Arcade, 8 In.	985.00
Tank, Army, Roadchamps, Olive Green, 1 1/4 In.	2.00
Tank, Bulldog, U.S. Army, Tin Lithograph, Rubber Wheels, Japan, 1950s, 5 1/2 In.	26.00
Tank, Centurion, Britains, All Yellow	385.00
Tank, Doughboy, Marx, Box	595.00
Tank, Friction, Tin, Camouflage, Modern Toys, Japan, 2 x 3 In.	120.00
Tank, Maroon, Gray, 1914, 12 In.	345.00
Tank, Rollover, Marx	100.00
Tank, Rollover, Windup, Marx, Box	235.00
Tank, World War II, Windup, 6 Wheels, Arnold, 7 In.	425.00
Tank, Zigzag, Windup, Tin Litho, Camouflage, Pre-World War II, Germany, 2 3/4 In.	70.00
Taxi, Dome Signal Light, Plastic, Motor Steering All Directions, Andy Bard, 1940s, 10 In.	95.00
Taxi, Ford, 1959 Model, Yellow, Toy, Master, Box, 8 In.	165.00
Taxi, Plymouth, Plastic, 1953, 7 In.	65.00
Taxi, Yellow Cab, Black Driver, License Plate, Cast Iron, Freidag, 7 1/2 In.	850.00
Taxi, Yellow Cab, Original Parts & Paint, Hubley, 8 In.	725.00
Taxi, Yellow Cab, Seated Driver, Orange, Black, Tin, 1924, 8 1/2 In.	1795.00
Taxi, Yellow Cab, Seated Driver, Orange, Black, White, Orange Disc Wheels, Tin, 7 In.	845.00
Tea Set, Doll's, Children At Picnic On Box Top, Porcelain, Violets, Vines, 10 Piece	475.00
Tea Set, Dresden Flowers, China, Open Sugar, Deep Saucer, Box, 13 Piece	145.00
Tea Set, Luster, Painted, Japan, Child's, 1930s, 16 Piece	65.00
Teakettle, Wagner, Iron	130.00
Teddy Bears are also listed in the Teddy Bear category.	
Telephone Switchboard, Plastic Handset, Dial & Connectors, Tinplate, 11 1/2 In.	69.00
Tent & Stove Set, Sargent Preston, Unused, Shipping Box	465.00
Thresher, McCormick-Deering, Cast Iron, Gray, Cream Wheels, Arcade, 12 In.	315.00
Thresher, McCormick-Deering, Chutes, Arcade Decal, Cast Iron, Arcade, 10 In.	1045.00
Tiger, Windup, Marx, 9 In.	95.00
Toilette Set, Doll's, Porcelain, In Lidded Basket, Germany, 7-In. Basket, 7 Piece	300.00
Top, Throw Type, 19th Century, 6 1/2-In. Handle, 4 In.	155.00
Topo Gigio, Baseball Player, Plastic, Huron Products Co., 10 In.	45.00
Topo Gigio, Football Player, Molded Plastic, Huron Products Co., 10 In.	48.00
Topo Gigio, U.S. Mail Carrier, Plastic, Red Mop Hair, Huron Product Co., 10 In.	42.00
Tower, Hoisting, Portable Chutes, Buddy L	5500.00
Tractor, Allis-Chalmers, WD Tractor, Box, 1977, 13 1/2 In.	475.00
Tractor, Bottom Plow, Clock Work, Green, Structo	845.00
Tractor, Caterpillar, Nickel Driver, Metal Tracks, Cast Iron, Arcade, 8 In.	550.00
Tractor, Corn Planter, Green, Driver On Tractor, Arcade, Box, 1940s, 8 In.	125.00
Tractor, Crawler, Windup, Woodhaver, Gray, Red Wheels, 10 In.	425.00
Tractor, Double-Action Side-Dumping Body, Girard, 11 In.	385.00
Tractor, Driver, Scoop, Earth Grader, Windup, Marx, Box, 1930s	395.00
Tractor, Ertl Cub, Die Cast Metal, Rubber Tires, Original Box, 1/16 Scale	65.00
Tractor, Ertl Farmall H, Die Cast Metal, Rubber Tires, Steerable, Box, 1/16 Scale	85.00
Tractor, Express, Red, Embossed Pacific Intermountain Express, Smith Miller, 28 In.	785.00
Tractor, Farm, Driver Behind Wheel, Forward & Back Motion, Marx, 7 In.	175.00
Tractor, Field Artillery, Olive-Drab Green, Rubber Wheels, Dinky Toys	40.00
Tractor, Ford 4000, Tinplate Trailer, Ertl, 23 In.	150.00
Tractor, Fordson F, Cast Iron, Red, Hubley, 6 In.	255.00
Tractor, Fordson, Gray, Red Wheels, Tootsie, 1928, 3 In.	195.00
Tractor, Green & Yellow Paint, Cast Iron, Arcade, 3 1/2 In.	70.00
Tractor, Manoil, Gasoline Tank, Gray, Wooden Wheels, 2 In.	22.00
Tractor, Massey Ferguson, Red, Yellow Wheels, Dinky	95.00
Tractor, Massey Harris, Red, Yellow Wheels, Man, Dinky	85.00
Tractor, Red Wheels, Nickel Driver, Cast Iron, Arcade, 5 1/2 In.	200.00
Tractor, Red, Aluminum Trailer Body, 14 Wheels, Miller Ironson Corp., 27 In.	665.00
Tractor, Ride-On, Red, 26 x 33 In.	80.00
Tractor, Sparking, Climbing, Windup, Marx	250.00
Tractor, Steel, Wooden Wheels, Chain Treads, Cast Iron Driver, Wilkins, 8 1/2 In.	115.00

Tractor, Trailer, Chipperfield's, With 6 Horses, Corgi 225.00
Tractor, Trailer, John Deere, No. 587, Box, 17 In. 190.00
Tractor, Tricky Tommy, Battery Operated, Box, 1950s 225.00
Tractor, Yellow, Black Wheels, Hubley, 5 In. 15.00
Tractor Plow, Massey-Harris, Reuhl Prod., Box, 1940s 585.00
Tractor Trailer Set, Union Sheep, U.S. Transportation Co., Friction, Daiya Co., 13 In. ... 175.00
Train, American Flyer, Automobile Car, Wide Gauge, No. 4018, c.1931 .... 275.00
Train, American Flyer, Circus, S-Gauge, Pacific Locomotive, Mid 1930s 2750.00
Train, American Flyer, Locomotive, Improved Presidents Special, No. 4689, c.1931 ..... 9350.00
Train, American Flyer, Lumber Unloading Car, Box, No. 971 S 100.00
Train, American Flyer, Pullman Cars, 1948 .... 60.00
Train, American Flyer, Steam Locomotive & Tender, New York Central No. 322, 19 In. ... 90.00
Train, American Flyer, Tanker, Wide Gauge, No. 4010, 1931 .... 880.00
Train, Arcade, Locomotive, Passenger, Observation Caboose, 14 In. 110.00
Train, Auburn No. 922 Express, 3 Piece, 19 In. 225.00
Train, Begg's & Co. No. 1, Locomotive, Tin, Brass, Painted, 12 In. 745.00
Train, Buddy L, Caboose, Pressed Steel, 20 In. 468.00
Train, Buddy L, Locomotive & Tender, Heavy Gauge Pressed Steel 5940.00
Train, Caney, Locomotive & Tender, Portable Trestle, 1898, 12 5/8 In. 2200.00
Train, Coal Tender, Passenger Car, American Tin Co., Painted, Tin, 3 Piece 688.00
Train, Cor-Cor, Red Locomotive, Black Tender, 4 Piece 475.00
Train, Ives, Caboose, No. 195, Red & Black 200.00
Train, Lionel, Crane, No. 219, c.1926 .... 184.00
Train, Lionel, Locomotive & Tender, Norfolk & Western Powhatan Arrow 455.00
Train, Lionel, Locomotive, Rail Chief, No. 709, 1937-1941 .... 6050.00
Train, Lionel, Searchlight Car, No. 520 .... 143.00
Train, Marklin, Flying Hamburger, Diesel-Electric Express, c.1935, 52 In. 920.00
Train, Marx, Locomotive, Sparking, Box 95.00
Train, Marx, Steam Engine, New York Central, Plastic, Metal Frame, 6 In. 21.00
Train, Painted, Black, Yellow, Red, Wooden, Late 19th Century, 54 3/8 In., 4 Piece 6900.00
Train, Passenger, Friction, Schieble, Red, Green, 1915, 15 In. 395.00
Train, Steam Engine, Cast Iron Base, 25 In. 2100.00
Train, Western Black Locomotive, No. 922, Red Wheels, Auburn, 2 Piece 50.00
Train Accessory, Billboard Blinker, No. 410, Lionel, c.1956 .... 45.00
Train Accessory, Bridge Set, Lionel, No. 103, 3 Center Span Section, c.1920-1931 ...... 825.00
Train Accessory, Casino, Contemporary, Canopy, With Tables, Chandelier, Germany 1375.00
Train Accessory, Durchgang Station, Marklin 2860.00
Train Accessory, Foot Bridge, Marklin 330.00
Train Accessory, Freight Shed, Bing 1210.00
Train Accessory, Hot Dog Grill Cart, Alcohol Burner, Kilbri 1070.00
Train Accessory, Newsstand, Bing 245.00
Train Accessory, Railroad Station, Lionel, No. 116, c.1935 .... 1705.00
Train Accessory, Station, Crossing, Twin Gates, Warning Bell, Marklin, No. 2195, 14 In. .. 488.00
Train Set, American Flyer, Engine & 3 Cars, Windup, 1914, 24 In. 575.00
Train Set, American Flyer, Engine, Tanker, Caboose & Gondola 325.00
Train Set, American Flyer, Gilbert, S-Gauge, Plastic, Box, 1960s 80.00
Train Set, American Flyer, Hiawatha, Bipolar Locomotive, 1928 .... 2090.00
Train Set, American Flyer, No. 312, Locomotive, Coal Tender, 4 Cars, Boxes, 1940s 200.00
Train Set, Cragstan, Freight, Locomotive, 2 Wagons, Accessories, Box 58.00
Train Set, Diesel Locomotive, Red Caboose, 6 Silver Tank Cars, Midgetoy, 1950s, 27 In. .. 45.00
Train Set, Hafner Streamliners, Accessories, Engine & 4 Cars, Tracks, Box 110.00
Train Set, Ives, Engine, Coal Tender, 1900s, 5 Piece 795.00
Train Set, Ives, No. 1134, Circus Set, Locomotive, 6 Cars, 1930s 5750.00
Train Set, Marx, Honeymoon Express, All Aboard, Figure, Standing, Tin, Box, 9 In. 425.00
Train Set, Marx, Steam Type, Tin, 3-Rail Track, Transformer, Instruction Sheet, Box 140.00
Train Set, Marx, Stream Line, Locomotive, 5 Cars, Transformer, Curved Track, Box 75.00
Train Set, Penny, Japan, Box, 11 In., 6 Piece 300.00
Train Set, Tyco, Petticoat Junction, HO Scale, Box, Early 1960s 250.00
Tricycle, Aerodynamic, Wheel Fenders, Headlight 2200.00
Tricycle, Circus, Celluloid, Tin, Windup, Occupied Japan, Box 225.00
Tricycle, Humphrey Mobile, 3-Wheel, Tin, Windup, Wyandotte, 1940s, 7 In. 525.00
Tricycle, Velocity Trike, Boy On Board, Gunthermann 6500.00
Trolley, Bowery & Central Park, Lithographed Paper On Wood, Bliss 5500.00

Trolley, Dayton, Red, Yellow, 23 1/2 In. 395.00
Trolley, Hill-Climber, Tin, 8 Children In Windows, Inertia Mechanical 1430.00
Trolley, Interurban, Red, Yellow & Black, Dayton, 1915, 23 In. 495.00
Trolley, Toonerville, Figure Standing On Platform, Red, Yellow, Tin, Fischer, 1922, 5 In. . 910.00
Trolley, Toonerville, Fontaine Fox, Dent, Reproduction, Box, 5 In. 895.00
Trolley, Toonerville, Fontaine Fox, Penny Toy, 1922, 2 In. 522.00
Trot-Away King, Push Toy, 1889 .... 1100.00
Truck, Army, American National, 27 In. 2195.00
Truck, Army, Canvas Covering Bed, Pressed Steel, Sturditoy, 1920s, 27 In. 3630.00
Truck, Army, Materiel, Load, Canvas Covering, Mack, Smith-Miller, 20 In. 1320.00
Truck, Auto, Green, Yellow Wheels, Hubley, 10 1/4 In. 975.00
Truck, Barrel, Red & Blue, Windup, 1950, 18 In. 110.00
Truck, Bucket Loader, Barber-Greene, Green, Doepke, 1948, 18 In. .... .395.00 to 425.00
Truck, Buckeye Ditch Digger, Cast Iron, 1930, Kenton, 12 In. 750.00
Truck, Canada Dry Delivery, 1950s 225.00
Truck, Car Carrier, 2 Cars, No. 2845, Tonka, Box, 27 In. 420.00
Truck, Car Carrier, 2 Firebird Cars, Cast Trailer, No. 3663, Ertl, Box, 20 In. 280.00
Truck, Car Carrier, 3 Cadillac Cars, Ramp, Wyandotte, 1952, 22 In. 450.00
Truck, Car Carrier, 3 Cars, Ideal, Box, 27 In. 275.00
Truck, Car Carrier, Metal, Aluminum Trailer With 4 Cars, Matchbox 95.00
Truck, Car Carrier, Model A Ford, With 3 Austin Coupes, Williams, 12 1/2 In. 895.00
Truck, Car Carrier, Trans Am & Z-28 Cars, Nylint, Box, 24 In. 210.00
Truck, Car Carrier, With 4 Cars, Battery Operated, Barclay, 4 1/2 In. 110.00
Truck, Cattle Transport, Ertl, Box, 22 In. 420.00
Truck, Cement Delivery, Albion Chieftan No. 51, Metal, Lesney Matchbox, 2 In. 30.00
Truck, Cement Mixer, Bronze, White Drum, Structo, 1950, 22 In. 85.00
Truck, Cement Mixer, Jaeger, Kenton, 1932, 6 1/2 In. 625.00
Truck, Cement Mixer, Jaeger, Kenton, 7 In. 585.00
Truck, Cement Mixer, Jeep, Red & White, Tonka, 1968, 9 In. 45.00
Truck, Cement Mixer, Mack Cab, Lithographed Tin, Chein 4100.00
Truck, Cement Mixer, Pressed Steel, Decals, Buddy L, 1920, 18 In. 690.00
Truck, Cement Mixer, Treads, 15 In. 2640.00
Truck, Cement Mixer, Yellow, Black Drum, Doepke, 1947, 15 In. 325.00
Truck, Circus, Chipperfields, Crane, Red, 1968 .... 75.00
Truck, City Dray, Green, Orange & White Painted, Buddy L, 19 1/2 In. 225.00
Truck, City Ice, Decals On Front & Sides Of Cab, Steelcraft, 4 In. 880.00
Truck, Coal, Cab Over Early Grille, Red, Buddy L, 13 1/2 In. 135.00
Truck, Contractor's, Dent, 1928, 11 In. 1900.00
Truck, Crane, Chipperfields, Red, Blue Logo, Corgi, 1968 .... 110.00
Truck, Delivery, Crown Oil, Model A Ford, Die Cast Metal, 7 1/2 In. 23.00
Truck, Delivery, CW Coffee, Black Cab, Green, Pressed Steel, Metalcraft, 11 In. . .330.00 to 825.00
Truck, Delivery, Fanny Farmer Candy, Japan, Red & White, 1960s, 8 1/4 In. 265.00
Truck, Delivery, Flivver, Black, Canopy Top, Pressed Steel, Buddy L, 14 In. 2180.00
Truck, Delivery, Ford, 1932 Model, 5 Spokes, Hot Wheels, No. 446 .... 140.00
Truck, Delivery, Heinz, White, Side Decals, Pressed Steel, Metalcraft, 12 1/2 In. 785.00
Truck, Delivery, Metalcraft, Black Cab, Green, Pressed Steel, 11 In. 454.00
Truck, Delivery, Names Of Many Toys On Rooftop & Sides, Tin, England, 10 In. 785.00
Truck, Delivery, Panel, Boston Store Embossed On Sides, Tin, Bing, Germany, 7 3/4 In. ... 2135.00
Truck, Delivery, Red Paint, Stake Side Body, Aluminum, Miller Ironson Corp., 18 In. 1030.00
Truck, Delivery, Werk's Tag Soap, Black Cab, Green, Pressed Steel, Metalcraft, 11 In. ... 1030.00
Truck, Delivery, Yellow Body, Buddy L, Steel, 1957, 14 1/2 In. 200.00
Truck, Digger, Hubley, 1930, 8 In. 475.00
Truck, Dodge, Armored, Contains A Safe, Japan, 7 In. .... , 135.00
Truck, Dump, 3-Way Clockwork, Structo 525.00
Truck, Dump, A-Frame, Buddy L, Box, 1920s 3300.00
Truck, Dump, Black Doorless Cab, Red Spoke Wheels, Rubber Tires, Kelmet, 26 In. 1450.00
Truck, Dump, Black, White Cab, Gray Tilting Tailgate, Pressed Steel, Kelmet, 25 In. 2180.00
Truck, Dump, Driver, Yellow Baby, 1923 Model, Cast Iron, Arcade, 10 1/2 In. 975.00
Truck, Dump, Flivver, Black, Aluminum Wheels, Pressed Steel, Buddy L, 11 In. 2905.00
Truck, Dump, Green & Red, Turner, 20 In. 395.00
Truck, Dump, Hydraulic, Red & White, Structo, 1957, 20 In. 235.00
Truck, Dump, Mack Jr., Metal, Green & Orange, Steelcraft, c.1930, 22 x 8 In. 460.00
Truck, Dump, Mack, Cast Iron, Arcade, 8 1/4 In. 305.00

Truck, Dump, Mack, Driver, Arcade, 1928, 12 In. 1695.00
Truck, Dump, Mighty Dump Truck, Friction, Y, Japan, Box, 1960s, 13 1/2 In. 200.00
Truck, Dump, Military, Tin, Friction, MAR, 1950s, 7 1/4 In. 110.00
Truck, Dump, Open Bed Dump Body, Disc Wheels, Tin, Ferdinand Strauss, 10 1/4 In. 1935.00
Truck, Dump, Packard, Black & Orange, Metal Wheels, Turner, 27 1/2 In. 660.00
Truck, Dump, Painted Metal, Steelcraft, c.1930, 23 In. 400.00
Truck, Dump, Plastic, Red, Yellow, Lever Lift Bed, 1950s, 6 x 2 In. 20.00
Truck, Dump, Republic Momentum, Steel, 1921, 20 In. 475.00
Truck, Dump, Robotoy, Electric Transformer, Buddy L, 1932 .... 895.00
Truck, Dump, Seated Driver, Gray Paint, Blue Trim, Gray Spoke Wheels, Tin, 5 1/4 In. .. 180.00
Truck, Dump, Side, Open Bench Seat, Brass Hood Plate, Tin, France, 8 1/2 In. 240.00
Truck, Dump, Steel, Ride Type, Buddy L, Box, 20 1/2 In. 245.00
Truck, Dump, Wooldridge Bottom, Yellow, Doepke No. 2000, 1946, 24 In. 375.00
Truck, Dump, World Transport, Friction, Tin, Orange, Y, Japan, 1960s, 11 In. 195.00
Truck, Dump, Yellow, Cab With Opening Doors, Die Cast, Miller, Ironson Corp, 17 In. .. 750.00
Truck, Excavating, Tin, Friction, MAR, 5 1/2 In. 65.00
Truck, Express Delivery, 1930s Model A, Red & Black, Bandai, 6 In. 125.00
Truck, Express, Black, Red Frame, Aluminum Spoke Wheels, Pressed Steel, Buddy L ... 2300.00
Truck, Express, Bunte Candies, Red Cab, White Body, Pressed Steel, Metalcraft, 12 In. .. 180.00
Truck, Express, Driver, Jones & Bixler, 15 1/2 In. 1295.00
Truck, Express, Flivver, One Ton, Black, Pressed Steel, Buddy L, 14 In. 2905.00
Truck, Figure Holding Steering Wheel On Top, Disc Wheels, Tin, F. Strauss, 9 In. 500.00
Truck, Fire Wrecking, Red, Open Drivers Seat, Ladders, Crane, Pressed Steel, Buddy L .. 3025.00
Truck, Frosty Bar Ice Cream, Tin, Friction, Automatic Bell, 7 1/2 In. 275.00
Truck, Good Humor, 4 In. 275.00
Truck, Grader, John Deere, Cast Iron, Ertl, 12 In. 250.00
Truck, Grain Hauler, Metal, Friction, Japan, 1950s 195.00
Truck, Gravel Mixer, Marx, 9 1/2 In. 395.00
Truck, Groceries Delivery, Windup, Chein 295.00
Truck, Hathaway Bread, Original Paint, Arcade, 1932, 9 1/2 In. 2600.00
Truck, Heinz Pickle, 1 Side In French, 1 Side In English, 1950s, 29 In. 1000.00
Truck, Heinz Pickle, White, Green, Metalcraft, 1933, 12 In. ....450.00 to 695.00
Truck, Hi-Way Express, Blue & Silver, Marx, 28 In. 245.00
Truck, Hydraulic, Red, Silver Extension Ladders, Spoke Wheels, Pressed Steel, Buddy L . 2905.00
Truck, Ice Cream, Tin Lithograph, Friction, Name Both Sides, 1960s, 4 In. 60.00
Truck, Ice Cream, Yellow & White, 1930s Model, Japan, 8 In. 235.00
Truck, Ice, Arcade, 1941, 6 3/4 In. 425.00
Truck, Ice, Red & White, Marx, 12 In. 125.00
Truck, International Dairy, Grade A Dairy, Japan, 1960s 265.00
Truck, Lincoln Transfer & Storage, Tinplate, Windup, Marx 1320.00
Truck, Livestock Van, Friction, Tin, Japan, 9 In. 165.00
Truck, Log, Orange, Hubley, Box, 10 In. 145.00
Truck, Log, Structo, 1950 .... 60.00
Truck, Lumber, Mack, Light Green Paint, Dark Green Frame, Smith Miller, 36 In. 785.00
Truck, Meat Stock, 1950s Chevy, Red, Yellow, Blue, Daiya, Box, 8 In. 110.00
Truck, Milk & Cream, Cast Iron, Orange, Hubley, 3 1/2 In. 435.00
Truck, Moving Van, Aero-Mayflower, 1951 .... 360.00
Truck, Moving Van, Pressed Steel, Rear Doors, Tonka, 22 In. 287.00
Truck, Moving Van, Sonny, Sheet Steel, Dayton Toy & Specialty Co., 25 3/4 In. 660.00
Truck, NBC Television Battery Operated, Screen Lights Up, Camera Man Moves, 1950 .. 625.00
Truck, NBC Television, Friction, Box, 6 In. 695.00
Truck, Pickup, Cast Iron, Tonka 60.00
Truck, Pickup, Flivver, Black, Red Spoke Wheels, Pressed Steel, Buddy L, 12 In. .825.00 to 905.00
Truck, Pickup, Motorcycle In Back, No. 2953, Tonka, Box, 15 In. 270.00
Truck, RCA-NBC Television, Battery Operated, Box 1295.00
Truck, Recovery Vehicle, Die Cast Metal, Rubber Tires, Olive Drab, Dinky Toy, 5 1/2 In. .. 50.00
Truck, Road Service, Tin, Friction, Japan, 1950s, 5 1/4 In. 45.00
Truck, Sand & Gravel, Buddy L 8250.00
Truck, Searchlight, Battery Light, Tecno, 6 1/2 In. 360.00
Truck, Sheffield Farms Select Milk, 4 Milk Cans, Decals 2200.00
Truck, Side Dump, Friction, Tinplate, Red & Cream, TN, Box, 11 In. 144.00
Truck, Side Dump, Green, Orange, 1 1/2 In. 11.00
Truck, Sprinkler, Tank Line, Filler Cap, Buddy L, 26 In. ....1380.00 to 1650.00

Truck, Stake, Black, Open Bench Seat, Flat Bed Body, Pressed Steel, Buddy L, 24 In. ... 1815.00
Truck, Stake, Coast To Coast, A.C. Williams, 1930s, 5 1/2 In. 375.00
Truck, Stake, International, Nickel Plated Grille, Arcade, c.1940, 9 1/2 In. 575.00
Truck, Stake, Take-Apart, 6 Original Tires, Hubley, 1930s, 5 In. 275.00
Truck, Stroh's Beer, With Gray Tavern, 16 In. 295.00
Truck, Tanker, Aero Oil Company, Marx, 5 In. 82.00
Truck, Tanker, Gasoline, Metal Wheels, A.C. Williams, 1930s, 5 1/8 In. 145.00
Truck, Tanker, Gasoline, Yellow Body, Red Lettering, Red Disc Wheels, Tin, 7 In. 2180.00
Truck, Tanker, GMC Triton Oil, Orange Cab, Smith Miller 385.00
Truck, Tanker, GMC, Texaco, Buddy L 255.00
Truck, Tanker, Kerosene, Packard, Keystone, 26 In. 2000.00
Truck, Tanker, Label, Buddy L, 24 In. 110.00
Truck, Tanker, Milk, Exclusive Dairies, Friction Power, Tin, Japan, 1960s, 7 1/2 In. 125.00
Truck, Tanker, Mobil Gas, Friction, Tin Lithograph, Flying Horse, Japan, 11 In. 240.00
Truck, Tanker, Oil & Gas, Dark Green, Yellow Wheels, Kenton, 8 In. 675.00
Truck, Tanker, Oil, Seated Driver, Green Body, Tin, Ferdinand Strauss, 10 1/2 In. 1150.00
Truck, Tanker, Shell Gas, Tonka, Box, 26 In. 350.00
Truck, Tanker, Texaco, Buddy L, Box, 25 In. 745.00
Truck, Timber, Seated Driver, Open Frame Body, Disc Wheels, Ferdinand Strauss, 18 In. . 725.00
Truck, Tow, BP, Dodge, No. 13, Die Cast, Matchbox, Lesney, Box 32.00
Truck, Tow, Dinky Service, Blue & Gray, No Hook, 1950s, 4 In. 65.00
Truck, Tow, GMC, White & Red, Smith Miller 450.00
Truck, Tow, Open Service Body, Tow-Crane Hook, White, Miller Ironson Corp., 16 In. .. 850.00
Truck, Tow, Plee-Zing, Black Cab, Yellow, Angled Tow Hook, Pressed Steel, Metalcraft .. 605.00
Truck, Tow, Red Body, Open, Gray, Blue, Tin, Ferdinand Strauss, 11 1/2 In. 195.00
Truck, Tow, Towing & Repairs, Black Cab, Orange, Pressed Steel, Metalcraft, 10 In. 305.00
Truck, Trailer, Red Cab, Rear Doors, Rubber Tires, Buddy L, 24 In. 605.00
Truck, Trailer, Toys R Us, Ertl, 1979, 20 In. 45.00
Truck, Transport, Ice Cream, Railway Express, Pressed Steel, Buddy L 2090.00
Truck, Troop, Open Cab, British Type, Olive Drab, Black Rubber Tires, Dinky Toys, 4 In. 77.00
Truck, U-Haul, Push Toy, Tootsietoy 175.00
Truck, U.S. Army Mobile Canteen, Plastic, Sliding Side Doors, Rubber Tires, 4 1/2 In. ... 25.00
Truck, U.S. Army, 5-Ton, Friction, Pressed Metal, Plastic Tires, Canvas Top, 1950s, 9 In. . 63.00
Truck, U.S. Army, Steel, Canvas Top, Marx, 1950, 18 In. 160.00
Truck, U.S. Mail, Opening Doors, Headlights, Rubber Tires, Buddy L, 22 In. 3410.00
Truck, U.S. Mail, Packard, Decals, Keystone, 1920s 1300.00
Truck, U.S. Mail, Packard, Pressed Steel, Opening Rear Doors, Black Tires, 1920s, 26 In. 798.00
Truck, U.S. Mail, Yellow, Black, Spoke Wheels, Tin Lithograph, 8 In. 335.00
Truck, Utility, Pressed Steel, Lifting Mechanism, No. 7, Structo, 21 In. 86.00
Truck, Water Tower, Buddy L, Red, Lattice Extension Tower, Disc Wheels, 36 1/2 In. ... 4235.00
Truck, Water Tower, Red, Disc Wheels, Rubber Tires, Pressed Steel, Sturditoy, 34 In. 1090.00
Truck, Zephyr Fuel, Hubley, 1930s, 5 1/2 In. 175.00
Trunk, Doll's, Flat Top 70.00
Trunk, Doll's, Louis Vuitton, Flat Top, Paper Cover, Brass Studs & Clasps, 11 In. 3300.00
Trunk, Doll's, Steamer, Canvas Cover, Lift-Out Tray, Louis Vuitton, Label, 14 x 20 In. 2600.00
Trunk, Doll, Domed, 2 Trays, Wooden, Canvas Cover, Lined, France, c.1885, 22 In. 550.00
Van, Market Gardener's, Yellow Paint, Dinky 125.00
Velocipede, Clockwork, Black Boy Rider, Cloth Body, Brass Shoes, Stevens & Brown ... 1980.00
View-Master Reel, Tom Corbett, Space Cadet, 1954, 3 Reels 25.00
Viewer, Charlie's Angels, 3-D, 24 Scenes, Kenner, 1973, 7 x 12 In. 48.00
Viewer, Ultra-Vue, Bakelite, Swirl Slide, Box 30.00
Village Set, Wooden, 12 Buildings, 4 Trees, Lighthouse, 16 Piece 220.00
Violin, Tin, Czechoslovkia, 10 In. 70.00
Waffle Iron, Stover, Jr., Iron 120.00
Waffle Iron, Wagner, Iron 110.00
Wagon, Dray, 2 Horses, Cast Iron, Kenton, 15 In. 250.00
Wagon, Duro-Bilt Racer, Orange Paint, Black Lettering, c.1920 .... 385.00
Wagon, Express, Wooden, Wooden Wheels, Iron Bindings, 19th Century, 48 In. 99.00
Wagon, Fleetwing, Metal Wheels, Hard Rubber Tires, Dark Brown, 15 x 13 x 39 In. 230.00
Wagon, Flyer, Express, Orange, Nickeled Pull Handle, Disc Wheels, Cast Iron, 7 3/4 In. ... 540.00
Wagon, Green Paint, Blue, Yellow Highlights, Chicago Farm Wagon, 37 In. 8800.00
Wagon, Horse Drawn, Milk, Cast Iron, Black, Gilt Harness, Yellow Wheel, 6 3/4 In. 145.00
Wagon, Log, 2 Oxen, Hubley, 1900s, 15 In. 1195.00

Wagon, Milk, Cast Iron Driver & 2 Horses, Tin 460.00
Wagon, Our Very Best, Mustard Paint, Metal Wheels & Spokes 750.00
Wagon, Poplar, Inscribed Bulletin, Floral Sprays, Iron Rimmed Wheels, Spokes, 40 In. ... 345.00
Wagon, Red, Wooden Bottom, Green Wheels, Metal Spoke Wheels, 1900, 16 In. 125.00
Wagon, Shopping News On Sides, Iron-Bound Wooden Spoke Wheels, 16 x 42 In. 795.00
Wagon, Wooden, Blue Paint, Wooden Spoke Wheels, Red Paint Traces 245.00
Wagon, Wooden, Iron Wheels, White Paint Traces, 19th Century, 31 x 85 x 19 In. 550.00
Walker, Barnacle Bill, Battery Operated, Chein 325.00
Walker, Boob McNutt, Windup, Strauss, 1920s 650.00
Walker, Dopey, Battery Operated, Marx 575.00
Walker, Doughboy, Battery Operated, Chein 125.00
Walker, Happy Hooligan, Windup, Chein, 1930s 550.00
Walker, Mammy's Boy, Wearing Colorful Suit, Cane In Hand, Tin, Louis Marx, 11 In. ... 1150.00
Walker, Penguin 24.00
Walkie-Talkie, Starsky & Hutch, LJN, Box, 8 x 13 In. 418.00
Walking Grandma, Gunthermann 565.00
Wallet, Li'l Abner 44.00
Washing Machine, 3 Little Pigs, Tin, Wringer, Pedestal Foot Base, Chein, 8 In. 360.00
Washing Machine, Ohio Art, Marx 295.00
Water Trailer, Military, Slush Mold, Silver Paint, Orange Spoke Wheels, Manoil, 2 In. ... 22.00
Wheelbarrow, Paris Mfg. Co. #4, Wooden, Red & Black Paint, 45 In. 240.00
Wheelbarrow, Salmon Paint, Black Handles, Penna., 19th Century, 5 1/2 x 12 In. 1650.00
Wiggle Fish, Paper, Heavy Roller Front, Pull String, Box, 1946, 14 In. 20.00
Wild Bill Hickok Bunkhouse Kit, 1950s 65.00
Wolf, Painted Brown, Sharp Snout, Open Mouth, Schoenhut, c.1912, 5 In. 805.00
Yo-Yo, Wooden, Duncan 10.00
Zepolay, Tin Lithograph, 4 Outboard Motors, Clockwork, Gunthermann, 13 In. 1295.00
Zeppelin, Pull Toy, Cast Iron, 1930s, 5 In. 115.00
Zeppelin, Tin Lithograph, Lehmann, 10 In. 1200.00
Zigzag, Black & White Man, On Wheeled Apparatus, Windup, Lehmann 1500.00
Zilotone, 6 Interchangeable Discs, Windup, Tin, Wolverine Supply Co., 1930s, 7 x 9 In. ... 995.00
Zilotone, With 3 Records, Wolverine 650.00

TRAMP ART is a form of folk art made since the Civil War. It is usually made from chip-carved cigar boxes. Examples range from small boxes and picture frames to full-sized pieces of furniture.

Bench, 2 Birds On Apron, Upholstered Seat, Gladys, Child's, 25 1/2 In. 1100.00
Box, 6 x 9 x 10 In. 250.00
Box, Bible, Hinged Lid, 3-Section Interior, Velvet Lined, 2 Drawers, Lock, 8 x 21 In. 286.00
Box, Green Material On Top Center, Wallpaper Interior, Walnut, Pine, 1899, 7 In. 201.00
Clock, Chrome, Green, Black & White, Wall 1800.00
Dollhouse, Symmetrical Shape, 2 Chimneys, Glass Windows, 10 x 10 x 8 In. 440.00
Dressing Stand, 5 Tiers, Swivel Mirror At Top, Raised Panel Design, 30 1/2 In. 1150.00
Frame, 12 1/2 x 10 1/4 In. 165.00
Frame, Block Trim, Original Finish, 20 1/4 x 18 1/4 In. 187.00
Frame, Gold Accents, 20 x 15 In. 385.00
Frame, Hearts & Circles, 23 1/2 x 16 1/4 In. 190.00
Humidor, Pine & Poplar, Geometric & Foliate, Hinged Slant Lid, Tin Lined, 10 In. 125.00
Mirror, 2 Turtledoves Top, 2 Lower Drawer & Comb Box, 28 x 16 In. 740.00
Mirror, Chip Carved, Ovolo Corners, Heart Shaped Spandrels, c.1900, 16 x 13 1/2 In. ... 633.00
Staff, Man's Head Top, Bead Eyes, Oversized Mouth & Nose, Wooden, 24 1/4 In. 110.00
Stand, Chip Carved Borders, Applied Half Globes & Diamonds, Square, 11 x 19 In. 65.00
Stool, Pine, Polychrome Design, Mirror Insets, 1900, 19 1/2 In. 825.00
Table, Projecting Top, Medial Shelf, Multilayered, Chip Carving, 26 x 16 x 15 3/4 In. ... 690.00

TRAPS for animals may be handmade. One of the most unusual is the mousetrap made so that when the mouse entered the trap, it was hit on the head with a mallet. Other traps were commercially manufactured and often are marked with the name of the manufacturer. Many traps were designed to be as humane as possible, and they would trap the live animal so it could be released in the woods.

Bear, Iron, Blacksmith Made 230.00
Bug, Tin, Screen, Dome Shape 40.00

 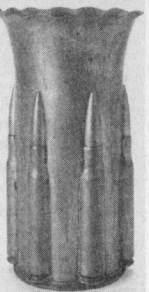

Trench Art, Vase,
Mermaids & Gulls,
Shell Casing,
Concrete Base, 16

Trench Art, Vase,
Shell Casing, Bullets,
Sgt. Paul L.
Knott, June 9, 1942,
7 3/4 In.

Never polish Trench art pieces made of brass shell casings. Collectors prefer the dark colored metal.

Fly, Blown Glass, 19th Century	203.00
Fly, Glass, Blown, 3 Applied Feet, Glass Stopper, Bubbles, 6 1/2 x 5 1/2 In.	75.00
Fly, Glass, Blown, Hanging, Cork, 4 1/2 x 3 1/2 In.	45.00
Fly, Glass, Blown, Hanging, Cork, Marked, Initials SJ In Circle, 6 x 4 In.	45.00
Fly, Screen, Table Type	265.00
Minnow, Wire Handle & Feet, C.F. Orvis	148.00

TREEN, see Wooden category.

TRENCH ART is a form of folk art made by soldiers. Metal casings from bullets and mortar shells were cut and decorated to form useful objects, such as vases.

Lighter, Aircraft Parts, Air Depot No. 17, World War I	11.00
Salt & Pepper, 1944	21.00
Vase, Mermaids & Gulls, Shell Casing, Concrete Base, 16 In. ....*Illus*	325.00
Vase, Shell Casing, Bullets, Sgt. Paul L. Knott, June 9, 1942, 7 3/4 In. ....*Illus*	250.00

TRIVETS are now used to hold hot dishes. Most trivets of the late nineteenth and early twentieth centuries were made to hold hot irons. Iron or brass reproductions are being made of many of the old styles.

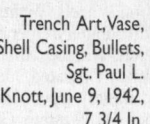

Brass, Fireplace, Turned Feet, Pierced Top, Lion, Crown & Plume Design, 17 x 7 1/4 In.	245.00
Brass, Ornate Shield Shape, Date 1872	95.00
Brass, Pierced, Sliding, On Iron Frame, Hanging	70.00
Brass, Reticulated Gallery, Turned Handle, 14 In.	275.00
Brass, Reticulated Scrolled Top, Turned Feet, 6 3/8 In.	187.00
Brass, Wrought Iron, England, 18th Century, 15 In.	121.00
Brass & Iron, Hearth, Pierced Top, Heart Handle, Brass Front Leg, England, 11 1/4 In.	575.00
California Faience, Cuenca, Flower Basket, Polychrome, Yellow, Round, 5 In.	305.00
California Faience, Stylized Peacock, Blue, Yellow & Turquoise, Round, 5 1/4 In.	330.00
Cast Iron, Benjamin Harrison Bust Inside Horseshoe, 5 In.	50.00
Cast Iron, Coffee, Griswold, No. 1759, Round	70.00
Cast Iron, Jenny Lind, 10 In.	165.00
Cast Iron, Revolving, Twisted Handle, Footed, 11 In.	75.00
Ceramic Tile, Copper Trim, Hand Painted Dutch Boy, Holland, Small	75.00
Copper, Pennsylvania Design, Openwork, Late 18th Century	2295.00
Fender, Lyre Form, Brass, Iron, Wooden Handle, Gray Birm	360.00
Hanging, Hand Forged, Iron, Early 1800s, 18 5/8 In.	290.00
Iron, Tall Legs, Shaped Handle, Lancaster County, Pa., 11 In.	95.00
Iron, Wooden Handle, 6 In.	49.00
Mahogany, Cat, Ring Turned, Spiral Arms, 3 Cabriole Legs, Pad Feet, 15 In.	460.00
Sadiron, Griswold, No. 1604	50.00
Sadiron, Iron, Wapak	75.00

TRUNKS of many types were made. The nineteenth-century sea chest was often handmade of unpainted wood. Brass-fitted camphorwood chests were brought back from the Orient. Leather-covered trunks were popular from the late eighteenth to mid-nineteenth centuries. By 1895, trunks were covered with canvas or decorated sheet metal. Embossed metal coverings were used from 1870 to 1910. By 1925, trunks were covered with vulcanized fiber or undecorated metal.

A.W. Dethloff & Co., Iron Mounts, Hinged Lid, Leather Strap Handle, Tray, 24 x 14 In.	125.00

Applied Tin Flowers & Birds, Mexico, 1950s, 20 x 39 In. 750.00
Camphor, Military, Hinged Top, Brass Bail Handles, Brassbound, 12 1/2 x 21 3/4 In. 200.00
Dome Top, Brass, Figures In Garden Landscape, Black Japanned, Handles, 19 In. 750.00
Dome Top, Dovetailed, Mustard Over White Pine, Mid 19th Century, 13 x 28 x 15 In. ... 365.00
Dome Top, Faux Tortoiseshell, 19th Century 198.00
Dome Top, Hide Covered, Brass Tacks, Initials EC, Paper Interior, 11 x 24 In. 275.00
Dome Top, Horsehair, Brass Tack Design, Early 19th Century, 16 In. 110.00
Dome Top, Leather Straps, Wrought Iron Lock With Hasp, Side Handles, 8 1/4 In. 330.00
Dome Top, Leather Trim, Original Brass Bail Handle, 18 x 9 x 8 1/2 In. 110.00
Dome Top, Leather, Painted Design, 19th Century, 20 x 20 x 35 In. 3900.00
Dome Top, Oak, Carved Ships, Cedar Interior, Hammered Strap Hinges, 23 x 36 x 17 In. . 138.00
Dome Top, Oak, Divided Tray, Hat Box, Metal Trim, Beveled Staves, 23 x 28 x 37 In. ... 425.00
Dome Top, Painted, Sponging & Stippling, 10 1/2 x 23 1/2 In. 220.00
Dome Top, Pine, Green Sponge Painted, c.1800, 36 x 17 1/4 In. 190.00
Dome Top, Pine, Iron Bound, 19th Century, 8 1/2 x 14 x 9 1/2 In. 88.00
Dome Top, Red Flowers, Garlands On Side, Exotic Birds On Front, Dark Green, Pine ... 3735.00
Dome Top, Slanted Sides, Iron Straps & Handles, Original Key, Mid 19th Century, 35 In. . 550.00
Dome Top, Yellow, Burnt Sienna Exterior, Green, Yellow Border Inlay, 12 x 28 x 14 In. ... 258.00
Geometric Design, Flower Sprays, Carved, Painted, Madura, 23 x 32 x 17 In. 201.00
Immigrant's, Dome Top, Green, Flowers, R.E. Cahoon Jr., 1950s, 21 x 46 1/2 x 20 In. .. 2860.00
Immigrant's, Scandinavian, Dome Top, Strap Hinges, Floral Design, 21 x 38 In. 140.00
Iron Bound, Hinged Vaulted Lid, Removable Tray, Late 19th Century, 37 x 31 In. 375.00
Leather Covered, Brass Tacks, 1840s, 17 x 32 1/2 In. 575.00
Leather Covered, Camphorwood, Brass Tack Design, Chinese, 19th Century, 15 x 35 In. . 490.00
Leather Covered, Tooled Design, Marked J. Gale, Mt. Holly, N.J., 18 x 30 In. 200.00
Leather Covered, Wrought Iron Lock, Brass Bail Handle, 12 In. 82.00
Liquor Case, Traveling, Tan Leatherette, 2 Bottles, Glasses, Shot Glass, Utensils, 1950s .. 45.00
Louis Vuitton, Garment Bag, Shoulder Strap, Leather, 27 x 15 x 14 In. 390.00
Louis Vuitton, Leather & Wood Strapping, Brass Mounts, 13 x 40 In. 1150.00
Louis Vuitton, Lower Document Drawer, 4 Drawers, 2 Upper Drawers, 12 1/2 x 24 In. 1650.00
Louis Vuitton, Metal Closures & Locks, Lift-Out Interior, Leather, Handles 1045.00
Louis Vuitton, Paris, 20 x 17 In. 500.00
Louis Vuitton, Stenciled H.P.H., 28 x 48 1/2 In. 2645.00
Louis Vuitton, Suitcase, On Wheels, Original Pull Strap, 1930s, Large 2800.00
Louis Vuitton, Valise, 9 x 17 In. 488.00
Louis Vuitton, Wardrobe, 1929, 21 1/2 x 44 In. 2530.00
Marquetry Floral Inlay, Lift-Out Tray, Period Wallpaper Lined, 30 1/2 x 45 In. 1650.00
Painted Leather, Hinged Cover, Floral Panels, Inner Well, Brassbound, 34 x 18 1/4 In. .. 220.00
Painted Leather On Camphor Wood, Floral On Red Ground, Brassbound, 10 x 24 In. 165.00
Red Lacquer, Bamboo, 19th Century, 31 1/2 In. 345.00
Red Lacquer With Gold, 2 Brass Hasp Latches, Leather, 14 1/2 x 35 1/2 In. 110.00
Shipping, Aluminum, 2 Clasps, Twist Knob, American Airlines Decal, 26 x 16 x 7 1/2 In. 20.00
Travel Chest, Bail Handles, Brass Studwork, 18th Century Style, 33 x 18 x 13 1/4 In. 92.00
Walnut, Hinged Top, Storage Well, Inlaid Floral Marquetry Panels, 29 1/2 x 41 3/4 In. ... 1380.00

TUTHILL Cut Glass Company of Middletown, New York, worked from
1902 to 1923. Of special interest are the finely cut pieces of stemware
and tableware.

Basket, Wild Rose, Handle, 5 x 6 1/2 In. 1150.00
Bowl, 6-Point Star, Filled With Hobstars, Intaglio Floral Border, Signed, 4 x 8 In. 595.00
Candlestick, Cut Glass, Teardrop Stem, Stara Clear Base, Signed, 9 x 4 In., Pair 850.00
Plate, Primrose, Center Hobstar, Signed, 8 In. 375.00
Sugar & Creamer, Vintage, Signed 300.00
Tray, Flowers, Frosted Ovals, Sawtooth, Signed, 10 x 4 1/4 In. 295.00
Vase, Butterfly & Flowers, Signed, 13 3/4 In. 650.00

TYPEWRITER collectors divide typewriters into two main classifica-
tions: the index machine, which has a pointer and a dial for letter selection, and the keyboard machine, most commonly seen today. The first
successful typewriter was made by Sholes and Glidden in 1874.

American Index, Wooden Baseboard & Tin Cover, 1893 .... 550.00
Blickensdorf No. 5, Dhiatensor Keyboard, Wooden Case, 1894 .... 70.00
Burnett, Chicago, Ill., 1907 ....*Illus* 7275.00

Typewriter, Burnett, Chicago, Ill., 1907

Typewriter, Williams, No. 1, Round Keyboard, 1891

Corona, Folding No. 3, Black, New Ribbon Feed Design, 1914 .... 48.00
Franklin, No. 7, 3-Row Curved Keyboard, 1891 .... 920.00
IBM Electromatic, 1933 .... 34.00
Marx 200, Manual, Yellow Plastic Case 25.00
National, Square Index, Hinged Frame, Mahogany Case 488.00
Oliver No. 5, 1907 .... 82.00
Remington No. 10, Visible Writer, Wide Carriage B, 1908 .... 48.00
Remington Portable, Early Version, Cover, 1920 .... 18.00
Smith Corona, Folding, Black, 1926 .... 49.00
Smith Premier No. 5, Wide Carriage, 1895 .... 138.00
Underwood, Black, Red, White & Gold Lettering, 1942, 16 In. 145.00
Underwood Portable, Shifts Left & Right, Cover, 1919 .... 41.00
VariTyper No. 410, Industrial Version Of Multiplex, 1935 .... 206.00
Williams, No. 1, Round Keyboard, 1891 ....*Illus* 6325.00

TYPEWRITER TINS

TYPEWRITER TINS are now being collected. The lithographed tin containers have been used since the 1870s. Most popular with collectors are tins with pictorial graphics.

Addressograph, Duro Clear, Silver & Black, 2 1/2 In. 7.00
Allied Carbon & Ribbon, White Sea Gull A, Gray & Black, 2 1/2 In. 10.00
American Writing Co., Roman Warrior, Invincible, 2 1/2 In. 10.00
Bell System, Cardboard, Blue, Logo, 2 In. 7.00
Black Hawk, Miller-Bryant-Pierce, Aurora, Ill. 27.00
Burroughs Corp., Adding Machine, Green, 2 1/4 In. 8.00
Carter Ink Co., Carter's Ideal, Nylon, 2 1/2 In. 6.00
Carter Ink Co., Silver Craft, Black, 2 1/2 In. 10.00
Carter's Guardian, 3 Planes 28.00
Cleaner, Carter, Dark Blue, Cylindrical, 2 x 3 In. 5.00
Cleaner, Eberhard Faber, Star, Gold Letters, Rectangular, 2 1/2 x 1 5/8 In. . 5.00
Cleaner, Norta, Brown, Plastic Type, Rectangular, 1 3/4 x 3 In. 5.00
Cleaner, Remitco, Plastic Type, Rectangular, 2 1/2 x 1 5/8 In. 10.00
Cleaner, Sanford's, Ink Eraser Kit, Rectangular, 3 In. 5.00
Columbia Carbon Co., Rainbow, Square, 2 1/4 In. 7.00
Cricco, Consolidated Ribbon & Carbon Co., Chicago, Square 27.00
Crowfoot, How Company, Old Town, Maine, Crow Picture, Square 84.00
Ditto Incorporated, Green, Square, 2 1/4 In. 10.00
Duroc Beaver, M.B. Cook Co., Chicago, 2 Beavers 60.00
F.W. Woolworth Co., Herald Square, Square, 2 1/2 In. 10.00
IBM, Typists, Orange, 2 1/2 In. 7.00
Kee-Lox Mfg. Co., Woman, Gold, Square, 1 1/2 In. 10.00
Miller-Bryant-Pierce, Carnation, Red, White & Black, 2 1/2 In. 5.00
Old Town Secretarial, Unopened, Key, Contents 43.00
Oliver Typewriter Co., Revilo, Dark Green, 2 In. 7.00
One Monarch Ribbon, American Can Co., Square 130.00
Paramount, Frye Manufacturing Co., Des Moines, Iowa 27.00

Pigeon Brand, Corona Typewriter Co., Inc., Groton, N.Y. 34.00
Plenty Copy, Mittag & Volger, Inc., Parkridge, N.J. 27.00
Rembrandco., S. Gomers, 3-Cent Stamp, Square Shipping Box 60.00
Remington Rand, Dur-Edge Silk, Cardboard, 2 1/2 In. 5.00
Royal Typewriter Co., Vogue, Salmon Color, 2 1/4 In. 5.00
Smith-Corona, Secretarial, Logo, Silver, 2 1/2 In. 7.00
True-Mark 28.00

UHL pottery was made in Evansville, Indiana, in 1854. The pottery moved to Huntingburg, Indiana, in 1908. Stoneware and glazed pottery were made until the mid-1940s.

Ashtray, Dog & Fire Hydrant, Butterscotch 210.00
Batter Bowl, Blue, Impressed B-8 .... 140.00
Casserole, Green, Marked, 3 Pt. 35.00
Churn, Blue & White, Red Dasher, Bail Handle, Marked, Miniature, 18 Oz. 1025.00
Crock, Commemorative, Uhl Collectors Society, 1993, Miniature 30.00
Jug, Acorn, Miniature 70.00
Jug, Brown Over White, Acorn Worms Logo 275.00
Jug, Canteen, Believe It Or Not 275.00
Jug, Christmas, 1939 .... 280.00
Jug, Grandpa Meiers, 1/2 Gal. 300.00
Jug, Merry Christmas, 1941 .... 220.00
Jug, Stoneware, Indian Transfer Decoration, Round Ink Mark, 8 1/2 x 6 In. 66.00
Lamp, Liberty Bell, 18 In. 230.00
Mug, Barrel, Tan, Miniature 75.00
Pitcher, Barrel, 1/4 Gal. 40.00
Pitcher, Cover, Grape, Blue, Squat 100.00
Pitcher, Grape, Blue & White, Large 125.00
Pitcher, Grape, Brown, Bulbous, No. 181 .... 70.00
Plaque, Lincoln Head, Brown, 6 In. 500.00

UMBRELLA collectors like rain or shine. The first known umbrella was owned by King Louis XIII of France in 1637. The earliest umbrellas were sunshades, not designed to be used in the rain. The umbrella was embellished and redesigned many times. In 1852, the fluted steel rib style was developed, and it has remained the most useful style.

Handle, Dog's Head, Bakelite 60.00
Soft Leather Shaft, England, 1920 .... 200.00

UNION PORCELAIN WORKS was established at Greenpoint, New York, in 1848 by Charles Cartlidge. The company went through a series of ownership changes and finally closed in the early 1900s. The company made a fine quality white porcelain that was often decorated in clear, bright colors.

Oyster Plate, 5 Wells, 8 5/8 In. ....*Illus* 375.00

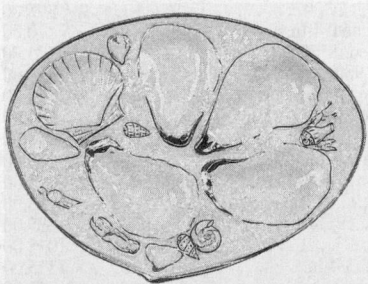

Union Porcelain Works, Oyster Plate,
5 Wells, 8 5/8 In.

**An unglazed rim on the bottom
of a plate usually indicates it
was made before 1850.**

Oyster Plate, Olive Green Seaweed, UPW, 8 1/2 In. 495.00
Oyster Plate, Shell & Sea Life, Polychrome, Gilt, Oval, N.Y., Pair 805.00
Pitcher, Parian Poets, Hexagonal, Gilt, Iron Red Inside, 1875, 9 In. 1955.00

UNIVERSITY OF NORTH DAKOTA, see North Dakota School of Mines category.

VAL ST. LAMBERT Cristalleries of Belgium was founded by Messieurs
Kemlin and Lelievre in 1825. The company is still in operation. All
types of table glassware and decorative glassware have been made.
Pieces are often decorated with cut designs.

Val St Lambert

Console, Leaf & Berry, Cameo, Marked, 15 In. 375.00
Paperweight, Quatrefoil, Garland, Cog Canes, Lace Filigree Loops, 3 1/2 In. 800.00
Paperweight, Umbrella, Compound Frit, Cog Canes, Twists, 3 11/16 In. 275.00
Plate, Relief Bust Of El Greco, Clear Opalescent, 1971, 8 In. 55.00
Rose Bowl, Spear & Oval Cuts, Green Panels, Signed, 20th Century, 7 In. 460.00
Vase, Applied Abstract Design, Satin Finish, Signed, 10 In. 795.00
Vase, Applied Cranberry Decoration, Satin Ground, Louis, LeLoup, 10 In. 795.00
Vase, Green Leaf Foliage, Etched, 10 In. 345.00
Vase, Green To Clear, Signed, 6 In. 65.00

VALLERYSTHAL Glassworks was founded in 1836 in Lorraine, France.
In 1854, the firm became Klenglin et Cie. It made table and decorative
glass, opaline, cameo, and art glass. A line of covered, pressed glass
animal dishes was made in the nineteenth century. The firm is still
working.

Vallerysthal

Bowl, Orange To Clear, Floral, Cameo, Marked, 9 In. 1000.00
Dish, Robin Dover, Pedestal, Marked 275.00
Sugar, Beehive, Milk Glass 85.00

VAN BRIGGLE pottery was made by Artus Van Briggle in Colorado
Springs, Colorado, after 1901. Van Briggle had been a decorator at
Rookwood Pottery of Cincinnati, Ohio. He died in 1904. His wares
usually had modeled relief decorations and a soft, dull glaze. The pottery is still working and still making some of the original designs.

Bowl, Blue, Green Matte Glaze, Incised Mark, 9 x 5 1/2 In. 45.00
Bowl, Dragonflies, Embossed, Blue & Burgundy Glaze, Incised, 1915, 3 x 6 In. 935.00
Bowl, Flower Shape, Blue Green, Matte, 3 1/4 In. 40.00
Bowl, Green, Brown Matte Glaze, Low Closed Form, 1916, 12 In. 525.00
Bowl, Lady Of The Lake, Turquoise, Kneeling Woman Looking In Pool, 15 In. ...258.00 to 310.00
Bowl, Leaf Design, Signed, 20th Century, 4 3/4 x 14 In. 300.00
Bowl, Multicolored, Matte Glaze, Signed, c.1916, 9 1/2 In. 330.00
Bowl, Pinecones & Needles, Blue, Green Glaze, 1912, 5 3/4 x 9 In. 2970.00
Bowl, Turquoise, Lily Pad Shape, Flower Frog, 3 x 16 x 9 In. 305.00
Compote, Maroon, 6 1/2 In. 100.00
Dish, Hopi, Maiden, Turquoise Matte Glaze, Incised Mark, 6 In. 140.00
Dish, Spider Design, Brown & Green Matte Glaze, 4 In. 305.00
Ewer, Maroon Glaze, 6 3/4 In. 33.00
Figurine, Cat, Blue, Purple Matte Glaze, 15 In. 395.00
Figurine, Deer, Reclining, Blue Green Matte Glaze, Signed, 4 In. 70.00
Figurine, Man & Woman, 18th Century Costume, Signed, 8 1/2 In., Pair 75.00
Jardiniere, Tulips, Blue Matte Glaze, Incised Mark, c.1909, 5 x 5 In. 1210.00
Jug, Fire Water, Indian Design, Blue To Lavender Matte Glaze, Stopper, 7 In. 2860.00
Lamp, Lady Of The Lake, Flower Frog, Rose, Colorado Springs, 21 In. 385.00
Mug, Eagle In Flight, Green Matte Glaze, Incised, 1906, 5 x 5 In. 440.00
Mug, Green Matte Glaze, Incised Mark, 1906, 4 1/4 x 5 1/4 In. 275.00
Paperweight, Horned Toad, Green Matte Glaze, Mustard Base, 1913, 6 x 4 In. 2090.00
Paperweight, Rabbit 185.00
Plate, Grapes & Leaves, Green, Maroon Matte Glaze, c.1912, 8 1/2 In. 825.00
Plate, Poppy, Blue & Tan Matte Glaze, 1902 .... 1045.00
Tile, Scenic, Oak Frame, Signed VBP Co., Impressed, 5 3/4 In. 1375.00
Vase, 2 Butterflies, Medium Blue Mottled Glaze, 2 3/4 In. 247.00
Vase, 3-Headed Indian, Mahogany & Blue Matte Glaze, 11 In. 440.00
Vase, 4 Leaves, Molded, Green Matte Glaze, Brown Ground, 1910, 5 In. 260.00
Vase, 4 Leaves, Molded, Yellow, Green Matte Glaze, 1902, 8 In. 2415.00

Vase, Anemone, Ming, Turquoise, 5 In. 65.00
Vase, Arrowroot, Leaves, Blossoms, Embossed, Turquoise Glaze, 1906, 9 x 9 In. 6600.00
Vase, Arrowroot, Leaves, Green Matte Glaze, 1905, 9 x 4 1/2 In. 2970.00
Vase, Blue Green Matte, Tan, Handles, Amphora, Marked, 1920, 12 1/4 x 6 In. 1295.00
Vase, Blue Matte Glaze, Bulbous, Incised Mark, 1905, 6 x 4 1/2 In. 465.00
Vase, Blue, Purple, Green Marbleized Crystalline Glaze, 1914, 9 1/2 x 4 In. 1210.00
Vase, Brown, Green Matte Glaze, 1905, 5 1/2 x 2 3/4 In. 715.00
Vase, Brown, Green Matte Glaze, Pre-1920, 11 x 5 In. 605.00
Vase, Bud, Dragonflies, Embossed, Burgundy Matte Glaze, 1915, 7 In. 330.00
Vase, Bud, Leaves, Embossed, Green Matte Glaze, Flared Rim, 6 1/2 In. 195.00
Vase, Butterflies, Blue Matte Glaze, Squat, 3 x 3 1/2 In. 275.00
Vase, Charcoal Matte Glaze, Tapered, Incised Mark, 1902, 6 1/2 x 4 3/4 In. 2640.00
Vase, Cherub Holding Cornucopia, Blue Green Matte Glaze, Incised MC, 9 In. 165.00
Vase, Child Holding Design Carved Pole, Pale Blue, 9 In., Pair 110.00
Vase, Cornflowers, Blue, Gray, Green Glaze, Small Handles, 1903, 9 1/2 x 7 In. 4400.00
Vase, Cornflowers, Embossed, Green Matte Glaze, 1911, 9 1/2 x 7 1/2 In. 2530.00
Vase, Cornflowers, Embossed, Persian Rose Glaze, 1911, 9 1/2 x 7 1/2 In. 1320.00
Vase, Cornflowers, Light Brown Glaze, 1906, 8 1/2 x 4 1/2 In. 2860.00
Vase, Cornflowers, Rose Glaze, Beige Clay, 11 1/4 In. 2640.00
Vase, Crocuses, Blue To Green, Crazing, 5 In. 70.00
Vase, Crocuses, Embossed, Green Matte Glaze, Incised, 2 1/2 In. 250.00
Vase, Crocuses, Embossed, Persian Rose Matte Glaze, 1920, 4 1/2 In. 165.00
Vase, Daffodils, Blue & Turquoise Matte Glaze, Mottled, 9 1/2 x 4 1/2 In. 330.00
Vase, Daffodils, Embossed, Persian Rose Glaze, 1915, 10 1/2 x 4 1/4 In. 770.00
Vase, Daisies, Around Rim, Brown Matte Glaze, Tapered, 1915, 7 x 4 In. 605.00
Vase, Daisies, Embossed, Burgundy & Blue Matte Glaze, Bulbous, 1930, 9 In. 550.00
Vase, Daisies, Mustard Glaze, Cylindrical, 1907-1911, 6 3/4 x 3 In. 1760.00
Vase, Dandelion, Stylized, Brown Glaze, Black Speckles, 1915, 6 In. 1540.00
Vase, Dark Green Matte Glaze, 14 x 9 1/2 In. 1210.00
Vase, Deep Rose, Green Matte Glaze, 1903, 10 x 9 In. 18700.00
Vase, Dragonflies, Green, Blue Matte Glaze, Dark Brown Body, 1912, 6 1/2 In. 1430.00
Vase, Echinacea, Embossed, Flowers, Blue & Mahogany Matte Glaze, 11 In. 305.00
Vase, Floral, Molded, Turquoise, 1921, 5 In. 135.00
Vase, Flower Design, Molded, 2-Tone Blue Matte Glaze, 9 1/2 x 9 1/2 In. 990.00
Vase, Flowers & Leaves, Molded, Blue, Green Glaze, c.1905, 4 3/4 In. 580.00
Vase, Flowers, Dark Blue Matte Glaze, Bulbous, 1903, 3 x 3 1/2 In. 715.00
Vase, Flowers, Embossed, Light Green Matte Glaze, 1903, 6 1/2 x 4 In. 1100.00
Vase, Flowers, Embossed, Mulberry, Signed, 8 3/8 In. 275.00
Vase, Flowers, Molded, Mulberry Matte, Squatty, Handles, Marked, 1920, 9 1/2 In. 995.00
Vase, Flowers, Molded, Multitoned Blue Matte Glaze, 1920, 7 1/2 In. 550.00
Vase, Flowers, Stylized, Black Glaze, 1907, 9 x 3 3/4 In. 1760.00
Vase, Flowers, Stylized, Green Matte Glaze, Incised Mark, 9 1/2 x 3 3/4 In. 1320.00
Vase, Flowers, Turquoise, 5 In. 55.00
Vase, Flowers, Yellow, Leaves, Green Matte Glaze, Embossed, 10 x 4 In. 470.00
Vase, Fronds, Stylized, Embossed, Matte Glaze, Oval, Incised, c.1915, 13 In. 1540.00
Vase, Gooseberries, Green Matte Glaze, Bulbous, Incised, 1907, 8 x 5 In. 1650.00
Vase, Grass Blades, Blue Matte Glaze, Clay Body, Footed Rim, 13 In. 550.00
Vase, Gray, Lavender Matte Glaze, 1905, 4 1/2 x 5 1/4 In. 1210.00
Vase, Gray, Pink Glaze, Vertical Ribs, 1912, 7 x 3 3/4 In. 1320.00
Vase, Green & Brown Matte Glaze, 2 Handles, Incised, 1904, 11 x 4 In. 2420.00
Vase, Green & Rose Matte Glaze, Bulbous, 1916, 9 1/2 x 4 1/2 In. 385.00
Vase, Green Matte Glaze, 1903, 11 x 3 3/4 In. 2530.00
Vase, Green Matte Glaze, 1916, 8 In. 605.00
Vase, Green Matte Glaze, c.1905, 7 x 3 1/4 In. 2640.00
Vase, Green Matte Glaze, Embossed Vertical Lines, 1906, 5 x 3 3/4 In. 853.00
Vase, Green, Burgundy Matte Glaze, 2 Handles, 1904, 10 1/2 x 4 1/4 In. 2420.00
Vase, Green, Yellow Matte Glaze, 1912, 7 1/2 In. 710.00
Vase, Irises, Blue Gray Glaze, Red Clay, c.1905, 13 In. 3850.00
Vase, Irises, Red, Chartreuse Glaze, Beige Clay, 1903, 14 x 5 In. 17600.00
Vase, Irises, Stylized, Turquoise Glaze, Bulbous, 1911, 10 In. 1100.00
Vase, Jonquils, Blue & Maroon Matte Glaze, Tapered, 5 1/2 In. 195.00
Vase, Jonquils, Trumpet Shape, Pink Matte Glaze, Embossed, 1906, 9 x 4 In. 2310.00
Vase, Lady Of The Lily, Light Green Glaze, Incised Mark, 1902, 11 x 9 1/2 In. 4130.00

Vase, Leaf, Blue & Maroon Matte Glaze, Signed, 5 In. 265.00
Vase, Leaves & Buds, Spade Shaped, Brown, Green Glaze, 1916, 7 1/4 x 3 3/4 In. 880.00
Vase, Leaves, Embossed, Green & Brown Glaze, Incised, c.1907, 4 x 6 In. 1650.00
Vase, Leaves, Embossed, Green, Brown Matte Glaze, 1918, 8 In. 297.00
Vase, Leaves, Spade Shape, Green Glaze, Beige Clay, c.1905, 10 In. 3575.00
Vase, Leaves, Spade Shape, Purple, Blue, Gray Matte Glaze, 1904, 4 x 3 In. 1760.00
Vase, Leaves, Stylized, Brown Matte Glaze, Incised, 1905, 9 3/4 x 5 In. 3080.00
Vase, Leaves, Stylized, Brown Matte Glaze, Squat, c.1906, 3 1/2 x 4 1/4 In. 1210.00
Vase, Leaves, Stylized, Brown, Green Matte Glaze, Cylindrical, c.1925, 7 In. 264.00
Vase, Leaves, Stylized, Copper Clad, Original Dark Patina, 1911, 2 x 3 In. 1760.00
Vase, Leaves, Stylized, Copper Clad, Original Dark Patina, 1911, 4 x 4 3/4 In. 3850.00
Vase, Leaves, Stylized, Embossed, Blue, Green Matte Glaze, 2 x 2 1/2 In. 550.00
Vase, Leaves, Stylized, Green Matte Crystalline Glaze, 1911, 6 1/2 x 3 3/4 In. 1760.00
Vase, Leaves, Stylized, Green Matte Glaze, Red Clay, 1905, 8 In. 3300.00
Vase, Leaves, Stylized, Persian Rose, 2 Handles, Impressed Logo, c.1925, 8 1/2 In. 168.00
Vase, Light Green, Yellow Matte Glaze, 2 Handles, 1903, 15 1/2 In. 15400.00
Vase, Lorelei, Maiden Wrapped Around Rim, Blue, Green Matte Glaze, 10 In. ....198.00 to 360.00
Vase, Lorelei, Medium Blue Glaze, 1919, 9 1/2 x 4 In. 2530.00
Vase, Ming Turquoise Glaze, 3 3/4 In. 50.00
Vase, Mistletoe & Berries, Embossed, Green, Mauve Matte Glaze, 3 In. 2750.00
Vase, Mistletoe, Dark Green Glaze, Brown Clay, 4 x 4 In. 770.00
Vase, Mistletoe, Green, Pink Matte Glaze, Closed-In Rim, 1906, 4 1/2 x 11 In. 2640.00
Vase, Morning Glories, Blue & Green Glaze, 1905, 6 1/2 x 7 1/2 In. 1540.00
Vase, Morning Glory, Embossed, Light Green, Yellow Matte Glaze, 12 x 4 In. 2200.00
Vase, Painted Floral, Embossed, Suspended Matte Glaze, Signed, c.1903, 9 In. 4975.00
Vase, Papyrus, Embossed, Green, Rose Matte Glaze, 1916, 6 1/2 x 4 1/2 In. 2090.00
Vase, Papyrus, Stylized, Turquoise Glaze, Bottle Shape, 7 In. 1045.00
Vase, Peacock Feathers, Stylized, Burgundy Ground, Incised, 1905, 11 3/4 In. 1980.00
Vase, Pinecones, Branches, Embossed, Persian Rose Glaze, c.1917, 4 x 10 In. 1045.00
Vase, Poppies, Blue, Deep Red Matte Ground, 1930, 8 1/2 In. 330.00
Vase, Poppy Pods, Embossed, Green, Black Matte Glaze, 1902, 4 1/4 x 3 In. 4675.00
Vase, Poppy Pods, Embossed, Purple Matte Glaze, 1903, 9 x 6 In. 2860.00
Vase, Poppy Pods, Turquoise Matte Glaze, Red Clay, 1906, 4 1/4 x 4 1/2 In. 1540.00
Vase, Poppy, Pods, Light Blue Glaze, Brown Clay, 1905, 3 x 6 In. 935.00
Vase, Purple Matte Glaze, Cylindrical, 1905, 6 In. 770.00
Vase, Shamrocks, Embossed, Mulberry Glaze, Signed, 5 7/8 In. 2750.00
Vase, Trefoils, Embossed, Curdled Brown Glaze, 1911, 3 x 3 In. 550.00
Vase, Trillium, Embossed, Green Matte Glaze, Incised, 1905, 7 1/2 x 3 3/4 In. 2090.00
Vase, Turquoise & Blue Matte Glaze, Squat, Incised Mark, 1906, 5 In. 550.00
Vase, Turquoise Matte Glaze, 1906, 4 x 6 In. 495.00
Vase, Turquoise Matte Glaze, Squat, 1905, 3 1/4 x 6 In. 275.00
Vase, Turquoise, Green Matte Glaze, Marked, 1905, 3 1/2 x 5 In. 522.00
Vase, Wreath Leaves, Embossed, Green & Mauve Matte Glaze, 1906, 3 x 3 1/4 In. 770.00
Vase, Yucca Plants, Light Green Matte Glaze, 1906, 12 3/4 x 5 1/2 In. 2200.00

VASA MURRHINA is the name of a glassware made by the Vasa Murrhina Art Glass Company of Sandwich, Massachusetts, about 1884.
The glassware was transparent and was embedded with small pieces of
colored glass and metallic flakes. The mica flakes were coated with silver, gold, copper, or nickel. Some of the pieces were cased. The same
type of glass was made in England. Collectors often confuse Vasa
Murrhina glass with aventurine, spatter, or spangle glass. There is
uncertainty about what actually was made by the Vasa Murrhina factory. Related pieces may be listed under Spangle Glass.

   Basket, Jack-In-The-Pulpit, Mica Flakes, Ruffled Edge, Clear Handle, 11 1/2 In. 295.00
   Vase, Blue, Silver Mica Branch Design, Ormolu Top & Foot, 7 1/4 In., Pair 265.00

VASELINE GLASS is a greenish-yellow glassware resembling petroleum
jelly. Some vaseline glass is still being made in old and new styles.
Pressed glass of the 1870s was often made of vaseline-colored glass.
Additional pieces of vaseline glass may also be listed under Pressed
Glass in this book.

   Tumble-Up Set, Crackle 88.00

Vase, Light Blue Stem, Flared, Applied Snake Banding, 10 1/2 In. 165.00
Vase, Opalescent Flared Opening, Circular Foot, 12 1/2 In. 190.00
Vase, Reeded Body, Fluted, Ruffled Edge, 11 In. 165.00
Vase, Spiral Banding, Cranberry & White Flared Top, Cylindrical, 7 In. 165.00
Vase, Tapered Body, Blue Opalescent Edge, Crimped Spiral Band, 10 1/2 In. 210.00

VENETIAN GLASS, see Glass-Venetian category.

VERLYS glass was made in France after 1931. It was made in the United
States from 1935 to 1951. The glass is either blown or molded. The
American glass is signed with a diamond-point-scratched name, but
the French pieces are marked with a molded signature. The designs
resemble those used by Lalique.

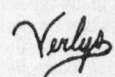

Vase, Alpine Thistle, Opalescent, Signed, 9 In. 725.00
Vase, Laurel, Opalescent, Incised Mark, 10 1/2 In. 445.00
Vase, Molded & Frosted Mermaids & Dolphins, Label, 10 1/4 In. 330.00
Vase, Thistle, Topaz, Molded Mark, 9 7/8 In. 220.00

VERNON KILNS was the name used after 1958 by Vernon Potteries, Ltd.
The company, which started in 1931 in Vernon, California, made dinnerware and figurines until it went out of business in 1958. The molds
were bought by Metlox and they continued to make some patterns.
Collectors search for the brightly colored dinnerware and the pieces
designed by Rockwell Kent, Walt Disney, and Don Blanding. For more
information, see *Kovels' Depression Glass & Dinnerware Price List.*

Hawaiian Coral, Platter, Large 35.00
Hawaiian Flowers, Chop Plate, Blue, 12 In. 165.00
Hawaiian Flowers, Salt & Pepper, Maroon, Pair 65.00
Lake Tahoe, Plate, 10 In. 15.00
Moby Dick, Plate, Rodney Kent 125.00
Moby Dick, Tumbler, Brown 195.00
Organdie, Bowl, 5 5/8 In. 5.00
Organdie, Casserole, Cover 25.00
Organdie, Plate, 9 3/4 In. 10.00
Organdie, Salt & Pepper 15.00
Organdie, Sugar & Creamer, Cover 20.00
Our America, Plate, Skyscraper & Drawbridge, Maroon, Ivory Ground, 9 In. 55.00
Tam O'Shanter, Plate, 9 1/2 In. 12.00
Tickled Pink, Pitcher, Tall 45.00

VERRE DE SOIE glass was first made by Frederick Carder at the
Steuben Glass Works from about 1905 to 1930. It is an iridescent glass
of soft white or very, very pale green. The name means *glass of silk,*
and it does resemble silk. Other factories have made verre de soie, and
some of the English examples were made of different colors. Verre de
soie is an art glass and is not related to the iridescent, pressed, white
carnival glass mistakenly called by its name. Related pieces may be
found in the Steuben category.

Perfume Bottle, Melon Ribs, Flame Stopper, Steuben, 7 In. 650.00
Tumbler, Floral Garland & Bow, Etched By Hawkes, 4 3/4 In. 138.00

VIENNA, see Beehive category.

VIENNA ART plates are round metal serving trays produced at the turn
of the century. The designs, copied from Royal Vienna porcelain
plates, usually featured a portrait of a woman encircled by a wide,
ornate border. Many were used as advertising or promotional items and
were produced in Coshocton, Ohio, by J.F. Meeks Tuscarora Advertising Co. and H.D. Beach's Standard Advertising Co.

Charger, Cupid & Venus In Landscape Setting, 11 3/4 In., Pair 690.00
Plate, Girl With Red Tam, 1910, 8 3/4 In. 220.00
Plate, Girl With White Tam, 1910, 7 1/2 In. 176.00
Plate, Joslin Dry Goods, Gypsy Type Woman, 10 In. 90.00

Plate, Malt Nutrine, Woman, Green Border, 1900s, 10 In. 90.00
Plate, Portrait Of Aida, Trailing Leaves, Cobalt Blue Rim, Gilt, 9 1/2 In. 345.00
Plate, Rising Sun Bottled Beer, Shamokin Brewing Co., Pa., 1905, 10 In. 75.00
Tray, Bust Of Maid, Plunging Neckline, 10 In. 90.00
Tray, Hotel Majestic, Lithograph Maiden, Gilt Border, 10 In. 150.00
Tray, Royal Saxony, Maid In White Gown, 10 In. 60.00

VILLEROY & BOCH Pottery of Mettlach was founded in 1836. The firm made many types of wares, including the famous Mettlach steins. Collectors can be confused because although Villeroy & Boch made most of its pieces in the city of Mettlach, Germany, they also had factories in other locations. The dating code impressed on the bottom of most pieces makes it possible to determine the age of the piece. Additional items, including steins and earthenware pieces marked with the famous castle mark or the word *Mettlach,* may be found in the Mettlach category.

Box, Dresser, Le Moineau Delachine Bird 20.00
Candlestick, Signed, 8 In., Pair 110.00
Mug, Hires Root Beer, 4 2/3 In. 105.00
Pitcher, Baseball Batter & Catcher, Enameled, 11 In. 2420.00
Pitcher, Baseball, Dresden, 11 In. 2420.00
Pitcher, Beer, Cream Body, Classical Figures, Swags On Coral Panels, 12 In. .. 209.00
Pitcher & Bowl, Green Transfer Hunting Scene, 11 1/2 x 15 In. 220.00
Plate, Baseball Catcher, Enameled, 8 1/2 In. 715.00
Plate, Snow White, Mettlach Society, 1st Issue, 1980 .... 85.00
Tray, Barmaid Serving In Elaborate Floral Design, Frame, 19 1/2 x 12 In. .. 288.00
Vase, Oval, Salt Glaze, Taupe Ground, Relief Figures, c.1860, 8 1/2 In. 125.00

VOLKMAR pottery was made by Charles Volkmar of New York from 1879 to about 1911. He was associated with several firms, including the Volkmar Ceramic Company, Volkmar and Cory, and Charles Volkmar and Son. Volkmar had been a painter, and his designs often look like oil paintings drawn on pottery.

Bowl, Green Matte Glaze, 5 3/4 In. 55.00
Vase, Black Gunmetal Glaze, 8 Sides, Signed, 4 In. 330.00
Vase, Dark Gray, Black Matte Glaze, 8 Sides, 4 In. 22.00
Vase, Incised Panels, Rust & Green Glaze, Signed, 8 In. 198.00
Vase, Incised Vertical Leaves, Allover Green Glaze, 9 1/2 In. 1760.00
Vase, Mottled & Frothy Purple Glaze, Bulbous, Incised, 1929, 6 1/2 x 4 In. ... 440.00
Vase, Pillow, Barbotine, Horses Pulling Carts, Sepia Tones, 12 1/4 x 7 In., Pair 5500.00

VOLKSTEDT was a soft-paste porcelain factory started in 1760 by Georg Heinrich Macheleid at Volkstedt, Thuringia. Volkstedt-Rudolstadt was a porcelain factory started at Volkstedt-Rudolstadt by Beyer and Bock in 1890. Most pieces seen in shops today are from the later factory.

Candelabrum, 4-Light, Flower Encrusted Tree, Winged Putti, 16 1/2 In., Pair 470.00
Group, 2 Cherubs Near Tree, 5 1/4 In. 55.00

WADE pottery is made by the Wade Group of Potteries started in 1810 near Burslem, England. Several potteries merged to become George Wade & Son, Ltd. early in the twentieth century, and other potteries have been added through the years. The best-known Wade pieces are the small figurines given away with Red Rose Tea and other promotional items. The Disney figures are listed in this book in the Disneyana category.

Figurine, Horse 200.00
Figurine, Irish Setter 250.00
Figurine, Jack Horner, Large 35.00
Figurine, King Cole, Large 45.00
Figurine, Little Miss Muffet, Large 40.00
Figurine, My Fair Ladies, Sarah, Large, 1992 .... 30.00
Figurine, Owl 45.00

Figurine, Queen Of Hearts, Large 65.00
Figurine, Wee Willie Winkie, Large 25.00
Pitcher, Water 20.00
Teapot, Clown 30.00

WAHPETON POTTERY, see Rosemeade category.

WALLACE NUTTING photographs are listed under Print, Nutting. His reproduction furniture is listed under Furniture.

WALRATH was a potter who worked in New York City; Rochester, New York; and at the Newcomb Pottery in New Orleans, Louisiana. Frederick Walrath died in 1920. Pieces listed here are from his Rochester period.

Walrath
Pottery

Bowl, Allover Gray Matte Glaze, Signed, 8 In. 120.00
Bowl, Flower Frog, Nude Maiden, Signed 400.00
Bowl, Green Matte Glaze, 2 x 8 In. 44.00
Bowl, Lavender Matte Glaze, 8 1/2 In. 165.00
Figurine, Kneeling Nude, Picking Rose, Green Glaze, Incised, 4 x 6 In. 330.00
Scarab, Blue Matte Glaze, 3 1/2 In. 187.00
Tile, Stylized Fish, Green, Blue Waves, 6 In. 385.00
Tile, Stylized Floral Design, Yellow & Brown, Blue Ground, 4 1/2 In. 305.00
Trivet, Seagulls, Ocean Scene, Violet Crystalline Glaze, Round, 6 In. 195.00
Vase, Cypress Trees, Ocher & Red, Blue Ground, Incised, 5 1/4 x 3 3/4 In. 5500.00
Vase, Frothy Ivory Vellum Over Celadon, Blue, Red, 3 3/4 x 3 1/4 In. 605.00
Vase, Landscape, Stylized Trees, Clouds, Moon, Dark Green, Orange, Blue, 7 x 4 In. 14300.00
Vase, Mottled Apple Green Matte Glaze, Bulbous, Incised Mark, 5 In. 440.00
Vase, Stylized Flowers, Gray Green Ground, Incised, 6 1/4 x 4 In. 4400.00

WALT DISNEY, see Disneyana category.

WALTER, see A. Walter category.

WARWICK china was made in Wheeling, West Virginia, in a pottery working from 1887 to 1951. Many pieces were made with hand painted or decal decorations. The most familiar Warwick has a shaded brown background. The name *Warwick* is part of the mark and sometimes the mysterious word *IOGA* is also included.

Vase, Bronze Model, 19th Century, England, 3 1/4 x 5 In. 258.00
Vase, Bronze Model, 19th Century, Italy, 4 1/2 x 7 In. 977.00
Vase, Bronze, Gilt, Continental, 8 x 13 In. 3220.00
Vase, Earthenware, Cylindrical, Flared Base, Woman, 2 Handles, c.1910, 10 1/2 In. 40.00
Vase, Masks Of Historical Figures, Entwined Vine Handles, Bronze, 9 1/2 x 14 In. 1150.00
Vase, Polychrome Transfer Of Girl, Twig Handles, IOGA, 10 1/2 In. 137.00

WATCH pockets held the pocket watch that was important in Victorian times because it was not until World War I that the wristwatch was used. All types of watches are collected: silver, gold, or plated. Watches are arranged by company name or by style. Pocket watches are listed here; wristwatches are a separate category.

Advertising, Ready Kilowatt, Compliments Of Philadelphia Power & Light 495.00
American Watch Co., Demihunter, Gold, Porcelain Dial, Roman Numerals, 1884 .... 750.00
Benrus, Gold Case, Gold Arabic Quarter Numerals, Monogram, Signed, c.1954 .... 402.00
Blinking Eye, Nickel, Celluloid Dial, Movable Eyes, Switzerland, 38 mm. 165.00
Bucherer, 25 Jewel, Gold Filled, Automatic 185.00
Case, Open Face, Roman Numerals, 18K Yellow Gold Dial, England 345.00
Case, Open Face, White Porcelain Dial, Arabic Numerals, Scrolled Hands, 14K Gold 632.00
Chain & Fob, 9 Gilded Buttons 33.00
Chatelaine, Waist Plaque, 3 Banded Agates, Gold Filled 495.00
Cherished Teddies, Musical, Package 25.00
Chinese, Mock Pendulum, Peacocks & Landscape, Silver, Shanghai, c.1875 .... 920.00
Columbia, White Gold Hunting Case, Attached Medallion Watch Fob 125.00
Dueber-Hampden, Open Face, Silverine, Safety Pinion, Enamel Dial, Size 18 .... 65.00
Elgin, 15 Jewel, Enameled Dial & Lines, 14K Gold 95.00

Elgin, 15 Jewel, Metal Dial Face, Havila Case, 2 In. 50.00
Elgin, Gold Tone Case, 7 Jewel, Seconds Dial, Pastoral Scene Reverse, 1920s, 1 3/4 In. ... 100.00
Elgin, Hunting Case, 15 Jewel, Yellow Gold Floral, Late 19th Century 200.00
Elgin, Hunting Case, Chased Rim, Enameled Dial, 14K Gold 145.00
Elgin, Hunting Case, Gold Filled, Engraved, Chain & Slide Set, Seed Pearls, c.1895 ..... 230.00
Elgin, Hunting Case, No. 1355971, Roman Numerals, Seconds Dial, 14K Gold Engraved . 290.00
Elgin, Open Face, Metal Figural, Floral Stand, Arabic Numerals, Pocket, 6 3/4 In. 403.00
Elgin, Presentation Hunter's Case, 17 Jewel, Stem Set, 14K Gold, 1899 .... 385.00
Elgin, Steel Hands, Seconds Dial, Metal, Roman Numerals, 14K Gold 80.00
Elgin, Yellow Gold Filled, Dust Cover, 1 3/4 In. 60.00
F. Kobel, Hunting Case, 21 Jewel, Monogram, Leather Case, 18K Gold, Switzerland 660.00
F. Putley, No. 2411, Open Face Pair Case, Fusee Movement, Roman Numerals, c.1810 ... 690.00
Fulton-Dueber, Open Face, Silverine, Safety Pinion, Enamel Dial, Size 18 .... 110.00
Gruen, Open Face, 19 Jewel, No. 150099, Seconds Dial, Diamonds, Enamel, Platinum ... 690.00
Hamilton, 23 Jewel, Presentation, Gold Tone Dial, 18K Gold 310.00
Hamilton, Lever Set, Porcelain Railroad Dial, 20 Year 90.00
Hamilton, Navigation, AN-5740-1, White Metal, Black Luminous Dial, 1958, 2 In. 210.00
Hamilton, Open Face, 17 Jewel, Gold Filled, Gold Tone Numerals, Gold Tone Dial 90.00
Hamilton, Open Face, 23 Jewel, Gold, Pearlized Dial, Arabic Numerals 365.00
Hamilton, Screw Bezel, Embossed Wreath Around Dial, Recessed Seconds Dial 80.00
Hampden, Lafayette, Open Face, Silveroid, Key Wind, Enamel Dial 90.00
Hampden, Open Face, Gold Filled, Engraved Floral, Enamel Dial, Dial Lines 45.00
Hampden, Woman's, Round Case, Blue Steel Handles, Seconds Dial, 14K Yellow Gold .. 155.00
Howard, Swing-Out Case, Porcelain Dial, Recessed Seconds Dial 105.00
Hunting Case, Philadelphia Watch Case, Engraved Dog, Enameled Dial 175.00
Illinois, Gold Filled Hunting Case, Scroll, Floral & Avian Design, 17 Jewel 95.00
Jasper Stone, Hunting Case, Fusee, Key Wind, Silver, Enameled Dial, 1855-1856 ...... 200.00
Jules Jurgensen, Hunting Case, 21 Jewel, Bow Setting, 18K Gold, Pat. 1867 .... 2000.00
Kelbert, Manual Minute Recorder, Chronograph 120.00
Keystone, Hunting Case, Gold Filled, Enameled Dial, Size 16 .... 145.00
Leonidas, 17 Jewel, Chronograph, Minute Recorder 180.00
Longines, Desk, Up & Down Indicator, 8-Day Calendar, c.1900, 5 x 6 In. 2070.00
Longines, Pendant, Gold Tone Dial, Enamel, Diamonds, Sapphire, Edwardian, 14K Gold . 865.00
Longines, Woman's, Peach Guilloche Enamel, Diamond Accents, Gold, Edwardian 460.00
Marc Chantre, Minute Repeater, Perpetual Calendar, Chronograph, 18K Gold, 1884 .... 9200.00
Movado, 17 Jewel, Date, Automatic 295.00
Movado, Lapel, Platinum, Onyx & Diamond, c.1920 .... 3450.00
Open Face, 17 Jewel, Gold Filled, Frank & Davis, Monogram 105.00
Open Face, Admiral, 7 Jewel, Gold Tone Case, Seconds Dial, Switzerland, 1926, 2 In. ... 53.00
Open Face, Burlington Special, Gold Filled, Enamel Dial, 19 Jewel 120.00
Open Face, Gold Porcelain Dial, Black Arabic Numerals, 18K Yellow Gold 5175.00
Open Face, White Porcelain Dial, Arabic Numerals, Second Dial, Blue Steel Hands 805.00
Open Face, White Porcelain Dial, Black Roman Numerals, 14K Yellow Gold 258.00
Patek Philippe, Case, Open Face, Black Arabic Numerals, 18K Yellow Gold 1265.00
Patek Philippe, Lapel, Bicycle Wheel & Wing Pin, Gold, Enamel, Diamonds, c.1900 .... 4485.00
Pavel Buhre, Hunting Case, Gold, Applied Imperial Eagle, 1900, 1 7/8 In. 2760.00
Pavel Buhre, Hunting Case, Gold, Niello, Imperial Eagle, 1900, 1 7/8 In. 2875.00
Pendant, Rose Cut Diamonds & Rubies, Diamonds & Rubies On Links, c.1900 .... 4025.00
Pendant, Silvertone Dial, Guilloche Enamel, Paperclip Links, Edwardian, 22 1/2 In. 920.00
Poll-Parrot Shoes, Embossed, 3 In. 110.00
Racine Perrot, Hunting Case, Gold, Inlaid Cobalt Blue Enamel, Gold Foliate Design 690.00
Rockford, Dueber Coin Silver, Enamel Dial, Key Or Stem Wind, Size 16 .... 180.00
Seth Thomas, Man's, White Porcelain Face, Nickel Case, 1905 .... 139.00
Silver Bronze Case, Open Face, Hebrew Characters & Coat Of Arms, Pocket, 2 1/2 In. ... 1955.00
Standard, Open Face, 15 Jewel, Silveroid, Inlaid Copper Locomotive 45.00
Tiffany, Open Face, White Porcelain Dial & Black Arabic Numerals, 18K Yellow Gold ... 3450.00
Tiffany, Pendant, Diamonds In Flower Design, Sapphires, Gold, Edwardian 8050.00
Tiffany, Pendant, Diamonds, Sapphires, Platinum, Seed Pearls, Chain, 19 In. 5465.00
Vacheron & Constantin, Gold Case, 17 Jewel, Silvered Dialbrushed Gold Bezel 575.00
Van Buren, Open Face, 6 Jewel, Nickel Case, Seconds Dial, Switzerland, 1 3/4 In. 70.00
Vincenz Boschofsky, Silver Fusee, Blue Enameled Hour Ring, Arabic Numerals 385.00
W.E. Huguenin, Hunting Case, Repeating, Enameled Dial, Second Hand, 14K Gold 2750.00
Waltham, 7 Jewel, Polished Nickel, White Face, Blue Hands, Numerals, 1902 .... 95.00

Waltham, Diver's, U.S. Navy, 8-Day Mechanism, 3 In. 230.00
Waltham, Engraved Gold Hunting Case, Porcelain Dial, Seconds Dial, Gold Hands 690.00
Waltham, Gunmetal Color Case, Porcelain Face, Woman's, Seconds Dial, 1 1/4 In. 70.00
Waltham, Hunting Case, 3 Colors, Monogram Reverse, Woman's Portrait, 18K Gold 685.00
Waltham, Hunting Case, Coin Silver, Engraved Border & Medallion, Key Wind 165.00
Waltham, Hunting Case, Gold, White Porcelain Dial, Black Roman Numerals, 14 In. 316.00
Waltham, Hunting Case, Stork Medallion Cover, Enameled Dial, 14K Gold 275.00
Waltham, Mahogany Case, 15 Jewel, Chronometer, 8-Day, Up & Down Indicator 910.00
Waltham, Maximus, 21 Jewel, Demihunting Case, Gold, Roman Numerals, 1899 .... 1150.00
Waltham, Overall Scroll Hunting Case, 15 Jewel, Monogram, 14K Gold, 1920s 175.00
Waltham, R.W. Co., White Enamel Face, Roman Numerals, Seconds Face, 1 7/8 In. 57.00
Waltham, Woman's, Hunting Case, Gold, White Porcelain Dial, Black Arabic Numerals .. 287.00
Westclox, Pocket Ben, Nickel Case, Black Luminescent Face, Box, 2 In. 29.00
Westclox, Pocket Ben, Polished Case, Silver Toned Face, Clip Style Fob, 2 In. 30.00
Windmill, Automated, Chinese Calligraphy, Chain, 19th Century 740.00
Woman's, Gold Hunting Case, Porcelain Dial, Seconds Dial, Roman Numerals, Chain ... 750.00
Woman's, White Porcelain Dial, Black Roman Numerals, 18K Yellow Gold, 1898 ...... 345.00

WATCH FOBS were worn on watch chains. They were popular during Victorian times and after. Many styles, especially advertising designs, are still made today.

2nd Annual Ohio & Michigan Land Products Farm Expo, 1915, 1 7/8 In. 25.00
Abraham Fur Co., St. Louis, U.S.A., Fox, Cast Bronze, Shield Shape, c.1900, 2 In. 30.00
Allis-Chalmers 38.00
American Occupation Vera Cruz, Mexico, Shoreline Scene, 1914, 1 1/2 In. 18.00
Americana Range & Foundry, 1 3/4 x 1 1/2 In. 66.00
Anheuser-Busch, Metal, Enameled, 1910s 100.00
Bulldog, Cabochon Red Eyes, Suspended From Swivel Hook, Sterling Silver 747.00
California Midwinter Fair, Name & Eagle On Medal, Columbus Landing, 5 1/2 In. 25.00
Caterpillar, Leather Strap, 1 1/2 x 5 In. ....*Illus* 25.00
Cleveland Bros. Equipment Co., Caterpillar, Tractor, White Metal, 1 3/4 In. 21.00
Columbus, Ohio Badge Co., Metal, Leather Band, Hunter Trader Trapper, 2 x 1 5/8 In. 107.00
DeLaval, Cloisonne & Enamel Inlay, Polished Metal, 2 1/4 In. 155.00
Enameled Kingfisher, Perching, Watered Silk Band, Victorian 35.00
Ford Mar Trac Inc., Industrial Farm Equipment, Enameled, Hudson, Oh., 1 3/4 In. 10.00
George N. Steere & Co., Dragon, Leaves, Painted Cabochons, Gold Plated, 3 In. 345.00
Green River Whiskey, Man & Horse In Horseshoe, Nickel, 1 5/8 In. 22.00
Green River Whiskey, She Was Bred In Old Kentucky, White, Metal, 1 1/2 In. 39.00
Heinz 57, Plated Brass, Image Of Factory On Back, 1 3/4 In. 27.00
Heiser Saddles, Lykes & Fernandez, Havana, Flowers, 3 1/4 x 1 3/4 In. 147.00
Horse Head, Horseshoes, Inset Horses, Stirrup & Saddle Bag, Composite, 1 In. 21.00
Illinois R.R., Bunn Special 100.00
Izaak Walton League Of America, Sterling Silver, Flying Duck, Buck Deer, Creel 155.00
Jess Willard, World's Champion, Brass Color, Boxing Glove Shape, 2 In. 100.00
John W. Albers, Blacksmith & Horseshoer, Celluloid, Horse & Anvil, 2 In. 93.00
Jordan, Leather Strap, 1 1/4 x 5 In. ....*Illus* 10.00
Leisy Brewing, Metal, Enameled, Peoria, Il., 1900s 70.00
Locket, Photo Of Boy, Gold Filled, Engraved Initials, Black Ribbon, Late 1800s, 1 In. ... 23.00
Macveagh's Baseball Sales League, Gold Tone, 1923, 1 1/4 In. 35.00
Manitowoc Speedcrane, Speedshovel, Steam Shovel On Front, Brass, 2 In. 25.00

Watch Fob,
Caterpillar,
Leather Strap,
1 1/2 x 5 In.

Watch Fob, Old
Home Week,
Bath, July 1914,
1 x 5 In.

Watch Fob,
Jordan,
Leather Strap,
1 1/4 x 5 In.

Watch Fob,
Speedshovel,
Leather Strap,
1 1/2 x 5 In.

National Sportsman Magazine, Buck Deer Head, Shotgun 27.00
Northwest Construction Equipment, Bronze, Brown Leather Strap, N.Y., 1 In. 20.00
Oakland, Porcelain, Leather Strap 65.00
Old Home Week, Bath, July 1914, 1 x 5 In. ....*Illus* 10.00
Paul Revere Life Ins. Co., Nickel, Worcester, Mass., 1 In. 20.00
Sante Fe Railroad Emblem, Enamel, Leather Strap 50.00
Southworth Mach Inc., Cat, Bulldozer & Scoop Loader, Brass, Albany, N.Y. 20.00
Speedshovel, Leather Strap, 1 1/2 x 5 In. ....*Illus* 30.00
Thew Automatic Shovel Co., Steam Electric, Gasoline Shovels, Lorain, Oh., 1 3/4 In. ... 50.00
Weinhards Beer, Metal, Enamel, Portland, Or., 1912 .... 135.00

WATERFORD type glass resembles the famous glass made from 1783 to
1851 in the Waterford Glass Works in Ireland. It is a clear glass that
was often decorated by cutting. Modern glass is being made again in
Waterford, Ireland, and is marketed under the name *Waterford*.

Biscuit Barrel, Colleen 87.00
Bowl, Allover Diamonds, 9 3/4 In. 345.00
Bowl, Diamonds, Vertical Notches Around Rim, 8 In. 145.00
Bowl, Linear Cut Rim, Wave & Diamond Bands, Footed, 11 In. 345.00
Bowl, Wedding, 12-Lobed Rim, Gothic Arch & Fan Above Diamonds, 9 1/2 In. 345.00
Bowl, Wedding, Diamonds, Linear Cut Band, Gothic Arch & Fan, Lobed Rim, 9 1/2 In. ... 345.00
Bowl, Wishing Well, 16-Lobed Rim, Diamond Line, Fan Cuts, 9 3/4 In. 230.00
Brandy, Lismore, Spiked Diamonds, 12 Piece 460.00
Candlestick, Crystal Stem, Brass Top, Box, 10 3/4 In., Pair 115.00
Castor, Silver Plated Top, 7 1/2 In., 3 Piece 138.00
Chandelier, 8-Light, 16 Hanging Teardrops, 2 From Each Arm, 48 In. 6325.00
Compote, Boat Shape, Diamonds, Knop Stem, 13 In. 690.00
Cordial, Kylemore, 7 Piece 230.00
Cordial, Lismore, 8 Piece 179.00
Decanter, Diamond & Stylized Fan, Stopper, 13 1/4 In. 230.00
Decanter, Lismore, Footed 139.00
Decanter, Ship's, Spiked Diamond Band, Paneled Neck, Faceted Stopper, 10 In. 230.00
Figurine, Cat Looking Down, Curled Tail, Box, 4 In. 80.00
Figurine, Leaping Salmon, Signed, Gene O'Shea, Box, 8 1/2 In. 80.00
Figurine, Swan, Roy Cunningham, Signed, 5 1/2 In. 315.00
Garniture Set, Diamond, Fan & Drapery Swag Cuts, 8 In., 3 Piece 315.00
Goblet, Lismore, Box, 10 Oz., 4 Piece 74.00
Lamp, Fan, Diamond & Linear Cut Shade & Base, 18 In. 230.00
Lamp, Votive, Spiked Diamond, Hourglass Shaped Base, Signed, 7 1/4 In. 130.00
Pitcher, Lismore, 6 In. ....110.00 to 132.00
Relish, Lismore, Cover 38.00
Sauce, Dessert, Lismore, Footed, 4 In., 8 Piece 220.00
Vase, Bluebell, Diamond & Feather, Baluster, Scalloped Rim, 14 In. 200.00
Vase, Celebration, Trumpet Shape, Bow & Diamond Cuts, 12 In. 175.00
Vase, Princess, Trumpet Form, Crown Rim, Fluted Body, Pedestal Foot, 12 3/4 In. 200.00
Vase, Scalloped Rim, Fan Cut Outer Edge, Diamond Cut Body, 8 In. 86.00
Vase, Stepped Rim, Linear & Star Design Above Linear & Diamond Cut Body, 8 In. 200.00
Vase, Swelled Oval, Diamond, Oval, Fan & Starburst Design, 9 In. 345.00
Vase, Trumpet Shape, Wheat Sheaf & Diamond Cuts, Script Signed, 12 In. 290.00
Wine, Lismore, Signed, 12 Piece 575.00

WATT family members bought the Globe pottery of Crooksville, Ohio,
in 1922. They made pottery mixing bowls and tableware of the type
made by Globe. In 1935 they changed the production and made the
pieces with the freehand decorations that are popular with collectors
today. Apple, Starflower, Rooster, Tulip, and Autumn Foliage are the
best-known patterns. Pansy, also called Rio Rose, was the earliest pattern. Apple, the most popular pattern, can be dated from the leaves.
Originally, the apples had three leaves; after 1958 two leaves were
used. The plant closed in 1965. For more information, see *Kovels'
Depression Glass & Dinnerware Price List*.

Apple, Bowl, 3-Leaf, No. 73 .... 125.00
Apple, Casserole, Cover, Double, No. 96 .... 265.00

Apple, Mixing Bowl, Ribbed No. 05 .... 45.00
Banded Ware, Bowl, White & Brown Stripe, c.1940, No. 05 .... 40.00
Eve-N-Bake, Mixing Bowl, Shaded Brown, 6 1/2 x 10 In. 25.00
Morning Glory, Creamer, No. 97 .... 750.00
Orchard Ware, Bowl, Baker, Westwood, Yellow, Brown Drip, Impressed Mark, No. 96 .. 45.00
Rooster, Pitcher, Refrigerator, No. 69 .... 325.00
Starflower, Bowl, Spaghetti, No. 39 .... 125.00
Starflower, Ice Bucket, Cover 185.00
Starflower, Plate, Dinner, 9 1/2 In. 225.00
Tulip, Baker, Cover, No. 600 .... 380.00

WAVE CREST glass is an opaque white glassware manufactured by the Pairpoint Manufacturing Company of New Bedford, Massachusetts, and some French factories. It was decorated by the C.F. Monroe Company of Meriden, Connecticut. The glass was painted in pastel colors and decorated with flowers. The name *Wave Crest* was used after 1898.

WAVE CREST WARE

Biscuit Jar, Pink & White, Blue Enameled Floral, 8 1/2 In. 300.00
Biscuit Jar, Yellow & White, Enameled Floral, Scroll Mold, Square, 9 In. 350.00
Biscuit Jar, Yellow Enameled, Daisy, Melon, Ribbed, 7 In. 275.00
Biscuit Jar, Yellow Enameled, Pink Floral, 8 In. 175.00
Box, Blue, Pink Enameled Blossoms, Footed, Key Lock, 6 x 5 In. 740.00
Box, Cover, Dresser, Blue Enameled Daisy Floral, White Enamel Accents, 4 x 7 In 330.00
Box, Cover, Dresser, Opal, Light Blue Enameled Floral, Gold Metal Rim, 3 1/4 In. 260.00
Box, Cover, Dresser, Pink, Blue & White Enameled Flowers, Brass Foliage, 3 In. 467.00
Box, Cover, Dresser, White, Satin, Gold Metal Rim, Marked, 3 In. 315.00
Box, Dresser, Enameled Maroon, Pink Wild Roses, Gray Foliage, 4 x 7 In. 220.00
Box, Dresser, Ivory, Enameled Floral, Brass Band, C.F.M. Co., 5 x 3 In. 415.00
Box, Helmschmied Swirl, Pink Floral, 5 In. 650.00
Box, Helmschmied Swirl, Yellow, 6 In. 345.00
Ewer, Pink, Blue Enameled Floral, Brass Foot & Rim, 13 In., Pair 325.00
Jar, Dresser, Helmschmied Swirl, Pink, Floral, 6 1/2 x 3 1/2 In. 330.00
Lamp, Oil, Blue & Pink Enameled, Boat & Lake Scene, 16 In. 300.00
Photo Receiver, Enameled Floral Sprays, Brass Ormolu, Footed, 5 1/4 x 6 In. 425.00
Pin Dish, White, Enameled Floral, Brass Rim, 3 In. 70.00
Pin Jar, Enameled Floral, 3 Gold Metal Legs, Rim, 3 1/2 In. 66.00
Sugar & Creamer, Enameled Floral, Silver Plated Handle & Rim 3350.00
Tobacco Jar, Helmschmied Swirl, Enameled Yellow Roses, Silver Plated, 6 1/2 In. 168.00
Vase, Blue, Enameled Pink Rose, Brass Foot & Rim, 5 In. 180.00
Vase, Scroll Mold, Light Blue, Enameled Floral, Brass Base & Rim, 6 1/2 In. 225.00
Vase, White & Pink, Enameled Yellow Daisy, Brass Handles & Feet, 12 In. 1100.00

WEAPONS listed here include instruments of combat other than guns, knives, rifles, or swords. Firearms are not listed in this book. Knives and swords are listed in their own categories.

Billy Club, Lignum Vitae, 19th Century, 13 1/2 In. 33.00
Brass Knuckles, 1 Aluminum, Other Cast Iron, Pair 55.00
Bullet Mold, 38 Smith & Wesson SPL, 38 WC, Winchester Rep Arms Co., 2 Piece 50.00
Cap Box, Pewter Finial, AVC Stamp On Flap, Confederate, 4 x 4 In. 798.00
Crossbow, Central Shaft, Iron Bow Strung With Sisal String, Dark Brown Patina, 26 In. ... 1063.00
Dagger, Ebony Handle, Original Scabbard, Revolutionary War Era 110.00
Pistol Belt, Stag Handled Knife, Sheath, 1930s, 2 x 44 In. 193.00
Spear, Bamboo, Hardwood Points, South America, 1920s, 65 In., 3 Piece 28.00
Spear, Wooden, Wrapped Copper, Iron Point, Africa, 66 1/2 In. 195.00
Swagger Stick, Marked CSN, Includes 1989 Letter, Stag Handle, Silver Ring 319.00
Trench Pike, Fort Ticonderoga, Civil War 285.00

WEATHER VANES were used in seventeenth-century Boston. The direction of the wind was an indication of coming weather, important to the seafaring and farming communities. By the mid-nineteenth century, commercial weather vanes were made of metal. Today's collectors often consider weather vanes to be examples of folk art, even though they may not have been handmade.

Arrow, Copper, 19th Century 450.00

Arrow, Copper, Rod Mounted, 12 x 54 In. 488.00
Bank, Paddy And The Pig, Original Paint, Patented 1882 .... 5500.00
Banner, Directionals, Copper, 70 x 32 In. 1090.00
Banner, Green, Blue Verdigris, 70 x 32 In. 785.00
Black Hawk, Copper, Allover Verdigris, Late 19th Century, 18 1/2 x 33 In. 6555.00
Black Hawk, Copper, With Directionals, Windham, Maine, 22 In. 3025.00
Bobtail Running Horse & Jockey, Full-Bodied Copper, 19th Century, 31 1/2 In. 4600.00
Bull, 2-Piece Molded Body, Wooden Base, 19th Century, 18 x 26 In. 85.00
Bull, Full-Bodied, Zinc Head, Copper Body, Rod, Base, 19th Century, 26 In. 4312.00
Bull, Silhouette, White & Black Paint, Rod Mounted, 25 In. 325.00
Butterfly, Copper, Stylized Flowers, Gilt Traces, J.W. Fiske, 35 x 36 In. 5463.00
Clipper Ship, Carved Wood, Tin, Wire & Copper 785.00
Cow, Beige Paint, 28 x 15 In. 3740.00
Cow, Full-Bodied, Gilt Copper, Rod Mounted, 19th Century, 18 1/2 x 33 In. 4400.00
Cow, Full-Bodied, Horned, Arrow Directional, 1870s, 50 1/2 x 49 1/2 In. 9775.00
Cow, Hollow Body, Cast Zinc Head, Bullet Hole, Legs Wired To Rod, 28 In. 2750.00
Cow, Hollow, Zinc, 14 1/2 x 9 In. 65.00
Cow, Sheet Zinc, 19th Century, 9 1/2 In. 2200.00
Cow, Silouette, Full-Bodied, Late 19th Century, 13 1/2 x 24 3/4 In. 6325.00
Dekalb, Winged Ear Of Corn, Die Cut Tin Lithograph, 8 x 18 In. 65.00
Dog, Hunting, 4 Hunting Dogs Surrounding Fox, Sheet Iron, 98 x 88 In. 5750.00
Dragon, Copper, Gilt, Molded 515.00
Eagle, Copper, Full-Bodied, Verdigris, 12 1/2 x 24 In. 1650.00
Eagle, Copper, Perched On Orb Above Rod, Black Painted Wood Base, 34 In. 1495.00
Eagle, On Ball, Copper, 19th Century, 26-In. Wingspan 785.00
Eagle, Wing, Spread, Copper, Iron Head ....*Illus* 4025.00
Eagle, Wing, Spread, Sheet Lead, 57 x 30 In. 385.00
Fish, Pike, Copper, Full-Bodied, Sheet Metal Fins, Black Metal Stand, 27 In. 9200.00
Fish, Wood, Lead, Copper, Iron Hook, 31 1/2 In. 522.00
Fox, Leaping, Copper, Zinc, Allover Verdigris, Rod Mounted, 11 In. 9200.00
Fox, Running, Copper, 1883, 22 In. 5750.00
Horse, 2-Piece Molded Zinc, Bullet Holes, 11 x 15 In. 110.00
Horse, Copper, Directionals, 1950s, 16 x 18 In. 195.00
Horse, Copper, Full-Bodied, Gilt, Late 19th Century, 22 x 34 In. 2420.00
Horse, Copper, Full-Bodied, Harris & Co., Boston, 1885, 18 x 33 In. 1045.00
Horse, Copper, Full-Bodied, Zinc Head, Late 19th Century, 31 x 33 In. 6900.00
Horse, Copper, Zinc Head, 16 In. 1100.00
Horse, Running, Cooper, Zinc Ears, 1880 .... 1120.00
Horse, Running, Copper, Bullet Holes, Missing Tail 1485.00
Horse, Running, Copper, Cast Iron Head, Directionals, Rod, 29 x 65 In. 1870.00
Horse, Running, Copper, Gilt, Directionals, N.H., 19th Century, 65 1/2 x 33 1/2 In. 2415.00
Horse, Running, Copper, Gilt, Late 19th Century, 30 In. 1840.00
Horse, Running, Copper, Gilt, Molded, 31 In. 1980.00
Horse, Running, Copper, Hollow Body, 31 In. 3080.00
Horse, Running, Copper, Late 19th Century, 25 1/2 In. 400.00
Horse, Running, Copper, Zinc Head, Mounted On Rod, Black Stand, 20 In. 9775.00
Horse, Running, Copper, Zinc, Full-Bodied, Allover Verdigris, 20 x 42 1/4 In. 3160.00

Weather Vane, Eagle,
Wing, Spread, Copper,
Iron Head

**To clean very dirty brass or copper,
boil it for two hours in a pan of
water with a tablespoon of salt and
a cup of white vinegar.**

Horse, Running, Copper, Zinc, Full-Bodied, Verdigris, 21 In. 18400.00
Horse, Running, Copper, Zinc, Swell-Bodied, Allover Verdigris, 18 x 30 In. 2875.00
Horse, Running, Copper, Zinc, Swell-Bodied, Driver, Yellow, Red, 21 1/2 In. 11500.00
Horse, Running, Zinc Head, Copper, Gilt, Directionals, 46 1/2 x 25 In. 530.00
Horse, Running, Zinc, Red Ball 1000.00
Horse, Standing, Copper, Full-Bodied, Raised Foreleg, Rod Mounted, 15 In. 3735.00
Horse, Standing, Copper, Zinc, Sheet Metal Ears, Tail, Wooden Base, 14 x 20 In. 11500.00
Horse, Standing, Sheet Metal, Pine Plank Base, Early 20th Century, 24 In., Pair 1380.00
Horse, Trotting, Copper, Allover Verdigris, Wooden Base, 49 1/2 In. 575.00
Horse, Trotting, Sheet Metal, Broom Form Terminal, Old Paint, Late 1800s, 47 In. 2875.00
Hunter, Black Hunter Taking Aim, Sheet Iron, 26 1/2 x 25 In. 1265.00
Indian Chief, Standing, Drawn Bow, Sheet Metal Arrow, Pine, 60 In. 3450.00
Leaping Stag, Copper, Gilt, Cast Iron Rod, Directionals, 29 1/2 In. 16100.00
Merino Ram, Standing, Copper, Zinc, Swell-Bodied, Sheet Copper Horns, 29 In. 1725.00
Pigeon, Copper, J.W. Fiske 8995.00
Rooster, Black Repainted, Directionals, Wooden Base, Primitive, 26 In. 135.00
Rooster, Copper, Full-Bodied, 30 x 25 In. 1430.00
Rooster, Copper & Zinc, Full-Bodied 6150.00
Rooster, On Ball, Molded, Gilt 1840.00
Rooster, Sheet Iron Tail, Cast Iron, Rochester Iron Works, 19th Century 4300.00
Rooster, Sheet Iron, Arched Tail Feathers, 21 x 24 In. 1760.00
Schooner, Painted Wood Hull, Copper Sails, Painted Base, 17 x 24 In. 633.00
Setter, Full-Bodied, Walking Dog, Gilded Copper, 1880s, 15 1/2 In. 6900.00
Sheep, Standing, Copper, Swell-Bodied, Sheet Metal Ears, Black Stand, 16 In. 3450.00
Sloop Shape, Sheet Brass, 10 In. 75.00
Stag, Sheet Metal, Standing, Early 20th Century 1265.00
Sulky & Driver, Copper, 4 Wheels, Mounted On Wooden Base, 19 In. 17250.00
Whale, Copper, Full-Bodied, Stand, 28 x 38 In. 1100.00

WEBB glass is made by Thomas Webb & Sons of Ambelcot, England.
Many types of art and cameo glass were made by them during the Victorian era. Production ceased by 1991, and the factory was demolished
in 1995. Webb Burmese and Webb Peachblow are special colored
glasswares of the Victorian era. They are listed at the end of this section. Glassware that is not Burmese or Peachblow is included here.

Webb

Bride's Bowl, Cranberry, Enameled Design, 13 In. 150.00
Finger Bowl, Underplate, Violet Blue To Amber, Ruffled Edge, 6 In. 1176.00
Inkwell, Cranberry, Wisteria Blossoms & Branches, Silver Plate Lid, 3 In. 747.00
Lamp, Kerosene, White To Amber, Brass Fittings 1045.00
Pitcher, Ivory, Apple Blossoms, Clear Handle, 10 x 5 1/2 In. 395.00
Scent Bottle, White Over Amber, Water Leaves, Silver Mount, Cameo, 6 3/4 In. 1430.00
Vase, Amber Iris, Cameo, Marked, 11 In. 1600.00
Vase, Deep Emerald Over White, Gold Grape, Glossy, Cameo, 7 1/4 In. 308.00
Vase, Enameled Apple Blossom, Blue Cased, 2 Handles, 12 1/2 In. 175.00
Vase, Enameled Gold & White Branches, White Interior, 11 3/4 In. 245.00
Vase, Enameled White Flowers & Leaves, Greek Key Border At Neck, c.1900, 8 In., Pair . 170.00
Vase, Flower-Form, Brown, Peacock Blue, Amethyst, Pale Yellow, 3 1/4 In. 650.00
Vase, Flowers, Russet, Satin Glass, Gold Trim Handles, 10 In. 202.00
Vase, Lavender Cut To Clear, Ribbed, Footed, Marked, 10 In. 350.00
Vase, Morning Glory, Pink & White Over Yellow, Cameo, 3 1/4 In. 185.00
Vase, Ruby Cased, Applied Bird On Branch, 2 Handles, Squat, Signed, 7 In. 250.00
Vase, Ruby Mother-Of-Pearl, Squat, 5 x 5 In. 450.00
Vase, Stick, Ivory, Beaded Design, 9 1/2 In. 200.00
Vase, White Over Blue, Floral & Butterfly, Signed, Gem Cameo, 11 In. 1800.00
Vase, White Over Ruby, Floral & Butterfly, Cameo, Marked, 9 In. 2250.00
Vase, White Over Sky Blue, Geranium, Leaves, Butterflies, Baluster, Cameo, 7 In. 1705.00

WEBB BURMESE is a colored Victorian glass made by Thomas Webb
& Sons of Stourbridge, England, from 1886.

Bowl, Ruffled Edge, 2 1/4 x 3 3/4 In. 235.00
Fairy Lamp, Clarke Base, 4 In. 200.00
Finger Bowl, Floral, Ruffled Edge, Marked, 4 In. 475.00
Rose Bowl, Enameled Flowers, Footed 430.00

Rose Bowl, Lavender Blue Flowers, Enameled, Scalloped Rim, 3 In. 325.00
Vase, Ivory Beading, Footed, Signed, 8 1/2 In. 900.00
Vase, Star Crimped, 3 1/2 In. 170.00

WEBB PEACHBLOW is a colored Victorian glass made by Thomas
Webb & Sons of Stourbridge, England, from 1885.
Vase, Enameled Bird & Blossom, 7 In., Pair 130.00
Vase, Enameled Birds, Flowers, 7 1/2 In., Pair 525.00
Vase, Enameled Stork & Branch, 13 In. 700.00
Vase, Enameled White Apple Blossom, 4 Sides, 11 1/2 In., Pair 600.00
Vase, Enameled, Signed, 8 In. 150.00
Vase, Footed, 9 In. 165.00
Vase, Gold Enameled, 9 In. 200.00
Vase, Stick, 9 In. 275.00
Vase, Stick, White Lining, 10 3/4 In. 350.00

WEDGWOOD, one of the world's most successful potteries, was
founded by Josiah Wedgwood, who was considered a cripple by his
brother and was forbidden to work at the family business. The pottery
was established in England in 1759. A large variety of wares has been
made, including the well-known jasper ware, basalt, cream ware, and
even a limited amount of porcelain. There are two kinds of jasper ware.
One is made from two colors of clay, the other is made from one color
of clay with a color dip to create the contrast in design. The firm is still
in business. Other Wedgwood pieces may be listed under Flow Blue,
Majolica, Tea Leaf Ironstone or in other porcelain categories.

WEDGWOOD

Ashtray, Churchill 80.00
Ashtray, Jasper Ware, Light Blue, White, 3 Piece 88.00
Basket, Cream Ware, Underplate, Reticulated, 10 1/2 In. 316.00
Basket, Jasper Dip, Dark Blue, Basket Weave Loop Handle, Openwork, Mark, 4 1/2 In. . . . 431.00
Bell, Dinner, Jasper Ware, Light Blue, White 55.00
Biscuit Jar, Black Basalt, Playing Children Relief Band, Silver Plated Rim, 5 1/2 In. 518.00
Biscuit Jar, Cover, Barrel, Light Blue Dip, Figures, Horses, Silver Plated Handle, 6 In. . . . 695.00
Biscuit Jar, Cover, Jasper Dip, Black, White Figures, Cherubs, Handle, 1880s, 7 In. 640.00
Biscuit Jar, Cover, Jasper Dip, Tricolor, Dark Blue Ground, Silver Rim, Handle, 5 In. 288.00
Biscuit Jar, Cover, Jasper Ware, Grecian Ladies, Silver Plated Rim, Handle, 6 1/2 In. . . . 165.00
Biscuit Jar, Cover, Silver Plated Band & Handle, Marbleized Glazes, c.1878, 6 1/2 In. . . . 288.00
Biscuit Jar, Jasper Ware, Green, White, Silver Plated Lid & Handle, 19th Century 305.00
Biscuit Jar, Stand, Jasper Dip, Black, White Classical Relief, England, c.1876, 7 3/4 In. . . 633.00
Bonbon, Lizard Form Handle, Chestnut & Leaf, 19th Century, 6 1/2 In., Pair 150.00
Book Slide, Calamander Case, Oval Medallion Ends, 19th Century, 15 3/4 In. 575.00
Bookcase, Mounted, Jasper Ware, Light Blue, England, c.1900, 8 1/4 x 3 3/8 x 5 In. 1610.00
Bottle, Cover, Jasper Dip, Dark Blue, Muse & Leaf Relief, England, c.1863, 5 3/4 In. . . . 460.00
Bottle, Solid Black, Glazed, White Grapevine Swags, Lion Masks, 11 3/4 In., Pair 374.00
Bough Pot, Jasper Ware, Solid Blue, Square, Arched Top, Classical, Late 1700s, 6 1/8 In. 259.00
Bouquetiere, Queen's Ware, Brown, Red Slip, Basket Weave, Late 18th Century, 5 In. 288.00
Bowl, Black & White, Boston, Massacre & Other Scenes, 9 1/2 x 4 1/2 In. 61.00
Bowl, Black Basalt, Flowers, Banded Leaves, 5 In. 103.00
Bowl, Black Basalt, Grape, Leaf Design, 10 In. 460.00
Bowl, Black Basalt, Polychrome Enamels, Cherubs Below, 1840s, 6 1/4 In. 460.00
Bowl, Black Basalt, Ribbed, Leaf Design, Goat Head Handles, 7 In. 126.00
Bowl, Black Basalt, Scrollwork, Floral Festoons, Basket Weave, Late 1800s, 8 5/8 In. 1035.00
Bowl, Cover, Stand, Cane Ware, Glazed, Blue Classical & Leaf Relief, 5 In. 374.00
Bowl, Dragon Luster, Dragon & Phoenix, 8 1/4 In. 200.00
Bowl, Fairyland Luster, Castle On Road, Fairy In Cage, 1920, 9 In. 3735.00
Bowl, Fairyland Luster, Poplar Trees Exterior, Fairy Interior, c.1920, 9 1/8 In. 6325.00
Bowl, Fruit, Jasper Dip, Dark Blue, Plated Rim, 14 Classical Figures, 4 1/2 In. 425.00
Bowl, Harvard, Red Shield & Architectural Designs, Fruit & Leaf Border, 12 1/4 In. 145.00
Bowl, Hummingbird Luster, Blue, 3 1/2 In., Pair 3500.00
Bowl, Jasper Dip, Yellow, Footed, Applied Black Classical & Leaf Relief, 8 1/8 In. 518.00
Bowl, Jasper Ware, Solid Blue, Dancing Hours, White Classical & Leaf Relief, 10 In. 460.00
Bowl, Salad, Black Basalt, Vintage Border, 9 3/4 In. 275.00
Bowl, Salad, Jasper Ware, Blue, White, Silver Plated Rim, 9 In. 220.00

Bowl, Salad, Servers, Majolica, Relief, Scrolled Feet, Silver Plate, c.1870, 7 3/4 In. 403.00
Bowl, Salad, Servers, Queen's Ware, Polychrome Transfer, Fowl, c.1863, 10 1/4 In. 489.00
Bowl, Whieldon, Pineapple Design, 1765 .... 700.00
Box, Cover, Blue, Hummingbird Luster, Widow's Finial, Marked, Round, 6 x 6 In. 795.00
Box, Cover, Jasper Dip, Crimson, White Classical Figures, Flowers, Square, c.1920, 4 In. . 1150.00
Box, Cover, Jasper Ware, Solid Light Blue, White Blind Man's Bluff Relief, c.1975, 6 In. . 144.00
Box, Sardine, Cover, Majolica, Trunk Shape, Shells & Coral Rim, c.1879, 8 1/8 In. 1725.00
Box, Sardine, Cover, Majolica, Wood Plank Boat Form, Fish At Ends, 1878, 9 3/4 In. 1725.00
Bread Tray, Majolica, Basket Weave Body, Flowers, Ears Of Corn, c.1882, 13 In. 603.00
Bust, Black Basalt, Laughing Boy, 19th Century 100.00
Bust, Classical Male, Intaglio, Black Basalt, Wedgwood & Bentley, 1/2 x 5/8 In., Pair ... 259.00
Butter Chip, Appledore, 3 1/4 In. 26.00
Butter Chip, Hague, 3 1/4 In. 10.00
Cachepot, Jasper Ware, Blue, Classical Figures, Muses, Grapevine, 9 x 8 1/4 In. 865.00
Cake Stand, Majolica, Pierced Border, 3 Dolphins Pedestal, 7 In., Pair 1955.00
Candlestick, Dolphin Form, Majolica, Shell Trim, c.1879, 9 1/2 In., Pair 1495.00
Candlestick, Jasper Dip, Black, Applied White Classical & Leaf Relief, 8 In., Pair 863.00
Candlestick, Jasper Dip, Black, Applied White Muses & Leaves Relief, 5 3/4 In., Pair ... 316.00
Candlestick, Jasper Ware, Blue, White, Pair 66.00
Candlestick, Reeded Stems, Wheat Designs, Impressed, Brown Stamp, 10 In., Pair 295.00
Charger, Queen's Ware, Female Figure, Holding Fan, c.1877, 15 1/8 In. 230.00
Cheese Dish, Cover, Jasper Dip, Blue, White Classical Figures, Oak Border, 1880s, 8 In. . 620.00
Cheese Dish, Cover, Jasper Dip, Dark Blue, Classical Figures, Oak Leaves, 7 1/2 In. 288.00
Clock, Jasper Ware, Blue, Round, Oval Medallion, Classical Figures, Art Deco, 6 In. 115.00
Clock Case, Jasper Dip, Dark Blue, Rectangular, Applied White Relief, c.1900, 6 In. 173.00
Clock Case, Jasper Dip, Dark Blue, Tempus Fugit, Father Time, c.1900, 8 In. 863.00
Clock Case, Jasper Dip, Dark Blue, White Classical & Leaf Relief, c.1900, 12 In. 690.00
Clock Case, Jasper Dip, Dark Blue, White Classical Relief, Urn On Top, c.1900, 8 5/8 In. . 863.00
Clock Case, Jasper Ware, Green, Classical Relief, Rhinestones, c.1900, 14 In. 805.00
Clock Case, Jasper Ware, Light Green, Classical & Leaf Relief, England, c.1900, 6 In. ... 316.00
Clock Case, Jasper Ware, Light Green, White Oak & Acanthus Leaves, c.1900, 8 In. 403.00
Clock Case, Mantel, Jasper Ware, Blue, White Garlands, Ram Heads, Brass Finial, 10 In. . 1955.00
Clock Face, Jasper Ware, Tricolor Medallions, Arabesque Floral, 1880s, 11 5/8 In. 1495.00
Coffee Cann & Saucer, Jasper Ware, Light Blue, Banding, Late 18th Century, 5 In. 259.00
Coffeepot, Black Basalt, Pear Shape, Fluted Base, 19th Century, 11 3/4 In. 175.00
Coffeepot, Cover, Black Basalt, Flowers, Enamel, England, c.1840, 8 3/4 In. 690.00
Coffeepot, Cover, Drab Ware, Glazed, Arabesque Floral Relief, 19th Century, 9 1/4 In. ... 230.00
Coffeepot, Queen's Ware, Pear Shape, Leaf Spout & Handle, c.1785, 10 5/8 In. 460.00
Creamer, Black Basalt, Iris Kenlock Ware, c.1800, 2 3/8 In. 977.00
Creamer, Classical Figures, Grape & Scroll Band, Cobalt Blue, Bulbous, 5 1/4 In. 50.00
Creamer, Jasper Ware, 2 Muses, Metal Hinged Lid, 4 3/4 In. 60.00
Creamer, Jasper Ware, Blue, Classical Figures Making Offerings Relief, c.1901, 4 In. 69.00
Crocus Pot, Stand, Stoneware, Smear Glaze, Basket Weave, Beehive Shape, 6 1/2 In. 575.00
Cup, Stemmed, Golconda, Glazed Cane Ground, Urn Finial, 2 Handles, England, 22 In. .. 575.00
Cup & Saucer, Jasper Ware, Dark Blue, 1850-1870, Miniature, 1 In. 285.00
Cup Plate, Strawberry, 3 3/4 In. 1100.00
Decanter, Black Basalt, Banded Key Design, Silver Rim, Spout, Stopper, 10 1/4 In. 690.00
Dish, Green Leaf, Majolica, 8 1/2 In. 75.00
Dish, Majolica, Leaf, Green, 8 1/2 x 8 3/4 In. ....*Illus* 121.00
Dish, Meat Pie, Underplate, Removable Rim, Terra-Cotta, 19th Century, 12 1/4 In. 275.00
Dish, Queen's Ware, Boat Shape, Grapevine, Bearded Mask Head Handles, 13 1/4 In. 316.00
Dish, Queen's Ware, Emile Lessore, Oval Shell Shape, Cherubs, Signed, c.1860, 13 In. ... 546.00
Dresser Set, Tray, Bacchanalian Boys, Blue Transfer, Leaf Design, c.1900, 5 Piece 515.00
Ewer, Black Basalt, Gilt, Bronze, Feather Mold Rim, Leaf Relief, 1800s, 7 3/4 In., Pair .. 1380.00
Figurine, Bacchanalian Boy, Holding Vase, Cobalt Blue Glaze, c.1871, 8 1/4 In. 431.00
Figurine, Bear, Black Basalt, Ernest Light, Impressed Mark, c.1915, 2 1/2 In. 489.00
Figurine, Cat, Glass Eyes, Ernest Light, c.1915, 4 1/2 In. 430.00
Figurine, Cybele, Black Basalt, Standing Figure With Lion, Round Base, 1800s, 9 In. 373.00
Figurine, Elephant, Black Basalt, Glass Eyes, Ernest Light, c.1915, 3 1/2 In. 805.00
Figurine, Fallow Deer, Black Basalt, Artist Mark, c.1930, 7 1/2 In. 632.00
Figurine, Ireland & Scotland, Black Basalt, W. Beattie Modeled, c.1860, 12 In., Pair 3105.00
Figurine, Kingfisher, Majolica, Pierced Rocky Base, Late 19th Century, 8 1/4 In. 2415.00
Figurine, Musician, Holding String Instrument, Pearl Ware, c.1800, 8 1/2 In. 862.00

Don't use old home-canning jars to preserve food. The jars with wire bails, glass caps, zinc porcelain-lined caps, or metal caps with rubber rings do not seal as well as the new two-piece vacuum-cap jars.

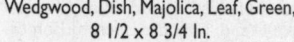

Wedgwood, Dish, Majolica, Leaf, Green, 8 1/2 x 8 3/4 In.

Figurine, Raven, Glass Eyes, Ernest Light, c.1915, 4 3/8 In.	287.00
Figurine, Spring, Black Basalt, Clutching Bird, Circular Plinth, Title, 1850s, 9 3/4 In.	1092.00
Figurine, Taurus The Bull, Signs Of Zodiac, c.1962, 14 1/2 In.	517.00
Figurine, Venus, Nude, Arms Posed, Title, 1850s, 9 1/2 In.	862.00
Flowerpot, Majolica, Flowering Pots, Banded Borders, Signed, c.1883, 7 3/4 In.	345.00
Footbath, Pearl Ware, Printed, Blue Transfer, Oval, Tower Of London Scene, 19 1/4 In.	1955.00
Garniture, Cane Ware, Bough Pot, Blue, Red White Enamel, Cartouches, 4 In., 3 Piece	2300.00
Goblet, Jasper Dip, Dice Ware, Light Blue, White, Green, Bicentennial, 1976, 4 3/4 In.	690.00
Incense Burner, Jasper Dip, Black, White Dolphin Shape Tripod Base, 4 1/8 In.	173.00
Inkstand, Black Basalt, 2 Pots, Central 2 Handles, Urn Shape, 19th Century, 3 3/4 In.	863.00
Inkstand, Medieval Maiden Cover, Train Forms Pen Tray, 1872, 9 In.	6325.00
Inkstand, Moonlight Luster, Candle Sconce To Top, c.1810, 4 1/2 In.	690.00
Inkstand, Queen's Ware, Bird's Head Handles, Delvaux R. Royale, 8 1/4 In.	2645.00
Inkwell, Black Basalt, Oil Lamp Form, Candle At Spout, Rosso Antico, 5 1/4 In.	1092.00
Inkwell, Jasper Ware, Tricolor, Pale Blue, Lavender, White, Leaf Relief, Oval, 4 1/8 In.	920.00
Jar, Cover, Jasper Dip, Blue, Classical & Leaf Relief, England, c.1900, 3 7/8 In., Pair	288.00
Jar, Cover, Queen's Ware, Floral Garlands, Acanthus Leaves, 19th Century, 4 In.	920.00
Jardiniere, Jasper Dip, Cylindrical, Crimson, White Muses, Grapevine, Masks, 7 1/4 In.	2415.00
Jardiniere, Jasper Ware, Classical Figures, Flower & Leaf Swags, Blue Ground, 6 In.	145.00
Jardiniere, Stand, Jasper Dip, Crimson, Applied White Classical Relief, c.1920, 3 1/2 In.	1840.00
Jug, Black Basalt, Dragon Kenlock Ware, Enamel, Rope Twist Handle, c.1900, 5 1/8 In.	316.00
Jug, Dragon Kenlock Ware, Rope Twist Handle, Enamel Titled, c.1900, 7 1/4 In.	287.00
Jug, Ivory, Raised Gilt Flower Design, Printed Mark, England, c.1885, 6 1/4 In.	173.00
Jug, Jasper Dip, Dark Blue Ground, Yellow Trellis, White Leaves, Pewter Lid, 6 1/8 In.	575.00
Jug, Jasper Dip, Dark Blue, Portland Shape, Hinged Pewter Cover, Mid 1800s, 8 In.	518.00
Jug, Jasper Dip, Green Ground, Yellow Trellis, White Leaves, Pewter Cover, 6 5/8 In.	518.00
Jug, Jasper Dip, Portland Shape, Dark Blue, Classical Relief, Pewter Rim & Cover, 9 In.	633.00
Jug, Jasper Dip, Tricolor, Blue Ground, Yellow Trellis, White Band, Pewter Cover, 6 In.	633.00
Jug, Majolica, Bird & Fan, Impressed Mark, England, c.1860, 6 1/4 In.	345.00
Jug, Majolica, Caterer, Raised Jeweling, Banded Motto Relief, c.1868, 7 1/2 In.	374.00
Jug, Queen's Ware, Portrait On Side, Armchair On Reverse, c.1896, 8 1/4 In.	258.00
Jug, Rosso Antico, Basalt, Pear Shape, Reeds, Foliage In Relief, Mark, 5 3/4 In.	403.00
Jug, Stoneware, White Smear Glazed, Blue Grapevine Banded Border, c.1840, 5 7/8 In.	230.00
Jug, Stoneware, White, Leafage, Impressed Mark, England, c.1830, 8 1/8 In.	287.00
Lamp Base, Jasper Dip, Light Blue, White Relief, Cupid & Psyche, c.1869, 10 3/8 In.	374.00
Lazy Susan, Pearl Ware, Gilt, Enamel, Panels, Insects, Foliage, c.1863, 18 5/8 In.	374.00
Match Holder, Basalt, Grape & Leaf Design, England, 2 1/4 In.	95.00
Matchbox, Cover, Jasper Dip, Yellow, White Classical & Leaf Relief, 3 3/4 In.	86.00
Medallion, Benjamin Franklin, Signed, Wedgwood & Bentley, c.1775, 2 1/4 In.	1265.00
Medallion, Galileo Galilei, Signed, Wedgwood & Bentley, c.1779, 3 1/8 In.	1725.00
Medallion, Jasper Dip, Green, Black, White Classical Relief, Octagon, 1 1/4 x 1 1/2 In.	230.00
Medallion, Jasper Dip, Multicolored, Early 19th Century, 3 1/8 In.	1000.00
Medallion, Jasper Dip, Yellow, Oval, White Classical Female, 1800s, 2 1/4 x 4 1/8 In.	460.00
Medallion, Jasper Ware, Tricolor, Green, Lilac, White, Polished Edge, Oval, 2 In., Pair	460.00
Medallion, Martin Heinrich Klaproth, Signed, c.1815, 3 1/4 In.	1035.00
Medallion, Portrait, Charlotte Augusta Matilda, Oval, 19th Century, 3 x 4 In.	430.00
Medallion, Samuel More, Gilt Wood Frame, Wedgwood & Bentley, c.1773, 3 3/8 In.	1667.00

Mug, Dark Blue, White Classical, Dip, W.M.I.E., 2 7/8 In. 195.00
Mug, Jasper Ware, Dark Green Handle, 5 3/8 In. 575.00
Mug, Jasper Ware, Piccadilly Circus, Christmas, 1971, Light Blue, White 66.00
Mug, Motto, Here's To Thee My Honest Friend, Harry Barnard, 1880s, 4 1/8 In. 460.00
Pail, Jasper Dip, Dark Blue, Silver Plated Rim & Handle, Raised Banding, 5 In. 259.00
Pestle, Wooden Handle, Size 6, 11 In. 32.00
Pie Dish, Game, Majolica, Oval, Domed Cover, Rabbit Finial, Painted, 1865, 10 1/4 In. . . . 725.00
Pitcher, Bird & Fan, Majolica, 6 1/2 In. 1045.00
Pitcher, Black Basalt, Polychrome Floral Enamel, Incised Mark, c.1920, 8 1/2 In. 745.00
Pitcher, Garfield, Garfield Year Of 1831, 7 1/2 In. 1210.00
Pitcher, Grecian Women, Lambs, 8 1/4 In. 350.00
Pitcher, Jasper Dip, Blue, Busts Of Washington & Franklin, 5 In. 137.00
Pitcher, Milk, Blue & White Classical Figures, 6 In. 55.00
Pitcher, Milk, Jasper Ware, Blue, White, Early 20th Century, 7 1/2 In. 275.00
Pitcher, Primrose, Cobalt Handle, Brown Ground, 7 In. 350.00
Pitcher, Primrose, White, 4 1/2 In. 100.00
Pitcher, Water, Orchids, Lily Of The Valley, Ferns, Flow Blue, Gold Trim, Lid 1250.00
Plaque, Black Basalt, 2 Hercules Portraits, 1 Strangling Nemean Lion, 7 In., Pair 750.00
Plaque, Black Basalt, 3 Graces, Oval, 19th Century, 6 x 8 In. 575.00
Plaque, Black Basalt, Gilt, Beloved Of The Great Enchantress, 1973, 8 x 8 1/2 In. 345.00
Plaque, Black Basalt, Gladiators, 19th Century, 10 3/4 x 12 3/8 In. 3220.00
Plaque, Black Basalt, Judgment Of Hercules, Oval, 19th Century, 8 3/4 x 11 3/4 In. 1035.00
Plaque, Black Basalt, Vulcan Forging Armor For Achilles, Rectangular, 6 x 9 1/2 In. 1265.00
Plaque, Fairyland Luster, River Scene, Elves, Dwarfs, Gilt, c.1920, 4 1/2 x 10 1/2 In. 8005.00
Plaque, Jasper Dip, Black, Blind Man's Bluff, c.1860, 3 3/4 x 11 1/4 In. 575.00
Plaque, Jasper Dip, Black, Dancing Hours, Rectangular, Classical Figures, 4 x 11 In. 633.00
Plaque, Jasper Dip, Black, Oval, White Dancing Hour Relief, 19th Century, 5 x 8 1/2 In. . . 403.00
Plaque, Jasper Dip, Black, Rectangular, Classical Figures Relief, 3 3/8 x 9 1/8 In. 374.00
Plaque, Jasper Dip, Dark Blue, Oval, Bacchanalian Boys, Late 1800s, 3 3/4 x 5 3/4 In. . . . 748.00
Plaque, Jasper Ware, Blue, White, Apotheosis Of Virgil, 15 1/4 x 24 1/2 In. 5000.00
Plaque, Jasper Ware, Light Blue, White Relief, Bacchanalian Boys, 6 1/2 In. 1400.00
Plaque, Jasper Ware, Solid Black, Rectangular, Blind Man's Bluff, c.1900, 6 x 18 In. 1150.00
Plaque, Jasper Ware, Solid Black, Rectangular, White Classical Relief, 2 1/2 x 7 In. 403.00
Plaque, Jasper Ware, Solid Light Blue, White Muses In Relief, Oval, 3 x 4 In., Pair 489.00
Plaque, Old Man, Majolica, Green Glaze, Rectangular, England, c.1860, 8 x 12 5/8 In. . . . 259.00
Plaque, Queen's Ware, Green, Shakespearean Characters, 3 1/2 x 9 1/8 In., 4 Piece 805.00
Plate, Basalt, Rosso Antico, Hieroglyph Band, Impressed Mark, 19th Century, 7 1/2 In. . . 402.00
Plate, Bird & Fan, 9 In. 150.00
Plate, Cabinet, Jasper Ware, Classical Design, Dark Blue, White, 9 In., Pair 220.00
Plate, Chapoo, Flow Blue, 1850, 9 In. 176.00
Plate, Fallow Deer, Flow Blue, Flowers On Edge, 10 In. 110.00
Plate, Faneuil Hall, Blue & White, 9 In. 70.00
Plate, Fruit Center, Cobalt Blue Border, Arthur Holland, 9 In. 125.00
Plate, Fruit, Turquoise, 8 3/4 In. 275.00
Plate, Green Cabbage Leaf, Wedgwood & Barlaston, 8 In., 12 Piece 258.00
Plate, High Rock Springs, Saratoga Springs, N.Y., Cobalt Blue Indian Design, 9 In. 20.00
Plate, Lobster, 8 1/2 In. 500.00
Plate, Majolica, Openwork Border, Mottled Enamel, Marked, c.1872, 8 5/8 In., Pair 173.00
Plate, Parrot & Butterfly, 9 In. 200.00
Plate, Portrait, Therese Lessore, Pearl Ware, Blue Underglaze, c.1921, 9 3/8 In. 518.00
Plate, Rosso Antico, Stoneware, White, Banded, Hieroglyph Band, Mark, 7 In. 690.00
Plate, Sandman, 6 In. 57.00
Plate, Strawberry Leaf, Turquoise, 9 In. 375.00
Plate, Strawberry, 19th Century, 10 In. 1870.00
Plate, Strawberry, 8 1/2 In. 465.00
Plate, Sunflower, 8 1/2 In. . . . . .200.00 to 225.00
Plate, Trout, Turquoise, 9 In. 550.00
Plate, Washington Bicentennial, Blue, Floral Border, Each Different, 12 Piece Set 165.00
Platter, Hibernia, Pale Blue Center Panel, Grape, Leaf Border, 1830, 13 In. 330.00
Platter, Oriental Design, Urn In Center, Blue Transfer, Oval, 20 3/4 In. 410.00
Platter, Salmon Resting On Bed Of Fern, Turquoise Ground, Signed, 25 In. 3737.00
Plinth, Jasper Ware, Light Green, Panels, Seasons, Bellflower Relief, 19th Century, 5 In. . 345.00
Pot, Hanging, Jasper Dip, Blue, Applied White Relief, England, Late 1800s, 6 1/2 In. 259.00

Potpourri, Pierced Cover, Jasper Dip, Blue, Arabesque Floral, Leaf, Urn Relief, 6 3/4 In. . 1725.00
Potpourri, Pierced Cover, Rosso Antico, Enamel, Allover Flowers, c.1830, 14 3/4 In. 3335.00
Punch Bowl, Butterfly Luster, Chinoiserie Border, Signed, 1920s, 11 In. 690.00
Punch Bowl, Cover, Black Basalt, Engine-Turned Band, Early 19th Century, 7 1/2 In. . . . 460.00
Punch Bowl, Ornamental Bands, Orange Interior, c.1920, 10 1/2 In. 805.00
Punch Bowl, Queen's Ware, Grapevine, Flaring Foot, 1890s, 14 1/4 In. 504.00
Salt Cellar, Majolica, Cobalt Blue Band, Yellow Beadwork, c.1867, 3 1/8 In., Pair 201.00
Scale, Jasper Ware, Pale Blue, Medallion Each Pan, 19th Century, 2 x 4 3/4 In. 862.00
Scent Bottle, Jasper Dip, Dark Blue, White Classical Relief, England, 3 1/4 In. 1035.00
Sconce, 3 Arms, Jasper Ware, Green, Ormolu, Classical Relief, c.1860, 22 1/4 In., Pair . . . 3738.00
Soup, Dish, Indiana, Flow Blue, 10 1/2 In. 125.00
Stirrup Cup, Cane Ware, Hare's Head Shape, Erect Ears, Delineated Fur, 6 In. 10925.00
Syrup, Jasper Ware, Blue & White, Pewter Lid, Signed, 6 1/2 In. 70.00
Tankard, Oak Leaf Body, Dimpled Ground, Silver Mounted, Signed, c.1880, 5 In. 287.00
Tea Infuser, Gilt Trim, Polychrome Leaves, Scroll Handles, Brass, Beanes, 13 1/4 In. 316.00
Tea Set, Black Basalt, Enamel Yellow & Purple Irises, 3 Piece, 3 1/2 x 5 1/2 In. 350.00
Tea Set, Bone China, Gilt, Red Transfer, Stylized Flower, Leaves, Late 1800s, 5 Piece . . . 489.00
Tea Set, Bone China, Green Transfer, Flower & Fruit Panels, Late 1800s, 10 Piece 863.00
Tea Set, Jasper Ware, Blue, Classical Figures, 6 1/2-In. Teapot, 20 Piece 290.00
Tea Set, Yellow Ware, Enameled Flowering Trees, Marked, 5-In. Pot, 3 Piece 55.00
Teakettle, Lobed Bail Handle, Foliate Boarder, Sibyl Finial, 18th Century, 6 1/2 In. 546.00
Teapot, Cover, Jasper Dip, White, Green & Lilac Leaves, Medallions, 4 In. 690.00
Teapot, Jasper Ware, Grecian Women, Children & Cupids, 5 1/2 In. 210.00
Tile, Federal Street Theater, Calendar, 1897 . . . . 135.00
Tray, Jasper Dip, Black, Oval, White Classical Relief, Frame, 1800s, 6 1/2 x 9 1/4 In. . . . 259.00
Tray, Tea, Jasper Dip, Green, Classical Figures, Scrolled Border, 1830s, 15 5/8 In. 747.00
Trophy Vase, Jasper Dip, Dark Blue, White Classical Relief, England, c.1900, 14 3/4 In. . . 978.00
Tureen, Soup, Leaf Form Handles, Mushroom Finial, c.1790, 12 x 16 1/2 In. 1035.00
Umbrella Stand, Majolica, Bonnet Form, Basket Weave Body, c.1879, 21 1/2 In. 2645.00
Urn, Black Basalt, Dancing Hours, Domed Lid, 20th Century, 13 In., Pair 868.00
Urn, Cover, Jasper Ware, Slate Blue, Hercules In Garden Of Hesperides, 22 In. 3900.00
Urn, Trophy, Jasper Ware, Terra-Cotta, White Classical, W. Mieng, 1957, 8 3/4 In. 675.00
Vase, Black Basalt, Classical Design, Cylindrical, 2 1/2 x 6 1/2 In. 57.00
Vase, Black Basalt, Classical Design, Cylindrical, 2 1/8 x 4 7/8 In. 575.00
Vase, Black Basalt, Classical Figural Design, Club Form, 5 In. 51.00
Vase, Blue Luster, Dragon Design, Mother-Of-Pearl Interior, Marked, 8 In. 475.00
Vase, Bone China, Yellow, Enamel, Glazed, Oriental Landscape, c.1915, Pair 431.00
Vase, Cover, Jasper Dip, Apollo, Latin Verse, 200th Anniversary, c.1930, 9 1/2 In. 633.00
Vase, Cover, Jasper Dip, Black, Arabesque Flowers, Cupid, Quiver Finial, 8 5/8 In., Pair . 1150.00
Vase, Cover, Jasper Dip, Black, Dancing Hours, Loop Handles, 7 5/8 In., Pair 460.00
Vase, Cover, Jasper Dip, Dark Blue, Trumpet Shape, Arabesque, Flowers, 7 In. 633.00
Vase, Cover, Jasper Dip, Dice Ware, Black, White, Yellow Quatrefoils, 12 3/4 In., Pair . . . 3680.00
Vase, Cover, Jasper Dip, Light Blue, White Dancing Hours, Lilac, c.1900, 9 5/8 In., Pair . . 1150.00
Vase, Cover, Jasper Ware, Black, Classical Medallions, Festoons, Ram's Head, 12 In. 546.00
Vase, Cover, Jasper Ware, Black, White Classical Figures, Scrolled Handles, 7 3/8 In. 633.00
Vase, Cover, Jasper Ware, Light Blue, Dancing Hours, Bacchus Handles, 8 1/4 In. 431.00
Vase, Cover, Jasper Ware, Light Blue, Dancing Hours, Bacchus Mask Handles, 15 In. 805.00
Vase, Cover, Jasper Ware, Light Blue, Dancing Hours, White Relief, c.1900, 8 3/4 In. 345.00
Vase, Cover, Jasper Ware, Tricolor, White, Mauve Medallions, Leaves, c.1900, 8 7/8 In. . . 978.00
Vase, Cover, Jasper Ware, White, Bacchus Head Handles, Light Blue Relief, 6 3/4 In. 633.00
Vase, Domed Cover, White Flower Swags, Teal Blue, 2 Handles, 1880, 12 In. 2300.00
Vase, Double Gourd Shape, Ivory, Gilt Birds, Porcelain, Enamel, 1800s, 5 In., Pair 316.00
Vase, Earthenware, Gilt, White Slip, 2 Handles, Harry Barnard, c.1900, 11 1/2 In. 345.00
Vase, Folded Rim, Blue Green Matte Glaze, Keith Murray, 10 1/2 In. 715.00
Vase, Glazed Stoneware, Portland, Black, Half-Length Figure, Phrygian Cap, 9 1/2 In. . . . 1035.00
Vase, Jasper Dip, 2 Handles, Classical Trophy & Foliate Relief, c.1900, 10 In., Pair 1840.00
Vase, Jasper Dip, Dark Blue, Portland Shape, White Classical Relief, Marks, 4 In., Pair . . 575.00
Vase, Jasper Dip, Dark Blue, White Classical & Leaf Relief, Mid 1800s, 7 1/2 In. 316.00
Vase, Jasper Dip, Dark Blue, White Classical, 2 Handles, W.M.I.E., 7 3/4 x 5 In., Pair . . . 695.00
Vase, Jasper Dip, Lilac, Drum Shape Plinth, Festoons, Ram's Heads, c.1864, 6 1/2 In. 403.00
Vase, Jasper Dip, Portland Shape, Dark Blue, White Classical Relief, Mid 1800s, 7 In. . . . 316.00
Vase, Jasper Dip, Tricolor, Blue, Lavender, White, Adams & Bromley, c.1875, 10 In. 259.00

Vase, Jasper Ware, Black, Bands Of Black & White Aquatic Plants Border, 3 In. 1300.00
Vase, Jasper Ware, Black, White Muses, Leaf Borders, England, Mid 19th Century, 8 In. .   863.00
Vase, Jasper Ware, Light Blue Ground, Lilac Medallions, White Portraits, 5 In. 345.00
Vase, Jasper Ware, Light Blue, Hand Painted Raised Gilt Design, 19th Century, 10 In. . . .   2875.00
Vase, Jasper Ware, Portland Shape, Solid Black, Half-Figure, Phrygian Cap, 10 1/4 In. . . .   863.00
Vase, Jasper Ware, Solid Pale Blue, Snake Handles, Late 18th Century, 14 In. 2415.00
Vase, Jasper Ware, White Classical Relief & Figure Wearing Phrygian Cap, 11 In. 2700.00
Vase, Krater, Black Basalt, Upturned Loop Handles, Impressed Mark, 1800s, 7 In. 690.00
Vase, Marsden Art Ware, Flowers, Leaves, Buff Ground, c.1885, 14 3/4 In., Pair 805.00
Vase, Marsden Art Ware, Scrolled Foliage, c.1885, 14 1/4 In. 345.00
Vase, Pierced Cover, Jasper Dip, 2 Handles, Light Blue, White Relief, c.1864, 8 1/4 In. . .   546.00
Vase, Portland, Black Basalt, c.1900, 10 1/4 In. 1400.00
Vase, Ships Sailing In Harbor, Blue Transfer Design, 9 1/4 In. 95.00
Vase, Spill, Jasper Dip, Black, Striping, Mid 19th Century, 4 In., Pair 1150.00
Vase, Veronese Ware, Green Ground, Silver Luster Flowers, Marked, c.1935, 8 1/2 In. 144.00
Wall Pocket, Nautilus Shell, Majolica, Insert Lid, c.1863, 10 In.   690.00

WELLER pottery was first made in 1872 in Fultonham, Ohio. The firm
moved to Zanesville, Ohio, in 1882. Art wares were introduced in
1893. Hundreds of lines of pottery were produced, including
Louwelsa, Eocean, Dickens Ware, and Sicardo, before the pottery
closed in 1948.

Alvin, Vase, Pastel, Yellow Ground, 12 In. 75.00
Arcadia, Wall Pocket, Turquoise, 9 1/2 In. 88.00
Ardsley, Planter, Irises, Incised, Pillow, Ink Kiln Mark, 7 x 7 In.   358.00
Ardsley, Wall Pocket, Double, Embossed Cattails & Water Lily, 11 1/2 x 9 1/2 In. 468.00
Art Nouveau, Vase, Birds Holding Lily Bud, Die Stamped, 7 1/4 x 3 1/4 In. 495.00
Art Nouveau, Vase, Embossed Flowers, 4 Sides, Die Stamped, 12 x 4 In. . . . . .220.00 to 320.00
Art Nouveau, Vase, Embossed Flowers, Scalloped Rim, 2 Handles, Pillow, 11 x 9 1/4 In. . .   385.00
Aurelian, Mug, Cherries, Charles Chilcote, c.1900, 6 1/8 In. 275.00
Aurelian, Umbrella Stand, Yellow Irises, Removable Metal Insert, 23 7/8 In. 1650.00
Aurelian, Vase, Yellow Daffodils, Brown, Yellow & Green Ground, Incised, 10 x 4 In. 165.00
Aurelian, Vase, Yellow Roses, Black & Mahogany Ground, Squat, Incised, 4 x 6 In. 358.00
Baldin, Lamp, Base, Tapered, Stamped, 9 x 8 1/2 In. . . . . .165.00 to 220.00
Baldin, Vase, Red, Yellow Apples, Branching, Green Leaves, Tan, Green Ground, 7 In. 175.00
Bank, Fox, Wearing Spectacles, Ceramic, 3 1/4 In. 935.00
Bedford Matte, Umbrella Stand, Embossed, Poppies, Tulips, Green Matte Glaze, 20 In. . . .   825.00
Blue Ware, Jardiniere, Ladies Dancing, Playing Instruments, 7 1/2 In. 286.00
Bouquet, Bowl, Green, 9 x 10 In. 175.00
Brighton, Figurine, Black Crow, 6 1/2 In. 1450.00
Brighton, Figurine, Kingfisher, 9 In. 300.00
Brighton, Figurine, Parakeets, 9 In. 675.00
Brighton, Figurine, Parrot, 12 1/2 In. 675.00
Brighton, Lamp, Mad Parrot 1100.00
Bronzeware, Lamp, Textured Iridescent Violet Glaze, Die Stamped, 10 x 14 In. 385.00
Burntwood, Jardiniere, California Missions Scenes, Brown Banding, 10 In. 175.00
Burntwood, Vase, Embossed, Chariots, Bands, Footed, Flared Rim, 13 x 5 1/2 In. 190.00
Camelot, Vase, Bulbous, Flared Rim, Incised, 4 x 3 1/2 In. 248.00
Camelot, Vase, Ivory, Light Green Matte Glaze, 6 1/2 In. 230.00
Chase, Vase, Cylindrical, Stilt-Pulls, Footed, Incised In Script, 11 3/4 x 6 1/2 In., Pair 358.00
Chengtu, Vase, 9 3/4 In. 135.00
Claywood, Vase, 10 In. 130.00
Coppertone, Bowl, Green & Brown Glaze, 9 In. 220.00
Coppertone, Bowl, Green, Brown Matte Glaze, 8 1/2 In. 330.00
Coppertone, Candlestick, Turtle, 3 In. 400.00
Coppertone, Candlestick, Turtle, Incised Weller Potter, 3 In., Pair 963.00
Coppertone, Console, Frog, 11 1/2 In. 650.00
Coppertone, Console, Perched Frog, Scalloped, 5 1/2 x 8 1/2 In.   1210.00
Coppertone, Console, Turtle, 17 1/2 In. 1300.00
Coppertone, Figure, Frog, Brass Sprinkler, 8 1/2 In. 3000.00
Coppertone, Figurine, Frog, 4 In. 225.00
Coppertone, Figurine, Frog, 6 In. 375.00

Coppertone, Figurine, Frog, Incised Weller Pottery, 2 1/4 In. . . . . .265.00 to 340.00
Coppertone, Figurine, Turtle, 5 1/2 In. . . . . .340.00 to 500.00
Coppertone, Figurine, Turtle, Incised, 4 In. 341.00
Coppertone, Fountain Figure, Frog, Artist's Initial B In Ink, 6 x 6 In. 660.00
Coppertone, Garden Ornament, Owl, Green, Blue Matte Glaze, Mottled, 9 In. 3300.00
Coppertone, Pitcher, Fish Handle, 7 1/2 In. 2000.00
Coppertone, Vase, Climbing Frog, No Mark, 9 3/4 In. 660.00
Coppertone, Vase, Deep Brown, Green Matte Glaze, 2 Handles, 8 In. 415.00
Coppertone, Vase, Flared Foot & Rim, Incised Script, 15 1/4 x 7 In. 1540.00
Coppertone, Vase, Frog Each Side, 8 In. 1700.00
Coppertone, Vase, Green, Brown Matte Glaze, 2 Closed Handles At Shoulder, 8 x 6 In. . . 660.00
Coppertone, Vase, Green, Copper Matte Glaze, 8 In. 495.00
Coppertone, Vase, With Frog, 26 In. 4300.00
Creamware, Basket, Hanging, 11 3/4 x 4 1/4 In. 33.00
Creamware, Vase, Fan, 8 In. 100.00
Dickens Ware I, Green Hydrangea, Dark Brown Ground, Frank Ferrel, 9 x 5 1/4 In. 412.00
Dickens Ware I, Jug, Mt. Vernon Bridge Co., African-American Face, Blue, 6 1/4 In. 385.00
Dickens Ware II, Pitcher, Incised Deer, Antlers, Tan Swirl Along Handle, 11 1/4 In. 660.00
Dickens Ware II, Tobacco Jar, Irishman, Incised Under Lid, 6 1/2 In. 248.00
Dickens Ware II, Tobacco Jar, Turk, Turquoise & Brown Turban, Incised, 7 x 5 In. 1045.00
Dickens Ware II, Vase, Deer Leaping In Woods, Signed Anthony Dunlavy, 7 x 7 1/4 In. . . 413.00
Dickens Ware II, Vase, Fish, Green Ground, 3 Sides, Impressed Mark, 6 3/4 x 5 In. 440.00
Dickens Ware II, Vase, Golfer, Polychrome Matte Glaze, Bottle Shape, 12 In. 1430.00
Dickens Ware II, Vase, Monk, Brown Glossy Glaze, Cylindrical, 10 1/4 x 3 1/2 In. 440.00
Dickens Ware II, Vase, Native American Chief, White Man, L.J. Burgess, 10 x 3 1/2 In. . . 1100.00
Dickens Ware II, Vase, Pillow, Ribbon Garland, 1903, 5 1/4 In. 550.00
Dickens Ware III, Vase, Fat Boy, Corseted, By E. Q., 6 3/4 x 3 In. 495.00
Dickens Ware III, Vase, Mr. Pickwick, Pickwick Papers, Lily Mitchell, 10 1/4 In. 880.00
Eocean, Jardiniere, Pink Nasturtium, Leaves, Celadon Ground, 6 In. 137.00
Eocean, Vase, Blue & Gray Hollyhock, Green Ground, 6 Handles, Signed, 15 1/4 In. 1320.00
Eocean, Vase, Cylinder, Ross, 9 In. 545.00
Eocean, Vase, Gooseberries, Bulbous, Green To Pink Ground, 8 1/4 x 4 1/2 In. 440.00
Eocean, Vase, Gooseberries, Gray Ground, Squat, 5 In. 275.00
Eocean, Vase, Lavender & Celadon Pears, Lavender Ground, Incised, 12 1/4 x 4 1/2 In. . . 880.00
Eocean, Vase, Red, Purple Berries, Celadon Ground, Metu, 10 In. 495.00
Eocean, Vase, Spaniel Portrait, Brown Eyes, Signed, No. 2 . . . . 1540.00
Eocean, Vase, White Clover, Blue Gray Ground, 6 1/2 x 5 In. 363.00
Eocean Rose, Vase, Oval, White Roses, Shaded Black To Gray Ground, 10 x 3 1/2 In. . . . 385.00
Eocean Rose, Vase, Red Roses, Celadon Ground, Cylindrical, 9 1/4 In. 165.00
Eocean Rose, Vase, Tapered, Ivory, Pink & Red Flowers, Shaded Gray Ground, 8 3/4 In. . . 165.00
Etna, Jardiniere, Embossed Blue Irises, Shaded Green Ground, Bulbous, 7 1/2 x 9 In. 193.00
Etna, Jardiniere, Embossed Red Pansies, Shaded Gray Ground, 5 x 6 In. 165.00
Etna, Vase, Flower Underglaze, Embossed Mark, 9 In. 190.00
Etna, Vase, Grapes & Leaves, Corseted, Stamped, 15 x 6 1/4 In. 220.00
Etna, Vase, Grapes, Shaded Green To Gray, Shoulders, 15 1/4 In. 500.00
Etna, Vase, Roses, Olive Branch, Cylindrical, 14 1/2 In. 1225.00
Etna, Vase, White & Yellow Daffodil, Gray To White Ground, Signed, 13 1/2 x 5 1/4 In. . . 715.00
Flemish, Jardiniere, 9 1/2 x 11 1/2 In. 300.00
Flemish, Jardiniere, Pedestal, Parrot 3200.00
Floretta, Vase, Pink Cyclamen, Ivory, Gray Ground, Bulbous, 6 In. 195.00
Forest, Jardiniere, Pedestal, 30 In. 650.00
Forest, Jardiniere, Woodland Scene, 7 x 8 In. 350.00
Forest, Vase, Embossed Trees, Landscape, Corseted, No Mark, 12 x 6 In. 250.00
Forest, Vase, Woodland Design, Blue, Tan, Green Matte Glaze, 8 1/2 In., Pair 230.00
Forest, Wall Pocket, Owl In Tree Trunk, Copper Liner, Die Stamp, 11 x 5 1/2 In. 300.00
Garden Ware, Figurine, Rabbit, 7 1/2 x 13 In. 2300.00
Glendale, Vase, Bird Nesting Beside Lake, Cattails, 12 7/8 In. 1540.00
Glendale, Vase, Embossed Quail & Nest In Glade, Polychrome, Tapered, 11 1/2 x 6 In. . . 825.00
Glendale, Wall Pocket, 2 Birds On Cherry Blossom, Ink Stamp, 7 1/4 x 7 In. 305.00
Glendale, Wall Pocket, Cornucopia, Nesting Birds, Polychrome, 12 1/2 x 6 1/4 In. 525.00
Glendale, Wall Pocket, Wrens On Branch, Polychrome, Cone Shape, 8 3/4 x 5 In. 358.00
Greora, Ginger Jar, Incised Mark, 6 1/4 x 5 In. 140.00

Greora, Vase, Copper, Brown, Green Matte Glaze, 5 1/2 In. 330.00
Greora, Vase, Green To Bronze Glaze, 2 Open Handles, 9 1/2 In. ....220.00 to 495.00
Holland, Vase, Dutch Mother & Child, Windmills & Sailing Ships, 4 Handles, 8 In. 3300.00
Hudson, Vase, Irises, Periwinkle Blue Ground, Signed H. Pillsbury, 9 1/4 x 4 3/4 In. 1100.00
Hudson, Vase, Irises, Yellow, Pink & Purple, Drilled, Signed Mae Timberlake, 15 In. 2310.00
Hudson, Vase, Nightscape, Owl, Full Moon, Stamped, 8 x 5 In. 5555.00
Hudson, Vase, Perfecto Style, Seagulls, Nude Sitting On Rock, Timberlake, 7 5/8 In. 2750.00
Hudson, Vase, Polychrome Iris, Signed Mae Timberlake, Incised, 9 1/2 x 3 1/2 In. 1760.00
Hudson, Vase, Red & Purple Grape Clusters, Blue Ground, Mae Timberlake, 27 x 11 In. . 14300.00
Hudson, Vase, Wild Roses, Sarah Timberlake, 8 5/8 In. 410.00
Hudson, Vase, Yellow & White Roses, Gray & Ivory Ground, Stamped, 13 x 6 1/2 In. ... 990.00
Ivory, Wall Pocket, Embossed Stag's Head, Stamped, 8 3/4 x 6 1/2 In. 250.00
Jap Birdimal, Mug, Blue Gray, Squeezebag, Stylized Cobalt Trees, Rhead, 5 x 4 In. 440.00
Jap Birdimal, Vase, Blue Carp, Green Ground, Squeezebag, Stamped, 6 x 3 1/4 In. 1100.00
Jap Birdimal, Vase, Geisha Playing Samisen, Bottle Shape, Squeezebag, 11 3/4 In. 1045.00
Jap Birdimal, Vase, Stylized Blue Roses, White Geese, Trees, Green Ground, 8 3/4 In. ... 2750.00
Jap Birdimal, Vase, Stylized Trees, Blue Green Ground, Many Sided, 3 In. 410.00
Knifewood, Vase, Embossed Daisies & Butterflies, Textured Ground, Oval, 7 1/4 In. 275.00
La Mar, Vase, Silhouetted Trees, Red Ground, No Mark, 10 1/4 x 4 In. 358.00
La Mar, Wall Pocket, Tree & Landscape, Chinese Orange, Cone Shape, 8 1/2 x 2 1/2 In. .. 330.00
LaSa, Vase, Cylindrical, Tropical Seascape, Iridescent Glaze, 8 1/2 x 3 In. 135.00
LaSa, Vase, Oak Trees In Landscape, Tapered, 6 1/4 x 2 1/2 In. 165.00
LaSa, Vase, Tropical Landscape, Oval, No Mark, 6 1/2 x 3 3/4 In. 495.00
Lavonia, Wall Pocket, Woman Figure, Matte Turquoise Glaze, 12 x 7 In. 330.00
Louwelsa, Bowl, Nasturtium, Marked, c.1905, 5 x 7 In. 50.00
Louwelsa, Ewer, Amber & Orange Corn, Brown Ground, 12 1/2 x 7 In. 248.00
Louwelsa, Ewer, Berry Design, Brown, Green, Orange Ground, 11 In. 165.00
Louwelsa, Ewer, Bulbous, Brown & Green Leaves, Stamped, 7 x 5 In. 275.00
Louwelsa, Ewer, Cascading Grapes, Wine Branch, Brown To Sage, Incised, 6 x 5 In. 220.00
Louwelsa, Ewer, Flower Spray, Stamped, 9 In. 45.00
Louwelsa, Jardiniere, Orange Poppies, Ruffled Rim, Dark Brown Ground, 7 1/4 In. 137.00
Louwelsa, Jardiniere, Orange Tulips, Brown Ground, 9 x 12 1/4 In. 330.00
Louwelsa, Pedestal, Yellow Chrysanthemums, Brown, Green Ground, 16 1/2 In. 247.00
Louwelsa, Vase, Blue Nasturtium, Shaded Blue Ground, Squat, Tapered, 6 1/4 x 8 In. 825.00
Louwelsa, Vase, Blue, Bottle Shape, Cherries & Leaves, Cobalt Ground, 8 1/2 In. 135.00
Louwelsa, Vase, Brown & Gold Crocuses, 9 In. 250.00
Louwelsa, Vase, Mums, Brown, 20 In. 800.00
Louwelsa, Vase, Pillow, Small House, Dirt Path, Clouds, Signed, 7 In. 1100.00
Louwelsa, Vase, Red & Purple Grapes, Hanging From Vine, Frank Ferrell, 18 1/2 In. 1540.00
Louwelsa, Vase, Stylized Leaves, Gray Ground, Bulbous, Stamped, 4 1/2 In. 220.00
Louwelsa, Vase, Wisteria, Shaded Brown Ground, Stilt Pull At Base, 10 3/4 In. 242.00
Louwelsa, Vase, Yellow & Orange Roses, Signed Helen Smith, 11 1/2 x 3 1/4 In. 275.00
Louwelsa, Vase, Yellow Roses, Brown, Yellow Ground, Josephine Inlay, 6 1/2 In. 220.00
Louwelsa, Wall Pocket, Shaded Blue Matte Ground, Roses, Die Stamp, 7 1/4 x 2 1/2 In .. 550.00
Malvern, Vase, Pillow, Bulbous, Stamped, 8 In. 120.00
Mammy, Cookie Jar, 11 In. 2000.00
Muskota, Figure, Fisher Boy, 20 5/8 In. 6325.00
Muskota, Figurine, Kingfisher Frog 125.00
Muskota, Fishing Boy, Flower Frog, Polychrome, 6 In. 330.00
Muskota, Flower Frog, Frog Emerging From Water Lily, No Mark, 4 1/2 x 4 1/2 In. 165.00
Muskota, Vase, Frog & Water Lily Relief, Green Matte Glaze, Bulbous, 7 x 5 1/2 In. 880.00
Novelty, Figurine, Dog, Pop-Eye, Black, 4 In. 650.00
Novelty, Figurine, Dog, Pop-Eye, White, 4 In. 450.00
Novelty, Figurine, Scottie Dog, 12 x 15 In. 2500.00
Novelty, Wall Pocket, Man's Face, White Glaze, 3 Sides, No Mark, 9 1/2 x 5 1/2 In. 195.00
Ollas, Water Bottle, Lid, Red, Cream, D. England, 11 In. 40.00
Perfecto, Tankard, Raspberries, Albert Jaisbroc, c.1900, 12 3/8 In. 660.00
Perfecto, Vase, Baluster, Daffodils, White To Green Ground, D. Laughead Initials, 13 In. . 415.00
Ragenda, Vase, Embossed Drape, Raspberry Matte Glaze, No Mark, 9 1/2 In. 154.00
Rochelle, Vase, Daisies, Lavender Ground, 6 In. 297.00
Roma, Vase, Double Bud, 8 In. 85.00
Roma, Wall Pocket, 10 In. 190.00

Roma, Wall Pocket, Incised Trellis, Pink Roses, 1 Bee, 5 1/2 In. 220.00
Rosemont, Vase, Cockatoos, Rose Clusters, Black Ground, Bulbous, 8 1/2 In. 798.00
Sabrinian, Box, Cover, Seahorse Finial, Signed, 8 1/4 In. 770.00
Sicardo, Jar, Cover, Clover, Purple, Green, Gold Nacreous Glaze, Marked, 4 In. 440.00
Sicardo, Tray, Ring, Abraham Lincoln Face Embossed, Iridescent Purple, 5 1/4 In. 605.00
Sicardo, Vase, Butterflies, Green Glaze, Bronze Ground, Marked, 5 1/2 x 3 In. 220.00
Sicardo, Vase, Cylindrical, 8 3/4 In. 525.00
Sicardo, Vase, Oval, Scrollwork, Purple & Green Glaze, Signed, 7 1/2 x 3 3/4 In. 660.00
Sicardo, Vase, Poppies, Iridescent Gold, Green, Purple, Organic Shape, 4 Lobes, 11 1/2 In. 2945.00
Sicardo, Vase, Squat, Abstract Flowers, Green & Purple Glaze, Signed, 3 1/2 x 5 3/4 In. . .   770.00
Sicardo, Vase, Stylized Flowers, Berries, Iridescent Green, Gold, Purple Glaze, 8 In. 440.00
Sicardo, Vessel, Stylized Flowers, 4 Squares On Each Panel, 4 1/4 In. 660.00
Silvertone, Vase, Pink Poppies, Lavender Ground, Mottled, 2 Handles, 8 1/4 x 7 3/4 In. . . .   275.00
Silvertone, Wall Pocket, Yellow Flowers, Lavender Ground, 10 1/2 In. 410.00
Souevo, Planter, Hanging, Banded Design, Umber, Terra-Cotta, Ivory, Chains, 7 In. 110.00
Stellar, Vase, Blue Ground, Factory Mark, 4 In. 60.00
Stellar, Vase, Blue Stars, White Matte Ground, Incised In Script, 5 1/4 x 5 3/4 In. 248.00
Sydonia, Candlestick, Mottled Green Glaze, Impressed Script Mark, 6 3/4 In., Pair 110.00
Sydonia, Vase, Flared, Mottled Blue Glaze, Green Base, 11 In. 110.00
Turada, Lamp Base, Scroll & Floral, Brown Glaze, Signed, 8 x 10 In. 440.00
Turada, Tobacco Jar, Reticulated Lid, 5 1/2 In. 605.00
Tutone, Wall Pocket, Rose, 11 In. 275.00
Warwick, Vase, Bud, Turquoise, Brown, 7 In. 33.00
Warwick, Wall Pocket, Brown, Green Leaves, 11 1/2 In. 137.00
Wild Rose, Console, Green, 18 x 6 In. 85.00
Wild Rose, Ewer, Peach, 6 3/4 In. 60.00
Woodcraft, Basket, Hanging, Fox Head, 4 1/2 x 9 In. 350.00
Woodcraft, Candlestick, Owl 550.00
Woodcraft, Flower Frog, 2 Fish, Log, 5 x 4 In. 413.00
Woodcraft, Jardiniere, Attached Woodpecker, 5 In. 600.00
Woodcraft, Lamp, Owl Figure, Branches, 2-Light, Stamped, 15 In. 506.00
Woodcraft, Planter, Foxes, With Flower Frog, 6 In. 275.00
Woodcraft, Planter, Spider Line To Base, Pale Green, Light Tan, 8 1/2 In. 192.00
Woodcraft, Smoker Set With Butterfly, 5 In. 675.00
Woodcraft, Tankard, Foxes, 12 1/2 In. 700.00
Woodcraft, Vase, Brown Glaze, Squirrel, Eating Nuts In Tree, 9 1/2 In. 275.00
Woodcraft, Vase, Signed, 10 In. 525.00
Woodcraft, Vase, Tree Trunk, Stamped, 8 1/2 In. 60.00
Woodcraft, Vase, With Crow, 9 In. 450.00
Woodcraft, Wall Pocket, 5 Branch Openings, Tree Trunk Form, 10 In. 75.00
Woodcraft, Wall Pocket, Birds & Flowers, 14 1/2 x 12 1/2 In. 1900.00
Woodcraft, Wall Pocket, Owl, 10 In. 300.00
Woodcraft, Wall Pocket, Squirrel, Kiln Mark, 9 1/2 x 4 1/2 In. 248.00
Woodrose, Vase, 2 Handles, 5 In. 33.00
Xenia, Vase, Red Flowers, Green Ground, Bulbous, Stamped, 5 1/2 In. 468.00
Xenia, Vase, Stylized Pink Flowers, Oval, Impressed Mark, 8 In. 1953.00
Zona, Creamer, Duck, Child's . . . . .75.00 to 150.00
Zona, Jardiniere, Moorish Pattern, Blue Ground, White, Stamped, 9 1/4 x 11 1/4 In. 193.00
Zona, Jardiniere, Pedestal, Kingfisher 2400.00
Zona, Pitcher, Apples, 6 In. 175.00
Zona, Pitcher, Flowers, 7 1/2 In. 175.00
Zona, Pitcher, Kingfisher, Cobalt Blue, 8 In. 125.00
Zona, Pitcher, Kingfisher, Embossed Panels, Polychrome, Ivory Ground, 8 In. 275.00
Zona, Pitcher, Kingfisher, Multicolored, 8 In. 225.00
Zona, Pitcher, Leaves, Frolicking Ducks, Olive Green, Ivory Ground, Bulbous, 7 3/4 In. . . .   230.00

WESTMORELAND GLASS was made by the Westmoreland Glass Company of Grapeville, Pennsylvania, from 1890 to 1984. They made clear and colored glass of many varieties, such as milk glass, pressed glass, and slag glass.

Beaded Edge, Bread Plate, Milk Glass 3.00
Beaded Edge, Enameled, Plate, Milk Glass, 7 In. 12.00
Beaded Edge, Plate, Milk Glass, 8 In. 4.00

Beaded Grape, Bowl, Wedding, Cover, Enameled Roses & Bows, Large 90.00
Beaded Grape, Cake Stand, Milk Glass, Square, 9 1/2 In. 70.00
Cat On Lattice Cover, Dish, Blue Glass Eyes, Milk Glass 110.00
Compote, Marigold, Milk Glass, Flared, Stemmed 175.00
Della Robbia, Candlestick, Ruby Stain, Pair 38.00
English Hobnail, Box, Cover, Milk Glass, 6 In. 20.00
English Hobnail, Cocktail, Round Base, 3 Oz. 8.00
English Hobnail, Cocktail, Square Base, 3 Oz. 8.00
Figurine, Owl, Glass Eyes, Cobalt, Satin 35.00
Figurine, Pouter Pigeon, 2 1/2 In. 25.00
Figurine, Pouter Pigeon, Apricot Mist, 2 1/2 In. 35.00
Lattice Edge, Plate, 10 1/2 In. 45.00
Old Quilt, Candy, Cover 15.00
Old Quilt, Candy, Cover, Milk Glass 22.00
Old Quilt, Cheese Dish, Cover, Milk Glass 55.00
Old Quilt, Compote 20.00
Old Quilt, Goblet, Water, Milk Glass 18.00
Paneled Grape, Ashtray, Milk Glass, Square, Large 18.00
Paneled Grape, Basket, Scalloped Edge, Footed, 10 1/2 In. 90.00
Paneled Grape, Celery Vase, 6 In. 35.00
Paneled Grape, Cup & Saucer 22.00
Paneled Grape, Gravy Boat, Underplate, Milk Glass 40.00
Paneled Grape, Ivy Ball 30.00
Paneled Grape, Pitcher, Milk Glass, 7 3/4 In. 32.00
Paneled Grape, Plate, 8 1/2 In. 18.00
Paneled Grape, Punch Set, Ladle, 16 Cups, 18 Piece 825.00
Paneled Grape, Salt & Pepper, Milk Glass 25.00
Paneled Grape, Sugar & Creamer, Milk Glass, Individual 25.00
Paneled Grape, Vase, Bell Shape, 11 1/2 In. 45.00
Princess Feather, Bowl, Milk Glass, 4 1/2 In. 16.00
Princess Feather, Plate, Milk Glass, 8 In. 8.00
Princess Feather, Wine, Milk Glass, 1 1/2 Oz. 18.00
Ribbon Candy, Compote 30.00
Viking, Sugar & Creamer 95.00

WHEATLEY Pottery was established in 1880. Thomas J. Wheatley had
worked in Cincinnati, Ohio, with the founders of the art pottery movement, including M. Louise McLaughlin of the Rookwood Pottery.
Wheatley Pottery was purchased by the Cambridge Tile Manufacturing Company in 1927.

Bowl, Corseted, Embossed Leaves, Thick Green Matte Glaze, Mark, 2 1/2 x 6 In. 165.00
Bowl, Frothy Green Matte Glaze, Low, 8 1/2 In. 220.00
Bowl, Lotus Leaves, Frothy Green Matte Glaze, 8 1/2 In. 550.00
Bust, Dante, Frothy Green Matte Glaze, 11 1/2 x 15 In. 990.00
Fountain, Frog, Green Matte Glaze, 7 3/4 x 11 1/2 x 8 1/4 In. 935.00
Jardiniere, Tapered Rim, Frothy Green Matte Glaze, 6 x 8 1/2 In. 875.00
Lamp, Black & Green Matte Glaze, Leaded Glass Shade, 21 x 16 In. 3850.00
Lamp, Floral Design, Green Floral Glass Shade, Green Matte Glaze, 16 x 15 In. 2310.00
Lamp, Green Matte Glaze, Slag White Floral Border Glass Shade, Label, 22 In. 6050.00
Pitcher, Pinched Waist, Embossed Grapes & Vines, Frothy Green Matte Glaze, 8 In. 770.00
Stein, Embossed Coat Of Arms, Pretzel Handle, Signed, Green Matte Glaze, 7 In. 165.00
Urn, Bulbous, 2 Handles, Collar Rim, Frothy Green Matte Glaze, 11 x 11 In. 495.00
Vase, Bulbous, Embossed Broad Leaves, Buds, Green Matte Glaze, Incised, 5 1/2 x 7 In. .. 1320.00
Vase, Bulbous, Frothy Green Matte Glaze, 10 x 7 1/2 In. 550.00
Vase, Bulbous, Reptile Around Pot, Hand Carved, Green Matte Glaze, 10 x 9 3/4 In. 1540.00
Vase, Bulbous, Tapered Rim, Frothy Green Matte Glaze, 8 1/4 x 5 1/2 In. 495.00
Vase, Chain Link, Green Organic Matte Glaze, 8 1/2 x 6 1/2 In. 467.00
Vase, Frothy Green Matte Glaze, Tapered Ribbed Rim, 9 3/4 x 6 In. 495.00
Vase, Green Matte Glaze, Stems Supporting Buds, 13 In. 3575.00
Vase, Green Matte Glaze, White, Art Pottery, 10 In. 60.00
Vase, Light Blue Matte Glaze, Dripping Over Exposed Clay, Signed, 26 In. 880.00
Vase, Molded Leaves & Buds On Stems, Green Matte Glaze, Signed, 9 In. 1320.00
Vase, Organic Form, Vertical Leaves Above 3 Flaring Buttresses, Deep Green, 6 In. ... 1320.00

Vase, Organic, 2 Handles, Frothy Green Matte Glaze, 5 3/4 x 7 3/4 In. 2200.00
Vase, Pink Roses, Green Leaves, Gray & Green Ground, Flask Shape, Valentien, 7 In. . . . 415.00
Vase, Pink, Yellow, White Cherry Blossoms, Ivory Mottled Ground, 1880, 7 x 4 In. 467.00

WHIELDON was an English potter who worked alone and with Josiah
Wedgwood in eighteenth-century England. Whieldon made many
pieces in natural shapes, like cauliflowers or cabbages.

Figurine, Swan, Brown & White, 1770, 3 1/2 In. 750.00
Figurine, Swan, Brown & White, c.1760, 3 3/4 In. 595.00
Plate, Mottled Colors, Gadrooned Edge, Creamware, c.1760, 9 1/2 In. 200.00

WILLETS Manufacturing Company of Trenton, New Jersey, began
work in 1879. The company made Belleek in the late 1880s and 1890s
in shapes similar to those used by the Irish Belleek factory. They
stopped working about 1912. A variety of marks were used, all including the name Willets.

Box, Heart Shape, Portrait Top, Belleek, 6 x 5 1/2 In. 195.00
Tankard, Blackberries, Belleek, 15 In. 825.00
Tankard, Grapes, Dragon Handle, Belleek, Signed, E.N. Baker, 11 1/4 In. 625.00
Teapot, Belleek, Ivory, Silver Overlay Windmill Scene 525.00
Vase, Art Nouveau Design, Belleek, 12 In. 325.00
Vase, Chrysanthemums, Belleek, 15 1/2 In. 1050.00
Vase, Roses, Belleek, 16 In. 995.00
Vase, Roses, Belleek, Signed, M. Malyom, 12 In. 1400.00

WILLOW pattern has been made in England since 1780. The pattern has
been copied by factories in many countries, including Germany, Japan,
and the United States. It is still being made. Willow was named for a
pattern that pictures a bridge, birds, willow trees, and a Chinese landscape. Most pieces are blue and white.

Bowl, 5 3/8 In. 2.00
Bowl, Cover, Potato, Shenango 150.00
Bowl, Homer Laughlin, 6 In. 14.00
Bowl, Homer Laughlin, 8 3/4 In. 23.00
Bowl, Vegetable, Oval, Japan, 10 1/2 In. 45.00
Bowl, Vegetable, Round, Homer Laughlin, 8 3/4 In. . . . . .30.00 to 39.00
Bread Plate, Homer Laughlin, 6 1/4 In. 8.00
Bread Plate, Occupied Japan, 6 1/4 In. 7.00
Candle Warmer 65.00
Casserole, Cover, England, 8 x 10 In. 160.00
Chop Plate, Shenango 22.00
Creamer, Homer Laughlin, 3 1/2 In. 22.00
Creamer, Individual 17.00
Cup & Saucer, 2 1/4 In. 11.00
Cup & Saucer, Child's 10.00
Cup & Saucer, Homer Laughlin, 1 3/8 In. 18.00
Cup & Saucer, Homer Laughlin, 2 3/8 In. 18.00
Cup & Saucer, Japan, 2 1/4 In. 12.00
Cup & Saucer, Occupied Japan, 2 1/4 In. 24.00
Ginger Jar, Brown 18.00
Ginger Jar, Japan, 5 1/2 In., Pair 220.00
Gravy Boat, Homer Laughlin . . . . .25.00 to 44.00
Grill Plate, 9 7/8 In. 15.00
Grill Plate, Japan, 10 1/2 In. 14.00
Pepper Shaker 17.00
Plate, 1908, 6 1/8 In. 28.00
Plate, 1915, 10 1/4 In. 100.00
Plate, 6 1/4 In. 6.00
Plate, 7 1/8 In. 8.00
Plate, 7 3/4 In. 14.00
Plate, 9 3/8 In. 8.00
Plate, H & A, 17 1/2 x 14 In. 155.00
Plate, Homer Laughlin, 9 7/8 In. 10.00

Plate, Homer Laughlin, 10 In.	19.00
Platter, 1890, 19 1/2 In.	165.00
Platter, 8 x 10 In.	95.00
Platter, England, 13 x 16 In.	55.00
Platter, England, 21 In.	275.00
Platter, H.A. & Co., England, 11 1/2 In.	110.00
Platter, Homer Laughlin, 15 1/2 In.	37.00
Platter, Ironstone, Marked, Semi-China, England, 13 3/4 In.	55.00
Platter, Oval, 12 3/4 In.	35.00
Platter, Oval, Homer Laughlin, 9 1/2 In.	9.00
Platter, Oval, Homer Laughlin, 11 3/4 In.	22.00
Platter, Oval, Japan, 12 3/4 In.	35.00
Saucer, Occupied Japan	8.00
Soup, Coupe, Homer Laughlin, 8 In.	9.00 to 18.00
Soup, Coupe, Japan, 7 1/2 In.	9.00
Soup, Dish, Homer Laughlin, 8 In.	14.00 to 17.00
Spice Mill	85.00
Sugar, Cover, Handle, Homer Laughlin	38.00
Sugar & Creamer, Tray, Lightning, 3 Piece	150.00
Tea Set, Child's, Occupied Japan	495.00
Undertray, Pierced, Gold Trim, Chinese Export, 19th Century, 11 x 9 1/2 In.	605.00

WINDOW glass that was stained and beveled was popular for houses during the late nineteenth and early twentieth centuries. The old windows became popular with collectors in the 1970s; today, old and new examples are seen.

Diamond Pattern, Amber, Painted Medallion, Gothic Style, 84 x 86 In.	25.00
Frame, Pine, Carved, Frank Lloyd Wright, Louis Sullivan Style, 1894	4400.00
Leaded, Birds Flying, Clouds, Water Lilies, Border, 20th Century, 47 x 21 In.	4025.00
Leaded, Cross & Flowers, John Held, 16 3/4 x 14 In.	300.00
Leaded, Grapevine, Green, Brown, Blue, 20 x 65 In., Pair	3575.00
Leaded, Landscape, Trees, Mountains, River, Slag Glass, Arts & Crafts, 80 x 47 In.	7700.00
Leaded, Memorial, Memory Of Ida R. Smith, Methodist Church, 10 x 51 In.	3630.00
Leaded, Scrolled Leaves, Strapwork, Flowers, Colored Cut Jewels, 43 x 35 In.	134.00
Leaded, Spring Flowers, Rippled Border, Tiffany, 10 1/4 x 13 1/2 In. ....*Illus*	13200.00
Leaded, Stylized Flowers, Clear Geometric Design, Frame, 46 x 23 In.	605.00
Leaded, Stylized Lilies & Tulips, Prairie School, 36 x 16 1/4 In., 5 Piece	4680.00
Leaded, Sunrise Between Mountains, Lake, Walnut Frame, Tiffany Style, 46 x 33 In.	3450.00
Leaded, Tinted & Clear, Green & Salmon, Frame, Prairie School, 65 x 21 In.	1760.00
Leaded, Urn, Floral, Swag, Ribbon Design, Multicolored, 60 x 37 3/4 In., Pair	2760.00
Leaded, Wisteria Branch, Green, Blue Striated Glass, Art Nouveau, 18 x 19 In., Pair	2875.00
Stained Glass, Green Transparent Ground, Mahogany Frame, c.1900, 24 x 18 In.	230.00
Stained Glass, Lyre, Tulips & Floral, Elongated Chain Border, Victorian, 24 x 35 In.	660.00
Stained Glass, Stylized Butterfly Wing, Roses, Oak Frame, 65 x 34 1/2 In., Pair	1815.00

Window, Leaded, Spring Flowers, Rippled Border, Tiffany, 10 1/4 x 13 1/2 In.

Permanent marker stains can be removed from most wood or textiles by wiping with a cloth soaked in rubbing alcohol.

WOOD CARVINGS and wooden pieces are listed separately in this book. Many of the wood carvings are figurines or statues. There are also wooden pieces found in other categories, such as Kitchen.

Alligator, Black, 73 In.	220.00
Angel, Mahogany, 7 1/2 x 12 3/8 In.	185.00
Apostle, Standing, Holding Bible, 15 In.	215.00
Bear, Brass Bowl, Glass Eyes, c.1910, 9 1/4 x 7 1/4 In.	405.00
Bear, Paws Outstretched, Glass Eyes, Painted Mouth, c.1910, 10 In.	1715.00
Bear, Sitting, Tree Trunk On Back, Glass Eyes, Painted Mouth, c.1910, 7 In.	1145.00
Bear, Squatting, Glass Eyes, Painted Mouth, c.1910, 5 In.	185.00
Bearded Man, With Staff, 2 Children, 20 In.	82.50
Bearded Man's Head, On Tree Stump, Young Man's Posterior On Reverse, 38 In.	385.00
Bird, Standing, Long Beak, 43 In.	345.00
Blue Whale, Mounted On Plaque, 8 x 24 In.	330.00
Boar, c.1920, 4 In.	255.00
Buffalo Bill Cody, Old Finish, 1800, Pair	770.00
Busk, Allover Geometric, Initials BC, Pennsylvania Dutch, 1789, 2 3/8 x 12 5/8 In.	285.00
Busk, Susannah Wiggin, Hardwood, Scratched Inscription, 1778, 13 In.	220.00
Bust, Woman, Walnut, Henry Sconbauer, 11 x 17 In.	1265.00
Canada Goose, Swimmer, Clem Widling, 31 In.	210.00
Cherub, Flying, Giltwood, Italy, Mid 19th Century, 11 1/2 In., Pair	990.00
Cherub, Painted, Gilt, Italy, 1700-1725, 20 In., Pair	4950.00
Cherub, Reaching Upward, Oak, Italy, 18th Century, 22 In.	1100.00
Chipmunk, Tack Eyes, Inscribed, Maueby. S P Ziratti, 696, 4 x 8 In.	99.00
Christ Child, Multicolored, Mexico, 19th Century, 6 1/4 In.	105.00
Christ Child, Painted, Glass Eyes, Continental, 22 In.	880.00
Christ With Staff, Olive Wood, Jerusalem On Back, 6 5/8 x 5 3/4 In.	95.00
Cigar Holder, Bulldog With Hat, Glass Eyes	132.00
Clown, Dunce Hat, Life Size, 87 In.	1870.00
Coat Of Arms, Royal, England, 19th Century, 34 1/2 x 26 In.	588.00
Dachshund, Collar With Pendant, c.1950, 8 1/2 x 5 1/4 In.	230.00
Deity, Root, Chinese, 21 In. *Illus*	400.00
Deity, Seated, Headdress, Ormolu, 22 1/2 In.	1380.00
Dignitary, Seated, Dragon Design On Robe, Painted, Chinese, 25 In.	750.00
Dog, Tack Eyes, Laika, Signed Pushinka, 5 x 3 1/2 In.	33.00
Dolphin, Wooden Base, Black, Robert Innis, Dennis, Mass., 11 In.	140.00
Dragon, Far East, 39 In., Pair	990.00
Eagle, 12-In. Wingspread, Fred Tilton, 12 In.	715.00
Eagle, American Shield, Bellamy Style, Painted, 38 In.	2310.00
Eagle, American, Perched On Rock, Glass Eyes, 1880, 32 x 10 In.	3850.00
Eagle, Extended Wings, Strawser, 11 x 21 In.	135.00
Eagle, Folded Wings, Multicolored, Strawser, 9 1/4 In.	85.00
Eagle, Gilt, 20th Century, 15 In.	110.00
Eagle, Multicolored, D.M. Ludwig, 18 x 12 In.	770.00
Eagle, Multicolored, Painted, 24 1/2 In.	1265.00
Eagle, Pine, Wings, Spread, Half Orb Base, 31 1/2 x 26 1/2 In.	3300.00
Female Graces, Children, Walnut, G. Derujinsky, c.1930, 15 1/2 In.	3450.00

**Wooden items should be kept off
a sunny windowsill. Direct sunlight
will harm wood finishes.**

Wood Carving, Deity,
Root, Chinese, 21 In.

Goat, Mahogany, Painted, 33 x 32 In., Pair 715.00
Greyhound, With Rabbit, 11 In. 1100.00
Groundhog, Sitting, 1971, 10 In. 100.00
Group, Madonna & Child, Standing, France, 19th Century, 32 In. 3080.00
Head, Hat Cover, Flowing Hair, Beard, Germany, 19th Century, 17 In. 476.00
Indian Bust, Headdress, Weathered, 13 In. 110.00
Lady Liberty, 19 1/2 In. 330.00
Lions, Reclining, Gilt, 1860, 7 1/2 x 15 1/2 In., Pair 3850.00
Lohan, With Staff & Peach, Root Carving, Chinese, 37 1/2 In. 315.00
Madonna, Anri, 10 3/4 In. 366.00
Madonna, Praying, Painted, Art Deco, France, c.1930, 8 1/2 In. 17.00
Madonna & Child, Seated, Painted, Italy, 19th Century, 53 In. 3575.00
Man, Holding Box, Root, Chinese, 13 In. 175.00
Man, Sitting, Paint Traces, Chinese, 18th Century, 17 x 8 1/4 In. 2000.00
Man, Top Hat, Harpoon, Whale Shape Base, 56 In. 2860.00
Man, Wearing Cape, Sitting On Post, 60 In. 1035.00
Mask, Buddha, Seated On Lotus Throne, Gold Lacquer, 19th Century, 11 1/2 In. 770.00
Mask, Man, Mustache, Painted, 10 1/2 In. 487.00
Mask, Oni, Grinning Expression, 1900, 8 In. 385.00
Mule, Andy Anderson, c.1930, 5 x 6 In. 605.00
Musician Playing Recorder, Gilt, 35 In. 175.00
Owl, Perched On Branch, Glass Eyes, Round Base, c.1910, 20 1/2 In. 1030.00
Plaque, American Eagle, Glass Eye, 14 x 12 1/2 In. 90.00
Plaque, Caesar, Profile, France, Early 20th Century, 14 In. 1760.00
Plaque, Indian, In Desert, Dee Flag, c.1940, 20 x 21 In. 250.00
Plaque, Maiden, Sleeping, 18 In., Pair 175.00
Plaque, Satyr, Fierce Expression, 29 x 20 In. 880.00
Rabbit, Wearing Apron, Early 1900s, 29 3/4 In. 285.00
Robin, James Lapham, Dennisport, Massachusetts 275.00
Rooster, Brown Patina, Orange, Red, Black, 25 1/2 x 15 In. 220.00
Rooster, Multicolored, D.M. Ludwig, 12 In. 165.00
Saint Francis, Pine, Holding Bird, Birds At Feet, Spanish Colonial, 39 In. 1265.00
Smoking Set, Boar Shape, Hinged, 19th Century, 4 In. 230.00
Soldier's Head, Plume Hat, Gold Braid, 20th Century, 36 In. 305.00
Sperm Whale, Robert Innis, Wooden Base, Dennis, Mass., 12 In. 300.00
Swan, Pine, Painted, 20th Century, 19 x 25 In. 3162.00
Tableau, Hunter, Bird In Tree, 10 In. 385.00
Torso, Nude, Leaves, Continental, 18th Century, 25 In., Pair 3080.00
Train, Steam Engine, Tender, Boston & Maine, Painted Black, 38 1/2 In. 1320.00
Warriors, In Battle, Gilt, Glass, Plinth Base, Siam, 53 In. 330.00
Wild Boar, Wooden Base, Continental, 8 1/2 x 8 In. 195.00
Wolf, Henry Larume, 1940s-1950s, 10 In. 385.00

WOODEN wares were used in all parts of the home. Wood was used for many containers and tools. Small wooden pieces are called *treenware* in England, but the term woodenware is more common in the United States. Additional pieces may be found in the Advertising, Kitchen, and Tool categories.

Beaker, Troika Scene, Painted, Russia, c.1900, 3 In. 110.00
Book Rack, Folding, Floral & Leaf Panels, Gilt Metal, England, 8 x 16 In. 1210.00
Bootjack, Tiger Maple, Brown Paint, Rosehead Nails, Inscribed AM 1763 .... 595.00
Bowl, Ash Burl, Dark Finish, 8 x 3 1/2 In. 220.00
Bowl, Ash Burl, Fissures, 16 x 6 In. 1210.00
Bowl, Burl, 4 x 9 1/4 In. 175.00
Bowl, Burl, Handles, 1700s, 24 1/2 x 21 1/2 x 6 1/2 In. 13225.00
Bowl, Burlwood, Turned, 6 In. 470.00
Bowl, Curly Maple, 19th Century, 21 x 12 In. 231.00
Bowl, Dough, Burl, 19th Century, 6 x 20 1/2 In. 805.00
Bowl, Dough, Fruitwood, Provincial, France, c.1900, 19 1/2 In. .... 165.00 to 250.00
Bowl, Flared, Green, Red Trim, 19th Century, 3 1/4 x 10 1/2 In. 315.00
Bowl, Globe, Zigzag Bands, Relief Figure, Dogon, Mali, 26 In. 430.00
Bowl, Hardwood, Treen, Footed, Provincial, France, 19th Century, 10 1/4 In. 99.00
Bowl, Hardwood, Treen, Provincial, France, 19th Century, 15 1/2 In. 88.00

Bowl, Hardwood, Treen, Provincial, France, 19th Century, 22 In. 99.00
Bowl, Koa, Oval, Hawaii, 2 x 4 In. 575.00
Bowl, Lignum Vitae, Cover, Finial, Pedestal, 11 x 8 1/4 In. 1200.00
Bowl, Painted, Green, Yellow Band, Handles, 3 x 10 x 6 In. 121.00
Bowl, Treen, Gray Patina, 20 x 21 x 7 In. 190.00
Bowl, Treen, Yellow, 13 3/4 x 4 In. 357.00
Bucket, Fir, Lacquered, Lotus Flower Handle, 11 x 13 x 13 In. 100.00
Bucket, Mahogany, Brass Bands, Liner, 1860s, 17 1/2 In. 2587.00
Bucket, Peat, Mahogany, Bail Handles, Lead Liner, 1830s, 14 In. 2185.00
Bucket, Red Paint, Hoops, Swing Handle, 12 x 9 1/4 In. 2185.00
Bucket, Sand, Good Girl, 4 x 5 1/2 In. 465.00
Bucket, Stave & Hoop, Pegged, Swing Handle, 16 x 12 1/4 In. 489.00
Bucket, Stave Construction, Bands, Cover 55.00
Bucket, Stave Construction, Tan & Yellow Grained, Handle, 11 1/2 x 9 In. 55.00
Bucket, Storage, Fir, Cover, Ching Dynasty, 10 x 10 x 9 In. 175.00
Bucket, Sugar, Cover, Green Paint, Handle 525.00
Bucket, Sugar, Flowers, Painted Iron Bands, Salmon Grained, Jos. Long Lehn, 8 1/2 In. . . . 1650.00
Bucket, Sugar, Grain, Vine & Berry, Iron Bands, Yellow & Red, 19th Century, 8 In. 1210.00
Bucket, Sugar, Stave Construction, 12 In. 138.00
Bucket, Sugar, Stave Construction, 14 In. 385.00
Bucket, Sugar, Stave Construction, Metal Bands, Wired Bail Handle, Grip, 9 1/2 In. 85.00
Bucket, Sugar, Stave Construction, Red, 13 In. 165.00
Bucket, Sugar, Stave Construction, Wooden Handle, Wire Bail, Label, 7 1/2 In. 120.00
Bucket, Well, Bamboo, Curved Handle, 20th Century, 30 x 16 In. 55.00
Bucket, Well, Bamboo, Red Tint, Oval, 22 3/4 x 16 1/2 In. 55.00
Butter Tub, Chip Carved Rim, Sycamore, c.1830, 4 1/8 In. 165.00
Canister, Flower, Trailing Vines, Salmon Ground, Jos. Long Lehn, 3 1/2 In. 1439.00
Canteen, Blue, Wrought Iron Bands & Chain, Revolutionary War, 5 1/2 In. 425.00
Canteen, Buttonholed Bands, Initials Each Side, Mid 18th Century 195.00
Canteen, Drum, Shaker Barrel Hoop Design, Pewter Neck, Late 1700s, 8 1/2 x 5 1/2 In. . . 688.00
Canteen, Oak, Iron Bands, Signed, 1805, 8 In. 295.00
Canteen, Red Paint, Original Bung, Revolutionary War, 18 1/2 In. 450.00
Card Case, Sandalwood, Floral, Sunken Medallions Reverse, 4 1/2 In. 120.00
Card Case, Sandalwood, Landscape Scene, Chinese, 1830, 4 1/2 In. 130.00
Carrier, Oak, Pegged, Handles, Oval, Norway, 30 x 18 x 7 In. 595.00
Cart, Peddler's, Forged Iron Fittings, Red Paint 467.00
Charger, Serving, Ash, Treen, Light Finish, 19th Century, 21 In. 225.00
Cheese Cradle, Mahogany, Leather Casters, Rosette Buttons, Regency, c.1820, 18 x 8 In. . . 2250.00
Chicken Coop, Mixed Woods, Provincial, France 385.00
Cigar Mold, American, 11 7/8 x 4 7/8 In. 85.00
Decanter Set, Treenware, Footed Cup, 9 Piece 850.00
Dipper, Burl, Carved, Pierced Handle, American, 19th Century, 8 In. 173.00
Dresser Set, Ebony, 3 Brushes, Shoehorn, Box With Pincushion Lid, France, 5 Piece 90.00
Dummy Board, Victorian Woman, 41 In. . . . . Illus 850.00
Eggcup, Strawberries, Salmon Ground, Emma, Jos. Long Lehn, 2 In. . . . . 1210.00 to 1870.00
Eggcup, Yellow, Salmon Ground, Leaves, Jos. Long Lehn, 3 In. 660.00
Firkin, Cover, Blue Paint, Swing Handle, 9 1/4 x 9 In. 245.00

To remove the odor from a wooden bowl, try washing it with baking soda or vinegar and then airing it in sunlight. As a last resort, use diluted household bleach. Soak the bowl for about 15 minutes, then rinse with full-strength vinegar, then clear water. If this does not remove the odor, repeat the process with a stronger solution of bleach.

Wooden, Dummy Board,
Victorian Woman, 41 In.

Firkin, Tapered Cylinder, Painted Green, American, Late 1800s, 12 x 12 1/4 In. 201.00
Frame, Heart Shape, Scrolled Arms Base, Varnish, 7 1/8 In., Pair 385.00
Frame, Rosewood, Ormolu, 8 Sides, A.F., 5 3/4 x 4 5/8 In. 220.00
Goblet, Brown Paint, 18th Century, 6 1/4 In. 195.00
Humidor, Oak, Silver Plate Trim, Ceramic Lining, 6 1/4 In. 70.00
Humidor, Walnut, Brass Inlay, Inlaid Plaque On Lid, Carry Handles, England, 7 x 14 In. . . 550.00
Humidor, Walnut, Top Over Doors, Opening To Drawers, Carrying Handles, 13 In. 1495.00
Jar, Cover, Poplar, Lehnware, Flowers, Strawberries, 5 1/8 In. 1070.00
Jar, Poplar, Brown Sponging, Yellow Ground, 4 3/4 In 165.00
Kovsh, Double Handle, Horse Heads, Carved, Russia, c.1910, 7 In. 140.00
Kovsh, Scrolling Foliage, Birds, Russia, c.1910, 12 In. 310.00
Measure, Green Paint, Metal Bands, Small 70.00
Mold, Gorilla Head, For Making Papier-Mache Mask, Late 1800s, 5 x 3 1/2 x 8 In. 110.00
Mortar, Ring-Turned Base, Early 19th Century, 10 1/4 In. 460.00
Mortar & Pestle, Burl, Mortar, 7 1/2 In. 360.00
Mug, Burl, Child's, New England, 18th Century, 2 3/8 In. 375.00
Page Turner, Walnut, Figural Handle, Confederate Soldier, 15 1/2 In. 83.00
Pail, Herring, Cover, Stave Construction, Varnished, 6 3/4 In. 25.00
Pencil Holder, Barrel Shape, Kremlin Walls, Incised, Painted, 3 1/2 In. 67.00
Pipe Holder, Brass Inlay, Applied Design, Continental, 18th Century, 9 In. 460.00
Pipe Holder, Brass Inlay, Continental, 18th Century, 11 1/2 In. 460.00
Pipe Holder, Figures, Animals, Flowers, Initials AHSW, Continental, 7 1/4 In. 1840.00
Pipe Holder, Snake Design, Continental, 18th Century, 11 In. 290.00
Planter, Floral & Scroll Design, Paw Feet, Tin Liner, 30 In. 1500.00
Plate, Treenware, 8 3/4 In. 330.00
Propeller, Airplane, 6 Ft. 675.00
Reliquary, Figural, Saint, Glazed Viewing Chamber In Chest, Giltwood, Italy, 13 In. 1980.00
Saki Set, Treen, Decanter, 6 Cups 27.50
Scoop, Brass Reinforcers, Treen Handle, 19th Century, 4 1/2 x 12 In. 85.00
Shadowbox, Pine, Painted Design, Bun Footed, 1840, 13 x 18 x 5 1/2 In. 1850.00
Shoes, Size 8, 12 1/4 In. 80.00
Spoon, Cream, Enameled, 19th Century, 7 1/4 In. 168.00
Stein, 2 Lions, Shield Shape, Pewter Lid, 1 Liter 632.00
Stein, Animals In Forest, Engraved, Wooden Lid, 1860, 1 Liter 880.00
Stein, Scroll Design, Pewter Coin In Center Of Lid, 1 Liter 632.00
Target, St. Hubertus & Floral Design, Painted, F.R. Fruchtl, 1898, 23 In. 750.00
Tea Tray, Inlaid Satinwood, Gilt Bronze Handles, Musical Design, George III, 26 In. 920.00
Tray, Cutlery, 2 Compartments, Divided, Handle, Blue, Red, 5 x 9 In. 977.00
Tray, Cutlery, Inlaid Mosaic, Eagle Heads, Flags, Divided, 5 1/2 x 13 x 9 In. 2530.00
Tray, Cutlery, Pine, Shaped Divider, Whimsical Painting, 12 3/4 x 11 In. 8625.00
Tray, Inlaid Design, Horse Center, Multicolored Wood, Mahogany Gallery, 14 x 24 In. . . . 330.00
Triptych, Carved, Brass Reserves, Inset Scenes, 19th Century, 17 1/4 x 22 3/4 In. 865.00
Tub, Coppered, Wooden Loops, Painted, Oval, 19th Century, 7 x 16 x 11 In. 315.00
Urn, Giltwood, Italy, 19 x 13 In., Pair 495.00
Urn, Knife, Checker, Crossbanded, Fitted Interior, George III, 25 1/2 In. 4600.00
Urn, Swag Design, Italy, 40 In., Pair 3630.00
Vase, Carved Chamois & Tree, White & Clear Glass Inserts, c.1910, 17 In. 450.00
Wall Box, Slanted Lift Top, Drawer, Red Paint, American, 19th Century, 13 1/2 In. 1610.00
Wall Bracket, Men, Ancient Clothes, Gessoed, Polychrome, Continental, Pair 3735.00
Wall Pocket, Snow Scene, Home Sweet Home, 19th Century, 22 x 23 In. 3410.00
Wall Pocket, Walnut, Open Work, Star, Hinges, Victorian 310.00
Wheelbarrow, Cranberry Worker's, Red Paint, Iron Wheel, 62 In. 300.00
Wheelbarrow, Red, Black Striping 1210.00
Wheelbarrow, Rosewood, Graining, Yellow Striping, 12 In. 70.00

WORCESTER porcelains were made in Worcester, England, from 1751.
The firm went through many name changes and eventually, in 1862,
became The Royal Worcester Porcelain Company Ltd. Collectors
often refer to *Dr. Wall*, Barr, *Flight*, and other names that indicate time
periods or artists at the factory. It became part of Royal Worcester
Spode Ltd. in 1976. Related pieces may be found in the Royal Worcester category.

Basket, Chestnut, Cover, Stand, Yellow Border, Yellow Twig Handles, 1765, 10 In. 2875.00

Basket, Floral Sprays & Sprigs, Iron Red, Purple, Green Floral Border, 1770, 7 In. 1610.00
Bowl, Slop, Japan, Floral, Flight, Barr & Barr, 1810, 7 1/2 In. 920.00
Candlesnuffer, Owl, Peeking Out, 3 1/8 In. 225.00
Creamer, Floral Finial, Blue Floral & Insect Designs, Cover, 18th Century, 5 In. 173.00
Creamer, Waiting Chinaman, Blue Decorated Underglaze, 18th Century, 6 1/2 In. 748.00
Cup & Saucer, Exotic Birds, Hand Painted, Blue Ground, 1755-1775, 5 In. 450.00
Cup & Saucer, Hop Trellis, Red Berry Leafy Swags, Puce, Gilt Trellis, 1770, 6 In. 1150.00
Dish, 4 Elephant-Head Feet, Scrolled Leaf Design, Cream Ground, Gilt Rim, 10 In. 575.00
Dish, Blue Chantilly Sprig Underglaze, Crescent Mark, 1700s, 9 1/2 In. 317.00
Dish, Dessert, Armorial, Square, Scalloped, Flight & Barr, 1801, 9 1/4 In. 2300.00
Dish, Sweetmeat, Blind Earl, 2 Oriental Figures Standing By Large Urn, 1758, 6 In. 920.00
Dish, Sweetmeat, Blind Earl, Cell-Diaper Border, Rose Branch Handle, 6 5/8 In. 1610.00
Dish, Sweetmeat, Oriental Flowering Plant Growing Amidst Grasses, 5 In., Pair 920.00
Dish, Vine Leaf, 2 Overlapping Leaves, Green, Brown Twig Handle, 8 In., Pair 4310.00
Inkstand, Panel Of Feathers, 3 Penholders, Sander, Dolphin Handle, c.1812, 6 In. 4025.00
Jug, Armorial, Cabbage Leaf Mask, Overlapping Leaves, Gilt Foliate, 1775, 10 In. 10060.00
Jug, Cream, Chelsea Ewer, Floral Sprays & Sprigs, Puce, Green Border, 3 3/8 In. 520.00
Jug, Milk, Japan, Oriental River Garden, Exotic Birds, Flight, Barr & Barr, 5 In. 2585.00
Mug, Parrot Perched Upon Branch, Above Row Of Fruit, Blue, White, 5 3/4 In. 287.00
Pitcher, Milk, Gilt Borders, Floral, Chamberlain, 1845, 5 1/2 In. 518.00
Plate, Blind Earl, Insects & Butterflies, Scalloped Rim, 1770, 7 5/8 In. 2300.00
Plate, Cabinet, Ornithological, Songbird, Turquoise & Gilt Edge, c.1840, 9 In., 8 Piece .. 1430.00
Plate, Central Flower Head Medallion, Flight, Barr & Barr, c.1820, 9 In., 12 Piece 1840.00
Plate, Central Spray Of Blackberries, 3 Exotic Birds, Perched, 1770, 9 In. 2875.00
Plate, Colorful Floral Sprays & Sprigs, Blue, Scalloped, 1770, 7 In. 1035.00
Plate, Loose Bouquet & Sprigs Of Summer Flowers, Scalloped, 1770, 7 In. 575.00
Plate, Pinecone, Blue Decorated Underglaze, 18th Century, 9 3/4 In. 173.00
Platter, Imari Palette, Flowering Plants, Flight, Barr & Barr, 10 In., Pair 1265.00
Platter, Royal Lily, Blue Radiating Foliate Panels, Blue Oval Medallion, 12 In. 460.00
Punch Bowl, House, Landscape Scenes, Latticework Band Rim, Blue, White, 9 In. 431.00
Sauceboat, Blue Flowers, Cell Border, Molded, 18th Century, 5 1/4 In. 288.00
Sauceboat, Fashionable Dressed Figure, Scattered Insects Interior, c.1754, 8 In. 2587.00
Sauceboat, Leaf Shape, Overlapping Rose Veined Leaves, Green, 1762, 7 In., Pair 1150.00
Soup, Dish, Chinese Pheasant-And-Flower, 1852, 10 In., 10 Piece 220.00
Sweetmeat, Stand, Shell Form, Modeled Shells, Coral, Seaweed, 1770, 6 In. 2585.00
Sweetmeat, Stand, Shell Form, Modeled Shells, Coral, Seaweed, 1770, 8 In. 5175.00
Teapot, Cover, Sprays & Sprigs, Orange, Blue, Yellow, Butterflies, Loop Handle, 5 In. 920.00
Teapot, Domed Cover, Sprays Of Flowers, Entwined Handle, Fluted Spout, 7 In. 805.00
Teapot, Vase Of Flowers, Bat, 5 In. 210.00
Teapot Stand, Bengal Tiger, 4 Alternating Panels Of Beasts, Gilt Rim, 1805, 7 In. 920.00
Tureen, Pinecone Underglaze, Artichoke Finial, Shell Handles, Stand, 1700s, 10 1/2 In. .. 805.00
Tureen, Soup, Cover, Underplate, Gothic Arch, Oval, 20th Century, 19 x 10 In. 390.00
Tureen, Soup, Stand, Pinecone, Shell Form Handles, Bud Knop, c.1775, 12 1/2 In. 1840.00
Vase, Bud, Yellow, Allover Gilt Vines, Squatty, Short Fluted Neck, 1887, 3 1/4 In. 245.00
Vase, C-Scroll, Still Life Surround, Cobalt Blue, Urn Shape, R. Sebright, 10 1/2 In. 905.00
Vase, Polychrome Floral, Dolphin Design, Cream Ground, 2 Handles, 11 In. 200.00

WORLD WAR I and World War II souvenirs are collected today. Be
careful not to store anything that includes live ammunition. Your local
police will tell you how to dispose of the explosives. See also Sword
and Trench Art.

WORLD WAR I, Badge, Wound, Die Struck, Magnetic Iron, Black, Germany 20.00
Banner, Welcome Veterans, Disabled American, Stiff Cotton, 11 x 17 In. 12.00
Button, Welcome Home, Liberty 79th Division, 1 1/4 In. 10.00
Canteen, Water, Tin, Connecting Chain 95.00
Chest, Handmade, Green, Lt. Col. James Cochrun, 2nd U.S. Army, 18 1/2 x 13 x 32 In. .. 66.00
Cigarette Holder Set, Kriegs, Celluloid, Paper Cones, Cellophane Package, 6 Piece 30.00
Coat, POW Issue, U.S. Army, Cotton, Standard M1917 Pattern 45.00
Dagger, Trench, French Nail, England 150.00
Hat, Campaign, Officer's 50.00
Medal, Goddess Comforting Mother With Child, Soldiers, Germany 25.00
Medal, Goetz Canine Service, Dog, Cross On Collar, German Inscription 200.00
Medal, Hofrat Dr. Carl Uhl, Goddess, With Snake, Wounded Soldier, 1916 .... 140.00

Medal, Medical Care, People Treating Wounded, Remenyi Jozsef, 1916 . . . . 150.00
Medal, Purple Heart 98.00
Medical Kit, Auxiliary Eye Case V. Mueller & Co., Original Case, 30 Tools, 1918 . . . . . . 310.00
Pants, Enlisted Man's 25.00
Photograph Album, German, 64th Feld Flieger Abteilung, 324 Photos, 1915-1916 . . . . . . 935.00
Poster, Buy U.S. Government Bonds, 3rd Liberty Loan, S. Riesenberg 345.00
Poster, For Action, Enlist In Air Service, Airplane, Propeller, 19 x 25 1/4 In. 630.00
Poster, Gee, I Wish I Were A Man, I'd Join The Navy, Female Sailor, 1918, 26 x 41 In. . . 1955.00
Poster, Help The Horse, Save The Soldier, Fortunino Matania, 1917, 20 x 30 In. 1265.00
Poster, I Want You For U.S. Army, James Montgomery Flagg, 1917, 30 x 40 In. 3910.00
Poster, Join Navy, Sailor In Blue, Riding Bareback, Orange Torpedo, 1917, 27 x 39 In. . . 630.00
Poster, Join The Air Service, Color 660.00
Poster, On The Job For Victory, Lithograph, 29 1/2 x 38 1/2 In. 250.00
Poster, Women Wanted Urgently, Enlisting In The WAACS, 19 x 29 In. 575.00
Pouch, Ammo, Rifle, 3 Pocket, Brown Leather 20.00
Print, American Soldiers On The Attack, Lithograph, 36 x 28 In. 330.00
Ribbon, Hungarian War Service, 16 In. 10.00
Ribbon, Karl Troop Cross, Red On White Design, 16 In. 8.00
Saber, U.S.M.C., Black Handguard, Black Checkered Handle, 34 3/4-In. Blade, 1918 . . . . 345.00
Shoe Polish, Froeschkoenig-Lederfett, Semisolid Compound 20.00
Sword, Officer's, French Infantry, Rhinoceros Horn Grip, 31 1/2-In. Blade 325.00
Wings, Pilot, U.S. In Shield 225.00
WORLD WAR II, Badge, German Armored Assault 750.00
Badge, Wound, Steel, Black Paint, Stamped 25.00
Bank, German Nazi Collection Canister, Handle, Tin, 6 1/2 In. 110.00
Bank, Hitler Pig, Composition, Otis Lawson Co., 1942, 4 1/2 In. 160.00
Bayonet, Leather & Steel Scabbard, Germany 140.00
Boots, Combat, Boondockers, U.S.M.C. 88.00
Boots, Paratrooper 300.00
Boots, Rubber, Black, Wehrmacht, Marked Gr. 9IX 1944, 16 In. 200.00
Box, Cigarette, Special Oriental Blend Tobaccos, Swastika, Eagle, 24 Piece 25.00
Box, Hairpin Kit, Vicky Victory, Help Uncle Sam Save Steel, 75 Piece 7.00
Bread Bag, Nazi, Rings & Buckles, Blue & Gray 45.00
Breeches, Riding, Gray Leather, Button Calves, Back Pocket 125.00
Broadside, Hindenburg's 1932 Campaign, Anti-Hitler, Multicolored 440.00
Buckle, Brazilian Army Officer, Stars, Leaves, Bronze Finish, 2 Piece 15.00
Buckle, Hitler Youth, Nickeled Steel, Inset, Celluloid, NSDAP Flag 75.00
Bugle, Japan 195.00
Canteen, Field, Germany 35.00
Canteen, Nazi, Gray Wool Cover, Leather Strap, Metal Cup 35.00
Card, Playing, Albina Hell Shipyard, Double, Box 45.00
Chamber Pot, Hitler Caricature, Chums, What Would You Do, England, 2 1/4 In. 68.00
Chamber Pot, Stalin, Caricature, Peace On Stalin, 1 7/8 In. 68.00
Clock, V For Victory, Eagle Top, Wooden, Howard Clock Co., 12 1/2 In. 50.00
Coat, POW, Cotton, US Issue 45.00
Compass, Wrist, Corps Of Engineers 50.00
Dagger, Luftwaffe 2nd, Alcosa Blade 295.00
Dagger, Nazi, Rad Hewer, Stag Handle, Eickhorn 575.00
Dagger & Scabbard, Hitler Youth, 5 1/2 In. 44.00
Decal, Police Vehicle, Silver Eagle, Swastika, Germany, 1933-1945, 5 In. 35.00
Dog Tag, Auschwitz, Serial Number On Reverse 450.00
First Aid Kit, Field 95.00
Flag, Keep 'Em Flying, Remember Pearl Harbor, Wooden Base, 9 In. 35.00
Flashlight, Sliding Lens Filters In Red, Blue & Green, Hanging Hook 50.00
Flight Helmet, Goggles, Type A-11 . . . . 215.00
Flight Helmet, Luftwaffe, Summer Issue 350.00
Game, Atomic Bomb, Heading Towards Japan, Under Glass, 3 1/4 In. 50.00
Goggles, Flight, U.S.N., Type M-1944 . . . . 25.00
Goggles, Flying, Gray Elastic Band, Adjustable, Rubber Cups, Germany 150.00
Helmet, Gladiator, Nazi Luftschutz, Gray Paint, 3 Piece 50.00
Helmet, Tanker, Green, Chin Strap & Liner, Ear Piece, Brazil 50.00
Jacket, 101st Air Borne, Major Oak Leaf, Airborne Wings, Patch 185.00
Jacket, Fighter Pilot's, USS Hornet, Leather, Reversible 1450.00

Jacket, Flight, 7th Bomber Group, Brown Leather, 48 Star Flag Back, Medium 460.00
Jacket, Flight, AAF, Type AN-J-4 .... 615.00
K Rations, Dinner 120.00
Medal, Czechoslovakian Occupation, Bronze, Ribbon 75.00
Medal, Service, Kriegsverdienst, Ribbon, Germany, 1939 .... 10.00
Mess Kit, Army, Metal, Handle, 3rd Reich 30.00
Microphone, T-17-D, Box 25.00
Mother's Cross, Bronze, Awarded To Woman Who Had Children, Germany 35.00
Oxygen Mask, Demand, Type A-14, 1944 .... 240.00
Oxygen Mask, Luftwaffe ....500.00 to 750.00
Oxygen Mask, Type A-10, 1944 .... 325.00
Pants, Don't Get Caught With Your Pants Down, Pearl Harbor, 5 1/2 In. 40.00
Pants, Shoot The Pants Off JapaNazi, Hitler & Tojo Picture, Silk, 5 3/4 In. 58.00
Parachute, U.S.N. 165.00
Parachute Harness, Pack, Irvin Chest Pack Pattern, AAF 455.00
Parka, Hood, National Flag On Sleeves, Polycotton Shell 35.00
Pillow, 5th Army, Italy, 1944 .... 25.00
Pin, God Bless Our Boys, For U.S.A. Let's All Help, Red, White & Blue, 3 3/8 In. 10.00
Pin, Kilroy Was Here, Cast Iron 75.00
Pin, Nazi Party Membership, Painted, RZM 14.00
Pin, Nazi, Plastic, Pinback, 1938, 1 1/2 In. 20.00
Pin, War Loan, 1944, 3/4 In. 5.00
Postcard, Hermann Goering, General Feld Marschall, Uniform 10.00
Postcard, V, Strive For Victory, Soldiers Marching On Beach, Battleships 15.00
Poster, Adolf Hitler, 1943, 33 x 23 In. 300.00
Poster, Confidence, Franklin D. Roosevelt, Boat Scene, 18 x 24 In. 9.00
Poster, Mein Kampf, Adolf Hitler Picture, Book, 1930s, 13 x 20 In. ....35.00 to 50.00
Poster, War Is Hell!, Black G.I. Cradling Wounded White G.I., 17 x 22 In. 258.00
Poster, Welcome Home, Herzlich Wilkommen, 1939 Iron Cross, Germany, 36 x 12 In. ... 75.00
Poster, When Women Decide, This War Should End, Orange, Blue, 11 x 17 In. 36.00
Pouch, Ammo, Black Leather, 3 Pocket, Riveted Straps, Germany 25.00
Purple Heart, Ribbon Bar, Lapel Device, Slot Brooch Mounted, Cased 28.00
Rain Cap, U-Boat, Rubberized Canvas, Gray, 3rd Reich 125.00
Scarf, Hitler Youth, Black, JH, DJ Tag 75.00
Sheet Music, Remember Pearl Harbor, Navy Bugler, War Planes, 1941 .... 23.00
Sheet Music, They Started Somethin', But We're Gonna End It, 1942, 9 x 12 In. 23.00
Sheet Music, You're A Sap, Mister Jap, Uncle Sam Smacking Tojo 25.00
Sign, Collection Jar, Regal Pale, Save Caps To Beat Japs, 1940s 18.00
Stamp, Hitler Cartoon, Help Lick 'Em, Red, Black, Kinsmen Club War Services 15.00
Uniform, Medical Corps, 1944 .... 35.00
Uniform, Nazi Army Generals 2500.00
Wings, Nurse, N In Center, On Card, N.S. Meyer, Inc., New York 145.00
Wings, Senior Pilot, Star Above Shield 285.00

WORLD'S FAIR souvenirs from all of the fairs are collected. The first
fair was the Great Exhibition of 1851 in London. Other important exhi-
bitions and fairs include Philadelphia, 1876 (Centennial); Chicago,
1893 (World's Columbian); Buffalo, 1901 (Pan-American); St. Louis,
1904 (Louisiana Purchase); San Francisco, 1915 (Panama-Pacific);
Philadelphia, 1926 (Sesquicentennial); Chicago, 1933 (Century of
Progress); Cleveland, 1936 (Great Lakes); San Francisco, 1939
(Golden Gate International); New York, 1939 (World of Tomorrow);
Seattle, 1962; New York, 1964; Montreal, 1967; New Orleans, 1984;
Tsukuba, Japan, 1985; Vancouver, B.C., 1986; Brisbane, Australia,
1988; Seville, Spain, 1992; and Genoa, Italy, 1992; Seoul, Korea,
1993; and Lisbon, Portugal, 1998. Memorabilia of fairs include direc-
tories, pictures, fabrics, ceramics, etc. Memorabilia from other similar
celebrations may be listed in the Souvenir category.

Album, 1893, Columbian Exposition 40.00
Ashtray, 1933, Chicago, Cauldron Shape, Glass Insert, Brass Stand, 4 1/4 In. 27.00
Ashtray, 1933, Chicago, Chrysler Exhibition Building, Stamped, Copper, 3 In. 20.00
Ashtray, 1939, New York, Communication Building, Syroco Wood, Box 27.00
Ashtray, 1962, Seattle, Century 21, Copper 10.00

World's Fair, Bank, 1893, Chicago,
Adminstration Building, Cast Iron, 6 In.

World's Fair, Cup, 1904, St. Louis,
Graniteware, 2 3/4 In.

Badge, 1876, Philadelphia, Legion Of Historic Military Commands, 1 3/8 In.	86.00
Badge, 1893, Chicago, Discovery Of America, Shield Shape, 3 In.	34.00
Badge, 1894, California Midwinter, Bear, Eagle & Wreath, Gold Ribbon, 4 1/2 In.	65.00
Badge, 1933, Chicago, Century Of Progress 1934, Globe, Bronze, 1 In.	30.00
Badge, 1939, New York, Man Shackled To Nazi Columns, Medal, Czechoslovakia	25.00
Bank, 1893, Chicago, Adminstration Building, Cast Iron, 6 In. . . . .*Illus*	2310.00
Bank, 1939, Block, Glass, Large, 5 1/2 In.	28.00
Bank, 1939, Book, World Of Tomorrow, Brass, Leatherette	66.00
Bank, 1939, Trylon & Perisphere, Tin, 12 In.	143.00
Bank, 1964-1965, New York, Embossed Scenes, Asymmetrical Base, 5 In.	88.00
Bank, 1964-1965, Register, Dime, Original Packaging, Tin, 2 1/2 In.	121.00
Book, 1893, Chicago, Fold-Out, Fair Views, 6 x 9 1/2 In.	20.00
Book, 1915, San Francisco, Exposition Palaces & Courts, Juliet James	35.00
Book, 1940, New York, Official Guide Book, Peace & Freedom, 159 Pages	40.00
Booklet, 1934, Chicago, Official Pictures	25.00
Bookmark, 1876, Philadelphia, Washington Bust, Flags, T. Stevens, England, 8 In.	90.00
Bookmark, 1893, Chicago, Columbian Exposition, Blue, Yellow, Red, Silk, 12 In.	80.00
Bookmark, 1933, Chicago, Century Of Progress, Painted, Leather, 1934, 10 In.	6.00
Bookmark, 1934, Chicago, Federal Bldg. In Center, 4 1/2 In.	10.00
Bookmark, 1939, Westinghouse, Orange Ribbon, 3/4 x 12 In.	3.00
Bottle Opener, 1933, Chicago, Federal Building, 7 1/2 In.	18.00
Bowl, 1904, St. Louis, Liberal Arts Building, Porcelain, Floral, Footed, 3 1/2 In.	220.00
Bracelet, 1934, Chicago, Metal, Scenes Of 1934 Chicago World's Fair, 1 1/4 In.	20.00
Card, 1901, Pan-American, Iron Clad Factories, N.Y., Nelly Bly, 2 3/8 x 4 In.	33.00
Cigar Case, 1904, St. Louis, Aluminum, Raised Letters, 2 1/2 x 5 In.	30.00
Cigarette Case, 1893, Columbian Exposition, Buffalo Bill, Legs, Silver, 3 3/4 x 6 In.	1413.00
Coin, 1904, St. Louis, Horseshoe, Mule, Napoleon Hat, Encased, Aluminum	33.00
Coin, 1939, New York, Elongated Cent, Administration Building	17.00
Compact, 1933, Chicago, Century Of Progress On Lid, Enamel, Mint Green, 3 In.	30.00
Compact, 1933, Chicago, Century Of Progress, Chicago On Lid, 1/2 x 1 3/4 In.	45.00
Compact, 1939, Golden Gate International Exposition, Enamel, Blue, White, 2 In.	46.00
Compact, 1939, New York, Mother-Of-Pearl Inlay, Cover, 2 3/4 In.	48.00
Compact, 1939, New York, Trylon & Perisphere On Lid, 3 In.	51.00
Compact, 1939, New York, Trylon & Perisphere On Lid, Blue Enamel, 2 1/2 In.	56.00
Compact, 1939, San Francisco International Exposition, Black, 2 3/4 In.	51.00
Conch Shell, 1904, St. Louis, Palace Of Education & Social Economy, 7 In.	40.00
Corkscrew, 1893, Chicago, Hail Columbia Chicago, Metal, Case, 3 In.	20.00
Cuff Links, 1939, New York, Swank, Box	60.00
Cup, 1894, California Midwinter, Ruby Flash, Boy's Name, Butterfly, 2 1/4 In.	25.00
Cup, 1901, Pan-American, Buffalo, Amber Glass, 3 1/2 In.	45.00
Cup, 1904, St. Louis, Graniteware, 2 3/4 In. . . . .*Illus*	25.00
Cup, 1909, Alaska-Yukon-Pacific, Aluminum, Collapsible, Logo, 2 1/2 In.	35.00
Cup & Saucer, 1893, Chicago, Ships, Shell, Blue, White, W.S. Baker	115.00
Dish, 1876, Philadelphia, Liberty Bell Center, Glass, 9 1/2 x 13 In.	10.00
Doll, 1926, Philadelphia, Liberty Belle, Bell Dress, Cloth, Annin & Co., N.Y., 13 In.	205.00

Doll, 1933, Chicago, Boy & Girl, Cloth Body, Costume, Czechoslovakia, 8 In., Pair 170.00
Egg, 1893, Chicago, Ceramic, Metal Shaker Top, 2 3/4 In. 125.00
Fan, 1893, Chicago, Aerial View, Fair Buildings, Sepia, 24 In. 200.00
Folder, 1939, New York, Kodak At The Fair, Owl Drug Co., 8 Pages 7.00
Frying Pan, 1894, California Midwinter, Home Comfort, 3 7/8 In. 33.00
Glass, 1901, Buffalo, U.S. Government Building, 3 1/2 In. 26.00
Glass, 1964, New York, 4 Piece 20.00
Handkerchief, 1893, Chicago, Embroidered, Globe, Folded, 15 In. 25.00
Handkerchief, 1893, Chicago, Embroidered, Man's Name, Folded, 19 In. 25.00
Handkerchief, 1904, St. Louis, Embroidered, Crossed Flags, Girl's Name, 12 In. 22.00
Handkerchief, 1915, Panama-Pacific, San Francisco, Embroidered, 16 In. 38.00
Handkerchief, 1933, Chicago, Name, Blimps, Child's, 11 1/2 In. 15.00
Handkerchief, 1939, New York, Trylon & Perisphere, Embroidered, 12 In. 20.00
Hat, 1933, Chicago, Green & Blue Felt, Name, Buildings Other Side 27.00
Hat, 1936, Texas Centennial Exposition, Rangers, Logo, Autographs, Certificate, Wool ... 345.00
Hatchet, 1893, Chicago, Glass, Libbey, George Washington Bust, 4 x 8 In. 81.00
Hatchet, 1893, Sapphire Blue, George Washington, Embossed Profile, 8 In. 55.00
Jar, 1893, Columbia Exposition, Teardrop, Swirled Stopper, 16 In. 286.00
Key, 1933, Chicago, Hall Of Science, Travel & Transportation, 8 1/2 In. 45.00
Knife, Pocket, 1933, Chicago, Mickey Mouse, Yellow 95.00
Lamp, 1926, Philadelphia, Metal Stand, Glass Bell Shade, 6 1/2 x 4 1/4 x 7 In. 200.00
Lighter, 1962, Seattle, Monorail, Fair Logo, Scripto Vue-Lighter 30.00
Map, 1904, St. Louis Fairgrounds, Gould Pumps Mfg. Co. 15.00
Map, 1933, Chicago, Chicago Surface Lines, Trolley Guide, Fair Attractions 30.00
Map, 1933, Chicago, Gray Line Bus Tours, Tour, Guide To Attractions 29.00
Match Holder, 1876, Philadelphia, Woman Bust, Glass, Frosted, 4 1/4 In. 50.00
Mirror, 1904, St. Louis, Ferris Wheel Picture, Color, 2 1/4 In. 145.00
Mirror, 1904, St. Louis, Observation Wheel, Ferris Wheel, Pocket, 2 1/8 In. 248.00
Mirror, 1904, St. Louis, Palace Of Varied Industries, Celluloid, Pocket 85.00
Mirror, 1926, Philadelphia, Liberty Bell, Oval, 46 x 68 mm. 42.00
Mirror, 1939, New York, Trylon & Perisphere, Pittsburgh Plate Glass Co., 2 1/2 In. 25.00
Mug, 1893, Chicago, Man's Name, 4 1/4 In. 70.00
Mug, 1893, Chicago, Ruby Flash, Woman's Name, 4 In. 35.00
Mug, 1915, San Diego Exposition, Bisque, Cuenca Design, Alberhill, 4 1/2 In. 1430.00
Paperweight, 1898, Trans-Mississippi, Government Bldg., Sepia, Glass, 2 x 4 In. 80.00
Paperweight, 1933, Chicago, Key Shape, 4 Fair Buildings 20.00
Pennant, 1964, New York, Hollywood U.S.A., Chinese Theater, 11 1/2 In. .... 13.00 to 21.00
Perfume Cache, 1939, New York, Woven Cane, Sticker On Top, 4 1/4 In. 55.00
Photo Booklet, 1901, Pan-American Expo, Buffalo Head, Indian Congress, 9 x 8 In. 85.00
Picture, 1904, St. Louis, Cascade Gardens, Terrace Of States, Reverse Painted, 5 In. 70.00
Pin, 1894, California Midwinter, Shovel, Groundbreaking Ceremony, 3 1/8 In. 68.00
Pin, 1898, Trans-Mississippi, Iowa Day, Building, Celluloid, 1 1/4 In. 42.00
Pin, 1901, Buffalo, Compliments Of Lion Brewery, Hot Air Balloon, 7/8 In. 39.00
Pin, 1904, St. Louis, Louisiana Purchase, 1803, Enameled, Shield Shape, 7/8 In. 60.00
Pin, 1904, St. Louis, Maine Building, Celluloid, 1 3/4 In. 30.00
Pin, 1933, Chicago, Rhinestone, Key Shape, Logo Overlay, 1 3/4 In. 12.00
Pin, 1939, New York, Gilt, Red, Blue Enamel, Chain With Smaller Pin, 3 Piece 42.00
Pin, 1939, New York, Heinz Pickle 30.00
Pin Tray, 1893, Columbian Exposition, Landing Of Columbus 35.00
Pin Tray, 1894, California Midwinter, Pot Metal, 4 1/4 In. 21.00
Pin Tray, 1904, St. Louis, Administration Building, Plated Brass, 2 1/8 x 3 In. 21.00
Pin Tray, 1904, St. Louis, Palace Of Electricity, Porcelain, Shell Shape, 5 In. 65.00
Pitcher, 1893, Chicago, Fisheries Building, Brown, White, Bridgwood, 5 1/2 In. 170.00
Plaque, 1904, St. Louis, William McKinley, Weller 120.00
Plate, 1893, Chicago, Art Building, Reticulated, Victoria Carlsbad, 8 3/4 In. 85.00
Plate, 1894, California, Midwinter, Bear In Wreath, Milk Glass, 9 1/2 In. 70.00
Plate, 1904, St. Louis, General Fred Grant & Friends On Art Hill, Carlsbad, 8 1/4 In. 120.00
Plate, 1904, St. Louis, Thomas Jefferson, Porcelain, Victoria Art Co., 7 In. 150.00
Plate, 1933, Chicago, Fair Building, Ceramic, Gold, 7 In. 55.00
Plate, 1939, New York, Anniversary Washington Inauguration, Homer Laughlin 130.00
Plate, 1939, New York, Gold Stamp 250.00
Plate, 1939, New York, Trylon & Perisphere, Blue & White, Adams, 10 5/8 In. 140.00
Postcard, 1909, Alaska-Yukon-Pacific, Agricultural Building, Color 8.00

Postcard, 1915, San Francisco, Mass. State Building, Panama Pacific, Unused 6.00
Postcard, 1933, Dallas World's Fair, Pioneer Days, Tex Cooper, 3 1/2 x 5 1/2 In. 85.00
Ribbon, 1885, New Orleans, Pennsylvania Presentation Day, 2 1/4 x 6 1/4 In. 27.00
Salt & Pepper, 1939, New York, Trylon & Perisphere, Plastic, 3 5/8 In. 12.00
Saucer, 1893, Chicago, Government Building, England, 4 3/4 In. 11.00
Saucer, 1893, Chicago, Porcelain, Mines Building, Bridgwood, 5 3/4 In. 55.00
Scarf, 1893, Chicago, 5 Fair Buildings, White Ground, Folded, 17 In. 12.00
Scarf, 1901, Buffalo, Embroidered Buffalo, Pink & White Border, 16 1/2 In. 25.00
Scarf, 1904, Pan-American, Temple Of Music, Silver & Black, 19 1/2 In. 30.00
Scarf, 1939, New York, Fair Buildings, Fuchsia, Pink & White, 17 1/2 x 20 In. 20.00
Serving Dish, 1939, New York, Syroco Wood, Enamel Trylon & Perisphere, 9 In. 22.00
Shaker, 1893, Chicago, Egg Shape, White Opaque, Embossed, Mt. Washington, 3 In. 156.80
Socks, 1933, Chicago, Red & White, Phoenix Hosiery Co., Size 9 .... 25.00
Spoon, 1894, California Midwinter, Building & Fair, Sterling Silver, 4 1/4 In. 25.00
Spoon, 1898, Trans-Mississippi, Administration Bldg. Bowl, Silver Plate 46.00
Spoon, 1898, Trans-Mississippi, Fleischmann & Co. Bowl, 4 1/2 In. 25.00
Spoon, 1901, Buffalo, 1901 N.Y., Buffalo In Bowl 17.00
Spoon, 1907, Norfolk, Jamestown, Silver Plate, Demitasse, Pier, Boats 12.00
Spoon, 1933, Chicago 10.00
Spoon, 1939, New York, Trylon & Perisphere In Bowl, Silver Plate 2.00
Stamp Case, 1904, St. Louis, Souvenir, Aluminum, 1 1/8 x 1 3/8 In. 50.00
Stein, 1904, St. Louis Exposition, Palace Of Electricity, Stoneware, 8 1/2 In. 138.00
Stein, 1904, St. Louis, Palace Of Varied Industries, Stoneware, Germany, 8 In. 105.00
Sticker, 1933, Chicago, Illinois Invites You, 4 x 7 1/2 In. 8.00
Sticker, 1939, San Francisco, Century Of Progress, Statue, 4 1/4 In. 8.00
Sugar, 1893, Chicago, Porcelain, Oriental, 5-Footed, Handles, 4 In. 800.00
Tankard, 1893, Chicago, Porcelain, Electrical Building, Germany, 2 In. 65.00
Tapestry, 1939, New York, Trylon & Perisphere, Statue Of Liberty, 21 x 41 In. 85.00
Teapot, 1939, New York, Trylon & Perisphere, Porcelain, 7 In. 230.00
Teaspoon, 1904, St. Louis, Machinery Hall In Bowl, Silver Plated, Imperial 21.00
Teaspoon, 1933, Chicago, Science Building In Bowl, Silver Plated, Winthrop 6.00
Textile, 1876, Philadelphia, Eagle & Shield, In God We Trust, 13 x 18 In. 130.00
Textile, 1876, Philadelphia, Memorial Hall Art Gallery, 18 1/2 x 24 1/2 In. 37.00
Thermometer, 1901, Buffalo, Pan Shape, Fried Egg Continents, Milk Glass, 6 In. 95.00
Thermometer, 1933, Chicago, Century Of Progress, Frame, 5 1/8 x 7 1/8 In. 45.00
Ticket, 1876, Admission, Philadelphia, Indian Maiden & Eagle Back, 3 13/16 In. 18.00
Ticket, 1894, California Midwinter, Bearded Man, Flag With Bear, 3 7/8 In. 80.00
Ticket, 1915, Admission, Panama-California, Green & White, 1 1/2 x 3 1/4 In. 20.00
Tie Rack, 1933, Chicago, Key Shape, Wooden, Bamboo Dowel, 11 1/2 In. 20.00
Tip Tray, 1904, St. Louis, Jergens Pumiss Chemical Soap, Aluminum, 3 x 4 1/2 In. 65.00
Token, 1964, New York, Lincoln Bust, Illinois Pavilion Info, Gilt Brass, 1 3/8 In. 15.00
Toy, Greyhound Bus, 1933, Chicago, Trailer Boy, 10 1/2 In., 2 Piece 105.00
Toy, Trolley, 1939, New York, Greyhound Lines, Arcade, 10 1/2 In. 1150.00
Trade Card, 1876, Philadelphia, New Jersey Mutual Life Insurance Co., 5 1/4 In. 13.00
Trade Card, 1894, California Midwinter, Mellin's Food, 4 x 5 3/4 In. 7.00
Tray, 1939, New York, DuPont Building, Art Deco 245.00
Viewer, 1939, New York, World Of Tomorrow, Panoramic View, Paper 115.00
Walking Stick, 1934, Chicago, Century Of Progress, Black Wood, 36 In. 29.00
Wallet, 1939, San Francisco, Leather, Colorful Logo 25.00
Watch, 1893, Chicago, Columbian Expo, Silver Half-Dollar, Swiss Movement 415.00
Whiskey, 1893, Portrait Of Columbus In Base 110.00
Yo-Yo, 1939, New York, Wooden, Gold Trylon & Perisphere Sticker, 2 In. 67.00

WPA is the abbreviation for Works Progress Administration, a program created by executive order in 1935 to provide jobs for millions of unemployed Americans. Artists were hired to create murals, paintings, drawings, and sculptures for public buildings. Pieces are marked WPA and may have the artist's name on them.

Figurine, Alice & Knight, Edris Eckhardt, 1941, 6 x 5 1/2 In. 1170.00
Figurine, Alice & Old Knight, Edris Eckhardt, 5 3/4 x 4 3/4 In. 1125.00
Figurine, Elephant & The Crocodile, Edris Eckhardt, 8 In. 530.00
Figurine, Fish Woman, Kneeling, Holding Fish, Terra-Cotta, Grace Luce, 12 1/2 In. 2700.00
Figurine, From David Copperfield, Edris Eckhardt, 8 1/2 In. 1015.00

Figurine, From Mother Goose Tales, Edris Eckhardt, 6 3/4 In. 790.00
Figurine, Mad Hatter & March Hare, Edris Eckhardt, 4 3/4 x 6 In. 1015.00
Figurine, Rima Purple Hair, Animals, Edris Eckhardt, 11 1/2 In. 1915.00
Figurine, Tiny Tim, Father & Sister, Edris Eckhardt, 9 1/2 In. 1125.00
Figurine, Tortoise & Hare, Edris Eckhardt, 1936, 6 x 6 1/2 In. 1350.00
Figurine, Tortoise & Hare, Stoneware, Edris Eckhardt, 6 In. 580.00
Figurine, Unicorn, Black Marble Base, Bronze, Edris Eckhardt, 8 1/2 In. 450.00
Puppet Set, 3 Little Pigs, Papier-Mache & Wood 4000.00

WRISTWATCHES came into use during World War I. Wristwatches are
listed here by manufacturer or as advertising or character watches.
Pocket watches are listed in the Watch category.

Advertising, Hot Wheels, Animated, Revolving Cars, 1970 .... 75.00
Advertising, Joe Boxer, Yellow Smiley Face, Nickel Case, Original Chain, 2 In. 28.00
Advertising, Tony The Tiger, Smiling, Kellogg's Cereal, Brown Leather Band 38.00
Baume & Mercier, Woman's, Covered, Diamonds, Platinum, c.1930, 6 In. 7475.00
Baume & Mercier, Woman's, Gold Dial, Diamond Bezel, Gold Mesh Bracelet 635.00
Bertolucci, Pulchra Mini Vir, Woman's, Integral 18K Gold Band, Box, Papers 3795.00
Bulgari, Tubogas, Engraved 18K Gold Frame, Spring Band, Signed 6900.00
Bulova, 17 Jewel, 6 Diamonds, 7 Rubies, 14K Rose Gold 210.00
Bulova, 23 Jewel, Calendar, Alligator 115.00
Bulova, Anah Temple, Bangor Shriner, 17 Jewel, Fez On Dial 45.00
Bulova, Aviator's, Nickel Case, Black Face, Sweep Seconds, Expandable Band 100.00
Bulova, Woman's, 10K White Gold Plated Case, Flex Style Wrist Band, 5 In. 22.00
Bulova, Woman's, Square Face, Spiedel Gold Tone Flex Band, 10K Gold, 1950 .... 62.00
C.H. Meylan, Brassus, Marcus & Co., Woman's, Painted Crystal, Gold Bracelet 1380.00
Cabo Watch Co., Mercier, Diamonds, Rubies, Gold, Chain Bracelet, Retro 920.00
Cartier, 8 Adjustments, Enamel On Bezel Of Bracelet, 18K Gold, 1920 .... 6610.00
Cartier, Diamond Dial, Gold Hands, Diamond & Gold Frame, Gold, Leather Band 8050.00
Cartier, Panther, Square Case, Silvered Dial, Bar Link Bracelet, 18K Gold, Signed 6900.00
Cartier, Santos Automatic, Stainless Steel, Roman Numerals, Deployment Clasp 750.00
Cartier, Tank, Self-Winding, White Dial, 18K Gold Bracelet & Buckle, c.1990 .... 5750.00
Chanel, Mother-Of-Pearl Dial, Leather & Gold Chain Bracelet, 6 3/4 In. 2990.00
Character, Alice In Wonderland, Child's, U.S. Time 85.00
Character, Alice In Wonderland, U.S. Time 75.00
Character, Bart Simpson, Silvertone, Black Leather Band, Tin Box 80.00
Character, Dukes Of Hazzard, LCD Quartz, Plastic Band, Digital, On Card, 1981 ...... 20.00
Character, Dukes Of Hazzard, Melody Alarm, Battery Operated, Box 25.00
Character, Ewoks, Bradley, Box, 1983 .... 30.00
Character, Fossil, Felix The Cat, Box 50.00
Character, Hazzard, Quartz, TV Series, Melody Alarm, Battery Operated, Box 25.00
Character, Jerry Lewis, 1960s 75.00
Character, Michael Jordan, No. 23, Signature As Sweep Hand, Ball-Shaped Case 44.00
Character, Muffy Vanderbear, Red Leather Band, Box 30.00
Character, Snoopy, Arms As Watch Hands, Gold Tone Case, Leather Band, 1968 .... 50.00
Character, Snoopy, Joe Cool, On Black Plastic Base & Snoopy Figure, Domed Top 38.00
Character, Snoopy, Tennis Outfit, Gilt Case, White Leather Strap, 1960s, 1 3/8 In. 40.00
Character, Zorro, Ingersoll 45.00
Chaumet, Transparent Back Case, Automatic Movement, Leather Band, Buckle 2300.00
Continental, Woman's, 1879 Coin, Ferencz Josep On Reverse, 1 1/8 In. 290.00
Elgin, Lord, Direct Reading, Gold Filled, Leather Band, Original Case, 1957 .... 310.00
Eloga, Incablock, 17 Jewel, Diamonds, Black Cord Band, Art Deco 865.00
Girard Perregaux, 17 Jewel, White Gold 60.00
Girard Perregaux, 18K Gold, Mesh Bracelet, Roman Numerals, Adjustable 460.00
Girard Perregaux, Woman's, White Dial, Abstract Indicators, Gold Mesh Bracelet 690.00
Gruen, Pearl White Face, Dark Brown Alligator Wristband, 1 x 3/4 In. 95.00
H. Moser, Enamel Dial, Subsidiary Seconds, Hinged Case, c.1920 .... 1610.00
Hamilton, Gilbert, 19 Jewel, 14K Gold 130.00
Hamilton, Hayden, 19 Jewel, 14K Gold 70.00
Hamilton, Woman's, 17 Jewel, Leaf Bezel Design, 6 Diamonds, 14K White Gold 130.00
Hamilton, Woman's, 46 Diamonds, Square Case, Steel Bracelet, 14K White Gold 92.00
Hamilton, Woman's, Covered Case, Platinum, Diamonds, Flexible Band, c.1950 .... 2645.00

Hamilton, Woman's, Diamonds, Platinum, Oval Case, Rectangular White Dial 920.00
Harman, Silver Plated, Black Face, Seconds Dial, Leather Band, Wooden Box, 1 In. 60.00
Heuer, Tag, Stainless Steel, Glow-In-The-Dark Abstract Indicators, Brushed Case 545.00
Illinois, 17 Jewel, Presentation, Gold Filled, Original Band, 1935 .... 250.00
LeCoultre, 17 Jewel, Ecru Dial, Gold Numerals, Leather Strap, Signed 290.00
LeCoultre, 17 Jewel, Futurematic, Gold Filled, Kreisler Spandex Band 440.00
Longines, 17 Jewel, Platinum Head, Diamond Numerals & Markers 1100.00
Longines, Abstract Indicators, Diamond Set Bezel, Textured Bracelet, 18K Gold 460.00
Longines, Chronograph, Tachometer, Telemeter & Register, 18K Pink Gold, 1945 .... 3450.00
Longines, Woman's, Diamonds Around Face & On Bracelet, 14K Gold 520.00
Longines, Woman's, Square Dial, Link Bracelet, 14K Gold, 1940s-1950s 175.00
Lucien Piccard, Woman's, Round Cut Diamonds, 14K Yellow Gold 690.00
Movado, Round Case, Seconds Dial, 14K Yellow Gold, Leather Band 185.00
Omega, Seamaster De Ville, Gold Tone Case, Speidel Flex Band, 1 1/4 In. 155.00
Omega, Seamaster, Calendar, Stainless Steel, Leather Strap 172.00
Omega, Tiger's-Eye Dial, Palm Tree, Diamonds, 14K Gold, Mesh Band, c.1970 .... 690.00
Omega, Woman's, 17 Jewel, Mesh Band, 18K Yellow Gold, 6 In. 145.00
Omega DeVille, Tank Style, Abstract Indicators, 18K Gold, Alligator Strap 230.00
Patek Philippe, Autowind Movement, 18K Yellow Gold, Goat Skin Band 4600.00
Patek Philippe, Bracelet, Ellipse, Gold Baton Numerals, 18K Gold, c.1970 .... 2875.00
Patek Philippe, Cushion, Blue Dial, Abstract Indicators, 18K Gold Bracelet 2875.00
Patek Philippe, Date, Nautilus, 18K Gold Bracelet & Buckle, c.1990 .... 8625.00
Patek Philippe, Stainless Steel, Seconds, Signed, c.1945 .... 8050.00
Patek Philippe, White Dial, Arc Lugs, 18K Gold, Lizard Strap, c.1940 .... 4025.00
Patek Philippe, Yellow Dial, Seconds Dial, 18K Yellow Gold Double Bezel, 1954 ...... 3565.00
Piaget, Cushion-Shaped Dial, Date On Right, Textured Bracelet, 18K White Gold 865.00
Rolex, Cream Dial, Nautical Flag Indicators, Gold, Stainless Steel Case 1035.00
Rolex, GMT-Master, Oyster, Perpetual, Stainless Steel, Black Dial, 1981 .... 1610.00
Rolex, Gold Dial, Diamond Chapters, Emerald & Diamond Bezel, 18K Gold 6325.00
Rolex, Oyster, Perpetual Datejust, Sweep Seconds Hand, Stainless Steel, 1970 .... 1092.00
Rolex, Oyster, Perpetual, Circular Gold Dial, 18K Yellow Gold 5290.00
Rolex, Oyster, Perpetual, Stainless Steel, 14K Gold Bezel, Gold & Steel Bracelet 1150.00
Rolex, Oyster, Perpetual, Tan Dial, Gold Abstract Indicators, Stainless Steel, Case 747.00
Rolex, Oyster, Stainless Steel 575.00
Rolex, Perpetual Day & Date, 18K Yellow Gold 3310.00
Royce, Second Hand, 14K Solid Gold 230.00
S. Kirk & Son, Woman's, No. 41507, 17 Jewel, Diamonds, Platinum, Art Deco 2300.00
Swatch, Cosmic Encounters 95.00
Tiffany, Meylan Brassus, Octagonal Dial, Diamonds, Platinum, Art Deco, 6 1/4 In. 865.00
Tiffany, Tank Style, Rectangular Case, Stainless Steel, Leather Band 315.00
Tiffany & Co., No. D286753, Silver, Atlas Style Case, Black Lizard Strap 635.00
Timex, Woman's, Bracelet, Gold Tone, Strand Link Chain, 3 In. 25.00
Universal Geneve, Chronograph, Tachometer, Telemeter & Register, c.1945 .... 1610.00
Vacheron & Constantin, 17 Jewel, Adjusted To Heart & Cold, 1970 .... 3160.00
Vacheron & Constantin, 20 Jewel, Gyromax Balance, Diamond Bezel, c.1960 .... 3160.00
Vacheron & Constantin, Day & Date, Abstract Indicators, 18K Gold, Leather Strap 3740.00
Vacheron & Constantin, Diamond Surround, Integral 18K Gold Band, Leather Box 3450.00
Vacheron & Constantin, Silvertone Metal Dial, Seconds Dial, 18K Gold, Lizard Strap ... 1610.00
Waltham, 14K Gold, Second Hand, Leather Strap 175.00
Waltham, 17 Jewel, Tin, Gold Tone Finish, Brick Design Band, Leatherette Box 36.00
Westclox, Woman's, Gold Toned Aluminum Case, Steel Flex Style Band, 1 x 5 In. 65.00
Woman's, 96 Diamonds, 4 Strands Of Pearls, Art Deco, Platinum Case, 5 3/4 In. 9200.00
Woman's, Cream Colored Dial, Gold Arabic Numerals, 14K Yellow Gold, 1942 .... 345.00
Woman's, Cream Dial, 18K Yellow Gold, Aubergine Lizard Strap 2185.00
Woman's, Cream Dial, Black Roman Numerals, Gold, Stainless Steel 1035.00
Woman's, Diamonds In Fan Design, Platinum, Oval Dial, Robert Cart, Art Deco 1035.00
Woman's, Diamonds, Platinum, Roman Numerals, Jules Robert, Art Deco 5405.00
Woman's, Roman Numerals, 18K Yellow Gold, Black Lizard Strap, France 920.00
Woman's, Silvertone Dial, Sapphires, Diamonds, Art Deco, White Gold, Mesh Band 520.00
Woman's, Tak Style, Diamonds, Blue Stones, White Gold, Art Deco, France, 6 3/8 In. ... 345.00
Woman's, Twisted Gold Wire Surround, 14K Gold, Leather Band, 5 1/4 In. 635.00
Zodiac, Swiss, SST 36000, Gold Tone Metal Case, Silver, Glass Face, 1970 .... 26.00

YELLOWWARE is a heavy earthenware made of a yellowish clay. It varies in color from light yellow to orange-yellow. Many nineteenth- and twentieth-century kitchen bowls and jugs were made of yellowware. It was made in England and in the United States. Another form of pottery that is sometimes classed as yellowware is listed in this book in the Mocha category.

Bank, Pig, Blue & White Sponge, 6 x 3 1/2 In.	210.00
Bank, Pig, Marbleized Glaze, Brown, Green & Cream, 6 1/4 In.	80.00
Bowl, Blue & White Stripes, 5 x 9 1/2 In.	192.00
Bowl, Brown Seaweed, White Band, Blue Border, 2 1/2 x 4 13/16 In.	335.00
Bowl, Cover, Blue Bands & Stripes, Crazing, 7 x 3 1/2 In.	220.00
Bowl, Vegetable, Marked Fire Proof, Oval, 13 3/8 In.	495.00
Bowl, With Spout, Seaweed, Blue, White Band, Blue Stripes, 4 1/2 In.	467.00
Bowl & Pitcher Set, Blue Sponging, 15 x 11 3/4 In.	275.00
Box, Desk, Gilded Vines, Sheaf, Ram's Head, 8 3/4 In.	137.00
Chamber Pot, Seaweed, Blue & White Band, Ribbed Handle, 5 3/4 x 9 In.	220.00
Chamber Pot, White Stripe, 2 5/8 In.	100.00
Cup & Saucer, Black Transfer, Black Banding, Demitasse	305.00
Desk Set, Shell Design, Dog, 7 In.	190.00
Dish, Game, Cabbage Leaf & Rabbit Design, Unglazed, Lid & Underplate, 6 1/4 In.	165.00
Figurine, Bear, Hanging On Tree, Nature's Sweetnin', 8 In.	225.00
Flask, Molded Morning Glories & Eagle, 7 3/8 In.	1210.00
Jar, Barrel Shape, Black Letters Cereal, Cover, 8 3/4 In.	60.00
Jar, Beater, 3 White Stripes	170.00
Jar, Bread, Straight Sides, 3 White Slip Bands, 9 x 9 3/16 In.	250.00
Jar, Canning, Paneled, High Neck, 6 In.	275.00
Jar, Cover, Seaweed, Blue & White Band, East Liverpool, Ohio, 6 In.	605.00
Jug, Blue Sponging, Mustard Glaze, Stepped Shoulder, 1 Gal.	120.00
Jug, Snake Form Handle, 11 3/4 In.	105.00
Match Holder, Lion, 5 7/8 x 7 7/8 In.	280.00
Mold, Ear Of Corn, 6 Piece	1175.00
Mold, Lamb, Reclining, 2 Piece	335.00
Mold, Pineapple	350.00
Mold, Sheaf Of Wheat, 7 5/8 x 5 7/8 In.	110.00
Mug, Blue Stripes, White Shaded Band, 2 In.	181.00
Mug, Frog, Rockingham Glaze	660.00
Mug, Rabbit For William, Russet Transfer, Child's, 2 x 2 1/2 In.	635.00
Mug, White Band, Applied Ribbed Handle, 3 1/4 In., Pair	635.00
Pan, Canted Sides, 11 x 8 In.	270.00
Pie Plate, 7 7/8 In.	550.00
Pipkin, Brown & Green Sponging, Chicken Wire Design, 5 1/2 In.	360.00
Pitcher, 8 Panels Of Raised Flowers & Stems, 5 1/2 In.	95.00
Pitcher, Blue & White Stripes, 7 3/4 In.	740.00
Pitcher, Blue Stripes, Strap Handle & Spout, 5 In.	375.00
Pitcher, Buff, Cobalt Band, 9 1/4 In.	135.00
Pitcher, Cows Under Tree Scene, Brown & Green, 8 In.	160.00
Pitcher, Earthworm, Cream, Brown, Yellow, Signed, McAllister, 6 In.	505.00
Pitcher, Gothic Design, Mary, John & Jesus, Charles Meigh, 1846, 8 7/8 In.	495.00
Pitcher, Grazing Cow, Tree, 7 1/4 In.	165.00
Pitcher, Man's Face In Relief, Partial Rockingham Glaze, England, 7 1/2 In.	525.00
Pitcher, White Bands, Black Stripes, Strap Handle, 6 1/8 In.	685.00
Pitcher, White Bands, Brown Stripes, Strap Handle, 5 1/2 In.	550.00
Pitcher, White Bands, Ribbed Handle, 8 1/2 In.	550.00
Pitcher, Yellow, Green, Brown Mottled Glaze, Applied Strap Handle, 6 In.	575.00
Pitcher & Bowl, Blue Sponging, Worn Gilt, 15 x 11 3/4 In.	275.00
Salt, Hanging, Brown & Green Sponging, 6 In.	470.00
Shaker, Blue, White & Black Stripes, 4 3/8 In.	577.00
Shaker, Pepper, Seaweed, Blue & White Bands, East Liverpool, Ohio, 4 3/8 In.	1320.00
Soap Dish, 5 5/8 In.	550.00
Tankard, Relief Lattice Design, Brown & Green Sponging, 9 1/4 In.	220.00
Teapot, Applied Flowers, Ribbed & Tooled Handle, Brown Sponging, 6 1/4 In.	140.00
Teapot, Blue & Green Sponging, 8 1/4 In.	220.00
Toby Jug, Man With Fiddle, Crazing, 8 1/2 In.	715.00

ZANE Pottery was founded in 1921 by Adam Reed and Harry McClelland in South Zanesville, Ohio, at the old Peters and Reed Building. Zane pottery is very similar to Peters and Reed pottery, but it is usually marked. The factory was sold in 1941 to Lawton Gonder.

Bowl, Molded Organic Design, Green Matte Glaze, 9 In.	220.00
Vase, Leaf, Vine Design, Tobacco Ground, Ivory Mark, 12 In.	175.00

ZANESVILLE Art Pottery was founded in 1900 by David Schmidt in Zanesville, Ohio. The firm made faience umbrella stands, jardinieres, and pedestals. The company closed in 1962. Many pieces are marked with just the words *La Moro.*

LA MORO

Pitcher, Brown & Green Rockingham Glaze, Impressed Bull, c.1910, 4 3/4 In.	75.00
Vase, Brown, Green Matte, Cream Ground, 6 In.	220.00

ZSOLNAY pottery was made in Hungary after 1862 and was characterized by Persian, Art Nouveau, or Hungarian motifs. A series of new Zsolnay figurines with green-gold luster finish is available in many shops today. Early Zsolnay was not marked, but by 1878 the tower trademark was used.

Boat, Flower, Polar Bear Peering Into Water, Waves & Fish, 1920s, 19 In.	690.00
Boat, Flower, Reticulated Floral Border, Oriental Flowers, Metal Cherubs, 13 1/2 In.	1150.00
Compote, Daisy, Pink, Footed, Oval, 12 In.	350.00
Figurine, Buffalo, 4 1/4 In.	80.00
Figurine, Buffalo, Sharp Horns, Muscular Legs, Iridescent Glaze, 9 1/2 In.	220.00
Figurine, Nude, Green & Yellow Lustered Glaze, Stamp Mark, 9 1/2 In.	140.00
Figurine, Peasant Girl Carrying Platter, Green, Yellow Glaze, Mark, 8 1/2 In.	120.00
Figurine, Polar Bear, Gold & Maroon, c.1890, 4 1/2 In.	990.00
Figurine, Stylized Animal, 1950s, 5 1/2 In.	57.00
Pitcher, Floral, Scroll Design, Hobnail Handle, 11 1/2 In.	230.00
Vase, Elongated Oval, Extended Neck, Handle, Flowers, Sunset, Trees, c.1900, 10 In.	1610.00
Vase, Enamel Design, Exotic Peacock, Surrounded By Bees, Gourd Form, 7 3/4 In.	880.00
Vase, Moth, Green, Gold Purple, Blue Iridescent, Deep Red Ground, 1901, 3 In.	1610.00
Vase, Peacock, Molded, Painted, Insects, Branches, Cylinder, c.1900, 14 1/4 In.	1235.00
Vase, Poppies, Green & Yellow Lustered Glaze, 2 Handles, Stamp Mark, 8 3/4 In.	99.00
Vase, Red Pomegranite, Eocin Ground, Gourd Shape, Marked, 10 x 5 In.	1100.00
Vase, Waves & Fish, Purple & Blue, Matte Luster, Trademark Stamp, 9 x 6 1/2 In.	690.00

INDEX

This index is computer-generated, making it as complete as possible. References in uppercase type are category listings. There is also an internal cross-referencing system used in the main part of the book, so if you look for a Kewpie doll in the Doll category, you will be told it is in its own category. There is additional information at the end of many paragraphs about where to find prices of pieces similar to yours.

K O V E L S

SEND ORDERS & INQUIRIES TO: **CROWN PUBLISHERS**
c/o RANDOM HOUSE, 400 HAHN ROAD, WESTMINSTER, MD 21157
   ATTN: ORDER DEPARTMENT
WEB SITE: www.randomhouse.com

Sales & Title Information:
1-800-733-3000
For order entry:
FAX# **1-800-659-2436**

NAME _____

ADDRESS _____

CITY & STATE _____ ZIP_____

Please send me the following books:

ITEM NO.	QTY.	TITLE		PRICE	TOTAL
0-609-80471-5	___	Kovels' Antiques & Collectibles Price List — 32nd Edition	PAPER	$15.95	_____
0-517-58012-8	___	Kovels' American Art Pottery: The Collector's Guide to Makers, Marks, and Factory Histories	HARDCOVER	$60.00	_____
0-517-70137-5	___	Dictionary of Marks—Pottery and Porcelain	HARDCOVER	$17.00	_____
0-517-55914-5	___	Kovels' New Dictionary of Marks	HARDCOVER	$19.00	_____
0-517-56882-9	___	Kovels' American Silver Marks	HARDCOVER	$40.00	_____
0-609-80312-3	___	Kovels' Bottles Price List—11th Edition	PAPER	$16.00	_____
0-609-80310-7	___	Kovels' Depression Glass & Dinnerware Price List — 6th Edition	PAPER	$16.00	_____
0-517-57806-9	___	Kovels' Know Your Antiques, Revised and Updated	PAPER	$17.00	_____
0-517-58840-4	___	Kovels' Know Your Collectibles Updated	PAPER	$16.00	_____
0-517-88381-3	___	Kovels' Quick Tips: 799 Helpful Hints on How to Care for Your Collectibles	PAPER	$12.00	_____
0-609-60168-7	___	The Label Made Me Buy It: From Aunt Jemima to Zonkers	HARDCOVER	$40.00	_____
0-609-80417-0	___	Kovels' Yellow Pages: A Collector's Directory of Names, Addresses, Telephone and Fax Numbers, E-Mail, and Internet Addresses to Make Selling, Fixing, and Pricing Your Antiques and Collectibles Easy	PAPER	$18.00	_____
	___	TOTAL ITEMS	TOTAL RETAIL VALUE		_____

CHECK OR MONEY ORDER ENCLOSED
MADE PAYABLE TO CROWN PUBLISHERS
or telephone 1-800-733-3000
(No cash or stamps, please)

Shipping & Handling Charge
$2.00 for one book;
50¢ for each additional book.
Please add applicable sales tax._____

CHARGE: ☐ Master Card ☐ Visa ☐ American Express
Account Number (include all digits) Expires: MO.____ YR.____

TOTAL AMOUNT DUE _____

_____

PRICES SUBJECT TO CHANGE WITHOUT
NOTICE. If a more recent edition of a price
list has been published at the same price, it
will be sent instead of the old edition.

Signature

Thank you for your order